P9-CJH-450

CASSELL'S CONCISE

German–English
English–German
Dictionary

CASSELL'S CONCISE

German–English
English–German
Dictionary

Compiled by
H.-C. SASSE, M.A. (ADEL.), **M.Litt.** (CANTAB.)
Lecturer in German in the
University of Newcastle upon Tyne

DR. J. HORNE
Formerly Lecturer in German in the
University of Birmingham

DR. CHARLOTTE DIXON

CASSELL LTD.   MACMILLAN PUBLISHING CO., INC.
London   New York

Cassell Ltd.
35 Red Lion Square, London, WCIR 4SG
and at Sydney, Toronto,
Johannesburg, Auckland
an affiliate of
Macmillan Publishing Co., Inc.,
866 Third Avenue, New York, N.Y. 10022

CASSELL'S NEW COMPACT GERMAN–ENGLISH
ENGLISH–GERMAN DICTIONARY
First edition 1966
Second edition 1966
Second edition, Second impression 1968
Second edition, Third impression 1969
Second edition, Fourth impression 1970
Second edition, Fifth impression 1971
Second edition, Sixth impression 1972
Second edition, Seventh impression 1974
Second edition, Eighth impression 1975
Second edition, Ninth impression 1976
Second edition, Tenth impression (title changed to CASSELL'S
CONCISE GERMAN–ENGLISH ENGLISH–GERMAN
DICTIONARY) 1977
Second edition, Eleventh impression 1979
I.S.B.N. 0 304 52265 1

Library of Congress Cataloging in Publication Data
Main entry under title:
Cassell's concise German–English, English–German Dictionary.
1. German Language–Dictionaries–English.
2. English Language–Dictionaries–German.
I. Sasse, H. C. II. Horne, Joseph. III. Dixon, Charlotte.
PF3640.C28 1977 433'.21 77–7567

Macmillan I.S.B.N. 0 02 522650 9

First Macmillan Edition 1977

Printed in Spain by Grijelmo, S.A., Bilbao

Contents

Preface

Among the difficulties that arise in the compilation of a
Concise Dictionary that of the selection of words is un-
doubtedly the most formidable one. The decision as to
what to include and, much more difficult, what to exclude,
must to a considerable extent depend on the type of student
of a foreign language who is most likely to use it. Primarily
a dictionary of this kind is intended for the student in the
earlier stages of learning German, whether at school or
university. As the study of German, even at an early stage,
is likely to include the reading of literary texts from the
eighteenth century onwards, it was felt that some attention
at least must be paid to the inclusion of words no longer in
common use today but frequently found in the prescribed
texts, whether poetry, drama or prose. That in this respect
severe limitations are imposed by the very concept of a
'Concise' Dictionary is of course obvious, but an attempt
has been made to include at least some of the most common
literary and poetical terms. However, the main emphasis
throughout must of course be on straightforward contemporary German. In addition to the needs of the student, those
of the traveller and the tourist, of the reader of contemporary
literature and of newspapers and magazines, have been kept
in mind. It is hoped that the student of science and technology too will find the dictionary useful, though in his case
additional reference must of course be made to one of the
growing number of specialized works dealing with the
technical vocabulary of his particular discipline.

The aim of a Concise Dictionary must be to achieve
some kind of viable compromise between conciseness on the
one hand and completeness on the other. To make the
dictionary as helpful as possible—given only a limited
amount of space—certain economies were called for. Omis-
sions were inevitable. What is similarly inevitable is that,
except in the most obvious cases, no two experts are likely

to agree as to what may safely be omitted unless (as was attempted here) one makes frequency of usage and general usefulness the main criteria.

It should be remembered, lastly, that this is a concise dictionary which cannot remotely hope to do justice to all the finer meanings and nuances of two highly developed and complex languages. But it is hoped that the student and reader of German, especially in the earlier stages of learning the language, will find here all the help he needs.

For more detailed reference the user will find Cassell's New German Dictionary (ed. Dr. H. T. Betteridge) of considerable help, while the Duden works of reference on German are regarded as the authoritative last word on matters of controversy. In the final analysis there will always be areas of doubt and dispute. That is the prerogative of a living and developing language.

Finally, thanks are due on behalf of the publishers to Prof. W. E. Collinson, late of the University of Liverpool, who acted in a consultative capacity.

H.-C. Sasse

Advice to the User

As a guide to the nature of words which have inevitably been omitted from a dictionary of this size, it may be helpful to state that, when a German *Fremdwort* is identical with the corresponding English term and possesses no grammatical peculiarities, it appears only in the English–German section. For example, it was felt that the word *Atom* (and *a fortiori* derivative compounds such as *Atomphysik*) was unlikely to perplex any English reader and it has therefore been omitted from the German–English, but included in the English–German, section. For the same reason, a somewhat similar plan has been followed with regard to the names of countries. These have mostly been given in German–English only, whereas the corresponding nouns and adjectives of nationality or race are given in English–German only.

Arrangement of Entries

Strict alphabetical order seemed to be most helpful in a dictionary intended primarily for readers in the earlier stages of acquiring a knowledge of German. Within the entries themselves literal meanings and frequency of usage determine the sequence of definitions. Admittedly the second criterion is to a considerable extent a matter of personal linguistic judgment, indeed of *Sprachgefühl*, but it is hoped that in most cases the reader will thereby more readily discover the meaning of any particular word. It can generally be assumed that definitions separated by commas have much the same meaning, whereas differences in meaning or usage are marked by semicolons. Where it was thought desirable and feasible to include idiomatic phrases, relative frequency of usage appeared a more helpful criterion than strict alphabetic sequence.

Words which are spelt alike but are etymologically distinct

Zur Benutzung des Wörterbuches

Ein Hinweis auf die Art der Wörter, auf die in einem Taschenwörterbuch unweigerlich verzichtet werden muss, wird dem Leser die Anwendung dieses Nachschlagwerkes gewiss erleichtern: Ein deutsches Fremdwort, das mit dem entsprechenden englischen Ausdruck identisch ist und keine grammatikalischen Besonderheiten aufweist, erscheint als Stichwort nicht in beiden Sprachen, sondern wird nur im englisch–deutschen Teil aufgeführt. Man darf wohl annehmen, dass ein Wort wie z.B. *Atom* (und *a fortiori* abgeleitete Zusammensetzungen wie *Atomphysik*) einen englischen Leser kaum verwirren wird, weshalb es denn auch im deutsch–englischen Teil weggelassen, indessen im englisch–deutschen Teil berücksichtigt wurde. Aus dem gleichen Grunde wurde bei den Namen von Ländern ein ähnliches Prinzip beachtet. Diese wurden in der Regel nur im deutsch–englischen Teil aufgeführt, während die entsprechenden Substantive und Adjektive der Nationalität oder Rasse nur im englisch–deutschen Teil erscheinen.

Anordnung der Stichwörter

Die strikte alphabetische Reihenfolge schien vorteilhaft für ein Nachschlagwerk, das in erster Linie für Lernende gedacht ist, die die deutsche Sprache noch nicht völlig beherrschen. Bei den gegebenen Übersetzungen eines Stichwortes bestimmen die wörtliche Übertragung sowie die Häufigkeit des Gebrauches die Folge der Definitionen. Gewiss ist das zweite Kriterium weitgehend eine Angelegenheit der persönlichen linguistischen Beurteilung, in der Tat des Sprachgefühls. Doch ist zu hoffen, dass der Leser in den meisten Fällen gerade dadurch der Bedeutung eines Begriffes näher kommt. Allgemein gilt, dass durch ein Komma getrennte Wörter eine annähernd gleiche Bedeutung haben, während Unterschiede in Bedeutung oder Anwendung

have been given separate, numbered entries for the sake of clarity.

A word should be added on the subject of compounds. Most students of German come to realize before long that the notoriously long German nouns, far from complicating the understanding of the language, are merely a matter of syntactical and grammatical convenience, a device for structural conciseness within a given sentence construction. In a 'Concise' Dictionary only such compounds can be given which have a meaning which can be arrived at only with difficulty or not at all. Where a compound is not given, the constituent parts of the word should be looked up. The meaning should then become self-evident.

Grammar

Parts of Speech. These are indicated by abbreviations in italics (*adj.*, *v.a.* etc.), the meaning of which will be found in the List of Abbreviations. It has not been felt necessary to indicate the nature of English proper names.

Genders. In the German-English section nouns are denoted by their gender (*m.*, *f.* or *n.*). In the English-German section gender is shown by the definite article preceding the noun; in a series of nouns the gender is sometimes omitted when it is the same as that of the preceding noun or nouns.

Declension. The Genitive singular and Nominative plural of German nouns are given in parentheses after the gender. The plurals of English nouns are not given, except for certain very irregular forms. The cases governed by prepositions have been included.

Verbs. In both German and English the indication *irr.* refers the user to the tables of Irregular Verbs. Where a compound irregular verb is not given, its forms are identical with those of the simple irregular verb in the table. "To" is omitted from English infinitives throughout. German inseparable verbs are described as such only when there is any possibility of doubt, *e.g.* in the case of prepositional prefixes. Where prefixes are axiomatically always part of an

durch ein Semikolon markiert sind. Wo es als notwendig und durchführbar erachtet wurde, idiomatische Redewendungen zu zitieren, schien die relative Häufigkeit der Anwendung ein nützlicheres Kriterium als die strenge alphabetische Folge. Orthographisch gleiche Wörter, die sich durch ihre etymologische Herkunft unterscheiden, wurden um der Klarheit willen als einzelne Stichwörter aufgeführt und mit Ziffern versehen. Noch ein Wort zum Thema der Wortzusammensetzungen: Die meisten Deutschlernenden werden bald erkennen, dass die berüchtigt langen deutschen Substantive das Verständnis der Sprache keineswegs erschweren. Sie sind lediglich eine Sache syntaktischer und grammatikalischer Vereinfachung, ein Hilfsmittel zu struktureller Kürze und Prägnanz innerhalb einer gegebenen Satzbildung. In einem Taschenwörterbuch können allein solche Wortverbindungen berücksichtigt werden, die nur mit Mühe oder überhaupt nicht abzuleiten sind. Ist eine Wortverbindung nicht angeführt, so sollten die einzelnen Bestandteile nachgesehen werden. Auf diese Weise wird sich der Sinn der Zusammensetzung von selbst ergeben.

Grammatik

Wortarten. Sie sind in abgekürzter Form durch Kursivschrift gekennzeichnet (*adj.*, *v.a.* etc.). Eine Erläuterung der Abkürzungen findet sich im Verzeichnis der Abkürzungen. Es wurde nicht für nötig befunden, die Zugehörigkeit von Eigennamen anzuzeigen.

Geschlecht. Im deutsch–englischen Teil sind die Substantive mit ihrem Geschlecht (*m.*, *f.* oder *n.*) gekennzeichnet. Im englisch–deutschen Teil ist das Geschlecht durch den bestimmten Artikel vor dem Substantiv angegeben. In einer Reihe aufeinanderfolgender Definitionen wurde der Artikel dort weggelassen, wo er mit dem vorhergehenden übereinstimmt.

Deklination. Die Endungen des Genitiv Singular und des Nominativ Plural deutscher Substantive sind in Klammern nach der Bezeichnung des Geschlechtes eingefügt. Der

inseparable verb (*be-*, *ent-*, *zer-* etc.) no such information is given, as it is assumed that the student will be familiar with the function of these prefixes long before he comes to use a dictionary.

Phonetics. Phonetic transcriptions, using the symbols of the International Phonetic Association, are given throughout for all entries in both sections of the dictionary as a help to correct pronunciation. The mark ′ precedes the syllable which carries the stress. The glottal stop is not indicated.

Numbers. Only the most common numerals appear in the body of the dictionary. However, fuller coverage is given in the separate Numerical Tables.

Zur Benutzung des Wörterbuches

Plural englischer Substantive wurde nicht berücksichtigt ausser bei einigen stark unregelmässigen Formen. Fälle, die von Präpositionen regiert werden, wurden aufgenommen.

Verben. Im Deutschen wie im Englischen weist die Anmerkung *irr.* den Leser auf die Tabellen unregelmässiger Verben hin. Ist ein zusammengesetztes Verb nicht angeführt, so sind seine Formen mit denen des einfachen Verbs in der Tabelle identisch. "To" vor englischen Infinitivformen wurde durchgehend weggelassen. Deutsche untrennbare Verben werden nur dort als solche gekennzeichnet, wo Zweifel möglich sind, also bei Verben mit präpositionalen Vorsilben. Wo Vorsilben grundsätzlich Teile eines untrennbaren Verbes (*be-*, *ent-*, *zer-* etc.) bilden, ist kein solcher Hinweis angebracht, da angenommen werden darf, dass der Lernende die Funktion dieser Vorsilben kennt, lange bevor er dazu kommt, ein Wörterbuch zu konsultieren.

Phonetik. Jedes einzelne Stichwort ist auch in seiner phonetischen Transkription wiedergegeben. Dabei wurden die phonetischen Symbole der *International Phonetic Association* benutzt. Der Akzent ' steht jeweils unmittelbar vor der betonten Silbe. Der Knacklaut ist indessen nicht markiert.

Zahlwörter. Nur die gebräuchlichsten Zahlen erscheinen im Hauptteil des Wörterbuches. Eine ausführliche Zusammenstellung findet sich in den besonderen Zahlentabellen.

Key to Pronunciation

Vowels

Phonetic Symbol	German Example	Phonetic Symbol	English Example
a	lassen ['lasən]	iː	seat [siːt]
aː	haben ['haːbən], Haar [haːr]	i	finish ['finiʃ], physic ['fizik]
ɛ	häßlich ['hɛslɪç], Geld [gɛlt]	e	neck [nek]
ɛː	Märchen ['mɛːrçən], Zähne ['tsɛːnə]	æ	man [mæn], malefactor ['mælifæktə]
e˙	Medizin [medi'tsiːn]	ɑ	father ['fɑːðə], task [tɑːsk]
eː	leben ['leːbən], See [zeː], lehnen ['leːnən]	ɔ	block [blɔk], waddle ['wɔdl]
ə	rufen ['ruːfən]	ɔː	shawl [ʃɔːl], tortoise ['tɔːtəs]
ɪ	Fisch [fɪʃ], Mystik ['mɪstɪk]	o	domain [do'mein]
i	Militär [mili'tɛːr]	u	good [gud], July [dʒu'lai]
iː	Berlin [bɛr'liːn], Liebe ['liːbə], ihm [iːm]	uː	moon [muːn], tooth [tuːθ]
ɔ	Kopf [kɔpf]	ʌ	cut [kʌt], somewhere ['sʌmweə]
o	mobil [mo'biːl]	əː	search [səːtʃ], surgeon ['səːdʒən]
oː	Rose ['roːzə], Boot [boːt], ohne ['oːnə]	ə	cathedral [kə'θiːdrəl], never ['nevə]
œ	Mörder ['mœrdər]		
ø	möblieren [mø'bliːrən]		
øː	Löwe ['løːvə], Röhre ['røːrə]		
u	Hund [hunt]		
uː	gut [guːt], Uhr [uːr]		
y	fünf [fynf], Symbol [zym'boːl]		
yː	Lübeck ['lyːbɛk], Mühe ['myːə]		

Diphthongs

aɪ	Eis [aɪs], Waise ['vaɪzə]	ei	great [greit]
au	Haus [haus]	ou	show [ʃou]
ɔy	Beute ['bɔytə], Gebäude [gə'bɔydə]	ai	high [hai]
		au	crowd [kraud]
		ɔi	boy [bɔi]
		iə	steer [stiə]
		ɛə	hair [hɛə]
		uə	moor [muə]

Key to Pronunciation

Consonants

Phonetic Symbol	German Example	Phonetic Symbol	English Example
ç	Blech [blɛç], ich [ɪç]	p	paper ['peipə]
f	Vater ['fa:tər]	b	ball [bɔ:l]
j	ja [ja:]	t	tea [ti:], train [trein]
ŋ	bringen ['brɪŋən]	d	deed [di:d]
s	beißen ['baɪsən], wißen ['vɪsən], los [lo:s]	k	cake [keik], quest [kwest]
ʃ	schon [ʃo:n]	g	game [geim]
ts	Cäcilie [tsɛ'tsi:ljə], Zimmer ['tsɪmər]	m	mammoth ['mæməθ]
		n	nose [nouz], nanny ['næni]
v	weiß [vaɪs]	ŋ	bring [briŋ], finger ['fiŋgə]
x	Bach [bax], kochen ['kɔxən], ruchbar ['ru:xba:r]	f	fair [fɛə], far [fɑ:]
		v	vine [vain]
z	lesen ['le:zən]	θ	thin [θin], bath [bɑ:θ]
b	Biene ['bi:nə]	ð	thine [ðain], bathe [beið]
d	Dach [dax]		
g	geben ['ge:bən]	s	since [sins]
h	hier [hi:r]	z	busy ['bizi]
k	Koch [kɔx], quartieren [kwar'ti:rən]	l	land [lænd], hill [hil]
		ʃ	shield [ʃi:ld], sugar ['ʃugə]
l	Lied [li:t]		
m	Mirakel [mi'ra:kəl]	ʒ	vision ['viʒən]
n	Nase ['na:zə]	r	rat [ræt], train [trein]
p	Probe ['pro:bə]	h	here [hiə], horse [hɔ:s]
r	rot [ro:t]	x	coronach ['kɔrənæx], loch [lɔx]
t	Tisch [tɪʃ]		

Semi-Consonants

j	yellow ['jelou], yes [jes]
w	wall [wɔ:l]

List of Abbreviations

abbr.	abbreviation (of), abbreviated	*m.*	masculine
Acc.	Accusative	*Maths.*	Mathematics
adj.	adjective	*Meas.*	Measurement
adv.	adverb	*Mech.*	Mechanics
Agr.	agriculture	*Med.*	Medicine
Am.	American(ism)	*Met.*	Meteorology
Anat.	Anatomy	*Metall.*	Metallurgy
Archæol.	Archæology	*Mil.*	Military
Archit.	Architecture	*Min.*	Mining
Arith.	Arithmetic	*Motor.*	Motoring
art.	article	*Mount.*	Mountaineering
Astrol.	Astrology	*Mus.*	Music
Astron.	Astronomy	*Myth.*	Mythology
Austr.	Austrian	*n.*	neuter
aux.	auxiliary	*Naut.*	Nautical
Aviat.	Aviation	*Nav.*	Navigation
Bibl.	Biblical	*o.('s)*	one('s)
Bot.	Botany	*o.s.*	oneself
Br.	British	*obs.*	obsolete
Build.	Building	*Orn.*	Ornithology
Carp.	Carpentry	*p.*	person
Chem.	Chemistry	*Parl.*	Parliament
coll.	colloquial	*part.*	particle
collec.	collective	*pej.*	pejorative
Comm.	Commerce	*pers.*	person(al)
comp.	comparative	*Phil.*	Philosophy
conj.	conjunction	*Phonet.*	Phonetics
Cul.	Culinary	*Phot.*	Photography
Dat.	Dative	*Phys.*	Physics
def.	definite	*Physiol.*	Physiology
defect.	defective	*pl.*	plural
dem.	demonstrative	*Poet.*	Poetical
dial.	dialect	*Pol.*	Political
Eccl.	Ecclesiastical	*poss.*	possessive
Econ.	Economics	*p.p.*	past participle
Elec.	Electricity	*prec.*	preceded
em.ph.	emphatic	*pred.*	predicative
Engin.	Engineering	*prep.*	preposition
Ent.	Entomology	*pron.*	pronoun
excl.	exclamation	*Psych.*	Psychology
f.	feminine	*r.*	reflexive
fig.	figurative	*Rad.*	Radio
Fin.	Finance	*Railw.*	Railways
Footb.	Football	*reg.*	regular
Genit.	Genitive	*Rel.*	Religion
Geog.	Geography	*rel.*	relative
Geol.	Geology	*s.*	substantive
Geom.	Geometry	*Sch.*	School
Gram.	Grammar	*Scot.*	Scottish
Gymn.	Gymnastics	*sing.*	singular
Her.	Heraldry	*sl.*	slang
Hist.	History	*s.th.*	something
Hunt.	Hunting	*Tail.*	Tailoring
imper.	imperative	*Tech.*	Technical
impers.	impersonal	*Teleph.*	Telephone
Ind.	Industry	*temp.*	temporal
indecl.	indeclinable	*Text.*	Textiles
indef.	indefinite	*Theat.*	Theatre
infin.	infinitive	*Theol.*	Theology
insep.	inseparable	*Transp.*	Transport
int.	interjection	*Typ.*	Typography
interr.	interrogative	*Univ.*	University
intim.	intimate	*us.*	usually
iron.	ironical	*v.a.*	active *or* transitive verb
irr.	irregular	*v.n.*	neuter *or* intransitive verb
Ling.	Linguistics	*v.r.*	reflexive verb
Lit.	Literary	*Vet.*	Veterinary Science
Log.	Logic	*vulg.*	vulgar
		Zool.	Zoology

Cassell's German-English Dictionary

A

A, a [a:], *n. das A* (*des* —**s, die** —**s**) the letter A; (*Mus.*) the note A; *A Dur*, A major; *A Moll*, A minor.

Aal [a:l], *m.* (—**s,** *pl.* —**e**) eel.

Aas [a:s], *n.* (—**es,** *pl.* **Äser** *or* —**e**) carcass, carrion.

ab [ap], *adv.* off; down; away; (*Theat.*) exit *or* exeunt, — *und zu*, now and again, occasionally; *auf und* —, up and down, to and fro. — *prep.* from; — *Hamburg*, from Hamburg.

abändern ['apɛndərn], *v.a.* alter.

Abart ['apaːrt], *f.* (—, *pl.* —**en**) variety, species.

Abbau ['apbau], *m.* (—**s,** *no pl.*) demolition, dismantling; reduction (of staff).

abberufen ['apbəruːfən], *v.a. irr.* recall.

abbestellen ['apbəʃtɛlən], *v.a.* countermand, annul, cancel (an order).

Abbild ['apbɪlt], *n.* (—**es,** *pl.* —**er**) copy, image.

Abbildung ['apbɪlduŋ], *f.* (—, *pl.* —**en**) illustration.

Abbitte ['apbɪtə], *f.* (—, *pl.* —**n**) apology; — *leisten,* — *tun,* apologise.

abblenden ['apblɛndən], *v.a.* dim (lights).

Abbruch ['apbrux], *m.* (—**s,** *pl.* ˙⁻**e**) breaking off; demolition; *einer Sache* — *tun,* damage s.th.

abdanken ['apdaŋkən], *v.n.* resign, abdicate, retire (from office).

abdecken ['apdɛkən], *v.a.* uncover, unroof; clear (the table).

Abdruck ['apdruk], *m.* (—**s,** *pl.* —**e**) impression, copy, reprint, cast.

Abend ['a:bənt], *m.* (—**s,** *pl.* —**e**) evening, eve.

Abendbrot ['a:bəntbro:t], *n.* (—**s,** *no pl.*) evening meal, (*Am.*) supper.

Abendland ['a:bəntlant], *n.* (—**es,** *no pl.*) occident, west.

Abendmahl ['a:bəntma:l], *n.* (—**s,** *no pl.*) supper; *das heilige* —, Holy Communion, the Lord's Supper.

abends ['a:bənts], *adv.* in the evening, of an evening.

Abenteuer ['a:bəntɔyər], *n.* (—**s,** *pl.* —**) adventure.

aber ['a:bər], *conj.* but, however; (*emphatic*) — *ja!* yes, indeed! of course! —*prefix.* again, once more.

Aberglaube ['a:bərglaubə], *m.* (—**ns,** *no pl.*) superstition.

abermals ['a:bərma:ls], *adv.* again, once more.

Abessinien [abɛ'si:njən], *n.* Abyssinia.

abfahren ['apfa:rən], *v.n. irr.* (*aux.* sein) set out, depart, drive off.

Abfall ['apfal], *m.* (—**s,** *pl.* ˙⁻**e**) scrap, remnant; secession; slope; (*pl.*) waste, refuse.

abfallen ['apfalən], *v.n. irr.* (*aux.* sein) fall off; desert; slope.

abfällig ['apfɛlɪç], *adj.* derogatory.

abfangen ['apfaŋən], *v.a. irr.* intercept, catch.

abfärben ['apfɛrbən], *v.n.* (*colours*) run; stain; lose colour.

abfassen ['apfasən], *v.a.* compose, draft.

abfertigen ['apfɛrtɪgən], *v.a.* despatch; deal with, serve (a customer *or* client).

abfeuern ['apfɔyərn], *v.a.* fire (off), launch (rocket, missile).

abfinden ['apfɪndən], *v.a. irr.* indemnify, compound with (o.'s creditors). — *v.r. sich* — *mit,* put up with, come to terms with.

Abflug ['apflu:k], *m.* (—**s,** *pl.* ˙⁻**e**) take-off, departure (by air).

Abfluß ['apflus], *m.* (—**sses,** *pl.* ˙⁻**sse**) flowing off; drain.

Abfuhr ['apfu:r], *f.* (—, *pl.* —**en**) removal, collection (of refuse); (*coll.*) rebuff.

abführen ['apfy:rən], *v.a.* arrest, lead away. —*v.n.* (*Med.*) act as a purgative.

Abführmittel ['apfy:rmɪtəl], *n.* (—**s,** *pl.* —**) purgative, laxative.

Abgabe ['apga:bə], *f.* (—, *pl.* —**n**) delivery, tax, duty, levy.

abgabepflichtig ['apga:bəpflɪçtɪç], *adj.* taxable, subject to duty.

Abgang ['apgaŋ], *m.* (—(**e**)**s,** *pl.* ˙⁻**e**) wastage, loss; departure; *Schul—,* school-leaving.

abgängig ['apgɛŋɪç], *adj.* lost, missing; (*of goods*) saleable.

abgeben ['apge:bən], *v.a. irr.* deliver, cede; give (an opinion). — *v.r. sich mit etwas,* — concern o.s. with s.th.

abgedroschen ['apgədrɔʃən], *adj.* (*phrases etc.*) trite, hackneyed.

abgefeimt ['apgəfaɪmt], *adj.* cunning, crafty.

abgegriffen ['apgəgrɪfən], *adj.* well thumbed, worn.

abgehen ['apge:ən], *v.n. irr.* (*aux.* sein) leave, retire; branch off; (*Theat.*) make an exit.

abgelebt ['apgəle:pt], *adj.* (*of humans*) decrepit, worn out.

abgelegen ['apgəle:gən], *adj.* remote, distant.

abgemacht ['apgəmaxt], *adj., int.* agreed! done!

abgeneigt ['apgənaɪkt], *adj.* disinclined, averse.

Abgeordnete ['apgəɔrdnətə], *m., f.* (—**n,** *pl.* —**n**) political representative, deputy, Member of Parliament.

Abgesandte ['apgəzantə], *m., f.* (—**n,** *pl.* —**n**) delegate, ambassador.

abgeschieden ['apgəʃi:dən], *adj.* secluded, remote; deceased.

abgeschmackt ['apgəʃmakt], *adj.* insipid.

abgesehen ['apgəze:ən], *adv.* — *von*, apart from, except for.

abgespannt ['apgəʃpant], *adj.* worn out, run down, exhausted.

abgestorben ['apgəʃtɔrbən], *adj.* dead, numb.

abgetan ['apgəta:n], *adj.* finished, over, done with; *damit ist die Sache* —, that finishes the matter.

abgetragen ['apgətra:gən], *adj.* (*clothes*) shabby, threadbare.

abgewöhnen ['apgəvø:nən], *v.a.* *einem etwas* —, free (rid) s.o. from (of) a habit, wean from.

abgrasen ['apgra:zən], *v.a.* (*animals*) graze.

Abgrund ['apgrunt], *m.* (—es, *pl.* ⸚e) abyss, precipice.

Abguss ['apgus], *m.* (—es, *pl.* ⸚e) cast, plaster-cast, mould.

abhalten ['aphaltən], *v.a.* *irr.* restrain, hold back; hold (meeting etc.).

abhandeln ['aphandəln], *v.a.* *einem etwas* —, bargain for s.th.

abhanden [ap'handən], *adv.* mislaid; — *kommen*, get lost.

Abhandlung ['aphandluŋ], *f.* (—, *pl.* —en) treatise, dissertation; (*pl.*) proceedings.

Abhang ['aphaŋ], *m.* (—es, *pl.* ⸚e) slope; declivity.

abhängen ['aphɛŋən], *v.a.* *irr.* take off, unhook; *von etwas oder jemandem* —, depend on s.th. *or* s.o.

abhärten ['aphɛrtən], *v.a.* inure against rigours, toughen.

abheben ['aphe:bən], *v.a.* *irr.* draw (money from bank).

abhold ['aphɔlt], *adj.* averse to (*Dat.*).

abholen ['apho:lən], *v.a.* *etwas* —, fetch, collect s.th.; *einen* —, meet s.o. (at the station etc.).

Abitur [abi'tu:r], *n.* (—s, *no pl.*) matriculation examination.

Abiturient [abitu'rjɛnt], *m.* (—en, *pl.* —en) matriculation candidate.

Abkehr ['apke:r], *f.* (—, *no pl.*) turning away, renunciation.

abklären ['apklɛ:rən], *v.a.* (*Chem.*) filter, clear.

Abkommen ['apkɔmən], *n.* (—s, *pl.* —) treaty, agreement, contract.

Abkömmling ['apkœmliŋ], *m.* (—s, *pl.* —e) descendant.

abkühlen ['apky:lən], *v.a.* cool, chill.

Abkunft ['apkunft], *f.* (—, *no pl.*) descent, origin.

abkürzen ['apkyrtsən], *v.a.* shorten, abridge, curtail.

abladen ['apla:dən], *v.a.* *irr.* unload, dump.

Ablaß ['aplas], *m.* (—sses, *pl.* ⸚sse) (*Eccl.*) indulgence.

ablassen ['aplasən], *v.n.* *irr.* *von etwas* —, desist from, refrain from s.th. — *v.a.* *einem etwas billig* —, reduce the price of s.th. for s.o.

Ablauf ['aplauf], *m.* (—es, *no pl.*) (*water*) drainage; (*ticket*) expiration; lapse (of time); (*bill*) maturity.

ablaufen ['aplaufən], *v.n.* *irr.* (*aux.* sein) (*water*) run off; (*ticket*) expire; *gut* —, turn out well.

Ableben ['aple:bən], *n.* (—s, *no pl.*) decease, death.

ablegen ['aple:gən], *v.a.* (*clothes*) take off; (*documents*) file; *Rechenschaft* —, account for; *eine Prüfung* —, take an examination.

Ableger ['aple:gər], *m.* (—s, *pl.* —) (*Hort.*) cutting.

Ablegung ['aple:guŋ], *f.* (—, *no pl.*) making (of a vow); taking (of an oath).

ablehnen ['aple:nən], *v.a.* refuse, decline.

ableiten ['aplaitən], *v.a.* divert, draw off; (*water*) drain; (*words*) derive from.

ablenken ['aplɛŋkən], *v.a.* (*aux.* haben) *einen von etwas* —, divert s.o.'s attention from s.th., distract.

ablesen ['aple:zən], *v.a.* *irr.* (*meter*) read off; (*field*) glean.

abliefern ['apli:fərn], *v.a.* deliver.

ablösen ['aplø:zən], *v.a.* *einen* —, take the place of s.o., (*Mil.*) relieve; detach (a stamp from a letter etc.).

abmachen ['apmaxən], *v.a.* undo, detach; settle, arrange.

abmagern ['apma:gərn], *v.n.* (*aux.* sein) get thinner, waste away.

Abmarsch ['apmarʃ], *m.* (—es, *no pl.*) (*Mil.*) marching off.

abmelden ['apmɛldən], *v.r.* *sich* —, give notice of departure.

abmessen ['apmɛsən], *v.a.* *irr.* measure (off), gauge.

abmühen ['apmy:ən], *v.r.* *sich* —, exert o.s., strive.

Abnahme ['apna:mə], *f.* (—, *pl.* —n) decline, loss of weight; (*moon*) waning; (*goods*) taking delivery.

abnehmen ['apne:mən], *v.n.* *irr.* lose weight; (*moon*) wane. — *v.a.* (*hat*) take off; *einem etwas* —, relieve s.o. of trouble *or* work).

Abneigung ['apnaiguŋ], *f.* (—, *pl.* —en) antipathy, dislike.

abnutzen ['apnutsən], *v.a.* wear out by use.

Abonnement [abɔnə'maŋ], *n.* (—s, *pl.* —s) (*newspaper*) subscription; (*railway*) season-ticket.

Abonnent [abɔ'nɛnt], *m.* (—en, *pl.* —en) subscriber.

abonnieren [abɔ'ni:rən], *v.a.* subscribe to (a paper).

Abordnung ['apɔrdnuŋ,] *f.* (—, *pl.* —en) delegation, deputation.

Abort [a'bɔrt], *m.* (—s, *pl.* —e) lavatory, toilet.

Abortus [a'bɔrtus], *m.* (—us, *no pl.*) (*Med.*) abortion.

abplagen ['appla:gən], *v.r.* *sich* —, slave, toil.

abprallen ['appralən], *v.n.* (*aux.* sein) *von etwas* —, bounce off, rebound.

abquälen ['apkvɛ:lən], v.r. sich —, toil, make o.s. weary (mit, with).

abraten ['apra:tən], v.n. irr. einem von etwas —, dissuade s.o. from, advise or warn s.o. against.

abräumen ['aprɔymən], v.a. remove; den Tisch —, clear the table.

abrechnen ['aprɛçnən], v.a. reckon up. — v.n. mit einem —, settle accounts with s.o., (coll.) get even with s.o.

Abrede ['apre:də], f. (—, pl. —n) agreement, arrangement; in — stellen, deny.

abreißen ['apraɪsən], v.a. irr. tear off.

abrichten ['aprɪçtən], v.a. (dogs) train, (horses) break in.

abriegeln ['apri:gəln], v.a. bolt, bar.

Abriß ['aprɪs], m. (—sses, pl. —sse) sketch; summary, synopsis.

abrollen ['aprɔlən], v.a. uncoil. — v.n. (aux. sein) roll off.

abrücken ['aprykən], v.a. move away. —v.n. (aux. sein) (Mil.) march off.

Abruf ['apru:f], m. (—es, no pl.) recall (from a post).

abrunden ['aprundən], v.a. round off.

abrupfen ['aprupfən], v.a. (feathers) pluck; (flowers) pluck off.

abrüsten ['aprystən], v.n. disarm.

Abrüstung ['aprystuŋ], f. (—, no pl.) disarmament.

abrutschen ['aprutʃən], v.n. (aux. sein) slide, slither down.

Absage ['apza:gə], f. (—, pl. —n) cancellation, refusal.

absagen ['apza:gən], v.n. refuse, beg to be excused, decline (an invitation).

Absatz ['apzats], m. (—es, pl. -e) (shoe) heel; (letter) paragraph; (Comm.) guter —, ready sale.

abschaffen ['apʃafən], v.a. abolish, do away with.

abschälen ['apʃɛ:lən], v.a. peel. — v.r. sich —, peel off.

abschätzen ['apʃɛtsən], v.a. estimate, appraise; (taxes) assess.

Abschaum ['apʃaum], m. (—es, no pl.) scum.

Abscheu ['apʃɔy], m. (—s, no pl.) abhorrence, detestation, loathing.

abscheulich ['apʃɔyliç], adj. abominable, repulsive.

abschieben ['apʃi:bən], v.a. irr. shove off, push off; schieb ab! scram!

Abschied ['apʃi:t], m. (—s, pl. —e) leave, departure, farewell; discharge; resignation.

abschießen ['apʃi:sən], v.a. irr. shoot off; discharge; (gun) fire; den Vogel —, win the prize.

abschinden ['apʃɪndən], v.r. irr. sich —, exhaust o.s. with hard work.

abschirren ['apʃɪrən], v.a. unharness.

abschlagen ['apʃla:gən], v.a. irr. (attack) beat off; (branches) lop off; einem etwas —, deny s.o. s.th.: eine Bitte —, refuse a request.

abschlägig ['apʃlɛ:giç], adj. negative.

Abschlagszahlung ['apʃla:kstsa:luŋ], f. (—, pl. —en) payment by instalments.

abschleifen ['apʃlaɪfən], v.a. irr. grind off.

abschleppen ['apʃlɛpən], v.a. (car) tow (away). — v.r. sich —, wear o.s. out by carrying heavy loads.

abschließen ['apʃli:sən], v.a. irr. lock up; (work) conclude; (accounts) balance; einen Vertrag —, conclude an agreement.

Abschluß ['apʃlus], m. (—sses, pl. -sse) settlement, winding-up.

abschneiden ['apʃnaɪdən], v.a. irr. cut off. — v.n. gut —, come off well.

Abschnitt ['apʃnɪt], m. (—es, pl. —e) section; (book) paragraph.

abschnüren ['apʃny:rən], v.a. lace up, tie up.

abschrecken ['apʃrɛkən], v.a. deter, frighten.

abschreiben ['apʃraɪbən], v.a. irr. copy, transcribe; crib; eine Schuld —, write off a debt.

Abschrift ['apʃrɪft], f. (—, pl. —en) copy, transcript, duplicate; beglaubigte —, certified copy.

Abschuß ['apʃus], m. (—sses, pl. -sse) act of firing (a gun), shooting down (aircraft).

abschüssig ['apʃysiç], adj. steep.

abschütteln ['apʃytəln], v.a. shake off, cast off.

abschwächen ['apʃvɛçən], v.a. weaken, diminish.

abschweifen ['apʃvaɪfən], v.n. (aux. sein) digress (from), deviate.

abschwenken ['apʃvɛŋkən], v.n. (aux. sein) wheel off (or aside).

abschwören ['apʃvø:rən], v.a. irr. abjure, renounce by oath.

absehbar ['apze:ba:r], adj. imaginable, conceivable, foreseeable.

absehen ['apze:ən], v.a., v.n. irr. einem etwas —, copy s.th. from s.o.; auf etwas —, aim at s.th.; von etwas —, waive s.th.; refrain from s.th.

abseits ['apzaɪts], adv., prep. (Genit.) aside; — von, away from.

Absender ['apzɛndər], m. (—s, pl.—) sender; (Comm.) consigner.

absetzen ['apzɛtsən], v.a. set down; dismiss, deprive of office; depose; (Comm.) sell, dispose of.

Absicht ['apzɪçt], f. (—, pl. —en) intention, purpose, aim.

absondern ['apzɔndərn], v.a. separate, set apart; (Med.) secrete. — v.r. sich —, seclude o.s. from.

abspannen ['apʃpanən], v.a. unharness.

absparen ['apʃpa:rən], v.n. sich etwas vom Munde —, stint o.s. for s.th.

abspenstig ['apʃpɛnstiç], adj. — machen, alienate s.o.'s affections, entice s.o. away; — werden, desert.

absperren ['apʃpɛrən], v.a. (door) lock, shut up; (street) close, barricade; (gas, water) turn off.

absprechen ['apʃprɛçən], v.a. irr. einem das Recht —, deprive s.o. of the right to do s.th.

3

abspülen

abspülen ['apʃpy:lən], *v.a.* wash up, rinse.
abstammen ['apʃtamən], *v.n. (aux.* sein) descend from, originate from.
Abstand ['apʃtant], *m.* (**—es,** pl. ⁀e) distance; *von etwas* **—** *nehmen,* refrain from doing s.th.
abstatten ['apʃtatən], *v.a. einen Besuch* **—,** pay a visit; *einen Bericht* **—,** report on; *Dank* **—,** return thanks.
abstechen ['abʃtɛçən], *v.a. irr. Tiere* **—,** slaughter animals. **—** *v.n. von etwas* **—,** contrast with s.th.
Abstecher ['apʃtɛçər], *m.* (**—s,** pl. **—**) short trip, excursion; detour.
abstecken ['apʃtɛkən], *v.a.* mark off, peg out.
absteigen ['apʃtaɪgən], *v.n. irr. (aux.* sein) descend, alight, dismount.
abstellen ['apʃtɛlən], *v.a.* put s.th. down; *(gas, water)* turn off.
absterben ['apʃtɛrbən], *v.n. irr. (aux.* sein) wither; die.
Abstieg ['apʃti:k], *m.* (**—es,** no pl.) descent.
Abstimmung ['apʃtɪmuŋ], *f.* (**—,** pl. **—en**) *(Parl.)* division; referendum, voting.
abstoßen ['apʃto:sən], *v.a. irr.* push off, kick off. **—** *v.n. (Naut.)* set sail.
abstoßend ['apʃto:sənt], *adj.* repulsive, repugnant.
abstreifen ['apʃtraɪfən], *v.a. irr.* strip off, pull off; cast, shed.
abstufen ['apʃtu:fən], *v.a.* grade.
abstumpfen ['apʃtumpfən], *v.a.* blunt, dull, take the edge off.
abstürzen ['apʃtyrtsən], *v.n. (aux.* sein) *(person)* fall; fall down; *(Aviat.)* crash.
Abt [apt], *m.* (**—es,** pl. ⁀e) abbot.
Abtei ['aptaɪ], *f.* (**—,** pl. **—en**) abbey.
Abteil ['aptaɪl], *n.* (**—s,** pl. **—e**) compartment.
abteilen ['aptaɪlən], *v.a.* divide, partition.
Abteilung [ap'taɪluŋ], *f.* (**—,** pl. **—en**) section, department.
Äbtissin [ɛp'tɪsɪn], *f.* (**—,** pl. **—nen**) abbess.
abtöten ['aptø:tən], *v.a.* mortify, deaden.
abtragen ['aptra:gən], *v.a. irr.* carry away; *(building)* demolish; *(dress, shoes)* wear out; *eine Schuld* **—,** pay a debt.
abtreiben ['aptraɪbən], *v.a. irr. (cattle)* drive off; procure an abortion. **—** *v.n. (aux.* sein) *(ship)* drift off.
Abtreibung ['aptraɪbuŋ], *f.* (**—,** pl. **—en**) abortion.
abtrennen ['aptrɛnən], *v.a. (s.th. sewn)* unpick; separate.
Abtretung ['aptre:tuŋ], *f.* (**—,** pl. **—en**) cession; conveyance.
Abtritt ['aptrɪt], *m.* (**—es,** pl. **—e**) W.C.; *(Theat.)* exit *or* exeunt.
abtrocknen ['aptrɔknən], *v.a.* dry.
abtrünnig ['aptrynɪç], *adj.* disloyal, faithless.
aburteilen ['apurtaɪlən], *v.a.* pass judgment on.
abwägen ['apvɛ:gən], *v.a. gegeneinander* **—,** weigh against each other.

abwälzen ['apvɛltsən], *v.a. etwas von sich* **—,** clear o.s. from s.th.
abwandeln ['apvandəln], *v.a.* change; *(verbs)* conjugate; *(nouns)* decline.
abwärts ['apvɛrts], *prep., adv.* downward.
abwaschen ['apvaʃən], *v.a. irr.* wash up.
abwechseln ['apvɛksəln], *v.a.* vary, alternate.
Abweg ['apve:k], *m.* (**—es,** pl. **—e**) wrong way; *auf* **—***e geraten,* go astray.
abwehren ['apve:rən], *v.a.* ward off, parry.
abweichen ['apvaɪçən], *v.n. irr. (aux.* sein) **—** *von,* deviate from.
abweisen ['apvaɪzən], *v.a. irr.* refuse admittance to, rebuff.
abwenden ['apvɛndən], *v.a. irr.* avert, prevent. **—** *v.r. sich* **—,** turn away from.
abwesend ['apve:zənt], *adj.* absent.
Abwesenheit ['apve:zənhaɪt], *f.* (**—,** pl. **—en**) absence.
abwickeln ['apvɪkəln], *v.a.* uncoil; *(business)* wind up.
abwischen ['apvɪʃən], *v.a.* wipe clean; *sich die Stirn* **—,** mop o.'s brow.
abzahlen ['aptsa:lən], *v.a.* pay off; pay by instalments.
abzehren ['aptse:rən], *v.n. (aux.* sein) waste away.
Abzeichen ['aptsaɪçən], *n.* (**—s,** pl. **—**) badge, insignia.
abzeichnen ['apsaɪçnən], *v.a.* sketch, draw from a model. **—** *v.r. sich* **—,** become clear.
abziehen ['aptsi:ən], *v.a. irr.* deduct, subtract; *(knife)* sharpen; strip (a bed). **—** *v.n. (aux.* sein) depart; *(Mil.)* march off.
Abzug ['aptsu:k], *m.* (**—es,** pl. ⁀e) retreat, departure; photographic copy; **—** *der Kosten,* deduction of charges; *(steam, air)* outlet.
abzweigen ['aptsvaɪgən], *v.n. (aux.* sein) fork off, branch off.
Achsel ['aksəl], *f.* (**—,** pl. **—n**) shoulder; *die* **—***n zucken,* shrug o.'s shoulders.
Acht [axt], *f.* (**—,** *no pl.)* attention, care, caution, heed; *acht geben,* pay attention; *sich in* **—** *acht nehmen,* be careful; ban, excommunication, outlawry; *in* **—** *und Bann tun,* outlaw, proscribe.
acht [axt], *num. adj.* eight; *in* **—** *Tagen,* in a week; *vor* **—** *Tagen,* a week ago.
achtbar ['axtba:r], *adj.* respectable.
achten ['axtən], *v.a.* hold in esteem, value; **—** *auf,* pay attention to, keep an eye on.
ächten ['ɛxtən], *v.a.* ban, outlaw, proscribe.
achtlos ['axtlo:s], *adj.* inattentive, negligent.
achtsam ['axtza:m], *adj.* attentive, careful.
Achtung ['axtuŋ], *f.* (**—,** *no pl.)* esteem, regard; *(Mil.)* attention!
Ächtung ['ɛxtuŋ], *f.* (**—,** *no pl.)* ban, proscription.
achtzehn ['axtse:n], *num. adj.* eighteen.

4

achtzig ['axtsɪç], *num. adj.* eighty.

ächzen ['ɛçtsən], *v.n.* groan.

Acker ['akər], *m.* (—s, *pl.* ∵) field, arable land; *den — bestellen,* till the soil.

ackern ['akərn], *v.n.* till (the land).

addieren [a'di:rən], *v.a.* add, add up.

Adel ['a:dəl], *m.* (—s, *no pl.*) nobility, aristocracy.

ad(e)lig ['a:dlɪç], *adj.* of noble birth, aristocratic.

Ader ['a:dər], *f.* (—, *pl.* —n) vein; *zu — lassen,* bleed s.o.

Adler ['a:dlər], *m.* (—s, *pl.* —) eagle.

Adresse [a'drɛsə], *f.* (—, *pl.* —n) address.

adrett [a'drɛt], *adj.* neat, adroit, smart.

Affe ['afə], *m.* (—n, *pl.* —n) ape, monkey; (*fig.*) fool.

affektiert [afɛk'ti:rt], *adj.* affected, giving o.s. airs.

äffen ['ɛfən], *v.a.* ape, mimic.

Afghanistan [af'ganɪstan], *n.* Afghanistan.

Afrika ['a:frika], *n.* Africa.

After ['aftər], *m.* (—s, *pl.* —) anus.

Agentur [agɛn'tu:r], *f.* (—, *pl.* —en) agency.

Agraffe [a'grafə], *f.* (—, *pl.* —n) brooch, clasp.

Agrarier [a'gra:rjər], *m.* (—s, *pl.* —) landed proprietor.

Ägypten [ɛ'gyptən], *n.* Egypt.

Ahle ['a:lə], *f.* (—, *pl.* —n) awl, bodkin.

Ahn [a:n], *m.* (—en, *pl.* —en) ancestor, forefather.

ahnden ['a:ndən], *v.a.* avenge, punish.

Ahne ['a:nə] *see* Ahn.

ähneln ['ɛ:nəln], *v.a.* resemble, look like.

ahnen ['a:nən], *v.a., v.n.* have a presentiment, foresee, have a hunch.

ähnlich ['ɛ:nlɪç], *adj.* resembling, like, similar.

Ahnung ['a:nuŋ], *f.* (—, *pl.* —en) foreboding, presentiment, idea, (*Am.*) hunch.

Ahorn ['a:hɔrn], *m.* (—s, *pl.* —e) (*Bot.*) maple.

Ähre ['ɛ:rə], *f.* (—, *pl.* —n) ear of corn.

Akademiker [aka'de:mɪkər], *m.* (—s, *pl.* —) university graduate.

akademisch [aka'de:mɪʃ], *adj.* academic; — *gebildet,* with a university education.

Akazie [a'ka:tsjə], *f.* (—, *pl.* —n) (*Bot.*) acacia.

akklimatisieren [aklimati'zi:rən], *v.r. sich —,* become acclimatised.

Akkord [a'kɔrt], *m.* (—es, *pl.* —e) (*Mus.*) chord; *in — arbeiten,* work on piece-rates.

Akt [akt], *m.* (—es, *pl.* —e) deed, action; (*Theat.*) act; (*Art*) (depiction of) the nude.

Akte ['aktə], *f.* (—, *pl.* —n) document, deed; (*pl.*) records, files; *zu den —n legen,* pigeonhole, shelve.

Aktenstück ['aktənʃtyk], *n.* (—es, *pl.* —e) official document, file.

Aktie ['aktsjə], *f.* (—, *pl.* —n) (*Comm.*) share, (*Am.*) stock.

Aktiengesellschaft ['aktsjəngəzɛlʃaft], *f.* (—, *pl.* —en) joint stock company.

Aktionär [aktsjo'nɛ:r], *m.* (—s, *pl.* —e) shareholder, (*Am.*) stockholder.

Aktiv ['akti:f], *n.* (—s, *pl.* —e) (*Gram.*) active voice.

Aktiva [ak'ti:va], *n. pl.* (*Comm.*) assets.

aktuell [aktu'ɛl], *adj.* topical.

akzentuieren [aktsɛntu'i:rən], *v.a.* accentuate, stress, emphasize.

Albanien [al'ba:njən], *n.* Albania.

albern ['albərn], *adj.* silly, foolish.

Aliment [ali'mɛnt], *n.* (—es, *pl.* —e) (*usually pl.*—e) alimony, maintenance.

Alkali [al'ka:li], *n.* (—s, *pl.* —en) alkali.

Alkohol ['alkoho:l], *m.* (—s, *no pl.*) alcohol.

Alkoholiker [alko'ho:likər], *m.* (—s, *pl.* —) drunkard, alcoholic.

All [al], *n.* (—s, *no pl.*) the universe, (outer) space.

all [al], *adj.* all, entire, whole; every, each, any.

alle ['alə], *adj.* all, everybody; — *beide,* both of them.

Allee [a'le:], *f.* (—, *pl.* —n) tree-lined walk, avenue.

allein [a'laɪn], *adj.* alone, sole. — *adv.* solely, only, merely. —*conj.* (*obs.*) only, but, however.

alleinig [a'laɪnɪç], *adj.* sole, only, exclusive.

allenfalls [alən'fals], *adv.* possibly, perhaps, if need be.

allenthalben [alənt'halbən], *adv.* everywhere, in all places.

allerdings [alər'dɪŋs], *adv.* of course, indeed, nevertheless.

allerhand [alər'hant], *adj.* of all sorts *or* kinds, various; *das ist ja —!* I say!

Allerheiligen [alər'haɪlɪgən], *pl.* All Saints' Day.

allerlei [alər'laɪ], *adj.* miscellaneous, various.

allerliebst [alər'li:pst], *adj.* (*Am.*) cute; charming.

allerseits ['alərzaɪts], *adv.* generally, on all sides, universally.

alles ['aləs], *adj.* everything, all.

allgemein [algə'maɪn], *adj.* universal, common, general.

alliieren [ali'i:rən], *v.a., v.n.* ally (o.s.).

allmächtig [al'mɛçtɪç], *adj.* omnipotent.

allmählich [al'mɛ:lɪç], *adj.* by degrees, gradual.

allseitig ['alzaɪtɪç], *adj.* universal, (*Am.*) all-round.

Alltag ['alta:k], *m.* (—s, *pl.* —e) working day, week-day.

allwissend [al'vɪsənt], *adj.* omniscient.

allzu ['altsu:], *adv.* too, much too.

Alm [alm], *f.* (—, *pl.* —en) Alpine meadow.

Almosen [al'mo:zən], *n.* (—s, *pl.* —) alms, charity.

Alp [alp], *f.* (—, *pl.* —en) (*mostly pl.*) mountain(s), Alps.

Alpdrücken ['alpdrykən], *n.* (—s, *no pl.*) nightmare.

als [als], *conj.* than; (*after comparatives*) than; as, like; but; *er hat nichts — Schulden,* he has nothing but debts; (*temp.*) when, as.

alsbald [als'balt], *adv.* forthwith.

also ['alzo:], *adv.* thus, so, in this manner. — *conj.* consequently, therefore.

Alt [alt], *m.* (**—s,** *pl.* **—e**) (*Mus.*) alto.

alt [alt], *adj.* old, ancient; aged; antique.

Altan [al'ta:n], *m.* (**—s,** *pl.* **—e**) balcony, gallery.

Altar [al'ta:r], *m.* (**—s,** *pl.* ⏑e) altar.

altbacken ['altbakən], *adj.* stale.

Alter ['altər], *n.* (**—s,** *no pl.*) age, old age; epoch.

altern ['altərn], *v.n.* (*aux.* sein) grow old.

Altertum ['altərtu:m], *n.* (**—s,** *pl.* ⏑er) antiquity.

Altistin [al'tıstın], *f.* (**—,** *pl.* **—nen**) (*Mus.*) contralto.

altklug ['altklu:k], *adj.* precocious.

ältlich ['eltlıç], *adj.* elderly.

Altweibersommer [alt'vaıbərzɔmər], *m.* (**—s,** *pl.* **—**) Indian summer.

Amboß ['ambɔs], *m.* (**—sses,** *pl.* **—sse**) anvil.

Ameise ['a:maızə], *f.* (**—,** *pl.* **—n**) (*Ent.*) ant.

Amerika [a'me:rika], *n.* America.

Amme ['amə], *f.* (**—,** *pl.* **—n**) wet nurse.

Ammoniak [amon'jak], *n.* (**—s,** *no pl.*) ammonia.

Ampel ['ampəl], *f.* (**—,** *pl.* **—n**) (hanging) light, lamp, lantern; traffic light.

Ampfer ['ampfər], *m.* (**—s,** *pl.* **—**) (*Bot.*) sorrel, dock.

Amsel ['amzəl], *f.* (**—,** *pl.* **—n**) (*Orn.*) blackbird.

Amt [amt], *n.* (**—es,** *pl.* ⏑er) office, post, employment; administration, domain, jurisdiction; place of public business.

amtlich ['amtlıç], *adj.* official.

Amtmann ['amtman], *m.* (**—s,** *pl.* ⏑er) bailiff.

Amtsblatt ['amtsblat], *n.* (**—es,** *pl.* ⏑er) official gazette.

Amtsgericht ['amtsgərıçt], *n.* (**—s,** *pl.* **—e**) county court; (*Am.*) district court.

amüsieren [amy'zi:rən], *v.a.* amuse.— *v.r. sich —,* enjoy o.s.

an [an], *prep.* (*Dat. or Acc.*), at, to, on.

analog [ana'lo:k], *adj.* analogous.

Ananas ['ananas], *f.* (**—,** *pl.* **—**) pineapple.

Anatom [ana'to:m], *m.* (**—en,** *pl.* **—en**) anatomist.

anbahnen ['anba:nən], *v.a.* initiate, open up, pave the way for.

anbändeln ['anbendəln], *v.n.* — *mit,* flirt with, make up to.

Anbau ['anbau], *m.* (**—s,** *pl.* **—ten**) (*grain*) cultivation; annex(e), wing (of building).

anbauen ['anbauən], *v.a.* cultivate; add to a building.

anbei [an'baı], *adv.* enclosed (in letter).

anbeißen ['anbaısən], *v.a. irr.* bite at, take a bite of. — *v.n.* (*fish*) bite; (*coll.*) take the bait.

anbelangen ['anbəlaŋən], *v.a.* concern.

anberaumen ['anbəraumən], *v.a.* fix (a date).

anbeten ['anbe:tən], *v.a.* worship, adore, idolise.

anbiedern ['anbi:dərn], *v.r. sich mit einem —,* chum up with s.o.

anbieten ['anbi:tən], *v.a. irr.* offer.

anbinden ['anbındən], *v.a. irr.* tie on, bind to; *kurz angebunden sein,* be curt.

Anblick ['anblık], *m.* (**—s,** *no pl.*) view, sight, aspect, spectacle.

anbrechen ['anbreçən], *v.a. irr.* begin; break; start on. —*v.n.* dawn.

anbrennen ['anbrenən], *v.a. irr.* light, set fire to, burn. — *v.n.* (*aux.* sein) catch fire; burn.

anbringen ['anbrıŋən], *v.a. irr.* fit to, place.

Anbruch ['anbrux], *m.* (**—s,** *no pl.*) beginning; — *der Nacht,* night-fall.

anbrüllen ['anbrylən], *v.a.* roar at.

Andacht ['andaxt], *f.* (**—,** *pl.* **—en**) (*Eccl.*) devotion(s).

andächtig ['andextıç], *adj.* devout.

andauern ['andauərn], *v.n.* last, continue.

Andenken ['andeŋkən], *n.* (**—s,** *pl.* **—**) memory; keepsake; souvenir.

anderer ['andərər], *adj.* other, different; *ein —,* another.

andermal ['andərma:l], *adv. ein —,* another time.

ändern ['endərn], *v.a.* alter, change.

andernfalls ['andərnfals], *adv.* otherwise, or else.

anders ['andərs], *adv.* differently, in another manner, otherwise.

anderthalb ['andərthalp], *adj.* one and a half.

anderweitig ['andərvaıtıç], *adj.* elsewhere.

andeuten ['andɔytən], *v.a.* hint at, intimate, indicate.

Andrang ['andraŋ], *m.* (**—es,** *no pl.*) throng, crowd.

aneignen ['anaıgnən], *v.r. sich etwas —,* appropriate s.th.; (*an opinion*) adopt.

anekeln ['ane:kəln], *v.a.* disgust.

Anerbieten ['anɛrbi:tən], *n.* (**—s,** *pl.* **—**) offer.

anerkennen ['anɛrkɛnən], *v.a. irr.* acknowledge, appreciate, recognize, accept.

anfachen ['anfaxən], *v.a.* kindle (a flame).

Anfahrt ['anfa:rt], *f.* (**—,** *pl.* **—en**) drive; (*down a mine*) descent; (*Am.*) drive-way.

Anfall ['anfal], *m.* (**—s,** *pl.* ⏑e) attack, assault; (*Med.*) seizure, fit; (*mood*) fit, burst.

anfallen ['anfalən], *v.a. irr. einen —,* attack s.o.

Anfang ['anfaŋ], *m.* (**—s,** *pl.* ⏑e) beginning, start, commencement.

anfangen [ˈanfaŋən], *v.a. irr.* begin, start. — *v.n.* begin, originate.

Anfänger [ˈanfɛŋər], *m.* (**—s,** *pl.* **—**) beginner, novice.

anfänglich [ˈanfɛŋlɪç], *adv.* in the beginning, at first, initially.

anfassen [ˈanfasən], *v.a.* take hold of; touch; seize.

anfechtbar [ˈanfɛçtbaːr], *adj.* disputable, refutable, debatable.

anfechten [ˈanfɛçtən], *v.a.* (*a will, a verdict*) contest; (*jurors*) challenge.

anfeinden [ˈanfaɪndən], *v.a.* show enmity to.

anfertigen [ˈanfɛrtɪgən], *v.a.* make, manufacture, prepare; (*a list*) draw up.

anflehen [ˈanfleːən], *v.a.* implore, beseech.

Anflug [ˈanfluːk], *m.* (**—s,** *pl.* ⁚e) (*Aviat.*) approach; (*beard*) down; touch.

anfordern [ˈanfɔrdərn], *v.a.* demand, claim.

Anfrage [ˈanfraːgə], *f.* (**—,** *pl.* **—n**) enquiry.

anfügen [ˈanfyːgən], *v.a.* join to, annex.

anführen [ˈanfyːrən], *v.a.* lead; adduce, quote (examples), cite; *einen* **—,** dupe s.o., take s.o. in.

Anführungszeichen [ˈanfyːruŋstsaɪçən], *n.* (**—s,** *pl.* **—**) inverted commas, quotation marks.

anfüllen [ˈanfylən], *v.a. wieder* **—,** replenish.

Angabe [ˈangaːbə], *f.* (**—,** *pl.* **—n**) declaration, statement; data; instruction; bragging.

angeben [ˈangeːbən], *v.a. irr.* declare, state; *den Ton* **—,** lead the fashion; *den Wert* **—,** declare the value of.— *v.n. groß* **—,** brag, show off.

Angeber [ˈangeːbər], *m.* (**—s,** *pl.* **—**) informer; braggart.

Angebinde [ˈangəbɪndə], *n.* (**—s,** *pl.* **—**) (*obs.*) present, gift.

angeblich [ˈangeːplɪç], *adj.* ostensible, alleged, so-called.

angeboren [ˈangəboːrən], *adj.* innate, inborn.

Angebot [ˈangəboːt], *n.* (**—es,** *pl.* **—e**) offer, tender, bid; (*Comm.*) — *und Nachfrage,* supply and demand.

angebracht [ˈangəbraxt], *adj.* apt, appropriate, opportune.

angedeihen [ˈangədaɪən], *v.n. einem etwas* — *lassen,* bestow s.th. on s.o.

angegossen [ˈangəgɔsən], *adj. das sitzt wie* **—,** it fits like a glove.

angehen [ˈangeːən], *v.a. irr. einen um etwas* **—,** apply to s.o. for s.th.; *das geht Dich nichts an,* that is none of your business.

angehören [ˈangəhøːrən], *v.n.* belong to.

Angehörige [ˈangəhøːrɪgə], *m., f.* (**—n,** *pl.* **—n**) near relative; next of kin.

Angeklagte [ˈangəklaːktə], *m., f.* (**—n,** *pl.* **—n**) the accused, defendant, prisoner at the bar.

Angel [ˈaŋəl], *f.* (**—,** *pl.* **—n**) fishing-rod;

(*door*) hinge, pivot; *zwischen Tür und* **—,** in passing.

angelegen [ˈangəleːgən], *adj. sich etwas* — *sein lassen,* interest o.s. in s.th., concern o.s. in s.th.; *ich werde es mir* — *sein lassen,* I shall make it my business.

Angelegenheit [ˈangəleːgənhaɪt], *f.* (**—,** *pl.* **—en**) concern, matter, affair.

angeln [ˈaŋəln], *v.a.* fish, angle.

angemessen [ˈangəmɛsən], *adj.* proper, suitable, appropriate.

angenehm [ˈangəneːm], *adj.* acceptable, agreeable, pleasing, pleasant.

angenommen [ˈangənɔmən], *conj.* — *daß,* given that, supposing that, say.

Anger [ˈaŋər], *m.* (**—s,** *pl.* **—**) grass-plot; green, common.

angesehen [ˈangəzeːən], *adj.* respected, esteemed, distinguished.

Angesicht [ˈangəzɪçt], *n.* (**—s,** *pl.* **—er**) face, countenance.

angestammt [ˈangəʃtamt], *adj.* ancestral, hereditary.

Angestellte [ˈangəʃtɛltə], *m., f.* (**—n,** *pl.* **—n**) employee; (*pl.*) staff.

Angler [ˈaŋlər], *m.* (**—s,** *pl.* **—**) angler, fisherman.

angliedern [ˈangliːdərn], *v.a.* annex, attach.

Anglist [aŋˈglɪst], *m.* (**—en,** *pl.* **—en**) (*Univ.*) professor *or* student of English.

angreifen [ˈangraɪfən], *v.a. irr.* handle, touch; (*capital*) break into; attack, assail; *es greift mich an,* it taxes my strength.

angrenzen [ˈangrɛntsən], *v.n.* border upon, adjoin.

Angriff [ˈangrɪf], *m.* (**—s,** *pl.* **—e**) offensive, attack, assault.

Angst [aŋst], *f.* (**—,** *pl.* ⁚e) anxiety; fear; anguish.

ängstigen [ˈɛŋstɪgən], *v.a.* alarm, frighten. — *v.r. sich* **—,** feel uneasy, be afraid.

angucken [ˈanguкən], *v.a.* look at.

anhaben [ˈanhaːbən], *v.a. irr.* have on, be dressed in, wear; *einem etwas* **—,** hold s.th. against s.o.

anhaften [ˈanhaftən], *v.n.* stick to, adhere to.

Anhalt [ˈanhalt], *m.* (**—es,** *no pl.*) support, basis.

anhalten [ˈanhaltən], *v.a. irr. einen* **—,** stop s.o. — *v.n.* stop, pull up, halt; *um ein Mädchen* **—,** ask for a girl's hand in marriage. — *v.r. sich an etwas halten,* cling to, hang on to s.th.

Anhaltspunkt [ˈanhaltspuŋkt], *m.* (**—es,** *pl.* **—e**) clue, (*Am.*) lead.

Anhang [ˈanhaŋ], *m.* (**—s,** *pl.* ⁚e) appendix, supplement.

anhängen [ˈanhɛŋən], *v.a. irr.* hang on, fasten to, attach.

Anhänger [ˈanhɛŋər], *m.* (**—s,** *pl.* **—**) follower, adherent; (*Footb.*) supporter; pendant (on a necklace); label; (*Transp.*) trailer.

anhänglich [ˈanhɛŋlɪç], *adj.* attached, affectionate.

7

Anhängsel [ˈanhɛŋsəl], *n.* (**—s,** *pl.* **—**) appendage.

anhauchen [ˈanhauxən], *v.a.* breathe upon.

anhäufen [ˈanhɔyfən], *v.a.* heap up, pile up, amass. **—***v.r. sich* **—,** accumulate.

anheben [ˈanheːbən], *v.a. irr.* lift. **—** *v.n.* (*obs.*) begin.

anheim [anˈhaɪm], *adv.* **—** *stellen,* leave to s.o.'s discretion.

anheimeln [ˈanhaɪməln], *v.a.* remind one of home.

anheischig [ˈanhaɪʃɪç], *adj. sich* **—** *machen,* undertake, pledge o.s.

Anhieb [ˈanhiːp], *m.* (**—s,** *pl.* **—e**) (*fencing*) first stroke; *auf* **—,** at the first attempt.

Anhöhe [ˈanhøːə], *f.* (**—,** *pl.* **—n**) hill, rising ground.

anhören [ˈanhøːrən], *v.a.* listen to; tell by s.o.'s voice *or* accent.

animieren [aniˈmiːrən], *v.a.* instigate, egg on.

ankämpfen [ˈankɛmpfən], *v.n. gegen etwas* **—,** struggle against s.th.

ankaufen [ˈankaufən], *v.a.* purchase, buy. **—** *v.r. sich irgendwo* **—,** buy land somewhere.

Anker [ˈaŋkər], *m.* (**—s,** *pl.* **—**) (*Naut.*) anchor; *den* **—** *auswerfen,* cast anchor.

ankern [ˈaŋkərn], *v.a., v.n.* anchor, cast anchor.

Anklage [ˈanklaːgə], *f.* (**—,** *pl.* **—n**) accusation; *gegen einen* **—** *erheben,* bring a charge against s.o.

Ankläger [ˈanklɛːgər], *m.* (**—s,** *pl.* **—**) accuser, prosecutor; plaintiff.

Anklang [ˈanklaŋ], *m.* (**—s,** *pl.* **—e**) reminiscence; **—** *finden,* please, meet with approval.

ankleben [ˈankleːbən], *v.a.* stick to, glue to, paste on.

ankleiden [ˈanklaɪdən], *v.a.* dress. **—** *v.r. sich* **—,** dress o.s., get dressed.

anklingeln [ˈanklɪŋəln], *v.a.* (*coll.*) *einen* **—,** ring s.o. up (on the telephone.)

anklopfen [ˈanklɔpfən], *v.n.* knock.

anknüpfen [ˈanknypfən], *v.a.* tie; join on to; *ein Gespräch* **—,** start a conversation; *wieder* **—,** resume.

ankommen [ˈankɔmən], *v.n. irr.* (*aux.* sein) arrive; *es kommt darauf an,* it depends upon.

ankreiden [ˈankraɪdən], *v.a.* chalk up.

ankündigen [ˈankyndɪgən], *v.a.* announce, advertise, give notice of, proclaim.

Ankunft [ˈankunft], *f.* (**—,** *no pl.*) arrival.

ankurbeln [ˈankurbəln], *v.a.* (*Motor.*) crank up.

Anlage [ˈanlaːgə], *f.* (**—,** *pl.* **—n**) (*capital*) investment; enclosure (*with a letter*); (*industrial*) plant; (*building*) lay-out; *öffentliche* **—,** pleasure grounds; talent.

anlangen [ˈanlaŋən], *v.n.* (*aux.* sein) arrive; concern; *was das anlangt,* as far as this is concerned.

Anlaß [ˈanlas], *m.* (**—sses,** *pl.* **—sse**) cause, occasion, motive.

anlassen [ˈanlasən], *v.a. irr.* keep on; (*Motor.*) start. **—** *v.r. sich gut* **—,** promise well.

Anlasser [ˈanlasər], *m.* (**—s,** *pl.* **—**) (*Motor.*) starter.

anläßlich [ˈanlɛslɪç], *prep.* (*Genit.*) à propos of, on the occasion of.

Anlauf [ˈanlauf], *m.* (**—s,** *pl.* **-e**) start, run, (*Aviat.*) take-off run.

anlaufen [ˈanlaufən], *v.n. irr.* tarnish; call at (port).

anlegen [ˈanleːgən], *v.a. Geld* **—,** invest money; *Kleider* **—,** don clothes; *einen Garten* **—,** lay out a garden; *Hand* **—,** give a helping hand; *auf einen* **—,** take aim at s.o.; (*Naut.*) land, dock.

Anlegestelle [ˈanleːgəʃtɛlə], *f.* (**—,** *pl.* **—n**) landing place.

anlehnen [ˈanleːnən], *v.r. sich an etwas* **—,** lean against s. th.

Anleihe [ˈanlaɪə], *f.* (**—,** *pl.* **—n**) loan, *öffentliche* **—,** government loan; *eine* **—** *machen,* raise a loan.

anleiten [ˈanlaɪtən], *v.a.* train, instruct.

anlernen [ˈanlɛrnən], *v.a. einen* **—,** train, apprentice s.o. (in a craft).

Anliegen [ˈanliːgən], *n.* (**—s,** *pl.* **—**) request, petition, concern.

anmachen [ˈanmaxən], *v.a.* fix, fasten; light (a fire).

anmaßen [ˈanmaːsən], *v.a. sich etwas* **—,** arrogate s.th.

anmaßend [ˈanmaːsənt], *adj.* arrogant.

anmelden [ˈanmɛldən], *v.a.* announce, (*claim*) give notice of. **—** *v.r. sich* **—,** notify o.'s arrival, make an appointment; *sich* **—** *lassen,* send in o.'s name.

Anmeldungsformular [anˈmɛlduŋsformulaːr], *n.* (**—s,** *pl.* **—e**) registration form.

Anmerkung [ˈanmɛrkuŋ], *f.* (**—,** *pl.* **—en**) remark, annotation, footnote.

anmessen [ˈanmɛsən], *v.a. irr.* measure (s.o. for a garment).

Anmut [ˈanmuːt], *f.* (**—,** *no pl.*) grace, charm.

annähen [ˈannɛːən], *v.a.* sew on (to).

annähern [ˈannɛːərn], *v.r. sich* **—,** approach, draw near; (*Maths.*) approximate.

Annäherung [ˈannɛːəruŋ], *f.* (**—,** *pl.* **—en**) approach; (*Maths.*) approximation.

Annahme [ˈannaːmə], *f.* (**—,** *pl.* **—n**) acceptance; assumption, hypothesis.

annehmbar [ˈannɛːmbaːr], *adj.* acceptable; *ganz* **—,** passable.

annehmen [ˈannɛːmən], *v.a. irr.* take, accept, take delivery of; suppose, assume, presume; *an Kindes Statt* **—,** adopt.

Annehmlichkeit [ˈannɛːmlɪçkaɪt], *f.* (**—,** *pl.* **—en**) amenity, comfort.

Annonce [anˈnõːsə], *f.* (**—,** *pl.* **—n**) (classified) advertisement (in newspaper).

anordnen [ˈanɔrdnən], *v.a.* arrange, regulate; order, direct.

anorganisch ['anɔrgaːnɪʃ], *adj.* inorganic.

anpacken ['anpakən], *v.a.* get hold of, seize, grasp.

anpassen ['anpasən], *v.a.* fit, suit. — *v.r. sich* —, adapt o.s.

anpflanzen ['anpflantsən], *v.a.* plant, grow.

Anprall ['anpral], *m.* (—s, *no pl.*) impact, bounce, shock.

anpumpen ['anpumpən], *v.a.* (*coll.*) *einen* —, borrow money from s.o.

anrechnen ['anrɛçnən], *v.a. einem etwas* —, charge s.o. with s.th.; *einem etwas hoch* —, think highly of a person for s.th.

Anrecht ['anrɛçt], *n.* (—es, *no pl.*) — *auf*, title to, claim to.

Anrede ['anreːdə], *f.* (—, *pl.* —**n**) (form of) address, title.

anreden ['anreːdən], *v.a.* address (s.o.).

anregen ['anreːgən], *v.a.* stimulate (s.o.); suggest (s.th.).

Anregung ['anreːguŋ], *f.* (—, *pl.* —**en**) suggestion, hint.

Anreiz ['anraits], *m.* (—es, *no pl.*) incentive; impulse.

Anrichte ['anrɪçtə], *f.* (—, *pl.* —**n**) dresser, sideboard.

anrichten ['anrɪçtən], *v.a.* (*meal*) prepare, serve (up); *Unheil* —, make mischief.

anrüchig ['anryːçɪç], *adj.* disreputable.

anrücken ['anrykən], *v.a.* bring near to. — *v.n.* (*aux.* sein) approach.

Anruf ['anruːf], *m.* (—s, *pl.* —**e**) (*by sentry*) challenge; telephone call.

anrufen ['anruːfən], *v.a. irr.* call to, challenge; implore; ring up; *Gott* —, invoke God.

anrühren ['anryːrən], *v.a.* handle, touch; (*Cul.*) mix.

Ansage ['anzaːgə], *f.* (—, *pl.* —**n**) announcement.

ansagen ['anzaːgən], *v.a.* announce, notify.

Ansager ['anzaːgər], *m.* (—s, *pl.* —) announcer; compere.

ansammeln ['anzaməln], *v.a.* accumulate, gather. — *v.r. sich* —, gather, foregather, congregate, collect.

ansässig ['anzɛsɪç], *adj.* domiciled, resident; *sich* — *machen*, settle.

Ansatz ['anzats], *m.* (—es, *pl.* —**:e**) start; (*Maths.*) construction; disposition (to), tendency (to).

anschaffen ['anʃafən], *v.a.* buy, purchase, get.

anschauen ['anʃauən], *v.a.* look at, view.

anschaulich ['anʃaulɪç], *adj.* clear; *einem etwas* — *machen*, give s.o. a clear idea of s.th.

Anschauung ['anʃauuŋ], *f.* (—, *pl.* —**en**) view, perception; *nach meiner* —, in my opinion.

Anschein ['anʃain], *m.* (—s, *no pl.*) appearance, semblance.

anscheinend ['anʃainənt], *adj.* apparent, ostensible, seeming.

anschicken ['anʃikən], *v.r. sich* — *zu*, prepare for, get ready for.

anschirren ['anʃɪrən], *v.a.* (*horses*) harness.

Anschlag ['anʃlaːk], *m.* (—s, *pl.* —**:e**) poster, placard; — *auf das Leben*, attempt at assassination.

Anschlagbrett ['anʃlaːkbrɛt], *n.* (—es, *pl.* —**er**) notice-board.

anschlagen ['anʃlaːgən], *v.a. irr.* (*keys of piano or typewriter*) strike, touch; (*knitting*) cast on; *zu hoch* —, overestimate.

anschließen ['anʃliːsən], *v.a. irr.* fasten with a lock. — *v.r. sich* —, join in; (*club*) join.

Anschluß ['anʃlus], *m.* (—**sses**, *pl.* —**:sse**) (*Railw., telephone*) connection; (*Pol.*) annexation.

Anschlußpunkt ['anʃluspuŋkt], *m.* (—**es**, *pl.* —**e**) junction; (*Elec.*) inlet point, power point.

anschmiegen ['anʃmiːgən], *v.r. sich* —, nestle closely to.

anschmieren ['anʃmiːrən], *v.a. einen* —, (*coll.*) deceive, cheat s.o.

anschnallen ['anʃnalən], *v.a.* buckle on.

anschnauzen ['anʃnautsən], *v.a.* snarl at, snap at.

anschneiden ['anʃnaidən], *v.a. irr.* cut into; *ein Thema* —, broach a subject.

Anschrift ['anʃrɪft], *f.* (—, *pl.* —**en**) address.

anschwellen ['anʃvɛlən], *v.n.* (*aux.* sein) swell.

Ansehen ['anzeːən], *n.* (—s, *no pl.*) respect; reputation; authority.

ansehen ['anzeːən], *v.a. irr.* look at *or* upon, consider, regard.

ansehnlich ['anzeːnlɪç], *adj.* considerable, appreciable.

anseilen ['anzailən], *v.a.* (*Mount.*) rope together.

ansetzen ['anzɛtsən], *v.a.* join to; (*Maths.*) start, write out (an equation).

Ansicht ['anzɪçt], *f.* (—, *pl.* —**en**) opinion; view; (*Comm.*) approval.

ansichtig ['anzɪçtɪç], *adj.* — *werden*, get a glimpse of.

Ansichts(post)karte ['anzɪçts(post)-kartə], *f.* (—, *pl.* —**n**) picture postcard.

ansiedeln ['anziːdəln], *v.r. sich* —, settle (down), colonize.

Ansinnen ['anzɪnən], *n.* (—s, *pl.* —) demand, suggestion.

anspannen ['anʃpanən], *v.a.* tighten yoke, stretch; harness.

anspielen ['anʃpiːlən], *v.n.* (*Game, Sport*) lead off; *auf etwas* —, allude to s.th.

Ansporn ['anʃpɔrn], *m.* (—s, *no pl.*) spur, incentive.

Ansprache ['anʃpraːxə], *f.* (—, *pl.* —**n**) address, speech, talk.

ansprechen ['anʃprɛçən], *v.a. irr.* address, accost; please.

anspringen ['anʃprɪŋən], *v.a. irr.* leap at. — *v.n.* (*Motor.*) start.

9

Anspruch ['anʃprux], *m.* (**—s**, *pl.* ⸚e) (*Law*) claim, title.

anspruchsvoll ['anʃpruxsfɔl], *adj.* demanding, hard to please.

anstacheln ['anʃtaxəln], *v.a.* goad, prod.

Anstalt ['anʃtalt], *f.* (—, *pl.* —en) institution, establishment; —*en treffen*, make arrangements (for).

Anstand ['anʃtant], *m.* (**—es**, *no pl.*) propriety; politeness, good manners, good grace; decency; (*Hunt.*) stand, butts.

anständig ['anʃtɛndɪç], *adj.* decent, proper, respectable.

Anstandsbesuch ['anʃtantsbəzu:x], *m.* (**—es**, *pl.* —e) formal visit.

anstandshalber ['anʃtantshalbər], *adv.* for decency's sake.

anstandslos ['anʃtantslo:s], *adv.* unhesitatingly.

anstarren ['anʃtarən], *v.a.* stare at.

anstatt [an'ʃtat], *prep.* (*Genit.*), *conj.* instead of, in lieu of, in the place of.

anstecken ['anʃtɛkən], *v.a.* pin on; set fire to; infect.

Ansteckung ['anʃtɛkuŋ], *f.* (—, *pl.* —en) infection, contagion.

anstehen ['anʃte:ən], *v.n. irr.* stand in a queue; — *lassen*, put off, delay.

ansteigen ['anʃtaɪgən], *v.n. irr.* (*aux.* sein) rise, increase.

anstellen ['anʃtɛlən], *v.a. einen* —, appoint s.o. to a post; employ; *Betrachtungen* —, speculate. — *v.r. sich* —, form a queue, line up.

anstellig ['anʃtɛlɪç], *adj.* able, skilful, adroit.

Anstellung ['anʃtɛluŋ], *f.* (—, *pl.* —en) appointment, employment.

anstiften ['anʃtɪftən], *v.a.* instigate.

anstimmen ['anʃtɪmən], *v.a.* intone.

Anstoß ['anʃto:s], *m.* (**—es**, *pl.* ⸚e) (*Footb.*) kick-off; — *erregen*, give offence; *den* — *geben zu*, initiate, give an impetus to; *Stein des* —*es*, stumbling block; — *nehmen*, take offence.

anstoßen ['anʃto:sən], *v.a. irr.* knock against, push against; give offence; clink (glasses); border on; *mit der Zunge* —, lisp.

anstößig ['anʃtø:sɪç], *adj.* shocking, offensive.

anstreichen ['anʃtraɪçən], *v.a. irr.* paint; *Fehler* —, mark wrong.

Anstreicher ['anʃtraɪçər], *m.* (**—s**, *pl.* —) house-painter.

anstrengen ['anʃtrɛŋən], *v.a.* strain exert; *eine Klage gegen einen* —, bring an action against s.o. — *v.r. sich* —, exert o.s.

Anstrengung ['anʃtrɛŋuŋ], *f.* (—, *pl.* —en) exertion, effort.

Anstrich ['anʃtrɪç], *m.* (**—s**, *pl.* —e) coat of paint.

Ansturm ['anʃturm], *m.* (**—s**, *no pl.*) attack, assault, charge.

Ansuchen ['anzu:xən], *n.* (**—s**, *pl.* —) application, request, petition.

ansuchen ['anzu:xən], *v.n. bei einem um etwas* —, apply to s.o. for s.th.

Anteil ['antaɪl], *m.* (**—s**, *pl.* —e) share, portion; sympathy.

Anteilnahme ['antaɪlna:mə], *f.* (—, *no pl.*) sympathy.

Antenne [an'tɛnə], *f.* (—, *pl.* —n) aerial; antenna.

antik [an'ti:k], *adj.* antique, ancient, classical.

Antike [an'ti:kə], *f.* (—, *pl.* —en) (classical) antiquity; ancient work of art (statue etc.).

Antiquar [anti'kva:r], *m.* (**—s**, *pl.* —e) second-hand dealer; antiquary.

Antiquariat [antikva'rja:t], *n.* (**—s**, *pl.* —e) second-hand bookshop.

antiquarisch [anti'kva:rɪʃ], *adj.* antiquarian, second-hand.

Antlitz ['antlɪts], *n.* (**—es**, *pl.* —e) countenance, (*Poet.*) face.

Antrag ['antra:k], *m.* (**—s**, *pl.* ⸚e) proposition, proposal, application; *einen* — *stellen*, bring in a motion; make application.

antragen ['antra:gən], *v.a. irr.* propose, make a proposal, offer to.

Antragsformular ['antra:ksfɔrmula:r], *n.* (**—s**, *pl.* —e) (*Insurance*) proposal form; application form.

Antragsteller ['antra:kʃtɛlər], *m.* (**—s**, *pl.* —) applicant, mover of a resolution.

antreten ['antre:tən], *v.a. irr. ein Amt* —, enter upon an office; *eine Reise* —, set out on a journey. — *v.n.* (*aux.* sein) (*Mil.*) fall in.

Antrieb ['antri:p], *m.* (**—s**, *pl.* —e) impulse, motive; incentive; *aus eigenem* —, voluntarily.

Antritt ['antrɪt], *m.* (**—s**, *no pl.*) start, commencement.

Antrittsvorlesung ['antrɪtsforle:zuŋ], *f.* (*Univ.*) inaugural lecture.

antun ['antu:n], *v.a. irr. einem etwas* —, do s.th. to s.o.

Antwort ['antvɔrt], *f.* (—, *pl.* —en) answer, reply; *abschlägige* —, refusal, rebuff.

antworten ['antvɔrtən], *v.a.* answer, reply to.

anvertrauen ['anfɛrtrauən], *v.a. einem etwas* —, entrust s.o. with s.th.; confide in s.o.

anverwandt ['anfɛrvant] *see* **verwandt**.

Anwalt ['anvalt], *m.* (**—s**, *pl.* ⸚e) lawyer, barrister, solicitor, attorney, advocate.

anwandeln ['anvandəln], *v.a.* befall.

Anwandlung ['anvandluŋ], *f.* (—, *pl.* —en) fit, turn.

Anwartschaft ['anvartʃaft], *f.* (—, *pl.* —en) (*Law*) reversion; candidacy.

anweisen ['anvaɪzən], *v.a. irr.* instruct, direct; *angewiesen sein auf*, depend upon.

Anweisung ['anvaɪzuŋ], *f.* (—, *pl.* —en) instruction, advice, method; (*Comm.*) voucher, credit voucher, cheque.

anwenden ['anvɛndən], *v.a. irr.* use, make use of, apply.

anwerben ['anvɛrbən], v.a. irr. (Mil.) recruit; sich — lassen, enlist.

anwesend ['anve:zənt], adj. at hand, present.

Anwesenheit ['anve:zənhaɪt], f. (—, no pl.) presence, attendance.

anwidern ['anvi:dərn], v.a. disgust.

Anzahl ['antsa:l], f. (—, no pl.) number, quantity.

anzahlen ['antsa:lən], v.a. pay a deposit.

Anzahlung ['antsa:luŋ], f. (—, pl. —en) deposit.

Anzeichen ['antsaɪçən], n. (—s, pl. —) indication, omen.

Anzeige ['antsaɪgə], f. (—, pl. —n) notice, (classified) advertisement; denunciation; — erstatten, to lay information.

anzeigen ['antsaɪgən], v.a. point out, indicate; announce; notify; advertise; denounce.

Anzeiger ['antsaɪgər], m. (—s, pl. —) indicator; (newspaper) advertiser.

anzetteln ['antsɛtəln], v.a. plot, contrive.

anziehen ['antsi:ən], v.a. irr. pull, draw tight, give a tug; attract; stretch; dress; (screws) tighten. —, v.r. sich —, dress, put on o.'s clothes.

anziehend ['antsi:ənt], adj. attractive.

Anziehung ['antsi:uŋ], f. (—, no pl.) attraction.

Anzug ['antsu:k], m. (—s, pl. ⁻e) (man's) suit; approach.

anzüglich ['antsy:klɪç],adj.allusive; suggestive; — werden, become offensive.

anzünden ['antsyndən], v.a. kindle, ignite.

apart [a'part], adj. charming, delightful; (Am.) cute.

Apfel ['apfəl], m. (—s, pl. ⁻) apple.

Apfelmost ['apfəlmɔst], m. (—s, no pl.) cider.

Apfelsine [apfəl'zi:nə], f. (—, pl. —n) orange.

Apostel [a'pɔstəl], m. (—s, pl. —) apostle.

Apotheke [apo'te:kə], f. (—, pl. —n) dispensary, pharmacy, chemist's shop; (Am.) drugstore.

Apparat [apa'ra:t], m. (—(e)s, pl. ⁻e) apparatus; radio or television set; telephone.

appellieren [apɛ'li:rən], v.n. — an, appeal to.

appetitlich [ape'ti:tlɪç], adj. appetising, dainty.

Aprikose [aprɪ'ko:zə], f. (—, pl. —en) apricot.

Aquarell [akva'rɛl], n. (—s, pl. —e) water-colour (painting).

Ära ['ɛ:ra], f. (—, no pl.) era.

Arabien [a'ra:bjən], n. Arabia.

Arbeit ['arbaɪt], f. (—, pl. —en) work, labour; job; employment; workmanship; an die — gehen, set to work.

arbeiten ['arbaɪtən], v.a., v.n. work, labour, toil.

Arbeiter ['arbaɪtər], m. (—s, pl. —) worker, workman, labourer, hand.

Arbeiterschaft ['arbaɪtərʃaft], f. (—, no pl.) working men; workers.

arbeitsam ['arbaɪtza:m], adj. industrious, diligent.

Arbeitsamt ['arbaɪtsamt], n. (—s, pl. ⁻er) labour exchange.

arbeitsfähig ['arbaɪtsfɛ:ɪç], adj. capable of working, able-bodied.

arbeitslos ['arbaɪtslo:s], adj. unemployed, out of work.

Arbeitslosigkeit ['arbaɪtslo:zɪçkaɪt], f. (—, no pl.) unemployment.

Arbeitsnachweis ['arbaɪtsnaxvaɪs], m. (—es, no pl.) labour exchange; (Am.) labour registry-office.

Arbeitssperre ['arbaɪtsʃpɛrə], f. (—, pl. —n) (Ind.) lock-out.

Archäologe [arçeo'lo:gə], m. (—n, pl. —n) archaeologist.

Arche ['arçə], f. (—, pl. —n) ark.

Archipel [arçi'pe:l], m. (—s, pl. —e) archipelago.

architektonisch [arçɪtɛk'to:nɪʃ], adj. architectural.

Archivar [arçi'va:r], m. (—s, pl. —e) keeper of archives.

arg [ark], adj. bad, wicked, mischievous.

Argentinien [argən'ti:njən], n. Argentina.

Ärger ['ɛrgər], m. (—s, no pl.) anger, annoyance.

ärgerlich ['ɛrgərlɪç], adj. annoying, aggravating, vexing; angry.

ärgern ['ɛrgərn], v.a. annoy, vex, make angry. — v.r. sich —, get annoyed.

Ärgernis ['ɛrgərnɪs], n. (—ses, pl. —se) scandal, nuisance.

arglistig ['arklɪstɪç], adj. crafty, sly.

arglos ['arklo:s], adj. unsuspecting, guileless, naive.

Argwohn ['arkvo:n], m. (—s, no pl.) mistrust, suspicion.

argwöhnisch ['arkvø:nɪʃ], adj. suspicious, distrustful.

Arie ['a:rjə], f. (—, pl. —n) (Mus.) aria.

Arm [arm], m. (—s, pl. —e) arm.

arm [arm], adj. poor, indigent, needy.

Armaturenbrett [arma'tu:rənbrɛt], n. (—s, no pl.) dashboard.

Armband ['armbant], n. (—s, pl. ⁻er) bracelet.

Armbanduhr ['armbantu:r], f. (—, pl. —en) wrist-watch.

Armbrust ['armbrust], f. (—, pl. —e) cross-bow.

Ärmel ['ɛrməl], m. (—s, pl. —) sleeve.

Ärmelkanal ['ɛrməlkana:l], m. (—s, no pl.) English Channel.

Armenien [ar'me:njən], n. Armenia.

Armenhaus ['armənhaus], n. (—es, pl. ⁻er) poor-house, almshouse.

Armenpfleger ['armənpfle:gər], m. (—s, pl. —) almoner.

Armesündermiene [armə'zyndərmi:nə], f. (—, pl. —n) hangdog look.

ärmlich ['ɛrmlɪç], adj. poor, shabby, scanty.

armselig ['armze:lɪç], adj. poor, miserable, wretched; paltry.

Armut ['armu:t], f. (—, no pl.) poverty; in — geraten, be reduced to penury.

Arsch [arʃ], m. (—es, ⁻e) (vulg.) arse.

Arsen(ik) [ar'ze:n(ik)], n. (—s, no pl.) arsenic.

Art [a:rt], f. (—, pl. —en) kind, species; race; sort; method, way, manner.

artig ['a:rtiç], adj. well-behaved, civil.

Artigkeit ['a:rtiçkait], f. (—, pl. —en) politeness, courtesy.

Artikel [ar'ti:kəl], m. (—s, pl. —) article; commodity.

Artist [ar'tist], m. (—en, pl. —en) artiste (circus, variety).

Arznei [arts'nai], f. (—, pl. —en) medicine.

Arzneimittel [arts'naimitəl], n. (—, pl.—) medicine, drug.

Arzt [artst], m. (—es, pl. ⁻e) doctor, physician; praktischer —, general practitioner.

ärztlich ['ɛrtstliç], adj. medical.

As (1) [as], n. (—ses, pl. —se) (Mus.) A flat; — Dur, A flat major, — Moll, A flat minor.

As (2) [as], n. (—sses, pl. —sse) (Sport, cards) ace.

Asbest [as'bɛst], m. (—s, no pl.) asbestos.

Asche ['aʃə], f. (—, no pl.) ashes.

Aschenbecher ['aʃənbɛçər], m. (—s, pl. —) ash-tray.

Aschenbrödel ['aʃənbrø:dəl] or **Aschenputtel** ['aʃənputəl], n. Cinderella.

Aschkraut ['aʃkraut], n. (—s, pl. ⁻er) (Bot.) cineraria.

Askese [as'ke:zə], f. (—, no pl.) asceticism.

Asket [as'ke:t], m. (—en, pl. —en) ascetic.

Assessor [a'sɛsɔr], m. (—s, pl. —en) assistant; assistant judge.

Ast [ast], m. (—es, pl. ⁻e) branch, bough.

Aster ['astər], f. (—, pl. —n) (Bot.) aster.

Astronaut [astro'naut], m. (—en, pl.—en) astronaut.

Astronom [astro'no:m], m. (—en, pl. —en) astronomer.

Asyl [a'zy:l], n. (—s, pl. —e) asylum, sanctuary.

Atem ['a:təm], m. (—s, no pl.) breath, breathing, respiration.

Atemzug ['a:təmtsu:k], m. (—s, pl. ⁻e) breath.

Äthiopien [ɛti'o:pjən], n. Ethiopia.

Atlas (1) ['atlas], m. (—sses, pl. —sse and **Atlanten**) atlas, book of maps.

Atlas (2) ['atlas], m. (—sses, pl. —asse) satin.

atmen ['a:tmən], v.n. breathe.

atomar [ato'ma:r], adj. atomic.

Attentat [atɛn'ta:t], n. (—s, pl. —e) attempt on s.o.'s life.

Attest [a'tɛst], n. (—s, pl. —e) (Med.) certificate.

ätzen ['ɛtsən], v.a. corrode; (Art) etch; (Med.) cauterise.

auch [aux], conj., adv. also, too, likewise, as well.

Au(e) ['au(ə)], f. (—, pl. —en) green meadow, pasture.

auf [auf], prep. on, upon; — der Straße, in the road; — deine Gefahr, at your own risk; — Befehl, by order; — einige Tage, for a few days; — dem Lande, in the country; — keinen Fall, on no account.

aufatmen ['aufa:tmən], v.n. breathe a sigh of relief.

Aufbau ['aufbau], m. (—s, no pl.) building; (Lit.) composition, structure.

aufbauen ['aufbauən], v.a. erect, build, construct.

aufbäumen ['aufbɔymən], v.r. sich —, (horses) rear.

aufbewahren ['aufbəva:rən], v.a. keep, store; (luggage) take charge of.

Aufbewahrung ['aufbəva:ruŋ], f. (—, pl. —en) storage, safe keeping.

aufbieten ['aufbi:tən], v.a. irr. call up for service; exert (energies).

aufbinden ['aufbindən], v.a. irr. untie; einem einen Bären —, to hoax s.o.

aufblähen ['aufblɛ:ən], v.a. puff up, swell, inflate.

aufblühen ['aufbly:ən], v.n. (aux. sein) flourish, unfold.

aufbrausen ['aufbrauzən], v.n. (aux. sein) fly into a rage.

aufbringen ['aufbriŋən], v.a. irr. bring up; afford; annoy (s.o.).

Aufbruch ['aufbrux], m. (—s, no pl.) departure.

aufbürden ['aufbyrdən], v.a. einem eine Last —, burden s.o. with a thing.

aufdecken ['aufdɛkən], v.a. uncover, unveil.

aufdonnern ['aufdɔnərn], v.r. sich — dress up showily.

aufdrängen ['aufdrɛŋən], v.a. einem etwas —, press s.th. upon s.o. — v.r. sich —, force o.'s company on.

aufdrehen ['aufdre:ən], v.a. (tap) turn on.

aufdringlich ['aufdriŋliç], adj. importunate, officious, obtrusive.

Aufdruck ['aufdruk], m. (—s, pl. —e) imprint.

aufdrücken ['aufdrykən], v.a. press open; press on s.th.

Aufenthalt ['aufɛnthalt], m. (—s, pl. —e) stay, sojourn; delay; stop.

auferlegen ['auferle:gən], v.a. impose; enjoin.

auferstehen ['auferʃte:ən], v.n. irr. (aux. sein) (Rel.) rise from the dead.

auffahren ['auffa:rən], v.n. irr. (aux. sein) start (from o.'s sleep); mount; flare up (in anger).

Auffahrt ['auffa:rt], f. (—, pl. —en) ascent; approach to a house, drive.

auffallen ['auffalən], v.n. irr. (aux. sein) strike the ground; einem —, strike s.o., astonish.

auffangen ['auffaŋən], v.a. irr. (ball) catch; (blow) parry, ward off; (letter) intercept.

auffassen ['auffasən], v.a. take in, comprehend.

Auffassung ['auffasuŋ], *f.* (—, *pl.* —en) conception, interpretation; view.

aufflackern ['aufflakərn],*v.n.* (*aux.* sein) flare up, flicker.

auffordern ['auffɔrdərn], *v.a.* summon, request, ask, invite.

aufforsten ['auffɔrstən], *v.a.* afforest.

auffressen ['auffrɛsən],*v.a. irr.* devour; (*of animals*) eat up.

auffrischen ['auffrɪʃən], *v.a.* renew, redecorate; (*fig.*) brush up.

aufführen ['auffy:rən], *v.a.* (*Theat.*) perform; *einzeln* —, specify, particularise. — *v.r. sich* —, behave, conduct o.s.

Aufführung ['auffy:ruŋ], *f.* (—, *pl.* —en) (*Theat.*) performance.

Aufgabe ['aufga:bə], *f.* (—, *pl.* —n) giving up, abandonment; (*letters, telegrams*) posting, despatch; (*work*) task; (*Sch.*) exercise; (*Maths.*) problem.

aufgabeln ['aufga:bəln], *v.a.* (*sl.*) pick up.

Aufgang ['aufgaŋ], *m.* (—s, *pl.* ⁻e) ascent, stairs.

aufgeben ['aufge:bən], *v.a. irr.* give up, abandon, relinquish; (*Am.*) quit; (*luggage*) check.

aufgeblasen ['aufgəbla:zən], *adj.* conceited, stuck up.

Aufgebot ['aufgəbo:t], *n.* (—s, *pl.* —e) (*marriage*) banns; (*Mil.*) levy; *mit — aller Kräfte*, with the utmost exertion.

aufgebracht ['aufgəbraxt], *adj.* angry, annoyed.

aufgedunsen ['aufgədunzən], *adj.* bloated, sodden.

aufgehen ['aufge:ən], *v.n. irr.* (*aux.* sein) (*knot*) come undone; (*sun*) rise; (*dough*) swell, rise; (*Maths.*) leave no remainder, cancel out.

aufgehoben ['aufgəho:bən], *adj. gut — sein*, be in good hands.

aufgelegt ['aufgəle:kt], *adj.* disposed, inclined.

aufgeräumt ['aufgərɔymt], *adj.* merry, cheerful, in high spirits.

aufgeweckt ['aufgəvɛkt], *adj.* bright, clever, intelligent.

aufgießen ['aufgi:sən], *v.a. irr. Kaffee* —, make coffee.

aufgreifen ['aufgraɪfən], *v.a. irr.* seize.

Aufguß ['aufgus], *m.* (—sses, *pl.* ⁻sse) infusion.

aufhalsen ['aufhalzən], *v.a. einem etwas* —, (*coll.*) saddle s.o. with s.th.

aufhalten ['aufhaltən], *v.a. irr.* (*door*) hold open; *einen* —, delay s.o. — *v.r. sich an einem Ort* —, stay at a place; *sich über etwas* —, find fault with s.th.

aufhängen ['aufhɛŋən], *v.a. irr.* hang (up).

aufhäufen ['aufhɔyfən], *v.a.* pile up. — *v.r. sich* —, accumulate.

Aufheben ['aufhe:bən], *n.* (—s, *no pl.*) lifting up; ado; *viel —s machen*, make a great fuss.

aufheben ['aufhe:bən], *v.a. irr.* lift (up), pick up; keep, preserve; (*laws*) repeal, abolish; (*agreements*) rescind, annul.

Aufhebung ['aufhe:buŋ], *f.* (—, *pl.* —en) abolition, abrogation, annulment, repeal.

aufheitern ['aufhaɪtərn], *v.a.* cheer up; amuse. — *v.r. sich* —, (*weather*) brighten, clear up.

aufhelfen ['aufhɛlfən], *v.n. irr. einem* —, help s.o. up.

aufhellen ['aufhɛlən], *v.r. sich* —, (*weather*) clear up; (*face*) brighten up.

aufhetzen ['aufhɛtsən],*v.a.* rouse (s.o.); *einen — gegen*, incite s.o. against.

aufhorchen ['aufhɔrçən], *v.n.* prick up o.'s ears.

aufhören ['aufhø:rən], *v.n.* cease, stop; (*Am.*) quit; *ohne aufzuhören*, incessantly; *da hört sich doch alles auf!* that is the limit!

aufklären ['aufklɛ:rən], *v.a.* enlighten; clear up; *einen* —, enlighten s.o. —*v.r. sich* —, (*weather*) brighten.

Aufklärung ['aufklɛ:ruŋ], *f.* (—, *no pl.*) (age of) Enlightenment.

aufknacken ['aufknakən], *v.a.* crack (open).

aufknöpfen ['aufknœpfən], *v.a.* unbutton; *aufgeknöpft sein*, be in a talkative mood.

aufkommen ['aufkɔmən], *v.n. irr.* (*aux.* sein) come into use, spring up; *für etwas* —, pay for s.th.; *einen nicht — lassen*, give s.o. no chance.

aufkrempeln ['aufkrɛmpəln],*v.a.* (*coll.*) roll up (o.'s sleeves).

aufkündigen ['aufkyndɪgən], *v.a.* (*money*) recall; *einem die Freundschaft* —, break with s.o.

Auflage ['aufla:gə], *f.* (—, *pl.* —n) (*tax*) impost, duty, levy; (*book*) edition, impression; circulation.

auflassen ['auflasən], *v.a. irr.* leave open; (*Law*) cede.

auflauern ['auflauərn], *v.n. einem* —, lie in wait for s.o., waylay s.o.

Auflauf ['auflauf], *m.* (—s, *pl.* ⁻e) tumult, noisy street gathering; soufflé.

auflaufen ['auflaufən], *v.n. irr.* (*aux.* sein) swell, increase; (*ship*) run aground.

aufleben ['aufle:bən], *v.n.* (*aux.* sein) *wieder* —, revive.

auflegen ['aufle:gən], *v.a. irr.* lay upon, put on; (*book*) publish; (*tax, punishment*) impose, inflict.

auflehnen ['aufle:nən], *v.r. sich gegen einen* (or *etwas*) —, rebel against, mutiny, oppose.

auflesen ['aufle:zən], *v.a. irr.* pick up, gather.

aufleuchten ['auflɔyçtən], *v.n.* light up; (*eyes*) shine.

auflockern ['auflɔkərn], *v.a.* loosen.

auflodern ['auflo:dərn], *v.n.* (*aux.* sein) flare up, blaze up.

auflösen

auflösen ['auflø:zən], v.a. dissolve, loosen; (puzzle) solve, guess; (meeting) break up; (business) wind up; (partnership) dissolve; (army) disband. — v.r. sich —, melt, dissolve, be broken up.

aufmachen ['aufmaxən], v.a. (door, packet) open; (knot) undo; gut —, pack nicely. — v.r. sich —, get going, set out for.

Aufmachung ['aufmaxuŋ], f. (—, pl. —en) outward appearance, make-up, get-up.

Aufmarsch ['aufmarʃ], m. (—es, pl. ⁻e) (Mil.) parade.

aufmerksam ['aufmɛrkza:m], adj. attentive, observant; civil, kind; einen — machen auf, draw s.o.'s attention to.

aufmuntern ['aufmuntərn], v.a. encourage, cheer up.

Aufnahme ['aufna:mə], f. (—, pl. —n) reception; (Phot.) snap, photograph; (Geog.) mapping out, survey; (Mus.) recording.

aufnehmen ['aufne:mən], v.a. irr. take up; receive, give shelter to; (Phot.) photograph, film; (Mus.) record; (money) raise, borrow; (minutes) draw up; den Faden wieder —, take up the thread; die Arbeit wieder —, return to work, resume work; die Fährte —, (Hunt.) recover the scent; es mit einem —, be a match for s.o.; (Comm.) Inventar —, take stock, draw up an inventory.

aufnötigen ['aufnø:tɪgən], v.a. einem etwas —, force s.th. upon s.o.

aufpassen ['aufpasən], v.n. attend to, pay attention to, take notice of, take care of.

aufpeitschen ['aufpaɪtʃən], v.a. whip up.

aufpflanzen ['aufpflantsən], v.a. mount, erect. — v.r. sich vor einem —, plant o.s. in front of s.o.; mit aufgepflanztem Bajonett, with bayonets fixed.

Aufputz ['aufputs], m. (—es, no pl.) finery, trimmings.

aufraffen ['aufrafən], v.a. snatch up, rake up. — v.r. sich wieder —, pull o.s. together.

aufräumen ['aufrɔymən], v.a. put in order, clear away; (room) tidy up; mit etwas —, make a clean sweep of s.th.; aufgeräumt sein, be in a jolly mood.

aufrechnen ['aufrɛçnən], v.a. reckon up; set off against.

aufrecht ['aufrɛçt], adj. upright, erect; etwas — erhalten, maintain s.th.; (opinion) stick to, adhere to, uphold.

Aufrechterhaltung ['aufrɛçtərhaltuŋ], f. (—, no pl.) maintenance, preservation.

aufregen ['aufre:gən], v.a. excite, enrage.

aufreiben ['aufraɪbən], v.a. irr. rub sore; (Mil.) destroy, wipe out. — v.r. sich —, exhaust o.s. with worry (or work).

aufreizen ['aufraɪtsən], v.a. incite, provoke.

aufrichten ['aufrɪçtən], v.a. raise, erect, set upright; (fig.) comfort, console. — v.r. sich —, rise, sit up.

aufrichtig ['aufrɪçtɪç], adj. sincere, frank.

aufriegeln ['aufri:gəln], v.a. unbolt.

Aufriß ['aufrɪs], m. (—sses, pl. —sse) sketch, draft; (Archit.) elevation, section.

aufrücken ['aufrykən], v.n. (aux. sein) rise, be promoted (in rank), advance.

Aufruf ['aufru:f], m. (—s, pl. —e) summons, proclamation, appeal; (Law) citation.

aufrufen ['aufru:fən], v.a. irr. summons; (Sch.) call upon.

Aufruhr ['aufru:r], m. (—s, pl. —e) uproar, riot, tumult, rebellion, mutiny.

aufrühren ['aufry:rən], v.a. stir up, agitate, rouse to rebellion.

Aufrüstung ['aufrystuŋ], f. (—, no pl.) (Mil.) (re-)armament.

aufrütteln ['aufrytəln], v.a. rouse, shake s.o. out of his lethargy.

aufsagen ['aufza:gən], v.a. recite.

aufsässig ['aufzɛsɪç], adj. refractory, rebellious.

Aufsatz ['aufzats], m. (—es, pl. ⁻e) top, head-piece, table centre-piece; (Sch.) composition, essay; (newspaper) article.

aufscheuchen ['aufʃɔyçən], v.a. flush (game), startle.

aufschichten ['aufʃɪçtən], v.a. stack, pile up in layers.

aufschieben ['aufʃi:bən], v.a. irr. push open; delay, postpone, adjourn; (Parl.) prorogue.

Aufschlag ['aufʃla:k], m. (—s, pl. ⁻e) impact, striking; (sleeve) cuff; turn-up; (uniform) facings; (Comm.) increase in price; (Tennis) service.

aufschlagen ['aufʃla:gən], v.n. irr. (aux. sein) hit, strike (open); (Tennis) serve. — v.a. die Augen —, open o.'s eyes; ein Lager —, pitch camp; ein Buch —, open a book.

aufschlitzen ['aufʃlɪtsən], v.a. rip open, slit open.

Aufschluß ['aufʃlus], m. (—sses, pl. ⁻sse) disclosure, information.

aufschneiden ['aufʃnaɪdən], v.a. irr. cut open. — v.n. brag, boast.

Aufschneider ['aufʃnaɪdər], m. (-s, pl. —) swaggerer, braggart.

Aufschnitt ['aufʃnɪt], m. (—s, no pl.) slice of cold meat or sausage.

aufschnüren ['aufʃny:rən], v.a. unlace, untie.

Aufschrei ['aufʃraɪ], m. (—s, pl. —e) outcry, screech, scream, shout, shriek.

Aufschrift ['aufʃrɪft], f. (—, pl. —en) inscription, address; heading.

Aufschub ['aufʃu:p], m. (—s, pl. ⁻e) delay, adjournment, postponement.

aufschütten ['aufʃytən], v.a. (liquid) pour upon; (dam) raise.

aufschwingen [ˈaufʃvɪŋən], *v.r. irr.*
sich —, soar, rise; *ich kann mich dazu
nicht* —, I cannot rise to that.
Aufschwung [ˈaufʃvuŋ], *m.* (—s, *no
pl.*) flight, rising; (*Comm.*) improvement, boom.
Aufsehen [ˈaufzeːən], *n.* (—s, *no pl.*)
sensation, stir.
Aufseher [ˈaufzeːər], *m.* (—s, *pl.* —)
overseer, inspector.
aufsein [ˈaufzaɪn], *v.n. irr.* (*aux.* sein)
be out of bed, be up and about.
aufsetzen [ˈaufzɛtsən], *v.a.* (*hat*) put on;
(*letter, essay*) draft.
Aufsicht [ˈaufzɪçt], *f.* (—, *no pl.*)
inspection, supervision, control.
Aufsichtsrat [ˈaufzɪçtsraːt], *m.* (—s,
pl. ⁇e) (*Comm.*) board of directors.
aufsitzen [ˈaufzɪtsən], *v.n. irr.* sit up,
wait up at night; (*horse*) mount.
aufspannen [ˈaufʃpanən], *v.a.* (*umbrella*)
put up; (*tent*) pitch.
aufspeichern [ˈaufʃpaɪçərn], *v.a.* store
(up), warehouse.
aufsperren [ˈaufʃpɛrən], *v.a.* open
wide, unlock.
aufspielen [ˈaufʃpiːlən], *v.n. zum Tanz*
—, play music for dancing. — *v.r.
sich groß* —, give o.s. airs.
aufspießen [ˈaufʃpiːsən], *v.a.* pieçce on
a spit; (*joint*) skewer.
aufspringen [ˈaufʃprɪŋən], *v.n. irr.*
(*aux.* sein) leap up, jump up; (*door*)
fly open; (*hands in winter*) chap.
aufspüren [ˈaufʃpyːrən], *v.a.* track, trace.
aufstacheln [ˈaufʃtaxəln], *v.a.* goad,
incite.
Aufstand [ˈaufʃtant], *m.* (—s, *pl.* ⁇e)
insurrection, revolt, sedition.
aufstapeln [ˈaufʃtaːpəln], *v.a.* pile up,
stack, store.
aufstechen [ˈaufʃtɛçən], *v.a. irr.* (*Med.*)
lance.
aufstehen [ˈaufʃteːən], *v.n. irr.* (*aux.*
sein) (*door*) stand open; stand up; get
up (from bed); rise (from a chair).
aufstellen [ˈaufʃtɛlən], *v.a.* set up,
arrange; erect; (*Pol.*) put forward
(candidate).
Aufstellung [ˈaufʃtɛluŋ], *f.* (—, *pl.*
—en) arrangement; statement; inventory; (*Pol.*) nomination.
aufstemmen [ˈaufʃtɛmən], *v.a.* prise
open.
Aufstieg [ˈaufʃtiːk], *m.* (—s, *pl.* —e)
ascent, rise.
aufstöbern [ˈaufʃtøːbərn], *v.a.* stir (up);
start; (*fig.*) discover, ferret out.
aufstoßen [ˈaufʃtoːsən], *v.a. irr.* push
open; bump against. — *v.n.* belch.
aufstreben [ˈaufʃtreːbən], *v.n.* soar;
(*fig.*) aspire.
aufstreichen [ˈaufʃtraɪçən], *v.a. irr.*
(*paint*) lay on; (*butter*) spread.
aufstülpen [ˈaufʃtylpən], *v.a.* turn up;
(*hat*) clap on o.'s head.
auftakeln [ˈaufzaːkəln], *v.a.* (*Naut.*)
rig.
Auftakt [ˈauftakt], *m.* (—s, *pl.* —e)
(*Mus.*) arsis; (*fig.*) opening, prelude.

auftauchen [ˈauftauxən], *v.n.* (*aux.*
sein) appear, emerge, surface.
auftauen [ˈauftauən], *v.n.* (*aux.* sein)
thaw; (*fig.*) lose o.'s reserve.
auftischen [ˈauftɪʃən], *v.a.* dish up.
Auftrag [ˈauftraːk], *m.* (—s, *pl.* ⁇e)
assignment, commission, errand; *im
— von*, on behalf of.
auftragen [ˈauftraːgən], *v.a. irr.* (*food*)
serve up; (*paint*) apply; *einem etwas
—*, charge s.o. with a job; *stark —*,
lay it on thick.
auftreiben [ˈauftraɪbən], *v.a. irr.* raise
(*money*); procure, obtain. — *v.n.*
(*aux.* sein) (*ship*) run aground.
auftrennen [ˈauftrɛnən], *v.a.* unstitch;
(*hem*) unpick.
Auftreten [ˈauftreːtən], *n.* (—s, *no pl.*)
(*Theat.*) appearance; behaviour.
auftreten [ˈauftreːtən], *v.n. irr.* (*aux.*
sein) tread upon, step upon; (*Theat.*)
appear, come on; *energisch —*, take
strong measures, put o.'s foot
down.
Auftritt [ˈauftrɪt], *m.* (—s, *pl.* —e)
(*Theat.*) scene; altercation, row.
auftun [ˈauftuːn], *v.a. irr.* open; *den
Mund —*, speak. — *v.r. sich —*, (*abyss*)
yawn.
auftürmen [ˈauftʏrmən], *v.a.* pile up,
heap up. — *v.r. sich —*, tower.
aufwachen [ˈaufvaxən], *v.n.* (*aux.* sein)
awake, wake up.
aufwallen [ˈaufvalən], *v.n.* (*aux.* sein)
boil up, bubble up, rage.
Aufwand [ˈaufvant], *m.* (—s, *no pl.*)
expense, expenditure; sumptuous-
ness.
aufwarten [ˈaufvartən], *v.n.* wait upon,
attend on.
aufwärts [ˈaufvɛrts], *adv.* upward(s),
aloft.
Aufwartung [ˈaufvartuŋ], *f.* (—, *pl.*
—en) attendance; *seine — machen*, pay
a (formal) visit.
aufwaschen [ˈaufvaʃən], *v.a. irr.* wash
the dishes.
aufweisen [ˈaufvaɪzən], *v.a. irr.* show,
produce.
aufwenden [ˈaufvɛndən], *v.a. irr.*
spend upon, expend upon.
aufwickeln [ˈaufvɪkəln], *v.a.* wind up;
unwind.
aufwiegeln [ˈaufviːgəln], *v.a.* stir up,
incite to rebellion.
aufwiegen [ˈaufviːgən], *v.a. irr.* outweigh, counter-balance, make up
for.
aufwischen [ˈaufvɪʃən], *v.a.* wipe away,
mop up.
aufwühlen [ˈaufvyːlən], *v.a.* dig, root
up, (*fig.*) stir.
aufzählen [ˈaufzɛːlən], *v.a.* count up,
enumerate, list.
aufzäumen [ˈaufzɔymən], *v.a.* bridle
(horses).
aufzehren [ˈaufzeːrən], *v.a.* eat up,
consume.
aufzeichnen [ˈaufzaɪçnən], *v.a.* write
down, take a note of, record.

aufziehen [´auftsi:ən], *v.a. irr.* draw up, pull up; pull open; (*pennant*) hoist; (*clock*) wind up; (*child*) bring up, rear; *einen* —, tease s.o.; *gelindere Saiten* —, be more lenient.

Aufzucht [´auftsuxt], *f.* (—, *no pl.*) breeding, rearing.

Aufzug [´auftsu:k], *m.* (—s, *pl.* ¨e) lift; (*Am.*) elevator; (*Theat.*) act; dress, array, attire.

aufzwingen [´auftsvɪŋən], *v.a. irr. einem etwas* —, force s.th. on s.o.

Augapfel [´augapfəl], *m.* (—s, *pl.* ¨) eye-ball; (*fig.*) apple of o.'s eye.

Auge [´augə], *n.* (—s, *pl.* —n) eye; *aus den* —*n, aus dem Sinn,* out of sight, out of mind; *mit einem blauen* — *davonkommen,* escape by the skin of o.'s teeth, get off cheaply; *es wird mir schwarz vor den* —*n,* I feel faint.

Augenblick [´augənblɪk], *m.* (—s, *pl.* —e) moment, instant; *jeden* —, at any moment.

augenblicklich [augən´blɪklɪç], *adj.* momentary, instantaneous.— *adv.* at present, for the moment, immediately.

Augenbraue [´augənbrauə], *f.* (—, *pl.* —n) eye-brow.

augenfällig [´augənfɛlɪç], *adj.* visible, evident, conspicuous.

Augenglas [´augənglas], *n.* (—es, *pl.* ¨er) eye-glass.

Augenhöhle [´augənhø:lə], *f.* (—, *pl.* —n) eye-socket.

Augenlicht [´augənlɪçt], *n.* (—s, *no pl.*) eye-sight.

Augenlid [´augənli:t], *n.* (—s, *pl.* —er) eye-lid.

Augenmaß [´augənma:s], *n.* (—es, *no pl.*) *gutes* —, good measuring ability with the eye, a sure eye.

Augenmerk [´augənmɛrk], *n.* (—s, *no pl.*) attention; *sein* — *auf etwas richten,* focus o.'s attention on s.th.

Augenschein [´augənʃain], *m.* (—s, *no pl.*) appearance; *in* — *nehmen,* view.

augenscheinlich [´augənʃainlɪç], *adj.* apparent, evident.

Augenweide [´augənvaidə], *f.* (—, *pl.* —n) delight to the eye, s.th. lovely to look at.

Augenwimper [´augənvɪmpər], *f.* (—, *pl.* —n) eye-lash.

Augenzeuge [´augəntsɔygə], *m.* (—n, *pl.* —n) eye-witness.

August [au´gust], *m.* (—s, *no pl.*) (*month*) August.

Augustiner [augus´ti:nər], *m.* (—s, *pl.* —) (*Eccl.*) Augustinian.

auktionieren [auktsjo´ni:rən], *v.a.* auction(eer), sell by auction.

Aula [´aula], *f.* (—, *pl.* —len) (*Sch., Univ.*) great hall; auditorium maximum.

Aurikel [au´ri:kəl], *f.* (—, *pl.* —n) (*Bot.*) auricula.

aus [aus], *prep.* (*Dat.*) from, out of, of, off. — *adv.* out, over, finished, done with, spent; *es ist alles* —, it is over and done with; *ich weiß weder ein noch* —, I am at my wits' end.

ausarten [´ausartən], *v.n.* (*aux.* sein) degenerate; (*fig.*) deteriorate.

Ausbau [´ausbau], *m.* (—s, *no pl.*) enlargement, extension.

ausbauen [´ausbauən], *v.a.* enlarge (a house); improve on.

ausbedingen [´ausbədɪŋən], *v.a. sich etwas* —, stipulate.

ausbessern [´ausbɛsərn], *v.a.* (*garment*) mend, repair.

Ausbeute [´ausbɔytə], *f.* (—, *no pl.*) gain, profit, produce.

Ausbeutung [´ausbɔytuŋ], *f.* (—, *no pl.*) exploitation, sweating; (*Min.*) working.

ausbezahlen [´ausbətsa:lən], *v.a.* pay in full.

ausbilden [´ausbɪldən], *v.a.* develop, train; (*Mil.*) drill.

Ausbildung [´ausbɪlduŋ], *f.* (—, *pl.* —en) training, education.

ausbleiben [´ausblaibən], *v.n. irr.* (*aux.* sein) fail to appear, be absent.

Ausblick [´ausblik], *m.* (—s, *pl.* —e) view (from window); (*fig.*) prospect, outlook.

ausborgen [´ausbɔrgən], *v.a.* (*sich*) *etwas* —, borrow s.th. from.

ausbreiten [´ausbraitən], *v.a.* spread (things); stretch out (o.'s arms). — *v.r. sich* —, spread, extend.

Ausbreitung [´ausbraituŋ], *f.* (—, *no pl.*) spreading, extension, distribution, expansion.

ausbringen [´ausbrɪŋən], *v.a. irr. einen Toast auf einen* —, drink s.o.'s health.

Ausbruch [´ausbrux], *m.* (—s, *pl.* ¨e) breaking out, outbreak, eruption, burst (of laughter).

ausbrüten [´ausbry:tən], *v.a.* hatch; (*fig.*) plot.

Ausbund [´ausbunt], *m.* (—s, *pl.* ¨e) paragon, embodiment.

Ausdauer [´ausdauər], *f.* (—, *no pl.*) perseverance, persistence, stamina.

ausdehnen [´ausde:nən], *v.a.* extend, stretch, distend; (*fig.*) prolong, protract. — *v.r. sich* —, expand, extend, stretch.

Ausdehnung [´ausde:nuŋ], *f.* (—, *pl.* —en) extension, expansion; dilation; (*Phys.*) dimension.

ausdenken [´ausdɛŋkən], *v.a. irr.* think out. — *v.r. sich etwas* —, devise s.th., invent s.th.; *das ist gar nicht auszudenken,* that is unimaginable, inconceivable.

Ausdeutung [´ausdɔytuŋ], *f.* (—, *pl.* —en) interpretation, explanation.

ausdörren [´ausdœrən], *v.a.* parch, dry (up).

ausdrehen [´ausdre:ən], *v.a.* (*gas, light, water*) turn off, switch off.

Ausdruck [´ausdruk], *m.* (—s, *pl.* ¨e) expression, phrase.

ausdrücken [´ausdrykən], *v.a.* squeeze out, press out; (*fig.*) express.

ausdrücklich [´ausdryklɪç], *adj.* express, explicit.

Ausdrucksweise ['ausdruksvaɪzə], *f.* (—, *pl.* —n) enunciation, manner of speech, (mode of) expression, style.

ausdünsten ['ausdynstən], *v.a.* exhale, perspire.

auseinander [ausaɪn'andər], *adv.* asunder, apart.

Auseinandersetzung [ausaɪn'andərzɛtsuŋ], *f.* (—, *pl.* —en) altercation; discussion, explanation.

auserkoren ['ausɛrko:rən], *adj.* elect, chosen, selected.

auserlesen ['ausɛrle:zən], *adj.* choice, picked, excellent, first class.

auserwählen ['ausɛrvɛ:lən], *v.a.* choose, select.

Ausfahrt ['ausfa:rt], *f.* (—, *pl.* —en) drive; gateway; exit.

Ausfall ['ausfal], *m.* (—s, *pl.* ⁝e) falling out; (*radioactivity*) fall-out; sortie, sally; deficiency, loss, cancellation; ·result, outcome.

ausfallen ['ausfalən], *v.n. irr.* (*aux.* sein) drop out, fall out; be cancelled, be omitted, fail to take place; turn out (well etc.).

ausfallend ['ausfalənt], *adj.* offensive, abusive; — *werden*, become insulting.

ausfertigen ['ausfɛrtɪgən], *v.a.* despatch, draw up, make out, issue.

ausfindig ['ausfɪndɪç], *adj.* — *machen*, find out, locate, discover.

ausflicken ['ausflɪkən], *v.a.* mend, patch.

Ausflucht ['ausfluxt], *f.* (—, *pl.* ⁝e) evasion, excuse, subterfuge.

Ausflug ['ausflu:k], *m.* (—s, *pl.* ⁝e) trip, excursion, outing.

Ausfluß ['ausflus], *m.* (—sses, *pl.* ⁝sse) (*Engin.*) outflow, outlet; (*Med.*) discharge, suppuration.

ausfragen ['ausfra:gən], *v.a. einen* —, question, quiz s.o.

Ausfuhr ['ausfu:r], *f.* (—, *pl.* —en) export.

ausführbar ['ausfy:rba:r], *adj.* practicable, feasible; exportable.

ausführen ['ausfy:rən], *v.a.* take out; lead out; export; carry out, perform, fulfil; point out.

ausführlich [aus'fy:rlɪç], *adj.* detailed, full.

Ausführung ['ausfy:ruŋ], *f.* (—, *pl.* —en) execution, carrying out; finish; workmanship.

ausfüllen ['ausfylən], *v.a.* (*forms*) fill up, fill in, complete.

ausfüttern ['ausfytərn], *v.a.* line (a dress).

Ausgabe ['ausga:bə], *f.* (—, *pl.* —en) issue, distribution; (*goods*) dispatch, issuing counter; delivery; (*book*) edition; (*pl.*) expenses, expenditure.

Ausgang ['ausgaŋ], *m.* (—s, *pl.* ⁝e) going out; exit; result, upshot; end, conclusion; time off (from duty).

Ausgangspunkt ['ausgaŋspuŋkt], *m.* (—s, *pl.* ⁝e) starting-point; point of departure.

ausgären ['ausgɛ:rən], *v.n. irr.* (*aux.* sein) ferment; *ausgegoren sein*, have fermented.

ausgeben ['ausge:bən], *v.a. irr.* (*work*) give out, distribute; (*money*) expend, spend; (*tickets*) issue. —*v.r. sich — für*, pass o.s. off as.

ausgebreitet ['ausgəbraɪtət], *adj.* extensive, widespread.

Ausgeburt ['ausgəburt], *f.* (—, *pl.* —en) monstrosity; — *des Hirns*, figment of the imagination.

ausgefahren ['ausgəfa:rən], *adj.* (*street*) rutted, well-worn.

ausgehen ['ausge:ən], *v.n. irr.* (*aux.* sein) go out; (*hair*) to fall out; (*colour*) come off, fade; (*breath, patience, money*) become exhausted; result, end in.

ausgelassen ['ausgəlasən], *adj.* boisterous, exuberant, frolicsome, merry, jolly, unbridled.

ausgemacht ['ausgəmaxt], *adj.* arranged, settled, decided; *eine —e Sache*, a matter of course, a foregone conclusion; *ein —er Schurke*, a downright scoundrel.

ausgeschlossen ['ausgəʃlɔsən], *p.p. das ist —*, that is impossible, out of the question.

ausgewachsen ['ausgəvaksən], *adj.* full-grown, fully grown.

ausgezeichnet ['ausgətsaɪçnət], *adj.* excellent, first rate, distinguished.

ausgiebig ['ausgi:bɪç], *adj.* abundant, plentiful; (*soil*) fertile, rich.

ausgießen ['ausgi:sən], *v.a. irr.* pour out.

Ausgleich ['ausglaɪç], *m.* (—s, *no pl.*) settlement, compromise, compensation, equalisation.

ausgleichen ['ausglaɪçən], *v.a. irr.* make even, balance, equalise, compensate; (*sport*) equalise, draw.

ausgraben ['ausgra:bən], *v.a. irr.* dig out, dig up, excavate, exhume.

Ausguck ['ausguk], *m.* (—s, *pl.* —e) look-out; (*Naut.*) crow's nest.

Ausguß ['ausgus], *m.* (—sses, *pl.* ⁝sse) sink, gutter.

aushalten ['aushaltən], *v.a. irr.* sustain, endure, bear, stand.

aushändigen ['aushɛndɪgən], *v.a.* deliver up, hand over.

Aushang ['aushaŋ], *m.* (—s, *pl.* ⁝e) sign, sign-board, placard.

ausharren ['ausharən], *v.n.* persevere, hold out, wait patiently.

aushecken ['aushɛkən], *v.a.* hatch (a plot).

aushelfen ['aushɛlfən], *v.n. irr.* help out.

Aushilfe ['aushɪlfə], *f.* (—, *pl.* —n) help, aid, assistance.

aushilfsweise ['aushɪlfsvaɪzə], *adv.* temporarily, as a stop-gap.

aushöhlen ['ausho:lən], *v.a.* hollow out, excavate.

ausholen ['ausho:lən], *v.a.* pump, sound s.o. — *v.n.* strike out; *weit —*, go far back (in a narration).

auskehren ['auske:rən], *v.a.* sweep out.

auskennen ['auskɛnən], *v.r. irr. sich in etwas* —, know all about s.th.

auskleiden ['ausklaIdən], *v.a.* undress.

ausklingen ['ausklɪŋən], *v.n. irr. (aux. sein) (sound)* die away.

ausklügeln ['auskly:gəln], *v.a.* puzzle out, contrive.

auskneifen ['ausknaIfən], *v.n. irr. (aux. sein) (coll.)* bolt, run away.

Auskommen ['auskɔmən], *n.* (—**s**, *no pl.*) sufficiency, subsistence, livelihood; *mit dem ist kein* —, there is no getting on with him.

auskommen ['auskɔmən], *v.n. irr. (aux. sein) mit etwas* —, have enough *or* sufficient of s.th., manage; *mit einem gut* —, be on good terms with s.o., get on well with s.o.

auskömmlich ['auskœmlɪç], *adj.* sufficient.

auskosten ['auskɔstən], *v.a.* taste *or* enjoy to the full.

auskramen ['auskra:mən], *v.a.* rummage out; *(fig.)* reminisce; talk freely.

auskundschaften ['auskuntʃaftən], *v.a.* spy out, reconnoitre, explore.

Auskunft ['auskunft], *f.* (—, *pl.* ‥e) information; *(Tel.)* enquiries; *(Mil.)* intelligence, enquiry.

auslachen ['auslaxən], *v.a.* laugh at, deride.

ausladen ['ausla:dən], *v.a. irr.* unload, discharge; cancel (invitation).

Auslage ['ausla:gə], *f.* (—, *pl.* —**n**) outlay, expenses, advance; shop-window display.

Ausland ['auslant], *n.* (—**s**, *no pl.*) foreign country; *ins* — *fahren*, go abroad.

Ausländer ['auslɛndər], *m.* (—**s**, *pl.* —) foreigner, alien.

auslassen ['auslasən], *v.a. irr.* let off (steam); let out (a dress); melt (butter); leave off, omit. — *v.r. sich über etwas* —, speak o.'s mind about s.th.

Auslassung ['auslasuŋ], *f.* (—, *pl.* —**en**) utterance; omission.

auslaufen ['auslaufən], *v.n. irr. (aux. sein)* run out, leak out; *(ship)* put to sea; *(result)* turn out.

Ausläufer ['auslɔyfər], *m.* (—**s**, *pl.* —) errand boy; *(mountain)* spur.

Auslaut ['auslaut], *m.* (—**s**, *pl.* —**e**) *(Phonet.)* final sound.

auslegen ['ausle:gən], *v.a.* lay out, spread out, display; interpret; *(money)* advance.

ausleihen ['auslaIən], *v.a. irr.* lend, hire out. — *v.r. sich etwas* —, borrow s.th.

auslernen ['auslɛrnən], *v.n.* end o.'s apprenticeship.

ausliefern ['ausli:fərn], *v.a.* hand over, deliver; surrender, give up, extradite.

auslöschen ['auslœʃən], *v.a.* extinguish, put out (fire).

auslosen ['auslo:zən], *v.a.* raffle, draw lots for.

auslösen ['auslø:zən], *v.a.* redeem, ransom, recover; *(fig.)* produce; arouse.

Auslosung ['auslo:zuŋ], *f.* (—, *pl.* —**en**) raffle, draw.

Auslösung ['auslø:zuŋ], *f.* (—, *pl.* —**en**) ransom.

auslüften ['auslyftən], *v.a.* air, ventilate.

ausmachen ['ausmaxən], *v.a.* decide, settle; amount to; *etwas mit einem* —, arrange s.th. with s.o.; *es macht nichts aus*, it does not matter; *wieviel macht das aus?* how much is this? *würde es Ihnen etwas* —? would you mind?

Ausmaß ['ausma:s], *n.* (—**es**, *pl.* —**e**) dimension, amount, extent, scale.

ausmeißeln ['ausmaIsəln], *v.a.* chisel out, carve out.

ausmerzen ['ausmertsən], *v.a.* expunge, eradicate.

ausmisten ['ausmIstən], *v.a.* clean, clear up (mess).

ausmustern ['ausmustərn], *v.a.* eliminate, reject; *(Mil.)* discharge.

Ausnahme ['ausna:mə], *f.* (—, *pl.* —**n**) exception.

ausnehmen ['ausne:mən], *v.a. irr.* except, exclude; *(poultry)* draw; *(fish)* clean.

ausnutzen ['ausnutsən], *v.a.* make the most of s.th.; take advantage of s.th.

ausnützen ['ausnytsən], *v.a.* exploit.

auspacken ['auspakən], *v.a.* unpack. — *v.n.* talk freely; *(coll.)* open up.

auspfeifen ['auspfaIfən], *v.a. irr.* *(Theat.)* hiss at, cat-call.

auspolstern ['auspɔlstərn], *v.a.* stuff.

ausprägen ['ausprɛ:gən], *v.a.* stamp, impress, coin.

ausprobieren ['ausprobi:rən], *v.a.* try out.

Auspuff ['auspuf], *m.* (—**s**, *no pl.*) *(Motor.)* exhaust.

auspusten ['auspu:stən], *v.a.* blow out.

ausputzen ['ausputsən], *v.a.* clean out; adorn.

ausquartieren ['auskvarti:rən], *v.a.* *(Mil.)* billet out.

ausquetschen ['auskvɛtʃən], *v.a.* squeeze out.

ausradieren ['ausradi:rən], *v.a.* erase.

ausrangieren ['ausranʒi:rən], *v.a.* cast off, sort out.

ausräuchern ['ausrɔyçərn], *v.a.* fumigate.

ausraufen ['ausraufən], *v.a. (obs.)* tear *or* pull out (hair).

ausräumen ['ausrɔymən], *v.a.* clear out, clear away.

ausrechnen ['ausrɛçnən], *v.a.* reckon, compute, calculate; *ausgerechnet du*, *(emph.)* you of all people.

ausrecken ['ausrɛkən], *v.a. sich den Hals* —, crane o.'s neck.

Ausrede ['ausre:də], *f.* (—, *pl.* —**n**) evasion, excuse, subterfuge.

ausreden ['ausre:dən], *v.a. einem etwas* —, dissuade s.o. from s.th. — *v.n.* finish speaking; *einen* — *lassen*, allow s.o. to finish speaking.

ausreichen ['ausraıçən], *v.n.* suffice.
ausreißen ['ausraısən], *v.a. irr.* pluck, pull out. — *v.n.* (*aux.* sein) run away, bolt.
ausrenken ['ausreŋkən], *v.a.* dislocate, sprain.
ausrichten ['ausrıçtən], *v.a.* adjust, make straight; deliver (a message); accomplish; (*Mil.*) dress.
ausrotten ['ausrɔtən], *v.a.* root up; exterminate, extirpate.
ausrücken ['ausrykən], *v.n.* (*aux.* sein) (*Mil.*) march out; (*coll.*) decamp.
Ausruf ['ausru:f], *m.* (—**s**, *pl.* —**e**) exclamation, interjection, outcry; (*public*) proclamation.
Ausruf(ungs)zeichen ['ausru:f(uŋs)-tsaıçən], *n.* (—**s**, *pl.* —) exclamation mark.
ausruhen ['ausru:ən], *v.r. sich* —, rest, take a rest.
ausrüsten ['ausrystən], *v.a.* furnish, fit out, equip.
Ausrutschen ['ausrutʃən], *v.n.* (*aux.* sein) slip.
Aussage ['ausza:gə], *f.* (—, *pl.* —**n**) declaration, statement, evidence; (*Law*) deposition, affidavit; (*Gram.*) predicate.
aussagen ['ausza:gən], *v.a.* say, state, utter, declare; (*Law*) depose, give evidence.
Aussatz ['auszats], *m.* (—**es**, *no pl.*) leprosy.
Aussätzige ['auszɛtsıgə], *m.* (—**n**, *pl.* —**n**) leper.
aussaugen ['auszaugən], *v.a.* suck dry.
ausschalten ['ausʃaltən], *v.a.* switch off.
Ausschank ['ausʃaŋk], *m.* (—**s**, *no pl.*) pub, bar.
Ausschau ['ausʃau], *f.* (—, *no pl.*) watch; — *halten*, look out for.
ausscheiden ['ausʃaıdən], *v.a. irr.* separate; (*Med.*) secrete. — *v.n.* (*aux.* sein) withdraw from, retire, secede.
Ausscheidung ['ausʃaıduŋ], *f.* (—, *pl.* —**en**) retirement, withdrawal; (*Med.*) secretion.
Ausschlag ['ausʃla:k], *m.* (—**s**, *pl.* —**e**) turn (of the scales); deflection (of the magnetic needle); (*Med.*) rash, eczema; *den* — *geben*, clinch the matter; give the casting vote.
ausschlagen ['ausʃla:gən], *v.a. irr.* knock out; refuse, decline (an invitation); *das schlägt dem Faß den Boden aus*, that is the last straw. — *v.n.* (*aux.* sein) (*Hort.*) bud, shoot; *gut* —, turn out well.
auschlaggebend ['ausʃla:kge:bənt], *adj.* decisive; (*vote*) casting.
ausschließen ['ausʃli:sən], *v.a. irr.* lock out; exclude.
ausschließlich ['ausʃli:slıç], *adj.* exclusive, sole.
ausschlüpfen ['ausʃlypfən], *v.n.* (*aux.* sein) hatch out.
Ausschluß ['ausʃlus], *m.* (—**sses**, *pl.* ·**sse**) exclusion; *unter* — *der Öffentlichkeit*, in camera.

ausschmücken ['ausʃmykən], *v.a.* adorn, decorate, embellish.
Ausschnitt ['ausʃnıt], *m.* (—**s**, *pl.* —**e**) cutting out; (*newspaper*) cutting; (*dress*) neck (line).
ausschreiben ['ausʃraıbən], *v.a. irr.* write down in full; make out a bill; advertise (post) as vacant.
ausschreiten ['ausʃraıtən], *v.n. irr.* (*aux.* sein) step out, stride along.
Ausschreitungen ['ausʃraıtuŋən], *f. pl.* rioting; excesses.
Ausschuß ['ausʃus], *m.* (—**sses**, *pl.* ·**sse**) dross, refuse, rejects, low quality goods; committee, commission, board.
ausschweifend ['ausʃvaıfənt], *adj.* extravagant; licentious, dissolute.
aussehen ['ausze:ən], *v.n. irr.* look; look like, appear.
außen ['ausən], *adv.* outside, abroad, outward, without.
Außenhandel ['ausənhandəl], *m.* (—**s**, *no pl.*) export trade.
Außenministerium .['ausənmınıste:r-jum], *n.* (—**s**, *pl.* —**terien**) Ministry of Foreign Affairs; (*U.K.*) Foreign Office, (*U.S.*) State Department.
Außenstände ['ausənʃtɛndə], *m. pl.* outstanding claims, liabilities.
außer ['ausər], *prep.* (*Dat.*) in addition to, besides, apart from; out of, at the outside of, beside, without; — *Dienst*, retired. — *conj.* except, save, but.
außerdem ['ausərde:m], *adv.* besides, moreover, furthermore.
Äussere ['ɔysərə], *n.* (—**n**, *no pl.*) exterior.
außerehelich ['ausəre:əlıç], *adj.* illegitimate.
außergewöhnlich ['ausərgəvø:nlıç], *adj.* unusual, exceptional.
außerhalb ['ausərhalp], *prep.* outside.
äußerlich ['ɔysərlıç], *adj.* external.
Äußerlichkeit ['ɔysərlıçkaıt], *f.* (—, —**en**) formality.
äußern ['ɔysərn], *v.a.* utter, express. — *v.r. sich zu etwas* —, give o.'s opinion on some question; express o.s. on some subject.
außerordentlich [ausər'ɔrdəntlıç], *adj.* extraordinary, unusual; (*Univ.*) —*er Professor*, senior lecturer or reader; (*Am.*) associate professor.
äußerst ['ɔysərst], *adj.* outermost, most remote; extreme, utmost.
außerstande ['ausərʃtandə], *adj.* unable.
Äußerung ['ɔysəruŋ], *f.* (—, *pl.* —**en**) utterance, remark, observation.
aussetzen ['auszɛtsən], *v.a.* set out, put out; offer (a reward); suspend; *etwas an einer Sache* —, find fault with s.th.; *sich einer Gefahr* —, expose o.s. to danger, run a risk. — *v.n.* pause, discontinue; (*Motor.*) stop, misfire.
Aussicht ['auszıçt], *f.* (—, *pl.* —**en**) view, panorama; prospect, chance; *etwas in* — *stellen*, hold out the prospect of s.th.; *in* — *nehmen*, intend.

aussinnen [ˈauszɪnən],*v. a. irr.* imagine, invent, devise.

aussöhnen [ˈauszøːnən], *v.r. sich mit einem —*, become reconciled with s.o.

aussondern [ˈauszɔndərn], *v.a.* single out.

ausspannen [ˈausʃpanən], *v.a. (animals)* unharness. — *v.n. (coll.)* relax.

ausspeien [ˈausʃpaɪən], *v.a.* spit out, vomit.

aussperren [ˈausʃpɛrən], *v.a.* shut out; *(industrial)* lock out.

ausspielen [ˈausʃpiːlən], *v.n.* finish playing; *(Sport, Game)* lead (off).

Aussprache [ˈausʃpraːxə], *f.* (—, *no pl.*) pronunciation; discussion; confidential talk.

aussprechen [ˈausʃprɛçən], *v.a. irr.* have o.'s say; utter; pronounce. — *v.r. sich —*, speak o.'s mind.

Ausspruch [ˈausʃprux], *m.* (—s, *pl.* ꞊e) utterance, dictum.

ausspüren [ˈausʃpyːrən], *v.a. (Hunt.)* track down.

ausstaffieren [ˈausʃtafiːrən],*v.a.*furnish, equip.

Ausstand [ˈausʃtant], *m.* (—s, *pl.* ꞊e) *(industry)* strike; *(pl.)* outstanding debts, arrears.

ausständig [ˈausʃtɛndɪç], *adj.* outstanding; on strike.

ausstatten [ˈausʃtatən], *v.a.* endow with, provide with, equip.

Ausstattung [ˈausʃtatuŋ], *f.* (—, *pl.* —en) outfit; (bridal) trousseau; *(coll.)* get-up.

ausstechen [ˈausʃtɛçən], *v.a. irr.* pierce; *einen —*, (*fig.*) excel s.o.

ausstehen [ˈausʃteːən], *v.n. irr.* stand out; *(money)* be overdue. — *v.a.* endure, suffer, bear, undergo; *ich kann ihn nicht —*, I cannot stand him.

aussteigen [ˈausʃtaɪɡən], *v.n. irr. (aux. sein)* get out, alight; disembark.

ausstellen [ˈausʃtɛlən], *v.a.* exhibit; display; make out (bill etc.).

Aussteller [ˈausʃtɛlər], *m.* (—s, *pl.* —) drawer (of a cheque); exhibitor.

Ausstellung [ˈausʃtɛluŋ], *f.* (—, *pl.* —en) exhibition; *(Am.)* exposition.

Aussteuer [ˈausʃtɔyər], *f.* (—, *pl.* —n) trousseau.

ausstopfen [ˈausʃtɔpfən], *v.a.* stuff.

ausstoßen [ˈausʃtoːsən], *v.a. irr.* push out, expel; utter.

Ausstrahlung [ˈausʃtraːluŋ], *f.* (—, *pl.* —en) radiation.

ausstrecken [ˈausʃtrɛkən], *v.a.* stretch out, reach out, extend.

ausstreichen [ˈausʃtraɪçən], *v.a. irr.* strike out, erase, delete; smoothe.

ausstreuen [ˈausʃtrɔyən], *v.a.* scatter, spread, sprinkle; *Gerüchte —*, circulate rumours.

ausstudieren [ˈausʃtudiːrən], *v.n.* finish o.'s studies, graduate.

aussuchen [ˈauszuːxən], *v.a.* select.

Austausch [ˈaustauʃ], *m.* (—es, *pl.* —e) barter, exchange; *(thoughts, letters)* interchange.

austauschen [ˈaustauʃən], *v.a.* barter, exchange; *(thoughts, letters)* interchange.

austeilen [ˈaustaɪlən], *v.a.* distribute, allocate.

Auster [ˈaustər], *f.* (—, *pl.* —n) oyster.

Austerbank [ˈaustərbaŋk], *f.* (—, *pl.* ꞊e) oyster-bed.

austilgen [ˈaustɪlɡən], *v.a.* exterminate, eradicate, extirpate.

Australien [auˈstraːljən], *n.* Australia.

austreiben [ˈaustraɪbən], *v.a. irr.* drive out, expel; exorcise.

austreten [ˈaustreːtən], *v.a. irr.* tread out; stretch (shoes) by walking; *ausgetretene Stufen*, worn steps. — *v.n. (aux. sein)* retire (from business); withdraw (from a club); *(coll.)* go to the lavatory.

Austritt [ˈaustrɪt], *m.* (—s, *pl.* —e) withdrawal, retirement.

ausüben [ˈausyːbən], *v.a.* exercise, practise; exert, commit.

Ausverkauf [ˈausfɛrkauf], *m.* (—s, *pl.* ꞊e) selling-off, clearance sale.

Auswahl [ˈausvaːl], *f.* (—, *pl.* —en) choice, selection.

Auswanderer [ˈausvandərər], *m.* (—s, *pl.* —) emigrant.

auswärtig [ˈausvɛrtɪç], *adj.* foreign, away.

auswärts [ˈausvɛrts], *adv.* outward(s), away from home.

auswechseln [ˈausvɛksəln], *v.a.* exchange; fit (spare parts).

Ausweg [ˈausveːk], *m.* (—s, *pl.* —e) expedient; way out; *ich weiß keinen —*, I am at my wits' end.

ausweichen [ˈausvaɪçən], *v.n. irr. (aux. sein)* give way; evade, parry.

Ausweis [ˈausvaɪs], *m.* (—es, *pl.* —e) proof of identity, identity card.

ausweisen [ˈausvaɪzən], *v.a. irr.* turn out, banish, exile, deport. — *v.r. (aux. haben) sich —*, show proof of o.'s identity.

auswendig [ˈausvɛndɪç], *adj.* by heart.

auswirken [ˈausvɪrkən], *v.r. sich gut —*, work out well, have a good effect.

Auswuchs [ˈausvuːks], *m.* (—es, *pl.* ꞊e) sprouting, outgrowth, (*fig.*) excrescence.

Auswurf [ˈausvurf], *m.* (—s, *pl.* ꞊e) excretion; expectoration; — *der Menschheit*, scum of the earth.

auszählen [ˈaustsɛːlən], *v.n.* count, number. — *v.a.* count out.

Auszahlung [ˈaustsaːluŋ], *f.* (—, *pl.* —en) payment.

auszanken [ˈaustsaŋkən], *v.a.* scold, chide.

auszehren [ˈaustseːrən], *v.n. (aux. sein)* waste away, be consumed.

auszeichnen [ˈaustsaɪçnən], *v.a.* mark out, honour, decorate. — *v.r. sich —*, distinguish o.s.

Auszeichnung [ˈaustsaɪçnuŋ], *f.* (—, *pl.* —en) distinction, medal.

ausziehen ['austsi:ən], *v.a. irr.* undress, take off (clothes); (*Chem.*) extract; stretch. — *v.n.* (*aux.* sein) move out. — *v.r. sich* —, undress.

auszischen ['austsɪʃən], *v.a.* (*Theat.*) hiss, cat-call.

Auszug ['austsu:k], *m.* (—s, *pl.* ⁻e) removal (from home); marching off; exodus; extract (from a book), abstract (from a deed).

Auto ['auto], *n.* (—s, *pl.* —s) motor-car, (*Am.*) automobile.

Autogramm [auto'gram], *n.* (—s, *pl.* —e) autograph.

Automat [auto'ma:t], *m.* (—en, *pl.* —en) slot machine.

Autor ['autɔr], *m.* (—s, *pl.* —en) author, writer.

Autorität [autori'tɛ:t], *f.* (—, *pl.* —en) authority.

avisieren [avɪ'zi:rən], *v.a.* notify, advise.

Axt [akst], *f.* (—, *pl.* ⁻e) axe.

Azur [a'tsu:r], *m.* (—s, *no pl.*) azure.

B

B [be:], *n.* (—s, *pl.*—s) the letter B; (*Mus.*) B flat; — *Dur,* B flat major; — *Moll,* B flat minor.

Bach [bax], *m.* (—es, *pl.* ⁻e) brook, rivulet.

Bachstelze ['baxʃtɛltsə], *f.* (—, *pl.* —n) wagtail.

Backe ['bakə], *f.* (—, *pl.* —n) cheek.

backen ['bakən], *v.a.* bake.

Backenstreich ['bakənʃtraɪç], *m.* (—s, *pl.* —e) box on the ear.

Bäcker ['bɛkər], *m.* (—s, *pl.* —) baker.

Backfisch ['bakfɪʃ], *m.* (—es, *pl.* —e) (*fig.*) teenage girl.

Backhuhn ['bakhu:n], *n.* (—s, *pl.* ⁻er) fried chicken.

Backobst ['bakopst], *n.* (—es, *no pl.*) dried fruit.

Backpfeife ['bakpfaɪfə], *f.* (—, *pl.* —n) box on the ear.

Backpflaume ['bakpflaumə], *f.* (—, *pl.* —n) prune.

Backstein ['bakʃtaɪn], *m.* (—s, *pl.* —e) brick.

Backwerk ['bakvɛrk], *n.* (—s, *no pl.*) pastry.

Bad [ba:t], *n.* (—es, *pl.* ⁻er) bath; spa, watering-place.

Badeanstalt ['ba:dəanʃtalt], *f.* (—, *pl.* —en) public baths.

baden ['ba:dən], *v.n.* bathe, have a bath.

Badewanne ['ba:dəvanə], *f.* (—, *pl.* —n) bath-tub.

Bagage [ba'ga:ʒə], *f.* (—, *no pl.*) luggage; (*Am.*) baggage; (*sl.*) mob, rabble.

Bagger ['bagər], *m.* (—s, *pl.* —) dredger, dredging-machine.

baggern ['bagərn], *v.a.* dredge.

Bahn [ba:n], *f.* (—, *pl.* —en) road, path, course; (*Astr.*) orbit; railway(-line); — *brechen,* open a path.

bahnbrechend ['ba:nbrɛçənt], *adj.* pioneering, epoch-making.

bahnen ['ba:nən], *v.a.* make passable; pave (the way).

Bahngleis ['ba:nglaɪs], *n.* (—es, *pl.* —e) railway-line, railway-track; (*Am.*) railroad-line, railroad-track.

Bahnhof ['ba:nho:f], *m.* (—s, *pl.* ⁻e) railway-station, (*Am.*) depot.

Bahnsteig ['ba:nʃtaɪk], *m.* (—s, *pl.* —e) platform.

Bahnwärter ['ba:nvɛrtər], *m.* (—s, *pl.* —) signal-man.

Bahre ['ba:rə], *f.* (—, *pl.* —n) litter, stretcher; bier.

Bahrtuch ['ba:rtu:x], *n.* (—s, *pl.* ⁻er) pall, shroud.

Bai [baɪ], *f.* (—, *pl.* —en) bay, cove.

Baisse ['bɛsə], *f.* (—, *pl.* —n) (*Comm.*) fall in share prices.

Bakkalaureat [bakalaurε'a:t], *n.* (—s, *pl.* —e) bachelor's degree.

Bakterie [bak'te:rjə], *f.* (—, *pl.* —n) bacterium.

bald [balt], *adv.* soon, shortly, directly, presently.

Baldachin ['baldaxɪn], *m.* (—s, *pl.* —e) canopy.

baldig ['baldɪç], *adj.* quick, speedy; *auf —es Wiedersehen,* see you again soon.

Baldrian ['baldria:n], *m.* (—s, *no pl.*) valerian.

Balearen, die [balε'a:rən, di:], *pl.* Balearic Islands.

Balg (1) [balk], *m.* (—s, *pl.* ⁻e) skin, slough, husk; bellows (of organ *or* forge).

Balg (2) [balk], *n.* (—s, *pl.* ⁻er) brat; naughty child.

balgen ['balgən], *v.r. sich* —, (*children*) fight, romp.

Balgerei ['balgəraɪ], *f.* (—, *pl.* —en) scuffle, scrimmage.

Balken ['balkən], *m.* (—s, *pl.* —) beam, joist, rafter.

Balkenwerk ['balkənvɛrk], *n.* (—s, *no pl.*) building-frame, timbers, woodwork.

Balkon [bal'kɔ̃], *m.* (—s, *pl.* —s, —e) balcony.

Ball [bal], *m.* (—s, *pl.* ⁻e) ball; globe; sphere; dance.

ballen ['balən], *v.a.* form into a ball; clench (o.'s fist).

Ballen ['balən], *m.* (—s, *pl.* —) bale, bundle, package; ball (of the hand *or* foot).

ballförmig ['balfœrmɪç], *adj.* spherical.

Ballistik [ba'lɪstɪk], *f.* (—, *no pl.*) ballistics.

Ballon [ba'lɔ̃], *m.* (—s, *pl.* —s, —e) balloon.

Balsam ['balza:m], *m.* (—s, *pl.* —e) balm, balsam.

Baltikum ['baltɪkum], *n.* (—s, *no pl.*) the Baltic countries.

Bambusrohr

Bambusrohr ['bambusro:r], *n.* (**—s**, *pl.* **—e**) bamboo (cane).

Banane [ba'na:nǝ], *f.* (**—**, *pl.* **—n**) banana.

Banause [ba'nauzǝ], *m.* (**—n**, *pl.* **—n**) narrow-minded person, philistine.

Band (1) [bant], *n.* (**—s**, *pl.* **ˮer**) ribbon, riband, tape; string; (*Bot.*) band; hoop (*for a cask*); (*Anat.*) ligament, tendon.

Band (2) [bant], *n.* (**—s**, *pl.* **—e**) (*fig.*) bond, fetter, chain, (*pl.*) bonds, ties (*of friendship*).

Band (3) [bant], *m.* (**—es**, *pl.* **ˮe**) volume.

Bändchen ['bɛntçǝn], *n.* (**—s**, *pl.* **—**) small ribbon, small piece of string; (*book*) small volume.

Bande ['bandǝ], *f.* (**—**, *pl.* **—n**) horde, gang, set.

bändigen ['bɛndɪgǝn], *v.a.* tame, subdue.

Bandmaß ['bantma:s], *n.* (**—es**, *pl.* **—e**) tape-measure.

Bandwurm ['bantvurm], *m.* (**—s**, *pl.* **ˮer**) (*Zool.*) tape-worm.

bange ['baŋǝ], *adj.* afraid, worried, alarmed.

Bangigkeit ['baŋɪçkaɪt], *f.* (**—**, *no pl.*) uneasiness, anxiety.

Bank (1) [baŋk], *f.* (**—**, *pl.* **ˮe**) bench, seat (in a park); *auf die lange — schieben*, delay, shelve; *durch die —*, without exception.

Bank (2) [baŋk], *f.* (**—**, *pl.* **—en**) bank; *die — sprengen*, break the bank.

Bänkelsänger ['bɛŋkǝlzɛŋǝr], *m.* (**—s**, *pl.* **—**) ballad singer.

bank(e)rott [baŋk'rɔt], *adj.* bankrupt.

Bankett [baŋ'kɛt], *n.* (**—s**, *pl.* **—e**) banquet.

Bankkonto ['baŋkkɔnto], *n.* (**—s**, *pl.* **—ten**) bank-account.

Bann [ban], *m.* (**—s**, *no pl.*) ban, exile; (*Eccl.*) excommunication; *in den — tun*, outlaw, (*Eccl.*) excommunicate; (*fig.*) charm, spell.

bannen [banǝn], *v.a.* banish, exile, cast out.

Banner ['banǝr], *n.* (**—s**, *pl.* **—**) banner, standard.

Bannmeile ['banmaɪlǝ], *f.* (**—**, *pl.* **—n**) boundary.

bar [ba:r], *adv.* in cash, ready money.

Bar [ba:r], *f.* (**—**, *pl.* **—s**) bar (for selling drinks etc.).

Bär [bɛ:r], *m.* (**—en**, *pl.* **—en**) (*Zool.*) bear; *einem einen —en aufbinden*, to lead s.o. up the garden-path.

Barauslagen ['barausla:gǝn], *f. pl.* cash expenses.

Barbar [bar'ba:r], *m.* (**—en**, *pl.* **—en**) barbarian, vandal.

barbarisch [bar'ba:rɪʃ], *adj.* barbarous.

Barbestand [bar'baʃtant], *m.* (**—s**, *pl.* **ˮe**) cash reserve, cash balance.

bärbeißig ['bɛ:rbaɪsɪç], *adj.* surly, morose.

Barchent ['barçǝnt], *m.* (**—s**, *no pl.*) fustian.

Barde ['bardǝ], *m.* (**—n**, *pl.* **—n**) bard, minstrel.

Bärenfell ['bɛ:rǝnfɛl], *n.* (**—s**, *pl.* **—e**) bear-skin.

Bärenmütze ['bɛ:rǝnmytsǝ], *f.* (**—**, *pl.* **—n**) (*Mil.*) busby.

Bärenzwinger ['bɛ:rǝntsvɪŋǝr], *m.* (**—s**, *pl.* **—**) bear-garden.

Barett [ba'rɛt], *n.* (**—s**, *pl.* **—e**) cap, beret; (*Eccl.*) biretta.

barfuß ['barfus], *adj.* barefoot(ed).

Bargeld ['bargɛlt], *n.* (**—(e)s**, *no pl.*) cash.

barhäuptig ['barhɔyptɪç], *adj.* bareheaded.

Barkasse [bar'kasǝ], *f.* (**—**, *pl.* **—n**) launch.

Barke ['barkǝ], *f.* (**—**, *pl.* **—n**) barge, lighter.

barmherzig [barm'hɛrtsɪç], *adj.* merciful, charitable, compassionate.

Barock [ba'rɔk], *n.* (**—s**, *no pl.*) Baroque.

Baronin [ba'ro:nɪn], *f.* (**—**, *pl.* **—nen**) baroness.

Barren ['barǝn], *m.* (**—s**, *pl.* **—**) parallel bars.

Barsch [barʃ], *m.* (**—es**, *pl.* **—e**) (*Zool.*) perch.

barsch [barʃ], *adj.* rough, harsh, sharp, abrupt, unfriendly.

Barschaft ['ba:rʃaft], *f.* (**—**, *pl.* **—en**) ready money.

Bart [ba:rt], *m.* (**—s**, *pl.* **ˮe**) beard; (*key*) ward.

Bartflechte ['ba:rtflɛçtǝ], *f.* (**—**, *pl.* **—n**) barber's itch.

bärtig ['bɛ:rtɪç], *adj.* bearded.

Basalt [ba'zalt], *m.* (**—s**, *pl.* **—e**) (*Min.*) basalt.

Base ['ba:zǝ], *f.* (**—**, *pl.* **—n**) female cousin; (*Chem.*) base.

Basis ['ba:zɪs], *f.* (**—**, *pl.* **Basen**) base, foundation.

Baskenmütze ['baskǝnmytsǝ], *f.* (**—**, *pl.* **—n**) tam-o'-shanter, beret.

Baß [bas], *m.* (**—sses**, *pl.* **ˮsse**) (*Mus.*) bass.

Baßschlüssel ['basʃlysǝl], *m.* (**—s**, *pl.* **—**) (*Mus.*) bass-clef.

Bassin [ba'sẽ], *n.* (**—s**, *pl.* **—s**) basin, reservoir.

Bast [bast], *m.* (**—es**, *pl.* **—e**) inner bark, fibre (*of trees etc.*); bast.

basta ['basta], *int.* and that's that!

Bastei [bas'taɪ], *f.* (**—**, *pl.* **—en**) bastion.

basteln ['bastǝln], *v.a.* work on a hobby, tinker.

Batist [ba'tɪst], *m.* (**—s**, *pl.* **—e**) cambric.

Bau [bau], *m.* (**—es**, *pl.* **—ten**) building, structure, edifice; act of building; *im — begriffen*, in course of construction.

Bauart ['bauart], *f.* (**—**, *pl.* **—en**) (architectural) style, structure.

Bauch [baux], *m.* (**—es**, *pl.* **ˮe**) belly, stomach.

Bauchfell ['bauxfɛl], *n.* (**—s**, *pl.* **—e**) peritoneum.

bauchig ['bauçıç], *adj.* bulgy.

Bauchredner ['bauxreːdnər], *m.* (—s, *pl.* —) ventriloquist.

bauen ['bauən], *v.a.* build, construct, erect. — *v.n. auf etwas* —, (*fig.*) rely on s.th., count on s.th.

Bauer (1) ['bauər], *m.* (—n, *pl.* —n) farmer, peasant; (*chess*) pawn.

Bauer (2) ['bauər], *n.* (—s, *pl.* —) (*bird*) cage.

Bauernfänger ['bauərnfɛɳər], *m.* (—s, *pl.* —) sharper, rook, confidence-trickster.

Bäuerin ['bɔyərın], *f.* (—, *pl.* —nen) farmer's wife.

Bauernstand ['bauərnʃtant], *m.* (—s, *pl.* ⁓e) peasantry.

baufällig ['baufɛlıç], *adj.* dilapidated, ramshackle.

Baugerüst ['baugəryst], *n.* (—s, *pl.* —e) scaffolding.

Baugewerbe ['baugəvɛrbə], *n.* (—s, *no pl.*) building trade.

Baukunst ['baukunst], *f.* (—, *no pl.*) architecture.

Baum [baum], *m.* (—(e)s, *pl.* ⁓e) tree.

Baumeister ['baumaıstər], *m.* (—s, *pl.* —) architect, master-builder.

baumeln ['bauməln], *v.n.* dangle.

Baumkuchen ['baumkuːxən], *m.* (—s, *pl.* —) pyramid-cake.

Baumschule ['baumʃuːlə], *f.* (—, *pl.* —n) plantation of trees, orchard, tree nursery.

Baumstamm ['baumʃtam], *m.* (—s, *pl.* ⁓e) stem, trunk.

Baumwolle ['baumvɔlə], *f.* (—, *pl.* —n) cotton.

Bauriß ['baurıs], *m.* (—sses, *pl.* —sse) plan, architect's drawing.

Bausch [bauʃ], *m.* (—es, *pl.* ⁓e) pad, bolster; *in* — *und Bogen*, in the lump: all at once.

bauschig ['bauʃıç], *adj.* baggy.

Bauwerk ['bauvɛrk] *see* **Gebäude**.

Bayern ['baıərn], *n.* Bavaria.

Bazar [ba'zaːr], *m.* (—s, *pl.* —e) bazaar, fair, emporium.

beabsichtigen [bə'apzıçtıgən], *v.a.* aim at, intend, have in view.

beachten [bə'axtən], *v.a.* observe, pay attention to.

Beamte [bə'amtə], *m.* (—n, *pl.* —n) official, officer, civil servant.

Beamtin [bə'amtın], *f.* (—, *pl.* —nen) female official, female civil servant.

beängstigen [bə'ɛɳstıgən], *v.a.* alarm, make afraid.

beanspruchen [bə'anʃpruxən], *v.a.* demand, claim, lay claim to.

beanstanden [bə'anʃtandən], *v.a.* object to, raise objections to, query.

beantragen [bə'antraːgən], *v.a.* move, apply, lodge an application.

beantworten [bə'antvɔrtən], *v.a.* answer, reply to.

bearbeiten [bə'arbaıtən], *v.a.* work (on); (*book, play*) adapt, arrange, revise; (*Agr.*) cultivate; (*fig.*) *einen* —, try to influence s.o., try to convince s.o.

Bearbeitung [bə'arbaıtuɳ], *f.* (—, *pl.* —en) working, manipulation, operation; (*Agr.*) culture, cultivation; (*book, play*) adaptation, revision, arrangement.

beargwöhnen [bə'arkvøːnən], *v.a.* suspect, view with suspicion.

beaufsichtigen [bə'aufzıçtıgən], *v.a.* control, supervise, superintend.

beauftragen [bə'auftraːgən], *v.a.* commission, charge, authorize.

bebauen [bə'bauən], *v.a.* build upon; (*Agr.*) cultivate.

beben ['beːbən], *v.n.* shake, quake, tremble; *vor Kälte* —, shiver with cold.

Becher ['bɛçər], *m.* (—s, *pl.* —) beaker, cup, goblet, mug; (*dice*) box.

Becken ['bɛkən], *n.* (—s, *pl.* —) basin, bowl; (*Anat.*) pelvis; (*Mus.*) cymbal.

Bedacht [bə'daxt], *m.* (—s, *no pl.*) consideration; *mit* —, deliberately; *ohne* —, thoughtlessly.

bedächtig [bə'dɛçtıç], *adj.* circumspect, deliberate, cautious, slow.

bedanken [bə'daɳkən], *v.r. sich für etwas* —, thank s.o. for s.th., decline with thanks (*also iron.*).

Bedarf [bə'darf], *m.* (—s, *no pl.*) need, requirement, demand.

bedauerlich [bə'dauərlıç], *adj.* regrettable, deplorable.

bedauern [bə'dauərn], *v.a.* pity, commiserate, regret; *ich bedaure, daß*, I am sorry that . . .

bedecken [bə'dɛkən], *v.a.* cover (up); *sich mit Ruhm* —, cover o.s. with glory.

bedeckt [bə'dɛkt], *adj.* (*sky*) overcast.

bedenken [bə'dɛɳkən], *v.a. irr.* consider, bear in mind. — *v.r. sich* —, deliberate, hesitate; *sich anders* —, change o.'s mind.

bedenklich [bə'dɛɳklıç], *adj.* (*persons*) doubtful, dubious; (*things*) risky, delicate, precarious; (*illness*) serious, grave.

Bedenkzeit [bə'dɛɳktsaıt], *f.* (—, *pl.* —en) time to consider, respite.

bedeuten [bə'dɔytən], *v.a.* signify, mean, imply; direct, order.

bedeutend [bə'dɔytənt], *adj.* important, eminent, considerable, outstanding.

bedeutsam [bə'dɔytzaːm], *adj.* significant.

Bedeutung [bə'dɔytuɳ], *f.* (—, *pl.* —en) significance, meaning; consequence, importance; *nichts von* —, nothing to speak of.

bedienen [bə'diːnən], *v.a.* serve, attend to, wait on; (*machine*) operate; (*Cards*) follow suit. — *v.r. sich* —, help o.s., make use of.

Bediente [bə'diːntə], *m.* (—n, *pl.* —n) servant, attendant, footman, lackey.

Bedienung [bə'diːnuɳ], *f.* (—, *pl.* —en) service, attendance.

bedingen [bə'dıɳən], *v.a.* stipulate, postulate, condition, cause.

bedingt

bedingt [bə'dıŋkt], *adj.* conditional.
Bedingung [bə'dıŋuŋ], *f.* (—, *pl.* —en) stipulation, condition, term; *unter keiner* —, on no account.
bedingungsweise [bə'dıŋuŋsvaızə], *adv.* on condition, conditionally.
bedrängen [bə'drɛŋən], *v.a.* oppress: press hard, afflict.
Bedrängnis [bə'drɛŋnıs], *n.* (—ses, *pl.* —se) oppression, distress.
bedrohen [bə'dro:ən], *v.a.* threaten, menace.
bedrohlich [bə'dro:lıç], *adj.* threatening, menacing, ominous.
bedrücken [bə'drykən], *v.a.* oppress, harass, depress.
Beduine [bedu'i:nə], *m.* (—n, *pl.* —n) Bedouin.
bedünken [bə'dyŋkən], *v.a.* appear, seem; *es bedünkt mich*, methinks.
bedürfen [bə'dyrfən], *v.n. irr.* want, need, be in need of.
Bedürfnis [bə'dyrfnıs], *n.* (—ses, *pl.* —se) want, need, requirement, necessity; *es ist mir ein* —, I cannot but: *einem dringenden* — *abhelfen*, meet an urgent want *or* need; *ein* — *haben*, (*coll.*) need to relieve o.s.
Bedürfnisanstalt [bə'dyrfnısanʃtalt], *f.* (—, *pl.* —en) public lavatory, public convenience.
bedürftig [bə'dyrftıç], *adj.* needy, indigent, poor.
beeidigen [bə'aıdıgən], *v.a.* confirm by oath, swear in.
beeifern [bə'aıfərn], *v.r. sich* —, exert o.s., strive, be zealous.
beeilen [bə'aılən], *v.r. sich* —, hurry, hasten, make haste.
beeindrucken [bə'aındrukən], *v.a.* impress.
beeinflussen [bə'aınflusən], *v.a.* influence.
beeinträchtigen [bə'aıntrɛçtıgən], *v.a.* injure, lessen, diminish, detract from, curtail.
beenden [bə'ɛndən], *v.a.* end, finish, terminate, conclude.
beendigen [bə'ɛndıgən], *v.a.* end, finish, terminate, conclude.
beengen [bə'ɛŋən], *v.a.* cramp, narrow.
beerben [bə'ɛrbən], *v.a. einen* —, inherit from s.o.
beerdigen [bə'e:rdıgən], *v.a.* bury, inter.
Beere ['be:rə], *f.* (—, *pl.* —n) berry.
Beet [be:t], *n.* (—es, *pl.* —e) (flower) bed.
befähigen [bə'fɛ:ıgən], *v.a.* fit, enable, qualify.
Befähigung [bə'fɛ:ıguŋ], *f.* (—, *pl.* —en) qualification, capacity, aptitude.
befahren [bə'fa:rən], *v.a. irr.* pass over, travel over; (*Naut.*) navigate.
befallen [bə'falən], *v.a. irr.* befall, fall on; *von Traurigkeit* — *sein*, be overcome by sadness.
befangen [bə'faŋən], *adj.* biased, prejudiced; bashful, embarrassed.

befassen [bə'fasən], *v.a.* touch, handle.
— *v.r. sich mit etwas* —, occupy o.s. with s.th.
befehden [bə'fe:dən], *v.a.* make war upon, show enmity towards.
Befehl [bə'fe:l], *m.* (—s, *pl.* —e) order, command; (*Mil.*) *zu* —, very good, sir; (*Mil.*) *den* — *führen über*, command.
befehlen [bə'fe:lən], *v.a. irr.* order, command.
befehligen [bə'fe:lıgən], *v.a.* (*Mil.*) command, head.
Befehlshaber [bə'fe:lsha:bər], *m.* (—s, *pl.* —) commander, commanding officer, chief.
befehlswidrig [bə'fe:lsvı:drıç], *adj.* contrary to orders.
befestigen [bə'fɛstıgən], *v.a.* fasten, fix, attach, affix; (*Mil.*) fortify; strengthen.
befeuchten [bə'fɔyçtən], *v.a.* wet, moisten, dampen.
Befinden [bə'fındən], *n.* (—s, *no pl.*) state of health.
befinden [bə'fındən], *v.a. irr.* think, deem, find. — *v.r. sich an einem Ort* —, be in some place; *sich wohl* —, feel well.
befindlich [bə'fıntlıç], *adj.* existing — *sein*, be contained in.
beflecken [bə'flɛkən], *v.a.* stain, spot, blot; defile, pollute.
befleißigen [bə'flaısıgən], *v.r. sich* —, devote o.s. to, take pains to.
beflissen [bə'flısən], *adj.* eager to serve, assiduous.
beflügeln [bə'fly:gəln], *v.a.* give wings; (*fig.*) accelerate, animate.
befolgen [bə'fɔlgən], *v.a.* follow, obey; *einen Befehl* —, comply with an order.
befördern [bə'fœrdərn], *v.a.* despatch, forward, send, post, mail, transmit; promote, advance.
Beförderung [bə'fœrdəruŋ], *f.* (—, *pl.* —en) forwarding, transmission; (*office*) promotion, advancement.
Beförderungsmittel [bə'fœrdəruŋsmıtəl], *n.* (—s, *pl.* —) conveyance, means of transport.
befragen [bə'fra:gən], *v.a.* question, interrogate, examine.
befreien [bə'fraıən], *v.a.* free, liberate.
befremden [bə'frɛmdən], *v.a.* appear strange, astonish, surprise.
befreunden [bə'frɔyndən], *v.a.* befriend. — *v.r. sich mit einem* —, make friends with s.o.
befriedigen [bə'fri:dıgən], *v.a.* content, satisfy; appease, calm.
befruchten [bə'fruxtən], *v.a.* fertilise; impregnate.
Befugnis [bə'fu:knıs], *f.* (—, *pl.* —se) authority, right, warrant.
Befund [bə'funt], *m.* (—s, *pl.* —e) (*Med.*) diagnosis, findings.
befürchten [bə'fyrçtən], *v.a.* fear, be afraid of.
befürworten [bə'fy:rvɔrtən], *v.a.* support, second.

begabt [bə'ga:pt], adj. gifted, talented, able.

Begabung [bə'ga:buŋ], f. (—, pl. —en) ability, talent, gift.

begaffen [bə'gafən], v.a. stare at, gape at.

begatten [bə'gatən], v.r. sich —, (Zool.) copulate.

begeben [bə'ge:bən], v.r. irr. sich an einen Ort —, go to a place, betake o.s. to a place; happen, occur.

Begebenheit [bə'ge:bənhaɪt], f. (—, pl. —en) happening, event, occurrence.

begegnen [bə'ge:gnən], v.n. (aux. sein) meet, meet with, encounter, befall, happen.

begehen [bə'ge:ən], v.a. irr. (road) walk along, go over; (festival) celebrate; (crime) commit, perpetrate.

begehren [bə'ge:rən], v.a. desire, wish, covet, want.—v.n. nach etwas —, long for s.th.

begehrlich [bə'ge:rlɪç], adj. covetous, greedy, desirous.

begeifern [bə'gaɪfərn], v.a. spit at; (fig.) vilify, besmirch.

begeistern [bə'gaɪstərn], v.a. inspire, fill with enthusiasm, enrapture.—v.r. sich für etwas —, become enthusiastic about s.th.

Begier(de) [bə'gi:r(də)], f. (—, pl. —den) desire, lust, appetite.

begierig [bə'gi:rɪç], adj. desirous, lustful; anxious; curious (for news).

begießen [bə'gi:sən], v.a. irr. (plants) water; (meat etc.) baste; etwas festlich —, celebrate s.th. by drinking; sich die Nase —, (coll.) get tight.

Beginn [bə'gɪn], m. (—s, no pl.) beginning, commencement, start.

beginnen [bə'gɪnən], v.a., v.n. irr. begin, commence, start.

beglaubigen [bə'glaubɪgən], v.a. attest; certify, verify; accredit (an ambassador).

Beglaubigungsschreiben [bə'glaubɪguŋsʃraɪbən], n. (—s, pl. —) credentials.

begleichen [bə'glaɪçən], v.a. irr. (bill) pay, settle.

begleiten [bə'glaɪtən], v.a. accompany, escort, see s.o. off, home etc.

Begleiter [bə'glaɪtər], m. (—s, pl. —) companion, escort; (Mus.) accompanist.

Begleiterscheinung [bə'glaɪtərʃaɪnuŋ], f. (—, pl. —en) concomitant; (Med.) complication, attendant symptom.

Begleitung [bə'glaɪtuŋ], f. (—, pl. —en) company; (Mus.) accompaniment.

beglücken [bə'glykən], v.a. make happy.

beglückwünschen [bə'glykvynʃən], v.a. congratulate.

begnadet [bə'gna:dət], adj. highly talented.

begnadigen [bə'gna:dɪgən], v.a. pardon, reprieve.

begnügen [bə'gny:gən], v.r. sich mit etwas —, content o.s. with s.th.

Begonie [bə'go:njə], f. (—, pl. —n) (Bot.) begonia.

begraben [bə'gra:bən], v.a. irr. bury, inter.

Begräbnis [bə'grɛ:pnɪs], n. (—ses, pl. —se) burial, funeral, interment.

begreifen [bə'graɪfən], v.a. irr. understand, comprehend, conceive.

begreiflich [bə'graɪflɪç], adj. comprehensible, conceivable, understandable.

begrenzen [bə'grɛntsən], v.a. bound, border, limit.

Begriff [bə'grɪf], m. (—s, pl. —e) notion, concept, idea, conception; im — sein, be about to . . . .

begriffen [bə'grɪfən], adj. — sein in, be engaged in.

begriffsstutzig [bə'grɪfsʃtutsɪç], adj. obtuse, dense, slow in the uptake.

begründen [bə'gryndən], v.a. base on, justify; found, establish.

begrüßen [bə'gry:sən], v.a. greet, salute, welcome.

begünstigen [bə'gynstɪgən], v.a. favour, prefer.

Begutachter [bə'gu:taxtər], m. (—s, pl. —) expert; (Sch.) assessor, second examiner.

Begutachtung [bə'gu:taxtuŋ], f. (—, pl. —en) expert opinion, assessment, report.

begütert [bə'gy:tərt], adj. wealthy, rich, well-to-do.

behaart [bə'ha:rt], adj. covered with hair, hairy.

behäbig [bə'hɛ:bɪç], adj. comfortable, corpulent, portly.

behaften [bə'haftən], v.a. charge, burden.

behagen [bə'ha:gən], v.n. please, be agreeable; es behagt mir nicht, I do not like it.

behaglich [bə'ha:klɪç], adj. cosy, comfortable, snug.

behalten [bə'haltən], v.a. irr. retain, keep.

Behälter [bə'hɛltər], m. (—s, pl. —) container; box, bin; (water) reservoir; tank.

behandeln [bə'handəln], v.a. treat, use; (Med.) treat; (subject) treat; handle.

Behandlung [bə'handluŋ], f. (—, pl. —en) treatment, use; (Med.) treatment.

Behang [bə'haŋ], m. (—es, pl. ⁀e) hanging(s); appendage.

behängen [bə'hɛŋən], v.a. irr. festoon with, drape.

beharren [bə'harən], v.n. persevere; persist, insist.

beharrlich [bə'harlɪç], adj. persevering, persistent, constant, firm.

behauen [bə'hauən], v.a. (stones) hew, cut.

behaupten [bə'hauptən], v.a. claim, assert, affirm, maintain.

Behauptung [bə'hauptuŋ], *f.* (—, *pl.* —en) claim, assertion, affirmation.

Behausung [bə'hauzuŋ], *f.* (—, *pl.* —en) habitation, housing.

behelfen [bə'hɛlfən], *v.r. irr. sich — mit*, make do with.

behelfsmäßig [bə'hɛlfsmɛːsɪç], *adj.* makeshift, temporary.

behelligen [bə'hɛlɪgən], *v.a.* trouble, molest, disturb.

behend(e) [bə'hɛndə], *adj.* quick, nimble, agile.

beherbergen [bə'hɛrbɛrgən], *v.a.* give shelter to, put up, harbour.

beherrschen [bə'hɛrʃən], *v.a.* rule, govern, dominate; *eine Sache —*, master a subject. *— v.r. sich —*, control o.s.

Beherrschung [bə'hɛrʃuŋ], *f.* (—, *pl.* (*rare*) —en) domination, sway; (*subject*) grasp; (*languages*) command.

beherzigen [bə'hɛrtsɪgən], *v.a.* take to heart, follow, heed.

Beherztheit [bə'hɛrtsthaɪt], *f.* (—, *no pl.*) courage, spirit.

behexen [bə'hɛksən], *v.a.* bewitch.

behilflich [bə'hɪlflɪç], *adj.* helpful, useful.

behindern [bə'hɪndərn], *v.a.* hinder, hamper.

Behörde [bə'hœrdə], *f.* (—, *pl.* —n) the authorities.

behufs [bə'huːfs], *prep.* (*Genit.*) in order to, with a view to.

behüten [bə'hyːtən], *v.a.* guard, protect; *Gott behüte!* Heaven forbid!

behutsam [bə'huːtzaːm], *adj.* careful, cautious.

bei [baɪ], *prep.* (*Dat.*) (*locally*) near by, close by, next to, at.

beibehalten [´baɪbəhaltən], *v.a. irr.* keep, retain.

Beiblatt [´baɪblat], *n.* (—s, *pl.* ⁐er) supplement (to a newspaper).

beibringen [´baɪbrɪŋən], *v.a. irr.* adduce (proof); produce (witnesses); (*fig.*) teach; impart to.

Beichte [´baɪçtə], *f.* (—, *pl.* —n) confession.

Beichtstuhl [´baɪçtʃtuːl], *m.* (—s, *pl.* ⁐e) confessional.

beide [´baɪdə], *adj.* both, either, the two.

beiderlei [´baɪdərlaɪ], *adj.* of both kinds.

beidrehen [´baɪdreːən], *v.n.* (*Naut.*) heave to.

Beifall [´baɪfal], *m.* (—s, *no pl.*) (*verbal*) approbation; (*shouting*) acclamation, acclaim; (*clapping*) applause.

beifällig [´baɪfɛlɪç], *adj.* favourable, approving, assenting.

beifügen [´baɪfyːgən], *v.a.* enclose, attach.

Beifuß [´baɪfuːs], *m.* (—es, *no pl.*) (*Bot.*) mugwort.

beigeben [´baɪgeːbən], *v.a. irr.* add, join to. *— v.n. klein —*, give in.

Beigeschmack [´baɪgəʃmak], *m.* (—s, *no pl.*) aftertaste, tang.

beigesellen [´baɪgəzɛlən], *v.r. sich —*, associate with.

Beihilfe [´baɪhɪlfə], *f.* (—, *pl.* —n) aid, assistance, subsidy.

beikommen [´baɪkəmən], *v.n. irr.* (*aux.* sein) *einer Sache —*, to grapple with s.th.; *ich kann ihm nicht —*, I cannot catch him out, get at him.

Beil [baɪl], *n.* (—s, *pl.* —e) hatchet, axe.

Beilage [´baɪlaːgə], *f.* (—, *pl.* —n) enclosure (with a letter); supplement (to a newspaper); *Braten mit —*, joint with vegetables.

beiläufig [´baɪlɔyfɪç], *adv.* by the way, incidentally.

beilegen [´baɪleːgən], *v.a.* add, join; enclose (in letter).

beileibe [baɪ'laɪbə], *int. — nicht!* on no account!

Beileid [´baɪlaɪt], *n.* (—s, *no pl.*) condolence, sympathy.

beiliegen [´baɪliːgən], *v.n. irr.* be enclosed with.

beimengen [´baɪmɛŋən], *v.a.* (*Cul.*) mix with, add.

beimessen [´baɪmɛsən], *v.a. irr. einem etwas —*, impute s.th. to s.o.; *einem Glauben —*, credit s.o., give credence to.

Bein [baɪn], *n.* (—s, *pl.* —e) leg; *einem auf die —e helfen*, give a helping hand to s.o.

beinahe [baɪ'naːə], *adv.* almost, nearly.

Beiname [´baɪnaːmə], *m.* (—ns, *pl.* —n) surname; nickname.

Beinbruch [´baɪnbrux], *m.* (—s, *pl.* ⁐e) fracture of the leg; (*coll.*) *Hals- und Beinbruch!* good luck!

Beinkleider [´baɪnklaɪdər], *n. pl.* (*obs.*) pants, trousers.

beipflichten [´baɪpflɪçtən], *v.n. einem —*, agree with s.o.

beirren [bə'ɪrən], *v.a. sich nicht — lassen*, not let o.s. be dissuaded *or* put off.

beisammen [baɪ'zamən], *adv.* together.

Beischlaf [´baɪʃlaːf], *m.* (—s, *no pl.*) cohabitation, coition.

Beisein [´baɪzaɪn], *n.* (—s, *no pl.*) *im — von*, in the presence of.

beiseite [baɪ'zaɪtə], *adv.* apart, aside; (*Theat.*) aside.

beisetzen [´baɪzɛtsən], *v.a.* bury, inter, entomb.

Beispiel [´baɪʃpiːl], *n.* (—s, *pl.* —e) example, instance; *zum —* (*abbr.* z.B.), for instance, for example.

beißen [´baɪsən], *v.a. irr.* bite; (*pepper, smoke*) burn, sting.

Beißzange [´baɪstsaŋə], *f.* (—, *pl.* —n) pair of pincers *or* nippers.

Beistand [´baɪʃtant], *m.* (—s, *pl.* ⁐e) assistance, help; (*Law*) counsel; *— leisten*, give assistance.

beistehen [´baɪʃteːən], *v.n. irr. einem —*, stand by s.o., help s.o.

beisteuern [´baɪʃtɔyərn], *v.a. zu etwas —*, contribute to s.th.

beistimmen [´baɪʃtɪmən], *v.n.* agree with, assent.

Beistrich ['baɪʃtrɪç], *m.* (—(e)s, *pl.* —e) comma.

beitragen ['baɪtraːgən], *v.a. irr.* contribute; be conducive to.

beitreten ['baɪtreːtən], *v.n. irr.* (*aux.* sein) join (a club); enter into partnership with (a firm).

Beitritt ['baɪtrɪt], *m.* (—s, *no pl.*) accession, joining.

Beiwagen ['baɪvaːgən], *m.* (—s, *pl.* —) trailer, sidecar (on motor cycle).

beiwohnen ['baɪvoːnən], *v.n.* be present at, attend.

Beiwort ['baɪvɔrt], *n.* (—s, *pl.* ˜er) adjective, epithet.

Beize ['baɪtsə], *f.* (—, *pl.* —n) caustic fluid; (*wood*) stain.

beizeiten [baɪ'tsaɪtən], *adv.* betimes, early, in good time.

beizen ['baɪtsən], *v.a.* cauterise; (*wood*) stain.

bejahen [bə'jaːən], *v.a.* answer in the affirmative.

bejahrt [bə'jaːrt], *adj.* aged, elderly, old.

bejammern [bə'jamərn], *v.a.* bemoan, bewail.

bekannt [bə'kant], *adj.* known, well-known; — machen, acquainted with.

Bekannte [bə'kantə], *m.* (—n, *pl.* —n) acquaintance.

bekanntlich [bə'kantlɪç], *adv.* as is well known.

Bekanntmachung [bə'kantmaxuŋ], *f.* (—, *pl.* —en) publication, announcement.

Bekanntschaft [bə'kantʃaft], *f.* (—, *pl.* —en) — mit einem machen, strike up an acquaintance with s.o.

bekehren [bə'keːrən], *v.a.* convert. — *v.r. sich* —, be converted *or* become a convert (*to*); reform.

bekennen [bə'kɛnən], *v.a. irr.* confess, profess; admit, own up to.

Bekenner [bə'kɛnər], *m.* (—s, *pl.* —) Confessor (as title).

Bekenntnis [bə'kɛntnɪs], *n.* (—ses, *pl.* —se) confession (of faith), avowal, creed.

beklagen [bə'klaːgən], *v.a.* lament, bewail, deplore. — *v.r. sich* — über, complain of.

Beklagte [bə'klaːktə], *m.* (—n, *pl.* —n) (*Law*) defendant.

bekleiden [bə'klaɪdən], *v.a.* clothe, dress, cover; (*office*) hold.

Bekleidung [bə'klaɪduŋ], *f.* (—, *no pl.*) clothing, clothes; (*office*) administration, holding, exercise.

beklemmen [bə'klɛmən], *v.a. irr.* oppress.

Beklemmung [bə'klɛmuŋ], *f.* (—, *pl.* —en) oppression, anguish.

beklommen [bə'klɔmən], *adj.* anxious, uneasy.

bekommen [bə'kɔmən], *v.a. irr.* obtain, get, receive.

bekömmlich [bə'kœmlɪç], *adj.* beneficial; digestible, wholesome.

beköstigen [bə'kœstɪgən], *v.a.* board; feed.

bekräftigen [bə'krɛftɪgən], *v.a.* aver, corroborate, confirm.

bekränzen [bə'krɛntsən], *v.a.* wreathe, crown (with a garland).

bekreuzigen [bə'krɔytsɪgən], *v.r. sich* —, make the sign of the cross, cross o.s.

bekriegen [bə'kriːgən], *v.a.* make war on.

bekritteln [bə'krɪtəln], *v.a.* criticise, carp at, find fault with.

bekritzeln [bə'krɪtsəln], *v.a.* scrawl on, doodle on.

bekümmern [bə'kymərn], *v.a.* grieve, distress, trouble. — *v.r.* trouble o.s. about, grieve over.

bekunden [bə'kundən], *v.a.* manifest, show; declare.

beladen [bə'laːdən], *v.a. irr.* load.

Belag [bə'laːk], *m.* (—s, *pl.* ˜e) covering, layer; spread (on sandwiches); fur (on the tongue).

belagern [bə'laːgərn], *v.a.* besiege.

Belang [bə'laŋ], *m.* (—s, *pl.* —e) importance; von —, of great moment *or* consequence; (*pl.*) concerns, interests.

• **belangen** [bə'laŋən], *v.a.* (*Law*) sue, prosecute.

belanglos [bə'laŋloːs], *adj.* of small account; irrelevant, unimportant.

belassen [bə'lasən], *v.a. irr. es dabei* —, leave things as they are.

belasten [bə'lastən], *v.a.* load, burden; (*Comm.*) debit, charge; (*Law*) incriminate.

belästigen [bə'lɛstɪgən], *v.a.* bother, pester, molest.

Belastung [bə'lastuŋ], *f.* (—, *pl.* —en) load, burden; (*Comm.*) debiting; (*house*) mortgage; erbliche —, hereditary disposition.

Belastungszeuge [bə'lastuŋstsɔygə], *m.* (—n, *pl.* —n) witness for the prosecution.

belaubt [bə'laupt], *adj.* covered with leaves, leafy.

belaufen [bə'laufən], *v.r. irr. sich* — auf, amount to, come to.

belauschen [bə'lauʃən], *v.a.* eavesdrop, overhear.

beleben [bə'leːbən], *v.a.* animate, enliven.

Belebtheit [bə'leːpthaɪt], *f.* (—, *no pl.*) animation, liveliness.

Beleg [bə'leːk], *m.* (—s, *pl.* —e) document, proof, receipt, voucher.

belegen [bə'leːgən], *v.a.* cover, overlay; reserve, book (*seat*); support by documents, authenticate, prove.

Belegschaft [bə'leːkʃaft], *f.* (—, *pl.* —en) workers, personnel, staff; (*Min.*) gang, shift.

belegt [bə'leːkt], *adj.* (*tongue*) furred; —es Brot, sandwich.

belehnen [bə'leːnən], *v.a.* enfeoff, invest (with a fief).

belehren [bə'leːrən], *v.a.* instruct, advise, inform.

Belehrung

Belehrung [bə'le:ruŋ], *f.* (—, *pl.* —en) information, instruction, advice.
beleibt [bə'laɪpt], *adj.* stout, corpulent, obese.
beleidigen [bə'laɪdɪgən], *v.a.* insult, offend, give offence to.
belesen [bə'le:zən], *adj.* well-read.
beleuchten [bə'lɔʏçtən], *v.a.* illumine, illuminate; (*fig.*) throw light on, elucidate.
Beleuchtungskörper [bə'lɔʏçtuŋskœr-pər], *m.* (—s, *pl.* —) lighting fixture, lamp.
Belgien ['bɛlgjən], *n.* Belgium.
belichten [bə'lɪçtən], *v.a.* (*Phot.*) expose.
belieben [bə'li:bən], *v.a., v.n.* please, like, choose.
beliebig [bə'li:bɪç], *adj.* optional; any, whatever.
beliebt [bə'li:pt], *adj.* popular, well-liked.
Beliebtheit ['bəli:pthaɪt], *f.* (—, *no pl.*) popularity.
bellen ['bɛlən], *v.n.* bark.
beloben [bə'lo:bən], *v.a.* praise, approve.
belohnen [bə'lo:nən], *v.a.* reward, recompense.
belügen [bə'ly:gən], *v.a. irr. einen* —, tell lies to s.o., deceive s.o. by lying.
belustigen [bə'lustɪgən], *v.a.* amuse, divert, entertain.
bemächtigen [bə'mɛçtɪgən], *v.r. sich einer Sache* —, take possession of s.th.
bemäkeln [bə'mɛ:kəln], *v.a.* find fault with.
bemalen [bə'ma:lən], *v.a.* paint (over).
bemängeln [bə'mɛŋəln], *v.a.* find fault with.
bemannen [bə'manən], *v.a.* man.
bemänteln [bə'mɛntəln], *v.a.* cloak, hide.
bemeistern [bə'maɪstərn], *v.a.* master.
bemerkbar [bə'mɛrkba:r], *adj.* perceptible, noticeable.
bemerken [bə'mɛrkən], *v.a.* observe, perceive, notice.
Bemerkung [bə'mɛrkuŋ], *f.* (—, *pl.* —en) remark, observation, note.
bemessen [bə'mɛsən], *v.a. irr.* measure; curtail.
bemitleiden [bə'mɪtlaɪdən], *v.a.* pity, be sorry for.
bemittelt [bə'mɪtəlt], *adj.* well-off, well-to-do.
bemoost [bə'mo:st], *adj.* mossy.
bemühen [bə'my:ən], *v.a.* trouble, give trouble (to). — *v.r. sich* —, take pains, strive, endeavour.
bemüht [bə'my:t], *adj.* studious; — *sein*, endeavour, try to.
bemuttern [bə'mutərn], *v.a.* mother.
benachbart [bə'naxba:rt], *adj.* neighbouring, adjacent.
benachrichtigen [bə'naxrɪçtɪgən], *v.a.* inform, give notice of, notify.
benachteiligen [bə'naxtaɪlɪgən], *v.a.* prejudice, discriminate against, handicap.

benagen [bə'na:gən], *v.a.* gnaw at.
benebeln [bə'ne:bəln], *v.a.* befog, cloud; (*fig.*) dim, intoxicate.
benedeien [bene'daɪən], *v.a.* bless, glorify.
Benediktiner [benedɪk'ti:nər], *m.* (—s, *pl.* —) (monk) Benedictine; Benedictine liqueur.
Benefiz [bene'fi:ts], *n.* (—es, *pl.* —e) benefit; benefit performance.
Benehmen [bə'ne:mən], *n.* (—s, *no pl.*) conduct, behaviour.
benehmen [bə'ne:mən], *v.r. irr. sich* —, behave, conduct o.s.
beneiden [bə'naɪdən], *v.a. einen* — *um*, envy s.o. (s.th.).
benennen [bə'nɛnən], *v.a.* name.
benetzen [bə'nɛtsən], *v.a.* moisten.
Bengel ['bɛŋəl], *m.* (—s, *pl.* —) naughty boy, scamp; rascal, lout.
benommen [bə'nɔmən], *adj.* dazed, giddy.
benötigen [bə'nø:tɪgən], *v.a.* be in need of, require.
benutzen [bə'nutsən], *v.a.* make use of, utilise.
Benzin [bɛnt'si:n], *n.* (—s, *no pl.*) benzine; (*Motor.*) petrol; (*Am.*) gas, gasoline.
beobachten [bə'o:baxtən], *v.a.* watch, observe.
bequem [bə'kve:m], *adj.* comfortable, easy; convenient; indolent, lazy.
bequemen [bə'kve:mən], *v.r. sich* —, condescend (to), comply (with).
Bequemlichkeit [bə'kve:mlɪçkaɪt], *f.* (—, *pl.* —en) convenience, ease; indolence.
beraten [bə'ra:tən], *v.a. irr.* advise, assist with advice, counsel. — *v.r. sich* — *mit*, confer with, consult with.
beratschlagen [bə'ra:tʃla:gən], *v.n.* deliberate with.
Beratung [bə'ra:tuŋ], *f.* (—, *pl.* —en) council, deliberation, consultation.
berauben [bə'raubən], *v.a.* rob, deprive (s.o.) of (s.th.).
berauschen [bə'rauʃən], *v.a.* intoxicate.
berechnen [bə'rɛçnən], *v.a.* compute, charge, calculate, estimate.
berechtigen [bə'rɛçtɪgən], *v.a. einen zu etwas* —, entitle s.o. to s.th.; authorise s.o. to have or do s.th.
beredsam [bə're:tza:m], *adj.* eloquent.
beredt [bə're:t], *adj.* eloquent.
Bereich [bə'raɪç], *m. & n.* (—s, *pl.* —e) extent, realm, sphere, scope.
bereichern [bə'raɪçərn], *v.a.* enrich, enlarge.
bereisen [bə'raɪzən], *v.a.* travel over *or* through, tour (a country).
bereit [bə'raɪt], *adj.* ready, prepared.
bereiten [bə'raɪtən], *v.a.* prepare, get ready.
bereits [bə'raɪts], *adv.* already.
Bereitschaft [bə'raɪtʃaft], *f.* (—, *no pl.*) readiness, preparedness.
bereitwillig [bə'raɪtvɪlɪç], *adj.* willing, ready, obliging.

bereuen [bəˈrɔyən], *v.a.* repent, be sorry for, regret.

Berg [bɛrk], *m.* (—es, *pl.* —e) mountain, hill.

bergab [bɛrkˈap], *adj.* downhill.

Bergamt [ˈbɛrkamt], *n.* (—s, *pl.* ˙er) mining-office, mine authority.

bergan [bɛrkˈan], *adj.* uphill.

Bergarbeiter [ˈbɛrkarbaitər], *m.* (—s, *pl.* —) miner, collier.

bergauf [bɛrkˈauf], *adj.* uphill.

Bergbau [ˈbɛrkbau], *m.* (—s, *no pl.*) mining, mining industry.

bergen [ˈbɛrgən], *v.a. irr.* shelter, protect, save; (*flotsam*) save, recover, salvage.

bergig [ˈbɛrgɪç], *adj.* mountainous, hilly.

Bergkristall [ˈbɛrkkrɪstal], *m.* (—s, *pl.* —e) rock-crystal.

Bergleute [ˈbɛrklɔytə], *pl.* miners, colliers.

Bergmann [ˈbɛrkman], *m.* (—s, *pl.* Bergleute) miner, collier.

Bergpredigt [ˈbɛrkpreːdɪçt], *f.* (—, *no pl.*) Sermon on the Mount.

Bergschlucht [ˈbɛrkʃluxt], *f.* (—, *pl.* —en) ravine, gorge.

Bergsteiger [ˈbɛrkʃtaigər], *m.* (—s, *pl.* —) mountaineer.

Bergstock [ˈbɛrkʃtɔk], *m.* (—s, *pl.* ˙e) alpenstock.

Bergsturz [ˈbɛrkʃturts], *m.* (—es, *pl.* ˙e) landslip, landslide.

Bergung [ˈbɛrgun], *f.* (—, *pl.* —en) sheltering, salvaging; rescue operation.

Bergwerk [ˈbɛrkvɛrk], *n.* (—s, *pl.* —e) mine, pit.

Bericht [bəˈrɪçt], *m.* (—s, *pl.* —e) report, account, statement;— *erstatten*, report, give an account of.

Berichterstatter [bəˈrɪçtɛrʃtatər], *m.* (—s, *pl.* —) reporter.

berichtigen [bəˈrɪçtɪgən], *v.a.* set right, correct, rectify, amend.

berieseln [bəˈriːzəln], *v.a.* irrigate.

beritten [bəˈrɪtən], *adj.* mounted on horseback.

Berlin [bɛrˈliːn], *n.* Berlin; —*er Blau*, Prussian blue.

Bern [bɛrn], *n.* Berne.

Bernhardiner [bɛrnharˈdiːnər], *m.* (—s, *pl.* —) Cistercian monk; Newfoundland dog, St. Bernard dog.

Bernstein [ˈbɛrnʃtain], *m.* (—s, *no pl.*) amber.

bersten [ˈbɛrstən], *v.n. irr.* (*aux.* sein) burst.

berüchtigt [bəˈryçtɪçt], *adj.* notorious, infamous.

berücken [bəˈrykən], *v.a.* enchant, fascinate.

berücksichtigen [bəˈrykzɪçtɪgən], *v.a.* have regard to, take into consideration, allow for.

Beruf [bəˈruːf], *m.* (—s, *pl.* —e) profession, occupation, calling, trade.

berufen [bəˈruːfən], *v.a. irr.* (*meeting*) call, convene; appoint (*to an office*). — *v.r.* sich — *auf*, appeal to, refer to. — *adj.* competent, qualified.

berufsmäßig [bəˈruːfsmɛːsɪç], *adj.* professional.

Berufung [bəˈruːfun], *f.* (—, *pl.* —en) call, vocation, appointment; (*Law*) appeal.

beruhen [bəˈruːən], *v.n. auf etwas* —, be based on, be founded on.

beruhigen [bəˈruːɪgən], *v.a.* calm, pacify; comfort, console, set at rest.

Beruhigung [bəˈruːɪgun], *f.* (—, *pl.* —en) reassurance, quieting, calming.

berühmt [bəˈryːmt], *adj.* famous, celebrated, illustrious, renowned.

berühren [bəˈryːrən], *v.a.* touch, handle; (*subject*) mention, touch upon; *peinlich berührt*, unpleasantly affected.

berußt [bəˈruːst], *adj.* sooty.

Beryll [beˈryl], *m.* (—s, *pl.* —e) beryl.

besagen [bəˈzaːgən], *v.a.* mean, signify.

besagt [bəˈzaːkt], *adj.* aforesaid, above-mentioned.

besaiten [bəˈzaitən], *v.a.* fit with strings.

Besan [bəˈzaːn], *m.* (—s, *pl.* —e) (*Naut.*) miz(z)en.

besänftigen [bəˈzɛnftɪgən], *v.a.* calm, appease, pacify.

Besatz [bəˈzats], *m.* (—es, *pl.* ˙e) trimming, border.

Besatzung [bəˈzatsun], *f.* (—, *pl.* —en) crew; (*Mil.*) garrison, occupation.

besaufen [bəˈzaufən], *v.r. irr.* (*vulg.*) sich —, get drunk.

beschädigen [bəˈʃɛːdɪgən], *v.a.* damage.

beschaffen [bəˈʃafən], *v.a.* procure, get. — *adj.* conditioned, constituted.

Beschaffenheit [bəˈʃafənhait], *f.* (—, *no pl.*) nature, kind, quality, condition.

beschäftigen [bəˈʃɛftɪgən], *v.a.* occupy, employ.

beschämen [bəˈʃɛːmən], *v.a.* make ashamed, shame.

beschatten [bəˈʃatən], *v.a.* shade, shadow; follow (s.o.).

Beschau [bəˈʃau], *f.* (—, *no pl.*) examination; inspection.

beschauen [bəˈʃauən], *v.a.* view, look at.

beschaulich [bəˈʃauliç], *adj.* tranquil, contemplative.

Beschaulichkeit [bəˈʃauliçkait], *f.* (—, *pl.* —en) tranquillity, contemplation.

Bescheid [bəˈʃait], *m.* (—s, *pl.* —e) answer, information; (*Law*) decision; — *wissen*, know o.'s way about; know what's what.

bescheiden [bəˈʃaidən], *v.a. irr.* inform (s.o.); *einen zu sich* —, send for s.o. — *adj.* modest, unassuming.

Bescheidenheit [bəˈʃaidənhait], *f.* (—, *no pl.*) modesty.

bescheinen [bəˈʃainən], *v.a. irr.* shine upon.

bescheinigen [bəˈʃainɪgən], *v.a. einem etwas* —, attest, certify.

beschenken [bəˈʃɛnkən], *v.a.* give a present to.

bescheren [bəˈʃeːrən], *v.a.* give (a present to), bestow (s.th. on s.o.).

Bescherung [bəˈʃeːruŋ], *f.* (—, *pl.* —en) giving (of present); *das ist eine schöne* —, (*fig.*) this is a nice mess!

beschicken [bəˈʃɪkən], *v.a. eine Ausstellung* —, contribute to an exhibition.

beschießen [bəˈʃiːsən], *v.a. irr.* shoot at, fire upon, bombard.

beschiffen [bəˈʃɪfən], *v.a.* navigate, sail.

beschimpfen [bəˈʃɪmpfən], *v.a.* insult, abuse, revile.

beschirmen [bəˈʃɪrmən], *v.a.* protect, shelter, defend.

Beschlag [bəˈʃlaːk], *m.* (—s, *pl.* ˙e) mounting; metal fitting; (*on stick*) ferrule; *etwas mit* — *belegen*, or *in* — *nehmen*, sequestrate, confiscate, seize.

beschlagen [bəˈʃlaːgən], *v.a. irr.* shoe (a horse). — *v.n.* (*window*) mist over.

Beschlagnahme [bəˈʃlaːknaːmə], *f.* (—, *pl.* —n) confiscation, seizure.

beschleunigen [bəˈʃlɔynɪgən], *v.a.* hasten, speed up, accelerate.

beschließen [bəˈʃliːsən], *v.a. irr.* shut, lock up; close, conclude, finish; decide, resolve upon.

Beschluß [bəˈʃlus], *m.* (—sses, *pl.* ˙sse) determination, resolution, decree.

beschmieren [bəˈʃmiːrən], *v.a.* soil, smear.

beschmutzen [bəˈʃmutsən], *v.a.* soil, dirty, foul.

beschneiden [bəˈʃnaɪdən], *v.a. irr.* cut, clip; (*Hort.*) lop, prune; (*animals*) crop; circumcise.

Beschneidung [bəˈʃnaɪduŋ], *f.* (—, *pl.* —en) lopping, pruning; circumcision.

beschönigen [bəˈʃøːnɪgən], *v.a.* palliate, excuse.

beschränken [bəˈʃrɛnkən], *v.a.* limit, restrict.

beschränkt [bəˈʃrɛŋkt], *adj.* limited; *etwas* —, a little stupid; *Gesellschaft mit* —*er Haftung*, limited (liability) company.

Beschränkung [bəˈʃrɛŋkuŋ], *f.* (—, *pl.* —en) limitation, restriction.

beschreiben [bəˈʃraɪbən], *v.a. irr.* describe; write upon.

beschreiten [bəˈʃraɪtən], *v.a. irr.* tread on.

beschuldigen [bəˈʃuldɪgən], *v.a.* charge (s.o.), accuse.

beschützen [bəˈʃytsən], *v.a.* protect, shelter, guard.

Beschützer [bəˈʃytsər], *m.* (—s, *pl.* —) protector, defender.

Beschwerde [bəˈʃveːrdə], *f.* (—, *pl.* —en) trouble, hardship, difficulty; complaint, grievance.

beschweren [bəˈʃveːrən], *v.a.* make heavier, weight. — *v.r. sich über etwas* —, complain of s.th.

beschwerlich [bəˈʃveːrlɪç], *adj.* burdensome, hard, troublesome.

beschwichtigen [bəˈʃvɪçtɪgən], *v.a.* soothe, appease, still.

beschwindeln [bəˈʃvɪndəln], *v.a.* cheat, swindle (s.o.).

beschwingt [bəˈʃvɪŋkt], *adj.* winged, light-footed.

beschwipst [bəˈʃvɪpst], *adj.* (*coll.*) tipsy.

beschwören [bəˈʃvøːrən], *v.a. irr.* testify on oath; *einen* —, implore s.o.; conjure (up) (ghosts etc.); exorcize.

beseelen [bəˈzeːlən], *v.a.* animate.

besehen [bəˈzeːən], *v.a. irr.* look at, inspect.

beseitigen [bəˈzaɪtɪgən], *v.a.* remove.

beseligt [bəˈzeːlɪçt], *adj.* enraptured, beatified.

Besen [ˈbeːzən], *m.* (—s, *pl.* —) broom, besom.

Besenstiel [ˈbeːzənʃtiːl], *m.* (—s, *pl.* —e) broom-stick.

besessen [bəˈzɛsən], *adj.* possessed, obsessed, mad.

besetzen [bəˈzɛtsən], *v.a.* (*dress*) trim, lace; (*Mil.*) occupy, garrison; (*office*) fill; (*Theat.*) cast; (*seat*) occupy, take; *besetzt*, engaged.

Besetzung [bəˈzɛtsuŋ], *f.* (—, *pl.* —en) lacing, trimming; appointment (to post); (*Theat.*) cast.

besichtigen [bəˈzɪçtɪgən], *v.a.* view, go over, inspect, examine.

besiedeln [bəˈziːdəln], *v.a.* colonise.

besiegeln [bəˈziːgəln], *v.a.* seal, set o.'s seal to.

besiegen [bəˈziːgən], *v.a.* vanquish, conquer, overcome.

besinnen [bəˈzɪnən], *v.r. irr.* reflect; *sich auf etwas* —, recollect, remember.

besinnungslos [bəˈzɪnuŋsloːs], *adj.* insensible, unconscious.

Besitz [bəˈzɪts], *m.* (—es, *no pl.*) possession, property.

besitzanzeigend [bəˈzɪtsantsaɪgənt], *adj.* (*Gram.*) possessive.

besitzen [bəˈzɪtsən], *v.a. irr.* possess, own, have.

Besitzergreifung [bəˈzɪtsɛrgraɪfuŋ], *f.* (—, *no pl.*) occupation, taking possession (of).

besoffen [bəˈzɔfən], *adj.* (*vulg.*) drunk.

besohlen [bəˈzoːlən], *v.a.* sole (shoes).

besolden [bəˈzɔldən], *v.a.* give a salary to, pay.

besonder [bəˈzɔndər], *adj.* special, particular.

Besonderheit [bəˈzɔndərhaɪt], *f.* (—, *pl.* —en) particularity, peculiarity, strangeness.

besonders [bəˈzɔndərs], *adv.* especially.

besonnen [bəˈzɔnən], *adj.* prudent, cautious, collected, circumspect.

besorgen [bəˈzɔrgən], *v.a.* take care of, provide, procure.

Besorgnis [bəˈzɔrknɪs], *f.* (—, *pl.* —se) care, concern, anxiety, fear.

besorgt [bəˈzɔrkt], *adj.* apprehensive, anxious, worried.

Besorgung [bə'zɔrguŋ], *f.* (—, *pl.* —en) care, management; purchase, commission; —en machen, go shopping.

bespannen [bə'ʃpanən], *v.a.* string (a musical instrument); put horses (to a carriage).

bespötteln [bə'ʃpœtəln], *v.a.* ridicule.

besprechen [bə'ʃprɛçən], *v.a. irr.* discuss, talk over; (book) review. — *v.r. sich* — *mit,* confer with.

bespritzen [bə'ʃprɪtsən], *v.a.* sprinkle, splash.

besser ['bɛsər], *adj.* better; um so —, so much the better; je mehr desto —, the more the better; — sein als, be better than, be preferable to; — werden, (weather) clear up; (health) improve.

bessern ['bɛsərn], *v.a.* better, improve. — *v.r. sich* —, reform, improve, mend o.'s ways.

Besserung ['bɛsəruŋ], *f.* (—pl. —en) improvement, amendment, reform; (Med.) recovery; gute —, get well soon.

Besserungsanstalt ['bɛsəruŋsanʃtalt], *f.* (—, *pl.* —en) reformatory.

best ['bɛst], *adj.* best.

bestallen [bə'ʃtalən], *v.a.* appoint.

Bestand [bə'ʃtant], *m.* (—s, *pl.* ˙˙e) continuance, duration; stock; balance of cash; — haben, endure.

Bestandaufnahme [bə'ʃtantaufna:mə], *f.* (—, *pl.* —n) (Comm.) stocktaking.

beständig [bə'ʃtɛndɪç], *adj.* continual, perpetual; (persons) steady, steadfast, constant.

Bestandteil [bə'ʃtanttaɪl], *m.* (—s, *pl.* —e) constituent part, component, ingredient, essential part.

bestärken [bə'ʃtɛrkən], *v.a.* confirm, strengthen.

bestätigen [bə'ʃtɛ:tɪgən], *v.a.* confirm, ratify, bear out, sanction; den Empfang eines Briefes —, acknowledge receipt of a letter.

bestatten [bə'ʃtatən], *v.a.* bury, inter.

bestäuben [bə'ʃtɔybən], *v.a.* cover with dust, spray; (Bot.) pollinate.

bestechen [bə'ʃtɛçən], *v.a. irr.* bribe, corrupt; (fig.) captivate.

bestechlich [bə'ʃtɛçlɪç], *adj.* corruptible.

Bestechung [bə'ʃtɛçuŋ], *f.* (—, *pl.* —en) corruption, bribery.

Besteck [bə'ʃtɛk], *n.* (—s, *pl.* —e) set of knife, fork and spoon; set or case (of instruments).

Bestehen [bə'ʃte:ən], *n.* (—s, *no pl.*) existence.

bestehen [bə'ʃte:ən], *v.a. irr.* undergo, endure, pass (an examination). — *v.n.* exist; aus etwas —, consist of s.th.; be composed of s.th.; auf (Dat.) —, insist upon s.th.

besteigen [bə'ʃtaɪgən], *v.a. irr.* ascend, mount, climb.

bestellen [bə'ʃtɛlən], *v.a.* order, book; appoint; put in order; (letter, message) deliver; (field) till.

Bestellung [bə'ʃtɛluŋ], *f.* (—, *pl.* —en) order, commission, delivery (of letter); tilling (of field); appointment; auf —, to order.

bestens ['bɛstəns], *adv.* in the best manner.

besteuern [bə'ʃtɔyərn], *v.a.* tax.

bestialisch [bɛsti'a:lɪʃ], *adj.* beastly, bestial.

Bestie ['bɛstjə], *f.* (—, *pl.* —n) beast, brute.

bestimmen [bə'ʃtɪmən], *v.a.* fix, settle; decide (s.th.); determine, define.

bestimmt [bə'ʃtɪmt], *adj.* decided, fixed, appointed; ganz —, positively, most decidedly.

Bestimmtheit [bə'ʃtɪmthaɪt], *f.* (—, *no pl.*) certainty.

Bestimmung [bə'ʃtɪmuŋ], *f.* (—, *pl.* —en) settlement, decision, determination; provision; destiny.

bestrafen [bə'ʃtra:fən], *v.a.* punish, chastise.

bestrahlen [bə'ʃtra:lən], *v.a.* irradiate; (Med.) treat by radiotherapy.

bestreben [bə'ʃtre:bən], *v.r. sich* —, exert o.s., strive (for); endeavour.

Bestrebung [bə'ʃtre:buŋ], *f.* (—, *pl.* —en) effort, endeavour, exertion.

bestreichen [bə'ʃtraɪçən], *v.a. irr.* spread.

bestreiten [bə'ʃtraɪtən], *v.a. irr.* contest, deny, dispute; defray (costs).

bestreuen [bə'ʃtrɔyən], *v.a.* sprinkle, strew, powder.

bestricken [bə'ʃtrɪkən], *v.a.* ensnare, entangle.

bestürmen [bə'ʃtyrmən], *v.a.* storm, assail; (fig.) importune.

bestürzen [bə'ʃtyrtsən], *v.a.* dismay, confound, perplex.

Besuch [bə'zu:x], *m.* (—s, *pl.* —e) visit; (person) visitor.

besuchen [bə'zu:xən], *v.a.* visit, call on; attend; frequent.

besudeln [bə'zu:dəln], *v.a.* soil, foul.

betagt [bə'ta:kt], *adj.* aged, elderly.

betätigen [bə'tɛ:tɪgən], *v.a.* practise, operate. — *v.r. sich* —, take an active part, work, participate (in).

betäuben [bə'tɔybən], *v.a.* deafen; stun, benumb, anaesthetize.

Betäubung [bə'tɔybuŋ], *f.* (—, *pl.* —en) stupor, stupefaction; örtliche —, local anaesthetic.

beteiligen [bə'taɪlɪgən], *v.a.* einen an etwas —, give s.o. a share of s.th. — *v.r. sich an etwas* —, participate in s.th.; (Comm.) have shares in s.th.

Beteiligte [bə'taɪlɪçtə], *m.* (—n, *pl.* —n) person concerned.

Beteiligung [bə'taɪlɪguŋ], *f.* (—, *pl.* —en) participation, interest.

beten ['be:tən], *v.n.* pray, say o.'s prayers.

beteuern [bə'tɔyərn], *v.a.* aver, affirm solemnly.

betiteln [bə'ti:təln], *v.a.* entitle, name.

Beton [be'tɔ̃], *m.* (—s, *no pl.*) concrete.

betonen [bə'to:nən], v.a. accentuate, stress, emphasise.

Betonung [bə'to:nuŋ], f. (—, pl. —en) accentuation, emphasis, stress.

betören [bə'tø:rən], v.a. delude, infatuate.

Betracht [bə'traxt], m. (—s, no pl.) consideration, respect, regard.

betrachten [bə'traxtən], v.a. consider, look at, view; etwas aufmerksam —, contemplate s.th.

beträchtlich [bə'trɛçtlɪç], adj. considerable.

Betrachtung [bə'traxtuŋ], f. (—, pl. —en) contemplation, consideration.

Betrag [bə'tra:k], m. (—s, pl. ˙-e) amount, sum total.

betragen [bə'tra:gən], v.a. irr. amount to, come to. — v.r. sich —, behave, conduct o.s.

Betragen [bə'tra:gən], n. (—s, no pl.) behaviour, conduct, demeanour.

betrauen [bə'trauən], v.a. einen mit etwas —, entrust s.o. with s.th.

betrauern [bə'trauərn], v.a. mourn for, bemoan.

Betreff [bə'trɛf], m. (—s, no pl.) reference; in —, with regard to.

betreffen [bə'trɛfən], v.a. irr. concern, affect, relate to.

Betreiben [bə'traɪbən], n. (—s, no pl.) auf — von, at the instigation of.

betreiben [bə'traɪbən], v.a. irr. (business) carry on; (factory) run; (trade) follow, practise.

Betreten [bə'tre:tən], n. (—s, no pl.) entry, entering.

betreten [bə'tre:tən], v.a. irr. step upon, set foot on, enter. — adj. disconcerted, embarrassed.

betreuen [bə'trɔyən], v.a. care for, attend to.

Betrieb [bə'tri:p], m. (—s, pl. —e) management, business, factory, plant; den — einstellen, close down; in — sein, be in operation; in — setzen, start working.

betriebsam [bə'tri:pza:m], adj. active, busy, industrious, diligent.

Betriebsamkeit [bə'tri:pza:mkaɪt], f. (—, pl. —en) activity, industry, bustle.

betriebsfertig [bə'tri:psfɛrtɪç], adj. ready for service; operational.

Betriebsmaterial [bə'tri:psmaterja:l], n. (—s, pl. —ien) (Railw.) rolling-stock; (factory) working-stock.

Betriebspersonal [bə'tri:pspɛrzona:l], n. (—s, no pl.) workmen, employees, staff.

betrinken [bə'trɪŋkən], v.r. irr. sich —, get drunk.

betroffen [bə'trɔfən], adj. perplexed, confounded.

betrüben [bə'try:bən], v.a. afflict, grieve.

Betrübnis [bə'try:pnɪs], f. (—ses, pl. —se) affliction, grief, distress, sorrow.

betrübt [bə'try:pt], adj. sad, grieved.

Betrug [bə'tru:k], m. (—s, pl. ˙-ereien) fraud, deceit, deception, imposture; einen — begehen, commit a fraud.

betrügen [bə'try:gən], v.a. irr. cheat, deceive.

Betrüger [bə'try:gər], m. (—s, —) swindler, cheat, deceiver, impostor.

betrunken [bə'truŋkən], adj. drunk, drunken, tipsy.

Bett [bɛt], n. (—(e)s, pl. —en) bed; (river) bed, channel.

Bettdecke ['bɛtdɛkə], f. (—, pl. —n) counterpane; (Am.) bedspread; wollene —, blanket; gesteppte —, quilt.

Bettel ['bɛtəl], m. (—s, no pl.) trash, trifle.

bettelarm ['bɛtəlarm], adj. destitute.

Bettelei [bɛtə'laɪ], f. (—, pl. —en) begging, beggary, penury.

betteln ['bɛtəln], v.a. beg, ask alms.

betten ['bɛtən], v.a. bed, lay to rest. — v.r. (fig.) sich —, make o.'s bed.

bettlägerig ['bɛtlɛgərɪç], adj. bedridden.

Bettlaken ['bɛtla:kən], n. (—s, pl. —) sheet.

Bettler ['bɛtlər], m. (—s, pl. —) beggar.

Bettstelle ['bɛtʃtɛlə], f. (—, pl. —n) bedstead.

Bettvorleger ['bɛtfo:rle:gər], m. (—s, pl. —s) bedside-carpet or rug.

Bettwäsche ['bɛtvɛʃə], f. (—, no pl.) bed linen, bed clothes.

Bettzeug ['bɛttsɔyk], n. (—s, no pl.) bedding.

beugen ['bɔygən], v.a. bend, bow. — v.r. sich —, bend down, stoop.

Beugung ['bɔyguŋ], f. (—, pl. —en) (Gram.) inflection.

Beule ['bɔylə], f. (—, pl. —n) bruise, bump, swelling, boil.

beunruhigen [bə'unru:ɪgən], v.a. alarm, trouble, disquiet.

beurkunden [bə'u:rkundən], v.a. authenticate, verify.

beurlauben [bə'u:rlaubən], v.a. grant leave of absence. — v.r. sich —, take leave.

beurteilen [bə'urtaɪlən], v.a. judge, criticise.

Beute ['bɔytə], f. (—, no pl.) booty, loot; (animals) prey; (Hunt.) bag.

Beutel ['bɔytəl], m. (—s, pl. —) bag; (money) purse; (Zool.) pouch.

Beuteltier ['bɔytəlti:r], n. (—s, pl. —e) marsupial.

bevölkern [bə'fœlkərn], v.a. people, populate.

Bevölkerung [bə'fœlkəruŋ], f. (—, pl. —en) population.

bevollmächtigen [bə'fɔlmɛçtɪgən], v.a. empower, authorise.

bevor [bə'fo:r], conj. before, ere, beforehand.

bevormunden [bə'fo:rmundən], v.a. insep. act as guardian to; (fig.) browbeat.

bevorrechtigt [bə'fo:rrɛçtɪçt], adj. privileged.

bevorstehen [bəˈfoːrʃteːən], *v.n. irr.* impend, lie ahead, be imminent; *einem —*, be in store for s.o.

bevorzugen [bəˈfoːrtsuːgən], *v.a. insep.* prefer, favour.

bewachen [bəˈvaxən], *v.a.* watch over, guard.

bewachsen [bəˈvaksən], *adj.* overgrown.

bewaffnen [bəˈvafnən], *v.a.* arm, supply with arms.

Bewahranstalt [bəˈvaːranʃtalt], *f.* (—, *pl.* —en) kindergarten, nursery.

bewahren [bəˈvaːrən], *v.a.* preserve, keep, take care of.

bewähren [bəˈvɛːrən], *v.r. sich —*, prove o.s.

bewahrheiten [bəˈvaːrhaɪtən], *v.r. sich —*, come true.

bewährt [bəˈvɛːrt], *adj.* proved.

Bewährung [bəˈvɛːruŋ], *f.* (—, *no pl.*) proof, verification.

Bewährungsfrist [bəˈvɛːruŋsfrɪst], *f.* (—, *no pl.*) probation.

bewaldet [bəˈvaldət], *adj.* wooded, woody.

bewältigen [bəˈvɛltɪgən], *v.a.* overcome; manage, master; cope *or* deal with.

bewandert [bəˈvandərt], *adj.* versed, skilled, experienced, conversant.

bewandt [bəˈvant], *adj.* such; *damit ist es so —*, it is like this.

Bewandtnis [bəˈvantnɪs], *f.* (—, *pl.* —se) circumstance, condition, state; *es hat damit folgende —*, the circumstances are as follows.

bewässern [bəˈvɛsərn], *v.a.* water, irrigate.

bewegen [bəˈveːgən], *v.a., v.r.* move, stir; take exercise. *— v.a. irr.* persuade, induce.

Beweggrund [bəˈveːkgrunt], *m.* (—es, *pl.* ⁻e) motive, reason, motivation.

beweglich [bəˈveːklɪç], *adj.* movable; agile, brisk, sprightly.

Bewegung [bəˈveːguŋ], *f.* (—, *pl.* —en) motion, movement; (*mind*) emotion, agitation.

beweinen [bəˈvaɪnən], *v.a.* lament, bemoan, deplore.

Beweis [bəˈvaɪs], *m.* (—es, *pl.* —e) proof, evidence; (*Maths.*) demonstration.

beweisen [bəˈvaɪzən], *v.a. irr.* prove, show, demonstrate.

Beweiskraft [bəˈvaɪskraft], *f.* (—, *no pl.*) (*Law*) probative force.

Beweismittel [bəˈvaɪsmɪtəl], *n.* (—s, *pl.* —) evidence, proof.

Bewenden [bəˈvɛndən], *n.* (—s, *no pl.*) *es hat damit sein —*, there the matter rests.

bewenden [bəˈvɛndən], *v.n. irr. es dabei — lassen*, leave it at that.

bewerben [bəˈvɛrbən], *v.r. irr. sich um etwas —*, apply for s.th.

Bewerber [bəˈvɛrbər], *m.* (—s, *pl.* —) applicant, candidate; (*marriage*) suitor.

Bewerbung [bəˈvɛrbuŋ], *f.* (—, *pl.* —en) application, candidature; (*marriage*) courtship.

bewerkstelligen [bəˈvɛrkʃtɛlɪgən], *v.a.* perform, bring about.

bewerten [bəˈvɛrtən], *v.a.* estimate, value.

bewilligen [bəˈvɪlɪgən], *v.a.* grant, allow, permit.

bewillkommnen [bəˈvɪlkɔmnən], *v.a.* welcome.

bewirken [bəˈvɪrkən], *v.a.* effect, bring about.

bewirten [bəˈvɪrtən], *v.a.* entertain, act as host (to).

bewirtschaften [bəˈvɪrtʃaftən], *v.a.* manage.

bewohnen [bəˈvoːnən], *v.a.* inhabit, occupy.

Bewohner [bəˈvoːnər], *m.* (—s, *pl.* —) inhabitant, tenant, resident.

bewölken [bəˈvœlkən], *v.r. sich —*, become overcast, become cloudy.

bewundern [bəˈvundərn], *v.a.* admire.

bewundernswert [bəˈvundərnsvɛrt], *adj.* admirable.

bewußt [bəˈvust], *adj.* conscious, aware; *es war mir nicht —*, I was not aware of.

bewußtlos [bəˈvustloːs], *adj.* unconscious; *— werden*, faint, lose consciousness.

Bewußtsein [bəˈvustzaɪn], *n.* (—s, *no pl.*) consciousness; *einem etwas zum — bringen*, bring s.th. home to s.o.

bezahlbar [bəˈtsaːlbaːr], *adj.* payable.

bezahlen [bəˈtsaːlən], *v.a.* pay; (*bill*) settle.

bezähmen [bəˈtsɛːmən], *v.a.* tame, restrain; *— v.r. sich —*, restrain o.s., control o.s.

bezaubern [bəˈtsaubərn], *v.a.* bewitch, enchant, fascinate.

bezeichnen [bəˈtsaɪçnən], *v.a.* mark, denote, indicate, designate.

bezeichnend [bəˈtsaɪçnənt], *adj.* indicative, characteristic, significant.

bezeigen [bəˈtsaɪgən], *v.a.* manifest, show.

bezeugen [bəˈtsɔygən], *v.a.* attest, bear witness, testify.

bezichtigen [bəˈtsɪçtɪgən], *v.a.* accuse (s.o.) of (s.th.).

beziehbar [bəˈtsiːbaːr], *adj.* (*goods*) obtainable; (*house*) ready for occupation.

beziehen [bəˈtsiːən], *v.a. irr.* cover; (*house etc.*) move into; (*instrument*) string; make up (a bed); *die Wache —*, mount guard. *— v.r. sich —*, (*sky*) cloud over; *sich auf etwas —*, refer to s.th.

Bezieher [bəˈtsiːər], *m.* (—s, *pl.* —) customer; (*newspaper*) subscriber.

Beziehung [bəˈtsiːuŋ], *f.* (—, *pl.* —en) relation, connection; reference, bearing; *in dieser —*, in this respect; (*Comm.*) *unter — auf*, with reference to.

beziehungsweise [bəˈtsiːuŋsvaɪzə], *adv.* respectively, as the case may be, or.

beziffern

beziffern [bə'tsɪfərn], *v.a.* number.

Bezirk [bə'tsɪrk], *m.* (—s, *pl.* —e) district; (*Am.*) precinct; (*Parl.*) constituency; (*Law*) circuit.

Bezirksgericht [bə'tsɪrksɡərɪçt], *n.* (—s, *pl.* —e) county court.

Bezug [bə'tsu:k], *m.* (—s, *pl.* ⁓e) (*pillow*) case, cover; (*goods*) order, purchase; (*fig.*) relation; — haben auf, refer to; mit — auf, referring to; (*pl.*) emoluments, income.

bezüglich [bə'tsy:klɪç], *adj.* with regard to, regarding.

Bezugnahme [bə'tsu:kna:mə], *f.* (—, *pl.* —n) reference; unter — auf, with reference to.

Bezugsbedingung [bə'tsu:ksbədɪŋuŋ], *f.* (—, *pl.* —en) (*usually pl.*) (*Comm.*) conditions *or* terms of delivery.

Bezugsquelle [bə'tsu:kskvɛlə], *f.* (—, *pl.* —n) source of supply.

bezwecken [bə'tsvɛkən], *v.a.* aim at, intend.

bezweifeln [bə'tsvaɪfəln], *v.a.* doubt, question.

bezwingen [bə'tsvɪŋən], *v.a. irr.* subdue, conquer. — *v.r.* sich —, restrain o.s.

Bibel ['bi:bəl], *f.* (—, *pl.* —n) Bible.

Bibelauslegung ['bi:bəlauslə:ɡuŋ], *f.* (—, *pl.* —en) (Biblical) exegesis.

Biber ['bi:bər], *m.* (—s, *pl.* —) (*Zool.*) beaver.

Bibliothek [biblio'te:k], *f.* (—, *pl.* —en) library.

Bibliothekar [bibliote'ka:r], *m.* (—s, *pl.* —e) librarian.

biblisch ['bi:blɪʃ], *adj.* biblical, scriptural.

Bickbeere ['bɪkbe:rə], *f.* (—, *pl.* —n) bilberry.

bieder ['bi:dər], *adj.* upright, honest, decent.

Biederkeit ['bi:dərkaɪt], *f.* (—, *no pl.*) uprightness, probity.

Biedermann ['bi:dərman], *m.* (—s, *pl.* ⁓er) honourable man; (*iron.*) Philistine.

biegen ['bi:ɡən], *v.a. irr.* bend, bow. — *v.n.* (*aux.* sein) um die Ecke —, turn the corner. — *v.r.* sich —, curve; — oder brechen, by hook or by crook.

biegsam ['bi:kza:m], *adj.* flexible, supple, pliant.

Biegung ['bi:ɡuŋ], *f.* (—, *pl.* —en) curve, bend; (*Gram.*) inflexion.

Biene ['bi:nə], *f.* (—, *pl.* —n) bee.

Bienenhaus ['bi:nənhaus], *n.* (—es, *pl.* ⁓er) apiary.

Bienenkorb ['bi:nənkɔrp], *m.* (—s, *pl.* ⁓e) beehive.

Bienenzüchter ['bi:nəntsyçtər], *m.* (—s, *pl.* —) apiarist, bee-keeper.

Bier ['bi:r], *n.* (—(e)s, *pl.* —e) beer.

Bierkanne ['bi:rkanə], *f.* (—, *pl.* —n) tankard.

Biest [bi:st], *n.* (—es, *pl.* —er) brute, beast.

bieten ['bi:tən], *v.a. irr.* offer; (*auction*) bid.

Bieter ['bi:tər], *m.* (—s, *pl.* —) (*auction*) bidder.

Bigotterie [bɪɡɔtə'ri:], *f.* (—, *no pl.*) bigotry.

Bijouterie [bɪʒutə'ri:], *f.* (—, *pl.* —n) trinkets, dress-jewellery.

Bilanz [bɪ'lants], *f.* (—, *pl.* —en) (*Comm.*) balance; (financial) statement.

Bild [bɪlt], *n.* (—es, *pl.* —er) picture, painting, portrait, image; idea; (*coins*) effigy; (*Cards*) court card; (*books*) illustration; (*speech*) figure of speech, metaphor.

bilden ['bɪldən], *v.c.* form, shape; (*mind*) cultivate. — *v.r.* sich —, improve o.'s mind, educate o.s.

bildend ['bɪldənt], *adj.* instructive, civilising; die —en Künste, the fine arts.

bilderreich ['bɪldəraɪç], *adj.* —e Sprache, flowery language, figurative style.

Bilderschrift ['bɪldərʃrɪft], *f.* (—, *pl.* —en) hieroglyphics.

Bilderstürmer ['bɪldərʃtyrmər], *m.* (—s, *pl.* —) iconoclast.

Bildhauer ['bɪlthauər], *m.* (—s, *pl.* —) sculptor.

bildhübsch ['bɪlthypʃ], *adj.* as pretty as a picture.

bildlich ['bɪltlɪç], *adj.* figurative.

Bildnis ['bɪltnɪs], *n.* (—ses, *pl.* —se) portrait, figure, image, effigy.

bildsam ['bɪltza:m], *adj.* plastic, ductile.

bildschön ['bɪltʃø:n], *adj.* very beautiful.

Bildseite ['bɪltzaɪtə], *f.* (—, *pl.* —n) (*coin*) face, obverse.

Bildung ['bɪlduŋ], *f.* (—, *pl.* (*rare*) —en) formation; (*mind*) education, culture; knowledge, learning, accomplishments, attainments.

Billard ['bɪljart], *n.* (—s, *pl.* —s) billiards.

Billett [bɪl'jɛt], *n.* (—s, *pl.* —s) ticket.

billig ['bɪlɪç], *adj.* cheap, inexpensive; equitable, just, fair, reasonable.

billigen ['bɪlɪɡən], *v.a.* sanction, approve of, consent to.

Billigkeit ['bɪlɪçkaɪt], *f.* (—, *no pl.*) cheapness; fairness, equitableness, reasonableness.

Billigung ['bɪlɪɡuŋ], *f.* (—, *no pl.*) approbation, approval, sanction.

Bilsenkraut ['bɪlzənkraut], *n.* (—s, *pl.* ⁓er) henbane.

bimmeln ['bɪməln], *v.n.* (*coll.*) tinkle.

Bimsstein ['bɪmsʃtaɪn], *m.* (—s, *pl.* —e) pumice stone.

Binde ['bɪndə], *f.* (—, *pl.* —n) band, bandage; tie; ligature; sanitary towel.

Bindeglied ['bɪndegli:t], *n.* (—s, *pl.* —er) connecting link.

Bindehaut ['bɪndəhaut], *f.* (—, *pl.* ⁓e) (*Anat.*) conjunctiva.

Bindehautentzündung ['bɪndəhautɛntsynduŋ], *f.* (—, *pl.* —en) conjunctivitis.

binden ['bɪndən], *v.a. irr.* bind, tie, fasten.

Bindestrich ['bɪndeʃtrɪç], *m.* (—(e)s, *pl.* —e) hyphen.

Bindewort ['bɪndəvɔrt], *n.* (—s, *pl.* ⁀er) conjunction.

Bindfaden ['bɪntfaːdən], *m.* (—s, *pl.* ⁀) string, twine.

Bindung ['bɪnduŋ], *f.* (—, *pl.* —en) binding, bond; obligation; (*Mus.*) ligature.

binnen ['bɪnən], *prep.* (*Genit. & Dat.*), *adv.* within.

Binnenhafen ['bɪnənhaːfən], *m.* (—s, *pl.* ⁀) inland harbour.

Binnenhandel ['bɪnənhandəl], *m.* (—s, *no pl.*) inland trade.

Binse ['bɪnzə], *f.* (—, *pl.* —n) (*Bot.*) rush, reed.

Biographie [biogra'fiː], *f.* (—, *pl.* —n) biography.

Birke ['bɪrkə], *f.* (—, *pl.* —n) (*Bot.*) birch, birch-tree.

Birma ['bɪrmaː], *n.* Burma.

Birnbaum ['bɪrnbaum], *m.* (—s, *pl.* ⁀e) pear-tree.

Birne ['bɪrnə], *f.* (—, *pl.* —n) pear; (*Elec.*) bulb.

birnförmig ['bɪrnfœrmɪç], *adj.* pear-shaped.

bis [bɪs], *prep.* (*time*) till, until; by; (*place*) to, up to; — *auf*, with the exception of. — *conj.* till, until.

Bisam ['biːzam], *m.* (—s, *pl.* —e) musk.

Bischof ['bɪʃɔf], *m.* (—s, *pl.* ⁀e) bishop.

bischöflich ['bɪʃœflɪç], *adj.* episcopal.

Bischofsstab ['bɪʃɔfsʃtaːp], *m.* (—s, *pl.* ⁀e) crosier.

bisher ['bɪsheːr], *adv.* hitherto, till now.

bisherig [bɪs'heːrɪç], *adj.* up to this time, hitherto existing.

Biskayischer Meerbusen [bɪs'kaːɪʃər 'meːrbuːzən]. Bay of Biscay.

Biß [bɪs], *m.* (—sses, *pl.* —sse) bite, sting.

Bißchen ['bɪsçən], *n.* (—s, *pl.* —) morsel; little bit.

Bissen ['bɪsən], *m.* (—s, *pl.* —) bite, morsel.

bissig ['bɪsɪç], *adj.* biting, cutting; sharp, vicious; sarcastic.

Bistum ['bɪstum], *n.* (—s, *pl.* ⁀er) bishopric, diocese; see.

bisweilen [bɪs'vaɪlən], *adv.* sometimes, now and then, occasionally.

Bitte ['bɪtə], *f.* (—, *pl.* —n) request, entreaty.

bitte ['bɪtə], *int.* please.

bitten ['bɪtən], *v.a. irr.* ask; request.

bitter ['bɪtər], *adj.* bitter.

Bitterkeit ['bɪtərkaɪt], *f.* (—, *no pl.*) bitterness.

bitterlich ['bɪtərlɪç], *adv.* (*fig.*) bitterly.

Bittersalz ['bɪtərzalts], *n.* (—es, *no pl.*) Epsom salts.

Bittgang ['bɪtgaŋ], *m.* (—(e)s, *pl.* ⁀e) (*Eccl.*) procession.

Bittsteller ['bɪtʃtɛlər], *m.* (—s, *pl.* —) petitioner, suppli(c)ant.

Biwak ['biːvak], *m.* (—s, *pl.* —s) bivouac.

blähen ['blɛːən], *v.a.* inflate, puff up, swell.

Blähung ['blɛːuŋ], *f.* (—, *pl.* —en) (*Med.*) flatulence.

blaken ['blaːkən], *v.n.* smoulder; smoke.

Blamage [bla'maːʒə], *f.* (—, *pl.* —n) shame, disgrace.

blamieren [bla'miːrən], *v.a.*, *v.r.* make (o.s.) ridiculous, make a fool of o.s.

blank [blaŋk], *adj.* shining, bright, smooth, polished.

Bläschen ['blɛːsçən], *n.* (—s, *pl.* —) little bubble, blister; (*Med.*) vesicle.

Blase ['blaːzə], *f.* (—, *pl.* —n) (*soap*) bubble; (*skin*) blister; (*Anat.*) bladder.

Blasebalg ['blaːzəbalk], *m.* (—s, *pl.* ⁀e) pair of bellows.

blasen ['blaːzən], *v.a. irr.* blow; (*Mus.*) sound.

Bläser ['blɛːzər], *m.* (—s, *pl.* —) (*glass*) blower; (*Mus.*) wind player.

blasiert [bla'ziːrt], *adj.* blasé, haughty.

Blasrohr ['blaːsroːr], *n.* (—s, *pl.* —e) blow-pipe, pea-shooter.

blaß [blas], *adj.* pale, wan, pallid.

Blässe ['blɛsə], *f.* (—, *no pl.*) paleness, pallor.

Blatt [blat], *n.* (—s, *pl.* ⁀er) leaf; (*paper*) sheet; blade.

Blatter ['blatər], *f.* (—, *pl.* —n) pustule; (*pl.*) smallpox.

blättern ['blɛtərn], *v.a.* turn the leaves (of a book).

Blätterteig ['blɛtərtaɪk], *m.* (—s, *no pl.*) puff pastry.

Blattgold ['blatgɔlt], *n.* (—es, *no pl.*) gold-leaf.

Blattlaus ['blatlaus], *f.* (—, *pl.* ⁀e) (*Ent.*) plant-louse.

Blattpflanze ['blatpflantsə], *f.* (—, *pl.* —n) leaf-plant.

blau [blau], *adj.* blue; —*en Montag machen*, stay away from work; *sein —es Wunder erleben*, be amazed.

blauäugig ['blauɔygɪç], *adj.* blue-eyed.

Blaubeere ['blaubeːrə], *f.* (—, *pl.* —n) bilberry, blueberry.

blaublütig ['blaublyːtɪç], *adj.* aristocratic.

bläuen ['blɔyən], *v.a.* dye blue, rinse in blue.

bläulich ['blɔylɪç], *adj.* pale blue, bluish.

Blausäure ['blauzɔyrə], *f.* (—, *no pl.*) prussic acid.

Blaustrumpf ['blauʃtrumpf], *m.* (—s, *pl.* ⁀e) blue-stocking.

Blech [blɛç], *n.* (—s, *pl.* —e) tinplate, sheet metal.

blechen ['blɛçən], *v.n.* (*coll.*) fork out money.

blechern ['blɛçərn], *adj.* made of tin, tinny.

Blechinstrument ['blɛçɪnstrumɛnt], *n.* (—s, *pl.* —e) (*Mus.*) brass instrument.

Blei [blaɪ], *n.* (—s, *no pl.*) lead.
bleiben ['blaɪbən], *v.n. irr.* (*aux.* sein) remain, stay.
bleich [blaɪç], *adj.* pale, wan, pallid.
Bleiche ['blaɪçə], *f.* (—, *pl.* —n) pallor; (*laundry*) bleaching-place.
bleichen ['blaɪçən], *v.a. irr.* bleach, whiten.
Bleichsucht ['blaɪçzuxt], *f.* (—, *no pl.*) chlorosis, anaemia.
bleiern ['blaɪərn], *adj.* leaden.
Bleiglanz ['blaɪglants], *m.* (—es, *no pl.*) (*Min.*) lead sulphide.
Bleisoldat ['blaɪzɔldaːt], *m.* (—en, *pl.* —en) tin soldier.
Bleistift ['blaɪʃtɪft], *m.* (—s, *pl.* —e) pencil.
Blende ['blɛndə], *f.* (—, *no pl.*) blind; (*Min.*) blende; (*Phot.*) shutter.
blenden ['blɛndən], *v.a.* dazzle, blind.
Blendlaterne ['blɛntlatɛrnə], *f.* (—, *pl.* —n) dark-lantern.
Blendung ['blɛnduŋ], *f.* (—, *pl.* —en) blinding, dazzling.
Blendwerk ['blɛntvɛrk], *n.* (—s, *no pl.*) (optical) illusion, false show.
Blick [blɪk], *m.* (—s, *pl.* —e) glance, look, glimpse.
blicken ['blɪkən], *v.n.* look, glance.
blind [blɪnt], *adj.* blind, sightless; —er Passagier, stowaway.
Blinddarm ['blɪntdarm], *m.* (—s, *pl.* —e) appendix.
Blinddarmentzündung ['blɪntdarmɛntsynduŋ], *f.* (—, *pl.* —en) appendicitis.
Blindekuh [blɪndə'kuː], *f.* (—, *no pl.*) blind man's buff.
Blindgänger ['blɪntgɛŋər], *m.* (—s, *pl.* —) misfire, dud, blind.
Blindheit ['blɪnthaɪt], *f.* (—, *no pl.*) blindness.
blindlings ['blɪntlɪŋs], *adv.* blindly; at random.
Blindschleiche ['blɪntʃlaɪçə], *f.* (—, *pl.* —n) (*Zool.*) blind-worm.
blinken ['blɪŋkən], *v.n.* blink, flash, glitter, gleam.
blinzeln ['blɪntsəln], *v.n.* blink.
Blitz [blɪts], *m.* (—es, *pl.* —e) lightning, flash.
Blitzableiter ['blɪtsaplaɪtər], *m.* (—s, *pl.* —) lightning-conductor.
blitzblank ['blɪtsblaŋk], *adj.* as bright as a new pin; shining.
blitzen ['blɪtsən], *v.n.* flash; *es blitzt*, it is lightning; glitter, shine.
Blitzesschnelle ['blɪtsəsʃnɛlə], *f.* (—, *no pl.*) lightning-speed.
Blitzlicht ['blɪtslɪçt], *n.* (—s, *no pl.*) flashlight.
Blitzschlag ['blɪtsʃlaːk], *m.* (—s, *pl.* —e) flash of lightning.
Blitzstrahl ['blɪtsʃtraːl], *m.* (—s, *pl.* —en) flash of lightning.
Block [blɔk], *m.* (—s, *pl.* —e) block, log; pad.
Blockhaus ['blɔkhaus], *n.* (—es, *pl.* —er) log-cabin.

blockieren [blɔ'kiːrən], *v.a.* block (up); (*Mil.*) blockade.
blöde ['bløːdə], *adj.* stupid, dull, thick-headed, dim.
Blödsinn ['bløːtsɪn], *m.* (—s, *no pl.*) nonsense, idiocy.
blöken ['bløːkən], *v.n.* bleat; (*cows*) low.
blond [blɔnt], *adj.* blond, fair, fair-headed.
bloß [bloːs], *adj.* naked, uncovered; bare, mere.
Blöße ['bløːsə], *f.* (—, *pl.* —n) nakedness, bareness; (*fig.*) weak point.
bloßlegen ['bloːsleːgən], *v.a.* uncover, lay bare; (*fig.*) reveal, expose.
bloßstellen ['bloːsʃtɛlən], *v.a.* compromise, show up. — *v.r. sich* —, compromise o.s.
blühen ['blyːən], *v.n.* bloom, blossom, flower, flourish.
Blümchen ['blyːmçən], *n.* (—s, *pl.* —) small flower.
Blume ['bluːmə], *f.* (—, *pl.* —n) flower, bloom; (*wine*) bouquet; (*beer*) froth.
Blumenblatt ['bluːmənblat], *n.* (—s, *pl.* —er) petal.
Blumenerde ['bluːmənerdə], *f.* (—, *no pl.*) garden mould.
Blumenkelch ['bluːmənkɛlç], *m.* (—es, *pl.* —e) calyx.
Blumenkohl ['bluːmənkoːl], *m.* (—s, *pl.* —e) cauliflower.
Blumenstaub ['bluːmənʃtaup], *m.* (—s, *no pl.*) pollen.
Blumenstrauß ['bluːmənʃtraus], *m.* (—es, *pl.* —e) bunch of flowers, posy, nosegay.
Blumenzucht ['bluːməntsuxt], *f.* (—, *no pl.*) floriculture.
Bluse ['bluːzə], *f.* (—, *pl.* —n) blouse.
Blut [bluːt], *n.* (—es, *no pl.*) blood.
blutarm ['bluːtarm], *adj.* anaemic; (*fig.*) very poor.
Blutbad ['bluːtbaːt], *n.* (—es, *pl.* —er) massacre.
blutdürstig ['bluːtdyrstɪç], *adj.* blood-thirsty.
Blüte ['blyːtə], *f.* (—, *pl.* —n) blossom, flower, bloom.
Blutegel ['bluːteːgəl], *m.* (—s, *pl.* —) leech.
bluten ['bluːtən], *v.n.* bleed.
Bluterguß ['bluːtɛrgus], *m.* (—es, *pl.* —e) effusion of blood.
Blutgefäß ['bluːtgəfɛːs], *n.* (—es, *pl.* —e) blood-vessel.
blutig ['bluːtɪç], *adj.* bloody; cruel.
blutjung ['bluːtjuŋ], *adj.* very young.
Blutkörperchen ['bluːtkœrpərçən], *n.* (—s, *pl.* —) blood-corpuscle.
Blutlassen ['bluːtlasən], *n.* (—s, *no pl.*) (*Med.*) bloodletting.
Blutrache ['bluːtraxə], *f.* (—, *no pl.*) vendetta.
Blutsauger ['bluːtzaugər], *m.* (—s, *pl.* —) vampire.
Blutschande ['bluːtʃandə], *f.* (—, *no pl.*) incest.

blutstillend ['blu:ʃtɪlənt], *adj.* styptic, blood-stanching.

Blutsturz ['blu:tʃturts], *m.* (—es, *no pl.*) haemorrhage; *einen — haben,* burst a blood-vessel.

Blutsverwandte ['blu:tsfɛrvantə], *m. or f.* (—n, *pl.* —n) blood-relation.

Blutvergießen ['blu:tfɛrgi:sən], *n.* (—s, *no pl.*) bloodshed.

Blutvergiftung ['blu:tfɛrgɪftuŋ], *f.* (—, *pl.* —en) blood poisoning.

Blutwurst ['blu:tvurst], *f.* (—, *pl.* ⁻e) black-pudding.

Blutzeuge ['blu:ttsɔygə], *m.* (—n, *pl.* —n) martyr.

Bö [bø:], *f.* (—, *pl.* —en) (*Naut.*) squall, gust of wind.

Bock [bɔk], *m.* (—s, *pl.* ⁻e) buck; he-goat; (*Gymn.*) horse; (*horse-drawn carriage*) box seat.

bockbeinig ['bɔkbaɪnɪç], *adj.* bow-legged; pigheaded, obstinate.

Bockbier ['bɔkbi:r], *n.* (—s, *no pl.*) bock beer.

bocken ['bɔkən], *v.n.* kick, be refractory; sulk.

Bockfell ['bɔkfɛl], *n.* (—s, *pl.* —e) buckskin.

bockig ['bɔkɪç], *adj.* pigheaded, obstinate.

Bocksbeutel ['bɔksbɔytəl], *m.* (—s, *pl.* —) leather bag; Franconian wine (bottle).

Bockshorn ['bɔkshɔrn], *n.* (—s, *pl.* ⁻er) buck horn; *einen ins — jagen,* intimidate s.o.

Boden ['bo:dən], *m.* (—s, *pl.* ⁻) ground, bottom, soil, floor; garret, loft.

Bodenfenster ['bo:dənfɛnstər], *n.* (—s, *pl.* —) attic window.

Bodenkammer ['bo:dənkamər], *f.* (—, *pl.* —n) garret, attic.

bodenlos ['bo:dənlo:s], *adj.* bottomless; (*fig.*) unimaginable, enormous.

Bodensatz ['bo:dənzats], *m.* (—es, *pl.* ⁻e) sediment, dregs, deposit.

Bodensee ['bo:dənze:], *m.* Lake Constance.

Bogen ['bo:gən], *m.* (—s, *pl.* —, ⁻) arch, vault, curve; (*Maths.*) arc; (*violin*) bow; (*paper*) sheet; (*Mus.*) ligature.

bogenförmig ['bo:gənfœrmɪç], *adj.* arch-shaped, arched.

Bogenführung ['bo:gənfy:ruŋ], *f.* (—, *no pl.*) (*Mus.*) bowing (technique).

Bogengang ['bo:gəngaŋ], *m.* (—es, *pl.* ⁻e) arcade.

Bogenlampe ['bo:gənlampə], *f.* (—, *pl.* —n) arc-lamp.

Bogenschütze ['bo:gənʃytsə], *m.* (—n, *pl.* —n) archer.

bogig ['bo:gɪç], *adj.* bent, curved, arched.

Bohle ['bo:lə], *f.* (—, *pl.* —n) board, plank.

Böhmen ['bø:mən], *n.* Bohemia.

Bohne ['bo:nə], *f.* (—, *pl.* —n) bean; *grüne —n,* French (*Am.* string) beans; *dicke —n,* broad beans; *blaue —n,* (*fig.*) bullets.

Bohnenstange ['bo:nənʃtaŋə], *f.* (— *pl.* —n) bean-pole.

Bohnerbürste ['bo:nərbyrstə], *f.* (—, *pl.* —n) polishing-brush.

bohnern ['bo:nərn], *v.a.* polish, wax.

bohren ['bo:rən], *v.a.* bore, pierce, drill.

Bohrer ['bo:rər], *m.* (—s, *pl.* —) gimlet; drill.

Bohrturm ['bo:rturm], *m.* (—s, *pl.* ⁻e) derrick.

Boje ['bo:jə], *f.* (—, *pl.* —n) (*Naut.*) buoy.

Bolivien [bo'li:vjən], *n.* Bolivia.

Böller ['bœlər], *m.* (—s, *pl.* —) (*Mil.*) small mortar.

Bollwerk ['bɔlvɛrk], *n.* (—s, *pl.* —e) bulwark.

Bolzen ['bɔltsən], *m.* (—s, *pl.* —) bolt, arrow, pin; (*smoothing iron*) heater.

Bombe ['bɔmbə], *f.* (—, *pl.* —n) bomb, bomb-shell.

Bombenerfolg ['bɔmbənɛrfɔlk], *m.* (—(e)s, *pl.* —e) (*Theat.*) smash hit.

Bonbon [bɔ̃'bɔ̃], *m.* (—s, *pl.* —s) sweet(s), bonbon; (*Am.*) candy.

Bonbonniere [bɔ̃bɔ'njɛ:rə], *f.* (—, *pl.* —n) box of sweets.

Bonze ['bɔntsə], *m.* (—n, *pl.* —n) (*coll.*) bigwig, (*Am.*) big shot.

Boot [bo:t], *n.* (—es, *pl.* —e) boat.

Bootsanker ['bo:tsaŋkər], *m.* (—s, *pl.* —) grapnel.

Bootsleine ['bo:tslaɪnə], *f.* (—, *pl.* —n) tow-rope.

Bor [bo:r], *n.* (—s, *no pl.*) (*Chem.*) boron.

Bord [bɔrt], *m.* (—s, *pl.* —e) rim; (*Naut.*) board.

Bordell [bɔr'dɛl], *n.* (—s, *pl.* —e) brothel.

borgen ['bɔrgən], *v.a., v.n.* borrow; borrow (*von,* from); lend (*Dat.,* to).

Borke ['bɔrkə], *f.* (—, *pl.* —n) bark, rind.

Born [bɔrn], *m.* (—es, —e) (*Poet.*) bourn, spring, well, source.

borniert [bɔr'ni:rt], *adj.* narrow-minded.

Borsäure ['bo:rzɔyrə], *f.* (—, *no pl.*) boric acid.

Börse ['bœrzə], *f.* (—, *pl.* —n) purse; (*Comm.*) stock-exchange, bourse.

Börsenbericht ['bœrzənbərɪçt], *m.* (—s, *pl.* —e) stock-market report.

Borste ['bɔrstə], *f.* (—, *pl.* —n) bristle.

borstig ['bɔrstɪç], *adj.* bristly; (*fig.*) irritable.

Borte ['bɔrtə], *f.* (—, *pl.* —n) order, trimming.

bösartig ['bø:sartɪç], *adj.* malevolent, malicious, vicious; (*disease*) malignant.

Böschung ['bøʃuŋ], *f.* (—, *pl.* —en) slope, scarp.

böse ['bø:zə], *adj.* bad, wicked; evil; angry, cross (with, *Dat.*); — *auf* (*Acc.*), angry with s.o., (*Am.*) mad at s.o.

Bösewicht ['bø:zəvɪçt], *m.* (—s, *pl.* —er) villain, ruffian; wretch.

boshaft ['bo:shaft], *adj.* spiteful, malicious.
Bosheit ['bo:shaɪt], *f.* (—, *pl.* —en) malice.
böswillig ['bø:svɪlɪç], *adj.* malevolent.
Botanik [bo'ta:nɪk], *f.* (—, *no pl.*) botany.
Botaniker [bo'ta:nɪkər], *m.* (—s, *pl.* —) botanist.
Botanisiertrommel [botanɪ'zi:rtrɔmǝl], *f.* (—, *pl.* —n) specimen-box.
Bote ['bo:tǝ], *m.* (—n, *pl.* —n) messenger.
Botengang ['bo:tǝŋgaŋ], *m.* (—s, *pl.* ⁻e) errand.
botmäßig [bo:tmɛ:sɪç], *adj.* subject, subordinate.
Botschaft ['bo:tʃaft], *f.* (—, *pl.* —en) message; (*Pol.*) embassy; *gute* —, glad tidings.
Botschafter ['bo:tʃaftǝr], *m.* (—s, *pl.* —) ambassador.
Böttcher ['bœtçǝr], *m.* (—s, *pl.* —) cooper.
Bottich [bɔtɪç], *m.* (—s, *pl.* —e) vat, tub.
Bouillon [bul'jɔ̃], *f.* (—, *no pl.*) broth, meat soup.
Bowle ['bo:lǝ], *f.* (—, *no pl.*) bowl; spiced wine.
boxen ['bɔksǝn], *v.n.* box.
brach [bra:x], *adj.* fallow, unploughed, untilled.
Brand [brant], *m.* (—es, *pl.* ⁻e) burning, fire, combustion, conflagration; (*Med.*) gangrene.
Brandblase ['brantbla:zǝ], *f.* (—, *pl.* —n) blister.
branden ['brandǝn], *v.n.* surge, break (waves).
brandig ['brandɪç], *adj.* blighted; (*Med.*) gangrenous.
Brandmal ['brantma:l], *n.* (—s, *pl.* —e) burn mark; brand (cattle); (*fig.*) stigma.
brandmarken ['brantmarkǝn], *v.a.* brand; (*fig.*) stigmatise.
Brandmauer ['brantmauǝr], *f.* (—, *pl.* —n) fire-proof wall.
brandschatzen ['brantʃatsǝn], *v.a.* levy contributions (from); pillage, plunder.
Brandsohle ['brantzo:lǝ], *f.* (—, *pl.* —n) inner sole, welt (of shoe).
Brandstifter ['brantʃtɪftǝr], *m.* (—s, *pl.* —) incendiary, fire-raiser.
Brandstiftung ['brantʃtɪftuŋ], *f.* (—, *pl.* —en) arson.
Brandung ['branduŋ], *f.* (—, *pl.* —en) breakers, surf, surge (of sea).
Branntwein ['brantvaɪn], *m.* (—s, *pl.* —e) brandy.
Brasilien [bra'zi:ljǝn], *n.* Brazil.
Braten ['bra:tǝn], *m.* (—s, *pl.* —) roast (meat), joint.
braten ['bra:tǝn], *v.a. reg. & irr.* roast, broil, bake, fry, grill. — *v.n.* (*coll.*) bask (in sun), roast.
Brathering ['bra:the:rɪŋ], *m.* (—s, *pl.* —e) grilled herring.

Brathuhn ['bra:thu:n], *n.* (—s, *pl.* ⁻er) roast chicken.
Bratkartoffeln ['bra:tkartɔfǝln], *f. pl.* roast *or* fried potatoes.
Bratpfanne ['bra:tpfanǝ], *f.* (—, *pl.* —n) frying pan.
Bratsche ['bra:tʃǝ], *f.* (—, *pl.* —n) (*Mus.*) viola.
Bratspieß ['bra:tʃpi:s], *m.* (—es, *pl.* —e) spit (roasting).
Bratwurst ['bra:tvurst], *f.* (—, *pl.* ⁻e) sausage for frying; fried sausage.
Brau [brau], **Bräu,** [brɔy], *n. & m.* (—s, *no pl.*) brew.
Brauch [braux], *m.* (—es, *pl.* ⁻e) usage, custom, habit.
brauchbar ['brauxba:r], *adj.* useful, serviceable.
brauchen ['brauxǝn], *v.a.* make use of, employ; need, require, want; (*time*) take.
Braue ['brauǝ], *f.* (—, *pl.* —n) brow, eye-brow.
brauen ['brauǝn], *v.a.* brew.
Brauer ['brauǝr], *m.* (—s, *pl.* —) brewer.
Brauerei ['brauǝraɪ], *f.* (—, *pl.* —en) brewery.
Brauhaus ['brauhaus], *n.* (—es, *pl.* ⁻er) brewery.
braun [braun], *adj.* brown.
bräunen ['brɔynǝn], *v.a.* make brown, tan.
Braunkohl ['braunko:l], *m.* (—s, *no pl.*) (*Bot.*) broccoli.
Braunschweig ['braunʃvaɪk], *n.* Brunswick.
Braus [braus], *m.* (—es, *no pl.*) bustle, tumult; *in Saus und — leben,* lead a riotous life.
Brause ['brauzǝ], *f.* (—, *pl.* —n) shower (bath); effervescence, (*coll.*) fizzy drink.
Brausekopf ['brauzǝkɔpf], *m.* (—es, *pl.* ⁻e) hothead.
Brauselimonade ['brauzǝlɪmona:dǝ], *f.* (—, *pl.* —n) effervescent *or* fizzy lemonade.
brausen ['brauzǝn], *v.n.* roar, bluster, rush; effervesce.
Brausepulver ['brauzǝpulvǝr], *n.* (—s, *pl.* —) effervescent powder.
Braut [braut], *f.* (—, *pl.* ⁻e) bride, betrothed, fiancée.
Brautführer ['brautfy:rǝr], *m.* (—s, *pl.* —) best man.
Bräutigam ['brɔytɪgam], *m.* (—s, *pl.* —e) bridegroom, betrothed, fiancé.
Brautjungfer ['brautjuŋfǝr], *f.* (—, *pl.* —n) bridesmaid.
bräutlich ['brɔytlɪç], *adj.* bridal.
Brautpaar ['brautpa:r], *n.* (—es, *pl.* —e) engaged couple.
Brautschau ['brautʃau], *f.* (—, *no pl.*) (*obs.*) search for a wife.
brav [bra:f], *adj.* honest, upright, worthy, honourable; well-behaved, good.
bravo! ['bra:vo], *int.* well done!

Bravourstück [bra'vu:rʃtyk], *n.* (**—s,** *pl.* **—e**) feat of valour.

Brechbohnen ['brɛçboːnən], *f. pl.* kidney-beans.

Brecheisen ['brɛçaɪzən], *n.* (**—s,** *pl.* **—**) jemmy.

brechen ['brɛçən], *v.a. irr.* break; *(flowers)* pluck, pick; vomit. — *v.n.* *(aux. sein)* break.

Brechmittel ['brɛçmɪtəl], *n.* (**—s,** *pl.* **—**) emetic.

Brechruhr ['brɛçruːr], *f.* (**—,** *no pl.*) cholera.

Brechstange ['brɛçʃtaŋə], *f.* (**—,** *pl.* **—n**) crow-bar.

Brechung ['brɛçuŋ], *f.* (**—,** *pl.* **—en**) breaking; *(Phys.)* refraction.

Brei [braɪ], *m.* (**—s,** *pl.* **—e**) pap, pulp, porridge.

breiartig ['braɪaːrtɪç], *adj.* pulpy.

breiig ['braɪɪç], *adj.* pappy.

breit [braɪt], *adj.* broad, wide.

breitbeinig ['braɪtbaɪnɪç], *adj.* straddle-legged.

Breite ['braɪtə], *f.* (**—,** *pl.* **—n**) breadth, width; *(Geog.)* latitude.

Breitengrad ['braɪtəngraːt], *m.* (**—es,** *pl.* **—e**) *(Geog.)* degree of latitude.

Breitenkreis ['braɪtənkraɪs], *m.* (**—es,** *pl.* **—e**) *(Geog.)* parallel.

breitschultrig ['braɪtʃultrɪç], *adj.* broad-shouldered.

Bremse ['brɛmzə], *f.* (**—.** *pl.* **—n**) *(Ent.)* gad-fly; *(Motor.)* brake; *(horse)* barnacle.

bremsen ['brɛmzən], *v.a.* brake, pull up.

brennbar ['brɛnbaːr], *adj.* combustible.

Brenneisen ['brɛnaɪzən], *n.* (**—s,** *pl.* **—**) branding iron.

brennen ['brɛnən], *v.a. irr.* burn; *(Med.)* cauterise; *(alcohol)* distil; *(hair)* curl; *(coffee)* roast; *(coal)* char; *(bricks)* bake. — *v.n.* burn; *(fig.)* sting; *(eyes)* smart.

Brenner ['brɛnər], *m.* (**—s,** *pl.* **—**) *(person)* distiller; *(Tech.)* burner.

Brennerei [brɛnə'raɪ], *f.* (**—,** *pl.* **—en**) distillery.

Brennessel ['brɛnnɛsəl], *f.* (**—,** *pl.* **—n**) stinging nettle.

Brennholz ['brɛnhɔlts], *n.* (**—es,** *no pl.*) firewood.

Brennmaterial ['brɛnmaterjaːl], *n.* (**—s,** *pl.* **—ien**) fuel.

Brennofen ['brɛnoːfən], *m.* (**—s,** *pl.* **—n**) kiln.

Brennpunkt ['brɛnpuŋkt], *m.* (**—s,** *pl.* **—e**) focus.

Brennschere ['brɛnʃeːrə], *f.* (**—,** *pl.* **—n**) curling-irons.

Brennstoff ['brɛnʃtɔf], *m.* (**—(e)s,** *pl.* **—e**) fuel.

brenzlich ['brɛntslɪç], *adj.* smelling (or tasting) of burning; *(fig.)* ticklish.

Bresche ['brɛʃə], *f.* (**—,** *pl.* **—n**) breach, gap.

Brett [brɛt], *n.* (**—s,** *pl.* **—er**) board, plank, shelf.

Brettspiel ['brɛtʃpiːl], *n.* (**—s,** *pl.* **—e**) table-game.

Brevier [bre'viːr], *n.* (**—s,** *pl.* *(rare)* **—e**) breviary.

Brezel ['breːtsəl], *f.* (**—,** *pl.* **—n**) cracknel, pretzel.

Brief [briːf], *m.* (**—es,** *pl.* **—e**) letter; epistle.

Briefanschrift ['briːfanʃrɪft], *f.* (**—,** *pl.* **—en**) address.

Briefbeschwerer ['briːfbəʃveːrər], *m.* (**—s,** *pl.* **—**) letter-weight, paper-weight.

Briefbogen ['briːfboːgən], *m.* (**—s,** *pl.* **—**) sheet of notepaper.

Briefkasten ['briːfkastən], *m.* (**—s,** *pl.* **⁻**) *(house)* letter-box; *(street)* pillar-box, *(Am.)* post-box.

brieflich ['briːflɪç], *adv.* by letter, in writing.

Briefmarke ['briːfmarkə], *f.* (**—,** *pl.* **—n**) postage stamp.

Briefpapier ['briːfpapiːr], *n.* (**—s,** *no pl.*) notepaper.

Briefporto ['briːfpɔrto], *n.* (**—s,** *pl.* **—ti**) postage.

Brieftasche ['briːftaʃə], *f.* (**—,** *pl.* **—n**) portfolio, wallet; *(Am.)* pocket-book.

Brieftaube ['briːftaubə], *f.* (**—,** *pl.* **—n**) carrier pigeon.

Briefträger ['briːftrɛːgər], *m.* (**—s,** *pl.* **—**) postman.

Briefumschlag ['briːfumʃlaːk], *m.* (**—s,** *pl.* **⁻e**) envelope.

Briefwechsel ['briːfvɛksəl], *m.* (**—s,** *no pl.*) correspondence.

Brillant [bril'jant], *m.* (**—en,** *pl.* **—en**) brilliant, diamond. — *adj.* brilliant.

Brille ['brilə], *f.* (**—** *pl.* **—n**) spectacles, glasses.

Brillenschlange ['brilənʃlaŋə], *f.* (**—,** *pl.* **—n**) *(Zool.)* hooded cobra.

bringen ['briŋən], *v.a. irr.* bring, fetch, carry to, take to, conduct to.

Brise ['briːzə], *f.* (**—,** *pl.* **—n**) breeze, light wind.

Britannien [bri'tanjən], *n.* Britain.

bröckeln ['brœkəln], *v.a., v.n.* crumble.

Brocken ['brɔkən], *m.* (**—s,** *pl.* **—**) bit, piece, fragment, scrap; *(bread)* crumb.

bröcklig ['brœklɪç], *adj.* crumbling.

brodeln ['broːdəln], *v.n.* bubble, simmer.

Brodem ['broːdəm], *m.* (**—s,** *no pl.*) *(Poet.)* steam, vapour, exhalation.

Brokat [bro'kaːt], *m.* (**—s,** *pl.* **—e**) brocade.

Brom [broːm], *n.* (**—s,** *no pl.*) *(Chem.)* bromine.

Brombeere ['brɔmbeːrə], *f.* (**—,** *pl.* **—n**) blackberry, bramble.

Bronze ['brɔ̃ːsə], *f.* (**—,** *pl.* **—n**) bronze.

Brosamen ['bro:zaːmən], *pl.* crumbs.

Brosche ['brɔʃə], *f.* (**—,** *pl.* **—n**) brooch.

Broschüre [brɔ'ʃyːrə], *f.* (**—,** *pl.* **—n**) pamphlet, brochure, folder.

Brösel ['brøːzəl], *m.* (**—s,** *pl.* **—**) crumb.

Brot [broːt], *n.* (**—es,** *pl.* **—e**) bread, loaf; *(fig.)* livelihood.

Brötchen ['brøːtçən], *n.* (**—s,** *pl.* **—**) roll, bread-roll.

Broterwerb [ˈbroːtərvɛrp], *m.* (—s, *no pl.*) livelihood.

Brotgeber [ˈbroːtgeːbər], *m.* (—s, *pl.* —) employer, master.

Brotherr [ˈbroːthɛr], *m.* (—n, *pl.* —en) employer, master.

Brotkorb [ˈbroːtkɔrp], *m.* (—s, *pl.* ⁻e) bread-basket.

brotlos [ˈbroːtloːs], *adj.* unemployed; *(fig.)* unprofitable.

Brotneid [ˈbroːtnaɪt], *m.* (—s, *no pl.*) professional jealousy.

Bruch [brux], *m.* (—s, *pl.* ⁻e) breakage; rupture; *(Med.)* fracture, rupture, hernia; *(Maths.)* fraction.

Bruchband [ˈbruxbant], *f.* (—es, *pl.* ⁻er) abdominal belt, truss.

brüchig [ˈbryçɪç], *adj.* brittle, full of flaws.

Bruchlandung [ˈbruxlanduŋ], *f.* (—, —en) *(Aviat.)* crash-landing.

Bruchrechnung [ˈbruxrɛçnuŋ], *f.* (—, *pl.* —en) *(Arith.)* fractions.

Bruchstück [ˈbruxʃtyk], *n.* (—s, *pl.* —e) fragment, scrap.

Bruchteil [ˈbruxtaɪl], *m.* (—s, *pl.* —e) fraction.

Brücke [ˈbrykə], *f.* (—, *pl.* —n) bridge.

Brückenpfeiler [ˈbrykənpfaɪlər], *m.* (—s, *pl.* —) pier.

Bruder [ˈbruːdər], *m.* (—s, *pl.* ⁻) brother; *(Eccl.)* friar.

brüderlich [ˈbryːdərlɪç], *adj.* fraternal, brotherly.

Bruderschaft [ˈbruːdərʃaft], *f.* (—, *pl.* —en) fraternity, brotherhood.

Brügge [ˈbrygə], *n.* Bruges.

Brühe [ˈbryːə], *f.* (—, *pl.* —n) broth, meat-soup.

brühen [ˈbryːən], *v.a.* scald.

Brühkartoffeln [ˈbryːkartɔfəln], *f. pl.* potatoes cooked in broth.

brüllen [ˈbrylən], *v.n.* roar, howl, yell; *(cows)* low, bellow.

Brummbaß [ˈbrumbas], *m.* (—sses, *pl.* ⁻sse) *(Mus.)* double-bass.

Brummeisen [ˈbrumaɪzən], *n.* (⁻s, *pl.* —) Jew's harp.

brummen [ˈbrumən], *v.n.* growl, grumble, hum.

Brummer [ˈbrumər], *n.* (—s, *pl.* —) *(Ent.)* blue-bottle.

Brunnen [ˈbrunən], *m.* (—s, *pl.* —) well, fountain, spring.

Brunnenkur [ˈbrunənkuːr], *f.* (—, *pl.* —en) taking of mineral waters.

Brunst [brunst], *f.* (—, *pl.* ⁻e) *(Zool.)* rut, heat.

Brust [brust], *f.* (—, *pl.* ⁻e) breast; chest; bosom.

Brustbein [ˈbrustbaɪn], *n.* (—s, *pl.* —e) breastbone, sternum.

Brustbild [ˈbrustbɪlt], *n.* (—s, *pl.* —er) half-length portrait.

brüsten [ˈbrystən], *v.r. sich* —, boast, brag, plume o.s.

Brustfell [ˈbrustfɛl], *n.* (—s, *pl.* —e) pleura.

Brustfellentzündung [ˈbrustfɛlɛntsynduŋ], *f.* (—, *no pl.*) pleurisy.

Brusthöhle [ˈbrusthøːlə], *f.* (—, *pl.* —n) thoracic cavity.

Brustkasten [ˈbrustkastən], *m.* (—s, *pl.* ⁻n) chest.

Brusttee [ˈbrustteː], *m.* (—s, *no pl.*) pectoral (herbal) tea.

Brüstung [ˈbrystuŋ], *f.* (—, *pl.* —en) parapet.

Brustwarze [ˈbrustvartsə], *f.* (—, *pl.* —n) nipple.

Brustwehr [ˈbrustveːr], *f.* (—, *pl.* —en) breastwork, parapet.

Brut [bruːt], *f.* (—, *no pl.*) brood; *(fish)* fry.

brutal [bruˈtaːl], *adj.* brutal.

brüten [ˈbryːtən], *v.a.* brood, hatch.

Brutofen [ˈbruːtoːfən], *m.* (—s, *pl.* ⁻) incubator.

brutto [ˈbruːto], *adv.* *(Comm.)* gross.

Bube [ˈbuːbə], *m.* (—n, *pl.* —n) boy, lad; *(cards)* knave, *(Am.)* jack; rogue, rascal.

Bubenstreich [ˈbuːbənʃtraɪç], *m.* (—s, *pl.* —e) boyish prank; knavish trick.

Bubikopf [ˈbuːbɪkɔpf], *m.* (—(e)s, *pl.* ⁻e) bobbed hair.

Buch [buːx], *n.* (—s, *pl.* ⁻er) book; quire (of paper).

Buchdruckerei [ˈbuːxdrukəraɪ], *f.* (—, —en) printing works, printing office.

Buche [ˈbuːxə], *f.* (—, *pl.* —n) beech (tree).

buchen [ˈbuːxən], *v.a.* book, enter, reserve; *(fig.)* score.

Bücherei [byːçəˈraɪ], *f.* (—, *pl.* —en) library.

Buchesche [ˈbuːxɛʃə], *f.* (—, *pl.* —n) hornbeam.

Buchfink [ˈbuːxfɪŋk], *m.* (—en, *pl.* —en) *(Orn.)* chaffinch.

Buchhalter [ˈbuːxhaltər], *m.* (—s, *pl.* —) book-keeper.

Buchhändler [ˈbuːxhɛndlər], *m.* (—s, *pl.* —) bookseller.

Buchmarder [ˈbuːxmardər], *m.* (—s, *pl.* —) *(Zool.)* pine-marten.

Buchsbaum [ˈbuksbaum], *m.* (—s, *pl.* ⁻e) *(Bot.)* box-tree.

Büchse [ˈbyksə], *f.* (—, *pl.* —n) box, case; tin, can; rifle, gun.

Büchsenfleisch [ˈbyksənflaɪʃ], *n.* (—es, *no pl.*) tinned meat.

Büchsenlauf [ˈbyksənlauf], *m.* (—s, *pl.* ⁻e) gun-barrel.

Büchsenöffner [ˈbyksənœfnər], *m.* (—s, *pl.*—) tin-opener.

Buchstabe [ˈbuːxʃtaːbə], *m.* (—n, *pl.* —n) letter, character; *großer* —, capital (letter).

Buchstabenrätsel [ˈbuːxʃtaːbənrɛtsəl], *n.* (—s, *pl.* —) anagram.

buchstabieren [buːxʃtaˈbiːrən], *v.a.* spell (out).

buchstäblich [ˈbuːxʃtɛplɪç], *adj.* literal.

Bucht [buxt], *f.* (—, *pl.* —en) inlet, bay, creek, bight.

Buchung [ˈbuːxuŋ], *f.* (—, *pl.* —en) *(Comm.)* entry (in a book); booking (of tickets).

Buchwissen ['bu:xvɪsən], *n.* (—s, *no pl.*) book-learning.
Buckel ['bukəl], *m.* (—s, *pl.* —) hump, humpback; boss, stud; (*coll.*) back.
bücken ['bykən], *v.r. sich* —, stoop, bow.
bucklig ['buklɪç], *adj.* humpbacked.
Bückling ['byklɪŋ], *m.* (—s, *pl.* —e) smoked herring; kipper.
buddeln ['budəln], *v.n.* (*coll.*) dig.
Bude ['bu:də], *f.* (—, *pl.* —n) shack, stall; (*coll.*) room; (*student's*) digs.
Büfett [by'fɛt], *n.* (—s, *pl.* —s) sideboard; buffet.
Büffel ['byfəl], *m.* (—s, *pl.* —) buffalo.
büffeln ['byfəln], *v.n.* (*coll.*) cram (for an examination), swot.
Bug [bu:k], *m.* (—s, *pl.* ·:e, —e) (*Naut.*) bow, (*Aviat.*) nose.
Buganker ['bu:kaŋkər], *m.* (—s, *pl.* —) bow-anchor.
Bügel ['bygəl], *m.* (—s, *pl.* —) coathanger; (*trigger*) guard; (*horse*) stirrup.
bügeln ['bygəln], *v.a.* iron, smoothe, press.
bugsieren [buk'si:rən], *v.a.* tow.
Bugspriet ['bu:kʃpri:t], *n.* (—s, *pl.* —e) bowsprit.
Buhle ['bu:lə], *m.* or *f.* (—n, *pl.* —n) (*Poet.*) paramour, lover.
buhlen ['bu:lən], *v.n.* (*Poet.*) woo, make love (to).
buhlerisch ['bu:lərɪʃ], *adj.* (*Poet.*) amorous, wanton, lewd.
Bühne ['by:nə], *f.* (—, *pl.* —n) (*Theat.*) stage; scaffold, platform.
Bühnenbild ['by:nənbɪlt], *n.* (—es, *pl.* —er) scenery.
Bukett [bu'kɛt], *n.* (—s, *pl.* —s) bunch of flowers, bouquet; bouquet (*wine*).
Bulgarien [bul'ga:rjən], *n.* Bulgaria.
Bulldogge ['buldɔgə], *f.* (—, *pl.* —n) bulldog.
Bulle (1) ['bulə], *m.* (—n, *pl.* —n) bull, bullock.
Bulle (2) ['bulə], *f.* (—, *pl.* —n) (*Eccl.*) (Papal) Bull.
bumm [bum], *int.* boom! bang!
Bummel ['buməl], *m.* (—s, *pl.* —) stroll.
Bummelei [bumə'lai], *f.* (—, *pl.* —en) idleness, negligence, casualness, carelessness.
bummeln ['buməln], *v.n.* lounge, waste o.'s time, dawdle; stroll.
Bummelzug ['buməltsu:k], *m.* (—s, *pl.* ·:e) slow train.
bums [bums], *int.* bang! crash!
Bund (1) [bunt], *m.* (—es, *pl.* ·:e) bond, tie, league, alliance, federation, confederacy; (*Eccl.*) covenant.
Bund (2) [bunt], *n.* (—es, *pl.* —e) bundle, bunch (of keys).
Bündel ['byndəl], *n.* (—s, *pl.* —) bundle, package.
Bundesgenosse ['bundəsgənɔsə], *m.* (—n, *pl.* —n) confederate, ally.
Bundesstaat ['bundəsʃta:t], *m.* (—es, *pl.* —en) federal state; federation.

Bundestag ['bundəsta:k], *m.* (—es, *pl.* —e) federal parliament.
Bundeswehr ['bundəsve:r], *f.* (—, *no pl.*) federal defence; armed forces.
bündig ['byndɪç], *adj.* binding; *kurz und* —, concise, terse, to the point.
Bündnis ['byntnɪs], *n.* (—ses, *pl.* —se) alliance.
Bundschuh ['buntʃu:], *m.* (—s, *pl.* —e) clog, sandal.
bunt [bunt], *adj.* many-coloured, chequered, variegated, motley; *das ist mir zu* —, this is going too far.
buntscheckig ['buntʃekɪç], *adj.* dappled, spotted.
Buntspecht ['buntʃpɛçt], *m.* (—s, *pl.* —e) (*Orn.*) (spotted) woodpecker.
Bürde ['byrdə], *f.* (—, *pl.* —n) load, burden.
Bure ['bu:rə], *m.* (—n, *pl.* —n) Boer.
Burg [burk], *f.* (—, *pl.* —en) castle, fortress, citadel, stronghold.
Bürge ['byrgə], *m.* (—n, *pl.* —n) surety, bail, guarantee; *einen* — *stellen*, offer bail.
bürgen ['byrgən], *v.n.* give security, vouch (for), go bail (for).
Bürger ['byrgər], *m.* (—s, *pl.* —) citizen, townsman, bourgeois, commoner.
bürgerlich ['byrgərlɪç], *adj.* civic; middle-class, bourgeois; —e *Küche*, plain cooking.
Bürgermeister ['byrgərmaistər], *m.* (—s, *pl.* —) burgomaster, mayor.
Burggraf ['burkgra:f], *m.* (—en, *pl.* —en) burgrave.
Bürgschaft ['byrkʃaft], *f.* (—, *pl.* —en) bail, surety, guarantee; — *leisten*, provide security.
Burgund [bur'gunt], *n.* Burgundy.
Burgvogt ['burkfo:kt], *m.* (—s, *pl.* —e) (*obs.*) castellan, bailiff.
Burgwarte ['burkvartə], *f.* (—, *pl.* —n) watch-tower.
Büro [by'ro:], *n.* (—s, *pl.* —s) office, bureau, (professional) chambers.
Bursche ['burʃə], *m.* (—n, *pl.* —n) lad, boy, fellow; student; (*Mil.*) batman.
Burschenschaft ['burʃənʃaft], *f.* (—, *pl.* —en) students' association.
Bürste ['byrstə], *f.* (—, *pl.* —n) brush.
Burundi [bu'rundi], *n.* Burundi.
Busch [buʃ], *m.* (—es, *pl.* ·:e) bush, shrub, copse, thicket.
Büschel ['byʃəl], *n.* (—s, *pl.* —) bunch; (*hair*) tuft.
buschig ['buʃɪç], *adj.* bushy, tufted.
Buschklepper ['buʃklɛpər], *m.* (—s, *pl.* —) bushranger.
Busen ['bu:zən], *m.* (—s, *pl.* —) bosom, breast; (*Geog.*) bay, gulf.
Bussard ['busart], *m.* (—s, *pl.* —e) (*Orn.*) buzzard.
Buße ['bu:sə], *f.* (—, *pl.* —n) penance; repentance; penalty.
büßen ['by:sən], *v.a., v.n.* repent, atone, expiate, make amends.
bußfertig ['bu:sfertɪç], *adj.* penitent, repentant.

Büste ['bystə], *f.* (—, *pl.* —**n**) bust.
Büstenhalter ['bystenhaltər], *m.* (—**s**, *pl.* —) brassière.
Bütte ['bytə], *f.* (—, *pl.* —**n**) tub.
Büttel ['bytəl], *m.* (—**s**, *pl.* —) beadle; bailiff.
Büttenpapier ['bytənpapi:r], *n.* (—**s**, *no pl.*) hand-made paper.
Butter ['butər], *f.* (—, *no pl.*) butter.
Butterblume ['butərblu:mə], *f.* (—, *pl.* —**n**) buttercup.
Butterbrot ['butərbro:t], *n.* (—**s**, *pl.* —**e**) bread and butter.
buttern ['butərn], *v.a., v.n.* smear with butter; churn.
Butterteig ['butərtaik], *m.* (—**es**, *pl.* —**e**) puff-pastry.
Butzenscheibe ['butsənʃaibə], *f.* (—, *pl.* —**n**) bull's-eyed pane.
Byzanz [by'tsants], *n.* Byzantium, Constantinople.

C

C [tse:], *n.* (—**s**, *pl.* —**s**) the letter C; (*Mus.*) C *dur*, C major; C *Moll*, C minor; C-*Schlüssel*, C clef.
Cäsar ['tsɛ:zar], *m.* Cæsar.
Ceylon ['tseilɔn], *n.* Ceylon.
Chaiselongue [ʃɛ:zə'lɔ̃:g], *f.* (—, *pl.* —**s**) couch, settee, sofa.
Champagner [ʃam'panjər], *m.* (—**s**, *pl.* —) champagne.
Champignon [ʃampiɲ'jɔ̃], *m.* (—**s**, *pl.* —**s**) mushroom.
chaotisch [ka'o:tiʃ], *adj.* chaotic.
Charakter [ka'raktər], *m.* (—**s**, *pl.* —**e**) character; mental make-up, disposition.
Charakteristik [karaktər'istik], *f.* (—, *pl.* —**en**) characterisation.
charakteristisch [karaktər'istiʃ], *adj.* characteristic; typical.
Charge ['ʃarʒə], *f.* (—, *pl.* —**n**) office, appointment; (*pl.*) (*Mil.*) non-commissioned officers.
Chaussee [ʃɔ'se:], *f.* (—, *pl.* —**n**) main road, highway.
Chef [ʃɛf], *m.* (—**s**, *pl.* —**s**) chief, head, employer; (*coll.*) boss.
Chefredakteur ['ʃɛfredaktø:r], *m.* (—**s**, *pl.* —**e**) editor-in-chief.
Chemie [çe'mi:], *f.* (—, *no pl.*) chemistry.
Chemikalien [çemi'ka:ljən], *f. pl.* chemicals.
Chemiker ['çe:mikər], *m.* (—**s**, *pl.* —) (analytical) chemist.
chemisch ['çe:miʃ], *adj.* chemical; — *gereinigt*, dry-cleaned.
Chiffre ['ʃifər], *f.* (—, *pl.* —**n**) cipher.
chiffrieren [ʃi'fri:rən], *v.a.* encipher.
Chile ['tʃi:lə, 'çi:lə], *n.* Chile.

China ['çi:na], *n.* China.
Chinarinde [çi:na'rində], *f.* (—, *no pl.*) Peruvian bark.
Chinin [çi'ni:n], *n.* (—**s**, *no pl.*) quinine.
Chirurg [çi'rurk], *m.* (—**en**, *pl.* —**en**) surgeon.
Chirurgie [çirur'gi:], *f.* (—, *no pl.*) surgery.
Chlor [klo:r], *n.* (—**s**, *no pl.*) chlorine.
Chlorkalk ['klo:rkalk], *m.* (—**s**, *no pl.*) chloride of lime.
Chlornatrium [klo:r'na:trjum], *n.* (—**s**, *no pl.*) sodium chloride.
Choleriker [ko'le:rikər], *m.* (—**s**, *pl.* —) irascible person.
Chor [ko:r], *m.* (—**s**, *pl.* ⁓**e**) chorus; choir; (*Archit.*) choir, chancel.
Choral [ko'ra:l], *m.* (—**s**, *pl.* ⁓**e**) hymn, chorale.
Choramt ['ko:ramt], *n.* (—**s**, *pl.* ⁓**er**) cathedral service.
Chorgesang ['ko:rgəsaŋ], *m.* (—**s**, *pl.* ⁓**e**) chorus, choral singing.
Chorhemd ['ko:rhɛmt], *n.* (—**s**, *pl.* —**en**) surplice.
Chorherr ['ko:rhɛr], *m.* (—**n**, *pl.* —**en**) canon, prebendary.
Christ [krist], *m.* (—**en**, *pl.* —**en**) Christian.
Christbaum ['kristbaum], *m.* (—**s**, *pl.* ⁓**e**) Christmas tree.
Christentum ['kristəntu:m], *n.* (—**s**, *no pl.*) Christendom, Christianity.
Christkind ['kristkint], *n.* (—**s**, *no pl.*) Infant Christ, Christ child.
christlich ['kristliç], *adj.* Christian.
Christmette ['kristmɛtə], *f.* (—, *pl.* —**n**) Christmas matins; midnight mass.
Christus ['kristus], *m.* (—**i**) Christ; *vor* —, B.C.; *nach* —, A.D.
Chrom [kro:m], *n.* (—**s**, *no pl.*) chrome.
chromatisch [kro'ma:tiʃ], *adj.* chromatic.
chromsauer ['kro:mzauər], *adj.* — chromate of; —*es Salz*, chromate.
Chronik ['kro:nik], *f.* (—, *pl.* —**en**) chronicle.
chronisch ['kro:niʃ], *adj.* chronic.
Chronist [kro'nist], *m.* (—**en**, *pl.* —**en**) chronicler.
Chrysantheme [kryzan'te:mə], *f.* (—, *pl.* —**n**) chrysanthemum.
Cis [tsis], (*Mus.*) C sharp.
Clique ['klikə], *f.* (—, *pl.* —**n**) clique, set.
Coeur [kø:r], *n.* (*Cards*) hearts.
coulant [ku'lant], *adj.* polite, friendly; (*Comm.*) fair, obliging.
Couleur [ku'lø:r], *f.* (—, *pl.* —**en**) colour; students' corporation.
Coupé [ku'pe:], *n.* (—**s**, *pl.* —**s**) (*train*) compartment.
Couplet [ku'ple:], *n.* (—**s**, *pl.* —**s**) comic song.
Coupon [ku'pɔ̃], *m.* (—**s**, *pl.* —**s**) coupon, check, dividend voucher.
Cour [ku:r], *f.* (—, *no pl.*) *einem Mädchen die* — *machen*, court a girl.

Courtage [kur'ta:ʒə], *f.* (—, *pl.* —n) brokerage.

Cousin [ku'zɛ̃], *m.* (—s, *pl.* —s) cousin.

Cousine [ku'zi:nə], *f.* (—, *pl.* —n) (female) cousin.

Cutaway ['katave:], *m.* (—s, *pl.* —s) morning coat.

Czar [tsa:r], *m.* (—en, *pl.* —en) Tsar, Czar.

D

D [de:], *n.* (—s, *pl.* —s) the letter D; (*Mus.*) *D dur*, D major; *D moll*, D minor; *D-Zug*, express train.

da [da:], *adv.* (*local*) there; here; (*temporal*) then, at that moment; (*Mil.*) *wer* —? who goes there? (*Poet. obs.*) where. — *conj.* (*temporal*) when, as; (*causal*) as, because, since.

dabei [da'baɪ], *adv.* nearby; besides, moreover; as well; —*sein*, be present, be about to (*infin.*); — *bleiben*, persist in.

Dach [dax], *n.* (—es, *pl.* ˙er) roof.

Dachboden ['daxbo:dən], *m.* (—s, *pl.* ˙) loft.

Dachdecker ['daxdɛkər], *m.* (—s, *pl.* —) slater, tiler.

Dachgiebel ['daxgi:bəl], *m.* (—s, *pl.* —) gable.

Dachluke ['daxlu:kə], *f.* (—, *pl.* —n) dormer window.

Dachpappe ['daxpapə], *f.* (—, *pl.* —n) roofing felt.

Dachrinne ['daxrɪnə], *f.* (—, *pl.* —n) gutter.

Dachs [daks], *m.* (—es, *pl.* —e) badger.

Dachstube ['daxʃtu:bə], *f.* (—, *pl.* —n) garret, attic (room).

Dachtraufe ['daxtraufə], *f.* (—, *pl.* —n) eaves.

dadurch [da'durç], *adv.* (*local*) through it; in that way; (*causal*) thereby.

dafür [da'fy:r], *adv.* for it; instead of it, in return for it; *ich kann nichts* —, it is not my fault, I can't help it.

Dafürhalten [da'fy:rhaltən], *n.* (—s, *no pl.*) opinion.

dagegen [da'ge:gən], *adv.* against it, compared to it. — *conj.* on the other hand.

daheim [da'haɪm], *adv.* at home.

daher [da'he:r], *adv.* thence, from that. — *conj.* therefore, for that reason.

dahin [da'hɪn], *adv.* thither, to that place; there; *bis* —, (*local*) thither; (*temporal*) till then; over, past, lost, gone.

dahinbringen [da'hɪnbrɪŋən], *v.a. irr. jemanden* —, induce s.o. to; *es* —, succeed in, manage to.

dahinsiechen [da'hɪnzi:çən], *v.n.* (*aux.* sein) pine away, ʰe failing (in health).

dahinter [da'hɪntər], *adv.* behind that.

Dahlie ['da:ljə], *f.* (—, *pl.* —n) (*Bot.*) dahlia.

Dahome ['daome:], *n.* Dahomey.

damalig ['da:maliç], *adj.* then; of that time; past.

damals ['da:mals], *adv.* then, at that time.

Damast [da'mast], *m.* (—s, *no pl.*) damask.

Damaszener [damas'tse:nər], *m.* (—s, *pl.* —) Damascene. — *adj.* — *Stahl*, Damascus steel, dagger.

Dame ['da:mə], *f.* (—, *pl.* —n) lady; (*cards, chess*) queen; draughts (*game*).

damit [da'mɪt], *adv.* therewith, with that, with it; *und* — *basta!* and that's all there is to it. — *conj.* in order that, so that; — *nicht*, lest.

dämlich ['dɛ:mlɪç], *adj.* (*coll.*) foolish, silly.

Damm [dam], *m.* (—es, *pl.* ˙e) dam, dyke, mole; (*street*) roadway, causeway; (*rail*) embankment.

dämmen ['dɛmən], *v.a.* dam; (*fig.*) stop, restrain.

dämmerig ['dɛmərɪç], *adj.* dusky.

dämmern ['dɛmərn], *v.n.* grow dusky; dawn.

dämonisch [dɛ'mo:nɪʃ], *adj.* demoniac-(al), demonlike.

Dampf [dampf], *m.* (—es, *pl.* ˙e) vapour, steam, mist, fume; smoke.

dampfen ['dampfən], *v.n.* smoke, fume, steam.

dämpfen ['dɛmpfən], *v.a.* damp, smother, steam; subdue, deaden, muffle, soften down.

Dampfer ['dampfər], *m.* (—s, *pl.* —) steamer.

Dämpfer ['dɛmpfər], *m.* (—s, *pl.* —) damper; (*Mus.*) mute.

Dampfkessel ['dampfkɛsəl], *m.* (—s, *pl.* —) boiler.

Dämpfung ['dɛmpfuŋ], *f.* (—, *pl.* —en) damping, smothering, suppression; (*Aviat.*) stabilization.

danach [da'na:x], *adv.* after that, thereafter; accordingly, according to that.

daneben [da'ne:bən], *adv.* near it, by it, close by; *es geht* —, it goes amiss. — *conj.* besides.

Dänemark ['dɛ:nəmark], *n.* Denmark.

Dank [daŋk], *m.* (—es, *no pl.*) thanks, gratitude; reward; *Gott sei* —, thank heaven!

dank [daŋk], *prep.* (*Dat.*) owing to, thanks to.

dankbar ['daŋkba:r], *adj.* grateful; thankful.

danken ['daŋkən], *v.n.* (*Dat.*) thank. — *v.a.* owe.

Dankgebet ['daŋkgəbe:t], *n.* (—s, *pl.* —e) (prayer of) thanksgiving.

dann [dan], *adv.* then, at that time, in that case; — *und wann*, now and then, occasionally.

Danzig ['dantsɪç], *n.* Dantzig.

43

daran

daran, dran [da′ran, dran], *adv.* on it, at it, near that; thereon, thereby; *was liegt —?* what does it matter?

darauf, drauf [da′rauf, drauf], *adv.* (*local*) upon it, on it; (*temporal*) thereupon, thereon, thereafter.

daraufhin [darauf′hɪn], *adv.* thereupon; on the strength of that.

daraus, draus [da′raus, draus], *adv.* therefrom, hence, from that; *ich mache mir nichts —,* I do not care for it.

darben [′darbən], *v.n.* suffer want, go short; famish.

darbieten [′da:rbi:tən], *v.a. irr.* offer, tender, present.

Darbietung [′da:rbi:tuŋ], *f.* (—, *pl.* —en) offering, presentation, performance.

darbringen [′da:rbrɪŋən], *v.a. irr.* bring, present, offer.

darein, drein [da′raɪn, draɪn], *adv.* into it, therein.

darin, drin [da′rɪn, drɪn], *adv.* therein, in it, within.

darinnen, drinnen [da′rɪnən, ′drɪnən], *adv.* inside, in there.

darlegen [′da:rle:gən], *v.a.* demonstrate, explain; expound.

Darlehen [′da:rle:ən], *n.* (—s, *pl.* —) loan.

Darm [darm], *m.* (—s, *pl.* ⁂e) gut; (*pl.*) intestines, bowels.

Darmsaite [′darmzaɪtə], *f.* (—, *pl.* —n) catgut, gut-string.

darob [da′rɔp], *adv.* (*obs.*) on that account, on account of it.

darreichen [′da:raɪçən], *v.a.* offer, tender, present; (*Eccl.*) administer (sacraments).

darstellen [′da:rʃtɛlən], *v.a.* represent, delineate; (*Theat.*) perform.

Darstellung [′da:rʃtɛluŋ], *f.* (—, *pl.* —en) representation, exhibition, presentation; (*Theat.*) performance.

dartun [′da:rtu:n], *v.a. irr.* prove, demonstrate.

darüber, drüber [dar′y:bər, ′dry:bər], *adv.* over that, over it; concerning that.

darum, drum [da′rum, drum], *adv.* around it, around that, thereabout; therefore, for that reason.

darunter, drunter [da′runtər, ′druntər], *adv.* under that; thereunder; among; — *und drüber,* topsy-turvy.

das [das], *def. art. n.* the. — *dem. pron., dem. adj.* that, this. —*rel. pron.* which.

Dasein [′da:zaɪn], *n.* (—s, *no pl.*) presence, being, existence.

daselbst [da′zɛlpst], *adv.* there, in that very place.

daß [das], *conj.* that; *es sei denn —,* unless; — *nicht,* lest.

dastehen [′da:ʃte:ən], *v.n. irr.* stand (there).

datieren [da′ti:rən], *v.a.* date, put a date to.

Dativ [′da:ti:f], *m.* (—s, *pl.* —e) dative.

dato [′da:to], *adv. bis —,* till now, hitherto.

Dattel [′datəl], *f.* (—, *pl.* —n) (*Bot.*) date.

Datum [′da:tum], *n.* (—s, *pl.* **Daten**) date (*calendar*).

Dauer [′dauər], *f.* (—, *no pl.*) duration, length of time; continuance; permanence.

dauerhaft [′dauərhaft], *adj.* durable, lasting; (*colours*) fast.

Dauerkarte [′dauərkartə], *f.* (—, *pl.* —n) season ticket; (*Am.*) commutation ticket.

dauern [′dauərn], *v.n.* continue, last, endure.— *v.a.* move to pity; *er dauert mich,* I am sorry for him.

Dauerpflanze [′dauərpflantsə], *f.* (—, *pl.* —n) perennial plant.

Dauerwelle [′dauərvɛlə], *f.* (—, *pl.* —n) permanent wave, (*coll.*) perm.

Daumen [′daumən], *m.* (—s, *pl.* —) thumb; *einem den — halten,* wish s.o. well, keep o.'s fingers crossed for s.o.

Daune [′daunə], *f.* (—, *pl.* —n) down.

davon [da′fɔn], *adv.* thereof, therefrom, from that; off, away.

davonkommen [da′fɔnkɔmən], *v.n. irr.* (*aux.* sein) get off; *mit einem blauen Auge —,* get off lightly.

davor [da′fo:r], *adv.* before that, before it.

dawider [da′vi:dər], *adv.* against it.

dazu [da′tsu:], *adv.* thereto, to that, to it; in addition to that; for that purpose; *noch —,* besides.

dazumal [da′tsuma:l], *adv.* then, at that time.

dazwischen [da′tsvɪʃən], *adv.* between, among; — *kommen,* intervene, interfere; — *treten,* intervene.

debattieren [debaˈti:rən], *v.a., v.n.* debate.

Debet [′de:bɛt], *n.* (—s, *pl.* —s) debit.

Debüt [de′by:], *n.* (—s, *pl.* —s) first appearance, début.

Dechant [de′çant], *m.* (—en, *pl.* —en) (*Eccl.*) dean.

dechiffrieren [deʃɪfˈri:rən], *v.a.* decode, decipher.

Deck [dɛk], *n.* (—s, *pl.* —e) (*Naut.*) deck.

Deckbett [′dɛkbɛt], *n.* (—s, *pl.* —en) coverlet.

Deckblatt [′dɛkblat], *n.* (—s, *pl.* ⁂er) (*Bot.*) bractea; (*cigar*) wrapper.

Decke [′dɛkə], *f.* (—, *pl.* —n) cover; blanket, rug; (*bed*) coverlet; (*room*) ceiling.

Deckel [′dɛkəl], *m.* (—s, *pl.* —) lid, top; (*book*) cover; (*coll.*) hat.

decken [′dɛkən], *v.a.* cover; (*Comm.*) secure, reimburse. — *v.r. sich —,* *Maths.*) coincide; (*fig.*) square, tally.

Deckfarbe [′dɛkfarbə], *f.* (—, *pl.* —n) body colour.

Deckmantel [′dɛkmantəl], *m.* (—s, *pl.* ⁂) cloak, disguise.

Deckung [′dɛkuŋ], *f.* (—, *pl.* —en) covering, protection; (*Comm.*) reimbursement; security; (*Mil.*) cover.

dedizieren [dedɪˈtsi:rən], *v.a.* dedicate.

44

deduzieren [dedu'tsi:rən], *v.a.* deduce.

defekt [de'fɛkt], *adj.* defective, incomplete, imperfect.

defilieren [defɪ'li:rən], *v.n.* (*Mil.*) pass in review, march past.

definieren [defɪ'ni:rən], *v.a.* define.

Degen ['de:gən], *m.* (—s, *pl.* —) sword; (*fig.*) brave warrior.

degradieren [degra'di:rən], *v.a.* degrade, demote.

dehnbar ['de:nba:r], *adj.* extensible, ductile.

dehnen ['de:nən], *v.a.* extend, expand, stretch. — *v.r. sich* —, stretch o.s.

Deich [daɪç], *m.* (—es, *pl.* —e) dike, dam, embankment.

Deichsel ['daɪksəl], *f.* (—, *pl.* —n) thill, shaft, pole.

deichseln ['daɪksəln], *v.a.* (*fig.*) engineer; (*coll.*) manage; wangle.

dein [daɪn], *poss. adj.* your; (*Poet.*) thy. — *poss. pron.* yours; (*Poet.*) thine.

deinesgleichen [daɪnəs'glaɪçən], *adj. pron.* the like of you, such as you.

deinethalben ['daɪnəthalbən], *adv.* on your account, for your sake, on your behalf.

deinetwegen ['daɪnətve:gən], *adv.* because of you, on your account, for your sake, on your behalf.

deinetwillen ['daɪnətvɪlən], *adv.* um —, on your account, for your sake, on your behalf.

deinige ['daɪnɪgə], *poss. adj.* your; (*Poet.*) thy. — *poss. pron.* yours; (*Poet.*) thine.

Dekan [de'ka:n], *m.* (—s, *pl.* —e) (*Eccl., Univ.*) dean.

Dekanat [deka'na:t], *n.* (—s, *pl.* —e) (*Eccl., Univ.*) deanery, office of dean.

deklamieren [dekla'mi:rən], *v.a., v.n.* recite, declaim.

deklarieren [dekla'ri:rən], *v.a.* declare (for customs duty).

Deklination [deklina'tsjo:n], *f.* (—, *pl.* —en) (*Gram.*) declension; (*Phys.*) declination.

deklinieren [deklɪ'ni:rən], *v.a.* (*Gram.*) decline.

dekolletiert [dekɔle'ti:rt], *adj.* décolleté, low-necked.

Dekret [de'kre:t], *n.* (—s, *pl.* —e) decree, edict, official regulation.

dekretieren [dekre'ti:rən], *v.a.* decree, ordain.

delegieren [dele'gi:rən], *v.a.* delegate.

Delegierte [dele'gi:rtə], *m.* (—n, *pl.* —n) delegate.

delikat [delɪ'ka:t], *adj.* subtle, dainty; tasty; (*coll.*) tricky, difficult.

Delikatesse [delɪka'tɛsə], *f.* (—, *pl.* —n) delicacy, dainty; (*pl.*) (*Am.*) delicatessen.

Delikt [de'lɪkt], *n.* (—s, *pl.* —e) (*Law*) crime; misdemeanour.

Delle ['dɛlə], *f.* (—, *pl.* —n) dent.

Delphin [dɛl'fi:n], *m.* (—s, *pl.* —e) dolphin.

deltaförmig ['dɛltafœrmɪç], *adj.* deltoid.

dem [de:m], *def. art. Dat.* to the. — *dem. adj.* to this, to that: — *dem. pron.* to this, to that; *wie* — *auch sei*, however that may be. — *rel. pron.* to whom, to which.

demarkieren [demar'ki:rən], *v.a.* mark, demarcate.

Dementi [de'mɛnti], *n.* (—s, *pl.* —s) (*official*) denial.

dementieren [demɛn'ti:rən], *v.a.* (*Pol.*) deny, contradict.

demgemäß ['de:mgəmɛ:s], *adv.* accordingly.

demnach ['de:mnax], *conj.* therefore, consequently, in accordance with that.

demnächst ['de:mnɛ:çst], *adv.* shortly, soon, in the near future.

demokratisch [demo'kra:tɪʃ], *adj.* democratic.

demolieren [demo'li:rən], *v.a.* demolish.

demonstrieren [demɔn'stri:rən], *v.a., v.n.* demonstrate.

Demut ['de:mu:t], *f.* (—, *no pl.*) humility, meekness.

demütig ['de:mytɪç], *adj.* humble, meek, submissive.

demütigen ['de:mytɪgən], *v.a.* humble, humiliate, subdue.

Denkart ['dɛŋka:rt], *f.* (—, *pl.* —en) way of thinking.

denken ['dɛŋkən], *v.a., v.n. irr.* think, reflect (upon); imagine; (*coll.*) guess.

Denker ['dɛŋkər], *m.* (—s, *pl.* —) thinker, philosopher.

Denkmal ['dɛŋkma:l], *n.* (—s, *pl.* ⸱er) monument.

Denkmünze ['dɛŋkmyntsə], *f.* (—, *pl.* —n) (commemorative) medal.

Denkschrift ['dɛŋkʃrɪft], *f.* (—, *pl.* —en) memorandum, memoir.

Denkspruch ['dɛŋkʃprux], *m.* (—s, *pl.* ⸱e) aphorism, maxim, motto.

Denkungsart ['dɛŋkuŋsart], *f.* (*pl.* —en) *see* Denkart.

Denkweise ['dɛŋkvaɪzə], *f.* (—, *pl.* —n) *see* Denkart.

denkwürdig ['dɛŋkvyrdɪç], *adj.* memorable.

Denkzettel ['dɛŋktsɛtəl], *m.* (—s, *pl.* —) (*fig.*) reminder, punishment, lesson; *einem einen* — *geben*, give s.o. s.th. to think about *or* a sharp reminder.

denn [dɛn], *conj.* for. — *adv.* then; (*after comparatives*) than; *es sei* — *dass*, unless.

dennoch ['dɛnɔx], *conj.* yet, nevertheless, notwithstanding.

Denunziant [denun'tsjant], *m.* (—en, *pl.* —en) informer.

denunzieren [denun'tsi:rən], *v.a.* inform against, denounce.

Depesche [de'pɛʃə], *f.* (—, *pl.* —n) dispatch; telegram, wire.

deponieren [depo'ni:rən], *v.a.* deposit; (*Law*) depose.

Depositenbank [depo'zi:tənbaŋk], *f.* (—, *pl.* —en) deposit-bank.

deprimieren

deprimieren [deprɪ'miːrən], *v.a.* depress.

Deputierte [depu'tiːrtə], *m.* (**—n,** *pl.* **—n**) deputy.

der [deːr], *def. art. m.* the. — *dem. adj., dem. pron.* this, that. — *rel. pron.* who, which, that.

derart ['deːraːrt], *adv.* so, in such a manner.

derartig ['deːraːrtɪç], *adj.* such.

derb [dɛrp], *adj.* firm, solid, coarse, blunt, uncouth; strong, robust.

dereinst [deːr'aɪnst], *adv.* one day (in future).

derenthalben ['deːrənthalbən], *adv.* for her (their) sake, on her (their) account, on whose account.

derentwegen ['deːrəntveːgən], *adv. see* **derenthalben.**

derentwillen ['deːrəntvɪlən], *adv. see* **derenthalben.**

dergestalt ['deːrgəʃtalt], *adv.* in such a manner; so.

dergleichen [deːr'glaɪçən], *adv.* such, such as, suchlike.

derjenige ['deːrjeːnɪgə], *dem. adj., dem. pron.* that, this; — *welcher,* he who.

derlei ['deːrlaɪ], *adj.* of that sort.

dermaßen ['deːrmaːsən], *adv.* to such an extent, to such a degree.

derselbe [deːr'zɛlbə], *pron.* the same.

derweilen [deːr'vaɪlən], *adv.* meanwhile.

Derwisch ['dɛrvɪʃ], *m.* (**—(e)s,** *pl.* **—e**) dervish.

derzeit ['deːrtsaɪt], *adv.* at present.

Des [dɛs], *n.* (**—,** *pl.* **—**) (*Mus.*) D flat; — *Dur,* D flat major; — *Moll,* D flat minor.

des [dɛs], *def. art. m. & n. Genit. sing.* of the.

desgleichen [dɛs'glaɪçən], *adj.* such, suchlike. — *adv.* likewise, ditto.

deshalb ['dɛshalp], *adv., conj.* therefore.

desinfizieren [dɛsɪnfit'siːrən], *v.a.* disinfect.

dessen ['dɛsən], *dem. pron. m & n. Genit. sing.* of it, of that. — *rel. pron. m. & n. Genit. sing.* whose, of whom, of which, whereof.

dessenungeachtet [dɛsənunge'axtət], *conj.* notwithstanding that, for all that, despite all that.

Destillateur [dɛstɪla'tøːr], *m.* (**—s,** *pl.* **—e**) distiller.

destillieren [dɛstɪ'liːrən], *v.a.* distil.

desto ['dɛsto], *adv.* the; — *besser,* so much the better; *je . . . —,* the . . . the.

deswegen ['dɛsveːgən], *adv., conj.* therefore.

Detaillist [deta'jɪst], *m.* (**—en,** *pl.* **—en**) retailer.

deucht [dɔyçt] *see* **dünken**; (*obs.*) *mich deucht,* methinks.

deuten ['dɔytən], *v.a.* point to, show; explain, interpret.

deutlich ['dɔytlɪç], *adj.* clear, distinct; evident, plain.

deutsch [dɔytʃ], *adj.* German.

Deutschland ['dɔytʃlant], *n.* Germany.

Deutschmeister ['dɔytʃmaɪstər], *m.* (**—s,** *pl.* **—**) Grand Master of the Teutonic Order.

Deutschtum ['dɔytʃtuːm], *n.* (**—s,** *no pl.*) German nationality, German customs, German manners.

Deutung ['dɔytuŋ], *f.* (**—,** *pl.* **—en**) explanation, interpretation.

Devise [de'viːzə], *f.* (**—,** *pl.* **—n**) device, motto; (*pl.*) foreign currency.

devot [de'voːt], *adj.* submissive, respectful, humble.

Dezember [de'tsɛmbər], *m.* December.

dezent [de'tsɛnt], *adj.* modest, decent; unobtrusive.

Dezernent [detsɛr'nɛnt], *m.* (**—en,** *pl.* **—en**) head of section in ministry or city administration.

dezimieren [detsi'miːrən], *v.a.* decimate, reduce.

Diagramm [dia'gram], *n.* (**—s,** *pl.* **—e**) diagram, graph.

Diakon [dia'koːn], *m.* (**—s,** *pl.* **—e**) (*Eccl.*) deacon.

Diakonisse, Diakonissin [diako'nɪsə, diako'nɪsɪn], *f.* (**—,** *pl.* **—nen**) deaconess.

Dialektik [dia'lɛktɪk], *f.* (**—,** *no pl.*) dialectics.

Diamant [dia'mant], *m.* (**—en,** *pl.* **—en**) diamond.

diametral [diame'traːl], *adj.* diametrical.

Diapositiv [diapozi'tiːf], *n.* (**—s,** *pl.* **—e**) (*lantern, Phot.*) slide.

Diät [di'ɛːt], *f.* (**—,** *pl.* **—en**) diet; (*pl.*) daily allowance.

dich [dɪç], *pers. pron.* you. — *refl. pron.* yourself.

dicht [dɪçt], *adj.* tight; impervious (to water); dense, compact, solid, firm; — *bei,* hard by, close to.

Dichte ['dɪçtə], *f.* (**—,** *no pl.*) density.

dichten ['dɪçtən], *v.a., v.n.* write poetry, compose (*verses etc.*); (*Tech.*) tighten; (*Naut.*) caulk.

Dichter ['dɪçtər], *m.* (**—s,** *pl.* **—**) poet.

dichterisch ['dɪçtərɪʃ], *adj.* poetic(al).

Dichtigkeit ['dɪçtɪçkaɪt], *f.* (**—,** *no pl.*) closeness, compactness, thickness, density.

Dichtkunst ['dɪçtkunst], *f.* (**—,** *no pl.*) (art of) poetry.

Dichtung ['dɪçtuŋ], *f.* (**—,** *pl.* **—en**) poetry, poem; fiction; (*Tech.*) caulking; washer, gasket.

dick [dɪk], *adj.* thick; fat; (*books*) bulky; voluminous, stout, obese, corpulent.

Dicke ['dɪkə], *f.* (**—,** *no pl.*) thickness, stoutness.

dickfellig ['dɪkfɛlɪç], *adj.* thick-skinned.

Dickicht ['dɪkɪçt], *n.* (**—s,** *pl.* **—e**) thicket.

die [diː], *def. art. f. & pl.* the. — *dem. adj., dem. pron. f. & pl.* this, these. — *rel. pron. f. & pl.* who, that which.

Dieb [diːp], *m.* (**—s,** *pl.* **—e**) thief.

Diebstahl ['diːpʃtaːl], *m.* (**—s,** *pl.* **⁚e**) theft.

dito

Diele ['di:lǝ], *f.* (—, *pl.* —n) floor; (entrance) hall; plank.
dielen ['di:lǝn], *v.a.* board, floor.
dienen ['di:nǝn], *v.n.* *einem* —, serve (s.o.); help (s.o.).
Diener ['di:nǝr], *m.* (—s, *pl.* —) servant, attendant; (*coll.*) bow.
dienlich ['di:nlɪç], *adj.* serviceable, useful; *für* — *halten*, think fit.
Dienst [di:nst], *m.* (—es, *pl.* —e) service, employment, duty; — *haben*, be on duty.
Dienstag ['di:nsta:k], *m.* (—s, *pl.* —e) Tuesday.
Dienstalter ['di:nstaltǝr], *n.* (—s, *pl.* —) seniority.
dienstbar ['di:nstba:r], *adj.* subject, subservient.
Dienstbarkeit ['di:nstba:rkaɪt], *f.* (—, *no pl.*) bondage, servitude.
dienstbeflissen ['di:nstbǝflɪsǝn], *adj.* assiduous.
Dienstbote ['di:nstbo:tǝ], *m.* (—n, *pl.* —n) domestic servant.
dienstfertig ['di:nstfɛrtɪç], *adj.* obliging, ready to serve.
Dienstleistung ['di:nstlaɪstuŋ], *f.* (—, *pl.* —en) service.
dienstlich ['di:nstlɪç], *adj.* official.
Dienstmädchen ['di:nstmɛ:tçǝn], *n.* (—s, pl. —) maidservant.
Dienstmann ['di:nstman], *m.* (—s, *pl.* ⁻er) commissionaire, porter.
Dienstpflicht ['di:nstpflɪçt], *f.* (—, *no pl.*) official duty, liability to serve; (*Mil.*) (compulsory) military service.
Dienststunden ['di:nstʃtundǝn], *f. pl.* office hours.
diensttauglich ['di:nsttauklɪç], *adj.* (*Mil.*) fit for service.
Dienstverhältnis ['di:nstfɛrhɛltnɪs], *n.* (—ses, *pl.* —se) (*pl.*) terms of service.
dies [di:s], *abbr.* **dieses.**
diesbezüglich ['di:sbǝtsy:klɪç], *adj.* concerning this, relating to this matter.
diese ['di:zǝ], *dem. adj., dem. pron. f. & pl.* this, these.
dieser ['di:zǝr], *dem. adj., dem. pron. m.* this.
dieses ['di:zǝs], *dem. adj., dem. pron. n.* this.
diesjährig ['di:sjɛ:rɪç], *adj.* of this year, this year's.
diesmal ['di:sma:l], *adv.* this time, for this once.
Dietrich (1) ['di:trɪç], *m.* Derek.
Dietrich (2) ['di:trɪç], *m.* (—s, *pl.* —e) pick lock, master-key, skeleton key.
Differentialrechnung [dɪfǝrɛnts'ja:l-rɛçnuŋ], *f.* (—, *pl.* —en) differential calculus.
Differenz [dɪfǝ'rɛnts], *f.* (—, *pl.* —en) difference; quarrel.
Diktat [dɪk'ta:t], *n.* (—s, *pl.* —e) dictation.
diktatorisch [dɪkta'to:rɪʃ], *adj.* dictatorial.
Diktatur [dɪkta'tu:r], *f.* (—, *pl.* —en) dictatorship.

diktieren [dɪk'ti:rǝn], *v.a.* dictate.
Ding [dɪŋ], *n.* (- -s, *pl.* —e) thing, object, matter.
dingen ['dɪŋǝn], *v.a.* hire, engage (a manual worker).
dingfest ['dɪŋfɛst], *adj.* — *machen*, arrest.
dinglich ['dɪŋlɪç], *adj.* real.
dinieren [di'ni:rǝn], *v.n.* dine.
Diözese [diø'tse:zǝ], *f.* (—, *pl.* —n) diocese.
Diphtherie [dɪftǝ'ri:], *f.* (—, *no pl.*) diphtheria.
Diplom [di'plo:m], *n.* (—s, *pl.* —e) diploma.
Diplomatie [dɪploma'ti:], *f.* (—, *no pl.*) diplomacy.
dir [di:r], *pers. pron. Dat.* to you.
direkt [di'rɛkt], *adj.* direct; —*er Wagen*, (*railway*) through carriage; — *danach*, immediately afterwards.
Direktion [dɪrɛk'sjo:n], *f.* (—, *pl.* —en) direction, management.
Direktor [di'rɛktɔr], *m.* (—s, *pl.* —en) (managing) director, manager; headmaster, principal.
Direktorium [dɪrɛk'to:rjum], *n.* (—s, *pl.* —rien) directorate, board of directors.
Direktrice [dɪrɛk'tri:sǝ], *f.* (—, *pl.* —n) manageress.
Dirigent [diri'gɛnt], *m.* (—en, *pl.* —en) (*Mus.*) conductor; (*Austr. Admin.*) head of section in Ministry.
dirigieren [diri'gi:rǝn], *v.a.* direct, manage; (*Mus.*) conduct.
Dirndl ['dɪrndl], *n.* (—s, *pl.* —) (*dial.*) young girl, country wench; (*fig.*) peasant dress, dirndl.
Dirne ['dɪrnǝ], *f.* (—, *pl.* —n) (*Poet.*) girl; prostitute.
Dis [dɪs], *n.* (—, *no pl.*) (*Mus.*) D sharp.
disharmonisch [dɪshar'mo:nɪʃ], *adj.* discordant.
Diskant [dɪs'kant], *m.* (—s, *pl.* —e) (*Mus.*) treble, soprano.
Diskont [dɪs'kɔnt], *m.* (—(e)s, *pl.* —e) discount, rebate.
diskret [dɪs'kre:t], *adj.* discreet.
Diskurs [dɪs'kurs], *m.* (—es, *pl.* —e) discourse.
diskutieren [dɪsku'ti:rǝn], *v.a.* discuss, debate.
Dispens [dɪs'pɛns], *m.* (—es, *pl.* —e) dispensation.
dispensieren [dɪspɛn'zi:rǝn], *v.a.* dispense (from); exempt (from).
disponieren [dɪspo'ni:rǝn], *v.n.* — *über*, dispose of; make plans about.
Dissident [dɪsi'dɛnt], *m.* (—en, *pl.* —en) dissenter, nonconformist.
distanzieren [dɪstan'tsi:rǝn], *v.r. sich* — *von*, keep o.'s distance from; dissociate o.s. from.
Distel ['dɪstǝl], *f.* (—, *pl.* —n) thistle.
Distelfink ['dɪstǝlfɪŋk], *m.* (—s, *pl.* —e) (*Orn.*) gold-finch.
disziplinarisch [dɪstsipli'na:rɪʃ], *adj.* diciplinary.
dito ['di:to], *adv.* ditto.

dividieren

dividieren [dɪvɪ'di:rən], *v.a.* divide.
Diwan ['di:van], *m.* (—s, *pl.* —e) divan, sofa, couch.
doch [dɔx], *adv., conj.* however, though, although, nevertheless, yet, but; after all, (*emphatic*) yes.
Docht [dɔxt], *m.* (—es, *pl.* —e) wick.
Dock [dɔk], *n.* (—s, *pl.* —s, —e) dock.
Dogge ['dɔgə], *f.* (—, *pl.* —n) bulldog, mastiff; Great Dane.
Dogmatiker [dɔg'ma:tɪkər], *m.* (—s, *pl.* —) dogmatist.
dogmatisch [dɔg'ma:tɪʃ], *adj.* dogmatic, doctrinal.
Dohle ['do:lə], *f.* (—, *pl.* —n) (*Orn.*) jackdaw.
Doktor ['dɔktər], *m.* (—s, *pl.* —en) doctor; physician, surgeon.
Dolch [dɔlç], *m.* (—es, *pl.* —e) dagger, dirk.
Dolde ['dɔldə], *f.* (—, *pl.* —n) (*Bot.*) umbel.
Dolmetscher ['dɔlmɛtʃər], *m.* (—s, *pl.* —) interpreter.
dolmetschen ['dɔlmɛtʃən], *v.a.* interpret.
Dolomiten [dolo'mi:tən], *pl.* Dolomites.
Dom [do:m], *m.* (—s, *pl.* —e) cathedral; dome, cupola.
Domherr ['do:mhɛr], *m.* (—n, *pl.* —en) canon, prebendary.
dominieren [domi'ni:rən], *v.a.* dominate, domineer.
Dominikaner [domini'ka:nər], *m.* (—s, *pl.* —) Dominican friar.
dominikanische Republik [domini'ka:nɪʃə repu'bli:k], *f.* Dominican Republic.
Domizil [domi'tsi:l], *n.* (—s, *pl.* —e) domicile, residence, address.
Domkapitel ['do:mkapɪtəl], *n.* (—s, *pl.* —) dean and chapter.
Dompfaff ['do:mpfaf], *m.* (—s, *pl.* —en) (*Orn.*) bullfinch.
Dompropst ['do:mpro:pst], *m.* (—es, *pl.* ⁻e) provost.
Donau ['do:nau], *f.* (—, *no pl.*) Danube.
Donner ['dɔnər], *m.* (—s, *no pl.*) thunder.
donnern ['dɔnərn], *v.n.* thunder; (*fig.*) storm, rage.
Donnerschlag ['dɔnərʃla:k], *m.* (—s, *pl.* ⁻e) thunderclap.
Donnerstag ['dɔnərsta:k], *m.* (—s, *pl.* —e) Thursday; *Grün* —, Maundy Thursday.
Donnerwetter ['dɔnərvɛtər], *m.* (—s, *pl.* —) thunderstorm; *zum* — (*nochmal*)! hang it all, confound it!
doppeldeutig ['dɔpəldɔytɪç], *adj.* ambiguous.
Doppelgänger ['dɔpəlgɛŋər], *m.* (—s, *pl.* —) double.
Doppellaut ['dɔpəllaut], *m.* (—s, *pl.* —e) diphthong.
doppeln ['dɔpəln] *see* **verdoppeln.**
doppelsinnig ['dɔpəlzɪnɪç] *see* **doppeldeutig.**
doppelt ['dɔpəlt], *adj.* double, twofold.

Doppelzwirn ['dɔpəltsvɪrn], *m.* (—s, *no pl.*) double-thread.
Dorf [dɔrf], *n.* (—es, *pl.* ⁻er) village.
dörflich ['dœrflɪç], *adj.* rural, rustic.
dorisch ['do:rɪʃ], *adj.* Doric.
Dorn [dɔrn], *m.* (—s, *pl.* —en) thorn, prickle; (*Bot.*) spine; (*buckle*) tongue.
dornig ['dɔrnɪç], *adj.* thorny.
Dornröschen ['dɔrnro:sçən], *n.* (—s, *pl.* —) Sleeping Beauty.
Dorothea [doro'te:a], *f.* Dorothea, Dorothy.
dorren ['dɔrən] *see* **verdorren.**
dörren ['dœrən], *v.a.* dry, make dry, parch.
Dörrobst ['dœrrobst], *n.* (—es, *no pl.*) dried fruit.
Dorsch [dɔrʃ], *m.* (—es, *pl.* —e) cod, codfish.
dort [dɔrt], (*Austr.*) **dorten** ['dɔrtən], *adv.* there, yonder; *von* — *aus*, from that point, from there.
dorther ['dɔrthe:r], *adv.* from there, therefrom, thence.
dorthin ['dɔrthɪn], *adv.* to that place, thereto, thither.
dortig ['dɔrtɪç], *adj.* of that place, local.
Dose ['do:zə], *f.* (—, *pl.* —n) box, tin, can.
dösen ['do:zən], *v.n.* doze, daydream.
Dosis ['do:zɪs], *f.* (—, *pl.* **Dosen**) dose.
Dotter ['dɔtər], *n.* (—s, *pl.* —) yolk (of egg).
Dozent [do'tsɛnt], *m.* (—en, *pl.* —en) university lecturer; (*Am.*) Assistant Professor.
dozieren [do'tsi:rən], *v.n.* lecture.
Drache ['draxə], *m.* (—n, *pl.* —n) dragon; kite; (*fig.*) termagant, shrew.
Dragoner [dra'go:nər], *m.* (—s, *pl.* —) dragoon.
Draht [dra:t], *m.* (—es, *pl.* ⁻e) wire.
drahten ['dra:tən], *v.a.* wire, telegraph.
Drahtgewebe [dra:tgəve:bə], *n.* (—s, *pl.* —) wire-gauze.
Drahtgitter ['dra:tgɪtər], *m.* (—s, *pl.* —) wire grating.
drahtlos ['dra:tlo:s], *adj.* wireless.
Drahtseilbahn ['dra:tzaɪlba:n], *f.* (—, *pl.* —en) cable (funicular) railway.
Drahtzange ['dra:ttsaŋə], *f.* (—, *pl.* —n) pliers.
drall [dral], *adj.* buxom, plump.
Drama ['dra:ma], *n.* (—s, *pl.* —men) drama.
Dramatiker [dra'ma:tɪkər], *m.* (—s, *pl.* —) dramatist.
dramatisch [dra'ma:tɪʃ], *adj.* dramatic.
dran [dran] *see* **daran.**
Drang [draŋ], *m.* (—s, *no pl.*) urge; rush; throng; pressure; impulse.
drängeln ['drɛŋəln], *v.a.* jostle.
drängen ['drɛŋən], *v.a.* press, urge; *die Zeit drängt*, time presses; *es drängt mich*, I feel called upon.
Drangsal ['draŋza:l], *f.* or *n.* (—s, *pl.* —e *or* —en) distress, misery.
drapieren [dra'pi:rən], *v.a.* drape.

drastisch ['drastɪʃ], *adj.* drastic.
drauf [drauf] *see* **darauf.**
Draufgänger ['draufgɛŋər], *m.* (—s, *pl.* —) daredevil.
draußen ['drausən], *adv.* outside, without, out of doors.
drechseln ['drɛksəln], *v.a.* turn (on a lathe); *Phrasen* —, turn phrases.
Drechsler ['drɛkslər], *m.* (—s, *pl.* —) turner.
Dreck [drɛk], *m.* (—s, *no pl.*) dirt, mire, dust, filth, dung.
dreckig ['drɛkɪç], *adj.* dirty, filthy, muddy.
drehbar ['dre:ba:r], *adj.* revolving, swivelling.
Drehbuch ['dre:bu:x], *n.* (—s, *pl.* ̈er) (*film*) script.
drehen ['dre:ən], *v.a.* turn; (*film*) shoot. — *v.n.* turn round, veer.
Drehorgel ['dre:ɔrgəl], *f.* (—, *pl.* —n) barrel-organ.
Drehrad ['dre:ra:t], *n.* (—s, *pl.* ̈er) fly-wheel.
Drehung ['dre:uŋ], *f.* (—, *pl.* —en) rotation, turn, revolution.
drei [draɪ], *num. adj.* three.
dreiblätterig ['draɪblɛtərɪç], *adj.* trifoliate.
Dreieck ['draɪɛk], *n.* (—s, *pl.* —e) triangle.
dreieckig ['draɪɛkɪç], *adj.* triangular, three-cornered.
dreieinig [draɪ'aɪnɪç], *adj.* (*Theol.*) triune.
dreifach ['draɪfax], *adj.* threefold, triple.
Dreifaltigkeit [draɪ'faltɪçkaɪt], *f.* (—, *no pl.*) (*Theol.*) Trinity.
Dreifuß ['draɪfu:s], *m.* (—es, *pl.* ̈e) tripod.
dreijährlich ['draɪjɛrlɪç], *adj.* triennial.
Dreikönigsfest [draɪ'kø:nɪksfɛst], *n.* (—es, *no pl.*) Epiphany.
dreimonatlich ['draɪmo:natlɪç], *adj.* quarterly.
Dreirad ['draɪra:t], *n.* (—s, *pl.* ̈er) tricycle.
dreiseitig ['draɪzaɪtɪç], *adj.* trilateral.
dreißig ['draɪsɪç], *num. adj.* thirty.
dreist [draɪst], *adj.* bold, audacious; impudent.
dreistellig ['draɪʃtɛlɪç], *adj.* —*e Zahl*, number of three figures.
dreistimmig ['draɪʃtɪmɪç], *adj.* for three voices.
Dreistufenrakete ['draɪʃtu:fənra'ke:tə], *f.* (—, *pl.* —n) three-stage rocket.
dreistündig ['draɪʃtyndɪç], *adj.* lasting three hours.
dreitägig ['draɪtɛ:gɪç], *adj.* lasting three days.
dreiteilig ['draɪtaɪlɪç], *adj.* tripartite; three-piece.
dreizehn ['draɪtse:n], *num. adj.* thirteen.
Drell [drɛl], *m.* (—s, *no pl.*) *see* **Drillich.**
Dresche ['drɛʃə], *f.* (—, *no pl.*) thrashing, beating.
dreschen ['drɛʃən], *v.a. irr.* (*corn*) thresh; (*person*) thrash.

Dreschflegel ['drɛʃfle:gəl], *m.* (—s, *pl.* —) flail.
dressieren [drɛ'si:rən], *v.a.* (*animal*) train; break in.
Dressur [drɛ'su:r], *f.* (—, *pl.* —en) training, breaking-in.
Drillbohrer ['drɪlbo:rər], *m.* (—s, *pl.* —) drill.
drillen ['drɪlən], *v.a.* (*a hole*) bore; (*soldiers*) drill.
Drillich ['drɪlɪç], *m.* (—s, *pl.* —e) drill, canvas.
Drilling ['drɪlɪŋ], *m.* (—s, *pl.* —e) three-barrelled gun; (*pl.*) triplets.
drin [drɪn] *see* **darin.**
dringen ['drɪŋən], *v.n. irr.* penetrate, force o.'s way through; *auf etwas* —, insist on s.th.
dringlich ['drɪŋlɪç], *adj.* urgent, pressing.
drinnen ['drɪnən], *adv.* inside, within.
drittens ['drɪtəns], *adv.* thirdly.
droben ['dro:bən], *adv.* up there, above, aloft, overhead.
Droge ['dro:gə], *f.* (—, *pl.* —n) drug.
Drogerie [dro:gə'ri:], *f.* (—, *pl.* —n) druggist's shop, chemist's; (*Am.*) drugstore.
drohen ['dro:ən], *v.a., v.n.* threaten, menace.
Drohne ['dro:nə], *f.* (—, *pl.* —n) drone.
dröhnen ['drø:nən], *v.n.* boom, roar.
Drohung ['dro:uŋ], *f.* (—, *pl.* —en) threat, menace.
drollig ['drɔlɪç], *adj.* droll, odd, quaint.
Dromedar [droma'da:r], *n.* (—s, *pl.* —e) dromedary.
Droschke ['drɔʃkə], *f.* (—, *pl.* —n) cab, hansom, taxi.
Drossel ['drɔsəl], *f.* (—, *pl.* —n) thrush.
Drosselader ['drɔsəla:dər], *f.* (—, *pl.* —n) jugular vein.
Drosselbein ['drɔsəlbaɪn], *n.* (—s, *pl.* —e) collar-bone.
drosseln ['drɔsəln], *v.a.* throttle. *See also* **erdrosseln.**
drüben ['dry:bən], *adv.* over there, on the other side.
drüber ['dry:bər] *see* **darüber.**
Druck [druk], *m.* (—s, *pl.* ̈e, —e) pressure, squeeze; (*Phys.*) compression; (*Typ.*) impression; print; (*fig.*) hardship.
Druckbogen ['drukbo:gən], *m.* (—s, *pl.* —) proof-sheet, proof.
Druckbuchstabe ['drukbu:xʃta:bə], *m.* (—n, *pl.* —n) letter, type.
Drückeberger ['drykəbɛrgər], *m.* (—s, *pl.* —) slacker, shirker.
drucken ['drukən], *v.a.* print.
drücken ['drykən], *v.a.* press, squeeze; trouble, oppress. — *v.r. sich* —, sneak away, shirk.
Drucker ['drukər], *m.* (—s, *pl.* —) printer.
Drücker ['drykər], *m.* (—s, *pl.* —) (*door*) handle, latch; (*gun*) trigger.
Druckerei ['drukəraɪ], *f.* (—, *pl.* —en) printing shop.

49

Druckerschwärze

Druckerschwärze ['drukərʃvɛrtsə], *f.* (—, *no pl.*) printing-ink.
Druckfehler ['drukfe:lər], *m.* (—s, *pl.* —) misprint, printer's error.
druckfertig ['drukfɛrtɪç], *adj.* ready for press.
Drucksache ['drukzaxə], *f.* (—, *pl.* —n) (*Postal*) printed matter.
drum [drum] *see* **darum.**
drunten ['druntən], *adv.* down there, below.
drunter ['druntər] *see* **darunter.**
Drüse ['dry:zə], *f.* (—, *pl.* —n) gland.
Dschungel ['dʒuŋəl], *m.* or *n.* (—s, *pl.* —) jungle.
du [du:], *pers. pron.* thou, you.
ducken ['dukən], *v.a.* bring down, humble. — *v.r. sich* —, duck, stoop, crouch.
dudeln ['du:dəln], *v.n.* play the bagpipes; tootle.
Dudelsack ['du:dəlzak], *m.* (—s, *pl.* ̈-e) bagpipe(s).
Duft [duft], *m.* (—s, *pl.* ̈-e) scent, odour, fragrance, aroma, perfume.
duften ['duftən], *v.n.* be fragrant.
duftig ['duftɪç], *adj.* fragrant, odoriferous, perfumed.
dulden ['duldən], *v.a.* suffer, endure, bear, tolerate.
duldsam ['dultza:m], *adj.* tolerant, indulgent, patient.
dumm [dum], *adj.* stupid, foolish, dull.
Dummheit ['dumhaɪt], *f.* (—, *pl.* —en) stupidity, folly.
dumpf [dumpf], *adj.* musty; (*air*) close; (*sound*) hollow; (*fig.*) gloomy.
dumpfig ['dumpfɪç], *adj.* damp, musty, stuffy.
Düne ['dy:nə], *f.* (—, *pl.* —n) dune, sand-hill.
Düngemittel ['dyŋəmɪtəl], *n.* (—s, *pl.* —) fertilizer.
düngen ['dyŋən], *v.a.* manure, fertilize.
Dünger ['dyŋər], *m.* (—s, *no pl.*) compost, artificial manure.
dunkel ['duŋkəl], *adj.* dark; (*fig.*) obscure, mysterious.
Dünkel ['dyŋkəl], *m.* (—s, *no pl.*) conceit, arrogance.
dünkelhaft ['dyŋkəlhaft], *adj.* conceited, arrogant.
Dunkelheit ['duŋkəlhaɪt], *f.* (—, *no pl.*) darkness, obscurity.
dunkeln ['duŋkəln], *v.n.* grow dark.
dünken ['dyŋkən], *v.n.* (*rare*) seem, appear. — *v.r. sich* —, fancy o.s., imagine o.s.
dünn [dyn], *adj.* thin, slim, weak.
Dunst [dunst], *m.* (—es, *pl.* ̈-e) vapour, fume; exhalation; haze; *einem blauen — vormachen,* humbug a p.
dünsten ['dynstən], *v.a.* stew.
dunstig ['dunstɪç], *adj.* misty, hazy.
Dunstkreis ['dunstkraɪs], *m.* (—es, *pl.* —e) atmosphere.
Dunstobst ['dunsto:pst], *n.* (—es, *no pl.*) stewed fruit.

duodez [duo'de:ts], *adj.* (*Typ.*) duodecimo (12mo).
Duodezfürst [duo'de:tsfyrst], *m.* (—en, *pl.* —en) petty prince, princeling.
Dur [du:r], *n.* (*Mus.*) major; sharp.
durch [durç], *prep.* (*Acc.*) (*local*) through, across; (*temporal*) during, throughout; (*manner*) by means of, by. — *adv.* thoroughly, through.
durchaus [durç'aus], *adv.* throughout, quite, by all means, absolutely.
Durchblick ['durçblɪk], *m.* (—s, *pl.* —e) vista, view.
durchbohren [durç'bo:rən], *v.a. insep.* perforate, pierce.
durchbrennen ['durçbrɛnən], *v.n. irr.* (*aux. sein*) abscond, bolt.
durchbringen ['durçbrɪŋən], *v.a. irr.* bring through, get through; squander (money); pull (a sick person) through. — *v.r. sich redlich* —, make an honest living.
Durchbruch ['durçbrux], *m.* (—s, *pl.* ̈-e) breach, break-through.
durchdrängen ['durçdrɛŋən], *v.r. sich* —, force o.'s way through.
durchdringen ['durçdrɪŋən], *v.n. irr. sep.* (*aux. sein*) get through. — [durç'drɪŋən], *v.a. irr. insep.* penetrate, pierce, permeate, pervade.
durchdrücken ['durçdrykən], *v.a.* press through; (*fig.*) carry through.
durcheilen [durç'aɪlən], *v.a. insep.* hurry through.
Durcheinander [durçaɪn'andər], *n.* (—s, *no pl.*) confusion, muddle.
durcheinander [durçaɪn'andər], *adv.* in confusion, pell-mell.
Durchfall ['durçfal], *m.* (—s, *no pl.*) diarrhoea; (*exams etc.*) failure.
durchfallen ['durçfalən], *v.n. irr.* (*aux. sein*) fall through, come to nought; (*exams etc.*) fail.
durchflechten [durç'flɛçtən], *v.a. irr.* interweave, intertwine.
durchfliegen [durç'fli:gən], *v.a. irr.* fly through; read superficially, skim through.
durchforschen [durç'fɔrʃən], *v.a. insep.* explore, scrutinise, examine thoroughly.
Durchfuhr ['durçfu:r], *f.* (—, *pl.* —en) passage, transit.
durchführbar ['durçfy:rba:r], *adj.* practicable, feasible.
durchführen ['durçfy:rən], *v.a.* escort through; (*fig.*) execute, bring about, carry through.
Durchgang ['durçgaŋ], *m.* (—s, *pl.* ̈-e) passage, thoroughfare; (*Comm.*) transit.
Durchgänger ['durçgɛŋər], *m.* (—s, *pl.* —) runaway horse, bolter; (*fig.*) hothead.
durchgängig ['durçgɛŋɪç], *adj.* general, universal.
durchgehen ['durçge:ən], *v.n. irr.* (*aux. sein*) go through, (*fig.*) abscond; (*horse*) bolt; (*proposal*) be carried. — *v.a. irr.* (*aux. sein*) peruse, review, go over.

durchgreifen ['durçgraɪfən], v.n. irr. act decisively, take strong action.
durchhauen ['durçhauən], v.a. cut through; einen —, flog s.o.
durchkommen ['durçkɔmən], v.n. irr. (aux. sein) get through; (exams etc.) pass.
durchkreuzen [durç'krɔytsən], v.a. insep. cross out; (fig.) thwart.
durchlassen ['durçlasən], v.a. irr. let pass.
Durchlaucht ['durçlauxt], f. (— pl. —en) Highness.
durchleuchten [durç'lɔyçtən], v.a. insep. (Med.) X-ray.
durchlöchern [durç'lœçərn], v.a. insep. perforate, riddle.
durchmachen ['durcmaxən], v.a. go through, suffer.
Durchmesser ['durcmɛsər], m. (—s, pl. —) diameter.
durchnässen [durç'nɛsən], v.a. insep. wet to the skin, soak.
durchnehmen ['durçne:mən], v.a. irr. go over or cover (a subject).
durchpausen ['durçpauzən], v.a. trace, copy.
durchqueren [durç'kve:rən], v.a. insep. cross, traverse.
Durchsage ['durçza:gə], f. (—, pl. —n) (radio) announcement.
durchschauen [durç'ʃauən], v.a. insep. einen —, see through s.o.
durchscheinend ['durçʃaɪnənt], adj. transparent, translucent.
Durchschlag ['durçʃla:k], m. (—s, pl. ⸚e) strainer, sieve, colander, filter; carbon copy.
durchschlagen ['durçʃla:gən], v.a. irr. insep. strain, filter. — v.r. irr. sich —, fight o.'s way through.
durchschlagend ['durçʃla:gənt], adj. thorough, complete, effective.
Durchschnitt ['durçʃnɪt], m. (—s, pl. —e) average; (Med. etc.) cross section.
durchschnittlich ['durçʃnɪtlɪç], adj. average; ordinary.
durchschossen [durç'ʃɔsən], adj. interleaved; interwoven.
durchseihen ['durçzaɪən], v.a. see durchsieben.
durchsetzen [durç'zɛtsən], v.a. insep. intersperse; ['durçzɛtsən], v.a. sep. have o.'s way (with s.o.). — v.r. sep. sich —, make o.'s way successfully, succeed.
Durchsicht ['durçzɪçt], f. (—, no pl.) revision, inspection, perusal.
durchsichtig ['durçzɪçtɪç], adj. transparent.
durchsickern ['durçzɪkərn], v.n. (aux. sein) trickle through, ooze through.
durchsieben ['durçzi:bən], v.a. strain, filter, sift.
durchsprechen ['durçʃprɛxən], v.a. irr. talk over, discuss.
durchstöbern [durç'ʃtø:bərn], v.a. insep. rummage through.
durchstreichen ['durçʃtraɪçən], v.a. irr. cross out, delete.

durchstreifen [durç'ʃtraɪfən], v.a. insep. roam (through).
durchströmen [durç'ʃtrø:mən], v.a. insep. flow through, permeate.
durchsuchen [durç'zu:xən], v.a. insep. search thoroughly, examine closely.
durchtrieben [durç'tri:bən], adj. artful, sly, cunning, crafty.
durchweben [durç've:bən], v.a. interweave.
durchweg(s) ['durçvɛk(s)], adv. without exception, every time, throughout.
durchwühlen [durç'vy:lən], v.a. insep. search; ransack.
durchziehen [durç'tsi:ən], v.a. irr. insep. wander through, traverse; ['durçtsi:ən], v.a. irr. sep. interlace (with threads); draw through.
durchzucken [durç'tsukən], v.a. insep. flash through, convulse.
Durchzug ['durçtsu:k], m. (—s, no pl.) passage, march through; (air) draught.
dürfen ['dyrfən], v.n. irr. be permitted; be allowed; dare; be likely.
dürftig ['dyrftɪç], adj. paltry, insufficient, poor.
dürr [dyr], adj. dry, arid, withered; (wood) dead; (persons) thin, gaunt.
Dürre ['dyrə], f. (—, pl. —n) aridity, dryness; drought; (persons) thinness.
Durst [durst], m. (—es, no pl.) thirst.
dürsten ['dyrstən], v.n. thirst.
durstig ['durstɪç], adj. thirsty.
Dusche ['du:ʃə], f. (—, pl. —n) shower (bath).
Düse ['dy:zə], f. (—, pl. —n) jet.
duselig ['du:zəlɪç], adj. drowsy; silly.
düster ['dy:stər], adj. dark, gloomy; sad, mournful; sombre.
Dutzend ['dutsənt], n. (—s, pl. —e) dozen.
Duzbruder ['du:tsbru:dər], m. (—s, pl. ⸚) crony, chum; close friend.
duzen ['du:tsen], v.a. be on close terms with.
dynamisch [dy'na:mɪʃ], adj. dynamic(al).

E

E [e:], n. (—s, pl. —s) the letter E; (Mus.) E Dur, E major; E Moll, E minor.
Ebbe ['ɛbə], f. (—, pl. —n) ebb, low tide; — und Flut, the tides.
ebben ['ɛbən], v.n. ebb.
eben ['e:bən], adj. even, level, plane; (fig.) plain. — adv. precisely, exactly.
Ebenbild ['e:bənbɪlt], n. (—es, pl. —er) likeness, image.
ebenbürtig ['e:bənbyrtɪç], adj. of equal birth or rank; equal.

51

ebenda

ebenda [ˈeːbəndaː], *adv.* in the same place.

ebendeswegen [ˈeːbəndɛsveːgən], *adv.* for that very reason.

Ebene [ˈeːbənə], *f.* (—, *pl.* —n) plain; level ground; (*Maths.*) plane; *schiefe* —, inclined plane.

ebenfalls [ˈeːbənfals], *adv.* likewise, also, too, as well.

Ebenholz [ˈeːbənhɔlts], *n.* (—es, *no pl.*) ebony.

Ebenmaß [ˈeːbənmaːs], *n.* (—es, *pl.* —e) symmetry.

ebenmäßig [ˈeːbənmɛːsɪç], *adj.* symmetrical.

ebenso [ˈeːbənzoː], *adv.* in the same way; — *wie*, just as ...

Eber [ˈeːbər], *m.* (—s, *pl.* —) (*Zool.*) boar.

Eberesche [ˈeːbərɛʃə], *f.* (—, *pl.* —n) (*Bot.*) mountain ash, rowan.

ebnen [ˈeːbnən], *v.a.* even out, level; smoothe.

echt [ɛçt], *adj.* genuine, real, true, authentic, pure.

Ecke [ˈɛkə], *f.* (—, *pl.* —en) corner, nook.

eckig [ˈɛkɪç], *adj.* angular.

Eckzahn [ˈɛktsaːn], *m.* (—s, *pl.* ⁻e) eye tooth; canine tooth.

Eckziegel [ˈɛktsiːgəl], *m.* (—s, *pl.* —) (*Build.*) header.

edel [ˈeːdəl], *adj.* noble; well-born, aristocratic; (*metal*) precious.

Edelmann [ˈeːdəlman], *m.* (—s, *pl.* **Edelleute**) nobleman, aristocrat.

Edelmut [ˈeːdəlmuːt], *m.* (—s, *no pl.*) generosity, magnanimity.

Edelstein [ˈeːdəlʃtain], *m.* (—s, *pl.* —e) precious stone, jewel.

Edeltanne [ˈeːdəltanə], *f.* (—, *pl.* —n) (*Bot.*) silver fir.

Edelweiß [ˈeːdəlvais], *n.* (—sses, *no pl.*) (*Bot.*) edelweiss; lion's foot.

Eduard [ˈeːduart], *m.* Edward.

Efeu [ˈeːfɔy], *m.* (—s, *no pl.*) (*Bot.*) ivy.

Effekten [eˈfɛktən], *m. pl.* goods and chattels; effects; stocks, securities.

Effektenbörse [eˈfɛktənbœrzə], *f.* (—, *pl.* —n) Stock Exchange.

Effekthascherei [eˈfɛkthaʃərai], *f.* (—, *pl.* —en) sensationalism, clap-trap.

effektuieren [efɛktuˈiːrən], *v.a.* (*Comm.*) execute, effectuate.

egal [eˈgaːl], *adj.* equal; all the same.

Egge [ˈɛgə], *f.* (—, *pl.* —n) harrow.

Egoismus [egoˈɪsmus], *m.* (—, *no pl.*) selfishness, egoism.

egoistisch [egoˈɪstɪʃ], *adj.* selfish, egoistic(al).

Ehe [ˈeːə], *f.* (—, *pl.* —n) marriage.

ehe [ˈeːə], *conj.* before; *adv.* formerly; *je —r, desto besser*, the sooner, the better.

Ehebrecher [ˈeːəbrɛçər], *m.* (—s, *pl.* —) adulterer.

Ehebruch [ˈeːəbrux], *m.* (—s, *pl.* ⁻e) adultery.

Ehefrau [ˈeːəfrau], *f.* (—, *pl.* —en) wife, spouse, consort.

Ehegatte [ˈeːəgatə], *m.* (—n, *pl.* —n) husband, spouse.

ehelich [ˈeːəlɪç], *adj.* matrimonial; (*children*) legitimate.

Ehelosigkeit [ˈeːəloːzɪçkait], *f.* (—, *no pl.*) celibacy.

ehemalig [ˈeːəmaːlɪç], *adj.* former, late.

ehemals [ˈeːəmaːls], *adv.* formerly, once, of old.

Ehemann [ˈeːəman], *m.* (—s, *pl.* ⁻er) husband.

ehern [ˈeːərn], *adj.* brazen; of brass, of bronze.

Ehestand [ˈeːəʃtant], *m.* (—s, *no pl.*) matrimony.

ehestens [ˈeːəstəns], *adv.* as soon as possible.

Ehre [ˈeːrə], *f.* (—, *pl.* —n) honour, reputation, respect, distinction, glory.

ehren [ˈeːrən], *v.a.* honour, respect, esteem; *sehr geehrter Herr*, dear Sir.

Ehrenbezeigung [ˈeːrənbətsaiguŋ], *f.* (—, *pl.* —en) mark of respect; (*Mil.*) salute.

Ehrenbürger [ˈeːrənbyrgər], *m.* (—s, *pl.* —) honorary citizen *or* freeman.

Ehrendame [ˈeːrəndaːmə], *f.* (—, *pl.* —n) maid of honour.

Ehrenerklärung [ˈeːrənɛrklɛːruŋ], *f.* (—, *pl.* —en) reparation, apology.

Ehrengericht [ˈeːrəngərɪçt], *n.* (—s, *pl.* —e) court of honour.

ehrenhaft [ˈeːrənhaft], *adj.* honourable, worthy.

Ehrenpreis [ˈeːrənprais], *m.* (—es, *pl.* —e) prize; (*no pl.*) (*Bot.*) speedwell.

Ehrenrettung [ˈeːrənrɛtuŋ], *f.* (—, *pl.* —en) vindication.

ehrenrührig [ˈeːrənryːrɪç], *adj.* defamatory, calumnious.

ehrenvoll [ˈeːrənfɔl], *adj.* honourable.

ehrenwert [ˈeːrənvɛrt], *adj.* honourable, respectable.

ehrerbietig [ˈeːrɛrbiːtɪç], *adj.* reverential, respectful.

Ehrfurcht [ˈeːrfurçt], *f.* (—, *no pl.*) reverence, awe.

Ehrgefühl [ˈeːrgəfyːl], *n.* (—s, *no pl.*) sense of honour.

Ehrgeiz [ˈeːrgaits], *m.* (—es, *no pl.*) ambition.

ehrlich [ˈeːrlɪç], *adj.* honest; — *währt am längsten*, honesty is the best policy.

ehrlos [ˈeːrloːs], *adj.* dishonourable, infamous.

ehrsam [ˈeːrzaːm], *adj.* respectable, honourable.

Ehrwürden [ˈeːrvyrdən], *m. & f.* (*form of address*) *Euer* —, Reverend Sir, Your Reverence.

ehrwürdig [ˈeːrvyrdɪç], *adj.* venerable, reverend.

Ei [ai], *n.* (—s, *pl.* —er) egg, ovum.

ei [ai], *int.* ay, indeed.

Eibe [ˈaibə], *f.* (—, *pl.* —n) (*Bot.*) yew.

Eichamt [ˈaiçamt], *n.* (—s, *pl.* ⁻er) office of weights and measures; (*Am.*) bureau of standards.

Eichapfel [ˈaɪçapfəl], m. (—s, pl. ¨) oak apple.

Eiche [ˈaɪçə], f. (—, pl. —n) (Bot.) oak.

Eichel [ˈaɪçəl], f. (—, pl. —n) acorn; (Anat.) glans; (Cards) clubs.

eichen [ˈaɪçən], v.a. gauge, calibrate. — adj. made of oak.

Eichhörnchen [ˈaɪçhœrnçən] or **Eichkätzchen** [ˈaɪçkɛtsçən], n. (—s, pl. —) squirrel.

Eid [aɪt], m. (—es, pl. —e) oath; falscher —, perjury.

Eidam [ˈaɪdam], m. (—s, pl. —e) (obs.) son-in-law.

eidbrüchig [ˈaɪtbryçɪç], adj. guilty of perjury.

Eidechse [ˈaɪdɛksə], f. (—, pl. —n) lizard.

Eidesleistung [ˈaɪdəslaɪstuŋ], f. (—, pl. —en) affidavit.

Eidgenosse [ˈaɪtgənɔsə], m. (—n, pl. —n) confederate.

Eidgenossenschaft [ˈaɪtgənɔsənʃaft], f. (—, pl. —en) confederacy.

eidlich [ˈaɪtlɪç], adj. by oath, sworn.

Eidotter [ˈaɪdɔtər], m. & n. (—s, pl. —) yolk of an egg.

Eierbecher [ˈaɪərbɛçər], m. (—s, pl. —) egg cup.

Eierkuchen [ˈaɪərkuːxən], m. (—s, pl. —) omelet(te), pancake.

Eierschale [ˈaɪərʃaːlə], f. (—, pl. —n) egg shell.

Eierspeise [ˈaɪərʃpaɪzə], f. (—, pl. —n) dish prepared with eggs.

Eierstock [ˈaɪərʃtɔk], m. (—s, pl. ¨e) ovary.

Eifer [ˈaɪfər], m. (—s, no pl.) zeal, eagerness, ardour, haste, passion, vehemence.

Eiferer [ˈaɪfərər], m. (—s, pl. —) zealot.

eifern [ˈaɪfərn], v.n. be zealous; gegen einen —, inveigh against s.o.

eiförmig [ˈaɪfœrmɪç], adj. oval, egg-shaped.

eifrig [ˈaɪfrɪç], adj. zealous, ardent, eager.

Eigelb [ˈaɪgɛlp], n. (—s, no pl.) yolk of (an) egg.

eigen [ˈaɪgən], adj. own; particular, peculiar.

Eigenart [ˈaɪgənaːrt], f. (—, pl. —en) peculiarity; idiosyncrasy.

eigenhändig [ˈaɪgənhɛndɪç], adj. with o.'s own hand.

Eigenheit [ˈaɪgənhaɪt], f. (—, pl. —en) peculiarity; idiosyncrasy.

eigenmächtig [ˈaɪgənmɛçtɪç], adj. arbitrary, autocratic, high-handed.

Eigenname [ˈaɪgənnaːmə], m. (—ns, pl. —n) proper name.

Eigennutz [ˈaɪgənnuts], m. (—es, no pl.) self-interest, selfishness.

eigennützig [ˈaɪgənnytsɪç], adj. selfish, self-interested, self-seeking.

eigens [ˈaɪgəns], adv. particularly, specially.

Eigenschaft [ˈaɪgənʃaft], f. (—, pl. —en) quality, peculiarity; property.

Eigenschaftswort [ˈaɪgənʃaftsvɔrt], n. (—s, pl. ¨er) (Gram.) adjective.

Eigensinn [ˈaɪgənzɪn], m. (—s, no pl.) obstinacy.

eigentlich [ˈaɪgəntlɪç], adj. true, real; exact, literal.

Eigentum [ˈaɪgəntuːm], n. (—s, pl. ¨er) property, possession, estate.

Eigentümer [ˈaɪgəntyːmər], m. (—s, pl. —) owner, proprietor.

eigenwillig [ˈaɪgənvɪlɪç], adj. self-willed.

eignen [ˈaɪgnən], v.r. sich — für (zu), suit, fit, be suitable or fit for (to).

Eilbote [ˈaɪlboːtə], m. (—n, pl. —n) special messenger.

Eile [ˈaɪlə], f. (—, no pl.) haste, hurry.

eilen [ˈaɪlən], v.n. (aux. sein), v.r. (sich —), hasten, hurry; be urgent.

eilends [ˈaɪlənts], adv. hastily.

eilfertig [ˈaɪlfɛrtɪç], adj. hasty.

Eilgut [ˈaɪlguːt], n. (—s, pl. ¨er) express goods.

eilig [ˈaɪlɪç], adj. hasty, speedy; pressing, urgent.

Eilzug [ˈaɪltsuːk], m. (—s, pl. ¨e) fast train.

Eimer [ˈaɪmər], m. (—s, pl. —) pail, bucket.

ein(e) [ˈaɪn(ə)], indef. art, a, an; was für —; what kind of a(n). — num. adj. one; — jeder, each one.

einander [aɪnˈandər], adv. each other, one another.

einarbeiten [ˈaɪnarbaɪtən], v.a. train, familiarise s.o. with. —v.r. (aux. haben) sich —, familiarize o.s.

einäschern [ˈaɪnɛʃərn], v.a. reduce to ashes, incinerate; cremate.

einatmen [ˈaɪnaːtmən], v.a. breathe in, inhale.

einätzen [ˈaɪnɛtsən], v.a. etch in.

einäugig [ˈaɪnɔygɪç], adj. one-eyed.

Einbahnstraße [ˈaɪnbaːnʃtraːsə], f. (—, pl. —n) one-way street.

Einband [ˈaɪnbant], m. (—s, pl. ¨e) binding, cover of book.

einbändig [ˈaɪnbɛndɪç], adj. in one volume.

einbauen [ˈaɪnbauən], v.a. build in.

einbegreifen [ˈaɪnbəgraɪfən], v.a. irr. include, comprise.

einberufen [ˈaɪnbəruːfən], v.a. irr. convene, convoke; (Mil.) call up.

einbeziehen [ˈaɪnbətsiːən], v.a. irr. include.

einbiegen [ˈaɪnbiːgən], v.n. irr. turn into (road).

einbilden [ˈaɪnbɪldən], v.r. sich —, imagine, fancy.

Einbildung [ˈaɪnbɪlduŋ], f. (—, no pl.) imagination, fancy, delusion; conceit.

einbinden [ˈaɪnbɪndən], v.a. irr. (book) bind.

Einblick [ˈaɪnblɪk], m. (—s, no pl.) insight.

Einbrecher [ˈaɪnbrɛçər], m. (—s, pl. —) burglar; intruder.

Einbrenne

Einbrenne ['aɪnbrɛnə], *f.* (—, *pl.* —n) thickening of soup.

einbringen ['aɪnbrɪŋən], *v.a. irr.* bring in, yield, fetch (a price); *wieder* —, retrieve.

einbrocken ['aɪnbrɔkən], *v.a.* crumble; *einem etwas* —, (*fig.*) get s.o. into trouble.

Einbruch ['aɪnbrux], *m.* (—s, *pl.* ⁻e) breaking-in; burglary, house-breaking.

Einbuchtung ['aɪnbuxtuŋ], *f.* (—, *pl.* —en) bight, bay.

einbürgern ['aɪnbyrgərn], *v.a.* naturalise.

Einbuße ['aɪnbu:sə], *f.* (—, *pl.* —n) loss.

einbüßen ['aɪnby:sən], *v.a.* suffer a loss from, lose, forfeit.

eindämmen ['aɪndɛmən], *v.a.* dam in (*or* up).

Eindecker ['aɪndɛkər], *m.* (—s, *pl.* —) (*Aviat.*) monoplane.

eindeutig ['aɪndɔytɪç], *adj.* unequivocal, unambiguous.

eindrängen ['aɪndrɛŋən], *v.r. sich* —, intrude (into), force o.'s way in(to), interfere.

eindrillen ['aɪndrɪlən], *v.a. einem etwas* —, drum s.th. into s.o.

eindringen ['aɪndrɪŋən], *v.n. irr.* (*aux.* sein) enter, intrude; invade; penetrate.

eindringlich ['aɪndrɪŋlɪç], *adj.* forceful, urgent; impressive.

Eindruck ['aɪndruk], *m.* (—s, *pl.* ⁻e) impression.

eindrücken ['aɪndrykən], *v.a.* press in, squeeze in.

eindrucksfähig ['aɪndruksfɛ:ɪç], *adj.* impressionable.

einengen ['aɪnɛŋən], *v.a.* compress, limit, confine, cramp.

Einer ['aɪnər], *m.* (—s, *pl.* —) (*Maths.*) digit, unit.

einerlei ['aɪnərlaɪ], *adj.* the same, all the same.

einerseits ['aɪnərzaɪts], *adv.* on the one hand.

einfach ['aɪnfax], *adj.* single; simple, plain, uncomplicated; modest, homely.

einfädeln ['aɪnfɛ:dəln], *v.a.* thread.

einfahren ['aɪnfa:rən], *v.n. irr.* (*aux.* sein) drive in, enter. — *v.a.* run in (new car).

Einfahrt ['aɪnfa:rt], *f.* (—, *pl.* —en) entrance, gateway, drive; (*Min.*) descent.

Einfall ['aɪnfal], *m.* (—s, *pl.* ⁻e) falling-in, downfall, fall; (*Mil.*) invasion; (*fig.*) idea, inspiration.

einfallen ['aɪnfalən], *v.n. irr.* (*aux.* sein) fall in, fall into; (*Mil.*) invade; (*fig.*) occur to s.o.

Einfalt ['aɪnfalt], *f.* (—, *no pl.*) simplicity; silliness.

Einfaltspinsel ['aɪnfaltspɪnzəl], *m.* (—s, *pl.* —) simpleton, dunce.

einfangen ['aɪnfaŋən], *v.a. irr.* catch, get hold of.

einfarbig ['aɪnfarbɪç], *adj.* of one colour; monochrome.

einfassen ['aɪnfasən], *v.a.* border, trim; (*diamonds*) set.

Einfassung ['aɪnfasuŋ], *f.* (—, *pl.* —en) bordering, trimming, edging, framing.

einfetten ['aɪnfɛtən], *v.a.* grease, lubricate.

einfinden ['aɪnfɪndən], *v.r. irr. sich* —, appear, be present.

einflechten ['aɪnflɛçtən], *v.a. irr.* plait; (*fig.*) insert.

einfließen ['aɪnfli:sən], *v.n. irr.* (*aux.* sein) flow in; — *lassen*, (*fig.*) mention casually, slip in (a word).

einflößen ['aɪnflø:sən], *v.a.* infuse; (*fig.*) instil, inspire with.

Einfluß ['aɪnflus], *m.* (—sses, *pl.* ⁻sse) influx; (*fig.*) influence.

einflußreich ['aɪnflusraɪç], *adj.* influential.

einflüstern ['aɪnflystərn], *v.n.* suggest, insinuate.

einförmig ['aɪnfœrmɪç], *adj.* uniform; monotonous.

einfriedigen ['aɪnfri:dɪgən], *v.a.* fence in, enclose.

einfügen ['aɪnfy:gən], *v.a.* insert, include, fit in. — *v.r. sich* —, adapt o.s., become a part of.

Einfühlungsvermögen ['aɪnfy:luŋsfɛr-mø:gən], *n.* (—s, *no pl.*) (*Phil.*) empathy, sympathetic understanding.

Einfuhr ['aɪnfu:r], *f.* (—, *pl.* —en) importation, import.

einführen ['aɪnfy:rən], *v.a.* introduce; (*goods*) import.

Einführung ['aɪnfy:ruŋ], *f.* (—, *pl.* —en) introduction; (*goods*) importation.

einfüllen ['aɪnfylən], *v.a.* fill in, pour into, bottle.

Eingabe ['aɪnga:bə], *f.* (—, *pl.* —n) petitition; application.

Eingang ['aɪngaŋ], *m.* (—s, *pl.* ⁻e) entry, entrance; arrival.

eingangs ['aɪngaŋs], *adv.* in *or* at the beginning.

eingeben ['aɪngə:bən], *v.a. irr.* inspire (with); (*petition*) present, deliver; (*claim*) file; (*complaint*) bring; (*medicine*) administer.

eingeboren ['aɪngəbo:rən], *adj.* native; (*Theol.*) only-begotten.

Eingeborene ['aɪngəbo:rənə], *m.* (—n, *pl.* —n) native.

Eingebrachte ['aɪngəbraxtə], *n.* (—n, *no pl.*) dowry.

Eingebung ['aɪngə:buŋ], *f.* (—, *pl.* —en) inspiration.

eingedenk ['aɪngədɛŋk], *prep.* (*Genit.*) mindful of, remembering.

eingefleischt ['aɪngəflaɪʃt], *adj.* inveterate, confirmed.

eingehen ['aɪngə:ən], *v.n. irr.* (*aux.* sein) (*Comm.*) arrive; *auf etwas* —, enter into s.th., agree to s.th.; *auf etwas näher* —, enter into the details of s.th.; (*animals, plants*) die; (*cloth*) shrink.

eingehend ['aɪngeːənt], *adj.* thorough, exhaustive.

Eingemachte ['aɪngəmaxtə], *n.* (—n, *no pl.*) preserve.

eingenommen ['aɪngənɔmən], *adj.* enthusiastic for, infatuated with; — *von sich,* conceited.

Eingeschlossenheit ['aɪngəʃlɔsənhaɪt], *f.* (—, *no pl.*) isolation, seclusion.

eingeschrieben ['aɪngəʃriːbən], *adj.* registered (letter).

eingesessen ['aɪngəzɛsən], *adj.* old-established; resident.

Eingeständnis ['aɪngəʃtɛntnɪs], *n.* (—ses, *pl.* —se) confession.

eingestehen ['aɪngəʃteːən], *v.a. irr.* confess to, avow.

Eingeweide ['aɪngəvaɪdə], *n. pl.* bowels, intestines.

eingewöhnen ['aɪngəvøːnən], *v.r. sich* —, accustom o.s. to, get used to.

eingießen ['aɪngiːsən], *v.a. irr.* pour in; pour out.

eingleisig ['aɪnglaɪzɪç], *adj.* single-track.

eingliedern ['aɪngliːdərn], *v.r. sich* —, adapt o.s., fit in.

eingreifen ['aɪngraɪfən], *v.n. irr.* intervene in; interfere with, encroach on.

Eingriff ['aɪngrɪf], *m.* (—s, *pl.* —e) intervention, encroachment, infringement; (*Med.*) operation.

Einguß ['aɪngus], *m.* (—sses, *pl.* ˙sse) infusion; enema.

einhaken ['aɪnhaːkən], *v.a.* hook in. — *v.r. sich* —, (*fig.*) take a p.'s arm.

Einhalt ['aɪnhalt], *m.* (—s, *no pl.*) stop, check, prohibition, cessation; — *gebieten,* check, suppress.

einhalten ['aɪnhaltən], *v.a. irr.* observe, adhere to.

einhändigen ['aɪnhɛndɪgən], *v.a.* hand in, deliver.

einhauen ['aɪnhauən], *v.a.* hew in, break open.

Einhebung ['aɪnheːbuŋ], *f.* (—, *pl.* —en) (*taxes*) collection.

einheften ['aɪnhɛftən], *v.a.* sew in, stitch in; (*papers*) file.

einhegen ['aɪnheːgən], *v.a.* fence in, hedge in.

einheimisch ['aɪnhaɪmɪʃ], *adj.* native; (*Bot.*) indigenous.

einheimsen ['aɪnhaɪmzən], *v.a.* reap.

Einheit ['aɪnhaɪt], *f.* (—, *pl.* —en) unit, unity.

einheitlich ['aɪnhaɪtlɪç], *adj.* uniform, consistent.

einheizen ['aɪnhaɪtsən], *v.a., v.n.* heat the stove, light the fire.

einhellig ['aɪnhɛlɪç], *adj.* unanimous, harmonious.

einher [aɪn'heːr], *adv.* forth, along, on.

einholen ['aɪnhoːlən], *v.a.* obtain; catch up with. — *v.n.* go shopping.

Einhorn ['aɪnhɔrn], *n.* (—s, *pl.* ˙er) unicorn.

einhüllen ['aɪnhylən], *v.a.* wrap up, cover, envelop.

einig ['aɪnɪç], *adj.* at one. — *adv.* in agreement.

einige ['aɪnɪgə], *adj.* some, several.

einigemal ['aɪnɪgəmaːl], *adv.* several times.

einigen ['aɪnɪgən], *v.a.* unite. — *v.r. sich* —, come to an agreement with.

einigermaßen [aɪnɪgər'maːsən], *adv.* to a certain extent.

Einigkeit ['aɪnɪçkaɪt], *f.* (—, *no pl.*) union; unity, unanimity, harmony.

Einigung ['aɪnɪguŋ], *f.* (—, *no pl.*) agreement.

einimpfen ['aɪnɪmpfən], *v.a.* inoculate, vaccinate.

einjährig ['aɪnjɛːrɪç], *adj.* one-year-old, annual.

einkassieren ['aɪnkasiːrən], *v.a.* cash (*cheque*), collect (*money*).

Einkauf ['aɪnkauf], *m.* (—s, *pl.* ˙e) purchase, buy.

einkaufen ['aɪnkaufən], *v.a.* purchase, buy. — *v.n.* go shopping.

Einkäufer ['aɪnkɔyfər], *m.* (—s, *pl.* —) (*Comm.*) purchaser, buyer.

Einkehr ['aɪnkeːr], *f.* (—, *no pl.*) stopping (at an inn); (*fig.*) meditation.

einkehren ['aɪnkeːrən], *v.n.* (*aux.* sein) stop *or* put up (at an inn).

einkerkern ['aɪnkɛrkərn], *v.a.* imprison.

einklagen ['aɪnklaːgən], *v.a.* (*Law*) sue for (money).

einklammern ['aɪnklamərn], *v.a.* bracket, enclose in brackets.

Einklang ['aɪnklaŋ], *m.* (—s, *no pl.*) accord, unison, harmony.

einkleben ['aɪnkleːbən], *v.a.* paste in.

einkleiden ['aɪnklaɪdən], *v.a.* clothe; (*fig.*) invest; *sich* — *lassen,* (*Eccl.*) take the veil.

einklemmen ['aɪnklɛmən], *v.a.* squeeze in, jam in.

einkochen ['aɪnkɔxən], *v.a.* preserve. — *v.n.* (*aux.* sein) boil down.

Einkommen ['aɪnkɔmən], *n.* (—s, *no pl.*) income, revenue.

einkommen ['aɪnkɔmən], *v.n. irr.* (*aux.* sein) *bei einem wegen etwas* —, apply to s.o. for s.th.

einkreisen ['aɪnkraɪzən], *v.a.* encircle, isolate.

Einkünfte ['aɪnkynftə], *pl.* income, revenue; emoluments.

einladen ['aɪnlaːdən], *v.a. irr.* load in; invite.

Einlage ['aɪnlaːgə], *f.* (—, *pl.* —en) (*letter*) enclosure; (*Theat.*) addition to programme; (*game*) stake; (*Comm.*) investment.

einlagern ['aɪnlaːgərn], *v.a.* (*goods*) store, warehouse; (*Mil.*) billet, quarter.

Einlaß ['aɪnlas], *m.* (—sses, *no pl.*) admission, admittance; (*water*) inlet.

einlassen ['aɪnlasən], *v.a. irr.* admit, allow in; let in. — *v.r. sich auf etwas* —, engage in s.th., enter into s.th.

Einlauf ['aɪnlauf], *m.* (—s, *no pl.*) entering; (*Med.*) enema.

55

einlaufen

einlaufen [ˈaɪnlaufən], *v.n. irr. (aux.* sein) *(Naut.)* enter harbour, put into port; *(materia¹)* shrink.

einleben [ˈaɪnleːbən], *v.r. sich —,* grow accustomed to, settle down, acclimatise o.s.

einlegen [ˈaɪnleːgən], *v.a.* put in, lay in; enclose; *(money)* deposit; *(food)* pickle, preserve; *Fürbitte —,* intercede; *eingelegte Arbeit,* inlaid work.

einleiten [ˈaɪnlaɪtən], *v.a.* begin, introduce; institute.

Einleitung [ˈaɪnlaɪtuŋ], *f. (—, pl. —en)* introduction; *(book)* preface; *(Mus.)* prelude; *(Law)* institution.

einlenken [ˈaɪnlɛŋkən], *v.n.* turn in; give in, come round.

einleuchten [ˈaɪnlɔyçtən], *v.n.* become clear.

einlösen [ˈaɪnløːzən], *v.a.* redeem; *(bill)* honour; *(cheque)* cash.

einmachen [ˈaɪnmaxən], *v.a.* preserve.

einmal [ˈaɪnmaːl], *adv.* once; *es war —,* once upon a time; *auf —,* suddenly; *noch —,* once more; *nicht —,* not even.

Einmaleins [ˈaɪnmaːlaɪns], *n. (—es, no pl.)* multiplication table.

einmalig [ˈaɪnmaːlɪç], *adv.* unique, unrepeatable.

Einmaster [ˈaɪnmastər], *m. (—s, pl. —)* *(Naut.)* brigantine, cutter.

einmauern [ˈaɪnmauərn], *v.a.* wall in, immure.

einmengen [ˈaɪnmɛŋən], *v.r. sich —,* meddle with, interfere.

einmieten [ˈaɪnmiːtən], *v.r. sich —,* take lodgings.

einmischen [ˈaɪnmɪʃən], *v.r. sich —,* meddle (with), interfere.

einmütig [ˈaɪnmyːtɪç], *adj.* unanimous, in harmony, united.

Einnahme [ˈaɪnnaːmə], *f. (—, pl. —n)* income, revenue; receipts; *(Mil.)* occupation, capture.

einnehmen [ˈaɪnneːmən], *v.a. irr.* take in; *(money)* receive; *(medicine)* take; *(taxes)* collect; *(place)* take up, occupy; *(Mil.)* occupy, conquer; *(fig.)* captivate, fascinate.

einnehmend [ˈaɪnneːmənt], *adj.* fetching, engaging, charming.

einnicken [ˈaɪnnɪkən], *v.n. (aux. sein)* nod *or* doze off.

einnisten [ˈaɪnnɪstən], *v.r. sich —,* nestle down; *(fig.)* settle in a place.

Einöde [ˈaɪnøːdə], *f. (—, pl. —n)* desert, solitude.

einordnen [ˈaɪnɔrdnən], *v.a.* place in order, file, classify.

einpauken [ˈaɪnpaukən], *v.a.* cram.

einpferchen [ˈaɪnpfɛrçən], *v.a.* pen in, coop up.

einpökeln [ˈaɪnpøːkəln], *v.a.* salt, pickle.

einprägen [ˈaɪnprɛːgən], *v.a.* imprint; impress.

einquartieren [ˈaɪnkvartiːrən], *v.a.* *(Mil.)* quarter, billet.

einrahmen [ˈaɪnraːmən], *v.a.* frame.

einräumen [ˈaɪnrɔymən], *v.a.* stow (things) away; *einem etwas —,* concede s.th. to s.o.

Einrede [ˈaɪnreːdə], *f. (—, pl. —n)* objection.

einreden [ˈaɪnreːdən], *v.a. einem etwas —,* persuade s.o. to. *— v.r. sich etwas —,* get s.th. into o.'s head.

einreichen [ˈaɪnraɪçən], *v.a.* hand in, deliver; tender.

einreihen [ˈaɪnraɪən], *v.a.* place in line, arrange.

einreihig [ˈaɪnraɪɪç], *adj.* consisting of a single row; *(Tail.)* single-breasted (suit).

einreißen [ˈaɪnraɪsən], *v.a. irr.* make a tear in; *(houses)* pull down. *— v.n. (fig.)* gain ground.

einrenken [ˈaɪnrɛŋkən], *v.a.* *(Med.)* set; *(fig.)* settle.

einrichten [ˈaɪnrɪçtən], *v.a.* put in order, arrange; equip, set up; furnish.

Einrichtung [ˈaɪnrɪçtuŋ], *f. (—, pl. —en)* arrangement, management; furnishing; *(pl.)* facilities; equipment, amenities.

einrücken [ˈaɪnrykən], *v.n. (aux. sein)* march in. *— v.a.* insert (in the newspaper).

Eins [aɪns], *f. (—, pl. —en, —er)* one; *(Sch.)* top marks.

eins [aɪns], *num.* one; *es ist mir alles —,* it is all the same to me.

einsalzen [ˈaɪnzaltsən], *v.a.* salt, pickle, cure.

einsam [ˈaɪnzaːm], *adj.* lonely, solitary, secluded.

Einsamkeit [ˈaɪnzaːmkaɪt], *f. (—, no pl.)* loneliness, solitude, seclusion.

Einsatz [ˈaɪnzats], *m. (—es, pl. ˙-e)* *(game)* stake, pool; *(dress)* lace inset; *(Mus.)* entry (of a voice), starting intonation; *(Mil.)* sortie, mission.

einsaugen [ˈaɪnzaugən], *v.a.* suck in; *(fig.)* imbibe.

einsäumen [ˈaɪnzɔymən], *v.a.* hem (in).

einschalten [ˈaɪnʃaltən], *v.a.* insert, interpolate; switch on; put in gear.

einschärfen [ˈaɪnʃɛrfən], *v.a.* impress s.th. on s.o.

einschätzen [ˈaɪnʃɛtsən], *v.a.* assess.

einschenken [ˈaɪnʃɛŋkən], *v.a.* pour in *or* out, fill.

einschieben [ˈaɪnʃiːbən], *v.a.* push in; interpolate, insert.

Einschiebsel [ˈaɪnʃiːpsəl], *n. (—s, pl. —)* interpolation; interpolated part.

einschiffen [ˈaɪnʃɪfən], *v.a.* embark; *(goods)* ship. *— v.r. sich —,* go aboard, embark.

einschlafen [ˈaɪnʃlaːfən], *v.n. irr. (aux. sein)* fall asleep, go to sleep.

einschläfern [ˈaɪnʃlɛːfərn], *v.a.* lull to sleep.

Einschlag [ˈaɪnʃlaːk], *m. (—s, pl. ˙-e)* cover, envelope; *(weaving)* woof, weft; explosion; strike; *(fig.)* streak *(of character)*; touch.

einschlagen [ˈaɪnʃlaːgən], *v.a. irr.* knock in; (*nail*) drive in; (*parcel*) wrap up; (*road*) take. — *v.n.* (*lightning*) strike; be a success.

einschlägig [ˈaɪnʃlɛːgɪç], *adj.* bearing on (the subject), pertinent.

einschleppen [ˈaɪnʃlɛpən], *v.a.* (*disease*) bring in, introduce.

einschließen [ˈaɪnʃliːsən], *v.a. irr.* lock in *or* up; (*enemy*) surround; (*fig.*) include.

einschlummern [ˈaɪnʃlumərn], *v.n.* (*aux.* sein) doze off, fall asleep.

Einschluß [ˈaɪnʃlus], *m.* (—sses, *pl.* -sse) inclusion; *mit* — *von*, inclusive of.

einschmeicheln [ˈaɪnʃmaɪçəln], *v.r. sich bei einem* —, ingratiate o.s. with s.o.

einschmelzen [ˈaɪnʃmɛltsən], *v.a. irr.* melt down.

einschmieren [ˈaɪnʃmiːrən], *v.a.* smear, grease, oil; (*sore*) put ointment on.

einschneidend [ˈaɪnʃnaɪdənt], *adj.* important, sweeping, incisive, trenchant.

einschneidig [ˈaɪnʃnaɪdɪç], *adj.* single-edged.

Einschnitt [ˈaɪnʃnɪt], *m.* (—s, *pl.* —e) incision, cut, notch; (*verse*) caesura.

einschnüren [ˈaɪnʃnyːrən], *v.a.* lace up; (*parcel*) tie up.

einschränken [ˈaɪnʃrɛŋkən], *v.a.* confine, limit, restrict. — *v.r. sich* —, curtail o.'s expenses, economize.

einschrauben [ˈaɪnʃraʊbən], *v.a.* screw in.

einschreiben [ˈaɪnʃraɪbən], *v.a. irr.* write in *or* down, inscribe; (*letter*) register. — *v.r. sich* —, enter o.'s name; enrol.

Einschreibesendung [ˈaɪnʃraɪbəzendʊŋ], *f.* (—, *pl.* —en) registered letter, registered parcel.

einschreiten [ˈaɪnʃraɪtən], *v.n. irr.* (*aux.* sein) step in, intervene.

einschrumpfen [ˈaɪnʃrʊmpfən], *v.n.* (*aux.* sein) shrink, shrivel.

einschüchtern [ˈaɪnʃyçtərn], *v.a.* intimidate, overawe.

Einschuß [ˈaɪnʃus], *m.* (—sses, *pl.* -sse) share, advance of capital; (*weaving*) woof, weft.

einsegnen [ˈaɪnzeːgnən], *v.a.* consecrate, bless; (*Eccl.*) confirm.

Einsehen [ˈaɪnzeːən], *n.* (—s, *no pl.*) realisation; *ein* — *haben*, be reasonable.

einsehen [ˈaɪnzeːən], *v.a. irr.* look into, glance over; (*fig.*) comprehend, realise.

einseifen [ˈaɪnzaɪfən], *v.a.* soap, lather; (*fig.*) take s.o. in.

einseitig [ˈaɪnzaɪtɪç], *adj.* one-sided; (*fig.*) one-track (mind).

Einsenkung [ˈaɪnzɛŋkʊŋ], *f.* (—, *pl.* —en) depression (of the ground).

einsetzen [ˈaɪnzɛtsən], *v.a.* put in, set in; institute, establish; (*money*) stake; (*Hort.*) plant; (*office*) install s.o. — *v.n.* begin.

Einsetzung [ˈaɪnzɛtsʊŋ], *f.* (—, *pl.* —en) (*office*) investiture, installation; institution.

Einsicht [ˈaɪnzɪçt], *f.* (—, *no pl.*) inspection, examination; insight, understanding.

einsichtig [ˈaɪnzɪçtɪç], *adj.* intelligent, sensible, judicious.

Einsichtnahme [ˈaɪnzɪçtnaːmə], *f. zur* —, (*Comm.*) on approval, for inspection.

Einsiedler [ˈaɪnziːdlər], *m.* (—s, *pl.* —) hermit, recluse.

einsilbig [ˈaɪnzɪlbɪç], *adj.* monosyllabic; (*fig.*) taciturn, laconic.

einspannen [ˈaɪnʃpanən], *v.a.* stretch in a frame; harness; (*coll.*) put to work.

Einspänner [ˈaɪnʃpɛnər], *m.* (—s, *pl.* —) one-horse vehicle; one-horse cab, fiacre.

einsperren [ˈaɪnʃpɛrən], *v.a.* lock in, shut up, imprison.

einspinnen [ˈaɪnʃpɪnən], *v.r. irr. sich* —, spin a cocoon.

einsprengen [ˈaɪnʃprɛŋən], *v.a.* sprinkle.

einspringen [ˈaɪnʃprɪŋən], *v.n. irr.* (*aux.* sein) *auf einen* —, leap at; (*lock*) catch, snap; *für einen* —, deputize for s.o.

Einspruch [ˈaɪnʃprux], *m.* (—s, *pl.* -e) objection, protest; — *erheben*, protest; (*Law*) appeal (against).

einspurig [ˈaɪnʃpuːrɪç], *adj.* (*Railw.*) single-track line.

einst [aɪnst], *adv.* (*past*) once, once upon a time; (*future*) some day.

Einstand [ˈaɪnʃtant], *m.* (—s, *no pl.*) (*Tennis*) deuce.

einstecken [ˈaɪnʃtɛkən], *v.a.* put in; pocket; post (a letter).

einstehen [ˈaɪnʃteːən], *v.a. irr. zu etwas* —, answer for s.th.; *für einen* —, stand security for s.o.

einsteigen [ˈaɪnʃtaɪgən], *v.n. irr.* (*aux.* sein) get in, climb on; board.

einstellen [ˈaɪnʃtɛlən], *v.a.* put in; (*persons*) engage, hire; adjust; (*work*) stop, strike; (*payments*) stop; (*hostilities*) suspend, cease fire. — *v.r. sich* —, turn up, appear.

einstellig [ˈaɪnʃtɛlɪç], *adj.* (*Maths.*) of one digit.

Einstellung [ˈaɪnʃtɛlʊŋ], *f.* (—, *pl.* —en) putting in; (*persons*) engagement, hiring; adjustment; (*work*) stoppage, strike; (*payments*) suspension; (*hostilities*) suspension, cessation; (*fig.*) opinion, attitude.

einstig [ˈaɪnstɪç], *adj.* (*past*) former, late, erstwhile; (*future*) future, to be, to come.

einstimmen [ˈaɪnʃtɪmən], *v.n.* join in, chime in.

einstimmig [ˈaɪnʃtɪmɪç], *adj.* (*Mus.*) (for) one voice, unison; (*fig.*) unanimous.

einstmals [ˈaɪnstmaːls], *adv.* once, formerly.

einstöckig

einstöckig [ˈaɪnʃtœkɪç], *adj.* one-storied.

einstreichen [ˈaɪnʃtraɪçən], *v.a.* irr. (*money*) take in, pocket.

einstreuen [ˈaɪnʃtrɔyən], *v.a.* strew; (*fig.*) intersperse.

einstudieren [ˈaɪnʃtudiːrən], *v.a.* study; (*Theat., Mus.*) rehearse.

einstürmen [ˈaɪnʃtyrmən], *v.n.* (*aux.* sein) *auf einen* —, rush at, fall upon.

Einsturz [ˈaɪnʃturts], *m.* (—es, *pl.* ⁔e) fall, crash: subsidence, collapse.

einstürzen [ˈaɪnʃtyrtsən], *v.n.* (*aux.* sein) fall in, fall into ruin, fall to pieces, collapse.

einstweilen [ˈaɪnstvaɪlən], *adv.* in the meantime, meanwhile, for the time being, provisionally.

einstweilig [ˈaɪnstvaɪlɪç], *adj.* temporary, provisional.

eintägig [ˈaɪntɛːgɪç], *adj.* one-day, ephemeral.

Eintagsfliege [ˈaɪntaːksfliːgə], *f.* (—, *pl.* —n) dayfly.

eintauschen [ˈaɪntauʃən], *v.a.* — *gegen*, exchange for, barter for.

einteilen [ˈaɪntaɪlən], *v.a.* divide; distribute; classify.

eintönig [ˈaɪntøːnɪç], *adj.* monotonous.

Eintracht [ˈaɪntraxt], *f.* (—, *no pl.*) concord, harmony.

einträchtig [ˈaɪntrɛçtɪç], *adj.* united, harmonious.

Eintrag [ˈaɪntraːk], *m.* (—s, *pl.* ⁔e) entry (in a book); prejudice, damage, detriment.

eintragen [ˈaɪntraːgən], *v.a.* irr. enter (in a book), register; bring in, yield.

einträglich [ˈaɪntrɛklɪç], *adj.* profitable, lucrative.

Eintragung [ˈaɪntraːguŋ], *f.* (—, *pl.* —en) entry (in a book); enrolment.

einträufeln [ˈaɪntrɔyfəln], *v.a.* instil.

eintreffen [ˈaɪntrɛfən], *v.n.* irr. (*aux.* sein) arrive; happen, come true.

eintreiben [ˈaɪntraɪbən], *v.a.* irr. drive home (*cattle*); collect (debts etc.).

eintreten [ˈaɪntreːtən], *v.n.* irr. (*aux.* sein) step in, enter; happen, take place; *in einen Verein* —, join a club; *für einen* —, speak up for s.o.

eintrichtern [ˈaɪntrɪçtərn], *v.a. einem etwas* —, cram s.th. into s.o.

Eintritt [ˈaɪntrɪt], *m.* (—s, *no pl.*) entry, entrance; beginning; *kein* —, no admission.

eintrocknen [ˈaɪntrɔknən], *v.n.* (*aux.* sein) shrivel, dry up.

einüben [ˈaɪnyːbən], *v.a.* practise, exercise.

einverleiben [ˈaɪnfɛrlaɪbən], *v.a.* incorporate in, embody in.

Einvernahme [ˈaɪnfɛrnaːmə], *f.* (—, *pl.* —n) (*Austr.*) see **Vernehmung**.

Einvernehmen [ˈaɪnfɛrneːmən], *n.* (—s, *no pl.*) understanding; *im besten* —, on the best of terms.

einvernehmen [ˈaɪnfɛrneːmən], *v.a.* (*aux.* haben) (*Austr.*) see **vernehmen**.

einverstanden [ˈaɪnfɛrʃtandən], (*excl.*)

agreed! — *adj.* — *sein*, agree.

Einverständnis [ˈaɪnfɛrʃtɛntnɪs], *n.* (—ses, *no pl.*) consent, agreement, accord.

Einwand [ˈaɪnvant], *m.* (—s, *pl.* ⁔e) objection, exception; — *erheben*, raise objections.

einwandern [ˈaɪnvandərn], *v.n.* (*aux.* sein) immigrate.

einwandfrei [ˈaɪnvantfraɪ], *adj.* irreproachable, unobjectionable.

einwärts [ˈaɪnvɛrts], *adv.* inward(s).

einwechseln [ˈaɪnvɛksəln], *v.a.* change, exchange.

einweichen [ˈaɪnvaɪçən], *v.a.* steep in water, soak.

einweihen [ˈaɪnvaɪən], *v.a.* dedicate; (*Eccl.*) consecrate; open (formally), inaugurate; initiate (into).

Einweihung [ˈaɪnvaɪuŋ], *f.* (—, *pl.* —en) (*Eccl.*) consecration; inauguration, formal opening; initiation.

einwenden [ˈaɪnvɛndən], *v.a.* irr. object to, raise objections, urge against.

einwerfen [ˈaɪnvɛrfən], *v.a.* irr. throw in; smash in; interject.

einwickeln [ˈaɪnvɪkəln], *v.a.* wrap up, envelop.

einwilligen [ˈaɪnvɪlɪgən], *v.n.* consent, assent, agree, accede.

einwirken [ˈaɪnvɪrkən], *v.n. auf einen* —, influence s.o.

Einwohner [ˈaɪnvoːnər], *m.* (—s, *pl.* —) inhabitant.

Einwohnerschaft [ˈaɪnvoːnərʃaft], *f.* (—, *no pl.*) population, inhabitants.

Einwurf [ˈaɪnvurf], *m.* (—s, *pl.* ⁔e) (*letter box*) opening, slit; slot; objection.

einwurzeln [ˈaɪnvurtsəln], *v.r. sich* —, take root; *eingewurzelt*, deep-rooted.

Einzahl [ˈaɪntsaːl], *f.* (—, *no pl.*) singular.

einzahlen [ˈaɪntsaːlən], *v.a.* pay in, deposit.

einzäunen [ˈaɪntsɔynən], *v.a.* fence in.

einzeichnen [ˈaɪntsaɪçnən], *v.a.* draw in, sketch in. — *v.r. sich* —, enter o.'s name, sign.

Einzelhaft [ˈaɪntsəlhaft], *f.* (—, *no pl.*) solitary confinement.

Einzelheit [ˈaɪntsəlhaɪt], *f.* (—, *pl.* —en) detail, particular.

einzeln [ˈaɪntsəln], *adj.* single; isolated; detached, apart.

einziehen [ˈaɪntsiːən], *v.a.* irr. draw in, retract; (*Law*) confiscate, impound; (*debts*) collect, call in; (*bill of sight*) discount, cash; (*money*) withdraw (from circulation); (*sails*) furl; (*Mil.*) call up.

einzig [ˈaɪntsɪç], *adj.* sole, single; unique, only.

Einzug [ˈaɪntsuːk], *m.* (—s, *pl.* ⁔e) entry, entrance; move (into new house).

einzwängen [ˈaɪntsvɛŋən], *v.a.* force in, squeeze in.

Eis [aɪs], *n.* (—es, *no pl.*) ice; ice-cream.

E-is [ˈeːɪs], *n.* (—, *pl.* —) (*Mus.*) E sharp.

58

Eisbahn ['aɪsbaːn], f. (—, pl. —en) ice-rink, skating-rink.
Eisbär ['aɪsbɛːr], m. (—en, pl. —en) polar bear, white bear.
Eisbein ['aɪsbaɪn], n. (—s, pl. —e) pig's trotters.
Eisberg ['aɪsbɛrk], m. (—s, pl. —e) iceberg.
Eisblumen ['aɪsbluːmən], f. pl. frost patterns (on glass).
Eisen ['aɪzən], n. (—s, pl. —) iron; altes —, scrap iron.
Eisenbahn ['aɪzənbaːn], f. (—, pl. —en) railway.
Eisenfleck ['aɪzənflɛk], m. (—s, pl. —e) iron mould.
Eisengießerei ['aɪzəngiːsəraɪ], f. (—, pl. —en) iron foundry, iron forge.
Eisenguß ['aɪzəngus], m. (—sses, pl. ⸚sse) cast-iron.
Eisenhändler ['aɪzənhɛndlər], m. (—s, pl. —) ironmonger.
Eisenhütte ['aɪzənhytə], f. (—, pl. —n) see **Eisengießerei**.
Eisenschlacke ['aɪzənʃlakə], f. (—, no pl.) iron dross, iron slag.
eisern ['aɪzərn], adj. made of iron; (coll. & fig.) strong; strict.
Eisgang ['aɪsgaŋ], m. (—s, pl. ⸚e) drift of ice.
eisgrau ['aɪsgrau], adj. hoary.
eiskalt ['aɪskalt], adj. icy cold.
Eislauf ['aɪslauf], m. (—s, no pl.) ice-skating.
Eismeer ['aɪsmeːr], n. (—s, pl. —e) polar sea; nördliches —, Arctic Ocean; südliches —, Antarctic Ocean.
Eispickel ['aɪspɪkəl], m. (—s, pl. —) ice axe.
Eisvogel ['aɪsfoːgəl], m. (—s, pl. ⸚) (Orn.) kingfisher.
Eiszapfen ['aɪstsapfən], m. (—s, pl. —) icicle.
eitel ['aɪtəl], adj. vain, frivolous, conceited; (obs.) pure.
Eiter ['aɪtər], m. (—s, no pl.) (Med.) pus, matter.
Eitergeschwür ['aɪtərgəʃvyːr], n. (—s, pl. —e) abscess.
eitern ['aɪtərn], v.n. suppurate.
Eiterung ['aɪtəruŋ], f. (—, pl. —en) suppuration.
eitrig ['aɪtrɪç], adj. purulent.
Eiweis ['aɪvaɪs], n. (—es, no pl.) white of egg; albumen.
Ekel ['eːkəl], m. (—s, no pl.) nausea, disgust, distaste, aversion.
ekelhaft ['eːkəlhaft], adj. loathsome, disgusting, nauseous.
ekeln ['eːkəln], v.r. sich — vor, be disgusted (by), feel sick, loathe.
Ekuador [ekua'doːr], n. Ecuador.
Elan [e'lã], m. (—s, no pl.) verve, vigour.
elastisch [e'lastɪʃ], adj. elastic, flexible, buoyant.
Elastizität [elastɪtsi'tɛːt], f. (—, no pl.) elasticity; (mind) buoyancy.
Elch [ɛlç], m. (—s, pl. —e) (Zool.) elk.
Elegie [ele'giː], f. (—, pl. —n) elegy.

elektrisieren [elɛktri'ziːrən], v.a. electrify.
Elektrizität [elɛktritsi'tɛːt], f. (—, no pl.) electricity.
Elend ['eːlɛnt], n. (—s, no pl.) misery, distress, wretchedness.
elend ['eːlɛnt], adj. miserable, wretched, pitiful; weak; sich — fühlen, feel poorly.
elendiglich ['eːlɛndɪklɪç], adv. miserably, wretchedly.
Elentier ['eːlɛntiːr], n. (—s, pl. —e) (Zool.) elk.
elf [ɛlf], num. adj. eleven.
Elfe ['ɛlfə], f. (—, pl. —n) fairy.
Elfenbein ['ɛlfənbaɪn], n. (—s, no pl.) ivory.
Elisabeth [e'liːzabɛt], f. Elizabeth.
Ellbogen ['ɛlboːgən], m. (—s, pl. —) elbow.
Elle ['ɛlə], f. (—, pl. —n) yard, ell.
Elritze ['ɛlrɪtsə], f. (—, pl. —n) minnow.
Elsaß ['ɛlzas], n. Alsace.
Elster ['ɛlstər], f. (—, pl. —n) magpie.
Eltern ['ɛltərn], pl. parents.
Emaille [e'maːj], n. (—s, no pl.) enamel.
emailliert [ema(l)'jiːrt], adj. covered with vitreous enamel, enamelled.
Empfang [ɛm'pfaŋ], m. (—s, pl. ⸚e) receipt; reception.
empfangen [ɛm'pfaŋən], v.a. irr. receive, accept, take.
Empfänger [ɛm'pfɛŋər], m. (—s, pl. —) recipient, receiver.
empfänglich [ɛm'pfɛŋlɪç], adj. susceptible, impressionable.
Empfängnis [ɛm'pfɛŋnɪs], f. (—, no pl.) conception.
empfehlen [ɛm'pfeːlən], v.a. irr. commend, recommend; give compliments to. — v.r. sich —, take leave.
empfinden [ɛm'pfɪndən], v.a. irr. feel, perceive.
empfindlich [ɛm'pfɪntlɪç], adj. sensitive, susceptible; touchy, thin-skinned.
empfindsam [ɛm'pfɪntsaːm], adj. sentimental.
Empfindung [ɛm'pfɪnduŋ], f. (—, pl. —en) sensation, feeling, sentiment.
empor [ɛm'poːr], adv. upward(s), up.
Empore [ɛm'poːrə], f. (—, pl. —n) gallery (in church).
empören [ɛm'pøːrən], v.a. excite, enrage, shock. — v.r. sich —, revolt, rebel.
Emporkömmling [ɛm'poːrkœmlɪŋ], m. (—s, pl. —e) upstart.
empört [ɛm'pøːrt], adj. furious, shocked, disgusted.
Empörung [ɛm'pøːruŋ], f. (—, pl. —en) rebellion, revolt, mutiny, insurrection; indignation, disgust.
emsig ['ɛmzɪç], adj. assiduous, industrious, busy.
Emsigkeit ['ɛmzɪçkaɪt], f. (—, no pl.) assiduity, diligence.
Ende ['ɛndə], n. (—s, pl. —n) end, conclusion.

enden ['ɛndən], *v.n.* end, finish, conclude. — *v.a.* terminate, put an end to.

endgültig ['ɛntgyltɪç], *adj.* definitive, final.

Endivie [ɛn'diːvjə], *f.* (—, *pl.* —n) (*Bot.*) endive.

endlich ['ɛntlɪç], *adj.* finite, final, ultimate. — *adv.* at last, at length, finally.

endlos ['ɛntloːs], *adj.* endless, neverending, boundless.

Endung ['ɛnduŋ], *f.* (—, *pl.* —en) (*Gram.*) ending, termination.

Endziel ['ɛntsiːl], *n.* (—s, *pl.* —e) final aim.

Energie [enɛr'giː], *f.* (—, *pl.* —n) energy.

energisch [e'nɛrgɪʃ], *adj.* energetic.

eng [ɛŋ], *adj.* narrow, tight; tight-fitting.

engagieren [ãga'ʒiːrən], *v.a.* engage, hire.

Enge ['ɛŋə], *f.* (—, *pl.* —n) narrowness, lack of space; *einen in die* — *treiben* drive s.o. into a corner.

Engel ['ɛŋəl], *m.* (—s, *pl.* —) angel.

engelhaft ['ɛŋəlhaft], *adj.* angelic.

Engelschar ['ɛŋəlʃaːr], *f.* (—, *pl.* —en) angelic host.

Engelwurzel ['ɛŋəlvurtsəl], *f.* (—, *pl.* —n) angelica.

engherzig ['ɛŋhɛrtsɪç], *adj.* narrow-minded.

England ['ɛŋlant], *n.* England.

englisch (1) ['ɛŋlɪʃ], *adj.* (*obs.*) angelic.

englisch (2) ['ɛŋlɪʃ], *adj.* English; —*e Krankheit*, rickets.

Engpaß ['ɛŋpas], *m.* (—sses, *pl.* ⁻e) defile, narrow pass; (*fig.*) bottleneck.

engros [ã'groː], *adj.* wholesale.

engstirnig ['ɛŋʃtɪrnɪç], *adj.* narrow-minded.

Enkel ['ɛŋkəl], *m.* (—s, *pl.* —) grandchild, grandson.

enorm [e'nɔrm], *adj.* enormous; (*coll.*) terrific.

entarten [ɛnt'artən], *v.n.* (*aux.* sein) degenerate.

entäußern [ɛnt'ɔysərn], *v.r. sich einer Sache* —, part with s.th.

entbehren [ɛnt'beːrən], *v.a.* lack, be in want of; spare.

entbehrlich [ɛnt'beːrlɪç], *adj.* dispensable, unnecessary, superfluous.

Entbehrung [ɛnt'beːruŋ], *f.* (—, *pl.* —en) privation, want.

entbieten [ɛnt'biːtən], *v.a. irr. Grüße* —, send o.'s respects.

entbinden [ɛnt'bɪndən], *v.a. irr. einen von etwas* —, release *or* dispense s.o. from s.th.; (*Med.*) deliver (a woman of a child).

Entbindung [ɛnt'bɪnduŋ], *f.* (—, *pl.* —en) (*Med.*) delivery, child-birth.

entblättern [ɛnt'blɛtərn], *v.a.* strip of leaves.

entblößen [ɛnt'bløːsən], *v.a., v.r.* (*sich*) —, uncover (o.s.), bare (o.s.).

entdecken [ɛnt'dɛkən], *v.a.* discover, detect.

Ente ['ɛntə], *f.* (—, *pl.* —n) duck; *junge* —, duckling; (*fig.*) hoax, fictitious newspaper report.

entehren [ɛnt'eːrən], *v.a.* dishonour, disgrace; deflower, ravish.

enterben [ɛnt'ɛrbən], *v.a.* disinherit.

Enterich ['ɛntərɪç], *m.* (—s, *pl.* —e) drake.

entfachen [ɛnt'faxən], *v.a.* set ablaze, kindle.

entfahren [ɛnt'faːrən], *v.n. irr.* (*aux.* sein) slip off, escape.

entfallen [ɛnt'falən], *v.n. irr.* (*aux.* sein) escape o.'s memory; be left off.

entfalten [ɛnt'faltən], *v.a.* unfold; display. — *v.r. sich* —, develop, open up, expand.

entfärben [ɛnt'fɛrbən], *v.r. sich* —, lose colour, grow pale.

entfernen [ɛnt'fɛrnən], *v.a.* remove. — *v.r. sich* —, withdraw.

Entfernung [ɛnt'fɛrnuŋ], *f.* (—, *pl.* —en) removal; distance.

entfesseln [ɛnt'fɛsəln], *v.a.* unfetter; let loose.

Entfettungskur [ɛnt'fɛtuŋskuːr], *f.* (—, —en) slimming-cure.

entflammen [ɛnt'flamən], *v.a.* inflame.

entfliegen [ɛnt'fliːgən], *v.n. irr.* (*aux.* sein) fly away.

entfliehen [ɛnt'fliːən], *v.n. irr.* (*aux.* sein) run away, escape, flee.

entfremden [ɛnt'frɛmdən], *v.a.* estrange, alienate.

entführen [ɛnt'fyːrən], *v.a.* abduct, carry off; kidnap; elope with.

entgegen [ɛnt'geːgən], *prep.* (*Dat.*), *adv.* against, contrary to; towards.

Entgegenkommen [ɛnt'geːgənkɔmən], *n.* (—s, *no pl.*) obliging behaviour, courtesy.

entgegenkommen [ɛnt'geːgənkɔmən], *v.n. irr.* (*aux.* sein) come towards s.o., come to meet s.o.; do a favour, oblige.

entgegennehmen [ɛnt'geːgənneːmən], *v.a. irr.* receive, accept.

entgegensehen [ɛnt'geːgənzeːən], *v.n. irr.* await, look forward to.

entgegnen [ɛnt'geːgnən], *v.a.* reply, retort.

Entgegnung [ɛnt'geːgnuŋ], *f.* (—, *pl.* —en) reply, retort, rejoinder.

entgehen [ɛnt'geːən], *v.n. irr.* (*aux.* sein) (*Dat.*) escape; — *lassen*, let slip.

Entgelt [ɛnt'gɛlt], *n.* (—s, *no pl.*) remuneration, recompense.

entgelten [ɛnt'gɛltən], *v.a. irr. einen etwas — lassen*, make s.o. pay for s.th. *or* suffer.

entgleisen [ɛnt'glaizən], *v.n.* (*aux.* sein) run off the rails, be derailed.

enthaaren [ɛnt'haːrən], *v.a.* depilate.

enthalten [ɛnt'haltən], *v.a. irr.* hold, contain. — *v.r. sich* —, abstain from, refrain from.

enthaltsam [ɛnt'haltzaːm], *adj.* abstinent, abstemious, temperate.

Enthaltung [ɛnt'haltuŋ], *f.* (—, *no pl.*) abstention.

enthaupten [ɛntʹhauptən], *v.a.* behead, decapitate.

entheben [ɛnʹheːbən], *v.a. irr. einen einer Sache* —, exempt or dispense from, suspend from, relieve of.

entheiligen [ɛntʹhaɪlɪgən], *v.a.* profane, desecrate.

enthüllen [ɛntʹhylən], *v.a.* unveil; (*fig.*) reveal.

entkleiden [ɛntʹklaɪdən], *v.a.* unclothe, undress, strip.

entkommen [ɛntʹkɔmən], *v.n. irr.* (*aux.* sein) escape, get off.

entkräften [ɛntʹkrɛftən], *v.a.* enfeeble, debilitate, weaken; (*fig.*) refute (an argument).

entladen [ɛntʹlaːdən], *v.a. irr.* unload, discharge. — *v.r. sich* —, burst; (*gun*) go off.

Entladung [ɛntʹlaːduŋ], *f.* (—, *pl.* —en) unloading, discharge, explosion.

entlang [ɛntʹlaŋ], *prep.* along.

entlarven [ɛntʹlarfən], *v.a.* unmask; expose.

Entlarvung [ɛntʹlarfuŋ], *f.* (—, *pl.* —en) unmasking, exposure.

entlassen [ɛntʹlasən], *v.a. irr.* dismiss; (*Am.*) fire; discharge; pension off.

Entlastung [ɛntʹlastuŋ], *f.* (—, *no pl.*) exoneration; credit (to s.o.'s bank account).

entlaufen [ɛntʹlaufən], *v.n. irr.* (*aux.* sein) run away.

entlausen [ɛntʹlauzən], *v.a.* delouse.

entledigen [ɛntʹleːdɪgən], *v.r. sich einer Sache* —, rid o.s. of or get rid of a thing; *sich einer Aufgabe* —, perform a task, discharge a commission.

entleeren [ɛntʹleːrən], *v.a.* empty.

entlegen [ɛntʹleːgən], *adj.* remote, distant, far off.

entlehnen [ɛntʹleːnən], *v.a.* borrow from.

entleihen [ɛntʹlaɪən], *v.a. irr.* borrow.

entlocken [ɛntʹlɔkən], *v.a.* elicit from.

entmannen [ɛntʹmanən], *v.a.* castrate, emasculate.

entmündigen [ɛntʹmyndɪgən], *v.a.* place under care of a guardian or (*Law*) trustees.

Entmündigung [ɛntʹmyndɪguŋ], *f.* (—, *no pl.*) placing under legal control.

entmutigen [ɛntʹmuːtɪgən], *v.a.* discourage, dishearten.

Entnahme [ɛntʹnaːmə], *f.* (—, *pl.* —n) (*money*) withdrawal.

entnehmen [ɛntʹneːmən], *v.a. irr.* (*money*) withdraw; understand, gather or infer from.

entnerven [ɛntʹnɛrfən], *v.a.* enervate.

entpuppen [ɛntʹpupən], *v.r. sich* —, burst from the cocoon; (*fig.*) turn out to be.

enträtseln [ɛntʹrɛːtsəln], *v.a.* decipher, make out.

entreißen [ɛntʹraɪsən], *v.a. irr.* snatch away from; *einer Gefahr* —, save or rescue from danger.

entrichten [ɛntʹrɪçtən], *v.a.* pay (off).

entrinnen [ɛntʹrɪnən], *v.n. irr.* (*aux.* sein) escape from.

entrückt [ɛntʹrykt], *adj.* enraptured.

entrüsten [ɛntʹrystən], *v.a.* make angry, exasperate. — *v.r. sich* —, become angry, fly into a passion.

entsagen [ɛntʹzaːgən], *v.n.* renounce; waive; abdicate.

Entsatz [ɛntʹzats], *m.* (—es, *no pl.*) (*Mil.*) relief.

entschädigen [ɛntʹʃɛːdɪgən], *v.a.* indemnify, compensate.

entscheiden [ɛntʹʃaɪdən], *v.a. irr.* decide. — *v.r. sich* — *für*, come to a decision for, decide in favour of.

Entscheidung [ɛntʹʃaɪduŋ], *f.* (—, *pl.* —en) decision; verdict.

entschieden [ɛntʹʃiːdən], *adj.* decided, determined, resolute, peremptory.

Entschiedenheit [ɛntʹʃiːdənhaɪt], *f.* (—, *no pl.*) resolution, firmness, determination.

entschlafen [ɛntʹʃlaːfən], *v.n. irr.* (*aux.* sein) fall asleep; (*fig.*) die, depart this life.

entschleiern [ɛntʹʃlaɪərn], *v.a.* unveil.

entschließen [ɛntʹʃliːsən], *v.r. irr. sich* —, decide (upon), resolve, make up o.'s mind.

Entschlossenheit [ɛntʹʃlɔsənhaɪt], *f.* (—, *no pl.*) resoluteness, determination.

entschlummern [ɛntʹʃlumərn], *v.n.* (*aux.* sein) fall asleep.

entschlüpfen [ɛntʹʃlypfən], *v.n.* (*aux.* sein) slip away; escape.

Entschluß [ɛntʹʃlus], *m.* (—sses, *pl.* ⸚sse) resolution; *einen* — *fassen*, resolve (to).

entschuldigen [ɛntʹʃuldɪgən], *v.a.* excuse. — *v.r. sich* —, apologise.

entschwinden [ɛntʹʃvindən], *v.n. irr.* (*aux.* sein) disappear, vanish.

entseelt [ɛntʹzeːlt], *adj.* inanimate, lifeless.

entsenden [ɛntʹzɛndən], *v.a. irr.* send off, despatch.

Entsetzen [ɛntʹzɛtsən], *n.* (—s, *no pl.*) horror, terror.

entsetzen [ɛntʹzɛtsən], *v.a.* (*Mil.*) relieve; frighten, shock, fill with horror. — *v.r. sich* — *über*, be horrified at.

entsetzlich [ɛntʹzɛtslɪç], *adj.* horrible, terrible, dreadful, awful.

entsiegeln [ɛntʹziːgəln], *v.a.* unseal.

entsinnen [ɛntʹzinən], *v.r. sich einer Sache* —, recollect, remember, call s.th. to mind.

entspannen [ɛntʹʃpanən], *v.a., v.r.* (*sich*) —, relax.

entspinnen [ɛntʹʃpinən], *v.r. irr. sich* —, arise, begin.

entsprechen [ɛntʹʃprɛçən], *v.n. irr.* respond to, correspond to, meet, suit.

entsprechend [ɛntʹʃprɛçənt], *adj.* corresponding, suitable.

entsprießen [ɛntʹʃpriːsən], *v.n. irr.* (*aux.* sein) spring up, sprout.

entspringen [ɛntʹʃpriŋən], *v.n. irr.* (*aux.* sein) escape, originate from; (*river*) have its source at, rise.

entstammen

entstammen [ɛnt'ʃtamən], *v.n.* (*aux.* sein) spring from, originate from.

entstehen [ɛnt'ʃteːən], *v.n. irr.* (*aux.* sein) arise, originate, begin, result, spring from.

Entstehung [ɛnt'ʃteːuŋ], *f.* (—, *no pl.*) origin, rise.

entstellen [ɛnt'ʃtɛlən], *v.a.* disfigure, deform, distort; (*fig.*) garble.

entsühnen [ɛnt'zyːnən], *v.a.* free from sin, purify, purge.

enttäuschen [ɛnt'tɔyʃən], *v.a.* disappoint.

entthronen [ɛnt'troːnən], *v.a.* dethrone.

entvölkern [ɛnt'fœlkərn], *v.a.* depopulate.

entwachsen [ɛnt'vaksən], *v.n. irr.* (*aux.* sein) grow out of, outgrow.

entwaffnen [ɛnt'vafnən], *v.a.* disarm.

entwässern [ɛnt'vɛsərn], *v.a.* drain.

entweder [ɛnt'veːdər], *conj.* either; — ......*oder*, either ...... or.

entweichen [ɛnt'vaɪçən], *v.n. irr.* escape, run away.

entweihen [ɛnt'vaɪən], *v.a.* profane, desecrate.

entwenden [ɛnt'vɛndən], *v.a.* take away, steal, embezzle.

entwerfen [ɛnt'vɛrfən], *v.a. irr.* design, sketch, plan, draw up.

entwerten [ɛnt'vɛrtən], *v.a.* reduce in value, depreciate; (*stamps*) cancel.

entwickeln [ɛnt'vɪkəln], *v.a.* unfold, develop; (*ideas*) explain, explicate. — *v.r. sich* —, develop (into), evolve.

Entwicklung [ɛnt'vɪkluŋ], *f.* (—, *pl.* —en) unfolding, development, evolution.

entwinden [ɛnt'vɪndən], *v.a. irr.* wrench from, wrest from.

entwirren [ɛnt'vɪrən], *v.a.* unravel, disentangle.

entwischen [ɛnt'vɪʃən], *v.n.* (*aux.* sein) slip away, escape.

entwöhnen [ɛnt'vøːnən], *v.a.* disaccustom; break off a habit; (*baby*) wean.

entwürdigen [ɛnt'vyrdɪgən], *v.a.* disgrace, degrade.

Entwurf [ɛnt'vurf], *m.* (—s, *pl.* ⸚e) sketch, design, draft, plan, project.

entwurzeln [ɛnt'vurtsəln], *v.a.* uproot.

entziehen [ɛnt'tsiːən], *v.a. irr.* withdraw, take away, deprive of.

entziffern [ɛnt'tsɪfərn], *v.a.* decipher.

entzücken [ɛnt'tsykən], *v.a.* enchant, delight, charm.

entzündbar [ɛnt'tsyntbaːr], *adj.* inflammable.

entzünden [ɛnt'tsyndən], *v.a.* set on fire, light the fire; (*fig.*) inflame. — *v.r. sich* —, catch fire, ignite; (*Med.*) become inflamed.

Entzündung [ɛnt'tsynduŋ], *f.* (—, *pl.* —en) kindling, setting on fire; (*Med.*) inflammation.

entzwei [ɛnt'tsvaɪ], *adv.* in two, broken.

entzweien [ɛnt'tsvaɪən], *v.a.* disunite.

Enzian ['ɛntsjan], *m.* (—s, *pl.* —e) (*Bot.*) gentian.

Enzyklopädie [ɛntsyklopɛ'diː], *f.* (—, *pl.* —n) encyclopædia.

Epidemie [epɪde'miː], *f.* (—, *pl.* —en) epidemic.

epidemisch [epɪ'deːmɪʃ], *adj.* epidemic(al).

Epik ['eːpɪk], *f.* (—, *no pl.*) epic poetry.

episch ['eːpɪʃ], *adj.* epic.

Epos ['eːpɔs], *n.* (—, *pl.* **Epen**) epic poem.

Equipage [ekvi'paːʒə], *f.* (—, *pl.* —n) carriage.

er [eːr], *pers. pron.* he.

Erachten [ɛr'axtən], *n.* (—s, *no pl.*) opinion, judgment; *meines* —s, in my opinion.

erachten [ɛr'axtən], *v.a.* think, consider.

erarbeiten [ɛr'arbaɪtən], *v.a.* gain *or* achieve by working.

erb ['ɛrb], *adj.* (*in compounds*) hereditary.

erbarmen [ɛr'barmən], *v.r. sich* —, have mercy (on), take pity (on).

erbärmlich [ɛr'bɛrmlɪç], *adj.* miserable, pitiful; contemptible.

erbauen [ɛr'bauən], *v.a.* build, erect; (*fig.*) edify.

erbaulich [ɛr'baulɪç], *adj.* edifying.

Erbauung [ɛr'bauuŋ], *f.* (—, *no pl.*) building, erection; (*fig.*) edification.

Erbbesitz ['ɛrpbazɪts], *m.* (—es, *pl.* —e) hereditary possession.

Erbe ['ɛrbə], *m.* (—n, *pl.* —n) heir. *n.* (—s, *no pl.*) inheritance; heritage.

erbeben [ɛr'beːbən], *v.n.* (*aux.* sein) shake, tremble, quake.

erbeigen ['ɛrpaɪgən], *adj.* inherited.

erben ['ɛrbən], *v.a.* inherit.

erbeten [ɛr'beːtən], *v.a. sich etwas* —, ask for s.th. by prayer; request.

erbetteln [ɛr'bɛtəln], *v.a.* obtain by begging.

erbeuten [ɛr'bɔytən], *v.a.* take as booty.

Erbfeind ['ɛrpfaɪnt], *m.* (—s, *pl.* —e) sworn enemy.

Erbfolge ['ɛrpfɔlgə], *f.* (—, *no pl.*) succession.

erbieten [ɛr'biːtən], *v.r. irr. sich* —, offer to do s.th.; volunteer; *Ehre* —, do homage.

Erbin ['ɛrbɪn], *f.* (—, *pl.* —nen) heiress.

erbitten [ɛr'bɪtən], *v.a. irr.* beg, request, ask for, gain by asking.

erbittern [ɛr'bɪtərn], *v.a.* embitter, anger, exasperate.

erblassen [ɛr'blasən], *v.n.* (*aux.* sein) turn pale.

Erblasser ['ɛrplasər], *m.* (—s, *pl.* —) testator.

erbleichen [ɛr'blaɪçən], *v.n. irr.* (*aux.* sein) turn pale, lose colour.

erblich ['ɛrplɪç], *adj.* hereditary, congenital.

erblicken [ɛr'blɪkən], *v.a.* perceive, behold, catch sight of.

erblinden [ɛr'blɪndən], *v.n.* (*aux.* sein) turn blind.

erblos ['ɛrploːs], *adj.* disinherited; without an heir.

erblühen [ɛr'bly:ən], *v.n.* (*aux.* sein) blossom (out).

Erbmasse ['ɛrpmasə], *f.* (—, *no pl.*) estate.

erbosen [ɛr'bo:zən], *v.a.* make angry. — *v.r. sich* —, become angry.

erbötig [ɛr'bø:tɪç], *adj.* — sein, be willing, be ready.

Erbpacht ['ɛrppaxt], *f.* (—, *pl.* —en) hereditary tenure.

erbrechen [ɛr'brɛçən], *v.a. irr.* break open, open by force. — *v.r. sich* —, vomit.

Erbrecht ['ɛrprɛçt], *n.* (—s, *no pl.*) law (*or* right) of succession.

Erbschaft ['ɛrpʃaft], *f.* (—, *pl.* —en) inheritance, heritage, legacy.

Erbse ['ɛrpsə], *f.* (—, *pl.* —n) pea.

Erbstück ['ɛrpʃtyk], *n.* (—s, *pl.* —e) heirloom.

Erbsünde ['ɛrpzyndə], *f.* (—, *no pl.*) original sin.

Erbteil ['ɛrptaɪl], *n.* (—s, *pl.* —e) portion of inheritance.

Erdapfel ['e:rtapfəl], *m.* (—s, *pl.* ⸚) (*Austr.*) potato.

Erdbahn ['e:rtba:n], *f.* (—, *no pl.*) orbit of the earth.

Erdball ['e:rtbal], *m.* (—s, *no pl.*) terrestrial globe.

Erdbeben ['e:rtbe:bən], *n.* (—s, *pl.* —) earthquake.

Erdbeere ['e:rtbe:rə], *f.* (—, *pl.* —n) strawberry.

Erde ['e:rdə], *f.* (—, *pl.* —n) earth, soil, ground.

erden ['e:rdən], *v.a.* (*Rad.*) earth.

erdenken [ɛr'dɛŋkən], *v.a. irr.* think out; invent. — *v.r. sich etwas* —, invent s.th., devise s.th.

erdenklich [ɛr'dɛŋklɪç], *adj.* imaginable, conceivable.

Erdenleben ['e:rdənle:bən], *n.* (—s, *no pl.*) life on this earth.

Erdfall ['e:rtfal], *m.* (—s, *pl.* ⸚e) landslip.

Erdfläche ['e:rtflɛçə], *f.* (—, *no pl.*) surface of the earth.

Erdgeschoß ['e:rtgəʃɔs], *n.* (—sses, *pl.* —sse) ground floor.

Erdhügel ['e:rthy:gəl], *m.* (—s, *pl.* —) mound of earth.

erdichten [ɛr'dɪçtən], *v.a.* think out, invent, feign.

Erdkunde ['e:rtkundə], *f.* (—, *no pl.*) geography.

Erdleitung ['e:rtlaɪtuŋ], *f.* (—, *pl.* —en) earth circuit, earth connexion.

Erdmaus ['e:rtmaus], *f.* (—, *pl.* ⸚e) field mouse.

Erdmolch ['e:rtmɔlç], *m.* (—s, *pl.* —e) salamander.

Erdnuß ['e:rtnus], *f.* (—, *pl.* ⸚sse) groundnut, peanut.

Erdöl ['e:rtø:l], *n.* (—s, *no pl.*) petroleum, mineral oil.

erdolchen [ɛr'dɔlçən], *v.a.* stab (with a dagger).

Erdpech ['e:rtpɛç], *n.* (—s, *no pl.*) bitumen.

erdreisten [ɛr'draɪstən], *v.r. sich* —, dare, have the audacity.

erdrosseln [ɛr'drɔsəln], *v.a.* strangle, throttle.

erdrücken [ɛr'drykən], *v.a.* crush to death.

Erdrutsch ['e:rtrutʃ], *m.* (—es, *no pl.*) landslip, landslide.

Erdschicht ['e:rtʃɪçt], *f.* (—, *pl.* —en) (*Geol.*) layer, stratum.

Erdschnecke ['e:rtʃnɛkə], *f.* (—, *pl.* —n) slug, snail.

Erdscholle ['e:rtʃɔlə], *f.* (—, *pl.* —n) clod (of earth).

Erdsturz ['e:rtʃturts], *m.* (—es, *no pl.*) landslide.

erdulden [ɛr'duldən], *v.a.* suffer, endure.

Erdumseg(e)lung ['e:rtumze:g(ə)luŋ], *f.* (—, *pl.* —en) circumnavigation of the earth.

ereifern [ɛr'aɪfərn], *v.r. sich* —, become heated, get excited.

ereignen [ɛr'aɪgnən], *v.r. sich* —, happen, come to pass.

Ereignis [ɛr'aɪknɪs], *n.* (—ses, *pl.* —se) event, occurrence, happening.

ereilen [ɛr'aɪlən], *v.a.* overtake, befall.

Eremit [ere'mi:t], *m.* (—en, *pl.* —en) hermit, recluse.

erfahren [ɛr'fa:rən], *v.a. irr.* learn, hear; experience. — *adj.* experienced, practised; conversant with, versed in.

Erfahrenheit [ɛr'fa:rənhaɪt], *f.* (—, *no pl.*) experience, skill.

Erfahrung [ɛr'fa:ruŋ], *f.* (—, *pl.* —en) experience, knowledge, expertness, skill; *in — bringen*, ascertain, come to know.

erfahrungsgemäß [ɛr'fa:ruŋsgəmɛ:s], *adj.* based on *or* according to experience.

erfahrungsmäßig [ɛr'fa:ruŋsmɛ:sɪç], *adj.* based on experience; empirical.

erfassen [ɛr'fasən], *v.a.* get hold of, seize, comprehend, grasp.

erfinden [ɛr'fɪndən], *v.a. irr.* invent, contrive.

erfinderisch [ɛr'fɪndərɪʃ], *adj.* inventive, ingenious.

Erfindung [ɛr'fɪnduŋ], *f.* (—, *pl.* —en) invention; contrivance.

Erfolg [ɛr'fɔlk], *m.* (—s, *pl.* —e) success; result; effect; — *haben*, succeed, be successful; *keinen — haben*, fail.

erfolgen [ɛr'fɔlgən], *v.n.* (*aux.* sein) ensue, follow, result.

erfolgreich [ɛr'fɔlkraɪç], *adj.* successful.

erforderlich [ɛr'fɔrdərlɪç], *adj.* necessary, required.

erfordern [ɛr'fɔrdərn], *v.a.* demand, require.

Erfordernis [ɛr'fɔrdərnɪs], *n.* (—ses, *pl.* —se) necessity, requirement, requisite.

erforschen [ɛr'fɔrʃən], *v.a.* explore, investigate, conduct research into.

erfragen [ɛr'fra:gən], *v.a.* find out by asking, ascertain.

erfreuen [ɛr'frɔyən], *v.a.* gladden, cheer, delight. — *v.r. sich — an*, enjoy, take pleasure in.

erfreulich [ɛr'frɔylɪç], *adj.* pleasing, gratifying.
erfrieren [ɛr'fri:rən], *v.n. irr. (aux.* sein) freeze to death, die of exposure; become numb.
erfrischen [ɛr'frɪʃən], *v.a.* refresh.
erfüllen [ɛr'fylən], *v.a.* fulfil, keep (promise); comply with; perform; *seinen Zweck* —, serve its purpose. — *v.r. sich* —, come true, be fulfilled.
Erfüllung [ɛr'fylʊŋ], *f.* (—, *no pl.*) fulfilment; granting; performance; *in* — *gehen,* come true, be realised.
ergänzen [ɛr'gɛntsən], *v.a.* complete, complement.
Ergänzung [ɛr'gɛntsʊŋ], *f.* (—, *pl.* —en) completion; complement, supplement.
ergattern [ɛr'gatərn], *v.a.* pick up.
ergeben [ɛr'ge:bən], *v.a. irr.* give, yield, prove, show. — *v.r. sich* —, surrender (to), acquiesce (in); happen, result, follow. — *adj.* devoted, submissive, humble, obedient.
Ergebenheit [ɛr'ge:bənhaɪt], *f.* (—, *no pl.*) devotion, obedience, humility, fidelity.
ergebenst [ɛr'ge:bənst], *adj. Ihr* —*er (letter ending),* yours very truly, your obedient servant. — *adv.* respectfully.
Ergebnis [ɛr'ge:pnɪs], *n.* (—**seś,** *pl.* —**se**) outcome, result; *(Agr.)* yield.
Ergebung [ɛr'ge:bʊŋ], *f.* (—, *no pl.*) submission, resignation; surrender.
Ergehen [ɛr'ge:ən], *n.* (—**s,** *no pl.*) health, condition, well-being.
ergehen [ɛr'ge:ən], *v.n. irr. (aux.* sein) be promulgated or issued; — *lassen,* issue, publish; *etwas über sich* — *lassen,* submit to or suffer s.th. patiently. — *v.r. sich* —, *(obs.)* take a stroll.
ergiebig [ɛr'gi:bɪç], *adj.* rich, productive, fertile, profitable.
ergießen [ɛr'gi:sən], *v.r. irr. sich* —, discharge, flow into.
erglänzen [ɛr'glɛntsən], *v.n. (aux.* sein) shine forth, sparkle.
erglühen [ɛr'gly:ən], *v.n. (aux.* sein) glow; blush.
ergötzen [ɛr'gœtsən], *v.a. (obs.)* amuse, delight. — *v.r. sich* — *an,* delight in.
ergrauen [ɛr'grauən], *v.n. (aux.* sein) become grey; grow old.
ergreifen [ɛr'graɪfən], *v.a. irr.* seize, grasp, get hold of; move, touch, affect; *Maßnahmen* —, take measures.
Ergreifung [ɛr'graɪfʊŋ], *f.* (—, *no pl.*) seizure; *(measure)* adoption.
ergriffen [ɛr'grɪfən], *adj.* moved, touched, impressed.
Ergriffenheit [ɛr'grɪfənhaɪt], *f.* (—, *no pl.*) emotion.
ergrimmen [ɛr'grɪmən], *v.n. (aux.* sein) grow angry, be enraged.
ergründen [ɛr'gryndən], *v.a.* get to the bottom of, investigate, fathom.
Erguß [ɛr'gus], *m.* (—**sses,** *pl.* ⸚**sse**) outpouring; *(fig.)* effusion.
erhaben [ɛr'ha:bən], *adj.* sublime, exalted; majestic, elevated.
Erhabenheit [ɛr'ha:bənhaɪt], *f.* (—, *no pl.*) majesty, sublimity.
erhalten [ɛr'haltən], *v.a. irr.* receive, obtain, get, preserve; maintain, keep up. — *v.r. sich* — *von,* subsist on.
erhältlich [ɛr'hɛltlɪç], *adj.* obtainable.
Erhaltung [ɛr'haltʊŋ], *f.* (—, *no pl.*) preservation, conservation; *(family)* maintenance.
erhärten [ɛr'hɛrtən], *v.a.* make hard; *(fig.)* prove, confirm.
erhaschen [ɛr'haʃən], *v.a.* catch, snatch.
erheben [ɛr'he:bən], *v.a. irr.* lift up, raise; *(fig.)* elevate, exalt; *Klage* —, bring an action; *Geld* —, raise money; *Steuern* —, levy taxes. — *v.r. sich* —, rise, stand up.
erheblich [ɛr'he:plɪç], *adj.* considerable, weighty, appreciable.
Erhebung [ɛr'he:bʊŋ], *f.* (—, *pl.* —en) elevation; *(taxes)* levying; revolt, rebellion, rising.
erheischen [ɛr'haɪʃən], *v.a. (rare)* require, demand.
erheitern [ɛr'haɪtərn], *v.a.* cheer, exhilarate.
erhellen [ɛr'hɛlən], *v.a.* light up, illuminate; *(fig.)* enlighten. — *v.n.* become evident.
erhitzen [ɛr'hɪtsən], *v.a.* heat; *(fig.)* inflame, excite. — *v.r. sich* —, grow hot; grow angry.
erhöhen [ɛr'hø:ən], *v.a.* heighten, raise, intensify, increase; *(value)* enhance.
erholen [ɛr'ho:lən], *v.r. sich* —, recover, get better; relax (after work); take a rest.
erholungsbedürftig [ɛr'ho:lʊŋsbədyrf-tɪç], *adj.* in need of a rest.
erhören [ɛr'hø:rən], *v.a.* hear, vouchsafe, grant.
Erich ['e:rɪç], *m.* Eric.
erinnerlich [ɛr'ɪnərlɪç], *adj.* remembered; *soweit mir* — *ist,* as far as I can remember.
erinnern [ɛr'ɪnərn], *v.a.* remind. — *v.r. sich* —, remember, recollect, recall, call to mind.
Erinnerung [ɛr'ɪnərʊŋ], *f.* (—, *pl.* —en) remembrance; recollection; reminiscences.
erjagen [ɛr'ja:gən], *v.a.* hunt (down), chase.
erkalten [ɛr'kaltən], *v.n. (aux.* sein) grow cold.
erkälten [ɛr'kɛltən], *v.r. sich* —, catch cold.
Erkältung [ɛr'kɛltʊŋ], *f.* (—, *pl.* —en) cold, chill.
erkämpfen [ɛr'kɛmpfən], *v.a.* obtain by fighting; obtain by great exertion.
erkaufen [ɛr'kaufən], *v.a.* purchase; bribe, corrupt.
erkennen [ɛr'kɛnən], *v.a. irr.* recognise; perceive, distinguish, discern; *(Comm.)* credit; *zu* — *geben,* give to understand; *sich zu* — *geben,* make o.s. known. — *v.n. (Law)* judge; — *auf,* *(Law)* announce verdict, pass sentence.

erkenntlich [ɛrˈkɛntlɪç], *adj.* grateful; (*fig.*) *sich — zeigen*, show o.s. grateful.
Erkenntlichkeit [ɛrˈkɛntlɪçkaɪt], *f.* (—, *no pl.*) gratitude.
Erkenntnis [ɛrˈkɛntnɪs], *f.* (—, *pl.* —e) perception, knowledge, comprehension, understanding; realisation, (*Phil.*) cognition.
Erkennung [ɛrˈkɛnuŋ], *f.* (—, *no pl.*) recognition.
Erker [ˈɛrkər], *m.* (—s, *pl.* —) alcove, bay, turret.
Erkerfenster [ˈɛrkərfɛnstər], *n.* (—s, *pl.* —) bay-window.
erklären [ɛrˈklɛːrən], *v.a.* explain, expound, account for; make a statement on, declare, state.
erklärlich [ɛrˈklɛːrlɪç], *adj.* explicable.
Erklärung [ɛrˈklɛːruŋ], *f.* (—, *pl.* —en) explanation; declaration, statement; (*income tax*) return.
erklecklich [ɛrˈklɛklɪç], *adj.* considerable.
erklettern [ɛrˈklɛtərn], *v.a.* climb.
erklimmen [ɛrˈklɪmən], *v.a. irr.* climb.
erklingen [ɛrˈklɪŋən], *v.n. irr.* (*aux.* sein) sound, resound.
erkoren [ɛrˈkoːrən], *adj.* select, chosen.
erkranken [ɛrˈkraŋkən], *v.n.* (*aux.* sein) fall ill.
erkühnen [ɛrˈkyːnən], *v.r. sich —*, dare, make bold, venture.
erkunden [ɛrˈkundən], *v.a.* explore, find out; (*Mil.*) reconnoitre.
erkundigen [ɛrˈkundɪgən], *v.r. sich —*, enquire (about), make enquiries.
erlaben [ɛrˈlaːbən], *v.r. sich —*, (*obs.*) refresh o.s.
erlahmen [ɛrˈlaːmən], *v.n.* (*aux.* sein) become lame; lose o.'s drive; grow tired.
erlangen [ɛrˈlaŋən], *v.a.* reach, gain, obtain; acquire; attain.
Erlaß [ɛrˈlas], *m.* (—sses, *pl.* ˉsse) remission, exemption, release, dispensation; (*Comm.*) deduction; (*Law, Pol.*) proclamation, edict, decree, writ; (*Eccl.*) indulgence; remission.
erlassen [ɛrˈlasən], *v.a. irr.* remit, release, let off; (*Law, Pol.*) enact, promulgate.
erläßlich [ɛrˈlɛslɪç], *adj.* remissible, dispensable, venial.
erlauben [ɛrˈlaubən], *v.a.* permit, allow; *sich etwas —*, take the liberty of, make bold to; have the impertinence to.
Erlaubnis [ɛrˈlaupnɪs], *f.* (—, *no pl.*) permission, leave, permit; *die — haben*, be permitted; *um — bitten*, beg leave; *mit Ihrer —*, by your leave.
erlaucht [ɛrˈlauxt], *adj.* illustrious, noble.
erlauschen [ɛrˈlauʃən], *v.a.* overhear.
erläutern [ɛrˈlɔytərn], *v.a.* explain, illustrate, elucidate.
Erle [ˈɛrlə], *f.* (—, *pl.* —n) (*Bot.*) alder.
erleben [ɛrˈleːbən], *v.a.* live to see; go through, experience.
Erlebnis [ɛrˈleːpnɪs], *n.* (—sses, *pl.* —sse) experience, adventure, occurrence.

erledigen [ɛrˈleːdɪgən], *v.a.* settle, finish off, clear up; dispatch; execute (commission etc.).
erledigt [ɛrˈleːdɪçt], *adj.* (*coll.*) worn-out; exhausted.
erlegen [ɛrˈleːgən], *v.a.* slay; pay down.
erleichtern [ɛrˈlaɪçtərn], *v.a.* lighten, ease, facilitate.
erleiden [ɛrˈlaɪdən], *v.a. irr.* suffer, endure, bear, undergo.
erlernen [ɛrˈlɛrnən], *v.a.* learn, acquire.
erlesen [ɛrˈleːzən], *v.a. irr.* select, choose. — *adj.* select, choice.
erleuchten [ɛrˈlɔyçtən], *v.a.* illumine, illuminate, floodlight; (*fig.*) enlighten, inspire.
erliegen [ɛrˈliːgən], *v.n. irr.* (*aux.* sein) succumb.
Erlkönig [ˈɛrlkøːnɪç], *m.* (—s, *pl.* —e) fairy-king, elf-king.
erlogen [ɛrˈloːgən], *adj.* false, untrue; trumped-up.
Erlös [ɛrˈløːs], *m.* (—es, *no pl.*) proceeds.
erlöschen [ɛrˈlœʃən], *v.n. irr.* (*aux.* sein) be extinguished, die out; (*fire*) go out; (*contract*) expire.
erlösen [ɛrˈløːzən], *v.a.* redeem; release, save, deliver.
ermächtigen [ɛrˈmɛçtɪgən], *v.a.* empower; authorise.
ermahnen [ɛrˈmaːnən], *v.a.* admonish, exhort, remind.
ermäßigen [ɛrˈmɛːsɪgən], *v.a.* reduce.
ermatten [ɛrˈmatən], *v.a.* weaken, weary, tire. — *v.n.* (*aux.* sein) grow weak, become tired.
Ermessen [ɛrˈmɛsən], *n.* (—s, *no pl.*) judgment, opinion.
ermitteln [ɛrˈmɪtəln], *v.a.* ascertain, find out.
ermöglichen [ɛrˈmøːklɪçən], *v.a.* make possible.
ermorden [ɛrˈmɔrdən], *v.a.* murder.
ermüden [ɛrˈmyːdən], *v.a.* tire, fatigue. — *v.n.* (*aux.* sein) get tired, grow weary.
ermuntern [ɛrˈmuntərn], *v.a.* encourage, cheer up.
ermutigen [ɛrˈmuːtɪgən], *v.a.* encourage.
ernähren [ɛrˈnɛːrən], *v.a.* nourish, feed.
ernennen [ɛrˈnɛnən], *v.a. irr.* nominate, appoint.
erneuern [ɛrˈnɔyərn], *v.a.* renew, repair, renovate.
erniedrigen [ɛrˈniːdrɪgən], *v.a.* humble, humiliate, degrade. — *v.r. sich —*, humble o.s., abase o.s.
Ernst (1) [ɛrnst], *m.* Ernest.
Ernst (2) [ɛrnst], *m.* (—es, *no pl.*) earnestness, seriousness.
ernst [ɛrnst], *adj.* earnest, serious.
Ernte [ˈɛrntə], *f.* (—, *pl.* —n) harvest, crop.
ernüchtern [ɛrˈnyçtərn], *v.a.* sober; (*fig.*) disenchant, disillusion.
erobern [ɛrˈoːbərn], *v.a.* (*Mil.*) conquer; take, win.
eröffnen [ɛrˈœfnən], *v.a.* open, inaugurate; inform, reveal.
erörtern [ɛrˈœrtərn], *v.a.* discuss, debate, argue.

erpicht [ɛr'pɪçt], *adj.* eager for, bent on.
erpressen [ɛr'prɛsən], *v.a.* extort, blackmail.
erquicken [ɛr'kvɪkən], *v.a.* refresh.
erraten [ɛr'ɪa:tən], *v.a.* irr. guess.
erregen [ɛr're:gən], *v.a.* cause; stir up, excite, agitate; provoke.
erreichen [ɛr'raɪçən], *v.a.* reach, arrive at; (*fig.*) attain, reach.
erretten [ɛr'rɛtən], *v.a.* save, rescue.
errichten [ɛr'rɪçtən], *v.a.* erect, raise, build.
erringen [ɛr'rɪŋən], *v.a.* irr. obtain (by exertion), achieve.
erröten [ɛr'rø:tən], *v.n.* (*aux.* sein) blush, redden.
Errungenschaft [ɛr'rʊŋənʃaft], *f.* (—, *pl.* —en) achievement, acquisition.
Ersatz [ɛr'zats], *m.* (—es, *no pl.*) substitute; compensation, amends: (*Mil. etc.*) replacement.
erschallen [ɛr'ʃalən], *v.n.* (*aux.* sein) resound, sound.
erschaudern [ɛr'ʃaudərn], *v.n.* (*aux.* sein) be seized with horror.
erscheinen [ɛr'ʃaɪnən], *v.n.* irr. (*aux.* sein) appear, make o.'s appearance; seem; be published.
erschießen [ɛr'ʃi:sən], *v.a.* irr. shoot dead.
erschlaffen [ɛr'ʃlafən], *v.n.* (*aux.* sein) flag, slacken.
erschlagen [ɛr'ʃla:gən], *v.a.* irr. slay, kill.
erschließen [ɛr'ʃli:sən], *v.a.irr.* open up.
erschöpfen [ɛr'ʃœpfən], *v.a.* exhaust.
erschrecken [ɛr'ʃrɛkən], *v.a.* irr. startle, shock, terrify. — *v.n.* (*aux.* sein) be startled, be frightened, be terrified.
erschüttern [ɛr'ʃytərn], *v.a.* shake; (*fig.*) move, affect strongly.
erschweren [ɛr'ʃve:rən], *v.a.* (*fig.*) aggravate, make more difficult.
erschwingen [ɛr'ʃvɪŋən], *v.a.irr.* afford, be able to pay.
erschwinglich [ɛr'ʃvɪŋlɪç], *adj.* attainable, within o.'s means.
ersehen [ɛr'ze:ən], *v.a.* irr. —*aus*, gather (from).
ersehnen [ɛr'ze:nən], *v.a.* long for, yearn for.
ersetzen [ɛr'zɛtsən], *v.a.* replace, take the place of; restore, make good; repair; (*money*) refund.
ersichtlich [ɛr'zɪçtlɪç], *adj.* evident.
ersinnen [ɛr'zɪnən], *v.a.* irr. think out; imagine, devise, contrive.
ersparen [ɛr'ʃpa:rən], *v.a.* save.
ersprießlich [ɛr'ʃpri:slɪç], *adj.* useful, profitable, beneficial.
erst [e:rst], *num. adj.* first. — *adv.* first, at first, only, but; — *jetzt*, only now; *nun* — *recht*, now more than ever.
erstatten [ɛr'ʃtatən], *v.a.* reimburse, compensate, repay; *Bericht* —, report.
Erstattung [ɛr'ʃtatʊŋ], *f.* (—, *pl.* —en) reimbursement, restitution.
Erstaufführung ['e:rstauffy:rʊŋ], *f.* (—, *pl.* —en) (*Theat.*) first night; première.

Erstaunen [ɛr'ʃtaunən], *n.* (—s, *no pl.*) amazement, astonishment, surprise.
erstechen [ɛr'ʃtɛçən], *v.a.* irr. stab.
erstehen [ɛr'ʃte:ən], *v.n.* irr. (*aux.* sein) rise, arise. — *v.a.* buy, purchase.
ersteigen [ɛr'ʃtaɪgən], *v.a.* irr. climb, mount, ascend.
ersticken [ɛr'ʃtɪkən], *v.a.* irr. choke, stifle, suffocate. — *v.n.* (*aux.* sein) choke, suffocate.
erstmalig ['e:rstma:lɪç], *adj.* first. — *adv.* for the first time.
erstreben [ɛr'ʃtre:bən], *v.a.* strive after.
erstrecken [ɛr'ʃtrɛkən], *v.r. sich* —, extend, reach to.
ersuchen [ɛr'zu:xən], *v.a.* request, ask.
ertappen [ɛr'tapən], *v.a.* catch, detect.
erteilen [ɛr'taɪlən], *v.a.* bestow, impart; *einen Auftrag* —, issue an order; *Unterricht* —, instruct; *die Erlaubnis* —, give permission.
ertönen [ɛr'tø:nən], *v.n.* (*aux.* sein) sound, resound.
Ertrag [ɛr'tra:k], *m.* (—s, *pl.* ⁻e) produce; returns, yield; output; (*sale*) proceeds.
ertragen [ɛr'tra:gən], *v.a.* irr. bear, suffer, endure.
ertränken [ɛr'trɛnkən], *v.a.* drown.
ertrinken [ɛr'trɪŋkən], *v.n.* irr. (*aux.* sein) drown, be drowned.
erübrigen [ɛr'y:brɪgən], *v.a.* save, spare.
erwachen [ɛr'vaxən], *v.n.* (*aux.* sein) awake, wake up.
erwachsen [ɛr'vaksən], *adj.* grown-up, adult. — *v.n.* irr. grow up; ensue, follow, arise.
erwägen [ɛr'vɛ:gən], *v.a.* irr. weigh, ponder, consider.
erwähnen [ɛr'vɛ:nən], *v.a.* mention.
erwärmen [ɛr'vɛrmən], *v.a.* warm (up), make warm.
erwarten [ɛr'vartən], *v.a.* expect, await.
Erwartung [ɛr'vartʊŋ], *f.* (—, *pl.* —en) expectation.
erwecken [ɛr'vɛkən], *v.a.* wake up, awaken, raise; rouse.
erwehren [ɛr've:rən], *v.r. sich* — (*Genit.*), defend o.s.; *ich kann mich des Lachens nicht* —, I cannot help laughing.
erweichen [ɛr'vaɪçən], *v.a.* soften.
erweisen [ɛr'vaɪzən], *v.a.* irr. prove, show; demonstrate.
erweitern [ɛr'vaɪtərn], *v.a.* widen, enlarge, expand.
erwerben [ɛr'vɛrbən], *v.a.* irr. acquire.
erwidern [ɛr'vi:dərn], *v.a.* reply, answer; return.
erwirken [ɛr'vɪrkən], *v.a.* effect, secure.
erwischen [ɛr'vɪʃən], *v.a.* see **ertappen**.
erwünschen [ɛr'vynʃən], *v.a.* desire, wish for.
erwürgen [ɛr'vyrgən], *v.a.* strangle, throttle.
Erz [ɛrts], (—es, *pl.* —e) ore; brass, bronze.

erzählen [ɛr'tsɛ:lən], *v.a.* narrate, relate, tell.
Erzbischof ['ɛrtsbɪʃɔf], *m.* (—s, *pl.* ⁻e) archbishop.
erzeugen [ɛr'tsɔygən], *v.a.* engender; beget; produce; (*Elec.*) generate.
Erzherzog ['ɛrtshɛrtso:k], *m.* (—s, *pl.* ⁻e) archduke.
erziehen [ɛr'tsi:ən], *v.a. irr.* educate, train, bring up, rear.
Erziehungsanstalt [ɛr'tsi:uŋsanʃtalt], *f.* (—, *pl.* —en) approved school, reformatory.
erzielen [ɛr'tsi:lən], *v.a.* obtain; fetch, realize (a price); *Gewinn* —, make a profit.
erzittern [ɛr'tsɪtərn], *v.n.* (*aux.* sein) tremble, shake.
Erzofen ['ɛrtso:fən], *m.* (—s, *pl.* ⁻n) furnace.
erzürnen [ɛr'tsyrnən], *v.a.* make angry. — *v.r. sich* —, grow angry.
Erzvater ['ɛrtsfa:tər], *m.* (—s, *pl.* ⁻) patriarch.
erzwingen [ɛr'tsvɪŋən], *v.a. irr.* enforce, force, compel.
es [ɛs], *pron.* it; — *gibt*, there is; — *sind*, there are; — *lebe*, long live!
Es [ɛs], *n.* (—, *pl.* —) (*Mus.*) E flat.
Esche ['ɛʃə], *f.* (—, *pl.* —n) (*Bot.*) ash, ashtree.
Esel ['e:zəl], *m.* (—s, *pl.* —) ass, donkey.
Eselsohr ['e:zəlso:r], *n.* (—s, *pl.* —en) (*fig.*) dog's ear.
Eskadron [ɛska'dro:n], *f.* (—, *pl.* —en) squadron.
Espe ['ɛspə], *f.* (—, *pl.* —n) (*Bot.*) asp, aspen.
eßbar ['ɛsba:r], *adj.* edible.
Esse ['ɛsə], *f.* (—, *pl.* —n) chimney, forge.
Essen ['ɛsən], *n.* (—s, *no pl.*) meal; eating.
essen ['ɛsən], *v.a. irr.* eat, have a meal.
Essenz [ɛ'sɛnts], *f.* (—, *pl.* —en) essence.
Essig ['ɛsɪç], *m.* (—s, *no pl.*) vinegar.
Eßlöffel ['ɛslœfəl], *m.* (—s, *pl.* —) table-spoon.
Estland ['ɛstlant], *n.* Estonia.
Estrade [ɛ'stra:də], *f.* (—, *pl.* —n) platform.
Estrich ['ɛstrɪç], *m.* (—s, *no pl.*) floor, flooring, plaster-floor.
etablieren [eta'bli:rən], *v.a.* establish, set up (business).
Etagenwohnung [e'ta:ʒənvo:nuŋ], *f.* (—, *pl.* —en) flat; (*Am.*) apartment.
Etappe [e'tapə], *f.* (—, *pl.* —n) stage; (*Mil.*) lines of communication.
Etat [e'ta:], *m.* (—s, *pl.* —s) (*Parl.*) estimates, budget; (*Comm.*) statement, balance sheet.
ethisch ['e:tɪʃ], *adj.* ethical.
Etikett [eti'kɛt], *n.* (—s, *pl.* —s) label, ticket, tag.
Etikette [eti'kɛtə], *f.* (—, *no pl.*) etiquette; ceremonial.
etikettieren [etikɛ'ti:rən], *v.a.* label.

etliche ['ɛtlɪçə], *pl. adj. & pron.* some, several, sundry.
Etui [e'tvi:], *n.* (—s, *pl.* —s) small case, small box.
etwa ['ɛtva], *adv.* nearly, about; perhaps, perchance, in some way.
etwaig ['ɛtvaɪç], *adj.* possible, any, eventual.
etwas ['ɛtvas], *indef. pron.* some, something. — *adj.* some, any. — *adv.* a little, somewhat.
Etzel ['ɛtsəl], *m.* Attila.
euch [ɔyç], *pers. pron. pl. Dat. & Acc.* you, yourselves.
euer ['ɔyər], *poss. adj.* your. — *poss. pron.* yours.
Eule ['ɔylə], *f.* (—, *pl.* —n) owl.
eurige ['ɔyrɪgə], *poss. pron. der, die, das* —, yours.
Europa [ɔy'ro:pa], *n.* Europe.
Euter ['ɔytər], *n.* (—s, *pl.* —) udder.
evangelisch [evan'ge:lɪʃ], *adj.* Evangelical, Protestant.
Evangelium [evan'ge:ljum], *n.* (—s, *pl.* —lien) gospel.
eventuell [evɛntu'ɛl], *adj.* possible.
ewig ['e:vɪç], *adj.* eternal; perpetual.
Ewigkeit ['e:vɪçkaɪt], *f.* (—, *pl.* —en) eternity.
explodieren [ɛksplo'di:rən], *v.n.* explode; detonate.
exponieren [ɛkspo'ni:rən], *v.a.* set forth, explain at length.
Extemporale [ɛkstɛmpo'ra:lə], *n.* (—s, *pl.* —lien) unprepared exercise.
extrahieren [ɛkstra'hi:rən], *v.a.* extract.
Extremitäten [ɛkstremɪ'tɛ:tən], *f. pl.* extremities.

F

F [ɛf], *n.* (—s, *pl.* —s) the letter F; (*Mus.*) *F Dur*, F major; *F Moll*, F minor.
Fabel ['fa:bəl], *f.* (—, *pl.* —n) fable; (*fig.*) tale, fiction; (*drama*) plot, story.
fabelhaft ['fa:bəlhaft], *adj.* fabulous; phenomenal, gorgeous.
fabeln ['fa:bəln], *v.n.* tell fables; talk nonsense.
Fabrik [fa'bri:k], *f.* (—, *pl.* —en) factory; plant, works.
Fabrikant [fabrɪ'kant], *m.* (—en, *pl.* —en) manufacturer.
fabrizieren [fabrɪ'tsi:rən], *v.a.* manufacture, make.
fabulieren [fabu'li:rən], *v.n.* tell fables; (*fig.*) tell tall stories.
Fach [fax], *n.* (—s, *pl.* ⁻er) compartment; pigeon-hole, drawer; (*fig.*) subject of study, department, branch.
Fachausdruck ['faxausdruk], *m.* (—s, *pl.* ⁻e) technical term.

Fächer

Fächer ['fɛçər], *m.* (—s, *pl.* —) fan.
Fächertaube ['fɛçərtaubə], *f.* (—, *pl.* —n) fantail.
Fachmann ['faxman], *m.* (—s, *pl.* ˙er *or* Fachleute) expert, specialist.
Fachschule ['faxʃuːlə], *f.* (—, *pl.* —n) technical school.
fachsimpeln ['faxzɪmpəln], *v.n.* talk shop.
Fachwerk ['faxvɛrk], *n.* (—s, *no pl.*) timbered framework.
Fackel ['fakəl], *f.* (—, *pl.* —n) torch.
fade ['faːdə], *adj.* tasteless; boring, insipid.
Faden ['faːdən], *m.* (—s, *pl.* ˙) thread; (*measure*) fathom.
fadenscheinig ['faːdənʃainɪç], *adj.* threadbare.
Fagott [fa'gɔt], *n.* (—s, *pl.* —'e) (*Mus.*) bassoon.
fähig ['fɛːɪç], *adj.* able, capable; talented, gifted, competent.
fahl [faːl], *adj.* pale, sallow.
Fähnchen ['fɛːnçən], *n.* (—s, *pl.* —) small banner; pennon; (*Mil.*) (*obs.*) small troop.
fahnden ['faːndən], *v.a.* search for (officially).
Fahne ['faːnə], *f.* (—, *pl.* —n) flag, banner, standard, colours; (*weather*) vane; (*Typ.*) galley proof.
Fahnenflucht ['faːnənfluxt], *f.* (—, *no pl.*) (*Mil.*) desertion.
Fähnrich ['fɛːnrɪç], *m.* (—s, *pl.* —e) ensign.
Fahrbahn ['faːrbaːn], *f.* (—, *pl.* —en) traffic lane, roadway.
fahrbar ['faːrbaːr], *adj.* passable, navigable, negotiable.
Fähre ['fɛːrə], *f.* (—, *pl.* —n) ferry, ferry-boat.
fahren. ['faːrən], *v.a. irr.* drive. — *v.n.* (*aux.* sein) (*vehicle*) ride (in), be driven; (*vessel*) sail; go, travel.
Fahrer ['faːrər], *m.* (—s, *pl.* —) driver, chauffeur.
Fahrgast ['faːrgast], *m.* (—s, *pl.* ˙e) passenger.
fahrig ['faːrɪç], *adj.* absent-minded, giddy, thoughtless.
Fahrkarte ['faːrkartə], *f.* (—, *pl.* —n) ticket.
fahrlässig ['faːrlɛsɪç], *adj.* negligent, careless.
Fährmann ['fɛːrman], *m.* (—s, *pl.* ˙er) ferry-man.
Fahrplan ['faːrplaːn], *m.* (—s, *pl.* ˙e) timetable, railway-guide.
fahrplanmäßig ['faːrplanmɛːsɪç], *adj.* according to the timetable, scheduled.
Fahrpreis ['faːrprais], *m.* (—es, *pl.* —e) cost of ticket, fare.
Fahrrad ['faːrraːt], *n.* (—s, *pl.* ˙er) cycle, bicycle.
Fahrschein ['faːrʃain], *m.* (—s, *pl.* —e) ticket.
Fahrstraße ['faːrʃtrasə], *f.* (—, *pl.* —n) roadway.
Fahrstuhl ['faːrʃtuːl], *m.* (—s, *pl.* ˙e) lift; (*Am.*) elevator.

Fahrt [faːrt], *f.* (—, *pl.* —en) drive, ride, journey; (*sea*) voyage, cruise.
Fährte ['fɛːrtə], *f.* (—, *pl.* —n) track, trace, trail.
Fahrzeug ['faːrtsɔyk], *n.* (—s, *pl.* —e) vehicle, conveyance; vessel, craft.
faktisch ['faktɪʃ], *adj.* real, actual.
Faktor ['faktɔr], *m.* (—s, *pl.* —en) foreman, overseer, factor; (*Maths.*) factor, component part.
Faktura [fak'tuːra], *f.* (—, *pl.* —ren) (*Comm.*) invoice.
fakturieren [faktuˈriːrən], *v.a.* (*Comm.*) invoice.
Fakultät [fakulˈtɛːt], *f.* (—, *pl.* —en) (*Univ.*) faculty.
fakultativ [fakultaˈtiːf], *adj.* optional.
Falbel ['falbəl], *f.* (—, *pl.* —n) flounce, furbelow.
Falke ['falkə], *m.* (—n, *pl.* —n) (*Orn.*) falcon, hawk.
Fall [fal], *m.* (—s, *pl.* ˙e) fall, falling; case; (*Geog.*) decline, incline, gradient; (*fig.*) fall, decline, downfall, failure.
Fallbaum ['falbaum], *m.* (—s, *pl.* ˙e) tollbar, turnpike.
Fallbeil ['falbail], *n.* (—s, *pl.* —e) guillotine.
Fallbrücke ['falbrykə], *f.* (—, *pl.* —n) draw-bridge.
Falle ['falə], *f.* (—, *pl.* —n) trap, snare.
fallen ['falən], *v.n. irr.* (*aux.* sein) fall, drop; (*Mil.*) be killed.
fällen ['fɛlən], *v.a.* fell, cut down, hew down; *ein Urteil —,* (*Law*) pronounce judgment.
Fallensteller ['falənʃtɛlər], *m.* (—s, *pl.* —) trapper.
fallieren [fa'liːrən], *v.n.* become bankrupt.
fällig ['fɛlɪç], *adj.* due, payable.
Fälligkeit ['fɛlɪçkait], *f.* (—, *pl.* —en) (*Comm.*) maturity.
Fallobst ['falopst], *n.* (—es, *no pl.*) windfall (of fruit).
falls [fals], *conj.* in case, if.
Fallschirm ['falʃɪrm], *m.* (—s, *pl.* —e) parachute.
Fallstrick ['falʃtrɪk], *m.* (—s, *pl.* —e) snare, trap.
Fallsucht ['falzuxt], *f.* (—, *no pl.*) (*Med.*) epilepsy.
Falltür ['faltyːr], *f.* (—, *pl.* —en) trap-door.
Fällung ['fɛluŋ], *f.* (—, *pl.* —en) cutting down.
falsch [falʃ], *adj.* false, incorrect, wrong; disloyal; counterfeit.
fälschen ['fɛlʃən], *v.a.* falsify, forge, tamper with.
Falschheit ['falʃhait], *f.* (—, *pl.* —en) falsehood, deceit, disloyalty.
fälschlich ['fɛlʃlɪç], *adv.* wrongly, falsely.
Fälschung ['fɛlʃuŋ], *f.* (—, *pl.* —en) falsification; forgery.
Falte ['faltə], *f.* (—, *pl.* —n) fold, pleat; (*face*) wrinkle.
falten ['faltən], *v.a.* fold, plait, pleat; wrinkle.

Falter ['faltər], *m.* (—s, *pl.* —) (*Ent.*) butterfly.

-fältig [fɛltɪç], *suffix* (*following numbers*). –fold (*e.g.* vierfältig, fourfold).

Falz [falts], *m.* (—es, *pl.* —e) groove, notch; joint.

Falzbein ['faltsbaɪn], *n.* (—s, *pl.* —e) paper-folder, paper-knife.

Falzmaschine ['faltsmaʃi:nə], *f.* (—, *pl.* —n) folding-machine.

familiär [famil'jɛ:r], *adj.* familiar, intimate.

Familie [fa'mi:ljə], *f.* (—, *pl.* —n) family.

famos [fa'mo:s], *adj.* (*coll.*) excellent, splendid.

fanatisch [fa'na:tɪʃ], *adj.* fanatic(al), bigoted.

Fanatismus [fana'tɪsmus], *m.* (—, *no pl.*) fanaticism.

Fang [faŋ], *m.* (—es, *pl.* ˙̈e) catch, capture; (*bird*) talon, claw.

fangen ['faŋən], *v.a. irr.* catch, seize.

Fangzahn ['faŋtsa:n], *m.* (—s, *pl.* ˙̈e) fang, tusk.

Fant [fant], *m.* (—s, *pl.* —e) fop, cockscomb.

Farbe ['farbə], *f.* (—, *pl.* —n) colour, hue, paint, dye.

färben ['fɛrbən], *v.a.* dye, stain.

Farbenbrett ['farbənbrɛt], *n.* (—s, *pl.* —er) palette.

Farb(en)druck ['farpdruk, farbəndruk], *m.* (—s, *pl.* —e) colour-printing.

Farbenspiel ['farbənʃpi:l], *n.* (—s, *no pl.*) iridescence.

Färber ['fɛrbər], *m.* (—s, *pl.* —) dyer.

farbig ['farbɪç], *adj.* coloured.

Farbstift ['farpʃtɪft], *m.* (—s, *pl.* —e) crayon.

Farbstoff ['farpʃtɔf], *m.* (—es, *pl.* —e) dye.

Farbton ['farpto:n], *m.* (—s, *pl.* ˙̈e) hue, tone, tinge, shade.

Farn [farn], *m.* (—s, *pl.* —e) (*Bot.*) fern.

Färse ['fɛrzə], *f.* (—, *pl.* —n) (*Zool.*) heifer.

Fasan [fa'za:n], *m.* (—s, *pl.* —e) (*Orn.*) pheasant.

Fasching ['faʃɪŋ], *m.* (—s, *no pl.*) (Shrovetide) carnival.

Faschismus [fa'ʃɪsmus], *m.* (—s, *no pl.*) fascism.

Faselei [fa:zə'laɪ], *f.* (—, *pl.* —en) silly talk, drivel.

faseln ['fa:zəln], *v.n.* drivel.

Faser ['fa:zər], *f.* (—, *pl.* —n) thread; string; fibre, filament.

fasern ['fa:zərn], *v.n.* fray.

Faß [fas], *n.* (—sses, *pl.* ˙̈sser) barrel, vat, tun, tub, cask, keg; *Bier vom* —, draught beer; *Wein vom* —, wine from the wood.

Fassade [fa'sa:də], *f.* (—, *pl.* —n) façade.

faßbar ['fasba:r], *adj.* tangible.

Faßbinder ['fasbɪndər], *m.* (—s, *pl.* —) cooper.

fassen ['fasən], *v.a.* seize, take hold of, grasp; (*jewels*) set; contain, hold. — *v.r.* (*aux.* haben) *sich* —, compose o.s.; *sich kurz* —, be brief.

faßlich ['faslɪç], *adj.* comprehensible, understandable.

Fasson [fa'sõ], *f.* (—, *pl.* —s) fashion; (*fig.*) cut, style.

Fassung ['fasuŋ], *f.* (—, *pl.* —en) (*jewels*) setting; (*speech*) wording, version; (*fig.*) composure.

fassungslos ['fasuŋslo:s], *adj.* bewildered, disconcerted; distraught, speechless.

fast [fast], *adv.* almost, nearly.

-fasten ['fastən], *v.n.* fast.

Fastenzeit ['fastəntsaɪt], *f.* (—, *pl.* —en) time of fasting; Lent.

Fastnacht ['fastnaxt], *f.* (—, *no pl.*) Shrove Tuesday; Shrovetide.

fauchen ['fauxən], *v.n.* spit, hiss.

faul [faul], *adj.* (*food*) rotten, putrid, decayed; (*persons*) lazy, idle.

Fäule ['fɔylə], *f.* (—, *no pl.*) rot.

faulen ['faulən], *v.n.* (*aux.* sein) rot.

faulenzen ['faulɛntsən], *v.n.* laze, idle.

Faulenzer ['faulɛntsər], *m.* (—s, *pl.* —) idler, sluggard, lazybones.

Faulenzerei ['faulɛntsəraɪ], *f.* (—, *pl.* —en) idleness, laziness.

Faulheit ['faulhaɪt], *f.* (—, *no pl.*) idleness, laziness, sluggishness.

faulig ['faulɪç], *adj.* putrid, rotten.

Fäulnis ['fɔylnɪs], *f.* (—, *no pl.*) rottenness, putridity.

Faust [faust], *f.* (—, *pl.* ˙̈e) fist.

Fäustchen ['fɔystçən], *n.* (—s, *pl.* —) small fist; *sich ins* — *lachen*, laugh in o.'s sleeve.

Faustkampf ['faustkampf], *m.* (—es, *pl.* ˙̈e) boxing (match).

Faxen ['faksən], *f. pl.* foolery; — *machen*, play the buffoon.

Fazit ['fatsɪt], *n.* (—s, *no pl.*) sum, amount.

Februar ['fe:brua:r], *m.* (—s, *no pl.*) February.

fechten ['fɛçtən], *v.n. irr.* fight; fence; (*fig.*) beg.

Feder ['fe:dər], *f.* (—, *pl.* —n) (*bird*) feather; (*hat*) plume; (*writing*) pen; (*antique*) quill; (*Tech.*) spring.

Federball ['fe:dərbal], *m.* (—s, *pl.* ˙̈e) shuttle-cock.

federig ['fe:dərɪç], *adj.* feathery; (*Tech.*) springy, resilient.

Federlesen(s) ['fe:dərle:zən(s)], *n.* (—s, *no pl.*) *nicht viel* — *machen*, make short work of.

Fee [fe:], *f.* (—, *pl.* —n) fairy.

feenhaft ['fe:ənhaft], *adj.* fairy-like, magical.

Fegefeuer ['fe:gəfɔyər], *n.* (—s, *no pl.*) purgatory.

fegen ['fe:gən], *v.a.* clean, sweep. — *v.n.* (*aux.* sein) tear along.

Fehde ['fe:də], *f.* (—, *pl.* —n) feud, quarrel.

Fehdehandschuh ['fe:dəhantʃu:], *m.* (—s, *pl.* —e) gauntlet.

69

fehlbar ['fe:lba:r], *adj.* fallible.
Fehlbetrag ['fe:lbətra:k], *m.* (—s, *pl.* ¨e) deficit.
fehlen ['fe:lən], *v.a.* miss. — *v.n.* err, do wrong; be absent; be wanting; *er fehlt mir,* I miss him.
Fehler ['fe:lər], *m.* (—s, *pl.* —) fault, defect; mistake, error.
Fehlgeburt ['fe:lgəburt], *f.* (—, *pl.* —en) miscarriage.
Fehlschlag ['fe:lʃla:k], *m.* (—s, *pl.* ¨e) failure, disappointment.
feien ['faɪən], *v.a. einen* — *gegen,* charm s.o. against; *gefeit,* proof.
Feier ['faɪər], *f.* (—, *pl.* —n) celebration, festival, holiday, festive day.
Feierabend ['faɪəra:bənt], *m.* (—s, *pl.* —e) time for leaving off work; — *machen,* knock off (work).
feierlich ['faɪərlɪç], *adj.* festive, solemn, stately.
feiern ['faɪərn], *v.a.* celebrate; honour, praise. — *v.n.* rest from work.
Feiertag ['faɪərta:k], *m.* (—s, *pl.* —e) holiday, festive day.
feig [faɪk], *adj.* cowardly.
Feige ['faɪgə], *f.* (—, *pl.* —n) (*Bot.*) fig.
Feigheit ['faɪkhaɪt], *f.* (—, *pl.* —en) cowardice, cowardliness.
Feigling ['faɪklɪŋ], *m.* (—s, *pl.* —e) coward.
Feigwurz ['faɪkvurts], *m.* (—es, *no pl.*) (*Bot.*) fennel.
feil [faɪl], *adj.* (*obs.*) for sale; venal.
feilbieten ['faɪlbi:tən], *v.a.* offer for sale.
Feile ['faɪlə], *f.* (—, *pl.* —n) file.
feilen ['faɪlən], *v.a.* file.
feilhalten ['faɪlhaltən], *v.a.* have for sale, be ready to sell.
feilschen ['faɪlʃən], *v.n.* bargain, haggle.
Feilspäne ['faɪlʃpɛ:nə], *m. pl.* filings.
fein [faɪn], *adj.* fine; neat, pretty, nice; delicate; (*clothes*) elegant; (*behaviour*) refined, polished.
Feinbäckerei ['faɪnbɛkəraɪ], *f.* (—, *pl.* —en) confectioner's shop.
Feind [faɪnt], *m.* (—es, *pl.* —e) enemy, foe, adversary.
Feindschaft ['faɪntʃaft], *f.* (—, *pl.* —en) enmity, hostility.
feindselig ['faɪntze:lɪç], *adj.* hostile, malignant.
feinfühlend ['faɪnfy:lənt], *adj.* delicate, sensitive.
Feinheit ['faɪnhaɪt], *f.* (—, *pl.* —en) fineness, elegance, politeness, delicacy.
Feinschmecker ['faɪnʃmɛkər], *m.* (—s, *pl.* —), gourmet.
Feinsliebchen ['faɪns'li:pçən], *n.* (—s, *pl.* —) (*Poet. obs.*) sweetheart.
feist [faɪst], *adj.* fat, obese.
Feld [fɛlt], *n.* (—es, *pl.* —er) field, plain; (*chess*) square; (*fig.*) sphere, province.
Feldbett ['fɛltbɛt], *n.* (—s, *pl.* —en) camp-bed.
Feldherr ['fɛlthɛr], *m.* (—n, *pl.* —en) commander, general.

Feldmesser ['fɛltmɛsər], *m.* (—s, *pl.* —) land-surveyor.
Feldscher ['fɛltʃe:r], *m.* (—s, *pl.* —e) army-surgeon.
Feldstecher ['fɛltʃtɛçər], *m.* (—s, *pl.* —) field-glass(es).
Feldwebel ['fɛltve:bəl], *m.* (—s, *pl.* —) sergeant-major.
Feldzug ['fɛlttsu:k], *m.* (—es, *pl.* ¨e) campaign, expedition.
Felge ['fɛlgə], *f.* (—, *pl.* —n) (*wheel*) felloe, felly, rim.
Fell [fɛl], *n.* (—s, *pl.* —e) hide, skin, pelt.
Felsabhang ['fɛlsaphaŋ], *m.* (—s, *pl.* ¨e) rocky slope.
Felsen ['fɛlzən], *m.* (—s, *pl.* —) rock, cliff.
Felsengebirge ['fɛlzəngəbɪrgə], *n.* Rocky Mountains.
Felsenriff ['fɛlzənrɪf], *n.* (—s, *pl.* —e) reef.
felsig ['fɛlzɪç], *adj.* rocky.
Feme ['fe:mə], *f.* (—, *pl.* —n) secret tribunal.
Fenchel ['fɛnçəl], *m.* (—s, *no pl.*) (*Bot.*) fennel.
Fenster ['fɛnstər], *n.* (—s, *pl.* —) window.
Fensterbrett ['fɛnstərbrɛt], *n.* (—s, *pl.* —er) window-sill.
Fensterflügel ['fɛnstərfly:gəl], *m.* (—s, *pl.* —) (window) casement.
Fensterladen ['fɛnstərla:dən], *m.* (—s, *pl.* ¨) shutter.
Fensterscheibe ['fɛnstərʃaɪbə], *f.* (—, *pl.* —n) pane.
Ferien ['fe:rjən], *pl.* holidays.
Ferkel ['fɛrkəl], *n.* (—s, *pl.* —) young pig, piglet.
Fermate [fɛr'ma:tə], *f.* (—, *pl.* —n) (*Mus.*) pause, fermata.
fern [fɛrn], *adj.* far, distant, remote.
Fernbleiben ['fɛrnblaɪbən], *n.* (—s, *no pl.*) absence.
Ferne ['fɛrnə], *f.* (—, *pl.* —n) distance, remoteness.
ferner ['fɛrnər], *adv.* further, furthermore, moreover.
fernerhin ['fɛrnərhɪn], *adv.* henceforth.
Ferngespräch ['fɛrngəʃprɛx], *n.* (—s, *pl.* —e) long-distance telephone call, trunk call.
Fernglas ['fɛrngla:s], *n.* (—es, *pl.* ¨er) binoculars.
fernhalten ['fɛrnhaltən], *v.a. irr.* keep away.
fernher ['fɛrnhe:r], *adv. von* —, from afar.
fernliegen ['fɛrnli:gən], *v.n. irr.* be far from.
Fernrohr ['fɛrnro:r], *n.* (—s, *pl.* —e) telescope.
Fernschreiber ['fɛrnʃraɪbər], *m.* (—s, *pl.* —) teleprinter.
Fernsehen ['fɛrnze:ən], *n.* (—s, *no pl.*) television.
fernsehen ['fɛrnze:ən], *v.n. irr.* watch television.

Fernsehgerät ['fɛrnzeːgərɛːt], *n.* (—s, —e) television set.
Fernsprechamt ['fɛrnʃprɛçamt], *n.* (—s, *pl.* ¨er) telephone exchange.
Fernsprecher ['fɛrnʃprɛçər], *m.* (—s, *pl.* —) telephone.
Fernstehende ['fɛrnʃteːəndə], *m.* (—n, *pl.* —n) outsider.
Fernverkehr ['fɛrnfɛrkeːr], *m.* (—s, *no pl.*) long-distance traffic.
Ferse ['fɛrzə], *f.* (—, *pl.* —n) heel.
Fersengeld ['fɛrzəngɛlt], *n.* (—s, *no pl.*) — *geben*, take to o.'s heels.
fertig ['fɛrtɪç], *adj.* ready, finished; (*coll.*) worn-out, ruined, done for.
Fertigkeit ['fɛrtɪçkaɪt], *f.* (—, *pl.* —en) dexterity, skill.
Fes [fɛs], *n.* (—, *pl.* —) (*Mus.*) F flat.
fesch [fɛʃ], *adj.* smart, stylish; (*dial.*) good-looking.
Fessel ['fɛsəl], *f.* (—, *pl.* —n) fetter, shackle.
Fesselballon ['fɛsəlbalɔ̃], *m.* (—s, *pl.* —s) captive balloon.
Fesselbein ['fɛsəlbaɪn], *n.* (—s, *pl.* —e) pastern-joint.
fesseln ['fɛsəln], *v.a.* fetter, shackle, chain; (*fig.*) captivate.
Fest [fɛst], *n.* (—es, *pl.* —e) feast, festival.
fest [fɛst], *adj.* fast, firm; solid, hard; sound; fixed; constant, steadfast.
Feste ['fɛstə], *f.* (—, *pl.* —n) fortress, stronghold.
festigen ['fɛstɪgən], *v.a.* make firm; strengthen.
Festland ['fɛstlant], *n.* (—es, *pl.* ¨er) continent.
festlich ['fɛstlɪç], *adj.* festive, solemn.
festmachen ['fɛstmaxən], *v.a.* fasten.
Festnahme ['fɛstnaːmə], *f.* (—, *no pl.*) apprehension, arrest.
festnehmen ['fɛstneːmən], *v.a. irr.* seize, arrest.
Festrede ['fɛstreːdə], *f.* (—, *pl.* —n) formal address.
festschnallen ['fɛstʃnalən], *v.a.* buckle on, fasten.
Festschrift ['fɛstʃrɪft], *f.* (—, *pl.* —en) commemorative volume (in honour of a person or an occasion).
festsetzen ['fɛstzɛtsən], *v.a.* fix, decree.
Festspiel ['fɛstʃpiːl], *n.* (—s, *pl.* —e) festival (play).
feststehen ['fɛstʃteːən], *v.n. irr.* stand firm; *es steht fest*, it is certain.
feststellen ['fɛstʃtelən], *v.a.* ascertain; state; find; determine; diagnose; establish.
Festtag ['fɛstaːk], *m.* (—s, *pl.* —e) feast-day, holiday.
Festung ['fɛstuŋ], *f.* (—, *pl.* —en) fortress, stronghold, citadel.
festziehen ['fɛsttsiːən], *v.a. irr.* tighten.
Festzug ['fɛsttsuːk], *m.* (—s, *pl.* ¨e) procession.
Fett [fɛt], *n.* (—s, *pl.* —e) fat, grease, lard.
fett [fɛt], *adj.* fat, greasy.
fettartig ['fɛtartɪç], *adj.* fatty.

fetten ['fɛtən], *v.a.* oil, grease.
Fettfleck ['fɛtflɛk], *m.* (—s, *pl.* —e) spot of grease.
fettgedruckt ['fɛtgədrukt], *adj.* in heavy type.
fetthaltig ['fɛthaltɪç], *adj.* greasy; adipose.
fettig ['fɛtɪç], *adj.* greasy.
fettleibig ['fɛtlaɪbɪç], *adj.* corpulent, obese.
Fetzen ['fɛtsən], *m.* (—s, *pl.* —) piece, rag, tatter, shred.
feucht [fɔʏçt], *adj.* moist; (*weather*) muggy, wet; (*room*) damp.
Feuchtigkeit ['fɔʏçtɪçkaɪt], *f.* (—, *no pl.*) moisture, humidity, dampness, wetness.
feudal [fɔʏ'daːl], *adj.* feudal; (*coll.*) distinguished, magnificent.
Feuer ['fɔʏər], *n.* (—s, *pl.* —) fire; (*jewels*) brilliancy; (*fig.*) ardour, passion.
feuerbeständig ['fɔʏərbəʃtɛndɪç], *adj.* fire-proof.
Feuerbestattung ['fɔʏərbəʃtatuŋ], *f.* (—, *pl.* —en) cremation.
Feuereifer ['fɔʏəraɪfər], *m.* (—s, *no pl.*) ardour.
feuerfest ['fɔʏərfɛst], *adj.* fire-proof, incombustible.
feuergefährlich ['fɔʏərgəfɛːrlɪç], *adj.* inflammable.
Feuerlilie ['fɔʏərliːljə], *f.* (—, *pl.* —n) tiger lily.
Feuermal ['fɔʏərmaːl], *n.* (—s, *pl.* —e) burn, burn-mark.
Feuermauer ['fɔʏərmaʊər], *f.* (—, *pl.* —n) fire-proof wall, party-wall.
Feuermelder ['fɔʏərmɛldər], *m.* (—s, *pl.* —) fire-alarm.
feuern ['fɔʏərn], *v.a.* (*Mil.*) fire, discharge; (*coll.*) fire, sack.
Feuerprobe ['fɔʏərproːbə], *f.* (—, *pl.* —n) ordeal by fire.
Feuerrad ['fɔʏərraːt], *n.* (—s, *pl.* ¨er) Catherine wheel.
Feuerrohr ['fɔʏərroːr], *n.* (—s, *pl.* —e) gun, matchlock.
Feuersbrunst ['fɔʏərsbrunst], *f.* (—, *pl.* ¨e) (*rare*) fire, conflagration.
Feuerspritze ['fɔʏərʃprɪtsə], *f.* (—, *pl.* —n) fire-engine.
Feuerstein ['fɔʏərʃtaɪn], *m.* (—s, *no pl.*) flint.
Feuertaufe ['fɔʏərtaʊfə], *f.* (—, *pl.* —n) baptism of fire.
Feuerwarte ['fɔʏərvartə], *f.* (—, *pl.* —en) beacon; lighthouse.
Feuerwehr ['fɔʏərveːr], *f.* (—, *no pl.*) fire-brigade.
Feuerwerk ['fɔʏərvɛrk], *n.* (—, *no pl.*) fireworks.
Feuerwerkskunst ['fɔʏərvɛrkskunst], *f.* (—, *no pl.*) pyrotechnics.
Feuerzange ['fɔʏərtsaŋə], *f.* (—, *pl.* —n) fire-tongs.
Feuerzeug ['fɔʏərtsɔʏk], *n.* (—s, *pl.* —e) match-box; cigarette-lighter.
feurig ['fɔʏrɪç], *adj.* fiery, burning; (*fig.*) ardent, impassioned, fervent; (*wine*) heady.

Fiaker [fi'akər], *m.* (—s, *pl.* —) (*Austr.*) cab, hansom; (*Am.*) coach.

Fiasko [fi'asko:], *n.* (—s, *pl.* —s) failure.

Fibel ['fi:bəl], *f.* (—, *pl.* —n) primer, spelling-book.

Fiber ['fi:bər], *f.* (—, *pl.* —n) fibre.

Fichte ['fıçtə], *f.* (—, *pl.* —n) (*Bot.*) pine, pine-tree.

fidel [fi'de:l], *adj.* merry, jolly.

Fidibus ['fi:dibus], *m.* (—ses, *pl.* —se) spill, fidibus.

Fidschi ['fıdʒi:], Fiji.

Fieber ['fi:bər], *n.* (—s, *no pl.*) fever.

fieberhaft ['fi:bərhaft], *adj.* feverish, vehement.

fieberig ['fi:bərıç], *adj.* feverish, racked by fever.

Fieberkälte ['fi:bərkɛltə], *f.* (—, *no pl.*) chill, shivering (fit).

fiebern ['fi:bərn], *v.n.* have a fever; (*fig.*) rave.

fiebrig ['fi:brıç], *see* **fieberig**.

Fiedel ['fi:dəl], *f.* (—, *pl.* —n) (*Mus.*) fiddle, violin.

Figur [fi'gu:r], *f.* (—, *pl.* —en) figure, statue, sculpture; chessman.

figürlich [fi'gy:rlıç], *adj.* figurative.

Filet [fi'le:], *n.* (—s, *pl.* —s) netting, net-work; (*meat*) fillet.

Filiale [fıl'ja:lə], *f.* (—, *pl.* —n) branch, branch-establishment, branch-office.

Filigran [fıli'gra:n], *n.* (—s, *no pl.*) filigree.

Film [fılm], *m.* (—s, *pl.* —e) film; (*motion*) picture.

Filter ['fıltər], *m.* (—s, *pl.* —) filter.

filtrieren [fıl'tri:rən], *v.a.* filter.

Filz [fılts], *m.* (—es, *pl.* —e) felt; (*fig.*) niggard, miser, skinflint.

Filzlaus ['fıltslaus], *f.* (—, *pl.* ¨e) crab-louse.

Finanzamt [fı'nantsamt], *n.* (—s, *pl.* ¨er) income-tax office; revenue-office.

Finanzen [fı'nantsən], *f. pl.* finances, revenue.

Findelkind ['fındəlkınt], *n.* (—s, *pl.* —er) foundling.

finden ['fındən], *v.a. irr.* find. — *v.r. sich* —, *das wird sich* —, we shall see.

Finder ['fındər], *m.* (—s, *pl.* —) finder.

findig ['fındıç], *adj.* resourceful, ingenious.

Findling ['fıntlıŋ], *m.* (—s, *pl.* —e) foundling.

Finger ['fıŋər], *m.* (—s, *pl.* —) finger.

Fingerabdruck ['fıŋərapdruk], *m.* (—s, *pl.* ¨e) finger-print.

fingerfertig ['fıŋərfɛrtıç], *adj.* nimble-fingered.

Fingerhut ['fıŋərhu:t], *m.* (—s, *pl.* ¨e) thimble; (*Bot.*) foxglove.

fingern ['fıŋərn], *v.a.* touch with the fingers, finger.

Fingersatz ['fıŋərzats], *m.* (—es, *pl.* ¨e) (*Mus.*) fingering.

Fingerspitze ['fıŋərʃpıtsə], *f.* (—, *pl.* —n) finger-tip.

Fingerzeig ['fıŋərtsaık], *m.* (—s, *pl.* —e) hint.

fingieren [fıŋ'gi:rən], *v.a.* sham.

fingiert [fıŋ'gi:rt], *adj.* fictitious.

Fink [fıŋk], *m.* (—en, *pl.* —en) (*Orn.*) finch.

Finne (1) ['fınə], *m.* (—n, *pl.* —n) Finn.

Finne (2) ['fınə], *f.* (—, *pl.* —n) pimple; (*fish*) fin.

finnig ['fınıç], *adj.* pimpled; (*fish*) finny.

Finnland ['fınlant], *n.* Finland.

finster ['fınstər], *adj.* dark, obscure; (*fig.*) gloomy, sinister.

Finsternis ['fınstərnıs], *f.* (—, *no pl.*) darkness, gloom.

Finte ['fıntə], *f.* (—, *pl.* —n) feint; (*fig.*) pretence, trick.

Firlefanz ['fırləfants], *m.* (—es, *no pl.*) foolery.

Firma ['fırma], *f.* (—, *pl.* —men) (*business*) firm, company.

Firmung ['fırmuŋ], *f.* (—, *pl.* —en) (*Eccl.*) confirmation.

Firnis ['fırnıs], *m.* (—ses, *pl.* —se) varnish.

firnissen ['fırnısən], *v.a.* varnish.

First [fırst], *m.* (—es, *pl.* —e) (*house*) roof-ridge; (*mountain*) top.

Fis [fıs], *n.* (—, *pl.* —) (*Mus.*) F sharp.

Fisch [fıʃ], *m.* (—es, *pl.* —e) fish.

Fischadler ['fıʃa:dlər], *m.* (—s, *pl.* —) osprey, sea-eagle.

Fischbein ['fıʃbaın], *n.* (—s, *no pl.*) whalebone.

fischen ['fıʃən], *v.a., v.n.* fish, angle.

Fischer ['fıʃər], *m.* (—s, *pl.* —) fisherman, fisher.

Fischerei [fıʃə'raı], *f.* (—, *no pl.*) fishing; fishery.

Fischergerät ['fıʃərgərɛ:t], *n.* (—s, *pl.* —e) fishing-tackle.

Fischgräte ['fıʃgrɛ:tə], *f.* (—, *pl.* —n) fish-bone.

Fischkelle ['fıʃkɛlə], *f.* (—, *pl.* —n) fish-slice.

Fischlaich ['fıʃlaıç], *m.* (—s, *no pl.*) spawn.

Fischmilch ['fıʃmılç], *f.* (—, *no pl.*) soft roe, milt.

Fischotter ['fıʃɔtər], *m.* (—, *pl.* —n) common otter.

Fischreiher ['fıʃraıər], *m.* (—s, *pl.* —) (*Orn.*) heron.

Fischreuse ['fıʃrɔyzə], *f.* (—, *pl.* —n) bow-net; weir.

Fischrogen ['fıʃro:gən], *m.* (—s, *no pl.*) roe.

Fischschuppe ['fıʃʃupə], *f.* (—, *pl.* —n) scale.

Fischtran ['fıʃtra:n], *m.* (—s, *no pl.*) train-oil.

Fischzucht ['fıʃtsuxt], *f.* (—, *no pl.*) fish-breeding, pisciculture.

Fiskus ['fıskus], *m.* (—, *pl.* —ken) Treasury, Exchequer.

Fisole [fi'zo:lə], *f.* (—, *pl.* —n) (*Austr.*) French bean.

Fistelstimme ['fɪstəlʃtɪmə], *f.* (—, *no pl.*) (*Mus.*) falsetto.

Fittich ['fɪtɪç], *m.* (—es, *pl.* —e) (*Poet.*) wing, pinion.

fix [fɪks], *adj.* quick, sharp; — *und fertig*, quite ready.

Fixum ['fɪksum], *n.* (—s, *pl.* —xa) fixed amount; regular salary.

flach [flax], *adj.* flat, plain, smooth, level; (*water*) shallow.

Fläche ['flɛçə], *f.* (—, *pl.* —n) plain; (*Maths.*) plane; (*crystal*) face.

Flächeninhalt ['flɛçənɪnhalt], *m.* (—s, *no pl.*) area.

Flächenmaß ['flɛçənma:s], *n.* (—es, *pl.* —e) square-measure.

Flächenraum ['flɛçənraum], *m.* (—es, *no pl.*) surface area.

Flachheit ['flaxhaɪt], *f.* (—, *no pl.*) flatness; (*fig.*) shallowness.

Flachs [[flaks], *m.* (—es, *no pl.*) flax.

flackern ['flakərn], *v.n.* flare, flicker.

Fladen ['fla:dən], *m.* (—s, *pl.* —) flat cake; cow-dung.

Flagge ['flagə], *f.* (—, *pl.* —n) flag.

Flame ['fla:mə], *m.* (—n, *pl.* —n) Fleming.

flämisch ['flɛ:mɪʃ], *adj.* Flemish.

Flamme ['flamə], *f.* (—, *pl.* —n) flame; blaze.

flammen ['flamən], *v.n.* flame, blaze, sparkle.

Flammeri ['flaməri:], *m.* (—s, *pl.* —s) blanc-mange.

Flandern ['flandərn], *n.* Flanders.

Flanell [fla'nɛl], *m.* (—s, *pl.* —e) flannel.

Flaneur [fla'nø:r], *m.* (—s, *pl.* —e) lounger, stroller.

flanieren [fla'ni:rən], *v.n.* lounge, stroll.

Flanke ['flaŋkə], *f.* (—, *pl.* —n) flank; *in die — fallen*, (*Mil.*) attack in the flank.

Flasche ['flaʃə], *f.* (—, *pl.* —en) bottle, flask.

Flaschenzug ['flaʃəntsu:k], *m.* (—es, *pl.* ⁻e) pulley.

flatterhaft ['flatərhaft], *adj.* fickle, inconstant, flighty.

flattern ['flatərn], *v.n.* flutter.

flau [flau], *adj.* insipid, stale; (*fig.*) dull.

Flaum [flaum], *m.* (—s, *no pl.*) down.

Flausch [flauʃ], *m.* (—es, *no pl.*) pilot-cloth.

Flaute ['flautə], *f.* (—, *pl.* —n) (*Nav.*) calm; (*fig.*) (*Comm.*) depression.

Flechte ['flɛçtə], *f.* (—, *pl.* —n) twist, plait, braid; (*Med.*) eruption, ringworm; (*Bot.*) lichen.

flechten ['flɛçtən], *v.a. irr.* plait; wreathe.

Flechtwerk ['flɛçtvɛrk], *n.* (—s, *no pl.*) wicker-work, basketry.

Fleck [flɛk], *m.* (—s, *pl.* —e) spot; place, piece (of ground); (*fig.*) stain, blemish.

Flecken ['flɛkən], *m.* (—s, *pl.* —) market town, small town.

fleckenlos ['flɛkənlo:s], *adj.* spotless.

fleckig ['flɛkɪç], *adj.* spotted, speckled.

Fledermaus ['fle:dərmaus], *f.* (—, *pl.* ⁻e) (*Zool.*) bat.

Flederwisch ['fle:dərvɪʃ], *m.* (—es, *pl.* —e) feather-duster.

Flegel ['fle:gəl], *m.* (—s, *pl.* —) flail; (*fig.*) boor.

flegelhaft ['fle:gəlhaft], *adj.* boorish, churlish, rude.

Flegeljahre ['fle:gəlja:rə], *n. pl.* years of indiscretion; teens, adolescence.

flehen ['fle:ən], *v.a., v.n.* implore, supplicate, entreat.

Fleisch [flaɪʃ], *n.* (—es, *no pl.*) (raw) flesh; (*for cooking*) meat; (*fruit*) pulp.

Fleischbrühe ['flaɪʃbry:ə], *f.* (—, *pl.* —n) broth, beef-tea.

Fleischer ['flaɪʃər], *m.* (—s, *pl.* —) butcher.

fleischfressend ['flaɪʃfrɛsənt], *adj.* carnivorous.

Fleischhacker ['flaɪʃhakər], **Fleischhauer** ['flaɪʃhauər], *m.* (—s, *pl.* —) butcher.

fleischlich ['flaɪʃlɪç], *adj.* fleshly, carnal.

fleischlos ['flaɪʃlo:s], *adj.* vegetarian.

Fleischpastete ['flaɪʃpaste:tə], *f.* (—, *pl.* —n) meat-pie.

Fleiß [flaɪs], *m.* (—es, *no pl.*) diligence, assiduity, industry.

fleißig ['flaɪsɪç], *adj.* diligent, assiduous, industrious, hard-working.

fletschen ['flɛtʃən], *v.a. die Zähne —*, show o.'s teeth.

Flicken ['flɪkən], *m.* (—s, *pl.* —) patch.

flicken ['flɪkən], *v.a.* patch, repair, mend; (*shoes*) cobble; (*stockings*) darn.

Flieder ['fli:dər], *m.* (—s, *pl.* —) (*Bot.*) elder, lilac.

Fliege ['fli:gə], *f.* (—, *pl.* —n) (*Ent.*) fly; (*beard*) imperial.

fliegen ['fli:gən], *v.n. irr.* (*aux.* sein) fly; (*coll.*) get the sack, be fired. — *v.a.* fly, pilot (an aircraft).

Flieger ['fli:gər], *m.* (—s, *pl.* —) airman, aviator; pilot.

fliehen ['fli:ən], *v.n. irr.* (*aux.* sein) flee, run away; *zu einem —*, take refuge with s.o. — *v.a. irr.* avoid, shun (s.o.).

Fliehkraft ['fli:kraft], *f.* (—, *no pl.*) centrifugal force.

Fliese ['fli:zə], *f.* (—, *pl.* —n) floor-tile, flagstone.

Fließband ['fli:sbant], *n.* (—(e)s, *pl.* ⁻er) (*Ind.*) assembly line.

fließen ['fli:sən], *v.n. irr.* (*aux.* sein) flow.

Fließpapier ['fli:spapi:r], *n.* (—s, *no pl.*) blotting-paper.

Flimmer ['flɪmər], *m.* (—s, *no pl.*) glittering, sparkling, glimmer.

flimmern ['flɪmərn], *v.n.* glisten, glitter.

flink [flɪŋk], *adj.* brisk, agile, quick, sharp, nimble.

73

Flinte

Flinte ['flɪntə], *f.* (—, *pl.* —n) gun, musket, rifle.

Flitter ['flɪtər], *m.* (—s, *no pl.*) tinsel, spangle, frippery.

Flitterwochen ['flɪtərvɔxən], *f. pl.* honeymoon.

flitzen ['flɪtsən], *v.n. (aux.* sein*)* *vorbei* —, flit *or* rush past, dash along.

Flocke ['flɔkə], *f.* (—, *pl.* —n) *(snow)* flake; *(wool)* flock.

Floh [floː], *m.* (—s, *pl.* ⁻e) *(Ent.)* flea.

Flor [floːr], *m.* (—s, *pl.* —e) bloom; gauze, crape; *in* —, blossoming, blooming.

Florenz [floˈrɛnts], *n.* Florence.

Florett [floˈrɛt], *n.* (—s, *pl.* —e) *(fencing)* foil.

florieren [floˈriːrən], *v.n.* flourish.

Florstrumpf ['floːrʃtrumpf], *m.* ⁻s, *pl.* ⁻e) lisle stocking.

Floskel ['flɔskəl], *f.* (—, *pl.* —n) rhetorical ornament; oratorical flourish; phrase.

Floß [floːs], *n.* (—es, *pl.* ⁻e) raft.

Flosse ['flɔsə], *f.* (—, *pl.* —n) fin.

flößen ['floːsən], *v.a.* float.

Flößer ['floːsər], *m.* (—s, *pl.* —) raftsman.

Flöte ['floːtə], *f.* (—, *pl.* —n) *(Mus.)* flute.

Flötenzug ['floːtəntsuːk], *m.* (—es, *pl.* ⁻e) *(organ)* flute-stop.

flott [flɔt], *adj. (Naut.)* afloat, floating; *(fig.)* gay, jolly, lively, smart; — *leben*, lead a fast life.

Flotte ['flɔtə], *f.* (—, *pl.* —n) fleet, navy.

Flottille [flɔˈtɪljə], *f.* (—, *pl.* —n) flotilla, squadron.

Flöz [floːts], *n.* (—es, *pl.* —e) layer, stratum; *(coal)* seam.

Fluch [fluːx], *m.* (—es, *pl.* ⁻e) curse, spell; *(verbal)* curse, oath, swear-word.

fluchen ['fluːxən], *v.n.* curse, swear.

Flucht [fluxt], *f.* (—, *pl.* —en) flight, fleeing; suite (of rooms).

flüchten ['flyçtən], *v.n. (aux.* sein*)*, *v.r.* flee, run away, escape.

flüchtig ['flyçtɪç], *adj.* fugitive; *(Chem.)* volatile; *(fig.)* superficial; evanescent; hasty; slight.

Flüchtling ['flyçtlɪŋ], *m.* (—s, *pl.* —e) fugitive, refugee.

Flug [fluːk], *m.* (—s, *pl.* ⁻e) *(Aviat.)* flight.

Flugblatt ['fluːkblat], *n.* (—s, *pl.* ⁻er) broadsheet, leaflet.

Flügel ['flyːgəl], *m.* (—s, *pl.* —) wing; *(Mus.)* grand piano; *(door)* leaf.

Flügelschlag ['flyːgəlʃlaːk], *m.* (—s, *pl.* ⁻e) wing-stroke.

Flügeltür ['flyːgəltyːr], *f.* (—, *pl.* —en) folding-door.

flügge ['flyɡə], *adj.* fledged.

Flughafen ['fluːkhaːfən], *m.* (—s, *pl.* ⁻) airport; aerodrome.

Flugpost ['fluːkpɔst], *f.* (—, *no pl.*) air mail.

flugs [fluks], *adv.* quickly, instantly; *(Lit., obs.)* anon.

Flugsand ['fluːkzant], *m.* (—s, *no pl.*) quicksand, drifting sand.

Flugzeug ['fluːktsɔyk], *n.* (—s, *pl.* —e) aeroplane; *(Am.)* airplane.

Flugzeugführer ['fluːktsɔykfyːrər], *m.* (—s, *pl.* —) *(Aviat.)* pilot.

Fluidum ['fluːidum], *n.* (—s, *pl.* —da) fluid; *(fig.)* atmosphere.

Flunder ['flundər], *f.* (—, *pl.* —n) *(fish)* flounder.

Flunkerer ['fluŋkərər], *m.* (—s, *pl.* —) *(coll.)* fibber, story-teller.

Flur (1) [fluːr], *f.* (—, *pl.* —en) field, plain; *auf weiter* —, in the open.

Flur (2) [fluːr], *m.* (—s, *pl.* —e) *(house)* hall, vestibule; corridor.

Flurschaden ['fluːrʃaːdən], *m.* (—s, *pl.* ⁻) damage to crops.

Fluß [flus], *m.* (—sses, *pl.* ⁻sse) river, stream; flow, flowing; flux.

Flußbett ['flusbet], *n.* (—s, *pl.* —en) channel, riverbed.

flüssig ['flysɪç], *adj.* fluid, liquid; —*e Gelder*, ready cash; liquid assets.

flüstern ['flystərn], *v.a.* whisper.

Flut [fluːt], *f.* (—, *pl.* —en) flood; high-tide, high water; torrent; deluge.

fluten ['fluːtən], *v.n.* flow.

Focksegel ['fɔkzeːgəl], *n.* (—s, *pl.* —) foresail.

Fockmast ['fɔkmast], *m.* (—s, *pl.* —en) foremast.

Föderalismus [fœdəraˈlɪsmus], *m.* (—, *no pl.*) federalism.

Fohlen ['foːlən], *n.* (—s, *pl.* —) foal.

fohlen ['foːlən], *v.n.* foal.

Föhn [foːn], *m.* (—s, *pl.* —e) (warm) Alpine wind.

Föhre ['føːrə], *f.* (—, *pl.* —n) *(Bot.)* fir, fir-tree.

Folge ['fɔlɡə], *f.* (—, *pl.* —n) succession; series, sequence; continuation; consequence.

folgen ['fɔlɡən], *v.n. (aux.* sein*)* follow; succeed; result from, be the consequence of; obey.

folgendermaßen ['fɔlɡəndərmaːsən], *adv.* as follows.

folgenschwer ['fɔlɡənʃveːr], *adj.* momentous, portentous.

folgerichtig ['fɔlɡərɪçtɪç], *adj.* consistent, logical.

folgern ['fɔlɡərn], *v.a.* draw a conclusion, infer, conclude, deduce.

Folgerung ['fɔlɡəruŋ], *f.* (—, *pl.* —en) induction, deduction, inference.

folglich ['fɔlklɪç], *conj.* consequently, therefore.

folgsam ['fɔlkzaːm], *adj.* obedient.

Foliant [foˈljant], *m.* (—en, *pl.* —en) folio-volume, tome.

Folie ['foːljə], *f.* (—, *pl.* —n) foil.

Folter ['fɔltər], *f.* (—, *pl.* —n) rack, torture.

Folterbank ['fɔltərbaŋk], *f.* (—, *pl.* ⁻e) rack.

Fond [fɔ̃], *m.* (—s, *pl.* —s) back seat.

Fontäne [fɔ'tɛ:nə], f. (—, pl. —n) fountain.

foppen ['fɔpən], v.a. chaff, banter, tease.

Fopperei ['fɔpə'raı], f. (—, pl. —en) chaff, banter, teasing.

forcieren [fɔr'si:rən], v.a. strain, overdo.

Förderer ['fœrdərər], m. (—s, pl. —) promoter, backer.

Förderkarren ['fœrdərkarən], m. (—s, pl. —) (Min.) truck, trolley.

förderlich ['fœrdərlıç], adj. useful, conducive (to).

Fördermaschine ['fœrdərmaʃi:nə], f. (—, pl. —n) hauling-machine.

fordern ['fɔrdərn], v.a. demand, claim, ask for; (duel) challenge.

fördern ['fœrdərn], v.a. further, advance, promote, back; hasten; (Min.) haul.

Förderschacht ['fœrdərʃaxt], m. (—s, pl. ⁻e) (Min.) winding shaft.

Forderung ['fɔrdəruŋ], f. (—, pl. —en) demand, claim; (duel) challenge.

Förderung ['fœrdəruŋ], f. (—, no pl.) furtherance, promotion, advancement; (Min.) hauling.

Forelle [fo'rɛlə], f. (—, pl. —n) trout.

Forke ['fɔrkə], f. (—, pl. —n) pitchfork, garden-fork.

Form [fɔrm], f. (—, pl. —en) form, shape, figure; manner; condition; (casting) mould; (grammar) form, voice.

Formalien [fɔr'ma:ljən], pl. formalities.

Formalität [fɔrmalı'tɛ:t], f. (—, pl. —en) formality, form.

Format [fɔr'ma:t], n. (—s, pl. —e) (book, paper) size; format; (fig.) stature.

Formel ['fɔrməl], f. (—, pl. —n) formula.

formell [fɔr'mɛl], adj. formal.

Formfehler ['fɔrmfe:lər], m. (—s, pl. —) faux pas, breach of etiquette.

formieren [fɔr'mi:rən], v.a. form. — v.r. sich —, fall into line.

förmlich ['fœrmlıç], adj. formal; downright.

formlos ['fɔrmlo:s], adj. shapeless; (fig.) unconventional, informal, unceremonious.

Formular [fɔrmu'la:r], n. (—s, pl. —e) (printed) form, schedule.

formulieren [fɔrmu'li:rən], v.a. formulate, word.

formvollendet ['fɔrmfɔlɛndət], adj. well-rounded, well-finished.

forsch [fɔrʃ], adj. dashing.

forschen ['fɔrʃən], v.n. search, enquire (after), do research.

Forschung ['fɔrʃuŋ], f. (—, pl. —en) research, investigation; search, exploration.

Forst [fɔrst], m. (—es, pl. —e) forest.

Förster ['fœrstər], m. (—s, pl. —) forester, forest-keeper; (Am.) ranger.

Forstfrevel ['fɔrstfre:fəl], m. (—s, no pl.) infringement of forest-laws.

Forstrevier ['fɔrstrevi:r], n. (—s, pl. —e) section of forest.

Forstwesen ['fɔrstve:zən], n. (—s, no pl.) forestry.

Forstwirtschaft ['fɔrstvırtʃaft], f. (—, no pl.) forestry.

fort [fɔrt], adv. away; lost, gone, forth, forward.

Fort [fo:rt], n. (—s, pl. —s) fort.

fortan [fɔrt'an], adv. henceforth.

fortbilden ['fɔrtbıldən], v.r. sich —, improve o.s., receive further education.

fortbleiben ['fɔrtblaıbən], v.n. irr. (aux. sein) stay away.

Fortdauer ['fɔrtdauər], f. (—, no pl.) continuance, duration.

fortfahren ['fɔrtfa:rən], v.n. irr. (aux. sein) drive off; (Naut.) set sail; (fig.) continue, go on.

Fortgang ['fɔrtgaŋ], m. (—s, no pl.) going away, departure; (fig.) continuation, progress.

Fortkommen ['fɔrtkɔmən], n. (—s, no pl.) advancement, progress; (fig.) livelihood.

fortkommen ['fɔrtkɔmən], v.n. irr. (aux. sein) get on, prosper, succeed.

fortlassen ['fɔrtlasən], v.a. irr. allow to go; leave out, omit; nicht —, detain.

fortlaufen ['fɔrtlaufən], v.n. irr. (aux. sein) run away.

fortpflanzen ['fɔrtpflantsən], v.r. sich —, propagate, multiply; (sickness) spread.

forträumen ['fɔrtrɔymən], v.a. clear away, remove.

fortschaffen ['fɔrtʃafən], v.a. carry away, get rid of.

fortscheren ['fɔrtʃe:rən], v.r. sich — (coll.) beat it, go away.

fortscheuchen ['fɔrtʃɔyçən], v.a. scare away.

fortschreiten ['fɔrtʃraıtən], v.n. irr. (aux. sein) progress, advance.

Fortschritt ['fɔrtʃrıt], m. (—s, pl. —e) progress, advancement, proficiency.

fortsetzen ['fɔrtzɛtsən], v.a. continue, carry on.

fortwährend ['fɔrtvɛ:rənt], adj. continual, perpetual, unceasing.

Fracht [fraxt], f. (—, pl. —en) freight, cargo, load.

Frack [frak], m. (—s, pl. —s, ⁻e) dress-suit, evening dress.

Frage ['fra:gə], f. (—, pl. —n) question, query.

Fragebogen ['fra:gəbo:gən], m. (—s, pl. —) questionnaire.

fragen ['fra:gən], v.a. ask, enquire, question.

Fragesteller ['fra:gəʃtɛlər], m. (—s, pl —) interrogator, questioner.

fraglich ['fra:klıç], adj. questionable, problematic(al).

fragwürdig ['fra:kvyrdıç], adj. doubtful, questionable.

Fraktion [frak'tsjo:n], f. (—, pl. —en) (Pol.) party group.

Frakturschrift [frak'tu:rʃrɪft], *f.* (—, *no pl.*) (*lettering*) Gothic type, Old English type, Black Letter type.
Frank [fraŋk], *m.* (—en, *pl.* —en) (*money*) franc.
Franke ['fraŋkə], *m.* (—n, *pl.* —n) Frank, Franconian.
frankieren [fraŋ'ki:rən], *v.a.* (*post*) prepay, frank.
franko ['fraŋko], *adj.* post-paid; *gratis und* —, gratuitously.
Frankreich ['frankraɪx], *n.* France.
Franse ['franzə], *f.* (—, *pl.* —n) fringe.
Franzose [fran'tso:zə], *m.* (—n, *pl.* —n) Frenchman.
französisch [fran'tsø:zɪʃ], *adj.* French.
frappant [fra'pant], *adj.* striking.
frappieren [fra'pi:rən], *v.a.* strike, astonish.
Fraß [fra:s], *m.* (—es, *no pl.*) (*animals*) feed, fodder; (*sl.*) grub.
Fratz [frats], *m.* (—es, *pl.* —en) brat, little monkey.
Fratze ['fratsə], *f.* (—, *pl.* —en) grimace, caricature.
Frau [frau], *f.* (—, *pl.* —en) woman, wife, lady; (*title*) Mrs.; *gnädige* —, Madam.
Frauenkirche ['frauənkɪrçə], *f.* (—, *no pl.*) Church of Our Lady.
Frauenzimmer ['frauəntsɪmər], *n.* (—s, *pl.* —) (*pej.*) woman, female.
Fräulein ['frɔylaɪn], *n.* (—s, *pl.* —) young lady; (*title*) Miss.
frech [frɛç], *adj.* insolent, impudent, cheeky, pert, saucy.
Frechheit ['frɛçhaɪt], *f.* (—, *pl.* —en) insolence, impudence.
Fregatte [fre'gatə], *f.* (—, *pl.* —n) frigate.
frei [fraɪ], *adj.* free, exempt, unhampered, independent, disengaged; vacant; candid, frank.
Freibeuter ['fraɪbɔytər], *m.* (—s, *pl.* —) freebooter, pirate.
Freibrief ['fraɪbri:f], *m.* (—s, *pl.* —e) patent, licence; permit.
freien ['fraɪən], *v.a.* woo, court.
Freier ['fraɪər], *m.* (—s, *pl.* —) (*obs.*) suitor.
Freigabe ['fraɪga:bə], *f.* (—, *no pl.*) release.
freigeben ['fraɪge:bən], *v.a. irr.* release.
freigebig ['fraɪge:bɪç], *adj.* liberal, generous.
Freigebigkeit ['fraɪgə:bɪçkaɪt], *f.* (—, *no pl.*) liberality, munificence, generosity.
Freigut ['fraɪgu:t], *n.* (—s, *pl.* ⁓er) freehold.
Freiheit ['fraɪhaɪt], *f.* (—, *pl.* —en) freedom, liberty, immunity, privilege.
Freiherr ['fraɪhɛr], *m.* (—n, *pl.* —en) baron.
Freikorps ['fraɪko:r], *n.* (—, *no pl.*) volunteer-corps.
Freilauf ['fraɪlauf], *m.* (—s, *no pl.*) (*bicycle*) free-wheel.

freilich ['fraɪlɪç], *adv.* to be sure, it is true, indeed, of course.
Freilicht- ['fraɪlɪxt], *adj.* (*in compounds*) open-air.
Freimarke ['fraɪmarkə], *f.* (—, *pl.* —n) postage stamp.
freimütig ['fraɪmy:tɪç], *adj.* frank, open, candid.
Freisprechung ['fraɪʃprɛçuŋ], *f.* (—, *no pl.*) acquittal; absolution.
Freistätte ['fraɪʃtɛtə], *f.* (—, *pl.* —n) refuge, asylum.
Freistoß ['fraɪʃto:s], *m.* (—es, *pl.* ⁓e) (*Footb.*) free-kick.
Freitag ['fraɪta:k], *m.* (—s, *pl.* —e) Friday.
Freitreppe ['fraɪtrɛpə], *f.* (—, *pl.* —n) outside staircase.
Freiübung ['fraɪy:buŋ], *f.* (—, *pl.* —en) (*mostly pl.*) physical exercises, gymnastics.
freiwillig ['fraɪvɪlɪç], *adj.* voluntary, of o.'s own accord; spontaneous.
Freiwillige ['fraɪvɪlɪgə], *m.* (—n, *pl.* —n) (*Mil.*) volunteer.
fremd [frɛmt], *adj.* strange, foreign, outlandish; odd.
fremdartig ['frɛmtartɪç], *adj.* strange, odd.
Fremde (1) ['frɛmdə], *f.* (—, *no pl.*) foreign country; *in die* — *gehen*, go abroad.
Fremde (2) ['frɛmdə], *m.* (—n, *pl.* —n) stranger, foreigner.
Fremdheit ['frɛmthaɪt], *f.* (—, *no pl.*) strangeness.
Freßbeutel ['frɛsbɔytəl], *m.* (—s, *pl.* —) nose-bag.
Fresse ['frɛsə], *f.* (—, *pl.* —n) (*vulg.*) mouth, snout.
fressen ['frɛsən], *v.a. irr.* (*animals*) eat; (*also fig.*) devour.
Fresserei ['frɛsəraɪ], *f.* (—, *no pl.*) gluttony.
Frettchen ['frɛtçən], *n.* (—s, *pl.* —) (*Zool.*) ferret.
Freude ['frɔydə], *f.* (—, *pl.* —n) joy, joyfulness, gladness, enjoyment, delight, pleasure.
Freudenfest ['frɔydənfɛst], *n.* (—s, *pl.* —e) feast, jubilee.
Freudenhaus ['frɔydənhaus], *n.* (—es, *pl.* ⁓er) brothel.
Freudenmädchen ['frɔydənmɛːtçən], *n.* (—s, *pl.* —) prostitute.
freudig ['frɔydɪç], *adj.* joyful, cheerful, glad.
freudlos ['frɔytlo:s], *adj.* joyless.
freuen ['frɔyən], *v.r. sich* —, rejoice (at), be glad (of); *sich auf etwas* —, look forward to s.th.
Freund [frɔynt], *m.* (—es, *pl.* —e) friend.
freundlich ['frɔyntlɪç], *adj.* friendly, kind, affable, pleasing, cheerful, pleasant, genial.
Freundschaft ['frɔyntʃaft], *f.* (—, *pl.* —en) friendship.
Frevel ['fre:fəl], *m.* (—s, *pl.* —) crime, misdeed, offence.

freveln ['fre:fəln], *v.n.* do wrong, trespass, commit an outrage.

Friede(n) ['fri:də(n)], *m.* (—ns, *no pl.*) peace.

friedfertig ['fri:fɛrtɪç], *adj.* peaceable.

Friedhof ['fri:tho:f], *m.* (—s, *pl.* ⸚e) churchyard, cemetery.

friedlich ['fri:tlɪç], *adj.* peaceful.

friedliebend ['fri:tli:bənt], *adj.* peaceable, peace-loving.

Friedrich ['fri:drɪç], *m.* Frederic(k).

friedselig ['fri:tze:lɪç], *adj.* peaceable.

frieren ['fri:rən], *v.n.* irr. feel cold, freeze.

Fries [fri:s], *m.* (—es, *pl.* —e) frieze.

Friese ['fri:zə], *m.* (—n, *pl.* —n) Frisian.

frisch [frɪʃ], *adj.* fresh; new; (*weather*) crisp; (*fig.*) lively, brisk, gay.

Frische ['frɪʃə], *f.* (—, *no pl.*) freshness, liveliness, gaiety.

Friseur [fri'zø:r], *m.* (—s, *pl.* —e) hairdresser, barber.

Friseuse [fri'zø:zə], *f.* (—, *pl.* —n) female hairdresser.

frisieren [fri'zi:rən], *v.a.* dress (s.o.'s) hair.

Frist [frɪst], *f.* (—, *pl.* —en) time, term, period; (fixed) term; delay, respite.

fristen ['frɪstən], *v.a. das Leben —,* gain a bare living.

Frisur [fri'zu:r], *f.* (—, *pl.* —en) coiffure, hair-style.

frivol [fri'vo:l], *adj.* frivolous.

Frivolität [frivo:li'tɛ:t], *f.* (—, *pl.* —en) frivolity.

froh [fro:], *adj.* glad, joyful, joyous.

frohgelaunt ['fro:gəlaunt], *adj.* good-humoured, cheerful.

fröhlich ['frø:lɪç], *adj.* gay, merry.

frohlocken [fro:'lɔkən], *v.n.* (*rare*) exult.

Frohsinn ['fro:zɪn], *m.* (—s, *no pl.*) good humour, gaiety.

fromm [frɔm], *adj.* pious, religious, devout.

frommen ['frɔmən], *v.n.* (*obs.*) be of advantage (to s.o.).

Frömmigkeit ['frœmɪçkaɪt], *f.* (—, *no pl.*) piety, devoutness.

Fron [fro:n], *f.* (—, *no pl.*) (feudal) service; statute labour.

frönen ['frø:nən], *v.n.* (*fig.*) be a slave to; indulge in (*Dat.*).

Fronleichnam [fro:n'laɪxna:m], *m.* (*Eccl.*) (feast of) Corpus Christi.

Front [frɔnt], *f.* (—, *pl.* —en) front, forepart; (*building*) elevation; (*Mil.*) front line.

Frosch [frɔʃ], *m.* (—es, *pl.* ⸚e) (*Zool.*) frog.

Frost [frɔst], *m.* (—es, *pl.* ⸚e) frost; coldness, chill.

Frostbeule ['frɔstbɔylə], *f.* (—, *pl.* —n) chilblain.

frösteln ['frœstəln], *v.n.* feel a chill, shiver.

frostig ['frɔstɪç], *adj.* frosty; cold, chilly.

frottieren [frɔ'ti:rən], *v.a.* rub (down).

Frottiertuch [frɔ'ti:rtu:x], *n.* (—s, *pl.* ⸚er) Turkish towel, bath towel.

Frucht [fruxt], *f.* (—, *pl.* ⸚e) fruit; (*fig.*) result, effect; (*Med.*) fœtus.

fruchtbar ['fruxtba:r], *adj.* fruitful, productive, fertile.

fruchten ['fruxtən], *v.n.* produce fruit; (*fig.*) be effectual.

Fruchtknoten ['fruxtkno:tən], *m.* (—s, *pl.* —) (*Bot.*) seed-vessel.

früh(e) [fry:(ə)], *adj.* early.

Frühe ['fry:ə], *f.* (—, *no pl.*) early morning, dawn.

früher ['fry:ər], *adv.* earlier (on), formerly.

frühestens ['fry:əstəns], *adv.* at the earliest (possible moment).

Frühjahr ['fry:ja:r], *n.,* **Frühling** ['fry:lɪŋ], *m.* (—s, *pl.* —e) spring.

frühreif ['fry:raɪf], *adj.* precocious.

Frühschoppen ['fry:ʃɔpən], *m.* (—s, *pl.* —) morning pint (beer *or* wine).

Frühstück ['fry:ʃtyk], *n.* (—s, *pl.* —e) breakfast; *zweites* —, lunch.

Fuchs [fuks], *m.* (—es, *pl.* ⸚e) fox; chestnut (horse); (*fig.*) cunning chap; (*student*) freshman.

Fuchsbau ['fuksbau], *m.* (—s, *pl.* —e) fox-hole.

Fuchseisen ['fuksaɪzən], *n.* (—s, *pl.* —) fox-trap.

fuchsen ['fuksən], *v.r. sich — über,* be annoyed about.

Fuchsie ['fuksjə], *f.* (—, *pl.* —n) (*Bot.*) fuchsia.

fuchsig ['fuksɪç], *adj.* (*coll.*) very angry.

Füchsin ['fyksɪn], *f.* (—, *pl.* —innen) vixen.

fuchsrot ['fuksro:t], *adj.* fox-coloured, sorrel.

Fuchsschwanz ['fuksʃvants], *m.* (—es, *pl.* ⸚e) fox-brush; pad saw.

Fuchtel ['fuxtəl], *f.* (—, *pl.* —n) sword blade; rod, whip.

Fuder ['fu:dər], *n.* (—s, *pl.* —) load, cart-load; wine measure (c. 270 gallons).

Fug ['fu:k], *m.* (—s, *no pl.*) (*rare*) right, justice; *mit — und Recht,* with every right.

Fuge (1) ['fu:gə], *f.* (—, *pl.* —n) joint, groove.

Fuge (2) ['fu:gə], *f.* (—, *pl.* —n) (*Mus.*) fugue.

fügen ['fy:gən], *v.a.* fit together, join, dovetail. — *v.r. sich —,* submit (to), accommodate o.s. (to).

fügsam ['fy:kza:m], *adj.* pliant, submissive, yielding.

Fügung ['fy:guŋ], *f.* (—, *pl.* —en) coincidence; dispensation (of Providence); Providence.

fühlbar ['fy:lba:r], *adj.* perceptible; tangible; *sich — machen,* make o.s. felt.

fühlen ['fy:lən], *v.a.* feel, touch, sense, be aware of.

Fühler ['fy:lər], *m.* (—s, *pl.* —) tentacle, feeler.

Fühlhorn

Fühlhorn ['fy:lhɔrn], *n.* (—s, *pl.* ⁻er) feeler, antenna, tentacle.

Fühlung ['fy:luŋ], *f.* (—, *no pl.*) — *haben mit*, be in touch with.

Fuhre ['fu:rə], *f.* (—, *pl.* —n) conveyance, vehicle, cart-load.

führen ['fy:rən], *v.a.* lead, guide, conduct, command; (*pen*) wield; (*law-suit*) carry on; (*conversation*) have, keep up; (*name, title*) bear; (*goods*) stock, deal in; *Krieg* —, wage war; *etwas im Schilde* —, have a plan; *das Wort* —, be spokesman; *einen hinters Licht* —, cheat s.o.

Führer ['fy:rər], *m.* (—s, *pl.* —) leader, guide; head, manager; conductor; driver, pilot.

Führerschaft ['fy:rərʃaft], *f.* (—, *no pl.*) leadership.

Führerschein ['fy:rərʃain], *m.* (—s, *pl.* —e) driving-licence.

Führersitz ['fy:rərzits], *m.* (—es, *pl.* —e) driver's seat; pilot's cockpit.

Fuhrlohn ['fu:rlo:n], *m.* (—s, *no pl.*) cartage, carriage.

Fuhrmann ['fu:rman], *m.* (—s, *pl.* ⁻er) carter, carrier.

Führung ['fy:ruŋ], *f.* (—, *no pl.*) guidance; leadership; conducted tour; management, direction; behaviour, conduct.

Führungszeugnis ['fy:ruŋstsɔyknis], *n.* (—sses, *pl.* —sse) certificate of good conduct.

Fuhrwerk ['fu:rvɛrk], *n.* (—s, *pl.* —e) carriage, vehicle, waggon.

Fuhrwesen ['fu:rve:zən], *n.* (—s, *no pl.*) transport services, transportation.

Fülle ['fylə], *f.* (—, *no pl.*) fullness; abundance, plenty.

Füllen ['fylən], *n.* (—s, *pl.* —) foal.

füllen ['fylən], *v.a.* fill, fill up; stuff.

Füllfederhalter ['fylfe:dərhaltər], *m.* (—s, *pl.* —) fountain-pen.

Füllung ['fyluŋ], *f.* (—, *pl.* —en) filling; stuffing; (*door*) panel.

fummeln ['fuməln], *v.n.* fumble.

Fund [funt], *m.* (—es, *pl.* —e) find; discovery.

Fundbüro ['funtbyro], *n.* (—s, *pl.* —s) lost property office.

Fundgrube ['funtgru:bə], *f.* (—, *pl.* —n) gold-mine, source, treasure-house.

fundieren [fun'di:rən], *v.a.* found; establish.

fünf [fynf], *num. adj.* five.

Fünfeck ['fynfɛk], *n.* (—s, *pl.* —e) pentagon.

Fünffüßler ['fynffy:slər], *m.* (—s, *pl.* —) (*Poet.*) pentameter.

fünfjährig ['fynfjɛ:riç], *num. adj.* five-year-old.

fünfjährlich ['fynfjɛ:rliç], *num. adj.* quinquennial, five-yearly.

fünfzehn ['fynftse:n], *num. adj.* fifteen.

fünfzig ['fynftsiç], *num. adj.* fifty.

fungieren [fuŋ'gi:rən], *v.n.* — *als*, act as, officiate as.

Funk [funk], *m.* (—s, *no pl.*) radio; wireless; telegraphy.

Funke ['funkə], *m.* (—n, *pl.* —n) spark, sparkle.

funkeln ['funkəln], *v.n.* sparkle, glitter; (*stars*) twinkle.

funkelnagelneu ['funkəlna:gəlnɔy], *adj.* (*coll.*) brand-new.

funken ['funkən], *v.a.* flash (messages); telegraph, broadcast.

Funker ['funkər], *m.* (—s, *pl.* —) wireless operator.

Funksender ['funkzɛndər], *m.* (—s, *pl.* —) radio-transmitter.

Funkspruch ['funkʃprux], *m.* (—s, *pl.* ⁻e) wireless-message.

Funktelegramm ['funktelegram], *n.* (—s, *pl.* —e) radio telegram.

für [fy:r], *prep.* (*Acc.*) for, instead of; *ein — allemal*, once and for all; *an und — sich*, in itself.

Fürbitte ['fy:rbitə], *f.* (—, *pl.* —n) intercession.

Furche ['furçə], *f.* (—, *pl.* —n) furrow; (*face*) wrinkle.

furchen ['furçən], *v.a.* furrow; (*face*) wrinkle.

Furcht [furçt], *f.* (—, *no pl.*) fear, worry, anxiety; dread, fright, terror, apprehension.

furchtbar ['furçtba:r], *adj.* dreadful, terrible, frightful.

fürchten ['fyrçtən], *v.a.* fear, be afraid of. — *v.r. sich — vor*, be afraid of.

fürchterlich ['fyrçtərliç], *adj.* terrible, horrible, awful.

furchtsam ['furçtza:m], *adj.* timid, fearful, apprehensive.

Furie ['fu:rjə], *f.* (—, *pl.* —n) fury, virago.

fürlieb [fyr'li:p], *adv. mit etwas — nehmen*, put up with, be content with s.th.

Furnier [fur'ni:r], *n.* (—s, *pl.* —e) veneer, inlay.

Furore [fu'ro:rə], *n.* (—s, *no pl.*) — *machen*, cause a sensation, create an uproar.

Fürsorge ['fy:rzɔrgə], *f.* (—, *no pl.*) solicitude; provision; welfare.

fürsorglich ['fy:rzɔrgliç], *adj.* thoughtful, with loving care.

Fürsprache ['fy:rʃpra:xə], *f.* (—, *no pl.*) advocacy, intercession.

Fürst [fyrst], *m.* (—en, *pl.* —en) prince, sovereign.

Furt [furt], *f.* (—, *pl.* —en) ford.

Furunkel [fu'runkəl], *m.* (—s, *pl.* —) furuncle, boil.

Fürwort ['fy:rvɔrt], *n.* (—s, *pl.* ⁻er) pronoun.

Fusel ['fu:zəl], *m.* (—s, *no pl.*) bad liquor, (*Am.*) hooch (*sl.*).

Fuß [fu:s], *m.* (—es, *pl.* ⁻e) (*human*) foot; (*object*) base.

Fußangel ['fu:saŋəl], *f.* (—, *pl.* —n) man-trap.

Fußball ['fu:sbal], *m.* (—s, *pl.* ⁻e) football.

Fußboden ['fu:sbo:dən], *m.* (—s, *pl.* ∵) floor.
fußen ['fu:sən], *v.n.* — *auf*, be based upon.
fußfrei ['fu:sfraɪ], *adj.* ankle-length.
Fußgänger ['fu:sgɛŋər], *m.* (—s, *pl.* —) pedestrian.
Fußgestell ['fu:sgəʃtɛl], *n.* (—s, *pl.* —e) pedestal.
Fußpflege ['fu:spfle:gə], *f.* (—, *no pl.*) chiropody.
Fußpunkt ['fu:spuŋkt], *m.* (—s, *no pl.*) nadir.
Fußtritt ['fu:strɪt], *m.* (—s, *pl.* —e) kick.
futsch [futʃ], *excl.* (*coll.*) gone, lost.
Futter ['futər], *n.* (—s, *no pl.*) (*dress*) lining; (*animals*) fodder, feed.
Futteral [futəˈra:l], *n.* (—s, *pl.* —e) case; sheath.
Futterkräuter ['futərkrɔytər], *n. pl.* herbage.
futtern ['futərn], *v.n.* (*coll.*) feed, stuff o.s.
füttern ['fytərn], *v.a.* feed; (*garment*) line.

G

G [ge:], *n.* (—s, *pl.* —s) the letter G; (*Mus.*) *G Dur*, G major; (*Mus.*) *G Moll*, G minor; (*Mus.*) — -*Saite*, G string.
Gabe ['ga:bə], *f.* (—, *pl.* —n) gift, present; donation; *barmherzige* —, alms; (*fig.*) gift, talent.
Gabel ['ga:bəl], *f.* (—, *pl.* —n) fork; (*deer*) antler; (*cart*) shafts.
gabelig ['ga:bəlɪç], *adj.* forked.
Gabelung ['ga:bəluŋ], *f.* (—, *pl.* —en) bifurcation, branching (of road).
Gabelzinke ['ga:bəltsɪŋkə], *f.* (—, *pl.* —n) prong, tine.
Gabun [ga'bu:n], *n.* Gaboon.
gackern ['gakərn], *v.n.* cackle; (*fig.*) chatter.
gaffen ['gafən], *v.n.* gape (at), stare.
Gage ['ga:ʒə], *f.* (—, *pl.* —n) salary, pay, fee.
gähnen ['gɛ:nən], *v.n.* yawn, gape.
Galan [ga'la:n], *m.* (—s, *pl.* —e) lover, gallant.
galant [ga'lant], *adj.* polite, courteous; —*es Abenteuer*, love affair.
Galanterie [galantə'ri:], *f.* (—, *pl.* —n) courtesy.
Galanteriewaren [galantə'ri:va:rən], *f. pl.* fancy goods.
Galeere [ga'le:rə], *f.* (—, *pl.* —n) galley.
Galerie [galə'ri:], *f.* (—, *pl.* —n) gallery.
Galgen ['galgən], *m.* (—s, *pl.* —) gallows, gibbet; scaffold.

Galgenfrist ['galgənfrɪst], *f.* (—, *no pl.*) short delay, respite.
Galgenhumor ['galgənhumo:r], *m.* (—s, *no pl.*) wry or grim humour.
Galgenvogel ['galgənfo:gəl], *m.* (—s, *pl.* ∵) gallows-bird.
Galizien [ga'li:tsjən], *n.* Galicia.
Gallapfel ['galapfəl], *m.* (—s, *pl.* ∵) gall-nut.
Galle ['galə], *f.* (—, *pl.* —n) gall, bile.
Gallenblase ['galənbla:zə], *f.* (—, *pl.* —n) gall-bladder.
Gallert ['galərt], *n.* (—s, *no pl.*) jelly.
Gallien ['galjən], *n.* Gaul.
gallig ['galɪç], *adj.* bilious.
galvanisieren [galvani'zi:rən], *v.a.* galvanize.
Gamaschen [ga'maʃən], *f. pl.* spats, gaiters.
Gang [gaŋ], *m.* (—es, *pl.* ∵e) walk, gait; (*horse*) pace; (*house*) passage, corridor; (*meal*) course, dish; (*action*) progress, course; (*sport*) round, bout; (*machine*) motion; stroke; (*Motor.*) gear.
gang [gaŋ], *adj.* — *und gäbe*, customary, usual, common.
Gangart ['gaŋa:rt], *f.* (—, *pl.* —en) gait; (*horse*) pace.
gangbar ['gaŋba:r], *adj.* marketable, saleable; (*road*) passable; practicable.
Gans [gans], *f.* (—, *pl.* ∵e) (*Orn.*) goose.
Gänseblümchen ['gɛnzəbly:mçən], *n.* (—s, *pl.* —) daisy.
Gänsefüßchen ['gɛnzəfy:sçən], *n. pl.* (*coll.*) inverted commas, quotation marks.
Gänsehaut ['gɛnzəhaut], *f.* (—, *no pl.*) goose-flesh, goose-pimples.
Gänserich ['gɛnzərɪç], *m.* (—s, *pl.* —e) (*Orn.*) gander.
ganz ['gants], *adj.* whole, entire, all; complete, total.
gänzlich ['gɛntslɪç], *adj.* whole, total, entire, full, complete.
gar [ga:r], *adj.* sufficiently cooked, done. — *adv.* very, quite.
garantieren [garan'ti:rən], *v.a.* guarantee, warrant.
Garaus ['ga:raus], *m.* (—, *no pl.*) *einem den* — *machen*, finish s.o., kill s.o.
Garbe ['garbə], *f.* (—, *pl.* —n) sheaf.
Garde ['gardə], *f.* (—, *pl.* —n) guard, guards.
Garderobe [gardə'ro:bə], *f.* (—, *pl.* —n) wardrobe; cloak-room; (*Theat.*) dressing-room.
Gardine [gar'di:nə], *f.* (—, *pl.* —n) curtain.
Gardist [gar'dɪst], *m.* (—en, *pl.* —en) guardsman.
gären ['gɛ:rən], *v.n.* ferment; effervesce.
Garn [garn], *n.* (—s, *pl.* —e) yarn, thread.
Garnele [gar'ne:lə], *f.* (—, *pl.* —n) (*Zool.*) shrimp; *große* —, prawn.
garnieren [gar'ni:rən], *v.a.* trim, garnish.
Garnison [garni'zo:n], *f.* (—, *pl.* —en) garrison.

Garnitur

Garnitur [garniˈtuːr], *f.* (—, *pl.* **—en**) trimming; set.

Garnröllchen [ˈgarnrœlçən], *n.* (**—s**, *pl.* —) reel of thread.

garstig [ˈgarstɪç], *adj.* nasty, loathsome, ugly.

Garten [ˈgartən], *m.* (**—s**, *pl.* ∵) garden.

Gartenlaube [ˈgartənlaubə], *f.* (—, *pl.* **—n**) bower, arbour.

Gärtner [ˈgɛrtnər], *m.* (**—s**, *pl.* —) gardener.

Gärtnerei [gɛrtnəˈraɪ], *f.* (—, *pl.* **—en**) horticulture; market-garden; (plant) nursery.

Gärung [ˈgɛːruŋ], *f.* (—, *pl.* **—en**) fermentation, effervescence.

Gas [gaːs], *n.* (**—es**, **—e**) gas; — *geben*, (*Motor.*) accelerate.

gasartig [ˈgaːsartɪç], *adj.* gaseous.

Gäßchen [ˈgɛsçən], *n.* (**—s**, *pl.* —) narrow alley; lane.

Gasse [ˈgasə], *f.* (—, *pl.* **—n**) alleyway, lane; (*rare*) street.

Gassenbube [ˈgasənbuːbə] *see* **Gassenjunge.**

Gassenhauer [ˈgasənhauər], *m.* (**—s**, *pl.* —), street-song, vulgar ballad; pop song.

Gassenjunge [ˈgasənjuŋə], *m.* (**—n**, *pl.* **—n**) street-urchin.

Gast [gast], *m.* (**—s**, *pl.* ∵e) guest, visitor.

gastfrei [ˈgastfraɪ], *adj.* hospitable.

Gastfreund [ˈgastfrɔynt], *m.* (**—s**, *pl.* **—e**) guest; host. .

Gastfreundschaft [ˈgastfrɔyntʃaft], *f.* (—, *no pl.*) hospitality.

Gastgeber [ˈgastgeːbər], *m.* (**—s**, *pl.* —) host.

Gasthaus [ˈgasthaus], *n.* (**—es**, *pl.* ∵er), **Gasthof** [ˈgasthoːf], *m.* (**—es**, *pl.* ∵e) inn, hotel, public house.

gastieren [gasˈtiːrən], *v.n.* (*Theat.*) appear as a guest artist; star.

gastlich [ˈgastlɪç], *adj.* hospitable.

Gastmahl [ˈgastmaːl], *n.* (**—s**, *pl.* **—e**) banquet, feast.

Gastrecht [ˈgastrɛçt], *n.* (**—s**, *no pl.*) right of hospitality.

Gastspiel [ˈgastʃpiːl], *n.* (**—s**, *pl.* **—e**) (*Theat.*) performance by visiting company.

Gaststätte [ˈgaststɛtə], *f.* (—, *pl.* **—n**) restaurant.

Gaststube [ˈgastʃtuːbə], *f.* (—, *pl.* **—n**) hotel lounge; guest room.

Gastwirt [ˈgastvɪrt], *m.* (**—s**, *pl.* **—e**) landlord.

Gastwirtin [ˈgastvɪrtɪn], *f.* (—, *pl.* **—nen**) landlady.

Gastzimmer [ˈgasttsɪmər], *n.* (**—s**, *pl.* —) *see* **Gaststube**; spare bedroom.

Gatte [ˈgatə], *m.* (**—n**, *pl.* **—n**) husband, spouse, consort.

Gatter [ˈgatər], *n.* (**—s**, *pl.* —) grate, lattice, grating.

Gattin [ˈgatɪn], *f.* (—, *pl.* **—nen**) wife, spouse, consort.

Gattung [ˈgatuŋ], *f.* (—, *pl.* **—en**) kind, species, sort, class; breed, genus; (*Lit.*) genre.

Gau [gau], *m.* (**—s**, *pl.* **—e**) district, province.

gaukeln [ˈgaukəln], *v.n.* juggle. — *v.a.* dazzle.

Gaul [gaul], *m.* (**—s**, *pl.* ∵e) (old) horse, nag; *einem geschenkten — sieht man nicht ins Maul*, never look a gift horse in the mouth.

Gaumen [ˈgaumən], *m.* (**—s**, *pl.* —) palate.

Gauner [ˈgaunər], *m.* (**—s**, *pl.* —) rogue, sharper, swindler, cheat.

gaunern [ˈgaunərn], *v.n.* cheat, trick, swindle.

Gaunersprache [ˈgaunərʃpraːxə], *f.* (—, *no pl.*) thieves' slang.

Gaze [ˈgaːzə], *f.* (—, *pl.* **—n**) gauze.

Gazelle [gaˈtsɛlə], *f.* (—, *pl.* **—n**) (*Zool.*) gazelle, antelope.

Geächtete [gəˈɛçtətə], *m.* (**—n**, *pl.* **—n**) outlaw.

Geächze [gəˈɛçtsə], *n.* (**—s**, *no pl.*) moaning, groaning.

Geäder [gəˈɛːdər], *n.* (**—s**, *no pl.*) veins, arteries; veining.

geädert [gəˈɛdərt], *adj.* veined, streaked; grained.

-geartet [gəˈaːrtət], *adj.* (*suffix in compounds*) -natured.

Gebäck [gəˈbɛk], *n.* (**—s**, *no pl.*) pastry, rolls, cakes.

Gebälk [gəˈbɛlk], *n.* (**—s**, *no pl.*) timberwork, timber-frame.

Gebärde [gəˈbɛːrdə], *f.* (—, *pl.* **—n**) gesture.

gebärden [gəˈbɛːrdən], *v.r. sich —*, behave.

Gebaren [gəˈbaːrən], *n.* (**—s**, *no pl.*) demeanour.

gebären [gəˈbɛːrən], *v.a. irr.* bear, bring forth, give birth to, be delivered of.

Gebärmutter [gəˈbɛːrmutər], *f.* (—, *no pl.*) womb, uterus.

Gebäude [gəˈbɔydə], *n.* (**—s**, *pl.* —) building, edifice.

Gebein [gəˈbaɪn], *n.* (**—s**, *pl.* **—e**) bones, skeleton; (*fig.*) remains.

Gebell [gəˈbɛl], *n.* (**—s**, *no pl.*) barking.

geben [ˈgeːbən], *v.a. irr.* give, present; confer, bestow; yield; (*cards*) deal. — *v.r. sich —*, show o.s., behave; abate; *das gibt sich*, that won't last long; *es gibt . . .*, there is . . .; *was gibt's?* what's the matter?

Geber [ˈgeːbər], *m.* (**—s**, *pl.* —) giver, donor.

Gebet [gəˈbeːt], *n.* (**—s**, *pl.* **—e**) prayer; *sein — verrichten*, say o.'s prayers; *ins — nehmen*, question s.o. thoroughly.

Gebiet [gəˈbiːt], *n.* (**—s**, *pl.* **—e**) district, territory; (*Am.*) precinct; jurisdiction; (*fig.*) province, field, sphere, domain.

gebieten [gəˈbiːtən], *v.a. irr.* command, order.

Gebieter [gəˈbiːtər], *m.* (**—s**, *pl.* —) lord, master, ruler.

Gebilde [gə'bɪldə], *n.* (**—s,** *pl.* **—**) form, thing; formation, structure; figment.

gebildet [gə'bɪldət], *adj.* educated, cultured, refined.

Gebirge [gə'bɪrgə], *n.* (**—s,** *pl.* **—**) mountains.

Gebirgskamm [gə'bɪrkskam], *m.* (**—s,** *pl.* ⁻e) mountain-ridge.

Gebiß [gə'bɪs], *n.* (**—sses,** *pl.* **—sse**) set of (false) teeth, denture; (*horse*) bit.

Gebläse [gə'blɛːzə], *n.* (**—s,** *pl.* **—**) bellows; blower.

Gebläsemaschine [gə'blɛːzəmaʃiːnə], *f.* (**—,** *pl.* **—n**) blower.

Gebläseofen [gə'blɛːzəoːfən], *m.* (**—s,** *pl.* ⁻) blast-furnace.

geblümt [gə'blyːmt], *adj.* flowered.

Geblüt [gə'blyːt], *n.* (**—s,** *no pl.*) blood; race, line, lineage, stock.

geboren [gə'boːrən], *adj.* born.

geborgen [gə'bɔrgən], *adj.* saved, hidden, sheltered, rescued.

Gebot [gə'boːt], *n.* (**—s,** *pl.* **—e**) order, decree, command; (*Bibl.*) Commandment.

geboten [gə'boːtən], *adj.* necessary, advisable.

Gebräu [gə'brɔy], *n.* (**—s,** *no pl.*) brew, concoction, mixture.

Gebrauch [gə'braux], *m.* (**—s,** *pl.* ⁻e) use; employment; custom, usage, habit, practice; (*rare*) rite.

gebrauchen [gə'brauxən], *v.a.* use, make use of, employ.

gebräuchlich [gə'brɔyçlɪç], *adj.* usual, customary, common.

Gebrauchsanweisung [gə'brauxsanvaɪzuŋ], *f.* (**—,** *pl.* **—en**) directions for use.

gebraucht [gə'brauxt], *adj.* used, second-hand.

Gebrechen [gə'brɛçən], *n.* (**—s,** *pl.* **—**) infirmity.

gebrechen [gə'brɛçən], *v.n. irr. es gebricht mir an,* I am in want of, I lack.

gebrechlich [gə'brɛçlɪç], *adj.* infirm, frail, weak.

gebrochen [gə'brɔxən], *adj.* broken; **—es Deutsch,** broken German.

Gebrüder [gə'bryːdər], *m. pl.* (*Comm.*) brothers.

Gebrüll [gə'bryl], *n.* (**—s,** *no pl.*) roaring; (*cows*) lowing.

Gebühr [gə'byːr], *f.* (**—,** *pl.* **—en**) charge, due; fee; tax, duty.

gebühren [gə'byːrən], *v.n.* be due to s.o. — *v.r. sich —, wie es sich gebührt,* as it ought to be, as is right and proper.

gebunden [gə'bundən], *adj.* (*fig.*) bound, committed; (*Poet.*) metrical.

Geburt [gə'buːrt], *f.* (**—,** *pl.* **—en**) birth.

gebürtig [gə'byrtɪç], *adj.* a native of.

Geburtsfehler [gə'buːrtsfeːlər], *m.* (**—s,** *pl.* **—**) congenital defect.

Geburtshelfer [gə'buːrtshɛlfər], *m.* (**—s,** *pl.* **—**) obstetrician.

Geburtshelferin [gə'buːrtshɛlfərɪn], *f.* (**—,** *pl.* **—nen**) midwife.

Geburtsort [gə'buːrtsɔrt], *m.* (**—s,** *pl.* **—e**) birthplace.

Geburtsschein [gə'buːrtsʃaɪn], *m.* (**—(e)s,** *pl.* **—e**) birth certificate.

Geburtswehen [gə'buːrtsveːən], *f. pl.* birthpangs; labour pains.

Gebüsch [gə'byʃ], *n.* (**—es,** *pl.* **—e**) bushes, thicket; underwood.

Geck [gɛk], *m.* (**—en,** *pl.* **—en**) fop, dandy; (*carnival*) fool.

geckenhaft ['gɛkənhaft], *adj.* foppish, dandyish.

Gedächtnis [gə'dɛçtnɪs], *n.* (**—ses,** *no pl.*) memory; remembrance, recollection; *im — behalten,* keep in mind.

Gedanke [gə'daŋkə], *m.* (**—ns,** *pl.* **—n**) thought, idea.

Gedankenfolge [gə'daŋkənfɔlgə], *f.* (**—,** *no pl.*), **Gedankengang** [gə'daŋkəngaŋ], *m.* (**—s,** *pl.* ⁻e) sequence of thought, train of thought.

Gedankenstrich [gə'daŋkənʃtrɪç], *m.* (**—s,** *pl.* **—e**) dash; hyphen.

Gedärm [gə'dɛrm], *n.* (**—s,** *pl.* **—e**) bowels, intestines, entrails.

Gedeck [gə'dɛk], *n.* (**—s,** *pl.* **—e**) cover; menu; place laid at a table.

gedeihen [gə'daɪən], *v.n. irr.* (*aux. sein*) thrive, prosper; progress.

gedeihlich [gə'daɪlɪç], *adj.* thriving, salutary.

gedenken [gə'dɛŋkən], *v.n. irr.* (*Genit.*) think of, remember; *— etwas zu tun,* intend to do s.th.

Gedenken [gə'dɛŋkən], *n.* (**—s,** *no pl.*) remembrance.

Gedenkfeier [gə'dɛŋkfaɪər], *f.* (**—,** *pl.* **—n**) commemoration.

Gedicht [gə'dɪçt], *n.* (**—s,** *pl.* **—e**) poem.

gediegen [gə'diːgən], *adj.* solid, sound, genuine, true, honourable, sterling.

Gedränge [gə'drɛŋə], *n.* (**—s,** *no pl.*) crowd, throng; crush.

Gedrängtheit [gə'drɛŋkthaɪt], *f.* (**—,** *no pl.*) conciseness.

gedrungen [gə'druŋən], *adj.* thick-set, stocky; compact; concise (style).

Geduld [gə'dult], *f.* (**—,** *no pl.*) patience, forbearance.

gedulden [gə'duldən], *v.r. sich —,* be patient.

geduldig [gə'duldɪç], *adj.* patient, forbearing, indulgent.

Geduld(s)spiel [gə'dult(s)ʃpiːl], *n.* (**—s,** *pl.* **—e**) puzzle; (*Cards*) patience.

gedunsen [gə'dunzən], *adj.* bloated.

geeignet [gə'aɪgnət], *adj.* suitable, fit, appropriate, apt.

Gefahr [gə'faːr], *f.* (**—,** *pl.* **—en**) danger, peril, hazard, risk; *— laufen,* run the risk.

gefährden [gə'fɛːrdən], *v.a.* endanger, imperil, jeopardize.

gefährlich [gə'fɛːrlɪç], *adj.* dangerous, perilous.

Gefährt [gə'fɛːrt], *n.* (**—s,** *pl.* **—e**) (*obs.*) vehicle, conveyance.

Gefährte [gə'fɛːrtə], *m.* (**—en,** *pl.* **—en**) comrade, companion, fellow.

Gefälle

Gefälle [gə'fɛlə], *n.* (—s, *pl.* —e) fall, descent, incline, gradient.

Gefallen [gə'falən], *m.* (—s, *no pl.*) pleasure, liking; favour, kindness.

gefallen (1) [gə'falən], *v.n. irr.* please; *es gefällt mir,* I like it; *wie gefällt Ihnen* ...; how do you like ....

gefallen (2) [gə'falən], *adj.* (*Mil.*) fallen, killed in action.

gefällig [gə'fɛlɪç], *adj.* pleasing, accommodating, obliging, anxious to please; *was ist* —? what can I do for you?

Gefälligkeit [gə'fɛlɪçkaɪt], *f.* (—, *pl.* —en) courtesy; favour, service, good turn.

gefälligst [gə'fɛlɪçst], *adv.* if you please.

Gefallsucht [gə'falzuxt], *f.* (—, *no pl.*) coquetry.

gefallsüchtig [gə'falzyçtɪç], *adj.* coquettish.

gefangen [gə'faŋən], *adj.* in prison, imprisoned, captive.

Gefangene [gə'faŋənə], *m.* (—n, *pl.* —n) prisoner, captive.

Gefangennahme [gə'faŋənna:mə], *f.* (—, *no pl.*) arrest, capture.

Gefangenschaft [gə'faŋənʃaft], *f.* (—, *no pl.*) captivity, imprisonment, detention; *in — geraten,* be taken prisoner.

Gefängnis [gə'fɛŋnɪs], *n.* (—sses, *pl.* —sse) prison, gaol.

Gefäß [gə'fɛ:s], *n.* (—es, *pl.* —e) vessel.

gefaßt [gə'fast], *adj.* collected, composed, ready; calm; *sich auf etwas — machen,* prepare o.s. for s.th.

Gefecht [gə'fɛçt], *n.* (—s, *pl.* —e) fight, battle, combat; action, engagement.

gefeit [gə'faɪt], *adj.* proof against.

Gefieder [gə'fi:dər], *n.* (—s, *no pl.*) plumage, feathers.

Gefilde [gə'fɪldə], *n.* (—s, *pl.* —) (*Poet.*) fields, plain.

Geflecht [gə'flɛçt], *n.* (—s, *no pl.*) wicker-work, texture.

geflissentlich [gə'flɪsəntlɪç], *adj.* intentional, wilful, with a purpose.

Geflügel [gə'fly:gəl], *n.* (—s, *no pl.*) fowls, poultry.

geflügelt [gə'fly:gəlt], *adj.* winged; *—e Worte,* household word, familiar quotation.

Geflüster [gə'flystər], *n.* (—s, *no pl.*) whispering, whisper.

Gefolge [gə'fɔlgə], *n.* (—s, *no pl.*) retinue, following.

gefräßig [gə'frɛ:sɪç], *adj.* voracious, gluttonous.

Gefreite [gə'fraɪtə], *m.* (—n, *pl.* —n) (*Mil.*) lance-corporal.

gefrieren [gə'fri:rən], *v.n. irr.* (*aux.* sein) freeze; congeal.

Gefrierpunkt [gə'fri:rpuŋkt], *m.* (—s, *no pl.*) freezing point, zero.

Gefrorene [gə'fro:rənə], *n.* (—n, *no pl.*) ice-cream.

Gefüge [gə'fy:gə], *n.* (—s, *no pl.*) joints, structure, construction; frame.

gefügig [gə'fy:gɪç], *adj.* pliant; docile; *einen — machen,* make s.o. amenable, persuade s.o.

Gefühl [gə'fy:l], *n.* (—s, *pl.* —e) feeling, sense, sensation.

gegen ['ge:gən], *prep.* (*Acc.*) against; towards; about, near; in comparison with; in the direction of; opposed to; in exchange for; — *Quittung,* against receipt. — *adv., prefix.* counter, opposing, contrary.

Gegend ['ge:gənt], *f.* (—, *pl.* —en) region, country, part.

Gegengewicht ['ge:gəngəvɪçt], *n.* (—s, *pl.* —e) counterweight, counterpoise.

Gegengift ['ge:gəngɪft], *n.* (—s, *pl.* —e) antidote.

Gegenleistung ['ge:gənlaɪstuŋ], *f.* (—, *pl.* —en) return; service in return; *Leistung und* —, give and take.

Gegenrede ['ge:gənre:də], *f.* (—, *pl.* —n) contradiction; objection.

Gegensatz ['ge:gənzats], *m.* (—es, *pl.* ⁝e) contrast, opposition, antithesis.

gegensätzlich ['ge:gənzɛtslɪç], *adj.* contrary, adverse.

Gegenseite ['ge:gənzaɪtə], *f.* (—, *pl.* —n) opposite side; (*coin*) reverse.

gegenseitig ['ge:gənzaɪtɪç], *adj.* reciprocal, mutual.

Gegenstand ['ge:gənʃtant], *m.* (—s, *pl.* ⁝e) object; subject, matter.

gegenstandslos ['ge:gənʃtantslo:s], *adj.* superfluous, irrelevant.

Gegenstück ['ge:gənʃtyk], *n.* (—s, *pl.* —e) counterpart.

Gegenteil ['ge:gəntaɪl], *n.* (—s, *no pl.*) contrary; *im* —, on the contrary.

gegenüber [ge:gən'y:bər], *prep.* (*Dat.*) opposite to, facing. — *adv.* opposite.

Gegenüberstellung [ge:gən'y:bərʃtelun], *f.* (—, *pl.* —en) confrontation.

Gegenwart ['ge:gənvart], *f.* (—, *no pl.*) presence; (*Gram.*) present tense.

Gegenwehr ['ge:gənve:r], *f.* (—, *no pl.*) defence, resistance.

Gegenwirkung ['ge:gənvɪrkuŋ], *f.* (—, *pl.* —en) reaction, counter-effect.

gegenzeichnen ['ge:gəntsaɪçnən], *v.a.* countersign.

Gegner ['ge:gnər], *m.* (—s, *pl.* —) opponent, adversary, antagonist.

gegnerisch [ge:'gnərɪʃ], *adj.* adverse, antagonistic.

Gegnerschaft ['ge:gnərʃaft], *f.* (—, *no pl.*) antagonism; opposition.

Gehalt (1) [gə'halt], *m.* (—s, *no pl.*) contents; (*fig.*) value, standard.

Gehalt (2) [gə'halt], *n.* (—s, *pl.* ⁝er) salary, stipend; pay.

Gehaltszulage [gə'haltstsu:la:gə], *f.* (—, *pl.* —n) rise (in salary); increment; (*Am.*) raise.

gehaltvoll [gə'haltfɔl], *adj.* substantial.

Gehänge [gə'hɛŋə], *n.* (—s, *pl.* —) slope; festoon, garland.

geharnischt [gə'harnɪʃt], *adj.* armoured, steel-clad; (*fig.*) severe.

gehässig [gə'hɛsɪç], *adj.* malicious, spiteful.

Gehäuse [gə'hɔyzə], *n.* (—s, *pl.* —) casing, case; (*snail*) shell.

Gehege [gə'he:gə], *n.* (—s, *pl.* —) enclosure; *einem ins — kommen*, trespass on s.o.'s preserves.

geheim [gə'haɪm], *adj.* secret, clandestine.

Geheimnis [gə'haɪmnɪs], *n.* (—ses, *pl.* —se) secret, mystery.

geheimnisvoll [gə'haɪmnɪsfɔl], *adj.* mysterious.

Geheimrat [gə'haɪmra:t], *m.* (—s, *pl.* ⁝e) Privy Councillor.

Geheimschrift [gə'haɪmʃrɪft], *f.* (—, *pl.* —en) cryptography.

Geheimsprache [gə'haɪmʃpra:xə], *f.* (—, *pl.* —en) cipher.

Geheiß [gə'haɪs], *n.* (—es, *no pl.*) command, order, bidding.

gehen ['ge:ən], *v.n. irr.* (*aux.* sein) go, walk; (*Mach.*) work, function; (*goods*) sell; (*dough*) rise; *er lässt sich —*, he lets himself go; *er lässt es sich gut —*, he enjoys himself; *einem an die Hand —*, lend s.o. a hand, assist s.o.; *in Erfüllung —*, come true; *in sich —*, reflect; *wie geht es dir?* how are you? *es geht mir gut*, I am well.

geheuer [gə'hɔyər], *adj.* (*only in neg.*) *nicht ganz —*, creepy, eerie, uncanny; (*coll.*) fishy.

Gehilfe [gə'hɪlfə], *m.* (—n, *pl.* —n) assistant, helper.

Gehirn [gə'hɪrn], *n.* (—s, *pl.* —e) brain, brains.

Gehirnhautentzündung [gə'hɪrnhaut-ɛntsynduŋ], *f.* (—, *pl.* —en) meningitis, cerebral inflammation.

Gehirnschlag [gə'hɪrnʃla:k], *m.* (—s, *pl.* ⁝e) apoplexy.

Gehöft [gə'hœft], *n.* (—es, *pl.* —e) farmstead.

Gehör [gə'hø:r], (—s, *no pl.*) hearing; *gutes —*, musical ear.

gehorchen [gə'hɔrçən], *v.n.* obey; *nicht —*, disobey.

gehören [gə'hø:rən], *v.n.* belong. — *v.r. sich —*, be the proper thing to do.

gehörig [gə'hø:rɪç], *adj. dazu —*, belonging to, referring to; due, fit, proper, thorough; (*fig.*) sound.

Gehörn [gə'hœrn], *n.* (—s, *pl.* —e) horns, antlers.

gehörnt [gə'hœrnt], *adj.* horned; (*fig.*) duped (husband).

Gehorsam [gə'ho:rza:m], *m.*(—s, *no pl.*) obedience; *— leisten*, show obedience; *den — verweigern*, refuse to obey.

gehorsam [gə'ho:rza:m], *adj.* obedient, dutiful, submissive.

Gehrock ['ge:rɔk], *m.* (—s, *pl.* ⁝e) frock-coat.

Geier ['gaɪər], *m.* (—s, *pl.* —) (*Orn.*) vulture.

Geifer ['gaɪfər], *m.* (—s, *no pl.*) saliva, drivel; (*animals*) foam; (*fig.*) venom, rancour.

geifern ['gaɪfərn], *v.n.* slaver, drivel; (*fig.*) foam at the mouth; give vent to o.'s anger.

Geige ['gaɪgə], *f.* (—, *pl.* —n) violin, fiddle.

Geigenharz ['gaɪgənha:rts], *n.* (—es, *no pl.*) colophony; rosin.

Geigensteg ['gaɪgənʃte:k], *m.* (—s, *pl.* —e) bridge of a violin.

Geiger ['gaɪgər], *m.* (—s, *pl.* —) violinplayer, violinist.

geil [gaɪl], *adj.* rank; lecherous, lascivious.

Geisel ['gaɪzəl], *f.* (—, *pl.* —n) hostage.

Geiß [gaɪs], *f.* (—, *pl.* —en) goat, shegoat.

Geißblatt ['gaɪsblat], *n.* (—s, *no pl.*) (*Bot.*) honeysuckle.

Geißbock ['gaɪsbɔk], *m.* (—s, *pl.* ⁝e) billy-goat.

Geißel ['gaɪsəl], *f.* (—, *pl.* —n) scourge.

geißeln ['gaɪsəln], *v.a.* scourge, whip, flagellate.

Geist [gaɪst], *m.* (—es, *pl.* —er) spirit, mind; brains, intellect; wit; apparition, ghost.

Geisterbeschwörung ['gaɪstərbəʃvø:-ruŋ], *f.* (—, *pl.* —en) evocation (of spirits); necromancy; exorcism.

geisterhaft ['gaɪstərhaft], *adj.* ghostly, spectral, weird.

Geisterwelt ['gaɪstərvɛlt], *f.* (—, *no pl.*) world of spirits.

geistesabwesend ['gaɪstəsapve:zənt], *adj.* absent-minded.

Geistesfreiheit ['gaɪstəsfraɪhaɪt], *f.* (—, *no pl.*) freedom of thought.

Geistesgegenwart ['gaɪstəsge:gənvart], *f.* (—, *no pl.*) presence of mind.

Geisteskraft ['gaɪstəskraft], *f.* (—, *pl.* ⁝e) faculty of the mind.

Geistesstörung ['gaɪstəsʃtø:ruŋ], *f.* (—, *pl.* —en) mental aberration.

Geistesverfassung ['gaɪstəsfɛrfasuŋ], *f.* (—, *no pl.*) state of mind.

geistesverwandt ['gaɪstəsfɛrvant], *adj.* congenial.

Geistesverwirrung ['gaɪstəsfɛrvɪruŋ], *f.* (—, *no pl.*) bewilderment.

Geisteswissenschaften ['gaɪstəsvɪsən-ʃaftən], *f.pl.* (*Univ.*) Arts, Humanities.

Geisteszerrüttung ['gaɪstəstsɛrytuŋ], *f.* (—, *no pl.*) mental derangement, insanity.

geistig ['gaɪstɪç], *adj.* intellectual, mental; spiritual; *—e Getränke*, alcoholic liquors.

geistlich ['gaɪstlɪç], *adj.* spiritual; religious; ecclesiastical, clerical; *—er Orden*, religious order; *—er Stand*, holy orders, the Clergy.

Geistliche ['gaɪstlɪçə], *m.* (—n, *pl.* —n) priest, clergyman, cleric; minister of religion.

Geistlichkeit ['gaɪstlɪçkaɪt], *f.* (—, *no pl.*) clergy.

geistlos ['gaɪstlo:s], *adj.* dull, stupid.

geistreich ['gaɪstraɪç], *adj.* clever, witty.

Geiz [gaɪts], *m.* (—es, *no pl.*) avarice, covetousness.

geizen ['gaɪtsən], *v.n.* be miserly.

Geizhals ['gaɪtshals], *m.* (—es, *pl.* ⸚e) miser, niggard.

Geizkragen ['gaɪtskra:gən], *m.* (—s, *pl.* —) *see* **Geizhals**.

Gekreisch [gə'kraɪʃ], *n.* (—es, *no pl.*) screaming, shrieks.

Gekritzel [gə'krɪtsəl], *n.* (—s, *no pl.*) scrawling, scribbling.

Gekröse [gə'krø:zə], *n.* (—s, *no pl.*) tripe; (*Anat.*) mesentery.

gekünstelt [gə'kynstəlt], *adj.* artificial, affected.

Gelächter [gə'lɛçtər], *n.* (—s, *no pl.*) laughter.

Gelage [gə'la:gə], *n.* (—s, *pl.* —) (*obs.*) feast, banquet.

Gelände [gə'lɛndə], *n.* (—s, *pl.* —) terrain, region; landscape.

Geländer [gə'lɛndər], *n.* (—s, *pl.* —) railing, balustrade, banister.

gelangen [gə'laŋən], *v.n.* (*aux.* sein) arrive, come (to).

Gelaß [gə'las], *n.* (—sses, *pl.* —sse) (*obs.*) room, chamber.

gelassen [gə'lasən], *adj.* calm, composed, collected.

geläufig [gə'lɔyfɪç], *adj.* fluent.

gelaunt [gə'launt], *adj.* disposed.

Geläute [gə'lɔytə], *n.* (—s, *no pl.*) ringing, chiming; bells.

geläutert [gə'lɔytərt], *adj.* purified, cleansed.

gelb [gɛlp], *adj.* yellow, amber.

Gelbschnabel ['gɛlpʃna:bəl], *m.* (—s, *pl.* ⸚) (*Orn.*) fledg(e)ling; greenhorn.

Gelbsucht ['gɛlpzuxt], *f.* (—, *no pl.*) jaundice.

Geld [gɛlt], *n.* (—es, *pl.* —er) money, currency, coin; *bares* —, ready money, hard cash; *kleines* —, small change.

Geldanweisung ['gɛltanvaɪzuŋ], *f.* (—*pl.* —en) money-order.

Geldbuße ['gɛltbu:sə], *f.* (—, *pl.* —n) fine.

Geldkurs ['gɛltkurs], *m.* (—es, *pl.* —e) rate of exchange.

Geldmittel ['gɛltmɪtəl], *n. pl.* pecuniary resources, financial resources.

Geldschrank ['gɛltʃraŋk], *m.* (—s, *pl.* ⸚e) safe.

Geldstrafe ['gɛltʃtra:fə], *f.* (—, *pl.* —n) fine.

Geldverlegenheit ['gɛltfɛrle:gənhaɪt], *f.* (—, *pl.* —en) pecuniary embarrassment, financial difficulty.

Geldwährung ['gɛltvɛ:ruŋ], *f.* (—, *pl.* —en) currency.

Geldwechsel ['gɛltvɛksəl], *m.* (—s, *no pl.*) exchange.

Gelee [ʒə'le:], *n.* (—s, *pl.* —s) jelly.

gelegen [gə'le:gən], *adj.* situated, situate; *das kommt mir gerade* —, that suits me; *mir ist daran* —, *dass*, I am anxious that.

Gelegenheit [gə'le:gənhaɪt], *f.* (—, *pl.* —en) occasion, chance, opportunity; facility; *bei* —, one of these days.

Gelegenheitskauf [gə'le:gənhaɪtskauf], *m.* (—s, *pl.* ⸚e) bargain.

gelegentlich [gə'le:gəntlɪç], *adj.* occasional.

gelehrig [gə'le:rɪç], *adj.* docile, tractable.

Gelehrsamkeit [gə'le:rza:mkaɪt], *f.* (—, *no pl.*) learning, erudition.

gelehrt [gə'le:rt], *adj.* learned, erudite.

Gelehrte [gə'le:rtə], *m.* (—n, *pl.* —n) scholar, man of learning, savant.

Geleise [gə'laɪzə], *n.* (—s, *pl.* —) *see* **Gleis**.

Geleit [gə'laɪt], *n.* (—s, *no pl.*) escort, accompaniment; (*Naut.*) convoy; *sicheres* —, safe conduct.

geleiten [gə'laɪtən], *v.a.* accompany, conduct, escort.

Gelenk [gə'lɛŋk], *n.* (—s, *pl.* —e) (*human*) joint; (*chain*) link.

Gelenkentzündung [gə'lɛŋkɛnttsyn-duŋ], *f.* (—, *pl.* —en) (*Med.*) arthritis.

gelenkig [gə'lɛŋkɪç], *adj.* flexible, pliant, nimble, supple.

Gelenkrheumatismus [gə'lɛŋkrɔyma-tɪsmus], *m.* (—, *no pl.*) (*Med.*) rheumatoid arthritis, rheumatic gout.

Gelichter [gə'lɪçtər], *n.* (—s, *no pl.*) riff-raff.

Geliebte [gə'li:ptə], *m.* (—n, *pl.* —n) lover, sweetheart, beloved. — *f.* (—n, *pl.* —n) mistress; beloved.

gelinde [gə'lɪndə], *adj.* soft, smooth, gentle, mild; *gesagt*, to say the least.

Gelingen [gə'lɪŋən], *n.* (—s, *no pl.*) success.

gelingen [gə'lɪŋən], *v.n. irr.* (*aux.* sein) succeed; *es gelingt mir*, I succeed.

gellen ['gɛlən], *v.n.* yell; shrill.

geloben [gə'lo:bən], *v.a.* (*aux.* haben) promise solemnly, vow; *das Gelobte Land*, the Promised Land.

Gelöbnis [gə'lø:pnɪs], *n.* (—ses, *pl.* —se) vow, promise.

gelt [gɛlt], *inter.* (*coll.*) isn't it? don't you think so?

gelten ['gɛltən], *v.a. irr.* be worth, cost. — *v.n.* count (as), be valid.

Geltung ['gɛltuŋ], *f.* (—, *no pl.*) value, importance.

Gelübde [gə'lypdə], *n.* (—s, *pl.* —) vow, solemn promise *or* undertaking.

gelungen [gə'luŋən], *adj.* (*coll.*) funny, capital.

Gelüst [gə'lyst], *n.* (—s, *pl.* —e) appetite, desire.

gelüsten [gə'lystən], *v.a.* — *nach*, long for, covet.

Gemach [gə'ma:x], *n.* (—es, *pl.* ⸚er) (*Poet.*) chamber, room; apartment.

gemach [gə'ma:x], *adv.* slowly, softly, by degrees.

gemächlich [gə'mɛçlɪç], *adj.* slow, soft, easy, unhurried, leisurely.

Gemahl [gə'ma:l], *m.* (—s, *pl.* —e) spouse, husband, consort.

Gemahlin [gə'ma:lɪn], *f.* (—, *pl.* —nen) spouse, wife, consort.

Gemälde [gə'mɛ:ldə], *n.* (—s, *pl.* —) picture, painting, portrait.

gemäß [gə'mɛ:s], *prep.* (*Dat.*) in accordance with, according to.

Genie

gemäßigt [gə'mɛ:sɪçt], *adj.* temperate, moderate; *—es Klima,* temperate climate.

Gemäuer [gə'mɔyər], *n.* (**—s,** *no pl.*) ancient walls, ruins.

gemein [gə'maɪn], *adj.* common, mean, low, vulgar, base.

Gemeinde [gə'maɪndə], *f.* (**—,** *pl.* **—n**) community, parish, municipality; (*Eccl.*) congregation.

Gemeindevorstand [gə'maɪndefor-ʃtant], *m.* (**—es,** *no pl.*) town or borough council.

gemeingefährlich [gə'maɪngəfɛ:rlɪç], *adj.* dangerous to the public.

Gemeinheit [gə'maɪnhaɪt], *f.* (**—,** *pl.* **—en**) meanness; baseness; dirty trick.

gemeinhin [gə'maɪnhɪn], *adv.* commonly.

Gemeinplatz [gə'maɪnplats], *m.* (**—es,** *pl.* ⸚e) commonplace, truism.

gemeinsam [gə'maɪnza:m], *adj.* common, joint; *der — Markt,* (*Pol.*) Common Market; *—e Sache machen,* make common cause. *— adv.* together.

Gemeinschaft [gə'maɪnʃaft], *f.* (**—,** *pl.* **—en**) community; association; *in — mit,* jointly; *in — haben,* hold in common.

gemeinschaftlich [gə'maɪnʃaftlɪç], *adj.* common. *— adv.* in common, together.

Gemeinsinn [gə'maɪnzɪn], *m.* (**—s,** *no pl.*) public spirit.

Gemeinwesen [gə'maɪnve:zən], *n.* (**—s,** *no pl.*) community.

Gemeinwohl [gə'maɪnvo:l], *n.* (**—s,** *no pl.*) common weal; common good.

Gemenge [gə'mɛŋə], *n.* (**—s,** *no pl.*) mixture, (*fig.*) scuffle.

Gemengsel [gə'mɛŋsəl], *n.* (**—s,** *no pl.*) medley, hotchpotch.

gemessen [gə'mɛsən], *adj.* deliberate.

Gemessenheit [gə'mɛsənhaɪt], *f.* (**—,** *no pl.*) precision, deliberation.

Gemetzel [gə'mɛtsəl], *n.* (**—s,** *no pl.*) slaughter, massacre.

Gemisch [gə'mɪʃ], *n.* (**—es,** *pl.* **—e**) mixture, motley.

Gemme ['gɛmə], *f.* (**—,** *pl.* **—n**) gem, cameo.

Gemse ['gɛmzə], *f.* (**—,** *pl.* **—n**) chamois.

Gemüse [gə'my:zə], *n.* (**—s,** *pl.* **—**) vegetables, greens.

Gemüsehändler [gə'my:zəhɛndlər], *m.* (**—s,** *pl.* **—**) greengrocer.

gemustert [gə'mustərt], *adj.* patterned, figured; (*Comm.*) *—e Sendung,* delivery as per sample.

Gemüt [gə'my:t], *n.* (**—s,** *pl.* **—er**) mind, soul, heart; disposition, nature, spirit, temper; feeling.

gemütlich [gə'my:tlɪç], *adj.* cosy, snug, comfortable; genial, friendly, pleasant.

Gemütlichkeit [gə'my:tlɪçkaɪt], *f.* (**—,** *no pl.*) cosiness, snugness; *da hört die — auf,* that is more than I will stand for.

gemütlos [gə'my:tlo:s], *adj.* unfeeling.

Gemütsart [gə'my:tsa:rt], *f.* (**—,** *no pl.*) disposition; character.

Gemütsbewegung [gə'my:tsbəve:guŋ], *f.* (**—,** *pl.* **—en**) emotion.

gemütskrank [gə'my:tskraŋk], *adj.* sick in mind; melancholy.

Gemütsleben [gə'my:tsle:bən], *n.* (**—s,** *no pl.*) emotional life.

Gemütsmensch [gə'my:tsmɛnʃ], *m.* (**—en,** *pl.* **—en**) man of feeling or sentiment; (*pej.*) sentimentalist.

gemütvoll [gə'my:tfɔl], *adj.* full of feeling, sympathetic.

gen [gɛn], *prep. contraction* of *gegen,* (*Poet.*) towards, to (*Acc.*).

Genannte [gə'nantə], *m.* (**—n,** *pl.* **—n**) named person, aforesaid.

genäschig [gə'nɛʃɪç], *adj.* fond of sweets, sweet-toothed.

genau [gə'nau], *adj.* precise, exact, accurate; strict, parsimonious.

Genauigkeit [gə'nauɪçkaɪt], *f.* (**—,** *no pl.*) accuracy, exactitude, precision.

Gendarm [ʒã'darm], *m.* (**—en,** *pl.* **—en**) policeman, constable.

genehm [gə'ne:m], *adj.* agreeable, acceptable, convenient.

genehmigen [gə'ne:mɪgən], *v.a.* approve of, agree to, permit; (*contract*) ratify.

geneigt [gə'naɪkt], *adj.* inclined (to), disposed (to), prone (to); *einem — sein,* be well disposed towards s.o.; (*Lit.*) *der —e Leser,* gentle reader.

Geneigtheit [gə'naɪkthaɪt], *f.* (**—,** *no pl.*) inclination, proneness, propensity; favour, kindness.

General [gena'ra:l], *m.* (**—s,** *pl.* ⸚e) general.

Generalfeldmarschall [gena'ra:lfɛltmarʃal], *m.* (**—s,** *pl.* ⸚e) field marshal.

Generalkommando [gena'ra:lkɔmando], *m.* (**—s,** *pl.* **—s**) general's headquarters; (corps) headquarters.

Generalkonsul [gena'ra:lkɔnzul], *m.* (**—s,** *pl.* **—e**) consul-general.

Generalnenner [gena'ra:lnɛnər], *m.* (**—s,** *pl.* **—**) (*Maths.*) common denominator.

Generalprobe [gena'ra:lpro:bə], *f.* (**—,** *pl.* **—n**) dress-rehearsal.

Generalvollmacht [gena'ra:lfɔlmaxt], *f.* (**—,** *pl.* **—en**) (*Law*) general power of attorney.

generell [genə'rɛl], *adj.* general, common.

generös [genə'rø:s], *adj.* generous, magnanimous.

genesen [gə'ne:zən], *v.n. irr.* (*aux.* sein) recover, be restored to health; convalesce.

Genf [gɛnf], *n.* Geneva.

genial [gen'ja:l], *adj.* ingenious; extremely gifted.

Genick [gə'nɪk], *n.* (**—s,** *pl.* **—e**) nape, neck.

Genickstarre [gə'nɪkʃtarə], *f.* (**—,** *no pl.*) (*Med.*) (cerebrospinal) meningitis.

Genie [ʒe'ni:], *n.* (**—s,** *pl.* **—s**) genius.

85

genieren

genieren [ʒeˈniːrən], *v.a.* trouble, embarrass, disturb. — *v.r. sich —*, feel embarrassed; *sich nicht —*, make o.s. at home.

genießbar [gəˈniːsbaːr], *adj.* eatable, edible, palatable; drinkable; (*fig.*) pleasant, agreeable.

genießen [gəˈniːsən], *v.a. irr.* enjoy; have the use of; (*food*) eat, partake of; *Ansehen —*, enjoy respect.

Geniestreich [ʒeˈniːʃtraɪç], *m.* (**—s**, *pl.* **—e**) stroke of genius.

Genitiv [ˈgeːnitiːf], *m.* (**—s**, *pl.* **—e**) (*Gram.*) genitive.

Genosse [gəˈnɔsə], *m.* (**—n**, *pl.* **—n**) comrade, mate, colleague; (*crime*) accomplice.

Genossenschaft [gəˈnɔsənʃaft], *f.* (**—**, *pl.* **—en**) association, company, confederacy, co-operative, union.

Genre [ˈʒãrə], *n.* (**—s**, *pl.* **—s**) genre; style, kind.

Gent [gɛnt], *n.* Ghent.

Genua [ˈgeːnua], *n.* Genoa.

genug [gəˈnuːk], *indecl. adj.* enough, sufficient; *—!* that will do!

Genüge [gəˈnyːgə], *f.* (**—**, *no pl.*) *zur —*, sufficiently; *einem — leisten*, give satisfaction to s.o.

genügen [gəˈnyːgən], *v.n.* be enough, suffice; *sich etwas — lassen*, be content with s.th.

genügsam [gəˈnyːkzaːm], *adj.* easily satisfied; temperate, sober.

Genügsamkeit [gəˈnyːkzaːmkaɪt], *f.* (**—**, *no pl.*) contentedness, moderation; temperateness, sobriety.

Genugtuung [gəˈnuːktuːuŋ], *f.* (**—**, *no pl.*) satisfaction; reparation; atonement.

Genuß [gəˈnus], *m.* (**—sses**, *pl.* **-̈sse**) enjoyment; use; (*food*) consumption.

Genußmittel [gəˈnusmitəl], *n.* (**—s**, *pl.* **—**) (*mostly pl.*) luxuries; (*Am.*) delicatessen.

genußreich [gəˈnusraɪç], *adj.* enjoyable, delightful.

Genußsucht [gəˈnusuxt], *f.* (**—**, *no pl.*) thirst for pleasure.

Geograph [geoˈgraːf], *m.* (**—en**, *pl.* **—en**) geographer.

Geographie [geograˈfiː], *f.* (**—**, *no pl.*) geography.

Geologe [geoˈloːgə], *m.* (**—n**, *pl.* **—n**) geologist.

Geologie [geoloˈgiː], *f.* (**—**, *no pl.*) geology.

Geometer [geoˈmeːtər], *m.* (**—s**, *pl.* **—**) geometrician; land-surveyor.

Geometrie [geomeˈtriː], *f.* (**—**, *no pl.*) geometry.

Georg [geˈɔrk], *m.* George.

Georgine [geˈɔrgiːnə], *f.* (**—**, *pl.* **—n**) (*Bot.*) dahlia.

Gepäck [gəˈpɛk], *n.* (**—s**, *no pl.*) luggage; (*Am.*) baggage.

Gepäckaufbewahrung [gəˈpɛkaufbəvaːruŋ], *f.* (**—**, *pl.* **—en**) left luggage office.

Gepäckträger [gəˈpɛktrɛːgər], *m.* (**—s**, *pl.* **—**) porter.

Gepflogenheit [gəˈpfloːgənhaɪt], *f.* (**—**, *pl.* **—en**) habit, custom, wont.

Geplänkel [gəˈplɛnkəl], *n.* (**—s**, *pl.* **—**) (*rare*) skirmish.

Geplärr [gəˈplɛr], *n.* (**—s**, *no pl.*) bawling.

Geplauder [gəˈplaudər], *n.* (**—s**, *no pl.*) chatting; small talk.

Gepräge [gəˈprɛːgə], *n.* (**—s**, *no pl.*) impression, stamp.

Gepränge [gəˈprɛŋə], *n.* (**—s**, *no pl.*) pomp, ceremony, splendour.

Ger [geːr], *m.* (**—s**, *pl.* **—e**) (*rare*) spear, javelin.

Gerade [gəˈraːdə], *f.* (**—n**, *pl.* **—n**) (*Maths.*) straight line.

gerade [gəˈraːdə], *adj.* straight, direct, erect, even; (*fig.*) upright, honest. — *adv.* quite, just; *jetzt —*, now more than ever; *fünf — sein lassen*, stretch a point; — *heraus*, in plain terms.

geradeaus [gəˈraːdəaus],*adv.*straight on.

gerädert [gəˈrɛːdərt], *adj.* (*fig.*) fatigued, exhausted, worn out.

geradeswegs [gəˈraːdəsveːks], *adv.* straightaway, immediately.

geradezu [gəˈraːdətsuː], *adv.* frankly, downright; *das ist — scheußlich*, this is downright nasty.

Geradheit [gəˈraːthaɪt], *f.* (**—**, *no pl.*) straightness; (*fig.*) straightforwardness.

geradlinig [gəˈraːtliniç], *adj.* rectilinear.

geradsinnig [gəˈraːtzɪniç], *adj.* honest, upright.

gerändert [gəˈrɛndərt], *adj.* with a milled edge.

Geranie [gəˈraːnjə], *f.* (**—**, *pl.* **—n**) (*Bot.*) geranium.

Gerät [gəˈrɛːt], *n.* (**—s**, *pl.* **—e**) tool, implement, device; appliance; (radio, television) set; apparatus.

geraten [gəˈraːtən], *v.n. irr.* (*aux. sein*) turn out; *gut —*, turn out well; — *auf*, come upon.

Geräteturnen [gəˈrɛːtəturnən], *n.* (**—s**, *no pl.*) gymnastics with apparatus.

Geratewohl [gəˈraːtəvoːl], *n.* (**—s**, *no pl.*) *aufs —*, at random.

geraum [gəˈraum], *adj.* *—e Zeit*, a long time.

geräumig [gəˈrɔymiç], *adj.* spacious, large, wide, roomy.

Geräusch [gəˈrɔyʃ], *n.* (**—es**, *pl.* **—e**) noise; sound.

gerben [ˈgɛrbən], *v.a.* tan, taw; *einem die Haut —*, give s.o. a hiding.

Gerber [ˈgɛrbər], *m.* (**—s**, *pl.* **—**) tanner.

Gerbsäure [ˈgɛrpsɔyrə], *f.* (**—**, *no pl.*) tannin.

gerecht [gəˈrɛçt], *adj.* just, fair; (*Bibl.*) righteous; *einem — werden*, do justice to s.o.

Gerechtigkeit [gəˈrɛçtiçkaɪt], *f.* (**—**, *no pl.*) justice, fairness; (*Bibl.*) righteousness.

Gerede [gə're:də], *n.* (**—s,** *no pl.*) talk, rumour, gossip.

gereichen [gə'raɪçən], *v.n.* turn out to be; *einem zur Ehre —,* redound to s.o.'s honour.

gereizt [gə'raɪtst], *adj.* irritated, annoyed.

gereuen [gə'rɔyən] *see* **reuen.**

Gerhard ['ge:rhart], *m.* Gerard, Gerald.

Gericht [gə'rɪçt], *n.* (**—s,** *pl.* **—e**) court of justice, tribunal; (*food*) course, dish; *das Jüngste —,* Last Judgment.

gerichtlich [gə'rɪçtlɪç], *adj.* judicial, legal; *einen — belangen,* sue s.o.

Gerichtsbarkeit [gə'rɪçtsbarkaɪt], *f.* (**—,** *no pl.*) jurisdiction.

Gerichtsdiener [gə'rɪçtsdi:nər], *m.* (**—s,** *pl.* **—**) (*law court*) usher.

Gerichtshof [gə'rɪçtsho:f], *m.* (**—es,** *pl.* **⁓e**) court of justice.

Gerichtskanzlei [gə'rɪçtskantslaɪ], *f.* (**—,** *pl.* **—en**) record office.

Gerichtskosten [gə'rɪçtskɔstən], *f. pl.* (*Law*) costs.

Gerichtsordnung [gə'rɪçtsɔrdnuŋ], *f.* (**—,** *pl* **—en**) legal procedure.

Gerichtstermin [gə'rɪçtstɛrmi:n], *m.* (**—s,** *pl.* **—e**) day fixed for a hearing.

Gerichtsverhandlung [gə'rɪçtsfɛrhandluŋ], *f.* (**—,** *pl.* **—en**) hearing; trial.

Gerichtsvollzieher [gə'rɪçtsfɔltsi:ər], *m.* (**—s,** *pl.* **—**) bailiff.

gerieben [gə'ri:bən], *adj.* ground; crafty, cunning.

gering [gə'rɪŋ], *adj.* small, little, mean, petty, unimportant, of little value, trifling; low, base.

geringfügig [gə'rɪŋfy:gɪç], *adj.* small, petty, insignificant.

geringschätzig [gə'rɪŋʃɛtsɪç], *adj.* contemptuous, disdainful, supercilious; derogatory.

gerinnen [gə'rɪnən], *v.n. irr.* (*aux.* sein) coagulate, clot; curdle.

Gerinnsel [gə'rɪnzəl], *n.* (**—s,** *pl.* **—**) embolism (of the blood); clot.

Gerippe [gə'rɪpə], *n.* (**—s,** *pl.* **—**) skeleton; frame; (*Aviat.*) air-frame.

gerippt [gə'rɪpt], *adj.* ribbed, fluted.

gerissen [gə'rɪsən], *adj.* (*coll.*) sharp, cunning.

Germane [gɛr'ma:nə], *m.* (**—n,** *pl.* **—n**) Teuton.

Germanist ['gɛrmanɪst], *m.* (**—en,** *pl.* **— en**) (*Univ.*) student of *or* expert in German language and/or literature.

gern [gɛrn], *adv.* gladly, willingly, readily, with pleasure; *— haben,* like.

Geröll [gə'rœl], *n.* (**—s,** *no pl.*) boulders, rubble.

Gerste ['gɛrstə], *f.* (**—,** *no pl.*) (*Bot.*) barley.

Gerstenschleim ['gɛrstənʃlaɪm], *m.* (**—s,** *no pl.*) barley water.

Gerte ['gɛrtə], *f.* (**—,** *pl.* **—n**) whip, switch, rod.

Geruch [gə'ru:x], *m.* (**—s,** *pl.* **⁓e**) smell, odour, scent; *guter —,* fragrance, aroma.

geruchlos [gə'ru:xlo:s], *adj.* scentless, odourless, without smell.

Geruchsinn [gə'ru:xzɪn], *m.* (**—es,** *no pl.*) sense of smell.

Gerücht [gə'ryçt], *n.* (**—s,** *pl.* **—e**) rumour, report.

Gerümpel [gə'rympəl], *n.* (**—s,** *no pl.*) lumber, trash.

Gerundium [gə'rundjum], *n.* (**—s,** *pl.* **—dien**) (*Gram.*) gerund.

Gerüst [gə'ryst], *n.* (**—es,** *pl.* **—e**) scaffolding.

Ges [gɛs], *n.* (**—,** *pl.* **—**) (*Mus.*) G flat.

gesamt [gə'zamt], *adj.* entire, all, complete.

Gesamtheit [gə'zamthaɪt], *f.* (**—,** *no pl.*) totality.

Gesandte [gə'zantə], *m.* (**—n,** *pl.* **—n**) messenger; ambassador, envoy; *päpstlicher —,* papal nuncio.

Gesandtschaft [gə'zantʃaft], *f.* (**—,** *pl.* **—en**) embassy, legation.

Gesang [gə'zaŋ], *m.* (**—s,** *pl.* **⁓e**) song, air; hymn; (*Lit.*) canto.

Gesangbuch [gə'zaŋbu:x], *n.* (**—s,** *pl.* **⁓er**) hymnal, hymn-book.

Gesäß [gə'zɛ:s], *n.* (**—es,** *pl.* **—e**) seat, buttocks.

Geschäft [gə'ʃɛft], *n.* (**—s,** *pl.* **—e**) business; trade, commerce; affairs; occupation; shop; (*Am.*) store.

geschäftig [gə'ʃɛftɪç], *adj.* active, bustling, busy.

geschäftlich [gə'ʃɛftlɪç], *adj.* concerning business. — *adv.* on business.

Geschäftsführer [gə'ʃɛftsfy:rər], *m.* (**—s,** *pl.* **—**) manager.

Geschäftshaus [gə'ʃɛftshaus], *n.* (**—es,** *pl.* **⁓er**) firm; business premises.

geschäftskundig [gə'ʃɛftskundɪç], *adj.* experienced in business.

Geschäftslokal [gə'ʃɛftsloka:l], *n.* (**—s,** *pl.* **—e**) business premises, shop.

Geschäftsordnung [gə'ʃɛftsɔrdnuŋ], *f.* (**—,** *pl.* **—en**) standing orders; agenda.

Geschäftsträger [gə'ʃɛftstrɛ:gər], *m.* (**—s,** *pl.* **—**) (*Comm.*) agent; (*Pol.*) chargé d'affaires.

Geschäftsverkehr [gə'ʃɛftsfɛrke:r], *m.* (**—s,** *no pl.*) business dealings.

Geschehen [gə'ʃe:ən], *n.* (**—s,** *no pl.*) happening.

geschehen [gə'ʃe:ən], *v.n. irr.* (*aux.* sein) happen, occur; take place; be done; *das geschieht dir recht,* it serves you right.

gescheit [gə'ʃaɪt], *adj.* clever, intelligent.

Geschenk [gə'ʃɛŋk], *n.* (**—s,** *pl.* **—e**) gift, present, donation.

Geschichte [gə'ʃɪçtə], *f.* (**—,** *pl.* **—n**) tale; story; history.

Geschichtenbuch [gə'ʃɪçtənbu:x], *n.* (**—es,** *pl.* **⁓er**) story-book.

geschichtlich [gə'ʃɪçtlɪç], *adj.* historical.

Geschichtsschreiber [gə'ʃɪçtsʃraɪbər], *m.* (**—s,** *pl.* **—**) historian.

Geschick [gə'ʃɪk], *n.* (**—es,** *no pl.*) fate, destiny; dexterity, skill, knack, aptitude.

Geschicklichkeit [gə'ʃɪklɪçkaɪt], *f.* (—, *pl.* —en) dexterity, adroitness, skill.

geschickt [gə'ʃɪkt], *adj.* skilled, skilful, clever, able.

Geschirr [gə'ʃɪr], *n.* (—s, *no pl.*) crockery, plates and dishes; (*horses*) harness.

Geschlecht [gə'ʃlɛçt], *n.* (—s, *pl.* —er) sex; kind, race, species, extraction, family; (*Gram.*) gender.

geschlechtlich [gə'ʃlɛçtlɪç], *adj.* sexual; generic.

Geschlechtsart [gə'ʃlɛçtsaːrt], *f.* (—, *pl.* —en) generic character.

Geschlechtskrankheit [gə'ʃlɛçtskraŋkhaɪt], *f.* (—, *pl.* —en) venereal disease.

Geschlechtskunde [gə'ʃlɛçtskundə], *f.* (—, *no pl.*) genealogy.

Geschlechtsreife [gə'ʃlɛçtsraɪfə], *f.* (—, *no pl.*) puberty.

Geschlechtsteile [gə'ʃlɛçtstaɪlə], *m. pl.* genitals.

Geschlechtstrieb [gə'ʃlɛçtstriːp], *m.* (—s, *no pl.*) sexual instinct.

Geschlechtswort [gə'ʃlɛçtsvɔrt], *n.* (—s, *pl.* ˙er) (*Gram.*) article.

geschliffen [gə'ʃlɪfən], *adj.* polished; (*glass*) cut.

Geschmack [gə'ʃmak], *m.* (—s, *pl.* ˙er) taste, flavour.

geschmacklos [gə'ʃmakloːs], *adj.* tasteless, insipid; in bad taste.

Geschmacksrichtung [gə'ʃmaksrɪçtuŋ], *f.* (—, *pl.* —en) prevailing taste; vogue; tendency.

Geschmeide [gə'ʃmaɪdə], *n.* (—s, *pl.* —) jewels, jewellery; trinkets.

geschmeidig [gə'ʃmaɪdɪç], *adj.* flexible, pliant, supple; (*Tech.*) malleable.

Geschmeiß [gə'ʃmaɪs], *n.* (—es, *no pl.*) dung; vermin; (*fig.*) rabble.

Geschnatter [gə'ʃnatər], *n.* (—s, *no pl.*) cackling.

geschniegelt [gə'ʃniːgəlt], *adj.* spruce, dressed up.

Geschöpf [gə'ʃœpf], *n.* (—es, *pl.* —e) creature.

Geschoß [gə'ʃɔs], *n.* (—sses, *pl.* —sse) shot, shell, projectile, missile; (*house*) storey.

Geschrei [gə'ʃraɪ], *n.* (—s, *no pl.*) shrieking, shouting, screaming; (*fig.*) stir, great noise.

Geschreibsel [gə'ʃraɪpsəl], *n.* (—s, *no pl.*) scrawl, scribbling.

Geschütz [gə'ʃyts], *n.* (—es, *pl.* —e) artillery, guns; *schweres — auffahren*, bring o.'s. guns into play.

Geschützweite [gə'ʃytsvaɪtə], *f.* (—, *no pl.*) calibre.

Geschwader [gə'ʃvaːdər], *n.* (—s, *pl.*—) squadron.

Geschwätz [gə'ʃvɛts], *n.* (—es, *no pl.*) chatter, gossip, prattle, tittle-tattle.

geschweige [gə'ʃvaɪgə], *adv.* let alone, to say nothing of.

geschwind [gə'ʃvɪnt], *adj.* quick, nimble, fast, swift, fleet.

Geschwindigkeitsmesser [gə'ʃvɪndɪçkaɪtsmɛsər], *m.* (—s, *pl.* —) (*Motor.*) speedometer.

Geschwister [gə'ʃvɪstər], *pl.* brothers and sisters.

geschwollen [gə'ʃvɔlən], *adj.* stilted, turgid, pompous.

Geschworene [gə'ʃvoːrənə], *m.* (—n, *pl.* —n), juror, juryman; (*pl.*) jury.

Geschwulst [gə'ʃvulst], *f.* (—, *pl.* ˙e) swelling, tumour.

Geschwür [gə'ʃvyːr], *n.* (—s, *pl.* —e) sore, ulcer, abscess.

Geselle [gə'zɛlə], *m.* (—n, *pl.* —n) journeyman; companion, comrade, mate.

gesellen [gə'zɛlən], *v.a.*, *v.r.* join, associate with, keep company with.

gesellig [gə'zɛlɪç], *adj.* sociable, companionable; gregarious.

Gesellschaft [gə'zɛlʃaft], *f.* (—, *pl.* —en) society; community; (formal) party; company, club; *geschlossene* —, private party; *einem* — *leisten*, keep s.o. company; (*Comm.*) — *mit beschränkter Haftung*, (abbr.) *GmbH*, limited company, (*abbr.*) Ltd.

gesellschaftlich [gə'zɛlʃaftlɪç], *adj.* social.

Gesellschaftsanzug [gə'zɛlʃaftsantsuːk], *m.* (—es, *pl.* ˙e) evening dress.

Gesellschaftsspiel [gə'zɛlʃaftsʃpiːl], *n.* (—s, *pl.* —e) round game, party game.

Gesellschaftsvertrag [gə'zɛlʃaftsfɛrtraːk], *m.* (—es, *pl.* ˙e) (*Law*) partnership agreement; deed of partnership.

Gesellschaftszimmer [gə'zɛlʃaftstsɪmər], *n.* (—s, *pl.* —) drawing-room, reception room.

Gesetz [gə'zɛts], *n.* (—es, *pl.* —e) law, statute, regulation.

Gesetzbuch [gə'zɛtsbuːx], *n.* (—es, *pl.* ˙er) code of laws; statute book.

Gesetzentwurf [gə'zɛtsɛntvurf], *m.* (—es, *pl.* ˙e) (*Parl.*) draft bill.

gesetzgebend [gə'zɛtsgeːbənt], *adj.* legislative.

gesetzlich [gə'zɛtslɪç], *adj.* lawful, legal.

Gesetzlichkeit [gə'zɛtslɪçkaɪt], *f.* (—, *no pl.*) lawfulness, legality.

gesetzlos [gə'zɛtsloːs], *adj.* lawless, anarchical.

gesetzmäßig [gə'zɛtsmɛːsɪç], *adj.* conforming to law, lawful, legitimate.

gesetzt [gə'zɛtst], *adj.* steady, sedate, staid; *von* —*em Alter*, of mature age; — *daß*, supposing that.

Gesetztheit [gə'zɛtsthaɪt], *f.* (—, *no pl.*) sedateness, steadiness.

gesetzwidrig [gə'zɛtsviːdrɪç], *adj.* illegal, unlawful.

Gesicht (1) [gə'zɪçt], *n.* (—s, *pl.* —er) face, physiognomy, look.

Gesicht (2) [gə'zɪçt], *n.* (—s, *pl.* —e) sight; vision, apparition.

Gesichtsausdruck [gə'zɪçtsausdruk], *m.* (—s, *no pl.*) face, mien; expression.

Gesichtsfeld [gə'zɪçtsfɛlt], *n.* (**—es,** *pl.* **—er**) field of vision.

Gesichtskreis [gə'zɪçtskraɪs], *m.* (**—es,** *pl.* **—e**) horizon.

Gesichtspunkt [gə'zɪçtspuŋkt], *m.* (**—es,** *pl.* **—e**) point of view.

Gesichtszug [gə'zɪçtstsu:k], *m.* (**—s,** *pl.* ⁻**e**) feature.

Gesims [gə'zɪms], *n.* (**—es,** *pl.* **—e**) cornice, moulding, ledge.

Gesinde [gə'zɪndə], *n.* (**—s,** *no pl.*) (domestic) servants.

Gesindel [gə'zɪndəl], *n.* (**—s,** *no pl.*) mob, rabble.

gesinnt [gə'zɪnt], *adj.* disposed.

Gesinnung [gə'zɪnuŋ], *f.* (**—,** *pl.* **—en**) disposition, sentiment; conviction.

gesinnungslos [gə'zɪnuŋslo:s], *adj.* unprincipled.

gesinnungstreu [gə'zɪnuŋstrɔy], *adj.* loyal, staunch.

Gesinnungswechsel [gə'zɪnuŋsvɛksəl], *m.* (**—s,** *no pl.*) change of opinion, volte-face.

gesittet [gə'zɪtət], *adj.* civilised, well-mannered.

Gesittung [gə'zɪtuŋ], *f.* (**—,** *no pl.*) (*rare*) civilisation, good manners.

gesonnen [gə'zɔnən] *see* **gesinnt.**

Gespann [gə'ʃpan], *n.* (**—s,** *pl.* **—e**) team, yoke (oxen etc.).

gespannt [gə'ʃpant], *adj.* stretched; intense, thrilled; tense; filled with suspense.

Gespanntheit [gə'ʃpanthaɪt], *f.* (**—,** *no pl.*) tension, strain, suspense.

Gespenst [gə'ʃpɛnst], *n.* (**—es,** *pl.* **—er**) ghost, spectre, apparition.

gespenstisch [gə'ʃpɛnstɪʃ], *adj.* ghostly, spectral.

Gespiele [gə'ʃpi:lə], *m.* (**—n,** *pl.* **—n**) playmate.

Gespielin [gə'ʃpi:lɪn], *f.* (**—,** *pl.* **—innen**) (girl) playmate.

Gespinst [gə'ʃpɪnst], *n.* (**—es,** *pl.* **—e**) web.

Gespött [gə'ʃpœt], *n.* (**—s,** *no pl.*) mocking, mockery, jeering, derision; (*fig.*) laughing stock.

Gespräch [gə'ʃprɛ:ç], *n.* (**—s,** *pl.* **—e**) conversation, discourse, talk; (*phone*) call; *ein — anknüpfen,* start a conversation.

gesprächig [gə'ʃprɛ:çɪç], *adj.* talkative, communicative.

gespreizt [gə'ʃpraɪtst], *adj.* wide apart; (*fig.*) affected, pompous.

gesprenkelt [gə'ʃprɛŋkəlt], *adj.* speckled.

gesprungen [gə'ʃpruŋən], *adj.* cracked (glass etc.).

Gestade [gə'ʃta:də], *n.* (**—s,** *pl.* **—**) shore, coast, bank.

Gestalt [gə'ʃtalt], *f.* (**—,** *pl.* **—en**) form, figure, shape; configuration; stature; fashion; manner, way.

gestalten [gə'ʃtaltən], *v.a.* form, shape, fashion, make. —*v.r. sich* —, turn out.

Gestaltung [gə'ʃtaltuŋ], *f.* (**—,** *pl.* **—en**) formation; arrangement; planning.

geständig [gə'ʃtɛndɪç], *adj.* confessing; — *sein,* confess.

Geständnis [gə'ʃtɛntnɪs], *n.* (**—ses,** *pl.* **—se**) confession, admission.

Gestank [gə'ʃtaŋk], *m.* (**—s,** *no pl.*) stink, stench.

gestatten [gə'ʃtatən], *v.a.* permit, allow, grant; *wir — uns,* we beg leave to; — *Sie !* pardon me, excuse me.

Geste ['gɛstə], *f.* (**—,** *pl.* **—n**) gesture, gesticulation.

gestehen [gə'ʃte:ən], *v.a. irr.* confess, admit, own; *offen gestanden,* quite frankly.

Gestein [gə'ʃtaɪn], *n.* (**—s,** *pl.* **—e**) (*Poet.*) rock; (*Geol.*) rocks, minerals.

Gestell [gə'ʃtɛl], *n.* (**—s,** *pl.* **—e**) rack, frame; (*table*) trestle; (*books*) stand.

Gestellung [gə'ʃtɛluŋ], *f.* (**—,** *no pl.*) (*Mil.*) reporting for service.

gestern ['gɛstərn], *adv.* yesterday; — *abend,* last night.

gestiefelt [gə'ʃti:fəlt], *adj.* booted; *der —e Kater,* Puss in Boots.

gestielt [gə'ʃti:lt], *adj.* (*axe*) helved; (*Bot.*) stalked, stemmed.

gestikulieren [gɛstiku'li:rən], *v.n.* gesticulate.

Gestirn [gə'ʃtɪrn], *n.* (**—s,** *pl.* **—e**) star, constellation.

gestirnt [gə'ʃtɪrnt], *adj.* starred, starry.

Gestöber [gə'ʃtø:bər], *n.* (**—s,** *pl.* **—**) (*snow, dust*) drift, storm, blizzard.

Gesträuch [gə'ʃtrɔyç], *n.* (**—es,** *no pl.*) bushes, shrubs; thicket.

gestreift [gə'ʃtraɪft], *adj.* striped.

gestreng [gə'ʃtrɛŋ], *adj.* (*obs.*) strict, severe.

gestrig ['gɛstrɪç], *adj.* of yesterday.

Gestrüpp [gə'ʃtryp], *n.* (**—s,** *no pl.*) bushes, underwood, shrubs, shrubbery.

Gestüt [gə'ʃty:t], *n.* (**—s,** *pl.* **—e**) stud (-farm).

Gestüthengst [gə'ʃty:thɛnst], *m.* (**—es,** *pl.* **—e**) stallion.

Gesuch [gə'zu:x], *n.* (**—s,** *pl.* **—e**) petition, request, application.

gesucht [gə'zu:xt], *adj.* in demand; (*style*) far-fetched; affected; studied.

gesund [gə'zunt], *adj.* healthy, wholesome; *der —e Menschenverstand,* common sense.

Gesundbrunnen [gə'zuntbrunən], *m.* (**—s,** *pl.* **—**) mineral waters; spa.

gesunden [gə'zundən], *v.n.* (*aux.* sein) recover o.'s health.

Gesundheit [gə'zunthaɪt], *f.* (**—,** *no pl.*) health.

Gesundheitslehre [gə'zunthaɪtsle:rə], *f.* (**—,** *no pl.*) hygiene.

Getäfel [gə'tɛ:fəl], *n.* (**—s,** *no pl.*) wainscot, wainscoting, panelling.

Getändel [gə'tɛndəl], *n.* (**—s,** *no pl.*) (*rare*) flirting, dallying.

Getier [gə'ti:r], *n.* (**—s,** *no pl.*) (*collective term*) animals.

Getöse [gə'tø:zə], *n.* (**—s,** *no pl.*) loud noise, din.

Getränk

Getränk [gə'trɛŋk], *n.* (—s, *pl.* —e) drink, beverage.

getrauen [gə'trauən], *v.r. sich* —, dare, venture.

Getreide [gə'traɪdə], *n.* (—s, *pl.* —) corn, grain.

getreu [gə'trɔy], *adj.* faithful, true, loyal.

getreulich [gə'trɔylɪç], *adv.* faithfully, truly, loyally.

Getriebe [gə'tri:bə], *n.* (—s, *pl.* —) machinery; (*Motor.*) gear; drive; *das — der Welt*, the bustle of life.

getrieben [gə'tri:bən], *adj.* (*Tech.*) chased (work.)

Getrödel [gə'trø:dəl], *n.* (—s, *no pl.*) dawdling.

getrost [gə'tro:st], *adj.* confident, cheerful; — *sein*, be of good cheer.

Getto ['gɛto], *n.* (—s, *pl.* —s) ghetto.

Getue [gə'tu:ə], *n.* (—s, *no pl.*) pretence, fuss.

Getümmel [gə'tymǝl], *n.* (—s, *no pl.*) bustle, turmoil.

geübt [gə'y:pt], *adj.* skilled, versed.

Geübtheit [gə'y:pthaɪt], *f.* (—, *no pl.*) skill, experience, dexterity.

Gevatter [gə'fatər], *m.* (—s, *pl.* —) (*obs.*) godfather.

gevierteilt [gə'fi:rtaɪlt], *adj.* quartered.

Gewächs [gə'vɛks], *n.* (—es, *pl.* —e) plant, growth; (*Med.*) excrescence.

gewachsen [gə'vaksən], *adj.* *einem* (*einer Sache*) — *sein*, be equal to s.o. (s.th.).

Gewächshaus [gə'vɛkshaus], *n.* (—es, *pl.* ̈er) green-house, hot-house, conservatory.

gewagt [gə'va:kt], *adj.* risky, hazardous; daring.

gewählt [gə've:lt], *adj.* choice, select.

gewahr [gə'va:r], *adj. einer Sache — werden*, become aware of s.th., perceive s.th.

Gewähr [gə'vɛ:r], *f.* (—, *no pl.*) surety; guarantee; warranty; — *leisten*, guarantee.

gewahren [gə'va:rən], *v.a.* perceive, see, become aware of.

gewähren [gə've:rən], *v.a.* allow, grant; *einen — lassen*, let s.o. do as he pleases, let be.

Gewährleistung [gə've:rlaɪstuŋ], *f.* (—, *pl.* —en) grant of security (*or* bail); guarantee.

Gewahrsam [gə'va:rza:m], *m.* (—s, *no pl.*) safe-keeping, custody.

Gewährsmann [gə've:rsman], *m.* (—es, *pl.* ̈er) authority; informant.

Gewährung [gə've:ruŋ], *f.* (—, *no pl.*) granting (of request).

Gewalt [gə'valt], *f.* (—, *pl.* —en) power, force, might; authority; violence; *höhere* —, act of God, force majeure; *sich in der — haben*, have control over o.s.

Gewalthaber [gə'valtha:bər], *m.* (—s, *pl.* —) tyrant; despot, autocrat; person in authority.

gewaltig [gə'valtɪç], *adj.* powerful, mighty, enormous, stupendous.

gewaltsam [gə'valtza:m], *adj.* forcible, violent.

Gewaltstreich [gə'valtʃtraɪç], *m.* (—s, *pl.* —e) bold stroke; coup d'état.

Gewalttat [gə'valtta:t], *f.* (—, *pl.* —en) violent action, violence, outrage.

gewalttätig [gə'valtte:tɪç], *adj.* violent, fierce, outrageous.

Gewand [gə'vant], *n.* (—es, *pl.* ̈er) (*Lit.*) garment, dress; (*Eccl.*) vestment.

gewandt [gə'vant], *adj.* nimble, deft, clever; (*mind*) versatile.

gewärtig [gə'vɛrtɪç], *adj. einer Sache — sein*, expect s.th. to happen.

Gewäsch [gə'vɛʃ], *n.* (—es, *no pl.*) stuff and nonsense; rubbish.

Gewässer [gə'vɛsər], *n.* (—s, *pl.* —) waters.

Gewebe [gə've:bə], *n.* (—s, *pl.* —) (*Physiol.*, *Text.*) tissue; web, weft, texture.

geweckt [gə'vɛkt], *adj.* smart, wideawake.

Gewehr [gə've:r], *n.* (—s, *pl.* —e) gun, fire-arm, rifle.

Gewehrlauf [gə've:rlauf], *m.* (—s, *pl.* ̈e) barrel.

Geweih [gə'vaɪ], *n.* (—s, *pl.* —e) horns, antlers.

geweiht [gə'vaɪt], *adj.* consecrated; holy.

gewellt [gə'vɛlt], *adj.* corrugated, wavy.

Gewerbe [gə'vɛrbə], *n.* (—s, *pl.* —) trade, profession, business; calling; industry.

Gewerbekunde [gə'vɛrbəkundə], *f.* (—, *no pl.*) technology.

Gewerbeschein [gə'vɛrbəʃaɪn], *m.* (—s, *pl.* —e) trade-licence.

gewerblich [gə'vɛrplɪç], *adj.* industrial.

gewerbsmäßig [gə'vɛrpsmɛ:sɪç], *adj.* professional.

Gewerkschaft [gə'vɛrkʃaft], *f.* (—, *pl.* —en) trade union.

Gewicht [gə'vɪçt], *n.* (—s, *pl.* —e) weight; *schwer ins — fallen*, carry great weight, weigh heavily.

gewichtig [gə'vɪçtɪç], *adj.* weighty, ponderous; (*fig.*) momentous, important, strong.

gewiegt [gə'vi:kt], *adj.* experienced, clever.

gewillt [gə'vɪlt], *adj.* willing.

Gewimmel [gə'vɪməl], *n.* (—s, *no pl.*) milling crowd, swarm, throng.

Gewinde [gə'vɪndə], *n.* (—s, *pl.* —) (*screw*) thread; (*flowers*) garland.

Gewinn [gə'vɪn], *m.* (—s, *pl.* —e) gain, profit; (*lottery*) prize; (*gambling*) winnings.

gewinnen [gə'vɪnən], *v.a. irr.* win, gain, obtain, get, earn.

gewinnend [gə'vɪnənt], *adj.* prepossessing; engaging.

Gewinnung [gə'vɪnuŋ], *f.* (—, *no pl.*) (*Ind.*, *Chem.*) extraction; output, production.

Gewinsel [gə'vɪnzəl], *n.* (—s, *no pl.*) whimpering.

Gewinst [gə'vɪnst], *m.* (—es, *pl.* —e) (*obs.*) gain, profit.

Gewirr [gə'vɪr], *n.* (—s, *no pl.*) entanglement, confusion.

gewiß [gə'vɪs], *adj.* (*Genit.*) certain, sure. — *adv.* indeed.

Gewissen [gə'vɪsən], *n.* (—s, *no pl.*) conscience.

gewissenhaft [gə'vɪsənhaft], *adj.* conscientious, scrupulous.

gewissenlos [gə'vɪsənlo:s], *adj.* unscrupulous.

Gewissensbiß [gə'vɪsənsbɪs],*m.*(—sses, *pl.* —sse) (*mostly pl.*) pangs of conscience.

gewissermaßen [gə'vɪsərma:sən], *adv.* to a certain extent, so to speak.

Gewißheit [gə'vɪshaɪt], *f.* (—, *no pl.*) certainty.

gewißlich [gə'vɪslɪç], *adv.* surely.

Gewitter [gə'vɪtər], *n.* (—s, *pl.* —) thunderstorm.

gewittern [gə'vɪtərn], *v.n.* thunder.

gewitzigt, gewitzt [gə'vɪtsɪçt, gə'vɪtst], *adj.* knowing, clever; shrewd.

gewogen [gə'vo:gən], *adj.* kindly disposed, favourable; *einem — sein,* be favourably inclined towards s.o.

Gewogenheit [gə'vo:gənhaɪt], *f.* (—, *no pl.*) kindness, favour.

gewöhnen [gə'vø:nən], *v.a.* accustom to. — *v.r. sich — an,* get used to, accustom o.s. to.

Gewohnheit [gə'vo:nhaɪt], *f.* (—, *pl.* —en) (*general*) custom, usage; (*personal*) habit.

gewohnheitsmäßig [gə'vo:nhaɪtsmɛ:sɪç], *adj.* habitual. — *adv.* by force of habit.

Gewohnheitsrecht [gə'vo:nhaɪtsrɛçt], *n.* (—s, *no pl.*) common law.

gewöhnlich [gə'vø:nlɪç],*adj.* customary, usual; (*fig.*) common, mean, vulgar.

gewohnt [gə'vo:nt], *adj.* accustomed to, used to.

Gewöhnung [gə'vø:nuŋ], *f.* (—, *no pl.*) habit, use, habituation.

Gewölbe [gə'vœlbə], *n.* (—s, *pl.* —) vault, arch.

Gewölk [gə'vœlk], *n.* (—s, *no pl.*) clouds, cloud formation.

Gewühl [gə'vy:l], *n.* (—s, *no pl.*) crowd, throng, bustle.

gewunden [gə'vundən], *adj.* tortuous.

Gewürm [gə'vyrm], *n.* (—s, *no pl.*) reptiles, worms; vermin.

Gewürz [gə'vyrts], *n.* (—es, *pl.* —e) spice.

Gewürznelke [gə'vyrtsnɛlkə], *f.* (—, *pl.* —n) clove.

Gezänk [gə'tsɛŋk], *n.* (—s, *no pl.*) quarrelling, bickering.

Gezeiten [gə'tsaɪtən], *f. pl.* tides.

Gezeter [gə'tse:tər], *n.* (—s, *no pl.*) screaming, yelling; (*fig.*) outcry.

geziemen [gə'tsi:mən], *v.r. sich. für einen —,* befit *or* become s.o.

geziert [gə'tsi:rt], *adj.* affected.

Gezischel [gə'tsɪʃəl], *n.* (—s, *no pl.*) whispering.

Gezücht [gə'tsyçt], *n.* (—s, *no pl.*) brood, breed.

Gezweig [gə'tsvaɪk], *n.* (—s, *no pl.*) branches, boughs.

Gezwitscher [gə'tsvɪtʃər], *n.* (—s, *no pl.*) chirping.

Gezwungenheit [gə'tsvuŋənhaɪt], *f.* (—, *no pl.*) constraint.

Gicht [gɪçt], *f.* (—, *no pl.*) (*Med.*) gout.

gichtbrüchig ['gɪçtbryçɪç], *adj.* (*obs.*) paralytic; gouty.

gichtig ['gɪçtɪç], *adj.* gouty.

Giebel ['gi:bəl], *m.* (—s, *pl.* —) gable.

Giebelfenster ['gi:bəlfɛnstər], *n.* (—s, *pl.*—) gable-window, dormer-window.

gieb(e)lig ['gi:b(ə)lɪç], *adj.* gabled.

Gier [gi:r], *f.* (—, *no pl.*) greediness, eagerness.

gieren ['gi:rən], *v.n.* (*rare*) — *nach,* thirst for, yearn for.

gierig ['gi:rɪç], *adj.* eager, greedy.

Gießbach ['gi:sbax], *m.* (—s, *pl.* ⸚e) mountain-torrent.

gießen ['gi:sən], *v.a. irr.* (*liquids*) pour, shed; (*metal*) cast, found.

Gießer ['gi:sər], *m.* (—s, *pl.* —) founder.

Gießerei [gi:sə'raɪ], *f.* (—, *pl.* —en) foundry.

Gießform ['gi:sfɔrm], *f.* (—, *pl.* —en) casting-mould.

Gießkanne ['gi:skanə], *f.* (—, *pl.* —n) watering-can.

Gift [gɪft], *n.* (—es, *pl.* —e) poison, venom; (*fig.*) virulence; (*coll.*) *darauf kannst du — nehmen,* you can bet your life on it.

Giftbaum ['gɪftbaum], *m.* (—s, *pl.* ⸚e) upas-tree.

Giftdrüse ['gɪftdry:zə], *f.* (—, *pl.* —n) poison-gland.

giftig ['gɪftɪç], *adj.* poisonous; (*fig.*) venomous; (*Med.*) toxic.

Giftlehre ['gɪftle:rə], *f.* (—, *no pl.*) toxicology.

Giftpilz ['gɪftpɪlts], *m.* (—es, *pl.* —e) poisonous toadstool.

Giftschlange ['gɪftʃlaŋə], *f.* (—, *pl.* —n) poisonous snake.

Giftstoff ['gɪftʃtɔf], *m.* (—es, *pl.* —e) poison, virus.

Gigant [gɪ'gant], *m.* (—en, *pl.* —en) giant.

Gigerl ['gi:gərl], *m.* (—s, *pl.* —) (*Austr. dial.*) fop, coxcomb.

Gilde ['gɪldə], *f.* (—, *pl.* —n) guild, corporation.

Gimpel ['gɪmpəl], *m.* (—s, *pl.* —) (*Orn.*) bullfinch, chaffinch; (*fig.*) simpleton.

Ginster ['gɪnstər], *m.* (—s, *no pl.*) (*Bot.*) gorse, furze, broom.

Gipfel ['gɪpfəl], *m.* (—s, *pl.* —) summit, peak; (*fig.*) acme, culmination, height.

gipfeln ['gɪpfəln], *v.n.* culminate.

Gips [gɪps], *m.* (—es, *no pl.*) gypsum, stucco, plaster of Paris.

Gipsabdruck ['gɪpsapdruk], *m.* (—s, *pl.* ⸚e) plaster-cast.

Gipsbild ['gɪpsbɪlt], *n.* (—s, *pl.* —er)
plaster-figure.
Gipsverband ['gɪpsfɛrbant], *m.* (—es,
pl. ⁻e) (*Med.*) plaster of Paris dressing.
girieren [ʒi'ri:rən], *v.a.* (*Comm.*) endorse (a bill).
Girlande [gɪr'landə], *f.* (—, *pl.* —n)
garland.
Girobank ['ʒi:robaŋk], *f.* (—, *pl.* —en)
transfer *or* clearing bank.
Gis [gɪs], *n.* (—, *pl.* —) (*Mus.*) G sharp;
— *Moll*, G sharp minor.
gischen ['gɪʃən], *v.n.* foam, froth.
Gischt [gɪʃt], *f.* (—, *pl.* —e) foam,
froth; spray.
Gitarre [gi'tarə], *f.* (—, *pl.* —n) guitar.
Gitter ['gɪtər], *n.* (—s, *pl.* —) trellis,
grate, fence; railing; lattice; (*colour-
printing*) screen.
Gitterwerk ['gɪtərverk], *n.* (—s, *no pl.*)
trellis-work.
Glacéhandschuh [gla'se:hantʃu:], *m.*
(—s, *pl.* —e) kid-glove.
Glanz [glants], *m.* (—es, *no pl.*) brightness, lustre, gloss; polish, sheen;
(*fig.*) splendour.
glänzen ['glɛntsən], *v.n.* shine, glitter,
glisten; (*fig.*) sparkle.
glänzend ['glɛntsənt], *adj.* glossy;
(*fig.*) splendid, magnificent.
Glanzfirnis ['glantsfɪrnɪs], *m.* (—ses,
pl. —se) glazing varnish.
Glanzleder ['glantsle:dər], *n.* (—s, *no
pl.*) patent leather.
Glanzleinwand ['glantslaɪnvant], *f.*
(—, *no pl.*) glazed linen.
glanzlos ['glantslo:s], *adj.* lustreless,
dull.
glanzvoll ['glantsfɔl], *adj.* splendid,
brilliant.
Glanzzeit ['glantstsaɪt], *f.* (—, *pl.* —en)
golden age.
Glas [gla:s], *n.* (—es, *pl.* ⁻er) glass,
tumbler.
glasartig ['gla:sa:rtɪç], *adj.* vitreous,
glassy.
Glaser ['gla:zər], *m.* (—s, *pl.* —)
glazier.
Glaserkitt ['gla:zərkɪt], *m.* (—s, *no
pl.*) putty.
gläsern ['glɛ:zərn], *adj.* vitreous, glassy,
made of glass.
Glashütte ['gla:shytə], *f.* (—, *pl.* —n)
glass-works.
glasieren [gla'zi:rən], *v.a.* glaze;
(*cake etc.*) ice.
glasiert [gla'zi:rt], *adj.* glazed; (*Cul.*)
frosted, iced; (*Art.*) varnished.
Glasröhre ['gla:srø:rə], *f.* (—, *pl.* —n)
glass-tube.
Glasscheibe ['gla:sʃaɪbə], *f.* (—, *pl.* —n)
glass-pane, sheet of glass.
Glassplitter ['gla:sʃplɪtər], *m.* (—s,
pl. —) splinter of glass.
Glasur [gla'zu:r], *f.* (—, *pl.* —en)
(*potter's*) glaze, glazing; enamel,
varnish; (*cake*) icing.
glatt [glat], *adj.* smooth, sleek; even,
plain, glossy; glib; downright. — *adv.*
entirely; — *rasiert*, close-shaven.

Glätte ['glɛtə], *f.* (—, *no pl.*) smooth-
ness, evenness, slipperiness; polish.
Glatteis ['glataɪs], *n.* (—es, *no pl.*)
slippery ice; sheet ice; (*Am.*) glaze;
einen aufs — führen, lead s.o. up
the garden path.
glätten ['glɛtən], *v.a.* smooth; (*dial.*)
iron.
Glatze ['glatsə], *f.* (—, *pl.* —n) bald
head.
glatzköpfig ['glatskœpfɪç], *adj.* bald,
bald-pated.
Glaube(n) ['glaubə(n)], *m.* (—ns, *no
pl.*) faith, belief; creed, religion.
glauben ['glaubən], *v.a.* believe; think,
suppose. — *v.n. an etwas* (*Acc.*) —,
believe in s.th.
Glaubensbekenntnis ['glaubənsbə-
kentnɪs], *n.* (—ses, *pl.* —se) confession of faith; creed.
Glaubensgericht ['glaubənsgərɪçt], *n.*
(—es, *no pl.*) inquisition.
Glaubersalz ['glaubərzalts], *n.* (—es,
no pl.) phosphate of soda, Glauber's
salts.
glaubhaft ['glauphaft], *adj.* credible,
authentic.
gläubig ['glɔybɪç], *adj.* believing, faithful; (*Eccl.*) *die Gläubigen*, the faithful.
Gläubiger ['glɔybɪgər], *m.* (—s, *pl.* —)
creditor.
glaublich ['glauplɪç], *adj.* credible,
believable.
glaubwürdig ['glaupvyrdɪç], *adj.*
authentic, worthy of belief; plausible.
gleich [glaɪç], *adj.* same, like, equal,
even; *auf —e Weise*, likewise; *es ist
mir ganz —*, it is all the same to me.
— *adv.* alike, at once; almost; just as;
ich komme —, I shall be there in a
moment; — *und — gesellt sich gern*,
birds of a feather flock together.
gleichaltrig ['glaɪçaltrɪç], *adj.* of the
same age.
gleichartig ['glaɪça:rtɪç], *adj.* of the
same kind, homogeneous.
gleichberechtigt ['glaɪçbərɛçtɪçt], *adj.*
entitled to equal rights.
Gleiche ['glaɪçə], *n.* (—n, *pl.* —n) the
like; the same; *etwas ins — bringen*,
straighten s.th. out.
gleichen ['glaɪçən], *v.n. irr.* be like,
resemble, be equal to.
gleichermaßen ['glaɪçərma:sən], *adv.*
in a like manner, likewise.
gleichfalls ['glaɪçfals], *adv.* likewise,
equally, as well; *danke —*, thanks,
the same to you.
gleichförmig ['glaɪçfœrmɪç], *adj.* uniform; monotonous.
gleichgesinnt ['glaɪçgəzɪnt], *adj.* congenial, of the same mind.
Gleichgewicht ['glaɪçgəvɪçt], *n.* (—s,
no pl.) balance, equilibrium.
gleichgültig ['glaɪçgyltɪç], *adj.* indifferent; *es ist mir —*, it's all the same
to me.
Gleichheit ['glaɪçhaɪt], *f.* (—, *pl.* —en)
equality, likeness.

Gleichklang ['glaɪçklaŋ], *m.* (—s, *pl.* ⸚e) consonance.

gleichmachen ['glaɪçmaxən], *v.a.* level, equate; *dem Erdboden —*, raze to the ground.

Gleichmaß ['glaɪçma:s], *n.* (—es, *no pl.*) proportion, symmetry.

gleichmäßig ['glaɪçmɛ:sɪç], *adj.* proportionate, symmetrical.

Gleichmut ['glaɪçmu:t], *m.* (—s, *no pl.*) equanimity, calm.

gleichmütig ['glaɪçmy:tɪç], *adj.* eventempered, calm.

gleichnamig ['glaɪçna:mɪç], *adj.* homonymous.

Gleichnis ['glaɪçnɪs], *n.* (—ses, *pl.* —se) simile; (*Bibl.*) parable.

gleichsam ['glaɪçza:m], *adv.* as it were, as if.

gleichschenklig ['glaɪçʃɛŋklɪç], *adj.* (*Maths.*) isosceles.

gleichseitig ['glaɪçzaɪtɪç], *adj.* (*Maths.*) equilateral.

Gleichsetzung ['glaɪçzɛtsuŋ], *f.* (—, *no pl.*), **Gleichstellung** ['glaɪçʃtɛluŋ], *f.* (—, *pl.* —en) equalisation.

Gleichstrom ['glaɪçʃtro:m], *m.* (—s, *no pl.*) (*Elec.*) direct current.

gleichtun ['glaɪçtu:n], *v.a.* irr. *es einem —*, emulate s.o.

Gleichung ['glaɪçuŋ], *f.* (—, *pl.* —en) (*Maths.*) equation.

gleichwohl ['glaɪçvo:l], *adv.*, *conj.* nevertheless, however, yet.

gleichzeitig ['glaɪçtsaɪtɪç], *adj.* simultaneous, contemporary.

Gleis [glaɪs], *n.* (—es, *pl.* —e) (*Railw.*) track; rails; (*Am.*) track.

gleiten ['glaɪtən], *v.n.* irr. (*aux.* sein) glide, slide, slip.

Gleitflug ['glaɪtflu:k], *m.* (—es, *pl.* ⸚e) (*Aviat.*) gliding.

Gletscher ['glɛtʃər], *m.* (—s, *pl.* —) glacier.

Gletscherspalte ['glɛtʃərʃpaltə], *f.* (—, *pl.* —n) crevasse.

Glied [gli:t], *n.* (—es, *pl.* —er) limb, joint; member; link; rank, file.

Gliederlähmung ['gli:dərlɛ:muŋ], *f.* (—, *no pl.*) paralysis.

gliedern ['gli:dərn], *v.a.* articulate, arrange, form.

Gliederreißen ['gli:dərraɪsən], *n.* (—s, *no pl.*) pain in the limbs, rheumatism, arthritis etc.

Gliederung ['gli:dəruŋ], *f.* (—, *pl.* —en) articulation, disposition, structure, arrangement, organisation.

Gliedmaßen ['gli:tma:sən], *f. pl.* limbs.

glimmen ['glɪmən], *v.n.* irr. glimmer, glow, burn faintly; —*de Asche*, embers.

Glimmer ['glɪmər], *m.* (—s, *no pl.*) (*Min.*) mica.

glimpflich ['glɪmpflɪç], *adj.* gentle.

glitschen ['glɪtʃən], *v.n.* (*aux.* sein) (*coll.*) slide.

glitschig ['glɪtʃɪç], *adj.* (*coll.*) slippery.

glitzern ['glɪtsərn], *v.n.* glisten, glitter.

Globus ['glo:bus], *m.* (—ses, *pl.* —se) globe.

Glöckchen ['glœkçən], *n.* (—s, *pl.* —) small bell; hand-bell.

Glocke ['glɔkə], *f.* (—, *pl.* —n) bell; *etwas an die große — hängen*, make a great fuss about s.th.

Glockenblume ['glɔkənblu:mə], *f.* (—, *pl.* —n) (*Bot.*) bluebell.

Glockengießer ['glɔkəngi:sər], *m.* (—s, *pl.* —) bell-founder.

glockenklar ['glɔkənkla:r], *adj.* as clear as a bell.

Glockenläuter ['glɔkənlɔytər], *m.* (—s, *pl.* —) bell-ringer.

Glockenspiel ['glɔkənʃpi:l], *n.* (—s, *pl.* —e) chime; (*Mus.*) glockenspiel, carillon.

Glockenstuhl ['glɔkənʃtu:l], *m.* (—s, *pl.* ⸚e) belfry.

Glockenzug ['glɔkəntsu:k], *m.* (—s, *pl.* ⸚e) bell-rope; (*Mus.*) bellstop.

Glöckner ['glœkner], *m.* (—s, *pl.* —) bellringer, sexton.

glorreich ['glo:raɪç], *adj.* glorious.

Glosse ['glɔsə], *f.* (—, *pl.* —n) gloss, comment, annotation; —*n machen über*, comment upon; find fault with; scoff at.

glotzen ['glɔtsən], *v.n.* stare wideeyed; gape.

Glück [glyk], *n.* (—s, *no pl.*) luck, good luck, fortune, happiness; — *haben*, be in luck; *auf gut —*, at random; *zum —*, fortunately, luckily; *viel —*, good luck.

Glucke ['glukə], *f.* (—, *pl.* —n) (sitting) hen.

glücken ['glykən], *v.n.* succeed; *es ist mir geglückt*, I have succeeded in.

glücklich ['glyklɪç], *adj.* fortunate, lucky, happy.

glückselig [glyk'ze:lɪç], *adj.* blissful, happy.

glucksen ['gluksən], *v.n.* gurgle.

Glücksfall ['glyksfal], *m.* (—es, *pl.* ⸚e) lucky chance, windfall, stroke of good fortune.

Glückspilz ['glykspɪlts], *m.* (—es, *pl.* —e) (*coll.*) lucky dog.

glückverheißend ['glykfɛrhaɪsənt], *adj.* auspicious, propitious.

Glückwunsch ['glykvunʃ], *m.* (—es, *pl.* ⸚e) congratulation; felicitation.

glühen ['gly:ən], *v.a.* make red-hot; (*wine*) mull. — *v.n.* glow, be red-hot.

glühend ['gly:ənt], *adj.* glowing, burning; red-hot; (*coal*) live; (*fig.*) ardent, fervent.

Glühstrumpf ['gly:ʃtrumpf], *m.* (—es, *pl.* ⸚e) incandescent mantle.

Glühwein ['gly:vaɪn], *m.* (—s, *no pl.*) mulled wine.

Glut [glu:t], *f.* (—, *no pl.*) glowing fire; heat; (*fig.*) ardour.

glutrot ['glu:tro:t], *adj.* fiery red.

Glyzerin ['glytsəri:n], *n.* (—s, *no pl.*) glycerine.

Gnade

Gnade ['gna:də], f. (—, pl. —n) grace; favour; pardon, clemency, mercy; kindness; *Euer —n*, Your Grace.

Gnadenakt ['gna:dənakt], m. (—s, pl. —e) act of grace.

Gnadenbrot ['gna:dənbro:t], n. (—s, *no pl.*) *das — eßen*, live on charity.

Gnadenfrist ['gna:dənfrɪst], f. (—, pl. —en) respite.

Gnadenort ['gna:dənɔrt], m. (—(e)s, pl. —e) place of pilgrimage.

Gnadenstoß ['gna:dənʃto:s], m. (—es, pl. ⁺e) finishing stroke, coup de grâce, death-blow.

gnadenvoll ['gna:dənfɔl], adj. merciful, gracious.

Gnadenweg ['gna:dənve:k], m. (—es, *no pl.*) act of grace; *auf dem —*, by reprieve (as an act of grace).

gnädig ['gnɛ:dɪç], adj. gracious, merciful, kind; *—e Frau*, Madam; *—er Herr*, Sir.

Gnostiker ['gnɔstɪkər], m. (—s, pl. —) gnostic.

Gnu [gnu:], n. (—s, pl. —s) (*Zool.*) gnu.

Gold [gɔlt], n. (—(e)s, *no pl.*) gold.

Goldammer ['gɔltamər], f. (—, pl. —n) (*Orn.*) yellow-hammer.

Goldamsel ['gɔltamzəl], f. (—, pl. —n) (*Orn.*) yellow-thrush.

Goldarbeiter ['gɔltarbaɪtər], m. (—s, pl. —) goldsmith.

Goldbarren ['gɔltbarən], m. (—s, pl. —) ingot of gold.

Goldbergwerk ['gɔltbɛrkvɛrk], n. (—s, pl. —e) gold-mine.

Goldfisch ['gɔltfɪʃ], m. (—es, pl. —e) goldfish.

Goldgewicht ['gɔltgəvɪçt], n. (—s, *no pl.*) gold-weight, troy-weight.

Goldgrube ['gɔltgru:bə], f. (—, pl. —n) gold-mine.

goldig ['gɔldɪç], adj. golden; (*fig.*) sweet, cute, charming.

Goldklumpen ['gɔltklumpən], m. (—s, pl. —) nugget (of gold).

Goldlack ['gɔltlak], m. (—s, *no pl.*) gold-coloured varnish; (*Bot.*) wallflower.

Goldmacher ['gɔltmaxər], m. (—s, pl. —) alchemist.

Goldregen ['gɔltre:gən], m. (—s, pl. —) (*Bot.*) laburnum.

Goldscheider ['gɔltʃaɪdər], m. (—s, pl. —) gold-refiner.

Goldschmied ['gɔltʃmi:t], m. (—s, pl. —e) goldsmith.

Goldschnitt ['gɔltʃnɪt], m. (—s, *no pl.*) gilt edge.

Golf (1) [gɔlf], m. (—s, pl. —e) gulf.

Golf (2) [gɔlf], n. (—s, *no pl.*) golf.

Gondel ['gɔndəl], f. (—, pl. —n) gondola.

gondeln ['gɔndəln], v.n. (*aux.* sein) ride in a gondola; (*coll.*) travel, get about.

gönnen ['gœnən], v.a. *einem etwas —*, not grudge s.o. s.th.; *wir — es ihm*, we are happy for him.

Gönner ['gœnər], m. (—s, pl. —) patron, protector.

gönnerhaft ['gœnərhaft], adj. patronising.

Gönnerschaft ['gœnərʃaft], f. (—, *no pl.*) patronage.

gordisch ['gɔrdɪʃ], adj. Gordian; *der —e Knoten*, the Gordian knot.

Göre ['gø:rə], f. (—, pl. —n) (*coll.*) brat; (*Am.*) kid.

Gosse ['gɔsə], f. (—, pl. —n) gutter.

Gote ['go:tə], m. (—n, pl. —n) Goth.

Gotik ['go:tɪk], f. (—, *no pl.*) Gothic style (architecture etc.).

gotisch ['go:tɪʃ], adj. Gothic.

Gott [gɔ:t], m. (—es, pl. ⁺er) God, god; *— befohlen*, goodbye; *grüß —!* (*Austr.*) good day; *— sei Dank*, thank God, thank heaven.

gottbegnadet ['gɔtbəgna:dət], adj. favoured by God, inspired.

Götterbild ['gœtərbɪlt], n. (—es, pl. —er) image of a god.

gottergeben ['gɔtɛrge:bən], adj. submissive to God's will, devout.

Götterlehre ['gœtərle:rə], f. (—, pl. —n) mythology.

Götterspeise ['gœtərʃpaɪzə], f. (—, pl. —n) ambrosia.

Götterspruch ['gœtərʃprux], m. (—s, *no pl.*) oracle.

Göttertrank ['gœtərtraŋk], m. (—s, pl. ⁺e) nectar.

Gottesacker ['gɔtəsakər], m. (—s, pl. —) God's acre, churchyard.

Gottesdienst ['gɔtəsdi:nst], m. (—es, pl. —e) divine service, public worship.

gottesfürchtig ['gɔtəsfyrçtɪç], adj. God-fearing, pious.

Gottesgelehrsamkeit ['gɔtəsgəle:rza:mkaɪt], f. (—, *no pl.*) (*rare*) theology, divinity.

Gottesgericht ['gɔtəsgərɪçt], n. (—s, pl. —e) ordeal.

Gotteshaus ['gɔtəshaus], n. (—es, pl. ⁺er) house of God; (*rare*) church.

Gotteslästerer ['gɔtəslɛstərər], m. (—s, pl. —) blasphemer.

Gottesleugner ['gɔtəslɔygnər], m. (—s, pl. —) atheist.

Gottfried ['gɔtfri:t], m. Godfrey, Geoffrey.

gottgefällig ['gɔtgəfɛlɪç], adj. pleasing to God.

Gottheit ['gɔthaɪt], f. (—, pl. —en) deity, divinity.

Göttin ['gœtɪn], f. (—, pl. —nen) goddess.

göttlich ['gœtlɪç], adj. divine, godlike; (*fig.*) heavenly.

gottlob! ['gɔt'lo:p]; *excl.* thank God!

gottlos ['gɔtlo:s], adj. godless, ungodly, impious; (*fig.*) wicked.

gottvergessen ['gɔtfɛrgɛsən], adj. reprobate, impious.

gottverlassen ['gɔtfɛrlasən], adj. God-forsaken.

Götze ['gœtsə], m. (—n, pl. —n) idol, false deity.

94

Götzenbild ['gœtsənbɪlt], *n.* (**—es,** *pl.* **—er**) idol.

Götzendienst ['gœtsəndi:nst], *m.* (**—es,** *no pl.*) idolatry.

Gouvernante [guvɛr'nantə], *f.* (**—,** *pl.* **—n**) governess.

Gouverneur [guvɛr'nø:r], *m.* (**—s,** *pl.* **—e**) governor.

Grab [gra:p], *n.* (**—s,** *pl.* ˙er) grave, tomb; sepulchre.

Graben ['gra:bən], *m.* (**—s,** *pl.* ˙) ditch, trench.

graben ['gra:bən], *v.a. irr.* dig.

Grabgeläute ['gra:pgələytə], *n.* (**—s,** *no pl.*) death-knell.

Grabhügel ['gra:phy:gəl], *m.* (**—s,** *pl.* **—**) tumulus, mound.

Grablegung ['gra:ple:guŋ], *f.* (**—,** *no pl.*) *(rare)* burial, interment.

Grabmal ['gra:pma:l], *n.* (**—s,** *pl.* **—e,** ˙er) tomb, sepulchre, monument.

Grabschrift ['gra:pʃrɪft], *f.* (**—,** *pl.* **—n**) epitaph.

Grabstichel ['gra:pʃtɪçəl], *m.* (**—s,** *pl.* **—**) graving-tool.

Grad [gra:t], *m.* (**—s,** *pl.* **—e**) degree; rank; grade; extent; point; *in gewissem* **—e,** to a certain degree; *im höchsten* **—e,** in the highest degree, extremely.

Gradeinteilung ['gra:taɪntaɪluŋ], *f.* (**—,** *pl* **—en**) gradation, graduation.

Gradmesser ['gra:tmɛsər], *m.* (**—s,** *pl.* **—**) graduator; (*fig.*) index.

gradweise ['gra:tvaɪzə], *adv.* gradually, by degrees.

Graf [gra:f], *m.* (**—en,** *pl.* **—en**) count, earl.

Gräfin ['grɛfɪn], *f.* (**—,** *pl.* **—en**) countess.

gräflich ['grɛflɪç], *adj.* belonging to a count *or* earl.

Grafschaft ['gra:fʃaft], *f.* (**—,** *pl.* **—en**) county, shire.

Gral [gra:l], *m.* (**—s,** *no pl.*) Holy Grail.

Gram [gra:m], *m.* (**—s,** *no pl.*) grief, sorrow.

grämen ['grɛ:mən], *v.a.* grieve. — *v.r. sich* **—,** grieve, fret, worry.

gramgebeugt ['gra:mgəbɔykt], *adj.* prostrate with grief.

grämlich ['grɛ:mlɪç], *adj.* sullen, morose, ill-humoured.

Gramm [gram], *n.* (**—s,** *pl.* **—e**) gramme (15.438 grains); *(Am.)* gram.

Grammatik [gra'matɪk], *f.* (**—,** *pl.* **—en**) grammar.

grammatikalisch, **grammatisch** [gramatɪ'ka:lɪʃ, gra'matɪʃ], *adj.* grammatical.

Gran [gra:n], *n.* (**—s,** *pl.* **—e**) *(weight)* grain.

Granat [gra'na:t], *m.* (**—s,** *pl.* **—e**) garnet.

Granatapfel [gra'na:tapfəl], *m.* (**—s,** *pl.* ˙e) *(Bot.)* pomegranate.

Granate [gra'na:tə], *f.* (**—,** *pl.* **—n**) shell, grenade.

Grande ['grandə], *m.* (**—n,** *pl.* **—n**) grandee.

Grandezza [gran'dɛtsa], *f.* (**—,** *no pl.*) grandeur; sententiousness; pomposity.

grandios [grandi'o:s], *adj.* grand.

Granit [gra'ni:t], *m.* (**—s,** *pl.* **—e**) granite.

Granne ['granə], *f.* (**—,** *pl.* **—n**) *(corn)* awn, beard.

graphisch ['gra:fɪʃ], *adj.* graphic.

Graphit [gra'fi:t], *m.* (**—s,** *no pl.*) blacklead.

Gras [gra:s], *n.* (**—es,** *pl.* ˙er) grass; *ins* **—** *beißen,* bite the dust.

grasartig ['gra:sa:rtɪç], *adj.* gramineous.

grasen ['gra:zən], *v.n.* graze.

Grasfleck ['gra:sflɛk], *m.* (**—s,** *pl.* **—e**) grass-stain.

Grashalm ['gra:shalm], *m.* (**—s,** *pl.* **—e**) grass-blade.

Grashüpfer ['gra:shypfər], *m.* (**—s,** *pl.* **—**) *(Ent.)* grass-hopper.

grasig ['gra:zɪç], *adj.* grassy.

Grasmäher ['gra:smɛ:ər], *m.* (**—s,** *pl.* **—**) lawn-mower.

Grasmücke ['gra:smykə], *f.* (**—,** *pl.* **—n**) *(Orn.)* hedge-sparrow.

grassieren [gra'si:rən], *v.n. (epidemics etc.)* spread, rage.

gräßlich ['grɛslɪç], *adj.* hideous, horrible, ghastly.

Grasweide ['gra:svaɪdə], *f.* (**—,** *pl.* **—n**) pasture.

Grat [gra:t], *m.* (**—s,** *pl.* **—e**) edge, ridge.

Gräte ['grɛ:tə], *f.* (**—,** *pl.* **—n**) fish-bone.

Grätenstich ['grɛ:tənʃtɪç], *m.* (**—s,** *pl.* **—e**) *(embroidery)* herring-bone stitch.

grätig ['grɛ:tɪç], *adj.* full of fishbones; (*fig.*) grumpy.

gratis ['gra:tɪs], *adj.* gratis; — *und franko,* for nothing.

Gratulation [gratula'tsjo:n], *f.* (**—,** *pl.* **—en**) congratulation.

gratulieren [gratu'li:rən], *v.n. einem zu etwas* **—,** congratulate s.o. on s.th.

grau [grau], *adj.* grey; *(Am.)* gray; *vor* **—***en Zeiten,* in times of yore.

Grauen ['grauən], *n.* (**—s,** *no pl.*) horror, aversion.

grauen ['grauən], *v.n. (morning)* dawn; *es graut mir vor,* I shudder at.

grauenhaft ['grauənhaft], *adj.* horrible, awful, ghastly.

graulen ['graulən], *v.r. sich* **—,** shudder, be afraid (of ghosts etc.).

graulich ['graulɪç], *adj. mir ist ganz* **—,** I shudder.

Graupe ['graupə], *f.* (**—,** *pl.* **—n**) groats, peeled barley.

graupeln ['graupəln], *v.n. imp. (coll.)* drizzle, sleet.

Graus [graus], *m.* (**—es,** *no pl.*) horror, dread.

grausam ['grauza:m], *adj.* cruel.

Grauschimmel ['grauʃɪməl], *m.* (**—s,** *pl.* **—**) grey (horse).

grausen ['grauzən], *v.n. es graust mir vor,* I shudder at.

grausig ['grauzɪç], *adj.* dread, gruesome, horrible.

Graveur [gra'vø:r], *m.* (—s, *pl.* —e) engraver.

gravieren [gra'vi:rən], *v.a.* engrave.

Gravität [gravi'tɛ:t], *f.* (—, *no pl.*) gravity.

gravitätisch [gravi'tɛ:tiʃ], *adj.* grave, solemn.

Grazie ['gra:tsjə], *f.* (—, *pl.* —n) grace, charm; (*goddess*) Grace.

graziös [gra'tsjø:s], *adj.* graceful.

Greif [graIf], *m.* (—(e)s, *pl.* —e) griffin.

greifbar ['graIfba:r], *adj.* to hand; (*fig.*) tangible, palpable.

greifen ['graIfən], *v.a. irr.* grasp, seize, touch, handle; *etwas aus der Luft —*, invent s.th.; *um sich —*, gain ground.

greinen ['graInən], *v.n.* (*dial. & coll.*) cry, blubber.

Greis [graIs], *m.* (—es, *pl.* —e) old man.

greisenhaft ['graIzənhaft], *adj.* senile.

grell [grɛl], *adj.* (*colour*) glaring; (*light*) dazzling; (*tone*) shrill, sharp.

Grenadier [grena'di:r], *m.* (—s, *pl.* —e) grenadier.

Grenadiermütze [grena'di:rmytsə], *f.* (—, *pl.* —n) busby, bearskin.

Grenze ['grɛntsə], *f.* (—, *pl.* —n) boundary; frontier; borders; (*fig.*) limit.

grenzen ['grɛntsən], *v.n. — an*, border on; (*fig.*) verge on.

Grenzlinie ['grɛntsli:njə], *f.* (—, *pl.* —n) boundary-line, line of demarcation.

· **Greuel** ['grɔyəl], *m.* (—s, *pl.* —) horror, abomination; *das ist mir ein —*, I abominate it.

Greueltat ['grɔyəlta:t], *f.* (—, *pl.* —en) atrocity.

greulich ['grɔylIç], *adj.* horrible, dreadful, shocking, heinous.

Griebe ['gri:bə], *f.* (—, *pl.* —n) (*mostly pl.*) greaves.

Griebs ['gri:ps], *m.* (—es, *pl.* —e) (*dial.*) (*apple*) core.

Grieche ['gri:çə], *m.* (—n, *pl.* —n) Greek.

Griechenland ['gri:çənlant], *n.* Greece.

Griesgram ['gri:sgra:m], *m.* (—s, *pl.* —e) grumbler.

griesgrämig ['gri:sgrɛ:mIç], *adj.* morose, grumbling.

Grieß ['gri:s], *m.* (—es, *no pl.*) groats, semolina.

Grießbrei ['gri:sbraI], *m.* (—s, *pl.* —e) gruel.

Griff [grIf], *m.* (—s, *pl.* —e) grip, hold, handle.

griffbereit ['grIfbəraIt], *adj.* handy.

Grille ['grIlə], *f.* (—, *pl.* —n) (*Ent.*) cricket; (*fig.*) whim; *—n haben*, be capricious; *—n fangen*, be crotchety, be depressed.

grillenhaft ['grIlənhaft], *adj.* whimsical; capricious.

Grimasse [gri'masə], *f.* (—, *pl.* —n) grimace.

Grimm [grIm], *m.* (—s, *no pl.*) fury, rage, wrath.

Grimmen ['grImən], *n.* (—s, *no pl.*) gripes; (*Med.*) colic.

grimmig ['grImIç], *adj.* fierce, furious, grim.

Grind [grInt], *m.* (—s, *pl.* —e) scab, scurf.

grinsen ['grInzən], *v.n.* grin.

Grippe ['grIpə], *f.* (—, *pl.* —n) influenza, grippe.

Grips [grIps], *m.* (—es, *no pl.*) (*coll.*) sense, brains; *einen — nehmen*, take s.o. by the scruff of his neck.

grob [grɔp], *adj.* coarse; rough; gross; rude, crude, uncouth, impolite; (*jewels*) rough, unpolished.

Grobheit ['grɔphaIt], *f.* (—, *pl.* —en) rudeness; abusive language.

Grobian ['gro:bja:n], *m.* (—s, *pl.* —e) boor, rude fellow.

Grobschmied ['grɔpʃmi:t], *m.* (—s, *pl.* —e) blacksmith.

Grog [grɔk], *m.* (—s, *pl.* —s) grog, toddy.

grölen ['grø:lən], *v.n.* (*coll.*) scream, squall, bawl.

Groll [grɔl], *m.* (—s, *no pl.*) resentment, anger, rancour; *einen — gegen einen haben*, bear s.o. a grudge.

grollen ['grɔlən], *v.n.* (*thunder*) rumble; *einen —, bear s.o. ill-will*; (*Poet.*) be angry (with).

Grönland ['grø:nlant], *n.* Greenland.

Gros (1) [grɔs], *m.* (—ses, *pl.* —se) gross; twelve dozen.

Gros (2) [gro:], *n.* (—s, *no pl.*) bulk, majority; *en —*, wholesale.

Groschen ['grɔʃən], *m.* (—s, *pl.* —) small coin, penny; one 100th of an Austrian shilling; ten-pfennig piece; *einen schönen — verdienen*, make good money.

groß [gro:s], *adj.* great, big, large; tall; vast; eminent, famous; intense; *ein Augen machen*, stare; *Grosser Ozean*, Pacific (Ocean).

großartig ['gro:sa:rtIç], *adj.* grand, sublime, magnificent, splendid.

Großbetrieb ['gro:sbətri:p], *m.* (—s, *pl.* —e) large business; large (industrial) concern.

Großbritannien [gro:sbri'tanjən], *n.* Great Britain.

Größe ['grø:sə], *f.* (—, *pl.* —n) size, largeness, greatness; height; quantity; power; celebrity, star; importance.

Großeltern ['gro:sɛltərn], *pl.* grandparents.

Großenkel ['gro:sɛŋkəl], *m.* (—s, *pl.* —) great-grandson.

Größenverhältnis ['grø:sənferhɛltnIs], *n.* (—ses, *pl.* —se) proportion, ratio.

Größenwahn ['grø:sənva:n], *m.* (—s, *no pl.*) megalomania; delusion of grandeur.

Großfürst ['gro:sfyrst], *m.* (—en, *pl.* —en) grand-duke.

Großfürstin ['groːsfyrstın], *f.* (—, *pl.* —nen) grand-duchess.

Großgrundbesitz ['groːsgruntbəzıts], *m.* (—es, *pl.* —e) large landed property, estates.

Großhandel ['groːshandəl], *m.* (—s, *no pl.*) wholesale business.

großherzig ['groːshɛrtsıç], *adj.* magnanimous.

Grossist [grɔ'sıst], *m.* (—en, *pl.* —en) wholesale merchant.

großjährig ['groːsjɛːrıç], *adj.* of age; — werden, come of age.

großmächtig ['groːsmɛçtıç], *adj.* (*fig.*) high and mighty.

großmäulig ['groːsmɔylıç], *adj.* bragging, swaggering.

Großmut ['groːsmuːt], *f.* (—, *no pl.*) magnanimity, generosity.

Großmutter ['groːsmutər], *f.* (—, *pl.* ⁻) grandmother.

Großsiegelbewahrer [groːsˈziːgəlbəvaːrər], *m.* (—s, *pl.* —) Lord Chancellor; Keeper of the Great Seal.

Großstadt ['groːsʃtat], *f.* (—, *pl.* ⁻e) large town, city, metropolis.

Großtat ['groːstaːt], *f.* (—, *pl.* —en) achievement, exploit, feat.

Großtuer ['groːstuːər], *m.* (—s, *pl.* —) boaster, braggart.

großtun ['groːstuːn], *v.r. irr.* sich — mit, brag of; show off, parade.

Großvater ['groːsfaːtər], *m.* (—s, *pl.* ⁻) grandfather.

großziehen ['groːstsiːən], *v.a. irr.* bring up, rear.

großzügig ['groːstsyːgıç], *adj.* boldly conceived; grand, generous.

Grotte ['grɔtə], *f.* (—, *pl.* —n) grotto.

Grübchen ['gryːpçən], *n.* (—s, *pl.* —) dimple.

Grube ['gruːbə], *f.* (—, *pl.* —n) hole, pit; (*Min.*) mine; in die — fahren, (*Bibl.*) go down to the grave.

Grübelei ['gryːbəlaɪ], *f.* (—, *pl.* —en) brooding, musing.

grübeln ['gryːbəln], *v.n.* brood (over s.th.)

Grubenarbeiter ['gruːbənarbaɪtər], *m.* (—s, *pl.* —) miner.

Grubengas ['gruːbəngaːs], *n.* (—es, *pl.* —e) fire-damp.

Grubenlampe ['gruːbənlampə], *f.* (—, *pl.* —n) miner's lamp.

Gruft [gruft], *f.* (—, *pl.* ⁻e) tomb, sepulchre; vault, mausoleum.

grün [gryːn], *adj.* green; *grüne Bohnen,* French beans, runner beans; (*fig.*) unripe, immature, inexperienced; *am —en Tisch,* at the conference table; (*fig.*) in theory; *auf einen —en Zweig kommen,* thrive, get on in the world; *einem wohl — sein,* dislike s.o.

Grund [grunt], *m.* (—s, *pl.* ⁻e) ground, soil; earth; land; bottom; foundation, basis; valley; reason, cause, argument; motive.

Grundbedeutung ['gruntbədɔytuŋ], *f.* (—, *pl.* —en) primary meaning, basic meaning.

Grundbesitz ['gruntbəzıts], *m.* (—es, *no pl.*) landed property.

Grundbuch ['gruntbuːx], *n.* (—s, *pl.* ⁻er) land register.

grundehrlich ['grunteːrlıç], *adj.* thoroughly honest.

Grundeigentum ['gruntaɪgəntuːm], *n.* (—s, *pl.* ⁻er) landed property.

Grundeis ['gruntaɪs], *n.* (—es, *no pl.*) ground-ice.

gründen ['gryndən], *v.a.* found, establish, float (a company). — *v.r.* sich — auf, be based on.

grundfalsch ['gruntfalʃ], *adj.* radically false.

Grundfarbe ['gruntfarbə], *f.* (—, *pl.* —n) primary colour.

Grundfläche ['gruntflɛçə], *f.* (—, *pl.* —n) basis, base.

Grundherr ['grunthɛr], *m.* (—n, *pl.* —en) lord of the manor, freeholder.

grundieren [grun'diːrən], *v.a.* prime, size, paint the undercoat.

Grundkapital ['gruntkapitaːl], *n.* (—s, *no pl.*) original stock.

Grundlage ['gruntlaːgə], *f.* (—, *pl.* —n) foundation, basis.

Grundlegung ['gruntleːguŋ], *f.* (— *no pl.*) laying the foundation.

gründlich ['gryntlıç], *adj.* thorough, solid.

grundlos ['gruntloːs], *adj.* bottomless; groundless, unfounded, without foundation.

Grundmauer ['gruntmauər], *f.* (—, *pl.* —n) foundation wall.

Gründonnerstag [gryːnˈdɔnərstaːk], *m.* (—s, *pl.* —e) Maundy Thursday.

Grundpfeiler ['gruntpfaɪlər], *m.* (—s, *pl.* —) (main) pillar.

Grundriß ['gruntrıs], *m.* (—sses, *pl.* —sse) design, groundplan; compendium, elements; blueprint.

Grundsatz ['gruntzats], *m.* (—es, *pl.* ⁻e) principle, maxim; axiom.

grundschlecht ['gruntʃlɛçt], *adj.* thoroughly bad.

Grundschuld ['gruntʃult], *f.* (—, *pl.* —en) mortgage (on land).

Grundstein ['gruntʃtaɪn], *m.* (—s, *pl.* —e) foundation-stone.

Grundsteuer ['gruntʃtɔyər], *f.* (—, *pl.* —n) land-tax.

Grundstoff ['gruntʃtɔf], *m.* (—es, *pl.* —e) raw material.

Grundstück ['gruntʃtyk], *n.* (—s, *pl.* —e) real estate; plot of land; lot.

Grundtugend ['grunttuːgənt], *f.* (— *pl.* —en) cardinal virtue.

Gründung ['grynduŋ], *f.* (—, *pl.* —en) foundation, establishment.

grundverschieden ['gruntfɛrʃiːdən], *adj.* radically different.

Grundwasser ['gruntvasər], *n.* (—s, *no pl.*) underground water.

Grundzahl ['grunttsaːl], *f.* (—, *pl.* —en) cardinal number.

Grundzug ['grunttsuːk], *m.* (—s, *pl.* ⁻e) characteristic; distinctive feature.

Grüne ['gry:nə], *n.* (**—n**, *no pl.*) greenness, verdure; *ins — gehen*, take a walk in the open country.

grünen ['gry:nən], *v.n.* become green; (*fig.*) flourish.

Grünfutter ['gry:nfutər], *n.* (**—s**, *no pl.*) green food.

Grünkohl ['gry:nko:l], *m.* (**—s**, *no pl.*) green kale.

Grünkramhändler ['gry:nkra:mhɛndlər], *m.* (**—s**, *pl.* **—**) greengrocer.

Grünschnabel ['gry:nʃna:bəl], *m.* (**—s**, *pl.* ˙:) greenhorn.

Grünspan ['gry:nʃpa:n], *m.* (**—s**, *no pl.*) verdigris.

Grünspecht ['gry:nʃpɛçt], *m.* (**—s**, *pl.* **—e**) (*Orn.*) green woodpecker.

grunzen ['gruntsən], *v.n.* grunt.

Grünzeug ['gry:ntsɔyk], *n.* (**—s**, *no pl.*) greens, herbs.

Gruppe ['grupə], *f.* (**—**, *pl.* **—n**) group.

gruppieren [gru'pi:rən], *v.a.* group.

gruselig ['gru:zəliç], *adj.* creepy, uncanny.

gruseln ['gru:zəln], *v.a.* *es gruselt mir* I shudder, it gives me the creeps.

Gruß [gru:s], *m.* (**—es**, *pl.* ˙:e) salutation, greeting; (*pl.*) greeting; *mit herzlichem —*, with kind regards; *einen — ausrichten*, convey s.o.'s regards.

grüßen ['gry:sən], *v.a.* greet; *einen lassen*, send o.'s regards to s.o.; *Sie ihn von mir*, remember me to him.

Grütze ['grytsə], *f.* (**—**, *pl.* **—n**) peeled grain, groats; (*fig.*) (*coll.*) gumption, brains.

Guatemala [guatə'ma:la], *n.* Guatemala.

gucken ['gukən], *v.n.* look, peep.

Guinea [gɪ'ne:a], *n.* Guinea.

Gulasch ['gulaʃ], *n.* (**—s**, *no pl.*) goulash.

Gulden ['guldən], *m.* (**—s**, *pl.* **—**) florin, guilder.

gülden ['gyldən], *adj.* (*Poet.*) golden.

gültig ['gyltiç], *adj.* valid; (*money*) current, legal (tender).

Gummi ['gumi:], *m.* (**—s**, *no pl.*) gum, rubber.

Gummiarabikum [gumia'ra:bɪkum], *n.* gum arabic.

gummiartig ['gumia:rtiç], *adj.* gummy; like rubber.

Gummiball ['gumibal], *m.* (**—s**, *pl.* ˙:e) rubber-ball.

Gummiband ['gumibant], *n.* (**—s**, *pl.* ˙:er) rubber-band, elastic.

Gummielastikum [gumie'lastikum], *n.* indiarubber.

gummieren [gu'mi:rən], *v.a.* gum.

Gummireifen ['gumiraɪfən], *m.* (**—s**, *pl.* **—**) tyre; (*Am.*) tire.

Gummischuhe ['gumiʃu:ə], *m. pl.* galoshes; (*Am.*) rubbers.

Gunst [gunst], *f.* (**—**, *no pl.*) favour; *zu seinen —*, in his favour.

Gunstbezeigung ['gunstbətsaɪguŋ], *f.* (**—**, *pl.* **—en**) favour, kindness, goodwill.

günstig ['gynstɪç], *adj.* favourable, propitious.

Günstling ['gynstlɪŋ], *m.* (**—s**, *pl.* **—e**) favourite.

Gurgel ['gurgəl], *f.* (**—**, *pl.* **—n**) gullet, throat.

gurgeln ['gurgəln], *v.n.* gargle; gurgle.

Gurke ['gurkə], *f.* (**—**, *pl.* **—n**) (*Bot.*) cucumber; (*pickled*) gherkin.

Gurt [gurt], *m.* (**—es**, *pl.* **—e**) belt; strap; harness.

Gürtel ['gyrtəl], *m.* (**—s**, *pl.* **—**) girdle, belt; (*Geog.*) zone.

Guß [gus], *m.* (**—sses**, *pl.* ˙:sse) gush, downpour; founding, cast; (*Cul.*) icing.

Gut [gu:t], *n.* (**—(e)s**, *pl.* ˙:er) good thing, blessing; property, possession; country seat; estate; (*pl.*) goods.

gut [gu:t], *adj.* good; beneficial; kind; virtuous. *— adv.* well; *es — haben*, be well off; *—er Dinge sein*, be of good cheer; *kurz und —*, in short.

Gutachten ['gu:taxtən], *n.* (**—s**, *pl.* **—**) expert opinion, expert evidence.

gutartig ['gu:ta:rtiç], *adj.* good-natured; benign.

Güte ['gy:tə], *f.* (**—**, *no pl.*) goodness, kindness, quality.

Güterabfertigung ['gy:tərapfɛrtiguŋ], *f.* (**—**, *pl.* **—en**) (*Railw.*) goods-depot, goods-office.

Güterabtretung ['gy:təraptre:tuŋ], *f.* (**—**, *pl.* **—en**) cession of goods; (*Law*) surrender of an estate.

gutgelaunt ['gu:tgəlaunt], *adj.* in good spirits, good-humoured.

gutgemeint ['gu:tgəmaɪnt], *adj.* well-meant, well-intentioned.

gutgesinnt ['gu:tgəzɪnt], *adj.* well-intentioned.

Guthaben ['gu:tha:bən], *n.* (**—s**, *pl.* **—**) credit-balance, assets.

gutheißen ['gu:thaɪsən], *v.a.* *irr.* approve.

gütig ['gy:tiç], *adj.* kind, benevolent.

gütlich ['gy:tlɪç], *adj.* amicable, friendly; *—er Vergleich*, amicable settlement; *sich — tun*, indulge o.s.

gutmachen ['gu:tmaxən], *v.a.* *etwas wieder —*, make amends for s.th., compensate.

gutmütig ['gu:tmy:tɪç], *adj.* good-natured, good-tempered.

Gutsbesitzer ['gu:tsbəzɪtsər], *m.* (**—s**, *pl.* **—**) landowner; proprietor of an estate.

gutschreiben ['gu:tʃraɪbən], *v.a.* *irr.* *einem etwas —*, enter a sum to s.o.'s credit.

Gutsverwalter ['gu:tsfɛrvaltər], *m.* (**—s**, *pl.* **—**) land-steward, agent, bailiff.

gutwillig ['gu:tvɪlɪç], *adj.* willing, of o.'s own free will.

Gymnasialbildung [gymnaz'ja:lbɪlduŋ], *f.* (**—**, *no pl.*) classical *or* grammar school education.

Gymnasiast [gymnaz'jast], *m.* (**—en**, *pl.* **—en**) grammar-school pupil.

Gymnasium [gym'na:zjum], *n.* (—s, *pl.* —sien) high school.
Gymnastik [gym'nastɪk], *f.* (—, *no pl.*) gymnastics.
gymnastisch [gym'nastɪʃ], *adj.* gymnastic(al); —e *Übungen*, physical exercises.

H

H [ha:], *n.* (—s, *pl.* —s) the letter H; (*Mus.*) *H Dur*, B major; *H Moll*, B minor.
ha! [ha:], *excl.* ha!
Haag, Den [ha:k, de:n], *m.* The Hague.
Haar [ha:r], *n.* (—s, *pl.* —e) hair; wool; nap; *aufs* —, exactly, to a hair; *um ein* —, very nearly, within a hair's breadth.
haaren ['ha:rən], *v.r. sich* —, shed o.'s hair.
haargenau ['ha:rgənau], *adj.* (very) exactly; to a nicety.
haarig ['ha:rɪç], *adj.* hairy.
Haarlocke ['ha:rlɔkə], *f.* (—, *pl.* —n) curl, ringlet.
Haarnadel ['ha:rna:dəl], *f.* (—, *pl.* —n) hairpin.
Haaröl ['ha:rø:l], *n.* (—s, *no pl.*) hair-oil.
Haarpinsel ['ha:rpɪnzəl], *m.* (—s, *pl.* —) camel-hair brush.
Haarröhrchen ['ha:rrø:rçən], *n.* (—s, *pl.* —) capillary tube.
Haarschleife ['ha:rʃlaifə], *f.* (—, *pl.* —en) bow in the hair.
Haarschnitt ['ha:rʃnɪt], *m.* (—s, *pl.* —e) hair-cut.
Haarschuppen ['ha:rʃupən], *f. pl.* dandruff.
Haarspalterei ['ha:rʃpaltərai], *f.* (—, *pl.* —en) hair-splitting.
haarsträubend ['ha:rʃtrɔybənt], *adj.* hair-raising, monstrous.
Haarwäsche ['ha:rvɛʃə], *f.* (—, *no pl.*) shampooing.
Haarwickel ['ha:rvɪkəl], *m.* (—s, *pl.* —) curler.
Haarzange ['ha:rtsaŋə], *f.* (—, *pl.* —n) tweezers.
Habe ['ha:bə], *f.* (—, *no pl.*) property, belongings, effects; *Hab und Gut*, all o.'s belongings, goods and chattels.
Haben ['ha:bən], *n.* (—s, *no pl.*) credit: *Soll und* —, debit and credit.
haben ['ha:bən], *v.a. irr.* have, possess; *da hast du's*, there you are; *es ist nicht zu* —, it is not available.
Habenichts ['ha:bənɪçts], *m.* (—es, *no pl.*) have-not.
Habgier ['ha:pgi:r], *f.* (—, *no pl.*) greediness, avarice, covetousness.

habhaft ['ha:phaft], *adj. einer Sache* — *werden*, get possession of a thing.
Habicht ['ha:bɪçt], *m.* (—s, *pl.* —e) (*Orn.*) hawk.
Habichtsinseln ['ha:bɪçtsɪnzəln], *f. pl.* the Azores.
Habichtsnase ['ha:bɪçtsna:zə], *f.* (—, *pl.* —n) hooked nose, aquiline nose.
Habilitation [habilita'tsjo:n], *f.* (—, *pl.* —en) admission *or* inauguration as a university lecturer.
habilitieren [habili'ti:rən], *v.r. sich* —, qualify as a university lecturer.
Habseligkeiten ['ha:pzelɪçkaitən], *f. pl.* property, effects, chattels.
Habsucht ['ha:pzuxt], *f.* (—, *no pl.*) avarice, greediness.
Hackbeil ['hakbail], *n.* (—s, *pl.* —e) cleaver, chopping-knife.
Hackbrett ['hakbrɛt], *n.* (—s, *pl.* —er) chopping-board.
Hacke ['hakə], *f.* (—, *pl.* —n) hoe, mattock; heel.
Hacken ['hakən], *m.* (—s, *pl.* —) heel; *sich auf die* — *machen*, be off, take to o.'s heels.
hacken ['hakən], *v.a.* hack, chop, hoe; mince; (*birds*) peck.
Hacker ['hakər], *m.* (—s, *pl.* —) chopper.
Häckerling ['hɛkərlɪŋ], *m.* (—s, *no pl.*) chopped straw.
Hackfleisch ['hakflaiʃ], *n.* (—es, *no pl.*) minced meat.
Häcksel ['hɛksəl], *n.* (—s, *no pl.*) chopped straw.
Hader ['ha:dər], *m.* (—s, *no pl.*) quarrel, dispute.
hadern ['ha:dərn], *v.n.* quarrel, have a dispute.
Hafen ['ha:fən], *m.* (—s, *pl.* ̈) harbour, port; refuge, haven.
Hafendamm ['ha:fəndam], *m.* (—s, *pl.* ̈e) jetty, mole, pier.
Hafensperre ['ha:fɛnʃpɛrə], *f.* (—, *pl.* —n) embargo, blockade.
Hafenzoll ['ha:fəntsɔl], *m.* (—s, *no pl.*) anchorage, harbour due.
Hafer ['ha:fər], *m.* (—s, *no pl.*) oats; *es sticht ihn der* —, he is getting cheeky, insolent.
Haferbrei ['ha:fərbrai], *m.* (—s, *no pl.*) porridge.
Hafergrütze ['ha:fərgrytsə], *f.* (—, *no pl.*) ground-oats, oatmeal.
Haferschleim ['ha:fərʃlaim], *m.* (—s, *no pl.*) oat-gruel, porridge.
Haff [haf], *n.* (—s, *pl.* —e) bay, lagoon.
Haft [haft], *f.* (—, *no pl.*) custody, imprisonment, arrest.
haftbar ['haftba:r], *adj.* answerable; (*Law*) liable.
Haftbefehl ['haftbəfe:l], *m.* (—s, *pl.* —e) warrant for arrest.
haften ['haftən], *v.n.* stick, cling, adhere; *für einen* —, go bail for s.o.; *für etwas* —, answer for, be liable for s.th.

Häftling

Häftling ['hɛftlɪŋ], *m.* (**—s**, *pl.* **—e**) prisoner.

Haftpflicht ['haftpflɪçt], *f.* (**—**, *no pl.*) liability.

Haftung ['haftuŋ], *f.* (**—**, *no pl.*) liability, security; (*Comm.*) *Gesellschaft mit beschränkter* **—**, limited liability company, (*abbr.*) Ltd.

Hag [ha:k], *m.* (**—es**, *pl.* **—e**) hedge, enclosure.

Hagebuche ['ha:gəbu:xə], *f.* (**—**, *pl.* **—n**) hornbeam.

Hagebutte ['ha:gəbutə], *f.* (**—**, *pl.* **—n**) (*Bot.*) hip, haw.

Hagedorn ['ha:gədɔrn], *m.* (**—s**, *no pl.*) (*Bot.*) hawthorn.

Hagel ['ha:gəl], *m.* (**—s**, *no pl.*) hail.

hageln ['ha:gəln], *v.n.* hail.

Hagelschauer ['ha:gəlʃauər], *m.* (**—s**, *pl.* **—**) hailstorm.

hager ['ha:gər], *adj.* thin, lean, lank, gaunt.

Häher ['hɛ:ər], *m.* (**—s**, *pl.* **—**) (*Orn.*) jay.

Hahn [ha:n], *m.* (**—s**, *pl.* **—e**) (*Orn.*) cockerel, cock; (*water, gas*) cock, tap, faucet; *— im Korbe sein*, rule the roost; *da kräht kein — danach*, nobody cares two hoots about it.

Hahnenbalken ['ha:nənbalkən], *m.* (**—s**, *pl.* **—**) cock-loft; hen-roost.

Hahnenfuß ['ha:nənfu:s], *m.* (**—es**, *no pl.*) (*Bot.*) crow-foot.

Hahnensporn ['ha:nɛnʃpɔrn], *m.* (**—s**, *no pl.*) cockspur.

Hahnentritt ['ha:nəntrɪt], *m.* (**—s**, *no pl.*) cock's tread.

Hahnrei ['ha:nraɪ], *m.* (**—s**, *pl.* **—e**) cuckold; *einen zum — machen*, cuckold s.o.

Hai [haɪ], *m.* (**—s**, *pl.* **—e**) (*Zool.*) shark.

Haifisch ['haɪfɪʃ], *m.* (**—es**, *pl.* **—e**) (*Zool.*) shark.

Hain [haɪn], *m.* (**—s**, *pl.* **—e**) (*Poet.*) grove, thicket.

Haiti [ha'ɪti], *n.* Haiti.

Häkchen ['hɛ:kçən], *n.* (**—s**, *pl.* **—**) small hook, crotchet; apostrophe.

häkeln ['hɛ:kəln], *v.a. v.n.* crochet; (*fig.*) tease; (*Am.*) needle (*coll.*).

Haken ['ha:kən], *m.* (**—s**, *pl.* **—**) hook, clasp; (*fig.*) hitch, snag.

Hakenkreuz ['ha:kənkrɔyts], *n.* (**—es**, *pl.* **—e**) swastika.

halb [halp], *adj.* half; *halb neun*, half past eight.

halbieren [hal'bi:rən], *v.a.* halve, divide into halves; (*Maths.*) bisect.

Halbinsel ['halpɪnzəl], *f.* (**—**, *pl.* **—n**) peninsula.

Halbmesser ['halpmɛsər], *m.* (**—s**, *pl.* **—**) radius.

halbpart ['halppart], *adj.* *— mit einem machen*, go halves with s.o.

halbstündig ['halpʃtyndɪç], *adj.* lasting half an hour.

halbstündlich ['halpʃtyntlɪç], *adj.* half-hourly, every half-hour.

halbwegs ['halpve:ks], *adv.* (*coll.*) reasonably, tolerably.

Halbwelt ['halpvɛlt], *f.* (**—**, *no pl.*) demi-monde.

halbwüchsig ['halpvy:ksɪç], *adj.* teenage.

Halde ['haldə], *f.* (**—**, *pl.* **—n**) declivity, hill; (*Min.*) waste-heap, slag-heap.

Hälfte ['hɛlftə], *f.* (**—**, *pl.* **—n**) half; (*obs.*) moiety.

Halfter ['halftər], *f.* (**—**, *pl.* **—n**) halter.

Hall [hal], *m.* (**—s**, *no pl.*) sound, echo.

Halle ['halə], *f.* (**—**, *pl.* **—n**) hall, vestibule; portico; porch.

hallen ['halən], *v.n.* sound, resound; clang.

Halm [halm], *m.* (**—es**, *pl.* **—e**) stalk; (*grass*) blade.

Hals [hals], *m.* (**—es**, *pl.* **—e**) neck, throat; *— über Kopf*, head over heels, hastily, hurriedly.

Halsader ['halsa:dər], *f.* (**—**, *pl.* **—n**) jugular vein.

Halsbinde ['halsbɪndə], *f.* (**—**, *pl.* **—n**) scarf, tie.

Halsentzündung ['halsɛntsynduŋ], *f.* (**—**, *pl.* **—en**) inflammation of the throat.

Halskrause ['halskrauzə], *f.* (**—**, *pl.* **—n**) frill, ruff.

halsstarrig ['halsʃtarɪç], *adj.* stubborn, obstinate.

Halsweh ['halsve:], *n.* (**—s**, *no pl.*) sore throat.

Halt [halt], *m.* (**—es**, *no pl.*) halt; stop; hold; (*also fig.*) support.

haltbar ['haltba:r], *adj.* durable, strong; tenable, valid.

halten ['haltən], *v.a. irr.* hold; keep; detain; deliver (speech, lecture); observe, celebrate. *— v.n.* stop; stand firm; insist; *halt!* stop! stop it! *— v.r. sich —*, hold out, keep, behave.

haltlos ['haltlo:s], *adj.* unprincipled; floundering, unsteady.

Haltung ['haltuŋ], *f.* (**—**, *pl.* **—en**) carriage, posture, attitude; (*fig.*) behaviour, demeanour; attitude.

Halunke [ha'luŋkə], *m.* (**—n**, *pl.* **—n**) scoundrel, rascal, scamp.

hämisch ['hɛ:mɪʃ], *adj.* malicious, spiteful.

Hammel ['haməl], *m.* (**—s**, *pl.* **—**) (*meat*) mutton.

Hammelkeule ['haməlkɔylə], *f.* (**—**, *pl.* **—n**) leg of mutton.

Hammer ['hamər], *m.* (**—s**, *pl.* **—**) hammer; *unter den — kommen*, be sold by auction.

Hämorrhoiden [hɛmo'ri:dən], *f.* (*Med.*) piles, haemorrhoids.

Hand [hant], *f.* (**—**, *pl.* **—e**) hand.

Handarbeit ['hantarbaɪt], *f.* (**—**, *pl.* **—en**) manual labour; needlework.

Handel ['handəl], *m.* (**—s**, *no pl.*) trade, commerce; *— treiben*, carry on trade, do business.

Händel ['hɛndəl], *m. pl.* quarrel, difference, dispute.

handeln ['handəln], *v.n.* act; — *in*, deal in; *es handelt sich um* . . . it is a question of . . . ; *es handelt von* . . ., it deals with . . . .
handelseinig ['handəlsaɪnɪç], *adj.* — *werden*, come to terms.
Handelsgenossenschaft ['handəlsgənɔsənʃaft], *f.* (—, *pl.* —en) trading company.
Handelsgeschäft ['handəlsgəʃɛft], *n.* (—es, *pl.* —e) commercial transaction.
Handelsgesellschaft ['handəlsgəzɛlʃaft], *f.* (—, *pl.* —en) trading company; joint-stock company.
Handelskammer ['handəlskamər], *f.* (—, *pl.* —n) chamber of commerce.
Handelsmarke ['handəlsmarkə], *f.* (—, *pl.* —n) trade-mark.
Handelsreisende ['handəlsraɪzəndə], *m.* (—n, *pl.* —n) commercial traveller.
händelsüchtig ['hɛndəlzyçtɪç], *adj.* quarrelsome; litigious.
Handelsvertrag ['handəlsfɛrtraːk], *m.* (—es, *pl.* ‍e) commercial treaty; contract.
Handelszweig ['handəlstsvaɪk], *m.* (—es, *pl.* —e) branch of trade.
Handfeger ['hantfeːgər], *m.* (—s, *pl.* —) hand-broom, handbrush.
Handfertigkeit ['hantfɛrtɪçkaɪt], *f.* (—, *no pl.*) dexterity, manual skill; handicrafts.
handfest ['hantfɛst], *adj.* robust, strong.
Handgeld ['hantgɛlt], *n.* (—es, *no pl.*) earnest; (*money*) advance.
Handgelenk ['hantgəlɛŋk], *n.* (—s, *pl.* —e) wrist.
handgemein ['hanɪgəmaɪn], *adj.* — *werden*, come to blows.
Handgemenge ['hantgəmɛŋə], *n.* (—s, *no pl.*) fray, scuffle.
handgreiflich ['hantgraɪflɪç], *adj.* palpable; evident, plain.
Handgriff ['hantgrɪf], *m.* (—es, *pl.* —e) handle; (*fig.*) knack.
Handhabe ['hantha:bə], *f.* (—, *pl.* —n) (*fig.*) hold, handle.
handhaben ['hantha:bən], *v.a.* handle, manage; operate.
Handlanger ['hantlaŋər], *m.* (—s, *pl.* —) helper, carrier.
Händler ['hɛndlər], *m.* (—s, *pl.* —) dealer, merchant.
handlich ['hantlɪç], *adj.* handy, manageable.
Handlung ['handluŋ], *f.* (—, *pl.* —en) shop; (*Am.*) store; commercial house, mercantile business; action, act, deed; (*Lit.*) plot.
Handrücken ['hantrykən], *m.* (—s, *pl.* —) back of the hand.
Handschelle ['hantʃɛlə], *f.* (—, *pl.* —n) manacle, handcuff.
Handschlag ['hantʃla:k], *m.* (—s, *pl.* ‍e) handshake.

Handschuh ['hantʃu:], *m.* (—s, *pl.* —e) glove; (*of iron*) gauntlet.
Handstreich ['hantʃtraɪç], *m.* (—es, *pl.* —e) (*Mil.*) surprise attack, coup de main.
Handtuch ['hanttu:x], *n.* (—es, *pl.* ‍er) towel.
Handumdrehen ['hantumdre:ən], *n.* (—s, *no pl.*) *im* —, in no time, in a jiffy.
Handwerk ['hantvɛrk], *n.* (—s, *pl.* —e) handicraft, trade, craft.
Handwörterbuch ['hantvœrtərbu:x], *n.* (—es, *pl.* ‍er) compact dictionary.
Handwurzel ['hantvurtsəl], *f.* (—, *pl.* —n) wrist.
Hanf [hanf], *m.* (—es, *no pl.*) hemp.
Hänfling ['hɛnflɪŋ], *m.* (—s, *pl.* —e) (*Orn.*) linnet.
Hang [haŋ], *m.* (—es, *pl.* ‍e) slope, declivity; (*fig.*) (*no pl.*) inclination, propensity.
Hängematte ['hɛŋəmatə], *f.* (—, *pl.* —n) hammock.
hängen ['hɛŋən], *v.a.* irr. hang, suspend. — *v.r. sich* —, hang o.s. — *v.n.* hang, be suspended; be hanged (*execution*).
Hannover [ha'no:fər], *n.* Hanover.
Hänselei ['hɛnzəlaɪ], *f.* (—, *pl.* —en) chaffing, leg-pulling, teasing.
hänseln ['hɛnzəln], *v.a.* tease, chaff.
Hantel ['hantəl], *f.* (—, *pl.* —n) dumbbell.
hantieren [han'ti:rən], *v.n.* busy o.s., work, occupy o.s. (with).
hapern ['ha:pərn], *v.n.* lack, be deficient; *da hapert es*, that's the snag.
Häppchen ['hɛpçən], *n.* (—s, *pl.* —) morsel.
Happen ['hapən], *m.* (—s, *pl.* —) mouthful.
happig ['hapɪç], *adj.* greedy; excessive.
Härchen ['hɛːrçən], *n.* (—s, *pl.* —) short hair.
Harfe ['harfə], *f.* (—, *pl.* —n) (*Mus.*) harp.
Harke ['harkə], *f.* (—, *pl.* —n) rake.
Harm [harm], *m.* (—es, *no pl.*) grief, sorrow; injury, wrong.
härmen ['hɛrmən], *v.r. sich* — *um*, grieve over.
harmlos ['harmlo:s], *adj.* harmless, innocuous.
Harmonielehre [harmo'ni:le:rə], *f.* (—, *pl.* —n) (*Mus.*) harmonics; harmony.
harmonieren [harmo'ni:rən], *v.n.* mit *einem* —, be in concord with s.o., agree with s.o.
Harmonika [har'mo:nɪka], *f.* (—, *pl.* —ken) (*Mus.*) accordion, concertina; mouth-organ.
Harn [harn], *m.* (—s, *no pl.*) urine.
Harnisch ['harnɪʃ], *m.* (—es, *pl.* —e) harness, armour; *in* — *bringen*, enrage.
Harpune [har'pu:nə], *f.* (—, *pl.* —n) harpoon.
harren ['harən], *v.n.* wait for, hope for.

harsch

harsch [harʃ], *adj.* harsh; rough; unfriendly.

hart [hart], *adj.* hard, severe, cruel, austere.

Härte [ˈhɛrtə], *f.* (—, *pl.* —n) hardness, severity.

härten [ˈhɛrtən], *v.a.* harden.

hartleibig [ˈhartlaɪbɪç], *adj.* constipated.

hartnäckig [ˈhartnɛkɪç], *adj.* stubborn, obstinate; undaunted.

Harz (1) [harts], *m.* (*Geog.*) (—es, *no pl.*) the Hartz mountains.

Harz (2) [harts], *n.* (—es, *pl.* —e) resin, rosin.

harzig [ˈhartsɪç], *adj.* resinous.

Hasardspiel [haˈzartʃpiːl], *n.* (—es, *pl.* —e) game of chance, gamble.

Haschee [haˈʃeː], *n.* (—s, *pl.* —s) puree, hash, mash.

haschen [ˈhaʃən], *v.a.* catch, snatch, seize. — *v.n.* — *nach,* strain after, snatch at.

Häschen [ˈhɛːsçən], *n.* (—s, *pl.* —) (*Zool.*) small hare, leveret.

Häscher [ˈhɛʃər], *m.* (—s, *pl.* —) bailiff.

Hase [ˈhaːzə], *m.* (—n, *pl.* —n) (*Zool.*) hare.

Haselrute [ˈhaːzəlruːtə], *f.* (—, *pl.* —n) hazel-switch.

Hasenfuß [ˈhaːzənfuːs], *m.* (—es, *no pl.*) coward.

Hasenklein [ˈhaːzənklaɪn], *n.* (—s, *no pl.*) jugged hare.

Hasenscharte [ˈhaːzənʃartə], *f.* (—, *pl.* —n) hare-lip.

Haspe [ˈhaspə], *f.* (—, *pl.* —n) hasp, hinge.

Haspel [ˈhaspəl], *f.* (—, *pl.* —n) reel.

haspeln [ˈhaspəln], *v.a.* wind on a reel; (*fig.*) rattle off.

Haß [has], *m.* (—sses, *no pl.*) hatred, hate, detestation.

hassen [ˈhasən], *v.a.* hate, detest.

haßerfüllt [ˈhasərfylt], *adj.* full of spite, full of hatred.

häßlich [ˈhɛslɪç], *adj.* ugly, repulsive; (*fig.*) unpleasant, unkind; unseemly.

Hast [hast], *f.* (—, *no pl.*) haste, hurry, hastiness, rashness.

hastig [ˈhastɪç], *adj.* hasty, hurried.

hätscheln [ˈhɛtʃəln], *v.a.* pamper, caress, fondle.

Hatz [hats], *f.* (—, *pl.* —en) baiting; hunt; revelry.

Haube [ˈhaubə], *f.* (—, *pl.* —n) bonnet, cap; (*Motor.*) bonnet, (*Am.*) hood.

Haubenlerche [ˈhaubənlɛrçə], *f.* (—, *pl.* —n) (*Orn.*) crested lark.

Haubitze [hauˈbɪtsə], *f.* (—, *pl.* —n) howitzer.

Hauch [haux], *m.* (—es, *no pl.*) breath, whiff; (*fig.*) touch, tinge.

hauchdünn [ˈhauxdyn], *adj.* extremely thin.

hauchen [ˈhauxən], *v.n.* breathe.

Hauchlaut [ˈhauxlaut], *m.* (—es, *pl.* —e) (*Phonet.*) aspirate.

Haudegen [ˈhaudeːgən], *m.* (—s, *pl.* —) broad-sword; *ein alter* —, an old bully.

Haue [ˈhauə], *f.* (—, *no pl.*) (*coll.*) thrashing.

hauen [ˈhauən], *v.a.* hew; cut; strike; hit; give a hiding to. — *v.n. über die Schnur* —, kick over the traces.

Hauer [ˈhauər], *m.* (—s, *pl.* —) hewer, cutter; (*animal*) fang, tusk.

Häuer [ˈhɔyər], *m.* (—s, *pl.* —) miner.

Haufen [ˈhaufən], *m.* (—s, *pl.* —) heap, pile.

häufen [ˈhɔyfən], *v.a.* heap, pile. — *v.r. sich* —, accumulate, multiply, increase.

häufig [ˈhɔyfɪç], *adj.* frequent, abundant. — *adv.* frequently, often.

Häufung [ˈhɔyfuŋ], *f.* (—, *pl.* —en) accumulation.

Haupt [haupt], *n.* (—es, *pl.* ⁝er) head; leader; chief, principal, (*compounds*) main—; *aufs* — *schlagen,* inflict a total defeat on; *ein bemoostes* —, an old student.

Hauptaltar [ˈhauptaltaːr], *m.* (—s, *pl.* —e) (*Eccl.*) high altar.

Hauptbuch [ˈhauptbuːx], *n.* (—es, *pl.* ⁝er) ledger.

Häuptling [ˈhɔyptlɪŋ], *m.* (—s, *pl.* —e) chieftain.

Hauptmann [ˈhauptman], *m.* (—s, *pl.* ⁝er, **Hauptleute**) (*Mil.*) captain.

Hauptnenner [ˈhauptnɛnər], *m.* (—s, *pl.* —) (*Maths.*) common denominator.

Hauptquartier [ˈhauptkvartiːr], *n.* (—es, *pl.* —e) headquarters.

Hauptsache [ˈhauptzaxə], *f.* (—, *pl.* —n) main thing, substance, main point; *in der* —, in the main.

hauptsächlich [ˈhauptzɛçlɪç], *adj.* chief, main, principal, essential.

Hauptsatz [ˈhauptzats], *m.* (—es, *pl.* ⁝e) (*Gram.*) principal sentence.

Hauptschriftleiter [ˈhauptʃrɪftlaɪtər], *m.* (—s, *pl.* —) editor-in-chief.

Hauptschule [ˈhauptʃuːlə], *f.* (—, *pl.* —n) intermediate school.

Hauptstadt [ˈhauptʃtat], *f.* (—, *pl.* ⁝e) capital, metropolis.

Hauptton [ˈhauptoːn], *m.* (—s, *pl.* ⁝e) (*Mus.*) key-note; (*Phonet.*) primary accent.

Haupttreffer [ˈhaupttrɛfər], *m.* (—s, *pl.* —) first prize; jackpot.

Hauptverkehrsstunden [ˈhauptfɛrkeːrsʃtundən], *f. pl.* (*traffic etc.*) rush-hour.

Hauptwache [ˈhauptvaxə], *f.* (—, *pl.* —n) central guardroom.

Hauptwort [ˈhauptvɔrt], *n.* (—es, *pl.* ⁝er) noun, substantive.

Hauptzahl [ˈhaupttsaːl], *f.* (—, *pl.* —en) cardinal number.

Haus [haus], *n.* (—es, *pl.* ⁝er) house, home; household; firm; *zu* —*e,* at home; *nach* —*e,* home.

Hausarbeit [ˈhausarbaɪt], *f.* (—, *pl.* —en) housework, domestic work; homework.

Hausarrest ['hausarɛst], *m.* (**—es**, *no pl.*) house arrest.

Hausarzt ['hausartst], *m.* (**—es**, *pl.* ˙e) family doctor.

hausbacken ['hausbakən], *adj.* homemade; homely; humdrum.

Häuschen ['hɔysçən], *n.* (**—s**, *pl.* —) small house, cottage; *ganz aus dem — sein*, be beside o.s.

Hausen ['hauzən], *m.* (**—s**, *pl.* —) sturgeon.

hausen ['hauzən], *v.n.* reside, be domiciled; *übel* —, play havoc among.

Hausflur ['hausflu:r], *m.* (**—s**, *pl.* —e) entrance hall (of a house), vestibule.

Hausfrau ['hausfrau], *f.* (—, *pl.* —en) housewife, mistress of the house.

Hausfriedensbruch ['hausfri:dənsbrux], *m.* (**—es**, *pl.* ˙e) (*Law*) intrusion, trespass.

Hausgenosse ['hausgənɔsə], *m.* (**—n**, *pl.* **—n**) fellow-lodger.

Haushalt ['haushalt], *m.* (**—es**, *no pl.*) household.

Haushaltung ['haushaltuŋ], *f.* (—, *no pl.*) housekeeping.

Hausherr ['hausher], *m.* (**—n**, *pl.* **—en**) master of the house, householder.

Haushofmeister ['haushofmaɪstər], *m.* (**—s**, *pl.* —) steward; butler.

hausieren [hau'zi:rən], *v.n.* peddle, hawk.

Hauslehrer ['hausle:rər], *m.* (**—s**, *pl.* —) private tutor.

Häusler ['hɔyslər], *m.* (**—s**, *pl.* —) cottager.

häuslich ['hɔyslɪç], *adj.* domestic, domesticated.

Hausmädchen ['hausmɛdçən], *n.* (**—s**, *pl.* —) housemaid.

Hausmannskost ['hausmanskɔst], *f.* (—, *no pl.*) plain fare.

Hausmeister ['hausmaɪstər], *m.* (**—s**, *pl.* —) house-porter, caretaker.

Hausmittel ['hausmɪtəl], *n.* (**—s**, *pl.* —) household remedy.

Hausrat ['hausra:t], *m.* (**—s**, *no pl.*) household furnishings, household effects.

Hausschlüssel ['hausʃlysəl], *m.* (**—s**, *pl.* —) latch-key.

Hausschuh ['hausʃu:], *m.* (**—s**, *pl.* —e) slipper.

Hausstand ['hausʃtant], *m.* (**—es**, *pl.* ˙e) household.

Haustier ['hausti:r], *m.* (**—es**, *pl.* —e) domestic animal.

Hausvater ['hausfa:tər], *m.* (**—s**, *pl.* ˙) paterfamilias.

Hausverwalter ['hausfɛrvaltər], *m.* (**—s**, *pl.* —) steward, caretaker; (*Am.*) janitor.

Hauswesen ['hausve:zən], *n.* (**—s**, *no pl.*) household management *or* affairs.

Hauswirt ['hausvɪrt], *m.* (**—es**, *pl.* —e) landlord.

Hauswirtin ['hausvɪrtɪn], *f.* (—, *pl.* **—nen**) landlady.

Hauswirtschaft ['hausvɪrtʃaft], *f.* (—, *no pl.*) housekeeping, domestic economy.

Haut [haut], *f.* (—, *pl.* ˙e) (*human*) skin; (*animal*) hide; (*fruit*) peel; (*on liquid*) skin; membrane; film; *aus der — fahren*, flare up.

Hautausschlag ['hautausʃla:k], *m.* (**—s**, *pl.* ˙e) rash, eczema.

Häutchen ['hɔytçən], *n.* (**—s**, *pl.* —) cuticle, pellicle, membrane.

häuten ['hɔytən], *v.a.* skin, flay, strip off the skin. — *v.r. sich* —, cast off (skin) *or* slough.

Hebamme ['he:pamə], *f.* (—, *pl.* **—n**) midwife.

Hebel ['he:bəl], *m.* (**—s**, *pl.* —) lever.

heben ['he:bən], *v.a. irr.* raise, lift, hoist, heave; elevate; improve; *aus der Taufe —*, be godfather (godmother) to (s.o.).

Heber ['he:bər], *m.* (**—s**, *pl.* —) siphon.

Hebräer [he'brɛ:ər], *m.* (**—s**, *pl.* —) Hebrew.

Hechel ['hɛçəl], *f.* (—, *pl.* **—n**) hackle, flax-comb.

hecheln ['hɛçəln], *v.a.* dress flax; hackle; (*fig.*) taunt, heckle.

Hecht [hɛçt], *m.* (**—es**, *pl.* —e) (*Zool.*) pike; (*swimming*) dive.

Hechtsprung ['hɛçtʃpruŋ], *m.* (**—s**, *pl.* ˙e) header.

Heck [hɛk], *n.* (**—s**, *pl.* —e) (*Naut.*) stern; (*Motor.*) rear; (*Aviat.*) tail.

Heckbord ['hɛkbɔrt], *m.* (**—s**, *pl.* —e) (*Naut.*) taffrail.

Hecke ['hɛkə], *f.* (—, *pl.* **—n**) hedge.

hecken ['hɛkən], *v.n.* breed, bring forth.

Heckpfennig ['hɛkpfɛnɪç], *m.* (**—s**, *pl.* —e) lucky sixpence.

heda! ['he:da:], *excl.* hey, you!

Heer [he:r], *n.* (**—es**, *pl.* —e) army; multitude; *stehendes —*, regular army.

Heeresmacht ['he:rəsmaxt], *f.* (—, *pl.* ˙e) armed forces, troops.

Heerschar ['he:rʃar], *f.* (—, *pl.* **—en**) host; corps, legion; (*Bibl.*) *der Herr der —en*, the Lord of Hosts.

Heerschau ['he:rʃau], *f.* (—, *pl.* **—en**) review, muster, parade.

Heerstraße ['he:rʃtra:sə], *f.* (—, *pl.* **—en**) military road; highway; (*Am.*) highroad.

Heerwesen ['he:rve:zən], *n.* (**—s**, *no pl.*) military affairs.

Hefe ['he:fə], *f.* (—, *no pl.*) yeast; dregs, sediment.

Hefeteig ['he:fataɪk], *m.* (**—s**, *pl.* —e) leavened dough.

Heft [hɛft], *n.* (**—es**, *pl.* —e) exercise-book, copy-book; haft, handle, hilt.

heften ['hɛftən], *v.a.* fasten; baste, stitch, fix, pin.

heftig ['hɛftɪç], *adj.* vehement, violent.

Heftnadel ['hɛftna:dəl], *f.* (—, *pl.* **—n**) stitching-needle.

hegen ['he:gən], *v.a.* enclose, protect, preserve; (*fig.*) cherish; entertain; hold; *— und pflegen*, nurse carefully.

Hehl

Hehl [heːl], *n.* (**—es**, *no pl.*) concealment, secret.
hehlen ['heːlən], *v.n.* receive stolen goods.
Hehler ['həːlər], *m.* (**—s**, *pl.* **—**) receiver of stolen goods, (*sl.*) fence.
hehr [heːr], *adj.* (*Lit.*) exalted, august, sublime.
Heide (1) ['haɪdə], *m.* (**—n**, *pl.* **—n**) heathen, pagan.
Heide (2) ['haɪdə], *f.* (**—**, *pl.* **—n**) heath.
Heidekraut ['haɪdəkraut], *n.* (**—es**, *no pl.*) heath, heather.
Heidelbeere ['haɪdəlbeːrə], *f.* (**—**, *pl.* **—n**) (*Bot.*) bilberry; (*Am.*) blueberry.
Heidenangst ['haɪdənaŋst], *f.* (**—**, *no pl.*) (*coll.*) mortal fear.
Heidenlärm ['haɪdənlɛrm], *m.* (**—es**, *no pl.*) hullaballoo.
Heidenröschen ['haɪdənrøːsçən], *n.* (**—s**, *pl.* **—**) (*Bot.*) sweet-briar.
Heidentum ['haɪdəntuːm], *n.* (**—s**, *no pl.*) paganism.
heidnisch ['haɪdnɪʃ], *adj.* pagan, heathen.
Heidschnuke ['haɪtʃnuːkə], *f.* (**—**, *pl.* **—n**) moorland sheep.
heikel ['haɪkəl], *adj.* delicate, sensitive, critical.
Heil [haɪl], *n.* (**—(e)s**, *no pl.*) safety, welfare; (*Theol.*) salvation; *sein — versuchen*, have a try, try o.'s luck. *— int.* hail! — *der Königin*, God save the Queen.
heil [haɪl], *adj.* unhurt, intact.
Heiland ['haɪlant], *m.* (**—s**, *no pl.*) Saviour, Redeemer.
Heilanstalt ['haɪlanʃtalt], *f.* (**—**, *pl.* **—en**) sanatorium, convalescent home; (*Am.*) sanitarium.
heilbar ['haɪlbaːr], *adj.* curable.
heilbringend ['haɪlbrɪŋənt], *adj.* salutary.
heilen ['haɪlən], *v.a.* cure, heal. *— v.n.* (*aux.* sein) heal.
heilig ['haɪlɪç], *adj.* holy, sacred; *der Heilige Abend*, Christmas Eve; *— sprechen*, canonise; (*before name*) *der*, *die —e*, Saint.
Heiligenschein ['haɪlɪgənʃaɪn], *m.* (**—s**, *pl.* **—e**) halo; (*clouds*) nimbus.
Heiligkeit ['haɪlɪçkaɪt], *f.* (**—**, *no pl.*) holiness, sanctity, sacredness.
Heiligtum ['haɪlɪçtuːm], *n.* (**—s**, *pl.* **-er**) sanctuary, shrine; holy relic.
Heiligung ['haɪlɪguŋ], *f.* (**—**, *pl.* **—en**) sanctification, consecration.
heilkräftig ['haɪlkrɛftɪç], *adj.* curative, salubrious.
Heilkunde ['haɪlkundə], *f.* (**—**, *no pl.*) therapeutics.
heillos ['haɪlloːs], *adj.* wicked, mischievous; (*fig.*) awful.
Heilmittel ['haɪlmɪtəl], *n.* (**—s**, *pl.* **—**) remedy.
heilsam ['haɪlzaːm], *adj.* salubrious, salutary.
Heilsamkeit ['haɪlzaːmkaɪt], *f.* (**—**, *no pl.*) salubrity, salubriousness.
Heilsarmee ['haɪlsarmeː], *f.* (**—**, *no pl.*) Salvation Army.

Heilslehre ['haɪlsleːrə], *f.* (**—**, *pl.* **—n**) doctrine of salvation.
Heiltrank ['haɪltraŋk], *m.* (**—es**, *no pl.*) (medicinal) potion.
Heim [haɪm], *n.* (**—es**, *pl.* **—e**) home.
heim [haɪm], *adv. prefix* (*to verbs*) home.
Heimat ['haɪmat], *f.* (**—**, *no pl.*) native place, home, homeland.
Heimatschein ['haɪmatʃaɪn], *m.* (**—es**, *pl.* **—e**) certificate of origin *or* domicile.
Heimchen ['haɪmçən], *n.* (**—s**, *pl.* **—**) (*Ent.*) cricket.
heimführen ['haɪmfyːrən], *v.a.* bring home (a bride); (*fig.*) marry.
Heimgang ['haɪmgaŋ], *m.* (**—es**, *no pl.*) going home; (*fig.*) decease, death.
heimisch ['haɪmɪʃ], *adj.* native, indigenous; *sich — fühlen*, feel at home.
heimkehren ['haɪmkeːrən], *v.n.* return (home).
heimleuchten ['haɪmləɪçtən], *v.n. einem —*, tell s.o. the plain truth, give s.o. a piece of o.'s mind.
heimlich ['haɪmlɪç], *adj.* secret, clandestine, furtive.
heimsuchen ['haɪmzuːxən], *v.a.* visit; afflict, punish.
Heimtücke ['haɪmtykə], *f.* (**—**, *no pl.*) malice.
heimwärts ['haɪmvɛrts], *adv.* homeward.
Heimweh ['haɪmveː], *n.* (**—s**, *no pl.*) homesickness; nostalgia.
heimzahlen ['haɪmtsaːlən], *v.a.* pay back, retaliate.
Hein [haɪn], *m.* (*coll.*) *Freund —*, Death.
Heinzelmännchen ['haɪntsəlmɛnçən], *n.* (**—s**, *pl.* **—**) goblin, brownie, imp.
Heirat ['haɪraːt], *f.* (**—**, *pl.* **—en**) marriage, wedding.
heiraten ['haɪraːtən], *v.a.* marry, wed.
Heiratsgut ['haɪraːtsguːt], *n.* (**—es**, *pl.* **-er**) dowry.
heischen ['haɪʃən], *v.a.* (*Poet.*) ask, demand.
heiser ['haɪzər], *adj.* hoarse.
heiß [haɪs], *adj.* hot; (*fig.*) ardent; (*climate*) torrid.
heißen ['haɪsən], *v.a. irr.* bid, command. *— v.n.* be called; be said; signify, mean; *es heißt*, it is said; *das heißt (d.h.)*, that is to say; *wie — Sie?* what is your name?
heißgeliebt ['haɪsgəliːpt], *adj.* dearly beloved.
heiter ['haɪtər], *adj.* clear; serene; cheerful.
Heiterkeit ['haɪtərkaɪt], *f.* (**—**, *no pl.*) serenity; cheerfulness.
heizen ['haɪtsən], *v.a. v.n.* heat.
Heizkissen ['haɪtskɪsən], *n.* (**—s**, *pl.* **—**) electric pad *or* blanket.
Heizkörper ['haɪtskœrpər], *m.* (**—s**, *pl.* **—**) radiator; heater.
Heizung ['haɪtsuŋ], *f.* (**—**, *pl.* **—en**) heating.
hektisch ['hɛktɪʃ], *adj.* hectic.

hektographieren [hɛktograˈfiːrən], *v.a.* stencil, duplicate.

Hektoliter [ˈhɛktoliːtər], *m.* (—s, *pl.* —) hectolitre (22 gallons).

Held [hɛlt], *m.* (—en, *pl.* —en) hero.

Heldengedicht [ˈhɛldəngədɪçt], *n.* (—es, *pl.* —e) heroic poem, epic.

heldenhaft [ˈhɛldənhaft], *adj.* heroic. — *adv.* heroically.

Heldenmut [ˈhɛldənmuːt], *m.* (—es, *no pl.*) heroism.

helfen [ˈhɛlfən], *v.n. irr.* (*Dat.*) help, aid, assist.

Helfershelfer [ˈhɛlfərshɛlfər], *m.* (—s, *pl.* —) accomplice, accessory.

Helgoland [ˈhɛlgolant], *n.* Heligoland.

hell [hɛl], *adj.* clear, bright, light; (*coll.*) clever, wide awake.

Helldunkel [ˈhɛldʊŋkəl], *n.* (—s, *no pl.*) twilight; (*Art*) chiaroscuro.

Helle [ˈhɛlə], *f.* (—, *no pl.*) clearness; brightness; daylight.

Heller [ˈhɛlər], *m.* (—s, *pl.* —) small coin, farthing.

hellhörig [ˈhɛlhøːrɪç], *adj.* keen of hearing.

Helligkeit [ˈhɛlɪçkaɪt], *f.* (—, *no pl.*) clearness; daylight.

Hellseher [ˈhɛlzeːər], *m.* (—s, *pl.* —) clairvoyant.

hellsichtig [ˈhɛlzɪçtɪç], *adj.* clairvoyant; clear-sighted.

Helm [hɛlm], *m.* (—es, *pl.* —e) helmet.

Helmbusch [ˈhɛlmbʊʃ], *m.* (—es, *pl.* ⁻e) crest (of helmet).

Helmgitter [ˈhɛlmgɪtər], *n.* (—s, *pl.* —) eye-slit (in helmet).

Helsingfors [ˈhɛlzɪŋfɔrs], *n.* Helsinki.

Helsingör [hɛlzɪŋˈøːr], *n.* Elsinore.

Hemd [hɛmt], *n.* (—es, *pl.* —en) shirt; vest.

Hemdenstoff [ˈhɛmdənʃtɔf], *m.* (—es, *pl.* —e) shirting.

hemmen [ˈhɛmən], *v.a.* stop, hamper, hinder, restrain; (*fig.*) inhibit.

Hemmschuh [ˈhɛmʃuː], *m.* (—s, *pl.* —e) brake; (*fig.*) drag, obstruction.

Hemmung [ˈhɛmʊŋ], *f.* (—, *pl.* —en) stoppage, hindrance, restraint; (*watch*) escapement; (*fig.*) inhibition, reluctance.

Hengst [hɛŋkst], *m.* (—es, *pl.* —e) stallion.

Henkel [ˈhɛŋkəl], *m.* (—s, *pl.* —) handle.

henken [ˈhɛŋkən], *v.a* hang (s.o.).

Henker [ˈhɛŋkər], *m.* (—s, *pl.* —) hangman, executioner.

Henne [ˈhɛnə], *f.* (—, *pl.* —n) (*Zool.*) hen; *junge —*, pullet.

her [heːr], *adv.* hither, here, to me; (*temp.*) since, ago; *von alters —*, from olden times; *von je —*, from time immemorial; *wo kommst du —?* where do you come from? *wie lange ist es —?* how long ago was it?

herab [hɛˈrap], *adv.* downwards, down to; *die Treppe —*, downstairs.

herablassen [hɛˈraplasən], *v.r. irr. sich — etwas zu tun*, condescend to do s.th.

herabsehen [hɛˈrapzeːən], *v.n. irr.* look down; (*fig.*) look down upon s.o.

herabsetzen [hɛˈrapzɛtsən], *v.a.* put down; degrade; (*value*) depreciate; (*price*) reduce, lower; (*fig.*) disparage.

herabwürdigen [hɛˈrapvyrdɪgən], *v.a.* degrade, abase.

herabziehen [hɛˈraptsiːən], *v.a. irr.* pull down.

Heraldik [heˈraldɪk], *f.* (—, *no pl.*) heraldry.

heran [hɛˈran], *adv.* up to, on, near.

heranbilden [hɛˈranbɪldən], *v.a.* train. — *v.r. sich —*, train, qualify.

herangehen [hɛˈrangeːən], *v.n. irr.* (*aux. sein*) approach, sidle up (to); *an etwas —*, set to work on s.th.

heranmachen [hɛˈranmaxən], *v.r. sich an etwas —*, set to work on s.th., set about s.th.

herannahen [hɛˈrannaːən], *v.n.* (*aux. sein*) approach, draw near.

heranrücken [hɛˈranrykən], *v.a.* move near. — *v.n.* (*aux. sein*) advance, draw near.

heranschleichen [hɛˈranʃlaɪçən], *v.r. irr. sich — an*, sneak up to.

heranwachsen [hɛˈranvaksən], *v.n. irr.* (*aux. sein*) grow up.

heranwagen [hɛˈranvaːgən], *v.r. sich —*, venture near.

heranziehen [hɛˈrantsiːən], *v.a. irr.* draw near; *als Beispiel —*, cite as an example; (*fig.*) enlist (s.o.'s aid). — *v.n.* (*aux. sein*) draw near, approach.

herauf [hɛˈrauf], *adv.* up, upwards.

heraufbeschwören [hɛˈraufbeʃvøːrən], *v.a.* conjure up.

heraus [hɛˈraus], *adv.* out, out of.

herausfordern [hɛˈrausfɔrdərn], *v.a.* challenge.

Herausgabe [hɛˈrausgaːbə], *f.* (—, *pl.* —n) delivery; (*book*) publication; editing.

herausgeben [hɛˈrausgeːbən], *v.a. irr.* give out, deliver; (*money*) give change; (*book*) publish, edit.

Herausgeber [hɛˈrausgeːbər], *m.* (—s, *pl.* —) publisher; editor.

heraushaben [hɛˈraushaːbən], *v.a. irr. etwas —*, have the knack of s.th.

herausputzen [hɛˈrausputsən], *v.r. sich —*, dress up.

herausrücken [hɛˈrausrykən], *v.n. mit Geld —*, fork out money; *mit der Sprache —*, speak out, come out with.

herausschlagen [hɛˈrausʃlaːgən], *v.a. irr. die Kosten —*, recover expenses; *viel —*, make the most of; profit by.

herausstellen [hɛˈrausʃtɛlən], *v.a.* put out, expose. — *v.r. sich — als*, turn out to be.

herausstreichen [hɛˈrausʃtraɪçən], *v.a. irr.* extol, praise.

heraussuchen [hɛˈrauszuːxən], *v.a.* pick out.

herauswollen [hɛˈrausvɔlən], *v.n. nicht mit der Sprache —*, hesitate to speak out.

herb [hɛrp], *adj.* sour, sharp, tart, acrid; (*fig.*) austere, harsh, bitter; (*wine*) dry.

herbei [hɛrˈbaɪ], *adv.* hither, near.

herbeischaffen [hɛrˈbaɪʃafən], *v.a.* procure.

herbeiströmen [hɛrˈbaɪʃtrøːmən], *v.n.* (*aux.* sein) crowd, flock.

Herberge [ˈhɛrbɛrgə], *f.* (—, *pl.* —n) shelter, lodging, inn.

Herbst [hɛrpst], *m.* (—es, *pl.* —e) autumn; (*Am.*) fall.

Herbstrose [ˈhɛrpstroːzə], *f.* (—, *pl.* —n) (*Bot.*) hollyhock.

Herbstzeitlose [ˈhɛrpsttsaɪtloːzə], *f.* (—, *pl.* —n) (*Bot.*) meadow-saffron.

Herd [heːrt], *m.* (—es, *pl.* —e) hearth, fireplace; cooking-stove; (*fig.*) focus.

Herde [ˈheːrdə], *f.* (—, *pl.* —n) flock, herd; (*fig.*) troop.

herein [heˈraɪn], *adv.* in, inside. — *int.* —! come in!

hereinbrechen [heˈraɪnbrɛçən], *v.n. irr.* (*aux.* sein) *über einen —*, befall s.o., overtake s.o.; (*night*) close in.

hereinfallen [heˈraɪnfalən], *v.n. irr.* (*aux.* sein) (*fig.*) be taken in, fall for s.th.

herfallen [ˈheːrfalən], *v.n. irr.* (*aux.* sein) *über einen —*, go for s.o., set upon s.o.

Hergang [ˈheːrgaŋ], *m.* (—es, *no pl.*) proceedings, course of events; circumstances; story, plot.

hergeben [ˈheːrgeːbən], *v.a. irr.* give up, surrender.

hergebracht [ˈheːrgəbraxt], *adj.* traditional, time-honoured.

hergehen [ˈheːrgeːən], *v.n. irr.* (*aux.* sein) proceed; *es geht lustig her*, they are having a gay time.

hergelaufen [ˈheːrgəlaufən], *adj. ein —er Kerl*, an adventurer, an upstart.

herhalten [ˈheːrhaltən], *v.n. irr.* suffer, serve (as a butt).

Hering [ˈheːrɪŋ], *m.* (—s, *pl.* —e) (*Zool.*) herring; *geräucherter —*, smoked herring, bloater; *gesalzener —*, pickled herring.

herkommen [ˈheːrkɔmən], *v.n. irr.* (*aux.* sein) come here; be derived from, descend from.

herkömmlich [ˈheːrkœmlɪç], *adj.* traditional, customary, usual.

Herkunft [ˈheːrkunft], *f.* (—, *no pl.*) descent, extraction; origin.

herleiern [ˈheːrlaɪərn], *v.a.* recite monotonously; reel off.

herleiten [ˈheːrlaɪtən], *v.a.* derive from.

Hermelin [hɛrməˈliːn], *m.* (—s, *no pl.*) ermine (*fur*).

hermetisch [hɛrˈmeːtɪʃ], *adj.* hermetical.

hernach [hɛrˈnaːx], *adv.* after, afterwards; hereafter.

hernehmen [ˈheːrneːmən], *v.a. irr.* take, get (from); take (s.o.) to task.

hernieder [hɛrˈniːdər], *adv.* down.

Herr [hɛr], *m.* (—n, *pl.* —en) master; lord; nobleman; gentleman; (*Theol.*) Lord; principal, governor; *mein —*, Sir; *meine Herren*, gentlemen; — *Schmidt*, Mr. Smith; *einer Sache — werden*, master s.th.

Herrenhaus [ˈhɛrənhaus], *n.* (—es, *pl.* ⁓er) mansion, manor house; (*Parl.*) House of Lords.

Herrenhof [ˈhɛrənhoːf], *m.* (—es, *pl.* ⁓e) manor, country-seat.

Herrenstand [ˈhɛrənʃtant], *m.* (—es, *no pl.*) nobility, gentry.

Herrenzimmer [ˈhɛrəntsɪmər], *n.* (—s, *pl.* —) study.

Herrgott [ˈhɛrgɔt], the Lord God.

herrichten [ˈheːrrɪçtən], *v.a.* prepare, fix up.

Herrin [ˈhɛrɪn], *f.* (—, *pl.* —innen) mistress, lady.

herrisch [ˈhɛrɪʃ], *adj.* imperious, lordly.

herrlich [ˈhɛrlɪç], *adj.* magnificent, splendid, glorious, excellent.

Herrnhuter [ˈhɛrnhuːtər], *m.* (—s, *pl.* —) Moravian; (*pl.*) Moravian brethren.

Herrschaft [ˈhɛrʃaft], *f.* (—, *pl.* —en) mastery, rule, dominion; master, mistress; *meine —en!* ladies and gentlemen!

herrschaftlich [ˈhɛrʃaftlɪç], *adj.* belonging to a lord; (*fig.*) elegant, fashionable, distinguished.

herrschen [ˈhɛrʃən], *v.n.* rule, govern, reign.

Herrscher [ˈhɛrʃər], *m.* (—s, *pl.* —) ruler.

herrühren [ˈheːrryːrən], *v.n.* come from, originate in.

hersagen [ˈheːrzaːgən], *v.a.* recite, reel off.

herschaffen [ˈheːrʃafən], *v.a.* procure.

herstammen [ˈheːrʃtamən], *v.n.* come from, stem from, originate from; be derived from.

herstellen [ˈheːrʃtɛlən], *v.a.* place here; manufacture; *wieder —*, restore; (*sick person*) restore to health.

Herstellung [ˈheːrʃtɛluŋ], *f.* (—, *no pl.*) manufacture, production.

herstürzen [ˈheːrʃtyrtsən], *v.n.* (*aux.* sein) *über einen —*, rush at s.o.

herüber [heˈryːbər], *adv.* over, across; — *und hinüber*, there and back.

herum [heˈrum], *adv.* round, about; around.

herumbalgen [heˈrumbalgən], *v.r. sich —*, scrap; scuffle.

herumbekommen [heˈrumbəkɔmən], *v.a. irr.* (*coll.*) talk s.o. over, win s.o. over.

herumbummeln [heˈrumbuməln], *v.n.* loaf about.

herumstreichen [heˈrumʃtraɪçən], *v.n. irr.* (*aux.* sein) gad about.

herumtreiben [heˈrumtraɪbən], *v.r. irr. sich —*, loaf about, gad about.

herumzanken [heˈrumtsaŋkən], *v.r. sich —*, squabble, quarrel; live like cat and dog.

herumziehen [hɛˈrumtsiːən], *v.a. irr.* drag about. — *v.n.* (*aux.* sein) wander about, move from place to place.

herunter [hɛˈruntər], *adj.* down, downward; *ich bin ganz* —, I feel poorly.

heruntergekommen [hɛˈruntərgəkomən], *adj.* decayed, broken down; in straitened circumstances; depraved.

herunterhandeln [hɛˈruntərhandəln], *v.a. einem etwas* —, beat s.o. down (in price).

herunterwürgen [hɛˈruntervyrgən], *v.a.* swallow s.th. with dislike.

hervor [hɛrˈfoːr], *adv.* forth, forward, out.

hervorheben [hɛrˈfoːrheːbən], *v.a. irr.* emphasize, stress.

hervorragen [hɛrˈfoːrraːgən], *v.n.* stand out, project; (*fig.*) be distinguished, excel.

hervorragend [hɛrˈfoːrraːgənt], *adj.* prominent; (*fig.*) outstanding, excellent.

hervorrufen [hɛrˈfoːrruːfən], *v.a. irr.* call forth; (*fig.*) evoke, bring about, create, cause.

hervorstechen [hɛrˈfoːrʃtɛçən], *v.n. irr.* be predominant, stand out.

hervortun [hɛrˈfoːrtuːn], *v.r. irr. sich* —, distinguish o.s.

Herz [hɛrts], *n.* (—ens, *pl.* —en) heart; courage; mind; spirit; feeling; core; (*Cards*) hearts; (*coll.*) darling; *einem etwas ans* — *legen*, impress s.th. upon s.o.; *von* —*en gern*, with all my heart; *sich etwas zu* —*en nehmen*, take s.th. to heart.

herzählen [ˈheːrtsɛːlən], *v.a.* enumerate.

Herzanfall [ˈhɛrtsanfal], *m.* (—s, *pl.* ˙-e) (*Med.*) heart attack.

Herzbube [ˈhɛrtsbuːbə], *m.* (—n, *pl.* —n) (*Cards*) knave *or* jack of hearts.

Herzdame [ˈhɛrtsdaːmə], *f.* (—, *pl.* —n) (*Cards*) queen of hearts.

Herzeleid [ˈhɛrtsəlait], *n.* (—es, *no pl.*) heartbreak, sorrow, anguish, grief.

herzen [ˈhɛrtsən], *v.a.* hug.

Herzenseinfalt [ˈhɛrtsənsainfalt], *f.* (—, *no pl.*) simple-mindedness.

Herzensgrund [ˈhɛrtsənsgrunt], *m.* (—es, *no pl.*) *aus* —, with all my heart.

Herzenslust [ˈhɛrtsənslust], *f.* (—, *no pl.*) heart's delight; *nach* —, to o.'s heart's content.

Herzfehler [ˈhɛrtsfeːlər], *m.* (—s, *pl.* —) (*Med.*) cardiac defect; organic heart disease.

Herzfell [ˈhɛrtsfɛl], *n.* (—s, *pl.* —e) pericardium.

herzförmig [ˈhɛrtsfœrmiç], *adj.* heart-shaped.

herzhaft [ˈhɛrtshaft], *adj.* stout-hearted; courageous, bold; resolute; hearty.

herzig [ˈhɛrtsiç], *adj.* lovely, charming, sweet; (*Am.*) cute.

Herzkammer [ˈhɛrtskamər], *f.* (—, *pl.* —n) ventricle (of the heart).

Herzklappe [ˈhɛrtsklapə], *f.* (—, *pl.* —n) valve of the heart.

Herzklopfen [ˈhɛrtsklɔpfən], *n.* (—s, *no pl.*) palpitations.

herzlich [ˈhɛrtsliç], *adj.* hearty, cordial, affectionate; — *gern*, with pleasure; —*e Grüße*, kind regards.

Herzog [ˈhɛrtsoːk], *m.* (—s, *pl.* ˙-e) duke.

Herzogtum [ˈhɛrtsoːktuːm], *n.* (—s, *pl.* ˙-er) duchy, dukedom.

Herzschlag [ˈhɛrtsʃlaːk], *m.* (—es, *pl.* ˙-e) heartbeat; (*Med.*) heart attack, cardiac failure.

Hetäre [heˈtɛːrə], *f.* (—, *pl.* —n) courtesan.

Hetzblatt [ˈhɛtsblat], *n.* (—s, *pl.* ˙-er) gutter press.

Hetze [ˈhɛtsə], *f.* (—, *pl.* —n) chase, hunt, hurry, rush; agitation.

hetzen [ˈhɛtsən], *v.a.* bait, fluster, chase, hunt, incite. — *v.n. herum* —, rush around.

Hetzer [ˈhɛtsər], *m.* (—s, *pl.* —) instigator, rabble-rouser.

Heu [hɔy], *n.* (—s, *no pl.*) hay.

Heuboden [ˈhɔyboːdən], *m.* (—s, *pl.* ˙-) hayloft.

Heuchelei [hɔyçəˈlai], *f.* (—, *pl.* —en) hypocrisy.

heucheln [ˈhɔyçəln], *v.n.* play the hypocrite, dissemble. — *v.a.* simulate, affect, feign.

Heuchler [ˈhɔyçlər], *m.* (—s, *pl.* —) hypocrite.

Heuer [ˈhɔyər], *f.* (—, *pl.* —n) (*Naut.*) engagement; hire, wages.

heuer [ˈhɔyər], *adv.* (*dial.*) this year, this season.

heuern [ˈhɔyərn], *v.a.* (*Naut.*) engage, hire.

Heugabel [ˈhɔygaːbəl], *f.* (—, *pl.* —n) pitchfork.

heulen [ˈhɔylən], *v.n.* howl; roar; cry, yell, scream.

Heupferd [ˈhɔypfɛrt], *n.* (—es, *pl.* —e) (*Ent.*) grasshopper.

heurig [ˈhɔyriç], *adj.* of this year, this year's (*wine etc.*).

Heuschnupfen [ˈhɔyʃnupfən], *m.* (—s, *no pl.*) hay-fever.

Heuschober [ˈhɔyʃoːbər], *m.* (—s, *pl.* —) hayrick.

Heuschrecke [ˈhɔyʃrɛkə], *f.* (—, *pl.* —n) (*Ent.*) locust.

heute [ˈhɔytə], *adv.* today, this day; — *in acht Tagen*, today week, a week today; — *abend*, tonight.

heutig [ˈhɔytiç], *adj.* today's, this day's; modern.

heutzutage [ˈhɔytsuːtaːgə], *adv.* nowadays.

Hexe [ˈhɛksə], *f.* (—, *pl.* —n) witch, sorceress, hag.

hexen [ˈhɛksən], *v.n.* use witchcraft; practise sorcery.

Hexenschuß [ˈhɛksənʃus], *m.* (—sses, *no pl.*) (*Med.*) lumbago.

Hexerei

Hexerei [hɛksə'raɪ], *f.* (—, *pl.* **—en**) witchcraft, sorcery, juggling.

hie [hi:], *adv.* (*dial.*) here.

Hieb [hi:p], *m.* (**—es**, *pl.* **—e**) cut, stroke; hit, blow; (*pl.*) a thrashing.

hienieden [hi:'ni:dən], *adv.* here below, down here.

hier [hi:r], *adv.* here, in this place.

Hiersein ['hi:rzaɪn], *n.* (**—s**, *no pl.*) presence, attendance.

hiesig ['hi:zɪç], *adj.* of this place, of this country, local.

Hifthorn ['hɪfthɔrn], *n.* (**—s**, *pl.* **—er**) hunting-horn.

Hilfe ['hɪlfə], *f.* (—, *pl.* **—n**) help, aid, assistance, succour, relief.

hilflos ['hɪlflo:s], *adj.* helpless.

hilfreich ['hɪlfraɪç], *adj.* helpful.

Hilfsmittel ['hɪlfsmɪtəl], *n.* (**—s**, *pl.* —) expedient, remedy.

Hilfsschule ['hɪlfsʃu:lə], *f.* (—, *pl.* **—n**) school for backward children.

Hilfszeitwort ['hɪlfstsaɪtvɔrt], *n.* (**—s**, *pl.* **-er**) (*Gram.*) auxiliary verb.

Himbeere ['hɪmbe:rə], *f.* (—, *pl.* **—n**) raspberry.

Himmel ['hɪməl], *m.* (**—s**, *pl.* —) heaven, heavens; sky; firmament.

himmelan [hɪməl'an], *adv.* heavenward.

himmelangst ['hɪməlaŋkst], *adv. ihm war —*, he was panic-stricken.

Himmelbett ['hɪməlbɛt], *n.* (**—s**, *pl.* **—en**) fourposter.

himmelblau ['hɪməlblau], *adj.* sky-blue.

Himmelfahrt ['hɪməlfa:rt], *f.* (—, *no pl.*) Ascension.

Himmelschlüssel ['hɪməlʃlysəl], *m.* (**—s**, *pl.* —) (*Bot.*) primrose.

himmelschreiend ['hɪməlʃraɪənt], *adj.* atrocious, revolting.

Himmelsgewölbe ['hɪməlsgəvœlbə], *n.* (**—s**, *pl.* —) firmament.

Himmelsstrich ['hɪməlsʃtrɪç], *m.* (**—s**, *pl.* **—e**) climate, zone.

Himmelszeichen ['hɪməlstsaɪçən], *n.* (**—s**, *pl.* —) sign of the zodiac.

himmelweit ['hɪməlvaɪt], *adj.* enormous; — *entfernt*, poles apart.

himmlisch ['hɪmlɪʃ], *adj.* celestial, heavenly.

hin [hɪn], *adv.* there, towards that place; finished, gone; ruined; — *und her*, to and fro.

hinab [hɪn'ap], *adv.* down.

hinan [hɪn'an], *adv.* up.

hinarbeiten ['hɪnarbaɪtən], *v.n. auf etwas —*, work towards s.th.

hinauf [hɪn'auf], *adv.* up, up to.

hinaus [hɪn'aus], *adv.* out, out of; *es kommt auf dasselbe —*, it comes to the same thing.

hinauswollen [hɪn'ausvɔlən], *v.n.* wish to go out; (*fig.*) *hoch —*, aim high.

hinausziehen [hɪn'austsi:ən], *v.a. irr.* draw out; drag on; (*fig.*) protract.

Hinblick ['hɪnblɪk], *m.* (**—es**, *no pl.*) *im — auf*, in consideration of, with regard to.

hinbringen ['hɪnbrɪŋən], *v.a. irr.* bring to; escort; *Zeit —*, while away time.

hinderlich ['hɪndərlɪç], *adj.* obstructive, cumbersome.

hindern ['hɪndərn], *v.a.* hinder, obstruct, hamper, impede.

hindeuten ['hɪndɔytən], *v.n. auf etwas —*, point to s.th., hint at s.th.

Hindin ['hɪndɪn], *f.* (—, *pl.* **—innen**) (*Poet.*) hind.

hindurch [hɪn'durç], *adv.* through; throughout; *die ganze Zeit —*, all the time.

hinein [hɪn'aɪn], *adv.* in, into; *in den Tag — leben*, live for the present, lead a life of carefree enjoyment.

hineinfinden [hɪn'aɪnfɪndən], *v.r. irr. sich in etwas —*, reconcile *or* adapt o.s. to s.th.

hinfällig ['hɪnfɛlɪç], *adj.* frail, feeble, weak; shaky, void, invalid.

Hingabe ['hɪnga:bə], *f.* (—, *no pl.*) surrender; (*fig.*) devotion.

hingeben ['hɪnge:bən], *v.a. irr.* give up, surrender. — *v.r. sich einer Sache —*, devote o.s. to a task.

hingegen [hɪn'ge:gən], *adv.* on the other hand.

hinhalten ['hɪnhaltən], *v.a. irr.* (*thing*) hold out; (*person*) keep in suspense, put off.

hinken ['hɪŋkən], *v.n.* limp.

hinlänglich ['hɪnlɛŋlɪç], *adj.* sufficient.

hinlegen ['hɪnle:gən], *v.a.* lay down, put away. — *v.r. sich —*, lie down, go to bed.

hinnehmen ['hɪnne:mən], *v.a. irr.* take, submit to, accept.

hinreichen ['hɪnraɪçən], *v.a.* pass to. — *v.n.* suffice, be sufficient.

Hinreise ['hɪnraɪzə], *f.* (—, *pl.* **—n**) outward journey.

hinreißen ['hɪnraɪsən], *v.r. irr. sich — lassen*, allow o.s. to be carried away.

hinreißend ['hɪnraɪsənt], *adj.* charming, ravishing, enchanting.

hinrichten ['hɪnrɪçtən], *v.a.* execute, put to death.

hinscheiden ['hɪnʃaɪdən], *v.n. irr.* die, pass away.

hinschlängeln ['hɪnʃlɛŋəln], *v.r. sich —*, meander, wind along.

Hinsicht ['hɪnzɪçt], *f.* (—, *no pl.*) view, consideration, regard.

hinsichtlich ['hɪnzɪçtlɪç], *prep.* (*Genit.*) with regard to.

hinstellen ['hɪnʃtɛlən], *v.a.* put down; make out to be.

hinten ['hɪntən], *adv.* behind; *von —*, from behind.

hinter ['hɪntər], *prep.* (*Dat.*) behind, after.

Hinterachse ['hɪntəraksə], *f.* (—, *pl.* **—n**) (*Motor.*) rear-axle.

Hinterbein ['hɪntərbaɪn], *n.* (**—s**, *pl.* **—e**) hind-leg; (*fig.*) *sich auf die —e stellen*, get up on o.'s hind-legs.

Hinterbliebene [hɪntər'bli:bənə], *m.* (—n, *pl.* —n) survivor; mourner; (*pl.*) the bereaved.

hinterbringen [hɪntər'brɪŋən], *v.a. irr.* give information about, (*coll.*) tell on.

Hinterdeck ['hɪntərdɛk], *n.* (—s, *no pl.*) (*Naut.*) quarter deck.

hinterdrein ['hɪntərdraɪn], *adv.* afterwards, after; behind.

hintereinander [hɪntəraɪn'andər], *adv.* in succession, one after another.

Hintergedanke ['hɪntərgədaŋkə], *m.* (—n, *pl.* —n) mental reservation, ulterior motive.

hintergehen [hɪntər'ge:ən], *v.a. irr.* deceive, circumvent.

Hintergrund ['hɪntərgrunt], *m.* (—es, *pl.* ⁻e) background; (*Theat.*) backcloth, back-drop.

Hinterhalt ['hɪntərhalt], *m.* (—s, *pl.* —e) ambush; (*fig.*) reserve.

hinterhältig ['hɪntərhɛltɪç], *adj.* furtive, secretive; insidious.

hinterher [hɪntər'he:r], *adv.* behind; in the rear; afterwards.

Hinterindien ['hɪntərɪndjən], *n.* Indo-China.

Hinterkopf ['hɪntərkɔpf], *m.* (—es, *pl.* ⁻e) occiput, back of the head.

Hinterlader ['hɪntərla:dər], *m.* (—s, *pl.* —) breech-loader.

hinterlassen [hɪntər'lasən], *v.a. irr.* leave (a legacy), bequeath; leave (word).

Hinterlassenschaft [hɪntər'lasənʃaft], *f.* (—, *pl.* —en) inheritance, bequest.

Hinterlegung [hɪntər'le:guŋ], *f.* (—, *pl.* —en) deposition.

Hinterlist ['hɪntərlɪst], *f.* (—, *no pl.*) fraud, deceit; cunning.

hinterrücks [hɪntər'ryks], *adv.* from behind; (*fig.*) treacherously, behind s.o.'s back.

Hintertreffen ['hɪntərtrɛfən], *n.* (—s, *no pl.*) ins — geraten, be left out in the cold, fall behind.

hintertreiben [hɪntər'traɪbən], *v.a. irr.* prevent, frustrate.

Hintertreppe ['hɪntərtrɛpə], *f.* (—, *pl.* —n) back-stairs.

Hintertreppenroman ['hɪntərtrɛpənroma:n], *m.* (—s, *pl.* —e) (*Lit.*) cheap thriller.

hinterziehen [hɪntərtsi:ən], *v.a. irr.* insep. defraud.

hinträumen ['hɪntrɔymən], *v.n. vor sich —*, daydream.

hinüber [hɪn'y:bər], *adv.* over, across.

hinunter [hɪn'untər], *adv.* down; *den Berg —*, downhill.

hinweg [hɪn'vɛk], *adv.* away, off.

hinwegsetzen [hɪn'vɛkzɛtsən], *v.r. sich über etwas —*, make light of s.th.

Hinweis ['hɪnvaɪs], *m.* (—es, *pl.* —e) hint, indication, reference; *unter — auf*, with reference to.

hinweisen ['hɪnvaɪzən], *v.a. irr. auf etwas —*, refer to, point to s.th.

hinwerfen ['hɪnvɛrfən], *v.a. irr.* throw down; *hingeworfene Bemerkung*, casual remark.

hinziehen ['hɪntsi:ən], *v.a. irr.* draw along; attract. — *v.n.* (*aux.* sein) march along. — *v.r. sich —*, drag on.

hinzielen ['hɪntsi:lən], *v.n. auf etwas —*, aim at s.th., have s.th. in mind.

hinzu [hɪn'tsu:], *adv.* to, near; besides, in addition.

hinzufügen [hɪn'tsu:fy:gən], *v.a.* add.

hinzukommen [hɪn'tsu:kɔmən], *v.n. irr.* (*aux.* sein) be added.

hinzuziehen [hɪn'tsutsi:ən], *v.a. irr.* include, add; call in (expert).

Hiobsbotschaft ['hi:ɔpsbo:tʃaft], *f.* (—, *no pl.*) bad news.

Hirn [hɪrn], *n.* (—es, *pl.* —e) brain, brains. *See also* **Gehirn.**

Hirngespinst ['hɪrngəʃpɪnst], *n.* (—es, *pl.* —e) fancy, chimera, illusion, figment of the imagination.

hirnverbrannt ['hɪrnfɛrbrant], *adj.* crazy, insane, mad; (*coll.*) crackbrained.

Hirsch [hɪrʃ], *m.* (—es, *pl.* —e) (*Zool.*) stag, hart.

Hirschbock ['hɪrʃbɔk], *m.* (—s, *pl.* ⁻e) (*Zool.*) stag.

Hirschfänger ['hɪrʃfɛŋər], *m.* (—s, *pl.* —) hunting-knife.

Hirschgeweih ['hɪrʃgəvaɪ], *n.* (—s, *pl.* —e) horns, antlers.

Hirschhorn ['hɪrʃhɔrn], *n.* (—s, *no pl.*) (*Chem.*) hartshorn.

Hirschkäfer ['hɪrʃkɛ:fər], *m.* (—s, *pl.* —) (*Ent.*) stag beetle.

Hirschkeule ['hɪrʃkɔylə], *f.* (—, *pl.* —n) haunch of venison.

Hirschkuh ['hɪrʃku:], *f.* (—, *pl.* ⁻e) (*Zool.*) hind, doe.

Hirse ['hɪrzə], *f.* (—, *no pl.*) (*Bot.*) millet.

Hirt [hɪrt], *m.* (—en, *pl.* —en) shepherd, herdsman.

Hirtenbrief ['hɪrtənbri:f], *m.* (—s, *pl.* —e) (*Eccl.*) pastoral letter.

His [hɪs], *n.* (—, *pl.* —) (*Mus.*) B sharp.

hissen ['hɪsən], *v.a.* hoist (the flag).

Historiker [hɪ'sto:rɪkər], *m.* (—s, *pl.* —) historian.

historisch [hɪ'sto:rɪʃ], *adj.* historical.

Hitzblase ['hɪtsbla:zə], *f.* (—, *pl.* —n) blister, heat-rash.

Hitze ['hɪtsə], *f.* (—, *no pl.*) heat, hot weather.

hitzig ['hɪtsɪç], *adj.* hot-headed, hasty, passionate.

Hitzschlag ['hɪtsʃla:k], *m.* (—es, *pl.* ⁻e) sunstroke, heat-stroke.

Hobel ['ho:bəl], *m.* (—s, *pl.* —) (*tool*) plane.

Hoch [ho:x], *n.* (—s, *no pl.*) toast (*drink*); (*Met.*) high.

hoch, hoh [ho:x, ho:], *adj.* high; (*fig.*) eminent, sublime.

Hochachtung ['ho:xaxtuŋ], *f.* (—, *no pl.*) esteem, regard, respect.

hochachtungsvoll ['ho:xaxtuŋsfɔl], *adj., adv.* (*letters*) yours faithfully.

109

Hochamt

Hochamt ['ho:xamt], *n.* (—es, *pl.* ⸗er) (*Eccl.*) High Mass.

Hochbau ['ho:xbau], *m.* (—s, *pl.* —ten) superstructure.

hochbetagt ['ho:xbəta:kt], *adj.* advanced in years.

Hochburg ['ho:xburk], *f.* (—, *pl.* —en) (*fig.*) stronghold, citadel.

Hochebene ['ho:xe:bənə], *f.* (—, *pl.* —n) table-land, plateau.

hochfahrend ['ho:xfa:rənt], *adj.* haughty, high-flown; (*coll.*) stuck-up.

Hochgefühl ['ho:xgəfy:l], *n.* (—s, *no pl.*) exaltation.

Hochgenuß ['ho:xgənus], *m.* (—sses, *pl.* ⸗sse) exquisite enjoyment; treat.

Hochgericht ['ho:xgərɪçt], *n.* (—s, *pl.* —e) place of execution, scaffold.

hochherzig ['ho:xhɛrtsɪç], *adj.* magnanimous.

Hochmeister ['ho:xmaɪstər], *m.* (—s, *pl.* —) Grand Master.

Hochmut ['ho:xmu:t], *m.* (—s, *no pl.*) haughtiness, pride.

hochnäsig ['ho:xnɛ:zɪç], *adj.* supercilious, stuck-up.

hochnotpeinlich ['ho:xno:tpaɪnlɪç], *adj.* (*obs.*) penal, criminal; —es Verhör, criminal investigation.

Hochofen ['ho:xo:fən], *m.* (—s, *pl.* ⸗) blast-furnace.

Hochschule ['ho:xʃu:lə], *f.* (—, *pl.* —n) academy; university.

Hochschüler ['ho:xʃy:lər], *m.* (—s, *pl.* —) student, undergraduate.

höchst [hœ:çst], *adj.* highest, most. — *adv.* most, extremely.

Hochstapler ['ho:xʃta:plər], *m.* (—s, *pl.* —) confidence trickster, swindler.

höchstens ['hœ:çstəns], *adv.* at most, at best.

hochtrabend ['ho:xtra:bənt], *adj.* (*horse*) high-stepping; (*fig.*) high-sounding, bombastic.

hochverdient ['ho:xfɛrdi:nt], *adj.* highly meritorious.

Hochverrat ['ho:xfɛra:t], *m.* (—s, *no pl.*) high treason.

Hochwild ['ho:xvɪlt], *n.* (—es, *no pl.*) deer; big game.

hochwohlgeboren ['ho:xvo:lgəbo:rən], *adj.* (*obs.*) noble; Euer Hochwohlgeboren, Right Honourable Sir.

hochwürden ['ho:xvyrdən], *adj.* Euer Hochwürden, Reverend Sir.

Hochzeit ['hɔxtsaɪt], *f.* (—, *pl.* —en) wedding; nuptials.

hochzeitlich ['hɔxtsaɪtlɪç], *adj.* nuptial, bridal.

Hochzeitsreise ['hɔxtsaɪtsraɪzə], *f.* (—, *pl.* —n) honeymoon.

Hocke ['hɔkə], *f.* (—, *pl.* —n) squatting posture; shock, stook.

hocken ['hɔkən], *v.n.* crouch, squat; zu Hause —, be a stay-at-home.

Hocker ['hɔkər], *m.* (—s, *pl.* —) stool.

Höcker ['hœkər], *m.* (—s, *pl.* —) hump.

höckerig ['hœkərɪç], *adj.* hump-backed, hunch-backed.

Hode ['ho:də], *f.* (—, *pl.* —n) testicle.

Hof [ho:f], *m.* (—es, *pl.* ⸗e) yard, courtyard; farm(stead); (*royal*) court; (*moon*) halo; einem den — machen, court s.o.

Hofarzt ['ho:fartst], *m.* (—es, *pl.* ⸗e) court physician.

hoffähig ['ho:ffɛ:ɪç], *adj.* presentable at court.

Hoffart ['hɔfart], *f.* (—, *no pl.*) pride, arrogance.

hoffärtig ['hɔfɛrtɪç], *adj.* proud, arrogant.

hoffen ['hɔfən], *v.n.* hope; fest auf etwas —, trust.

hoffentlich ['hɔfəntlɪç], *adv.* as I hope, I trust that.

Hoffnung ['hɔfnuŋ], *f.* (—, *pl.* —en) hope, expectation, anticipation, expectancy; guter — sein, be full of hope; be expecting a baby; sich — machen auf, cherish hopes of.

hoffnungslos ['hɔfnuŋslo:s], *adj.* hopeless, past hope.

hofieren [ho'fi:rən], *v.a.* court.

höfisch ['hø:fɪʃ], *adj.* courtlike, courtly.

höflich ['hø:flɪç], *adj.* courteous, civil, polite.

Hoflieferant ['ho:fli:fərant], *m.* (—en, *pl.* —en) purveyor to His or Her Majesty.

Höfling ['hø:flɪŋ], *m.* (—s, *pl.* —e) courtier.

Hofmarschall ['ho:fmarʃal], *m.* (—s, *pl.* —e) Lord Chamberlain.

Hofmeister ['ho:fmaɪstər], *m.* (—s, *pl.* —) (*obs.*) steward; tutor.

Hofnarr ['ho:fnar], *m.* (—en, *pl.* —en) court jester, court fool.

Hofrat ['ho:fra:t], *m.* (—s, *pl.* ⸗e) Privy Councillor.

Hofschranze ['ho:fʃrantsə], *m.* (—n, *pl.* —n) courtier; flunkey.

Hofsitte ['ho:fzɪtə], *f.* (—, *pl.* —n) court etiquette.

Höhe ['hø:ə], *f.* (—, *pl.* —n) height, altitude; bis zur — von, up to the level of; in die —, upwards; in die — fahren, give a start, get excited.

Hoheit ['ho:haɪt], *f.* (—, *pl.* —en) grandeur; sovereignty; (*title*) Highness.

Hohelied [ho:ə'li:t], *n.* (—s, *no pl.*) Song of Solomon.

Höhenmesser ['hø:ənmɛsər], *m.* (—s, *pl.* —) (*Aviat.*) altimeter.

Höhensonne ['hø:ənzɔnə], *f.* (—, *pl.* —n) Alpine sun; (*Med.*) ultra-violet lamp.

Höhenzug ['hø:əntsu:k], *m.* (—s, *pl.* ⸗e) mountain range.

Höhepunkt ['hø:əpuŋkt], *m.* (—s, *pl.* —e) climax, culmination, acme; peak.

höher ['hø:ər], *comp. adj.* higher.

hohl [ho:l], *adj.* hollow; (*tooth*) decayed, hollow.

Höhle ['hø:lə], *f.* (—, *pl.* —n) cave, cavern, den.

110

hohlgeschliffen ['ho:lgəʃlɪfən], *adj.* concave, hollow-ground.
Hohlheit ['ho:lhaɪt], *f.* (—, *no pl.*) hollowness.
Hohlleiste ['ho:llaɪstə], *f.* (—, *pl.* —n) groove, channel.
Hohlmaß ['ho:lma:s], *n.* (—es, *pl.* —e) dry measure.
Hohlmeißel ['ho:lmaɪsəl], *m.* (—s, *pl.* —) gouge.
Hohlsaum ['ho:lzaum], *m.* (—s, *pl.* ⁓e) hemstitch.
Hohlspiegel ['ho:lʃpi:gəl], *m.* (—s, *pl.* —) concave mirror.
Höhlung ['hø:luŋ], *f.* (—, *pl.* —en) hollow, cavity.
Hohlziegel ['ho:ltsi:gəl], *m.* (—s, *pl.* —) hollow brick.
Hohn [ho:n], *m.* (—s, *no pl.*) scorn, derision, mockery; sneer.
höhnen ['hø:nən], *v.a.* deride, sneer at; *see* **verhöhnen**.
Höker ['hø:kər], *m.* (—s, *pl.* —) hawker, huckster.
hold [hɔlt], *adj.* kind, friendly; gracious; graceful; sweet.
Holder ['hɔldər] *see* **Holunder**.
holdselig ['hɔltze:lɪç], *adj.* sweet, charming, gracious.
holen ['ho:lən], *v.a.* fetch, collect, get.
Holland ['hɔlant], *n.* Holland.
Hölle ['hœlə], *f.* (—, *no pl.*) hell.
Holm [hɔlm], *m.* (—es, *pl.* —e) islet, holm; (*Gymn.*) bar.
holperig ['hɔlpərɪç], *adj.* rough, bumpy.
holpern ['hɔlpərn], *v.n.* jolt, stumble; (*fig.*) falter.
Holunder [ho'lundər], *m.* (—s, *pl.* —) (*Bot.*) elder; *spanischer* —, lilac.
Holz [hɔlts], *n.* (—es, *pl.* ⁓er) wood, timber; (*Am.*) lumber; (*no pl.*) forest; bush.
Holzapfel ['hɔltsapfəl], *m.* (—s, *pl.* ⁓) (*Bot.*) crab-apple.
holzartig ['hɔltsartɪç], *adj.* woody, ligneous.
holzen ['hɔltsən], *v.a.* cut *or* gather wood.
hölzern ['hœltsərn], *adj.* wooden; (*fig.*) stiff.
Holzhändler ['hɔltshɛndlər], *m.* (—s, *pl.* —) timber-merchant; (*Am.*) lumber merchant.
Holzhauer ['hɔltshauər], *m.* (—s, *pl.* —) wood-cutter.
holzig ['hɔltsɪç], *adj.* woody, wooded; (*asparagus*) woody, hard; (*beans*) stringy.
Holzkohle ['hɔltsko:lə], *f.* (—, *no pl.*) charcoal.
Holzscheit ['hɔltsʃaɪt], *n.* (—s, *pl.* —e) log of wood.
Holzschlag ['hɔltsʃla:k], *m.* (—es, *pl.* ⁓e) clearing; felling area.
Holzschnitt ['hɔltsʃnɪt], *m.* (—es, *pl.* —e) wood-cut.
Holzschuh ['hɔltsʃu:], *m.* (—s, *pl.* —e) clog.

Holzweg ['hɔltsve:k], *m.* (—s, *pl.* —e) timbertrack; (*fig.*) *auf dem* — *sein*, be on the wrong tack.
Holzwolle ['hɔltsvɔlə], *f.* (—, *no pl.*) wood shavings.
homogen [homo'ge:n], *adj.* homogeneous.
homolog [homo'lo:g], *adj.* homologous.
honett [ho'nɛt], *adj.* (*obs.*) respectable, genteel.
Honig ['ho:nɪç], *m.* (—s, *no pl.*) honey.
Honigkuchen ['ho:nɪçku:xən], *m.* (—s, *pl.* —) ginger-bread.
Honigwabe ['ho:nɪçva:bə], *f.* (—, *pl.* —n) honeycomb.
Honorar [hono'ra:r], *n.* (—s, *pl.* —e) remuneration; (*professional*) fee; honorarium.
Honoratioren [honora'tsjo:rən], *m. pl.* people of rank; dignitaries.
honorieren [hono'ri:rən], *v.a.* pay a fee to, remunerate.
Hopfen ['hɔpfən], *m.* (—s, *no pl.*) (*Bot.*) hop, hops; *an dem ist* — *und Malz verloren*, he is beyond help.
Hopfenstange ['hɔpfənʃtaŋə], *f.* (—, *pl.* —n) hop-pole; (*fig.*) tall thin person.
hopsen ['hɔpsən], *v.n.* (*aux.* sein) (*coll.*) hop, jump.
hörbar ['hø:rba:r], *adj.* audible.
horchen ['hɔrçən], *v.n.* listen, eavesdrop.
Horde ['hɔrdə], *f.* (—, *pl.* —n) horde.
hören ['hø:rən], *v.a., v.n.* hear.
Hörer ['hø:rər], *m.* (—s, *pl.* —) listener; (*Univ.*) student; (*telephone*) receiver.
Hörerin ['hø:rərɪn], *f.* (—, *pl.* —innen) female listener; (*Univ.*) woman student.
Hörerschaft ['hø:rərʃaft], *f.* (—, *no pl.*) audience.
Hörgerät ['hø:rgerɛ:t], *n.* (—es, *pl.* —e) hearing aid.
hörig ['hø:rɪç], *adj.* in bondage, a slave to.
Horizont [hori'tsɔnt], *m.* (—es, *pl.* —e) horizon.
Horizontale [horitsɔn'ta:lə], *f.* (—, *pl.* —n) horizontal line.
Horn [hɔrn], *n.* (—s, *pl.* ⁓er) horn; (*Mus.*) French horn.
Hörnchen ['hœrnçən], *n.* (—s, *pl.* —) French roll, croissant.
hörnern ['hœrnərn], *adj.* horny, made of horn.
Hornhaut ['hɔrnhaut], *f.* (—, *pl.* ⁓te) horny skin; (*eye*) cornea.
Hornhautverpflanzung ['hɔrnhautfɛrpflantsuŋ], *f.* (—, *no pl.*) corneal graft.
hornig ['hɔrnɪç], *adj.* hard, horny.
Hornisse [hɔr'nɪsə], *f.* (—, *pl.* —n) (*Ent.*) hornet.
horrend [hɔ'rɛnt], *adj.* exorbitant; stupendous.
Hörrohr ['hø:rro:r], *n.* (—s, *pl.* —e) ear trumpet.
Hörsaal ['hø:rza:l], *m.* (—s, *pl.* —säle) auditorium, lecture room.

Hörspiel ['hø:rʃpi:l], *n.* (—s, *pl.* —e) radio play.

Horst [hɔrst], *m.* (—es, *pl.* —e) eyrie.

Hort [hɔrt], *m.* (—es, *pl.* —e) (*Poet.*) treasure; stronghold.

Hortensie [hɔr'tɛnzjə], *f.* (—, *pl.* —n) (*Bot.*) hydrangea.

Hose ['ho:zə], *f.* (—, *pl.* —n) trousers, pants, breeches; (*women*) slacks.

Hosenband ['ho:zənbant], *n.* (—es, *pl.* ⸚er) garter.

Hosenträger ['ho:zəntrɛgər], *m. pl.* braces, suspenders.

Hospitant [hɔspi'tant], *m.* (—en, *pl.* —en) (*Univ.*) temporary student, non-registered student.

hospitieren [hɔspi'ti:rən], *v.n.* attend lectures as a visitor.

Hostie ['hɔstjə], *f.* (—, *pl.* —n) (*Eccl.*) the Host.

hüben ['hy:bən], *adv.* on this side; — *und drüben*, on either side.

hübsch [hypʃ], *adj.* pretty, attractive; handsome; good-looking.

Hubschrauber ['hu:pʃraubər], *m.* (—s, *pl.* —) (*Aviat.*) helicopter.

huckepack ['hukəpak], *adv.* — *tragen*, carry pick-a-back.

Huf [hu:f], *m.* (—es, *pl.* —e) hoof.

Hufe ['hu:fə], *f.* (—, *pl.* —n) hide (of land).

Hufeisen ['hu:faizən], *n.* (—s, *pl.* —) horseshoe.

Huflattich ['hu:flatiç], *m.* (—s, *pl.* —e) (*Bot.*) colt's foot.

Hufschlag ['hu:fʃla:k], *m.* (—s, *pl.* ⸚e) (*of a horse*) hoof-beat.

Hüfte ['hyftə], *f.* (—, *pl.* —n) (*Anat.*) hip; (*animals*) haunch.

Hügel ['hy:gəl], *m.* (—s, *pl.* —) hill, hillock.

hügelig ['hy:gəliç], *adj.* hilly.

Huhn [hu:n], *n.* (—s, *pl.* ⸚er) fowl; hen.

Hühnchen ['hy:nçən], *n.* (—s, *pl.* —) pullet, chicken.

Hühnerauge ['hy:nəraugə], *n.* (—s, *pl.* —n) corn (*on the foot*).

Huld [hult], *f.* (—, *no pl.*) grace, favour.

huldigen ['huldigən], *v.n.* pay homage.

huldvoll ['hultfɔl], *adj.* gracious.

Hülle ['hylə], *f.* (—, *pl.* —n) cover, covering; veil; *in — und Fülle*, in abundance, in profusion.

hüllen ['hylən], *v.a.* cover, veil, wrap.

Hülse ['hylzə], *f.* (—, *pl.* —n) hull, husk, shell; cartridge-case.

Hülsenfrucht ['hylzənfruxt], *f.* (—, *pl.* ⸚e) (*Bot.*) leguminous plant.

human [hu'ma:n], *adj.* humane.

humanistisch [huma'nistiʃ], *adj.* classical; humanistic.

Hummel ['huməl], *f.* (—, *pl.* —n) (*Ent.*) bumble-bee.

Hummer ['humər], *m.* (—s, *pl.* —) (*Zool.*) lobster.

Humor [hu'mo:r], *m.* (—s, *no pl.*) humour.

humoristisch [humo'ristiʃ], *adj.* humorous, witty.

humpeln ['humpəln], *v.n.* hobble, limp.

Humpen ['humpən], *m.* (—s, *pl.* —) deep drinking-cup, bowl, tankard.

Humus ['hu:mus], *m.* (—, *no pl.*) garden-mould, humus.

Hund [hunt], *m.* (—es, *pl.* —e) dog; (*hunting*) hound; (*fig.*) rascal, scoundrel.

Hundehaus ['hundəhaus], *n.* (—es, *pl.* ⸚er) dog-kennel.

hundert ['hundərt], *num. adj.* a hundred, one hundred.

Hündin ['hyndin], *f.* (—, *pl.* —innen) bitch.

Hundstage ['huntsta:gə], *m. pl.* dog days (July to August).

Hundszahn ['huntstsa:n], *m.* (—es, *pl.* ⸚e) (*Bot.*) dandelion.

Hüne ['hy:nə], *m.* (—n, *pl.* —n) giant, colossus; (*fig.*) tall man.

Hünengrab ['hy:nəngra:p], *n.* (—es, *pl.* ⸚er) tumulus, burial mound, barrow, cairn.

Hunger ['huŋər], *m.* (—s, *no pl.*) hunger; starvation.

hungern ['huŋərn], *v.n.* hunger, be hungry.

Hungertuch ['huŋərtu:x], *n.* (—es, *no pl.*) *am — nagen*, go without food; live in poverty.

hungrig ['huŋriç], *adj.* hungry; (*fig.*) desirous (of).

Hupe ['hu:pə], *f.* (—, *pl.* —n) motor-horn, hooter (of a car).

hüpfen ['hypfən], *v.n.* (*aux.* sein) hop, skip.

Hürde ['hyrdə], *f.* (—, *pl.* —n) hurdle.

Hure ['hu:rə], *f.* (—, *pl.* —n) whore, prostitute, harlot; (*coll.*) tart.

hurtig ['hurtiç], *adj.* nimble, agile; quick, speedy, swift.

Husar [hu'za:r], *m.* (—en, *pl.* —en) hussar.

husch! [huʃ], *excl.* quick!

huschen ['huʃən], *v.n.* (*aux.* sein) scurry, slip away.

hüsteln ['hystəln], *v.n.* cough slightly; clear o.'s throat.

husten ['hu:stən], *v.n.* cough.

Hut (1) [hu:t], *m.* (—es, *pl.* ⸚e) hat; *steifer —*, bowler.

Hut (2) [hu:t], *f.* (—, *no pl.*) guard, keeping, care.

hüten ['hy:tən], *v.a.* guard, tend, care for; *Kinder —*, baby-sit; *das Bett —*, be confined to o.'s bed, be ill in bed. — *v.r. sich — vor*, be on o.'s guard against, beware of.

Hüter ['hy:tər], *m.* (—s, *pl.* —) guardian, keeper; (*cattle*) herdsman.

Hutkrempe ['hu:tkrɛmpə], *f.* (—, *pl.* —n) hat-brim.

Hütte ['hytə], *f.* (—, *pl.* —n) hut, cottage; (*Tech.*) furnace, forge, foundry.

Hüttenarbeiter ['hytənarbaitər], *m.* (—s, *pl.* —) smelter, foundry worker.

Hyäne [hy'ɛ:nə], *f.* (—, *pl.* —n) (*Zool.*) hyena.

Hyazinthe [hyat'sɪntə], *f.* (—, *pl.* —n) (*Bot.*) hyacinth.
Hyperbel [hy'pɛrbəl], *f.* (—, *pl.* —n) hyperbola.
hypnotisch [hyp'no:tɪʃ], *adj.* hypnotic.
hypnotisieren [hypnoti'zi:rən], *v.a.* hypnotise.
Hypochonder [hypo'xɔndər], *m.* (—s, *pl.* —) hypochondriac.
Hypothek [hypo'te:k], *f.* (—, *pl.* —en) mortgage.
Hysterie [hyste'ri:], *f.* (—, *no pl.*) hysterics, hysteria.
hysterisch [hys'te:rɪʃ], *adj.* hysterical.

I

I [i:], *n.* (—, *no pl.*) the letter I. — *excl.* *i wo!* (*dial.*) certainly not, of course not.
ich [ɪç], *pers. pron.* I, myself.
ideal [ide'a:l], *adj.* ideal.
idealisieren [ideali'zi:rən], *v.a.* idealise.
Idealismus [idea'lɪsmus], *m.* (—, *no pl.*) idealism.
Idee [i'de:], *f.* (—, *pl.* —n) idea, notion, conception.
identifizieren [identifi'tsi:rən], *v.a.* identify.
identisch [i'dɛntɪʃ], *adj.* identical.
Identität [identi'tɛ:t], *f.* (—, *no pl.*) identity.
idiomatisch [idio'ma:tɪʃ], *adj.* idiomatic.
Idyll [i'dyl], *n.* (—s, *pl.* —e) idyll.
Idylle [i'dylə], *f.* (—, *pl.* —n) idyll.
idyllisch [i'dylɪʃ], *adj.* idyllic.
Igel ['i:gəl], *m.* (—s, *pl.* —) (*Zool.*) hedgehog.
ignorieren [ɪgno'ri:rən], *v.a.* ignore, take no notice of.
ihm [i:m], *pers. pron. Dat.* to him, it.
ihn [i:n], *pers. pron. Acc.*, him, it.
Ihnen ['i:nən], *pers. pron. Dat.* you, to you.
ihnen ['i:nən], *pers. pron. pl. Dat.* them, to them.
Ihr [i:r], *poss. adj.* your; of your. —, *poss. pron.* yours.
ihr [i:r], *pers. pron.* to her; (*pl.*) (*intim.*) you. — *poss. adj.* her, their. — *poss. pron.* hers, theirs.
Ihrer ['i:rər], *pers. pron.* of you. — *poss. adj.* of your.
ihrer ['i:rər], *pers. pron.* of her, of it; (*pl.*) of them. — *poss. adj* of her; to her; (*pl.*) of their.
ihresgleichen ['i:rəsglaɪçən], *adv.* of her, its *or* their kind.
ihrethalben ['i:rəthalbən], *adv.* for her sake, for their sake, on her account, on their account.

ihretwegen ['i:rətve:gən] *see* **ihrethalben.**
ihretwillen ['i:rətvɪlən] *see* **ihrethalben.**
Ihrige [i:rɪgə], *poss. pron.* yours.
ihrige ['i:rɪgə], *poss. pron.* hers, its, theirs.
illegitim [ɪlegi'ti:m], *adj.* illegitimate.
illuminieren [ɪlumi'ni:rən], *v.a.* illuminate, floodlight.
illustrieren [ɪlu'stri:rən], *v.a.* illustrate.
Iltis ['ɪltɪs], *m.* (—ses, *pl.* —se) (*Zool.*) polecat, fitchet.
im [ɪm], *contraction of* **in dem,** in the.
Imbiß ['ɪmbɪs], *m.* (—sses, *pl.* —sse) snack, refreshment, light meal.
Imker ['ɪmkər], *m.* (—s, *pl.* —) bee-keeper.
immatrikulieren [ɪmmatriku'li:rən], *v.a.* (*Univ.*) matriculate, enrol.
Imme ['ɪmə], *f.* (—, *pl.* —n) (*dial.*, *Poet.*) bee.
immer ['ɪmər], *adv.* always, ever; — *mehr,* more and more; — *noch,* still; — *wieder,* time and again: — *größer,* larger and larger; *auf* —, for ever.
immerdar ['ɪmərda:r], *adv.* for ever.
immerhin ['ɪmərhɪn], *adv.* nevertheless, still, after all.
immerzu ['ɪmərtsu:], *adv.* always, constantly.
Immobilien [ɪmo'bi:ljən], *pl.* real estate.
Immortelle [ɪmɔr'tɛlə], *f.* (—, *pl.* —n) (*Bot.*) everlasting flower.
immun [ɪ'mu:n], *adj.* immune.
impfen ['ɪmpfən], *v.a.* vaccinate, inoculate; (*Hort.*) graft.
imponieren [ɪmpo'ni:rən], *v.n.* impress.
Import [ɪm'pɔrt], *m.* (—s, *pl.* —e) import, importation.
imposant [ɪmpo'zant], *adj.* imposing, impressive.
imstande [ɪm'ʃtandə], *adv.* capable, able; — *sein,* be able.
in [ɪn], *prep.* (*Dat., Acc.*) in, into; at; within.
Inangriffnahme [ɪn'angrɪfna:mə], *f.* (—, *no pl.*) start, beginning, inception.
Inbegriff ['ɪnbəgrɪf], *m.* (—es, *no pl.*) essence, epitome.
inbegriffen ['ɪnbəgrɪfən], *adv.* inclusive.
Inbrunst ['ɪnbrunst], *f.* (—, *no pl.*) ardour, fervour.
indem [ɪn'de:m], *adv.* meanwhile. — *conj.* while, whilst; as, because, in that.
indessen [ɪn'dɛsən], *adv.* meanwhile, in the meantime. — *conj.* however, nevertheless, yet.
Indien ['ɪndjən], *n.* India.
Individualität [ɪndividuali'tɛ:t], *f.* (—, *pl.* —en) individuality, personality.
individuell [ɪndividu'ɛl], *adj.* individual.
Individuum [ɪndi'vi:duum], *n.* (—s, *pl.* —duen) individual.

Indizienbeweis [ɪn'di:tsjənbəvaɪs], *m.* (—es, *pl.* —e) (*Law*) circumstantial evidence *or* proof.

indossieren [ɪndɔ'si:rən], *v.a.* endorse.

Industrie [ɪndus'tri:], *f.* (—, *pl.* —n) industry; manufacture.

industriell [ɪndustri'ɛl], *adj.* industrial.

Industrielle [ɪndustri'ɛlə], *m.* (—n, *pl.* —n) manufacturer, industrialist.

ineinander [ɪnaɪ'nandər], *adv.* into each other, into one another.

infam [ɪn'fa:m], *adj.* infamous.

Infantin [ɪn'fantɪn], *f.* (—, *pl.* —en) Infanta.

infizieren [ɪnfi'tsi:rən], *v.a.* infect.

infolge [ɪn'fɔlgə], *prep.* (*Genit.*) in consequence of, owing to.

informieren [ɪnfɔr'mi:rən], *v.a.* inform, advise.

Ingenieur [ɪnʒen'jø:r], *m.* (—s, *pl.* —e) engineer.

Ingrimm ['ɪngrɪm], *m.* (—s, *no pl.*) anger, rage, wrath.

Ingwer ['ɪŋvər], *m.* (—s, *no pl.*) ginger.

Inhaber ['ɪnha:bər], *m.* (—s, *pl.* —) possessor, owner; proprietor; occupant.

inhaftieren [ɪnhaf'ti:rən], *v.a.* imprison; arrest.

inhalieren [ɪnha'li:rən], *v.a.* inhale.

Inhalt ['ɪnhalt], *m.* (—(e)s, *no pl.*) content; contents; tenor.

Inhaltsverzeichnis ['ɪnhaltsfɛrtsaɪçnɪs], *n.* (—ses, *pl.* —se) (table of) contents; index.

inhibieren [ɪnhi'bi:rən], *v.a.* inhibit, prevent.

Inkasso [ɪn'kaso], *n.* (—s, *pl.* —s) encashment.

inklinieren [ɪnkli'ni:rən], *v.n.* be inclined to.

inklusive [ɪnklu'zi:və], *adv.* inclusive of, including.

inkonsequent ['ɪnkɔnzəkvɛnt], *adj.* inconsistent.

Inkrafttreten [ɪn'krafttre:tən], *n.* (—s, *no pl.*) enactment; coming into force.

Inland ['ɪnlant], *n.* (—s, *no pl.*) inland, interior.

Inländer ['ɪnlɛndər], *m.* (—s, *pl.* —) native.

Inlett ['ɪnlɛt], *n.* (—s, *pl.* —e) bed-tick, ticking.

inliegend ['ɪnli:gənt], *adj.* enclosed.

inmitten [ɪn'mɪtən], *prep.* (*Genit.*) in the midst of.

innehaben ['ɪnəha:bən], *v.a.* *irr.* possess; occupy; hold.

innehalten ['ɪnəhaltən], *v.a. irr.* (*conditions*) keep to, observe; (*time*) come promptly at. — *v.n.* stop, pause.

innen ['ɪnən], *adv.* within; *nach* —, inwards; *von* —, from within.

Innenminister ['ɪnənmɪnɪstər], *m.* (—s, *pl.* —) Minister for Internal Affairs; Home Secretary; (*Am.*) Secretary of the Interior.

inner ['ɪnər], *adj.* inner, interior, internal; intrinsic.

innerhalb ['ɪnərhalp], *prep.* (*Genit.*) within.

innerlich ['ɪnərlɪç], *adj.* internal; inside o.s.; inward.

innerste ['ɪnərstə], *adj.* inmost, innermost.

innewerden [ɪnəve:rdən], *v.a. irr.* (*aux.* sein) perceive, become aware of.

innewohnen ['ɪnəvo:nən], *v.n.* be inherent in.

innig ['ɪnɪç], *adj.* heartfelt, cordial.

Innung ['ɪnuŋ], *f.* (—, *pl.* —en)guild, corporation.

Insasse ['ɪnzasə], *m.* (—n, *pl.* —n) inmate; occupant.

insbesondere [ɪnsbə'zɔndərə], *adv.* especially, particularly, in particular.

Inschrift ['ɪnʃrɪft], *f.* (—, *pl.* —en) inscription.

Insel ['ɪnzəl], *f.* (—, *pl.* —n) island.

Inserat [ɪnzə'ra:t], *n.* (—es, *pl.* —e) classified advertisement; (*coll.*) (small) ad.

inserieren [ɪnzə'ri:rən], *v.a.* advertise; insert.

insgeheim [ɪnsgə'haɪm], *adv.* privately, secretly.

insgesamt [ɪnsgə'zamt], *adv.* altogether, in a body.

insofern [ɪnzo'fɛrn], *conj.* — *als*, in so far as, inasmuch as, so far as.

inspirieren [ɪnspi'ri:rən], *v.a.* inspire.

installieren [ɪnsta'li:rən], *v.a.* install, fit.

instandhalten [ɪn'ʃtanthaltən], *v.a. irr.* maintain, preserve, keep in repair.

inständig ['ɪnʃtɛndɪç], *adj.* urgent; fervent.

instandsetzen [ɪn'ʃtantzɛtsən], *v.a.* restore, repair; *einen* — *etwas zu tun*, enable s.o. to do s.th.

Instanz [ɪn'stants], *f.* (—, *pl.* —en) (*Law*) instance; *letzte* —, highest court of appeal, last resort.

Institut [ɪnsti'tu:t], *n.* (—es, *pl.* —e) institute, institution, establishment; (*Univ.*) department.

instruieren [ɪnstru'i:rən], *v.a.* instruct.

Insulaner [ɪnzu'la:nər], *m.* (—s, *pl.* —) islander.

inszenieren [ɪnstse'ni:rən], *v.a.* put on the stage, produce.

Inszenierung [ɪnstse'ni:ruŋ], *f.* (—, *pl.* —en) (*Theat.*) production, staging.

intellektuell [ɪntɛlɛktu'ɛl], *adj.* intellectual.

Intendant [ɪntɛn'dant], *m.* (—en, *pl.* —en) (*Theat.*) director.

interessant [ɪntərɛ'sant], *adj.* interesting.

Interesse [ɪntə'rɛsə], *n.* (—s, *pl.* —n) interest.

Interessent [ɪntərɛ'sɛnt], *m.* (—en, *pl.* —en) interested party.

interessieren [ɪntərɛ'si:rən], *v.a.* interest. — *v.r. sich* —, be interested (in).

intern [ɪn'tɛrn], *adj.* internal.

Internat [ɪntɛr'na:t], *n.* (—es, *pl.* —e) boarding-school.

Interne [ɪn'tɛrnə], *m.* (**—n,** *pl.* **—n**) resident (pupil *or* doctor), boarder.
Internist [ɪntɛr'nɪst], *m.* (**—en,** *pl.* **—en**) specialist in internal diseases.
interpunktieren [ɪntərpuŋk'tiːrən], *v.a.* punctuate.
Interpunktion [ɪntərpuŋkts'joːn], *f.* (**—,** *pl.* **—en**) punctuation.
intim [ɪn'tiːm], *adj.* intimate; *mit einem — sein,* b : on close terms with s.o.
intonieren [ɪnto'niːrən], *v.n.* intone.
Intrigant [ɪntri'gant], *m.* (**—en,** *pl.* **—en**) intriguer, schemer.
intrigieren [ɪntri'giːrən], *v.n.* intrigue, scheme.
Inventar [ɪnvɛn'taːr], *n.* (**—s,** *pl.* **—e**) inventory; *ein — aufnehmen,* draw up an inventory.
Inventur [ɪnvɛn'tuːr], *f.* (**—,** *pl.* **—en**) stock-taking.
inwärts ['ɪnvɛrts], *adv.* inwards.
inwendig ['ɪnvɛndɪç], *adj.* inward, internal, inner.
inwiefern [ɪnviːˈfɛrn], *adv.* to what extent.
inwieweit [ɪnviːˈvaɪt], *adv.* how far.
Inzucht ['ɪntsuxt], *f.* (**—,** *no pl.*) inbreeding.
inzwischen [ɪn'tsvɪʃən], *adv.* meanwhile, in the meantime.
Irak [i'raːk], *m.,* *n.* Iraq.
Iran [i'raːn], *n.* Iran.
irden ['ɪrdən], *adj.* earthen.
irdisch ['ɪrdɪʃ], *adj.* earthly, worldly; terrestrial, temporal.
irgend ['ɪrgənt], *adv.* any, some; *wenn es — geht,* if it can possibly be done.
irgendein [ɪrgənt'aɪn], *pron.* any, some.
Irland ['ɪrlant], *n.* Ireland.
ironisch [i'roːnɪʃ], *adj.* ironic, ironical.
Irre (1) ['ɪrə], *f.* (**—,** *no pl.*) *in die — gehen,* go astray.
Irre (2) ['ɪrə], *m.* (**—n,** *pl.* **—n**) madman, lunatic.
irre ['ɪrə], *adj.* astray; wrong, confused; crazy, demented.
irren ['ɪrən], *v.n.* err, go astray, be wrong. — *v.r. sich —,* be mistaken.
Irrenarzt ['ɪrənartst], *m.* (**—es,** *pl.* ˝e) psychiatrist.
Irrenhaus ['ɪrənhaus], *n.* (**—es,** *pl.* ˝er) lunatic asylum, mental hospital.
Irrfahrt ['ɪrfaːrt], *f.* (**—,** *pl.* **—en**) wandering.
Irrglaube ['ɪrglaubə], *m.* (**—ns,** *no pl.*) heresy.
irrig ['ɪrɪç], *adj.* erroneous.
irritieren [ɪri'tiːrən], *v.a.* irritate.
Irrlicht ['ɪrlɪçt], *n.* (**—s,** *pl.* **—er**) will-o'-the-wisp.
Irrsinn ['ɪrzɪn], *m.* (**—s,** *no pl.*) madness, insanity, lunacy.
irrsinnig ['ɪrzɪnɪç], *adj.* insane, deranged.
Irrtum ['ɪrtuːm], *m.* (**—s,** *pl.* ˝er) error, mistake, fault, oversight.
Irrweg ['ɪrveːk], *m.* (**—s,** *pl.* **—e**) wrong track.
Irrwisch ['ɪrvɪʃ], *m.* (**—es,** *pl.* **—e**) will-o'-the-wisp.

Ischias ['ɪsçias], *f., m.* (*Med.*) sciatica.
Isegrim ['iːzəgrɪm], *m.* (**—s,** *pl.* **—e**) (*fable*) the wolf; a bear (with a sore head) (*also fig.*).
Island ['iːslant], *n.* Iceland.
isolieren [izo'liːrən], *v.a.* (*Electr.*) insulate; (*fig.*) isolate.
Isolierung [izo'liːruŋ], *f.* (**—,** *pl.* **—en**) (*Electr.*) insulation; (*fig.*) isolation.
Italien [i'taːljən], *n.* Italy.

J

J [jɔt], *n.* (**—,** *no pl.*) the letter J.
ja [jaː], *adv., part.* yes; indeed, certainly; even; *— doch,* to be sure; *— freilich,* certainly.
Jacht [jaxt], *f.* (**—,** *pl.* **—en**) yacht.
Jacke ['jakə], *f.* (**—,** *pl.* **—n**) jacket, tunic.
Jackett [ja'kɛt], *n.* (**—s,** *pl.* **—s**) jacket, short coat.
Jagd [jaːkt], *f.* (**—,** *pl.* **—en**) hunt, hunting; shooting; chase.
Jagdhund ['jaːkthunt], *m.* (**—es,** *pl.* **—e**) retriever, setter; hound.
Jagdrevier ['jaːktreviːr], *n.* (**—s,** *pl.* **—e**) hunting-ground.
jagen ['jaːgən], *v.a.* hunt; chase; (*fig.*) tear along.
Jäger ['jɛːgər], *m.* (**—s,** *pl.* **—**) hunter, huntsman; game-keeper.
Jägerei [jɛːgə'raɪ], *f.* (**—,** *no pl.*) huntsmanship.
jäh [jɛː], *adj.* abrupt; steep, precipitous; (*fig.*) hasty, rash, sudden.
jählings ['jɛːlɪŋs], *adv.* abruptly, suddenly, hastily.
Jahr [jaːr], *n.* (**—es,** *pl.* **—e**) year.
jähren ['jɛːrən], *v.r. sich —,* (*anniversary*) come round.
Jahresfeier [ja:rəsfaɪər], *f.* (**—,** *pl.* **—n**) anniversary.
Jahresrente ['jaːrəsrɛntə], *f.* (**—,** *pl.* **—n**) annuity.
Jahreszeit ['jaːrəstsaɪt], *f.* (**—,** *pl.* **—en**) season.
Jahrgang ['jaːrgaŋ], *m.* (**—s,** *pl.* ˝e) age group; class; year of publication; vintage.
Jahrhundert [jaːr'hundərt], *n.* (**—s,** *pl.* **—e**) century.
jährig ['jɛːrɪç], *adj.* year-old.
jährlich ['jɛːrlɪç], *adj.* yearly, annual. *— adv.* every year.
Jahrmarkt ['jaːrmarkt], *m.* (**—s,** *pl.* ˝e) annual fair.
Jahrtausend [jaːr'tauzənt], *n.* (**—s,** *pl.* **—e**) millennium.
Jahrzehnt [jaːr'tseːnt], *n.* (**—s,** *pl.* **—e**) decade.
Jähzorn ['jɛːtsɔrn], *m.* (**—s,** *no pl.*) irascibility.

Jalousie

Jalousie [ʒalu'zi:], *f.* (—, *pl.* —n) Venetian blind.

Jamaika [ja'maika], *n.* Jamaica.

Jambus ['jambus], *m.* (—, *pl.* —ben) (*Poet.*) iambic foot.

Jammer ['jamər], *m.* (—s, *no pl.*) lamentation; misery; (*fig.*) pity.

jämmerlich ['jɛmərlɪç], *adj.* lamentable, miserable, wretched, piteous.

jammerschade ['jamərʃa:də], *adv.* a thousand pities.

Jänner ['jɛnər] (*Austr.*) *see* **Januar**.

Januar ['janua:r], *m.* (—s, *pl.* —e) January.

Japan ['ja:pan], *n.* Japan.

Jaspis ['jaspɪs], *m.* (—ses, *pl.* —se) jasper.

jäten ['jɛ:tən], *v.a.* weed.

Jauche ['jauxə], *f.* (—, *pl.* —n) liquid manure.

jauchzen ['jauxtsən], *v.n.* exult, shout with joy.

Jauchzer ['jauxtsər], *m.* (—s, *pl.* —) shout of joy.

jawohl [ja'vo:l], *int.* yes, indeed! certainly, of course.

je [je:], *adv.* ever; at any time; at a time; each; *von — her*, always; — *nachdem*, it depends; — *zwei*, in twos; — *eher — besser*, the sooner the better.

jedenfalls ['je:dənfals], *adv.* at all events, in any case, at any rate, anyway.

jeder, -e, -es ['je:dər], *adj.* every, each; — *beliebige*, any. — *pron.* each, each one; everybody.

jederlei ['je:dərlai], *adj.* of every kind.

jedoch [je'dɔx], *adv.*, however, nevertheless, yet, notwithstanding.

jeglicher, -e, -es ['je:klɪçər], *adj.* every, each. — *pron.* every man, each.

jemals ['je:mals], *adv.* ever, at any time.

jemand ['je:mant], *pron.* somebody, someone; anybody, anyone.

Jemen ['je:mən], *n.* Yemen.

jener, -e, -es ['je:nər], *dem. adj.* that, (*Poet.*) yonder. — *dem. pron.* that one, the former.

Jenseits ['jɛnzaɪts], *n.* (—, *no pl.*) the next world, the hereafter, the life to come.

jenseits ['jɛnzaɪts], *prep.* (*Genit.*) on the other side, beyond.

jetzig ['jetsɪç], *adj.* present, now existing, current, extant.

jetzt [jetst], *adv.* now, at this time, at present.

jeweilig ['je:vaɪlɪç], *adj.* momentary; actual, for the time being.

Joch [jɔx], *n.* (—es, *pl.* —e) yoke.

Jochbein ['jɔxbaɪn], *n.* (—s, *pl.* —e) cheek-bone.

Jockei ['jɔkaɪ], *m.* (—s, *pl.* —s) jockey.

Jod [jo:t], *n.* (—s, *no pl.*) iodine.

jodeln ['jo:dəln], *v.n.* yodel.

Jodler ['jo:dlər], *m.* (—s, *pl.* —) (*person*) yodeler; (*sound*) yodelling.

Johannisbeere [jo'hanɪsbe:rə], *f.* (—, *pl.* —n) (*Bot.*) red currant.

Johannisfest [jo'hanɪsfɛst], *n.* (—s, *pl.* —e) Midsummer Day, St. John the Baptist's Day (June 24th).

Johanniskäfer [jo'hanɪskɛ:fər], *m.* (—s, *pl.* —) (*Ent.*) glow-worm.

Johannisnacht [jo'hanɪsnaxt], *f.* (—, *pl.* -̈e) Midsummer Eve.

johlen ['jo:lən], *v.n.* bawl.

Joppe ['jɔpə], *f.* (—, *pl.* —n) shooting jacket.

Jota ['jo:ta], *n.* (—s, *pl.* —s) iota, jot.

Journalismus [ʒurna'lɪsmus], *m. see* **Journalistik**.

Journalistik [ʒurna'lɪstɪk], *f.* (—, *no pl.*) journalism.

jubeln ['ju:bəln], *v.n.* rejoice, exult.

Jubilar [ju:bi'la:r], *m.* (—s, *pl.* —e) person celebrating a jubilee.

Jubiläum [ju:bi'lɛ:um], *n.* (—s, *pl.* —läen) jubilee.

jubilieren [ju:bi'li:rən], *v.n.* exult, ● shout with glee.

juchhe [jux'he:], *excl.* hurrah!

Juchten ['juxtən], *m.* (—, *no pl.*) Russian leather.

jucken ['jukən], *v.a.* scratch. — *v.n.* itch.

Jude ['ju:də], *m.* (—n, *pl.* —n) Jew, Israelite.

Judentum ['ju:dəntu:m], *n.* (—s, *no pl.*) Judaism.

Judenviertel ['ju:dənfi:rtəl], *n.* (—s, *pl.* —) Jewish quarter, ghetto.

Jüdin ['jy:dɪn], *f.* (—, *pl.* —innen) Jewess.

jüdisch ['jy:dɪʃ], *adj.* Jewish.

Jugend ['ju:gənt], *f.* (—, *no pl.*) youth.

jugendlich ['ju:gəntlɪç], *adj.* youthful, juvenile.

Jugoslawien [ju:go'sla:vjən], *n.* Jugoslavia.

Julfest ['ju:lfɛst], *n.* (—es, *pl.* —e) Yule.

Juli ['ju:li], *m.* (—s, *pl.* —s) July.

jung [juŋ], *adj.* young.

Junge (1) ['juŋə], *m.* (—n, *pl.* —n) boy, lad.

Junge (2) ['juŋə], *n.* (—n, *pl.* —n) young animal.

jungenhaft ['juŋənhaft], *adj.* boyish.

Jünger ['jyŋər], *m.* (—s, *pl.* —) disciple, devotee, follower.

Jungfer ['juŋfər], *f.* (—, *pl.* —n) (*obs.*) virgin, maid, maiden; lady's maid.

jüngferlich ['jyŋfərlɪç], *adj.* maidenly, coy, prim.

Jungfrau ['juŋfrau], *f.* (—, *pl.* —en) virgin.

Junggeselle ['juŋgəzɛlə], *m.* (—n, *pl.* —n) bachelor; *eingefleischter —*, confirmed bachelor.

Jüngling ['jyŋlɪŋ], *m.* (—s, *pl.* —e) young man.

jüngst [jyŋst], *adv.* lately, recently.

Juni ['ju:ni], *m.* (—s, *pl.* —s) June.

Junker ['juŋkər], *m.* (—s, *pl.* —) country squire; titled landowner.

Jura ['ju:ra], *n. pl.* jurisprudence, law; (*Univ.*) — *studieren*, read law.

Jurisprudenz [ju:rɪspru'dɛnts], *f.* (—, *no pl.*) jurisprudence.

Jurist [ju:'rɪst], *m.* (—en, *pl.* —en) lawyer, jurist.

juristisch [juːˈrɪstɪʃ], *adj.* juridical; legal.
just [just], *adv.* just now.
Justiz [jusˈtiːts], *f.* (—, *no pl.*) administration of the law *or* of justice.
Justizrat [jusˈtiːtsraːt], *m.* (—s, ¨e) (*Law*) Counsellor; King's (Queen's) Counsel.
Jute [ˈjuːtə], *f.* (—, *no pl.*) jute.
Juwel [juˈveːl], *n.* (—s, *pl.* —en) jewel; (*pl.*) jewellery; (*Am.*) jewelry.
Juwelier [juvəˈliːr], *m.* (—s, *pl.* —e) jeweller, goldsmith.

K

K [kaː], *n.* (—, *no pl.*) the letter K.
Kabel [ˈkaːbəl], *n.* (—s, *pl.* —) cable.
Kabeljau [kabəlˈjau], *m.* (—s, *pl.* —e) (*Zool.*) cod, codfish.
kabeln [ˈkaːbəln], *v.n.* cable, send a cablegram.
Kabine [kaˈbiːnə], *f.* (—, *pl.* —n) cabin, cubicle.
Kabinett [kabiˈnɛt], *n.* (—s, *pl.* —e) closet; cabinet.
Kabinettsrat [kabiˈnɛtsraːt], *m.* (—s, *pl.* ¨e) cabinet *or* ministerial committee; political adviser.
Kabüse [kaˈbyːzə], *f.* (—, *pl.* —n) ship's galley.
Kachel [ˈkaxəl], *f.* (—, *pl.* —n) glazed tile.
Kadaver [kaˈdaːvər], *m.* (—s, *pl.* —) carrion, carcass; corpse.
Kadenz [kaˈdɛnts], *f.* (—, *pl.* —en) (*Mus.*) cadenza.
Kadett [kaˈdɛt], *m.* (—en, *pl.* —en) cadet.
Käfer [ˈkɛːfər], *m.* (—s, *pl.* —) (*Ent.*) beetle, (*Am.*) bug.
Kaffee [ˈkafe], *m.* (—s, *no pl.*) coffee.
Käfig [ˈkɛːfɪç], *m.* (—s, *pl.* —e) cage.
kahl [kaːl], *adj.* bald; (*trees*) leafless; (*landscape*) barren; — *geschoren*, close-cropped.
Kahn [kaːn], *m.* (—s, *pl.* ¨e) boat; punt.
Kai [kaɪ], *m.* (—s, *pl.* —s) quay, wharf, landing-place.
Kaimeister [ˈkaɪmaɪstər], *m.* (—s, *pl.* —) wharfinger.
Kaiser [ˈkaɪzər], *m.* (—s, *pl.* —) emperor; *um des* —s *Bart streiten*, quarrel about nothing.
kaiserlich [ˈkaɪzərlɪç], *adj.* imperial.
Kaiserschnitt [ˈkaɪzərʃnɪt], *m.* (—es, *pl.* —e) (*Med.*) Caesarean operation.
Kajüte [kaˈjyːtə], *f.* (—, *pl.* —n) cabin.
Kakadu [ˈkakaduː], *m.* (—s, *pl.* —s) (*Orn.*) cockatoo.
Kakao [kaˈkaːo], *m.* (—s, *no pl.*) cocoa.
Kalauer [ˈkaːlauər], *m.* (—s, *no pl.*) pun; stale joke.

Kalb [kalp], *n.* (—es, *pl.* ¨er) calf; (*roe*) fawn; (*fig.*) colt, calf.
Kalbfleisch [ˈkalpflaɪʃ], *n.* (—es, *no pl.*) veal.
Kälberei [kɛlbəˈraɪ], *f.* (—, *pl.* —en) friskiness.
kälbern [ˈkɛlbərn], *v.n.* frisk, frolic.
Kalbsbraten [ˈkalpsbraːtən], *m.* (—s, *pl.* —) roast veal.
Kalbshaxe [ˈkalpshaksə], *f.* (—, *pl.* —n) knuckle of veal.
Kalbskeule [ˈkalpskɔylə], *f.* (—, *pl.* —n) leg of veal.
Kalbsmilch [ˈkalpsmɪlç], *f.* (—, *no pl.*) sweetbread.
Kaldaunen [kalˈdaunən], *f. pl.* (*dial.*) tripe.
Kalesche [kaˈlɛʃə], *f.* (—, *pl.* —n) chaise, light carriage.
Kali [ˈkaːli], *n.* (—s, *no pl.*) potash.
Kaliber [kaˈliːbər], *n.* (—s, *pl.* —) calibre; (*fig.*) sort, quality.
kalibrieren [kaliˈbriːrən], *v.a.* (*Tech.*) calibrate, graduate, gauge.
Kalifornien [kaliˈfɔrnjən], *n.* California.
Kalium [ˈkaːljum], *n.* (—s, *no pl.*) (*Chem.*) potassium.
Kalk [kalk], *m.* (—s, *pl.* —e) lime; *gebrannter* —, quicklime; *mit* — *bewerfen*, rough-cast.
kalkartig [ˈkalkaːrtɪç], *adj.* calcareous.
Kalkbewurf [ˈkalkbəvurf], *m.* (—es, *pl.* ¨e) coat of plaster.
kalken [ˈkalkən], *v.a.* whitewash; (*Agr.*) lime.
kalkig [ˈkalkɪç], *adj.* limy, calcareous.
kalkulieren [kalkuˈliːrən], *v.n.* calculate, reckon.
kalt [kalt], *adj.* cold, frigid; *mir ist* —, I am cold.
kaltblütig [ˈkaltblyːtɪç], *adj.* cold-blooded, cool.
Kälte [ˈkɛltə], *f.* (—, *no pl.*) cold, coldness.
Kaltschale [ˈkaltʃaːlə], *f.* (—, *pl.* —n) cold beer (*or* wine) soup.
Kambodscha [kamˈbɔtʃa], *f.* Cambodia.
Kamee [kaˈmeː], *f.* (—, *pl.* —n) cameo.
Kamel [kaˈmeːl], *n.* (—s, *pl.* —e) (*Zool.*) camel.
Kamelziege [kaˈmeːltsiːgə], *f.* (—, *pl.* —n) (*Zool.*) Angora-goat, llama.
Kamerad [kaməˈraːt], *m.* (—en, *pl.* —en) comrade, companion, mate.
Kameradschaft [kaməˈraːtʃaft], *f.* (—, *pl.* —en) comradeship, fellowship.
Kamerun [kaməˈruːn], *n.* the Cameroons.
Kamille [kaˈmɪlə], *f.* (—, *pl.* —n) camomile.
Kamin [kaˈmiːn], *m.* (—s, *pl.* —e) chimney; funnel; fireplace, fireside.
Kaminaufsatz [kaˈmiːnaufzats], *m.* (—es, *pl.* ¨e) mantel-piece, overmantel.
Kaminfeger [kaˈmiːnfeːgər], *m.* (—s, *pl.* —) chimney-sweep.

Kaminsims

Kaminsims [ka'mi:nzɪms], *m.* or *n.* (—es, *pl.* —e) mantel-piece.

Kamm [kam], *m.* (—es, *pl.* ˙:e) comb; (*cock*) crest; (*mountains*) ridge.

kämmen ['kɛmən], *v.a.* comb; (*wool*) card.

Kammer ['kamər], *f.* (—, *pl.* —n) chamber, small room; (*Am.*) closet; (*authority*) board; (*Parl. etc.*) chamber.

Kammerdiener ['kamərdi:nər], *m.* (—s, *pl.* —) valet.

Kämmerer ['kɛmərər], *m.* (—s, *pl.* —) Chamberlain, Treasurer.

Kammergericht ['kamərgərɪçt], *n.* (—s, *pl.* —e) Supreme Court of Justice.

Kammergut ['kamərgu:t], *n.* (—s, *pl.* ˙:er) domain, demesne; crown land.

Kammerherr ['kamərhɛr], *m.* (—n, *pl.* —en) chamberlain.

Kammersänger ['kamərzɛŋər], *m.* (—s, *pl.* —) court singer; title given to prominent singers.

Kammgarn ['kamgarn], *n.* (—s, *no pl.*) worsted.

Kammwolle ['kamvɔlə], *f.* (—, *no pl.*) carded wool.

Kampagne [kam'panjə], *f.* (—, *pl.* —n) (*Mil.*) campaign.

Kämpe ['kɛmpe], *m.* (—n, *pl.* —n) (*Poet.*) champion, warrior; *alter* —, old campaigner.

Kampf [kampf], *m.* (—es, *pl.* ˙:e) combat, fight, struggle; (*fig.*) conflict.

kämpfen ['kɛmpfən], *v.n.* fight, combat, struggle.

Kampfer ['kampfər], *m.* (—s, *no pl.*) camphor.

Kämpfer ['kɛmpfər], *m.* (—s, *pl.* —) fighter, combatant.

kampfunfähig ['kampfunfɛ:ɪç], *adj.* (*Mil.*) disabled; — *machen*, disable, put out of action.

kampieren [kam'pi:rən], *v.n.* be encamped, camp.

Kanada ['kanada], *n.* Canada.

Kanal [ka'na:l], *m.* (—s, *pl.* ˙:e) (*natural*) channel; (*artificial*) canal; sewer; *der Ärmelkanal*, the English Channel.

kanalisieren [kanali'zi:rən], *v.a.* canalise; (*streets*) drain by means of sewers.

Kanapee ['kanape:], *n.* (—s, *pl.* —s) sofa, divan.

Kanarienvogel [ka'na:rjənfo:gəl], *m.* (—s, *pl.* ˙:) (*Orn.*) canary.

Kanarische Inseln [ka'na:rɪʃə 'ɪnzəln], *f.pl.* Canary Islands.

Kandare [kan'da:rə], *f.* (—, *pl.* —n) bridle, bit.

Kandelaber [kandə'la:bər], *m.* (—s, *pl.* —) candelabrum, chandelier.

kandidieren [kandi'di:rən], *v.n.* be a candidate (for), apply (for) (*post*); (*Parl.*) stand (for), (*Am.*) run (for election).

kandieren [kan'di:rən], *v.a.* candy.

Kandiszucker ['kandɪstsukər], *m.* (—, *no pl.*) sugar-candy.

Kanevas ['kanəvas], *m.* (—ses, *pl.* —se) canvas.

Känguruh ['kɛŋguru:], *n.* (—s, *pl.* —s) (*Zool.*) kangaroo.

Kaninchen [ka'ni:nçən], *n.* (—s, *pl.* —) (*Zool.*) rabbit.

Kaninchenbau [ka'ni:nçənbau], *m.* (—s, *pl.* —e) rabbit-warren, burrow.

Kanne ['kanə], *f.* (—, *pl.* —n) can, tankard, mug; jug; pot; quart.

Kannegießer ['kanəgi:sər], *m.* (—s, *pl.* —) pot-house politician.

kannelieren [kanə'li:rən], *v.a.* flute; channel.

Kannibale [kani'ba:lə], *m.* (—n, *pl.* —n) cannibal.

Kanoe [ka'nu:], *n. see* **Kanu**.

Kanone [ka'no:nə], *f.* (—, *pl.* —n) cannon, gun; *unter aller* —, beneath contempt; beneath criticism.

Kanonier [kano'ni:r], *m.* (—s, *pl.* —e) gunner.

Kanonikus [ka'no:nikus], *m.* (—, *pl.* —ker) canon, prebendary.

kanonisieren [kanoni'zi:rən], *v.a.* canonise.

Kante ['kantə], *f.* (—, *pl.* —n) edge, rim, brim, brink, ledge; (*cloth*) list, selvedge.

Kanten ['kantən], *m.* (—s, *pl.* —) (*bread*) crust.

kanten ['kantən], *v.a.* edge, tilt.

Kanthaken ['kantha:kən], *m.* (—s, *pl.* —) cant-hook; grapple; grappling hook.

kantig ['kantɪç], *adj.* angular.

Kantine [kan'ti:nə], *f.* (—, *pl.* —n), canteen, mess.

Kanton [kan'to:n], *m.* (—s, *pl.* —e) (*Swiss*) canton; district, region.

Kantonist [kanto'nɪst], *m.* (—en, *pl.* —en) *unsicherer* —, shifty fellow.

Kantor ['kantər], *m.* (—s, *pl.* —en) precentor; organist; cantor.

Kanu [ka'nu:], *n.* (—s, *pl.* —s) canoe.

Kanzel ['kantsəl], *f.* (—, *pl.* —n) pulpit; (*Aviat.*) cockpit.

Kanzlei [kants'lai], *f.* (—, *pl.* —en) office, secretariat; chancellery; chancery office; lawyer's office.

Kanzleipapier [kants'laipapi:r], *n.* (—s, *no pl.*) foolscap (paper).

Kanzleistil [kants'laiʃti:l], *m.* (—s, *no pl.*) legal jargon.

Kanzler ['kantslər], *m.* (—s, *pl.* —) Chancellor.

Kanzlist [kants'lɪst], *m.* (—en, *pl.* —en) chancery clerk; copying clerk.

Kap [kap], *n.* (—s, *pl.* —s) (*Geog.*) cape, promontory.

Kapaun [ka'paun], *m.* (—s, *pl.* —e) capon.

Kapazität [kapatsi'tɛ:t], *f.* (—, *pl.* —en) capacity; (*fig.*) (*person*) authority.

Kapelle [ka'pɛlə], *f.* (—, *pl.* —n) chapel; (*Mus.*) band.

Kapellmeister [ka'pɛlmaistər], *m.* (—s, *pl.* —) (*Mus.*) band leader, conductor.

Kaper ['ka:pər], *f.* (—, *pl.* —n) (*Bot.*) caper.

kapern ['ka:pərn], *v.a.* capture, catch.
kapieren [ka'pi:rən], *v.a.* (*coll.*) understand, grasp.
Kapital [kapi'ta:l], *n.* (**—e**, *pl.* **—ien**) (*money*) capital, stock.
Kapitäl, Kapitell [kapı'tɛ:l, kapı'tɛl], *n.* (**—s**, *pl.* **—e**) (*Archit.*) capital.
Kapitalanlage [kapi'talanla:gə], *f.* (— *pl.* **—n**) investment.
kapitalisieren [kapitali'zi:rən], *v.a.* capitalise.
kapitalkräftig [kapi'ta:lkrɛftıç], *adj.* wealthy, moneyed, affluent; (*business, firm*) sound.
Kapitalverbrechen [kapi'ta:lfɛrbrɛçən], *n.* (**—s**, *pl.* —) capital offence.
Kapitän [kapi'tɛ:n], *m.* (**—s**, *pl.* **—e**) captain (of a ship), master.
Kapitel [ka'pıtəl], *n.* (**—s**, *pl.* —) chapter.
Kapitulation [kapitulats'jo:n], *f.* (—, *pl.* **—en**) surrender.
kapitulieren [kapitu'li:rən], *v.n.* surrender; capitulate.
Kaplan [kap'la:n], *m.* (**—s**, *pl.* **ˑ·e**) chaplain; assistant priest.
Kapotte [ka'pɔtə], *f.* (—, *pl.* **—n**) hood.
Kappe ['kapə], *f.* (—, *pl.* **—n**) cap, bonnet; (*shoe*) toe-cap.
Käppi ['kɛpi], *n.* (**—s**, *pl.* **—s**) military cap.
Kapriole [kapri'o:lə], *f.* (—, *pl.* **—n**) caper.
kaprizieren [kapri'tsi:rən], *v.r. sich auf etwas* —, set o.'s heart on s.th., be obstinate about s.th.
kapriziös [kapri'tsjø:s], *adj.* whimsical, capricious.
Kapsel ['kapzəl], *f.* (—, *pl.* **—n**) capsule.
kaputt [ka'put], *adj.* broken, ruined, done for; — *machen*, break, ruin.
Kapuze [ka'pu:tsə], *f.* (—, *pl.* **—n**) hood; monk's cowl.
Kapuziner [kaput'si:nər], *m.* (**—s**, *pl.* —) Capuchin (friar); (*coffee*) cappuccino.
Kapuzinerkresse [kaput'si:nərkrɛsə], *f.* (—, *no pl.*) (*Bot.*) nasturtium.
Karabiner [kara'bi:nər], *m.* (**—s**, *pl.* —) (*rifle*) carbine.
Karaffe [ka'rafə], *f.* (—, *pl.* **—n**) carafe; decanter.
Karambolage [karambo'la:ʒə], *f.* (—, *pl.* **—n**) collision; (*billiards*) cannon.
Karawane [kara'va:nə], *f.* (—, *pl.* **—n**) convoy; caravan.
Karbol [kar'bo:l], *n.* (**—s**, *no pl.*) carbolic acid.
Karbunkel [kar'buŋkəl], *m.* (**—s**, *pl.* —) (*Med.*) carbuncle.
Karfreitag [kar'fraɪta:k], *m.* Good Friday.
Karfunkel [kar'fuŋkəl], *m.* (**—s**, *pl.* —) (*Min.*) carbuncle.
karg [kark], *adj.* scant; meagre; parsimonious.
kargen ['kargən], *v.n.* be stingy, be niggardly.
kärglich ['kɛrklıç], *adj.* sparing, scanty, poor, paltry.

karieren [ka'ri:rən], *v.a.* checker.
kariert [ka'ri:rt], *adj.* checked, checkered.
Karikatur [karika'tu:r], *f.* (—, *pl.* **—en**) caricature, cartoon.
karikieren [kari'ki:rən], *v.a.* caricature, distort.
Karl [karl], *m.* Charles; — *der Grosse*, Charlemagne.
Karmeliter [karme'li:tər], *m.* (**—s**, *pl.* —) Carmelite (friar).
karminrot [kar'mi:nro:t], *adj.* carmine.
karmoisin [karmoa'zi:n], *adj.* crimson.
Karneol [karne'o:l], *m.* (**—s**, *pl.* **—e**) (*Min.*) cornelian, carnelian.
Karneval ['karnəval], *m.* (**—s**, *pl.* **—s**) carnival; Shrovetide festivities.
Karnickel [kar'nıkəl], *n.* (**—s**, *pl.* —) rabbit; *er war das* —, he was to blame.
Kärnten ['kɛrntən], *n.* Carinthia.
Karo ['ka:ro], *n.* (**—s**, *pl.* **—s**) check, square; (*cards*) diamonds.
Karosse [ka'rɔsə], *f.* (—, *pl.* **—n**) statecoach.
Karosserie [karɔsə'ri:], *f.* (—, *pl.* **—n**) (*Motor.*) body(-work).
Karotte [ka'rɔtə], *f.* (—, *pl.* **—n**) (*Bot.*) carrot.
Karpfen ['karpfən], *m.* (**—s**, *pl.* —) (*fish*) carp.
Karre ['karə], *f.* (—, *pl.* **—n**) cart, wheelbarrow.
Karren ['karən], *m.* (**—s**, *pl.* —) cart, wheelbarrow, dray.
Karrete [ka're:tə], *f.* (—, *pl.* —) (*Austr.*) rattletrap, rickety coach.
Karriere [ka'rjɛ:rə], *f.* (—, *pl.* **—n**) career; — *machen*, get on well.
Kärrner ['kɛrnər], *m.* (**—s**, *pl.* —) (*obs.*) carter.
Karst [karst], *m.* (**—s**, *pl.* **—e**) mattock.
Karthago [kar'ta:go], *n.* Carthage.
Kartätsche [kar'tɛ:tʃə], *f.* (—, *pl.* **—n**) grape-shot, shrapnel.
Kartäuser [kar'tɔyzər], *m.* (**—s**, *pl.* —) Carthusian (monk).
Karte ['kartə], *f.* (—, *pl.* **—n**) card; ticket; map; chart; (*pl.*) pack ((*Am.*) deck) of cards.
Kartei [kar'taɪ], *f.* (—, *pl.* **—en**) card index.
Kartell [kar'tɛl], *n.* (**—s**, *pl.* **—e**) cartel; ring; syndicate.
Kartoffel [kar'tɔfəl], *f.* (—, *pl.* **—n**) (*Bot.*) potato.
Kartoffelpuffer [kar'tɔfəlpufər], *m.* **—s**, *pl.* —) potato-pancake.
Karton [kar'tɔŋ], *m.* (**—s**, *pl.* **—s**) carton, cardboard-box; (*material*) cardboard, paste-board; cartoon.
Kartusche [kar'tuʃə], *f.* (—, *pl.* **—n**) cartridge.
Karussell [karu'sɛl], *n.* (**—s**, *pl.* **—e**) merry-go-round.
Karwoche ['ka:rvɔxə], *f.* Holy Week.
Karzer ['kartsər], *m.* (**—s**, *pl.* —) lock-up, prison.
Kaschmir ['kaʃmi:r], *m.* (**—s**, *no pl.*) cashmere.

Käse

Käse ['kɛːzə], m. (—s, pl. —) cheese.
käseartig ['kɛːzəaːrtɪç], adj. like cheese; caseous.
Kaserne [ka'zɛrnə], f. (—, pl. —n) barracks.
kasernieren [kazɛr'niːrən], v.a. put into barracks.
Käsestoff ['kɛːzəʃtɔf], m. (—s, pl. —e) casein.
käseweiß ['kɛːzəvaɪs], adj. deathly pale.
käsig ['kɛːzɪç], adj. cheese-like, cheesy, caseous; (fig.) sallow.
Kasperle ['kaspɛrlə], n. (—s, pl. —) Punch.
Kasperl(e)theater ['kaspərl(ə)teaːtər], n. (—s, pl. —) Punch-and-Judy show.
Kaspisches Meer ['kaspɪʃəsmeːr], n. Caspian Sea.
Kasse ['kasə], f. (—, pl. —n) money-box, till; cash-desk; box-office; cash, ready money.
Kassenanweisung ['kasənanvaɪzuŋ], f. (—, pl. —en) treasury-bill; cash voucher.
Kassenbuch ['kasənbuːx], n. (—es, pl. ⁓er) cash-book.
Kassenschrank ['kasənʃraŋk], m. (—s, pl. ⁓e) strong-box, safe.
Kasserolle [kasə'rɔlə], f. (—, pl. —n) stew-pot, casserole.
Kassette [ka'sɛtə], f. (—, pl. —n) deed-box; casket; (Phot.) plate-holder.
kassieren [ka'siːrən], v.a. cash, collect (money); cashier, annul, discharge.
Kassierer [ka'siːrər], m. (—s, pl. —) cashier; teller.
Kastanie [kas'taːnjə], f. (—, pl. —n) (Bot.) chestnut, (coll.) conker; chest-nut-tree.
Kästchen ['kɛstçən], n. (—s, pl. —) casket, little box.
Kaste ['kastə], f. (—, pl. —n) caste.
kasteien [ka'staɪən], v.r. sich —, castigate or mortify o.s.
Kastell [ka'stɛl], n. (—s, pl. —e) citadel, small fort; castle.
Kastellan [kastɛ'laːn], m. (—s, pl. —e) castellan; caretaker.
Kasten ['kastən], m. (—s, pl. ⁓) box, chest, case, crate.
Kastengeist ['kastəngaɪst], m. (—es, no pl.) exclusiveness; class consciousness.
Kastilien [ka'stiːljən], n. Castile.
Kastrat [ka'straːt], m. (—en, pl. —en) eunuch.
kastrieren [ka'striːrən], v.a. castrate.
Katafalk [kata'falk], m. (—s, pl. —e) catafalque.
katalogisieren [katalogi'ziːrən], v.a. catalogue.
Katarakt [kata'rakt], m. (—es, pl. —e) cataract; waterfall.
Katasteramt [ka'tastəramt], n. (—es, pl. ⁓er) land-registry office.
katechisieren [kateçi'ziːrən], v.a. catechise, instruct.

kategorisch [kate'goːrɪʃ], adj. categorical, definite.
Kater ['kaːtər], m. (—s, pl. —) tom-cat; (fig.) hangover; der gestiefelte —, Puss-in-Boots.
Katheder [ka'teːdər], n. (—s, pl. —) desk; rostrum; lecturing-desk; (fig.) professorial chair.
Kathedrale [kate'draːlə], f. (—, pl. —n) cathedral.
Katholik [kato'liːk], m. (—en, pl. —en) (Roman) Catholic.
katholisch [ka'toːlɪʃ], adj. (Roman) Catholic.
Kattun [ka'tuːn], m. (—s, pl. —e) calico, cotton.
Kätzchen ['kɛtsçən], n. (—s, pl. —) kitten; (Bot.) catkin.
Katze ['katsə], f. (—, pl. —n) cat; die — im Sack kaufen, buy a pig in a poke; für die —, no good at all, useless.
katzenartig ['katsənaːrtɪç], adj. cat-like, feline.
Katzenauge ['katsənaugə], n. (—s, pl. —n) cat's-eye.
Katzenbuckel ['katsənbukəl], m. (—s, pl. —) arched back of a cat.
Katzenjammer ['katsənjamər], m. (—s, pl. —) hangover.
Katzenmusik ['katsənmuziːk], f. (—, no pl.) caterwauling; cacophony, discordant music.
Katzensprung ['katsənʃpruŋ], m. (—es, no pl.) (fig.) stone's throw
Kauderwelsch ['kaudərvɛlʃ], n. (—es, no pl.) gibberish, double-Dutch.
kauen ['kauən], v.a., v.n. chew.
kauern ['kauərn], v.n. cower, squat, crouch.
Kauf [kauf], m. (—es, pl. ⁓e) purchase, buy; bargain.
Kaufbummel ['kaufbuməl], m. (—s, no pl.) shopping-spree.
kaufen ['kaufən], v.a. (things) buy, purchase; (persons) bribe.
Käufer ['kɔyfər], m. (—s, pl. —) buyer, purchaser.
Kaufhaus ['kaufhaus], n. (—es, pl. ⁓er) department store, emporium.
Kaufladen ['kaufla:dən], m. (—s, pl. ⁓) shop.
käuflich ['kɔyflɪç], adj. (things) purchasable, marketable; (persons) open to bribery, venal.
Kaufmann ['kaufman], m. (—s, pl. Kaufleute) merchant; shopkeeper; (Am.) store-keeper.
kaufmännisch ['kaufmɛnɪʃ], adj. commercial, mercantile.
Kaugummi ['kaugumi], m. (—s, no pl.) chewing gum.
Kaukasus ['kaukazus], m. Caucasus (Mountains).
Kaulquappe ['kaulkvapə], f. (—, pl. —n) (Zool.) tadpole.
kaum [kaum], adv. scarcely, hardly; no sooner.
Kaurimuschel ['kaurimuʃəl], f. (—, pl. —n) (Zool.) cowrie shell.

120

Kautabak ['kautabak], *m.* (**—s**, *no pl.*) chewing-tobacco.
Kaution [kau'tsjo:n], *f.* (**—**, *pl.* **—en**) security, bail, surety; *eine* **—** *stellen,* go, give *or* stand bail.
Kautschuk ['kautʃuk], *m.* (**—s**, *no pl.*) caoutchouc, India-rubber.
Kauz [kauts], *m.* (**—es**, *pl.* **˸e**) (*Orn.*) screech-owl; (*fig.*) *komischer* **—**, queer customer.
Käuzchen ['kɔytsçən], *n.* (**—s**, *pl.* **—**) little owl; (*fig.*) imp.
Kavalier [kava'li:r], *m.* (**—s**, *pl.* **—e**) gentleman; lady's man.
keck [kɛk], *adj.* bold, daring; pert, saucy.
Kegel ['ke:gəl], *m.* (**—s**, *pl.* **—**) ninepin, skittle; (*Geom.*) cone; *mit Kind und* **—**, bag and baggage.
Kegelbahn ['ke:gəlba:n], *f.* (**—**, *pl.* **—en**) skittle-alley, bowling-alley.
kegelförmig ['ke:gəlfœrmiç], *adj.* conical.
kegeln ['ke:gəln], *v.n.* bowl, play at ninepins.
Kehle ['ke:lə], *f.* (**—**, *pl.* **—n**) throat, windpipe.
Kehlkopf ['ke:lkɔpf], *m.* (**—es**, *pl.* **˸e**) larynx.
Kehllaut ['ke:llaut], *m.* (**—es**, *pl.* **—e**) (*Phonet.*) guttural sound.
Kehlung ['ke:luŋ], *f.* (**—**, *pl.* **—en**) channel, flute, groove.
Kehraus ['ke:raus], *m.* (**—**, *no pl.*) last dance; (*fig.*) break-up, end.
kehren ['ke:rən], *v.a.* sweep; turn; *den Rücken* **—**, turn o.'s back. — *v.r. sich* **—** *an,* pay attention to, regard.
Kehricht ['ke:riçt], *m.* (**—s**, *no pl.*) sweepings; rubbish.
Kehrreim ['ke:rraim], *m.* (**—s**, *pl.* **—e**) refrain.
Kehrseite ['ke:rzaitə], *f.* (**—**, *pl.* **—n**) reverse.
kehrtmachen ['ke:rtmaxən], *v.n.* turn around; (*Mil.*) face about; turn back.
keifen ['kaifən], *v.n.* scold, nag.
Keil [kail], *m.* (**—s**, *pl.* **—e**) wedge.
Keile ['kailə], *f.* (**—**, *no pl.*) blows; (*coll.*) hiding; **—** *kriegen,* get a thrashing.
keilen ['kailən], *v.a.* wedge; (*coll.*) thrash.
Keilerei [kailə'rai], *f.* (**—**, *pl.* **—en**) brawl, fight.
keilförmig ['kailfœrmiç], *adj.* wedge-shaped.
Keilschrift ['kailʃrift], *f.* (**—**, *pl.* **—en**) cuneiform writing.
Keim [kaim], *m.* (**—es**, *pl.* **—e**) germ, seed.
keimen ['kaimən], *v.n.* germinate.
keimfrei ['kaimfrai], *adj.* sterile, germ-free.
keiner, -e, -es [kainər], *adj.* no, not a, not any. — *pron.* no one, none.
keinerlei ['kainərlai], *adj.* no, of no sort, no ... whatever.
keineswegs ['kainəsve:ks], *adv.* by no means, on no account.

Keks [ke:ks], *m.* (**—es**, *pl.* **—e**) biscuit.
Kelch [kɛlç], *m.* (**—es**, *pl.* **—e**) cup; (*Eccl.*) chalice; (*Bot.*) calyx.
Kelchblatt ['kɛlçblat], *n.* (**—es**, *pl.* **˸er**) sepal.
kelchförmig ['kɛlçfœrmiç], *adj.* cup-shaped.
Kelle ['kɛlə], *f.* (**—**, *pl.* **—n**) ladle; (*mason*) trowel.
Keller ['kɛlər], *m.* (**—s**, *pl.* **—**) cellar, basement.
Kellergewölbe ['kɛlərgəvœlbə], *n.* (**—s**, *pl.* **—**) vault.
Kellner ['kɛlnər], *m.* (**—s**, *pl.* **—**) waiter.
keltern ['kɛltərn], *v.a.* press (*grapes*).
Kenia ['ke:nja], *n.* Kenya.
kennbar ['kɛnba:r], *adj.* recognisable, conspicuous.
kennen ['kɛnən], *v.a. irr.* know, be acquainted with.
Kenner ['kɛnər], *m.* (**—s**, *pl.* **—**) connoisseur, expert.
Kennkarte ['kɛnkartə], *f.* (**—**, *pl.* **—n**) identity card.
kenntlich ['kɛntliç], *adj.* distinguishable.
Kenntnis ['kɛntnis], *f.* (**—**, *pl.* **—se**) knowledge; (*language*) command.
Kennzeichen ['kɛntsaixən], *n.* (**—s**, *pl.* **—**) characteristic, distinguishing mark; sign; symptom; criterion.
Kenterhaken ['kɛntərha:kən], *m.* (**—s**, *pl.* **—**) grappling-iron.
kentern ['kɛntərn], *v.n.* (*aux.* sein) capsize.
keramisch [ke'ra:miʃ], *adj.* ceramic.
Kerbe ['kɛrbə], *f.* (**—**, *pl.* **—n**) notch, indentation.
kerben ['kɛrbən], *v.a.* notch.
Kerbholz ['kɛrphɔlts], *n.* (**—es**, *no pl.*) tally; *auf dem* **—**, on o.'s conscience, charged against o.
Kerbtier ['kɛrpti:r], *n.* (**—es**, *pl.* **—e**) insect.
Kerker ['kɛrkər], *m.* (**—s**, *pl.* **—**) prison, jail, gaol; dungeon.
Kerl [kɛrl], *m.* (**—s**, *pl.* **—e**) fellow, chap; (*Am.*) guy (*coll.*).
Kern [kɛrn], *m.* (**—es**, *pl.* **—e**) (*nut*) kernel; (*fruit*) stone; (*fig.*) heart, crux; pith; (*Phys.*) nucleus.
kerngesund ['kɛrngəzunt], *adj.* hale and hearty, fit as a fiddle.
kernig ['kɛrniç], *adj.* solid, pithy.
Kernphysik ['kɛrnfyzi:k], *f.* (**—**, *no pl.*) nuclear physics.
Kernpunkt ['kɛrnpuŋkt], *m.* (**—es**, *pl.* **—e**) gist, essential point.
Kernwaffe ['kɛrnvafə], *f.* (**—**, *pl.* **—n**) nuclear weapon.
Kerze ['kɛrtsə], *f.* (**—**, *pl.* **—n**) candle.
Kessel ['kɛsəl], *m.* (**—s**, *pl.* **—**) kettle, cauldron; (*steam*) boiler.
Kesselschmied ['kɛsəlʃmi:t], *m.* (**—s**, *pl.* **—e**) boiler maker.
Kesselstein ['kɛsəlʃtain], *m.* (**—s**, *no pl.*) fur, deposit, scale (on boiler).
Kette ['kɛtə], *f.* (**—**, *pl.* **—n**) chain.
ketten ['kɛtən], *v.a.* chain, fetter.
Kettenstich ['kɛtənʃtiç], *m.* (**—es**, *pl.* **—e**) chain stitch; (*Naut.*) chain knot.

Ketzer

Ketzer ['kɛtsər], *m.* (—s, *pl.* —) heretic.
Ketzerei [kɛtsə'raɪ], *f.* (—, *pl.* —en) heresy.
ketzerisch ['kɛtsərɪʃ], *adj.* heretical.
keuchen ['kɔyçən], *v.n.* pant, puff, gasp.
Keuchhusten ['kɔyçhu:stən], *m.* (—s, *no pl.*) whooping-cough.
Keule ['kɔylə], *f.* (—, *pl.* —n) club; (*meat*) leg.
keusch [kɔyʃ], *adj.* chaste, pure.
kichern ['kɪçərn], *v.n.* titter, giggle.
Kiebitz ['ki:bɪts], *m.* (—es, *pl.* —e) (*Orn.*) lapwing, peewit; (*fig.*) on-looker; (*coll.*) rubber-neck (at chess or cards).
Kiefer (1) ['ki:fər], *m.* (—s, *pl.* —) jaw, jaw-bone.
Kiefer (2) ['ki:fər], *f.* (—, *pl.* —n) (*Bot.*) pine.
Kiel [ki:l], *m.* (—es, *pl.* —e) keel; (*pen*) quill.
Kielwasser ['ki:lvasər], *n.* (—s, *no pl.*) wake.
Kieme ['ki:mə], *f.* (—, *pl.* —n) (*fish*) gill.
Kien [ki:n], *m.* (—s, *no pl.*) pine-resin, resinous pinewood.
Kienspan ['ki:nʃpa:n], *m.* (—s, *pl.* ∵e) pine-splinter.
Kiepe ['ki:pə], *f.* (—, *pl.* —n) (*dial.*) creel, wicker basket.
Kies [ki:s], *m.* (—es, *no pl.*) gravel.
Kiesel ['ki:zəl], *m.* (—s, *pl.* —) pebble; flint.
Kieselsäure ['ki:zəlzɔyrə], *f.* (—, *no pl.*) silicic acid.
Kieselstein ['ki:zəlʃtaɪn], *m.* (—s, *pl.* —e) pebble.
Kilogramm ['ki:logram], *n.* (—s, *pl.* —e) kilogram (1000 grammes).
Kilometer ['ki:lome:tər], *m.* (—s, *pl.* —) kilometre; (*Am.*) kilometer (1000 metres).
Kimme ['kɪmə], *f.* (—, *pl.* —n) notch.
Kind [kɪnt], *n.* (—es, *pl.* —er) child; (*law*) infant; — *und Kegel*, bag and baggage.
Kind(e)l ['kɪnd(ə)l], *n.* (—s, *pl.* —) (*dial.*) small child, baby; *Münchner* —, Munich beer.
Kinderei [kɪndə'raɪ], *f.* (—, *pl.* —) childishness; childish prank.
Kinderfräulein ['kɪndərfrɔylaɪn], *n.* (—s, *pl.* —) nurse, (*coll.*) nannie.
Kindergarten ['kɪndərgartən], *m.* (—s, *pl.* ∵) kindergarten, infant-school.
Kinderhort ['kɪndərhɔrt], *m.* (—s, *pl.* —e) crèche.
kinderleicht ['kɪndərlaɪçt], *adj.* extremely easy, child's play.
Kindermärchen ['kɪndərmɛ:rçən], *n.* (—s, *pl.* —) fairy-tale.
Kinderstube ['kɪndərʃtu:bə], *f.* (—, *pl.* —n) nursery; *eine gute* —, a good upbringing.
Kinderwagen ['kɪndərva:gən], *m.* (—s, *pl.* —) perambulator, pram.
Kindesbeine ['kɪndəsbaɪnə], *n. pl. von* —*n an*, from infancy.

Kindeskind ['kɪndəskɪnt], *n.* (—es, *pl.* —er) (*obs.*) grandchild.
Kindheit ['kɪnthaɪt], *f.* (—, *no pl.*) childhood, infancy.
kindisch ['kɪndɪʃ], *adj.* childish.
kindlich ['kɪntlɪç], *adj.* childlike; naïve.
Kinn [kɪn], *n.* (—s, *pl.* —e) chin.
Kinnbacken ['kɪnbakən], *m.* (—s, *pl.* —) (*Anat.*) jaw-bone.
Kinnbackenkrampf ['kɪnbakənkrampf], *m.* (—s, *pl.* ∵e) (*Med.*) lock-jaw.
Kinnlade ['kɪnla:də], *f.* (—, *pl.* —n) (*Anat.*) jaw-bone.
Kino ['ki:no], *n.* (—s, *pl.* —s) cinema; (*coll.*) pictures; (*Am.*) motion picture theatre; motion pictures, (*coll.*) movies.
Kipfel ['kɪpfəl], *n.* (—s, *pl.* —) (*dial.*) roll, croissant.
kippen ['kɪpən], *v.a.* tilt, tip over.
Kirche ['kɪrçə], *f.* (—, *pl.* —n) church.
Kirchenbann ['kɪrçənban], *m.* (—s, *no. pl.*) excommunication.
Kirchenbuch ['kɪrçənbu:x], *n.* (—es, *pl.* ∵er) parish-register.
Kirchengut ['kɪrçəngu:t], *n.* (—es, *pl.* ∵er) church-property.
Kirchenlicht ['kɪrçənlɪçt], *n.* (—es, *pl.* —er) (*fig.*) shining light, bright spark.
Kirchenrecht ['kɪrçənrɛçt], *n.* (—es, *no pl.*) canon law.
Kirchenschiff ['kɪrçənʃɪf], *n.* (—es, *pl.* —e) nave.
Kirchenstuhl ['kɪrçənʃtu:l], *m.* (—es, *pl.* ∵e) pew.
Kirchenversammlung ['kɪrçənferzamluŋ], *f.* (—, *pl.* —en) synod; convocation.
Kirchenvorsteher ['kɪrçənforʃte:ər], *m.* (—s, *pl.* —) churchwarden.
kirchlich ['kɪrçlɪç], *adj.* ecclesiastic(al), religious.
Kirchspiel ['kɪrçʃpi:l], *n.* (—es, *pl.* —e) parish.
Kirchsprengel ['kɪrçʃprɛŋəl], *m.* (—s, *pl.* —) diocese.
Kirchturm ['kɪrçturm], *m.* (—es, *pl.* ∵e) steeple.
Kirchweih ['kɪrçvaɪ], *f.* (—, *pl.* —en) consecration (of a church); church fair.
Kirmes ['kɪrmɛs], *f.* (—, *pl.* —sen) *see* **Kirchweih.**
kirre ['kɪrə], *adj.* tame; (*fig.*) amenable.
kirren ['kɪrən], *v.a.* tame, allure. — *v.n.* coo.
Kirsch(branntwein) [kɪrʃ(brantvaɪn)], *m.* (—s, *no pl.*) cherry-brandy.
Kirsche ['kɪrʃə], *f.* (—, *pl.* —n) (*Bot.*) cherry; *mit ihr ist nicht gut* —*n essen*, she is hard to get on with *or* not pleasant to deal with.
Kirschsaft ['kɪrʃzaft], *m.* (—es, *no pl.*) cherry-juice.
Kirschwasser ['kɪrʃvasər], *n.* (—s, *no pl.*) cherry-brandy.
Kissen ['kɪsən], *n.* (—s, *pl.* —) cushion, pillow.

Kiste ['kɪstə], *f.* (—, *pl.* —n) box, case, chest; crate; coffer.

Kitsch [kɪtʃ], *m.* (—es, *no pl.*) trash; rubbish.

Kitt [kɪt], *m.* (—s, *pl.* —e) cement; (*Glazing*) putty.

Kittel ['kɪtəl], *m.* (—s, *pl.* —) smock; overall, tunic; frock.

kitten ['kɪtən], *v.a.* cement, glue.

Kitzchen ['kɪtsçən], *n.* (—s, *pl.* —) kid; fawn; kitten.

Kitzel ['kɪtsəl], *m.* (—s, *no pl.*) tickling, titillation; itch; (*fig.*) desire, appetite.

kitzeln ['kɪtsəln], *v.a.* tickle, titillate.

kitzlich ['kɪtslɪç], *adj.* ticklish; (*fig.*) delicate.

Kladderadatsch ['kladəradatʃ], *m.* (—es, *no pl.*) bang; mess, muddle.

klaffen ['klafən], *v.n.* gape, yawn.

kläffen ['klɛfən], *v.n.* bark, yelp.

Klafter ['klaftər], *f.* (—, *pl.* —n) fathom; (*wood*) cord.

klagbar ['kla:kba:r], *adj.* (*Law*) actionable.

Klage ['kla:gə], *f.* (—, *pl.* —n) complaint; (*Law*) suit, action.

Klagelied ['kla:gəli:t], *n.* (—es, *pl.* —er) dirge, lamentation.

klagen ['kla:gən], *v.n.* complain, lament; (*Law*) sue.

Kläger ['klɛ:gər], *m.* (—s, *pl.* —) complainant; (*Law*) plaintiff.

Klageschrift ['kla:gəʃrɪft], *f.* (—, *pl.* —en) bill of indictment; written complaint.

kläglich ['klɛ:klɪç], *adj.* woeful, pitiful, deplorable.

klaglos ['kla:klo:s], *adj.* uncomplaining.

Klamm [klam], *f.* (—, *pl.* —en) gorge, ravine.

klamm [klam], *adj.* tight, narrow; numb; clammy.

Klammer ['klamər], *f.* (—, *pl.* —n) clamp, clasp, hook; peg; clip; bracket, parenthesis.

klammern ['klamərn], *v.a.* fasten, peg. — *v.r. sich* — *an*, cling to.

Klang [klaŋ], *m.* (—es, *pl.* ⁻e) sound, tone; *ohne Sang und* —, unheralded and unsung.

klanglos ['klaŋlo:s], *adj.* soundless.

klangnachahmend ['klaŋnaxa:mənt], *adj.* onomatopoeic.

klangvoll ['klaŋfɔl], *adj.* sonorous.

Klappe ['klapə], *f.* (—, *pl.* —en) flap; (*Tech.*) valve; (*vulg.*) *halt die* —*!* shut up!

klappen ['klapən], *v.n.* flap; (*fig.*) tally, square; *es hat geklappt*, it worked.

Klapper ['klapər], *f.* (—, *pl.* —n) rattle.

klappern ['klapərn], *v.n.* rattle; (*teeth*) chatter.

Klapperschlange ['klapərʃlaŋə], *f.* (—, *pl.* —n) (*Zool.*) rattle-snake.

Klapphut ['klaphu:t], *m.* (—es, *pl.* ⁻e) opera-hat; chapeau-claque.

Klapps [klaps], *m.* (—es, *pl.* ⁻e) slap, smack; (*fig.*) touch of madness, kink.

Klappstuhl ['klapʃtu:l], *m.* (—s, *pl.* ⁻e) camp-stool, folding-chair.

Klapptisch ['klaptɪʃ], *m.* (—es, *pl.* —e) folding-table.

klar [kla:r], *adj.* clear; bright; (*fig.*) evident; plain, distinct.

Kläranlage ['klɛ:ranla:gə], *f.* (—, *pl.* —n) sewage-farm; filter plant.

klären ['klɛ:rən], *v.a.* clear.

Klarheit ['kla:rhaɪt], *f.* (—, *no pl.*) clearness, plainness.

Klarinette [klari'nɛtə], *f.* (—, *pl.* —n) (*Mus.*) clarinet.

Klärmittel ['klɛ:rmɪtəl], *n.* (—s, *pl.* —) clarifier.

Klärung ['klɛ:ruŋ], *f.* (—, *pl.* —en) clarification; (*fig.*) elucidation.

Klasse ['klasə], *f.* (—, *pl.* —n) class, order; (*Sch.*) form.

klassifizieren [klasifi'tsi:rən], *v.a.* classify.

Klassiker ['klasɪkər], *m.* (—s, *pl.* —) classic.

klassisch ['klasɪʃ], *adj.* classic(al), standard.

Klatsch [klatʃ], *m.* (—es, *no pl.*) gossip, scandal.

klatschen ['klatʃən], *v.n.* clap; gossip; (*rain*) patter; *Beifall* —, applaud.

Klatscherei [klatʃə'raɪ], *f.* (—, *pl.* —en) gossip, scandalmongering.

klauben ['klaubən], *v.a.* pick.

Klaue ['klauə], *f.* (—, *pl.* —n) claw, talon; paw.

klauen ['klauən], *v.a.* steal, (*coll.*) pinch.

Klauenseuche ['klauənzɔyçə], *f.* (—, *pl.* —n) *Maul und* —, foot and mouth disease.

Klause ['klauzə], *f.* (—, *pl.* —n) cell, hermitage; (*coll.*) den.

Klausel ['klauzəl], *f.* (—, *pl.* —n) clause, paragraph.

Klausner ['klausnər], *m.* (—s, *pl.* —) hermit, recluse, anchorite.

Klausur [klau'zu:r], *f.* (—, *pl.* —en) seclusion; written examination.

Klaviatur [klavja'tu:r], *f.* (—, *pl.* —en) keyboard.

Klavier [kla'vi:r], *n.* (—s, *pl.* —e) piano, pianoforte.

Klavierstück [kla'vi:rʃtyk], *n.* (—s, *pl.* —e) piece of piano music.

Klebemittel ['kle:bəmɪtəl], *n.* (—s, *pl.* —) adhesive, glue.

kleben ['kle:bən], *v.a.* paste, stick, glue. — *v.n.* stick, adhere.

klebrig ['kle:brɪç], *adj.* sticky; clammy.

Klebstoff ['kle:pʃtɔf], *m.* (—es, *no pl.*) gum; glue.

Klecks [klɛks], *m.* (—es, *pl.* —e) blot; blotch.

Kleckser ['klɛksər], *m.* (—s, *pl.* —) scrawler; (*painter*) dauber.

Klee [kle:], *m.* (—s, *no pl.*) (*Bot.*) clover, trefoil.

Kleid [klaɪt], *n.* (—es, *pl.* —er) frock, garment, dress, gown; (*Poet.*) garb; (*pl.*) clothes; —*er machen Leute*, clothes make the man.

Kleidchen ['klaɪtçən], *n.* (—s, *pl.* —) child's dress.

kleiden ['klaɪdən], *v.a.* dress, clothe.

Kleiderbügel

Kleiderbügel ['klaɪdərby:gəl], *m.* (—s, *pl.* —) coat-hanger.

Kleiderpuppe ['klaɪdərpupə], *f.* (—, *pl.* —n) tailor's dummy.

Kleiderschrank ['klaɪdərʃraŋk], *m.* (—s, *pl.* ̈e) wardrobe.

kleidsam ['klaɪtza:m], *adj.* becoming; well-fitting, a good fit.

Kleidung ['klaɪduŋ], *f.* (—, *no pl.*) clothing, clothes, dress.

Kleie ['klaɪə], *f.* (—, *no pl.*) bran.

klein [klaɪn], *adj.* little, small; minute; petty; *ein — wenig*, a little bit.

Kleinasien [klaɪn'a:zjən], *n.* Asia Minor.

Kleinbahn ['klaɪnba:n], *f.* (—, *pl.* —en) narrow-gauge railway.

kleinbürgerlich ['klaɪnbyrgərlɪç], *adj.* (petit) bourgeois.

Kleingeld ['klaɪngɛlt], *n.* (—(e)s, *no pl.*) small change.

kleingläubig ['klaɪnglɔybɪç], *adj.* fainthearted.

Kleinhandel ['klaɪnhandəl], *m.* (—s, *no pl.*) retail-trade.

Kleinigkeit ['klaɪnɪçkaɪt], *f.* (—, *pl.* —en) trifle, small matter.

Kleinkram ['klaɪnkra:m], *m.* (—s, *no pl.*) trifles.

kleinlaut ['klaɪnlaut], *adj.* subdued, dejected, low-spirited.

kleinlich ['klaɪnlɪç], *adj.* petty; mean; narrow-minded; pedantic.

Kleinmut ['klaɪnmu:t], *m.* (—es, *no pl.*) faint-heartedness; dejection.

Kleinod ['klaɪno:t], *n.* (—s, *pl.* —ien) jewel; trinket.

Kleinstadt ['klaɪnʃtat], *f.* (—, *pl.* ̈e) small town.

Kleister ['klaɪstər], *m.* (—s, *no pl.*) paste.

Klemme ['klɛmə], *f.* (—, *pl.* —n) (*Tech.*) vice; clamp; (*fig.*) difficulty, straits; (*coll.*) fix, jam.

klemmen ['klɛmən], *v.a.* pinch, squeeze, jam.

Klemmer ['klɛmər], *m.* (—s, *pl.*—) (*eye*) glasses, pince-nez.

Klempner ['klɛmpnər], *m.* (—s, *pl.*—) tin-smith; plumber.

Klerus ['kle:rus], *m.* (—, *no pl.*) clergy.

Klette ['klɛtə], *f.* (—, *pl.* —n) burdock, bur(r); (*fig.*) hanger-on.

klettern ['klɛtərn], *v.n.* (*aux.* sein) climb, clamber.

Klima ['kli:ma], *n.* (—s, *pl.* —s) climate.

Klimaanlage ['kli:maanla:gə], *f.* (—, *pl.* —n) air conditioning plant.

Klimbim ['klɪm'bɪm], *m.* (—s, *no pl.*) goings-on; festivity; fuss; *der ganze —*, the whole caboodle.

klimpern ['klɪmpərn], *v.n.* (*piano*) strum; (*money*) jingle.

Klinge ['klɪŋə], *f.* (—, *pl.* —n) blade.

Klingel ['klɪŋəl], *f.* (—, *pl.* —n) (*door, telephone*) bell.

Klingelbeutel ['klɪŋəlbɔytəl], *m.* (—s, *pl.*—) collecting-bag.

klingeln ['klɪŋəln], *v.n.* ring, tinkle.

Klingelzug ['klɪŋəltsu:k], *m.* . (—es, *pl.* ̈e) bell-rope, bell-pull.

klingen ['klɪŋən], *v.n. irr.* sound; (*metals*) clang; (*ears*) tingle; —*de Münze*, hard cash, ready money.

Klinke ['klɪŋkə], *f.* (—, *pl.* —en) (*door*) handle, latch.

klipp [klɪp], *adv.* — *und klar*, as clear as daylight.

Klippe ['klɪpə], *f.* (—, *pl.* —n) cliff, crag, rock.

klirren ['klɪrən], *v.n.* clatter, rattle.

Klischee [kli'ʃe:], *n.* (—s, *pl.* —s) (*Typ.*) plate, printing-block; (*fig.*) cliché, hackneyed expression, tag.

Klistier [klɪ'sti:r], *n.* (—s, *pl.* —e) (*Med.*) enema.

Kloake [klo'a:kə], *f.* (—, *pl.* —n) sewer, drain.

Kloben ['klo:bən], *m.* (—s, *pl.* —) log, block (of wood); pulley.

klopfen ['klɔpfən], *v.a., v.n.* knock, beat.

Klöppel ['klœpəl], *m.* (—s, *pl.* —) mallet; (*bell*) tongue, clapper; (*drum*) stick; (*lace*) bobbin.

klöppeln ['klœpəln], *v.a* make (bone) lace.

Klöppelspitze ['klœpəlʃpɪtsə], *f.* (—, *no pl.*) bone-lace.

Klops [klɔps], *m.* (—es, *pl.* —e) meat-dumpling.

Klosett [klo'zɛt], *n.* (—s, *pl.* —e) lavatory, water-closet, toilet.

Kloß [klo:s], *m.* (—es, *pl.* ̈e) dumpling.

Kloster ['klo:stər], *n.* (—s, *pl.* ̈) cloister; monastery; convent.

Klostergang ['klo:stərgaŋ], *m.* (—es, *pl.* ̈e) cloisters.

Klotz [klɔts], *m.* (—es, *pl.* ̈e) block, trunk, stump; (*fig.*) *ein grober —*, a great lout.

klotzig ['klɔtsɪç], *adj.* cloddy; lumpish; (*sl.*) enormous.

Klub [klup], *m.* (—s, *pl.* —s) club.

Kluft [kluft], *f.* (—, *pl.* ̈e) gap; gulf, chasm; (*fig.*) cleavage.

klug [klu:k], *adj.* clever, wise, prudent, judicious, sagacious; *ich kann daraus nicht — werden*, I cannot make head nor tail of it.

klügeln ['kly:gəln], *v.n.* ponder; quibble.

Klugheit ['klu:khaɪt], *f.* (—, *no pl.*) cleverness, wisdom, prudence, judiciousness.

Klumpfuß ['klumpfu:s], *m.* (—es, *pl.* ̈e) club-foot.

Klumpen ['klumpən], *m.* (—s, *pl.* —) lump, mass, clod; (*blood*) clot; (*metal*) ingot; (*gold*) nugget.

Klüngel ['klyŋəl], *m.* (—s, *pl.* —) clique, set.

knabbern ['knabərn], *v.n.* nibble.

Knabe ['kna:bə], *m.* (—n, *pl.* —n) boy.

Knäblein ['knɛ:blaɪn], *n.* (—s, *pl.* —) (*Poet.*) baby boy, small boy.

knack [knak], *int.* crack! snap!

Knäckebrot ['knɛkəbro:t], *n.* (—es, *no pl.*) crispbread.

knacken ['knakən], *v.a.* crack.

Knackmandel ['knakmandəl], *f.* (—, *pl.* —n) shell-almond.

Knackwurst ['knakvurst], *f.* (—, *pl.* ̈e) saveloy.

Knacks [knaks], *m.* (—es, *pl.* —e) crack.

knacksen ['knaksən], *v.n.* (*coll.*) crack.

Knall [knal], *m.* (—es, *pl.* —e) report, bang, detonation; — *und Fall,* quite suddenly, then and there.

Knallbüchse ['knalbyksə], *f.* (—, *pl.* —n) pop-gun.

Knalleffekt ['knalɛfɛkt], *m.* (—s, *pl.* —e) coup de théâtre; sensation.

knallen ['knalən], *v.n.* pop, explode, crack.

Knallgas ['knalga:s], *n.* (—es, *no pl.*) oxyhydrogen gas.

knallrot ['knalro:t], *adj.* scarlet; glaring red.

knapp [knap], *adj.* tight; scarce, insufficient; (*style*) concise; (*majority*) narrow, bare.

Knappe ['knapə], *m.* (—n, *pl.* —n) esquire, shield-bearer; miner.

Knappheit ['knaphaɪt], *f.* (—, *no pl.*) scarcity, shortage.

Knappschaft ['knapʃaft], *f.* (—, *pl.* —en) miners' association.

Knarre ['knarə], *f.* (—, *pl.* —n) rattle.

knarren ['knarən], *v.n.* rattle, creak.

Knaster ['knastər], *m.* (—s, *pl.* —) tobacco.

knattern ['knatərn], *v.n.* crackle.

Knäuel ['knɔyəl], *m., n.* (—s, *pl.* —) skein, clew, ball.

Knauf [knauf], *m.* (—es, *pl.* ̈e) (*stick*) knob, head; (*Archit.*) capital.

Knauser ['knauzər], *m.* (—s, *pl.* —) niggard, skinflint.

knausern ['knauzərn], *v.n.* be stingy, scrimp.

Knebel ['kne:bəl], *m.* (—s, *pl.* —) cudgel; gag.

knebeln ['kne:bəln], *v.a.* tie, bind; gag; (*fig.*) muzzle.

Knecht [knɛçt], *m.* (—es, *pl.* —e) servant, farm hand, menial; vassal, slave.

Knechtschaft ['knɛçtʃaft], *f.* (—, *no pl.*) servitude, slavery.

kneifen ['knaɪfən], *v.a. irr.* pinch. — *v.n.* (*fig. coll.*) back out (of), shirk.

Kneifer ['knaɪfər], *m.* (—s, *pl.* —) pince-nez.

Kneifzange ['knaɪftsaŋə], *f.* (—, *pl.* —n) pincers.

Kneipe ['knaɪpə], *f.* (—, *pl.* —n) pub; saloon.

kneten ['kne:tən], *v.a.* knead; massage.

knick(e)beinig ['knɪk(ə)baɪnɪç], *adj.* knock-kneed.

knicken ['knɪkən], *v.a.* crack, break.

Knicks [knɪks], *m.* (—es, *pl.* —e) curtsy.

knicksen ['knɪksən], *v.n.* curtsy.

Knie [kni:], *n.* (—s, *pl.* —) knee; *etwas übers — brechen,* make short work of.

Kniekehle ['kni:ke:lə], *f.* (—, *pl.* —n) hollow of the knee.

knien ['kni:ən], *v.n.* kneel.

Kniescheibe ['kni:ʃaɪbə], *f.* (—, *pl.* —n) knee-cap.

Kniff [knɪf], *m.* (—es, *pl.* —e) fold; (*fig.*) trick, knack, dodge.

knipsen ['knɪpsən], *v.a.* (*tickets*) clip, punch; (*Phot.*) take a snap of.

Knirps [knɪrps], *m.* (—es, *pl.* —e) pigmy; (*fig.*) urchin.

knirschen ['knɪrʃən], *v.n.* crunch, grate, gnash (teeth).

knistern ['knɪstərn], *v.n.* crackle.

knittern ['knɪtərn], *v.a.* rumple, wrinkle, crinkle, crease.

Knobel ['kno:bəl], *m. pl.* dice.

Knoblauch ['kno:blaux], *m.* (—s, *no pl.*) (*Bot.*) garlic.

Knöchel ['knœçəl], *m.* (—s, *pl.* —) knuckle, joint; ankle.

Knochen ['knɔxən], *m.* (—s, *pl.* —) bone.

Knochengerüst ['knɔxəngəryst], *n.* (—es, *pl.* —e) skeleton.

knöchern ['knœçərn], *adj.* made of bone.

knochig ['knɔxɪç], *adj.* bony.

Knödel ['knø:dəl], *m.* (—s, *pl.* —) dumpling.

Knollen ['knɔlən], *m.* (—s, *pl.* —) lump, clod; (*Bot.*) tuber, bulb.

knollig ['knɔlɪç], *adj.* knobby, bulbous.

Knopf [knɔpf], *m.* (—es, *pl.* ̈e) button; stud; (*stick*) head, knob.

knöpfen ['knœpfən], *v.a.* button.

Knorpel ['knɔrpəl], *m.* (—s, *pl.* —) gristle, cartilage.

knorplig ['knɔrplɪç], *adj.* gristly.

knorrig ['knɔrɪç], *adj.* knotty, gnarled.

Knospe ['knɔspə], *f.* (—, *pl.* —n) bud.

Knote ['kno:tə], *m.* (—n, *pl.* —n) (*fig.*) bounder; lout.

Knoten ['kno:tən], *m.* (—s, *pl.* —) knot; (*fig.*) difficulty; (*Theat.*) plot.

Knotenpunkt ['kno:tənpuŋkt], *m.* (—es, *pl.* —e) (*Railw.*) junction.

Knotenstock ['kno:tənʃtɔk], *m.* (—es, *pl.* ̈e) knotty stick.

knotig ['kno:tɪç], *adj.* knotty, nodular.

knüllen ['knylən], *v.a.* crumple.

knüpfen ['knypfən], *v.a.* tie; knot; form (a friendship etc.).

Knüppel ['knypəl], *m.* (—s, *pl.* —) cudgel.

knurren ['knurən], *v.n.* grunt, snarl; (*fig.*) growl, grumble.

knurrig ['knurɪç], *adj.* surly, grumpy.

knusprig ['knusprɪç], *adj.* crisp, crunchy.

Knute ['knu:tə], *f.* (—, *pl.* —n) knout.

knutschen ['knu:tʃən], *v.r. sich* —, (*coll.*) cuddle; (*Am.*) neck.

Knüttel [knytəl], *m.* (—s, *pl.* —) cudgel, bludgeon.

Knüttelvers ['knytəlfɛrs], *m.* (—es, *pl.* —e) doggerel, rhyme.

Kobalt ['ko:balt], *m.* (—s, *no pl.*) cobalt.

Kobaltblau ['ko:baltblau], *n.* (—s, *no pl.*) smalt.

Koben

Koben ['ko:bən], *m.* (—s, *pl.* —)
pig-sty.
Kober ['ko:bər], *m.* (—s, *pl.* —) (*dial.*)
basket, hamper.
Kobold ['ko:bɔlt], *m.* (—(e)s, *pl.* —e)
goblin, hobgoblin.
Koch [kɔx], *m.* (—es, *pl.* ⁻e) cook, chef.
kochen ['kɔxən], *v.a.* cook, boil. —
v.n. boil; (*fig.*) seethe.
Kocher ['kɔxər], *m.* (—s, *pl.* —) boiler.
Köcher ['kœçər], *m.* (—s, *pl.* —)
quiver.
Köchin ['kœçɪn], *f.* (—, *pl.* —innen)
(female) cook.
Kochsalz ['kɔxzalts], *n.* (—es, *no pl.*)
common salt.
Köder ['kø:dər], *m.* (—s, *no pl.*) bait,
lure; (*fig.*) decoy.
ködern ['kø:dərn], *v.a.* bait; (*fig.*)
decoy.
Kodex ['ko:dɛks], *m.* (—es, *pl.* —e)
codex; old MS.; (*Law*) code.
kodifizieren [ko:difi'tsi:rən], *v.a.*
codify.
Koffein [kɔfə'i:n], *n.* (—s, *no pl.*)
caffeine.
Koffer ['kɔfər], *m.* (—s, *pl.* —) box,
trunk, suitcase, portmanteau.
Kofferradio ['kɔfɔrra:djo], *n.* (—s,
pl. —s) portable radio.
Kofferraum ['kɔfərraum], *m.* (—s, *no
pl.*) (*Motor.*) boot, (*Am.*) trunk.
Kohl [ko:l], *m.* (—s, *no pl.*) (*Bot.*) cabbage; (*fig.*) nonsense, rot.
Kohle ['ko:lə], *f.* (—, *pl.* —n) coal.
Kohlenflöz ['ko:lənflø:ts], *n.* (—es,
pl. —e) coal-seam.
Kohlenoxyd ['ko:lənɔksy:t], *n.* (—s,
no pl.) carbon monoxide.
Kohlensäure ['ko:lənzɔyrə], *f.* (—, *no
pl.*) carbonic acid.
Kohlenstift ['ko:lənʃtɪft], *m.* (—es,
pl. —e) charcoal-crayon.
Köhler ['kø:lər], *m.* (—s, *pl.* —) char-
coal-burner.
Koje ['ko:jə], *f.* (—, *pl.* —n) (*Naut.*)
berth, bunk.
Kokarde [kɔ'kardə], *f.* (—, *pl.* —n)
cockade.
kokett [ko'kɛt], *adj.* coquettish.
Kokette [ko'kɛtə], *f.* (—, *pl.* —n)
coquette, flirt.
kokettieren [kokɛ'ti:rən], *v.n.* flirt.
Kokon [ko'kɔ̃], *m.* (—s, *pl.* —s) cocoon.
Kokosnuß ['ko:kɔsnus], *f.* (—, *pl.* ⁻sse)
(*Bot.*) coconut.
Koks [ko:ks], *m.* (—es, *no pl.*) coke.
Kolben ['kɔlbən], *m.* (—s, *pl.* —) club;
(*rifle*) butt-end; (*engine*) piston;
(*Chem.*) retort.
Kolbenstange ['kɔlbənʃtaŋə], *f.* (—,
pl. —n) piston-rod.
Kolibri ['ko:libri:], *m.* (—s, *pl.* —s)
(*Orn.*) humming-bird.
Kolkrabe ['kɔlkra:bə], *m.* (—n, *pl.* —n)
(*Orn.*) raven.
Kolleg [kɔ'le:k], *n.* (—s, *pl.* —ien)
course of lectures; lecture.
Kollege [kɔ'le:gə], *m.* (—n, *pl.* —n)
colleague.

Kollekte [kɔ'lɛktə], *f.* (—, *pl.* —n)
collection; (*Eccl.*) collect.
Koller ['kɔlər], *m.* (—s, *no pl.*) frenzy,
rage.
kollidieren [kɔli'di:rən], *v.n.* collide.
Köln [kœln], *n.* Cologne.
kölnisch ['kœlnɪʃ], *adj.* of Cologne;
— *Wasser*, eau de Cologne.
kolonisieren [koloni'zi:rən], *v.a.*
colonise.
Kolonnade [kolo'na:də], *f.* (— *pl.* —n)
colonnade.
Koloratur [kolora'tu:r], *f.* (—, *pl.* —n)
coloratura.
kolorieren [kolo'ri:rən], *v.a.* colour.
Koloß [ko'lɔs], *m.* (—sses, *pl.* —sse)
colossus.
Kolportage [kɔlpɔr'ta:ʒə], *f.* (—, *pl.*
—n) colportage, door-to-door sale of
books; sensationalism.
Kolportageroman [kɔlpɔr'ta:ʒəro-
ma:n], *m.* (—s, *pl.* —e) penny
dreadful, shocker.
kolportieren [kɔlpɔr'ti:rən], *v.a.* hawk;
spread, disseminate.
Kombinationsgabe [kɔmbina'tsjo:ns-
ga:bə], *f.* (—, *pl.* —en) power of
deduction.
kombinieren [kɔmbi'ni:rən], *v.a.* combine; deduce.
Kombüse [kɔm'by:zə], *f.* (— *pl.* —n)
galley, caboose.
Komik ['ko:mɪk], *f.* (—, *no pl.*) comical-
ity; humour; funny side.
Komiker ['ko:mɪkər], *m.* (—s, *pl.* —)
comedian.
komisch ['ko:mɪʃ], *adj.* comical, funny;
peculiar, strange, odd.
Kommandantur [kɔmandan'tu:r], *f.*
(—, *pl.* —en) commander's office;
garrison headquarters.
kommandieren [kɔman'di:rən], *v.a.*
command.
Kommanditgesellschaft [kɔman'di:t-
gəzɛlʃaft], *f.* (—, *pl.* —en) limited partnership.
Kommando [kɔ'mando], *n.* (—s, *pl.*
—s) command.
kommen ['kɔmən], *v.n. irr.* (*aux.* sein)
come, arrive; come about; *um etwas*
—, lose s.th.; *zu etwas* —, come by
s.th.; *zu sich* —, come to, regain
consciousness.
Kommentar [kɔmɛn'ta:r], *m.* (—s, *pl.*
—e) comment, commentary.
Kommers [kɔ'mɛrs], *m.* (—es, *pl.* —e)
students' festivity; drinking party.
Kommersbuch [kɔ'mɛrsbu:x], *n.* (—es,
pl. ⁻er) students' song-book.
kommerziell [kɔmɛrts'jɛl], *adj.* commercial.
Kommerzienrat [kɔ'mɛrtsjənra:t], *m.*
(—s, *pl.* ⁻e) Councillor to the Chamber of Commerce.
Kommilitone [kɔmili'to:nə], *m.* (—n,
pl. —n) fellow-student.
Kommis [kɔ'mi:], *m.* (—, *pl.* —) clerk.
Kommiß [kɔ'mɪs], *m.* (—sses, *pl.* —)
military fatigue-dress; (*fig.*) military
service.

Kommißbrot [kɔ'mɪsbroːt], n. (—es, no pl.) (coarse) army bread.
Kommissar [kɔmɪ'saːr], m. (—s, pl. —e) commissioner.
Kommissariat [kɔmɪsar'jaːt], n. (—s, pl. —e) commissioner's office.
Kommission [kɔmɪs'joːn], f. (—, pl. —en) commission, mission, committee.
kommod [kɔ'moːd], adj. (coll.) snug, comfortable.
Kommode [kɔ'moːdə], f. (—, pl. —n) chest of drawers.
Kommune [kɔ'muːnə], f. (—, pl. —n) (coll.) Communist Party; Reds.
Kommunismus [kɔmu'nɪsmus], m. (—, no pl.) Communism.
kommunistisch [kɔmu'nɪstɪʃ], adj. Communist.
Komödiant [kɔmød'jant], m. (—en, pl. —en) comedian, player; humbug.
Komödie [kɔ'møːdjə], f. (—, pl. —n) comedy, play; make-believe; — spielen, (fig.) sham, pretend, playact.
Kompagnon ['kɔmpanjɔ̃], m. (—s, pl. —s) partner, associate.
Kompanie [kɔmpa'niː], f. (—, pl. —n) (Mil.) company; (Comm.) partnership, company.
Kompaß ['kɔmpas], m. (—sses, pl. —sse) compass.
Kompaßrose ['kɔmpasroːzə], f. (—, pl. —n) compass-card.
kompensieren [kɔmpɛn'ziːrən], v.a. compensate.
komplementär [kɔmpləmɛn'tɛːr], adj. complementary.
komplett [kɔm'plɛt], adj. complete.
komplimentieren [kɔmplimɛn'tiːrən], v.a. compliment, flatter.
Komplize [kɔm'pliːtsə], m. (—n, pl. —n) accomplice.
kompliziert [kɔmpli'tsiːrt], adj. complicated.
Komplott [kɔm'plɔt], n. (—s, pl. —e) plot, conspiracy.
Komponente [kɔmpo'nɛntə], f. (—, pl. —n) component part; constituent.
komponieren [kɔmpo'niːrən], v.a. compose, set to music.
Komponist [kɔmpo'nɪst], m. (—en, pl. —en) composer.
Kompositum [kɔm'poːzɪtum], n. (—s, pl. —ta) (Gram.) compound word.
Kompott [kɔm'pɔt], n. (—s, pl. —e) stewed fruit, compote; sweet, dessert.
Kompresse [kɔm'prɛsə], f. (—, pl. —n) compress.
komprimieren [kɔmpri'miːrən], v.a. compress.
Kompromiß [kɔmpro'mɪs], m. (—sses, pl. —sse) compromise, settlement.
kompromittieren [kɔmprɔmɪ'tiːrən], v.a. compromise. — v.r. sich —, compromise o.s.
kondensieren [kɔndɛn'ziːrən], v.a. condense.
Konditor [kɔn'diːtɔr], m. (—s, pl. —en) confectioner, pastry-cook.

Konditorei [kɔnditɔ'raɪ], f. (—, pl. —en) confectioner's shop, pastry-shop; café.
kondolieren [kɔndo'liːrən], v.n. condole with s.o.
Kondukteur [kɔnduk'tøːr], m. (—s, pl. —e) (Swiss & Austr. dial.) guard (on train), conductor (on tram or bus).
Konfekt [kɔn'fɛkt], n. (—s, pl. —e) chocolates; (Am.) candy.
Konfektion [kɔnfɛk'tsjoːn], f. (—, no pl.) ready-made clothes; outfitting.
Konfektionär [kɔnfɛktsjo'nɛːr], m. (—s, pl. —e) outfitter.
Konferenz [kɔnfe'rɛnts], f. (—, pl. —en) conference.
konfessionell [kɔnfɛsjo'nɛl], adj. denominational, confessional.
Konfirmand [kɔnfɪr'mant], m. (—en, pl. —en) confirmation candidate.
konfirmieren [kɔnfɪr'miːrən], v.a. (Eccl.) confirm.
konfiszieren [kɔnfɪs'tsiːrən], v.a. confiscate.
Konfitüren [kɔnfɪ'tyːrən], f. pl. confectionery, candied fruit, preserves.
konform [kɔn'fɔrm], adj. in comformity (with).
konfus [kɔn'fuːs], adj. confused, puzzled, disconcerted.
Kongo ['kɔŋgo], m. Congo.
Kongruenz [kɔŋgru'ɛnts], f. (—, no pl.) congruity.
König ['køːnɪç], m. (—s, pl. —e) king.
Königin ['køːnɪgɪn], f. (—, pl. —nen) queen.
königlich ['køːnɪglɪç], adj. royal, regal, kingly, king-like.
Königreich ['køːnɪçraɪç], n. (—(e)s, pl. —e) kingdom.
Königsadler ['køːnɪçsaːdlər], m. (—s, pl. —) golden eagle.
Königsschlange ['køːnɪçsʃlaŋə], f. (—, pl. —n) (Zool.) boa constrictor.
Königstiger ['køːnɪçstiːgər], m. (—s, pl. —) (Zool.) Bengal tiger.
Königtum ['køːnɪçtuːm], n. (—s, no pl.) kingship.
Konjunktur [kɔnjuŋk'tuːr], f. (—, pl. —en) state of the market, (coll.) boom.
Konkordat [kɔnkɔr'daːt], n. (—s, pl. —e) concordat.
konkret [kɔn'kreːt], adj. concrete.
Konkurrent [kɔnku'rɛnt], m. (—en, pl. —en) competitor, (business) rival.
Konkurrenz [kɔnku'rɛnts], f. (—, no pl.) competition.
konkurrieren [kɔnku'riːrən], v.n. compete.
Konkurs [kɔn'kurs], m. (—es, pl. —e) bankruptcy.
Konkursmasse [kɔn'kursmasə], f. (—, pl. —n) bankrupt's estate, bankrupt's stock.
Können ['kœnən], n. (—s, no pl.) ability; knowledge.
können ['kœnən], v.a., v.n. irr. be able to, be capable of; understand; ich kann, I can; er kann Englisch, he speaks English.

konsequent

konsequent [kɔnzeˈkvɛnt], *adj.* consistent.

Konsequenz [kɔnzeˈkvɛnts], *f.* (—, *pl.* —en) (*characteristic*) consistency; (*result*) consequence.

Konservatorium [kɔnzɛrvaˈtoːrjum], *n.* (—s, *pl.* —rien) (*Mus.*) conservatoire, conservatorium.

Konserve [kɔnˈzɛrvə], *f.* (—, *pl.* —n) preserve; tinned, *or* (*Am.*) canned food.

konservieren [kɔnzɛrˈviːrən], *v.a.* preserve.

Konsistorium [kɔnzɪsˈtoːrjum], *n.* (—s, *pl.* —rien) (*Eccl.*) consistory.

Konsole [kɔnˈzoːlə], *f.* (—, *pl.* —n) bracket.

konsolidieren [kɔnzoliˈdiːrən], *v.a.* consolidate.

Konsonant [kɔnzoˈnant], *m.* (—en, *pl.* —en) (*Phonet.*) consonant.

Konsorte [kɔnˈzɔrtə], *m.* (—n, *pl.* —n) associate, accomplice.

Konsortium [kɔnˈzɔrtsjum], *n.* (—s, *pl.* —tien) syndicate.

konstatieren [kɔnstaˈtiːrən], *v.a.* state, note, assert.

konsternieren [kɔnstɛrˈniːrən], *v.a.* dismay, disconcert.

konstituieren [kɔnstituˈiːrən], *v.a.* constitute.

konstitutionell [kɔnstitutsjoˈnɛl], *adj.* constitutional.

konstruieren [kɔnstruˈiːrən], *v.a.* construct; (*Gram.*) construe.

konsularisch [kɔnzuˈlaːrɪʃ], *adj.* consular.

Konsulat [kɔnzuˈlaːt], *n.* (—s, *pl.* —e) consulate.

Konsulent [kɔnzuˈlɛnt], *m.* (—en, *pl.* —en) (*Law*) counsel; consultant.

konsultieren [kɔnzulˈtiːrən], *v.a.* consult.

Konsum [kɔnˈzuːm], *m.* (—s, *no pl.*) (*Econ.*) consumption.

Konsumverein [kɔnˈzuːmfɛraɪn], *m.* (—s, *pl.* —e) cooperative society.

konsumieren [kɔnzuˈmiːrən], *v.a.* consume.

Konterbande [kɔntərˈbandə], *f.* (—, *no pl.*) contraband.

Konterfei [kɔntərˈfaɪ], *n.* (—s, *pl.* —e) (*obs.*) portrait, likeness.

Kontertanz [ˈkɔntərtants], *m.* (—es, *pl.* ⸚e) square dance, quadrille.

kontinuierlich [kɔntinuˈiːrlɪç], *adj.* continuous.

Kontinuität [kɔntinuiˈtɛːt], *f.* (—, *no pl.*) continuity.

Konto [ˈkɔnto], *n.* (—s, *pl.* —ten) (*bank*) account; à —, on account.

Kontokorrent [kɔntokoˈrɛnt], *n.* (—s, *pl.* —e) current account.

Kontor [kɔnˈtoːr], *n.* (—s, *pl.* —e) (*obs.*) office.

Kontorist [kɔntoˈrɪst], *m.* (—en, *pl.* —en) clerk.

Kontrabaß [ˈkɔntrabas], *m.* (—sses, *pl.* ⸚sse) double-bass.

Kontrapunkt [ˈkɔntrapuŋkt], *m.* (—es, *pl.* —e) (*Mus.*) counterpoint.

kontrastieren [kɔntrasˈtiːrən], *v.a., v.n.* contrast.

kontrollieren [kɔntrɔˈliːrən], *v.a.* check, verify.

Kontroverse [kɔntroˈvɛrzə], *f.* (—, *pl.* —n) controversy.

Kontur [kɔnˈtuːr], *f.* (—, *pl.* —en) outline, (*pl.*) contours.

Konvent [kɔnˈvɛnt], *m.* (—s, *pl.* —e) convention, assembly, congress.

konventionell [kɔnvɛntsjoˈnɛl], *adj.* conventional, formal.

Konversationslexikon [kɔnvɛrzaˈtsjoːnslɛksɪkɔn], *n.* (—s, *pl.* —s) encyclopaedia.

konvertieren [kɔnvɛrˈtiːrən], *v.a., v.n.* convert.

Konvertit [kɔnvɛrˈtɪt], *m.* (—en, *pl.* —en) convert.

Konvolut [kɔnvoˈluːt], *n.* (—s, *pl.* —e) bundle; scroll.

konvulsivisch [kɔnvulˈziːvɪʃ], *adj.* convulsive.

konzentrieren [kɔntsɛnˈtriːrən], *v.a., v.r.* concentrate; *auf etwas* —, centre upon.

konzentrisch [kɔnˈtsɛntrɪʃ], *adj.* concentric.

Konzept [kɔnˈtsɛpt], *n.* (—es, *pl.* —e) rough draft, sketch; *aus dem — bringen*, unsettle, disconcert.

Konzeptpapier [kɔnˈtsɛptpapiːr], *n.* (—s, *no pl.*) scribbling paper.

Konzern [kɔnˈtsɛrn], *m.* (—s, *pl.* —e) (*Comm.*) combine.

Konzert [kɔnˈtsɛrt], *m.* (—es, *pl.* —e) concert, (musical) recital.

Konzertflügel [kɔnˈtsɛrtflyːgəl], *m.* (—s, *pl.* —) grand piano.

konzertieren [kɔntsɛrˈtiːrən], *v.n.* give recitals; play in a concert.

Konzertmeister [kɔnˈtsɛrtmaɪstər], *m.* (—s, *pl.* —) impresario.

Konzession [kɔntseˈsjoːn], *f.* (—, *pl.* —en) concession, licence.

konzessionieren [kɔntsesjoˈniːrən], *v.a.* license.

Konzil [kɔnˈtsiːl], *n.* (—s, *pl.* —ien) (*Eccl.*) council.

konzipieren [kɔntsiˈpiːrən], *v.a.* draft, plan.

Koordinierung [koːɔrdiˈniːruŋ], *f.* (—, *pl.* —en) co-ordination.

Kopf [kɔpf], *m.* (—es, *pl.* ⸚e) head; top ⸚ heading; (*fig.*) mind, brains, judgment; *aus dem —*, by heart.

köpfen [ˈkœpfən], *v.a.* behead, decapitate; (*Bot.*) lop.

Kopfhaut [ˈkɔpfhaut], *f.* (—, *no pl.*) scalp.

Kopfhörer [ˈkɔpfhøːrər], *m.* (—s, *pl.* —) headphone, receiver.

Kopfkissen [ˈkɔpfkɪsən], *n.* (—s, *pl.* —) pillow.

Kopfsalat [ˈkɔpfzalaːt], *m.* (—s, *pl.* —e) (garden) lettuce.

kopfscheu [ˈkɔpfʃɔy], *adj.* afraid; alarmed, timid; *— machen*, scare; *— werden*, take fright, jib.

Kopfschmerz ['kɔpfʃmɛrts], *m.* (**—es,** *pl.* **—en**) (*mostly pl.*) headache.
Kopfsprung ['kɔpfʃpruŋ], *m.* (**—s,** *pl.* **:e**) (*diving*) header.
kopfüber [kɔpf'yːbər], *adv.* head over heels; headlong.
Kopfweh ['kɔpfveː], *n.* (**—s,** *no pl.*) headache.
Kopfzerbrechen ['kɔpftsɛrbrɛçən], *n.* (**—s,** *no pl.*) racking o.'s brains.
Kopie [ko'piː] *f.* (**—,** *pl.* **—n**) copy, duplicate.
kopieren [ko'piːrən], *v.a.* copy, ape, mimic, take off.
Koppe ['kɔpə], *f. see* **Kuppe.**
Koppel ['kɔpəl], *f.* (**—,** *pl.* **—n**) (*dogs*) couple, leash; (*ground*) enclosure, paddock.
koppeln ['kɔpəln], *v.a.* couple, leash.
kopulieren [kopu'liːrən], *v.a.* (*obs.*) marry; pair; (*Hort.*) graft.
Koralle [ko'ralə], *f.* (**—,** *pl.* **—n**) coral.
Korallenriff [ko'ralənrif], *n.* (**—es,** *pl.* **—e**) coral-reef.
Korb [kɔrp], *m.* (**—s,** *pl.* **:e**) basket, hamper; *einen — geben,* turn s.o. down, refuse an offer of marriage.
Korbweide ['kɔrpvaidə], *f.* (**—,** *pl.* **—n**) (*Bot.*) osier.
Kord [kɔrt], *m.* (**—s,** *no pl.*) corduroy.
Kordel ['kɔrdəl], *f.* (**—,** *pl.* **—n**) cord, twine, thread.
Korea [ko'reːa], *n.* Korea.
Korinthe [ko'rɪntə], *f.* (**—,** *pl.* **—n**) (*Bot.*) currant.
Korken ['kɔrkən], *m.* (**—s,** *pl.* **—**) cork, stopper.
Korkenzieher ['kɔrkəntsiːər], *m.* (**—s,** *pl.* **—**) cork-screw.
Korn [kɔrn], *n.* (**—s,** *pl.* **—e, :er**) (*Bot.*) corn, grain, cereal, rye; (*gun*) sight, *aufs — nehmen,* take aim at.
Kornblume ['kɔrnbluːmə], *f.* (**—,** *pl.* **—n**) (*Bot.*) corn-flower.
Kornbranntwein ['kɔrnbrantvain], *m.* (**—s,** *no pl.*) corn-brandy, whisky.
Kornett [kɔr'nɛt], *m.* (**—s,** *pl.* **—e**) (*Mil., Mus.*) cornet.
körnig ['kœrnɪç], *adj.* granular, granulous; grained.
Kornrade ['kɔrnraːdə], *f.* (**—,** *pl.* **—n**) (*Bot.*) corn-cockle.
Kornspeicher ['kɔrnʃpaiçər], *m.* (**—s,** *pl.* **—**) granary, corn-loft.
Körper ['kœrpər], *m.* (**—s,** *pl.* **—**) body; (*Phys.*) solid.
Körperbau ['kœrpərbau], *m.* (**—s,** *no pl.*) build, frame.
Körpergeruch ['kœrpərgəruːx], *m.* (**—s,** *no pl.*) body odour.
körperlich ['kœrpərlɪç], *adj.* bodily, physical; *—e Züchtigung,* corporal punishment.
Körpermaß ['kœrpərmaːs], *n.* (**—es,** *pl.* **—e**) cubic measure.
Körperschaft ['kœrpərʃaft], *f.* (**—,** *pl.* **—en**) corporation.
Korps [koːr], *n.* (**—,** *pl.* **—**) (*Mil.*) corps; students' corporation.

Korrektheit [kɔ'rɛkthait], *f.* (**—,** *no pl.*) correctness.
Korrektionsanstalt [kɔrɛk'tsjoːnsanʃtalt], *f.* (**—,** *pl.* **—en**) penitentiary, Borstal institution.
Korrektor [kɔ'rɛktor], *m.* (**—s,** *pl.* **—en**) proof-reader.
Korrektur [kɔrɛk'tuːr], *f.* (**—,** *pl.* **—en**) correction; proof-correction; revision.
Korrekturbogen [kɔrɛk'tuːrboːgən], *m.* (**—s,** *pl.* **—**) (*Typ.*) proof-sheet, galley.
Korrespondenzkarte [kɔrɛspɔn'dɛntskartə], *f.* (**—,** *pl.* **—n**) post-card.
korrigieren [kɔri'giːrən], *v.a.* correct, revise; read (proofs).
Korsett [kɔr'zɛt], *m.* (**—s,** *pl.* **—s**) corset, bodice, stays.
Koryphäe [kɔri'fɛːə], *m.* (**—n,** *pl.* **—n**) celebrity, authority, master mind.
Koseform ['koːzəfɔrm], *f.* (**—,** *pl.* **—en**) term of endearment, pet-name, diminutive.
kosen ['koːzən], *v.a., v.n.* caress, fondle; make love (to).
Kosinus ['koːzinus], *m.* (**—,** *pl.* **—**) (*Maths.*) cosine.
Kosmetik [kɔs'meːtik], *f.* (**—,** *no pl.*) cosmetics.
kosmetisch [kɔs'meːtiʃ], *adj.* cosmetic.
kosmisch ['kɔzmiʃ], *adj.* cosmic.
Kosmopolit [kɔsmopo'liːt], *m.* (**—en,** *pl.* **—en**) cosmopolitan.
kosmopolitisch [kɔsmopo'liːtiʃ], *adj.* cosmopolitan.
Kost [kɔst], *f.* (**—,** *no pl.*) food, fare; board.
Kostarika [kɔsta'rika], *n.* Costa Rica.
kostbar ['kɔstbaːr], *adj.* valuable, precious, costly.
Kostbarkeit ['kɔstbaːrkait], *f.* (**—,** *pl.* **—en**) costliness, preciousness; (*pl.*) (*goods*) valuables.
Kosten ['kɔstən], *pl.* cost(s), expenses, charges; (*Law*) costs.
kosten ['kɔstən], *v.a.* taste; (*money*) cost; take, require; *was kostet das?* how much is this?
Kosten(vor)anschlag ['kɔstən(for)anʃlaːk], *m.* (**—s,** *pl.* **:e**) estimate.
Kostenaufwand ['kɔstənaufvant], *m.* (**—s,** *pl.* **:e**) expenditure.
Kostenersatz ['kɔstənɛrzats], *m.* (**—es,** *no pl.*) refund of expenses, compensation.
kostenfrei ['kɔstənfrai], *adj.* free (of charge), gratis.
kostenlos ['kɔstənloːs], *see* **kostenfrei.**
Kostgänger ['kɔstgɛŋər], *m.* (**—s,** *pl.* **—**) boarder.
Kostgeld ['kɔstgɛlt], *n.* (**—es,** *no pl.*) maintenance or board allowance.
köstlich ['kœstlɪç], *adj.* excellent, precious; delicious; *ein —er Witz,* a capital joke.
kostspielig ['kɔstʃpiːlɪç], *adj.* expensive, costly.
Kostüm [kɔ'styːm], *n.* (**—s,** *pl.* **—e**) costume; fancy dress.
Kostümfest [kɔ'styːmfɛst], *n.* (**—s,** *pl.* **—e**) fancy-dress ball.

kostümieren [kɔsty'miːrən], *v.a.* dress up.

Kot [koːt], *m.* (**—es**, *no pl.*) mud, dirt; filth, mire; excrement.

Kotelett [kɔt'let], *n.* (**—s**, *pl.* **—s**) cutlet.

Köter [ˈkøːtər], *m.* (**—s**, *pl.* **—**) cur, mongrel.

Koterie [koːtə'riː], *f.* (**—**, *pl.* **—n**) clique, set, coterie.

Kotflügel [ˈkoːtflyːgəl], *m.* (**—s**, *pl.* **—**) (*Motor.*) mudguard.

kotig [ˈkoːtiç], *adj.* dirty, miry.

kotzen [ˈkɔtsən], *v.n.* (*vulg.*) vomit.

Koweit [ˈkɔvaɪt], *n.* Kuwait.

Krabbe [ˈkrabə], *f.* (**—**, *pl.* **—n**) (*Zool.*) crab; shrimp; (*fig.*) brat, imp.

krabbeln [ˈkrabəln], *v.n.* crawl.

Krach [krax], *m.* (**—es**, *pl.* **—e**) crack, crash; din, noise; (*Comm.*) slump; quarrel, row.

krachen [ˈkraxən], *v.n.* crack, crash.

krächzen [ˈkrɛçtsən], *v.n.* croak.

Kraft [kraft], *f.* (**—**, *pl.* **—e**) strength, vigour; force; power, energy; intensity; *in — treten*, come into force.

kraft [kraft], *prep.* (*Genit.*) by virtue of, by authority of, on the strength of.

Kraftausdruck [ˈkraftausdruk], *m.* (**—s**, *pl.* **—e**) forcible expression; expletive.

Kraftbrühe [ˈkraftbryːə], *f.* (**—**, *pl.* **—n**) meat-soup, beef-tea.

Kraftfahrer [ˈkraftfaːrər], *m.* (**—s**, *pl.* **—**) motorist.

kräftig [ˈkrɛftiç], *adj.* strong, powerful, vigorous, energetic; (*food*) nourishing.

Kraftlehre [ˈkraftleːrə], *f.* (**—**, *no pl.*) dynamics.

kraftlos [ˈkraftloːs], *adj.* weak, feeble.

Kraftwagen [ˈkraftvaːgən], *m.* (**—s**, *pl.* **—**) motor car, automobile, car; lorry, truck.

Kragen [ˈkraːgən], *m.* (**—s**, *pl.* **—**) collar; *es geht mir an den —*, it will cost me dearly.

Krähe [ˈkrɛːə], *f.* (**—**, *pl.* **—n**) (*Orn.*) crow.

krähen [ˈkrɛːən], *v.n.* crow.

Krähenfüße [ˈkrɛːənfyːsə], *m. pl.* crow's feet (wrinkles).

Krakau [ˈkraːkau], *n.* Cracow.

krakeelen [kra'keːlən], *v.n.* (*coll.*) kick up a row.

Kralle [ˈkralə], *f.* (**—**, *pl.* **—n**) claw, talon.

Kram [kraːm], *m.* (**—s**, *no pl.*) small wares (trade); stuff, rubbish, litter; *es paßt mir nicht in den —*, it does not suit my purpose.

kramen [ˈkraːmən], *v.n.* rummage.

Krämer [ˈkrɛːmər], *m.* (**—s**, *pl.* **—**) retailer, general dealer, shopkeeper.

Kramladen [ˈkraːmlaːdən], *m.* (**—s**, *pl.* **—**) small retail-shop, general shop *or* store.

Krampe [ˈkrampə], *f.* (**—**, *pl.* **—n**) staple.

Krampf [krampf], *m.* (**—es**, *pl.* **—**) cramp, spasm, convulsion.

Krampfader [ˈkrampfaːdər], *f.* (**—**, *pl.* **—n**) varicose vein.

krampfartig [ˈkrampfaːrtiç], *adj.* spasmodic.

krampfhaft [ˈkrampfhaft], *adj.* convulsive.

Kran [kraːn], *m.* (**—s**, *pl.* **—e**) (*Engin.*) crane.

Kranich [ˈkraːniç], *m.* (**—s**, *pl.* **—e**) (*Orn.*) crane.

krank [kraŋk], *adj.* sick, ill.

kränkeln [ˈkrɛŋkəln], *v.n.* be ailing, be in poor health.

kranken [ˈkraŋkən], *v.n.* an etwas —, suffer from s.th., be afflicted with s.th.

kränken [ˈkrɛŋkən], *v.a.* vex, grieve; offend, insult.

Krankenbahre [ˈkraŋkənbaːrə], *f.* (**—**, *pl.* **—n**) stretcher.

Krankenhaus [ˈkraŋkənhaus], *n.* (**—es**, *pl.* **—er**) hospital.

Krankenkasse [ˈkraŋkənkasə], *f.* (**—**, *pl.* **—n**) sick-fund; health insurance.

Krankenkost [ˈkraŋkənkɔst], *f.* (**—**, *no pl.*) invalid diet.

Krankenschwester [ˈkraŋkənʃvɛstər], *f.* (**—**, *pl.* **—n**) nurse.

Krankenstuhl [ˈkraŋkənʃtuːl], *m.* (**—s**, *pl.* **—e**) invalid chair.

Krankenversicherung [ˈkraŋkənfɛrziçəruŋ], *f.* (**—**, *pl* **—en**) health insurance.

Krankenwärter [ˈkraŋkənvɛrtər], *m.* (**—s**, *pl.* **—**) attendant, male nurse.

krankhaft [ˈkraŋkhaft], *adj.* morbid.

Krankheit [ˈkraŋkhaɪt], *f.* (**—**, *pl.* **—en**) illness, sickness, disease, malady; complaint; *englische —*, rickets.

Krankheitserscheinung [ˈkraŋkhaɪtsɛrʃaɪnuŋ], *f.* (**—**, *pl.* **—en**) symptom.

kränklich [ˈkrɛŋkliç], *adj.* sickly, infirm, in poor health.

Kränkung [ˈkrɛŋkuŋ], *f.* (**—**, *pl.* **—en**) grievance, annoyance; offence, insult.

Kranz [krants], *m.* (**—es**, *pl.* **—e**) wreath, garland.

Kränzchen [ˈkrɛntsçən], *n.* (**—s**, *pl.* **—**) little garland; (*fig.*) (ladies') weekly tea party; circle, club.

kränzen [ˈkrɛntsən], *v.a.* garland, wreathe.

Krapfen [ˈkrapfən], *m.* (**—s**, *pl.* **—**) doughnut.

kraß [kras], *adj.* crass, crude.

Krater [ˈkraːtər], *m.* (**—s**, *pl.* **—**) crater.

Kratzbürste [ˈkratsbyrstə], *f.* (**—**, *pl.* **—n**) scraper; (*fig.*) cross-patch, irritable person.

Krätze [ˈkrɛtsə], *f.* (**—**, *no pl.*) (*Med.*) scabies, itch, mange.

kratzen [ˈkratsən], *v.a., v.n.* scratch, scrape, itch.

krauen [ˈkrauən], *v.a.* scratch softly.

kraus [kraus], *adj.* frizzy, curly; crisp, fuzzy; creased; (*fig.*) abstruse; *die Stirn — ziehen*, frown, knit o.'s brow.

Krause [ˈkrauzə], *f.* (**—**, *pl.* **—n**) ruff.

kräuseln [ˈkrɔyzəln], *v.a., v.r.* crisp, curl; ripple.

Krauskohl [ˈkrauskoːl], *m.* (**—s**, *no pl.*) Savoy cabbage.

Kraut [kraut], *n.* (—es, *pl.* ⸚er) herb; plant; (*dial.*) cabbage; *wie — und Rüben*, higgledy-piggledy.

krautartig [ˈkrautaːrtiç], *adj.* herbaceous.

Kräuterkäse [ˈkrɔytɛrkɛːzə], *m.* (—s, *pl.* —) green cheese.

Kräutertee [ˈkrɔytɛrteː], *m.* (—s, *no pl.*) herb-tea, infusion of herbs.

Krawall [kraˈval], *m.* (—s, *pl.* —e) (*coll.*) row, uproar; shindy.

Krawatte [kraˈvatə], *f.* (—, *pl.* —n) cravat, tie.

kraxeln [ˈkraksəln], *v.n.* (*coll.*) climb, clamber.

Krebs [kreːps], *m.* (—es, *pl.* —e) (*Zool.*) crayfish, crab; (*Med.*) cancer, carcinoma; (*Geog.*) Tropic of Cancer.

krebsartig [ˈkreːpsaːrtiç], *adj.* cancerous.

Krebsbutter [ˈkreːpsbutər], *f.* (—, *no pl.*) crab-cheese.

Krebsgang [ˈkreːpsɡaŋ], *m.* (—es, *no pl.*) crab's walk, sidling; *den — gehen*, retrograde, decline.

Krebsschaden [ˈkreːpsʃaːdən], *m.* (—s, *pl.* ⸚) cancerous sore *or* affection; (*fig.*) canker, inveterate evil.

Kredenz [kreˈdɛnts], *f.* (—, *pl.* —en) buffet, serving table, sideboard.

kredenzen [kreˈdɛntsən], *v.a.* taste (*wine*); (*obs.*) present, offer.

kreditieren [krediˈtiːrən], *v.a. einem etwas —*, credit s.o. with s.th.

Kreide [ˈkraidə], *f.* (—, *pl.* —n) chalk; (*Art*) crayon.

kreieren [kreˈiːrən], *v.a.* create.

Kreis [krais], *m.* (—es, *pl.* —e) circle; (*Astron.*) orbit; district; range; sphere.

Kreisabschnitt [ˈkraisapʃnit], *m.* (—s, *pl.* —e) segment.

Kreisausschnitt [ˈkraisausʃnit], *m.* (—s, *pl.* —e) sector.

Kreisbogen [ˈkraisboːɡən], *m.* (—s, *pl.* ⸚) arc.

kreischen [ˈkraiʃən], *v.n.* scream, shriek.

Kreisel [ˈkraizəl], *m.* (—s, *pl.* —) (*toy*) (spinning) top; gyroscope.

kreisen [ˈkraizən], *v.n.* circle, revolve; circulate.

Kreislauf [ˈkraislauf], *m.* (—es, *pl.* ⸚e) circular course; (*Astron.*) orbit; (*blood*) circulation.

kreißen [ˈkraisən], *v.n.* (*Med.*) be in labour.

Kreisstadt [ˈkraisʃtat], *f.* (—, *pl.* ⸚e) county town.

Kreisumfang [ˈkraisumfaŋ], *m.* (—s, *pl.* ⸚e) circumference.

Kreml [krɛml], *m.* (—s, *no pl.*) the Kremlin.

Krempe [ˈkrɛmpə], *f.* (—, *pl.* —n) (*hat*) brim.

Krempel [ˈkrɛmpəl], *m.* (—s, *no pl.*) (*coll.*) refuse, rubbish; stuff.

Kren [kreːn], *m.* (—s, *no pl.*) (*Austr.*) horse-radish.

krepieren [kreˈpiːrən], *v.n.* (*aux.* sein) (*animals*) die; (*humans*) (*coll.*) perish miserably; explode.

Krepp [krɛp], *m.* (—s, *no pl.*) crape, crêpe.

Kresse [ˈkrɛsə], *f.* (—, *pl.* —n) cress.

Kreta [ˈkreːta], *n.* Crete.

Kreuz [krɔyts], *n.* (—es, *pl.* —e) cross, crucifix; (*Anat.*) small of the back; (*fig.*) calamity; affliction; *kreuz und quer*, in all directions.

Kreuzband [ˈkrɔytsbant], *n.* (—es, *pl.* ⸚er) wrapper (for printed matter).

kreuzbrav [ˈkrɔytsbraːf], *adj.* as good as gold.

kreuzen [ˈkrɔytsən], *v.a.* cross. — *v.r. sich —*, make the sign of the cross.

Kreuzfahrer [ˈkrɔytsfaːrər], *m.* (—s, *pl.* —) crusader.

kreuzfidel [ˈkrɔytsfideːl], *adj.* jolly, merry, as merry as a cricket.

Kreuzgang [ˈkrɔytsɡaŋ], *m.* (—es, *pl.* ⸚e) cloisters.

kreuzigen [ˈkrɔytsiɡən], *v.a.* crucify.

Kreuzritter [ˈkrɔytsritər], *m.* (—s, *pl.* —) Knight of the Cross; crusader.

Kreuzschmerzen [ˈkrɔytsʃmɛrtsən], *m. pl.* lumbago.

Kreuzstich [ˈkrɔytsʃtiç], *m.* (—es, *no pl.*) (*Embroidery*) cross-stitch.

Kreuzung [ˈkrɔytsuŋ], *f.* (—, *pl.* —en) (*road*) crossing; (*animals*) cross-breeding.

Kreuzverhör [ˈkrɔytsfɛrhøːr], *n.* (—s, *pl.* —e) cross-examination.

Kreuzweg [ˈkrɔytsveːk], *m.* (—s, *pl.* —e) crossroads; (*Eccl.*) Stations of the Cross.

Kreuzworträtsel [ˈkrɔytsvɔrtrɛːtsəl], *n.* (—s, *pl.* —) crossword-puzzle.

Kreuzzug [ˈkrɔytstsuːk], *m.* (—es, *pl.* ⸚e) crusade.

kriechen [ˈkriːçən], *v.n. irr.* (*aux.* sein) creep, crawl; (*fig.*) cringe, fawn.

kriecherisch [ˈkriːçəriʃ], *adj.* fawning, cringing.

Kriechtier [ˈkriːçtiːr], *n.* (—s, *pl.* —e) reptile.

Krieg [kriːk], *m.* (—es, *pl.* —e) war.

kriegen [ˈkriːɡən], *v.a.* get, obtain.

Krieger [ˈkriːɡər], *m.* (—s, *pl.* —) warrior.

kriegerisch [ˈkriːɡəriʃ], *adj.* warlike, martial.

kriegführend [ˈkriːkfyːrənt], *adj.* belligerent.

Kriegsfuß [ˈkriːksfuːs], *m.* (—es, *no pl.*) *auf —*, at logger-heads.

Kriegsgewinnler [ˈkriːksɡəvinlər], *m.* (—s, *pl.* —) war-profiteer.

Kriegslist [ˈkriːkslist], *f.* (—, *pl.* —en) stratagem.

Kriegsschauplatz [ˈkriːksʃauplats], *m.* (—es, *pl.* ⸚e) theatre of war.

Kriegsschiff [ˈkriːksʃif], *n.* (—es, *pl.* —e) man-of-war, warship.

Kriegswesen [ˈkriːksveːzən], *n.* (—s, *no pl.*) military affairs.

Kriegszug [ˈkriːkstsuːk], *m.* (—es, *pl.* ⸚e) campaign.

Krim [krim], *f.* the Crimea.

Kriminalbeamte [krimiˈnaːlbəamtə], *m.* (—n, *pl.* —n) crime investigator.

131

Kriminalprozeß [krɪmi'naːlprotsɛs], *m.* (**—sses**, *pl.* **—sse**) criminal procedure *or* trial.

Krimskrams ['krɪmskrams], *m.* (**—**, *no pl.*) whatnots, knick-knacks, medley.

Krippe ['krɪpə], *f.* (**—**, *pl.* **—n**) crib, manger; crèche.

Krise ['kriːzə], *f.* (**—**, *pl.* **—n**) crisis.

Kristall [krɪ'stal], *m.* (**—s**, *pl.* **—e**) crystal; cut glass.

kristallartig [krɪ'stalaːrtɪç], *adj.* crystalline.

kristallisieren [krɪstali'ziːrən], *v.a., v.n.* (*aux.* sein), crystallise.

Kristallkunde [krɪ'stalkundə], *f.* (**—**, *no pl.*) crystallography.

Kriterium [kri'teːrjum], *n.* (**—s**, *pl.* **—rien**) criterion, test.

Kritik [kri'tiːk], *f.* (**—**, *pl.* **—en**) criticism, review; *unter aller —*, extremely bad.

Kritiker ['kriːtɪkər], *m.* (**—s**, *pl.* **—**) critic.

kritisch ['kriːtɪʃ], *adj.* critical; precarious, crucial.

kritisieren [kriti'ziːrən], *v.a.* criticise; review; censure.

kritteln ['krɪtəln], *v.n.* cavil (at), find fault.

Krittler ['krɪtlər], *m.* (**—s**, *pl.* **—**) caviller, fault-finder.

Kritzelei [krɪtsə'laɪ], *f.* (**—**, *pl.* **—en**) scrawling, scribbling.

kritzeln ['krɪtsəln], *v.a.* scrawl, scribble.

Kroatien [kro'aːtsjən], *n.* Croatia.

Krokodil [kroko'diːl], *n.* (**—s**, *pl.* **—e**) (*Zool.*) crocodile.

Kronbewerber ['kroːnbevɛrbər], *m.* (**—s**, *pl.* **—**) aspirant to the crown, pretender.

Krone ['kroːnə], *f.* (**—**, *pl.* **—n**) crown; (*Papal*) tiara; (*fig.*) head, top, flower.

krönen ['krøːnən], *v.a.* crown.

Kronerbe ['kroːnɛrbə], *m.* (**—n**, *pl.* **—n**) heir apparent.

Kronleuchter ['kroːnlɔyçtər], *m.* (**—s**, *pl.* **—**) chandelier.

Kronsbeere ['kroːnsbeːrə], *f.* (**—**, *pl.* **—n**) (*Bot.*) cranberry.

Krönung ['krøːnuŋ], *f.* (**—**, *pl.* **—en**) coronation.

Kropf [krɔpf], *m.* (**—es**, *pl.* **⸚e**) (*human*) goitre, wen; (*birds*) crop, craw.

kropfartig ['krɔpfaːrtɪç], *adj.* goitrous.

kröpfen ['krœpfən], *v.a.* (*birds*) cram.

Kropftaube ['krɔpftaubə], *f.* (**—**, *pl.* **—n**) (*Orn.*) pouter-pigeon.

Kröte ['krøːtə], *f.* (**—**, *pl.* **—n**) toad.

Krücke ['krykə], *f.* (**—**, *pl.* **—n**) crutch; (*fig.*) rake.

Krückstock ['krykʃtɔk], *m.* (**—s**, *pl.* **⸚e**) crutch.

Krug [kruːk], *m.* (**—es**, *pl.* **⸚e**) jug, pitcher, mug; (*fig.*) pub, inn.

Krüger ['kryːgər], *m.* (**—s**, *pl.* **—**) pub-keeper, tapster.

Krume ['kruːmə], *f.* (**—**, *pl.* **—n**) crumb.

krüm(e)lig ['kryːm(ə)lɪç], *adj.* crumbly, crumby.

krümeln ['kryːmeln], *v.n.* crumble.

krumm [krum], *adj.* crooked, curved; *etwas — nehmen*, take s.th. amiss.

krummbeinig ['krumbaɪnɪç], *adj.* bandy-legged.

krümmen ['krymən], *v.a.* crook, bend, curve. *— v.r. sich —*, (*fig.*) writhe, cringe.

Krummholz ['krumhɔlts], *n.* (**—es**, *no pl.*) (*Bot.*) dwarf-pine.

Krummschnabel ['krumʃnaːbəl], *m.* (**—s**, *pl.* **⸚**) (*Orn.*) curlew, crook-bill.

Krümmung ['krymuŋ], *f.* (**—**, *pl.* **—en**) curve; turning, winding.

Krüppel ['krypəl], *m.* (**—s**, *pl.* **—**) cripple.

krüppelhaft ['krypəlhaft], *adj.* crippled, lame.

krüpp(e)lig ['kryp(ə)lɪç], *adj.* crippled, lame.

Kruste ['krustə], *f.* (**—**, *pl.* **—n**) crust.

Kübel ['kyːbəl], *m.* (**—s**, *pl.* **—**) tub, bucket.

Kubikfuß [ku'biːkfuːs], *m.* (**—es**, *pl.* **—**) cubic foot.

Kubikinhalt [ku'biːkɪnhalt], *m.* (**—s**, *no pl.*) cubic content.

Kubismus [ku'bɪsmus], *m.* (**—**, *no pl.*) cubism.

Küche ['kyçə], *f.* (**—**, *pl.* **—n**) (*room*) kitchen; (*food*) cooking, cookery, cuisine.

Kuchen ['kuːxən], *m.* (**—s**, *pl.* **—**) cake.

Küchengeschirr ['kyçəngəʃɪr], *n.* (**—s**, *no pl.*) kitchen utensils.

Küchenherd ['kyçənheːrt], *m.* (**—es**, *pl.* **—e**) kitchen-range.

Küchenlatein ['kyçənlataɪn], *n.* (**—s**, *no pl.*) dog-Latin.

Küchenmeister ['kyçənmaɪstər], *m.* (**—s**, *pl.* **—**) chef, head cook.

Küchenschrank ['kyçənʃraŋk], *m.* (**—s**, *pl.* **⸚e**) dresser.

Kuchenteig ['kuːxəntaɪk], *m.* (**—s**, *pl.* **—e**) dough (for cake).

Küchenzettel ['kyçəntsɛtəl], *m.* (**—s**, *pl.* **—**) bill of fare.

Küchlein ['kyːçlaɪn], *n.* (**—s**, *pl.* **—**) young chicken, pullet.

Kücken ['kykən], *n.* (**—s**, *pl.* **—**) young chicken, pullet.

Kuckuck ['kukuk], *m.* (**—s**, *pl.* **—e**) (*Orn.*) cuckoo; *scher Dich zum —! * go to blazes!

Kufe ['kuːfə], *f.* (**—**, *pl.* **—n**) tub, vat; (*sleigh*) runner; (*cradle*) rocker.

Küfer ['kyːfər], *m.* (**—s**, *pl.* **—**) cooper.

Kugel ['kuːgəl], *f.* (**—**, *pl.* **—n**) ball, bullet, sphere; globe.

kugelfest ['kuːgəlfest], *adj.* bullet-proof.

kugelförmig ['kuːgəlfœrmɪç], *adj.* spherical, globular.

Kugelgelenk ['kuːgəlgəleŋk], *n.* (**—s**, *pl.* **—e**) ball and socket joint.

Kugellager ['kuːgəllaːgər], *n.* (**—s**, *pl.* **—**) ball-bearing.

Kugelmaß ['kuːgəlmaːs], *n.* (**—es**, *pl.* **—e**) ball-calibre.

kugeln ['kuːgəln], *v.a.* roll; bowl.

Kugelregen ['ku:gəlre:gən], *m.* (**—s**, *no pl.*) hail of bullets.

kugelrund ['ku:gəlrunt], *adj.* round as a ball, well-fed.

Kugelschreiber ['ku:gəlʃraɪbər], *m.* (**—s**, *pl.* **—**) ball-point pen.

Kuh [ku:] *f.* (**—**, *pl.* ¨e) cow; *junge* **—**, heifer.

Kuhblattern ['ku:blatərn], *f. pl.* cowpox.

Kuhblume ['ku:blu:mə], *f.* (**—**, *pl.* **—n**) (*Bot.*) marigold.

Kuhfladen ['ku:fla:dən], *m.* (**—s**, *pl.* **—**) cow-dung.

Kuhhaut ['ku:haut], *f.* (**—**, *pl.* ¨e) cowhide; *das geht auf keine* **—**, that defies description.

kühl [ky:l], *adj.* cool, fresh; (*behaviour*) reserved.

Kühle ['ky:lə], *f.* (**—**, *no pl.*) coolness, freshness; (*behaviour*) reserve.

kühlen ['ky:lən], *v.a.* cool, freshen.

Kühlraum ['ky:lraum], *m.* (**—es**, *pl.* ¨e) refrigerating-chamber.

Kühlschrank ['ky:lʃraŋk], *m.* (**—s**, *pl.* ¨e) refrigerator, (*coll.*) fridge.

Kühltruhe ['ky:ltru:ə], *f.* (**—**, *pl.* **—n**) deep freeze.

Kühlung ['ky:luŋ], *f.* (**—**, *pl.* **—en**) refrigeration.

Kuhmist ['ku:mɪst], *m.* (**—s**, *no pl.*) cow-dung.

kühn [ky:n], *adj.* bold, daring, audacious.

Kühnheit ['ky:nhaɪt], *f.* (**—**, *no pl.*) boldness, daring, audacity.

Kujon [ku'jo:n], *m.* (**—s**, *pl.* **—e**) bully, scoundrel.

kujonieren [kujo'ni:rən], *v.a.* bully, exploit.

Kukuruz ['kukuruts], *m.* (**—es**, *no pl.*) (*Austr.*) maize.

kulant [ku'lant], *adj.* obliging; (*terms*) easy.

Kulanz [ku'lants], *f.* (**—**, *no pl.*) accommodating manner.

Kuli ['ku:li:], *m.* (**—s**, *pl.* **—s**) coolie.

kulinarisch [kuli'na:rɪʃ], *adj.* culinary.

Kulisse [ku'lɪsə], *f.* (**—**, *pl.* **—n**) (*Theat.*) back-drop, side-scene, wings.

Kulissenfieber [ku'lɪsənfi:bər], *n.* (**—s**, *no pl.*) stage-fright.

kulminieren [kulmi'ni:rən], *v.n.* culminate.

kultivieren [kulti'vi:rən], *v.a.* cultivate.

Kultur [kul'tu:r], *f.* (**—**, *pl.* **—en**) (*Agr.*) cultivation; (*fig.*) culture, civilization.

Kultus ['kultus], *m.* (**—**, *pl.* **Kulte**) cult, worship.

Kultusministerium ['kultusmɪnɪste:-rjum], *n.* (**—s**, *pl.* **—rien**) Ministry of Education.

Kümmel ['kyməl], *m.* (**—s**, *no pl.*) caraway-seed; (*drink*) kümmel.

Kummer ['kumər], *m.* (**—s**, *no pl.*) grief, sorrow, trouble.

kümmerlich ['kymərlɪç], *adj.* miserable, pitiful.

kummerlos ['kumərlo:s], *adj.* untroubled.

kümmern ['kymərn], *v.r. sich* **— um**, mind, look after, be worried about, care for.

Kümmernis ['kymərnɪs], *f.* (**—**, *pl.* **—se**) grief, sorrow.

kummervoll ['kumərfɔl], *adj.* sorrowful, painful, grievous.

Kumpan [kum'pa:n], *m.* (**—s**, *pl.* **—e**) companion; mate; *lustiger* **—**, jolly fellow, good companion.

kund [kunt], *adj.* known, public; *etwas* **— tun**, make s.th. public; **— und zu** *wissen sei hiermit*, (*obs.*) we hereby give notice.

kundbar ['kuntba:r], *adj.* known; *etwas* **— machen**, announce s.th., make s.th. known.

kündbar ['kyntba:r], *adj.* (*loan, capital etc.*) redeemable; capable of being called in, terminable.

Kunde (1) ['kundə], *m.* (**—n**, *pl.* **—n**) customer; *ein schlauer* **—**, an artful dodger.

Kunde (2) ['kundə], *f.* (**—**, *pl.* **—n**) news; information, notification; (*compounds*) science.

Kundgebung ['kuntge:buŋ], *f.* (**—**, *pl.* **—en**) publication; rally; demonstration.

kundig ['kundɪç], *adj.* versed in, conversant with.

Kundige ['kundɪgə], *m.* (**—n**, *pl.* **—n**) expert, initiate.

kündigen ['kyndɪgən], *v.n.* give notice (*Dat.*).

Kundmachung ['kuntmaxuŋ], *f.* (**—**, *pl.* **—en**) publication.

Kundschaft ['kuntʃaft], *f.* (**—**, *no pl.*) clientele, customers; information, reconnaissance.

kundschaften ['kuntʃaftən], *v.n.* reconnoitre, scout.

künftig ['kynftɪç], *adj.* future, prospective, to come.

Kunst [kunst], *f.* (**—**, *pl.* ¨e) art; skill.

Kunstbutter ['kunstbutər], *f.* (**—**, *no pl.*) margarine.

Künstelei [kynstə'laɪ], *f.* (**—**, *pl.* **—en**) affectation, mannerism.

kunstfertig ['kunstfertɪç], *adj.* skilled, skilful.

Kunstfreund ['kunstfrɔynt], *m.* (**—es**, *pl.* **—e**) art-lover.

kunstgerecht ['kunstgəreçt], *adj.* workmanlike.

Kunstgewerbe ['kunstgəverbə], *n.* (**—s**, *no pl.*) arts and crafts.

Kunstgriff ['kunstgrɪf], *m.* (**—es**, *pl.* **—e**) trick, dodge, artifice, knack.

Kunsthändler ['kunsthendlər], *m.* (**—s**, *pl.* **—**) art-dealer.

Kunstkenner ['kunstkenər], *m.* (**—s**, *pl.* **—**) connoisseur.

Künstler ['kynstlər], *m.* (**—s**, *pl.* **—**) artist, performer.

künstlerisch ['kynstlərɪʃ], *adj.* artistic, elaborate, ingenious.

künstlich ['kynstlɪç], *adj.* artificial.

kunstlos ['kunstlo:s], *adj.* artless, unaffected.

kunstreich ['kunstraɪç], *adj.* ingenious.
Kunstseide ['kunstzaɪdə], *f.* (—, *no pl.*) artificial silk.
Kunststickerei ['kunstʃtɪkəraɪ], *f.* (—, *no pl.*) art needlework.
Kunststoff ['kunstʃtɔf], *m.* (—es, *pl.* —e) plastics.
Kunststopfen ['kunstʃtɔpfən], *n.* (—s, *no pl.*) invisible mending.
Kunststück ['kunstʃtyk], *n.* (—es, *pl.* —e) trick, feat.
Kunstverständige ['kunstfɛrʃtɛndɪgə], *m.* (—n, *pl.* —n) art expert.
Küpe ['ky:pə], *f.* (—, *pl.* —n) large tub; (dyeing) copper.
Kupfer ['kupfər], *n.* (—s, *no pl.*) copper.
Kupferblech ['kupfərblɛç], *n.* (—es, *no pl.*) copper-sheet.
Kupferdraht ['kupfərdra:t], *m.* (—es, *pl.* ∵e) copper-wire.
kupferhaltig ['kupfərhaltɪç], *adj.* containing copper.
Kupferrost ['kupfərrɔst], *m.* (—es, *no pl.*) verdigris.
Kupferstecher ['kupfərʃtɛçər], *m.* (—s, *pl.* —) (copperplate) engraver.
kupieren [ku'pi:rən], *v.a.* (*rare*) (*ticket*) punch; (*Austr.*) (*horse*) dock.
Kuppe ['kupə], *f.* (—, *pl.* —n) (*hill*) top, summit.
Kuppel ['kupəl], *f.* (—, *pl.* —n) cupola, dome.
kuppeln ['kupəln], *v.n.* procure, pimp; make a match.
Kuppler ['kuplər], *m.* (—s, *pl.* —) procurer, pimp; matchmaker.
Kupplung ['kupluŋ], *f.* (—, *pl.* —en) (*Railw.*) coupling, joint; (*Motor.*) clutch.
Kur [ku:r], *f.* (—, *pl.* —en) cure; *eine — machen*, undergo medical treatment.
Kuranstalt ['ku:ranʃtalt], *f.* (—, *pl.* —en) sanatorium; (*Am.*) sanatorium.
Küraß ['ky:ras], *m.* (—sses, *pl.* —sse) cuirass.
Kuratel [kura'tel], *f.* (—, *pl.* —en) guardianship, trusteeship.
Kuratorium [kura'to:rjum], *n.* (—s, *pl.* —rien) board of guardians *or* trustees; council, governing body.
Kurbel ['kurbəl], *f.* (—, *pl.* —n) crank, winch.
Kurbelstange ['kurbəlʃtaŋə], *f.* (—, *pl.* —n) connecting rod.
Kurbelwelle ['kurbəlvɛlə], *f.* (—, *pl.* —n) crankshaft.
Kürbis ['kyrbɪs], *m.* (—ses, *pl.* —se) (*Bot.*) pumpkin, gourd.
küren ['ky:rən], *v.a. irr.* (*Poet.*) choose, elect.
Kurfürst ['ku:rfyrst], *m.* (—en, *pl.* —en) Elector (of the Holy Roman Empire).
Kurhaus ['ku:rhaus], *n.* (—es, *pl.* ∵er) spa; hotel; pump room.
Kurie ['ku:rjə], *f.* (—, *pl.* —n) (*Eccl.*) Curia; Papal Court.

Kurier [ku'ri:r], *m.* (—s, *pl.* —e) courier.
kurieren [ku'ri:rən], *v.a.* cure.
kurios [kur'jo:s], *adj.* curious, queer, strange.
Kuriosität [kurjozi'tɛ:t], *f.* (—, *pl.* —en) curio, curiosity.
Kurort ['ku:rɔrt], *m.* (—es, *pl.* —e) spa, watering-place, health-resort.
Kurrentschrift [ku'rɛntʃrɪft], *f.* (—, *no pl.*) running hand, cursive writing.
Kurs [kurs], *m.* (—es, *pl.* —e) rate of exchange; quotation; circulation; course.
Kursaal ['ku:rza:l], *m.* (—s, *pl.* —säle) hall, (*spa*) pump-room, casino.
Kursbericht ['kursbərɪçt], *m.* (—es, *pl.* —e) market report.
Kursbuch ['kursbu:x], *n.* (—es, *pl.* ∵er) railway-guide, time-table.
Kürschner ['kyrʃnər], *m.* (—s, *pl.* —) furrier, skinner.
kursieren [kur'zi:rən], *v.n.* be current, circulate.
Kursivschrift [kur'zi:fʃrɪft], *f.* (—, *no pl.*) italics.
Kursstand ['kursʃtant], *m.* (—es, *no pl.*) rate of exchange.
Kursus ['kurzus], *m.* (—, *pl.* **Kurse**) course (of lectures).
Kurszettel ['kurstsɛtəl], *m.* (—s, *pl.* —) quotation-list.
Kurve ['kurvə], *f.* (—, *pl.* —n) curve.
kurz [kurts], *adj.* short, brief, concise; curt, abrupt.
kurzangebunden [kurts'angəbundən], *adj.* terse, abrupt, curt.
kurzatmig ['kurtsa:tmɪç], *adj.* short-winded, short of breath.
Kürze ['kyrtsə], *f.* (—, *no pl.*) shortness, brevity.
kürzen ['kyrtsən], *v.a.* shorten, abbreviate, condense; (*Maths.*) reduce.
kürzlich ['kyrtslɪç], *adv.* lately, recently, the other day.
Kurzschluß ['kurtsʃlus], *m.* (—sses, *pl.* ∵sse) short circuit.
Kurzschrift ['kurtsʃrɪft], *f.* (—, *no pl.*) shorthand.
kurzsichtig ['kurtszɪçtɪç], *adj.* short-sighted.
kurzum [kurts'um], *adv.* in short.
Kürzung ['kyrtsuŋ], *f.* (—, *pl.* —en) abbreviation, abridgement.
Kurzwaren ['kurtsva:rən], *f. pl.* haberdashery.
kurzweg [kurts've:k], *adv.* simply, offhand, briefly.
Kurzweil ['kurtsvaɪl], *f.* (—, *no pl.*) pastime.
kurzweilig ['kurtsvaɪlɪç], *adj.* amusing, diverting, entertaining.
kusch! [kuʃ], *excl.* (*to dogs*) lie down!
kuschen ['kuʃən], *v.n.*, *v.r.* crouch, lie down.
Kuß [kus], *m.* (—sses, *pl.* ∵sse) kiss.
küssen ['kysən], *v.a.*, *v.n.*, *v.r.* kiss.
Küste ['kystə], *f.* (—, *pl.* —n) coast, shore.

Küstenstadt ['kystənʃtat], *f.* (—, *pl.* ˑe) seaside town.

Küster ['kystər], *m.* (—s, *pl.* —) sacristan, sexton, verger.

Kustos ['kustɔs], *m.* (—, *pl.* —oden) custodian; director of museum.

Kutschbock ['kutʃbɔk], *m.* (—s, *pl.* ˑe) box(-seat).

Kutsche ['kutʃə], *f.* (—, *pl.* —n) coach, carriage.

kutschieren [kut'ʃiːrən], *v.n.* drive a coach.

Kutte ['kutə], *f.* (—, *pl.* —n) cowl.

Kutter ['kutər], *m.* (—s, *pl.* —) (*Naut.*) cutter.

Kuvert [ku'vɛːr], *n.* (—s, *pl.* —s) envelope; (*dinner*) place laid.

kuvertieren [kuvɛr'tiːrən], *v.a.* envelop, wrap.

Kux [kuks], *m.* (—es, *pl.* —e) share in a mining concern.

Kybernetik [kyːbɛr'neːtɪk], *f.* (—, *no pl.*) cybernetics.

L

L [ɛl], *n.* (—, *pl.* —) the letter L.

Lab [laːp], *n.* (—es, *pl.* —e) rennet.

labbern ['labərn], *v.a.*, *v.n.* dribble, slobber; blab.

Labe ['laːbə], *f.* (—, *no pl.*) (*Poet.*) refreshment; comfort.

laben ['laːbən], *v.a.* refresh, restore, revive.

labil [la'biːl], *adj.* unstable.

Laborant [labo'rant], *m.* (—en, *pl.* —en) laboratory assistant.

Laboratorium [labora'toːrjum], *n.* (—s, *pl.* —rien) laboratory.

laborieren [labo'riːrən], *v.n.* experiment; suffer (from).

Labsal ['laːpzaːl], *n.* (—s, *pl.* —e) restorative, refreshment.

Labung ['laːbuŋ], *f.* (—, *pl.* —en) refreshment, comfort.

Lache ['laxə], *f.* (—, *pl.* —n) pool, puddle.

Lächeln ['lɛçəln], *n.* (—s, *no pl.*) smile; *albernes* —, smirk; *höhnisches* —, sneer.

lächeln ['lɛçəln], *v.n.* smile.

Lachen ['laxən], *n.* (—s, *no pl.*) laugh, laughter.

lachen ['laxən], *v.n.* laugh.

lächerlich ['lɛçərlɪç], *adj.* laughable, ridiculous; preposterous; ludicrous; *sich — machen*, make a fool of o.s.; *etwas — machen*, ridicule s.th.

Lachgas ['laxgaːs], *n.* (—es, *no pl.*) nitrous oxide, laughing-gas.

lachhaft ['laxhaft], *adj.* laughable, ridiculous.

Lachkrampf ['laxkrampf], *m.* (—es, *pl.* ˑe) hysterical laughter, a fit of laughter.

Lachs [laks], *m.* (—es, *pl.* —e) salmon.

Lachsalve ['laxzalvə], *f.* (—, *pl.* —n) peal of laughter.

Lack [lak], *m.* (—s, *pl.* —e) lac, lacquer, varnish.

lackieren [la'kiːrən], *v.a.* lacquer, varnish.

Lackmus ['lakmus], *n.* (—, *no pl.*) litmus.

Lackschuh ['lakʃuː], *m.* (—s, *pl.* —e) patent-leather shoe.

Lackwaren ['lakvaːrən], *f. pl.* japanned goods.

Lade ['laːdə], *f.* (—, *pl.* —n) box, chest, case, drawer.

Ladebaum ['laːdəbaum], *m.* derrick.

Ladefähigkeit ['laːdəfɛːɪçkaɪt], *f.* (—, *pl.* —en), carrying capacity, loading capacity; tonnage.

Ladegeld ['laːdəgɛlt], *n.* (—es, *pl.* —er) loading charges.

Laden ['laːdən], *m.* (—s, *pl.* ˑ) (*window*) shutter; shop, store.

laden ['laːdən], *v.a. irr.* load; (*Elec.*) charge; (*Law*) summon, (*fig.*) incur.

Ladenhüter ['laːdənhyːtər], *m.* (—s, *pl.* —) unsaleable article.

Ladenpreis ['laːdənpraɪs], *m.* (—es, *pl.* —e) retail-price.

Ladentisch ['laːdəntɪʃ], *m.* (—es, *pl.* —e) counter.

Ladeschein ['laːdəʃaɪn], *m.* (—s, *pl.* —e) bill of lading.

Ladestock ['laːdəʃtɔk], *m.* (—es, *pl.* ˑe) ramrod.

Ladung ['laːduŋ], *f.* (—, *pl.* —en) loading, lading, freight; shipment, cargo; (*gun*) charge; (*Law*) summons.

Laffe ['lafə], *m.* (—n, *pl.* —n) fop.

Lage ['laːgə], *f.* (—, *pl.* —n) site, position, situation; state, condition; stratum, layer.

Lager ['laːgər], *n.* (—s, *pl.* —) couch, bed, divan; (*Geol.*) seam, vein; (*Tech.*) bearing; (*Comm.*) warehouse, store; camp.

Lageraufnahme ['laːgəraufnaːmə], *f.* (—, *pl.* —n) stock-taking, inventory.

Lager(bier) ['laːgər(biːr)], *n.* (—s, *pl.* —e) lager.

Lagergeld ['laːgərgɛlt], *n.* (—es, *pl.* —er) storage charge.

Lagerist [laːgə'rɪst], *m.* (—en, *pl.* —en) warehouse-clerk.

lagern ['laːgərn], *v.a.* store, warehouse.

Lagerstätte ['laːgərʃtɛtə], *f.* (—, *pl.* —n) couch, resting-place; camp site.

Lagerung ['laːgəruŋ], *f.* (—, *pl.* —en) encampment; storage; stratification.

Lagune [la'guːnə], *f.* (—, *pl.* —n) lagoon.

lahm [laːm], *adj.* lame, paralysed, crippled.

lahmen ['laːmən], *v.n.* be lame, limp.

lähmen ['lɛːmən], *v.a.* paralyse.

lahmlegen ['laːmleːgən], *v.a.* paralyse.

Lähmung ['lɛ:muŋ], *f.* (—, *pl.* —en) paralysis.

Laib [laɪp], *m.* (—es, *pl.* —e) (*bread*) loaf.

Laich [laɪç], *m.* (—es, *pl.* —e) spawn.

laichen ['laɪçən], *v.n.* spawn.

Laie ['laɪə], *m.* (—n, *pl.* —n) layman, (*pl.*) laity.

Lakai [la'kaɪ], *m.* (—en, *pl.* —en) lackey, flunkey, footman.

Lake ['la:kə], *f.* (—, *pl.* —n) brine, pickle.

Laken ['la:kən], *n.* (—s, *pl.* —) (*bed*) sheet.

lakonisch [la'ko:nɪʃ], *adj.* laconic.

Lakritze [la'krɪtsə], *f.* (—, *pl.* —n) liquorice.

lallen ['lalən], *v.a.*, *v.n.* stammer; babble.

Lama (1) ['la:ma:], *n.* (—s, *pl.* —s) (*animal*) llama.

Lama (2) ['la:ma:], *m.* (—s, *pl.* —s) (*priest*) lama.

lamentieren [lamɛn'ti:rən], *v.n.* lament, wail.

Lamm [lam], *n.* (—es, *pl.* ˙er) (*Zool.*) lamb.

Lämmchen ['lɛmçən], *n.* (—s, *pl.* —) (*Zool.*) lambkin.

Lämmergeier ['lɛmərgaɪər], *m.* (—s, *pl.* —) (*Orn.*) great bearded vulture.

Lampe ['lampə], *f.* (—, *pl.* —n) lamp.

Lampenfieber ['lampənfi:bər], *n.* (—s, *no pl.*) stage-fright.

Lampenputzer ['lampənputsər], *m.* (—s, *pl.* —) lamplighter.

Lampenschirm ['lampənʃɪrm], *m.* (—s, *pl.* —e) lampshade.

Lampion [lam'pjɔ], *m. & n.* (—s, *pl.* —s) Chinese lantern.

lancieren [lã'si:rən], *v.a.* thrust; launch.

Land [lant], *n.* (—es, *pl.* —e (*Poet.*) and ˙er) land, country; state; ground, soil; *das Gelobte* —, the Promised Land; *an* — *gehen*, go ashore; *aufs* — *gehen*, go into the country.

Landadel ['lanta:dəl], *m.* (—s, *no pl.*) landed gentry.

Landarbeiter ['lantarbaɪtər], *m.* (—s, *pl.* —) farm-worker.

Landauer ['landauər], *m.* (—s, *pl.* —) landau.

Landebahn ['landəba:n], *f.* (—, *pl.* —en) (*Aviat.*) runway.

landen ['landən], *v.n.* (*aux. sein*) land, disembark; (*aircraft*) land, touch down.

Landenge ['lantɛŋə], *f.* (—, *pl.* —n) isthmus.

Ländereien ['lɛndəraɪən], *f. pl.* landed property, estate.

Landeserzeugnis ['landəsɛrtsɔyknɪs], *n.* (—sses, *pl.* —sse) home produce.

Landesfürst ['landəsfyrst], *m.* (—en, *pl.* —en) sovereign.

Landesherr ['landəshɛr], *m.* (—n, *pl.* —en) (reigning) prince; sovereign.

Landeshoheit ['landəshohaɪt], *f.* (—, *no pl.*) sovereignty.

Landeskirche ['landəskɪrçə], *f.* (—, *pl.* —n) established church; national church.

Landesschuld ['landəsʃult], *f.* (—, *no pl.*) national debt.

Landessprache ['landəsʃpra:xə], *f.* (—, *pl.* —n) vernacular.

Landestracht ['landəstraxt], *f.* (—, *pl.* —en) national costume.

landesüblich ['landəsy:plɪç], *adj.* conventional, usual, customary.

Landesverweisung ['landəsfɛrvaɪzuŋ], *f.* (—, *pl.* —en) exile, banishment.

landflüchtig ['lantflyçtɪç], *adj.* fugitive.

Landfrieden ['lantfri:dən], *m.* (—s, *no pl.*) King's (*or* Queen's) peace; (*medieval*) public peace.

Landgericht ['lantgərɪçt], *n.* (—es, *pl.* —e) district court; county court.

Landgraf ['lantgra:f], *m.* (—en, *pl.* —en) landgrave, count.

Landhaus ['lanthaus], *n.* (—es, *pl.* ˙er) country house.

Landjunker ['lantjuŋkər], *m.* (—s, *pl.* —) country squire.

Landkarte ['lantkartə], *f.* (—, *pl.* —n) map.

landläufig ['lantlɔyfɪç], *adj.* customary, conventional.

ländlich ['lɛntlɪç], *adj.* rural, rustic.

Landmann ['lantman], *m.* (—es, *pl.* **Landleute**) rustic, peasant.

Landmesser ['lantmɛsər], *m.* (—s, *pl.* —) surveyor.

Landpartie ['lantparti:], *f.* (—, *pl.* —n) country excursion, picnic.

Landplage ['lantpla:gə], *f.* (—, *pl.* —n) scourge, calamity; *eine richtige* —, a public nuisance.

Landrat ['lantra:t], *m.* (—s, *pl.* ˙e) district president *or* magistrate.

Landratte ['lantratə], *f.* (—, *pl.* —n) landlubber.

Landrecht ['lantrɛçt], *n.* (—es, *no pl.*) common law.

Landregen ['lantre:gən], *m.* (—s, *no pl.*) steady downpour; persistent rain.

Landschaft ['lantʃaft], *f.* (—, *pl.* —en) landscape.

landschaftlich ['lantʃaftlɪç], *adj.* scenic.

Landsknecht ['lantsknɛçt], *m.* (—es, *pl.* —e) mercenary; hired soldier.

Landsmann ['lantsman], *m.* (—es, *pl.* **Landsleute**) fellow-countryman, compatriot.

Landspitze ['lantʃpɪtsə], *f.* (—, *pl.* —n) cape, headland, promontory.

Landstraße ['lantʃtra:sə], *f.* (—, *pl.* —n) open road, main road, highway.

Landstreicher ['lantʃtraɪçər], *m.* (—s, *pl.* —s) vagabond, tramp, (*Am.*) hobo.

Landstrich ['lantʃtrɪç], *m.* (—es, *pl.* —e) tract of land.

Landsturm ['lantʃturm], *m.* (—s, *no pl.*) (*Milit.*) militia; Home Guard.

Landtag ['lantta:k], *m.* (—s, *pl.* —e) (*Parl.*) diet.

Landung ['landuŋ], *f.* (—, *pl.* —en) landing.

Landvermesser *see* **Landmesser**.

Landvogt ['lantfo:kt], m. (—es, pl. ⸚e) (provincial) governor.
Landweg ['lantve:k], m. (—s, pl. —e) overland route.
Landwehr ['lantve:r], f. (—, pl. —en) militia.
Landwirt ['lantvɪrt], m. (—s, pl. —e) farmer, husbandman.
Landwirtschaft ['lantvɪrtʃaft], f. (—, no pl.) agriculture.
Landzunge ['lanttsuŋə], f. (—, pl. —n) spit of land.
lang [laŋ], adj. long, tall. — adv., prep. (prec. by Acc.) for, during, long.
langatmig ['laŋa:tmɪç], adj. long-winded.
lange ['laŋə], adv. a long time; wie —? how long? so — wie, as long as.
Länge ['lɛŋə], f. (—, pl. —n) length; (Geog.) longitude.
langen ['laŋən], v.a. reach, hand, give s.o. s.th. — v.n. suffice, be enough.
Längengrad ['lɛŋəngra:t], m. (—s, pl. —e) degree of longitude.
Längenkreis ['lɛŋənkraɪs], m. (—es, pl. —e) meridian.
Längenmaß ['lɛŋənma:s], n. (—es, pl. —e) linear measure.
Langeweile ['laŋəvaɪlə], f. (—, no pl.) boredom, ennui.
Langfinger ['laŋfɪŋər], m. (—s, pl. —) pickpocket.
langjährig ['laŋjɛːrɪç], adj. of long standing.
Langlebigkeit ['laŋle:bɪçkaɪt], f. (—, no pl.) longevity.
länglich ['lɛŋlɪç], adj. oblong.
Langmut ['laŋmu:t], f. (—, no pl.) forbearance, patience.
längs [lɛŋs], prep. (Genit., Dat.) along.
langsam ['laŋza:m], adj. slow; deliberate.
längst [lɛŋst], adv. long ago, long since.
längstens ['lɛŋstəns], adv. at the longest; at the latest.
Languste [la'ŋʊstə], f. (—, pl. —n) (Zool.) spiny lobster.
langweilen ['laŋvaɪlən], v.a.(insep.) bore, tire. — v.r. sich —, feel bored, be bored.
langwierig ['laŋvi:rɪç], adj. lengthy, protracted, wearisome.
Lanze ['lantsə], f. (—, pl. —n) lance, spear; eine — brechen, take up the cudgels, stand up for (s.th. or s.o.).
Lanzenstechen ['lantsənʃteçən], n. (—s, no pl.) tournament.
Lanzette [lan'tsetə], f. (—, pl. —n) lancet.
Lanzknecht ['lantsknɛçt], m. (—es, pl. —e) see **Landsknecht**.
Laos ['la:ɔs], n. Laos.
Lappalie [la'paljə], f. (—, pl. —n) trifle.
Lappen ['lapən], m. (—s, pl. —) rag, duster, patch; (ear) lobe.
Läpperschulden ['lɛpərʃuldən], f. pl. petty debts.
läppisch ['lɛpɪʃ], adj. silly, foolish, trifling.
Lappland ['lapland], n. Lapland.

Lärche ['lɛrçə], f. (—, pl. —n) (Bot.) larch.
Lärm [lɛrm], m. (—s, no pl.) noise, din.
lärmen ['lɛrmən], v.n. make a noise, brawl.
Larve ['larfə], f. (—, pl. —n) mask; (Ent.) grub, larva.
lasch [laʃ], adj. limp; insipid.
Lasche ['laʃə], f. (—, pl. —n) flap; (shoe) gusset, strip.
lassen ['lasən], v.a., v.n. irr. let, allow, suffer, permit; leave; make, cause; order, command; desist.
läßlich ['lɛslɪç], adj. (Eccl.) venial (sin).
lässig ['lɛsɪç], adj. indolent, sluggish, inactive.
Lässigkeit ['lɛsɪçkaɪt], f. (—, no pl.) lassitude, inaction, indolence; negligence.
Last [last], f. (—, pl. —en) load, burden, weight, charge.
lasten ['lastən], v.n. be heavy; weigh (on).
lastenfrei ['lastənfraɪ], adj. unencumbered.
Laster ['lastər], n. (—s, pl. —) vice.
Lästerer ['lɛstərər], m. (—s, pl. —) slanderer, calumniator; blasphemer.
lasterhaft ['lastərhaft], adj. vicious, wicked; corrupt.
Lasterhöhle ['lastərhø:lə], f. (—, pl. —n) den of vice.
lästerlich ['lɛstərlɪç], adj. blasphemous.
lästern ['lɛstərn], v.a. slander, defame; blaspheme.
lästig ['lɛstɪç], adj. tiresome, troublesome.
Lasttier ['lastti:r], n. (—es, pl. —e) beast of burden.
Lastwagen ['lastva:gən], m. (—s, pl. —) lorry, (Am.) truck.
Lasur [la'zu:r], m. (—s, pl. —e) lapis-lazuli; ultramarine.
Latein [la'taɪn], n. (—s, no pl.) Latin.
lateinisch [la'taɪnɪʃ], adj. Latin.
Laterne [la'tɛrnə], f. (—, pl. —n) lantern; (street) lamp.
latschen ['la:tʃən], v.n. shuffle along.
Latte ['latə], f. (—, pl. —n) lath, batten; eine lange —, lanky person.
Lattich ['latɪç], m. (—s, pl. —e) lettuce.
Latz [lats], m. (—es, pl. ⸚e) flap, bib; pinafore.
lau [lau], adj. tepid, lukewarm, insipid; (fig.) half-hearted.
Laub [laup], n. (—es, no pl.) foliage, leaves.
Laube ['laubə], f. (—, pl. —n) arbour, summer-house.
Laubengang ['laubəngaŋ], m. (—es, pl. ⸚e) arcade, covered walk.
Laubfrosch ['laupfrɔʃ], m. (—es, pl. ⸚e) (Zool.) tree-frog.
Laubsäge ['laupzɛ:gə], f. (—, pl. —n) fret-saw.
Lauch [laux], m. (—s, no pl.) (Bot.) leek.
Lauer ['lauər], f. (—, no pl.) ambush, hiding-place; auf der — sein, lie in wait.

lauern ['lauərn], v.n. lurk, lie in wait (for), watch (for).

Lauf [lauf], m. (—es, pl. ·̈e) course, run; running; operation; (river) current; (gun) barrel; (fig.) rein.

Laufbahn ['laufba:n], f. (—, pl. —en) career, die medizinische — einschlagen, enter upon a medical career.

Laufband ['laufbant], n. (—s, pl. ·̈er) (baby) rein, leading-string; (Tech.) conveyor-belt.

Laufbrücke ['laufbrykə], f. (—, pl. —n) gangway.

Laufbursche ['laufburʃə], m. (—n, pl. —n) errand-boy.

laufen ['laufən], v.n. irr. (aux. sein) run; walk; (wheel) turn; flow, trickle down.

laufend ['laufənt], adj. current.

Läufer ['lɔyfər], m. (—s, pl. —) runner; (carpet) rug; (Chess) bishop; (Footb.) half-back.

Lauffeuer ['lauffɔyər], n. (—s, no pl.) wildfire.

Laufgraben ['laufgra:bən], m. (—s, pl. ·̈) trench.

läufig ['lɔyfɪç], adj. (animals) ruttish.

Laufpaß ['laufpas], m. (—sses, no pl.) den — geben, give (s.o.) the sack.

Laufschritt ['laufʃrɪt], m. (—es, pl. —e) march; im —, at the double.

Laufzeit ['lauftsaɪt], f. (—, pl. —en) running-time; currency; (animals) rutting time.

Lauge ['laugə], f. (—, pl. —n) (Chem.) lye, alkali.

Lauheit ['lauhaɪt], f. (—, no pl.) tepidity, lukewarmness; (fig.) half-heartedness.

Laune ['launə], f. (—, pl. —n) humour, temper, mood, whim.

launenhaft ['launənhaft], adj. moody.

launig ['launɪç], adj. humorous.

launisch ['launɪʃ], adj. moody, fitful, bad-tempered.

Laus [laus], f. (—, pl. ·̈e) (Zool.) louse.

Lausbub ['lausbu:p], m. (—en, pl. —en) young scamp, rascal.

lauschen ['lauʃən], v.n. listen, eavesdrop.

Lausejunge ['lauzəjuŋə], m. (—n, pl. —n) rascal, lout.

lausig ['lauzɪç], adj. (vulg.) sordid, lousy.

laut [laut], adj. loud, noisy, audible, clamorous. — prep. (Genit.) as per, according to, in virtue of.

Laut [laut], m. (—es, pl. —e) sound.

lautbar ['lautba:r], adj. — machen, make known.

Laute ['lautə], f. (—, pl. —n) (Mus.) lute.

lauten ['lautən], v.n. purport, run, read.

läuten ['lɔytən], v.a., v.n. ring; toll; es läutet, the bell is ringing.

lauter ['lautər], adj. clear, pure; (fig.) single-minded; genuine; nothing but. — adv. merely.

Lauterkeit ['lautərkaɪt], f. (—, no pl.) clearness, purity; (fig.) single-mindedness, integrity.

läutern ['lɔytərn], v.a. clear, purify; refine.

Läuterung ['lɔytəruŋ], f. (—, pl. —en) clearing, purification; refinement.

lautieren [lau'ti:rən], v.a. read phonetically.

Lautlehre ['lautle:rə], f. (—, no pl.) phonetics.

lautlich ['lautlɪç], adj. phonetic.

lautlos ['lautlo:s], adj. mute, silent; noiseless.

Lautmalerei ['lautma:ləraɪ], f. (—, no pl.) onomatopoeia.

Lautsprecher ['lautʃprɛçər], m. (—s, pl. —) loudspeaker.

Lautverschiebung ['lautfɛrʃi:buŋ], f. (—, pl. —en) sound shift.

lauwarm ['lauvarm], adj. lukewarm, tepid; (fig.) half-hearted.

Lava ['la:va], f. (—, no pl.) lava.

Lavendel [la'vɛndəl], m. (—s, no pl.) (Bot.) lavender.

lavieren [la'vi:rən], v.n. tack; (fig.) wangle.

Lawine [la'vi:nə], f. (—, pl. —n) avalanche.

lax [laks], adj. lax, loose.

Laxheit ['lakshaɪt], f. (—, pl. —en) laxity.

Laxiermittel [lak'si:rmɪtəl], n. (—s, pl. —) laxative, aperient.

Lazarett [latsa'rɛt], n. (—s, pl. —e) infirmary, military hospital.

Lebemann ['le:bəman], m. (—es, pl. ·̈er) man about town.

Leben ['le:bən], n. (—s, pl. —) life; (fig.) existence;·activity; animation, bustle, stir.

leben ['le:bən], v.n. live, be alive.

lebend ['le:bənt], adj. alive, living; (language) modern.

lebendig [le'bɛndɪç], adj. living, alive, quick.

Lebensanschauung ['le:bənsanʃauuŋ], f. (—, pl. —en) conception of life, philosophy of life.

Lebensart ['le:bənsa:rt], f. (—, no pl.) way of living; (fig.) behaviour; gute —, good manners.

lebensfähig ['le:bənsfɛ:ɪç], adj. capable of living, viable.

lebensgefährlich ['le:bənsgəfɛ:rlɪç], adj. perilous, extremely dangerous.

Lebensgeister ['le:bənsgaɪstər], m. pl. spirits.

lebensgroß ['le:bənsgro:s], adj. life-size.

lebenslänglich ['le:bənslɛŋlɪç], adj. lifelong, for life; —e Rente, life annuity.

Lebenslauf ['le:bənslauf], m. (—es, pl. ·̈e) curriculum vitae.

Lebensmittel ['le:bənsmɪtəl], n. pl. food, provisions, victuals.

lebensmüde ['le:bənsmy:də], adj. weary of life.

Lebensunterhalt ['le:bənsuntərhalt], m. (—s, no pl.) livelihood.

Lebenswandel ['le:bənsvandəl], m. (—s, no pl.) conduct, mode of life.

Lebensweise ['le:bənsvaɪzə], *f.* (—, *no pl.*) habits, way of life.

Leber ['le:bər], *f.* (—, *pl.* —n) liver; *frisch von der — weg,* frankly, without mincing matters.

Leberblümchen ['le:bərbly:mçən], *n.* (—s, *pl.* —) (*Bot.*) liverwort.

Leberfleck ['le:bərflɛk], *m.* (—s, *pl.* —e) mole.

Lebertran ['le:bərtra:n], *m.* (—s, *no pl.*) cod-liver oil.

Leberwurst ['le:bərvurst], *f.* (—, *pl.* ·e) liver sausage.

Lebewesen ['le:bəve:zən], *n.* (—s, *pl.* —) living creature.

Lebewohl ['le:bəvo:l], *n., excl.* farewell, good-bye; — *sagen,* bid farewell.

lebhaft ['le:phaft], *adj.* lively, vivacious, brisk, animated.

Lebkuchen ['le:pku:xən], *m.* (—s, *pl.* —) gingerbread.

Lebzeiten ['le:ptsaɪtən], *f. pl.* zu von (*Genit.*), in the lifetime of.

lechzen ['lɛçtsən], *v.n.* be parched with thirst; *nach etwas —,* (*fig.*) long for s.th., pine for s.th.

Leck [lɛk], *n.* (—s, *pl.* —e) leak; *ein — bekommen,* spring a leak.

leck [lɛk], *adj.* leaky.

lecken ['lɛkən], *v.a.* lick, lap.

lecker ['lɛkər], *adj.* delicate, delicious, dainty.

Leckerbissen ['lɛkərbɪsən], *m.* (—s, *pl.* —) delicacy; dainty, tit-bit.

Leckerei [lɛkə'raɪ], *f.* (—, *pl.* —en) delicacy.

Leder ['le:dər], *n.* (—s, *no pl.*) leather.

ledern ['le:dərn], *adj.* (of) leather, leathery; (*fig.*) dull, boring.

ledig ['le:dɪç], *adj.* unmarried, single; (*fig.*) rid of, free from.

lediglich ['le:dɪklɪç], *adv.* merely, only, solely.

leer [le:r], *adj.* empty, void; blank; (*fig.*) hollow, futile, empty, vain, inane.

Leere ['le:rə], *f.* (—, *no pl.*) emptiness, void, vacuum.

leeren ['le:rən], *v.a.* empty, evacuate.

Leerlauf ['le:rlauf], *m.* (—s, *no pl.*) (*Motor.*) idling; (*gear*) neutral.

legalisieren [legali'zi:rən], *v.a.* legalise, authenticate.

Legat (1) [le'ga:t], *m.* (—en, *pl.* —en) legate.

Legat (2) [le'ga:t], *n.* (—s, *pl.* —e) legacy, bequest.

Legationsrat [lega'tsjo:nsra:t], *m.* (—s, *pl.* ·e) counsellor in a legation.

legen ['le:gən], *v.a.* lay, put, place. — *v.r. sich —,* lie down; cease, subside.

Legende [le'gɛndə], *f.* (—, *pl.* —n) legend.

Legierung [lə'gi:ruŋ], *f.* (—, *pl.* —en) alloy.

Legion [le'gjo:n], *f.* (—, *pl.* —en) legion.

Legionär [le:gjo'nɛ:r], *m.* (—s, *pl.* —e) legionary.

legitim [legi'ti:m], *adj.* legitimate.

Legitimation [legitima'tsjo:n], *f.* (—, *pl.* —en) proof of identity.

legitimieren [legiti'mi:rən], *v.a.* legitimise. — *v.r. sich —,* prove o.'s identity.

Lehen ['le:ən], *n.* (—s, *pl.* —) fief; *zu — geben,* invest with, enfeoff; *zu — tragen,* hold in fee.

Lehensdienst *see* **Lehnsdienst.**

Lehenseid *see* **Lehnseid.**

Lehensmann *see* **Lehnsmann.**

Lehm [le:m], *m.* (—s, *no pl.*) loam, clay, mud.

lehmig ['le:mɪç], *adj.* clayey, loamy.

Lehne ['le:nə], *f.* (—, *pl.* —n) support, prop; (*chair*) back, arm-rest.

lehnen ['le:nən], *v.a., v.n.* lean. — *v.r. sich — an,* lean against.

Lehnsdienst ['le:nsdi:nst], *m.* (—es, *pl.* —e) feudal service.

Lehnseid ['le:nsaɪt], *m.* (—es, *pl.* —e) oath of allegiance.

Lehnsmann ['le:nsman], *m.* (—es, *pl.* ·er) feudal tenant, vassal.

Lehnstuhl ['le:nʃtu:l], *m.* (—s, *pl.* ·e) armchair, easy chair.

Lehramt ['le:ramt], *n.* (—es, *pl.* ·er) professorship; teaching post *or* profession.

Lehrbrief ['le:rbri:f], *m.* (—es, *pl.* —e) apprentice's indentures; certificate of apprenticeship.

Lehrbuch ['le:rbu:x], *n.* (—es, *pl.* ·er) textbook, manual.

Lehre ['le:rə], *f.* (—, *pl.* —n) teaching, advice, rule, doctrine, dogma, moral; (*craft*) apprenticeship.

lehren ['le:rən], *v.a.* teach, inform, instruct; profess.

Lehrer ['le:rər], *m.* (—s, *pl.* —) teacher, instructor, schoolmaster.

Lehrgang ['le:rgaŋ], *m.* (—es, *pl.* ·e) course (of instruction).

Lehrgegenstand ['le:rge:gənʃtant], *m.* (—es, *pl.* ·e) subject of instruction; branch of study.

Lehrgeld ['le:rgɛlt], *n.* (—es, *pl.* —er) premium for apprenticeship; — *zahlen,* (*fig.*) pay for o.'s experience.

Lehrkörper ['le:rkœrpər], *m.* (—s, *no pl.*) teaching staff; (*Univ.*) faculty.

Lehrling ['le:rlɪŋ], *m.* (—s, *pl.* —e) apprentice.

Lehrmädchen ['le:rmɛ:tçən], *n.* (—s, *pl.* —) girl apprentice.

Lehrmeister ['le:rmaɪstər], *m.* (—s, *pl.* —) teacher, instructor, master.

Lehrmittel ['le:rmɪtəl], *n.* (—s, *pl.* —) teaching appliance *or* aid.

lehrreich ['le:rraɪç], *adj.* instructive.

Lehrsatz ['le:rzats], *m.* (—es, *pl.* ·e) tenet, dogma, rule; (*Maths.*) theorem.

Lehrstuhl ['le:rʃtu:l], *m.* (—s, *pl.* ·e) (*Univ.*) chair; professorship.

Lehrzeit ['le:rtsaɪt], *f.* (—, *pl.* —en) apprenticeship.

Leib [laɪp], *m.* (—es, *pl.* —er) body; abdomen; womb.

Leibarzt ['laɪpa:rtst], *m.* (—es, *pl.* ·e) court surgeon.

Leibbinde ['laɪpbɪndə], f. (—, pl. —n) abdominal belt.

Leibchen ['laɪpçən], n. (—s, pl. —) bodice, corset; vest.

leibeigen [laɪp'aɪgən], adj. in bondage, in thraldom, in serfdom.

Leibeserbe ['laɪbəsɛrbə], m. (—n, pl. —n) heir, descendant, offspring; (pl.) issue.

Leibesfrucht ['laɪbəsfruxt], f. (—, pl. ⁼e) embryo, foetus.

Leibeskraft ['laɪbəskraft], f. (—, pl. ⁼e) bodily strength; aus —en, with might and main.

Leibesübung ['laɪbəsy:buŋ], f. (—, pl. —en) physical exercise; (pl.) gymnastic exercises.

Leibgericht ['laɪpgərɪçt], n. (—s, pl. —e) favourite dish.

leibhaftig [laɪp'haftɪç], adj. real, incarnate, in person.

leiblich ['laɪplɪç], adj. bodily, corporeal.

Leibrente ['laɪprɛntə], f. (—, pl. —n) life-annuity.

Leibschmerzen ['laɪpʃmɛrtsən], m. pl. stomach-ache.

Leibspeise ['laɪpʃpaɪzə], f. (—, pl. —n) favourite dish.

Leibwache ['laɪpvaxə], f. (—, no pl.) body-guard.

Leibwäsche ['laɪpvɛʃə], f. (—, no pl.) underwear.

Leiche ['laɪçə], f. (—, pl. —n) (dead) body, corpse; (dial.) funeral.

Leichenbegängnis ['laɪçənbəgɛŋnɪs], n. (—ses, pl. —se) funeral, burial, interment.

Leichenbeschauer ['laɪçənbəʃauər], m. (—s, pl. —) coroner.

Leichenbestatter ['laɪçənbəʃtater], m. (—s, pl. —) undertaker; (Am.) mortician.

leichenhaft ['laɪçenhaft], adj. corpselike, cadaverous.

Leichenschau ['laɪçənʃau], f. (—, no pl.) post mortem (examination), (coroner's) inquest.

Leichentuch ['laɪçəntu:x], n. (—es, pl. ⁼er) shroud, pall.

Leichenverbrennung ['laɪçənfɛrbrɛnuŋ], f. (—, pl. —en) cremation.

Leichenwagen ['laɪçənva:gən], m. (—s, pl. —) hearse.

Leichenzug ['laɪçəntsu:k], m. (—es, pl. ⁼e) funeral procession.

Leichnam ['laɪçna:m], m. (—s, pl. —e) (dead) body, corpse.

leicht [laɪçt], adj. light; slight; weak; easy.

leichtfertig ['laɪçtfɛrtɪç], adj. frivolous, irresponsible.

leichtgläubig ['laɪçtglɔybɪç], adj. credulous, gullible.

leichthin ['laɪçthɪn], adv. lightly.

Leichtigkeit ['laɪçtɪçkaɪt], f. (—, no pl.) ease, facility.

Leichtsinn ['laɪçtsɪn], m. (—s, no pl.) thoughtlessness, carelessness; frivolity.

Leid [laɪt], n. (—es, no pl.) sorrow, grief; harm, hurt; einem etwas zu —e tun, harm s.o.

leid [laɪt], adj. es tut mir —, I am sorry; du tust mir —, I am sorry for you.

Leiden ['laɪdən], n. (—s, pl. —) suffering, misfortune; (illness) affliction, complaint; das — Christi, the Passion.

leiden ['laɪdən], v.a., v.n. irr. suffer, bear, endure, undergo.

Leidenschaft ['laɪdənʃaft], f. (—, pl. —en) passion.

leider ['laɪdər], adv. unfortunately.

leidig ['laɪdɪç], adj. tiresome, unpleasant.

leidlich ['laɪtlɪç], adj. tolerable, moderate.

leidtragend ['laɪttra:gənt], adj. in mourning.

Leidtragende ['laɪttra:gəndə], m. or f. (—n, pl. —n) mourner.

Leidwesen ['laɪtve:zən], n. (—s, no pl.) zu meinem —, to my regret.

Leier ['laɪər], f. (—, pl. —n) lyre.

Leierkasten ['laɪərkastən], m. (—s, pl. ⁼) barrel organ.

leiern ['laɪərn], v.n. drone, drawl on.

leihen ['laɪən], v.a. irr. einem etwas —, lend s.o. s.th.; von einem etwas —, borrow s.th. from s.o.

Leim [laɪm], m. (—s, no pl.) glue; einem auf den — gehen, be taken in by s.o., fall for s.th.

Leimfarbe ['laɪmfarbə], f. (—, pl. —en) water-colour, distemper.

Lein [laɪn], m. (—s, pl. —e) linseed, flax.

Leine ['laɪnə], f. (—, pl. —n) line, cord.

Leinen ['laɪnən], n. (—s, no pl.) linen.

Leinöl ['laɪnø:l], n. (—s, no pl.) linseed oil.

Leintuch ['laɪntu:x], n. (—es, pl. ⁼er) linen sheet, sheeting.

Leinwand ['laɪnvant], f. (—, no pl.) linen, sheeting; (Art) canvas; (film) screen.

leise ['laɪzə], adj. low, soft, gentle, faint, slight; delicate.

Leiste ['laɪstə], f. (—, pl. —n) ledge, border; groin.

Leisten ['laɪstən], m. (—s, pl. —) (shoe) last, form.

leisten ['laɪstən], v.a. do, perform; accomplish; ich kann es mir nicht —, I cannot afford it.

Leistenbruch ['laɪstənbrux], m. (—es, pl. ⁼e) hernia, rupture.

Leistung ['laɪstuŋ], f. (—, pl. —en) performance, accomplishment, achievement.

leistungsfähig ['laɪstuŋksfɛ:ɪç], adj. efficient.

leiten ['laɪtən], v.a. lead, guide, manage; preside over.

Leiter (1) ['laɪtər], m. (—s, pl. —) leader, manager; conductor; head.

Leiter (2) ['laɪtər], f. (—, pl. —n) ladder.

Leiterwagen ['laɪtərva:gən], m. (—s, pl. —) rack-wagon; (Austr.) small hand-cart.

Leitfaden ['laɪtfa:dən], m. (—s, pl. ⁝) (book) manual, textbook, guide.

Leitstern ['laɪtʃtɛrn], m. (—s, pl. —e) pole-star; (fig.) lodestar, guiding star.

Leitung ['laɪtuŋ], f. (—, pl. —en) management, direction; (Elec.) lead, connection; line; (water- or gas-) main(s); pipeline; eine lange — haben, be slow in the uptake.

Leitungsvermögen ['laɪtuŋsfɛrmø:-gən], n. (—s, no pl.) conductivity.

Leitwerk ['laɪtvɛrk], n. (—s, no pl.) (Aviat.) tail unit.

Lektion [lɛkts'jo:n], f. (—, pl. —en) lesson; einem eine — geben, lecture s.o.

Lektor ['lɛktɔr], m. (—s, pl. —en) publisher's reader; teacher, lector.

Lektüre [lɛk'ty:rə], f. (—, pl. —n) reading matter, books.

Lende ['lɛndə], f. (—, pl. —n) (Anat.) loin.

lendenlahm ['lɛndənla:m], adj. weak-kneed, lame.

lenkbar ['lɛŋkba:r], adj. dirigible, manageable, tractable, governable.

lenken ['lɛŋkən], v.a. drive, steer; (fig.) direct, rule, manage.

Lenkstange ['lɛŋkʃtaŋə], f. (—, pl. —n) connecting-rod; (bicycle) handle-bar.

Lenz [lɛnts], m. (—es, pl. —e) (Poet.) spring.

Lepra ['le:pra], f. (—, no pl.) leprosy.

Lerche ['lɛrçə], f. (—, pl. —n) (Orn.) lark, skylark.

lernbegierig ['lɛrnbəgi:rɪç], adj. studious, eager to learn.

lernen ['lɛrnən], v.a. learn; study; einen kennen —, make s.o.'s acquaintance; auswendig —, learn by heart.

Lesart ['le:sa:rt], f. (—, pl. —en) reading, version.

lesbar ['le:sba:r], adj. legible; readable.

Lese ['le:zə], f. (—, pl. —n) gathering (of fruit); vintage.

lesen ['le:zən], v.a. irr. gather; glean; read; die Messe —, celebrate or say mass; über etwas —, (Univ.) lecture on s.th.

lesenswert ['le:zənsvɛrt], adj. worth reading.

Leser ['le:zər], m. (—s, pl. —) gatherer, gleaner; reader.

leserlich ['le:zərlɪç], adj. legible.

Lettland ['lɛtlant], n. Latvia.

letzen ['lɛtsən], v.a. (Poet.) comfort, cheer, refresh.

letzt [lɛtst], adj. last, extreme, ultimate, final.

letztens ['lɛtstəns], adv. lastly, in the end.

letztere ['lɛtstərə], adj. latter.

letzthin ['lɛtsthɪn], adv. (rare) lately, the other day, recently.

Leu [lɔy], m. (—en, pl. —en) (Poet.) lion.

Leuchte ['lɔyçtə], f. (—, pl. —n) light, lamp, lantern; (fig.) luminary, star.

leuchten ['lɔyçtən], v.n. light, shine.

leuchtend ['lɔyçtənt], adj. shining, bright; luminous.

Leuchter ['lɔyçtər], m. (—s, pl. —) candlestick, candelabrum.

Leuchtrakete ['lɔyçtrake:ta], f. (—, pl. —n) Roman candle; flare.

Leuchtturm ['lɔyçtturm], m. (—s, pl. ⁝e) lighthouse.

leugnen ['lɔygnən], v.a. deny, disclaim; nicht zu —, undeniable.

Leumund ['lɔymunt], m. (—es, no pl.) renown, reputation.

Leute ['lɔytə], pl. persons, people, men; servants, domestic staff.

Leutnant ['lɔytnant], m. (—s, pl. —s) lieutenant.

leutselig ['lɔytze:lɪç], adj. affable, friendly; condescending.

Levkoje [lɛf'ko:jə], f. (—, pl. —n) (Bot.) stock.

Lexikon ['lɛksɪkɔn], n. (—s, pl. —s, —ka) dictionary, lexicon, encyclopaedia.

Libanon ['li:banɔn], m. Lebanon.

Libelle [li'bɛlə], f. (—, pl. —n) (Ent.) dragonfly.

Liberia [li'be:rja], n. Liberia.

Libyen ['li:bɪən], n. Libya.

Licht [lɪçt], n. (—es, pl. —er) light, candle; luminary.

licht [lɪçt], adj. light, clear, open.

Lichtbild ['lɪçtbɪlt], n. (—es, pl. —er) photograph.

Lichtbrechung ['lɪçtbrɛçuŋ], f. (—, pl. —en) refraction of light.

lichten ['lɪçtən], v.a. clear, thin; den Anker —, weigh anchor.

lichterloh ['lɪçtərlo:], adj. blazing, ablaze.

Lichthof ['lɪçtho:f], m. (—s, pl. ⁝e) well of a court, quadrangle.

Lichtmeß ['lɪçtmɛs], f. (—, no pl.) (Eccl.) Candlemas.

Lichtschirm ['lɪçtʃɪrm], m. (—s, pl. —e) screen, lamp-shade.

Lichtspieltheater ['lɪçtʃpi:ltea:tər], n. (—s, pl. —) cinema.

Lichtung ['lɪçtuŋ], f. (—, pl. —en) glade, clearing.

Lid [li:t], n. (—s, pl. —er) eye-lid.

lieb [li:p], adj. dear; beloved; good; das ist mir —, I am glad of it; der —e Gott, God; unsere —e Frau, Our Lady; bei einem — Kind sein, be a favourite with s.o., curry favour with s.o.

liebäugeln ['li:pɔygəln], v.n. insep. ogle.

Liebchen ['li:pçən], n. (—s, pl. —) sweetheart, love, darling.

Liebe ['li:bə], f. (—, no pl.) love.

Liebelei [li:bə'laɪ], f. (—, pl. —en) flirtation.

lieben ['li:bən], v.a. love, like, be fond of.

liebenswürdig ['li:bənsvyrdɪç], adj. amiable, kind, charming.

lieber ['li:bər], adv. rather, better, sooner; etwas — tun, prefer to do s.th.

Liebhaber ['li:pha:bər], m. (—s, pl. —) lover; (fig.) amateur, dilettante; (Theat.) leading man.

Liebhaberin ['li:phabərɪn], f. leading lady.

141

liebkosen

liebkosen ['li:pko:zən], _v.a. insep._ fondle, caress.

lieblich ['li:plɪç], _adj._ lovely, charming, sweet.

Liebling ['li:plɪŋ], _m._ (—s, _pl._ —e) darling, favourite.

lieblos ['li:plo:s], _adj._ hard-hearted; unkind.

Liebreiz ['li:praɪts], _m._ (—es, _no pl._) charm, attractiveness.

liebreizend ['li:praɪtsənt], _adj._ charming.

Liebschaft ['li:pʃaft], _f._ (—, _pl._ —en) love affair.

Lied [li:t], _n._ (—es, _pl._ —er) song, air, tune; _geistliches_ —, hymn.

liederlich ['li:dərlɪç], _adj._ careless, slovenly; dissolute, debauched; —es _Leben_, profligacy.

Lieferant [li:fə'rant], _m._ (—en, _pl._ —en) supplier, purveyor, contractor; _Eingang für_ —en, tradesmen's entrance.

liefern ['li:fərn], _v.a._ deliver, furnish, supply.

Lieferschein ['li:fərʃaɪn], _m._ (—s, _pl._ —e) delivery note.

liegen ['li:gən], _v.n. irr._ lie; be situated; _es liegt mir daran_, it is of importance to me, I have it at heart; _es liegt mir nichts daran_, it is of no consequence to me.

Liegenschaft ['li:gənʃaft], _f._ (—, _pl._ —en) landed property, real estate.

Liga ['li:ga:], _f._ (—, _pl._ —gen) league.

Liguster [li'gustər], _m._ (—s, _no pl._) privet.

liieren [li'i:rən], _v.r._ (_aux._ haben) _sich — mit_, unite with, combine with.

Likör [li'kø:r], _m._ (—s, _pl._ —e) liqueur.

lila ['li:la:] _adj._ (_colour_) lilac.

Lilie ['li:ljə], _f._ (—, _pl._ —n) (_Bot._) lily.

Limonade [limo'na:də], _f._ (—, _pl._ —n) lemonade.

lind [lɪnt], _adj._ soft, gentle, mild.

Linde ['lɪndə], _f._ (—, _pl._ —n) (_Bot._) lime-tree, linden.

lindern ['lɪndərn], _v.a._ soften, assuage, mitigate, soothe, allay.

Lindwurm ['lɪntvurm], _m._ (—s, _pl._ —er) (_Poet._) dragon.

Lineal [line'a:l], _n._ (—s, _pl._ —e) ruler, rule.

Linie ['li:njə], _f._ (—, _pl._ —n) line; lineage, descent; _in erster_ —, in the first place.

Linienschiff ['li:njənʃɪf], _n._ (—es, _pl._ —e) (_Naut._) liner.

lin(i)ieren [lin'(j)i:rən], _v.a._ rule.

linkisch ['lɪŋkɪʃ], _adj._ awkward, clumsy.

links [lɪŋks], _adv._ to the left, on the left-hand side; _—um!_ left about turn!

Linnen ['lɪnən], _n._ (—s, _no pl._) (_Poet._) linen.

Linse ['lɪnzə], _f._ (—, _pl._ —n) (_vegetable_) lentil; (_optical_) lens.

linsenförmig ['lɪnzənfœrmɪç], _adj._ lens-shaped.

Linsengericht ['lɪnzəngərɪçt], _n._ (—s, _pl._ —e) (_Bibl._) mess of pottage.

Lippe ['lɪpə], _f._ (—, _pl._ —n) lip; (_coll._) _eine — riskieren_, be cheeky.

Lippenlaut ['lɪpənlaut], _m._ (—s, _pl._ —e) (_Phonet._) labial.

Lippenstift ['lɪpənʃtɪft], _m._ (—s, _pl._ —e) lipstick.

liquidieren [lɪkvi'di:rən], _v.a._ liquidate, wind up, settle; charge.

lispeln ['lɪspəln], _v.n._ lisp.

Lissabon [lɪsa'bɔn], _n._ Lisbon.

List [lɪst], _f._ (—, _pl._ —en) cunning, craft; trick, stratagem, ruse.

Liste ['lɪstə], _f._ (—, _pl._ —n) list, roll, catalogue.

listig ['lɪstɪç], _adj._ cunning, crafty, sly.

Listigkeit ['lɪstɪçkaɪt], _f._ (—, _no pl._) slyness, craftiness.

Litanei [lita'naɪ], _f._ (—, _pl._ —en) litany.

Litauen ['lɪtauən], _n._ Lithuania.

Liter ['li:tər], _m. & n._ (—s, _pl._ —) litre.

literarisch [lita'ra:rɪʃ], _adj._ literary.

Literatur [litəra'tu:r], _f._ (—, _pl._ —en) literature, letters.

Litfaßsäule ['lɪtfaszɔylə], _f._ (—, _pl._ —n) advertisement pillar.

Liturgie [litur'gi:], _f._ (—, _pl._ —n) liturgy.

Litze ['lɪtsə], _f._ (—, _pl._ —n) lace, braid, cord; (_Elec._) flex.

Livland ['li:flant], _n._ Livonia.

Livree [li'vre:], _f._ (—, _pl._ —n) livery.

Lizenz [li'tsɛnts], _f._ (—, _pl._ —en) licence.

Lob [lo:p], _n._ (—es, _no pl._) praise, commendation.

loben ['lo:bən], _v.a._ praise, commend.

lobesam ['lo:bəza:m], _adj._ (_Poet._) worthy, honourable.

Lobgesang ['lo:pgəzaŋ], _m._ (—s, _pl._ —e) hymn of praise.

Lobhudelei ['lo:phu:də'laɪ], _f._ (—, _pl._ —en) adulation, flattery, toadying.

löblich ['lø:plɪç], _adj._ laudable, commendable, meritorious.

lobpreisen ['lo:ppraɪzən], _v.a._ insep. eulogise, extol.

Lobrede ['lo:pre:də], _f._ (—, _pl._ —n) panegyric, eulogy.

Loch [lɔx], _n._ (—es, _pl._ —er) hole.

Lochbohrer ['lɔxbo:rər], _m._ (—s, _pl._—) auger.

lochen ['lɔxən], _v.a._ perforate, punch.

Locher ['lɔxər], _m._ (—s, _pl._ —) perforator, punch.

löcherig ['lœçərɪç], _adj._ full of holes.

Lochmeißel ['lɔxmaɪsəl], _m._ (—s, _pl._ —) mortice-chisel.

Locke ['lɔkə], _f._ (—, _pl._ —n) curl, lock, ringlet, tress.

locken ['lɔkən], _v.a._ allure, decoy, entice.

locker ['lɔkər], _adj._ loose; slack; spongy; dissolute; _nicht — lassen_, stick to o.'s guns.

lockern ['lɔkərn], _v.a._ loosen.

lockig ['lɔkɪç], _adj._ curled, curly.

Lockmittel ['lɔkmɪtəl], _n._ (—s, _pl._ —) inducement, lure, bait.

Lockspeise ['lɔkʃpaɪzə], _f._ (—, _pl._ —n) lure, bait.

Lockung ['lɔkuŋ], f. (—, pl. —en) allurement, enticement.

Lockvogel ['lɔkfo:gəl], m. (—s, pl. ∵) decoy-bird.

Loden ['lo:dən], m. (—s, pl. —) coarse cloth, frieze.

lodern ['lo:dərn], v.n. blaze, flame.

Löffel ['lœfəl], m. (—s, pl. —) spoon; (animal) ear; einen über den — barbieren, take s.o. in.

Logarithmus [loga'rItmus], m. (—, pl. —men) logarithm.

Logbuch ['lɔkbu:x], n. (—es, pl. ∵er) logbook.

Loge ['lo:ʒə], f. (—, pl. —n) (Theat.) box; (Freemasonry) lodge.

Logenschließer ['lo:ʒənʃli:sər], m. (—s, pl. —) (Theat.) attendant.

logieren [lo'ʒi:rən], v.n. board (with).

Logis [lo'ʒi:], n. (—, pl. —) lodgings.

logisch ['lo:gIʃ], adj. logical.

Lohe ['lo:hə], f. (—, pl. —n) tanning bark; flame.

Lohgerber ['lo:gɛrbər], m. (—s, pl. —) tanner.

Lohn [lo:n], m. (—s, pl. ∵e) wages, pay; reward; recompense.

lohnen ['lo:nən], v.a. reward, recompense, remunerate; pay wages to; es lohnt sich nicht, it is not worth while.

Lohnstopp ['lo:nʃtɔp], m. (—s, pl. —s) pay pause, wage freeze.

Löhnung ['lø:nuŋ], f. (—, pl. —en) pay, payment.

Lokal [lo'ka:l], n. (—s, pl —e) locality, premises; inn, pub, café.

lokalisieren [lokali'zi:rən], v.a. localise.

Lokalität [lokali'tɛ:t], f. (—, pl. —en) see Lokal.

Lokomotive [lokomo'ti:və], f. (—, pl. —n) (Railw.) locomotive, engine.

Lokomotivführer [lokomo'ti:ffy:rər], m. (—s, pl. —) (Railw.) engine-driver.

Lombard [lɔm'bart], m. (—s, pl. —e) deposit-bank, loan bank.

Lombardei [lɔmbar'daɪ], f. Lombardy.

Lorbeer ['lɔrbe:r], m. (—s, pl. —en) laurel.

Lorbeerbaum ['lɔrbe:rbaum], m. (—s, pl. ∵e) laurel-tree, bay-tree.

Lorbeerspiritus ['lɔrbe:rʃpi:ritus], m. (—, no pl.) bay rum.

Lorgnon [lɔrn'jɔ̃], n. (—s, pl. —s) monocle, eye-glass.

Los [lo:s], n. (—es, pl. —e) share, ticket; lot, fate; das große —, first prize.

los [lo:s], adj. loose, untied; free from, released from, rid of; (Am.) quit of; was ist los? what is going on? what's the matter? etwas — werden, get rid of s.th.; schieß los! fire away!

lösbar ['lø:sba:r], adj. (question, riddle) soluble.

losbinden ['lo:sbIndən], v.a. irr. untie, unbind, loose.

losbrechen ['lo:sbrɛçən], v.a. irr. break off. — v.n. (aux. sein) break loose.

Löschblatt ['lœʃblat], n. (—es, pl. ∵er) blotting-paper.

Löscheimer ['lœʃaɪmər], m. (—s, pl. —) fire-bucket.

löschen ['lœʃən], v.a. put out; extinguish; (debt) cancel; (writing) efface, blot; (freight) (Naut.) unload; (thirst) quench.

Löschpapier ['lœʃpapi:r], n. (—s, no pl.) blotting-paper.

Löschung ['lœʃuŋ], f. (—, pl. —en) (freight) (Naut.) discharging, landing, unloading.

losdrücken ['lo:sdrykən], v.n. discharge, fire.

lose ['lo:zə], adj. loose, slack; (fig.) dissolute; —s Maul, malicious tongue.

Lösegeld ['lø:zəgɛlt], n. (—es, pl. —er) ransom.

losen ['lo:zən], v.n. draw lots.

lösen ['lø:zən], v.a. loosen, untie; absolve, free, deliver; dissolve; solve; (relations) break off; (tickets) take, buy.

losgehen ['lo:sge:ən], v.n. irr. (aux. sein) begin; (gun) go off; auf einen —, go for s.o.; jetzt kann's —, now for it.

loskaufen ['lo:skaufən], v.a. redeem, ransom.

loskommen ['lo:skɔmən], v.n. irr. (aux. sein) come loose; von etwas —, get rid of s.th.

löslich ['lø:slIç], adj. (Chem.) soluble.

loslösen ['lo:slø:zən], v.a. detach.

losmachen ['lo:smaxən], v.a. free from. — v.r. sich — von, disengage o.s. from.

losreißen ['lo:sraɪsən], v.a. irr. pull away, separate. — v.n. (aux. sein), break loose. — v.r. sich — von, tear o.s. away from.

lossagen ['lo:sza:gən], v.r. sich — von, renounce s.th., dissociate o.s. from s.th.

losschlagen ['lo:sʃla:gen], v.a. knock loose; let fly; (fig.) sell, dispose of.

lossprechen ['lo:sʃprɛçən], v.a. irr. (Eccl.) absolve; (Law) acquit.

lossteuern ['lo:sʃtɔyərn], v.n. — auf, make for.

Losung ['lo:zuŋ], f. (—, pl. —en) watchword, motto, password, slogan.

Lösung ['lø:zuŋ], f. (—, pl. —en) loosening; solution.

losziehen ['lo:stsi:ən], v.n. irr. (Mil.) set out; gegen einen —, inveigh against s.o.; (fig., coll.) run s.o. down.

Lot [lo:t], n. (—s, pl. —e) lead, plummet; (weight) half an ounce; (Maths.) perpendicular (line).

Löteisen ['lø:taɪzən], n. (—s, pl. —) soldering iron.

loten ['lo:tən], v.a., v.n. (Naut.) take soundings, plumb.

löten ['lø:tən], v.a. solder.

Lothringen ['lo:trIŋən], n. Lorraine.

Lötkolben ['lø:tkɔlbən], m. (—s, pl. —) soldering iron.

Lotleine ['lo:tlaɪnə], f. (—, pl. —n) sounding-line.

Lotrechtstarter ['lo:trɛçtʃtartər], m. (—s, pl. —) (Aviat.) vertical take-off plane (V.T.O.L.).

Lötrohr

Lötrohr ['lø:tro:r], *n.* (—s, *pl.* —e) soldering-pipe.

Lotse ['lo:tsə], *m.* (—n, *pl.* —n) (*Naut.*) pilot.

Lotterbett ['lɔtərbɛt], *n.* (—es, *pl.*—en) bed of idleness; (*obs.*) couch.

Lotterie [lɔtə'ri:], *f.* (—, *pl.* —n) lottery, sweep-stake.

Lotterleben ['lɔtərle:bən], *n.* (—s, *no pl.*) dissolute life.

Löwe ['lø:və], *m.*(—n,*pl.*—n)(*Zool.*)lion.

Löwenbändiger ['lø:vənbɛndigər], *m.* (—s, *pl.*—) lion tamer.

Löwengrube ['lø:vəngru:bə], *f.* (—, *pl.* —n) lion's den.

Löwenmaul ['lø:vənmaul], *n.* (—s, *no pl.*) (*Bot.*) snapdragon.

Löwenzahn ['lø:vəntsa:n], *m.* (—s, *no pl.*) (*Bot.*) dandelion.

Löwin ['lø:vɪn], · *f.* (—, *pl.* —nen) (*Zool.*) lioness.

Luchs [luks], *m.* (—es, *pl.* —e) lynx.

Lücke ['lykə], *f.* (—, *pl.* —n) gap, breach; (*fig.*) omission, defect, blank.

Lückenbüßer ['lykənby:sər], *m.* (—s, *pl.* —) stop-gap, stand-in.

lückenhaft ['lykənhaft], *adj.* fragmentary, incomplete, imperfect.

Luder ['lu:dər], *n.* (—s, *pl.* —) (*rare*) carrion; (*vulg.*) beast, trollop; *dummes* —, silly ass, fathead.

Luderleben ['lu:dərle:bən], *n.* (—s, *no pl.*) dissolute life.

ludern ['lu:dərn], *v.n.* lead a dissolute life.

Luft [luft], *f.* (—, *pl.* ·'e) air.

Luftbrücke ['luftbrykə], *f.* (—, *no pl.*) air-lift.

Lüftchen ['lyftçən], *n.* (—s, *pl.* —) gentle breeze.

luftdicht ['luftdɪçt], *adj.* airtight.

Luftdruck ['luftdruk], *m.* (—s, *no pl.*) air pressure, atmospheric pressure; blast.

Luftdruckmesser ['luftdrukmɛsər], *m.* (—s, *pl.* —) barometer, pressure-gauge.

lüften ['lyftən], *v.a.* air, ventilate.

luftförmig ['luftfœrmɪç], *adj.* gaseous.

luftig ['luftɪç], *adj.* airy, windy.

Luftklappe ['luftklapə], *f.* (—, *pl.* —n) air-valve.

Luftkurort ['luftku:rɔrt], *m.* (—s, *pl.* —e) health resort.

Luftlinie ['luftli:njə], *f.* (—,*pl.*—n)bee-line; *in der* —, as the crow flies; (*Aviat.*) airline.

Luftloch ['luftlɔx], *m.* (—s, *pl.* ·'er) air-pocket.

Luftraum ['luftraum], *m.* (—s, *no pl.*) atmosphere; air space.

Luftröhre ['luftrø:rə], *f.* (—, *pl.* —n) windpipe.

Luftschiff ['luftʃɪf], *n.* (—es, *pl.* —e) air-ship.

Luftschiffahrt ['luftʃifa:rt], *f.* (—, *no pl.*) aeronautics.

Luftspiegelung ['luftʃpi:gəluŋ], *f.* (—, *pl.* —en) mirage.

Luftsprung ['luftʃpruŋ], *m.* (—s, *pl.* ·'e) caper, gambol; ·'e *machen*, caper, gambol.

Lüftung ['lyftuŋ], *f.* (—, *no pl.*) airing, ventilation.

Lug [lu:k], *m.* (—s, *no pl.*) (*obs.*) lie; — *und Trug*, a pack of lies.

Lüge ['ly:gə], *f.* (—, *pl.* —n) lie, falsehood, fib; *einen — strafen*, give s.o. the lie.

lügen ['ly:gən], *v.n. irr.* lie, tell a lie.

lügenhaft ['ly:gənhaft], *adj.* lying, false, untrue.

Lügner ['ly:gnər], *m.* (—s, *pl.* —) liar.

Luke ['lu:kə], *f.* (—, *pl.* —n) dormer-window; (*ship*) hatch.

Lümmel ['lyməl], *m.* (—s, *pl.* —) lout; hooligan.

Lump ['lump], *m.* (—s, *pl.* —en, *pl.* —e,· —en) scoundrel, blackguard.

Lumpen ['lumpən], *m.* (—s, *pl.* —) rag, tatter.

Lumpengesindel ['lumpəngəzɪndəl], *n.* (—s, *no pl.*) rabble, riffraff.

Lumpenpack ['lumpənpak], *n.* (—s, *no pl.*) rabble, riffraff.

Lumpensammler ['lumpənzamlər], *m.* (—s, *pl.* —) rag-and-bone-man.

Lumperei [lumpə'rai], *f.* (—, *pl.* —en) shabby trick; meanness; trifle.

lumpig ['lumpɪç], *adj.* ragged; (*fig.*) shabby, mean.

Lunge ['luŋə], *f.* (—, *pl.* —n) (*human*) lung; (*animals*) lights.

Lungenentzündung ['luŋənɛntsynduŋ], *f.* (—, *pl.* —en) pneumonia.

Lungenkrankheit ['luŋənkraŋkhait], *f.* (—, *pl.* —en) pulmonary disease.

Lungenkraut ['luŋənkraut], *n.* (—s, *pl.* ·'er) lungwort.

Lungenschwindsucht ['luŋənʃvɪntzuxt], *f.* (—, *no pl.*) pulmonary consumption, tuberculosis.

lungern ['luŋərn], *v.n.* idle, loiter.

Lunte ['luntə], *n.*, *pl.* —n) fuse, slow-match; — *riechen*, smell a rat.

Lupe ['lu:pə], *f.* (—, *pl.* —n) magnifying glass, lens; *etwas durch die — besehen*, examine s.th. closely, scrutinise s.th.; *unter die — nehmen*, examine closely.

lüpfen ['lypfən], *v.a.* lift.

Lupine [lu'pi:nə], *f.* (—, *pl.* —n) (*Bot.*) lupin.

Lust [lust], *f.* (—, *pl.* ·'e) enjoyment, pleasure, delight; desire, wish, inclination, liking; — *bekommen zu*, feel inclined to; — *haben auf*, have a mind to, feel like; *nicht übel — haben*, have half a mind to.

Lustbarkeit ['lustba:rkait], *f.* (—, *pl.* —en) amusement, diversion, entertainment, pleasure.

Lustdirne ['lustdɪrnə], *f.* (—, *pl.* —n) prostitute.

lüstern ['lystərn], *adj.* lustful, lascivious.

lustig ['lustɪç], *adj.* gay, merry, cheerful, amusing, funny; — *sein*, make merry; *sich über einen — machen*, poke fun at s.o.

Lüstling ['lystlɪŋ], *m.* (—s, *pl.* —e) libertine, lecher.

Lustmord ['lustmɔrt], *m.* (—es, *pl.* —e) sex murder.

Lustreise ['lustraɪzə], *f.* (—, *pl.* —n) pleasure trip.

Lustschloß ['lustʃlɔs], *n.* (—sses, *pl.* ⁻sser) country house, country seat.

Lustspiel ['lustʃpi:l], *n.* (—s, *pl.* —e) comedy.

lustwandeln ['lustvandəln], *v.n. insep.* (*aux.* sein) stroll, promenade.

Lutherisch ['lutərɪʃ], *adj.* Lutheran.

lutschen ['lutʃən], *v.a.* suck.

Lüttich ['lytɪç], *n.* Liège.

Luxus ['luksus], *m.* (—, *no pl.*) luxury.

Luzern [lu'tsɛrn], *n.* Lucerne.

Luzerne [lu'sɛrnə], *f.* (—, *pl.* —n) (*Bot.*) lucerne.

Lymphe ['lymfə], *f.* (—, *pl.* —n) lymph.

lynchen ['lynçən], *v.a.* lynch.

Lyrik ['ly:rɪk], *f.* (—, *no pl.*) lyric poetry.

lyrisch ['ly:rɪʃ], *adj.* lyric(al).

Lyzeum [ly'tse:um], *n.* (—s, *pl.* **Lyzeen**) lyceum, grammar school *or* high school for girls.

M

M [ɛm], *n.* (—s, *pl.* —s) the letter M.

Maas [ma:s], *f.* River Meuse.

Maat [ma:t], *m.* (—s, *pl.* —s, —en) (*Naut.*) mate.

Mache ['maxə], *f.* (—, *no pl.*) put-up job, humbug, sham, eyewash.

machen ['maxən], *v.a.* make, do, produce, manufacture; cause; amount to; *mach schon*, be quick; *das macht nichts*, it does not matter; *mach's kurz*, cut it short; *etwas — lassen*, have s.th. made; *sich auf den Weg —*, set off; *sich viel (wenig) aus etwas —*, care much (little) for s.th.; *mach, daß du fortkommst!* get out! scram!

Macherlohn ['maxərlo:n], *m.* (—es, *pl.* ⁻e) charge for making s.th.

Macht [maxt], *f.* (—, *pl.* ⁻e) might, power; force, strength; authority; *mit aller —*, with might and main.

Machtbefugnis ['maxtbəfu:knɪs], *f.* (—, *pl.* —se) competence.

Machtgebot ['maxtgəbo:t], *n.* (—s, *pl.* —e) authoritative order.

Machthaber ['maxtha:bər], *m.* (—s, *pl.* —) potentate, ruler.

mächtig ['mɛçtɪç], *adj.* mighty, powerful; *einer Sache — sein*, to have mastered s.th.

machtlos ['maxtlo:s], *adj.* powerless.

Machtspruch ['maxtʃprux], *m.* (—s, *pl.* ⁻e) authoritative dictum; command; decree.

Machtvollkommenheit ['maxtfɔlkəmənhaɪt], *f.* (—, *pl.* —en) absolute power; sovereignty; *aus eigner —*, of o.'s own authority.

Machtwort ['maxtvɔrt], *n.* (—es, *pl.* —e) word of command, fiat; *ein — sprechen*, bring o.'s authority to bear, speak with authority.

Machwerk ['maxvɛrk], *n.* (—s, *pl.* —e) shoddy product; bad job; concoction; (*story*) pot-boiler.

Madagaskar [mada'gaskar], *n.* Madagascar.

Mädchen ['mɛ:tçən], *n.* (—s, *pl.* —) girl; (*servant*) maid; *— für alles*, maid-of-all-work.

mädchenhaft ['mɛ:tçənhaft], *adj.* girlish, maidenly.

Mädchenhandel ['mɛ:tçənhandəl], *m.* (—s, *no pl.*) white slave trade.

Made ['ma:də], *f.* (—, *pl.* —n) maggot, mite.

Mädel ['mɛ:dəl], *n.* (—s, *pl.* —) (*coll.*) see **Mädchen**.

madig ['ma:dɪç], *adj.* maggoty.

Magazin [maga'tsi:n], *n.* (—s, *pl.* —e) warehouse, storehouse; journal.

Magd [ma:kt], *f.* (—, *pl.* ⁻e) maid, maidservant; (*Poet.*) maiden.

Magen ['ma:gən], *m.* (—s, *pl.* —) (*human*) stomach; (*animals*) maw.

Magengrube ['ma:gəngru:bə], *f.* (—, *pl.* —n) pit of the stomach.

Magensaft ['ma:gənzaft], *m.* (—es, *pl.* ⁻e) gastric juice.

mager ['ma:gər], *adj.* lean, thin, slender, slim; (*fig.*) meagre.

Magerkeit ['ma:gərkaɪt], *f.* (—, *no pl.*) leanness, thinness, slenderness.

Magie [ma'gi:], *f.* (—, *no pl.*) magic.

Magier ['ma:gjər], *m.* (—s, *pl.* —) magician.

Magister [ma'gɪstər], *m.* (—s, *pl.* —) schoolmaster; (*Univ.*) Master; *— der freien Künste*, Master of Arts.

Magistrat [magɪs'tra:t], *m.* (—s, *pl.* —e) municipal board, local authority.

magnetisch [mag'ne:tɪʃ], *adj.* magnetic.

magnetisieren [magneti'zi:rən], *v.a.* magnetise.

Magnetismus [magne'tɪsmus], *m.* (—, *pl.* —men) magnetism; (*person*) mesmerism; *Lehre vom —*, magnetics.

Magnifizenz [magnifi'tsɛnts], *f.* (—, *pl.* —en) magnificence; *seine —*, (*Univ.*) title of Vice-Chancellor.

Mahagoni [maha'go:ni], *n.* (—s, *no pl.*) mahogany.

Mahd [ma:t], *f.* (—, *pl.* —en) mowing.

mähen ['mɛ:ən], *v.a.* mow.

Mäher ['mɛ:ər], *m.* (—s, *pl.* —) mower.

Mahl [ma:l], *n.* (—s, *pl.* —e, ⁻er) meal, repast.

mahlen ['ma:lən], *v.a.* grind.

Mahlstrom ['ma:lʃtro:m], *m.* (—s, *no pl.*) maelstrom, whirlpool, eddy.

Mahlzahn ['ma:ltsa:n], *m.* (—s, *pl.* ⁻e) molar, grinder.

145

Mahlzeit ['ma:ltsaɪt], f. (—, pl. —en) meal, repast.

Mähmaschine ['mɛ:maʃi:nə], f. (—, pl. —n) reaping-machine; lawn-mower.

Mähne ['mɛ:nən], f. (—, pl. —n) mane.

mahnen ['ma:nən], v.a. remind, admonish, warn; (debtor) demand payment, dun.

Mähre ['mɛ:rə], f. (—, pl. —n) mare.

Mähren ['mɛ:rən], n. Moravia.

Mai [maɪ], m. (—s, pl. —e) May.

Maid [maɪt], f. (—, no pl.) (Poet.) maiden.

Maiglöckchen ['maɪɡlœkçən], n. (—s, pl. —) (Bot.) lily of the valley.

Maikäfer ['maɪkɛ:fər], m. (—s, pl. —) (Ent.) cockchafer.

Mailand ['maɪlant], n. Milan.

Mais [maɪs], m. (—es, no pl.) (Bot.) maize, Indian corn.

Majestät [majɛs'tɛ:t], f. (—, pl. —en) majesty.

majestätisch [majɛs'tɛ:tiʃ], adj. majestic.

Major [ma'jo:r], m. (—s, pl. —e) (Mil.) major.

Majoran [majo'ra:n], m. (—s, no pl.) (Bot.) marjoram.

Majorat [majo'ra:t], n. (—s, pl. —e) primogeniture; entail.

majorenn [majo'rɛn], adj. (obs.) of age, over twenty-one.

Majorität [majori'tɛ:t], f. (—, pl. —en) majority.

Makel ['ma:kəl], m. (—s, pl. —) spot, blot; (fig.) blemish, flaw, defect.

Mäkelei [mɛ:kə'laɪ], f. (—, pl. —en) fault-finding, carping; fastidiousness.

makellos ['ma:kəllo:s], adj. spotless, immaculate.

mäkeln ['mɛ:kəln], v.n. find fault (with), cavil (at).

Makkabäer [maka'bɛ:ər], m. Maccabee.

Makler ['ma:klər], m. (—s, pl. —) broker.

Mäkler ['mɛ:klər], m. (—s, pl. —) fault-finder, caviller.

Maklergebühr ['ma:klərɡəby:r], f. (—, pl. —en) brokerage.

Makrele [ma'kre:lə], f. (—, pl. —n) (Zool.) mackerel.

Makrone [ma'kro:nə], f. (—, pl. —n) macaroon.

Makulatur [makula'tu:r], f. (—, no pl.) waste paper.

Mal [ma:l], n. (—s, pl. —e) mark, sign, token; monument; mole, birth-mark; stain; time; dieses —, this time, this once; manches —, sometimes; mehrere —e, several times; mit einem —, all of a sudden.

mal [ma:l], adv. & part. once; noch—, once more; (coll.) hör —, I say.

Malaya [ma'laɪa], n. Malaya.

malen ['ma:lən], v.a. paint.

Maler ['ma:lər], m. (—s, pl. —) painter.

Malerei [ma:lə'raɪ], f. (—, pl. —en) painting; picture.

malerisch ['ma:lərɪʃ], adj. picturesque.

Malerleinwand ['ma:lərlaɪnvant], f. (—, no pl.) canvas.

Malheur [ma'lø:r], n. (—s, pl. —e) misfortune, mishap.

Mali [ma:li] n. Mali.

maliziös [mali'tsjø:s], adj. malicious.

Malkasten ['ma:lkastən], m. (—s, pl. ⁚) paint-box.

Malstein ['ma:lʃtaɪn], m. (—s, pl. —e) monument; boundary stone.

Malstock ['ma:lʃtɔk], m. (—s, pl. ⁚e) maulstick, mahlstick.

Malteserorden [mal'te:zərɔrdən], m. (—s, no pl.) Order of the Knights of Malta.

malträtieren [maltrɛ'ti:rən], v.a. illtreat.

Malve ['malvə], f. (—, pl. —n) (Bot.) mallow.

Malz [malts], n. (—es, no pl.) malt; an ihm ist Hopfen und — verloren, he is hopeless.

Malzbonbon ['maltsbɔbɔ], m. (—s, pl. —s) cough-lozenge, malt drop.

Mälzer ['mɛltsər], m. (—s, pl. —) maltster.

Mama [ma'ma:], f. (—, pl. —s) (fam.) mummy, mum, (Am.) ma.

Mammon ['mamɔn], m. (—s, no pl.) mammon; schnöder —, filthy lucre.

Mammut ['mamut], n. (—s, pl. —e) mammoth.

Mamsell [mam'zɛl], f. (—, pl. —en) housekeeper.

man [man], indef. pron. one, they, people, men; — sagt, they say.

manch [manç], pron. (—er, —e, —es) many a, some, several.

mancherlei [mançər'laɪ], adj. several; of several kinds.

Manchester [man'çɛstər], m. (—s, no pl.) corduroy.

manchmal ['mançma:l], adv. sometimes.

Mandant [man'dant], m. (—en, pl. —en) client.

Mandantin [man'dantin], f. (—, pl. —innen) female client.

Mandarine [manda'ri:nə], f. (—, pl. —n) mandarin (orange), tangerine.

Mandat [man'da:t], n. (—s, pl. —e) mandate.

Mandel ['mandəl], f. (—, pl. —n) almond; (Anat.) tonsil; (quantity) fifteen; eine — Eier, fifteen eggs.

Mandoline [mando'li:nə], f. (—, pl. —n) mandolin.

Mangan [maŋ'ga:n], n. (—s, no pl.) (Chem.) manganese.

Mangel (1) ['maŋəl], f. (—, pl. —n) mangle, wringer.

Mangel (2) ['maŋəl], m. (—s, pl. ⁚) deficiency, defect; blemish; lack, shortage, want; aus — an, for want of; — haben an, be short of, lack (s.th.).

mangelhaft ['maŋəlhaft], adj. defective, imperfect.

mangeln (1) ['maŋəln], v.a. (laundry) mangle.

146

mangeln (2) ['maŋəln], *v.n.* be in want of, be short of; *es —t uns an . . .*, we lack . . . .

mangels ['maŋəls], *prep.* (*Genit.*) for lack of, for want of.

Mangold ['maŋɔlt], *m.* (**—s**, *no pl.*) (*Bot.*) beet, mangel-wurzel.

Manie [ma'ni:], *f.* (**—**, *pl.* **—n**) mania, craze.

Manier [ma'ni:r], *f.* (**—**, *pl.* **—en**) manner, habit; *gute —en · haben*, have good manners.

manieriert [mani'ri:rt], *adj.* affected; (*Art*) mannered.

manierlich [ma'ni:rlɪç], *adj.* well behaved, civil, polite.

manipulieren [manipu'li:rən], *v.a.* manipulate.

Manko ['maŋko:], *n.* (**—s**, *pl.* **—s**) deficit, deficiency.

Mann [man], *m.* (**—(e)s**, *pl.* ˙˙er, (*Poet.*) **—en**) man; husband; *etwas an den — bringen*, get s.th. off o.'s hands, dispose of s.th.; *seinen — stellen*, hold o.'s own; *bis auf den letzten —*, to a man.

Mannbarkeit ['manba:rkaɪt], *f.* (**—**, *no pl.*) puberty; marriageable age.

Männchen ['mɛnçən], *n.* (**—s**, *pl.* **—**) little man, manikin; (*Zool.*) male; *mein —*, (*coll.*) my hubby; *— machen*, (*dogs*) sit on the hindlegs, beg.

mannhaft ['manhaft], *adj.* manly, stout, valiant.

mannigfaltig ['manɪçfaltɪç], *adj.* manifold, multifarious.

männlich ['mɛnlɪç], *adj.* male; (*fig.*) manly; (*Gram.*) masculine.

Mannsbild ['mansbɪlt], *n.* (**—es**, *pl.* **—er**) (*coll.*) man, male person.

Mannschaft ['manʃaft], *f.* (**—**, *pl.* **—en**) men; crew, team.

mannstoll ['manstɔl], *adj.* man-mad.

Mannszucht ['manstsuxt], *f.* (**—**, *no pl.*) discipline.

Manöver [ma'nøːvər], *n.* (**—s**, *pl.* **—**) manoeuvre.

manövrieren [manø'vri:rən], *v.a.* manoeuvre.

Mansarde [man'zardə], *f.* (**—**, *pl.* **—n**) garret, attic.

manschen ['manʃən], *v.a.*, *v.n.* dabble; splash (about).

Manschette [man'ʃɛtə], *f.* (**—**, *pl.* **—n**) cuff.

Mantel ['mantəl], *m.* (**—s**, *pl.* ˙˙) cloak, overcoat, coat, mantle, wrap; *den — nach dem Winde hängen*, be a timeserver.

Manufaktur [manufak'tu:r], *f.* (**—**, *pl.* **—en**) manufacture.

Mappe ['mapə], *f.* (**—**, *pl.* **—n**) portfolio, case, file.

Mär [mɛ:r], *f.* (**—**, *pl.* **—en**) (*Poet.*) tale, tidings, legend.

Märchen ['mɛ:rçən], *n.* (**—s**, *pl.* **—**) fairy-tale, fable; fib.

märchenhaft ['mɛ:rçənhaft], *adj.* fabulous, legendary; (*coll.*) marvellous.

Marder ['mardər], *m.* (**—s**, *pl.* **—**) (*Zool.*) marten.

Maria [ma'ri:a], *f.* Mary; *die Jungfrau —*, the Virgin Mary.

Marienbild [ma'ri:ənbɪlt], *n.* (**—es**, *pl.* **—er**) image of the Virgin Mary.

Marienblume [ma'ri:ənblu:mə], *f.* (**—**, *pl.* **—n**) (*Bot.*) daisy.

Marienglas [ma'ri:ənglas], *n.* (**—es**, *no pl.*) mica.

Marienkäfer [ma'ri:ənkɛ:fər], *m.* (**—s**, *pl.* **—**) (*Ent.*) lady-bird.

Marine [ma'ri:nə], *f.* (**—**, *pl.* **—n**) navy.

marinieren [mari'ni:rən], *v.a.* pickle.

Marionette [mario'nɛtə], *f.* (**—**, *pl.* **—n**) puppet, marionette.

Mark (1) [mark], *n.* (**—s**, *no pl.*) (*bone*) marrow; (*fruit*) pith, pulp.

Mark (2) [mark], *f.* (**—**, *pl.* **—en**) boundary, frontier province.

Mark (3) [mark], *f.* (**—**, *pl.* **—**) (*coin*) mark.

markant [mar'kant], *adj.* striking, prominent; (*remark*) pithy.

Marke ['markə], *f.* (**—**, *pl.* **—n**) (*trade*) mark, brand; (*postage*) stamp; (*game*) counter.

markieren [mar'ki:rən], *v.a.* mark.

markig ['markɪç], *adj.* marrowlike; (*fig.*) pithy, strong.

Markise [mar'ki:zə], *f.* (**—**, *pl.* **—n**) (sun)blind, awning.

Markt [markt], *m.* (**—es**, *pl.* ˙˙e) market, market-square, fair.

Marktflecken ['marktflɛkən], *m.* (**—s**, *pl.* **—**) borough; (small) market town.

Marktschreier ['marktʃraɪər], *m.* (**—s**, *pl.* **—**) cheap-jack, quack, charlatan.

Markus ['markus], *m.* Mark.

Marmel ['marməl], *f.* (**—**, *pl.* **—n**) (*obs.*) marble.

Marmelade [marmə'la:də], *f.* (**—**, *pl.* **—n**) marmalade, jam.

Marmor ['marmɔr], *m.* (**—s**, *no pl.*) marble.

Marokko [ma'rɔko], *n.* Morocco.

Marone [ma'ro:nə], *f.* (**—**, *pl.* **—n**) sweet chestnut.

Maroquin [maro'kɛ̃], *n.* (**—s**, *no pl.*) Morocco leather.

Marotte [ma'rɔtə], *f.* (**—**, *pl.* **—n**) whim; fad.

Marquise [mar'ki:zə], *f.* (**—**, *pl.* **—n**) marchioness.

Marsch (1) [marʃ], *m.* (**—es**, *pl.* ˙˙e) march; *sich in — setzen*, set out; march off.

Marsch (2) [marʃ], *f.* (**—**, *pl.* **—en**) fen, marsh.

marsch! [marʃ], *int.* march! be off! get out!

Marschboden ['marʃbo:dən], *m.* (**—s**, *no pl.*) marshy soil, marshland.

marschieren [mar'ʃi:rən], *v.n.* (*aux.* sein) march.

Marstall ['marʃtal], *m.* (**—s**, *pl.* ˙˙e) royal stud.

Marter ['martər], *f.* (**—**, *pl.* **—n**) torture, torment.

martern

martern ['martərn], *v.a.* torture, torment.

Märtyrer ['mɛrtyrər], *m.* (—s, *pl.* —) martyr.

Martyrium [mar'ty:rjum], *n.* (—s, *pl.* —rien) martyrdom.

März [mɛrts], *m.* (—es, *pl.* —e) (*month*) March.

Masche ['maʃə], *f.* (—, *pl.* —n) mesh; (*knitting*) stitch; (*dial.*) bow tie; (*coll.*) racket.

Maschine [ma'ʃi:nə], *f.* (—, *pl.* —n) machine; engine; *mit der — geschrieben,* typewritten.

Maschinengarn [ma'ʃi:nəngarn], *n.* (—s, *no pl.*) twist.

Maschinerie [maʃinə'ri:], *f.* (—, *pl.* —en) machinery.

Maser ['ma:zər], *f.* (—, *pl.* —n) (*wood*) vein, streak.

Masern ['ma:zərn], *f. pl.* measles.

Maske ['maskə], *f.* (—, *pl.* —n) mask, visor.

Maskerade [maskə'ra:də], *f.* (—, *pl.* —n) masquerade.

maskieren [mas'ki:rən], *v.a.* mask. — *v.r. sich —,* put on a mask.

Maß (1) [ma:s], *n.* (—es, *pl.* —e) measure, size; moderation, propriety; degree, extent; proportion; — *halten,* be moderate; *einem — nehmen,* measure s.o. (for); *in starkem —,* to a high degree; *mit —,* in moderation; *nach —,* to measure; *ohne — und Ziel,* immoderately, with no holds barred; *über alle —en,* exceedingly.

Maß (2) [ma:s], *m. & f.* (—, *pl.* —e) (*drink*) quart.

massakrieren [masa'kri:rən], *v.a.* massacre, slaughter.

Maßarbeit ['ma:sarbaɪt], *f.* (—, *pl.* —en) (*work*) made to measure; bespoke tailoring.

Masse ['masə], *f.* (—, *pl.* —n) mass, bulk; multitude; *eine —,* a lot.

Maßeinheit ['ma:saɪnhaɪt], *f.* (—, *pl.* —n) measuring-unit.

massenhaft ['masənhaft], *adj.* abundant.

Maßgabe ['ma:sga:bə], *f.* (—, *pl.* —n) *nach —,* according to, in proportion to.

maßgebend ['ma:sge:bənt], *adj.* standard; (*fig.*) authoritative.

massieren [ma'si:rən], *v.a.* massage.

mäßig ['mɛ:sɪç], *adj.* moderate, temperate, frugal.

Mäßigkeit ['mɛ:sɪçkaɪt], *f.* (—, *no pl.*) moderation, temperance, frugality.

Mäßigung ['mɛ:sɪguŋ], *f.* (—, *no pl.*) moderation.

Massiv [ma'si:f], *n.* (—s, *pl.* —e) (*mountains*) massif, range.

Maßliebchen ['ma:sli:pçən], *n.* (—s, *pl.* —) (*Bot.*) daisy.

maßlos ['ma:slo:s], *adj.* immoderate; (*fig.*) extravagant.

Maßnahme ['ma:sna:mə], *f.* (—, *pl.* —n) measure; *—n ergreifen,* take steps.

Maßregel ['ma:sre:gəl], *f.* (—, *pl.* —n) measure.

maßregeln ['ma:sre:gəln], *v.a.* reprove, reprimand.

Maßstab ['ma:sʃta:p], *m.* (—es, *pl.* ⁻e) standard; (*maps*) scale; *in kleinem (großem) —,* on a small (large) scale.

maßvoll ['ma:sfɔl], *adj.* moderate.

Mast (1) [mast], *m.* (—es, *pl.* —e) mast; pylon.

Mast (2) [mast], *f.* (—, *no pl.*) fattening.

Mastbaum ['mastbaum], *m.* (—s, *pl.* ⁻e) mast.

Mastdarm ['mastdarm], *m.* (—s, *pl.* ⁻e) rectum.

mästen ['mɛstən], *v.a.* feed, fatten.

Mastkorb ['mastkɔrp], *m.* (—s, *pl.* ⁻e) masthead.

Mästung ['mɛstuŋ], *f.* (—, *no pl.*) fattening, cramming.

Materialwaren [mate'rjalva:rən], *f. pl.* groceries; household goods.

materiell [mate'rjɛl], *adj.* material, real; materialistic.

Mathematik [matema'ti:k], *f.* (—, *no pl.*) mathematics.

mathematisch [mate'ma:tiʃ], *adj.* mathematical.

Matratze [ma'tratsə], *f.* (—, *pl.* —n) mattress.

Matrikel [ma'tri:kəl], *f.* (—, *pl.* —n) register, roll.

Matrize [ma'tri:tsə], *f.* (—, *pl.* —n) matrix, die, stencil.

Matrose [ma'tro:zə], *m.* (—n, *pl.* —n) sailor, seaman.

Matsch [matʃ], *m.* (—es, *no pl.*) slush; mud.

matt [mat], *adj.* tired, exhausted, spent; languid; weak, feeble; (*light*) dim; (*gold*) dull; (*silver*) tarnished; (*Chess*) (check-)mate; — *setzen,* (*Chess*) to (check-)mate.

Matte ['matə], *f.* (—, *pl.* —n) mat, matting.

Matthäus [ma'tɛ:us], *m.* Matthew.

Mattheit ['mathaɪt], *f.* (—, *no pl.*) tiredness, exhaustion, languor, feebleness; (*light*) dimness; (*gold*) dullness.

mattherzig ['mathɛrtsɪç], *adj.* poor-spirited, faint-hearted.

Matura [ma'tu:ra], *f.* (—, *pl.* —en) (*Austr.*) school-leaving *or* matriculation examination.

Mätzchen ['mɛtsçən], *n.* (—s, *pl.* —) nonsense; trick; *mach keine —,* don't be silly.

Mauer ['mauər], *f.* (—, *pl.* —n) wall.

Mauerkelle ['mauərkɛlə], *f.* (—, *pl.* —n) trowel.

mauern ['mauərn], *v.a.* build. — *v.n.* lay bricks, construct a wall.

Mauerwerk ['mauərvɛrk], *n.* (—s, *no pl.*) brick-work.

Maul [maul], *n.* (—es, *pl.* ⁻er) (*animals*) mouth, muzzle; (*vulg.*) mouth; *das — halten,* shut up, hold o.'s tongue; *ein loses — haben,* have a loose tongue; *nicht aufs — gefallen sein,* have a quick tongue; (*vulg.*) *halt's —,* shut up.

Maulaffe ['maulafə], *m.* (**—n,** *pl.* **—n**) booby; **—***n feilhalten,* stand gaping.
Maulbeere ['maulbɛːrə], *f.* (**—,** *pl.* **—n**) (*Bot.*) mulberry.
maulen ['maulən], *v.n.* pout, sulk.
Maulesel ['mauleːzəl], *m.* (**—s,** *pl.* **—**) (*Zool.*) mule.
maulfaul ['maulfaul], *adj.* tongue-tied; taciturn.
Maulheld ['maulhɛlt], *m.* (**—en** *pl.* **—en**) braggart.
Maulkorb ['maulkɔrp], *m.* (**—s,** *pl.* **ẅe**) muzzle.
Maulschelle ['maulʃɛlə], *f.* (**—,** *pl.* **—n**) box on the ear.
Maultier ['maultiːr], *n.* (**—s,** *pl.* **—e**) (*Zool.*) mule.
Maulwerk ['maulvɛrk], *n.* (**—s,** *no pl.*) *ein großes — haben,* (*coll.*) have the gift of the gab.
Maulwurf ['maulvurf], *m.* (**—s,** *pl.* **ẅe**) (*Zool.*) mole.
Maurer ['maurər], *m.* (**—s,** *pl.* **—**) mason, bricklayer.
Maus [maus], *f.* (**—,** *pl.* **ẅe**) mouse.
Mausefalle ['mauzəfalə], *f.* (**—,** *pl.* **—n**) mouse-trap.
mausen ['mauzən], *v.n.* catch mice. **—** *v.a.* (*fig.*) pilfer, pinch.
Mauser ['mauzər], *f.* (**—,** *no pl.*) moulting.
mausern ['mauzərn], *v.r. sich —,* moult.
mausetot ['mauzətoːt], *adj.* dead as a door-nail.
mausig ['mauzɪç], *adj. sich — machen,* put on airs.
Maxime [mak'siːmə], *f.* (**—,** *pl.* **—n**) maxim, motto, device.
Mazedonien [matsə'doːnjən], *n.* Macedonia.
Mäzen [mɛː'tseːn], *m.* (**—s,** *pl.* **—e**) patron of the arts, Maecenas.
Mechanik [me'çaːnɪk], *f.* (**—,** *no pl.*) mechanics.
Mechaniker [me'çaːnɪkər], *m.* (**—s,** *pl.* **—**) mechanic.
mechanisch [me'çaːnɪʃ], *adj.* mechanical.
meckern ['mɛkərn], *v.n.* bleat; (*fig.*) grumble, complain.
Medaille [me'daljə], *f.* (**—,** *pl.* **—n**) medal.
Medaillon [medal'jɔ̃], *n.* (**—s,** *pl.* **—s**) locket.
meditieren [medi'tiːrən], *v.n.* meditate.
Medizin [medi'tsiːn], *f.* (**—,** *pl.* **—en**) medicine, physic.
Mediziner [medi'tsiːnər], *m.* (**—s,** *pl.* **—**) physician, medical practitioner, student of medicine.
medizinisch [medi'tsiːnɪʃ], *adj.* medical, medicinal.
Meer [meːr], *n.* (**—es,** *pl.* **—e**) sea, ocean; *offnes —,* high seas; *am —,* at the seaside; *auf dem —,* at sea; *übers —,* overseas.
Meerbusen ['meːrbuːzən], *m.* (**—s,** *pl.* **—**) bay, gulf, bight.

Meerenge ['meːrɛŋə], *f.* (**—,** *pl.* **—n**) straits.
Meeresspiegel ['meːrəsʃpiːgəl], *m.* (**—s,** *no pl.*) sea-level.
Meerkatze ['meːrkatsə], *f.* (**—,** *pl.* **—n**) long-tailed monkey.
Meerrettich ['meːrrɛtɪç], *m.* (**—s,** *pl.* **—e**) (*Bot.*) horse-radish.
Meerschaum ['meːrʃaum], *m.* (**—s,** *no pl.*) sea-foam; (*pipe*) meerschaum.
Meerschwein ['meːrʃvain], *n.* (**—s,** *pl.* **—e**) (*Zool.*) porpoise.
Meerschweinchen ['meːrʃvainçən], *n.* (**—s,** *pl.* **—**) (*Zool.*) guinea-pig.
Mehl [meːl], *n.* (**—es,** *no pl.*) flour; meal; dust, powder.
Mehlkleister ['meːlklaistər], *m.* (**—s,** *no pl.*) flour paste.
Mehlspeise ['meːlʃpaizə], *f.* (**—,** *pl.* **—n**) (*dial.*) pudding, sweet.
mehr [meːr], *indecl. adj., adv.* more; *umso —,* all the more; *immer —,* more and more; *— als genug,* enough and to spare.
Mehrbetrag ['meːrbətraːk], *m.* (**—s,** *pl.* **ẅe**) surplus.
mehrdeutig ['meːrdɔytɪç], *adj.* ambiguous.
mehren ['meːrən], *v.r. sich —,* multiply, increase in numbers.
mehrere ['meːrərə], *pl. adj.* several.
mehrfach ['meːrfax], *adj.* repeated.
Mehrheit ['meːrhait], *f.* (**—,** *pl.* **—en**) majority.
mehrmals ['meːrmaːls], *adv.* several times.
Mehrzahl ['meːrtsaːl], *f.* (**—,** *no pl.*) (*Gram.*) plural; majority, bulk.
meiden ['maidən], *v.a. irr.* shun, avoid.
Meierei [maiə'rai], *f.* (**—,** *pl.* **—en**) (*dairy*) farm.
Meile ['mailə], *f.* (**—,** *pl.* **—n**) mile; league.
Meiler ['mailər], *m.* (**—s,** *pl.* **—**) charcoal-kiln, charcoal-pile.
mein(e) ['main(ə)], *poss. adj.* my; *—poss. pron.* mine.
Meineid ['mainait], *m.* (**—s,** *pl.* **—e**) perjury; *einen — schwören,* perjure o.s.
meineidig ['mainaidɪç], *adj.* perjured, forsworn.
meinen ['mainən], *v.a.* mean, intend, think.
meinerseits ['mainərzaits], *adv.* I, for my part.
meinethalben ['mainəthalbən], *adv.* on my account, speaking for myself, for my sake; I don't care, I don't mind.
meinetwegen ['mainətveːgən], *adv. see* **meinethalben**.
meinetwillen ['mainətvilən], *adv. um —,* for my sake, on my behalf.
meinige ['mainigə], *poss. pron.* mine.
Meinung ['mainuŋ], *f.* (**—,** *pl.* **—en**) opinion; meaning; notion; *öffentliche —,* public opinion; *der — sein,* be of the opinion, hold the opinion; *einem die — sagen,* give s.o. a piece of o.'s mind; *meiner — nach,* in my opinion.

Meinungsverschiedenheit [ˈmaɪnuŋs-ferʃiːdənhaɪt], *f.* (—, *pl.* —en) difference of opinion, disagreement.

Meise [ˈmaɪzə], *f.* (—, *pl.* —n) (*Orn.*) titmouse.

Meißel [ˈmaɪsəl], *m.* (—s, *pl.* —) chisel.

meißeln [ˈmaɪsəln], *v.a.* chisel, sculpt.

meist [maɪst], *adj.* most. — *adv.* usually, generally.

meistens [ˈmaɪstəns], *adv.* mostly.

Meister [ˈmaɪstər], *m.* (—s, *pl.* —) (*craft*) master; (*sport*) champion; *seinen — finden,* meet o.'s match.

meisterhaft [ˈmaɪstərhaft], *adj.* masterly.

meisterlich [ˈmaɪstərlɪç], *adj.* masterly.

meistern [ˈmaɪstərn], *v.a.* master.

Meisterschaft [ˈmaɪstərʃaft], *f.* (—, *pl.* —en) mastery; (*sport*) championship.

Mekka [ˈmɛka], *n.* Mecca.

Meldeamt [ˈmɛldəamt], *n.* (—s, *pl.* ·er) registration office.

melden [ˈmɛldən], *v.a.* announce, inform, notify; (*Mil.*) report. — *v.r. sich —,* answer the phone; *sich — lassen,* send in o.'s name, have o.s. announced; *sich zu etwas —,* apply for s.th.

Meldezettel [ˈmɛldətsɛtəl], *m.* (—s, *pl.* —) registration form.

meliert [meˈliːrt], *adj.* mixed; (*hair*) iron grey, streaked with grey.

melken [ˈmɛlkən], *v.a. irr.* milk.

Melodie [meloˈdiː], *f.* (—, *pl.* —n) melody, tune.

Melone [meˈloːnə], *f.* (—, *pl.* —n) (*Bot.*) melon; (*coll.*) bowler hat.

Meltau [ˈmeːltau], *m.* (—s, *no pl.*) mildew.

Membrane [mɛmˈbraːnə], *f.* (—, *pl.* —n) membrane, diaphragm.

Memme [ˈmɛmə], *f.* (—, *pl.* —n) coward, poltroon.

memorieren [memoˈriːrən], *v.a.* memorise, learn by heart.

Menage [meˈnaːʒə], *f.* (—, *pl.* —n) household.

Menge [ˈmɛŋə], *f.* (—, *pl.* —n) quantity, amount; multitude, crowd; *eine —,* a lot.

mengen [ˈmɛŋən], *v.a.* mix. — *v.r. sich — in,* interfere in.

Mensch (1) [mɛnʃ], *m.* (—en, *pl.* —en) human being; man; person; *kein —,* nobody.

Mensch (2) [mɛnʃ], *n.* (—es, *pl.* —er) (*vulg.*) wench.

Menschenfeind [ˈmɛnʃənfaɪnt], *m.* (—es, *pl.* —e) misanthropist.

Menschenfreund [ˈmɛnʃənfrɔynt], *m.* (—es, *pl.* —e) philanthropist.

Menschengedenken [ˈmɛnʃəngədɛŋkən], *n.* (—s, *no pl.*) *seit —,* from time immemorial.

Menschenhandel [ˈmɛnʃənhandəl], *m.* (—s, *no pl.*) slave-trade.

Menschenkenner [ˈmɛnʃənkɛnər], *m.* (—s, *pl.* —) judge of character.

Menschenmenge [ˈmɛnʃənmɛŋə], *f.* (—, *no pl.*) crowd.

Menschenraub [ˈmɛnʃənraup], *m.* (—s, *no pl.*) kidnapping.

Menschenverstand [ˈmɛnʃənfɛrʃtant], *m.* (—es, *no pl.*) human understanding; *gesunder —,* common-sense.

Menschheit [ˈmɛnʃhaɪt], *f.* (—, *no pl.*) mankind, human race.

menschlich [ˈmɛnʃlɪç], *adj.* human.

Menschwerdung [ˈmɛnʃverduŋ], *f.* (—, *no pl.*) incarnation.

Mensur [mɛnˈzuːr], *f.* (—, *pl.* —en) students' duel.

Mergel [ˈmɛrgəl], *m.* (—s, *no pl.*) marl.

merkbar [ˈmɛrkbaːr], *adj.* perceptible, noticeable.

merken [ˈmɛrkən], *v.a.* note, perceive, observe, notice; *sich etwas —,* bear in mind; *sich nichts — lassen,* show no sign.

merklich [ˈmɛrklɪç], *adj.* perceptible, appreciable.

Merkmal [ˈmɛrkmaːl], *n.* (—s, *pl.* —e) mark, characteristic, feature.

merkwürdig [ˈmɛrkvyrdɪç], *adj.* remarkable, curious, strange.

Merle [ˈmɛrlə], *f.* (—, *pl.* —n) (*dial.*) blackbird.

Mesner [ˈmɛsnər], *m.* (—s, *pl.* —) sexton, sacristan.

meßbar [ˈmɛsbaːr], *adj.* measurable.

Meßbuch [ˈmɛsbuːx], *n.* (—es, *pl.* ·er) missal.

Messe [ˈmɛsə], *f.* (—, *pl.* —n) (*Eccl.*) Mass; *stille —,* Low Mass; (*Comm.*) fair; (*Mil.*) mess.

messen [ˈmɛsən], *v.a. irr.* measure, gauge. — *v.r. sich mit einem —,* pit oneself against s.o.

Messer (1) [ˈmɛsər], *m.* (—s, *pl.* —) gauge, meter.

Messer (2) [ˈmɛsər], *n.* (—s, *pl.* —) knife.

Messerheld [ˈmɛsərhɛlt], *m.* (—en, *pl.* —en) cut-throat, hooligan, rowdy.

Messias [meˈsiːas], *m.* Messiah.

Meßgewand [ˈmɛsgəvant], *n.* (—es, *pl.* ·er) chasuble, vestment.

Meßkunst [ˈmɛskunst], *f.* (—, *no pl.*) surveying.

Messing [ˈmɛsɪŋ], *n.* (—s, *no pl.*) brass; *aus —,* brazen.

Metall [meˈtal], *n.* (—s, *pl.* —e) metal; *unedle —e,* base metals.

Metallkunde [meˈtalkundə], *f.* (—, *no pl.*) metallurgy.

meteorologisch [meteoroˈloːgɪʃ], *adj.* meteorological.

Meter [ˈmeːtər], *n. & m.* (—s, *pl.* —) (*linear measure*) metre; (*Am.*) meter; (*Poet.*) metre.

methodisch [meˈtoːdɪʃ], *adj.* methodical.

Metrik [ˈmeːtrɪk], *f.* (—, *no pl.*) prosody, versification.

Mette [ˈmɛtə], *f.* (—, *pl.* —n) (*Eccl.*) matins.

Metze [ˈmɛtsə], f. (—, pl. —n) (obs.) prostitute.

Metzelei [mɛtsəˈlaɪ], f. (—, pl. —en) slaughter, massacre.

metzeln [ˈmɛtsəln], v.a. massacre, butcher.

Metzger [ˈmɛtsɡər], m. (—s, pl. —) butcher.

Meuchelmörder [ˈmɔʏçəlmœrdər], m. (—s, pl. —) assassin.

meucheln [ˈmɔʏçəln], v.a. assassinate.

meuchlings [ˈmɔʏçlɪŋs], adv. treacherously, insidiously.

Meute [ˈmɔʏtə], f. (—, pl. —n) pack of hounds; (fig.) gang.

Meuterei [mɔʏtəˈraɪ], f. (—, pl. —en) mutiny, sedition.

meutern [ˈmɔʏtərn], v.n. mutiny.

Mezzanin [ˈmɛtsanɪn], n. (—s, pl. —e) half-storey, mezzanine.

miauen [miˈauən], v.n. mew.

mich [mɪç], pers. pron. me, myself.

Michaeli(s) [mɪçaˈeːli(s)], n. Michaelmas.

Michel [ˈmɪçəl], m. Michael; deutscher —, plain honest German.

Mieder [ˈmiːdər], n. (—s, pl. —) bodice.

Miene [ˈmiːnə], f. (—, pl. —n) mien, air; (facial) expression.

Miete [ˈmiːtə], f. (—, pl. —n) rent; hire; (corn) rick, stack.

mieten [ˈmiːtən], v.a. rent, hire.

Mieter [ˈmiːtər], m. (—s, pl. —) tenant, lodger.

Mietskaserne [ˈmiːtskazɛrnə], f. (—, pl. —en) tenement house.

Mietszins [ˈmiːtstsɪns], m. (—es, pl. —e) rent.

Milbe [ˈmɪlbə], f. (—, pl. —n) mite.

Milch [mɪlç], f. (—, no pl.) milk; (fish) soft roe; abgerahmte —, skim(med) milk; geronnene —, curdled milk.

Milchbart [ˈmɪlçbaːrt], m. (—s, pl. ⁻e) milksop.

Milchbruder [ˈmɪlçbruːdər], m. (—s, pl. ⁻) foster-brother.

milchen [ˈmɪlçən], v.n. yield milk.

Milcher [ˈmɪlçer], m. (—s, pl. —) (fish) milter.

Milchgesicht [ˈmɪlçɡəzɪçt], n. (—s, pl. —er) baby face; smooth complexion.

Milchglas [ˈmɪlçɡlas], n. (—es, no pl.) opalescent glass, frosted glass.

Milchstraße [ˈmɪlçʃtraːsə], f. (—, no pl.) Milky Way.

Milde [ˈmɪldə], f. (—, no pl.) mildness, softness; (fig.) gentleness, (rare) charity, generosity.

mildern [ˈmɪldərn], v.a. soften, alleviate, mitigate, soothe, allay; —de Umstände, extenuating circumstances.

Milderung [ˈmɪldəruŋ], f. (—, pl. —en) mitigation, moderation; soothing.

mildtätig [ˈmɪltteːtɪç], adj. charitable, benevolent, munificent.

Militär [miliˈtɛːr], n. (—s, no pl. military, army ; beim — sein, serve in the army.

Miliz [miˈliːts], f. (—, no pl.) militia.

Milliarde [mɪlˈjardə], f. (—, pl. —n) a thousand millions; (Am.) billion.

Million [mɪlˈjoːn], f. (—, pl. —en) million.

Millionär [mɪljoˈnɛːr], m. (—s, pl. —e) millionaire.

Milz [mɪlts], f. (—, pl. —en) spleen.

Mime [ˈmiːmə], m. (—n, pl. —n) mime, actor.

Mimik [ˈmiːmɪk], f. (—, no pl.) mime, miming.

Mimiker [ˈmiːmɪkər], m. (—s, pl. —) mimic.

Mimose [miˈmoːzə], f. (—, pl. —n) (Bot.) mimosa.

minder [ˈmɪndər], adj. lesser, smaller, minor, inferior.

Minderheit [ˈmɪndərhaɪt], f. (—, pl. —en) minority.

minderjährig [ˈmɪndərjɛːrɪç], adj. (Law) under age.

mindern [ˈmɪndərn], v.a. diminish, lessen.

minderwertig [ˈmɪndərvɛrtɪç], adj. inferior, of poor quality.

Minderwertigkeitskomplex [ˈmɪndərvɛrtɪçkaɪtskɔmplɛks], m. (—es, pl. —e) inferiority complex.

mindest [ˈmɪndəst], adj. least, smallest, minimum, lowest; nicht im —en, not in the least, not at all.

mindestens [ˈmɪndəstəns], adv. at least.

Mine [ˈmiːnə], f. (—, pl. —n) mine; (ball point pen) refill; (pencil) lead.

minimal [miniˈmaːl], adj. infinitesimal, minimum.

Ministerialrat [minɪsterˈjaːlraːt], m. (—s, pl. ⁻e) senior civil servant.

ministeriell [minɪsterˈjɛl], adj. ministerial.

Ministerium [minɪsteˈrjum], n. (—s, pl. —rien) ministry.

Ministerpräsident [miˈnɪstərprɛːzidɛnt], m. (—en, pl. —en) prime minister; premier.

Ministerrat [miˈnɪstərraːt], m. (—s, pl. ⁻e) cabinet, council of ministers.

Ministrant [minɪˈstrant], m. (—en, pl. —en) acolyte; sacristan.

Minne [ˈmɪnə], f. (—, no pl.) (obs., Poet.) love.

Minnesänger [mɪnəˈzɛŋər], m. (—s, pl. —) minnesinger; troubadour, minstrel.

Minus [ˈmiːnus], n. (—, no pl.) deficit.

Minze [ˈmɪntsə], f. (—, pl. —n) (Bot.) mint.

mir [miːr], pers. pron. to me.

Mirakel [miˈraːkəl], n. (—s, pl. —) miracle, marvel, wonder.

mischen [ˈmɪʃən], v.a. mix; (Cards) shuffle; (coffee, tea) blend.

Mischling [ˈmɪʃlɪŋ], m. (—s, pl. —e) mongrel, hybrid.

Mischrasse

Mischrasse ['mɪʃrasə], f. (—, pl. —n) cross-breed.

Mischung ['mɪʃuŋ], f. (—, pl. —en) mixture, blend.

Misere [mi'ze:rə], f. (—, no pl.) unhappiness, misery.

Mispel ['mɪspəl], f. (—, pl. —n) (Bot.) medlar (tree).

mißachten [mɪs'axtən], v.a. disregard, despise.

mißarten [mɪs'a:rtən], v.n. (aux. sein) degenerate.

Mißbehagen [mɪsbəha:gən], n. (—s, no pl.) displeasure, uneasiness.

mißbilligen [mɪs'bɪlɪgən], v.a. object (to), disapprove (of).

Mißbrauch ['mɪsbraux], m. (—s, pl. ⁻e) abuse, misuse.

missen ['mɪsən], v.a. lack, be without, feel the lack of.

Missetat ['mɪsəta:t], f. (—, pl. —en) misdeed, felony.

mißfallen [mɪs'falən], v.n. irr. displease.

mißförmig ['mɪsfœrmɪç], adj. deformed, misshapen.

Mißgeburt ['mɪsgəburt], f. (—, pl. —en) abortion; monster.

mißgelaunt ['mɪsgəlaunt], adj. illhumoured.

Mißgeschick ['mɪsgəʃɪk], n. (—s, no pl.) mishap, misfortune.

mißgestimmt ['mɪsgəʃtɪmt], adj. grumpy, out of sorts.

mißglücken [mɪs'glʏkən], v.n. (aux. sein) fail, be unsuccessful.

Mißgriff ['mɪsgrɪf], m. (—s, pl. —e) blunder, mistake.

Mißgunst ['mɪsgunst], f. (—, no pl.) jealousy, envy.

mißhandeln [mɪs'handəln], v.a. illtreat.

Missionar [mɪsjo'na:r], m. (—s, pl. —e) missionary.

mißlich ['mɪslɪç], adj. awkward; difficult, unpleasant.

mißliebig ['mɪsli:bɪç], adj. unpopular, odious.

mißlingen [mɪs'lɪŋən], v.n. irr. (aux. sein) miscarry, go wrong, misfire, prove a failure, turn out badly.

mißraten [mɪs'ra:tən], v.n. irr. (aux. sein) miscarry, turn out badly.

Mißstand ['mɪsʃtant], m. (—es, pl. ⁻e) grievance, abuse.

Mißton ['mɪsto:n], m. (—s, pl. ⁻e) dissonance.

mißtrauen [mɪs'trauən], v.n. distrust, mistrust.

Mißverhältnis ['mɪsfɛrhɛltnɪs], n. (—ses, no pl.) disproportion.

Mißverständnis ['mɪsfɛrʃtɛntnɪs], n. (—ses, pl. —se) misunderstanding.

Mist [mɪst], m. (—es, no pl.) dung, manure, muck; (fig.) rubbish.

Mistel ['mɪstəl], f. (—, pl. —n) (Bot.) mistletoe.

Mistfink ['mɪstfɪŋk], m. (—s, pl. —e) (fig.) dirty child; mudlark.

mit [mɪt], prep. (Dat.) with. — adv. also, along with.

mitarbeiten ['mɪtarbaItən], v.n. collaborate, cooperate; (lit. work) contribute.

mitbringen ['mɪtbrɪŋən], v.a. irr. bring along.

Mitbürger ['mɪtbyrgər], m. (—s, pl. —) fellow-citizen.

mitempfinden ['mɪtɛmpfɪndən], v.a. irr. sympathise with.

Mitesser ['mɪtɛsər], m. (—s, pl. —) (Med.) blackhead.

mitfahren ['mɪtfa:rən], v.n. irr. (aux. sein) ride with s.o.; einen — lassen, give s.o. a lift.

mitfühlen ['mɪtfy:lən], v.n. sympathise.

mitgehen ['mɪtge:ən], v.n. irr. (aux. sein) go along (with), accompany (s.o.); etwas — heißen or lassen, pilfer, pocket, pinch.

Mitgift ['mɪtgɪft], f. (—, no pl.) dowry.

Mitglied ['mɪtgli:t], n. (—s, pl. —er) member, fellow, associate.

mithin [mɪt'hɪn], adv., conj. consequently, therefore.

Mitläufer ['mɪtlɔyfər], m. (—s, pl. —) (Polit.) fellow-traveller.

Mitlaut ['mɪtlaut], m. (—s, pl. —e) (Phonet.) consonant.

Mitleid ['mɪtlaIt], n. (—s, no pl.) compassion, sympathy, pity; mit einem — haben, take pity on s.o.

Mitleidenschaft ['mɪtlaIdənʃaft], f. (—, no pl.) einen in — ziehen, involve s.o., implicate s.o.

mitmachen ['mɪtmaxən], v.a., v.n. join in, participate (in), do as others do; go through, suffer.

Mitmensch ['mɪtmɛnʃ], m. (—en, pl. —en) fellow-man; fellow-creature.

mitnehmen ['mɪtne:mən], v.a. irr. take along, take with o.; strain, take it out of o., weaken.

mitnichten [mɪt'nɪçtən], adv. by no means.

mitreden ['mɪtre:dən], v.n. join in a conversation; contribute.

mitsamt [mɪt'zamt], prep. (Dat.) together with.

Mitschuld ['mɪtʃult], f. (—, no pl.) complicity.

Mitschüler ['mɪtʃy:lər], m. (—s, pl. —) schoolfellow, fellow-pupil, fellowstudent, classmate.

Mittag ['mɪta:k], m. (—s, pl. —e) midday, noon, noontide; zu — essen, have dinner or lunch.

Mittagessen ['mɪta:kɛsən], n. (—s, pl. —) lunch, luncheon.

Mittagsseite ['mɪta:kszaItə], f. (—, no pl.) south side.

Mittäter ['mɪttɛːtər], m. (—s, pl. —) accomplice.

Mitte ['mɪtə], f. (—, no pl.) middle, midst.

mitteilen ['mɪttaIlən], v.a. (Dat.) communicate, inform, impart.

mitteilsam ['mɪttaɪlzaːm], *adj.* communicative.
Mitteilung ['mɪttaɪluŋ], *f.* (—, *pl.* —en) communication.
Mittel ['mɪtəl], *n.* (—s, *pl.*) means, expedient, way, resource; remedy; (*pl.*) money, funds; *als* — *zum Zweck*, as a means to an end; *sich ins* — *legen*, mediate, intercede.
Mittelalter ['mɪtəlaltər], *n.* (—s, *no pl.*) Middle Ages.
mittelbar ['mɪtəlbaːr], *adj.* indirect.
Mittelding ['mɪtəldɪŋ], *n.* (—s, *pl.* —e) medium; something in between.
Mittelgebirge ['mɪtəlgəbɪrgə], *n.* (—s, *pl.* —) hills; (subalpine) mountains.
mittelländisch ['mɪtəllendɪʃ], *adj.* Mediterranean.
mittellos ['mɪtəloːs], *adj.* penniless, impecunious.
Mittelmaß ['mɪtəlmaːs], *n.* (—es, *pl.* —e) average.
mittelmäßig ['mɪtəlmɛːsɪç], *adj.* mediocre.
Mittelmeer ['mɪtəlmeːr], *n.* (—s, *no pl.*) Mediterranean.
Mittelpunkt ['mɪtəlpuŋkt], *m.* (—s, *pl.* —e) centre; focus.
mittels ['mɪtəls], *prep.* (Genit.) by means of.
Mittelschule ['mɪtəlʃuːlə], *f.* (—, *pl.* —n) secondary (intermediate) school; (*Austr.*) grammar school; (*Am.*) high school.
Mittelstand ['mɪtəlʃtant], *m.* (—es, *no pl.*) middle class.
mittelste ['mɪtəlstə], *adj.* middlemost, central.
Mittelstürmer ['mɪtəlʃtyrmər], *m.* (—s, *pl.* ⫤) (Footb.) centre-forward.
Mittelwort ['mɪtəlvɔrt], *n.* (—es, *pl.* ⫤er) (Gram.) participle.
mitten ['mɪtən], *adv.* in the midst; — *am Tage*, in broad daylight.
Mitternacht ['mɪtərnaxt], *f.* (—, *no pl.*) midnight.
Mittler ['mɪtlər], *m.* (—s, *pl.* —) mediator.
mittlere ['mɪtlərə], *adj.* middle; average; mean.
Mittwoch ['mɪtvɔx], *m.* (—s, *pl.* —e) Wednesday.
mitunter [mɪt'untər], *adv.* now and then, occasionally, sometimes.
mitunterzeichnen ['mɪtuntərtsaɪçnən], *v.a., v.n.* countersign; add o.'s signature (to).
Miturheber ['mɪtuːrheːbər], *m.* (—s, *pl.* —) co-author.
Mitwelt ['mɪtvɛlt], *f.* (—, *no pl.*) the present generation, contemporaries, our own times; the world outside.
mitwirken ['mɪtvɪrkən], *v.n.* cooperate.
Mnemotechnik [mne:mo'tɛçnɪk], *f.* (—, *no pl.*) mnemonics.
Möbel ['møːbəl], *n.* (—s, *pl.* —) piece of furniture; (*pl.*) furniture.
mobil [mo'biːl], *adj.* mobile, active, quick; — *machen*, mobilise, put in motion.

Mobiliar [mobil'jaːr], *n.* (—s, *pl.* **Mobilien**) furniture, movables.
mobilisieren [mobili'ziːrən], *v.a.* mobilise.
möblieren [mø'bliːrən], *v.a.* furnish; *neu* —, refurnish.
Mode ['moːdə], *f.* (—, *pl.* —n) mode, fashion; custom, use; *in der* —, in fashion, in vogue.
Modell [mo'dɛl], *n.* (—s, *pl.* —e) model; — *stehen*, model; (*fig.*) be the prototype.
modellieren [modɛ'liːrən], *v.a.* (*dresses*) model; (*Art*) mould.
Moder ['moːdər], *m.* (—s, *no pl.*) mould.
moderig ['moːdrɪç] *see* **modrig**.
modern(1) ['moːdərn], *v.n.* moulder, rot.
modern(2) [mo'dɛrn], *adj.* modern, fashionable, up-to-date.
modernisieren [modɛrni'ziːrən], *v.a.* modernise.
modifizieren [modifi'tsiːrən], *v.a.* modify.
modisch ['moːdɪʃ], *adj.* stylish, fashionable.
Modistin [mo'dɪstɪn], *f.* (—, *pl.* —nen) milliner.
modrig ['moːdrɪç], *adj.* mouldy.
modulieren [modu'liːrən], *v.a.* modulate.
Modus ['moːdus], *m.* (—, *pl.* **Modi**) (Gram.) mood; mode, manner.
mogeln ['moːgəln], *v.n.* cheat.
mögen ['møːgən], *v.n. irr.* like, desire, want, be allowed, have a mind to; (*modal auxiliary*) may, might; *ich möchte gern*, I should like to.
möglich ['møːklɪç], *adj.* possible, practicable; feasible; *sein* —*stes tun*, do o.'s utmost; *nicht* —*!* you don't say (so)!
Möglichkeit ['møːklɪçkaɪt], *f.* (—, *pl.* —en) possibility, feasibility, practicability; (*pl.*) potentialities; contingencies; prospects (of career).
Mohn [moːn], *m.* (—es, *no pl.*) poppy(-seed).
Mohr [moːr], *m.* (—en, *pl.* —en) Moor; negro.
Möhre ['møːrə], *f.* (—, *pl.* —n) carrot.
Mohrenkopf ['moːrənkɔpf], *m.* (—es, *pl.* ⫤e) chocolate éclair.
Mohrrübe ['moːrryːbə], *f.* (—, *pl.* —n) carrot.
mokieren [mɔ'kiːrən], *v.r. sich* — *über*, sneer at, mock at, be amused by.
Mokka ['mɔka], *m.* (—s, *no pl.*) Mocha coffee.
Molch [mɔlç], *m.* (—es, *pl.* —e) (Zool.) salamander.
Moldau ['mɔldau], *f.* Moldavia.
Mole ['moːlə], *f.* (—, *pl.* —n) breakwater, jetty, pier.
Molekül [mole'kyːl], *n.* (—s, *pl.* —e) molecule.
Molke ['mɔlkə], *f.* (—, *pl.* —n) whey.
Molkerei [mɔlkə'raɪ], *f.* (—, *pl.* —en) dairy.
moll [mɔl], *adj.* (Mus.) minor.

Molluske

Molluske [mɔ'luskə], *f.* (—, *pl.* —n) (*Zool.*) mollusc.

Moment (1) [mo'mɛnt], *m.* (—s, *pl.* —e) moment, instant.

Moment (2) [mo'mɛnt], *n.* motive, factor; (*Phys.*) momentum.

Momentaufnahme [mo'mɛntaufna:-mə], *f.* (—, *pl.* —n) snapshot.

momentan [momɛn'ta:n], *adv.* at the moment, for the present, just now.

Monarch [mo'narç], *m.* (—en, *pl.* —en) monarch.

Monarchie [monar'çi:], *f.* (—, *pl.* —n) monarchy.

Monat [mo'na:t], *m.* (—s, *pl.* —e) month.

monatlich ['mo:natlɪç], *adj.* monthly.

Monatsfluß ['mo:natsflus], *m.* (—sses, *pl.* -sse) menses.

Monatsschrift ['mo:natsʃrɪft], *f.* (—, *pl.* —en) monthly (*journal*).

Mönch [mœnç], *m.* (—es, *pl.* —e) monk, friar.

Mönchskappe ['mœnçskapə], *f.* (—, *pl.* —n) cowl, monk's hood.

Mönchskutte ['mœnçskutə], *f.* (—, *pl.* —n) cowl.

Mond [mo:nt], *m.* (—es, *pl.* —e) moon; *zunehmender* —, waxing moon; *abnehmender* —, waning moon.

Mondfinsternis ['mo:ntfɪnstərnɪs], *f.* (—, *pl.* —se) eclipse of the moon.

mondsüchtig ['mo:ntzyçtɪç], *adj.* given to sleep-walking; (*fig.*) moon-struck.

Mondwandlung ['mo:ntvandluŋ], *f.* (—, *pl.* —en) phase of the moon.

Moneten [mo'ne:tən], *pl.* (*sl.*) money, cash, funds.

Mongolei [mɔŋgo'laɪ], *f.* Mongolia.

monieren [mo'ni:rən], *v.a.* remind (a debtor); censure.

monogam [mono'ga:m], *adj.* monogamous.

Monopol [mono'po:l], *n.* (—s, *pl.* —e) monopoly.

monoton [mono'to:n], *adj.* monotonous.

Monstrum ['mɔnstrum], *n.* (—s, *pl.* **Monstra**) monster, monstrosity.

Monsun [mɔn'zu:n], *m.* (—s, *pl.* —e) monsoon.

Montag ['mo:nta:k], *m.* (—s, *pl.* —e) Monday; *blauer* —, Bank Holiday Monday.

Montage [mɔn'ta:ʒə], *f.* (—, *pl.* —n) fitting (up), setting up, installation, assembling.

Montanindustrie [mɔn'ta:nɪndustri:], *f.* (—, *no pl.*) mining industry.

Montanunion [mɔn'ta:nunjo:n], *f.* (—, *no pl.*) (*Pol.*) European Coal and Steel Community.

Monteur [mɔn'tø:r], *m.* (—s, *pl.* —e) fitter.

montieren [mɔn'ti:rən], *v.a.* fit (up), set up, mount, install.

Montur [mɔn'tu:r], *f.* (—, *pl.* —en) uniform, livery.

Moor [mo:r], *n.* (—es, *pl.* —e) swamp, fen, bog.

Moos [mo:s], *n.* (—es, *pl.* —e) moss; (*sl.*) cash.

Moped ['mo:pɛt], *n.* (—s, *pl.* —s) moped, motorised pedal cycle.

Mops [mɔps], *m.* (—es, *pl.* -e) pug (dog).

mopsen ['mɔpsən], *v.r. sich* —, feel bored.

Moral [mo'ra:l], *f.* (—, *no pl.*) moral, morals.

moralisch [mo'ra:lɪʃ], *adj.* moral.

Morast [mo'rast], *m.* (—es, *pl.* -e) morass, bog, fen, mire.

Moratorium [mora'to:rjum], *n.* (—s, *pl.* **-rien**) (*payments etc.*) respite.

Morchel ['mɔrçəl], *f.* (—, *pl.* —n) (*Bot.*) morel (edible fungus).

Mord [mɔrt], *m.* (—es, *pl.* —e) murder.

morden ['mɔrdən], *v.a., v.n.* murder.

Mörder ['mœrdər], *m.* (—s, *pl.* —) murderer.

Mordsgeschichte ['mɔrtsgəʃɪçtə], *f.* (—, *pl.* —n) (*coll.*) cock-and-bull story.

Mordskerl ['mɔrtskɛrl], *m.* (—s, *pl.* —e) devil of a fellow; (*Am.*) great guy.

Mordtat ['mɔrtta:t], *f.* (—, *pl.* —en) murder.

Morelle [mo'rɛlə], *f.* (—, *pl.* —n) (*Bot.*) morello cherry.

Morgen ['mɔrgən], *m.* (—s, *pl.* —) morning, daybreak; (*Poet.*) east; measure of land; *eines* —s, one morning.

morgen ['mɔrgən], *adv.* tomorrow; — *früh*, tomorrow morning; *heute* —, this morning.

Morgenblatt ['mɔrgənblat], *n.* (—s, *pl.* -er) morning paper.

morgendlich ['mɔrgəntlɪç], *adj.* of *or* in the morning; matutinal.

Morgenland ['mɔrgənlant], *n.* (—es, *pl.* —) orient, east.

Morgenrot ['mɔrgənro:t], *n.* (—s, *no pl.*) dawn, sunrise.

morgens ['mɔrgəns], *adv.* in the morning.

morgig ['mɔrgɪç], *adj.* tomorrow's.

Morphium ['mɔrfjum], *n.* (—s, *no pl.*) morphia, morphine.

morsch [mɔrʃ], *adj.* brittle, rotten, decayed.

Mörser ['mœrzər], *m.* (—s, *pl.* —) mortar.

Mörserkeule ['mœrzərkɔylə], *f.* (—, *pl.* —n) pestle.

Mörtel ['mœrtəl], *m.* (—s, *no pl.*) mortar, plaster.

Mörtelkelle ['mœrtəlkɛlə], *f.* (—, *pl.* —n) trowel.

Mosaik [moza'i:k], *n.* (—s, *pl.* —e) mosaic (work); inlaid work.

mosaisch [mo'za:ɪʃ], *adj.* Mosaic.

Moschee [mo'ʃe:], *f.* (—, *pl.* —n) mosque.

Moschus ['mɔʃus], *m.* (—, *no pl.*) musk.

Mosel ['mo:zəl], *f.* Moselle.

Moskau ['mɔskau], *n.* Moscow.

Moskito [mɔs'ki:to], *m.* (—s, *pl.* —s) (*Ent.*) mosquito.

Most [mɔst], *m.* (—es, *no pl.*) new wine, cider.

Mostrich ['mɔstriç], *m.* (—s, *no pl.*) mustard.

Motiv [mo'ti:f], *n.* (—es, *pl.* —e) motive; (*Mus., Lit.*) motif, theme.

motivieren [moti'vi:rən], *v.a.* motivate.

Motorrad ['mo:tɔrra:t], *n.* (—es, *pl.* ̈er) motor-cycle.

Motte ['mɔtə], *f.* (—, *pl.* —n) (*Ent.*) moth.

moussieren [mu'si:rən], *v.n.* effervesce, sparkle.

Möwe ['mø:və], *f.* (—, *pl.* —n) (*Orn.*) seagull.

Mucke ['mukə], *f.* (—, *pl.* —n) whim, caprice; obstinacy.

Mücke ['mykə], *f.* (—, *pl.* —n) (*Ent.*) gnat, fly, mosquito.

Muckerei [mukə'raɪ], *f.* (—, *pl.* —en) cant.

mucksen ['muksən], *v.n.* stir, move, budge.

müde ['my:də], *adj.* tired, weary; — *machen*, tire.

Muff [muf], *m.* (—es, *pl.* —e) muff.

muffig ['mufiç], *adj.* musty, fusty, stuffy.

Mühe ['my:ə], *f.* (—, *pl.* —n) trouble, pains; effort, labour, toil; *sich — geben*, take pains.

mühelos ['my:əlo:s], *adj.* effortless, easy.

mühen ['my:ən], *v.r. sich* —, exert o.s., take pains.

Mühewaltung ['my:əvaltuŋ], *f.* (—, *pl.* —en) exertion, effort.

Mühle ['my:lə], *f.* (—, *pl.* —n) (*flour*) mill; (*coffee*) grinder; game.

Muhme ['mu:mə], *f.* (—, *pl.* —n) (*obs.*) aunt.

Mühsal ['my:za:l], *f.* (—, *pl.* —e) hardship, misery, toil.

mühsam ['my:za:m], *adj.* troublesome, laborious.

mühselig ['my:ze:liç], *adj.* painful, laborious; miserable.

Mulatte [mu'latə], *m.* (—n, *pl.* —n) mulatto.

Mulde ['muldə], *f.* (—, *pl.* —n) trough.

muldenförmig ['muldənfœrmiç], *adj.* trough-shaped.

Mull [mul], *m.* (—s, *no pl.*) Indian muslin.

Müll [myl], *m.* (—s, *no pl.*) dust, rubbish; (*Am.*) garbage.

Müller ['mylər], *m.* (—s, *pl.* —) miller.

mulmig ['mulmiç], *adj.* dusty, mouldy, decayed.

multiplizieren [multipli'tsi:rən], *v.a.* multiply.

Mumie ['mu:mjə], *f.* (—, *pl.* —n) (*Archæol.*) mummy.

Mummenschanz ['mumənʃants], *m.* (—es, *no pl.*) mummery, masquerade.

München ['mynçən], *n.* Munich.

Mund [munt], *m.* (—es, *pl.* —e, ̈er) mouth; *den — halten*, keep quiet; *einen großen — haben*, talk big; *sich den — verbrennen*, put o.'s foot in it.

Mundart ['munta:rt], *f.* (—, *pl.* —en) (local) dialect.

Mündel ['myndəl], *m., f. & n.* (—s, *pl.* —) ward, minor, child under guardianship.

mündelsicher ['myndəlzɪçər], *adj.* gilt-edged.

munden ['mundən], *v.n. es mundet mir*, I like the taste, I relish it.

münden ['myndən], *v.n.* discharge (into), flow (into).

mundfaul ['muntfaul], *adj.* tonguetied; taciturn.

mundgerecht ['muntgərɛçt], *adj.* palatable; (*fig.*) suitable.

Mundharmonika ['muntharmo:nika], *f.* (—, *pl.* —kas, —ken) mouth organ.

mündig ['myndiç], *adj.* of age; — *werden*, come of age.

mündlich ['myntliç], *adj.* verbal, oral, by word of mouth; (*examination*) viva voce.

Mundschenk ['muntʃɛŋk], *m.* (—s, *pl.* —e) cupbearer.

mundtot ['muntto:t], *adj.* — *machen*, silence, gag.

Mündung ['mynduŋ], *f.* (—, *pl.* —en) (*river*) estuary, mouth; (*gun*) muzzle.

Mundvorrat ['muntfɔrra:t], *m.* (—s, *pl.* ̈e) provisions, victuals.

Mundwerk ['muntvɛrk], *n.* (—s, *no pl.*) mouth; (*fig.*) gift of the gab.

Munition [muni'tsjo:n], *f.* (—, *no pl.*) ammunition.

munkeln ['muŋkəln], *v.n.* whisper; *man munkelt*, it is rumoured.

Münster ['mynstər], *n.* (—s, *pl.* —) minster, cathedral.

munter ['muntər], *adj.* awake; lively, active, sprightly, vivacious, cheerful, gay.

Münze ['myntsə], *f.* (—, *pl.* —n) coin.

Münzeinheit ['myntsaɪnhaɪt], *f.* (—, *no pl.*) monetary unit.

Münzfälscher ['myntsfɛlʃər], *m.* (—s, *pl.* —) (counterfeit) coiner.

Münzkunde ['myntskundə], *f.* (—, *no pl.*) numismatics.

Münzprobe ['myntspro:bə], *f.* (—, *pl.* —n) assay of a coin.

mürbe ['myrbə], *adj.* mellow; (*meat*) tender; (*cake*) crisp; brittle; *einen — machen*, soften s.o. up, force s.o. to yield.

Murmel ['murməl], *f.* (—, *pl.* —n) (*toy*) marble.

murmeln ['murməln], *v.n.* murmur, mutter.

Murmeltier ['murməlti:r], *n.* (—s, *pl.* —e) (*Zool.*) marmot; *wie ein — schlafen*, sleep like a log.

murren ['murən], *v.n.* grumble, growl.

mürrisch ['myrɪʃ], *adj.* morose, surly, sulky, peevish, sullen.

Mus [mu:s], *n.* (**—es,** *no pl.*) purée, (apple) sauce; pulp.

Muschel [ˈmuʃəl], *f.* (**—,** *pl.* **—n**) mussel, shell; (*telephone*) ear-piece.

Muse [ˈmu:zə], *f.* (**—,** *pl.* **—n**) muse.

Muselman [ˈmu:zəlman], *m.* (**—en,** *pl.* **—en**) Muslim, Moslem.

Musik [muˈzi:k], *f.* (**—,** *no pl.*) music.

musikalisch [muziˈka:liʃ], *adj.* musical.

Musikant [muziˈkant], *m.* (**—en,** *pl.* **—en**) musician; performer.

Musiker [ˈmu:zɪkər], *m.* (**—s,** *pl.* **—**) musician.

musizieren [muziˈtsi:rən], *v.n.* play music.

Muskateller [muskaˈtɛlər], *m.* (**—s,** *no pl.*) muscatel (wine).

Muskatnuß [musˈka:tnus], *f.* (**—,** *pl.* **-̈sse**) nutmeg.

Muskel [ˈmuskəl], *m.* (**—s,** *pl.* **—n**) muscle.

muskelig [ˈmusklɪç] *see* **musklig**.

Muskete [musˈke:tə], *f.* (**—,** *pl.* **—n**) musket.

Musketier [muskeˈti:r], *m.* (**—s,** *pl.* **—e**) musketeer.

musklig [ˈmusklɪç], *adj.* muscular.

muskulös [muskuˈlø:s], *adj.* muscular.

Muße [ˈmu:sə], *f.* (**—,** *no pl.*) leisure; *mit* **—,** leisurely, at leisure.

Musselin [musəˈli:n], *m.* (**—s,** *pl.* **—e**) muslin.

müssen [ˈmysən], *v.n. irr.* have to, be forced, be compelled, be obliged; *ich muß,* I must, I have to.

müßig [ˈmy:sɪç], *adj.* idle, lazy, unemployed.

Müßiggang [ˈmy:sɪçɡaŋ], *m.* (**—s,** *no pl.*) idleness, laziness, sloth.

Muster [ˈmustər], *n.* (**—s,** *pl.* **—**) sample; pattern; (proto-)type; (*fig.*) example.

Musterbild [ˈmustərbɪlt], *n.* (**—s,** *pl.* **—er**) paragon.

mustergültig [ˈmustərɡyltɪç], *adj.* exemplary; standard; excellent.

musterhaft [ˈmustərhaft], *adj.* exemplary.

mustern [ˈmustərn], *v.a.* examine, muster, scan; (*troops*) review, inspect.

Musterung [ˈmustəruŋ], *f.* (**—,** *pl.* **—en**) review; examination, inspection.

Mut [ˈmu:t], *m.* (**—es,** *no pl.*) courage, spirit; — *fassen,* take heart, muster up courage.

Mutation [mutaˈtsjo:n], *f.* (**—,** *pl.* **—en**) change.

mutieren [muˈti:rən], *v.n.* change; (*voice*) break.

mutig [ˈmu:tɪç], *adj.* courageous, brave.

mutlos [ˈmu:tlo:s], *adj.* discouraged, dejected, despondent.

mutmaßen [ˈmu:tma:sən], *v.a. insep.* surmise, suppose, conjecture.

Mutter [ˈmutər], *f.* (**—,** *pl.* **-̈**) mother; (*screw*) nut.

Mutterkorn [ˈmutərkɔrn], *n.* (**—s,** *no pl.*) ergot.

Mutterkuchen [ˈmutərku:xən], *m.* (**—s,** *pl.* **—**) placenta, after-birth.

Mutterleib [ˈmutərlaɪp], *m.* (**—s,** *no pl.*) womb, uterus.

Muttermal [ˈmutərma:l], *n.* (**—s,** *pl.* **—e**) birth-mark.

Mutterschaft [ˈmutərʃaft], *f.* (**—,** *no pl.*) motherhood, maternity.

mutterseelenallein [ˈmutərze:lənalaɪn], *adj.* quite alone; (*coll.*) all on o.'s own.

Muttersöhnchen [ˈmutərzø:nçən], *n.* (**—s,** *pl.* **—**) mother's darling, spoilt child.

Mutterwitz [ˈmutərvɪts], *m.* (**—es,** *no pl.*) mother-wit, native wit, common sense.

Mutwille [ˈmu:tvɪlə], *m.* (**—ns,** *no pl.*) mischievousness, wantonness.

Mütze [ˈmytsə], *f.* (**—,** *pl.* **—n**) cap; bonnet; beret.

Myrrhe [ˈmɪrə], *f.* (**—,** *pl.* **—n**) myrrh.

Myrte [ˈmɪrtə], *f.* (**—,** *pl.* **—n**) (*Bot.*) myrtle.

Mysterium [mɪsˈte:rjum], *n.* (**—s,** *pl.* **—rien**) mystery.

Mystik [ˈmɪstɪk], *f.* (**—,** *no pl.*) mysticism.

Mythologie [mytoloˈgi:], *f.* (**—,** *pl.* **—n**) mythology.

Mythus [ˈmytus], *m.* (**—,** *pl.* **Mythen**) myth.

N

N [ɛn], *n.* (**—s,** *pl.* **—s**) the letter N.

na [na], *int.* well, now; —*nu!* well, I never! — *und?* so what?

Nabe [ˈna:bə], *f.* (**—,** *pl.* **—n**) hub.

Nabel [ˈna:bəl], *m.* (**—s,** *pl.* **—**) navel.

Nabelschnur [ˈna:bəlʃnu:r], *f.* (**—,** *pl.* **-̈e**) umbilical cord.

nach [na:x], *prep.* (*Dat.*) after, behind, following; to, towards; according to, in conformity *or* accordance with; in imitation of. — *adv., prefix.* after, behind; afterwards, later; — *und* —, little by little, by degrees, gradually.

nachäffen [ˈna:xɛfən], *v.a.* ape, mimic, imitate; (*coll.*) take off.

nachahmen [ˈna:xa:mən], *v.a.* imitate, copy; counterfeit.

nacharbeiten [ˈna:xarbaɪtən], *v.n.* work after hours *or* overtime. — *v.a.* copy (*Dat.*).

nacharten [ˈna:xa:rtən], *v.n.* (*aux.* sein) resemble, (*coll.*) take after.

Nachbar [ˈnaxba:r], *m.* (**—s, —n,** *pl.* **—n**) neighbour.

Nachbarschaft [ˈnaxba:rʃaft], *f.* (**—,** *no pl.*) neighbourhood, vicinity; (*people*) neighbours.

nachbestellen [ˈna:xbəʃtɛlən], *v.a.* order more, re-order.

nachbilden ['naːxbɪldən], *v.a.* copy, reproduce.

nachdem [naːxˈdeːm], *adv.* afterwards, after that. — *conj.* after, when; *je —*, according to circumstances, that depends.

nachdenken ['naːxdɛŋkən], *v.n. irr.* think (over), meditate, muse, ponder.

nachdenklich ['naːxdɛŋklɪç], *adj.* reflective, pensive, wistful; — *stimmen*, set thinking.

Nachdruck ['naːxdruk], *m.* (**—s**, *pl.* **—e**) reprint; stress, emphasis.

nachdrucken ['naːxdrukən], *v.a.* reprint.

nachdrücklich ['naːxdryklɪç], *adj.* emphatic; — *betonen*, emphasise.

nacheifern ['naːxaɪfərn], *v.n. einem —*, emulate s.o.

nacheinander ['naːxaɪnandər], *adv.* one after another.

nachempfinden ['naːxɛmpfɪndən], *v.a. irr.* sympathize with, feel for.

Nachen ['naxən], *m.* (**—s**, *pl.* **—**) (*Poet.*) boat, skiff.

Nachfolge ['naːxfɔlgə], *f.* (**—**, *pl.* **—n**) succession.

nachfolgend ['naːxfɔlgənt], *adj.* following, subsequent.

Nachfolger ['naːxfɔlgər], *m.* (**—s**, *pl.* **—**) successor.

nachforschen ['naːxfɔrʃən], *v.a.* search after; enquire into, investigate.

Nachfrage ['naːxfraːgə], *f.* (**—**, *no pl.*) enquiry; (*Comm.*) demand; *Angebot und —*, supply and demand.

nachfühlen ['naːxfyːlən], *v.a. einem etwas —*, enter into s.o.'s feelings, sympathize with s.o.

nachfüllen ['naːxfylən], *v.a.* replenish, fill up.

nachgeben ['naːxgeːbən], *v.n. irr.* relax, slacken, yield; give in, relent, give way.

nachgehen ['naːxgeːən], *v.n. irr.* (*aux. sein*) *einem —*, follow s.o., go after s.o.; (*clock*) be slow; follow up, investigate.

nachgerade ['naːxgəraːdə], *adv.* by this time, by now; gradually.

nachgiebig ['naːxgiːbɪç], *adj.* yielding, compliant.

nachgrübeln ['naːxgryːbəln], *v.n.* speculate.

Nachhall ['naːxhal], *m.* (**—s,** *no pl.*) echo, resonance.

nachhaltig ['naːxhaltɪç], *adj.* lasting, enduring.

nachhängen ['naːxhɛŋən], *v.n. irr. seinen Gedanken —*, muse.

nachher ['naːxheːr], *adv.* afterwards, later on.

nachherig ['naːxheːrɪç], *adj.* subsequent, later.

Nachhilfestunde ['naːxhɪlfəʃtundə], *f.* (**—**, *pl.* **—n**) private coaching.

nachholen ['naːxhoːlən], *v.a.* make good; make up for.

Nachhut ['naːxhuːt], *f.* (**—**, *no pl.*) (*Mil.*) rearguard.

nachjagen ['naːxjaːgən], *v.n.* (*aux sein*) pursue.

Nachklang ['naːxklaŋ], *m.* (**—s**, *pl.* **—e**) echo; (*fig.*) after-effect, reminiscence.

Nachkomme ['naːxkɔmə], *m.* (**—n**, *pl.* **—n**) descendant, offspring.

nachkommen ['naːxkɔmən], *v.n. irr.* (*aux. sein*) come after, follow; *seiner Pflicht —*, do o.'s duty; comply with; *einem Versprechen —*, keep a promise; *seinen Verpflichtungen nicht — können*, be unable to meet o.'s commitments.

Nachkommenschaft ['naːxkɔmənʃaft], *f.* (**—**, *no pl.*) descendants, offspring, issue, progeny.

Nachlaß ['naːxlas], *m.* (**—sses**, *pl.* **—sse**) inheritance, estate, bequest; remission, discount, allowance.

nachlassen ['naːxlasən], *v.a. irr.* leave behind, bequeath; (*trade*) give a discount of. — *v.n.* abate, subside, slacken.

nachlässig ['naːxlɛsɪç], *adj.* negligent, remiss, careless.

nachlaufen ['naːxlaufən], *v.n. irr.* (*aux. sein*) *einem —*, run after s.o.

Nachlese ['naːxleːzə], *f.* (**—**, *pl.* **—n**) gleaning.

nachliefern ['naːxliːfərn], *v.a.* supply subsequently, complete delivery of.

nachmachen ['naːxmaxən], *v.a.* copy, imitate; counterfeit, forge.

nachmals ['naːxmaːls], *adv.* afterwards, subsequently.

Nachmittag ['naːxmɪtaːk], *m.* (**—s**, *pl.* **—e**) afternoon.

Nachnahme ['naːxnaːmə], *f.* (**—**, *no pl.*) *per —*, cash *or* (*Am.*) collect (payment) on delivery (*abbr.* C.O.D.).

nachplappern ['naːxplapərn], *v.a.* repeat mechanically.

Nachrede ['naːxreːdə], *f.* (**—**, *pl.* **—n**) epilogue; *üble —*, slander.

Nachricht ['naːxrɪçt], *f.* (**—**, *pl.* **—en**) news, information; (*Mil.*) intelligence; — *geben*, send word.

nachrücken ['naːxrykən], *v.n.* (*aux. sein*) move up.

Nachruf ['naːxruːf], *m.* (**—s**, *pl.* **—e**) obituary.

nachrühmen ['naːxryːmən], *v.a. einem etwas —*, speak well of s.o.

Nachsatz ['naːxzats], *m.* (**—es**, *pl.* **—e**) concluding clause; postscript.

nachschauen ['naːxʃauən], *v.n. jemandem —*, gaze after s.o.

nachschlagen ['naːxʃlaːgən], *v.a. irr.* look up, consult (a book).

Nachschlagewerk ['naːxʃlaːgəverk], *n.* (**—s**, *pl.* **—e**) work of reference, reference book.

Nachschlüssel ['naːxʃlysəl], *m.* (**—s**, *pl.* **—**) master-key, skeleton-key.

Nachschrift ['naːxʃrɪft], *f.* (**—**, *pl.* **—en**) postscript, (*abbr.* P.S.).

Nachschub ['naːxʃuːp], *m.* (**—s**, *pl.* **—e**) (fresh) supply; (*Mil.*) reinforcements.

Nachsehen ['naːxzeːən], *n.* (**—s**, *no pl.*) *das — haben*, be left out in the cold.

nachsehen ['na:xze:ən], *v.a., v.n. irr.*
look for, look s.th. up, refer to s.th.;
einem etwas —, be indulgent with s.o.
Nachsicht ['na:xzɪçt], *f.* (—, *no pl.*)
forbearance, indulgence.
Nachsilbe ['na:xzɪlbə], *f.* (—, *pl.* —n)
suffix.
nachsinnen ['na:xzɪnən], *v.n.* muse,
reflect.
nachsitzen ['na:xzitsən], *v.n.* be kept
in after school.
Nachsommer ['na:xzɔmər], *m.* (—s,
pl. —) Indian summer.
Nachspeise ['na:xʃpaɪzə], *f.* (—, *pl.* —n)
dessert.
nachspüren ['na:xʃpy:rən], *v.n. einem*
—, trace, track.
nächst [nɛ:çst], *prep.* (*Dat.*) next to,
nearest to. — *adj.* next.
Nächste ['nɛ:çstə], *m.* (—n, *pl.* —n)
fellow-man, neighbour.
nachstehen ['na:xʃte:ən], *v.n. irr.*
einem —, be inferior to s.o.; *keinem*
—, be second to none.
nachstehend ['na:xʃte:ənt], *adv.* below,
hereinafter. — *adj.* following.
nachstellen ['na:xʃtelən], *v.n. einem* —,
lie in wait for s.o.
Nachstellung ['na:xʃtɛluŋ], *f.* (—, *pl.*
—en) persecution, ambush; (*Gram.*)
postposition.
nächstens ['nɛ:çstəns], *adv.* soon,
shortly.
nachstöbern ['na:xʃtø:bərn], *v.n.* rummage.
nachströmen ['na:xʃtrø:mən], *v.n.*
(*aux.* sein) crowd after.
Nacht [naxt], *f.* (—, *pl.* ⁻e) night;
die ganze — *hindurch*, all night;
bei —, at night; *gute* — *wünschen*,
bid goodnight; *über* —, overnight;
in der —, during the night; *bei* — *und
Nebel*, in the dead of night.
Nachteil ['na:xtaɪl], *m.* (—s, *pl.* —e)
disadvantage, damage.
Nachtessen ['naxtɛsən], *n.* (—s, *pl.* —)
supper; evening meal.
Nachtfalter ['naxtfaltər], *m.* (—s, *pl.* —)
(*Ent.*) moth.
Nachtgeschirr ['naxtgəʃɪr], *n.* (—s,
pl. —e) chamber-pot.
Nachtgleiche ['naxtglaɪçə], *f.* (—, *pl.*
—n) equinox.
Nachthemd ['naxthɛmt], *n.* (—es, *pl.*
—en) night-dress, night-gown.
Nachtigall ['naxtɪgal], *f.* (—, *pl.* —en)
(*Orn.*) nightingale.
nächtigen ['nɛçtɪgən], *v.n.* spend the
night.
Nachtisch ['naxtɪʃ], *m.* (—es, *pl.* —e)
dessert.
Nachtlager ['naxtla:gər], *n.* (—s, *pl.*
—) lodgings for the night; (*Mil.*)
bivouac.
Nachtmahl ['naxtma:l], *n.* (—s, *pl.*
—e) (*Austr.*) supper.
nachtönen ['naxtø:nən], *v.n.* resound.
Nachtrag ['na:xtra:k], *m.* (—s, *pl.* ⁻e)
supplement, postscript, addition; (*pl.*)
addenda.

nachtragen ['na:xtra:gən], *v.a. irr.*
carry after; add; (*fig.*) *einem etwas* —,
bear s.o. a grudge.
nachträglich ['na:xtrɛ:klɪç], *adj.* subsequent; supplementary; additional;
further; later.
Nachtrupp ['na:xtrup], *m.* (—s, *no pl.*)
rearguard.
Nachtschwärmer ['naxtʃvɛrmər], *m.*
(—s, *pl.* —) night-reveller.
Nachttisch ['naxttɪʃ], *m.* (—es, *pl.* —e)
bedside-table.
nachtun ['na:xtu:n], *v.a. irr. einem
etwas* —, imitate s.o., emulate s.o.
Nachtwächter ['naxtvɛçtər], *m.* (—s,
pl. —) night-watchman.
Nachtwandler ['naxtvandlər], *m.* (—s,
pl. —) sleep-walker, somnambulist.
Nachwahl ['na:xva:l], *f.* (—, *pl.* —en)
by(e)-election.
Nachwehen ['na:xve:ən], *f. pl.* after-
math; unpleasant consequences.
Nachweis ['na:xvaɪs], *m.* (—es, *pl.*
—e) proof; (*Lit.*) reference; agency.
nachweisen ['na:xvaɪzən], *v.a. irr.*
prove, establish; (*Lit.*) refer.
Nachwelt ['na:xvɛlt], *f.* (—, *no pl.*)
posterity.
Nachwort ['na:xvɔrt], *n.* (—es, *pl.* —e)
epilogue.
Nachwuchs ['na:xvu:ks], *m.* (—es, *no
pl.*) coming generation; recruits.
Nachzahlung ['na:xtsa:luŋ], *f.* (—, *pl.*
—en) additional payment, supplementary payment.
Nachzählung ['na:xtsɛ:luŋ], *f.* (—, *pl.*
—en) recount.
nachziehen ['na:xtsi:ən], *v.a. irr.*
drag, tow; tighten; trace, pencil. —
v.n. follow.
Nachzügler ['na:xtsy:glər], *m.* (—s, *pl.*
—) straggler.
Nacken ['nakən], *m.* (—s, *pl.* —) nape,
scruff of the neck.
nackend ['nakənt], *adj.* naked.
nackt [nakt], *adj.* nude, naked; (*bird*)
callow; (*fig.*) bare; *sich* — *ausziehen*,
strip.
Nadel ['na:dəl], *f.* (—, *pl.* —n) needle,
pin; *wie auf* —*n sitzen*, be on tenterhooks.
Nadelöhr ['na:dəlø:r], *n.* (—s, *pl.* —e)
eye of a needle.
Nagel ['na:gəl], *m.* (—s, *pl.* ⁻) nail;
(*wooden*) peg; (*ornament*) stud; *etwas
an den* — *hängen*, lay s.th. aside, give
s.th. up.
nagelneu ['na:gəlnɔy], *adj.* brand new.
nagen ['na:gən], *v.a., v.n.* gnaw; (*fig.*)
rankle.
Näharbeit ['nɛ:arbaɪt], *f.* (—, *pl.* —en)
sewing, needlework.
nahe ['na:ə], *adj., adv.* near, close, nigh;
— *bei*, close to; — *daran sein*, be on
the point of; *es geht mir* —, it grieves
me, it touches me; *einem zu* —
treten, hurt s.o.'s feelings; *es liegt* —,
it is obvious, it suggests itself.
Nähe ['nɛ:ə], *f.* (—, *no pl.*) nearness,
proximity; *in der* —, at hand, close by.

nahen ['na:ən], v.n. (aux. sein) draw near, approach.

nähen ['nɛ:ən], v.a. sew, stitch.

Nähere ['nɛ:ərə], n. (—n, no pl.) details, particulars.

Näherin ['nɛ:ərɪn], f. (—, pl. — innen) seamstress, needlewoman.

nähern ['nɛ:ərn], v.r. sich —, draw near, approach.

nahestehen ['na:əʃte:ən], v.n. be closely connected or friendly (with s.o.).

Nährboden ['nɛ:rbo:dən], m. (—s, pl. ˙) rich soil; (Med., Biol.) culture-medium.

nähren ['nɛ:rən], v.a. nourish, feed. — v.r. sich — von, feed on; (fig.) gain a livelihood.

nahrhaft ['na:rhaft], adj. nourishing, nutritive, nutritious.

Nährstand ['nɛ:rʃtant], m. (—es, no pl.) peasants, producers.

Nahrung ['na:ruŋ], f. (—, no pl.) nourishment.

Nahrungsmittel ['na:ruŋsmɪtəl], n. (—s, pl. —) food, provisions, victuals.

Naht [na:t], f. (—, pl. ˙e) seam.

Nähzeug ['nɛ:tsɔyk], n. (—s, no pl.) sewing kit, work box.

naiv [na'i:f], adj. naïve, artless, guileless.

Naivität [naivi'tɛ:t], f. (—, no pl.) artlessness, guilelessness, naiveté.

Name ['na:mə], m. (—ns, pl. —n) name; guter —, good name, renown, reputation; dem —n nach, by name; etwas beim rechten —n nennen, call a spade a spade.

namens ['na:məns], adv. called; by the name of.

Namensvetter ['na:mənsfɛtər], m. (—s, pl. —n) namesake.

namentlich ['na:məntlɪç], adj. by name; particularly.

Namenverzeichnis ['na:menfɛrtsaɪç-nɪs], n. (—ses, pl. —se) list of names; (scientific) nomenclature.

namhaft ['na:mhaft], adj. distinguished, renowned; considerable; — machen, name.

nämlich ['nɛ:mlɪç], adv. namely, to wit.

Napf [napf], m. (—es, pl. ˙e) bowl, basin.

Napfkuchen ['napfku:xən], m. (—s, pl. —) pound-cake, large cake.

Narbe ['narbə], f. (—, pl. —n) scar; (leather) grain.

Narkose [nar'ko:zə], f. (—, pl. —n) anaesthesia; narcosis.

Narr [nar], m. (—en, pl. —en) fool; jester, buffoon; einen zum —en haben, make a fool of s.o.; an einem einen —en gefressen haben, dote on, be infatuated with s.o.

Narrheit ['narhaɪt], f. (—, pl. —en) foolishness, folly.

närrisch ['nɛrɪʃ], adj. foolish, comical; odd; merry; eccentric, mad; — werden, go mad.

Narzisse [nar'tsɪsə], f. (—, pl. —n) (Bot.) narcissus; gelbe —, daffodil.

naschen ['naʃən], v.a., v.n. pilfer titbits; nibble at, eat sweets.

Näscherei [nɛʃər'aɪ], f. (—, pl. —en) sweets, dainties, sweetmeats.

naschhaft ['naʃhaft], adj. sweet-toothed.

Naschkatze ['naʃkatsə], f. (—, pl. —n) sweet tooth.

Nase ['na:zə], f. (—, pl. —n) nose; (animal) snout; scent; stumpfe —, snub nose; gebogene —, Roman nose; immer der — nach, follow your nose; die — hoch tragen, be stuck-up; eine feine (gute) — haben, be good at; not miss much; die — rümpfen, turn up o.'s nose; seine — in alles stecken, poke o.'s nose into everything; einem etwas unter die — reiben, bring s.th. home to s.o.

näseln ['nɛ:zəln], v.n. speak with a twang.

Nasenbein ['na:zənbaɪn], n. (—s, pl. —e) nasal bone.

Nasenbluten ['na:zənblu:tən], n. (—s, no pl.) nose-bleed.

Nasenflügel ['na:zənfly:gəl], m. (—s, pl. —) side of the nose; nostril.

naseweis ['na:zəvaɪs], adj. pert, saucy.

Nashorn ['na:shɔrn], n. (—s, pl. ˙er) (Zool.) rhinoceros.

Naß [nas], n. (—sses, no pl.) (Poet.) fluid.

naß [nas], adj. wet, moist, damp.

Nässe ['nɛsə], f. (—, no pl.) wetness, dampness, moisture, humidity.

nationalisieren [natsjonali'zi:rən], v.a. nationalise.

Nationalität [natsjonali'tɛ:t], f. (—, pl. —en) nationality.

Natrium ['na:trjum], n. (—s, no pl.) sodium.

Natron ['natrɔn], n. (—s, no pl.) sodium carbonate; doppelkohlensaures —, sodium bicarbonate; bicarbonate of soda.

Natter ['natər,] f. (—, pl. —n) (Zool.) adder, viper.

Natur [na'tu:r], f. (—, pl. —en) nature; (body) constitution; (mind) disposition; von —, by nature, constitutionally; nach der — zeichnen, draw from nature.

naturalisieren [naturali'zi:rən], v.a. naturalise.

Naturalleistung [natu'ra:llaɪstuŋ], f. (—, pl. —en) payment in kind.

Naturell [natu'rɛl], n. (—s, pl. —e) natural disposition, temper.

Naturforscher [na'tu:rfɔrʃər], m. (—s, pl. —) naturalist.

naturgemäß [na'tu:rgəmɛ:s], adj. natural.

Naturgeschichte [na'tu:rgəʃɪçtə], f. (—, no pl.) natural history.

naturgetreu [na'tu:rgətrɔy], adj. true to nature, lifelike.

Naturkunde [na'tu:rkundə], f. (—, no pl.) natural history.

Naturlehre [na'tu:rle:rə], f. (—, no pl.) natural philosophy; physics.

natürlich

natürlich [na'ty:rlɪç], *adj.* natural; innate, inherent; unaffected, artless. — *adv.* of course, naturally.

Naturspiel [na'tu:rʃpi:l], *n.* (—s, *pl.* —e) freak of nature.

Naturtrieb [na'tu:rtri:p], *m.* (—s, *no pl.*) natural impulse, instinct.

naturwidrig [na'tu:rvi:drɪç], *adj.* contrary to nature, unnatural.

Naturwissenschaft [na'tu:rvɪsənʃaft], *f.* (—, *pl.* —en) (natural) science.

naturwüchsig [na'tu:rvy:ksɪç], *adj.* original; unsophisticated.

Nautik ['nautɪk], *f.* (—, *no pl.*) nautical science.

nautisch ['nautɪʃ], *adj.* nautical.

Nazi ['na:tsi], *abbr.* National Socialist.

Neapel [ne'a:pəl], *n.* Naples.

Nebel ['ne:bəl], *m.* (—s, *pl.* —) fog; *leichter —,* haze, mist; *dichter —,* (*London*) pea-souper; (*with soot*) smog.

Nebelschicht ['ne:bəlʃɪçt], *f.* (—, *pl.* —n) fog-bank.

neben ['ne:bən], *prep.* (*Dat., Acc.*) near, by, beside, besides, close to, next to; (*in compounds*) secondary, subsidiary, side-. — *adv.* beside, besides.

nebenan [ne:bən'an], *adv.* next door, nearby.

nebenbei [ne:bən'bai], *adv.* besides, by the way, incidentally.

Nebenbuhler ['ne:bənbu:lər], *m.* (—s, *pl.* —) rival.

nebeneinander [ne:bənain'andər], *adv.* side by side, abreast.

Nebenfluß ['ne:bənflus], *m.* (—sses, *pl.* ⸚sse) tributary, affluent.

nebenher [ne:bən'he:r], *adv.* by the side of, along with.

Nebenmensch ['ne:bənmɛnʃ], *m.* (—en, *pl.* —en) fellow creature.

Nebensatz ['ne:bənzats], *m.* (—es, *pl.* ⸚e) (*Gram.*) subordinate clause.

Nebenzimmer ['ne:bəntsimər], *n.* (—s, *pl.* —) adjoining room.

neblig ['ne:blɪç], *adj.* foggy, misty, hazy.

nebst [ne:pst], *prep.* (*Dat.*) together with, including.

necken ['nɛkən], *v.a.* tease, chaff, banter.

neckisch ['nɛkɪʃ], *adj.,* droll, playful, arch.

Neffe ['nɛfə], *m.* (—n, *pl.* —n) nephew.

Neger ['ne:gər], *m.* (—s, *pl.* —) Negro.

negerartig ['ne:gəra:rtɪç], *adj.* Negroid.

negieren [ne'gi:rən], *v.a.* deny, negate, negative.

nehmen ['ne:mən], *v.a. irr.* take, seize; receive, accept; *einem etwas —,* take s.th. from s.o.; *das lasse ich mir nicht —,* I insist on that, I am not to be done out of that; *ein Ende —,* come to an end; *etwas in die Hand —,* take s.th. in hand; *Schaden —,* suffer damage; *einen beim Wort —,* take s.o. at his word; *sich in acht —,* take care.

Nehrung ['ne:ruŋ], *f.* (—, *pl.* —en) narrow tongue of land, spit.

Neid [nait], *m.* (—es, *no pl.*) envy, grudge.

Neidhammel ['naithaməl], *m.* (—s, *pl.* —) dog in the manger.

neidisch ['naidɪʃ], *adj.* envious, grudging, jealous.

Neige ['naigə], *f.* (—, *pl.* —n) remnant, sediment; *zur — gehen,* be on the decline, run short, dwindle.

neigen ['naigən], *v.a., v.n.* incline, bow, bend; *zu etwas —,* be inclined to, be prone to. — *v.r. sich —,* bow.

Neigung ['naiguŋ], *f.* (—, *pl.* —en) inclination, proneness; affection; (*ground*) dip, slope, gradient; (*ship*) list.

Neigungsfläche ['naiguŋsflɛçə], *f.* (—, *pl.* —n) inclined plane.

nein [nain], *adv.* no.

Nekrolog [nekro'lo:k], *m.* (—(e)s, *pl.* —e) obituary.

Nelke ['nɛlkə], *f.* (—, *pl.* —n) (*Bot.*) pink, carnation; (*condiment*) clove.

nennen ['nɛnən], *v.a. irr.* name, call by name, term, style.

Nenner ['nɛnər], *m.* (—s, *pl.* —) denominator.

Nennung ['nɛnuŋ], *f.* (—, *pl.* —en) naming, mentioning.

Nennwert ['nɛnve:rt], *m.* (—s, *pl.* —e) nominal value.

Nepal ['ne:pal], *n.* Nepal.

Nerv [nɛrf], *m.* (—s, *pl.* —en) nerve, sinew; *einem auf die —en gehen,* get on s.o.'s nerves.

Nervenlehre ['nɛrfənle:rə], *f.* (—, *no pl.*) neurology.

nervig ['nɛrvɪç], *adj.* strong; (*fig.*) pithy.

nervös [nɛr'vø:s], *adj.* nervous, irritable, fidgety.

Nerz [nɛrts], *m.* (—es, *pl.* —e) mink.

Nessel ['nɛsəl], *f.* (—, *pl.* —n) nettle.

Nesseltuch ['nɛsəltu:x], *n.* (—es, *no pl.*) muslin.

Nest [nɛst], *n.* (—es, *pl.* —er) nest; (*eagle*) eyrie; *kleines —,* small town.

Nesthäkchen ['nɛsthɛ:kçən], *n.* (—s, *pl.* —) youngest child.

nett [nɛt], *adj.* nice, kind, friendly; neat, trim.

netto ['nɛto], *adv.* (*Comm.*) net, clear.

Netz [nɛts], *n.* (—es, *pl.* —e) net; (*Electr.*) grid; *Eisenbahn —,* railway network or system.

netzen ['nɛtsən], *v.a.* (*obs., Poet.*) wet, moisten.

Netzhaut ['nɛtshaut], *f.* (—, *pl.* ⸚e) retina.

neu [nɔy], *adj.* new, fresh; modern; recent; *aufs —e, von ..—em,* anew, afresh; *—e, —ere Sprachen,* modern languages.

Neuenburg ['nɔyənburk], *n.* Neuchâtel.

neuerdings ['nɔyərdɪŋs], *adv.* newly, lately.

Neuerer ['nɔyərər], *m.* (—s, *pl.* —) innovator.

neuerlich ['nɔyərlɪç], *adj.* late, repeated.

Neufundland [nɔy'funtlant], *n.* Newfoundland.

Neugier(de) ['nɔygiːr(də)], *f.* (—, *no pl.*) inquisitiveness, curiosity.

neugierig ['nɔygiːrɪç], *adj.* curious, inquisitive.

Neuheit ['nɔyhaɪt], *f.* (—, *pl.* —en) novelty.

Neuigkeit ['nɔyɪçkaɪt], *f.* (—, *pl.* —en) piece of news.

neulich ['nɔylɪç], *adv.* lately, recently.

Neuling ['nɔylɪŋ], *m.* (—s, *pl.* —e) novice, beginner, tyro, newcomer; (*Am.*) greenhorn.

neumodisch ['nɔymoːdɪʃ], *adj.* newfangled, in vogue.

Neumond ['nɔymoːnt], *m.* (—s, *pl.* —e) new moon.

neun [nɔyn], *num. adj.* nine.

Neunauge ['nɔynaugə], *n.* (—s, *pl.* —n) river lamprey.

neunzehn ['nɔyntseːn], *num. adj.* nineteen.

neunzig ['nɔyntsɪç], *num. adj.* ninety.

Neuregelung ['nɔyreːgəluŋ], *f.* (—, *pl.* —en) rearrangement.

Neuseeland [nɔy'zeːlant], *n.* New Zealand.

neutralisieren [nɔytrali'ziːrən], *v.a.* neutralise.

Neutralität [nɔytrali'tɛːt], *f.* (—, *no pl.*) neutrality.

Neutrum ['nɔytrum], *n.* (—s, *pl.* —ren) (*Gram.*) neuter.

Neuzeit ['nɔytsaɪt], *f.* (—, *no pl.*) modern times.

nicht [nɪçt], *adv.* not; *auch* —, nor; — *doch,* don't; — *einmal,* not even; *durchaus* —, not at all, by no means; — *mehr,* no more, no longer; not any more; *noch* —, not yet; — *wahr?* isn't it? aren't you? (*in compounds*) non–, dis–, a– (*negativing*).

Nichte ['nɪçtə], *f.* (—, *pl.* —n) niece.

nichten ['nɪçtən], *adv.* (*obs.*) *mit*—, by no means, not at all.

nichtig ['nɪçtɪç], *adj.* null, void, invalid.

Nichtigkeit ['nɪçtɪçkaɪt], *f.* (—, *no pl.*) invalidity, nullity.

nichts [nɪçts], *pron.* nothing, nought; — *als,* nothing but.

nichtsdestoweniger [nɪçtsdɛsto'veːnɪgər], *adv.* nevertheless.

Nichtsnutz ['nɪçtsnuts], *m.* (—es, *pl.* —e) good for nothing.

Nickel ['nɪkəl], *n.* (—s, *no pl.*) (*metal*) nickel.

nicken ['nɪkən], *v.n.* nod.

nie [niː], *adv.* never, at no time.

nieder ['niːdər], *adj.* low, lower, nether; mean, inferior. — *adv.* down.

niedergeschlagen ['niːdərgəʃlaːgən], *adj.* dejected, low-spirited, depressed.

niederkommen ['niːdərkɔmən], *v.n. irr.* (*aux.* sein) (*rare*) be confined.

Niederkunft ['niːdərkunft], *f.* (—, *no pl.*) confinement, childbirth.

Niederlage ['niːdərlaːgə], *f.* (—, *pl.* —n) (*enemy*) defeat, overthrow; (*goods*) depot, warehouse; agency.

Niederlande ['niːdərlandə], *n. pl.* the Netherlands.

niederlassen ['niːdərlasən], *v.a. irr.* let down. — *v.r. sich* —, sit down, take a seat; settle; establish o.s. in business.

Niederlassung ['niːdərlasuŋ], *f.* (—, *pl.* —en) establishment; settlement, colony; branch, branch establishment.

niederlegen ['niːdərleːgən], *v.a.* lay down, put down; (*office*) resign, abdicate. — *v.r. sich* —, lie down.

Niederschlag ['niːdərʃlaːk], *m.* (—s, *pl.* ⸚e) precipitation, sediment, deposit; rain.

niederschlagen ['niːdərʃlaːgən], *v.a. irr.* strike down; (*fig.*) depress, discourage; (*Law*) quash, cancel; (*eyes*) cast down; (*Chem.*) precipitate; (*Boxing*) knock out.

Niedertracht ['niːdərtraxt], *f.* (—, *no pl.*) baseness, meanness, villainy, beastliness.

Niederung ['niːdəruŋ], *f.* (—, *pl.* —en) low ground, marsh.

niedlich ['niːtlɪç], *adj.* pretty, dainty; (*Am.*) cute.

niedrig ['niːdrɪç], *adj.* low; (*fig.*) base, vile.

niemals ['niːmaːls], *adv.* never, at no time.

niemand ['niːmant], *pron.* nobody, no one.

Niere ['niːrə], *f.* (—, *pl,* —n) kidney.

Nierenbraten ['niːrənbraːtən], *m.* (—s, *no pl.*) roast loin.

Nierenfett ['niːrənfɛt], *n.* (—s, *no pl.*) suet.

nieseln ['niːzəln], *v.n. imp.* drizzle.

niesen ['niːzən], *v.n.* sneeze.

Nießbrauch ['niːsbraux], *m.* (—s, *no pl.*) usufruct, benefit.

Niete ['niːtə], *f.* (—, *pl.* —n) blank; (*Engin.*) rivet; failure.

Niger ['niːgər], *n.* Niger.

Nigeria [ni'geːrja], *n.* Nigeria.

Nikaragua [nika'raːgua], *n.* Nicaragua.

Nikolaus ['niːkolaus], *m.* Nicholas; *Sankt* —, Santa Claus.

Nil [niːl], *m.* (—s, *no pl.*) Nile.

Nilpferd ['niːlpfɛrt], *n.* (—s, *pl.* —e) (*Zool.*) hippopotamus.

nimmer (mehr) ['nɪmər (meːr)], *adv.* never, never again.

nippen ['nɪpən], *v.a., v.n.* sip, (take a) nip (of).

Nippsachen ['nɪpzaxən], *f. pl.* knickknacks.

nirgends ['nɪrgənts], *adv.* nowhere.

Nische ['niːʃə], *f.* (—, *pl.* —n) niche.

Nisse ['nɪsə], *f.* (—, *pl.* —n) nit.

nisten ['nɪstən], *v.n.* nest.

Niveau [ni'voː], *n.* (—s, *pl.* —s) level, standard.

nivellieren [nivɛ'liːrən], *v.a.* level.

Nixe ['nɪksə], *f.* (—, *pl.* —n) waternymph, mermaid, water-sprite.

Nizza

Nizza ['nɪtsa], *n.* Nice.
nobel ['no:bəl], *adj.* noble, smart; (*Am.*) swell; munificent, open-handed, magnanimous.
noch [nɔx], *adv.* still, yet; — *einmal,* — *mals,* once more; *weder . . . — . . .,* neither . . . nor . . .; — *nicht,* not yet; — *nie,* never yet, never before.
nochmalig ['nɔxma:lɪç], *adj.* repeated.
Nomade [no'ma:də], *m.* (—n, *pl.* —n) nomad.
nominell [nomi'nɛl], *adj.* nominal.
nominieren [nomi'ni:rən], *v.a.* nominate.
Nonne ['nɔnə], *f.* (—, *pl.* —n) nun.
Noppe ['nɔpə], *f.* (—, *pl.* —n) nap.
Norden ['nɔrdən], *m.* (—s, *no pl.*) north.
nördlich ['nœrtlɪç], *adj.* northern, northerly.
Nordsee ['nɔrtze:], *f.* North Sea.
nörgeln ['nœrgəln], *v.n.* find fault, cavil, carp, nag.
Norm ['nɔrm], *f.* (—, *pl.* —en) standard, rule, norm.
normal [nɔr'ma:l], *adj.* normal, standard.
Norwegen ['nɔrve:gən], *n.* Norway.
Not [no:t], *f.* (—, *pl.* ⁻e) need, necessity; misery, want, trouble, distress; (*in compounds*) emergency.
not [no:t], *pred. adj.* — *tun,* be necessary.
Nota ['no:ta], *f.* (—, *pl.* —s) bill, statement.
Notar [no'ta:r], *m.* (—s, *pl.* —e) notary.
Notdurft ['no:tdurft], *f.* (—, *pl.* ⁻e) want, necessaries, necessity; *seine — verrichten,* ease o.s.
notdürftig ['no:tdyrftɪç], *adj.* scanty, makeshift.
Note ['no:tə], *f.* (—, *pl.* —n) note; (*Mus.*) note; (*School*) mark(s); *nach —n,* (*fig.*) with a vengeance.
Notenbank ['no:tənbaŋk], *f.* (—, *pl.* —en) bank of issue.
Notenblatt ['no:tənblat], *n.* (—s, *pl.* ⁻er) sheet of music.
notgedrungen ['no:tgədruŋən], *adj.* compulsory, forced; perforce.
Nothelfer ['no:thɛlfər], *m.* (—s, *pl.* —) helper in time of need.
notieren [no'ti:rən], *v.a.* note, book; (*Comm.*) quote.
notifizieren [notifi'tsi:rən], *v.a.* notify.
nötig ['nø:tɪç], *adj.* necessary; — *haben,* want, need.
nötigen ['nø:tɪgən], *v.a.* compel, press, force, urge; necessitate; *sich — lassen,* stand upon ceremony.
Notiz [no'ti:ts], *f.* (—, *pl.* —en) note, notice; — *nehmen von,* take notice of; (*pl.*) notes, jottings.
notleidend ['no:tlaɪdənt], *adj.* financially distressed, indigent, needy.
notorisch [no'to:rɪʃ], *adj.* notorious.
Notstand ['no:tʃtant], *m.* (—s, *no pl.*) state of distress; emergency.

Notverband ['no:tfɛrbant], *m.* (—es, *pl.* ⁻e) first-aid dressing.
Notwehr ['no:tve:r], *f.* (—, *no pl.*) self-defence.
notwendig ['no:tvɛndɪç], *adj.* necessary, essential, needful.
Notzucht ['no:ttsuxt], *f.* (—, *no pl.*) rape, violation.
Novelle [no'vɛlə], *f.* (—, *pl.* —n) (*Lit.*) novella, short story, short novel.
Novize [no'vi:tsə], *m.* (—n, *pl.* —n) or *f.* (—, *pl.* —n) novice.
Nu [nu:], *m. & n.* (—, *no pl.*) moment; *im —,* in no time, in an instant.
Nubien ['nu:bjən], *n.* Nubia.
nüchtern ['nʏçtərn], *adj.* fasting; sober; jejune; (*fig.*) dry, matter-of-fact, realistic.
Nüchternheit ['nʏçtərnhaɪt], *f.* (—, *no pl.*) sobriety; (*fig.*) dryness.
Nudel ['nu:dəl], *f.* (—, *pl.* —n) noodles, macaroni, vermicelli; *eine komische —,* a funny person.
Null [nul], *f.* (—, *pl.* —en) nought, zero; (*fig.*) nonentity.
null [nul], *adj.* null; nil; — *und nichtig,* null and void; *etwas für — und nichtig erklären,* annul.
numerieren [nume'ri:rən], *v.a.* number.
Nummer ['numər], *f.* (—, *pl.* —n) number, size, issue.
nun [nu:n], *adv., conj.* now, at present; since; —*!* now! well! *von — an,* henceforth; — *und nimmermehr,* nevermore; *was —?* what next?
nunmehr ['nu:nme:r], *adv.* now, by this time.
Nunzius ['nuntsjus], *m.* (—, *pl.* —zien) (Papal) nuncio.
nur [nu:r], *adv.* only, solely, merely, but; *wenn —,* if only, provided that; — *das nicht,* anything but that; — *zu,* go to it!
Nürnberg ['nʏrnbɛrk], *n.* Nuremberg.
Nuß [nus], *f.* (—, *pl.* ⁻sse) nut.
Nußhäher ['nushɛ:ər], *m.* (—s, *pl.* —) (*Orn.*) jay.
Nüster ['nʏstər], *f.* (—, *pl.* —n) (*horse*) nostril.
Nutzanwendung ['nutsanvɛnduŋ], *f.* (—, *pl.* —en) practical application.
nutzbar ['nutsba:r], *adj.* useful, usable, productive.
nütze ['nʏtsə], *adj.* useful, of use.
Nutzen ['nutsən], *m.* (—s, *pl.* —) use, utility; profit, gain, advantage, benefit; — *bringen,* yield profit; — *ziehen aus,* derive profit from.
nützen ['nʏtsən], *v.a.* make use of, use. — *v.n.* be of use, serve, be effective, work.
nützlich ['nʏtslɪç], *adj.* useful.
nutzlos ['nutslo:s], *adj.* useless.
Nutznießer ['nutsni:sər], *m.* (—s, *pl.* —) beneficiary, usufructuary.
Nymphe ['nʏmfə], *f.* (—, *pl.* —en) nymph.

O

O [o:], *n*, (**—s**, *pl.* **—s**) the letter O.
o! [o:], *excl.* oh!
Oase [o'a:zə], *f.* (**—**, *pl.* **—n**) oasis.
ob [ɔp], *conj.*, whether; if; *als* **—**, as if; *und* **—!** rather! yes, indeed! **—** *prep.* (*Genit., Dat.*) on account of; upon, on.
Obacht ['o:baxt], *f.* (**—**, *no pl.*) heed, care; **—** *geben*, pay attention, look out.
Obdach ['ɔpdax], *n.* (**—es**, *no pl.*) shelter, lodging.
Obduktion ['ɔpdukts'jo:n], *f.* (**—**, *pl.* **—en**) post-mortem examination.
oben [o:bən], *adv.* above, aloft, on top; (*house*) upstairs; (*water*) on the surface; *von* **—** *bis unten*, from top to bottom; *von* **—** *herab*, from above; (*fig.*) haughtily, superciliously.
obendrein [o:bən'draɪn], *adv.* besides, into the bargain.
obengenannt ['o:bəngənant], *adj.* above-mentioned.
Ober ['o:bər], *m.* (**—s**, *pl.* **—**) head waiter; *Herr* **—!**, waiter!; (*in compounds*) upper, chief.
ober ['o:bər], *adj.* upper, higher; chief; superior.
Oberfläche ['o:bərflɛçə], *f.* (**—**, *pl.* **—n**) surface.
oberflächlich ['o:bərflɛçlɪç], *adj.* superficial, casual.
oberhalb ['o:bərhalp], *adv.*, *prep.* (*Genit.*) above.
Oberin ['o:bərɪn], *f.* (**—**, *pl.* **—innen**) (*Eccl.*) Mother Superior; hospital matron.
Oberschule ['o:bərʃu:lə], *f.* (**—**, *pl.* **—n**) high school, secondary school.
Oberst ['o:bərst], *m.* (**—en**, *pl.* **—en**) colonel.
Oberstaatsanwalt ['o:bərʃta:tsanvalt], *m.* (**—s**, *pl.* **⁻e**) Attorney-General.
oberste ['o:bərstə], *adj.* uppermost, highest, supreme.
Oberstimme ['o:bərʃtɪmə], *f.* (**—**, *pl.* **—n**) (*Mus.*) treble, soprano.
Oberstübchen ['o:bərʃty:pçən], *n.* (**—s**, *pl.* **—**) (*fig.*) *nicht richtig im* **—** *sein*, have bats in the belfry.
Obervolta ['o:bərvɔlta], *n.* Upper Volta.
obgleich [ɔp'glaɪç], *conj.* though, although.
Obhut ['ɔphu:t], *f.* (**—**, *no pl.*) keeping, care, protection.
obig ['o:bɪç], *adj.* foregoing, above-mentioned, aforementioned, aforesaid.
objektiv [ɔpjɛk'ti:f], *adj.* objective, impartial, unprejudiced.
Oblate [o'bla:tə], *f.* (**—**, *pl.* **—n**) wafer; (*Eccl.*) Host.

obliegen ['ɔpli:gən], *v.n. irr.* be incumbent upon s.o.; be o.'s duty; apply o.s. to.
Obmann ['ɔpman], *m.* (**—es**, *pl.* **⁻er**) chairman; (*jury*) foreman.
Obrigkeit ['o:brɪçkaɪt], *f.* (**—**, *pl.* **—en**) authorities.
obschon [ɔp'ʃo:n] *see under* **obwohl**.
Observatorium ['ɔpzɛrva'to:rjum], *n.* (**—s**, *pl.* **—rien**) observatory.
obsiegen ['ɔpzi:gən], *v.n.* (*rare*) be victorious.
Obst [o:pst], *n.* (**—es**, *no pl.*) fruit.
obszön [ɔps'tsø:n], *adj.* obscene.
obwalten ['ɔpvaltən], *v.n.* (*rare*) exist, prevail, obtain; *unter den* **—den** *Umständen*, in the circumstances, as matters stand.
obwohl [ɔp'vo:l] '(also **obschon** [ɔp'ʃo:n], **obzwar** [ɔp'tsva:r]), *conj.* though, although.
Ochse ['ɔksə], *m.* (**—n**, *pl.* **—n**) (*Zool.*) ox; bullock; (*fig.*) blockhead.
ochsen ['ɔksən], *v.n.* (*sl.*) swot, cram.
Ochsenauge ['ɔksənaugə], *n.* (**—s**, *pl.* **—n**) ox-eye, bull's eye; (*Archit.*) oval dormer window; porthole light.
Ochsenziemer ['ɔksəntsi:mər], *m.* (**—s**, *pl.* **—**) (*obs.*) horse-whip.
Ocker ['ɔkər], *m.* (**—s**, *no pl.*) ochre.
Öde ['ø:də], *f.* (**—**, *pl.* **—n**) wilderness.
öde ['ø:də], *adj.* desolate, bleak, dreary.
Odem ['o:dəm], *m.* (**—s**, *no pl.*) (*Poet.*) breath.
oder ['o:dər], *conj.* or; **—** *aber*, or else; **—** *auch*, or rather.
Ofen ['o:fən], *m.* (**—s**, *pl.* **⁻**) stove; oven, furnace.
Ofenpest [o:fən'pɛst], *n.* Budapest.
offen ['ɔfən], *adj.* open; (*fig.*) candid, sincere, frank; **—** *gestanden*, frankly speaking.
offenbar [ɔfən'ba:r], *adj.* obvious, manifest, evident.
offenbaren [ɔfən'ba:rən], *v.a. insep.* make known, reveal, disclose. **—** *v.r. sich einem* **—**, open o.'s heart to s.o.; unbosom o.s.
Offenheit ['ɔfənhaɪt], *f.* (**—**, *pl.* **—en**) frankness, candour.
offenkundig ['ɔfənkundɪç], *adj.* obvious, manifest.
offensichtlich ['ɔfənzɪçtlɪç], *adj.* obvious; apparent.
öffentlich ['œfəntlɪç], *adj.* public.
offerieren [ɔfe'ri:rən], *v.a.* offer.
Offerte [ɔ'fɛrtə], *f.* (**—**, *pl.* **—n**) offer, tender.
offiziell [ɔfi'tsjɛl], *adj.* official.
Offizier [ɔfi'tsi:r], *m.* (**—s**, *pl.* **—e**) officer, lieutenant.
Offizierspatent [ɔfi'tsi:rspatɛnt], *n.* (**—s**, *pl.* **—e**) (*Mil.*) commission.
offiziös [ɔfi'tsjø:s], *adj.* semi-official.
öffnen ['œfnən], *v.a.* open.
oft [ɔft], **oftmals** ['ɔftma:ls], *adv.* often, frequently.
öfters ['œftərs], *adv.* often, frequently.

Oheim

Oheim ['o:haɪm], *m.* (**—s**, *pl.* **—e**) (*Poet.*) uncle.

ohne ['o:nə], *prep.* (*Acc.*) without, but for, except.

ohnehin ['o:nəhɪn], *adv.* as it is.

Ohnmacht ['o:nmaxt], *f.* (**—**, *pl.* **—en**) fainting-fit, swoon; impotence; *in — fallen*, faint.

Ohr [o:r], *n.* (**—es**, *pl.* **—en**) ear; *bis über beide —en*, head over heels; *die —en spitzen*, prick up o.'s ears.

Ohrenbläser ['o:rənblɛ:zər], *m.* (**—s**, *pl.* **—**) tale-bearer.

Ohrensausen ['o:rənzauzən], *n.* (**—s**, *no pl.*) humming in the ears.

Ohrenschmaus ['o:rənʃmaus], *m.* (**—es**, *no pl.*) musical treat.

Ohrfeige ['o:rfaɪgə], *f.* (**—**, *pl.* **—n**) box on the ear.

Ohrläppchen ['o:rlɛpçən], *n.* (**—s**, *pl.* **—**) lobe of the ear.

Ohrmuschel ['o:rmuʃəl], *f.* (**—**, *pl.* **—n**) auricle.

oktav [ɔk'ta:f], *adj.* octavo.

Oktober [ɔk'to:bər], *m.* (**—s**, *pl.* **—**) October.

oktroyieren [ɔktroa'ji:rən], *v.a.* dictate, force s.th. upon s.o.

okulieren [oku'li:rən], *v.a.* (*trees*) graft.

Öl [ø:l], *n.* (**—s**, *pl.* **—e**) oil; (*rare*) olive-oil.

Ölanstrich ['ø:lanʃtriç], *m.* (**—s**, *pl.* **—e**) coat of oil-paint.

ölen ['ø:lən], *v.a.* oil, lubricate; (*rare*) anoint.

Ölgemälde ['ø:lgəmɛ:ldə], *n.* (**—s**, *pl.* **—**) oil painting.

Ölung ['ø:luŋ], *f.* (**—**, *pl.* **—en**) oiling; anointing; (*Eccl.*) *die letzte —*, Extreme Unction.

Olymp [o'lymp], *m.* Mount Olympus.

olympisch [o'lympɪʃ], *adj.* Olympian.

Omelett [ɔmə'lɛt], *n.* (**—s**, *pl.* **—s**) omelette.

Onkel ['ɔŋkəl], *m.* (**—s**, *pl.* **—**) uncle.

Oper ['o:pər], *f.* (**—**, *pl.* **—n**) opera.

operieren [opə'ri:rən], *v.a.*, *v.n.* operate (on); *sich — lassen*, be operated on; undergo an operation.

Opfer ['ɔpfər], *n.* (**—s**, *pl.* **—**) sacrifice; victim.

opfern ['ɔpfərn], *v.a.*, *v.n.* offer (up), sacrifice, immolate.

opponieren [ɔpo'ni:rən], *v.n.* oppose.

Optiker ['ɔptɪkər], *m.* (**—s**, *pl.* **—**) optician.

oratorisch [ora'to:rɪʃ], *adj.* oratorical.

Orchester [ɔr'kɛstər], *n.* (**—s**, *pl.* **—**) orchestra, band.

orchestrieren [ɔrkɛs'tri:rən], *v.a.* orchestrate, score for orchestra.

Orchidee [ɔrçi'de:], *f.* (**—**, *pl.* **—n**) (*Bot.*) orchid.

Orden ['ɔrdən], *m.* (**—s**, *pl.* **—**) medal; (*Eccl.*) (religious) order.

ordentlich ['ɔrdəntlɪç], *adj.* orderly, tidy, methodical, neat; regular; respectable, steady; sound; *—er Professor*, (full) professor.

Order ['ɔrdər], *f.* (**—**, *pl.* **—s**) (*Comm.*) order.

Ordinarius [ɔrdi'na:rjus], *m.* (**—**, *pl.* **—ien**) (*Univ.*) professor; (*Eccl.*) ordinary.

ordinär [ɔrdi'nɛ:r], *adj.* common, vulgar.

ordnen ['ɔrdnən], *v.a.* put in order, tidy, arrange, dispose.

Ordnung ['ɔrdnuŋ], *f.* (**—**, *pl.* **—en**) order, arrangement, disposition, routine; tidiness; class, rank; *in —*, all right, in good trim; *nicht in —*, out of order, wrong.

ordnungsgemäß ['ɔrdnuŋsgəmɛ:s], *adv.* duly.

ordnungsmäßig ['ɔrdnuŋsmɛsɪç], *adj.* regular.

ordnungswidrig ['ɔrdnuŋsvi:drɪç], *adj.* irregular.

Ordnungszahl ['ɔrdnuŋstsa:l], *f.* (**—**, *pl.* **—en**) ordinal number.

Ordonnanz [ɔrdɔ'nants], *f.* (**—**, *pl.* **—en**) ordinance; (*Mil.*) orderly.

Organ [ɔr'ga:n], *n.* (**—s**, *pl.* **—e**) organ.

organisieren [ɔrgani'zi:rən], *v.a.* organise.

Orgel ['ɔrgəl], *f.* (**—**, *pl.* **—n**) (*Mus.*) organ.

Orgelzug ['ɔ:rgəltsu:k], *m.* (**—s**, *pl.* **-̈e**) organ-stop.

Orgie ['ɔrgjə], *f.* (**—**, *pl.* **—n**) orgy.

orientalisch [ɔrjɛn'ta:lɪʃ], *adj.* oriental, eastern.

orientieren [ɔrjɛn'ti:rən], *v.a.* inform, orientate; set s.o. right. — *v.r. sich — über*, orientate o.s., find out about; get o.'s bearings.

Orkan [ɔr'ka:n], *m.* (**—s**, *pl.* **—e**) hurricane, gale, typhoon.

Ornat [ɔr'na:t], *m.* (**—es**, *pl.* **—e**) official robes; vestments.

Ort [ɔrt], *m.* (**—es**, *pl.* **—e**, **-̈er**) place, spot; region; (*in compounds*) local.

örtlich ['œrtlɪç], *adj.* local.

Ortschaft ['ɔrtʃaft], *f.* (**—**, *pl.* **—en**) place, township, village.

Öse ['ø:zə], *f.* (**—**, *pl.* **—n**) loop; *Haken und —n*, hooks and eyes.

Ostasien ['ɔsta:zjən], *n.* Eastern Asia, the Far East.

Ost(en) ['ɔst(ən)], *n.* (**—s**, *no pl.*) east.

ostentativ [ɔstɛnta'ti:f], *adj.* ostentatious.

Osterei ['o:stəraɪ], *n.* (**—s**, *pl.* **—er**) Easter egg.

Ostern ['o:stərn], *f. pl.* (used as *n. sing.*) Easter.

Österreich ['ø:stərraɪç], *n.* Austria.

Ostindien ['ɔstɪndjən], *n.* the East Indies.

östlich ['œstlɪç], *adj.* eastern, easterly.

Oxyd [ɔk'sy:t], *n.* (**—es**, *pl.* **—e**) oxide.

oxydieren [ɔksy'di:rən], *v.a.*, *v.n.* oxidise.

Ozean ['o:tsea:n], *m.* (**—s**, *pl.* **—e**) ocean, sea; *Grosser —*, Pacific (Ocean).

Ozon [o'tso:n], *n.* (**—s**, *no pl.*) ozone.

P

P [pe:], *n.* (—s, *pl.* —s) the letter P.
Paar [pa:r], *n.* (—es, *pl.* —e) pair, couple.
paar [pa:r], *adj. ein* —, a few, some.
Pacht [paxt], *f.* (—, *pl.* —en) lease; *in* — *nehmen,* take on lease.
Pachthof ['paxtho:f], *m.* (—s, *pl.* ⸚e) leasehold estate, farm.
Pack (1) [pak], *m.* (—s, *pl.* ⸚e) pack, bale, packet; *mit Sack und* —, (with) bag and baggage.
Pack (2) [pak], *n.* (—s, *no pl.*) rabble, mob.
Päckchen ['pɛkçən], *n.* (—s, *pl.* —) pack, packet; (small) parcel.
packen ['pakən], *v.a.* pack; seize; (*fig.*) —*d,* thrilling; *pack dich!* be off! scram!
pädagogisch [pɛ:da'go:gɪʃ], *adj.* educational, pedagogic(al).
paddeln ['padəln], *v.n.* paddle.
paff [paf], *excl.* bang! *ich bin ganz* —, I am astounded.
paffen ['pafən], *v.n.* puff; draw (at a pipe).
Page ['pa:ʒə], *m.* (—n, *pl.* —n) page-boy.
Paket [pa'ke:t], *n.* (—s, *pl.* —e) packet, package, parcel.
paktieren [pak'ti:rən], *v.n.* come to terms.
Palast [pa'last], *m.* (—es, *pl.* ⸚e) palace.
Palästina [palɛ'sti:na], *n.* Palestine.
Paletot ['paləto:], *m.* (—s, *pl.* —s) overcoat.
Palisanderholz [pali'zandərhɔlts], *n.* (—es, *no pl.*) rosewood.
Palme ['palmə], *f.* (—, *pl.* —n) (*Bot.*) palm-tree.
Palmkätzchen ['palmkɛtsçən], *n.* (—s, *pl.* —) (*Bot.*) catkin.
Palmwoche ['palmvɔxə], *f.* Holy Week.
Pampelmuse ['pampəlmu:zə], *f.* (—, *pl.* —n) (*Bot.*) grapefruit.
Panama ['pa:nama], *n.* Panama.
Panier [pa'ni:r], *n.* (—s, *pl.* —e) standard, banner.
panieren [pa'ni:rən], *v.a.* dress (*meat etc.*), roll in bread-crumbs.
Panne ['panə], *f.* (—, *pl.* —n) puncture; (*Motor.*) break-down; mishap.
panschen ['panʃən], *v.n.* splash about in water. —*v.a.* adulterate.
Pantoffel [pan'tɔfəl], *m.* (—s, *pl.* —n) slipper; *unter dem* — *stehen,* be henpecked.
Pantoffelheld [pan'tɔfəlhɛlt], *m.* (—en, *pl.* —en) henpecked husband.

Panzer ['pantsər], *m.* (—s, *pl.* —) armour, breast-plate, coat of mail; (*Mil.*) tank.
Papagei [papa'gaɪ], *m.* (—s, *pl.* —en) (*Orn.*) parrot.
Papier [pa'pi:r], *n.* (—s, *pl.* —e) paper; (*Comm.*) stocks; (*pl.*) papers, documents; *ein Bogen* —, a sheet of paper.
Papierkrieg [pa'pi:rkri:k], *m.* (—s, *no pl.*) (*coll.*) red tape.
Papierwaren [pa'pi:rva:rən], *f. pl.* stationery.
Pappdeckel ['papdɛkəl], *m.* (—s, *pl.* —) pasteboard.
Pappe ['papə], *f.* (—, *no pl.*) paste, cardboard, pasteboard.
Pappel ['papəl], *f.* (—, *pl.* —n) poplar.
pappen ['papən], *v.a.* stick; glue, paste.
Pappenstiel ['papənʃti:l], *m.* (—s, *pl.* —e) trifle.
papperlapapp ['papərlapap], *excl.* fiddlesticks! nonsense!
Papst [pa:pst], *m.* (—es, *pl.* ⸚e) Pope.
päpstlich ['pɛ:pstlɪç], *adj.* papal; —*er als der Papst,* fanatically loyal, outheroding Herod; over-zealous.
Parabel [pa'ra:bəl], *f.* (—, *pl.* —n) parable; (*Maths.*) parabola.
paradieren [para'di:rən], *v.n.* parade, make a show.
Paradies [para'di:s], *n.* (—es, *pl.* —e) paradise.
paradox [para'dɔks], *adj.* paradoxical.
Paragraph [para'gra:f], *m.* (—en, *pl.* —en) paragraph, article, clause, section.
Paraguay ['paragvaɪ, para'gua:ɪ], *n.* Paraguay.
Paralyse [para'ly:zə], *f.* (—, *pl.* —n) paralysis.
parat [pa'ra:t], *adj.* prepared, ready.
Pardon [par'dɔ̃], *m.* (—s, *no pl.*) pardon, forgiveness.
Parfüm [par'fy:m], *n.* (—s, *pl.* —e) perfume, scent.
pari ['pa:ri:], *adv.* at par.
parieren [pa'ri:rən], *v.a.* parry, keep off. —*v.n.* obey; *aufs Wort* —. obey implicitly *or* to the letter.
Parität [pari'tɛ:t], *f.* (—, *no pl.*) parity; (religious) equality.
Parkanlagen [park'anla:gən], *f. pl.* parks; public gardens.
parken ['parkən], *v.a.* park.
Parkett [par'kɛt], *n.* (—s, *pl.* —e) parquet flooring; (*Theat.*) stalls.
Parkuhr [park'u:r], *f.* (—, *pl.* —en) parking-meter.
Parlament [parla'mɛnt], *n.* (—s, *pl.* —e) parliament.
Parlamentär [parlamɛn'tɛ:r], *m.* (—s, *pl.* —e) officer negotiating a truce.
Parlamentarier [parlamɛn'ta:rjər], *m.* (—s, *pl.* —) parliamentarian, member of a parliament.
Parole [pa'ro:lə], *f.* (—, *pl.* —n) watchword, cue, motto, slogan, password.

Partei

Partei [par'taɪ], *f.* (—, *pl.* **—en**) party, faction; — *nehmen für*, side with.

Parteigänger [par'taɪgɛŋər], *m.* (—s, *pl.* —) partisan.

Parteigenosse [par'taɪgənɔsə], *m.* (—n, *pl.* —n) party member (especially National Socialist); comrade.

parteiisch [par'taɪɪʃ], *adj.* partial, biased, prejudiced.

Parteinahme [par'taɪna:mə], *f.* (—, *no pl.*) partisanship.

Parteitag [par'taɪta:k], *m.* (—s, *pl.* —e) party conference; congress.

Parterre [par'tɛrə], *n.* (—s, *pl.* —s) ground floor; (*Theat.*) pit; stalls.

Partie [par'ti:], *f.* (—, *pl.* —n) (*Comm.*) parcel; (*marriage*) match; (*chess etc.*) game; (*bridge*) rubber; outing, excursion, trip.

Partitur [parti'tu:r], *f.* (—, *pl.* —en) (*Mus.*) score.

Partizip [parti'tsi:p], *n.* (—s, *pl.* —e, —ien) (*Gram.*) participle.

Parzelle [par'tsɛlə], *f.* (—, *pl.* —n) allotment, lot, parcel.

paschen ['paʃən], *v.a.* smuggle.

Paß [pas], *m.* (—sses, *pl.* ⁓sse) (*mountain*) pass; (*travelling*) passport; (*horse*) amble.

Passagier [pasa'ʒi:r], *m.* (—s, *pl.* —e) passenger; *blinder* —, stowaway.

Passant [pa'sant], *m.* (—en, *pl.* —en) passer-by.

Passatwind [pa'sa:tvɪnt], *m.* (—s, *pl.* —e) trade-wind.

passen ['pasən], *v.n.* fit, suit, be suitable, be convenient; (*Cards*) pass.

passieren [pa'si:rən], *v.a.* sieve; (*road*) pass, cross, negotiate. — *v.n.* (*aux.* sein) pass; happen, take place, come about.

Passif, Passivum [pa'si:f *or* 'pasi:f, pa'si:vum], *n.* (—s, *pl.* —e; —, *pl.* —va) (*Gram.*) passive voice; (*Comm.*) (*pl.*) debts, liabilities.

Passus ['pasus], *m.* (—, *pl.* —) passage (in book).

Pasta, Paste ['pasta, 'pastə], *f.* (—, *pl.* —ten) paste.

Pastell [pa'stɛl], *m.* (—s, *pl.* —e) pastel, crayon; — *malen*, draw in pastel.

Pastete [pa'ste:tə], *f.* (—, *pl.* —n) pie, pastry.

Pastille [pa'stɪlə], *f.* (—, *pl.* —n) lozenge, pastille.

Pastor ['pastɔr], *m.* (—s, *pl.* —en) minister, pastor; parson; vicar, rector.

Pate ['pa:tə], *m.* (—n, *pl.* —n) godparent; — *stehen*, be godfather to.

patent [pa'tent], *adj.* fine, grand, (*sl.*) smashing.

Patent [pa'tent], *n.* (—(e)s, *pl.* —e) patent; charter, licence.

patentieren [paten'ti:rən], *v.a.* patent, license.

pathetisch [pa'te:tɪʃ], *adj.* elevated, solemn, moving.

Patin ['pa:tɪn], *f.* (—, *pl.* **—innen**) godmother.

patriotisch [patri'o:tɪʃ], *adj.* patriotic.

Patrone [pa'tro:nə], *f.* (—, *pl.* —n) cartridge; stencil, pattern.

Patrouille [pa'truljə], *f.* (—, *pl.* —n) (*Mil.*) patrol.

Patsche ['patʃə], *f.* (—, *pl.* —n) (*dial.*) hand; (*fig.*) mess, pickle; *in eine — geraten*, get into a jam.

patschen ['patʃən], *v.n.* (*aux.* sein) splash.

Patt [pat], *n.* (—s, *pl.* —s) (*Chess*) stalemate.

patzig ['patsɪç], *adj.* rude; cheeky, saucy.

Pauke ['paukə], *f.* (—, *pl.* —n) kettledrum; *mit —n und Trompeten*, with drums beating and colours flying.

pauken ['paukən], *v.n.* beat the kettledrum; (*coll.*) swot, plod, grind; fight a duel.

pausbackig ['pausbakɪç], *adj.* chubbyfaced, bonny.

Pauschale [pau'ʃa:lə], *f.* (—, *pl.* —n) lump sum.

Pause ['pauzə], *f.* (—, *pl.* —n) pause, stop; (*Theat.*) interval; (*Sch.*) playtime, break; (*Tech.*) tracing.

pausen ['pauzən], *v.a.* trace.

pausieren [pau'zi:rən], *v.n.* pause.

Pavian ['pa:vja:n], *m.* (—s, *pl.* —e) (*Zool.*) baboon.

Pech [pɛç], *n.* (—es, *no pl.*) pitch; (*shoemaker's*) wax; (*fig.*) bad luck, rotten luck.

pechschwarz ['pɛçʃvarts], *adj.* black as pitch.

Pechvogel ['pɛçfo:gəl], *m.* (—s, *pl.* ⁓) unlucky fellow.

Pedell [pe'dɛl], *m.* (—s, *pl.* —e) beadle; porter, caretaker; (*Univ. sl.*) bulldog.

Pegel ['pe:gəl], *m.* (—s, *pl.* —) watergauge.

peilen ['paɪlən], *v.a.*, *v.n.* sound, measure, take bearings (of).

Pein [paɪn], *f.* (—, *no pl.*) pain, torment.

peinigen ['paɪnɪgən], *v.a.* torment; harass, distress.

peinlich ['paɪnlɪç], *adj.* painful, disagreeable; embarrassing; delicate; strict, punctilious; (*Law*) capital, penal.

Peitsche ['paɪtʃə], *f.* (—, *pl.* —n) whip.

pekuniär [pekun'jɛ:r], *adj.* financial.

Pelerine [pelə'ri:nə], *f.* (—, *pl.* —n) cape.

Pelle ['pɛlə], *f.* (—, *pl.* —n) peel, husk.

Pellkartoffeln ['pɛlkartɔfəln], *f. pl.* potatoes in their jackets.

Pelz [pɛlts], *m.* (—es, *pl.* —e) pelt, fur; fur coat.

pelzig ['pɛltsɪç], *adj.* furry.

Pendel ['pɛndəl], *n.* (—s, *pl.* —) pendulum.

pendeln ['pɛndəln], *v.n.* swing, oscillate; commute.

pennen ['pɛnən], *v.n.* (*sl.*) sleep.

Pension [pɑ̃'sjoːn], f. (—, pl. —en) pension; boarding-house; board and lodging.

Pensionat [pɑ̃sjo'naːt], n. (—s, pl. —e) boarding-school.

pensionieren [pɑ̃sjo'niːrən], v.a. pension off; sich — lassen, retire.

Pensum ['pɛnzum], n. (—s, pl. —sen) task; curriculum, syllabus.

per [pɛr], prep. — Adresse, care of.

Perfekt [pɛr'fɛkt], n. (—s, pl. —e) (Gram.) perfect (tense).

perforieren [pɛrfo'riːrən], v.a. perforate, punch.

Pergament [pɛrga'mɛnt], n. (—s, pl. —e) parchment, vellum.

Perle ['pɛrlə], f. (—, pl. —n) pearl; (glass) bead; (fig.) gem, treasure.

perlen ['pɛrlən], v.n. sparkle.

Perlgraupe ['pɛrlgraupə], f. (—, no pl.) (Bot.) pearl-barley.

Perlhuhn ['pɛrlhuːn], n. (—s, pl. ⁻er) (Zool.) guinea-fowl.

Perlmutter ['pɛrlmutər], f. (—, no pl.) mother-of-pearl.

Perpendikel [pɛrpən'diːkəl], m. & n. (—s, pl. —) pendulum.

Perser ['pɛrzər], m. (—s, pl. —) Persian; echter —, genuine Persian carpet.

Persien ['pɛrzjən], n. Persia.

Personal [pɛrzo'naːl], n. (—s, no pl.) personnel, staff.

Personalien [pɛrzo'naːljən], n. pl. particulars (of a person).

Personenverkehr [pɛr'zoːnənfɛrkeːr], m. (—s, no pl.) passenger-traffic.

Personenzug [pɛr'zoːnəntsuːk], m. (—s, pl. ⁻e) (slow) passenger train.

personifizieren [pɛrzonifi'tsiːrən], v.a. personify, embody, impersonate.

Persönlichkeit [pɛr'zøːnlɪçkaɪt], f. (—, pl. —en) personality, person.

perspektivisch [pɛrspɛk'tiːvɪʃ], adj. perspective.

Peru [pe'ruː], n. Peru.

Perücke [pe'rykə], f. (—, pl. —n) wig.

Pest [pɛst], f. (—, no pl.) plague, pestilence.

pestartig ['pɛsta:rtɪç], adj. pestilential.

Petersilie [pe:tər'ziːljə], f. (—, no pl.) (Bot.) parsley.

petitionieren [petitsjo'niːrən], v.a. petition.

Petschaft ['pɛtʃaft], n. (—s, pl. —e) seal, signet.

Petz [pɛts], m. (—es, pl. —e) Meister —, Bruin (the bear).

petzen ['pɛtsən], v.n. tell tales (about), sneak.

Pfad [pfaːt], m. (—es, pl. —e) path.

Pfadfinder ['pfaːtfɪndər], m. (—s, pl. —) Boy Scout.

Pfaffe ['pfafə], m. (—n, pl. —n) (pej.) cleric, priest.

Pfahl [pfaːl], m. (—s, pl. ⁻e) post, stake.

Pfahlbauten ['pfaːlbautən], m. pl. lake dwellings.

pfählen ['pfɛːlən], v.a. fasten with stakes; impale.

Pfand [pfant], n. (—s, pl. ⁻er) pawn, pledge; security; (game) forfeit; ein — einlösen, redeem a pledge.

pfänden ['pfɛndən], v.a. take in pledge; seize.

Pfänderspiel ['pfɛndərʃpiːl], n. (—s, pl. —e) game of forfeits.

Pfandgeber ['pfantgeːbər], m. (—s, pl. —) pawner.

Pfandleiher ['pfantlaɪər], m. (—s, pl. —) pawnbroker.

Pfandrecht ['pfantrɛçt], n. (—s, no pl.) lien.

Pfändung ['pfɛnduŋ], f. (—, pl. —en) seizure, attachment, distraint.

Pfanne ['pfanə], f. (—, pl. —n) pan, frying-pan.

Pfannkuchen ['pfanku:xən], m. (—s, pl. —) pancake; Berliner —, doughnut.

Pfarre ['pfarə], f. (—, pl. —n) living, parish; (house) vicarage, parsonage, manse.

Pfarrer ['pfarər], m. (—s, pl. —) parson; vicar, (parish) priest.

Pfau [pfau], m. (—en, pl. —en) (Orn.) peacock.

Pfauenauge ['pfauənaugə], n. (—s, pl. —n) (Ent.) peacock butterfly.

Pfeffer ['pfɛfər], m. (—s, no pl.) pepper; spanischer —, red pepper, cayenne.

Pfefferkuchen ['pfɛfərku:xən], m. (—s, pl. —) gingerbread, spiced cake.

Pfefferminz ['pfɛfərmɪnts], n. (—, no pl.) peppermint.

Pfeife ['pfaɪfə], f. (—, pl. —n) whistle, fife; pipe.

pfeifen ['pfaɪfən], v.a., v.n. irr. whistle, play the fife; (Theat.) boo, hiss; (bullets) whiz(z).

Pfeifenrohr ['pfaɪfənro:r], n. (—s, pl. —e) pipe-stem.

Pfeil [pfaɪl], m. (—es, pl. —e) arrow, dart, bolt.

Pfeiler ['pfaɪlər], m. (—s, pl. —) pillar.

Pfeilwurz ['pfaɪlvurts], f. (—, no pl.) (Bot.) arrow root.

Pfennig ['pfɛnɪç], m. (—s, pl. —e) one hundredth of a mark; (loosely) penny.

Pferch [pfɛrç], m. (—es, pl. —e) fold, pen.

Pferd [pfeːrt], n. (—es, pl. —e) horse; zu —, on horseback; vom — steigen, dismount.

Pferdeknecht ['pfeːrdəknɛçt], m. (—es, pl. —e) groom.

Pferdestärke ['pfeːrdəʃtɛrkə], f. (—, no pl.) horse-power (abbr. PS).

Pfiff [pfɪf], m. (—s, pl. —e) whistle.

Pfifferling ['pfɪfərlɪŋ], m. (—s, pl. —e) (Bot.) mushroom; chanterelle; einen — wert, worthless.

pfiffig ['pfɪfɪç], adj. cunning, sly, crafty.

Pfiffikus ['pfɪfɪkus], m. (—, pl. —se) (coll.) sly dog.

Pfingsten ['pfɪŋkstən], *n.* Whitsun (-tide), Pentecost.
Pfingstrose ['pfɪŋkstroːzə], *f.* (—, *pl.* (*Bot.*) peony.
Pfirsich ['pfɪrzɪç], *m.* (—s, *pl.* —e) (*Bot.*) peach.
Pflanze ['pflantsə], *f.* (—, *pl.* —n) plant.
pflanzen ['pflantsən], *v.a.* plant.
Pflanzer ['pflantsər], *m.* (—s, *pl.* —) planter.
pflanzlich ['pflantslɪç], *adj.* vegetable, botanical.
Pflänzling ['pflɛntslɪŋ], *m.* (—s, *pl.* —e) seedling, young plant.
Pflanzung ['pflantsuŋ], *f.* (—, *pl.* —en) plantation.
Pflaster ['pflastər], *n.* (—s, *pl.* —) (*Med.*) plaster; (*street*) pavement; *ein teures* —, an expensive place to live in.
Pflaume ['pflaumə], *f.* (—, *pl.* —n) plum; *getrocknete* —, prune.
Pflege ['pfleːgə], *f.* (—, *no pl.*) care, attention, nursing, fostering.
Pflegeeltern ['pfleːgəɛltərn], *pl.* foster-parents.
pflegen ['pfleːgən], *v.a.* nurse, look after, take care of; *Umgang* — *mit*, associate with. — *v.n.* be used to, be in the habit of.
Pflegling ['pfleːklɪŋ], *m.* (—s, *pl.* —e) foster-child, ward.
Pflicht [pflɪçt], *f.* (—, *pl.* —en) duty, obligation.
Pflichtgefühl ['pflɪçtgəfyːl], *n.* (—s, *no pl.*) sense of duty.
pflichtgemäß ['pflɪçtgəmɛːs], *adj.* dutiful.
pflichtschuldig ['pflɪçtʃuldɪç], *adj.* in duty bound.
Pflock [pflɔk], *m.* (—s, *pl.* ⁻e) plug, peg.
pflücken ['pflykən], *v.a.* pluck, pick, gather.
Pflug [pfluːk], *m.* (—es, *pl.* ⁻e) plough.
Pflugschar ['pfluːkʃaːr], *f.* (—, *pl.* —en) ploughshare.
Pforte ['pfɔrtə], *f.* (—, *pl.* —n) gate, door, porch.
Pförtner ['pfœrtnər], *m.* (—s, *pl.* —) door-keeper, porter.
Pfosten ['pfɔstən], *m.* (—s, *pl.* —) post, stake; (*door*) jamb.
Pfote ['pfoːtə], *f.* (—, *pl.* —n) paw.
Pfriem [pfriːm], *m.* (—es, *pl.* —e) awl.
Pfropf(en) ['pfrɔpf(ən)], *m.* (—s, *pl.* —en) cork, stopper; (*gun*) wad.
pfropfen ['pfrɔpfən], *v.a.* graft; cork.
Pfründe ['pfryndə], *f.* (—, *pl.* —n) living, benefice.
Pfuhl [pfuːl], *m.* (—es, *pl.* —e) pool, puddle.
Pfühl [pfyːl], *m.* (—es, *pl.* —e) (*Poet.*) bolster, pillow, cushion.
pfui! [pfui], *excl.* shame! ugh! — *Teufel!* shame! a damned shame!
Pfund [pfunt], *n.* (—es, *pl.* —e) pound.
pfuschen ['pfuʃən], *v.n.* botch; *einem ins Handwerk* —, poach on s.o. else's preserve.

Pfütze ['pfytsə], *f.* (—, *pl.* —n) puddle.
Phänomen [fɛːnoˈmeːn], *n.* (—s, *pl.* —e) phenomenon.
Phantasie [fantaˈziː], *f.* (—, *pl.* —n) fancy, imagination; (*Mus.*) fantasia.
phantasieren [fantaˈziːrən], *v.n.* indulge in fancies; (*sick person*) rave, wander, be delirious; (*Mus.*) improvise.
Phantast [fanˈtast], *m.* (—en, *pl.* —en) dreamer, visionary.
Pharisäer [fariˈzɛːər], *m.* (—s, *pl.* —) Pharisee.
Phase ['faːzə], *f.* (—, *pl.* —n) phase, stage (of process *or* development).
Philippinen [filiˈpiːnən], *f. pl.* Philippines.
Philister [fiˈlɪstər], *m.* (—s, *pl.* —) Philistine.
philisterhaft [fiˈlɪstərhaft], *adj.* philistine, narrow-minded, conventional.
Philologie [filoloˈgiː], *f.* (—, *no pl.*) philology; study of languages.
Philosoph [filoˈzoːf], *m.* (—en, *pl.* —en) philosopher.
Philosophie [filozoˈfiː], *f.* (—, *pl.* —n) philosophy.
Phiole [fiˈoːlə], *f.* (—, *pl.* —n) phial, vial.
Phlegma ['flɛgma], *n.* (—s, *no pl.*) phlegm.
Phonetik [foˈneːtɪk], *f.* (—, *no pl.*) phonetics.
photogen [fotoˈgeːn], *adj.* photogenic.
Photograph [fotoˈgraːf], *m.* (—en, *pl.* —en) photographer.
Photographie [fotograˈfiː], *f.* (—, *pl.* —n) photograph, photo; (*Art*) photography.
photographieren [fotograˈfiːrən], *v.a.* photograph.
Physik [fyˈziːk], *f.* (—, *no pl.*) physics.
physikalisch [fyziˈkaːlɪʃ], *adj.* physical (of physics).
Physiker ['fyːzɪkər], *m.* (—s, *pl.* —) physicist.
Physiologe [fyːzjoˈloːgə], *m.* (—en, *pl.* —en) physiologist.
physiologisch [fyːzjoˈloːgɪʃ], *adj.* physiological.
physisch ['fyːzɪʃ], *adj.* physical.
Picke ['pɪkə], *f.* (—, *pl.* —n) pickaxe, axe.
Pickel ['pɪkəl], *m.* (—s, *pl.* —) pimple.
Piedestal ['pjeːdɛstaːl], *n.* (—s, *pl.* —e) pedestal.
piepen ['piːpən], *v.n.* squeak, chirp.
piepsen ['piːpsən], *v.n.* squeak, chirp.
Pietät [pieˈtɛːt], *f.* (—, *no pl.*) piety, reverence.
Pik [piːk], *n.* (—s, *pl.* —s) (*cards*) spades.
pikant [piˈkant], *adj.* piquant, spicy; (*fig.*) risqué.
Pikee [piˈkeː], *m.* (—s, *pl.* —s) piqué.
pikiert [piˈkiːrt], *adj.* irritated, annoyed, piqued.
Pikkolo ['pɪkolo], *m.* (—s, *pl.* —s) apprentice waiter, boy (waiter); (*Mus.*) piccolo, flute.

pochen

Pilger ['pɪlgər], *m.* (—s, *pl.* —) pilgrim.
Pille ['pɪlə], *f.* (—, *pl.* —n) pill.
Pilz [pɪlts], *m.* (—es, *pl.* —e) fungus, mushroom.
Piment [pi'mɛnt], *n.* (—s, *pl.* —e) pimento, Jamaican pepper, all-spice.
pimplig ['pɪmplɪç], *adj.* effeminate.
Pinguin ['pɪŋgu'i:n], *m.* (—s, *pl.* —e) (*Orn.*) penguin.
Pinie ['pi:njə], *f.* (—, *pl.* —n) (*Bot.*) stone-pine.
Pinne ['pɪnə], *f.* (—, *pl.* —n) drawing-pin; peg.
Pinscher ['pɪnʃər], *m.* (—s, *pl.* —) terrier.
Pinsel ['pɪnzəl], *m.* (—s, *pl.* —) (*Painting*) brush, pencil; (*fig.*) simpleton.
Pinzette [pɪn'tsɛtə], *f.* (—, *pl.* —n) pincers, tweezers.
Pirsch [pɪrʃ], *f.* (—, *no pl.*) (deer-)stalking.
Piste ['pɪstə], *f.* (—, *pl.* —n) track; (*Aviat.*) runway.
pittoresk [pɪto'rɛsk], *adj.* picturesque.
placken ['plakən], *v.r. sich* —, toil, drudge.
plädieren [plɛ'di:rən], *v.n.* plead.
Plädoyer [plɛ:doa'je:], *n.* (—s, *pl.* —s) speech for the prosecution *or* the defence (in a court of law), plea, pleading.
Plage ['pla:gə], *f.* (—, *pl.* —n) torment, trouble; calamity; plague.
plagen ['pla:gən], *v.a.* plague, trouble, torment, vex. — *v.r. sich* —, toil.
Plagiat [plag'ja:t], *n.* (—es, *pl.* —e) plagiarism.
Plaid [ple:t], *n.* (—s, *pl.* —s) travelling-rug.
Plakat [pla'ka:t], *n.* (—(e)s, *pl.* —e) poster, placard, bill.
Plan [pla:n], *n.* (—es, *pl.* ̈e) plan, scheme, plot; map, ground-plan.
Plane ['pla:nə], *f.* (—, *pl.* —n) awning, cover.
planieren [pla'ni:rən], *v.a.* level, plane down; bulldoze, flatten.
Planke ['plaŋkə], *f.* (—, *pl.* —n) plank, board.
Plänkelei [plɛnkə'laɪ], *f.* (—, *pl.* —en) skirmish.
planmäßig ['pla:nmɛ:sɪç], *adj.* according to plan.
planschen ['planʃən], *v.n.* splash; paddle.
Plantage [plan'ta:ʒə], *f.* (—, *pl.* —n) plantation.
planvoll ['pla:nfɔl], *adj.* systematic, well-planned.
Planwagen ['pla:nva:gən], *m.* (—s, *pl.* —) tilt-cart.
plappern ['plapərn], *v.n.* prattle, chatter.
plärren ['plɛrən], *v.n.* blubber, bawl.
Plastik ['plastɪk], *f.* (—, *pl.* —en) plastic art; plastic (material).
Platane [pla'ta:nə], *f.* (—, *pl.* —n) plane-tree.

Platin ['pla:ti:n], *n.* (—s, *no pl.*) platinum.
platonisch [pla'to:nɪʃ], *adj.* platonic.
plätschern ['plɛtʃərn], *v.n.* splash about.
platt [plat], *adj.* flat, level, even; insipid; downright; —e *Redensart*, commonplace, platitude; (*coll.*) *ich bin ganz* —, I am astonished *or* dumbfounded.
Plättbrett ['plɛtbrɛt], *n.* (—es, *pl.* —er) ironing board.
plattdeutsch ['platdɔytʃ], *adj.* Low German.
Platte ['platə], *f.* (—, *pl.* —n) plate; dish; board; slab; sheet; ledge; (*fig.*) bald head; (*Mus.*) (gramophone) record.
plätten ['plɛtən], *v.a.* iron (clothes).
Plattfisch ['platfɪʃ], *m.* (—es, *pl.* —e) (*Zool.*) plaice.
Plattfuß ['platfu:s], *n.* (—es, *pl.* ̈e) flat foot.
Plattheit ['plathaɪt], *f.* (—, *pl.* —en) flatness; (*fig.*) platitude.
Platz [plats], *m.* (—es, *pl.* ̈e) place, town, spot, site; space, room; (*town*) square; seat; — *nehmen*, take a seat, be seated.
Platzanweiserin ['platsanvaɪzərɪn], *f.* (—, *pl.* —nen) usherette.
Plätzchen ['plɛtsçən], *n.* (—s, *pl.* —) small place; drop; biscuit.
platzen ['platsən], *v.n.* (*aux.* sein) burst, explode.
Platzregen ['platsre:gən], *m.* (—s, *no pl.*) downpour, heavy shower.
Plauderei [plaudə'raɪ], *f.* (—, *pl.* —en) chat.
Plaudertasche ['plaudərtaʃə], *f.* (—, *pl.* —n) chatterbox.
Pleite ['plaɪtə], *f.* (—, *pl.* —n) (*coll.*) bankruptcy; — *machen*, go bankrupt.
Plenum ['ple:num], *n.* (—s, *no pl.*) plenary session.
Pleuelstange ['plɔyəlʃtaŋə], *f.* (—, *pl.* —n) connecting-rod.
Plinsen ['plɪnzən], *f. pl.* (*Austr.*) fritters.
Plissee [plɪ'se:], *n.* (—s, *pl.* —s) pleating.
Plombe ['plɔmbə], *f.* (—, *pl.* —n) lead, seal; (*teeth*) filling.
plombieren [plɔm'bi:rən], *v.a.* seal with lead; (*teeth*) fill.
plötzlich ['plœtslɪç], *adj.* sudden.
plump [plump], *adj.* clumsy, ungainly, awkward; crude, coarse.
plumps [plumps], *excl.* bump! oops!
Plunder ['plundər], *m.* (—s, *no pl.*) lumber, trash.
plündern ['plyndərn], *v.a.* plunder, pillage.
Plüsch [ply:ʃ], *m.* (—es, *no pl.*) plush.
pneumatisch [pnɔy'ma:tɪʃ], *adj.* pneumatic.
Pöbel ['pø:bəl], *m.* (—s, *no pl.*) mob, rabble.
pochen ['pɔxən], *v.a., v.n.* knock, beat, throb.

Pocke

Pocke ['pɔkə], *f.* (—, *pl.* —n) pockmark; (*pl.*) smallpox.

pockennarbig ['pɔkənnarbɪç], *adj.* pockmarked.

Podagra ['po:dagra:], *n.* (—s, *no pl.*) (*Med.*) gout.

Pointe [po'ɛ̃tə], *f.* (—, *pl.* —n) (*of a story*) point.

Pokal [po'ka:l], *m.* (—s, *pl.* —e) goblet, cup; trophy.

Pökelfleisch ['pø:kəlflaɪʃ], *n.* (—es, *no pl.*) salted meat.

Pol [po:l], *m.* (—s, *pl.* —e) pole.

polemisch [po'le:mɪʃ], *adj.* polemic(al), controversial.

Polen ['po:lən], *n.* Poland.

Police [po'li:sə], *f.* (—, *pl.* —n) insurance policy.

polieren [po'li:rən], *v.a.* polish, furbish, burnish.

Poliklinik ['po:likli:nɪk], *f.* (—, *pl.* —en) (*Med.*) out-patients' department.

Politik [poli'ti:k], *f.* (—, *no pl.*) politics; policy.

politisieren [politi'zi:rən], *v.n.* talk politics.

Politur [poli'tu:r], *f.* (—, *no pl.*) polish, gloss.

Polizei [poli'tsaɪ], *f.* (—, *no pl.*) police.

polizeilich [poli'tsaɪlɪç], *adj.* of the police.

Polizeistunde [poli'tsaɪʃtundə], *f.* (—, *no pl.*) closing time.

Polizeiwache [poli'tsaɪvaxə], *f.* (—, *pl.* —n) police station.

Polizist [poli'tsɪst], *m.* (—en, *pl.* —en) policeman, constable.

Polizze [po'lɪtsə], *f.* (—, *pl.* —n) (*Austr. dial.*) insurance policy.

polnisch ['pɔlnɪʃ], *adj.* Polish.

Polster ['pɔlstər], *n.* (—s, *pl.* —) cushion, bolster.

Polterabend ['pɔltəra:bənt], *m.* (—s, *pl.* —e) wedding-eve party.

Poltergeist ['pɔltərgaɪst], *m.* (—es, *pl.* —er) poltergeist, hobgoblin.

poltern ['pɔltərn], *v.n.* rumble; make a noise; bluster.

Polyp [po'ly:p], *m.* (—en, *pl.* —en) (*Zool.*) polyp; (*Med.*) polypus.

Pomeranze [pomə'rantsə], *f.* (—, *pl.* —n) (*Bot.*) orange.

Pommern ['pɔmərn], *n.* Pomerania.

Pope [po:'pə], *m.* (—n, *pl.* —n) Greek Orthodox priest.

Popo [po'po:], *m.* (—s, *pl.* —s) (*coll.*) backside, bottom.

populär [popu'lɛ:r], *adj.* popular.

porös [po'rø:s], *adj.* porous.

Porree ['pɔre:], *m.* (—s, *no pl.*) leek.

Portefeuille [pɔrt'fœj], *n.* (—s, *pl.* —s) portfolio.

Portier [pɔr'tje:], *m.* (—s, *pl.* —s) doorkeeper, caretaker; porter.

Porto ['pɔrto:], *n.* (—s, *pl.* **Porti**) postage.

Porzellan [pɔrtsɛ'la:n], *n.* (—s, *pl.* —e) china, porcelain; *Meißner —*, Dresden china.

Posamenten [poza'mɛntən], *n. pl.* trimmings.

Posaune [po'zaunə], *f.* (—, *pl.* —n) (*Mus.*) trombone.

Positur [pozi'tu:r], *f.* (—, *pl.* —en) posture; *sich in — setzen*, strike an attitude.

Posse ['pɔsə], *f.* (—, *pl.* —n) (*Theat.*) farce, skit.

Possen ['pɔsən], *m.* (—s, *pl.* —) trick; *einem qinen — spielen*, play a trick on s.o.

possierlich [pɔ'si:rlɪç], *adj.* droll, funny, comic(al).

Post [pɔst], *f.* (—, *pl.* —en) post, mail; (*building*) post-office.

Postament [pɔsta'mɛnt], *n.* (—s, *pl.* —e) plinth, pedestal.

Postanweisung ['pɔstanvaɪzuŋ], *f.* (—, *pl.* —en) postal order, money order.

Posten ['pɔstən], *m.* (—s, *pl.* —) post, station; place; (*goods*) parcel, lot, job lot; (*Comm.*) item; (*Mil.*) outpost; *— stehen*, stand sentry; *nicht auf dem — sein*, be unwell.

Postfach ['pɔstfax], *n.* (—es, *pl.* ̈er) post-office box.

postieren [pɔs'ti:rən], *v.a.* post, place, station.

postlagernd ['pɔstla:gərnt], *adj.* poste restante, to be called for.

Postschalter ['pɔstʃaltər], *m.* (—s, *pl.* —) post-office counter.

postulieren [pɔstu'li:rən], *v.a.* postulate.

postwendend ['pɔstvɛndənt], *adj.* by return of post.

Postwertzeichen ['pɔstve:rttsaɪçən], *n.* (—s, *pl.* —) stamp.

Potenz [po'tɛnts], *f.* (—, *pl.* —en) (*Maths.*) power; *zur dritten —*, cubed, to the power of three.

potenzieren [potɛn'tsi:rən], *v.a.* (*Math.*) raise; intensify.

Pottasche ['pɔtaʃə], *f.* (—, *no pl.*) potash.

potzblitz ['pɔtsblɪts], *excl.* good Heavens! good gracious!

potztausend ['pɔtstauzənt], *excl.* great Scott! good Heavens!

Pracht [praxt], *f.* (—, *no pl.*) splendour, magnificence; (*in compounds*) de luxe.

prächtig ['prɛ:çtɪç], *adj.* splendid, magnificent, sumptuous.

prachtvoll ['praxtfɔl], *adj.* gorgeous, magnificent.

Prädikat [prɛ:di'ka:t], *n.* (—s, *pl.* —e) mark; (*Gram.*) predicate.

Prag [pra:k], *n.* Prague.

prägen ['prɛ:gən], *v.a.* coin, mint, stamp.

prägnant [prɛg'nant], *adj.* meaningful, precise.

prahlen ['pra:lən], *v.n.* boast, brag, talk big, show off.

Praktikant [praktɪ'kant], *m.* (—en, *pl.* —en) probationer; apprentice.

Praktiken ['praktɪkən], *f. pl.* machinations.

praktisch ['praktɪʃ], *adj.* practical; —*er Arzt*, general practitioner.
praktizieren [prakti'tsi:rən], *v.a.* practise.
Prall [pral], *m.* (—**es**, *pl.* —**e**) impact.
prall [pral], *adj.* tense, tight; (*cheeks*) chubby.
prallen ['pralən], *v.n.* (*aux.* sein) *auf etwas* —, bounce against s.th.
Prämie ['prɛ:mjə], *f.* (—, *pl.* —**n**) prize; (*insurance*) premium; (*dividend*) bonus.
prangen ['praŋən], *v.n.* shine, glitter, make a show.
Pranger ['praŋər], *m.* (—**s**, *pl.* —) pillory; *etwas an den* — *stellen*, expose s.th., pillory.
präparieren [prɛpa'ri:rən], *v.a., v.r.* prepare.
Präsens ['prɛ:zɛns], *n.* (—, *pl.* —**ntia**) (*Gram.*) present tense.
präsentieren [prɛzɛn'ti:rən], *v.a.* present; *präsentiert das Gewehr!* present arms!
prasseln ['prasəln], *v.n.* (*fire*) crackle; rattle.
prassen ['prasən], *v.n.* revel, gorge (o.s.), guzzle, feast.
Prätendent [prɛtɛn'dɛnt], *m.* (—**en**, *pl.* —**en**) pretender, claimant.
Präteritum [prɛ'te:ritum], *n.* (—**s**, *pl.* —**ta**) (*Gram.*) preterite, past tense.
Praxis ['praksɪs], *f.* (—, *no pl.*) practice.
präzis [prɛ'tsi:s], *adj.* precise, exact.
präzisieren [prɛtsi'zi:rən], *v.a.* define exactly.
predigen ['pre:dɪɡən], *v.a., v.n.* preach.
Predigt ['pre:dɪçt], *f.* (—, *pl.* —**en**) sermon; (*fig.*) homily, lecture.
Preis [praɪs], *m.* (—**es**, *pl.* —**e**) price, rate, value; (*reward*) prize; praise; *um jeden* —, at any price, at all costs; *um keinen* —, not for all the world; *feste* —*e*, fixed prices; no rebate, no discount.
Preisausschreiben ['praɪsausʃraɪbən], *n.* (—**s**, *pl.* —) prize competition.
Preiselbeere ['praɪzɛlbe:rə], *f.* (—, *pl.* —**n**) (*Bot.*) bilberry, cranberry.
preisen ['praɪzən], *v.a. irr.* praise, laud; glorify.
preisgeben ['praɪsɡe:bən], *v.a. irr.* give up, abandon, part with; *dem Spott preisgegeben sein*, become a laughing-stock.
Preisunterbietung ['praɪsuntərbi:tuŋ], *f.* (—, *pl.* —**en**) under-cutting.
Prellbock ['prɛlbɔk], *m.* (—**s**, *pl.* —**e**) buffer (-block).
prellen ['prɛlən], *v.a.* cheat, defraud.
Prellstein ['prɛlʃtaɪn], *m.* (—**s**, *pl.* —**e**) kerbstone.
pressant [prɛ'sant], *adj.* (*Austr.*) urgent.
Presse ['prɛsə], *f.* (—, *pl.* —**n**) press; newspapers; (*coll.*) coaching establishment, crammer.
pressieren [prɛ'si:rən], *v.n.* be urgent.
Preßkohle ['prɛsko:lə], *f.* (—, *no pl.*) briquette(s).

Preßkolben ['prɛskɔlbən], *m.* (—**s**, *pl.* —) piston.
Preßluft ['prɛsluft], *f.* (—, *no pl.*) compressed air.
Preußen ['prɔysən], *n.* Prussia.
prickeln ['prɪkəln], *v.n.* prick, prickle, sting, tickle.
Prieme ['pri:mə], *f.* (—, *pl.* —**n**) chew, quid.
Priester ['pri:stər], *m.* (—**s**, *pl.* —) priest; *zum* — *weihen*, ordain to the priesthood.
Prima ['pri:ma:], *f.* (—, *pl.* **Primen**) highest form at a grammar school (sixth form).
prima ['pri:ma:], *adj.* excellent, splendid, first-rate.
Primaner [pri'ma:nər], *m.* (—**s**, *pl.* —) pupil in the highest form at a grammar school, sixth form boy.
Primel ['pri:məl], *f.* (—, *pl.* —**n**) (*Bot.*) primrose, primula.
Primus ['pri:mus], *m.* (—, *no pl.*) (*School*) head boy, captain of the school.
Prinzip [prɪnt'si:p], *n.* (—**s**, *pl.* —**ien**) principle.
Priorität [priori'tɛ:t], *f.* (—, *no pl.*) priority, precedence.
Prise ['pri:zə], *f.* (—, *pl.* —**n**) pinch of snuff.
Prisma ['prɪsma:], *n.* (—**s**, *pl.* —**men**) prism.
Pritsche ['prɪtʃə], *f.* (—, *pl.* —**n**) plank-bed.
Privatdozent [pri'va:tdotsɛnt], *m.* (—**en**, *pl.* —**en**) (*Univ.*) (unsalaried) lecturer.
privatisieren [privati'zi:rən], *v.n.* have private means.
Probe ['pro:bə], *f.* (—, *pl.* —**n**) experiment, trial, probation, test; (*Theat., Mus.*) rehearsal; sample, pattern; *auf* —, on trial; *auf die* — *stellen*, put to the test *or* on probation.
Probeabzug ['pro:bəaptsu:k], *m.* (—**s**, *pl.* —**e**) (*Printing*) proof.
proben ['pro:bən], *v.a.* rehearse.
probieren [pro'bi:rən], *v.a.* try, attempt; taste.
Probst [pro:pst], *m.* (—**es**, *pl.* —**e**) provost.
Produzent [produ'tsɛnt], *m.* (—**en**, *pl.* —**en**) producer (of goods), manufacturer.
produzieren [produ'tsi:rən], *v.a.* produce (goods). — *v.r. sich* —, perform, show off.
profanieren [profa'ni:rən], *v.a.* desecrate, profane.
Professur [profɛ'su:r], *f.* (—, *pl.* —**en**) (*Univ.*) professorship, Chair.
profitieren [profi'ti:rən], *v.a., v.n.* profit (by), take advantage (of).
projizieren [proji'tsi:rən], *v.a.* project.
Prokura [pro'ku:ra:], *f.* (—, *no pl.*) (*Law*) power of attorney.
Prokurist [proku'rɪst], *m.* (—**en**, *pl.* —**en**) confidential clerk; company secretary.

171

prolongieren

prolongieren [prolɔŋˈgiːrən], *v.a.* prolong, extend.

promenieren [proməˈniːrən], *v.n.* take a stroll.

Promotion [promoˈtsjoːn], *f.* (—, *pl.* —en) graduation, degree ceremony.

promovieren [promoˈviːrən], *v.n.* graduate, take a degree.

promulgieren [promulˈgiːrən], *v.a.* promulgate.

Pronomen [proˈnoːmən], *n.* (—s, *pl.* —mina) (*Gram.*) pronoun.

prophezeien [profeˈtsaiən], *v.a.* prophesy, predict, forecast.

prophylaktisch [profyˈlaktɪʃ], *adj.* preventive, prophylactic.

Propst [proːpst], *m.* (—es, *pl.* ⁻e) provost.

Prosa [ˈproːzaː], *f.* (—, *no pl.*) prose.

prosit [ˈproːzɪt], *excl.* cheers! here's to you! your health!

Prospekt [proˈspɛkt], *m.* (—es, *pl.* —e) prospect; (*booklet*) prospectus.

Prostituierte [prostituˈiːrtə], *f.* (—n, *pl.* —n) prostitute; (*coll.*) tart.

protegieren [proteˈʒiːrən], *v.a.* favour, patronize.

Protektion [protɛkˈtsjoːn], *f.* (—, *no pl.*) patronage, favouritism.

protestieren [protɛsˈtiːrən], *v.n.* make a protest, protest (against s.th.).

Protokoll [protoˈkɔl], *n.* (—s, *pl.* —e) minutes, record; protocol; regulations.

Protokollführer [protoˈkɔlfyːrər], *m.* (—s, *pl.* —) recorder, clerk of the minutes.

Protz [prɔts], *m.* (—en, *pl.* —en) snob, upstart; show-off.

Proviant [proˈvjant], *m.* (—s, *no pl.*) provisions, stores.

provinziell [provɪnˈtsjɛl], *adj.* provincial.

Provinzler [proˈvɪntslər], *m.* (—s, *pl.* —) provincial.

Provision [proviˈzjoːn], *f.* (—, *pl.* —en) (*Comm.*) commission, brokerage.

Provisor [proˈviːzɔr], *m.* (—s, *pl.* —en) dispenser.

provisorisch [proviˈzoːrɪʃ], *adj.* provisional, temporary.

provozieren [provoˈtsiːrən], *v.a.* provoke.

Prozedur [protseˈduːr], *f.* (—, *pl.* —en) proceedings, procedure.

Prozent [proˈtsɛnt], *m. & n.* (—s, *pl.* —e) per cent.

Prozentsatz [proˈtsɛntzats], *m.* (—es, *pl.* ⁻e) percentage, rate of interest.

Prozeß [proˈtsɛs], *m.* (—es, *pl.* —e) process; lawsuit, litigation; trial; *mit etwas kurzen — machen,* deal summarily with.

Prozeßwesen [proˈtsɛsveːzən], *n.* (—s, *no pl.*) legal procedure.

prüde [ˈpryːdə], *adj.* prudish, prim.

prüfen [ˈpryːfən], *v.a.* test, examine.

Prüfung [ˈpryːfuŋ], *f.* (—, *pl.* —en) trial, test; examination; (*fig.*) temptation, affliction.

Prügel [ˈpryːgəl], *m.* (—s, *pl.*—) cudgel; (*pl.*) thrashing; *eine Tracht* —, a good hiding.

prügeln [ˈpryːgəln], *v.a.* beat, give a hiding to.

Prunk [pruŋk], *m.* (—(e)s, *no pl.*) splendour, ostentation, pomp.

prusten [ˈpruːstən], *v.n.* snort.

Psalm [psalm], *m.* (—es, *pl.* —e) psalm.

Psalter [ˈpsaltər], *m.* (—s, *pl.* —) (*book*) psalter; (*instrument*) psaltery.

Psychiater [psyçiˈaːtər], *m.* (—s, *pl.* —) psychiatrist.

Psychologe [psyçoˈloːgə], *m.* (—n, *pl.* —n) psychologist.

Pubertät [puberˈtɛːt], *f.* (—, *no pl.*) puberty.

Publikum [ˈpuːblɪkum], *n.* (—s, *no pl.*) public; (*Theat.*) audience.

publizieren [publiˈtsiːrən], *v.a.* publish; promulgate.

Pudel [ˈpuːdəl], *m.* (—s, *pl.* —) poodle; *des —s Kern,* the gist of the matter.

Puder [ˈpuːdər], *m.* (—s, *no pl.*) powder, face-powder.

pudern [ˈpuːdərn], *v.a.* powder.

Puff [puf], *m.* (—es, *pl.* ⁻e) cuff, thump.

puffen [ˈpufən], *v.a.* cuff, thump.

Puffer [ˈpufər], *m.* (—s, *pl.* —) buffer.

Puffspiel [ˈpufʃpiːl], *n.* (—s, *pl.* —e) backgammon.

pullen [ˈpulən], *v.n.* rein in (a horse); (*coll.*) piddle.

Pulsader [ˈpulsaːdər], *f.* (—, *pl.* —n) artery; aorta.

pulsieren [pulˈziːrən], *v.n.* pulsate; pulse, throb.

Pulsschlag [ˈpulsʃlaːk], *m.* (—s, *pl.* ⁻e) pulse-beat; pulsation.

Pult [pult], *n.* (—es, *pl.* —e) desk, writing-table; lectern.

Pulver [ˈpulvər], *n.* (—s, *pl.* —) powder.

Pump [pump], *m.* (—s, *no pl.*) (*sl.*) credit; *auf* —, on tick.

pumpen [ˈpumpən], *v.a., v.n.* pump; (*fig.*) (*sl.*) *sich etwas* —, borrow s.th., touch s.o. for s.th.; lend.

Pumpenschwengel [ˈpumpənʃvɛŋəl], *m.* (—s, *pl.* —) pump-handle.

Pumpernickel [ˈpumpərnɪkəl], *m.* (—s, *pl.* —) black bread, Westphalian rye-bread.

Pumphosen [ˈpumphoːzən], *f. pl.* plusfours.

Punkt [puŋkt], *m.* (—es, *pl.* —e) point, dot, spot; (*Gram.*) full stop.

punktieren [puŋkˈtiːrən], *v.a.* dot; punctuate.

pünktlich [ˈpyŋktlɪç], *adj.* punctual.

punktum [ˈpuŋktum], *excl. und damit* —, that's the end of it; that's it.

Puppe [ˈpupə], *f.* (—, *pl.* —n) doll; (*Ent.*) pupa, chrysalis.

pur [puːr], *adj.* pure, sheer; (*drink*) neat.

Puritaner [puri'ta:nər], *m.* (—s, *pl.* —) puritan.

Purpur ['purpur], *m.* (—s, *no pl.*) purple.

Purzelbaum ['purtsəlbaum], *m.* (—s, *pl.* ⁻e) somersault.

purzeln ['purtsəln], *v.n.* tumble.

Pustel ['pustəl], *f.* (—, *pl.* —n) pustule.

pusten ['pu:stən], *v.n.* puff, blow.

Pute ['pu:tə], *f.* (—, *pl.* —n) (*Orn.*) turkey-hen; *dumme* —, silly goose.

Puter ['pu:tər], *m.* (—s, *pl.* —) turkeycock.

puterrot ['pu:tərro:t], *adj.* as red as a turkey-cock.

Putsch [putʃ], *m.* (—es, *pl.* —e) coup de main, insurrection, riot.

Putz [puts], *m.* (—es, *no pl.*) finery; cleaning; rough-cast.

putzen ['putsən], *v.a.* polish, shine; clean. — *v.r. sich* —, dress up.

Putzfrau ['putsfrau], *f.* (—, *pl.* —en) charwoman.

Putzmacherin ['putsmaxərɪn], *f.* (—, *pl.* —nen) milliner.

Pyramide [pyra'mi:də], *f.* (—, *pl.* —n) pyramid.

Pyrenäen [pyrə'nɛ:ən], *pl.* Pyrenees; —*halbinsel*, Iberian Peninsula.

Q

Q [ku:], *n.* (—s, *pl.* —s) the letter Q.

quabbeln ['kvabəln], *v.n.* shake, wobble.

Quacksalber ['kvakzalbər], *m.* (—s, *pl.* —) quack, mountebank.

Quacksalberei [kvakzalbə'raɪ], *f.* (—, *pl.* —en) quackery.

Quaderstein ['kva:dərʃtaɪn], *m.* (—s, *pl.* —e) ashlar, hewn stone.

Quadrat [kva'dra:t], *n.* (—es, *pl.* —e) square; *zum* (or *ins*) — *erheben*, square (a number).

Quadratur [kvadra'tu:r], *f.* (—, *pl.* —en) quadrature; *die* — *des Kreises finden*, square the circle.

quadrieren [kva'dri:rən], *v.a.* square.

quaken ['kva:kən], *v.n.* (*frog*) croak; (*duck*) quack.

quäken ['kvɛ:kən], *v.n.* squeak.

Quäker ['kvɛ:kər], *m.* (—s, *pl.* —) Quaker.

Qual [kva:l], *f.* (—, *pl.* —en) anguish, agony, torment.

quälen ['kvɛ:lən], *v.a.* torment, torture, vex. — *v.r. sich* —, toil.

qualifizieren [kvalifi'tsi:rən], *v.a.* qualify.

Qualität [kvali'tɛ:t], *f.* (—, *pl.* —en) quality.

Qualle ['kvalə], *f.* (—, *pl.* —n) (*Zool.*) jelly-fish.

Qualm [kvalm], *m.* (—es, *no pl.*) dense smoke.

Quantität [kvanti'tɛ:t], *f.* (—, *pl.* —en) quantity.

Quantum ['kvantum], *n.* (—s, *pl.* —ten) portion, quantity.

Quappe ['kvapə], *f.* (—, *pl.* —n) (*Zool.*) tadpole.

Quarantäne [kvaran'tɛ:nə], *f.* (—, *no pl.*) quarantine.

Quark [kvark], *m.* (—s, *no pl.*) curds; cream-cheese; (*fig.*) trash, rubbish, nonsense, bilge.

Quarta ['kvarta:], *f.* (—, *no pl.*) fourth form.

Quartal [kvar'ta:l], *n.* (—s, *pl.* —e) quarter of a year; term.

Quartier [kvar'ti:r], *n.* (—s, *pl.* —e) quarters, lodging; (*Mil.*) billet.

Quarz [kvarts], *m.* (—es, *no pl.*) quartz.

Quaste ['kvastə], *f.* (—, *pl.* —n) tassel.

Quatember [kva'tɛmbər], *m.* (—s, *pl.* —) quarter day; (*Eccl.*) Ember Day.

Quatsch [kvatʃ], *m.* (—es, *no pl.*) nonsense, drivel.

Quecke ['kvɛkə], *f.* (—, *pl.* —n) couch-grass, quick-grass.

Quecksilber ['kvɛkzɪlbər], *n.* (—s, *no pl.*) quicksilver, mercury.

Quelle ['kvɛlə], *f.* (—, *pl.* —n) well, spring, fountain; (*fig.*) source; *aus sicherer* —, on good authority.

Quentchen ['kvɛntçən], *n.* (—s, *pl.* —) small amount, dram.

quer [kve:r], *adj.* cross, transverse, oblique, diagonal. — *adv.* across; *kreuz und* —, in all directions.

Querbalken ['kve:rbalkən], *m.* (—s, *pl.* —) cross-beam.

querdurch ['kve:rdurç], *adv.* across.

querfeldein ['kve:rfɛltaɪn], *adv.* crosscountry.

Querkopf ['kve:rkɔpf], *m.* (—es, *pl.* ⁻e) crank.

Quersattel ['kve:rzatəl], *m.* (—s, *pl.* ⁻) side-saddle.

Querschiff ['kve:rʃɪf], *n.* (—es, *pl.* —e) (*church*) transept.

Querschnitt ['kve:rʃnɪt], *m.* (—s, *pl.* —e) cross-section; (*fig.*) average.

Querulant [kveru'lant], *m.* (—en, *pl.* —en) grumbler.

quetschen ['kvɛtʃən], *v.a.* squeeze, crush, mash; bruise.

Queue [kø:], *n.* (—s, *pl.* —s) (*Billiards*) cue.

quieken ['kvi:kən], *v.n.* squeak.

Quinta ['kvɪnta:], *f.* (—, *no pl.*) fifth form.

Quinte ['kvɪntə], *f.* (—, *pl.* —n) (*Mus.*) fifth.

Quirl [kvɪrl], *m.* (—s, *pl.* —e) whisk; (*Bot.*) whorl.

quitt [kvɪt], *adj.* — *sein*, be quits.

Quitte ['kvɪtə], *f.* (—, *pl.* —n) (*Bot.*) quince.

173

quittegelb [ˈkvɪtəgɛlp], *adj.* bright
yellow.
quittieren [kvɪˈtiːrən], *v.a.* receipt;
give a receipt; *den Dienst —,* leave the
service.
Quittung [ˈkvɪtuŋ], *f.* (—, *pl.* —en)
receipt.
Quodlibet [ˈkvɔdlɪbɛt], *n.* (—s, *pl.* —s)
medley.
Quote [ˈkvoːtə], *f.* (—, *pl.* —n) quota,
share.
quotieren [kvoˈtiːrən], *v.a.* (*stock
exchange*) quote (prices).

R

R [ɛr], *n.* (—s, *pl.* —s) the letter R.
Rabatt [raˈbat], *m.* (—s, *pl.* —e)
rebate, discount.
Rabatte [raˈbatə], *f.* (—, *pl.* —n)
flower-border.
Rabbiner [raˈbiːnər], *m.* (—s, *pl.* —)
rabbi.
Rabe [ˈraːbə], *m.* (—n, *pl.* —n) (*Orn.*)
raven; *ein weißer —,* a rare bird.
Rabenaas [ˈraːbənaːs], *n.* (—es, *pl.*
—e) carrion.
rabiat [raˈbjaːt], *adj.* furious, rabid.
Rache [ˈraxə], *f.* (—, *no pl.*) revenge,
vengeance.
Rachen [ˈraxən], *m.* (—s, *pl.* —) jaws,
throat.
rächen [ˈrɛːçən], *v.a.* avenge. — *v.r.
sich —,* avenge o.s., take vengeance.
Rachenbräune [ˈraxənbrɔynə], *f.* (—,
no pl.) croup, quinsy.
Rachitis [raˈxiːtɪs], *f.* (—, *no pl.*)
(*Med.*) rickets.
rachsüchtig [ˈraxzyçtɪç], *adj.* vindictive, vengeful.
rackern [ˈrakərn], *v.r. sich —,* (*coll.*)
toil, work hard.
Rad [raːt], *n.* (—es, *pl.* ⸚er) wheel;
bicycle; *ein — schlagen,* turn a
cart-wheel; (*peacock*) spread the tail.
Radau [raˈdau], *m.* (—s, *no pl.*) noise,
din, shindy.
Rade [ˈraːdə], *f.* (—, *pl.* —n) corn-
cockle.
radebrechen [ˈraːdəbrɛçən], *v.a. insep.*
murder a language.
radeln [ˈraːdəln], *v.n.* (*aux.* sein) (*coll.*)
cycle.
Rädelsführer [ˈrɛːdəlsfyːrər], *m.* (—s,
pl. —) ringleader.
rädern [ˈrɛːdərn], *v.a.* break on the
wheel; *gerädert sein,* (*fig.*) ache in all
o.'s bones, be exhausted.
Radfahrer [ˈraːtfaːrər], *m.* (—s, *pl.* —)
cyclist.
radieren [raˈdiːrən], *v.n.* erase; etch.
Radierung [raˈdiːruŋ], *f.* (—, *pl.* —en)
etching.

Radieschen [raˈdiːsçən], *n.* (—s, *pl.*
—) (*Bot.*) radish.
Radio [ˈraːdjo], *n.* (—s, *pl.* —s)
wireless, radio.
raffen [ˈrafən], *v.a.* snatch up, gather
up.
Raffinade [rafiˈnaːdə], *f.* (—, *no pl.*)
refined sugar.
Raffinement [rafinəˈmã], *n.* (—s, *no
pl.*) elaborateness.
raffinieren [rafiˈniːrən], *v.a.* refine.
raffiniert [rafiˈniːrt], *adj.* refined;
elaborate, crafty, wily, cunning.
ragen [ˈraːgən], *v.n.* tower, soar.
Rahm [raːm], *m.* (—es, *no pl.*) cream;
den — abschöpfen, skim; (*fig.*) skim
the cream off.
Rahmen [ˈraːmən], *m.* (—s, *pl.* —)
frame; milieu, limit, scope, compass;
im — von, within the framework of.
rahmig [ˈraːmɪç], *adj.* creamy.
raisonnieren [rɛzɔˈniːrən], *v.n.* reason,
argue; (*fig.*) grumble, answer back.
Rakete [raˈkeːtə], *f.* (—, *pl.* —n) rocket,
sky-rocket.
Rakett [raˈkɛt], *n.* (—s, *pl.* —s) (*tennis*)
racket.
rammen [ˈramən], *v.a.* ram.
Rampe [ˈrampə], *f.* (—, *pl.* —n)
ramp, slope; platform; (*Theat.*)
apron.
ramponiert [rampoˈniːrt], *adj.*
battered, damaged.
Ramsch [ramʃ], *m.* (—es, *pl.* ⸚e)
odds and ends; (*Comm.*) job lot.
Rand [rant], *m.* (—es, *pl.* ⸚er) edge,
border, verge, rim; (*book*) margin;
(*hat*) brim; *am — des Grabes,* with one
foot in the grave; *außer — und Band
geraten,* get completely out of hand.
randalieren [randaˈliːrən], *v.n.* kick
up a row.
Randbemerkung [ˈrantbəmɛrkuŋ], *f.*
(—, *pl.* —en) marginal note, gloss.
rändern [ˈrɛndərn], *v.a.* border, edge,
mill.
Ränftchen [ˈrɛnftçən], *n.* (—s, *pl.* —)
crust (of bread).
Rang [raŋ], *m.* (—es, *pl.* ⸚e) rank,
grade, rate; order, class; standing (in
society); (*Theat.*) circle, tier, gallery.
Range [ˈraŋə], *m.* (—n, *pl.* —n)
scamp, rascal. — *f.* (—, *pl.* —n) tomboy, hoyden.
rangieren [rãˈʒiːrən], *v.a.* (*Railw.*)
shunt. — *v.n.* rank.
Ranke [ˈraŋkə], *f.* (—, *pl.* —n) tendril,
shoot.
Ränke [ˈrɛŋkə], *m. pl.* intrigues,
tricks.
ranken [ˈraŋkən], *v.r.* (*aux.* haben)
sich —, (*plant*) climb (with
tendrils).
Ränkeschmied [ˈrɛŋkəʃmiːt], *m.* (—es,
pl. —e) plotter, intriguer.
Ranzen [ˈrantsən], *m.* (—s, *pl.* —)
satchel, knapsack, rucksack.
ranzig [ˈrantsɪç], *adj.* rancid, rank.
Rappe [ˈrapə], *m.* (—n, *pl.* —n) black
horse.

Raute

Rappel ['rapəl], *m.* (—s, *no pl.*) (*coll.*) slight madness; rage, fit.

Rappen ['rapən], *m.* (—s, *pl.* —) small Swiss coin; centime.

rapportieren [rapɔr'tiːrən], *v.a.* report.

Raps [raps], *m.* (—es, *no pl.*) rapeseed.

rar [raːr], *adj.* rare, scarce; exquisite.

rasch [raʃ], *adj.* quick, swift.

rascheln ['raʃəln], *v.n.* rustle.

Rasen ['raːzən], *m.* (—s, *pl.* —) lawn, turf, sod.

rasen ['raːzən], *v.n.* rave, rage, be delirious; rush, speed; *in —der Eile,* in a tearing hurry.

Raserei [raːzə'raɪ], *f.* (—, *pl.* —en) madness; (*fig.*) fury.

Rasierapparat [ra'ziːrapaːt], *m.* (—s, *pl.* —e) (safety-)razor; shaver.

rasieren [ra'ziːrən], *v.a.* shave; *sich — lassen,* be shaved, get a shave.

Rasierzeug [ra'ziːrtsɔyk], *n.* (—s, *no pl.*) shaving-tackle.

Raspel ['raspəl], *f.* (—, *pl.* —n) rasp.

Rasse ['rasə], *f.* (—, *pl.* —n) race; breed; *reine —,* thoroughbred; *ge-kreuzte —,* cross-breed.

Rassel ['rasəl], *f.* (—, *pl.* —n) rattle.

rasseln ['rasəln], *v.n.* rattle, clank.

Rassendiskriminierung ['rasəndɪskrimini:ruŋ], *f.* (—, *no pl.*) racial discrimination.

Rast [rast], *f.* (—, *no pl.*) rest, repose.

rasten ['rastən], *v.n.* rest, take a rest; halt.

Raster ['rastər], *m.* (—s, *pl.* —) (*Phot.*) screen.

rastlos ['rastloːs], *adj.* restless.

Rat (1) [raːt], *m.* (—es, *pl.* —schläge) advice, counsel; deliberation.

Rat (2) [raːt], *m.* (—es, *pl.* ¨e) council, councillor; *mit — und Tat,* with advice and assistance; *einem einen — geben,* give s.o. advice, counsel s.o.; *einen um — fragen,* consult s.o.; *— schaffen,* find ways and means.

Rate ['raːtə], *f.* (—, *pl.* —n) instalment, rate.

raten ['raːtən], *v.a.,* *v.n. irr.* advise; guess, conjecture.

Ratgeber ['raːtgeːbər], *m.* (—s, *pl.* —) adviser, counsellor.

Rathaus ['raːthaus], *n.* (—es, *pl.* ¨er) town-hall.

Ratifizierung [ratifi'tsiːruŋ], *f.* (—, *pl.* —en) ratification.

Ration [ra'tsjoːn], *f.* (—, *pl.* —en) ration, share, portion.

rationell [ratsjo'nɛl], *adj.* rational.

ratlos ['raːtloːs], *adj.* helpless, perplexed.

ratsam ['raːtzaːm], *adj.* advisable.

Ratschlag ['raːtʃlaːk], *m.* (—s, *pl.* ¨e) advice, counsel.

Ratschluß ['raːtʃlus], *m.* (—sses, *pl.* ¨sse) decision, decree.

Ratsdiener ['raːtsdiːnər], *m.* (—s, *pl.* —) beadle, tipstaff, summoner.

Rätsel ['rɛːtsəl], *n.* (—s, *pl.* —) riddle, puzzle, mystery, enigma, conundrum.

Ratsherr ['raːtshɛr], *m.* (—n, *pl.* —en) alderman, (town-)councillor, senator.

Ratte ['ratə], *f.* (—, *pl.* —n) (*Zool.*) rat.

Raub [raup], *m.* (—es, *no pl.*) robbery; booty, prey.

rauben ['raubən], *v.a.* rob, plunder; *es raubt mir den Atem,* it takes my breath away.

Räuber ['rɔybər], *m.* (—s, *pl.* —) robber, thief; highwayman; *— und Gendarm,* cops and robbers.

Raubgier ['raupgiːr], *f.* (—, *no pl.*) rapacity.

Rauch [raux], *m.* (—s, *no pl.*) smoke, vapour.

Rauchen ['rauxən], *n.* (—s, *no pl.*) smoking; *— verboten,* no smoking.

rauchen ['rauxən], *v.a., v.n.* smoke.

räuchern ['rɔyçərn], *v.a.* (*meat, fish*) smoke-dry, cure; (*disinfect*) fumigate. — *v.n.* (*Eccl.*) burn incense.

Rauchfang ['rauxfaŋ], *m.* (—s, *pl.* ¨e) chimney-flue.

Räude ['rɔydə], *f.* (—, *no pl.*) mange.

Raufbold ['raufbɔlt], *m.* (—s, *pl.* —e) brawler, bully.

raufen ['raufən], *v.a.* (*hair*) tear out, pluck. — *v.n.* fight, brawl. — *v.r. sich — mit,* scuffle with, fight, have a scrap with.

rauh [rau], *adj.* rough; (*fig.*) harsh, rude; hoarse; (*weather*) raw, inclement.

Rauheit ['rauhaɪt], *f.* (—, *no pl.*) roughness; hoarseness; (*fig.*) harshness, rudeness; (*weather*) inclemency; (*landscape*) ruggedness.

rauhen ['rauən], *v.a.* (*cloth*) nap.

Raum [raum], *m.* (—es, *pl.* ¨e) space, room; outer space; (*fig.*) scope; *dem Gedanken — geben,* entertain an idea.

räumen ['rɔymən], *v.a.* clear, empty; quit, leave; *das Feld —,* abandon the field, clear out.

Rauminhalt ['rauminhalt], *m.* (—s, *no pl.*) volume.

räumlich ['rɔymlɪç], *adj.* spatial; (*in compounds*) space-.

Räumlichkeiten ['rɔymlɪçkaɪtən], *f. pl.* premises.

Raumschiff ['raumʃif], *n.* (—es, *pl.* —e) spaceship, spacecraft.

Räumung ['rɔymuŋ], *f.* (—, *pl.* —en) evacuation.

raunen ['raunən], *v.a., v.n.* whisper.

Raupe ['raupə], *f.* (—, *pl.* —n) (*Ent.*) caterpillar.

Rausch [rauʃ], *m.* (—es, *pl.* ¨e) intoxication; delirium, frenzy; *einen — haben,* be drunk, intoxicated; *seinen — ausschlafen,* sleep it off.

rauschen ['rauʃən], *v.n.* rustle, rush, roar.

Rauschgift ['rauʃgift], *n.* (—s, *pl.* —e) drug; narcotic.

Rauschgold ['rauʃgɔlt], *n.* (—es, *no pl.*) tinsel.

räuspern ['rɔyspərn], *v.r. sich —,* clear o.'s throat.

Raute ['rautə], *f.* (—, *pl.* —n) (*Maths.*) rhombus; lozenge; (*Bot.*) rue.

Razzia

Razzia ['ratsja], *f.* (—, *pl.* **—zzien**) (police-)raid, swoop.

reagieren [rea'gi:rən], *v.n.* react (on).

realisieren [reali'zi:rən], *v.a.* convert into money, realise.

Realschule [re'a:lʃu:lə], *f.* (—, *pl.* **—n**) technical grammar school; secondary modern school.

Rebe ['re:bə], *f.* (—, *pl.* **—n**) vine.

Rebell [re'bɛl], *m.* (**—en**, *pl.* **—en**) rebel, mutineer, insurgent.

Rebensaft ['re:bənzaft], *m.* (**—s**, *pl.* ⁻e) grape-juice, wine.

Rebhuhn ['re:phu:n], *n.* (**—s**, *pl.* ⁻er) (*Orn.*) partridge.

Reblaus ['re:plaus], *f.* (—, *pl.* ⁻e) (*Ent.*) phylloxera.

Rechen ['rɛçən], *m.* (**—s**, *pl.* —) (*garden*) rake; (*clothes*) rack.

Rechenaufgabe ['rɛçənaufga:bə], *f.* (—, *pl.* **—n**) sum; mathematical *or* arithmetical problem.

Rechenmaschine ['rɛçənmaʃi:nə], *f.* (—, *pl.* **—n**) calculating machine, adding-machine.

Rechenschaft ['rɛçənʃaft], *f.* (—, *no pl.*) account; — *ablegen,* account for; *zur — ziehen,* call to account.

Rechenschieber ['rɛçənʃi:bər], *m.* (**—s**, *pl.* —) slide-rule.

Rechentabelle ['rɛçəntabɛlə], *f.* (—, *pl.* **—n**) ready reckoner.

rechnen ['rɛçnən], *v.a.,* *v.n.* reckon, calculate, do sums, compute; *auf etwas —,* count on s.th.; *auf einen —,* rely on s.o.

Rechnung ['rɛçnuŋ], *f.* (—, *pl.* **—en**) reckoning, account, computation; (*document*) invoice, bill, statement, account; *einer Sache — tragen,* make allowances for s.th.; take s.th. into account; *einem einen Strich durch die — machen,* put a spoke in s.o.'s wheel; *eine — begleichen,* settle an account.

Rechnungsabschluß ['rɛçnuŋsapʃlus], *m.* (**—sses**, *pl.* ⁻sse) balancing of accounts, balance-sheet.

Rechnungsprüfer ['rɛçnuŋspry:fər], *m.* (**—s**, *pl.* —) auditor.

Rechnungsrat ['rɛçnuŋsra:t], *m.* (**—s**, *pl.* ⁻e) member of the board of accountants, (senior government) auditor.

Recht [rɛçt], *n.* (**—es**, *pl.* **—e**) right, justice; claim on, title to; law, jurisprudence; *von —s wegen,* by right; — *sprechen,* administer justice; *die —e studieren,* study law.

recht [rɛçt], *adj.* right; just; real, true; suitable; proper; *zur —en Zeit,* in time; *es geht nicht mit —en Dingen zu,* there is s.th. queer about it; *was dem einen —, ist dem andern billig,* what is sauce for the goose is sauce for the gander; *einem — geben,* agree with s.o.; — *haben,* be (in the) right.

Rechteck ['rɛçtɛk], *n.* (**—s**, *pl.* **—e**) rectangle.

rechten ['rɛçtən], *v.n. mit einem —,* dispute, remonstrate with s.o.

rechtfertigen ['rɛçtfɛrtigən], *v.a. insep.* justify. — *v.r. sich —,* exculpate o.s.

rechtgläubig ['rɛçtglɔybiç], *adj.* orthodox.

rechthaberisch ['rɛçtha:bərɪʃ], *adj.* stubborn, obstinate.

rechtlich ['rɛçtliç], *adj.* legal, lawful, legitimate; (*Law*) judicial, juridical.

rechtmäßig ['rɛçtmɛ:sɪç], *adj.* lawful, legitimate, legal.

rechts [rɛçts], *adv.* to the right, on the right.

Rechtsabtretung ['rɛçtsaptre:tuŋ], *f.* (—, *pl.* **—en**) cession, assignment.

Rechtsanwalt ['rɛçtsanvalt], *m.* (**—s**, *pl.* ⁻e) lawyer, solicitor, attorney.

Rechtsbeistand ['rɛçtsbaɪʃtant], *m.* (**—s**, *pl.* ⁻e) (legal) counsel.

rechtschaffen ['rɛçtʃafən], *adj.* upright, honest, righteous.

Rechtschreibung ['rɛçtʃraɪbuŋ], *f.* (—, *no pl.*) orthography, spelling.

Rechtshandel ['rɛçtshandəl], *m.* (**—s**, *pl.* ⁻) action, case, lawsuit.

rechtskräftig ['rɛçtskrɛftɪç], *adj.* legal, valid.

Rechtslehre ['rɛçtsle:rə], *f.* (—, *pl.* **—n**) jurisprudence.

Rechtsspruch ['rɛçtsʃprux], *m.* (**—(e)s**, *pl.* ⁻e) verdict.

Rechtsverhandlung ['rɛçtsfɛrhandluŋ], *f.* (—, *pl.* **—en**) legal proceedings.

Rechtsweg ['rɛçtsve:k], *m.* (**—(e)s**, *pl.* **—e**) course of law.

rechtswidrig ['rɛçtsvi:drɪç], *adj.* against the law, illegal.

Rechtszuständigkeit ['rɛçtstsu:ʃtendɪçkaɪt], *f.* (—, *pl.* **—en**) (legal) competence.

rechtwinklig ['rɛçtvɪŋklɪç], *adj.* rectangular.

rechtzeitig ['rɛçttsaɪtɪç], *adj.* opportune. — *adv.* in time, at the right time.

Reck [rɛk], *n.* (**—s**, *pl.* **—e**) horizontal bar.

Recke ['rɛkə], *m.* (**—n**, *pl.* **—n**) (*Poet.*) hero.

recken ['rɛkən], *v.a.* stretch, extend.

Redakteur [redak'tø:r], *m.* (**—s, *pl.* —e**) editor (newspaper, magazine).

Redaktion [redak'tsjo:n], *f.* (—, *pl.* **—en**) editorship, editorial staff; (*room*) editorial office.

Rede ['re:də], *f.* (—, *pl.* **—n**) speech, oration; address; *es geht die —,* people say; *es ist nicht der — wert,* is not worth mentioning; *eine — halten,* deliver a speech; *zur — stellen,* call to account.

reden ['re:dən], *v.a.* speak, talk, discourse; *einem nach dem Munde —,* humour s.o.; *in den Wind —,* speak in vain, preach to the winds; *mit sich — lassen,* be amenable to reason.

Redensart ['re:dənsa:rt], *f.* (—, *pl.* —en) phrase, idiom; cliché; *einen mit leeren —en abspeisen*, put s.o. off with fine words.

Redewendung ['re:dəvendun], *f.* (—, *pl.* —en) turn of phrase.

redigieren [redi'gi:rən], *v.a.* edit.

redlich ['re:tliç], *adj.* honest, upright.

Redner ['re:dnər], *m.* (—s, *pl.* —) speaker, orator.

Reede ['re:də], *f.* (—, *pl.* —n) (*Naut.*) roadstead.

Reederei [re:də'raɪ], *f.* (—, *pl.* —en) shipping-business.

reell [re'ɛl], *adj.* honest, fair, sound, bona fide.

Reep [re:p], *n.* (—s, *pl.* —e) (*Naut.*) rope.

Referat [refe'ra:t], *n.* (—s, *pl.* —e) report; paper (to a learned society), lecture.

Referendar [referɛn'da:r], *m.* (—s, *pl.* —e) junior barrister *or* teacher.

Referent [refe'rɛnt], *m.* (—en, *pl.* —en) reporter, reviewer; lecturer; expert (adviser).

Referenz [refe'rɛnts], *f.* (—, *pl.* —en) reference (to s.o. *or* s.th.).

referieren [refe'ri:rən], *v.a., v.n.* report (on), give a paper (on).

reflektieren [reflɛk'ti:rən], *v.a.* reflect. — *v.n. auf etwas* —, be a prospective buyer of s.th., have o.'s eye on s.th.

Reformator [refor'ma:tɔr], *m.* (—s, *pl.* —en) reformer.

reformieren [refor'mi:rən], *v.a.* reform.

Regal [re'ga:l], *n.* (—s, *pl.* —e) shelf.

rege ['re:gə], *adj.* brisk, lively, animated.

Regel ['re:gəl], *f.* (—, *pl.* —n) rule, precept, principle; *in der* —, as a rule, generally.

regelmäßig ['re:gəlmɛ:siç], *adj.* regular.

regeln ['re:gəln], *v.a.* regulate, arrange, order.

Regelung ['re:gəlun], *f.* (—, *pl.* —en) regulation.

regelwidrig ['re:gəlvi:driç], *adj.* contrary to rule, irregular, foul.

Regen ['re:gən], *m.* (—s, *no pl.*) rain.

regen ['re:gən], *v.r. sich* —, move, stir.

Regenbogen ['re:gənbo:gən], *m.* (—s, *pl.* —) rainbow.

Regenbogenhaut ['re:gənbo:gənhaut], *f.* (—, *pl.* ⁻e) (*eye*) iris.

Regenguß ['re:gəngus], *m.* (—sses, *pl.* ⁻sse) downpour, violent shower.

Regenmantel ['re:gənmantəl], *m.* (—s, *pl.* ⁻) waterproof, raincoat, mac.

Regenpfeifer ['re:gənpfaɪfər], *m.* (—s, *pl.* —) (*Orn.*) plover.

Regenrinne ['re:gənrinə], *f.* (—, *pl.* —n) eaves.

Regenschirm ['re:gənʃirm], *m.* (—s, *pl.* —e) umbrella.

Regentschaft [re'gɛntʃaft], *f.* (—, *pl.* —en) regency.

Regie [re'ʒi:], *f.* (—, *pl.* —n) stage management, production, direction.

regieren [re'gi:rən], *v.a.* rule, reign over, govern. — *v.n.* reign; (*fig.*) prevail, predominate.

Regierung [re'gi:run], *f.* (—, *pl.* —en) government; reign.

Regierungsrat [re'gi:runsra:t], *m.* (—s, *pl.* ⁻e) government adviser.

Regiment (1) [regi'mɛnt], *n.* (—s, *pl.* —e) rule, government.

Regiment (2) [regi'mɛnt], *n.* (—s, *pl.* —er) (*Mil.*) regiment.

Regisseur [reʒi'sø:r], *m.* (—s, *pl.* —e) stage-manager, producer, director.

Registrator [regis'tra:tɔr], *m.* (—s, *pl.* —en) registrar, recorder; registering machine.

Registratur [registra'tu:r], *f.* (—, *pl.* —en) record office, registry; filing-cabinet.

registrieren [regis'tri:rən], *v.a.* register, record, file.

reglos ['re:klo:s], *adj.* motionless.

regnen ['re:gnən], *v.n.* rain; *es regnet in Strömen*, it is raining cats and dogs.

Regreß [re'grɛs], *m.* (—sses, *pl.* —sse) recourse, remedy.

regsam ['re:kza:m], *adj.* quick, alert, lively.

regulieren [regu'li:rən], *v.a.* regulate.

Regung ['re:gun], *f.* (—, *pl.* —en) movement; impulse.

Reh [re:], *n.* (—(e)s, *pl.* —e) doe, roe.

rehabilitieren [rehabili'ti:rən], *v.a.* rehabilitate.

Rehbock ['re:bɔk], *m.* (—s, *pl.* ⁻e) (*Zool.*) roe-buck.

Rehkeule ['re:kɔylə], *f.* (—, *pl.* —n) haunch of venison.

reiben ['raɪbən], *v.a. irr.* rub, grate, grind; *einem etwas unter die Nase* —, throw s.th. in s.o.'s teeth, bring s.th. home to s.o.

Reibung ['raɪbun], *f.* (—, *pl.* —en) friction.

Reich [raɪç], *n.* (—(e)s, *pl.* —e) kingdom, realm, empire, state.

reich [raɪç], *adj.* rich, wealthy, opulent.

reichen ['raɪçən], *v.a.* reach, pass, hand; *einem die Hand* —, shake hands with s.o. — *v.n.* reach, extend; be sufficient.

reichhaltig ['raɪçhaltiç], *adj.* abundant, copious.

reichlich ['raɪçliç], *adj.* ample, plentiful.

Reichskammergericht [raɪçs'kamərgəriçt], *n.* (—s, *no pl.*) Imperial High Court of Justice (*Holy Roman Empire*).

Reichskanzlei ['raɪçskantslaɪ], *f.* (—, *pl.* —en) (Imperial) Chancery.

Reichskanzler ['raɪçskantslər], *m.* (—s, *pl.* —) (Imperial) Chancellor.

Reichsstände ['raɪçsʃtɛndə], *m. pl.* Estates (of the Holy Roman Empire).

Reichstag ['raɪçsta:k], *m.* (—s, *pl.* —e) Imperial Parliament, Reichstag, Diet.

Reichtum

Reichtum ['raɪçtuːm], *m.* (—s, *pl.* ⸚er) riches, wealth, opulence.

Reif (1) [raɪf], *m.* (—s, *no pl.*) hoar-frost.

Reif (2) [raɪf], *m.* (—s, *pl.* —e) ring.

reif [raɪf], *adj.* ripe, mature.

Reifen ['raɪfən], *m.* (—s, *pl.* —) hoop; tyre; — *schlagen*, trundle a hoop.

reifen ['raɪfən], *v.n.* (*aux.* sein) ripen, mature, grow ripe.

Reifeprüfung ['raɪfəpryːfuŋ], *f.* (—, *pl.* —en) matriculation examination.

reiflich ['raɪflɪç], *adj. sich etwas — überlegen*, give careful consideration to s.th.

Reigen ['raɪgən], *m.* (—s, *pl.* —) round-dance, roundelay.

Reihe ['raɪə], *f.* (—, *pl.* —n) series; file; row; progression, sequence; (*Theat.*) tier; *in — und Glied*, in closed ranks; *nach der —*, in turns; *ich bin an der —*, it is my turn.

Reihenfolge ['raɪənfɔlgə], *f.* (—, *no pl.*) succession.

Reiher ['raɪər], *m.* (—s, *pl.* —) (*Orn.*) heron.

Reim [raɪm], *m.* (—(e)s, *pl.* —e) rhyme.

rein [raɪn], *adj.* clean, pure, clear, neat; *—e Wahrheit*, plain truth; *ins —e bringen*, settle, clear up; *ins —e schreiben*, make a fair copy of; *einem —en Wein einschenken*, have a straight talk with s.o.

Reineke ['raɪnəkə], *m.* (—, *no pl.*) — *Fuchs*, Reynard the Fox.

Reinertrag ['raɪnɛrtraːk], *m.* (—(e)s, *pl.* ⸚e) net proceeds.

Reinfall ['raɪnfal], *m.* (—s, *pl.* ⸚e) sell, wild-goose chase; disappointment.

reinfallen ['raɪnfalən], *v.n. irr.* (*aux.* sein) be unsuccessful.

Reingewinn ['raɪngəvɪn], *m.* (—s, *pl.* —e) net proceeds.

Reinheit ['raɪnhaɪt], *f.* (—, *no pl.*) purity.

reinigen ['raɪnɪgən], *v.a.* clean, cleanse; dry-clean; purge.

Reinigung ['raɪnɪguŋ], *f.* (—, *pl.* —en) cleaning; (*fig.*) purification, cleansing; *chemische —*, dry-cleaning.

reinlich ['raɪnlɪç], *adj.* clean, neat.

Reis (1) [raɪs], *m.* (—es, *no pl.*) rice.

Reis (2) [raɪs], *n.* (—es, *pl.* —er) twig; sprig; scion; cutting.

Reisbesen ['raɪsbeːzən], *m.* (—s, *pl.* —) birch-broom, besom.

Reise ['raɪzə], *f.* (—, *pl.* —n) tour, trip, journey, travels; voyage; *gute —!* bon voyage!

reisefertig ['raɪzəfɛrtɪç], *adj.* ready to start.

Reisegeld ['raɪzəgɛlt], *n.* (—es, *pl.* —er) travel allowance.

reisen ['raɪzən], *v.n.* (*aux.* sein) travel, tour, journey, take a trip.

Reisende ['raɪzəndə], *m.* (—n, *pl.* —n) traveller; commercial traveller.

Reisig ['raɪzɪç], *n.* (—s, *no pl.*) brush-wood.

Reisige ['raɪzɪgə], *m.* (—n, *pl.* —n) (*obs.*) trooper, horseman.

Reißaus [raɪs'aus], *n.* (—, *no pl.*) — *nehmen*, take to o.'s heels.

Reißbrett ['raɪsbrɛt], *n.* (—es, *pl.* —er) drawing-board.

reißen ['raɪsən], *v.a. irr.* tear; rend; pull; snatch; *etwas an sich —*, seize s.th., usurp.

reißend ['raɪsənt], *adj.* rapid; ravening; carnivorous; (*Comm.*) brisk, rapid (sales).

Reißnagel ['raɪsnaːgəl], *m. see* **Reißzwecke**.

Reißschiene ['raɪsʃiːnə], *f.* (—, *pl.* —n) T-square.

Reißverschluß ['raɪsfɛrʃlus], *m.* (—sses, *pl.* ⸚sse) zip-fastener.

Reißzwecke ['raɪstsvɛkə], *f.* (—, *pl.* —n) drawing-pin.

reiten ['raɪtən], *v.a. irr.* ride (a horse). — *v.n.* (*aux.* sein) ride, go on horse-back.

Reiterei [raɪtə'raɪ], *f.* (—, *pl.* —en) cavalry.

Reitknecht ['raɪtknɛçt], *m.* (—es, *pl.* —e) groom.

Reiz [raɪts], *m.* (—es, *pl.* —e) charm, attraction, fascination, allure; stimulus; irritation; (*Phys.*) impulse.

reizbar ['raɪtsbaːr], *adj.* susceptible; irritable.

reizen ['raɪtsən], *v.a.* irritate; stimulate, charm, entice.

reizend ['raɪtsənt], *adj.* charming.

Reizmittel ['raɪtsmɪtəl], *n.* (—s, *pl.* —) stimulant; irritant.

rekeln ['reːkəln], *v.r.* (*dial.*) sich —, loll about.

Reklame [re'klaːmə], *f.* (—, *pl.* —n) propaganda, advertisement, advertising, publicity.

reklamieren [rekla'miːrən], *v.a.* claim, reclaim. — *v.n.* complain.

rekognoszieren [rekɔgnɔs'tsiːrən], *v.a.* reconnoitre.

rekommandieren [rekɔman'diːrən], *v.a.* (*Austr.*) register (a letter).

Rekonvaleszent [rekɔnvalɛs'tsɛnt], *m.* (—en, *pl.* —en) convalescent.

Rekrut [re'kruːt], *m.* (—en, *pl.* —en) recruit.

rekrutieren [rekru'tiːrən], *v.a.* recruit. — *v.r. sich — aus*, be recruited from.

rektifizieren [rɛktifi'tsiːrən], *v.a.* rectify.

Rektor ['rɛktɔr], *m.* (—s, *pl.* —en) (school) principal; (*Univ.*) president.

Rektorat [rɛkto'raːt], *n.* (—es, *pl.* —e) rectorship, presidency.

relativ [rela'tiːf], *adj.* relative, comparative.

relegieren [rele'giːrən], *v.a.* expel; (*Univ.*) send down, rusticate.

Relief [rel'jɛf], *n.* (—s, *pl.* —s) (*Art*) relief.

religiös [reli'gjøːs], *adj.* religious.

Reliquie [re'liːkvjə], *f.* (—, *pl.* —n) (*Rel.*) relic.

Remise [re'mi:zə], *f.* (—, *pl.* —n) coach-house.

Remittent [rɛmɪ'tɛnt], *m.* (—en, *pl.* —en) remitter.

Renegat [rene'ga:t], *m.* (—en, *pl.* —en) renegade.

Renette [re'nɛtə], *f.* (—, *pl.* —n) rennet(-apple).

renken ['rɛŋkən], *v.a.* wrench, bend, twist.

Rennbahn ['rɛnba:n], *f.* (—, *pl.* —en) race-course; (cinder)-track; (*Motor.*) racing-circuit.

rennen ['rɛnən], *v.n. irr.* (*aux.* sein) run, race, rush.

Renommé [renɔ'me:], *n.* (—s, *no pl.*) renown, repute, reputation.

renommieren [renɔ'mi:rən], *v.n.* brag, boast.

renovieren [reno'vi:rən], *v.a.* renovate, restore, redecorate, renew.

rentabel [rɛn'ta:bəl], *adj.* profitable, lucrative.

Rente ['rɛntə], *f.* (—, *pl.* —n) pension, annuity.

Rentier [rɛn'tje:], *m.* (—s, *pl.* —s) rentier, person of independent means.

rentieren [rɛn'ti:rən], *v.r. sich* —, be profitable, be worthwhile, pay.

Rentner ['rɛntnər], *m.* (—s, *pl.* —) pensioner.

Reparatur [repara'tu:r], *f.* (—, *pl.* —en) repair.

reparieren [repa'ri:rən], *v.a.* repair.

Repräsentant [reprɛzɛn'tant], *m.* (—en, *pl.* —en) representative.

Repräsentantenkammer [reprɛzɛn'tantənkamər], *f.* (—, *pl.* —n) (*Am.*) House of Representatives.

Repressalien [reprɛ'sa:ljən], *f. pl.* reprisals, retaliation.

reproduzieren [reprodu'tsi:rən], *v.a.* reproduce.

Republikaner [republi'ka:nər], *m.* (—s, *pl.* —) republican.

requirieren [rekvi'ri:rən], *v.a.* requisition.

Reseda [re'ze:da], *f.* (—, *pl.* —s) (*Bot.*) mignonette.

Reservat [rezɛr'va:t], *n.* (—es, *pl.* —e) reservation, reserve.

Residenz [rezi'dɛnts], *f.* (—, *pl.* —en) residence, seat of the Court.

residieren [rezi'di:rən], *v.n.* reside.

Residuum [re'zi:duum], *n.* (—s, *pl.* —duen) residue, dregs.

resignieren [rezɪg'ni:rən], *v.n., v.r.* resign; be resigned (to s.th.); give up.

Respekt [re'spɛkt], *m.* (—es, *no pl.*) respect, regard; *mit* — *zu sagen*, with all due respect.

respektieren [respɛk'ti:rən], *v.a.* respect, honour.

Ressort [re'so:r], *n.* (—s, *pl.* —s) department, domain.

Rest [rɛst], *m.* (—es, *pl.* —e) rest, residue, remainder; remnant; (*money*) balance.

restaurieren [rɛsto'ri:rən], *v.a.* restore, renovate.

Resultat [rezul'ta:t], *n.* (—es, *pl.* —e) result, outcome.

Resümee [rezy'me:], *n.* (—s, *pl.* —s) résumé, précis, digest, summary, synopsis, abstract.

retten ['rɛtən], *v.a.* save, preserve; rescue, deliver; *die Ehre* —, vindicate o.'s honour.

Rettich ['rɛtɪç], *m.* (—s, *pl.* —e) radish.

Rettung ['rɛtuŋ], *f.* (—, *pl.* —en) saving, rescue, deliverance.

retuschieren [retu'ʃi:rən], *v.a.* retouch.

Reue ['rɔyə], *f.* (—, *no pl.*) repentance, remorse, contrition.

reuen ['rɔyən], *v.a., v.n.* repent, regret; *es reut mich*, I am sorry.

Reugeld ['rɔygɛlt], *n.* (—es, *pl.* —er) forfeit-money, penalty.

reüssieren [rey'si:rən], *v.n.* succeed.

Revanche [re'vã:ʃə], *f.* (—, *pl.* —n) revenge; (*fig.*) return.

revanchieren [revã'ʃi:rən], *v.r. sich* —, repay a service, have *or* take o.'s revenge.

Reverenz [reve'rɛnts], *f.* (—, *pl.* —en) bow, curtsy.

revidieren [revi'di:rən], *v.a.* revise, check.

Revier [re'vi:r], *n.* (—s, *pl.* —e) district, precinct, quarter; preserve.

Revisor [re'vi:zɔr], *m.* (—s, *pl.* —en) accountant, auditor.

revoltieren [revɔl'ti:rən], *v.n.* rise, revolt.

revolutionieren [revolutsjo'ni:rən], *v.a.* revolutionise.

Revolverblatt [re'vɔlvərblat], *n.* (—s, *pl.* ⸚er) gutter press.

Revue [re'vy:], *f.* (—, *pl.* —n) revue; review; — *passieren lassen*, pass in review.

Rezensent [retsɛn'zɛnt], *m.* (—en, *pl.* —en) reviewer, critic.

rezensieren [retsɛn'zi:rən], *v.a.* review.

Rezept [re'tsɛpt], *n.* (—es, *pl.* —e) (*Med.*) prescription; (*Cul.*) recipe.

rezitieren [retsi'ti:rən], *v.a.* recite.

Rhabarber [ra'barbər], *m.* (—s, *no pl.*) (*Bot.*) rhubarb.

Rhein [rain], *m.* (—s, *no pl.*) (River) Rhine.

Rhodesien [ro'de:zjən], *n.* Rhodesia.

Rhodus ['ro:dus], *n.* Rhodes.

Rhythmus ['rytmus], *m.* (—, *pl.* —men) rhythm.

Richtbeil ['rɪçtbail], *n.* (—s, *pl.* —e) executioner's axe.

richten ['rɪçtən], *v.a., v.n.* direct, point at; prepare; *die Augen* — *auf*, fix o.'s eyes upon; *einen zugrunde* —, ruin s.o.; judge, try, pass sentence on, condemn. —*v.r. sich nach* (*Dat.*) —, be guided by.

Richter ['rɪçtər], *m.* (—s, *pl.* —) judge; justice.

richtig ['rɪçtɪç], *adj.* right, correct, exact, true; *nicht ganz* — *sein*, be not quite right in the head.

Richtlot ['rɪçtlo:t], *n.* (—s, *pl.* —e) plumb-line.

Richtschnur ['rɪçtʃnu:r], *f.* (—, *pl.* —en) plumb-line; (*fig.*) rule, precept.

Richtung ['rɪçtuŋ], *f.* (—, *pl.* —en) direction.

riechen ['ri:çən], *v.a.*, *v.n. irr.* smell, scent, reek; *Lunte* —, smell a rat.

Riege ['ri:gə], *f.* (—, *pl.* —n) row, section.

Riegel ['ri:gəl], *m.* (—s, *pl.* —) bar, bolt; *ein* — *Schokolade,* a bar of chocolate.

Riemen ['ri:mən], *m.* (—s, *pl.* —) strap, thong; oar.

Ries [ri:s], *n.* (—es, *pl.* —e) (*paper*) ream.

Riese ['ri:zə], *m.* (—n, *pl.* —n) giant.

rieseln ['ri:zəln], *v.n.* murmur, babble, ripple, trickle; drizzle.

Riesenschlange ['ri:zənʃlaŋə], *f.* (—, *pl.* —n) anaconda.

Riff [rɪf], *n.* (—es, *pl.* —e) reef.

rigoros [rigo'ro:s], *adj.* strict, rigorous.

Rille ['rɪlə], *f.* (—, *pl.* —n) groove, small furrow; (*Archit.*) flute, chamfer.

Rind [rɪnt], *n.* (—es, *pl.* —er) ox, cow; (*pl.*) cattle, horned cattle, head of cattle.

Rinde ['rɪndə], *f.* (—, *pl.* —n) rind, bark, peel; (*bread*) crust.

Rinderbraten ['rɪndərbra:tən], *m.* (—s, *pl.* —n) roast beef.

Rindfleisch ['rɪntflaɪʃ], *n.* (—es, *no pl.*) beef.

Rindvieh ['rɪntfi:], *n.* (—s, *no pl.*) cattle; (*fig.*) blockhead, ass.

Ring [rɪŋ], *m.* (—(e)s, *pl.* —e) ring; (*chain*) link; (*under the eye*) dark circle; (*Comm.*) syndicate, trust.

Ringelblume ['rɪŋəlblu:mə], *f.* (—, *pl.* —n) (*Bot.*) marigold.

ringeln ['rɪŋəln], *v.r. sich* —, curl.

ringen ['rɪŋən], *v.a. irr.* wring. — *v.n.* wrestle.

Ringer ['rɪŋər], *m.* (—s, *pl.* —) wrestler.

Ringmauer ['rɪŋmauər], *f.* (—, *pl.* —n) city *or* town wall.

rings [rɪŋs], *adv.* around.

ringsum(her) [rɪŋ'sum(he:r)], *adv.* round about.

Rinne ['rɪnə], *f.* (—, *pl.* —n) furrow, gutter; groove.

rinnen ['rɪnən], *v.n. irr.* (*aux,* sein) run, leak, drip.

Rinnsal ['rɪnza:l], *n.* (—s, *pl.* —e) channel, water-course.

Rinnstein ['rɪnʃtain], *m.* (—s, *pl.* —e) gutter.

Rippe ['rɪpə], *f.* (—, *pl.* —n) rib.

Rippenfellentzündung ['rɪpənfɛlɛnt-tsynduŋ], *f.* (—, *pl.* —en) pleurisy.

Rippenspeer ['rɪpənʃpe:r], *m.* (—s, *pl.* —e) (*Casseler* —), spare-rib, ribs of pork.

Rippenstoß ['rɪpənʃto:s], *m.* (—es, *pl.* ⸚e) dig in the ribs, nudge.

Rips [rɪps], *m.* (—es, *no pl.*) rep.

Risiko ['ri:ziko], *n.* (—s, *pl.* —ken) risk.

riskant [rɪs'kant], *adj.* risky.

riskieren [rɪs'ki:rən], *v.a.* risk.

Riß [rɪs], *m.* (—sses, *pl.* —sse) rent, tear; sketch, design, plan.

rissig ['rɪsɪç], *adj.* cracked, torn.

Ritt [rɪt], *m.* (—(e)s, *pl.* —e) ride.

Ritter ['rɪtər], *m.* (—s, *pl.* —) knight; *einen zum* — *schlagen,* dub s.o. a knight.

ritterlich ['rɪtərlɪç], *adj.* knightly; (*fig.*) chivalrous, valiant, gallant.

Ritterschlag ['rɪtərʃla:k], *m.* (—(e)s, *pl.* ⸚e) accolade.

Rittersporn ['rɪtərʃpɔrn], *m.* (—s, *pl.* —e) (*Bot.*) larkspur.

rittlings ['rɪtlɪŋs], *adv.* astride.

Rittmeister ['rɪtmaistər], *m.* (—s, *pl.* —) captain (of cavalry).

Ritus ['ri:tus], *m.* (—, *pl.* **Riten**) rite.

Ritz [rɪts], *m.* (—es, *pl.* —e) chink, fissure, cleft, crevice; (*glacier*) crevasse.

ritzen ['rɪtsən], *v.a.* scratch.

Rivale [ri'va:lə], *m.* (—n, *pl.* —n) rival.

Rivalität [rivali'tɛ:t], *f.* (—, *pl.* —en) rivalry.

Rizinusöl ['ri:tsinusø:l], *n.* (—s, *no pl.*) castor oil.

Robbe ['rɔbə], *f.* (—, *pl.* —n) (*Zool.*) seal.

Robe ['ro:bə], *f.* (—, *pl.* —n) dress, robe; gown.

röcheln ['rœçəln], *v.n.* rattle in o.'s throat.

rochieren [rɔ'xi:rən], *v.n.* (*Chess*) castle.

Rock [rɔk], *m.* (—(e)s, *pl.* ⸚e) (*woman*) skirt; (*man*) coat.

rodeln ['ro:dəln], *v.n.* (*aux.* haben & sein) toboggan.

roden ['ro:dən], *v.a.* clear, weed, thin out (plants).

Rogen ['ro:gən], *m.* (—s, *no pl.*) (*fish*) roe, spawn.

Roggen ['rɔgən], *m.* (—s, *no pl.*) rye.

roh [ro:], *adj.* raw; rough, rude, coarse, crude; *ein* —*er Mensch,* a brute; (*in compounds*) rough-; preliminary, unrefined.

Rohbilanz ['ro:bilants], *f.* (—, *pl.* —en) trial balance.

Roheisen ['ro:aɪzən], *n.* (—s, *no pl.*) pig-iron.

Roheit ['ro:hait], *f.* (—, *pl.* —en) coarseness, rudeness, crudity.

Rohr [ro:r], *n.* (—es, *pl.* —e, ⸚en) tube, pipe; reed, cane; (*gun*) barrel.

Rohrdommel ['ro:rdɔməl], *f.* (—, *pl.* —n) (*Orn.*) bittern.

Röhre ['rø:rə], *f.* (—, *pl.* —n) tube, pipe; (*Radio*) valve.

Röhricht ['rø:rɪçt], *n.* (—s, *pl.* —e) reeds.

Rohrpfeife ['ro:rpfaifə], *f.* (—, *pl.* —n) reed-pipe.

Rohrpost ['ro:rpɔst], *f.* (—, *no pl.*) pneumatic post.

Rohrzucker ['ro:rtsukər], *m.* (—s, *no pl.*) cane-sugar.

Rolladen ['rɔladən], *m.* (**—s**, *pl.*) sliding shutter, roller blind.

Rollbahn ['rɔlbaːn], *f.* (**—**, *pl.* **—en**) (*Aviat.*) runway.

Rolle ['rɔlə], *f.* (**—**, *pl.* **—n**) reel, roll; pulley; (*Theat.*) part; rôle; (*laundry*) mangle.

rollen ['rɔlən], *v.a.* roll, reel; (*laundry*) mangle. — *v.n.* (*aux.* sein) roll (along); (*thunder*) roar, roll.

Roller ['rɔlər], *m.* (**—s**, *pl.* **—**) scooter.

Rollmops ['rɔlmɔps], *m.* (**—es**, *pl.* ¨e) soused herring.

Rollschuh ['rɔlʃuː], *m.* (**—s**, *pl.* **—e**) roller-skate.

Rollstuhl ['rɔlʃtuːl], *m.* (**—s**, *pl.* ¨e) wheel-chair, bath-chair.

Rolltreppe ['rɔltrɛpə], *f.* (**—**, *pl.* **—n**) escalator, moving staircase.

Rom [roːm], *n.* Rome.

Roman [ro'maːn], *m.* (**—s**, *pl.* **—e**) novel.

romanisch [ro'maːnɪʃ], *adj.* Romanesque.

Romanliteratur [ro'maːnlitəratuːr], *f.* (**—**, *no pl.*) fiction.

Romanschriftsteller [ro'maːnʃrɪftʃtɛlər], *m.* (**—s**, *pl.* **—**) novelist.

Römer ['røːmər], *m.* (**—s**, *pl.* **—**) Roman; (*glass*) rummer.

Rondell [rɔn'dɛl], *n.* (**—s**, *pl.* **—e**) circular flower-bed.

Röntgenstrahlen ['rœntɡənʃtraːlən], *m. pl.* X-rays.

rosa ['roːzaː], *adj.* pink, rose-coloured.

Rose ['roːzə], *f.* (**—**, *pl.* **—n**) rose.

Rosenkranz ['roːzənkrants], *m.* (**—es**, *pl.* ¨e) garland of roses; (*Eccl.*) rosary.

Rosenkreuzer ['roːzənkrɔytsər], *m.* (**—s**, *pl.* **—**) Rosicrucian.

Rosine [ro'ziːnə], *f.* (**—**, *pl.* **—n**) sultana, raisin.

Rosmarin ['rɔsmariːn], *m.* (**—s**, *no pl.*) (*Bot.*) rosemary.

Roß [rɔs], *n.* (**—sses**, *pl.* **—sse**) horse, steed.

Roßbremse ['rɔsbrɛmzə], *f.* (**—**, *pl.* **—n**) (*Ent.*) horsefly, gadfly.

Rössel ['rœsəl], *n.* (**—s**, *pl.* **—**) (*Chess*) knight.

Roßhaarmatratze ['rɔshaːrmatratsə], *f.* (**—**, *pl.* **—n**) hair-mattress.

Roßkastanie ['rɔskastaːnjə], *f.* (**—**, *pl.* **—n**) (*Bot.*) horse-chestnut.

Rost (1) [rɔst], *m.* (**—es**, *no pl.*) rust.

Rost (2) [rɔst], *m.* (**—es**, *pl.* **—e**) grate; gridiron.

Rostbraten ['rɔstbraːtən], *m.* (**—s**, *pl.* **—**) roast meat.

rosten ['rɔstən], *v.n.* go rusty; rust; *alte Liebe rostet nicht*, love that's old rusts not away.

rösten ['røːstən], *v.a.* toast, roast, grill.

rot [roːt], *adj.* red; **— werden**, redden, blush.

Rotauge ['roːtauɡə], *n.* (**—s**, *pl.* **—n**) (*Zool.*) roach.

Röte ['røːtə], *f.* (**—**, *no pl.*) redness, red colour.

Röteln ['røːtəln], *m. pl.* (*Med.*) German measles, rubella.

Rotfink ['roːtfɪŋk], *m.* (**—en**, *pl.* **—en**) (*Orn.*) bullfinch.

Rotfuchs ['roːtfuks], *m.* (**—es**, *pl.* ¨e) (*Zool.*) sorrel horse.

rotieren [ro'tiːrən], *v.n.* rotate.

Rotkäppchen ['roːtkɛpçən], *n.* Little Red Riding Hood.

Rotkehlchen ['roːtkeːlçən], *n.* (**—s**, *pl.* **—**) robin.

Rotlauf ['roːtlauf], *m.* (**—s**, *no pl.*) (*Med.*) erysipelas.

Rotschimmel ['roːtʃɪməl], *m.* (**—s**, *pl.* **—**) roan-horse.

Rotspon ['roːtʃpoːn], *m.* (**—s**, *no pl.*) (*dial.*) claret.

Rotte ['rɔtə], *f.* (**—**, *pl.* **—n**) band, gang, rabble; (*Mil.*) file, squad.

Rotwild ['roːtvɪlt], *n.* (**—s**, *no pl.*) red deer.

Rotz [rɔts], *m.* (**—es**, *no pl.*) (*vulg.*) mucus; snot.

Rouleau [ru'loː], *n.* (**—s**, *pl.* **—s**) sun-blind, roller-blind.

routiniert [ruti'niːrt], *adj.* smart; experienced.

Rübe ['ryːbə], *f.* (**—**, *pl.* **—n**) (*Bot.*) turnip; *rote* **—**, beetroot; *gelbe* **—**, carrot.

Rubel ['ruːbəl], *m.* (**—s**, *pl.* **—**) rouble.

Rübenzucker ['ryːbəntsukər], *m.* (**—s**, *no pl.*) beet-sugar.

Rubin [ru'biːn], *m.* (**—s**, *pl.* **—e**) ruby.

Rubrik [ru'briːk], *f.* (**—**, *pl.* **—en**) rubric; title, heading, category, column.

Rübsamen ['ryːpzaːmən], *m.* (**—s**, *no pl.*) rape-seed.

ruchbar ['ruːxbaːr], *adj.* manifest, known, notorious.

ruchlos ['ruːxloːs], *adj.* wicked, profligate, vicious.

Ruck [ruk], *m.* (**—(e)s**, *pl.* **—e**) pull, jolt, jerk.

Rückblick ['rykblɪk], *m.* (**—s**, *pl.* **—e**) retrospect, retrospective view.

Rücken ['rykən], *m.* (**—s**, *pl.* **—**) back; (*mountains*) ridge; *einem den* **— kehren**, turn o.'s back upon s.o.

rücken ['rykən], *v.a.* move, push. — *v.n.* move along.

Rückenmark ['rykənmark], *n.* (**—s**, *no pl.*) spinal marrow.

Rückenwirbel ['rykənvɪrbəl], *m.* (**—s**, *pl.* **—**) dorsal vertebra.

rückerstatten ['rykarʃtatən], *v.a.* refund.

Rückfahrkarte ['rykfaːrkartə], *f.* (**—**, *pl.* **—n**) return ticket.

Rückfall ['rykfal], *m.* (**—s**, *pl.* ¨e) relapse.

rückgängig ['rykɡɛnɪç], *adj.* **— machen**, cancel, annul, reverse (a decision).

Rückgrat ['rykɡraːt], *n.* (**—s**, *pl.* **—e**) backbone, spine.

Rückhalt ['rykhalt], *m.* (**—s**, *no pl.*) reserve; support, backing.

Rückkehr

Rückkehr ['rykke:r], *f.* (—, *no pl.*) return.

Rücklicht ['ryklıçt], *n.* (—s, *pl.* —er) (*Motor. etc.*) tail-light.

rücklings ['ryklıŋks], *adv.* from behind.

Rucksack ['rukzak], *m.* (—s, *pl.* ¨e) rucksack; knapsack.

Rückschritt ['rykʃrıt], *m.* (—es, *pl.* —e) step backward, retrograde step, regression.

Rücksicht ['rykzıçt], *f.* (—, *pl.* —en) consideration, regard.

Rücksprache ['rykʃpra:xə], *f.* (—, *pl.* —n) conference, consultation; — *nehmen mit*, consult, confer with.

rückständig ['rykʃtɛndıç], *adj.* outstanding; old-fashioned; backward.

Rücktritt ['ryktrıt], *m.* (—s, *no pl.*) resignation.

ruckweise ['rukvaızə], *adv.* by fits and starts; jerkily.

Rückwirkung ['rykvırkuŋ], *f.* (—, *pl.* —en) reaction, retroaction.

Rüde ['ry:də], *m.* (—n, *pl.* —n) male (dog, fox etc.).

Rudel ['ru:dəl], *n.* (—s, *pl.* —) flock, herd, pack.

Ruder ['ru:dər], *n.* (—s, *pl.* —) oar, rudder, paddle; *am — sein*, be at the helm; (*Pol.*) be in power.

rudern ['ru:dərn], *v.a., v.n.* row.

Ruf [ru:f], *m.* (—(e)s, *pl.* —e) call; shout; reputation, renown; *einen guten (schlechten) — haben*, have a good (bad) reputation, be well (ill) spoken of.

rufen ['ru:fən], *v.a., v.n. irr.* call, shout; *einen — lassen*, send for s.o.

Rüffel ['ryfəl], *m.* (—s, *pl.* —) (*coll.*) reprimand; (*sl.*) rocket.

Rüge ['ry:gə], *f.* (—, *pl.* —n) censure, blame, reprimand.

Ruhe ['ru:ə], *f.* (—, *no pl.*) rest, repose; quiet, tranquillity; *sich zur — setzen*, retire (from business etc.).

Ruhegehalt ['ru:əgəhalt], *n.* (—es, *pl.* ¨er) retirement pension, superannuation.

ruhen ['ru:ən], *v.n.* rest, repose, take a rest.

Ruhestand ['ru:əʃtant], *m.* (—es, *no pl.*) retirement.

ruhig ['ru:ıç], *adj.* quiet, tranquil, peaceful, calm; *sich — verhalten*, keep quiet.

Ruhm [ru:m], *m.* (—(e)s, *no pl.*) glory, fame, renown; *einem zum — gereichen*, be *or* redound to s.o.'s credit.

rühmen ['ry:mən], *v.a.* praise, extol, glorify. — *v.r. sich —*, boast.

Ruhr (1) [ru:r], *f.* (River) Ruhr.

Ruhr (2) [ru:r], *f.* (—, *no pl.*) dysentery.

Rührei ['ry:raı], *n.* (—s, *pl.* —er) scrambled egg.

rühren ['ry:rən], *v.a.* stir, move, touch. — *v.r. sich —*, move, stir; get a move on.

rührig ['ry:rıç], *adj.* active, alert.

rührselig ['ry:rze:lıç], *adj.* oversentimental; lachrymose.

Rührung ['ry:ruŋ], *f.* (—, *no pl.*) emotion.

Ruin [ru'i:n], *m.* (—s, *no pl.*) (*fig.*) ruin; decay; bankruptcy.

Ruine [ru'i:nə], *f.* (—, *pl.* —n) ruin(s).

rülpsen ['rylpsən], *v.n.* belch.

Rum [rum], *m.* (—s, *no pl.*) rum.

Rumänien [ru'mɛ:njən], *n.* Rumania.

Rummel ['ruməl], *m.* (—s, *no pl.*) tumult, row, hubbub.

Rumor [ru'mo:r], *m.* (—s, *no pl.*) noise; rumour.

rumoren [ru'mo:rən], *v.n.* make a noise.

Rumpelkammer ['rumpəlkamər], *f.* (—, *pl.* —n) lumber-room, junkroom.

rumpeln ['rumpəln], *v.n.* rumble.

Rumpf [rumpf], *m.* (—(e)s, *pl.* ¨e) (*Anat.*) trunk; (*ship*) hull; (*Aviat.*) fuselage.

rümpfen ['rympfən], *v.a. die Nase —*, turn up o.'s nose.

rund [runt], *adj.* round, rotund; — *heraus*, flatly; *etwas — abschlagen*, refuse s.th. flatly; — *herum*, round about.

Runde ['rundə], *f.* (—, *pl.* —n) round; (*Sport*) round, bout; *die — machen*, (*watchman*) patrol.

Rundfunk ['runtfuŋk], *m.* (—s, *no pl.*) broadcasting, wireless; radio.

Rundgang ['runtgaŋ], *m.* (—s, *pl.* ¨e) round, tour (of inspection).

rundlich ['runtlıç], *adj.* plump.

Rundschau ['runtʃau], *f.* (—, *no pl.*) panorama; review, survey.

Rundschreiben ['runtʃraıbən], *n.* (—s, *pl.* —) circular letter.

rundweg ['runtve:k], *adv.* flatly, plainly.

Rune ['ru:nə], *f.* (—, *pl.* —n) rune; runic writing.

Runkelrübe ['ruŋkəlry:bə], *f.* (—, *pl.* —n) beetroot.

Runzel ['runtsəl], *f.* (—, *pl.* —n) wrinkle, pucker.

Rüpel ['ry:pəl], *m.* (—s, *pl.* —) bounder, lout.

rupfen ['rupfən], *v.a.* pluck; *einen —*, (*fig.*) fleece s.o.

Rupie ['ru:pjə], *f.* (—, *pl.* —n) rupee.

ruppig ['rupıç], *adj.* unfriendly, rude; scruffy.

Ruprecht ['ru:prɛçt], *m. Knecht —*, Santa Claus.

Rüsche ['ry:ʃə], *f.* (—, *pl.* —n) ruche.

Ruß [ru:s], *m.* (—es, *no pl.*) soot.

Rüssel ['rysəl], *m.* (—s, *pl.* —) snout; (*elephant*) trunk.

Rußland ['ruslant], *n.* Russia.

rüsten ['rystən], *v.a.* prepare, fit (out); equip; (*Mil.*) arm, mobilise.

Rüster ['rystər], *f.* (—, *pl.* —n) elm.

rüstig ['rystıç], *adj.* vigorous, robust.

Rüstung ['rystuŋ], *f.* (—, *pl.* —en) armour; preparation; (*Mil.*) armament.

Rüstzeug ['rysttsɔyk], *n.* (—s, *no pl.*) equipment.
Rute ['ru:tə], *f.* (—, *pl.* —n) rod, twig; (*fox*) brush.
Rutengänger ['ru:tənɡɛŋər], *m.* (—s, *pl.* —) water-diviner.
rutschen ['rutʃən], *v.n.* (*aux.* sein) slip, slide, skid, slither.
rütteln ['rytəln], *v.a., v.n.* shake, jolt.

S

S [ɛs], *n.* (—s, *pl.* —s) the letter S.
Saal [za:l], *m.* (—(e)s, *pl.* **Säle**) hall, large room.
Saat [za:t], *f.* (—, *pl.* —en) seed; sowing; standing corn.
Sabbat ['zabat], *m.* (—s, *pl.* —e) sabbath.
sabbern ['zabərn], *v.n.* (*sl.*) slaver, drivel.
Säbel ['zɛ:bəl], *m.* (—s, *pl.* —) sabre; *krummer* —, falchion, scimitar.
säbeln ['zɛ:bəln], *v.a.* sabre, hack at.
sachdienlich ['zaxdi:nlɪç], *adj.* relevant, pertinent.
Sache ['zaxə], *f.* (—, *pl.* —n) thing, matter, affair; (*Law*) action, case; *die — ist (die) daß*, the fact is that; *das gehört nicht zur —*, that is beside the point; *bei der — sein*, pay attention to the matter in hand; *das ist meine —*, that is my business; *die — der Unterdrückten verteidigen*, take up the cause of the oppressed.
Sachlage ['zaxla:ɡə], *f.* (—, *no pl.*) state of affairs.
sachlich ['zaxlɪç], *adj.* pertinent; objective.
sächlich ['zɛçlɪç], *adj.* (*Gram.*) neuter.
Sachse ['zaksə], *m.* (—n, *pl.* —n) Saxon.
Sachsen ['zaksən], *n.* Saxony.
sachte ['zaxtə], *adj.* soft, slow, quiet, careful, gentle.
Sachverhalt ['zaxfɛrhalt], *m.* (—s, *no pl.*) facts (of a case), state of things, circumstances.
sachverständig ['zaxfɛrʃtɛndɪç], *adj.* expert, competent, experienced.
Sachwalter ['zaxvaltər], *m.* (—s, *pl.* —) manager, counsel, attorney.
Sack [zak], *m.* (—(e)s, *pl.* ⸚e) sack, bag; *mit — und Pack*, (with) bag and baggage.
Säckel ['zɛkəl], *m.* (—s, *pl.* —) purse.
Sackgasse ['zakɡasə], *f.* (—, *pl.* —n) cul-de-sac, blind alley; *einen in eine — treiben*, corner s.o.
Sackpfeife ['zakpfaifə], *f.* (—, *pl.* —n) bagpipe.
Sacktuch ['zaktu:x], *n.* (—es, *pl.* ⸚er) sacking; (*dial.*) pocket-handkerchief.

säen ['zɛ:ən], *v.a.* sow.
Saffian ['zafja:n], *m.* (—s, *no pl.*) morocco-leather.
Saft [zaft], *m.* (—(e)s, *pl.* ⸚e) juice; (*tree*) sap; (*meat*) gravy; *ohne — und Kraft*, insipid; *im eigenen — schmoren*, stew in o.'s own juice.
Sage ['za:ɡə], *f.* (—, *pl.* —n) legend, fable, myth; *es geht die —*, it is rumoured.
Säge ['zɛ:ɡə], *f.* (—, *pl.* —n) saw.
sagen ['za:ɡən], *v.a.* say, tell; *einem etwas — lassen*, send word to s.o.; *es hat nichts zu —*, it does not matter; *was Du nicht sagst!* you don't say (so)!
sägen ['zɛ:ɡən], *v.a., v.n.* saw; (*fig.*) snore.
sagenhaft ['za:ɡənhaft], *adj.* legendary, mythical; (*fig.*) fabulous.
Sahne ['za:nə], *f.* (—, *no pl.*) cream.
Saite ['zaitə], *f.* (—, *pl.* —n) string; *strengere —n aufziehen*, (*fig.*) take a stricter line.
Sakko ['zako], *m.* (—s, *pl.* —s) lounge jacket.
Sakristei [zakrɪ'stai], *f.* (—, *pl.* —en) vestry.
Salat [za'la:t], *m.* (—(e)s, *pl.* —e) salad; (*plant*) lettuce; (*sl.*) mess.
salbadern ['zalba:dərn], *v.n.* prate, talk nonsense.
Salbe ['zalbə], *f.* (—, *pl.* —n) ointment, salve.
Salbei ['zalbai], *m.* (—s, *no pl.*) (*Bot.*) sage.
salben ['zalbən], *v.a.* anoint.
salbungsvoll ['zalbuŋsfɔl], *adj.* unctuous.
Saldo ['zaldo], *m.* (—s, *pl.* —s) balance.
Saline [za'li:nə], *f.* (—, *pl.* —n) salt-mine, salt-works.
Salkante ['za:lkantə], *f.* (—, *pl.* —n) selvedge, border.
Salm [zalm], *m.* (—s, *pl.* —e) (*Zool.*) salmon.
Salmiakgeist ['zalmjakɡaist], *m.* (—s, *no pl.*) ammonia.
Salon [za'lɔ̃], *m.* (—s, *pl.* —s) salon; saloon; drawing-room.
salonfähig [za'lɔ̃fɛ:ɪç], *adj.* presentable, socially acceptable.
salopp [za'lɔp], *adj.* careless, slovenly, shabby, sloppy.
Salpeter [zal'pe:tər], *m.* (—s, *no pl.*) nitre, saltpetre.
salutieren [zalu'ti:rən], *v.a., v.n.*, salute.
Salve ['zalvə], *f.* (—, *pl.* —n) volley, discharge, salute.
Salz [zalts], *n.* (—es, *pl.* —e) salt.
Salzfaß ['zaltsfas], *n.* (—sses, *pl.* ⸚sser) salt-cellar.
Salzlake ['zaltsla:kə], *f.* (—, *pl.* —n) brine.
Salzsäure ['zaltszɔyrə], *f.* (—, *no pl.*) hydrochloric acid.
Sämann ['zɛ:man], *m.* (—s, *pl.* ⸚ner) sower.
Sambia ['zambia], *n.* Zambia.

Same(n)

Same(n) ['zaːmə(n)], *m.* (**—ns,** *pl.* **—n**) seed; sperm; spawn.

Samenstaub ['zaːmənʃtaup], *m.* (**—s,** *no pl.*) pollen.

Sämereien [zɛːməˈraɪən], *f. pl.* seeds, grain.

sämisch ['zɛːmiʃ], *adj.* chamois.

Sammelband ['zaməlbant], *m.* (**—es,** *pl.* **‥e**) miscellany, anthology.

sammeln ['zaməln], *v.a.* collect, gather. — *v.r.* **sich** —, meet; collect o.'s thoughts, compose o.s.

Sammler ['zamlər], *m.* (**—s,** *pl.* **—**) collector; accumulator.

Samstag ['zamstaːk], *m.* (**—s,** *pl.* **—e**) Saturday.

Samt [zamt], *m.* (**—(e)s,** *pl.* **—e**) velvet.

samt [zamt], *adv.* together, all together; — *und sonders,* jointly and severally. — *prep.* (*Dat.*) together with.

sämtlich ['zɛmtlɪç], *adj.* each and every.

Sand [zant], *m.* (**—es,** *no pl.*) sand; *feiner* —, grit; *grober* —, gravel.

Sandtorte ['zanttɔrtə], *f.* (**—,** *pl.* **—n**) sponge-cake, madeira-cake.

Sanduhr ['zantuːr], (**—,** *pl.* **—en**) hour-glass.

sanft [zanft], *adj.* soft, gentle.

Sänfte ['zɛnftə], *f.* (**—,** *pl.* **—n**) sedan-chair.

Sang [zaŋ], *m.* (**—es,** *pl.* **Gesänge**) song; *ohne — und Klang,* (*fig.*) unostentatiously, without fuss, without ceremony.

sanieren [zaˈniːrən], *v.a.* cure; (*company*) reconstruct, put on a sound financial basis.

sanitär [zaniˈtɛːr], *adj.* sanitary.

Sanitäter [zaniˈtɛːtər], *m.* (**—s,** *pl.*—) medical orderly; ambulance man.

Sankt [zaŋkt], *indecl. adj.* Saint; (*abbr.*) St.

sanktionieren [zaŋktsjoˈniːrən], *v.a.* sanction.

Sansibar ['zanziːbaːr], *n.* Zanzibar.

Sardelle [zarˈdɛlə], *f.* (**—,** *pl.* **—n**) (*Zool.*) anchovy.

Sardinien [zarˈdiːnjən], *n.* Sardinia.

Sarg [zark], *m.* (**—es,** *pl.* **‥e**) coffin.

sarkastisch [zarˈkastiʃ], *adj.* sarcastic.

Satellit [zatəˈliːt], *m.* (**—en,** *pl.* **—en**) satellite.

Satiriker [zaˈtiːrɪkər], *m.* (**—s,** *pl.* **—**) satirist.

satt [zat], *adj.* sated, satiated, satisfied; (*colours*) deep, rich; *sich — essen,* eat o.'s fill; *einer Sache — sein,* be sick of s.th., have had enough of s.th.

Sattel ['zatəl], *m.* (**—s,** *pl.* **‥**) saddle; *einen aus dem — heben,* (*fig.*) oust s.o.; *fest im — sitzen,* (*fig.*) be master of a situation; *in allen ‥n gerecht,* versatile.

satteln ['zatəln], *v.a.* saddle.

Sattheit ['zathaɪt], *f.* (**—,** *no pl.*) satiety.

sättigen ['zɛtɪgən], *v.a.* satisfy, sate, satiate; (*Chem.*) saturate.

sattsam ['zatsaːm], *adv.* enough, sufficiently.

saturieren [zatuˈriːrən], *v.a.* (*Chem.*) saturate.

Satz [zats], *m.* (**—es,** *pl.* **‥e**) sentence; proposition; thesis; (*Mus.*) movement; (*Typ.*) composition; (*dregs*) sediment; (*gambling*) stake; *mit einem* —, with one leap (*or* jump *or* bound).

Satzbildung ['zatsbɪlduŋ], *f.* (**—,** *pl.* **—en**) (*Gram.*) construction; (*Chem.*) sedimentation.

Satzlehre ['zatsleːrə], *f.* (**—,** *no pl.*) syntax.

Satzung ['zatsuŋ], *f.* (**—,** *pl.* **—en**) statute.

Satzzeichen ['zatstsaɪçən], *n.* (**—s,** *pl.* **—**) punctuation-mark.

Sau [zau], *f.* (**—,** *pl.* **‥e**) sow; (*vulg.*) dirty person, slut.

sauber ['zaubər], *adj.* clean, neat, tidy.

säubern ['zyːbərn], *v.a.* clean, cleanse; (*fig.*) purge.

Saubohne ['zauboːnə], *f.* (**—,** *pl.* **—n**) broad bean.

Saudiarabien ['zaudiaraːbjən], *n.* Saudi Arabia.

sauer ['zauər], *adj.* sour, acid; (*fig.*) troublesome; morose.

Sauerbrunnen ['zauərbrunən], *m.* (**—s,** *pl.* **—**) mineral water.

Sauerei [zauəˈraɪ], *f.* (**—,** *pl.* **—en**) (*sl.*) filthiness; mess.

Sauerkraut ['zauərkraut], *n.* (**—s,** *no pl.*) pickled cabbage.

säuerlich ['zɔyərlɪç], *adj.* acidulous.

Sauerstoff ['zauərʃtɔf], *m.* (**—(e)s,** *no pl.*) oxygen.

Sauerteig ['zauərtaɪk], *m.* (**—(e)s,** *pl.* **—e**) leaven.

sauertöpfisch ['zauərtœpfiʃ], *adj.* morose, peevish.

saufen ['zaufən], *v.a., v.n. irr.* (*animals*) drink; (*humans*) drink to excess.

Säufer ['zɔyfər], *m.* (**—s,** *pl.* —) drunkard, drinker, alcoholic.

saugen ['zaugən], *v.a., v.n.* suck.

säugen ['zɔygən], *v.a.* suckle.

Säugetier ['zɔygətiːr], *n.* (**—s,** *pl.* **—e**) mammal.

Saugheber ['zaukheːbər], *m.* (**—s,** *pl.* —) suction-pump; siphon.

Säugling ['zɔyklɪŋ], *m.* (**—s,** *pl.* **—e**) suckling, baby.

Saugwarze ['zaukvartsə], *f.* (**—,** *pl.* **—n**) nipple.

Säule ['zɔylə], *f.* (**—,** *pl.* **—n**) pillar, column.

Säulenbündel ['zɔylənbyndəl], *n.* (**—s,** *pl.* —) (*Archit.*) clustered column.

Säulenfuß ['zɔylənfuːs], *m.* (**—es,** *pl.* **‥e**) (*Archit.*) base, plinth.

Säulengang ['zɔyləngaŋ], *m.* (**—s,** *pl.* **‥e**) colonnade.

Saum [zaum], *m.* (**—(e)s,** *pl.* **‥e**) seam, hem, border, edge; selvedge.

saumäßig ['zaumɛːsɪç], *adj.* (*sl.*) beastly, filthy, piggish; enormous.

säumen (1) ['zɔymən], *v.a.* hem.

säumen (2) ['zɔymən], *v.n.* delay, tarry.

säumig ['zɔymɪç], *adj.* tardy, slow, dilatory.

Saumpferd [ˈzaumpfeːrt], n. (—s, pl. —e) pack-horse.

saumselig [ˈzaumzeːlɪç], adj. tardy, dilatory.

Säure [ˈzɔyrə], f. (—, pl. —n) acid; (Med.) acidity.

Saurier [ˈzaurjər], m. (—s, pl. —) saurian.

Saus [zaus], m. (—es, no pl.) rush; revel, riot; in — und Braus leben, live a wild life, live riotously.

säuseln [ˈzɔyzəln], v.n. rustle, murmur.

sausen [ˈzauzən], v.n. bluster, blow, howl, whistle; (coll.) rush, dash.

Saustall [ˈzauʃtal], m. (—s, pl. ⸚e) pigsty.

Schabe [ˈʃaːbə], f. (—, pl. —n) (Ent.) cockroach.

schaben [ˈʃaːbən], v.a. scrape, shave, rub.

Schabernack [ˈʃaːbərnak], m. (—s, pl. —e) practical joke, trick.

schäbig [ˈʃɛːbɪç], adj. shabby.

Schablone [ʃaˈbloːnə], f. (—, pl. —n) model, mould, pattern, stencil; (fig.) routine.

Schach [ʃax], n. (—(e)s, no pl.) chess; — bieten, check; — spielen, play chess; in — halten, keep in check.

Schacher [ˈʃaxər], m. (—s, no pl.) haggling, bargaining, barter.

Schächer [ˈʃɛçər], m. (—s, pl. —) wretch, felon, robber.

Schacht [ʃaxt], m. (—(e)s, pl. ⸚e) shaft.

Schachtel [ˈʃaxtəl], f. (—, pl. —n) box, (cardboard) box, (small) case.

Schachtelhalm [ˈʃaxtəlhalm], m. (—s, pl. —e) (grass) horse-tail.

Schächter [ˈʃɛçtər], m. (—s, pl. —) (kosher) butcher.

schade [ˈʃaːdə], int. a pity, a shame, unfortunate; wie —, what a pity; sehr —, a great pity.

Schädel [ˈʃɛːdəl], m. (—s, pl. —) skull.

Schaden [ˈʃaːdən], m. (—s, pl. ⸚) damage, injury, detriment; zu — kommen, come to grief.

schaden [ˈʃaːdən], v.n. do harm, do damage, do injury; es schadet nichts, it does not matter.

Schadenersatz [ˈʃaːdənɛrzats], m. (—es, no pl.) indemnity, compensation, indemnification; (money) damages.

Schadenfreude [ˈʃaːdənfrɔydə], f. (—, no pl.) malicious pleasure.

Schadensforderung [ˈʃaːdənsfordərʊŋ], f. (—, pl. —en) claim (for damages).

schadhaft [ˈʃaːthaft], adj. defective, faulty.

schädlich [ˈʃɛːtlɪç], adj. injurious, noxious, pernicious, noisome.

schadlos [ˈʃaːtloːs], adj. indemnified; einen — halten, indemnify s.o., compensate s.o.; sich an einem — halten, recoup o.s. from s.o.

Schadlosigkeit [ˈʃaːtloːzɪçkaɪt], f. (—, no pl.) harmlessness.

Schaf [ʃaːf], n. (—(e)s, pl. —e) sheep.

Schafblattern [ˈʃaːfblatərn], f. pl. (Med.) chicken-pox.

Schafdarm [ˈʃaːfdarm], m. (—s, pl. ⸚e) sheep-gut.

Schäfer [ˈʃɛːfər], m. (—s, pl. —) shepherd.

Schäferstündchen [ˈʃɛːfərʃtyntçən], n. (—s, pl. —) tryst; rendezvous.

schaffen [ˈʃafən], v.a., v.n. irr. make, produce, create. — v.a. reg. provide; manage; aus dem Wege —, remove. — v.n. reg. work; einem zu — machen, give s.o. trouble.

Schaffner [ˈʃafnər], m. (—s, pl. —) (Railw. etc.) guard, conductor.

Schafgarbe [ˈʃaːfgarbə], f. (—, pl. —n) (Bot.) common yarrow.

Schafhürde [ˈʃaːfhyrdə], f. (—, pl. —n) sheep-fold.

Schafott [ʃaˈfɔt], n. (—(e)s, pl. —e) scaffold.

Schafschur [ˈʃaːfʃuːr], f. (—, pl. —en) sheep-shearing.

Schaft [ʃaft], m. (—(e)s, pl. ⸚e) shaft; (gun) stock.

Schafwolle [ˈʃaːfvɔlə], f. (—, no pl.) sheep's wool, fleece.

Schakal [ʃaˈkaːl], m. (—s, pl. —e) (Zool.) jackal.

Schäkerei [ʃɛːkəˈraɪ], f. (—, pl. —en) playfulness, teasing, dalliance, flirtation.

Schal [ʃaːl], m. (—s, pl. —e) scarf, shawl.

schal [ʃaːl], adj. stale, flat, insipid.

Schale [ˈʃaːlə], f. (—, pl. —n) (nut, egg) shell; (fruit) peel, rind; dish, bowl; (Austr.) cup; (fig.) outside.

schälen [ˈʃɛːlən], v.a. shell; peel.

Schalk [ʃalk], m. (—s, pl. —e) knave; rogue; wag, joker.

Schall [ʃal], m. (—(e)s, no pl.) sound.

Schallbecken [ˈʃalbɛkən], n. (—s, pl. —) cymbal.

Schallehre [ˈʃalleːrə], f. (—, no pl.) acoustics.

schallen [ˈʃalən], v.n. sound, reverberate.

Schalmei [ʃalˈmaɪ], f. (—, pl. —en) (Poet., Mus.) shawm.

Schallplatte [ˈʃalplatə], f. (—, pl. —n) (gramophone) record.

schalten [ˈʃaltən], v.n. rule; switch; (Motor.) change gear; — und walten, manage.

Schalter [ˈʃaltər], m. (—s, pl. —) (Elec.) switch; booking-office; counter.

Schalthebel [ˈʃaltheːbəl], m. (—s, pl. —) (Motor.) gear lever.

Schaltier [ˈʃaltiːr], n. (—s, pl. —e) (Zool.) crustacean.

Schaltjahr [ˈʃaltjaːr], n. (—s, pl. —e) leap year.

Schalttafel [ˈʃalttaːfəl], f. (—, pl. —n) switch-board.

Scham [ʃaːm], f. (—, no pl.) shame, modesty; private parts.

schämen [ˈʃɛːmən], v.r. sich —, be ashamed (of).

schamlos [ˈʃaːmloːs], adj. shameless.

schamrot [ˈʃaːmroːt], adj. blushing; — werden, blush.

schandbar ['ʃantbaːr], *adj.* ignominious, infamous.
Schande ['ʃandə], *f.* (—, *no pl.*) shame, disgrace; dishonour, ignominy.
schänden ['ʃɛndən], *v.a.* dishonour, disgrace; violate, ravish.
Schandfleck ['ʃantflɛk], *m.* (—s, *pl.* —e) stain, blemish.
schändlich ['ʃɛntliç], *adj.* shameful, disgraceful, infamous.
Schändung ['ʃenduŋ], *f.* (—, *pl.* —en) violation.
Schank ['ʃaŋk], *m.* (—s, *no pl.*) sale of liquor.
Schanzarbeiter ['ʃantsarbaɪtər], *m.* (—s, *pl.* —) sapper.
Schanze ['ʃantsə], *f.* (—, *pl.* —n) redoubt, bulwark; *in die — schlagen*, risk, venture.
Schar [ʃaːr], *f.* (—, *pl.* —en) troop, band; host.
Scharade [ʃaˈraːdə], *f.* (—, *pl.* —n) charade.
scharen ['ʃaːrən], *v.r. sich — um*, assemble, congregate, gather round.
Schären ['ʃɛːrən], *f. pl.* reefs, skerries.
scharf [ʃarf], *adj.* sharp, keen, acute, acrid, pungent; piercing; (*fig.*) severe, rigorous.
Schärfe ['ʃɛrfə], *f.* (—, *no pl.*) sharpness, keenness, acuteness; pungency, acridness; severity, rigour.
schärfen ['ʃɛrfən], *v.a.* sharpen, whet; (*fig.*) strengthen, intensify.
Scharfrichter ['ʃarfriçtər], *m.* (—s, *pl.* —) executioner.
scharfsichtig ['ʃarfziçtiç], *adj.* sharp-eyed, (*fig.*) penetrating, astute.
scharfsinnig ['ʃarfzɪnɪç], *adj.* clear-sighted, sagacious, ingenious.
Scharlach ['ʃarlax], *m.* (—s, *no pl.*) scarlet; (*Med.*) scarlet-fever.
Scharlatan ['ʃarlataːn], *m.* (—s, *pl.* —e) charlatan, humbug.
scharmant [ʃarˈmant], *adj.* charming.
Scharmützel [ʃarˈmytsəl], *n.* (—s, *pl.* —) skirmish.
Scharnier [ʃarˈniːr], *n.* (—s, *pl.* —e) hinge, joint.
Schärpe ['ʃɛrpə], *f.* (—, *pl.* —n) sash.
Scharpie [ʃarˈpiː], *f.* (—, *no pl.*) lint.
scharren ['ʃarən], *v.a., v.n.* scrape, rake.
Scharte ['ʃartə], *f.* (—, *pl.* —n) notch, crack; *eine — auswetzen*, repair a mistake, make up for s.th.
Scharteke [ʃarˈteːkə], *f.* (—, *pl.* —n) worthless book, trash; *eine alte —*, an old fuddy-duddy, frump.
scharwenzeln [ʃarˈvɛntsəln], *v.n.* dance attendance, be obsequious.
Schatten ['ʃatən], *m.* (—s, *pl.* —) shade, shadow.
Schattenbild ['ʃatənbɪlt], *n.* (—s, *pl.* —er) silhouette.
Schattenriß ['ʃatənrɪs], *m.* (—sses, *pl.* —sse) silhouette.
schattieren [ʃaˈtiːrən], *v.a.* shade (drawing).
schattig ['ʃatɪç], *adj.* shady.

Schatulle [ʃaˈtulə], *f.* (—, *pl.* —n) cash-box; privy purse.
Schatz [ʃats], *m.* (—es, *pl.* ⸚e) treasure; (*fig.*) sweetheart, darling.
Schatzamt ['ʃatsamt], *n.* (—s, *pl.* ⸚er) Treasury, Exchequer.
schätzbar ['ʃɛtsbaːr], *adj.* estimable.
Schätzchen ['ʃɛtsçən], *n.* (—s, *pl.* —) (*coll.*) sweetheart.
schätzen ['ʃɛtsən], *v.a.* value, estimate; esteem; reckon at.
Schatzkammer ['ʃatskamər], *f.* (—, *pl.* —n) treasury.
Schatzmeister ['ʃatsmaɪstər], *m.* (—s, *pl.* —) treasurer.
Schätzung ['ʃɛtsuŋ], *f.* (—, *pl.* —en) valuation, estimate; (*fig.*) esteem.
Schau [ʃau], *f.* (—, *pl.* —en) show, view, spectacle; *zur — stellen*, display; parade.
Schauder ['ʃaudər], *m.* (—s, *pl.* —) shudder, shiver; horror.
schaudern ['ʃaudərn], *v.n.* shudder, shiver.
schauen ['ʃauən], *v.a.* see, view. — *v.n.* look, gaze (*auf*, at), *schau mal*, look here.
Schauer ['ʃauər], *m.* (—s, *pl.* —) shiver, paroxysm; (*fig.*) thrill, awe; (*rain*) shower.
schauern ['ʃauərn], *v.n.* shudder, shiver; (*rain*) shower.
Schauerroman ['ʃauərroːmaːn], *m.* (—s, *pl.* —e) (*novel*) penny dreadful, thriller.
Schaufel ['ʃaufəl], *f.* (—, *pl.* —n) shovel.
Schaufenster ['ʃaufɛnstər], *n.* (—s, *pl.* —) shop-window.
Schaukel ['ʃaukəl], *f.* (—, *pl.* —n) swing.
schaulustig ['ʃaulustiç], *adj.* curious.
Schaum [ʃaum], *m.* (—es, *pl.* ⸚e) foam, froth; bubbles; scum; *— schlagen*, whip cream.
schäumen ['ʃɔymən], *v.n.* foam, froth, sparkle.
Schauplatz ['ʃauplats], *m.* (—es, *pl.* ⸚e) scene, stage.
schaurig ['ʃauriç], *adj.* grisly, horrid, horrible.
Schauspiel ['ʃauʃpiːl], *n.* (—s, *pl.* —e) spectacle; drama, play.
Schauspieler ['ʃauʃpiːlər], *m.* (—s, *pl.* —) actor, player.
Schaustellung ['ʃauʃtɛluŋ], *f.* (—, *pl.* —en) exhibition.
Scheck [ʃɛk], *m.* (—s, *pl.* —s) cheque.
scheckig ['ʃɛkɪç], *adj.* piebald, spotted, dappled.
scheel [ʃeːl], *adj.* squint-eyed; envious; *einen — ansehen*, look askance at s.o.
Scheffel ['ʃɛfəl], *m.* (—s, *pl.* —) bushel.
scheffeln ['ʃɛfəln], *v.a.* rake in; accumulate.
Scheibe ['ʃaɪbə], *f.* (—, *pl.* —n) disc; (*window*) pane; (*shooting*) target; (*bread*) slice.
Scheibenhonig ['ʃaɪbənhoːnɪç], *m.* (—s, *no pl.*) honey in the comb.

Scheibenschießen ['ʃaɪbənʃiːsən], *n.* (—s, *no pl.*) target-practice.
Scheich [ʃaɪç], *m.* (—s, *pl.* —e) sheikh.
Scheide ['ʃaɪdə], *f.* (—, *pl.* —n) sheath, scabbard; (*Anat.*) vagina.
Scheidemünze ['ʃaɪdəmyntsə], *f.* (—, *pl.* —n) small coin, change.
scheiden ['ʃaɪdən], *v.a. irr.* divide; separate, divorce; *sich — lassen*, obtain a divorce. — *v.n.* (*aux.* sein) part, depart; *aus dem Amte —*, resign office.
Scheidewand ['ʃaɪdəvant], *f.* (—, *pl.* ⁻e) partition-wall.
Scheideweg ['ʃaɪdəveːk], *m.* (—s, *pl.* —e) cross-roads; *am — stehen*, be at the parting of the ways.
Scheidung ['ʃaɪduŋ], *f.* (—, *pl.* —en) divorce.
Schein [ʃaɪn], *m.* (—(e)s, *no pl.*) shine, sheen, lustre, splendour; semblance, pretence; *den — wahren*, keep up appearances; *der — trügt*, appearances are deceptive; (*in compounds*) mock, would-be, apparent; (*pl.* —e) (piece of) paper, chit, note; (*fig.*) attestation, certificate.
scheinbar ['ʃaɪnbaːr], *adj.* apparent; ostensible, specious. — *adv.* seemingly.
scheinen ['ʃaɪnən], *v.n. irr.* shine, sparkle; seem, appear.
scheinheilig ['ʃaɪnhaɪlɪç], *adj.* hypocritical.
Scheinheiligkeit ['ʃaɪnhaɪlɪçkaɪt], *f.* (—, *no pl.*) hypocrisy.
scheintot ['ʃaɪntoːt], *adj.* in a cataleptic trance; seemingly dead.
Scheinwerfer ['ʃaɪnvɛrfər], *m.* (—s, *pl.* —) headlight; searchlight; floodlight.
Scheit [ʃaɪt], *n.* (—(e)s, *pl.* —e) piece of wood, billet.
Scheitel ['ʃaɪtəl], *m.* (—s, *pl.* —) (*hair*) parting; top, vertex.
Scheiterhaufen ['ʃaɪtərhaufən], *m.* (—s, *pl.* —) stake; funeral pyre.
scheitern ['ʃaɪtərn], *v.n.* (*aux.* sein) (*ship*) founder, be wrecked; (*fig.*) miscarry, fail.
Schelle ['ʃɛlə], *f.* (—, *pl.* —n) bell.
Schellen ['ʃɛlən], *f. pl.* (*Cards*) diamonds.
schellen ['ʃɛlən], *v.n.* ring the bell.
Schellfisch ['ʃɛlfɪʃ], *m.* (—es, *pl.* —e) (*Zool.*) haddock.
Schelm [ʃɛlm], *m.* (—(e)s, *pl.* —e) rogue, knave, villain.
schelten ['ʃɛltən], *v.a. irr.* scold, chide, rebuke, reprimand.
Schema ['ʃeːma], *n.* (—s, *pl.* —s) schedule, model, plan, scheme.
Schemel ['ʃeːməl], *m.* (—s, *pl.* —) foot-stool.
Schenk [ʃɛŋk], *m.* (—en, *pl.* —en) cupbearer; publican.
Schenke ['ʃɛŋkə], *f.* (—, *pl.* —n) alehouse, tavern, pub.
Schenkel ['ʃɛŋkəl], *m.* (—s, *pl.* —) thigh; (*Geom.*) side of triangle.

schenken ['ʃɛŋkən], *v.a.* present s.o. with, donate, give.
Schenkstube ['ʃɛŋkʃtuːbə], *f.* (—, *pl.* —n) tap-room.
Scherbe ['ʃɛrbə], *f.* (—, *pl.* —n) potsherd; fragment of glass etc.
Schere ['ʃeːrə], *f.* (—, *pl.* —n) scissors; (*garden*) shears; (*crab*) claw.
scheren ['ʃeːrən], *v.a.* shave; clip, shear; bother, concern. — *v.r. sich —*, clear off; *scher dich zum Teufel!* go to blazes!
Scherereien [ʃerəˈraɪən], *f. pl.* vexation, bother, trouble.
Scherflein ['ʃɛrflaɪn], *n.* (—s, *pl.* —) mite; *sein — beitragen*, contribute o.'s share.
Scherge ['ʃɛrgə], *m.* (—n, *pl.* —n) (*obs.*) beadle.
Scherz [ʃɛrts], *m.* (—es, *pl.* —e) jest, joke; —*beiseite*, joking apart.
scheu [ʃɔy], *adj.* shy, bashful, timid; skittish.
scheuchen ['ʃɔyçən], *v.a.* scare away.
scheuen ['ʃɔyən], *v.a.* shun, avoid, fight shy of, fear. — *v.n.* take fright.
Scheuer ['ʃɔyər], *f.* (—, *pl.* —n) barn.
scheuern ['ʃɔyərn], *v.a.* scour, scrub.
Scheuklappe ['ʃɔyklapə], *f.* (—, *pl.* —n) blinker.
Scheune ['ʃɔynə], *f.* (—, *pl.* —n) barn.
Scheusal ['ʃɔyzaːl], *n.* (—s, *pl.* —e) monster.
scheußlich ['ʃɔyslɪç], *adj.* frightful, dreadful, abominable, hideous.
Schicht [ʃɪçt], *f.* (—, *pl.* —en) layer, stratum, seam; (*society*) class; (*work*) shift.
schick [ʃɪk], *adj.* stylish, chic.
schicken ['ʃɪkən], *v.a.* send, despatch, convey. — *v.r. sich —*, be proper; *sich in etwas —*, put up with s.th., resign o.s. to s.th.
schicklich ['ʃɪklɪç], *adj.* proper, becoming, suitable, seemly.
Schicksal ['ʃɪkzaːl], *n.* (—s, *pl.* —e) fate, destiny, lot.
Schickung ['ʃɪkuŋ], *f.* (—, *pl.* —en) Divine Will, Providence.
schieben ['ʃiːbən], *v.a. irr.* shove, push; *die Schuld auf einen —*, put the blame on s.o.
Schieber ['ʃiːbər], *m.* (—s, *pl.* —) bolt, slide; (*fig.*) profiteer, spiv.
Schiedsgericht ['ʃiːtsgərɪçt], *n.* (—es, *pl.* —e) arbitration tribunal.
Schiedsrichter ['ʃiːtsrɪçtər], *m.* (—s, *pl.* —) referee, umpire, arbiter.
schief [ʃiːf], *adj.* slanting, oblique, bent, crooked; wry; — *Ebene*, inclined plane; — *gehen*, go wrong.
Schiefe ['ʃiːfə], *f.* (—, *no pl.*) obliquity.
Schiefer ['ʃiːfər], *m.* (—s, *no pl.*) slate.
schiefrig ['ʃiːfrɪç], *adj.* slaty.
schielen ['ʃiːlən], *v.n.* squint, be cross-eyed.
Schienbein ['ʃiːnbaɪn], *n.* (—s, *pl.* —e) shin-bone, shin.

Schiene

Schiene ['ʃiːnə], *f.* (—, *pl.* —n) rail; (*Med.*) splint.
schier [ʃiːr], *adj.* (*rare*) sheer, pure. — *adv.* almost, very nearly.
Schierling ['ʃiːrlɪŋ], *m.* (—s, *pl.* —e) (*Bot.*) hemlock.
schießen ['ʃiːsən], *v.a., v.n. irr.* shoot, fire, discharge; (*fig.*) rush; *etwas — lassen*, let go of s.th.; *die Zügel — lassen*, loosen o.'s hold on the reins; *ein Kabel — lassen*, pay out a cable; *das ist zum —*, that's very funny.
Schiff [ʃɪf], *n.* (—(e)s, *pl.* —e) ship, vessel, boat; (*church*) nave.
schiffbar ['ʃɪfbaːr], *adj.* navigable.
Schiffbruch ['ʃɪfbrux], *m.* (—s, *pl* ⁝e) shipwreck.
Schiffbrücke ['ʃɪfbrykə], *f.* (—, *pl.* —n) pontoon-bridge.
schiffen ['ʃɪfən], *v.n.* sail; navigate.
Schiffsboden ['ʃɪfsboːdən], *m.* (—s, *pl.* ⁝) (ship's) hold.
Schiffsmaat ['ʃɪfsmaːt], *m.* (—s, *pl.* —e) shipmate.
Schiffsrumpf ['ʃɪfsrumpf], *m.* (—es, *pl.* ⁝e) hull.
Schiffsschnabel ['ʃɪfsʃnaːbəl], *m.* (—s, *pl.* ⁝) prow, bows.
Schiffsvorderteil ['ʃɪfsfɔrdərtaɪl], *n.* (—s, *pl.* —e) forecastle, prow.
Schiffszwieback ['ʃɪfstsviːbak], *m.* (—s, *no pl.*) ship's biscuit.
Schikane [ʃiˈkaːnə], *f.* (—, *pl.* —n) chicanery.
Schild (1) [ʃɪlt], *m.* (—(e)s, *pl.* —e) shield, buckler, escutcheon; *etwas im — führen*, have designs on s.th., plan s.th.
Schild (2) [ʃɪlt], *n.* (—s, *pl.* —er) signboard, plate.
Schilderhaus ['ʃɪldərhaus], *n.* (—es, *pl.* ⁝er) sentry-box.
Schildermaler ['ʃɪldərmaːlər], *m.* (—s, *pl.* —) sign-painter.
schildern ['ʃɪldərn], *v.a.* describe, depict.
Schildknappe ['ʃɪltknapə], *m.* (—n, *pl.* —n) shield-bearer, squire.
Schildkrot ['ʃɪltkroːt], *n.* (—s, *no pl.*) tortoise-shell.
Schildkröte ['ʃɪltkrøːtə], *f.* (—, *pl.* —n) (*Zool.*) turtle, tortoise.
Schildpatt ['ʃɪltpat], *n.* (—s, *no pl.*) tortoise-shell.
Schildwache ['ʃɪltvaxə], *f.* (—, *pl.* —n) sentinel, sentry; — *stehen*, be on sentry duty, stand guard.
Schilf(rohr) ['ʃɪlf(roːr)], *n.* (—(e)s, *no pl.*) (*Bot.*) reed, rush, sedge.
schillern ['ʃɪlərn], *v.n.* opalesce, glitter, change colour, be iridescent.
Schilling ['ʃɪlɪŋ], *m.* (—s, *pl.* —e) Austrian coin; shilling.
Schimmel (1) ['ʃɪməl], *m.* (—s, *pl.* —) white horse.
Schimmel (2) ['ʃɪməl], *m.* (—s, *no pl.*) mould, mustiness.
schimmeln ['ʃɪməln], *v.n.* (*aux.* sein) go mouldy, moulder.

Schimmer ['ʃɪmər], *m.* (—s, *pl.* —) glitter, gleam; *ich habe keinen —*, I haven't a clue.
schimmlig ['ʃɪmlɪç], *adj.* mouldy, musty, mildewed.
Schimpanse [ʃɪmˈpanzə], *m.* (—n, *pl.* —n) (*Zool.*) chimpanzee.
Schimpf [ʃɪmpf], *m.* (—es, *no pl.*) abuse, affront, insult; *mit — und Schande*, in disgrace.
schimpfen ['ʃɪmpfən], *v.n.* curse, swear; — *auf*, (*fig.*) run (s.o.) down. — *v.a.* insult (s.o.), call (s.o.) names; scold.
Schindel ['ʃɪndəl], *f.* (—, *pl.* —n) shingle.
schinden ['ʃɪndən], *v.a. irr.* flay; (*fig.*) grind, oppress, sweat. — *v.r. sich —*, slave, drudge.
Schindluder ['ʃɪntluːdər], *n.* (—s, *pl.* —) worn-out animal; *mit einem — treiben*, exploit s.o.
Schinken ['ʃɪŋkən], *m.* (—s, *pl.* —) ham.
Schinkenspeck ['ʃɪŋkənʃpɛk], *m.* (—s, *no pl.*) bacon.
Schippe ['ʃɪpə], *f.* (—, *pl.* —n) shovel, spade.
Schirm [ʃɪrm], *m.* (—(e)s, *pl.* —e) screen; umbrella; parasol, sunshade; lampshade; (*fig.*) shield, shelter, cover.
schirmen ['ʃɪrmən], *v.a.* protect (from), shelter.
Schirmherr ['ʃɪrmhɛr], *m.* (—n, *pl.* —en) protector, patron.
Schlacht [ʃlaxt], *f.* (—, *pl.* —en) battle; fight; *eine — liefern*, give battle; *die — gewinnen*, carry the day, win the battle.
Schlachtbank ['ʃlaxtbaŋk], *f.* (—, *pl.* ⁝e) shambles; *zur — führen*, lead to the slaughter.
schlachten ['ʃlaxtən], *v.a.* kill, butcher, slaughter.
Schlachtenbummler ['ʃlaxtənbumlər], *m.* (—s, *pl.* —) camp follower.
Schlachtfeld ['ʃlaxtfɛlt], *n.* (—s, *pl.* —er) battlefield.
Schlachtruf ['ʃlaxtruːf], *m.* (—s, *pl.* —e) battle-cry.
Schlacke ['ʃlakə], *f.* (—, *pl.* —n) slag, clinker, dross.
Schlackwurst ['ʃlakvurst], *f.* (—, *pl.* ⁝e) (*North German*) sausage.
Schlaf [ʃlaːf], *m.* (—(e)s, *no pl.*) sleep; slumber, rest; *in tiefem —*, fast asleep; *in den — wiegen*, rock to sleep.
Schläfchen ['ʃlɛːfçən], *n.* (—s, *pl.* —) nap; *ein — machen*, have forty winks.
Schläfe ['ʃlɛːfə], *f.* (—, *pl.* —n) temple.
schlafen ['ʃlaːfən], *v.n. irr.* sleep; *schlaf wohl*, sleep well; — *gehen*, go to bed.
schlaff [ʃlaf], *adj.* slack, loose, lax, flabby; weak; remiss.
schlaflos ['ʃlaːfloːs], *adj.* sleepless.
Schlafmittel ['ʃlaːfmɪtəl], *n.* (—s, *pl.* —) soporific, sleeping tablet, sleeping draught.
schläfrig ['ʃlɛːfrɪç], *adj.* drowsy, sleepy.

Schlafrock [ˈʃlaːfrɔk], s. (—s, pl. ⸚e) dressing-gown; *Äpfel im* —, apple fritters.

schlafwandeln [ˈʃlaːfvandəln], v.n. (aux. sein) walk in o.'s sleep, sleepwalk.

Schlag [ʃlaːk], m. (—(e)s, pl. ⸚e) blow, stroke; beat; (Elec.) shock; *ein Mann von gutem* —, a good type of man; *vom* — *gerührt*, struck by apoplexy; — *fünf*, at five o'clock sharp.

Schlagader [ˈʃlaːkaːdər], f. (—, pl. —n) artery.

Schlaganfall [ˈʃlaːkanfal], m. (—s, pl. ⸚e) stroke, apoplexy.

Schlagballspiel [ˈʃlaːkbalʃpiːl], n. (—s, pl. —e) rounders.

Schlagbaum [ˈʃlaːkbaum], m. (—s, pl. ⸚e) turnpike.

schlagen [ˈʃlaːgən], v.a. irr. beat, strike, hit; (tree) fell; (money) coin; *Alarm* —, sound the alarm; *ans Kreuz* —, crucify; *ein Kreuz* —, make the sign of the cross. — v.n. (clock) strike; (birds) warble; *aus der Art* —, degenerate. — v.r. *sich* —, fight; *sich auf Säbel* —, fight with sabres; *sich an die Brust* —, beat o.'s breast.

Schlager [ˈʃlaːgər], m. (—s, pl. —) hit, pop song; (fig.) success.

Schläger [ˈʃlɛːgər], m. (—s, pl. —) rapier; bat; (tennis-)racket; (golf-)club.

Schlägerei [ʃlɛːgəˈraɪ], f. (—, pl. —en) fray, scuffle.

schlagfertig [ˈʃlaːkfɛrtiç], adj. quick-witted.

Schlagkraft [ˈʃlaːkkraft], f. (—, no pl.) striking power.

Schlaglicht [ˈʃlaːklɪçt], n. (—s, pl. —er) strong direct light.

Schlagsahne [ˈʃlaːkzaːnə], f. (—, no pl.) double cream, raw cream; whipped cream.

Schlagschatten [ˈʃlaːkʃatən], m. (—s, pl. —) deep shadow.

Schlagseite [ˈʃlaːkzaɪtə], f. (—, no pl.) — *bekommen*, (Naut.) list.

Schlagwort [ˈʃlaːkvɔrt], n. (—s, pl. ⸚er) catchword, slogan; trite saying.

Schlagzeile [ˈʃlaːktsaɪlə], f. (—, pl. —n) headline.

Schlamm [ʃlam], m. (—(e)s, no pl.) mud, mire.

Schlampe [ˈʃlampə], f. (—, pl. —n) slut.

Schlange [ˈʃlaŋə], f. (—, pl. —n) snake, serpent; (fig.) queue.

schlängeln [ˈʃlɛŋəln], v.r. sich —, wind, meander.

schlangenartig [ˈʃlaŋənaːrtɪç], adj. snaky, serpentine.

schlank [ʃlaŋk], adj. slim, slender.

schlapp [ʃlap], adj. limp, tired, weak, slack; — *machen*, break down, collapse.

Schlappe [ˈʃlapə], f. (—, pl. —n) reverse, defeat; *eine* — *erleiden*, suffer a setback.

Schlappschwanz [ˈʃlapʃvants], m. (—es, pl. ⸚e) weakling; milksop.

Schlaraffenland [ʃlaˈrafənlant], n. (—(e)s, pl. ⸚er) land of milk and honey.

schlau [ʃlau], adj. cunning, crafty, sly, shrewd.

Schlauch [ʃlaux], m. (—(e)s, pl. ⸚e) hose; tube.

Schlaukopf [ˈʃlaukɔpf], m. (—(e)s, pl. ⸚e) slyboots; (Am.) wiseacre.

schlecht [ʃlɛçt], adj. bad, evil, wicked; poor; *mir ist* —, I feel ill; —*e Zeiten*, hard times; —*es Geld*, base money.

schlechterdings [ˈʃlɛçtərdɪŋs], adv. simply, positively, absolutely.

schlechthin [ˈʃlɛçthɪn], adv. simply, plainly.

Schlechtigkeit [ˈʃlɛçtɪçkaɪt], f. (—, pl. —en) wickedness, baseness.

Schlegel [ˈʃleːgəl], m. (—s, pl. —) mallet; drumstick; (bell) clapper.

Schlehdorn [ˈʃleːdɔrn], m. (—s, pl. —e) blackthorn, sloe-tree.

schleichen [ˈʃlaɪçən], v.n. irr. (aux. sein) sneak, prowl, slink; —*de Krankheit*, lingering illness.

Schleichhandel [ˈʃlaɪçhandəl], m. (—s, pl. ⸚) smuggling, black marketeering.

Schleie [ˈʃlaɪə], f. (—, pl. —n) tench.

Schleier [ˈʃlaɪər], m. (—s, pl. —) veil.

Schleife [ˈʃlaɪfə], f. (—, pl. —n) bow, loop, noose.

schleifen [ˈʃlaɪfən], v.a. irr. drag along, trail; grind, polish, sharpen, whet, hone; cut.

Schleim [ʃlaɪm], m. (—(e)s, no pl.) slime, mucus, phlegm.

Schleimhaut [ˈʃlaɪmhaut], f. (—, pl. ⸚e) mucous membrane.

Schleimsuppe [ˈʃlaɪmzupə], f. (—, pl. —n) gruel.

schleißen [ˈʃlaɪsən], v.a. irr. split, slit; (feathers) strip.

schlemmen [ˈʃlɛmən], v.n. carouse, gormandise.

schlendern [ˈʃlɛndərn], v.n. (aux. sein) saunter along, stroll.

Schlendrian [ˈʃlɛndriaːn], m. (—s, no pl.) old jog-trot, routine.

schlenkern [ˈʃlɛŋkərn], v.a. dangle, swing.

Schleppdampfer [ˈʃlɛpdampfər], m. (—s, pl. —) steam-tug, tug-boat, tow-boat.

Schleppe [ˈʃlɛpə], f. (—, pl. —n) train (of a dress).

schleppen [ˈʃlɛpən], v.a. carry (s.th. heavy), drag, tow.

Schleppenträger [ˈʃlɛpəntrɛːgər], m. (—s, pl. —) train-bearer.

Schleppnetz [ˈʃlɛpnɛts], n. (—es, pl. —e) dragnet.

Schlesien [ˈʃleːzjən], n. Silesia.

Schleuder [ˈʃlɔydər], f. (—, pl. —n) sling; catapult.

schleudern [ˈʃlɔydərn], v.a. sling, throw, fling away. — v.n. (Motor.) skid; (Comm.) sell cheaply, undersell.

schleunigst [ˈʃlɔynɪçst], *adv.* very quickly, with the utmost expedition, promptly.
Schleuse [ˈʃlɔyzə], *f.* (—, *pl.* —n) sluice, flood-gate, lock.
Schlich [ʃlɪç], *m.* (—es, *pl.* —e) trick, dodge; *einem hinter seine —e kommen*, be up to s.o.'s tricks.
schlicht [ʃlɪçt], *adj.* plain, simple, homely; *—er Abschied*, curt dismissal.
schlichten [ˈʃlɪçtən], *v.a.* level; (*argument*) settle; adjust, compose.
Schlichtheit [ˈʃlɪçthaɪt], *f.* (—, *no pl.*) plainness, simplicity, homeliness.
schließen [ˈʃliːsən], *v.a. irr.* shut, close; contract; *etwas — aus*, conclude s.th. from; (*meeting*) close; *Frieden —*, make peace; *einen in die Arme —*, embrace s.o.; *etwas in sich —*, imply, entail.
Schließer [ˈʃliːsər], *m.* (—s, *pl.* —) doorkeeper; (*prison*) jailer, turnkey.
schließlich [ˈʃliːslɪç], *adv.* lastly, finally, in conclusion.
Schliff [ʃlɪf], *m.* (—(e)s, *no pl.*) polish, refinement.
schlimm [ʃlɪm], *adj.* bad, evil, ill; sad; serious, sore; disagreeable; naughty; *um so —er*, so much the worse, worse luck.
Schlinge [ˈʃlɪŋə], *f.* (—, *pl.* —n) loop, knot; noose, snare.
Schlingel [ˈʃlɪŋəl], *m.* (—s, *pl.* —) little rascal.
schlingen [ˈʃlɪŋən], *v.a. irr.* sling, wind; swallow, devour.
Schlips [ʃlɪps], *m.* (—es, *pl.* —e) (neck-)tie, cravat.
Schlitten [ˈʃlɪtən], *m.* (—s, *pl.* —) sledge, sled, sleigh.
Schlittschuh [ˈʃlɪtʃuː], *m.* (—s, *pl.* —e) skate; *— laufen*, skate.
Schlitz [ʃlɪts], *m.* (—es, *pl.* —e) slit.
schlohweiß [ˈʃloːvaɪs], *adj.* white as sloe-blossom, snow-white.
Schloß [ʃlɔs], *n.* (—sses, *pl.* ⁻sser) (*door*) lock, padlock; (*gun*) lock; palace, castle; *unter — und Riegel*, under lock and key.
Schloße [ˈʃloːsə], *f.* (—, *pl.* —n) hailstone.
Schlosser [ˈʃlɔsər], *m.* (—s, *pl.* —) locksmith.
Schlot [ʃloːt], *m.* (—(e)s, *pl.* —e) chimney, funnel.
schlottern [ˈʃlɔtərn], *v.n.* wobble, dodder; tremble.
Schlucht [ʃluxt], *f.* (—, *pl.* —en) deep valley, defile, cleft, glen, ravine, gorge.
schluchzen [ˈʃluxtsən], *v.n.* sob.
schlucken [ˈʃlukən], *v.a.* gulp down, swallow. — *v.n.* hiccup.
Schlucker [ˈʃlukər], *m.* (—s, *pl.* —) *armer —*, poor wretch.
Schlummer [ˈʃlumər], *m.* (—s, *no pl.*) slumber.
Schlumpe [ˈʃlumpə], *f.* (—, *pl.* —n) slut, slattern.

Schlund [ʃlunt], *m.* (—(e)s, *pl.* ⁻e) throat, gorge, gullet; gulf, abyss.
schlüpfen [ˈʃlypfən], *v.n.* (*aux.* sein) slip, slide, glide.
Schlüpfer [ˈʃlypfər], *m. pl.* knickers.
schlüpfrig [ˈʃlypfrɪç], *adj.* slippery; (*fig.*) obscene, indecent.
schlürfen [ˈʃlyrfən], *v.a.* drink noisily, lap up. — *v.n.* (*aux.* sein) (*dial.*) shuffle along.
Schluß [ʃlus], *m.* (—sses, *pl.* ⁻sse) end, termination; conclusion.
Schlüssel [ˈʃlysəl], *m.* (—s, *pl.* —) key; (*Mus.*) clef.
Schlüsselbein [ˈʃlysəlbaɪn], *n.* (—s, *pl.* —e) collar-bone.
Schlüsselblume [ˈʃlysəlbluːmə], *f.* (—, *pl.* —n) (*Bot.*) cowslip, primrose.
Schlußfolgerung [ˈʃlusfɔlgəruŋ], *f.* (—, *pl.* —en) conclusion, inference, deduction.
schlüssig [ˈʃlysɪç], *adj.* resolved, determined; sure; (*Law*) well-grounded; *sich — werden über*, resolve on.
Schmach [ʃmaːx], *f.* (—, *no pl.*) disgrace, ignominy.
schmachten [ˈʃmaxtən], *v.n.* languish, pine.
schmächtig [ˈʃmɛçtɪç], *adj.* slender, slim, spare.
schmackhaft [ˈʃmakhaft], *adj.* tasty, savoury.
schmähen [ˈʃmɛːən], *v.a.* revile, abuse, calumniate.
Schmähschrift [ˈʃmɛːʃrɪft], *f.* (—, *pl.* —en) lampoon.
schmal [ʃmaːl], *adj.* narrow.
schmälen [ˈʃmɛːlən], *v.a.* chide, scold.
schmälern [ˈʃmɛːlərn], *v.a.* lessen, diminish, curtail; detract from, belittle.
Schmalz [ʃmalts], *n.* (—es, *no pl.*) grease, lard, fat.
schmarotzen [ʃmaˈrɔtsən], *v.n.* sponge on others.
Schmarren [ˈʃmarən], *m.* (—s, *pl.* —) trash; (*dial.*) omelette.
Schmatz [ʃmats], *m.* (—es, *pl.* ⁻e) (*dial.*) smacking kiss.
schmauchen [ˈʃmauxən], *v.a., v.n.* smoke.
Schmaus [ʃmaus], *m.* (—es, *pl.* ⁻e) feast, banquet.
schmecken [ˈʃmɛkən], *v.a.* taste. — *v.n.* taste; *es schmeckt mir*, I like it.
Schmeichelei [ʃmaɪçəˈlaɪ], *f.* (—, *pl.* —en) flattery, adulation.
schmeicheln [ˈʃmaɪçəln], *v.n.* flatter; fondle, pet.
schmeißen [ˈʃmaɪsən], *v.a. irr.* throw, hurl, fling; (*sl.*) *ich werde die Sache schon —*, I shall pull it off.
Schmeißfliege [ˈʃmaɪsfliːgə], *f.* (—, *pl.* —n) (*Ent.*) bluebottle.
Schmelz [ʃmɛlts], *m.* (—es, *no pl.*) enamel; melting; (*voice*) mellowness.
schmelzbar [ˈʃmɛltsbaːr], *adj.* fusible.
schmelzen [ˈʃmɛltsən], *v.a. irr.* smelt, melt. — *v.n.* (*aux.* sein) (*ice*) melt; (*fig.*) decrease, diminish.

Schmelztiegel [ˈʃmɛltsti:gəl], *m.* (—s, *pl.* —) crucible; melting pot.
Schmelztopf [ˈʃmɛltstɔpf], *m. see* **Schmelztiegel**.
Schmerbauch [ˈʃme:rbaux], *m.* (—(e)s, *pl.* ̈-e) (*coll.*) paunch, belly.
Schmerz [ʃmɛrts], *m.* (—es, *pl.* —en) ache, pain; grief, sorrow; *einem —en verursachen*, give *or* cause s.o. pain.
schmerzlich [ˈʃmɛrtslɪç], *adj.* painful, distressing.
Schmetterling [ˈʃmɛtərlɪŋ], *m.* (—s, *pl.* —e) (*Ent.*) butterfly, moth.
schmettern [ˈʃmɛtərn], *v.n.* resound; (*trumpets*) blare; (*bird*) warble.
Schmied [ʃmi:t], *m.* (—s, *pl.* —e) (black)smith.
Schmiede [ˈʃmi:də], *f.* (—, *pl.* —n) forge, smithy.
schmiegen [ˈʃmi:gən], *v.r. sich —*, bend, yield; *sich an einen —*, cling to s.o., nestle against s.o.
Schmiere [ˈʃmi:rə], *f.* (—, *pl.* —n) grease, salve; (*Theat.*) troop of strolling players.
schmieren [ˈʃmi:rən], *v.a.* smear, grease, spread; (*fig.*) bribe; (*bread*) butter. — *v.n.* scrawl, scribble.
Schmierfink [ˈʃmi:rfɪŋk], *m.* (—en, *pl.* —en) dirty person; muckraker.
Schmiermittel [ˈʃmi:rmɪtəl], *n.* (—s, *pl.* —) lubricant.
Schmierseife [ˈʃmi:rzaɪfə], *f.* (—, *no pl.*) soft soap.
Schminke [ˈʃmɪŋkə], *f.* (—, *pl.* —n) greasepaint; rouge; make-up, cosmetics.
Schmirgel [ˈʃmɪrgəl], *m.* (—s, *no pl.*) emery.
Schmiß [ʃmɪs], *m.* (—sses, *pl.* —sse) cut in the face, (duelling) scar; (*fig.*) smartness, verve.
Schmöker [ˈʃmø:kər], *m.* (—s, *pl.* —) trashy book.
schmollen [ˈʃmɔlən], *v.n.* sulk, pout.
Schmorbraten [ˈʃmo:rbra:tən], *m.* (—s, *pl.* —) stewed meat.
Schmuck [ʃmuk], *m.* (—(e)s, *pl.* —stücke) ornament, jewels, jewellery; (*Am.*) jewelry.
schmuck [ʃmuk], *adj.* neat, spruce, dapper, smart.
schmücken [ˈʃmykən], *v.a.* adorn, embellish.
Schmucksachen [ˈʃmukzaxən], *f. pl.* jewels, finery, jewellery, articles of adornment; (*Am.*) jewelry.
schmuggeln [ˈʃmugəln], *v.a.* smuggle.
schmunzeln [ˈʃmuntsəln], *v.n.* smirk, grin.
Schmutz [ʃmuts], *m.* (—es, *no pl.*) dirt, filth.
schmutzen [ˈʃmutsən], *v.n.* get soiled, get dirty.
Schmutzkonkurrenz [ˈʃmutskɔnkurɛnts], *f.* (—, *no pl.*) unfair competition.
Schnabel [ˈʃna:bəl], *m.* (—s, *pl.* ̈-) bill, beak; (*ship*) prow; *halt den —*, keep your mouth shut; *er spricht, wie ihm*

der — gewachsen ist, he calls a spade a spade.
Schnabeltier [ˈʃna:bəlti:r], *n.* (—s, *pl.* —e) duck-bill, duck-billed platypus.
Schnaderhüpfel [ˈʃna:dərhypfəl], *n.* (—s, *pl.* —) (*dial.*) Alpine folk-song.
Schnalle [ˈʃnalə], *f.* (—, *pl.* —n) buckle.
schnalzen [ˈʃnaltsən], *v.n.* click; snap.
schnappen [ˈʃnapən], *v.n.* snap; snatch at s.th.; *nach Luft —*, gasp for breath.
Schnaps [ʃnaps], *m.* (—es, *pl.* ̈-e) spirits, brandy, gin.
schnarchen [ˈʃnarçən], *v.n.* snore.
Schnarre [ˈʃnarə], *f.* (—, *pl.* —n) rattle.
schnattern [ˈʃnatərn], *v.n.* cackle; gabble; chatter.
schnauben [ˈʃnaubən], *v.n.* puff and blow; snort; *vor Zorn —*, fret and fume.
schnaufen [ˈʃnaufən], *v.n.* breathe heavily, pant.
Schnauze [ˈʃnautsə], *f.* (—, *pl.* —n) (*animals*) snout; (*vulg.*) mouth, trap; nozzle.
schnauzen [ˈʃnautsən], *v.n.* snarl, shout (at).
Schnecke [ˈʃnɛkə], *f.* (—, *pl.* —n), (*Zool.*) snail, slug.
Schnee [ʃne:], *m.* (—s, *no pl.*) snow.
Schneegestöber [ˈʃne:gəʃtø:bər], *n.* (—s, *pl.* —) snow-storm.
Schneeglöckchen [ˈʃne:glœkçən], *n.* (—s, *pl.* —) (*Bot.*) snowdrop.
Schneeschläger [ˈʃne:ʃlɛ:gər], *m.* (—s, *pl.* —) whisk.
Schneetreiben [ˈʃne:traɪbən], *n.* (—s, *no pl.*) snow-storm, blizzard.
Schneewittchen [ʃne:ˈvɪtçən], *n.* (—s, *no pl.*) Snow White.
Schneid [ʃnaɪt], *m.* (—s, *no pl.*) go, push, dash, courage.
Schneide [ˈʃnaɪdə], *f.* (—, *pl.* —n) edge.
Schneidebohne [ˈʃnaɪdəbo:nə], *f.* (—, *pl.* —n) French bean, string-bean.
Schneidemühle [ˈʃnaɪdəmy:lə], *f.* (—, *pl.* —n) saw mill.
schneiden [ˈʃnaɪdən], *v.a. irr.* cut, trim, carve; (*fig.*) ignore, cut; *Gesichter —*, make faces. — *v.r. sich —*, cut o.s.; (*Maths.*) intersect; *sich die Haare — lassen*, have o.'s hair cut.
Schneider [ˈʃnaɪdər], *m.* (—s, *pl.* —) tailor.
Schneiderei [ʃnaɪdeˈraɪ], *f.* (—, *no pl.*) tailoring; dressmaking.
Schneidezahn [ˈʃnaɪdətsa:n], *m.* (—s, *pl.* ̈-e) incisor.
schneidig [ˈʃnaɪdɪç], *adj.* dashing.
schneien [ˈʃnaɪən], *v.n.* snow.
Schneise [ˈʃnaɪzə], *f.* (—, *pl.* —n) (*forest*) glade, cutting.
schnell [ʃnɛl], *adj.* quick, swift, speedy, fast, rapid; *mach —*, hurry up.
Schnelle [ˈʃnɛlə], *f.* (—, *pl.* —n) (*river*) rapids.
schnellen [ˈʃnɛlən], *v.n.* spring, jump.

Schnelligkeit

Schnelligkeit ['ʃnɛlɪçkaɪt], *f.* (—, *no pl.*) quickness, speed, swiftness, rapidity; (*Tech.*) velocity.

Schnepfe ['ʃnɛpfə], *f.* (—, *pl.* —n) (*Orn.*) snipe, woodcock.

schneuzen ['ʃnɔytsən], *v.r.* sich (*die Nase*) —, blow o.'s nose.

schniegeln ['ʃniːgəln], *v.r.* sich —, (*coll.*) dress up, deck out; *geschniegelt und gebügelt*, spick and span.

Schnippchen ['ʃnɪpçən], *n.* (—s, *pl.* —) *einem ein* — *schlagen*, play a trick on s.o.

schnippisch ['ʃnɪpɪʃ], *adj.* pert, perky.

Schnitt [ʃnɪt], *m.* (—(e)s, *pl.* —e) cut, incision; section; (*beer*) small glass; (*dress*) cut-out pattern; (*book*) edge.

Schnittbohne ['ʃnɪtboːnə], *f.* (—, *pl.* —n) (*Bot.*) French bean.

Schnitte ['ʃnɪtə], *f.* (—, *pl.* —n) slice (of bread).

Schnitter ['ʃnɪtər], *m.* (—s, *pl.* —) reaper.

Schnittlauch ['ʃnɪtlaux], *m.* (—s, *no pl.*) (*Bot.*) chives.

Schnittmuster ['ʃnɪtmustər], *n.* (—s, *pl.* —) cut-out pattern.

Schnittwaren ['ʃnɪtvaːrən], *f. pl.* dry goods, drapery.

Schnitzel ['ʃnɪtsəl], *n.* (—s, *pl.* —) (*Cul.*) cutlet; *Wiener* —, veal cutlet; snip; (*pl.*) shavings.

schnitzen ['ʃnɪtsən], *v.a.* carve (in wood).

schnodd(e)rig ['ʃnɔd(ə)rɪç], *adj.* (*coll.*) cheeky, insolent.

schnöde ['ʃnøːdə], *adj.* base, heinous, mean, vile; —*r Mammon*, filthy lucre; —*r Undank*, rank ingratitude.

Schnörkel ['ʃnœrkəl], *m.* (—s, *pl.* —) (*writing*) flourish.

schnorren ['ʃnɔrən], *v.n.* (*rare*) cadge, beg.

schnüffeln ['ʃnyfəln], *v.n.* sniff; (*fig.*) pry, snoop.

Schnuller ['ʃnulər], *m.* (—s, *pl.* —) baby's dummy; (*Am.*) pacifier.

Schnupfen ['ʃnupfən], *m.* (—s, *pl.* —) cold (in the head); *den* — *haben*, have a (running) cold; *den* — *bekommen*, catch cold.

schnupfen ['ʃnupfən], *v.a.*, *v.n.* take snuff.

Schnupftuch ['ʃnupftuːx], *n.* (—(e)s, *pl.* ̈er) (*dial.*) (pocket-) handkerchief.

schnuppe ['ʃnupə], *adj.* (*sl.*) *mir ist alles* —, it is all the same to me, I don't care.

schnuppern ['ʃnupərn], *v.n.* smell, snuffle.

Schnur [ʃnuːr], *f.* (—, *pl.* —en, ̈e) twine, cord, string; (*Elec.*) lead, extension cord.

Schnurrbart ['ʃnurbaːrt], *m.* (—s, *pl.* ̈e) moustache; *sich einen* — *wachsen lassen*, grow a moustache.

Schnürchen ['ʃnyːrçən], *n.* (—s, *pl.* —) *wie am* —, like clockwork.

schnüren ['ʃnyːrən], *v.a.* lace, tie up; *sein Ränzel* —, pack o.'s bag.

Schnurre ['ʃnurə], *f.* (—, *pl.* —n) funny story, yarn.

schnurren ['ʃnurən], *v.n.* purr.

Schnürsenkel ['ʃnyːrzɛŋkəl], *m.* (—s, *pl.* —) (*shoe*) lace.

schnurstracks ['ʃnuːrʃtraks], *adv.* directly, immediately, on the spot.

Schober ['ʃoːbər], *m.* (—s, *pl.* —) stack, rick.

Schock (1) [ʃɔk], *n.* (—(e)s, *pl.* —e) sixty, three score.

Schock (2) [ʃɔk], *m.* (—(e)s, *pl.* —s) shock; blow; stroke.

Schöffe ['ʃœfə], *m.* (—n, *pl.* —n) (*Law*) juror; member of jury.

Schokolade [ʃokoˈlaːdə], *f.* (—, *pl.* —n) chocolate; *eine Tafel* —, a bar of chocolate.

Scholle ['ʃɔlə], *f.* (—, *pl.* —n) plaice; (*ice*) floe; clod; soil.

schon [ʃoːn], *adv.* already; indeed; yet; *na wenn* —, so what; — *gut*, that'll do; — *gestern*, as early as yesterday.

schön [ʃøːn], *adj.* beautiful, fair, handsome, lovely; —*e Literatur*, belleslettres, good books.

schonen ['ʃoːnən], *v.a.* spare, save; treat considerately.

Schoner ['ʃoːnər], *m.* (—s, *pl.* —) antimacassar; (*Naut.*) schooner.

Schönheit ['ʃøːnhaɪt], *f.* (—, *no pl.*) beauty.

Schonung ['ʃoːnuŋ], *f.* (—, *pl.* —en) forbearance, considerate treatment; (*forest*) plantation of young trees.

Schonzeit ['ʃoːntsaɪt], *f.* (—, *pl.* —en) close season.

Schopf [ʃɔpf], *m.* (—es, *pl.* ̈e) tuft, head of hair; (*bird*) crest; *das Glück beim* —*e fassen*, take time by the forelock, make hay while the sun shines.

Schöpfbrunnen ['ʃœpfbrunən], *m.* (—s, *pl.* —) (draw-)well.

schöpfen ['ʃœpfən], *v.a.* (*water*) draw; derive; *Verdacht* —, become suspicious; *frische Luft* —, get a breath of fresh air; *Mut* —, take heart.

Schöpfer ['ʃœpfər], *m.* (—s, *pl.* —) creator.

Schöpfkelle ['ʃœpfkɛlə], *f.* (—, *pl.* —n) scoop.

Schopflerche ['ʃɔpflɛrçə], *f.* (—, *pl.* —n) (*Orn.*) crested lark.

Schöpfung ['ʃœpfuŋ], *f.* (—, *pl.* —en) creation.

Schoppen ['ʃɔpən], *m.* (—s, *pl.* —) (*approx.*) half a pint.

Schöps [ʃœps], *m.* (—es, *pl.* —e) (*Zool.*) wether; (*fig.*) simpleton.

Schorf [ʃɔrf], *m.* (—(e)s, *pl.* —e) scab, scurf.

Schornstein ['ʃɔrnʃtaɪn], *m.* (—s, *pl.* —e) chimney; (*ship*) funnel.

Schoß [ʃoːs], *m.* (—es, *pl.* ̈e) (*Poet.*) womb; skirt; tail; *die Hände in den* — *legen*, be idle, fold o.'s arms, twiddle o.'s thumbs.

Schößling ['ʃœslɪŋ], *m.* (**—s**, *pl.* **—e**) shoot, sprig.
Schote ['ʃo:tə], *f.* (**—**, *pl.* **—n**) pod, husk, shell; (*pl.*) green peas.
Schotter ['ʃɔtər], *m.* (**—s**, *no pl.*) road-metal, broken stones, gravel.
Schottland ['ʃɔtlant], *n.* Scotland.
schraffieren [ʃraˈfiːrən], *v.a.* (*Art*) hatch.
schräg ['ʃrɛːk], *adj.* oblique, sloping, slanting, diagonal.
Schramme ['ʃramə], *f.* (**—**, *pl.* **—n**) scratch, scar.
Schrank [ʃraŋk], *m.* (**—(e)s**, *pl.* ˝e) cupboard, wardrobe.
Schranken ['ʃraŋkən], *f. pl.* barriers, (level crossing) gates, limits, bounds; *in — halten*, limit, keep within bounds.
schränken ['ʃrɛŋkən], *v.a.* cross; fold.
Schranze ['ʃrantsə], *m.* (**—n**, *pl.* **—n**) sycophant, toady.
Schraube ['ʃraubə], *f.* (**—**, *pl.* **—n**) screw; bolt; propeller.
Schraubengewinde ['ʃraubəngəvɪndə], *n.* (**—s**, *pl.* **—**) thread of a screw.
Schraubenmutter ['ʃraubənmutər], *f.* (**—**, *pl.* **—n**) female screw, nut.
Schraubenzieher ['ʃraubəntsiːər], *m.* (**—s**, *pl.* **—**) screw-driver.
Schraubstock ['ʃraupʃtɔk], *m.* (**—s**, *pl.* ˝e) (*tool*) vise.
Schreck(en) ['ʃrɛk(ən)], *m.* (**—s**, *pl.* **—**) fright, terror, alarm, horror; shock.
Schrecknis ['ʃreknɪs], *n.* (**—ses**, *pl.* **—se**) terror, horror.
Schrei [ʃrai], *m.* (**—s**, *pl.* **—e**) cry; scream.
Schreiben ['ʃraibən], *n.* (**—s**, *pl.* **—**) letter, missive.
schreiben ['ʃraibən], *v.a. irr.* write; *ins Reine —*, make a fair copy.
Schreibfehler ['ʃraipfeːlər], *m.* (**—s**, *pl.* **—**) slip of the pen.
Schreibkrampf ['ʃraipkrampf], *m.* (**—(e)s**, *pl.* ˝e) writer's cramp.
Schreibmaschine ['ʃraipmaʃiːnə], *f.* (**—**, *pl.* **—n**) typewriter.
Schreibwaren ['ʃraipvaːrən], *f. pl.* stationery.
Schreibweise ['ʃraipvaizə], *f.* (**—**, *pl.* **—n**) style; spelling.
schreien ['ʃraiən], *v.a., v.n. irr.* cry, shout, scream, yell.
Schreihals ['ʃraihals], *m.* (**—es**, *pl.* ˝e) cry-baby, noisy child.
Schrein [ʃrain], *m.* (**—(e)s**, *pl.* **—e**) box, chest; shrine.
schreiten ['ʃraitən], *v.n. irr.* (*aux.* sein) stride, step, pace.
Schrift [ʃrɪft], *f.* (**—**, *pl.* **—en**) writing; handwriting, calligraphy; publication; type; *Heilige —*, Holy Writ, Holy Scripture.
Schriftführer ['ʃrɪftfyːrər], *m.* (**—s**, *pl.* **—**) secretary.
Schriftgießerei ['ʃrɪftgiːsərai], *f.* (**—**, *pl.* **—en**) type-foundry.
Schriftleiter ['ʃrɪftlaitər], *m.* (**—s**, *pl.* **—**) editor.

schriftlich ['ʃrɪftlɪç], *adj.* written. — *adv.* in writing, by letter.
Schriftsetzer ['ʃrɪftzɛtsər], *m.* (**—s**, *pl.* **—**) compositor.
Schriftsteller ['ʃrɪftʃtɛlər], *m.* (**—s**, *pl.* **—**) writer, author.
Schriftstück ['ʃrɪftʃtyk], *n.* (**—s**, *pl.* **—e**) document, deed.
Schriftwechsel ['ʃrɪftvɛksəl], *m.* (**—s**, *no pl.*) exchange of notes, correspondence.
Schriftzeichen ['ʃrɪftsaiçən], *n.* (**—s**, *pl.* **—**) character, letter (of alphabet).
schrill [ʃrɪl], *adj.* shrill.
Schritt [ʃrɪt], *m.* (**—(e)s**, *pl.* **—e**) step, pace, move; *lange —e machen*, stride; *— halten*, keep pace; *— fahren*, drive slowly, drive at walking pace; *aus dem —*, out of step; *in einer Sache —e tun*, make a move *or* take steps about s.th.
schrittweise ['ʃritvaizə], *adv.* step by step, gradually.
schroff ['ʃrɔf], *adj.* steep, precipitous; (*fig.*) gruff, blunt, rough, harsh.
schröpfen ['ʃrœpfən], *v.a.* (*Med.*) cup; (*fig.*) fleece.
Schrot [ʃro:t], *m. & n.* (**—(e)s**, *pl.* **—e**) grape-shot, small shot; *ein Mann vom alten —*, a man of the utmost probity.
Schrotbrot ['ʃro:tbro:t], *n.* (**—es**, *no pl.*) wholemeal bread.
Schrott [ʃrɔt], *m.* (**—(e)s**, *pl.* **—e**), old iron, scrap metal.
Schrulle ['ʃrulə], *f.* (**—**, *pl.* **—n**) fad, whim.
schrumpfen ['ʃrumpfən], *v.n.* (*aux.* sein) shrink, shrivel.
Schub [ʃup], *m.* (**—s**, *pl.* ˝e) shove, push; batch.
Schubkarren ['ʃupkarən], *m.* (**—s**, *pl.* **—**) wheelbarrow.
Schublade ['ʃupla:də], *f.* (**—**, *pl.* **—n**) drawer.
schüchtern ['ʃyçtərn], *adj.* shy, bashful, timid.
Schuft [ʃuft], *m.* (**—(e)s**, *pl.* **—e**) blackguard, scoundrel.
schuften ['ʃuftən], *v.n.* work hard, toil.
Schufterei [ʃuftəˈrai], *f.* (**—**, *no pl.*) drudgery.
schuftig ['ʃuftɪç], *adj.* rascally, mean.
Schuh [ʃu:], *m.* (**—s**, *pl.* **—e**) shoe; *einem etwas in die — schieben*, lay the blame at s.o.'s door.
Schuhwerk ['ʃu:vɛrk], *n.* (**—s**, *no pl.*) footwear.
Schuhwichse ['ʃu:vɪksə], *f.* (**—**, *no pl.*) shoe-polish.
Schuld [ʃult], *f.* (**—**, *pl.* **—en**) guilt, offence, sin; fault; blame; cause; (*money*) debt; *in —en geraten*, run into debt.
schuld [ʃult], *adj. ich bin —*, it is my fault, I am to blame.
schulden ['ʃuldən], *v.a.* owe, be indebted to.
schuldig ['ʃuldɪç], *adj.* guilty, culpable; *sich — bekennen*, plead guilty; *einen — sprechen*, pronounce s.o. guilty;

ihm ist Anerkennung —, appreciation is due to him.
Schuldigkeit ['ʃuldɪçkaɪt], *f.* (—, *no pl.*) obligation, duty.
schuldlos ['ʃultlo:s], *adj.* innocent, guiltless.
Schuldner ['ʃuldnər], *m.* (—s, *pl.* —) debtor.
Schule ['ʃu:lə], *f.* (—, *pl.* —n) school; *in die* — *gehen*, go to school, attend school; *die* — *schwänzen*, play truant; *hohe* —, (*Riding*) advanced horsemanship.
schulen ['ʃu:lən], *v.a.* train, instruct.
Schüler ['ʃy:lər], *m.* (—s, *pl.* —) schoolboy, pupil, student, scholar.
Schulklasse ['ʃu:lklasə], *f.* (—, *pl.* —n) class, form.
Schulleiter ['ʃu:llaɪtər], *m.* (—s, *pl.* —) headmaster.
Schulrat ['ʃu:lra:t], *m.* (—s, *pl.* ⁓e) school-inspector.
Schulter ['ʃultər], *f.* (—, *pl.* —n) shoulder.
Schulterblatt ['ʃultərblat], *n.* (—s, *pl.* ⁓er) shoulder-blade.
Schultheiß ['ʃulthaɪs], *m.* (—en, *pl.* —en) village magistrate, mayor.
Schulunterricht ['ʃu:lʊntərrɪçt], *m.* (—s, *no pl.*) school teaching, lessons.
schummeln ['ʃuməln], *v.n.* (*coll.*) cheat.
Schund [ʃunt], *m.* (—(e)s, *no pl.*) trash.
Schuppe ['ʃupə], *f.* (—, *pl.* —n) scale; (*pl.*) dandruff.
Schuppen ['ʃupən], *m.* (—s, *pl.* —) shed.
Schuppentier ['ʃupənti:r], *n.* (—s, *pl.* —e) (*Zool.*) armadillo.
Schur [ʃu:r], *f.* (—, *pl.* —en) shearing.
schüren ['ʃy:rən], *v.a.* (*fire*) poke, rake; (*fig.*) stir up, fan, incite.
schürfen ['ʃyrfən], *v.a.* scratch. — *v.n.* (*Min.*) prospect.
schurigeln ['ʃu:rɪgəln], *v.a.* bully, pester.
Schurke ['ʃurkə], *m.* (—n, *pl.* —n) scoundrel, villain, blackguard.
Schurz [ʃurts], *m.* (—es, *pl.* —e) apron, overall.
Schürze ['ʃyrtsə], *f.* (—, *pl.* —n) apron, pinafore.
schürzen ['ʃyrtsən], *v.a.* tuck up, pin up.
Schürzenjäger ['ʃyrtsənjɛ:gər], *m.* (—s, *pl.* —) ladies' man.
Schurzfell ['ʃurtsfɛl], *n.* (—s, *pl.* —e) leather apron.
Schuß [ʃus], *m.* (—sses, *pl.* ⁓sse) shot, report; dash; *weit vom* —, out of harm's way; wide of the mark.
Schüssel ['ʃysəl], *f.* (—, *pl.* —n) dish.
Schußwaffe ['ʃusvafə], *f.* (—, *pl.* —n) fire-arm.
Schuster ['ʃu:stər], *m.* (—s, *pl.* —) shoemaker, cobbler; *auf* —*s Rappen*, on Shanks's pony.
schustern ['ʃu:stərn], *v.n.* cobble, make or mend shoes.
Schutt [ʃut], *m.* (—(e)s, *no pl.*) rubbish, refuse; rubble; — *abladen,*

dump refuse.
Schütte ['ʃytə], *f.* (—, *pl.* —n) (*dial.* bundle, truss.
schütteln ['ʃytəln], *v.a.* shake, jolt.
schütten ['ʃytən], *v.a.* shoot, pour; pour out.
schütter ['ʃytər], *adj.* (*dial.*) (*hair*) thin; scarce.
Schutz [ʃuts], *m.* (—es, *no pl.*) protection, shelter, cover; *einen in* — *nehmen gegen*, defend s.o. against.
Schutzbefohlene ['ʃutsbəfo:lənə], *m.* (—n, *pl.* —n) charge, person in o.'s care, ward.
Schutzbündnis ['ʃutsbyntnɪs], *n.* (—ses, *pl.* —se) defensive alliance.
Schütze ['ʃytsə], *m.* (—n, *pl.* —n) rifleman, sharpshooter, marksman; (*Astrol.*) Sagittarius.
schützen ['ʃytsən], *v.a.* protect, shelter, defend. — *v.r. sich* — *vor*, guard o.s. against.
Schützengraben ['ʃytsəngra:bən], *m.* (—s, *pl.* ⁓) trench.
Schutzgebiet ['ʃutsgəbi:t], *n.* (—s, *pl.* —e) protectorate.
Schutzgitter ['ʃutsgɪtər], *n.* (—s, *pl.* —) grid, guard.
Schutzheilige ['ʃutshaɪlɪgə], *m.* (—n, *pl.* —n) patron saint.
Schützling ['ʃytslɪŋ], *m.* (—s, *pl.* —e) protégé, charge.
Schutzmann ['ʃutsman], *m.* (—s, *pl.* ⁓er, **Schutzleute**) policeman, constable.
Schutzmarke ['ʃutsmarkə], *f.* (—, *pl.* —n) trade-mark.
Schutzzoll ['ʃutstsɔl], *m.* (—s, *pl.* ⁓e) protective duty, tariff.
Schwaben ['ʃva:bən], *n.* Swabia.
Schwabenstreich ['ʃva:bənʃtraɪç], *m.* (—s, *pl.* —e) tomfoolery.
schwach [ʃvax], *adj.* weak, frail, feeble; (*noise*) faint; (*pulse*) low; —*e Seite*, foible; —*e Stunde*, unguarded moment.
Schwäche ['ʃvɛçə], *f.* (—, *pl.* —n) weakness, faintness; infirmity.
schwächen ['ʃvɛçən], *v.a.* weaken, debilitate.
Schwächling ['ʃvɛçlɪŋ], *m.* (—s, *pl.* —e) weakling.
Schwachsinn ['ʃvaxzɪn], *m.* (—s, *no pl.*) feeble-mindedness.
Schwächung ['ʃvɛçuŋ], *f.* (—, *pl.* —en) weakening, lessening.
Schwadron [ʃva'dro:n], *f.* (—, *pl.* —en) squadron.
Schwadroneur [ʃvadro'nø:r], *m.* (—s, *pl.* —e) swaggerer.
schwadronieren [ʃvadro'ni:rən], *v.n.* talk big, swagger.
schwafeln ['ʃva:fəln], *v.n.* (*sl.*) talk nonsense, waffle.
Schwager ['ʃva:gər], *m.* (—s, *pl.* ⁓) brother-in-law.
Schwägerin ['ʃvɛ:gərɪn], *f.* (—, *pl.* —nen) sister-in-law.
Schwalbe ['ʃvalbə], *f.* (—, *pl.* —n) (*Orn.*) swallow.

Schwalbenschwanz ['ʃvalbənʃvants], *m.* (**—es,** *pl.* ⁀e) (*butterfly*) swallow's tail; (*joinery*) dovetail.

Schwall [ʃval], *m.* (**—(e)s,** *no pl.*) flood; (*fig.*) deluge, torrent.

Schwamm [ʃvam], *m.* (**—(e)s,** *pl.* ⁀e) sponge; fungus, mushroom; dry rot.

schwammig ['ʃvamɪç], *adj.* spongy, fungous.

Schwan [ʃvaːn], *m.* (**—(e)s,** *pl.* ⁀e) swan; *junger* —, cygnet.

schwanen ['ʃvaːnən], *v.n. imp. es schwant mir,* I have a foreboding.

Schwang [ʃvaŋ], *m. im* —*e sein,* be in fashion, be the rage.

schwanger ['ʃvaŋər], *adj.* pregnant.

schwängern ['ʃvɛŋərn], *v.a.* make pregnant, get with child; (*fig.*) impregnate.

Schwangerschaft ['ʃvaŋərʃaft], *f.* (**—,** *pl.* **—en**) pregnancy.

Schwank [ʃvaŋk], *m.* (**—(e)s,** *pl.* ⁀e) funny story, joke; (*Theat.*) farce.

schwank [ʃvaŋk], *adj.* flexible, supple; *ein* —*es Rohr,* a reed shaken by the wind.

schwanken ['ʃvaŋkən], *v.n.* totter, stagger; (*fig.*) waver, vacillate; (*prices*) fluctuate.

Schwanz [ʃvants], *m.* (**—es,** *pl.* ⁀e) tail.

schwänzeln ['ʃvɛntsəln], *v.n.* (*animal*) wag the tail; (*fig.*) fawn, cringe.

schwänzen ['ʃvɛntsən], *v.a. die Schule* —, play truant.

Schwären ['ʃvɛːrən], *m.* (**—s,** *pl.* —) ulcer, abscess.

schwären ['ʃvɛːrən], *v.n.* fester, suppurate.

Schwarm [ʃvarm], *m.* (**—(e)s,** *pl.* ⁀e) (*insects*) swarm; (*humans*) crowd; (*birds*) flight.

Schwärmerei [ʃvɛrmə'raɪ], *f.* (**—,** *pl.* **—en**) enthusiasm, passion, craze.

Schwarte ['ʃvartə], *f.* (**—,** *pl.* **—n**) rind; crust; *alte* —, (*fig.*) old volume; tome.

schwarz [ʃvarts], *adj.* black.

Schwarzamsel ['ʃvartsamzəl], *f.* (**—,** *pl.* **—n**) (*Orn.*) blackbird.

Schwarzdorn ['ʃvartsdɔrn], *m.* (**—s,** *no pl.*) (*Bot.*) blackthorn, sloe.

Schwärze ['ʃvɛrtsə], *f.* (**—,** *no pl.*) blackness; printer's ink.

schwärzen ['ʃvɛrtsən], *v.a.* blacken.

Schwarzkünstler ['ʃvartskynstlər], *m.* (**—s,** *pl.* **—)** magician, necromancer.

Schwarzwald ['ʃvartsvalt], *m.* Black Forest.

Schwarzwild ['ʃvartsvɪlt], *n.* (**—(e)s,** *no pl.*) wild boar.

schwatzen ['ʃvatsən], *v.n.* chat, chatter, prattle.

Schwätzer ['ʃvɛtsər], *m.* (**—s,** *pl.* **—)** chatterbox.

Schwatzhaftigkeit ['ʃvatshaftɪçkaɪt], *f.* (**—,** *no pl.*) loquacity, talkativeness.

Schwebe ['ʃveːbə], *f.* (**—,** *pl.* **—n**) suspense; suspension.

Schwebebaum ['ʃveːbəbaum], *m.* (**—s,** *pl.* ⁀e) horizontal bar.

schweben ['ʃveːbən], *v.n.* be suspended, hover; (*fig.*) be pending; *in Gefahr* —, be in danger; *es schwebt mir auf der Zunge,* it is on the tip of my tongue.

Schwede ['ʃveːdə], *m.* (**—n,** *pl.* **—n**) Swede; *alter* —, (*fig.*) old boy.

Schweden ['ʃveːdən], *n.* Sweden.

Schwedenhölzer ['ʃveːdənhœltsər], *n. pl.* (*rare*) matches.

Schwefel ['ʃveːfəl], *m.* (**—s,** *no pl.*) sulphur, brimstone.

Schwefelhölzchen ['ʃveːfəlhœltsçən], *n.* (**—s,** *pl.* **—)** (*obs.*) match.

schwefeln ['ʃveːfəln], *v.a.* impregnate with sulphur, fumigate.

Schwefelsäure ['ʃveːfɔlzɔyrə], *f.* (**—,** *no pl.*) sulphuric acid.

Schweif [ʃvaɪf], *m.* (**—(e)s,** *pl.* **—e**) tail.

schweifen ['ʃvaɪfən], *v.n.* (*aux. sein*) ramble, stray, wander.

schweifwedeln ['ʃvaɪfveːdəln], *v.n.* fawn.

Schweigegeld ['ʃvaɪgəgɛlt], *n.* (**—(e)s,** *pl.* **—er**) (*coll.*) hush-money.

Schweigen ['ʃvaɪgən], *n.* (**—s,** *no pl.*) silence.

schweigen ['ʃvaɪgən], *v.n. irr.* be silent; be quiet; *ganz zu* — *von,* to say nothing of.

schweigsam ['ʃvaɪkzaːm], *adj.* taciturn.

Schwein [ʃvaɪn], *n.* (**—(e)s,** *pl.* **—e**) pig, hog; swine; *wildes* —, boar; (*fig.*) luck, fluke; — *haben,* be lucky.

Schweinekoben ['ʃvaɪnəkoːbən], *m.* (**—s,** *pl.* **—)** pigsty.

Schweinerei [ʃvaɪnə'raɪ], *f.* (**—,** *pl.* **—en**) filth; (*fig.*) smut, filthiness, obscenity; mess.

Schweineschmalz ['ʃvaɪnəʃmalts], *n.* (**—es,** *no pl.*) lard.

Schweinigel ['ʃvaɪnɪgəl], *m.* (**—s,** *pl.* **—)** (*Zool.*) hedgehog, porcupine; (*fig.*) dirty pig, filthy wretch.

Schweinskeule ['ʃvaɪnskɔylə], *f.* (**—,** *pl.* **—n**) leg of pork.

Schweiß [ʃvaɪs], *m.* (**—es,** *no pl.*) sweat, perspiration.

schweißen ['ʃvaɪsən], *v.a.* weld, solder.

Schweiz [ʃvaɪts], *f.* Switzerland.

Schweizer ['ʃvaɪtsər], *m.* (**—s,** *pl.* **—)** Swiss; (*fig.*) dairyman.

Schweizerei [ʃvaɪtsə'raɪ], *f.* (**—,** *pl.* **—en**) dairy.

schwelen ['ʃveːlən], *v.n.* burn slowly, smoulder.

schwelgen ['ʃvɛlgən], *v.n.* carouse, revel.

Schwelgerei [ʃvɛlgə'raɪ], *f.* (**—,** *pl.* **—en**) revelry.

schwelgerisch ['ʃvɛlgərɪʃ], *adj.* luxurious, voluptuous.

Schwelle ['ʃvɛlə], *f.* (**—,** *pl.* **—n**) threshold; (*Railw.*) sleeper, tie.

schwellen ['ʃvɛlən], *v.n. irr.* (*aux. sein*) swell; (*water*) rise.

Schwellung ['ʃvɛluŋ], *f.* (**—,** *pl.* **—en**) swelling.

schwemmen

schwemmen [ˈʃvɛmən], *v.a.* wash, soak, carry off.
Schwengel [ˈʃvɛŋəl], *m.* (—s, *pl.* —) *(bell)* clapper; *(pump)* handle.
schwenken [ˈʃvɛŋkən], *v.a.* swing; shake, brandish; *(glasses)* rinse.
Schwenkung [ˈʃvɛŋkuŋ], *f.* (—, *pl.* —en) change; *(Mil.)* wheeling.
schwer [ʃveːr], *adj.* heavy; difficult, hard; ponderous; severe; — *von Begriff*, obtuse, slow in the uptake; —*e Speise*, indigestible food; *einem das Herz — machen*, grieve s.o.
schwerblütig [ˈʃveːrblyːtiç], *adj.* phlegmatic.
Schwere [ˈʃveːrə], *f.* (—, *no pl.*) weight, heaviness; gravity.
Schwerenöter [ˈʃveːrənøːtər], *m.* (—s, *pl.* —) gay dog, ladies' man.
schwerfällig [ˈʃveːrfɛliç], *adj.* ungainly, cumbrous, unwieldy; *(fig.)* thickheaded, dense.
Schwergewicht [ˈʃveːrgəviçt], *n.* (—s, *no pl.*) *(Sport)* heavyweight; *(fig.)* emphasis.
schwerhörig [ˈʃveːrhøːriç], *adj.* hard of hearing, deaf.
Schwerkraft [ˈʃveːrkraft], *f.* (—, *no pl.*) gravity.
schwerlich [ˈʃveːrliç], *adv.* hardly, scarcely.
schwermütig [ˈʃveːrmyːtiç], *adj.* melancholy.
Schwerpunkt [ˈʃveːrpuŋkt], *m.* (—s, *pl.* —e) centre of gravity.
Schwert [ʃveːrt], *n.* (—(e)s, *pl.* —er) sword.
Schwertgriff [ˈʃveːrtgrif], *m.* (—s, *pl.* —e) hilt.
Schwertlilie [ˈʃveːrtliːljə], *f.* (—, *pl.* —n) *(Bot.)* iris; fleur-de-lys.
Schwertstreich [ˈʃveːrtʃtraiç], *m.* (—(e)s, *pl.* —e) sword-blow, swordstroke.
schwerwiegend [ˈʃveːrviːgənt], *adj.* weighty.
Schwester [ˈʃvɛstər], *f.* (—, *pl.* —n) sister; *barmherzige* —, sister of mercy.
Schwesternschaft [ˈʃvɛstərnʃaft], *f.* (—, *pl.* —en) sisterhood; *(Am.)* sorority.
Schwibbogen [ˈʃvɪpboːgən], *m.* (—s, *pl.* —) *(Archit.)* flying buttress.
Schwiegersohn [ˈʃviːgərzoːn], *m.* (—s, *pl.* ⁓e) son-in-law.
Schwiegertochter [ˈʃviːgərtɔxtər], *f.* (—, *pl.* ⁓) daughter-in-law.
Schwiele [ˈʃviːlə], *f.* (—, *pl.* —n) hard skin, callus, weal.
schwielig [ˈʃviːliç], *adj.* callous, horny.
schwierig [ˈʃviːriç], *adj.* difficult, hard.
Schwierigkeit [ˈʃviːriçkait], *f.* (—, *pl.* —en) difficulty; *auf* —*en stoßen*, meet with difficulties.
schwimmen [ˈʃvɪmən], *v.n. irr.* *(aux.* sein) swim, float.
Schwimmer [ˈʃvɪmər], *m.* (—s, *pl.* —) swimmer.

Schwimmgürtel [ˈʃvɪmgyrtəl], *m.* (—s, *pl.* —) life-belt.
Schwindel [ˈʃvɪndəl], *m.* (—s, *pl.* —) giddiness, dizziness, vertigo; swindle, fraud.
Schwindelanfall [ˈʃvɪndəlanfal], *m.* (—s, *pl.* ⁓e) attack of giddiness, vertigo.
Schwindelei [ʃvɪndəˈlai], *f.* (—, *pl.* —en) swindle, fraud, deceit.
schwindelhaft [ˈʃvɪndəlhaft], *adj.* fraudulent.
schwinden [ˈʃvɪndən], *v.n. irr.* *(aux.* sein) dwindle; disappear, vanish.
Schwindler [ˈʃvɪndlər], *m.* (—s, *pl.* —) swindler, humbug, cheat.
schwindlig [ˈʃvɪndliç], *adj.* dizzy, giddy.
Schwindsucht [ˈʃvɪntzuxt], *f.* (—, *no pl.*) *(Med.)* tuberculosis, consumption.
schwindsüchtig [ˈʃvɪntzyçtiç], *adj.* *(Med.)* tubercular.
Schwinge [ˈʃvɪŋə], *f.* (—, *pl.* —n) wing.
schwingen [ˈʃvɪŋən], *v.a. irr.* brandish. — *v.n.* swing, vibrate. — *v.r. sich* —, vault; *sich auf den Thron* —, usurp or take possession of the throne.
Schwingung [ˈʃvɪŋuŋ], *f.* (—, *pl.* —en) vibration, oscillation.
Schwips [ʃvɪps], *m.* (—es, *pl.* —e) *(coll.)* tipsiness; *einen* — *haben*, be tipsy.
schwirren [ˈʃvɪrən], *v.n.* whir, buzz.
Schwitzbad [ˈʃvɪtsbaːt], *n.* (—es, *pl.* ⁓er) Turkish bath, steam-bath.
schwitzen [ˈʃvɪtsən], *v.n.* sweat, perspire.
schwören [ˈʃvøːrən], *v.a., v.n. irr.* swear, take an oath; *darauf kannst du* —, you can be quite sure of that, you bet; *falsch* —, forswear o.s., perjure o.s.
schwül [ʃvyːl], *adj.* sultry, close.
Schwüle [ˈʃvyːlə], *f.* (—, *no pl.*) sultriness.
Schwulst [ʃvulst], *m.* (—es, *no pl.*) bombast.
schwülstig [ˈʃvylstiç], *adj.* bombastic, turgid.
Schwülstigkeit [ˈʃvylstiçkait], *f.* (—, *pl.* —en) bombastic style, turgidity.
Schwund [ʃvunt], *m.* (—(e)s, *no pl.*) dwindling, decline; shrinkage.
Schwung [ʃvuŋ], *m.* (—(e)s, *pl.* ⁓e) swing, leap, bound; *(fig.)* verve, élan; *(Poet.)* flight, soaring.
schwunghaft [ˈʃvuŋhaft], *adj.* flourishing, soaring.
Schwungkraft [ˈʃvuŋkraft], *f.* (—, *no pl.*) centrifugal force; *(mental)* resilience.
Schwungrad [ˈʃvuŋraːt], *n.* (—s, *pl.* ⁓er) fly-wheel.
schwungvoll [ˈʃvuŋfɔl], *adj.* spirited.
Schwur [ʃvuːr], *m.* (—(e)s, *pl.* ⁓e) oath.
Schwurgericht [ˈʃvuːrgəriçt], *n.* (—s, *pl.* —e) *(Law)* assizes.
sechs [zɛks], *num. adj.* six.
Sechseck [ˈzɛksɛk], *n.* (—s, *pl.* —e) hexagon.
sechseckig [ˈzɛksɛkiç], *adj.* hexagonal.

Sechser ['zɛksər], *m.* (**—s**, *pl.* **—**) coin of small value.

sechsspännig ['zɛksʃpɛnɪç], *adj.* drawn by six horses.

sechzehn ['zɛçtseːn], *num. adj.* sixteen.

sechzig ['zɛçtsɪç], *num. adj.* sixty.

Sediment [zediˈmɛnt], *n.* (**—s**, *pl.* **—e**) sediment.

See (1) [zeː], *m.* (**—s**, *pl.* **—n**) lake, pool.

See (2) [zeː], *f.* (**—**, *no pl.*) sea, ocean; *hohe* **—**, high seas; *zur* **—** *gehen*, go to sea, become a sailor.

Seeadler ['zeːadlər], *m.* (**—s**, *pl.* **—**) (*Orn.*) osprey.

Seebad ['zeːbaːt], *n.* (**—s**, *pl.* ˙ˈer) seaside resort; bathe in the sea.

Seebär ['zeːbɛːr], *m.* (**—en**, *pl.* **—en**) (*fig.*) old salt.

Seefahrer ['zeːfaːrər], *m.* (**—s**, *pl.* **—**) mariner, navigator.

Seefahrt ['zeːfaːrt], *f.* (**—**, *pl.* **—en**) seafaring; voyage, cruise.

seefest ['zeːfɛst], *adj.* (*ship*) seaworthy; (*person*) a good sailor.

Seefischerei ['zeːfɪʃəraɪ], *f.* (**—**, *no pl.*) deep-sea fishing.

Seeflotte ['zeːflɔtə], *f.* (**—**, *pl.* **—n**) navy, fleet.

Seegang ['zeːgaŋ], *m.* (**—s**, *no pl.*) swell.

Seegras ['zeːgraːs], *n.* (**—es**, *no pl.*) seaweed.

Seehandel ['zeːhandəl], *m.* (**—s**, *no pl.*) maritime trade.

Seehund ['zeːhunt], *m.* (**—s**, *pl.* **—e**) (*Zool.*) seal.

Seeigel ['zeːiːgəl], *m.* (**—s**, *pl.* **—**) (*Zool.*) sea-urchin.

Seejungfrau ['zeːjuŋfrau], *f.* (**—**, *pl.* **—en**) mermaid.

Seekadett ['zeːkadɛt], *m.* (**—en**, *pl.* **—en**) midshipman; (naval) cadet.

Seekarte ['zeːkartə], *f.* (**—**, *pl.* **—n**) chart.

seekrank ['zeːkraŋk], *adj.* seasick.

Seekrieg ['zeːkriːk], *m.* (**—s**, *pl.* **—e**) naval war.

Seeküste ['zeːkystə], *f.* (**—**, *pl.* **—n**) sea-coast, shore, beach.

Seele ['zeːlə], *f.* (**—**, *pl.* **—n**) soul; *mit ganzer* **—**, with all my heart.

Seelenamt ['zeːlənamt], *n.* (**—s**, *pl.* ˙ˈer) (*Eccl.*) office for the dead, requiem.

Seelenangst ['zeːlənaŋkst], *f.* (**—**, *pl.* ˙ˈe) anguish, agony.

Seelenheil ['zeːlənhaɪl], *n.* (**—s**, *no pl.*) (*Theol.*) salvation.

Seelenhirt ['zeːlənhɪrt], *m.* (**—en**, *pl.* **—en**) pastor.

seelenlos ['zeːlənloːs], *adj.* inanimate.

Seelenmesse ['zeːlənmɛsə], *f.* (**—**, *pl.* **—n**) requiem; Mass for the dead.

Seelenruhe ['zeːlənruːə], *f.* (**—**, *no pl.*) tranquillity of mind.

seelenruhig ['zeːlənruːɪç], *adj.* cool, calm, collected, unperturbed.

Seelenstärke ['zeːlənʃtɛrkə], *f.* (**—**, *no pl.*) fortitude; composure.

seelenvergnügt ['zeːlənfɛrgnyːkt], *adj.* blissfully happy.

Seelenverwandtschaft ['zeːlənfɛrvantʃaft], *f.* (**—**, *pl.* **—en**) mental affinity, (mutual) understanding.

seelenvoll ['zeːlənfɔl], *adj.* wistful, soulful.

Seelenwanderung ['zeːlənvandəruŋ], *f.* (**—**, *no pl.*) transmigration of souls, metempsychosis.

Seeleute ['zeːlɔytə] *see under* **Seemann.**

seelisch ['zeːlɪʃ], *adj.* mental, psychological, psychic(al).

Seelsorge ['zeːlsɔrgə], *f.* (**—**, *no pl.*) (*Eccl.*) cure of souls; pastoral duties or work.

Seemann ['zeːman], *m.* (**—s**, *pl.* ˙ˈer, **Seeleute**) seaman, sailor, mariner.

Seemeile ['zeːmaɪlə], *f.* (**—**, *pl.* **—n**) knot, nautical mile.

Seemöwe ['zeːmøːvə], *f.* (**—**, *pl.* **—n**) (*Orn.*) seagull.

Seemuschel ['zeːmuʃəl], *f.* (**—**, *pl.* **—n**) sea-shell.

Seepflanze ['zeːpflantsə], *f.* (**—**, *pl.* **—n**) marine plant.

Seerabe ['zeːraːbə], *m.* (**—n**, *pl.* **—n**) (*Orn.*) cormorant.

Seeräuber ['zeːrɔybər], *m.* (**—s**, *pl.* **—**) pirate.

Seerose ['zeːroːzə], *f.* (**—**, *pl.* **—n**) (*Bot.*) water-lily.

Seesalz ['zeːzalts], *n.* (**—es**, *no pl.*) bay salt, sea salt.

Seeschlacht ['zeːʃlaxt], *f.* (**—**, *pl.* **—en**) naval engagement, naval battle.

Seestern ['zeːʃtɛrn], *m.* (**—s**, *pl.* **—e**) (*Zool.*) starfish.

Seestille ['zeːʃtɪlə], *f.* (**—**, *no pl.*) calm (at sea).

Seetang ['zeːtaŋ], *m.* (**—s**, *no pl.*) (*Bot.*) seaweed.

seetüchtig ['zeːtyçtɪç], *adj.* seaworthy.

Seeuhr ['zeːuːr], *f.* (**—**, *pl.* **—en**) marine chronometer.

Seeuntüchtigkeit ['zeːuntyçtɪçkaɪt], *f.* (**—**, *no pl.*) unseaworthiness.

Seewasser ['zeːvasər], *n.* (**—s**, *no pl.*) sea-water, brine.

Seewesen ['zeːvezən], *n.* (**—s**, *no pl.*) naval affairs.

Seezunge ['zeːtsuŋə], *f.* (**—**, *pl.* **—n**) sole (*fish*).

Segel ['zeːgəl], *n.* (**—s**, *pl.* **—**) sail; *großes* **—**, mainsail; *unter* **—** *gehen*, set sail, put to sea; *die* **—** *streichen*, strike sail.

segelfertig ['zeːgəlfɛrtɪç], *adj.* ready to sail; *sich* **—** *machen*, get under sail.

Segelflugzeug ['zeːgəlfluːktsɔyk], *n.* (**—s**, *pl.* **—e**) glider(-plane).

Segelschiff ['zeːgəlʃɪf], *n.* (**—s**, *pl.* **—e**) sailing-vessel.

Segelstange ['zeːgəlʃtaŋə], *f.* (**—**, *pl.* **—n**) sail-yard.

Segen ['zeːgən], *m.* (**—s**, *no pl.*) blessing, benediction; (*fig.*) abundance; **—** *sprechen*, give the blessing, say grace.

segensreich

segensreich ['ze:gənsraɪç], *adj.* blessed, full of blessings; prosperous.
Segenswunsch ['ze:gənsvunʃ], *m.* (—es, *pl.* ˙e) good wish.
segnen ['ze:gnən], *v.a.* bless.
sehen ['ze:ən], *v.a. irr.* see, behold, perceive; *etwas gern* —, like s.th., approve of s.th. — *v.n.* look, see; *sich lassen*, parade, show o.s., *wir werden* —, that remains to be seen, we shall see.
sehenswert ['ze:ənsve:rt], *adj.* worth seeing.
Sehenswürdigkeit ['ze:ənsvyrdɪçkaɪt], *f.* (—, *pl.* —en) curiosity, object of interest, tourist attraction; (*pl.*) sights.
Seher ['ze:ər], *m.* (—s, *pl.* —) seer, prophet.
Sehne ['ze:nə], *f.* (—, *pl.* —n) sinew, tendon; string.
sehnig ['ze:nɪç], *adj.* sinewy, muscular; (*meat*) tough.
sehnlich ['ze:nlɪç], *adj.* earnest, passionate, eager.
Sehnsucht ['ze:nzuxt], *f.* (—, *no pl.*) longing, yearning, desire.
sehr [ze:r], *adv.* very, much, greatly, very much; *zu* —, too much; — *gut*, very good; — *wohl*, very well.
Schweite ['ze:vaɪtə], *f.* (—, *no pl.*) range of vision.
seicht [zaɪçt], *adj.* shallow, superficial.
Seide ['zaɪdə], *f.* (—, *pl.* —n) silk.
Seidel ['zaɪdəl], *n.* (—s, *pl.* —) (*dial.*) mug, tankard; pint.
seiden ['zaɪdən], *adj.* silk, silken, silky.
Seidenpapier ['zaɪdənpapiːr], *n.* (—s, *no pl.*) tissue-paper.
Seidenraupe ['zaɪdənraupə], *f.* (—, *pl.* —n) (*Ent.*) silkworm.
Seidenstoff ['zaɪdənʃtɔf], *m.* (—es, *pl.* —e) spun silk.
Seife ['zaɪfə], *f.* (—, *pl.* —n) soap; *ein Stück* —, a cake of soap.
seifen ['zaɪfən], *v.a.* soap.
Seifenschaum ['zaɪfənʃaum], *m.* (—s, *no pl.*) lather.
Seifenwasser ['zaɪfənvasər], *n.* (—s, *no pl.*) soap-suds.
seifig ['zaɪfɪç], *adj.* soapy, saponaceous.
seihen ['zaɪən], *v.a.* strain, filter.
Seil [zaɪl], *n.* (—(e)s, *pl.* —e) rope; *straffes* —, taut rope, tight rope; *schlaffes* —, slack rope.
Seilbahn ['zaɪlbaːn], *f.* (—, *pl.* —en) funicular railway; cable car.
Seilbrücke ['zaɪlbrykə], *f.* (—, *pl.* —n) rope bridge.
Seiltänzer ['zaɪltɛntsər], *m.* (—s, *pl.* —) tight-rope walker.
Seilziehen ['zaɪltsiːən], *n.* (—s, *no pl.*) tug of war.
Seim [zaɪm], *m.* (—(e)s, *pl.* —e) strained honey.
Sein [zaɪn], *n.* (—s, *no pl.*) being, existence.
sein (1) [zaɪn], *v.n. irr.* (*aux.* sein) be, exist.
sein (2) [zaɪn], *poss. adj.* his, her, its; one's. — *pers. pron.* his.

seinerseits ['zaɪnərzaɪts], *adv.* for his part.
seinerzeit ['zaɪnərtsaɪt], *adv.* at that time, at the time, formerly.
seinesgleichen ['zaɪnəsglaɪçən], *indecl. adj. & pron.* of his sort, such as he.
seinethalben ['zaɪnəthalbən], *adv.* on his account, for his sake, on his behalf.
seinetwegen ['zaɪnətveːgən], *adv.* on his account, for his sake, on his behalf.
Seinige ['zaɪnɪgə], *n.* (—n, *pl.* —n) his, his property; (*pl.*) his family, his people; *das* — *tun*, do o.'s share.
seit [zaɪt], *prep.* (*Dat.*) since, for; — *gestern*, since yesterday, from yesterday onwards; — *einiger Zeit*, for some time past. — *conj. see* **seitdem**.
seitdem [zaɪt'deːm], *adv.* since then, since that time. — *conj.* since.
Seite ['zaɪtə], *f.* (—, *pl.* —n) side, flank; (*book*) page; *etwas auf die* — *bringen*, put s.th. aside; *ich bin auf seiner* —, I side with him, I am on his side; *er hat seine guten* —n, he has his good points.
Seitenansicht ['zaɪtənanzɪçt], *f.* (—, *pl.* —en) profile.
Seitengleis ['zaɪtənglaɪs], *n.* (—es, *pl.* —e) (railway) siding.
Seitenhieb ['zaɪtənhiːp], *m.* (—s, *pl.* —e) innuendo, sly hit, dig.
seitens ['zaɪtəns], *prep.* (*Genit.*) on the part of.
Seitensprung ['zaɪtənʃprun], *m.* (—s, *pl.* ˙e) side-leap, caper; (*fig.*) (amorous) escapade.
Seitenstraße ['zaɪtənʃtraːsə], *f.* (—, *pl.* —n) side-street.
Seitenstück ['zaɪtənʃtyk], *n.* (—s, *pl.* —e) companion-piece.
Seitenzahl ['zaɪtəntsaːl], *f.* (—, *pl.* —en) page-number; number of pages.
seither ['zaɪtheːr], *adv.* since that time, since then.
seitlich ['zaɪtlɪç], *adj.* lateral.
Sekretär [zekreˈtɛːr], *m.* (—s, *pl.* —e) secretary.
Sekretariat [zekretaˈrjaːt], *n.* (—s, *pl.* —e) secretariat, secretary's office.
Sekt [zɛkt], *m.* (—s, *pl.* —e) champagne.
Sekte ['zɛktə], *f.* (—, *pl.* —n) sect.
Sektierer [zɛkˈtiːrər], *m.* (—s, *pl.* —) sectarian.
Sektion [zɛkˈtsjoːn] *f.* (—, *pl.* —en) section; (*Med.*) dissection.
Sekundaner [zekunˈdaːnər], *m.* (—s, *pl.* —) pupil in the second (highest) form.
Sekundant [zekunˈdant], *m.* (—en, *pl.* —en) (*Duelling*) second.
sekundär [zekunˈdɛːr], *adj.* secondary.
Sekunde [zeˈkundə], *f.* (—, *pl.* —n) (*time*) second.
Sekundenzeiger [zeˈkundəntsaɪgər], *m.* (—s, *pl.* —) (*clock*) second-hand.
sekundieren [zekunˈdiːrən], *v.n. einem* —, second s.o.
selber ['zɛlbər], *indecl. adj. & pron.* self.
selb(ig) ['zɛlb(ɪg)], *adj.* the same.

198

selbst [zɛlpst], *indecl. adj. & pron.* self; — *ist der Mann*, depend on yourself; *von* —, of its own accord, spontaneously. — *adv.* even; — *wenn*, even if, even though; — *dann nicht*, not even then.

selbständig ['zɛlpʃtɛndɪç], *adj.* independent.

Selbstbestimmung ['zɛlpstbəʃtɪmuŋ], *f.* (—, *no pl.*) self-determination, autonomy.

selbstbewußt ['zɛlpstbəvust], *adj.* self-assertive, self-confident, conceited.

selbstherrlich ['zɛlpstherlɪç], *adj.* autocratic, tyrannical.

Selbstlaut ['zɛlpstlaut], *m.* (—s, *pl.* —e) vowel.

selbstlos ['zɛlpstlo:s], *adj.* unselfish, selfless, altruistic.

Selbstlosigkeit [zɛlpst'lo:zɪçkaɪt], *f.* (—, *no pl.*) unselfishness, altruism.

Selbstmord ['zɛlpstmɔrt], *m.* (—s, *pl.* —e) suicide.

selbstredend ['zɛlpstre:dənt], *adj.* self-evident, obvious.

Selbstsucht ['zɛlpstzuxt], *f.* (—, *no pl.*) selfishness, ego(t)ism.

selbstsüchtig ['zɛlpstzyçtɪç], *adj.* selfish, ego(t)istic(al).

selbstverständlich ['zɛlpstferʃtɛntlɪç], *adj.* self-evident. — *adv.* of course, obviously.

Selbstzweck ['zɛlpsttsvɛk], *m.* (—s, *no pl.*) end in itself.

selig ['ze:lɪç], *adj.* blessed, blissful; (*fig.*) delighted; deceased, late; — *sprechen*, beatify.

Seligkeit ['ze:lɪçkaɪt], *f.* (—, *pl.* —en) bliss, blissfulness; (*Eccl.*) salvation, beatitude.

Seligsprechung ['ze:lɪçʃprɛçuŋ], *f.* (—, *pl.* —en) beatification.

Sellerie ['zɛləri:], *m.* (—s, *pl.* —s) (*Bot.*) celery.

selten ['zɛltən], *adj.* rare, scarce; (*fig.*) remarkable. — *adv.* seldom, rarely, infrequently.

Seltenheit ['zɛltənhaɪt], *f.* (—, *pl.* —en) rarity, curiosity, scarcity; (*fig.*) remarkableness.

Selterwasser ['zɛltərvasər], *n.* (—s, *no pl.*) soda-water.

seltsam ['zɛltza:m], *adj.* strange, unusual, odd, curious.

Semester [ze'mɛstər], *n.* (—s, *pl.* —) university term, semester.

Semit [ze'mi:t], *m.* (—en, *pl.* —en) Semite, Jew.

semmelblond ['zɛməlblɔnt], *adj.* flaxen-haired.

Semmelkloß ['zɛməlklo:s], *m.* (—es, *pl.* ⸚e) bread dumpling.

Senator [ze'na:tɔr], *m.* (—s, *pl.* —en) senator.

senden ['zɛndən], *v.a. irr.* send, despatch; (*money*) remit. — *v.a. reg.* (*Rad.*) broadcast.

Sender ['zɛndər], *m.* (—s, *pl.* —) sender; (*Rad.*) (broadcasting) station, transmitter.

Sendling ['zɛntlɪŋ], *m.* (—s, *pl.* —e) (*Poet.*) emissary.

Sendschreiben ['zɛntʃraɪbən], *n.* (—s, *pl.* —) epistle, missive.

Sendung ['zɛnduŋ], *f.* (—, *pl.* —en) (*Comm.*) shipment, consignment; (*fig.*) mission; (*Rad.*) broadcast, transmission.

Senegal ['ze:nəgal], *n.* Senegal.

Senf [zɛnf], *m.* (—s, *no pl.*) mustard.

sengen ['zɛŋən], *v.a.* singe, scorch; — *und brennen*, lay waste.

Senkblei ['zɛŋkblaɪ], *n.* (—s, *pl.* —e) plummet.

Senkel ['zɛŋkəl], *m.* (—s, *pl.* —) shoe-lace.

senken ['zɛŋkən], *v.a.* lower, sink. — *v.r. sich* —, sink, go down; dip, slope, subside.

senkrecht ['zɛŋkrɛçt], *adj.* perpendicular.

Senkung ['zɛŋkuŋ], *f.* (—, *pl.* —en) depression, dip, subsidence.

Senn(e) ['zɛn(ə)], *m.* (—n, *pl.* —(e)n) Alpine herdsman.

Sennerin ['zɛnərɪn], *f.* (—, *pl.* —nen) Alpine dairy-woman.

Senneschoten ['zɛnəʃo:tən], *f. pl.* senna pods.

Sennhütte ['zɛnhytə], *f.* (—, *pl.* —n) Alpine dairy; chalet.

sensationell [zɛnzatsjo'nɛl], *adj.* sensational.

Sense ['zɛnzə], *f.* (—, *pl.* —n) scythe.

sensibel [zɛn'zi:bəl], *adj.* sensitive.

Sentenz [zɛn'tɛnts], *f.* (—, *pl.* —en) aphorism.

sentimental [zɛntimɛn'ta:l], *adj.* sentimental.

separat [zepa'ra:t], *adj.* separate, special.

September [zɛp'tɛmbər], *m.* (—s, *pl.* —) September.

Serbien ['zɛrbjən], *n.* Serbia.

Serie ['ze:rjə], *f.* (—, *pl.* —n) series.

Service [zɛr'vi:s], *n.* (—s, *pl.* —) dinner-set, dinner-service.

servieren [zɛr'vi:rən], *v.a., v.n.* serve, wait at table.

Serviertisch [zɛr'vi:rtɪʃ], *m.* (—es, *pl.* —e) sideboard.

Sessel ['zɛsəl], *m.* (—s, *pl.* —) armchair, easy-chair; (*Austr. dial.*) chair.

seßhaft ['zɛshaft], *adj.* settled, domiciled.

setzen ['zɛtsən], *v.a.* set, put, place; (*monument*) erect; (*bet*) stake; (*Typ.*) compose. — *v.r. sich* —, sit down; (*coffee*) settle; *sich bei einem in Gunst* —, ingratiate o.s. with s.o.

Setzer ['zɛtsər], *m.* (—s, *pl.* —) compositor.

Setzling ['zɛtslɪŋ], *m.* (—s, *pl.* —e) young tree, young plant.

Seuche ['zɔyçə], *f.* (—, *pl.* —n) pestilence; epidemic.

seufzen ['zɔyftsən], *v.n.* sigh.

Seufzer ['zɔyftsər], *m.* (—s, *pl.* —) sigh.

Sexta ['zɛksta:], *f.* (—, *pl.* —s) (*Sch.*) sixth form, lowest form.

Sextant [zɛks'tant], *m.* (**—en**, *pl.* **—en**) sextant.
sexuell [zɛksu'ɛl], *adj.* sexual.
sezieren [ze'tsi:rən], *v.a.* dissect.
Seziersaal [ze'tsi:rza:l], *m.* (**—s**, *pl.* **—säle**) dissecting-room.
Sibirien [zi'bi:rjən], *n.* Siberia.
sich [zɪç], *pron.* oneself, himself, herself, itself, themselves; each other.
Sichel [ˈzɪçəl], *f.* (**—**, *pl.* **—n**) sickle.
sicher [ˈzɪçər], *adj.* certain, sure, secure, safe; confident, positive; *seiner Sache — sein*, be sure of o.'s ground; *— stellen*, secure.
Sicherheit [ˈzɪçərhaɪt], *f.* (**—**, *pl.* **—en**) certainty; security, safety; confidence, positiveness; *in — bringen*, secure.
sichern [ˈzɪçərn], *v.a.* secure, make secure; assure, ensure.
Sicherung [ˈzɪçəruŋ], *f.* (**—**, *pl.* **—en**) securing; (*Elec.*) fuse; (*gun*) safety-catch.
Sicht [zɪçt], *f.* (**—**, *no pl.*) sight.
sichtbar [ˈzɪçtba:r], *adj.* visible; conspicuous.
sichten [ˈzɪçtən], *v.a.* sift, sort out; sight.
sichtlich [ˈzɪçtlɪç], *adv.* visibly.
Sichtwechsel [ˈzɪçtvɛksəl], *m.* (**—s**, *pl.* **—**) (*Banking*) sight-bill, bill payable on sight.
Sichtweite [ˈzɪçtvaɪtə], *f.* (**—**, *no pl.*) range of vision.
sickern [ˈzɪkərn], *v.n.* (*aux.* sein) leak, ooze, seep.
Sie [zi:], *pron.* (*formal*) you.
sie [zi:], *pers. pron.* she, her; they, them.
Sieb [zi:p], *n.* (**—(e)s**, *pl.* **—e**) sieve; riddle; colander.
sieben (1) [ˈzi:bən], *v.a.* (*Cul.*) sift, strain.
sieben (2) [ˈzi:bən], *num. adj.* seven; *meine — Sachen*, my belongings.
Siebeneck [ˈzi:bənɛk], *n.* (**—s**, *pl.* **—e**) heptagon.
Siebengestirn [ˈzi:bəngəʃtɪrn], *n.* (**—s**, *no pl.*) Pleiades.
siebenmal [ˈzi:bənma:l], *adv.* seven times.
Siebenmeilenstiefel [zi:bən'maɪlənʃti:fəl], *m. pl.* seven-league boots.
Siebenschläfer [ˈzi:bənʃle:fər], *m.* (**—s**, *pl.* **—**) lazy-bones.
siebzehn [ˈzi:ptse:n], *num. adj.* seventeen.
siebzig [ˈzi:ptsɪç], *num. adj.* seventy.
siech [zi:ç], *adj.* (*rare*) sick, infirm.
siechen [ˈzi:çən], *v.n.* be in bad health.
sieden [ˈzi:dən], *v.a., v.n.* boil, seethe.
siedeln [ˈzi:dəln], *v.n.* settle.
Siedlung [ˈzi:dluŋ], *f.* (**—**, *pl.* **—en**) settlement; housing estate.
Sieg [zi:k], *m.* (**—(e)s**, *pl.* **—e**) victory; *den — davontragen*, win the day.
Siegel [ˈzi:gəl], *n.* (**—s**, *pl.* **—**) seal; *Brief und —*, sign and seal.
Siegelbewahrer [ˈzi:gəlbəva:rər], *m.* (**—s**, *pl.* **—**) Lord Privy Seal; keeper of the seal.

Siegellack [ˈzi:gəllak], *n.* (**—s**, *no pl.*) sealing wax.
siegeln [ˈzi:gəln], *v.a.* seal.
siegen [ˈzi:gən], *v.n.* conquer, win, be victorious, triumph (over).
Sieger [ˈzi:gər], *m.* (**—s**, *pl.* **—**) victor, conqueror.
Siegesbogen [ˈzi:gəsbo:gən], *m.* (**—s**, *pl.* **⸚**) triumphal arch.
Siegeszeichen [ˈzi:gəstsaɪçən], *n.* (**—s**, *pl.* **—**) sign of victory, trophy.
sieghaft [ˈzi:khaft], *adj.* victorious, triumphant.
siegreich [ˈzi:kraɪç], *adj.* victorious, triumphant.
siehe! [ˈzi:ə], *excl.* see! look! lo and behold!
Sierra Leone [ˈsiɛra le'o:nə], *f.* Sierra Leone.
Signal [zɪg'na:l], *n.* (**—s**, *pl.* **—e**) signal.
Signalement [zɪgnalə'mã], *n.* (**—s**, *pl.* **—s**) personal description.
Signalglocke [zɪg'na:lglɔkə], *f.* (**—**, *pl.* **—n**) warning-bell.
signalisieren [zɪgnali'zi:rən], *v.a.* signal.
Signatarmacht [zɪgna'ta:rmaxt], *f.* (**—**, *pl.* **⸚e**) signatory power.
signieren [zɪg'ni:rən], *v.a.* sign.
Silbe [ˈzɪlbə], *f.* (**—**, *pl.* **—n**) syllable.
Silbenmaß [ˈzɪlbənma:s], *n.* (**—es**, *pl.* **—e**) (*Poet.*) metre.
Silbenrätsel [ˈzɪlbənrɛ:tsəl], *n.* (**—s**, *pl.* **—**) charade.
Silber [ˈzɪlbər], *n.* (**—s**, *no pl.*) silver; plate.
Silberbuche [ˈzɪlbərbu:xə], *f.* (**—**, *pl.* **—n**) white beech(-tree).
Silberfuchs [ˈzɪlbərfuks], *m.* (**—es**, *pl.* **⸚e**) (*Zool.*) silver fox.
silbern [ˈzɪlbərn], *adj.* made of silver, silvery.
Silberpappel [ˈzɪlbərpapəl], *f.* (**—**, *pl.* **—n**) (*Bot.*) white poplar(-tree).
Silberschimmel [ˈzɪlbərʃɪməl], *m.* (**—s**, *pl.* **—**) grey-white horse.
Silberzeug [ˈzɪlbərtsɔyk], *n.* (**—s**, *no pl.*) (silver) plate.
Silvester [zɪl'vɛstər], *n.* (**—s**, *pl.* **—**) New Year's Eve.
Similistein [ˈzi:milɪʃtaɪn], *m.* (**—s**, *pl.* **—e**) imitation *or* paste jewellery.
Sims [zɪms], *m.* (**—es**, *pl.* **—e**) cornice, moulding, shelf, ledge.
Simulant [zimu'lant], *m.* (**—en**, *pl.* **—en**) malingerer.
simulieren [zimu'li:rən], *v.a.* simulate.
simultan [zimul'ta:n], *adj.* simultaneous.
Singapur [zɪŋga'pu:r], *n.* Singapore.
Singdrossel [ˈzɪŋdrɔsəl], *f.* (**—**, *pl.* **—n**) (*Orn.*) common thrush.
singen [ˈzɪŋən], *v.a., v.n. irr.* sing.
Singspiel [ˈzɪŋʃpi:l], *n.* (**—s**, *pl.* **—e**) musical comedy, light opera, opera buffa.
Singular [ˈzɪŋgula:r], *m.* (**—s**, *pl.* **—e**) singular.

sinken ['zɪŋkən], *v.n. irr. (aux.* sein) sink; *(price)* decline, drop, fall; *den Mut — lassen,* lose heart.

Sinn [zɪn], *m.* (—(e)s, *pl.* —e) sense; intellect, mind; consciousness, memory; taste, meaning, purport; wish; *etwas im — haben,* have s.th. in mind, intend s.th.; *leichter —,* lightheartedness; *andern —es werden,* change o's mind; *das hat keinen —,* there is no sense in that; *von —en sein,* be out of o.'s senses; *seine fünf —e beisammen haben,* be in o.'s right mind; *sich etwas aus dem — schlagen,* dismiss s.th. from o.'s mind; *es kommt mir in den —,* it occurs to me.

Sinnbild ['zɪnbɪlt], *n.* (—s, *pl.* —er) symbol, emblem.

sinnen ['zɪnən], *v.n. irr.* meditate, reflect.

Sinnesänderung ['zɪnəsɛndərʊŋ], *f.* (—, *pl.* —en) change of mind.

Sinnesart ['zɪnəsaːrt], *f.* (—, *no pl.*) disposition, character.

Sinnesorgan ['zɪnəsɔrgaːn], *n.* (—s, *pl.* —e) sense-organ.

Sinnestäuschung ['zɪnəstɔyʃʊŋ], *f.* (—, *pl.* —en) illusion, hallucination.

sinnfällig ['zɪnfɛlɪç], *adj.* obvious, striking.

Sinngedicht ['zɪngədɪçt], *n.* (—es, *pl.* —e) epigram.

sinnig ['zɪnɪç], *adj.* thoughtful, meaningful; judicious, fitting.

sinnlich ['zɪnlɪç], *adj.* sensual, sensuous.

Sinnlichkeit ['zɪnlɪçkaɪt], *f.* (—, *no pl.*) sensuality, sensuousness.

sinnlos ['zɪnloːs], *adj.* senseless, meaningless, pointless.

sinnreich ['zɪnraɪç], *adj.* ingenious.

Sinnspruch ['zɪnʃprʊx], *m.* (—es, *pl.* —e) sentence, maxim, device, motto.

sinnverwandt ['zɪnfɛrvant], *adj.* synonymous.

sinnvoll ['zɪnfɔl], *adj.* meaningful, significant.

sinnwidrig ['zɪnviːdrɪç], *adj.* nonsensical, absurd.

Sintflut ['zɪntfluːt], *f.* (—, *no pl.*) *(Bibl.)* the Flood.

Sinus ['ziːnus], *m.* (—, *pl.* —se) *(Maths.)* sine.

Sippe ['zɪpə], *f.* (—, *pl.* —n) kin, tribe, family, clan.

Sippschaft ['zɪpʃaft], *f.* (—, *pl.* —en) kindred; *die ganze —,* the whole caboodle.

Sirene [ziˈreːnə], *f.* (—, *pl.* —n) siren.

Sirup ['ziːrup], *m.* (—s, *no pl.*) syrup, treacle.

Sitte ['zɪtə], *f.* (—, *pl.* —n) custom, mode, fashion; *(pl.)* manners, morals; *—n und Gebräuche,* manners and customs.

Sittengesetz ['zɪtəngəzɛts], *n.* (—es, *pl.* —e) moral law.

Sittenlehre ['zɪtənleːrə], *f.* (—, *no pl.*) moral philosophy, ethics.

sittenlos ['zɪtənloːs], *adj.* immoral, profligate, licentious.

Sittenprediger ['zɪtənpreːdɪgər], *m.* (—s, *pl.* —) moraliser.

Sittich ['zɪtɪç], *m.* (—s, *pl.* —e) *(Orn.)* budgerigar; parakeet.

sittig ['zɪtɪç], *adj.* well-behaved.

sittlich ['zɪtlɪç], *adj.* moral.

Sittlichkeit ['zɪtlɪçkaɪt], *f.* (—, *no pl.*) morality, morals.

sittsam ['zɪtzaːm], *adj.* modest, demure.

situiert [zituˈiːrt], *adj. gut (schlecht) —,* well (badly) off.

Sitz [zɪts], *m.* (—es, *pl.* —e) seat, chair; residence, location, place; *(Eccl.)* see.

Sitzarbeit ['zɪtsarbaɪt], *f.* (—, *pl.* —en) sedentary work.

Sitzbad ['zɪtsbaːt], *n.* (—(e)s, *pl.* —er) hip bath.

sitzen ['zɪtsən], *v.n. irr.* sit, be seated; *(fig.)* be in prison; *(dress)* fit; *— lassen,* throw over, jilt; *— bleiben,* remain seated; *(school)* stay in the same class, not be moved up; be a wallflower; remain unmarried.

Sitzfleisch ['zɪtsflaɪʃ], *n.* (—es, *no pl.*) *(coll.) kein — haben,* be restless, lack application.

Sitzplatz ['zɪtsplats], *m.* (—es, *pl.* —e) seat.

Sitzung ['zɪtsʊŋ], *f.* (—, *pl.* —en) meeting, sitting, session.

Sitzungsprotokoll ['zɪtsʊŋsprotokɔl], *n.* (—s, *pl.* —e) minutes (of a meeting).

Sitzungssaal ['zɪtsʊŋszaːl], *m.* (—s, *pl.* —säle) board-room, conference room.

Sizilien [ziˈtsiːljən], *n.* Sicily.

Skala ['skaːla], *f.* (—, *pl.* —len) scale; *(Mus.)* gamut.

Skandal [skanˈdaːl], *m.* (—s, *pl.* —e) scandal; row, riot; *— machen,* kick up a row.

skandalös [skandaˈløːs], *adj.* scandalous.

skandieren [skanˈdiːrən], *v.a. (Poet.)* scan.

Skandinavien [skandiˈnaːvjən], *n.* Scandinavia.

Skelett [skeˈlɛt], *n.* (—s, *pl.* —e) skeleton.

Skepsis ['skɛpzɪs], *f.* (—, *no pl.*) scepticism, doubt.

skeptisch ['skɛptɪʃ], *adj.* sceptical, doubtful.

Skizze ['skɪtsə], *f.* (—, *pl.* —n) sketch.

skizzieren [skɪˈtsiːrən], *v.a.* sketch.

Sklave ['sklaːvə], *m.* (—n, *pl.* —n) slave; *zum —n machen,* enslave.

Sklavendienst ['sklaːvəndiːnst], *m.* (—es, *no pl.*) slavery.

Sklaverei [sklaːvəˈraɪ], *f.* (—, *no pl.*) slavery, thraldom.

Skonto ['skɔnto], *m. & n.* (—s, *pl.* —s) discount.

Skrupel ['skruːpəl], *m.* (—s, *pl.* —) scruple; *sich — machen,* have scruples.

skrupulös [skrupuˈløːs], *adj.* scrupulous, meticulous.

201

Skulptur [skulp'tu:r], *f.* (—, *pl.* —en) sculpture.

skurril [sku'ri:l], *adj.* ludicrous.

Slawe ['sla:və], *m.* (—n, *pl.* —n) Slav.

slawisch ['sla:vɪʃ], *adj.* Slav, Slavonic.

Slowake [slo'va:kə], *m.* (—n, *pl.* —n) Slovakian.

Slowene [slo've:nə], *m.* (—n, *pl.* —n) Slovenian.

Smaragd [sma'rakt], *m.* (—(e)s, *pl.* —e) emerald.

smaragden [sma'raktən], *adj.* emerald.

Smoking ['smo:kɪŋ], *m.* (—s, *pl.* —s) dinner-jacket.

so [zo:], *adv.* so, thus, in this way, like this; — ? really? — *ist es*, that is how it is; — *daß*, so that; — . . . *wie*, as . . . as; *na — was!* well, I never! — *conj.* then, therefore.

sobald [zo'balt], *conj.* as soon as, directly.

Socke ['zɔkə], *f.* (—, *pl.* —n) sock.

Sockel ['zɔkəl], *m.* (—s, *pl.* —) pedestal, plinth, stand, base.

Soda ['zo:da], *n.* (—s, *no pl.*) (carbonate of) soda.

sodann [zo'dan], *adv. conj.* then.

Sodbrennen ['zo:tbrɛnən], *n.* (—s, *no pl.*) heartburn.

soeben [zo'e:bən], *adv.* just now.

sofern [zo'fɛrn], *conj.* if, in case, so far as.

sofort [zo'fɔrt], *adv.* at once, immediately.

Sog [zo:k], *m.* (—(e)s, *pl.* —e) undertow, suction.

sogar [zo'ga:r], *adv.* even.

sogenannt [zogə'nant], *adj.* so-called, would-be.

sogleich [zo'glaɪç], *adv.* at once, immediately.

Sohle ['zo:lə], *f.* (—, *pl.* —n) sole; (*mine*) floor.

Sohn [zo:n], *m.* (—(e)s, *pl.* ¨e) son; *der verlorene* —, the prodigal son.

solange [zo'laŋə], *conj.* as long as.

Solbad ['zo:lba:t], *n.* (—s, *pl.* ¨er) saline bath.

solch [zɔlç], *adj., dem. pron.* such.

solcherlei ['zɔlçərlaɪ], *adj.* of such a kind, suchlike.

Sold [zɔlt], *m.* (—(e)s, *no pl.*) army pay.

Soldat [zɔl'da:t], *m.* (—en, *pl.* —en) soldier.

Soldateska [zɔlda'tɛska], *f.* (—, *pl.* —s) soldiery.

Söldner ['zœldnər], *m.* (—s, *pl.* —) mercenary, hireling.

Sole ['zo:lə], *f.* (—, *pl.* —n) salt-water, brine.

Solei ['zo:laɪ], *n.* (—s, *pl.* —er) pickled egg.

solidarisch [zoli'da:rɪʃ], *adj.* joint, jointly responsible; unanimous.

Solidarität [zolidari'tɛ:t], *f.* (—, *no pl.*) solidarity.

Solist [zo'lɪst], *m.* (—en, *pl.* —en) soloist.

Soll [zɔl], *n.* (—s, *no pl.*) debit; — *und Haben*, debit and credit.

sollen ['zɔlən], *v.n. irr.* be obliged, be compelled; have to; be supposed to; (*aux.*) shall, should etc.; *ich soll*, I must, I am to; *er soll krank sein*, he is said to be ill; *ich sollte eigentlich*, I really ought to.

Söller ['zœlər], *m.* (—s, *pl.* —) loft, garret, balcony.

Somali [zo'ma:li], *n.* Somalia.

somit [zo'mɪt], *adv.* consequently, therefore, accordingly.

Sommer ['zɔmər], *m.* (—s, *pl.* —) summer.

Sommerfäden ['zɔmərfɛ:dən], *m. pl.* gossamer.

Sommerfrische ['zɔmərfrɪʃə], *f.* (—, *pl.* —n) holiday resort.

Sommergetreide ['zɔmərgətraɪdə], *n.* (—s, *no pl.*) spring corn.

Sommersonnenwende ['zɔmərzɔnənvɛndə], *f.* (—, *pl.* —n) summer solstice.

Sommersprosse ['zɔmərʃprɔsə], *f.* (—, *pl.* —n) freckle.

sonach [zo'na:x], *adv.* therefore, consequently.

Sonate [zo'na:tə], *f.* (—, *pl.* —n) sonata.

Sonde ['zɔndə], *f.* (—, *pl.* —n) sounding-lead, plummet; probe.

sonder ['zɔndər], (*obs.*) *prep.* (*Acc.*) without.

Sonderausgabe ['zɔndərausga:bə], *f.* (—, *pl.* —n) separate edition; special edition.

Sonderausschuß ['zɔndərausʃus], *m.* (—sses, *pl.* ¨sse) select committee.

sonderbar ['zɔndərba:r], *adj.* strange, odd, queer, singular, peculiar.

sonderlich ['zɔndərlɪç], *adj.* special, especial, particular. — *adv. nicht* —, not much.

Sonderling ['zɔndərlɪŋ], *m.* (—s, *pl.* —e) freak, odd character, crank.

sondern ['zɔndərn], *v.a.* separate, distinguish, differentiate. — *conj.* but; *nicht nur*, . . . — *auch*, not only . . . but also.

Sonderrecht ['zɔndərrɛçt], *n.* (—s, *pl.* —e) special privilege.

sonders ['zɔndərs], *adv. samt und* —, all and each, all and sundry.

Sonderstellung ['zɔndərʃtɛluŋ], *f.* (—, *no pl.*) exceptional position.

Sonderung ['zɔndəruŋ], *f.* (—, *pl.* —en) separation.

Sonderzug ['zɔndərtsu:k], *m.* (—s, *pl.* ¨e) special train.

sondieren [zɔn'di:rən], *v.a.* (*wound*) probe; (*ocean*) plumb; (*fig.*) sound.

Sonett [zo'nɛt], *n.* (—(e)s, *pl.* —e) sonnet.

Sonnabend ['zɔna:bənt], *m.* (—s, *pl.* —e) Saturday.

Sonne ['zɔnə], *f.* (—, *pl.* —n) sun.

sonnen ['zɔnən], *v.r. sich* —, sun o.s., bask in the sun, sunbathe.

Sonnenaufgang ['zɔnənaufgaŋ], *m.* (—s, *pl.* ¨e) sunrise.

Sonnenbrand ['zɔnənbrant], *m.* (—s, *pl.* ¨e) sunburn.

Sonnendeck [ˈzɔnəndɛk], *n.* (**—s,** *pl.* **—e**) awning.

Sonnenfinsternis [ˈzɔnənfɪnstərnɪs], *f.* (**—,** *pl.* **—se**) eclipse of the sun.

sonnenklar [ˈzɔnənklaːr], *adj.* very clear, as clear as daylight.

Sonnenschirm [ˈzɔnənʃɪrm], *m.* (**—s,** *pl.* **—e**) parasol, sunshade.

Sonnenstich [ˈzɔnənʃtɪç], *n.* (**—(e)s,** *no pl.*) sunstroke.

Sonnenuhr [ˈzɔnənuːr], *f.* (**—,** *pl.* **—en**) sundial.

Sonnenuntergang [ˈzɔnənuntərɡaŋ], *m.* (**—s,** *pl.* **⸚e**) sunset.

Sonnenwende [ˈzɔnənvɛndə], *f.* (**—,** *no pl.*) solstice.

Sonntag [ˈzɔntaːk], *m.* (**—s,** *pl.* **—e**) Sunday.

sonntags [ˈzɔntaːks], *adv.* on Sundays, of a Sunday.

Sonntagsjäger [ˈzɔntaːksjɛːɡər], *m.* (**—s,** *pl.* **—**) amateur sportsman.

sonor [zoˈnoːr], *adj.* sonorous.

sonst [zɔnst], *adv.* else, otherwise, besides, at other times; — *noch etwas?* anything else?

sonstig [ˈzɔnstɪç], *adj.* other, existing besides.

sonstwo [ˈzɔnstvo], *adv.* elsewhere, somewhere else.

Sopran [zoˈpraːn], *m.* (**—s,** *pl.* **—e**) soprano.

Sorbett [ˈzɔrbɛt], *n.* (**—s,** *pl.* **—s**) sherbet.

Sorge [ˈzɔrɡə], *f.* (**—,** *pl.* **—n**) care; grief, worry; sorrow; anxiety; concern; (*pl.*) troubles, worries; — *tragen dass . . .* , see to it that . . . ; — *tragen zu,* take care of ; — *um,* concern for.

sorgen [ˈzɔrɡən], *v.n.* — *für,* care for, provide for, look after. — *v.r. sich* — *um,* worry about.

sorgenvoll [ˈzɔrɡənfɔl], *adj.* uneasy, troubled, anxious.

Sorgfalt [ˈzɔrkfalt], *f.* (**—,** *no pl.*) care, attention.

sorgfältig [ˈzɔrkfɛltɪç], *adj.* careful, painstaking; elaborate.

sorglos [ˈzɔrkloːs], *adj.* careless, irresponsible, unconcerned, indifferent; carefree.

sorgsam [ˈzɔrkzaːm], *adj.* careful, heedful.

Sorte [ˈzɔrtə], *f.* (**—,** *pl.* **—n**) sort, kind, species, brand.

sortieren [zɔrˈtiːrən], *v.a.* sort (out).

Sortiment [zɔrtiˈmɛnt], *n.* (**—s,** *pl.* **—e**) assortment; bookshop.

Sortimentsbuchhändler [zɔrtiˈmɛntsbuːxhɛndlər], *m.* (**—s,** *pl.* **—**) retail bookseller.

Soße [ˈzoːsə], *f.* (**—,** *pl.* **—n**) sauce, gravy.

Souffleur [sufˈløːr], *m.* (**—s,** *pl.* **—e**) prompter.

Soutane [suˈtaːnə], *f.* (**—,** *pl.* **—n**) cassock, soutane.

Souterrain [sutɛˈrɛ̃], *n.* (**—s,** *pl.* **—s**) basement.

souverän [suːvəˈrɛːn], *adj.* sovereign; (*fig.*) supremely good.

Souveränität [suːvərɛːniˈtɛːt], *f.* (**—,** *no pl.*) sovereignty.

soviel [zoˈfiːl], *adv.* so much; — *wie,* as much as. — *conj.* so far as; — *ich weiß,* as far as I know.

sowie [zoˈviː], *conj.* as, as well as, as soon as.

Sowjet [sɔvˈjɛt], *m.* (**—s,** *pl.* **—s**) Soviet.

sowohl [zoˈvoːl], *conj.* — *wie,* as well as.

sozial [zoˈtsjaːl], *adj.* social.

sozialisieren [zotsjaliˈziːrən], *v.a.* nationalise.

Sozialwissenschaft [zoˈtsjaːlvɪsənʃaft], *f.* (**—,** *pl.* **—en**) sociology; social science.

Sozietät [zotsjeˈtɛːt], *f.* (**—,** *pl.* **—en**) partnership.

Sozius [ˈzotsjus], *m.* (**—,** *pl.* **—se, Socii**) partner; pillion-rider; —*sitz,* (*motor cycle*) pillion (seat).

sozusagen [ˈzoːtsuzaːɡən], *adv.* as it were, so to speak.

Spagat [ʃpaˈɡaːt], *m.* (**—(e)s,** *no pl.*) (*dial.*) string, twine; (*Dancing*) the splits.

spähen [ˈʃpɛːən], *v.n.* look out, watch; (*Mil.*) scout; spy.

Späher [ˈʃpɛːər], *m.* (**—s,** *pl.* **—**) scout; spy.

Spalier [ʃpaˈliːr], *n.* (**—s,** *pl.* **—e**) trellis; — *bilden,* form a lane (*of people*).

Spalierobst [ʃpaˈliːroːpst], *n.* (**—(e)s,** *no pl.*) wall-fruit.

Spalt [ʃpalt], *m.* (**—(e)s,** *pl.* **—e**) crack, rift, cleft, rent; (*glacier*) crevasse.

Spalte [ˈʃpaltə], *f.* (**—,** *pl.* **—n**) (*newspaper*) column.

spalten [ˈʃpaltən], *v.a.* split, cleave, slit. — *v.r. sich* —, divide, break up, split up; (*in two*) bifurcate.

Spaltholz [ˈʃpalthɔlts], *n.* (**—es,** *no pl.*) fire-wood.

Spaltpilz [ˈʃpaltpɪlts], *m.* (**—es,** *pl.* **—e**) fission-fungus.

Spaltung [ˈʃpaltuŋ], *f.* (**—,** *pl.* **—en**) cleavage; (*atomic*) fission; (*fig.*) dissension, rupture; (*Eccl.*) schism.

Span [ʃpaːn], *m.* (**—(e)s,** *pl.* **⸚e**) chip, chippings, shavings.

Spange [ˈʃpaŋə], *f.* (**—,** *pl.* **—n**) clasp, buckle.

Spanien [ˈʃpaːnjən], *n.* Spain.

spanisch [ˈʃpaːnɪʃ], *adj.* Spanish; —*e Wand,* folding screen; *es kommt mir* — *vor,* it is Greek to me.

Spann [ʃpan], *m.* (**—(e)s,** *pl.* **—e**) instep.

Spanne [ˈʃpanə], *f.* (**—,** *pl.* **—n**) span; *eine* — *Zeit,* a short space of time.

spannen [ˈʃpanən], *v.a.* stretch, strain, span.

spannend [ˈʃpanənt], *adj.* thrilling, tense.

Spannkraft [ˈʃpankraft], *f.* (**—,** *no pl.*) elasticity.

Spannung [ˈʃpanuŋ], *f.* (**—,** *pl.* **—en**) tension, suspense, strain; (*fig.*) eager expectation, curiosity, suspense, close attention; (*Elec.*) voltage.

Sparbüchse

Sparbüchse [ˈʃpaːrbyksə], *f.* (—, *pl.* —n) money-box.

sparen [ˈʃpaːrən], *v.a.*, *v.n.* save, economise, put by, lay by.

Spargel [ˈʃpargəl], *m.* (—s, *pl.* —) asparagus.

Spargelder [ˈʃpaːrgɛldər], *n. pl.* savings.

Sparkasse [ˈʃpaːrkasə], *f.* (—, *pl.* —n) savings bank.

spärlich [ˈʃpɛːrlɪç], *adj.* scant, scanty, sparse.

Sparpfennig [ˈʃpaːrpfɛnɪç], *m.* (—s, *pl.* —e) nest-egg.

Sparren [ˈʃparən], *m.* (—s, *pl.* —) spar, rafter; *er hat einen* —, he has a screw loose.

sparsam [ˈʃpaːrzaːm], *adj.* economical, thrifty, frugal.

Spaß [ʃpaːs], *m.* (—es, *pl.* ⸚e) jest, fun, joke; *aus* —, *im* —, *zum* —, in fun; — *verstehen*, take a joke; *es macht mir* —, it amuses me, it is fun for me.

spaßen [ˈʃpaːsən], *v.n.* jest, joke.

spaßhaft [ˈʃpaːshaft], *adj.* funny, facetious, jocular.

Spaßverderber [ˈʃpaːsfɛrdɛrbər], *m.* (—s, *pl.* —) spoil-sport.

Spaßvogel [ˈʃpaːsfoːgəl], *m.* (—s, *pl.* ⸚) wag.

Spat [ʃpaːt], *m.* (—(e)s, *pl.* —e) (*Min.*) spar.

spät [ʃpɛːt], *adj.* late; *wie* — *ist es?* what is the time? *zu* — *kommen*, be late.

Spätabend [ˈʃpɛːtaːbənt], *m.* (—s, *pl.* —e) latter part of the evening, late evening.

Spatel [ˈʃpaːtəl], *m.* (—s, *pl.* —) spatula.

Spaten [ˈʃpaːtən], *m.* (—s, *pl.* —) spade.

Spatenstich [ˈʃpaːtənʃtɪç], *m.* (—(e)s, *pl.* —e) *den ersten* — *tun*, turn the first sod.

später [ˈʃpɛːtər], *adv.* later (on), afterwards.

spätestens [ˈʃpɛːtəstəns], *adv.* at the latest.

Spätling [ˈʃpɛːtlɪŋ], *m.* (—s, *pl.* —e) late arrival; late fruit.

Spätsommer [ˈʃpɛːtzɔmər], *m.* (—s, *pl.* —) Indian summer.

Spatz [ʃpats], *m.* (—en *pl.* —en) (*Orn.*) sparrow.

spazieren [ʃpaˈtsiːrən], *v.n.* (*aux.* sein) walk leisurely, stroll; — *gehen*, go for a walk, take a stroll; — *führen*, take for a walk.

Spazierfahrt [ʃpaˈtsiːrfaːrt], *f.* (—, *pl.* —en) (pleasure-)drive.

Spazierstock [ʃpaˈtsiːrʃtɔk], *m.* (—s, *pl.* ⸚e) walking-stick.

Spazierweg [ʃpaˈtsiːrveːk], *m.* (—s, *pl.* —e) walk, promenade.

Specht [ʃpɛçt], *m.* (—(e)s, *pl.* —e) (*Orn.*) woodpecker.

Speck [ʃpɛk], *m.* (—(e)s, *no pl.*) bacon; *eine Scheibe* —, a rasher of bacon.

speckig [ˈʃpɛkɪç], *adj.* fat.

Speckschwarte [ˈʃpɛkʃvartə], *f.* (—, *pl.* —n) bacon-rind.

Speckseite [ˈʃpɛkzaɪtə], *f.* (—, *pl.* —n) flitch of bacon.

spedieren [ʃpeˈdiːrən], *v.a.* forward; despatch.

Spediteur [ʃpediˈtøːr], *m.* (—s, *pl.* —e) forwarding agent, furniture-remover, carrier.

Spedition [ʃpediˈtsjoːn], *f.* (—, *pl.* —en) conveyance; forwarding agency.

Speer [ʃpeːr], *m.* (—(e)s, *pl.* —e) spear, lance.

Speiche [ˈʃpaɪçə], *f.* (—, *pl.* —n) spoke.

Speichel [ˈʃpaɪçəl], *m.* (—s, *no pl.*) spittle, saliva.

Speicher [ˈʃpaɪçər], *m.* (—s, *pl.* —) granary; warehouse, storehouse; loft.

speien [ˈʃpaɪən], *v.a.*, *v.n. irr.* spit; vomit, be sick.

Speise [ˈʃpaɪzə], *f.* (—, *pl.* —n) food, nourishment, dish.

Speisekammer [ˈʃpaɪzəkamər], *f.* (—, *pl.* —n) larder, pantry.

Speisekarte [ˈʃpaɪzəkartə], *f.* (—, *pl.* —n) bill of fare, menu.

speisen [ˈʃpaɪzən], *v.a.* feed, give to eat. — *v.n.* eat, dine, sup, lunch.

Speiseröhre [ˈʃpaɪzərøːrə], *f.* (—, *pl.* —n) gullet.

Speisewagen [ˈʃpaɪzəvaːgən], *m.* (—s, *pl.* —) (*Railw.*) dining-car.

Spektakel [ʃpɛkˈtaːkəl], *m.* (—s, *no pl.*) uproar, hubbub; shindy, rumpus; noise, row.

Spektrum [ˈʃpɛktrum], *n.* (—s, *pl.* **Spektren**) spectrum.

Spekulant [ʃpekuˈlant], *m.* (—en, *pl.* —en) speculator.

spekulieren [ʃpekuˈliːrən], *v.n.* speculate; theorise.

Spende [ˈʃpɛndə], *f.* (—, *pl.* —n) gift, donation; bounty.

spenden [ˈʃpɛndən], *v.a.* bestow, donate, contribute.

Spender [ˈʃpɛndər], *m.* (—s, *pl.* —) donor, giver, benefactor.

spendieren [ʃpɛnˈdiːrən], *v.a.* (give a) treat, pay for, stand.

Sperber [ˈʃpɛrbər], *m.* (—s, *pl.* —) (*Orn.*) sparrow-hawk.

Sperling [ˈʃpɛrlɪŋ], *m.* (—s, *pl.* —e) (*Orn.*) sparrow.

sperrangelweit [ˈʃpɛraŋəlvaɪt], *adv.* wide open.

Sperre [ˈʃpɛrə], *f.* (—, *pl.* —n) shutting, closing, blockade, blocking; closure; ban; (*Railw.*) barrier.

sperren [ˈʃpɛrən], *v.a.* spread out; (*Typ.*) space; shut, close, block; cut off; *ins Gefängnis* —, put in prison. — *v.r. sich* — *gegen*, offer resistance to.

Sperrhaken [ˈʃpɛrhaːkən], *m.* (—s, *pl.* —) catch, ratchet.

Sperrsitz [ˈʃpɛrzɪts], *m.* (—es, *pl.* —e) (*Theat.*) stall.

Sperrung [ˈʃpɛruŋ], *f.* (—, *pl.* —en) barring, obstruction, block, blockade; (*Comm.*) embargo.

Sperrzeit [ˈʃpɛrtsaɪt], *f.* (—, *pl.* —en) closing-time.

Spesen [ˈʃpeːzən], *f. pl.* charges, expenses.

spesenfrei ['ʃpeːzənfraɪ], *adj.* free of charge; expenses paid.

Spezereien [ʃpeːtsəˈraɪən], *f. pl.* spices.

spezial [ʃpeˈtsjaːl], *adj.* special, particular.

spezialisieren [ʃpetsjaliˈziːrən], *v.a.* specify. — *v.r. sich* —, specialise.

Spezialist [ʃpetsjaˈlɪst], *m.* (—**en**, *pl.* —**en**) specialist, expert.

Spezialität [ʃpetsjaliˈtɛːt], *f.* (—, *pl.* —**en**) speciality, (*Am.*) specialty.

Spezies ['ʃpeːtsjɛs], *f.* (—, *pl.* —) species; (*Maths.*) rule.

Spezifikation [ʃpetsifikaˈtsjoːn], *f.* (—, *pl.* —**en**) specification.

spezifisch [ʃpeˈtsiːfɪʃ], *adj.* specific.

spezifizieren [ʃpetsifiˈtsiːrən], *v.a.* specify.

Spezifizierung [ʃpetsifiˈtsiːruŋ], *f.* (— *pl.* —**en**) specification.

Spezimen ['ʃpeːtsimən], *n.* (—**s**, *pl.* —**mina**) specimen.

Sphäre ['sfɛːrə], *f.* (—, *pl.* —**n**) sphere.

sphärisch ['sfɛːrɪʃ], *adj.* spherical.

Spickaal ['ʃpɪkaːl], *m.* (—**s**, *pl.* —**e**) smoked eel.

spicken ['ʃpɪkən], *v.a.* lard; *den Beutel* —, fill o.'s purse.

Spiegel ['ʃpiːɡəl], *m.* (—**s**, *pl.* —) mirror, looking-glass.

spiegelblank ['ʃpiːɡəlblaŋk], *adj.* sparkling, shiny, polished.

Spiegelei ['ʃpiːɡəlaɪ], *n.* (—**s**, *pl.* —**er**) fried egg.

Spiegelfechterei ['ʃpiːɡəlfɛçtəraɪ], *f.* (—, *pl.* —**en**) shadow-boxing, make-believe.

Spiegelfenster ['ʃpiːɡəlfɛnstər], *n.* (—**s**, *pl.* —) plate-glass window.

spiegeln ['ʃpiːɡəln], *v.n.* glitter, shine. — *v.a.* reflect. — *v.r. sich* —, be reflected.

Spiegelscheibe ['ʃpiːɡəlʃaɪbə], *f.* (—, *pl.* —**n**) plate-glass pane.

Spiegelung ['ʃpiːɡəluŋ], *f.* (—, *pl.* —**en**) reflection; mirage.

Spiel [ʃpiːl], *n.* (—(**e**)**s**, *pl.* —**e**) play; game; sport; (*Theat.*) acting, performance; (*Mus.*) playing; *ehrliches (unehrliches)* —, fair (foul) play; *leichtes* —, walk-over; *auf dem* — *stehen*, be at stake; *aufs* — *setzen*, stake, risk; *die Hand im* — *haben*, have a finger in the pie; *gewonnenes* — *haben*, gain o.'s point; *ein gewagtes* — *treiben*, play a bold game; *sein* — *mit einem treiben*, trifle with s.o.

Spielart ['ʃpiːlaːrt], *f.* (—, *pl.* —**en**) manner of playing; variety.

Spielbank ['ʃpiːlbaŋk], *f.* (—, *pl.* —**en**) casino; gambling-table.

Spieldose ['ʃpiːldoːzə], *f.* (—, *pl.* —**n**) musical box.

spielen ['ʃpiːlən], *v.a., v.n.* play; gamble; (*Mus.*) play; (*Theat.*) act; *eine Rolle* —, play a part; *mit dem Gedanken* —, toy with the idea.

spielend ['ʃpiːlənt], *adv.* easily.

Spieler ['ʃpiːlər], *m.* (—**s**, *pl.* —) player; gambler; gamester.

Spielerei [ʃpiːləˈraɪ], *f.* (—, *pl.* —**en**) child's play; trivialities.

Spielhölle ['ʃpiːlhœlə], *f.* (—, *pl.* —**n**) gambling-den.

Spielmann ['ʃpiːlman], *m.* (—**s**, *pl.* **Spielleute**) musician, fiddler; (*Middle Ages*) minstrel.

Spielmarke ['ʃpiːlmarkə], *f.* (—, *pl.* —**n**) counter, chip.

Spielplan ['ʃpiːlplaːn], *m.* (—**s**, *pl.* ¨**e**) (*Theat.*) repertory.

Spielplatz ['ʃpiːlplats], *m.* (—**es**, *pl.* ¨**e**) playground.

Spielraum ['ʃpiːlraum], *m.* (—**s**, *no pl.*) elbow-room; (*fig.*) scope; margin; clearance.

Spielsache ['ʃpiːlzaxə], *f.* (—, *pl.* —**n**) toy, plaything.

Spielschule ['ʃpiːlʃuːlə], *f.* (—, *pl.* —**n**) infant-school, kindergarten.

Spieltisch ['ʃpiːltɪʃ], *m.* (—**es**, *pl.* —**e**) card-table.

Spieluhr ['ʃpiːluːr], *f.* (—, *pl.* —**en**) musical clock.

Spielverderber ['ʃpiːlfɛrdɛrbər], *m.* (—**s**, *pl.* —) spoilsport.

Spielwaren ['ʃpiːlvaːrən], *f. pl.* toys.

Spielzeit ['ʃpiːltsaɪt], *f.* (—, *pl.* —**en**) playtime; (*Theat.*) season.

Spielzeug ['ʃpiːltsɔyk], *n.* (—**s**, *pl.* —**e**) plaything, toy.

Spieß [ʃpiːs], *m.* (—**es**, *pl.* —**e**) spear, pike; (*Cul.*) spit.

Spießbürger ['ʃpiːsbyrɡər], *m.* (—**s**, *pl.* —) Philistine.

spießen ['ʃpiːsən], *v.a.* spear, pierce.

Spießer ['ʃpiːsər], *m.* (—**s**, *pl.* —) Philistine.

Spießgeselle ['ʃpiːsɡəzɛlə], *m.* (—**n**, *pl.* —**n**) accomplice, companion *or* partner in crime.

spießig ['ʃpiːsɪç], *adj.* (*coll.*) Philistine, uncultured, narrow-minded.

Spießruten ['ʃpiːsruːtən], *f. pl.* — *laufen*, run the gauntlet.

Spinat [ʃpiˈnaːt], *m.* (—**s**, *no pl.*) spinach.

Spind [ʃpɪnt], *n.* (—(**e**)**s**, *pl.* —**e**) cupboard.

Spindel ['ʃpɪndəl], *f.* (—, *pl.* —**n**) spindle; distaff; (*staircase*) newel.

spindeldürr ['ʃpɪndəldyr], *adj.* as thin as a lath.

Spindelholz ['ʃpɪndəlhɔlts], *n.* (—**es**, *no pl.*) spindle-tree wood.

Spinett [ʃpiˈnɛt], *n.* (—**s**, *pl.* —**e**) spinet.

Spinne ['ʃpɪnə], *f.* (—, *pl.* —**n**) spider.

spinnefeind ['ʃpɪnəfaɪnt], *adj. einander* — *sein*, hate each other like poison.

spinnen ['ʃpɪnən], *v.a. irr.* spin. — *v.n.* (*coll.*) be off o.'s head; be crazy.

Spinnerei [ʃpɪnəˈraɪ], *f.* (—, *pl.* —**en**) spinning-mill.

Spinngewebe ['ʃpɪnɡəveːbə], *n.* (—**s**, *pl.* —) cobweb.

Spinnrocken ['ʃpɪnrɔkən], *m.* (—**s**, *pl.* —) distaff.

spintisieren [ʃpɪntiˈziːrən], *v.n.* muse, meditate.

Spion

Spion [ʃpi'oːn], *m.* (**—s**, *pl.* **—e**) spy.

spionieren [ʃpio'niːrən], *v.n.* spy, pry.

Spirale [ʃpi'raːlə], *f.* (**—**, *pl.* **—n**) spiral.

Spirituosen [ʃpiritu'oːzən], *pl.* spirits, liquors.

Spiritus [ʃpiːritus], *m.* (**—**, *pl.* **—se**) alcohol, spirits of wine; *denaturierter* **—**, methylated spirits.

Spiritusbrennerei [ʃpiːritusbrɛnərai], *f.* (**—**, *pl.* **—en**) distillery.

Spiritusgehalt [ʃpiːritusgəhalt], *m.* (**—s**, *pl.* **—e**) (*alcoholic*) strength, proof.

Spital [ʃpi'taːl], *n.* (**—s**, *pl.* **·er**) infirmary; hospital.

Spitz [ʃpits], *m.* (**—es**, *pl.* **—e**) Pomeranian dog; *einen — haben*, (*coll.*) be slightly tipsy.

spitz [ʃpits], *adj.* pointed; (*fig.*) snappy, biting.

Spitzbart [ʃpitsbaːrt], *m.* (**—s**, *pl.* **·e**) imperial (beard), pointed beard.

Spitzbogen [ʃpitsboːgən], *m.* (**—s**, *pl.* **—**) pointed arch, Gothic arch.

Spitzbogenfenster [ʃpitsboːgənfɛnstər], *n.* (**—s**, *pl.* **—**) lancet window.

Spitzbube [ʃpitsbuːbə], *m.* (**—n**, *pl.* **—n**) rogue; rascal; scamp.

Spitzbubenstreich [ʃpitsbuːbənʃtraiç], *m.* (**—(e)s**, *pl.* **—e**) act of roguery, knavery.

spitzbübisch [ʃpitsbyːbiʃ], *adj.* roguish.

Spitze [ʃpitsə], *f.* (**—**, *pl.* **—n**) point; tip; top, peak; extremity; (*pipe*) mouthpiece; (*cigarette*) holder; (*pen*) nib; lace; *etwas auf die — treiben*, carry s.th. to extremes; *an der — stehen*, be at the head of.

Spitzel [ʃpitsəl], *m.* (**—s**, *pl.* **—**) policeagent; informer.

spitzen [ʃpitsən], *v.a.* sharpen; *die Ohren —*, prick up o.'s ears; *sich auf etwas —*, await s.th. eagerly, be all agog for s.th.

Spitzenbelastung [ʃpitsənbəlastuŋ], *f.* (**—**, *pl.* **—en**) peak load.

Spitzenleistung [ʃpitsənlaistuŋ], *f.* (**—**, *pl.* **—en**) maximum output; peak performance.

Spitzentuch [ʃpitsəntuːx], *n.* (**—(e)s**, *pl.* **·er**) lace scarf.

spitzfindig [ʃpitsfindiç], *adj.* subtle, crafty; hair-splitting.

Spitzhacke [ʃpitshakə], *f.* (**—**, *pl.* **—n**) pickaxe.

spitzig [ʃpitsiç], *adj.* pointed, sharp; (*fig.*) biting, poignant.

Spitzmaus [ʃpitsmaus], *f.* (**—**, *pl.* **·e**) (*Zool.*) shrew.

Spitzname [ʃpitsnaːmə], *m.* (**—ns**, *pl.* **—n**) nickname.

spitzwinklig [ʃpitsviŋkliç], *adj.* acute-angled.

spleißen [ʃplaisən], *v.a. irr.* split, cleave.

Splitter [ʃplitər], *m.* (**—s**, *pl.* **—**) splinter, chip.

splitternackt [ʃplitərnakt], *adj.* stark naked.

splittern [ʃplitərn], *v.n.* (*aux.* sein) splinter.

spontan [ʃpɔn'taːn], *adj.* spontaneous.

sporadisch [ʃpo'raːdiʃ], *adj.* sporadic.

Spore [ʃpoːrə], *f.* (**—**, *pl.* **—n**) spore.

Sporn [ʃpɔrn], *m.* (**—s**, *pl.* **Sporen**) spur.

spornstreichs [ʃpɔrnʃtraiçs], *adv.* posthaste, at once.

Sportler [ʃpɔrtlər], *m.* (**—s**, *pl.* **—**) athlete, sportsman.

sportlich [ʃpɔrtliç], *adj.* athletic; sporting.

sportsmäßig [ʃpɔrtsmɛːsiç], *adj.* sportsmanlike.

Spott [ʃpɔt], *m.* (**—(e)s**, *no pl.*) mockery; scorn; *Gegenstand des —s*, laughing-stock; *— treiben mit*, mock, deride; *zum Schaden den — hinzufügen*, add insult to injury.

spottbillig [ʃpɔtbiliç], *adj.* ridiculously cheap, dirt-cheap.

Spöttelei [ʃpœtə'lai], *f.* (**—**, *pl.* **—en**) sarcasm.

spötteln [ʃpœtəln], *v.n.* mock, jeer.

spotten [ʃpɔtən], *v.a.*, *v.n.* deride, scoff (at); *es spottet jeder Beschreibung*, it defies description.

Spötter [ʃpœtər], *m.* (**—s**, *pl.* **—**) mocker, scoffer.

Spötterei [ʃpœtə'rai], *f.* (**—**, *pl.* **—en**) mockery, derision.

Spottgedicht [ʃpɔtgədiçt], *n.* (**—(e)s**, *pl.* **—e**) satirical poem.

spöttisch [ʃpœtiʃ], *adj.* mocking, satirical, ironical, scoffing.

spottlustig [ʃpɔtlustiç], *adj.* flippant, satirical.

Spottschrift [ʃpɔtʃrift], *f.* (**—**, *pl.* **—en**) satire, lampoon.

Sprache [ʃpraːxə], *f.* (**—**, *pl.* **—n**) speech, language, tongue; expression; diction; discussion; *etwas zur — bringen*, bring a subject up; *zur — kommen*, come up for discussion; *heraus mit der —!* speak out!

Sprachfehler [ʃpraːxfeːlər], *m.* (**—s**, *pl.* **—**) impediment in o.'s speech.

sprachfertig [ʃpraːxfɛrtiç], *adj.* having a ready tongue; a good linguist, fluent.

Sprachgebrauch [ʃpraːxgəbraux], *m.* (**—(e)s**, *no pl.*) (linguistic) usage.

Sprachkenner [ʃpraːxkɛnər], *m.* (**—s**, *pl.* **—**) linguist.

sprachkundig [ʃpraːxkundiç], *adj.* proficient in languages.

Sprachlehre [ʃpraːxleːrə], *f.* (**—**; *no pl.*) grammar.

sprachlich [ʃpraːxliç], *adj.* linguistic.

sprachlos [ʃpraːxloːs], *adj.* speechless, tongue-tied; *— dastehen*, be dumbfounded.

Sprachrohr [ʃpraːxroːr], *n.* (**—s**, *pl.* **—e**) megaphone, speaking-tube; (*fig.*) mouthpiece.

Sprachschatz [ʃpraːxʃats], *m.* (**—es**, *no pl.*) vocabulary.

Sprachvergleichung [ʃpraːxfɛrglaiçuŋ], *f.* (**—**, *no pl.*) comparative philology.

Sprachwerkzeug ['ʃpra:xvərktsɔyk], *n.* (—s, *pl.* —e) organ of speech.
Sprachwissenschaft ['ʃpra:xvisənʃaft], *f.* (—, *pl.* —en) linguistics, philology.
sprechen ['ʃprɛçən], *v.a.,v.n. irr.* speak, declare, say; talk; *für einen* —, put in a good word for s.o., speak up for s.o.; *er ist nicht zu* —, he is not available; *auf einen gut zu* — *sein*, feel well disposed towards s.o.; *schuldig* —, pronounce guilty; *das Urteil* —, pass sentence.
sprechend ['ʃprɛçənt], *adj.* expressive; — *ähnlich*, strikingly alike.
Sprecher ['ʃprɛçər], *m.* (—s, *pl.* —) speaker, orator, spokesman; (*Rad.*) announcer.
Sprechstunde ['ʃprɛçʃtundə], *f.* (—, *pl.* —n) consulting hours, surgery hours; office hours.
Sprechzimmer ['ʃprɛçtsimər], *n.* (—s, *pl.*—) consulting-room.
spreizen ['ʃpraɪtsən], *v.a.* spread open; *die Beine* —, plant o.'s legs wide apart, straddle. — *v.r. sich* —, give o.s. airs.
Sprengbombe ['ʃprɛŋbɔmbə], *f.* (—, *pl.* —n) (high explosive) bomb.
Sprengel ['ʃprɛŋəl], *m.* (—s, *pl.* —) diocese.
sprengen ['ʃprɛŋən], *v.a.* sprinkle; water; burst, explode; burst open, blow up; *eine Versammlung* —, break up a meeting. — *v.n.* (*aux.* sein) ride at full speed, gallop.
Sprengpulver ['ʃprɛŋpulvər], *n.* (—s, *no pl.*) blasting-powder.
Sprengstoff ['ʃprɛŋʃtɔf], *m.* (—es, *pl.* —e) explosive.
Sprengwagen ['ʃprɛŋva:gən], *m.* (—s, *pl.* —) sprinkler; water-cart.
sprenkeln ['ʃprɛŋkəln], *v.a.* speckle.
Spreu [ʃprɔy], *f.* (—, *no pl.*) chaff.
Sprichwort ['ʃprɪçvɔrt], *n.* (—s, *pl.* ̈er) proverb, adage, saying.
sprießen ['ʃpri:sən], *v.n. irr.* sprout, shoot, germinate.
Springbrunnen ['ʃprɪŋbrunən], *m.* (—s, *pl.* —) fountain.
springen ['ʃprɪŋən], *v.n. irr.* (*aux.* sein) spring, leap, jump; (*glass*) burst; *etwas* — *lassen*, (*coll.*) treat s.o. to s.th.
Springer ['ʃprɪŋər], *m.* (—s, *pl.* —) jumper, acrobat; (*Chess*) knight.
Springflut ['ʃprɪŋflu:t], *f.* (—, *pl.* —en) spring-tide.
Springtau ['ʃprɪŋtau], *n.* (—s, *pl.* —e) skipping-rope; (*Naut.*) slip-rope.
Sprit [ʃprɪt], *m.* (—s, *pl.* —e) spirit alcohol; (*sl.*) fuel, petrol.
Spritze ['ʃprɪtsə], *f.* (—, *pl.* —n) squirt, syringe; fire-engine; (*coll.*) injection.
spritzen ['ʃprɪtsən], *v.a.* squirt, spout, spray, sprinkle; (*coll.*) inject. — *v.n.* gush forth.
Spritzkuchen ['ʃprɪtsku:xən], *m.* (—s, *pl.* —) fritter.
Spritztour ['ʃprɪtstu:r], *f.* (—, *pl.* —en) (*coll.*) pleasure trip, outing; (*coll.*) spin.

spröde ['ʃprø:də], *adj.* (*material*) brittle; (*person*) stubborn; coy, prim, prudish.
Sprödigkeit ['ʃprø:dɪçkaɪt], *f.* (—, *no pl.*) (*material*) brittleness; (*person*) stubbornness; coyness, primness, prudery.
Sproß [ʃprɔs], *m.* (—sses, *pl.* —sse) sprout, shoot, germ; (*fig.*) scion, offspring.
Sprosse ['ʃprɔsə], *f.* (—, *pl.* —n) (*ladder*) step, rung.
Sprößling ['ʃprœslɪŋ], *m.* (—s, *pl.* —e) scion, offspring.
Sprotte ['ʃprɔtə], *f.* (—, *pl.* —n) sprat.
Spruch [ʃprux], *m.* (—(e)s, *pl.* ̈e) saying, aphorism; proverb; (*obs.*) saw; (*judge*) sentence, verdict.
spruchreif ['ʃpruxraɪf], *adj.* ripe for judgment; ready for a decision.
Sprudel ['ʃpru:dəl], *m.* (—s, *pl.* —) bubbling spring; (*coll.*) soda water.
sprudeln ['ʃpru:dəln], *v.n.* bubble, gush.
sprühen ['ʃpry:ən], *v.a.* sprinkle, scatter, spray. — *v.n.* sparkle, emit sparks; (*rain*) drizzle.
sprühend ['ʃpry:ənt], *adj.* (*fig.*) sparkling, scintillating, brilliant.
Sprühregen ['ʃpry:re:gən], *m.* (—s, *no pl.*) drizzling rain, drizzle.
Sprung [ʃpruŋ], *m.* (—(e)s, *pl.* ̈e) leap, bound, jump; chink, crack; *nur auf einen* — *zu Besuch kommen*, pay a flying visit; *auf dem* — *sein zu*, be on the point of; *sich auf den* — *machen*, cut and run, (*coll.*) fly; *große* ̈e *machen*, (*coll.*) live it up, cut a dash.
Sprungfeder ['ʃpruŋfe:dər], *f.* (—, *pl.* —n) spring.
Sprungkraft ['ʃpruŋkraft], *f.* (—, *no pl.*) springiness, elasticity, buoyancy.
Spucke ['ʃpukə], *f.* (—, *no pl.*) spittle, saliva.
spucken ['ʃpukən], *v.a.,v.n.* spit.
Spuk [ʃpu:k], *m.* (—s, *pl.* —e) haunting; ghost, spectre, apparition; (*coll.*) spook.
spuken ['ʃpu:kən], *v.n.* haunt; be haunted.
spukhaft ['ʃpu:khaft], *adj.* uncanny, phantom-like, ghost-like, spooky.
Spule ['ʃpu:lə], *f.* (—, *pl.* —n) spool; (*Elec.*) coil.
Spüleimer ['ʃpy:laɪmər], *m.* (—s, *pl.* —) slop-pail.
spülen ['ʃpy:lən], *v.a.* rinse, wash.
Spülicht ['ʃpy:lɪçt], *n.* (—s, *no pl.*) dish-water.
Spund [ʃpunt], *m.* (—(e)s, *pl.* ̈e) bung.
Spundloch ['ʃpuntlɔx], *n.* (—s, *pl.* ̈er) bung-hole.
Spur [ʃpu:r], *f.* (—, *pl.* —en) footprint, track, trail; spoor; (*fig.*) trace, vestige; *frische* —, hot scent; *einer Sache auf die* — *kommen*, be on the track of s.th.; *keine* — *von*, not a trace of, not an inkling of.
spüren ['ʃpy:rən], *v.a.* trace, track (down); feel, sense, notice.
Spürhund ['ʃpy:rhunt], *m.* (—s, *pl.* —e) tracker dog, setter, beagle; (*fig.*) spy, sleuth.

spurlos

spurlos ['ʃpuːrloːs], *adj.* trackless, without a trace; *es ging — an ihm vorüber,* it left no mark on him; *— verschwinden,* vanish into thin air.

Spürsinn ['ʃpyːrzɪn], *m.* (**—s,** *no pl.*) scent; flair; sagacity, shrewdness.

Spurweite ['ʃpuːrvaɪtə], *f.* (**—,** *pl.* **—n**) gauge, width of track.

sputen ['ʃpuːtən], *v.r. sich —,* make haste, hurry.

Staat [ʃtaːt], *m.* (**—(e)s,** *pl.* **—en**) state; government; pomp, show, parade; *— machen,* make a show of.

Staatenbund ['ʃtaːtənbunt], *m.* (**—(e)s,** *pl.* ˙e) confederacy, federation.

staatlich ['ʃtaːtlɪç], *adj.* belonging to the state, public, national.

Staatsangehörige ['ʃtaːtsangəhøːrɪgə], *m.* (**—n,** *pl.* **—n**) citizen (of a country), subject, national.

Staatsangehörigkeit ['ʃtaːtsangəhøːrɪçkaɪt], *f.* (**—,** *pl.* **—en**) nationality.

Staatsanwalt ['ʃtaːtsanvalt], *m.* (**—s,** *pl.* ˙e) public prosecutor, Attorney-General.

Staatsbeamte ['ʃtaːtsbəamtə], *m.* (**—n,** *pl.* **—n**) civil servant, employee of the state.

Staatsbürger ['ʃtaːtsbyrgər], *m.* (**—s,** *pl.* **—**) citizen, national.

Staatsdienst ['ʃtaːtsdiːnst], *m.* (**—(e)s,** *pl.* **—e**) civil service, government service.

Staatseinkünfte ['ʃtaːtsaɪnkynftə], *f. pl.* public revenue.

Staatsgesetz ['ʃtaːtsgəzɛts], *n.* (**—es,** *pl.* **—e**) statute law.

Staatsgewalt ['ʃtaːtsgəvalt], *f.* (**—,** *no pl.*) executive power.

Staatshaushalt ['ʃtaːtshaushalt], *m.* (**—s,** *no pl.*) state finances, budget.

Staatshaushaltsanschlag ['ʃtaːtshaushaltsanʃlaːk], *m.* (**—s,** *pl.* ˙e) budget estimates.

Staatskanzler ['ʃtaːtskantslər], *m.* (**—s,** *pl.* **—**) Chancellor.

Staatskasse ['ʃtaːtskasə], *f.* (**—,** *no pl.*) public exchequer, treasury.

Staatskörper ['ʃtaːtskœrpər], *m.* (**—s,** *pl.* **—**) body politic.

Staatskosten ['ʃtaːtskɔstən], *f. pl. auf* **—,** at (the) public expense.

Staatskunst ['ʃtaːtskunst], *f.* (**—,** *no pl.*) statesmanship; statecraft.

Staatsminister ['ʃtaːtsmɪnɪstər], *m.* (**—s,** *pl.* **—**) cabinet minister; minister of state.

Staatsrat ['ʃtaːtsraːt], *m.* (**—s,** *no pl.*) council of state; (*pl.* ˙e) councillor of state.

Staatsrecht ['ʃtaːtsrɛçt], *n.* (**—(e)s,** *no pl.*) constitutional law.

Staatssiegel ['ʃtaːtsziːgəl], *n.* (**—s,** *pl.* **—**) Great Seal, official seal.

Staatsstreich ['ʃtaːtsʃtraɪç], *m.* (**—(e)s,** *pl.* **—e**) coup d'état.

Staatswirtschaft ['ʃtaːtsvɪrtʃaft], *f.* (**—,** *no pl.*) political economy.

Staatszimmer ['ʃtaːtstsɪmər], *n.* (**—s,** *pl.* **—**) state apartment.

Stab [ʃtaːp], *m.* (**—(e)s,** *pl.* ˙e) staff; stick, rod, pole; crosier; mace; (*Mil.*) field-officers, staff; *den — über einen brechen,* condemn s.o. (to death).

stabil [ʃtaˈbiːl], *adj.* steady, stable, firm.

stabilisieren [ʃtabiliˈziːrən], *v.a.* stabilise.

Stabreim ['ʃtaːpraɪm], *m.* (**—s,** *no pl.*) alliteration.

Stabsarzt ['ʃtaːpsartst], *m.* (**—es,** *pl.* ˙e) (*Mil.*) medical officer.

Stabsquartier ['ʃtaːpskvartiːr], *n.* (**—s,** *pl.* **—e**) (*Mil.*) headquarters.

Stachel ['ʃtaxəl], *m.* (**—s,** *pl.* **—n**) (*animal*) sting; (*plant*) prickle, thorn; (*fig.*) keen edge, sting; stimulus; *wider den — löcken,* kick against the pricks.

Stachelbeere ['ʃtaxəlbeːrə], *f.* (**—,** *pl.* **—n**) (*Bot.*) gooseberry.

Stachelschwein ['ʃtaxəlʃvaɪn], *n.* (**—s,** *pl.* **—e**) (*Zool.*) hedgehog, porcupine.

stachlig ['ʃtaxlɪç], *adj.* prickly, thorny; (*fig.*) disagreeable.

Stadion ['ʃtaːdjɔn], *n.* (**—s,** *pl.* **—dien**) sports-arena, stadium.

Stadium ['ʃtaːdjum], *n.* (**—s,** *pl.* **—dien**) stage (of development), phase.

Stadt [ʃtat], *f.* (**—,** *pl.* ˙e) town; city.

Stadtbahn ['ʃtatbaːn], *f.* (**—,** *pl.* **—en**) metropolitan railway.

Städtchen ['ʃtɛtçən], *n.* (**—s,** *pl.* **—**) small town, township.

Städter ['ʃtɛtər], *m.* (**—s,** *pl.* **—**) townsman.

Stadtgemeinde ['ʃtatgəmaɪndə], *f.* (**—,** *pl.* **—n**) municipality.

städtisch ['ʃtɛtɪʃ], *adj.* municipal.

Stadtmauer ['ʃtatmauər], *f.* (**—,** *pl.* **—n**) town wall, city wall.

Stadtrat ['ʃtatraːt], *m.* (**—s,** *no pl.*) town council; (*pl.* ˙e) town councillor; alderman.

Stadtteil ['ʃtattaɪl], *m.* (**—s,** *pl.* **—e**) ward, district, part of a town.

Stadttor ['ʃtattoːr], *n.* (**—s,** *pl.* **—e**) city-gate.

Stadtverordnete ['ʃtatferɔrdnətə], *m.* (**—n,** *pl.* **—n**) town councillor.

Stafette [ʃtaˈfɛtə], *f.* (**—,** *pl.* **—n**) courier; relay.

Staffel ['ʃtafəl], *f.* (**—,** *pl.* **—n**) step, rundle, rung, round; relay; (*fig.*) degree; (*Aviat.*) squadron.

Staffelei [ʃtafəˈlaɪ], *f.* (**—,** *pl.* **—en**) easel.

staffeln ['ʃtafəln], *v.a.* grade; differentiate; stagger.

Staffelung ['ʃtafəluŋ], *f.* (**—,** *pl.* **—en**) gradation.

stagnieren [ʃtagˈniːrən], *v.n.* stagnate.

Stahl [ʃtaːl], *m.* (**—(e)s,** *pl.* ˙e) steel.

stählen ['ʃtɛːlən], *v.a.* steel, harden, temper; brace.

stählern ['ʃtɛːlərn], *adj.* made of steel, steely.

Stahlquelle ['ʃtaːlkvɛlə], *f.* (**—,** *pl.* **—n**) chalybeate spring; mineral spring.

Stahlstich ['ʃtaːlʃtɪç], *m.* (**—(e)s,** *pl.* **—e**) steel-engraving.

Stählung ['ʃtɛːluŋ], *f.* (—, *no pl.*) steeling; (*fig.*) bracing.

Stahlwaren ['ʃtaːlvaːrən], *f. pl.* hardware, cutlery.

Stall [ʃtal], *m.* (—(e)s, *pl.* ·̈e) stable; (*pig*) sty; (*dog*) kennel.

Stallbursche ['ʃtalburʃə], *m.* (—n, *pl.* —n) stable-boy, groom.

Stallungen ['ʃtaluŋən], *f. pl.* stabling, stables.

Stambul ['stambul], *n.* Istanbul.

Stamm [ʃtam], *m.* (—(e)s, *pl.* ·̈e) (*tree*) trunk; (*people*) tribe, family, race; (*words*) stem; root.

Stammaktie ['ʃtamaktsjə], *f.* (—, *pl.* —n) (*Comm.*) original share.

Stammbaum ['ʃtambaum], *m.* (—s, *pl.* ·̈e) pedigree; family tree.

Stammbuch ['ʃtambuːx], *n.* (—(e)s, *pl.* ·̈er) album.

stammeln ['ʃtaməln], *v.a., v.n.* stammer, stutter; falter.

stammen ['ʃtamən], *v.n.* (*aux.* sein) be descended from, spring from, originate from, stem from; be derived from.

Stammesgenosse ['ʃtaməsgənɔsə], *m.* (—n, *pl.* —n) kinsman, clansman.

Stammgast ['ʃtamgast], *m.* (—es, *pl.* ·̈e) regular customer.

Stammgut ['ʃtamguːt], *n.* (—s, *pl.* ·̈er) family estate.

Stammhalter ['ʃtamhaltər], *m.* (—s, *pl.* —) son and heir; eldest son.

Stammhaus ['ʃtamhaus], *n.* (—es, *pl.* ·̈er) ancestral mansion; (*royalty*) dynasty; (*Comm.*) business headquarters, head office.

stämmig ['ʃtɛmɪç], *adj.* sturdy, strong.

Stammler ['ʃtamlər], *m.* (—s, *pl.* —) stammerer, stutterer.

Stammsilbe ['ʃtamzɪlbə], *f.* (—, *pl.* —n) (*Ling.*) radical syllable.

Stammtafel ['ʃtamtaːfəl], *f.* (—, *pl.* —n) genealogical table.

Stammvater ['ʃtamfaːtər], *m.* (—s, *pl.* ·̈) ancestor, progenitor.

stammverwandt ['ʃtamfɛrvant], *adj.* cognate, kindred.

stampfen ['ʃtampfən], *v.a.* stamp, pound, ram down. — *v.n.* stamp, trample.

Stand [ʃtant], *m.* (—(e)s, *pl.* ·̈e) stand; (*market*) stall; situation, state (of affairs); condition; reading, position; rank, station (in life); (*pl.*) the classes, the estates.

Standarte [ʃtan'dartə], *f.* (—, *pl.* —n) standard, banner.

Standbild ['ʃtantbɪlt], *n.* (—(e)s, *pl.* —er) statue.

Ständchen ['ʃtɛntçən], *n.* (—s, *pl.* —) serenade; *einem ein — bringen*, serenade s.o.

Ständehaus ['ʃtɛndəhaus], *n.* (—es, *pl.* ·̈er) state assembly-hall.

Ständer ['ʃtɛndər], *m.* (—s, *pl.* —) stand, pedestal; post; (upright) desk.

Standesamt ['ʃtandəsamt], *n.* (—s, *pl.* ·̈er) registry office.

Standesbeamte ['ʃtandəsbəamtə], *m.* (—n, *pl.* —n) registrar (of births, marriages and deaths).

Standesbewußtsein ['ʃtandəsbəvustzaɪn], *n.* (—s, *no pl.*) class-feeling, class-consciousness.

Standesperson ['ʃtandəspɛrzoːn], *f.* (—, *pl.* —en) person of rank.

Standgericht ['ʃtantgərɪçt], *n.* (—es, *pl.* —e) court-martial; summary court of justice.

standhaft ['ʃtanthaft], *adj.* constant, firm, steadfast.

standhalten ['ʃtanthaltən], *v.n.* *irr.* bear up, stand o.'s ground, withstand, resist.

ständig ['ʃtɛndɪç], *adj.* permanent.

ständisch ['ʃtɛndɪʃ], *adj.* relating to the estates (of the realm).

Standort ['ʃtantɔrt], *m.* (—s, *pl.* —e) location; station.

Standpauke ['ʃtantpaukə], *f.* (—, *pl.* —n) (*coll.*) harangue; severe reprimand.

Standpunkt ['ʃtantpuŋkt], *m.* (—(e)s, *pl.* —e) standpoint; point of view; *den — vertreten*, take the line; *einem den — klar machen*, give s.o. a piece of o.'s mind.

Standrecht ['ʃtantrɛçt], *n.* (—(e)s, *no pl.*) martial law.

Standuhr ['ʃtantuːr], *f.* (—, *pl.* —en) grandfather-clock.

Stange ['ʃtaŋə], *f.* (—, *pl.* —n) stick, pole; *bei der — bleiben*, stick to the point, persevere.

Stank [ʃtaŋk], .*m.* (—s, *no pl.*) (*dial.*) stench; discord, trouble.

Stänker ['ʃtɛŋkər], *m.* (—s, *pl.* —) (*coll.*) mischief-maker, quarrelsome person.

stänkern ['ʃtɛŋkərn], *v.n.* pick quarrels; ferret about, make trouble.

Stanniol [ʃta'njoːl], *n.* (—s, *no pl.*) tinfoil.

stanzen ['ʃtantsən], *v.a.* punch, stamp.

Stapel ['ʃtaːpəl], *m.* (—s, *pl.* —) pile, heap; (*Naut.*) slipway; *ein Schiff vom — lassen*, launch a ship.

Stapellauf ['ʃtaːpəllauf], *m.* (—s, *pl.* ·̈e) (*Naut.*) launch, launching.

stapeln ['ʃtaːpəln], *v.a.* pile up.

Stapelnahrung ['ʃtaːpəlnaːruŋ], *f.* (—, *no pl.*) staple diet.

Stapelplatz ['ʃtaːpəlplats], *m.* (—es, *pl.* ·̈e) mart, emporium.

Stapelware ['ʃtaːpəlvaːrə], *f.* (—, *pl.* —n) staple goods.

Stapfen ['ʃtapfən], *m.* or *f. pl.* footsteps.

Star (1) [ʃtaːr], *m.* (—(e)s, *pl.* —e) (*Med.*) cataract; *einem den — stechen*, operate for cataract; (*fig.*) open s.o's eyes.

Star (2) [ʃtaːr], *m.* (—(e)s, *pl.* —en) (*Orn.*) starling.

stark [ʃtark], *adj.* strong, stout; robust; vigorous; heavy; considerable; *—er Esser*, hearty eater. — *adv.* very much.

Stärke [ˈʃtɛrkə], f. (—, no pl.) strength, vigour, robustness; strong point; starch.

Stärkekleister [ˈʃtɛrkəklaɪstər], m. (—s, no pl.) starch-paste.

Stärkemehl [ˈʃtɛrkəmeːl], n. (—s, no pl.) starch-flour.

stärken [ˈʃtɛrkən], v.a. strengthen; corroborate; starch. — v.r. sich —, take some refreshment.

stärkend [ˈʃtɛrkənt], adj. strengthening, restorative; —es Mittel, tonic.

starkleibig [ˈʃtarklaɪbɪç], adj. corpulent, stout, obese.

Stärkung [ˈʃtɛrkuŋ], f. (—, pl. —en) strengthening, invigoration; refreshment.

starr [ʃtar], adj. stiff, rigid; fixed; inflexible; stubborn; einen — ansehen, stare at s.o.

starren [ˈʃtarən], v.n. stare.

Starrheit [ˈʃtarhaɪt], f. (—, no pl.) stiffness, rigidity; fixedness; inflexibility; stubbornness.

starrköpfig [ˈʃtarkœpfɪç], adj. headstrong, stubborn, obstinate, pigheaded.

Starrkrampf [ˈʃtarkrampf], m. (—(e)s, no pl.) (Med.) tetanus.

Starrsinn [ˈʃtarzɪn], m. (—s, no pl.) stubbornness, obstinacy.

Station [ʃtaˈtsjoːn], f. (—, pl. —en) (Railw.) station; (main) terminus; stop, stopping-place; (hospital) ward; freie —, board and lodging found.

stationär [ʃtatsjoˈnɛːr], adj. stationary.

stationieren [ʃtatsjoˈniːrən], v.a. station.

Stationsvorsteher [ʃtaˈtsjoːnsfɔrʃteːər], m. (—s, pl. —) station-master.

statisch [ˈʃtaːtɪʃ], adj. static.

Statist [ʃtaˈtɪst], m. (—en, pl. —en) (Theat.) extra, walking-on part; (pl.) supers.

Statistik [ʃtaˈtɪstɪk], f. (—, pl. —en) statistics.

Statistiker [ʃtaˈtɪstɪkər], m. (—s, pl. —) statistician.

Stativ [ʃtaˈtiːf], n. (—s, pl. —e) stand, tripod.

Statt [ʃtat], f. (—, no pl.) place, stead; an seiner —, in his place.

statt [ʃtat], prep. (Genit.) instead of, in lieu of.

Stätte [ˈʃtɛtə], f. (—, pl. —n) place, abode.

stattfinden [ˈʃtatfɪndən], v.n. irr. take place.

stattgeben [ˈʃtatgeːbən], v.n. irr. einer Bitte —, grant a request.

statthaft [ˈʃtathaft], adj. admissible, allowable, lawful.

Statthalter [ˈʃtathaltər], m. (—s, pl. —) governor.

stattlich [ˈʃtatlɪç], adj. stately, handsome, distinguished, comely; portly; considerable; eine —e Summe, a tidy sum.

statuieren [ʃtatuˈiːrən], v.a. decree; ein Exempel —, make an example of.

Statut [ʃtaˈtuːt], n. (—s, pl. —en) statute, regulation.

Staub [ʃtaup], m. (—(e)s, no pl.) dust, powder; sich aus dem — machen, take French leave; abscond.

Stäubchen [ˈʃtɔypçən], n. (—s, pl. —) mote, particle of dust.

stauben [ˈʃtaubən], v.n. es staubt, it is dusty.

Staubgefäß [ˈʃtaupɡəfɛːs], n. (—es, pl. —e) stamen.

staubig [ˈʃtaubɪç], adj. dusty.

Staubkamm [ˈʃtaupkam], m. (—s, pl. ⸚e) fine-tooth comb.

Staublappen [ˈʃtauplapən], m. (—s, pl. —) duster.

Staubmantel [ˈʃtaupmantəl], m. (—s, pl. ⸚) overall, smock; dust(er)coat, (Am.) duster.

Staubsauger [ˈʃtaupzaugər], m. (—s, pl. —) vacuum cleaner.

Staubtuch [ˈʃtauptuːx], n. (—es, pl. ⸚er) duster.

Staubwedel [ˈʃtaupveːdəl], m. (—s, pl. —) feather duster.

Staubwolke [ˈʃtaupvɔlkə], f. (—, pl. —n) cloud of dust.

Staubzucker [ˈʃtauptsukər], m. (—s, no pl.) castor-sugar, icing-sugar.

Staudamm [ˈʃtaudam], m. (—s, pl. ⸚e) dam, dyke.

Staude [ˈʃtaudə], f. (—, pl. —n) shrub, bush.

stauen [ˈʃtauən], v.a. stow; (water) dam. — v.r. sich —, be congested.

staunen [ˈʃtaunən], v.n. be astonished, be surprised, wonder (at).

Staupe [ˈʃtaupə], f. (—, pl. —n) (animals) distemper.

stäupen [ˈʃtɔypən], v.a. (obs.) scourge, flog.

Stauung [ˈʃtauuŋ], f. (—, pl. —en) stowage; (water) damming-up, swell, rising; (blood) congestion; (traffic) jam, build-up.

stechen [ˈʃteçən], v.a. irr. prick, sting; stab; (cards) trump.

stechend [ˈʃteçənt], adj. pungent, biting.

Stechmücke [ˈʃteçmykə], f. (—, pl. —n) (Ent.) gnat, mosquito.

Stechpalme [ˈʃteçpalmə], f. (—, pl. —n) (Bot.) holly.

Steckbrief [ˈʃtɛkbriːf], m. (—s, pl. —e) warrant (for arrest).

stecken [ˈʃtɛkən], v.a. stick into, put, place, fix; (plants) set, plant; in Brand —, set on fire, set fire to. — v.n. irgendwo —, be about somewhere; — bleiben, get stuck, break down; er steckt dahinter, he is at the bottom of it. — v.r. sich hinter einen —, shelter behind s.o.

Stecken [ˈʃtɛkən], m. (—s, pl. —) stick, staff.

Stecker [ˈʃtɛkər], m. (—s, pl. —) (Elec.) plug.

Steckkontakt [ˈʃtɛkkɔntakt], m. (—(e)s, pl. —e) (Elec.) plug, point.

Stecknadel [ˈʃtɛknaːdəl], f. (—, pl. —n) pin.

Steg [ʃteːk], m. (—(e)s, pl. —e) plank, foot-bridge; jetty; (violin) bridge.

Stegreif [´ʃteːkraɪf], m. (—s, pl. —e) (obs.) stirrup; aus dem — sprechen, extemporise, improvise.

stehen [´ʃteːən], v.n. irr. stand; be; stand still; einem gut —, fit or suit s.o. well; mit einem gut —, be on good terms with s.o.; gut —, be in a fair way, look promising; was steht zu Diensten? what can I do for you? — bleiben, stand still, stop, pull up.

stehlen [´ʃteːlən], v.a. irr. steal.

Steiermark [´ʃtaɪərmark], f. Styria.

steif [ʃtaɪf], adj. stiff; (grog) strong; awkward; ceremonious, punctilious, formal. — adv. etwas — und fest behaupten, swear by all that's holy.

steifen [´ʃtaɪfən], v.a. stiffen, starch.

Steifheit [´ʃtaɪfhaɪt], f. (—, no pl.) stiffness; (fig.) formality.

Steifleinen [´ʃtaɪflaɪnən], n. (—s, no pl.) buckram.

Steig [ʃtaɪk], m. (—(e)s, pl. —e) path, (mountain) track.

Steigbügel [´ʃtaɪkbyːgəl], m. (—s, pl. —) stirrup.

Steigen [´ʃtaɪgən], n. (—s, no pl.) rising, increase; (price) advance, rise; im —, on the increase.

steigen [´ʃtaɪgən], v.n. irr. (aux. sein) climb, mount, ascend; (barometer) rise; (population) increase; (horse) rear; (price) advance, rise.

Steiger [´ʃtaɪgər], m. (—s, pl. —) climber, mountaineer; mining-surveyor, overseer.

steigern [´ʃtaɪgərn], v.a. (price) raise; (fig.) enhance, increase. — v.r. sich —, increase.

Steigerung [´ʃtaɪgəruŋ], f. (—, pl. —en) raising; (fig.) enhancement; increase; (Gram.) comparison.

Steigung [´ʃtaɪguŋ], f. (—, pl. —en) gradient.

steil [ʃtaɪl], adj. steep.

Stein [ʃtaɪn], m. (—(e)s, pl. —e) stone, rock; flint; jewel, gem; monument; (Chess) piece, chessman; (Draughts) man; (fruit) stone, kernel; — des Anstoßes, stumbling block; mir fällt ein — vom Herzen, it is a load off my mind; bei einem einen — im Brett haben, be in s.o.'s good books; einem —e in den Weg legen, put obstacles in s.o.'s way; der — des Weisen, the philosopher's stone.

Steinadler [´ʃtaɪnaːdlər], m. (—s, pl. —) (Orn.) golden eagle.

steinalt [´ʃtaɪnalt], adj. very old.

Steinbock [´ʃtaɪnbɔk], m. (—s, pl. ¨e) ibex; (Astrol.) Capricorn.

Steinbruch [´ʃtaɪnbrux], m. (—s, pl. ¨e) stone-pit, quarry.

Steinbutt [´ʃtaɪnbut], m. (—s, pl. —e) (Zool.) turbot.

Steindruck [´ʃtaɪndruk], m. (—s, no pl.) lithography.

steinern [´ʃtaɪnərn], adj. stony; built of stone.

Steingut [´ʃtaɪnguːt], n. (—s, no pl.) earthenware, stoneware, pottery.

Steinhagel [´ʃtaɪnhaːgəl], m. (—s, no pl.) shower of stones.

Steinhaue [´ʃtaɪnhauə], f. (—, pl. —n) pickaxe.

Steinhügel [´ʃtaɪnhyːgəl], m. (—s, pl. —) cairn.

steinig [´ʃtaɪnɪç], adj. stony, rocky.

steinigen [´ʃtaɪnɪgən], v.a. stone, rock.

Steinkalk [´ʃtaɪnkalk], m. (—s, no pl.) quicklime.

Steinkohle [´ʃtaɪnkoːlə], f. (—, no pl.) pit-coal.

Steinkrug [´ʃtaɪnkruːk], m. (—s, pl. ¨e) stone jar.

Steinmarder [´ʃtaɪnmardər], m. (—s, pl. —) (Zool.) stone-marten.

Steinmetz [´ʃtaɪnmɛts], m. (—es, pl. —e) stone-cutter, stone-mason.

Steinobst [´ʃtaɪnoːpst], n. (—es, no pl.) stone-fruit.

Steinplatte [´ʃtaɪnplatə], f. (—, pl. —n) slab, flagstone.

steinreich [´ʃtaɪnraɪç], adj. as rich as Croesus.

Steinsalz [´ʃtaɪnzalts], n. (—es, no pl.) rock-salt, mineral-salt.

Steinwurf [´ʃtaɪnvurf], m. (—s, pl. ¨e) einen — entfernt, within a stone's throw.

Steiß [ʃtaɪs], m. (—es, pl. —e) rump; (coll.) buttocks, posterior.

Stellage [ʃtɛ´laːʒə], f. (—, pl. —n) stand, frame.

Stelldichein [´ʃtɛldɪçaɪn], n. (—s, no pl.) assignation, rendezvous, tryst; (coll.) date.

Stelle [´ʃtɛlə], f. (—, pl. —n) place, spot; job, position; situation; (book) passage; figure, digit; department; offene —, vacancy; auf der —, at once, immediately; an deiner —, if I were you; nicht von der — kommen, remain stationary; zur — sein, be at hand.

stellen [´ʃtɛlən], v.a. put, place, set; richtig —, regulate, correct, amend; (clock) set right; seinen Mann —, play o.'s part, pull o.'s weight. — v.r. sich —, come forward; pretend; sich krank —, feign illness, malinger, pretend to be ill.

Stellenbewerber [´ʃtɛlənbəvɛrbər], m. (—s, pl. —) applicant (for a job).

Stellengesuch [´ʃtɛləngəzuːx], n. (—s, pl. —e) application (for a job).

Stellenvermittlung [´ʃtɛlənfɛrmɪtluŋ], f. (—, pl. —en) employment office, employment exchange.

stellenweise [´ʃtɛlənvaɪzə], adv. in parts, here and there.

Stellmacher [´ʃtɛlmaxər], m. (—s, pl. —) wheelwright.

Stellung [´ʃtɛluŋ], f. (—, pl. —en) position, posture; attitude; situation; job; (Mil.) trenches; — nehmen zu, express o.'s views on.

Stellvertreter [´ʃtɛlfɛrtreːtər], m. (—s, pl. —) representative, deputy; substitute, supply, proxy, relief; (doctor) locum.

Stelzbein [´ʃtɛltsbaɪn], n. (—s, pl. —e) wooden leg.

211

Stemmeisen

Stemmeisen ['ʃtɛmaɪzən], *n.* (**—s,** *pl.* **—**) crowbar.

stemmen ['ʃtɛmən], *v.a.* (*water*) stem, dam; (*weight*) lift. — *v.r.* sich — gegen, resist fiercely.

Stempel ['ʃtɛmpəl], *m.* (**—s,** *pl.* **—**) stamp, rubber-stamp, die; pounder; (*Bot.*) pistil.

Stempelgebühr ['ʃtɛmpəlgəby:r], *f.* (**—,** *pl.* **—en**) stamp-duty.

stempeln ['ʃtɛmpəln], *v.a.* stamp, hallmark; brand; cancel (*postage stamp*). — *v.n.* (*coll.*) — gehen, be on the dole.

Stengel ['ʃtɛŋəl], *m.* (**—s,** *pl.* **—**) stalk.

Stenografie [ʃtenogra'fi:], *f.* (**—,** *no pl.*) stenography, shorthand.

stenografisch [ʃteno'gra:fɪʃ], *adj.* in shorthand.

Stenogramm [ʃteno'gram], *n.* (**—s,** *pl.* **—e**) shorthand-note.

Stenotypistin [ʃtenoty'pɪstɪn], *f.* (**—,** *pl.* **—nen**) shorthand-typist.

Stephan ['ʃtɛfan], *m.* Stephen.

Steppdecke ['ʃtɛpdɛkə], *f.* (**—,** *pl.* **—n**) quilt.

Steppe ['ʃtɛpə], *f.* (**—,** *pl.* **—n**) steppe.

steppen ['ʃtɛpən], *v.a.* stitch, quilt.

Sterbeglocke ['ʃtɛrbəglɔkə], *f.* (**—,** *pl.* **—n**) passing bell, death bell.

Sterbehemd ['ʃtɛrbəhɛmt], *n.* (**—(e)s,** *pl.* **—en**) shroud, winding-sheet.

sterben ['ʃtɛrbən], *v.n. irr.* (*aux.* sein) die.

Sterbenswörtchen ['ʃtɛrbənsvœrtçən], *n.* (**—s,** *pl.* **—**) nicht ein —, not a syllable.

Sterbesakramente['ʃtɛrbəzakramɛntə], *n. pl.* (*Eccl.*) last sacraments, last rites.

sterblich ['ʃtɛrplɪç], *adj.* mortal; — verliebt, desperately in love.

Sterblichkeit ['ʃtɛrplɪçkaɪt], *f.* (**—,** *no pl.*) mortality.

stereotyp [stereo'ty:p], *adj.* stereotyped.

sterilisieren [sterili'zi:rən], *v.a.* sterilise.

Sterilität [sterili'tɛ:t], *f.* (**—,** *no pl.*) sterility.

Stern [ʃtɛrn], *m.* (**—(e)s,** *pl.* **—e**) star; (*Typ.*) asterisk.

Sternbild ['ʃtɛrnbɪlt], *n.* (**—s,** *pl.* **—er**) constellation.

Sterndeuter ['ʃtɛrndɔytər], *m.* (**—s,** *pl.* **—**) astrologer.

Sterndeutung ['ʃtɛrndɔytuŋ], *f.* (**—,** *no pl.*) astrology.

Sternenschimmer ['ʃtɛrnənʃɪmər], *m.* (**—s,** *no pl.*) starlight.

sternförmig ['ʃtɛrnfœrmɪç], *adj.* star-like, star-shaped.

Sterngucker ['ʃtɛrngukər], *m.* (**—s,** *pl.* **—**) stargazer.

sternhagelvoll ['ʃtɛrnha:gəlfɔl], *adj.* (*coll.*) as drunk as a lord.

Sternkunde ['ʃtɛrnkundə], *f.* (**—,** *no pl.*) astronomy.

Sternkundige ['ʃtɛrnkundɪgə], *m.* (**—n,** *pl.* **—n**) astronomer.

Sternschnuppe ['ʃtɛrnʃnupə], *f.* (**—** *pl.* **—n**) falling star, shooting star meteorite.

Sternwarte ['ʃtɛrnvartə], *f.* (**—,** *pl.* **—n** observatory.

stetig ['ʃte:tɪç], *adj.* continual, continuous, constant.

stets [ʃte:ts], *adv.* always, ever, continually.

Steuer (1) ['ʃtɔyər], *n.* (**—s,** *pl.* **—** rudder, helm, steering wheel.

Steuer (2) ['ʃtɔyər], *f.* (**—,** *pl.* **—n**) tax (*local*) rate; (*import*) customs duty.

Steueramt ['ʃtɔyəramt], *n.* (**—s,** *pl* **—er**) inland revenue office, tax office

Steuerbeamte ['ʃtɔyərbaamtə], *m.* (**—n,** *pl.* **—n**) revenue officer, tax collector.

Steuerbord ['ʃtɔyərbɔrt], *n.* (**—s,** *n pl.*) starboard.

Steuereinnehmer ['ʃtɔyəraɪnne:mər] *m.* (**—s,** *pl.* **—**) tax collector.

steuerfrei ['ʃtɔyərfraɪ], *adj.* duty-free exempt from taxes.

Steuerhinterziehung ['ʃtɔyərhɪntərtsi: uŋ], *f.* (**—,** *pl.* **—en**) tax evasion.

steuerlos ['ʃtɔyərlo:s], *adj.* rudderless adrift.

Steuermann ['ʃtɔyərman], *m.* (**—s** *pl.* **—er**) mate; helmsman.

steuern ['ʃtɔyərn], *v.a.* steer; einen Unheil —, avoid or steer clear of an evil.

steuerpflichtig ['ʃtɔyərpflɪçtɪç], *adj* taxable, liable to tax, dutiable.

Steuerrad ['ʃtɔyərra:t], *n.* (**—s,** *pl.* **—er** steering-wheel.

Steuerung ['ʃtɔyəruŋ], *f.* (**—,** *no pl.* steering, controls.

Steuerveranlagung ['ʃtɔyərfəranla: guŋ], *f.* (**—,** *pl.* **—en**) tax-assessment

stibitzen [ʃti'bɪtsən], *v.a.* (*coll.*) pilfer filch.

Stich [ʃtɪç], *m.* (**—(e)s,** *pl.* **—e**) sting prick; stitch; stab; (*Cards*) trick (*Art*) engraving; einen im — lassen leave s.o. in the lurch.

Stichel ['ʃtɪçəl], *m.* (**—s,** *pl.* **—**) (*Art* graver.

Stichelei [ʃtɪçə'laɪ], *f.* (**—,** *pl.* **—en** taunt, sneer, gibe.

sticheln ['ʃtɪçəln], *v.a.* taunt, nag.

stichhaltig ['ʃtɪçhaltɪç], *adj.* valid sound.

Stichhaltigkeit ['ʃtɪçhaltɪçkaɪt], *f.* (**—** *no pl.*) validity, cogency.

Stichprobe ['ʃtɪçpro:bə], *f.* (**—,** *p* **—n**) sample taken at random, sam pling.

Stichwahl ['ʃtɪçva:l], *f.* (**—,** *pl.* **—en** second ballot.

Stichwort ['ʃtɪçvɔrt], *n.* (**—s,** *pl.* **—e** key-word; (*Theat.*) cue.

sticken ['ʃtɪkən], *v.a., v.n.* embroider.

Stickerei [ʃtɪkə'raɪ], *f.* (**—,** *pl.* **—en** embroidery.

Stickgarn ['ʃtɪkgarn], *n.* (**—s,** *pl.* **—** embroidery cotton or silk.

Stickhusten ['ʃtɪkhu:stən], *m.* (**—s** *no pl.*) choking cough.

212

Stock

stickig [ˈʃtɪkɪç], *adj.* stuffy.
Stickmuster [ˈʃtɪkmustər], *n.* (—s, *pl.* —) embroidery-pattern.
Stickstoff [ˈʃtɪkʃtɔf], *m.* (—(e)s, *no pl.*) nitrogen.
stieben [ˈʃtiːbən], *v.n.* (*aux.* sein) scatter, spray; *auseinander* —, disperse.
Stiefbruder [ˈʃtiːfbruːdər], *m.* (—s, *pl.* ˙˙) step-brother.
Stiefel [ˈʃtiːfəl], *m.* (—s, *pl.* —) boot.
Stiefelknecht [ˈʃtiːfəlknɛçt], *m.* (—(e)s, *pl.* —e) boot-jack.
Stiefelputzer [ˈʃtiːfəlputsər], *m.* (—s, *pl.* —) shoe-black; (*Am.*) shoe-shine; (*hotel*) boots.
Stiefeltern [ˈʃtiːfɛltern], *pl.* stepparents.
Stiefmütterchen [ˈʃtiːfmytərçən], *n.* (—s, *pl.* —) (*Bot.*) pansy.
stiefmütterlich [ˈʃtiːfmytərlɪç], *adj.* like a stepmother; niggardly.
Stiefsohn [ˈʃtiːfzoːn], *m.* (—s, *pl.* ˙˙e) stepson.
Stiege [ˈʃtiːgə], *f.* (—, *pl.* —n) staircase.
Stieglitz [ˈʃtiːglɪts], *m.* (—es, *pl.* —e) goldfinch.
Stiel [ʃtiːl], *m.* (—(e)s, *pl.* —e) handle; (*plant*) stalk.
Stier [ʃtiːr], *m.* (—(e)s, *pl.* —e) bull; *junger* —, bullock; (*Astrol.*) Taurus.
stieren [ˈʃtiːrən], *v.n.* stare (at), goggle.
Stift (1) [ʃtɪft], *m.* (—(e)s, *pl.* —e) tack, pin, peg; pencil; (*coll.*) apprentice; young chap.
Stift (2) [ʃtɪft], *n.* (—(e)s, *pl.* —e) charitable *or* religious foundation.
stiften [ˈʃtɪftən], *v.a.* establish, give, donate; found, set on foot, originate; *Frieden* —, bring about peace.
Stifter [ˈʃtɪftər], *m.* (—s, *pl.* —) founder, originator, donor.
Stiftung [ˈʃtɪftuŋ], *f.* (—, *pl.* —en) establishment, foundation; institution; charitable foundation; endowment, donation.
Stil [ʃtiːl], *m.* (—(e)s, *pl.* —e) style; (*fig.*) manner.
stilisieren [ʃtiːliˈziːrən], *v.a.* word, draft.
Stilistik [ʃtiːˈlɪstɪk], *f.* (—, *no pl.*) art of composition.
stilistisch [ʃtiːˈlɪstɪʃ], *adj.* stylistic.
still [ʃtɪl], *adj.* quiet, still, silent; calm; —*er Teilhaber*, sleeping partner; *im* —*en*, secretly, on the sly.
Stille [ˈʃtɪlə], *f.* (—, *no pl.*) silence, quietness, tranquillity; calm, calmness; *in der* —, silently; *in der* — *der Nacht*, at dead of night.
stillen [ˈʃtɪlən], *v.a.* allay; (*blood*) staunch; (*baby*) suckle, feed, nurse; (*thirst*) quench; (*hunger*) appease.
stillos [ˈʃtiːloːs], *adj.* incongruous; in bad taste.
Stillung [ˈʃtɪluŋ], *f.* (—, *no pl.*) allaying; (*blood*) staunching; (*baby*) suckling, feeding, nursing; (*thirst*) quenching; (*hunger*) appeasing.

stilvoll [ˈʃtiːlfɔl], *adj.* harmonious; stylish; in good taste.
Stimmband [ˈʃtɪmbant], *n.* (—s, *pl.* ˙˙er) vocal chord.
stimmberechtigt [ˈʃtɪmbərɛçtɪçt], *adj.* entitled to vote, enfranchised.
Stimmbruch [ˈʃtɪmbrux], *m.* (—s, *no pl.*) breaking of the voice.
Stimme [ˈʃtɪmə], *f.* (—, *pl.* —n) voice; (*election*) vote, suffrage; *die* — *abgeben*, vote.
stimmen [ˈʃtɪmən], *v.a.* (*piano*) tune; *einen günstig* —, dispose s.o. favourably towards s.th. — *v.n.* agree, tally (with), square (with), accord (with); vote.
Stimmeneinheit [ˈʃtɪmənaɪnhaɪt], *f.* (—, *no pl.*) unanimity.
Stimmengleichheit [ˈʃtɪmənɡlaɪçhaɪt], *f.* (—, *no pl.*) equality of votes, tie.
Stimmer [ˈʃtɪmər], *m.* (—s, *pl.* —) (*piano*) tuner.
Stimmführer [ˈʃtɪmfyːrər], *m.* (—s, *pl.* —) leader, spokesman.
Stimmgabel [ˈʃtɪmɡaːbəl], *f.* (—, *pl.* —n) tuning fork.
stimmhaft [ˈʃtɪmhaft], *adj.* (*Phonet.*) voiced.
Stimmlage [ˈʃtɪmlaːɡə], *f.* (—, *pl.* —n) (*Mus.*) register.
stimmlos [ˈʃtɪmloːs], *adj.* voiceless; (*Phonet.*) unvoiced.
Stimmrecht [ˈʃtɪmrɛçt], *n.* (—s, *no pl.*) suffrage, right to vote; *allgemeines* —, universal suffrage.
Stimmung [ˈʃtɪmuŋ], *f.* (—, *no pl.*) tuning; (*fig.*) disposition, humour, mood; atmosphere; *in guter* —, in high spirits; *in gedrückter* —, in low spirits.
stimmungsvoll [ˈʃtɪmuŋsfɔl], *adj.* impressive, full of atmosphere.
Stimmwechsel [ˈʃtɪmvɛksəl], *m.* (—s, *no pl.*) breaking of the voice.
Stimmzettel [ˈʃtɪmtsɛtəl], *m.* (—s, *pl.* —) ballot-paper.
stinken [ˈʃtɪŋkən], *v.n. irr.* stink, reek, smell.
Stinktier [ˈʃtɪŋktiːr], *n.* (—s, *pl.* —e) (*Zool.*) skunk.
Stipendium [ʃtiˈpɛndjum], *n.* (—s, *pl.* —dien) scholarship.
Stirn [ʃtɪrn], *f.* (—, *pl.* —en) forehead, brow; *die* — *runzeln*, frown, knit o.'s brow; *die* — *haben zu*, have the cheek to; *einem die* — *bieten*, face s.o., defy s.o.
Stirnhöhle [ˈʃtɪrnhøːlə], *f.* (—, *pl.* —en) frontal cavity.
Stirnseite [ˈʃtɪrnzaɪtə], *f.* (—, *pl.* —n) front.
stöbern [ˈʃtøːbərn], *v.n.* rummage about; (*snow*) drift.
stochern [ˈʃtɔxərn], *v.a., v.n.* (*food*) pick (at); (*teeth*) pick.
Stock (1) [ʃtɔk], *m.* (—(e)s, *pl.* ˙˙e) stick, cane, walking-stick; *über* — *und Stein*, over hedges and ditches.
Stock (2) [ʃtɔk], *m.* (—es, *pl.* —werke) storey, floor.

stocken ['ʃtɔkən], *v.n.* stop; (*blood*) run cold; (*linen*) go mildewed; hesitate, falter; (*conversation*) flag.

stockfinster ['ʃtɔkfɪnstər], *adj.* pitch dark.

Stockfisch ['ʃtɔkfɪʃ], *m.* (—es, *pl.* —e) dried cod; dried fish.

stöckisch ['ʃtœkɪʃ], *adj.* obstinate, stubborn.

Stockrose ['ʃtɔkro:zə], *f.* (—, *pl.* —n) (*Bot.*) hollyhock.

Stockschnupfen ['ʃtɔkʃnupfən], *m.* (—s, *no pl.*) heavy *or* chronic cold.

stocksteif ['ʃtɔkʃtaɪf], *adj.* stiff as a poker.

stockstill ['ʃtɔkʃtɪl], *adj.* quite still, stock-still.

stocktaub ['ʃtɔktaup], *adj.* deaf as a post.

Stockung ['ʃtɔkuŋ], *f.* (—, *pl.* —en) stagnation; hesitation; block, blockage; stopping, standstill.

Stockwerk ['ʃtɔkvɛrk], *n.* (—s, *pl.* —e) storey, floor.

Stoff [ʃtɔf], *m.* (—(e)s, *pl.* —e) fabric, material; substance; subject matter.

Stoffwechsel ['ʃtɔfvɛksəl], *m.* (—s, *no pl.*) metabolism.

stöhnen ['ʃtø:nən], *v.n.* groan, moan.

Stoiker ['sto:ɪkər], *m.* (—s, *pl.* —) stoic.

Stola ['sto:la:], *f.* (—, *pl.* —len) (*Eccl.*) stole.

Stollen ['ʃtɔlən], *m.* (—s, *pl.* —) fruit-cake; (*Min.*) gallery, adit.

stolpern ['ʃtɔlpərn], *v.n.* (*aux.* sein) stumble, trip.

Stolz [ʃtɔlts], *m.* (—es, *no pl.*) haughtiness, pride.

stolz [ʃtɔlts], *adj.* haughty, proud; stuck-up, conceited; (*fig.*) majestic.

stolzieren [ʃtɔl'tsi:rən], *v.n.* (*aux.* sein) strut; prance.

stopfen ['ʃtɔpfən], *v.a.* stuff; fill; darn, mend; *einem den Mund* —, cut s.o. short.

Stopfgarn ['ʃtɔpfgarn], *n.* (—s, *pl.* —e) darning-thread.

Stoppel ['ʃtɔpəl], *f.* (—, *pl.* —n) stubble.

stoppeln ['ʃtɔpəln], *v.a.* glean; *etwas zusammen* —, compile s.th. badly.

Stöpsel ['ʃtœpsəl], *m.* (—s, *pl.* —) stopper, cork; *kleiner* —, little mite.

stöpseln ['ʃtœpsəln], *v.a.* cork.

Stör [ʃtø:r], *m.* (—(e)s, *pl.* —e) (*Zool.*) sturgeon.

Storch [ʃtɔrç], *m.* (—(e)s, *pl.* ⁻e) (*Orn.*) stork.

Storchschnabel ['ʃtɔrçʃna:bəl], *m.* (—s, *pl.* ⁻) stork's bill; (*Tech.*) pantograph.

stören ['ʃtø:rən], *v.a.* disturb, trouble; (*Rad.*) jam. — *v.n.* intrude, be in the way.

Störenfried ['ʃtø:rənfri:d], *m.* (—s, *pl.* —e) intruder, mischief-maker, nuisance.

Störer ['ʃtø:rər], *m.* (—s, *pl.* —) disturber.

stornieren [stɔr'ni:rən], *v.a.* cancel, annul.

störrisch ['ʃtœrɪʃ], *adj.* stubborn, obstinate.

Störung ['ʃtø:ruŋ], *f.* (—, *pl.* —en) disturbance, intrusion; (*Rad.*) jamming.

Stoß [ʃto:s], *m.* (—es, *pl.* ⁻e) push, thrust; impact; blow, stroke, jolt; (*papers*) heap, pile; (*documents*) bundle.

Stoßdegen ['ʃto:sde:gən], *m.* (—s, *pl.* —) rapier.

Stößel ['ʃtø:səl], *m.* (—s, *pl.* —) pestle; (*Motor.*) tappet.

stoßen ['ʃto:sən], *v.a. irr.* thrust, push; pound; *vor den Kopf* —, offend. — *v.n.* bump, jolt; — *an*, border upon; *auf etwas* —, come across s.th., stumble on s.th.; *ins Horn* —, blow a horn. — *v.r. sich* —, hurt o.s.; *sich an etwas* —, take offence at s.th., take exception to s.th.

Stoßseufzer ['ʃto:szɔyftsər], *m.* (—s, *pl.* —) deep sigh.

Stoßwaffe ['ʃto:svafə], *f.* (—, *pl.* —n) thrusting *or* stabbing weapon.

stoßweise ['ʃto:svaɪzə], *adv.* by fits and starts.

Stotterer ['ʃtɔtərər], *m.* (—s, *pl.* —) stutterer, stammerer.

stottern ['ʃtɔtərn], *v.n.* stutter, stammer.

stracks [ʃtraks], *adv.* straight away, directly.

Strafanstalt ['ʃtra:fanʃtalt], *f.* (—, *pl.* —en) penitentiary, prison.

Strafarbeit ['ʃtra:farbaɪt], *f.* (—, *pl.* —en) (*Sch.*) imposition.

strafbar ['ʃtra:fba:r], *adj.* punishable, criminal, culpable.

Strafbarkeit ['ʃtra:fba:rkaɪt], *f.* (—, *no pl.*) culpability.

Strafe ['ʃtra:fə], *f.* (—, *pl.* —n) punishment; (*money*) fine, penalty; *bei* — *von*, on pain of.

strafen ['ʃtra:fən], *v.a.* punish, rebuke; (*money*) fine.

Straferlaß ['ʃtra:fərlas], *m.* (—sses, *pl.* —sse) remission of penalty, amnesty.

straff [ʃtraf], *adj.* tight, tense, taut.

Strafgericht ['ʃtra:fgərɪçt], *n.* (—es, *no pl.*) punishment; judgment; (*Law*) Criminal Court.

Strafgesetzbuch ['ʃtra:fgəzɛtsbu:x], *n.* (—(e)s, *pl.* ⁻er) penal code.

sträflich ['ʃtrɛ:flɪç], *adj.* punishable; culpable; reprehensible, blameworthy.

Sträfling ['ʃtrɛ:flɪŋ], *m.* (—s, *pl.* —e) convict.

Strafporto ['ʃtra:fpɔrto], *n.* (—s, *pl.* —ti) excess postage.

Strafpredigt ['ʃtra:fpre:dɪçt], *f.* (—, *pl.* —en) severe admonition, stern reprimand.

Strafprozéss ['ʃtra:fprotsɛs], *m.* (—es, *pl.* —e) criminal proceedings.

Strafrecht ['ʃtra:frɛçt], *n.* (—(e)s, *no pl.*) criminal law.

Strafverfahren ['ʃtra:fferfa:rən], *n.* (—s, *pl.* —) criminal procedure.

Strahl [ʃtraːl], *m.* (—(e)s, *pl.* —en)
beam, ray; (*water etc.*) jet, spout;
(*lightning*) flash; —en werfen, emit
rays.

Strahlantrieb [ʃtraːlantriːp], *m.* (—s,
no pl.) (*Aviat.*) jet propulsion.

strahlen [ʃtraːlən], *v.n.* radiate, shine,
beam, emit rays; (*fig.*) beam (with
joy).

strählen [ʃtrɛːlən], *v.a.* (*rare*) comb.

Strahlenbrechung [ʃtraːlənbrɛçuŋ],
f. (—, *pl.* —en) refraction.

strahlenförmig [ʃtraːlənfœrmɪç], *adj.*
radiate.

Strahlenkrone [ʃtraːlənkroːnə], *f.* (—,
pl. —n) aureole, halo.

Strahlung [ʃtraːluŋ], *f.* (—, *pl.* —en)
radiation; (*fig.*) radiance.

Strähne [ʃtrɛːnə], *f.* (—, *pl.* —n)
skein, hank; *eine* — *Pech*, a spell of
bad luck.

Stramin [ʃtraˈmiːn], *m.* (—s, *pl.* —e)
embroidery canvas.

stramm [ʃtram], *adj.* tight; rigid;
sturdy, strapping.

strampeln [ʃtrampəln], *v.n.* struggle;
(*baby*) kick.

Strand [ʃtrant], *m.* (—(e)s, *pl.* —e)
shore, beach, strand.

stranden [ʃtrandən], *v.n.* be stranded,
founder.

Strandkorb [ʃtrantkɔrp], *m.* (—s,
pl. ̈e) beach-chair.

Strandwache [ʃtrantvaxə], *f.* (—, *no
pl.*) coast-guard.

Strang [ʃtraŋ], *m.* (—(e)s, *pl.* ̈e) rope,
cord; *über die* ̈e *schlagen*, kick over
the traces; *zum* — *verurteilen*, condemn to be hanged.

strangulieren [ʃtraŋguˈliːrən], *v.a.*
strangle.

Strapaze [ʃtraˈpatsə], *f.* (—, *pl.* —n)
over-exertion, fatigue, hardship.

strapazieren [ʃtrapaˈtsiːrən], *v.a.* overexert, fatigue.

strapaziös [ʃtrapaˈtsjøːs], *adj.* fatiguing,
exacting.

Straße [ʃtraːsə], *f.* (—, *pl.* —n) (*city*)
street; (*country*) road, highway; (*sea*)
strait; *auf der* —, in the street; *über
die* — *gehen*, cross the street.

Straßenbahn [ʃtraːsənbaːn], *f.* (—,
pl. —en) tram; tramcar, (*Am.*) streetcar.

Straßendamm [ʃtraːsəndam], *m.* (—s,
pl. ̈e) roadway.

Straßendirne [ʃtraːsəndɪrnə], *f.* (—,
pl. —n) prostitute, street-walker.

Straßenfeger [ʃtraːsənfeːgər], *m.* (—s,
pl. —) roadman, road-sweeper,
scavenger, crossing-sweeper.

Straßenpflaster [ʃtraːsənpflastər], *n.*
(—s, *no pl.*) pavement.

Straßenraub [ʃtraːsənraup], *m.* (—s,
no pl.) highway-robbery.

Stratege [ʃtraˈteːgə], *m.* (—n, *pl.* —n)
strategist.

träuben [ʃtrɔybən], *v.r. sich* —,
bristle; (*fig.*) struggle (against),
oppose.

Strauch [ʃtraux], *m.* (—(e)s, *pl.* ̈er)
bush, shrub.

straucheln [ʃtrauxəln], *v.n.* (*aux.* sein)
stumble.

Strauchritter [ʃtrauxrɪtər], *m.* (—s,
pl. —) footpad, vagabond, highwayman.

Strauß (1) [ʃtraus], *m.* (—es, *pl.* ̈e)
(*Poet.*) fight, tussle; (*flowers*) bunch,
bouquet, nosegay.

Strauß (2) [ʃtraus], *m.* (—es, *pl.* —e)
(*Orn.*) ostrich.

Sträußchen [ʃtrɔysçən], *n.* (—s,
pl. —) small bunch of flowers, nosegay.

Straußfeder [ʃtrausfeːdər], *f.* (—,
pl. —n) ostrich-feather.

Strazze [ʃtratsə], *f.* (—, *pl.* —n)
scrapbook.

Strebe [ʃtreːbə], *f.* (—, *pl.* —n) buttress, prop, stay.

Strebebogen [ʃtreːbəboːgən], *m.* (—s,
pl. —) (*Archit.*) arch, buttress; flying
buttress.

Streben [ʃtreːbən], *n.* (—s, *no pl.*)
ambition, aspiration; effort, endeavour, striving.

streben [ʃtreːbən], *v.n.* strive, aspire,
endeavour.

Streber [ʃtreːbər], *m.* (—s, *pl.* —)
pushing person, (social) climber. (*Am.
coll.*) go-getter.

strebsam [ʃtreːpzaːm], *adj.* ambitious,
assiduous, industrious.

streckbar [ʃtrɛkbaːr], *adj.* ductile,
extensible.

Streckbett [ʃtrɛkbɛt], *n.* (—s, *pl.* —en)
orthopaedic bed.

Strecke [ʃtrɛkə], *f.* (—, *pl.* —n) stretch,
reach, extent; distance; tract; line;
zur — *bringen*, (*Hunt.*) bag, run to
earth.

strecken [ʃtrɛkən], *v.a.* stretch, extend; (*metal*) hammer out, roll; make
(s.th.) last; *die Waffen* —, lay down
arms.

Streich [ʃtraɪç], *m.* (—(e)s, *pl.* —e)
stroke, blow; (*fig.*) prank; trick;
dummer —, piece of folly, lark.

streicheln [ʃtraɪçəln], *v.a.* stroke,
caress.

streichen [ʃtraɪçən], *v.a. irr.* stroke,
touch; paint, spread; cancel; strike;
(*sail*) lower. — *v.n.* move past, fly
past; wander.

Streichholz [ʃtraɪçhɔlts], *n.* (—es,
pl. ̈er) match.

Streichinstrument [ʃtraɪçɪnstru-
mɛnt], *n.* (—s, *pl.* —e) stringed
instrument.

Streif [ʃtraɪf], *m.* (—(e)s, *pl.* —e)
stripe, strip, streak.

Streifband [ʃtraɪfbant], *n.* (—s, *pl.*
̈er) wrapper.

Streifblick [ʃtraɪfblɪk], *m.* (—s, *pl.*
—e) glance.

Streife [ʃtraɪfə], *f.* (—, *pl.* —n) raid;
patrol (*police etc*).

Streifen [ʃtraɪfən], *m.* (—s, *pl.* —)
stripe, streak; (*Mil.*) bar.

streifen

streifen ['ʃtraɪfən], *v.a.* graze, touch in passing; take off (*remove*). — *v.n.* (*aux.* sein) ramble, roam, rove.

streifig ['ʃtraɪfɪç], *adj.* striped, streaky.

Streik [ʃtraɪk], *m.* (—(e)s, *pl.* —s) strike; *in den* — *treten*, go on strike.

Streikbrecher ['ʃtraɪkbrɛçər], *m.* (—s, *pl.* —) blackleg.

streiken ['ʃtraɪkən], *v.n.* (*workers*) strike, be on strike.

Streit [ʃtraɪt], *m.* (—(e)s, *pl.* —e) dispute, quarrel, conflict; (*words*) argument; *einen* — *anfangen*, pick a quarrel.

Streitaxt ['ʃtraɪtakst], *f.* (—, *pl.* ̈e) battle-axe.

streitbar ['ʃtraɪtba:r], *adj.* warlike, martial.

streiten ['ʃtraɪtən], *v.n.* irr. quarrel, fight; —*de Kirche*, Church Militant.

Streitfrage ['ʃtraɪtfra:gə], *f.* (—, *pl.* —n) moot point, point at issue; controversy.

Streithammel ['ʃtraɪthaməl], *m.* (—s, *pl.* —) squabbler.

Streithandel ['ʃtraɪthandəl], *m.* (—s, *pl.* ̈) law-suit.

streitig ['ʃtraɪtɪç], *adj.* disputable, doubtful, at issue; *einem etwas* — *machen*, contest s.o.'s right to s.th.

Streitkräfte ['ʃtraɪtkrɛftə], *f. pl.* (*Mil.*) forces.

streitlustig ['ʃtraɪtlustɪç], *adj.* argumentative.

Streitschrift ['ʃtraɪtʃrɪft], *f.* (—, *pl.* —en) pamphlet, polemical treatise.

Streitsucht ['ʃtraɪtzuxt], *f.* (—, *no pl.*) quarrelsomeness; (*Law*) litigiousness.

streitsüchtig ['ʃtraɪtzyçtɪç], *adj.* quarrelsome, litigious.

streng [ʃtrɛŋ], *adj.* severe, strict, rigorous; —*e Kälte*, biting cold; *im* —*sten Winter*, in the depth of winter. — *adv.* —*genommen*, strictly speaking.

Strenge ['ʃtrɛŋə], *f.* (—, *no pl.*) severity, rigour.

strenggläubig ['ʃtrɛŋɡləybɪç], *adj.* strictly orthodox.

Streu [ʃtrɔy], *f.* (—, *pl.* —en) litter, bed of straw.

Streubüchse ['ʃtrɔybyksə], *f.* (—, *pl.* —n) castor.

streuen ['ʃtrɔyən], *v.a.* strew, scatter, sprinkle.

streunen ['ʃtrɔynən], *v.n.* roam (about).

Streuung ['ʃtrɔyuŋ], *f.* (—, *pl.* —en) strewing; (*shot*) dispersion.

Streuzucker ['ʃtrɔytsukər], *m.* (—s, *no pl.*) castor-sugar.

Strich [ʃtrɪç], *m.* (—(e)s, *pl.* —e) stroke, line, dash; (*land*) tract; (*Art*) touch; region; *gegen den* —, against the grain; *einem einen* — *durch die Rechnung machen*, put a spoke in s.o.'s wheel, frustrate s.o.

Strichpunkt ['ʃtrɪçpuŋkt], *m.* (—s, *pl.* —e) semicolon.

Strichregen ['ʃtrɪçre:gən], *m.* (—s. *pl.* —) passing shower.

Strick [ʃtrɪk], *m.* (—(e)s, *pl.* —e) cord, line, rope; *du* —, (*fig.*) you scamp! *einem einen* — *drehen*, give s.o. enough rope to hang himself, lay a trap for s.o.

stricken ['ʃtrɪkən], *v.a., v.n.* knit.

Strickerei [ʃtrɪkə'raɪ], *f.* (—, *pl.* —en) knitting; knitting business, workshop.

Strickleiter ['ʃtrɪklaɪtər], *f.* (—, *pl.* —n) rope-ladder.

Strickzeug ['ʃtrɪktsɔyk], *n.* (—s, *pl.* —e) knitting.

Striegel ['ʃtri:gəl], *m.* (—s, *pl.* —) curry-comb.

striegeln ['ʃtri:gəln], *v.a.* curry.

Strieme ['ʃtri:mə], *f.* (—, *pl.* —n) weal, stripe.

Strippe ['ʃtrɪpə], *f.* (—, *pl.* —n) strap, band, string; cord.

strittig ['ʃtrɪtɪç], *adj.* contentious, debatable.

Stroh [ʃtro:], *n.* (—s, *no pl.*) straw; (*roof*) thatch; *mit* — *decken*, thatch; *leeres* — *dreschen*, beat the air.

Strohfeuer ['ʃtro:fɔyər], *n.* (—s, *no pl.*) (*fig.*) flash in the pan; short-lived enthusiasm.

Strohhalm ['ʃtro:halm], *m.* (—s, *pl.* —e) straw.

Strohhut ['ʃtro:hu:t], *m.* (—s, *pl.* ̈e) straw-hat.

Strohkopf ['ʃtro:kɔpf], *m.* (—(e)s, *pl.* ̈e) (*coll.*) stupid person.

Strohmann ['ʃtro:man], *m.* (—s, *pl.* ̈er) (*coll.*) man of straw; (*Cards*) dummy.

Strohmatte ['ʃtro:matə], *f.* (—, *pl.* —n) straw-mat.

Strohwitwe ['ʃtro:vɪtvə], *f.* (—, *pl.* —n) grass-widow.

Strolch [ʃtrɔlç], *m.* (—(e)s, *pl.* —e) vagabond; (*fig.*) scamp.

Strom [ʃtro:m], *m.* (—(e)s, *pl.* ̈e) river torrent; (*also fig.*) flood; stream (*also Elec.*) current; (*coll.*) electricity *gegen den* — *schwimmen*, swim against the current, be an individualist.

stromab ['ʃtro:map], *adv.* downstream.

stromauf ['ʃtro:mauf], *adv.* upstream.

strömen ['ʃtrø:mən], *v.n.* (*aux.* sein flow, stream; (*rain*) pour; (*people* flock.

Stromer ['ʃtro:mər], *m.* (—s, *pl.* —vagabond, tramp, vagrant.

Stromkreis ['ʃtro:mkraɪs], *m.* (—es *pl.* —e) (*Elec.*) circuit.

Stromschnelle ['ʃtro:mʃnɛlə], *f.* (— *pl.* —n) rapids.

Strömung ['ʃtrø:muŋ], *f.* (—, *pl.* —en current; (*fig.*) tendency.

Strophe ['ʃtro:fə], *f.* (—, *pl.* —n) verse stanza.

strotzen ['ʃtrɔtsən], *v.n.* be puffed up overflow, burst, teem.

strotzend ['ʃtrɔtsənt], *adj. vor Gesund heit* —, bursting with health.

Strudel ['ʃtru:dəl], *m.* (—s, *pl.* — whirl, whirlpool, vortex, eddy; pastry

Struktur [ʃtruk'tu:r], *f.* (—, *pl.* —en structure.

Strumpf [ʃtrumpf], *m.* (—(e)s, *pl.* ⁻e) stocking; (*short*) sock.
Strumpfband [ˈʃtrumpfbant], *n.* (—(e)s, *pl.* ⁻er) garter.
Strumpfwaren [ˈʃtrumpfvaːrən], *f. pl.* hosiery.
Strumpfwirker [ˈʃtrumpfvɪrkər], *m.* (—s, *pl.* —) stocking-weaver.
Strunk [ʃtruŋk], *m.* (—(e)s, *pl.* ⁻e) (*tree*) stump, trunk; (*plant*) stalk.
struppig [ˈʃtrupɪç], *adj.* rough, unkempt, frowsy.
Stube [ˈʃtuːbə], *f.* (—, *pl.* —n) room, chamber; *gute* —, sitting-room.
Stubenarrest [ˈʃtuːbənarɛst], *m.* (—s, *pl.* —e) confinement to quarters.
Stubenhocker [ˈʃtuːbənhɔkər], *m.* (—s, *pl.* —) stay-at-home.
Stubenmädchen [ˈʃtuːbənmɛːtçən], *n.* (—s, *pl.* —) housemaid.
Stuck [ʃtuk], *m.* (—(e)s, *no pl.*) stucco, plaster.
Stück [ʃtyk], *n.* (—(e)s, *pl.* —e) piece; part; lump; (*Theat.*) play; *aus freien —en*, of o.'s own accord; *große —e auf einen halten*, think highly of s.o.
Stückarbeit [ˈʃtykarbaɪt], *f.* (—, *pl.* —en) piece-work.
Stückchen [ˈʃtykçən], *n.* (—s, *pl.* —) small piece, morsel, bit.
stückeln [ˈʃtykəln], *v.a.* cut in(to) pieces; patch, mend.
stückweise [ˈʃtykvaɪzə], *adv.* piecemeal.
Stückwerk [ˈʃtykvɛrk], *n.* (—s, *no pl.*) (*fig.*) patchy *or* imperfect work, a bungled job.
Stückzucker [ˈʃtyktsukər], *m.* (—s, *no pl.*) lump sugar.
Student [ʃtuˈdɛnt], *m.* (—en, *pl.* —en) (*Univ.*) student, undergraduate.
studentenhaft [ʃtuˈdɛntənhaft], *adj.* student-like.
Studentenverbindung [ʃtuˈdɛntənfɛrbɪnduŋ], *f.* (—, *pl.* —en) students' association *or* union.
Studie [ˈʃtuːdjə], *f.* (—, *pl.* —n) study, (*Art*) sketch; (*Lit.*) essay; (*pl.*) studies.
Studienplan [ˈʃtuːdjənplaːn], *m.* (—s, *pl.* ⁻e) curriculum.
Studienrat [ˈʃtuːdjənraːt], *m.* (—s, *pl.* ⁻e) grammar school teacher, assistant master.
studieren [ʃtuˈdiːrən], *v.a., v.n.* study, read (a subject); be at (the) university.
studiert [ʃtuˈdiːrt], *adj.* educated; (*fig.*) affected, deliberate, studied.
Studierte [ʃtuˈdiːrtə], *m.* (*coll.*) egghead.
Studium [ˈʃtuːdjum], *n.* (—s,) *pl.* —dien) study, pursuit; university education.
Stufe [ˈʃtuːfə], *f.* (—, *pl.* —n) step; (*fig.*) degree; *auf gleicher — mit*, on a level with.
stufenweise [ˈʃtuːfənvaɪzə], *adv.* gradually, by degrees.
Stuhl [ʃtuːl], *m.* (—s, *pl.* ⁻e) chair, seat; *der Heilige —*, the Holy See.
Stuhlgang [ˈʃtuːlgaŋ], *m.* (—s, *no pl.*) (*Med.*) stool, evacuation (of the bowels), movement, motion.

Stukkatur [ʃtukaˈtuːr], *f.* (—, *no pl.*) stucco-work.
Stulle [ˈʃtulə], *f.* (—, *pl.* —n) (*dial.*) slice of bread and butter.
Stulpe [ˈʃtulpə], *f.* (—, *pl.* —n) cuff.
stülpen [ˈʃtylpən], *v.a.* turn up, invert.
Stulpnase [ˈʃtulpnaːzə], *f.* (—, *pl.* —n) turned-up nose, pug-nose.
Stulpstiefel [ˈʃtulpʃtiːfəl], *m.* (—s, *pl.* —) top-boot.
stumm [ʃtum], *adj.* mute, dumb, silent.
Stumme [ˈʃtumə], *m. & f.* (—n, *pl.* —n) dumb person, mute.
Stummel [ˈʃtuməl], *m.* (—s, *pl.* —) stump; (*cigarette*) end, butt.
Stummheit [ˈʃtumhaɪt], *f.* (—, *no pl.*) dumbness.
Stümper [ˈʃtympər], *m.* (—s, *pl.* —) bungler, botcher.
stümperhaft [ˈʃtympərhaft], *adj.* bungling, botchy.
stümpern [ˈʃtympərn], *v.a., v.n.* bungle, botch.
Stumpf [ʃtumpf], *m.* (—(e)s, *pl.* ⁻e) stump, trunk; *mit — und Stiel ausrotten*, destroy root and branch.
stumpf [ʃtumpf], *adj.* blunt; (*angle*) obtuse; (*fig.*) dull; *— machen*, blunt, dull.
Stumpfsinn [ˈʃtumpfzɪn], *m.* (—s, *no pl.*) stupidity, dullness.
stumpfwinklig [ˈʃtumpfvɪŋklɪç], *adj.* obtuse-angled.
Stunde [ˈʃtundə], *f.* (—, *pl.* —n) hour; lesson.
stunden [ˈʃtundən], *v.a.* give a respite, allow time (to pay up).
Stundenglas [ˈʃtundənglas], *n.* (—es, *pl.* ⁻er) hour-glass.
Stundenplan [ˈʃtundənplaːn], *m.* (—s, *pl.* ⁻e) (*Sch.*) schedule.
Stundenzeiger [ˈʃtundəntsaɪgər], *m.* (—s, *pl.* —) hour-hand.
Stündlein [ˈʃtyntlaɪn], *n.* (—s, *pl.* —) *sein — hat geschlagen*, his last hour has come.
Stundung [ˈʃtunduŋ], *f.* (—, *pl.* —en) respite, grace.
stupend [ʃtuˈpɛnt], *adj.* stupendous.
stur [ʃtuːr], *adj.* obdurate, unwavering, stolid, dour, stubborn.
Sturm [ʃturm], *m.* (—(e)s, *pl.* ⁻e) storm, gale, tempest, hurricane; (*Mil.*) attack, assault; *— und Drang*, (*Lit.*) Storm and Stress; *— im Wasserglas*, storm in a teacup; *— laufen gegen*, storm against.
Sturmband [ˈʃturmbant], *n.* (—s, *pl.* ⁻er) chinstrap.
Sturmbock [ˈʃturmbɔk], *m.* (—s, *pl.* ⁻e) battering-ram.
stürmen [ˈʃtyrmən], *v.a.* storm, take by assault. *— v.n.* be violent, be stormy; (*Mil.*) advance.
Stürmer [ˈʃtyrmər], *m.* (—s, *pl.* —) assailant; (*football*) centre-forward.
Sturmglocke [ˈʃturmglɔkə], *f.* (—, *pl.* —n) tocsin, alarm-bell.

Sturmhaube

Sturmhaube [ˈʃturmhaubə], *f.* (—, *pl.* **—en**) (*Mil.*) morion, helmet.

stürmisch [ˈʃtyrmɪʃ], *adj.* stormy, tempestuous; (*fig.*) boisterous, turbulent, tumultuous, impetuous; —*er Beifall*, frantic applause; —*e Überfahrt*, rough crossing.

Sturmschritt [ˈʃturmʃrɪt], *m.* (—s, *no pl.*) double march.

Sturmvogel [ˈʃturmfoːɡəl], *m.* (—s, *pl.* —) (*Orn.*) stormy petrel.

Sturz [ʃturts], *m.* (—es, *pl.* ⸚e) fall, tumble; crash; collapse; (*Comm.*) failure, smash; (*government*) overthrow.

Sturzacker [ˈʃturtsakər], *m.* (—s, *pl.* ⸚) freshly ploughed field.

Sturzbach [ˈʃturtsbax], *m.* (—(e)s, *pl.* ⸚e) torrent.

Stürze [ˈʃtyrtsə], *f.* (—, *pl.* —n) pot-lid, cover.

stürzen [ˈʃtyrtsən], *v.a.* hurl, overthrow; ruin. — *v.n.* (*aux.* sein) (*person*) have a fall; (*object*) tumble down; (*business*) fail; crash; plunge; (*water*) rush. — *v.r.* throw oneself; *sich — auf*, rush at, plunge into.

Sturzhelm [ˈʃturtshɛlm], *m.* (—s, *pl.* —e) crash-helmet.

Sturzsee [ˈʃturtszeː], *f.* (—, *no pl.*) heavy sea.

Sturzwelle [ˈʃturtsvɛlə], *f.* (—, *pl.* —n) breaker, roller.

Stute [ˈʃtuːtə], *f.* (—, *pl.* —n) mare.

Stutzbart [ˈʃtutsbaːrt], *m.* (—s, *pl.* ⸚e) short beard.

Stütze [ˈʃtytsə], *f.* (—, *pl.* —n) prop, support, stay.

Stutzen [ˈʃtutsən], *m.* (—s, *pl.* —) short rifle, carbine.

stutzen [ˈʃtutsən], *v.a.* (*hair*) clip, trim; (*horse*) dock, crop; (*tree*) prune, lop. — *v.n.* be taken aback, hesitate.

stützen [ˈʃtytsən], *v.a.* prop, support; base *or* found (on). — *v.r. sich — auf*, lean upon; (*fig.*) rely upon.

Stutzer [ˈʃtutsər], *m.* (—s, *pl.* —) dandy, fop, beau.

stutzerhaft [ˈʃtutsərhaft], *adj.* dandified.

stutzig [ˈʃtutsɪç], *adj.* startled, puzzled; — *werden*, be non-plussed, be taken aback *or* puzzled.

Stützmauer [ˈʃtytsmauər], *f.* (—, *pl.* —n) buttress, retaining wall.

Stützpunkt [ˈʃtytspuŋkt], *m.* (—s, *pl.* —e) point of support; foothold; (*Mil.*) base; (*Tech.*) fulcrum.

Subjekt [zupˈjɛkt], *n.* (—s, *pl.* —e) subject; (*fig.*) creature.

subjektiv [zupjɛkˈtiːf], *adj.* subjective, personal, prejudiced.

sublimieren [zubliˈmiːrən], *v.a.* sublimate.

Substantiv [zupstanˈtiːf], *n.* (—(e)s, *pl.* —e) (*Gram.*) substantive, noun.

subtil [zupˈtiːl], *adj.* subtle.

subtrahieren [zuptraˈhiːrən], *v.a.* subtract.

Subvention [zupvɛnˈtsjoːn], *f.* (—, *pl.* —en) subsidy, grant-in-aid.

Suche [ˈzuːxə], *f.* (—, *no pl.*) search quest; *auf der — nach*, in quest of.

suchen [ˈzuːxən], *v.a., v.n.* seek, look for; attempt, endeavour.

Sucht [zuxt], *f.* (—, *pl.* ⸚e) mania addiction, passion.

süchtig [ˈzyxtɪç], *adj.* addicted (to).

Sud [zuːd], *m.* (—(e)s, *pl.* —e) boiling brewing; suds.

Sudan [ˈzuːdan], *m.* the Sudan.

sudeln [ˈzuːdəln], *v.a., v.n.* smear daub, make a mess (of).

Süden [ˈzyːdən], *m.* (—s, *no pl.*) south

Südfrüchte [ˈzyːtfryçtə], *f. pl.* Mediterranean *or* tropical fruit.

südlich [ˈzyːtlɪç], *adj.* southern, southerly; *in —er Richtung*, southward.

Südosten [zyːtˈʔɔstən], *m.* (—s, *no pl.* south-east.

Suff [zuf], *m.* (—(e)s, *no pl.*) (*sl.* boozing, tippling.

suggerieren [zuɡeˈriːrən], *v.a.* suggest

Sühne [ˈzyːnə], *f.* (—, *no pl.*) expiation atonement.

sühnen [ˈzyːnən], *v.a.* expiate, atone for

Sühneopfer [ˈzyːnəʔɔpfər], *n.* (—s *pl.* —) expiatory sacrifice; atonement

Suite [ˈsviːtə], *f.* (—, *pl.* —n) retinue, train

sukzessiv [zuktseˈsiːf], *adj.* gradual successive.

Sülze [ˈzyltsə], *f.* (—, *pl.* —n) brawn aspic, jelly.

Summa [zuˈmaː], *f.* (—, *pl.* **Summen** — *summarum*, sum total.

summarisch [zuˈmaːrɪʃ], *adj.* summary.

Summe [ˈzumə], *f.* (—, *pl.* —n) sum amount.

summen [ˈzumən], *v.a.* hum. — *v.n* buzz, hum.

summieren [zuˈmiːrən], *v.a.* sum up add up. — *v.r. sich —*, mount up.

Sumpf [zumpf], *m.* (—(e)s, *pl.* ⸚e) bog morass, marsh, moor, swamp.

sumpfig [ˈzumpfɪç], *adj.* boggy, marshy

Sund [zunt], *m.* (—(e)s, *pl.* —e) straits sound.

Sünde [ˈzyndə], *f.* (—, *pl.* —n) sin.

Sündenbock [ˈzyndənbɔk], *m.* (—s *pl.* ⸚e) scapegoat.

Sündenfall [ˈzyndənfal], *m.* (—s, *no pl.*) (*Theol.*) the Fall (*of man*).

Sündengeld [ˈzyndənɡɛlt], *n.* (—(e)s *no pl.*) ill-gotten gains; (*coll.*) vas sum of money.

sündenlos [ˈzyndənloːs], *adj.* sinless impeccable.

Sündenpfuhl [ˈzyndənpfuːl], *m.* (—s *pl.* —e) sink of iniquity.

Sünder [ˈzyndər], *m.* (—s, *pl.* — sinner; *armer —*, poor devil; *du alter —*, you old scoundrel.

sündhaft [ˈzynthaft], *adj.* sinful, iniquitous.

sündig [ˈzyndɪç], *adj.* sinful.

sündigen [ˈzyndɪɡən], *v.n.* sin, err.

Sündigkeit [ˈzyndɪçkaɪt], *f.* (—, *no pl.* sinfulness.

Superlativ [ˈzuːpərlatiːf], *m.* (—s *pl.* —e) superlative (degree).

Suppe ['zupə], *f.* (—, *pl.* —n) soup; *eingebrannte* —, thick soup; *einem edi — versalzen*, spoil s.o.'s little game.
Suppenfleisch ['zupənflaɪʃ], *n.* (—es, *no pl.*) stock-meat.
Suppenkelle ['zupənkɛlə], *f.* (—, *pl.* —n) soup ladle.
Suppenterrine ['zupəntɛri:nə], *f.* (—, *pl.* —n) tureen.
Surrogat [zuro'ga:t], *n.* (—s, *pl.* —e) substitute.
süß [zy:s], *adj.* sweet.
Süße ['zy:sə], *f.* (—, *no pl.*) sweetness.
süßen ['zy:sən], *v.a.* sweeten.
Süßholz ['zy:shɔlts], *n.* (—es, *no pl.*) liquorice; — *raspeln*, talk sweet nothings, pay compliments.
Süßigkeit ['zy:sɪçkaɪt], *f.* (—, *pl.* —en) sweetness; (*pl.*) sweets.
süßlich ['zy:slɪç], *adj.* sweetish; (*fig.*) fulsome, mawkish, cloying.
Süßspeise ['zy:sʃpaɪzə], *f.* (—, *pl.* —n) dessert.
Süßwasser ['zy:svasər], *n.* (—s, *no pl.*) fresh water.
Symbolik [zym'bo:lɪk], *f.* (—, *no pl.*) symbolism.
symbolisch [zym'bo:lɪʃ], *adj.* symbolic(al).
symbolisieren [zymbɔli'zi:rən], *v.a.* symbolize.
symmetrisch [zy'me:trɪʃ], *adj.* symmetrical.
Sympathie [zympa'ti:], *f.* (—, *no pl.*) sympathy.
sympathisch [zym'pa:tɪʃ], *adj.* congenial, likeable.
Synagoge [zyna'go:gə], *f.* (—, *pl.* —n) synagogue.
synchronisieren [zynkroni'zi:rən], *v.a.* synchronise.
Syndikus ['zyndikus], *m.* (—, *pl.* **Syndizi**) syndic.
Synode [zy'no:də], *f.* (—, *pl.* —n) synod.
synthetisch [zyn'te:tɪʃ], *adj.* synthetic.
Syrien [zy:rjən], *n.* Syria.
systematisch [zyste'ma:tɪʃ], *adj.* systematic(al).
Szenarium [stse'na:rjum], *n.* (—s, *pl.* —rien) scenario, stage, scene.
Szene ['stse:nə], *f.* (—, *pl.* —n) scene; *in — setzen*, stage, produce; (*coll.*) *get up; sich in — setzen*, show off.
Szenerie [stsenə'ri:], *f.* (—, *pl.* —n) scenery.
szenisch ['stse:nɪʃ], *adj.* scenic.
Szepter ['stsɛptər], *n.* (—s, *pl.* —) sceptre, mace.

T

T [te:], *n.* (—, *pl.* —) the letter T.
Tabak ['ta:bak], *m.* (—s, *pl.* —e) tobacco.

Tabaksbeutel ['ta:baksbɔytəl], *m.* (—s, *pl.* —) tobacco-pouch.
Tabatiere [ta:ba'tjɛ:rə], *f.* (—, *pl.* —n) snuff-box.
tabellarisch [tabɛ'la:rɪʃ], *adj.* in tables, tabular.
Tabelle [ta'bɛlə], *f.* (—, *pl.* —n) table, index, schedule.
Tablett [ta'blɛt], *n.* (—s, *pl.* —s) tray.
Tablette [ta'blɛtə], *f.* (—, *pl.* —n) tablet, pill.
Tabulatur [tabula'tu:r], *f.* (—, *pl.* —en) tablature, tabling, index.
Tadel ['ta:dəl], *m.* (—s, *pl.* —) blame, censure, reproach; (*Sch.*) bad mark; *ohne* —, blameless.
tadellos ['ta:dəllo:s], *adj.* blameless, faultless, impeccable.
tadeln ['ta:dəln], *v.a.* blame, censure, find fault with; reprimand.
tadelnswert ['ta:dəlnsve:rt], *adj.* blameworthy, culpable.
Tafel ['ta:fəl], *f.* (—, *pl.* —n) board; (*Sch.*) blackboard; slate; (*fig.*) (*obs.*) dinner, banquet; festive fare; (*chocolate*) slab, bar.
Täfelchen ['tɛ:fəlçən], *n.* (—s, *pl.* —) tablet.
tafelförmig ['ta:fəlfœrmɪç], *adj.* tabular.
tafeln ['ta:fəln], *v.n.* dine, feast.
täfeln ['tɛ:fəln], *v.a.* wainscot, panel.
Täfelung ['tɛ:fəluŋ], *f.* (—, *pl.* —en) wainscoting, panelling.
Taft, Taffet [taft, 'tafət], *m.* (—(e)s, *pl.* —e) taffeta.
Tag [ta:k], *m.* (—(e)s, *pl.* —e) day; (*fig.*) light; *der jüngste* —, Doomsday; *bei —e*, in the daytime, by daylight; *sich etwas bei —e besehen*, examine s.th. in the light of day; — *für* —, day by day; *von — zu* —, from day to day; *dieser —e*, one of these days, shortly; *etwas an den — bringen*, bring s.th. to light; *in den — hinein leben*, live improvidently; *— und Nachtgleiche*, equinox.
Tagbau ['ta:kbau], *m.* (—s, *no pl.*) opencast mining.
Tageblatt ['ta:gəblat], *n.* (—s, *pl.* ̈er) daily paper.
Tagebuch ['ta:gəbu:x], *n.* (—(e)s, *pl.* ̈er) diary, journal.
Tagedieb ['ta:gədi:p], *m.* (—(e)s, *pl.* —e) idler, wastrel.
Tagelöhner ['ta:gəlø:nər], *m.* (—s, *pl.* —) day-labourer.
tagen ['ta:gən], *v.n.* dawn; (*gathering*) meet; (*Law*) sit.
Tagesanbruch ['ta:gəsanbrux], *m.* (—s, *pl.* ̈e) daybreak, dawn.
Tagesbericht ['ta:gəsbərɪçt], *m.* (—(e)s, *pl.* —e) daily report.
Tagesgespräch ['ta:gəsgəʃprɛ:ç], *n.* (—(e)s, *pl.* —e) topic of the day.
Tagesordnung ['ta:gəsɔrdnuŋ], *f.* (—, *pl.* —en) agenda.
Tagewerk ['ta:gəvɛrk], *n.* (—s, *no pl.*) day's work, daily round.
täglich ['tɛ:klɪç], *adj.* daily.

tagsüber ['ta:ksy:bər], *adv.* in the daytime, during the day.

Taille ['taljə], *f.* (—, *pl.* —n) waist.

takeln ['ta:kəln], *v.a.* tackle, rig.

Takelwerk ['ta:kəlvɛrk], *n.* (—s, *no pl.*) rigging.

Takt (1) [takt], *m.* (—es, *pl.* —e) (*Mus.*) time, measure, bar; — *schlagen*, beat time.

Takt (2) [takt], *m.* (—es, *no pl.*) tact, discretion.

taktfest ['taktfɛst], *adj.* (*Mus.*) good at keeping time; (*fig.*) firm.

taktieren [tak'ti:rən], *v.n.* (*Mus.*) beat time.

Taktik ['taktɪk], *f.* (—, *pl.* —en) tactics.

Taktiker ['taktɪkər], *m.* (—s, *pl.* —) tactician.

taktisch ['taktɪʃ], *adj.* tactical.

taktlos ['taktlo:s], *adj.* tactless.

Taktmesser ['taktmɛsər], *m.* (—s, *pl.* —) metronome.

Taktstock ['taktʃtɔk], *m.* (—s, *pl.* ⁓e) baton.

Tal [ta:l], *n.* (—(e)s, *pl.* ⁓er) valley, dale, glen.

talab [ta:l'ap], *adv.* downhill.

Talar [ta'la:r], *m.* (—s, *pl.* —e) gown.

Talent [ta'lɛnt], *n.* (—(e)s, *pl.* —e) talent, accomplishment, gift.

talentiert [talən'ti:rt], *adj.* talented, gifted, accomplished.

talentvoll [ta'lɛntfəl], *adj.* talented, gifted, accomplished.

Taler ['ta:lər], *m.* (—s, *pl.* —) old German coin; thaler.

Talfahrt ['ta:lfa:rt], *f.* (—, *pl.* —en) descent.

Talg [talk], *m.* (—(e)s, *no pl.*) tallow.

Talk [talk], *m.* (—(e)s, *no pl.*) talc.

Talkerde ['talke:rdə], *f.* (—, *no pl.*) magnesia.

Talkessel ['ta:lkɛsəl], *m.* (—s, *pl.* —) (*Geog.*) hollow, narrow valley.

Talmulde ['ta:lmuldə], *f.* (—, *pl.* —n) narrow valley, trough.

Talschlucht ['ta:lʃluxt], *f.* (—, *pl.* —en) glen.

Talsohle ['ta:lzo:lə], *f.* (—, *pl.* —n) floor of a valley.

Talsperre ['ta:lʃpɛrə], *f.* (—, *pl.* —n) dam (across valley); barrage.

Tambour ['tambu:r], *m.* (—s, *pl.* —e) drummer.

Tamtam ['tamtam], *n.* (—s, *no pl.*) tom-tom; (*fig.*) palaver.

Tand [tant], *m.* (—(e)s, *no pl.*) knick-knack, trifle; rubbish.

Tändelei [tɛndə'laɪ], *f.* (—, *pl.* —en) trifling, toying; (*fig.*) flirting.

Tändelmarkt ['tɛndəlmarkt], *m.* (—s, *pl.* ⁓e) rag-fair.

tändeln ['tɛndəln], *v.n.* trifle, dally, toy; (*fig.*) flirt.

Tang [taŋ], *m.* (—s, *pl.* —e) (*Bot.*) seaweed.

Tanganjika [taŋga'nji:ka], *n.* Tanganyika.

Tangente [taŋ'gɛntə], *f.* (—, *pl.* —n) tangent.

Tanger ['taŋər], *n.* Tangier.

Tank [taŋk], *m.* (—(e)s, *pl.* —e) tank.

tanken ['taŋkən], *v.n.* refuel; fill up (with petrol).

Tankstelle ['taŋkʃtɛlə], *f.* (—, *pl.* —n) filling-station.

Tanne ['tanə], *f.* (—, *pl.* —n) (*Bot.*) fir.

Tannenbaum ['tanənbaum], *m.* (—s, *pl.* ⁓e) (*Bot.*) fir-tree.

Tannenholz ['tanənhɔlts], *n.* (—es, *no pl.*) (*timber*) deal.

Tannenzapfen ['tanəntsapfən], *m.* (—s, *pl.* —) (*Bot.*) fir-cone.

Tansania [tanza'ni:a], *n.* Tanzania.

Tante ['tantə], *f.* (—, *pl.* —n) aunt.

Tantieme [tã'tjɛ:mə], *f.* (—, *pl.* —n) royalty, share (in profits), percentage.

Tanz [tants], *m.* (—es, *pl.* ⁓e) dance.

Tanzboden ['tantsbo:dən], *m.* (—s, *pl.* ⁓) ballroom, dance-hall.

tänzeln ['tɛntsəln], *v.n.* skip about, frisk; (*horses*) amble.

tanzen ['tantsən], *v.a., v.n.* dance.

tanzlustig ['tantslustɪç], *adj.* fond of dancing.

Tapet [ta'pe:t], *n.* (—s, *no pl.*) *aufs* — *bringen*, broach, bring up for discussion.

Tapete [ta'pe:tə], *f.* (—, *pl.* —n) wall-paper.

tapezieren [tape'tsi:rən], *v.a.* paper.

Tapezierer [tape'tsi:rər], *m.* (—s, *pl.* —) paperhanger; upholsterer.

tapfer ['tapfər], *adj.* brave, valiant, gallant, courageous.

Tapferkeit ['tapfərkaɪt], *f.* (—, *no pl.*) valour, bravery, gallantry.

Tapisserie [tapsɪə'ri:], *f.* (—, *no pl.*) needlework; tapestry.

tappen ['tapən], *v.n.* grope about.

täppisch ['tɛpɪʃ], *adj.* clumsy, awkward, unwieldy.

tarnen ['tarnən], *v.a.* camouflage.

Tasche ['taʃə], *f.* (—, *pl.* —n) pocket; bag, pouch; *in die* — *stecken*, pocket; *in die* — *greifen*, pay, fork out, put o.'s hand in o.'s pocket.

Taschendieb ['taʃəndi:p], *m.* (—(e)s, *pl.* —e) pickpocket; *vor* —*en wird gewarnt*, beware of pickpockets.

Taschenformat ['taʃənfɔrma:t], *n.* (—s, *no pl.*) pocket-size.

Taschenspieler ['taʃənʃpi:lər], *m.* (—s, *pl.* —) juggler, conjurer.

Taschentuch ['taʃəntu:x], *n.* (—s, *pl.* ⁓er) (pocket-)handkerchief.

Taschenuhr ['taʃənu:r], *f.* (—, *pl.* —en) pocket-watch.

Tasse ['tasə], *f.* (—, *pl.* —n) cup.

Tastatur [tasta'tu:r], *f.* (—, *pl.* —en) keyboard.

Taste ['tastə], *f.* (—, *pl.* —n) (*Mus.*) key.

tasten ['tastən], *v.n.* grope about, feel o.'s way.

Tastsinn ['tastzɪn], *m.* (—s, *no pl.*) sense of touch.

Tat [ta:t], *f.* (—, *pl.* —en) deed, act, action; feat, exploit; *in der* —, in fact, indeed; *auf frischer* —, in the very act; *einem mit Rat und* — *beistehen*, give s.o. advice and guidance, help by word and deed.

Tatbestand ['ta:tbəʃtant], *m.* (—es, *pl.* —e) (*Law*) facts of the case.

Tatendrang ['ta:təndraŋ], *m.* (—(e)s, *no pl.*) urge for action; impetuosity.

tatenlos ['ta:tənlo:s], *adj.* inactive.

Täter ['tɛ:tər], *m.* (—s, *pl.* —) perpetrator, doer; culprit.

tätig ['tɛ:tɪç], *adj.* active, busy.

Tätigkeit ['tɛ:tɪçkaɪt], *f.* (—, *pl.* —en) activity.

Tätigkeitswort ['tɛ:tɪçkaɪtsvɔrt], *n.* (—(e)s, *pl.* ⁀er) (*Gram.*) verb.

Tatkraft ['ta:tkraft], *f.* (—, *no pl.*) energy.

tätlich ['tɛ:tlɪç], *adj.* — *werden*, become violent.

tätowieren [tɛ:to'vi:rən], *v.a.* tattoo.

Tatsache ['ta:tzaxə], *f.* (—, *pl.* —en) fact, matter of fact.

tatsächlich ['ta:tzɛçlɪç], *adj.* actual. — *excl.* really!

tätscheln ['tɛ:tʃəln], *v.a.* fondle.

Tatterich ['tatərɪç], *m.* (—s, *no pl.*) (*coll.*) trembling, shakiness.

Tatze ['tatsə], *f.* (—, *pl.* —n) paw.

Tau (1) [tau], *m.* (—s, *no pl.*) thaw; dew.

Tau (2) [tau], *n.* (—s, *pl.* —e) rope, cable.

taub [taup], *adj.* deaf; (*nut*) hollow, empty; — *machen*, deafen; — *sein gegen*, turn a deaf ear to.

Täubchen ['tɔypçən], *n.* (—s, *pl.* —) little dove; (*fig.*) sweetheart.

Taube ['taubə], *f.* (—, *pl.* —n) (*Orn.*) pigeon, dove.

Taubenschlag ['taubənʃla:k], *m.* (—s, *pl.* ⁀e) dovecote.

Taubenschwanz ['taubənʃvants], *m.* (—es, *pl.* ⁀e) (*Ent.*) hawkmoth.

Tauber ['taubər], *m.* (—s, *pl.* —) (*Orn.*) cock-pigeon.

Taubheit ['tauphaɪt], *f.* (—, *no pl.*) deafness.

Taubnessel ['taupnɛsəl], *f.* (—, *pl.* —n) (*Bot.*) deadnettle.

taubstumm ['taupʃtum], *adj.* deaf and dumb, deaf-mute.

tauchen ['tauçən], *v.n.* (*aux.* haben & sein) dive, plunge. — *v.a.* immerse, dip.

Tauchsieder ['tauçzi:dər], *m.* (—s, *pl.* —) (*Elec.*) immersion heater.

tauen ['tauən], *v.a., v.n.* thaw, melt.

Taufbecken ['taufbɛkən], *n.* (—s, *pl.* —) (baptismal) font.

Taufe ['taufə], *f.* (—, *pl.* —n) baptism, christening; *aus der* — *heben*, stand godparent.

taufen ['taufən], *v.a.* baptise, christen.

Taufkleid ['taufklaɪt], *n.* (—s, *pl.* —er) christening robe.

Täufling ['tɔyflɪŋ], *m.* (—s, *pl.* —e) infant presented for baptism; neophyte.

Taufname ['taufna:mə], *n.* (—ns, *pl.* —n) Christian name.

Taufpate ['taufpa:tə], *m.* (—n, *pl.* —n) godfather, godmother.

Taufstein ['taufʃtaɪn], *n.* (—s, *pl.* —e) (baptismal) font.

taugen ['taugən], *v.n.* be good for, be fit for; *nichts* —, be good for nothing.

Taugenichts ['taugənɪçts], *m.* (—, *pl.* —e) ne'er-do-well, scapegrace, good-for-nothing.

tauglich ['tauklɪç], *adj.* able; useful, fit, suitable.

Taumel ['tauməl], *m.* (—s, *no pl.*) giddiness, dizziness, staggering; (*fig.*) whirl; ecstasy, frenzy, delirium, intoxication.

taumeln ['tauməln], *v.n.* (*aux.* sein) reel, stagger.

Tausch [tauʃ], *m.* (—es, *no pl.*) exchange, barter.

tauschen ['tauʃən], *v.a.* exchange for, barter against, swop; *die Rollen* —, change places.

täuschen ['tɔyʃən], *v.a.* deceive, delude. — *v.r. sich* —, be mistaken.

Tauschhandel ['tauʃhandəl], *m.* (—s, *no pl.*) barter.

Tauschmittel ['tauʃmɪtəl], *n.* (—s, *pl.* —) medium of exchange.

Täuschung ['tɔyʃuŋ], *f.* (—, *pl.* —en) deceit, deception; illusion.

Täuschungsversuch ['tɔyʃuŋsfɛrzu:ç], *m.* (—es, *pl.* —e) attempt at deception; (*Mil.*) diversion.

tausend ['tauzənt], *num. adj.* a thousand.

tausendjährig ['tauzəntjɛ:rɪç], *adj.* millennial, of a thousand years; *das* —*e Reich*, the millennium.

Tausendsasa ['tauzəntzasa], *m.* (—s, *pl.* —) devil of a fellow.

Tautropfen ['tautrɔpfən], *m.* (—s, *pl.* —) dew-drop.

Tauwetter ['tauvɛtər], *n.* (—s, *no pl.*) thaw.

Taxameter [taksa'me:tər], *m.* (—s, *pl.* —) taximeter.

Taxe ['taksə], *f.* (—, *pl.* —n) set rate, tariff; (taxi)cab; *nach der* — *verkauft werden*, be sold *ad valorem*.

taxieren [tak'si:rən], *v.a.* appraise, value.

Taxus ['taksus], *m.* (—, *pl.* —) (*Bot.*) yew(-tree).

Technik ['tɛçnɪk], *f.* (—, *pl.* —en) technology, engineering; technique; skill, execution.

Techniker ['tɛçnɪkər], *m.* (—s, *pl.* —) technician, technical engineer.

Technikum ['tɛçnɪkum], *n.* (—s, *pl.* —s) technical school, college.

technisch ['tɛçnɪʃ], *adj.* technical; —*er Ausdruck*, technical term; —*e Störung*, technical hitch *or* breakdown.

technologisch [tɛçno'lo:gɪʃ], *adj.* technological.

221

Techtelmechtel

Techtelmechtel ['tɛçtəlmɛçtəl], *n.* (**—s,** *pl.* **—**) (*coll.*) love affair, flirtation.
Tee [te:], *m.* (**—s,** *no pl.*) tea.
Teedose ['te:do:zə], *f.* (**—,** *pl.* **—n**) tea-caddy.
Teekanne ['te:kanə], *f.* (**—,** *pl.* **—n**) tea-pot.
Teelöffel ['te:lœfəl], *m.* (**—s,** *pl.* **—**) tea-spoon.
Teemaschine ['te:maʃi:nə], *f.* (**—,** *pl.* **—n**) tea-urn.
Teer [te:r], *m.* (**—(e)s,** *no pl.*) tar.
Teerleinwand ['te:rlaɪnvant], *f.* (**—,** *no pl.*) tarpaulin.
Teerose ['te:ro:zə], *f.* (**—,** *pl.* **—n**) (*Bot.*) tea rose.
Teerpappe ['te:rpapə], *f.* (**—,** *no pl.*) roofing-felt.
teeren ['te:rən], *v.a.* tar.
Teesieb ['te:zi:p], *n.* (**—(e)s,** *pl.* **—e**) tea-strainer.
Teich [taɪç], *m.* (**—es,** *pl.* **—e**) pond.
Teig [taɪk], *m.* (**—(e)s,** *pl.* **—e**) dough, paste.
teigig ['taɪgɪç], *adj.* doughy.
Teigrolle ['taɪkrɔlə], *f.* (**—,** *pl.* **—n**) rolling-pin.
Teil [taɪl], *m. & n.* (**—(e)s,** *pl.* **—e**) part; portion; piece, component; share; *edler* **—,** vital part; *zum* **—,** partly; *zu gleichen* **—en,** share and share alike.
teilbar ['taɪlba:r], *adj.* divisible.
Teilchen ['taɪlçən], *n.* (**—s,** *pl.* **—**) particle.
teilen ['taɪlən], *v.a.* divide; share; partition off. **—** *v.r. sich* **—,** share in; (*road*) fork.
Teiler ['taɪlər], *m.* (**—s,** *pl.* **—**) divider; (*Maths.*) divisor.
teilhaben ['taɪlha:bən], *v.n. irr.* (have a) share in, participate in.
Teilhaber ['taɪlha:bər], *m.* (**—s,** *pl.* **—**) partner.
teilhaftig ['taɪlhaftɪç], *adj.* sharing, participating; *einer Sache* **—** *werden,* partake of s.th., come in for s.th.
Teilnahme ['taɪlna:mə], *f.* (**—,** *no pl.*) participation; (*fig.*) sympathy, interest.
teilnahmslos ['taɪlna:mslo:s], *adj.* unconcerned, indifferent.
Teilnahmslosigkeit ['taɪlna:mslo:zɪçkaɪt], *f.* (**—,** *no pl.*) unconcern; listlessness, indifference.
teilnahmsvoll ['taɪlna:msfɔl], *adj.* solicitous.
teilnehmen ['taɪlne:mən], *v.n. irr.* take part (in), participate, partake; (*fig.*) sympathise.
Teilnehmer ['taɪlne:mər], *m.* (**—s,** *pl.* **—**) member, participant; (*telephone*) subscriber.
teils [taɪls], *adv.* partly.
Teilstrecke ['taɪlʃtrɛkə], *f.* (**—,** *pl.* **—n**) section (of a railway).
Teilung ['taɪluŋ], *f.* (**—,** *pl.* **—en**) division, partition; distribution.
Teilungszahl ['taɪluŋstsa:l], *f.* (**—,** **—en**) (*Maths.*) dividend; quotient.

teilweise ['taɪlvaɪzə], *adv.* partly, in part.
Teilzahlung ['taɪltsa:luŋ], *f.* (**—,** *pl.* **—en**) part-payment, instalment.
Teint [tɛ̃], *m.* (**—s,** *no pl.*) complexion.
telephonieren [telefo'ni:rən], *v.a., v.n.* telephone.
Telegraphie [telegra'fi:], *f.* (**—,** *no pl.* telegraphy.
telegraphisch [tele'gra:fɪʃ], *adj.* telegraphic, by telegraph.
Telegramm [tele'gram], *n.* (**—s,** *pl.* **—e**) telegram, wire, cable.
Telegrammadresse [tele'gramadrɛsə] *f.* (**—,** *pl.* **—n**) telegraphic address.
Telegrammformular [tele'gramfor mula:r], *n.* (**—s,** *pl.* **—e**) telegram form.
Teleskop [telɛs'ko:p], *n.* (**—s,** *pl.* **—e**) telescope.
Teller ['tɛlər], *m.* (**—s,** *pl.* **—**) plate.
Tempel ['tɛmpəl], *m.* (**—s,** *pl.* **—**) temple.
Temperament [tɛmpəra'mɛnt], *n.* (**—s,** *pl.* **—e**) temperament, disposition; (*fig.*) spirits.
temperamentvoll [tɛmpəra'mɛntfɔl] *adj.* full of spirits, vivacious; lively.
Temperatur [tɛmpəra'tu:r], *f.* (**—,** *pl.* **—en**) temperature.
Temperenzler [tɛmpə'rɛntslər], *m.* (**—s,** *pl.* **—**) total abstainer, teetotaller.
temperieren [tɛmpə'ri:rən], *v.a.* temper.
Tempo ['tɛmpo:], *n.* (**—s,** *pl.* **—s** *Tempi*) time, measure, speed.
temporisieren [tɛmpori'zi:rən], *v.n.* temporise.
Tendenz [tɛn'dɛnts], *f.* (**—,** *pl.* **—en**) tendency.
tendenziös [tɛndɛn'tsjø:s], *adj.* biased, coloured, tendentious.
Tender ['tɛndər], *m.* (**—s,** *pl.* **—**) (*Railw.*) tender.
Tenne ['tɛnə], *f.* (**—,** *pl.* **—n**) threshing floor.
Tenor [te'no:r], *m.* (**—s,** *pl.* **⸚e**) (*Mus.* tenor.
Teppich ['tɛpɪç], *m.* (**—s,** *pl.* **—e**) carpet.
Termin [tɛr'mi:n], *m.* (**—s,** *pl.* **—e** time, date, appointed day; *einen ansetzen,* fix a day (for a hearing examination etc.).
Termingeschäft [tɛr'mi:ngəʃɛft], *n.* (**—s,** *pl.* **—e**) (business in) futures.
Terminologie [tɛrminolo'gi:], *f.* (**—** *pl.* **—n**) terminology.
Terpentin [tɛrpɛn'ti:n], *n.* (**—s,** *no pl.* turpentine.
Terrain [tɛ'rɛ̃], *n.* (**—s,** *pl.* **—s**) ground terrain.
Terrasse [tɛ'rasə], *f.* (**—,** *pl.* **—n** terrace.
Terrine [tɛ'ri:nə], *f.* (**—,** *pl.* **—n** tureen.
territorial [tɛrɪto'rja:l], *adj.* territorial
Territorium [tɛrɪ'to:rjum], *n.* (**—s** *pl.* **—torien**) territory.

tertiär [tɛr'tsjɛːr], *adj.* tertiary.
Terzett [tɛr'tsɛt], *n.* (—s, *pl.* —e) trio.
Testament [tɛsta'mɛnt], *n.* (—s, *pl.* —e) testament, will; (*Bibl.*) Testament; *ohne* —, intestate.
testamentarisch [tɛstamɛn'taːrɪʃ], *adj.* testamentary.
Testamentseröffnung [tɛsta'mɛntsɛrœfnuŋ], *f.* (—, *pl.* —en) reading of the will.
Testamentsvollstrecker [tɛsta'mɛntsfɔlʃtrɛkər], *m.* (—s, *pl.* —) executor.
teuer ['tɔyər], *adj.* dear; costly, expensive; *einem* — *zu stehen kommen*, cost s.o. dear.
Teuerung ['tɔyəruŋ], *f.* (—, *pl.* —en) scarcity, dearth.
Teufel ['tɔyfəl], *m.* (—s, *pl.* —) devil, fiend; *armer* —, poor devil; *scher dich zum* —, go to blazes; *den* — *an die Wand malen*, talk of the devil.
Teufelei [tɔyfə'laɪ], *f.* (—, *pl.* —en) devilry, devilish trick.
teuflisch ['tɔyflɪʃ], *adj.* devilish, diabolical.
Thailand ['taɪlant], *n.* Thailand.
Theater [te'aːtər], *n.* (—s, *pl.* —) theatre, stage.
Theaterkarte [te'aːtərkartə], *f.* (—, *pl.* —n) theatre-ticket.
Theaterkasse [te'aːtərkasə], *f.* (—, *pl.* —n) box-office.
Theaterstück [te'aːtərʃtyk], *n.* (—(e)s, *pl.* —e) play, drama.
Theatervorstellung [te'aːtərfoːrʃtɛluŋ], *f.* (—, *pl.* —en) theatre performance.
Theaterzettel [te'aːtərtsɛtəl], *m.* (—s, *pl.* —) play-bill.
theatralisch [tea'traːlɪʃ], *adj.* theatrical; dramatic; histrionic.
Thema ['teːmaː], *n.* (—s, *pl.* —men, **Themata**) theme, subject, topic.
Themse ['tɛmzə], *f.* Thames.
Theologe [teo'loːgə], *m.* (—n, *pl.* —n) theologian.
Theologie [teolo'giː], *f.* (—, *no pl.*) theology, divinity.
theorrtisch [teo'reːtɪʃ], *adj.* theoretical.
theoretisieren [teoreti'ziːrən], *v.n.* theorise.
Theorie [teo'riː], *f.* (—, *pl.* —n) theory.
Therapie [tera'piː], *f.* (—, *no pl.*) therapy.
Therme ['tɛrmə], *f.* (—, *pl.* —n) hot spring.
Thermometer [tɛrmo'meːtər], *n.* (—s, *pl.* —) thermometer.
Thermosflasche ['tɛrmɔsflaʃə], *f.* (—, *pl.* —n) thermos-flask.
These ['teːzə], *f.* (—, *pl.* —n) thesis.
Thron [troːn], *m.* (—(e)s, *pl.* —e) throne; *auf den* — *setzen*, place on the throne, enthrone; *vom* — *stoßen*, dethrone, depose.
Thronbesteigung ['troːnbəʃtaɪguŋ], *f.* (—, *pl.* —en) accession (to the throne).
Thronbewerber ['troːnbəvɛrbər], *m.* (—s, *pl.* —) claimant to the throne, pretender.
thronen ['troːnən], *v.n.* sit enthroned.

Thronerbe ['troːnɛrbə], *m.* (—n, *pl.* —n) heir apparent, crown prince.
Thronfolge ['troːnfɔlgə], *f.* (—, *no pl.*) line *or* order of succession.
Thronfolger ['troːnfɔlgər], *m.* (—s, *pl.* —) heir to the throne, heir apparent.
Thronhimmel ['troːnhɪməl], *m.* (—s, *pl.* —s) canopy.
Thronrede ['troːnreːdə], *f.* (—, *pl.* —n) speech from the throne.
Thunfisch ['tuːnfɪʃ], *m.* (—es, *pl.* —e) (*Zool.*) tunny, (*Am.*) tuna.
Thüringen ['tyːrɪŋən], *n.* Thuringia.
Thymian ['tyːmjaːn], *m.* (—s, *no pl.*) (*Bot.*) thyme.
ticken ['tɪkən], *v.n.* tick.
tief [tiːf], *adj.* deep, profound, low; far; extreme; (*voice*) bass; (*fig.*) profound; *in* —*ster Nacht*, in the dead of night; *aus* —*stem Herzen*, from the bottom of o.'s heart. — *adv.* — *atmen*, take a deep breath; — *in Schulden*, head over ears in debt; — *verletzt*, cut to the quick.
Tiefbau ['tiːfbau], *m.* (—s, *no pl.*) underground workings.
tiefbedrückt ['tiːfbədrykt], *adj.* deeply distressed; very depressed.
tiefbewegt ['tiːfbəveːkt], *adj.* deeply moved.
Tiefe ['tiːfə], *f.* (—, *pl.* —en) depth; (*fig.*) profundity.
tiefgebeugt ['tiːfgəbɔykt], *adj.* bowed down.
tiefgreifend ['tiːfgraɪfənt], *adj.* radical, sweeping.
tiefschürfend ['tiːfʃyrfənt], *adj.* profound; thoroughgoing.
Tiefsee ['tiːfzeː], *f.* (—, *no pl.*) deep sea.
Tiefsinn ['tiːfzɪn], *m.* (—s, *no pl.*) pensiveness, melancholy.
tiefsinnig ['tiːfzɪnɪç], *adj.* pensive, melancholy, melancholic(al).
Tiegel ['tiːgəl], *m.* (—s, *pl.* —) crucible; saucepan.
Tier [tiːr], *n.* (—(e)s, *pl.* —e) animal, beast; *ein großes* —, (*coll.*) a V.I.P., a bigwig; (*Am.*) a swell, a big shot.
Tierart ['tiːraːrt], *f.* (—, *pl.* —en) (*Zool.*) species.
Tierarzt ['tiːraːrtst], *m.* (—es, *pl.* ⸚e) veterinary surgeon.
Tierbändiger ['tiːrbɛndɪgər], *m.* (—s, *pl.* —) animal-tamer.
Tiergarten ['tiːrgartən], *m.* (—s, *pl.* ⸚) zoological gardens, zoo.
tierisch ['tiːrɪʃ], *adj.* animal, brute, brutal, bestial.
Tierkreis ['tiːrkraɪs], *m.* (—es, *no pl.*) zodiac.
Tierkunde ['tiːrkundə], *f.* (—, *no pl.*) zoology.
Tierquälerei ['tiːrkvɛːləraɪ], *f.* (—, *pl.* —en) cruelty to animals.
Tierreich ['tiːrraɪç], *n.* (—(e)s, *no pl.*) animal kingdom.
Tierschutzverein ['tiːrʃutsfəraɪn], *m.* (—s, *pl.* —e) society for the prevention of cruelty to animals.

Tierwärter ['ti:rvɛrtər], m. (—s, pl. —) keeper (at a zoo).

Tiger ['ti:gər], m. (—s, pl. —) (Zool.) tiger.

Tigerin ['ti:gərɪn], f. (—, pl. —nen) (Zool.) tigress.

tilgbar ['tɪlkba:r], adj. extinguishable; (debt) redeemable.

tilgen ['tɪlgən], v.a. strike out, efface, annul; (debt) discharge; (sin) expiate, atone for.

Tilgung ['tɪlguŋ], f. (—, pl. —en) striking out, obliteration; annulment, payment; redemption.

Tilgungsfonds ['tɪlguŋsfɔ], m. (—, pl. —) sinking fund.

Tingeltangel ['tɪŋəltaŋəl], m. & n. (—s, pl. —) (coll.) music-hall.

Tinktur [tɪŋk'tu:r], f. (—, pl. —en) tincture.

Tinte ['tɪntə], f. (—, pl. —n) ink; in der — sein, be in a jam, be in the soup.

Tintenfaß ['tɪntənfas], n. (—sses, pl. –sser) ink-pot, ink-stand.

Tintenfisch ['tɪntənfɪʃ], m. (—es, pl. —e) (Zool.) cuttle-fish.

Tintenfleck ['tɪntənflɛk], m. (—s, pl. —e) blot, ink-spot.

Tintenklecks ['tɪntənklɛks], m. (—es, pl. —e) blot.

Tintenstift ['tɪntənʃtɪft], m. (—s, pl. —e) indelible pencil.

Tintenwischer ['tɪntənvɪʃər], m. (—s, pl. —) pen-wiper.

tippen ['tɪpən], v.a. tap; (coll.) type.

Tirol [ti'ro:l], n. Tyrol.

Tisch [tɪʃ], m. (—es, pl. —e) table, board; den — decken, lay the table; zu — gehen, sit down to dinner.

Tischdecke ['tɪʃdɛkə], f. (—, pl. —n) tablecloth.

Tischgebet ['tɪʃgəbe:t], n. (—s, pl. —e) grace.

Tischler ['tɪʃlər], m. (—s, pl. —) joiner, cabinet-maker, carpenter.

Tischlerei [tɪʃlə'raɪ], f. (—, no pl.) joinery, cabinet-making, carpentry.

Tischrede ['tɪʃre:də], f. (—, pl. —n) after-dinner speech.

Tischrücken ['tɪʃrykən], n. (—s, no pl.) table-turning.

Tischtennis ['tɪʃtɛnɪs], n. (—, no pl.) table-tennis, ping-pong.

Tischtuch ['tɪʃtu:x], n. (—(e)s, pl. –er) tablecloth.

Tischzeit ['tɪʃtsaɪt], f. (—, pl. —en) mealtime.

Titane [ti'ta:nə], m. (—n, pl. —n) Titan.

titanenhaft [ti'ta:nənhaft], adj. titanic.

Titel ['ti:təl], m. (—s, pl. —) title; claim; heading, headline.

Titelbild ['ti:təlbɪlt], n. (—(e)s, pl. —er) frontispiece.

Titelblatt ['ti:təlblat], n. (—(e)s, pl. –er) title page.

Titelrolle ['ti:təlrɔlə], f. (—, pl. —n) title role.

titulieren [titu'li:rən], v.a. style, address.

toben ['to:bən], v.n. rave; rage, roar; be furious; be wild.

tobsüchtig ['to:pzyçtɪç], adj. raving, mad.

Tochter ['tɔxtər], f. (—, pl. ¨) daughter.

töchterlich ['tœçtərlɪç], adj. filial, daughterly.

Tod [to:t], m. (—es, pl. —esfälle or (rare) —e) death, decease, demise; dem — geweiht, doomed; Kampf auf — und Leben, fight to the death; zum — verurteilen, condemn to death.

Todesangst ['to:dəsaŋst], f. (—, pl. ¨e) agony, mortal terror.

Todesanzeige ['to:dəsantsaɪgə], f. (—, pl. —n) announcement of death; obituary notice.

Todesfall ['to:dəsfal], m. (—(e)s, pl. ¨e) death, decease; fatality.

Todesgefahr ['to:dəsgəfa:r], f. (—, pl. —en) mortal danger.

Todeskampf ['to:dəskampf], m. (—(e)s, pl. ¨e) death agony.

todesmutig ['to:dəsmu:tɪç], adj. death-defying.

Todesstoß ['to:dəsʃto:s], m. (—es, pl. ¨e) death-blow.

Todesstrafe ['to:dəsʃtra:fə], f. (—, no pl.) capital punishment.

Todfeind ['to:tfaɪnt], m. (—es, pl. —e) mortal enemy.

todkrank ['to:tkraŋk], adj. sick unto death, dangerously or mortally ill.

tödlich ['tœ:tlɪç], adj. mortal, deadly, fatal.

todmüde ['to:tmy:də], adj. tired to death.

Todsünde ['to:tzyndə], f. (—, pl. —n) mortal sin.

Togo ['to:go], n. Togo.

Toilette [toa'lɛtə], f. (—, pl. —n) lavatory, toilet; (fig.) dress.

tolerant [tole'rant], adj. tolerant.

Toleranz [tole'rants], f. (—, no pl.) toleration; tolerance.

tolerieren [tole'ri:rən], v.a. tolerate.

toll [tɔl], adj. mad, frantic; wild; —er Streich, mad prank; zum — werden, enough to drive o. mad.

Tolle ['tɔlə], f. (—, pl. —n) (dial.) forelock, tuft of hair, top-knot.

Tollhaus ['tɔlhaus], n. (—es, pl. ¨er) madhouse, lunatic asylum.

Tollheit ['tɔlhaɪt], f. (—, pl. —en) foolhardiness, mad prank.

Tollkirsche ['tɔlkɪrʃə], f. (—, pl. —n) belladonna, deadly nightshade.

Tollwut ['tɔlvu:t], f. (—, no pl.) frenzy; rabies.

Tolpatsch ['tɔlpatʃ], m. (—es, pl. —e) clumsy person.

Tölpel ['tœlpəl], m. (—s, pl. —) blockhead, lout, hobbledehoy.

Tölpelei [tœlpə'laɪ], f. (—, pl. —en) clumsiness, awkwardness.

tölpelhaft ['tœlpəlhaft], adj. clumsy, doltish, loutish.

Tomate [to'ma:tə], f. (—, pl. —n) tomato.

Ton (1) [to:n], *m.* (—(e)s, *pl.* ⸚e) sound, tone, accent, note; shade; manners; *guter* (*schlechter*) —, good (bad) form, etiquette; *den* — *angeben*, set the fashion.

Ton (2) [to:n], *m.* (—s, *no pl.*) clay, potter's earth.

Tonabnehmer ['to:nabne:mər], *m.* (—s, *pl.* —) (*gramophone*) pick-up.

tonangebend ['to:nange:bənt], *adj.* leading in fashion, setting the pace; leading, fashionable.

Tonart ['to:na:rt], *f.* (—, *pl.* —en) (*Mus.*) key.

Tonbandgerät ['to:nbantgɛrɛ:t], *n.* (—s, *pl.* —e) tape-recorder.

tönen ['tø:nən], *v.n.* sound.

Tonerde ['to:ne:rdə], *f.* (—, *no pl.*) clay.

tönern ['tø:nərn], *adj.* earthen.

Tonfall ['to:nfal], *m.* (—s, *no pl.*) cadence, intonation (of voice).

Tonfolge ['to:nfɔlgə], *f.* (—, *pl.* —n) (*Mus.*) succession of notes.

Tonführung ['to:nfy:ruŋ], *f.* (—, *no pl.*) modulation.

Tonkunst ['to:nkunst], *f.* (—, *no pl.*) music.

Tonkünstler ['to:nkynstlər], *m.* (—s, *pl.* —) musician.

Tonleiter ['to:nlaItər], *f.* (—, *pl.* —n) scale, gamut.

Tonne ['tɔnə], *f.* (—, *pl.* —n) tun, cask, barrel; ton.

Tonnengewölbe ['tɔnəngəvœlbə], *n.* (—s, *pl.* —) cylindrical vault.

Tonpfeife ['to:npfaIfə], *f.* (—, *pl.* —n) clay-pipe.

Tonsatz ['to:nzats], *m.* (—es, *pl.* ⸚e) (*Mus.*) composition.

Tonsur [tɔn'zu:r], *f.* (—, *pl.* —en) tonsure.

Tonwelle ['to:nvɛlə], *f.* (—, *pl.* —n) sound-wave.

Topas [to'pa:s], *m.* (—es, *pl.* —e) topaz.

Topf [tɔpf], *m.* (—(e)s, *pl.* ⸚e) pot; *alles in einen* — *werfen*, lump everything together.

Topfblume ['tɔpfblu:mə], *f.* (—, *pl.* —n) pot-plant.

Topfdeckel ['tɔpfdɛkəl], *m.* (—s, *pl.* —) lid of a pot.

Töpfer ['tœpfər], *m.* (—s, *pl.* —) potter.

Töpferarbeit ['tœpfərarbaIt], *f.* (—, *pl.* —en) pottery.

Töpferscheibe ['tœpfərʃaIbə], *f.* (—, *pl.* —n) potter's wheel.

Töpferware ['tœpfərva:rə], *f.* (—, *pl.* —n) pottery, earthenware.

Topfgucker ['tɔpfgukər], *m.* (—s, *pl.* —) busybody; inquisitive person.

Topographie [topogra'fi:], *f.* (—, *no pl.*) topography.

Tor (1) [to:r], *m.* (—en, *pl.* —en) (*obs.*) fool, simpleton.

Tor (2) [to:r], *n.* (—(e)s, *pl.* —e) gate; (*Footb.*) goal.

Torangel ['to:raŋəl], *f.* (—, *pl.* —n) hinge.

Tor(es)schluß ['to:r(əs)ʃlus], *m.* (—es, *no pl.*) shutting of the gate; *noch gerade vor* —, at the eleventh hour.

Torf [tɔrf], *m.* (—(e)s, *no pl.*) peat, turf.

Torfgrube ['tɔrfgru:bə], *f.* (—, *pl.* —n) turf-pit.

Torfmoor ['tɔrfmo:r], *n.* (—s, *pl.* —e) peat-bog.

Torfstecher ['tɔrfʃtɛçər], *m.* (—s, *pl.* —) peat-cutter.

Torheit ['to:rhaIt], *f.* (—, *pl.* —en) foolishness, folly.

Torhüter ['to:rhy:tər], *m.* (—s, *pl.* —) gate-keeper.

töricht ['tø:rIçt], *adj.* foolish, silly.

Törin ['tø:rIn], *f.* (—, *pl.* —nen) (*rare*) foolish woman.

torkeln ['tɔrkəln], *v.n.* (*aux.* sein) (*coll.*) stagger, reel.

Tornister [tɔr'nIstər], *m.* (—s, *pl.* —) knapsack, satchel.

Torpedo [tɔr'pe:do], *m.* (—s, *pl.* —s) torpedo.

Torso ['tɔrzo], *m.* (—s, *pl.* —s) trunk, torso.

Tort [tɔrt], *m.* (—s, *no pl.*) injury, wrong; *einem einen* — *antun*, wrong s.o.; play a trick on s.o.

Torte ['tɔrtə], *f.* (—, *pl.* —n) cake, pastry, tart.

Tortur [tɔr'tu:r], *f.* (—, *pl.* —en) torture.

Torwächter ['to:rvɛçtər], *m.* (—s, *pl.* —) gate-keeper; porter.

tosen ['to:zən], *v.n.* roar.

tot [to:t], *adj.* dead, deceased.

total [to'ta:l], *adj.* total, complete.

Totalisator [totali'za:tɔr], *m.* (—s, *pl.* —en) totalisator; (*coll.*) tote.

Totalleistung [to'ta:llaIstuŋ], *f.* (—, *pl.* —en) full effect; total output.

Tote ['to:tə], *m., f.* (—n, *pl.* —n) dead person, the deceased.

töten ['tø:tən], *v.a.* kill, put to death.

Totenacker ['to:tənakər], *m.* (—s, *pl.* ⸚) churchyard, cemetery.

Totenamt ['to:tənamt], *n.* (—s, *no pl.*) office for the dead, requiem, Mass for the dead.

Totenbahre ['to:tənba:rə], *f.* (—, *pl.* —n) bier.

Totengräber ['to:təngrɛ:bər], *m.* (—s, *pl.* —) grave-digger.

Totenhemd ['to:tənhɛmt], *n.* (—(e)s, *pl.* —en) shroud, winding-sheet.

Totenklage ['to:tənkla:gə], *f.* (—, *no pl.*) lament.

Totenschein ['to:tənʃaIn], *m.* (—(e)s, *pl.* —e) death-certificate.

Totenstille ['to:tənʃtIlə], *f.* (—, *no pl.*) dead calm.

Totenwache ['to:tənvaxə], *f.* (—, *no pl.*) wake.

totgeboren ['to:tgəbo:rən], *adj.* still-born, born dead.

Totschlag ['to:tʃla:k], *m.* (—s, *no pl.*) manslaughter.

totschlagen ['to:tʃla:gən], *v.a.* *irr.* kill, strike dead.

225

Totschläger

Totschläger ['to:tʃlɛ:gər], *m.* (—s, *pl.* —) loaded cane, cudgel.
totschweigen ['to:tʃvaɪgən], *v.a. irr.* hush up.
Tötung ['tø:tuŋ], *f.* (—, *pl.* —en) killing.
Tour [tu:r], *f.* (—, *pl.* —en) tour, excursion; *in einer* —, ceaselessly; *auf* —en *bringen,(coll.) (Motor.)* rev up.
Tournee [tur'ne:], *f.* (—, *pl.* —n) (*Theat.*) tour.
Trab [tra:p], *m.* (—(e)s, *no pl.*) trot.
Trabant [tra'bant], *m.* (—en, *pl.* —en) satellite.
traben ['tra:bən], *v.n.* (*aux.* sein) trot.
Trabrennen ['tra:prɛnən], *n.* (—s, *pl.* —) trotting-race.
Tracht [traxt], *f.* (—, *pl.* —en) dress, costume; national costume; native dress; *eine* — *Prügel*, a good hiding.
trachten ['traxtən], *v.n.* strive, aspire, endeavour; *einem nach dem Leben* —, seek to kill s.o.
trächtig ['trɛçtɪç], *adj.* (*animal*) pregnant, with young.
Trafik [tra'fik], *m.* (—s, *pl.* —s) (*Austr.*) tobacco-kiosk.
Tragbahre ['tra:kba:rə], *f.* (—, *pl.* —n) stretcher.
Tragbalken ['tra:kbalkən], *m.* (—s *pl.*, —) girder.
tragbar ['tra:kba:r], *adj.* portable; tolerable.
träge ['trɛ:gə], *adj.* lazy, indolent, inert, sluggish.
tragen ['tra:gən], *v.a. irr.* bear, carry; (*dress*) wear; (*fig.*) bear, endure; *Bedenken* —, hesitate, have doubts; *Zinsen* —, yield interest; *einen auf Händen* —, care lovingly for s.o.
Träger ['trɛ:gər], *m.* (—s, *pl.* —) porter, carrier; girder.
Trägheit ['trɛ:khaɪt], *f.* (—, *no pl.*) indolence, laziness, inertia.
tragisch ['tra:gɪʃ], *adj.* tragic(al).
Tragkraft ['tra:kkraft], *f.* (—, *no pl.*) carrying *or* load capacity; lifting power.
Tragödie [tra'gø:djə], *f.* (—, *pl.* —n) tragedy.
Tragsessel ['tra:kzɛsəl], *m.* (—s, *pl.* —) sedan-chair.
Tragweite ['tra:kvaɪtə], *f.* (—, *no pl.*) significance, importance, range.
trainieren [trɛ'ni:rən], *v.a.* train.
Traktat [trak'ta:t], *n.* (—s, *pl.* —e) treatise, tract.
Traktätchen [trak'tɛ:tçən], *n.* (—s, *pl.* —) (short) tract.
traktieren [trak'ti:rən], *v.a.* treat; treat badly.
trällern ['trɛlərn], *v.n.* trill, hum.
Trambahn ['tramba:n], *f.* (—, *pl.* —en) tram; (*Am.*) streetcar.
Trampel ['trampəl], *n.* (—s, *pl.* —) clumsy person, bumpkin; (*Am.*) hick.
trampeln ['trampəln], *v.n.* trample.
Trampeltier ['trampəlti:r], *n.* (—s, *pl.* —e) camel; (*fig.*) clumsy person.
Tran [tra:n], *m.* (—(e)s, *no pl.*) whale-oil.

tranchieren [trã'ʃi:rən], *v.a.* carve.
Tranchiermesser [trã'ʃi:rmɛsər], *n.* (—s, *pl.* —) carving-knife.
Träne ['trɛ:nə], *f.* (—, *pl.* —n) tear, teardrop; *zu* —n *gerührt*, moved to tears.
tränen ['trɛ:nən], *v.n.* (*eyes*) water.
Tränendrüse ['trɛ:nəndry:zə], *f.* (—, *pl.* —n) lachrymal gland.
tränenleer ['trɛ:nənle:r], *adj.* tearless.
Tränenstrom ['trɛ:nənʃtro:m], *m.* (—s, *pl.* ⁓e) flood of tears.
tränenvoll ['trɛ:nənfɔl], *adj.* tearful.
tranig ['tra:nɪç], *adj.* dull, slow.
Trank [traŋk], *m.* (—(e)s, *pl.* ⁓e) drink, beverage, potion.
Tränke ['trɛŋkə], *f.* (—, *pl.* —n) (*horse*) watering-place.
tränken ['trɛŋkən], *v.a.* give to drink, water; impregnate, saturate.
transitiv ['tranziti:f], *adj.* transitive.
Transitlager ['tranzitla:gər], *n.* (—s, *pl.* —) bonded warehouse; transit camp.
transitorisch [tranzi'to:rɪʃ], *adj.* transitory.
transpirieren [transpi'ri:rən], *v.n.* perspire.
transponieren [transpo'ni:rən], *v.a.* transpose.
Transportkosten [trans'pɔrtkɔstən], *f. pl.* shipping charges.
Transportmittel [trans'pɔrtmɪtəl], *n.* (—s, *pl.* —) means of carriage, conveyance, transport.
Trapez [tra'pe:ts], *n.* (—es, *pl.* —e) trapeze; (*Maths.*) trapezoid.
Tratsch [tra:tʃ], *m.* (—es, *no pl.*) (*coll.*) gossip, tittle-tattle.
tratschen ['tra:tʃən], *v.n.* (*coll.*) gossip.
Tratte ['tratə], *f.* (—, *pl.* —n) (*Comm.*) draft, bill of exchange.
Traube ['traubə], *f.* (—, *pl.* —n) (*Bot.*) grape, bunch of grapes.
Traubensaft ['traubənzaft], *m.* (—s, *pl.* ⁓e) grape-juice; (*Poet.*) wine.
traubig ['traubɪç], *adj.* clustered, grape-like.
trauen ['trauən], *v.a.* marry; join in marriage; *sich* — *lassen*, get married. — *v.n. einem* —, trust s.o., confide in s.o. — *v.r. sich* —, dare, venture.
Trauer ['trauər], *f.* (—, *no pl.*) mourning; sorrow, grief.
Trauermarsch ['trauərmarʃ], *m.* (—es, *pl.* ⁓e) funeral march.
trauern ['trauərn], *v.n.* mourn, be in mourning.
Trauerspiel ['trauərʃpi:l], *n.* (—s, *pl.* —e) tragedy.
Trauerweide ['trauərvaɪdə], *f.* (—, *pl.* —n) (*Bot.*) weeping willow.
Traufe ['traufə], *f.* (—, *pl.* —n) eaves; *vom Regen in die* —, out of the frying pan into the fire.
träufeln ['trɔyfəln], *v.a.* drip, drop.
Traufröhre ['traufrø:rə], *f.* (—, *pl.* —n) gutter-pipe.

traulich ['traulɪç], *adj.* familiar, homely, cosy.

Traum [traum], *m.* (—(e)s, *pl.* ⁻e) dream; *das fällt mir nicht im —e ein*, I should not dream of it.

Traumbild ['traumbɪlt], *n.* (—s, *pl.* —er) vision.

Traumdeutung ['traumdɔytuŋ], *f.* (—, *no pl.*) interpretation of dreams.

träumen ['trɔymən], *v.n.* dream; *sich etwas nicht — lassen*, have no inkling of, not dream of s.th.; not believe s.th.

Träumer ['trɔymər], *m.* (—s, *pl.* —) dreamer; (*fig.*) visionary.

Träumerei [trɔymə'raɪ], *f.* (—, *pl.* —en) dreaming, reverie.

traumhaft ['traumhaft], *adj.* dream-like.

traurig ['traurɪç], *adj.* sad, mournful, sorrowful.

Traurigkeit ['traurɪçkaɪt], *f.* (—, *no pl.*) sadness, melancholy.

Trauring ['trauⁿrɪŋ], *m.* (—s, *pl.* —e) wedding-ring.

Trauschein ['trauʃaɪn], *m.* (—s, *pl.* —e) marriage certificate.

traut [traut], *adj.* dear, beloved; cosy; *—es Heim Glück allein*, east, west, home's best; there's no place like home.

Trauung ['trauuŋ], *f.* (—, *pl.* —en) marriage ceremony.

Trauzeuge ['trautsɔygə], *m.* (—n, *pl.* —n) witness to a marriage.

trecken ['trɛkən], *v.a.* (*dial.*) draw, drag, tug.

Trecker ['trɛkər], *m.* (—s, *pl.* —) tractor.

Treff [trɛf], *n.* (—s, *no pl.*) (*Cards*) clubs.

Treffen ['trɛfən], *n.* (—s, *pl.* —) action, battle, fight; meeting, gathering; *etwas ins — führen*, put s.th. forward, urge s.th.

treffen ['trɛfən], *v.a. irr.* hit, meet; *nicht —*, miss; *wie vom Donner getroffen*, thunderstruck; *ins Schwarze —*, hit the mark, score a bull's eye. *— v.r. sich —*, happen.

treffend ['trɛfənt], *adj.* appropriate, pertinent.

Treffer ['trɛfər], *m.* (—s, *pl.* —) (*lottery*) win, prize; (*Mil.*) hit.

trefflich ['trɛflɪç], *adj.* excellent.

Treffpunkt ['trɛfpuŋkt], *m.* (—s, *pl.* —e) meeting-place.

Treffsicherheit ['trɛfzɪçərhaɪt], *f.* (—, *no pl.*) accurate aim.

Treibeis ['traɪpaɪs], *n.* (—es, *no pl.*) floating-ice, ice floe.

treiben ['traɪbən], *v.a. irr.* drive, urge; incite; (*trade*) carry on, ply; *Studien —*, study; *was treibst du?* what are you doing? *etwas zu weit —*, carry s.th. too far; *einen in die Enge —*, drive s.o. into a corner. *— v.n.* be adrift, drift.

Treiben ['traɪbən], *n.* (—s, *no pl.*) driving; doings; bustle.

Treiber ['traɪbər], *m.* (—s, *pl.* —) (*Hunt.*) driver; beater.

Treibhaus ['traɪphaus], *n.* (—es, *pl.* ⁻er) hothouse, greenhouse.

Treibkraft ['traɪpkraft], *f.* (—, *no pl.*) impulse, driving power.

Treibriemen ['traɪpriːmən], *m.* (—s, *pl.* —) driving-belt.

Treibsand ['traɪpzant], *m.* (—s, *no pl.*) quicksand, shifting sand.

Treibstange ['traɪpʃtaŋə], *f.* (—, *pl.* —en) main rod, connecting-rod.

Treibstoff ['traɪpʃtɔf], *m.* (—(e)s, *pl.* —e) fuel.

treideln ['traɪdəln], *v.a.* (*Naut.*) tow.

Treidelsteig ['traɪdəlʃtaɪk], *m.* (—s, *pl.* —e) towpath.

trennbar ['trɛnbaːr], *adj.* separable.

trennen ['trɛnən], *v.a.* separate, sever. *— v.r. sich —*, part.

Trennung ['trɛnuŋ], *f.* (—, *pl.* —en) separation, segregation; parting; division.

Trennungsstrich ['trɛnuŋsʃtrɪç], *m.* (—es, *pl.* —e) hyphen, dash.

treppab [trɛp'ap], *adv.* downstairs.

treppauf [trɛp'auf], *adv.* upstairs.

Treppe ['trɛpə], *f.* (—, *pl.* —n) stairs, staircase, flight of stairs.

Treppenabsatz ['trɛpənapzats], *m.* (—es, *pl.* ⁻e) (*staircase*) landing.

Treppengeländer ['trɛpəngəlɛndər], *n.* (—s, *pl.* —) balustrade, banisters.

Treppenhaus ['trɛpənhaus], *n.* (—es, *pl.* ⁻er) stair-well, staircase.

Treppenläufer ['trɛpənlɔyfər], *m.* (—s, *pl.* —) stair-carpet.

Treppenstufe ['trɛpənʃtuːfə], *f.* (—, *pl.* —n) step, stair.

Treppenwitz ['trɛpənvɪts], *m.* (—es, *no pl.*) afterthought, esprit de l'escalier.

Tresor [tre'zoːr], *m.* (—s, *pl.* —e) safe, strongroom.

Tresse ['trɛsə], *f.* (—, *pl.* —n) braid, lace, galloon.

treten ['treːtən], *v.a., v.n. irr.* tread, step, trample upon; go; *— Sie näher*, step this way; *in Verbindung — mit*, make contact with; *in den Ehestand —*, get married; *einem zu nahe —*, offend s.o., tread on s.o.'s toes.

treu [trɔy], *adj.* faithful, loyal, true; conscientious.

Treubruch ['trɔybrux], *m.* (—(e)s, *pl.* ⁻e) breach of faith, disloyalty.

Treue ['trɔyə], *f.* (—, *no pl.*) faithfulness, loyalty, fidelity; *meiner Treu!* upon my soul! *auf Treu und Glauben*, on trust.

Treueid ['trɔyaɪt], *m.* (—s, *pl.* —e) oath of allegiance.

Treuhänder ['trɔyhɛndər], *m.* (—s, *pl.* —) trustee.

treuherzig ['trɔyhɛrtsɪç], *adj.* guileless, trusting.

treulich ['trɔylɪç], *adv.* faithfully.

treulos ['trɔyloːs], *adj.* faithless, perfidious; unfaithful.

Treulosigkeit

Treulosigkeit ['trɔylo:zɪçkaɪt], *f.* (—, *no pl.*) faithlessness, perfidy, disloyalty.

Tribüne [tri'by:nə], *f.* (—, *pl.* —n) tribune, platform; (*racing*) grandstand.

Tribut [tri'bu:t], *m.* (—s, *pl.* —e) tribute.

tributpflichtig [tri'bu:tpflɪçtɪç], *adj.* tributary.

Trichter ['trɪçtər], *m.* (—s, *pl.* —) funnel.

trichterförmig ['trɪçtərfœrmɪç], *adj.* funnel-shaped.

Trieb [tri:p], *m.* (—(e)s, *pl.* —e) (*plant*) shoot, growth; instinct, bent, propensity, inclination; (*Psych.*) drive.

Triebfeder ['tri:pfe:dər], *f.* (—, *pl.* —n) mainspring; (*fig.*) motive, guiding principle.

Triebkraft ['tri:pkraft], *f.* (—, *pl.* ⁻e) motive power.

Triebwagen ['tri:pva:gən], *m.* (—s, *pl.* —) rail-car.

Triebwerk ['tri:pvɛrk], *n.* (—s, *pl.* —e) power unit, drive.

triefen ['tri:fən], *v.n. irr. & reg.* trickle, drip; be wet through, be soaking wet.

Trient [tri'ɛnt], *n.* Trent.

Trier [tri:r], *n.* Treves.

Triest [tri'ɛst], *n.* Trieste.

Trift [trɪft], *f.* (—, *pl.* —en) pasture, pasturage, common, meadow.

triftig ['trɪftɪç], *adj.* weighty, valid, conclusive, cogent.

Trikot [tri'ko:], *m. & n.* (—s, *pl.* —s) stockinet; (*circus, ballet*) tights.

Triller ['trɪlər], *m.* (—s, *pl.* —) (*Mus.*) trill, shake.

trillern ['trɪlərn], *v.n.* trill, quaver, shake; warble.

Trinität [trini'tɛ:t], *f.* (—, *no pl.*) Trinity.

trinkbar ['trɪŋkba:r], *adj.* drinkable.

Trinkbecher ['trɪŋkbɛçər], *m.* (—s, *pl.* —) drinking-cup.

trinken ['trɪŋkən], *v.a., v.n. irr.* drink.

Trinker ['trɪŋkər], *m.* (—s, *pl.* —) drinker, drunkard.

Trinkgelage ['trɪŋkgəla:gə], *n.* (—s, *pl.* —) drinking-bout.

Trinkgeld ['trɪŋkgɛlt], *n.* (—s, *pl.* —er) tip, gratuity.

Trinkhalle ['trɪŋkhalə], *f.* (—, *pl.* —n) (*spa*) pump-room.

Trinkspruch ['trɪŋkʃprux], *m.* (—(e)s, *pl.* ⁻e) toast.

Trinkstube ['trɪŋkʃtu:bə], *f.* (—, *pl.* —n) tap-room.

Tripolis ['tri:polɪs], *n.* Tripoli.

trippeln ['trɪpəln], *v.n.* trip (daintily), patter.

Tripper ['trɪpər], *m.* (—s, *no pl.*) (*Med.*) gonorrhœa.

Tritt [trɪt], *m.* (—(e)s, *pl.* —e) step, pace; kick.

Trittbrett ['trɪtbrɛt], *n.* (—s, *pl.* —er) foot-board; carriage-step; (*organ*) pedal.

Triumph [tri'umf], *m.* (—(e)s, *pl.* —e) triumph.

Triumphzug [tri'umftsu:k], *m.* (—(e)s, *pl.* ⁻e) triumphal procession.

Trivialität [trivjali'tɛ:t], *f.* (—, *pl.* —en) triviality, platitude.

trocken ['trɔkən], *adj.* dry, arid; (*fig.*) dull, dry as dust; (*wine*) dry.

Trockenfäule ['trɔkənfɔylə], *f.*, **Trockenfäulnis** ['trɔkənfɔylnɪs], *f.* (—, *no pl.*) dry rot.

Trockenboden ['trɔkənbo:dən], *m.* (—s, *pl.* ⁻) loft.

Trockenfutter ['trɔkənfutər], *n.* (—s, *no pl.*) fodder.

Trockenfütterung ['trɔkənfytəruŋ], *f.* (—, *pl.* —en) dry feeding.

Trockenhaube ['trɔkənhaubə], *f.* (—, *pl.* —n) hair drier.

Trockenheit ['trɔkənhaɪt], *f.* (—, *no pl.*) dryness; drought.

Trockenschleuder ['trɔkənʃlɔydər], *f.* (—, *pl.* —n) spin-drier.

trocknen ['trɔknən], *v.a., v.n.* dry, air.

Troddel ['trɔdəl], *f.* (—, *pl.* —n) tassel.

Trödel ['trø:dəl], *m.* (—s, *no pl.*) junk, lumber, rubbish.

Trödelladen ['trø:dəlla:dən], *m.* (—s, *pl.* ⁻) junk-shop.

Trödelmarkt ['trø:dəlmarkt], *m.* (—s, *no pl.*) kettle market, jumble sale.

trödeln ['trø:dəln], *v.n.* dawdle, loiter.

Trödler ['trø:dlər], *m.* (—s, *pl.* —) second-hand dealer; (*coll.*) dawdler, loiterer.

Trog [tro:k], *m.* (—(e)s, *pl.* ⁻e) trough.

Troja ['tro:ja], *n.* Troy.

trollen ['trɔlən], *v.r. sich* —, decamp, toddle off, make o.s. scarce.

Trommel ['trɔməl], *f.* (—, *pl.* —n) drum; cylinder, barrel; tin box; *die* — *rühren,* beat the big drum.

Trommelfell ['trɔməlfɛl], *n.* (—s, *pl.* —e) drum-skin; ear-drum.

trommeln ['trɔməln], *v.n.* drum, beat the drum.

Trommelschlegel ['trɔməlʃle:gəl], *m.* (—s, *pl.* —) drumstick.

Trommelwirbel ['trɔməlvɪrbəl], *m.* (—s, *pl.* —) roll of drums.

Trommler ['trɔmlər], *m.* (—s, *pl.* —) drummer.

Trompete [trɔm'pe:tə], *f.* (—, *pl.* —n) trumpet; *die* — *blasen,* blow the trumpet.

trompeten [trɔm'pe:tən], *v.n.* trumpet, sound the trumpet.

Trompetengeschmetter [trɔm'pe:təngəʃmɛtər], *n.* (—s, *no pl.*) flourish of trumpets.

Tropen ['tro:pən], *f. pl.* the tropics.

Tropenfieber ['tro:pənfi:bər], *n.* (—s, *no pl.*) tropical fever.

tröpfeln ['trœpfəln], *v.a., v.n.* trickle, sprinkle.

Tropfen ['trɔpfən], *m.* (—s, *pl.* —) drop; *steter* — *höhlt den Stein,* constant dripping wears away a stone.

tropfen ['trɔpfən], *v.n.* drop, drip.

Trophäe [tro'fɛə], *f.* (—, *pl.* —n) trophy.

tropisch ['tro:pɪʃ], *adj.* tropical, tropic.

Troß [trɔs], *m.* (—sses, *pl.* -sse) (*Mil.*) baggage-train; (*fig.*) hangers-on, camp-followers.

Troßpferd ['trɔspfe:rt], *n.* (—s, *pl.* —e) pack-horse.

Trost [tro:st], *m.* (—es, *no pl.*) consolation, comfort; *geringer* —, cold comfort; *du bist wohl nicht bei* —? have you taken leave of your senses?

trösten ['trø:stən], *v.a.* comfort, console; *tröste dich*, cheer up.

Tröster ['trø:stər], *m.* (—s, *pl.* —) comforter, consoler; (*Theol.*) Holy Ghost, Comforter.

tröstlich ['trø:stlɪç], *adj.* consoling, comforting.

trostlos ['tro:stlo:s], *adj.* disconsolate, inconsolable; desolate, bleak.

Trostlosigkeit ['tro:stlo:zɪçkaɪt], *f.* (—, *no pl.*) disconsolateness; (*fig.*) wretchedness; dreariness.

Trott [trɔt], *m.* (—s, *no pl.*) trot.

Trottel ['trɔtəl], *m.* (—s, *pl.* —) (*coll.*) idiot.

Trottoir [trɔto'a:r], *n.* (—s, *pl.* —e) pavement, footpath; (*Am.*) sidewalk.

trotz ['trɔts], *prep.* (*Genit., Dat.*) in spite of, despite; — *alledem*, all the same.

Trotz [trɔts], *m.* (—es, *no pl.*) defiance, obstinacy, refractoriness; *einem* — *bieten*, defy s.o.; *einem etwas zum* — *machen*, do s.th. in defiance of s.o.

trotzdem [trɔts'de:m], *conj.* notwithstanding that, albeit, although. — *adv.* nevertheless.

trotzen ['trɔtsən], *v.n.* defy; sulk, be obstinate; *Gefahren* —, brave dangers.

trotzig ['trɔtsɪç], *adj.* defiant; sulky, refractory; headstrong, stubborn, obstinate.

Trotzkopf ['trɔtskɔpf], *m.* (—(e)s, *pl.* ⁻e) obstinate child; pig-headed person.

trübe ['try:bə], *adj.* dim, gloomy; (*weather*) dull, cloudy, overcast; (*water*) troubled; (*glass*) misted; —*s Lächeln*, wan smile.

Trubel ['tru:bəl], *m.* (—s, *no pl.*) tumult, turmoil, disturbance.

trüben ['try:bən], *v.a.* darken, sadden, trouble; (*glass*) mist; (*metal*) tarnish; (*fig.*) obscure.

Trübsal ['try:pza:l], *f.* (—, *pl.* —e), *n.* (—s, *pl.* —e) misery, trouble, distress; — *blasen*, mope.

trübselig ['try:pze:lɪç], *adj.* woeful, lamentable; woebegone, forlorn.

Trübsinn ['try:pzɪn], *m.* (—s, *no pl.*) sadness, dejection.

trübsinnig ['try:pzɪnɪç], *adj.* sad, dejected.

Trüffel ['tryfəl], *f.* (—, *pl.* —n) truffle.

Trug [tru:k], *m.* (—(e)s, *no pl.*) deceit, fraud; *Lug und* —, a pack of lies.

Trugbild ['tru:kbɪlt], *n.* (—es, *pl.* —er) phantom.

trügen ['try:gən], *v.a. irr.* deceive.

trügerisch ['try:gərɪs], *adj.* deceptive, illusory, fallacious.

Truggewebe ['tru:kgəve:bə], *n.* (—s, *pl.* —) tissue of lies.

Trugschluß ['tru:kʃlus], *m.* (—sses, *pl.* -sse) fallacy, false deduction.

Truhe ['tru:ə], *f.* (—, *pl.* —n) chest, trunk, coffer.

Trumm [trum], *m.* (—s, *pl.* ⁻er) lump, broken piece.

Trümmer ['trymər], *m. pl.* fragments, debris, ruins; *in* — *gehen*, go to wrack and ruin; *in* — *schlagen*, wreck.

Trümmerhaufen ['trymərhaufən], *m.* (—s, *pl.* —) heap of ruins, heap of rubble.

Trumpf [trumpf], *m.* (—(e)s, *pl.* ⁻e) trump, trump-card.

trumpfen ['trumpfən], *v.a.* trump.

Trumpffarbe ['trumpffarbə], *f.* (—, *pl.* —n) trump-suit.

Trunk [truŋk], *m.* (—(e)s, *pl.* ⁻e) draught, potion, drinking; *sich dem* — *ergeben*, take to drink.

trunken ['truŋkən], *adj.* drunk, intoxicated; (*fig.*) elated.

Trunkenbold ['truŋkənbɔlt], *m.* (—s, *pl.* —e) drunkard.

Trunkenheit ['truŋkənhaɪt], *f.* (—, *no pl.*) drunkenness, intoxication.

Trunksucht ['truŋkzuxt], *f.* (—, *no pl.*) dipsomania, alcoholism.

trunksüchtig ['truŋkzyçtɪç], *adj.* dipsomaniac, addicted to drinking.

Trupp [trup], *m.* (—s, *pl.* —s) troop, band.

Truppe ['trupə], *f.* (—, *pl.* —n) (*Mil.*) company, troops, forces; (*actors*) troupe.

Truppengattung ['trupəngatuŋ], *f.* (—, *pl.* —en) branch of the armed forces.

Truthahn ['tru:tha:n], *m.* (—s, *pl.* ⁻e) (*Orn.*) turkey cock.

Truthenne ['tru:thɛnə], *f.* (—, *pl.* —n) (*Orn.*) turkey hen.

Trtuhühner ['tru:thy:nər], *n. pl.* (*Orn.*) turkey-fowl.

Trutz [truts], *m.* (—es, *no pl.*) (*Poet.*) defiance; *zum Schutz und* —, offensively and defensively.

Tschad [tʃat], *n.* Chad.

Tschechoslowakei [tʃɛçoslova'kaɪ], *f.* Czechoslovakia.

Tuch (1) [tu:x], *n.* (—(e)s, *pl.* ⁻er) shawl, wrap.

Tuch (2) [tu:x], *n.* (—s, *pl.* —e) cloth, fabric.

Tuchhändler ['tu:xhɛndlər], *m.* (—s, *pl.* —) draper, clothier.

tüchtig ['tyçtɪç], *adj.* able, competent, efficient. — *adv.* largely, much, heartily.

Tüchtigkeit ['tyçtɪçkaɪt], *f.* (—, *no pl.*) ability, competence, efficiency.

Tücke ['tykə], *f.* (—, *pl.* —n) malice, spite.

tückisch

tückisch ['tykɪʃ], *adj.* malicious, insidious.

Tugend ['tu:gənt], *f.* (—, *pl.* —en) virtue.

Tugendbold ['tu:gəntbɔlt], *m.* (—s, *pl.* —e) paragon.

tugendhaft ['tu:gənthaft], *adj.* virtuous.

Tugendlehre ['tu:gəntle:rə], *f.* (—, *no pl.*) ethics, morals.

Tüll [tyl], *m.* (—s, *pl.* —e) tulle.

Tulpe ['tulpə], *f.* (—, *pl.* —n) (*Bot.*) tulip.

Tulpenzwiebel ['tulpəntsvi:bəl], *f.* (—, *pl.* —n) tulip-bulb.

tummeln ['tuməln], *v.r. sich* —, romp about; make haste.

Tummelplatz ['tuməlplats], *m.* (—es, *pl.* -e) playground, fairground.

Tümpel ['tympəl], *m.* (—s, *pl.* —) pond, pool, puddle.

Tun [tu:n], *n.* (—s, *no pl.*) doing; *sein — und Lassen*, his conduct.

tun [tu:n], *v.a. irr.* do, make; put; *tut nichts*, it does not matter; *viel zu — haben*, have a lot to do, be busy; *not —*, be necessary; *Buße —*, repent.

Tünche ['tynçə], *f.* (—, *pl.* —n) whitewash.

tünchen ['tynçən], *v.a.* whitewash.

Tunichtgut ['tu:nɪçtgu:t], *m.* (—s, *no pl.*) ne'er-do-well, scamp.

Tunke ['tuŋkə], *f.* (—, *pl.* —n) sauce, gravy.

tunken ['tuŋkən], *v.a.* dip, steep; (*Am.*) dunk.

tunlich ['tu:nlɪç], *adj.* feasible, practicable, expedient.

tunlichst ['tu:nlɪçst], *adv.* if possible, possibly.

Tunnel ['tunəl], *m.* (—s, *pl.* —) tunnel.

Tunnelbau ['tunəlbau], *m.* (—s, *no pl.*) tunnelling.

tüpfeln ['typfəln], *v.a.* dot, spot.

Tupfen ['tupfən], *m.* (—s, *pl.* —) dot, polka-dot.

Tür [ty:r], *f.* (—, *pl.* —en) door; *einem die — weisen*, show s.o. the door; *vor der — stehen*, be imminent; *kehr vor deiner eigenen —*, mind your own business; put your own house in order; *offene —en einrennen*, flog a willing horse; *zwischen — und Angel stecken*, be undecided.

Türangel ['ty:raŋəl], *f.* (—, *pl.* —n) door-hinge.

Türhüter ['ty:rhy:tər], *m.* (—s, *pl.* —) doorkeeper.

Türkei [tyr'kai], *f.* Turkey.

Türkensäbel ['tyrkənze:bəl], *m.* (—s, *pl.* —) scimitar.

Türkis [tyr'ki:s], *m.* (—es, *pl.* —e) turquoise.

Türklinke ['ty:rklɪŋkə], *f.* (—, *pl.* —n) door-handle.

Turm [turm], *m.* (—(e)s, *pl.* -e) tower; spire, steeple; belfry; (*Chess*) castle.

Turmalin [turma'li:n], *m.* (—s, *pl.* —e) tourmaline.

Türmchen ['tyrmçən], *n.* (—s, *pl.* —) turret.

türmen ['tyrmən], *v.a.* pile up. — *v.n.* (*coll.*) bolt, run away. — *v.r. sich —*, rise high, be piled high.

Turmspitze ['turmʃpɪtsə], *f.* (—, *pl.* —n) spire.

turnen ['turnən], *v.n.* do exercises *or* gymnastics.

Turnen ['turnən], *n.* (—s, *no pl.*) gymnastics, physical training.

Turner ['turnər], *m.* (—s, *pl.* —) gymnast.

Turngerät ['turngəre:t], *n.* (—es, *pl.* —e) gymnastic apparatus.

Turnhalle ['turnhalə], *f.* (—, *pl.* —n) gymnasium.

Turnier [tur'ni:r], *n.* (—s, *pl.* —e) tournament.

Turnübung ['turny:buŋ], *f.* (—, *pl.* —en) gymnastic exercise.

Turnverein ['turnfərain], *m.* (—s, *pl.* —e) athletics club, gymnastics club.

Türpfosten ['ty:rpfɔstən], *m.* (—s, *pl.* —) door-post.

Türriegel ['ty:rri:gəl], *m.* (—s, *pl.* —) bolt.

Türschild ['ty:rʃɪlt], *n.* (—(e)s, *pl.* —e) (door)plate.

Türschloß ['ty:rʃlɔs], *n.* (—sses, *pl.* -sser) lock.

Türschlüssel ['ty:rʃlysəl], *m.* (—s, *pl.* —) door-key, latch-key.

Türschwelle ['ty:rʃvelə], *f.* (—, *pl.* —n) threshold.

Tusch [tuʃ], *m.* (—es, *pl.* —e) (*Mus.*) flourish.

Tusche ['tuʃə], *f.* (—, *pl.* —n) water-colour; Indian ink.

tuscheln ['tuʃəln], *v.n.* whisper.

tuschen ['tuʃən], *v.a.* draw in Indian ink.

Tuschkasten ['tuʃkastən], *m.* (—s, *pl.* -) paint-box.

Tüte ['ty:tə], *f.* (—, *pl.* —n) paper bag.

Tutel [tu'te:l], *f.* (—, *no pl.*) guardianship.

tuten ['tu:tən], *v.n.* hoot, honk, blow a horn.

Tütendreher ['ty:təndre:ər], *m.* (—s, *pl.* —) (*sl.*) small shopkeeper.

Typ [ty:p], *m.* (—s, *pl.* —en) type.

Type ['ty:pə], *f.* (—, *pl.* —n) (*Typ.*) type; (*fig.*) queer fish.

Typhus ['ty:fus], *m.* (—, *no pl.*) (*Med.*) typhoid (fever).

typisch ['ty:pɪʃ], *adj.* typical.

Typus ['ty:pus], *m.* (—, *pl.* **Typen**) type.

Tyrann [ty'ran], *m.* (—en, *pl.* —en) tyrant.

Tyrannei [tyra'nai], *f.* (—, *pl.* —en) tyranny, despotism.

tyrannisch [ty'ranɪʃ], *adj.* tyrannical, despotic.

tyrannisieren [tyrani'zi:rən], *v.a.* tyrannize over, oppress, bully.

230

U

U [u:], *n.* (—**s**, *pl.* —**s**) the letter U.

U-Bahn ['u:ba:n], *f.* (—, *no pl.*) underground (railway);(*Am.*)subway.

Übel ['y:bəl], *n.* (—**s**, *pl.* —) evil, trouble; misfortune; disease.

übel ['y:bəl], *adj.* evil, ill, bad; *mir ist* —, I feel sick; *nicht* —, not too bad; — *daran sein*, be in a bad way, be in a mess.

übelgesinnt ['y:bəlgəzɪnt], *adj.* evil-minded; ill-disposed; *einem* — *sein*, bear s.o. a grudge.

Übelkeit ['y:bəlkaɪt], *f.* (—, *pl.* —**en**) nausea, sickness.

übellaunig ['y:bəllaunɪç], *adj.* ill-humoured, bad-tempered.

übelnehmen ['y:bəlne:mən], *v.a. irr.* take amiss, resent, be offended at.

übelnehmerisch ['y:bəlne:mərɪʃ], *adj.* touchy, easily offended.

Übelstand ['y:bəlʃtant], *m.* (—(**e**)**s**, *pl.* ⸚**e**) inconvenience, drawback; (*pl.*) abuses.

Übeltat ['y:bəlta:t], *f.* (—, *pl.* —**en**) misdeed.

Übeltäter ['y:bəltɛ:tər], *m.* (—**s**, *pl.* —) evildoer, malefactor.

übelwollend ['y:bəlvɔlənt], *adj.* malevolent.

üben ['y:bən], *v.a.* practise, exercise; *Rache* —, wreak vengeance.

über ['y:bər], *prep.* (*Dat.*, *Acc.*) over, above; across; about; more than, exceeding; via, by way of; concerning, on. — *adv.* over, above; — *und* —, all over; — *kurz oder lang*, sooner or later; *heute* —**s** *Jahr*, a year from today.

überall ['y:bəral], *adv.* everywhere, anywhere.

überanstrengen [y:bər'anʃtrɛŋən], *v.a. insep.* overtax s.o.'s strength, strain. — *v.r. sich* —, overtax o.'s strength, overexert o.s.

Überanstrengung [y:bər'anʃtrɛŋuŋ], *f.* (—, *pl.* —**en**) over-exertion, strain.

überantworten [y:bər'antvɔrtən], *v.a. insep.* deliver up, surrender.

überarbeiten [y:bər'arbaɪtən], *v.a. insep.* revise, do again. — *v.r. sich* —, overwork o.s.

überarbeitet [y:bər'arbaɪtət], *adj.* over-wrought, overworked.

überaus ['y:bəraus], *adv.* exceedingly, extremely.

überbauen [y:bər'bauən], *v.a. insep.* build over.

überbieten [y:bər'bi:tən], *v.a. irr. insep.* outbid (s.o.); (*fig.*) surpass.

Überbleibsel ['y:bərblaɪpsəl], *n.* (—**s**, *pl.* —) remainder, remnant, residue, rest.

Überblick ['y:bərblɪk], *m.* (—(**e**)**s**, *pl.* —**e**) survey, general view.

überblicken [y:bər'blɪkən], *v.a. insep.* survey, look over.

überbringen [y:bər'brɪŋən], *v.a. irr. insep.* bear, deliver, hand in.

Überbringung [y:bər'brɪŋuŋ], *f.* (—, *no pl.*) delivery.

überbrücken [y:bər'brykən], *v.a. insep.* bridge, span.

überdachen [y:bər'daxən], *v.a. insep.* roof (over).

überdauern [y:bər'dauərn], *v.a. insep.* outlast; tide over.

überdenken [y:bər'dɛŋkən], *v.a. irr. insep.* think over, consider.

überdies [y:bər'di:s], *adv.* besides, moreover.

überdrucken [y:bər'drukən], *v.a. insep.* overprint.

Überdruß ['y:bərdrus], *m.* (—**sses**, *no pl.*) weariness; disgust; *zum* —, ad nauseam.

überdrüssig ['y:bərdrysɪç],*adj.* weary of.

Übereifer ['y:bəraɪfər], *m.* (—**s**, *no pl.*) excessive zeal.

übereifrig ['y:bəraɪfrɪç], *adj.* excessively zealous, officious.

übereilen [y:bər'aɪlən], *v.r. insep. sich* —, hurry too much, overshoot the mark.

übereilt [y:bər'aɪlt], *adj.* overhasty, rash.

übereinkommen [y:bər'aɪnkɔmən], *v.n. irr.* (*aux.* sein) agree.

Übereinkunft [y:bər'aɪnkunft], *f.* (—, *pl.* ⸚**e**) agreement, convention.

übereinstimmen [y:bər'aɪnʃtɪmən], *v.n.* agree, concur, harmonize, be of one mind, be of the same opinion; (*things*) tally, square.

Übereinstimmung [y:bər'aɪnʃtɪmuŋ], *f.* (—, *no pl.*) accord, agreement, conformity, harmony.

überfahren (1) [y:bər'fa:rən], *v.a. irr. insep.* traverse, pass over; run over (s.o.).

überfahren (2) ['y:bərfa:rən], *v.a. irr.* ferry across. — *v.n.* (*aux.* sein) cross.

überfahren (3) ['y:bərfa:rən], *v.n.* (*aux.* sein) cross.

Überfahrt ['y:bərfa:rt], *f.* (—, *pl.* —**en**) passage, crossing.

Überfall ['y:bərfal], *m.* (—**s**, *pl.* ⸚**e**) sudden attack, raid.

überfallen (1) ['y:bərfalən], *v.n. irr.* (*aux.* sein) (*p.p.* übergefallen) fall over.

überfallen (2) [y:bər'falən], *v.a. irr. insep.* (*p.p.* überfallen) attack suddenly, raid.

überfliegen [y:bər'fli:gən], *v.a. irr. insep.* fly over; (*fig.*) glance over, skim.

überfließen ['y:bərfli:sən], *v.n. irr.* (*aux.* sein) overflow.

überflügeln [y:bər'fly:gəln], v.a. insep. surpass, outstrip.

Überfluß ['y:bərflus], m. (—sses, no pl.) abundance, plenty, profusion; surplus; — haben an, abound in, have too much of.

überflüssig ['y:bərflysıç], adj. superfluous, unnecessary.

überfluten [y:bər'flu:tən], v.a. insep. overflow, flood.

überführen (1) ['y:bərfy:rən], v.a. convey, conduct (across).

überführen (2) [y:bər'fy:rən], v.a. insep. convict; transport a coffin.

Überführung [y:bər'fy:ruŋ], f. (—, pl. —en) conviction (for a crime); transport (of a coffin).

Überfüllung [y:bər'fyluŋ], f. (—, no pl.) overcrowding.

Übergabe ['y:bərga:bə], f. (—, no pl.) surrender, yielding up; delivery, handing over.

Übergang ['y:bərgaŋ], m. (—s, pl. ⸗e) passage; (Railw.) crossing; (fig.) change-over, transition.

übergeben [y:bər'ge:bən], v.a. irr. insep. deliver up, hand over. — v.r. sich —, vomit.

übergehen (1) ['y:bərge:ən], v.n. irr. (aux. sein) (p.p. übergegangen) go over, change over, turn (into); zum Feinde —, go over to the enemy; in andre Hände —, change hands.

übergehen (2) [y:bər'ge:ən], v.a. irr. insep. (p.p. übergangen) pass over, pass by.

Übergehung [y:bər'ge:uŋ], f. (—, no pl.) omission; passing over.

übergeordnet ['y:bərgəordnət], adj. superior.

Übergewicht ['y:bərgəvıçt], n. (—(e)s, no pl.) overweight; (fig.) preponderance, superiority.

übergießen [y:bər'gi:sən], v.a. irr. insep. pour over, douse with.

überglücklich ['y:bərglyklıç], adj. overjoyed.

übergreifen [y:bərgraıfən], v.n. irr. overlap; encroach (upon); spread.

Übergriff ['y:bərgrıf], m. (—(e)s, pl. —e) encroachment.

übergroß ['y:bərgro:s], adj. excessively large, overlarge.

überhaben ['y:bərha:bən], v.a. irr. have enough of, be sick of.

überhandnehmen [y:bər'hantne:mən], v.n. irr. gain the upper hand; run riot.

überhangen ['y:bərhaŋən], v.n. irr. hang over.

überhängen ['y:bərhɛŋən], v.a. irr. cover, hang upon.

überhäufen [y:bər'hoyfən], v.a. insep. overwhelm.

überhaupt [y:bər'haupt], adv. in general, altogether, at all.

überheben [y:bər'he:bən], v.r. irr. insep. sich —, strain o.s. by lifting; (fig.) be overbearing.

überheblich [y:bər'he:plıç], adj. overbearing, arrogant.

überheizen [y:bər'haıtsən], v.a. insep. overheat.

überhitzt [y:bər'hıtst], adj. overheated; impassioned.

überholen [y:bər'ho:lən], v.a. insep. overtake, out-distance; (fig.) overhaul.

überhören [y:bər'hø:rən], v.a. insep. hear s.o.'s lessons; ignore, miss (s.th.).

überirdisch ['y:bərɪrdıʃ], adj. celestial, superterrestrial.

Überkleid ['y:bərklaıt], n. (—(e)s, pl. —er) outer garment; overall.

überklug ['y:bərklu:k], adj. too clever by half, conceited.

überkochen ['y:bərkɔxən], v.n. (aux. sein) boil over.

überkommen [y:bər'kɔmən], adj. — sein von, be seized with.

überladen [y:bər'la:dən], v.a. irr. insep. overload. — adj. overdone, too elaborate; bombastic.

überlassen [y:bər'lasən], v.a. irr. insep. leave, relinquish, give up, yield.

überlasten [y:bər'lastən], v.a. insep. overburden.

überlaufen (1) ['y:bərlaufən], v.a. irr. run over; (to the enemy) desert.

überlaufen (2) [y:bər'laufən], v.a. insep. (p.p. überlaufen) overrun.

Überläufer ['y:bərlɔyfər], m. (—s, pl. —) deserter, runaway.

überleben [y:bər'le:bən], v.a. insep. survive, outlive; (fig.) live (s.th.) down; sich überlebt haben, be out of date, be dated.

Überlebende [y:bər'le:bəndə], m. (—n, pl. —n) survivor.

überlegen (1) ['y:bərle:gən], v.a. lay over, cover.

überlegen (2) [y:bər'le:gən], v.a. insep. (p.p. überlegt) think over, consider, turn over in o.'s mind. — adj. superior; — sein, outdo, be superior to.

Überlegenheit [y:bər'le:gənhaıt], f. (—, no pl.) superiority.

Überlegung [y:bər'le:guŋ], f. (—, pl. —en) consideration, deliberation; bei näherer —, on second thoughts, on thinking it over.

überliefern [y:bər'li:fərn], v.a. insep. hand down (to posterity), hand on, pass on.

Überlieferung [y:bər'li:fəruŋ], f. (—, pl. —en) tradition.

überlisten [y:bər'lıstən], v.a. insep. outwit.

Übermacht ['y:bərmaxt], f. (—, no pl.) superiority, superior force.

übermalen [y:bər'ma:lən], v.a. insep. paint over.

übermangansauer [y:bərmaŋ'ga:nzauər], adj. permanganate of; —saueres Kali, permanganate of potash.

übermannen [y:bər'manən], v.a. insep. overpower.

Übermaß ['y:bərma:s], n. (—es, no pl.) excess; im —, to excess.

übermäßig ['y:bərmɛ:sıç], *adj.* excessive, immoderate.

Übermensch ['y:bərmɛnʃ], *m.* (**—en**, *pl.* **—en**) superman.

übermenschlich ['y:bərmɛnʃlıç], *adj.* superhuman.

übermitteln [y:bər'mıtəln], *v.a. insep.* convey.

übermorgen ['y:bərmɔrgən], *adv.* the day after tomorrow.

Übermut ['y:bərmu:t], *m.* (**—s**, *no pl.*) wantonness; high spirits.

übermütig ['y:bərmy:tıç], *adj.* wanton; full of high spirits.

übernachten [y:bər'naxtən], *v.n. insep.* pass *or* spend the night.

übernächtig [y:bər'nɛçtıç], *adj.* haggard, tired by a sleepless night.

Übernahme ['y:bərna:mə], *f.* (**—**, *no pl.*) taking possession, taking charge.

übernatürlich ['y:bərnaty:rlıç], *adj.* supernatural.

übernehmen [y:bər'ne:mən], *v.a. irr. insep.* take possession of, take upon o.s., take over. — *v.r. sich —*, overtax o.'s strength.

überordnen ['y:bərɔrdnən], *v.a.* place above.

überprüfen [y:bər'pry:fən], *v.a. insep.* examine, overhaul.

überquellen ['y:bərkvɛlən], *v.n. irr. insep.* (*aux.* sein) bubble over.

überqueren [y:bər'kve:rən], *v.a. insep.* cross.

überragen [y:bər'ra:gən], *v.a. insep.* tower above, overtop; (*fig.*) surpass, outstrip.

überraschen [y:bər'raʃən], *v.a. insep.* surprise, take by surprise.

Überraschung [y:bər'raʃuŋ], *f.* (**—**, *pl.* **—en**) surprise.

überreden [y:bər're:dən], *v.a. insep.* persuade, talk s.o. into (s.th.).

Überredung [y:bər're:duŋ], *f.* (**—**, *no pl.*) persuasion.

überreichen [y:bər'raıçən], *v.a. insep.* hand over, present formally.

überreichlich ['y:bərraıçlıç], *adj.* superabundant.

Überreichung [y:bər'raıçuŋ], *f.* (**—**, *no pl.*) formal presentation.

überreizen [y:bər'raıtsən], *v.a. insep.* over-excite, over-stimulate.

überrennen [y:bər'rɛnən], *v.a. irr. insep.* take by storm, overrun.

Überrest [y:bərrɛst], *m.* (**—es**, *pl.* **—e**) remainder, remnant, residue.

überrumpeln [y:bər'rumpəln], *v.a. insep.* catch unawares, surprise.

übersättigen [y:bər'zɛtıgən], *v.a. insep.* saturate, surfeit, cloy.

Übersättigung [y:bər'zɛtıguŋ], *f.* (**—**, *no pl.*) saturation; surfeit.

Überschallgeschwindigkeit ['y:bər-ʃalgəʃvındıçkaıt], *f.* (**—**, *no pl.*) supersonic speed.

überschatten [y:bər'ʃatən], *v.a. insep.* overshadow.

überschätzen [y:bər'ʃɛtsən], *v.a. insep.* overrate, over-estimate.

überschauen [y:bər'ʃauən], *v.a. insep.* survey.

überschäumen ['y:bərʃɔymən], *v.n.* (*aux.* sein) bubble over.

überschäumend ['y:bərʃɔymənt], *adj.* ebullient, exuberant.

Überschlag ['y:bərʃla:k], *m.* (**—s**, *pl.* **—e**) somersault; estimate.

überschlagen ['y:bərʃla:gən], *v.a. irr. insep.* (*pages*) miss, skip; estimate, compute. — *v.r. sich —*, turn a somersault, overturn. — *adj.* tepid, lukewarm.

überschnappen ['y:bərʃnapən], *v.n.* (*aux.* sein) snap; (*fig., coll.*) go out of o.'s mind.

überschreiben [y:bər'ʃraıbən], *v.a. irr. insep.* superscribe, entitle.

überschreiten [y:bər'ʃraıtən], *v.a. irr. insep.* cross; go beyond, exceed.

Überschrift ['y:bərʃrıft], *f.* (**—**, *pl.* **—en**) heading, headline.

Überschuß ['y:bərʃus], *m.* (**—sses**, *pl.* **—sse**) surplus.

überschüssig ['y:bərʃysıç], *adj.* surplus, remaining.

überschütten [y:bər'ʃytən], *v.a. insep.* shower with, overwhelm with.

Überschwang ['y:bərʃvaŋ], *m.* (**—s**, *no pl.*) exaltation, rapture.

überschwemmen [y:bər'ʃvɛmən], *v.a. insep.* flood, inundate.

Überschwemmung [y:bər'ʃvɛmuŋ], *f.* (**—**, *pl.* **—en**) inundation, flood, deluge.

überschwenglich [y:bər'ʃvɛŋlıç], *adj.* exuberant, exalted.

Übersee ['y:bərze:], *f.* (**—**, *no pl.*) overseas.

übersehen [y:bər'ze:ən], *v.a. irr. insep.* survey, look over; overlook, disregard.

übersenden [y:bər'zɛndən], *v.a. irr. insep.* send, forward, transmit; (*money*) remit.

Übersendung [y:bər'zɛnduŋ], *f.* (**—**, *pl.* **—en**) sending, forwarding, transmission; remittance.

übersetzen (1) ['y:bərzɛtsən], *v.a.* (*p.p.* übergesetzt) ferry across, cross (a river).

übersetzen (2) [y:bər'zɛtsən], *v.a. insep.* (*p.p.* übersetzt) translate.

Übersetzer [y:bər'zɛtsər], *m.* (**—s**, *pl.* **—**) translator.

Übersetzung [y:bər'zɛtsuŋ], *f.* (**—**, *pl.* **—en**) translation.

Übersicht ['y:bərzıçt], *f.* (**—**, *pl.* **—en**) survey, summary; epitome.

übersichtlich ['y:bərzıçtlıç], *adj.* clearly arranged, readable at a glance, lucid.

übersiedeln [y:bər'zi:dəln], *v.n.* (*aux.* sein) remove, move, settle in a different place.

Übersiedlung [y:bər'zi:dluŋ], *f.* (**—**, *pl.* **—en**) removal.

überspannen [y:bər'ʃpanən], *v.a. insep.* overstretch.

überspannt [y:bər'ʃpant], *adj.* eccentric, extravagant.

Überspanntheit

Überspanntheit [y:bər'ʃpanthaɪt], *f.* (—, *pl.* —en) eccentricity.

überspringen [y:bər'ʃprɪŋən], *v.a. irr. insep.* jump over; (*fig.*) skip.

übersprudeln ['y:bərʃpru:dəln], *v.n.* (*aux.* sein) bubble over.

überstechen [y:bər'ʃtɛçən], *v.a. irr.* (*cards*) trump higher.

überstehen [y:bər'ʃte:ən], *v.a. irr. insep.* overcome, endure, get over, weather.

übersteigen [y:bər'ʃtaɪgən], *v.a. irr. insep.* exceed, surpass.

überstrahlen [y:bər'ʃtra:lən], *v.a. insep.* outshine, surpass in splendour.

überstreichen [y:bər'ʃtraɪçən], *v.a. irr. insep.* paint over.

überströmen [y:bər'ʃtrø:mən], *v.a. insep.* flood, overflow.

Überstunde ['y:bərʃtundə], *f.* (—, *pl.* —n) extra working time, overtime.

überstürzen [y:bər'ʃtyrtsən], *v.r. insep. sich* —, act in haste.

übertäuben [y:bər'tɔybən], *v.a. insep.* deafen.

überteuern [y:bər'tɔyərn], *v.a. insep.* overcharge.

übertölpeln [y:bər'tœlpəln], *v.a. insep.* cheat.

übertönen [y:bər'tø:nən], *v.a. insep.* (*sound*) drown.

übertragen [y:bər'tra:gən], *v.a. irr. insep.* transfer, hand over; convey; broadcast; translate; (*Comm.*) carry over; *einem ein Amt* —, confer an office on s.o.

Übertragung [y:bər'tra:guŋ], *f.* (—, *pl.* —en) cession; transference; handing over; (*Comm.*) carrying over; (*Rad.*) transmission; (*Med.*) transfusion.

übertreffen [y:bər'trɛfən], *v.a. irr. insep.* surpass, excel, outdo.

übertreiben [y:bər'traɪbən], *v.a. irr. insep.* exaggerate.

Übertreibung [y:bər'traɪbuŋ], *f.* (—, *pl.* —en) exaggeration.

übertreten (1) ['y:bərtre:tən], *v.n. irr.* (*aux.* sein) go over to; (*river*) overflow; (*religion*) change to, join (*church, party*).

übertreten (2) [y:bər'tre:tən], *v.a. irr. insep.* transgress, trespass against, infringe, violate.

Übertretung [y:bər'tre:tuŋ], *f.* (—, *pl.* —en) transgression, trespass, violation, infringement.

übertrieben [y:bər'tri:bən], *adj.* excessive, immoderate, exaggerated.

Übertritt ['y:bərtrɪt], *m.* (—s, *no pl.*) defection, going over; (*Rel.*) change, conversion.

übertünchen [y:bər'tynçən], *v.a. insep.* whitewash, rough-cast; (*fig.*) gloss over.

Übervölkerung [y:bər'fœlkəruŋ], *f.* (—, *no pl.*) overpopulation.

übervoll ['y:bərfɔl], *adj.* overful, brimful, chock-full.

übervorteilen [y:bər'fo:rtaɪlən], *v.a. insep.* cheat, defraud.

überwachen [y:bər'vaxən], *v.a. insep.* watch over, superintend, supervise.

Überwachung [y:bər'vaxuŋ], *f.* (—, *no pl.*) superintendence, supervision.

überwachsen [y:bər'vaksən], *v.a. irr. insep.* overgrow.

überwältigen [y:bər'vɛltɪgən], *v.a. insep.* overcome, overpower, subdue.

überwältigend [y:bər'vɛltɪgənt], *adj.* overwhelming.

Überwältigung [y:bər'vɛltɪguŋ], *f.* (—, *no pl.*) overpowering.

überweisen [y:bər'vaɪzən], *v.a. irr. insep.* assign; (*money*) remit.

Überweisung [y:bər'vaɪzuŋ], *f.* (—, *pl.* —en) assignment; (*money*) remittance.

überwerfen (1) ['y:bərvɛrfən], *v.a. irr.* throw over; (*clothes*) slip on.

überwerfen (2) [y:bər'vɛrfən], *v.r. insep. sich* — *mit*, fall out with s.o.

überwiegen [y:bər'vi:gən], *v.n. irr. insep.* prevail.

überwiegend [y:bər'vi:gənt], *adj.* paramount, overwhelming, predominant.

überwinden [y:bər'vɪndən], *v.a. irr. insep.* overcome, conquer. — *v.r. sich* —, prevail upon o.s., bring o.s. (to).

Überwindung [y:bər'vɪnduŋ], *f.* (—, *no pl.*) conquest; reluctance.

überwintern [y:bər'vɪntərn], *v.n. insep.* winter, hibernate.

Überwinterung [y:bər'vɪntəruŋ], *f.* (—, *no pl.*) hibernation.

überwölkt [y:bər'vœlkt], *adj.* overcast.

Überwurf ['y:bərvurf], *m.* (—s, *pl.* ⸚e) wrap, shawl, cloak.

Überzahl ['y:bərtsa:l], *f.* (—, *no pl.*) *in der* —, in the majority.

überzählig ['y:bərtsɛ:lɪç], *adj.* supernumerary, surplus.

überzeichnen ['y:bərtsaɪçnən], *v.a. insep.* (*Comm.*) over-subscribe.

überzeugen [y:bər'tsɔygən], *v.a. insep.* convince. — *v.r. sich* —, satisfy o.s.

Überzeugung [y:bər'tsɔyguŋ], *f.* (—, *no pl.*) conviction.

überziehen (1) ['y:bərtsi:ən], *v.a. irr.* put on (a garment).

überziehen (2) [y:bər'tsi:ən], *v.a. irr. insep.* cover; (*bed*) put fresh linen on; (*Bank*) overdraw.

Überzieher ['y:bərtsi:ər], *m.* (—s, *pl.* —) overcoat.

Überzug ['y:bərtsu:k], *m.* (—s, *pl.* ⸚e) case, cover; bed-tick; coating.

üblich ['y:blɪç], *adj.* usual, customary; *nicht mehr* —, out of use, obsolete.

übrig ['y:brɪç], *adj.* remaining, left over; *die* —en, the others; — *bleiben*, be left, remain; — *haben*, have left; — *sein*, be left; *im* —en, for the rest; *ein* —es *tun*, stretch a point; *für einen etwas* — *haben*, like s.o.

übrigens ['y:brɪgəns], *adv.* besides, moreover; by the way.

Übung ['y:buŋ], *f.* (—, *pl.* —en) exercise, practice.

Ufer ['u:fər], *n.* (—s, *pl.* —) (*river*) bank; (*sea*) shore, beach.

Uganda [u'ganda], *n.* Uganda.

Uhr [u:r], *f.* (—, *pl.* —en) clock; watch; *elf* —, eleven o'clock; *wieviel — ist es?* what is the time?

Uhrmacher ['u:rmaxər], *m.* (—s, *pl.* —) watchmaker, clockmaker.

Uhrwerk ['u:rverk], *n.* (—s, *pl.* —e) clockwork.

Uhrzeiger ['u:rtsaɪgər],·*m.* (—s, *pl.* —) hand (of clock *or* watch).

Uhu ['u:hu:], *m.* (—s, *pl.* —s) (*Orn.*) eagle-owl.

ulkig ['ulkɪç], *adj.* funny.

Ulme ['ulmə], *f.* (—, *pl.* —en) (*Bot.*) elm, elm-tree.

Ultrakurzwelle ['ultrakurtsvɛlə], *f.* (—, *pl.* —n) ultra-short wave.

ultrarot ['ultraro:t], *adj.* infra-red.

Ultrastrahlung ['ultraʃtra:luŋ], *f.* (—, *pl.* —en) cosmic radiation.

ultraviolett ['ultraviolet], *adj.* ultra-violet.

um [um], *prep.* (*Acc.*) about, around; approximately, near; for, because of; by; — *Geld bitten*, ask, for money; — *5 Uhr*, at five o'clock. — *conj.* to, in order to. — *adv.* up, past, upside down; round about; around.

umarbeiten ['umarbaɪtən], *v.a.* do again, remodel, revise; recast.

umarmen [um'armən], *v.a. insep.* embrace.

Umarmung [um'armuŋ], *f.* (—, *pl.* —en) embrace.

umbauen (1) ['umbauən], *v.a.* rebuild.

umbauen (2) [um'bauən], *v.a. insep.* surround with buildings.

umbiegen ['umbi:gən], *v.a. irr.* bend.

umbilden ['umbɪldən], *v.a.* transform, reform, recast, remould.

umbinden ['umbɪndən], *v.a. irr. sich etwas* —, tie s.th. around o.s.

umblicken ['umblɪkən], *v.r. sich* —, look round.

umbringen ['umbrɪŋən], *v.a. irr.* kill, slay, murder.

umdrehen ['umdre:ən], *v.a.* turn over, turn round, revolve. — *v.r. sich* —, turn round.

Umdrehung [um'dre:uŋ], *f.* (—, *pl.* —en) revolution, rotation.

umfahren (1) [um'fa:rən], *v.a. irr. insep.* drive round, circumnavigate.

umfahren (2) ['umfa:rən], *v.a. irr.* run down.

umfallen ['umfalən], *v.n. irr.* (*aux.* sein) fall down, fall over.

Umfang ['umfaŋ], *m.* (—s, *pl.* ⸚e) circumference; (*fig.*) extent.

umfangen [um'faŋən], *v.a. irr. insep.* encircle, embrace.

umfangreich ['umfaŋraɪç], *adj.* extensive, voluminous.

umfassen [um'fasən], *v.a. insep.* comprise, contain.

umfassend [um'fasənt], *adj.* comprehensive.

umfließen [um'fli:sən], *v.a. irr. insep.* surround by water.

umformen ['umfɔrmən], *v.a.* transform, remodel.

Umformung ['umfɔrmuŋ], *f.* (—, *pl.* —en) transformation, remodelling.

Umfrage ['umfra:gə], *f.* (—, *pl.* —n) enquiry, poll, quiz.

Umfriedung [um'fri:duŋ], *f.* (—, *pl.* —en) enclosure.

Umgang ['umgaŋ], *m.* (—s, *pl.* ⸚e) circuit, procession; (*fig.*) acquaintance, association; relations, connection; — *haben mit*, associate with.

umgänglich ['umgɛŋlɪç], *adj.* sociable, companionable.

Umgangsformen ['umgaŋsfɔrmən], *f. pl.* manners.

Umgangssprache ['umgaŋsʃpra:xə], *f.* (— *pl.* —en) colloquial speech.

umgeben [um'ge:bən], *v.a. irr. insep.* surround.

Umgebung [um'ge:buŋ], *f.* (—, *pl.* —en) environment, surroundings.

umgehen (1) ['umge:ən], *v.n. irr.* (*aux.* sein) associate with s.o.; handle s.th.; — *in*, haunt.

umgehen (2) [um'ge:ən], *v.a. irr. insep.* go round; (*flank*) turn; (*fig.*) evade, shirk.

umgehend ['umge:ənt], *adv.* immediately; (*letter*) by return mail.

Umgehung [um'ge:uŋ], *f.* (—, *pl.* —en) shirking, evasion; detour; (*Mil.*) flank movement, turning.

umgekehrt ['umgəke:rt], *adj.* reverse. — *adv.* conversely.

umgestalten ['umgəʃtaltən], *v.a.* transform, recast.

Umgestaltung ['umgəʃtaltuŋ], *f.* (—, *pl.* —en) transformation; recasting.

umgraben ['umgra:bən], *v.a. ·irr.* dig up.

umgrenzen [um'grɛntsən], *v.a. insep.* limit, set bounds to.

Umgrenzung [um'grɛntsuŋ], *f.* (—, *pl.* —en) boundary; limitation.

umgucken ['umgukən], *v.r. sich* —, look about o.

umhalsen [um'halzən], *v.a. insep.* hug, embrace.

Umhang ['umhaŋ], *m.* (—s, *pl.* ⸚e) shawl, cloak.

umher [um'he:r], *adv.* around, round, about.

umherblicken [um'he:rblɪkən], *v.n.* look round.

umherflattern [um'he:rflatərn], *v.n.* (*aux.* sein) flutter about.

umherlaufen [um'he:rlaufən], *v.n. irr.* (*aux.* sein) run about; roam about, ramble, wander.

umherziehend [um'he:rtsi:ənt], *adj.* itinerant.

umhüllen [um'hylən], *v.a. insep.* envelop, wrap up.

Umkehr ['umke:r], *f.* (—, *no pl.*) return; change; (*fig.*) conversion.

umkehren

umkehren [ˈumkeːrən], *v.a.* turn (back), upset, overturn. — *v.n.* (*aux.* sein) turn back, return.

Umkehrung [ˈumkeːruŋ], *f.* (—, *pl.* —en) inversion.

umkippen [ˈumkɪpən], *v.a.* upset, overturn. — *v.n.* (*aux.* sein) capsize, tilt over.

umklammern [umˈklamərn], *v.a. insep.* clasp; clutch; (*fig.*) cling to.

umkleiden (1) [ˈumklaɪdən], *v.r. sich* —, change o.'s clothes.

umkleiden (2) [umˈklaɪdən], *v.a. insep.* cover.

umkommen [ˈumkɔmən], *v.n. irr.* (*aux.* sein) perish.

Umkreis [ˈumkraɪs], *m.* (—es, *pl.* —e) circumference, compass.

Umlauf [ˈumlauf], *m.* (—s, *no pl.*) circulation; *in* — *bringen*, put into circulation.

Umlaut [ˈumlaut], *m.* (—s, *pl.* —e) (*Phonet.*) modification of vowels.

umlegen [ˈumleːgən], *v.a.* lay down, move, shift, put about; (*sl.*) kill.

umleiten [ˈumlaɪtən], *v.a.* (*traffic*) divert.

umlernen [ˈumlɛrnən], *v.a., v.n.* relearn; retrain (for new job).

umliegend [ˈumliːgənt], *adj.* surrounding.

ummodeln [ˈummoːdəln], *v.a.* remodel, recast, change, fashion differently.

Umnachtung [umˈnaxtuŋ], *f.* (—, *no pl.*) mental derangement.

umpacken [ˈumpakən], *v.a.* repack.

umpflanzen [ˈumpflantsən], *v.a.* transplant.

Umpflanzung [ˈumpflantsuŋ], *f.* (—, *pl.* —en) transplantation.

umrahmen [ˈumraːmən], *v.a. insep.* frame, surround.

umrändern [umˈrɛndərn], *v.a. insep.* border, edge.

umrechnen [ˈumrɛçnən], *v.a.* (*figures*) reduce, convert.

umreißen (1) [ˈumraɪsən], *v.a. irr.* pull down, break up.

umreißen (2) [umˈraɪsən], *v.a. irr. insep.* sketch, outline.

umrennen [ˈumrɛnən], *v.a. irr.* run down, knock over.

umringen [umˈrɪŋən], *v.a. insep.* encircle, surround.

Umriß [ˈumrɪs], *m.* (—sses, *pl.* —sse) outline, contour.

umrühren [ˈumryːrən], *v.a.* (*Cul.*) stir.

umsatteln [ˈumzatəln], *v.n.* (*fig.*) change o.'s profession.

Umsatz [ˈumzats], *m.* (—es, *pl.* ⸚e) turnover.

umschalten [ˈumʃaltən], *v.a.* (*Elec.*) switch (over); reverse (current).

Umschau [ˈumʃau], *f.* (—, *no pl.*) review, survey; — *halten*, look round, muster, review.

umschauen [ˈumʃauən], *v.r. sich* —, look round.

umschichtig [ˈumʃɪçtɪç], *adv.* turn and turn about, in turns.

umschiffen (1) [ˈumʃɪfən], *v.a.* tranship, transfer (cargo, passengers).

umschiffen (2) [umˈʃɪfən], *v.a. insep.* sail round, circumnavigate.

Umschlag [ˈumʃlaːk], *m.* (—(e)s, *pl.* ⸚e) (*weather*) break, sudden change; (*letter*) envelope; (*Med.*) poultice, compress.

umschlagen [ˈumʃlaːgən], *v.n. irr.* (*aux.* sein) (*weather*) change suddenly; capsize; turn sour.

umschließen [umˈʃliːsən], *v.a. irr. insep.* enclose, surround; comprise.

umschlingen [umˈʃlɪŋən], *v.a. irr. insep.* embrace.

umschnallen [ˈumʃnalən], *v.a.* buckle on.

umschreiben (1) [ˈumʃraɪbən], *v.a. irr. insep.* rewrite, write differently.

umschreiben (2) [umˈʃraɪbən], *v.a. irr. insep.* circumscribe, paraphrase.

Umschreibung [umˈʃraɪbuŋ], *f.* (—, *pl.* —en) paraphrase.

Umschweife [ˈumʃvaɪfə], *m.pl.* fuss, talk; circumlocution; *ohne* —, point-blank.

Umschwung [ˈumʃvuŋ], *m.* (—s, *no pl.*) sudden change, revolution.

umsegeln [umˈzeːgəln], *v.a. insep.* sail round.

umsehen [ˈumzeːən], *v.r. irr. sich* —, look round; look out (for), cast about (for).

Umsicht [ˈumzɪçt], *f.* (—, *no pl.*) circumspection.

umsichtig [ˈumzɪçtɪç], *adj.* cautious, circumspect.

umsinken [ˈumzɪŋkən], *v.n. irr.* (*aux.* sein) sink down.

umsonst [umˈzɔnst], *adv.* without payment, gratis, for nothing; in vain, vainly, to no purpose.

umspannen (1) [ˈumʃpanən], *v.a.* change horses.

umspannen (2) [umˈʃpanən], *v.a. insep.* encompass, span.

umspringen [ˈumʃprɪŋən], *v.n. irr.* (*aux.* sein) (*wind*) change suddenly; *mit einem* —, (*fig.*) deal with s.o.

Umstand [ˈumʃtant], *m.* (—s, *pl.* ⸚e) circumstance; fact; factor; (*pl.*) fuss; *in anderen* ⸚*en sein*, be expecting a baby; *unter keinen* ⸚*en*, on no account.

umständlich [ˈumʃtɛntlɪç], *adj.* circumstantial, ceremonious, complicated, fussy.

Umstandswort [ˈumʃtantsvɔrt], *n.* (—es, *pl.* ⸚er) (*Gram.*) adverb.

umstehend [ˈumʃteːənt], *adv.* on the next page.

Umstehenden [ˈumʃteːəndən], *pl.* bystanders.

umsteigen [ˈumʃtaɪgən], *v.n. irr.* (*aux.* sein) change (trains etc.).

umstellen (1) [ˈumʃtɛlən], *v.a.* place differently, transpose, change over.

umstellen (2) [umˈʃtɛlən], *v.a. insep.* surround, beset.

Umstellung [ˈumʃtɛluŋ], *f.* (—, *pl.*
—en) transposition; (*Gram.*) inversion; change of position in team.

umstimmen [ˈumʃtɪmən], *v.a.* turn
s.o. from his opinion, bring s.o.
round to (s.th.).

umstoßen [ˈumʃtoːsən], *v.a. irr.* knock
down, upset, overthrow; (*judgment*)
reverse.

umstricken [umˈʃtrɪkən], *v.a. insep.*
ensnare.

umstritten [umˈʃtrɪtən], *adj.* controversial, disputed.

umstülpen [ˈumʃtylpən], *v.a.* turn up,
turn upside down.

Umsturz [ˈumʃturts], *m.* (—es, *no pl.*)
downfall; subversion; revolution.

umstürzen [ˈumʃtyrtsən], *v.a.* upset,
overturn; overthrow.

umtaufen [ˈumtaufən], *v.a.* rename,
rechristen.

Umtausch [ˈumtauʃ], *m.* (—s, *no pl.*)
exchange.

umtauschen [ˈumtauʃən], *v.a.* exchange, change.

Umtriebe [ˈumtriːbə], *m. pl.* plots,
goings-on, intrigues.

umtun [ˈumtuːn], *v.r. irr. sich — nach*,
look for, cast about for.

Umwälzung [ˈumvɛltsuŋ], *f.* (—, *pl.*
—en) turning-about; (*fig.*) revolution.

umwandeln [ˈumvandəln], *v.a.* change,
transform; (*Gram.*) inflect.

umwechseln [ˈumvɛksəln], *v.a.* exchange.

Umweg [ˈumveːk], *m.* (—s, *pl.* —e)
roundabout way, detour.

Umwelt [ˈumvɛlt], *f.* (—, *no pl.*)
environment, milieu.

umwenden [ˈumvɛndən], *v.a. irr.* turn
round; turn over. — *v.r. sich —*, turn
round.

umwerben [umˈvɛrbən], *v.a. irr. insep.*
court.

umwerfen [ˈumvɛrfən], *v.a. irr.* overturn, knock over, upset.

umwickeln [umˈvɪkəln], *v.a. insep.*
wrap round, wind round.

umwölken [umˈvœlkən], *v.r. insep.
sich —*, (*sky*) darken, become overcast.

umzäunen [umˈtsɔynən], *v.a. insep.*
hedge in, fence in, enclose.

umziehen (1) [ˈumtsiːən], *v.a. irr.*
change (clothes). — *v.n.* (*aux.* scin)
move (abode).— *v.r. sich —*, change o.'s
clothes.

umziehen (2) [umˈtsiːən], *v.r. irr.
insep. sich —*, get overcast, cloud over.

umzingeln [umˈtsɪŋəln], *v.a. insep.*
surround.

Umzug [ˈumtsuːk], *m.* (—s, *pl.* ⁓e)
procession; removal; move.

unabänderlich [unapˈɛndərlɪç], *adj.*
unalterable, irrevocable.

Unabänderlichkeit [ˈunapɛndərlɪçkaɪt], *f.* (—, *no pl.*) unchangeableness,
irrevocability.

unabhängig [ˈunaphɛŋɪç], *adj.* independent, autonomous; unrelated.

Unabhängigkeit [ˈunaphɛŋɪçkaɪt], *f.*
(—, *no pl.*) independence, self-sufficiency.

unabkömmlich [ˈunapkœmlɪç], *adj.*
indispensable.

unablässig [ˈunaplɛsɪç], *adj.* unceasing, continual, unremitting.

unabsehbar [ˈunapzeːbaːr], *adj.* immeasurable, immense; unfathomable.

unabsichtlich [ˈunapzɪçtlɪç], *adj.* unintentional, accidental.

unabwendbar [unapˈvɛntbaːr], *adj.*
irremediable; unavoidable.

unachtsam [ˈunaxtzaːm], *adj.* inattentive, inadvertent, negligent, careless.

Unachtsamkeit [ˈunaxtzaːmkaɪt], *f.*
(—, *pl.* —en) inadvertence, inattention, negligence, carelessness.

unähnlich [ˈunɛːnlɪç], *adj.* unlike,
dissimilar.

unanfechtbar [ˈunanfɛçtbaːr], *adj.* indisputable, incontestable.

unangebracht [ˈunangəbraxt], *adj.*
out of place, inapposite.

unangefochten [ˈunangəfɔxtən], *adj.*
undisputed, uncontested.

unangemeldet [ˈunangəmɛldət], *adj.*
unannounced, unheralded.

unangemessen [ˈunangəmɛsən], *adj.*
unsuitable, inappropriate, inadequate.

unangenehm [ˈunangəneːm], *adj.* disagreeable, unpleasant; *einen —
berühren*, jar, grate on s.o.

unangetastet [ˈunangətastət], *adj.* untouched.

unangreifbar [ˈunangraɪfbaːr], *adj.*
unassailable, secure.

unannehmbar [ˈunanneːmbaːr], *adj.*
unacceptable.

Unannehmlichkeit [ˈunanneːmlɪçkaɪt], *f.* (—, *pl.* —en) unpleasantness,
annoyance.

unansehnlich [ˈunanzeːnlɪç], *adj.* insignificant; unattractive.

unanständig [ˈunanʃtɛndɪç], *adj.* improper, indecent.

Unanständigkeit [ˈunanʃtɛndɪçkaɪt], *f.*
(—, *pl.* —en) indecency, immodesty,
impropriety.

unantastbar [ˈunantastbaːr], *adj.* unimpeachable.

unappetitlich [ˈunapeti:tlɪç], *adj.* distasteful, unsavoury, unappetising.

Unart [ˈunaːrt], *f.* (—, *pl.* —en) bad
habit, naughtiness.

unartig [ˈunaːrtɪç], *adj.* ill-behaved,
naughty.

unästhetisch [ˈunɛstetɪʃ], *adj.* offensive, coarse; inartistic.

unauffällig [ˈunauffɛlɪç], *adj.* unobtrusive.

unaufgefordert [ˈunaufgəfɔrdərt], *adj.*
unbidden.

unaufgeklärt [ˈunaufgəkleːrt], *adj.* unexplained, unsolved.

unaufgeschnitten [ˈunaufgəʃnɪtən],
adj. uncut.

unaufhaltsam [ˈunaufhaltzaːm], *adj.*
incessant, irresistible.

unaufhörlich

unaufhörlich ['unaufhøːrlıç], *adj.* incessant, continual.

unauflöslich ['unaufløːslıç], *adj.* indissoluble.

unaufmerksam ['unaufmɛrkzaːm], *adj.* inattentive.

unaufrichtig ['unaufrıçtıç], *adj.* insincere.

unaufschiebbar ['unaufʃiːpbaːr], *adj.* urgent, pressing, brooking no delay.

unausbleiblich ['unausblaıplıç], *adj.* inevitable, unfailing.

unausführbar ['unausfyːrbaːr], *adj.* impracticable.

unausgebildet ['unausgəbıldət], *adj.* untrained, unskilled.

unausgefüllt ['unausgəfylt], *adj.* not filled up; (*form*) blank.

unausgegoren ['unausgəgoːrən], *adj.* crude; (*wine*) unfermented.

unausgesetzt ['unausgəzɛtst], *adj.* continual, continuous.

unausgesprochen ['unausgəʃprɔxən], *adj.* unsaid; (*fig.*) implied.

unauslöschlich ['unauslø:ʃlıç], *adj.* indelible, inextinguishable.

unaussprechlich ['unausʃprɛçlıç], *adj.* inexpressible, unspeakable.

unausstehlich ['unausʃteːlıç], *adj.* insufferable.

unausweichlich ['unausvaıçlıç], *adj.* inevitable.

unbändig ['unbɛndıç], *adj.* intractable, unmanageable; (*fig.*) extreme.

unbarmherzig ['unbarmhɛrtsıç], *adj.* merciless.

unbeabsichtigt ['unbəapzıçtıçt], *adj.* unintentional.

unbeanstandet ['unbəanʃtandət], *adj.* unexceptionable; unopposed; with impunity.

unbeantwortlich ['unbəantvɔrtlıç], *adj.* unanswerable.

unbeaufsichtigt ['unbəaufzıçtıçt], *adj.* unattended to, not looked after; without supervision.

unbebaut ['unbəbaut], *adj.* (*Agr.*) uncultivated; undeveloped (by building).

unbedacht ['unbədaxt], *adj.* thoughtless.

unbedenklich ['unbədɛŋklıç], *adj.* harmless, innocuous. — *adv.* without hesitation.

unbedeutend ['unbədɔytənt], *adj.* insignificant.

unbedingt ['unbədıŋkt], *adj.* unconditional, unlimited, absolute. — *adv.* quite definitely; without fail.

unbeeinflußt ['unbəaınflust], *adj.* uninfluenced.

unbefahrbar ['unbəfaːrbaːr], *adj.* impassable, impracticable.

unbefangen ['unbəfaŋən], *adj.* unbiased, unprejudiced; easy, unselfconscious, unembarrassed, uninhibited; natural.

Unbefangenheit ['unbəfaŋənhaıt], *f.*

(—, *no pl.*) impartiality; ease of manner, unselfconsciousness, openness, naturalness.

unbefestigt ['unbəfɛstıçt], *adj.* unfortified.

unbefleckt ['unbəflɛkt], *adj.* immaculate; —*e Empfängnis*, Immaculate Conception.

unbefriedigend ['unbəfriːdıgənt], *adj.* unsatisfactory.

unbefriedigt ['unbəfriːdıçt], *adj.* not satisfied, unsatisfied.

unbefugt ['unbəfuːkt], *adj.* unauthorised.

unbegreiflich ['unbəgraıflıç], *adj.* incomprehensible, inconceivable.

unbegrenzt ['unbəgrɛntst], *adj.* unlimited, unbounded.

unbegründet ['unbəgryndət], *adj.* unfounded, groundless.

Unbehagen ['unbəhaːgən], *n.* (—**s**, *no pl.*) uneasiness, discomfort.

unbehaglich ['unbəha:klıç], *adj.* uncomfortable; *sich — fühlen*, feel ill at ease.

unbehelligt ['unbəhɛlıçt], *adj.* unmolested.

unbeholfen ['unbəhɔlfən], *adj.* awkward, clumsy.

unbeirrt ['unbəırt], *adj.* unswerving, uninfluenced, unperturbed.

unbekannt ['unbəkant], *adj.* unknown, unacquainted; *ich bin hier —*, I am a stranger here.

unbekümmert ['unbəkymərt], *adj.* unconcerned, careless, indifferent.

unbelehrt ['unbəleːrt], *adj.* uninstructed.

unbeliebt ['unbəliːpt], *adj.* unpopular.

unbemannt ['unbəmant], *adj.* without crew, unmanned.

unbemerkbar ['unbəmɛrkbaːr], *adj.* unnoticeable, imperceptible.

unbemerkt ['unbəmɛrkt], *adj.* unnoticed.

unbemittelt ['unbəmıtəlt], *adj.* impecunious, poor.

unbenommen ['unbənɔmən], *adj. es bleibt dir —*, you are free to.

unbenutzt ['unbənutst], *adj.* unused.

unbequem ['unbəkveːm], *adj.* uncomfortable, inconvenient, troublesome.

Unbequemlichkeit ['unbəkveːmlıçkaıt], *f.* (—, *pl.* —**en**) inconvenience.

unberechenbar ['unbərɛçənbaːr], *adj.* incalculable; (*fig.*) erratic.

unberechtigt ['unbərɛçtıçt], *adj.* unwarranted, unjustified.

unberücksichtigt ['unbərykzıçtıçt], *adj.* disregarded; — *lassen*, ignore.

unberufen ['unbəruːfən], *adj.* unauthorized. — *excl.* touch wood!

unbeschadet ['unbəʃaːdət], *prep.* (*Genit.*) without prejudice to.

unbeschädigt ['unbəʃɛːdıçt], *adj.* undamaged.

unbeschäftigt ['unbəʃɛftıçt], *adj.* unemployed, disengaged.

unbescheiden ['unbəʃaɪdən], *adj.* presumptuous, greedy, immodest; unblushing; exorbitant; arrogant.
Unbescheidenheit ['unbəʃaɪdənhaɪt], *f.* (—, *no pl.*) presumptuousness, greed.
unbescholten ['unbəʃɔltən], *adj.* irreproachable, of unblemished character.
Unbescholtenheit ['unbəʃɔltənhaɪt], *f.* (—, *no pl.*) blamelessness, good character, unsullied reputation.
unbeschränkt ['unbəʃrɛŋkt], *adj.* unlimited, unbounded; —e *Monarchie,* absolute monarchy.
unbeschreiblich ['unbəʃraɪplɪç], *adj.* indescribable.
unbeschrieben ['unbəʃriːbən], *adj.* unwritten; *ein* —es *Papier,* a blank sheet of paper.
unbeschwert ['unbəʃveːrt], *adj.* unburdened; easy.
unbeseelt ['unbəzeːlt], *adj.* inanimate.
unbesiegbar [unbə'ziːkbaːr], *adj.* invincible.
unbesoldet ['unbəzɔldət], *adj.* unpaid, unsalaried.
unbesonnen ['unbəzɔnən], *adj.* thoughtless, rash.
Unbesonnenheit ['unbəzɔnənhaɪt], *f.* (—, *pl.* —en) thoughtlessness.
unbesorgt ['unbəzɔrkt], *adj.* unconcerned; *sei* —, never fear.
unbeständig ['unbəʃtɛndɪç], *adj.* fickle, inconstant; (*weather*) unsettled.
unbestechlich ['unbəʃtɛçlɪç], *adj.* incorruptible.
unbestellbar ['unbəʃtɛlbaːr], *adj.* not deliverable; (*letters etc.*) address(ee) unknown.
unbestellt ['unbəʃtɛlt], *adj.* not ordered; (*Agr.*) uncultivated, untilled.
unbestimmt ['unbəʃtɪmt], *adj.* uncertain, not settled; indefinite; irresolute; vague.
unbestraft ['unbəʃtraːft], *adj.* unpunished; without previous conviction.
unbestreitbar ['unbəʃtraɪtbaːr], *adj.* indisputable, incontestable.
unbestritten ['unbəʃtrɪtən], *adj.* uncontested, undoubted, undisputed.
unbeteiligt ['unbətaɪlɪçt], *adj.* unconcerned, indifferent.
unbeträchtlich ['unbətrɛçtlɪç], *adj.* inconsiderable, trivial.
unbetreten ['unbətreːtən], *adj.* untrodden, untouched.
unbeugsam ['unbɔykzaːm], *adj.* inflexible, unyielding.
unbewacht ['unbəvaxt], *adj.* unguarded.
unbewaffnet ['unbəvafnət], *adj.* unarmed; *mit* —em *Auge,* with the naked eye.
unbewandert ['unbəvandərt], *adj.* unversed in, unfamiliar with.
unbezahlt ['unbətsaːlt], *adj.* unpaid.
unbezähmbar ['unbətsɛːmbaːr], *adj.* uncontrollable; indomitable.

unbezwinglich ['unbətsvɪŋlɪç], *adj.* invincible, unconquerable.
Unbildung ['unbɪlduŋ], *f.* (—, *no pl.*) lack of education *or* knowledge *or* culture.
Unbill ['unbɪl], *f.* (—, *pl.* **Unbilden**) injustice, wrong, injury; (*weather*) inclemency.
unbillig ['unbɪlɪç], *adj.* unreasonable, unfair.
Unbilligkeit ['unbɪlɪçkaɪt], *f.* (—, *no pl.*) unreasonableness, injustice, unfairness.
unbotmäßig ['unboːtmɛːsɪç], *adj.* unruly, insubordinate.
unbußfertig ['unbuːsfɛrtɪç], *adj.* impenitent, unrepentant.
und [unt], *conj.* and; — *nicht,* nor; — *so weiter* (abbr. *u.s.w.*), etc., and so on, and so forth; — *wenn,* even if.
Undank ['undaŋk], *m.* (—s, *no pl.*) ingratitude.
undankbar ['undaŋkbaːr], *adj.* ungrateful; *eine* —e *Aufgabe,* a thankless task.
Undankbarkeit ['undaŋkbaːrkaɪt], *f.* (—, *no pl.*) ingratitude.
undenkbar ['undɛŋkbaːr], *adj.* unthinkable, unimaginable, inconceivable.
undenklich ['undɛŋklɪç], *adj. seit* —en *Zeiten,* from time immemorial.
undeutlich ['undɔytlɪç], *adj.* indistinct; inarticulate; (*fig.*) unintelligible.
Unding ['undɪŋ], *n.* (—s, *no pl.*) absurdity.
unduldsam ['undultzaːm], *adj.* intolerant.
undurchdringlich ['undurçdrɪŋlɪç], *adj.* impenetrable.
undurchführbar ['undurçfyːrbaːr], *adj.* impracticable, unworkable.
undurchsihtig ['undurçzɪçtɪç], *adj.* opaque, not transparent.
uneben ['uneːbən], *adj.* uneven, rugged; (*coll.*) *nicht* —, not bad.
unecht ['unɛçt], *adj.* false, not genuine, spurious, counterfeit.
unedel ['uneːdəl], *adj.* (*metal*) base.
unehelich ['uneːəlɪç], *adj.* illegitimate.
Unehre ['uneːrə], *f.* (—, *no pl.*) dishonour, disgrace, discredit.
unehrlich ['uneːrlɪç], *adj.* dishonest.
Unehrlichkeit ['uneːrlɪçkaɪt], *f.* (—, *pl.* —en) dishonesty.
uneigennützig ['unaɪgənnytsɪç], *adj.* unselfish, disinterested, public-spirited.
uneingedenk ['unaɪŋədɛŋk], *adj.* (*Genit.*) unmindful, forgetful.
uneingeschränkt ['unaɪŋəʃrɛŋkt], *adj.* unrestrained, unlimited.
uneinig ['unaɪnɪç], *adj.* disunited, divided; — *werden,* fall out; — *sein,* disagree.
Uneinigkeit ['unaɪnɪçkaɪt], *f.* (—, *pl.* —en) disharmony, discord.
uneinnehmbar ['unaɪnneːmbaːr], *adj.* unconquerable, impregnable.

uneins

uneins see under **uneinig**.

unempfänglich ['unɛmpfɛŋlıç], adj. insusceptible; unreceptive.

unempfindlich ['unɛmpfɪntlıç], adj. insensitive, indifferent; unfeeling.

unendlich [un'ɛntlıç], adj. endless, infinite.

unentbehrlich ['unɛntbeːrlıç], adj. indispensable, (absolutely) essential.

unentgeltlich [unɛnt'gɛltlıç], adj. free (of charge).

unentschieden ['unɛntʃiːdən], adj. undecided, undetermined; irresolute; (game) drawn, tied.

unentschlossen ['unɛntʃlɔsən], adj. irresolute.

Unentschlossenheit ['unɛntʃlɔsənhaɪt], f. (—, no pl.) irresolution, indecision.

unentschuldbar ['unɛntʃultbaːr], adj. inexcusable.

unentstellt ['unɛntʃtɛlt], adj. undistorted.

unentwegt ['unɛntveːkt], adj. steadfast, unflinching, unswerving.

unentwickelt ['unɛntvɪkəlt], adj. undeveloped; —e Länder, underdeveloped countries.

unentwirrbar ['unɛntvɪrbaːr], adj. inextricable.

unentzifferbar ['unɛntsɪfərbaːr], adj. indecipherable.

unentzündbar ['unɛnttsyntbaːr], adj. non-inflammable.

unerachtet ['unɛraxtət], prep. (Genit.) (obs.) notwithstanding.

unerbeten ['unɛrbeːtən], adj. unsolicited.

unerbittlich ['unɛrbɪtlıç], adj. inexorable.

unerfahren ['unɛrfaːrən], adj. inexperienced.

unerforschlich ['unɛrfɔrʃlıç], adj. inscrutable.

unerfreulich ['unɛrfrɔylıç], adj. unpleasant, displeasing, disagreeable.

unerfüllbar ['unɛrfylbaːr], adj. unrealisable.

unerfüllt ['unɛrfylt], adj. unfulfilled.

unergründlich ['unɛrgryntlıç], adj. unfathomable, impenetrable.

unerheblich ['unɛrheːplıç], adj. trifling, unimportant.

unerhört ['unɛrhøːrt], adj. unprecedented, unheard of, shocking, outrageous; not granted; turned down.

unerkannt ['unɛrkant], adj. unrecognised.

unerkennbar ['unɛrkɛnbaːr], adj. unrecognisable.

unerklärlich ['unɛrklɛːrlıç], adj. inexplicable.

unerläßlich ['unɛrlɛslıç], adj. indispensable.

unerlaubt ['unɛrlaupt], adj. unlawful, illicit.

unermeßlich ['unɛrmɛslıç], adj. immense, vast.

unermüdlich ['unɛrmyːtlıç], adj. untiring, indefatigable.

unerquicklich ['unɛrkvɪklıç], adj. unedifying, disagreeable.

unerreichbar ['unɛrraɪçbaːr], adj. unattainable, inaccessible.

unerreicht ['unɛrraɪçt], adj. unequalled.

unersättlich ['unɛrzɛtlıç], adj. insatiable, greedy.

unerschöpflich ['unɛrʃœpflıç], adj. inexhaustible.

unerschöpft ['unɛrʃœpft], adj. unexhausted.

unerschrocken ['unɛrʃrɔkən], adj. intrepid, undaunted.

unerschütterlich ['unɛrʃytərlıç], adj. imperturbable.

unerschüttert ['unɛrʃytərt], adj. unshaken, unperturbed.

unerschwinglich ['unɛrʃvɪŋlıç], adj. prohibitive, exorbitant, unattainable.

unersetzlich ['unɛrzɛtslıç], adj. irreplaceable.

unersprießlich ['unɛrʃpriːslıç], adj. unprofitable.

unerträglich ['unɛrtrɛːklıç], adj. intolerable, insufferable.

unerwartet ['unɛrvartət], adj. unexpected.

unerwidert ['unɛrvɪːdərt], adj. (love) unrequited; (letter) unanswered.

unerwünscht ['unɛrvynʃt], adj. undesirable, unwelcome.

unerzogen ['unɛrtsoːgən], adj. uneducated; ill-bred, unmannerly.

unfähig ['unfɛːıç], adj. incapable, unable, unfit.

Unfähigkeit ['unfɛːıçkaɪt], f. (—, no pl.) incapability, inability, unfitness.

Unfall ['unfal], m. (—s, pl. ⁻e) accident.

unfaßbar ['unfasbaːr], adj. incomprehensible, inconceivable.

unfehlbar ['unfɛːlbaːr], adj. inevitable, infallible.

Unfehlbarkeit ['unfɛːlbarkaɪt], f. (—, no pl.) infallibility.

unfein ['unfaɪn], adj. indelicate, coarse, impolite.

unfern ['unfɛrn], prep. (Genit., Dat.) not far from.

unfertig ['unfɛrtıç], adj. unfinished, unready.

unflätig ['unflɛːtıç], adj. obscene, nasty, filthy.

unfolgsam ['unfɔlkzaːm], adj. disobedient, recalcitrant.

unförmig ['unfœrmıç], adj. deformed, ill-shaped, misshapen.

unförmlich ['unfœrmlıç], adj. shapeless; free and easy, unceremonious.

unfrankiert ['unfraŋkiːrt], adj. (letter) not prepaid, unstamped, unfranked.

unfrei ['unfraɪ], adj. not free; subjugated; constrained.

unfreiwillig ['unfraɪvɪlıç], adj. involuntary.

unfreundlich ['unfrɔyntlıç], *adj.* unfriendly, unkind; (*weather*) inclement.

Unfreundlichkeit ['unfrɔyntlıçkaıt], *f.* (—, *pl.* —en) unfriendliness, unkindness; (*weather*) inclemency.

Unfrieden ['unfri:dən], *m.* (—s, *no pl.*) discord, dissension.

unfruchtbar ['unfruxtba:r], *adj.* barren, sterile; (*fig.*) fruitless.

Unfug ['unfu:k], *m.* (—s, *no pl.*) disturbance, misconduct; mischief; *grober* —, public nuisance.

unfühlbar ['unfy:lba:r], *adj.* imperceptible.

ungangbar ['unganba:r], *adj.* impassable.

Ungarn ['ungarn], *n.* Hungary.

ungastlich ['ungastlıç], *adj.* inhospitable.

ungeachtet ['ungəaxtət], *prep.* (*Genit.*) notwithstanding.

ungeahndet ['ungəa:ndət], *adj.* unpunished, with impunity.

ungeahnt ['ungəa:nt], *adj.* unexpected, unsuspected, undreamt of.

ungebändigt ['ungəbɛndıçt], *adj.* untamed.

ungebärdig ['ungəbɛːrdıç], *adj.* unmannerly, refractory.

ungebeten ['ungəbe:tən], *adj.* uninvited, unbidden.

ungebleicht ['ungəblaıçt], *adj.* unbleached.

ungebraucht ['ungəbrauxt], *adj.* unused.

Ungebühr ['ungəby:r], *f.* (—, *no pl.*) unseemliness, impropriety, excess.

ungebührlich ['ungəby:rlıç], *adj.* unseemly.

ungebunden ['ungəbundən], *adj.* unbound, in sheets; unrestrained, loose; unlinked; —*e Rede*, prose.

Ungeduld ['ungədult], *f.* (—, *no pl.*) impatience.

ungeduldig ['ungəduldıç], *adj.* impatient.

ungeeignet ['ungəaıgnət], *adj.* unfit, unsuitable.

ungefähr ['ungəfɛːr], *adj.* approximate, rough. — *adv.* approximately, roughly, about, round.

ungefährlich ['ungəfɛːrlıç], *adj.* not dangerous, harmless, safe.

ungefällig ['ungəfɛlıç], *adj.* ungracious, disobliging.

ungefärbt ['ungəfɛrpt], *adj.* uncoloured; (*fig.*) unvarnished.

ungefüge ['ungəfy:gə], *adj.* clumsy.

ungehalten ['ungəhaltən], *adj.* indignant, angry.

ungeheißen ['ungəhaısən], *adj.* unbidden. — *adv.* of o.'s own accord.

ungehemmt ['ungəhɛmt], *adj.* unchecked, uninhibited.

ungeheuchelt ['ungəhɔyçəlt], *adj.* unfeigned.

Ungeheuer ['ungəhɔyər], *n.* (—s, *pl.* —) monster, monstrosity.

ungeheuer ['ungəhɔyər], *adj.* huge, immense; atrocious, frightful.

ungehobelt ['ungəho:bəlt], *adj.* unplaned; (*fig.*) boorish, uncultured, unpolished.

ungehörig ['ungəhøːrıç], *adj.* unseemly, improper.

Ungehorsam ['ungəho:rza:m], *m.* (—s, *no pl.*) disobedience.

ungehorsam ['ungəho:rza:m], *adj.* disobedient; — *sein*, disobey.

Ungehorsamkeit ['ungəho:rza:mkaıt], *f.* (—, *pl.* —en) disobedience, insubordination.

ungekämmt ['ungəkɛmt], *adj.* unkempt.

ungekünstelt ['ungəkynstəlt], *adj.* artless, unstudied.

ungeladen ['ungəla:dən], *adj.* (*gun*) unloaded, not charged; uninvited.

ungeläutert ['ungələytərt], *adj.* unrefined; unpurified.

ungelegen ['ungəle:gən], *adj.* inconvenient, inopportune.

Ungelegenheit ['ungəle:gənhaıt], *f.* (—, *pl.* —en) inconvenience, trouble.

ungelehrig ['ungəle:rıç], *adj.* intractable, unintelligent.

ungelenk ['ungəlɛŋk], *adj.* clumsy, awkward; ungainly.

ungelöscht ['ungəlœʃt], *adj.* unquenched; (*lime*) unslaked; (*mortgage*) unredeemed.

Ungemach ['ungəma:x], *n.* (—(e)s, *no pl.*) adversity, toil, privation.

ungemein ['ungəmaın], *adj.* uncommon, extraordinary. — *adv.* very much, exceedingly.

ungemütlich ['ungəmy:tlıç], *adj.* uncomfortable, cheerless, unpleasant.

ungeniert ['unʒeni:rt], *adj.* free and easy, unceremonious, unabashed.

ungenießbar ['ungə'ni:sba:r], *adj.* unpalatable, uneatable, inedible.

ungenügend ['ungənygənt], *adj.* insufficient, unsatisfactory.

ungenügsam ['ungəny:kza:m], *adj.* insatiable, greedy.

ungeordnet ['ungəɔrdnət], *adj.* illassorted, confused.

ungepflegt ['ungəpfle:kt], *adj.* uncared for, neglected.

ungerade ['ungəra:də], *adj.* uneven; — *Zahl*, odd number.

ungeraten ['ungəra:tən], *adj.* abortive, unsuccessful, spoiled; undutiful; illbred.

ungerecht ['ungərɛçt], *adj.* unjust, unfair.

ungerechtfertigt ['ungərɛçtfɛrtıçt], *adj.* unwarranted, unjustified.

Ungerechtigkeit ['ungərɛçtıçkaıt], *f.* (—, *pl.* —en) injustice.

ungeregelt ['ungəre:gəlt], *adj.* not regulated, irregular.

ungereimt ['ungəraımt], *adj.* rhymeless; —*es Zeug*, nonsense, absurdity.

ungern ['ungɛrn], *adv.* unwillingly, reluctantly.

ungerufen

ungerufen [ˈungəruːfən], *adj.* un-bidden.
ungerührt [ˈungəryːrt], *adj.* unmoved.
ungesäumt [ˈungəzɔymt], *adj.* un-seamed, unhemmed; (*fig.*) im-mediate. — *adv.* immediately, without delay.
ungeschehen [ˈungəʃeːən], *adj.* un-done; — *machen*, undo.
Ungeschick [ˈungəʃɪk], *n.* (—s, *no pl.*) awkwardness, clumsiness.
Ungeschicklichkeit [ˈungəʃɪklɪçkaɪt], *f.* (—, *pl.* —en) awkwardness, clumsi-ness.
ungeschickt [ˈungəʃɪkt], *adj.* awkward, clumsy, unskilful.
ungeschlacht [ˈungəʃlaxt], *adj.* un-couth, unwieldy; coarse, rude.
ungeschliffen [ˈungəʃlɪfən], *adj.* un-polished; (*fig.*) coarse.
Ungeschliffenheit [ˈungəʃlɪfənhaɪt], *f.* (—, *no pl.*) coarseness, uncouthness.
ungeschmälert [ˈungəʃmɛːlərt], *adj.* undiminished, unimpaired.
ungeschminkt [ˈungəʃmɪŋkt], *adj.* without cosmetics *or* make-up, not made up; (*truth*) plain, unvarnished.
ungeschoren [ˈungəʃoːrən], *adj.* un-shorn; *laß mich* —, leave me alone.
ungeschult [ˈungəʃuːlt], *adj.* un-trained.
ungeschwächt [ˈungəʃvɛçt], *adj.* un-impaired.
ungesellig [ˈungəzɛlɪç], *adj.* unsociable.
ungesetzlich [ˈungəzɛtslɪç], *adj.* illegal, unlawful, illicit.
ungesetzmäßig [ˈungəzɛtsmɛːsɪç], *adj.* illegitimate, lawless; exceptional; not regular.
ungesiegelt [ˈungəziːgəlt], *adj.* un-sealed.
Ungestalt [ˈungəʃtalt], *f.* (—, *no pl.*) deformity.
ungestalt [ˈungəʃtalt], *adj.* misshapen, deformed.
ungestempelt [ˈungəʃtɛmpəlt], *adj.* unstamped, uncancelled, not post-marked.
ungestillt [ˈungəʃtɪlt], *adj.* unquenched, unslaked; not fed, unsatisfied.
ungestört [ˈungəʃtøːrt], *adj.* undis-turbed.
ungestraft [ˈungəʃtraːft], *adj.* un-punished. — *adv.* with impunity.
ungestüm [ˈungəʃtyːm], *adj.* im-petuous.
Ungestüm [ˈungəʃtyːm], *m. & n.* (—s, *no pl.*) impetuosity.
ungesund [ˈungəzunt], *adj.* unwhole-some, unhealthy, sickly; (*fig.*) un-natural, morbid.
ungetan [ˈungətaːn], *adj.* not done, left undone.
ungetreu [ˈungətrɔy], *adj.* disloyal, faithless.
ungetrübt [ˈungətryːpt], *adj.* un-troubled.
ungewandt [ˈungəvant], *adj.* unskilful.
ungewaschen [ˈungəvaʃən], *adj.* un-washed; (*sl.*) —*es Mundwerk*, mal-icious tongue.
ungeweiht [ˈungəvaɪt], *adj.* uncon-secrated.
ungewiß [ˈungəvɪs], *adj.* uncertain, doubtful.
Ungewißheit [ˈungəvɪshaɪt], *f.* (—, *no pl.*) uncertainty, suspense.
Ungewitter [ˈungəvɪtər], *n.* (—s, *pl.* —) storm, thunderstorm.
ungewöhnlich [ˈungəvøːnlɪç], *adj.* un-usual, uncommon.
Ungewohntheit [ˈungəvoːnthaɪt], *f.* (—, *no pl.*) strangeness; want of practice.
ungezähmt [ˈungətsɛːmt], *adj.* un-tamed; (*fig.*) uncurbed.
Ungeziefer [ˈungətsiːfər], *n.* (—s, *pl.* —) vermin.
ungeziert [ˈungətsiːrt], *adj.* unaffected, natural.
ungezogen [ˈungətsoːgən], *adj.* ill-mannered, naughty.
ungezügelt [ˈungətsyːgəlt], *adj.* un-bridled; (*fig.*) unruly.
ungezwungen [ˈungətsvuŋən], *adj.* unforced; (*fig.*) unaffected.
Ungezwungenheit [ˈungətsvuŋənhaɪt], *f.* (—, *no pl.*) naturalness, ease.
Unglaube [ˈunglaubə], *m.* (—ns, *no pl.*) disbelief.
unglaubhaft [ˈunglaubhaft], *adj.* un-authenticated, incredible.
ungläubig [ˈunglɔybɪç], *adj.* incredu-lous, disbelieving.
Ungläubige [ˈunglɔybɪgə], *m.* (—n, *pl.* —n) unbeliever.
unglaublich [ˈunglauplɪç], *adj.* in-credible, unbelievable.
unglaubwürdig [ˈunglaupvyrdɪç], *adj.* unauthenticated, incredible.
ungleichartig [ˈunglaɪçaːrtɪç], *adj.* dissimilar, heterogeneous.
ungleichförmig [ˈunglaɪçfœrmɪç], *adj.* not uniform; dissimilar.
Ungleichheit [ˈunglaɪçhaɪt], *f.* (—, *pl.* —en) inequality; unlikeness, dis-similarity; unevenness.
ungleichmäßig [ˈunglaɪçmɛːsɪç], *adj.* unequal, irregular; changeable, fitful.
Unglimpf [ˈunglɪmpf], *m.* (—(e)s, *no pl.*) harshness; insult.
Unglück [ˈunglyk], *n.* (—s, *pl.* —sfälle) misfortune, adversity, ill-luck; acci-dent, disaster; distress, sorrow, affliction.
unglückbringend [ˈunglykbrɪŋənt], *adj.* disastrous, unpropitious.
unglücklich [ˈunglyklɪç], *adj.* un-fortunate, unhappy, unlucky; —*e Liebe*, unrequited love.
unglücklicherweise [ˈunglyklɪçər-vaɪzə], *adv.* unfortunately, unluckily.
Unglücksbotschaft [ˈunglyksboːtʃaft], *f.* (—, *pl.* —en) bad news.
unglückselig [ˈunglykzeːlɪç], *adj.* luck-less, wretched, unfortunate, calamitous.
Unglücksfall [ˈunglyksfal], *m.* (—(e)s, *pl.* ⸚e) accident.

Unordnung

Unglücksgefährte [ˈunɡlyksɡəfɛːrtə], *m.* (—n, *pl.* —n) companion in misfortune.
Ungnade [ˈunɡnaːdə], *f.* (—, *no pl.*) disgrace.
ungültig [ˈunɡyltɪç], *adj.* invalid, void; — machen, invalidate, annul.
Ungunst [ˈunɡunst], *f.* (—, *no pl.*) disfavour; unpropitiousness; (*weather*) inclemency.
ungünstig [ˈunɡynstɪç], *adj.* unfavourable, adverse.
ungut [ˈunɡuːt], *adv.* etwas für — nehmen, take s.th. amiss.
unhaltbar [ˈunhaltbaːr], *adj.* untenable.
Unheil [ˈunhaɪl], *n.* (—s, *no pl.*) mischief, harm; disaster.
unheilbar [ˈunhaɪlbaːr], *adj.* incurable.
unheilbringend [ˈunhaɪlbrɪŋənt], *adj.* ominous, unlucky; disastrous.
Unheilstifter [ˈunhaɪlʃtɪftər], *m.* (—s, *pl.* —) mischief-maker.
unheilvoll [ˈunhaɪlfɔl], *adj.* calamitous, disastrous.
unheimlich [ˈunhaɪmlɪç], *adj.* weird, eerie, uncanny.
unhöflich [ˈunhøːflɪç], *adj.* impolite, uncivil, discourteous.
Unhold [ˈunhɔlt], *m.* (—s, *pl.* —e) fiend, monster.
Unhörbarkeit [ˈunhøːrbaːrkaɪt], *f.* (—, *no pl.*) inaudibility.
Uniformität [uniformiˈtɛːt], *f.* (—, *no pl.*) uniformity.
Unikum [ˈuːnikum], *n.* (—s, *pl.* —s) unique thing *or* person; eccentric.
Universalmittel [univɛrˈzaːlmɪtəl], *n.* (—s, *pl.* —) panacea, universal remedy.
Universität [univɛrziˈtɛːt], *f.* (—, *pl.* —en) university.
Universitätsdozent [univɛrziˈtɛːtsdotsɛnt], *m.* (—en, *pl.* —en) university lecturer.
Universum [uniˈvɛrzum], *n.* (—s, *no pl.*) universe.
unkaufmännisch [ˈunkaufmɛnɪʃ], *adj.* unbusinesslike.
Unke [ˈuŋkə], *f.* (—, *pl.* —n) (*Zool.*) toad; (*fig.*) grumbler, pessimist.
unken [ˈuŋkən], *v.n.* grumble, grouse.
unkenntlich [ˈunkɛntlɪç], *adj.* indiscernible, unrecognisable.
Unkenntlichkeit [ˈunkɛntlɪçkaɪt], *f.* (—, *no pl.*) bis zur —, past recognition.
Unkenntnis [ˈunkɛntnɪs], *f.* (—, *no pl.*) ignorance.
unklug [ˈunkluːk], *adj.* imprudent.
Unkosten [ˈunkɔstən], *f. pl.* expenses, costs, charges; overheads.
Unkraut [ˈunkraut], *n.* (—s, *no pl.*) weed(s).
unkündbar [ˈunkyntbaːr], *adj.* irredeemable; irrevocable, permanent.
unkundig [ˈunkundɪç], *adj.* ignorant (of), unacquainted (with).
unlängst [ˈunlɛŋst], *adv.* recently, lately, not long ago.

unlauter [ˈunlautər], *adj.* sordid squalid; unfair.
unleidlich [ˈunlaɪtlɪç], *adj.* intolerable.
unleserlich [ˈunleːzərlɪç], *adj.* illegible.
unleugbar [ˈunlɔykbaːr], *adj.* undeniable, indisputable.
unlieb [ˈunliːp], *adj.* disagreeable.
unliebenswürdig [ˈunliːbənsvyrdɪç], *adj.* sullen, surly.
unlösbar [ˈunløːsbaːr], *adj.* insoluble.
unlöslich [ˈunløːslɪç], *adj.* (*substance*) indissoluble, insoluble.
Unlust [ˈunlust], *f.* (—, *no pl.*) aversion, disinclination; slackness.
unlustig [ˈunlustɪç], *adj.* averse, disinclined.
unmanierlich [ˈunmaniːrlɪç], *adj.* illmannered.
unmännlich [ˈunmɛnlɪç], *adj.* unmanly, effeminate.
Unmaß [ˈunmaːs], *n.* (—es, *no pl.*) excess.
Unmasse [ˈunmasə], *f.* (—, *pl.* —n) vast quantity.
unmaßgeblich [ˈunmaːsɡeːplɪç], *adj.* unauthoritative, open to correction; (*fig.*) humble.
unmäßig [ˈunmɛːsɪç], *adj.* intemperate, excessive.
Unmenge [ˈunmɛŋə], *f.* (—, *pl.* —n) vast quantity.
Unmensch [ˈunmɛnʃ], *m.* (—en, *pl.* —en) brute.
unmenschlich [ˈunmɛnʃlɪç], *adj.* inhuman, brutal; (*coll.*) vast.
unmerklich [ˈunmɛrklɪç], *adj.* imperceptible.
unmeßbar [ˈunmɛsbaːr], *adj.* immeasurable.
unmittelbar [ˈunmɪtəlbaːr], *adj.* immediate, direct.
unmöglich [ˈunmøːklɪç], *adj.* impossible.
unmündig [ˈunmyndɪç], *adj.* under age, minor.
Unmündige [ˈunmyndɪɡə], *m.* (—n, *pl.* —n) (*Law*) minor.
Unmündigkeit [ˈunmyndɪçkaɪt], *f.* (—, *no pl.*) minority.
Unmut [ˈunmuːt], *m.* (—s, *no pl.*) ill-humour; displeasure, indignation, petulance.
unmutig [ˈunmuːtɪç], *adj.* illhumoured, petulant, indignant.
unnachahmlich [ˈunnaxaːmlɪç], *adj.* inimitable.
unnachgiebig [ˈunnaxɡiːbɪç], *adj.* relentless, unyielding.
unnachsichtig [ˈunnaxzɪçtɪç], *adj.* unrelenting, relentless.
unnahbar [ˈunnaːbaːr], *adj.* unapproachable, stand-offish.
unnennbar [ˈunnɛnbaːr], *adj.* unutterable.
unnütz [ˈunnyts], *adj.* useless.
unordentlich [ˈunɔrdəntlɪç], *adj.* untidy, slovenly.
Unordnung [ˈunɔrdnuŋ], *f.* (—, *no pl.*) disorder, untidiness, muddle, confusion.

243

unparteiisch ['unpartaιıʃ], *adj.* impartial, unbiased, objective.
unpassend ['unpasənt], *adj.* unsuitable, inappropriate; improper.
unpassierbar ['unpasi:rba:r], *adj.* impassable.
unpäßlich ['unpɛslıç], *adj.* indisposed, unwell, out of sorts.
Unpäßlichkeit ['unpɛslıçkaιt], *f.* (—, *pl.* —en) indisposition.
unproportioniert ['unproportsjoni:rt], *adj.* disproportionate; unshapely.
unqualifizierbar ['unkvalifitsi:rba:r], *adj.* unspeakable, nameless.
Unrat ['unra:t], *m.* (—(e)s, *no pl.*) dirt, rubbish.
unratsam ['unra:tza:m], *adj.* inadvisable.
Unrecht ['unrɛçt], *n.* (—(e)s, *no pl.*) wrong, injustice; — haben, be in the wrong.
unrecht ['unrɛçt], *adj.* wrong, unjust.
unrechtmäßig ['unrɛçtmɛ:sıç], *adj.* unlawful, illegal.
unredlich ['unre:tlıç], *adj.* dishonest.
unregelmäßig ['unre:gəlmɛ:sıç], *adj.* irregular.
unreif ['unraıf], *adj.* unripe, immature; (*fig.*) crude, raw.
Unreife ['unraıfə], *f.* (—, *no pl.*) immaturity.
unrein ['unraın], *adj.* unclean; (*fig.*) impure.
Unreinheit ['unraınhaιt], *f.* (—, *pl.* —en) impurity.
Unreinlichkeit ['unraınlıçkaιt], *f.* (—, *no pl.*) uncleanliness.
unrentabel ['unrɛnta:bəl], *adj.* unprofitable.
unrettbar ['unrɛtba:r], *adj.* irretrievable, hopelessly lost.
unrichtig ['unrıçtıç], *adj.* incorrect, erroneous, wrong.
Unrichtigkeit ['unrıçtıçkaιt], *f.* (—, *no pl.*) error, falsity, incorrectness.
Unruhe ['unru:ə], *f.* (—, *pl.* —en) unrest, restlessness; disquiet, uneasiness; riot, disturbance; (*clock*) balance.
Unruhestifter ['unru:əʃtıftər], *m.* (—s, *pl.* —) disturber (of the peace); troublemaker.
unruhig ['unru:ıç], *adj.* restless; troublesome, turbulent, uneasy (about), fidgety.
unrühmlich ['unry:mlıç], *adj.* inglorious.
uns [uns], *pers. pron.* us, ourselves; to us.
unsachlich ['unzaxlıç], *adj.* subjective; irrelevant.
unsagbar ['unza:kba:r], *adj.* unutterable, unspeakable.
unsanft ['unzanft], *adj.* harsh, violent.
unsauber ['unzaubər], *adj.* unclean, dirty; (*fig.*) squalid.
unschädlich ['unʃɛ:tlıç], *adj.* harmless, innocuous.

unschätzbar ['unʃɛtsba:r], *adj.* invaluable.
unscheinbar ['unʃaınba:r], *adj.* plain, homely, insignificant.
unschicklich ['unʃıklıç], *adj.* unbecoming, indecent, improper, unseemly.
unschlüssig ['unʃlysıç], *adj.* irresolute, undecided.
Unschuld ['unʃult], *f.* (—, *no pl.*) innocence; verfolgte —, injured innocence.
unschuldig ['unʃuldıç], *adj.* innocent, guiltless; chaste; —es Vergnügen, harmless pleasure.
unschwer ['unʃve:r], *adv.* easily.
Unsegen ['unze:gən], *m.* (—s, *no pl.*) misfortune; curse.
unselbständig ['unzɛlpʃtɛndıç], *adj.* dependent.
unselig ['unze:lıç], *adj.* unfortunate, luckless, fatal.
unser ['unzər], *poss. adj.* our. — *pers. pron.* of us.
unsereiner ['unzəraınər], *pron.* s.o. in our position; one of us, people in our position.
unserthalben, unsertwegen ['unzərthalbən, 'unzərtve:gən], *adv.* for our sake, on our account.
unsertwillen ['unzərtvılən], *adv. um —,* for our sake, on our account.
unsicher ['unzıçər], *adj.* unsafe; uncertain, doubtful; (*route*) precarious; (*hand*) unsteady; (*legs*) shaky.
unsichtbar ['unzıçtba:r], *adj.* invisible.
Unsinn ['unzın], *m.* (—s, *no pl.*) nonsense.
unsinnig ['unzınıç], *adj.* nonsensical; mad, insane.
Unsitte ['unzıtə], *f.* (—, *pl.* —n) abuse, nuisance; bad habit.
unsittlich ['unzıtlıç], *adj.* immoral.
unstät, unstet ['unʃtɛ:t, 'unʃte:t], *adj.* unsteady, inconstant; restless.
unstatthaft ['unʃtathaft], *adj.* illicit.
unsterblich ['unʃtɛrplıç], *adj.* immortal.
Unsterblichkeit ['unʃtɛrplıçkaιt], *f.* (—, *no pl.*) immortality.
unstillbar ['unʃtılba:r], *adj.* unappeasable, unquenchable.
unstreitig ['unʃtraıtıç], *adj.* indisputable, unquestionable.
Unsumme ['unzumə], *f.* (—, *pl.* —n) vast amount (of money).
unsympathisch ['unzympa:tıʃ], *adj.* uncongenial, disagreeable; er ist mir —, I dislike him.
untadelhaft, untadelig ['unta:dəlhaft, 'unta:dəlıç], *adj.* blameless, irreproachable, unimpeachable.
Untat ['unta:t], *f.* (—, *pl.* —en) misdeed, crime.
untätig ['unte:tıç], *adj.* inactive, idle, supine.
untauglich ['untauklıç], *adj.* unfit, useless; incompetent; (*Mil.*) disabled.
unteilbar ['un'taılba:r], *adj.* indivisible.

unten ['untən], *adv.* below, beneath; (*house*) downstairs.

unter ['untər], *prep.* (*Dat.*, *Acc.*) under, beneath, below, among, between.

Unterbau ['untərbau], *m.* (—s, *pl.* —ten) substructure, foundation.

Unterbewußtsein ['untərbəvustzaɪn], *n.* (—s, *no pl.*) subconscious mind, subconsciousness.

unterbieten [untər'bi:tən], *v.a. irr. insep.* underbid, undersell.

Unterbilanz ['untərbilants], *f.* (—, *pl.* —en) deficit.

unterbinden [untər'bɪndən], *v.a. irr. insep.* tie up, bind up; (*fig.*) prevent, check.

unterbleiben [untər'blaɪbən], *v.n. irr. insep.* (*aux.* sein) remain undone, be left undone, cease.

unterbrechen [untər'brɛçən], *v.a. irr. insep.* interrupt; (*journey*) break; (*speech*) cut short.

Unterbrechung [untər'brɛçuŋ], *f.* (—, *pl.* —en) interruption.

unterbreiten (1) ['untərbraɪtən], *v.a.* spread under.

unterbreiten (2) [untər'braɪtən], *v.a. insep.* submit, lay before.

unterbringen ['untərbrɪŋən], *v.a. irr.* provide (*a place*) for; (*goods*) dispose of; (*money*) invest; (*people*) accommodate, put up.

Unterbringung ['untərbrɪŋuŋ], *f.* (—, *no pl.*) provision for; (*goods*) disposal of; (*money*) investment; (*people*) accommodation.

unterdessen [untər'dɛsən], *adv., conj.* in the meantime, meanwhile.

unterdrücken [untər'drykən], *v.a. insep.* suppress, curb, check; oppress.

Unterdrückung [untər'drykuŋ], *f.* (—, *no pl.*) oppression, suppression.

untereinander [untəraɪn'andər], *adv.* with each other, mutually, among themselves.

unterfangen [untər'faŋən], *v.r. irr. insep. sich* —, dare, venture, presume.

Untergang ['untərgaŋ], *m.* (—s, *pl.* ⁻e) (*sun*) setting; (*ship*) sinking; (*fig.*) decline.

untergeben [untər'ge:bən], *adj.* subject, subordinate.

Untergebene [untər'ge:bənə], *m.* (—n, *pl.* —n) subordinate.

untergehen ['untərge:ən], *v.n. irr.* (*aux.* sein) (*sun*) go down, set; (*ship*) sink; (*fig.*) perish; decline.

Untergeschoß ['untərgəʃɔs], *n.* (—sses, *pl.* —sse) ground floor; basement.

Untergestell ['untərgəʃtɛl], *n.* (—s, *pl.* —e) undercarriage, chassis.

untergraben [untər'gra:bən], *v.a. irr. insep.* undermine.

unterhalb ['untərhalp], *prep.* (*Genit.*) below, under.

Unterhalt ['untərhalt], *m.* (—s, *no pl.*) maintenance, support, livelihood.

unterhalten (1) ['untərhaltən], *v.a. irr.* hold under.

unterhalten (2) [untər'haltən], *v.a. irr. insep.* maintain, keep, support; entertain. — *v.r. sich* —, converse, make conversation; *sich gut* —, enjoy o.s.

unterhaltend [untər'haltənt], *adj.* entertaining, amusing, lively.

Unterhaltskosten ['untərhaltskɔstən], *f. pl.* maintenance; (*house*) cost of repairs.

Unterhaltung [untər'haltuŋ], *f.* (—, *pl.* —en) maintenance; conversation; amusement, entertainment.

Unterhaltungslektüre [untər'haltuŋslɛkty:rə], *f.* (—, *no pl.*) light reading, fiction.

unterhandeln [untər'handəln], *v.n. insep.* negotiate.

Unterhändler ['untərhɛndlər], *m.* (—s, *pl.* —) negotiator, mediator.

Unterhandlung [untər'handluŋ], *f.* (—, *pl.* —en) negotiation.

Unterhaus ['untərhaus], *n.* (—es, *pl.* ⁻er) ground floor; (*Parl.*) lower house; House of Commons.

Unterhemd ['untərhɛmt], *n.* (—(e)s, *pl.* —en) vest.

unterhöhlen [untər'hø:lən], *v.a. insep.* undermine.

Unterholz ['untərhɔlts], *n.* (—es, *no pl.*) undergrowth, underwood.

Unterhosen ['untərho:zən], *f. pl.* (*women*) briefs; (*men*) underpants.

unterirdisch ['untərɪrdɪʃ], *adj.* subterranean, underground.

unterjochen [untər'jɔxən], *v.a. insep.* subjugate, subdue.

Unterkiefer ['untərki:fər], *m.* (—s, *pl.* —) lower jaw.

Unterkleid ['untərklaɪt], *n.* (—s, *pl.* —er) under-garment.

unterkommen ['untərkɔmən], *v.n. irr.* (*aux.* sein) find accommodation *or* shelter; (*fig.*) find employment.

Unterkommen ['untərkɔmən], *n.* (—s, *no pl.*) shelter, accommodation; (*fig.*) employment, place.

Unterkörper ['untərkœrpər], *m.* (—s, *pl.* —) lower part of the body.

unterkriegen ['untərkri:gən], *v.a.* get the better of; *lass dich nicht* —, stand firm.

Unterkunft ['untərkunft], *f.* (—, *pl.* ⁻e) shelter, accommodation; employment.

Unterlage ['untərla:gə], *f.* (—, *pl.* —n) foundation, base; blotting pad; (*pl.*) documents, files.

unterlassen [untər'lasən], *v.a. irr. insep.* omit (to do), fail (to do), neglect; forbear.

Unterlassung [untər'lasuŋ], *f.* (—, *pl.* —en) omission, neglect.

Unterlassungssünde [untər'lasuŋzyndə], *f.* (—, *pl.* —n) sin of omission.

Unterlauf ['untərlauf], *m.* (—(e)s, *pl.* ⁻e) (*river*) lower course.

Unterlaufen

unterlaufen [untər'laufən], *v.n. irr. insep. (aux.* sein) run under; (*mistake*) creep in. — *adj.* suffused, blood-shot.

unterlegen (1) ['untərle:gən], *v.a.* lay under; *einen anderen Sinn* —, put a different construction upon.

unterlegen (2) [untər'le:gən], *adj.* inferior.

Unterleib ['untərlaip], *m.* (—s, *no pl.*) abdomen.

unterliegen [untər'li:gən], *v.n. irr. insep. (aux.* sein) succumb, be overcome; be subject (to).

Untermieter ['untərmi:tər], *m.* (—s, *pl.* —) subtenant.

unterminieren [untərmi'ni:rən], *v.a. insep.* undermine.

unternehmen [untər'ne:mən], *v.a. irr. insep.* undertake, take upon o.s., attempt.

Unternehmen [untər'ne:mən], *n.* (—s, *pl.* —) enterprise, undertaking.

unternehmend [untər'ne:mənt], *adj.* bold, enterprising.

Unternehmer [untər'ne:mər], *m.* (—s, *pl.* —) contractor, entrepreneur.

Unteroffizier ['untərɔfitsi:r], *m.* (—s, *pl.* —e) (*army*) non-commissioned officer; (*navy*) petty officer.

unterordnen ['untərɔrdnən], *v.a.* subordinate. — *v.r. sich* —, submit (to).

Unterordnung ['untərɔrdnuŋ], *f.* (—, *no pl.*) subordination, submission; (*Biol.*) sub-order.

Unterpacht ['untərpaxt], *f.* (—, *no pl.*) sublease.

Unterpfand ['untərpfant], *n.* (—(e)s, *no pl.*) (*obs.*) pawn, pledge.

Unterredung [untər're:duŋ], *f.* (—, *pl.* —en) conference, interview, talk.

Unterricht ['untərrɪçt], *m.* (—(e)s, *no pl.*) instruction, tuition, teaching.

unterrichten [untər'rɪçtən], *v.a. insep.* instruct, teach.

Unterrichtsanstalt ['untərrɪçtsanʃtalt], *f.* (—, *pl.* —en) educational establishment *or* institution.

Unterrichtsgegenstand ['untərrɪçtsge:gənʃtant], *m.* (—s, *pl.* ˙e) subject of instruction.

Unterrock ['untərrɔk], *m.* (—s, *pl.* ˙e) petticoat, slip; underskirt.

untersagen [untər'za:gən], *v.a. insep.* forbid; *Rauchen untersagt*, smoking prohibited.

Untersatz ['untərzats], *m.* (—es, *pl.* ˙e) basis, holder, stand, trestle; saucer.

unterschätzen [untər'ʃɛtsən], *v.a. insep.* underrate, underestimate.

unterscheiden [untər'ʃaɪdən], *v.a. irr. insep.* distinguish, discriminate, discern, differentiate. — *v.r. sich* —, differ; *ich kann sie nicht* —, I cannot tell them apart.

Unterscheidung [untər'ʃaɪdun], *f.* (—, *pl.* —en) distinction, differentiation.

Unterscheidungsmerkmal [untər-'ʃaɪduŋsmɛrkma:l], *n.* (—s, *pl.* —e) distinctive mark, characteristic.

Unterscheidungsvermögen [untər-'ʃaɪduŋsfɛrmø:gən], *n.* (—s, *no pl.*) power of discrimination.

Unterscheidungszeichen [untər'ʃaɪduŋstsaɪçən], *n.* (—s, *pl.* —) criterion.

Unterschenkel ['untərʃɛŋkəl], *m.* (—s, *pl.* —) shank, lower part of the thigh.

Unterschicht ['untərʃɪçt], *f.* (—, *pl.* —en) substratum, subsoil.

unterschieben (1) ['untərʃi:bən], *v.a. irr.* substitute; interpolate; forge; foist upon.

unterschieben (2) [untər'ʃi:bən], *v.a. irr. insep.* (*fig.*) attribute falsely, pass s.o. off as.

Unterschiebung [untər'ʃi:buŋ], *f.* (—, *pl.* —en) substitution; forgery.

Unterschied ['untərʃi:t], *m.* (—(e)s, *pl.* —e) difference.

unterschiedlich ['untərʃi:tlɪç], *adj.* different, diverse.

unterschiedslos ['untərʃi:tslo:s], *adv.* indiscriminately.

unterschlagen [untər'ʃla:gən], *v.a. irr. insep.* embezzle, intercept.

Unterschlagung [untər'ʃla:guŋ], *f.* (—, *pl.* —en) embezzlement.

Unterschlupf ['untərʃlupf], *m.* (—es, *pl.* ˙e) shelter, refuge.

unterschlüpfen ['untərʃlypfən], *v.n. (aux.* sein) find shelter, slip away; (*fig.*) hide.

unterschreiben [untər'ʃraɪbən], *v.a. irr. insep.* sign, subscribe to.

Unterschrift ['untərʃrɪft], *f.* (—, *pl.* —en) signature.

Unterseeboot ['untərze:bo:t], *n.* (—s, *pl.* —e) submarine.

untersetzt [untər'zɛtst], *adj.* thickset, dumpy.

untersinken ['untərzɪŋkən], *v.n. irr. (aux.* sein) go down.

unterst ['untərst], *adj.* lowest, undermost, bottom.

Unterstaatssekretär [untər'ʃta:tszekretɛ:r], *m.* (—s, *pl.* —e) under-secretary of state.

unterstehen (1) [untər'ʃte:ən], *v.n. irr. (aux.* sein) find shelter (under).

unterstehen (2) [untər'ʃte:ən], *v.n. irr. insep.* be subordinate. — *v.r. sich* —, dare, venture.

unterstellen (1) ['untərʃtɛlən], *v.a.* place under. — *v.r. sich* —, take shelter (under).

unterstellen (2) [untər'ʃtɛlən], *v.a. insep.* put under the authority of; impute (s.th. to s.o.).

Unterstellung [untər'ʃtɛluŋ], *f.* (—, *pl.* —en) imputation, insinuation.

unterstreichen [untər'ʃtraɪçən], *v.a. irr. insep.* underline.

Unterstreichung [untər'ʃtraɪçuŋ], *f.* (—, *pl.* —en) underlining.

Unterströmung ['untərʃtrø:muŋ], *f.* (—, *pl.* —en) undercurrent.

unterstützen [untər'ʃtytsən], *v.a. insep.* support, assist, aid; (*fig.*) countenance.

Unterstützung [untər'ʃtytsuŋ], *f.* (—, *pl.* —en) support, aid, assistance, relief.

Unterstützungsanstalt [untər'ʃtytsuŋsanʃtalt], *f.* (—, *pl.* —en) charitable institution.

unterstützungsbedürftig [untər'ʃtytsuŋsbədyrftɪç], *adj.* indigent.

untersuchen [untər'zu:xən], *v.a. insep.* investigate, examine, look over.

Untersuchung [untər'zu:xuŋ], *f.* (—, *pl.* —en) investigation, inquiry; (*medical*) examination.

Untersuchungshaft [untər'zu:xuŋshaft], *f.* (—, *no pl.*) imprisonment pending investigation.

Untersuchungsrichter [untər'zu:xuŋsrɪçtər], *m.* (—s, *pl.* —) examining magistrate.

Untertan ['untərta:n], *m.* (—s, *pl.* —en) subject, vassal.

untertan ['untərta:n], *adj.* subject.

untertänig ['untərtɛ:nɪç], *adj.* humble, obsequious, submissive, servile.

Untertasse ['untərtasə], *f.* (—, *pl.* —n) saucer.

untertauchen ['untərtauxən], *v.a.* dip, duck, submerge. — *v.n.* (*aux.* sein) dive.

unterwegs [untər've:ks], *adv.* on the way.

unterweisen [untər'vaɪzən], *v.a. irr. insep.* teach, instruct.

Unterweisung [untər'vaɪzuŋ], *f.* (—, *pl.* —en) instruction, teaching.

Unterwelt ['untərvɛlt], *f.* (—, *no pl.*) Hades, the underworld.

unterwerfen [untər'vɛrfən], *v.a. irr. insep.* subject, subdue. — *v.r. sich* —, submit (to), resign o.s. (to).

Unterwerfung [untər'vɛrfuŋ], *f.* (—, *no pl.*) subjection, submission.

unterwühlen [untər'vy:lən], *v.a. insep.* root up; (*fig.*) undermine.

unterwürfig [untər'vyrfɪç], *adj.* submissive, subject; obsequious.

Unterwürfigkeit [untər'vyrfɪçkaɪt], *f.* (—, *no pl.*) submissiveness; obsequiousness.

unterzeichnen [untər'tsaɪçnən], *v.a. insep.* sign.

Unterzeichner [untər'tsaɪçnər], *m.* (—s, *pl.* —) signatory; (*insurance*) underwriter.

Unterzeichnete [untər'tsaɪçnətə], *m.* (—n, *pl.* —n) undersigned.

Unterzeichnung [untər'tsaɪçnuŋ], *f.* (—, *pl.* —en) signature.

unterziehen [untər'tsi:ən], *v.r. irr. insep. sich* —, submit to, undertake; (*operation*) undergo.

Untiefe ['unti:fə], *f.* (—, *pl.* —n) shallow water, flat, shoal, sands.

Untier ['unti:r], *n.* (—s, *pl.* —e) monster.

untilgbar ['untɪlkba:r], *adj.* indelible; (*debt*) irredeemable.

untrennbar ['untrɛnba:r], *adj.* inseparable.

untreu ['untrɔy], *adj.* faithless, unfaithful, disloyal, perfidious.

Untreue ['untrɔyə], *f.* (—, *no pl.*) faithlessness, unfaithfulness, disloyalty, perfidy.

untröstlich ['untrø:stlɪç], *adj.* inconsolable, disconsolate.

untrüglich ['untry:klɪç], *adj.* unmistakable, infallible.

untüchtig ['untyçtɪç], *adj.* inefficient; incompetent.

unüberlegt ['uny:bərle:kt], *adj.* inconsiderate, thoughtless; rash.

unübersehbar ['uny:bərze:ba:r], *adj.* immense, vast.

unübersteiglich ['uny:bərʃtaɪklɪç], *adj.* insurmountable.

unübertrefflich ['uny:bərtrɛflɪç], *adj.* unsurpassable, unequalled, unrivalled.

unübertroffen ['uny:bərtrɔfən], *adj.* unsurpassed. .

unüberwindlich ['uny:bərvɪntlɪç], *adj.* invincible, unconquerable.

unumgänglich ['unumgɛŋlɪç], *adj.* indispensable, unavoidable, inevitable.

unumschränkt ['unumʃrɛŋkt], *adj.* unlimited, absolute.

unumstößlich ['unumʃtø:slɪç], *adj.* irrefutable.

unumwunden ['unumvundən], *adj.* frank, plain.

ununterbrochen ['ununtərbrɔxən], *adj.* uninterrupted, unremitting.

unveränderlich ['unfɛrɛndərlɪç], *adj.* unchangeable, unalterable.

unverändert ['unfɛrɛndərt], *adj.* unchanged, unaltered.

unverantwortlich ['unfɛrantvɔrtlɪç], *adj.* irresponsible, inexcusable, unjustifiable.

unveräußerlich ['unfɛrɔysərlɪç], *adj.* not for sale; inalienable.

unverbesserlich ['unfɛrbɛsərlɪç], *adj.* incorrigible.

unverbindlich ['unfɛrbɪntlɪç], *adj.* not binding, without prejudice, without obligation.

unverblümt ['unfɛrblymt], *adj.* blunt, point-blank.

unverbrennlich ['unfɛrbrɛnlɪç], *adj.* incombustible.

unverbrüchlich ['unfɛrbryçlɪç], *adj.* inviolable.

unverbürgt ['unfɛrbyrkt], *adj.* unwarranted, unofficial; unconfirmed.

unverdaulich ['unfɛrdaulɪç], *adj.* indigestible.

unverdaut ['unfɛrdaut], *adj.* undigested.

unverdient ['unfɛrdi:nt], *adj.* unmerited, undeserved.

unverdientermaßen ['unfɛrdi:ntərma:sən], *adv.* undeservedly.

unverdorben ['unfɛrdɔrbən], *adj.* unspoiled, uncorrupted, innocent.

unverdrossen ['unfɛrdrɔsən], *adj.* indefatigable.

unvereidigt ['unfɛraɪdɪçt], *adj.* unsworn.

unvereinbar ['unfɛraɪnba:r], *adj.* incompatible, inconsistent.

Unvereinbarkeit [ˈunfɛraɪnbaːrkaɪt], *f.* (—, *no pl.*) incompatibility, inconsistency.
unverfälscht [ˈunfɛrfɛlʃt], *adj.* unadulterated, genuine, pure.
unverfänglich [ˈunfɛrfɛŋlɪç], *adj.* harmless.
unverfroren [ˈunfɛrfroːrən], *adj.* cheeky, impudent.
unvergeßlich [ˈunfɛrgɛslɪç], *adj.* memorable, not to be forgotten, unforgettable.
unvergleichlich [ˈunfɛrglaɪçlɪç], *adj.* incomparable.
unverhältnismäßig [ˈunfɛrhɛltnɪsmɛːsɪç], *adj.* disproportionate.
unverheiratet [ˈunfɛrhaɪraːtət], *adj.* unmarried.
unverhofft [ˈunfɛrhɔft], *adj.* unexpected.
unverhohlen [ˈunfɛrhoːlən], *adj.* unconcealed, undisguised, candid.
unverkennbar [ˈunfɛrkɛnbaːr], *adj.* unmistakable.
unverlangt [ˈunfɛrlaŋkt], *adj.* unsolicited, not ordered.
unverletzlich [ˈunfɛrlɛtslɪç], *adj.* invulnerable; (*fig.*) inviolable.
unverletzt [ˈunfɛrlɛtst], *adj.* (*persons*) unhurt; (*things*) undamaged, intact.
unvermeidlich [ˈunfɛrmaɪtlɪç], *adj.* inevitable, unavoidable.
unvermindert [ˈunfɛrmɪndərt], *adj.* undiminished.
unvermittelt [ˈunfɛrmɪtəlt], *adj.* sudden, abrupt.
Unvermögen [ˈunfɛrmøːgən], *n.* (—s, *no pl.*) inability, incapacity.
unvermögend [ˈunfɛrmøːgənt], *adj.* incapable; impecunious.
unvermutet [ˈunfɛrmuːtət], *adj.* unexpected, unforeseen.
unverrichtet [ˈunfɛrrɪçtət], *adj.* —*er Sache*, empty-handed; unsuccessfully.
unverschämt [ˈunfɛrʃɛːmt], *adj.* impudent, brazen.
unverschuldet [ˈunfɛrʃuldət], *adj.* not in debt, unencumbered; (*fig.*) undeserved.
unversehens [ˈunfɛrzeːəns], *adv.* unexpectedly, unawares.
unversehrt [ˈunfɛrzeːrt], *adv.* (*persons*) unhurt, safe; (*things*) undamaged.
unversiegbar [ˈunfɛrziːkbaːr], *adj.* inexhaustible.
unversiegt [ˈunfɛrziːkt], *adj.* unexhausted.
unversöhnlich [ˈunfɛrzøːnlɪç], *adj.* implacable, irreconcilable.
unversöhnt [ˈunfɛrzøːnt], *adj.* unreconciled.
unversorgt [ˈunfɛrzɔrkt], *adj.* unprovided for.
Unverstand [ˈunfɛrʃtant], *m.* (—(e)s, *no pl.*) want of judgment, indiscretion.
unverständig [ˈunfɛrʃtɛndɪç], *adj.* foolish, unwise, imprudent.
unverständlich [ˈunfɛrʃtɛntlɪç], *adj.* unintelligible, incomprehensible.

unversteuert [ˈunfɛrʃtɔyərt], *adj.* with duty *or* tax unpaid.
unversucht [ˈunfɛrzuːxt], *adj.* untried; *nichts* — *lassen*, leave no stone unturned.
unverträglich [ˈunfɛrtrɛːklɪç], *adj.* quarrelsome.
unverwandt [ˈunfɛrvant], *adj.* unrelated; fixed, constant; immovable.
unverwundbar [ˈunfɛrvuntbaːr], *adj.* invulnerable.
unverwüstlich [ˈunfɛrvyːstlɪç], *adj.* indestructible.
unverzagt [ˈunfɛrtsaːkt], *adj.* undaunted, intrepid.
unverzeihlich [ˈunfɛrtsaɪlɪç], *adj.* unpardonable.
unverzinslich [ˈunfɛrtsɪnslɪç], *adj.* (*money*) gaining no interest.
unverzollt [ˈunfɛrtsɔlt], *adj.* duty unpaid.
unverzüglich [ˈunfɛrtsyːklɪç], *adj.* immediate.
unvollendet [ˈunfɔlɛndət], *adj.* unfinished.
unvollständig [ˈunfɔlʃtɛndɪç], *adj.* incomplete.
unvorbereitet [ˈunfoːrbəraɪtət], *adj.* unprepared.
unvordenklich [ˈunfoːrdɛŋklɪç], *adj.* *seit* —*en Zeiten*, from time immemorial.
unvorhergesehen [ˈunfoːrheːrgəzeːən], *adj.* unforeseen, unlooked for.
unvorsichtig [ˈunfoːrzɪçtɪç], *adj.* imprudent, incautious, careless.
unvorteilhaft [ˈunfɔrtaɪlhaft], *adj.* unprofitable, disadvantageous; — *aussehen*, not look o.'s best.
unwägbar [ˈunvɛːkbaːr], *adj.* imponderable.
unwahr [ˈunvaːr], *adj.* untrue, false.
Unwahrhaftigkeit [ˈunvaːrhaftɪçkaɪt], *f.* (—, *no pl.*) want of truthfulness, unreliability, dishonesty.
Unwahrheit [ˈunvaːrhaɪt], *f.* (—, *pl.* —*en*) lie, untruth, falsehood.
unwegsam [ˈunveːkzaːm], *adj.* impassable, impracticable.
unweigerlich [ˈunvaɪgərlɪç], *adj.* unhesitating, unquestioning. — *adv.* without fail.
unweit [ˈunvaɪt], *prep.* (*Genit.*) not far from, near.
Unwesen [ˈunveːzən], *n.* (—s, *no pl.*) nuisance; *sein* — *treiben*, be up to o.'s tricks.
Unwetter [ˈunvɛtər], *n.* (—s, *pl.* —) bad weather, thunderstorm.
unwichtig [ˈunvɪçtɪç], *adj.* unimportant; insignificant, of no consequence.
unwiderleglich [ˈunviːdərleːklɪç], *adj.* irrefutable.
unwiderruflich [ˈunviːdərruːflɪç], *adj.* irrevocable.
unwidersprechlich [ˈunviːdərʃprɛçlɪç], *adj.* incontestable.
unwidersprochen [ˈunviːdərʃprɔxən], *adj.* uncontradicted.

unwiderstehlich ['unvi:dərʃteːlɪç], *adj.* irresistible.

unwiederbringlich ['unvi:dərbrɪŋlɪç], *adj.* irrecoverable, irretrievable.

Unwille ['unvːlə], *m.* (—ns, *no pl.*) displeasure, indignation.

unwillkürlich ['unvɪlkyːrlɪç], *adj.* involuntary; instinctive.

unwirsch ['unvɪrʃ], *adj.* petulant, testy; curt, uncivil.

unwirtlich ['unvɪrtlɪç], *adj.* inhospitable.

unwirtschaftlich ['unvɪrtʃaftlɪç], *adj.* not economic, uneconomic.

unwissend ['unvɪsənt], *adj.* illiterate, ignorant.

Unwissenheit ['unvɪsənhaɪt], *f.* (—, *no pl.*) ignorance.

unwissenschaftlich ['unvɪsənʃaftlɪç], *adj.* unscholarly; unscientific.

unwissentlich ['unvɪsəntlɪç], *adv.* unknowingly, unconsciously.

unwohl ['unvoːl], *adj.* unwell, indisposed.

Unwohlsein ['unvoːlzaɪn], *n.* (—s, *no pl.*) indisposition.

unwürdig ['unvyrdɪç], *adj.* unworthy, undeserving.

Unzahl ['untsaːl], *f.* (—, *no pl.*) vast number.

unzählbar [un'tsɛːlbaːr], *adj.* innumerable, numberless.

unzählig [un'tsɛːlɪç], *adj.* innumerable; —*e Male*, over and over again.

unzart ['untsaːrt], *adj.* indelicate, rude, rough; unceremonious.

Unzeit ['untsaɪt], *f.* (—, *no pl.*) *zur* —, out of season, inopportunely.

unzeitgemäß ['untsaɪtɡəmɛːs], *adj.* out of date, behind the times; unfashionable.

unzeitig ['untsaɪtɪç], *adj.* unseasonable; untimely, inopportune.

unziemlich ['untsiːmlɪç], *adj.* unseemly, unbecoming.

Unzier ['untsiːr], *f.* (—, *no pl.*) disfigurement; flaw.

Unzucht ['untsuxt], *f.* (—, *no pl.*) unchastity; lewdness; fornication.

unzüchtig ['untsyçtɪç], *adj.* unchaste, lascivious, lewd.

unzufrieden ['untsufriːdən], *adj.* discontented, dissatisfied.

unzugänglich ['untsuɡɛŋlɪç], *adj.* inaccessible.

unzulänglich ['untsulɛŋlɪç], *adj.* inadequate, insufficient.

Unzulänglichkeit ['untsulɛŋlɪçkaɪt], *f.* (—, *no pl.*) inadequacy.

unzulässig ['untsulɛsɪç], *adj.* inadmissible.

unzurechnungsfähig ['untsurɛçnuŋsfɛːɪç], *adj.* not accountable (for o.'s actions), non compos mentis, insane.

Unzurechnungsfähigkeit ['untsurɛçnuŋsfɛːɪçkaɪt], *f.* (—, *no pl.*) irresponsibility; feeblemindedness.

unzusammenhängend ['untsuzamənhɛŋənt], *adj.* incoherent.

unzuständig ['untsuʃtɛndɪç], *adj.* incompetent, not competent (*Law etc.*).

unzuträglich ['untsutrɛːklɪç], *adj.* unwholesome.

unzutreffend ['untsutrɛfənt], *adj.* inapposite; unfounded; inapplicable.

unzuverlässig ['untsufɛrlɛsɪç], *adj.* unreliable.

unzweckmäßig ['untsvɛkmɛːsɪç], *adj.* inexpedient.

unzweideutig ['untsvaɪdɔytɪç], *adj.* unequivocal, explicit, unambiguous.

üppig ['ʏpɪç], *adj.* abundant; opulent, luxurious, luxuriant, voluptuous.

uralt ['uːralt], *adj.* very old, old as the hills; ancient.

uranfänglich ['uːranfɛŋlɪç], *adj.* primordial, primeval.

Uraufführung ['urauffyːruŋ], *f.* (—, *pl.* —en) (*Theat.*) first night, première.

urbar ['uːrbaːr], *adj.* arable, under cultivation; — *machen*, cultivate.

Urbarmachung ['uːrbaːrmaxuŋ], *f.* (—, *no pl.*) cultivation.

Urbild ['uːrbɪlt], *n.* (—(e)s, *pl.* —er) prototype; (*fig.*) ideal.

ureigen ['uːraɪɡən], *adj.* quite original; idiosyncratic.

Ureltern ['uːrɛltərn], *pl.* ancestors.

Urenkel ['uːrɛŋkəl], *m.* (—s, *pl.* —) great-grandson, great-grandchild.

Urenkelin ['uːrɛŋkəlɪn], *f.* (—, *pl.* —nen) great-granddaughter.

Urfehde ['uːrfeːdə], *f.* (—, *no pl.*) oath to keep the peace.

Urform ['uːrfɔrm], *f.* (—, *pl.* —en) primitive form; original form; archetype.

Urgroßmutter ['uːrɡroːsmutər], *f.* (—, *pl.* ⸚) great-grandmother.

Urgroßvater ['uːrɡroːsfaːtər], *m.* (—s, *pl.* ⸚) great-grandfather.

Urheber ['uːrheːbər], *m.* (—s, *pl.* —) author, originator.

Urheberrecht ['uːrheːbərrɛçt], *n.* (—s, *pl.* —e) copyright.

Urheberschaft ['uːrheːbərʃaft], *f.* (—, *no pl.*) authorship.

Urin [u'riːn], *m.* (—s, *no pl.*) urine.

Urkunde ['uːrkundə], *f.* (—, *pl.* —n) document, deed, charter; *zur dessen*, (*obs.*) in witness whereof.

Urkundenbeweis ['uːrkundənbavaɪs], *m.* (—es, *pl.* —e) documentary evidence.

urkundlich ['uːrkuntlɪç], *adj.* documentary.

Urlaub ['uːrlaup], *m.* (—s, *pl.* —e) leave of absence; vacation; (*Mil.*) furlough.

urplötzlich ['uːrplœtslɪç], *adj.* sudden. — *adv.* all at once, suddenly.

Urquell ['uːrkvɛl], *m.* (—s, *pl.* —en) fountain-head, original source.

Ursache ['uːrzaxə], *f.* (—, *pl.* —n) cause; *keine* —, don't mention it.

Urschrift ['uːrʃrɪft], *f.* (—, *pl.* —en) original text.

Ursprache ['uːrʃpraːxə], *f.* (—, *pl.* —n) original language.

Ursprung ['uːrʃpruŋ], *m.* (—s, *pl.* ⸚e) origin; extraction.

ursprünglich [ˈuːrʃpryŋlɪç], *adj.* original.

Urteil [ˈurtaɪl], *n.* (—s, *pl.* —e) opinion; (*Law*) judgment, verdict, sentence; *ein — fällen*, pass judgment on; *nach meinem —*, in my opinion.

urteilen [ˈurtaɪlən], *v.n.* judge.

Urteilsspruch [ˈurtaɪlsʃprux], *m.* (—s, *pl.* ·· e) judgment, sentence.

Uruguay [uruˈgwaːɪ], *n.* Uruguay.

Urureltern [ˈuːruːrɛltərn], *pl.* ancestors.

Urvater [ˈuːrfaːtər], *m.* (—s, *pl.* ··) forefather.

Urvolk [ˈuːrfɔlk], *n.* (—(e)s, *pl.* ··er) primitive people, aborigines.

Urwald [ˈuːrvalt], *m.* (—(e)s, *pl.* ··er) primæval forest, virgin forest.

Urwelt [ˈuːrvɛlt], *f.* (—, *no pl.*) primæval world.

Urzeit [ˈuːrtsaɪt], *f.* (—, *pl.* —en) prehistoric times.

V

V [fau], *n.* (—s, *pl.* —s) the letter V.

Vagabund [vagaˈbunt], *m.* (—en, *pl.* —en) vagabond, tramp; (*Am.*) hobo.

vag [vaːk], *adj.* vague.

Vakuumbremse [ˈvaːkuumbrɛmzə], *f.* (—, *pl.* —n) air-brake, vacuum-brake.

Vase [ˈvaːzə], *f.* (—, *pl.* —n) vase.

Vater [ˈfaːtər], *m.* (—s, *pl.* ··) father.

Vaterland [ˈfaːtərlant], *n.* (—(e)s, *pl.* ··er) mother-country, native country; *—sliebe*, patriotism.

vaterländisch [ˈfaːtərlɛndɪʃ], *adj.* patriotic.

vaterlandslos [ˈfaːtərlantsloːs], *adj.* having no mother country; unpatriotic.

väterlich [ˈfɛːtərlɪç], *adj.* fatherly, paternal. *— adv.* like a father.

vaterlos [ˈfaːtərloːs], *adj.* fatherless.

Vatermord [ˈfaːtərmɔrt], *m.* (—(e)s, *pl.* —e) parricide; patricide.

Vatermörder [ˈfaːtərmœrdər], *m.* (—s, *pl.* —) parricide; (*fig.*) high *or* stand-up collar.

Vaterschaft [ˈfaːtərʃaft], *f.* (—, *no pl.*) paternity.

Vatersname [ˈfaːtərsnaːmə], *m.* (—ns, *pl.* —n) surname, family name.

Vaterstadt [ˈfaːtərʃtat], *f.* (—, *pl.* ··e) native town.

Vaterstelle [ˈfaːtərʃtɛlə], *f.* (—, *pl.* —n) *— vertreten*, act as a father, be a father (to).

Vaterunser [faːtərˈunzər], *n.* (—s, *pl.* —s) Lord's Prayer.

Vatikan [vatiˈkaːn], *m.* (—s, *no pl.*) Vatican.

vegetieren [vegeˈtiːrən], *v.n.* vegetate.

Veilchen [ˈfaɪlçən], *n.* (—s, *pl.* —) (*Bot.*) violet.

Vene [ˈveːnə], *f.* (—, *pl.* —n) vein.

Venezuela [vɛnətsuˈeːla], *n.* Venezuela.

Ventil [vɛnˈtiːl], *n.* (—s, *pl.* —e) valve.

ventilieren [vɛntiˈliːrən], *v.a.* ventilate, air; (*fig.*) discuss, ventilate.

verabfolgen [fɛrˈapfɔlgən], *v.a.* deliver, hand over, remit; serve.

Verabfolgung [fɛrˈapfɔlguŋ], *f.* (—, *no pl.*) delivery.

verabreden [fɛrˈapreːdən], *v.a.* agree (upon); stipulate; *etwas mit einem —*, agree on s.th. with s.o. — *v.r. sich mit einem —*, make an appointment with s.o.; (*coll.*) have a date.

Verabredung [fɛrˈapreːduŋ], *f.* (—, *pl.* —en) agreement, arrangement, appointment; (*coll.*) date.

verabreichen [fɛrˈapraɪçən], *v.a.* deliver, dispense.

verabsäumen [fɛrˈapzɔymən], *v.a.* neglect, omit.

verabscheuen [fɛrˈapʃɔyən], *v.a.* detest, loathe, abhor.

Verabscheuung [fɛrˈapʃɔyuŋ], *f.* (—, *no pl.*) abhorrence, detestation, loathing.

verabscheuungswürdig [fɛrˈapʃɔyuŋsvyrdɪç], *adj.* abominable, detestable.

verabschieden [fɛrˈapʃiːdən], *v.a.* dismiss, discharge. — *v.r. sich —*, take leave, say good-bye; (*Pol.*) pass (of an Act).

Verabschiedung [fɛrˈapʃiːduŋ], *f.* (—, *no pl.*) dismissal; discharge; (*Pol.*) passing (of an Act).

verachten [fɛrˈaxtən], *v.a.* despise, scorn.

verächtlich [fɛrˈɛçtlɪç], *adj.* despicable, contemptible; contemptuous, scornful.

Verachtung [fɛrˈaxtuŋ], *f.* (—, *no pl.*) contempt, disdain, scorn.

verallgemeinern [fɛralgəˈmaɪnərn], *v.a., v.n.* generalise.

veralten [fɛrˈaltən], *v.n.* (*aux.* sein) become obsolete, date.

veraltet [fɛrˈaltət], *adj.* obsolete.

Veranda [veˈranda], *f.* (—, *pl.* —den) verandah, porch.

veränderlich [fɛrˈɛndərlɪç], *adj.* changeable, variable; (*fig.*) inconstant, fickle.

verändern [fɛrˈɛndərn], *v.a.* change, alter. — *v.r. sich —*, change, vary; change o.'s job.

verankern [fɛrˈaŋkərn], *v.a.* anchor.

veranlagt [fɛrˈanlaːkt], *adj.* inclined; gifted; having a propensity (to); *gut —*, talented; (*tax*) assessed.

Veranlagung [fɛrˈanlaːguŋ], *f.* (—, *pl.* —en) bent; talent · predisposition; (*tax*) assessment.

veranlassen [fɛrˈanlasən], *v.a.* bring about, cause, motivate; *einen —*, induce s.o., cause s.o.; *etwas —*, bring s.th. about, cause s.th.

Veranlassung [fɛr'anlasuŋ], *f.* (—, *no pl.*) cause, motive; occasion; inducement; *auf seine* —, at his suggestion; *ohne irgend eine* —, without the slightest provocation.

veranschaulichen [fɛr'anʃaulıçən], *v.a.* illustrate, make clear.

veranschlagen [fɛr'anʃla:gən], *v.a.* estimate, assess.

Veranschlagung [fɛr'anʃla:guŋ], *f.* (—, *pl.* —en) estimate.

veranstalten [fɛr'anʃtaltən], *v.a.* organise, arrange.

Veranstalter [fɛr'anʃtaltər], *m.* (—s, *pl.* —) organiser.

Veranstaltung [fɛr'anʃtaltuŋ], *f.* (—, *pl.* —en) arrangement; entertainment; show; event; (sporting) fixture.

verantworten [fɛr'antvɔrtən], *v.a.* account for. — *v.r. sich* —, answer (for), justify o.s.

verantwortlich [fɛr'antvɔrtlıç], *adj.* responsible, answerable, accountable.

Verantwortlichkeit [fɛr'antvɔrtlıçkaɪt], *f.* (—, *no pl.*) responsibility.

Verantwortung [fɛr'antvɔrtuŋ], *f.* (—, *no pl.*) responsibility, justification, excuse; defence; *auf deine* —, at your own risk; *einen zur — ziehen*, call s.o. tc account.

verantwortungsvoll [fɛr'antvɔrtuŋsfɔl], *adj.* responsible.

verarbeiten [fɛr'arbaɪtən], *v.a.* manufacture, process; (*fig.*) digest.

Verarbeitung [fɛr'arbaɪtuŋ], *f.* (—, *no pl.*) manufacture; process; finish; (*fig.*) digestion.

verargen [fɛr'argən], *v.a.* einem etwas —, blame *or* reproach s.o. for s.th.

verärgern [fɛr'ɛrgərn], *v.a.* annoy, make angry.

Verarmung [fɛr'armuŋ], *f.* (—, *no pl.*) impoverishment.

verausgaben [fɛr'ausga:bən], *v.r. sich* —, overspend, run short of money; spend o.s., wear o.s. out.

veräußern [fɛr'ɔysərn], *v.a.* dispose of, sell.

Veräußerung [fɛr'ɔysəruŋ], *f.* (—, *no pl.*) sale; alienation.

Verband [fɛr'bant], *m.* (—s, *pl.* ˙e) bandage, dressing; association, union; unit.

verbannen [fɛr'banən], *v.a.* banish, exile, outlaw.

Verbannte [fɛr'bantə], *m.* (—n, *pl.* —n) exile, outlaw.

Verbannung [fɛr'banuŋ], *f.* (—, *pl.* —en) banishment, exile.

verbauen [fɛr'bauən], *v.n.* obstruct; build up; use up *or* spend in building.

verbeißen [fɛr'baɪsən], *v.a. irr. sich etwas* —, suppress s.th.; *sich das Lachen* —, stifle a laugh. — *v.r. sich in etwas* —, stick doggedly to s.th.

verbergen [fɛr'bɛrgən], *v.a. irr.* conceal, hide.

verbessern [fɛr'bɛsərn], *v.a.* improve, correct, mend.

Verbesserung [fɛr'bɛsəruŋ], *f.* (—, *pl.* —en) improvement; correction.

verbeugen [fɛr'bɔygən], *v.r. sich* —, bow.

Verbeugung [fɛr'bɔyguŋ], *f.* (—, *pl.* —en) bow, obeisance.

verbiegen [fɛr'bi:gən], *v.a. irr.* twist, distort, bend the wrong way.

verbieten [fɛr'bi:tən], *v.a. irr.* forbid, prohibit.

verbilligen [fɛr'bıllıgən], *v.a.* cheapen, reduce the price of.

verbinden [fɛr'bındən], *v.a. irr.* tie up, bind up, connect; (*Med.*) dress, bandage; unite, join; *die Augen* —, blindfold. — *v.r. sich* —, unite, join; (*Chem.*) combine.

verbindlich [fɛr'bındlıç], *adj.* binding; obligatory; obliging; *—en Dank*, my best thanks.

Verbindlichkeit [fɛr'bındlıçkaɪt], *f.* (—, *pl.* —en) liability, obligation; compliment.

Verbindung [fɛr'bınduŋ], *f.* (—, *pl.* —en) connexion, connection, junction; association; alliance; (*Railw.*) connection; (*Chem.*) compound.

Verbindungsglied [fɛr'bınduŋsgli:t], *n.* (—(e)s, *pl.* —er) connecting link.

Verbindungslinie [fɛr'bınduŋsli:njə], *f.* (—, *pl.* —n) line of communication.

verbissen [fɛr'bısən], *adj.* obstinate, grim; soured. — *adv.* doggedly.

verbitten [fɛr'bıtən], *v.a. irr. sich etwas* —, forbid s.th. determinedly; insist on s.th. not being done, object to.

verbittern [fɛr'bıtərn], *v.a.* embitter.

Verbitterung [fɛr'bıtəruŋ], *f.* (—, *no pl.*) exasperation.

verblassen [fɛr'blasən], *v.n.* (*aux.* sein) turn pale.

Verbleib [fɛr'blaɪp], *m.* (—(e)s, *no pl.*) whereabouts.

verbleiben [fɛr'blaɪbən], *v.n. irr.* (*aux.* sein) remain.

verblenden [fɛr'blɛndən], *v.a.* dazzle, delude, blind.

Verblendung [fɛr'blɛnduŋ], *f.* (—, *no pl.*) infatuation; delusion.

verblüffen [fɛr'blyfən], *v.n.* amaze, stagger, dumbfound.

Verblüffung [fɛr'blyfuŋ], *f.* (—, *no pl.*) bewilderment.

verblühen [fɛr'bly:ən], *v.n.* (*aux.* sein) wither, fade.

verblümt [fɛr'bly:mt], *adj.* veiled.

verbluten [fɛr'blu:tən], *v.n.* (*aux.* sein) bleed to death.

verborgen (1) [fɛr'bɔrgən], *v.a.* lend out.

verborgen (2) [fɛr'bɔrgən], *adj.* concealed, hidden; *im —en*, secretly.

Verborgenheit [fɛr'bɔrgənhaɪt], *f.* (—, *no pl.*) concealment, seclusion.

Verbot [fɛr'bo:t], *n.* (—(e)s, *pl.* —e) prohibition.

verboten [fɛr'bo:tən], *adj.* forbidden, prohibited.

verbrämen [fɛr'brɛ:mən], *v.a.* (*garment*) edge, border.

251

verbrauchen

verbrauchen [fɛr'brauxən], *v.a.* consume, use up; spend.

Verbraucher [fɛr'brauxər], *m.* (—s, *pl.* —) consumer.

Verbrechen [fɛr'brɛçən], *n.* (—s, *pl.* —) crime.

verbrechen [fɛr'brɛçən], *v.a. irr.* commit, perpetrate.

Verbrecher [fɛr'brɛçər], *m.* (—s, *pl.* —) criminal.

Verbrecheralbum [fɛr'brɛçəralbum], *n.* (—s, *no pl.*) rogues' gallery.

verbreiten [fɛr'braɪtən], *v.a.* spread, diffuse.

verbreitern [fɛr'braɪtərn], *v.a.* widen.

Verbreitung [fɛr'braɪtuŋ], *f.* (—, *no pl.*) spread(ing), propaganda, extension.

verbrennbar [fɛr'brɛnba:r], *adj.* combustible.

verbrennen [fɛr'brɛnən], *v.a. irr.* burn; cremate; *von der Sonne verbrannt,* sunburnt. — *v.n.* (*aux.* sein) get burnt. — *v.r. sich* —, scald o.s., burn o.s.

Verbrennung [fɛr'brɛnuŋ], *f.* (—, *pl.* —en) burning, combustion; cremation.

verbrieft [fɛr'bri:ft], *adj.* vested; documented.

verbringen [fɛr'brɪŋən], *v.a. irr.* (*time*) spend, pass.

verbrüdern [fɛr'bry:dərn], *v.r. sich* —, fraternise.

verbrühen [fɛr'bry:ən], *v.a.* scald.

verbummeln [fɛr'buməln], *v.a. die Zeit* —, fritter the time away.

verbunden [fɛr'bundən], *adj. einem* — *sein,* be obliged to s.o.

verbünden [fɛr'byndən], *v.r. sich* — *mit,* ally o.s. with.

Verbündete [fɛr'byndətə], *m.* (—n, *pl.* —n) ally, confederate.

verbürgen [fɛr'byrgən], *v.a.* warrant, guarantee. — *v.r. sich für etwas* —, vouch for s.th.; guarantee s.th.

Verdacht [fɛr'daxt], *m.* (—(e)s, *no pl.*) suspicion.

verdächtig [fɛr'dɛçtɪç], *adj.* suspicious, doubtful, questionable.

verdächtigen [fɛr'dɛçtɪgən], *v.a.* throw suspicion on, suspect.

verdammen [fɛr'damən], *v.a.* condemn, damn.

verdammenswert [fɛr'damənsve:rt], *adj.* damnable.

Verdammung [fɛr'damuŋ], *f.* (—, *no pl.*) condemnation.

verdampfen [fɛr'dampfən], *v.n.* (*aux.* sein) evaporate.

verdanken [fɛr'daŋkən], *v.a. einem etwas* —, be indebted to s.o. for s.th.; owe s.th. to s.o.

verdauen [fɛr'dauən], *v.a.* digest.

verdaulich [fɛr'daulɪç], *adj.* digestible.

Verdauung [fɛr'dauuŋ], *f.* (—, *no pl.*) digestion.

Verdauungsstörung [fɛr'dauuŋsʃtø:-ruŋ], *f.* (—, *pl.* —en) indigestion.

Verdeck [fɛr'dɛk], *n.* (—s, *pl.* —e) awning; (*Naut.*) deck.

verdecken [fɛr'dɛkən], *v.a.* cover, hide.

verdenken [fɛr'dɛŋkən], *v.a. irr. einem etwas* —, blame s.o. for s.th.

Verderb [fɛr'dɛrp], *m.* (—s, *no pl.*) ruin, decay.

verderben [fɛr'dɛrbən], *v.a. irr.* spoil, corrupt, pervert. — *v.n.* (*aux.* sein) decay, go bad.

Verderben [fɛr'dɛrbən], *n.* (—s, *no pl.*) corruption, ruin.

Verderber [fɛr'dɛrbər], *m.* (—s, *pl.*—) corrupter, perverter.

verderblich [fɛr'dɛrplɪç], *adj.* ruinous, pernicious, destructive; (*goods*) perishable.

Verderbnis [fɛr'dɛrpnɪs], *f.* (—, *no pl.*) corruption, depravity; perversion; perdition.

Verderbtheit [fɛr'dɛrpthaɪt], *f.* (—, *no pl.*) corruption, perversion, depravity.

verdeutlichen [fɛr'dɔytlɪçən], *v.a.* illustrate, clarify.

verdichten [fɛr'dɪçtən], *v.a.*, *v.r.* thicken, condense, liquefy.

Verdichtung [fɛr'dɪçtuŋ], *f.* (—, *no pl.*) condensation; solidification.

verdicken [fɛr'dɪkən], *v.a.* thicken; solidify.

verdienen [fɛr'di:nən], *v.a.* earn; deserve.

Verdienst (1) [fɛr'di:nst], *m.* (—es, *pl.* —e) profit, gain, earnings.

Verdienst (2) [fɛr'di:nst], *n.* (—es, *pl.* —e) merit, deserts.

verdienstvoll [fɛr'di:nstfɔl], *adj.* meritorious, deserving; distinguished.

verdient [fɛr'di:nt], *adj. sich* — *machen um,* deserve well of, serve well (a cause etc.).

verdientermaßen [fɛr'di:ntərmasən], *adv.* deservedly.

verdingen [fɛr'dɪŋən], *v.r. irr. sich* —, enter service (with), take a situation (with).

verdolmetschen [fɛr'dɔlmɛtʃən], *v.a.* interpret, translate.

verdoppeln [fɛr'dɔpəln], *v.a.* double.

verdorben [fɛr'dɔrbən], *adj.* spoilt; corrupted, depraved, debauched.

verdrängen [fɛr'drɛŋən], *v.a.* crowd out; (*Phys.*) displace; (*fig.*) supplant, supersede; (*Psych.*) inhibit, repress.

Verdrängung [fɛr'drɛŋuŋ], *f.* (—, *no pl.*) supplanting; (*Phys.*) displacement; (*Psych.*) inhibition, repression.

verdrehen [fɛr'dre:ən], *v.a.* twist (the wrong way); (*fig.*) misrepresent, distort.

verdreht [fɛr'dre:t], *adj.* cracked, cranky, crazy, queer.

Verdrehtheit [fɛr'dre:thaɪt], *f.* (—, *no pl.*) crankiness.

Verdrehung [fɛr'dre:uŋ], *f.* (—, *pl.* —en) distortion; (*fig.*) misrepresentation.

verdrießen [fɛr'dri:sən], *v.a. irr.* vex, annoy.

verdrießlich [fɛr'dri:slɪç], *adj.* (*thing*) vexatious, tiresome; (*person*) morose, peevish.

verdrossen [fɛr'drɔsən], *adj.* annoyed; fretful, sulky.

Verdrossenheit [fɛr'drɔsənhaɪt], *f.* (—, *no pl.*) annoyance ; fretfulness, sulkiness.

verdrücken [fɛr'drykən], *v.a.* (*sl.*) eat o.'s fill of. — *v.r.* (*coll.*) *sich* —, slink away ; sneak away.

Verdruß [fɛr'drus], *m.* (—sses, *no pl.*) vexation, annoyance; — *bereiten*, give trouble, cause annoyance.

verduften [fɛr'duftən], *v.n.* (*aux.* sein) evaporate; (*fig.*) (*coll.*) take French leave, clear out.

verdummen [fɛr'dumən], *v.n.* (*aux.* sein) become stupid.

verdunkeln [fɛr'duŋkəln], *v.a.* blackout, obscure; (*fig.*) eclipse.

Verdunk(e)lung [fɛr'duŋk(ə)luŋ], *f.* (—, *no pl.*) darkening, eclipse; blackout.

Verdunk(e)lungsgefahr [vɛr'duŋk(ə)luŋsgəfaːr], *f.* (—, *no pl.*) (*Law*) danger of prejudicing the course *or* administration of justice.

verdünnen [fɛr'dynən], *v.a.* thin out, dilute.

Verdünnung [fɛr'dynuŋ], *f.* (—, *no pl.*) attenuation; dilution.

verdunsten [fɛr'dunstən], *v.n.* (*aux.* sein) evaporate.

verdursten [fɛr'durstən], *v.n.* (*aux.* sein) die of thirst, perish with thirst.

verdüstern [fɛr'dyːstərn], *v.a.* darken, make gloomy.

verdutzen [fɛr'dutsən], *v.a.* disconcert, bewilder, nonplus.

Veredlung [fɛr'eːdluŋ], *f.* (—, *no pl.*) improvement, refinement.

verehelichen [fɛr'eːəlɪçən], *v.r.* (*obs.*) *sich* —, get married.

verehren [fɛr'eːrən], *v.a.* respect, revere, esteem; worship, adore.

Verehrer [fɛr'eːrər], *m.* (—s, *pl.* —) admirer; lover.

verehrlich [fɛr'eːrlɪç], *adj.* venerable.

verehrt [fɛr'eːrt], *adj.* honoured; *sehr —er Herr*, dear Sir.

Verehrung [fɛr'eːruŋ], *f.* (—, *no pl.*) reverence, veneration; worship, adoration.

verehrungswürdig [fɛr'eːruŋsvyrdɪç], *adj.* venerable.

vereidigt [fɛr'aɪdɪçt], *adj.* sworn in, bound by oath, under oath; *—er Bücherrevisor*, chartered accountant.

Vereidigung [fɛr'aɪdɪguŋ], *f.* (—, *no pl.*) swearing in; oathtaking.

Verein [fɛr'aɪn], *m.* (—s, *pl.* —e) union, association, society; club.

vereinbar [fɛr'aɪnbaːr], *adj.* compatible.

vereinbaren [fɛr'aɪnbaːrən], *v.a.* agree upon, arrange.

Vereinbarung [fɛr'aɪnbaːruŋ], *f.* (—, *pl.* —en) arrangement, agreement.

vereinen [fɛr'aɪnən], *v.a.* unite.

vereinfachen [fɛr'aɪnfaxən], *v.a.* simplify.

vereinigen [fɛr'aɪnɪgən], *v.a.* unite. — *v.r. sich — mit*, associate o.s. with, join with.

Vereinigung [fɛr'aɪnɪguŋ], *f.* (—, *pl.* —en) union; association.

vereinnahmen [fɛr'aɪnnaːmən], *v.a.* receive, take (*money*).

vereinsamen [fɛr'aɪnzaːmən], *v.n.* (*aux.* sein) become isolated, become lonely.

vereint [fɛr'aɪnt], *adj.* united, joined. — *adv.* in concert, (all) together.

vereinzelt [fɛr'aɪntsəlt], *adj.* sporadic, isolated. — *adv.* here and there, now and then.

Vereinzelung [fɛr'aɪntsəluŋ], *f.* (—, *pl.* —en) isolation; individualization.

vereisen [fɛr'aɪzən], *v.n.* become frozen, freeze; congeal.

Vereisung [fɛr'aɪzuŋ], *f.* (—, *pl.* —en) freezing, icing (up).

vereiteln [fɛr'aɪtəln], *v.a.* frustrate, thwart.

Vereitelung [fɛr'aɪtəluŋ], *f.* (—, *pl.* —en) frustration, thwarting.

vereitern [fɛr'aɪtərn], *v.n.* suppurate.

Vereiterung [fɛr'aɪtəruŋ], *f.* (—, *pl.* —en) suppuration.

verenden [fɛr'ɛndən], *v.n.* (*aux.* sein) (*animal*) die.

verengen [fɛr'ɛŋən], *v.a.* narrow, straighten, constrict.

Verengung [fɛr'ɛŋuŋ], *f.* (—, *pl.* —en) narrowing, straightening, contraction.

vererben [fɛr'ɛrbən], *v.a.* leave (by will), bequeath. — *v.r. sich — auf*, devolve upon, be hereditary.

vererblich [fɛr'ɛrplɪç], *adj.* (in)heritable, hereditary.

Vererbung [fɛr'ɛrbuŋ], *f.* (—, *no pl.*) heredity.

verewigen [fɛr'eːvɪgən], *v.a.* immortalise.

Verewigte [fɛr'eːvɪçtə], *m.* (—n, *pl.* —n) (*Poet.*) deceased.

Verfahren [fɛr'faːrən], *n.* (—s, *pl.* —) process; (*Law*) procedure; proceedings; *das — einstellen*, quash proceedings.

verfahren [fɛr'faːrən], *v.n. irr.* (*aux.* sein) proceed, act, operate. — *v.a.* spend (*money etc.*) on travelling. — *v.r. sich —*, (*Motor.*) lose o.'s way.

Verfall [fɛr'fal], *m.* (—s, *no pl.*) decay, decline; downfall, ruin; (*Comm.*) expiration, maturity; *in — geraten*, fall into ruin, decay.

verfallen [fɛr'falən], *v.n. irr.* (*aux.* sein) decay; go to ruin; lapse; (*Comm.*) fall due, expire; (*pledge*) become forfeit; *einem —*, become the property of, accrue to, devolve upon s.o.; (*fig.*) become the slave of s.o.; (*health*) decline, fail; *auf etwas —*, hit upon an idea. — *adj.* decayed, ruined.

Verfalltag [fɛr'faltaːk], *m.* (—s, *pl.* —e) day of payment; maturity.

verfälschen [fɛr'fɛlʃən], *v.a.* falsify; adulterate.

Verfälschung [fɛr'fɛlʃuŋ], *f.* (—, *pl.* —en) falsification; adulteration.

verfangen

verfangen [fɛr'faŋən], v.r. irr. sich —, get entangled; *sich in ein Lügennetz* —, entangle o.s. in a tissue of lies.

verfänglich [fɛr'fɛŋlɪç], adj. risky; insidious.

verfärben [fɛr'fɛrbən], v.r. sich —, change colour.

verfassen [fɛr'fasən], v.a. compose, write, be the author of.

Verfasser [fɛr'fasər], m. (—s, pl. —) author, writer.

Verfassung [fɛr'fasuŋ], f. (—, pl. —en) composition; (state) constitution; state, condition, disposition.

verfassungsgemäß [fɛr'fasuŋsgəmɛːs], adj. constitutional.

verfassungswidrig [fɛr'fasuŋsviːdrɪç], adj. unconstitutional.

verfaulen [fɛr'faulən], v.n. (aux. sein) rot, putrefy.

verfechten [fɛr'fɛçtən], v.a. irr. defend, advocate; maintain.

verfehlen [fɛr'feːlən], v.a. fail, miss; fail to meet; fail to do; *den Weg* —, lose o.'s way.

verfehlt [fɛr'feːlt], adj. unsuccessful, false, abortive; *eine —e Sache*, a failure.

Verfehlung [fɛr'feːluŋ], f. (—, pl. —en) lapse.

verfeinern [fɛr'fainərn], v.a. refine, improve.

Verfeinerung [fɛr'fainəruŋ], f. (—, pl. —en) refinement, polish.

verfertigen [fɛr'fɛrtɪgən], v.a. make, manufacture.

verfilmen [fɛr'fɪlmən], v.a. make a film of, film.

verfinstern [fɛr'fɪnstərn], v.r. sich —, get dark; be eclipsed.

verflechten [fɛr'flɛçtən], v.a. irr. interweave, interlace. — v.r. sich —, (fig.) become entangled, become involved.

verfließen [fɛr'fliːsən], v.n. irr. (aux. sein) flow away; (time) elapse, pass.

verflossen [fɛr'flɔsən], adj. past, bygone.

verfluchen [fɛr'fluːxən], v.a. curse, execrate.

verflucht [fɛr'fluːxt], excl. damn!

verflüchtigen [fɛr'flyçtɪgən], v.r. sich —, become volatile; evaporate; (coll.) make off, make o.s. scarce.

Verfluchung [fɛr'fluːxuŋ], f. (—, pl. —en) malediction, curse.

Verfolg [fɛr'fɔlk], m. (—(e)s, no pl.) progress, course.

verfolgen [fɛr'fɔlgən], v.a. pursue; persecute; prosecute.

Verfolger [fɛr'fɔlgər], m. (—s, pl. —) pursuer; persecutor.

Verfolgung [fɛr'fɔlguŋ], f. (—, pl. —en) pursuit; persecution; prosecution.

Verfolgungswahn [fɛr'fɔlguŋsvaːn], m. (—s, no pl.) persecution mania.

verfrüht [fɛr'fryːt], adj. premature.

verfügbar [fɛr'fyːkbaːr], adj. available.

verfügen [fɛr'fyːgən], v.a. decree, order. — v.n. — *über etwas*, have control of s.th, have s.th. at o.'s disposal.

Verfügung [fɛr'fyːguŋ], f. (—, pl. —en) decree, ordinance; disposition, disposal; *einem zur* — *stehen*, be at s.o.'s service or disposal.

verführen [fɛr'fyːrən], v.a. seduce.

verführerisch [fɛr'fyːrərɪʃ], adj. seductive, alluring; (coll.) fetching.

Verführung [fɛr'fyːruŋ], f. (—, no pl.) seduction.

vergällen [fɛr'gɛlən], v.a. spoil, mar.

vergallopieren [fɛrgalo'piːrən], v.r. (coll.) sich —, blunder, overshoot the mark.

vergangen [fɛr'gaŋən], adj. past, gone, last.

Vergangenheit [fɛr'gaŋənhait], f. (—, no pl.) past, time past; (Gram.) past tense.

vergänglich [fɛr'gɛŋlɪç], adj. transient, transitory.

Vergaser [fɛr'gaːzər], m. (—s, pl. —) (Motor.) carburettor.

vergeben [fɛr'geːbən], v.a. irr. give away; forgive, pardon; confer, bestow.

vergebens [fɛr'geːbəns], adv. in vain, vainly.

vergeblich [fɛr'geːplɪç], adj. vain, futile, fruitless. — adv. in vain.

Vergebung [fɛr'geːbuŋ], f. (—, no pl.) forgiveness, pardon; (office) bestowal.

vergegenwärtigen [fɛrge:gən'vɛrtɪgən], v.a. bring to mind, imagine.

Vergehen [fɛr'ge:ən], n. (—s, pl. —) offence lapse.

vergehen [fɛr'ge:ən], v.n. irr. (aux. sein) go away, pass (away); elapse; perish; (time) pass. — v.r. sich —, go wrong; offend; violate (Law, person).

vergelten [fɛr'gɛltən], v.a. irr. repay, reward, recompense.

Vergeltung [fɛr'gɛltuŋ], f. (—, no pl.) requital, retribution; reward, recompense.

vergessen [fɛr'gɛsən], v.a. irr. forget; *bei einem* —, leave behind.

Vergessenheit [fɛr'gɛsənhait], f. (—, no pl.) oblivion.

vergeßlich [fɛr'gɛslɪç], adj. forgetful.

vergeuden [fɛr'gɔydən], v.a. waste, squander.

vergewaltigen [fɛrgə'valtɪgən], v.a. assault criminally, rape, violate; (fig.) coerce, force.

Vergewaltigung [fɛrgə'valtɪguŋ], f. (—, no pl.) criminal assault, rape; (fig.) coercion.

vergewissern [fɛrgə'vɪsərn], v.r. sich —, ascertain, make sure.

vergießen [fɛr'giːsən], v.a. irr. spill; shed.

vergiften [fɛr'gɪftən], v.a. poison.

Vergiftung [fɛr'gɪftuŋ], f. (—, pl. —en) poisoning.

vergilbt [fɛr'gɪlpt], adj. yellow with age.

Vergißmeinnicht [fɛr'gɪsmainnɪçt], n. (—s, pl. —e) (Bot.) forget-me-not.

Vergleich [fɛr'glaɪç], *m.* (—(e)s, *pl.* —e) comparison; agreement; (*Law*) compromise.

vergleichbar [fɛr'glaɪçba:r], *adj.* comparable.

vergleichen [fɛr'glaɪçən], *v.a. irr.* compare.

vergleichsweise [fɛr'glaɪçsvaɪzə], *adv.* by way of comparison; comparatively; (*Law*) by way of agreement.

Vergnügen [fɛr'gny:gən], *n.* (—s, *no pl.*) pleasure, enjoyment, fun.

vergnügen [fɛr'gny:gən], *v.a.* amuse, delight.

Vergnügung [fɛr'gny:guŋ], *f.* (—, *pl.* —en) entertainment, amusement.

vergönnen [fɛr'gœnən], *v.a.* grant, allow; not (be)grudge.

vergöttern [fɛr'gœtərn], *v.a.* idolise, worship.

vergraben [fɛr'gra:bən], *v.a. irr.* hide in the ground, bury.

vergrämt [fɛr'grɛ:mt], *adj.* careworn.

vergreifen [fɛr'graɪfən], *v.r. irr. sich — an,* lay violent hands on, violate.

vergriffen [fɛr'grɪfən], *adj.* out of stock, out of print.

vergrößern [fɛr'grø:sərn], *v.a.* enlarge, expand; increase; magnify; (*fig.*) exaggerate.

Vergrößerung [fɛr'grø:sərun], *f.* (—, *pl.* —en) magnification, enlargement, increase.

Vergrößerungsglas [fɛr'grø:səruŋsglas], *n.* (—es, *pl.* ˙-er) magnifying glass.

Vergünstigung [fɛr'gynstɪguŋ], *f.* (—, *pl.* —en) privilege, favour, special facility, concession.

vergüten [fɛr'gy:tən], *v.a. einem etwas —,* compensate s.o. for s.th.; reimburse s.o. for s.th.

Vergütung [fɛr'gy:tuŋ], *f.* (—, *pl.* —en) indemnification, compensation, reimbursement.

verhaften [fɛr'haftən], *v.a.* arrest.

Verhaftung [fɛr'haftuŋ], *f.* (—, *pl.* —en) arrest.

verhallen [fɛr'halən], *v.n.* (*aux. sein*) (*sound*) fade, die away.

verhalten [fɛr'haltən], *v.r. irr. sich —,* act, behave.

Verhalten [fɛr'haltən], *n.* (—s, *no pl.*) behaviour, conduct, demeanour.

Verhältnis [fɛr'hɛltnɪs], *n.* (—ses, *pl.* —se) (*Maths.*) proportion, ratio; relation; footing; love-affair, liaison; (*coll.*) mistress.

verhältnismäßig [fɛr'hɛltnɪsmɛsɪç], *adj.* proportionate, comparative.

Verhältniswort [fɛr'hɛltnɪsvɔrt], *n.* (—es, *pl.* ˙-er) preposition.

Verhältniszahl [fɛr'hɛltnɪstsa:l], *f.* (—, *pl.* —en) proportional number.

Verhaltungsmaßregel [fɛr'haltuŋsma:sre:gəl], *f.* (—, *pl.* —n) rule of conduct; instruction.

verhandeln [fɛr'handəln], *v.a.* discuss, transact. — *v.n.* negotiate.

Verhandlung [fɛr'handluŋ], *f.* (—, *pl.* —en) discussion, negotiation, transaction; (*Law*) proceedings.

verhängen [fɛr'hɛŋən], *v.a.* cover with; decree; inflict (a penalty) on s.o.

Verhängnis [fɛr'hɛŋnɪs], *n.* (—ses, *pl.* —se) fate, destiny; misfortune.

Verhängnisglaube [fɛr'hɛŋnɪsglaubə], *m.* (—ns, *no pl.*) fatalism.

verhängnisvoll [fɛr'hɛŋnɪsfɔl], *adj.* fateful, portentous; fatal.

verhärmt [fɛr'hɛrmt], *adj.* careworn.

verharren [fɛr'harən], *v.n.* remain; persist.

Verhärtung [fɛr'hɛrtuŋ], *f.* (—, *pl.* —en) hardening, hardened state; (*skin*) callosity; (*fig.*) obduracy.

verhaßt [fɛr'hast], *adj.* hated, odious.

verhätscheln [fɛr'hɛtʃəln], *v.a.* pamper, coddle.

verhauen [fɛr'hauən], *v.a.* beat, thrash.

Verheerung [fɛr'he:ruŋ], *f.* (—, *pl.* —en) devastation.

verhehlen [fɛr'he:lən], *v.a.* conceal, hide.

verheilen [fɛr'haɪlən], *v.n.* (*aux. sein*) heal.

verheimlichen [fɛr'haɪmlɪçən], *v.a.* keep secret, hush up.

verheiraten [fɛr'haɪra:tən], *v.a.* give in marriage, marry off. — *v.r. sich —,* marry, get married.

verheißen [fɛr'haɪsən], *v.a. irr.* promise.

Verheißung [fɛr'haɪsuŋ], *f.* (—, *pl.* —en) promise.

verhelfen [fɛr'hɛlfən], *v.n. irr. einem zu etwas —,* help s.o. to s.th.

Verherrlichung [fɛr'hɛrlɪçuŋ], *f.* (—, *no pl.*) glorification.

Verhetzung [fɛr'hɛtsuŋ], *f.* (—, *pl.* —en) incitement, instigation.

verhexen [fɛr'hɛksən], *v.a.* bewitch.

verhindern [fɛr'hɪndərn], *v.a.* hinder, prevent.

Verhinderung [fɛr'hɪndəruŋ], *f.* (—, *pl.* —en) prevention, obstacle.

verhöhnen [fɛr'hø:nən], *v.a.* deride, scoff at, jeer at.

Verhöhnung [fɛr'hø:nuŋ], *f.* (—, *pl.* —en) derision.

Verhör [fɛr'hø:r], *n.* (—s, *pl.* —e) hearing; (judicial) examination; *ins — nehmen,* question, interrogate, cross-examine.

verhören [fɛr'hø:rən], *v.a.* examine judicially, interrogate. — *v.r. sich —,* misunderstand.

verhüllen [fɛr'hylən], *v.a.* cover, wrap up, veil.

verhungern [fɛr'huŋərn], *v.n.* (*aux. sein*) starve.

verhungert [fɛr'huŋərt], *adj.* famished.

verhunzen [fɛr'huntsən], *v.a.* spoil, bungle.

verhüten [fɛr'hy:tən], *v.a.* prevent, avert.

Verhütung [fɛr'hy:tuŋ], *f.* (—, *no pl.*) prevention, warding off.

verirren [fɛr'ɪrən], *v.r. sich —,* go astray, lose o.'s way.

verirrt [fɛrˈɪrt], *adj.* stray, straying, lost.

verjagen [fɛrˈjaːgən], *v.a.* drive away, chase away.

verjährt [fɛrˈjɛːrt], *adj.* statute-barred; prescriptive; obsolete; old.

verjubeln [fɛrˈjuːbəln], *v.a.* play ducks and drakes with; squander.

verjüngen [fɛrˈjʏŋən], *v.a.* make younger; (*Archit.*) taper. — *v.r. sich* —, grow younger.

Verjüngung [fɛrˈjʏŋuŋ], *f.* (—, *pl.* —en) rejuvenation.

verkannt [fɛrˈkant], *adj.* misunderstood.

verkappt [fɛrˈkapt], *adj.* disguised, secret, in disguise.

Verkauf [fɛrˈkauf], *m.* (—(e)s, *pl.* ⁻e) sale.

verkaufen [fɛrˈkaufən], *v.a.* sell.

Verkäufer [fɛrˈkɔyfər], *m.* (—s, *pl.* —) seller; shop assistant, salesman.

verkäuflich [fɛrˈkɔyflɪç], *adj.* for sale, saleable; mercenary.

Verkaufspreis [fɛrˈkaufsprais], *m.* (—es, *pl.* —e) selling-price.

Verkehr [fɛrˈkeːr], *m.* (—s, *no pl.*) traffic; commerce; intercourse; communication; — *mit*, association with; service (*trains, buses etc.*), transport.

verkehren [fɛrˈkeːrən], *v.a.* turn upside down; transform; pervert. — *v.n.* frequent (a place), visit, associate (with); run, operate.

Verkehrsstraße [fɛrˈkeːrsʃtraːsə], *f.* (—, *pl.* —n) thoroughfare.

Verkehrsstockung [fɛrˈkeːrsʃtɔkuŋ], *f.* (—, *pl.* —en) traffic jam.

verkehrt [fɛrˈkeːrt], *adj.* upside down; (*fig.*) wrong.

Verkehrtheit [fɛrˈkeːrthait], *f.* (—, *pl.* —en) absurdity, piece of folly.

Verkehrung [fɛrˈkeːruŋ], *f.* (—, *pl.* —en) turning; inversion; perversion; misrepresentation; (*Gram.*) inversion.

verkennen [fɛrˈkɛnən], *v.a. irr.* mistake, fail to recognize; misjudge (s.o.'s intentions).

verklagen [fɛrˈklaːgən], *v.a.* sue; accuse.

verklären [fɛrˈklɛːrən], *v.a.* transfigure, illumine.

verklärt [fɛrˈklɛːrt], *adj.* transfigured; radiant.

verkleben [fɛrˈkleːbən], *v.a.* paste over.

verkleiden [fɛrˈklaidən], *v.a., v.r.* disguise (o.s.).

Verkleidung [fɛrˈklaiduŋ], *f.* (— *pl.* —en) disguise.

verkleinern [fɛrˈklainərn], *v.a.* make smaller, diminish, reduce; belittle, disparage.

Verkleinerung [fɛrˈklainəruŋ], *f.* (—, *pl.* —en) diminution, reduction; belittling, detraction.

Verkleinerungswort [fɛrˈklainəruŋsvɔrt], *n.* (—s, *pl.* ⁻er) (*Gram.*) diminutive.

verkneifen [fɛrˈknaifən], *v.r. irr.* (*coll.*) *sich etwas* —, deny o.s. s.th.

verkniffen [fɛrˈknɪfən], *adj.* pinched; shrewd; hard-bitten.

verknöchern [fɛrˈknœçərn], *v.n.* (*aux.* sein) ossify; (*fig.*) become fossilised *or* inflexible.

Verknöcherung [fɛrˈknœçəruŋ], *f.* (—, *pl.* —en) ossification; (*fig.*) fossilisation.

verknüpfen [fɛrˈknʏpfən], *v.a.* tie, connect, link.

verkochen [fɛrˈkɔxən], *v.n.* (*aux.* sein) boil away.

verkommen [fɛrˈkɔmən], *v.n. irr.* (*aux.* sein) go from bad to worse, go to seed, decay, become depraved. — *adj.* demoralised, down and out, depraved.

Verkommenheit [fɛrˈkɔmənhait], *f.* (—, *no pl.*) demoralisation; depravity.

verkörpern [fɛrˈkœrpərn], *v.a.* embody.

verkrachen [fɛrˈkraxən], *v.r. sich* —, quarrel, (*coll.*) have a row.

verkriechen [fɛrˈkriːçən], *v.r. irr. sich* —, creep *or* crawl away; slink away, lie low.

verkümmern [fɛrˈkʏmərn], *v.n.* (*aux.* sein) wear away, waste away; pine away.

verkünden [fɛrˈkʏndən], *v.a.* proclaim, announce, publish, prophesy.

Verkündigung [fɛrˈkʏndiguŋ], *f.* (—, *pl.* —en) announcement, proclamation; prediction.

Verkündung [fɛrˈkʏnduŋ], *f.* (—, *pl.* —en) publication, proclamation.

Verkürzung [fɛrˈkʏrtsuŋ], *f.* (—, *pl.* —en) shortening, curtailment.

verlachen [fɛrˈlaxən], *v.a.* laugh at, deride.

verladen [fɛrˈlaːdən], *v.a. irr.* load, ship, freight.

Verladung [fɛrˈlaːduŋ], *f.* (—, *pl.* —en) loading, shipping.

Verlag [fɛrˈlaːk], *m.* (—(e)s, *pl.* —e) publication; publishing-house, (firm of) publishers.

Verlagsrecht [fɛrˈlaːksrɛçt], *n.* (—s, *pl.* —e) copyright.

Verlangen [fɛrˈlaŋən], *n.* (—s, *no pl.*) demand, request; longing, desire.

verlangen [fɛrˈlaŋən], *v.a.* ask, demand, request.

verlängern [fɛrˈlɛŋərn], *v.a.* lengthen, prolong, extend.

Verlängerung [fɛrˈlɛŋəruŋ], *f.* (—, *pl.* —en) lengthening; (*period*) prolongation, extension.

verlangsamen [fɛrˈlaŋzaːmən], *v.a.* slow down, slacken, decelerate.

Verlaß [fɛrˈlas], *m.* (—sses, *no pl.*) *es ist kein* — *auf dich*, you cannot be relied on.

verlassen [fɛrˈlasən], *v.a. irr.* leave, abandon. — *v.r. sich* — *auf*, rely on, depend upon. — *adj.* forlorn, forsaken, deserted, desolate, lonely.

Verlassenheit [fɛrˈlasənhait], *f.* (—, *no pl.*) desolation, loneliness, solitude.

verläßlich [fɛrˈlɛslɪç], *adj.* reliable, trustworthy.

Verlauf [fɛr'lauf], *m.* (—(e)s, *no pl.*) lapse, expiration; course.

verlaufen [fɛr'laufən], *v.n. irr.* (*aux. sein*) (*time*) pass; (*period*) expire, elapse; develop(e), turn out. — *v.r. sich* —, lose o.'s way; (*colour*) run.

verlauten [fɛr'lautən], *v.n.* transpire.

verleben [fɛr'le:bən], *v.a.* pass, spend.

verlebt [fɛr'le:pt], *adj.* worn out; spent; (*Am.*) played out.

verlegen [fɛr'le:gən], *v.a.* (*domicile*) move, remove; (*things*) mislay; (*books*) publish; obstruct; adjourn; change to another date *or* place. — *v.r. sich auf etwas* —, devote o.s. to s.th. — *adj.* embarrassed, ill at ease.

Verlegenheit [fɛr'le:gənhaIt], *f.* (—, *pl.* —en) embarrassment, perplexity; predicament, difficulty.

Verleger [fɛr'le:gər], *m.* (—s, *pl.* —) publisher.

verleiden [fɛr'laIdən], *v.a. einem etwas* —, spoil s.th. for s.o.

verleihen [fɛr'laIən], *v.a. irr.* lend; (*honour, title*) confer; bestow, award.

Verleiher [fɛr'laIər], *m.* (—s, *pl.* —) lender.

Verleihung [fɛr'laIuŋ], *f.* (—, *pl.* —en) lending, loan; (*medal, prize*) investiture; grant, conferring.

verleiten [fɛr'laItən], *v.a.* mislead, entice, induce; seduce.

Verleitung [fɛr'laItuŋ], *f.* (—, *no pl.*) misleading, enticement, inducement; seduction.

verlernen [fɛr'lɛrnən], *v.a.* unlearn; forget.

verlesen [fɛr'le:zən], *v.a. irr.* read aloud, read out, recite. — *v.r. sich* —, misread.

verletzen [fɛr'lɛtsən], *v.a.* injure, hurt, wound, violate.

verletzend [fɛr'lɛtsənt], *adj.* offensive, insulting; cutting.

verletzlich [fɛr'lɛtslɪç], *adj.* vulnerable.

Verletzlichkeit [fɛr'lɛtslɪçkaIt], *f.* (—, *no pl.*) vulnerability.

Verletzung [fɛr'lɛtsuŋ], *f.* (—, *pl.* —en) hurt, wound; (*Law*) violation.

verleugnen [fɛr'lɔygnən], *v.a.* deny, renounce, disown.

Verleugnung [fɛr'lɔygnuŋ], *f.* (—, *pl.* —en) denial, abnegation.

verleumden [fɛr'lɔymdən], *v.a.* slander, calumniate, traduce.

Verleumdung [fɛr'lɔymduŋ], *f.* (—, *pl.* —en) slander, libel, calumny.

verlieben [fɛr'li:bən], *v.r. sich* — *in*, fall in love with.

Verliebte [fɛr'li:ptə], *m. or f.* (—n, *pl.* —n) person in love, lover.

Verliebtheit [fɛr'li:pthaIt], *f.* (—, *no pl.*) infatuation, amorousness.

verlieren [fɛr'li:rən], *v.a. irr.* lose.

Verlierer [fɛr'li:rər], *m.* (—s, *pl.* —) loser.

Verlies [fɛr'li:s], *n.* (—(s)es, *pl.* —(s)e) dungeon.

verloben [fɛr'lo:bən], *v.r. sich* — *mit*, become engaged to.

Verlöbnis [fɛr'lø:pnIs], *n.* (—ses, *pl.* —se) (*rare*) engagement.

Verlobte [fɛr'lo:ptə], *m.* (—n, *pl.* —n) and *f.* (—n, *pl.* —n) fiancé(e), betrothed.

Verlobung [fɛr'lo:buŋ], *f.* (—, *pl.* —en) engagement, betrothal.

verlocken [fɛr'lɔkən], *v.a.* tempt, entice.

verlogen [fɛr'lo:gən], *adj.* lying, mendacious.

Verlogenheit [fɛr'lo:gənhaIt], *f.* (—, *no pl.*) mendacity.

verlohnen [fɛr'lo:nən], *v. impers.* be worth while.

verlöschen [fɛr'lœʃən], *v.a.* extinguish.

verlosen [fɛr'lo:zən], *v.a.* raffle; draw *or* cast lots for.

Verlosung [fɛr'lo:zuŋ], *f.* (—, *pl.* —en) raffle, lottery.

verlöten [fɛr'lø:tən], *v.a.* solder.

verlottern [fɛr'lɔtərn], *v.n.* (*aux. sein*) go to the dogs.

Verlust [fɛr'lust], *m.* (—es, *pl.* —e) loss; (*death*) bereavement; (*Mil.*) casualty.

verlustig [fɛr'lustɪç], *adj.* — *gehen*, lose s.th., forfeit s.th.

vermachen [fɛr'maxən], *v.a. einem etwas* —, bequeath s.th. to s.o.

Vermächtnis [fɛr'mɛçtnIs], *n.* (—ses, *pl.* —sse) will; legacy, bequest; (*fig.*) *heiliges* —, sacred trust.

vermahlen [fɛr'ma:lən], *v.a.* grind (down).

Vermählung [fɛr'mɛ:luŋ], *f.* (—, *pl.* —en) marriage, wedding.

Vermahnung [fɛr'ma:nuŋ], *f.* (—, *pl.* —en) admonition, exhortation.

vermauern [fɛr'mauərn], *v.a.* wall up.

vermehren [fɛr'me:rən], *v.a.* augment, multiply, increase. — *v.r. sich* —, multiply.

Vermehrung [fɛr'me:ruŋ], *f.* (—, *pl.* —en) increase, multiplication.

vermeiden [fɛr'maIdən], *v.a. irr.* avoid, shun, shirk.

vermeidlich [fɛr'maItlɪç], *adj.* avoidable.

Vermeidung [fɛr'maIduŋ], *f.* (—, *no pl.*) avoidance.

vermeintlich [fɛr'maIntlɪç], *adj.* supposed, alleged, pretended; (*heir*) presumptive.

vermelden [fɛr'mɛldən], *v.a.* announce, notify.

vermengen [fɛr'mɛŋən], *v.a.* mingle, mix.

Vermerk [fɛr'mɛrk], *m.* (—s, *pl.* —e) entry, notice, note.

vermerken [fɛr'mɛrkən], *v.a.* observe, jot down.

vermessen [fɛr'mɛsən], *v.a. irr.* measure; (*land*) survey. — *adj.* bold, daring, audacious; arrogant.

Vermessenheit [fɛr'mɛsənhaIt], *f.* (—, *no pl.*) boldness, audacity; arrogance.

Vermesser [fɛr'mɛsər], *m.* (—s, *pl.* —) (*land*) surveyor.

257

Vermessung

Vermessung [fɛr'mɛsuŋ], f. (—, pl. —en) (*land*) survey; measuring.

vermieten [fɛr'mi:tən], v.a. let, lease, hire out.

Vermieter [fɛr'mi:tər], m. (—s, pl. —) landlord; hirer.

vermindern [fɛr'mɪndərn], v.a. diminish, lessen.

Verminderung [fɛr'mɪndəruŋ], f. (—, pl. —en) diminution, reduction, decrease, lessening.

vermischen [fɛr'mɪʃən], v.a. mix, mingle, blend.

vermissen [fɛr'mɪsən], v.a. miss; *vermißt sein*, be missing; *vermißt werden*, be missed.

vermitteln [fɛr'mɪtəln], v.n. mediate. — v.a. adjust; negotiate, secure.

Vermittler [fɛr'mɪtlər], m. (—s, pl. —) mediator; agent, middleman.

Vermittlung [fɛr'mɪtluŋ], f. (—, pl. —en) mediation, intervention.

vermöbeln [fɛr'mø:bəln], v.a. (*sl.*) *einen* —, thrash s.o.

vermodern [fɛr'mo:dərn], v.n. (*aux.* sein) moulder, rot.

vermöge [fɛr'mø:gə], prep. (*Genit.*) by virtue of, by dint of, on the strength of.

Vermögen [fɛr'mø:gən], n. (—s, pl. —) faculty, power; means, assets; fortune, wealth, riches; *er hat* —, he is a man of property; *nach bestem* —, to the best of o.'s ability.

vermögen [fɛr'mø:gən], v.a. irr. be able to, have the power to, be capable of.

vermögend [fɛr'mø:gənt], adj. wealthy.

Vermögensbestand [fɛr'mø:gənsbəʃtant], m. (—s, pl. ·̈e) assets.

Vermögenssteuer [fɛr'mø:gənsʃtɔyər], f. (—, pl. —n) property tax.

vermorscht [fɛr'mɔrʃt], adj. mouldering, rotten.

vermuten [fɛr'mu:tən], v.a. suppose, conjecture, surmise, presume; guess.

vermutlich [fɛr'mu:tlɪç], adj. likely, probable.

Vermutung [fɛr'mu:tuŋ], f. (—, pl. —en) guess, supposition, conjecture.

vernachlässigen [fɛr'naxlɛsɪgən], v.a. neglect.

Vernachlässigung [fɛr'naxlɛsɪguŋ], f. (—, pl. —en) neglect, negligence.

vernarren [fɛr'narən], v.r. *sich* — (*in*, *Acc.*), become infatuated (with).

vernarrt [fɛr'nart], adj. madly in love.

vernaschen [fɛr'naʃən], v.a. squander (money) on sweets.

vernehmbar [fɛr'ne:mba:r], adj. audible; *sich* — *machen*, make o.s. heard.

Vernehmen [fɛr'ne:mən], n. (—s, no pl.) *dem* — *nach*, from what o. hears.

vernehmen [fɛr'ne:mən], v.a. irr. hear, learn; (*Law*) examine, interrogate.

vernehmlich [fɛr'ne:mlɪç], adj. audible, distinct, clear.

Vernehmlichkeit [fɛr'ne:mlɪçkaɪt], f. (—, no pl.) audibility.

Vernehmung [fɛr'ne:muŋ], f. (—, pl. —en) (*Law*) interrogation, examination.

verneigen [fɛr'naɪgən], v.r. *sich* —, curts(e)y, bow.

Verneigung [fɛr'naɪguŋ], f. (—, pl. —en) curts(e)y, bow.

verneinen [fɛr'naɪnən], v.a. deny, answer in the negative.

Verneinung [fɛr'naɪnuŋ], f. (—, pl. —en) negation, denial; (*Gram.*) negation, negative.

vernichten [fɛr'nɪçtən], v.a. annihilate, destroy utterly, exterminate.

Vernichtung [fɛr'nɪçtuŋ], f. (—, no pl.) annihilation, extinction, destruction.

vernieten [fɛr'ni:tən], v.a. rivet.

Vernunft [fɛr'nunft], f. (—, no pl.) reason, sense, intelligence, judgment; *gesunde* —, common sense; — *annehmen*, listen to reason; *einen zur* — *bringen*, bring s.o. to his senses.

vernünftig [fɛr'nynftɪç], adj. sensible, reasonable, rational.

veröden [fɛr'ø:dən], v.n. (*aux.* sein) become desolate, become devastated.

Verödung [fɛr'ø:duŋ], f. (—, no pl.) devastation, desolation.

veröffentlichen [fɛr'œfəntlɪçən], v.a. publish.

Veröffentlichung [fɛr'œfəntlɪçuŋ], f. (—, pl. —en) publication.

verordnen [fɛr'ɔrdnən], v.a. order, command, ordain; (*Med.*) prescribe.

Verordnung [fɛr'ɔrdnuŋ], f. (—, pl. —en) order; (*Law*) decree, edict, statute; (*Med.*) prescription.

verpassen [fɛr'pasən], v.a. lose by delay, let slip; (*train etc.*) miss.

verpfänden [fɛr'pfɛndən], v.a. pawn, pledge.

Verpfänder [fɛr'pfɛndər], m. (—s, pl. —) mortgager.

Verpfändung [fɛr'pfɛnduŋ], f. (—, pl. —en) pawning, pledging.

verpflanzen [fɛr'pflantsən], v.a. transplant.

Verpflanzung [fɛr'pflantsuŋ], f. (—, pl. —en) transplantation.

verpflegen [fɛr'pfle:gən], v.a. board, provide food for, feed; nurse.

Verpflegung [fɛr'pfle:guŋ], f. (—, no pl.) board, catering; food.

Verpflegungskosten [fɛr'pfle:guŋskostən], f. pl. (cost of) board and lodging.

verpflichten [fɛr'pflɪçtən], v.a. bind, oblige, engage.

verpflichtend [fɛr'pflɪçtənt], adj. obligatory.

Verpflichtung [fɛr'pflɪçtuŋ], f. (—, pl. —en) obligation, duty; liability, engagement.

verplaudern [fɛr'plaudərn], v.a. spend (time) chatting.

verplempern [fɛr'plɛmpərn], v.a. (*coll.*) spend foolishly, fritter away.

verpönt [fɛr'pø:nt], adj. frowned upon; taboo.

verprassen [fɛr'prasən], v.a. squander (money) in riotous living.

Verschickung

verpuffen [fɛr'pufən], *v.n.* (*aux.* sein) (*coll.*) fizzle out.
verpulvern [fɛr'pulvərn], *v.a.* fritter away.
Verputz [fɛr'puts], *m.* (—es, *no pl.*) plaster.
verquicken [fɛr'kvɪkən], *v.a.* amalgamate; mix up.
Verrat [fɛr'ra:t], *m.* (—(e)s, *no pl.*) treachery, treason.
verraten [fɛr'ra:tən], *v.a. irr.* betray; disclose; *das verrät die Hand des Künstlers*, this proclaims the hand of the artist.
Verräter [fɛr'rɛ:tər], *m.* (—s, *pl.* —) traitor.
verräterisch [fɛr'rɛ:tərɪʃ], *adj.* treacherous, treasonable, perfidious; (*fig.*) tell-tale.
verrauchen [fɛr'rauxən], *v.n.* (*aux.* sein) evaporate; (*fig.*) blow over; cool down.
verräuchern [fɛr'rɔyçərn], *v.a.* smoke, fill with smoke.
verräumen [fɛr'rɔymən], *v.a.* misplace, mislay.
verrauschen [fɛr'rauʃən], *v.n.* (*aux.* sein) (*sound*) die away; pass away.
verrechnen [fɛr'rɛçnən], *v.a.* reckon up. — *v.r. sich* —, miscalculate.
Verrechnung [fɛr'rɛçnuŋ], *f.* (—, *pl.* — en) reckoning-up.
Verrechnungsscheck [fɛr'rɛçnuŋsʃɛk], *m.* (—s, *pl.* —e, —s) crossed cheque. non-negotiable cheque.
verregnen [fɛr're:gnən], *v.a.* spoil by rain.
verreiben [fɛr'raɪbən], *v.a. irr.* rub away; rub hard.
verreisen [fɛr'raɪzən], *v.n.* (*aux.* sein) go on a journey.
verrenken [fɛr'rɛŋkən], *v.a.* sprain, dislocate.
Verrenkung [fɛr'rɛŋkuŋ], *f.* (—, *pl.* —en) sprain, dislocation.
verrichten [fɛr'rɪçtən], *v.a.* do, perform, acquit o.s. of; execute; (*prayer*) say.
verriegeln [fɛr'ri:gəln], *v.a.* bolt.
verringern [fɛr'rɪŋərn], *v.a.* reduce, diminish.
Verringerung [fɛr'rɪŋəruŋ], *f.* (—, *no pl.*) diminution, reduction.
verrinnen [fɛr'rɪnən], *v.n. irr.* (*aux.* sein) run off; (*fig.*) pass, elapse.
verrosten [fɛr'rɔstən], *v.n.* (*aux.* sein) rust.
verrottet [fɛr'rɔtət], *adj.* rotten.
verrucht [fɛr'ru:xt], *adj.* villainous, atrocious, heinous, infamous.
Verruchtheit [fɛr'ru:xthaɪt], *f.* (—, *no pl.*) villainy.
verrücken [fɛr'rykən], *v.a.* shift, displace.
verrückt [fɛr'rykt], *adj.* crazy, mad.
Verrückte [fɛr'ryktə], *m.* (—n, *pl.* —n) madman — *f.* (—n, *pl.* —n) madwoman.
Verrücktheit [fɛr'rykthaɪt], *f.* (—, *pl.* —en) craziness; mad act.
Verruf [fɛr'ru:f], *m.* (—s, *no pl.*) discredit, ill repute.

verrufen [fɛr'ru:fən], *adj.* notorious, of ill repute.
Vers [fɛrs], *m.* (—es, *pl.* —e) verse.
versagen [fɛr'za:gən], *v.a. einem etwas* —, deny s.o. s.th., refuse s.o. s.th. — *v.n.* fail, break down; (*voice*) falter; *sich etwas* —, abstain from s.th., deny o.s. s.th.
Versager [fɛr'za:gər], *m.* (—s, *pl.* —) misfire; failure, unsuccessful person, flop.
versammeln [fɛr'zaməln], *v.a.* gather around, convene. — *v.r. sich* —, assemble, meet.
Versammlung [fɛr'zamluŋ], *f.* (—, *pl.* —en) assembly, meeting, gathering, convention.
Versand [fɛr'zant], *m.* (—s, *no pl.*) dispatch, forwarding, shipping, shipment.
versanden [fɛr'zandən], *v.n.* (*aux.* sein) silt up.
Versandgeschäft [fɛr'zantgəʃɛft], *n.* (—s, *pl.* —e) export business; mail order business.
Versatzamt [fɛr'zatsamt], *n.* (—s, *pl.* ⁻er) pawn-shop.
versauen [fɛr'zauən], *v.a.* (*sl.*) make a mess of.
versauern [fɛr'zauərn], *v.n.* (*aux.* sein) turn sour; (*fig.*) become morose.
versaufen [fɛr'zaufən], *v.a. irr.* (*sl.*) squander (money) on drink, drink away.
versäumen [fɛr'zɔymən], *v.a.* miss, omit, lose by delay; leave undone; neglect.
Versäumnis [fɛr'zɔymnɪs], *n.* (—ses, *pl.* —se) neglect, omission; (*time*) loss.
Versbau ['fɛrsbau], *m.* (—s, *no pl.*) versification; verse structure.
verschachern [fɛr'ʃaxərn], *v.a.* barter away.
verschaffen [fɛr'ʃafən], *v.a.* provide, procure, obtain, get.
verschämt [fɛr'ʃɛ:mt], *adj.* shamefaced, bashful.
verschanzen [fɛr'ʃantsən], *v.a.* fortify.
Verschanzung [fɛr'ʃantsuŋ], *f.* (—, *pl.* —en) fortification, entrenchment.
verschärfen [fɛr'ʃɛrfən], *v.a.* heighten, intensify, sharpen.
verscharren [fɛr'ʃarən], *v.a.* cover with earth; bury hurriedly.
verscheiden [fɛr'ʃaɪdən], *v.n. irr.* (*aux.* sein) die, pass away.
verschenken [fɛr'ʃɛŋkən], *v.a.* make a present of, give away.
verscherzen [fɛr'ʃɛrtsən], *v.a. sich etwas* —, forfeit s.th.
verscheuchen [fɛr'ʃɔyçən], *v.a.* scare away, frighten away; *Sorgen* —, banish care.
verschicken [fɛr'ʃɪkən], *v.a.* send on, send out, forward, transmit; evacuate.
Verschickung [fɛr'ʃɪkuŋ], *f.* (—, *no pl.*) forwarding, transmission; evacuation; banishment, exile.

verschieben

verschieben [fɛrˈʃiːbən], *v.a. irr.* shift, move; delay, put off, defer, postpone.
Verschiebung [fɛrˈʃiːbuŋ], *f.* (—, *pl.* —en) removal; postponement; (*fig.*) black marketeering.
verschieden [fɛrˈʃiːdən], *adj.* different, diverse, deceased, departed; (*pl.*) some, several, sundry.
verschiedenartig [fɛrˈʃiːdənaːrtɪç], *adj.* varied, various, heterogeneous.
verschiedenerlei [fɛrˈʃiːdənərlaɪ], *indecl. adj.* diverse, of various kinds.
Verschiedenheit [fɛrˈʃiːdənhaɪt], *f.* (—, *pl.* —en) difference; diversity, variety.
verschiedentlich [fɛrˈʃiːdəntlɪç], *adv.* variously, severally; repeatedly.
verschiffen [fɛrˈʃɪfən], *v.a.* export, ship.
verschimmeln [fɛrˈʃɪməln], *v.n.* (*aux.* sein) go mouldy.
verschlafen [fɛrˈʃlaːfən], *v.a. irr.* sleep through, sleep away. — *v.r. sich* —, oversleep. — *adj.* sleepy, drowsy.
Verschlag [fɛrˈʃlaːk], *m.* (—s, *pl.* ⁻e) partition, box, cubicle.
verschlagen [fɛrˈʃlaːgən], *v.a. irr.* es *verschlägt mir den Atem*, it takes my breath away. — *adj.* cunning, crafty, sly.
verschlechtern [fɛrˈʃlɛçtərn], *v.a.* worsen, make worse. — *v.r. sich* —, deteriorate.
Verschlechterung [fɛrˈʃlɛçtəruŋ], *f.* (—, *no pl.*) deterioration.
verschleiern [fɛrˈʃlaɪərn], *v.a.* veil.
Verschleierung [fɛrˈʃlaɪəruŋ], *f.* (—, *pl.* —en) veiling, concealment; camouflage.
verschleißen [fɛrˈʃlaɪsən], *v.a. irr.* wear out, waste.
verschlemmen [fɛrˈʃlɛmən], *v.a.* squander on eating and drinking.
verschleppen [fɛrˈʃlɛpən], *v.a.* carry off, deport; kidnap; protract, spread; put off, procrastinate.
verschleudern [fɛrˈʃlɔydərn], *v.a.* waste; sell at cut prices.
verschließen [fɛrˈʃliːsən], *v.a. irr.* lock, lock up.
verschlimmern [fɛrˈʃlɪmərn], *v.a.* make worse. — *v.r. sich* —, get worse, worsen, deteriorate.
Verschlimmerung [fɛrˈʃlɪməruŋ], *f.* (—, *no pl.*) worsening, deterioration.
verschlingen [fɛrˈʃlɪŋən], *v.a. irr.* swallow up, devour.
verschlossen [fɛrˈʃlɔsən], *adj.* reserved, uncommunicative, withdrawn.
Verschlossenheit [fɛrˈʃlɔsənhaɪt], *f.* (—, *no pl.*) reserve.
verschlucken [fɛrˈʃlukən], *v.a.* swallow, gulp down; (*fig.*) suppress. — *v.r. sich* —, swallow the wrong way.
verschlungen [fɛrˈʃluŋən], *adj.* intricate, complicated.
Verschluß [fɛrˈʃlus], *m.* (—sses. *pl.* ⁻sse) lock; clasp; fastening; *unter* — *haben*, keep under lock and key.
Verschlußlaut [fɛrˈʃluslaut], *m.* (—s, *pl.* —e) (*Phon.*) explosive, plosive, stop.

verschmachten [fɛrˈʃmaxtən], *v.n.* (*aux.* sein) languish, pine; be parched.
Verschmähung [fɛrˈʃmɛːuŋ], *f.* (—, *no pl.*) disdain, scorn, rejection.
Verschmelzung [fɛrˈʃmɛltsuŋ], *f.* (—, *no pl.*) coalescence, fusion, blending.
verschmerzen [fɛrˈʃmɛrtsən], *v.a.* get over; bear stoically, make the best of.
verschmitzt [fɛrˈʃmɪtst], *adj.* cunning, crafty, mischievous.
verschmutzen [fɛrˈʃmutsən], *v.n.* (*aux.* sein) get dirty.
verschnappen [fɛrˈʃnapən], *v.r. sich* —, blurt out a secret, give o.s. away, let the cat out of the bag.
verschneiden [fɛrˈʃnaɪdən], *v.a. irr.* (*wings*) clip; (*trees*) prune; (*animals*) castrate; (*wine*) blend.
verschneien [fɛrˈʃnaɪən], *v.n.* (*aux.* sein) be snowed up, be covered with snow, be snowbound.
Verschnitt [fɛrˈʃnɪt], *m.* (—s, *no pl.*) blended wine, blend.
Verschnittene [fɛrˈʃnɪtənə], *m.* (—n, *pl.* —n) eunuch.
verschnörkelt [fɛrˈʃnœrkəlt], *adj.* adorned with flourishes.
verschnupft [fɛrˈʃnupft], *adj.* — *sein*, have a cold in the head; (*fig.*) be vexed.
verschnüren [fɛrˈʃnyːrən], *v.a.* (*shoes*) lace up; (*parcel*) tie up.
verschonen [fɛrˈʃoːnən], *v.a.* spare, exempt from.
verschönern [fɛrˈʃøːnərn], *v.a.* embellish, beautify.
Verschönerung [fɛrˈʃøːnəruŋ], *f.* (—, *pl.* —en) embellishment, adornment.
Verschonung [fɛrˈʃoːnuŋ], *f.* (—, *no pl.*) exemption; forbearance.
verschossen [fɛrˈʃɔsən], *adj.* faded, discoloured; (*fig.*) madly in love.
verschreiben [fɛrˈʃraɪbən], *v.a. irr.* prescribe. — *v.r. sich* —, make a mistake in writing.
verschrien [fɛrˈʃriːən], *adj.* notorious.
verschroben [fɛrˈʃroːbən], *adj.* cranky, eccentric.
Verschrobenheit [fɛrˈʃroːbənhaɪt], *f.* (—, *pl.* —en) crankiness, eccentricity.
verschrumpfen [fɛrˈʃrumpfən], *v.n.* (*aux.* sein) shrivel up.
verschüchtern [fɛrˈʃyçtərn], *v.a.* intimidate.
verschulden [fɛrˈʃuldən], *v.a.* bring on, be the cause of; be guilty of.
verschuldet [fɛrˈʃuldət], *adj.* in debt.
Verschuldung [fɛrˈʃulduŋ], *f.* (—, *no pl.*) indebtedness.
verschütten [fɛrˈʃytən], *v.a.* spill; bury alive.
verschwägern [fɛrˈʃvɛːgərn], *v.r. sich* —, become related by marriage.
Verschwägerung [fɛrˈʃvɛːgəruŋ], *f.* (—, *no pl.*) relationship by marriage.
verschwatzen [fɛrˈʃvatsən], *v.a.* gossip (the time) away, spend o.'s time gossiping.
verschweigen [fɛrˈʃvaɪgən], *v.a. irr.* keep secret, keep (news) from, hush up.

verschwenden [fɛrˈʃvɛndən], *v.a.* squander, waste.

verschwenderisch [fɛrˈʃvɛndərɪʃ], *adj.* prodigal, profuse, lavish; wasteful.

Verschwendung [fɛrˈʃvɛnduŋ], *f.* (—, *no pl.*) waste, extravagance.

Verschwendungssucht [fɛrˈʃvɛnduŋszuxt], *f.* (—, *no pl.*) prodigality; extravagance.

verschwiegen [fɛrˈʃviːgən], *adj.* discreet, close, secretive.

Verschwiegenheit [fɛrˈʃviːgənhaɪt], *f.* (—, *no pl.*) discretion, secrecy.

verschwimmen [fɛrˈʃvɪmən], *v.n. irr.* (*aux.* sein) become blurred.

verschwinden [fɛrˈʃvɪndən], *v.n. irr.* (*aux.* sein) disappear, vanish.

verschwommen [fɛrˈʃvɔmən], *adj.* vague, blurred.

verschwören [fɛrˈʃvøːrən], *v.r. irr. sich* —, plot, conspire.

Verschwörer [fɛrˈʃvøːrer], *m.* (—s, *pl.* —) conspirator.

Verschwörung [fɛrˈʃvøːruŋ], *f.* (—, *pl.* —en) conspiracy.

Versehen [fɛrˈzeːən], *n.* (—s, *pl.* —) error, mistake, oversight.

versehen [fɛrˈzeːən], *v.a. irr.* provide; perform; fill (an office); *einen — mit,* furnish s.o. with. — *v.r. sich* —, make a mistake.

versehren [fɛrˈzeːrən], *v.a.* wound; disable.

versenden [fɛrˈzɛndən], *v.a. irr.* forward, consign, send off.

Versender [fɛrˈzɛndər], *m.* (—s, *pl.*—) consigner, exporter.

Versendung [fɛrˈzɛnduŋ], *f.* (—, *no pl.*) transmission, shipping.

Versendungskosten [fɛrˈzɛnduŋskɔstən], *f. pl.* forwarding charges.

versengen [fɛrˈzɛŋən], *v.a.* singe, scorch.

versenken [fɛrˈzɛŋkən], *v.a.* sink; (*ship*) scuttle.

Versenkung [fɛrˈzɛŋkuŋ], *f.* (—, *no pl.*) sinking; hollow; (*ship*) scuttling; (*Theat.*) trap-door.

versessen [fɛrˈzɛsən], *adj.* — *sein auf,* be bent upon, be mad on.

versetzen [fɛrˈzɛtsən], *v.a.* transplant, remove; give; pawn, pledge; transfer; (*pupil*) promote to a higher form. — *v.r. sich in die Lage eines anderen* —, put o.s. in s.o. else's position.

versichern [fɛrˈzɪçərn], *v.a.* assert, declare, aver, assure (s.o. of s.th); insure (s.th.).

Versicherung [fɛrˈzɪçəruŋ], *f.* (—, *pl.* —en) assurance, assertion; insurance.

Versicherungsgesellschaft [fɛrˈzɪçəruŋsgəzɛlʃaft], *f.* (—, *pl.* —en) insurance company.

Versicherungsprämie [fɛrˈzɪçəruŋsprɛːmjə], *f.* (—, *pl.* —n) insurance premium.

versiegbar [fɛrˈziːkbaːr], *adj.* exhaustible.

versiegeln [fɛrˈziːgəln], *v.a.* seal (up).

versiegen [fɛrˈziːgən], *v.n.* (*aux.* sein) dry up, be exhausted.

versilbern [fɛrˈzɪlbərn], *v.a.* plate with silver; (*fig.*) convert into money.

versinken [fɛrˈzɪŋkən], *v.n. irr.* sink; (*ship*) founder; sink; *versunken sein,* be absorbed (in s.th.).

Versmaß [ˈfɛrsmaːs], *n.* (—es, *pl.* —e) metre.

versoffen [fɛrˈzɔfən], *adj.* (*vulg.*) drunken.

versohlen [fɛrˈzoːlən], *v.a.* (*coll.*) thrash (s.o.).

versöhnen [fɛrˈzøːnən], *v.r. sich mit einem* —, become reconciled with s.o.

versöhnlich [fɛrˈzøːnlɪç], *adj.* propitiatory, conciliatory.

Versöhnung [fɛrˈzøːnuŋ], *f.* (—, *no pl.*) reconciliation.

versorgen [fɛrˈzɔrgən], *v.a.* provide with; take care of; support, maintain.

Versorger [fɛrˈzɔrgər], *m.* (—s, *pl.* —) provider.

Versorgung [fɛrˈzɔrguŋ], *f.* (—, *no pl.*) provision, maintenance.

verspäten [fɛrˈʃpɛːtən], *v.r. sich* —, be late, be behind time; (*train*) be overdue.

Verspätung [fɛrˈʃpɛːtuŋ], *f.* (—, *no pl.*) delay; lateness.

verspeisen [fɛrˈʃpaɪzən], *v.a.* eat up.

versperren [fɛrˈʃpɛrən], *v.a.* block up, barricade, close.

verspielen [fɛrˈʃpiːlən], *v.a.* lose (at play); gamble away. — *v.r. sich* —, play wrong.

verspielt [fɛrˈʃpiːlt], *adj.* playful.

verspotten [fɛrˈʃpɔtən], *v.a.* deride, scoff at.

versprechen [fɛrˈʃprɛçən], *v.a. irr.* promise. — *v.r. sich* —, make a slip of the tongue.

Versprechen [fɛrˈʃprɛçən], *n.* (—s, *pl.* —) promise.

versprengen [fɛrˈʃprɛŋən], *v.a.* disperse.

verspüren [fɛrˈʃpyːrən], *v.a.* feel, perceive.

verstaatlichen [fɛrˈʃtaːtlɪçən], *v.a.* nationalise.

Verstand [fɛrˈʃtant], *m.* (—(e)s, *no pl.*) intellect, intelligence, sense; understanding, reason, mind.

verstandesmäßig [fɛrˈʃtandəsmɛːsɪç], *adj.* rational, reasonable.

Verstandesschärfe [fɛrˈʃtandəsʃɛrfə], *f.* (—, *no pl.*) penetration, acumen.

verständig [fɛrˈʃtɛndɪç], *adj.* judicious, sensible, reasonable.

verständigen [fɛrˈʃtɛndɪgən], *v.a.* inform, notify. — *v.r. sich mit einem* —, come to an agreement with s.o.

Verständigung [fɛrˈʃtɛndɪguŋ], *f.* (—, *pl.* —en) understanding, agreement; information; arrangement.

verständlich [fɛrˈʃtɛntlɪç], *adj.* intelligible, clear, understandable.

Verständnis [fɛrˈʃtɛntnɪs], (—ses, *no pl.*) comprehension, understanding, perception, insight.

verständnisinnig

verständnisinnig [fɛrˈʃtɛntnɪsɪnɪç], *adj.* sympathetic; having profound insight.

verstärken [fɛrˈʃtɛrkən], *v.a.* strengthen, reinforce, intensify.

Verstärker [fɛrˈʃtɛrkər], *m.* (**—s,** *pl.* **—**) amplifier; magnifier.

Verstärkung [fɛrˈʃtɛrkuŋ], *f.* (**—,** *pl.* **—en**) strengthening, intensification, amplification; (*Mil.*) reinforcements.

verstauben [fɛrˈʃtaubən], *v.n.* (*aux.* sein) get dusty.

verstauchen [fɛrˈʃtauxən], *v.a.* wrench, sprain, dislocate.

verstauen [fɛrˈʃtauən], *v.a.* stow away.

Versteck [fɛrˈʃtɛk], *n.* (**—s,** *pl.* **—e**) hiding-place; place of concealment; **—(en)** spielen, play hide-and-seek.

verstecken [fɛrˈʃtɛkən], *v.a.* hide, conceal.

versteckt [fɛrˈʃtɛkt], *adj.* indirect, veiled.

verstehen [fɛrˈʃteːən], *v.a. irr.* understand, comprehend.

versteigen [fɛrˈʃtaɪgən], *v.r. irr. sich —*, climb too high; (*fig.*) go too far.

versteigern [fɛrˈʃtaɪgərn], *v.a.* sell by auction.

Versteigerung [fɛrˈʃtaɪgəruŋ], *f.* (**—,** *pl.* **—en**) auction, public sale.

versteinern [fɛrˈʃtaɪnərn], *v.n.* (*aux.* sein) turn into stone, petrify.

verstellbar [fɛrˈʃtɛlbaːr], *adj.* adjustable.

verstellen [fɛrˈʃtɛlən], *v.a.* adjust; (*voice*) disguise. — *v.r. sich —,* sham, pretend.

versterben [fɛrˈʃtɛrbən], *v.n. irr.* (*aux.* sein) (*Poet.*) die.

versteuern [fɛrˈʃtɔyərn], *v.a.* pay tax on.

verstiegen [fɛrˈʃtiːgən], *adj.* eccentric, extravagant.

verstimmen [fɛrˈʃtɪmən], *v.a.* (*Mus.*) put out of tune; (*fig.*) put out of humour, annoy.

Verstimmtheit [fɛrˈʃtɪmthaɪt], *f.* (**—,** *no pl.*) ill-humour, ill-temper, pique.

Verstimmung [fɛrˈʃtɪmuŋ], *f.* (**—,** *pl.* **—en**) bad temper, ill-feeling.

verstockt [fɛrˈʃtɔkt], *adj.* stubborn, obdurate.

Verstocktheit [fɛrˈʃtɔkthaɪt], *f.* (**—,** *no pl.*) stubbornness, obduracy.

verstohlen [fɛrˈʃtoːlən], *adj.* surreptitious, clandestine, furtive.

verstopfen [fɛrˈʃtɔpfən], *v.a.* stop up; block (up); *verstopft sein*, be constipated.

Verstopfung [fɛrˈʃtɔpfuŋ], *f.* (**—,** *pl.* **—en**) obstruction, constipation.

verstorben [fɛrˈʃtɔrbən], *adj.* deceased, late.

verstört [fɛrˈʃtøːrt], *adj.* troubled, worried; distracted.

Verstörtheit [fɛrˈʃtøːrthaɪt], *f.* (**—,** *no pl.*) consternation, agitation; distraction; haggardness.

Verstoß [fɛrˈʃtoːs], *m.* (**—es,** *pl.* **⸚e**) blunder, mistake; offence.

verstoßen [fɛrˈʃtoːsən], *v.a. irr.* cast off, disown, repudiate. — *v.n. —*

gegen, offend against, act in a manner contrary to.

verstreichen [fɛrˈʃtraɪçən], *v.n. irr.* (*aux.* sein) (*time*) elapse, pass away.

verstricken [fɛrˈʃtrɪkən], *v.a.* entangle, ensnare.

Verstrickung [fɛrˈʃtrɪkuŋ], *f.* (**—,** *pl.* **—en**) entanglement.

verstümmeln [fɛrˈʃtyməln], *v.a.* mutilate, mangle.

verstummen [fɛrˈʃtumən], *v.n.* (*aux.* sein) grow silent; become speechless.

Verstümmlung [fɛrˈʃtymluŋ], *f.* (**—,** *pl.* **—en**) mutilation.

Versuch [fɛrˈzuːx], *m.* (**—s,** *pl.* **—e**) attempt, trial, endeavour; (*science*) experiment; (*Lit.*) essay.

versuchen [fɛrˈzuːxən], *v.a.* try, attempt, endeavour; (*food*) taste; *einen —,* tempt s.o.

Versucher [fɛrˈzuːxər], *m.* (**—s,** *pl.* **—**) tempter.

Versuchskaninchen [fɛrˈzuːxskaniːnçən], *n.* (**—s,** *pl.* **—**) (*fig.*) guinea-pig.

Versuchung [fɛrˈzuːxuŋ], *f.* (**—,** *pl.* **—en**) temptation.

versündigen [fɛrˈzyndɪgən], *v.r. sich —,* sin (against).

Versunkenheit [fɛrˈzuŋkənhaɪt], *f.* (**—,** *no pl.*) absorption, preoccupation.

vertagen [fɛrˈtaːgən], *v.a.* adjourn, prorogue.

Vertagung [fɛrˈtaːguŋ], *f.* (**—,** *pl.* **—en**) adjournment, prorogation.

vertauschen [fɛrˈtauʃən], *v.a.* exchange, barter, mistake, confuse.

verteidigen [fɛrˈtaɪdɪgən], *v.a.* defend, uphold, vindicate; (*fig.*) maintain.

Verteidiger [fɛrˈtaɪdɪgər], *m.* (**—s,** *pl.* **—**) defender; (*Law*) counsel for the defence.

Verteidigung [fɛrˈtaɪdɪguŋ], *f.* (**—,** *no pl.*) defence; justification.

Verteidigungskrieg [fɛrˈtaɪdɪguŋskriːk], *m.* (**—(e)s,** *pl.* **—e**) defensive war.

verteilen [fɛrˈtaɪlən], *v.a.* distribute, allot, allocate.

Verteilung [fɛrˈtaɪluŋ], *f.* (**—,** *pl.* **—en**) distribution, apportionment.

verteuern [fɛrˈtɔyərn], *v.a.* make dearer, raise the price of.

verteufelt [fɛrˈtɔyfəlt], *adj.* devilish. — *adv.* (*coll.*) awfully, infernally.

vertiefen [fɛrˈtiːfən], *v.a.* deepen.

vertieft [fɛrˈtiːft], *adj.* absorbed, deep in thought.

Vertiefung [fɛrˈtiːfuŋ], *f.* (**—,** *pl.* **—en**) cavity, recess, hollow; (*knowledge*) deepening; (*fig.*) absorption.

vertilgen [fɛrˈtɪlgən], *v.a.* wipe out, exterminate; (*food*) (*coll.*) polish off.

Vertilgung [fɛrˈtɪlguŋ], *f.* (**—,** *no pl.*) extermination, extirpation.

Vertrag [fɛrˈtraːk], *m.* (**—(e)s,** *pl.* **⸚e**) contract, agreement; (*Pol.*) treaty, pact, convention.

vertragen [fɛrˈtraːgən], *v.a. irr.* suffer, endure; (*food*) digest. — *v.r. sich — mit,* get on well with.

262

vertraglich [fɛr'traːklɪç], *adj.* as per contract, according to agreement.

verträglich [fɛr'trɛːklɪç], *adj.* accommodating, peaceable.

vertragsmäßig [fɛr'traːksmɛːsɪç], *adj.* according to contract.

vertragswidrig [fɛr'traːksviːdrɪç], *adj.* contrary to contract.

vertrauen [fɛr'trauən], *v.n.* rely (upon), trust (in).

Vertrauen [fɛr'trauən], *n.* (—s, *no pl.*) confidence, trust, reliance.

vertrauenerweckend [fɛr'trauənɛrvɛkənt], *adj.* inspiring confidence.

Vertrauensbruch [fɛr'trauənsbrux], *m.* (—es, *pl.* ̈-e) breach of faith.

Vertrauensmann [fɛr'trauənsman], *m.* (—s, *pl.* ̈er) confidant; delegate; person entrusted with s.th.; (*Ind.*) shop steward.

vertrauensselig [fɛr'trauənszeːlɪç], *adj.* confiding, trusting.

Vertrauensvotum [fɛr'trauənsvoːtum], *n.* (—s, *pl.* —ten) vote of confidence.

vertrauenswürdig [fɛr'trauənsvyrdɪç], *adj.* trustworthy.

vertraulich [fɛr'traulɪç], *adj.* confidential; familiar.

Vertraulichkeit [fɛr'traulɪçkaɪt], *f.* (—, *pl.* —en) familiarity.

verträumt [fɛr'trɔymt], *adj.* dreamy.

vertraut [fɛr'traut], *adj.* intimate, familiar; conversant.

Vertraute [fɛr'trautə], *m.* (—n, *pl.* —n) close friend, confidant.

Vertrautheit [fɛr'trauthaɪt], *f.* (—, *no pl.*) familiarity.

vertreiben [fɛr'traɪbən], *v.a. irr.* drive away, expel; eject; (*person*) banish; (*time*) pass, kill; (*goods*) sell.

Vertreibung [fɛr'traɪbuŋ], *f.* (—, *no pl.*) expulsion; banishment.

vertreten [fɛr'treːtən], *v.a. irr.* represent (s.o.), deputise for (s.o.).

Vertreter [fɛr'treːtər], *m.* (—s, *pl.* —) representative, deputy; (*Comm.*) agent.

Vertretung [fɛr'treːtuŋ], *f.* (—, *pl.* —en) representation, agency.

Vertrieb [fɛr'triːp], *m.* (—s, *pl.* —e) sale; distribution.

vertrinken [fɛr'trɪŋkən], *v.a. irr.* spend *or* waste money on drink.

vertrocknen [fɛr'trɔknən], *v.n.* (*aux.* sein) dry up, wither.

vertrödeln [fɛr'trøːdəln], *v.a.* fritter (o.'s time) away.

vertrösten [fɛr'trøːstən], *v.a.* console; put off; put (s.o.) off with fine words; fob (s.o.) off with vain hopes.

Vertröstung [fɛr'trøːstuŋ], *f.* (—, *pl.* —en) comfort; empty promises.

vertun [fɛr'tuːn], *v.a. irr.* squander, waste.

vertuschen [fɛr'tuʃən], *v.a.* hush up.

verübeln [fɛr'yːbəln], *v.a.* take amiss.

verüben [fɛr'yːbən], *v.a.* commit, perpetrate.

verunehren [fɛr'uneːrən], *v.a.* dishonour, disgrace.

verunglimpfen [fɛr'unɡlɪmpfən], *v.a.* bring into disrepute; defame, calumniate.

Verunglimpfung [fɛr'unɡlɪmpfuŋ], *f.* (—, *pl.* —en) defamation, detraction, calumny.

verunglücken [fɛr'unɡlykən], *v.n.* (*aux.* sein) (*person*) meet with an accident; be killed; (*thing*) misfire, fail.

verunreinigen [fɛr'unraɪnɪɡən], *v.a.* contaminate.

Verunreinigung [fɛr'unraɪnɪɡuŋ], *f.* (—, *pl.* —en) contamination.

verunstalten [fɛr'unʃtaltən], *v.a.* disfigure, deface.

Verunstaltung [fɛr'unʃtaltuŋ], *f.* (—, *pl.* —en) disfigurement.

Veruntreuung [fɛr'untrɔyuŋ], *f.* (—, *pl.* —en) embezzlement, misappropriation.

verunzieren [fɛr'untsiːrən], *v.a.* disfigure, spoil.

verursachen [fɛr'uːrzaxən], *v.a.* cause, occasion.

verurteilen [fɛr'urtaɪlən], *v.a.* condemn; (*Law*) sentence.

Verurteilung [fɛr'urtaɪluŋ], *f.* (—, *no pl.*) condemnation; (*Law*) sentence.

vervielfältigen [fɛr'fiːlfɛltɪɡən], *v.a.* multiply; duplicate, make copies of.

Vervielfältigung [fɛr'fiːlfɛltɪɡuŋ], *f.* (—, *pl.* —en) multiplication; duplication, copying.

vervollkommnen [fɛr'fɔlkɔmnən], *v.a.* improve, perfect.

Vervollkommnung [fɛr'fɔlkɔmnuŋ], *f.* (—, *no pl.*) improvement, perfection.

vervollständigen [fɛr'fɔlʃtɛndɪɡən], *v.a.* complete.

Vervollständigung [fɛr'fɔlʃtɛndɪɡuŋ], *f.* (—, *no pl.*) completion.

verwachsen [fɛr'vaksən], *v.n. irr.* (*aux.* sein) grow together; be overgrown. — *adj.* deformed.

verwahren [fɛr'vaːrən], *v.a.* take care of, preserve, secure. — *v.r.* sich — gegen, protest against.

verwahrlosen [fɛr'vaːrloːzən], *v.a.* neglect. — *v.n.* (*aux.* sein) be in need of care and protection, be neglected.

Verwahrlosung [fɛr'vaːrloːzuŋ], *f.* (—, *no pl.*) neglect.

Verwahrung [fɛr'vaːruŋ], *f.* (—, *no pl.*) keeping; charge; *in* — *geben*, deposit, give into s.o.'s charge; — *einlegen gegen*, enter a protest against.

verwalten [fɛr'valtən], *v.a.* manage, administer.

Verwalter [fɛr'valtər], *m.* (—s, *pl.* —) administrator, manager; steward, bailiff.

Verwaltung [fɛr'valtuŋ], *f.* (—, *pl.* —en) administration, management; Civil Service.

Verwaltungsbezirk [fɛr'valtuŋsbətsɪrk], *m.* (—s, *pl.* —e) administrative district.

Verwandlung [fɛr'vandluŋ], *f.* (—, *pl.* —en) alteration, transformation.

Verwandlungskünstler [fɛr'vandluŋs-kynstlər], *m.* (**—s,** *pl.* **—**) quick-change artist.

verwandt [fɛr'vant], *adj.* related; cognate; congenial.

Verwandte [fɛr'vantə], *m.* (**—n,** *pl.* **—n**) relative, relation; kinsman; *der nächste* **—**, next of kin.

Verwandtschaft [fɛr'vantʃaft], *f.* (**—,** *pl.* **—en**) relationship; relations, family; congeniality, sympathy.

verwarnen [fɛr'varnən], *v.a.* admonish, forewarn.

Verwarnung [fɛr'varnuŋ], *f.* (**—,** *pl.* **—en**) admonition.

Verwässerung [fɛr'vɛsəruŋ], *f.* (**—,** *pl.* **—en**) dilution.

verwechseln [fɛr'vɛksəln], *v.a.* confuse; mistake for.

Verwechslung [fɛr'vɛksluŋ], *f.* (**—,** *pl.* **—en**) confusion, mistake.

verwegen [fɛr've:gən], *adj.* bold, audacious.

Verwegenheit [fɛr've:gənhaɪt], *f.* (**—,** *pl.* **—en**) boldness, audacity.

verweichlichen [fɛr'vaɪçlıçən], *v.a.* coddle. **—** *v.n.* (*aux.* sein) become effeminate.

verweigern [fɛr'vaɪgərn], *v.a.* refuse, deny; reject.

Verweigerung [fɛr'vaɪgəruŋ], *f.* (**—,** *pl.* **—en**) refusal, denial; rejection.

verweilen [fɛr'vaɪlən], *v.n.* remain; tarry; stay (with), dwell (on).

verweint [fɛr'vaɪnt], *adj.* (*eyes*) red with weeping.

Verweis [fɛr'vaɪs], *m.* (**—es,** *pl.* **—e**) reproof, reprimand, rebuke.

verweisen [fɛr'vaɪzən], *v.a. irr.* reprimand; banish, exile; **—** *auf etwas,* refer to s.th., hint at s.th.

Verweisung [fɛr'vaɪzuŋ], *f.* (**—,** *pl.* **—en**) banishment, exile; reference.

verweltlichen [fɛr'vɛltlıçən], *v.a.* secularise, profane.

verwenden [fɛr'vɛndən], *v.a.* use, make use of; apply to, employ in, utilize.

Verwendung [fɛr'vɛnduŋ], *f.* (**—,** *pl.* **—en**) application, use, expenditure, employment.

verwerfen [fɛr'vɛrfən], *v.a. irr.* reject, disapprove of.

verwerflich [fɛr'vɛrflıç], *adj.* objectionable.

Verwertung [fɛr've:rtuŋ], *f.* (**—,** *no pl.*) utilisation.

verwesen [fɛr've:zən], *v.a.* administer. **—** *v.n.* (*aux.* sein) rot, decompose, putrefy.

Verweser [fɛr've:zər], *m.* (**—s,** *pl.* **—**) administrator.

Verwesung [fɛr've:zuŋ], *f.* (**—,** *no pl.*) (*office*) administration; putrefaction, rotting.

verwickeln [fɛr'vıkəln], *v.a.* entangle, involve.

verwickelt [fɛr'vıkəlt], *adj.* intricate, complicated, involved.

Verwicklung [fɛr'vıkluŋ], *f.* (**—,** *pl.* **—en**) entanglement, involvement, complication.

verwildern [fɛr'vıldərn], *v.n.* (*aux.* sein) run wild.

verwildert [fɛr'vıldərt], *adj.* wild, uncultivated, overgrown; (*fig.*) intractable.

Verwilderung [fɛr'vıldəruŋ], *f.* (**—,** *no pl.*) running wild, growing wild.

verwirken [fɛr'vırkən], *v.a.* forfeit.

verwirklichen [fɛr'vırklıçən], *v.a.* realise. **—** *v.r. sich* **—**, materialise, come true.

Verwirklichung [fɛr'vırklıçuŋ], *f.* (**—,** *no pl.*) realisation, materialisation.

Verwirkung [fɛr'vırkuŋ], *f.* (**—,** *no pl.*) forfeiture.

verwirren [fɛr'vırən], *v.a.* disarrange, throw into disorder, entangle; puzzle, bewilder, confuse, disconcert.

Verwirrung [fɛr'vıruŋ], *f.* (**—,** *pl.* **—en**) bewilderment, confusion.

verwischen [fɛr'vıʃən], *v.a.* blot out, smudge, obliterate.

verwittern [fɛr'vıtərn], *v.n.* (*aux.* sein) be weather-beaten.

verwöhnen [fɛr'vø:nən], *v.a.* spoil, pamper, coddle.

verworfen [fɛr'vɔrfən], *adj.* profligate; rejected, reprobate.

verworren [fɛr'vɔrən], *adj.* confused, perplexed; intricate; (*speech*) rambling.

verwundbar [fɛr'vuntba:r], *adj.* vulnerable.

verwunden [fɛr'vundən], *v.a.* wound, hurt, injure.

verwundern [fɛr'vundərn], *v.r. sich* **—**, be surprised, wonder, be amazed.

Verwunderung [fɛr'vundəruŋ], *f.* (**—,** *no pl.*) surprise, astonishment, amazement.

Verwundung [fɛr'vunduŋ], *f.* (**—,** *pl.* **—en**) wounding, wound, injury.

verwunschen [fɛr'vunʃən], *adj.* enchanted, spellbound, bewitched.

verwünschen [fɛr'vynʃən], *v.a.* curse; cast a spell on, bewitch.

verwünscht [fɛr'vynʃt], *excl.* confound it!

Verwünschung [fɛr'vynʃuŋ], *f.* (**—,** *pl.* **—en**) curse, malediction.

verwüsten [fɛr'vy:stən], *v.a.* devastate, ravage, lay waste.

Verwüstung [fɛr'vy:stuŋ], *f.* (**—,** *pl.* **—en**) devastation.

verzagen [fɛr'tsa:gən], *v.n.* (*aux.* sein) lose heart, lose courage.

verzagt [fɛr'tsa:kt], *adj.* fainthearted, discouraged.

Verzagtheit [fɛr'tsa:kthaɪt], *f.* (**—,** *no pl.*) faintheartedness.

verzählen [fɛr'tsɛ:lən], *v.r. sich* **—**, miscount.

verzapfen [fɛr'tsapfən], *v.a.* sell (liquor) on draught; (*fig.*) tell (a story), talk (nonsense).

verzärteln [fɛr'tsɛ:rtəln], *v.a.* pamper, coddle; spoil.

verzaubern [fɛr'tsaubərn], *v.a.* bewitch, charm, put a spell on.

verzehren [fɛr'tse:rən], *v.a.* consume, eat. — *v.r. sich* — *in*, pine away with, be consumed with.

Verzehrung [fɛr'tse:ruŋ], *f.* (—, *no pl.*) (*obs.*) consumption, tuberculosis.

verzeichnen [fɛr'tsaiçnən], *v.a.* draw badly; note down, register, record.

Verzeichnis [fɛr'tsaiçnis], *n.* (—ses, *pl.* —se) catalogue, list, register.

verzeihen [fɛr'tsaiən], *v.a. irr.* forgive, pardon.

verzeihlich [fɛr'tsailiç], *adj.* pardonable, forgivable, excusable, venial.

Verzeihung [fɛr'tsaiuŋ], *f.* (—, *no pl.*) pardon, forgiveness; *ich bitte um* —, I beg your pardon.

verzerren [fɛr'tsɛrən], *v.a.* distort.

Verzerrung [fɛr'tsɛruŋ], *f.* (—, *pl.* —en) distortion; (*face*) grimace.

verzetteln [fɛr'tsɛtəln], *v.a.* disperse, scatter.

Verzicht [fɛr'tsiçt], *m.* (—(e)s, *no pl.*) renunciation, resignation.

verzichten [fɛr'tsiçtən], *v.n.* forgo, renounce.

verziehen [fɛr'tsi:ən], *v.a. irr.* distort; spoil (*child*). — *v.n.* (*aux.* sein) go away, move away.

Verzierung [fɛr'tsi:ruŋ], *f.* (—, *pl.* —en) decoration, ornament.

verzögern [fɛr'tsø:gərn], *v.a.* delay, defer, retard, protract, procrastinate. — *v.r. sich* —, be delayed.

Verzögerung [fɛr'tsø:gəruŋ], *f.* (—, *pl.* —en) delay, retardation, procrastination; time-lag.

verzollen [fɛr'tsɔlən], *v.a.* pay duty on.

Verzücktheit [fɛr'tsykthait], *f.* (—, *no pl.*) ecstasy, rapture.

Verzug [fɛr'tsu:k], *m.* (—s, *no pl.*) delay.

verzweifeln [fɛr'tsvaifəln], *v.n.* despair, be desperate.

Verzweiflung [fɛr'tsvaifluŋ], *f.* (—, *no pl.*) despair.

verzwickt [fɛr'tsvikt], *adj.* complicated, intricate, tricky.

Vesuv [ve'zu:f], *m.* Mount Vesuvius.

Vetter ['vɛtər], *m.* (—s, *pl.* —n) cousin.

Vetternwirtschaft ['vɛtərnvirtʃaft], *f.* (—, *no pl.*) nepotism.

Vexierbild [vɛ'ksi:rbilt], *n.* (—s, *pl.* —er) picture-puzzle.

Vexierspiegel [vɛ'ksi:rʃpi:gəl], *m.* (—s, *pl.*—) distorting mirror.

vibrieren [vi'bri:rən], *v.n.* vibrate.

Vieh [fi:], *n.* (—s, *no pl.*) cattle, livestock.

Viehfutter ['fi:futər], *n.* (—s, *no pl.*) forage, fodder, feeding-stuff.

viehisch ['fi:iʃ], *adj.* beastly, brutal.

Viehwagen ['fi:va:gən], *m.* (—s, *pl.* —) cattle-truck.

Viehweide ['fi:vaidə], *f.* (—, *pl.* —n) pasture, pasturage.

Viehzüchter ['fi:tsyçtər], *m.* (—s, *pl.* —) cattle-breeder.

viel [fi:l], *adj.* much, a great deal, a lot; (*pl.*) many.

vielartig ['fi:lartiç], *adj.* multifarious.

vieldeutig ['fi:ldɔytiç], *adj.* ambiguous, equivocal.

Vieleck ['fi:lɛk], *n.* (—s, *pl.* —e) polygon.

vielerlei ['fi:lərlai], *adj.* of many kinds, various.

vielfältig ['fi:lfɛltiç], *adj.* manifold.

vielfarbig ['fi:lfarbiç], *adj.* multicoloured, variegated.

Vielfraß ['fi:lfra:s], *m.* (—es, *pl.* —e) glutton.

vielgeliebt ['fi:lɡəli:pt], *adj.* much loved.

vielgereist ['fi:lɡəraist], *adj.* much travelled.

vielleicht [fi'laiçt], *adv.* perhaps, maybe.

vielmals ['fi:lma:ls], *adv.* many times, frequently, much.

Vielmännerei [fi:lmɛnə'rai], *f.* (—, *no pl.*) polyandry.

vielmehr [fi:l'me:r], *adv.* rather, much more. — *conj.* rather, on the other hand.

vielsagend ['fi:lza:gənt], *adj.* expressive, full of meaning.

vielseitig ['fi:lzaitiç], *adj.* multilateral; (*fig.*) versatile.

Vielseitigkeit ['fi:lzaitiçkait], *f.* (—, *no pl.*) versatility.

vielverheißend ['fi:lfɛrhaisənt], *adj.* promising, auspicious.

Vielweiberei [fi:lvaibə'rai], *f.* (—, *no pl.*) polygamy.

vier [fi:r], *num. adj.* four.

Viereck ['fi:rɛk], *n.* (—s, *pl.* —e) square, quadrangle.

viereckig ['fi:rɛkiç], *adj.* square.

vierfüßig ['fi:rfy:siç], *adj.* four-footed.

vierhändig ['fi:rhɛndiç], *adj.* fourhanded; — *spielen*, (*piano*) play duets.

vierschrötig ['fi:rʃrø:tiç], *adj.* robust, thick-set, stocky.

vierseitig ['fi:rzaitiç], *adj.* quadrilateral.

vierstimmig ['fi:rʃtimiç], *adj.* (*Mus.*) four-part; for four voices.

vierteilen ['fi:rtailən], *v.a.* quarter, divide into four parts.

Viertel ['firtəl], *n.* (—s, *pl.* —) quarter, fourth part.

Viertelstunde [firtəl'ʃtundə], *f.* (—, *pl.* —n) quarter of an hour.

viertens ['fi:rtəns], *num. adv.* fourthly, in the fourth place.

Vierwaldstättersee [fi:r'valtʃtɛtərze:], *m.* Lake Lucerne.

vierzehn ['firtse:n], *num. adj.* fourteen; — *Tage*, a fortnight.

vierzig ['firtsiç], *num. adj.* forty.

Vietnam [viɛt'na:m], *n.* Vietnam.

Vikar [vi'ka:r], *m.* (—s, *pl.* —e) curate.

Violinschlüssel [vio'li:nʃlysəl], *m.* (—s, *pl.* —) (*Mus.*) treble clef.

Virtuosität [virtuozi'tɛ:t], *f.* (—, *no pl.*) mastery, virtuosity.

Visage [vi'za:ʒə], *f.* (—, *pl.* —n) (*coll.*) face.

Visier [vi'zi:r], *n.* (—, *pl.* —e) visor; (*gun*) sight.

Vision [vi'zjo:n], *f.* (—, *pl.* —en) vision.

Visionär

Visionär [vizjo'nɛ:r], *m.* (—s, *pl.* —e) visionary.
Visitenkarte [vi'zi:tənkartə], *f.* (—, *pl.* —n) card, visiting card.
Visum ['vi:zum], *n.* (—s, *pl.* Visa) visa.
Vizekönig ['vi:tsəkø:nɪç], *m.* (—s, *pl.* —e) viceroy.
Vlies [fli:s], *n.* (—es, *pl.* —e) fleece.
Vogel ['fo:gəl], *m.* (—s, *pl.* ∺) bird; (*coll.*) fellow; *einen — haben*, be off o.'s head.
Vogelbauer ['fo:gəlbauər], *n.* (—s, *pl.* —) bird-cage.
Vogelfänger ['fo:gəlfɛŋər], *m.* (—s, *pl.* —) fowler, bird-catcher.
vogelfrei ['fo:gəlfraɪ], *adj.* outlawed, proscribed.
Vogelfutter ['fo:gəlfutər], *n.* (—s, *no pl.*) bird-seed.
Vogelhändler ['fo:gəlhɛndlər], *m.* (—s, *pl.* —) bird-dealer.
Vogelhaus ['fo:gəlhaus], *n.* (—es, *pl.* ∺er) aviary.
Vogelkenner ['fo:gəlkɛnər], *m.* (—s, *pl.* —) ornithologist.
Vogelkunde ['fo:gəlkundə], *f.* (—, *no pl.*) ornithology.
Vogelperspektive ['fo:gəlpɛrspɛkti:və], *f.* (—, *no pl.*) bird's-eye view.
Vogelschau ['fo:gəlʃau], *f.* (—, *no pl.*) bird's-eye view.
Vogelsteller ['fo:gəlʃtɛlər], *m.* (—s, *pl.* —) fowler, bird-catcher.
Vogesen [vo'ge:zən], *pl.* Vosges Mountains.
Vogler ['fo:glər], *m.* (—s, *pl.* —) fowler.
Vogt [fo:kt], *m.* (—(e)s, *pl.* ∺e) prefect, bailiff, steward, provost.
Vogtei [fo:k'taɪ], *f.* (—, *pl.* —en) prefecture, bailiwick.
Vokabel [vo'ka:bəl], *f.* (—, *pl.* —n) word, vocable.
Vokabelbuch [vo'ka:bəlbu:x], *n.* (—(e)s, *pl.* ∺er) vocabulary (book).
Vokal [vo'ka:l], *m.* (—s, *pl.* —e) vowel.
Vokativ [voka'ti:f], *m.* (—s, *pl.* —e) (*Gram.*) vocative.
Volk [fɔlk], *n.* (—(e)s, *pl.* ∺er) people, nation; *das gemeine —,* mob, the common people.
Völkerkunde ['fœlkərkundə], *f.* (—, *no pl.*) ethnology.
Völkerrecht ['fœlkərrɛçt], *n.* (—s, *no pl.*) international law.
Völkerschaft ['fœlkərʃaft], *f.* (—, *pl.* —en) tribe, people.
Völkerwanderung ['fœlkərvandəruŋ], *f.* (—, *pl.* —en) mass migration.
Volksabstimmung ['fɔlksapʃtɪmuŋ], *f.* (—, *pl.* —en) referendum.
Volksausgabe ['fɔlksausga:bə], *f.* (—, *pl.* —n) popular edition.
Volksbeschluß ['fɔlksbəʃlus], *m.* (—sses, *pl.* ∺sse) plebiscite.
Volksbibliothek ['fɔlksbiblio:k], *f.* (—, *pl.* —en) public library.
Volkscharakter ['fɔlkskaraktər], *m.* (—s, *no pl.*) national character.

Volksentscheid ['fɔlksɛntʃaɪt], *m.* (—s, *pl.* —e) plebiscite.
Volksführer ['fɔlksfy:rər], *m.* (—s, *pl.* —) demagogue.
Volksheer ['fɔlkshe:r], *n.* (—s, *pl.* —e) national army.
Volksherrschaft ['fɔlksherʃaft], *f.* (—, *no pl.*) democracy.
Volkshochschule ['fɔlkshoxʃu:lə], *f.* (—, *no pl.*) adult education (classes).
Volksjustiz ['fɔlksjusti:ts], *f.* (—, *no pl.*) lynch-law.
Volkskunde ['fɔlkskundə], *f.* (—, *no pl.*) folklore.
Volkslied ['fɔlksli:t], *n.* (—s, *pl.* —er) folk-song.
Volksschicht ['fɔlksʃɪçt], *f.* (—, *pl.* —en) class.
Volksschule ['fɔlksʃu:lə], *f.* (—, *pl.* —n) primary school; elementary school.
Volkssitte ['fɔlkszɪtə], *f.* (—, *pl.* —n) national custom.
Volkssprache ['fɔlksʃpra:xə], *f.* (—, *pl.* —n) vernacular.
Volksstamm ['fɔlksʃtam], *m.* (—s, *pl.* ∺e) tribe.
Volkstracht ['fɔlkstraxt], *f.* (—, *pl.* —en) national costume.
volkstümlich ['fɔlksty:mlɪç], *adj.* national, popular.
Volksvertretung ['fɔlksfɛrtre:tuŋ], *f.* (—, *no pl.*) representation of the people, parliamentary representation.
Volkswirt ['fɔlksvɪrt], *m.* (—s, *pl.* —e) political economist.
Volkswirtschaft ['fɔlksvɪrtʃaft], *f.* (—, *no pl.*) political economy.
Volkszählung ['fɔlkstse:luŋ], *f.* (—, *pl.* —en) census.
voll [fɔl], *adj.* full, filled; whole, complete, entire.
vollauf ['fɔlauf], *adv.* abundantly.
Vollbart ['fɔlba:rt], *m.* (—s, *pl.* ∺e) beard.
vollberechtigt ['fɔlbərɛçtɪçt], *adj.* fully entitled.
Vollbild ['fɔlbɪlt], *n.* (—s, *pl.* —er) full-length portrait, full-page illustration.
Vollblut ['fɔlblu:t], *n.* (—s, *pl.* ∺er) thoroughbred.
vollblütig ['fɔlbly:tɪç], *adj.* full-blooded, thoroughbred.
vollbringen [fɔl'brɪŋən], *v.a. irr.* accomplish, achieve, complete.
Vollbringung [fɔl'brɪŋuŋ], *f.* (—, *no pl.*) achievement.
Volldampf ['fɔldampf], *m.* (—es, *no pl.*) full steam.
vollenden [fɔl'ɛndən], *v.a.* finish, complete.
vollendet [fɔl'ɛndət], *adj.* finished; accomplished.
vollends ['fɔlɛnts], *adv.* quite, altogether, wholly, entirely, moreover.
Vollendung [fɔl'ɛnduŋ], *f.* (—, *no pl.*) completion; perfection.
Völlerei [fœlə'raɪ], *f.* (—, *pl.* —en) gluttony.

266

Vorbereitung

vollführen [fɔl'fy:rən], *v.a.* execute, carry out.

Vollgefühl ['fɔlgəfy:l], *n.* (—s, *no pl.*) consciousness, full awareness.

Vollgenuß ['fɔlgənus], *m.* (—sses, *no pl.*) full enjoyment.

vollgültig ['fɔlgyltɪç], *adj.* fully valid; unexceptionable.

Vollheit ['fɔlhaɪt], *f.* (—, *no pl.*) fullness, plenitude.

völlig ['fœlɪç], *adj.* entire, whole, complete.

vollinhaltlich ['fɔlɪnhaltlɪç], *adv.* to its full extent.

volljährig ['fɔljɛːrɪç], *adj.* of age.

Volljährigkeit ['fɔljɛːrɪçkaɪt], *f.* (—, *no pl.*) adult years, majority.

vollkommen ['fɔlkɔmən], *adj.* perfect. — *adv.* entirely.

Vollkommenheit [fɔl'kɔmənhaɪt], *f.* (—, *no pl.*) perfection.

Vollmacht ['fɔlmaxt], *f.* (—, *pl.* —en) authority; fullness of power; power of attorney.

vollsaftig ['fɔlzaftɪç], *adj.* juicy, succulent.

vollständig ['fɔlʃtɛndɪç], *adj.* complete, full. — *adv.* entirely.

vollstrecken [fɔl'ʃtrɛkən], *v.a.* execute, carry out.

Vollstrecker [fɔl'ʃtrɛkər], *m.* (—s, *pl.* —) executor.

volltönig ['fɔltøːnɪç], *adj.* sonorous.

vollwertig ['fɔlvɛrtɪç], *adj.* standard, sterling.

vollzählig ['fɔltsɛːlɪç], *adj.* complete.

vollziehen [fɔl'tsiːən], *v.a. irr.* execute, carry out, ratify.

vollziehend [fɔl'tsiːənt], *adj.* executive.

Vollziehungsgewalt [fɔl'tsiːuŋsgəvalt], *f.* (—, *no pl.*) executive power.

Vollzug [fɔl'tsuːk], *m.* (—s, *no pl.*) execution; fulfilment.

Volontär [volɔ'tɛːr], *m.* (—s, *pl.* —e) volunteer.

von [fɔn] (*von dem* becomes **vom**), *prep.* (*Dat.*) by, from; of; on; concerning, about; — *Shakespeare*, by Shakespeare; — *Beruf*, by profession; *er kommt* — *London*, he comes from London; — *fern*, from afar; —*jetzt an*, from now on; — *einem sprechen*, speak of s.o.; *dein Brief vom 15.*, your letter of the 15th.

vonnöten [fɔn'nøːtən], *adv.* — *sein*, be necessary.

vonstatten [fɔn'ʃtatən], *adv.* — *gehen*, progress; go off.

vor [foːr], *prep.* (*Dat., Acc.*) (*place*) before, ahead of, in front of; (*time*) before, prior to, earlier than; (*from*; of; with; above; in presence of, because of; more than; — *dem Hause*, in front of the house; — *Sonnenaufgang*, before sunrise; —*zwei Tagen*, two days ago; *sich — einem verstecken*, hide from s.o.; *sich hüten* —, beware of; *starr* — *Kälte*, stiff with cold; — *allem*, above all. — *adv.* before; *nach wie* —, now as before.

Vorabend ['foːraːbənt], *m.* (—s, *pl.* —e) eve.

Vorahnung ['foːraːnuŋ], *f.* (—, *pl.* —en) presentiment, foreboding.

voran [fo'ran], *adv.* before, in front, forward, on.

vorangehen [fo'ranɡeːən], *v.n. irr.* (*aux. sein*) take the lead, go ahead.

Voranzeige ['foːrantsaɪɡə], *f.* (—, *pl.* —n) advance notice; (*film*) trailer.

Vorarbeiter ['foːrarbaɪtər], *m.* (—s, *pl.* —) foreman.

voraus [fo'raus], *adv.* before, in front, foremost; in advance; *im* or *zum* —, beforehand; (*thanks*) in anticipation.

vorauseilen [fo'rausaɪlən], *v.n.* (*aux. sein*) run ahead.

vorausgehen [fo'rausɡeːən], *v.n.* (*aux. sein*) walk ahead; *einem* —, go before; precede s.o.

voraushaben [fo'rausha:bən], *v.n. irr.* *etwas vor einem* —, have the advantage over s.o.

Voraussage [fo'rauzaːɡə], *f.* (—, *pl.* —n) prediction, prophecy; (*weather*) forecast.

voraussagen [fo'rauzaːɡən], *v.a.* predict, foretell; (*weather*) forecast.

voraussehen [fo'rauzeːən], *v.a. irr.* foresee.

voraussetzen [fo'rauzɛtsən], *v.a.* presuppose, take for granted.

Voraussetzung [fo'rauzɛtsuŋ], *f.* (—, *pl.* —en) supposition, presupposition; *unter der* —, on the understanding.

Voraussicht [fo'rauzɪçt], *f.* (—, *no pl.*) foresight, forethought; *aller* — *nach*, in all probability.

voraussichtlich [fo'rauzɪçtlɪç], *adj.* prospective, presumptive, probable, expected. — *adv.* probably, presumably.

Vorbau ['foːrbau], *m.* (—s, *pl.* —ten) frontage.

Vorbedacht ['foːrbədaxt], *m.* (—s, *no pl.*) premeditation; *mit* —, on purpose, deliberately.

vorbedacht ['foːrbədaxt], *adj.* premeditated.

Vorbedeutung ['foːrbədɔytuŋ], *f.* (—, *pl.* —en) omen.

Vorbehalt ['foːrbəhalt], *m.* (—s, *pl.* —e) reservation, proviso.

vorbehalten ['foːrbəhaltən], *v.a. irr.* reserve; make reservation that.

vorbehaltlich ['foːrbəhaltlɪç], *prep.* (*Genit.*) with the proviso that.

vorbei [foːr'baɪ], *adv.* by; along; past, over, finished, gone.

vorbeigehen [foːr'baɪɡeːən], *v.n. irr.* (*aux. sein*) pass by; go past; march past.

vorbeilassen [foːr'baɪlasən], *v.a. irr.* let pass.

Vorbemerkung ['foːrbəmɛrkuŋ], *f.* (—, *pl.* —en) preface, prefatory note.

vorbereiten ['foːrbəraɪtən], *v.a.* prepare.

Vorbereitung ['foːrbəraɪtuŋ], *f.* (—, *pl.* —en) preparation.

Vorbesitzer ['fo:rbəzɪtsər], *m.* (**—s,** *pl.* **—**) previous owner.
Vorbesprechung ['fo:rbəʃprɛçuŋ], *f.* (**—,** *pl.* **—en**) preliminary discussion.
vorbestimmen ['fo:rbəʃtɪmən], *v.a.* predestine, predetermine.
Vorbestimmung ['fo:rbəʃtɪmuŋ], *f.* (**—,** *no pl.*) predestination.
vorbestraft ['fo:rbəʃtra:ft], *adj.* previously convicted.
vorbeten ['fo:rbe:tən], *v.n.* lead in prayer.
vorbeugen ['fo:rbɔygən], *v.n.* prevent, preclude, obviate. — *v.r. sich* —, bend forward.
Vorbeugung ['fo:rbɔyguŋ], *f.* (**—,** *no pl.*) prevention; prophylaxis.
Vorbeugungsmaßnahme ['fo:rbɔyguŋsma:sna:mə], *f.* (**—,** *pl.* **—n**) preventive measure.
Vorbild ['fo:rbɪlt], *n.* (**—s,** *pl.* **—er**) model, example, pattern, ideal.
vorbildlich ['fo:rbɪltlɪç], *adj.* exemplary; typical; — *sein,* be a model.
Vorbildung ['fo:rbɪlduŋ], *f.* (**—,** *no pl.*) preparatory training.
Vorbote ['fo:rbo:tə], *m.* (**—n,** *pl.* **—n**) herald, precursor, forerunner.
vorbringen ['fo:rbrɪŋən], *v.a. irr.* produce, proffer; advance, utter, allege, assert, claim.
vordatieren ['fo:rdati:rən], *v.a.* antedate.
vordem [for'de:m], *adv.* (*obs.*) formerly, once.
Vorderachse ['fordəraksə], *f.* (**—,** *pl.* **—n**) front axle.
Vorderansicht ['fordəranzɪçt], *f.* (**—,** *pl.* **—en**) front view.
Vorderarm ['fordərarm], *m.* (**—s,** *pl.* **—e**) forearm.
Vordergrund ['fordərgrʊnt], *m.* (**—s,** *pl.* **-e**) foreground
vorderhand ['fordərhant], *adv.* for the present.
Vorderseite ['fordərzaɪtə], *f.* (**—,** *pl.* **—n**) front.
vorderst ['fordərst], *adj.* foremost, first.
Vordertür ['fordərty:r], *f.* (**—,** *pl.* **—en**) front door.
Vordertreffen ['fordərtrɛfən], *n.* (**—s,** *no pl.*) *ins* — *kommen,* be in the vanguard, come to the fore.
vordrängen ['fo:rdrɛŋən], *v.r. sich* —, press forward, jump the queue.
vordringen ['fo:rdrɪŋən], *v.n. irr.* (*aux.* sein) advance, push forward.
vordringlich ['fo:rdrɪŋlɪç], *adj.* urgent; forward, importunate.
Vordruck ['fo:rdruk], *m.* (**—s,** *pl.* **—e**) (*printed*) form.
voreilen ['fo:raɪlən], *v.n.* (*aux.* sein) rush forward.
voreilig ['fo:raɪlɪç], *adj.* over-hasty, rash.
Voreiligkeit ['fo:raɪlɪçkaɪt], *f.* (**—,** *no pl.*) hastiness, rashness.
voreingenommen ['fo:raɪŋənɔmən], *adj.* biased, prejudiced.

Voreingenommenheit ['fo:raɪŋənɔmənhaɪt], *f.* (**—,** *no pl.*) bias, prejudice.
Voreltern ['fo:rɛltərn], *pl.* forefathers, ancestors.
vorenthalten ['fo:rɛnthaltən], *v.a. irr. sep. & insep.* withhold.
Vorentscheidung ['fo:rɛntʃaɪduŋ], *f.* (**—,** *pl.* **—en**) preliminary decision.
vorerst [fo:r'e:rst], *adv.* first of all, firstly; for the time being.
vorerwähnt ['fo:rɛrvɛ:nt], *adj.* aforementioned.
Vorfahr ['fo:rfa:r], *m.* (**—en,** *pl.* **—en**) ancestor.
vorfahren ['fo:rfa:rən], *v.n. irr.* (*aux.* sein) drive up (to a house *etc.*).
Vorfall ['fo:rfal], *m.* (**—s,** *pl.* **-e**) occurrence, incident.
vorfinden ['fo:rfɪndən], *v.a. irr.* find, find present, meet with.
Vorfrage ['fo:rfra:gə], *f.* (**—,** *pl.* **—n**) preliminary question.
vorführen ['fo:rfy:rən], *v.a.* bring forward, produce.
Vorführung ['fo:rfy:ruŋ], *f.* (**—,** *pl.* **—en**) production, presentation; performance.
Vorgang ['fo:rgaŋ], *m.* (**—s,** *pl.* **-e**) occurrence, event, happening; proceeding, precedent; procedure.
Vorgänger ['fo:rgɛŋər], *m.* (**—s,** *pl.* **—**) predecessor.
Vorgarten ['fo:rgartən], *m.* (**—s,** *pl.* **-**) front garden.
vorgeben ['fo:rge:bən], *v.a. irr.* pretend; allow (in advance).
Vorgebirge ['fo:rgəbɪrgə], *n.* (**—s,** *no pl.*) cape, promontory.
vorgeblich ['fo:rge:plɪç], *adj.* pretended; ostensible.
vorgefaßt ['fo:rgəfast], *adj.* preconceived.
Vorgefühl ['fo:rgəfy:l], *n.* (**—s,** *pl.* **—e**) presentiment.
vorgehen ['fo:rge:ən], *v.n. irr.* (*aux.* sein) advance, walk ahead; proceed; (*clock*) be fast, gain; (*fig.*) take precedence; occur, happen; *was geht hier vor?* what's going on here?
Vorgehen ['fo:rge:ən], *n.* (**—s,** *no pl.*) (course of) action, (manner of) procedure.
vorgenannt ['fo:rgənant], *adj.* aforenamed.
Vorgericht ['fo:rgərɪçt], *n.* (**—s,** *pl.* **—e**) hors d'œuvre, entrée.
Vorgeschichte ['fo:rgəʃɪçtə], *f.* (**—,** *no pl.*) prehistory; early history; antecedents.
vorgeschichtlich ['fo:rgəʃɪçtlɪç], *adj.* prehistoric.
Vorgeschmack ['fo:rgəʃmak], *m.* (**—s,** *no pl.*) foretaste.
Vorgesetzte ['fo:rgəzɛtstə], *m.* (**—n,** *pl.* **—n**) superior, senior; boss.
vorgestern ['fo:rgɛstərn], *adv.* the day before yesterday.
vorgreifen ['fo:rgraɪfən], *v.n. irr.* anticipate, forestall.

Vorhaben ['fo:rha:bən], m. (—s, no pl.) intention, purpose, design.

vorhaben ['fo:rha:bən], v.a. irr. intend; be busy with; etwas mit einem —, have designs on s.o.; have plans for s.o.

Vorhalle ['fo:rhalə], f. (—, pl. —n) vestibule, hall, porch.

vorhalten ['fo:rhaltən], v.a. irr. hold s.th. before s.o.; (fig.) remonstrate (with s.o. about s.th.); reproach. — v.n. last.

Vorhaltungen ['fo:rhaltuŋən], f. pl. remonstrances, expostulations.

vorhanden [for'handən], adj. at hand, present, in stock, on hand.

Vorhandensein [for'handənzaın], n. (—s, no pl.) existence; availability.

Vorhang ['fo:rhaŋ], m. (—s, pl. ⁀e) curtain.

Vorhängeschloß ['fo:rhɛŋəʃlɔs], n. (—sses, pl. ⁀sser) padlock.

vorher ['fo:rhe:r], adv. before, beforehand, in advance.

vorhergehen [fo:r'he:rge:ən], v.n. irr. (aux. sein) go before, precede.

vorhergehend [fo:r'he:rge:ənt], adj. foregoing, aforesaid, preceding.

vorherig [fo:r'he:rɪç], adj. preceding, previous, former.

vorherrschen ['fo:rhɛrʃən], v.n. prevail, predominate.

vorhersagen [fo:r'he:rza:gən], v.a. predict, foretell.

vorhersehen [fo:r'he:rze:ən], v.a. irr. foresee.

vorheucheln ['fo:rhɔyçəln], v.a. einem etwas —, pretend s.th. to s.o.

vorhin [fo:r'hɪn], adv. just before, a short while ago.

Vorhof ['fo:rho:f], m. (—s, pl. ⁀e) forecourt.

Vorhölle ['fo:rhœlə], f. (—, no pl.) limbo.

Vorhut ['fo:rhu:t], f. (—, no pl.) vanguard.

vorig ['fo:rɪç], adj. former, preceding.

Vorjahr ['fo:rja:r], n. (—s, pl. —e) preceding year.

vorjammern ['fo:rjamərn], v.n. einem etwas —, moan to s.o. about s.th.

Vorkämpfer ['fo:rkɛmpfər], m. (—s, pl. —) champion; pioneer.

vorkauen ['fo:rkauən], v.a. (fig.) predigest; spoon-feed.

Vorkaufsrecht ['fo:rkaufsrɛçt], n. (—s, no pl.) right of first refusal, right of pre-emption.

Vorkehrung ['fo:rke:ruŋ], f. (—, pl. —en) preparation; precaution; (pl.) arrangements.

Vorkenntnisse ['fo:rkɛntnɪsə], f. pl. rudiments, elements, grounding; previous knowledge.

vorkommen ['fo:rkɔmən], v.n. irr. (aux. sein) occur, happen; be found.

Vorkommnis ['fo:rkɔmnɪs], n. (—ses, pl. —se) occurrence, event, happening.

Vorkriegs- ['fo:rkri:ks], prefix. prewar.

Vorladung ['fo:rla:duŋ], f. (—, pl. —en) summons, writ, subpœna.

Vorlage ['fo:rla:gə], f. (—, pl. —n) pattern, master-copy.

vorlagern ['fo:rla:gərn], v.n. (aux. sein) extend (in front of).

Vorland ['fo:rlant], n. (—s, pl. ⁀er) cape, foreland, foreshore.

vorlassen ['fo:rlasən], v.a. irr. give precedence to; admit, show in.

Vorläufer ['fo:rlɔyfər], m. (—s, pl. —) forerunner, precursor.

vorläufig ['fo:rlɔyfɪç], adj. provisional, preliminary, temporary. — adv. for the time being.

vorlaut ['fo:rlaut], adj. pert, forward.

Vorleben ['fo:rle:bən], n. (—s, no pl.) antecedents, past life.

vorlegen ['fo:rle:gən], v.a. put before s.o.; submit, propose; (food) serve.

Vorleger ['fo:rle:gər], m. (—s, pl. —) rug, mat.

Vorlegeschloß ['fo:rle:gəʃlɔs], n. (—sses, pl. ⁀sser) padlock.

vorlesen ['fo:rle:zən], v.a. irr. read aloud, read out.

Vorlesung ['fo:rle:zuŋ], f. (—, pl. —en) lecture.

vorletzte ['fo:rlɛtstə], adj. last but one, penultimate.

Vorliebe ['fo:rli:bə], f. (—, no pl.) predilection, partiality.

vorliebnehmen [for'li:pne:mən], v.n. — mit etwas, be content with s.th., take pot luck.

vorliegen ['fo:rli:gən], v.n. irr. (aux. sein) be under consideration.

vorlügen ['fo:rly:gən], v.a. irr. einem etwas —, tell lies to s.o.

vormachen ['fo:rmaxən], v.a. einem etwas —, show s.o. how a thing is done; (fig.) play tricks on s.o., deceive s.o.

vormalig ['fo:rma:lɪç], adj. former, erstwhile, late.

vormals ['fo:rma:ls], adv. formerly.

Vormarsch ['fo:rmarʃ], m. (—es, pl. ⁀e) (Mil.) advance.

vormerken ['fo:rmɛrkən], v.a. make a note of, take down; book.

Vormittag ['fo:rmɪta:k], m. (—s, pl. —e) morning, forenoon.

vormittags ['fo:rmɪta:ks], adv. in the morning; before noon.

Vormund ['fo:rmunt], m. (—s, pl. ⁀er) guardian.

Vormundschaft ['fo:rmuntʃaft], f. (—, pl. —en) guardianship.

Vormundschaftsgericht ['fo:rmuntʃaftsgərɪçt], n. (—s, pl. —e) Court of Chancery.

vorn [fɔrn], adv. before, in front of; in front; (Naut.) fore.

Vorname ['fo:rna:mə], m. (—ns, pl. —n) first name, Christian name.

vornehm ['fo:rne:m], adj. of noble birth, refined; distinguished, elegant.

vornehmen ['fo:rne:mən], v.a. irr. take in hand; sich etwas —, undertake s.th.; plan or intend to do s.th.

Vornehmheit ['foːrneːmhaɪt], *f.* (—, *no pl.*) refinement, distinction.
vornehmlich ['foːrneːmlɪç], *adv.* chiefly, principally, especially.
vornherein ['fɔrnhɛraɪn], *adv. von* —, from the first; from the beginning.
Vorort ['foːrɔrt], *m.* (—s, *pl.* —e) suburb.
Vorortsbahn ['foːrɔrtsbaːn], *f.* (—, *pl.* —en) suburban (railway) line.
Vorplatz ['foːrplats], *m.* (—es, *pl.* ⁓e) forecourt.
Vorposten ['foːrpɔstən], *m.* (—s, *pl.* —) (*Mil.*) outpost, pickets.
Vorpostengefecht ['foːrpɔstəngəfɛçt], *n.* (—s, *pl.* —e) outpost skirmish.
Vorprüfung ['foːrpryːfuŋ], *f.* (—, *pl.* —en) preliminary examination.
Vorrang ['foːrraŋ], *m.* (—s, *no pl.*) precedence, first place, priority.
Vorrat ['foːrraːt], *m.* (—s, *pl.* ⁓e) store, stock, provision.
Vorratskammer ['foːrraːtskamər], *f.* (—, *pl.* —n) store-room; larder.
Vorrecht ['foːrrɛçt], *n.* (—s, *pl.* —e) privilege, prerogative.
Vorrede ['foːrreːdə], *f.* (—, *pl.* —n) preface; introduction.
Vorredner ['foːrreːdnər], *m.* (—s, *pl.* —) previous speaker.
vorrichten ['foːrrɪçtən], *v.a.* prepare, fix up, get ready.
Vorrichtung ['foːrrɪçtuŋ], *f.* (—, *pl.* —en) appliance, device, contrivance.
vorrücken ['foːrrykən], *v.a.* move forward, advance; (*clock*) put on. — *v.n.* (*aux.* sein) (*Mil.*) advance.
Vorsaal ['foːrzaːl], *m.* (—s, *pl.* —säle) hall, entrance hall.
Vorsatz ['foːrzats], *m.* (—es, *pl.* ⁓e) purpose, design, intention.
vorsätzlich ['foːrzɛtslɪç], *adj.* intentional, deliberate.
Vorschein ['foːrʃaɪn], *m.* *zum* — *kommen*, turn up; appear.
vorschießen ['foːrʃiːsən], *v.a.* irr. (*money*) advance, lend.
Vorschlag ['foːrʃlaːk], *m.* (—s, *pl.* ⁓e) proposal, offer, proposition.
vorschlagen ['foːrʃlaːgən], *v.a.* irr. put forward, propose, suggest; recommend.
vorschnell ['foːrʃnɛl], *adj.* hasty, rash, precipitate.
vorschreiben ['foːrʃraɪbən], *v.a.* irr. write out (for s.o.); (*fig.*) prescribe, order.
Vorschrift ['foːrʃrɪft], *f.* (—, *pl.* —en) prescription, direction, order, command, regulation.
vorschriftsmäßig ['foːrʃrɪftsmɛːsɪç], *adj.* according to regulations.
vorschriftswidrig ['foːrʃrɪftsviːdrɪç], *adj.* contrary to regulations.
Vorschub ['foːrʃuːp], *m.* (—s, *no pl.*) aid, assistance; — *leisten*, countenance, encourage, abet.
Vorschule ['foːrʃuːlə], *f.* (—, *pl.* —n) preparatory school.
Vorschuß ['foːrʃus], *m.* (—sses, *pl.* ⁓sse) advance (of cash).

vorschützen ['foːrʃytsən], *v.a.* use as a pretext, pretend, plead.
vorschweben ['foːrʃveːbən], *v.n.* be present in o.'s mind.
vorsehen ['foːrzeːən], *v.r.* irr. *sich* —, take heed, be careful, look out, beware.
Vorsehung ['foːrzeːuŋ], *f.* (—, *no pl.*) Providence.
vorsetzen ['foːrzɛtsən], *v.a.* set before; serve; (*word*) prefix.
Vorsicht ['foːrzɪçt], *f.* (—, *no pl.*) care, precaution, caution, circumspection.
vorsichtig ['foːrzɪçtɪç], *adj.* cautious, careful, circumspect.
vorsichtshalber ['foːrzɪçtshalbər], *adv.* as a precautionary measure.
Vorsichtsmaßnahme ['foːrzɪçtsmaːs-naːmə], *f.* (—, *pl.* —n) precautionary measure, precaution.
Vorsilbe ['foːrzɪlbə], *f.* (—, *pl.* —n) prefix.
vorsintflutlich ['foːrzɪntfluːtlɪç], *adj.* antediluvian; (*fig.*) out-of-date.
Vorsitzende ['foːrzɪtsəndə], *m.* (—n, *pl.* —n) chairman, president.
Vorsorge ['foːrzɔrgə], *f.* (—, *no pl.*) care, precaution.
vorsorglich ['foːrzɔrklɪç], *adj.* provident, careful.
vorspiegeln ['foːrʃpiːgəln], *v.a. einem etwas* —, deceive s.o.; pretend.
Vorspiegelung ['foːrʃpiːgəluŋ], *f.* (—, *pl.* —en) pretence; — *falscher Tatsachen*, false pretences.
Vorspiel ['foːrʃpiːl], *n.* (—s, *pl.* —e) prelude; overture.
vorsprechen ['foːrʃprɛçən], *v.n.* irr. *bei einem* —, call on s.o. — *v.a. einem etwas* —, say s.th. for s.o.; repeat.
vorspringen ['foːrʃprɪŋən], *v.n.* irr. (*aux.* sein) leap forward; jut out, project.
Vorsprung ['foːrʃpruŋ], *m.* (—s, *pl.* ⁓e) projection, prominence; (*fig.*) advantage (over), start, lead.
Vorstadt ['foːrʃtat], *f.* (—, *pl.* ⁓e) suburb.
vorstädtisch ['foːrʃtɛtɪʃ], *adj.* suburban.
Vorstand ['foːrʃtant], *m.* (—s, *pl.* ⁓e) board of directors; director, principal.
Vorstandssitzung ['foːrʃtantszɪtsuŋ], *f.* (—, *pl.* —en) board meeting.
vorstehen ['foːrʃteːən], *v.n.* irr. project, protrude; (*office*) administer, govern, direct, manage.
vorstehend ['foːrʃteːənt], *adj.* projecting, protruding; above-mentioned, foregoing.
Vorsteher ['foːrʃteːər], *m.* (—s, *pl.* —) director, manager; supervisor.
Vorsteherdrüse ['foːrʃteːərdryːzə], *f.* (—, *pl.* —n) prostate gland.
vorstellbar ['foːrʃtɛlbaːr], *adj.* imaginable.
vorstellen ['foːrʃtɛlən], *v.a.* (*thing*) put forward; (*person*) present, introduce; (*Theat.*) impersonate; represent; (*clock*) put on; *sich etwas* —, visualise s.th., imagine s.th.

vorstellig ['fo:rʃtɛlıç], *adj.* — *werden*, petition; lodge a complaint.

Vorstellung ['fo:rʃtɛluŋ], *f.* (—, *pl.* —en) (*person*) presentation, introduction; (*Theat.*) performance; idea, notion, image; representation.

Vorstellungsvermögen ['fo:rʃtɛluŋs-fɛr'mø:gən], *n.* (—s, *no pl.*) imagination, imaginative faculty.

Vorstoß ['fo:rʃto:s], *m.* (—es, *pl.* ⁻e) (*Mil.*) sudden advance, thrust.

vorstoßen ['fo:rʃto:sən], *v.a. irr.* push forward. — *v.n.* (*aux.* sein) (*Mil.*) advance suddenly.

Vorstrafe ['fo:rʃtra:fə], *f.* (—, *pl.* —n) previous conviction.

vorstrecken ['fo:rʃtrɛkən], *v.a.* stretch forward, protrude; (*money*) advance.

Vorstufe ['fo:rʃtu:fə], *f.* (—, *pl.* —n) first step.

Vortänzerin ['fo:rtɛntsərin], *f.* (—, *pl.* —nen) prima ballerina.

Vorteil ['fɔrtaıl], *m.* (—s, *pl.* —e) advantage, profit.

vorteilhaft ['fɔrtaılhaft], *adj.* advantageous, profitable, lucrative.

Vortrag ['fo:rtra:k], *m.* (—s, *pl.* ⁻e) recitation, delivery, rendering; statement, report; talk, speech, lecture.

vortragen ['fo:rtra:gən], *v.a. irr.* make a report; (*poem*) recite, declaim; make a request; (*Comm.*) carry forward; lecture on.

Vortragskunst ['fo:rtra:kskunst], *f.* (—, *no pl.*) elocution; (art of) public speaking.

vortrefflich [for'trɛflıç], *adj.* excellent, splendid.

Vortrefflichkeit [for'trɛflıçkaıt], *f.* (—, *no pl.*) excellence.

vortreten ['fo:rtre:tən], *v.n. irr.* (*aux.* sein) step forward.

Vortritt ['fo:rtrıt], *m.* (—s, *no pl.*) precedence.

vorüber [for'y:bər], *adv.* past, gone, over, finished, done with.

vorübergehen [for'y:bərge:ən], *v.n. irr.* (*aux.* sein) pass by, pass, go past.

vorübergehend [for'y:bərge:ənt], *adj.* passing, temporary, transitory.

Vorübung ['fo:ry:buŋ], *f.* (—, *pl.* —en) preliminary exercise.

Voruntersuchung ['fo:runtərzu:xuŋ], *f.* (—, *pl.* —en) preliminary inquiry; trial in magistrate's court.

Vorurteil ['fo:rurtaıl], *n.* (—s, *pl.* —e) bias, prejudice.

vorurteilslos ['fo:rurtaılslo:s], *adj.* impartial, unprejudiced, unbiased.

Vorvater ['fo:rfa:tər], *m.* (—s, *pl.* ⁻) progenitor, ancestor.

Vorverkauf ['fo:rfɛrkauf], *m.* (—s, *pl.* ⁻e) booking in advance, advance booking.

vorwagen ['fo:rva:gən], *v.r. sich* —, dare to go (*or* come) forward.

vorwaltend ['fo:rvaltənt], *adj.* prevailing, predominating.

Vorwand ['fo:rvant], *m.* (—s, *pl.* ⁻e) pretence, pretext · *unter dem* —, under pretence of.

vorwärts ['fɔrvɛrts], *adv.* forward.

vorwärtskommen ['fɔrvɛrtskɔmən], *v.n. irr.* (*aux.* sein) make headway, get on.

vorweg [for'vɛk], *adv.* before.

vorwegnehmen [for'vɛkne:mən], *v.a. irr.* anticipate.

vorweisen ['fo:rvaızən], *v.a. irr.* show, produce, exhibit.

Vorwelt ['fo:rvɛlt], *f.* (—, *no pl.*) primitive world; former ages.

vorweltlich ['fo:rvɛltlıç], *adj.* primæval, prehistoric.

vorwerfen ['fo:rvɛrfən], *v.a. irr. einem etwas* —, blame s.o. for s.th.; charge s.o. with s.th., tax s.o. with s.th.

vorwiegen ['fo:rvi:gən], *v.n. irr.* prevail.

vorwiegend ['fo:rvi:gənt], *adv.* mostly, for the most part.

Vorwissen ['fo:rvısən], *n.* (—s, *no pl.*) foreknowledge, prescience.

Vorwitz ['fo:rvıts], *m.* (—es, *no pl.*) pertness.

vorwitzig ['fo:rvıtsıç], *adj.* forward, pert, meddlesome.

Vorwort (1) ['fo:rvɔrt], *n.* (—s, *pl.* —e) preface.

Vorwort (2) ['fo:rvɔrt], *n.* (—s, *pl.* ⁻er) (*Gram.*) preposition.

Vorwurf ['fo:rvurf], *m.* (—s, *pl.* ⁻e) reproach; theme, subject.

vorwurfsfrei ['fo:rvurfsfraı], *adj.* free from blame, irreproachable.

vorwurfsvoll ['fo:rvurfsfɔl], *adj.* reproachful.

Vorzeichen ['fo:rtsaıxən], *n.* (—s, *pl.* —) omen, token; (*Maths.*) sign.

vorzeigen ['fo:rtsaıgən], *v.a.* show, produce, exhibit, display.

Vorzeit ['fo:rtsaıt], *f.* (—, *no pl.*) antiquity, olden times.

vorzeiten [for'tsaıtən], *adv.* (*Poet.*) in olden times, formerly.

vorzeitig ['fo:rtsaıtıç], *adj.* premature.

vorziehen ['fo:rtsi:ən], *v.a. irr.* prefer.

Vorzimmer ['fo:rtsımər], *n.* (—s, *pl.* —) anteroom, antechamber.

Vorzug ['fo:rtsu:k], *m.* (—s, *pl.* ⁻e) preference, advantage; excellence, superiority.

vorzüglich [for'tsy:klıç], *adj.* superior, excellent, exquisite.

Vorzüglichkeit [for'tsy:klıçkaıt], *f.* (—, *no pl.*) excellence, superiority.

Vorzugsaktie ['fo:rtsu:ksaktsjə], *f.* (—, *pl.* —n) preference share.

vorzugsweise ['fo:rtsu:ksvaızə], *adv.* for choice, preferably.

vulgär [vul'gɛ:r], *adj.* vulgar.

Vulkan [vul'ka:n], *m.* (—s, *pl.* —e) volcano.

vulkanisch [vul'ka:nıʃ], *adj.* volcanic. ⁻

271

W

W [ve:] *n.* (—**s**, *pl.* —**s**) the letter W.

Waage ['va:gə], *f.* (—, *pl.* —**n**) balance, pair of scales.

waag(e)recht ['va:g(ə)rɛçt], *adj.* horizontal.

Waagschale ['va:kʃa:lə], *f.* (—, *pl.* —**n**) pan of a balance.

Wabe ['va:bə], *f.* (—, *pl.* —**n**) honeycomb.

Waberlohe ['va:bərlo:ə], *f.* (—, *no pl.*) (*Poet.*) flickering flames, magic fire.

wach [vax], *adj.* awake; alert; *völlig* —, wide awake.

Wachdienst ['vaxdi:nst], *m.* (—**es**, *no pl.*) guard, sentry duty.

Wache ['vaxə], *f.* (—, *pl.* —**n**) guard, watch; (*person*) sentry, sentinel.

wachen ['vaxən], *v.n.* be awake; guard; — *über*, watch, keep an eye on.

Wacholder [va'xɔldər], *m.* (—**s**, *pl.* —) (*Bot.*) juniper.

wachrufen [vax'ru:fən], *v.a. irr.* (*fig.*) call to mind.

Wachs [vaks], *n.* (—**es**, *no pl.*) wax.

wachsam ['vaxza:m], *adj.* watchful, vigilant.

Wachsamkeit ['vaxza:mkaɪt], *f.* (—, *no pl.*) watchfulness, vigilance.

Wachsbild ['vaksbɪlt], *n.* (—**s**, *pl.* —**er**) waxen image.

wachsen ['vaksən], *v.n. irr.* (*aux.* sein) grow, increase.

wächsern ['vɛksərn], *adj.* waxen, made of wax.

Wachsfigur ['vaksfigu:r], *f.* (—, *pl.* —**en**) wax figure.

Wachsfigurenkabinett ['vaksfigu:rənkabinɛt], *n.* (—**s**, *pl.* —**e**) waxworks.

Wachsleinwand ['vakslaɪnvant], *f.* (—, *no pl.*) oil-cloth.

Wachstuch ['vakstu:x], *n.* (—(**e**)**s**, *no pl.*) oil-cloth; American cloth.

Wachstum ['vakstu:m], *n.* (—**s**, *no pl.*) growth, increase.

Wacht [vaxt], *f.* (—, *pl.* —**en**) watch, guard.

Wachtdienst ['vaxtdi:nst] *see* **Wachdienst**.

Wachtel ['vaxtəl], *f.* (—, *pl.* —**n**) (*Orn.*) quail.

Wachtelhund ['vaxtəlhunt], *m.* (—(**e**)**s**, *pl.* —**e**) (*Zool.*) spaniel.

Wächter ['vɛçtər], *m.* (—**s**, *pl.* —) watchman, warder, guard.

wachthabend ['vaxtha:bənt], *adj.* on duty.

Wachtmeister ['vaxtmaɪstər], *m.* (—**s**, *pl.* —) sergeant.

Wachtparade [vaxtpara:də], *f.* (—, *pl.* —**n**) mounting of the guard.

Wachtposten ['vaxtpɔstən], *m.* (—**s**, *pl.* —) guard, picket.

Wachtraum ['vaxtraum], *m.* (—**s**, *pl.* ⁻e) day-dream, waking dream.

Wachtturm ['vaxtturm], *m.* (—**s**, *pl.* ⁻e) watch-tower.

wackeln ['vakəln], *v.n.* totter, shake, wobble.

wacker ['vakər], *adj.* gallant, brave, valiant; upright.

wacklig ['vaklɪç], *adj.* tottering, shaky; (*furniture*) rickety; (*tooth*) loose.

Wade ['va:də], *f.* (—, *pl.* —**n**) calf (of the leg).

Wadenbein ['va:dənbaɪn], *n.* (—**s**, *pl.* —**e**) shin-bone.

Waffe ['vafə], *f.* (—, *pl.* —**n**) weapon, arm; *die* —*n strecken*, surrender.

Waffel ['vafəl], *f.* (—, *pl.* —**n**) wafer; waffle.

Waffeleisen ['vafəlaɪzən], *n.* (—**s**, *pl.* —) waffle-iron.

Waffenbruder ['vafənbru:dər], *m.* (—**s**, *pl.* ⁻) brother-in-arms, comrade.

waffenfähig ['vafənfɛ:ɪç], *adj.* able to bear arms.

Waffengewalt ['vafəngəvalt], *f.* (—, *no pl.*) *mit* —, by force of arms.

Waffenglück ['vafənglyk], *n.* (—**s**, *no pl.*) fortunes of war.

Waffenrock ['vafənrɔk], *m.* (—**s**, *pl.* ⁻e) tunic.

Waffenruf ['vafənru:f], *m.* (—**s**, *no pl.*) call to arms.

Waffenschmied [vafənʃmi:t], *m.* (—**s**, *pl.* —**e**) armourer.

Waffenstillstand ['vafənʃtɪlʃtant], *m.* (—**s**, *no pl.*) armistice, truce.

waffnen ['vafnən], *v.a.* arm.

Wage *see* **Waage**.

Wagebalken ['va:gəbalkən], *m.* (—**s**, *pl.* —) scale-beam.

Wagen ['va:gən], *m.* (—**s**, *pl.* —) vehicle, conveyance, carriage, coach, car, cab, wagon, cart, truck, van, dray.

wagen ['va:gən], *v.a., v.n.* dare, venture, risk.

wägen ['vɛ:gən], *v.a., irr.* weigh, balance; (*words*) consider.

Wagenverkehr ['va:gənfɛrke:r], *m.* (—**s**, *no pl.*) vehicular traffic.

wagerecht *see* **waagerecht**.

Waggon [va'gɔ̃], *m.* (—**s**, *pl.* —**s**) railway car, goods van, freight car.

waghalsig ['va:khalzɪç], *adj.* foolhardy, rash, daring.

Wagnis ['va:knɪs], *n.* (—**ses**, *pl.* —**se**) venture, risky undertaking; risk.

Wagschale *see* **Waagschale**.

Wahl [va:l], *f.* (—, *pl.* —**en**) choice; election; selection; alternative.

Wahlakt ['va:lakt], *m.* (—**s**, *pl.* —**e**) poll, election.

Wahlaufruf ['va:laufru:f], *m.* (—**s**, *pl.* —**e**) manifesto, election address.

wählbar ['vɛ:lba:r], *adj.* eligible.

Wählbarkeit ['vɛ:lba:rkaɪt], *f.* (—, *no pl.*) eligibility.

wahlberechtigt ['va:lbərɛçtɪçt], *adj.*
entitled to vote.

wählen ['vɛ:lən], *v.a.* choose; (*Parl.*)
elect; (*Telephone*) dial.

Wähler ['vɛ:lər], *m.* (**—s**, *pl.* **—**)
elector; constituent.

wählerisch ['vɛ:lərɪʃ], *adj.* fastidious,
particular.

Wählerschaft ['vɛ:lərʃaft], *f.* (**—**,
pl. **—en**) constituency.

wahlfähig ['va:lfɛ:ɪç], *adj.* eligible.

Wahlliste ['va:llɪstə], *f.* (**—**, *pl.* **—n**)
electoral list, register (of electors).

wahllos ['va:llo:s], *adj.* indiscriminate.

Wahlrecht ['va:lrɛçt], *n.* (**—s**, *no pl.*)
franchise.

Wahlspruch ['va:lʃprux], *m.* (**—s**,
pl. ˙**e**) device, motto.

wahlunfähig ['va:lunfɛ:ɪç], *adj.* ineligible.

Wahlurne ['va:lurnə], *f.* (**—**, *pl.* **—n**)
ballot-box.

Wahlverwandtschaft ['va:lfɛrvantʃaft],
f. (**—**, *no pl.*) elective affinity, congeniality.

Wahlzettel ['va:ltsɛtəl], *m.* (**—s**, *pl.* **—**)
ballot-paper.

Wahn [va:n], *m.* (**—(e)s**, *no pl.*) delusion.

Wahnbild ['va:nbɪlt], *n.* (**—s**, *pl.* **—er**)
hallucination, delusion; phantasm.

wähnen ['vɛ:nən], *v.a.* fancy, believe.

Wahnsinn ['va:nzɪn], *m.* (**—s**, *no pl.*)
madness, lunacy.

wahnsinnig ['va:nzɪnɪç], *adj.* insane,
mad, lunatic; (*coll.*) terrific.

Wahnsinnige ['va:nzɪnɪgə], *m.* (**—n**,
pl. **—n**) madman, lunatic.

Wahnwitz ['va:nvɪts], *m.* (**—es**, *no pl.*)
madness.

wahnwitzig ['va:nvɪtsɪç], *adj.* mad.

wahr [va:r], *adj.* true, real, genuine.

wahren ['vɛ:rən], *v.a.* guard, watch
over.

währen ['vɛ:rən], *v.n.* last.

während ['vɛ:rənt], *prep.* (*Genit.*)
during. — *conj.* while, whilst; whereas.

wahrhaft ['va:rhaft], *adj.* truthful,
veracious.

wahrhaftig [va:r'haftɪç], *adv.* truly,
really, in truth.

Wahrhaftigkeit [va:r'haftɪçkaɪt], *f.*
(**—**, *no pl.*) truthfulness, veracity.

Wahrheit ['va:rhaɪt], *f.* (**—**, *pl.* **—en**)
truth; reality; *die — sagen*, tell the
truth.

Wahrheitsliebe ['va:rhaɪtsli:bə], *f.* (**—**,
no pl.) love of truth, truthfulness.

wahrlich ['va:rlɪç], *adv.* truly, in truth.

wahrnehmbar ['va:rne:mba:r], *adj.*
perceptible.

wahrnehmen ['va:rne:mən], *v.a. irr.*
perceive, observe.

Wahrnehmung ['va:rne:muŋ], *f.* (**—**,
pl. **—en**) perception, observation.

wahrsagen ['va:rza:gən], *v.n.* prophesy;
tell fortunes.

Wahrsager ['va:rza:gər], *m.* (**—s**,
pl. **—**) fortune-teller, soothsayer.

wahrscheinlich [va:r'ʃaɪnlɪç], *adj.*
likely, probable; *es wird — regnen*, it
will probably rain.

Wahrscheinlichkeit [va:r'ʃaɪnlɪçkaɪt],
f. (**—**, *pl.* **—en**) likelihood, probability.

Wahrung ['va:ruŋ], *f.* (**—**, *no pl.*)
protection, preservation, maintenance.

Währung ['vɛ:ruŋ], *f.* (**—**, *pl.* **—en**)
currency, standard.

Wahrzeichen ['va:rtsaɪçən], *n.* (**—s**,
pl. **—**) landmark; (*fig.*) sign, token.

Waibling(er) ['vaɪblɪŋ(ər)], *m.* Ghibelline.

Waidmann ['vaɪtman], *m.* (**—s**, *pl.*
˙**er**) huntsman, hunter.

waidmännisch ['vaɪtmɛnɪʃ], *adj.* sportsmanlike.

Waise ['vaɪzə], *f.* (**—**, *pl.* **—n**) orphan.

Waisenhaus ['vaɪzənhaus], *n.* (**—es**,
pl. ˙**er**) orphanage.

Waisenmutter ['vaɪzənmutər], *f.* (**—**,
pl. ˙) foster-mother.

Waisenvater ['vaɪzənfa:tər], *m.* (**—s**,
pl. ˙) foster-father.

Wald [valt], *m.* (**—es**, *pl.* ˙**er**) wood,
forest; woodland.

Waldbrand ['valtbrant], *m.* (**—s**, *pl.*
˙**e**) forest-fire.

Waldlichtung ['valtlɪçtuŋ], *f.* (**—**,
pl. **—en**) forest glade, clearing.

Waldmeister ['valtmaɪstər], *m.* (**—s**,
no pl.) (*Bot.*) woodruff.

Waldung ['valduŋ], *f.* (**—**, *pl.* **—en**)
woods, woodland.

Waldwiese ['valtvi:zə], *f.* (**—**, *pl.* **—en**)
forest-glade.

Walfisch ['va:lfɪʃ], *m.* (**—es**, *pl.* **—e**)
whale.

Walfischfang ['va:lfɪʃfaŋ], *m.* (**—s**, *no
pl.*) whaling.

Walfischfänger ['va:lfɪʃfɛŋər], *m.* (**—s**,
pl. **—**) whaler, whale fisher.

Walfischtran ['va:lfɪʃtra:n], *m.* (**—s**,
no pl.) train-oil.

Walküre [val'ky:rə], *f.* (**—**, *pl.* **—n**)
Valkyrie.

Wall [val], *m.* (**—(e)s**, *pl.* ˙**e**) rampart,
dam, vallum; mound.

Wallach ['valax], *m.* (**—s**, *pl.* **—e**)
castrated horse, gelding.

wallen ['valən], *v.n.* bubble, boil up;
wave, undulate.

Wallfahrer ['valfa:rər], *m.* (**—s**, *pl.* **—**)
pilgrim.

Wallfahrt ['valfa:rt], *f.* (**—**, *pl.* **—en**)
pilgrimage.

wallfahrten ['valfa:rtən], *v.n.* (*aux.*
sein) go on a pilgrimage.

Walnuß ['valnus], *f.* (**—**, *pl.* ˙**sse**)
(*Bot.*) walnut.

Walpurgisnacht [val'purgɪsnaxt], *f.*
witches' sabbath.

Walroß ['valrɔs], *n.* (**—sses**, *pl.* **—sse**)
sea-horse, walrus.

Walstatt ['valʃtat], *f.* (**—**, *pl.* ˙**en**)
(*Poet.*) battlefield.

walten ['valtən], *v.n.* rule; *seines Amtes
—*, do o.'s duty, carry out o.'s duties.

Walze ['valtsə], *f.* (**—**, *pl.* **—n**) roller,
cylinder.

walzen ['valtsən], *v.a.* roll. — *v.n.* waltz.

wälzen ['vɛltsən], *v.a.* roll, turn about.

walzenförmig ['valtsənfœrmɪç], *adj.* cylindrical.

Walzer ['valtsər], *m.* (—s, *pl.* —) waltz.

Wälzer ['vɛltsər], *m.* (—s, *pl.* —) tome; thick volume.

Walzwerk ['valtsvɛrk], *n.* (—s, *pl.* —e) rolling-mill.

Wams [vams], *n.* (—es, *pl.* ⸚e) (*obs.*) doublet, jerkin.

Wand [vant], *f.* (—, *pl.* ⸚e) wall; side.

Wandbekleidung ['vantbəklaɪduŋ], *f.* (—, *pl.* —en) wainscot, panelling.

Wandel ['vandəl], *m.* (—s, *no pl.*) mutation, change; behaviour, conduct; *Handel und* —, trade and traffic.

wandelbar ['vandəlbaːr], *adj.* changeable, inconstant.

Wandelgang ['vandəlgaŋ], *m.* (—s, *pl.* ⸚e) lobby; lounge, foyer; (*in the open*) covered way, covered walk.

wandeln ['vandəln], *v.a.* (*aux.* haben) change. — *v.n.* (*aux.* sein) walk, wander. — *v.r. sich* —, change.

Wanderbursche ['vandərburʃə], *m.* (—n, *pl.* —n) travelling journeyman.

Wanderer ['vandərər], *m.* (—s, *pl.* —) wanderer, traveller; hiker.

Wanderleben ['vandərleːbən], *n.* (—s, *no pl.*) nomadic life.

Wanderlehrer ['vandərleːrər], *m.* (—s, *pl.* —) itinerant teacher.

Wanderlust ['vandərlust], *f.* (—, *no pl.*) urge to travel; call of the open.

wandern ['vandərn], *v.n.* (*aux.* sein) wander, travel; migrate.

Wanderschaft ['vandərʃaft], *f.* (—, *no pl.*) wanderings.

Wandersmann ['vandərsman], *m.* (—s, *pl.* ⸚er) wayfarer.

Wandertruppe ['vandərtrupə], *f.* (—, *pl.* —n) (*Theat.*) strolling players.

Wanderung ['vandəruŋ], *f.* (—, *pl.* —en) walking tour; hike.

Wandervolk ['vandərfɔlk], *n.* (— (e)s, *pl.* ⸚er) nomadic tribe.

Wandgemälde ['vantgəmɛːldə], *n.* (—s, *pl.* —) mural painting, mural.

Wandlung ['vandluŋ], *f.* (—, *pl.* —en) transformation; (*Theol.*) transubstantiation.

Wandspiegel ['vantʃpiːgəl], *m.* (—s, *pl.* —) pier-glass.

Wandtafel ['vanttaːfəl], *f.* (—, *pl.* —n) blackboard.

Wange ['vaŋə], *f.* (—, *pl.* —n) cheek.

Wankelmut ['vaŋkəlmuːt], *m.* (—s, *no pl.*) fickleness, inconstancy.

wankelmütig ['vaŋkəlmyːtɪç], *adj.* inconstant, fickle.

wanken ['vaŋkən], *v.n.* totter, stagger; (*fig.*) waver, be irresolute.

wann [van], *adv.* when; *dann und* —, now and then, sometimes.

Wanne ['vanə], *f.* (—, *pl.* —n) tub, bath.

wannen ['vanən], *adv.* (*obs.*) *von* —, whence.

Wannenbad ['vanənbaːt], *n.* (—s, *pl.* ⸚er) bath.

Wanst [vanst], *m.* (—es, *pl.* ⸚e) belly, paunch.

Wanze ['vantsə], *f.* (—, *pl.* —n) (*Ent.*) bug.

Wappen ['vapən], *n.* (—s, *pl.* —) crest, coat-of-arms.

Wappenbild ['vapənbɪlt], *n.* (—s, *pl.* —er) heraldic figure.

Wappenkunde ['vapənkundə], *f.* (—, *no pl.*) heraldry.

Wappenschild ['vapənʃɪlt], *m.* (—s, *pl.* —e) escutcheon.

Wappenspruch ['vapənʃprux], *m.* (—(e)s, *pl.* ⸚e) motto, device.

wappnen ['vapnən], *v.a.* arm.

Ware ['vaːrə], *f.* (—, *pl.* —n) article, commodity; (*pl.*) merchandise, goods, wares.

Warenausfuhr ['vaːrənausfuːr], *f.* (—, *no pl.*) exportation, export.

Warenbörse ['vaːrənbœrzə], *f.* (—, *pl.* —n) commodity exchange.

Wareneinfuhr ['vaːrənaɪnfuːr], *f.* (—, *no pl.*) importation, import.

Warenhaus ['vaːrənhaus], *n.* (—es, *pl.* ⸚er) department store, emporium; (*Am.*) store.

Warenlager ['vaːrənlaːgər], *n.* (—s, *pl.* —) magazine; stock; warehouse.

Warensendung ['vaːrənzɛnduŋ], *f.* (—, *pl.* —en) consignment of goods.

Warentausch ['vaːrəntauʃ], *m.* (—es, *no pl.*) barter.

warm [varm], *adj.* warm, hot.

warmblütig ['varmblyːtɪç], *adj.* warm-blooded.

Wärme ['vɛrmə], *f.* (—, *no pl.*) warmth; heat.

Wärmeeinheit ['vɛrməaɪnhaɪt], *f.* (—, *pl.* —en) thermal unit; calorie.

Wärmegrad ['vɛrməgraːt], *m.* (—s, *pl.* —e) degree of heat; temperature.

Wärmeleiter ['vɛrmələɪtər], *m.* (—s, *pl.* —) conductor of heat.

Wärmemesser ['vɛrməmɛsər], *m.* (—s, *pl.* —) thermometer.

wärmen ['vɛrmən], *v.a.* warm, heat.

Wärmflasche ['vɛrmflaʃə], *f.* (—, *pl.* —n) hot-water bottle.

warnen ['varnən], *v.a.* warn; caution.

Warnung ['varnuŋ], *f.* (—, *pl.* —en) warning, caution, admonition; notice.

Warschau ['varʃau], *n.* Warsaw.

Warte ['vartə], *f.* (—, *pl.* —n) watchtower, belfry, look-out.

Wartegeld ['vartəgɛlt], *n.* (—s, *pl.* —er) half pay; (*ship*) demurrage charges.

warten ['vartən], *v.n.* wait; — *auf* (*Acc.*), wait for, await. — *v.a.* tend, nurse.

Wärter ['vɛrtər], *m.* (—s, *pl.* —) keeper, attendant; warder; male nurse.

Wartesaal ['vartəzaːl], *m.* (—s, *pl.* —säle) (*Railw.*) waiting-room.

Wartung ['vartuŋ], *f.* (—, *no pl.*) nursing, attendance; servicing; maintenance.

warum [va′rum], *adv., conj.* why, for what reason.
Warze [′vartsə], *f.* (—, *pl.* —n) wart.
was [vas], *interr. pron.* what? — *rel. pron.* what, that which.
Waschanstalt [′vaʃanʃtalt], *f.* (—, *pl.* —en) laundry.
waschbar [′vaʃbaːr], ·*adj.* washable.
Waschbär [′vaʃbɛːr], *m.* (—en, *pl.* —en) (*Zool.*) raccoon.
Waschbecken [′vaʃbɛkən], *n.* (—s, *pl.* —) wash-basin.
Wäsche [′vɛʃə], *f.* (—, *no pl.*) washing, wash, laundry; linen.
waschecht [′vaʃɛçt], *adj.* washable; (*fig.*) genuine.
waschen [′vaʃən], *v.a. irr.* wash.
Wäscherin [′vɛʃərɪn], *f.* (—, *pl.* —nen) washerwoman, laundress.
Waschhaus [′vaʃhaus], *n.* (—es, *pl.* ·er) wash-house, laundry; (*reg. trade name*) launderette.
Waschkorb [′vaʃkɔrp], *m.* (—s, *pl.* ·e) clothes-basket.
Waschküche [′vaʃkyçə], *f.* (—, *pl.* —en) wash-house.
Waschlappen [′vaʃlapən], *m.* (—s, *pl.* —) face-flannel, face-cloth, face-washer; (*fig.*) milksop.
Waschleder [′vaʃleːdər], *n.* (—s, *no pl.*) chamois leather, wash-leather.
Waschmaschine [′vaʃmaʃiːnə], *f.* (—, *pl.* —n) washing-machine.
Waschtisch [′vaʃtɪʃ], *m.* (—es, *pl.* —e) wash-stand.
Waschwanne [′vaʃvanə], *f.* (—, *pl.* —n) wash-tub.
Wasser [′vasər], *n.* (—s, *pl.* —) water; *stille — sind tief*, still waters run deep.
wasserarm [′vasərarm], *adj.* waterless, dry, arid.
Wasserbehälter [′vasərbəhɛltər], *m.* (—s, *pl.* —) reservoir, cistern, tank.
Wasserblase [′vasərblaːzə], *f.* (—, *pl.* —en) bubble.
Wässerchen [′vɛsərçən], *n.* (—s, *pl.* —) brook, streamlet; *er sieht aus, als ob er kein — trüben könnte*, he looks as if butter would not melt in his mouth.
Wasserdampf [′vasərdampf], *m.* (—(e)s, *no pl.*) steam.
wasserdicht [′vasərdɪçt], *adj.* water-proof.
Wasserdruck [′vasərdruk], *m.* (—s, *no pl.*) hydrostatic pressure, hydraulic pressure.
Wassereimer [′vasəraimər], *m.* (—s, *pl.* —) pail, water-bucket.
Wasserfall [′vasərfal], *m.* (—s, *pl.* ·e) waterfall, cataract, cascade.
Wasserfarbe [′vasərfarbə], *f.* (—, *pl.* —n) water-colour.
Wasserheilanstalt [′vasərhailanʃtalt], *f.* (—, *pl.* —en) spa.
wässerig [′vɛsərɪç], *adj.* watery; (*fig.*) insipid, flat, diluted.
Wasserkanne [′vasərkanə], *f.* (—, *pl.* —n) pitcher, ewer.
Wasserkessel [′vasərkɛsəl], *m.* (—s, *pl.* —) boiler; kettle.

Wasserkopf [′vasərkɔpf], *m.* (—(e)s, *pl.* ·e) (*Med.*) hydrocephalus.
Wasserkur [′vasərkuːr], *f.* (—, *pl.* —en) hydropathic treatment.
Wasserleitung [′vasərlaituŋ], *f.* (—, *pl.* —en) aqueduct; water main.
Wasserlinsen [′vasərlɪnzən], *f. pl.* (*Bot.*) duck-weed.
Wassermann [′vasərman], *m.* (—s, *no pl.*) (*Astron.*) Aquarius.
wässern [′vɛsərn], *v.a.* water, irrigate, soak.
Wassernixe [′vasərnɪksə], *f.* (—, *pl.* —n) water nymph.
Wassernot [′vasərnoːt], *f.* (—, *no pl.*) drought, scarcity of water.
Wasserrabe [′vasərraːbə], *m.* (—n, *pl.* —n) (*Orn.*) cormorant.
Wasserrinne [′vasərrinə], *f.* (—, *pl.* —n) gutter.
Wasserröhre [′vasərrøːrə], *f.* (—, *pl.* —n) water-pipe.
Wasserscheide [′vasərʃaidə], *f.* (—, *pl.* —n) watershed.
Wasserscheu [′vasərʃɔy], *f.* (—, *no pl.*) hydrophobia.
Wasserspiegel [′vasərʃpiːgəl], *m.* (—s, *pl.* —) water-level.
Wasserspritze [′vasərʃpritsə], *f.* (—, *pl.* —n) squirt; sprinkler.
Wasserstand [′vasərʃtant], *m.* (—s, *no pl.*) water-level.
Wasserstiefel [′vasərʃtiːfəl], *m.* (—s, *pl.* —) wader, gumboot.
Wasserstoff [′vasərʃtɔf], *m.* (—(e)s, *no pl.*) hydrogen.
Wassersucht [′vasərzuxt], *f.* (—, *no pl.*) dropsy.
Wassersuppe [′vasərzupə], *f.* (—, *pl.* —n) water-gruel.
Wässerung [′vɛsəruŋ], *f.* (—, *pl.* —en) watering, irrigation.
Wasserverdrängung [′vasərfɛrdrɛŋuŋ], *f.* (—, *no pl.*) displacement (of water).
Wasserwaage [′vasərvaːgə], *f.* (—, *pl.* —n) water-balance, water-level; hydrometer.
Wasserweg [′vasərveːk], *m.* (—s, *pl.* —e) waterway; *auf dem* —, by water, by sea.
Wasserzeichen [′vasərtsaiçən], *n.* (—s, *pl.* —) watermark.
waten [′vaːtən], *v.n.* (*aux.* sein) wade.
watscheln [′vaːtʃəln], *v.n.* (*aux.* sein) waddle.
Watt (1) [vat], *n.* (—s, *pl.* —e) sand-bank; (*pl.*) shallows.
Watt (2) [vat], *n.* (—s, *pl.* —) (*Elec.*) watt.
Watte [′vatə], *f.* (—, *no pl.*) wadding, cotton-wool.
wattieren [va′tiːrən], *v.a.* pad.
Webe [′veːbə], *f.* (—, *pl.* —n) web, weft.
weben [′veːbən], *v.a.* weave.
Weber [′veːbər], *m.* (—s, *pl.* —) weaver.
Weberei [veːbə′rai], *f.* (—, *pl.* —en) weaving-mill.

Weberschiffchen [ˈveːbərʃɪfçən], *n.* (—s, *pl.* —) shuttle.

Wechsel [ˈvɛksəl], *m.* (—s, *pl.* —) change; turn, variation; vicissitude; (*Comm.*) bill of exchange.

Wechselbalg [ˈvɛksəlbalk], *m.* (—s, *pl.* ̈e) changeling.

Wechselbank [ˈvɛksəlbaŋk], *f.* (—, *pl.* ̈e) discount-bank.

Wechselbeziehung [ˈvɛksəlbətsiːuŋ], *f.* (—, *pl.* —en) reciprocal relation, correlation.

Wechselfälle [ˈvɛksəlfɛlə], *m. pl.* vicissitudes.

Wechselfieber [ˈvɛksəlfiːbər], *n.* (—s, *pl.* —) intermittent fever.

Wechselfolge [ˈvɛksəlfɔlgə], *f.* (—, *no pl.*) rotation, alternation.

Wechselgeld [ˈvɛksəlgɛlt], *n.* (—(e)s, *no pl.*) change.

wechseln [ˈvɛksəln], *v.a.* change, exchange. — *v.n.* change, alternate, change places.

wechselseitig [ˈvɛksəlzaɪtɪç], *adj.* reciprocal, mutual.

Wechselstrom [ˈvɛksəlʃtroːm], *m.* (—s, *no pl.*) alternating current.

Wechselstube [ˈvɛksəlʃtuːbə], *f.* (—, *pl.* —n) exchange office.

wechselvoll [ˈvɛksəlfɔl], *adj.* eventful, chequered; changeable.

wechselweise [ˈvɛksəlvaɪzə], *adv.* reciprocally, mutually; by turns, alternately.

Wechselwinkel [ˈvɛksəlvɪŋkəl], *m.* (—s, *pl.* —) alternate angle.

Wechselwirkung [ˈvɛksəlvɪrkuŋ], *f.* (—, *pl.* —en) reciprocal effect.

Wechselwirtschaft [ˈvɛksəlvɪrtʃaft], *f.* (—, *no pl.*) rotation of crops.

Wecken [ˈvɛkən], *m.* (—s, *pl.* —) (*dial.*) bread-roll.

wecken [ˈvɛkən], *v.a.* wake, rouse, awaken.

Wecker [ˈvɛkər], *m.* (—s, *pl.* —) alarm-clock.

Weckuhr [ˈvɛkuːr], *f.* (—, *pl.* —en) alarm-clock.

Wedel [ˈveːdəl], *m.* (—s, *pl.* —) feather-duster, fan; tail.

wedeln [ˈveːdəln], *v.n. mit dem Schwanz* —, wag its tail.

weder [ˈveːdər], *conj.* neither; — . . . *noch,* neither . . . nor.

Weg [veːk], *m.* (—(e)s, *pl.* —e) way, path, route, road; walk, errand; *am* —, by the wayside.

weg [vɛk], *adv.* away, gone, off, lost.

wegbegeben [ˈvɛkbəgeːbən], *v.r. irr. sich* —, go away, leave.

wegbekommen [ˈvɛkbəkɔmən], *v.a. irr. etwas* —, get the hang of s.th.; get s.th. off *or* away.

Wegbereiter [ˈveːkbəraɪtər], *m.* (—s, *pl.* —) forerunner, pathfinder, pioneer.

wegblasen [ˈvɛkblaːzən], *v.a. irr.* blow away; *wie weggeblasen,* without leaving a trace.

wegbleiben [ˈvɛkblaɪbən], *v.n. irr.* (*aux.* sein) stay away.

wegblicken [ˈvɛkblɪkən], *v.n.* look the other way.

wegbringen [ˈvɛkbrɪŋən], *v.a. irr. einen* —, get s.o. away.

wegdrängen [ˈvɛkdrɛŋən], *v.a.* push away.

Wegebau [ˈveːgəbau], *m.* (—s, *no pl.*) road-making.

wegeilen [ˈvɛkaɪlən], *v.n.* (*aux.* sein) hasten away, hurry off.

wegelagern [ˈveːgəlaːgərn], *v.a.* waylay.

wegen [ˈveːgən], *prep.* (*Genit., Dat.*) because of, on account of, owing to, by reason of.

Wegfall [ˈvɛkfal], *m.* (—s, *no pl.*) omission.

wegfallen [ˈvɛkfalən], *v.n. irr.* (*aux.* sein) fall off; be omitted; cease.

Weggang [ˈvɛkgaŋ], *m.* (—s, *no pl.*) departure, going away.

weggießen [ˈvɛkgiːsən], *v.a. irr.* pour away.

weghaben [ˈvɛkhaːbən], *v.a. irr. etwas* —, understand how to do s.th, have the knack of doing s.th.

wegkommen [ˈvɛkkɔmən], *v.n. irr.* (*aux.* sein) get away; be lost.

wegkönnen [ˈvɛkkœnən], *v.n. irr. nicht* —, not be able to get away.

Weglassung [ˈveːklasuŋ], *f.* (—, *pl.* —en) omission.

wegmachen [ˈvɛkmaxən], *v.r. sich* —, decamp, make off.

wegmüssen [ˈvɛkmysən], *v.n. irr.* be obliged to go; have to go.

Wegnahme [ˈvɛknaːmə], *f.* (—, *no pl.*) taking, seizure, capture.

Wegreise [ˈvɛkraɪzə], *f.* (—, *no pl.*) departure.

Wegscheide [ˈveːkʃaɪdə], *f.* (—, *pl.* —n) crossroads, crossways.

wegscheren [ˈvɛkʃeːrən], *v.a.* clip; shave off. — *v.r. sich* —, be off.

wegschnappen [ˈvɛkʃnapən], *v.a.* snatch away.

wegsehnen [ˈvɛkzeːnən], *v.r. sich* —, wish o.s. far away; long to get away.

wegsein [ˈvɛkzaɪn], *v.n. irr.* (*aux.* sein) (*person*) be gone, be away; have gone off; (*things*) be lost; *ganz* —, (*coll.*) be beside o.s. *or* amazed.

wegsetzen [ˈvɛkzɛtsən], *v.a.* put away.

wegspülen [ˈvɛkʃpyːlən], *v.a.* wash away.

Wegstunde [ˈveːkʃtundə], *f.* (—, *pl.* —n) an hour's walk.

Wegweiser [ˈveːkvaɪzər], *m.* (—s, *pl.* —) signpost, road-sign.

wegwenden [ˈvɛkvɛndən], *v.r. irr. sich* —, turn away.

wegwerfen [ˈvɛkvɛrfən], *v.a. irr.* throw away.

wegwerfend [ˈvɛkvɛrfənt], *adj.* disparaging, disdainful.

Wegzehrung [ˈveːktseːruŋ], *f.* (—, *no pl.*) food for the journey; (*Eccl.*) viaticum.

wegziehen ['vɛktsi:ən], *v.a. irr.* draw away, pull away. — *v.n. (aux.* sein) march away; (*fig.*) move, remove.

Wegzug ['vɛktsu:k], *m.* (—s, *no pl.*) removal; moving away.

Weh [ve:], *n.* (—s, *no pl.*) pain; grief, pang; misfortune.

weh [ve:], *adj.* painful, sore; *mir ist — ums Herz,* I am sick at heart; my heart aches. — *adv.* — *tun,* ache; pain, hurt, offend, distress, grieve. — *int.* — *mir!* woe is me!

Wehen ['ve:ən], *n. pl.* birth-pangs, labour-pains.

wehen ['ve:ən], *v.n. (wind)* blow.

Wehgeschrei ['ve:gəʃraɪ], *n.* (—s, *no pl.*) wailings.

Wehklage ['ve:kla:gə], *f.* (—, *pl.* —n) lamentation.

wehklagen ['ve:kla:gən], *v.n. insep.* lament, wail.

wehleidig ['ve:laɪdɪç], *adj.* tearful; easily hurt; self-pitying.

wehmütig ['ve:my:tɪç], *adj.* sad, melancholy, wistful.

Wehr (1) [ve:r], *n.* (—s, *pl.* —e) weir.

Wehr (2) [ve:r], *f.* (—, *pl.* —en) defence, bulwark.

wehren ['ve:rən], *v.r. sich —,* defend o.s., offer resistance.

wehrhaft ['ve:rhaft], *adj.* capable of bearing arms, able-bodied.

wehrlos ['ve:rlo:s], *adj.* defenceless, unarmed; (*fig.*) weak, unprotected.

Wehrpflicht ['ve:rpflɪçt], *f.* (—, *no pl.*) compulsory military service, conscription.

Wehrstand ['ve:rʃtant], *m.* (—s, *no pl.*) the military.

Weib [vaɪp], *n.* (—(e)s, *pl.* —er) woman; (*Poet.*) wife.

Weibchen ['vaɪpçən], *n.* (—s, *pl.* —) (*animal*) female.

Weiberfeind ['vaɪbərfaɪnt], *m.* (—s, *pl.* —e) woman-hater, misogynist.

Weiberherrschaft ['vaɪbərhɛrʃaft], *f.* (—, *no pl.*) petticoat rule.

weibisch ['vaɪbɪʃ], *adj.* womanish, effeminate.

weiblich ['vaɪplɪç], *adj.* female, feminine; womanly.

Weiblichkeit ['vaɪplɪçkaɪt], *f.* (—, *no pl.*) womanliness, femininity.

Weibsbild ['vaɪpsbɪlt], *n.* (—s, *pl.* —er) (*sl.*) female; wench.

weich [vaɪç], *adj.* weak; soft; tender, gentle; effeminate; sensitive; — *machen,* soften; — *werden,* relent.

Weichbild ['vaɪçbɪlt], *n.* (—s, *no pl.*) precincts; city boundaries.

Weiche ['vaɪçə], *f.* (—, *pl.* —n) (*Railw.*) switch, points.

weichen (1) ['vaɪçən], *v.a.* steep, soak, soften.

weichen (2) ['vaɪçən], *v.n. irr. (aux.* sein) yield away, make way, give ground.

Weichensteller ['vaɪçənʃtɛlər], *m.* (—s, *pl.* —) (*Railw.*) pointsman, signalman.

Weichheit ['vaɪçhaɪt], *f.* (—, *no pl.*) softness; (*fig.*) weakness, tenderness.

weichherzig ['vaɪçhɛrtsɪç], *adj.* softhearted, tender-hearted.

weichlich ['vaɪçlɪç], *adj.* soft; (*fig.*) weak, effeminate.

Weichling ['vaɪçlɪŋ], *m.* (—s, *pl.* —e) weakling.

Weichsel ['vaɪksəl], *f.* Vistula.

Weichselkirsche ['vaɪksəlkɪrʃə], *f.* (—, *pl.* —n) sour cherry; morello.

Weide ['vaɪdə], *f.* (—, *pl.* —n) pasture, pasturage; (*Bot.*) willow.

Weideland ['vaɪdəlant], *n.* (—s, *pl.* ⁺er) pasture-ground.

weiden ['vaɪdən], *v.a.,v.n.* pasture, feed.

Weidenbaum ['vaɪdənbaum], *m.* (—s, *pl.* ⁺e) willow-tree.

Weiderich ['vaɪdərɪç], *m.* (—s, *pl.* —e) willow-herb, loose-strife, rose bay.

Weidgenosse ['vaɪtgənɔsə], *m.* (—en, *pl.* —en) fellow huntsman.

weidlich ['vaɪtlɪç], *adv. (rare)* greatly, thoroughly.

Weidmann ['vaɪtman], *m.* (—s, *pl.* ⁺er) sportsman, huntsman.

Weidmannsheil! ['vaɪtmanshaɪl], *excl.* tally-ho!

weigern ['vaɪgərn], *v.r. sich —,* refuse, decline.

Weigerung ['vaɪgəruŋ], *f.* (—, *pl.* —en) refusal, denial.

Weih [vaɪ], *m.* (—en, *pl.* —en) (*Orn.*) kite.

Weihbischof ['vaɪbɪʃɔf], *m.* (—s, *pl.* ⁺e) suffragan bishop.

Weihe ['vaɪə], *f.* (—, *pl.* —en) consecration; (*priest*) ordination; initiation; (*fig.*) solemnity.

weihen ['vaɪən], *v.a.* bless, consecrate; ordain. — *v.r. sich —,* devote o.s. (to).

Weiher ['vaɪər], *m.* (—s, *pl.* —e) pond, fishpond.

weihevoll ['vaɪəfɔl], *adj.* solemn.

Weihnachten ['vaɪnaxtən], *n. or f.* Christmas.

Weihnachtsabend ['vaɪnaxtsa:bənt], *m.* (—s, *pl.* —e) Christmas Eve.

Weihnachtsfeiertag ['vaɪnaxtsfaɪərta:k], *m.* (—s, *pl.* —e) Christmas Day; *zweiter —,* Boxing Day.

Weihnachtsgeschenk ['vaɪnaxtsgəʃɛŋk], *n.* (—s, *pl.* —e) Christmas box, Christmas present.

Weihnachtslied ['vaɪnaxtsli:t], *n.* (—(e)s, *pl.* —er) Christmas carol.

Weihnachtsmann ['vaɪnaxtsman], *m.* (—(e)s, *pl.* ⁺er) Santa Claus, Father Christmas.

Weihrauch ['vaɪraux], *m.* (—s, *no pl.*) incense.

Weihwasser ['vaɪvasər], *n.* (—s, *no pl.*) holy water.

weil [vaɪl], *conj.* because, as, since.

weiland ['vaɪlant], *adv. (obs.)* formerly, once.

Weile ['vaɪlə], *f.* (—, *no pl.*) while, short time; leisure.

weilen ['vaɪlən], *v.n.* tarry, stay, abide.

Wein [vaɪn], *m.* (—en *pl.* —e) wine; (*plant*) vine; *einem reinen — einschenken,* tell s.o. the truth.

Weinbau ['vaɪnbau], m. (—s, no pl.) vine growing, viticulture.

Weinbeere ['vaɪnbeːrə], f. (—, pl. —n) grape.

Weinberg ['vaɪnbɛrk], m. (—s, pl. —e) vineyard.

Weinbrand ['vaɪnbrant], m. (—s, no pl.) brandy.

weinen ['vaɪnən], v.n. weep, cry.

Weinernte ['vaɪnɛrntə], f. (—, pl. —n) vintage.

Weinessig ['vaɪnɛsɪç], m. (—s, no pl.) (wine) vinegar.

Weinfaß ['vaɪnfas], n. (—sses, pl. ⸚sser) wine-cask.

Weingeist ['vaɪngaɪst], m. (—es, no pl.) spirits of wine, alcohol.

Weinhändler ['vaɪnhɛndlər], m. (—s, pl. —) wine merchant.

Weinkarte ['vaɪnkartə], f. (—, pl. —n) wine-list.

Weinkeller ['vaɪnkɛlər], m. (—s, pl. —) wine-cellar; wine-tavern.

Weinkellerei ['vaɪnkɛlərai], f. (—, pl. —en) wine-store.

Weinkelter ['vaɪnkɛltər], f. (—, pl. —n) wine-press.

Weinkneipe ['vaɪnknaɪpə], f. (—, pl. —n) wine-tavern.

Weinkoster ['vaɪnkɔstər], m. (—s, pl. —) wine-taster.

Weinlaub ['vaɪnlaup], n. (—s, no pl.) vine-leaves.

Weinlese ['vaɪnleːzə], f. (—, pl. —n) vintage, grape harvest.

Weinranke ['vaɪnraŋkə], f. (—, pl. —n) vine-branch, tendril.

Weinschenke ['vaɪnʃɛŋkə], f. (—, pl. —) wine-house, tavern.

weinselig ['vaɪnzeːlɪç], adj. tipsy.

Weinstein ['vaɪnʃtaɪn], m. (—s, no pl.) tartar.

Weinsteinsäure ['vaɪnʃtaɪnzɔyrə], f. (—, no pl.) tartaric acid.

Weinstock ['vaɪnʃtɔk], m. (—s, pl. ⸚e) vine.

Weintraube ['vaɪntraubə], f. (—, pl. —n) grape, bunch of grapes.

weinumrankt ['vaɪnumraŋkt], adj. vine-clad.

weise ['vaɪzə], adj. wise, prudent.

Weise (1) ['vaɪzə], m. (—n, pl. —n) wise man, sage.

Weise (2) ['vaɪzə], f. (—, pl. —n) manner, fashion; method, way; tune, melody.

weisen ['vaɪzən], v.a. irr. point to, point out, show.

Weiser ['vaɪzər], m. (—s, pl. —) signpost; indicator; (clock) hand.

Weisheit ['vaɪshaɪt], f. (—, pl. —en) wisdom, prudence.

Weisheitszahn ['vaɪshaɪtstsaːn], m. (—s, pl. ⸚e) wisdom tooth.

weislich ['vaɪslɪç], adv. wisely, prudently, advisedly.

weismachen ['vaɪsmaxən], v.a. einem etwas —, (coll.) spin a yarn to s.o.; laß dir nichts —, don't be taken in.

weissagen ['vaɪszaːgən], v.a. insep. prophesy, foretell.

Weissager ['vaɪszaːgər], m. (—s, pl. —) prophet, soothsayer.

Weissagung ['vaɪszaːguŋ], f. (—, pl. —en) prophecy.

weiß [vaɪs], adj. white, clean, blank.

Weißbuche ['vaɪsbuːxə], f. (—, pl. —n) (Bot.) hornbeam.

Weiße ['vaɪsə], f. (—, no pl.) whiteness; (fig.) (dial.) pale ale.

weißglühend ['vaɪsglyːənt], adj. at white heat, incandescent, white hot.

Weißnäherin ['vaɪsnɛːərɪn], f. (—, pl. —nen) seamstress.

Weißwaren ['vaɪsvaːrən], f. pl. linen.

Weisung ['vaɪzuŋ], f. (—, pl. —en) order, direction, instruction; directive.

weit [vaɪt], adj. distant, far, far off; wide, broad, vast, extensive; (clothing) loose, too big.

weitab [vaɪt'ap], adv. far away.

weitaus [vaɪt'aus], adv. by far.

weitblickend ['vaɪtblɪkənt], adj. far-sighted.

Weite ['vaɪtə], f. (—, pl. —n) width, breadth; distance.

weiten ['vaɪtən], v.a. widen, expand.

weiter ['vaɪtər], adj. further, farther, wider.

weiterbefördern ['vaɪtərbəfœrdərn], v.a. send, forward, send on.

weiterbilden ['vaɪtərbɪldən], v.a. improve, develop(e), extend.

Weitere ['vaɪtərə], n. (—n, no pl.) rest, remainder.

weiterführen ['vaɪtərfyːrən], v.a. continue, carry on.

weitergeben ['vaɪtərgeːbən], v.a. irr. pass on.

weitergehen ['vaɪtərgeːən], v.n. irr. (aux. sein) walk on.

weiterhin ['vaɪtərhɪn], adv. furthermore; in time to come; in future.

weiterkommen ['vaɪtərkɔmən], v.n. irr. (aux. sein) get on, advance.

Weiterung ['vaɪtəruŋ], f. (—, pl. —en) widening, enlargement.

weitgehend ['vaɪtgeːənt], adj. far-reaching, sweeping.

weitläufig ['vaɪtlɔyfɪç], adj. ample, large; detailed, elaborate; distant, widespread; diffuse, long-winded.

weitschweifig ['vaɪtʃvaɪfɪç], adj. prolix, diffuse, rambling.

weitsichtig ['vaɪtzɪçtɪç], adj. long-sighted.

weittragend ['vaɪttraːgənt], adj. portentous, far-reaching.

weitverbreitet ['vaɪtfɛrbraɪtət], adj. widespread.

Weizen ['vaɪtsən], m. (—s, no pl.) wheat.

Weizengrieß ['vaɪtsəngriːs], m. (—es, no pl.) semolina; grits.

welch [vɛlç], pron. what (a).

welcher, -e, -es ['vɛlçər], interr. pron. which ? what ? — rel. pron. who which, that; (indef.) (coll.) some.

welcherlei ['vɛlçərlaɪ], *indecl. adj.* of what kind.

Welfe ['vɛlfə], *m.*(—**n**, *pl.* —**n**) Guelph.

welk [vɛlk], *adj.* faded, withered; — *werden*, fade, wither.

welken ['vɛlkən], *v.n.* (*aux.* sein) wither, fade, decay.

Wellblech ['vɛlblɛç], *n.* (—**s**, *no pl.*) corrugated iron.

Welle ['vɛlə], *f.* (—, *pl.* —**n**) wave, billow.

wellen ['vɛlən], *v.a.* wave.

Wellenbewegung ['vɛlənbəve:guŋ], *f.* (—, *pl.* —**en**) undulation.

Wellenlinie ['vɛlənli:njə], *f.* (—, *pl.* —**n**) wavy line.

wellig ['vɛlɪç], *adj.* wavy, undulating.

welsch [vɛlʃ], *adj.* foreign; Italian; French.

Welschkohl ['vɛlʃko:l], *m.* (—**s**, *no pl.*) (*Bot.*) savoy cabbage.

Welschkorn ['vɛlʃkɔrn], *n.* (—**s**, *no pl.*) (*Bot.*) Indian corn.

Welt [vɛlt], *f.* (—, *pl.* —**en**) world, earth; universe; society.

Weltall ['vɛltal], *n.* (—**s**, *no pl.*) universe, cosmos; (outer) space.

Weltanschauung ['vɛltanʃauuŋ], *f.* (—, *pl.* —**en**) view of life, philosophy of life, ideology.

Weltbeschreibung ['vɛltbəʃraɪbuŋ], *f.* (—, *no pl.*) cosmography.

Weltbürger ['vɛltbyrgər], *m.* (—**s**, *pl.* —) cosmopolitan.

welterschütternd ['vɛltɛrʃytərnt], *adj.* world-shaking.

weltfremd ['vɛltfrɛmt], *adj.* unwordly, unsophisticated.

Weltgeschichte ['vɛltgəʃɪçtə], *f.* (—, *no pl.*) world history.

Weltherrschaft ['vɛlthɛrʃaft], *f.* (—, *no pl.*) world dominion.

Weltkenntnis ['vɛltkɛntnɪs], *f.* (—, *no pl.*) worldly wisdom.

weltklug ['vɛltklu:k], *adj.* astute, worldly-wise.

Weltkrieg ['vɛltkri:k], *m.* (—**es**, *pl.* —**e**) world war.

weltlich ['vɛltlɪç], *adj.* worldly; (*Eccl.*) temporal, secular.

Weltmacht ['vɛltmaxt], *f.* (—, *pl.* —**e**) world power, great power.

Weltmeer ['vɛltme:r], *n.* (—**s**, *pl.* —**e**) ocean.

Weltmeisterschaft ['vɛltmaɪstərʃaft], *f.* (—, *pl.* —**en**) world championship.

Weltordnung ['vɛltɔrdnuŋ], *f.* (— *pl.* —**en**) cosmic order.

Weltraum ['vɛltraum], *m.* (—**s**, *no pl.*) space.

Weltraumflug ['vɛltraumflu:k], *m.* (—(**e**)**s**, *pl.* —**e**) space flight.

Weltraumforschung ['vɛltraumfɔrʃuŋ], *f.* (—, *no pl.*) space exploration.

Weltraumgeschoss ['vɛltraumgəʃo:s], *n.* (—**es**, *pl.* —**e**) space rocket.

Weltruf ['vɛltru:f], *m.* (—**s**, *no pl.*) world-wide renown.

Weltschmerz ['vɛltʃmɛrts], *m.* (—**es**, *no pl.*) world-weariness, Wertherism; melancholy.

Weltsprache ['vɛltʃpra:xə], *f.* (—, *pl.* —**en**) universal language; world language.

Weltstadt ['vɛltʃtat], *f.* (—, *pl.* —**e**) metropolis.

Weltumsegelung ['vɛltumze:gluŋ], *f.* (—, *pl.* —**en**) circumnavigation (of the globe).

Weltuntergang ['vɛltuntərgaŋ], *m.* —**s**, *no pl.*) end of the world.

Weltwirtschaft ['vɛltvɪrtʃaft], *f.* (—, *no pl.*) world trade.

wem [ve:m], *pers. pron.* (*Dat. of* **wer**) to whom — *interr. pron.* to whom?

wen [ve:n], *pers. pron.* (*Acc. of* **wer**) whom — *interr. pron.* whom?

Wende ['vɛndə], *f.* (—, *pl.* —**n**) turn, turning(point).

Wendekreis ['vɛndəkraɪs], *m.* (—**es**, *pl.* —**e**) tropic.

Wendeltreppe ['vɛndəltrɛpə], *f.* (—, *pl.* —**n**) spiral staircase.

wenden ['vɛndən], *v.a. reg. & irr.* turn.

Wendepunkt ['vɛndəpuŋkt], *m.* (—**es**, *pl.* —**e**) turning point; crisis.

Wendung ['vɛnduŋ], *f.* (—, *pl.* —**en**) turn, turning; crisis; (*speech*) phrase.

wenig ['ve:nɪç], *adj.* little, few; *ein* —, a little.

weniger ['ve:nɪgər], *adj.* less, fewer.

wenigstens ['ve:nɪçstəns], *adv.* at least.

wenn [vɛn], *conj.* if; when; whenever, in case; — *nicht*, unless.

wenngleich [vɛn'glaɪç], *conj.* though, although.

wer [ve:r], *rel. pron.* who, he who; — *auch*, whoever. — *interr. pron.* who? which? — *da?* who goes there?

Werbekraft ['vɛrbəkraft], *f.* (—, *no pl.*) (*Advertising*) attraction; appeal; publicity value.

werben ['vɛrbən], *v.n. irr.* advertise, canvass; court, woo. — *v.a.* (*soldiers*) recruit.

Werbung ['vɛrbuŋ], *f.* (—, *pl.* —**en**) advertising, publicity, propaganda, recruiting; courtship.

Werdegang ['ve:rdəgaŋ], *m.* (—**s**, *no pl.*) evolution, development.

werden ['ve:rdən], *v.n. irr.* (*aux.* sein) become, get; grow; turn; *Arzt* — become a doctor; *alt* —, grow old; *bleich* —, turn pale.

werdend ['ve:rdənt], *adj.* becoming; nascent, incipient, budding.

werfen ['vɛrfən], *v.a. irr.* throw, cast.

Werft (1) [vɛrft], *m.* (—(**e**)**s**, *pl.* —**e**) warp.

Werft (2) [vɛrft], *f.* (—, *pl.* —**en**) dockyard, shipyard, wharf.

Werk [vɛrk], *n.* (— (**e**)**s**, *pl.* —**e**) work, action, deed; undertaking; (*Ind.*) works, plant, mill, factory.

Werkführer ['vɛrkfy:rər], *m.* (—**s**, *pl.* —) foreman.

Werkleute ['vɛrkləytə], *pl.* workmen.

Werkmeister ['vɛrkmaɪstər], *m.* (—**s**, *pl.* —) overseer.

werktätig ['vɛrktɛ:tɪç], *adj.* active, practical; hard-working.

279

Werkzeug

Werkzeug ['vɛrktsɔyk], *n.* (**—s,** *pl.* **—e**) implement, tool, jig, instrument.

Wermut ['ve:rmu:t], *m.* (**—s,** *no pl.*) absinthe, vermouth.

Wert [ve:rt], *m.* (**—(e)s,** *pl.* **—e**) value, worth, price; use; merit; importance.

wert [ve:rt], *adj.* valuable; worth; dear, esteemed.

Wertangabe ['ve:rtanga:bə], *f.* (**—,** *pl.* **—n**) valuation; declared value.

Wertbestimmung ['ve:rtbəʃtimuŋ], *f.* (**—,** *no pl.*) appraisal, assessment, valuation.

Wertbrief ['ve:rtbri:f], *m.* (**—s,** *pl.* **—e**) registered letter.

werten ['ve:rtən], *v.a.* value.

Wertgegenstand ['ve:rtgeːgənʃtant], *m.* (**—s,** *pl.* ¨**e**) article of value.

Wertmesser ['ve:rtmɛsər], *m.* (**—s,** *pl.* **—**) standard.

Wertpapiere ['ve:rtpapiːrə], *n. pl.* securities.

Wertsachen ['ve:rtzaxən], *f. pl.* valuables.

wertschätzen ['ve:rtʃɛtsən], *v.a.* esteem (highly).

wertvoll ['ve:rtfɔl], *adj.* of great value, valuable.

Wertzeichen ['ve:rttsaiçən], *n.* (**—s,** *pl.* **—**) stamp; coupon.

wes [vɛs], *pers. pron.* (*obs.*) whose.

Wesen ['ve:zən], *n.* (**—s,** *pl.* **—**) being, creature; reality; essence, nature, substance; character, demeanour; (*in compounds*) organisation, affairs.

wesenlos ['ve:zənloːs], *adj.* disembodied, unsubstantial, shadowy; trivial.

wesensgleich ['ve:zənsglaiç], *adj.* identical, substantially the same.

wesentlich ['ve:zəntliç], *adj.* essential, material.

weshalb [vɛs'halp], *conj., adv.* wherefore, why; therefore.

Wespe ['vɛspə], *f.* (**—,** *pl.* **—n**) (*Ent.*) wasp.

Wespennest ['vɛspənnɛst], *n.* (**—s,** *pl.* **—er,**) wasp's nest; *in ein — stechen,* stir up a hornet's nest.

wessen ['vɛsən], *pers .pron.* (*Genit. of* **wer**) whose. *— interr. pron.* whose ?

Weste ['vɛstə], *f.* (**—,** *pl.* **—n**) waistcoat.

Westen ['vɛstən], *m.* (**—s,** *no pl.*) west; *nach —,* westward.

Westfalen [vɛst'faːlən], *n.* Westphalia.

Westindien [vɛst'ʔndjən], *n.* the West Indies.

weswegen [vɛsˈve:gən] *see* **weshalb.**

Wettbewerb ['vɛtbəvɛrp], *m.* (**—s,** *pl.* **—e**) competition, rivalry; *unlauterer —,* unfair competition.

Wettbewerber ['vɛtbəvɛrbər], *m.* (**—s,** *pl.* **—**) rival, competitor.

Wette ['vɛtə], *f.* (**—,** *pl.* **—n**) bet, wager; *um die — laufen,* race one another.

Wetteifer ['vɛtaifər], *m.* (**—s,** *no pl.*) rivalry.

wetteifern ['vɛtaifərn], *v.n. insep.* vie (with), compete.

wetten ['vɛtən], *v.a., v.n.* bet, lay a wager, wager.

Wetter ['vɛtər], *n.* (**—s,** *pl.* **—**) weather; bad weather, storm; *schlagende —,* (*Min.*) fire-damp.

Wetterbeobachtung ['vɛtərbəobaxtuŋ], *f.* (**—,** *pl.* **—en**) meteorological observation.

Wetterbericht ['vɛtərbəriçt], *m.* (**—s,** *pl.* **—e**) weather report *or* forecast.

Wetterfahne ['vɛtərfaːnə], *f.* (**—,** *pl.* **—en**) weather-cock, vane; (*fig.*) turncoat.

wetterfest ['vɛtərfɛst], *adj.* weatherproof.

Wetterglas ['vɛtərglaːs], *n.* (**—es,** *pl.* ¨**er**) barometer.

Wetterhahn ['vɛtərhaːn], *m.* (**—s,** *pl.* ¨**e**) weather-cock.

Wetterkunde ['vɛtərkundə], *f.* (**—,** *no pl.*) meteorology.

Wetterleuchten ['vɛtərlɔyçtən], *n.* (**—s,** *no pl.*) summer lightning; sheet lightning.

wettern ['vɛtərn], *v.n.* be stormy; (*fig.*) curse, swear, thunder (against), storm.

Wettervorhersage ['vɛtərfoːrheːrzaːgə], *f.* (**—,** *pl.* **—n**) weather forecast.

wetterwendisch ['vɛtərvɛndiʃ], *adj.* changeable; irritable, peevish.

Wettkampf ['vɛtkampf], *m.* (**—(e)s,** *pl.* ¨**e**) contest, tournament.

Wettlauf ['vɛtlauf], *m.* (**—s,** *pl.* ¨**e**) race.

wettmachen ['vɛtmaxən], *v.a.* make up for.

Wettrennen ['vɛtrɛnən], *n.* (**—s,** *pl.* **—**) racing, race.

Wettstreit ['vɛtʃtrait], *m.* (**—s,** *pl.* **—e**) contest, contention.

wetzen ['vɛtsən], *v.a.* whet, hone, sharpen.

Wichse ['vɪksə], *f.* (**—,** *pl.* **—n**) blacking, shoe-polish; (*fig.*) thrashing.

wichsen ['vɪksən], *v.a.* black, shine; (*fig.*) thrash.

Wicht [vɪçt], *m.* (**—(e)s,** *pl.* **—e**) creature; (*coll.*) chap.

Wichtelmännchen ['vɪçtəlmɛnçən], *n.* (**—s,** *pl.* **—**) pixie, goblin.

wichtig ['vɪçtiç], *adj.* important; weighty; significant; *sich — machen,* put on airs.

Wichtigkeit ['vɪçtiçkait], *f.* (**—,** *no pl.*) importance; significance.

Wicke ['vɪkə], *f.* (**—,** *pl.* **—n**) (*Bot.*) vetch.

Wickel ['vɪkəl], *m.* (**—s,** *pl.* **—**) roller; (*hair*) curler; (*Med.*) compress.

Wickelkind ['vɪkəlkint], *n.* (**—s,** *pl.* **—er**) babe in arms.

wickeln ['vɪkəln], *v.a.* roll, coil; wind; wrap (up); (*babies*) swaddle; (*hair*) curl.

Widder ['vɪdər], *m.* (**—s,** *pl.* **—**) ram; (*Astrol.*) Aries.

wider ['viːdər], *prep.* (*Acc.*) against, in opposition to, contrary to.

widerfahren [vi:dər'fa:rən], *v.n. irr. insep. (aux.* sein) happen to s.o.; befall s.o.; *einem Gerechtigkeit — lassen,* give s.o. his due.

Widerhaken ['vi:dərha:kən], *m.* (—s, *pl.* —) barb.

Widerhall ['vi:dərhal], *m.* (—s, *pl.* —e) echo, resonance; *(fig.)* response.

widerlegen [vi:dər'le:gən], *v.a. insep.* refute, disprove, prove (s.o.) wrong.

Widerlegung [vi:dər'le:guŋ], *f.* (—, *pl.* —en) refutation, rebuttal.

widerlich ['vi:dərlɪç], *adj.* disgusting, nauseating, repulsive.

widernatürlich ['vi:dərnaty:rlɪç], *adj.* unnatural; perverse.

widerraten [vi:dər'ra:tən], *v.a. irr. insep.* advise against; dissuade from.

widerrechtlich ['vi:dərrɛçtlɪç], *adj.* illegal, unlawful.

Widerrede ['vi:dərre:də], *f.* (—, *pl.* —n) contradiction.

Widerruf ['vi:dərru:f], *m.* (—s, *pl.* —e) revocation, recantation.

widerrufen [vi:dər'ru:fən], *v.a. irr. insep.* recant, retract, revoke.

Widersacher ['vi:dərzaxər], *m.* (—s, *pl.* —) adversary, antagonist.

Widerschein ['vi:dərʃain], *m.* (—s, *no pl.*) reflection.

widersetzen [vi:dər'zɛtsən], *v.r. insep. sich —,* resist, *(Dat.)* oppose.

widersetzlich [vi:dər'zɛtslɪç], *adj.* refractory, insubordinate.

Widersinn [vi:dər'zɪn], *m.* (—s, *no pl.*) nonsense, absurdity; paradox.

widersinnig ['vi:dərzɪnɪç], *adj.* nonsensical, absurd; paradoxical.

widerspenstig ['vi:dərʃpɛnstɪç], *adj.* refractory, rebellious, obstinate, stubborn.

widerspiegeln [vi:dər'ʃpi:gəln], *v.a.* reflect, mirror.

widersprechen [vi:dər'ʃprɛçən], *v.n. irr. insep. (Dat.)* contradict, gainsay.

Widerspruch ['vi:dərʃprux], *m.* (—es, *pl.* ⁺e) contradiction.

widerspruchsvoll ['vi:dərʃpruxsfɔl], *adj.* contradictory.

Widerstand ['vi:dərʃtant], *m.* (—s, *pl.* ⁺e) resistance, opposition.

widerstandsfähig ['vi:dərʃtantsfɛ:ɪç], *adj.* resistant, hardy.

widerstehen [vi:dər'ʃte:ən], *v.n. irr. insep. (Dat.)* resist, withstand; be distasteful (to).

Widerstreben [vi:dər'ʃtre:bən], *n.* (—s, *no pl.*) reluctance.

widerstreben [vi:dər'ʃtre:bən], *v.n. insep. (Dat.)* strive against, oppose; be distasteful to a p.

Widerstreit ['vi:dərʃtrait], *m.* (—s, *no pl.*) contradiction, opposition; conflict.

widerwärtig ['vi:dərvɛrtɪç], *adj.* unpleasant, disagreeable, repugnant, repulsive; hateful, odious.

Widerwille ['vi:dərvɪlə], *m.* (—ns, *no pl.*) aversion (to).

widmen ['vɪdmən], *v.a.* dedicate.

Widmung ['vɪdmuŋ], *f.* (—, *pl.* —en) dedication.

widrig ['vi:drɪç], *adj.* contrary, adverse, inimical, unfavourable.

widrigenfalls ['vi:drɪgənfals], *adv.* failing this, otherwise, else.

wie [vi:], *adv.* how. — *conj.* as, just as, like; — *geht's?* how are you?

wieder ['vi:dər], *adv.* again, anew, afresh; back, in return.

Wiederabdruck ['vi:dərapdruk], *m.* (—s, *pl.* —e) reprint.

Wiederaufbau [vi:dər'aufbau], *m.* (—s, *no pl.*) rebuilding.

Wiederaufnahme [vi:dər'aufna:mə], *f.* (—, *no pl.*) resumption.

Wiederbelebungsversuch ['vi:dərbəle:buŋsfɛrzu:x], *m.* (—es, *pl.* —e) attempt at resuscitation.

Wiederbezahlung ['vi:dərbətsa:luŋ], *f.* (—, *pl.* —en) reimbursement.

wiederbringen ['vi:dərbrɪŋən], *v.a. irr.* bring back, restore.

Wiedereinrichtung ['vi:dəraɪnrɪçtuŋ], *f.* (—, *no pl.*) reorganisation, re-establishment.

Wiedereinsetzung ['vi:dəraɪnzɛtsuŋ], *f.* (—, *pl.* —en) restoration, reinstatement, rehabilitation.

wiedererkennen ['vi:dərɛrkɛnən], *v.a. irr.* recognise.

Wiedererstattung ['vi:dərɛrʃtatuŋ], *f.* (—, *no pl.*) restitution.

Wiedergabe ['vi:dərga:bə], *f.* (—, *no pl.*) restitution, return; *(fig.)* rendering, reproduction.

wiedergeben ['vi:dərge:bən], *v.a. irr.* return, give back; *(fig.)* render.

Wiedergeburt ['vi:dərgəbu:rt], *f.* (—, *no pl.*) rebirth, regeneration, renascence.

Wiedergutmachung [vi:dər'gu:tmaxuŋ], *f.* (—, *no pl.*) reparation.

Wiederherstellung [vi:dər'he:rʃtɛluŋ], *f.* (—, *no pl.*) restoration; recovery.

Wiederherstellungsmittel [vi:dər'he:rʃtɛluŋsmɪtəl], *n.* (—s, *pl.* —) restorative, tonic.

wiederholen [vi:dər'ho:lən], *v.a. insep.* repeat, reiterate.

Wiederholung [vi:dər'ho:luŋ], *f.* (—, *pl.* —en) repetition.

Wiederkäuer ['vi:dərkɔyər], *m.* (—s, *pl.* —) ruminant.

Wiederkehr ['vi:dərke:r], *f.* (—, *no pl.*) return; recurrence.

wiederkehren ['vi:dərke:rən], *v.n. (aux.* sein) return.

wiederklingen ['vi:dərklɪŋən], *v.n. irr.* reverberate.

wiederkommen ['vi:dərkɔmən], *v.n. irr. (aux.* sein) return, come back.

Wiedersehen ['vi:dərze:ən], *n.* (—s, *no pl.*) reunion, meeting after separation; *auf —,* good-bye; so long! see you again!

wiedersehen ['vi:dərze:ən], *v.a. irr.* see again, meet again.

wiederum

wiederum ['vi:dərum], *adv.* again, anew, afresh.

Wiedervereinigung ['vi:dərfɛraɪnɪ-guŋ], *f.* (—, *pl.* —en) reunion, reunification.

Wiedervergeltung ['vi:dərfɛrgɛltuŋ], *f.* (—, *no pl.*) requital, retaliation, reprisal.

Wiederverkauf ['vi:dərfɛrkauf], *m.* (—s, *no pl.*) resale.

Wiederverkäufer ['vi:dərfɛrkɔyfər], *m.* (—s, *pl.* —) retailer.

Wiederversöhnung ['vi:dərfɛrzø:nuŋ], *f.* (—, *no pl.*) reconciliation.

Wiederwahl ['vi:dərva:l], *f.* (—, *no pl.*) re-election.

Wiege ['vi:gə], *f.* (—, *pl.* —n) cradle.

wiegen ['vi:gən], *v.a.* rock (the cradle). — *v.r. sich* — *in*, delude o.s. with. — *v.a., v.n. irr.* weigh.

Wiegenfest ['vi:gənfɛst], *n.* (—es, *pl.* —e) (*Poet., Lit.*) birthday.

Wiegenlied ['vi:gənli:t], *n.* (—s, *pl.* —er) cradle-song, lullaby.

wiehern ['vi:ərn], *v.n.* neigh.

Wien [vi:n], *n.* Vienna.

Wiese ['vi:zə], *f.* (—, *pl.* —n) meadow.

Wiesel ['vi:zəl], *n.* (—s, *pl.* —) (*Zool.*) weasel.

wieso [vi'zo:] *adv.* why? how do you mean? in what way?

wieviel [vi'fi:l], *adv.* how much, how many; *den* —*ten haben wir heute?* what is the date today?

wiewohl [vi'vo:l], *conj.* although, though.

Wild [vɪlt], *n.* (—(e)s, *no pl.*) game; venison.

wild [vɪlt], *adj.* wild, savage, fierce; furious.

Wildbach ['vɪltbax], *m.* (—s, *pl.* ⸚e) (mountain) torrent.

Wilddieb ['vɪltdi:p], *m.* (—(e)s, *pl.* —e) poacher.

Wilde ['vɪldə], *m.* (—n, *pl.* —n) savage.

wildern ['vɪldərn], *v.n.* poach.

Wildfang ['vɪltfaŋ], *m.* (—s, *pl.* ⸚e) scamp, tomboy.

wildfremd ['vɪltfrɛmt], *adj.* completely strange.

Wildhüter ['vɪlthy:tər], *m.* (—s, *pl.* —) gamekeeper.

Wildleder ['vɪltle:dər], *n.* (—s, *no pl.*) suède, doeskin, buckskin.

Wildnis ['vɪltnɪs], *f.* (—, *pl.* —se) wilderness, desert.

Wildpark ['vɪltpark], *m.* (—s, *pl.* —s) game-reserve.

Wildpret ['vɪltprɛt], *n.* (—s, *no pl.*) game; venison.

Wildschwein ['vɪltʃvaɪn], *n.* (—s, *pl.* —e) wild boar.

Wille ['vɪlə], *m.* (—ns, *no pl.*) will, wish, design, purpose.

willenlos ['vɪlənlo:s], *adj.* weak-minded.

willens ['vɪləns], *adv.* — *sein*, be willing, have a mind to.

Willenserklärung ['vɪlənsɛrklɛ:ruŋ], *f.* (—, *pl.* —en) (*Law*) declaratory act.

Willensfreiheit ['vɪlənsfraɪhaɪt], *f.* (—, *no pl.*) free will.

Willenskraft ['vɪlənskraft], *f.* (—, *no pl.*) strength of will, will-power.

willentlich ['vɪləntlɪç], *adv.* purposely, on purpose, intentionally, wilfully.

willfahren [vɪl'fa:rən], *v.n. insep.* (*Dat.*) comply with, gratify.

willfährig ['vɪlfɛ:rɪç], *adj.* compliant, complaisant.

willig ['vɪlɪç], *adj.* willing, ready, docile.

willkommen [vɪl'kɔmən], *adj.* welcome; — *heißen*, welcome.

Willkür ['vɪlky:r], *f.* (—, *no pl.*) free will; discretion; caprice, arbitrariness.

willkürlich ['vɪlky:rlɪç], *adj.* arbitrary.

wimmeln ['vɪməln], *v.n.* swarm, teem (with).

wimmern ['vɪmərn], *v.n.* whimper.

Wimpel ['vɪmpəl], *m.* (—s, *pl.* —) pennon, pennant, streamer.

Wimper ['vɪmpər], *f.* (—, *pl.* —n) eyelash; *ohne mit der* — *zu zucken*, without turning a hair, without batting an eyelid.

Wind [vɪnt], *m.* (—(e)s, *pl.* —e) wind, breeze; *von etwas* — *bekommen*, get wind of.

Windbeutel ['vɪntbɔytəl], *m.* (—s, *pl.* —) cream puff; (*fig.*) windbag.

Windbüchse ['vɪntbyksə], *f.* (—, *pl.* —n) air-gun.

Winde ['vɪndə], *f.* (—, *pl.* —n) (*Tech.*) windlass; (*Bot.*) bindweed.

Windel ['vɪndəl], *f.* (—, *pl.* —n) (baby's) napkin; (*Am.*) diaper.

windelweich ['vɪndəlvaɪç], *adj.* very soft, limp; *einen* — *schlagen*, beat s.o. to a jelly.

winden ['vɪndən], *v.a. irr.* wind, reel; wring; (*flowers*) make a wreath of. — *v.r. sich* —, writhe.

Windeseile ['vɪndəsaɪlə], *f.* (—, *no pl.*) lightning speed.

Windfahne ['vɪntfa:nə], *f.* (—, *pl.* —n) weather-cock, vane.

windfrei ['vɪntfraɪ], *adj.* sheltered.

Windhund ['vɪnthunt], *m.* (—s, *pl.* —e) greyhound; (*fig.*) windbag.

windig ['vɪndɪç], *adj.* windy.

Windklappe ['vɪntklapə], *f.* (—, *pl.* —n) air-valve.

Windlicht ['vɪntlɪçt], *n.* (—s, *pl.* —er) torch; storm lantern.

Windmühle ['vɪntmy:lə], *f.* (—, *pl.* —n) windmill.

Windpocken ['vɪntpɔkən], *f. pl.* (*Med.*) chicken-pox.

Windrichtung ['vɪntrɪçtuŋ], *f.* (—, *pl.* —en) direction of the wind.

Windrose ['vɪntro:zə], *f.* (—, *pl.* —n) compass card; windrose.

Windsbraut ['vɪntsbraut], *f.* (—, *no pl.*) gust of wind, squall; gale.

windschief ['vɪntʃi:f], *adj.* warped, bent.

Windschutzscheibe ['vɪntʃutsʃaɪbə], *f.* (—, *pl.* —n) (*Motor.*) windscreen.

Windseite ['vɪntsaɪtə], *f.* (—, *pl.* —n) windward side.

Windspiel ['vɪntʃpiːl], *n.* (—s, *pl.* —e) greyhound.

windstill ['vɪntʃtɪl], *adj.* calm.

Windung ['vɪnduŋ], *f.* (—, *pl.* —en) winding; convolution; twist, loop; coil; meandering.

Wink [vɪŋk], *m.* (—(e)s, *pl.* —e) sign, nod; (*fig.*) hint, suggestion.

Winkel ['vɪŋkəl], *m.* (—s, *pl.* —) corner; (*Maths.*) angle.

Winkeladvokat ['vɪŋkəlatvokaːt], *m.* (—en, *pl.* —en) quack lawyer.

Winkelmaß ['vɪŋkəlmaːs], *n.* (—es, *pl.* —e) set-square.

Winkelmesser ['vɪŋkəlmɛsər], *m.* (—s, *pl.* —) protractor.

Winkelzug ['vɪŋkəltsuːk], *m.* (—s, *pl.* ˙e) evasion, trick, shift.

winken ['vɪŋkən], *v.n.* signal, nod, beckon, wave.

winklig ['vɪŋklɪç], *adj.* angular.

winseln ['vɪnzəln], *v.n.* whimper, whine, wail.

Winter ['vɪntər], *m.* (—s, *pl.* —) winter.

Wintergarten ['vɪntərgartən], *m.* (—s, *pl.* ˙) conservatory.

Wintergewächs ['vɪntərgəvɛks], *n.* (—es, *pl.* —e) perennial plant.

Wintergrün ['vɪntərgryːn], *n.* (—s, *no pl.*) evergreen; wintergreen.

wintern ['vɪntərn], *v.n.* become wintry.

Winterschlaf ['vɪntərʃlaːf], *m.* (—s, *no pl.*) hibernation; *den* — *halten*, hibernate.

Winzer ['vɪntsər], *m.* (—s, *pl.* —) vine-grower.

winzig ['vɪntsɪç], *adj.* tiny, diminutive.

Wipfel ['vɪpfəl], *m.* (—s, *pl.* —) top (of a tree), tree-top.

Wippe ['vɪpə], *f.* (—, *pl.* —n) seesaw.

wippen ['vɪpən], *v.n.* balance, see-saw.

wir [viːr], *pers. pron.* we.

Wirbel ['vɪrbəl], *m.* (—s, *pl.* —) (*water*) whirlpool, eddy; whirlwind; (*drum*) roll; (*head*) crown; (*back*) vertebra.

wirbeln ['vɪrbəln], *v.a., v.n.* whirl.

Wirbelsäule ['vɪrbəltsɔylə], *f.* (—, *pl.* —n) spine, vertebral column.

Wirbelwind ['vɪrbəlvɪnt], *m.* (—s, *pl.* —e) whirlwind.

Wirken ['vɪrkən], *n.* (—s, *no pl.*) activity.

wirken ['vɪrkən], *v.a.* effect, work; bring to pass; (*materials*) weave; (*dough*) knead. — *v.n.* work.

Wirker ['vɪrkər], *m.* (—s, *pl.* —) weaver.

wirklich ['vɪrklɪç], *adj.* real, actual; true, genuine.

Wirklichkeit ['vɪrklɪçkaɪt], *f.* (—, *no pl.*) reality.

wirksam ['vɪrkzaːm], *adj.* effective, efficacious.

Wirksamkeit ['vɪrkzaːmkaɪt], *f.* (—, *no pl.*) efficacy, efficiency.

Wirkung ['vɪrkuŋ], *f.* (—, *pl.* —en) working, operation; reaction; efficacy; effect, result, consequence; force, in-

fluence; *eine* — *ausüben auf*, have an effect on; influence s.o. *or* s.th.

Wirkungskreis ['vɪrkuŋskraɪs], *m.* —es, *pl.* —e) sphere of activity.

wirkungslos ['vɪrkuŋsloːs], *adj.* ineffectual.

wirkungsvoll ['vɪrkuŋsfɔl], *adj.* effective, efficacious; (*fig.*) impressive.

wirr [vɪr], *adj.* tangled, confused; — *durcheinander*, higgledy-piggledy; *mir ist ganz* — *im Kopf*, my head is going round.

Wirren ['vɪrən], *f. pl.* troubles, disorders, disturbances.

wirrköpfig ['vɪrkœpfɪç], *adj.* muddle-headed.

Wirrsal ['vɪrzaːl], *n.* (—s, *pl.* —e) confusion, disorder.

Wirrwarr ['vɪrvar], *m.* (—s, *no pl.*) jumble, hurly-burly, hubbub.

Wirt [vɪrt], *m.* (—(e)s, *pl.* —e) host; innkeeper; landlord.

Wirtin ['vɪrtɪn], *f.* (—, *pl.* —innen) hostess, landlady, innkeeper's wife.

wirtlich ['vɪrtlɪç], *adj.* hospitable.

Wirtschaft ['vɪrtʃaft], *f.* (—, *pl.* —en) housekeeping; administration; economy; household; housekeeping; inn, ale-house; (*coll.*) mess.

wirtschaften ['vɪrtʃaftən], *v.n.* keep house, housekeep; administer, run; (*coll.*) rummage.

Wirtschafterin ['vɪrtʃaftərɪn], *f.* (—, *pl.* —innen) housekeeper.

wirtschaftlich ['vɪrtʃaftlɪç], *adj.* economical, thrifty.

Wirtschaftlichkeit ['vɪrtʃaftlɪçkaɪt], *f.* (—, *no pl.*) economy; profitability.

Wirtschaftsgeld ['vɪrtʃaftsgɛlt], *n.* (—s, *pl.* —er) housekeeping-money.

Wirtshaus ['vɪrtshaus], *n.* (—es, *pl.* ˙er) inn.

Wisch [vɪʃ], *m.* (—es, *pl.* —e) scrap of paper, rag.

wischen ['vɪʃən], *v.a.* wipe.

wispern ['vɪspərn], *v.a., v.n.* whisper.

Wißbegier(de) ['vɪsbəgiːr(də)], *f.* (—, *no pl.*) craving for knowledge; curiosity.

Wissen ['vɪsən], *n.* (—s, *no pl.*) knowledge, learning, erudition.

wissen ['vɪsən], *v.a. irr.* know, be aware of (a fact); be able to.

Wissenschaft ['vɪsənʃaft], *f.* (—, *pl.* —en) learning, scholarship; science.

wissenschaftlich ['vɪsənʃaftlɪç], *adj.* learned, scholarly; scientific.

wissenswert ['vɪsənsveːrt], *adj.* worth knowing.

Wissenszweig ['vɪsənstsvaɪk], *m.* (—s, *pl.* —e) branch of knowledge.

wissentlich ['vɪsəntlɪç], *adj.* deliberate, wilful. — *adv.* knowingly.

wittern ['vɪtərn], *v.a.* scent, smell; (*fig.*) suspect.

Witterung ['vɪtəruŋ], *f.* (—, *no pl.*) weather; trail; scent.

Witterungsverhältnisse ['vɪtəruŋsfərhɛltnɪsə], *n. pl.* atmospheric conditions.

Witterungswechsel ['vɪtərunsvɛksəl], *m.* (**—s**, *no pl.*) change in the weather.

Witwe ['vɪtvə], *f.* (**—**, *pl.* **—n**) widow.

Witwer ['vɪtvər], *m.* (**—s**, *pl.* **—**) widower.

Witz [vɪts], *m.* (**—es**, *pl.* **—e**) wit, brains; joke, jest, witticism; funny story.

Witzblatt ['vɪtsblat], *n.* (**—s**, *pl.* ⁻**er**) satirical *or* humorous journal.

Witzbold ['vɪtsbɔlt], *m.* (**—es**, *pl.* **—e**) wag; wit.

witzeln ['vɪtsəln], *v.n.* poke fun (at).

witzig ['vɪtsɪç], *adj.* witty; funny, comical; bright.

wo [vo:], *interr. adv.* where? — *conj.* when.

wobei [vo:'baɪ], *adv.* by which, at which, in connection with which; whereby; in doing so.

Woche ['vɔxə], *f.* (**—**, *pl.* **—n**) week.

Wochenbericht ['vɔxənbərɪçt], *m.* (**—s**, *pl.* **—e**) weekly report.

Wochenbett ['vɔxənbɛt], *n.* (**—s**, *no pl.*) confinement.

Wochenblatt ['vɔxənblat], *n.* (**—s**, *pl.* ⁻**er**) weekly (paper).

Wochenlohn ['vɔxənlo:n], *m.* (**—s**, *pl.* ⁻**e**) weekly wage(s).

Wochenschau ['vɔxənʃau], *f.* (**—**, *no pl.*) newsreel.

Wochentag ['vɔxənta:k], *m.* (**—s**, *pl.* **—e**) week-day.

wöchentlich ['vœçəntlɪç], *adj.* weekly, every week.

wodurch [vo:'durç], *adv.* whereby, by which, through which; (*interr.*) by what?

wofern [vo:'fɛrn], *conj.* if, provided that.

wofür [vo:'fy:r], *adv.* for what, for which, wherefore.

Woge ['vo:gə], *f.* (**—**, *pl.* **—n**) wave, billow.

wogegen [vo:'ge:gən], *adv.* against what, against which, in return for which.

wogen ['vo:gən], *v.n.* heave, sway; (*fig.*) fluctuate.

woher [vo:'he:r], *adv.* whence, from what place, how.

wohin [vo:'hɪn], *adv.* whither, where.

wohingegen [vo:hɪn'ge:gən], *conj.* (*obs.*) whereas.

Wohl [vo:l], *n.* (**—(e)s**, *no pl.*) welfare, health; *auf dein —*, your health! cheers!

wohl [vo:l], *adv.* well, fit; indeed, doubtless, certainly; *ja —*, to be sure.

wohlan! [vo:l'an], *excl.* well! now then!

wohlauf! [vo:l'auf], *excl.* cheer up! — *sein*, be in good health.

wohlbedacht ['vo:lbədaxt], *adj.* well considered.

Wohlbefinden ['vo:lbəfɪndən], *n.* (**—s**, *no pl.*) good health.

Wohlbehagen ['vo:lbəha:gən], *n.* (**—s**, *no pl.*) comfort, ease, wellbeing.

wohlbehalten ['vo:lbəhaltən], *adj.* safe.

wohlbekannt ['vo:lbəkant], *adj.* well known.

wohlbeleibt ['vo:lbəlaɪpt], *adj.* corpulent, stout.

wohlbestallt ['vo:lbəʃtalt], *adj.* duly installed.

Wohlergehen ['vo:lɛrge:ən], *n.* (**—s**, *no pl.*) welfare, wellbeing.

wohlerhalten ['vo:lɛrhaltən], *adj.* well preserved.

wohlerzogen ['vo:lɛrtso:gən], *adj.* well bred, well brought up.

Wohlfahrt ['vo:lfa:rt], *f.* (**—**, *no pl.*) welfare, prosperity.

wohlfeil ['vo:lfaɪl], *adj.* cheap, inexpensive.

Wohlgefallen ['vo:lgəfalən], *n.* (**—s**, *no pl.*) pleasure, delight, approval.

wohlgefällig ['vo:lgəfɛlɪç], *adj.* pleasant, agreeable.

Wohlgefühl ['vo:lgəfy:l], *n.* (**—s**, *no pl.*) comfort, ease.

wohlgelitten ['vo:lgəlɪtən], *adj.* popular.

wohlgemeint ['vo:lgəmaɪnt], *adj.* well meant.

wohlgemerkt ['vo:lgəmɛrkt], *adv.* mind you! mark my words!

wohlgemut ['vo:lgəmu:t], *adj.* cheerful, merry.

wohlgeneigt ['vo:lgənaɪkt], *adj.* well disposed (towards).

wohlgepflegt ['vo:lgəpfle:kt], *adj.* well kept.

wohlgeraten ['vo:lgəra:tən], *adj.* successful; well turned out; good, well behaved.

Wohlgeruch ['vo:lgəru:x], *m.* (**—es**, *pl.* ⁻**e**) sweet scent, perfume, fragrance.

Wohlgeschmack ['vo:lgəʃmak], *m.* (**—s**, *no pl.*) pleasant flavour, agreeable taste.

wohlgesinnt ['vo:lgəzɪnt], *adj.* well disposed.

wohlgestaltet ['vo:lgəʃtaltət], *adj.* well shaped.

wohlgezielt ['vo:lgətsi:lt], *adj.* well aimed.

wohlhabend ['vo:lha:bənt], *adj.* well-to-do, wealthy, well off.

wohlig ['vo:lɪç], *adj.* comfortable, cosy.

Wohlklang ['vo:lklaŋ], *m.* (**—s**, *pl.* ⁻**e**) harmony, euphony.

wohlklingend ['vo:lklɪŋənt], *adj.* harmonious, euphonious, sweet-sounding.

Wohlleben ['vo:lle:bən], *n.* (**—s**, *no pl.*) luxurious living.

wohllöblich ['vo:llø:plɪç], *adj.* worshipful.

wohlmeinend ['vo:lmaɪnənt], *adj.* well-meaning.

wohlschmeckend ['vo:lʃmɛkənt], *adj.* savoury, tasty, delicious.

Wohlsein ['vo:lzaɪn], *n.* (**—s**, *no pl.*) good health, wellbeing.

Wohlstand ['vo:lʃtant], *m.* (**—s**, *no pl.*) prosperity.

Wohltat ['vo:lta:t], *f.* (**—**, *pl.* **—en**) benefit; kindness; (*pl.*) benefaction, charity; (*fig.*) treat.

Wohltäter ['vo:ltɛ:tər], *m.* (—s, *pl.* —) benefactor.
Wohltätigkeit ['vo:ltɛ:tɪçkaɪt], *f.* (—, *no pl.*) charity.
wohltuend ['vo:ltu:ənt], *adj.* soothing.
wohltun ['vo:ltu:n], *v.n. irr.* do good; be comforting.
wohlweislich ['vo:lvaɪslɪç], *adj.* wisely.
Wohlwollen ['vo:lvɔlən], *n.* (—s, *no pl.*) benevolence; favour, patronage.
wohnen ['vo:nən], *v.n.* reside, dwell, live.
wohnhaft ['vo:nhaft], *adj.* domiciled, resident; — *sein*, reside, be domiciled.
Wohnhaus ['vo:nhaus], *n.* (—es, *pl.* ∸er) dwelling-house.
wohnlich ['vo:nlɪç], *adj.* comfortable; cosy.
Wohnort ['vo:nɔrt], *m.* (—s, *pl.* —e) place of residence.
Wohnsitz ['vo:nzɪts], *m.* (—es, *pl.* —e) domicile, abode, residence.
Wohnstätte ['vo:nʃtɛtə], *f.* (—, *pl.* —n) abode, home.
Wohnung ['vo:nuŋ], *f.* (—, *pl.* —en) residence, dwelling; house, flat, lodging; apartment.
Wohnungsmangel ['vo:nuŋsmaŋəl], *m.* (—s, *no pl.*) housing shortage.
Wohnwagen ['vo:nva:gən], *m.* (—s, *pl.* —) caravan.
Wohnzimmer ['vo:ntsɪmər], *n.* (—s, *pl.* —) sitting-room, living-room.
wölben ['vœlbən], *v.r. sich* —, vault, arch.
Wölbung ['vœlbuŋ], *f.* (—, *pl.* —en) vault, vaulting.
Wolf [vɔlf], *m.* (—(e)s, *pl.* ∸e) wolf.
Wolke ['vɔlkə], *f.* (—, *pl.* —n) cloud.
Wolkenbruch ['vɔlkənbrux], *m.* (—s, *pl.* ∸e) cloudburst, violent downpour.
Wolkenkratzer ['vɔlkənkratsər], *m.* (—s, *pl.* —) sky-scraper.
Wolkenkuckucksheim [vɔlkən'kukukshaɪm], *n.* (—s, *no pl.*) Utopia, cloud cuckoo land.
Wolldecke ['vɔldɛkə], *f.* (—, *pl.* —n) blanket.
Wolle ['vɔlə], *f.* (—, *pl.* —n) wool.
wollen (1) ['vɔlən], *v.a., v.n. irr.* wish, want to, be willing, intend; *was — Sie*, what do you want?
wollen (2) ['vɔlən], *ad* . woollen, made of wool.
Wollgarn ['vɔlgarn], *n.* (—s, *pl.* —e) woollen yarn.
Wollhandel ['vɔlhandəl], *m.* (—s, *no pl.*) wool-trade.
wollig ['vɔlɪç], *adj.* woolly.
Wollsamt ['vɔlzamt], *m.* (—s, *no pl.*) plush, velveteen.
Wollust ['vɔlust], *f.* (—, *pl.* ∸e) voluptuousness; lust.
wollüstig ['vɔlystɪç], *adj.* voluptuous.
Wollwaren ['vɔlva:rən], *f. pl.* woollen goods.
Wollzupfen ['vɔltsupfən], *n.* (—s, *no pl.*) wool-picking.
womit [vo:'mɪt], *adv.* wherewith, with which; (*interr.*) with what?

womöglich [vo:'mø:klɪç], *adv.* if possible, perhaps.
wonach [vo:'na:x], *adv.* whereafter, after which; according to which.
Wonne ['vɔnə], *f.* (—, *pl.* —n) delight, bliss, rapture.
wonnetrunken ['vɔnətruŋkən], *adj.* enraptured.
wonnig ['vɔnɪç], *adj.* delightful.
woran [vo:'ran], *adv.* whereat, whereby; (*interr.*) by what? at what?
worauf [vo:'rauf], *adv.* upon which, at which; whereupon; (*interr.*) on what?
woraufhin [vo:rauf'hɪn], *conj.* whereupon.
woraus [vo:'raus], *adv.* (*rel. & interr.*) whence, from which; by or out of which.
worein [vo:'raɪn], *adv.* (*rel. & interr.*) into which; into what.
worin [vo:'rɪn], *adv.* (*rel.*) wherein; (*interr.*) in what?
Wort [vɔrt], *n.* (—(e)s, *pl.* ∸er, —e) word, term; expression, saying.
wortarm ['vɔrtarm], *adj.* poor in words, deficient in vocabulary.
Wortarmut ['vɔrtarmu:t], *f.* (—, *no pl.*) paucity of words, poverty of language.
Wortbildung ['vɔrtbɪlduŋ], *f.* (—, *pl.* —en) word-formation.
wortbrüchig ['vɔrtbryçɪç], *adj.* faithless, disloyal.
Wörterbuch ['vœrtərbu:x], *n.* (—(e)s, *pl.* ∸er) dictionary.
Worterklärung ['vɔrtɛrklɛ:ruŋ], *f.* (—, *pl.* —en) definition.
Wortforschung ['vɔrtfɔrʃuŋ], *f.* (—, *no pl.*) etymology.
Wortfügung ['vɔrtfy:guŋ], *f.* (—, *no pl.*) syntax.
Wortführer ['vɔrtfy:rər], *m.* (—s, *pl.* —) spokesman.
Wortgefecht ['vɔrtgəfɛçt], *n.* (—es, *pl.* —e) verbal battle.
wortgetreu ['vɔrtgətrɔy], *adj.* literal, verbatim.
wortkarg ['vɔrtkark], *adj.* laconic, sparing of words, taciturn.
Wortlaut ['vɔrtlaut], *m.* (—s, *pl.* —e) wording, text.
wörtlich ['vœrtlɪç], *adj.* verbal; literal; word for word.
wortlos ['vɔrtlo:s], *adj.* speechless. — *adv.* without uttering a word.
wortreich ['vɔrtraɪç], *adj.* (*language*) rich in words; (*fig.*) verbose, wordy.
Wortreichtum ['vɔrtraɪçtum], *m.* (—s, *no pl.*) (*language*) wealth of words; (*fig.*) verbosity, wordiness.
Wortschwall ['vɔrtʃval], *m.* (—s, *no pl.*) bombast; torrent of words.
Wortspiel ['vɔrtʃpi:l], *n.* (—s, *pl.* —e) pun.
Wortversetzung ['vɔrtfɛrzetsuŋ], *f.* (—, *pl.* —en) inversion (of words).
Wortwechsel ['vɔrtvɛksəl], *m.* (—s, *pl.* —) dispute, altercation.
worüber [vo:'ry:bər], *adv.* (*rel.*) about which, whereof; (*interr.*) about what?

worunter [vo'rʊntər], adv. (rel.) whereunder; (interr.) under what?

woselbst [vo:'zɛlpst], adv. where.

wovon [vo:'fɔn], adv. (rel.) whereof; (interr.) of what?

wovor [vo:'fo:r], adv. (rel.) before which; (interr.) before what?

wozu [vo:'tsu:], adv. (rel.) whereto; (interr.) why? for what purpose? to what end?

Wrack [vrak], n. (—s, pl. —s) wreck.

wringen ['vrɪŋən], v.a. wring.

Wringmaschine ['vrɪŋmaʃi:nə], f. (—, pl. —n) wringer, mangle.

Wucher ['vu:xər], m. (—s, no pl.) usury.

wucherisch ['vu:xərɪʃ], adj. usurious, extortionate.

wuchern ['vu:xərn], v.n. practise usury; (plants) luxuriate, grow profusely.

Wucherungen ['vu:xəruŋən], f. pl. (Med.) excrescence, growth.

Wuchs [vu:ks], m. (—es, no pl.) growth; shape, build.

Wucht [vuxt], f. (—, no pl.) power, force; weight; impetus.

wuchten ['vuxtən], v.n. (Poet.) press heavily. — v.a. prise up.

wuchtig ['vuxtɪç], adj. weighty, forceful.

Wühlarbeit ['vy:larbaɪt], f. (—, pl. —en) subversive activity.

wühlen ['vy:lən], v.a., v.n. dig, burrow; (fig.) agitate.

Wühler ['vy:lər], m. (—s, pl. —) agitator, demagogue.

Wühlmaus ['vy:lmaus], f. (—, pl. ⁻e) (Zool.) vole.

Wulst [vulst], m. (—es, pl. ⁻e) roll, pad; swelling.

wülstig ['vylstɪç], adj. padded, stuffed, swollen.

wund [vunt], adj. sore, wounded.

Wundarzt ['vuntartst], m. (—es, pl. ⁻e) (obs.) surgeon.

Wundbalsam ['vuntbalzam], m. (—s, pl. —e) balm.

Wunde ['vundə], f. (—, pl. —n) wound, hurt.

Wunder ['vundər], n. (—s, pl. —) marvel, wonder, miracle.

wunderbar ['vundərba:r], adj. wonderful, marvellous.

Wunderding ['vundərdɪŋ], n. (—s, pl. —e) marvel.

Wunderdoktor ['vundərdɔktər], m. (—s, pl. —en) quack doctor.

Wunderglaube ['vundərglaubə], m. (—ns, no pl.) belief in miracles.

wunderhübsch [vundər'hypʃ], adj. exceedingly pretty.

Wunderkind ['vundərkɪnt], n. (—s, pl. —er) infant prodigy.

Wunderlampe ['vundərlampə], f. (—, pl. —n) magic lantern.

wunderlich ['vundərlɪç], adj. strange, odd, queer.

wundern ['vundərn], v.r. sich — über, be surprised at, be astonished at.

wundersam ['vundərza:m], adj. wonderful, strange.

wunderschön ['vundərʃø:n], adj. lovely, gorgeous; exquisite.

Wundertat ['vundərta:t], f. (—, pl. —en) miraculous deed.

wundertätig ['vundərtɛ:tɪç], adj. miraculous.

Wundertier ['vundərti:r], n. (—s, pl. —e) monster; (fig.) prodigy.

Wunderwerk ['vundərvɛrk], n. (—s, pl. —e) miracle.

Wundmal ['vuntma:l], n. (—s, pl. —e) scar.

Wunsch [vunʃ], m. (—es, pl. ⁻e) wish, desire, aspiration.

Wünschelrute ['vynʃəlru:tə], f. (—, pl. —n) divining-rod.

wünschen ['vynʃən], v.a. wish, desire, long for.

wünschenswert ['vynʃənsve:rt], adj. desirable.

Wunschform ['vunʃfɔrm], f. (—, no pl.) (Gram.) optative form.

wuppdich! ['vupdɪç], excl. here goes!

Würde ['vyrdə], f. (—, pl. —n) dignity, honour.

Würdenträger ['vyrdəntrɛ:gər], m. (—s, pl. —) dignitary.

würdevoll ['vyrdəfɔl], adj. dignified.

würdig ['vyrdɪç], adj. worthy (of), deserving, meritorious.

würdigen ['vyrdɪgən], v.a. honour; ich weiss es zu —, I appreciate it.

Würdigung ['vyrdɪguŋ], f. (—, pl. —en) appreciation.

Wurf [vurf], m. (—(e)s, pl. ⁻e) cast, throw.

Würfel ['vyrfəl], m. (—s, pl. —) die; (Geom.) cube; — spielen, play at dice.

würfelförmig ['vyrfəlfœrmɪç], adj. cubic, cubiform.

würfeln ['vyrfəln], v.n. play at dice.

Wurfgeschoß ['vurfgəʃo:s], n. (—sses, pl. —sse) missile, projectile.

Wurfmaschine ['vurfmaʃi:nə], f. (—, pl. —n) catapult.

Wurfscheibe ['vurfʃaɪbə], f. (—, pl. —n) discus, quoit.

Wurfspieß ['vurfʃpi:s], m. (—es, pl. —e) javelin.

würgen ['vyrgən], v.a. strangle, throttle. — v.n. choke.

Würgengel ['vyrgɛŋəl], m. (—s, no pl.) avenging angel.

Würger ['vyrgər], m. (—s, pl. —) strangler, murderer; (Poet.) slayer; (Orn.) shrike, butcher-bird.

Wurm [vurm], m. (—(e)s, pl. ⁻er) worm; (apple) maggot.

wurmen ['vurmən], v.a. vex.

wurmstichig ['vurmʃtɪçɪç], adj. worm-eaten.

Wurst [vurst], f. (—, pl. ⁻e) sausage.

wurstig ['vurstɪç], adj. (sl.) quite indifferent.

Wurstigkeit ['vurstɪçkaɪt], f. (—, no pl.) callousness, indifference.

Würze ['vyrtsə], f. (—, pl. —n) seasoning, spice, condiment.

Wurzel ['vurtsəl], f. (—, pl. —n) root.

wurzeln ['vurtsəln], v.n. be rooted.

würzen ['vyrtsən], v.a. season, spice.

würzig ['vyrtsɪç], adj. spicy, fragrant.

Wust [vust], *m.* (**—es,** *no pl.*) chaos, trash.
wüst [vy:st], *adj.* waste, desert; desolate; dissolute.
Wüste ['vy:stə], *f.* (**—,** *pl.* **—n**) desert, wilderness.
Wüstling ['vy:stlɪŋ], *m.* (**—s,** *pl.* **—e**) profligate, libertine.
Wut [vu:t], *f.* (**—,** *no pl.*) rage, fury, passion.
wüten ['vy:tən], *v.n.* rage, storm, fume.
wutentbrannt ['vu:təntbrant], *adj.* enraged, infuriated.
Wüterich ['vy:tərɪç], *m.* (**—s,** *pl.* **—e**) tyrant; ruthless fellow.
Wutgeschrei ['vu:tgəʃraɪ], *n.* (**—s,** *no pl.*) yell of rage.
wutschnaubend ['vu:tʃnaubənt], *adj.* foaming with rage.

X

X [ɪks], *n.* (**—s,** *pl.* **—s**) the letter X.
X-Beine ['ɪksbaɪnə], *n. pl.* knock-knees.
x-beliebig ['ɪksbəli:bɪç], *adj.* any, whatever (one likes).
Xenie ['kse:njə], *f.* (**—,** *pl.* **—n**) epigram.
Xereswein ['kse:rəsvaɪn], *m.* (**—s,** *pl.* **—e**) sherry.
x-mal ['ɪksma:l], *adv.* (*coll.*) so many times, umpteen times.
X-Strahlen ['ɪksʃtra:lən], *m. pl.* X-rays.
Xylographie [ksylogra'fi:], *f.* (**—,** *no pl.*) wood-engraving.
Xylophon [ksylo'fo:n], *n.* (**—s,** *pl.* **—e**) (*Mus.*) xylophone.

Y

Y ['ypsilɔn], *n.* (**—s,** *pl.* **—s**) the letter Y.
Yak [jak], *m.* (**—s,** *pl.* **—s**) (*Zool.*) yak.
Yamswurzel ['jamsvurtsəl], *f.* (**—,** *pl.* **—n**) yam.
Ysop [y'zo:p], *m.* (**—s,** *no pl.*) hyssop.

Z

Z [tsɛt], *n.* (**—s,** *pl.* **—s**) the letter Z.
Zabel ['tsa:bəl], *m.* (**—s,** *pl.* **—**) (*obs.*) chess-board.

Zacke ['tsakə], *f.* (**—,** *pl.* **—n**) tooth, spike; (*fork*) prong.
zackig ['tsakɪç], *adj.* pronged, toothed, indented; (*rock*) jagged; (*sl.*) smart.
zagen ['tsa:gən], *v.n.* quail, blench, be disheartened, be fainthearted.
zaghaft ['tsa:khaft], *adj.* faint-hearted.
Zaghaftigkeit ['tsa:khaftɪçkaɪt], *f.* (**—,** *no pl.*) faintheartedness, timidity.
zäh [tsɛ:], *adj.* tough.
Zähigkeit ['tsɛ:ɪçkaɪt], *f.* (**—,** *no pl.*) toughness.
Zahl [tsa:l], *f.* (**—,** *pl.* **—en**) number, figure.
zahlbar ['tsa:lba:r], *adj.* payable, due.
zählbar ['tsɛ:lba:r], *adj.* calculable.
zahlen ['tsa:lən], *v.a.* pay; *Ober!* **—,** waiter! the bill, please.
zählen ['tsɛ:lən], *v.a.*, *v.n.* count, number.
Zahlenfolge ['tsa:lənfɔlgə], *f.* (**—,** *no pl.*) numerical order.
Zahlenlehre ['tsa:lənle:rə], *f.* (**—,** *no pl.*) arithmetic.
Zahlenreihe ['tsa:lənraɪə], *f.* (**—,** *pl.* **—n**) numerical progression.
Zahlensinn ['tsa:lənzɪn], *m.* (**—s,** *no pl.*) head for figures.
Zahler ['tsa:lər], *m.* (**—s,** *pl.* **—**) payer.
Zähler ['tsɛ:lər], *m.* (**—s,** *pl.* **—**) counter, teller; meter; (*Maths.*) numerator.
Zahlkellner ['tsa:lkɛlnər], *m.* (**—s,** *pl.* **—**) head waiter.
Zahlmeister ['tsa:lmaɪstər], *m.* (**—s,** *pl.* **—**) paymaster, treasurer, bursar.
zahlreich ['tsa:lraɪç], *adj.* numerous.
Zahltag ['tsa:lta:k], *m.* (**—s,** *pl.* **—e**) pay-day.
Zahlung ['tsa:luŋ], *f.* (**—,** *pl.* **—en**) payment; — *leisten,* make payment; *die —en einstellen,* stop payment.
Zählung ['tsɛ:luŋ], *f.* (**—,** *pl.* **—en**) counting, computation; census.
Zahlungseinstellung ['tsa:luŋsaɪnʃtɛluŋ], *f.* (**—,** *pl.* **—en**) suspension of payment.
zahlungsfähig ['tsa:luŋsfɛ:ɪç], *adj.* solvent.
Zahlungsmittel ['tsa:luŋsmɪtəl], *n.* (**—s,** *pl.* **—**) means of payment; *gesetzliches —,* legal tender.
Zahlungstermin ['tsa:luŋstɛrmi:n], *m.* (**—s,** *pl.* **—e**) time of payment.
zahlungsunfähig ['tsa:luŋsunfɛ:ɪç], *adj.* insolvent.
Zahlwort ['tsa:lvɔrt], *n.* (**—s,** *pl.* **⸚er**) (*Gram.*) numeral.
zahm [tsa:m], *adj.* tame; domestic(ated); — *machen,* tame.
zähmen ['tsɛ:mən], *v.a.* tame, domesticate.
Zähmer ['tsɛ:mər], *m.* (**—s,** *pl.* **—**) tamer.
Zahmheit ['tsa:mhaɪt], *f.* (**—,** *no pl.*) tameness.
Zähmung ['tsɛ:muŋ], *f.* (**—,** *no pl.*) taming, domestication.
Zahn [tsa:n], *m.* (**—(e)s,** *pl.* **⸚e**) tooth; (*wheel*) cog.

287

Zahnarzt ['tsa:nartst], *m.* (**—es**, *pl.* ⁀**e**) dentist, dental surgeon.

Zahnbürste ['tsa:nbyrstə], *f.* (**—**, *pl.* **—n**) tooth-brush.

Zähneklappern ['tsɛ:nəklapərn], *n.* (**—s**, *no pl.*) chattering of teeth.

Zähneknirschen ['tsɛ:nəknɪrʃən], *n.* (**—s**, *no pl.*) gnashing of teeth.

zahnen ['tsa:nən], *v.n.* teethe, cut o.'s teeth.

zähnen ['tsɛ:nən], *v.a.* indent, notch.

Zahnfleisch ['tsa:nflaɪʃ], *n.* (**—es**, *no pl.*) gums.

Zahnfüllung ['tsa:nfylun], *f.* (**—**, *pl.* **—en**) filling, stopping (of tooth).

Zahnheilkunde ['tsa:nhaɪlkundə], *f.* (**—**, *no pl.*) dentistry, dental surgery.

Zahnlücke ['tsa:nlykə], *f.* (**—**, *pl.* **—n**) gap in the teeth.

Zahnpaste ['tsa:npastə], *f.* (**—**, *no pl.*) tooth-paste.

Zahnpulver ['tsa:npulvər], *n.* (**—s**, *no pl.*) tooth-powder.

Zahnrad ['tsa:nra:t], *n.* (**—s**, *pl.* ⁀**er**) cog-wheel.

Zahnradbahn ['tsa:nra:tba:n], *f.* (**—**, *pl.* **—en**) rack-railway.

Zahnschmerzen ['tsa:nʃmɛrtsən], *m. pl.* toothache.

Zahnstocher ['tsa:nʃtɔxər], *m.* (**—s**, *pl.* **—**) tooth-pick.

Zähre ['tsɛ:rə], *f.* (**—**, *pl.* **—n**) (*Poet.*) tear.

Zander ['tsandər], *m.* (**—s**, *pl.* **—**) (*fish*) pike.

Zange ['tsaŋə], *f.* (**—**, *pl.* **—n**) tongs; pincers; tweezers; nippers; (*Med.*) forceps.

Zank [tsaŋk], *m.* (**—es**, *pl.* ⁀**ereien**) quarrel, altercation, tiff.

Zankapfel ['tsaŋkapfəl], *m.* (**—s**, *pl.* ⁀) bone of contention.

zanken ['tsaŋkən], *v.r. sich* **—**, quarrel, dispute.

zänkisch ['tsɛnkɪʃ], *adj.* quarrelsome.

Zanksucht ['tsaŋkzuxt], *f.* (**—**, *no pl.*) quarrelsomeness.

zanksüchtig ['tsaŋkzyctɪç], *adj.* quarrelsome, cantankerous.

Zapfen ['tsapfən], *m.* (**—s**, *pl.* **—**) pin, peg; (*cask*) bung, spigot; (*fir*) cone.

zapfen ['tsapfən], *v.a.* tap, draw.

Zapfenstreich ['tsapfənʃtraɪç], *m.* (**—s**, *no pl.*) (*Mil.*) tattoo, retreat.

zapp(e)lig ['tsap(ə)lɪç], *adj.* fidgety.

zappeln ['tsapəln], *v.n.* kick, struggle, wriggle.

Zar [tsa:r], *m.* (**—en**, *pl.* **—en**) Czar, Tsar.

zart [tsart], *adj.* tender, sensitive, delicate, gentle; **—** *besaitet*, (*iron.*) sensitive, highly strung.

Zartgefühl ['tsartgəfy:l], *n.* (**—s**, *no pl.*) delicacy, sensitivity.

Zartheit ['tsarthaɪt], *f.* (**—**, *no pl.*) tenderness, gentleness.

zärtlich ['tsɛ:rtlɪç], *adj.* loving, amorous, tender.

Zärtlichkeit ['tsɛ:rtlɪçkaɪt], *f.* (**—**, *pl.* **—en**) tenderness, caresses.

Zartsinn ['tsartzɪn], *m.* (**—s**, *no pl.*) delicacy.

Zauber ['tsaubər], *m.* (**—s**, *no pl.*) charm, spell, enchantment; magic; fascination.

Zauberei [tsaubə'raɪ], *f.* (**—**, *pl.* **—en**) magic, witchcraft, sorcery.

Zauberer ['tsaubərər], *m.* (**—s**, *pl.* **—**) magician, sorcerer, wizard.

zauberisch ['tsaubərɪʃ], *adj.* magical; (*fig.*) enchanting.

Zauberkraft ['tsaubərkraft], *f.* (**—**, *no pl.*) magic power, witchcraft.

Zaubermittel ['tsaubərmɪtəl], *n.* (**—s**, *pl.* **—**) charm.

zaubern ['tsaubərn], *v.n.* practise magic; conjure.

Zauberspruch ['tsaubərʃprux], *m.* (**—s**, *pl.* ⁀**e**) spell, charm.

Zauberstab ['tsaubərʃta:p], *m.* (**—s**, *pl.* ⁀**e**) magic wand.

Zauderer ['tsaudərər], *m.* (**—s**, *pl.* **—**) loiterer, temporizer, procrastinator.

zaudern ['tsaudərn], *v.n.* delay; hesitate, procrastinate.

Zaum [tsaum], *m.* (**—(e)s**, *pl.* ⁀**e**) bridle; *im* **—** *halten*, check, restrain.

zäumen ['tsɔymən], *v.a.* bridle.

Zaun [tsaun], *m.* (**—(e)s**, *pl.* ⁀**e**) hedge, fence; *einen Streit vom* **—** *brechen*, pick a quarrel.

Zaungast ['tsaungast], *m.* (**—s**, *pl.* ⁀**e**) onlooker, outsider; intruder.

Zaunkönig ['tsaunkø:nɪç], *m.* (**—s**, *pl.* **—e**) (*Orn.*) wren.

Zaunpfahl ['tsaunpfa:l], *m.* (**—s**, *pl.* ⁀**e**) pale, hedge-pole; *mit dem* **—** *winken*, give s.o. a broad hint.

Zaunrebe ['tsaunre:bə], *f.* (**—**, *pl.* **—n**) (*Bot.*) Virginia creeper.

zausen ['tsauzən], *v.a.* tousle; (*hair*) disarrange, ruffle.

Zechbruder ['tsɛçbru:dər], *m.* (**—s**, *pl.* ⁀) tippler, toper.

Zeche ['tsɛçə], *f.* (**—**, *pl.* **—n**) bill (in a restaurant); mine; *die* **—** *bezahlen*, foot the bill, pay the piper.

Zeder ['tse:dər], *f.* (**—**, *pl.* **—n**) (*Bot.*) cedar.

zedieren [tsɛ'di:rən], *v.a.* cede.

Zehe ['tse:ə], *f.* (**—**, *pl.* **—n**) toe.

Zehenspitze ['tse:ənʃpɪtsə], *f.* (**—**, *pl.* **—n**) tip of the toe, tiptoe.

zehn [tse:n], *num. adj.* ten.

Zehneck ['tse:nɛk], *n.* (**—s**, *pl.* **—e**) decagon.

Zehnte ['tse:ntə], *m.* (**—n**, *pl.* **—n**) tithe.

zehren ['tse:rən], *v.n. von etwas* **—**, live on s.th., prey upon s.th.

Zehrfieber ['tse:rfi:bər], *n.* (**—s**, *no pl.*) hectic fever.

Zehrgeld ['tse:rgɛlt], *n.* (**—s**, *pl.* **—er**) subsistence, allowance.

Zehrvorrat ['tse:rfo:rra:t], *m.* (**—s**, *pl.* ⁀**e**) provisions.

Zehrung ['tse:run], *f.* (**—**, *pl.* **—en**) consumption; victuals; (*Eccl.*) *letzte* **—**, viaticum.

Zeichen ['tsaɪçən], *n.* (**—s**, *pl.* **—**) sign, token, symbol, omen; indication; badge; signal.

Zeichenbrett ['tsaɪçənbrɛt], *n.* (**—s,** *pl.* **—er**) drawing-board.
Zeichendeuter ['tsaɪçəndɔytər], *m.* (**—s,** *pl.* **—**) astrologer.
Zeichendeuterei [tsaɪçəndɔytə'raɪ], *f.* (**—,** *no pl.*) astrology.
Zeichenerklärung ['tsaɪçənɛrklɛ:ruŋ], *f.* (**—** *pl.*—**en**) legend, key.
Zeichensprache ['tsaɪçənʃpra:xə], *f.* (**—,** *no pl.*) sign-language.
Zeichentinte ['tsaɪçəntintə], *f.* (**—,** *no pl.*) marking ink.
zeichnen ['tsaɪçnən], *v.a.* draw; mark; (*money*) subscribe; (*letter*) sign.
Zeichner ['tsaɪçnər], *m.* (**—s,** *pl.* **—**) draughtsman, designer.
Zeichnung ['tsaɪçnuŋ], *f.* (**—,** *pl.* **—en**) drawing.
Zeigefinger ['tsaɪgəfiŋər], *m.* (**—s,** *pl.* **—**) forefinger, index finger.
zeigen ['tsaɪgən], *v.a.* show, point to, prove.
Zeiger ['tsaɪgər], *m.* (**—s,** *pl.* **—**) indicator; hand (of watch, clock).
zeihen ['tsaɪən], *v.a. irr. einen einer Sache —,* tax s.o. with s.th.
Zeile ['tsaɪlə], *f.* (**—,** *pl.* **—n**) line; furrow; (*pl.*) letter.
Zeisig ['tsaɪzɪç], *m.* (**—s,** *pl.* **—e**) (*Orn.*) siskin.
Zeit [tsaɪt], *f.* (**—,** *pl.* **—en**) time; *zur —,* at present; *auf —,* on credit.
Zeitabschnitt ['tsaɪtapʃnɪt], *m.* (**—s,** *pl.*—**e**) period; epoch.
Zeitalter ['tsaɪtaltər], *n.* (**—s,** *pl.* **—**) age, era.
Zeitdauer ['tsaɪtdauər], *f.* (**—,** *no pl.*) space of time.
Zeitfrage ['tsaɪtfra:gə], *f.* (**—,** *pl.* **—n**) topical question; question of time.
Zeitgeist ['tsaɪtgaɪst], *m.* (**—s,** *no pl.*) spirit of the age.
zeitgemäß ['tsaɪtgəmɛ:s], *adj.* timely, seasonable, opportune, modern.
Zeitgenosse ['tsaɪtgənɔsə], *m.* (**—n,** *pl.* **—n**) contemporary.
zeitig ['tsaɪtɪç], *adj.* early, timely.
zeitigen ['tsaɪtɪgən], *v.a.* engender, generate. — *v.n.* mature, ripen.
Zeitkarte ['tsaɪtkartə], *f.* (**—,** *pl.* **—n**) season ticket.
Zeitlauf ['tsaɪtlauf], *m.* (**—s,** *pl.* ̈**e**) course of time, conjuncture.
zeitlebens ['tsaɪtle:bəns], *adv.* for life, (for) all his (*or her*) life.
zeitlich ['tsaɪtlɪç], *adj.* temporal, earthly; secular; temporary, transient.
zeitlos ['tsaɪtlo:s], *adj.* lasting, permanent.
Zeitmangel ['tsaɪtmaŋəl], *m.* (**—s,** *no pl.*) lack of time.
Zeitmesser ['tsaɪtmɛsər], *m.* (**—s,** *pl.* **—**) chronometer, timepiece; metronome.
Zeitpunkt ['tsaɪtpuŋkt], *m.* (**—s,** *pl.*—**e**) moment, date; point of time.
zeitraubend ['tsaɪtraubənt], *adj.* time-consuming.
Zeitraum ['tsaɪtraum], *m.* (**—s,** *pl.* ̈**e**) space of time, period.

Zeitschrift ['tsaɪtʃrɪft], *f.* (**—,** *pl.* **—en**) periodical, journal, magazine.
Zeitung ['tsaɪtuŋ], *f.* (**—,** *pl.* **—en**) newspaper.
Zeitungsente ['tsaɪtuŋsɛntə], *f.* (**—,** *pl.* **—n**) canard, newspaper hoax.
Zeitungskiosk ['tsaɪtuŋskiɔsk], *m.* (**—s,** *pl.* **—e**) newspaper-stall.
Zeitungsnachricht ['tsaɪtuŋsna:xrɪçt], *f.* (**—,** *pl.* **—en**) newspaper report.
Zeitungswesen ['tsaɪtuŋsve:zən], *n.* (**—s,** *no pl.*) journalism.
Zeitverlust ['tsaɪtfɛrlust], *m.* (**—s,** *no pl.*) loss of time; *ohne —,* without delay.
Zeitvertreib ['tsaɪtfɛrtraɪp], *m.* (**—s,** *no pl.*) pastime, amusement; *zum —,* to pass the time.
zeitweilig ['tsaɪtvaɪlɪç], *adj.* temporary.
zeitweise ['tsaɪtvaɪzə], *adv.* from time to time.
Zeitwort ['tsaɪtvɔrt], *n.* (**—s,** *pl.* ̈**er**) (*Gram.*) verb.
Zelle ['tsɛlə], *f.* (**—,** *pl.* **—n**) cell; booth.
Zelt [tsɛlt], *n.* (**—(e)s,** *pl.* **—e**) tent.
Zeltdecke ['tsɛltdɛkə], *f.* (**—,** *pl.* **—n**) awning, marquee.
Zement [tse'mɛnt], *m.* (**—s,** *no pl.*) cement.
Zenit [tse'ni:t], *m.* (**—s,** *no pl.*) zenith.
zensieren [tsɛn'zi:rən], *v.a.* review, censure; (*Sch.*) mark.
Zensor ['tsɛnzɔr], *m.* (**—s,** *pl.* **—en**) censor.
Zensur [tsɛn'zu:r], *f.* (**—,** *pl.* **—en**) censure; (*Sch.*) report, mark; censorship.
Zentimeter ['tsɛntime:tər], *m.* (**—s,** *pl.* **—**) centimetre.
Zentner ['tsɛntnər], *m.* (**—s,** *pl.* **—**) hundredweight.
zentral [tsɛn'tra:l], *adj.* central.
Zentrale [tsɛn'tra:lə], *f.* (**—,** *pl.* **—n**) control room; head office.
zentralisieren [tsɛntrali'zi:rən], *v.a.* centralise.
Zentrum ['tsɛntrum], *n.* (**—s,** *pl.* **—tren**) centre; (*Am.*) center.
Zephir ['tsɛ:fi:r], *m.* (**—s,** *pl.* **—e**) zephyr.
Zepter ['tsɛptər], *m. & n.* (**—s,** *pl.* **—**) sceptre, mace.
zerbrechen [tsɛr'brɛçən], *v.a., v.n. irr.* (*aux.* se**in**) break to pieces; shatter; *sich den Kopf —,* rack o.'s brains.
zerbrechlich [tsɛr'brɛçlɪç], *adj.* brittle, fragile.
zerbröckeln [tsɛr'brœkəln], *v.a., v.n.* (*aux.* sein) crumble.
zerdrücken [tsɛr'drykən], *v.a.* crush, bruise.
Zeremonie [tseremo'ni:], *f.* (**—,** *pl.* **—n**) ceremony.
zeremoniell [tseremo'njɛl], *adj.* ceremonial, formal.
Zerfahrenheit [tsɛr'fa:rənhaɪt], *f.* (**—,** *no pl.*) absent-mindedness.
Zerfall [tsɛr'fal], *m.* (**—s,** *no pl.*) disintegration; decay.
zerfallen [tsɛr'falən], *v.n. irr.* (*aux.* sein) fall to pieces. — *adj.* in ruins.

zerfleischen

zerfleischen [tsɛr'flaɪʃən], *v.a.* lacerate, tear to pieces.

zerfließen [tsɛr'fli:sən], *v.n. irr. (aux.* sein) dissolve, melt.

zerfressen [tsɛr'frɛsən], *v.a. irr.* gnaw, corrode.

zergehen [tsɛr'ge:ən], *v.n. irr. (aux.* sein) dissolve, melt.

zergliedern [tsɛr'gli:dərn], *v.a.* dissect; (*fig.*) analyse.

zerhauen [tsɛr'hauən], *v.a.* hew in pieces, chop up.

zerkauen [tsɛr'kauən], *v.a.* chew.

zerkleinern [tsɛr'klaɪnərn], *v.a.* cut into small pieces; (*firewood*) chop.

zerklüftet [tsɛr'klyftət], *adj.* rugged.

zerknirscht [tsɛr'knɪrʃt], *adj.* contrite.

Zerknirschung [tsɛr'knɪrʃuŋ], *f.* (—, *no pl.*) contrition.

zerknittern [tsɛr'knɪtərn], *v.a.* crumple.

zerknüllen [tsɛr'knylən], *v.a.* rumple.

zerlassen [tsɛr'lasən], *v.a. irr.* melt, liquefy.

zerlegen [tsɛr'le:gən], *v.a.* resolve; take to pieces; cut up, carve; (*fig.*) analyse.

zerlumpt [tsɛr'lumpt], *adj.* ragged, tattered.

zermahlen [tsɛr'ma:lən], *v.a.* grind to powder.

zermalmen [tsɛr'malmən], *v.a.* crush.

zermartern [tsɛr'martərn], *v.a.* torment; *sich das Hirn* —, rack o.'s brains.

zernagen [tsɛr'na:gən], *v.a.* gnaw (away).

zerquetschen [tsɛr'kvɛtʃən], *v.a.* squash, crush.

zerraufen [tsɛr'raufən], *v.a.* dishevel.

Zerrbild ['tsɛrbɪlt], *n.* (—s, *pl.* —er) caricature.

zerreiben [tsɛr'raɪbən], *v.a. irr.* grind to powder, pulverise.

zerreißen [tsɛr'raɪsən], *v.a. irr.* tear, rend, tear up; break; rupture. — *v.n.* (*aux.* sein) be torn; (*clothes*) wear out.

zerren ['tsɛrən], *v.a.* pull, tug, drag; strain.

zerrinnen [tsɛr'rɪnən], *v.n. irr. (aux.* sein) dissolve, melt; (*fig.*) vanish.

zerrütten [tsɛr'rytən], *v.a.* unsettle, disorder, unhinge; ruin, destroy.

zerschellen [tsɛr'ʃɛlən], *v.n. (aux.* sein) be dashed to pieces, be wrecked.

zerschlagen [tsɛr'ʃla:gən], *v.a. irr.* break, smash to pieces, batter.

zerschmettern [tsɛr'ʃmɛtərn], *v.a.* dash to pieces, break, crush; shatter, overwhelm.

zersetzen [tsɛr'zɛtsən], *v.a., v.r.* break up; disintegrate.

zerspalten [tsɛr'ʃpaltən], *v.a.* cleave, split, slit.

zersprengen [tsɛr'ʃprɛŋən], *v.a.* explode, burst; (*crowd*) disperse; (*Mil.*) rout.

zerspringen [tsɛr'ʃprɪŋən], *v.n. irr.* (*aux.* sein) crack; fly to pieces, split.

zerstampfen [tsɛr'ʃtampfən], *v.a.* crush, pound.

zerstäuben [tsɛr'ʃtɔybən], *v.a.* spray, atomize.

zerstörbar [tsɛr'ʃtø:rba:r], *adj.* destructible.

zerstören [tsɛr'ʃtø:rən], *v.a.* destroy, devastate.

Zerstörer [tsɛr'ʃtø:rər], *m.* (—s, *pl.* —) destroyer.

Zerstörung [tsɛr'ʃtø:ruŋ], *f.* (—, *pl.* —en) destruction.

Zerstörungswut [tsɛr'ʃtø:ruŋsvu:t], *f.* (—, *no pl.*) vandalism.

zerstoßen [tsɛr'ʃto:sən], *v.a. irr.* bruise, pound.

zerstreuen [tsɛr'ʃtrɔyən], *v.a.* scatter, disperse; divert.

zerstreut [tsɛr'ʃtrɔyt], *adj.* absent-minded.

Zerstreuung [tsɛr'ʃtrɔyuŋ], *f.* (—, *pl.* —en) dispersion; amusement, diversion, distraction.

zerstückeln [tsɛr'ʃtykəln], *v.a.* dismember.

Zerstückelung [tsɛr'ʃtykəluŋ], *f.* (—, *no pl.*) dismemberment.

zerteilen [tsɛr'taɪlən], *v.a.* divide, separate; disperse, dissipate. — *v.r. sich* —, dissolve.

Zertifikat [tsɛrtifi'ka:t], *n.* (—s, *pl.* —e) certificate, attestation.

zertrennen [tsɛr'trɛnən], *v.a.* rip up, unstitch.

zertrümmern [tsɛr'trymərn], *v.a.* destroy, break up, demolish.

Zerwürfnis [tsɛr'vyrfnɪs], *n.* (—ses, *pl.* —se) discord, dissension.

zerzausen [tsɛr'tsauzən], *v.a.* dishevel, tousle.

zerzupfen [tsɛr'tsupfən], *v.a.* pick to pieces, pluck.

Zession [tsɛs'jo:n], *f.* (—, *pl.* —en) cession, assignment, transfer.

Zetergeschrei ['tse:tərgəʃraɪ], *n.* (—s, *no pl.*) outcry, hullabaloo.

zetern ['tse:tərn], *v.n.* yell; (*coll.*) kick up a row.

Zettel ['tsɛtəl], *m.* (—s, *pl.* —) slip of paper; label, chit.

Zettelkasten ['tsɛtəlkastən], *m.* (—s, *pl.* ˸) card-index, filing cabinet.

Zeug [tsɔyk], *n.* (—(e)s, *no pl.*) stuff, material; implements, kit, utensils; (*coll.*) things.

Zeuge ['tsɔygə], *m.* (—n, *pl.* —n) witness; *zum* —*n aufrufen,* call to witness.

zeugen ['tsɔygən], *v.a.* beget, generate, engender. — *v.n.* give evidence.

Zeugenaussage ['tsɔygənausza:gə], *f.* (—, *pl.* —n) evidence, deposition.

Zeugenbeweis ['tsɔygənbəvaɪs], *m.* (—es, *pl.* —e) evidence, proof.

Zeugeneid ['tsɔygənaɪt], *m.* (—s, *pl.* —e) oath of a witness.

Zeughaus ['tsɔykhaus], *n.* (—es, *pl.* ˸er) (*obs.*) arsenal.

Zeugin ['tsɔygɪn], *f.* (—, *pl.* —innen) female witness.

Zeugnis ['tsɔyknɪs], *n.* (**—ses,** *pl.* **—se**) (*Law.*) deposition; testimonial, certificate, reference; character; school report; — *ablegen,* give evidence, bear witness; *einem ein gutes — ausstellen,* give s.o. a good reference.

Zeugung ['tsɔygun], *f.* (—, *pl.* **—en**) procreation, generation.

Zeugungskraft ['tsɔygunskraft], *f.* (—, *no pl.*) generative power.

Zeugungstrieb ['tsɔygunstri:p], *m.* (**—s,** *no pl.*) procreative instinct.

Zichorie [tsɪ'çoːrjə], *f.* (—, *pl.* **—n**) chicory.

Zicke ['tsɪkə], *f.* (—, *pl.* **—n**) dial. for **Ziege**.

Ziege ['tsiːgə], *f.* (—, *pl.* **—n**) goat.

Ziegel ['tsiːgəl], *m.* (**—s,** *pl.* —) (*roof*) tile; (*wall*) brick.

Ziegelbrenner ['tsiːgəlbrɛnər], *m.* (**—s,** *pl.* —) tile-maker, tiler; brickmaker.

Ziegelbrennerei [tsiːgəlbrɛnə'raɪ], *f.* (—, *pl.* **—en**) tile-kiln; brickyard.

Ziegeldach ['tsiːgəldax], *n.* (**—s,** *pl.* **⸚er**) tiled roof.

Ziegeldecker ['tsiːgəldɛkər], *m.* (**—s,** *pl.* —) tiler.

Ziegelei [tsiːgə'laɪ], *f.* (—, *pl.* **—en**) brickyard, brickworks.

Ziegelerde ['tsiːgəleːrdə], *f.* (—, *no pl.*) brick-clay.

Ziegenbart ['tsiːgənbaːrt], *m.* (**—s,** *pl.* **⸚e**) goat's beard; (*human*) goatee.

Ziegenleder ['tsiːgənleːdər], *n.* (**—s,** *no pl.*) kid (leather).

Ziegenpeter ['tsiːgənpeːtər], *m.* (**—s,** *no pl.*) (*Med.*) mumps.

ziehen ['tsiːən], *v.a. irr.* draw, pull, drag; pull out; cultivate; breed; (*game*) move. — *v.n.* draw, be an attraction; (*aux.* sein) go, move. — *v.r. sich —,* extend.

Ziehkind ['tsiːkɪnt], *n.* (**—s,** *pl.* **—er**) foster-child.

Ziehmutter ['tsiːmutər], *f.* (—, *pl.* **⸚**) foster-mother.

Ziehung ['tsiːun], *f.* (—, *pl.* **—en**) draw (in a lottery).

Ziehvater ['tsiːfaːtər], *m.* (**—s,** *pl.* **⸚**) foster-father.

Ziel [tsiːl], *n.* (**—s,** *pl.* **—e**) goal, aim, purpose, intention, end; butt, target; (*Mil.*) objective; (*sports*) winning-post.

zielbewußt ['tsiːlbəvust], *adj.* purposeful; systematic.

zielen ['tsiːlən], *v.n.* aim (at), take aim (at).

Ziellosigkeit ['tsiːlloːzɪçkaɪt], *f.* (—, *no pl.*) aimlessness.

Zielscheibe ['tsiːlʃaɪbə], *f.* (—, *pl.* **—en**) target, butt.

ziemen ['tsiːmən], *v.r. sich —,* become s.o., behove s.o., be proper for, befit.

Ziemer ['tsiːmər], *n. & m.* (**—s,** *pl.* —) whip.

ziemlich ['tsiːmlɪç], *adj.* moderate, tolerable, middling, fairly considerable, fair. — *adv.* rather, fairly.

Zier [tsiːr], *f.* (—, *pl.* **—den**) ornament.

Zieraffe ['tsiːrafə], *m.* (**—n,** *pl.* **—n**) fop, affected person.

Zierat ['tsiːraːt], *m.* (**—s,** *no pl.*) ornament, finery.

Zierde ['tsiːrdə], *f.* (—, *pl.* **—n**) decoration, embellishment; (*fig.*) credit, pride.

Ziererei [tsiːrə'raɪ], *f.* (—, *pl.* **—en**) affectation.

Ziergarten ['tsiːrgartən], *m.* (**—s,** *pl.* **⸚**) flower-garden, ornamental garden.

zierlich ['tsiːrlɪç], *adj.* dainty, graceful, pretty.

Zierpflanze ['tsiːrpflantsə], *f.* (—, *pl.* **—n**) ornamental plant.

Zierpuppe ['tsiːrpupə], *f.* (—, *pl.* **—n**) overdressed woman.

Ziffer ['tsɪfər], *f.* (—, *pl.* **—n**) figure, numeral.

Zifferblatt ['tsɪfərblat], *n.* (**—s,** *pl.* **⸚er**) dial, face.

ziffernmäßig ['tsɪfərnmɛːsɪç], *adj.* statistical.

Ziffernschrift ['tsɪfərnʃrɪft], *f.* (—, *pl.* **—en**) code.

Zigarette [tsiga'rɛtə], *f.* (—, *pl.* **—n**) cigarette.

Zigarettenetui [tsiga'rɛtənɛtvi:], *n.* (**—s,** *pl.* **—s**) cigarette-case.

Zigarettenspitze [tsiga'rɛtənʃpɪtsə], *f.* (—, *pl.* **—n**) cigarette-holder.

Zigarettenstummel [tsiga'rɛtənʃtuməl], *m.* (**—s,** *pl.* —) cigarette-end.

Zigarre [tsi'garə], *f.* (—, *pl.* **—n**) cigar.

Zigarrenkiste [tsi'garənkɪstə], *f.* (—, *pl.* **—n**) cigar-box.

Zigarrenstummel [tsi'garənʃtuməl], *m.* (**—s,** *pl.* —) cigar-end.

Zigeuner [tsi'gɔynər], *m.* (**—s,** *pl.* —) gipsy.

Zikade [tsi'kaːdə], *f.* (—, *pl.* **—n**) (*Ent.*) grasshopper.

Zimmer ['tsɪmər], *n.* (**—s,** *pl.* —) room.

Zimmermädchen ['tsɪmərmɛːtçən], *n.* (**—s,** *pl.* —) chambermaid.

Zimmermann ['tsɪmərman], *m.* (**—s,** *pl.* **Zimmerleute**) carpenter, joiner.

zimmern ['tsɪmərn], *v.a.* carpenter, construct, build.

Zimmernachweis ['tsɪmərnaːxvaɪs], *m.* (**—es,** *pl.* **—e**) accommodation bureau.

Zimmerreihe ['tsɪmərraɪə], *f.* (—, *pl.* **—n**) suite of rooms.

Zimmervermieter ['tsɪmərfɛrmiːtər], *m.* (**—s,** *pl.* —) landlord.

zimperlich ['tsɪmpərlɪç], *adj.* simpering; prim; finicky, hypersensitive.

Zimt [tsɪmt], *m.* (**—(e)s,** *no pl.*) cinnamon.

Zink [tsɪŋk], *n.* (**—s,** *no pl.*) zinc.

Zinke ['tsɪŋkə], *f.* (—, *pl.* **—n**) prong, tine.

Zinn [tsɪn], *n.* (**—s,** *no pl.*) tin; pewter.

Zinnblech ['tsɪnblɛç], *n.* (**—s,** *no pl.*) tin-plate.

Zinne ['tsɪnə], *f.* (—, *pl.* **—n**) battlement, pinnacle.

zinnern

zinnern ['tsɪnern], *adj.* made of pewter, of tin.

Zinnober [tsɪn'oːbər], *m.* (—s, *no pl.*) cinnabar; (*coll.*) fuss.

Zinnsäure ['tsɪnzɔyrə], *f.* (—, *no pl.*) stannic acid.

Zins [tsɪns], *m.* (—es, *pl.* —en) duty, tax; rent; (*pl.*) interest.

zinsbar ['tsɪnsbaːr], *adj.* tributary; — *anlegen*, invest at interest; — *machen*, force to pay a tribute.

Zinsen ['tsɪnzən], *m. pl.* interest.

zinsentragend ['tsɪnzəntraːgənt], *adj.* interest-bearing.

Zinseszins ['tsɪnzəstsɪns], *m.* (—, *no pl.*) compound interest.

Zinsfuß ['tsɪnsfuːs], *m.* (—es, *pl.* ⁻e) rate of interest.

zinspflichtig ['tsɪnspflɪçtɪç], *adj.* subject to tax.

Zinsrechnung ['tsɪnsrɛçnuŋ], *f.* (—, *pl.* —en) interest account, calculation of interest.

Zinsschein ['tsɪnsʃaɪn], *m.* (—s, *pl.* —e) coupon, dividend warrant.

Zipfel ['tsɪpfəl], *m.* (—s, *pl.* —) tassel, edge, point, tip.

Zipperlein ['tsɪpərlaɪn], *n.* (—s, *no pl.*) (*coll.*) gout.

zirka ['tsɪrka], *adv.* circa, about, approximately.

Zirkel ['tsɪrkəl], *m.* (—s, *pl.* —) circle; (*Maths.*) pair of compasses; gathering.

zirkulieren [tsɪrku'liːrən], *v.n.* circulate; — *lassen*, put in circulation.

Zirkus ['tsɪrkus], *m.* (—, *pl.* —se) circus.

zirpen ['tsɪrpən], *v.n.* chirp.

zischeln ['tsɪʃəln], *v.n.* whisper.

zischen ['tsɪʃən], *v.n.* hiss, sizzle.

Zischlaut ['tsɪʃlaut], *m.* (—s, *pl.* —e) (*Phon.*) sibilant.

Zisterne [tsɪs'tɛrnə], *f.* (—, *pl.* —n) cistern.

Zisterzienser [tsɪstɛr'tsjɛnzər], *m.* (—s, *pl.* —) Cistercian (monk).

Zitadelle [tsɪta'dɛlə], *f.* (—, *pl.* —n) citadel.

Zitat [tsi'taːt], *n.* (—(e)s, *pl.* —e) quotation, reference; *falsches —*, misquotation.

Zither ['tsɪtər], *f.* (—, *pl.* —n) zither.

zitieren [tsi'tiːrən], *v.a.* cite, quote; *falsch —*, misquote.

Zitronat [tsitro'naːt], *n.* (—s, *no pl.*) candied lemon peel.

Zitrone [tsi'troːnə], *f.* (—, *pl.* —n) lemon.

Zitronenlimonade [tsi'troːnənlimonaːdə], *f.* (—, *pl.* —n) lemonade, lemon drink.

Zitronensaft [tsi'troːnənzaft], *m.* (—s, *pl.* ⁻e) lemon-juice.

Zitronensäure [tsi'troːnənzɔyrə], *f.* (—, *no pl.*) citric acid.

Zitronenschale [tsi'troːnənʃaːlə], *f.* (—, *pl.* —n) lemon-peel.

zitterig ['tsɪtərɪç], *adj.* shaky, shivery.

zittern ['tsɪtərn], *v.n.* tremble, shiver, quake.

Zitterpappel ['tsɪtərpapəl], *f.* (—, *pl.* —n) (*Bot.*) aspen-tree.

Zivil [tsi'viːl], *n.* (—s, *no pl.*) civilians, *in —*, in plain clothes; (*coll.*) in civvies *or* mufti.

Zivilbeamte [tsi'viːlbəamtə], *m.* (—n, *pl.* —n) civil servant.

Zivildienst [tsi'viːldiːnst], *m.* (—es, *no pl.*) civil service.

Zivilehe [tsi'viːleːə], *f.* (—, *pl.* —n) civil marriage.

Zivilgesetzbuch [tsi'viːlgəzɛtsbuːx], *n.* (—s, *pl.* ⁻er) code of civil law.

Zivilingenieur [tsi'viːlɪnʒenjøːr], *m.* (—s, *pl.* —e) civil engineer.

Zivilisation [tsiviliza'tsjoːn], *f.* (—, *pl.* —en) civilisation.

zivilisatorisch [tsiviliza'toːrɪʃ], *adj.* civilising.

zivilisieren [tsivili'ziːrən], *v.a.* civilise.

Zivilist [tsivi'lɪst], *m.* (—en, *pl.* —en) civilian.

Zivilkleidung [tsi'viːlklaɪduŋ], *f.* (—, *no pl.*) civilian dress, plain clothes.

Zobel ['tsoːbəl], *m.* (—s, *pl.* —) sable.

Zobelpelz ['tsoːbəlpɛlts], *m.* (—es, *pl.* —e) sable fur; sable-coat.

Zofe ['tsoːfə], *f.* (—, *pl.* —n) lady's maid.

zögern ['tsøːgərn], *v.n.* hesitate, tarry, delay.

Zögerung ['tsøːgəruŋ], *f.* (—, *pl.* —en) hesitation, delay.

Zögling ['tsøːklɪŋ], *m.* (—s, *pl.* —e) pupil, charge.

Zölibat [tsøːli'baːt], *m. & n.* (—s, *no pl.*) celibacy.

Zoll (1) [tsɔl], *m.* (—s, *no pl.*) inch.

Zoll (2) [tsɔl], *m.* (—s, *pl.* ⁻e) customs duty; (*bridge*) toll.

Zollabfertigung ['tsɔlapfɛrtiguŋ], *f.* (—, *no pl.*) customs clearance.

Zollamt ['tsɔlamt], *n.* (—s, *pl.* ⁻er) custom house.

Zollaufschlag ['tsɔlauf ʃlaːk], *m.* (—s, *pl.* ⁻e) additional duty.

Zollbeamte ['tsɔlbəamtə], *m.* (—n, *pl.* —n) customs officer.

zollbreit ['tsɔlbraɪt], *adj.* one inch wide.

zollen ['tsɔlən], *v.a. Ehrfurcht —*, pay o.'s respects; *Beifall —*, applaud; *Dank —*, show gratitude.

zollfrei ['tsɔlfraɪ], *adj.* duty-free, exempt from duty.

Zöllner ['tsœlnər], *m.* (—s, *pl.* —) tax-gatherer.

zollpflichtig ['tsɔlpflɪçtɪç], *adj.* liable to duty, dutiable.

Zollsatz ['tsɔlzats], *m.* (—es, *pl.* ⁻e) customs tariff.

Zollverein ['tsɔlfəraɪn], *m.* (—s, *no pl.*) customs union.

Zollverschluß ['tsɔlfɛrʃlus], *m.* (—sses, *pl.* ⁻sse) bond.

Zone ['tsoːnə], *f.* (—, *pl.* —n) zone.

Zoologe [tsoːo'loːgə], *m.* (—n, *pl.* —n) zoologist.

Zoologie [tsoːolo'giː], *f.* (—, *no pl.*) zoology.

zoologisch [tso:oʹlo:gɪʃ], *adj.* zoological; —*er Garten*, zoological gardens, zoo.

Zopf [tsɔpf], *m.* (—(e)s, *pl.* ʹ̣e) plait, pigtail; (*coll.*) (old-fashioned) pedantry.

Zorn [tsɔrn], *m.* (—(e)s, *no pl.*) wrath, anger, indignation; *seinen — auslassen*, vent o.'s anger; *in — geraten*, get angry.

zornglühend [ʹtsɔrngly:ənt], *adj.* boiling with rage.

zornig [ʹtsɔrnɪç], *adj.* angry, wrathful, irate; — *werden*, get angry.

Zote [ʹtso:tə], *f.* (—, *pl.* —n) smutty story, ribaldry, bawdiness.

zotig [ʹtso:tɪç], *adj.* loose, ribald, smutty.

zottig [ʹtsɔtɪç], *adj.* shaggy.

zu [tsu:], *prep.* (*Dat.*) to, towards; in addition to; at, in, on; for; — *Anfang*, in the beginning; — *Fuß*, on foot; — *Hause*, at home; — *Wasser*, at sea, by sea; — *deinem Nutzen*, for your benefit. — *adv. & prefix*, to, towards; closed; too; — *sehr*, too; — *viel*, too much.

Zubehör [ʹtsu:bəhø:r], *n.* (—s, *no pl.*) accessory, appurtenance.

zubekommen [ʹtsu:bəkɔmən], *v.a. irr.* get in addition.

Zuber [ʹtsu:bər], *m.* (—s, *pl.* —) tub.

zubereiten [ʹtsu:bəraɪtən], *v.a.* prepare.

Zubereitung [ʹtsu:bəraɪtuŋ], *f.* (—, *no pl.*) preparation.

zubilligen [ʹtsu:bɪlɪgən], *v.a.* allow, grant.

zubleiben [ʹtsu:blaɪbən], *v.n. irr.* (*aux.* sein) remain shut.

zubringen [ʹtsu:brɪŋən], *v.a. irr. die Zeit —*, spend the time.

Zubringerdienst [ʹtsu:brɪŋərdi:nst], *m.* (—es, *pl.* —) shuttle-service, tender-service.

Zubuße [ʹtsu:bu:sə], *f.* (—, *pl.* —e) (additional) contribution.

Zucht [tsuxt], *f.* (—, *no pl.*) race, breed; discipline; breeding, rearing; education, discipline; (good) manners; *in — halten*, keep in hand.

züchten [ʹtsyçtən], *v.a.* cultivate; rear, breed; grow.

Züchter [ʹtsyçtər], *m.* (—s, *pl.* —) (*plants*) nurseryman; (*animals*) breeder.

Zuchthaus [ʹtsuxthaus], *n.* (—es, *pl.* ʹ̣er) penitentiary, convict prison.

Zuchthäusler [ʹtsuxthɔyslər], *m.* (—s, *pl.* —) convict.

Zuchthengst [ʹtsuxthɛŋst], *m.* (—es, *pl.* —e) stallion.

züchtig [ʹtsyçtɪç], *adj.* modest, chaste.

züchtigen [ʹtsyçtɪgən], *v.a.* chastise, lash.

Züchtigkeit [ʹtsyçtɪçkaɪt], *f.* (—, *no pl.*) modesty, chastity.

Züchtigung [ʹtsyçtɪguŋ], *f.* (—, *pl.* —en) chastisement; *körperliche —*, corporal punishment.

Zuchtlosigkeit [ʹtsuxtlo:zɪçkaɪt], *f.* (—, *no pl.*) want of discipline.

Zuchtmeister [ʹtsuxtmaɪstər], *m.* (—s, *pl.* —) disciplinarian, taskmaster.

Zuchtochse [ʹtsuxtɔksə], *m.* (—n, *pl.* —n) bull.

Zuchtstute [ʹtsuxtʃtu:tə], *f.* (—, *pl.* —n) brood-mare.

Züchtung [ʹtsyçtuŋ], *f.* (—, *pl.* —en) (*plants*) cultivation; (*animals*) rearing, breeding.

Zuchtvieh [ʹtsuxtfi:], *n.* (—s, *no pl.*) breeding stock.

Zuchtwahl [ʹtsuxtva:l], *f.* (—, *no pl.*) (*breeding*) selection.

zucken [ʹtsukən], *v.n.* quiver, twitch; wince; start, jerk.

Zucken [ʹtsukən], *n.* (—s, *no pl.*) palpitation, convulsion, twitch, tic.

Zucker [ʹtsukər], *m.* (—s, *no pl.*) sugar.

Zuckerbäcker [ʹtsukərbɛkər], *m.* (—s, *pl.* —) confectioner.

Zuckerguß [ʹtsukərgus], *m.* (—es, *no pl.*) (sugar-)icing.

Zuckerkandis [ʹtsukərkandɪs], *m.* (—, *no pl.*) sugar-candy.

zuckerkrank [ʹtsukərkraŋk], *adj.* (*Med.*) diabetic.

Zuckerkrankheit [ʹtsukərkraŋkhaɪt], *f.* (—, *no pl.*) (*Med.*) diabetes.

zuckern [ʹtsukərn], *v.a.* sugar.

Zuckerpflanzung [ʹtsukərpflantsuŋ], *f.* (—, *pl.* —en) sugar-plantation.

Zuckerraffinerie [ʹtsukərrafinəri:], *f.* (—, *pl.* —n) sugar-refinery.

Zuckerrohr [ʹtsukərro:r], *n.* (—s, *no pl.*) sugar-cane.

Zuckerrübe [ʹtsukərry:bə], *f.* (—, *pl.* —n) sugar-beet.

Zuckerwerk [ʹtsukərvɛrk], *n.* (—s, *no pl.*) confectionery.

Zuckerzange [ʹtsukərtsaŋə], *f.* (—, *pl.* —n) sugar-tongs.

Zuckung [ʹtsukuŋ], *f.* (—, *pl.* —en) convulsion, spasm.

zudecken [ʹtsu:dɛkən], *v.a.* cover up.

zudem [tsuʹde:m], *adv.* besides, moreover.

Zudrang [ʹtsu:draŋ], *m.* (—s, *no pl.*) crowd(ing); rush (on), run (on).

zudrehen [ʹtsu:dre:ən], *v.a.* turn off.

zudringlich [ʹtsu:drɪŋlɪç], *adj.* importunate; intruding.

zudrücken [ʹtsu:drykən], *v.a.* close (by pressing), shut.

zueignen [ʹtsu:aɪgnən], *v.a.* dedicate.

zuerkennen [ʹtsu:ɛrkɛnən], *v.a. irr.* award, adjudicate.

zuerst [tsuʹe:rst], *adv.* at first, first, in the first instance.

Zufahrt [ʹtsu:fa:rt], *f.* (—, *no pl.*) approach, drive.

Zufall [ʹtsu:fal], *m.* (—s, *pl.* ʹ̣e) chance, coincidence; *durch —*, by chance.

zufallen [ʹtsu:falən], *v.n. irr.* (*aux.* sein) close, fall shut; *einem —*, devolve upon s.o., fall to s.o.'s lot.

zufällig [ʹtsu:fɛlɪç], *adj.* accidental, casual, fortuitous. — *adv.* by chance.

Zuflucht [ʹtsu:fluxt], *f.* (—, *no pl.*) refuge, shelter, haven, recourse.

Zufluchtsort ['tsu:fluxtsɔrt], *m.* (—(e)s, *pl.* —e) asylum, shelter, place of refuge.

Zufluß ['tsu:flus], *m.* (—sses, *pl.* ⁻sse) supply; influx.

zuflüstern ['tsu:flystərn], *v.a. einem etwas* —, whisper s.th. to s.o.

zufolge [tsu'fɔlgə], *prep.* (*Genit., Dat.*) in consequence of, owing to, due to, on account of.

zufrieden [tsu'fri:dən], *adj.* content, contented, satisfied; — *lassen*, leave alone.

zufriedenstellen [tsu'fri:dənʃtɛlən], *v.a.* satisfy.

zufügen ['tsu:fy:gən], *v.a.* add (to); inflict.

Zufuhr ['tsu:fu:r], *f.* (—, *pl.* —en) (*goods*) supplies.

Zug [tsu:k], *m.* (—(e)s, *pl.* ⁻e) drawing, pull, tug; draught; march, procession; (*Railw.*) train; (*face*) feature; (*chess*) move; (*character*) trait; (*pen*) stroke; (*birds*) flight; migration; (*mountains*) range.

Zugabe ['tsu:ga:bə], *f.* (—, *pl.* —n) addition, make-weight, extra; (*concert*) encore; *als* —, into the bargain.

Zugang ['tsu:gaŋ], *m.* (—s, *pl.* ⁻e) approach, entry, entrance, admittance, access.

zugänglich ['tsu:gɛŋlɪç], *adj.* accessible, available; (*person*) affable.

Zugbrücke ['tsu:kbrykə], *f.* (—, *pl.* —n) drawbridge.

zugeben ['tsu:ge:bən], *v.a. irr.* give in addition; concede, admit.

zugegen [tsu'ge:gən], *adv.* present.

zugehen ['tsu:ge:ən], *v.n. irr.* (*aux.* sein) (*door*) shut (of itself), close; happen; *auf einen* —, walk towards s.o.; *so geht es im Leben zu,* such is life; *das geht nicht mit rechten Dingen zu,* there is something uncanny about it.

zugehörig ['tsu:gəhø:rɪç], *adj.* belonging, appertaining.

zugeknöpft ['tsu:gəknœpft], *adj.* reserved, taciturn.

Zügel ['tsy:gəl], *m.* (—s, *pl.* —) rein, bridle.

zügeln ['tsy:gəln], *v.a.* bridle, curb, check.

zugesellen ['tsu:gəzɛlən], *v.r. sich* —, associate with, join.

Zugeständnis ['tsu:gəʃtɛntnɪs], *n.* (—sses, *pl.* —sse) admission; concession.

zugestehen ['tsu:gəʃte:ən], *v.a. irr.* admit; concede; *einem etwas* —, allow s.o. s.th.

zugetan ['tsu:gəta:n], *adj.* attached, devoted.

Zugführer ['tsu:kfy:rər], *m.* (—s, *pl.* —) (*Railw.*) guard; (*Mil.*) platoon commander.

zugießen ['tsu:gi:sən], *v.a. irr.* fill up, pour on.

zugig ['tsu:gɪç], *adj.* windy, draughty.

Zugkraft ['tsu:kkraft], *f.* (—, *no pl.*) tractive power, magnetic attraction;

(*fig.*) pull, attraction; publicity value.

zugleich [tsu'glaɪç], *adv.* at the same time; — *mit*, together with.

Zugluft ['tsu:kluft], *f.* (—, *no pl.*) draught (of air).

zugreifen ['tsu:graɪfən], *v.n. irr.* grab; lend a hand; (*at table*) help o.s.

Zugrolle ['tsu:krɔlə], *f.* (—, *pl.* —n) pulley.

zugrunde [tsu'grundə], *adv.* — *gehen*, perish, go to ruin, go to the dogs; — *legen*, base upon.

Zugstück ['tsu:kʃtyk], *n.* (—s, *pl.* —e) (*Theat.*) popular show; (*coll.*) success, hit.

zugucken ['tsu:gukən], *v.n.* look on, watch.

zugunsten [tsu'gunstən], *prep.* (*Genit.*) for the benefit of.

zugute [tsu'gu:tə], *adv.* — *halten*, make allowances.

Zugvogel ['tsu:kfo:gəl], *m.* (—s, *pl.* ⁻) bird of passage.

zuhalten ['tsu:haltən], *v.a. irr.* keep closed.

Zuhälter ['tsu:hɛltər], *m.* (—s, *pl.* —) souteneur; pimp.

Zuhilfenahme [tsu'hɪlfəna:mə], *f.* (—, *no pl.*) *unter* —, with the help of, by means of.

zuhören ['tsu:hø:rən], *v.n.* listen to, attend to.

Zuhörerschaft ['tsu:hø:rərʃaft], *f.* (—, *pl.* —en) audience.

zujubeln ['tsu:ju:bəln], *v.n. einem* —, acclaim s.o., cheer s.o.

zukehren ['tsu:ke:rən], *v.a. einem den Rücken* —, turn o.'s back on s.o.

zuknöpfen ['tsu:knœpfən], *v.a.* button (up).

zukommen ['tsu:kɔmən], *v.n. irr.* (*aux.* sein) *auf einen* —, advance towards s.o.; *einem* —, be due to s.o.; become s.o.; reach s.o.

Zukost ['tsu:kɔst], *f.* (—, *no pl.*) (*food*) trimmings, extras.

Zukunft ['tsu:kunft], *f.* (—, *no pl.*) future; prospects.

zukünftig ['tsu:kynftɪç], *adj.* future, prospective.

Zukunftsmusik ['tsu:kunftsmuzi:k], *f.* (—, *no pl.*) daydreams, pipedreams.

zulächeln ['tsu:lɛçəln], *v.a. einem* —, smile at s.o.

Zulage ['tsu:la:gə], *f.* (—, *pl.* —n) addition; increase of salary, rise; (*Am.*) raise.

zulangen ['tsu:laŋən], *v.n.* be sufficient; (*at table*) help o.s.

zulänglich ['tsu:lɛŋlɪç], *adj.* sufficient, adequate.

zulassen ['tsu:lasən], *v.a. irr.* leave unopened; allow; admit; permit.

zulässig ['tsu:lɛsɪç], *adj.* admissible; *das ist nicht* —, that is not allowed.

Zulassung ['tsu:lasuŋ], *f.* (—, *pl.* —en) admission.

Zulauf ['tsu:lauf], *m.* (—s, *no pl.*) run (of customers); crowd, throng.

zulaufen ['tsu:laufən], *v.n. irr.* (*aux.* sein) *auf einen* —, run towards s.o.; *spitz* —, taper, come to a point.

zulegen ['tsu:le:gən], *v.a.* add; increase; *sich etwas* —, make o.s. a present of s.th.; get s.th.

zuletzt [tsu'lɛtst], *adv.* last, at last, lastly, finally, eventually, in the end.

zuliebe [tsu'li:bə], *adv. einem etwas* — *tun*, oblige s.o.; do s.th. for s.o.'s sake.

zum = **zu dem**.

zumachen ['tsu:maxən], *v.a.* shut, close.

zumal [tsu'ma:l], *adv.* especially, particularly. — *conj.* especially since.

zumeist [tsu'maɪst], *adv.* mostly, for the most part.

zumute [tsu'mu:tə], *adv. mir ist nicht gut* —, I don't feel well.

zumuten ['tsu:mu:tən], *v.a. einem etwas* —, expect *or* demand s.th. of s.o.

Zumutung ['tsu:mu:tuŋ], *f.* (—, *pl.* —en) unreasonable demand.

zunächst [tsu'nɛ:çst], *adv.* first, above all.

Zunahme ['tsu:na:mə], *f.* (—, *pl.* —n) increase.

Zuname ['tsu:na:mə], *m.* (—ns, *pl.* —n) surname, family name.

zünden ['tsyndən], *v.n.* catch fire, ignite.

Zunder ['tsundər], *m.* (—s, *no pl.*) tinder.

Zünder ['tsyndər], *m.* (—s, *pl.* —) lighter, detonator, fuse.

Zündholz ['tsynthɔlts], *n.* (—es, *pl.* ⁻er) match.

Zündkerze ['tsyntkɛrtsə], *f.* (—, *pl.* —n) (*Motor.*) sparking-plug.

Zündstoff ['tsyntʃtɔf], *m.* (—s, *pl.* —e) fuel.

Zündung ['tsynduŋ], *f.* (—, *pl.* —en) ignition; detonation.

zunehmen ['tsu:ne:mən], *v.n. irr.* increase, put on weight; (*moon*) wax.

zuneigen ['tsu:naɪgən], *v.r. sich* —, incline towards.

Zuneigung ['tsu:naɪguŋ], *f.* (—, *pl.* —en) affection, inclination.

Zunft [tsunft], *f.* (—, *pl.* ⁻e) company, guild, corporation; (*fig.*) brotherhood.

Zunftgenosse ['tsunftgənɔsə], *m.* (—n, *pl.* —n) member of a guild.

zünftig ['tsynftɪç], *adj.* professional; proper.

zunftmäßig ['tsunftmɛ:sɪç], *adj.* professional; competent.

Zunge ['tsuŋə], *f.* (—, *pl.* —n) tongue; (*buckle*) catch; (*fig.*) language; (*fish*) sole.

züngeln ['tsyŋəln], *v.n.* (*flame*) shoot out, lick.

Zungenband ['tsuŋənbant], *n.* (—s, *pl.* ⁻er) ligament of the tongue.

zungenfertig ['tsuŋənfɛrtɪç], *adj.* voluble, glib.

Zungenlaut ['tsuŋənlaut], *m.* (—s, *pl.* —e) (*Phon.*) lingual sound.

Zungenspitze ['tsuŋənʃpɪtsə], *f.* (—, *pl.* —n) tip of the tongue.

zunichte [tsu'nɪçtə], *adv.* — *machen*, ruin, undo, destroy; — *werden*, come to nothing.

zupfen ['tsupfən], *v.a.* pick, pluck.

zurechnungsfähig ['tsu:rɛçnuŋsfɛ:ɪç], *adj.* accountable, of sane mind, compos mentis.

zurecht [tsu'rɛçt], *adv.* aright, right(ly), in order.

zurechtfinden [tsu'rɛçtfɪndən], *v.r. irr. sich* —, find o.'s way about.

zurechtkommen [tsu'rɛçtkɔmən], *v.n. irr.* (*aux.* sein) arrive in (good) time; *mit einem gut* —, get on well with s.o.

zurechtlegen [tsu'rɛçtle:gən], *v.a.* put in order, get ready.

zurechtmachen [tsu'rɛçtmaxən], *v.a.* get s.th. ready, prepare s.th. — *v.r. sich*—, prepare o.s.; (*women*) make up; (*coll.*) put on o.'s face.

zurechtweisen [tsu'rɛçtvaɪzən], *v.a. irr.* reprove (s.o.), set (s.o.) right; direct.

Zurechtweisung [tsu'rɛçtvaɪzuŋ], *f.* (—, *pl.* —en) reprimand.

Zureden ['tsu:re:dən], *n.* (—s, *no pl.*) encouragement; entreaties.

zureden ['tsu:re:dən], *v.n.* encourage (s.o.), persuade (s.o.)

zureichen ['tsu:raɪçən], *v.a.* reach, hand. — *v.n.* be sufficient, be enough, suffice.

zurichten ['tsu:rɪçtən], *v.a. etwas* (*einen*) *übel* —, maltreat s.th. (s.o.).

zürnen ['tsyrnən], *v.n.* be angry (with).

zurück [tsu'ryk], *adv.* back; behind; backwards; — *excl.* stand back!

zurückbegeben [tsu'rykbəge:bən], *v.r. irr. sich* —, go back, return.

zurückbehalten [tsu'rykbəhaltən], *v.a. irr.* retain, keep back.

zurückbekommen [tsu'rykbəkɔmən], *v.a. irr.* get back, recover (s.th.).

zurückberufen [tsu'rykbəru:fən], *v.a. irr.* recall.

zurückfordern [tsu'rykfɔrdərn], *v.a.* demand back, demand the return of.

zurückführen [tsu'rykfy:rən], *v.a.* lead back; *auf etwas* —, attribute to; trace back to.

zurückgeblieben [tsu'rykgəbli:bən], *adj.* retarded, mentally deficient, backward.

zurückgezogen [tsu'rykgətso:gən], *adj.* secluded, retired.

zurückhalten [tsu'rykhaltən], *v.a. irr.* keep back, retain.

zurückhaltend [tsu'rykhaltənt], *adj.* reserved.

zurückkehren [tsu'rykke:rən], *v.n.* (*aux.* sein) return.

zurückkommen [tsu'rykkɔmən], *v.n. irr.* (*aux.* sein) come back.

zurücklassen [tsu'ryklasən], *v.a. irr.* leave behind, abandon.

zurücklegen

zurücklegen [tsuˈrykleːɡən], *v.a.* lay aside, put by; *eine Strecke* —, cover a distance. — *v.r. sich* —, lean back; *zurückgelegter Gewinn*, undistributed profits.

zurückmüssen [tsuˈrykmysən], *v.n. irr.* be obliged to return.

zurücknehmen [tsuˈrykneːmən], *v.a. irr.* take back.

zurückschrecken [tsuˈrykʃrɛkən], *v.a.* frighten away. — *v.n. irr.* (*aux.* sein) recoil (from).

zurücksehnen [tsuˈrykzeːnən], *v.r. sich* —, long to return, wish o.s. back.

zurücksetzen [tsuˈrykzɛtsən], *v.a.* put back; slight; discriminate against; neglect.

Zurücksetzung [tsuˈrykzɛtsuŋ], *f.* (—, *pl.* **—en**) slight, rebuff.

zurückstrahlen [tsuˈrykʃtraːlən], *v.a.* reflect.

zurücktreten [tsuˈryktreːtən], *v.n. irr.* (*aux.* sein) stand back, withdraw; resign.

zurückverlangen [tsuˈrykfɛrlaŋən], *v.a.* demand back, request the return of.

zurückversetzen [tsuˈrykfɛrzɛtsən], *v.a.* (*Sch.*) put in a lower form. — *v.r. sich* —, turn o.'s thoughts back (to), hark back.

zurückweichen [tsuˈrykvaɪçən], *v.n. irr.* (*aux.* sein) withdraw, retreat.

zurückweisen [tsuˈrykvaɪzən], *v.a. irr.* refuse, reject, repulse.

zurückwollen [tsuˈrykvɔlən], *v.n.* wish to return.

zurückziehen [tsuˈryktsiːən], *v.a. irr.* draw back; (*fig.*) withdraw, retract, countermand. — *v.r. sich* —, retire, withdraw.

Zuruf [ˈtsuːruːf], *m.* (**—s,** *pl.* **—e**) call, acclaim, acclamation.

Zusage [ˈtsuːzaːɡə], *f.* (—, *pl.* **—n**) promise; acceptance.

zusagen [ˈtsuːzaːɡən], *v.a.* promise; *es sagt mir zu,* I like it. — *v.n.* accept.

zusagend [ˈtsuːzaːɡənt], *adj.* affirmative; agreeable.

zusammen [tsuˈzamən], *adv.* together, jointly.

zusammenbeißen [tsuˈzamənbaɪsən], *v.a. irr. die Zähne* —, set o.'s teeth.

zusammenbetteln [tsuˈzamənbɛtəln], *v.a. sich etwas* —, collect (by begging).

zusammenbrechen [tsuˈzamənbrɛçən], *v.n. irr.* (*aux.* sein) break down, collapse.

Zusammenbruch [tsuˈzamənbrux], *m.* (**—s,** *pl.* **⸚e**) breakdown, collapse, débâcle.

zusammendrängen [tsuˈzaməndrɛŋən], *v.a.* press together; (*fig.*) abridge, condense.

zusammendrücken [tsuˈzaməndrykən], *v.a.* compress.

zusammenfahren [tsuˈzamənfaːrən], *v.n. irr.* (*aux.* sein) collide; give a start.

zusammenfallen [tsuˈzamənfalən], *v.n. irr.* (*aux.* sein) collapse.

zusammenfassen [tsuˈzamənfasən], *v.a.* sum up, summarize.

Zusammenfassung [tsuˈzamənfasuŋ], *f.* (—, *no pl.*) summing-up, summary.

zusammenfinden [tsuˈzamənfɪndən], *v.r. irr. sich* —, discover a mutual affinity, come together.

Zusammenfluß [tsuˈzamənflus], *m.* (**—sses,** *pl.* **⸚sse**) confluence.

zusammengeben [tsuˈzaməngeːbən], *v.a. irr.* join in marriage.

Zusammengehörigkeit [tsuˈzamənɡəhøːrɪçkaɪt], *f.* (—, *no pl.*) solidarity; (*Am.*) togetherness.

zusammengesetzt [tsuˈzaməngəzɛtst], *adj.* composed (of), consisting (of); complicated; (*Maths.*) composite.

zusammengewürfelt [tsuˈzaməngəvyrfəlt], *adj.* motley, mixed.

Zusammenhalt [tsuˈzamənhalt], *m.* (**—s,** *no pl.*) holding together; unity.

Zusammenhang [tsuˈzamənhaŋ], *m.* (**—s,** *pl.* **⸚e**) coherence; connection, context.

zusammenhängen [tsuˈzamənhɛŋən], *v.n. irr.* hang together, cohere; (*fig.*) be connected (with).

Zusammenklang [tsuˈzamənklaŋ], *m.* (**—s,** *pl.* **⸚e**) unison, harmony.

Zusammenkunft [tsuˈzamənkunft], *f.* (—, *pl.* **⸚e**) meeting, convention, conference; reunion.

zusammenlaufen [tsuˈzamənlaufən], *v.n. irr.* (*aux.* sein) crowd together, converge; flock together; (*milk*) curdle; (*material*) shrink.

zusammenlegen [tsuˈzamənleːɡən], *v.a.* put together; (*money*) collect; (*letter*) fold up.

zusammennehmen [tsuˈzamənneːmən], *v.a. irr.* gather up. — *v.r. sich* —, get a firm grip on o.s., pull o.s. together.

zusammenpassen [tsuˈzamənpasən], *v.n.* fit together, match; agree; be compatible.

zusammenpferchen [tsuˈzamənpfɛrçən], *v.a.* pen up, crowd together in a small space.

zusammenpressen [tsuˈzamənprɛsən], *v.a.* squeeze together.

zusammenraffen [tsuˈzamənrafən], *v.a.* gather up hurriedly, collect. — *v.r. sich* —, pluck up courage; pull o.s. together.

zusammenrechnen [tsuˈzamənrɛçnən], *v.a.* add up.

zusammenreimen [tsuˈzamənraɪmən], *v.a. sich etwas* —, figure s.th. out.

zusammenrücken [tsuˈzamənrykən], *v.a.* move together, draw closer. — *v.n.* move closer together, move up.

zusammenschießen [tsuˈzamənʃiːsən], *v.a. irr.* shoot to pieces, shoot down; *Geld* —, club together, raise a subscription.

zusammenschlagen [tsuˈzamənʃlaːɡən], *v.a. irr.* beat up; strike together; clap, fold.

Zustimmung

zusammenschließen [tsu'zamənʃli:-sən], *v.r. irr. sich* —, join, unite, ally o.s. (with).

zusammenschweißen [tsu'zamənʃvai-sən], *v.a.* weld together.

Zusammensein [tsu'zamənzaɪn], *n.* (—s, *no pl.*) meeting, social gathering.

Zusammensetzung [tsu'zamənzɛtsuŋ], *f.* (—, *no pl.*) construction; composition.

Zusammenspiel [tsu'zamənʃpi:l], *n.* (—s, *no pl.*) (*Theat., Mus.*) ensemble.

zusammenstellen [tsu'zamənʃtɛlən], *v.a.* compose, concoct; put together, compile.

Zusammenstellung [tsu'zamənʃtɛluŋ], *f.* (—, *pl.* —en) combination, compilation; juxtaposition.

zusammenstoppeln [tsu'zamənʃtɔp-əln], *v.a.* string together, patch up.

Zusammenstoß [tsu'zamənʃto:s], *m.* (—es, *pl.* ⸚e) clash, conflict; collision.

zusammenstoßen [tsu'zamənʃto:sən], *v.n. irr.* (*aux.* sein) clash; crash, come into collision, collide.

zusammentragen [tsu'zaməntra:gən], *v.a. irr.* collect, compile.

zusammentreffen [tsu'zaməntrɛfən], *v.n. irr.* meet; coincide.

zusammentreten [tsu'zaməntre:tən], *v.n. irr.* (*aux.* sein) meet.

zusammentun [tsu'zamntu:n], *v.r. irr. sich* — *mit*, associate with, join.

zusammenwirken [tsu'zamənvɪrkən], *v.n.* cooperate, collaborate.

zusammenwürfeln [tsu'zamənvyr-fəln], *v.a.* jumble up.

zusammenzählen [tsu'zaməntsɛ:lən], *v.a.* add up.

zusammenziehen [tsu'zaməntsi:ən], *v.n. irr.* (*aux.* sein) move in together. — *v.a.* draw together, contract. — *v.r. sich* —, shrink; (*storm*) gather; *Zahlen* —, add up.

Zusammenziehung [tsu'zaməntsi:uŋ], *f.* (—, *no pl.*) contraction.

Zusatz [' tsu:zats], *m.* (—es, *pl.* ⸚e) addition, supplement, admixture; (*will*) codicil.

zuschanzen [tsu'ʃantsən], *v.a. einem etwas* —, obtain s.th. for s.o.

zuschauen [' tsu:ʃauən], *v.n.* look on, watch.

Zuschauer [' tsu:ʃauər], *m.* (—s, *pl.* —) onlooker, spectator.

Zuschauerraum [' tsu:ʃauərraum], *m.* (—s, *pl.* ⸚e) (*Theat.*) auditorium.

zuschaufeln [' tsu:ʃaufəln], *v.a.* shovel in, fill up.

zuschieben [' tsu:ʃi:bən], *v.a. irr.* push towards; shut; *einem etwas* —, shove (blame) on to s.o.

zuschießen [' tsu:ʃi:sən], *v.a. irr. Geld* —, put money into (an undertaking).

Zuschlag [' tsu:ʃla:k], *m.* (—s, *pl.* ⸚e) addition; (*Railw.*) excess fare.

zuschlagen [' tsu:ʃla:gən], *v.a. irr.* add; (*door*) bang; (*auction*) knock down to (s.o.). — *v.n.* strike hard.

zuschlag(s)pflichtig [' tsu:ʃla:k(s)pflɪç-tɪç], *adj.* liable to a supplementary charge.

zuschmeißen [' tsu:ʃmaisən], *v.a. irr.* (*door*) slam to, bang.

zuschneiden [' tsu:ʃnaidən], *v.a. irr.* (*pattern*) cut out; cut up.

Zuschneider [' tsu:ʃnaidər], *m.* (—s, *pl.*—) (*Tail.*) cutter.

Zuschnitt [' tsu:ʃnɪt], *m.* (—s, *no pl.*) (*clothing*) cut.

zuschreiben [' tsu:ʃraibən], *v.a. irr. einem etwas* —, impute s.th. to s.o.; attribute *or* ascribe s.th. to s.o.

Zuschrift [' tsu:ʃrɪft], *f.* (—, *pl.* —en) communication, letter.

Zuschuß [' tsu:ʃus], *m.* (—sses, *pl.* ⸚sse) additional money, supplementary allowance, subsidy.

zuschütten [' tsu:ʃytən], *v.a.* fill up.

Zusehen [' tsu:ze:ən], *n.* (—s, *no pl.*) *das* — *haben*, be left out in the cold.

zusehen [' tsu:ze:ən], *v.n. irr.* look on, watch; be a spectator; see to it.

zusehends [' tsu:ze:ənts], *adv.* visibly.

zusetzen [' tsu:zɛtsən], *v.a.* add to, admix; lose. — *v.n. einem* —, pester s.o.; attack s.o.

zusichern [' tsu:zɪçərn], *v.a.* promise, assure.

Zusicherung [' tsu:zɪçəruŋ], *f.* (—, *pl.* —en) promise, assurance.

Zuspeise [' tsu:ʃpaizə], *f.* (—, *no pl.*) (*dial.*) (*food*) trimmings; vegetables.

zusperren [' tsu:ʃpɛrən], *v.a.* shut, close, lock up.

zuspitzen [' tsu:ʃpɪtsən], *v.a.* sharpen to a point. — *v.r. sich* —, come to a climax.

zusprechen [' tsu:ʃprɛçən], *v.n. irr. dem Wein* —, drink heavily. — *v.a. Mut* —, comfort.

Zuspruch [' tsu:ʃprux], *m.* (—s, *pl.* ⸚e) exhortation; consolation.

Zustand [' tsu:ʃtant], *m.* (—s, *pl.* ⸚e) condition, state of affairs, situation.

zustande [tsu'ʃtandə], *adv.* — *kommen*, come off, be accomplished; — *bringen*, accomplish.

zuständig [' tsu:ʃtɛndɪç], *adj.* competent; appropriate.

Zuständigkeit [' tsu:ʃtɛndɪçkait], *f.* (—, *no pl.*) competence.

zustecken [' tsu:ʃtɛkən], *v.a.* pin up; *einem etwas* —, slip s.th. into s.o.'s hand.

zustehen [' tsu:ʃte:ən], *v.n. irr.* be due to, belong to; be s.o.'s business to.

zustellen [' tsu:ʃtɛlən], *v.a.* deliver, hand over; (*Law*) serve (a writ).

Zustellung [' tsu:ʃtɛluŋ], *f.* (—, *pl.* —en) delivery; (*Law*) service.

zusteuern [' tsu:ʃtɔyərn], *v.a.* contribute. — *v.n.* (*aux.* sein) steer for; (*fig.*) aim at.

zustimmen [' tsu:ʃtɪmən], *v.n.* agree to.

Zustimmung [' tsu:ʃtɪmuŋ], *f.* (—, *pl.* —en) assent, consent, agreement.

zustopfen

zustopfen ['tsu:ʃtɔpfən], v.a. fill up, stop up, plug; darn, mend.

zustoßen ['tsu:ʃtoːsən], v.a. irr. push to, shut.

zustürzen ['tsu:ʃtyrtsən], v.n. (aux. sein) auf einen —, rush at or towards s.o.

Zutaten ['tsu:taːtən], f. pl. ingredients, garnishings.

zuteil [tsu'taɪl], adv. — werden, fall to s.o.'s share.

zutragen ['tsu:traːgən], v.a. irr. report, tell. — v.r. sich —, happen.

Zuträger ['tsu:trɛːgər], m. (—s, pl. —) informer, tale-bearer.

zuträglich ['tsu:trɛːklɪç], adj. advantageous, wholesome.

Zutrauen ['tsu:trauən], n. (—s, no pl.) confidence.

zutrauen ['tsu:trauən], v.a. einem etwas —, credit s.o. with s.th.

zutraulich ['tsu:traulɪç], adj. trusting; familiar, intimate; tame.

zutreffen ['tsu:trɛfən], v.n. irr. prove correct, take place.

zutreffend ['tsu:trɛfənt], adj. apposite, pertinent.

Zutritt ['tsu:trɪt], m. (—s, no pl.) entry; access, admittance; — verboten, no admittance.

zutunlich ['tsu:tuːnlɪç], adj. confiding; obliging.

zuverlässig ['tsu:fɛrlɛsɪç], adj. reliable; authentic.

Zuversicht ['tsu:fɛrzɪçt], f. (—, no pl.) trust, confidence.

zuversichtlich ['tsu:fɛrzɪçtlɪç], adj. confident.

zuvor [tsu'foːr], adv. before, first, formerly.

zuvorkommend [tsu'foːrkɔmənt], adj. obliging, polite.

Zuwachs ['tsu:vaks], m. (—es, no pl.) increase, accretion, growth.

zuwachsen ['tsu:vaksən], v.n. irr. (aux. sein) become overgrown.

zuwandern ['tsu:vandərn], v.n. (aux. sein) immigrate.

zuwegebringen [tsu've:gəbrɪŋən], v.a. irr. bring about, effect.

zuweilen [tsu'vaɪlən], adv. sometimes, at times.

zuweisen ['tsu:vaɪzən], v.a. irr. assign, apportion.

zuwenden ['tsu:vɛndən], v.a. turn towards; give.

zuwerfen ['tsu:vɛrfən], v.a. irr. throw towards, cast; (door) slam.

zuwider ['tsu:viːdər], prep. (Dat.) against, contrary to. — adv. repugnant.

Zuwiderhandlung [tsu'viːdərhandluŋ], f. (—, pl. —en) contravention.

zuwiderlaufen [tsu'viːdərlaufən], v.n. irr. (aux. sein) be contrary to, fly in the face of.

zuzählen ['tsu:tsɛːlən], v.a. add to.

zuziehen ['tsu:tsiːən], v.a. irr. draw together; tighten; consult; (curtain) draw. — v.r. sich eine Krankheit —, catch a disease.

Zuzug ['tsu:tsuːk], m. (—s, no pl.) immigration; population increase.

zuzüglich ['tsu:tsyːklɪç], prep. (Genit.) in addition to, including, plus.

Zwang [tsvaŋ], m. (—s, no pl.) coercion, force; compulsion; (fig.) constraint; sich — auferlegen, restrain o.s.; tu deinen Gefühlen keinen — an, let yourself go.

zwanglos ['tsvaŋloːs], adj. informal, free and easy.

Zwangsarbeit ['tsvaŋsarbaɪt], f. (—, pl. —en) forced labour.

Zwangsjacke ['tsvaŋsjakə], f. (—, pl. —en) strait-jacket.

Zwangsmaßnahme ['tsvaŋsmaːsnaːmə], f. (—, pl. —en) compulsory measure, compulsion.

Zwangsversteigerung ['tsvaŋsfɛrʃtaɪgəruŋ], f. (—, pl. —en) enforced sale.

Zwangsvollstreckung ['tsvaŋsfɔlʃtrɛkuŋ], f. (—, pl. —en) distraint.

zwangsweise ['tsvaŋsvaɪzə], adv. by force, compulsorily.

Zwangswirtschaft ['tsvaŋsvɪrtʃaft], f. (—, no pl.) price control, controlled economy.

zwanzig ['tsvantsɪç], num. adj. twenty.

zwar [tsvaːr], adv. to be sure, indeed, it is true, true; (Am.) sure.

Zweck [tsvɛk], m. (—(e)s, —e) end, object, purpose.

zweckdienlich ['tsvɛkdiːnlɪç], adj. useful, expedient.

Zwecke ['tsvɛkə], f. (—, pl. —n) tack, drawing-pin.

zwec_entsprechend ['tsvɛkɛntʃprɛçant], adj. suitable, appropriate.

zweckmäßig ['tsvɛkmɛːsɪç], adj. expedient, suitable, proper.

zwecks [tsvɛks], prep. (Genit.) for the purpose of.

zwei [tsvaɪ], num. adj. two.

zweibändig ['tsvaɪbɛndɪç], adj. in two volumes.

zweideutig ['tsvaɪdɔytɪç], adj. ambiguous, equivocal; (fig.) suggestive.

Zweideutigkeit ['tsvaɪdɔytɪçkaɪt], f. (—, pl. —en) ambiguity.

Zweifel ['tsvaɪfəl], m. (—s, pl. —) doubt, scruple; ohne —, no doubt.

zweifelhaft ['tsvaɪfəlhaft], adj. doubtful, dubious.

zweifellos ['tsvaɪfəlloːs], adv. doubtless.

zweifeln ['tsvaɪfəln], v.n. doubt, question; ich zweifle nicht daran, I have no doubt about it.

Zweifelsfall ['tsvaɪfəlsfal], m. (—s, pl. ⸚e) doubtful matter; im —, in case of doubt.

Zweifler ['tsvaɪflər], m. (—s, pl. —) doubter, sceptic.

Zweig [tsvaɪk], m. (—(e)s, pl. —e) twig, bough, branch.

zweigen ['tsvaɪgən], v.r. sich —, bifurcate, fork, branch.

Zweigniederlassung ['tsvaɪkniːdərlasuŋ], f. (—, pl. —en) branch establishment.

zweihändig ['tsvaɪhɛndɪç], *adj.* two-handed; (*keyboard music*) solo.

Zweihufer ['tsvaɪhu:fər], *m.* (—**s**, *pl.* —) cloven-footed animal.

zweijährig ['tsvaɪjɛːrɪç], *adj.* two-year-old; of two years' duration.

zweijährlich ['tsvaɪjɛːrlɪç], *adj.* biennial. — *adv.* every two years.

Zweikampf ['tsvaɪkampf], *m.* (— (e)s, *pl.* ⁻e) duel.

zweimal ['tsvaɪmal], *adv.* twice; — *soviel*, twice as much.

zweimotorig ['tsvaɪmoto:rɪç], *adj.* twin-(*or* two-) engined.

Zweirad ['tsvaɪra:t], *n.* (—**s**, *pl.* ⁻er) bicycle.

zweireihig ['tsvaɪraɪç], *adj.* (*suit*) double-breasted.

zweischneidig ['tsvaɪʃnaɪdɪç], *adj.* two-edged.

zweiseitig ['tsvaɪzaɪtɪç], *adj.* two-sided, bilateral.

zweisprachig ['tsvaɪʃpra:xɪç], *adj.* bilingual, in two languages.

zweitälteste ['tsvaɪtɛltstə], *adj.* second (eldest).

zweitbeste ['tsvaɪtbɛstə], *adj.* second best.

zweite ['tsvaɪtə], *num. adj.* second; *aus* —*r Hand*, secondhand; *zu zweit*, in twos, two of (us, them).

Zweiteilung ['tsvaɪtaɪluŋ], *f.* (—, *pl.* —**en**) bisection.

zweitens ['tsvaɪtəns], *adv.* secondly, in the second place.

zweitletzte ['tsvaɪtlɛtstə], *adj.* last but one, penultimate.

zweitnächste ['tsvaɪtnɛçstə], *adj.* next but one.

Zwerchfell ['tsvɛrçfɛl], *n.* (—**s**, *pl.* —**e**) diaphragm, midriff.

zwerchfellerschütternd ['tsvɛrçfɛlerʃytərnt], *adj.* side-splitting.

Zwerg [tsvɛrk], *m.* (—**s**, *pl.* —**e**) dwarf, pigmy.

zwerghaft ['tsvɛrkhaft], *adj.* dwarfish.

Zwetsche ['tsvɛtʃə], *f.* (—, *pl.* —**n**) (*Bot.*) damson.

Zwickel ['tsvɪkəl], *m.* (—**s**, *pl.* —) gusset; *komischer* —, (*coll.*) queer fish.

zwicken ['tsvɪkən], *v.a.* pinch, nip.

Zwicker ['tsvɪkər], *m.* (—**s**, *pl.* —) pince-nez.

Zwickmühle ['tsvɪkmy:lə], *f.* (—, *pl.* —**n**) *in der* — *sein*, be on the horns of a dilemma, be in a jam.

Zwickzange ['tsvɪktsaŋə], *f.* (—, *pl.* —**n**) pincers.

Zwieback ['tsvi:bak], *m.* (—**s**, *pl.* —**e**) rusk.

Zwiebel ['tsvi:bəl], *f.* (—, *pl.* —**n**) onion; bulb.

zwiebelartig ['tsvi:bəla:rtɪç], *adj.* bulbous.

zwiebeln ['tsvi:bəln], *v.a. einen* —, bully, torment s.o.

Zwielicht ['tsvi:lɪçt], *n.* (—**s**, *no pl.*) twilight.

Zwiespalt ['tsvi:ʃpalt], *m.* (—**s**, *pl.* —**e**) difference, dissension; schism.

Zwiesprache ['tsvi:ʃpra:xə], *f.* (—, *pl.* —**n**) dialogue; discussion.

Zwietracht ['tsvi:traxt], *f.* (—, *no pl.*) discord, disharmony.

zwieträchtig ['tsvi:trɛçtɪç], *adj.* discordant, at variance.

Zwillich ['tsvɪlɪç], *m.* (—**s**, *pl.* —**e**) ticking.

Zwilling ['tsvɪlɪŋ], *m.* (—**s**, *pl.* —**e**) twin; (*pl.*) (*Astron.*) Gemini.

Zwingburg ['tsvɪŋburk], *f.* (—, *pl.* —**en**) stronghold.

Zwinge ['tsvɪŋə], *f.* (—, *pl.* —**n**) ferrule.

zwingen ['tsvɪŋən], *v.a. irr.* force, compel; master, overcome, get the better of. — *v.r. sich* —, force o.s. (to), make a great effort (to).

zwingend ['tsvɪŋənt], *adj.* cogent, imperative, convincing.

Zwinger ['tsvɪŋər], *m.* (—**s**, *pl.* —) keep, donjon, fort; bear-pit.

Zwingherrschaft ['tsvɪŋhɛrʃaft], *f.* (—, *pl.* —**en**) despotism, tyranny.

zwinkern ['tsvɪŋkərn], *v.n.* wink; (*stars*) twinkle.

Zwirn [tsvɪrn], *m.* (—(e)s, *pl.* —**e**) thread, sewing cotton.

Zwirnrolle ['tsvɪrnrɔlə], *f.* (—, *pl.* —**n**) ball of thread, reel of cotton.

zwischen ['tsvɪʃən], *prep.* (*Dat.*, *Acc.*) between; among, amongst.

Zwischenakt ['tsvɪʃənakt], *m.* (—**s**, *pl.* —**e**) (*Theat.*) interval.

Zwischenbemerkung ['tsvɪʃənbəmɛrkuŋ], *f.* (—, *pl.* —**en**) interruption, digression.

Zwischendeck ['tsvɪʃəndɛk], *n.* (—**s**, *pl.* —**e**) (*ship*) steerage, between decks.

zwischendurch ['tsvɪʃəndurç], *adv.* in between, at intervals.

Zwischenfall ['tsvɪʃənfal], *m.* (—**s**, *pl.* ⁻e) incident; episode.

Zwischengericht ['tsvɪʃəngərɪçt], *n.* (—**s**, *pl.* —**e**) (*food*) entrée, entremets.

Zwischenglied ['tsvɪʃəngli:t], *n.* (—**s**, *pl.* —**er**) link.

Zwischenhändler ['tsvɪʃənhɛndlər], *m.* (—**s**, *pl.* —) middleman.

Zwischenpause ['tsvɪʃənpauzə], *f.* (—, *pl.* —**n**) interval; pause.

Zwischenraum ['tsvɪʃənraum], *m.* (—**s**, *pl.* ⁻e) intermediate space, gap.

Zwischenrede ['tsvɪʃənre:də], *f.* (—, *pl.* —**n**) interruption.

Zwischenruf ['tsvɪʃənru:f], *m.* (—**s**, *pl.* —**e**) interruption, interjection.

Zwischensatz ['tsvɪʃənzats], *m.* (—**es**, *pl.* ⁻e) parenthesis; interpolation.

Zwischenspiel ['tsvɪʃənʃpi:l], *n.* (—**s**, *pl.* —**e**) interlude, intermezzo.

Zwischenzeit ['tsvɪʃəntsaɪt], *f.* (—, *no pl.*) interval, interim, meantime; *in der* —, meanwhile.

Zwist [tsvɪst], *m.* (—**es**, *pl.* —**e**) discord, quarrel, dispute.

Zwistigkeiten ['tsvɪstɪçkaɪtən], *f. pl.* hostilities.

zwitschern ['tsvɪtʃərn], *v.n.* chirp, twitter.

Zwitter ['tsvɪtər], *m.* (—s, *pl.* —) hybrid, cross-breed, mongrel; hermaphrodite.

zwitterhaft ['tsvɪtərhaft], *adj.* hybrid; bisexual.

zwölf [svœlf], *num. adj.* twelve.

Zwölffingerdarm ['tsvœlffɪŋərdarm], *m.* (—s, *pl.* ⁓e) duodenum.

Zyankali [tsy:anˈkaːli], *n.* (—s, *no pl.*) potassium cyanide.

Zyklon [tsyˈkloːn], *m.* (—s, *pl.* —e) cyclone.

Zyklus ['tsyklus], *m.* (—, *pl.* **Zyklen**) cycle; course, series.

zylinderförmig [tsyˈlɪndərfœrmɪç], *adj.* cylindric(al).

Zylinderhut [tsyˈlɪndərhuːt], *m.* (—s, *pl.* ⁓e) top-hat, silk-hat.

zylindrisch [tsyˈlɪndrɪʃ], *adj.* cylindric(al).

Zyniker ['tsyːnɪkər], *m.* (—s, *pl.* —) cynic.

zynisch ['tsyːnɪʃ], *adj.* cynical.

Zynismus [tsyˈnɪsmus], *m.* (—, *no pl.*) cynicism.

Zypern ['tsyːpərn], *n.* Cyprus.

Zypresse [tsyˈprɛsə], *f.* (—, *pl.* —n) (*Bot.*) cypress.

Cassell's English-German Dictionary

A

A [ei]. das A (*also Mus.*).
a [ə, ei] (**an** [ən, æn] *before vowel or silent* h), *indef. art.* ein, eine, ein; *two at a time*, zwei auf einmal; *many a*, mancher; *two shillings a pound*, zwei Schilling das Pfund.
abacus ['æbəkəs], *s.* das Rechenbrett.
abandon [ə'bændən], *v.a.* (*give up*) aufgeben; (*forsake*) verlassen; (*surrender*) preisgeben.
abandonment [ə'bændənmənt], *s.* das Verlassen (*active*); das Verlassensein (*passive*); die Wildheit, das Sichgehenlassen.
abasement [ə'beismənt], *s.* die Demütigung, Erniedrigung.
abash [ə'bæʃ], *v.a.* beschämen.
abate [ə'beit], *v.n.* nachlassen.
abbess ['æbes], *s.* die Äbtissin.
abbey ['æbi], *s.* die Abtei.
abbot ['æbət], *s.* der Abt.
abbreviate [ə'bri:vieit], *v.a.* abkürzen.
abbreviation [əbri:vi'eiʃən], *s.* die Abkürzung.
abdicate ['æbdikeit], *v.a.*, *v.n.* entsagen (*Dat.*), abdanken.
abdomen [æb'doumən, 'æbdəmən], *s.* (*Anat.*) der Unterleib, Bauch.
abdominal [æb'dɔminəl], *adj.* (*Anat.*) Bauch-, Unterleibs-.
abduct [æb'dʌkt], *v.a.* entführen.
abed [ə'bed], *adv.* zu Bett, im Bett.
aberration [æbə'reiʃən], *s.* die Abirrung; die Verirrung; (*Phys.*) die Strahlenbrechung.
abet [ə'bet], *v.a.* helfen (*Dat.*), unterstützen.
abeyance [ə'beiəns], *s.* die Unentschiedenheit, (der Zustand der) Ungewißheit; *in* —, unentschieden.
abhor [əb'hɔ:], *v.a.* verabscheuen.
abhorrence [əb'hɔrəns], *s.* die Abscheu (*of*, vor, *Dat.*).
abhorrent [əb'hɔrənt], *adj.* widerlich, ekelhaft.
abide [ə'baid], *v.n. irr.* bleiben, verweilen; (*last*) dauern. — *v.a.* aushalten.
ability [ə'biliti], *s.* die Fähigkeit, Tüchtigkeit; (*pl.*) die Geisteskräfte, *f. pl.*
abject ['æbdʒekt], *adj.* elend; (*submissive*) unterwürfig, verächtlich.
ablaze [ə'bleiz], *adj.*, *adv.* in Flammen.
able [eibl], *adj.* fähig; (*clever*) geschickt; (*efficient*) tüchtig.
ablution [ə'blu:ʃən], *s.* die Abwaschung, Waschung.
abnormal [æb'nɔ:məl], *adj.* abnorm, ungewöhnlich.

abnormality [æbnɔ:'mæliti], *s.* die Ungewöhnlichkeit.
aboard [ə'bɔ:d], *adv.* an Bord.
abode [ə'boud], *s.* der Wohnsitz, Wohnort.
abolish [ə'bɔliʃ], *v.a.* aufheben, abschaffen.
abolition [æbo'liʃən], *s.* die Abschaffung, Aufhebung.
abominable [ə'bɔminəbl], *adj.* abscheulich, scheußlich.
abominate [ə'bɔmineit], *v.a.* verabscheuen.
abomination [əbɔmi'neiʃən], *s.* der Abscheu, Greuel.
aboriginal [æbə'ridʒinəl], *adj.* eingeboren, einheimisch. — *s.* der Eingeborene.
aborigines [æbə'ridʒini:z], *s. pl.* die Eingeborenen, Ureinwohner.
abortion [ə'bɔ:ʃən], *s.* die Fehlgeburt; die Abtreibung.
abortive [ə'bɔ:tiv], *adj.* mißlungen.
abound [ə'baund], *v.n.* wimmeln von (*Dat.*).
about [ə'baut], *prep.* um; (*toward*) gegen; *about 3 o'clock*, gegen drei; (*concerning*) über, betreffend. — *adv.* umher, herum; (*round*) rund herum; (*nearly*) etwa, ungefähr; (*everywhere*) überall; *to be* — *to*, im Begriffe sein or stehen zu . . .
above [ə'bʌv], *prep.* über; — *all things*, vor allen Dingen; *this is* — *me*, das ist mir zu hoch; — *board*, offen, ehrlich. — *adv.* oben, darüber, *over and* —, obendrein; — *mentioned*, obenerwähnt.
abrade [ə'breid], *v.a.* abschaben, abschürfen.
abrasion [ə'breiʒən], *s.* die Abschürfung; Abnutzung.
abreast [ə'brest], *adj.*, *adv.* nebeneinander, Seite an Seite; *keep* —, (sich) auf dem Laufenden halten; Schritt halten (mit).
abridge [ə'bridʒ], *v.a.* (ab)kürzen.
abridgement [ə'bridʒmənt], *s.* die (Ab)kürzung; (*book etc.*) der Auszug.
abroad [ə'brɔ:d], *adv.* im Ausland, auswärts; *to go* —, ins Ausland reisen.
abrogate ['æbrogeit], *v.a.* abschaffen.
abrogation [æbro'geiʃən], *s.* (*Pol.*) die Abschaffung.
abrupt [ə'brʌpt], *adj.* plötzlich; (*curt*) schroff; kurz; jäh.
abruptness [ə'brʌptnis], *s.* (*speech*) die Schroffheit; (*suddenness*) die Plötzlichkeit; (*drop*) die Steilheit.
abscess ['æbses], *s.* das Geschwür, die Schwellung, der Abszeß.

abscond

abscond [əb'skɔnd], *v.n.* sich davonmachen.
absence ['æbsəns], *s.* die Abwesenheit; *leave of* —, der Urlaub.
absent (1) ['æbsənt], *adj.* abwesend; — *minded*, zerstreut.
absent (2) [æb'sent], *v.r.* — *oneself*, fehlen, fernbleiben; (*go away*) sich entfernen.
absentee [æbsən'ti:], *s.* der Abwesende.
absolute ['æbsɔlu:t], *adj.* absolut, unumschränkt.
absolve [əb'zɔlv], *v.a.* freisprechen (*from*, von), lossprechen, entbinden.
absorb [əb'sɔ:b], *v.a.* absorbieren, aufsaugen; (*attention*) in Anspruch nehmen.
absorbed [əb'sɔ:bd], *adj.* versunken.
absorbent [əb'sɔ:bənt], *adj.* absorbierend.
absorption [əb'sɔ:pʃən], *s.* (*Chem.*) die Absorption; (*attention*) das Versunkensein.
abstain [əb'stein], *v.n.* sich enthalten; — *from voting*, sich der Stimme enthalten.
abstainer [əb'steinə], *s.* der Abstinenzler, Antialkoholiker.
abstemious [əb'sti:miəs], *adj.* enthaltsam.
abstention [əb'stenʃən], *s.* die Enthaltung.
abstinence ['æbstinəns], *s.* die Enthaltsamkeit, das Fasten (*food*).
abstract [æb'strækt], *v.a.* abstrahieren, abziehen; (*summarize*) kürzen, ausziehen. —['æbstrækt], *adj.* abstrakt; (*Maths.*) rein. — *s.* der Auszug, Abriß (*of article, book, etc.*).
abstracted [æb'stræktid], *adj.* zerstreut, geistesabwesend.
abstraction [æb'strækʃən], *s.* die Abstraktion; der abstrakte Begriff.
abstruse [æb'stru:s], *adj.* schwerverständlich, tiefsinnig.
absurd [əb'sɔ:d], *adj.* absurd, töricht; (*unreasonable*) unvernünftig, gegen alle Vernunft; (*laughable*) lächerlich.
absurdity [əb'sɔ:diti], *s.* die Torheit, Unvernünftigkeit.
abundance [ə'bʌndəns], *s.* die Fülle, der Überfluß.
abundant [ə'bʌndənt], *adj.* reichlich.
abuse [ə'bju:z], *v.a.* mißbrauchen; (*insult*) beschimpfen; (*violate*) schänden. —[ə'bju:s], *s.* der Mißbrauch; (*language*) die Beschimpfung; (*violation*) die Schändung.
abusive [ə'bju:siv], *adj.* (*language*) grob; schimpfend, schmähend.
abut [ə'bʌt], *v.n.* anstoßen, angrenzen.
abysmal [ə'bizməl], *adj.* bodenlos.
abyss [ə'bis], *s.* der Abgrund, Schlund.
Abyssinian [æbi'sinjən], *adj.* abessinisch. — *s.* der Abessinier.
acacia [ə'keiʃə], *s.* (*Bot.*) die Akazie.
academic [ækə'demik], *adj.* akademisch. — *s.* der Akademiker.
academy [ə'kædəmi], *s.* die Akademie.
acajon ['ækəʒu:], *s.* (*Bot.*) der Nierenbaum.

accede [æk'si:d], *v.n.* beistimmen; einwilligen; — *to the throne*, den Thron besteigen.
accelerate [æk'seləreit], *v.a.* beschleunigen. — *v.n.* schneller fahren.
acceleration [æksələ'reiʃən], *s.* die Beschleunigung.
accelerator [æk'seləreitə], *s.* (*Motor.*) der Gashebel, das Gaspedal.
accent (1), **accentuate** [æk'sent, æk'sentjueit], *v.a.* akzentuieren, betonen.
accent (2) ['æksənt], *s.* (*Phon.*) der Ton, Wortton, die Betonung; der Akzent (*dialect*), die Aussprache.
accentuation [æksentju'eiʃən], *s.* die Aussprache, Akzentuierung, Betonung.
accept [æk'sept], *v.a.* annehmen.
acceptable [æk'septəbl], *adj.* angenehm, annehmbar, annehmlich.
acceptance [æk'septəns], *s.* die Annahme; (*Comm.*) das Akzept.
access ['ækses], *s.* der Zugang, Zutritt.
accessible [æk'sesibl], *adj.* erreichbar, zugänglich.
accession [æk'seʃən], *s.* der Zuwachs; — *to the throne*, die Thronbesteigung.
accessory [æk'sesəri], *adj.* zugehörig; hinzukommend; (*Law*) mitschuldig; (*subsidiary*) nebensächlich. — *s.* (*Law*) der Mitschuldige; (*pl.*) das Zubehör.
accidence ['æksidəns], *s.* (*Gram.*) die Flexionslehre.
accident ['æksidənt], *s.* (*chance*) der Zufall; (*mishap*) der Unfall, Unglücksfall.
accidental [æksi'dentəl], *adj.* zufällig; (*inessential*) unwesentlich; durch Unfall.
acclaim [ə'kleim], *v.a.* akklamieren, mit Beifall aufnehmen. — *v.n.* zujubeln. — *s.* der Beifall.
acclamation [æklə'meiʃən], *s.* der Beifall, Zuruf.
acclimatize [ə'klaimətaiz], *v.a.*, *v.r.* akklimatisieren; sich anpassen, eingewöhnen.
accommodate [ə'kɔmədeit], *v.a.* (*adapt*) anpassen; (*lodge*) unterbringen, beherbergen, aufnehmen; einem aushelfen; (*with money*) jemandem Geld leihen. — *v.r.* — *oneself to*, sich an etwas anpassen, sich in etwas fügen.
accommodating [ə'kɔmədeitiŋ], *adj.* gefällig, entgegenkommend.
accommodation [əkɔmə'deiʃən], *s.* (*adaptation*) die Anpassung; (*dispute*) die Beilegung; (*room*) die Unterkunft.
accompaniment [ə'kʌmpənimənt], *s.* die Begleitung.
accompany [ə'kʌmpəni], *v.a.* begleiten.
accomplice [ə'kʌmplis *or* ə'kɔmplis], *s.* der Komplize, Mitschuldige, Mittäter.
accomplish [ə'kʌmpliʃ *or* ə'kɔmpliʃ], *v.a.* vollenden, zustandebringen, vollbringen; (*objective*) erreichen.
accomplished [ə'kʌmpliʃd *or* ə'kɔmpliʃd], *adj.* vollendet.

accomplishment [əˈkʌmpliʃmənt *or* əˈkɔmpliʃmənt], *s.* (*of project*) die Ausführung; (*of task*) die Vollendung; (*of prophecy*) die Erfüllung; (*pl.*) die Talente, *n. pl.*, Gaben, Kenntnisse, *f. pl.*

accord [əˈkɔːd], *s.* (*agreement*) die Übereinstimmung; (*unison*) die Eintracht. — *v.n.* übereinstimmen (*with*, mit) — *v.a.* bewilligen.

accordance [əˈkɔːdəns], *s.* die Übereinstimmung.

according [əˈkɔːdiŋ], *prep.* — *to*, gemäß, nach, laut.

accordingly [əˈkɔːdiŋli], *adv.* demgemäß, demnach, folglich.

accordion [əˈkɔːdiən], *s.* (*Mus.*) die Ziehharmonika, das Akkordeon.

accost [əˈkɔst], *v.a.* ansprechen, anreden.

account [əˈkaunt], *s.* die Rechnung; (*report*) der Bericht; (*narrative*) die Erzählung; (*importance*) die Bedeutung; (*Fin.*) das Konto, Guthaben; *cash* —, die Kassenrechnung; *on no* —, auf keinen Fall; *on his* —, seinetwegen, um seinetwillen; *on* — *of*, wegen (*Genit.*); *on that* —, darum; *of no* —, unbedeutend. — *v.n.* — *for*, Rechenschaft ablegen über (*Acc.*); (*explain*) erklären.

accountable [əˈkauntəbl], *adj.* verrechenbar (*item*); verantwortlich (*person*).

accountant [əˈkauntənt], *s.* der Bücherrevisor, Rechnungsführer; *junior* —, der Buchhalter.

accredit [əˈkredit], *v.a.* akkreditieren, beglaubigen; (*authorize*) ermächtigen, bevollmächtigen.

accretion [əˈkriːʃən], *s.* der Zuwachs.

accrue [əˈkruː], *v.n.* (*Comm.*) zuwachsen, erwachsen, zufallen.

accumulate [əˈkjuːmjuleit], *v.a.*, *v.n.* anhäufen; sich anhäufen, zunehmen, sich ansammeln.

accumulation [əkjuːmjuˈleiʃən], *s.* die Ansammlung, Anhäufung.

accuracy [ˈækjurəsi], *s.* die Genauigkeit.

accurate [ˈækjurit], *adj.* genau, richtig.

accursed [əˈkɔːsid], *adj.* verflucht, verwünscht.

accusation [ækjuˈzeiʃən], *s.* die Anklage.

accusative [əˈkjuːzətiv], *s.* (*Gram.*) der Akkusativ.

accuse [əˈkjuːz], *v.a.* anklagen, beschuldigen (*of*, *Genit.*).

accustom [əˈkʌstəm], *v.a.* gewöhnen (*to*, an, *Acc.*).

ace [eis], *s.* (*Cards*) das As, die Eins.

acerbity [əˈsəːbiti], *s.* die Rauheit, Herbheit; (*manner*) die Grobheit.

acetate [ˈæsiteit], *s.* das Azetat; essigsaures Salz.

acetic [əˈsiːtik, əˈsetik], *adj.* essigsauer.

acetylene [əˈsetiliːn], *s.* das Azetylen.

ache [eik], *s.* der Schmerz. — *v.n.* schmerzen, weh(e)tun.

achieve [əˈtʃiːv], *v.a.* erreichen, erlangen; (*accomplish*) vollenden; (*perform*) ausführen; (*gain*) erlangen, erwerben.

achievement [əˈtʃiːvmənt], *s.* (*accomplishment*) die Leistung, der Erfolg; die Errungenschaft; (*gain*) die Erwerbung.

achromatic [ækroˈmætik], *adj.* achromatisch, farblos.

acid [ˈæsid], *adj.* sauer, scharf. — *s.* (*Chem.*) die Säure.

acidulated [əˈsidjuleitid], *adj.* (*Chem.*) angesäuert.

acknowledge [ækˈnɔlidʒ], *v.a.* anerkennen; (*admit*) zugeben; (*confess*) bekennen; (*letter*) den Empfang bestätigen.

acknowledgement [ækˈnɔlidʒmənt], *s.* die Anerkennung, (*receipt*) Bestätigung, Quittung; (*pl.*) die Dankesbezeigung; die Erkenntlichkeit.

acme [ˈækmi], *s.* der Gipfel, Höhepunkt.

acorn [ˈeikɔːn], *s.* (*Bot.*) die Eichel.

acoustics [əˈkuːstiks], *s. pl.* die Akustik; (*subject*, *study*) die Schallehre.

acquaint [əˈkweint], *v.a.* bekanntmachen; (*inform*) mitteilen (*Dat.*), informieren; unterrichten.

acquaintance [əˈkweintəns], *s.* die Bekanntschaft; der Bekannte, die Bekannte (*person*); die Kenntnis (*with*, von).

acquiesce [ækwiˈes], *v.n.* einwilligen, sich fügen.

acquiescence [ækwiˈesəns], *s.* die Einwilligung (*in*, in, *Acc.*), Zustimmung (*in*, zu, *Dat.*).

acquiescent [ækwiˈesənt], *adj.* fügsam.

acquire [əˈkwaiə], *v.a.* erlangen, erwerben; (*language*) erlernen.

acquisition [ækwiˈziʃən], *s.* die Erlangung, Erwerbung.

acquit [əˈkwit], *v.a.* freisprechen.

acre [ˈeikə], *s.* der Acker (*appr.* 0.4 Hektar).

acrid [ˈækrid], *adj.* scharf, beißend.

acrimonious [ækriˈmouniəs], *adj.* scharf, bitter.

across [əˈkrɔs, əˈkrɔːs], *adv.* kreuzweise, (*quer*) hinüber. — *prep.* quer durch, über; *come* —, (*zufällig*) treffen, *come* — *a problem*, auf ein Problem stoßen.

act [ækt], *s.* (*deed*) die Tat; (*Theat.*) der Akt; (*Parl. etc.*) die Akte. — *v.a.* (*Theat.*) spielen. — *v.n.* handeln (*do something*); sich benehmen or tun, als ob (*act as if*, *pretend*); (*Theat.*) spielen; (*Chem.*) wirken (*react*).

action [ˈækʃən], *s.* die Handlung (*play*, *deed*), Wirkung (*effect*); (*Law*) der Prozeß; der Gang.

active [ˈæktiv], *adj.* (*person*, *Gram.*) aktiv; tätig; rührig (*industrious*); wirksam (*effective*).

activity [ækˈtiviti], *s.* die Tätigkeit; (*Chem.*) Wirksamkeit.

actor [ˈæktə], *s.* der Schauspieler.

actress [ˈæktrəs], die Schauspielerin.

actual [ˈæktjuəl], *adj.* tatsächlich, wirklich.

actuality [æktju'æliti], s. die Wirklichkeit.

actuary ['æktjuəri], s. der Aktuar, Versicherungsbeamte.

actuate ['æktjueit], v.a. betreiben, in Bewegung setzen.

acuity [ə'kju:iti], s. der Scharfsinn (mind), die Schärfe (vision etc.).

acute [ə'kju:t], adj. scharf, scharfsinnig (mind); spitz (angle); fein (sense); — accent, der Akut.

adage ['ædidʒ], s. das Sprichwort.

adamant ['ædəmənt], adj. sehr hart, unerbittlich (inexorable).

adapt [ə'dæpt], v.a. anpassen, angleichen; bearbeiten.

adaptable [ə'dæptəbl], adj. anpassungsfähig.

adaptation [ædæp'teiʃən], s. die Anpassung, die Bearbeitung (of book).

adaptive [ə'dæptiv], adj. anpassungsfähig.

add [æd], v.a. hinzufügen, (Maths.) addieren.

adder ['ædə], s. (Zool.) die Natter.

addict ['ædikt], s. der Süchtige.

addiction [ə'dikʃən], s. die Sucht.

addicted [ə'diktid], adj. verfallen.

addition [ə'diʃən], s. die Hinzufügung, Zugabe, (Maths.) Addition.

additional [ə'diʃənəl], adj. zusätzlich, nachträglich.

address [ə'dres], s. die Anschrift, Adresse (letter); die Ansprache (speech). — v.a. (letter) adressieren, richten an (Acc.).

addressee [ædre'si:], s. der Adressat, der Empfänger.

adduce [ə'dju:s], v.a. anführen (proof, Beweis).

adenoid ['ædinɔid], s. (usually pl.) (Med.) die Wucherung.

adept ['ædept], adj. geschickt, erfahren.

adequacy ['ædikwəsi], s. die Angemessenheit, das Gewachsensein, die Zulänglichkeit.

adequate ['ædikwət], adj. gewachsen (Dat.); angemessen, hinreichend (sufficient).

adhere [əd'hiə], v.n. haften, anhängen; — to one's opinion, bei seiner Meinung bleiben.

adherence [əd'hiərəns], s. das Festhalten (an, Dat.).

adhesion [əd'hi:ʒən], s. (Phys.) die Adhäsion; das Anhaften.

adhesive [əd'hi:ziv], adj. haftend, klebrig; — plaster, das Heftpflaster.

adipose ['ædipous], adj. fett, feist.

adjacent [ə'dʒeisənt], adj. naheliegend, benachbart, angrenzend.

adjective ['ædʒəktiv], s. (Gram.) das Adjektiv; Eigenschaftswort.

adjoin [ə'dʒɔin], v.a. anstoßen, angrenzen.

adjourn [ə'dʒə:n], v.a. vertagen, aufschieben.

adjudicate [ə'dʒu:dikeit], v.a. beurteilen, richten.

adjunct ['ædʒʌŋkt], s. der Zusatz.

adjust [ə'dʒʌst], v.a. ordnen; (adapt) anpassen; regulieren, einstellen.

adjustable [ə'dʒʌstəbl], adj. verstellbar, einstellbar.

adjustment [ə'dʒʌstmənt], s. die Einstellung, Anpassung; (Law) Schlichtung; Berichtigung.

administer [əd'ministə], v.a. verwalten (an enterprise); verabreichen (medicine); abnehmen (an oath, einen Eid).

administration [ədminis'treiʃən], s. die Verwaltung, Regierung; die Darreichung (sacraments).

administrative [əd'ministrətiv], adj. Verwaltungs-; verwaltend.

admirable ['ædmirəbl], adj. bewundernswert.

admiral ['ædmirəl], s. der Admiral.

Admiralty ['ædmirəlti], s. die Admiralität.

admiration [ædmi'reiʃən], s. die Bewunderung.

admire [əd'maiə], v.a. bewundern, verehren.

admirer [əd'maiərə], s. der Bewunderer, Verehrer.

admissible [əd'misibl], adj. zulässig.

admission [əd'miʃən], s. die Zulassung; (entry) der Eintritt; Zutritt; (confession) das Eingeständnis, Zugeständnis.

admit [əd'mit], v.a. zulassen; aufnehmen; zugeben (deed); gelten lassen (argument).

admittance [əd'mitəns], s. der Zugang, Eintritt, Zutritt.

admixture [əd'mikstʃə], s. die Beimischung, Beigabe.

admonish [əd'mɔniʃ], v.a. ermahnen, mahnen, warnen.

admonition [ædmə'niʃən], s. die Ermahnung, Warnung.

ado [ə'du:], s. der Lärm, das Tun, das Treiben; without further —, ohne weiteres.

adolescence [ædo'lesəns], s. die Adoleszenz, Jugend, Jugendzeit.

adolescent [ædo'lesənt], s. der Jugendliche. — adj. jugendlich.

adopt [ə'dɔpt], v.a. (Law) annehmen, adoptieren.

adoption [ə'dɔpʃən], s. (Law) die Annahme, Adoption.

adoptive [ə'dɔptiv], adj. Adoptiv-, angenommen.

adorable [ə'dɔ:rəbl], adj. anbetungswürdig; (coll.) wunderbar, schön.

adoration [ædo'reiʃən], s. die Anbetung.

adore [ə'dɔ:], v.a. anbeten; verehren.

adorn [ə'dɔ:n], v.a. (aus)schmücken, zieren.

Adriatic (Sea) [eidri'ætik (si:)]. das adriatische Meer.

adrift [ə'drift], adv. treibend; cut o.s. —, sich absondern.

adroit [ə'drɔit], adj. gewandt, geschickt.

adroitness [ə'drɔitnis], s. die Gewandtheit, die Geschicklichkeit.

adulation [ædju'leiʃən], *s.* die Schmeichelei.
adulator ['ædjuleitə], *s.* der Schmeichler.
adulatory ['ædjuleitəri], *adj.* schmeichlerisch.
adult [ə'dʌlt *or* 'ædʌlt], *adj.* erwachsen. — *s.* der Erwachsene.
adulterate [ə'dʌltəreit], *v.a.* verfälschen; verwässern.
adulterer [ə'dʌltərə], *s.* der Ehebrecher.
adultery [ə'dʌltəri], *s.* der Ehebruch.
adumbrate [ə'dʌmbreit *or* 'æd-], *v.a.* skizzieren, entwerfen, andeuten.
advance [əd'vɑːns], *v.a.* fördern (*a cause*); vorschießen (*money*); geltend machen (*claim*). — *v.n.* vorrücken, vorstoßen; (*make progress, gain promotion*) aufsteigen. — *s.* der Fortschritt (*progress*); der Vorschuß (*money*); *in —*, im voraus.
advancement [əd'vɑːnsmənt], *s.* der Fortschritt (*progress*), der Aufstieg, die Beförderung (*promotion*); die Förderung (*of a cause*).
advantage [əd'vɑːntidʒ], *s.* der Vorteil, Nutzen; (*superiority*) die Überlegenheit.
Advent ['ædvənt]. (*Eccl.*) der Advent.
advent ['ædvənt], *s.* die Ankunft.
adventitious [ædvən'tiʃəs], *adj.* zufällig.
adventure [əd'ventʃə], *s.* das Abenteuer. — *v.n.* auf Abenteuer ausgehen, wagen.
adventurer [əd'ventʃərə], *s.* der Abenteurer.
adventurous [əd'ventʃərəs], *adj.* abenteuerlich, unternehmungslustig.
adverb ['ædvəːb], *s.* (*Gram.*) das Adverb(ium), Umstandswort.
adverbial [əd'vəːbiəl], *adj.* adverbial.
adversary ['ædvəsəri], *s.* der Gegner, Widersacher.
adverse ['ædvəːs], *adj.* widrig, feindlich, ungünstig.
adversity [əd'vəːsiti], *s.* das Unglück, Mißgeschick; *in —*, im Unglück.
advert [əd'vəːt], *v.n.* hinweisen.
advertise ['ædvətaiz], *v.a.* anzeigen; annoncieren (*in press*), Reklame machen.
advertisement [əd'vəːtizmənt], *s.* die Anzeige, Annonce; Reklame.
advertiser ['ædvətaizə], *s.* der Anzeiger.
advice [əd'vais], *s.* der Rat, Ratschlag; die Nachricht (*information*).
advise [əd'vaiz], *v.a.* raten (*Dat.*), beraten; benachrichtigen (*inform*); verständigen.
advisable [əd'vaizəbl], *adj.* ratsam.
advisedly [əd'vaizidli], *adv.* absichtlich, mit Bedacht.
adviser [əd'vaizə], *s.* der Berater.
advisory [əd'vaizəri], *adj.* beratend, ratgebend, Rats-.
advocacy ['ædvəkəsi], *s.* (*Law*) die Verteidigung; die Fürsprache (*championing of*, für, *Acc.*); die Vertretung (*of view*).

Aegean (**Sea**) [iː'dʒiːən (siː)]. das ägäische Meer.
aerated ['ɛəreitid], *adj.* kohlensauer.
aerial ['ɛəriəl], *s.* (*Rad.*) die Antenne. — *adj.* luftig, Luft-.
aerie ['ɛəri, 'iəri], *s. see* **eyrie**.
aerodrome ['ɛərodroum], *s.* der Flugplatz, Flughafen.
aeronautical [ɛəro'nɔːtikəl], *adj.* aeronautisch.
aeronautics [ɛəro'nɔːtiks], *s. pl.* die Aeronautik, Luftfahrt.
aeroplane, (*Am.*) **airplane** ['ɛəroplein, 'ɛərplein], *s.* das Flugzeug.
aesthetic(al) [iːs'θetik(əl)], *adj.* ästhetisch.
aesthetics [iːs'θetiks], *s.* die Ästhetik.
afar [ə'fɑː], *adv.* fern, weit entfernt; *from —*, von weitem, (von) weit her.
affability [æfə'biliti], *s.* die Leutseligkeit, Freundlichkeit.
affable ['æfəbl], *adj.* freundlich, leutselig.
affair [ə'fɛə], *s.* die Affäre; die Angelegenheit (*matter*); das Anliegen (*concern*).
affect [ə'fekt], *v.a.* beeinflußen; rühren; wirken auf; vortäuschen (*pretend*); zur Schau tragen (*exhibit*).
affectation [æfek'teiʃən], *s.* die Ziererei, das Affektieren, die Affektiertheit.
affected [ə'fektid], *adj.* affektiert, geziert; befallen, angegriffen (*illness*).
affection [ə'fekʃən], *s.* die Zuneigung, Zärtlichkeit.
affectionate [ə'fekʃnit], *adj.* zärtlich, liebevoll; (*in letters*) yours *—ly*, herzlichst.
affinity [ə'finiti], *s.* (*Chem.*) die Affinität; die Verwandtschaft (*relationship*).
affirm [ə'fəːm], *v.a.* behaupten, bestätigen, versichern; bekräftigen (*confirm*).
affirmation [æfə'meiʃən], *s.* die Behauptung, Bekräftigung.
affirmative [ə'fəːmətiv], *adj.* bejahend, positiv; *in the —*, bejahend.
affix [ə'fiks], *v.a.* anheften, aufkleben (*stick*); anbringen (*join to*, an, *Acc.*).
afflict [ə'flikt], *v.a.* quälen, plagen.
affliction [ə'flikʃən], *s.* die Plage, Qual; das Mißgeschick; die Not; das Leiden.
affluence ['æfluəns], *s.* der Überfluß (*abundance*); der Reichtum.
affluent ['æfluənt], *adj.* reich, wohlhabend. — *s.* der Nebenfluß (*tributary*).
afford [ə'fɔːd], *v.a.* geben, bieten; (sich) leisten (*have money for*); gewähren (*give*); hervorbringen (*yield*).
afforest [ə'fɔrist], *v.a.* aufforsten.
affray [ə'frei], *s.* die Schlägerei.
African ['æfrikən], *adj.* afrikanisch. — *s.* der Afrikaner.
affront [ə'frʌnt], *s.* die Beleidigung. — *v.a.* beleidigen.
Afghan ['æfgæn], *adj.* afghanisch. — *s.* der Afghane.
afield [ə'fiːld], *adj., adv.* im Felde; weit umher; weit weg.
afire [ə'faiə], *adv., adv.* in Flammen.

305

aflame

aflame [ə'fleim], *adj., adv.* in Flammen.
afloat [ə'flout], *adj., adv.* schwimmend, dahintreibend.
afoot [ə'fut], *adj., adv.* im Gange.
afore [ə'fɔ:], *adv.* vorher.
aforesaid [ə'fɔ:sed], *adj. the* —, das Obengesagte, der Vorhergenannte.
afraid [ə'freid], *adj.* ängstlich, furchtsam; *be* —, fürchten (*of s.th.*, etwas, *Acc.*); sich fürchten.
afresh [ə'freʃ], *adv.* von neuem.
aft [ɑ:ft], *adv.* (*Naut.*) achtern.
after ['ɑ:ftə], *prep.* nach (*time*); nach, hinter (*place*); *the day* — *tomorrow*, übermorgen. — *adj.* hinter, später. — *adv.* hinterher, nachher (*time*); darauf, dahinter (*place*). — *conj.* nachdem.
afternoon [ɑ:ftə'nu:n], *s.* der Nachmittag.
afterwards ['ɑ:ftəwədz], *adv.* nachher, daraufhin, später.
again [ə'gein], *adv.* wieder, abermals, noch einmal; zurück (*back*); dagegen (*however*); *as much* —, noch einmal soviel; — *and* —, immer wieder.
against [ə'geinst], *prep.* gegen, wider; nahe bei (*near*, *Dat.*); bis an (*up to*, *Acc.*); — *the grain*, wider or gegen den Strich.
agate ['ægeit], *s.* der Achat.
agave [ə'geivi], *s.* (*Bot.*) die Agave.
age [eidʒ], *s.* das Alter (*person*); das Zeitalter (*period*); die Reife; *come of* —, volljährig werden; mündig werden; *old* —, das Greisenalter; *for* —*s*, seit einer Ewigkeit. — *v.n.* altern, alt werden.
aged ['eidʒid], *adj.* bejahrt.
agency ['eidʒənsi], *s.* die Agentur (*firm*); die Mitwirkung (*participation*); die Hilfe (*assistance*); die Vermittlung (*mediation*).
agenda [ə'dʒendə], *s.* das Sitzungsprogramm; die Tagesordnung.
agent ['eidʒənt], *s.* der Agent, Vertreter.
agglomerate [ə'gləməreit], *v.a.* zusammenhäufen. — *v.n.* sich zusammenhäufen, sich ballen.
aggrandisement [ə'grændizmənt], *s.* die Überhebung, Übertreibung, Erweiterung.
aggravate ['ægrəveit], *v.a.* verschlimmern; ärgern.
aggravation [ægrə'veiʃən], *s.* die Verschlimmerung (*of condition*); der Ärger (*annoyance*).
aggregate ['ægrigit], *adj.* gesamt, vereinigt, vereint. — *s.* das Aggregat.
aggregation [ægri'geiʃən], *s.* (*Geol.*, *Chem.*) die Vereinigung, Anhäufung, Ansammlung.
aggression [ə'greʃən], *s.* der Angriff, Überfall.
aggressive [ə'gresiv], *adj.* aggressiv, angreifend.
aggressor [ə'gresə], *s.* der Angreifer.
aggrieve [ə'gri:v], *v.a.* kränken.

aghast [ə'gɑ:st], *adj.* bestürzt; sprachlos; entsetzt.
agile ['ædʒail], *adj.* behend, flink, beweglich.
agitate ['ædʒiteit], *v.a.* bewegen; beunruhigen; aufrühren; stören.
agitation [ædʒi'teiʃən], *s.* (*Pol.*) die Agitation; die Unruhe (*unrest*); der Aufruhr (*revolt*).
agitator ['ædʒiteitə], *s.* (*Pol.*) der Agitator; der Aufwiegler (*inciter*).
aglow [ə'glou], *adv.* glühend.
agnostic [æg'nɔstik], *s.* der Agnostiker.
ago [ə'gou], *adv.* vor; *long* —, vor langer Zeit; *not long* —, kürzlich; *a month* —, vor einem Monat.
agog [ə'gɔg], *adv.* erregt, gespannt, neugierig (*for*, auf, *Acc.*).
agonize ['ægənaiz], *v.a.* quälen, martern. — *v.n.* Qual erleiden; mit dem Tode ringen or kämpfen.
agonising ['ægənaiziŋ], *adj.* schmerzhaft, qualvoll.
agony ['ægəni], *s.* die Pein, Qual; der Todeskampf; — *column*, die Seufzerspalte.
agrarian [ə'grɛəriən], *adj.* landwirtschaftlich; — *party*, die Bauernpartei.
agree [ə'gri:], *v.n.* übereinstimmen (*be in agreement*); übereinkommen (*come to an agreement*), sich einigen.
agreeable [ə'gri:əbl], *adj.* angenehm, gefällig.
agreement [ə'gri:mənt], *s.* die Übereinstimmung, das Übereinkommen; der Vertrag, die Verständigung (*understanding*).
agricultural [ægri'kʌltʃərəl], *adj.* landwirtschaftlich.
agriculture ['ægrikʌltʃə], *s.* die Landwirtschaft.
aground [ə'graund], *adj., adv.* (*Naut.*) gestrandet; *to run* —, stranden.
ague ['eigju:], *s.* (*Med.*) der Schüttelfrost.
ah! [ɑ:], *interj.* ach!; aha! (*surprise*).
aha! [ɑ'hɑ:], *interj.* ach so!
ahead [ə'hed], *adv.* vorwärts, voran (*movement*), voraus (*position*), *go* — (*carry on*), fortfahren; *go* — (*make progress*), vorwärtskommen.
ahoy! [ə'hɔi], *interj.* (*Naut.*) ahoi!
aid [eid], *v.a.* helfen (*Dat.*), unterstützen (*Acc.*), beistehen (*Dat.*). — *s.* die Hilfe, der Beistand.
aide-de-camp ['eiddə'kɑ̃], *s.* der Adjutant (eines Generals).
ail [eil], *v.n.* schmerzen; krank sein.
ailing ['eiliŋ], *adj.* kränklich, leidend.
ailment ['eilmənt], *s.* das Leiden.
aim [eim], *v.a.* (*weapon, blow etc.*) richten (*at*, auf). — *v.n.* zielen (auf, *Acc.*); trachten (nach, *strive for*). — *s,* das Ziel, der Zweck (*purpose*); die Absicht (*intention*).
aimless ['eimlis], *adj.* ziellos, zwecklos.

air [εə], s. die Luft; die Melodie (*tune*); die Miene (*mien*); *air force*, die Luftwaffe; *air pocket*, das Luftloch; *air raid*, der Luftangriff; *in the open* —, im Freien; *on the* —, im Rundfunk; *to give oneself* —*s*, vornehm tun. — *v.a.* lüften (*room*); trocknen (*washing*); aussprechen (*views*).

airbase ['εəbeis], s. der Fliegerstützpunkt.

airconditioning ['εəkəndiʃəniŋ], s. die Klimaanlage.

aircraft ['εəkrɑːft], s. das Luftfahrzeug, Flugzeug.

airgun ['εəgʌn], s. die Windbüchse, das Luftgewehr.

airiness ['εərinis], s. die Luftigkeit, Leichtigkeit.

airletter ['εəletə], s. der Luftpostbrief.

airliner ['εəlainə], s. das Verkehrsflugzeug.

airmail ['εəmeil], s. die Luftpost.

airman ['εəmən], s. der Flieger.

airplane *see* **aeroplane**.

airport ['εəpɔːt], s. der Flughafen.

airtight ['εətait], *adj.* luftdicht.

airy ['εəri], *adj.* luftig.

aisle [ail], s. das Seitenschiff (*church*); der Gang.

Aix-la-Chapelle ['eikslaʃæ'pel], Aachen, *n.*

ajar [ə'dʒɑː], *adv.* angelehnt, halb offen.

akimbo [ə'kimbou], *adv.* Hände an den Hüften, Arme in die Seiten gestemmt.

akin [ə'kin], *adj.* verwandt (*to*, mit, *Dat.*).

alack [ə'læk], *interj.* ach! oh, weh! *alas and* —, ach und wehe!

alacrity [ə'lækriti], s. die Bereitwilligkeit; Munterkeit.

alarm [ə'lɑːm], s. der Alarm; Lärm (*noise*); die Warnung; Angst, Bestürzung; — *clock*, der Wecker. — *v.a.* erschrecken.

alas! [ə'læs], *interj.* ach, wehe!

Albanian [æl'beiniən], *adj.* albanisch. — *s.* der Albanier.

album ['ælbəm], s. das Album.

albumen [æl'bjuːmən], s. das Eiweiß, (*Chem.*) der Eiweißstoff.

albuminous [æl'bjuːminəs], *adj.* eiweißhaltig, Eiweiß-.

alchemist ['ælkimist], s. der Alchimist.

alchemy ['ælkimi], s. die Alchimie.

alcohol ['ælkəhɔl], s. der Alkohol.

alcoholic [ælkə'hɔlik], *adj.* alkoholisch. — *s.* der Trinker, Alkoholiker.

alcove ['ælkouv], s. der Alkoven.

alder ['ɔːldə], s. (*Bot.*) die Erle.

alderman ['ɔːldəmən], s. der Ratsherr, der Stadtrat.

ale [eil], s. englisches Bier.

alert [ə'ləːt], *adj.* wachsam, aufmerksam; *on the* —, auf der Hut.

algebra ['ældʒibrə], s. die Algebra.

Algerian [æl'dʒiəriən], *adj.* algerisch. — *s.* der Algerier.

Algiers [æl'dʒiəz]. Algier, *n.*

alias ['eiliəs], *adv.* sonst genannt.

alien ['eiliən], *adj.* fremd, ausländisch. — *s.* der Fremde, Ausländer.

alienate ['eiliəneit], *v.a.* entfremden.

alienation [eiliə'neiʃən], s. die Entfremdung; — *of mind*, die Geisteskrankung, Geistesgestörtheit.

alienist ['eiliənist], s. der Irrenarzt.

alight (1) [ə'lait], *v.n.* absteigen (*from horse*); aussteigen (*from carriage etc.*).

alight (2) [ə'lait], *adj.* brennend, in Flammen.

alike [ə'laik], *adj.* gleich, ähnlich. — *adv. great and small* —, sowohl große wie kleine.

alimentary [æli'mentəri], *adj.* Nahrungs-, Verdauungs-; — *canal*, (*Anat.*) der Darmkanal.

alimentation [ælimen'teiʃən], s. die Beköstigung; (*Law*) der Unterhalt.

alimony ['æliməni], s. der Unterhaltsbeitrag; (*pl.*) Alimente. , *n.pl.*

alive [ə'laiv], *adj.* lebendig; — *and kicking*, wohlauf, munter; — *to*, empfänglich für.

alkali ['ælkəlai], s. (*Chem.*) das Laugensalz, Alkali.

alkaline ['ælkəlain], *adj.* (*Chem.*) alkalisch, laugensalzig.

all [ɔːl], *adj., pron.* all, ganz (*whole*); sämtliche, alle; *above* —, vor allem; *once and for* —, ein für allemal; *not at* —, keineswegs; *All Saints*, Allerheiligen; *All Souls*, Allerseelen. — *adv.* ganz, gänzlich, völlig; — *the same*, trotzdem; — *the better*, umso besser.

allay [ə'lei], *v.a.* lindern, beruhigen, unterdrücken.

allegation [æli'geiʃən], s. die Behauptung.

allege [ə'ledʒ], *v.a.* behaupten, aussagen.

allegiance [ə'liːdʒəns], s. die Treue, Ergebenheit; Untertanenpflicht.

allegorical [æli'gɔrikəl], *adj.* allegorisch, sinnbildlich.

alleviate [ə'liːvieit], *v.a.* erleichtern, mildern.

alleviation [əliːvi'eiʃən], s. die Erleichterung, Milderung.

alley ['æli], s. die Gasse; Seitenstraße; *bowling* —, die Kegelbahn.

alliance [ə'laiəns], s. (*Pol.*) die Allianz, das Bündnis (*treaty*); der Bund (*league*).

allied [ə'laid, 'ælaid], *adj.* verbündet, vereinigt; alliiert; verwandt.

alliteration [əlitə'reiʃən], s. die Alliteration, der Stabreim.

allocate ['ælokeit], *v.a.* zuweisen, zuteilen.

allot [ə'lɔt], *v.a.* zuteilen (*assign*); verteilen (*distribute*).

allotment [ə'lɔtmənt], s. der Anteil; die Zuteilung; die Landparzelle; die Laubenkolonie, der Schrebergarten (*garden*).

allow [ə'lau], *v.a.* gewähren (*grant*); erlauben (*permit*); zulassen (*admit*). — *v.n.* — *for*, Rücksicht nehmen auf (*Acc.*); in Betracht ziehen.

allowance [ə'lauəns], s. die Rente; das Taschengeld (*money*); die Erlaubnis (*permission*); die Genehmigung (*approval*); die Nachsicht (*indulgence*).

alloy [ə'lɔi, 'æləi], s. die Legierung. — v.a. (*Metall.*) legieren.

allude [ə'lu:d], v.a. anspielen (*to*, auf).

allure [ə'ljuə], v.a. locken, anlocken.

allurement [ə'ljuəmənt], s. der Reiz, die Lockung.

allusion [ə'lu:ʒən], s. die Anspielung.

alluvial [ə'lu:viəl], adj. angeschwemmt.

alluvium [ə'lu:viəm], s. das Schwemmgebiet, Schwemmland.

ally ['ælai], s. der Verbündete, Bundesgenosse, Alliierte. — [ə'lai], v.a., v.r. (sich) vereinigen, (sich) verbünden.

almanac ['ɔ:lmənæk], s. der Almanach.

almighty [ɔ:l'maiti], adj. allmächtig; *God Almighty!* allmächtiger Gott!

almond ['a:mənd], s. (*Bot.*) die Mandel.

almoner ['ælmənə], s. der Wohlfahrtsbeamte, die Fürsorgerin.

almost ['ɔ:lmoust], adv. fast, beinahe.

alms [a:mz], s. das Almosen.

aloe ['ælou], s. (*Bot.*) die Aloe.

aloft [ə'lɔft], adv. droben, (hoch) oben; empor.

alone [ə'loun], adj., adv. allein; *all —,* ganz allein; *leave —,* in Ruhe lassen; *let —,* geschweige (denn).

along [ə'lɔŋ], adv. längs, der Länge nach; entlang, weiter; *come —!* komm mit!; *get — (with),* auskommen. — prep. längs; entlang.

alongside [ə'lɔŋ'said], adv. nebenan. — [ə'lɔŋsaid], prep. neben.

aloof [ə'lu:f], adj., adv. fern, weitab; *keep —,* sich fernhalten.

aloofness [ə'lu:fnis], s. das Sichfernhalten; das Vornehmtun.

aloud [ə'laud], adj., adv. laut; hörbar.

alphabet ['ælfəbet], s. das Alphabet, Abc.

Alpine ['ælpain], adj. alpinisch, Alpen-.

Alps, The ['ælps, ði], die Alpen, pl.

already [ɔ:l'redi], adv. schon, bereits.

Alsatian [æl'seiʃən], adj. elsässisch. — s. der Elsässer; (*dog*) der Wolfshund, deutscher Schäferhund.

also ['ɔ:lsou], adv. (*likewise*) auch, ebenfalls; (*moreover*) ferner.

altar ['ɔ:ltə], s. der Altar.

alter ['ɔ:ltə], v.a. ändern, verändern. — v.n. sich (ver)ändern.

alterable ['ɔ:ltərəbl], adj. veränderlich.

alteration [ɔ:ltə'reiʃən], s. die Änderung, Veränderung.

altercation [ɔ:ltə'keiʃən], s. der Zank, Streit; Wortwechsel.

alternate [ɔ:l'təneit], v.a., v.n. abwechseln lassen, abwechseln.

alternative [ɔ:l'tə:nətiv], adj. abwechselnd, alternativ, zur Wahl gestellt. — s. die Alternative, die Wahl.

although [ɔ:l'ðou], conj. obgleich, obwohl, obschon.

altimeter ['æltimi:tə], s. der Höhenmesser.

altitude ['æltitju:d], s. die Höhe.

alto ['æltou], s. (*Mus.*) die Altstimme, der Alt.

altogether [ɔ:ltu'geðə], adv. zusammen, zusammengenommen, allesamt; (*wholly*) ganz und gar, durchaus.

alum ['æləm], s. (*Chem.*) der Alaun.

aluminium [ælju'minjəm], (*Am.*) **aluminum** [ə'lu:minəm], s. das Aluminium.

always ['ɔ:lweiz], adv. immer, stets.

am [æm] *see* **be.**

amalgamate [ə'mælgəmeit], v.a. amalgamieren. — v.n. sich vereinigen, vermischen.

amalgamation [əmælgə'meiʃən], s. die Verbindung, Vereinigung.

amass [ə'mæs], v.a. anhäufen, zusammentragen.

amateur [æmə'tə: *or* 'æmətjuə], s. der Amateur, Liebhaber.

amatory ['æmətəri], adj. Liebes-, verliebt, sinnlich.

amaze [ə'meiz], v.a. erstaunen, in Erstaunen versetzen; verblüffen (*baffle*).

amazement [ə'meizmənt], s. das Erstaunen, Staunen, die Verwunderung.

amazing [ə'meizin], adj. erstaunlich, wunderbar.

Amazon (1) ['æməzən], s. (*Myth.*) die Amazone.

Amazon (2) ['æməzən], s. (*river*) der Amazonas.

ambassador [æm'bæsədə], s. der Botschafter.

ambassadorial [æmbæsə'dɔ:riəl], adj. Botschafts-, gesandtschaftlich.

amber ['æmbə], s. der Bernstein.

ambidextrous [æmbi'dekstrəs], adj. (mit beiden Händen gleich) geschickt.

ambiguity [æmbi'gju:iti], s. die Zweideutigkeit, der Doppelsinn.

ambiguous [æm'bigjuəs], adj. zweideutig; dunkel (*sense*).

ambit ['æmbit], s. der Umkreis, die Umgebung.

ambition [æm'biʃən], s. die Ambition, der Ehrgeiz.

ambitious [æm'biʃəs], adj. ehrgeizig.

amble [æmbl], v.n. schlendern, (gemächlich) spazieren.

ambulance ['æmbjuləns], s. der Krankenwagen.

ambush ['æmbuʃ], v.a. überfallen (*Acc.*), auflauern (*Dat.*). — s. die Falle, der Hinterhalt.

ameliorate [ə'mi:liəreit], v.a. verbessern.

amenable [ə'mi:nəbl], adj. zugänglich; unterworfen.

amend [ə'mend], v.a. verbessern, berichtigen; ändern.

amendment [ə'mendmənt], s. die Verbesserung, der Zusatz, die zusätzliche Änderung (*proposal*).

amends [ə'mendz], s. pl. der Schadenersatz; *make —,* Schadenersatz leisten; wiedergutmachen.

amenity [ə'mi:niti or ə'meniti], s. die Behaglichkeit, Annehmlichkeit; (pl.) die Vorzüge, m pl.; die Einrichtungen, f. pl.

American [ə'merikən], adj. amerikanisch; — cloth, das Wachstuch. — s. der Amerikaner.

amiability [eimjə'biliti], s. die Liebenswürdigkeit.

amiable ['eimjəbl], adj. liebenswürdig.

amicable ['æmikəbl], adj. freundschaftlich.

amidst [ə'midst], prep. mitten in, mitten unter (Dat.), inmitten (Gen.).

amiss [ə'mis], adj., adv. übel; verkehrt; take —, übelnehmen.

amity ['æmiti], s. die Freundschaft.

ammonia [ə'mouniə], s. das Ammoniak; liquid —, der Salmiakgeist.

ammunition [æmju'niʃən], s. die Munition.

amnesty ['æmnisti], s. die Amnestie, Begnadigung.

among(st) [ə'mʌŋ(st)], prep. (mitten) unter, zwischen, bei.

amorous ['æmərəs], adj. verliebt.

amorphous [ə'mɔ:fəs], adj. amorph, gestaltlos, formlos.

amortization [əmɔ:ti'zeiʃən], s. die Amortisierung (debt); (Comm.) Tilgung, Abtragung.

amount [ə'maunt], s. der Betrag (sum of money); die Menge (quantity). — v.n. betragen; — to, sich belaufen auf (Acc.).

amphibian [æm'fibiən], adj. amphibisch. — s. (Zool.) die Amphibie.

amphibious [æm'fibiəs], adj. amphibienhaft.

ample [æmpl], adj. weit, breit (scope); voll, reichlich; ausgebreitet; genügend.

amplification [æmplifi'keiʃən], s. die Ausbreitung; Verbreiterung, Erklärung, Erweiterung; (Elec.) die Verstärkung (sound).

amplifier ['æmplifaiə], s. der Verstärker; der Lautsprecher.

amplify ['æmplifai], v.a. erweitern, ausführen, vergrößern; verstärken (sound).

amputate ['æmpjuteit], v.a. amputieren.

amputation [æmpju'teiʃən], s. die Amputation.

amuck [ə'mʌk], adv. amok.

amulet ['æmjulit], s. das Amulett.

amuse [ə'mju:z], v.a. unterhalten, amüsieren.

amusement [ə'mju:zmənt], s. die Unterhaltung, das Vergnügen.

an see under a.

Anabaptist [ænə'bæptist], s. der Wiedertäufer.

anachronism [ə'nækrənizm], s. der Anachronismus.

anaemia [ə'ni:miə], s. (Med.) die Blutarmut.

anaemic [ə'ni:mik], adj. (Med.) blutarm.

anaesthetic [ænəs'θetik], adj. schmerzbetäubend. — s. die Narkose.

analogous [ə'næləgəs], adj. analog.

analogy [ə'nælədʒi], s. die Analogie.

analyse ['ænəlaiz], v.a. analysieren.

analysis [ə'nælisis], s. die Analyse.

anarchic(al) [ə'na:kik(əl)], adj. anarchisch.

anarchy ['ænəki], s. die Anarchie.

anathema [ə'næθimə], s. (Eccl.) der Kirchenbann.

anatomical [ænə'tɔmikəl], adj. anatomisch.

anatomist [ə'nætəmist], s. der Anatom.

anatomize [ə'nætəmaiz], v.a. zergliedern, zerlegen.

anatomy [ə'nætəmi], s. die Anatomie.

ancestor ['ænsəstə], s. der Vorfahre, Ahnherr.

ancestry ['ænsəstri], s. die Ahnenreihe, Herkunft, der Stammbaum (family tree).

anchor ['æŋkə], s. der Anker. — v.a. verankern. — v.n. ankern.

anchorage ['æŋkəridʒ], s. die Verankerung; der Ankerplatz.

anchovy [æn'tʃouvi or 'æntʃəvi], s. (Zool.) die Sardelle.

ancient ['einʃənt], adj. alt, uralt, antik; althergebracht (traditional). — s. (pl.) die Alten (Griechen und Römer).

and [ænd], conj. und.

Andes, the ['ændi:z, ði]. die Anden, pl.

anecdote ['ænekdout], s. die Anekdote.

anemone [ə'neməni], s. (Bot.) die Anemone, das Windröschen; (Zool.) sea —, die Seeanemone.

anew [ə'nju:], adv. von neuem.

angel ['eindʒəl], s. der Engel.

angelic [æn'dʒelik], adj. engelhaft, engelgleich.

anger ['æŋgə], s. der Zorn, Unwille, Ärger. — v.a. erzürnen, verärgern, ärgerlich machen.

angle [æŋgl], s. (Geom.) der Winkel; die Angel (fishing). — v.n. angeln (for, nach).

Angles [æŋglz], s. pl. die Angeln, m. pl.

Anglo-Saxon [æŋglou'sæksən], adj. angelsächsisch. — s. der Angelsachse.

anglicism ['æŋglisizm], s. der Anglizismus (style).

anguish ['æŋgwiʃ], s. die Qual, Pein.

angular ['æŋgjulə], adj. winklig, eckig.

anhydrous [æn'haidrəs], adj. wasserfrei, (Chem.) wasserlos.

aniline ['ænilain], s. das Anilin. — adj. — dye, die Anilinfarbe.

animal ['æniməl], s. das Tier, Lebewesen.

animate ['ænimeit], v.a. beleben, beseelen; (fig.) anregen.

animated ['ænimeitid], adj. belebt; munter.

animation [æni'meiʃən], s. die Belebung.

animosity [æni'mɔsiti], s. die Feindseligkeit, Abneigung, Erbitterung.

anise ['ænis], s. (Bot.) der Anis.

ankle

ankle [æŋkl], s. (*Anat.*) der Fußknöchel; — *socks*, kurze Socken.
anklet ['æŋklit], s. der Fußring.
annalist ['ænəlist], s. der Chronist, Geschichtsschreiber.
annals ['ænəlz], s. pl. die Annalen (f. pl.); die Chronik (*sing.*).
anneal [ə'ni:l], v.a. ausglühen.
annex [ə'neks], v.a. annektieren, angliedern, sich aneignen.
annex(e) ['æneks], s. der Anhang, der Anbau.
annexation [ænek'seiʃən], s. die Angliederung, Aneignung.
annihilate [ə'naiileit], v.a. vernichten, zerstören.
annihilation [ənaii'leiʃən], s. die Vernichtung, Zerstörung.
anniversary [æni'və:səri], s. der Jahrestag, die Jahresfeier.
annotate ['ænoteit], v.a. anmerken, mit Anmerkungen versehen.
annotation [æno'teiʃən], s. die Anmerkung, Notiz.
announce [ə'nauns], v.a. melden, ankündigen; anzeigen; (*Rad.*) ansagen.
announcement [ə'naunsmənt], s. die Ankündigung, Bekanntmachung; (*Rad.*) die Ansage.
announcer [ə'naunsə], s. (*Rad.*) der Ansager.
annoy [ə'nɔi], v.a. ärgern; belästigen.
annoyance [ə'nɔiəns], s. das Ärgernis; die Belästigung.
annual ['ænjuəl], adj. jährlich, Jahres-. — s. der Jahresband (*serial publication*); das Jahrbuch; (*Bot.*) die einjährige Pflanze.
annuity [ə'nju:iti], s. die Jahresrente, Lebensrente.
annul [ə'nʌl], v.a. annullieren, ungültig machen, für ungültig erklären.
annulment [ə'nʌlmənt], s. die Annullierung, Ungültigkeitserklärung.
Annunciation [ənʌnsi'eiʃən], s. (*Eccl.*) die Verkündigung.
anode ['ænoud], s. die Anode.
anodyne ['ænodain], adj. schmerzstillend.
anoint [ə'nɔint], v.a. salben.
anomalous [ə'nɔmələs], adj. abweichend, unregelmäßig, anomal.
anomaly [ə'nɔməli], s. die Anomalie, Abweichung, Unregelmäßigkeit.
anon [ə'nɔn], adv. sogleich, sofort.
anonymous [ə'nɔniməs], adj. (*abbr. anon.*) anonym; namenlos; unbekannt.
anonymity [ænə'nimiti], s. die Anonymität.
another [ə'nʌðə], adj. & pron. ein anderer; ein zweiter; noch einer; one —, einander.
answer ['ɑ:nsə], v.a. beantworten. — v.n. antworten. — s. die Antwort, Erwiderung.
answerable ['ɑ:nsərəbl], adj. verantwortlich (*responsible*); beantwortbar (*capable of being answered*).
ant [ænt], s. (*Ent.*) die Ameise.

antagonise [æn'tægənaiz], v.a. sich (*Dat.*) jemanden zum Gegner machen.
antagonism [æn'tægənizm], s. der Widerstreit, Konflikt; der Antagonismus.
Antarctic [ænt'ɑ:ktik], adj. Südpol-, antarktisch. — s. der südliche Polarkreis.
antecedence [ænti'si:dəns], s. der Vortritt (*rank*).
antecedent [ænti'si:dənt], s. (*pl.*) das Vorhergehende, die Vorgeschichte.
antedate ['æntideit], v.a. vordatieren.
antediluvian [æntidi'lu:viən], adj. vorsintflutlich; (*fig.*) überholt; altmodisch.
antelope ['æntiloup], s. (*Zool.*) die Antilope.
antenna [æn'tenə], s. (*Ent.*) der Fühler; (*Rad.*) die Antenne.
anterior [æn'tiəriə], adj. vorder (*in space*), älter, vorherig, vorhergehend, (*in time*).
anteroom ['æntiru:m], s. das Vorzimmer.
anthem ['ænθəm], s. die Hymne, der Hymnus.
anther ['ænθə], s. (*Bot.*) der Staubbeutel.
antic ['æntik], s. die Posse; (*pl.*) komisches Benehmen.
anticipate [æn'tisipeit], v.a. vorwegnehmen; zuvorkommen; ahnen (*guess*); erwarten (*await*); vorgreifen.
anticipation [æntisi'peiʃən], s. die Vorwegnahme; die Erwartung.
antidote ['æntidout], s. das Gegengift.
antipathy [æn'tipəθi], s. die Antipathie, der Widerwille.
antipodal [æn'tipədəl], adj. antipodisch; entgegengesetzt.
antiquarian [ænti'kwɛəriən], adj. altertümlich; antiquarisch.
antiquary ['æntikwəri], s. der Altertumsforscher, Antiquar.
antiquated ['æntikweitid], adj. überholt, unmodern, veraltet.
antique [æn'ti:k], s. die Antike; das alte Kunstwerk. — adj. alt, antik; altmodisch.
antiquity [æn'tikwiti], s. die Antike, das Altertum; die Vorzeit (*period of history*).
antiseptic [ænti'septik], s. antiseptisch — s. das antiseptische Mittel.
antler ['æntlə], s. die Geweihsprosse; (*pl.*) das Geweih.
anvil ['ænvil], s. der Amboß.
anxiety [æŋ'zaiəti], s. die Angst (*fear*); Besorgnis (*uneasiness*); Unruhe.
anxious ['æŋkʃəs], adj. ängstlich (*afraid*); besorgt (*worried*); eifrig bemüht (*keen, um, on, Acc.*).
any ['eni], adj. & pron. jeder; irgendein; etwas; (*pl.*) einige; (*neg.*) not —, kein.
anybody, anyone ['enibɔdi, 'eniwʌn], pron. irgendeiner, jemand; jeder.
anyhow, anyway ['enihau, 'eniwei], adv. irgendwie, auf irgendeine Weise; auf alle Fälle.
anyone see under **anybody**.

anything ['eniθiŋ], s. irgend etwas; alles.

anyway see under **anyhow.**

anywhere ['enihwɛə], adv. irgendwo; überall; not —, nirgends.

apace [ə'peis], adv. geschwind, hurtig, flink.

apart [ə'pɑ:t], adv. für sich, abgesondert; einzeln; poles —, weit entfernt; take —, zerlegen; — from, abgesehen von.

apartment [ə'pɑ:tmənt], s. das Zimmer; (Am.) die Wohnung (flat).

apathy ['æpəθi], s. die Apathie, Interesselosigkeit, Gleichgültigkeit.

apathetic [æpə'θetik], adj. apathisch, uninteressiert; teilnahmslos.

ape [eip], s. (Zool.) der Affe. — v.a. nachäffen, nachahmen.

aperient [ə'piəriənt], adj. (Med.) abführend. — s. (Med.) das Abführmittel.

aperture ['æpətʃə], s. die Öffnung.

apex ['eipeks], s. die Spitze, der Gipfel.

aphorism ['æfərizm], s. der Aphorismus.

apiary ['eipiəri], s. das Bienenhaus.

apiece [ə'pi:s], adv. pro Stück, pro Person.

apologetic [əpɔlə'dʒetik], adj. entschuldigend, reumütig; verteidigend.

apologize [ə'pɔlədʒaiz], v.n. sich entschuldigen (for, wegen; to, bei).

apology [ə'pɔlədʒi], s. die Entschuldigung; Abbitte; Rechtfertigung.

apoplectic [æpə'plektik], adj. (Med.) apoplektisch.

apoplexy ['æpəpleksi], s. (Med.) der Schlagfluß, Schlaganfall (fit).

apostle [ə'pɔsl], s. der Apostel.

apostolic [æpəs'tɔlik], adj. apostolisch.

apostrophe [ə'pɔstrəfi], s. der Apostroph (punctuation); die Anrede (speech).

apostrophize [ə'pɔstrəfaiz], v.a. apostrophieren; anreden (speak to).

apotheosis [əpɔθi'ousis], s. die Apotheose.

appal [ə'pɔ:l], v.a. erschrecken.

appalling [ə'pɔ:liŋ], adj. schrecklich.

apparatus [æpə'reitəs], s. das Gerät, die Apparatur; (coll.) der Apparat.

apparel [ə'pærəl], s. die Kleidung.

apparent [ə'pærənt], adj. scheinbar; offensichtlich; augenscheinlich; heir —, der rechtmäßige Erbe.

apparition [æpə'riʃən], s. die Erscheinung; der Geist, das Gespenst (ghost).

appeal [ə'pi:l], v.n. appellieren (make an appeal); gefallen (please). — s. (public, Mil.) der Appell; die Bitte (request).

appear [ə'piə], v.n. erscheinen; scheinen; auftreten.

appearance [ə'piərəns], s. die Erscheinung; das Auftreten (stage, etc.); der Schein (semblance); keep up —s, den Schein wahren; to all —s, allem Anschein nach.

appease [ə'pi:z], v.a. besänftigen.

appeasement [ə'pi:zmənt], s. die Besänftigung, (Pol.) die Befriedung.

appellation [æpe'leiʃən], s. die Benennung.

append [ə'pend], v.a. anhängen, beifügen.

appendicitis [əpendi'saitis], s. (Med.) die Blinddarmentzündung.

appendix [ə'pendiks], s. der Anhang; (Med.) der Blinddarm.

appertain [æpə'tein], v.n. gehören (to, zu).

appetite ['æpitait], s. der Appetit.

appetizing ['æpitaiziŋ], adj. appetitlich, appetitanregend.

applaud [ə'plɔ:d], v.a., v.n. applaudieren, Beifall klatschen (Dat.).

applause [ə'plɔ:z], s. der Applaus, Beifall.

apple [æpl], s. der Apfel.

appliance [ə'plaiəns], s. das Gerät, die Vorrichtung.

applicable ['æplikəbl], adj. anwendbar, passend (to, auf).

applicant ['æplikənt], s. der Bewerber (for, um).

application [æpli'keiʃən], s. die Bewerbung (for, um); das Gesuch; die Anwendung (to, auf); letter of —, der Bewerbungsbrief; — form, das Bewerbungsformular.

apply [ə'plai], v.a. anwenden (auf, to, Acc.); gebrauchen. — v.n. sich bewerben (um, for, Acc.); (Dat.) this does not —, das trifft nicht zu; — within, drinnen nachfragen.

appoint [ə'pɔint], v.a. bestimmen; ernennen; ausrüsten.

appointment [ə'pɔintmənt], s. die Festsetzung; die Ernennung; die Bestellung, die Stellung (position); make an —, jemanden ernennen (fill a post), sich verabreden (arrange to meet); by —, Hoflieferant (to, Genit.).

apportion [ə'pɔ:ʃən], v.a. zuteilen, zuweisen, zumessen.

apposite ['æpəzit], adj. passend, angemessen.

appositeness ['æpəzitnis], s. die Angemessenheit.

appraise [ə'preiz], v.a. beurteilen.

appraisal [ə'preizəl], s. die Beurteilung, Abschätzung.

appreciable [ə'pri:ʃəbl], adj. merklich; nennenswert.

appreciate [ə'pri:ʃieit], v.a. würdigen, schätzen.

appreciation [əpri:ʃi'eiʃən], s. die Schätzung, Würdigung.

apprehend [æpri'hend], v.a. verhaften, ergreifen (arrest); befürchten (fear).

apprehension [æpri'henʃən], s. die Verhaftung (arrest); die Befürchtung (fear).

apprehensive [æpri'hensiv], adj. besorgt, in Furcht (for, um), furchtsam.

apprentice [ə'prentis], s. der Lehrling; Praktikant. — v.a. in die Lehre geben (with, bei, Dat.).

apprenticeship

apprenticeship [ə'prentiʃip], *s.* die Lehre, Lehrzeit, Praktikantenzeit; *student* —, die Studentenpraxis.

apprise [ə'praiz], *v.a.* benachrichtigen, informieren.

approach [ə'prout∫], *v.a., v.n.* sich nähern (*Dat.*). — *s.* die Annäherung, das Herankommen, Näherrücken.

approachable [ə'prout∫əbl], *adj.* zugänglich, freundlich.

approbation [æpro'beiʃən], *s.* die (offizielle) Billigung, Zustimmung.

appropriate [ə'proupriit], *adj.* angemessen, gebührend, geeignet (*suitable*). — [ə'prouprieit], *v.a.* requirieren, sich aneignen.

appropriation [əproupri'eiʃən], *s.* die Requisition, Aneignung, Übernahme, Besitznahme.

approval [ə'pru:vəl], *s.* die Billigung, der Beifall, die Zustimmung.

approve [ə'pru:v], *v.a.* loben, billigen; genehmigen; annehmen (*work*).

approved [ə'pru:vd], *adj.* anerkannt.

approximate [ə'prɔksimit], *adj.* ungefähr, annähernd. —*v.n. & a.*[ə'prɔksimeit], sich nähern.

approximation [əprɔksi'meiʃən], *s.* die Annäherung.

approximative [ə'prɔksimətiv], *adj.* annähernd.

appurtenance [ə'pə:tənəns], *s.* das (*or der*) Zubehör.

appurtenant [ə'pə:tənənt], *adj.* zugehörig.

apricot ['eiprikɔt], *s.* (*Bot.*) die Aprikose.

April ['eipril]. der April.

apron ['eiprən], *s.* die Schürze; der Schurz; — *stage*, die Vorbühne, das Proszenium.

apropos [ɑ:prɔ'pou], *adv.* beiläufig; mit Bezug auf, diesbezüglich.

apse [æps], *s.* (*Archit.*) die Apsis.

apt [æpt], *adj.* geeignet, passend; fähig.

aptitude ['æptitju:d], *s.* die Eignung, Fähigkeit.

aptness ['æptnis], *s.* die Angemessenheit, Eignung.

aquatic [ə'kwɔtik *or* ə'kwætik], *adj.* Wasser-, wasser-; — *display*, Wasserkünste. — *s.* (*pl.*) der Wassersport.

aqueduct ['ækwidʌkt], *s.* die Wasserleitung; der Aquädukt.

aqueous ['eikwiəs], *adj.* (*Chem.*) wässerig.

aquiline ['ækwilain], *adj.* adlerartig, Adler-.

Arab ['ærəb], *s.* der Araber.

Arabian [ə'reibiən], *adj.* arabisch; — *Nights*, Tausend-und-eine-Nacht.

Arabic ['ærəbik], *adj.* arabisch (*language, literature*).

arable ['ærəbl], *adj.* pflügbar, bestellbar.

arbiter ['ɑ:bitə], *s.* der Schiedsrichter.

arbitrary ['ɑ:bitrəri], *adj.* willkürlich.

arbitrate ['ɑ:bitreit], *v.n.* vermitteln.

arbitration [ɑ:bi'treiʃən], *s.* die Vermittlung; Entscheidung; (*Comm.*) Arbitrage.

arboriculture ['ɑ:bɔrikʌlt∫ə], *s.* die Baumzucht.

arbour ['ɑ:bə], *s.* die Laube, Gartenlaube.

arc [ɑ:k], *s.* (*Geom.*) der Bogen; — *lamp*, die Bogenlampe; — *welding*, das Lichtschweißen.

arcade [ɑ:'keid], *s.* die Arkade.

Arcadian [ɑ:'keidiən], *adj.* arkadisch. — *s.* der Arkadier.

arch [ɑ:t∫], *s.* der Bogen, die Wölbung; —*way*, der Bogengang. — *v.a., v.n.* wölben, sich wölben. — *adj.* schelmisch, listig. — *prefix* oberst; erst Haupt-; — *-enemy*, der Erzfeind.

archaeological [ɑ:kiə'lɔdʒikəl], *adj.* archäologisch.

archaeologist [ɑ:ki'ɔlədʒist], *s.* der Archäologe.

archaeology [ɑ:ki'ɔlədʒi], *s.* die Archäologie.

archaic [ɑ:'keiik], *adj.* altertümlich.

archaism ['ɑ:keiizm], *s.* der Archaismus (*style*).

archbishop [ɑ:t∫'biʃəp], *s.* der Erzbischof.

archduke [ɑ:t∫'dju:k], *s.* der Erzherzog.

archer ['ɑ:t∫ə], *s.* der Bogenschütze.

archery ['ɑ:t∫əri], *s.* das Bogenschießen.

architect ['ɑ:kitekt], *s.* der Architekt, Baumeister.

architecture ['ɑ:kitekt∫ə], *s.* die Architektur, Baukunst.

archives ['ɑ:kaivz], *s. pl.* das Archiv.

Arctic ['ɑ:ktik], *adj.* arktisch. — *s.* die Nordpolarländer, *n. pl.*

ardent ['ɑ:dənt], *adj.* heiß, glühend, brennend.

ardour ['ɑ:də], *s.* die Hitze, die Inbrunst, der Eifer.

arduous ['ɑ:djuəs], *adj.* schwierig; mühsam.

area ['ɛəriə], *s.* das Areal (*measurement*); das Gebiet, die Zone; die Fläche (*region*).

arena [ə'ri:nə], *s.* die Arena, der Kampfplatz.

Argentine ['ɑ:dʒəntain], *adj.* argentinisch. — (*Republic*), Argentinien, *n.*

Argentinian [ɑ:dʒən'tiniən], *adj.* argentinisch. — *s.* der Argentin(i)er.

argue ['ɑ:gju:], *v.n. irr.* disputieren, streiten; folgern, schließen.

argument ['ɑ:gjumənt], *s.* das Argument; (*Log.*) der Beweis; der Streit (*dispute*).

argumentative [ɑ:gju'mentətiv], *adj.* streitsüchtig.

arid ['ærid], *adj.* trocken, dürr.

aright [ə'rait], *adv.* richtig, zurecht.

arise [ə'raiz], *v.n. irr.* aufstehen; sich erheben; entstehen (*originate*); *arising from the minutes*, es ergibt sich aus dem Protokoll.

aristocracy [æris'tɔkrəsi], *s.* die Aristokratie, der Adel.

aristocratic [æris'o'krætik], *adj.* aristokratisch, adlig.

arithmetic [ə'riθmətik], *s.* die Arithmetik.

Asiatic

arithmetical [æriθ'metikəl], *adj.* arithmetisch.

ark [a:k], *s.* die Arche; — *of the Covenant,* die Bundeslade.

arm (1) [a:m], *s.* (*Anat.*) der Arm.

arm (2) [a:m], *s.* die Waffe; *up in —s,* in Aufruhr. — *v.a., v.n.* bewaffnen, sich bewaffnen, rüsten, sich rüsten.

armament ['a:məmənt], *s.* die Rüstung, Bewaffnung.

armature ['a:mətiuə], *s.* die Armatur.

armchair ['a:mtʃɛə], *s.* der Lehnstuhl; der Sessel.

Armenian [a:'mi:niən], *adj.* armenisch. — *s.* der Armenier.

armistice ['a:mistis], *s.* der Waffenstillstand.

armour ['a:mə], *s.* die Rüstung, der Harnisch; *—plated,* gepanzert; *—ed car,* der Panzerwagen.

armourer ['a:mərə], *s.* der Waffenschmied.

armoury ['a:məri], *s.* die Rüstkammer, Waffenschmiede.

army ['a:mi], *s.* die Armee, das Heer.

aroma [ə'roumə], *s.* das Aroma, der Duft.

aromatic [ærə'mætik], *adj.* aromatisch. —*s.* (*Chem.*) das Aromat.

around [ə'raund], *adv.* herum, rund-, ringsherum, umher, im Kreise; *stand —,* herumstehen; *be —,* sich in der Nähe halten. — *prep.* um; bei, um ... herum.

arouse [ə'rauz], *v.a.* aufwecken, aufrütteln.

arraignment [ə'reinmənt], *s.* die Anklage.

arrange [ə'reindʒ], *v.a.* anordnen, arrangieren, einrichten, vereinbaren.

arrangement [ə'reindʒmənt], *s.* die Anordnung; die Einrichtung; die Vereinbarung (*agreement*); (*Law*) die Vergleichung, der Vergleich.

arrant ['ærənt], *adj.* durchtrieben.

array [ə'rei], *v.a.* schmücken, aufstellen. — *s.* die Ordnung; Aufstellung.

arrears [ə'riəz], *s. pl.* der Rückstand, die Schulden.

arrest [ə'rest], *v.a.* (*Law*) festnehmen, verhaften; festhalten; aufhalten (*hinder*). — *s.* die Festnahme; die Festhaltung.

arrival [ə'raivəl], *s.* die Ankunft.

arrive [ə'raiv], *v.n.* ankommen.

arrogance ['ærəgəns], *s.* die Anmaßung, Überheblichkeit.

arrogant ['ærəgənt], *adj.* anmaßend, hochfahrend, überheblich.

arrow ['ærou], *s.* der Pfeil.

arrowroot ['ærouru:t], *s.* (*Bot.*) die Pfeilwurz.

arsenal ['a:sinəl], *s.* das Arsenal, Zeughaus.

arsenic ['a:sənik], *s.* das Arsen.

arson ['a:sən], *s.* die Brandstiftung.

art [a:t], *s.* die Kunst; *fine —,* schöne Kunst; (*Univ.*) *—s faculty,* die philosophische Fakultät; *—s* (*subject*), das humanistische Fach, die Geisteswissenschaften.

arterial [a:'tiəriəl], *adj.* Pulsader-, Schlagader-; — *road,* die Hauptverkehrsader, die Hauptstraße.

artery ['a:təri], *s.* die Pulsader, Schlagader; der Hauptverkehrsweg.

artesian [a:'ti:zən], *adj.* artesisch.

artful ['a:tful], *adj.* listig, schlau.

article ['a:tikl], *s.* (*Gram., Law, Press*) der Artikel; der Posten (*item in list*). — *v.a. be —d to a solicitor,* bei einem Advokaten assistieren.

articulate [a:'tikjuleit], *v.a.* artikulieren (*pronounce clearly*). — [—lit], *adj.* deutlich (*speech*).

articulation [a:tikju'leiʃən], *s.* die Artikulation, deutliche Aussprache.

artifice ['a:tifis], *s.* der Kunstgriff, die List.

artificer [a:'tifisə], *s.* der Handwerker.

artificial [a:ti'fiʃəl], *adj.* künstlich, Kunst-; — *silk,* die Kunstseide.

artillery [a:'tiləri], *s.* die Artillerie.

artisan [a:ti'zæn], *s.* der Handwerker.

artist ['a:tist], *s.* der Künstler, die Künstlerin.

artistic [a:'tistik], *adj.* künstlerisch.

artless ['a:tlis], *adj.* arglos, natürlich, naiv.

Aryan ['ɛəriən], *adj.* arisch. — *s.* der Arier.

as [æz], *adv., conj.* so, als, wie, ebenso; als, während, weil; — *big —,* so groß wie; — *well —,* sowohl als auch; *such —,* wie; — *it were,* gleichsam.

asbestos [æz'bestəs], *s.* der Asbest.

ascend [ə'send], *v.a., v.n.* ersteigen, besteigen; emporsteigen.

ascendancy, -ency [ə'sendənsi], *s.* der Aufstieg; der Einfluß; das Übergewicht.

ascendant, -ent [ə'sendənt], *s. in the —,* aufsteigend.

ascent [ə'sent], *s.* der Aufstieg, die Besteigung.

ascension [ə'senʃən], *s.* (*Astron.*) das Aufsteigen; *Ascension Day,* Himmelfahrt(stag).

ascertain [æsə'tein], *v.a.* in Erfahrung bringen, erkunden, feststellen.

ascertainable [æsə'teinəbl], *adj.* erkundbar, feststellbar.

ascetic [ə'setik], *adj.* asketisch.

asceticism [ə'setisizm], *s.* die Askese.

ascribe [ə'skraib], *v.a.* zuschreiben.

ascribable [ə'skraibəbl], *adj.* zuzuschreiben, zuschreibbar.

ash (1) [æʃ], *s.* (*Bot.*) die Esche.

ash (2) [æʃ], *s.* die Asche.

ashamed [ə'ʃeimd], *adj.* beschämt; *be —,* sich schämen.

ashcan ['æʃkæn] (*Am.*) see dustbin.

ashen ['æʃən], *adj.* aschgrau, aschfarben.

ashore [ə'ʃɔ:], *adv.* am Land; am Ufer, ans Ufer *or* Land.

ashtray ['æʃtrei], *s.* der Aschenbecher.

Ash Wednesday [æʃ'wenzdei], *s.* der Aschermittwoch.

Asiatic [eiʃi'ætik], *adj.* asiatisch. — *s.* der Asiat.

313

aside

aside [ə′said], *adv.* seitwärts, zur Seite; abseits.

ask [ɑːsk], *v.a.*, *v.n.* fragen (*question*); bitten (*request*); fordern (*demand*); einladen (*invite*).

asleep [ə′sliːp], *pred. adj.*, *adv.* schlafend, im Schlaf; eingeschlafen.

asp [æsp], *s.* (*Zool.*) die Natter.

asparagus [æs′pærəgəs], *s.* (*Bot.*) der Spargel.

aspect [′æspekt], *s.* der Anblick, die Ansicht (*view*, *angle*); der Gesichtspunkt.

aspen [′æspən], *s.* (*Bot.*) die Espe.

asperity [æs′periti], *s.* die Härte; Rauheit.

aspersion [æs′pəːʃən], *s.* die Verleumdung; Schmähung.

asphalt [′æsfælt], *s.* der Asphalt.

asphyxia [æs′fiksjə], *s.* (*Med.*) die Erstickung. ◂

aspirant [ə′spaiərənt, ′æsp-], *s.* der Bewerber, Anwärter.

aspirate [′æspireit], *v.a.* (*Phon.*) aspirieren. — [—rit] *adj.* aspiriert. — *s.* der Hauchlaut.

aspiration [æspi′reiʃən], *s.* der Atemzug; das Streben (*striving*) ; (*Phon.*) die Aspiration.

aspire [ə′spaiə], *v.n.* streben, verlangen.

ass [æs], *s.* der Esel.

assail [ə′seil], *v.a.* angreifen, anfallen.

assailable [ə′seiləbl], *adj.* angreifbar.

assassin [ə′sæsin], *s.* der Meuchelmörder.

assassinate [ə′sæsineit], *v.a.* meuchlings ermorden.

assassination [əsæsi′neiʃən], *s.* der Meuchelmord, die Ermordung.

assault [ə′sɔːlt], *v.a.* angreifen, überfallen. — *s.* der Überfall, Angriff.

assay [ə′sei], *s.* die Metallprobe. — *v.a.* (auf Edelmetall hin) prüfen.

assemble [ə′sembl], *v.a.*, *v.n.* versammeln, sich versammeln.

assembly [ə′sembli], *s.* die Versammlung (*assemblage*); — *line*, das laufende Band, das Fließband.

assent [ə′sent], *v.n.* beistimmen (*Dat.*), billigen (*Acc.*). — *s.* die Zustimmung (zu, *Dat.*), Billigung (*Genit.*).

assert [ə′səːt], *v.a.* behaupten.

assertion [ə′səːʃən], *s.* die Behauptung.

assess [ə′ses], *v.a.* schätzen, beurteilen.

assessment [ə′sesmənt], *s.* die Beurteilung, Schätzung, Wertung.

assessor [ə′sesə], *s.* der Beurteiler, Einschätzer, Bewerter, Assessor; der Beisitzer (*second examiner*).

assets [′æsets], *s. pl.* (*Comm.*) die Aktiva; Vorzüge (*personal*).

assiduity [æsi′djuːiti], *s.* der Fleiß, die Emsigkeit.

assiduous [ə′sidjuəs], *adj.* fleißig, unablässig, emsig.

assign [ə′sain], *v.a.* zuteilen, anweisen, zuweisen (*apportion*), festsetzen (*fix*).

assignable [ə′sainəbl], *adj.* zuteilbar; bestimmbar.

assignation [æsig′neiʃən], *s.* die Zuweisung; (*Law*) die Übertragung; die Verabredung.

assignment [ə′sainmənt], *s.* die Zuweisung, Übertragung; die Aufgabe.

assimilate [ə′simileit], *v.a.*, *v.n.* assimilieren, angleichen; sich assimilieren, sich angleichen, ähnlich werden.

assist [ə′sist], *v.a.*, *v.n.* beistehen (*Dat.*), helfen (*Dat.*), unterstützen (*Acc.*).

assistance [ə′sistəns], *s.* der Beistand, die Hilfe; die Aushilfe; (*financial*) der Zuschuß.

assistant [ə′sistənt], *s.* der Assistent, Helfer.

assize [ə′saiz], *s.* die Gerichtssitzung; (*pl.*) das Schwurgericht.

associate [ə′souʃieit], *v.a.* verbinden (*link*). — *v.n.* verkehren (*company*); sich verbinden; (*Comm.*) sich vereinigen. — [—iit], *s.* (*Comm.*) der Partner.

association [əsousi′eiʃən], *s.* die Vereinigung, der Bund, Verein; die Gesellschaft; der Verkehr.

assonance [′æsənəns], *s.* (*Phon.*) die Assonanz, der Gleichklaut.

assort [ə′sɔːt], *v.a.* ordnen, aussuchen, sortieren; —*ed sweets*, gemischte Bonbons.

assortment [ə′sɔːtmənt], *s.* die Sammlung, Mischung, Auswahl.

assuage [ə′sweidʒ], *v.a.* mildern, besänftigen, stillen.

assume [ə′sjuːm], *v.a.* annehmen; übernehmen, ergreifen.

assuming [ə′sjuːmiŋ], *adj.* anmaßend; — *that*, angenommen daß . . ., gesetzt den Fall.

assumption [ə′sʌmpʃən], *s.* die Annahme (*opinion*); Übernahme (*taking up*); Aneignung (*appropriation*); *Assumption of the Blessed Virgin*, Mariä Himmelfahrt.

assurance [ə′ʃuərəns], *s.* die Versicherung; Sicherheit (*manner*).

assure [ə′ʃuə], *v.a.* versichern, sicher stellen, ermutigen.

assuredly [ə′ʃuəridli], *adv.* sicherlich, gewiß.

aster [′æstə], *s.* (*Bot.*) die Aster.

asterisk [′æstərisk], *s.* (*Typ.*) das Sternchen.

astern [ə′stəːn], *adv.* (*Naut.*) achteraus.

asthma [′æsθmə], *s.* das Asthma.

asthmatic [æsθ′mætik], *adj.* asthmatisch.

astir [ə′stəː], *adv.* wach, in Bewegung.

astonish [ə′stɔniʃ], *v.a.* in Erstaunen versetzen, verblüffen.

astonishment [ə′stɔniʃmənt], *s.* das Erstaunen, die Verwunderung; die Bestürzung.

astound [ə′staund], *v.a.* in Erstaunen versetzen, bestürzen.

astounding [ə′staundiŋ], *adj.* erstaunlich, verblüffend.

astral [′æstrəl], *adj.* Stern(en)-, gestirnt.

astray [ə'strei], *pred. adj., adv.* irre; *go* —, sich verirren; (*fig.*) abschweifen.

astride[ə'straid], *pred.adj.,adv.*rittlings.

astringent [ə'strindȝənt], *adj.* zusammenziehend.

astrologer [ə'strɔlədȝə], *s.* der Sterndeuter, Astrolog(e).

astrological [æstrə'lɔdȝikəl], *adj.* astrologisch.

astrology [æ'strɔlədȝi], *s.* die Astrologie, Sterndeuterei.

astronaut['æstrənɔːt], *s.* der Astronaut.

astronomer [ə'strɔnəmə], *s.* der Astronom.

astronomical[æstrə'nɔmikəl], *adj.*astronomisch.

astronomy [ə'strɔnəmi], *s.* die Astronomie, Sternkunde.

astute [ə'stjuːt], *adj.* listig, schlau.

astuteness [ə'stjuːtnis], *s.* die Schlauheit, Listigkeit, der Scharfsinn.

asunder [ə'sʌndə], *adv.* auseinander, entzwei.

asylum [ə'sailəm], *s.* das Asyl, der Zufluchtsort (*refuge*); *lunatic* —, das Irrenhaus.

at [æt], *prep.* an; auf; bei, für; in, nach; mit, gegen; um, über; von, aus, zu; — *my expense*, auf meine Kosten; — *all*, überhaupt; — *first*, zuerst; — *last*, zuletzt, endlich; — *peace*, in Frieden; *what are you driving* —? worauf wollen sie hinaus?

atheism ['eiθiizm], *s.* der Atheismus.

atheist ['eiθiist], *s.* der Atheist.

atheistic [eiθi'istik], *adj.* atheistisch, gottlos.

Athens ['æθənz], Athen, *n.*

Athenian [ə'θiːnjən], *s.* der Athener. — *adj.* athenisch.

athlete ['æθliːt], *s.* der Athlet.

athletic [æθ'letik], *adj.* athletisch.

athletics [æθ'letiks], *s. pl.* die Leichtathletik, Athletik.

Atlantic (**Ocean**) [ət'læntik ('oufən)], der Atlantik.

atlas ['ætləs], *s.* der Atlas.

atmosphere ['ætməsfiə], *s.* die Atmosphäre.

atmospheric(**al**) [ætməs'ferik(əl)], *adj.* atmosphärisch. — *s.* (*pl.*) atmosphärische Störungen, *f. pl.*

atoll[ə'tɔl], *s.* die Koralleninsel,das Atoll.

atom ['ætəm], *s.* das Atom.

atomic [ə'tɔmik], *adj.* (*Phys.*) Atom-, atomisch, atomar; (*theory*) atomistisch; — *bomb*, die Atombombe; — *pile*, der Atomreaktor; — *armament*, die atomare Aufrüstung.

atone [ə'toun], *v.n.* sühnen, büßen.

atonement [ə'tounmənt], *s.* die Buße, Sühne, Versöhnung.

atonic [ei'tɔnik], *adj.* tonlos, unbetont.

atrocious [ə'troufəs], *adj.* gräßlich, schrecklich, entsetzlich.

atrocity [ə'trɔsiti], *s.* die Gräßlichkeit, Grausamkeit, Greueltat.

atrophy ['ætrəfi], *s.* (*Med.*) die Abmagerung, Atrophie. — ['ætrəfai], *v.n.* absterben, auszehren.

attach [ə'tætʃ], *v.a.* anheften, beilegen, anhängen; (*fig.*) beimessen (*attribute*).

attachment [ə'tætʃmənt], *s.* das Anhaften (*sticking to*, an, *Acc.*); das Anhängsel (*appendage*); die Freundschaft (*to*, für, *Acc.*); die Anhänglichkeit (*loyalty*, an, *Acc.*).

attack [ə'tæk], *v.a.* angreifen. — *s.* die Attacke, der Angriff; (*Med.*) der Anfall.

attain [ə'tein], *v.a.* erreichen, erlangen.

attainable [ə'teinəbl], *adj.* erreichbar.

attainment [ə'teinmənt], *s.* die Erlangung, Erreichung; Errungenschaft; (*pl.*) Kenntnisse, *f. pl.*

attempt [ə'tempt], *s.* der Versuch. — *v.a.* versuchen.

attend [ə'tend], *v.a., v.n.* begleiten, anwesend sein (*be present, at*, bei, *Dat.*); beiwohnen (*be present as guest*); zuhören (*listen to*); bedienen (*customer*); behandeln (*patient*).

attendance [ə'tendəns], *s.* die Begleitung (*accompaniment*); die Anwesenheit (*presence*); die Zuhörerschaft (*audience*); *to be in* —, Dienst tun (*at*, bei); anwesend sein (*be present*).

attendant [ə'tendənt], *s.* der Diener, Wärter.

attention [ə'tenʃən], *s.* die Aufmerksamkeit, Achtung.

attentive [ə'tentiv], *adj.* aufmerksam.

attenuate [ə'tenjueit], *v.a.* verdünnen (*dilute*). — *v.n.* abmagern.

attest [ə'test], *v.a.* attestieren, bezeugen, bescheinigen.

attestation [ætes'teiʃən], *s.* die Bescheinigung; das Zeugnis.

Attic ['ætik], *adj.* attisch, klassisch.

attic ['ætik], *s.* die Dachkammer, die Dachstube.

attire [ə'taiə], *v.a.* ankleiden, kleiden. — *s.* die Kleidung.

attitude ['ætitjuːd], *s.* die Haltung, Stellung (*toward*, zu), Einstellung.

attorney [ə'tɔːni], *s.* der Anwalt; *Attorney-General*, der Kronanwalt; (*Am.*) der Staatsanwalt; — *at law*, Rechtsanwalt.

attract [ə'trækt], *v.a.* anziehen.

attraction [ə'trækʃən], *s.* die Anziehung; der Reiz (*appeal*); die Anziehungskraft.

attractive [ə'træktiv], *adj.* anziehend, reizvoll.

attribute [ə'tribjuːt], *v.a.* zuschreiben, beimessen. — *s.* ['ætribjuːt], (*Gram.*) das Attribut, die Eigenschaft.

attributive [ə'tribjutiv], *adj.* (*Gram.*) attributiv; beilegend.

attrition [ə'triʃən], *s.* die Zermürbung, Aufreibung, Reue.

attune [ə'tjuːn], *v.a.* (*Mus.*) stimmen, anpassen (*adapt to*, an, *Acc.*).

auburn ['ɔːbən], *adj.* rotbraun.

auction [ɔːk'ʃən], `s.` die Auktion, die Versteigerung.

auctioneer [ɔːkʃə'niə], *s.* der Auktionator, Versteigerer.

audacious [ɔ:'deiʃəs], adj. waghalsig, kühn, dreist.
audacity [ɔ:'dæsiti], s. die Kühnheit (valour); Frechheit (impudence).
audible ['ɔ:dibl], adj. hörbar.
audibility [ɔ:di'biliti], s. die Hörbarkeit, Vernehmbarkeit.
audience ['ɔ:djəns], s. die Audienz (of the Pope, beim Papst); (Theat.) das Publikum; (listeners) die Zuhörer.
audit ['ɔ:dit], s. die Rechnungsprüfung, Revision. — v.a. revidieren, prüfen.
auditor ['ɔ:ditə], s. der Rechnungsrevisor, Buchprüfer.
auditory ['ɔ:ditəri], adj. Gehör-, Hör-.
auditorium [ɔ:di'tɔ:riəm], s. der Hörsaal, Vortragssaal.
auger ['ɔ:gə], s. der (große) Bohrer.
aught [ɔ:t], pron. (obs.) irgend etwas (opp. to naught).
augment [ɔ:g'ment], v.a., v.n. vermehren, vergrößern; zunehmen.
augmentation [ɔ:gmen'teiʃən], s. die Vergrößerung, Erhöhung, Zunahme.
augur ['ɔ:gə], v.a. weissagen, prophezeien.
August ['ɔ:gəst]. der August.
august [ɔ:'gʌst], adj. erhaben.
aunt [ɑ:nt], s. die Tante.
aurora [ɔ:'rɔ:rə], s. die Morgenröte.
auscultation [ɔ:skəl'teiʃən], s. (Med.) die Auskultation, Untersuchung.
auspices ['ɔ:spisiz], s.pl. die Auspizien.
auspicious [ɔ:'spiʃəs], adj. unter glücklichem Vorzeichen, verheißungsvoll, günstig.
austere [ɔ:s'tiə], adj. streng, ernst, schmucklos.
austerity [ɔ:s'teriti], s. die Strenge.
Australian [ɔ'streiljən], adj. australisch. — s. der Australier.
Austrian ['ɔ:striən], adj. österreichisch. — s. der Österreicher.
authentic [ɔ:'θentik], adj. authentisch, echt.
authenticity [ɔ:θen'tisiti], s. die Authentizität, Echtheit.
author, authoress ['ɔ:θə, ɔ:'θər'es], s. der Autor, die Autorin; der Verfasser, die Verfasserin.
authoritative [ɔ:'θɔritətiv], adj. autoritativ, maßgebend.
authority [ɔ:'θɔriti], s. die Autorität, Vollmacht (power of attorney); das Ansehen; the authorities, die Behörden.
authorization [ɔ:θɔrai'zeiʃən], s. die Bevollmächtigung, Befugnis.
authorize ['ɔ:θəraiz], v.a. autorisieren, bevollmächtigen, berechtigen.
authorship ['ɔ:θəʃip], s. die Autorschaft.
autobiographical [ɔ:tobaiə'græfikl], adj. autobiographisch.
autobiography [ɔ:tobai'ɔgrəfi], s. die Autobiographie.
autocracy [ɔ:'tɔkrəsi], s. die Selbstherrschaft.
autocrat ['ɔ:tokræt], s. der Autokrat, Selbstherrscher.

autograph ['ɔ:tograef, -grɑ:f], s. die eigene Handschrift, Unterschrift; das Autogramm.
automatic [ɔ:to'mætik], adj. automatisch.
automatize [ɔ:'tɔmətaiz], v.a. automatisieren, auf Automation umstellen.
automation [ɔ:to'meiʃən], s. (Engin.) die Automation; Automatisierung.
automaton [ɔ:'tɔmətən], s. der Automat.
automobile ['ɔ:tomobi:l], s. der Kraftwagen, das Auto.
autonomous [ɔ:'tɔnəməs], adj. autonom, unabhängig.
autonomy [ɔ:'tɔnəmi], s. die Autonomie, Unabhängigkeit.
autopsy ['ɔ:tɔpsi], s. die Autopsie; Obduktion, Leichenschau.
autumn ['ɔ:təm], s. der Herbst.
autumnal [ɔ:'tʌmnəl], adj. herbstlich.
auxiliary [ɔ:g'ziljəri], adj. Hilfs-.
avail [ə'veil], v.n. nützen, helfen, von Vorteil sein. — v.r. — o.s<of a th., sich einer Sache bedienen. — s. der Nutzen; of no —, nutzlos.
available [ə'veiləbl], adj. vorrätig, verfügbar, zur Verfügung (stehend).
avalanche ['ævəlɑ:nʃ], s. die Lawine.
avarice ['ævəris], s. der Geiz, die Habsucht, Gier.
avaricious [ævə'riʃəs], adj. geizig, habsüchtig, habgierig.
avenge [ə'vendʒ], v.a. rächen.
avenue ['ævənju:], s. die Allee; der Zugang.
average ['ævəridʒ], adj. durchschnittlich; not more than —, mäßig. — s. der Durchschnitt; on an —, durchschnittlich, im Durchschnitt. — v.a. den Durchschnitt nehmen.
averse [ə'və:s], adj. abgeneigt (to, Dat.).
aversion [ə'və:ʃən], s. die Abneigung, der Widerwille.
avert [ə'və:t], v.a. abwenden.
aviary ['eiviəri], s. das Vogelhaus.
aviation [əivi'eiʃən], s. das Flugwesen.
aviator ['eivieitə], s. der Flieger.
avid [ə'vid], adj. begierig (of or for, nach).
avidity [æ'viditi], s. die Begierde, Gier (for, nach).
avoid [ə'vɔid], v.a. vermeiden.
avoidable [ə'vɔidəbl], adj. vermeidlich, vermeidbar.
avoidance [ə'vɔidəns], s. die Vermeidung, das Meiden.
avow [ə'vau], v.a. eingestehen, anerkennen (acknowledge).
avowal [ə'vauəl], s. das Geständnis; die Erklärung.
await [ə'weit], v.a. erwarten, warten auf (Acc.).
awake(n) [ə'weik(ən)], v.a., v.n. irr. aufwecken, wecken; aufwachen (wake up). — adj. wide awake, schlau, auf der Hut.

award [ə'wɔ:d], s. die Zuerkennung, Auszeichnung; Belohnung (money); (Law) das Urteil. — v.a. zuerkennen; — damages, Schadenersatz zusprechen; verleihen (grant).
aware [ə'wɛə], adj. gewahr, bewußt (Genit.).
away [ə'wei], adv. weg; hinweg, fort.
awe [ɔ:], s. die Ehrfurcht; Furcht.
awful ['ɔ:ful], adj. furchtbar, schrecklich.
awhile [ə'wail], adv. eine Weile, eine kurze Zeit.
awkward ['ɔ:kwəd], adv. ungeschickt, unbeholfen, ungelenk; unangenehm (difficult); — situation, peinliche Situation, Lage.
awkwardness ['ɔkwədnis], s. die Ungeschicklichkeit, Unbeholfenheit.
awl [ɔ:l], s. die Ahle, der Pfriem.
awning ['ɔ:niŋ], s. die Plane; das Sonnendach.
awry [ə'rai], adj. schief, verkehrt.
axe [æks], s. die Axt, das Beil.
axiom ['æksiəm], s. das Axiom, der Satz, Lehrsatz, Grundsatz.
axiomatic [æksiə'mætik], adj. axiomatisch, grundsätzlich; gewiß.
axis ['æksis], s. die Achse.
axle [æksl], s. die Achse.
ay(e) (1) [ai], adv. ja, gewiß.
ay(e) (2) [ei], adv. ständig, ewig.
azalea [ə'zeiliə], s. (Bot.) die Azalie.
azure ['æʒə, 'eiʒə], adj. himmelblau, azurblau.

B

B [bi:]. das B; (Mus.) das H.
baa [ba:], v.n. blöken.
babble [bæbl], v.n. schwatzen, schwätzen. — s. das Geschwätz; das Murmeln (water).
babe, baby [beib, 'beibi], s. der Säugling, das Baby, das kleine Kind, das Kindlein.
baboon [bə'bu:n], s. (Zool.) der Pavian.
bachelor ['bætʃələ], s. der Junggeselle; (Univ.) Bakkalaureus.
back [bæk], s. der Rücken, die Rückseite. — adj. Hinter-, Rück-; — door, die Hintertür; — stairs, die Hintertreppe. — adv. rückwärts, zurück. — v.a. unterstützen; (Comm.) indossieren; gegenzeichnen; wetten auf (Acc.) (bet on).
backbone ['bækboun], s. (Anat.) das Rückgrat.
backfire ['bækfaiə], s. (Motor.) die Frühzündung; (gun) die Fehlzündung. — [bæk'faiə], v.n. (Motor.) frühzünden; (gun) fehlzünden.

backgammon [bæk'gæmən], s. das Bordspiel, das Puffspiel.
background ['bækgraund], s. der Hintergrund.
backhand ['bækhænd], s. (Sport) die Rückhand; —ed compliment, eine verblümte Grobheit.
backside [bæk'said], s. (vulg.) der Hintere.
backslide [bæk'slaid], v.n. abfallen, abtrünnig werden.
backward ['bækwəd], adj. zurückgeblieben. **backward(s)** adv. rückwärts, zurück.
backwater ['bækwɔ:tə], s. das Stauwasser.
backwoods ['bækwudz], s. pl. der Hinterwald.
bacon ['beikən], s. der Speck.
bad [bæd], adj. schlecht, schlimm; böse (immoral); (coll.) unwohl (unwell); not too —, ganz gut; from — to worse, immer schlimmer; — language, unanständige Worte, das Fluchen; — luck, Unglück, Pech; want —ly, nötig brauchen.
badge [bædʒ], s. das Abzeichen; Kennzeichen (mark).
badger (1) ['bædʒə], s. (Zool.) der Dachs.
badger (2) ['bædʒə], v.a. ärgern, stören, belästigen.
badness ['bædnis], s. die Schlechtigkeit, Bosheit, das schlechte Wesen, die Bösartigkeit.
baffle [bæfl], v.a. täuschen, verblüffen. — s. (obs.) die Täuschung; (Build.) Verkleidung; (Elec.) Verteilerplatte.
bag [bæg], s. der Sack, Beutel; die Tasche; shopping —, Einkaufstasche; travelling —, Reisehandtasche. — v.a. einstecken, als Beute behalten (hunt).
bagatelle [bægə'tel], s. die Bagatelle, Lappalie, Kleinigkeit; das Kugelspiel (pin-table ball-game).
baggage ['bægidʒ], s. das Gepäck.
bagging ['bægiŋ], s. die Sackleinwand.
baggy ['bægi], adj. ungebügelt; bauschig.
bagpipe ['bægpaip], s. der Dudelsack.
bagpiper ['bægpaipə], s. der Dudelsackpfeifer.
bail [beil], s. der Bürge; die Bürgschaft; stand —, für einen bürgen; allow —, Bürgschaft zulassen. — v.a. Bürgschaft leisten; — out, (durch Kaution) in Freiheit setzen.
bailiff ['beilif], s. der Amtmann; Gerichtsvollzieher.
bait [beit], s. der Köder. — v.a. ködern, locken (attract).
baiter ['beitə], s. der Hetzer, Verfolger.
baiting ['beitiŋ], s. die Hetze.
bake [beik], v.a., v.n. backen.
baker ['beikə], s. der Bäcker; —'s dozen, 13 Stück.
bakery ['beikəri], s. die Bäckerei.
baking ['beikiŋ], s. das Backen.

balance

balance ['bæləns], s. die Waage (scales); die Bilanz (audit); das Gleichgewicht (equilibrium); (Comm.) der Saldo, der Überschuß (profit); die Unruhe (watch). — v.a., v.n. wägen, abwägen (scales); ausgleichen (— up), einen Saldo ziehen (— an account); ins Gleichgewicht bringen (bring into equilibrium).
balcony ['bælkəni], s. der Balkon, der Söller (castle); Altan (villa).
bald [bɔːld], adj. kahl, haarlos; (fig.) armselig, schmucklos.
baldness ['bɔːldnis], s. die Kahlheit (hairlessness); Nacktheit (bareness).
bale (1) [beil], s. der Ballen.
bale (2) [beil], v.n. — out, abspringen; aussteigen.
Balearic Islands [bæli'ærik ailəndz], s. pl. die Balearen, Balearischen Inseln. — adj. balearisch.
baleful ['beilful], adj. unheilvoll.
balk [bɔːk], v.a. aufhalten, hemmen. — v.n. scheuen, zurückscheuen (at, vor).
ball (1) [bɔːl], s. der Ball; die Kugel; — cock, der Absperrhahn; —point pen, der Kugelschreiber.
ball (2) [bɔːl], s. der Ball (dance).
ballad ['bæləd], s. die Ballade.
ballast ['bæləst], s. der Ballast.
ballet ['bælei], s. das Ballett.
balloon [bə'luːn], s. der Ballon.
ballot ['bælət], s. die geheime Wahl, Abstimmung; —-box, die Wahlurne; —-paper, der Stimmzettel. —v.n. wählen, abstimmen.
balm [bɑːm], s. der Balsam.
balsam ['bɔːlsəm], s. der Balsam.
Baltic ['bɔːltik], adj. baltisch. — (Sea), die Ostsee; — Provinces, das Baltikum, die baltischen Provinzen.
balustrade ['bæləstreid], s. die Balustrade, das Geländer.
bamboo [bæm'buː], s. (Bot.) der Bambus.
bamboozle [bæm'buːzl], v.a. verblüffen; beschwindeln (cheat).
ban [bæn], v.a. bannen, verbannen; verbieten. — s. der Bann, das Verbot.
banal [bæ'næl, 'beinəl], adj. banal.
banality [bæ'næliti], s. die Banalität, Trivialität.
banana [bə'nɑːnə], s. die Banane.
band [bænd], s. das Band (ribbon etc.); (Mus.) die Kapelle; die Bande (robbers). — v.n. — together, sich verbinden; sich zusammentun.
bandage ['bændidʒ], s. der Verband, die Bandage.
bandit ['bændit], s. der Bandit.
bandmaster ['bændmɑːstə], s. der Kapellmeister.
bandstand ['bændstænd], s. der Musikpavillon.
bandy ['bændi], adj. -legged, krummbeinig. — v.a. — words, Worte wechseln; streiten.
bane [bein], s. das Gift; (fig.) Verderben.
baneful ['beinful], adj. verderblich.

bang [bæŋ], s. der Knall (explosion), das Krachen (clap). — v.n. knallen, krachen lassen. — v.a. — a door, eine Türe zuwerfen.
banish ['bæniʃ], v.a. verbannen, bannen.
banisters ['bænistəz], s. pl. das Treppengeländer.
bank [bæŋk], s. (Fin.) die Bank; das Ufer (river); der Damm (dam). — v.a. einlegen, einzahlen, auf die Bank bringen (sum of money); eindämmen (dam up). — v.n. ein Konto haben (have an account, with, bei).
banker ['bæŋkə], s. der Bankier.
bankrupt ['bæŋkrʌpt], adj. bankrott; zahlungsunfähig; (coll.) pleite.
bankruptcy ['bæŋkrʌptsi], s. der Bankrott.
banns [bænz], s. pl. das Heiratsaufgebot.
banquet ['bæŋkwit], s. das Bankett, Festessen.
bantam ['bæntəm], s. das Bantamhuhn, Zwerghuhn; (Boxing) —-weight, das Bantamgewicht.
banter ['bæntə], v.n. scherzen, necken. — s. das Scherzen, der Scherz.
baptism ['bæptizm], s. die Taufe.
Baptist ['bæptist], s. der Täufer; Baptist.
baptize [bæp'taiz], v.a. taufen.
bar [bɑː], s. die Barre, Stange (pole); der Riegel; Balken; Schlagbaum (barrier); (fig.) das Hindernis; der Schanktisch (in public house); prisoner at the —, Gefangener vor (dem) Gericht; call to the —, zur Gerichtsadvokatur (or als Anwalt) zulassen; (Mus.) der Takt. — v.a. verriegeln (door); (fig.) hindern (from action); verbieten (prohibit); ausschließen (exclude).
barb [bɑːb], s. die Spitze (of wire); der Widerhaken (hook).
barbed [bɑːbd], adj. spitzig; — remark, die spitze Bemerkung; — wire, der Stacheldraht.
barbarian [bɑː'bɛəriən], s. der Barbar. — adj. barbarisch.
barbarism ['bɑːbərizm], s. die Roheit; der Barbarismus.
barber ['bɑːbə], s. der Barbier, Friseur.
barberry ['bɑːbəri], s. (Bot.) die Berberitze.
bard [bɑːd], s. der Barde, Sänger.
bare [bɛə], adj. nackt, bloß; — -headed, barhäuptig. —v.a. entblößen.
barefaced ['bɛəfeisd], adj. schamlos.
barely ['bɛəli], adv. kaum.
bargain ['bɑːgin], s. der Kauf, Gelegenheitskauf; der Handel (trading); das Geschäft; into the —, noch dazu, obendrein. — v.n. feilschen, handeln (haggle) (for, um).
barge [bɑːdʒ], s. der Lastkahn, die Barke. — v.n. (coll.) — in, stören.
bargee [bɑː'dʒiː], s. der Flußschiffer, Bootsmann.
baritone ['bæritoun], s. (Mus.) der Bariton.

beam

bark (1) [ba:k], *s.* die Rinde (*of tree*).
bark (2) [ba:k], *v.n.* bellen (*dog*); — *up the wrong tree*, auf falscher Fährte sein. — *s.* das Gebell (*dog*).
barley ['ba:li], *s.* (*Bot.*) die Gerste.
barmaid ['ba:meid], *s.* die Kellnerin.
barman ['ba:mən], *s.* der Kellner.
barn [ba:n], *s.* die Scheune; — *owl*, die Schleiereule.
barnacle ['ba:nəkl], *s.* die Entenmuschel; die Klette.
barnstormer ['ba:nstɔ:mə], *s.* der Schmierenkomödiant.
barometer [bə'rɔmitə], *s.* das Barometer.
baron ['bærən], *s.* der Baron, Freiherr.
barony ['bærəni], *s.* die Baronswürde.
baroque [bə'rɔk], *adj.* barock. — *s.* das Barock.
barque [ba:k], *s.* die Bark.
barracks ['bærəks], *s. pl.* die Kaserne.
barrage ['bæra:ʒ, 'bæridʒ], *s.* das Sperrfeuer (*firing*); das Wehr, der Damm.
barrel ['bærəl], *s.* das Faß (*vat*), die Tonne (*tun*); der Gewehrlauf (*rifle*); die Trommel (*cylinder*); — *organ*, die Drehorgel.
barren ['bærən], *adj.* unfruchtbar, dürr.
barrenness ['bærənnis], *s.* die Unfruchtbarkeit.
barricade [bæri'keid], *s.* die Barrikade. — *v.a.* verrammeln, verschanzen.
barrier ['bæriə], *s.* die Barriere, der Schlagbaum; das Hindernis; (*Railw.*) die Schranke.
barrister ['bæristə], *s.* der Rechtsanwalt, Advokat.
barrow (1) ['bærou], *s.* der Schubkarren, Handkarren; — *-boy*, der Höker, Schnellverkäufer.
barrow (2) ['bærou], *s.* (*Archaeol.*) das Hünengrab, Heldengrab.
barter ['ba:tə], *v.a.* tauschen, austauschen. — *s.* der Tauschhandel.
Bartholomew [ba:'θɔləmju:]. Bartholomäus, *m.*; *Massacre of St. Bartholomew's Eve*, Bartholomäusnacht, Pariser Bluthochzeit.
basalt ['bæsɔ:lt, bæ'sɔ:lt], *s.* der Basalt.
base [beis], *s.* die Basis, Grundlage; der Sockel; (*Chem.*) die Base. — *adj.* niedrig, gemein; (*Metall.*) unedel. — *v.a.* basieren, beruhen, fundieren (*upon*, auf).
baseless ['beislis], *adj.* grundlos.
basement ['beismənt], *s.* das Kellergeschoß.
baseness ['beisnis], *s.* die Gemeinheit, Niedrigkeit.
bashful ['bæʃful], *adj.* verschämt, schamhaft, schüchtern.
basic ['beisik], *adj.* grundlegend.
basin ['beisən], *s.* das Becken.
basis ['beisis], *s.* die Basis, Grundlage.
bask [ba:sk], *v.n.* sich sonnen.
basket ['ba:skit], *s.* der Korb.
bass (1) [beis], *s.* (*Mus.*) der Baß, die Baßstimme.

bass (2) [bæs], *s.* (*Zool.*) der Barsch.
bassoon [bə'su:n], *s.* (*Mus.*) das Fagott.
bastard ['bæstəd], *s.* der Bastard.
baste [beist], *v.a.* mit Fett begießen (*roast meat*); (*coll.*) prügeln.
bastion ['bæstiən], *s.* die Bastion, Festung, das Bollwerk.
bat (1) [bæt], *s.* die Fledermaus.
bat (2) [bæt], *s.* der Schläger. — *v.n.* (den Ball) schlagen; (*cricket*) am Schlagen sein (*be batting*).
batch [bætʃ], *s.* der Stoß (*pile*); di‘ Menge (*people*); (*Mil.*) der Trupp.
bath [ba:θ], *s.* das Bad; (*Am.*) — *robe*, der Schlafrock, Bademantel; — *tub*, die Badewanne.
bathe [beið], *v.n.* baden; *bathing pool*, das Schwimmbad; *bathing suit*, der Badeanzug.
batman ['bætmən], *s.* der Offiziersbursche.
baton ['bætən], *s.* der Stab.
batsman ['bætsmən], *s.* der Schläger (*cricket*).
batten [bætn], *s.* die Holzlatte. — *v.a.* mästen, füttern. — *v.n.* fett werden.
batter ['bætə], *s.* der Schlagteig. — *v.a.* schlagen, zertrümmern; —*ing ram*, (*Mil.*) der Sturmbock.
battery ['bætəri], *s.* die Batterie.
battle [bætl], *s.* die Schlacht; —*cruiser*, der Schlachtkreuzer; —*ship*, das Schlachtschiff. — *v.n.* kämpfen (*for*, um).
Bavarian [bə'vɛəriən], *adj.* bayrisch. — *s.* der Bayer.
bawl [bɔ:l], *v.n.* plärren, schreien.
bay (1) [bei], *adj.* rötlich braun.
bay (2) [bei], *s.* die Bucht, Bai; — *window*, das Erkerfenster.
bay (3) [bei], *s. keep at —*, in Schach halten, *stand at —*, sich zur Wehr setzen.
bay (4) [bei], *s.* (*Bot.*) der Lorbeer.
bay (5) [bei], *v.n.* bellen, heulen; — *for the moon*, das Unmögliche wollen.
bayonet ['beiənet], *s.* das Bajonett.
bazaar [bə'za:], *s.* der Basar.
be [bi:], *v.n. irr.* sein, existieren; sich befinden; vorhanden sein; — *off*, sich fortmachen (*move*); ungenießbar sein (*meat, food*); nicht mehr da sein (— *off the menu*).
beach [bi:tʃ], *s.* der Strand, die Gestade.
beacon ['bi:kən], *s.* das Leuchtfeuer; der Leuchtturm; das Lichtsignal.
bead [bi:d], *s.* das Tröpfchen (*drop*); die Perle (*pearl*); (*pl.*) die Perlschnur; der Rosenkranz.
beadle [bi:dl], *s.* (*Univ.*) der Pedell; (*Eccl.*) Kirchendiener.
beagle [bi:gl], *s.* der Jagdhund, Spürhund.
beak [bi:k], *s.* der Schnabel.
beaker ['bi:kə], *s.* der Becher.
beam [bi:m], *s.* der Balken (*wood*); der Strahl (*ray*), Glanz. — *v.n.* strahlen.

319

bean [biːn], *s.* (*Bot.*) die Bohne; *not* a —, keinen Heller *or* Pfennig.
bear (1) [bɛə], *s.* (*Zool.*) der Bär.
bear (2) [bɛə], *v.a. irr.* tragen, ertragen; gebären (*a child*); hegen (*sorrow etc.*). — *v.n.* — *upon*, drücken auf (*pressure*), Einfluß haben (*effect*); — *up*, geduldig sein.
bearable [ˈbɛərəbl], *adj.* tragbar, erträglich.
beard [biəd], *s.* der Bart. — *v.a.* trotzen (*Dat.*).
bearded [ˈbiədid], *adj.* bärtig.
bearer [ˈbɛərə], *s.* der Träger, Überbringer.
bearing [ˈbɛəriŋ], *s.* das Benehmen, die Haltung (*manner*); (*pl.*) (*Geog.*) die Richtung; *lose o.'s* —*s*, sich verlaufen; *ball* —*s*, (*Engin.*) das Kugellager.
bearpit [ˈbɛəpit], *s.* der Bärenzwinger.
beast [biːst], *s.* das Tier; die Bestie.
beastliness [ˈbiːstlinis], *s.* das tierische Benehmen; die Grausamkeit (*cruelty*); die Gemeinheit.
beastly [ˈbiːstli], *adj.* grausam, (*coll.*) schrecklich.
beat [biːt], *s.* der Schlag, das Schlagen; (*Mus.*) der Takt; die Runde, das Revier (*patrol district*). — *v.a. irr.* schlagen; — *time*, den Takt schlagen; — *carpets*, Teppich klopfen. — *v.n.* — *it*, sich davonmachen.
beater [ˈbiːtə], *s.* (*Hunt.*) der Treiber.
beatify [biːˈætifai], *v.a.* seligsprechen.
beau [bou], *s.* der Stutzer, Geck.
beautiful [ˈbjuːtiful], *adj.* schön.
beautify [ˈbjuːtifai], *v.a.* schön machen, verschönern.
beauty [ˈbjuːti], *s.* die Schönheit; — *salon*, der Schönheitssalon; *Sleeping Beauty*, das Dornröschen.
beaver [ˈbiːvə], *s.* (*Zool.*) der Biber.
becalm [biˈkɑːm], *v.a.* besänftigen.
because [biˈkɔz], *conj.* weil, da; — *of*, wegen, um ... willen.
beck [bek], *s.* der Wink; *be at s.o.'s* — *and call*, jemandem zu Gebote stehen.
beckon [ˈbekən], *v.a., v.n.* winken, heranwinken, zuwinken (*Dat.*).
become [biˈkʌm], *v.n. irr.* werden. — *v.a.* anstehen, sich schicken, passen (*Dat.*).
becoming [biˈkʌmiŋ], *adj.* passend, kleidsam.
bed [bed], *s.* das Bett; Beet (*flowers*); (*Geol.*) das Lager, die Schicht. — *v.a.* betten, einbetten.
bedaub [biˈdɔːb], *v.a.* beflecken, beschmieren.
bedding [ˈbediŋ], *s.* das Bettzeug.
bedevil [biˈdevəl], *v.a.* behexen, verhexen.
bedew [biˈdjuː], *v.a.* betauen.
bedlam [ˈbedləm], *s.* (*coll.*) das Irrenhaus; *this is* —, die Hölle ist los.
Bedouin [ˈbeduin], *s.* der Beduine.
bedpost [ˈbedpoust], *s.* der Bettpfosten.
bedraggle [biˈdrægl], *v.a.* beschmutzen.

bedridden [ˈbedridn], *adj.* bettlägerig, ans Bett gefesselt.
bedroom [ˈbedruːm], *s.* das Schlafzimmer.
bedtime [ˈbedtaim], *s.* die Schlafenszeit.
bee [biː], *s.* (*Ent.*) die Biene; *have a* — *in o.'s bonnet*, einen Vogel haben.
beech [biːtʃ], *s.* (*Bot.*) die Buche.
beef [biːf], *s.* das Rindfleisch; — *tea*, die Fleischbrühe.
beehive [ˈbiːhaiv], *s.* der Bienenkorb.
beeline [ˈbiːlain], *s.* die Luftlinie, gerade Linie; *make a* — *for s.th.*, schnurstracks auf etwas losgehen.
beer [biə], *s.* das Bier; *small* —, Dünnbier, (*fig.*) unbedeutend.
beet [biːt], *s.* (*Bot.*) die Runkelrübe; *sugar* —, die Zuckerrübe.
beetle [biːtl], *s.* (*Ent.*) der Käfer; — *brows*, buschige Augenbrauen.
beetroot [ˈbiːtruːt], *s.* (*Bot.*) die rote Rübe.
befall [biˈfɔːl], *v.a. irr.* widerfahren (*Dat.*). — *v.n.* zustoßen (*happen, Dat.*).
befit [biˈfit], *v.a.* sich geziemen, sich gebühren.
befog [biˈfɔg], *v.a.* in Nebel hüllen; umnebeln.
before [biˈfɔː], *adv.* vorn; voraus, voran; (*previously*) vorher, früher; (*already*) bereits, schon. — *prep.* vor. — *conj.* bevor, ehe.
beforehand [biˈfɔːhænd], *adv.* im voraus, vorher.
befoul [biˈfaul], *v.a.* beschmutzen.
befriend [biˈfrend], *v.a.* befreunden, unterstützen (*request*).
beg [beg], *v.a., v.n.* betteln (um, *for*); ersuchen, bitten (*request*).
beget [biˈget], *v.a. irr.* zeugen.
beggar [ˈbegə], *s.* der Bettler.
begin [biˈgin], *v.a., v.n. irr.* beginnen, anfangen.
beginner [biˈginə], *s.* der Anfänger.
beginning [biˈginiŋ], *s.* der Anfang.
begone ! [biˈgɔn], *interj.* hinweg! fort! mach dich fort!
begrudge [biˈgrʌdʒ], *v.a.* nicht gönnen, mißgönnen.
beguile [biˈgail], *v.a.* bestricken, betrügen; — *the time*, die Zeit vertreiben.
behalf [biˈhɑːf], *s. on* — *of*, um ... (*Genit.*) willen; im Interesse von, im Namen von.
behave [biˈheiv], *v.n.* sich benehmen, sich betragen.
behaviour [biˈheivjə], *s.* das Benehmen, Gebaren.
behead [biˈhed], *v.a.* enthaupten.
behind [biˈhaind], *adv.* hinten, zurück, hinterher. — *prep.* hinter.
behindhand [biˈhaindhænd], *adj., adv.* im Rückstand (*in arrears*); zurück (*backward*).
behold [biˈhould], *v.a. irr.* ansehen; er blicken; *lo and* — *!* siehe da!
beholden [biˈhouldən], *adj.* verpflichtet (*to, Dat.*).
beholder [biˈhouldə], *s.* der Zuschauer.

behove [bi'houv], v.a. sich geziemen, ziemen, gebühren.

being ['bi:iŋ], pres. part for the time —, vorläufig, für jetzt. — s. das Sein, die Existenz; das Wesen (creature).

belated [bi'leitid], adj. verspätet.

belch [beltʃ], v.n. rülpsen, aufstoßen.

belfry ['belfri], s. der Glockenturm.

Belgian ['beldʒən], adj. belgisch. — s. der Belgier.

belie [bi'lai], v.a. täuschen, Li.gen strafen.

belief [bi'li:f], s. der Glaube, die Meinung.

believable [bi'li:vəbl], adj. glaubhaft, glaublich.

believe [bi'li:v], v.a., v.n. glauben (an, Acc.), vertrauen (Dat.).

believer [bi'li:və], s. der Gläubige.

belittle [bi'litl], v.a. schmälern, verkleinern, verächtlich machen.

bell [bel], s. die Glocke; Schelle, Klingel; — -founder, der Glockengießer; — -boy, (Am.) — -hop, der Hotelpage.

belligerent [bi'lidʒərənt], adj. kriegführend. — s. der Kriegführende.

bellow ['belou], v.n. brüllen. — s. das Gebrüll.

bellows ['belouz], s. der Blasebalg.

belly ['beli], s. der Bauch.

belong [bi'lɔŋ], v.n. gehören (Dat.), angehören (Dat.).

belongings [bi'lɔŋiŋz], s. pl. die Habe, das Hab und Gut, der Besitz.

beloved [bi'lʌvd, -vid], adj. geliebt, lieb.

below [bi'lou], adv. unten. — prep. unterhalb (Genit.), unter (Dat.).

Belshazzar [bel'ʃæzə]. Belsazar, m.

belt [belt], s. der Gürtel, Gurt; der Riemen; (Tech.) Treibriemen; below the —, unfair. — v.a. umgürten; (coll.) prügeln.

bemoan [bi'moun], v.a. beklagen.

bench [bentʃ], s. die Bank; der Gerichtshof (court of law); Queen's Bench, der oberste Gerichtshof.

bend [bend], v.a., v.n. irr. biegen; beugen; sich krümmen. — s. die Biegung, Krümmung, Kurve.

bendable ['bendəbl], adj. biegsam.

beneath [bi'ni:θ] see below.

Benedictine [beni'dikti:n], s. der Benediktiner.

benediction [beni'dikʃən], s. der Segensspruch, der Segen; die Segnung.

benefaction [benif'ækʃən], s. die Wohltat.

benefactor ['benifæktə], s. der Wohltäter.

benefactress ['benifæktris], s. die Wohltäterin.

beneficent [be'nefisənt], adj. wohltätig.

beneficial [beni'fiʃəl], adj. vorteilhaft, gut (for, für), wohltuend.

benefit ['benifit], s. der Vorteil, Nutzen. — v.n. Nutzen ziehen. — v.a. nützen.

benevolence [be'nevələns], s. das Wohlwollen.

benevolent [be'nevələnt], adj. wohlwollend; — society, der Unterstützungsverein, — fund, der Unterstützungsfond.

Bengali [ben'gɔ:li], adj. bengalisch. — s. der Bengale.

benign [bi'nain], adj. gütig, mild.

bent [bent], adj. gebogen, krumm; — on something, versessen auf etwas. — s. die Neigung, der Hang; — for, Vorliebe für.

benzene ['benzi:n], s. das Benzol, Kohlenbenzin.

benzine ['benzi:n], s. das Benzin.

bequeath [bi'kwi:θ], v.a. vermachen, hinterlassen.

bequest [bi'kwest], s. das Vermächtnis.

bereave [bi'ri:v], v.a. irr. berauben (durch Tod).

bereavement [bi'ri:vmənt], s. der Verlust (durch Tod).

beret ['berei], s. die Baskenmütze.

Bernard ['bə:nəd]. Bernhard, m.; St. — dog, der Bernhardiner.

berry ['beri], s. die Beere.

berth [bə:θ], s. (Naut.) der Ankerplatz; die Koje. — v.a., v.n. anlegen; vor Anker gehen (boat).

beseech [bi'si:tʃ], v.a. irr. bitten, anflehen.

beset [bi'set], v.a. irr. bedrängen, bedrücken, umringen.

beside [bi'said], prep. außer, neben, nahe bei; — the point, unwesentlich; quite — the mark, weit vom Schuß.

besides [bi'saidz], adv. überdies, außerdem.

besiege [bi'si:dʒ], v.a. belagern.

besmirch [bi'smə:tʃ], v.a. besudeln.

besom ['bi:zəm], s. der Besen.

bespatter [bi'spætə], v. a. bespritzen.

bespeak [bi'spi:k], v.a. irr. bestellen; (Tail.) bespoke, nach Maß gemacht or gearbeitet.

best [best], adj. (superl. of good) best; — adv. am besten. — s. want the — of both worlds, alles haben wollen; to the — of my ability, nach besten Kräften; to the — of my knowledge, soviel ich weiß.

bestial ['bestjəl], adj. bestialisch, tierisch.

bestow [bi'stou], v.a. verleihen, erteilen.

bet [bet], s. die Wette. — v.a., v.n. irr. wetten.

betray [bi'trei], v.a. verraten.

betrayal [bi'treiəl], s. der Verrat.

betrayer [bi'treiə], s. der Verräter.

betroth [bi'trouð], v.a. verloben.

betrothal [bi'trouðəl], s. die Verlobung.

better ['betə], adj. (comp. of good) besser. — adv. you had — go, es wäre besser, Sie gingen; think — of it, sich eines Besseren besinnen, sich's überlegen. — s. get the — of, überwinden; so much the —, desto or umso besser. — v.a. verbessern; — oneself, seine Lage verbessern.

betterment

betterment ['betəmənt], s. die Verbesserung.
between [bi'twi:n], adv. dazwischen. — prep. zwischen; unter (among).
bevel ['bevəl], s. der Winkelpasser; die Schräge. — v.a. abkanten.
beverage ['bevəridʒ], s. das Getränk.
bevy ['bevi], s. die Schar (of beauties, von Schönen).
bewail [bi'weil], v.a., v.n. betrauern, beweinen; trauern um.
beware [bi'wɛə], v.n. sich hüten (of, vor).
bewilder [bi'wildə], v.a. verwirren.
bewitch [bi'witʃ], v.a. bezaubern.
beyond [bi'jɔnd], adv. jenseits, drüben. — prep. über ... hinaus; jenseits; außer.
biannual [bai'ænjuəl], adj. halbjährlich.
bias ['baiəs], s. die Neigung; das Vorurteil (prejudice). — v.a. beeinflussen.
bias(s)ed ['baiəsd], adj. voreingenommen.
bib [bib], s. der Schürzenlatz; das Lätzchen.
Bible [baibl], s. die Bibel.
Biblical ['biblikəl], adj. biblisch.
bibliography [bibli'ɔgrəfi], s. die Bibliographie.
bibliophile ['bibliɔfail], s. der Bücherfreund.
biceps ['baiseps], s. der Bizeps, Armmuskel.
bicker ['bikə], v.n. zanken, hadern.
bickering ['bikəriŋ], s. das Gezänk, Hadern, der Hader.
bicycle ['baisikl], (coll.) **bike** [baik], s. das Fahrrad.
bicyclist ['baisiklist], s. der Radfahrer.
bid [bid], v.a., v.n. irr. gebieten, befehlen (Dat.) (order); bieten (at auction); — farewell, Lebewohl sagen. — s. das Gebot, Angebot (at auction).
bidding ['bidiŋ], s. der Befehl (order); das Bieten (at auction); die Einladung (invitation).
bide [baid], v.n. irr. verbleiben, verharren (in, by, bei).
biennial [bai'eniəl], adj. zweijährig, alle zwei Jahre.
bier [biə], s. die Bahre, Totenbahre.
big [big], adj. groß, dick (fat); talking —, großsprecherisch; talk —, prahlen.
bigamy ['bigəmi], s. die Bigamie, die Doppelehe.
bigness ['bignis], s. die Größe, Dicke.
bigoted ['bigətid], adj. bigott, fanatisch.
bigotry ['bigətri], s. die Bigotterie.
bigwig ['bigwig], s. (coll.) die vornehme Person, der Würdenträger.
bike see **bicycle**.
bilberry ['bilbəri], s. (Bot.) die Heidelbeere.
bile [bail], s. die Galle.
bilge [bildʒ], s. die Bilge, der Schiffsboden; (coll.) Unsinn (nonsense).
bilious ['biljəs], adj. gallig.
bill (1) [bil], s. der Schnabel (bird).

bill (2) [bil], die Rechnung (account); — of exchange, der Wechsel; — of entry, die Zolldeklaration; — of fare, die Speisekarte; (Parl.) der Gesetzentwurf; das Plakat (poster). — v.a. anzeigen.
billboard ['bilbɔ:d], s. (Am.) das Anschlagbrett.
billet ['bilit], s. das Billett (card); Quartier, die Unterkunft (army).
billfold ['bilfould], s. (Am.) die Brieftasche.
billhook ['bilhuk], s. die Hippe.
billiards ['biljədz], s. das Billardspiel.
billow ['bilou], s. die Woge. — v.n. wogen.
bin [bin], s. der Behälter.
bind [baind], v.a. irr. binden, verpflichten; (Law) — over, zu gutem Benehmen verpflichten.
binder ['baində], s. der Binder, Buchbinder.
bindery ['baindəri], s. die Buchbinderei, Binderwerkstatt.
binding ['baindiŋ], s. der Einband.
binnacle ['binəkl], s. das Kompaßhäuschen.
binocular [bi'nɔkjulə], adj. für beide Augen. — s. (pl.) das Fernglas, der Feldstecher.
binomial [bai'noumiəl], adj. binomisch. — s. (pl.) (Maths.) das Binom, der zweigliedrige Ausdruck.
biochemical [baio'kemikəl], adj. biochemisch.
biochemistry [baio'kemistri], s. die Biochemie.
biographer [bai'ɔgrəfə], s. der Biograph.
biographical [baio'græfikəl], adj. biographisch.
biography [bai'ɔgrəfi], s. die Biographie, die Lebensbeschreibung.
biological [baio'lɔdʒikəl], adj. biologisch.
biology [bai'ɔlədʒi], s. die Biologie.
biometric(al) [baio'metrik(əl)], adj. biometrisch.
biometry [bai'ɔmitri], s. die Biometrie.
biophysical [baio'fizikəl], adj. biophysisch.
biophysics [baio'fiziks], s. die Biophysik.
biped ['baiped], s. der Zweifüßler.
biplane ['baiplein], s. (Aviat.) der Doppeldecker.
birch [bə:tʃ], s. (Bot.) die Birke; die Birkenrute, Rute (cane). — v.a. (mit der Rute) züchtigen.
bird [bə:d], s. der Vogel; — of passage, der Wandervogel, Zugvogel; —cage, der Vogelkäfig, das Vogelbauer; —fancier, der Vogelzüchter; —'s-eye view, die Vogelperspektive.
birth [bə:θ], s. die Geburt; — certificate, der Geburtsschein.
birthday ['bə:θdei], s, der Geburtstag.
biscuit ['biskit], s. der or das Keks; der Zwieback.

bisect [bai'sekt], *v.a.* entzweischneiden, halbieren.

bisection [bai'sekʃən], *s.* die Zweiteilung, Halbierung.

bishop ['biʃəp], *s.* der Bischof; (*Chess*) der Läufer.

bishopric ['biʃəprik], *s.* das Bistum.

bismuth ['bizməθ], *s.* der *or* das Wismut.

bison ['baisən], *s.* (*Zool.*) der Bison.

bit [bit], *s.* der Bissen (*bite*), das Bißchen (*little* —); das Gebiß (*bridle*); der Bart (*of key*).

bitch [bitʃ], *s.* die Hündin.

bite [bait], *v.a. irr.* beißen. — *s.* das Beißen (*mastication*); der Biß (*morsel*).

biting ['baitiŋ], *adj.* (*also fig.*) beißend, scharf. — *adv.* — *cold*, bitterkalt.

bitter ['bitə], *adj.* bitter.

bitterness ['bitənis], *s.* die Bitterkeit.

bittern ['bitə:n], *s.* (*Orn.*) die Rohrdommel.

bitumen [bi'tju:mən], *s.* der Bergteer, Asphalt.

bivouac ['bivuæk], *s.* (*Mil.*) das Biwak, Lager.

bizarre [bi'za:], *adj.* bizarr, wunderlich.

blab [blæb], *v.a., v.n.* schwatzen, ausplaudern (*give away*).

blabber ['blæbə], *s.* (*coll.*) der Schwätzer.

black [blæk], *adj.* schwarz; — *sheep*, der Taugenichts; — *pudding*, die Blutwurst; *Black Forest*, der Schwarzwald; *Black Maria*, der Polizeiwagen; (*coll.*) die grüne Minna; *Black Sea*, das schwarze Meer.

blackberry ['blækbəri], *s.* (*Bot.*) die Brombeere.

blackbird ['blækbə:d], *s.* (*Orn.*) die Amsel.

blackguard ['blæga:d], *s.* der Spitzbube, Schurke.

blackmail ['blækmeil], *v.a.* erpressen. — *s.* die Erpressung.

bladder ['blædə], *s.* (*Anat.*) die Blase.

blacksmith ['blæksmiθ], *s.* der Grobschmied.

blade [bleid], *s.* die Klinge (*razor*); der Halm (*grass*); *shoulder* —, das Schulterblatt.

blamable ['bleiməbl], *adj.* tadelnswert, tadelhaft.

blame [bleim], *s.* der Tadel, die Schuld. — *v.a.* tadeln, beschuldigen, die Schuld zuschreiben (*Dat.*).

blameless ['bleimlis], *adj.* tadellos, schuldlos.

blanch [bla:ntʃ], *v.n.* erbleichen, weiß werden. — *v.a.* weiß machen.

bland [blænd], *adj.* mild, sanft.

blandish ['blændiʃ], *v.a.* schmeicheln (*Dat.*).

blandishment ['blændiʃmənt], *s.* (*mostly in pl.*) die Schmeichelei.

blandness ['blændnis], *s.* die Milde, Sanftheit.

blank [blæŋk], *adj.* blank, leer; reimlos (*verse*); *leave a* —, einen Raum freilassen; — *cartridge*, die Platzpatrone.

blanket ['blæŋkit], *s.* die Decke; (*coll.*) *a wet* —, ein langweiliger Kerl, der Spielverderber.

blare [blɛə], *v.n.* schmettern.

blaspheme [blæs'fi:m], *v.a., v.n.* lästern, fluchen.

blasphemous ['blæsfiməs], *adj.* lästerlich.

blasphemy ['blæsfəmi], *s.* die Gotteslästerung.

blast [bla:st], *v.a.* sprengen, zerstören. — *s.* der Windstoß (*gust*); der Stoß (*trumpets*); die Explosion (*bomb*); — *furnace*, der Hochofen. — *excl.* (*sl.*) —! zum Teufel!

blasting ['bla:stiŋ], *s.* das Sprengen.

blatant ['bleitənt], *adj.* laut, lärmend; dreist.

blaze [bleiz], *s.* die Flamme (*flame*); das Feuer; der Glanz (*colour etc.*). — *v.n.* flammen; leuchten (*shine*). — *v.a.* ausposaunen, bekannt machen (*make known*).

blazer ['bleizə], *s.* die Sportjacke, Klubjacke.

blazon ['bleizən], *v.a.* verkünden.

bleach [bli:tʃ], *v.a.* bleichen. — *s.* das Bleichmittel.

bleak [bli:k], *adj.* öde, rauh; trübe, freudlos.

bleakness ['bli:knis], *s.* die Öde (*scenery*); Traurigkeit, Trübheit.

bleary ['bliəri], *adj.* trübe; — *eyed*, triefäugig.

bleat [bli:t], *v.n.* blöken.

bleed [bli:d], *v.n. irr.* bluten. — *v.a.* bluten lassen; erpressen (*blackmail*).

blemish ['blemiʃ], *s.* der Makel, der Fehler. — *v.a.* schänden, entstellen.

blench [blentʃ], *v.n.* zurückweichen, stutzen.

blend [blend], *v.a., v.n.* mischen, vermengen; sich mischen. — *s.* die Mischung, Vermischung.

bless [bles], *v.a.* segnen; beglücken; loben.

blessed [blest, 'blesid], *adj.* gesegnet, selig.

blessing ['blesiŋ], *s.* der Segen.

blight [blait], *s.* der Meltau. — *v.a.* verderben.

blind [blaind], *adj.* blind; — *man's buff*, Blinde Kuh; — *spot*, der schwache Punkt. — *s.* die Blende, das Rouleau; *Venetian* —, die Jalousie. — *v.a.* blind machen, täuschen.

blindfold ['blaindfould], *adj.* mit verbundenen Augen.

blindness ['blaindnis], *s.* die Blindheit.

blindworm ['blaindwə:m], *s.* (*Zool.*) die Blindschleiche.

blink [bliŋk], *s.* das Blinzeln. — *v.n.* blinzeln, blinken. — *v.a.* nicht sehen wollen.

blinkers ['bliŋkəz], *s. pl.* die Scheuklappen.

bliss [blis], *s.* die Wonne, Seligkeit.

blissful ['blisful], *adj.* wonnig, selig.

blister ['blistə], *s.* die Blase. — *v.n.* Blasen ziehen, Blasen bekommen.

blithe [blaið], *adj.* munter, lustig, fröhlich.
blitheness ['blaiðnis], *s.* die Munterkeit, Fröhlichkeit.
blizzard ['blizəd], *s.* der Schneesturm.
bloated ['bloutid], *adj.* aufgeblasen, aufgedunsen.
bloater ['bloutə], *s.* (*Zool.*) der Bückling.
blob [blɔb], *s.* der Kleks.
block [blɔk], *s.* der Block, Klotz (*wood*); Häuserblock (*houses*); — *letters*, große Druckschrift. — *v.a.* blockieren, hemmen (*hinder*); sperren (*road*).
blockade [blɔ'keid], *s.* die Blockade.
blockhead ['blɔkhed], *s.* der Dummkopf.
blonde [blɔnd], *adj.* blond. — *s.* die Blondine.
blood [blʌd], *s.* das Blut; — *vessel*, das Blutgefäß.
bloodcurdling ['blʌdkə:dliŋ], *adj.* haarsträubend.
bloodless ['blʌdlis], *adj.* blutlos, unblutig.
bloodthirsty ['blʌdθə:sti], *adj.* blutdürstig.
bloody ['blʌdi], *adj.* blutig; (*vulg.*) verflucht.
bloom [blu:m], *s.* die Blüte; die Blume. — *v.n.* blühen.
bloomers ['blu:məz], *s. pl.* altmodische Unterhosen für Damen.
blooming ['blu:miŋ], *adj.* blühend.
blossom ['blɔsəm], *s.* die Blüte. — *v.n.* blühen, Blüten treiben.
blot [blɔt], *s.* der Klecks; Fleck; (*fig.*) der Schandfleck. — *v.a.* beflecken; löschen (*ink*); — *out*, ausmerzen, austilgen; *blotting paper*, das Löschpapier.
blotch [blɔtʃ], *s.* der Hautfleck; die Pustel; der Klecks (*blot*).
blotter ['blɔtə], *s.* der Löscher.
blouse [blauz], *s.* die Bluse.
blow (1) [blou], *s.* der Schlag.
blow (2) [blou], *v.a. irr.* blasen; wehen; — *o.'s own trumpet*, prahlen; anfachen (*fire*); — *o.'s nose*, sich schneuzen. — *v.n.* schnaufen, keuchen; — *up*, in die Luft sprengen.
blower ['blouə], *s.* das Gebläse; der Bläser.
blowpipe ['bloupaip], *s.* das Lötrohr.
blubber ['blʌbə], *s.* der Walfischspeck, der Tran. — *v.n.* schluchzen, heulen, flennen.
bludgeon ['blʌdʒən], *s.* der Knüppel; die Keule (*club*). — *v.a.* niederschlagen.
blue [blu:], *adj.* blau; schwermütig (*sad*); — *blooded*, aus edlem Geblüte.
bluebell ['blu:bel], *s.* (*Bot.*) die Glockenblume.
bluebottle ['blu:bɔtl], *s.* (*Ent.*) die Schmeißfliege.
bluestocking ['blu:stɔkiŋ], *s.* der Blaustrumpf.

bluff [blʌf], *adj.* grob, schroff. — *s.* der Bluff, die Täuschung, der Trick. — *v.a.*, *v.n.* vortäuschen (*pretend*), bluffen; verblüffen (*deceive*).
blunder ['blʌndə], *s.* der Fehler, Schnitzer. — *v.n.* einen Fehler machen.
blunderer ['blʌndərə], *s.* der Tölpel.
blunderbuss ['blʌndəbʌs], *s.* die Donnerbüchse.
blunt [blʌnt], *adj.* stumpf (*edge*); offen (*speech*). — *v.a.* abstumpfen; verderben (*appetite*).
bluntness ['blʌntnis], *s.* die Stumpfheit (*edge*); die Derbheit (*speech*).
blur [blə:], *s.* der Fleck. — *v.a.* verwischen.
blurt [blə:t], *v.a.* — *out*, herausplatzen.
blush [blʌʃ], *v.n.* erröten. — *s.* die Schamröte, das Erröten.
bluster ['blʌstə], *s.* das Toben, Brausen. — *v.n.* toben, brausen.
blustering ['blʌstəriŋ], *adj.* lärmend, tobend.
boa ['bouə], *s.* (*Zool.*) die Boa.
boar [bɔ:], *s.* (*Zool.*) der Eber.
board [bɔ:d], *s.* das Brett (*wood*); die Tafel (*notice —*); die Verpflegung (*food*); — *and lodging*, die Vollpension; die Behörde, der Ausschuß (*officials*). — *v.a.* — *up*, vernageln, zumachen; — *someone*, verpflegen; — *a steamer*, an Bord gehen; — *ing school*, das Internat, das Pensionat.
boarder ['bɔ:də], *s.* der Internatsschüler; der Pensionär.
boast [boust], *v.n.* prahlen, sich rühmen. — *s.* der Stolz (*pride*).
boastful ['boustful], *adj.* prahlerisch.
boat [bout], *s.* das Boot; *rowing- —*, das Ruderboot; der Kahn.
bob [bɔb], *s.* der Knicks; (*coll.*) der Schilling. — *v.n.* baumeln; springen; *bobbed hair*, der Bubikopf.
bobbin ['bɔbin], *s.* die Spule, der Klöppel.
bobsleigh ['bɔbslei], *s.* der Bob(sleigh), Rennschlitten.
bodice ['bɔdis], *s.* das Mieder, Leibchen.
bodied ['bɔdid], *adj. suffix; able- —*, gesund, stark.
body ['bɔdi], *s.* der Körper; die Körperschaft (*organisation*).
bodyguard ['bɔdiga:d], *s.* die Leibwache.
Boer ['bouə], *s.* der Bure.
bog [bɔg], *s.* der Sumpf. — *v.a.* (*coll.*) — *down*, einsinken.
Bohemian [bo'hi:mjən], *s.* der Böhme. — *adj.* böhmisch; künstlerhaft.
boil (1) [bɔil], *v.a.*, *v.n.* kochen, sieden. — *s.* das Kochen; *—ing point*, der Siedepunkt.
boil (2) [bɔil], *s.* (*Med.*) die Beule, der Furunkel.
boisterous ['bɔistərəs], *adj.* ungestüm; laut (*noisy*).
boisterousness ['bɔistərəsnis], *s.* die Heftigkeit, Lautheit.

bold [bould], *adj.* kühn, dreist; *make —*, sich erkühnen.

boldness ['bouldnis], *s.* die Kühnheit, Dreistigkeit.

Bolivian [bə'livjən], *adj.* bolivianisch. *—s.* der Bolivianer.

bolster ['boulstə], *s.* das Polster, Kissen.

bolt [boult], *s.* der Bolzen, Riegel (*on door*); der Pfeil (*arrow*). *— v.a.* verriegeln (*bar*); verschlingen (*devour*). *— v.n.* davonlaufen (*run away*), durchgehen (*abscond*).

bomb [bɔm], *s.* die Bombe. *— v.a.* bombardieren.

bombard [bɔm'baːd], *v.a.* bombardieren.

bombardment [bɔm'baːdmənt], *s.* die Beschießung.

bombastic [bɔm'bæstik], *adj.* schwülstig, bombastisch (*style*).

bombproof ['bɔmpruːf], *adj.* bombensicher.

bond [bɔnd], *s.* das Band (*link*); die Schuldverschreibung (*debt*); *in —*, unter Zollverschluß; (*pl.*) die Fesseln (*fetters*). *— v.a.* (*Chem.*) binden; (*Comm.*) zollpflichtig erklären (*declare dutiable*).

bondage ['bɔndidʒ], *s.* die Knechtschaft.

bone [boun], *s.* der Knochen; die Gräte (*fish*); *— china*, feines Geschirr, das Porzellan; *— of contention*, der Zankapfel; *— dry*, staubtrocken; *— idle*, stinkfaul; *— lace*, die Klöppelspitze. *— v.a.* Knochen oder Gräten entfernen.

bonfire ['bɔnfaiə], *s.* das Freudenfeuer.

bonnet ['bɔnit], *s.* die Haube, das Häubchen.

bonny ['bɔni], *adj.* hübsch, nett.

bony ['bouni], *adj.* beinern, knöchern.

book [buk], *s.* das Buch. *— v.a.* belegen (*seat*); eine Karte lösen (*ticket*); engagieren (*engage*).

bookbinder ['bukbaində], *s.* der Buchbinder.

bookcase ['bukkeis], *s.* der Bücherschrank.

bookie see **bookmaker**.

booking-office ['bukiɳɔfis], *s.* der Fahrkartenschalter; die Kasse (*Theat. etc.*)

book-keeper ['bukiːpə], *s.* der Buchhalter.

book-keeping ['bukiːpiɳ], *s.* die Buchhaltung; *double entry —*, doppelte Buchführung, *single entry —*, einfache Buchführung.

bookmaker ['bukmeikə] (*abbr.* **bookie** ['buki]), *s.* (*Racing*) der Buchmacher.

bookmark(er) ['bukmaːk(ə)], *s.* das Lesezeichen.

bookseller ['buksɛlə], *s.* der Buchhändler.

bookshop ['bukʃɔp], *s.* die Buchhandlung.

bookstall ['bukstɔːl], *s.* der Bücherstand.

bookworm ['bukwəːm], *s.* der Bücherwurm.

boom (1) [buːm], *s.* der Aufschwung; Boom; (*Comm.*) die Konjunktur; Hausse.

boom (2) [buːm], *v.n.* dröhnen, (dumpf) schallen.

boon [buːn], *s.* die Wohltat.

boor [buə], *s.* der Lümmel.

boorish ['buəriʃ], *adj.* lümmelhaft.

boot [buːt], *s.* der Stiefel, hohe Schuh. *— v.a.* mit dem Stiefel stoßen, kicken.

booth [buːð], *s.* die Bude, Zelle (*Teleph.*).

bootlace ['buːtleis], *s.* der Schnürsenkel, der Schnürriemen.

booty ['buːti], *s.* die Beute.

booze [buːz], *v.n.* (*coll.*) saufen.

boozy ['buːzi], *adj.* (*coll.*) angeheitert, leicht betrunken.

border ['bɔːdə], *s.* der Rand; die Grenze. *— v.a.* angrenzen (*on*); einsäumen (*surround*).

borderer ['bɔːdərə], *s.* der Grenzbewohner.

bore [bɔː], *v.a.* bohren; langweilen (*be boring*). *— s.* das Bohrloch (*drill-hole*), die Bohrung (*drilling*); der langweilige Kerl (*person*).

boredom ['bɔːdəm], *s.* die Langeweile.

borer ['bɔːrə], *s.* der Bohrer (*drill*).

born [bɔːn], *adj.* geboren.

borrow ['bɔrou], *v.a.* borgen, entlehnen.

borrowing ['bɔrouiɳ], *s.* das Borgen, Entlehnen.

bosom ['buzəm], *s.* der Busen.

boss [bɔs], *s.* der Beschlag, der Buckel; (*coll.*) der Chef.

botanical [bɔ'tænikəl], *adj.* botanisch.

botanist ['bɔtənist], *s.* der Botaniker.

botany ['bɔtəni], *s.* die Botanik.

botch [bɔtʃ], *s.* das Flickwerk. *— v.a.* verderben, verhunzen.

both [bouθ], *adj.,* *pron.* beide, beides; *— of them*, beide. *— conj.* *. . . and*, sowohl *. . .* als auch.

bother ['bɔðə], *v.a.* plagen, stören, belästigen; *— it!* zum Henker damit! *— v.n.* sich bemühen. *— s.* die Belästigung, das Ärgernis.

bottle ['bɔtl], *s.* die Flasche. *— v.a.* in Flaschen abfüllen.

bottom ['bɔtəm], *s.* der Boden, Grund (*ground*); die Ursache (*cause*); (*Naut.*) der Schiffsboden.

bottomless ['bɔtəmlis], *adj.* grundlos, bodenlos.

bough [bau], *s.* der Zweig, Ast.

boulder ['bouldə], *s.* der Felsblock.

bounce [bauns], *v.a.* aufprallen lassen (*ball*). *— v.n.* aufprallen. *— s.* der Rückprall, Aufprall.

bound (1) [baund], *s.* der Sprung; *by leaps and —s*, sehr schnell, sprunghaft. *— v.n.* springen, prallen.

bound (2) [baund], *v.a.* begrenzen, einschränken. *— adj.* verpflichtet; *— to* (*inf.*), wird sicherlich *. . .*

bound

bound (3) [baund], *adj. — for*, auf dem Wege nach.
boundary ['baundəri], *s.* die Grenzlinie, Grenze.
bounder ['baundə], *s.* der ungezogene Bursche.
boundless ['baundlis], *adj.* grenzenlos, unbegrenzt.
bounteous ['bauntiəs], *adj.* freigebig; reichlich (*plenty*).
bounty ['baunti], *s.* die Freigebigkeit (*generosity*); (*Comm.*) Prämie.
bouquet [bu'kei], *s.* das Bukett, der Blumenstrauß; die Blume (*wine*).
bourgeois ['buəʒwa:], *s.* der Bürger; Philister. — *adj.* kleinbürgerlich, philisterhaft.
bow (1) [bau], *s.* (*Naut.*) der Bug; —*sprit*, das Bugspriet.
bow (2) [bau], *s.* die Verbeugung, Verneigung. — *v.n.* sich verneigen, sich verbeugen. — *v.a.* neigen.
bow (3) [bou], *s.* (*Mus.*) der Bogen; die Schleife (*ribbon*). — *v.a.* streichen (*violin*).
bowel ['bauəl], *s.* der Darm; (*pl.*) die Eingeweide.
bowl (1) [boul], *s.* die Schale, der Napf, die Schüssel.
bowl (2) [boul], *s.* die Holzkugel; (*pl.*) das Rasenkugelspiel, Bowlingspiel. — *v.n.* (*Cricket*) den Ball werfen.
bowler (1) ['boulə], *s.* (*hat*) der steife Hut, die Melone.
bowler (2) ['boulə], *s.* (*Sport*) der Ballmann.
box (1) [bɔks], *s.* (*Bot.*) der Buchsbaum.
box (2) [bɔks], *s.* die Büchse, Dose, Schachtel, der Kasten; (*Theat.*) die Loge; — *office*, die Theaterkasse.
box (3) [bɔks], *s.* der Schlag; — *on the ear*, die Ohrfeige. — *v.n.* boxen.
boxer ['bɔksə], *s.* der Boxer; Boxkämpfer.
Boxing Day ['bɔksiŋ'dei], der zweite Weihnachtstag.
boy [bɔi], *s.* der Junge, Knabe; Diener (*servant*).
boyish ['bɔiiʃ], *adj.* knabenhaft.
boyhood ['bɔihud], *s.* das Knabenalter.
brace [breis], *s.* das Band; die Klammer (*clamp*); — *of partridges*, das Paar Rebhühner; die Spange (*denture*). — *v.a.* spannen, straffen. — *v.r.* — *yourself!* stähle dich!
bracelet ['breislit], *s.* das Armband.
braces ['breisiz], *s. pl.* die Hosenträger.
bracken ['brækən], *s.* (*Bot.*) das Farnkraut.
bracket ['brækit], *s.* die Klammer; *income* —, die Einkommensgruppe. — *v.a.* (ein-)klammern; (*Maths.*) in Klammern setzen.
brackish ['brækiʃ], *adj.* salzig.
brad [bræd], *s.* der kopflose Nagel; — *awl*, der Vorstechbohrer.
brag [bræg], *v.n.* prahlen.

braggart ['brægət], *s.* der Prahlhans.
Brahmin ['bra:min], *s.* der Brahmane.
braid [breid], *s.* die Borte; der Saumbesatz. — *v.a.* (mit Borten) besetzen.
Braille [breil], *s.* die Blindenschrift.
brain [brein], *s.* das Gehirn, Hirn; *scatter- —ed*, zerstreut.
brainwave ['breinweiv], *s.* der Geistesblitz.
brake [breik], *s.* die Bremse. — *v.a.* bremsen.
bramble [bræmbl], *s.* der (*Bot.*) Brombeerstrauch.
bran [bræn], *s.* die Kleie.
branch [bra:ntʃ], *s.* der Ast, Zweig; (*Comm.*) die Zweigstelle, Filiale. — *v.n.* — *out*, sich verzweigen; — *out into*, sich ausbreiten, etwas Neues anfangen; — *off*, abzweigen.
brand [brænd], *s.* der (Feuer) Brand; das Brandmal (*on skin*); die Sorte, Marke (*make*); — *new*, funkelnagelneu. — *v.a.* brandmarken, kennzeichnen.
brandish ['brændiʃ], *v.a.* schwingen, herumschwenken.
brandy ['brændi], *s.* der Branntwein, Kognac, Weinbrand.
brass [bra:s], *s.* das Messing; — *band*, die Blechmusik, Militärmusikkapelle; — *founder*, Erzgießer, Gelbgießer; (*sl.*) die Frechheit (*impudence*).
brassiere ['bræsiεə], *s.* der Büstenhalter.
brat [bræt], *s.* (*coll.*) das Kind, der Balg.
brave [breiv], *adj.* tapfer, kühn. — *v.a.* trotzen, standhalten (*Dat.*). — *s.* der Held, Krieger; der Indianer (*redskin*).
bravery ['breivəri], *s.* die Tapferkeit.
brawl [brɔ:l], *s.* der Krawall, die Rauferei. — *v.n.* zanken, lärmen.
brawn [brɔ:n], *s.* die Sülze; (*fig.*) die Körperkraft, Stärke.
brawny ['brɔ:ni], *adj.* stark, sehnig.
bray [brei], *v.n.* iah sagen, Eselslaute von sich geben (*donkey*). — *s.* das Iah des Esels, das Eselsgeschrei.
brazen [breizn], *adj.* (*Metall.*) aus Erz; unverschämt (*shameless*).
brazenfaced ['breiznfeisd], *adj.* unverschämt.
brazier ['breiziə], *s.* der Kupferschmied; die Kohlenpfanne.
Brazil [brə'zil]. Brasilien, *n.*; — *nut*, die Paranuß.
Brazilian [brə'ziliən], *adj.* brasilianisch. — *s.* der Brasilianer.
breach [bri:tʃ], *s.* die Bresche; der Bruch (*break*); die Verletzung; der Vertragsbruch (*of contract*); der Verstoß (*of*, gegen, *etiquette etc.*).
bread [bred], *s.* das Brot; *brown —*, das Schwarzbrot; — *and butter*, das Butterbrot.
breadth [bretθ], *s.* die Breite, Weite.

break [breik], *s.* der Bruch (*breach*); die Lücke (*gap*); die Chance (*chance*); *a lucky —*, ein glücklicher Zufall, ein Glücksfall; die Pause (*from work*). — *v.a.*, *v.n. irr.* brechen; — *off*, Pause machen; — *in*, unterbrechen (*interrupt*); — *in*, (*horse*) einschulen, zureiten; — *up*, abbrechen (*school, work*); — *away*, sich trennen, absondern; — *down*, zusammenbrechen (*health*); (*Am.*) analysieren; auflösen.

breakage ['breikidʒ], *s.* der Bruch, der Schaden (*damage*).

breakdown ['breikdoun], *s.* der Zusammenbruch (*health*); die Panne (*car*); (*Am.*) die Analyse (*analysis*).

breaker ['breikə], *s.* die Brandungswelle, Brandung.

breakfast ['brekfəst], *s.* das Frühstück. *v.n.* frühstücken.

breast [brest], *s.* die Brust.

breath [breθ], *s.* der Atem; der Hauch (*exhalation*); *with bated —*, mit verhaltenem Atem.

breathe [bri:ð], *v.n.* atmen.

breathing ['bri:ðiŋ], *s.* die Atmung.

breathless ['breθlis], *adj.* atemlos.

breech [bri:tʃ], *s.* der Boden; (*pl.*) die Reithosen, *f. pl.*

breed [bri:d], *v.a. irr.* zeugen, züchten (*cattle, etc.*). — *v.n.* sich vermehren. — *s.* die Zucht, die Art (*type*); die Rasse (*race*).

breeder ['bri:də], *s.* der Züchter.

breeding ['bri:diŋ], *s.* die gute Kinderstube (*manners*); die Erziehung; das Züchten (*of plants, cattle etc.*).

breeze [bri:z], *s.* die Briese.

breezy ['bri:zi], *adj.* windig; lebhaft (*manner*), beschwingt (*tone*).

brethren ['breðrən], *s. pl.* (*obs.*) die Brüder.

Breton [bretn], *adj.* bretonisch. — *s.* der Bretagner, Bretone.

brevet ['brevit], *s.* das Patent.

breviary ['bri:viəri], *s.* das Brevier.

brevity ['breviti], *s.* die Kürze.

brew [bru:], *v.a.* brauen. — *s.* das Gebräu, Bräu (*beer*).

brewer ['bru:ə], *s.* der Brauer, Bierbrauer.

brewery ['bru:əri], *s.* die Brauerei, das Brauhaus.

briar, brier ['braiə], *s.* (*Bot.*) der Dornstrauch, die wilde Rose.

bribe [braib], *v.a.* bestechen. — *s.* das Bestechungsgeld.

bribery ['braibəri], *s.* die Bestechung.

brick [brik], *s.* der Ziegel, Backstein; *drop a —*, eine Taktlosigkeit begehen, einen Schnitzer machen.

bricklayer ['brikleiə], *s.* der Maurer.

bridal [braidl], *adj.* bräutlich.

bride [braid], *s.* die Braut.

bridegroom ['braidgru:m], *s.* der Bräutigam.

bridesmaid ['braidzmeid], *s.* die Brautjungfer.

bridge [bridʒ], *s.* die Brücke. — *v.a.* überbrücken; — *the gap*, die Lücke füllen.

bridle [braidl], *s.* der Zaum, Zügel. — *v.a.* aufzäumen. — *v.n.* sich brüsten.

brief [bri:f], *adj.* kurz, bündig, knapp. — *s.* der Schriftsatz, der Rechtsauftrag, die Instruktionen, *f. pl.* (*instructions*). — *v.a.* instruieren, beauftragen; informieren (*inform*).

brigade [bri'geid], *s.* die Brigade.

brigand ['brigənd], *s.* der Brigant, Straßenräuber.

bright [brait], *adj.* hell, glänzend (*shiny*); klug, intelligent (*clever*).

brighten [braitn], *v.a.* glänzend machen (*polish etc.*); erhellen, aufheitern (*cheer*).

brightness ['braitnis], *s.* der Glanz; die Helligkeit; die Klugheit (*cleverness*).

brill [bril], *s.* (*Zool.*) der Glattbutt.

brilliance, brilliancy ['briljəns, -jənsi], *s.* der Glanz, die Pracht.

brim [brim], *s.* der Rand (*glass*); die Krempe (*hat*). — *v.n.* — (*over*) *with*, überfließen von.

brimful ['brimful], *adj.* übervoll.

brimstone ['brimstoun], *s.* der Schwefel; — *butterfly*, der Zitronenfalter.

brindled ['brindld], *adj.* scheckig, gefleckt.

brine [brain], *s.* die Salzsole, das Salzwasser.

bring [briŋ], *v.a. irr.* bringen; — *about*, zustande bringen; — *forth*, hervorbringen; gebären; — *forward*, fördern; anführen; — *on*, herbeiführen; — *up*, erziehen, aufziehen.

brink [briŋk], *s.* (*fig.*) der Rand, — *of a precipice*, Rand eines Abgrundes.

briny ['braini], *adj.* salzig.

brisk [brisk], *adj.* frisch, munter, feurig (*horse*).

brisket ['briskit], *s.* die Brust (eines Tieres).

briskness ['brisknis], *s.* die Lebhaftigkeit.

bristle [brisl], *s.* die Borste. — *v.n.* sich sträuben.

British ['britiʃ], *adj.* britisch.

Britisher, Briton ['britiʃə, 'britən], *s.* der Brite.

brittle [britl], *adj.* zerbrechlich, spröde.

brittleness ['britlnis], *s.* die Sprödigkeit, Zerbrechlichkeit.

broach [broutʃ], *v.a.* anzapfen, anschneiden; — *a subject*, ein Thema berühren.

broad [brɔːd], *adj.* breit, weit; ordinär, derb (*joke*); — *-minded*, duldsam, weitherzig.

broadcast ['brɔːdkɑːst], *v.a.* senden, übertragen (*radio*). — *s.* die Sendung, das Programm.

broadcaster ['brɔːdkɑːstə], *s.* der im Radio Vortragende *or* Künstler (*artist*); Ansager.

broadcasting ['brɔːdkɑːstiŋ], *s.* das Senden, der Rundfunk; — *station*, der Sender, die Rundfunkstation.

broadcloth

broadcloth ['brɔ:dclɔθ], *s.* das feine Tuch.

broaden [brɔ:dn], *v.a.* erweitern, verbreitern.

brocade [bro'keid], *s.* der Brokat.

brogue [broug], *s.* der grobe Schuh; der irische Akzent.

broil ['brɔil], *v.a.* braten, rösten.

broke [brouk], *adj.* (*coll.*) pleite.

broken ['broukən], *adj.* gebrochen; zerbrochen; unterbrochen (*interrupted*).

broker ['broukə], *s.* der Makler.

bronchial ['brɔŋkjəl], *adj.* (*Anat.*) bronchial, in *or* von der Luftröhre, Luftröhren-.

bronchitis [brɔŋ'kaitis], *s.* (*Med.*) die Luftröhrenentzündung, Bronchitis.

bronze [brɔnz], *s.* (*Metall.*) die Bronze, Bronzefarbe.

brooch [broutʃ], *s.* die Brosche.

brood [bru:d], *s.* die Brut. — *v.n.* brüten; grübeln (*meditate*).

brook (1) [bruk], *s.* der Bach.

brook (2) [bruk], *v.a.* ertragen, leiden.

brooklet ['bruklit], *s.* das Bächlein.

broom [bru:m], *s.* der Besen; (*Bot.*) der Ginster.

broth [brɔθ], *s.* die Brühe; *meat* —, Fleischbrühe.

brothel ['brɔθəl], *s.* das Bordell.

brother ['brʌðə], *s.* der Bruder; — *-in-law*, der Schwager.

brotherhood ['brʌðəhud], *s.* die Bruderschaft.

brotherly ['brʌðəli], *adj.* brüderlich.

brow [brau], *s.* die Braue, Augenbraue; der Kamm (*hill*); die Stirn(e) (*forehead*).

browbeat ['braubi:t], *v.a.* einschüchtern.

brown [braun], *adj.* braun; *in a* — *study*, in tiefem Nachsinnen.

browse [brauz], *v.n.* weiden (*cattle*); stöbern, (durch-)blättern (*in books etc.*).

Bruin ['bru:in]. Braun, Meister Petz, der Bär.

bruise [bru:z], *v.a.* quetschen, stoßen; (wund) schlagen. — *s.* die Quetschung.

Brunswick ['brʌnzwik]. Braunschweig, *n.*

brunt [brʌnt], *s.* der Anprall; *bear the* —, der Wucht ausgesetzt sein, den Stoß auffangen.

brush [brʌʃ], *s.* die Bürste (*clothes*); der Pinsel (*paint, painting*); — *stroke*, der Pinselstrich. — *v.a., v.n.* bürsten, abbürsten; — *against s.o.*, mit jemandem zusammenstoßen, streifen (*an, Acc.*); — *up one's English*, das Englisch auffrischen; — *off*, abschütteln.

brushwood ['brʌʃwud], *s.* das Gestrüpp.

brusque [brusk], *adj.* brüsk, barsch.

Brussels ['brʌsəlz]. Brüssel, *n.*; — *sprouts*, (*Bot.*) der Rosenkohl.

brutal [bru:tl], *adj.* brutal, grausam.

brutality [bru:'tæliti], *s.* die Brutalität.

brute [bru:t], *s.* der Unmensch.

bubble [bʌbl], *s.* die Blase; (*fig.*) der Schwindel (*swindle*). — *v.n.* sprudeln, wallen, schäumen.

buccaneer [bʌkə'niə], *s.* der Seeräuber.

buck [bʌk], *s.* (*Zool.*) der Bock; (*Am. sl.*) der Dollar. — *v.a.* — *up*, aufmuntern. — *v.n.* — *up*, sich zusammenraffen.

bucket ['bʌkit], *s.* der Eimer, Kübel.

buckle [bʌkl], *s.* die Schnalle. — *v.a.* zuschnallen; biegen. — *v.n.* sich krümmen.

buckler ['bʌklə], *s.* der Schild.

buckram ['bʌkrəm], *s.* die Steifleinwand.

buckskin ['bʌkskin], *s.* das Wildleder.

buckwheat ['bʌkwi:t], *s.* (*Bot.*) der Buchweizen.

bucolic [bju:'kɔlik], *adj.* bukolisch, ländlich, Schäfer-.

bud [bʌd], *s.* (*Bot.*) die Knospe. — *v.n.* knospen.

buddy ['bʌdi], *s.* (*coll. Am.*) der Freund, Kamerad.

budge [bʌdʒ], *v.n.* sich rühren, sich regen.

budget ['bʌdʒit], *s.* das Budget; der Haushaltsplan; der Etat; *present the* —, den Staatsetat vorlegen. — *v.n.* voranschlagen (*for*), planen.

buff [bʌf], *adj.* ledergelb.

buffalo ['bʌfəlou], *s.* (*Zool.*) der Büffel.

buffer ['bʌfə], *s.* der Puffer.

buffet (1) ['bʌfit], *s.* der Puff, Faustschlag (*blow*). — *v.a.* schlagen, stoßen.

buffet (2) ['bufei], *s.* das Buffet, der Anrichtetisch.

buffoon [bʌ'fu:n], *s.* der Possenreißer.

buffoonery [bʌ'fu:nəri], *s.* die Possen, *f. pl.*; das Possenreißen.

bug [bʌg], *s.* (*Ent.*) die Wanze; (*Am.*) der Käfer; (*coll.*) das Insekt.

buggy ['bʌgi], *s.* der Einspänner.

bugle [bju:gl], *s.* (*Mus.*) das Signalhorn, die Signaltrompete.

bugler ['bju:glə], *s.* (*Mus.*) der Trompeter.

build [bild], *v.a., v.n. irr.* bauen; errichten; — *on*, sich verlassen auf (*rely on*). — *s.* die Statur, Figur (*figure*).

builder ['bildə], *s.* der Bauherr, Baumeister (*employer*); Bauarbeiter (*worker*).

building ['bildiŋ], *s.* das Gebäude, der Bau; — *site*, der Bauplatz.

bulb [bʌlb], *s.* (*Bot.*) der Knollen, die Zwiebel; *Dutch* —, die Tulpe; (*Elec.*) die Birne.

bulbous ['bʌlbəs], *adj.* zwiebelartig; dickbäuchig.

Bulgarian [bʌl'gɛəriən], *adj.* bulgarisch. — *s.* der Bulgare.

bulge [bʌldʒ], *s.* die Ausbauchung; die Ausbuchtung (*in fighting line*). — *v.n.* herausragen, anschwellen.

bulk [bʌlk], *s.* die Masse, Menge; *buy in* —, im Großen einkaufen.

bulky ['bʌlki], *adj.* schwer (*heavy*); massig (*stodgy*); unhandlich.

bull (1) [bul], *s.* (*Zool.*) der Bulle, Stier; —'s eye, das Schwarze (*target*).

bull (2) [bul], *s.* (*Papal*) die Bulle, der Erlass.

bulldog ['buldɔg], *s.* der Bullenbeißer.

bullet ['bulit], *s.* die Kugel, das Geschoß.

bulletin ['bulitin], *s.* das Bulletin, der Tagesbericht.

bullfight ['bulfait], *s.* der Stierkampf.

bullfinch ['bulfintʃ], *s.* (*Orn.*) der Dompfaff.

bullfrog ['bulfrɔg], *s.* (*Zool.*) der Ochsenfrosch.

bullion ['buljən], *s.* das Goldbarren, Silberbarren.

bullock ['bulək], *s.* (*Zool.*) der Ochse.

bully ['buli], *s.* der Raufbold, Angeber, Großtuer (*braggart*); der Tyrann. — *v.a.* tyrannisieren, einschüchtern.

bulrush ['bulrʌʃ], *s.* (*Bot.*) die Binse.

bulwark ['bulwək], *s.* das Bollwerk, die Verteidigung.

bump [bʌmp], *s.* der Schlag, der Stoß. — *v.a.* stoßen.

bun [bʌn], *s.* das Rosinenbrötchen; das süße Brötchen; (*hair*) der Knoten.

bunch [bʌntʃ], *s.* der Bund (*keys*); der Strauß (*flowers*); die Traube (*grapes*). — *v.a.* zusammenfassen, zusammenbinden, zusammenraffen.

bundle [bʌndl], *s.* das Bündel.

bung [bʌŋ], *s.* der Spund (*in barrel*).

bungle [bʌŋgl], *v.a.* verpfuschen, verderben.

bungler ['bʌŋglə], *s.* der Stümper.

bunion ['bʌnjən], *s.* die Fußschwiele.

bunk (1) [bʌŋk], *s.* die (Schlaf-)Koje.

bunk (2) [bʌŋk], *s.* (*coll.*) der Unsinn.

bunker ['bʌŋkə], *s.* der Kohlenraum, Bunker.

bunting ['bʌntiŋ], *s.* das Flaggentuch.

buoy [bɔi], *s.* die Boje.

buoyant ['bɔiənt], *adj.* schwimmend; lebhaft, heiter.

buoyancy ['bɔiənsi], *s.* die Schwimmkraft; die Schwungkraft.

burden (1) [bə:dn], *s.* die Bürde, Last. — *v.a.* belasten, beladen.

burden (2) [bə:dn], *s.* der Refrain; der Hauptinhalt.

burdensome ['bə:dnsəm], *adj.* beschwerlich.

bureau [bjuə'rou], *s.* der Schreibtisch; das Büro.

bureaucracy [bjuə'rɔkrəsi], *s.* die Bürokratie.

burgess ['bə:dʒis], *s.* der Bürger.

burglar ['bə:glə], *s.* der Einbrecher.

burglary ['bə:gləri], *s.* der Einbruch, der Diebstahl.

burgomaster ['bə:gomɑ:stə], *s.* der Bürgermeister.

Burgundian [bə:'gʌndiən], *adj.* burgundisch. —*s.* der Burgunder.

Burgundy (1) ['bə:gəndi], das Burgund.

Burgundy (2) ['bə:gəndi], *s.* der Burgunder(-wein).

burial ['beriəl], *s.* das Begräbnis; — ground, der Kirchhof, Friedhof; — service, die Totenfeier, Trauerfeier.

burlesque [bə:'lesk], *s.* die Burleske, Posse.

burly ['bə:li], *adj.* dick, stark.

Burmese [bə:'mi:z], *adj.* birmesisch. — *s.* der Birmese.

burn [bə:n], *v.a.*, *v.n.* *irr.* brennen, verbrennen. — *s.* das Brandmal.

burner ['bə:nə], *s.* der Brenner.

burnish ['bə:niʃ], *v.a.* polieren.

burred [bə:d], *adj.* überliegend; (*Metall.*) ausgehämmert; — over, (*Metall.*) breitgeschmiedet.

burrow ['bɑrou], *s.* der Bau, (*rabbits etc.*). —*v.n.* sich eingraben; wühlen.

burst [bə:st], *v.a.*, *v.n.* *irr.* bersten, platzen, explodieren (*explode*); — out laughing, laut auflachen; — into tears, in Tränen ausbrechen; — into flames, aufflammen; sprengen (*blow up*). — *s.* der Ausbruch; die Explosion.

bury ['beri], *v.a.* begraben; beerdigen.

bus [bʌs], *s.* der Autobus, Omnibus.

busby ['bʌzbi], *s.* (*Mil.*) die Bärenmütze.

bush [buʃ], *s.* der Busch.

bushel ['buʃl], *s.* der Scheffel.

bushy ['buʃi], *adj.* buschig.

business ['biznis], *s.* das Geschäft; die Beschäftigung, die Tätigkeit (*activity*); Aufgabe, Obliegenheit; der Handel (*trade*); on —, geschäftlich.

businesslike ['biznislaik], *adj.* geschäftsmäßig, nüchtern, praktisch.

businessman ['biznismæn], *s.* der Geschäftsmann.

bust (1) [bʌst], *s.* die Büste.

bust (2) [bʌst], *v.a.*, *v.n.* (*coll.*) sprengen; go —, bankrott machen.

bustard ['bʌstəd], *s.* (*Orn.*) die Trappe.

bustle [bʌsl], *s.* der Lärm, die Aufregung. — *v.n.* aufgeregt umherlaufen; rührig sein (*be active*).

busy ['bizi], *adj.* geschäftig (*active*); beschäftigt (*engaged*, mit, *in*); be —, zu tun haben.

but [bʌt], *conj.* aber, jedoch; sondern. — *adv.* nur, bloß; — yesterday, erst gestern. — *prep.* außer; all — two, alle außer zwei.

butcher ['butʃə], *s.* der Metzger, Fleischer; —'s knife, das Fleischmesser.

butchery ['butʃəri], *s.* die Schlächterei; das Blutbad, das Gemetzel.

butler ['bʌtlə], *s.* der oberste Diener; Kellermeister.

butt [bʌt], *s.* das dicke Ende; der Kolben (*rifle*); der Stoß (*blow*); die Zielscheibe (*target*). — *v.a.* stoßen, spießen.

butter ['bʌtə], *s.* die Butter. — *v.a.* mit Butter bestreichen; — up, schmeicheln (*Dat.*).

butterfly ['bʌtəflai], *s.* (*Ent.*) der Schmetterling.

buttery ['bʌtəri], *s.* die Speisekammer.

buttock(s) [ˈbʌtək(s)], *s.* der Hintere, das Gesäß (*usually pl.*) (*vulg.*).
button [bʌtn], *s.* der Knopf. — *v.a.* — *up*, knöpfen, zumachen.
buttress [ˈbʌtris], *s.* der Strebepfeiler.
buxom [ˈbʌksəm], *adj.* drall, gesund.
buy [bai], *v.a. irr.* kaufen.
buzz [bʌz], *s.* das Summen. — *v.n.* summen.
buzzard [ˈbʌzəd], *s.* (*Orn.*) der Bussard.
by [bai], *prep.* (*beside*) neben, an; (*near*) nahe; (*before*) gegen, um, bei; (*about*) bei; (*from*, *with*) durch, von, mit; — *the way*, nebenbei bemerkt; — *way of*, mittels. — *adv.* (*nearby*) nahe; nebenan.
by-election [ˈbaiilekʃən], *s.* die Nachwahl; Ersatzwahl.
bygone [ˈbaigɔn], *adj.* vergangen.
bylaw, byelaw [ˈbailɔ:], *s.* die Bestimmung.
Byzantine [baiˈzæntain], *adj.* byzantinisch.

C

C [si:]. das C (*also Mus.*).
cab [kæb], *s.* (*horse-drawn*) die Droschke, der Wagen; das Taxi; —*stand*, der Droschkenhalteplatz; (*Motor.*) der Taxiplatz, Taxistand.
cabaret [ˈkæbərei], *s.* das Kabarett, die Kleinbühne.
cabbage [ˈkæbidʒ], *s.* (*Bot.*) der Kohl.
cabin [ˈkæbin], *s.* die Kabine (*boat*); die Hütte (*hut*); —*boy*, der Schiffsjunge.
cabinet [ˈkæbinet], *s.* das Kabinett (*government*); der Schrank (*cupboard*); das kleine Zimmer *or* Nebenzimmer (*mainly Austr.*); (*Rad.*) das Gehäuse; — *maker*, der Kunsttischler.
cable [keibl], *s.* das Kabel (*of metal*), das Seil (*metal or rope*); das Telegramm. — *v.a.* kabeln, telegraphieren.
cablegram [ˈkeiblgræm], *s.* die (Kabel-) Depesche.
cabman [ˈkæbmən], *s.* der Taxichauffeur.
caboose [kəˈbu:s], *s.* die Schiffsküche.
cabriolet [kæbrioˈlei], *s.* das Kabriolett.
cackle [kækl], *v.n.* gackern (*hens*); schnattern (*geese*); (*fig.*) schwatzen.
cacophony [kəˈkɔfəni], *s.* der Mißklang.
cad [kæd], *s.* der gemeine Kerl, Schuft.
cadaverous [kəˈdævərəs], *adj.* leichenhaft.
caddie [ˈkædi], *s.* der Golfjunge.
caddy [ˈkædi], *s. tea* —, die Teebüchse, Teedose.
cadence [ˈkeidəns], *s.* (*Phonet.*) der Tonfall; (*Mus.*) die Kadenz.
cadet [kəˈdet], *s.* (*Mil.*) der Kadett.
cadge [kædʒ], *v.a.* erbetteln.

Caesar [ˈsi:zə]. Cäsar, *m.*
Caesarean [si:ˈzɛəriən], *adj.* cäsarisch; *operation* or *section*, (*Med.*) der Kaiserschnitt.
cafeteria [kæfəˈtiəriə], *s.* das Selbstbedienungsrestaurant.
cage [keidʒ], *s.* (*Zool.*) der Käfig; (*Orn.*) das Vogelbauer. — *v.a.* einfangen, einsperren.
cagey [ˈkeidʒi], *adj.* (*coll.*) argwöhnisch, zurückhaltend; schlau.
cairn [kɛən], *s.* (*Archaeol.*) der Steinhaufen, der Grabhügel.
caitiff [ˈkeitif], *adj.* niederträchtig. — *s.* der Schuft.
cajole [kəˈdʒoul], *v.a.* schmeicheln (*Dat.*).
cake [keik], *s.* der Kuchen; — *of soap*, das Stück Seife; *have o.'s* — *and eat it*, alles haben. — *v.a., v.n.* zusammenbacken; —*d with dirt*, mit Schmutz beschmiert.
calamity [kəˈlæmiti], *s.* das Unheil, Unglück; Elend.
calcareous [kælˈkɛəriəs], *adj.* (*Geol.*) kalkartig.
calculate [ˈkælkjuleit], *v.a.* berechnen.
calculation [kælkjuˈleiʃən], *s.* die Berechnung.
calendar [ˈkæləndə], *s.* der Kalender.
calf [kɑ:f], *s.* (*Zool.*) das Kalb; (*Anat.*) die Wade; — *love*, die Jugendliebe.
calibre [ˈkælibə], *s.* das Kaliber.
calico [ˈkælikou], *s.* der Kaliko, Kattun.
Caliph [ˈkeilif], *s.* der Kalif.
calk (1) [kɔ:k], *v.a.* beschlagen (*horse*).
calk (2), **caulk** [kɔ:k], *v.a.* (*Naut.*) abdichten.
call [kɔ:l], *v.a., v.n.* rufen, herbeirufen; (*Am.*) antelefonieren, anrufen (*ring up*); (*name*) nennen; — *to account*, zur Rechenschaft ziehen; (*summon*) kommen lassen; — *for*, abholen; *this* —*s for*, das berechtigt zu. — *s.* der Ruf, Anruf; die (innere) Berufung, der Beruf.
callbox [ˈkɔ:lbɔks] *see* **phone box**.
calling [ˈkɔ:liŋ], *s.* der Beruf, das Gewerbe (*occupation*).
callous [ˈkæləs], *adj.* schwielig (*hands*); (*fig.*) unempfindlich, hart, gemein.
callow [ˈkælou], *adj.* ungefiedert (*bird*); (*fig.*) unerfahren.
calm [kɑ:m], *adj.* ruhig, still; gelassen. — *s.* die Ruhe; (*Naut.*) Windstille. — *v.a.* beruhigen. — *v.n.* — *down*, sich beruhigen, sich legen (*storm etc.*).
caloric [kæˈlɔrik], *adj.* Wärme-, warm; (*Chem.*) kalorisch.
calorie, calory [ˈkæləri], *s.* die Kalorie.
calumny [ˈkæləmni], *s.* die Verleumdung.
calve [kɑ:v], *v.n.* kalben, Kälber kriegen.
cambric [ˈkæmbrik], *s.* der Batist (*textile*).
camel [ˈkæməl], *s.* (*Zool.*) das Kamel.
cameo [ˈkæmiou], *s.* die Kamee.
camera [ˈkæmərə], *s.* (*Phot.*) die Kamera.
camomile [ˈkæməmail], *s.* (*Bot.*) die Kamille.

captain

camp [kæmp], *s.* das Lager; Zeltlager.
— *v.n.* sich lagern, ein Lager aufschlagen, zelten.

campaign [kæm'pein], *s.* der Feldzug.
— *v.n.* einen Feldzug mitmachen;
(*fig.*) Propaganda machen.

camphor ['kæmfə], *s.* der Kampfer.

camping ['kæmpiŋ], *s.* die Lagerausrüstung (*equipment*); das Lagern (*activity*), das Zelten.

can (1) [kæn], *s.* die Kanne; die Büchse;
watering —, die Gießkanne. — *v.a.*
(*Am.*) einmachen, einkochen (*fruit*).

can (2) [kæn], *v. aux. irr.* können,
imstande sein, vermögen.

Canadian [kə'neidiən], *adj.* kanadisch.
— *s.* der Kanadier.

canal [kə'næl], *s.* der Kanal; — *lock*,
die Kanalschleuse.

canalize ['kænəlaiz], *v.a.* kanalisieren,
leiten.

cancel ['kænsəl], *v.a.* widerrufen, absagen
(*show*); aufheben, ungültig machen.

cancellation [kænsə'leiʃən], *s.* die
Aufhebung, Absage, Widerrufung.

cancer ['kænsə], *s.* (*Med., Astron.*) der
Krebs.

cancerous ['kænsərəs], *adj.* (*Med.*)
krebsartig.

candelabra [kændi'lɑ:brə], *s.* der
Kandelaber, Leuchter.

candid ['kændid], *adj.* offen, aufrichtig.

candidate ['kændideit], *s.* der Kandidat, Bewerber.

candidature ['kændiditʃə], *s.* die
Kandidatur, die Bewerbung.

candied · ['kændid], *adj.* gezuckert,
kandiert (*fruit*).

candle [kændl], *s.* die Kerze, das Licht.

Candlemas ['kændlməs], *s.* (*Eccl.*)
Lichtmeß.

candlestick ['kændlstik], *s.* der Kerzenleuchter.

candlewick ['kændlwik], *s.* der Kerzendocht (*textile*).

candour ['kændə], *s.* die Offenheit,
Aufrichtigkeit.

candy ['kændi], *s.* (*Am.*) das Zuckerwerk, (*pl.*) Süßigkeiten. — *v.a.*
verzuckern.

cane [kein], *s.* (*Bot.*) das Rohr, der
Rohrstock; Spazierstock. — *v.a.* (mit
· dem Stock) schlagen.

canine ['kænain], *adj.* Hunde-, hündisch; — *tooth*, der Eckzahn.

canister ['kænistə], *s.* die Blechbüchse,
der Kanister.

canker ['kæŋkə], *s.* (*Bot.*) der Brand;
(*Bot.*) der Pflanzenrost; (*fig.*) eine
zerfressende Krankheit.

cannibal ['kænibəl], *s.* der Kannibale,
Menschenfresser.

cannon ['kænən], *s.* die Kanone, das
Geschütz.

canoe [kə'nu], *s.* das Kanu.

canon ['kænən], *s.* (*Mus., Eccl.*) der
Kanon; die Regel; (*Eccl.*) der Domherr; — *law*, das kanonische Recht.

canonize ['kænənaiz], *v.a.* (*Eccl.*)
kanonisieren, heiligsprechen.

canopy ['kænəpi], *s.* der Baldachin.

cant [kænt], *s.* die Heuchelei.

can't, cannot [kɑ:nt,'kænət] see **can** (2).

cantankerous [kæn'tæŋkərəs], *adj.*
zänkisch, mürrisch.

cantata [kæn'tɑ:tə], *s.* (*Mus.*) die
Kantate.

canteen [kæn'ti:n], *s.* die Kantine (*restaurant*); die Besteckgarnitur (*set of cutlery*).

canter ['kæntə], *s.* der Galopp, der
Kurzgalopp.

canticle ['kæntikl], *s.* (*Eccl.*) der
Lobgesang, das Loblied.

canto ['kæntou], *s.* (*Lit.*) der Gesang.

canton ['kæntən], *s.* (*Pol.*) der Kanton,
der Bezirk.

canvas ['kænvəs], *s.* das Segeltuch;
(*Art*) die Malerleinwand; die Zeltplane (*tent*).

canvass ['kænvəs], *v.a., v.n.* (*Pol.*)
um Stimmen werben.

canvasser ['kænvəsə], *s.* (*Pol.*) der
Werber, Stimmensammler.

cap [kæp], *s.* die Kappe, Mütze; die
Haube; der Deckel. — *v.a.* übertreffen.

capability [keipə'biliti], *s.* die Fähigkeit.

capable ['keipəbl], *adj.* fähig (*Genit.*),
imstande (*of*, zu); tüchtig.

capacious [kə'peiʃəs], *adj.* geräumig.

capacity [kə'pæsiti], *s.* der Inhalt, die
Geräumigkeit; die Fassungskraft
(*intellect*); die Leistungsfähigkeit
(*ability*); der Fassungsraum (*space*).

cape (1) [keip], *s.* (*Tail.*) der Kragenmantel.

cape (2) [keip], *s.* (*Geog.*) das Kap, das
Vorgebirge.

caper ['keipə], *s.* der Sprung, Luftsprung. — *v.n.* in die Luft springen.

capillary [kə'piləri], *adj.* haarfein; —
tubing, die Haarröhre, die Kapillarröhre.

capital ['kæpitl], *s.* (*Comm.*) das
Kapital; die Hauptstadt (*capital city*);
— *punishment*, die Todesstrafe; —
letter, der Großbuchstabe. — *adj.*
(*coll.*) ausgezeichnet, vorzüglich.

capitalize ['kæpitəlaiz], *v.a.* (*Comm.*)
kapitalisieren; ausnutzen.

capitation [kæpi'teiʃən], *s.* die Kopfsteuer.

capitulate [kə'pitjuleit], *v.n.* kapitulieren.

capon ['keipən], *s.* (*Zool.*) der Kapaun.

caprice [kə'pri:s], *s.* die Kaprize, Laune.

capricious [kə'priʃəs], *adj.* launenhaft,
eigensinnig.

Capricorn ['kæprikɔ:n]. (*Astron.*) der
Steinbock; *tropic of* —, der Wendekreis des Steinbocks.

capriole ['kæprioul], *s.* der Luftsprung.

capsize [kæp'saiz], *v.n.* umkippen,
kentern (*boat*).

capstan ['kæpstən], *s.* (*Engin.*) die
Ankerwinde; (*Mech.*) die Erdwinde;
(*Naut.*) das Gangspill.

capsular ['kæpsjulə], *adj.* kapselförmig.

capsule ['kæpsju:l], *s.* die Kapsel.

captain ['kæptin], *s.* (*Naut.*) der
Kapitän; (*Mil.*) der Hauptmann.

331

captious

captious ['kæpʃəs], *adj.* zänkisch, streitsüchtig; verfänglich.

captivate ['kæptiveit], *v.a.* einnehmen, gewinnen.

captive ['kæptiv], *s.* der Gefangene. — *adj.* gefangen.

capture ['kæptʃə], *s.* die Gefangennahme (*men*); Erbeutung (*booty*).

Capuchin ['kæputʃin], *s.* (*Eccl.*) der Kapuziner.

car [ka:], *s.* (*Motor.*) der Wagen; das Auto; (*Am.*) der Eisenbahnwagen.

carafe [kæ'ræf], *s.* die Karaffe, Wasserflasche.

caravan ['kærəvæn], *s.* die Karawane; der Wohnwagen.

caraway ['kærəwei], *s.* (*Bot.*) der Kümmel.

carbine ['ka:bain], *s.* der Karabiner.

carbolic [ka:'bolik], *adj.* — *acid*, (*Chem.*) die Karbolsäure.

carbon ['ka:bən], *s.* (*Chem.*) der Kohlenstoff.

carbonate ['ka:bəneit], *s.* (*Chem.*) das kohlensaure Salz, Karbonat.

carbonize ['ka:bənaiz], *v.a.* verkohlen. — *v.n.* (*Chem.*, *Geol.*) zu Kohle werden.

carbuncle ['ka:bʌŋkl], *s.* (*Min.*) der Karfunkel; (*Med.*) der Karbunkel.

carburettor [ka:bju'retə], *s.* (*Motor.*) der Vergaser.

carcase, carcass ['ka:kəs], *s.* der Kadaver.

card (1) [ka:d], *s.* die Karte, Postkarte; *playing* —, die Spielkarte; *put your* —*s on the table*, rück mit der Wahrheit heraus!

card (2) [ka:d], *v.a.* krempeln (*wool*); kardätschen (*cotton*).

cardboard ['ka:dbɔ:d], *s.* die Pappe, der Pappendeckel.

cardiac ['ka:diæk], *adj.* (*Med.*) Herz-.

cardinal ['ka:dinl], *s.* (*Eccl.*) der Kardinal. — *adj.* Kardinal-, grundlegend.

cardiogram ['ka:diogræm], *s.* (*Med.*) das Kardiogramm.

cardsharper ['ka:dʃa:pə], *s.* der Falschspieler.

care [kɛə], *s.* die Sorge (*anxiety*, um, *for*); *with* —, mit Sorgfalt, genau; *care of* (*abbr.* c/o *on letters*), bei; *take* —, sich in acht nehmen. — *v.n.* — *for*, sich interessieren, gern haben.

careen [kə'ri:n], *v.a.* (*Naut.*) kielholen, umlegen.

career [kə'riə], *s.* die Karriere, Laufbahn.

careful ['kɛəful], *adj.* sorgfältig, vorsichtig, umsichtig.

carefulness ['kɛəfulnis], *s.* die Vorsicht, Sorgfalt, Umsicht.

careless ['kɛəlis], *adj.* unachtsam, nachlässig.

carelessness ['kɛəlisnis], *s.* die Nachlässigkeit, Unachtsamkeit.

caress [kə'res], *v.a.* liebkosen, herzen. — *s.* die Liebkosung, die Zärtlichkeit.

caretaker ['kɛəteikə], *s.* der Hausmeister.

careworn ['kɛəwɔ:n], *adj.* abgehärmt, von Sorgen gebeugt.

cargo ['ka:gou], *s.* die Fracht, die Ladung.

caricature [kærikə'tjuə *or* 'kærikətʃə], *s.* die Karikatur. — *v.a.* karikieren, verzerren.

Carinthian [kə'rinθjən], *adj.* kärntnerisch.

carmine ['ka:main], *s.* der Karmin.

carnage ['ka:nidʒ], *s.* das Blutbad.

carnal [ka:nl], *adj.* fleischlich, sinnlich.

carnation [ka:'neiʃən], *s.* (*Bot.*) die Nelke.

carnival ['ka:nivl], *s.* der Karneval.

carnivorous [ka:'nivərəs], *adj.* fleischfressend.

carol ['kærəl], *s. Christmas* —, das Weihnachtslied.

carotid [kə'rɔtid], *s.* (*Anat.*) die Halspulsader.

carousal [kə'rauzəl], *s.* das Gelage, das Gezeche.

carouse [kə'rauz], *v.n.* zechen, schmausen.

carp (1) [ka:p], *s.* (*Zool.*) der Karpfen.

carp (2) [ka:p], *v.n.* bekritteln, tadeln.

Carpathian Mountains [ka:'peiθjən 'mauntinz], die Karpathen, *f. pl.*

carpenter ['ka:pəntə], *s.* der Zimmermann; Tischler.

carpentry ['ka:pəntri], *s.* die Tischlerei, das Zimmerhandwerk.

carpet ['ka:pit], *s.* der Teppich; — *bag*, die Reisetasche.

carriage ['kæridʒ], *s.* der Wagen, Waggon; das Verhalten, die Haltung (*bearing*); (*Comm.*) — *paid*, einschließlich Zustellung; — *way*, die Straßendamm.

carrier ['kæriə], *s.* der Fuhrmann, Fuhrunternehmer.

carrion ['kæriən], *s.* das Aas.

carrot ['kærət], *s.* (*Bot.*) die Mohrrübe; die Karotte.

carry ['kæri], *v.a.* tragen; bringen; führen (*on vehicle*), fahren (*convey*); — *interest*, Zinsen tragen; (*Comm.*) — *forward*, übertragen; — *two* (*in adding up*), zwei weiter; — *on*, weitermachen, fortfahren; — *through*, durchführen, durchhalten. — *v.n.* vernehmbar sein (*of sound*); — *on*, weiterarbeiten, weiterexistieren.

cart [ka:t], *s.* der Karren, Frachtwagen.

cartel [ka:'tel], *s.* (*Comm.*) das Kartell.

Carthage ['ka:θidʒ]. Karthago, *n.*

carthorse [ka:thɔ:s], *s.* das Zugpferd.

cartilage ['ka:tilidʒ], *s.* der Knorpel.

carton ['ka:tən], *s.* (*cardboard box*) der Karton, die Schachtel.

cartoon [ka:'tu:n], *s.* die Karikatur; — *film*, der Trickfilm.

cartridge ['ka:tridʒ], *s.* die Patrone.

cartwright ['ka:trait], *s.* der Stellmacher, Wagenbauer.

carve [ka:v], *v.a.* schneiden (*cut*); schnitzen (*wood*), meißeln (*stone*), tranchieren (*meat*).

carver ['kɑːvə], s. der Schnitzer (wood); das Tranchiermesser (carving knife).

cascade [kæs'keid], s. der Wasserfall.

case (1) [keis], s. der Kasten, Behälter; das Futteral, Etui (spectacles); das Gehäuse (watch); die Kiste (wooden box); (Typ.) der Schriftkasten.

case (2) [keis], s. der Fall (event); (Law) der Rechtsfall, der Umstand (circumstance); in —, falls.

casement ['keismənt], s. der Fensterflügel, das Fenster (frame).

caseous ['keisjəs], adj. käsig.

cash [kæʃ], s. bares Geld; die Barzahlung; — box, die Kasse. — v.a. einlösen (cheque).

cashier [kæ'ʃiə], s. der Kassierer. — v.a. (Mil.) entlassen.

cashmere ['kæʃmiə], s. die Kaschmirwolle (wool).

casing ['keisiŋ], s. die Hülle; das Gehäuse (case); die Haut (sausage skin).

cask ['kɑːsk], s. das Faß.

casket ['kɑːskit], s. das Kästchen; (Am.) der Sarg.

Caspian (Sea) ['kæspiən (siː)]. das kaspische Meer.

cassock ['kæsək], s. die Soutane.

cast [kɑːst], v.a. irr. werfen (throw); (Metall.) gießen; (Theat.) besetzen; (plaster) formen; — off, abwerfen; — anchor, ankern; — o.'s skin, sich häuten; — down, niederschlagen; — a vote, die Stimme abgeben. — s. der Wurf; (Metall.) der Guß; (Theat.) die Besetzung; der Abguß (plaster). — adj. — iron, das Gusseisen; — steel, der Gußstahl.

castanets [kæstə'nets], s. pl. (Mus.) die Kastagnetten, f. pl.

castaway ['kɑːstəwei], adj. weggeworfen; (Naut.) schiffbrüchig.

caste [kɑːst], s. die Kaste.

caster ['kɑːstə], s. der Streuer, die Streubüchse; — sugar, Streuzucker.

casting ['kɑːstiŋ], s. (Metall.) das Gießen, der Guß.

castle [kɑːsl], s. die Burg, das Schloß; (Chess) der Turm.

castor (1) ['kɑːstə], s. (Zool.) der Biber.

castor (2) ['kɑːstə] see **caster**.

castor (3) **oil** ['kɑːstər 'ɔil], s. das Rizinusöl.

castrate [kæs'treit], v.a. kastrieren.

castration [kæs'treiʃən], s. die Kastration.

casual ['kæʒjuəl], adj. zufällig; gelassen (manner); gelegentlich; flüchtig.

casualty ['kæʒjualti], s. der Unglücksfall; — ward, die Unfallstation; (pl.) die Verluste, m. pl.

cat [kæt], s. die Katze; tom —, der Kater; — burglar, der Fassadenkletterer; —'s eye, das Katzenauge, der Rückstrahler, der Reflektor.

cataclysm ['kætəklizm], s. die Sintflut, die Überschwemmung.

catacomb ['kætəkuːm], s. die Katakombe.

catalogue ['kætələg], s. der Katalog, das Verzeichnis. — v.a. im Katalog verzeichnen, katalogisieren.

catapult ['kætəpult], s. die Schleuder (hand); (Mil.) die Wurfmaschine. — v.a. schleudern.

cataract ['kætərækt], s. der Wasserfall (water); (Med.) der Star.

catarrh [kə'tɑː], s. (Med.) der Katarrh.

catastrophe [kə'tæstrəfi], s. die Katastrophe, das Unglück.

catastrophic [kætəs'trofik], adj. katastrophal, unheilvoll.

catch [kætʃ], v.a. irr. fangen, auffangen, fassen; überfallen (— unawares, ambush); — a cold, sich einen Schnupfen zuziehen, sich erkälten; erreichen (train, etc.); — redhanded, bei frischer Tat ertappen. — s. der Fang (fish); die Beute (prey, booty); der Haken (hook, also fig.).

catchpenny ['kætʃpeni], s. der Flitterkram, Lockartikel. — adj. marktschreierisch.

catchphrase, catchword ['kætʃfreiz, 'kætʃwɔːd], s. das (billige) Schlagwort.

catechism ['kætikizm], s. der Katechismus.

categorical [kæti'gɔrikəl], adj. kategorisch, entschieden.

category ['kætigəri], s. die Kategorie, Klasse, Gruppe, Gattung.

cater ['keitə], v.n. Lebensmittel einkaufen; verpflegen; (fig.) sorgen (for, für).

caterer ['keitərə], s. der Lebensmittellieferant.

catering ['keitəriŋ], s. die Verpflegung.

caterpillar ['kætəpilə], s. (Ent.) die Raupe; (Mech.) der Raupenschlepper.

caterwaul ['kætəwɔːl], v.n. miauen.

cathedral [kə'θiːdrəl], s. der Dom, die Kathedrale.

Catholic ['kæθəlik], adj. katholisch. — s. der Katholik.

catholic ['kæθəlik], adj. allumfassend.

Catholicism [kə'θɔlisizm], s. der Katholizismus.

catkin ['kætkin], s. (Bot.) das Kätzchen; pussy-willow —, das Palmkätzchen.

cattle [kætl], s. pl. das Vieh; — plague, die Rinderpest; — show, die Viehausstellung.

caucus ['kɔːkəs], s. die Wahlversammlung; der Wahlausschuß.

caul [kɔːl], s. das Haarnetz; (Anat.) die Eihaut.

cauldron ['kɔːldrən], s. der Kessel.

cauliflower ['kɔliflauə], s. (Bot.) der Blumenkohl.

caulk [kɔːk], v.a. kalfatern (see under **calk** (2)).

causal ['kɔːzəl], adj. ursächlich.

causality [kɔː'zæliti], s. der ursächliche Zusammenhang; (Log.) die Kausalität.

cause [kɔːz], s. die Ursache. — v.a. verursachen.

causeway ['kɔːzwei], s. der Damm.

caustic ['kɔːstik], adj. ätzend; beißend.

cauterize

cauterize ['kɔːtəraiz], *v.a. (Med.)* ätzen, ausbrennen.

caution ['kɔːʃən], *s.* die Vorsicht (*care*); die Warnung (*warning*). — *v.a. (Law)* ermahnen; warnen.

cautionary ['kɔːʃənəri], *adj.* warnend.

cautious ['kɔːʃəs], *adj.* vorsichtig, behutsam.

cautiousness ['kɔːʃəsnis], *s.* die Vorsicht, Behutsamkeit.

cavalcade [kævəl'keid], *s.* die Kavalkade; (*Mil.*) der Reiterzug.

cavalry ['kævəlri], *s.* die Kavallerie, die Reiterei.

cave [keiv], *s.* die Höhle. — *v.a.* aushöhlen. — *v.n.* — *in*, einstürzen, einfallen.

caveat ['keiviæt], *s. (Law)* die Warnung; der Vorbehalt.

cavern ['kævən], *s.* die Höhle.

cavernous ['kævənəs], *adj. (Geog., Geol.)* voll Höhlen.

caviare [kævi'ɑː], *s.* der Kaviar.

cavil ['kævil], *v.n.* nörgeln (*at*, über), tadeln (*Acc.*).

cavity ['kæviti], *s.* die Höhlung.

caw [kɔː], *v.n. (Orn.)* krächzen.

cease [siːs], *v.a.* einstellen. — *v.n.* aufhören.

ceaseless ['siːslis], *adj.* unaufhörlich.

cedar ['siːdə], *s. (Bot.)* die Zeder.

cede [siːd], *v.a.* überlassen. — *v.n.* nachgeben.

ceiling ['siːlin], *s.* die Decke (*room*); (*Comm.*) die Preisgrenze.

celebrate ['selibreit], *v.a.* feiern; zelebrieren.

celebrated ['selibreitid], *adj.* berühmt.

celebration [seli'breiʃən], *s.* die Feier.

celebrity [si'lebriti], *s.* die Berühmtheit; der „Star".

celerity [si'leriti], *s.* die Behendigkeit, Schnelligkeit.

celery ['seləri], *s. (Bot.)* der Sellerie.

celestial [si'lestjəl], *adj.* himmlisch.

celibacy ['selibəsi], *s.* die Ehelosigkeit; (*Eccl.*) das Zölibat.

celibate ['selibit], *adj.* unverheiratet.

cell [sel], *s.* die Zelle.

cellar ['selə], *s.* der Keller; salt —, das Salzfaß.

cellarage ['seləridʒ], *s.* die Kellerei; die Einkellerung (*storage*).

cellarer ['selərə], *s.* der Kellermeister.

cellular ['seljulə], *adj.* zellartig, Zell-.

Celt [kelt, selt], *s.* der Kelte.

Celtic ['keltik, 'seltik], *adj.* keltisch.

cement [si'ment], *s.* der Zement, Mörtel. — *v.a.* auszementieren, verkitten.

cemetery ['semətri], *s.* der Kirchhof, der Friedhof.

cenotaph ['senotæf *or* -tɑːf], *s.* das Ehrengrabmal, Ehrendenkmal.

censer ['sensə], *s. (Eccl.)* das Weihrauchfaß.

censor ['sensə], *s.* der Zensor.

censorious [sen'sɔːriəs], *adj.* kritisch, tadelsüchtig.

censure ['senʃə], *s.* der Tadel, Verweis. — *v.a.* tadeln.

census ['sensəs], *s.* die Volkszählung.

cent [sent], *s. (Am.)* der Cent (*coin*); (*Comm.*) per —, das Prozent.

centenarian [senti'nɛəriən], *adj.* hundertjährig. — *s.* der Hundertjährige.

centenary [sen'tiːnəri], *s.* die Hundertjahrfeier.

centennial [sen'tenjəl], *adj.* alle hundert Jahre, hundertjährig.

centipede ['sentipiːd], *s. (Zool.)* der Tausendfüßler.

central ['sentrəl], *adj.* zentral.

centralize ['sentrəlaiz], *v.a.* zentralisieren.

centre ['sentə], *s.* das Zentrum, der Mittelpunkt; die Mitte.

centric(al) ['sentrik(əl)], *adj. (Engin., Maths.)* zentral.

centrifugal [sen'trifjugəl], *adj.* zentrifugal.

centrifuge [sen'trifjuːdʒ], *s.* die Zentrifuge.

centripetal [sen'tripitl], *adj.* zentripetal, zum Mittelpunkt hinstrebend.

century ['sentʃuri], *s.* das Jahrhundert.

cereal ['siəriəl], *adj.* vom Getreide, Getreide—. — *s.* die Kornmehlspeise.

cerebral ['seribrəl], *adj.* Gehirn-.

ceremonial [seri'mounjəl], *adj.* feierlich, förmlich (*formal*). — *s.* das Zeremoniell.

ceremonious [seri'mounjəs], *adj.* feierlich, zeremoniell.

ceremony ['seriməni], *s.* die Zeremonie, die Feier.

certain ['səːtin], *adj.* sicher, gewiß.

certainty ['səːtinti], *s.* die Gewißheit.

certificate [səː'tifikit], *s.* das Zeugnis, die Bescheinigung.

certification [səːtifi'keiʃən], *s.* die Bescheinigung, Bezeugung.

certify ['səːtifai], *v.a.* bescheinigen, bezeugen, beglaubigen.

certitude ['səːtitjuːd], *s.* die Gewißheit.

cerulean [si'ruːljən], *adj.* himmelblau.

cesspool ['sespuːl], *s.* die Senkgrube.

cessation [se'seiʃən], *s.* das Aufhören; (*of hostilities*) der Waffenstillstand.

cession ['seʃən], *s.* die Abtretung, der Verzicht (*of*, auf).

chafe [tʃeif], *v.a.* wärmen, warmreiben; erzürnen (*annoy*); wundreiben (*skin*). — *v.n.* toben, wüten.

chafer ['tʃeifə], *s. (Ent.)* der Käfer.

chaff [tʃɑːf], *s.* die Spreu; die Neckerei (*teasing*). — *v.a.* necken.

chaffer ['tʃæfə], *v.n.* handeln, schachern (*haggle*).

chaffinch ['tʃæfintʃ], *s. (Orn.)* der Buchfink.

chagrin [ʃæ'griːn], *s.* der Verdruß, der Ärger.

chain [tʃein], *s.* die Kette. — *v.a.* anketten.

chair [tʃɛə], *s.* der Stuhl; (*Univ.*) Lehrstuhl. — *v.a.* vorsitzen (*Dat.*).

chairman ['tʃɛəmən], *s.* der Vorsitzende.

chalice ['tʃælis], *s. (Eccl.)* der Kelch.

chalk [tʃɔ:k], s. die Kreide. — v.a. — up, ankreiden, anschreiben.

chalky ['tʃɔ:ki], adj. (Geol.) kreidig, kreideartig.

challenge ['tʃælindʒ], v.a. herausfordern; in Frage stellen (question); anhalten (of a sentry). — s. die Herausforderung; das Anhalten (by a sentry); die Einwendung.

chalybeate [kə'libiət], adj. (Med.) eisenhaltig.

chamber ['tʃeimbə], s. das Zimmer, die Kammer.

chamberlain ['tʃeimbəlin], s. der Kammerherr.

chambermaid ['tʃeimbəmeid], s. das Zimmermädchen, Kammermädchen.

chameleon [kə'mi:ljən], s. (Zool.) das Chamäleon.

chamois ['ʃæmwa:], s. (Zool.) die Gemse.

champagne [ʃæm'pein], s. der Champagner, der Sekt.

champion ['tʃæmpjən], s. der Meister, Verteidiger. — v.a. vertreten (cause); beschützen (person).

chance [tʃa:ns], s. der Zufall; die Gelegenheit (opportunity); die Möglichkeit (possibility); take a —, es darauf ankommen lassen; by —, zufällig. — v.a. zufällig tun, geraten; riskieren (risk).

chancel ['tʃa:nsəl], s. (Eccl.) der Chor, der Altarplatz.

chancellor ['tʃa:nsələ], s. der Kanzler.

chancery ['tʃa:nsəri], s. das Kanzleigericht.

chandelier [ʃændə'liə], s. der Armleuchter, Kronleuchter.

chandler ['tʃa:ndlə], s. der Lichtzieher; Krämer; (corn merchant) der Kornhändler.

change [tʃeindʒ], s. die Änderung; das Umsteigen (trains); small —, das Kleingeld; die Veränderung; Abwechslung. — v.a. ändern (alter); wechseln (money); umsteigen (trains); eintauschen, umtauschen (exchange); sich umziehen (clothes). — v.n. sich (ver)ändern, anders werden, umschlagen; (Railw.) — for, umsteigen nach.

changeable ['tʃeindʒəbl], adj. veränderlich.

changeling ['tʃeindʒliŋ], s. der Wechselbalg.

changeover ['tʃeindʒouvə], s. der Wechsel; der Umschalter; die Umstellung.

channel ['tʃænəl], s. der Kanal. — v.a. leiten, kanalisieren.

chant [tʃa:nt], v.a., v.n. (Eccl.) singen. — s. (Mus.) der Kantus, der liturgische Gesang.

chaos ['keiɔs], s. das Chaos.

chaotic [kei'ɔtik], adj. chaotisch.

chap (1) [tʃæp], s. der Riss (skin etc.). — v.n. Risse bekommen.

chap (2) [tʃæp], s. (usually in pl.) der Kinnbacken.

chap (3) [tʃæp], s. (coll.) der Kerl, der Bursche.

chapel ['tʃæpəl], s. (Eccl.) die Kapelle.

chaperon ['ʃæpəroun], s. die Anstandsdame. — v.a. begleiten, bemuttern.

chaplain ['tʃæplin], s. der Kaplan.

chapter ['tʃæptə], s. das Kapitel.

char [tʃa:], v.a. verkohlen. — v.n. (coll.) putzen, Hausarbeit verrichten (do housework). — s. (coll.) die Haushilfe, die Hausgehilfin, Putzfrau.

character ['kærəktə], s. der Charakter (personality); das Zeichen (sign, symbol); (Maths.) die Ziffer; das Zeugnis (testimonial).

characteristic [kærəktə'ristik], adj. charakteristisch, typisch.

characterize ['kærəktəraiz], v.a. charakterisieren, kennzeichnen.

charade [ʃə'ra:d], s. die Scharade, das Silbenrätsel.

charcoal ['tʃa:koul], s. die Holzkohle; — burner, der Köhler.

charge [tʃa:dʒ], v.a. laden, aufladen; (Law) beschuldigen; (Mil.) angreifen; belasten (with a bill); — up to s.o., jemandem etwas anrechnen; verlangen (price). — s. die Ladung, der Auftrag (order); die Aufsicht; to be in —, die Aufsicht haben; (Law) die Beschuldigung, Anklage; das Mündel (of a guardian); (pl.) die Kosten, Spesen.

chargeable ['tʃa:dʒəbl], adj. anzurechnend; steuerbar (of objects).

charger ['tʃa:dʒə], s. das Schlachtroß.

chariness ['tʃɛərinis], s. die Behutsamkeit.

chariot ['tʃæriət], s. der Kriegswagen.

charioteer [tʃæriə'tiə], s. der Wagenlenker.

charitable ['tʃæritəbl], adj. wohltätig, mild, mildtätig.

charitableness ['tʃæritəblnis], s. die Wohltätigkeit, Milde.

charity ['tʃæriti], s. die Güte; Nächstenliebe; Mildtätigkeit (alms); die Barmherzigkeit (charitableness); der wohltätige Zweck (cause); sister of —, barmherzige Schwester.

charlatan ['ʃa:lətən], s. der Scharlatan, Pfuscher.

charm [tʃa:m], s. der Zauber (magic); der Reiz. — v.a. bezaubern.

chart [tʃa:t], s. (Geog.) die Karte. — v.a. auf der Karte einzeichnen.

charter ['tʃa:tə], s. die Urkunde; (Naut.) die Schiffsmiete. — v.a. mieten, chartern, heuern (ship, plane); ein Privileg geben, bevorrechtigen.

charwoman ['tʃa:wumən], s. die Putzfrau, Reinemacherin.

chary ['tʃɛəri], adj. behutsam; vorsichtig (cautious); sparsam (thrifty).

chase [tʃeis], v.a. jagen, verfolgen. — s. die Jagd (hunt); das Gehege (game preserve).

chaser ['tʃeisə], s. der Verfolger (pursuer); die Schiffskanone (gun).

chasm [kæzm], s. die Kluft; der Abgrund.

chassis ['ʃæsi], s. (Motor.) das Fahrgestell.

335

chaste [tʃeist], *adj.* keusch, züchtig.
chasten [tʃeisn], *v.a.* züchtigen; reinigen.
chastize [tʃæs'taiz], *v.a.* züchtigen.
chastity ['tʃæstiti], *s.* die Keuschheit, Züchtigkeit.
chasuble ['tʃæzjubl], *s.* (*Eccl.*) das Meßgewand.
chat [tʃæt], *v.n.* plaudern. — *s.* das Geplauder.
chattel [tʃætl], *s.* (*usually in pl.*) die Habe; *goods and* —s, Hab und Gut.
chatter ['tʃætə], *v.n.* schwätzen; schnattern. — *s.* das Geschwätz (*talk*).
chatterbox ['tʃætəbɔks], *s.* die Plaudertasche.
chatty ['tʃæti], *adj.* geschwätzig.
chauffeur ['ʃoufə, ʃou'fəː], *s.* (*Motor.*) der Fahrer.
chauffeuse [ʃou'fəːz], *s.* die Fahrerin.
chauvinism ['ʃouvinizm], *s.* der Chauvinismus.
cheap [tʃiːp], *adj.* billig.
cheapen ['tʃiːpən], *v.a.* herabsetzen, erniedrigen (*value*).
cheapness ['tʃiːpnis], *s.* die Billigkeit (*price*).
cheat [tʃiːt], *v.a.*, *v.n.* betrügen. — *s.* der Betrüger.
cheating ['tʃiːtiŋ], *s.* das Betrügen; der Betrug.
check [tʃek], *s.* der Einhalt, der Halt; die Kontrolle; das Hindernis (*obstacle*); (*Chess*) Schach; (*Am.*) *see* **cheque.** — *v.a.* zurückhalten, aufhalten (*stop*); überprüfen. — *v.n.* Schach bieten (*Dat.*).
checker *see under* **chequer.**
checkmate ['tʃekmeit], *s.* das Schachmatt.
cheek [tʃiːk], *s.* die Wange, die Backe; die Unverschämtheit (*impertinence*). — *v.a.* unverschämt sein *or* handeln (*s.o.*, an jemandem).
cheeky ['tʃiːki], *adj.* frech, unverschämt.
cheer [tʃiə], *v.a.* anfeuern, anspornen; zujubeln; — *up*, aufmuntern. — *v.n.* — *up*, Mut fassen. — *s.* der Zuruf; der Beifallsruf (*acclaim*); *three* —s, ein dreifaches Hoch (*for*, auf).
cheerful ['tʃiəful], *adj.* fröhlich, froh.
cheerless ['tʃiəlis], *adj.* unfreundlich, freudlos.
cheese [tʃiːz], *s.* der Käse; — *straw*, die Käsestange.
cheesecloth ['tʃiːzklɔθ], *s.* (*Am.*) das Nesseltuch.
cheeseparing ['tʃiːzpɛəriŋ], *adj.* knauserig.
cheesy ['tʃiːzi], *adj.* käsig; (*sl.*) schlecht aussehend.
cheetah ['tʃiːtə], *s.* (*Zool.*) der Jagdleopard.
chemical ['kemikəl], *adj.* chemisch. — *s.* die Chemikalie, das chemische Element; das chemische Produkt.
chemise [ʃi'miːz], *s.* das Frauenhemd.
chemist ['kemist], *s.* der Chemiker; Drogist; Apotheker (*dispenser*).

chemistry ['kemistri], *s.* die Chemie.
cheque, (*Am.*) **check** [tʃek], *s.* (*Fin.*) der Scheck.
chequer, checker ['tʃekə], *s.* das scheckige Muster, Würfelmuster. — *v.a.* würfelig machen, bunt machen.
cherish ['tʃeriʃ], *v.a.* hegen, wertschätzen, lieben.
cherry ['tʃeri], *s.* (*Bot.*) die Kirsche; — *brandy*, das Kirschwasser.
chess [tʃes], *s.* das Schachspiel; —*man*, die Schachfigur; —*board*, das Schachbrett.
chest [tʃest], *s.* die Truhe (*box*); die Kiste; (*Anat.*) Brust; — *of drawers*, die Kommode.
chestnut ['tʃestnʌt], *s.* (*Bot.*) die Kastanie; (*horse*) der Braune. — *adj.* kastanienbraun.
chew [tʃuː], *v.a.* kauen; —*ing gum*, der Kaugummi.
chic [ʃiːk], *adj.* elegant, schick.
chicanery [ʃi'keinəri], *s.* die Schikane, Haarspalterei, Kleinlichkeit.
chicken ['tʃikin], *s.* das Huhn, Kücken; — *soup*, die Hühnersuppe.
chickenpox ['tʃikinpɔks], *s.* (*Med.*) die Windpocken.
chicory ['tʃikəri], *s.* (*Bot.*) die Zichorie.
chide [tʃaid], *v.a. irr.* schelten.
chief [tʃiːf], *s.* der Häuptling (*of tribe*); (*Am. coll.*) der Chef (*boss*). — *adj.* hauptsächlich, Haupt-, oberst.
chieftain ['tʃiːftin], *s.* der Häuptling (*of tribe*); Anführer (*leader*).
chilblain ['tʃilblein], *s.* die Frostbeule.
child [tʃaild], *s.* das Kind.
childbirth ['tʃaildbəːθ], *s.* die Niederkunft.
childhood ['tʃaildhud], *s.* die Kindheit.
childish ['tʃaildiʃ], *adj.* kindisch.
childlike ['tʃaildlaik], *adj.* kindlich, wie ein Kind.
Chilean ['tʃiliən], *adj.* chilenisch. — *s.* der Chilene.
chill [tʃil], *s.* die Kälte, der Frost; die Erkältung. — *v.a.* kalt machen (*freeze*); erstarren lassen (*make rigid*); entmutigen (*discourage*).
chilly ['tʃili], *adj.* frostig, eisig, eiskalt.
chime [tʃaim], *s.* das Glockengeläute. — *v.n.* klingen, läuten.
chimera [ki'miərə], *s.* das Hirngespinst, das Trugbild.
chimney ['tʃimni], *s.* der Kamin, der Schornstein; —*pot*, —*stack*, der Schornstein; —*sweep*, der Kaminfeger, Schornsteinfeger.
chimpanzee [tʃimpæn'ziː], *s.* (*Zool.*) der Schimpanse.
chin [tʃin], *s.* (*Anat.*) das Kinn.
china ['tʃainə], *s.* das Porzellan; — *ware*, das Küchengeschirr.
chine (1) [tʃain], *s.* das Rückgrat.
chine (2) [tʃain], *s.* (*Geog.*) der Kamm.
Chinaman ['tʃainəmən], *s.* (*obs.*) der Chinese.
Chinese [tʃai'niːz], *adj.* chinesisch. — *s.* der Chinese.
chink [tʃink], *s.* die Ritze, der Spalt.

chip [tʃip], *v.a.* schnitzeln (*wood*); ausbrechen (*stone*); in kleine Stücke schneiden. — *v.n.* — *off*, abbröckeln; — *in*, (*coll.*) sich hineinmischen. —*s.* der Span (*wood*); der Splitter (*glass, stone*); (*pl.*) Pommes frites (*pl.*) (*potatoes*).

chiromancy ['kaiərəmænsi], *s.* das Handlesen.

chiropodist [ki'rɔpədist], *s.* der Fußpfleger.

chirp [tʃəːp], *v.n.* zwitschern (*birds*), zirpen (*crickets*).

chirping ['tʃəːpiŋ], *s.* das Gezwitscher (*birds*), das Gezirpe (*crickets*).

chisel [tʃizl], *s.* der Meißel. — *v.a.* meißeln.

chit [tʃit], *s.* das Stück Papier; (*coll.*) junges Ding; —*chat*, das Geplauder.

chivalrous ['ʃivəlrəs], *adj.* ritterlich; tapfer (*brave*).

chivalry ['ʃivəlri], *s.* die Ritterlichkeit (*courtesy*); Tapferkeit (*bravery*).

chive [tʃaiv], *s.* (*Bot.*) der Schnittlauch.

chlorate ['klɔːreit], *s.* (*Chem.*) das Chlorsalz.

chlorine ['klɔːriːn], *s.* (*Chem.*) das Chlor, Chlorgas.

chloroform ['klɔrəfɔːm], *s.* das Chloroform. — *v.a.* chloroformieren.

chocolate ı'tʃɔkəlit], *s.* die Schokolade. — *adj.* schokoladenfarben.

choice [tʃɔis], *s.* die Wahl; Auswahl (*selection*). — *adj.* auserlesen.

choir ['kwaiə], *s.* der Chor.

choke [tʃouk], *v.a., v.n.* ersticken; verstopfen (*block*). — *s.* (*Elec.*) die Drosselspule; (*Motor.*) die Starterklappe.

choler ['kɔlə], *s.* die Galle; (*fig.*) der Zorn (*anger*).

cholera ['kɔlərə], *s.* (*Med.*) die Cholera.

choleric ['kɔlərik], *adj.* jähzornig, cholerisch.

choose [tʃuːz], *v.a. irr.* wählen, auswählen (*select*).

choosy ['tʃuːzi], *adj.* wählerisch.

chop [tʃɔp], *v.a.* abhacken (*cut off*), hacken (*meat*). — *s.* das Kotelett (*meat*).

chopper ['tʃɔpə], *s.* das Hackbeil (*axe*); das Hackmesser (*knife*).

choppy ['tʃɔpi], *adj.* bewegt (*sea*), stürmisch.

chopstick ['tʃɔpstik], *s.* das Eßstäbchen.

choral ['kɔːrəl], *adj.* Chor-; — *society*, der Gesangverein.

chorale [kɔ'rɑːl], *s.* (*Eccl., Mus.*) der Choral.

chord [kɔːd], *s.* die Saite; (*Geom.*) die Sehne; (*Mus.*) der Akkord.

chorister ['kɔristə], *s.* der Chorknabe (*boy*), Chorsänger.

chorus ['kɔːrəs], *s.* der Chor (*opera*); der Refrain (*song*).

Christ [kraist]. Christus, *m.*

christen [krisn], *v.a.* taufen (*baptize*); nennen (*name*).

Christendom ['krisndəm], *s.* die Christenheit.

christening ['krisniŋ], *s.* die Taufe

Christian ['kristjən], *s.* der Christ (*believer in Christ*). — *adj.* christlich; — *name*, der Vorname.

Christianity [kristi'æniti], *s.* die christliche Religion, das Christentum.

Christmas ['krisməs], *s.* (die) Weihnachten; das Weihnachtsfest; — *Eve*, der heilige Abend.

chromatic [kro'mætik], *adj.* (*Mus.*) chromatisch.

chrome [kroum], *s.* das Chrom.

chronic ['krɔnik], *adj.* chronisch.

chronicle ['krɔnikl], *s.* die Chronik. — *v.a.* (in einer Chronik) verzeichnen.

chronological [krɔnə'lɔdʒikəl], *adj.* chronologisch.

chronology [krɔ'nɔlədʒi], *s.* die Chronologie.

chronometer [krɔ'nɔmitə], *s.* das Chronometer.

chrysalis ['krisəlis], *s.* (*Ent.*) die Puppe.

chrysanthemum [kri'zænθəməm], *s.* (*Bot.*) die Chrysantheme.

chub [tʃʌb], *s.* (*Zool.*) der Döbel.

chubby ['tʃʌbi], *adj.* pausbäckig, plump.

chuck [tʃʌk], *v.a.* (*coll.*) — *out*, hinauswerfen. — *v.n.* glucken (*chicken*).

chuckle [tʃʌkl], *v.n.* kichern. — *s.* das Kichern.

chum [tʃʌm], *s.* (*coll.*) der Freund, Kamerad. — *v.n.* (*coll.*) — *up*, sich befreunden (*with*, mit).

chump [tʃʌmp], *s.* der Klotz (*wood*).

chunk [tʃʌnk], *s.* das große Stück (*meat etc.*).

church [tʃəːtʃ], *s.* die Kirche.

churchwarden [tʃəːtʃ'wɔːdn], *s.* der Kirchenvorsteher.

churchyard ['tʃəːtʃjɑːd], *s.* der Friedhof.

churl [tʃəːl], *s.* der Grobian, der grobe Kerl.

churlish ['tʃəːliʃ], *adj.* grob, unfein.

churn [tʃəːn], *s.* das Butterfaß. — *v.a.* mischen, schütteln (*butter etc.*); — *up*, aufwühlen (*stir up*).

chute [ʃuːt], *s.* die Gleitbahn.

cider ['saidə], *s.* der Apfelmost.

cigar [si'gɑː], *s.* die Zigarre; — *case*, das Zigarrenetui.

cigarette [sigə'ret], *s.* die Zigarette; — *holder*, die Zigarettenspitze; — *lighter*, das Feuerzeug.

cinder ['sində], *s.* (*usually in pl.*) die Asche (*fire*); die Schlacke (*furnace*).

Cinderella [sində'relə]. das Aschenbrödel, Aschenputtel.

cinema ['sinimə], *s.* das Kino.

cinematography [sinimə'tɔgrəfi], *s.* die Filmkunst.

Cingalese *see* **Singhalese**.

cinnamon ['sinəmən], *s.* der Zimt.

cipher ['saifə], *s.* die Ziffer; die Geheimschrift (*code*). — *v.n.* rechnen. — *v.a.* chiffrieren (*code*).

Circassian [səː'kæsiən], *adj.* tscherkessisch. — *s.* der Tscherkesse.

circle

circle [səːkl], s. der Zirkel, Kreis; (social) Gesellschaftskreis; (Theat.) der Rang. — v.a. umringen. — v.n. umkreisen; sich drehen (revolve).

circuit ['səːkit], s. der Kreislauf; (Elec.) der Stromkreis.

circuitous [səː'kjuːitəs], adj. weitschweifig, weitläufig.

circular ['səːkjulə], adj. rund, kreisförmig, Rund-; — tour, die Rundreise. — s. das Rundschreiben (letter); der Werbebrief (advertising).

circulate ['səːkjuleit], v.a. in Umlauf setzen. — v.n. umlaufen, kreisen, zirkulieren.

circulation [səːkju'leiʃən], s. die Zirkulation, der Kreislauf (blood); die Verbreitung, Auflage (newspaper); der Umlauf (banknotes).

circumcise ['səːkəmsaiz], v.a. beschneiden.

circumference [səː'kʌmfərəns], s. der Umfang.

circumscribe ['səːkəmskraib], v.a. beschränken, einengen (narrow down); umschreiben (paraphrase).

circumspect ['səːkəmspekt], adj. umsichtig, vorsorglich.

circumspection [səːkəm'spekʃən], s. die Umsicht, Vorsicht.

circumstance ['səːkəmstæns, -staːns], s. der Umstand; pomp and —, großer Aufmarsch.

circumstantial [səːkəm'stænʃəl], adj. umständlich; zu einem Umstand gehörig; eingehend; — evidence, der Indizienbeweis.

circumvent [səːkəm'vent], v.a. überlisten, hintergehen.

circus ['səːkəs], s. der Zirkus; der Platz.

cirrhus ['sirəs], s. die Federwolke.

Cistercian [sis'təːʃən], s. der Zisterzienser (monk).

cistern ['sistən], s. die Zisterne, der Wasserbehälter.

citadel ['sitədəl], s. die Zitadelle, die Burg.

citation [sai'teiʃən], s. das Zitat; (Law) die Zitierung, Vorladung; (Mil.) die rühmliche Erwähnung.

cite [sait], v.a. zitieren (quote); (Law) vorladen.

citizen ['sitizən], s. der Bürger, Staatsbürger (national); fellow —, der Mitbürger.

citizenship ['sitizənʃip], s. das Bürgerrecht, die Staatsangehörigkeit.

citrate ['sitreit], s. (Chem.) das Zitrat.

citric ['sitrik], adj. (Chem.) Zitronen-.

citron ['sitrən], s. die Zitrone. — adj. zitronenfarben.

city ['siti], s. die Stadt; die Großstadt; die City. — adj. städtisch.

civic ['sivik], adj. Stadt-, städtisch (ceremonial); bürgerlich.

civil ['sivil], adj. zivil; höflich (polite); — engineer, der Zivilingenieur; — service, der Beamtendienst, die Beamtenlaufbahn, der Staatsdienst; — war, der Bürgerkrieg.

civilian [si'viljən], s. der Zivilist.

civility [si'viliti], s. die Höflichkeit.

civilization [sivilai'zeiʃən], s. die Zivilisation.

civilize ['sivilaiz], v.a. zivilisieren, verfeinern (refine).

clack [klæk], v.n. klappern (wood etc.); plaudern, plappern.

clad [klæd], adj. gekleidet.

claim [kleim], v.a. Anspruch erheben (to, auf); fordern (demand); behaupten (assert). — s. der Anspruch; die Forderung (demand); das Recht.

claimant ['kleimənt], s. der Beanspruchende, Ansprucherheber. ·

clairvoyance [klɛə'vɔiəns], s. das Hellsehen.

clairvoyant [klɛə'vɔiənt], s. der Hellseher.

clam [klæm], s. (Zool.) die Venusmuschel; shut up like a —, verschwiegen sein.

clamber ['klæmbə], v.n. klettern.

clamminess ['klæminis], s. die Feuchtigkeit, Klebrigkeit.

clammy ['klæmi], adj. feucht, klebrig.

clamorous ['klæmərəs], adj. lärmend, laut, ungestüm.

clamour ['klæmə], s. das Geschrei, der Lärm. — v.n. laut schreien (for, nach, Dat.).

clamp [klæmp], s. die Klammer, die Klampe. — v.a. festklammern.

clan [klæn], s. die Sippe, die Familie.

clandestine [klæn'destin], adj. heimlich, verstohlen.

clang [klæŋ], s. der Schall, das Geklirr. — v.n. erschallen. — v.a. erschallen lassen.

clangour ['klæŋə], s. das Getöse, der Lärm.

clank [klæŋk], s. das Geklirre, das Gerassel (metal).

clannish ['klæniʃ], adj. stammesbewußt; engherzig (narrow).

clap [klæp], v.a. schlagen, zusammenschlagen (hands). — v.n. Beifall klatschen (dates).

clapperboard ['klæpəbɔːd], s. (Film) das Klappbrett, die Klapptafel; der Klöppel (beater, in lacemaking).

claptrap ['klæptræp], s. der billige Effekt, das eitle Geschwätz (gossip).

claret ['klærit], s. der Rotwein.

clarification [klærifi'keiʃən], s. die Klarstellung, Aufklärung.

clarify ['klærifai], v.a. klarstellen.

clari(o)net [klæri(ə)'net], s. (Mus.) die Klarinette.

clarion ['klæriən], s. (Mus.) die Zinke, Trompete; — call, der laute Ruf.

clash [klæʃ], v.a. zusammenschlagen. — v.n. aufeinanderprallen, zusammenfallen (dates); widerstreiten (views). — s. (fig.) der Zusammenstoß, der Widerstreit.

clasp [klaːsp], v.a. ergreifen, festhalten. — s. der Haken (hook); die Schnalle, die Spange (buckle, brooch); — knife, das Taschenmesser.

class [klɑːs], *s.* die Klasse.
classic(al) [ˈklæsik(əl)], *adj.* klassisch.
classics [ˈklæsiks], *s. pl.* die Klassiker, *m. pl.*; die klassische Philologie (*subject of study*).
classification [klæsifiˈkeiʃən], *s.* die Klassifizierung.
classify [ˈklæsifai], *v.a.* klassifizieren.
clatter [ˈklætə], *s.* das Getöse, Geklirr. — *v.a., v.n.* klappern, klirren.
Claus [klɔːz]. Claus, Nicholas, *m.*; *Santa* —, der heilige Nikolaus, Knecht Ruprecht, Weihnachtsmann.
clause [klɔːz], *s.* (*Gram.*) der Nebensatz; die Klausel (*contract*); (*Law*) der Vertragspunkt.
claw [klɔː], *s.* die Klaue, die Kralle. — *v.a.* kratzen.
clay [klei], *s.* der Ton, Lehm.
clayey [kleii], *adj.* lehmig, tonig.
clean [kliːn], *adj.* rein, reinlich (*habits*); sauber; — *shaven*, glattrasiert. — *v.a.* reinigen, putzen.
cleaner [ˈkliːnə], *s.* die Reinemacherin, die Putzfrau.
cleanliness [ˈklenlinis], *s.* die Reinlichkeit, Sauberkeit.
cleanse [klenz], *v.a.* reinigen.
clear [kliə], *adj.* klar, hell; deutlich (*meaning*); schuldlos (*not guilty*). — *s.* *in the* —, nicht betroffen, schuldlos. — *v.a.* (*Chem.*) klären; (*Law*) für unschuldig erklären; verzollen (*pass through customs*); springen (über, *Acc.*). — *v.n.* (— *up*), sich aufklären, aufhellen (*weather*).
clearance [ˈkliərəns], *s.* die Räumung; — *sale*, der Ausverkauf; die Verzollung (*customs*).
clearing [ˈkliərin], *s.* die Lichtung (*in wood*); (*Comm.*) die Verrechnung.
clearness [ˈkliənis], *s.* die Deutlichkeit, die Klarheit, Helle.
cleave [kliːv], *v.a. irr.* spalten (*wood*). — *v.n.* sich spalten.
cleaver [ˈkliːvə], *s.* das Hackmesser.
cleek [kliːk], *s.* der Golfschläger.
clef [klef], *s.* (*Mus.*) der Schlüssel.
cleft [kleft], *s.* der Spalt. — *adj.* — *palate*, die Gaumenspalte.
clemency [ˈklemənsi], *s.* die Milde, Gnade (*mercy*).
clement [ˈklemənt], *adj.* mild (*climate*); gnädig (*merciful*).
clench [klentʃ], *v.a.* zusammenpressen; ballen (*fist*).
clergy [ˈkləːdʒi], *s.* (*Eccl.*) die Geistlichkeit.
clergyman [ˈkləːdʒimən], *s.* (*Eccl.*) der Geistliche.
clerical [ˈklerikl], *adj.* (*Eccl.*) geistlich; beamtlich, Beamten-, Büro- (*office*); — *work*, die Büroarbeit.
clerk [klɑːk], *s.* der Schreiber, der Bürogehilfe (*junior*), der Bürobeamte, Büroangestellte (*senior*); *bank* —, der Bankbeamte.
clever [ˈklevə], *adj.* klug; intelligent; geschickt (*deft*); gewandt, listig (*cunning*).

cleverness [ˈklevənis], *s.* die Klugheit (*intelligence*); die Schlauheit (*cunning*); die Begabung (*talent*); die Geschicklichkeit (*skill*).
clew [kluː] *see* clue.
click [klik], *v.a., v.n.* einschnappen (*lock*); zusammenschlagen (*o.'s heels*, die Hacken); schnalzen (*o.'s tongue*); (*sl.*) zusammenpassen (*of two people*). — *s.* das Einschnappen (*lock*); das Zusammenschlagen (*heels*); das Schnalzen (*tongue*).
client [ˈklaiənt], *s.* (*Law*) der Klient; (*Comm.*) der Kunde.
clientele [kliːənˈtel], *s.* die Klientel, die Kundschaft.
cliff [klif], *s.* die Klippe.
climate [ˈklaimit], *s.* das Klima.
climatic [klaiˈmætik], *adj.* klimatisch.
climax [ˈklaimæks], *s.* der Höhepunkt.
climb [klaim], *v.a.* erklettern, erklimmen. — *v.n.* klettern, bergsteigen; (*Aviat.*) steigen. — *s.* der Aufstieg, die Ersteigung.
climber [ˈklaimə], *s.* der Bergsteiger (*mountaineer*); (*Bot.*) die Schlingpflanze.
clinch [klintʃ], *v.a.* vernieten, befestigen; — *a deal*, einen Handel abschließen. — *s.* der feste Griff; die Umklammerung (*boxing*).
cling [klin], *v.n. irr.* sich anklammern, festhalten (*to*, an).
clinic [ˈklinik], *s.* die Klinik.
clinical [ˈklinikl], *adj.* klinisch.
clink [klink], *s.* das Geklirre; (*coll.*) das Gefängnis. — *v.a.* — *glasses*, mit den Gläsern anstoßen.
clinker [ˈklinkə], *s.* der Backstein; die Schlacke.
clip [klip], *v.a.* stutzen, beschneiden; lochen (*ticket*).
clip (2) [klip], *v.a.* befestigen. — *s.* *paper* —, die Büroklammer.
clippings [ˈklipinz], *s. pl.* die Abschnitte; die Schnitzel (*waste*); Zeitungsausschnitte, *m. pl.*
cloak [klouk], *s.* der Mantel, der Deckmantel (*cover*). — *v.a.* verbergen.
cloakroom [ˈkloukruːm], *s.* die Garderobe; — *free*, keine Garderobegebühr; (*Railw.*) die Gepäckaufbewahrung.
clock [klɔk], *s.* die (große) Uhr, Wanduhr; — *face*, das Zifferblatt. — *v.n.* — *in*, die Zeitkarte (Kontrollkarte) stempeln lassen, eintreffen (*arrive*).
clockwise [ˈklɔkwaiz], *adv.* im Uhrzeigersinne.
clod [klɔd], *s.* die Erdscholle, der Erdklumpen; (*sl.*) der Lümmel (*lout*).
clog [klɔg], *v.a.* belasten, hemmen, verstopfen. — *v.n.* sich verstopfen. — *s.* der Holzschuh.
cloisters [ˈklɔistəz], *s. pl.* (*Eccl.*, *Archit.*) der Kreuzgang.

close

close [klouz], *v.a.* schließen, verschließen; beenden (*meeting etc.*). — *v.n.* — *in on*, über einen hereinbrechen, umzingeln. — *s.* das Ende, der Schluß; [klous] der Domplatz. — [klous], *adj.* nahe (*near*); knapp (*narrow*); nahestehend, vertraut (*friend*); schwül (*weather*); geizig (*miserly*).

closeness ['klousnis], *s.* die Nähe (*nearness*); die Schwüle (*weather*); die Vertrautheit (*familiarity*).

closet ['klɔzit], *s.* der Wandschrank (*cupboard*); das kleine Zimmer; das Klosett (*W.C.*). — *v.r.* — *o.s. with*, sich mit jemandem zurückziehen, sich vertraulich beraten.

closure ['klouʒə], *s.* der Schluß; der Abschluß (einer Debatte).

clot [klɔt], *s.* das Klümpchen. — *v.n.* sich verdicken, gerinnen; —*ted cream*, dicke Sahne.

cloth [klɔθ], *s.* das Tuch; der Stoff; die Leinwand (*bookbinding*); *American* —, das Wachstuch; — *printing*, der Zeugdruck.

clothe [klouð], *v.a.* kleiden. — *v.r.* sich kleiden.

clothes [klouðz], *s. pl.* die Kleider, *n. pl.*; die Kleidung; die Wäsche (*washing*); — *basket*, der Wäschekorb; — *press*, der Kleiderschrank.

clothier ['klouðiə], *s.* der Tuchmacher (*manufacturer*); der Tuchhändler (*dealer*).

clothing ['klouðiŋ], *s.* die Kleidung.

cloud [klaud], *s.* die Wolke; *under a —*, in Ungnade; —*burst*, der Wolkenbruch. — *v.a.* bewölken, verdunkeln. — *v.n.* — *over*, sich umwölken.

cloudiness ['klaudinis], *s.* die Umwölkung, der Wolkenhimmel.

cloudy ['klaudi], *adj.* wolkig, bewölkt, umwölkt.

clout [klaut], *s.* (*obs.*) der Lappen (*rag*); (*coll.*) der Schlag (*hit*). — *v.a.* schlagen (*hit*).

clove [klouv], *s.* die Gewürznelke (*spice*).

clove(n) [klouv(n)], *adj.* gespalten.

clover ['klouvə], *s.* (*Bot.*) der Klee; *to be in* —, Glück haben, es gut haben.

clown [klaun], *s.* der Hanswurst. — *v.n.* den Hanswurst spielen.

clownish ['klauniʃ], *adj.* tölpelhaft.

clownishness ['klauniʃnis], *s.* die Derbheit, Tölpelhaftigkeit.

cloy [klɔi], *v.n.* übersättigen, anwidern, anekeln.

club (1) [klʌb], *s.* die Keule (*stick*). — *v.a.* (einen) mit einer Keule schlagen.

club (2) [klʌb], *s.* der Klub, der Verein. — *v.n.* — *together*, zusammen beitragen, zusammensteuern (*contribute jointly*).

club (3) [klʌb], *s.* (*cards*) das Treff, die Eichel (*German cards*).

clubfoot ['klʌbfut], ∴ der Klumpfuß.

cluck [klʌk], *v.n.* glucken (*hen*).

clue [klu:], *s.* der Anhaltspunkt, Leitfaden, die Richtlinie, die Angabe (*crossword*); *no* —, keine blasse Ahnung.

clump [klʌmp], *s.* der Klumpen; die Gruppe.

clumsiness ['klʌmzinis], *s.* die Unbeholfenheit, Ungeschicklichkeit.

clumsy ['klʌmzi], *adj.* unbeholfen, schwerfällig, ungeschickt.

Cluniac ['klu:njæk]. (*Eccl.*) der Kluniazenser.

cluster ['klʌstə], *s.* die Traube (*grapes*), der Büschel. — *v.n.* in Büschen wachsen oder stehen, sich gruppiert sein.

clutch [klʌtʃ], *v.a.* ergreifen, packen (*grip*). — *s.* der Griff; (*Motor.*) die Kupplung.

coach [koutʃ], *s.* die Kutsche; der Wagen, der Autobus; der Privatlehrer (*teacher*). — *v.a.* unterrichten, vorbereiten (*for examinations etc.*).

coachman ['koutʃmən], *s.* der Kutscher.

coagulate [kou'ægjuleit], *v.a.* gerinnen lassen. — *v.n.* gerinnen.

coagulation [kouægju'leiʃən], *s.* das Gerinnen.

coal [koul], *s.* die Kohle; — *mine*, das Kohlenbergwerk; die Kohlengrube; — *miner*, der Bergmann.

coalesce [kouə'les], *v.n.* zusammenwachsen, sich vereinigen.

coalescence [kouə'lesəns], *s.* die Verschmelzung.

coalition [kouə'liʃən], *s.* (*Pol.*) die Koalition, das Bündnis.

coarse [kɔ:s], *adj.* grob; gemein (*manner*).

coarseness ['kɔ:snis], *s.* die Grobheit, Unfeinheit.

coast [koust], *s.* die Küste. — *v.n.* (an der Küste) entlangfahren; gleiten, rodeln.

coat [kout], *s.* der Mantel, Rock; die Jacke (*jacket*); das Fell (*animal*); — *of arms*, das Wappenschild; — *of mail*, das Panzerhemd; — *of paint*, der Anstrich. — *v.a.* überziehen, bemalen (*paint*).

coathanger ['kouthæŋə], *s.* der Kleiderbügel.

coating ['koutiŋ], *s.* der Überzug.

coax [kouks], *v.a.* beschwatzen; überreden (*persuade*).

cob (1) [kɔb], *s.* der Gaul.

cob (2) [kɔb], *s.* (*Orn.*) der Schwan.

cob (3) [kɔb], *s.* der (Mais)Kolben (*corn on the —*).

cobble [kɔbl], *v.a.* flicken (*shoes*).

cobbled ['kɔbld], *adj.* mit Kopfsteinen gepflastert.

cobbler ['kɔblə], *s.* der Schuhflicker.

cobble(stone) ['kɔbl(stoun)], *s.* das Kopfsteinpflaster.

cobweb ['kɔbweb], *s.* das Spinngewebe.

cock [kɔk], *s.* (*Orn.*) der Hahn; (*Engin.*) der Sperrhahn, Hahn; — *sparrow*, das Sperlingsmännchen; —*-a-doodle-doo!* kikeriki!

cockade [kɔ'keid], *s.* die Kokarde.

cockatoo [kɔkə'tu:], *s.* (*Orn.*) der Kakadu.

340

cockchafer ['kɔktʃeifə], *s.* (*Ent.*) der Maikäfer.

cockerel ['kɔkərəl], *s.* (*Orn.*) der junge Hahn.

cockswain [kɔksn] *see* **coxswain**.

cockle [kɔkl], *s.* (*Zool.*) die Herzmuschel.

cockney ['kɔkni], *s.* der geborene Londoner.

cockpit ['kɔkpit], *s.* (*Aviat.*) der Pilotensitz, die Kanzel, der Führerraum.

cockroach ['kɔkroutʃ], *s.* (*Ent.*) die Schabe.

cocksure ['kɔkʃuə], *adj.* zuversichtlich, allzu sicher.

cocoa ['koukou], *s.* der Kakao.

coconut ['koukonʌt], *s.* die Kokosnuß.

cocoon [kə'ku:n], *s.* der Kokon, die Puppe (*of silkworm*).

cod [kɔd], *s.* der Kabeljau, Dorsch; — *liver oil*, der Lebertran; *dried* —, der Stockfisch.

coddle [kɔdl], *v.a.* verhätscheln, verweichlichen.

code [koud], *s.* das Gesetzbuch, der Kodex; die Chiffre (*cipher*). — *v.a.* chiffrieren, schlüsseln.

codify ['koudifai], *v.a.* kodifizieren.

coerce [kou'ə:s], *v.a.* zwingen.

coercion [kou'ə:ʃn], *s.* der Zwang.

coercive [kou'ə:siv], *adj.* zwingend.

coeval [kou'i:vəl], *adj.* gleichaltrig, gleichzeitig.

coexist [kouig'zist], *v.n.* zugleich existieren, nebeneinander leben.

coffee ['kɔfi], *s.* der Kaffee; — *grinder*, die Kaffeemühle; — *grounds*, der Kaffeesatz; — *pot*, die Kaffeekanne; — *set*, das Kaffee service.

coffer ['kɔfə], *s.* der Kasten, die Truhe.

coffin ['kɔfin], *s.* der Sarg.

cog [kɔg], *s.* der Zahn (*on wheel*); — *wheel*, das Zahnrad.

cogency ['koudʒənsi], *s.* die zwingende Kraft, Triftigkeit.

cogent ['koudʒənt], *adj.* zwingend, triftig.

cogitate ['kɔdʒiteit], *v.n.* nachdenken.

cogitation [kɔdʒi'teiʃən], *s.* die Überlegung, das Nachdenken.

cognate ['kɔgneit], *adj.* verwandt.

cognisance ['kɔgnizəns], *s.* die Erkenntnis; die Kenntnisnahme; (*Law*) die gerichtliche Kenntnisnahme.

cognisant ['kɔgnizənt], *adj.* wissend, in vollem Wissen (*of, Genit.*).

cognition [kɔg'niʃən], *s.* die Kenntnis, das Erkennen.

cohabit [kou'hæbit], *v.n.* zusammenleben.

cohabitation [kouhæbi'teiʃən], *s.* das Zusammenleben.

coheir [kou'εə], *s.* der Miterbe.

cohere [kou'hiə], *v.n.* zusammenhängen.

coherence [kou'hiərəns], *s.* der Zusammenhang.

coherent [kou'hiərənt], *adj.* zusammenhängend.

cohesion [kou'hi:ʒən], *s.* (*Phys.*) die Kohäsion.

coiffure [kwæ'fjuə], *s.* die Frisur, die Haartracht.

coil [kɔil], *s.* (*Elec.*) die Spule; die Windung. — *v.a.* aufwickeln; umwickeln, (auf)spulen. — *v.n.* sich winden.

coin [kɔin], *s.* die Münze, das Geldstück. — *v.a.* münzen, prägen; — *a phrase*, eine Redewendung prägen.

coinage ['kɔinidʒ], *s.* die Prägung.

coincide [kouin'said], *v.n.* zusammenfallen, zusammentreffen.

coincidence [kou'insidəns], *s.* das Zusammenfallen, Zusammentreffen; der Zufall (*chance*).

coincident [kou'insidənt], *adj.* zusammentreffend.

coke [kouk], *s.* der Koks. — *v.a.* (*Chem.*, *Engin.*) verkoken.

cold [kould], *adj.* kalt; gefühllos, kühl. — *s.* die Kälte (*temperature*); die Erkältung (*indisposition*).

coldish ['kouldiʃ], *adj.* kühl.

coldness ['kouldnis], *s.* die Kälte (*temperature*); die Kaltherzigkeit (*heartlessness*).

colic ['kɔlik], *s.* die Kolik.

collaborate [kə'læbəreit], *v.n.* zusammenarbeiten.

collaboration [kəlæbə'reiʃən], *s.* die Zusammenarbeit; die Mitwirkung, Mitarbeit (*assistance*).

collaborator [kə'læbəreitə], *s.* der Mitarbeiter.

collapse [kə'læps], *s.* der Zusammenbruch. — *v.n.* zusammenbrechen (*disintegrate*); zerfallen, einstürzen.

collapsible [kə'læpsibl], *adj.* zerlegbar, zusammenlegbar, zusammenklappbar.

collar ['kɔlə], *s.* der Kragen; —*bone*, das Schlüsselbein (*Anat.*); *dog* —, das Halsband; (*coll.*) der Priesterkragen; —*stud*, der Kragenknopf. — *v.a.* beim Kragen fassen, ergreifen.

collate [kɔ'leit], *v.a.* vergleichen (*texts etc.*).

collateral [kɔ'lætərəl], *adj.* Seiten-, von beiden Seiten. — *s.* (*Am.*) die Garantie, Bürgschaft.

collation [kɔ'leiʃən], *s.* die Vergleichung, der Vergleich (*texts etc.*); der Imbiß.

colleague ['kɔli:g], *s.* der Kollege, die Kollegin.

collect [kə'lekt], *v.a.* sammeln, zusammenbringen. — *v.n.* sich versammeln. — ['kɔlikt], *s.* (*Eccl.*) die Kollekte.

collection [kə'lekʃən], *s.* die Sammlung.

collective [kə'lektiv], *adj.* kollektiv, gemeinsam. — *s.* (*Pol.*) das Kollektiv.

collector [kə'lektə], *s.* der Sammler.

college ['kɔlidʒ], *s.* das Kollegium; das College; die Hochschule, Universität.

collide [kə'laid], *v.n.* zusammenstoßen.

collie ['kɔli], *s.* der Schäferhund.

collier ['kɔliə], *s.* der Kohlenarbeiter; das Kohlenfrachtschiff (*boat*).

collision

collision [kə'liʒən], s. der Zusammenstoß, Zusammenprall.
collocate ['kɔləkeit], v.a. ordnen.
collodion [kə'loudjən], s. (*Chem.*) das Kollodium.
colloquial [kə'loukwiəl], adj. umgangssprachlich, Umgangs-.
colloquy ['kɔlekwi], s. die Unterredung, das Gespräch (*formal*).
collusion [kə'luːʒən], s. das heimliche Einverständnis, die unstatthafte Partnerschaft; die Verdunkelung.
collusive [kə'luːziv], adj. abgekartet.
Cologne [kə'loun]. Köln, n.; *eau de* —, Kölnisch Wasser.
Colombian [kɔ'lɔmbjən], adj. kolumbisch. — s. der Kolumbier.
colon (1) ['koulən], s. das Kolon, der Doppelpunkt.
colon (2) ['koulɔn], s. (*Med.*) der Dickdarm.
colonel [kə:nl], s. (*Mil.*) der Oberst; — -*in-chief*, der Generaloberst, der oberste .Befehlshaber; *lieutenant-* —, der Oberstleutnant.
colonial [kə'lounjəl], adj. kolonial, aus den Kolonien.
colonist ['kɔlənist], s. der Siedler; Ansiedler.
colonization [kɔlənai'zeiʃən], s. die Kolonisierung, Besiedelung.
colonize ['kɔlənaiz], v.a. besiedeln, kolonisieren.
colonnade [kɔlə'neid], s. die Kolonnade, der Säulengang.
colony ['kɔləni], s. die Kolonie.
colophony [kɔ'lɔfəni], s. das Kolophonium (*resin*).
coloration [kʌlə'reiʃən], s. die Färbung, Tönung.
colossal [kə'lɔsəl], adj. kolossal, riesig, riesenhaft.
colour ['kʌlə], s. die Farbe; (*complexion*) die Gesichtsfarbe; (*paint*) die Farbe, der Anstrich; (*dye*) die Färbung. — v.a. färben; anstreichen (*paint house etc.*).
colt [koult], s. das Füllen.
columbine ['kɔləmbain], s. (*Bot.*) die Akelei.
column ['kɔləm], s. die Säule; die Spalte (*press*); (*also Mil.*) die Kolonne.
colza ['kɔlzə], s. (*Bot.*) der Raps.
coma ['koumə], s. (*Med.*) das Koma, die Schlafsucht.
comb [koum], s. der Kamm. — v.a. kämmen; (*fig.*) genau untersuchen.
combat ['kʌmbət, 'kɔmbət], s. der Kampf, das Gefecht; *in single* —, im Duell, Zweikampf. — v.a. kämpfen, bekämpfen.
combatant ['kʌmbətənt, 'kɔmb-], s. der Kämpfer.
comber ['koumə], s. der Wollkämmer.
combination [kɔmbi'neiʃən], s. die Kombination, die Verbindung.
combine [kəm'bain], v.a. kombinieren, verbinden. — v.n. sich verbinden. — ['kɔmbain], s. (*Comm.*) der Trust, Ring.

combustible [kəm'bʌstibl], adj. verbrennbar; feuergefährlich.
combustion [kəm'bʌstʃən], s. die Verbrennung.
come [kʌm], v.n. irr. kommen; — *about*, sich ereignen (*event*); — *across*, stoßen auf (*Acc.*); — *by* (*s.th.*), ergattern, erwerben; — *for*, abholen; — *forth*, *forward*, hervorkommen, hervortreten; — *from*, herkommen von, — *in*, hereinkommen; — *off*, (*of object*) loskommen, (*succeed*) glücken; — *out* (*appear*), herauskommen; — *to o.s.*, zu sich kommen; — *of age*, mündig werden; — *to o.'s senses*, zur Besinnung *or* Vernunft kommen; *that is still to* —, das steht uns noch bevor.
comedian [kə'miːdjən], s. der Komödiant, Komiker (*stage*).
comedy ['kɔmədi], s. die Komödie, das Lustspiel.
comeliness ['kʌmlinis], s. die Anmut, Schönheit.
comely ['kʌmli], adj. anmutig, schön.
comestible [kə'mestibl], s. (*usually pl.*) die Eßwaren, f. pl.
comet ['kɔmit], s. der Komet.
comfit ['kʌmfit], s. das Konfekt, die Bonbons.
comfort ['kʌmfət], s. der Trost (*solace*); der Komfort, die Bequemlichkeit. — v.a. trösten.
comforter ['kʌmfətə], s. der Tröster; (*Am.*) die Steppdecke.
comfortless ['kʌmfətlis], adj. trostlos, unbehaglich.
comic ['kɔmik], adj. komisch; — *writer*, humoristischer Schriftsteller. — s. die Bilderzeitung (*children's paper*).
comical ['kɔmikl], adj. lächerlich, zum Lachen, komisch.
comma ['kɔmə], s. das Komma, der Beistrich; *inverted* —s, die Anführungszeichen.
command [kə'maːnd], v.a., v.n. (*Mil.*) kommandieren; über jemanden verfügen (*have s.o. at o.'s disposal*). — s. der Befehl.
commandant [kɔmən'dænt], s. der Kommandant, Befehlshaber.
commander [kə'maːndə], s. der Befehlshaber.
commandment [kə'maːndmənt], s. (*Rel.*) das Gebot.
commemorate [kə'meməreit], v.a. feiern, gedenken (*Genit.*).
commemoration [kəmemə'reiʃən], s. die Feier, die Gedächtnisfeier.
commemorative [kə'memərətiv], adj. Gedächtnis-.
commence [kə'mens], v.a., v.n. beginnen, anfangen.
commencement [kə'mensmənt], s. der Anfang, der Beginn.
commend [kə'mend], v.a. empfehlen, loben (*praise*).
commendable [kə'mendəbl], adj. empfehlenswert.

commendation [kɔmen'deiʃən], *s.* die Empfehlung.

commensurable, commensurate [kə'menʃərəbl, kə'menʃərit], *adj.* kommensurabel, entsprechend; angemessen.

comment ['kɔment], *v.n.* kommentieren (*on*, zu, *Dat.*). — *s.* der Kommentar; die Bemerkung (*remark*).

commentary ['kɔmantari], *s.* der Kommentar.

commentator ['kɔmanteita], *s.* der Kommentator, Berichterstatter.

commerce ['kɔmaːs], *s.* der Handel; *college of* —, die Handelsschule.

commercial [kə'məːʃəl], *adj.* kommerziell, kaufmännisch, Handels-; — *traveller*, der Handelsreisende, Vertreter; — *manager*, der geschäftliche Leiter.

commingle [kə'miŋgl], *v.a.* vermischengefühl.

commiserate [kə'mizəreit], *v.n.* bemitleiden; — *with s.o.*, mit einem Mitgefühl haben.

commissariat [kɔmi'sɛəriət], *s.* (*Pol.*) das Kommissariat.

commissary ['kɔmisəri], *s.* der Kommissar. — *adj.* kommissarisch.

commission [kə'miʃən], *s.* die Kommission; (*Mil.*) der Offiziersrang; die Begehung (*of crime*); (*Law*) die (offizielle) Kommission; der Auftrag, die Bestellung (*order*).

commissionaire [kəmiʃən'ɛə], *s.* der Portier.

commissioned [kə'miʃənd], *adj.* bevollmächtigt.

commissioner [kə'miʃənə], *s.* (*Pol.*) der Kommissar, der Bevollmächtigte.

commit [kə'mit], *v.a.* begehen (*do*); übergeben (*consign*); anvertrauen (*entrust*). — *v.r.* sich verpflichten.

committal [kə'mitl], *s.* das Übergeben; die Überantwortung.

committee [kə'miti], *s.* das Komitee, der Ausschuß.

commodious [kə'moudiəs], *adj.* bequem, geräumig.

commodity [kə'mɔditi], *s.* (*Comm.*) die Ware, der Artikel.

commodore ['kɔmədɔː], *s.* (*Naut.*) der Kommodore, der Kommandant eines Geschwaders.

common ['kɔmən], *adj.* gewöhnlich (*usual*); gemein (*vulgar*); allgemein (*general*); *in* —, gemeinschaftlich; — *sense*, der gesunde Menschenverstand; *the — man*, der kleine Mann. — *n. pl. House of Commons*, das Unterhaus.

commoner ['kɔmənə], *s.* der Bürger; (*Parl.*) Mitglied des Unterhauses.

commonness ['kɔmənnis], *s.* die Gemeinheit (*vulgarity*); das häufige Vorkommen (*frequency*).

commonplace ['kɔmənpleis], *adj.* alltäglich. — *s.* der Gemeinplatz.

commonwealth ['kɔmənwelθ], *s.* die Staatengemeinschaft, der Staatenbund; das Commonwealth.

commotion [kə'mouʃən], *s.* die Erschütterung; der Aufruhr; der Lärm.

communal ['kɔmjunəl], *adj.* gemeinschaftlich, allgemein; (*Pol.*) Kommunal-.

commune ['kɔmjuːn], *s.* (*Pol.*) die Kommune. — [kə'mjuːn], *v.n.* sich unterhalten.

communicable [kə'mjuːnikəbl], *adj.* mitteilbar; übertragbar.

communicate [kə'mjuːnikeit], *v.a.* mitteilen; verkünden (*proclaim*); benachrichtigen. — *v.n.* in Verbindung stehen.

communication [kəmjuːni'keiʃən], *s.* die Mitteilung; Verlautbarung; die Verkündigung (*proclamation*); die Information; (*Elec.*) die Verbindung; (*pl.*), die Verbindungslinie; —*s engineering*, Fernmeldetechnik.

communion [kə'mjuːnjən], *s.* (*Eccl.*) die Kommunion; das heilige Abendmahl; die Gemeinschaft (*fellowship*).

Communism ['kɔmjunizm], *s.* (*Pol.*) der Kommunismus.

Communist ['kɔmjunist], *s.* der Kommunist. — *adj.* kommunistisch.

community [kə'mjuːniti], *s.* die Gemeinschaft.

commutable [kə'mjuːtəbl], *adj.* umtauschbar, auswechselbar.

commutation [kɔmju'teiʃən], *s.* der Austausch; (*Law*) die Herabsetzung (*of sentence*).

commutator ['kɔmjuteita], *s.* (*Elec.*) der Umschalter.

commute [kə'mjuːt], *v.n.* hin und her fahren, pendeln, mit Zeitkarte fahren (*travel*). — *v.a.* herabsetzen (*sentence*).

compact ['kɔmpækt], *adj.* kompakt, fest; gedrängt (*succinct*); kurz, bündig (*short*).

companion [kəm'pænjən], *s.* der Gefährte, die Gefährtin.

companionable [kəm'pænjənəbl], *adj.* gesellig, freundlich.

companionship [kəm'pænjənʃip], *s.* die Geselligkeit; die Gesellschaft.

company ['kʌmpəni], *s.* die Gesellschaft; (*Mil.*) die Kompanie; der Freundeskreis (*circle of friends*); (*Comm.*) die Handelsgesellschaft; *limited* (*liability*) —, Gesellschaft mit beschränkter Haftung; *public* (*private*) —, Gesellschaft des öffentlichen (privaten) Rechtes.

comparative [kəm'pærətiv], *adj.* vergleichend, relativ. — *s.* (*Gram.*) der Komparativ.

compare [kəm'pɛə], *v.a.* vergleichen. — *v.n.* sich vergleichen lassen.

comparison [kəm'pærisən], *s.* der Vergleich; das Gleichnis (*simile*).

compartment [kəm'pɑːtmənt], *s.* (*Railw.*) das Abteil; die Abteilung.

compass ['kʌmpəs], *s.* der Umkreis, Umfang (*scope*); (*Naut.*) der Kompaß; *point of the* —, der Kompaßstrich; (*Engin.*) der Zirkel.

343

compassion [kəm'pæʃən], s. die Barmherzigkeit, das Mitleid, das Erbarmen.
compassionate [kəm'pæʃənit], adj. mitleidig; (Mil.) — leave, der Sonderurlaub.
compatibility [kəmpæti'biliti], s. die Verträglichkeit, Vereinbarkeit.
compatible [kəm'pætibl], adj. verträglich, vereinbar.
compatriot [kəm'peitriət], s. der Landsmann.
compel [kəm'pel], v.a. zwingen, nötigen.
compendium [kəm'pendjəm], s. das Kompendium, die kurze Schrift, die kurze Darstellung.
compensate ['kɔmpənseit], v.a. kompensieren, einem Ersatz leisten.
compensation [kɔmpən'seiʃən], s. der Ersatz, die Wiedergutmachung.
compensatory [kɔmpən'seitəri], adj. ausgleichend, Ersatz-.
compete [kəm'pi:t], v.n. wetteifern, konkurrieren.
competence, competency ['kɔmpitəns, -nsi], s. die Kompetenz; Zuständigkeit; Befähigung (capability); Tüchtigkeit (ability).
competent ['kɔmpitənt], adj. kompetent; zuständig; fähig (capable); tüchtig (able).
competition [kɔmpi'tiʃən], s. die Konkurrenz; die Mitbewerbung (for job).
competitive [kəm'petitiv], adj. Konkurrenz-, konkurrierend.
competitor [kəm'petitə], s. (Comm.) der Konkurrent; der Mitbewerber (fellow applicant), Teilnehmer (sport).
complacent [kəm'pleisənt], adj. selbstzufrieden, selbstgefällig.
complain [kəm'plein], v.n. sich beklagen (of, über, Acc.).
complaint [kəm'pleint], s. die Klage; Beschwerde (grievance); das Leiden (illness).
complement ['kɔmplimənt], s. die Ergänzung, Gesamtzahl. — [-'ment], v.a. ergänzen.
complementary [kɔmpli'mentəri], adj. Ergänzungs-, ergänzend.
complete [kəm'pli:t], adj. komplett; voll (full up); vollkommen (perfect). — v.a. vollenden (end); ergänzen (make whole).
completeness [kəm'pli:tnis], s. die Vollendung (condition); Ganzheit (wholeness).
completion [kəm'pli:ʃən], s. die Vollendung (fulfilment); die Beendigung (ending); der Abschluß.
complex ['kɔmpleks], adj. (Maths.) komplex; kompliziert (complicated). — s. der Komplex (Archit., Psych.).
complexion [kəm'plekʃən], s. die Gesichtsfarbe; (fig.) das Aussehen.
complexity [kəm'pleksiti], s. die Kompliziertheit; die Schwierigkeit.
compliance [kəm'plaiəns], s. die Willfährigkeit, Einwilligung.
compliant [kəm'plaiənt], adj. willig, willfährig.

complicate ['kɔmplikeit], v.a. komplizieren, erschweren.
complication [kɔmpli'keiʃən], s. die Komplikation, die Erschwerung.
complicity [kəm'plisiti], s. (Law) die Mitschuld.
compliment ['kɔmplimənt], s. das Kompliment. — [-'ment], v.n. Komplimente machen.
complimentary [kɔmpli'mentəri], adj. lobend; — ticket, die Freikarte.
comply [kəm'plai], v.n. einwilligen (with, in, Acc.); sich halten (an, Acc.).
compose [kəm'pouz], v.a., v.n. (Mus.) komponieren; beruhigen (the mind); (Lit.) verfassen; (Typ.) setzen.
composed [kəm'pouzd], adj. ruhig, gefaßt.
composer [kəm'pouzə], s. (Mus.) der Komponist.
composite ['kɔmpəzit], adj. zusammengesetzt.
composition [kɔmpə'ziʃən], s. (Mus. etc.) die Komposition; Beschaffenheit Zusammensetzung.
compositor [kəm'pɔzitə], s. (Typ.) der Schriftsetzer.
compost ['kɔmpɔst], s. (Agr.) der Dünger, Kompost.
composure [kəm'pouʒə], s. die Gelassenheit, die Gemütsruhe, die Fassung.
compound ['kɔmpaund], s. (Chem.) die Verbindung; die Zusammensetzung. — adj. zusammengesetzt; kompliziert; (Comm.) — interest, die Zinszinsen. — [kəm'paund], v.a. (Chem.) mischen, zusammensetzen.
comprehend [kɔmpri'hend], v.a. verstehen (understand); einschließen (include).
comprehensible [kɔmpri'hensibl], adj. verständlich, begreiflich.
comprehension [kɔmpri'henʃən], s. das Verstehen, das Erfassen; (Psych.) — tests, die Verständnisprüfung.
comprehensive [kɔmpri'hensiv], adj. umfassend.
compress [kəm'pres], v.a. komprimieren; zusammendrücken (press together). — ['kɔmpres], s. (Med.) die Kompresse, der Umschlag (poultice).
compression [kəm'preʃən], s. der Druck; das Zusammendrücken (pressing together); die Kürzung (abridgment).
comprise [kəm'praiz], v.a. umfassen, einschließen.
compromise ['kɔmprəmaiz], v.a. kompromittieren. — v.n. einen Kompromiß schließen. — s. der or das Kompromiß.
compulsion [kəm'pʌlʃən], s. der Zwang.
compulsory [kəm'pʌlsəri], adj. zwingend; Zwangs-; — subject, das obligatorische Fach.
compunction [kəm'pʌnkʃən], s. die Gewissensbisse, m. pl.
computation [kɔmpju'teiʃən], s. die Berechnung.

compute [kəm'pju:t], *v.a.*, *v.n.* berechnen.

computer [kəm'pju:tə], *s.* die automatische Rechenmaschine.

comrade ['kɔmrid], *s.* der Kamerad.

comradeship ['kɔmridʃip], *s.* die Kameradschaft.

con [kɔn], *v.a.* genau betrachten, studieren; (*ship*) steuern.

concave ['kɔnkeiv], *adj.* (*Phys.*) konkav.

conceal [kən'si:l], *v.a.* verbergen, verstecken.

concealment [kən'si:lmənt], *s.* die Verhehlung, die Verheimlichung (*act of concealing*); *place of* —, das Versteck.

concede [kən'si:d], *v.a.* zugestehen, einräumen.

conceit [kən'si:t], *s.* die Einbildung, der Eigendünkel (*presumption*); (*obs.*) die Idee; (*Lit.*) die (gedankliche) Spielerei.

conceited [kən'si:tid], *adj.* eingebildet, eitel.

conceivable [kən'si:vəbl], *adj.* denkbar; begreiflich (*understandable*).

conceive [kən'si:v], *v.a.*, *v.n.* empfangen (*become pregnant*); begreifen (*understand*).

concentrate ['kɔnsəntreit], *v.a.* konzentrieren. — *v.n.* sich konzentrieren (*on*, auf, *Acc.*). — *s.* (*Chem.*) das Konzentrat.

concentrated ['kɔnsəntreitid], *adj.* konzentriert.

concentration [kɔnsən'treiʃən], *s.* die Konzentration.

concentric [kən'sentrik], *adj.* (*Geom.*) konzentrisch.

conception [kən'sepʃən], *s.* die Vorstellung, der Begriff (*idea*); die Empfängnis (*of a child*).

concern [kən'sə:n], *v.a.* (*affect*) betreffen, angehen; *be concerned with*, zu tun haben (mit, *Dat.*). — *s.* die Angelegenheit (*affair*); die Sorge (*care, business*); das Geschäft, das Unternehmen; *cause grave* —, tiefe Besorgnis erregen.

concerned [kən'sə:nd], *adj.* (*worried*) besorgt; (*involved*) interessiert (*in*, an, *Dat.*).

concerning [kən'sə:niŋ], *prep.* betreffend (*Acc.*), hinsichtlich (*Genit.*).

concert ['kɔnsət], *s.* (*Mus.*) das Konzert; Einverständnis.

concerted [kən'sə:tid], *adj.* gemeinsam, gemeinschaftlich.

concertina [kɔnsə'ti:nə], *s.* (*Mus.*) die Ziehharmonika.

concerto [kən'tʃə:tou], *s.* (*Mus.*) das Konzert.

concession [kən'seʃən], *s.* die Konzession (*licence*); das Zugeständnis.

conch [kɔŋk], *s.* die (große) Muschel.

conciliate [kən'silieit], *v.a.* versöhnen.

conciliation [kansili'eiʃən], *s.* die Versöhnung.

conciliatory [kən'siliətəri], *adj.* versöhnlich.

concise [kən'sais], *adj.* kurz, knapp.

conciseness [kən'saisnis], *s.* die Kürze, Knappheit.

conclave ['kɔnkleiv], ·. (*Eccl.*) das Konklave.

conclude [kən'klu:d], *v.a.*, *v.n.* schließen, beenden (*speech etc.*); (*infer*) folgern (*from*, aus, *Dat.*); abschließen (*treaty*).

conclusion [kən'klu:ʒən], *s.* der Abschluß (*treaty*); die Folgerung (*inference*); der Beschluß (*decision*).

conclusive [kən'klu:siv], *adj.* entscheidend, überzeugend.

concoct [kən'kɔkt], *v.a.* zusammenbrauen, aushecken.

concoction [kən'kɔkʃən], *s.* das Gebräu, die Mischung.

concomitant [kən'kɔmitənt], *adj.* begleitend; Begleit-, Neben-. — *s.* der Begleitumstand.

concord ['kɔnkɔ:d], *s.* die Eintracht, die Harmonie.

concordance [kən'kɔ:dəns], *s.* die Übereinstimmung; die Konkordanz (*of Bible etc.*).

concordant [kən'kɔ:dənt], *adj.* in Eintracht (mit), übereinstimmend (mit) (*Dat.*).

concordat [kən'kɔ:dæt], *s.* (*Eccl., Pol.*) das Konkordat.

concourse ['kɔnkɔ:s], *s.* das Gedränge (*crowd*).

concrete ['kɔnkri:t], *s.* (*Build.*) der Beton; (*Log.*) das Konkrete. — *adj.* konkret, wirklich.

concur [kən'kə:], *v.n.* übereinstimmen (*with*, mit, *Dat.*).

concurrence [kən'kʌrəns], *s.* die Übereinstimmung.

concurrent [kən'kʌrənt], *adj.* gleichzeitig (*simultaneous*); mitwirkend (*accompanying*).

concussion [kən'kʌʃən], *s.* (*Med.*) die (Gehirn)Erschütterung.

condemn [kən'dem], *v.a.* verurteilen, verdammen.

condemnable [kən'demnəbl], *adj.* verwerflich, verdammenswert.

condemnation [kɔndem'neiʃən], *s.* die Verurteilung, die Verdammung.

condensate ['kɔndenseit], *s.* (*Chem.*) das Kondensat, das Ergebnis der Kondensation.

condensation [kɔnden'seiʃən], *s.* die Kondensation; Verdichtung.

condensed [kən'densd], *adj.* (*Chem.*) kondensiert; (*Chem., Engin.*) verdichtet; gekürzt (*abridged*).

condenser [kən'densə], *s.* (*Chem., Engin.*) der Kondensator; (*Elec.*) der Verstärker.

condescend [kɔndi'send], *v.n.* sich herablassen.

condescending [kɔndi'sendiŋ], *adj.* herablassend.

condescension [kɔndi'senʃən], *s.* die Herablassung.

condiment ['kɔndimənt], *s.* die Würze.

condition [kən'diʃən], *s.* der Zustand; Umstand; die Bedingung (*proviso*); der Gesundheitszustand (*physical state*).

conditional [kən'diʃənəl], *adj.* bedingt; unter der Bedingung; konditionell.

conditioned [kən'diʃənd], *adj.* vorbereitet (*for action*); geartet.

condole [kən'doul], *v.n.* Beileid ausdrücken (*with*, *Dat.*), kondolieren (*with*, *Dat.*).

condolence [kən'douləns], *s.* das Beileid.

condone [kən'doun], *v.a.* verzeihen.

conducive [kən'dju:siv], *adj.* förderlich, dienlich, nützlich (*to*, *Dat.*).

conduct [kən'dʌkt], *v.a.* leiten, führen; (*Phys.*) ein Leiter sein; (*Mus.*) dirigieren. — *v.r.* sich aufführen, sich benehmen. — ['kɔndʌkt], *s.* das Benehmen (*behaviour*); — *of a war*, die Kriegsführung.

conductive [kən'dʌktiv], *adj.* (*Elec.*) leitend.

conductor [kən'dʌktə], *s.* der Leiter, Führer (*leader*); (*Phys.*, *Elec.*) der Leiter; (*Am.*) der Schaffner (*train*); (*Mus.*) der Dirigent.

conduit ['kʌn-, 'kɔndit], *s.* die Leitung, die Röhre.

cone [koun], *s.* (*Geom.*) der Kegel; (*Bot.*) der Zapfen.

coney ['kouni], *s.* (*Zool.*) das Kaninchen.

confection [kən'fekʃən], *s.* das Konfekt.

confectioner [kən'fekʃənə], *s.* der Zuckerbäcker, Konditor.

confectionery [kən'fekʃənəri], *s.* die Zuckerwaren, *f.pl.* (*sweets*); Konditoreiwaren, *f.pl.* (*cakes*); die Zuckerbäckerei (*sweet shop*); die Konditorei.

confederacy [kən'fedərəsi], *s.* der Bund (*of states*); das Bündnis (*treaty*).

confederate [kən'fedərit], *s.* der Bundesgenosse, der Verbündete. — *adj.* verbündet; — *state*, der Bundesstaat. — [-reit], *v.n.* sich verbünden (*with*, mit, *Dat.*).

confederation [kənfedə'reiʃən], *s.* das Bündnis (*treaty*); der Bund (*state*).

confer [kən'fə:], *v.a.* verleihen (*degree*, *title*). — *v.n.* beraten (*with*, mit, *Dat.*), unterhandeln (*negotiate*).

conference ['kɔnfərəns], *s.* die Konferenz, die Besprechung, die Beratung, Tagung.

confess [kən'fes], *v.a.* bekennen; beichten (*sin*); zugestehen (*acknowledge*).

confession [kən'feʃən], *s.* das Bekenntnis; die Beichte (*sin*); das Glaubensbekenntnis (*creed*).

confessor [kən'fesə], *s.* der Bekenner; *father* —, der Beichtvater.

confidant [kɔnfi'dænt], *s.* der Vertraute.

confide [kən'faid], *v.a.* anvertrauen. — *v.n.* vertrauen (*Dat.*).

confidence ['kɔnfidəns], *s.* das Vertrauen; die Zuversicht; — *trick*, die Bauernfängerei, der Schwindel.

confident ['kɔnfidənt], *adj.* zuversichtlich; dreist (*bold*).

confidential [kɔnfi'denʃəl], *adj.* vertraulich, privat.

confine [kən'fain], *v.a.* einschränken (*hem in*); einsperren; *be* —*d to bed*, bettlägerig sein.

confinement [kən'fainmənt], *s.* die Einschränkung (*limitation*); das Wochenbett, die Niederkunft (*childbirth*).

confines ['kɔnfainz], *s. pl.* die Grenzen, *f. pl.* (*physical*); die Einschränkungen, *f. pl.* (*limitations*).

confirm [kən'fə:m], *v.a.* bestätigen, bekräftigen (*corroborate*); (*Eccl.*) firmen, konfirmieren.

confirmation [kɔnfə'meiʃən], *s.* die Bestätigung (*corroboration*); (*Eccl.*) die Firmung, Konfirmation.

confirmed [kən'fə:md], *adj.* eingefleischt; unverbesserlich.

confiscate ['kɔnfiskeit], *v.a.* konfiszieren, einziehen, beschlagnahmen.

confiscation [kɔnfis'keiʃən], *s.* die Konfiszierung, die Einziehung, die Beschlagnahme (*customs etc.*).

conflagration [kɔnflə'greiʃən], *s.* der (große) Brand.

conflict ['kɔnflikt], *s.* der Konflikt, der Zusammenstoß. — [kən'flikt], *v.n.* in Konflikt geraten; in Widerspruch stehen.

confluence ['kɔnfluəns], *s.* (*Geog.*) der Zusammenfluß.

confluent ['kɔnfluənt], *adj.* zusammenfließend. — *s.* der Nebenfluß (*tributary*).

conform [kən'fɔ:m], *v.n.* sich anpassen.

conformation [kɔnfɔ:'meiʃən], *s.* die Anpassung.

conformist [kən'fɔ:mist], *adj.* fügsam. — *s.* das Mitglied der Staatskirche.

conformity [kən'fɔ:miti], *s.* die Gleichförmigkeit; *in* — *with*, gerade so; gemäß (*Dat.*); die Gleichheit (*equality*.)

confound [kən'faund], *v.a.* verwirren (*confuse*); vernichten (*overthrow*).

confounded [kən'faundid], *adj.* verdammt, verwünscht.

confront [kən'frʌnt], *v.a.* (*Law*) — *s.o. with*, gegenüberstellen (*put in front of*); gegenüberstehen (*stand in front of*).

confrontation [kɔnfrʌn'teiʃən], *s.* die Gegenüberstellung.

confuse [kən'fju:z], *v.a.* verwirren (*muddle*); bestürzen (*perplex*); verwechseln (*mix up*).

confusion [kən'fju:ʒən], *s.* die Verwirrung, das Durcheinander (*muddle*); die Bestürzung (*astonishment*); die Verlegenheit (*dilemma*).

confutation [kɔnfju:'teiʃən], *s.* die Widerlegung.

confute [kən'fju:t], *v.a.* widerlegen.

congeal [kən'dʒi:l], *v.n.* gefrieren (*freeze*); gerinnen.

congenial [kən'dʒi:niəl], *adj.* geistesverwandt, geistig ebenbürtig, sympathisch.

congeniality [kəndʒi:ni'æliti], *s.* die Geistesverwandtschaft.

conger ['kɔŋgə], *s.* (*Zool.*) der Meeraal.

congest [kən'dʒest], v.a. anhäufen, überfüllen.

congestion [kən'dʒestʃən], s. die Überfüllung; Stauung; die Übervölkerung (*overpopulation*); (*Med.*) der Blutandrang.

conglomerate [kən'glɔməreit], v.n. sich zusammenballen. — [–rit], s. das Konglomerat, die Ballung.

conglomeration [kənglɔmə'reiʃən], s. die Zusammenhäufung, Zusammenballung.

Congolese [kɔŋgo'li:z], adj. kongolesisch. — s. der Kongolese.

congratulate [kən'grætjuleit], v.n. gratulieren (*on*, zu, *Dat.*).

congratulation [kəngrætju'leiʃən], s. (*usually pl.*) die Glückwünsche.

congratulatory [kən'grætjuleitəri], adj. Glückwunsch-.

congregate ['kɔŋgrigeit], v.a. versammeln. — v.n. sich versammeln, sich scharen (*round*, um, *Acc.*).

congregation [kɔŋgri'geiʃən], s. die Versammlung, die Schar; (*Eccl.*) die Gemeinde.

congregational [kɔŋgri'geiʃənəl], adj. (*Eccl.*) Gemeinde-; *Congregational Church*, unabhängige Gemeindekirche.

congress ['kɔŋgres], s. der Kongreß.

congruence ['kɔŋgruəns], s. (*Geom.*) die Kongruenz.

congruent ['kɔŋgruənt], adj. (*Geom.*) kongruent.

congruity [kɔŋ'gru:iti], s. (*Geom.*) die Übereinstimmung, die Kongruenz.

congruous ['kɔŋgruəs], adj. übereinstimmend, angemessen.

conic(al) ['kɔnik(əl)], adj. konisch, kegelförmig; (*Geom.*) — *section*, der Kegelschnitt.

conifer ['kɔnifə], s. (*Bot.*) der Nadelbaum.

conjecture [kən'dʒektʃə], s. die Mutmaßung, die Annahme. — v.a. mutmaßen, annehmen.

conjoin [kən'dʒɔin], v.a. (*Law*) verbinden.

conjugal ['kɔndʒugəl], adj. ehelich.

conjugate ['kɔndʒugeit], v.a. (*Gram.*) konjugieren.

conjugation [kɔndʒu'geiʃən], s. (*Gram.*) die Konjugation.

conjunction [kən'dʒʌŋkʃən], s. (*Gram.*) das Bindewort.

conjunctive [kən'dʒʌŋktiv], adj. verbindend; (*Gram.*) — *mood*, der Konjunktiv.

conjunctivitis [kən'dʒʌŋktivaitis], s. (*Med.*) die Bindehautentzündung.

conjuncture [kən'dʒʌŋktʃə], s. der Wendepunkt; die Krise (*of events*).

conjure ['kʌndʒə], v.a. beschwören; — *up*, heraufbeschwören. — v.n. zaubern.

conjurer ['kʌndʒərə], s. der Zauberer.

connect [kə'nekt], v.a. verbinden, in Zusammenhang bringen.

connection, connexion [kə'nekʃən], s. die Verbindung, der Zusammenhang.

connivance [kə'naivəns], s. die Nachsicht, das Gewährenlassen.

connive [kə'naiv], v.n. nachsichtig sein (*at*, bei, *Dat.*); gewähren lassen.

connoisseur [kɔne'sə:], s. der Kenner.

connubial [kə'nju:biəl], adj. ehelich.

conquer ['kɔŋkə], v.a. besiegen (*foe*); erobern (*place*).

conqueror ['kɔŋkərə], s. der Eroberer, der Sieger.

conquest ['kɔŋkwest], s. der Sieg, die Eroberung.

consanguinity [kɔnsæŋ'gwiniti], s. die Blutsverwandtschaft.

conscience ['kɔnʃəns], s. das Gewissen; *in all* — wahrhaftig.

conscientious [kɔnʃi'enʃəs], adj. gewissenhaft.

conscientiousness [kɔnʃi'enʃəsnis], s. die Gewissenhaftigkeit.

conscious ['kɔnʃəs], adj. bewußt (*Genit.*).

consciousness ['kɔnʃəsnis], s. das Bewußtsein.

conscript [kən'skript], v.a. (*Mil.*) einziehen, einberufen. — ['kɔnskript], s. (*Mil.*) der Rekrut, der Dienstpflichtige.

conscription [kən'skripʃən], s. die allgemeine Wehrpflicht.

consecrate ['kɔnsikreit], v.a. weihen, widmen.

consecrated ['kɔnsikreitid], adj. geweiht (*Dat.*).

consecration [kɔnsi'kreiʃən], s. die Weihe, Einweihung (*of church*); die Weihung.

consecutive [kən'sekjutiv], adj. aufeinanderfolgend, fortlaufend.

consecutiveness [kən'sekjutivnis], s. die Aufeinanderfolge.

consent [kən'sent], v.n. zustimmen, beistimmen (*to*, *Dat.*). — s. die Zustimmung, die Einwilligung.

consequence ['kɔnsikwəns], s. die Konsequenz; (*Log.*) Folgerung; die Folge; die Wichtigkeit (*importance*).

consequent ['kɔnsikwənt], adj. folgend, nachfolgend.

consequential [kɔnsi'kwenʃəl], adj. wichtigtuend, anmaßend; (*Log.*) folgerichtig.

consequently ['kɔnsikwəntli], adv. folglich, infolgedessen.

conservatism [kən'sə:vətizm], s. (*Pol.*) der Konservatismus; die konservative Denkweise.

conservative [kən'sə:vətiv], adj. (*Pol.*) konservativ.

conservatoire [kən'sə:vatwa:], s. (*Mus.*) das Konservatorium, die Musikhochschule.

conservatory [kən'sə:vətəri], s. (*Bot.*) das Gewächshaus.

conserve [kən'sə:v], v.a. konservieren, erhalten, einmachen. — s. (*fruit*) das Eingemachte.

consider [kən'sidə], v.a. betrachten, in Betracht ziehen (*think over, look at*); berücksichtigen (*have regard to*); nachdenken über (*Acc.*) (*ponder*).

considerable

considerable [kən'sidərəbl], *adj.* beträchtlich, ansehnlich.

considerate [kən'sidərit], *adj.* rücksichtsvoll (*thoughtful*).

consideration [kənsidə'reiʃən], *s.* die Betrachtung (*contemplation*); die Rücksicht (*regard*) (*for*, auf, *Acc.*); die Entschädigung (*compensation*); die Belohnung (*reward*).

considering [kən'sidəriŋ], *prep.* in Anbetracht (*Genit.*).

consign [kən'sain], *v.a.* überliefern (*hand over*); übersenden (*remit*).

consignee [kənsai'ni:], *s.* (*Comm.*) der Empfänger, der Adressat (*recipient*).

consigner [kən'sainə], *s.* der Absender (*of goods*).

consignment [kən'sainmənt], *s.* die Sendung (*of goods*).

consist [kən'sist], *v.n.* bestehen (*of*, aus, *Dat.*).

consistency [kən'sistənsi], *s.* die Festigkeit, Dichtigkeit; (*Chem.*) die Konsistenz.

consistent [kən'sistənt], *adj.* konsequent; — *with*, übereinstimmend, gemäß (*Dat.*); (*Chem.*) dicht, fest.

consistory [kən'sistəri], *s.* (*Eccl.*) das Konsistorium.

consolable [kən'souləbl], *adj.* tröstlich, zu trösten.

consolation [kənso'leiʃən], *s.* der Trost; *draw* —, Trost schöpfen.

console (1) [kən'soul], *v.a.* trösten.

console (2) ['kɔnsoul], *s.* (*Archit.*) die Konsole.

consolidate [kən'sɔlideit], *v.a.* befestigen, konsolidieren. — *v.n.* fest werden.

consolidation [kənsɔli'deiʃən], *s.* die Befestigung; Festigung, Bestärkung (*confirmation*).

consonance ['kɔnsənəns], *s.* (*Phonet.*) die Konsonanz; der Einklang, die Harmonie.

consonant ['kɔnsənənt], *adj.* in Einklang (*with*, mit, *Dat.*). — *s.* der Konsonant.

consort ['kɔnsɔːt], *s.* der Gemahl, Gatte; die Gemahlin, die Gattin. — [kən'sɔːt], *v.n.* verkehren (*with*, mit, *Dat.*).

conspicuous [kən'spikjuəs], *adj.* auffallend, deutlich sichtbar, hervorragend.

conspiracy [kən'spirəsi], *s.* die Verschwörung.

conspirator [kən'spirətə], *s.* der Verschwörer.

conspire [kən'spaiə], *v.n.* sich verschwören.

constable ['kʌnstəbl], *s.* der Polizist, der Schutzmann.

Constance ['kɔnstəns]. Konstanze *f.* (*name*); Konstanz (*town*); *Lake* —, der Bodensee.

constancy ['kɔnstənsi], *s.* die Beständigkeit, Treue.

constant ['kɔnstənt], *adj.* (*Chem.*) konstant; treu, beständig.

constellation [kɔnste'leiʃən], *s.* die Konstellation; das Sternbild.

consternation [kɔnstə'neiʃən], *s.* die Bestürzung.

constipation [kɔnsti'peiʃən], *s.* die Verstopfung.

constituency [kən'stitjuənsi], *s.* der Wahlkreis (*electoral district*); die Wählerschaft (*voters*).

constituent [kən'stitjuənt], *adj.* wesentlich. — *s.* der Bestandteil (*component*); (*Pol.*) der Wähler.

constitute ['kɔnstitjuːt], *v.a.* ausmachen (*make up*); bilden (*form*); festsetzen (*establish*); (*Pol.*) errichten (*set up*).

constitution [kɔnsti'tjuːʃən], *s.* die Konstitution (*physique*); die Errichtung (*establishment*); die Beschaffenheit, Natur (*nature*); (*Pol.*) die Verfassung.

constitutional [kɔnsti'tjuːʃənəl], *adj.* körperlich bedingt; (*Pol.*) verfassungsmäßig.

constrain [kən'strein], *v.a.* nötigen, zwingen.

constraint [kən'streint], *s.* der Zwang.

constrict [kən'strikt], *v.a.* zusammenziehen.

constriction [kən'strikʃən], *s.* die Zusammenziehung, Beengtheit.

construct [kən'strʌkt], *v.a.* errichten, bauen, konstruieren.

construction [kən'strʌkʃən], *s.* die Errichtung, der Bau, die Konstruktion.

constructive [kən'strʌktiv], *adj.* (*Engin.*) konstruktiv; behilflich (*positive*).

constructor [kən'strʌktə], *s.* der Konstrukteur, der Erbauer (*builder*).

construe [kən'struː], *v.a.* konstruieren, deuten (*interpret*).

consul ['kɔnsəl], *s.* der Konsul; — *general*, der Generalkonsul.

consular ['kɔnsjulə], *adj.* konsularisch.

consulate ['kɔnsjulit], *s.* das Konsulat; — *general*, das Generalkonsulat.

consult [kən'sʌlt], *v.a.* konsultieren, zu Rate ziehen; nachschlagen (*a book*). — *v.n.* sich beraten (*with*, mit, *Dat.*); (*Comm.*) als Berater hinzuziehen.

consultant [kən'sʌltənt], *s.* (*Med.*) der Facharzt; der Berater.

consultation [kɔnsʌl'teiʃən], *s.* die Beratung (*advice*); die Besprechung (*discussion*); (*Med.*, *Engin.*) die Konsultation.

consume [kən'sjuːm], *v.a.* verzehren (*eat up*); verbrauchen (*use up*).

consumer [kən'sjuːmə], *s.* der Verbraucher; (*Comm.*) der Konsument.

consummate [kən'sʌmit], *adj.* vollendet. — ['kɔnsəmeit], *v.a.* vollenden, vollziehen.

consummation [kɔnsə'meiʃən], *s.* die Vollziehung, Vollendung.

consumption [kən'sʌmpʃən], *s.* (*Comm.*) der Verbrauch; (*Med.*) die Schwindsucht.

consumptive [kən'sʌmptiv], *adj.* (*Med.*) schwindsüchtig.

contact ['kɔntækt], *v.a.* berühren (*touch*); in Verbindung treten (mit) (*get into touch* (*with*)). — *s.* (*Elec.*) der Kontakt; die Berührung (*touch*); die Verbindung (*connexion*).

contagion [kən'teidʒən], *s.* (*Med.*) die Ansteckung.

contagious[kən'teidʒəs],*adj.*ansteckend.

contain [kən'tein], *v.a.* enthalten (*hold*); zurückhalten (*restrain*).

container [kən'teinə], *s.* der Behälter.

contaminate [kən'tæmineit], *v.a.* verunreinigen; vergiften.

contemplate ['kɔntəmpleit], *v.a.* betrachten (*consider*). — *v.n.* nachdenken (*ponder*).

contemplation [kɔntəm'pleiʃən], *s.* die Betrachtung (*consideration*); das Sinnen (*pondering*).

contemplative [kən'templətiv], *adj.* nachdenklich, kontemplativ.

contemporaneous [kəntempə'reiniəs], *adj.* gleichzeitig.

contemporary [kən'tempərəri], *adj.* zeitgenössisch. — *s.* der Zeitgenosse.

contempt [kən'tempt], *s.* die Verachtung; — *of court*, die Gerichtsbeleidigung.

contemptible [kən'temptibl], *adj.* verächtlich, verachtungswert.

contemptibleness [kən'temptiblnis], *s.* die Verächtlichkeit.

contemptuous [kən'temptjuəs], *adj.* höhnisch, verachtungsvoll.

contemptuousness [kən'temptjuəsnis], *s.* der Hohn, der verachtungsvolle Ton, der Hochmut.

contend [kən'tend], *v.n.* streiten; bestreiten, behaupten.

content [kən'tent], *adj.* zufrieden. — *v.a.* zufriedenstellen. — ['kɔntent], *s.* (*often pl.*) der Inhalt.

contented [kən'tentid], *adj.* zufrieden.

contentedness, contentment [kən'tentidnis, kən'tentmənt], *s.* die Zufriedenheit.

contention [kən'tenʃən], *s.* der Streit, die Behauptung.

contentious [kən'tenʃəs], *adj.* streitsüchtig (*person*); strittig (*question*).

contest ['kɔntest], *s.* der Streit, Wettstreit, Wettkampf. — [kən'test], *v.a.* um etwas streiten, bestreiten.

context ['kɔntekst], *s.* der Zusammenhang.

contexture [kən'tekstʃə], *s.* (*Engin.*) der Bau, die Zusammensetzung; das Gewebe (*textile*).

contiguity [kɔnti'gju:iti], *s.* die Berührung; die Nachbarschaft.

contiguous [kən'tigjuəs], *adj.* anstossend, anliegend.

continence ['kɔntinəns], *s.* die Mäßigung (*moderation*); die Enthaltsamkeit (*abstemiousness*).

continent (1) ['kɔntinənt], *adj.* enthaltsam, mässig.

continent (2) ['kɔntinənt], *s.* das Festland, der Kontinent.

contingency [kən'tindʒənsi], *s.* der Zufall; die Möglichkeit (*possibility*).

contingent [kən'tindʒənt], *s.* der Beitrag, das Kontingent (*share*). — *adj.* möglich.

continual [kən'tinjuəl], *adj.* fortwährend, beständig.

continuance [kən'tinjuəns], *s.* die Fortdauer.

continuation [kəntinju'eiʃən], *s.* die Fortsetzung.

continue [kən'tinju:], *v.a.* fortsetzen (*go on with*); verlängern (*prolong*). — *v.n.* weitergehen, weiterführen (*of story*).

continuity [kɔnti'nju:iti], *s.* der Zusammenhang, die ununterbrochene Folge, Kontinuität (*Film*); — *girl*, die Drehbuchsekretärin.

continuous [kən'tinjuəs], *adj.* zusammenhängend, ununterbrochen, andauernd.

contort [kən'tɔ:t], *v.a.* verdrehen.

contortion [kən'tɔ:ʃən], *s.* die Verdrehung, Verkrümmung, Verzerrung.

contortionist [kən'tɔ:ʃənist], *s.* der Schlangenmensch.

contour ['kɔntuə], *s.* die Kontur, der Umriß.

contraband ['kɔntrəbænd], *adj.* Schmuggel-, geschmuggelt. — *s.* die Bannware, Schmuggelware.

contract [kən'trækt], *v.a.* zusammenziehen (*pull together*); verengen (*narrow down*); verkürzen (*shorten*); sich eine Krankheit zuziehen (— *a disease*); Schulden machen (— *debts*). — *v.n.* sich zusammenziehen, kürzer werden; einen Kontrakt abschließen (*come to terms*). — ['kɔntrækt], *s.* der Vertrag (*pact*); (*Comm.*) der Kontrakt.

contraction [kən'trækʃən], *s.* die Zusammenziehung; (*Phonet.*) die Kürzung. .

contractor [kən'træktə], *s.* (*Comm.*) der Kontrahent; der Lieferant (*supplier*); *building* —, der Bauunternehmer.

contradict [kɔntrə'dikt], *v.n.* widersprechen (*Dat.*).

contradiction [kɔntrə'dikʃən], *s.* der Widerspruch.

contradictory [kɔntrə'diktəri], *adj.* in Widerspruch stehend, widersprechend.

contrarily ['kɔntrərili], *adv.* im Gegensatz dazu, hingegen, dagegen.

contrary ['kɔntrəri], *adj.* entgegengesetzt, *on the* —, im Gegenteil; [kən'treəri], widersprechend.

contrast [kən'trɑ:st], *v.a.* einander entgegenstellen, gegenüberstellen. — *v.n.* einen Gegensatz darstellen *or* bilden. — ['kɔntrɑ:st], *s.* der Kontrast (*colours*); der Gegensatz.

contravene [kɔntrə'vi:n], *v.a.* übertreten, zuwiderhandeln (*Dat.*).

contribute [kən'tribju:t], *v.a.* beitragen; beisteuern (*money, energy*).

contribution [kɔntri'bju:ʃən], *s.* der Beitrag.

349

contributive

contributive, contributory [kənˈtri-bjutiv, kənˈtribjutəri], *adj.* beitragend, Beitrags-.

contributor [kənˈtribjutə], *s.* der Beitragende, der Spender (*of money*); der Mitarbeiter (*journalist etc.*).

contrite [ˈkɔntrait], *adj.* zerknirscht, reuevoll.

contrition [kənˈtriʃən], *s.* die Zerknirschung, die Reue.

contrivance [kənˈtraivəns], *s.* die Vorrichtung, die Erfindung.

contrive [kənˈtraiv], *v.a.* ausdenken, erfinden; fertigbringen (*accomplish*).

control [kənˈtroul], *v.a.* kontrollieren (*check*); die Leitung haben (*have command of*); die Aufsicht führen (*supervise*). — *s.* die Kontrolle; die Aufsicht; die Leitung; (*pl.*) (*Motor.*) die Steuerung; (*Aviat.*) das Leitwerk.

controller [kənˈtroulə], *s.* der Aufseher (*supervisor*); der Direktor (*of corporation*); der Revisor (*examiner, auditor*).

controversial [kɔntroˈvəːʃəl], *adj.* umstritten, strittig.

controversy [ˈkɔntrovəːsi], *s.* die Kontroverse, die Streitfrage.

controvert [ˈkɔntrovəːt], *v.a.* bestreiten, widersprechen (*Dat.*).

contumacious [kɔntjuˈmeiʃəs], *adj.* widerspenstig, halsstarrig.

contumacy [ˈkɔntjuməsi], *s.* die Widerspenstigkeit (*obstreperousness*); der Ungehorsam (*disobedience*).

contumelious [kɔntjuˈmiːliəs], *adj.* frech, unverschämt (*insolent*).

contuse [kənˈtjuːz], *v.a.* quetschen.

conundrum [kəˈnʌndrəm], *s.* das Scherzrätsel.

convalescence [kɔnvəˈlesəns], *s.* die Gesundung, die Genesung.

convalescent [kɔnvəˈlesənt], *adj.* genesend. — *s.* der Genesende, der Rekonvaleszent.

convene [kənˈviːn], *v.a.* zusammenrufen, versammeln. — *v.n.* zusammentreten, sich versammeln.

convenience [kənˈviːniəns], *s.* die Bequemlichkeit; *at your early* —, umgehend; *public* —, öffentliche Bedürfnisanstalt.

convenient [kənˈviːniənt], *adj.* bequem, gelegen; passend (*time*).

convent [ˈkɔnvənt], *s.* das (Nonnen)-Kloster.

convention [kənˈvenʃən], *s.* die Konvention, der Kongress (*meeting*); der Vertrag (*treaty*); die Sitte (*tradition, custom*).

conventional [kənˈvenʃənəl], *adj.* herkömmlich, traditionell.

conventual [kənˈventjuəl], *adj.* klösterlich.

conversation [kɔnvəˈseiʃən], *s.* die Konversation, Unterhaltung; das Gespräch.

conversational [kɔnvəˈseiʃənəl], *adj.* gesprächig, umgangssprachlich.

converse (1) [kənˈvəːs], *v.n.* sich unterhalten (*with*, mit, *Dat.*).

converse (2) [ˈkɔnvəːs], *adj.* umgekehrt.

conversely [ˈkɔnvəːsli], *adv.* hingegen, dagegen.

conversion [kənˈvəːʃən], *s.* die Umkehrung (*reversal*); (*Rel.*) die Bekehrung; (*Comm.*) die Umwechslung.

convert [ˈkɔnvəːt], *s.* (*Rel.*) der Bekehrte, die Bekehrte; der Konvertit. — [kɔnˈvəːt], *v.a.* (*Rel.*) bekehren; (*Comm.*) umwechseln.

converter [kənˈvəːtə], *s.* (*Rel.*) der Bekehrer; (*Metall., Elec.*) der Umformer.

convertible [kənˈvəːtibl], *adj.* umwandelbar. — *s.* (*Motor.*) der or das Konvertible.

convex [ˈkɔnveks], *adj.* (*Phys.*) konvex.

convey [kənˈvei], *v.a.* transportieren; führen (*bear, carry*); mitteilen (*impart*).

conveyance [kənˈveiəns], *s.* die Beförderung (*transport*); das Fuhrwerk (*vehicle*); die Übertragung; (*Law*) das Übertragungsdokument.

conveyancing [kənˈveiənsiŋ], *s.* (*Law*) die legale or rechtliche Übertragung.

convict [ˈkɔnvikt], *s.* der Sträfling. — [kɔnˈvikt], *v.a.* für schuldig erklären.

conviction [kənˈvikʃən], *s.* die Überzeugung; (*Law*) die Überführung, die Schuldigsprechung.

convince [kənˈvins], *v.a.* überzeugen.

convivial [kənˈviviəl], *adj.* gesellig (*sociable*).

conviviality [kənviviˈæliti], *s.* die Geselligkeit.

convocation [kɔnvəˈkeiʃən], *s.* die Zusammenberufung, Festversammlung; (*Eccl.*) die Synode.

convoke [kənˈvouk], *v.a.* zusammenberufen.

convolvulus [kənˈvɔlvjuləs], *s.* (*Bot.*) die Winde.

convoy [ˈkɔnvɔi], *s.* das Geleit, die Bedeckung; (*Mil.*) der Begleitzug. — [kɔnˈvɔi], *v.a.* geleiten; (*Mil.*) im Geleitzug mitführen.

convulse [kənˈvʌls], *v.a.* erschüttern.

convulsion [kənˈvʌlʃən], *s.* der Krampf, die Zuckung.

convulsive [kənˈvʌlsiv], *adj.* krampfhaft, zuckend.

coo [kuː], *v.n.* girren (*of birds*); *bill and* —, schnäbeln.

cook [kuk], *v.a., v.n.* kochen; (*coll.*) — *the books*, die Bücher(Bilanz)fälschen (*or* frisieren. — *s.* der Koch, die Köchin; *too many cooks* (*spoil the broth*), zu viele Köche (verderben den Brei).

cookery [ˈkukəri], *s.* die Kochkunst; — *school*, die Kochschule.

cool [kuːl], *adj.* kühl (*climate*); kaltblütig (*coldblooded*); unverschämt (*brazen*). — *s.* die Kühle. — *v.a.* abkühlen; (*fig.*) besänftigen. — *v.n.* sich abkühlen.

cooler [ˈkuːlə], *s.* (*Chem.*) das Kühlfaß; (*coll.*) das Gefängnis; (*sl.*) das Kittchen.

coop [ku:p], *s.* die Kufe; das Faß; *hen* —, der Hühnerkorb. — *v.a.* — *up*, einsperren.

cooper ['ku:pə], *s.* der Böttcher, der Faßbinder.

cooperate [kou'ɔpəreit], *v.n.* zusammenarbeiten; mitarbeiten, mitwirken.

cooperation [kouɔpə'reiʃən], *s.* die Zusammenarbeit, die Mitarbeit.

cooperative [kou'ɔpərətiv], *adj.* willig; mitwirkend. — *s.* die Konsumgenossenschaft, der Konsum.

coordinate [kou'ɔ:dineit], *v.a.* koordinieren, beiordnen. — [-nit], *adj.* (*Gram.*) koordiniert.

coordination [kouɔ:di'neiʃən], *s.* die Koordinierung.

coot [ku:t], *s.* (*Orn.*) das Wasserhuhn.

copartnership [kou'pɑ:tnəʃip], *s.* die Teilhaberschaft; die Partnerschaft in der Industrie.

cope (1) [koup], *s.* (*Eccl.*) das Pluviale, der Priesterrock; (*Build.*) die Decke.

cope (2) [koup], *v.n.* — *with s.th.*, mit etwas fertig werden, es schaffen.

coping ['koupiŋ], *s.* (*Build.*) die Kappe; — *-stone* or *copestone*, der Firststein, Schlußstein, Kappstein.

copious ['koupiəs], *adj.* reichlich; wortreich (*style*).

copiousness ['koupiəsnis], *s.* die Reichhaltigkeit, Fülle.

copper ['kɔpə], *s.* (*Metall.*) das Kupfer; (*sl.*) der Polizist; (*coll.*) der Penny, das Pennystück. — *adj.* kupfern.

copperplate ['kɔpəpleit], *s.* der Kupferstich (*etching*); (*Typ.*) die Kupferplatte.

coppery ['kɔpəri], *adj.* Kupfer-, kupfern, kupferfarben (*colour*).

coppice, copse ['kɔpis, kɔps], *s.* das Unterholz, das Dickicht.

copulate ['kɔpjuleit], *v.n.* sich paaren, begatten.

copulation [kɔpju'leiʃən], *s.* die Paarung; der Beischlaf (*human*).

copy ['kɔpi], *v.a.* kopieren, abschreiben (*write*); imitieren, nachahmen (*imitate*). — *s.* die Kopie; *carbon* —, die Durchschrift; Abschrift; die Nachahmung (*imitation*); die Fälschung (*forgery*).

copybook ['kɔpibuk], *s.* das Heft.

copyist ['kɔpiist], *s.* der Kopist.

coquet, coquette (1) [kɔ'ket], *v.n.* kokettieren.

coquette (2) [kɔ'ket], *s.* die Kokette.

coquettish [kɔ'ketiʃ], *adj.* kokett.

coral ['kɔrəl], *s.* die Koralle. — *adj.* Korallen-.

cord [kɔ:d], *s.* die Schnur, der Strick (*rope*); (*Am.*) der Bindfaden (*string*); die Klafter (*wood measure*); der Kordstoff (*textile*); *vocal* —, das Stimmband.

cordage ['kɔ:didʒ], *s.* (*Naut.*) das Tauwerk.

cordial (1) ['kɔ:diəl], *adj.* herzlich.

cordial (2) ['kɔ:diəl], *s.* der Fruchtsaft (konzentriert), Magenlikör.

cordiality [kɔ:di'æliti], *s.* die Herzlichkeit.

corduroy ['kɔ:djurɔi], *s.* der Kordsamt.

core [kɔ:], *s.* der Kern; das Innere (*innermost part*).

cork [kɔ:k], *s.* der Kork, der Korken. — *v.a.* verkorken.

corkscrew ['kɔ:kskru:], *s.* der Korkzieher.

cormorant ['kɔ:mərənt], *s.* (*Orn.*) der Kormoran, die Scharbe.

corn (1) [kɔ:n], *s.* das Korn, das Getreide (*wheat etc.*); (*Am.*) *sweet* —, der Mais.

corn (2) [kɔ:n], *s.* das Hühnerauge (*on foot*).

corned [kɔ:nd], *adj.* eingesalzt; — *beef*, das Pökelrindfleisch.

cornea ['kɔ:niə], *s.* (*Anat.*) die Hornhaut.

cornel-tree ['kɔ:nəltri:], *s.* (*Bot.*) der Kornelkirschbaum.

cornelian [kɔ:'ni:liən], *s.* (*Geol.*) der Karneol.

corner ['kɔ:nə], *s.* die Ecke; (*Footb.*) der Eckstoß. — *v.a.* in eine Ecke treiben; in die Enge treiben (*force*).

cornered ['kɔ:nəd], *adj.* eckig (*angular*); in die Enge getrieben, gefangen (*caught*).

cornet ['kɔ:nit], *s.* (*Mus.*) die Zinke, das Flügelhorn; (*Mil.*) der Kornett, der Fähnrich.

cornflower ['kɔ:nflauə], *s.* (*Bot.*) die Kornblume.

cornice ['kɔ:nis], *s.* (*Archit.*) das Gesims.

cornucopia [kɔ:nju'koupjə], *s.* das Füllhorn.

corollary [kə'rɔləri], *s.* (*Log.*) der Folgesatz; die Folgeerscheinung (*consequence*).

corona [kə'rounə], *s.* (*Astron.*) der Hof, Lichtkranz.

coronation [kɔrə'neiʃən], *s.* die Krönung.

coroner ['kɔrənə], *s.* der Leichenbeschauer.

coronet ['kɔrənet], *s.* die Adelskrone.

corporal (1) ['kɔ:pərəl], *s.* (*Mil.*) der Korporal, der Unteroffizier, Obergefreite.

corporal (2) ['kɔ:pərəl], *adj.* körperlich; — *punishment*, die Züchtigung.

corporate ['kɔ:pərit], *adj.* (*Law, Comm.*) als Körperschaft; gemeinschaftlich, einheitlich (*as a group or unit.*)

corporation [kɔ:pə'reiʃən], *s.* (*Law, Comm.*) die Körperschaft; die Korporation; die Gemeinde (*municipal*); (*sl.*) der Schmerbauch (*stoutness*).

corps [kɔ:], *s.* das Korps.

corpse [kɔ:ps], *s.* der Leichnam.

corpulence ['kɔ:pjuləns], *s.* die Korpulenz, die Beleibtheit.

corpulent ['kɔ:pjulənt], *adj.* korpulent, dick.

Corpus Christi ['kɔ:pəs 'kristi]. (der) Fronleichnam, das Fronleichnamsfest.

corpuscle ['kɔ:pʌsl], *s.* (*Anat.*) das Körperchen.

correct

correct [kə'rekt], *v.a.* korrigieren (*remove mistakes*); verbessern; tadeln (*reprove*); berichtigen (*rectify*). — *adj.* korrekt, tadellos, richtig.

correction [kə'rekʃən], *s.* die Korrektur (*of mistakes*); die Verbesserung (*improvement*); die Richtigstellung (*restoration*); der Verweis (*censure*).

corrective [kə'rektiv], *adj.* zur Besserung. — *s.* das Korrektiv.

correctness [kə'rektnis], *s.* die Korrektheit (*of manner, action etc.*).

corrector [kə'rektə], *s.* der Korrektor (*proof reader etc.*).

correlate [ˈkɔrileit], *v.a.* in Beziehung setzen, aufeinander beziehen. — [-lit], *s.* (*Log.*) das Korrelat.

correlative [kɔ'relətiv], *adj.* in Wechselbeziehung stehend.

correspond [kɔris'pɔnd], *v.n.* korrespondieren (*exchange letters*); entsprechen (*to, Dat.*).

correspondence [kɔris'pɔndəns], *s.* die Korrespondenz; der Briefwechsel (*letters*); die Übereinstimmung (*harmony*).

correspondent [kɔris'pɔndənt], *s.* der Korrespondent (*letter-writer*); der Journalist, Berichterstatter (*newspaper*).

corridor [ˈkɔridɔ:], *s.* der Korridor; der Gang.

corrigible [ˈkɔridʒibl], *adj.* verbesserlich.

corroborate [kə'rɔbəreit], *v.a.* bestätigen (*confirm*); bestärken (*strengthen*).

corroboration [kərɔbə'reiʃən], *s.* die Bestätigung, die Bekräftigung.

corroborative [kə'rɔbərətiv], *adj.* bekräftigend.

corrode [kə'roud], *v.a.* zerfressen, zersetzen, ätzen (*acid*).

corrosion [kə'rouʒən], *s.* die Anfressung, Ätzung.

corrosive [kə'rouziv], *adj.* ätzend.

corrugated [ˈkɔrugeitid], *adj.* gewellt, Well-; — *iron*, das Wellblech; — *paper*, die Wellpappe.

corrupt [kə'rʌpt], *v.a.* verderben (*spoil*); bestechen (*bribe*). — *adj.* korrupt (*morals*); verdorben (*spoilt*).

corruptible [kə'rʌptibl], *adj.* verderblich; bestechlich.

corruption [kə'rʌpʃən], *s.* die Korruption; die Bestechung (*bribery*).

corruptness [kə'rʌptnis], *s.* die Verdorbenheit, der Verfall.

corsair [ˈkɔ:sɛə], *s.* der Korsar, der Seeräuber.

corset [ˈkɔ:sit], *s.* das Korsett.

coruscate [ˈkɔrəskeit], *v.n.* schimmern, leuchten.

corvette [kɔ:'vet], *s.* (*Naut.*) die Korvette.

cosine [ˈkousain], *s.* (*Maths.*) der Kosinus.

cosiness [ˈkouzinis], *s.* die Bequemlichkeit, die Behaglichkeit (*comfort*).

cosmetic [kɔz'metik], *adj.* kosmetisch. — *s.* (*pl.*) das *or* die (*pl.*) Schönheitsmittel.

cosmic [ˈkɔzmik], *adj.* kosmisch.

cosmopolitan [kɔzmo'pɔlitən], *adj.* kosmopolitisch, weltbürgerlich. — *s.* der Kosmopolit, der Weltbürger.

Cossack [ˈkɔsæk], *s.* der Kosak.

cost [kɔst], *v.a. irr.* kosten. — *v.n. irr.* zu stehen kommen. —*s.* die Kosten, *f. pl.* (*expenses*); *at all* —s, um jeden Preis.

costermonger [ˈkɔstəmʌŋgə], *s.* der Straßenhändler.

costly [ˈkɔstli], *adj.* kostspielig.

costume [ˈkɔstju:m], *s.* das Kostüm; — *play*, das Zeitstück.

cosy [ˈkouzi], *adj.* behaglich, bequem.

cot (1) [kɔt], *s.* das Bettchen, Kinderbett.

cot (2) [kɔt], *s.* (*obs.*) die Hütte (*hut*).

cottage [ˈkɔtidʒ], *s.* die Hütte, das Häuschen.

cottager [ˈkɔtidʒə], *s.* der Kleinhäusler.

cotton [kɔtn], *s.* die Baumwolle. — *v.n.* — *on to*, (*coll.*) sich anhängen, sich anschließen (*Dat.*); — *on*, folgen können (*understand*).

couch [kautʃ], *s.* die Chaiselongue; der Diwan. — *v.a.* (*express*) in Worte fassen.

cough [kɔf], *v.n.* husten. — *s.* der Husten; *whooping* —, der Keuchhusten.

council [ˈkaunsil], *s.* der Rat (*body*); die Ratsversammlung.

councillor [ˈkaunsilə], *s.* der Rat, das Ratsmitglied; der Stadtrat.

counsel [ˈkaunsəl], *s.* der Rat (*advice*); der Berater (*adviser*); der Anwalt (*lawyer*). — *v.a.* einen Rat geben, beraten (*Acc.*).

counsellor [ˈkaunsələ], *s.* der Ratgeber; der Ratsherr; (*Am.*) der Anwalt (*lawyer*).

count (1) [kaunt], *v.a., v.n.* zählen; — *on s.o.*, sich auf jemanden verlassen. — *s.* die Zählung.

count (2) [kaunt], *s.* der Graf.

countenance [ˈkauntənəns], *s.* das Gesicht, die Miene. — *v.a.* begünstigen, unterstützen, zulassen.

counter (1) [ˈkauntə], *s.* der Rechner, der Zähler (*chip*); die Spielmarke; der Zahltisch (*desk*); Ladentisch (*in shop*); Schalter (*in office*).

counter (2) [ˈkauntə], *adv.* entgegen.

counteract [kauntə'rækt], *v.a.* entgegenwirken (*Dat.*).

counteraction [kauntə'rækʃən], *s.* die Gegenwirkung; der Widerstand (*resistance*).

counterbalance [ˈkauntəbæləns], *s.* das Gegengewicht. — [-'bæləns], *v.a.* ausbalancieren, ausgleichen.

countercharge [ˈkauntətʃɑ:dʒ], *s.* die Gegenklage.

counterfeit [ˈkauntəfi:t, -fit], *s.* die Fälschung (*forgery*); die Nachahmung (*imitation*). — *adj.* gefälscht, falsch.

counterfoil [ˈkauntəfɔil], *s.* das Kontrollblatt; der Kupon.
counter–intelligence [ˈkauntərintelidʒəns], *s.* die Spionageabwehr.
countermand [kauntəˈmɑːnd], *v.a.* widerrufen.
counterpane [ˈkauntəpein], *s.* die Steppdecke.
counterpart [ˈkauntəpɑːt], *s.* das Gegenbild, das Gegenstück.
counterplot [ˈkauntəplɔt], *s.* der Gegenplan. — *v.n.* einen Gegenplan machen.
counterpoint [ˈkauntəpɔint], *s.* (*Mus.*) der Kontrapunkt.
counterpoise [ˈkauntəpɔiz], *s.* das Gegengewicht. — *v.a.* das Gleichgewicht halten.
countersign [ˈkauntəsain], *v.a.* gegenzeichnen, mitunterschreiben. — *s.* das Gegenzeichen.
countess [ˈkauntes], *s.* die Gräfin.
counting-house [ˈkauntiŋhaus], *s.* das Kontor.
countless [ˈkauntlis], *adj.* zahllos.
country [ˈkʌntri], *s.* das Land. — *adj.* ländlich, Bauern-.
county [ˈkaunti], *s.* die Grafschaft (*British*); der Landbezirk (*U.S.A.*).
couple [kʌpl], *s.* das Paar. — *v.a.* paaren, verbinden. — *v.n.* sich paaren (*pair*); sich verbinden.
couplet [ˈkʌplit], *s.* das Verspaar.
coupling [ˈkʌpliŋ], *s.* (*Mech.*) die Kupplung.
courage [ˈkʌridʒ], *s.* der Mut.
courageous [kəˈreidʒəs], *adj.* mutig, tapfer.
courier [ˈkuriə], *s.* der Eilbote (*messenger*); der Reisebegleiter (*tour leader*).
course [kɔːs], *s.* der Kurs; der Lauf (*time*); der Ablauf (*lapse of a period etc.*); die Bahn (*racing track*); *in due* —, zu gegebener Zeit; *of* —, natürlich.
courser [ˈkɔːsə], *s.* das schnelle Pferd.
court [kɔːt], *s.* der Hof (*royal etc.*); (*Law*) der Gerichtshof. — *v.a.* (*a lady*) den Hof machen (*Dat.*); — *disaster*, das Unglück herausfordern.
courteous [ˈkɔːtiəs], *adj.* höflich.
courtesan [ˈkɔːtizən *or* kɔːtiˈzæn], *s.* die Kurtisane, die Buhlerin.
courtesy [ˈkɔːtəsi], *s.* die Höflichkeit; *by* — *of*, mit freundlicher Erlaubnis von.
courtier [ˈkɔːtiə], *s.* der Höfling.
courtly [ˈkɔːtli], *adj.* höfisch, Hof-.
court-martial [kɔːtˈmɑːʃəl], *s.* das Kriegsgericht.
courtship [ˈkɔːtʃip], *s.* das Werben, die Werbung, das Freien.
courtyard [ˈkɔːtjɑːd], *s.* der Hof, der Hofraum.
cousin [kʌzn], *s.* der Vetter (*male*); die Kusine (*female*).
cove [kouv], *s.* die (kleine) Bucht.
covenant [ˈkʌvənənt], *s.* (*Bibl.*) der Bund; (*Comm.*) der Vertrag.

cover [ˈkʌvə], *v.a.* decken, bedecken (*table etc.*); schützen (*protect*); — *up*, bemänteln. — *s.* die Decke (*blanket*); der Deckel (*lid*); der Einband (*book*); das Gedeck (*table*); (*Comm.*) die Deckung; — *point*, (*Cricket*) die Deckstellung; *under* —, (*Mil.*) verdeckt, unter Deckung; — *girl*, das Mädchen auf dem Titelblatt (einer Illustrierten.)
covering [ˈkʌvəriŋ], *s.* die Bedeckung, die Bekleidung (*clothing*).
coverlet, coverlid [ˈkʌvəlit, ˈkʌvəlid], *s.* die Bettdecke.
covert [ˈkʌvəːt], *s.* der Schlupfwinkel (*hideout*); das Dickicht (*thicket*). — *adj.* verborgen, bedeckt (*covered*); heimlich (*secret*).
covet [ˈkʌvit], *v.a.*, *v.n.* begehren (*Acc.*), gelüsten (nach (*Dat.*)).
covetous [ˈkʌvitəs], *adj.* begierig, habsüchtig.
covetousness [ˈkʌvitəsnis], *s.* die Begierde, die Habsucht.
covey [ˈkʌvi], *s.* der Flug *or* die Kette (Rebhühner, *partridges*).
cow (1) [kau], *s.* die Kuh; — *-shed*, der Kuhstall.
cow (2) [kau], *v.a.* einschüchtern.
coward [ˈkauəd], *s.* der Feigling.
cowardice [ˈkauədis], *s.* die Feigheit.
cower [ˈkauə], *v.n.* sich kauern.
cowherd [ˈkauhəːd], *s.* der Kuhhirt.
cowl [kaul], *s.* die Kappe (*of monk*), die Kapuze (*hood*).
cowslip [ˈkauslip], *s.* (*Bot.*) die Primel, die Schlüsselblume.
coxswain [ˈkɔksn], *s.* (*Naut.*) der Steuermann.
coy [kɔi], *adj.* scheu, spröde, zurückhaltend.
coyness [ˈkɔinis], *s.* die Sprödigkeit.
crab [kræb], *s.* (*Zool.*) die Krabbe; — *apple*, (*Bot.*) der Holzapfel.
crabbed [kræbd], *adj.* mürrisch (*temper*); unleserlich (*handwriting*).
crack [kræk], *s.* der Riß (*fissure*); der Krach, Schlag; der Sprung; die komische Bemerkung (*remark*). — *adj.* (*coll.*) erstklassig; — *shot*, der Meisterschütze. — *v.a.* aufbrechen; aufknacken (*nut, safe*); — *a joke*, eine witzige Bemerkung machen. — *v.n.* — *under strain*, unter einer Anstrengung zusammenbrechen; bersten (*break*).
cracked, crackers [krækd, ˈkrækəz], *adj.* (*coll.*) verrückt.
cracker [ˈkrækə], *s.* der Keks; der Frosch (*firework*).
crackle [krækl], *v.n.* knistern, prasseln (*fire*); knallen, platzen (*rocket*).
cracknel [ˈkræknəl], *s.* die Brezel.
crackpot [ˈkrækpɔt], *s.* (*coll.*) der verrückte Kerl.
cradle [kreidl], *s.* die Wiege. — *v.a.* einwiegen.
craft [krɑːft], *s.* die Fertigkeit (*skill*); das Handwerk (*trade*); die List (*cunning*); *arts and* —*s*, die Handwerkskünste.

353

craftsman

craftsman ['krɑ:ftsmən], s. der (gelernte) Handwerker.
crafty ['krɑ:fti], adj. listig, schlau.
crag [kræg], s. die Klippe.
cragged, craggy [krægd, 'krægi], adj. felsig, schroff.
cram [kræm], v.a. vollstopfen (stuff full); (coll.) pauken (coach). — v.n. büffeln.
crammer ['kræmə], s. (coll.) der Einpauker, Privatlehrer (tutor).
cramp [kræmp], s. (Med.) der Krampf; die Klammer (tool). — v.a. einengen (narrow); verkrampfen.
cramped [kræmpd], adj. krampfhaft; eingeengt, beengt (enclosed).
cranberry ['krænbəri], s. (Bot.) die Preiselbeere.
crane [krein], s. (Orn.) der Kranich; (Engin.) der Kran. — v.a. — o.'s neck, den Hals ausrecken.
crank (1) [kræŋk], s. (Motor.) die Kurbel; — -handle, die Andrehwelle; (Motor., Engin.) —shaft, die Kurbelwelle, die Kurbel.
crank (2) [kræŋk], s. der Sonderling, der sonderbare Kauz (eccentric).
cranky ['kræŋki], adj. sonderbar.
cranny ['kræni], s. der Spalt, der Riß; nook and —, Eck und Spalt.
crape [kreip], s. der Krepp, Flor.
crash [kræʃ], s. der Krach; (Motor.) Zusammenstoß; (Aviat.) Absturz. — v.n. krachen (noise); stürzen, abstürzen (fall).
crass [kræs], adj. derb, grob, kraß.
crate [kreit], s. der Packkorb (basket); die Kiste (wood).
crater ['kreitə], s. (Geol.) der Krater.
cravat [krə'væt], s. die breite Halsbinde, das Halstuch (scarf); die Krawatte.
crave [kreiv], v.a. (dringend) verlangen (for, nach, Dat.).
craven ['kreivn], adj. feig, mutlos. — s. der Feigling.
craving ['kreiviŋ], s. das starke Verlangen.
craw [krɔ:], s. (Zool.) der Vogelkropf.
crawl [krɔ:l], v.n. kriechen; kraulen (swim).
crawling ['krɔ:liŋ], s. das Kriechen; das Kraulschwimmen.
crayon ['kreiən], s. der Farbstift, der Pastellstift.
craze [kreiz], s. die Manie; die verrückte Mode (fashion).
craziness ['kreizinis], s. die Verrücktheit.
crazy ['kreizi], adj. verrückt.
creak [kri:k], v.n. knarren.
cream [kri:m], s. der Rahm, die Sahne; whipped —, die Schlagsahne, (Austr.) der Schlagobers. — v.a. — off, (die Sahne) abschöpfen; (fig.) das Beste abziehen.
creamery ['kri:məri], s. die Molkerei.
creamy ['kri:mi], adj. sahnig.
crease [kri:s], s. die Falte (trousers etc.); — -resistant, knitterfrei. — v.a. falten (fold). — v.n. knittern.

create [kri'eit], v.a. erschaffen, schaffen.
creation [kri'eiʃən], s. die Schöpfung.
creative [kri'eitiv], adj. schöpferisch.
creator [kri'eitə], s. der Schöpfer.
creature ['kri:tʃə], s. das Geschöpf.
credence ['kri:dəns], s. der Glaube.
credentials [kri'denʃəlz], s. pl. das Zeugnis, das Beglaubigungsschreiben; die Legitimation (proof of identity).
credibility [kredi'biliti], s. die Glaubwürdigkeit.
credible ['kredibl], adj. glaubwürdig, glaublich.
credit ['kredit], s. (Comm.) der Kredit; der gute Ruf (reputation); das Guthaben (assets). — v.a. — s.o. with s.th., jemandem etwas gutschreiben; glauben (believe).
creditable ['kreditəbl], adj. ehrenwert, lobenswert.
creditor ['kreditə], s. (Comm.) der Gläubiger.
credulity [kre'dju:liti], s. die Leichtgläubigkeit.
credulous ['kredjuləs], adj. leichtgläubig.
creed [kri:d], s. das Glaubensbekenntnis.
creek [kri:k], s. die kleine Bucht; das Flüßchen (small river).
creel [kri:l], s. der Fischkorb.
creep [kri:p], s. (Geol.) der Rutsch; (pl., coll.) the —s, die Gänsehaut, das Gruseln. — v.n.irr. kriechen; (furtively) sich einschleichen.
creeper ['kri:pə], s. die Schlingpflanze, das Rankengewächs; (Sch.) der Kriecher; Virginia —, der wilde Wein.
creepy ['kri:pi], adj. kriechend; gruselig (frightening).
cremate [kri'meit], v.a. einäschern.
cremation [kri'meiʃən], s. die Verbrennung, Einäscherung.
crematorium, (Am.) **crematory** [kremə'tɔ:riəm, 'kremətəri], s. das Krematorium.
Creole ['kri:oul], s. der Kreole.
crepuscular [kri'pʌskjulə], adj. dämmerig.
crescent ['kresənt], adj. wachsend, zunehmend. — s. der (zunehmende) Mond, die Mondsichel; das Hörnchen.
cress [kres], s. (Bot.) die Kresse; mustard and —, die Gartenkresse.
crest [krest], s. der Kamm (cock); der Gipfel (hill); der Kamm (wave); der Busch (helmet); das Wappenschild (Heraldry).
crestfallen ['krestfɔ:lən], adj. entmutigt, mutlos, niedergeschlagen.
Cretan ['kri:tən], adj. kretisch. — s. der Kreter, die Kreterin.
cretonne ['kretɔn], s. die Kretonne.
crevasse [krə'væs], s. die Gletscherspalte.
crevice ['krevis], s. der Riß.
crew (1) [kru:], s. (Naut., Aviat.) die Besatzung; (Naut.) die Schiffsmannschaft; die Mannschaft (team); (Am.) — cut, die Bürstenfrisur.

crew (2) [kru:] *see* **crow**.
crib [krib], *s.* die Krippe (*Christmas*); die Wiege (*cradle*); (*Sch.*) die Eselsbrücke. — *v.a.* (*Sch.*) abschreiben (*copy*).
crick [krik], *s.* (*in neck*) der steife Hals.
cricket ['krikit], *s.* (*Ent.*) das Heimchen, die Grille; (*Sport*) das Cricket(spiel).
crime [kraim], *s.* das Verbrechen; — *fiction*, die Detektivromane, *m. pl.*
criminal ['kriminəl], *s.* der Verbrecher. — *adj.* — *case*, der Kriminalfall; verbrecherisch (*act*); — *investigation*, die Fahndung.
crimp [krimp], *v.a.* kräuseln (*hair*).
crimson ['krimzən], *adj.* karmesinrot.
cringe [krindʒ], *v.n.* kriechen.
crinkle [kriŋkl], *v.a., v.n.* kräuseln. — *s.* die Falte.
crinoline ['krinəlin], *s.* der Reifrock.
cripple [kripl], *s.* der Krüppel. — *v.a.* verkrüppeln; lahmlegen (*immobilize*).
crisis ['kraisis], *s.* die Krise, der Wendepunkt; die Notlage.
crisp [krisp], *adj.* kraus (*hair*); knusperig (*bread*); frisch.
criss-cross ['kriskrɔs], *adv.* kreuz und quer.
criterion [krai'tiəriən], *s.* das Kennzeichen, das Kriterium.
critic ['kritik], *s.* der Kritiker; Rezensent (*reviewer*).
critical ['kritikəl], *adj.* kritisch.
criticism ['kritisizm], *s.* die Kritik (*of, an, Dat.*); Rezension, Besprechung (*review*).
criticize ['kritisaiz], *v.a.* kritisieren.
croak [krouk], *v.n.* krächzen (*raven*); quaken (*frog*).
croaking ['kroukiŋ], *s.* das Krächzen, das Gekrächze (*raven*); das Quaken (*frog*).
Croat ['krouæt]. *s.* der Kroate.
Croatian [krou'eiʃən], *adj.* kroatisch.
crochet ['krouʃei], *s.* die Häkelei; — *hook*, die Häkelnadel. — *v.a., v.n.* häkeln.
crock [krɔk], *s.* der Topf, der irdene Krug; der alte Topf; (*coll.*) *old* —, der Invalide, Krüppel.
crockery ['krɔkəri], *s.* (*Comm.*) die Töpferware; das Geschirr (*household*).
crocodile ['krɔkədail], *s.* das Krokodil.
crocus ['kroukəs], *s.* (*Bot.*) der Krokus, die Safranblume.
croft [krɔft], *s.* das Kleinbauerngut.
crofter ['krɔftə], *s.* der Kleinbauer.
crone [kroun], *s.* das alte Weib; die Hexe (*witch*).
crony ['krouni], *s.* (*coll.*) *old* —, der alte Freund.
crook [kruk], *s.* der Krummstab (*staff*); der Schwindler (*cheat*). — *v.a.* krümmen, beugen.
crooked ['krukid], *adj.* krumm; (*fig.*) schwindlerisch, verbrecherisch.
crookedness ['krukidnis], *s.* die Krummheit; die Durchtriebenheit (*slyness*).
croon [kru:n], *v.n.* leise singen; (*Am.*) im modernen Stil singen.

crooner ['kru:nə], *s.* der Jazzsänger.
crop [krɔp], *s.* der Kropf (*bird*); die Ernte (*harvest*); der (kurze) Haarschnitt; *riding* —, die Reitpeitsche. — *v.a.* stutzen (*cut short*). — *v.n.* — *up*, auftauchen.
crosier ['krouziə], *s.* (*Eccl.*) der Bischofsstab.
cross [krɔs], *s.* das Kreuz. — *v.a.* (*Zool., Bot.*) kreuzen; überqueren (*road, on foot*); — *s.o.'s path*, einem in die Quere kommen. — *v.n.* überfahren (übers Wasser); hinübergehen; — *over*, übersetzen (*on boat or ferry*). — *v.r.* sich bekreuzigen. — *adj.* mürrisch (*grumpy*), verstimmt; *at* — *purposes*, ohne einander zu verstehen; *make* —, verstimmen. — *adv.* kreuzweise; — *-eyed*, schielend; — *-grained*, wider den Strich, schlecht aufgelegt.
crossbow ['krɔsbou], *s.* die Armbrust.
crossbreed ['krɔsbri:d]. *s.* die Mischrasse, der Mischling.
cross-examine [krɔsig'zæmin], *v.a., v.n.* (*Law*) ins (Kreuz-)Verhör nehmen.
crossing ['krɔsiŋ], *s.* die Straßenkreuzung; (*Naut.*) die Überfahrt; der Straßenübergang; Kreuzweg.
crossroads ['krɔsroudz], *s.* der Kreuzweg, die Kreuzung.
crossword ['krɔswə:d], *s.* das Kreuzworträtsel.
crotch [krɔtʃ], *s.* der Haken.
crotchet ['krɔtʃit], *s.* (*Mus.*) die Viertelnote; die Grille (*mood*).
crotchety ['krɔtʃiti], *adj.* grillenhaft, verschroben.
crouch [krautʃ], *v.n.* sich ducken (*squat*); sich demütigen (*cringe*).
croup (1) [kru:p], *s.* (*Med.*) der Krupp.
croup (2) [kru:p], *s.* die Kruppe.
crow [krou], *s.* (*Orn.*) die Krähe; das Krähen (*of cock*). — *v.n. irr.* krähen (*cock*).
crowbar ['krouba:], *s.* das Brecheisen.
crowd [kraud], *s.* die Menge (*multitude*); das Gedränge (*throng*). — *v.n.* — *in*, sich hineindrängen, dazudrängen; — *around*, sich herumscharen um (*Acc.*).
crown [kraun], *s.* die Krone (*diadem or coin*); der Gipfel (*mountain*); (*Anat.*) der Scheitel; — *lands*, Krongüter (*n. pl.*), Landeigentum der Krone, *n.*; — *prince*, der Kronprinz; — *of thorns*, die Dornenkrone. — *v.a.* krönen.
crucial ['kru:ʃəl], *adj.* entscheidend, kritisch.
crucifix ['kru:sifiks], *s.* das Kruzifix.
crucify ['kru:sifai], *v.a.* kreuzigen.
crude [kru:d], *adj.* roh, ungekocht, unreif; grob (*manners*), ungeschliffen.
crudity ['kru:diti], *s.* die Rohheit; Grobheit (*manners*).
cruel ['kru:əl], *adj.* grausam.
cruelty ['kru:əlti], *s.* die Grausamkeit.
cruet ['kru:it], *s.* das Salz- *oder* Pfefferfäßchen; das Fläschchen.

cruise

cruise [kru:z], v.n. (Naut.) kreuzen. — s. die Seefahrt, die Seereise; pleasure —, die Vergnügungsreise (zu Wasser).

cruiser ['kru:zə], s. (Naut.) der Kreuzer; battle —, der Panzerkreuzer.

crumb [krʌm], s. die Krume. — v.a. zerbröckeln, zerkrümeln.

crumble [krʌmbl], v.n. zerfallen, zerbröckeln.

crumpet ['krʌmpit], s. das Teebrötchen, das Teeküchlein.

crumple [krʌmpl], v.a. zerknittern (material). — v.n. — up, zusammenbrechen.

crunch [krʌntʃ], v.a. zerstoßen, zermalmen. — v.n. knirschen.

crusade [kru:'seid], s. der Kreuzzug.

crusader [kru:'seidə], s. der Kreuzfahrer.

crush [krʌʃ], v.a. zerdrücken; zerstoßen (pulverize); drängen (crowd); zertreten (tread down); (fig.) vernichten. — s. das Gedränge (throng); (coll.) have a — on, verknallt sein, in einen verliebt sein.

crust [krʌst], s. die Kruste, die Rinde (bread). — v.a. mit einer Kruste bedecken. — v.n. verkrusten.

crustaceous [krʌs'teiʃəs], adj. (Zool.) krustenartig, Krustentier-.

crusty ['krʌsti], adj. krustig, knusperig (pastry, bread); mürrisch (grumpy).

crutch [krʌtʃ], s. die Krücke.

crux [krʌks], s. der entscheidende Punkt, der springende Punkt, die Schwierigkeit.

cry [krai], v.n. schreien, rufen; weinen (weep). — v.a. — down, niederschreien. — s. der Schrei; der Zuruf (call).

crypt [kript], s. (Eccl.) die Krypta, die Gruft.

crystal ['kristəl], s. der Kristall.

crystallize ['kristəlaiz], v.n. sich kristallisieren, Kristalle bilden.

cub [kʌb], s. (Zool.) das Junge. — v.n. Junge haben, Junge werfen.

Cuban ['kju:bən], adj. kubanisch. — s. der Kubaner.

cube [kju:b], s. der Würfel; (Maths.) — root, die Kubikwurzel. — v.a. zur Dritten (Potenz) erheben; kubieren.

cubic(al) ['kju:bik(əl)], adj. kubisch, zur dritten Potenz.

cubit ['kju:bit], s. die Elle.

cuckoo ['kuku:], s. (Orn.) der Kuckuck.

cucumber ['kju:kʌmbə], s. (Bot.) die Gurke; cool as a —, ruhig und gelassen.

cud [kʌd], s. das wiedergekäute Futter; chew the —, wiederkauen (also fig.).

cuddle ['kʌdl], v.a. liebkosen, an sich drücken. — v.n. sich anschmiegen.

cudgel ['kʌdʒəl], s. der Knüttel; take up the —s for, sich für etwas einsetzen.

cue (1) [kju:], s. (Theat.) das Stichwort. — v.a. einem (Theat.) das Stichwort or (Mus.) den Einsatz geben.

cue (2) [kju:], s. der Billardstock. — v.a. (Billiards) abschießen.

cuff (1) [kʌf], s. die Manschette, der Aufschlag (shirt); —links, die Manschettenknöpfe.

cuff (2) [kʌf], s. der Schlag. — v.a. schlagen, puffen.

culinary ['kju:linəri], adj. kulinarisch; Küchen-, Eß-, Speisen-.

cull [kʌl], v.a. auswählen, auslesen (from books).

culminate ['kʌlmineit], v.n. kulminieren, den Höhepunkt erreichen.

culpable ['kʌlpəbl], adj. schuldig; strafbar.

culprit ['kʌlprit], s. der Schuldige, Verbrecher.

cult [kʌlt], s. der Kult, die Verehrung; der Kultus.

cultivate ['kʌltiveit], v.a. kultivieren; (Agr.) anbauen; pflegen (acquaintance); bilden (mind).

cultivation [kʌlti'veiʃən], s. (Agr.) der Anbau; die Bildung (mind).

culture ['kʌltʃə], s. die Kultur, die Bildung.

cumbersome ['kʌmbəsəm], adj. beschwerlich, lästig.

cunning ['kʌniŋ], s. die List, die Schlauheit. — adj. listig, schlau.

cup [kʌp], s. die Tasse (tea—); der Becher (handleless); (Eccl.) der Kelch; der Pokal (sports); — final, das Endspiel. — v.a. (Med.) schröpfen.

cupboard ['kʌbəd], s. der Schrank.

cupola ['kju:polə], s. (Archit., Metall.) die Kuppel.

cur [kə:], s. der Köter; (fig). der Schurke.

curable ['kjuərəbl], adj. heilbar.

curate ['kjuərit], s. der Hilfsgeistliche.

curative ['kjuərətiv], adj. heilsam, heilend.

curator [kjuə'reitə], s. der Kurator, Verwalter, Direktor.

curb [kə:b], v.a. zügeln, bändigen. — s. der Zaum (bridle).

curd [kə:d], s. der Rahmkäse, der Milchkäse; (pl.) der Quark.

curdle [kə:dl], v.a. gerinnen lassen. — v.n. gerinnen; erstarren.

cure [kjuə], s. die Kur, die Heilung. — v.a. kurieren, wieder gesundmachen; einpökeln (foodstuffs).

curfew ['kə:fju:], s. die Abendglocke (bells); das Ausgehverbot, die Polizeistunde (police).

curio ['kjuəriou], s. die Kuriosität, das Sammlerstück; die Rarität.

curiosity [kjuəri'ositi], s. die Neugier; Merkwürdigkeit.

curious ['kjuəriəs], adj. neugierig (inquisitive); seltsam, sonderbar (strange).

curl [kə:l], v.a. kräuseln, (in Locken) wickeln. — v.n. sich kräuseln. — s. die Haarlocke.

curler ['kə:lə], s. der Lockenwickler.

curlew ['kə:lju:], s.(Orn.) der Brachvogel.

curly ['kə:li], adj. lockig.

currant ['kʌrənt], s. (Bot.) die Korinthe, die Johannisbeere.

currency ['kʌrənsi], *s.* die Währung (*money*); der Umlauf (*circulation*).

current ['kʌrənt], *adj.* im Umlauf; allgemein gültig, eben gültig; jetzig (*modern*). — *s.* (*Elect.*) der Strom; die Strömung (*river*); der Zug (*air*).

curry (1) ['kʌri], *v.a.* gerben (*tan*); — *comb*, der Pferdestriegel; — *favour*, sich einschmeicheln.

curry (2) ['kʌri], *s.* das indische Ragout. — *v.a.* würzen.

curse [kəːs], *v.a.*, *v.n.* verfluchen; verwünschen. — *s.* der Fluch; die Verwünschung.

cursive ['kəːsiv], *adj.* kursiv, Kursiv-.

cursory ['kəːsəri], *adj.* kursorisch, oberflächlich.

curt [kəːt], *adj.* kurz angebunden (*speech, manner*).

curtail [kəː'teil], *v.a.* stutzen, beschränken (*scope*); verkürzen (*time*).

curtain ['kəːtin], *s.* die Gardine; der Vorhang; (*Mil.*) — *fire*, das Sperrfeuer; — *lecture*, die Gardinenpredigt; — *speech*, die Ansprache vor dem Vorhang. — *v.a.* verhüllen (*hide*); mit Vorhängen versehen (*hang curtains*).

curtness ['kəːtnis], *s.* die Kürze; die Barschheit.

curts(e)y ['kəːtsi], *s.* der Knicks. — *v.n.* knicksen, einen Knicks machen.

curve [kəːv], *s.* die Krümmung; (*Geom.*) die Kurve. — *v.a.* krümmen, biegen. — *v.n.* sich biegen.

curved [kəːvd], *adj.* krumm, gebogen.

cushion ['kuʃən], *s.* das Kissen. — *v.a.* polstern.

custody ['kʌstədi], *s.* die Obhut; Bewachung, Haft.

custom ['kʌstəm], *s.* die Sitte, die Tradition; der Gebrauch, Brauch (*usage*); die Kundschaft (*trade*); (*pl.*) der Zoll (*duty*).

customary ['kʌstəməri], *adj.* gewohnt, althergebracht, gebräuchlich.

customer ['kʌstəmə], *s.* der Kunde, die Kundin.

cut [kʌt], *v.a. irr.* schneiden; — (*s.o.*), ignorieren; — *o.'s teeth*, zahnen; *this won't* — *any ice*, das wird nicht viel nützen; — *both ways*, das ist ein zweischneidiges Schwert; — *a lecture*, eine Vorlesung schwänzen; — *short*, unterbrechen. — *adj.* — *out for*, wie gerufen zu *or* für; — *to the quick*, aufs tiefste verletzt; — *glass*, das geschliffene Glas; — *price*, verbilligt. — *s.* der Schnitt (*section*); der Hieb (*gash*); (*Art*) der Stich; — *in salary*, eine Gehaltskürzung; die Abkürzung, die Kürzung (*abridgement*).

cute [kjuːt], *adj.* klug, aufgeweckt; (*Am.*) süß, niedlich.

cutler ['kʌtlə], *s.* der Messerschmied.

cutlery ['kʌtləri], *s.* das Besteck (*tableware*); (*Comm.*) die Messerschmiedwaren, *f. pl.*

cutlet ['kʌtlit], *s.* das Kotelett, das Rippchen.

cut-throat ['kʌtθrout], *s.* der Halsabschneider; — *competition*, Konkurrenz auf Leben und Tod.

cuttie [kʌti], *s.* (*Zool.*) der Tintenfisch.

cyanide ['saiənaid], *s.* (*Chem.*) zyanidsaures Salz; das Zyanid, die Blausäure.

cyclamen ['sikləmən], *s.* (*Bot.*) das Alpenveilchen.

cycle [saikl], *s.* (*Geom.*) der Kreis; (*Mus., Zool.*) der Zyklus; (*coll.*) das Fahrrad. — *v.n.* (*coll.*) radfahren; zirkulieren (*round*, um, *Acc.*).

cyclone ['saikloun], *s.* der Wirbelwind, der Wirbelsturm.

cyclopaedia [saiklo'piːdjə] *see* **encyclopædia**.

cylinder ['silində], *s.* der Zylinder; die Walze.

cymbal ['simbəl], *s.* (*Mus.*) die Zimbel, das Becken.

cynic ['sinik], *s.* der Zyniker.

cynical ['sinikəl], *adj.* zynisch.

cypress ['saiprəs], *s.* (*Bot.*) die Zypresse.

Cypriot ['sipriət], *adj.* zyprisch. — *s.* der Zypriote.

czar [zaː], *s.* der Zar.

Czech, Czechoslovak(ian) [tʃek, tʃeko'slouvæk, tʃekoslo'vækjən], *adj.* tschechisch. — *s.* der Tscheche.

D

D [diː]. das D (*also Mus.*).

dab [dæb], *v.a.* leicht berühren. — *s.* der leichte Schlag (*blow*).

dabble [dæbl], *v.n.* sich in etwas versuchen, pfuschen (*in*, in, *Dat.*).

dabbler ['dæblə], *s.* der Pfuscher, Stümper.

dace [deis], *s.* (*Zool.*) der Weißfisch.

dad, daddy [dæd, 'dædi], *s.* der Papa; Vati; *daddy longlegs*, die Bachmücke, die langbeinige Mücke.

dado ['deidou], *s.* die Täfelung.

daffodil ['dæfədil], *s.* (*Bot.*) die Narzisse.

dagger ['dægə], *s.* der Dolch; *at* —*s drawn*, spinnefeind; *look* —*s*, mit Blicken durchbohren.

dahlia ['deiliə], *s.* (*Bot.*) die Dahlie, die Georgine.

daily ['deili], *adj.* täglich; Tages-. — *s.* (*newspaper*) die Tageszeitung; (*woman*) die Putzfrau.

dainties ['deintiz], *s. pl.* das Backwerk, das kleine Gebäck, das Teegebäck.

daintiness ['deintinis], *s.* die Feinheit; die Kleinheit; die Leckerhaftigkeit.

dainty ['deinti], *adj.* fein, klein, zierlich; lecker (*food*).

dairy ['dɛəri], *s.* die Molkerei, die Meierei.

dairyman ['dɛərimən], *s.* der Milchmann; der Senne (*in Alps*).

dais [deis, 'deiis], *s.* das Podium.

daisy

daisy [ˈdeizi], s. (*Bot.*) das Gänseblümchen, das Marienblümchen.
dale [deil], s. das Tal.
dalliance [ˈdæliəns], s. die Tändelei, Liebelei; Verzögerung.
dally [ˈdæli], v.n. die Zeit vertrödeln.
dam (1) [dæm], s. der Damm. — v.a. eindämmen, abdämmen.
dam (2) [dæm], s. (*Zool.*) die Tiermutter.
damage [ˈdæmidʒ], s. der Schaden; der Verlust (*loss*); (*pl.*) (*Law*) der Schadenersatz. — v.a. beschädigen.
damageable [ˈdæmidʒəbl], adj. leicht zu beschädigen.
damask [ˈdæməsk], s. der Damast (*textile*). — adj. damasten, aus Damast.
dame [deim], s. die Dame (*title*); (*Am.*) (*coll.*) die junge Dame, das Fräulein.
damn [dæm], v.a. verdammen.
damnable [ˈdæmnəbl], adj. verdammenswert, verdammt.
damnation [dæmˈneiʃən], s. die Verdammung, Verdammnis.
damn(ed) [dæm(d)], adj. & adv. verwünscht, verdammt.
damp [dæmp], adj. feucht, dumpfig. — s. die Feuchtigkeit; (*Build.*) — *course*, die Schutzschicht. — v.a. dämpfen, befeuchten; — *the spirits*, die gute Laune verderben.
damsel [ˈdæmzəl], s. die Jungfer; das Mädchen.
damson [ˈdæmzən], s. (*Bot.*) die Damaszenerpflaume.
dance [dɑːns], v.a., v.n. tanzen. — s. der Tanz; *lead s.o. a* —, einem viel Mühe machen.
dandelion [ˈdændilaiən], s. (*Bot.*) der Löwenzahn.
dandle [dændl], v.a. hätscheln; schaukeln.
dandy [ˈdændi], s. der Geck, der Stutzer.
Dane [dein], s. der Däne.
dane [dein], s. *great* —, die Dogge.
Danish [ˈdeiniʃ], adj. dänisch.
danger [ˈdeindʒə], s. die Gefahr.
dangerous [ˈdeindʒərəs], adj. gefährlich.
dangle [dæŋgl], v.a. baumeln lassen. — v.n. baumeln, hängen.
dank [dæŋk], adj. feucht, naßkalt.
Danube [ˈdænjuːb]. die Donau.
dapper [ˈdæpə], adj. schmuck; niedlich; elegant.
dappled [dæpld], adj. scheckig, bunt.
Dardanelles, The [dɑːdəˈnelz]. die Dardanellen, *pl.*
dare [dɛə], v.n. irr. wagen; *I* — *say*, das meine ich wohl, ich gebe zu.
daredevil [ˈdɛədevl], s. der Wagehals, der Draufgänger.
daring [ˈdɛəriŋ], s. die Kühnheit.
dark [dɑːk], adj. dunkel, finster. — s. die Dunkelheit; *shot in the* —, ein Schuß aufs Geratewohl, ins Blaue.
darken [ˈdɑːkən], v.a. verdunkeln, verfinstern. — v.n. dunkel werden.

darkish [ˈdɑːkiʃ], adj. nahezu dunkel.
darkness [ˈdɑːknis], s. die Dunkelheit, Finsternis.
darkroom [ˈdɑːkruːm], s. die Dunkelkammer.
darling [ˈdɑːliŋ], s. der Liebling. — adj. lieb, teuer.
darn (1) [dɑːn], v.a. stopfen.
darn (2) [dɑːn], v.a. verdammen.
darn(ed) [dɑːn(d)], (*excl.*) verdammt.
darning [ˈdɑːniŋ], s. das Stopfen; — *needle*, die Stopfnadel.
dart [dɑːt], s. der Pfeil; der Spieß (*spear*); (*pl.*) das Pfeilwurfspiel. — v.n. losstürmen, sich stürzen.
dash [dæʃ], v.a. zerschmettern, zerstören (*hopes*). — v.n. stürzen. — s. der Schlag (*blow*); die Eleganz; (*Typ.*) der Gedankenstrich; (*Motor.*) —*board*, das Schaltbrett, Armaturenbrett.
dashing [ˈdæʃiŋ], adj. schneidig.
dastard [ˈdæstəd], s. der Feigling, die Memme.
dastardly [ˈdæstədli], adj., adv. feige.
data [ˈdeitə], s. pl. (*Science*) die Angaben, die Daten.
date (1) [deit], s. das Datum; (*Am.*) die Verabredung; *out of* —, vertetal (*antiquated*), altmodisch (*out of fashion*). — v.a. datieren; (*Am.*) ausführen. — v.n. das Datum tragen.
date (2) [deit], s. (*Bot.*) die Dattel.
dative [ˈdeitiv], s. (*Gram.*) der Dativ.
daub [dɔːb], v.a. bekleksen; (*coll.*) bemalen. — s. die Klekserei; (*coll.*) die Malerei.
daughter [ˈdɔːtə], s. die Tochter; — -*inlaw*, die Schwiegertochter.
daunt [dɔːnt], v.a. einschüchtern.
dauphin [ˈdɔːfin], s. der Dauphin.
daw [dɔː], s. (*Orn.*) die Dohle.
dawdle [dɔːdl], v.n. trödeln, die Zeit vertrödeln.
dawdler [ˈdɔːdlə], s. der Trödler, Tagedieb, die Schlafmütze.
dawn [dɔːn], s. das Morgengrauen, die Morgendämmerung. — v.n. dämmern, tagen.
day [dei], s. der Tag; *the other* —, neulich; *every* —, täglich; *one* —, eines Tages; *by* —, bei *or* am Tage.
daybreak [ˈdeibreik], s. der Tagesanbruch.
daytime [ˈdeitaim], s. *in the* —, bei Tage.
daze [deiz], v.a. blenden (*dazzle*); betäuben (*stupefy*).
dazzle [dæzl], v.a. blenden.
deacon [ˈdiːkən], s. (*Eccl.*) der Diakon.
deaconess [ˈdiːkənes], s. (*Eccl.*) die Diakonisse.
dead [ded], adj. tot; *stop* —, plötzlich anhalten; *as* — *as mutton*, mausetot; — *from the neck up*, (*coll.*) dumm wie die Nacht. — adv. — *beat*, erschöpft; (*Am.*) — *sure*, ganz sicher. — s. *in the* — *of night*, in tiefster Nacht; (*pl.*) die Toten.

deaden [dedn], *v.a.* abschwächen (*weaken*); abtöten (*anæsthetise*).

deadly ['dedli], *adj.* tödlich.

deadness ['dednis], *s.* die Leblosigkeit; Mattheit (*tiredness*).

deaf [def], *adj.* taub; — *and dumb*, taubstumm.

deafen [defn], *v.a.* betäuben.

deafmute ['defmju:t], *s.* der Taubstumme.

deal (1) [di:l], *s.* das Geschäft; die Anzahl; *a fair* or *square* —, eine anständige Behandlung; *a good* —, beträchtlich; *a great — of*, sehr viel; *make a* —, ein Geschäft abschliessen; *it's a* —*!* abgemacht! — *v.a. irr.* austeilen; Karten geben (*cards*); — *a blow*, einen Schlag erteilen. — *v.n. irr.* — *with s.th.*, etwas behandeln.

deal (2) [di:l], *s.* der (*Bot.*) das Kiefernholz, die Kiefer; — *board*, das Kiefernholzbrett.

dealer ['di:lə], *s.* der Händler.

dean [di:n], *s.* der Dekan.

dear [diə], *adj.* teuer, lieb (*beloved*); teuer, kostspielig (*expensive*); — *me!* ach, Du lieber Himmel! —, —*!* du liebe Zeit! — *John !* Lieber Hans!

dearness ['diənis], *s.* die Teuerung, das Teuersein.

dearth [də:θ], *s.* der Mangel (*of*, an, *Dat.*).

death [deθ], *s.* der Tod; der Todesfall; — *penalty*, die Todesstrafe; — *warrant*, das Todesurteil.

deathbed ['deθbed], *s.* das Totenbett, Sterbebett.

deathblow ['deθblou], *s.* der Todesstoß.

deathless ['deθlis], *adj.* unsterblich.

debar [di'ba:], *v.a.* ausschließen (*from*, von, *Dat.*).

debase [di'beis], *v.a.* erniedrigen, verschlechtern.

debatable [di'beitəbl], *adj.* strittig.

debate [di'beit], *s.* die Debatte. — *v.a., v.n.* debattieren.

debauch [di'bɔ:tʃ], *v.a., v.n.* verführen; verderben.

debauchee [di'bɔ:tʃi:],*s.* der Schwelger, der Wüstling.

debenture [di'bentʃə], *s.* der Schuldschein.

debilitate [di'biliteit], *v.a.* schwächen.

debit ['debit], *s.* die Schuldseite, das Soll (*in account*). — *v.a.* belasten.

debt [det], *s.* die Schuld; *run into* — or *incur* —, Schulden machen.

debtor ['detə], *s.* der Schuldner.

decade ['dekəd, 'dekeid], *s.* das Jahrzehnt; die Dekade.

decadence ['dekədəns], *s.* die Dekadenz, der Verfall.

decalogue ['dekələg], *s.* (*Bibl.*) die zehn Gebote.

decamp [di'kæmp], *v.n.* aufbrechen, ausreißen.

decant [di'kænt], *v.a.* abfüllen, abgießen.

decanter [di'kæntə], *s.* die Karaffe.

decapitate [di'kæpiteit], *v.a.* enthaupten köpfen.

decapitation [di:kæpi'teiʃən], *s.* die Enthauptung.

decay [di'kei], *v.n.* in Verfall geraten. — *s.* der Verfall, die Verwesung.

decease [di'si:s], *s.* das Hinscheiden, der Tod. — *v.n.* sterben, dahinscheiden, verscheiden.

deceit [di'si:t], *s.* der Betrug; die List (*cunning*).

deceive [di'si:v], *v.a.* betrügen.

deceiver [di'si:və], *s.* der Betrüger.

December [di'sembə]. der Dezember.

decency [di'sənsi], *s.* der Anstand; die Anständigkeit, Ehrlichkeit; die Schicklichkeit.

decent ['di:sənt], *adj.* anständig.

decentralize [di:'sentrəlaiz], *v.a.* dezentralisieren.

deception [di'sepʃən], *s.* der Betrug.

deceptive [di'septiv], *adj.* trügerisch.

decide [di'said], *v.a., v.n.* entscheiden; bestimmen (*determine*).

decimal ['desiməl], *adj.* dezimal.

decimate ['desimeit], *v.a.* dezimieren, herabsetzen (*reduce*).

decipher [di'saifə],*v.a.* entziffern (*read*); dechiffrieren (*decode*).

decision [di'siʒən], *s.* die Entscheidung, der Beschluß (*resolution*); die Entschlossenheit (*decisiveness*).

decisive [di'saisiv], *adj.* entscheidend.

decisiveness [di'saisivnis], *s.* die Entschiedenheit.

deck [dek], *s.* (*Naut.*) das Deck; — *chair*, der Liegestuhl. — *v.a.* — (*out*), ausschmücken.

declaim [di'kleim], *v.a.* deklamieren.

declamation [deklə'meiʃən], *s.* die Deklamation.

declamatory [di'klæmətəri], *adj.* Deklamations-, deklamatorisch, Vortrags-.

declaration [deklə'reiʃən], *s.* die Erklärung; die Deklaration.

declare [di'kleə], *v.a.* erklären. — *v.n.* sich erklären.

declared [di'kleəd], *adj.* erklärt, offen.

declension [di'klenʃən], *s.* (*Gram.*) die Deklination, die Abwandlung.

declinable [di'klainəbl], *adj.* (*Gram.*) deklinierbar.

declination [dekli'neiʃən], *s.* (*Phys.*) die Abweichung, Deklination.

decline [di'klain], *v.n.* abweichen (*deflect*); abnehmen (*decrease*); sich weigern (*refuse*); fallen (*price*). — *v.a.* (*Gram.*) deklinieren; ablehnen (*turn down*). — *s.* die Abnahme (*decrease*); der Verfall (*decadence*); der Abhang (*slope*).

declivity [di'kliviti], *s.* der Abhang.

decode [di:'koud], *v.a.* entziffern, dechiffrieren.

decompose [di:kəm'pouz], *v.n.* verwesen; zerfallen, sich zersetzen. — *v.a.* auflösen.

decorate

decorate ['dekəreit], *v.a.* dekorieren (*honour*); ausschmücken (*beautify*); ausmalen (*paint*).

decoration [dekə'reiʃən], *s.* die Dekoration, der Orden (*medal*); die Ausschmückung (*ornamentation*); die Ausmalung (*décor*).

decorator ['dekəreitə], *s.* der Zimmermaler.

decorous ['dekərəs *or* di'kɔːrəs], *adj.* anständig, sittsam.

decorum [di'kɔːrəm], *s.* das Dekorum, das anständige Benehmen.

decoy [di'kɔi], *s.* der Köder (*bait*). — *v.a.* locken, verlocken.

decrease [di'kriːs], *v.a.* vermindern, verringern. — *v.n.* abnehmen. — ['diːkriːs], *s.* die Abnahme, die Verringerung.

decree [di'kriː], *s.* der Beschluß (*resolution*); (*Law*) das Urteil; — *nisi*, das provisorische Scheidungsurteil. — *v.a.*, *v.n.* eine Verordnung erlassen; beschließen (*decide*).

decrepit [di'krepit], *adj.* abgelebt; gebrechlich (*frail*).

decry [di'krai], *v.a.* verrufen; in Verruf bringen.

dedicate ['dedikeit], *v.a.* widmen, weihen, zueignen (*to, Dat.*).

dedication [dedi'keiʃən], *s.* die Widmung, Weihung; die Zueignung.

dedicatory ['dedikeitəri], *adj.* zueignend.

deduce [di'djuːs], *v.a.* schließen (*conclude*); ableiten (*derive*).

deduct [di'dʌkt], *v.a.* abziehen (*subtract*); abrechnen (*take off*).

deduction [di'dʌkʃən], *s.* der Abzug (*subtraction*); die Folgerung (*inference*); der Rabatt (*in price*).

deductive [di'dʌktiv], *adj.* (*Log.*) deduktiv.

deed [diːd], *s.* die Tat, die Handlung (*action*); (*Law*) die Urkunde, das Dokument.

deem [diːm], *v.a.* erachten, halten für.

deep [diːp], *adj.* tief; — *freeze*, die Tiefkühlung; (*fig.*) dunkel. — *s.* die Tiefe (*des Meeres*).

deepen [diːpn], *v.a.* vertiefen — *v.n.* tiefer werden; sich vertiefen.

deer [diə], *s.* (*Zool.*) das Rotwild, der Hirsch; — *stalking*, die Pirsch.

deface [di'feis], *v.a.* entstellen, verunstalten.

defalcate [di'fælkeit], *v.n.* Gelder unterschlagen.

defamation [defə'meiʃən], *s.* die Verleumdung.

defamatory [di'fæmətəri], *adj.* verleumderisch.

defame [di'feim], *v.a.* verleumden.

default [di'fɔːlt], *v.n.* (vor Gericht) ausbleiben. — *s.* der Fehler (*error*); die Unterlassung (*omission*).

defaulter [di'fɔːltə], *s.* der Pflichtvergessene; (*Law*) der Schuldige.

defeat [di'fiːt], *v.a.* schlagen, besiegen. — *s.* die Niederlage.

---

defect [di'fekt], *s.* der Fehler, Makel. — *v.n.* abfallen (*desert, from,* von, *Dat.*).

defection [di'fekʃən], *s.* der Abfall.

defective [di'fektiv], *adj.* fehlerhaft, mangelhaft.

defectiveness [di'fektivnis], *s.* die Mangelhaftigkeit, die Fehlerhaftigkeit.

defence [di'fens], *s.* die Verteidigung.

defenceless [di'fenslis], *adj.* wehrlos.

defencelessness [di'fenslisnis], *s.* die Wehrlosigkeit.

defend [di'fend], *v.a.* verteidigen.

defendant [di'fendənt], *s.* (*Law*) der Angeklagte.

defensive [di'fensiv], *adj.* verteidigend. — *s.* die Defensive; *be on the* —, sich verteidigen.

defer [di'fəː], *v.a.* aufschieben (*postpone*). — *v.n.* sich unterordnen, sich fügen (*to, Dat.*).

deference ['defərəns], *s.* der Respekt, die Achtung (*to,* vor, *Dat.*).

deferential [defə'renʃəl], *adj.* ehrerbietig, respektvoll.

defiance [di'faiəns], *s.* der Trotz, die Herausforderung.

defiant [di'faiənt], *adj.* trotzig, herausfordernd.

deficiency [di'fiʃənsi], *s.* die Unzulänglichkeit, der Mangel (*quantity*); die Fehlerhaftigkeit (*quality*).

deficient [di'fiʃənt], *adj.* unzulänglich (*quantity*); fehlerhaft (*quality*).

deficit ['defisit], *s.* das Defizit, der Fehlbetrag.

defile (1) [di'fail], *v.a.* schänden, beflecken.

defile (2) ['diːfail], *v.n.* vorbeimarschieren (*march past*) (an, *Dat.*). — *s.* der Engpaß.

defilement [di'failmənt], *s.* die Schändung.

define [di'fain], *v.a.* definieren, begrenzen; bestimmen (*determine*).

definite ['definit], *adj.* bestimmt (*certain*); klar, deutlich (*clear*); endgültig (*final*).

definition [defi'niʃən], *s.* die Definition, die Klarheit; (*Maths.*) die Bestimmung.

definitive [di'finitiv], *adj.* definitiv, endgültig (*final*); bestimmt (*certain*).

deflect [di'flekt], *v.a.* ablenken (*divert*). — *v.n.* abweichen (von, *Dat.*).

defoliation [diːfouli'eiʃən], *s.* der Blätterfall.

deform [di'fɔːm], *v.a.* verunstalten, entstellen. — *v.n.* (*Metall.*) sich verformen.

deformity [di'fɔːmiti], *s.* die Entstellung; die Häßlichkeit (*ugliness*).

defraud [di'frɔːd], *v.a.* betrügen.

defray [di'frei], *v.a.* bestreiten, bezahlen (*costs*).

deft [deft], *adj.* geschickt, gewandt.

deftness ['deftnis], *s.* die Gewandtheit, die Geschicktheit.

defunct [di'fʌŋkt], *adj.* verstorben. — *s.* der Verstorbene.

defy [di'fai], *v.a.* trotzen (*Dat.*).

degenerate [di'dʒenəreit], *v.n.* entarten; herabsinken (*sink low*). —[-rit], *adj.* degeneriert, entartet.

degradation [degri'deiʃən], *s.* die Absetzung, Entsetzung, Degradierung.

degrade [di'greid], *v.a.* (*Mil.*) degradieren; entwürdigen; vermindern.

degraded [di'greidid], *adj.* heruntergekommen.

degrading [di'greidiŋ], *adj.* entehrend.

degree [di'gri:], *s.* (*Meas., Univ.*) der Grad; (*Univ.*) die akademische Würde; die Stufe (*step, stage*); die Ordnung, die Klasse (*order, class*); by —s, nach und nach, allmählich.

deify ['di:ifai], *v.a.* vergöttern.

deign [dein], *v.n.* geruhen, belieben.

deity ['di:iti], *s.* die Gottheit.

dejected [di'dʒektid], *adj.* niedergeschlagen.

dejection [di'dʒekʃən], *s.* die Niedergeschlagenheit.

delay [di'lei], *v.a., v.n.* aufschieben (*put off*); verzögern (*retard*). — *s.* der Aufschub; die Verzögerung.

delectable [di'lektəbl], *adj.* erfreulich, köstlich.

delectation [delek'teiʃən], *s.* die Freude, das Ergötzen (*in*, an, *Dat.*).

delegate ['deligit], *s.* der Delegierte, Abgeordnete; der Vertreter. — ['deligeit], *v.a.* delegieren, entsenden.

delegation [deli'geiʃən], *s.* die Delegation, die Abordnung.

delete [di'li:t], *v.a.* tilgen, (aus-)streichen, auslöschen (*writing*).

deletion [di'li:ʃən], *s.* die Tilgung, die Auslöschung.

deleterious [deli'tiəriəs], *adj.* schädlich.

delf [delf], *s.* das Delfter Porzellan.

deliberate [di'libərit], *adj.* absichtlich (*intentional*), vorsichtig (*careful*); bedächtig (*thoughtful*). — [-reit], *v.n.* beratschlagen, Rat halten. — *v.a.* überlegen, bedenken.

deliberateness [di'libəritnis], *s.* die Bedächtigkeit (*thoughtfulness*); die Absichtlichkeit (*intention*).

deliberation [dilibə'reiʃən], *s.* die Überlegung, die Beratung.

delicacy ['delikəsi], *s.* die Feinheit, Zartheit (*manner*); der Leckerbissen (*luxury food*); die Schwächlichkeit (*health*).

delicate ['delikit], *adj.* fein (*manner*); schwächlich (*sickly*); kitzlig, heikel (*difficult*).

delicious [di'liʃəs], *adj.* köstlich (*food*).

deliciousness [di'liʃəsnis], *s.* die Köstlichkeit.

delight [di'lait], *s.* das Entzücken, das Vergnügen; *Turkish* —, türkisches Konfekt; *take* — *in*, an etwas Gefallen finden, sich freuen (an, über). — *v.a., v.n.* entzücken, erfreuen (*in*, an, *Dat.*).

delightful [di'laitful], *adj.* entzückend, bezaubernd.

delimit [di:'limit], *v.a.* abgrenzen, begrenzen.

delimitation [di:limi'teiʃən], *s.* die Begrenzung, Abgrenzung.

delineate [di'linieit], *v.a.* umreißen, entwerfen, skizzieren (*draft, sketch*); schildern, beschreiben (*describe*).

delineation [dilini'eiʃən], *s.* die Skizze, der Entwurf (*sketch, draft*); die Schilderung (*description*).

delinquency [di'liŋkwənsi], *s.* das Verbrechen.

delinquent [di'liŋkwənt], *adj.* verbrecherisch. — *s.* der Verbrecher, Missetäter (*criminal*).

deliquesce [deli'kwes], *v.n.* (*Chem.*) zergehen, zerschmelzen.

deliquescence [deli'kwesəns], *s.* das Zerschmelzen, die Schmelzbarkeit.

deliquescent [deli'kwesənt], *adj.* leicht schmelzbar (*melting*); leicht zerfliessend (*butter etc.*).

delirious [di'liriəs], *adj.* (*Med.*) phantasierend, wahnsinnig.

delirium [di'liriəm], *s.* (*Med.*) das Delirium; der Wahnsinn (*madness*); das Phantasieren (*raving*); — *tremens*, der Säuferwahnsinn.

deliver [di'livə], *v.a.* abliefern, überreichen (*hand over*); liefern (*goods*); befreien (*free*); erlösen (*redeem*); zustellen (*letters etc.*); entbinden (*woman of child*).

deliverance [di'livərəns], *s.* die Erlösung (*redemption*); die Befreiung (*liberation*); die Übergabe.

delivery [di'livəri], *s.* die Befreiung (*liberation*); (*Med.*) die Niederkunft, Entbindung; der Vortrag (*speech*); die Lieferung, die Zustellung (*goods*); — *man*, der Zustellbote; — *van*, der Lieferwagen.

dell [del], *s.* das enge Tal.

delude [di'lu:d], *v.a.* betrügen, täuschen.

deluge ['delju:dʒ], *s.* die Überschwemmung. — *v.a.* überschwemmen.

delusion [di'lu:ʒən], *s.* die Täuschung, das Blendwerk.

delusive, delusory [di'lu:ziv, di'lu:zəri], *adj.* täuschend, trügerisch.

delve [delv], *v.n.* graben.

demagogic(al) [demə'gɔdʒik(əl)], *adj.* demagogisch.

demagogue ['deməgɔg], *s.* der Demagoge, der Aufrührer.

demand [di'ma:nd], *v.a.* verlangen, fordern. — *s.* die Forderung; das Begehren (*desire*); on —, auf Verlangen; *in great* —, viel gefragt; *supply and* —, Angebot und Nachfrage.

demarcate [di:'ma:keit], *v.a.* abgrenzen; abstecken (*field*).

demarcation [di:mə'keiʃən], *s.* die Abgrenzung; — *line*, die Grenzlinie.

demeanour [di'mi:nə], *s.* das Benehmen.

demented [di'mentid], *adj.* wahnsinnig, von Sinnen, toll.

demerit [di:'merit], *s.* der Fehler.

demesne [di'mi:n *or* -'mein], *s.* das Erbgut; die Domäne.
demi- ['demi], *prefix.* halb-.
demigod ['demigɔd], *s.* der Halbgott.
demijohn ['demidʒɔn], *s.* der Glasballon.
demise [di'maiz], *s.* der Tod, das Hinscheiden. — *v.a.* (*Law*) vermachen.
demisemiquaver ['demisemikweivə], *s.* (*Mus.*) die Zweiunddreißigstelnote.
demobilize [di:'moubilaiz], *v.a.* demobilisieren.
democracy [di'mɔkrəsi], *s.* die Demokratie.
democratic [demo'krætik], *adj.* demokratisch.
demolish [di'mɔliʃ], *v.a.* demolieren, zerstören, niederreißen.
demon ['di:mən], *s.* der Dämon, der Teufel; *a — for work,* ein unersättlicher Arbeiter.
demoniac [di'mouniæk], **demoniacal** [di:mə'naiəkl], *adj.* besessen, teuflisch.
demonstrable [di'mɔnstrəbl], *adj.* beweisbar, nachweislich (*verifiable*).
demonstrate ['demənstreit], *v.a., v.n.* beweisen (*prove*); demonstrieren.
demonstration [demən'streiʃən], *s.* der Beweis (*theoretical*); die Demonstration (*practical*); (*Pol.*) Kundgebung.
demonstrative [di'mɔnstrətiv], *adj.* (*Gram.*) demonstrativ; überschwenglich (*emotional*).
demoralize [di:'mɔrəlaiz], *v.a.* demoralisieren.
demote [di:'mout], *v.a.* (*Mil., official*) degradieren.
demotion [di:'mouʃən], *s.* (*Mil., official*) die Degradierung.
demur [di'mə:], *v.n.* Anstand nehmen; Einwendungen machen (*raise objections*); zögern, zaudern (*hesitate*). — *s.* der Zweifel, der Skrupel.
demure [di'mjuə], *adj.* sittsam, zimperlich; spröde (*prim*).
demureness [di'mjuənis], *s.* die Sittsamkeit; die Sprödigkeit (*primness*).
den [den], *s.* die Höhle, Grube; *lion's —,* die Löwengrube.
denial [di'naiəl], *s.* die Verneinung, das Dementi (*negation*); das Ableugnen (*disclaimer*); die Absage (*refusal*).
denizen ['denizən], *s.* der Bürger, der Alteingesessene.
denominate [di'nɔmineit], *v.a.* nennen, benennen (*name*).
denomination [dinɔmi'neiʃən], *s.* die Bezeichnung; der Nennwert (*currency*); (*Rel.*) das Bekenntnis.
denominational [dinɔmi'neiʃənəl], *adj.* konfessionell.
denominator [di'nɔmineitə], *s.* (*Maths.*) der Nenner.
denote [di'nout], *v.a.* bezeichnen, kennzeichnen.
dénouement [dei'nu:mã], *s.* die Entwicklung, die Darlegung, die Lösung.
denounce [di'nauns], *v.a.* denunzieren, angeben; (*Law*) anzeigen.

dense [dens], *adj.* dicht; (*coll.*) beschränkt (*stupid*).
density ['densiti], *s.* die Dichte; — *of population,* die Bevölkerungsdichte.
dent (1) [dent], *s.* die Beule.
dent (2) [dent], *s.* die Kerbe (*in wood*); der Einschnitt (*cut*).
dental [dentl], *adj.* Zahn-; — *studies,* zahnärztliche Studien; — *treatment,* die Zahnbehandlung. — *s.* (*Phonet.*) der Zahnlaut.
dentist ['dentist], *s.* der Zahnarzt.
dentistry ['dentistri], *s.* die Zahnheilkunde.
denude [di'nju:d], *v.a.* entblößen; berauben (*of, Genit.*).
denunciation [dinʌnsi'eiʃən], *s.* die Denunzierung, die Anzeige.
deny [di'nai], *v.a.* verneinen (*negate*); abschlagen (*refuse*); verleugnen (*refuse to admit*).
deodorant, deodorizer [di:'oudərənt, di:'oudəraizə], *s.* der Geruchsentzieher (*apparatus*); der Deodorant.
deodorize [di:'oudəraiz], *v.a.* geruchlos machen.
depart [di'pɑ:t], *v.n.* abreisen, abfahren (*for,* nach, *Dat.*); scheiden.
department [di'pɑ:tmənt], *s.* die Abteilung; — *store,* das Kaufhaus.
departmental [di:pɑ:t'mentl], *adj.* Abteilungs-.
departure [di'pɑ:tʃə], *s.* die Abreise, die Abfahrt.
depend [di'pend], *v.n.* abhängen, abhängig sein (*upon,* von, *Dat.*); sich verlassen (*upon,* auf, *Acc.*); *that —s,* das kommt darauf an.
dependable [di'pendəbl], *adj.* verläßlich, zuverlässig.
dependant [di'pendənt], *s.* das abhängige Familienmitglied (*member of family*); der Angehörige, Abhängige.
dependence [di'pendəns], *s.* die Abhängigkeit (*need*); das Vertrauen, der Verlaß (*reliance*).
dependency [di'pendənsi], *s.* (*Pol.*) die abhängige Kolonie.
dependent [di'pendənt], *adj.* abhängig (*upon,* von, *Dat.*).
depict [di'pikt], *v.a.* schildern, beschreiben.
deplete [di'pli:t], *v.a.* entleeren (*make empty*); erschöpfen (*exhaust*).
depletion [di'pli:ʃən], *s.* die Entleerung.
deplorable [di'plɔ:rəbl], *adj.* bedauernswert, bedauerlich.
deplore [di'plɔ:], *v.a.* beklagen.
deploy [di'plɔi], *v.a.* entfalten. — *v.n.* sich entfalten; (*Mil.*) aufmarschieren.
deployment [di'plɔimənt], *s.* (*Mil.*) das Deployieren; die Entfaltung.
deponent [di'pounənt], *s.* (*Law*) der vereidigte Zeuge. — *adj.* (*Gram.*) (*verb*) das Deponens.
depopulate [di:'pɔpjuleit], *v.a.* entvölkern.
deport [di'pɔ:t], *v.a.* deportieren.
deportation [di:pɔ:'teiʃən], *s.* die Deportation.

deportment [di'pɔ:tmənt], s. die körperliche Haltung (*physical*); das Benehmen (*social*).

depose [di'pouz], v.a. absetzen (*remove from office*); (*Law*) zu Papier bringen (*write down*); schriftlich erklären (*declare in writing*).

deposit [di'pɔzit], s. (*Comm.*) die Anzahlung; (*Geol.*, *Chem.*) der Niederschlag; (*Geol.*) die Ablagerung; (*Comm.*) — *account*, das Depositenkonto. — v.a. (*Geol.*, *Chem.*) absetzen; (*Comm.*) anzahlen, einzahlen.

deposition [di:pə'ziʃən], s. die Niederschrift, die schriftliche Erklärung; die Absetzung (*removal from office*).

depositor [di'pɔzitə], s. (*Comm.*) der Einzahler.

depository [di'pɔzitəri], s. das Lagerhaus.

depot ['depou], s. das Depot, das Lagerhaus (*store*); (*Am.*) der Bahnhof.

deprave [di'preiv], v.a. verderben.

depraved [di'preivd], adj. (moralisch) verdorben.

depravity [di'præviti], s. die Verdorbenheit, die Verworfenheit.

deprecate ['deprikeit], v.a. mißbilligen (*disapprove of*; *Acc.*); sich verbitten.

deprecation [depri'keiʃən], s. die Abbitte; die Mißbilligung (*disapproval*).

depreciate [di'pri:ʃieit], v.a. abwerten, herabwürdigen. — v.n. an Wert verlieren, im Wert sinken.

depreciation [dipri:ʃi'eiʃən], s. die Abwertung; der Verlust (*loss*); (*Pol.*, *Comm.*) die Entwertung.

depredation [depri'deiʃən], s. das Plündern, der Raub.

depress [di'pres], v.a. niederdrücken (*press down*); deprimieren (*morale*).

depressed [di'prest], adj. niedergeschlagen.

depression [di'preʃən], s. das Niederdrücken (*action*); (*Pol.*) die Depression; die Niedergeschlagenheit (*despondency*); das Tief (*weather*).

deprivation [depri'veiʃən], s. der Verlust (*lack*); die Beraubung (*robbery*).

deprive [di'praiv], v.a. berauben (*of*, *Genit.*); wegnehmen (*of*, *Acc.*).

depth [depθ], s. die Tiefe; — *charge*, die Unterwasserbombe; *in the* —*s of night*, in tiefster Nacht; (*Phys.*) — *of focus*, die Tiefenschärfe; *be out of o.'s* —, den Grund unter seinen Füßen verloren haben, ratlos sein (*be helpless*); — *sounder*, das Echolot.

deputation [depju'teiʃən], s. die Deputation, die Abordnung.

depute [di'pju:t], v.a. abordnen, entsenden.

deputize ['depjutaiz], v.n. vertreten (*for*, *Acc.*).

deputy ['depjuti], s. der Abgeordnete, der Deputierte (*delegate*); der Vertreter (*replacement*).

derail [di:'reil], v.a. zum Entgleisen bringen. — v.n. entgleisen.

derailment [di:'reilmənt], s. die Entgleisung.

derange [di'reindʒ], v.a. verwirren, stören.

derangement [di'reindʒmənt], s. die Verwirrung; die Geistesstörung (*madness*).

derelict ['derilikt], adj. verlassen.

dereliction [deri'likʃən], s. das Verlassen; — *of duty*, die Pflichtvergessenheit.

deride [di'raid], v.a. verlachen, verhöhnen.

derision [di'riʒən], s. die Verhöhnung.

derisive [di'raisiv], adj. höhnisch, spöttisch.

derivable [di'raivəbl], adj. ableitbar.

derivation [deri'veiʃən], s. die Ableitung.

derivative [di'rivətiv], adj. abgeleitet. — s. das abgeleitete Wort.

derive [di'raiv], v.a., v.n. ableiten, herleiten.

derogation [dero'geiʃən], s. die Herabsetzung.

derrick ['derik], s. der Ladebaum.

dervish ['də:viʃ], s. der Derwisch.

descant ['deskænt], s. (*Mus.*) der Diskant *or* der Sopran. — [dis'kænt], v.n. sich verbreiten (*on*, über, *Acc.*).

descend [di'send], v.n. hinab- *or* herabsteigen (*go down*); abstammen (*stem from*).

descendant [di'sendənt], s. der Nachkomme.

descent [di'sent], s. der Abstieg (*going down*); der Fall (*decline*); die Abstammung (*forebears*); der Abhang (*slope*); (*Aviat.*) die Landung.

describable [dis'kraibəbl], adj. zu beschreiben, beschreibbar.

describe [dis'kraib], v.a. beschreiben, schildern.

description [dis'kripʃən], s. die Beschreibung; *of any* —, jeder Art.

descriptive [dis'kriptiv], adj. schildernd, beschreibend.

desecrate ['desikreit], v.a. entweihen, entheiligen.

desecration [desi'kreiʃən], s. die Entweihung, die Schändung.

desert (1) ['dezət], s. die Wüste.

desert (2) [di'zə:t], v.a. verlassen, im Stiche lassen. — v.n. desertieren.

desert (3) [di'zə:t], s. (*usually pl.*) das Verdienst.

desertion [di'zə:ʃən], s. (*Mil.*) die Fahnenflucht.

deserve [di'zə:v], v.a. verdienen.

deserving [di'zə:viŋ], adj. verdienstvoll.

design [di'zain], v.a. entwerfen (*plan*); vorhaben (*intend*); bestimmen (*determine*). — s. der Entwurf (*sketch*); der Plan (*draft*); die Absicht, das Vorhaben (*intention*); das Muster (*pattern*).

designate

designate ['dezigneit], *v.a.* bezeichnen (*mark*); ernennen (*appoint*). — [-nit], *adj.* ernannt; *chairman* —, der künftige Vorsitzende.

designation [dezig'neiʃən], *s.* die Bestimmung, Ernennung (*appointment*); die Bezeichnung (*mark*).

designer [di'zainə], *s.* der Zeichner, der Graphiker (*artist*); der Ränkeschmied (*schemer*).

designing [di'zainiŋ], *adj.* hinterlistig, schlau.

desirable [di'zaiərəbl], *adj.* erwünscht, wünschenswert.

desire [di'zaiə], *s.* der Wunsch, die Begierde; das Verlangen, die Sehnsucht (*longing*). — *v.a.* verlangen, begehren.

desirous [di'zaiərəs], *adj.* begierig (*of, inf.*).

desist [di'zist], *v.n.* ablassen, aufhören.

desk [desk], *s.* der Schreibtisch; das Pult; — *lamp*, die Tischlampe *or* Bürolampe.

desolate ['desəlit], *adj.* verlassen, öde; trostlos (*sad*). — [-leit], *v.a.* verwüsten (*lay waste*).

desolation [desə'leiʃən], *s.* die Verwüstung (*of land*); die Trostlosigkeit (*sadness*).

despair [dis'pɛə], *v.n.* verzweifeln (*of, an, Dat.*). — *s.* die Verzweiflung.

despatch, dispatch [dis'pætʃ], *v.a.* absenden, befördern (*post*); abfertigen (*send*); erledigen (*deal with*); töten (*kill*). — *s.* die Abfertigung (*clearance*); die Eile (*speed*); die Depesche (*message*).

desperado [despə'reidou, -'raːdou], *s.* der Wagehals, der Draufgänger.

desperate ['despərit], *adj.* verzweifelt.

desperation [despə'reiʃən], *s.* die Verzweiflung.

despicable ['despikəbl], *adj.* verächtlich.

despise [dis'paiz], *v.a.* verachten.

despite [dis'pait], *prep.* trotz (*Genit., Dat.*).

despoil [dis'pɔil], *v.a.* plündern, ausrauben.

despondency [dis'pɔndənsi], *s.* die Verzweiflung, Verzagtheit.

despondent [dis'pɔndənt], *adj.* verzagend, verzweifelnd, mutlos.

despot ['despɔt], *s.* der Despot, der Tyrann.

despotic [des'pɔtik], *adj.* despotisch.

despotism ['despətizm], *s.* (*Pol.*) der Despotismus.

dessert [di'zəːt], *s.* das Dessert, der Nachtisch.

destination [desti'neiʃən], *s.* die Bestimmung, das Ziel; der Bestimmungsort (*address*); das Reiseziel (*journey*).

destine ['destin], *v.a.* bestimmen.

destiny ['destini], *s.* das Geschick; das Schicksal, das Verhängnis (*fate*).

destitute ['destitjuːt], *adj.* verlassen (*deserted*); hilflos, mittellos (*poor*); in bitterer Not (*in great distress*).

destitution [desti'tjuːʃən], *s.* die Notlage, die bittere Not.

destroy [dis'trɔi], *v.a.* zerstören (*buildings*); verwüsten; vernichten (*lives*).

destroyer [dis'trɔiə], *s.* der Zerstörer.

destructible [dis'trʌktibl], *adj.* zerstörbar.

destruction [dis'trʌkʃən], *s.* die Zerstörung (*of buildings*), die Verwüstung; die Vernichtung.

destructive [dis'trʌktiv], *adj.* zerstörend, verderblich.

destructiveness [dis'trʌktivnis], *s.* die Zerstörungswut, der Zerstörungssinn.

desultory ['dezəltəri], *adj.* unmethodisch, sprunghaft; oberflächlich (*superficial*).

detach [di'tætʃ], *v.a.* absondern, trennen.

detachment [di'tætʃmənt], *s.* die Absonderung (*separation*); (*Mil.*) das Kommando.

detail [di'teil], *v.a.* im einzelnen beschreiben (*describe minutely*); (*Mil.*) abkommandieren. — ['diːteil], *s.* die Einzelheit.

detailed ['diːteild], *adj.* ausführlich; detailliert, ins Einzelne gehend (*report etc.*); [di'teild], (*Mil.*) abkommandiert.

detain [di'tein], *v.a.* aufhalten, zurückhalten; festhalten (*in prison*).

detect [di'tekt], *v.a.* entdecken, aufdecken.

detection [di'tekʃən], *s.* die Entdeckung, die Aufdeckung.

detective [di'tektiv], *s.* der Detektiv.

detention [di'tenʃən], *s.* (*Law*) die Haft; die Vorenthaltung (*of articles*).

deter [di'təː], *v.a.* abschrecken.

detergent [di'təːdʒənt], *s.* das Reinigungsmittel.

deteriorate [di'tiəriəreit], *v.n.* sich verschlimmern, verschlechtern.

deterioration [ditiəriə'reiʃən], *s.* die Verschlimmerung.

determinable [di'təːminəbl], *adj.* bestimmbar.

determinate [ditə'minit], *adj.* festgesetzt, bestimmt.

determination [di'təːmi'neiʃən], *s.* die Entschlossenheit (*resoluteness*); die Bestimmung (*identification*); der Entschluß (*resolve*).

determine [di'təːmin], *v.a.* bestimmen (*ascertain*); beschließen (*resolve*).

deterrent [di'terənt], *s.* das Abschreckungsmittel.

detest [di'test], *v.a.* verabscheuen.

detestable [di'testəbl], *adj.* abscheulich.

detestation [detes'teiʃən], *s.* der Abscheu (*of, vor, Dat.*).

dethrone [di:'θroun], *v.a.* entthronen, vom Thron verdrängen.

detonate ['diː- *or* 'detoneit], *v.n.* detonieren, explodieren. — *v.a.* explodieren, detonieren lassen, zum Detonieren bringen.

detonation [deto′neiʃən], s. die Detonation, die Explosion.
detonator [′detoneitə], s. der Zünder, die Zündpatrone; (Railw.) die Knallpatrone.
detour [′deituə or di′tuə], s. der Umweg; (Civil Engin.) die Umleitung. — v.n. (Am.) einen Umweg machen. — v.a. (Am.) umleiten (re-route).
detract [di′trækt], v.a., v.n. abziehen; schmälern.
detraction [di′trækʃən], s. die Schmälerung, die Verleumdung (slander).
detractive [di′træktiv], adj. verleumderisch.
detractor [di′træktə], s. der Verleumder.
detriment [′detrimənt], s. der Nachteil, der Schaden.
detrimental [detri′mentl], adj. nachteilig; abträglich; schädlich (harmful).
deuce (1) [dju:s], s. die Zwei (game); (Tennis) der Einstand.
deuce (2) [dju:s], s. (coll.) der Teufel.
devastate [′devəsteit], v.a. verwüsten, verheeren.
devastating [′devəsteitiŋ], adj. schrecklich, verheerend.
devastation [devəs′teiʃən], s. die Verheerung, die Verwüstung.
develop [di′veləp], v.a. entwickeln. — v.n. sich entwickeln; sich entfalten (prove, turn out).
developer [di′veləpə], s. (Phot.) das Entwicklungsmittel.
development [di′veləpmənt], s. die Entwicklung.
developmental [diveləp′mentl], adj. Entwicklungs-.
deviate [′di:vieit], v.n. abweichen.
deviation [di:vi′eiʃən], s. die Abweichung.
device [di′vais], s. die Vorrichtung (equipment); der Kungstgriff (trick).
devil [devl], s. der Teufel; der Lehrling, Laufbursche (printer′s, lawyer′s); the — take the hindmost! der Teufel hol was dann kommt! — v.n. in der Lehre sein (for, bei, Dat.).
devilish [′devəliʃ], adj. teuflisch.
devilment, devilry [′devəlmənt, ′devəlri], s. die Teufelei, die Teufelslaune.
devious [′di:viəs], adj. abweichend; abgelegen; abwegig.
deviousness [′di:viəsnis], s. die Abschweifung, Verirrung.
devise [di′vaiz], v.a. erfinden (invent); ersinnen (think out).
deviser, devisor [di′vaizə], s. der Erfinder (inventor); der Erblasser (testator).
devoid [di′vɔid], adj. frei (of, von, Dat.); ohne (Acc.).
devolve [di′vɔlv], v.a. übertragen (transfer); abwälzen (pass on burden) (to, auf, Acc.). — v.n. zufallen (Dat.).
devote [di′vout], v.a. widmen; aufopfern (sacrifice).

devoted [di′voutid], adj. ergeben (affectionate); geweiht (consecrated).
devotee [devo′ti:], s. der Anhänger; der Verehrer (fan).
devotion [di′vouʃən], s. die Hingabe; die Aufopferung (sacrifice); die Andacht (prayer).
devotional [di′vouʃənəl], adj. Andachts-.
devour [di′vauə], v.a. verschlingen.
devout [di′vaut], adj. andächtig, fromm.
devoutness [di′vautnis], s. die Frömmigkeit.
dew [dju:], s. der Tau.
dewy [dju:i], adj. betaut, taufeucht.
dexterity [deks′teriti], s. die Gewandtheit, die Fertigkeit.
dexterous [′dekstərəs], adj. gewandt, geschickt.
diabetes [daiə′bi:ti:z], s. (Med.) die Zuckerkrankheit.
diabetic [daiə′betik], s. (Med.) der Zuckerkranke. — adj. zuckerkrank.
diabolic(al) [daiə′bɔlik(əl)], adj. teuflisch.
diadem [′daiədem], s. das Diadem, das Stirnband.
diæresis [dai′iərəsis], s. die Diärese.
diagnose [daiəg′nouz], v.a. diagnostizieren, als Diagnose finden, befinden.
diagnosis [daiəg′nousis], s. die Diagnose, der Befund.
diagonal [dai′ægənəl], adj. diagonal, schräg. — s. (Geom.) die Diagonale.
diagram [′daiəgræm], s. das Diagramm.
dial [′daiəl], s. das Zifferblatt; (Teleph.) die Wählerscheibe. — v.a., v.n. (Teleph.) wählen.
dialect [′daiəlekt], s. der Dialekt, die Mundart.
dialectic [daiə′lektik], s. (Phil.) die Dialektik.
dialektical [daiə′lektikəl], adj. dialektisch, logisch.
dialogue [′daiəlɔg], s. der Dialog, das Zwiegespräch.
diameter [dai′æmitə], s. der Durchmesser.
diametrical [daiə′metrikəl], adj. diametral; gerade entgegengesetzt.
diamond [′daiəmənd], s. der Diamant; (Cards) das Karo.
diaper [′daiəpə], s. (Am.) die Windel.
diaphragm [′daiəfræm], s. (Anat.) das Zwerchfell; (Phys.) die Membran.
diarrhœa [daiə′riə], s. (Med.) der Durchfall.
diary [′daiəri], s. das Tagebuch, der Kalender.
diatribe [′daiətraib], s. der Tadel, der Angriff (verbal), die Schmähschrift (written).
dibble [dibl], s. der Pflanzstock. — v.n. Pflanzen stecken, anpflanzen.
dice [dais], s. pl. die Würfel (sing. **die**). — v.a. würfeln, werfen.

dicker

dicker [ˈdikə], *v.n.* (*Am.*) feilschen, handeln.
dicky [ˈdiki], *s.* das Vorhemd.
dictate [dikˈteit], *v.a.*, *v.n.* diktieren, vorschreiben.
dictation [dikˈteiʃən], *s.* (*Sch.*) das Diktat.
dictator [dikˈteitə], *s.* der Diktator.
dictatorship [dikˈteitəʃip], *s.* die Diktatur.
diction [ˈdikʃən], *s.* die Ausdrucksweise (*speech*).
dictionary [ˈdikʃənri], *s.* das Wörterbuch.
didactic [diˈdæktik], *adj.* lehrhaft, Lehr-.
die (1) [dai], *v.n.* sterben (*of*, an, *Dat.*); — *away*, verebben.
die (2) [dai], *s.* der Würfel (*cube*); die Gießform (*mould*); der Stempel (*punch*); (*Metall.*) das Gesenk (*swage*); — *casting*, der Spritzguß; — *castings*, die Spritzgußteile, Gußteile; — *forging*, das Gesenkschmiedestück.
die (3) [dai] *see under* **dice**.
dielectric [daiiˈlektrik], *adj.* dielektrisch.
diet (1) [ˈdaiət], *s.* (*Pol.*) der Landtag, Reichstag.
diet (2) [ˈdaiət], *s.* (*Med.*) die Diät. — *v.n.* (*Med.*) eine Diät halten. — *v.a.* (*Med.*) eine Diät vorschreiben.
dietary, dietetic [ˈdaiətəri, daiəˈtetik], *adj.* diätetisch.
differ [ˈdifə], *v.n.* sich unterscheiden (*be different from*, von, *Dat.*); anderer Meinung sein (*be of different opinion*).
difference [ˈdifərəns], *s.* (*Maths.*) die Differenz; der Unterschied (*discrepancy*); die Meinungsverschiedenheit (*divergence of opinion*).
different [ˈdifərənt], *adj.* verschieden, verschiedenartig.
differentiate [difəˈrenʃieit], *v.n.* (*Maths.*) differenzieren; einen Unterschied machen (*between*, zwischen, *Dat.*).
difficult [ˈdifikəlt], *adj.* schwierig, schwer.
difficulty [ˈdifikəlti], *s.* die Schwierigkeit.
diffidence [ˈdifidəns], *s.* die Schüchternheit.
diffident [ˈdifidənt], *adj.* schüchtern.
diffraction [diˈfrækʃən], *s.* die Ablenkung, (*Phys.*, *Optics*) die Brechung.
diffuse [diˈfjuːz], *v.a.* ausgießen (*pour*); verbreiten (*spread*). — [diˈfjuːs], *adj.* verbreitet, weitschweifig (*style*); zerstreut.
diffuseness [diˈfjuːsnis], *s.* die Weitläufigkeit (*style*).
diffusion [diˈfjuːʒən], *s.* (*Phys.*) die Diffusion, die Zerstreuung, die Verbreitung.
dig (1) [dig], *v.a. irr.* graben; — *in the ribs*, in die Rippen stoßen. — *v.n.* (*coll.*) wohnen (*live in lodgings*).
dig (2) [dig], *v.a.* (*coll.*) verstehen.

digger [ˈdigə], *s.* der Gräber; (*coll.*) der Australier.
digest [diˈdʒest], *v.a.* (*Anat.*) verdauen. — [ˈdaidʒest], *s.* (*Am.*) die Sammlung von Auszügen; (*pl.*) Pandekten.
digestibility [didʒestiˈbiliti], *s.* die Verdaulichkeit.
digestible [diˈdʒestibl], *adj.* verdaulich.
digestion [diˈdʒestʃən], *s.* die Verdauung.
digestive [diˈdʒestiv], *adj.* Verdauungs-; — *biscuit*, das Kornmehlkeks; — *organs*, die Verdauungsorgane.
digit [ˈdidʒit], *s.* (*Maths.*) die (einstellige) Zahl; der Zahlenwert.
digitalis [didʒiˈteilis], *s.* (*Bot.*) der Fingerhut.
dignified [ˈdignifaid], *adj.* würdig, würdevoll.
dignify [ˈdignifai], *v.a.* ehren (*honour*); zieren (*decorate*).
dignitary [ˈdignitəri], *s.* der Würdenträger.
dignity [ˈdigniti], *s.* die Würde.
digress [daiˈgres], *v.n.* abweichen, abschweifen.
digression [daiˈgreʃən], *s.* die Abweichung, die Abschweifung.
digressive [daiˈgresiv], *adj.* abschweifend (*style*).
digs [digz], *s. pl.* (*coll.*) das (möblierte) Zimmer, die Wohnung.
dike [daik], *s.* der Graben, der Deich. — *v.a.* eindeichen, eindämmen.
dilapidated [diˈlæpideitid], *adj.* baufällig.
dilapidation [dilæpiˈdeiʃən], *s.* die Baufälligkeit, der Verfall.
dilate [d(a)iˈleit], *v.a.* erweitern, ausdehnen. — *v.n.* sich ausdehnen; sich auslassen (*speak*) (*on*, über, *Acc.*).
dilation [d(a)iˈleiʃən], *s.* die Erweiterung (*expansion*); die Auslassung (*speaking*).
dilatoriness [ˈdilətərinis], *s.* die Saumseligkeit.
dilatory [ˈdilətəri], *adj.* zögernd, aufschiebend, saumselig.
dilemma [d(a)iˈlemə], *s.* das Dilemma, die Klemme.
diligence [ˈdilidʒəns], *s.* der Fleiß, die Emsigkeit.
diligent [ˈdilidʒənt], *adj.* fleißig, arbeitsam.
dilly-dally [ˈdiliˈdæli], *v.n.* tändeln, zaudern, Zeit vertrödeln.
dilute [d(a)iˈljuːt], *v.a.* (*Chem.*) verdünnen; schwächen (*weaken*).
dilution [d(a)iˈljuːʃən], *s.* die Verdünnung.
diluvial, diluvian [d(a)iˈljuːviəl, -iən], *adj.* Diluvial-, des Diluviums; sintflutlich.
dim [dim], *adj.* trübe, unklar; (*Phys.*) abgeblendet. — *v.a.* abdunkeln, abblenden.
dimension [d(a)iˈmenʃən], *s.* die Dimension, das Maß.
dimensional [d(a)iˈmenʃənəl], *adj.* dimensional.

366

diminish [dɪ'miniʃ], v.a. vermindern. — v.n. sich vermindern.

diminution [dimi'njuːʃən], s. die Verringerung, die Verminderung.

diminutive [di'minjutiv], adj. verkleinernd, klein. — s. (Gram.) das Verkleinerungswort.

dimness ['dimnis], s. die Trübheit; die Düsterkeit (dark).

dimple [dimpl], s. das Grübchen.

dimpled [dimpld], adj. mit einem Grübchen.

din [din], s. das Getöse, der Lärm.

dine [dain], v.n. speisen, essen.

dinginess ['dindʒinis], s. die Dunkelheit, die Schäbigkeit.

dingy ['dindʒi], adj. dunkel, schäbig.

dinner ['dinə], s. das Essen; das Festessen (formal); — jacket, der Smoking.

dint [dint], s. der Nachdruck, der Schlag; by — of, mittels (Genit.).

diocesan [dai'ɔsisən], adj. (Eccl.) einer Diözese angehörig, Diözesan–.

diocese ['daiəsis], s. (Eccl.) die Diözese.

dip [dip], v.a. eintauchen, eintunken; abblenden (lights). — v.n. (unter)tauchen, sinken; sich flüchtig einlassen (into, in). — s. die Senke; der Abhang (slope).

diphtheria [dif'θiəriə], s. (Med.) die Diphtherie.

diphthong ['difθɔŋ], s. (Phonet.) der Diphthong.

diploma [di'ploumə], s. das Diplom; teaching —, das Lehrerdiplom.

diplomacy [di'plouməsi], s. die Diplomatie.

diplomatic [diplə'mætik], adj. diplomatisch, taktvoll; urkundlich (documents). — s. (pl.) das Studium der Urkunden.

diplomat(ist) ['diplomæt, di'ploumətist], s. (Pol.) der Diplomat.

dipper ['dipə], s. der Taucher.

dire [daiə], adj. fürchterlich, schrecklich; — necessity, bittere Not.

direct [d(a)i'rekt], adj. direkt, unmittelbar. — v.a. leiten (be in charge of); hinweisen, hinlenken; den Weg zeigen (tell the way to); anordnen (arrange for).

direction [d(a)i'rekʃən], s. die Leitung (management); (Geog.) die Richtung, Himmelsrichtung; die Anordnung (arrangement, order); —s for use, die Gebrauchsanweisung.

director [d(a)i'rektə], s. der Direktor; der Leiter.

directory [d(a)i'rektəri], s. das Adreßbuch; das Telephonbuch.

dirge [dəːdʒ], s. der Trauergesang.

dirigible ['diridʒibl], adj. lenkbar, leitbar.

dirt [dəːt], s. der Schmutz, der Kot, Dreck. — adj. — cheap, spottbillig.

dirty ['dəːti], adj. schmutzig; gemein (joke).

disability [disə'biliti], s. die Unfähigkeit, das Unvermögen (inability); die Schädigung (impairment of health).

disable [dis'eibl], v.a. unfähig or untauglich machen.

disablement [dis'eiblmənt], s. die Versehrung, die Verkrüppelung.

disabuse [disə'bjuːz], v.a. aufklären, eines Besseren belehren.

disaccustom [disə'kʌstəm], v.a. entwöhnen, abgewöhnen.

disadvantage [disəd'vɑːntidʒ], s. der Nachteil.

disaffection [disə'fekʃən], s. die Abneigung; der Widerwille.

disagree [disə'griː], v.n. nicht übereinstimmen, nicht einer Meinung sein.

disagreeable [disə'griəbl], adj. unangenehm, verdrießlich; unfreundlich.

disagreement [disə'griːmənt], s. die Uneinigkeit (disunity); die Meinungsverschiedenheit (difference of opinion).

disallow [disə'lau], v.a. nicht gestatten; in Abrede stellen.

disappear [disə'piə], v.n. verschwinden.

disappearance [disə'piərəns], s. das Verschwinden.

disappoint [disə'pɔint], v.a. enttäuschen.

disappointment [disə'pɔintmənt], s. die Enttäuschung.

disapprobation [disæpro'beiʃən], s. die Mißbilligung.

disapproval [disə'pruːvəl], s. die Mißbilligung.

disapprove [disə'pruːv], v.a. mißbilligen (of, Acc.).

disarm [dis'ɑːm], v.a. entwaffnen. — v.n. abrüsten.

disarmament [dis'ɑːməmənt], s. die Abrüstung.

disarray [disə'rei], v.a. in Unordnung bringen. — s. die Unordnung (disorder); die Verwirrung (confusion).

disaster [di'zɑːstə], s. das Unglück; das Unheil, die Katastrophe.

disastrous [di'zɑːstrəs], adj. unheilvoll, schrecklich.

disavow [disə'vau], v.a. ableugnen.

disavowal [disə'vauəl], s. das Ableugnen.

disband [dis'bænd], v.a. entlassen (dismiss); auflösen (dissolve).

disbar [dis'bɑː], v.a. (Law) von der Rechtspraxis ausschließen.

disbelief [disbi'liːf], s. der Unglaube (incredulity); der Zweifel (doubt).

disbelieve [disbi'liːv], v.a. nicht glauben; bezweifeln.

disburse [dis'bəːs], v.a. auszahlen, ausgeben.

disbursement [dis'bəːsmənt], s. die Auszahlung, die Ausgabe.

disc [disk], s. (also Med.) die Scheibe; die Platte (record).

discard [dis'kɑːd], v.a. ablegen, beiseite legen, aufgeben.

discern [di'zəːn or di'səːn], v.a. unterscheiden; wahrnehmen, bemerken.

discernment [di'səːnmənt], s. die Urteilskraft (powers of judgment); die Einsicht.

discharge [dis'tʃɑ:dʒ], *v.a.* entlassen (*dismiss*); abfeuern (*pistol*); abladen, ausladen (*cargo*); bezahlen (*debt*); tun, erfüllen (*duty*). — *s.* die Entladung (*gun*); die Entlassung (*dismissal*); die Bezahlung (*debt*); die Erfüllung (*duty*).

disciple [di'saipl], *s.* (*Bibl.*) der Jünger; der Schüler.

disciplinarian [disipli'nɛəriən], *s.* der Zuchtmeister.

disciplinary ['disiplinəri], *adj.* disziplinarisch.

discipline ['disiplin], *s.* die Disziplin, die Zucht. — *v.a.* disziplinieren, züchtigen.

disclaim [dis'kleim], *v.a.* verleugnen (*deny*); nicht anerkennen (*refuse to acknowledge*); verzichten (*renounce*).

disclaimer [dis'kleimə], *s.* der Widerruf.

disclose [dis'klouz], *v.a.* eröffnen, enthüllen.

disclosure [dis'klouʒə], *s.* die Eröffnung, die Enthüllung.

discoloration [diskʌlə'reiʃən], *s.* die Entfärbung, Verfärbung.

discomfiture [dis'kʌmfitʃə], *s.* die Verwirrung.

discomfort [dis'kʌmfət], *s.* das Unbehagen; die Beschwerde.

disconcert [diskən'sə:t], *v.a.* außer Fassung bringen (*upset*); vereiteln (*frustrate*).

disconnect [diskə'nekt], *v.a.* trennen (*separate*); abstellen.

disconsolate [dis'kɔnsəlit], *adj.* trostlos, untröstlich.

discontent [diskən'tent], *s.* die Unzufriedenheit, das Mißvergnügen. — *v.a.* mißvergnügt stimmen.

discontinuance [diskən'tinjuəns], *s.* die Beendigung (*finish*); das Aufhören (*suspension*); die Unterbrechung (*interruption*).

discontinue [diskən'tinju:], *v.a.* nicht fortsetzen; unterbrechen (*interrupt*); einstellen.

discord ['diskɔ:d], *s.* die Zwietracht (*disagreement*); (*Mus.*) der Mißklang.

discordance [dis'kɔ:dəns], *s.* die Uneinigkeit.

discordant [dis'kɔ:dənt], *adj.* uneinig, widersprechend.

discount ['diskaunt], *s.* (*Comm.*) der Abzug, der Rabatt; *allow a* —, einen Rabatt gewähren; *be at a* —, unbeliebt sein, nicht geschätzt sein; *sell at a* —, unter dem Preis verkaufen. — [dis'kaunt], *v.a.* (*Comm.*) diskontieren, einen Rabatt gewähren; nur mit Vorsicht aufnehmen (*accept with doubt*).

discountable [dis'kauntəbl], *adj.* diskontierbar, in Abzug zu bringen.

discountenance [dis'kauntinəns], *v.a.* mißbilligen.

discourage [dis'kʌridʒ], *v.a.* entmutigen; abraten (*from*, von, *Dat.*).

discouragement [dis'kʌridʒmənt], *s.* die Entmutigung.

discourse [dis'kɔ:s], *v.n.* einen Vortrag halten (*on*, über, *Acc.*); sprechen. — ['diskɔ:s], *s.* der Vortrag; das Gespräch, die Rede.

discourteous [dis'kə:tiəs], *adj.* unhöflich.

discourtesy [dis'kə:təsi], *s.* die Unhöflichkeit.

discover [dis'kʌvə], *v.a.* entdecken.

discovery [dis'kʌvəri], *s.* die Entdeckung.

discredit [dis'kredit], *s.* der üble Ruf; die Schande. — *v.a.* in schlechten Ruf bringen; diskreditieren.

discreditable [dis'kreditəbl], *adj.* schimpflich.

discreet [dis'kri:t], *adj.* diskret, verschwiegen; vorsichtig (*cautious*).

discrepancy [dis'krepənsi], *s.* die Diskrepanz, der Widerspruch; der Unterschied (*difference*).

discretion [dis'kreʃən], *s.* die Diskretion; die Klugheit; der Takt (*tact*); die Verschwiegenheit (*silence*); *at your* —, nach Ihrem Belieben; *use your* —, handle nach deinem Ermessen; handeln Sie nach Ihrem Ermessen.

discretionary [dis'kreʃənəri], *adj.* willkürlich, uneingeschränkt.

discriminate [dis'krimineit], *v.a.*, *v.n.* unterscheiden (*distinguish*); absondern (*separate*).

discriminating [dis'krimineitiŋ], *adj.* scharfsinnig; einsichtig.

discriminatory [dis'krimineitəri], *adj.* einen Unterschied machend; — *legislation*, das Ausnahmegesetz.

discursive [dis'kə:siv], *adj.* diskursiv, ohne Zusammenhang.

discuss [dis'kʌs], *v.a.* besprechen, erörtern.

discussion [dis'kʌʃən], *s.* die Diskussion, das Gespräch.

disdain [dis'dein], *s.* die Verachtung. — *v.a.* verachten, verschmähen; herabsetzen (*belittle*).

disdainful [dis'deinful], *adj.* geringschätzig, verächtlich.

disease [di'zi:z], *s.* die Krankheit.

diseased [di'zi:zd], *adj.* krank.

disembark [disim'bɑ:k], *v.n.* aussteigen, landen. — *v.a.* aussteigen lassen, ausschiffen.

disembarkation [disembɑ:'keiʃən], *s.* die Ausschiffung; die Landung.

disenchant [disin'tʃɑ:nt], *v.a.* ernüchtern.

disenchantment [disin'tʃɑ:ntmənt], *s.* die Ernüchterung.

disengage [disin'geidʒ], *v.a.* losmachen, befreien (*release*); freigeben. — *v.n.* (*Mil.*) sich absetzen.

disengaged [disin'geidʒd], *adj.* frei (*unoccupied*).

disentangle [disin'tæŋgl], *v.a.* entwirren; befreien (*free*).

~ **disentanglement** [disin'tæŋglmənt], *s.* die Entwirrung, die Befreiung.

disfavour [dis′feivə], s. die Ungunst, die Ungnade.

disfigure [dis′figə], v.a. entstellen, verunstalten.

disfiguration [disfigjuə′reiʃən], s. die Entstellung, die Verunstaltung.

disfranchise [dis′fræntʃaiz], v.a. das Wahlrecht entziehen (Dat.).

disgorge [dis′gɔ:dʒ], v.a. ausspeien.

disgrace [dis′greis], v.a. entehren, Schande bringen. — s. die Ungnade, Schande (shame); die Entehrung (putting to shame).

disgraceful [dis′greisful], adj. schändlich, entehrend.

disgruntled [dis′grʌntld], adj. verstimmt, unzufrieden.

disguise [dis′gaiz], v.a. verkleiden (dress); (fig.) verstellen. — s. die Verkleidung, die Verstellung.

disgust [dis′gʌst], s. der Ekel, der Widerwille. — v.a. anekeln; be —ed, sehr ärgerlich sein; be —ed with s. th., etwas verabscheuen.

dish [diʃ], s. die Schüssel (bowl); das Gericht (food). — v.a. (coll.) abtun (frustrate); — up, auftragen (food).

dishcloth [′diʃklɔθ], s. das Wischtuch; der Abwaschlappen.

dishearten [dis′ha:tn], v.a. entmutigen, verzagt machen.

dishevelled [di′ʃevəld], adj. aufgelöst (hair); zerzaust (hair, clothes).

dishonest [dis′ɔnist], adj. unehrlich.

dishonesty [dis′ɔnisti], s. die Unehrlichkeit.

dishonour [dis′ɔnə], s. die Schande. — v.a. schänden, Schande bringen (über, Acc.).

dishonourable [dis′ɔnərəbl], adj. ehrlos, schimpflich.

dishwater [′diʃwɔ:tə], s. das Spülwasser.

disillusion [disi′lu:ʒən], s. die Enttäuschung, die Ernüchterung. — v.a. enttäuschen, ernüchtern.

disinclination [disinkli′neiʃən], s. die Abneigung.

disincline [disin′klain], v.a. abgeneigt machen (Dat.).

disinfect [disin′fekt], v.a. desinfizieren.

disinfectant [disin′fektənt], s. das Desinfektionsmittel.

disinfection [disin′fekʃən], s. die Desinfektion.

disingenuous [disin′dʒenjuəs], adj. unaufrichtig, unredlich.

disinherit [disin′herit], v.a. enterben.

disinter [disin′tə:], v.a. exhumieren, ausgraben.

disinterested [dis′intrəstid], adj. uneigennützig.

disinterestedness [dis′intrəstidnis], s. die Selbstlosigkeit, die Uneigennützigkeit.

disjoin [dis′dʒɔin], v.a. trennen.

disjoint [dis′dʒɔint], v.a. zerlegen, zerstückeln.

disjointedness [dis′dʒɔintidnis], s. die Zerstückheit, die Zusammenhangslosigkeit (style of writing etc.).

disjunction [dis′dʒʌŋkʃən], s. die Trennung, die Abtrennung.

disjunctive [dis′dʒʌŋktiv], adj. (Gram.) trennend, disjunktiv.

disk [disk] see **disc.**

dislike [dis′laik], v.a. nicht leiden mögen, nicht gerne haben. — s. die Abneigung (of, gegen, Acc.).

dislocate [′dislokeit], v.a. verrenken (bone); (fig.) in Unordnung bringen.

dislocation [dislo′keiʃən], s. (Med.) die Verrenkung; die Verwirrung (traffic etc.).

dislodge [dis′lɔdʒ], v.a. vertreiben (drive out); entfernen (remove).

disloyal [dis′lɔiəl], adj. ungetreu; verräterisch.

disloyalty [dis′lɔiəlti], s. die Untreue (sentiment); der Verrat (act).

dismal [′dizməl], adj. trostlos, traurig (mood); düster, trüb (weather).

dismantle [dis′mæntl], v.a. niederreißen, zerlegen; abbauen.

dismay [dis′mei], v.a. erschrecken, entmutigen. — s. die Furcht, der Schrecken, die Bangigkeit.

dismember [dis′membə], v.a. zerstückeln.

dismemberment [dis′membəmənt], s. die Zerstückelung, die Aufteilung.

dismiss [dis′mis], v.a. entlassen (person); aufgeben (idea).

dismissal [dis′misəl], s. die Entlassung; (Law) die Abweisung.

dismount [dis′maunt], v.n. vom Pferd absteigen. — v.a. (die Truppen) absteigen lassen.

disobedience [diso′bi:djəns], s. der Ungehorsam.

disobedient [diso′bi:djənt], adj. ungehorsam.

disobey [diso′bei], v.a., v.n. nicht gehorchen.

disoblige [diso′blaidʒ], v.a. verletzen, unhöflich behandeln.

disorder [dis′ɔ:də], s. die Unordnung; der Aufruhr (riot). — v.a. verwirren, in Unordnung bringen.

disorderliness [dis′ɔ:dəlinis], s. die Unordentlichkeit.

disorderly [dis′ɔ:dəli], adj. unordentlich (unsystematic); aufrührerisch, liederlich.

disorganization [disɔ:gəni′zeiʃən or -nai′zeiʃən], s. die Zerrüttung, die Auflösung (dissolution).

disorganize [dis′ɔ:gənaiz], v.a. auflösen.

disown [dis′oun], v.a. verleugnen.

disparage [dis′pæridʒ], v.a. verunglimpfen (slight); herabsetzen (minimize).

disparagement [dis′pæridʒmənt], s. die Herabsetzung.

disparity [dis′pæriti], s. die Ungleichheit.

dispatch [dis′pætʃ] see **despatch.**

dispel [dis′pel], v.a. vertreiben, verscheuchen.

dispensable [dis'pensəbl], *adj.* erläßlich, entbehrlich.

dispensation [dispen'seiʃən], *s.* die Austeilung; (*Eccl.*) die Dispensation.

dispensary [dis'pensəri], *s.* die Apotheke.

dispense [dis'pens], *v.a.* ausgeben, austeilen (*distribute*); — *with*, entbehren können, verzichten (auf, *Acc.*).

dispenser [dis'pensə], *s.* der Apotheker, der Pharmazeut.

dispersal [dis'pɔːsəl], *s.* das Zerstreuen, die Verteilung.

disperse [dis'pɔːs], *v.a.* zerstreuen. — *v.n.* sich zerstreuen, sich verteilen.

dispirit [dis'pirit], *v.a.* mutlos machen, entmutigen.

displace [dis'pleis], *v.a.* verlegen, versetzen; (*Phys.*) verdrängen; —*d person*, der Heimatlose, der Verschleppte, der Flüchtling.

displacement [dis'pleismənt], *s.* die Versetzung (*from one place to another*); die Entwurzelung (*uprooting*); (*Phys.*) die Verdrängung; (*Naut.*) das Deplacement.

display [dis'plei], *v.a.* entfalten, ausstellen, zur Schau stellen (*show*). — *s.* die Entfaltung (*showing*), die Schaustellung, Ausstellung (*exhibition*).

displease [dis'pliːz], *v.a.* mißfallen (*Dat.*).

displeased [dis'pliːzd], *adj.* ungehalten (*at*, über, *Acc.*).

displeasure [dis'pleʒə], *s.* das Mißvergnügen, das Mißfallen (— *at*, an, *Dat.*).

disposable [dis'pouzəbl], *adj.* (*Comm.*) disponibel; zur Verfügung stehend.

disposal [dis'pouzl], *s.* die Verfügung (*ordering*); die Übergabe (*handing over*); *at o.'s* —, zur Verfügung; *bomb* —, die Unschädlichmachung der Bomben.

dispose [dis'pouz], *v.a.* einrichten (*thing*); geneigt machen (*person*); — *of*, etwas loswerden (*Acc.*). — *v.n.* anordnen (*ordain*).

disposed [dis'pouzd], *adj.* geneigt; *be well — towards s.o.*, jemandem zugeneigt sein *or* wohlwollend gegenüberstehen; *well —*, (in) guter Laune.

disposition [dispə'ziʃən], *s.* (*Psych.*) die Anlage; die Gemütsart (*temperament*); die Anordnung (*sequence*); der Plan, die Anlage (*of book etc.*); die Verfügung (*arrangement*).

dispossess [dispə'zes], *v.a.* enteignen, (des Besitzes) berauben (*Genit.*).

disproof [dis'pruːf], *s.* die Widerlegung.

disproportion [disprə'pɔːʃən], *s.* das Mißverhältnis.

disproportionate [disprə'pɔːsənit], *adj.* unverhältnismäßig.

disprove [dis'pruːv], *v.a.* widerlegen.

disputable [dis'pjuːtəbl], *adj.* bestreitbar.

disputant ['dispjutənt], *s.* der Opponent, der Disputant.

disputation [dispjuː'teiʃən], *s.* der gelehrte Streit, die Disputation.

dispute [dis'pjuːt], *s.* der Disput, die Meinungsverschiedenheit. — *v.a.*, *v.n.* streiten, verschiedener Ansicht sein; disputieren (*debate*); mit Worten streiten (*argue*).

disqualification [diskwɔlifi'keiʃən], *s.* die Disqualifizierung.

disqualify [dis'kwɔlifai], *v.a.* disqualifizieren, ausschließen.

disquiet [dis'kwaiət], *v.a.* beunruhigen, stören. — *s.* die Unruhe, die Störung.

disquisition [diskwi'ziʃən], *s.* die (lange) Abhandlung *or* Rede.

disregard [disri'gaːd], *v.a.* mißachten, nicht beachten. — *s.* die Außerachtlassung, die Mißachtung.

disreputable [dis'repjutəbl], *adj.* verrufen, in üblem Rufe stehend.

disrepute [disri'pjuːt], *s.* der schlechte Name, der üble Ruf.

disrespect [disris'pekt], *s.* die Geringschätzung, der Mangel an Respekt. — *v.a.* (*obs.*) mißachten, geringschätzen, respektlos behandeln.

disrespectful [disris'pektful], *adj.* respektlos, unhöflich.

disrobe [dis'roub], *v.a.* entkleiden. — *v.n.* sich entkleiden.

disrupt [dis'rʌpt], *v.a.* abreißen, unterbrechen, stören (*disturb*).

disruption [dis'rʌpʃən], *s.* die Störung, die Unterbrechung (*interruption*); der Bruch.

dissatisfaction [dissætis'fækʃən], *s.* die Unzufriedenheit.

dissatisfied [dis'sætisfaid], *adj.* unzufrieden, unbefriedigt.

dissatisfy [dis'sætisfai], *v.a.* unzufrieden lassen.

dissect [di'sekt], *v.a.* zergliedern, zerlegen; (*Anat.*) sezieren.

dissection [di'sekʃən], *s.* die Zergliederung; (*Anat.*) die Sektion.

dissemble [di'sembl], *v.a.*, *v.n.* heucheln; sich verstellen.

disseminate [di'semineit], *v.a.* verbreiten.

dissemination [disemi'neiʃən], *s.* die Verbreitung.

dissension [di'senʃən], *s.* die Uneinigkeit, der Zwist (*conflict*).

dissent [di'sent], *v.n.* anderer Meinung sein; abweichen (*from*, von, *Dat.*). — *s.* die Abweichung, die abweichende Meinung.

dissenter [di'sentə], *s.* der Dissenter, das Mitglied der Freikirche.

dissertation [disə'teiʃən], *s.* die Dissertation, die Abhandlung.

dissever [di'sevə], *v.a.* trennen (*separate*); zerteilen (*divide*).

dissidence ['disidəns], *s.* die Uneinigkeit.

dissident ['disidənt], *adj.* uneinig, anders denkend.

dissimilar [di'similə], *adj.* unähnlich, ungleichartig.

dissimilarity [disimi'læriti], *s.* die Unähnlichkeit, die Ungleichartigkeit.

dissimulate [di'simjuleit], *v.a.* verhehlen (*conceal*). — *v.n.* sich verstellen, heucheln.

dissimulation [disimju'leiʃən], *s.* die Verstellung, Heuchelei, das Vorgeben (*pretence*).

dissipate ['disipeit], *v.a.* zerstreuen (*spread*); verschwenden (*waste*).

dissipation [disi'peiʃən], *s.* die Zerstreuung, die Verschwendung; die Ausschweifung.

dissociate [di'souʃieit], *v.a.* trennen, lösen. — *v.r.* abrücken (von).

dissociation [disouʃi'eiʃən], *s.* die Trennung; die Dissoziation.

dissolubility [disɔlju'biliti], *s.* die Auflösbarkeit.

dissoluble [di'sɔljubl], *adj.* auflösbar.

dissolute ['disɔlju:t], *adj.* ausschweifend, lose, liederlich.

dissolution [disə'lju:ʃən], *s.* die Auflösung; der Tod (*death*).

dissolvable [di'zɔlvəbl], *adj.* auflösbar, löslich.

dissolve [di'zɔlv], *v.a.* auflösen; lösen. — *v.n.* sich auflösen, zergehen (*melt*).

dissonance ['disənəns], *s.* die Dissonanz, der Mißklang.

dissonant ['disənənt], *adj.* (*Mus.*) dissonant; mißhellig (*discordant*).

dissuade [di'sweid], *v.a.* abraten (*from*, von, *Dat.*).

dissuasion [di'sweiʒən], *s.* das Abraten.

dissuasive [di'sweisiv], *adj.* abratend.

distaff ['distɑ:f], *s.* der Spinnrocken (*spinning*); on the — side, auf der weiblichen Linie.

distance ['distəns], *s.* die Entfernung; die Ferne (*remoteness*). — *v.a.* hinter sich lassen, sich distanzieren (von, *Dat.*)

distant ['distənt], *adj.* entfernt, fern (*space*); kühl (*manner*).

distaste [dis'teist], *s.* die Abneigung (vor, *Dat.*); der Widerwille (gegen, *Acc.*).

distasteful [dis'teistful], *adj.* widerwärtig, zuwider.

distastefulne s [dis'teistfulnis], *s.* die Widerwärtigkeit.

distemper (1) [dis'tempə], *s.* die Krankheit; die Staupe (*dogs*).

distemper (2) [dis'tempə], *s.* die Wasserfarbe (*paint*). — *v.a.* mit Wasserfarbe streichen.

distend [dis'tend], *v.a.* (*Med.*) ausdehnen, strecken. — *v.n.* sich ausdehnen.

distension, distention [dis'tenʃən], *s.* das Dehnen; (*Med.*) die Ausdehnung, die Streckung.

distich ['distik], *s.* (*Poet.*) das Distichon.

distil [dis'til], *v.a.* destillieren. — *v.n.* (*Chem.*) destillieren, herauströpfeln.

distillation [disti'leiʃən], *s.* die Destillierung, (*Chem.*) der Destilliervorgang.

distiller [dis'tilə], *s.* der Branntweinbrenner.

distillery [dis'tiləri], *s.* die (Branntwein)brennerei.

distinct [dis'tiŋkt], *adj.* deutlich, klar; — from, verschieden von (*Dat.*).

distinction [dis'tiŋkʃən], *s.* der Unterschied, die Unterscheidung (*differentiation*); die Auszeichnung (*eminence*).

distinctive [dis'tiŋktiv], *adj.* unterscheidend (*differentiating*); deutlich (*clear*); leicht zu unterscheiden (*easy to distinguish*).

distinctiveness [dis'tiŋktivnis], *s.* die Deutlichkeit (*of voice etc.*); die Eigenart, Eigentümlichkeit (*peculiarity*).

distinguish [dis'tiŋgwiʃ], *v.a.* unterscheiden. — *v.r.* — *o.s.*, sich auszeichnen.

distinguishable [dis'tiŋgwiʃəbl], *adj.* unterscheidbar.

distinguished [dis'tiŋgwiʃd], *adj.* berühmt, vornehm.

distort [dis'tɔ:t], *v.a.* verdrehen; verzerren, verrenken.

distortion [dis'tɔ:ʃən], *s.* die Verdrehung, Verzerrung; (*fig.*) die Entstellung (*of truth etc.*).

distract [dis'trækt], *v.a.* abziehen, ablenken (*divert*); stören (*disturb*).

distracted [dis'træktid], *adj.* zerstreut; verrückt (*mentally deranged*).

distraction [dis'trækʃən], *s.* die Ablenkung; die Störung (*disturbance*); to —, bis zur Raserei.

distrain [dis'trein], *v.a.* beschlagnahmen, in Beschlag nehmen.

distraint [dis'treint], *s.* die Beschlagnahme.

distress [dis'tres], *s.* die Not, die Trübsal. — *v.a.* betrüben (*sadden*); quälen (*torture*).

distribute [dis'tribju:t], *v.a.* verteilen, austeilen (*among*, unter, *Acc.*).

distribution [distri'bju:ʃən], *s.* die Verteilung; die Austeilung (*giving out*); (*Comm.*) der Vertrieb.

distributive [dis'tribjutiv], *adj.* (*Gram.*) distributiv; — trades, die Vertriebsgewerbe.

district ['distrikt], *s.* (*Geog., Pol.*) der Bezirk; die Gegend (*region*); der Kreis (*administrative*); — commissioner, der Kreisbeamte, Kreisvorsteher.

distrust [dis'trʌst], *v.a.* mißtrauen (*Dat.*). — *s.* das Mißtrauen (*of*, gegen, *Acc.*).

distrustful [dis'trʌstful], *adj.* mißtrauisch (*of*, gegen, *Acc.*).

disturb [dis'tə:b], *v.a.* stören (*trouble*); in Unordnung bringen (*disorder*).

disturbance [dis'tə:bəns], *s.* die Störung (*interruption etc.*); der Aufruhr (*riot*).

disunion [dis'ju:njən], *s.* die Entzweiung, die Zwietracht.

disunite [disju'nait], *v.a.* entzweien, Zwietracht säen zwischen. — *v.n.* sich trennen.

disuse [dis'ju:z], *v.a.* außer Gebrauch setzen. — [-'ju:s], *s.* der Nichtgebrauch (*abeyance*); die Entwöhnung (*cessation of practice*).

ditch [ditʃ], *s.* der Graben; *dull as —water*, uninteressant, langweilig. — *v.a.* mit einem Graben umgeben (*dig around*); graben.

ditto ['ditou], *adv.* desgleichen, dito.

ditty ['diti], *s.* das Liedchen.

diurnal [dai'ə:nəl], *adj.* täglich.

divan [di'væn], *s.* der Diwan.

dive [daiv], *v.n.* tauchen, springen (ins Wasser); (*Aviat.*) sturzfliegen, einen Sturzflug machen. — *s.* der Hechtsprung (ins Wasser); der Wassersprung; der Kopfsprung; (*Aviat.*) der Sturzflug.

diver ['daivə], *s.* (*Sport, Orn.*) der Taucher.

diverge [dai'və:dʒ], *v.n.* abweichen, auseinandergehen.

divergence [dai'və:dʒəns], *s.* die Abweichung, die Divergenz, Meinungsverschiedenheit.

divergent [dai'və:dʒənt], *adj.* auseinandergehend, abweichend.

divers ['daivəz], *adj. pl.* etliche, verschiedene.

diverse [dai'və:s], *adj.* verschieden, mannigfaltig.

diversify [dai'və:sifai], *v.a.* verschieden machen.

diversion [dai'və:ʃən], *s.* die Zerstreuung; (*Traffic*) die Umleitung.

diversity [dai'və:siti], *s.* die Verschiedenheit; die Ungleichheit (*disparity*).

divert [dai'və:t], *v.a.* ablenken, zerstreuen.

divest [di'vest *or* dai'-], *v.a.* entkleiden, berauben (*of office*, eines Amtes). — *v.r.* — *o.s. of*, auf etwas verzichten (*give up*).

divide [di'vaid], *v.a.* (*Maths.*) dividieren; teilen (*share*); aufteilen (*proportion*); sondern, trennen (*separate*). — *v.n.* sich teilen; (*Maths.*) sich dividieren lassen.

dividend ['dividənd], *s.* (*Comm.*) die Dividende; (*Maths.*) der Dividend.

dividers [di'vaidəz], *s.pl.* der Stechzirkel.

divination [divi'neiʃən], *s.* die Wahrsagung (*prophecy*); die Ahnung.

divine [di'vain], *v.a.* weissagen (*prophesy*); erraten (*guess*). — *adj.* göttlich; (*coll.*) herrlich. —*s.* (*obs.*) der Geistliche (*clergyman*).

divinity [di'viniti], *s.* die Göttlichkeit; die Gottheit (*deity*); die Theologie.

divisibility [divizi'biliti], *s.* (*Maths.*) die Teilbarkeit.

divisible [di'vizibl], *adj.* teilbar.

division [di'viʒən], *s.* (*Maths., Mil.*) die Division; die Teilung (*partition*); die Abteilung (*department*); (*Parl.*) die Abstimmung.

divisor [di'vaizə], *s.* (*Maths.*) der Divisor; der Teiler.

divorce [di'vɔ:s], *s.* (*Law*) die Scheidung; die Trennung (*separation*). — *v.a.* sich von einem scheiden lassen.

divulge [dai'vʌldʒ], *v.a.* ausplaudern; verraten (*betray*); verbreiten (*spread*).

dizziness ['dizinis], *s.* der Schwindel.

dizzy ['dizi], *adj.* schwindlig.

do [du:], *v.a. irr.* tun, machen; — *o.'s duty*, seine Pflicht erfüllen; — *o.'s bit*, das Seinige leisten; — *o.'s homework*, seine Aufgaben machen; — *a favour*, einen Gefallen erweisen; vollbringen (*accomplish*); — *away with*, abschaffen (*Acc.*); einpacken. — *v.n. this will —*, das genügt; *this won't —*, so geht's nicht; — *without*, ohne etwas auskommen; *how — you — ?* sehr angenehm (*on introduction to people*).

docile ['dousail], *adj.* gelehrig, lenksam, fügsam.

docility [do'siliti], *s.* die Gelehrigkeit, die Fügsamkeit.

dock (1) [dɔk], *s.* (*Bot.*) das Ampferkraut; — *leaf*, das Ampferblatt.

dock (2) [dɔk], *s.* (*Naut.*) das Dock; —*yard*, die Schiffswerft; (*Law*) die Anklagebank. — *v.a.* (*Naut.*) ein Schiff ins Dock bringen.

dock (3) [dɔk], *v.a.* stutzen (*clip*); kürzen (*wages*).

docket ['dɔkit], *s.* der Zettel (*chit*); der Lieferschein.

doctor ['dɔktə], *s.* (*Med.*) der Arzt, der Doktor. — *v.a.* operieren, kastrieren (*a cat etc.*).

doctorate ['dɔktərit], *s.* das Doktorat, die Doktorwürde.

doctrinaire [dɔktri'nɛə], *s.* der Doktrinär. — *adj.* doktrinär.

doctrinal [dɔk'trainəl], *adj.* Lehr-.

doctrine ['dɔktrin], *s.* die Lehre, die Doktrin.

document ['dɔkjumənt], *s.* das Dokument, die Urkunde.

documentary [dɔkju'mentəri], *adj.* Dokumentar- (*film*); dokumentarisch (*evidence*).

documentation [dɔkjumen'teiʃən], *s.* die Dokumentation, Heranziehung von Dokumenten.

dodge [dɔdʒ], *v.a.* ausweichen (*Dat.*). — *s.* der Kniff.

dodger ['dɔdʒə], *s.* der Schwindler.

doe [dou], *s.* (*Zool.*) das Reh.

doeskin ['douskin], *s.* das Rehleder.

doff [dɔf], *v.a.* abnehmen, ablegen (*clothes*).

dog [dɔg], *s.* der Hund; —*'s ear*, das Eselsohr (*in book*). — *v.a.* verfolgen, auf Schritt und Tritt folgen (*Dat.*) (*follow closely*).

dogfish ['dɔgfiʃ], *s.* (*Zool.*) der Dornhai.

dogged ['dɔgid], *adj.* unverdrossen, zäh.

doggedness ['dɔgidnis], *s.* die Zähigkeit.

doggerel ['dɔgərəl], *s.* der Knüttelvers.

dogma ['dɔgmə], *s.* das Dogma, der Glaubenssatz.

dower

dogmatic [dɔg'mætik], *adj.* dogmatisch.
dogmatism ['dɔgmətizm], *s.* der Dogmatismus.
dogmatize ['dɔgmətaiz], *v.n.* dogmatisieren.
doldrums ['douldrəmz], *s. pl.* die Schwermut, die Depression; (*Naut.*) die Windstillen, *f.pl.*
dole [doul], *s.* das Almosen; die Arbeitslosenunterstützung (*unemployment benefit*); *be on the* —, stempeln gehen, Arbeitslosenunterstützung beziehen. — *v.a.* — *out*, austeilen, verteilen.
doleful ['doulful], *adj.* traurig, bekümmert.
doll [dɔl], *s.* die Puppe.
dollar ['dɔlə], *s.* der Dollar.
dolman ['dɔlmən], *s.* der Dolman.
dolorous ['dɔlərəs], *adj.* (*Lit.*) schmerzlich, schmerzhaft.
dolphin ['dɔlfin], *s.* (*Zool.*) der Delphin.
dolt [doult], *s.* der Tölpel.
doltish ['doultiʃ], *adj.* tölpelhaft.
doltishness ['doultiʃnis], *s.* die Tölpelhaftigkeit.
domain [do'mein], *s.* das Gebiet, der Bereich.
dome [doum], *s.* (*Archit.*) die Kuppel, die Wölbung; der Dom.
domed [doumd], *adj.* gewölbt.
domestic [do'mestik], *adj.* Haus-, häuslich; — *animal*, das Haustier.
domesticate [do'mestikeit], *v.a.* zähmen (*tame*), zivilisieren.
domesticity [domes'tisiti], *s.* die Häuslichkeit.
domicile ['dɔmisail], *s.* das Domizil; der Wohnort.
domiciled ['dɔmisaild], *adj.* wohnhaft (*at*, in, *Dat.*).
dominant ['dɔminənt], *adj.* vorherrschend. — *s.* (*Mus.*) die Dominante.
dominate ['dɔmineit], *v.a.* beherrschen. — *v.n.* herrschen.
domination [dɔmi'neiʃən], *s.* die Herrschaft.
domineer [dɔmi'niə], *v.n.* tyrannisieren.
domineering [dɔmi'niəriŋ], *adj.* überheblich, gebieterisch.
Dominican [do'minikən], *s.* der Dominikaner (*friar*).
dominion [do'minjən], *s.* die Herrschaft (*rule*); das Dominion (*Br. Commonwealth*).
domino ['dɔminou], *s.* (*pl.* —**noes**) der Domino (*mask*); (*pl.*) das Domino (*game*).
don (1) [dɔn], *s.* der Universitätsgelehrte, Universitätsdozent (*scholar*); Don (*Spanish nobleman*).
don (2) [dɔn], *v.a.* anziehen.
donate [do'neit], *v.a.* schenken, stiften.
donation [do'neiʃən], *s.* die Schenkung, die Stiftung; die Gabe (*gift*).
donkey ['dɔŋki], *s.* (*Zool.*) der Esel; — *engine*, die Hilfsmaschine.
donor ['dounə], *s.* der Spender, der Stifter: *blood* —, der Blutspender.

doom [du:m], *s.* die Verurteilung (*judgment*); der Untergang; das jüngste Gericht.
doomed [du:md], *adj.* verurteilt, verdammt (*to*, zu, *Dat.*).
Doomsday ['du:msdei]. der jüngste Tag, der Tag des jüngsten Gerichtes.
door [dɔ:], *s.* die Tür(e); *next* —, nebenan; *out of* —*s*, draußen, im Freien; —*bell*, die Türklingel; — *latch*, die Klinke.
doorman ['dɔ:mæn], *s.* der Türsteher, der Pförtner.
dormant ['dɔ:mənt], *adj.* schlafend; unbenutzt.
dormer window ['dɔ:mə 'windou], *s.* das Dachfenster.
dormitory ['dɔ:mitri], *s.* der Schlafsaal.
dormouse ['dɔ:maus], *s.* (*Zool.*) die Haselmaus.
dose [dous], *s.* (*Med.*) die Dosis. — *v.a.* dosieren.
dot [dɔt], *s.* der Punkt, das Tüpfel. — *v.a.* punktieren; *sign on the* —*ted line*, unterschreiben; — *the i's and cross the i's*, äußerst genau sein.
dotage ['doutidʒ], *s.* die Altersschwäche, das Greisenalter.
dotard ['doutəd], *s.* der alte Dummkopf.
dote [dout], *v.n.* vernarrt sein (*on*, in, *Acc.*).
double ['dʌbl], *adj.* (*Maths.*) doppelt; zweideutig (*meaning*); falsch (*false*); — *entry book-keeping*, doppelte Buchführung. — *s.* der Doppelgänger, die Doppelgängerin; *at the* —, im Sturmschritt. — *v.a.* (*Maths.*) verdoppeln; zusammenlegen (*fold in two*). — *v.n.* — *up with pain*, sich vor Schmerzen winden *or* krümmen.
doublet ['dʌblit], *s.* der Wams; — *and hose*, Wams und Hosen; der Pasch (*dice*); (*Ling.*) die Dublette, Doppelform.
doubt [daut], *s.* der Zweifel. — *v.a.* zweifeln (an, *Dat.*); bezweifeln.
doubtful ['dautful], *adj.* zweifelhaft, fraglich (*uncertain*).
doubtless ['dautlis], *adj.* zweifellos, ohne Zweifel.
douche [du:ʃ], *s.* die Dusche.
dough [dou], *s.* der Teig.
doughnut ['dounʌt], *s.* der Krapfen, Pfannkuchen.
doughy ['doui], *adj.* weich, teigig.
douse [daus], *v.a.* begießen, mit Wasser beschütten.
dove [dʌv], *s.* (*Orn.*) die Taube.
dovecote ['dʌvkɔt], *s.* der Taubenschlag.
dovetail ['dʌvteil], *v.a.*, *v.n.* einpassen; fügen; —*ing*, die Einpassung, die Verzinkung.
dowager ['dauədʒə], *s.* die Witwe (*of noble family*, von Stande).
dowdy ['daudi], *adj.* schlampig, unordentlich, unelegant.
dower ['dauə], *s.* die Mitgift, die Ausstattung.

down

down (1) [daun], *s.* der Flaum, die Daune.

down (2) [daun], *s.* das Hügelland.

down (3) [daun], *adv.* hinunter, herunter; nieder; unter; hinab. — *prep.* herab; hinunter. — *adj. the — train,* der Zug aus London. — *v.a.* niederzwingen, hinunterstürzen.

downcast ['daunkɑ:st], *adj.* niedergeschlagen.

downfall ['daunfɔ:l], *s.* der Sturz.

downhill [daun'hil], *adv.* bergab. — ['daunhil], *adj.* abschüssig.

downpour ['daunpɔ:], *s.* der Platzregen.

downright ['daunrait], *adj.* völlig. — *adv.* geradezu.

downward ['daunwəd], *adj.* abschüssig. — *adv.* (*also* **downwards**) *see* **down.**

dowry ['dauri] *see* **dower.**

doze [douz], *v.n.* dösen, schlummern.

dozen ['dʌzn], *s.* das Dutzend.

drab [dræb], *adj.* eintönig; langweilig (*boring*).

draft [drɑ:ft], *s.* (*Comm.*) die Tratte; der Entwurf (*sketch*); (*Mil.*) das Detachement. — *v.a.* entwerfen (*sketch*); (*Mil.*) abordnen; (*Am.*) einziehen.

drag [dræg], *v.a.* schleppen. — *s.* (*Engin.*) die Schleppbremse, der Dregghaken; der Hemmschuh (*wedge*); —*net,* das Schleppnetz; —*wheel,* das Schlepprad.

dragoman ['drægomən], *s.* der Dolmetscher.

dragon ['drægən], *s.* der Drache.

dragonfly ['drægənflai], *s.* (*Ent.*) die Libelle.

dragoon [drə'gu:n], *v.a.* unterdrücken. — *s.* (*Mil.*) der Dragoner.

drain [drein], *v.a.* entwässern, austrocknen; trockenlegen. — *v.n.* ablaufen, abfließen, auslaufen. — *s.* der Abguß, Abzug, die Gosse (*in street*); (*Engin.*) die Dränage; —*ing board,* das Ablauf- *or* Abwaschbrett; (*Phot.*) —*ing rack,* der Trockenständer; *a — on o.'s income,* eine Belastung des Einkommens.

drainage ['dreinidʒ], *s.* die Trockenlegung, die Kanalisierung.

drainpipe ['dreinpaip], *s.* das Abflußrohr; — *trousers,* die Röhrenhosen, *f. pl.*

drake [dreik], *s.* (*Orn.*) der Enterich.

dram [dræm], *s.* der Trunk; Schluck (*spirits*).

drama ['drɑ:mə], *s.* das Drama, das Schauspiel.

dramatic [drə'mætik], *adj.* dramatisch.

dramatist ['drɑ:m- *or* 'dræmətist], *s.* der Dramatiker.

dramatize ['dræmətaiz], *v.a.* dramatisieren.

drape [dreip], *v.a.* drapieren, bedecken; einhüllen (*wrap*). — *s.* (*Am.*) der Vorhang.

draper ['dreipə], *s.* der Stoffhändler, der Tuchhändler.

drapery ['dreipəri], *s.* — *department,* die Stoff- *or* Tuchabteilung; die Tuchhandlung (*shop*).

drastic ['drɑ:stik *or* 'dræstik], *adj.* drastisch, radikal.

draught [drɑ:ft], *s.* der Zug (*air*); der Tiefgang (— *of ship*); der Schluck (*drink*); der Schlaftrunk (*sleeping* —); — *horse,* das Zugpferd; — *beer,* das Faßbier; —*board,* das Damespielbrett; (*pl.*) das Damespiel.

draw [drɔ:], *v.a. irr.* ziehen (*pull*); zeichnen (*sketch*); anlocken (*attract*); ausschreiben (*cheque*); —*well,* der Ziehbrunnen. — *s.* das Los, die Verlosung (*lottery*); (*Sport*) das Unentschieden.

drawback ['drɔ:bæk], *s.* der Nachteil, die Schattenseite.

drawbridge ['drɔ:bridʒ], *s.* die Zugbrücke.

drawer ['drɔ:ə], *s.* die Schublade; *chest of* —*s,* die Kommode; (*pl.*) die Unterhosen, *f.pl.*

drawing ['drɔ:iŋ], *s.* (*Art*) die Zeichnung; —*board,* das Reißbrett; —*office,* das Zeichenbüro, der Zeichensaal.

drawing room ['drɔ:iŋ rum], *s.* das Wohnzimmer, der Salon.

drawl [drɔ:l], *v.n.* gedehnt sprechen. — *s.* die gedehnte Sprechweise.

drawn [drɔ:n], *adj.* (*Sport*) unentschieden.

dray [drei], *s.* der Rollwagen, der Karren; —*man,* der Kutscher, der Fuhrmann.

dread [dred], *s.* der Schrecken. — *adj.* schrecklich. — *v.a.* fürchten. — *v.n.* sich fürchten (vor, *Dat.*).

dreadful ['dredful], *adj.* schrecklich, furchtbar.

dreadnought ['drednɔ:t], *s.* (*Naut.*) das große Schlachtschiff.

dream [dri:m], *s.* der Traum. — *v.n. irr.* träumen; *I would not — of it,* es würde mir nicht im Traum einfallen, ich denke nicht daran.

dreamt [dremt] *see* **dream.**

dreamy ['dri:mi], *adj.* verträumt, träumerisch.

dreariness ['driərinis], *s.* die Öde.

dreary ['driəri], *adj.* traurig, öde.

dredge [dredʒ], *s.* das Schleppnetz. — *v.a.* (*Engin.*) ausbaggern; (*Naut.*) dreggen.

dredger ['dredʒə], *s.* der Bagger, das Baggerschiff; (*Cul.*) die Streubüchse.

dregs [dregz], *s. pl.* der Bodensatz (*in cup etc.*); die Hefe (*yeast*).

drench [drentʃ], *v.a.* durchnässen, tränken.

Dresden ['drezdən]. (*china*) das Meißner Porzellan.

dress [dres], *s.* das Kleid; die Kleidung; *evening* —, die Abendkleidung; *full* —, die Gala(kleidung); — *circle,* erster Rang; —*maker,* die Schneiderin; — *rehearsal,* die Generalprobe; — *shirt,* das Frackhemd; — *suit,* der Frackanzug. — *v.a., v.n.* (sich) anziehen.

dresser ['dresə], s. der Ankleider (*valet*); der Anrichtetisch (*table*).

dressing ['dresiŋ], s. (*Build.*) die Verkleidung; der Verband (*bandage*); der Verputz (*interior decoration*); — *gown*, der Schlafrock, Bademantel; (*Theat.*) — *room*, das Künstlerzimmer; Ankleidezimmer; — *table*, der Toilettentisch.

dressy ['dresi], adj. elegant; modesüchtig.

dribble [dribl], v.n. tröpfeln (*trickle*); geifern (*slaver*); dribbeln.

driblet ['driblit], s. die Kleinigkeit, die Lappalie.

drift [drift], s. die Richtung (*direction*); die Strömung (*stream*); das Treiben; Gestöber (*snow*). — v.a. treiben. — v.n. dahintreiben.

drill (1) [dril], v.a. drillen, bohren (*bore*); (*Mil.*) exerzieren; (*Agr.*) eine Furche ziehen; einstudieren (*coach*). — s. (*Mil.*) das Exerzieren; (*Agr.*) die Furche; der Bohrer (*tool*); — *hall*, die Übungs- or Exerzierhalle.

drill (2) [dril], s. der Drillich (*textile*).

drily ['draili], adv. trocken.

drink [driŋk], v.a., v.n. irr. trinken. — s. das Getränk, der Trank (*potion*); etwas zum Trinken (a —); *come, have a* —, trinken wir ein Glas (zusammen); *strong* —, geistiges Getränk.

drinkable ['driŋkəbl], adj. trinkbar; zum Trinken.

drinker ['driŋkə], s. der Trinker, Säufer; der Zecher; der Trunkenbold (*drunkard*).

drip [drip], v.n. tröpfeln. — s. das Tröpfeln.

dripping ['dripiŋ], s. (*Cul.*) das Bratenfett, das Schmalz.

drive [draiv], v.a. irr. treiben (*sheep etc.*); fahren (a *car*). — v.n. fahren; dahinfahren (— *along*). — s. die Ausfahrt, Fahrt (*trip*); die Einfahrt (*approach to house*).

driving ['draiviŋ], s. das Fahren; — *licence*, der Führerschein; — *school*, die Fahrschule; — *test*, die Fahrprüfung.

drivel [drivl], s. der Geifer; der Unsinn (*nonsense*). — v.n. Unsinn reden.

driver ['draivə], s. der Fahrer, der Chauffeur; (*Railw.*) Führer; (*Hunt.*) der Treiber.

drizzle [drizl], v.n. rieseln; leicht regnen. — s. das Rieseln, der feine Regen, der Sprühregen.

droll [droul], adj. drollig, possierlich.

drollery ['drouləri], s. die Possierlichkeit; die Schnurre.

dromedary ['drʌmədəri or 'drɔm-], s. (*Zool.*) das Dromedar.

drone (1) [droun], s. das Gedröhn, das Gesumme (*noise*). — v.n. dröhnen, summen (*hum loudly*).

drone (2) [droun], s. (*Ent.*) die Drohne; der Faulpelz (*lazybones*).

droop [dru:p], v.a. hängen lassen. — v.n. herabhängen; verwelken (*flowers*); ermatten (*tire*).

drop [drɔp], s. der Tropfen (*liquid*); das Fallen (*fall*). — v.a. fallen lassen; — *a brick*, eine taktlose Bemerkung machen; — *a hint*, andeuten, auf etwas hindeuten. — v.n. fallen.

droppings ['drɔpiŋz], s. pl. der Mist, Dünger (*of animals*).

dropsical ['drɔpsikəl], adj. (*Med.*) wassersüchtig.

dropsy ['drɔpsi], s. (*Med.*) die Wassersucht.

dross [drɔs], s. (*Metall.*) die Schlacke; der Unrat, das wertlose Zeug.

drought [draut], s. die Dürre, die Trockenheit.

drove [drouv], s. die Herde, die Trift (*cattle*).

drover ['drouvə], s. der Viehtreiber.

drown [draun], v.a. ertränken; überschwemmen (*flood*); übertönen (*noise*). — v.n. ertrinken.

drowse [drauz], v.n. schlummern, schläfrig sein.

drowsy ['drauzi], adj. schläfrig.

drub [drʌb], v.a. prügeln.

drudge [drʌdʒ], s. das Packtier; der Sklave, der Knecht.

drudgery ['drʌdʒəri], s. die Plackerei, die Plagerei (*hard toil*).

drug [drʌg], s. die Droge; die Medizin; das Rauschgift. — v.a. betäuben.

drugget ['drʌgit], s. der (grobe) Wollstoff.

drum [drʌm], s. die Trommel. — v.n. trommeln, austrommeln.

drunk [drʌŋk], adj. betrunken.

drunkard ['drʌŋkəd], s. der Trunkenbold.

drunkenness ['drʌŋkənnis], s. die Trunkenheit.

dry [drai], adj. trocken, dürr; ausgetrocknet, durstig (*thirsty*). — v.a. austrocknen, trocken machen, dörren. — v.n. trocken werden, trocknen.

dryad ['draiæd], s. die Baumnymphe Dryade.

dryness ['drainis], s. die Trockenheit, die Dürre.

dual ['dju:əl], adj. doppelt; Zwei-.

dub (1) [dʌb], v.a. zum Ritter schlagen; nennen (*name*).

dub (2) [dʌb], v.a. (*Films*) synchronisieren.

dubious ['dju:bjəs], adj. zweifelhaft.

ducal ['dju:kəl], adj. herzoglich.

duchess ['dʌtʃis], s. die Herzogin.

duchy ['dʌtʃi], s. das Herzogtum.

duck (1) [dʌk], s. (*Orn.*) die Ente.

duck (2) [dʌk], v.n. sich ducken, sich bücken; untertauchen (*in water*).— v.a. untertauchen, ins Wasser tauchen.

duckling ['dʌkliŋ], s. (*Orn.*) das Entchen.

duct [dʌkt], s. (*Anat.*) der Kanal; die Röhre.

ductile ['dʌktail], adj. dehnbar; fügsam.

375

dud [dʌd], s. (Mil.) der Blindgänger; der Fehlschlag.
dude [dju:d], s. (Am.) der Geck.
dudgeon [ˈdʌdʒən], s. der Groll, der Unwille; *in high* —, sehr aufgebracht.
due [dju:], adj. gebührend, fällig, schuldig (*to,Dat.*); angemessen, recht; *this is* — *to carelessness*, das ist auf Nachlässigkeit zurückzuführen. — adv. direkt, gerade. — s. (pl.) die Gebühren.
duel [ˈdju:əl], s. das Duell. — v.n. sich duellieren (mit, *Dat.*).
duet [dju:ˈet], s. (Mus.) das Duett.
duffer [ˈdʌfə], s. der Tölpel; (*obs.*) der Hausierer.
duffle, duffel [dʌfl], s. der Düffel, das Düffeltuch.
dug [dʌg], s. die Zitze.
dug-out [ˈdʌg-aut], s. der Unterstand, der Bunker.
duke [dju:k], s. der Herzog; *Grand Duke*, der Großherzog.
dukedom [ˈdju:kdəm], s. das Herzogtum.
dull [dʌl], adj. fade, langweilig (*boring*); träge, schwerfällig (*slow to grasp*); stumpfsinnig (*obtuse*); schal, abgeschmackt (*tasteless*); schwach (*perception*); dumpf (*thud, noise*); matt (*colour*); trüb, überwölkt (*weather*); flau (*trade*). — v.a. abstumpfen (*senses*).
dullness [ˈdʌlnis], s. die Stumpfheit (*senses*); die Langweile (*boredom*); die Schwerfälligkeit (*stolidity*); die Schwäche (*vision etc.*); die Stumpfsinnigkeit (*stupidity*).
dumb [dʌm], adj. stumm; (*sl.*) dumm; —*founded*, verblüfft; — *show*, die Pantomime; —*bell* (*Gymn.*) die Hantel.
dumbness [ˈdʌmnis], s. die Stummheit.
dummy [ˈdʌmi], s. der Strohmann (*cards*); die Kleiderpuppe (*wax figure*); der Blindgänger (*dud shell*); der Schnuller (*baby's*).
dump [dʌmp], v.a. kippen, abladen; —*ing ground*, der Abladeplatz. — s. (*Am. coll.*) das Bumslokal.
dumpling [ˈdʌmpliŋ], s. der Kloß, (*Austr.*) der Knödel.
dumps [dʌmps], s. pl. der Unmut, der Mißmut, die Depression.
dumpy [ˈdʌmpi], adj. untersetzt, kurz und dick.
dun (1) [dʌn], adj. schwarzbraun.
dun (2) [dʌn], s. der Gläubiger. — v.a. energisch mahnen.
dunce [dʌns], s. der Dummkopf.
dune [dju:n], s. die Düne.
dung [dʌŋ], s. der Dünger. — v.n. düngen.
dungeon [ˈdʌndʒən], s. der Kerker.
dupe [dju:p], s. der Betrogene. — v.a. betrügen.
duplicate [ˈdju:plikeit], v.a. verdoppeln; doppelt schreiben or ausfüllen (*write twice*); vervielfältigen (*stencil*). — [-kit], s. das Duplikat.
duplicity [dju:ˈplisiti], s. die Falschheit, die Doppelzüngigkeit.
durability [djuərəˈbiliti], s. die Dauerhaftigkeit.

durable [ˈdjuərəbl], adj. dauerhaft.
duration [djuəˈreiʃən], s. die Dauer, die Länge (*time*).
duress [djuəˈres], s. der Zwang; *under* —, zwangsweise.
during [ˈdjuəriŋ], prep. während.
dusk [dʌsk], s. die Dämmerung.
dusky [ˈdʌski], adj. dunkel, trüb; düster.
dust [dʌst], s. der Staub. — v.a. abstauben (*clean*); bestäuben (*pollinate*); bestreuen.
dustbin [ˈdʌstbin], s. der Mülleimer.
dusty [ˈdʌsti], adj. staubig; *not so* —, (*coll.*) nicht so übel.
Dutch [dʌtʃ], adj. holländisch; niederländisch; — *treat*, auf getrennte Kosten; *double* —, Kauderwelsch, Unsinn.
Dutchman [ˈdʌtʃmən], s. der Holländer, der Niederländer.
dutiful [ˈdju:tiful], adj. gehorsam, pflichttreu, pflichtbewußt.
duty [ˈdju:ti], s. die Pflicht; die Abgabe (*tax*); *customs* —, der Zoll; *be on* —, Dienst haben; (*being*) *on* —, diensthabend; *off* —, dienstfrei; — *free*, zollfrei; *in* — *bound*, von Rechts wegen, pflichtgemäß.
dwarf [dwɔ:f], s. der Zwerg. — v.a. am Wachstum hindern (*stunt*); klein erscheinen lassen (*overshadow*).
dwell [dwel], v.n. irr. wohnen (*be domiciled*); verweilen (*remain*).
dwelling [ˈdweliŋ], s. die Wohnung; — *place*, der Wohnort.
dwindle [dwindl], v.n. abnehmen, kleiner werden.
dye [dai], v.a. färben. — s. die Farbe; (*Chem.*) der Farbstoff.
dyeing [ˈdaiiŋ], s. das Färben; Färbereigewerbe.
dyer [ˈdaiə], s. der Färber.
dying [ˈdaiiŋ], s. das Sterben; *the* —, (*pl.*) die Sterbenden, pl. — adj. sterbend.
dynamic [daiˈnæmik], adj. dynamisch.
dynamics [daiˈnæmiks], s. pl. die Dynamik.
dynamite [ˈdainəmait], s. das Dynamit.
dynamo [ˈdainəmou], s. der Dynamo, die Dynamomaschine.
dynasty [ˈdinəsti], s. die Dynastie.
dysentery [ˈdisəntri], s. (*Med.*) die Ruhr.
dyspepsia [disˈpepsiə], s. (*Med.*) der Magenverstimmung.
dyspeptic [disˈpeptik], adj. mit verstimmtem Magen; schlecht aufgelegt (*grumpy*).

E

E [i:]. das E (*also Mus.*); *E flat*, Es; *E sharp*, Eis; *E minor*, E-moll.

each [i:tʃ], *adj.*, *pron.* jeder, jede, jedes; — *other*, einander; — *one*, jeder einzelne.

eager ['i:gə], *adj.* eifrig, begierig.

eagerness ['i:gənis], *s.* der Eifer, die Begierde.

eagle [i:gl], *s.* (*Orn.*) der Adler; (*Am.*) das Zehndollarstück.

ear [iə], *s.* das Ohr; —*lap*, das Ohrläppchen; —*phones*, die Kopfhörer; — *piece*, die Hörmuschel; —*drum*, das Trommelfell; — *of corn*, die Ähre.

earl [ə:l], *s.* der Graf.

earldom ['ə:ldəm], *s.* die (englische) Grafschaft.

early ['ə:li], *adj.* früh, frühzeitig.

earmark ['iəmɑ:k], *v.a.* kennzeichnen, bezeichnen.

earn [ə:n], *v.a.* verdienen; erwerben.

earnest ['ə:nist], *s.* der Ernst; der ernste Beweis, das Handgeld; (*Comm.*) die Anzahlung; (*fig.*) der Vorgeschmack. — *adj.* ernst, ernsthaft.

earnings ['ə:niŋz], *s.* das Einkommen.

earshot ['iəʃɔt], *s.* die Hörweite.

earth [ə:θ], *s.* die Erde; der Erdboden (*soil*); der Fuchsbau (*of fox*); *down to* —, praktisch denkend; *move heaven and* —, alles daransetzen; *where on* —, wo in aller Welt.

earthen ['ə:θən], *adj.* irden, aus Erde; —*ware*, das Steingut.

earthquake ['ə:θkweik], *s.* das Erdbeben.

earthly ['ə:θli], *adj.* irdisch.

earthworm ['ə:θwə:m], *s.* (*Zool.*) der Regenwurm.

earthy ['ə:θi], *adj.* erdig; irdisch.

earwig ['iəwig], *s.* (*Ent.*) der Ohrwurm.

ease [i:z], *s.* die Leichtigkeit (*facility*); die Bequemlichkeit (*comfort*); *feel at* —, sich wie zu Hause fühlen; (*Mil.*) *stand at* —! rührt euch! *ill at* —, unbehaglich. — *v.a.* erleichtern, leichter machen; lindern (*pain*). — *v.n.* — *off*, (*Mil.*) sich auflockern.

easel [i:zl], *s.* das Gestell; die Staffelei.

easiness ['i:zinis], *s.* die Leichtigkeit, die Ungezwungenheit.

east [i:st], *adj.*, *adv.* Ost-, ostwärts (*direction*). — *s.* der Osten, der Orient.

Easter ['i:stə]. das *or* (*n. or f. pl.*) die Ostern.

eastern ['i:stən], *adj.* östlich; morgenländisch, orientalisch (*oriental*).

easy ['i:zi], *adj.* leicht, frei; — *chair*, der Lehnstuhl, Sessel; *stand* —! rührt Euch! *take it* —, nimm's nicht so ernst; es sich (*Dat.*) bequem machen (*make o.s. comfortable*); (*Comm.*) — *terms*, Zahlungserleichterungen; —*going*, gemütlich.

eat [i:t], *v.a.*, *v.n.* irr. essen, speisen (*dine*); fressen (*of animals*); — *humble pie*, sich demütigen; — *o.'s hat*, einen Besen fressen; — *o.'s words* seine Worte bereuen.

eatable ['i:təbl], *adj.* genießbar, eßbar.

eaves [i:vz], *s. pl.* die Dachrinne, die Traufe.

eavesdrop ['i:vzdrɔp], *v.n.* belauschen (*on s.o., Acc.*).

eavesdropper ['i:vzdrɔpə], *s.* der Lauscher.

ebb [eb], *s.* die Ebbe. — *v.n.* nachlassen, abebben, abfließen.

ebonize ['ebənaiz], *v.a.* wie Ebenholz *or* schwarz beizen.

ebony ['ebəni], *s.* das Ebenholz.

ebullient [i'bʌljənt], *adj.* aufwallend.

eccentric [ik'sentrik], *adj.* exzentrisch, überspannt, wunderlich.

eccentricity [eksen'trisiti], *s.* die Exzentrizität, die Überspanntheit.

ecclesiastic [ikli:zi'æstik], *s.* der Geistliche. — *adj.* (*also* -**ical**) geistlich, kirchlich.

echo ['ekou], *s.* das Echo, der Widerhall. — *v.a.*, *v.n.* widerhallen (*resound*); wiederholen (*repeat*).

eclectic [i'klektik], *adj.* eklektisch. — *s.* der Eklektiker.

eclecticism [i'klektisizm], *s.* (*Phil.*) der Eklektizismus.

eclipse [i'klips], *s.* die Verfinsterung, Finsternis (*darkness*); die Verdunklung (*darkening*). — *v.a.* verdunkeln.

ecliptic [i'kliptik], *s.* die Ekliptik, die Sonnenbahn.

economic [i:kə'nɔmik], *adj.* ökonomisch, wirtschaftlich.

economical [i:kə'nɔmikl], *adj.* (*frugal*) sparsam, wirtschaftlich.

economics [i:kə'nɔmiks], *s.* (*pl.*) die Wirtschaftslehre, die Ökonomie.

economist [i'kɔnəmist], *s.* der Ökonom der Wirtschaftsfachmann.

economize [i'kɔnəmaiz], *v.n.* sparen (*on*, mit, *Dat.*); sparsam sein mit (*Dat.*).

economy [i'kɔnəmi], *s.* die Wirtschaft; *political* —, die Nationalökonomie, Staatswirtschaftslehre.

ecstasy ['ekstəsi], *s.* die Ekstase, die Entzückung, die Verzückung.

ecstatic [iks'tætik], *adj.* ekstatisch, verzückt; entzückt (*delighted*).

Ecuadorean [ekwə'dɔ:riən], *adj.* ekuadorianisch. — *n.* der Ekuadorianer.

ecumenical [i:kju'menikəl], *adj.* ökumenisch.

eddy ['edi], *s.* der Wirbel, Strudel. — *v.n.* wirbeln.

edge [edʒ], *s.* die Schärfe, die Schneide (*blade*); die Kante (*ledge*); der Rand (*brink*); der Saum (*border*); die Ecke (*corner*); der Schnitt (*book*); die Schärfe (*wit, keenness*); *put an* — *on*, schärfen; *be on* —, nervös sein. — *v.a.* besetzen (*decorate*); umgeben; *double*— *d*, zweischneidig; *two*— *d*, zweischneidig, zweikantig; — *d with lace*, mit Spitze eingefaßt. — *v.n.* sich bewegen; — *forward*, langsam vorrücken; — *off*, sich abseits halten, sich drücken; — *away from*, abrücken.

edgy ['edʒi], *adj.* kantig, eckig; (*fig.*) nervös, reizbar.

edible ['edibl], *adj.* eßbar.

edict

edict ['i:dikt], *s.* die Verordnung.
edification [edifi'keiʃən], *s.* die Erbauung.
edifice ['edifis], *s.* der Bau, das Gebäude.
edify ['edifai], *v.a.* erbauen.
edit ['edit], *v.a.* herausgeben (*book etc.*).
edition [i'diʃən], *s.* die Ausgabe.
editor ['editə], *s.* der Herausgeber, der Schriftleiter; (*newspaper*) der Redakteur.
editorial [edi'tɔ:riəl], *adj.* Redaktions-. — *s.* der Leitartikel.
editorship ['editəʃip], *s.* die Redaktion; die Schriftleitung.
educate ['edjukeit], *v.a.* erziehen, (heran)bilden.
education [edju'keiʃən], *s.* die Erziehung (*upbringing*); die Bildung (*general culture*); das Bildungswesen, das Schulwesen (*educational system*); *primary* —, die Grundschulung, das Volksschulwesen; *secondary* —, das Mittelschulwesen, das höhere Schulwesen; *university* —, das Hochschulwesen (*system*), die Universitätsbildung (*of individual*); *local* — *authority*, das Schulamt, die Schulbehörde; *Professor of Education*, Professor der Pädagogik; *further* —, *adult* —, weitere Ausbildung, Erwachsenenbildung.
educational [edju'keiʃənəl], *adj.* erzieherisch (*educative*); Bildungs-, Unterrichts- (*for education*); — *attainment*, der Bildungsgrad, die Schulstufe (*grade*); — *facilities*, die Lehrmittel, Bildungs- or Schulungsmöglichkeiten, *f. pl.*
education(al)ist [edju'keiʃən(əl)ist], *s.* der Erzieher, der Pädagoge; der Erziehungsfachmann (*theorist*).
eel [i:l], *s.* (*Zool.*) der Aal.
eerie ['iəri], *adj.* gespenstisch, unheimlich.
efface [i'feis], *v.a.* auslöschen, austilgen.
effacement [i'feismənt], *s.* die Austilgung; *self-* —, die Selbstaufopferung.
effect [i'fekt], *s.* die Wirkung; die Folge, das Ergebnis (*consequence*); der Eindruck (*impression*); *of no* —, ohne jede Wirkung; *carry into* —, ausführen; *take* — *from*, vom . . . in Kraft treten. — *v.a.* bewirken (*bring about*).
effective [i'fektiv], *adj.* wirksam (*having an effect*); gültig (*in force*); dienstfähig (*usable*); wirklich (*actual*).
effectual [i'fektjuəl], *adj.* wirksam (*effective*); kräftig, energisch (*strong*).
effectuate [i'fektjueit], *v.a.* bewerkstelligen (*get done*); bewirken (*bring about*).
effeminacy [i'feminəsi], *s.* die Verweichlichung.
effeminate [i'feminit], *adj.* weichlich, verweichlicht.
effervescence [efə'vesəns], *s.* das Aufbrausen, Schäumen.
effervescent [efə'vesənt], *adj.* aufbrausend, aufschäumend.

effete [i'fi:t], *adj.* abgenutzt, erschöpft.
efficacious [efi'keiʃəs], *adj.* wirksam. energisch.
efficacy ['efikəsi], *s.* die Wirksamkeit, die Energie.
efficiency [i'fiʃənsi], *s.* die Tüchtigkeit (*of person*); die Wirksamkeit; die Leistung.
efficient [i'fiʃənt], *adj.* tüchtig; leistungsfähig; wirksam (*drug etc.*).
effigy ['efidʒi], *s.* das Bild, das Abbild.
efflorescent [eflɔ:'resənt], *adj.* aufblühend.
effluent ['efluənt], *adj.* ausfließend.
effluvium [i'flu:viəm], *s.* die Ausdünstung.
effort ['efət], *s.* die Anstrengung, die Bemühung; *make an* —, sich bemühen, sich anstrengen; *make every* —, alle Kräfte anspannen.
effrontery [i'frʌntəri], *s.* die Frechheit (*cheek*); die Unverschämtheit (*impertinence*).
effortless ['efətlis], *adj.* mühelos.
effulgence [i'fʌldʒəns], *s.* der Glanz, das Strahlen.
effulgent [i'fʌldʒənt], *adj.* schimmernd, strahlend.
effusion [i'fju:ʒən], *s.* die Ausgießung; der Erguß (*verse etc.*); der Überschwang.
effusive [i'fju:ziv], *adj.* überschwenglich.
egg [eg], *s.* das Ei; *fried* —, das Spiegelei; *scrambled* —, das Rührei; — *flip*, der Eierpunsch; —*shell*, die Eierschale. — *v.a.* — *on*, anspornen, anreizen.
eglantine ['egləntain], *s.* (*Bot.*) die wilde Rose.
egoism ['egouizm], *s.* der Egoismus.
ego(t)ist ['ego(t)ist], *s.* der Egoist.
egregious [i'gri:dʒəs], *adj.* ungeheuer(lich).
egress ['i:gres], *s.* der Ausgang, der Ausfluß (*water etc.*).
Egyptian [i'dʒipʃən], *adj.* ägyptisch. — *s.* der Ägypter.
eiderdown ['aidədaun], *s.* die Daunendecke, Steppdecke.
eiderduck ['aidədʌk], *s.* (*Orn.*) die Eidergans.
eight [eit], *num. adj.* acht.
eighteen [ei'ti:n], *num. adj.* achtzehn.
eighty ['eiti], *num. adj.* achtzig.
either ['aiðə], *adj.*, *pron.* einer von beiden. — *conj.* entweder (*or*, oder).
ejaculate [i'dʒækjuleit], *v.a.*, *v.n.* ausstoßen.
eject [i'dʒekt], *v.a.* hinauswerfen; ausstoßen.
ejection [i'dʒekʃən], *s.* die Ausstoßung.
eke [i:k], *v.a.* — *out*, verlängern, ergänzen; — *out an existence*, ein spärliches Auskommen finden.
elaborate [i'læbəreit], *v.a.* ausarbeiten, im einzelnen ausarbeiten. — [-rit], *adj.* detailliert, ausgearbeitet; kunstvoll (*intricate*); umständlich (*involved*).

elaboration [ilæbə'reiʃən], s. die Ausarbeitung (im einzelnen); die Detailarbeit.

elapse [i'læps], v.n. verstreichen, verfließen (time).

elastic [i'læstik], adj. elastisch. — s. das Gummiband.

elasticity [elæs'tisiti], s. (Phys.) die Elastizität.

elate [i'leit], v.a. stolz machen; ermutigen.

elated [i'leitid], adj. in gehobener Stimmung.

elation [i'leiʃən], s. der Stolz; die Begeisterung.

elbow ['elbou], s. (Anat.) der Ellenbogen; at o.'s —, bei der Hand; — room, der Spielraum. — v.a. — o.'s way through, sich durchdrängen.

elder (1) ['eldə], comp. adj. älter. — s. der Alte, der Älteste; Kirchenälteste.

elder (2) ['eldə], s. (Bot.) der Holunder.

elderly ['eldəli], adj. älter; alt; ältlich.

elect [i'lekt], v.a. erwählen (to, zu, Dat.); auswählen (choose). — adj. erwählt, auserwählt; chairman —, der gewählte Vorsitzende.

election [i'lekʃən], s. die Auswahl (selection); (Pol.) die Wahlen, f. pl.; die Wahl (choice); by(e) —, die Bezirkswahl, die Neuwahl; — broadcast, eine Radiowahlrede.

electioneering [ilekʃən'iəriŋ], s. das Wahlmanöver, die Wahlpropaganda, der Wahlkampf.

elective [i'lektiv], adj. durch Wahl bestimmt; Wahl-.

elector [i'lektə], s. (Pol.) der Wähler; das Mitglied eines Wahlausschusses (academic etc.); der Kurfürst (prince).

electorate [i'lektərit], s. die Wählerschaft.

electress [i'lektrəs], s. die Kurfürstin (princess).

electric(al) [i'lektrik(əl)], adj. elektrisch; electrical engineer, der Elektrotechniker; der Student der Elektrotechnik (trainee); electric switch, der elektrische Schalter; — razor, der elektrische Rasierapparat.

electrician [elek'triʃən], s. der Elektriker.

electricity [ilek- or elek'trisiti], s. die Elektrizität.

electrocution [ilektro'kjuːʃən], s. die Hinrichtung or der Unfall (accidental) durch Elektrizität.

electron [i'lektrɔn], s. das Elektron.

electroplate [i'lektropleit], v.a. galvanisch versilbern.

electrotype [i'lektrotaip], s. der galvanische Abdruck, die Galvanographie.

elegance ['eligəns], s. die Eleganz.

elegant ['eligənt], adj. elegant, fein.

elegy ['elidʒi], s. (Lit.) die Elegie.

element ['elimənt], s. das Element; der Bestandteil (component).

elemental [eli'mentl], adj. elementar.

elementary [eli'mentri], adj. einfach (simple); elementar (for beginners).

elephant ['elifənt], s. (Zool.) der Elefant.

elevate ['eliveit], v.a. erheben, erhöhen.

elevation [eli'veiʃən], s. die Erhebung (lifting); (Geom.) die Elevation; die Erhöhung (rise); der Aufriß (Engin. drawing).

elevator ['eliveitə], s. (Am.) der Lift, der Aufzug, der Fahrstuhl; (Agr.) der Getreideheber.

eleven [i'levn], num. adj. elf.

elf [elf], s. der Elf, der Kobold.

elfin ['elfin], adj. Elfen-, elfenhaft.

elicit [i'lisit], v.a. herauslocken, entlocken.

eligibility [elidʒi'biliti], s. die Wählbarkeit.

eligible ['elidʒibl], adj. wählbar, passend.

eliminate [i'limineit], v.a. ausschalten, ausscheiden, eliminieren.

elimination [ilimi'neiʃən], s. die Ausschaltung, die Ausscheidung.

elision [i'liʒən], s. (Phonet.) die Auslassung, die Weglassung.

elixir [i'liksə], s. das Elixier.

elk [elk], s. (Zool.) der Elch.

ell [el], s. die Elle.

ellipse [i'lips], s. (Geom.) die Ellipse.

ellipsis [i'lipsis], s. (Gram.) die Ellipse.

elliptic(al) [i'liptik(əl)], adj. (Gram., Geom.) elliptisch.

elm [elm], s. (Bot.) die Ulme.

elocution [elə'kjuːʃən], s. der Vortrag (delivery); die Vortragskunst.

elocutionist [elə'kjuːʃənist], s. der Vortragskünstler.

elongate ['iːlɔŋgeit], v.a. verlängern.

elongation [iːlɔŋ'geiʃən], s. die Verlängerung.

elope [i'loup], v.n. entlaufen, von zu Hause fliehen.

elopement [i'loupmənt], s. das Entlaufen, die Flucht von zu Hause.

eloquence ['eləkwəns], s. die Beredsamkeit.

eloquent ['eləkwənt], adj. beredt, redegewandt.

else [els], adv. sonst, außerdem, anders; or —, sonst . . . ; how —? wie denn sonst? nobody —, sonst niemand; anyone —? sonst noch jemand? — conj. sonst.

elsewhere [els'weə], adv. anderswo; anderswohin.

Elsinore ['elsinɔː]. Helsingör, n.

elucidate [i'ljuːsideit], v.a. erläutern, erklären (to s.o., Dat.).

elucidation [iljuːsi'deiʃən], s. die Erläuterung, die Erklärung.

elude [i'ljuːd], v.a. ausweichen, entgehen (Dat.).

elusive [i'ljuːsiv], adj. schwer faßbar, täuschend.

Elysian [i'lizian], adj. elysisch.

emaciate [i'meiʃieit], v.a. abmagern, dünn werden.

emaciation [imeiʃi'eiʃən], s. die Abmagerung.

emanate ['emǝneit], v.n. ausgehen, herrühren (derive); ausstrahlen (radiate).

emancipate [i'mænsipeit], v.a. befreien, emanzipieren.

emancipation [imænsi'peiʃǝn], s. die Emanzipation.

embalm [im'bɑ:m], v.a. einbalsamieren.

embankment [im'bæŋkmǝnt], s. der Flußdamm, der Eisenbahndamm; die Eindämmung.

embarcation see **embarkation**.

embargo [im'bɑ:gou], s. die Handelssperre.

embark [im'bɑ:k], v.a. einschiffen. — v.n. sich einschiffen; — upon s.th., an etwas herangehen, unternehmen.

embarkation [embɑ:'keiʃǝn], s. die Einschiffung.

embarrass [im'bærǝs], v.a. verlegen machen, in Verlegenheit bringen.

embarrassment [im'bærǝsmǝnt], s. die Verlegenheit.

embassy ['embǝsi], s. (Pol.) die Botschaft, die Gesandtschaft.

embed [im'bed], v.a. einbetten.

embellish [im'beliʃ], v.a. verschönern, ausschmücken; ausmalen (story).

embers ['embǝz], s. pl. die glühende Asche; die Kohlen, f. pl.; Ember Days, (Eccl.) die Quatembertage, m. pl.

embezzle [im'bezl], v.a. veruntreuen, unterschlagen.

embitter [im'bitǝ], v.a. verbittern.

emblazon [im'bleizn], v.a. ausmalen, auf ein Schild setzen.

emblem ['emblǝm], s. das Emblem, das Abzeichen.

emblematic(al) [emblǝ'mætik(ǝl)], adj. sinnbildlich, symbolisch.

embodiment [im'bɔdimǝnt], s. die Verkörperung.

embody [im'bɔdi], v.a. verkörpern.

embolden [im'bouldn], v.a. erkühnen, anfeuern, anspornen; be emboldened, sich erkühnen.

emboss [im'bɔs], v.a. in getriebener Arbeit verfertigen, prägen.

embossed [im'bɔst], adj. getrieben, in erhabener Arbeit; gestanzt.

embrace [im'breis], v.a. (fig.) umarmen, umfassen. — s. die Umarmung.

embrasure [im'breiʒǝ], s. die Schießscharte.

embrocation [embro'keiʃǝn], s. die Einreibung (act); (Pharm.) die Einreibsalbe.

embroider [im'brɔidǝ], v.a. sticken; verzieren, ausschmücken (adorn).

embroidery [im'brɔidǝri], s. die Stickerei; die Verzierung, Ausschmückung (of story etc.).

embroil [im'brɔil], v.a. verwickeln.

embryo ['embriou], s. der Keim; Embryo.

embryonic [embri'ɔnik], adj. im Embryostadium, im Werden.

emend [i'mend], v.a. verbessern (text), berichtigen.

emendation [i:men'deiʃǝn], s. die Textverbesserung.

emendator ['i:mendeitǝ], s. der Berichtiger.

emerald ['emǝrǝld], s. der Smaragd.

emerge [i'mǝ:dʒ], v.n. auftauchen, hervortreten, an den Tag kommen.

emergence [i'mǝ:dʒǝns], s. das Auftauchen, das Hervortreten.

emergency [i'mǝ:dʒǝnsi], s. der Notfall; die kritische Lage; in case of —, im Notfalle; — exit, der Notausgang; — landing, die Notlandung; — measures, Notmaßnahmen; — brake, die Notbremse.

emery ['emǝri], s. — paper, das Schmirgelpapier.

emetic [i'metik], s. das Brechmittel.

emigrant ['emigrǝnt], s. der Auswanderer.

emigrate ['emigreit], v.n. auswandern.

emigration [emi'greiʃǝn], s. die Auswanderung.

eminence ['eminǝns], s. die Anhöhe; die Eminenz, der hohe Ruf (fame); die eminente Stellung, die Autorität (authority); Your Eminence, Eure Eminenz.

eminent ['eminǝnt], adj. eminent, hervorragend.

emissary ['emisǝri], s. der Abgesandte, der Sendbote.

emission [i'miʃǝn], s. die Aussendung (sending out); die Ausstrahlung (radiation).

emit [i'mit], v.a. aussenden; ausstrahlen; ausströmen.

emolument [i'mɔljumǝnt], s. das (Neben)einkommen, das Zusatzgehalt, das Honorar (fee).

emotion [i'mouʃǝn], s. die Rührung, die Bewegung, das Gefühl, die Gemütsbewegung.

emotional [i'mouʃǝnǝl], adj. gefühlvoll.

emperor ['empǝrǝ], s. der Kaiser.

emphasis ['emfǝsis], s. der Nachdruck.

emphasize ['emfǝsaiz], v.a. betonen.

empire ['empaiǝ], s. das Reich, das Kaiserreich.

empiric(al) [emp'irik(ǝl)], adj. (Phil.) empirisch.

empiricism [em'pirisizm], s. (Phil.) der Empirizismus.

employ [im'plɔi], v.a. benutzen (thing); beschäftigen, anstellen (person).

employee [im'plɔii:], s. der Angestellte.

employer [im'plɔiǝ], s. der Arbeitgeber.

employment [im'plɔimǝnt], s. die Beschäftigung, die Arbeit.

emporium [em'pɔ:riǝm], s. der Handelsplatz; (Naut.) der Stapelplatz; das Warenhaus (stores).

empower [em'pauǝ], v.a. bevollmächtigen.

empress ['empres], s. die Kaiserin.

emptiness ['emptinis], s. die Leere, die Öde.

empty ['empti], adj. leer; — -headed, geistlos.

emulate ['emjuleit], *v.a.* nacheifern (*Dat.*).

emulation [emju'leiʃən], *s.* der Wetteifer, das Nacheifern.

emulous ['emjuləs], *adj.* nacheifernd, wetteifernd; eifersüchtig (*jealous*).

emulsion [i'mʌlʃən], *s.* (*Pharm.*) die Emulsion.

enable [i'neibl], *v.a.* befähigen; ermächtigen (*empower*).

enact [i'nækt], *v.a.* (*Pol.*) verordnen; verfügen (*order*); darstellen, aufführen (*on stage*).

enactment [i'næktmənt], *s.* die Verordnung.

enamel [i'næml], *v.a.* emaillieren. — *s.* die Emaille; (*Med.*) der Schmelz.

enamour [i'næmə], *v.a.* verliebt machen.

encamp [in'kæmp], *v.n.* (sich) lagern, das Lager aufschlagen.

encampment [in'kæmpmənt], *s.* das Lager.

encase [in'keis], *v.a.* einschließen, in ein Gehäuse schließen.

encashment [in'kæʃmənt], *s.* (*Comm.*) das Inkasso, die Einkassierung.

enchain [in'tʃein], *v.a.* in Ketten legen, anketten.

enchant [in'tʃɑ:nt], *v.a.* bezaubern.

enchantment [in'tʃɑ:mənt], *s.* die Bezauberung; der Zauber (*spell*).

encircle [in'sə:kl], *v.a.* umringen, umkreisen; (*Mil.*) einkreisen.

encirclement [in'sə:klmənt], *s.* die Einkreisung.

enclose [in'klouz], *v.a.* einschließen; einlegen (*in letter*).

enclosure [in'klouʒə], *s.* die Einfriedigung; die Beilage, Einlage (*in letter*).

encompass [in'kʌmpəs], *v.a.* umfassen, umspannen (*comprise*).

encore ['ɔnkɔ:, ɔn'kɔ:], *int.* noch einmal! — *s.* die Wiederholung, Zugabe.

encounter [in'kauntə], *v.a.* treffen, begegnen (*Dat.*). — *s.* das Zusammenmentreffen.

encourage [in'kʌridʒ], *v.a.* ermutigen; anspornen.

encouragement [in'kʌridʒmənt], *s.* die Ermutigung; die Förderung (*promotion*).

encroach [in'kroutʃ], *v.n.* eingreifen (*interfere*); übergreifen.

encroachment [in'kroutʃmənt], *s.* der Eingriff, der Übergriff.

encrust [in'krʌst], *v.a.* inkrustieren; verkrusten.

encumber [in'kʌmbə], *v.a.* belasten.

encumbrance [in'kʌmbrəns], *s.* die Belastung, das Hindernis.

encyclical [en'siklikl], *s.* das (päpstliche) Rundschreiben, die Enzyklika.

encylopaedia [insaiklo'pi:djə], *s.* das Lexikon, die Enzyklopädie.

encyclopaedic [insaiklo'pi:dik], *adj.* enzyklopädisch.

end [end], *s.* das Ende; der Schluß; das Ziel (*aim*); die Absicht (*intention*); *in the —,* am Ende, letzten Endes; *to*

that —, zu dem Zweck; *put an — to,* einer Sache ein Ende machen; *make —s meet,* sein Auskommen finden; *burn the candle at both —s,* seine Kräfte verschwenden. — *v.a.* beenden. — *v.n.* enden, Schluß machen.

ending ['endiŋ], *s.* das Ende (*of play etc.*); (*Gram.*) die Endung.

endanger [in'deindʒə], *v.a.* gefährden, in Gefahr bringen.

endear [in'diə], *v.a.* beliebt machen. — *v.r.* — *o.s. to,* sich lieb Kind machen bei.

endearment [in'diəmənt], *s. term of —,* ein Kosewort.

endeavour [in'devə], *v.n.* sich bemühen, sich bestreben. — *s.* das Streben, die Bestrebung, die Bemühung.

endemic(al) [en'demik(əl)], *adj.* einheimisch; endemisch.

endive ['endiv], *s.* (*Bot.*) die Endivie.

endless ['endlis], *adj.* unendlich, endlos.

endorse [in'dɔ:s], *v.a.* bestätigen (*confirm*); beipflichten; (*Fin.*) indossieren (*cheque*).

endorsement [in'dɔ:smənt], *s.* die Bestätigung (*confirmation*); (*Fin.*) das Indossament (*cheque*).

endow [en'dau], *v.a.* begaben (*talents*); ausstatten (*equip*); stiften.

endowment [en'daumənt], *s.* die Begabung (*talents*); die Stiftung; — *policy,* die abgekürzte Lebensversicherung.

endurable [in'djuərəbl], *adj.* erträglich.

endurance [in'djuərəns], *s.* die Ausdauer (*toughness*); die Dauer, Fortdauer (*time*); das Ertragen (*suffering*); — *test,* die Dauerprüfung; (*fig.*) die Geduldsprobe (*patience*).

endure [in'djuə], *v.a.* aushalten, ertragen; leiden (*suffer*).

endways, endwise ['endweiz, -waiz], *advs.* mit dem Ende nach vorne; aufrecht (*vertical*).

enemy ['enəmi], *s.* der Feind, der Gegner.

energetic [enə'dʒetik], *adj.* energisch, tatkräftig.

energy ['enədʒi], *s.* die Energie, die Tatkraft; der Nachdruck (*vehemence*).

enervate ['enə:veit], *v.a.* entkräften, schwächen.

enervation [enə:'veiʃən], *s.* die Entkräftigung, die Schwächung.

enfeeble [in'fi:bl], *v.a.* entkräften, schwächen.

enfold [in'fould], *v.a.* umschließen, umfassen; einhüllen (*veil*).

enforce [in'fɔ:s], *v.a.* erzwingen, durchsetzen.

enforcement [in'fɔ:smənt], *s.* die Erzwingung, die Durchsetzung.

enfranchise [in'fræntʃaiz], *v.a.* freilassen, befreien (*emancipate*); (*Pol.*) das Stimmrecht geben.

enfranchisement [in'fræntʃizmənt], *s.* die Befreiung, die Gewährung des Stimmrechts.

engage [in'geidʒ], v.a. verpflichten, engagieren (pledge, bind); anstellen (employ); verwickeln (in conversation); become —d, sich verloben. — v.n. — in, sich einlassen in (Acc.), sich befassen mit (Dat.).

engagement [in'geidʒmənt], s. die Verpflichtung (pledge); die Verlobung (betrothal); die Verabredung (appointment); das Gefecht (with enemy).

engaging [in'geidʒiŋ], adj. freundlich, verbindlich (smile etc.); einnehmend.

engender [in'dʒendə], v.a. erzeugen, hervorrufen (cause).

engine [endʒin], s. die Maschine; der Motor; (Railw.) die Lokomotive; fire —, die Feuerspritze; — driver, (Railw.) der Lokomotivführer.

engineer [endʒi'niə], s. der Ingenieur (professional); der Techniker (technician); (Am.) der Lokomotivführer (engine driver).

engineering [endʒi'niəriŋ], s. das Ingenieurwesen; der Maschinenbau; chemical —, die chemische Technik or Technologie; civil —, das Zivilingenieurwesen; electrical —, die Elektrotechnik or die Elektrotechnologie; mechanical —, der Maschinenbau, die Strukturtechnik; — laboratory, das technische Labor; — workshop, die technische Werkstatt.

English ['iŋgliʃ], adj. englisch; britisch. — s. die englische Sprache, das Englisch; (pl.) the —, die Engländer, m. pl.

Englishman ['iŋgliʃmən], s. der Engländer.

Englishwoman ['iŋgliʃwumən], s. die Engländerin.

engrain [in'grein], v.a. tief einprägen.

engrave [in'greiv], v.a. gravieren, eingravieren (art); einprägen (impress).

engraver [in'greivə], s. der Graveur, der Kupferstecher.

engraving [in'greiviŋ], s. der Kupferstich.

engross [in'grous], v.a. ganz in Anspruch nehmen, gefangen halten (mind).

engulf [in'gʌlf], v.a. verschlingen.

enhance [in'haːns], v.a. erhöhen (raise); steigern (increase).

enhancement [in'haːnsmənt], s. die Erhöhung (pleasure); die Steigerung (growth).

enigma [i'nigmə], s. das Rätsel.

enigmatic(al) [enig'mætik(əl)], adj. rätselhaft (puzzling); dunkel (obscure).

enjoin [in'dʒɔin], v.a. (an)befehlen (s.o., Dat.), einschärfen (s.o., Dat.).

enjoy [in'dʒɔi], v.a. genießen (Acc.); sich freuen (über, Acc.). — v.r. — o.s., sich amüsieren.

enjoyable [in'dʒɔiəbl], adj. erfreulich, angenehm, genießbar.

enjoyment [in'dʒɔimənt], s. der Genuß, die Freude (of, an, Dat.).

enlarge [in'laːdʒ], v.a. vergrößern (premises etc.); erweitern (expand). —

v.n. sich verbreiten (on or upon, über, Acc.).

enlargement [in'laːdʒmənt], s. die Vergrößerung (also Phot.).

enlighten [in'laitn], v.a. erleuchten, aufklären (explain to).

enlightenment [in'laitnmənt], s. (Eccl.) die Erleuchtung; (Phil.) die Aufklärung.

enlist [in'list], v.a. anwerben (Mil.); gewinnen (cooperation). — v.n. (Mil.) sich anwerben lassen.

enliven [in'laivn], v.a. beleben, aufmuntern.

enmity ['enmiti], s. die Feindschaft.

ennoble [i'noubl], v.a. adeln; veredeln.

enormity [i'nɔːmiti], s. die Ungeheuerlichkeit.

enormous [i'nɔːməs], adj. ungeheuer; ungeheuerlich.

enough [i'nʌf], adj., adv. genug; ausreichend; sure —, gewiß!; well —, ziemlich gut.

enquire see under **inquire**.

enquiry see under **inquiry**.

enrage [in'reidʒ], v.a. wütend machen.

enraged [in'reidʒd], adj. wütend, entrüstet.

enrapture [in'ræptʃə], v.a. in Entzückung versetzen, entzücken (delight).

enrich [in'ritʃ], v.a. bereichern; (Chem.) verbessern.

enrol [in'roul], v.a. einschreiben (inscribe); (Mil.) anwerben. — v.n. sich einschreiben; beitreten (Dat.).

enrolment [in'roulmənt], s. die Einschreibung; — form, das Einschreibeformular.

ensconce [in'skɔns], v.r. — o.s., sich niederlassen.

enshrine [in'ʃrain], v.a. umhüllen, einschließen; in einem Schrein aufbewahren.

enshroud [in'ʃraud], v.a. einhüllen.

ensign ['ensin or 'enzən, 'ensain], s. (Naut.) die Fahne, die Flagge; (Mil. rank) der Fähnrich.

enslave [in'sleiv], v.a. unterjochen, versklaven.

ensnare [in'snɛə], v.a. umgarnen, verführen (seduce).

ensue [in'sjuː], v.n. folgen.

ensure [in'ʃuə], v.a. versichern (assure); sicherstellen (make sure).

entail [in'teil], v.a. zur Folge haben, mit sich bringen.

entangle [in'tæŋgl], v.a. verwickeln, verwirren (confuse).

ntanglement [in'tæŋglmənt], s. die Verwicklung; die Verwirrung (confusion).

enter ['entə], v.a. betreten; eintreten; — o.'s name, seinen Namen einschreiben. — v.n. eintreten (in, in, Acc.); — into agreement, einen Vertrag eingehen; — on, sich einlassen in (Acc.); — upon a career, eine Laufbahn antreten.

enterprise ['entəpraiz], s. das Unternehmen; das Wagnis (daring); private —, das Privatunternehmen; (Econ.)

die freie Wirtschaft; *public —*, das staatliche *or* Staatsunternehmen.

enterprising ['entəpraiziŋ], *adj.* unternehmungslustig.

entertain [entə'tein], *v.a.* unterhalten (*amuse*); zu Tisch haben (*person*); hegen (*opinion*).

entertaining [entə'teiniŋ], *adj.* amüsant, unterhaltend.

entertainment [entə'teinmənt], *s.* die Unterhaltung, Vergnügung.

enthral [in'θrɔːl], *v.a.* fesseln, bannen.

enthrone [in'θroun], *v.a.* auf den Thron bringen *or* setzen.

enthusiasm [in'θjuːziæzm], *s.* die Begeisterung; die Schwärmerei.

enthusiast [in'θjuːziæst], *s.* der Enthusiast, der Schwärmer.

enthusiastic [inθjuːzi'æstik], *adj.* enthusiastisch, begeistert, schwärmerisch.

entice [in'tais], *v.a.* locken, anlocken, verlocken (*lure*).

enticement [in'taismənt], *s.* die Lockung.

entire [in'taiə], *adj.* gesamt, ganz; völlig; vollständig (*complete*).

entirety [in'taiəriti], *s.* die Gesamtheit (*totality*); das Ganze (*total*).

entitle [in'taitl], *v.a.* berechtigen; betiteln (*title*).

entitlement [in'taitlmənt], *s.* die Berechtigung.

entity ['entiti], *s.* das Wesen.

entomb [in'tuːm], *v.a.* begraben.

entomologist [entə'mɔlədʒist], *s.* der Entomologe.

entomology [entə'mɔlədʒi], *s.* die Entomologie.

entrails ['entreilz], *s. pl.* die Eingeweide, *n.pl.*

entrain [in'trein], *v.a.* (*Railw., Mil.*) einsteigen lassen. — *v.n.* (*Railw.*) (in den Zug) einsteigen.

entrance (1) ['entrəns], *s.* der Eingang (*door*); — *fee*, der Eintritt; — *hall*, der Hausflur, die Vorhalle; *university* —, Zulassung zur Universität.

entrance (2) [in'trɑːns], *v.a.* entzücken, hinreißen.

entrant ['entrənt], *s.* (*to school, university etc.*) der (neu) Zugelassene; Teilnehmer.

entrap [in'træp], *v.a.* fangen, verstricken.

entreat [in'triːt], *v.a.* anflehen, ersuchen.

entreaty [in'triːti], *s.* die flehentliche *or* dringende Bitte, (*obs.*) das Ansuchen.

entrench [in'trentʃ], *v.a.* verschanzen, festsetzen.

entrenchment [in'trentʃmənt], *s.* (*Mil.*) die Verschanzung.

entrust [in'trʌst], *v.a.* anvertrauen (*s. th.*); betreuen (*s.o. with*, mit, *Dat.*).

entry ['entri], *s.* das Eintreten, der Eintritt; der Eingang (*house*); (*Comm.*) die Eintragung (*book-keeping*); *double* —, doppelte Buchführung; die Einfuhr (*import*); — *permit*, die

Einreisebewilligung; *no —*, Eintritt verboten!

entwine [in'twain], *v.a.* verflechten, herumwickeln.

enumerate [i'njuːməreit], *v.a.* aufzählen.

enumeration [injuːmə'reiʃən], *s.* die Aufzählung.

enunciate [i'nʌnsieit], *v.a.* aussprechen.

enunciation [inʌnsi'eiʃən], *s.* (*Phonet.*) die Aussprache; die Kundgebung (*declaration*).

envelop [in'veləp], *v.a.* einhüllen, umhüllen.

envelope ['enviloup, 'ɔnvəloup], *s.* die Hülle; der Umschlag, Briefumschlag (*letter*).

enviable ['enviəbl], *adj.* beneidenswert.

envious ['enviəs], *adj.* neidisch (*of s.o.*, auf, *Acc.*).

environment [in'vaiərənmənt], *s.* die Umgebung; (*Geog., Zool.*) die Umwelt.

environs [in'vaiərənz], *s. pl.* die Umgebung, die Umgegend.

envisage [in'vizidʒ], *v.a.* sich vorstellen.

envoy ['envɔi], *s.* (*Pol.*) der Gesandte, der Bote.

envy ['envi], *s.* der Neid. — *v.a.* beneiden.

epaulette [epɔ:'let], *s.* (*Mil.*) das Achselstück, die Epaulette.

ephemeral [i'femərəl], *adj.* Eintags-, Tages-; eintägig, vergänglich (*transient*).

epic ['epik], *adj.* episch. — *s.* das Epos.

epicure ['epikjuə], *s.* der Epikureer, der Feinschmecker, der Genießer.

epidemic [epi'demik], *s.* die Epidemie.

epigram ['epigræm], *s.* das Epigramm.

epigrammatic [epigrə'mætik], *adj.* epigrammatisch, kurz; treffend (*apt*).

epilepsy ['epilepsi], *s.* (*Med.*) die Epilepsie, die Fallsucht.

epileptik [epi'leptik], *s.* (*Med.*) der Epileptiker.

epilogue ['epilɔg], *s.* der Epilog.

Epiphany [i'pifəni]. (*Eccl.*) das Fest der heiligen drei Könige, Epiphanias.

episcopal [i'piskəpəl], *adj.* bischöflich.

episcopate [i'piskəpit], *s.* die Bischofswürde, das Episkopat (*collective*).

episode ['episoud], *s.* die Episode.

epistle [i'pisl], *s.* die Epistel, das Sendschreiben.

epistolary [i'pistələri], *adj.* brieflich, Brief-.

epitaph ['epitɑːf], *s.* die Grabschrift.

epithet ['epiθet], *s.* das Beiwort, die Benennung.

epitome [i'pitəmi], *s.* die Epitome, der Auszug; der Abriß (*summary*).

epitomize [i'pitəmaiz], *v.a.* kürzen; einen Auszug machen von (*Dat.*).

epoch ['iːpɔk], *s.* die Epoche; — *-making*, bahnbrechend.

equable ['ekwəbl], *adj.* gleich, gleichmäßig; gleichmütig (*tranquil*).

equal ['iːkwəl], *adj.* gleich, ebenbürtig (*to, Dat.*).

equality [i'kwɔliti], *s.* die Gleichheit, Ebenbürtigkeit.

equalization [i:kwəlai'zeiʃən], *s.* der Ausgleich; — *of burdens,* der Lastenausgleich.

equalize ['i:kwəlaiz], *v.a.* gleichmachen. — *v.n.* (*Footb.*) ausgleichen.

equanimity [i:kwə'nimiti], *s.* der Gleichmut.

equate [i'kweit], *v.a.* (*Maths.*) gleichsetzen.

equation [i'kweiʃən], *s.* die Gleichung.

equator [i'kweitə], *s.* (*Geog.*)der Äquator.

equatorial [ekwə'tɔːriəl], *adj.* (*Geog.*) äquatorial.

equerry ['ekwəri], *s.* der Stallmeister; diensttuender Kammerherr (*of King*).

equestrian [i'kwestriən], *adj.* beritten; Reit-; — *art,* die Reitkunst.

equidistant [i:kwi'distənt], *adj.* gleich weit entfernt.

equilateral [i:kwi'lætərəl], *adj.* gleichseitig.

equilibrium [i:kwi'libriəm], *s.* das Gleichgewicht.

equine ['i:kwain], *adj.* Pferd-, pferdeartig.

equinoctial [i:kwi'nɔkʃəl], *adj.* äquinoktial.

equinox ['i:kwinɔks], *s.* die Tag- und Nachtgleiche.

equip [i'kwip], *v.a.* (*Mil.*) ausrüsten; ausstatten (*furnish*).

equipment [i'kwipmənt], *s.* die Ausrüstung, die Ausstattung; das Zeug.

equitable ['ekwitəbl], *adj.* unparteiisch, gerecht, billig.

equity ['ekwiti], *s.* die Billigkeit, die Unparteilichkeit.

equivalence [i'kwivələns], *s.* die Gleichwertigkeit, die Gleichheit.

equivalent [i'kwivələnt], *adj.* gleichwertig. — *s.* das Äquivalent, der gleiche Wert, der Gegenwert.

equivocal [i'kwivəkəl], *adj.* zweideutig, doppelsinnig, zweifelhaft.

era ['iərə], *s.* die Ära, die Zeitrechnung.

eradicate [i'rædikeit], *v.a.* ausrotten, austilgen, vertilgen.

eradication [irædi'keiʃən], *s.* die Ausrottung, die Vertilgung.

erase [i'reiz], *v.a.* ausradieren.

eraser [i'reizə], *s.* der Radiergummi (*India rubber*).

erasure [i'reiʒə], *s.* die Ausradierung; die Auskratzung (*scratching*).

ere [ɛə], *prep.* (*obs.*) vor. — *conj.* (*obs.*) ehe, bevor.

erect [i'rekt], *adj.* aufrecht, gerade. — *v.a.* aufrichten; errichten (*build*).

erection [i'rekʃən], *s.* die Errichtung (*structure*); die Aufrichtung (*putting up*).

ermine ['əːmin], *s.* der *or* das Hermelin.

erode [i'roud], *v.a.* (*Geog., Geol.*) ausfressen.

erosion [i'rouʒən], *s.* die Erosion.

erotic [i'rɔtik], *adj.* erotisch.

err [əː], *v.n.* irren.

errand ['erənd], *s.* der Auftrag, Gang;

der Botengang; — *boy,* der Laufbursche.

errant ['erənt], *adj.* herumstreifend; *knight* —, fahrender Ritter.

errata *see under* **erratum**.

erratic [i'rætik], *adj.* regellos, unberechenbar, ohne Verlaß.

erratum [e'reitəm, e'rɑːtəm], *s.* (*pl.* **errata** [e'reitə, e'rɑːtə]) der Druckfehler.

erroneous [i'rouniəs], *adj.* irrig, irrtümlich.

error ['erə], *s.* der Irrtum, der Fehler.

erudite ['erudait], *adj.* gelehrt.

erudition [eru'diʃən], *s.* die Gelehrsamkeit.

erupt [i'rʌpt], *v.n.* ausbrechen.

eruption [i'rʌpʃən], *s.* der Ausbruch.

eruptive [i'rʌptiv], *adj.* Ausbruchs-, ausbrechend.

escalator ['eskəleitə], *s.* die Rolltreppe.

escapade [eskə'peid], *s.* der Streich (*prank*).

escape [is'keip], *v.a.*, *v.n.* entkommen, entgehen, entfliehen.

escapism [is'keipizm], *s.* die Philosophie der Weltflucht.

escapist [is'keipist], *s.* der Weltflüchtling.

escarpment [is'kɑːpmənt], *s.* die Böschung.

eschew [is'tʃuː], *v.a.* vermeiden.

escort [is'kɔːt], *v.a.* geleiten; decken (*cover*). — ['eskɔːt], *s.* (*Mil.*) die Garde, die Deckung; Begleitung (*persons*); (*Mil.*) das Geleit (*conduct*).

escutcheon [is'kʌtʃən], *s.* das Wappenschild.

esoteric [eso'terik], *adj.* (*Phil.*) esoterisch, geheim, dunkel.

espalier [es'pæljə], *s.* (*Mil.*) das Spalier.

especial [is'peʃəl], *adj.* besonder, außergewöhnlich.

espionage ['espiənɑːʒ *or* -nidʒ], *s.* die Spionage, das Spionieren.

espouse [is'pauz], *v.a.* (ver)-heiraten; (*fig.*) eintreten (für, *Acc.*).

espy [is'pai], *v.a.* ausspähen, erspähen.

essay [e'sei], *v.a.* versuchen, probieren. — ['esei], *s.* der Versuch; der Aufsatz, Essay (*composition*).

essayist ['eseiist], *s.* der Essayist.

essence ['esəns], *s.* (*Phil., Chem.*) die Essenz.

essential [i'senʃəl], *adj.* wesentlich; wichtig (*important*).

establish [is'tæbliʃ], *v.a.* feststellen, (*ascertain*); gründen (*found*); —*ed Church,* die englische Staatskirche.

establishment [is'tæbliʃmənt], *s.* die Feststellung (*ascertainment*); die Gründung (*foundation*); die Unternehmung, das Geschäft (*business*); (*Mil.*) die Aufstellung, der Bestand; (*Eccl.*) die Staatskirche.

estate [is'teit], *s.* (*Pol.*) der Stand; das Vermögen; das Gut; (*property*) — *duty,* die Vermögenssteuer; — *manager,* der Gutsverwalter; — *agent,* der

Grundstückmakler; *real* —, der Grundbesitz; (*pl.*) Immobilien, *pl.*

esteem [is'ti:m], *v.a.* schätzen (*value*); achten (*respect*). — *s.* die Wertschätzung, die Achtung.

estimable ['estimabl], *adj.* schätzenswert.

estimate ['estimeit], *v.a.* schätzen (*evaluate*); berechnen (*calculate*). — ['estimit], *s.* die Schätzung, der Voranschlag.

estimation [esti'meiʃən], *s.* die Wertschätzung; die Achtung (*respect*).

Estonian [es'tounian], *adj.* estnisch, estländisch. — *s.* der Este, Estländer.

estrange [is'treindʒ], *v.a.* entfremden.

estrangement [is'treindʒmənt], *s.* die Entfremdung.

estuary ['estjuari], *s.* die Mündung (*river*); der Meeresarm (*bay*).

etch [etʃ], *v.a.* (*Metall.*) ätzen; (*Art*) radieren.

etching ['etʃiŋ], *s.* (*Art*) die Radierung.

eternal [i'tə:nl], *adj.* ewig; immerwährend.

eternity [i'tə:niti], *s.* die Ewigkeit.

ether ['i:θə], *s.* der Äther.

ethereal [i'θiəriəl], *adj.* ätherisch, luftig.

ethical ['eθikl], *adj.* ethisch, sittlich.

ethics ['eθiks], *s. pl.* die Ethik, die Sittenlehre; *professional* —, das Berufsethos.

Ethiopian [i:θi'oupiən], *adj.* äthiopisch. — *s.* der Äthiopier.

ethnography [eθ'nɔgrəfi], *s.* die Ethnographie, die Völkerkunde.

etymology [eti'mɔlədʒi], *s.* die Etymologie, die Wortableitung.

eucharist ['ju:karist], *s.* (*Eccl.*) die Eucharistie; das heilige Abendmahl.

eulogize ['ju:lədʒaiz], *v.a.* loben, preisen.

euphonium [ju'founiəm], *s.* (*Mus.*) das Bombardon, Baritonhorn.

euphony ['ju:fəni], *s.* der Wohlklang.

European [juərə'piən], *adj.* europäisch. — *s.* der Europäer.

euphemism ['ju:fimizm], *s.* der Euphemismus.

euphuism ['ju:fjuizm], *s.* (*Lit.*) die gezierte Stilart.

evacuate [i'vækjueit], *v.a.* evakuieren, räumen.

evacuation [ivækju'eiʃən], *s.* die Evakuierung, die Räumung.

evade [i'veid], *v.a.* ausweichen (*Dat.*); entgehen (*escape, Dat.*).

evanescent [evæ'nesənt], *adj.* verschwindend.

evangelical [i:væn'dʒelikəl], *adj.* evangelisch.

evangelist [i'vændʒəlist], *s.* der Evangelist.

evangelize [i'vændʒəlaiz], *v.a., v.n.* das Evangelium lehren *or* predigen.

evaporate [i'væpəreit], *v.a.* verdunsten lassen, verdampfen lassen. — *v.n.* (*Chem.*) verdunsten.

evaporation [ivæpə'reiʃən], *s.* die Verdampfung, die Verdunstung.

evasion [i'veiʒən], *s.* die Flucht (*escape*) (*from, von, Dat.*); die Ausflucht, das Ausweichen.

evasive [i'veiziv], *adj.* ausweichend.

eve, even (1) [i:v,i:vn], *s.* (*Poet.*) der Vorabend; Abend.

even (2) [i:vn], *adj.* eben, glatt (*smooth*); gerade (*number*); quitt (*quits*); gelassen (*temper*); gleich (*equal*). — *v.a.* — *out*, gleichmachen, ebnen.

even (3) [i:vn], *adv.* gerade, selbst, sogar (*emphatic*); *not* —, nicht einmal; — *though*, obwohl.

evening ['i:vniŋ], *s.* der Abend; — *gown*, das Abendkleid; — *dress*, der Abendanzug; der Smoking (*dinner jacket*); der Frack (*tails*).

evenness ['i:vənnis], *s.* die Ebenheit (*of surface*); die Gelassenheit (*of temper*).

event [i'vent], *s.* die Begebenheit, der Vorfall (*happening*); das (große) Ereignis (*state occasion*); *at all* —*s*, auf alle Fälle; *in the* —, im Falle, daß.

eventful [i'ventful], *adj.* ereignisreich.

eventual [i'ventjuəl], *adj.* schließlich, endlich.

ever ['evə], *adv.* je; immer, stets; nur, überhaupt; *for* —, für immer; — *so*, so sehr, sehr; — *since*, seitdem.

evergreen ['evəgri:n], *adj.* immergrün. —*s.* (*Bot.*) das Immergrün.

everlasting [evə'la:stiŋ], *adj.* ewig; dauernd; fortwährend (*continual*).

every ['evri], *adj.* jeder, jeder einzelne (*pl.* alle); — *one*, jeder einzelne; — *now and then*, dann und wann; — *other day*, jeden zweiten Tag; — *day*, alle Tage.

everybody, everyone ['evribɔdi, 'evriwʌn], *s.* jedermann, ein jeder.

everyday ['evridei], *adj.* alltäglich.

everyone *see under* **everybody**.

everything ['evriθiŋ], *s.* alles.

everywhere ['evrihwɛə], *adv.* überall.

evict [i'vikt], *v.a.* vertreiben (*eject*); (*Law*) (gerichtlich) kündigen (*Dat.*).

eviction [i'vikʃən], *s.* die Kündigung, die Vertreibung.

evidence ['evidəns], *s.* der Beweis (*proof*); (*Law*) das Zeugnis; *documentary* —, (*Law*) das Beweisstück; (*Law*) *give* —, eine Zeugenaussage machen.

evident ['evidənt], *adj.* klar, deutlich (*obvious*); augenscheinlich (*visible*); *self-* —, selbstverständlich.

evil ['i:vil], *s.* das Übel, das Böse. — *adj.* übel, böse; — *speaking*, die üble Nachrede.

evildoer ['i:vildu:ə], *s.* der Übeltäter.

evince [i'vins], *v.a.* zeigen, dartun, an den Tag legen.

evocation [i:vo'keiʃən], *s.* die Beschwörung (*magic*), das Hervorrufen.

evocative [i'vɔkətiv], *adj.* hervorrufend, voll Erinnerungen (*of, Genit.*).

evoke [i'vouk], *v.a.* hervorrufen (*call forth*); beschwören (*conjure up*).

evolution [i:və'lju:ʃən, ev–], *s.* die Entwicklung, Evolution.

evolutionary

evolutionary [i:və'lju:ʃənri], *adj.* Evolutions-, Entwicklungs-.
evolve [i'vɔlv], *v.a.* entwickeln. — *v.n.* sich entwickeln.
ewe [ju:], *s.* (*Zool.*) das Mutterschaf.
ewer ('juə], *s.* die Wasserkanne.
exact [ig'zækt], *adj.* genau, gewissenhaft, exakt. — *v.a.* fordern; erpressen; eintreiben (*dept.*).
exacting [ig'zæktiŋ], *adj.* genau, anspruchsvoll.
exactitude [ig'zæktitju:d], *s.* die Genauigkeit.
exactly [ig'zæktli], *adv.* (*coll.*) ganz richtig!
exactness [ig'zæktnis], *s.* die Genauigkeit.
exaggerate [ig'zædʒəreit], *v.a.* übertreiben.
exaggeration [igzædʒə'reiʃən], *s.* die Übertreibung.
exalt [ig'zɔ:lt], *v.a.* erhöhen, erheben.
exaltation [egzɔ:l'teiʃən], *s.* die Erhöhung, die Erhebung.
exalted [ig'zɔ:ltid], *adj.* erhaben, hoch.
examination [igzæmi'neiʃən], *s.* die Prüfung; (*Med.*) die Untersuchung; (*Law*) das Verhör, das Untersuchungsverhör; die Ausfragung (*scrutiny*); — *board*, die Prüfungskommission.
examine [ig'zæmin], *v.a.* prüfen; (*Med.*) untersuchen; (*Law*) verhören; ausfragen.
examiner [ig'zæminə], *s.* der Examinator.
example [ig'zɑ:mpl], *s.* das Beispiel; *for* —, zum Beispiel; *set an* —, ein Beispiel geben.
exasperate [ig'zæspəreit], *v.a.* aufreizen; ärgern, aufbringen.
exasperation [igzæspə'reiʃən], *s.* die Entrüstung, die Erbitterung.
excavate ['ekskəveit], *v.a.* ausgraben.
excavation [ekskə'veiʃən], *s.* die Ausgrabung.
exceed [ik'si:d], *v.a.* überschreiten (*go beyond*); übertreffen (*surpass*). — *v.n.* zu weit gehen.
exceeding [ik'si:diŋ], *adj.* (*obs.*) übermäßig, übertrieben.
exceedingly [ik'si:diŋli], *adv.* außerordentlich; äußerst.
excel [ik'sel], *v.a.* übertreffen. — *v.n.* sich auszeichnen (*in*, in, *Dat.*).
excellence ['eksələns], *s.* die Vortrefflichkeit.
excellent ['eksələnt], *adj.* ausgezeichnet, hervorragend.
except [ik'sept], *v.a.* ausnehmen, ausschließen. — *conj.* außer (es sei denn) daß. — *prep.* ausgenommen, mit Ausnahme von (*Dat.*).
exception [ik'sepʃən], *s.* die Ausnahme (*exemption*); der Einwand, Einwurf (*objection*).
exceptionable [ik'sepʃənəbl], *adj.* anfechtbar (*disputable*); anstößig.
exceptional [ik'sepʃənəl], *adj.* außergewöhnlich.

exceptionally [ik'sepʃənəli], *adv.* ausnahmsweise.
excerpt [ik'sə:pt], *v.a.* ausziehen, exzerpieren. — ['eksə:pt], *s.* der Auszug, das Exzerpt.
excess [ik'ses], *s.* das Übermaß; *carry to* —, übertreiben; — *fare*, der Zuschlag; — *luggage*, das Übergewicht.
excessive [ik'sesiv], *adj.* übermäßig, allzuviel.
exchange [iks'tʃeindʒ], *s.* der Austausch; *stock* —, die Börse; *rate of* —, der Kurs; *bill of* —, der Wechsel; der Tausch (*barter*). — *v.a.* wechseln; tauschen (*barter*) (*against*, für, *Acc.*); austauschen (*messages etc.*).
exchangeable [iks'tʃeindʒəbl], *adj.* (*Comm.*) austauschbar.
exchequer [iks'tʃekə], *s.* die Staatskasse; das Finanzamt (*office*); *Chancellor of the Exchequer*, der Schatzkanzler.
excise (1) ['eksaiz], *s.* die Aksize; *customs and* —, das Zollamt, der Zoll; — *officer*, der Zollbeamte, Steuerbeamte.
excise (2) [ek'saiz], *v.a.* (her)ausschneiden.
excision [ek'siʒən], *s.* das Ausschneiden, die Entfernung.
excitable [ik'saitəbl], *adj.* erregbar, reizbar.
excitation [eksi'teiʃən], *s.* (*Phys.*, *Chem.*) die Erregung.
excitement [ik'saitmənt], *s.* die Erregung, Aufregung (*mood*).
exciting [ik'saitiŋ], *adj.* erregend, aufregend, packend (*thrilling*).
exclaim [iks'kleim], *v.a.* ausrufen.
exclamation [ekskla'meiʃən], *s.* der Ausruf (*interjection*); das Geschrei (*shouting*).
exclude [iks'klu:d], *v.a.* ausschließen.
exclusion [iks'klu:ʒən], *s.* der Ausschluß.
exclusive [iks'klu:siv], *adj.* ausschließlich (*sole*); exklusiv (*select*).
exclusiveness [iks'klu:sivnis], *s.* der exklusive Charakter, die Exklusivität.
excommunicate [ekskə'mju:nikeit], *v.a.* (*Eccl.*) von der Kirchengemeinde ausschließen, bannen, exkommunizieren.
excommunication [ekskəmju:ni'keiʃən], *s.* (*Eccl.*) die Exkommunikation, der Bann.
excoriate [eks'kɔ:rieit], *v.a.* häuten; abschälen (*peel*).
excrement ['ekskrimənt], *s.* das Exkrement, der Kot.
excrescence [iks'kresəns], *s.* der Auswuchs.
excretion [eks'kri:ʃən], *s.* die Ausscheidung, der Auswurf.
excruciate [iks'kru:ʃieit], *v.a.* martern, peinigen; *excruciatingly funny*, furchtbar komisch.
exculpate ['ekskʌlpeit], *v.a.* rechtfertigen, entschuldigen.

exculpation [ekskʌl'peiʃən], s. die Entschuldigung, die Rechtfertigung.

excursion [iks'kə:ʃən], s. der Ausflug, die Exkursion (*outing*); die Digression (*irrelevance*); der Abstecher (*deviation*).

excusable [iks'kju:zəbl], adj. entschuldbar, verzeihlich.

excuse [iks'kju:s], s. die Entschuldigung. — [-'kju:z], v.a. entschuldigen (*Acc.*), verzeihen (*Dat.*).

execrable ['eksikrəbl], adj. abscheulich.

execrate ['eksikreit], v.a. verfluchen, verwünschen.

execute ['eksikju:t], v.a. ausführen (*carry out*); (*Law*) hinrichten (*kill*).

execution [eksi'kju:ʃən], s. die Ausführung (*of an order*); (*Law*) die Hinrichtung; die Pfändung (*official forfeit*).

executioner [eksi'kju:ʃənə], s. der Henker, der Scharfrichter.

executive [ik'sekjutiv], adj. ausübend, vollziehend (*of power etc.*). — s. (*Pol.*) die Exekutive; (*Comm.*) das Direktionsmitglied.

executor [ik'sekjutə], s. der Testamentsvollstrecker (*of a will*).

exemplar [ig'zemplə], s. das Muster, das Beispiel.

exemplary [ig'zempləri], adj. musterhaft, vorbildlich.

exemplify [ig'zemplifai], v.a. durch Beispiel(e) erläutern.

exempt [ig'zempt], v.a. ausnehmen, befreien, verschonen (*spare*).

exemption [ig'zempʃən], s. die Ausnahme.

exequies ['eksikwiz], s. pl. das Leichenbegängnis, die Totenfeier.

exercise ['eksəsaiz], s. die Übung (*practice*); die körperliche Betätigung (*exertion*). — v.a. üben; — o.'s rights, von seinen Rechten Gebrauch machen; — discretion, Diskretion walten lassen; (*Mil.*) — troops, exerzieren.

exert [ig'zə:t], v.a. ausüben; — pressure, Druck ausüben (*upon*, auf, *Acc.*). — v.r. — o.s., sich anstrengen.

exertion [ig'zə:ʃən], s. die Anstrengung, die Bemühung.

exhale [eks'heil], v.a. ausatmen; aushauchen; ausdünsten.

exhalation [eksha'leiʃən], s. die Ausatmung, die Ausdünstung.

exhaust [ig'zɔ:st], v.a. erschöpfen. — s. (*Motor.*) der Auspuff.

exhaustible [ig'zɔ:stibl], adj. erschöpflich.

exhaustion [ig'zɔ:stʃən], s. die Erschöpfung.

exhibit [ig'zibit], v.a. ausstellen (*display*); zeigen (*demonstrate*). — ['eksibit], s. das Ausstellungsobjekt; (*Law*) das Beweisstück.

exhibition [eksi'biʃən], s. die Ausstellung (*display*); (*Films*) die Vorführung (*showing*); das Stipendium (*scholarship*).

exhibitioner [eksi'biʃənə], s. der Stipendiat.

exhilarate [ig'ziləreit], v.a. aufheitern.

exhila.ation [igzilə'reiʃən], s. die Aufheiterung.

exhort [ig'zɔ:t], v.a. ermahnen.

exhortation [egzɔ:'teiʃən], s. die Ermahnung.

exigence, exigency ['eksidʒəns, -si], s. das Bedürfnis, Erfordernis (*necessity*); der dringende Notfall (*emergency*).

exigent ['eksidʒənt], adj. dringend.

exile ['eksail], s. der Verbannte (*person*); das Exil, die Verbannung (*state*). — v.a. verbannen; des Landes verweisen.

exist [ig'zist], v.n. existieren.

existence [ig'zistəns], s. das Dasein, die Existenz.

existent [ig'zistənt], adj. seiend, wirklich, existierend.

existentialism [egzis'tenʃəlizm], s. der Existentialismus.

exit ['eksit], s. der Ausgang; (*Theat.*) der Abgang.

exonerate [ig'zɔnəreit], v.a. entlasten.

exorbitant [ig'zɔ:bitənt], adj. übertrieben, übermäßig.

exorcise ['eksɔ:saiz], v.a. bannen, beschwören.

exorcism ['eksɔ:sizm], s. die Geisterbeschwörung.

exotic [ig'zɔtik], adj. exotisch.

expand [iks'pænd], v.a. erweitern, ausbreiten, ausdehnen. — v.n. sich erweitern (*broaden*); sich ausdehnen (*stretch*).

expansion [iks'pænʃən], s. die Ausdehnung, die Ausbreitung.

expansive [iks'pænsiv], adj. ausgedehnt; Ausdehnungs- (*forces*); (*fig.*) mitteilsam.

expatiate [iks'peiʃieit], v.n. sich verbreiten (*on*, über, *Acc.*).

expatriate [eks'peitrieit], v.a. verbannen.

expect [iks'pekt], v.a. erwarten (*wait for*); glauben (*believe*); hoffen (*hope for*); — a baby, ein Kind erwarten.

expectant [iks'pektənt], adj. schwanger (*with child*); voll Erwartung.

expectation [ekspek'teiʃən], s. die Erwartung, die Hoffnung.

expedience, expediency [iks'pi:diəns, -si], s. die Zweckmäßigkeit, die Schicklichkeit.

expedient [iks'pi:diənt], adj. zweckmäßig, schicklich, ratsam. — s. das Mittel; der Ausweg.

expedite ['ekspidait], v.a. beschleunigen.

expedition [ekspi'diʃən], s. (*Mil. etc.*) die Expedition; die schnelle Abfertigung.

expeditious [ekspi'diʃəs], adj. schleunig, schnell.

expel [iks'pel], v.a. vertreiben, austreiben; (*Sch.*) verweisen (*from*, von, aus).

expend [iks'pend], v.a. ausgeben.

expenditure [iks'penditʃə], s. (*Comm.*) die Ausgabe; der Aufwand (*of energy*).

expense

expense [iks'pens], *s.* die Ausgabe; (*pl.*) die Kosten, Auslagen, Spesen, *f. pl.*

expensive [iks'pensiv], *adj.* teuer, kostspielig.

experience [iks'piəriəns], *s.* die Erfahrung, das Erlebnis. — *v.a.* erfahren.

experienced [iks'piəriənsd], *adj.* erfahren.

experiment [iks'perimənt], *s.* das Experiment, der Versuch. — *v.n.* experimentieren, Versuche machen.

experimental [iksperi'mentl], *adj.* Probe-, probeweise, experimentell.

expert ['ekspə:t], *s.* der Fachmann; der Sachverständige.

expertise [ekspə'ti:z], *s.* die Expertise, die Fachkenntnis.

expertness [iks'pə:tnis], *s.* die Gewandtheit.

expiable ['ekspiəbl], *adj.* sühnbar.

expiation [ekspi'eiʃən], *s.* die Sühnung, die Sühne.

expiration [ekspi'reiʃən], *s.* das Ausatmen; (*fig.*) der Tod; der Ablauf (*time*); die Verfallszeit (*lapse of validity*).

expire [iks'paiə], *v.n.* aushauchen (*breathe*); ablaufen (*run out*); sterben (*die*).

expiry [iks'pairi], *s.* die Ablaufsfrist (*of papers*).

explain [iks'plein], *v.a.* erklären, erläutern.

explanation [eksplə'neiʃən], *s.* die Erklärung, Erläuterung.

expletive [iks'pli:tiv], *s.* das Fluchwort, der Kraftausdruck.

explicable ['eksplikəbl], *adj.* erklärlich, erklärbar.

explication [ekspli'keiʃən], *s.* die Erklärung.

explicit [iks'plisit], *adj.* ausdrücklich, deutlich.

explicitness [iks'plisitnis], *s.* die Deutlichkeit, die Bestimmtheit.

explode [iks'ploud], *v.n.* explodieren; (*Mil.*) platzen (*of a shell*). — *v.a.* explodieren lassen.

exploit [iks'plɔit], *v.a.* ausbeuten; ausnützen (*utilize*). — ['eksplɔit], *s.* die Heldentat, die Großtat.

exploitation [eksplɔi'teiʃən], *s.* die Ausbeutung, die Ausnützung.

exploration [eksplɔ:'reiʃən], *s.* die Erforschung.

explore [iks'plɔ:], *v.a.* erforschen, untersuchen (*investigate*).

explosion [iks'plouʒən], *s.* die Explosion.

explosive [iks'plousiv], *adj.* explosiv. — *s.* der Sprengstoff.

exponent [iks'pounənt], *s.* (*Maths.*) der Exponent; der Vertreter (*of a theory*).

export [eks'pɔ:t], *v.a.* ausführen, exportieren. — ['ekspɔ:t], *s.* der Export, die Ausfuhr.

exporter [eks'pɔ:tə], *s.* der Exporteur, der Ausfuhrhändler, der Exportkaufmann.

expose [iks'pouz], *v.a.* entblößen; aussetzen (*to cold etc.*); bloßstellen (*display*); (*Phot.*) belichten; darlegen (*set forth*); ausstellen (*exhibit*).

exposition [ekspo'ziʃən], *s.* die Aussetzung; die Auslegung (*interpretation*); die Darlegung (*deposition, declaration*); die Ausstellung (*exhibition*).

exposure [iks'pouʒə], *s.* die Aussetzung (*to cold etc.*); die Bloßstellung; (*Phot.*) die Belichtung.

expostulate [iks'pɔstjuleit], *v.n.* zur Rede stellen.

expound [iks'paund], *v.a.* auslegen, darlegen.

express [iks'pres], *v.a.* ausdrücken; zum Ausdruck bringen. — *adj.* ausdrücklich, eilig, Eil-; besonder; — *letter*, der Eilbrief; — *train*, der Schnellzug. — *s.* der Eilzug.

expression [iks'preʃən], *s.* der Ausdruck.

expressive [iks'presiv], *adj.* ausdrucksvoll.

expressly [iks'presli], *adv.* ausdrücklich, besonders.

expropriate [eks'prouprieit], *v.a.* enteignen.

expropriation [eksproupri'eiʃən], *s.* die Enteignung.

expulsion [iks'pʌlʃən], *s.* die Ausstoßung; der Ausschluß; die Vertreibung (*of a large number*).

expunge [iks'pʌndʒ], *v.a.* austilgen, auslöschen.

expurgate ['ekspə:geit], *v.a.* reinigen.

exquisite ['ekskwizit], *adj.* auserlesen, vortrefflich.

extant ['ekstənt, ek'stænt], *adj.* noch vorhanden, existierend.

extempore [eks'tempəri], *adv.* aus dem Stegreif, extemporiert.

extemporize [eks'tempəraiz], *v.a.* extemporieren, improvisieren.

extend [iks'tend], *v.a.* ausdehnen (*boundaries etc.*); ausstrecken (*a helping hand*); verlängern (*time*); bieten (*a welcome*); erweitern (*enlarge*). — *v.n.* sich erstrecken, sich ausdehnen; dauern (*time*).

extensible [iks'tensibl], *adj.* ausdehnbar.

extension [iks'tenʃən], *s.* die Ausdehnung; die Verlängerung (*time*); *university — classes*, Abendkurse, *m.pl.* (der Erwachsenenbildung); (*Telephone*) der Apparat.

extensive [iks'tensiv], *adj.* ausgedehnt, umfassend.

extent [iks'tent], *s.* die Ausdehnung, die Weite; die Größe (*size*); *to a certain —*, bis zu einem gewissen Grade; *to the — of £x*, bis zu einem Betrage von x Pfund.

extenuate [iks'tenjueit], *v.a.* beschönigen; mildern; *extenuating circumstances*, (*Law*) mildernde Umstände, *m. pl.*

extenuation [ikstenju'eiʃən], *s.* die Beschönigung, die Abschwächung.

exterior [eks'tiəriə], *adj.* äußerlich. — *s.* das Äußere.

exterminate [iks'tə:mineit], *v.a.* ausrotten, vertilgen.

extermination [ikstə:mi'neiʃən], *s.* die Ausrottung, die Vertilgung.

external [eks'tə:nl], *adj.* äußerlich; auswärtig.

extinct [iks'tiŋkt], *adj.* ausgestorben.

extinction [iks'tiŋkʃən], *s.* das Erlöschen (*dying*); die Vernichtung (*annihilation*); das Aussterben.

extinguish [iks'tiŋgwiʃ], *v.a.* auslöschen; vernichten (*annihilate*). — *v.n.* auslöschen, ausgehen (*of fire or life*).

extirpate ['ekstə:peit], *v.a.* ausrotten.

extol [iks'toul], *v.a.* preisen, erheben.

extort [iks'tə:t], *v.a.* erpressen.

extortion [iks'tə:ʃən], *s.* die Erpressung.

extortionate [iks'tə:ʃənit], *adj.* erpresserisch.

extra ['ekstrə], *adj.* zusätzlich. — *s.* (*pl.*) die Nebenausgaben, *f. pl.*

extract [iks'trækt], *v.a.* (aus)ziehen (*pull out*). — ['ekstrækt], *s.* (*Chem.*) der Extrakt; der Auszug (*book*).

extraction [iks'trækʃən], *s.* das Ausziehen (*pulling out*); das Zahnziehen (*tooth*); das Verfertigen eines Auszuges (*book*); die Herkunft (*origin*).

extradite ['ekstrədait], *v.a.* (*Pol.*) ausliefern.

extradition [ekstrə'diʃən], *s.* (*Pol.*) die Auslieferung.

extraneous [eks'treiniəs], *adj.* nicht zur Sache gehörig, unwesentlich.

extraordinary [iks'trə:dnəri], *adj.* außerordentlich.

extravagance [iks'trævəgəns], *s.* die Extravaganz, die Verschwendung (*waste*).

extravagant [iks'trævəgənt], *adj.* extravagant; verschwenderisch.

extravaganza [ikstrævə'gænzə], *s.* fantastisches Werk, die Burleske, Posse.

extreme [iks'tri:m], *adj.* äußerst (*uttermost*); höchst (*highest*); extrem (*stringent*); letzt (*last*); — *unction*, (*Eccl.*) die Letzte Ölung; *in the* —, äußerst.

extremity [iks'tremiti], *s.* die äußerste Grenze (*limit*); die Notlage (*straits*, *emergency*); (*pl.*) die Extremitäten, *f. pl.*

extricate ['ekstrikeit], *v.a.* herauswinden, herauswickeln (*disentangle*), befreien.

extrude [eks'tru:d], *v.a.* ausstoßen; (*Metall.*) ausziehen.

extrusion [eks'tru:ʒən], *s.* die Ausstoßung; die Ausziehung (*of steel etc.*).

exuberant [ig'zju:bərənt], *adj.* überschwenglich, überschäumend.

exude [ik'sju:d], *v.a.* ausschwitzen; von sich geben (*give out*).

exult [ig'zʌlt], *v.n.* frohlocken.

exultant [ig'zʌltənt], *adj.* triumphierend.

exultation [egzʌl'teiʃən], *s.* das Frohlocken, der Jubel.

eye [ai], *v.a.* ansehen, betrachten. — *s.* das Auge; — *of a needle*, das Nadelöhr; *an* — *for an* —, Aug' um Auge; — *witness*, der Augenzeuge.

eyeball ['aibɔ:l], *s.* der Augapfel.

eyebrow ['aibrau], *s.* die Augenbraue.

eyeglass ['aigla:s], *s.* der Zwicker, Klemmer.

eyelash ['ailæʃ], *s.* die Augenwimper.

eyelid ['ailid], *s.* das Augenlid.

eyesight ['aisait], *s.* die Sehkraft, das Augenlicht.

eyrie ['ɛəri, 'iəri], *s.* der Adlerhorst.

F

F [ef], das F (*also Mus.*).

fable [feibl], *s.* die Fabel; das Märchen.

fabric ['fæbrik], *s.* das Gewebe, der Stoff.

fabricate ['fæbrikeit], *v.a.* herstellen; (*fig.*) fabrizieren; erfinden.

fabrication [fæbri'keiʃən], *s.* (*fig.*) die Erdichtung, die Erfindung.

fabulous ['fæbjuləs], *adj.* fabelhaft; wunderbar.

façade [fə'sa:d], *s.* die Fassade.

face [feis], *v.a.* jemandem ins Gesicht sehen (*s.o.*); gegenüberstehen, gegenüberliegen (*lie opposite, Dat.*); — *west*, nach Westen gehen (*of house*, *window*). — *v.n.* — *about*, sich umdrehen. — *s.* das Gesicht, (*Poet.*) das Angesicht; — *to* — *with*, gegenüber (*Dat.*); *on the* — *of it*, auf den ersten Blick; *lose* —, sich blamieren; *have the* — *to*, die Frechheit haben etwas zu tun.

facet ['fæsit], *s.* die Facette; der Zug (*feature*).

facetious [fə'si:ʃəs], *adj.* scherzhaft.

facetiousness [fə'si:ʃəsnis], *s.* die Scherzhaftigkeit, die Witzigkeit.

facile [f'æsail], *adj.* leicht.

facilitate [fə'siliteit], *v.a.* erleichtern, leicht machen.

facility [fə'siliti], *s.* die Leichtigkeit (*ease*); die Gewandtheit (*deftness*); die Möglichkeit (*possibility*); (*pl.*) die Einrichtungen, die Möglichkeiten, *f. pl.* (*amenities*).

facing ['feisiŋ], *s.* (*Tail.*) der Besatz, der Aufschlag; (*Build.*) die Verkleidung; (*Mil.*) die Schwenkung, die Wendung.

facsimile [fæk'simili], *s.* das Faksimile.

fact [fækt], *s.* die Tatsache; *as a matter of* —, tatsächlich, in Wirklichkeit; —*s and figures*, der Bericht mit Tatsachen und Zahlen; *in* —, tatsächlich; *in point of* —, in der Tat, in Wirklichkeit.

faction ['fækʃən], *s.* (*Pol.*) die Partei, die Fraktion.

factitious [fæk'tiʃəs], *adj.* nachgemacht, künstlich.

factor ['fæktə], *s.* der Faktor; (*Comm.*) der Agent; der Umstand (*fact*).

factory

factory ['fæktəri], s. die Fabrik; — *hand*, der Fabrikarbeiter.
factual ['fæktjuəl], *adj.* Tatsachen-, tatsächlich.
faculty ['fækəlti], s. (*Univ.*) die Fakultät; die Fähigkeit (*sense*); (*pl.*) die Talente, *n. pl.*, die Begabung; Kräfte *f. pl.*
fad [fæd], s. die Grille, die Laune; die Marotte.
faddy ['fædi], *adj.* schrullig.
fade [feid], *v.n.* verschießen (*colour*); verwelken (*flower*); vergehen.
fag [fæg], *v.a.* ermüden. — *v.n.* (*Sch.*) Dienste tun, Diener sein (*for*, für). — *s.* die Plackerei; (*coll.*) die Zigarette; (*Sch.*) der Fuchs, der neue Schüler; — *end*, der Zigarettenstummel; (*Naut.*) das offene Tauende; der letze Rest (*remnant*).
faggot ['fægət], s. das Reisigbündel.
fail [feil], *v.a.* im Stiche lassen (*let down*); (*Sch.*) durchfallen (*an examination*, in einer Prüfung. — *v.n.* — *to do*, etwas nicht tun, fehlgehen, scheitern; versagen.
failing ['feiliŋ], *adj.* schwach, versagend. — *s.* der Mangel, Fehler.
failure ['feiljə], s. der Fehlschlag; das Versagen (*weakness*); das Nichteinhalten (*non-compliance*); das Durchfallen (*in examinations*); der Versager (*person*).
fain [fein], *adv.* (*obs.*) gern, gerne.
faint [feint], *v.n.* in Ohnmacht fallen, ohnmächtig werden. — *adj.* leise, schwach (*noise etc.*); — *hearted*, kleinmütig.
fair (1) [fɛə], *adj.* hübsch, schön (*beautiful*); unparteiisch, fair (*impartial*); anständig, angemessen (*equitable*); blond.
fair (2) [fɛə], s. der Jahrmarkt (*market*); (*Comm.*) die Messe, die Handelsmesse.
fairness ['fɛənis], s. die Schönheit (*beauty*); die Unparteilichkeit, Fairneß (*objectivity*); die Sportlichkeit (*sportsmanship*); die Anständigkeit (*equity*).
fairy ['fɛəri], s. die Fee.
faith [feiθ], s. der Glaube; die Treue (*loyalty*); das Vertrauen (*trust*).
faithful ['feiθful], *adj.* (*Rel.*) gläubig; treu (*loyal*); ergeben (*devoted*).
faithless ['feiθlis], *adj.* (*Rel.*) ungläubig; treulos, untreu (*disloyal*).
fake [feik], s. der Schwindel.
falcon ['fɔ:(l)kən], s. (*Orn.*) der Falke.
falconer ['fɔ:(l)knə], s. der Falkner.
falconry ['fɔ:(l)kənri], s. die Falknerei.
fall [fɔ:l], *v.n. irr.* fallen, abfallen (*leaves*); einbrechen (*night*); sich legen (*wind*); heruntergehen, sinken (*price*); geboren werden (*pigs, lambs*); — *through*, mißlingen, zunichte werden. — *s.* der Fall; (*Am.*) der Herbst (*autumn*); der Abhang (*precipice*); der Verfall(*decay*);der Untergang(*decline*).
fallacious [fə'leiʃəs], *adj.* trügerisch, trüglich, falsch (*assumption etc.*).

fallacy ['fæləsi], s. die Täuschung, der Irrtum, Trugschluß.
fallible ['fælibl], *adj.* fehlbar.
falling ['fɔ:liŋ], s. das Fallen; — *sickness*, die Fallsucht; — *off*, das Abnehmen (*decrease*); — *out*, der Zwist, der Streit (*disunity*). — *adj.* — *star*, die Sternschnuppe.
fallow ['fælou], *adj.* brach, fahl.
false [fɔ:ls], *adj.* falsch, unrichtig (*untrue*); — *alarm*, der blinde Alarm; — *bottom*, der Doppelboden; — *start*, der Fehlstart; — *step*, der Fehltritt; — *verdict*, das Fehlurteil; — *pretences*, die Vorspiegelung falscher Tatsachen.
falsehood ['fɔ:lshud], s. die Lüge, die Unwahrheit.
falseness ['fɔ:lsnis], s. die Falschheit; die Unaufrichtigkeit (*insincerity*).
falsify ['fɔ:lsifai], *v.a.* fälschen, verfälschen.
falsity ['fɔ:lsiti] *see* **falseness**.
falter ['fɔ:ltə], *v.n.* straucheln (*stumble*); stammeln (*stammer*).
fame [feim], s. der Ruhm; der Ruf; *ill* —, der üble Ruf.
familiar [fə'miljə], *adj.* vertraut, wohlbekannt, intim; gewohnt (*habitual*); *be on* — *terms*, auf vertrautem Fuß stehen.
familiarity [fəmili'æriti], s.die Vertrautheit, die Vertraulichkeit (*intimacy*).
familiarize [fə'miljəraiz], *v.a.* vertraut machen, bekannt machen.
family ['fæmili], s. die Familie; — *doctor*, der Hausarzt; (*Chem.*) die Gruppe; *be in the* — *way*, in anderen Umständen sein, guter Hoffnung sein, schwanger sein; — *tree*, der Stammbaum.
famine ['fæmin], s. die Hungersnot; — *relief*, Hilfe für die Hungernden.
famish ['fæmiʃ], *v.n.* verhungern, hungern; verschmachten.
famous ['feiməs], *adj.* berühmt, wohlbekannt (*for*, wegen).
fan [fæn], s. der Fächer (*lady's*); der Ventilator; (*sl.*) der leidenschaftliche Anhänger, der Fan; (*coll.*) Fanatiker (*admirer*). — *v.a.* fächeln; anfachen (*flames*); entfachen (*hatred*). — *v.n.* (*Mil.*) — *out*, sich ausbreiten, ausschwärmen.
fanatic [fə'nætik], s. der Fanatiker.
fanatical [fə'nætikəl], *adj.* fanatisch.
fanaticism [fə'nætisizm], s. der Fanatismus, die Schwärmerei.
fancier ['fænsiə], s. *pigeon* —, der Taubenzüchter; *bird* —, der Vogelzüchter.
fanciful ['fænsiful], *adj.* schwärmerisch, wunderlich.
fancy ['fænsi], s. die Vorliebe (*preference*); die Phantasie; die Laune (*whim*); *take a* — *to*, liebgewinnen. — *adj.* — *dress*, der Maskenanzug, das Kostüm; — *goods*, Galanteriewaren; — *cakes*, Torten, *f.pl.*; das Feingebäck. — *v.a.* denken, gern haben; (*coll.*) — *oneself as*, sich einbilden, man sei; *just* —!denk doch mal; denk mal an!

fanfare ['fænfɛə], s. (Mus.) die Fanfare, der Tusch.

fang [fæŋ], s. (Zool.) der Hauzahn, der Giftzahn (of snake); (Engin.) der Zapfen. — v.a. (Engin.) vollpumpen, aufpumpen und in Tätigkeit setzen.

fanlight ['fænlait], s. die Lünette, das Lichtfenster.

fantastic(al) [fæn'tæstik(əl)], adj. fantastisch.

fantasy ['fæntəsi], s. (Poet., Mus.) die Phantasie; das Hirngespinst (chimæra).

far [fɑ:], adj. weit; fern, entfernt (distant). — adv. — and wide, weit und breit; by —, bei weitem; go too —, zu weit gehen; he will go —, er wird seinen Weg machen; — sighted, weitsichtig.

farce [fɑ:s], s. die Farce, die Posse.

fare [fɛə], s. das Fahrgeld; der Fahrpreis (of taxi etc.); der Fahrgast (one travelling in taxi); — stage, die Fahror Teilstrecke; das Essen, die Kost (food); bill of —, die Speisekarte. — v.n. ergehen (Dat.), daran sein.

farewell [fɛə'wel], interj. lebewohl! — dinner, das Abschiedsessen; — party, die Abschiedsgesellschaft.

farinaceous [færi'neiʃəs], adj. mehlig, aus Mehl.

farm [fɑ:m], s. der Pachthof, der Bauernhof; die Farm; — hand, der Landarbeiter, der Farmarbeiter; — bailiff, der Gutsverwalter. — v.a. bebauen; — out, verpachten. — v.n. Landwirt sein.

farmer ['fɑ:mə], s. der Bauer, Landwirt; der Pächter (tenant).

farmland ['fɑ:mlænd], s. das Ackerland.

farmyard ['fɑ:mjɑ:d], s. der Bauernhof, Gutshof.

farrier ['færiə], s. der Hufschmied.

farrow ['færou], s. der Wurf (pigs). — v.n. ferkeln, Junge haben.

farther ['fɑ:ðə], comp. adj., adv. ferner, weiter.

farthest ['fɑ:ðist], superl. adj., adv. fernst, weitest.

farthing ['fɑ:ðiŋ], s. der Farthing, der Heller.

fascinate ['fæsineit], v.a. bezaubern, faszinieren.

fascination [fæsi'neiʃən], s. die Bezauberung; der Reiz; der Zauberbann (spell).

fascism ['fæʃizm], s. (Pol.) der Faschismus.

fashion ['fæʃən], s. die Mode; out of —, außer Mode; die Art und Weise (manner). — v.a. gestalten, bilden (shape); fully —ed, vollgeformt or geformt, angepaßt.

fashionable ['fæʃnəbl], adj. modisch, modern; elegant.

fast (1) [fɑ:st], adj. schnell (runner); fest (firm); my watch is —, meine Uhr geht vor; a — woman, eine leichtlebige Frau; — train, der Schnellzug; — and furious, schnell wie der Wind. — adv. fest.

fast (2) [fɑ:st], v.n. (Rel.) fasten; (Rel.) — day, der Fasttag.

fasten [fɑ:sn], v.a. festbinden, festmachen (fix). — v.n. sich festhalten (on to, an, Dat.).

fastidious [fəs'tidiəs], adj. wählerisch, anspruchsvoll.

fastidiousness [fəs'tidiəsnis], s. die anspruchsvolle Art.

fat [fæt], adj. fett; dick (person). — s. das Fett; (Cul.) das Speisefett.

fatal ['feitəl], adj. tödlich (lethal); verhängnisvoll.

fatalism ['feitəlizm], s. der Fatalismus.

fatality [fə'tæliti], s. das Verhängnis; der Todesfall; der tödliche Unfall.

fate [feit], s. das Schicksal, Geschick; das Verhängnis (doom, destiny).

fated ['feitid], adj. dem Verderben (Untergang) geweiht.

fateful ['feitful], adj. verhängnisvoll, unselig.

father ['fɑ:ðə], s. der Vater; (Eccl.) Pater; — -in-law, der Schwiegervater. — v.a. Vater sein or werden von (Dat.); zeugen (procreate).

fatherland ['fɑ:ðəlænd], s. das Vaterland.

fatherly ['fɑ:ðəli], adj. väterlich; wie ein Vater.

fathom ['fæðəm], s. die Klafter. — v.a. ergründen, erforschen.

fatigue [fə'ti:g], s. die Ermüdung, die Erschöpfung; (Mil.) der Arbeitsdienst. — v.a. ermüden, erschöpfen.

fatling ['fætliŋ], s. (Agr.) das Mastvieh.

fatness ['fætnis], s. die Beleibtheit (person); die Fettheit (animals).

fatten [fætn], v.a. — up, mästen (animals); fett werden lassen. — v.n. fett werden, sich mästen (an, Dat.).

fatty ['fæti], adj. (Chem.) fett, fettig. — s. (coll.) der Dickwanst.

fatuity [fə'tju:iti], s. die Albernheit, die Dummheit.

fatuous ['fætjuəs], adj. albern, dumm, nichtssagend.

faucet ['fɔ:sit], s. der Zapfen, der Hahn.

fault [fɔ:lt], s. der Fehler; die Schuld; find — with, etwas kritisieren; tadeln; it is my —, es ist meine Schuld; at —, im Irrtum.

faultless ['fɔ:ltlis], adj. fehlerlos, fehlerfrei.

faultlessness ['fɔ:ltlisnis], s. die Fehlerlosigkeit, die fehlerlose Ausführung.

faulty ['fɔ:lti], adj. fehlerhaft, mangelhaft.

faun [fɔ:n], s. (Myth.) der Faun.

fauna ['fɔ:nə], s. die Fauna, die Tierwelt.

favour ['feivə], s. die Gunst, das Wohlwollen; (Comm.) in — of, zugunsten; do a —, einen Gefallen tun or erweisen; be in —, sehr begehrt sein, in hoher Gunst stehen. — v.a. bevorzugen, begünstigen, wohlwollend gegenüberstehen (Dat.).

favourable ['feivərəbl], adj. günstig, vorteilhaft.

favourite

favourite ['feivərit], *s.* der Favorit, der Liebling; der Günstling (*of kings*). — *adj.* Lieblings-, bevorzugt.

fawn (1) [fɔ:n], *s.* (*Zool.*) das junge Reh, das Rehkalb; — *coloured*, rehfarben. — *adj.* rehfarben, hellbraun.

fawn (2) [fɔ:n], *v.n.* schmeicheln, kriecherisch sein ((*up*)*on*, *Dat.*).

fawning ['fɔ:niŋ], *adj.* kriecherisch, kriechend.

fear [fiə], *s.* die Furcht, die Angst; *stand in — of s.o.*, sich vor jemandem fürchten; *for — of*, aus Angst vor (*Dat.*). — *v.a.* fürchten, befürchten.

fearful ['fiəful], *adj.* furchtsam (*full of fear*); furchtbar (*causing fear*).

fearless ['fiəlis], *adj.* furchtlos (*of*, vor, *Dat.*).

fearlessness ['fiəlisnis], *s.* die Furchtlosigkeit.

feasibility [fi:zi'biliti], *s.* die Tunlichkeit, die Möglichkeit.

feasible ['fi:zibl], *adj.* tunlich, möglich.

feast [fi:st], *s.* das Fest, der Festtag; der Schmaus (*good meal*). — *v.n.* schmausen (*upon*, von, *Dat.*). — *v.a.* festlich bewirten.

feat [fi:t], *s.* die Tat, die Heldentat; das Kunststück.

feather ['feðə], *s.* die Feder; *show the white —*, Feigheit an den Tag legen; — *bed*, das Federbett. — *v.a.* federn; — *o.'s nest*, sein Schäfchen ins Trockene bringen.

feature ['fi:tʃə], *s.* der Zug (*characteristic*); der Gesichtszug (*facial*). — *v.a.* charakterisieren, (*Film*) in der Hauptrolle zeigen.

February ['februəri], der Februar.

feckless ['feklis], *adj.* hilflos, unfähig.

feculence ['fekjuləns], *s.* (*Chem.*) der Bodensatz, der Hefesatz.

fecund ['fekənd], *adj.* fruchtbar.

fecundate ['fekəndeit], *v.a.* fruchtbar machen, befruchten.

fecundity [fi'kʌnditi], *s.* die Fruchtbarkeit.

federacy ['fedərəsi], *s.* der Bund, die Föderation.

federal ['fedərəl], *adj.* Bundes-, föderativ.

federalism ['fedərəlizm], *s.* der Föderalismus.

federalize ['fedərəlaiz], *v.a.* verbünden.

federation [fedə'reiʃən], *s.* die Föderation, die Verbündung; (*Pol.*) der Bund.

fee [fi:], *s.* die Gebühr (*official dues*); das Honorar (*of doctor etc.*); (*pl.*) (*Sch.*) das Schulgeld.

feeble ['fi:bl], *adj.* schwach, matt; — *minded*, schwachsinnig.

feed [fi:d], *v.a. irr.* füttern; verköstigen (*humans*); unterhalten (*maintain*); zuführen (*into machine*, *Dat.*); *be fed up with*, etwas satt haben; — *pipe*, die Speiseröhre. — *v.n.* sich nähren (*on*, von, *Dat.*); weiden (*graze*).

feeder ['fi:də], *s.* der Kinderlatz (*bib*); (*Tech.*) der Zubringer.

feel [fi:l], *v.n. irr.* sich fühlen (*sense*); meinen (*think*). — *v.a.* berühren, betasten (*touch*); empfinden (*be aware of*).

feeler ['fi:lə], *s.* der Fühler; *put out a —*, einen Fühler ausstrecken.

feeling ['fi:liŋ], *s.* das Gefühl; *with —*, bewegt, gerührt (*moved*); grimmig (*in anger*).

feign [fein], *v.a.* vortäuschen, heucheln.

feint [feint], *s.* die Verstellung (*disguise*); die Finte (*fencing*).

felicitate [fi'lisiteit], *v.a.* Glück wünschen (*upon*, zu, *Dat.*), beglückwünschen (*Acc.*).

felicitation [filisi'teiʃən], *s.* die Beglückwünschung, der Glückwunsch.

felicitous [fi'lisitəs], *adj.* glücklich ausgedrückt, gut gesagt (*in speaking*).

felicity [fi'lisiti], *s.* die Glückseligkeit; die glückliche Ausdrucksweise (*style*).

feline ['fi:lain], *adj.* Katzen-, katzenartig.

fell (1) [fel], *adj.* grausam; *at one — swoop*, mit einem wilden Schwung.

fell (2) [fel], *v.a.* fällen (*timber*); töten (*kill*).

fell (3) [fel], *s.* das Gebirge, das Felsengelände.

fell (4) [fel], *s.* das Fell, die Haut (*skin*).

fellow ['felou], *s.* der Gefährte, Genosse (*companion*); das Mitglied eines College *or* einer Universität; (*coll.*) der Kerl; *queer —*, seltsamer Kauz; — *feeling*, das Mitgefühl; — *traveller*, der Weggenosse; (*Pol.*) der Mitläufer.

fellowship ['felouʃip], *s.* die Mitgliedschaft (*einer Hochschule etc.*) (*membership*); die Freundschaft (*friendship*); *good —*, die Geselligkeit.

felly, felloe ['feli,'felou], *s.* die Radfelge.

felon ['felən], *s.* der Verbrecher.

felonious [fi'louniəs], *adj.* verbrecherisch.

felt [felt], *s.* der Filz.

female ['fi:meil], *adj.* weiblich. — *s.* (*Zool.*) das Weibchen.

feminine ['feminin], *adj.* weiblich. — *s.* (*Gram.*) das weibliche Geschlecht; das Weibliche.

fen [fen], *s.* das Moor, das Marschland.

fence [fens], *s.* der Zaun, das Staket. — *v.a.* umzäunen, einzäunen (*enclose*). — *v.n.* fechten (*fight with rapiers*).

fencing ['fensiŋ], *s.* die Einzäunung (*fence*); das Fechten (*with rapiers*); — *master*, der Fechtmeister.

fend [fend], *v.a.* — *off*, abwehren, parieren. — *v.n.* — *for oneself*, sich allein behelfen.

fennel [fenl], *s.* (*Bot.*) der Fenchel.

ferment [fə:'ment], *v.a.* zur Gärung bringen. — *v.n.* gären, fermentieren. — ['fə:ment], *s.* das Gärmittel (*also fig.*); (*Chem.*) das Gärungsprodukt.

fermentation [fə:men'teiʃən], *s.* die Gärung.

fern [fə:n], *s.* (*Bot.*) das Farnkraut.

ferocious [fə'rouʃəs], *adj.* wild, grimmig.

ferocity [fə'rɔsiti], *s.* die Wildheit.
ferret ['ferit], *s.* (*Zool.*) das Frett, das Frettchen. — *v.a.* — *out*, ausspüren.
ferry ['feri], *s.* die Fähre. — *v.a.* — *across*, hinüberrudern, hinüberfahren, übersetzen.
fertile ['fə:tail], *adj.* fruchtbar.
fertility [fə:'tiliti], *s.* die Fruchtbarkeit.
fertilize ['fə:tilaiz], *v.a.* befruchten.
fertilizer ['fə:tilaizə], *s.* das Düngemittel, der Dünger.
fervent ['fə:vənt], *adj.* inbrünstig (*prayer*); heiß (*wish*).
fervid ['fə:vid], *adj.* glühend, heiß (*with zeal*).
fervour ['fə:və], *s.* die Inbrunst (*prayer*); die Sehnsucht (*wish*).
fester ['festə], *v.n.* schwären, eitern.
festival ['festivəl], *s.* das Fest, die Festspiele, *n. pl.*
festive ['festiv], *adj.* festlich, Fest-.
festivity [fes'tiviti], *s.* die Festlichkeit.
festoon [fes'tu:n], *s.* die Girlande. — *v.a.* behängen, mit Girlanden verzieren, schmücken.
fetch [fetʃ], *v.a.* holen, bringen.
fetching ['fetʃiŋ], *adj.* einnehmend.
fetter ['fetə], *v.a.* fesseln, binden. — *s.* (*pl.*) die Fesseln, *f. pl.*
feud [fju:d], *s.* die Fehde.
feudal ['fju:dl], *adj.* feudal, Lehns-.
fever ['fi:və], *s.* das Fieber.
few [fju:], *adj.* einige; wenige; *a* —, ein paar.
fiancé [fi'ɔ:nsei], *s.* der Verlobte, Bräutigam.
fiancée [fi'ɔ:nsei], *s.* die Verlobte, Braut.
fib [fib], *s.* (*coll.*) die Lüge. — *v.n.* (*coll.*) lügen.
fibre ['faibə], *s.* die Fiber, Faser.
fibrous ['faibrəs], *adj.* faserartig.
fickle [fikl], *adj.* unbeständig, wankelmütig.
fiction ['fikʃən], *s.* die Erdichtung (*figment*); (*Lit.*) die Romanliteratur.
fictitious [fik'tiʃəs], *adj.* erdichtet, in der Phantasie.
fiddle [fidl], *s.* (*coll.*) die Geige, Fiedel, Violine. — *v.n.* (*coll., Mus.*) geigen; schwindeln (*cheat*).
fiddlesticks! ['fidlstiks], *int.* Unsinn!
fidelity [fi'deliti], *s.* die Treue (*loyalty*); Genauigkeit; (*Engin.*) high —, Präzision, High Fidelity.
fidget ['fidʒit], *v.n.* unruhig sein.
fidgety ['fidʒiti], *adj.* nervös.
fie! [fai], *int.* pfui!
field [fi:ld], *s.* das Feld; (*fig.*) das Gebiet; — *glass*, der Feldstecher; (*Hunt.*) — *sports*, die Feldübungen, der Jagdsport. — *v.a., v.n.* abfangen, abpassen (*cricket*).
fiend [fi:nd], *s.* der Unhold, böse Geist; *fresh air* —, ein Freund der frischen Luft.
fiendish ['fi:ndiʃ], *adj.* teuflisch, boshaft.
fierce [fiəs], *adj.* wild, wütend (*beast*); — *weather*, — *cold*, die grimmige Kälte, der grimmige Winter.

fiery ['faiəri], *adj.* feurig; hitzig.
fife [faif], *s.* (*Mus.*) die Querpfeife.
fifteen [fif'ti:n], *num. adj.* fünfzehn.
fifth [fifθ], *num. adj.* der fünfte.
fifty ['fifti], *num. adj.* fünfzig.
fig [fig], *s.* (*Bot.*) die Feige.
fight [fait], *v.a., v.n. irr.* kämpfen, bekämpfen (*in battle*); raufen (*of boys*). — *s.* der Kampf; die Rauferei.
figment ['figmənt], *s.* die Erdichtung.
figurative ['figjuərətiv], *adj.* bildlich (*style*).
figure ['figə], *s.* die Figur (*body*); die Gestalt, Form (*shape*); (*Maths.*) die Zahl, die Ziffer; *cut a* —, einen Eindruck machen; *a fine* — *of a man!* ein fabelhafter Kerl! — *v.a.* — *out*, ausdenken, ausrechnen. — *v.n.* eine Rolle spielen, rangieren.
figured ['figəd], *adj.* figuriert.
figurehead ['figəhed], *s.* der scheinbare Leiter, die Repräsentationsfigur.
filament ['filəmənt], *s.* der Faden, der Glühfaden (*bulb*).
filbert ['filbə:t], *s.* (*Bot.*) die Haselnuß.
filch [filtʃ], *v.a.* stehlen, klauen.
file [fail], *s.* (*Engin.*) die Feile; (*Mil.*) die Reihe; (*Comm.*) der Aktenstoß, das Aktenbündel, der Ordner; (*pl.*) die Akten, *f. pl.*; *single* —, im Gänsemarsch; *rank and* —, die große Masse; *on the* —, in den Akten. — *v.a.* feilen (*metal*); zu den Akten legen (*papers*); einreichen (*petition*).
filial ['filiəl], *adj.* kindlich.
filibuster ['filibʌstə], *s.* der Freibeuter; (*Am.*) (*Pol.*) die Obstruktion.
filigree ['filigri:], *s.* die Filigranarbeit.
filing ['failiŋ], *s.* (*pl.*) die Feilspäne; das Einheften (*of papers*); — *cabinet*, die Kartei.
fill [fil], *v.a.* füllen; ausfüllen (*place, job*); plombieren (*tooth*); — *up*, tanken (*with petrol*). — *s.* das volle Maß; *eat o.'s* —, sich satt essen.
fillet ['filit], *s.* das Filet (*meat*); das Band, die Binde (*band*).
filling ['filiŋ], *s.* die Plombe (*in tooth*); — *station*, die Tankstelle.
filly ['fili], *s.* das Füllen.
film [film], *s.* der Film (*cinema, Phot.*); die Haut, das Häutchen (*skin*); der Belag (*coating*). — *v.a.* aufnehmen, verfilmen, filmen (*photograph*).
filter ['filtə], *v.a.* filtrieren, filtern. — *v.n.* durchfiltern. — *s.* das Filter.
filth [filθ], *s.* der Schmutz.
filthy ['filθi], *adj.* schmutzig.
filtration [fil'treiʃən], *s.* das Filtrieren, das Durchsickern.
fin [fin], *s.* (*Zool.*) die Finne, die Flosse.
final [fainl], *adj.* letzt, endlich; endgültig. — *s.* (*Sport*) die Endrunde, das Endspiel.
finale [fi'nɑ:li], *s.* (*Mus.*) das Finale.
finality [fai'næliti], *s.* die Endgültigkeit.
finance [fi'næns *or* 'fai-], *s.* die Finanz, das Finanzwesen. — *v.a.* finanzieren.

financial [fi'nænʃəl], *adj.* finanziell, Geld-, Finanz-.

finch [fintʃ], *s.* (*Orn.*) der Fink.

find [faind], *v.a. irr.* finden; — *fault with*, jemanden kritisieren; *all found*, volle Verpflegung (inbegriffen). — *s.* der Fund.

finding ['faindiŋ], *s.* das Finden, der Befund; (*Law*) der Wahrspruch.

fine (1) [fain], *adj.* fein (*delicate*); dünn (*thin*); schön (*beautiful*); scharf (*distinct*); großartig(*splendid*).

fine (2) [fain], *v.a.* zu einer Geldstrafe verurteilen. — *s.* die Geldstrafe.

finery ['fainəri], *s.* der Putz; (*Engin.*) der Frischofen.

finger ['fiŋgə], *s.* der Finger; *have a — in the pie*, die Hand im Spiel haben. — *v.a.* berühren, antasten.

finish ['finiʃ], *v.a.* beenden, fertig machen, vollenden; —*ing touch*, die lezte Hand. — *v.n.* aufhören, enden. — *s.* das Ende (*end*); der letzte Schliff; die Appretur, die Fertigung.

finite ['fainait], *adj.* endlich.

Finn [fin], *s.* der Finne.

Finnish ['finiʃ], *adj.* finnisch.

fir [fə:], *s.* (*Bot.*) die Föhre, die Tanne; — *cone*, der Tannenzapfen.

fire [faiə], *s.* das Feuer; — *brigade*, die Feuerwehr; — *damp*, (*Min.*) schlagende Wetter, *n.pl.*; — *engine*, die Feuerspritze; — *extinguisher*, der Löschapparat, Feuerlöscher; — *escape*, die Rettungsleiter. — *v.a.* brennen (*clay*); anzünden, in Gang setzen (*furnace*); anspornen (*enthuse*); (*coll.*) entlassen (*dismiss*). — *v.n.* feuern (*at, auf, Acc.*).

firebrand ['faiəbrænd], *s.* der Aufwiegler.

fireman ['faiəmən], *s.* der Heizer.

fireplace ['faiəpleis], *s.* der Kamin.

fireproof ['faiəpru:f], *adj.* feuerfest.

fireside ['faiəsaid], *s.* der (häusliche) Herd, der Kamin.

firewood ['faiəwud], *s.* das Brennholz.

firework ['faiəwə:k], *s.* (*usually pl.*) das Feuerwerk.

firm [fə:m], *adj.* fest, hart (*solid*); entschlossen (*decided*). — *s.* die Firma.

firmament ['fə:məmənt], *s.* das Firmament, Himmelsgewölbe; der Sternenhimmel.

firmness ['fə:mnis], *s.* die Festigkeit, Entschlossenheit.

first [fə:st], *num. adj., adv.* erst; zuerst; — *of all*, zuallererst; — *born*, erstgeboren; — *rate*, erstklassig. — *s. from the —*, von Anfang an.

fiscal ['fiskəl], *adj.* fiskalisch, von der Staatskasse, Finanz-.

fish [fiʃ], *s.* der Fisch; *like a — out of water*, nicht in seinem Element; *a queer —*, ein seltsamer Kauz; —*bone*, die Gräte. — *v.n.* fischen; — *for compliments*, nach Lob haschen, nach Komplimenten fischen.

fisherman ['fiʃəmən], *s.* der Fischer.

fishery ['fiʃəri], *s.* der Fischfang.

fishing ['fiʃiŋ], *s.* das Fischen, der Fischfang; — *fly*, die Angelfliege; — *line*, die Angelschnur; — *rod*, die Angelrute; — *tackle*, das Angelgerät.

fishy ['fiʃi], *adj.* (*coll.*) anrüchig, verdächtig.

fissile ['fisail], *adj.* (*Phys.*) spaltbar.

fission ['fiʃ(ə)n], *s.* (*Phys.*) die Spaltung.

fist [fist], *s.* die Faust; *hand over —*, im Überfluß; *tight —ed*, geizig.

fisticuffs ['fistikʌfs], *s.* die Schlägerei, das Raufen.

fistula ['fistjulə], *s.* (*Anat.*) die Fistel.

fit (1) [fit], *v.a.* passen, anpassen (*Dat.*); einfügen (— *into s.th.*); — *in*, hineinpassen; — *on a suit*, einen Anzug anprobieren (*Dat.*); — *for a career*, zu einer Laufbahn vorbereiten; — *out*, ausrüsten. — *v.n.* passen, sich fügen (— *into*); — *in*, passen (*in, zu, Dat.*). — *adj.* geeignet, fähig (*suitable*); — *to drop*, todmüde; gesund, stark (*healthy*); schicklich (*proper*); (*Sport*) in guter Form.

fit (2) [fit], *s.* der Anfall; *by —s and starts*, ruckweise.

fitful ['fitful], *adj.* launenhaft; unbeständig.

fitness ['fitnis], *s.* die Tauglichkeit (*health*); die Schicklichkeit (*propriety*); die Fähigkeit (*ability*); (*Sport*) die gute Form.

fitter ['fitə], *s.* der Monteur.

fitting, fitment ['fitiŋ, 'fitmənt], *s.* die Armatur; die Montage. — *adj.* passend (*suitable*); geeignet (*appropriate*).

five [faiv], *num. adj.* fünf.

fiver ['faivə], *s.* (*coll.*) die Fünfpfundnote.

fix [fiks], *v.a.* festmachen, befestigen (*make firm*); festsetzen (*a time*); (*Am.*) herrichten, anrichten (*a meal*); — *with a glare or stare*, mit den Augen fixieren, scharf ansehen; — *up* (*coll.*), etwas erledigen (*something*); bedienen (*serve s.o.*). — *s.* (*coll.*) die Klemme, die Schwierigkeit, das Dilemma.

fixture ['fikstʃə], *s.* (*Sport*) die Veranstaltung; das Inventarstück (*furniture*).

fizz [fiz], *v.n.* brausen (*drink*).

fizzle [fizl], *v.n.* zischen (*flame*); — *out*, verebben, ausgehen, zunichte werden; (*Am., coll.*) durchfallen (*fail in school*).

fizzy ['fizi], *adj.* mit Kohlensäure, sprudelnd.

flabbergast ['flæbəga:st], *v.a.* (*coll.*) verblüffen.

flabby ['flæbi], *adj.* schlaff.

flaccid ['flæksid], *adj.* schlapp, schlaff.

flag (1) [flæg], *s.* (*Mil.*) die Flagge; die Fahne; — *officer*, der Flaggoffizier; —*staff*, die Fahnenstange.

flag (2) [flæg], *v.n.* ermatten, erschlaffen.

flag (3) [flæg], *s.* (—*stone*) der Fliessstein, die Fliese. — *v.a.* mit Fliesen auslegen, mit Fliesteinen pflastern.

flagon ['flægən], *s.* die Doppelflasche.
flagrant ['fleigrənt], *adj.* entsetzlich
(*shocking*); schamlos (*impudent*).
flail [fleil], *s.* der Dreschflegel.
flair [flɛə], *s.* der Instinkt; (*coll.*) die
Nase (*for*, für, *Acc.*).
flake [fleik], *s.* die Flocke. — *v.n.* — *off*,
abblättern.
flame [fleim], *s.* die Flamme; (*coll.*) *old*
—, die (alte) Liebe, Geliebte(r), die
Flamme. — *v.n.* flammen, lodern.
flamingo [flə'miŋgou], *s.* (*Orn.*) der
Flamingo.
flange [flændʒ], *s.* (*Engin.*) der
Flan(t)sch.
flank [flæŋk], *s.* die Flanke, die Seite;
die Weiche (*of animal*). — *v.a.*
flankieren.
flannel [flænl], *s.* der Flanell.
flap [flæp], *s.* die Klappe; das Ohrläppchen (*earlobe*); der Flügelschlag (—
of wings).
flare [flɛə], *v.n.* flammen, flackern; —
up, aufbrausen (*in temper*). — *s.* das
Aufflammen, das Aufflackern; die
Leuchtkugel.
flash [flæʃ], *s.* der Blitz (*of lightning*); das
Aufflammen; (*Phot.*) —*light*, das
Blitzlicht. — *v.a.* aufflammen lassen,
aufblitzen lassen. — *v.n.* aufflammen,
aufblitzen.
flashy ['flæʃi], *adj.* großtuend, angeberisch (*bragging*); buntfarbig (*gaudy*).
flask [flɑːsk], *s.* die kleine Flasche, das
Fläschchen.
flat [flæt], *adj.* flach, eben; abgestanden,
schal (*drink*); — *footed*, plattfüßig;
(*Mus.*) zu tief, vermindert; platt;
albern (*conversation*); — *tyre*, die
Panne. — *adv.* — *out*, ausgepumpt,
erschöpft. — *s.* die Mietwohnung,
Wohnung (*lodgings*); (*Mus.*) das B;
(*pl.*) das Flachland; (*Theat.*) (*pl.*) die
Bühnenbilder.
flatness ['flætnis], *s.* die Flachheit, die
Plattheit (*of conversation etc.*).
flatten ['flætn], *v.a.* flach machen;
glätten (*smooth*).
flatter ['flætə], *v.a.* schmeicheln (*Dat.*).
flattery ['flætəri], *s.* die Schmeichelei.
flaunt [flɔːnt], *v.a.* prahlen, prunken
(*s.th.*, mit, *Dat.*).
flavour ['fleivə], *s.* der Geschmack, die
Würze; das Aroma; die Blume
(*bouquet of wine*). — *v.a.* würzen.
flaw [flɔː], *s.* der Riß (*chink*); der Fehler
(*fault*).
flawless ['flɔːlis], *adj.* fehlerlos.
flax [flæks], *s.* (*Bot.*) der Flachs.
flay [flei], *v.a.* schinden, die Haut
abziehen (*Dat.*).
flea [fliː], *s.* (*Ent.*) der Floh.
fleck [flek], *v.a.* sprenkeln.
fledge [fledʒ], *v.a.* befiedern; *fully* —*d*,
flügge; selbständig.
fledgling ['fledʒliŋ], *s.* der Grünschnabel, der Novize.
flee [fliː], *v.a.*, *v.n. irr.* fliehen, entfliehen (*from*, von, *Dat.*); flüchten
(vor, *Dat.*).

fleece [fliːs], *s.* das Vlies. — *v.a.* scheren
(*sheep*); ausnützen (*exploit*); berauben.
fleet [fliːt], *s.* die Flotte. — *adj.* (*Poet.*)
schnellfüßig.
Fleming ['flemiŋ], *s.* der Flame.
Flemish ['flemiʃ], *adj.* flämisch.
flesh [fleʃ], *s.* das (lebende) Fleisch;
die Frucht (*of fruit*).
flex [fleks], *s.* (*Elec.*) die Kontaktschnur.
flexible ['fleksibl], *adj.* biegsam; (*fig.*)
anpassungsfähig.
flexion ['flekʃən], *s.* (*Gram.*) die Flexion,
die Biegung.
flick [flik], *s.* der leichte Schlag. — *v.a.*
leicht schlagen, berühren.
flicker ['flikə], *s.* das Flackern, das
Flimmern. — *v.n.* flackern, flimmern.
flight [flait], *s.* (*Aviat.*) der Flug; die
Flucht (*escape*); — *of stairs*, die
Treppe, Treppenflucht.
flimsy ['flimzi], *adj.* hauchdünn (*material*); schwach (*argument*).
flinch [flintʃ], *v.n.* zurückweichen,
zurückzucken (*from*, vor, *Dat.*).
fling [fliŋ], *v.a. irr.* schleudern, werfen.
— *s.* der Wurf; *highland* —, schot-
tischer Tanz; *have a last* —, sich
zum letzten Mal austoben.
flint [flint], *s.* der Feuerstein.
flippancy ['flipənsi], *s.* die Leichtfertigkeit.
flippant ['flipənt], *adj.* leichtfertig,
leichtsinnig, schnippisch.
flirt [fləːt], *v.n.* flirten, liebeln, (*with*,
Dat.).
flirtation [fləː'teiʃən], *s.* die Liebelei.
flit [flit], *v.n.* hin und her flitzen;
huschen.
flitch [flitʃ], *s.* die Speckseite.
flitter ['flitə], *v.n.* flattern.
float [flout], *v.n.* obenauf schwimmen,
dahingleiten; —*ing ice*, das Treibeis.
— *v.a.* schwimmen lassen; (*Naut.*)
flott machen; (*Comm.*) gründen (*a
company*); ausgeben (*a loan*). — *s.* das
Floß (*raft*); der ausgeschmückte
Wagen (*decorated vehicle*).
flock [flɔk], *s.* die Herde (*sheep*). —
v.n. zusammenlaufen, sich scharen.
floe [flou], *s.* die Eisscholle.
flog [flɔg], *v.a.* peitschen (*whip*); antreiben; — *a dead horse*, sich umsonst
bemühen; (*coll.*) verkaufen.
flood [flʌd], *s.* die Flut (*das Hochwasser*,
die Überschwemmung (*flooding*); (*fig.*)
die Fülle; — *gate*, die Schleuse.
— *v.a.* überfluten, überschütten (*with
requests*). — *v.n.* überschwemmen (*of
river*).
floodlight ['flʌdlait], *s.* das Flutlicht,
Scheinwerferlicht.
floor [flɔː], *s.* der Boden, der Fußboden;
das Stockwerk, der Stock (*storey*);
from the —, aus dem Plenum; —
walker, die Aufsicht (*in stores*). —
v.a. zu Boden strecken, überrumpeln
(*surprise*).
flop [flɔp], *v.n.* (*coll.*) hinsinken, hin-
plumpsen; versagen (*fail*). — *s.* das
Hinfallen; der Versager (*play, film etc.*).

Florentine

Florentine ['florəntain], *adj.* florentinisch. — *s.* der Florentiner.
florid ['flɔrid], *adj.* blühend; überladen.
florin ['flɔrin], *s.* das Zweischillingstück.
florist ['flɔrist], *s.* der Blumenhändler.
flotsam ['flɔtsəm], *s.* das Strandgut, Wrackgut.
flounce (1) [flauns], *v.n.* hastig bewegen.
flounce (2) [flauns], *v.a.* mit Falbeln besetzen (*dress*). — *s.* die Falbel (*on dress*).
flounder (1) ['flaundə], *v.n.* umhertappen, unsicher sein.
flounder (2) ['flaundə], *s.* (*Zool.*) die Flunder.
flour ['flauə], *s.* das Mehl.
flourish ['flʌriʃ], *v.n.* blühen; wirken; gedeihen (*thrive*); schnörkeln, verzieren (*in writing*); Fanfaren blasen, schmettern (*trumpets*). — *s.* der Schnörkel; der Trompetenstoß, Tusch (*of trumpets*).
flout [flaut], *v.a.* verhöhnen, verspotten. — *s.* der Hohn, der Spott.
flow [flou], *v.n. irr.* fließen, strömen. — *s.* der Fluß (*of water, goods etc.*); — *of words*, der Redeschwall.
flower ['flauə], *s.* die Blume; die Blüte (*blossom*). — *v.n.* blühen, in Blüte stehen.
flowery ['flauəri], *adj.* gewählt, umständlich, geziert (*style*).
fluctuate ['flʌktjueit], *v.n.* schwanken.
fluctuation [flʌktju'eiʃənʃ, *s.* das Schwanken.
flue [fluː], *s.* der Rauchfang (*of chimney*).
fluency ['fluːənsi], *s.* das fließende Sprechen, die Geläufigkeit.
fluent ['fluːənt], *adj.* geläufig, fließend.
fluid ['fluːid], *adj.* fließend, flüssig (*liquid*). — *s.* die Flüssigkeit.
fluke [fluːk], *s.* der glückliche Zufall (*chance*).
flunkey ['flʌŋki], *s.* der Diener, der Bediente.
flurry ['flʌri], *s.* die Unruhe; die Aufregung (*excitement*).
flush (1) [flʌʃ], *s.* das Erröten (*blushing*); die Aufwallung (*of anger*). — *v.a.* nachspülen (*basin*); erröten machen (*make blush*). — *v.n.* erröten.
flush (2) [flʌʃ], *adj.* in gleicher Ebene, eben.
flush (3) [flʌʃ], *v.a.* (*Hunt.*) aufscheuchen.
fluster ['flʌstə], *v.a.* verwirren (*muddle*); aufregen (*excite*).
flute [fluːt], *s.* (*Mus.*) die Flöte; (*Carp.*) die Hohlkehle. — *v.a.* (*Carp., Archit.*) aushöhlen. — *v.n.* (*Mus.*) flöten, Flöte spielen.
flutter ['flʌtə], *v.n.* flattern, unruhig sein. — *s.* die Unruhe.
flux [flʌks], *s.* das Fließen; *be in* —, in der Schwebe sein.
fly [flai], *v.a. irr.* wehen lassen, hissen (*flag*). — *v.n. irr.* (*Aviat.*) fliegen;

fliehen (*escape*); eilen (*hurry*). — *s.* (*Ent.*) die Fliege.
flyleaf ['flailiːf], *s.* das Vorsatzblatt.
flying ['flaiiŋ], *adj.* fliegend, Flug-; — *squad*, das Überfallkommando.
flyover ['flaiouvə], *s.* die Brückenkreuzung, Überführung.
flywheel ['flaiwiːl], *s.* das Schwungrad.
foal [foul], *s.* (*Zool.*) das Füllen. — *v.n.* fohlen.
foam [foum], *s.* der Schaum; — *rubber*, das Schaumgummi. — *v.n.* schäumen.
fob [fɔb], *v.a.* — *off*, abfertigen, abspeisen.
focus ['foukəs], *s.* der Brennpunkt; der Mittelpunkt (*of interest*). — *v.a.* (*Phot.*) einstellen. — *v.n.* — *upon*, sich konzentrieren auf (*Acc.*).
fodder ['fɔdə], *s.* das Futter.
foe [fou], *s.* der Feind.
fog [fɔg], *s.* der Nebel.
fogey ['fougi], *s.* der Kerl, Kauz.
foible ['fɔibl], *s.* die Schwäche, die schwache Seite.
foil (1) [fɔil], *v.a.* vereiteln. — *s.* das Florett (*fencing rapier*).
foil (2) [fɔil], *s.* die Folie; der Hintergrund (*background*).
foist [fɔist], *v.a.* aufschwatzen (*upon, Dat.*).
fold (1) [fould], *v.a.* falten (*clothes etc.*); umarmen (*in o.'s arms*). — *v.n.* schließen, sich falten. — *s.* die Falte; (*Geol.*) die Vertiefung.
fold (2) [fould], *s.* die Herde (*sheep*); *return to the* —, zu den Seinen zurückkehren.
folder ['fouldə], *s.* die Mappe (*papers*); das Falzbein.
folding ['fouldiŋ], *adj.* Klapp-; — *chair*, der Klappstuhl; — *door*, die Flügeltür.
foliage ['fouljidʒ], *s.* (*Bot.*) das Laub.
folio ['fouliou], *s.* das Folio, der Foliant.
folk [fouk], *s.* (*also pl.*) die Leute; (*pl.*) (*Am.*) Freunde (*mode of address*).
folklore ['fouklɔː], *s.* die Volkskunde.
folksong ['fouksɔŋ], *s.* das Volkslied.
follow ['fɔlou], *v.a., v.n.* folgen (*Dat.*); — *suit*, dasselbe tun, Farbe bekennen.
follower ['fɔlouə], *s.* der Anhänger (*supporter*); der Nachfolger (*successor*); *camp* —, der Mitläufer.
folly ['fɔli], *s.* die Narrheit; die törichte Handlung (*action*).
foment [fo'ment], *v.a.* anregen (*stimulate*); pflegen (*cultivate*); warm baden.
fond [fɔnd], *adj.* zärtlich, lieb; *be* — *of*, gern haben.
fondle [fɔndl], *v.a.* liebkosen.
fondness ['fɔndnis], *s.* die Zärtlichkeit, die (Vor-)liebe.
font [fɔnt], *s.* der Taufstein (*baptismal*).
food [fuːd], *s.* die Nahrung, Speise (*nourishment*); Lebensmittel (*n.pl.*); das Futter (*for animals*); *some* —, etwas zum Essen; — *store*, das Lebensmittelgeschäft.
fool [fuːl], *s.* der Narr, Tor. — *v.a.* zum Narren halten, übertölpeln.

foolish ['fu:liʃ], *adj.* töricht, albern, närrisch (*person*); unsinnig (*act*).

foolscap ['fu:lskæp], *s.* das Kanzleipapier.

foot [fut], *s.* der Fuß; *on* —, zu Fuß; — *board*, das Trittbrett; *put o.'s* — *in it*, eine taktlose Bemerkung fallen lassen, ins Fettnäpfchen treten. — *v.a.* — *the bill*, bezahlen.

footage ['futidʒ], *s.* die Länge in Fuß.

football ['futbɔ:l], *s.* der Fußball.

footbridge ['futbridʒ], *s.* der Steg.

footing ['futiŋ], *s.* die Grundlage, Basis.

footlight ['futlait], *s.* (*usually pl.*) die Rampenlichter, *n. pl.*

footman ['futmən], *s.* der Bediente.

footprint ['futprint], *s.* die Fußstapfe.

footstool ['futstu:l], *s.* der Schemel.

fop [fɔp], *s.* der Geck.

for [fɔ:], *prep.* für (*Acc.*); anstatt (*Genit.*) (*instead of*); *in exchange* —, für, um; — *example*, zum Beispiel; — *heaven's sake*, um Himmels willen; — *two days*, zwei Tage lang; auf zwei Tage; seit zwei Tagen; *now you are* — *it!* jetzt has du's! *as* — *me*, meinetwegen, was mich anbelangt; — *all that*, trotz alledem. — *conj.* denn, weil.

forage ['fɔridʒ], *s.* das Futter. — *v.n.* furagieren.

forasmuch [fɔrəz'mʌtʃ], *conj.* (*obs.*) — *as*, insofern als.

foray ['fɔrei], *s.* der Raubzug.

forbear [fɔ:'bɛə], *v.a. irr.* vermeiden, unterlassen (*avoid*); sich enthalten (*abstain*). — *v.n.* (geduldig) hinnehmen, ertragen.

forbid [fə'bid], *v.a. irr.* verbieten; *God* —*!* Gott behüte!

forbidding [fə'bidiŋ], *adj.* abschreckend.

force [fɔ:s], *s.* (*Phys.*) die Kraft; die Macht (*might*); die Gewalt (*brute* —); (*pl.*) die Streitkräfte, *f. pl.*; (*Phys.*) die Kräfte. — *v.a.* zwingen, nötigen.

forceful ['fɔ:sful], *adj.* kräftig, energisch, kraftvoll.

forceps ['fɔ:seps], *s.* (*Med.*) die Zange; die Pinzette.

forcible ['fɔ:sibl], *adj.* heftig, stark (*strong*); gewaltsam (*violent*).

ford [fɔ:d], *s.* die Furt.

fore- [fɔ:], *pref.* Vorder-, vorder.

forebear ['fɔ:bɛə], *s.* der Vorfahre.

forebode [fɔ:'boud], *v.a.* voraussagen, vorbedeuten.

forecast [fɔ:'ka:st], *v.a.* vorhersagen, voraussagen. — [fɔ:ka:st], *s.* die Vorhersage.

foreclose [fɔ:'klouz], *v.a.* ausschließen.

forefather ['fɔ:fɑ:ðə], *s.* der Ahne, der Vorvater.

forefinger ['fɔ:fiŋgə], *s.* (*Anat.*) der Zeigefinger.

forego [fɔ:'gou], *v.a. irr.* vorhergehen.

foreground ['fɔ:graund], *s.* der Vordergrund.

forehead ['fɔrid], *s.* die Stirne.

foreign ['fɔrin], *adj.* fremd; ausländisch.

foreigner ['fɔrinə], *s.* der Fremde, der Ausländer.

foreland ['fɔ:lənd], *s.* das Vorgebirge.

foreman ['fɔ:mən], *s.* der Werkführer, Vorarbeiter.

foremast ['fɔ:mɑ:st], *s.* (*Naut.*) der Fockmast.

foremost ['fɔ:moust], *adj.* vorderst, vornehmlichst, führend. — *adv.* zuerst; *first and* —, zuallererst.

forenoon ['fɔ:nu:n], *s.* der Vormittag.

forensic [fɔ'rensik], *adj.* forensisch, gerichtsmedizinisch.

forerunner ['fɔ:rʌnə], *s.* der Vorläufer.

foresail ['fɔ:seil, 'fɔ:səl], *s.* (*Naut.*) das Focksegel.

foresee [fɔ:'si:], *v.a. irr.* vorhersehen.

foreshadow [fɔ:'ʃædou], *v.a.* vorher andeuten.

foreshorten [fɔ:'ʃɔ:tn], *v.a.* verkürzen.

foresight ['fɔ:sait], *s.* die Vorsorge, der Vorbedacht.

forest ['fɔrist], *s.* der Wald; der Urwald (*jungle*).

forestall [fɔ:'stɔ:l], *v.a.* vorwegnehmen, zuvorkommen (*Dat.*).

forester ['fɔristə], *s.* der Förster.

forestry ['fɔristri], *s.* die Forstwissenschaft (*science*); das Forstwesen (*management*).

foretaste ['fɔ:teist], *s.* der Vorgeschmack.

foretell [fɔ:'tel], *v.a. irr.* voraussagen.

forethought ['fɔ:θɔ:t], *s.* der Vorbedacht.

forewarn [fɔ:'wɔ:n], *v.a.* warnen.

forfeit ['fɔ:fit], *s.* das Pfand (*pledge*); die Einbuße (*fine*); (*pl.*) das Pfänderspiel. — *v.a.* verwirken, verwirken.

forfeiture ['fɔ:fitʃə], *s.* die Verwirkung, die Einbuße, der Verlust.

forge [fɔ:dʒ], *v.a.* schmieden (*iron*); fälschen (*falsify*). — *v.n.* — *ahead*, sich vorwärtsarbeiten. — *s.* die Schmiede (*iron*); der Eisenhammer (*hammer*).

forget [fə'get], *v.a., v.n. irr.* vergessen; — *-me-not*, das Vergißmeinnicht.

forgetful [fə'getful], *adj.* vergeßlich.

forgive [fə'giv], *v.a., v.n. irr.* vergeben, verzeihen.

forgo [fɔ:'gou], *v.a. irr.* verzichten; aufgeben.

fork [fɔ:k], *s.* die Gabel; die Abzweigung (*road*). — *v.n.* sich gabeln, sich spalten.

forlorn [fɔ:'lɔ:n], *adj.* verlassen, verloren, elend.

form [fɔ:m], *s.* die Form, die Gestalt (*shape*); die Formalität (*formality*); das Formular (*document*); *in good* —, (*Sport*) in guter Form; *bad* —, gegen den guten Ton; *a matter of* —, eine Formsache. — *v.a.* bilden, gestalten (*shape*); bilden (*an association etc. of*, über, *Acc.*).

formal ['fɔ:məl], *adj.* formal, äußerlich; formell.

formality [fɔ:'mæliti], *s.* die Formalität.

formation

formation [fɔː'meiʃən], s. (Mil.) die Formation; (Geol.) die Bildung; die Formung; die Aufstellung (sports team).

former ['fɔːmə], adj. früher, vorig.

formidable ['fɔːmidəbl], adj. schrecklich, furchtbar.

formula ['fɔːmjulə], s. die Formel.

formulate ['fɔːmjuleit], v.a. formulieren.

forsake [fɔː'seik], v.a. irr. verlassen, im Stich lassen.

forsooth [fɔː'suːθ], adv. (Poet.) wahrlich, wirklich!

forswear [fɔː'swɛə], v.a. irr. abschwören; — oneself, einen Meineid schwören.

fort, fortress [fɔːt, 'fɔːtris], s. das Fort, die Festung.

forth [fɔːθ], adv. vorwärts; weiter (further); and so —, und so weiter (u.s.w.); fort (away).

forthcoming ['fɔːθkʌmiŋ], adj. bevorstehend.

forthwith [fɔːθ'wiθ], adv. sogleich.

fortieth ['fɔːtiəθ], num. adj. vierzigst. — s. der Vierzigste.

fortification [fɔːtifi'keiʃən], s. die Befestigung.

fortify ['fɔːtifai], v.a. befestigen; bestärken.

fortitude ['fɔːtitjuːd], s. die Tapferkeit.

fortnight ['fɔːtnait], s. vierzehn Tage, m. pl.

fortuitous [fɔː'tjuːitəs], adj. zufällig.

fortunate ['fɔːtʃənit], adj. glücklich, günstig.

fortune ['fɔːtjuːn], s. das Glück, das Schicksal; das Vermögen (wealth); — teller, die Wahrsagerin.

forty ['fɔːti], num. adj. vierzig.

forward ['fɔːwəd], adj. vorder (in front); voreilig, vorlaut (rash); früh (early). — adv. vorne; — march! vorwärts! carry —, (Comm.) übertragen. — s. (Footb.) der Stürmer; — line, der Angriff. — v.a. weiterleiten, expedieren; (letter) please —, bitte nachsenden.

forwardness ['fɔːwədnis], s. die Frühreife; die Voreiligkeit, Dreistigkeit.

fossil ['fɔsil], s. das Fossil.

foster ['fɔstə], v.a. nähren (feed); aufziehen (bring up); — a thought, einen Gedanken hegen; — mother, die Pflegemutter; — brother, der Pflegebruder.

foul [faul], adj. schmutzig; faul (rotten). — v.a. beschmutzen. — v.n. (Footb.) einen Verstoß begehen. — s. (Footb.) der Verstoß.

found (1) [faund], v.a. gründen, begründen.

found (2) [faund], v.a. (Metall.) gießen (cast).

foundation [faun'deiʃən], s. das Fundament; die Unterlage; die Begründung, die Gründung (initiation); die Stiftung (establishment); — stone, der Grundstein.

founder (1) ['faundə], s. der Gründer, Stifter.

founder (2) ['faundə], v.n. scheitern, Schiffbruch erleiden (on, an, Dat.).

foundling ['faundliŋ], s. das Findelkind, der Findling.

foundry ['faundri], s. (Metall.) die Gießerei.

fount (1) [faunt], s. (Typ.) der Schriftguss.

fount (2) [faunt] (Poet.) see **fountain**.

fountain ['fauntin], s. die Quelle, der Brunnen; der Springbrunnen; — pen, die Füllfeder; — head, der Urquell.

four [fɔː], num. adj. vier; — -in-hand, das Viergespann.

fowl [faul], s. (Orn.) das Huhn, das Geflügel.

fowler ['faulə], s. der Vogelsteller, Vogelfänger.

fox [fɔks], s. (Zool.) der Fuchs; (fig.) der listige Kauz, Schlauberger (cunning fellow). — v.a. (coll.) überlisten, täuschen.

fraction ['frækʃən], s. (Maths.) der Bruch; (Mech.) der Bruchteil.

fractional ['frækʃənəl], adj. (Maths.) Bruch-, gebrochen.

fractionate ['frækʃəneit], v.a. (Chem.) fraktionieren (oil).

fractious ['frækʃəs], adj. zänkisch, streitsüchtig.

fracture ['fræktʃə], s. (Med.) der Bruch. — v.a. brechen; — o.'s leg, sich das Bein brechen.

fragile ['frædʒail], adj. zerbrechlich; gebrechlich (feeble).

fragment ['frægmənt], s. das Bruchstück, das Fragment.

fragrance ['freigrəns], s. der Wohlgeruch, Duft.

fragrant ['freigrənt], adj. wohlriechend, duftend.

frail [freil], adj. gebrechlich, schwach (feeble).

frailty ['freilti], s. die Schwäche.

frame [freim], s. der Rahmen (of picture); das Gerüst (scaffold); die Form (shape). — v.a. einrahmen (a picture); (Am.) in die Enge treiben, reinlegen (get s.o. wrongly blamed); (Comm.) entwerfen (a letter).

framework ['freimwəːk], s. der Rahmen (outline); das Fachwerk (construction).

franchise ['fræntʃaiz], s. das Wahlrecht.

Franciscan [fræn'siskən], s. der Franziskaner (friar).

frank [fræŋk], adj. offen, aufrichtig. — v.a. frankieren (letter). — s. der Frankovermerk.

frankincense ['fræŋkinsens], s. der Weihrauch.

frantic ['fræntik], adj. wahnsinnig, außer sich.

fraternal [frə'təːnəl], adj. brüderlich.

fraternity [frə'təːniti], s. die Bruderschaft; (Am.) der Studentenbund, -klub.

fraternize ['frætənaiz], v.n. sich verbrüdern, fraternisieren.
fraud [frɔːd], s. der Betrug.
fraudulent ['frɔːdjulənt], adj. betrügerisch.
fraught [frɔːt], adj. voll (with, von, Dat.).
fray (1) [frei], v.a. abnutzen; — the nerves, auf die Nerven gehen (Dat.).
fray (2) [frei], s. der Kampf, die Schlägerei.
freak [friːk], s. das Monstrum, die Mißgeburt.
freakish ['friːkiʃ], adj. seltsam; grotesk.
freckle [frekl], s. die Sommersprosse.
freckled [frekld], adj. sommersprossig.
free [friː], adj. frei; offen (frank); — trade area, die Freihandelszone; of my own — will, aus freien Stücken. — v.a. befreien.
freebooter ['friːbuːtə], s. der Freibeuter.
freedom ['friːdəm], s. die Freiheit; — of a city, das Ehrenbürgerrecht.
freehold ['friːhould], s. der freie Grundbesitz, der Freigrundbesitz.
freeholder ['friːhouldə], s. der (freie) Grundbesitzer.
freeman ['friːmən], s. der Freibürger, Ehrenbürger.
freemason ['friːmeisn], s. der Freimaurer.
freewheel ['friːˈwiːl], s. der Freilauf, das Freilaufrad. — v.n. mit Freilauf fahren.
freeze [friːz], v.a. irr. gefrieren lassen. — v.n. frieren, gefrieren; — up, zufrieren.
freight [freit], s. die Fracht. — v.a. verfrachten.
freighter ['freitə], s. (Naut.) der Frachtdampfer.
French [frentʃ], adj. französisch; — bean, die Schnittbohne; — horn, (Mus.) das Horn.
Frenchman ['frentʃmən], s. der Franzose.
Frenchwoman ['frentʃwumən], s. die Französin.
frenzied ['frenzid], adj. wahnsinnig, außer sich.
frequency ['friːkwənsi], s. (Phys.) die Frequenz; die Häufigkeit (of occurrence).
frequent ['friːkwənt], adj. häufig. — [friˈkwent], v.a. (häufig) besuchen.
fresh [freʃ], adj. frisch, neu; ungesalzen (water); (sl.) frech; — water, das Süßwasser.
fresher, freshman ['freʃə, 'freʃmən], s. der Neuankömmling; (Univ.) der Fuchs, Anfänger.
fret (1) [fret], s. (Carp.) das Gitterwerk, Laubsägewerk. — v.a. (Carp.) durchbrochen verzieren.
fret (2) [fret], s. der Verdruß, Ärger. — v.n. sich Sorgen machen.
fretful ['fretful], adj. verdrießlich, ärgerlich, mißmutig.

fretsaw ['fretsɔː], s. (Carp.) die Laubsäge.
friar ['fraiə], s. (Eccl.) der Mönch, Bettelmönch.
friction ['frikʃən], s. die Reibung; (fig.) die Unstimmigkeit.
Friday ['fraid(e)i]. der Freitag; Good —, der Karfreitag.
friend [frend], s. der (die) Freund(in).
friendly ['frendli], adj. freundlich.
friendship ['frendʃip], s. die Freundschaft.
frigate ['frigit], s. (Naut.) die Fregatte.
fright [frait], s. die Furcht, der Schreck, das Entsetzen.
frighten [fraitn], v.a. erschrecken (s.o.).
frightful ['fraitful], adj. schrecklich.
frigid ['fridʒid], adj. kalt, frostig; kühl.
frill [fril], s. die Krause; die Ausschmückung (style).
frilly ['frili], adj. gekräuselt, geziert.
fringe [frindʒ], s. die Franse (fringed edge); der Rand (edge, brink). — v.a. mit Fransen besetzen, einsäumen. — v.n. — on, grenzen an (Acc.).
Frisian ['friːʒən], adj. friesisch.
frisk [frisk], v.a. (sl.) durchsuchen (search). — v.n. hüpfen (of animals). — s. der Sprung (of animals).
frisky ['friski], adj. lebhaft, munter.
fritter ['fritə], s. der Pfannkuchen; apple —, Äpfel im Schlafrock. — v.a. zerstückeln (cut up); vertrödeln (waste), vergeuden.
frivolity [friˈvɔliti], s. der Leichtsinn, die Leichtfertigkeit.
frivolous ['frivələs], adj. leichtsinnig, leichtfertig.
fro [frou], adv. to and —, auf und ab, hin und her.
frock [frɔk], s. der Kittel, das Kleid; (Eccl.) die Soutane, Kutte.
frog [frɔg], s. (Zool.) der Frosch.
frogman ['frɔgmən], s. der Tauchschwimmer, Froschmann.
frolic ['frɔlik], s. der Scherz; der Spaß. — v.n. scherzen, ausgelassen sein.
from [frɔm], prep. von; von ... her (hence); aus ... heraus (out of); von ... an (starting —); vor (in the face of).
front [frʌnt], s. die Stirn; die Vorderseite; (Mil.) die Front; in — of, vor (Dat.); — door, die Haustür.
frontage ['frʌntidʒ], s. die Front, Vorderfront (of building).
frontal ['frʌntl], adj. Stirn-, Vorder-; (Mil.) — attack, der Frontalangriff. — s. (Eccl.) die Altardecke.
frontier ['frʌntjə], s. die Grenze; — police, die Grenzpolizei.
frontispiece ['frʌntispiːs], s. das Titelbild.
frost [frɔst], s. der Frost, der Reif.
frostbite ['frɔstbait], s. die Frostbeule.
frosted ['frɔstid], adj. bereift.
froth [frɔθ], s. der Schaum. — v.n. schäumen.

frown [fraun], *v.n.* die Stirn runzeln, finster dreinschauen. — *s.* das Stirnrunzeln.

frugal ['fru:gəl], *adj.* frugal, sparsam, einfach.

fruit [fru:t], *s.* die Frucht (*singular*); das Obst (*plural or collective*). — *v.n.* (*Bot.*) Früchte tragen.

frustrate [frʌs'treit], *v.a.* verhindern; vereiteln (*bring to nought*).

fry (1) [frai], *v.a.* braten; *fried potatoes*, Bratkartoffeln, *f. pl.*

fry (2) [frai], *s.* der Rogen (*of fish*); (*fig.*) die Brut, Menge.

frying pan ['fraiiŋpæn], *s.* die Bratpfanne; *out of the — into the fire*, vom Regen in die Traufe.

fuchsia ['fju:ʃə], *s.* (*Bot.*) die Fuchsie.

fudge [fʌdʒ], *s.* weiches Zuckerwerk; (*coll.*) Unsinn!

fuel ['fjuəl], *s.* der Brennstoff, Treibstoff; das Heizmaterial. — *v.a., v.n.* tanken.

fugitive ['fju:dʒitiv], *adj.* flüchtig, auf der Flucht. — *s.* der Flüchtling.

fugue [fju:g], *s.* (*Mus.*) die Fuge.

fulcrum ['fʌlkrəm], *s.* der Stützpunkt, Hebelpunkt.

fulfil [ful'fil], *v.a.* erfüllen; — *a requirement*, einem Gesetz genüge tun.

full [ful], *adj.* voll; vollständig (*complete*); *—time*, hauptberuflich.

fuller ['fulə], *s.* der Walker.

fullness ['fulnis], *s.* die Fülle.

fulsome ['fulsəm], *adj.* widerlich, ekelhaft; übermäßig.

fumble [fʌmbl], *v.n.* tappen (*for*, nach, *Dat.*).

fume [fju:m], *s.* der Rauch, Dunst; der Zorn (*anger*). — *v.n.* zornig sein, wüten (*be angered*).

fun [fʌn], *s.* der Spaß, Scherz; *have —*, sich gut unterhalten, sich amüsieren; *make —*, zum besten haben.

function ['fʌŋkʃən], *s.* (*also Maths.*) die Funktion; das Amt (*office*); die Feier(lichkeit) (*formal occasion*). — *v.n.* funktionieren (*be in working order*); fungieren (*officiate*).

fund [fʌnd], *s.* der Fonds (*financial*); (*fig.*) die Fülle (*of*, an); *public —s*, die Staatsgelder.

fundamental [fʌndə'mentl], *adj.* grundsätzlich, wesentlich. — *s.* (*pl.*) die Grundlagen, *f.pl.*

funeral ['fju:nərəl], *s.* die Bestattung, Beerdigung.

funereal [fju:'niəriəl], *adj.* wie bei einem Begräbnis, betrübt, traurig.

fungus ['fʌŋgəs], *s.* (*Bot.*) der Pilz; der Schwamm (*mushroom*).

funk [fʌŋk], *s.* (*sl.*) die Angst, Panik. — *v.a.* fürchten.

funnel [fʌnl], *s.* der Trichter.

funny ['fʌni], *adj.* spaßhaft, komisch.

fur [fə:], *s.* der Pelz, das Fell (*coat of animal*); (*Med.*) der Belag (*on tongue*).

furbelow ['fə:bilou], *s.* die Falbel.

furbish ['fə:biʃ], *v.a.* aufputzen.

furious ['fjuəriəs], *adj.* wild, rasend, wütend.

furl [fə:l], *v.a.* (zusammen-)rollen; (*Naut.*) aufrollen.

furlong ['fə:lɔŋ], *s.* ein Achtel einer englischen Meile.

furlough ['fə:lou], *s.* der Urlaub.

furnace ['fə:nis], *s.* der Ofen, Hochofen (*steel*); (*Metall.*) der Schmelzofen.

furnish ['fə:niʃ], *v.a.* ausstatten, versehen (*equip*); möblieren (*a room etc.*).

furnisher ['fə:niʃə], *s.* der Möbelhändler; der Lieferant.

furniture ['fə:nitʃə], *s.* die Möbel, *n. pl.*; die Einrichtung.

furrier ['fʌriə], *s.* der Kürschner.

furrow ['fʌrou], *s.* die Furche (*field*); die Runzel (*brow*). — *v.a.* runzeln (*brow*); Furchen ziehen (*plough up*).

further ['fə:ðə], *comp. adj., adv. see* **farther**. — *v.a.* fördern (*advance*).

furtherance ['fə:ðərəns], *s.* die Förderung (*advancement*).

furthermore ['fə:ðəmɔ:], *adv.* ferner.

furthest ['fə:ðist], *superl. adj., adv. see* **farthest**.

furtive ['fə:tiv], *adj.* verstohlen, heimlich.

fury ['fjuəri], *s.* die Wut; (*Myth.*) die Furie.

furze [fə:z], *s.* (*Bot.*) der Stechginster.

fuse [fju:z], *v.a., v.n.* schmelzen (*melt*); vereinigen (*unite*). — *s.* (*Elec.*) die Sicherung; *blow a —*, eine Sicherung durchbrennen; — *box*, der Sicherungskasten; — *wire*, der Schmelzdraht.

fuselage ['fju:zila:ʒ *or* -lidʒ], *s.* (*Aviat.*) der (Flugzeug-)rumpf.

fusible ['fju:zibl], *adj.* schmelzbar.

fusilier [fju:zi'liə], *s.* (*Mil.*) der Füsilier.

fusion ['fju:ʒən], *s.* die Verschmelzung; die Vereinigung.

fuss [fʌs], *s.* das Getue, die Umständlichkeit; *make a — about*, viel Aufhebens machen.

fussy ['fʌsi], *adj.* übertrieben genau; umständlich; geschäftig (*busy*); — *about*, genau in (*Dat.*).

fusty ['fʌsti], *adj.* moderig, muffig.

futile ['fju:tail], *adj.* nutzlos, vergeblich.

futility [fju:'tiliti], *s.* die Nutzlosigkeit.

future ['fju:tʃə], *s.* die Zukunft. — *adj.* (zu-)künftig.

fuzzy ['fʌzi], *adj.* kraus.

G

G [dʒi:]. das G (*also Mus.*); — *sharp*, das Gis; — *flat*, das Ges; *key of —*, der G Schlüssel, Violinschlüssel.

gab [gæb], *s.* das Geschwätz; *the gift of the —,* ein gutes Mundwerk.
gabble [gæbl], *v.n.* schwatzen.
gable [geibl], *s.* der Giebel.
gad [gæd], *v.n. — about,* umherstreifen.
gadfly ['gædflai], *s. (Ent.)* die Bremse.
gag [gæg], *s.* der Knebel; *(sl.)* der Witz. *— v.a.* knebeln.
gaiety ['geiəti], *s.* die Fröhlichkeit.
gain [gein], *v.a.* gewinnen, erwerben *(earn); — possession,* Besitz ergreifen. *— s.* der Gewinn, Vorteil.
gainful ['geinful], *adj. — employment,* die einträgliche Beschäftigung.
gainsay ['geinsei *or* gein'sei], *v.a.* widersprechen *(pers., Dat.).*
gait [geit], *s.* das Schreiten, der Schritt, Gang.
gaiter ['geitə], *s.* die Gamasche.
galaxy ['gæləksi], *s. (Astron.)* die Milchstraße; *(fig.)* die glänzende Versammlung.
gale [geil], *s.* der Sturm.
gall [gɔ:l], *s.* die Galle. *— v.a.* verbittern, ärgern.
gallant ['gælənt], *adj.* tapfer *(of soldier);* gallant, höflich *(polite).*
gallantry ['gæləntri], *s.* die Tapferkeit; die Höflichkeit, Galanterie.
gallery ['gæləri], *s.* die Gallerie.
galley ['gæli], *s. (Naut.)* die Galeere; *(Typ.) — proof,* der Fahnenabzug.
gallon ['gælən], *s.* die Gallone.
gallop ['gæləp], *v.n.* galoppieren. *— s.* der Galopp.
gallows ['gælouz], *s.* der Galgen.
galosh [gə'lɔʃ], *s.* die Galosche.
galvanic [gæl'vænik], *adj.* galvanisch.
galvanize ['gælvənaiz], *v.a.* galvanisieren.
gamble [gæmbl], *v.n.* um Geld spielen; *— away,* verspielen. *— s.* das Risiko.
gambol [gæmbl], *v.n.* herumspringen.
game [geim], *s.* das Spiel *(play);* das Wild, Wildbret *(pheasants etc.); fair —,* Freiwild, *n.,* offene Beute, *f.*
gamecock ['geimkɔk], *s. (Orn.)* der Kampfhahn.
gamekeeper ['geimki:pə], *s.* der Wildhüter.
gammon ['gæmən], *s.* der (geräucherte) Schinken *(bacon).*
gamut ['gæmət], *s.* die Tonleiter.
gander ['gændə], *s. (Orn.)* der Gänserich.
gang [gæŋ], *s.* die Bande; die Mannschaft *(workmen). — v.n. — up,* eine Bande bilden; *— up on s.o.,* sich gegen jemanden verbünden.
gangrene ['gæŋgri:n], *s. (Med.)* der Brand; die Fäulnis.
gangway ['gæŋwei], *s.* die Planke, der Laufgang *(on boat);* der Durchgang.
gaol, jail [dʒeil], *s.* das Gefängnis. *— v.a.* einsperren.
gaoler, jailer ['dʒeilə], *s.* der Kerkermeister.
gap [gæp], *s.* die Lücke; die Bresche *(breach).*
gape [geip], *v.n.* gähnen, *(fig.)* klaffen.

garage ['gærɑ:ʒ *or* 'gæridʒ], *s.* die Garage, die Tankstelle.
garb [gɑ:b], *s.* die Tracht, Kleidung.
garbage ['gɑ:bidʒ], *s.* der Abfall; *(Am.) — can,* der Mülleimer.
garble [gɑ:bl], *v.a.* verstümmeln.
garden [gɑ:dn], *s.* der Garten. *— v.n.* im Garten arbeiten.
gardener ['gɑ:dnə], *s.* der Gärtner.
gargle [gɑ:gl], *v.n.* gurgeln, spülen.
gargoyle ['gɑ:gɔil], *s. (Archit.)* der Wasserspeier.
garish ['gɛəriʃ], *adj.* grell, auffallend.
garland ['gɑ:lənd], *s.* der Blumenkranz, die Girlande.
garlic ['gɑ:lik], *s. (Bot.)* der Knoblauch.
garment ['gɑ:mənt], *s.* das Gewand.
garner ['gɑ:nə], *v.a.* aufspeichern *(store).*
garnet ['gɑ:nit], *s.* der Granat.
garnish ['gɑ:niʃ], *v.a.* ausschmücken, verzieren.
garret ['gærət], *s.* die Dachkammer.
garrison ['gærisən], *s. (Mil.)* die Garnison. *— v.a.* stationieren.
garrulity [gæ'ru:liti], *s.* die Schwatzhaftigkeit.
garter ['gɑ:tə], *s.* das Strumpfband, das Hosenband; *Order of the Garter,* der Hosenbandorden.
gas [gæs], *s.* das Gas; *(Am.) see* **gasoline**.
gaseous ['geisiəs], *adj.* gasförmig, gasartig.
Gascon ['gæskən], *s.* der Gaskogner.
gasoline ['gæsoli:n], *s. (Am.)* das Benzin.
gash [gæʃ], *s.* die Schnittwunde.
gasp [gɑ:sp], *v.n.* keuchen; nach Luft schnappen. *— s.* das Keuchen, das Luftschnappen.
gastric ['gæstrik], *adj. (Anat.)* gastrisch; *— ulcer,* das Magengeschwür.
gate [geit], *s.* das Tor, der Eingang. *— v.a.* einsperren, Hausarrest geben *(Dat.).*
gateway ['geitwei], *s.* die Einfahrt.
gather ['gæðə], *v.a.* sammeln, einsammeln *(collect);* versammeln *(assemble). — v.n.* entnehmen, schließen *(infer);* sich versammeln *(come together);* aufziehen *(storm).*
gathering ['gæðəriŋ], *s.* die Versammlung *(meeting).*
gauche [gouʃ], *adj.* linkisch, ungeschickt.
gaudy ['gɔ:di], *adj.* übertrieben, grell, prunkhaft.
gauge [geidʒ], *v.a. (Engin.)* ausmessen, kalibrieren; eichen *(officially). — s.* der Maßstab *(scale); (Railw.)* die Spurweite.
gauger ['geidʒə], *s.* der Eichmeister.
Gaul [gɔ:l], *s.* der Gallier.
gaunt [gɔ:nt], *adj.* mager; hager.
gauntlet ['gɔ:ntlit], *s.* der (Panzer)handschuh.
gauze [gɔ:z], *s.* die Gaze.
gavotte [gə'vɔt], *s. (Mus.)* die Gavotte.

gay [gei], *adj.* fröhlich, heiter; bunt (*colour*).

gaze [geiz], *v.n.* starren.

gazelle [gə'zel], *s.* (*Zool.*) die Gazelle.

gazette [gə'zet], *s.* die (amtliche) Zeitung; das Amtsblatt.

gear [giə], *s.* das Gerät; (*Mech.*) das Triebwerk; (*Naut.*) das Geschirr; *switch*—, das Schaltgerät; (*Motor.*) der Gang; — *ratio*, die Übersetzung; *differential* —, der Achsenantrieb; *steering* —, die Lenkung (*of car*); — *box*, das Schaltgetriebe, die Gangschaltung; *out of* —, in Unordnung; *in top* —, mit Höchstgeschwindigkeit; *change to bottom* —, auf erste Geschwindigkeit (*or*, auf langsam) einschalten. — *v.a.* — *down*, herabsetzen; (*Engin.*) — *up*, übersetzen; — *to*, anpassen.

gelatine ['dʒelətiːn], *s.* die Gallerte, die Geleemasse.

gem [dʒem], *s.* die Gemme, der Edelstein.

gender ['dʒendə], *s.* (*Gram.*) das Geschlecht.

gene [dʒiːn], *s.* (*Biol.*) das Gen.

geneaology [dʒiːni'ælədʒi], *s.* die Genealogie; der Stammbaum (*family tree*).

general ['dʒenərəl], *s.* (*Mil.*) der General; *lieutenant*- —, der Generalleutnant. — *adj.* allgemein, General-; — *-purpose*, für alle Zwecke; Allzweck-.

generalization [dʒenərəlai'zeiʃən], *s.* die Verallgemeinerung.

generalize ['dʒenərəlaiz], *v.a.* verallgemeinern.

generate ['dʒenəreit], *v.a.* erzeugen; (*Elec.*) Strom erzeugen.

generation [dʒenə'reiʃən], *s.* die Generation (*contemporaries*); das Zeugen (*production*); (*Elec.*) die Stromerzeugung.

generosity [dʒenə'rositi], *s.* die Großmut (*magnanimity*); die Freigebigkeit (*liberality*).

generous ['dʒenərəs], *adj.* großmütig; freigebig (*with gifts*).

Genevan [dʒi'niːvən], *adj.* genferisch. — *s.* der Genfer.

genitive ['dʒenitiv], *s.* (*Gram.*) der Wesfall, Genitiv.

genial ['dʒiːniəl], *adj.* freundlich, mild.

geniality [dʒiːni'æliti], *s.* die Freundlichkeit, Leutseligkeit.

genital ['dʒenitəl], *adj.* Zeugungs-. — *s.* (*pl.*) die Geschlechtsteile, Genitalien, *pl.*

genius ['dʒiːniəs], *s.* das Genie; der Genius.

Genoese [dʒenou'iːz], *adj.* genuesisch. — *s.* der Genuese.

Gentile ['dʒentail], *s.* heidnisch; nicht jüdisch.

gentility [dʒen'tiliti], *s.* die Herkunft aus vornehmem Haus, Vornehmheit.

gentle [dʒentl], *adj.* sanft, mild; gelind (*breeze*).

gentlefolk ['dʒentlfouk], *s.* bessere *or* vornehme Leute, *pl.*

gentleman ['dʒentlmən], *s.* der Gentleman, Herr; feiner Herr.

gentleness ['dʒentlnis], *s.* die Milde, Sanftheit.

gentry ['dʒentri], *s.* der niedere Adel.

genuine ['dʒenjuin], *adj.* echt.

genus ['dʒenəs], *s.* (*Biol.*) die Gattung.

geographer [dʒi'ɔgrəfə], *s.* der Geograph.

geographical [dʒi'o'græfikəl], *adj.* geographisch.

geography [dʒi'ɔgrəfi], die Geographie, Erdkunde.

geological [dʒi'o'lɔdʒikəl], *adj.* geologisch.

geologist [dʒi'ɔlədʒist], *s.* der Geologe.

geology [dʒi'ɔlədʒi], *s.* die Geologie.

geometric(al) [dʒi'o'metrik(əl)], *adj.* geometrisch.

geometrist [dʒi'ɔmətrist], *s.* der Geometer.

geometry [dʒi'ɔmətri], *s.* die Geometrie.

geranium [dʒə'reiniəm], *s.* (*Bot.*) die Geranie, das Germaniu.

germ [dʒəːm], *s.* der Keim; (*pl.*) die Bakterien, *f. pl.*

German ['dʒəːmən], *adj.* deutsch. — *s.* der, die Deutsche.

germane [dʒəː'mein], *adj.* zur Sache gehörig, zugehörig.

germinate ['dʒəːmineit], *v.n.* keimen.

Germanic [dʒəː'mænik], *adj.* germanisch.

gerund ['dʒerənd], *s.* (*Gram.*) das Gerundium.

gerundive [dʒe'rʌndiv], *s.* (*Gram.*) das Gerundiv(um).

gesticulate [dʒes'tikjuleit], *v.n.* Gebärden machen, gestikulieren.

gesture ['dʒestʃə], *s.* die Geste; der Gebärde.

get [get], *v.a. irr.* bekommen, (*coll.*) kriegen; erhalten (*receive*); erwischen (*catch up with*); einholen (*fetch*); — *over* or *across*, klar machen. — *v.n.* gelangen (*arrive*); werden (*become*); — *along*, weiterkommen; — *on* or (*Am.*) *along with s.o.*, mit jemandem auskommen; — *on in the world*, Karriere machen; — *away*, entkommen; — *down to it*, zur Sache kommen; — *in*, hineinkommen; — *off*, aussteigen; *show s.o. where he* —*s off*, jemandem seine Meinung sagen; (*Sch.*) — *through*, durchkommen (*in examination*); — *up*, aufstehen.

get-up ['getʌp], *s.* das Kostüm; die Ausstattung (*attire*).

Ghanaian [gɑː'neiən], *adj.* ghanaisch. — *s.* der Ghanaer.

ghastly ['gɑːstli], *adj.* furchtbar, schrecklich.

gherkin ['gəːkin], *s.* (*Bot.*) die Essiggurke.

ghost [goust], *s.* der Geist, das Gespenst.

giant ['dʒaiənt], *s.* der Riese.

gibberish ['dʒibəriʃ], *s.* das Kauderwelsch.

gibbet ['dʒibit], *s.* der Galgen.

gibe [dʒaib], *v.n.* spotten, höhnen (*at*, über, *Acc.*). — *s.* der Spott, Hohn; die spöttische Bemerkung (*remark*).

giblets ['dʒiblits], *s. pl.* das Gänseklein.

giddiness ['gidinis], *s.* das Schwindelgefühl.

giddy ['gidi], *adj.* schwindelig.

gift [gift], *s.* die Gabe, das Geschenk.

gifted ['giftid], *adj.* begabt.

gig [gig], *s.* der leichte Wagen; (*Naut.*) der Nachen, das Gig.

gigantic [dʒai'gæntik], *adj.* riesig, riesengroß.

giggle [gigl], *v.n.* kichern. — *s.* das Kichern, Gekicher.

gild [gild], *v.a.* vergolden; verschönern; —*ing the pill*, etwas Unangenehmes (die Pille) versüßen.

gill (1) [gil], *s.* (*Biol.*) die Kieme.

gill (2) [dʒil], *s.* das Viertel einer Pinte (0.14 *l.*).

gilt [gilt], *s.* die Vergoldung; — *edged*, mit Goldschnitt; (*Comm.*) hochwertige *or* mündelsichere Staatspapiere.

gimlet ['gimlit], *s.* (*Carp.*) der Handbohrer.

gin [dʒin], *s.* der Gin, der Wacholderbranntwein; — *and tonic*, Gin und Tonic.

ginger ['dʒindʒə], *s.* der Ingwer; — -*haired*, rothaarig; — *nut*, das Ingweror Pfeffernüßchen, Ingwerkeks; — *beer*, Ingwerbier. — *v.a.* — *up*, aufstacheln, anreizen.

gingerbread ['dʒindʒəbred], *s.* der Lebkuchen, Pfefferkuchen.

gipsy ['dʒipsi], *s.* der Zigeuner.

giraffe [dʒi'rɑːf], *s.* (*Zool.*) die Giraffe.

gird [gəːd], *v.a.* reg. & irr. (*Poet.*) gürten.

girder ['gəːdə], *s.* der Balken, Träger.

girdle [gəːdl], *v.a.* gürten, umgürten; — *the earth*, die Erde umkreisen.

girl [gəːl], *s.* das Mädchen.

girlhood ['gəːlhud], *s.* die Mädchenzeit, die Mädchenjahre, *n. pl.*

girlish ['gəːliʃ], *adj.* mädchenhaft, wie ein Mädchen.

gist [dʒist], *s.* das Wesentliche.

give [giv], *v.a. irr.* geben; — *out*, bekanntgeben, bekanntmachen; — *up*, aufgeben; — *way to*, Platz machen. — *v.n.* sich dehnen, sich strecken (*of wood, metal etc.*); — *in*, nachgeben (*to, Dat.*).

glacial ['gleiʃəl], *adj.* eisig, Gletscher-.

glacier ['glæsiə], *s.* der Gletscher.

glad [glæd], *adj.* froh, erfreut (*at*, über, *Acc.*).

gladden [glædn], *v.a.* erheitern, erfreuen.

glade [gleid], *s.* die Lichtung.

glamorous ['glæmərəs], *adj.* bezaubernd, blendend glanzvoll.

glamour ['glæmə], *s.* der Zauber; der Glanz.

glance [glɑːns], *s.* der Blick; *at a —*, auf den ersten Blick. — *v.n.* flüchtig blicken.

gland [glænd], *s.* (*Anat.*) die Drüse.

glandular ['glændjulə], *adj.* Drüsen-, drüsig.

glare [glɛə], *s.* der blendende Glanz, das Schimmern; der (scharf) durchbohrende Blick (*stare*).

glaring ['glɛəriŋ], *adj.* schreiend (*of colour*); auffallend (*obvious*).

glass [glɑːs], *s.* das Glas; der Spiegel (*mirror*); das Wetterglas (*barometer*); (*pl.*) die Brille (*spectacles*).

glassblower ['glɑːsblouə], *s.* der Glasbläser.

glassworks ['glɑːswəːks], *s.* die Glashütte.

glassy ['glɑːsi], *adj.* gläsern.

glaze [gleiz], *s.* die Glasur. — *v.a.* glasieren; verglasen.

glazier ['gleiziə], *s.* der Glaser.

gleam [gliːm], *v.n.* strahlen, glänzen (*with*, vor, *Dat.*). — *s.* der Glanz, das Strahlen.

glean [gliːn], *v.a.* auflesen; erfahren (*learn*).

glebe [gliːb], *s.* das Pfarrgut.

glee (1) [gliː], *s.* die Freude, Heiterkeit.

glee (2) [gliː], *s.* (*Mus.*) der Rundgesang; — *club*, die Liedertafel.

glen [glen], *s.* das enge Tal.

glib [glib], *adj.* glatt, geläufig, zungenfertig.

glide [glaid], *v.n.* gleiten. — *s.* das Gleiten.

glider ['glaidə], *s.* (*Aviat.*) das Segelflugzeug.

glimmer ['glimə], *s.* der Schimmer, Glimmer. — *v.n.* schimmern, glimmen.

glimpse [glimps], *s.* der (flüchtige) Blick; *catch a —*, einen Blick erhaschen. — *v.a.* flüchtig blicken (auf, *Acc.*).

glisten [glisn], *v.n.* glitzern, glänzen.

glitter ['glitə], *v.n.* glänzen, schimmern.

gloaming ['gloumiŋ], *s.* die Dämmerung.

globe [gloub], *s.* der Globus, der Erdball; die Kugel.

globular ['glɔbjulə], *adj.* kugelförmig.

gloom [gluːm], *s.* das Dunkel; der Trübsinn, die Traurigkeit.

gloomy ['gluːmi], *adj.* deprimiert, trübsinnig, düster.

glorify ['glɔːrifai], *v.a.* verherrlichen.

glorious ['glɔːriəs], *adj.* herrlich; (*Mil.*) glorreich.

glory ['glɔːri], *s.* die Herrlichkeit, der Ruhm. — *v.n.* frohlocken (*in*, über, *Acc.*).

gloss [glɔs], *s.* der Glanz; (*Lit.*) die Glosse, Anmerkung. — *v.a. — over*, beschönigen; (*Lit.*) glossieren, mit Anmerkungen versehen.

glossary ['glɔsəri], *s.* das Glossar, die Spezialwörterliste; das Wörterbuch.

glossy ['glɔsi], *adj.* glänzend.

glove [glʌv], *s.* der Handschuh.

glow [glou], *v.n.* glühen. — *s.* die Glut, das Glühen; Wohlbehagen.

glower ['glauə], *v.n.* — *at*, feindselig ansehen, anstarren.

glue

glue [glu:], *s.* der Leim. — *v.a.* leimen, zusammenleimen.

glum [glʌm], *adj.* mürrisch, finster.

glut [glʌt], *s.* die Überfülle. — *v.a.* überladen, überfüllen.

glutinous [ˈgluːtinəs], *adj.* zähe, klebrig.

glutton [glʌtn], *s.* der Vielfraß.

gluttony [ˈglʌtəni], *s.* die Schwelgerei, Gefräßigkeit.

glycerine [ˈglisəriːn], *s.* das Glyzerin.

gnarled [nɑːld], *adj.* knorrig.

gnash [næʃ], *v.a.* knirschen (*teeth*).

gnat [næt], *s.* (*Ent.*) die Mücke.

gnaw [nɔː], *v.a., v.n.* nagen (an, *Dat.*), zernagen, zerfressen (at, *Acc.*).

gnome [noum], *s.* der Erdgeist, der Zwerg, Gnom.

go [gou], *v.n. irr.* gehen, fahren, laufen; arbeiten (*engine*); verlaufen (*event*); sich erstrecken (*distance*); — *down in the general esteem*, in der Achtung sinken; — *on*, fortfahren; — *mad*, verrückt werden; — *bald*, die Haare verlieren; — *without*, leer ausgehen, entbehren; *let* —, loslassen; — *for*, auf jemanden losgehen; — *in for*, sich interessieren für (*Acc.*); — *all out for*, energisch unternehmen; *a* —*ing concern*, ein gutgehendes Unternehmen; —*ing on for 20*, fast 20 Jahre. — *s.* der Versuch; (*coll.*) *plenty of* —, recht lebhaft, voller Schwung.

goad [goud], *v.a.* anstacheln.

goal [goul], *s.* das Ziel; (*Footb.*) das Tor.

goalkeeper [ˈgoulkiːpə], *s.* der Torwart.

goalpost [ˈgoulpoust], *s.* der Torpfosten.

goat [gout], *s.* (*Zool.*) die Geiß, Ziege; *billy* —, der Ziegenbock; *nanny* —, die Geiß.

gobble [gɔbl], *v.a.* verschlingen, gierig essen.

goblet [ˈgɔblit], *s.* der Becher.

goblin [ˈgɔblin], *s.* der Kobold, der Gnom; der Schelm.

go-cart [ˈgouкɑːt], *s.* der Kinderwagen, Gängelwagen.

God [gɔd], *s.* Gott.

god [gɔd], *s.* der Gott.

godchild [ˈgɔdtʃaild], *s.* das Patenkind.

goddess [ˈgɔdes], *s.* die Göttin.

godfather [ˈgɔdfɑːðə], *s.* der Pate.

godhead [ˈgɔdhed], *s.* die Gottheit.

godless [ˈgɔdlis], *adj.* gottlos, ungläubig.

godmother [ˈgɔdmʌðə], *s.* die Patin.

goggle [gɔgl], *v.n.* glotzen, starren (*stare*). — *s.* (*pl.*) die Schutzbrille.

going [ˈgouiŋ], *s.* das Gehen, das Funktionieren (*of machinery*); *while the* — *is good*, zur rechten Zeit.

gold [gould], *s.* das Gold; (*Fin.*) — *standard*, die Goldwährung.

goldfinch [ˈgouldfintʃ], *s.* (*Orn.*) der Stieglitz.

goldsmith [ˈgouldsmiθ], *s.* der Goldschmied.

gondola [ˈgɔndələ], *s.* die Gondel.

good [gud], *adj.* gut; artig, brav; *for* —, auf immer; *in* — *time*, rechtzeitig; — *and proper*, (*coll.*) wie es sich gehört, anständig; *as* — *as*, so gut wie; — *looking*, hübsch; — *natured*, gutmütig. — *s.* *for your own* —, in Ihrem eigenen Interesse; *that's no* —, das taugt nichts; (*pl.*) die Güter, *n.pl.*, Waren, *f.pl.*; *goods station*, der Frachtbahnhof; *goods train*, der Güterzug; *goods yard*, der Güterstapelplatz.

goodbye [gudˈbai], *interj.*, *s.*—*!* leb wohl! auf Wiedersehen!

goodness [ˈgudnis], *s.* die Güte.

goodwill [gudˈwil], *s.* das Wohlwollen; (*Comm.*) die Kundschaft.

goose [guːs], *s.* (*Orm.*) die Gans.

gooseberry [ˈguzbəri], *s.* (*Bot.*) die Stachelbeere.

gore [gɔː], *s.* das geronnene Blut. — *v.a.* durchbohren (*pierce*, *stab*).

gorge [gɔːdʒ], *s.* die Felsenschlucht (*ravine*); (*Anat.*) die Kehle. — *v.a.* gierig verschlingen.

gorgeous [ˈgɔːdʒəs], *adj.* prachtvoll, prächtig.

gorse [gɔːs], *s.* (*Bot.*) der Stechginster.

gory [ˈgɔːri], *adj.* blutig.

goshawk [ˈgɔshɔːk], *s.* (*Orn.*) der Hühnerhabicht.

gosling [ˈgɔzliŋ], *s.* (*Orn.*) das Gänschen.

gospel [ˈgɔspəl], *s.* das Evangelium; *the*— *according to*, das Evangelium des...

gossamer [ˈgɔsəmə], *s.* das feine Gewebe; die Sommerfäden.

gossip [ˈgɔsip], *v.n.* klatschen; schwatzen, plaudern. — *s.* der Klatsch; der Schwätzer; die Klatschbase.

Gothic [ˈgɔθik], *adj.* gotisch.

gouge [gaudʒ], *s.* der Hohlmeißel. — *v.a.* aushöhlen, ausstechen.

gourd [ˈguəd], *s.* der Kürbis.

gout [gaut], *s.* (*Med.*) die Gicht.

govern [ˈgʌvən], *v.a., v.n.* (*Pol.*) regieren; beherrschen; (*fig.*) leiten, herrschen.

governable [ˈgʌvənəbl], *adj.* lenkbar, lenksam.

governess [ˈgʌvənis], *s.* die Erzieherin, die Gouvernante.

government [ˈgʌvənmənt], *s.* die Regierung; (*Pol.*) — *benches*, die Regierungssitze; — *loan*, die Staatsanleihe.

governor [ˈgʌvənə], *s.* der Gouverneur, Statthalter.

gown [gaun], *s.* das Kleid (*lady's*); (*Univ.*) der Talar; (*official robe*) die Amtstracht.

grab [græb], *v.a.* packen, ergreifen. — *s.* der Zugriff.

grace [greis], *s.* die Gnade; Gunst (*favour*); die Anmut (*gracefulness*); *Your Grace*, Euer Gnaden; das Tischgebet (*prayer at table*); (*Mus.*) — *note*, die Fermate; *ten minutes'* —, zehn Minuten Aufschub. — *v.a.* schmücken, zieren, ehren.

graceful [ˈgreisful], *adj.* anmutig, reizend; graziös (*movement*).

graceless ['greislis], *adj.* ungraziös.
gracious ['greiʃəs], *adj.* gnädig, huldreich.
gradation [grə'deiʃən], *s.* die Abstufung, die Stufenleiter.
grade [greid], *s.* der Grad, Rang (*rank*); (*Am.*) (*Sch.*) die Klasse. — *v.a.* sortieren, ordnen.
•**gradient** ['greidiənt], *s.* (*Geog.*) die Steigung; der Steigungswinkel (*angle*).
gradual ['grædjuəl], *adj.* allmählich.
graduate ['grædjueit], *v.n.* promovieren (*receive degree*); — *as a doctor*, als Doktor promovieren, den Doktor machen. — [-djuit], *s.* der Akademiker, Graduierte.
graft (1) [grɑ:ft], *s.* (*Hort., Med.*) die (Haut)übertragung. — *v.a.* (*Hort., Med.*) übertragen, anheften (*on to*, auf, *Acc.*).
graft (2) [grɑ:ft], *s.* (*Am.*) der unerlaubte Gewinn; das Schmiergeld; der Betrug (*swindle*).
grain [grein], *s.* das Korn, Samenkorn; das Getreide; das Gran (= 0·065 *gramme*); die Maserung (*in wood*); *against the* —, gegen den Strich.
grammar ['græmə], *s.* die Grammatik; — *school*, das Gymnasium.
grammatical [grə'mætikəl], *adj.* grammatisch.
gramme [græm], *s.* das Gramm.
gramophone ['græməfoun], *s.* das Grammophon.
granary ['grænəri], *s.* der (Korn)speicher, die Kornkammer.
grand [grænd], *adj.* groß, großartig; wunderbar; *Grand Duke*, der Großherzog. — *s.* (*Am.*) (*sl.*) 1000 Dollar; (*piano*) der Flügel; *baby* —, der Stutzflügel.
grandchild ['græntʃaild], *s.* der Enkel, die Enkelin.
grandee [græn'di:], *s.* der spanische Grande.
grandeur ['grændjə], *s.* die Größe, Pracht.
grandfather ['grændfɑ:ðə], *s.* der Großvater.
grandiloquent [græn'dilokwənt], *adj.* großsprecherisch.
grandmother ['grændmʌðə], *s.* die Großmutter.
grange [greindʒ], *s.* der Meierhof, das Landhaus.
granite ['grænit], *s.* der Granit.
grannie, granny ['græni], *s.* (*coll.*) die Oma.
grant [grɑ:nt], *s.* die Gewährung (*of permission etc.*); die Zuwendung (*subsidy*); (*Sch.*) das Stipendium. — *v.a.* geben, gewähren; *take for* —*ed*, als selbstverständlich hinnehmen.
granular ['grænjulə], *adj.* körnig.
granulated ['grænjuleitid], *adj.* feinkörnig, Kristall- (*sugar*).
grape [greip], *s.* (*Bot.*) die Weinbeere; die Traube; — *sugar*, der Traubenzucker; *bunch of* —*s*, Weintrauben, *f. pl.*
grapefruit ['greipfru:t], *s.* die Pampelmuse.

graphic ['græfik], *adj.* (*Art*) graphisch; deutlich, bildhaft, anschaulich.
grapnel ['græpnəl], *s.* (*Naut.*) der Dreganker.
grapple [græpl], *v.n.* — *with*, raufen, (miteinander) ringen.
grasp [grɑ:sp], *v.a.* (mit der Hand) ergreifen, erfassen. — *s.* das Fassungsvermögen, die Auffassung; der Griff (*hand*).
grasping ['grɑ:spiŋ], *adj.* habgierig, gewinnsüchtig.
grass [grɑ:s], *s.* (*Bot.*) das Gras; der Rasen (*lawn*); — *widow*, die Strohwitwe.
grasshopper ['grɑ:shɔpə], *s.* (*Ent.*) die Heuschrecke.
grate (1) [greit], *s.* der Feuerrost, der Kamin.
grate (2) [greit], *v.a.* reiben (*cheese*); schaben, kratzen. — *v.n.* knirschen; auf die Nerven gehen.
grateful ['greitful], *adj.* dankbar.
grater ['greitə], *s.* das Reibeisen; die Reibe (*electrical*).
gratification [grætifi'keiʃən], *s.* die Genugtuung, Befriedigung.
gratify ['grætifai], *v.a.* befriedigen, erfreuen.
grating ['greitiŋ], *s.* das Gitter.
gratis ['greitis], *adv.* gratis, umsonst, frei, unentgeltlich.
gratitude ['grætitju:d], *s.* die Dankbarkeit.
gratuitous [grə'tju:itəs], *adj.* frei, freiwillig (*voluntary*); unentgeltlich (*free of charge*); grundlos (*baseless*).
gratuity [grə'tju:iti], *s.* das Trinkgeld (*tip*); die Gratifikation.
grave (1) [greiv], *adj.* schwer, ernst (*serious*); feierlich (*solemn*). — *s.* (*Mus.*) das Grave.
grave (2) [greiv], *s.* das Grab (*tomb*).
gravel [grævl], *s.* der Kies.
graveyard ['greivjɑ:d], *s.* der Friedhof.
gravitate ['græviteit], *v.n.* gravitieren, hinstreben.
gravitation [grævi'teiʃən], *s.* die Schwerkraft.
gravitational [grævi'teiʃənəl], *adj.* (*Phys.*) Schwerkrafts-.
gravity ['græviti], *s.* der Ernst (*seriousness*); (*Phys.*) die Schwere, Schwerkraft.
gravy ['greivi], *s.* die Sauce, Soße; der Saft des Fleisches, des Bratens; — *boat*, die Sauciere.
gray, grey [grei], *adj.* grau.
graze (1) [greiz], *v.n.* weiden.
graze (2) [greiz], *v.a.* streifen (*pass closely*), abschürfen.
grazier ['greiziə], *s.* der Viehzüchter.
grease [gri:s], *s.* das Fett; das Schmieröl (*machine*). — *v.a.* einfetten (*pans*); schmieren, einschmieren (*machinery*).
greasy ['gri:si], *adj.* fett, schmierig, ölig.
great [greit], *adj.* groß, bedeutend, wichtig; (*Am.*) wundervoll, wunderbar.

greatcoat ['greitcout], s. der Winter-
mantel.

great-grandfather [greit'grændfɑ:ðə],
s. der Urgroßvater.

greatly ['greitli], adv. stark, sehr.

greatness ['greitnis], s. die Größe,
Bedeutung.

greedy ['gri:di], adj. gierig; gefräßig
(eater).

Greek [gri:k], adj. griechisch. — s. der
Grieche.

green [gri:n], adj. grün; neu (new),
frisch (fresh).

greengage ['gri:ngeidʒ], s. (Bot.) die
Reineclaude.

greengrocer ['gri:ngrousə], s. der
Grünwarenhändler, Gemüsehändler.

greenhorn ['gri:nhɔ:n], s. der Grünschnabel.

greenhouse ['gri:nhaus], s. das Gewächshaus, Treibhaus.

Greenlander ['gri:nləndə], s. der Grön-
länder.

greet [gri:t], v.a. grüßen, begrüßen.

greeting ['gri:tiŋ], s. die Begrüßung;
(pl.) Grüße, m. pl.

gregarious [gri'gɛəriəs], adj. gesellig.

grenade [gri'neid], s. die Granate.

grey see under **gray**.

greyhound ['greihaund], s. (Zool.) das
Windspiel, der Windhund.

grid [grid], s. (Elec.) das Stromnetz;
(Phys.) das Gitter.

gridiron ['gridaiən], s. der Bratrost, das
Bratrostgitter.

grief [gri:f], s. der Kummer, die Trauer.

grievance ['gri:vəns], s. die Klage,
Beschwerde.

grieve [gri:v], v.a. kränken. — v.n.
sich grämen, sich kränken (over, über,
Acc., wegen, Genit.).

grievous ['gri:vəs], adj. schmerzlich.

grill [gril], s. der Rostbraten, Bratrost.
— v.a. grillieren, rösten (meat);
verhören (question closely).

grilling ['griliŋ], s. das Verhör.

grim [grim], adj. grimmig, finster.

grimace [gri'meis], s. die Grimasse, die
Fratze.

grime [graim], s. der Schmutz, der Ruß.

grimy ['graimi], adj. schmutzig, rußig.

grin [grin], v.n. grinsen; (coll.) —
and bear it, mach gute Miene zum
bösen Spiel. — s. das Grinsen.

grind [graind], v.a. irr. zerreiben (rub);
schleifen (sharpen); mahlen (pulverize); — o.'s teeth, mit den Zähnen
knirschen. — s. (coll.) die ungeheuere
Anstrengung, die Plackerei.

grinder ['graində], s. coffee —, die
Kaffeemühle; knife —, der Schleifer,
Wetzer; der Backzahn (molar).

grindstone ['graindstoun], s. der Schleif-
stein; keep o.'s nose to the —, fest bei
der Arbeit bleiben.

grip [grip], s. der Griff; lose o.'s —,
nicht mehr bewältigen können (wie
bisher); (Tech.) der Handgriff (handle).
— v.a. ergreifen, festhalten.

gripe [graip], v.n. (sl.) meckern.

gripes [graips], s. pl. (Med.) das Bauch-
grimmen, die Kolik.

gripping ['gripiŋ], adj. fesselnd (story).

grisly ['grizli], adj. scheußlich, gräßlich.

grist [grist], s. das Mahlgut, Gemah-
lene; — to o.'s mill, Wasser auf seine
Mühle.

gristle [grisl], s. der Knorpel.

grit [grit], s. das Schrot, der Kies; der
Mut (courage).

gritty ['griti], adj. körnig, kiesig,
sandig.

grizzled [grizld], adj. grau, grau-
meliert.

groan [groun], v.n. stöhnen.

groats [grouts], s. pl. die Hafergrütze.

grocer ['grousə], s. der Kolonialwaren-
händler, Feinkosthändler.

groin [groin], s. (Anat.) die Leiste;
(Archit.) die Gewölbekante, Rippe.

groom [gru:m], s. der Stallknecht
(stables); (obs.) der Junge (inn). — v.a.
schniegeln, bürsten; schön machen.

groove [gru:v], s. die Rinne; die Rille
(of gramophone record). — v.a. rillen;
furchen (dig a furrow).

grope [group], v.n. tappen, tasten
(around, umher).

gross [grous], adj. dick (fat); plump
(heavy-handed); grob (ill-mannered);
— weight, das Bruttogewicht; ungeheuer (error).

grotto ['grotou], s. die Grotte.

ground [graund], s. der Grund, Boden
(also pl.); die Ursache (cause); —
floor, das Erdgeschoß. — v.n. stranden
(of ship).

groundwork ['graundwə:k], s. die
Grundlagen, f. pl.

group [gru:p], s. die Gruppe. — v.a.
gruppieren, anordnen.

grouse (1) [graus], v.n. (coll.) meckern,
sich beklagen. — s. der Grund zur
Klage, die Beschwerde.

grouse (2) [graus], s. (Orn.) das Birk-
huhn, Moorhuhn.

grove [grouv], s. der Hain, das Wäld-
chen.

grovel [grɔvl], v.n. kriechen, schöntun
(Dat.).

grow [grou], v.n. irr. wachsen, sich
mehren (increase); werden (become).
— v.a. anbauen, anpflanzen.

growl [graul], v.n. brummen, knurren.
— s. das Gebrumme, Geknurre.

grown-up [groun'ʌp], s. der Erwachsene. — adj. erwachsen.

growth [grouθ], s. das Anwachsen
(increase); das Wachstum (growing).

grub [grʌb], s. (Zool.) die Larve; (coll.)
das Essen. — v.n. — about, wühlen.

grudge [grʌdʒ], s. der Groll; Neid
(jealousy). — v.a. mißgönnen (envy).
— v.n. — doing s.th., etwas ungerne
tun.

gruel ['gru:əl], s. der Haferschleim.

gruesome ['gru:səm], adj. schauerlich,
schrecklich.

gruff [grʌf], adj. mürrisch.

grumble [grʌmbl], v.n. murren, klagen.

grumbler ['grʌmblə], s. der Unzufriedene, Nörgler.
grunt [grʌnt], v.n. grunzen. — s. das Grunzen.
guarantee [gærən'ti:], v.a. bürgen, garantieren. — s. die Bürgschaft; (Comm.) die Garantie.
guarantor ['gærəntɔː], s. der Bürge; (Comm.) der Garant.
guard [gɑːd], s. die Wache (watch or watchman); (Railw.) der Schaffner; die Schutzvorrichtung (protective device); (fire) —, das Kamingitter ; (for sword) das Stichblatt. — v.a. bewachen; behüten (protect). — v.n. auf der Hut sein; — against, sich hüten (vor, Dat.); vorbeugen.
guarded ['gɑːdid], adj. behutsam, vorsichtig.
guardian ['gɑːdjən], s. der Vormund (of child); der Wächter.
guardianship ['gɑːdjənʃip], s. (Law) die Vormundschaft.
Guatemalan [gwæti'mɑːlən], adj. guatemaltekisch. — s. der Guatemalteke.
Guelph [gwelf], s. der Welfe.
guess [ges], v.a. raten (a riddle). — v.n. (Am.) glauben, meinen. — s. die Vermutung; have a —, rate mal!
guest [gest], s. der Gast; paying —, der Pensionär.
guffaw [gʌ'fɔː], s. das (laute) Gelächter.
guidance ['gaidəns], s. die Führung, Anleitung.
guide [gaid], s. der Führer, Wegweiser, Reiseführer; (Phot.) die Führung. — v.a. führen, anleiten.
guided ['gaidid], adj. gelenkt; — missile, das Ferngeschoß, die Rakete.
guild [gild], s. die Gilde, Zunft, Innung.
guildhall ['gildhɔːl], s. das Rathaus.
guile [gail], s. der Betrug, die Arglist.
guileless ['gaillis], adj. arglos.
guilt [gilt], s. die Schuld.
guilty ['gilti], adj. schuldig.
guinea ['gini], s. die Guinee (21 shillings); — fowl, das Perlhuhn; — pig, das Meerschweinchen.
guise [gaiz], s. die Verkleidung (costume); die Erscheinung (appearance).
guitar [gi'tɑː], s. (Mus.) die Gitarre.
gulf [gʌlf], s. der Meerbusen, Golf; der Abgrund (abyss).
gull [gʌl], s. (Orn.) die Möwe.
gullet [gʌlit], s. (Anat.) der Schlund, die Gurgel.
gullible ['gʌlibl], adj. leichtgläubig.
gully ['gʌli], s. die Schlucht (abyss).
gulp [gʌlp], v.a. schlucken. — s. der Schluck, Zug.
gum (1) [gʌm], s. (Bot.) das Gummi. — v.a. gummieren; (coll.) — up, verderben (spoil).
gum (2) [gʌm], s. (Anat.) das Zahnfleisch.
gun [gʌn], s. das Gewehr (rifle); die Kanone (cannon); — carriage, die Lafette.

gunpowder ['gʌnpaudə], s. das Schießpulver.
gunsmith ['gʌnsmiθ], s. der Büchsenmacher.
gurgle [gəːgl], v.n. glucksen.
gush [gʌʃ], v.n. sich ergießen; schwärmen.
gusset ['gʌsit], s. (Tail.) der Zwickel.
gust [gʌst], s. der Windstoß.
gut [gʌt], s. (Anat.) der Darm; (pl.) die Eingeweide, n. pl.; (coll.) der Mut. — v.a. ausnehmen; ausleeren.
gutter ['gʌtə], s. die Rinne, Gosse.
guttersnipe ['gʌtəsnaip], s. der Lausbube.
guttural ['gʌtərəl], adj. Kehl-. — s. (Phon.) der Kehllaut.
guy [gai], s. die Vogelscheuche, die verkleidete Puppe; (Am.) der Kerl.
guzzle [gʌzl], v.n. schlemmen.
gymnasium [dʒim'neiziəm], s. die Turnhalle.
gymnastics [dʒim'næstiks], s. pl. das Turnen; die Gymnastik.
gypsum ['dʒipsəm], s. der Gips; der schwefelsaure Kalk.
gyrate [dʒaiə'reit], v.n. sich im Kreise bewegen, sich drehen, kreisen.

H

H [eitʃ]. das H.
haberdasher ['hæbədæʃə], s. der Kurzwarenhändler.
haberdashery ['hæbədæʃəri], s. die Kurzwarenhandlung.
habit ['hæbit], s. die Gewohnheit (custom); force of —, aus Gewohnheit, die Macht der Gewohnheit; die Kleidung (costume); riding —, das Reitkostüm.
habitable ['hæbitəbl], adj. bewohnbar.
habitation [hæbi'teiʃən], s. die Wohnung.
habitual [hə'bitjuəl], adj. gewohnheitsmäßig.
habituate [hə'bitjueit], v.a. gewöhnen.
hack (1) [hæk], v.a. hacken (wood); treten.
hack (2) [hæk], s. der Lohnschreiber; der (alte) Gaul, das Mietpferd (horse).
hackle [hækl], v.a. hecheln.
hackney ['hækni], s. — carriage, die Mietskutsche; das Taxi.
haddock ['hædək], s. (Zool.) der Schellfisch.
haemorrhage ['heməridʒ], s. (Med.) die Blutung, der Blutsturz.
haemorrhoids ['hemərɔidz], s.pl.(Med.) die Hämorrhoiden, f. pl.
hag [hæg], s. das alte Weib; die Hexe (witch).

haggard

haggard ['hægəd], *adj.* hager (*lean*); häßlich, abgehärmt.
haggle [hægl], *v.n.* feilschen.
haggler ['hæglə], *s.* der Feilscher.
hail (1) [heil], *s.* der Hagel. — *v.n.* hageln.
hail (2) [heil], *v.a.* (mit einem Ruf) begrüßen; rufen. — *interj.* Heil, willkommen! — *s.* der Zuruf, Gruß.
hair [hɛə], *s.* das Haar; *split* —*s,* Haarspalterei treiben.
haircut ['hɛəkʌt], *s.* der Haarschnitt.
hairdresser ['hɛədresə], *s.* der Friseur.
hale [heil], *adj.* — *and hearty,* frisch und gesund, rüstig.
half [hɑːf], *adj.* halb. — *adv.* — *baked,* unreif; unterentwickelt (*stupid*); (*coll.*) *not* —, und wie! sehr gern. — *s.* die Hälfte; *too clever by* —, allzu gescheit.
halfcaste ['hɑːfkɑːst], *s.* der Mischling.
halfpenny ['heipni], *s.* der halbe Penny.
halfwit ['hɑːfwit], *s.* der Dummkopf.
halibut ['hælibət], *s.* (*Zool.*) der Heilbutt.
hall [hɔːl], *s.* der Saal; die Halle; der Hausflur (*entrance* —); (*Univ.*) (*of residence*), das Studentenheim; — *porter,* der Portier.
hallmark ['hɔːlmɑːk], *s.* das Kennzeichen.
hallow ['hælou], *v.a.* weihen, heiligen.
Halloween [hælou'iːn]. der Allerheiligenabend.
halo ['heilou], *s.* der Heiligenschein (*of saint*); der Hof (*round the moon*).
hallucination [həluːsi'neiʃən], *s.* die Halluzination.
halt [hɔːlt], *v.n.* halten, haltmachen; — *!* Halt! zögern (*tarry*); — *ing speech,* die Sprechhemmung. — *v.a.* anhalten, zum Halten bringen. — *s.* (*Railw.*) die (kleine) Haltestelle.
halve [hɑːv], *v.a.* halbieren.
ham [hæm], *s.* (*Cul.*) der Schinken; (*Anat.*) der Schenkel; — *acting,* das Schmierentheater.
hammer ['hæmə], *s.* der Hammer. — *v.a., v.n.* hämmern; — *away at,* an etwas emsig arbeiten; — *out a problem,* ein Problem zur Lösung bringen.
hammock ['hæmək], *s.* die Hängematte.
hamper (1) ['hæmpə], *s.* der Packkorb.
hamper (2) ['hæmpə], *v.a.* behindern.
hand [hænd], *s.* die Hand; *a fair* —, eine gute Handschrift; der Uhrzeiger (*on watch, clock*); die Seite (*right, left* —); die Karten, *f. pl.* (*card game*); *play a strong* —, starke Karten halten *or* spielen; *on* —, vorrätig, *or* Lager; *get out of* —, unkontrollierbar werden. — *v.a.* — *in,* einhändigen, einreichen; — *out,* austeilen; — *over,* übergeben, einhändigen.
handbag ['hændbæg], *s.* die Handtasche.
handbill ['hændbil], *s.* der Zettel, Reklamezettel (*advertising*).

handful ['hændful], *s.* die Handvoll; *to be quite a* —, genug zu schaffen geben; das Sorgenkind.
handicap ['hændikæp], *s.* das Hindernis. — *v.a.* hindern, behindern.
handicraft ['hændikrɑːft], *s.* das Handwerk; Kunsthandwerk.
handkerchief ['hæŋkətʃif], *s.* das Taschentuch.
handle [hændl], *s.* der Griff; der Henkel (*pot, vase*). — *v.a.* handhaben (*machine*); behandeln (*person*); anpacken (*problem*).
handlebar ['hændlbɑː], *s.* die Lenkstange (*bicycle*).
handmaid(en) ['hændmeid(n)], *s.* (*obs.*) die Magd.
handrail ['hændreil], *s.* das Geländer.
handshake ['hændʃeik], *s.* der Händedruck.
handsome ['hænsəm], *adj.* hübsch, schön, stattlich.
handy ['hændi], *adj.* geschickt; — *man,* der Gelegenheitsarbeiter, Mann für alles.
hang [hæŋ], *v.a. reg. & irr.* hängen; aufhängen (*suspend*); — *it!* zum Henker; — *paper,* ein Zimmer austapezieren; — *dog expression,* den Kopf hängen lassen, die betrübte Miene. — *v.n.* hängen; (*coll.*) — *on!* warte einen Moment! — *about,* herumstehen; herumlungern (*loiter*).
hanger-on [hæŋər'ɔn], *s.* der Anhänger, Mitläufer.
hangman ['hæŋmən], *s.* der Henker.
hanker ['hæŋkə], *v.n.* sich sehnen.
Hanoverian [hæno'viəriən], *adj.* hannöversch. — *s.* der Hannoveraner.
hansom ['hænsəm], *s.* die zweirädrige Droschke.
haphazard [hæp'hæzəd], *s.* der Zufall, das Geratewohl.
hapless ['hæplis], *adj.* unglücklich.
happen [hæpn], *v.n.* sich ereignen, passieren; — *to . . .,* zufällig . . .
happiness ['hæpinis], *s.* das Glück; die Glückseligkeit.
happy ['hæpi], *adj.* glücklich, glückselig.
harangue [hə'ræŋ], *s.* die Ansprache. — *v.a.* einsprechen (auf, *Acc.*); anreden.
harass ['hærəs], *v.a.* plagen, quälen.
harbinger ['hɑːbindʒə], *s.* der Vorbote, Bote.
harbour ['hɑːbə], *s.* der Hafen. — *v.a.* beherbergen (*shelter*); hegen (*cherish*).
hard [hɑːd], *adj.* schwer (*difficult*); hart (*tough*); hartherzig (*miserly*); — *up,* in Not, in Geldverlegenheit; — *of hearing,* schwerhörig.
harden [hɑːdn], *v.a.* härten. — *v.n.* hart werden.
hardiness ['hɑːdinis], *s.* die Kraft, Stärke; die Rüstigkeit.
hardly ['hɑːdli], *adv.* kaum.
hardship ['hɑːdʃip], *s.* die Not, Bedrängnis (*need*); die Beschwerde (*complaint*).

hardware ['hɑːdwɛə], s. die Eisenware(n).

hardy ['hɑːdi], adj. abgehärtet, stark; (Bot.) — annual, ein widerstandsfähiges Jahresgewächs.

hare [hɛə], s. (Zool.) der Hase; — brained, unbedacht, gedankenlos; — lip, die Hasenscharte.

harebell ['hɛəbel], s. (Bot.) die Glockenblume.

haricot ['hærikou], s. (Bot.) — bean, die welsche Bohne.

hark [hɑːk], v.n. horchen.

harlequin ['hɑːlikwin], s. der Harlekin.

harlot ['hɑːlət], s. die Hure.

harm [hɑːm], s. das Leid, Unrecht; do — to, Schaden zufügen (Dat.). — v.a. verletzen (hurt); schaden (damage, Dat.).

harmful ['hɑːmful], adj. schädlich.

harmless ['hɑːmlis], adj. harmlos.

harmonious [hɑː'mouniəs], adj. harmonisch; einmütig (of one mind).

harmonize ['hɑːmənaiz], v.a. in Einklang bringen. — v.n. harmonieren, in Einklang stehen.

harmony ['hɑːməni], s. (Mus.) die Harmonie; (fig.) der Einklang, die Einmütigkeit.

harness ['hɑːnis], s. der Harnisch. — v.a. anschirren, anspannen (horse); (fig.) nutzbar machen.

harp [hɑːp], s. (Mus.) die Harfe. — v.n. (coll.) — upon, herumreiten auf (Dat.).

harpoon [hɑː'puːn], s. die Harpune. — v.a. harpunieren.

harrow ['hærou], s. die Egge, Harke. — v.a. harken, eggen; quälen.

harry ['hæri], v.a. verheeren, quälen.

harsh [hɑːʃ], adj. herb, rauh (rough); streng (severe).

hart [hɑːt], s. (Zool.) der Hirsch.

harvest ['hɑːvist], s. die Ernte; — home, das Erntefest.

hash [hæʃ], v.a. zerhacken; vermischen (mix up). — s. das Hackfleisch; make a — of things, verpfuschen, alles verderben.

hasp [hæsp or hɑːsp], s. der Haken, die Spange.

haste [heist], s. die Hast, Eile (hurry); die Voreiligkeit (rashness).

hasten [heisn], v.n. eilen, sich beeilen.

hasty ['heisti], adj. voreilig.

hat [hæt], s. der Hut; (coll.) talk through o.'s —, Unsinn reden.

hatch (1) [hætʃ], s. die Brut (chickens). — v.a., v.n. (aus-)brüten; ausshecken (cunning).

hatch (2) [hætʃ], s. das Servierfenster (for serving food); (Naut.) die Luke.

hatch (3) [hætʃ], v.a. (Art) schraffieren.

hatchet ['hætʃit], s. das Beil, die Axt; bury the —, das Kriegsbeil begraben.

hate [heit], v.a., v.n. hassen; — to ..., nicht ... wollen. — s. der Haß, Widerwille, die Abneigung.

hateful ['heitful], adj. verhaßt (hated); gehässig (hating).

hatred ['heitrid], s. der Haß.

hatter ['hætə], s. der Hutmacher.

haughty ['hɔːti], adj. übermütig (supercilious); hochmütig, stolz (proud); hochnäsig (giving o.s. airs).

haul [hɔːl], v.a. schleppen, ziehen. — s. das Schleppen; (coll.) die Beute.

haulage ['hɔːlidʒ], s. der Schleppdienst, die Spedition.

haunch [hɔːntʃ], s. (Anat.) die Hüfte; der Schenkel (horse); die Keule (venison).

haunt [hɔːnt], v.a. heimsuchen, spuken (in, Dat.); it is —ed, hier spuktes.

have [hæv], v.a. irr. haben, besitzen (possess); erhalten; lassen; — to, müssen; — s.th. made, done, etwas machen lassen.

haven [heivn], s. der Zufluchtsort.

haversack ['hævəsæk], s. der Brotbeutel.

havoc ['hævək], s. die Verwüstung, Verheerung.

hawk (1) [hɔːk], s. (Orn.) der Habicht; der Falke (falcon).

hawk (2) [hɔːk], v.a. hausieren.

hawker ['hɔːkə], s. der Hausierer.

hawthorn ['hɔːθɔːn], s. (Bot.) der Hagedorn.

hay [hei], s. das Heu; — fever, der Heuschnupfen; — loft, der Heuboden; — rick, der Heuschober.

hazard ['hæzəd], s. der Zufall (chance); die Gefahr (danger); das Risiko (risk). — v.a. aufs Spiel setzen, riskieren.

hazardous ['hæzədəs], adj. gefährlich, gewagt.

haze [heiz], s. der Dunst, Nebeldunst.

hazel [heizl], s. (Bot.) die Haselstaude; — nut, die Haselnuß.

hazy ['heizi], adj. dunstig, nebelig.

he [hiː] pers. pron. er; — who, derjenige, welcher, wer.

head [hed], s. der Kopf; die Spitze (of arrow); der Leiter (of firm); (Sch.) der Direktor; die Überschrift (heading); die Krisis (climax); (Pol.) der Führer, das (Staats-)Oberhaupt. — v.a. anführen, führen; (Mil.) befehligen; — v.n. (Naut.) — for, Kurs nehmen auf (Acc.).

headache ['hedeik], s. (Med.) die Kopfschmerzen, m. pl.

headlamp ['hedlæmp], s. der Scheinwerfer.

headphone ['hedfoun], s. (usually pl.) der Kopfhörer.

headstrong ['hedstrɔŋ], adj. halsstarrig.

heady ['hedi], adj. hastig, ungestüm; berauschend (liquor).

heal [hiːl], v.a. heilen. — v.n. (zu)heilen, verheilen.

health [helθ], s. die Gesundheit; — resort, der Kurort; your (good) —! Gesundheit! auf Ihr Wohl! Prosit! (drinking toast).

healthy ['helθi], adj. gesund.

heap [hiːp], s. der Haufen, die Menge. — v.a. häufen, aufhäufen.

hear

hear [hiə], v.a., v.n. irr. hören; erfahren (learn); (Law) verhören (evidence).
hearing ['hiəriŋ], s. das Gehör (auditory perception); within —, in Hörweite; (Law) das Verhör.
hearsay ['hiəsei], s. das Hörensagen.
hearse [həːs], s. der Leichenwagen.
heart [haːt], s. das Herz; der Mut (courage); das Innerste (core); by —, auswendig; take to —, beherzigen; take — from, Mut fassen (aus, Dat.).
heartburn ['haːtbəːn], s. (Med.) das Sodbrennen.
heartfelt ['haːtfelt], adj. herzlich.
hearth [haːθ], s. der Herd.
hearty ['haːti], adj. herzlich; aufrichtig (sincere); herzhaft.
heat [hiːt], s. die Hitze, Wärme; die Brunst (animals). — v.a. heizen (fuel); erhitzen (make hot).
heath [hiːθ], s. die Heide.
heathen [hiːðən], s. der Heide, Ungläubige.
heather ['heðə], s. (Bot.) das Heidekraut.
heating ['hiːtiŋ], s. die Heizung.
heave [hiːv], v.a. reg. & irr. heben, hieben. — v.n. sich heben und senken.
heaven [hevn], s. der Himmel; good —s! ach, du lieber Himmel!
heaviness ['hevinis], s. die Schwere.
heavy ['hevi], adj. schwer; schwerwiegend (grave).
Hebrew ['hiːbruː], adj. hebräisch. — s. der Hebräer, der Jude.
hectic ['hektik], adj. hektisch, aufgeregt.
hector ['hektə], v.a. tyrannisieren (bully). — v.n. renommieren, prahlen.
hedge [hedʒ], s. die Hecke. — v.a. einhegen, einzäunen.
hedgehog ['hedʒhɔg], s. (Zool.) der Igel.
hedgerow ['hedʒrou], s. die Baumhecke.
heed [hiːd], s. die Hut, Aufmerksamkeit. — v.a. beachten.
heedless ['hiːdlis], adj. unachtsam.
heel [hiːl], s. die Ferse (foot); der Absatz (shoe); take to o.'s —s, die Flucht ergreifen; (Am. sl.) der Lump.
heifer ['hefə], s. (Zool.) die junge Kuh.
height [hait], s. die Höhe, Anhöhe; die Größe (tallness); der Hügel (hill).
heighten [haitn], v.a. erhöhen.
heir [ɛə], s. der Erbe (to, Genit.).
heiress ['ɛəres], s. die Erbin.
heirloom ['ɛəluːm], s. das Erbstück.
helicopter ['helikɔptə], s. (Aviat.) der Hubschrauber.
hell [hel], s. die Hölle. — interj. zum Teufel!
hellish ['heliʃ], adj. höllisch.
helm [helm], s. das Steuer, Steuerruder.
helmet ['helmit], s. der Helm.
helmsman ['helmzmən], s. (Naut.) der Steuermann.
help [help], v.a., v.n. helfen (Dat.); I cannot — laughing, ich muß lachen; I cannot — it, ich kann nichts dafür. — v.r. — o.s., sich bedienen. — s. die Hilfe, Unterstützung.

helpful ['helpful], adj. behilflich, hilfreich.
helping ['helpiŋ], s. die Portion.
helpless ['helplis], adj. hilflos.
helpmate, helpmeet ['helpmeit, -miːt], s. der Gehilfe, die Gehilfin.
helter-skelter ['heltə'skeltə], adv. Hals über Kopf.
hem [hem], s. der Saum. — v.a. (Tail.) einsäumen, säumen.
hemisphere ['hemisfiə], s. die Halbkugel, Hemisphäre.
hemlock ['hemlɔk], s. der Schierling.
hemp [hemp], s. der Hanf.
hemstitch ['hemstitʃ], s. der Hohlsaum.
hen [hen], s. die Henne (poultry); das Weibchen (other birds).
hence [hens], adv. von hier; von jetzt an.
henceforth ['hens'fɔːθ], adv. fortan, von nun an.
henpecked ['henpekd], adj. unter dem Pantoffel stehend.
her [həː], pers. pron. sie (Acc.), ihr (Dat.). — poss. adj. ihr.
herald ['herəld], s. der Herold. — v.a. ankündigen.
heraldry ['herəldri], s. die Wappenkunde.
herb [həːb], s. (Bot.) das Kraut.
herbaceous [həː'beiʃəs], adj. krautartig.
herbage ['həːbidʒ], s. das Gras; (Law) das Weiderecht.
herbal ['həːbəl], adj. krautartig, Kräuter-, Kraut-.
herd [həːd], s. die Herde. — v.n. sich zusammenfinden.
here [hiə], adv. hier.
hereafter [hiər'aːftə], adv. hernach, künftig. — s. die Zukunft; das Jenseits.
hereby [hiə'bai], adv. hiermit.
hereditary [hi'reditəri], adj. erblich.
heredity [hi'rediti], s. (Biol.) die Erblichkeit, Vererbung.
heresy ['herisi], s. die Ketzerei.
heretic ['heritik], s. der Ketzer.
heretofore ['hiətuːfɔː], adv. zuvor, vormals.
heritage ['heritidʒ], s. die Erbschaft.
hermetic [həː'metik], adj. luftdicht.
hermit ['həːmit], s. der Eremit, Einsiedler.
hero ['hiərou], s. der Held.
heroic [hi'rouik], adj. heldenhaft, heldenmütig.
heroine ['heroin], s. die Heldin.
heroism ['heroizm], s. der Heldenmut.
heron ['herən], s. (Orn.) der Reiher.
herring ['heriŋ], s. (Zool.) der Hering; red —, die Ablenkungsfinte, das Ablenkungsmanöver; — bone, die Gräte; pickled —, der eingemachte Hering.
hers [həːz], poss. pron. ihr, der ihre, der ihrige.
herself [həː'self], pers. pron. sich; sie selbst.
hesitate ['heziteit], v.n. zögern, zaudern; unschlüssig sein (be undecided).

hesitation [hezi'teiʃən], s. das Zögern, Zaudern; das Bedenken (deliberation).

Hessian ['heʃən], adj. hessisch. — s. der Hesse.

hessian ['hesiən], s. die Sackleinwand (textile).

heterodox ['hetərədɔks], adj. irrgläubig.

heterogeneous [hetəro'dʒi:niəs], adj. heterogen, ungleichartig.

hew [hju:], v.a. irr. hauen.

hexagonal [hek'sægənəl], adj. sechseckig.

hiatus [hai'eitəs], s. die Lücke.

hibernate ['haibəneit], v.n. überwintern.

hibernation [haibə'neiʃən], s. der Winterschlaf.

hiccup ['hikʌp], s. (usually pl.) (Med.) der Schlucken, Schluckauf.

hickory ['hikəri], s. (Bot.) das Hickoryholz.

hide (1) [haid], v.a. irr. verstecken, verbergen. — v.n. irr. sich verbergen; — and seek, das Versteckspiel.

hide (2) [haid], s. die Haut (of animal), das Fell, (tanned) das Leder.

hideous ['hidiəs], adj. häßlich, scheußlich, furchtbar.

hiding (1) ['haidiŋ], s. das Versteck.

hiding (2) ['haidiŋ], s. die Tracht Prügel.

hierarchy ['haiərɑ:ki], s. die Hierarchie.

higgle [higl] see **haggle**.

higgledy-piggledy ['higldi'pigldi], adv. wüst durcheinander.

high [hai], adj. hoch; erhaben, vornehm; angegangen (meat); — school, die höhere Schule; — time, höchste Zeit; (Am.) vergnügliche Zeit; High Church, die Hochkirche. — s. (Meteor.) das Hoch.

Highness ['hainis], s. die Hoheit (title).

highroad, highway ['hairoud, 'haiwei], s. die Haupt- or Landstraße.

highwayman ['haiweimən], s. der Straßenräuber.

hike [haik], v.n. wandern, einen Ausflug machen. — s. die Wanderung, der Ausflug.

hilarious [hi'lɛəriəs], adj. fröhlich, lustig, ausgelassen.

hill [hil], s. der Hügel, Berg.

hilt [hilt], s. der Griff.

him [him], pers. pron. ihn, ihm.

himself [him'self], pers. pron. sich; er selbst.

hind [haind], s. (Zool.) die Hirschkuh, Hindin.

hinder ['hində], v.a. hindern.

hindmost ['haindmoust], adj. hinterst; the devil take the —, den letzten hol der Teufel! nach mir die Sintflut!

hindrance ['hindrəns], s. das Hindernis; (Law) without let or —, ohne Hinderung.

Hindu [hin'du:], s. der Hindu.

hinge [hindʒ], s. die Angel, der Angelpunkt. — v.n. sich um etwas drehen; von etwas abhängen (on, Dat.).

hint [hint], v.n. zu verstehen geben, auf etwas hindeuten (at, auf, Acc.), andeuten. — s. die Andeutung, der Fingerzeig.

hip (1) [hip], s. (Anat.) die Hüfte.

hip (2) [hip], s. (Bot.) die Hagebutte.

hire ['haiə], v.a. (ver-)mieten (car etc.); anstellen (man etc.). — s. die Miete; der Lohn (wage); — purchase, der Abzahlungskauf, die Ratenzahlung.

hireling ['haiəliŋ], s. der Mietling.

hirsute ['hə:sju:t], adj. behaart, haarig.

his [hiz], poss. adj. sein, seine. — poss. pron. sein, der seinige, der seine.

hiss [his], v.n. zischen (at, auf, Acc.). — s. das Zischen.

historian [his'tɔ:riən], s. der Historiker, der Geschichtsschreiber.

historical [his'tɔrikəl], adj. historisch, geschichtlich.

history ['histəri], s. die Geschichte, die Geschichtswissenschaft.

histrionic [histri'ɔnik], adj. schauspielerisch.

hit [hit], v.a. irr. schlagen, stoßen. — s. der Schlag, der Treffer (on the target); (Am.) der Schlager, Erfolg (success); — parade, die Schlagerparade.

hitch [hitʃ], v.a. anhaken (hook); anhängen; — a lift, — hike, per Anhalter fahren. — s. der Nachteil, der Haken.

hither ['hiðə], adv. hierher.

hitherto [hiðə'tu:], adv. bisher.

hive [haiv], s. der Bienenkorb; Bienenstock; — of bees, der Schwarm.

hoar [hɔ:], adj. eisgrau, weißlich; — frost, der Reif.

hoard [hɔ:d], v.a. hamstern. — s. der Vorrat, Schatz.

hoarding ['hɔ:diŋ], s. die Umzäunung, die Bretterwand; die Reklamewand.

hoarse [hɔ:s], adj. heiser.

hoarseness ['hɔ:snis], s. die Heiserkeit.

hoax [houks], s. der Betrug, die Irreführung; der Schabernack (in fun). — v.a. betrügen; foppen (in fun).

hobble [hɔbl], v.n. humpeln. — v.a. an den Füßen fesseln.

hobby ['hɔbi], s. das Steckenpferd, Hobby, die Liebhaberei.

hobgoblin [hɔb'gɔblin], s. der Kobold.

hobnail ['hɔbneil], s. der Hufnagel.

hobnailed ['hɔbneild], adj. — boots, genagelte Stiefel, m. pl.

hobnob [hɔb'nɔb], v.n. (coll.) vertraulich sein.

hock (1) [hɔk], s. (Anat.) das Sprunggelenk.

hock (2) [hɔk], s. (wine) der Rheinwein.

hod [hɔd], s. (Build.) der Trog; der Eimer (coal).

hodge-podge see under **hotchpotch**.

hoe [hou], s. die Hacke, Harke. — v.a., v.n. hacken, harken.

hog [hɔg], s. das Schwein. — v.a. verschlingen (food); an sich reißen (grasp).

hogshead ['hɔgzhed], s. das Oxhoft.

hoist [hɔist], v.a. hissen.

hold

hold [hould], *v.a.*, *v.n. irr.* halten (*keep*); enthalten (*contain*); behaupten (*assert*); meinen (*think*); gelten (*be valid*); — *forth*, deklamieren; — *good*, sich bewähren; — *out*, hinhalten (*hope*); (*endure*) aushalten;—*up*, aufhalten. — *s.* (*Naut.*) der Schiffsraum; die Macht (*power*).

holder ['houldə], *s.* der Inhaber, Besitzer.

holding ['houldiŋ], *s.* das Pachtgut (*farm*); der Besitz (*property*); (*Comm.*) der Trust.

hole [houl], *s.* das Loch; die Höhle (*cavity*). — *v.a.* aushöhlen; (*Golf*) ins Loch spielen.

holiday ['holidei], *s.* der Feiertag; der Urlaub (*vacation*); (*pl.*) die Ferien, *pl.*

holiness ['houlinis], *s.* die Heiligkeit.

hollow ['holou], *adj.* hohl. — *s.* die Höhlung; die Höhle.

holly ['holi], *s.* (*Bot.*) die Stechpalme.

hollyhock ['holihok], *s.* (*Bot.*) die Stockrose.

holocaust ['holokɔ:st], *s.* das Brandopfer; die Katastrophe.

holster ['houlstə], *s.* die Pistolentasche, die Halfter.

holy ['houli], *adj.* heilig; *Holy Week*, die Karwoche.

homage ['homidʒ], *s.* die Huldigung; *pay — to*, huldigen (*Dat.*).

home [houm], *s.* das Heim, die Wohnung; die Heimat; *at —*, zu Hause; *Home Office*, das Innenministerium; — *Rule*, (*Pol.*) die Selbstverwaltung.

homer ['houmə] (*Am.*) *see* **homing pigeon**.

homesick ['houmsik], *adj.* an Heimweh leidend.

homestead ['houmsted], *s.* der Bauernhof.

homicide ['homisaid], *s.* der Mord (*crime*); der Mörder (*killer*).

homily ['homili], *s.* die Predigt; Moralpredigt.

homing pigeon ['houmiŋ'pidʒən], *s.* die Brieftaube.

homogeneous [homə'dʒi:niəs], *adj.* homogen; gleichartig.

hone [houn], *s.* der Wetzstein. — *v.a.* (*blade, knife*) abziehen.

honest ['onist], *adj.* ehrlich, aufrichtig.

honesty ['onisti], *s.* die Ehrlichkeit.

honey ['hʌni], *s.* der Honig; (*Am., coll.*) Liebling!

honeycomb ['hʌnikoum], *s.* die Honigwabe.

honeymoon ['hʌnimu:n], *s.* die Flitterwochen.

honorarium [onə'rɛəriəm], *s.* das Honorar.

honorary ['onərəri], *adj.* Ehren-, ehrenamtlich.

honour ['onə], *s.* die Ehre; *your —*, Euer Ehrwürden, Euer Gnaden (*title*). — *v.a.* ehren, auszeichnen.

honourable ['onərəbl], *adj.* ehrenwert, ehrenvoll; Hochwohlgeboren (*title*).

hood [hud], *s.* die Kapuze; das akademische Gradabzeichen über dem Talar; (*Hunt.*) die Haube; —*ed falcon*, der Jagdfalke (mit Haube).

hoodwink ['hudwiŋk], *v.a.* täuschen.

hoof [hu:f *or* huf], *s.* der Huf (*horse*); die Klaue.

hook [huk], *s.* der Haken; *by — or by crook*, mit allen Mitteln. — *v.a.* angeln, fangen.

hooked [hukd], *adj.* gekrümmt, hakenförmig.

hooligan ['hu:ligən], *s.* der Rowdy.

hoop [hu:p], *s.* der Reifen. — *v.a.* (ein Faß) binden.

hooper ['hu:pə], *s.* der Böttcher.

hoopoe ['hu:pou], *s.* (*Orn.*) der Wiedehopf.

hoot [hu:t], *v.n.* schreien (*owl*); ertönen (*siren*); hupen (*car*).

hooter ['hu:tə], *s.* die Sirene (*siren*); die Hupe (*car*).

hop (1) [hop], *v.n.* hüpfen, tanzen; —*ping mad*, ganz verrückt.

hop (2) [hop], *s.* (*Bot.*) der Hopfen. — *v.a.* (*beer*) hopfen, Hopfen zusetzen (*Dat.*). — *v.n.* Hopfen ernten.

hope [houp], *s.* die Hoffnung. — *v.n.* hoffen (*for, aff, Acc.*).

hopeless ['houplis], *adj.* hoffnungslos.

horizon [hə'raizən], *s.* der Horizont.

horizontal [hori'zontl], *adj.* horizontal, waagrecht.

horn [hɔ:n], *s.* das Horn; (*Mus.*) *French —*, das Waldhorn, Horn; (*Motor.*) die Hupe.

hornet ['hɔ:nit], *s.* (*Ent.*) die Hornisse.

hornpipe ['hɔ:npaip], *s.* (*Mus.*) der Matrosentanz; die Hornpfeife.

horrible ['horibl], *adj.* schrecklich.

horrid ['horid], *adj.* abscheulich.

horrific [hɔ'rifik], *adj.* schrecklich, schreckenerregend.

horror ['horə], *s.* der Schrecken, das Entsetzen; (*fig.*) der Greuel.

horse [hɔ:s], *s.* das Pferd, Roß; *on —back*, zu Pferd.

horseman ['hɔ:smən], *s.* der Reiter.

horsepower ['hɔ:spauə], *s.* die Pferdestärke.

horseradish ['hɔ:srædiʃ], *s.* der Meerrettich.

horseshoe ['hɔ:sʃu:], *s.* das Hufeisen.

horticulture ['hɔ:tikʌltʃə], *s.* der Gartenbau.

hose [houz], *s.* die Strümpfe, *m. pl.* (*stockings*); der Schlauch (*water pipe*).

hosiery ['houʒəri], *s.* die Strumpfwarenindustrie; die Strumpfwaren.

hospitable [hos'pitəbl], *adj.* gastlich, gastfreundlich.

hospital ['hospitl], *s.* das Krankenhaus.

hospitality [hospi'tæliti], *s.* die Gastlichkeit, Gastfreundschaft.

host (1) [houst], *s.* der Gastwirt (*landlord*); der Gastgeber.

host (2) [houst], *s.* (*Rel.*) *angelic —*, die Engelschar; (*Mil.*) das Heer, die Heerschar.

host (3) [houst], *s.* (*Eccl.*) die Hostie.

hostage ['hɔstidʒ], s. die Geisel.
hostess ['houstis *or* -tes], s. die Gast-geberin; *air* —, die Stewardeß.
hostile ['hɔstail], *adj.* feindlich; feind-selig (*inimical*).
hot [hɔt], *adj.* heiß; hitzig (*tempera-ment*); scharf, gewürzt (*of spices*); (*fig.*) heftig, erbittert.
hotchpotch, hodge-podge ['hɔtʃpɔtʃ, 'hɔdʒpɔdʒ], s. das Mischmasch.
hotel [ho(u)'tel],s.das Hotel,der Gasthof.
hothouse ['hɔthaus], s. das Treibhaus.
hound [haund], s. (*Zool.*) der Jagdhund. — *v.a.* hetzen.
hour ['auə], s. die Stunde; — *hand*, der Stundenzeiger; *keep early (late)* —*s*, früh (spät) zu Bett gehen.
hourglass ['auəglɑ:s], s. die Sanduhr.
hourly ['auəli], *adj., adv.,* stündlich.
house [haus], s. das Haus; (*Comm.*) die Firma. — [hauz], *v.a.* beherbergen, unterbringen.
houseboat ['hausbout], s. das Wohn-boot.
housebreaking ['hausbreikiŋ], s. der Einbruch.
household ['haushould], s. der Haus-halt.
housekeeper ['hauski:pə], s. die Haus-hälterin.
housewife ['hauswaif], s. die Hausfrau.
housing ['hauziŋ], s. die Unterbring-ung; — *department*, das Wohnungs-amt.
hovel ['hɔvl *or* hʌvl], s. die Hütte.
hover ['hɔvə *or* 'hʌvə], *v.n.* schweben, schwanken.
how [hau], *adv.* wie; — *do you do?* (*in introduction*) sehr angenehm; — *are you?* wie geht es Ihnen, Dir?
however [hau'evə], *adv.* wie immer, wie auch immer, wie sehr auch. — *conj.* doch, jedoch, dennoch.
howl [haul], *v.n.* heulen. — *s.* das Geheul.
hoyden ['hɔidn], s. das wilde Mäd-chen.
hub [hʌb], s. die Nabe (am Rad); — *of the universe*, die Mitte der Welt.
hubbub ['hʌbʌb], s. der Tumult, Lärm.
huckaback ['hʌkəbæk], s. der Zwillich (*textile*).
huckle [hʌkl], s. die Hüfte.
huddle [hʌdl], *v.n.* sich drängen, sich zusammenducken. — *s.* das Ge-dränge.
hue [hju:], s. der Farbton, die Tönung.
huff [hʌf], s. die schlechte Laune, die Mißstimmung.
huffy ['hʌfi], *adj.* mißmutig, übel gelaunt.
hug [hʌg], *v.a.* umarmen. — *s.* die Umarmung.
huge [hju:dʒ], *adj.* riesig, groß, unge-heuer.
Huguenot ['hju:gənou *or* -nɔt], s. der Hugenotte. — *adj.* hugenottisch, Hugenotten-.

hulk [hʌlk], s. (*Naut.*) das Schiffsinnere, der Schiffsrumpf; der schwerfällige Mensch.
hull [hʌl], s. die Hülse, Schale; (*Naut., Aviat.*) der Rumpf. — *v.a.* (*Engin.*) hülsen.
hullo! [hə'lou], *interj.* hallo!
hum [hʌm], *v.n.* summen, brummen. — *s.* das Summen, Brummen, Gemur-mel (*murmuring*).
human ['hju:mən], *adj.* menschlich. — *s.* der Mensch.
humane [hju:'mein], *adj.* menschen-freundlich.
humanity [hju:'mæniti], s. die Mensch-heit (*mankind*); die Menschlichkeit (*compassion*); (*pl.*) die klassischen Fächer, *n. pl.*, die humanistischen Wissenschaften, *f. pl.*
humanize ['hju:mənaiz], *v.a.* mensch-lich oder gesittet machen.
humble [hʌmbl], *adj.* demütig; be-scheiden (*modest*); unterwürfig (*ser-vile*). — *v.a.* erniedrigen (*humiliate*).
humbug ['hʌmbʌg], s. die Schwindelei (*swindle*); der Schwindler (*crook*); der Unsinn (*nonsense*).
humdrum ['hʌmdrʌm], *adj.* langwei-lig, eintönig.
humid ['hju:mid], *adj.* feucht.
humidity [hju:'miditi], s. die Feuchtig-keit.
humiliate [hju:'milieit], *v.a.* ernie-drigen.
humility [hju:'militi], s. die Demut.
humming-bird ['hʌmiŋbə:d], s. (*Orn.*) der Kolibri.
humming-top ['hʌmiŋtɔp], s. der Brummkreisel.
humorous ['hju:mərəs], *adj.* humori-stisch, spaßhaft, komisch.
humour ['hju:mə], s. der Humor, die (gute) Laune. — *v.a.* in guter Laune erhalten, gut stimmen; willfahren (*Dat.*).
hump [hʌmp], s. der Buckel, der Höcker.
hunch [hʌntʃ], s. der Buckel; *have a* —, das Gefühl haben.
hunchback ['hʌntʃbæk], s. der Bucklige.
hundred ['hʌndrəd], *num. adj. a* —, hundert.
hundredweight ['hʌndrədweit], s. der (englische) Zentner.
Hungarian [hʌŋ'gɛəriən],*adj.*ungarisch. — *s.* der Ungar.
hunger ['hʌŋgə], s. der Hunger.
hungry ['hʌŋgri], *adj.* hungrig.
hunt [hʌnt], s. die Jagd. — *v.a., v.n.* jagen.
hunter ['hʌntə], s. der Jäger.
hurdle [hə:dl], s. die Hürde.
hurdy-gurdy ['hə:digə:di], s. der Leierkasten.
hurl [hə:l], *v.a.* schleudern, werfen.
hurly-burly ['hə:libə:li], s. der Wirr-warr.
hurricane ['hʌrikin], s. der Orkan; — *lamp*, die Sturmlaterne.
hurried ['hʌrid], *adj.* eilig, hastig.

hurry

hurry ['hʌri], *v.n.* eilen, sich beeilen; — *to do*, eiligst tun. — *v.a.* beschleunigen. — *s.* die Eile, Hast, Beschleunigung.

hurt [həːt], *v.a. irr.* verletzen; wehetun (*Dat.*); (*verbally*) kränken. — *s.* die Verletzung, Kränkung.

hurtful ['həːtful], *adj.* schädlich, kränkend.

husband ['hʌzbənd], *s.* der Mann, Ehemann, Gemahl. — *v.a.* verwalten, sparsam verfahren mit (*Dat.*).

husbandman ['hʌzbəndmən], *s.* der Landwirt.

husbandry ['hʌzbəndri], *s.* die Landwirtschaft.

hush [hʌʃ], *v.a.* zum Schweigen bringen. — *s.* die Stille; — *money*, das Schweigegeld.

husky (1) ['hʌski], *adj.* heiser (*voice*).

husky (2) ['hʌski], *s.* (*Zool.*) der Eskimohund.

hussy ['hʌzi], *s.* (*coll.*) das Frauenzimmer.

hustings ['hʌstiŋz], *s.* die Wahltribüne.

hustle [hʌsl], *v.a.* drängen, stoßen. — *s.* das Gedränge.

hut [hʌt], *s.* die Hütte, Baracke.

hutch [hʌtʃ], *s.* der Trog, Kasten (*chest*).

hybrid ['haibrid], *adj.* Bastard-. — *s.* der Bastard.

hydraulic [hai'drɔːlik], *adj.* hydraulisch.

hydrogen ['haidrədʒən], *s.* der Wasserstoff.

hydroelectric [haidroui'lektrik], *adj.* hydroelektrisch.

hyena [hai'iːnə], *s.* (*Zool.*) die Hyäne.

hygiene ['haidʒiːn], *s.* die Hygiene, Gesundheitslehre.

hymn [him], *s.* die Hymne, das Kirchenlied.

hymnal ['himnəl], *s.* das Gesangbuch.

hyper- ['haipə], *prefix.* über-.

hyperbole [hai'pəːbəli], *s.* die Übertreibung.

hyphen ['haifən], *s.* der Bindestrich.

hypnosis [hip'nousis], *s.* die Hypnose.

hypochondriac [haipo'kɔndriæk], *adj.* hypochondrisch. — *s.* der Hypochonder.

hypocrisy [hi'pɔkrisi], *s.* die Heuchelei.

hypocrite ['hipəkrit], *s.* der Heuchler.

hypothesis [hai'pɔθisis], *s.* die Hypothese.

hypothetical [haipə'θetikəl], *adj.* hypothetisch, angenommen.

hysteria [his'tiəriə], *s.* die Hysterie.

I

I [ai]. das I.
I [ai], *pers. pron.* ich.

ice [ais], *s.* das Eis; — *bound*, eingefroren; (*Naut.*) — *breaker*, der Eisbrecher; (*Am.*) — *box*, der Kühlschrank; — *cream*, das Eis; das Gefrorene. — *v.a.* (*confectionery*) verzuckern; (*cake*) glasieren.

Icelander ['aislændə], *s.* der Isländer.

Icelandic [ais'lændik], *adj.* isländisch.

icicle ['aisikl], *s.* der Eiszapfen.

icy ['aisi], *adj.* eisig.

idea [ai'diə], *s.* die Idee.

ideal [ai'diəl], *adj.* ideal. — *s.* das Ideal.

idealize [ai'diəlaiz], *v.a.* idealisieren.

identical [ai'dentikəl], *adj.* identisch, gleich.

identification [aidentifi'keiʃən], *s.* die Gleichsetzung, Identifizierung.

identify [ai'dentifai], *v.a.* identifizieren, gleichsetzen.

identity [ai'dentiti], *s.* die Identität, Gleichheit.

idiocy ['idiəsi], *s.* die Blödsinn.

idiom ['idiəm], *s.* das Idiom, die sprachliche Eigentümlichkeit.

idiomatic [idio'mætik], *adj.* idiomatisch.

idiosyncrasy [idio'siŋkrəsi], *s.* die Empfindlichkeit; die Abneigung (gegen, *Acc.*); die Idiosynkrasie.

idle [aidl], *adj.* unnütz (*useless*); müßig, faul (*lazy*). — *v.n.* träge sein.

idleness ['aidlnis], *s.* der Müßiggang, die Faulheit.

idiot ['idiət], *s.* der Idiot.

idol [aidl], *s.* das Götzenbild; das Idol.

idolatry [ai'dɔlətri], *s.* die Götzenverehrung.

idolize ['aidolaiz], *v.a.* vergöttern, abgöttisch lieben.

idyll ['aidil *or* 'idil], *s.* die Idylle, das Idyll.

idyllic [ai'dilik *or* i'dilik], *adj.* idyllisch.

if [if], *conj.* wenn, falls (*in case*); ob (*whether*).

igneous ['igniəs], *adj.* feurig.

ignite [ig'nait], *v.a.* entzünden. — *v.n.* zur Entzündung kommen, sich entzünden.

ignition [ig'niʃən], *s.* die Zündung.

ignoble [ig'noubl], *adj.* unedel, gemein.

ignominious [igno'miniəs], *adj.* schimpflich, schmählich.

ignominy ['ignomini], *s.* die Schande, Schmach.

ignoramus [ignə'reiməs], *s.* der Unwissende.

ignorance ['ignərəns], *s.* die Unwissenheit, Unkenntnis.

ignorant ['ignərənt], *adj.* unwissend.

ignore [ig'nɔː], *v.a.* ignorieren, nicht beachten.

ill [il], *adj.* böse, schlimm (*bad*); krank (*sick*); — *feeling*, die Verstimmung. — *adv.* — *at ease*, unbequem, verlegen; *can* — *afford*, kann sich kaum leisten …; — *timed*, zu unrechter Zeit.

illbred [il'bred], *adj.* ungezogen.

illegal [i'liːgəl], *adj.* illegal, ungesetzlich.

illegibility [iledʒi'biliti], *s.* die Unleserlichkeit.

illegible [i'ledʒibl], *adj.* unleserlich.
illegitimacy [ili'dʒitiməsi], *s.* die Unehelichkeit, Illegitimität.
illegitimate [ili'dʒitimit], *adj.* illegitim, unehelich.
illicit [[i'lisit], *adj.* unerlaubt.
illiteracy [i'litərəsi], *s.* die Unkenntnis des Schreibens und Lesens, das Analphabetentum.
illiterate [i'litərit], *s.* der Analphabet.
illness ['ilnis], *s.* die Krankheit.
illogical [i'lɔdʒikəl], *adj.* unlogisch.
illuminate [i'lju:mineit], *v.a.* erleuchten; (*fig.*) aufklären.
illuminating [i'lju:mineitiŋ], *adj.* aufschlußreich.
illumination [ilju:mi'neiʃən], *s.* die Erleuchtung; die Erklärung (*explanation*).
illusion [i'lju:ʒən], *s.* die Illusion, Täuschung.
illusive, illusory [i'lju:ziv, i'lju:zəri], *adj.* trügerisch, täuschend.
illustrate ['iləstreit], *v.a.* erläutern; illustrieren (*with pictures*).
illustration [iləs'treiʃən], *s.* die Illustration (*pictorial*); Erläuterung, Erklärung; das Beispiel (*instance*).
illustrious [i'lʌstriəs], *adj.* glänzend, berühmt.
image ['imidʒ], *s.* das Bild; das Ebenbild; die Erscheinung (*appearance*).
imagery ['imidʒəri], *s.* der Gebrauch von Stilbildern (*style*), die Bildersprache.
imaginable [i'mædʒinəbl], *adj.* denkbar.
imaginary [i'mædʒinəri], *adj.* eingebildet, nicht wirklich, vermeintlich.
imagination [imædʒi'neiʃən], *s.* die Einbildung; die Vorstellung; die Phantasie.
imaginative [i'mædʒinətiv], *adj.* erfinderisch, voll Phantasie.
imagine [i'mædʒin], *v.a.* sich vorstellen, sich denken.
imbecile ['imbisail *or* 'imbisi:l], *adj.* schwachsinnig. — *s.* der Idiot.
imbecility [imbi'siliti], *s.* der Schwachsinn.
imbibe [im'baib], *v.a.* trinken; (*fig.*) in sich aufnehmen.
imbroglio [im'brouliou], *s.* die Verwicklung.
imbue [im'bju:], *v.a.* erfüllen, sättigen (*fig.*).
imitate ['imiteit], *v.a.* nachahmen, imitieren.
imitation [imi'teiʃən], *s.* die Nachahmung, Imitation; — *leather*, das Kunstleder.
immaculate [i'mækjulit], *adj.* unbefleckt, makellos.
immaterial [imə'tiəriəl], *adj.* unwesentlich, unwichtig.
immature [imə'tjuə], *adj.* unreif.
immeasurable [i'meʒərəbl], *adj.* unermeßlich, unmeßbar.
immediate [i'mi:djit], *adj.* unmittelbar, direkt, sofortig.

immediately [i'mi:djətli], *adv.* sofort.
immemorial [imi'mɔ:riəl], *adj.* undenklich, ewig.
immense [i'mens], *adj.* unermeßlich, ungeheuer.
immerse [i'mə:s], *v.a.* eintauchen.
immersion [i'mə:ʃən], *s.* das Eintauchen, die Versenkung; — *heater*, der Tauchsieder.
immigrant ['imigrənt], *s.* der Einwanderer.
imminent ['iminənt], *adj.* bevorstehend.
immobile [i'moubail], *adj.* unbeweglich.
immoderate [i'mɔdərit], *adj.* unmäßig.
immodest [i'mɔdist], *adj.* unbescheiden; unsittlich, unanständig (*immoral*).
immodesty [i'mɔdisti], *s.* die Unanständigkeit (*indecency*); Unbescheidenheit (*presumption*).
immolate ['iməleit], *v.a.* opfern.
immoral [i'mɔrəl], *adj.* unsittlich, unmoralisch.
immortal [i'mɔ:tl], *adj.* unsterblich.
immortalize [i'mɔ:təlaiz], *v.a.* verewigen, unsterblich machen.
immovable [i'mu:vəbl], *adj.* unbeweglich (*fig.*).
immunity [i'mju:niti], *s.* die Freiheit, Straffreiheit; Immunität.
immutable [im'ju:təbl], *adj.* unabänderlich; unveränderlich.
imp [imp], *s.* der Knirps, Kobold, kleine Schelm.
impair [im'pɛə], *v.a.* beeinträchtigen; vermindern (*reduce*).
impale [im'peil], *v.a.* aufspießen; durchbohren.
impalpable [im'pælpəbl], *adj.* unfühlbar, unmerklich.
impart [im'pɑ:t], *v.a.* erteilen; verleihen (*confer*); mitteilen (*inform*).
impartial [im'pɑ:ʃəl], *adj.* unparteiisch.
impartiality [impɑ:ʃi'æliti], *s.* die Unparteilichkeit, Objektivität.
impassable [im'pɑ:səbl], *adj.* unwegsam, unpassierbar.
impasse [im'pæs], *s.* der völlige Stillstand.
impassioned [im'pæʃənd], *adj.* leidenschaftlich.
impassive [im'pæsiv], *adj.* unempfindlich.
impatience [im'peiʃəns], *s.* die Ungeduld.
impatient [im'peiʃənt], *adj.* ungeduldig.
impeach [im'pi:tʃ], *v.a.* anklagen.
impeachment [im'pi:tʃmənt], *s.* die Anklage.
impecunious [impi'kju:niəs], *adj.* unbemittelt, mittellos.
impede [im'pi:d], *v.a.* behindern, verhindern.
impediment [im'pedimənt], *s.* das Hindernis.
impel [im'pel], *v.a.* antreiben; zwingen (*force*).

415

impending

impending [im'pendiŋ], *adj.* bevorstehend, drohend.

impenetrable [im'penitrəbl], *adj.* undurchdringlich, unerforschlich.

impenitent [im'penitənt], *adj.* reuelos, unbußfertig.

imperative [im'perətiv], *adj.* zwingend (*cogent*); dringend notwendig. — *s.* (*Gram.*) der Imperativ, die Befehlsform.

imperceptible [impə'septibl], *adj.* unmerklich.

imperfect [im'pə:fikt], *adj.* unvollständig, unvollkommen; fehlerhaft (*goods etc.*). — *s.* (*Gram.*) das Imperfekt.

imperial [im'piəriəl], *adj.* kaiserlich, Kaiser-, Reichs-.

imperil [im'peril], *v.a.* gefährden; in Gefahr bringen, einer Gefahr aussetzen.

imperious [im'piəriəs], *adj.* gebieterisch.

imperishable [im'periʃəbl], *adj.* unverwüstlich, unvergänglich.

impermeable [im'pə:miəbl], *adj.* undurchdringlich.

impersonal [im'pə:sənəl], *adj.* unpersönlich.

impersonate [im'pə:səneit], *v.a.* verkörpern, darstellen; sich ausgeben als.

impertinence [im'pə:tinəns], *s.* die Anmaßung, Frechheit, Unverschämtheit.

impertinent [im'pə:tinənt], *adj.* anmaßend, frech, unverschämt.

imperturbable [impə'tə:bəbl], *adj.* unerschütterlich, ruhig, gelassen.

impervious [im'pə:viəs], *adj.* unwegsam, undurchdringlich.

impetuous [im'petjuəs], *adj.* ungestüm, heftig.

impetus [im'pitəs], *s.* die Triebkraft, der Antrieb.

impinge [im'pindʒ], *v.n.* verstoßen (*on*, gegen); übergreifen (*on*, in).

implacable [im'plækənt], *adj.* unversöhnlich.

implement ['implimənt], *s.* das Gerät. — [impli'ment], *v.a.* (*Law*) erfüllen, in Wirkung setzen, in Kraft treten lassen.

implementation [implimen'teiʃən], *s.* das Inkrafttreten, die Erfüllung, Ausführung.

implicate ['implikeit], *v.a.* verwickeln.

implicit [im'plisit], *adj.* unbedingt; einbegriffen.

implore [im'plɔ:], *v.a.* anflehen.

imply [im'plai], *v.a.* besagen, meinen; andeuten.

impolite [impə'lait], *adj.* unhöflich, grob.

impolitic [im'pɔlitik], *adj.* unklug, unpolitisch, undiplomatisch.

imponderable [im'pɔndərəbl], *adj.* unwägbar. — *s. pl.* unwägbare, unvorhersehbare Umstände, *m.pl.*

import [im'pɔ:t], *v.a.* einführen, importieren; bedeuten, besagen. — ['impɔ:t], *s.* (*Comm.*) die Einfuhr, der Import; die Bedeutung (*importance, meaning*), Wichtigkeit (*significance*); (*Comm.*) — *licence,* die Einfuhrgenehmigung.

importance [im'pɔ:təns], *s.* die Bedeutung, Wichtigkeit.

important [im'pɔ:tənt], *adj.* bedeutend, wichtig.

importation [impɔ:'teiʃən], *s.* die Einfuhr.

importune [impɔ:'tju:n], *v.a.* belästigen, angehen, dringend bitten.

impose [im'pouz], *v.a.* aufbürden, auferlegen. — *v.n.* — *upon s.o.,* einen belästigen.

imposition [impə'ziʃən], *s.* die Belästigung; (*Sch.*) die Strafarbeit.

impossible [im'pɔsibl], *adj.* unmöglich.

impostor [im'pɔstə], *s.* der Schwindler, Betrüger.

impotent ['impətənt], *adj.* schwach, machtlos; impotent (*sexually*).

impound [im'paund], *v.a.* beschlagnahmen, in Beschlag nehmen.

impoverish [im'pɔvəriʃ], *v.a.* arm machen.

impoverished [im'pɔvəriʃd], *adj.* verarmt, armselig.

impracticability [impræktikə'biliti], *s.* die Unmöglichkeit, Unausführbarkeit.

impracticable [im'præktikəbl], *adj.* unausführbar.

imprecate ['imprikeit], *v.a.* verwünschen.

impregnable [im'pregnəbl], *adj.* uneinnehmbar, unbezwinglich.

impregnate [im'pregneit], *v.a.* impregnieren; (*Chem.*) sättigen.

impress [im'pres], *v.a.* beeindrucken, imponieren (*fig.*); einprägen, einpressen (*print*). — ['impres], *s.* der Eindruck, (*Typ.*) Abdruck.

impression [im'preʃən], *s.* (*fig.*) der Eindruck; die Auflage (*books*).

impressionable [im'preʃənəbl], *adj.* eindrucksfähig, empfänglich.

impressive [im'presiv], *adj.* ergreifend, eindrucksvoll.

imprint ['imprint], *s.* der Name des Verlags oder Druckers. — [im'print], *v.a.* drucken.

imprison [im'prizn], *v.a.* gefangensetzen, in Haft nehmen.

imprisonment [im'priznmənt], *s.* die Haft; (*Law*) der Arrest.

improbability [imprɔbə'biliti], *s.* die Unwahrscheinlichkeit.

improbable [im'prɔbəbl], *adj.* unwahrscheinlich.

improbity [im'proubiti], *s.* die Unredlichkeit.

impromptu [im'prɔmptju:], *adj., adv.* aus dem Stegreif, unvorbereitet.

improper [im'prɔpə], *adj.* unpassend; unanständig (*indecent*).

impropriety [impro'praiiti], *s.* die Unanständigkeit (*indecency*); die Ungehörigkeit.

include

improve [im'pru:v], *v.a.* verbessern; (*Hort.*) veredeln. — *v.n.* besser werden, sich bessern; (*Med.*) sich erholen.

improvement [im'pru:vmənt], *s.* die Verbesserung; (*Med.*) die Besserung, der Fortschritt.

improvident [im'prɔvidənt], *adj.* unvorsichtig, nicht auf die Zukunft bedacht.

improvise ['imprəvaiz], *v.a.* improvisieren.

imprudent [im'pru:dənt], *adj.* unklug, unvorsichtig.

impudent ['impjudənt], *adj.* unverschämt.

impugn [im'pju:n], *v.a.* anfechten, angreifen.

impulse ['impʌls], *s.* der Impuls; der Anstoß.

impulsive [im'pʌlsiv], *adj.* impulsiv.

impunity [im'pju:niti], *s.* die Straffreiheit.

impure [im'pjuə], *adj.* (*also Metall.,* *Chem.*) unrein, unedel; unsauber.

impute [im'pju:t], *v.a.* beimessen; zurechnen, die Schuld geben für.

in [in], *prep.* in; an; zu, auf; bei; nach, unter; über; von; mit; — *the morning,* vormittags; — *case,* falls; — *any case,* auf jeden Fall; — *German,* auf deutsch; — *my opinion,* meiner Meinung nach; — *the street,* auf der Straße; — *time,* rechtzeitig. — *adv.* drinnen, innen; herein, hinein; zu Hause.

inability [inə'biliti], *s.* die Unfähigkeit.

inaccessible [inæk'sesibl], *adj.* unzugänglich.

inaccurate [i'nækjurit], *adj.* ungenau.

inaction [i'nækʃən], *s.* die Untätigkeit.

inactive [i'næktiv], *adj.* untätig.

inadequate [i'nædikwit], *adj.* unzulänglich.

inadmissible [inəd'misibl], *adj.* unzulässig.

inadvertent [inəd'və:tənt], *adj.* unbeabsichtigt; unachtsam.

inadvertently [inəd'və:təntli], *adv.* unversehens; versehentlich.

inalienable [in'eiliənəbl], *adj.* unveräußerlich.

inane [i'nein], *adj.* hohl, leer, sinnlos.

inanimate [i'nænimit], *adj.* unbeseelt, leblos.

inanity [i'næniti], *s.* die Leere, Nichtigkeit.

inapplicable [i'næplikəbl], *adj.* unanwendbar; unzutreffend.

inappropriate [inə'proupriit], *adj.* unpassend.

inarticulate [ina:'tikjulit], *adj.* unartikuliert.

inasmuch [inəz'mʌtʃ], *adv.* insofern (als).

inattentive [inə'tentiv], *adj.* unaufmerksam.

inaudible [i'nɔ:dibl], *adj.* unhörbar.

inaugural [i'nɔ:gjurəl], *adj.* Inaugural-, Eröffnungs-, Antritts-.

inaugurate [i'nɔ:gjureit], *v.a.* einweihen, eröffnen.

inauspicious [inɔ:'spiʃəs], *adj.* ungünstig.

inborn ['inbɔ:n], *adj.* angeboren.

inbred ['inbred], *adj.* in Inzucht geboren; angeboren, ererbt.

inbreeding ['inbri:diŋ], *s.* die Inzucht.

incalculable [in'kælkjuləbl], *adj.* unberechenbar.

incandescence [inkæn'desəns], *s.* die Weißglut.

incandescent [inkæn'desənt], *adj.* weißglühend.

incantation [inkæn'teiʃən], *s.* die Beschwörung.

incapable [in'keipəbl], *adj.* unfähig (*of doing s.th.,* etwas zu tun).

incapacitate [inkə'pæsiteit], *v.a.* unfähig machen.

incapacity [inkə'pæsiti], *s.* die Unfähigkeit.

incarcerate [in'ka:səreit], *v.a.* einkerkern, einsperren.

incarnate [in'ka:nit], *adj.* eingefleischt; (*Theol.*) verkörpert.

incarnation [inka:'neiʃən], *s.* die Verkörperung; (*Theol.*) Menschwerdung.

incautious [in'kɔ:ʃəs], *adj.* unvorsichtig.

incendiary [in'sendjəri], *adj.* Brand-, brennend. — *s.* der Brandstifter.

incense [in'sens], *v.a.* aufregen, erzürnen (*make angry*); (*Eccl.*) beweihräuchern. — ['insens], *s.* (*Eccl.*) der Weihrauch.

incentive [in'sentiv], *adj.* Ansporn-, Anreiz-. — *s.* der Ansporn, Anreiz; (*Comm.*) — *scheme,* das Inzentivsystem, Akkordsystem.

incessant [in'sesənt], *adj.* unaufhörlich, ununterbrochen.

incest ['insest], *s.* die Blutschande.

incestuous [in'sestjuəs], *adj.* blutschänderisch.

inch [intʃ], *s.* der Zoll. — *v.n.* — *away,* abrücken.

incident ['insidənt], *s.* der Vorfall, Zwischenfall; das Ereignis.

incidental [insi'dentl], *adj.* zufällig. — *s.* (*pl.*) zufällige Ausgaben, *f. pl.*; das Zusätzliche, Nebenausgaben, *f. pl.*

incipient [in'sipiənt], *adj.* beginnend, anfangend.

incise [in'saiz], *v.a.* einschneiden, (*Med.*) einen Einschnitt machen.

incision [in'siʒən], *s.* der Einschnitt.

incisive [in'saisiv], *adj.* einschneidend; energisch (*person*).

incite [in'sait], *v.a.* aufreizen, anspornen.

incivility [insi'viliti], *s.* die Unhöflichkeit.

inclement [in'klemənt], *adj.* unfreundlich (*weather, climate*).

inclination [inkli'neiʃən], *s.* die Neigung (*also fig.*).

incline [in'klain], *v.n.* neigen, sich neigen. — ['inklain], *s.* der Neigungswinkel; der Abhang.

include [in'klu:d], *v.a.* einschließen (*contain*); umfassen (*enclose*).

417

including

including [in'klu:diŋ], *prep.* einschließlich.

inclusive [in'klu:siv], *adj.* einschließlich, mitgerechnet.

incoherent [inko'hiərənt], *adj.* unzusammenhängend.

incombustible [inkəm'bʌstibl], *adj.* unverbrennbar.

income ['inkʌm], *s.* das Einkommen.

incommensurable, incommensurate [inkə'menʃərəbl, inkə'menʃərit], *adj.* unvereinbar, unmeßbar.

incomparable [in'kɔmpərəbl], *adj.* unvergleichlich.

incompatible [inkəm'pætibl], *adj.* unvereinbar.

incompetence, incompetency [in'kɔmpitəns, -tənsi], *s.* die Inkompetenz; Unzulänglichkeit.

incompetent [in'kɔmpitənt], *adj.* unzuständig, inkompetent; unzulänglich.

incomplete [inkəm'pli:t], *adj.* unvollständig.

incomprehensible [inkɔmpri'hensibl], *adj.* unverständlich.

inconceivable [inkən'si:vəbl], *adj.* unbegreiflich.

inconclusive [inkən'klu:siv], *adj.* unvollständig (*incomplete*); unüberzeugend; ergebnislos.

incongruity [inkɔŋ'gru:iti], *s.* (*Maths.*) die Inkongruenz; (*fig.*) die Unangemessenheit.

incongruous [in'kɔŋgruəs], *adj.* inkongruent; unangemessen.

inconsequent [in'kɔnsikwənt], *adj.* folgewidrig.

inconsequential [inkɔnsi'kwenʃəl], *adj.* inkonsequent (*inconsistent*); unzusammenhängend.

inconsiderate [inkən'sidərit], *adj.* rücksichtslos, unbedachtsam.

inconsistent [inkən'sistənt], *adj.* inkonsequent.

inconsolable [inkən'souləbl], *adj.* untröstlich.

inconstancy [in'kɔnstənsi], *s.* die Unbeständigkeit; Untreue (*fickleness*).

incontestable [inkən'testəbl], *adj.* unanfechtbar, unbestreitbar.

incontinent [in'kɔntinənt], *adj.* unenthaltsam.

incontrovertible [inkɔntro'və:tibl], *adj.* unstreitig, unanfechtbar.

inconvenience [inkən'vi:niəns], *s.* die Unbequemlichkeit, Unannehmlichkeit.

inconvenient [inkən'vi:niənt], *adj.* unangenehm, unpassend.

inconvertible [inkən'və:tibl], *adj.* unveränderlich; (*Comm.*) unumsetzbar.

incorporate [in'kɔ:pəreit], *v.a.* einverleiben (*Dat.*), eingliedern (*Acc.*).

incorporated [in'kɔ:pəreitid], *adj.* (*Am.*) eingetragene Körperschaft, eingetragener Verein.

incorrect [inkə'rekt], *adj.* unrichtig, fehlerhaft; unschicklich, unpassend.

incorrigible [in'kɔridʒibl], *adj.* unverbesserlich.

incorruptible [inkə'rʌptibl], *adj.* unbestechlich.

increase [in'kri:s], *v.a.* vermehren, vergrößern (*size, volume*); steigern (*heat, intensity*); erhöhen (*price*). — *v.n.* sich vermehren, sich erhöhen; wachsen (*grow*). — ['inkri:s], *s.* die Zunahme; der Zuwachs (*family*); die Erhöhung.

incredible [in'kredibl], *adj.* unglaublich.

incredulity [inkre'dju:liti], *s.* die Ungläubigkeit, der Unglaube.

incredulous [in'kredjuləs], *adj.* ungläubig, schwer zu überzeugen.

increment ['inkrimənt], *s.* (*Comm.*) die Zulage, Gehaltserhöhung.

incriminate [in'krimineit], *v.a.* beschuldigen, inkriminieren.

incubate ['inkjubeit], *v.a.* brüten, ausbrüten. — *v.n.* brüten.

incubator ['inkjubeitə], *s.* der Brutapparat.

inculcate ['inkʌlkeit], *v.a.* einprägen.

inculpate ['inkʌlpeit], *v.a.* beschuldigen.

incumbent [in'kʌmbənt], *adj.* (*upon, Dat.*) obliegend, nötig. — *s.* der Pfründner, Amtsinhaber.

incur [in'kə:], *v.a.* auf sich laden, sich zuziehen.

incurable [in'kjuərəbl], *adj.* unheilbar.

incursion [in'kə:ʃən], *s.* der Einfall, Streifzug.

indebted [in'detid], *adj.* verpflichtet, dankbar (*grateful*); verschuldet (*in debt*).

indecent [in'di:sənt], *adj.* unschicklich, unanständig.

indecision [indi'siʒən], *s.* die Unentschlossenheit.

indecisive [indi'saisiv], *adj.* unentschlossen.

indeclinable [indi'klainəbl], *adj.* (*Gram.*) undeklinierbar.

indecorous [indi'kɔ:rəs *or* in'dekɔrəs], *adj.* unrühmlich, unanständig.

indeed [in'di:d], *adv.* in der Tat, tatsächlich.

indefatigable [indi'fætigəbl], *adj.* unermüdlich.

indefensible [indi'fensibl], *adj.* unhaltbar; unverzeihlich (*unforgivable*).

indefinable [indi'fainəbl], *adj.* unbestimmbar, undefinierbar.

indefinite [in'definit], *adj.* unbestimmt.

indelible [in'delibl], *adj.* unauslöschlich.

indelicate [in'delikit], *adj.* unfein.

indemnify [in'demnifai], *v.a.* entschädigen.

indemnity [in'demniti], *die* Entschädigung.

indent [in'dent], *v.a.* auszacken, einschneiden.

indenture [in'dentʃə], *s.* der Lehrbrief (*apprentice*); Vertrag.

independence [indi'pendəns], *s.* die Unabhängigkeit, Freiheit.

independent [indi'pendənt], *adj.* unabhängig, frei.

inexhaustible

indescribable [indi'skraibəbl], *adj.*
unbeschreiblich.
indestructible [indi'strʌktibl], *adj.*
unverwüstlich; unzerstörbar.
indeterminable [indi'tə:minəbl], *adj.*
unbestimmbar.
indeterminate [indi'tə:minit], *adj.* unbestimmt.
index ['indeks], *s.* (*pl.* **indexes**) das
Inhaltsverzeichnis; (*pl.* **indices**)
(*Maths.*) der Exponent; — *finger*, der
Zeigefinger; (*pl.*) die Finger, Zeiger,
m. pl. (*pointers*).
India ['indjə], das Indien; — *paper*, das
Dünnpapier.
Indian ['indjən], *adj.* indisch; — *ink*,
die Tusche. — *s.* der Ind(i)er.
indiarubber ['indjə'rʌbə], *s.* der
Radiergummi.
indicate ['indikeit], *v.a.* anzeigen, angeben.
indication [indi'keiʃən], *s.* das Anzeichen, Merkmal, der Hinweis.
indicative [in'dikativ], *adj.* bezeichnend (für, *Acc.*). — *s.* (*Gram.*) der
Indikativ.
indict [in'dait], *v.a.* anklagen.
indictment [in'daitmənt], *s.* die Anklage.
indifference [in'difrəns], *s.* die Gleichgültigkeit.
indifferent [in'difrənt], *adj.* gleichgültig.
indigence ['indidʒəns], *s.* die Armut.
indigenous [in'didʒinəs], *adj.* eingeboren, einheimisch.
indigent ['indidʒənt], *adj.* arm,
dürftig.
indigestible [indi'dʒestibl], *adj.* unverdaulich.
indigestion [indi'dʒestʃən], *s.* die
Magenbeschwerden, *f. pl.*; die Magenverstimmung.
indignant [in'dignənt], *adj.* empört,
unwillig, entrüstet.
indignation [indig'neiʃən], *s.* die
Entrüstung, der Unwille.
indignity [in'digniti], *s.* die Schmach,
der Schimpf.
indirect [indi'rekt], *adj.* indirekt,
mittelbar.
indiscreet [indis'kri:t], *adj.* indiskret,
unvorsichtig; unbescheiden (*im-
modest*); taktlos.
indiscretion [indis'kreʃən], *s.* die In-
diskretion, Taktlosigkeit.
indiscriminate [indis'kriminit], *adj.*
ohne Unterschied, wahllos, kritiklos.
indispensable [indis'pensəbl], *adj.* unerläßlich, unentbehrlich.
indisposed [indis'pouzd], *adj.* unwohl
(*health*); unwillig (*unwilling*).
indisposition [indispə'ziʃən], *s.* das
Unwohlsein (*health*); das Abgeneigt-
sein (*disinclination*).
indisputable [indis'sɔljutəbl], *adj.* unbestreitbar.
indissoluble [indi'sɔljubl], *adj.* unauflöslich.
indistinct [indis'tiŋkt], *adj.* undeutlich.

indistinguishable [indis'tiŋgwiʃəbl],
adj. nicht zu unterscheiden, ununter-
scheidbar.
individual [indi'vidjuəl], *adj.* individuell, persönlich; einzeln (*single*). —
s. das Individuum, Einzelwesen.
individuality [individju'æliti], *s.* die
Individualität.
indivisible [indi'vizibl], *adj.* unteilbar.
Indo-Chinese [indotʃai'ni:z], *adj.* hin-
terindisch. — *s.* der Hinterind(i)er.
indolent ['indələnt], *adj.* indolent, träge.
Indonesian [indo'ni:ʒən], *adj.* indo-
nesisch. — *s.* der Indonesier.
indoor ['indɔ:], *adj.* im Haus; drinnen
(*inside*).
indoors [in'dɔ:z], *adv.* im Hause, zu
Hause.
indubitable [in'dju:bitəbl], *adj.* zweifellos, unzweifelhaft.
induce [in'dju:s], *v.a.* veranlassen, bewegen, verleiten (*incite*).
inducement [in'dju:smənt], *s.* der Beweggrund (*cause*); der Anlaß (*reason*);
die Verleitung (*incitement*).
induction [in'dʌkʃən], *s.* die Einführung; (*Elec.*) die Induktion.
inductive [in'dʌktiv], *adj.* (*Log.*, *Elec.*)
induktiv.
indulge [in'dʌldʒ], *v.a.* nachgeben
(*Dat.*); verwöhnen. — *v.n.* — *in*,
frönen (*Dat.*).
indulgence [in'dʌldʒəns], *s.* die Nachsicht; das Wohlleben; (*Eccl.*) der
Ablaß.
industrial [in'dʌstriəl], *adj.* industriell,
Industrie-.
industrious [in'dʌstriəs], *adj.* fleißig,
arbeitsam.
industry ['indəstri], *s.* die Industrie
(*production*); der Fleiß (*industrious-
ness*).
inebriate [i'ni:brieit], *v.a.* berauschen.
— [-iit], *adj.* berauscht.
ineffable [i'nefəbl], *adj.* unaussprechlich.
ineffective, ineffectual [ini'fektiv,
ini'fektjuəl], *adj.* unwirksam, wirkungslos; unfähig.
inefficiency [ini'fiʃənsi], *s.* die Erfolg-
losigkeit, Untauglichkeit.
inefficient [ini'fiʃənt], *adj.* untauglich,
untüchtig.
ineligible [in'elidʒibl], *adj.* nicht wählbar.
inept [i'nept], *adj.* untüchtig, albern,
dumm.
ineptitude [i'neptitju:d], *s.* die Unfähigkeit; die Dummheit (*stupidity*).
inequality [ini'kwɔliti], *s.* die Ungleichheit.
inert [i'nə:t], *adj.* träg.
inestimable [in'estiməbl], *adj.* unschätzbar.
inevitable [in'evitəbl], *adj.* unumgänglich, unvermeidlich.
inexcusable [iniks'kju:zəbl], *adj.* unverzeihlich, unentschuldbar.
inexhaustible [inig'zɔ:stibl], *adj.* unerschöpflich.

419

inexpedient [iniks'pi:djənt], *adj.* unzweckmäßig, unpraktisch, unpassend.
inexpensive [iniks'pensiv], *adj.* billig, nicht kostspielig.
inexperience [iniks'piəriəns], *s.* die Unerfahrenheit, Naivität.
inexpert [iniks'pə:t], *adj.* ungeübt, unerfahren.
inexpiable [i'nekspiəbl], *adj.* unsühnbar, nicht wieder gut zu machen.
inexplicable [i'neksplikəbl], *adj.* unerklärlich.
inexpressible [iniks'presibl], *adj.* unaussprechlich.
inexpressive [iniks'presiv], *adj.* ausdruckslos.
inextinguishable [iniks'tiŋgwiʃəbl], *adj.* unauslöschlich.
inextricable [i'nekstrikəbl], *adj.* unentwirrbar.
infallible [in'fælibl], *adj.* unfehlbar.
infamous ['infəməs], *adj.* verrufen, abscheulich, berüchtigt.
infamy ['infəmi], *s.* die Schande; Ehrlosigkeit (*dishonour*).
infancy ['infənsi], *s.* die Kindheit, Unmündigkeit; (*fig.*) der Anfang.
infant ['infənt], *s.* das Kind; (*Law*) der Unmündige, das Mündel.
infantry ['infəntri], *s.* die Infanterie.
infatuate [in'fætjueit], *v.a.* betören.
infect [in'fekt], *v.a.* anstecken, infizieren.
infection [in'fekʃən], *s.* (*Med.*) die Ansteckung, Infektion.
infectious [in'fekʃəs], *adj.* (*Med.*) ansteckend.
infer [in'fə:], *v.a.* schließen, herleiten, folgern.
inference ['infərəns], *s.* die Folgerung.
inferior [in'fiəriə], *comp. adj.* geringer; untergeordnet (*subordinate*); schlechter (*worse*).
inferiority [infiəri'ɔriti], *s.* die Inferiorität, Minderwertigkeit.
infernal [in'fə:nəl], *adj.* höllisch.
infest [in'fest], *v.a.* heimsuchen, plagen.
infidel ['infidəl], *adj.* ungläubig. — *s.* der Heide, Ungläubige.
infiltrate ['infiltreit], *v.n.* durchsickern, durchdringen, infiltrieren.
infinite ['infinit], *adj.* unendlich.
infinitive [in'finitiv], *s.* (*Gram.*) der Infinitiv, die Nennform.
infirm [in'fə:m], *adj.* gebrechlich, schwach; siech (*sick*).
infirmary [in'fə:məri], *s.* das Krankenhaus.
infirmity [in'fə:miti], *s.* die Schwäche, Gebrechlichkeit.
inflame [in'fleim], *v.a.* entzünden.
inflammation [inflə'meiʃən], *s.* die Entzündung.
inflate [in'fleit], *v.a.* aufblasen, aufblähen; (*Comm.*) künstlich erhöhen (*values*).
inflation [in'fleiʃən], *s.* die Aufblähung; (*Comm.*) die Inflation.

inflect [in'flekt], *v.a.* (*Gram.*) biegen, flektieren, deklinieren, konjugieren.
inflection [in'flekʃən], *s.* (*Gram.*) die Biegung; (*Phonet.*) der Tonfall.
inflexible [in'fleksibl], *adj.* unbiegsam.
inflexion *see* **inflection.**
inflict [in'flikt], *v.a.* auferlegen (*impose*); beibringen (*administer*).
infliction [in'flikʃən], *s.* die Verhängung, das Beibringen.
influence ['influəns], *v.a.* beeinflussen. — *s.* der Einfluß.
influential [influ'enʃəl], *adj.* einflußreich.
influenza [influ'enzə], *s.* (*Med.*) die Grippe.
inform [in'fɔ:m], *v.a., v.n.* informieren, benachrichtigen; — *against,* jemanden denunzieren.
informal [in'fɔ:məl], *adj.* nicht formell; ungezwungen, zwanglos.
informant [in'fɔ:mənt], *s.* der Angeber.
information [infə'meiʃən], *s.* die Information, Nachricht, Auskunft.
infrequent [in'fri:kwənt], *adj.* selten.
infringe [in'frindʒ], *v.a.* übertreten.
infuriate [in'fjuərieit], *v.a.* wütend machen.
infuse [in'fju:z], *v.a.* einflößen, aufgießen, begießen.
infusion [in'fju:ʒən], *s.* die Eingießung; der Aufguß (*tea*); (*Chem.*) die Infusion.
ingenious [in'dʒi:niəs], *adj.* geistreich, genial.
ingenuity [indʒi'nju:iti], *s.* der Scharfsinn.
ingenuous [in'dʒenjuəs], *adj.* offen, unbefangen, arglos.
ingot ['iŋgət], *s.* der Barren.
ingrained [in'greind], *adj.* eingefleischt.
ingratiate [in'greiʃieit], *v.r.* — *o.s.,* sich beliebt machen, sich einschmeicheln (*with,* bei).
ingratitude [in'grætitju:d], *s.* die Undankbarkeit.
ingredient [in'gri:diənt], *s.* der Bestandteil, die Zutat.
inhabit [in'hæbit], *v.a.* bewohnen.
inhabitant [in'hæbitənt], *s.* der Bewohner; Einwohner.
inhale [in'heil], *v.a.* einatmen.
inherent [in'hiərənt], *adj.* eigen, angeboren (*innate*); in der Sache selbst (*intrinsic*).
inherit [in'herit], *v.a.* erben.
inheritance [in'heritəns], *s.* die Erbschaft, das Erbgut (*patrimony*); (*fig.*) das Erbe.
inhibit [in'hibit], *v.a.* hindern; —*ing factor,* der Hemmfaktor.
inhibition [ini'biʃən], *s.* (*Psych.*) die Hemmung.
inhospitable [inhɔs'pitəbl], *adj.* ungastlich, ungastfreundlich.
inhuman [in'hju:mən], *adj.* unmenschlich.
inhume [in'hju:m], *v.a.* beerdigen.
inimical [i'nimikəl], *adj.* feindlich (gesinnt), feindselig.

inimitable [i'nimitəbl], *adj.* unnachahmlich.

iniquitous [i'nikwitəs], *adj.* ungerecht, schlecht, boshaft.

iniquity [i'nikwiti], *s.* die Ungerechtigkeit (*injustice*); die Schändlichkeit (*shame*).

initial [i'niʃəl], *adj.* anfänglich. — *s.* (*Typ.*) der Anfangsbuchstabe.

initiate [i'niʃieit], *v.a.* einweihen, anfangen.

initiative [i'niʃiətiv], *s.* die Initiative; der erste Anstoß (*impulse*).

injection [in'dʒekʃən], *s.* (*Med.*) die Einspritzung, Injektion.

injudicious [indʒu'diʃəs], *adj.* unbedacht, unbesonnen; übereilt (*rash*).

injunction [in'dʒʌŋkʃən], *s.* die Vorschrift, (*Law*) die gerichtliche Verfügung.

injure ['indʒə], *v.a.* verletzen.

injurious [in'dʒuəriəs], *adj.* verletzend; schädlich (*harmful*).

injury ['indʒəri], *s.* die Verletzung, Verwundung; der Schaden (*damage*).

injustice [in'dʒʌstis], *s.* die Ungerechtigkeit.

ink [iŋk], *s.* die Tinte.

inkling ['iŋkliŋ], *s.* die Ahnung.

inkstand ['iŋkstænd], *s.* das Schreibzeug.

inlaid [in'leid], *adj.* eingelegt.

inland ['inlənd], *adj.* inländisch, Binnen-; — *revenue office*, das Steueramt, Finanzamt.

inlet ['inlit], *s.* (*Geog.*) die kleine Bucht.

inmate ['inmeit], *s.* der Insasse, Bewohner.

inmost ['inmoust], *adj.* innerst.

inn [in], *s.* der Gasthof, das Wirtshaus; *Inns of Court*, die Londoner Rechtskammern, *f. pl.*

innate [i'neit], *adj.* angeboren.

inner ['inə], *adj.* inner; geheim (*secret*).

innings ['iniŋz], *s.* das Daransein (*in Cricket*); die Reihe.

innocence ['inəsəns], *s.* die Unschuld.

innocuous [i'nɔkjuəs], *adj.* unschädlich.

innovate ['inoveit], *v.a.*, *v.n.* als Neuerung einführen, Neuerungen machen.

innovation [ino'veiʃən], *s.* die Neuerung.

innuendo [inju'endou], *s.* das Innuendo, die Anspielung.

innumerable [i'nju:mərəbl], *adj.* unzählig, unzählbar.

inoculate [i'nɔkjuleit], *v.a.* impfen.

inoffensive [ino'fensiv], *adj.* harmlos, unschädlich.

inopportune [in'ɔpətju:n], *adj.* ungelegen.

inordinate [i'nɔ:dinit], *adj.* unmäßig.

inorganic [inɔ:'gænik], *adj.* anorganisch.

inquest ['inkwest], *s.* die gerichtliche Untersuchung (*Law*); *coroner's* —, die Leichenschau.

inquire, enquire [in'kwaiə], *v.n.* sich erkundigen (*after*, nach, *Dat.*), nachfragen.

inquiry, enquiry [in'kwaiəri], *s.* die Nachfrage; — *office*, die Auskunftsstelle.

inquisition [inkwi'ziʃən], *s.* (*Eccl.*) die Inquisition; die gerichtliche Untersuchung.

inquisitive [in'kwizitiv], *adj.* neugierig.

inquisitiveness [in'kwizitivnis], *s.* die Neugier(de).

inroad ['inroud], *s.* der Eingriff, Überfall.

insane [in'sein], *adj.* wahnsinnig.

insanity [in'sæniti], *s.* der Wahnsinn.

insatiable [in'seiʃəbl], *adj.* unersättlich.

inscribe [in'skraib], *v.a.* einschreiben (*enrol*); widmen (*book*).

inscription [in'skripʃən], *s.* die Inschrift.

inscrutable [in'skru:təbl], *adj.* unergründlich, unerforschlich.

insect ['insekt], *s.* das Insekt, Kerbtier.

insecure [insi'kjuə], *adj.* unsicher.

insensate [in'sensit], *adj.* unsinnig (*senseless*); gefühllos..

insensible [in'sensibl], *adj.* unempfindlich; gefühllos.

insensitive [in'sensitiv], *adj.* ohne feineres Gefühl, unempfindlich.

inseparable [in'sepərəbl], *adj.* unzertrennlich, untrennbar.

insert [in'sə:t], *v.a.* einsetzen, einschalten (*add*); inserieren (*in newspaper*).

insertion [in'sə:ʃən], *s.* die Einschaltung (*addition*); die Annonce, das Inserat (*press*).

inside [in'said], *adj.* inner. — *adv.* im Innern. — *prep.* innerhalb. — *s.* das Innere.

insidious [in'sidiəs], *adj.* heimtückisch.

insight ['insait], *s.* der Einblick.

insignia [in'signiə], *s. pl.* die Insignien.

insignificance [insig'nifikəns], *s.* die Geringfügigkeit, Bedeutungslosigkeit.

insignificant [insig'nifikənt], *adj.* unbedeutend, geringfügig.

insincere [insin'siə], *adj.* unaufrichtig.

insincerity [insin'seriti], *s.* die Unaufrichtigkeit.

insinuate [in'sinjueit], *v.a.* zu verstehen geben, andeuten, anspielen auf (*Acc.*).

insinuation [insinju'eiʃən], *s.* der Wink, die Andeutung, Anspielung.

insipid [in'sipid], *adj.* schal, geschmacklos.

insist [in'sist], *v.n.* bestehen (*upon*, auf, *Dat.*).

insistence [in'sistəns], *s.* das Bestehen, Beharren.

insolence ['insələns], *s.* die Frechheit.

insolent ['insələnt], *adj.* frech, unverschämt.

insoluble [in'sɔljubl], *adj.* unlösbar; (*Chem.*) unlöslich.

insolvent [in'sɔlvənt], *adj.* insolvent, zahlungsunfähig, bankrott.

inspect [in'spekt], *v.a.* inspizieren; besichtigen.

inspection

inspection [in'spekʃən], *s.* die Inspektion; Besichtigung.

inspiration [inspi'reiʃən], *s.* die Inspiration, Erleuchtung, Begeisterung.

inspire [in'spaiə], *v.a.* inspirieren, begeistern.

instability [instə'biliti], *s.* die Unbeständigkeit, Labilität.

install [in'stɔ:l], *v.a.* einsetzen (*in office*); einbauen.

installation [instə'leiʃən], *s.* die Einsetzung (*inauguration*); die Installation.

instalment [in'stɔ:lmənt], *s.* die Rate; *by* —s, auf Abzahlung; die Fortsetzung (*serial*).

instance ['instəns], *s.* das Beispiel (*example*); (*Law*) die Instanz; *at my* —, auf meine dringende Bitte; *for* —, zum Beispiel. — *v.a.* als Beispiel anführen.

instant ['instənt], *s.* der Augenblick. — *adj.* gegenwärtig; sofortig; laufend (*current month*).

instantaneous [instən'teiniəs], *adj.* augenblicklich, sofortig.

instead [in'sted], *adv.* dafür, stattdessen; — *of*, (an)statt (*Genit.*).

instep ['instep], *s.* (*Anat.*) der Rist.

instigate ['instigeit], *v.a.* aufhetzen, anreizen, anstiften.

instil [in'stil], *v.a.* einflößen.

instinct ['instiŋkt], *s.* der Instinkt, Naturtrieb.

institute ['institju:t], *s.* das Institut. — *v.a.* einrichten (*install*); stiften (*found*).

institution [insti'tju:ʃən], *s.* die Stiftung (*foundation*); die Anstalt (*establishment*).

instruct [in'strʌkt], *v.a.* unterrichten, unterweisen.

instruction [in'strʌkʃən], *s.* der Unterricht (*in schools etc.*); (*pl.*) die Instruktionen, *f. pl.*; die Direktive.

instructive [in'strʌktiv], *adj.* instruktiv, lehrreich.

instrument ['instrumənt], *s.* das Instrument; Werkzeug (*tool*).

insubordination [insəbɔ:di'neiʃən], *s.* der Ungehorsam.

insufferable [in'sʌfərəbl], *adj.* unerträglich.

insufficient [insə'fiʃənt], *adj.* ungenügend, unzulänglich.

insular ['insjulə], *adj.* Insel-; insular (*narrow-minded*).

insulate ['insjuleit], *v.a.* absondern (*separate*); (*Elec.*) isolieren; *insulating tape*, das Isolierband.

insult [in'sʌlt], *v.a.* beleidigen.

insuperable [in'sju:pərəbl], *adj.* unüberwindlich.

insupportable [insə'pɔ:təbl], *adj.* unhaltbar (*argument*); unerträglich (*insufferable*).

insurance [in'ʃuərəns], *s.* die Versicherung; — *policy*, die Police; — *premium*, die Prämie; — *broker*, der Versicherungsmakler.

insure [in'ʃuə], *v.a.* versichern.

insurgent [in'sə:dʒənt], *s.* der Aufständische, Aufrührer.

insurmountable [insə'mauntəbl], *adj.* unüberwindlich.

insurrection [insə'rekʃən], *s.* der Aufstand, Aufruhr; die Empörung.

intact [in'tækt], *adj.* unversehrt, intakt.

intangible [in'tændʒibl], *adj.* unberührbar (*untouchable*); (*Log.*) abstrakt. — *s. pl.* (*Log.*) die Intangibilien, *pl.*

integer ['intidʒə], *s.* (*Maths.*) das Ganze, die ganze Zahl.

integral ['intigrəl], *adj.* wesentlich; vollständig. — *s.* (*Maths.*) das Integral.

integrate ['intigreit], *v.a.* (*Maths.*) integrieren.

integration [inti'greiʃən], *s.* (*Maths.*) die Integrierung; (*fig.*) die Integration, das völlige Aufgehen.

integrity [in'tegriti], *s.* die Rechtschaffenheit, Redlichkeit (*probity*).

intellect ['intilekt], *s.* der Geist, Intellekt, Verstand.

intellectual [inti'lektjuəl], *adj.* intellektuell. — *s.* der Intellektuelle.

intelligence [in'telidʒəns], *s.* die Intelligenz; die Nachricht (*news*).

intelligent [in'telidʒənt], *adj.* intelligent.

intelligible [in'telidʒibl], *adj.* verständlich.

intemperance [in'tempərəns], *s.* die Unmäßigkeit.

intemperate [in'tempərit], *adj.* unmäßig.

intend [in'tend], *v.a.* beabsichtigen, vorhaben.

intendant [in'tendənt], *s.* der Intendant, Verwalter.

intense [in'tens], *adj.* intensiv, heftig.

intent [in'tent], *adj.* gespannt, begierig, bedacht (*on*, auf, *Acc.*). — *s.* die Absicht.

intention [in'tenʃən], *s.* die Absicht.

intentioned [in'tenʃənd], *adj.* *well-* —, wohlgesinnt.

inter [in'tə:], *v.a.* beerdigen.

intercede [intə'si:d], *v.n.* vermitteln (*between*); sich verwenden (*on behalf of*, für, *Acc.*).

intercept [intə'sept], *v.a.* abfangen, auffangen, hemmen.

intercession [intə'seʃən], *s.* die Vermittlung, Fürsprache, Fürbitte.

interchange ['intətʃeindʒ], *s.* der Austausch. — [-'tʃeindʒ], *v.a.* austauschen.

intercourse ['intəkɔ:s], *s.* der Verkehr, Umgang.

interdict [intə'dikt], *v.a.* untersagen, verbieten.

interest ['intrəst], *s.* das Interesse; die Beteiligung; (*Comm.*) die Zinsen, *m. pl.*; *compound* —, die Zinseszinsen, *m. pl.* — *v.a.* interessieren.

interested ['intrəstid], *adj.* (*in*, an, *Dat.*) interessiert; *be* — *in*, sich interessieren für.

interesting ['intrəstiŋ], *adj.* interessant.
interfere [intə'fiə], *v.n.* sich einmischen, eingreifen *(in,* in, *Acc.)*
interference [intə'fiərəns]; *s.* die Einmischung; *(Rad.)* die Störung.
interim ['intərim], *adj.* vorläufig, Zwischen-.
interior [in'tiəriə], *adj.* innerlich. — *s.* das Innere; das Binnenland; — *decorator,* der Innenraumgestalter, der Innenarchitekt; *Ministry of the Interior,* das Innenministerium.
interjection [intə'dʒekʃən], *s.* die Interjektion; der Ausruf.
interlace [intə'leis], *v.a.* einflechten.
interleave [intə'li:v], *v.a.* durchschießen *(a book).*
interlinear [intə'liniə], *adj.* zwischenzeilig.
interlocutor [intə'lɔkjutə], *s.* der Gesprächspartner.
interloper ['intəloupə], *s.* der Eindringling.
interlude ['intəlju:d], *s.* das Zwischenspiel.
intermarry [intə'mæri], *v.n.* untereinander heiraten.
intermediate [intə'mi:diit],*adj.* Mittel-; *(Sch.)* — *certificate,* das Mittelstufenzeugnis.
interment [in'tə:mənt], *s.* die Beerdigung.
interminable [in'tə:minəbl], *adj.* endlos, langwierig.
intermingle [intə'miŋgl], *v.n.* sich vermischen.
intermission [intə'miʃən], *s.* die Pause, Unterbrechung.
intermit [intə'mit], *v.a.* unterbrechen.
intermittent [intə'mitənt], *adj.* Wechsel-, aussetzend.
internal [in'tə:nl], *adj.* intern, innerlich.
international [intə'næʃənəl], *adj.* international; — *law,* das Völkerrecht.
interpolate [in'tə:poleit], *v.a.* interpolieren, einschalten.
interpose [intə'pouz], *v.a.* dazwischenstellen. — *v.n.* vermitteln *(mediate).*
interpret [in'tə:prit], *v.a.* verdolmetschen; erklären *(explain);* auslegen, interpretieren.
interpretation [intə:pri'teiʃən], *s.* die Auslegung, Interpretation.
interpreter [in'tə:pritə], *s.* der Dolmetscher.
interrogate [in'terogeit], *v.a.* ausfragen, befragen, vernehmen.
interrogation [intero'geiʃən], *s.* die Befragung; *(Law)* das Verhör, die Vernehmung.
interrogative [intə'rɔgətiv], *adj. (Gram.)* Frage-, Interrogativ-.
interrupt [intə'rʌpt], *v.a.* unterbrechen, stören *(disturb).*
interruption [intə'rʌpʃən], *s.* die Unterbrechung; Störung *(disturbance).*
intersect [intə'sekt], *v.a.* durchschneiden.

intersperse [intə'spə:s], *v.a.* untermengen, vermischen, einstreuen.
intertwine [intə'twain], *v.a., v.n.* (sich) durchflechten.
interval ['intəvəl], *s.* der Zwischenraum; die Pause; *(Mus.)* das Interval.
intervene [intə'vi:n], *v.n.* eingreifen; als Vermittler dienen *(act as mediator).*
intervention [intə'venʃən], *s.* die Vermittlung, Intervention.
interview ['intəvju:], *v.a.* zur Vorsprache einladen *(a candidate);* interviewen. — *s.* die Vorsprache, das Interview.
intestate [in'testit], *adj.* ohne Testament.
intestines [in'testinz], *s. pl. (Anat.)* die Eingeweide, *n. pl.*
intimacy ['intiməsi], *s.* die Vertraulichkeit, Intimität.
intimate ['intimit], *adj.* intim, vertraut, vertraulich. — [-meit], *v.a.* andeuten, zu verstehen geben.
intimation [inti'meiʃən], *s.* der Wink, die Andeutung.
intimidate [in'timideit], *v.a.* einschüchtern.
into ['intu], *prep. (Acc.)* in, in ... hinein *(towards).*
intolerable [in'tɔlərəbl], *adj.* unerträglich.
intolerance [in'tɔlərəns], *s.* die Unduldsamkeit, Intoleranz.
intonation [into'neiʃən], *s. (Phonet.)* die Intonation; *(Mus.)* das Anstimmen, der Tonansatz *(of instruments).*
intoxicate [in'tɔksikeit], *v.a.* berauschen.
intractable [in'træktəbl], *adj.* unbändig, unlenksam.
intransitive [in'trænsitiv *or* in'trɑ:ns-], *adj. (Gram.)* intransitiv.
intrepid [in'trepid], *adj.* unerschrocken, furchtlos.
intricacy ['intrikəsi], *s.* die Verwicklung *(tangle),* Schwierigkeit *(difficulty).*
intricate ['intrikit], *adj.* verwickelt, schwierig.
intrigue [in'tri:g], *s.* die Intrige. — *v.n.* intrigieren.
intrinsic [in'trinsik], *adj.* wesentlich; innerlich *(inner).*
introduce [intrə'dju:s], *v.a.* einführen, einleiten *(book etc.);* vorstellen *(person).*
introduction [intrə'dʌkʃən], *s.* die Einführung, das Bekanntmachen; die Einleitung *(preface);* die Vorstellung *(presentation to s.o., Dat.).*
introductory [intrə'dʌktəri], *adj.* einführend.
introspection [intrə'spekʃən], *s.* die Selbstbetrachtung, Introspektion.
introspective [intrə'spektiv], *adj.* nachdenklich, beschaulich.
intrude [in'tru:d], *v.n.* eindringen, sich eindrängen; stören *(be in the way).*
intrusion [in'tru:ʒən], *s.* das Eindringen.

intuition

intuition [intju'iʃən], *s.* die Intuition, Eingebung.
intuitive [in'tju:itiv], *adj.* intuitiv, gefühlsmäßig.
inundate ['inʌndeit], *v.a.* überschwemmen.
inure [i'njuə], *v.a.* gewöhnen; abhärten (*harden*).
invade [in'veid], *v.a.* angreifen, einfallen (in, *Dat.*).
invalid [in'vælid], *adj.* ungültig (*void*); ['invəlid] krank (*sick*). — *s.* der Kranke, Invalide.
invalidate [in'vælideit], *v.a.* ungültig machen, für ungültig erklären.
invalidity [invə'liditi], *s.* die Ungültigkeit.
invaluable [in'væljuəbl], *adj.* von hohem Wert, wertvoll, unschätzbar.
invariable [in'vɛəriəbl], *adj.* unveränderlich. — *s.* (*Maths.*) die unveränderliche Größe, die Konstante, Unveränderliche.
invasion [in'veiʒən], *s.* die Invasion, der Einfall; Angriff (*of,* auf, *Acc.*).
invective [in'vektiv], *adj.* schmähend. — *s.* die Schmähung.
inveigh [in'vei], *v.n.* schmähen, losziehen (gegen); schimpfen (auf, *Acc.*).
inveigle [in'veigl], *v.a.* verleiten, verführen.
invent [in'vent], *v.a.* erfinden.
invention [in'venʃən], *s.* die Erfindung.
inventor [in'ventə], *s.* der Erfinder.
inventory ['invəntri], *s.* der Bestand, das Inventar; die Liste (*list*).
inverse [in'və:s, 'invə:s], *adj.* umgekehrt.
inversion [in'və:ʃən], *s.* die Umkehrung; (*Gram., Maths.*) die Inversion.
invert [in'və:t], *v.a.* umstellen, umkehren. — ['invə:t], *s.* (*Chem.*) — *sugar,* der Invertzucker.
invest [in'vest], *v.a.* bekleiden; bedecken; (*Comm.*) investieren, anlegen.
investigate [in'vestigeit], *v.a.* untersuchen, erforschen.
investiture [in'vestitʃə], *s.* die Investitur; die Belehnung.
investment [in'vestmənt], *s.* die Investierung, Kapitalanlage.
inveterate [in'vetərit], *adj.* eingewurzelt, eingefleischt.
invidious [in'vidiəs], *adj.* neiderregend, verhaßt.
invigorate [in'vigəreit], *v.a.* stärken, beleben.
invincible [in'vinsibl], *adj.* unbesiegbar, unüberwindlich.
inviolable [in'vaiələbl], *adj.* unverletzlich.
invisible [in'vizibl], *adj.* unsichtbar.
invitation [invi'teiʃən], *s.* die Einladung.
invite [in'vait], *v.a.* einladen.
invocation [invo'keiʃən], *s.* die Anrufung.
invoice ['invɔis], *s.* die Rechnung, Faktura. — *v.a.* fakturieren.
invoke [in'vouk], *v.a.* anrufen.
involuntary [in'vɔləntri], *adj.* unfreiwillig (*unwilling*); unwillkürlich (*reflex*).

involve [in'vɔlv], *v.a.* verwickeln.
involved [in'vɔlvd], *adj.* schwierig, verwickelt, kompliziert.
invulnerable [in'vʌlnərəbl], *adj.* unverwundbar, unverletzlich.
inward ['inwəd], *adj.* inner(lich). — *adv.* (*also* **inwards**) einwärts, nach innen, ins Innere.
iodine ['aiədain *or* 'aiədi:n], *s.* (*Chem.*) das Jod.
Iraki, Iraqi [i'ra:ki], *adj.* irakisch. — *s.* der Iraker.
Iranian [i'reinjən], *adj.* iranisch. — *s.* der Iranier.
irascible [i'ræsibl], *adj.* jähzornig, aufbrausend.
irate [ai'reit], *adj.* erzürnt, zornig.
ire [aiə], *s.* (*Poet.*) der Zorn.
iridescent [iri'desənt], *adj.* irisierend, schillernd.
iris ['aiəris], *s.* (*Anat.*) die Regenbogenhaut; (*Bot.*) die Schwertlilie.
Irish ['airiʃ], *adj.* irisch, ersisch. — *s.* (*pl.*) die —, die Irländer, Iren, *pl.*
Irishman ['airiʃmən], *s.* der Irländer, Ire.
irk [ə:k], *v.a.* verdrießen, verärgern.
irksome ['ə:ksəm], *adj.* lästig, ärgerlich.
iron ['aiən], *s.* (*Metall.*) das Eisen; (*pl.*) die eisernen Fesseln. — *adj.* eisern, Eisen-. — *v.a.* bügeln, plätten; — *out,* schlichten, beilegen.
ironical [ai'rɔnikəl], *adj.* ironisch.
ironmonger ['aiənmʌŋgə], *s.* der Eisenhändler.
ironmould ['aiənmould], *s.* der Rostfleck.
irony ['aiərəni], *s.* die Ironie.
irradiate [i'reidieit], *v.a.* bestrahlen.
irrational [i'ræʃənəl], *adj.* (*Log., Maths.*) irrational; unvernünftig (*without reason*).
irreconcilable [irekən'sailəbl], *adj.* unversöhnlich; unvereinbar (*incompatible*).
irregular [i'regjulə], *adj.* unregelmäßig, gegen die Regel.
irrelevant [i'reləvənt], *adj.* belanglos.
irremediable [iri'mi:diəbl], *adj.* unheilbar; nicht wieder gut zu machen.
irreparable [i'repərəbl], *adj.* unersetzlich.
irrepressible [iri'presibl], *adj.* nicht zu unterdrücken, unbezähmbar.
irreproachable [iri'proutʃəbl], *adj.* untadelhaft, tadellos.
irresistible [iri'zistibl], *adj.* unwiderstehlich.
irresolute [i'rezolju:t], *adj.* unschlüssig, unentschlossen.
irrespective [iris'pektiv], *adj.* ohne Rücksicht (*of,* auf, *Acc.*).
irresponsible [iris'pɔnsibl], *adj.* unverantwortlich.
irretrievable [iri'tri:vəbl], *adj.* unersetzlich, unwiederbringlich.
irreverent [i'revərənt], *adj.* unehrerbietig.
irrevocable [i'revəkəbl], *adj.* unwiderruflich.

irrigate ['irigeit], *v.a.* bewässern.
irritable ['iritəbl], *adj.* reizbar.
irritant ['iritənt], *s.* das Reizmittel.
irritation [iri'teiʃən], *s.* die Reizung, das Reizen; die Erzürnung.
irruption [i'rʌpʃən], *s.* der Einbruch.
island ['ailənd], *s.* die Insel.
isle [ail], *s.* (*Poet.*) die Insel.
isolate ['aisəleit], *v.a.* (*Med.*) isolieren; absondern; (*Chem.*) darstellen.
isolation [aisə'leiʃən], *s.* die Absonderung, Isolierung.
Israeli [iz'reili], *adj.* den Staat Israel betreffend. — *s.* der Israeli.
Israelite ['izreiəlait], *adj.* israelitisch. — *s.* der Israelit.
issue ['isju: *or* 'iʃu:], *s.* der Ausgang, Erfolg (*result*); *main* —, der Hauptpunkt; die Nachkommenschaft (*children*); die Ausgabe (*edition*); Herausgabe (*publication*). — *v.a.* herausgeben; erlassen (*proclaim*); veröffentlichen (*publish*). — *v.n.* herrühren, stammen (*from*).
isthmus ['isθməs], *s.* die Landenge.
it [it], *pron.* es; *with* —, damit.
Italian [i'tæljən], *adj.* italienisch. — *s.* der Italiener.
italics [i'tæliks], *s. pl.* (*Typ.*) der Kursivdruck, die Kursivschrift.
itch [itʃ], *s.* das Jucken. — *v.n.* jucken; — *to do s.th.*, (*coll.*) darauf brennen, etwas zu tun.
item ['aitəm], *s.* der Posten (*in bill*); der Programmpunkt (*agenda*); die Einzelheit.
itemize ['aitəmaiz], *v.a.* (*Comm.*) aufführen; verzeichnen.
iterate ['itəreit], *v.a.* wiederholen.
itinerant [i'tinərənt], *adj.* wandernd.
its [its], *poss. adj.* sein, ihr; dessen, deren.
itself [it'self], *pron.* selber, sich; *of* —, von selbst.
ivory ['aivəri], *s.* das Elfenbein. — *adj.* aus Elfenbein, elfenbeinern.
ivy ['aivi], *s.* (*Bot.*) der Efeu.

J

J [dʒei]. das J.
jabber ['dʒæbə], *v.n.* schnattern.
Jack [dʒæk]. Hans; *Union* —, die britische Flagge; (*Cards*) der Bube.
jack [dʒæk], *s.* (*Motor.*) der Wagenheber. — *v.a.* — *up*, (*Motor.*) hochwinden.
jackal ['dʒækɔ:l], *s.* (*Zool.*) der Schakal.
jackass ['dʒækæs], *s.* (*Zool.*) der Esel.
jackdaw ['dʒækdɔ:], *s.* (*Orn.*) die Dohle.
jacket ['dʒækit], *s.* das Jackett, die Jacke; *dinner* —, der Smoking;

potatoes in their —*s*, Kartoffeln in der Schale, *f. pl.*
jade [dʒeid], *s.* der Nierenstein.
jaded ['dʒeidid], *adj.* abgeplagt, abgehärmt, ermüdet.
jag [dʒæg], *s.* die Kerbe. — *v.a.* kerben, zacken.
jagged ['dʒægid], *adj.* zackig.
jail *see under* **gaol.**
jailer *see under* **gaoler.**
jam (1) [dʒæm], *s.* die Marmelade, Konfitüre.
jam (2) [dʒæm], *s. traffic* —, die Verkehrsstauung; (*coll.*) *in a* —, in der Klemme. — *v.a.* zusammenpressen (*press together*); (*Rad.*) stören.
Jamaican [dʒə'meikən], *adj.* jamaikanisch. — *s.* der Jamaikaner.
jamb [dʒæm], *s.* der Türpfosten.
jangle ['dʒæŋgl], *v.n.* klirren, rasseln. — *s.* das Geklirr, Gerassel.
janitor ['dʒænitə], *s.* der Portier.
January ['dʒænjuəri]. der Januar.
japan [dʒə'pæn], *s.* lackierte Arbeit. — *v.a.* lackieren.
Japanese [dʒæpə'ni:z], *adj.* japanisch. — *s.* der Japaner.
jar (1) [dʒɑ:], *s.* der Topf, das Glas (*preserves*).
jar (2) [dʒɑ:], *v.n.* offenstehen (*door*); mißtönen, knarren.
jargon ['dʒɑ:gən], *s.* der Jargon.
jasmine ['dʒæzmin], *s.* (*Bot.*) der Jasmin.
jasper ['dʒæspə], *s.* der Jaspis.
jaundice ['dʒɔ:ndis], *s.* (*Med.*) die Gelbsucht; (*fig.*) der Neid (*envy*); —*d outlook*, die Verbitterung, Mißstimmung.
jaunt [dʒɔ:nt], *s.* der Ausflug, Spaziergang. — *v.n.* herumstreifen, spazieren.
jaunty ['dʒɔ:nti], *adj.* leicht, munter, lebhaft.
jaw [dʒɔ:], *s.* (*Anat.*) der Kinnbacken; der Rachen (*animals*).
jay [dʒei], *s.* (*Orn.*) der Häher.
jazz [dʒæz], *s.* die Jazzmusik.
jealous ['dʒeləs], *adj.* eifersüchtig.
jealousy ['dʒeləsi], *s.* die Eifersucht.
jeer ['dʒiə], *v.a.*, *v.n.* spotten, verhöhnen.
jejune [dʒi'dʒu:n], *adj.* nüchtern, trocken.
jelly ['dʒeli], *s.* das Gelee.
jellyfish ['dʒelifiʃ], *s.* (*Zool.*) die Qualle.
jeopardize ['dʒepədaiz], *v.a.* gefährden.
jeopardy ['dʒepədi], *s.* die Gefahr.
jerk [dʒɔ:k], *v.a.* rucken, stoßen (*push*); plötzlich bewegen (*move suddenly*). — *v.n.* zusammenzucken. — *s.* (*Am. coll.*) der Kerl; der Ruck, Stoß.
jersey ['dʒɔ:zi], *s.* die Wolljacke.
jessamine ['dʒesəmin], *s.* (*Bot.*) der Jasmin.
jest [dʒest], *s.* der Spaß, Scherz. — *v.n.* scherzen.
jester ['dʒestə], *s.* der Spaßmacher, Hofnarr.

jet

jet (1) [dʒet], *s.* der Strahl, Wasserstrahl; (*Aviat.*) die Düse; — *engine*, der Düsenmotor; — *plane*, das Düsenflugzeug. — *v.n.* hervorspringen.

jet (2) [dʒet], *s.* der Gagat; — *black*, pechschwarz.

jetsam [ˈdʒetsəm], *s.* das Strandgut.

jetty [ˈdʒeti], *s.* der Hafendamm, die Landungsbrücke (*landing stage*).

Jew [dʒuː], *s.* der Jude.

jewel [ˈdʒuəl], *s.* das Juwel, der Edelstein.

jewel(le)ry [ˈdʒuəlri], *s.* der Schmuck; die Juwelen, *n. pl.*

Jewish [ˈdʒuːiʃ], *adj.* jüdisch.

Jewry [ˈdʒuəri], *s.* die Judenschaft, das Judentum.

jiffy [ˈdʒifi], *s.* (*coll.*) der Augenblick.

jig (1) [dʒig], *s.* die Gigue (*dance*).

jig (2) [dʒig], *s.* das Werkzeug (*tool*); —*saw*, die Säge; —*saw puzzle*, das Zusammenlegspiel, -setzspiel.

jilt [dʒilt], *v.a.* sitzen lassen.

jingle [dʒiŋgl], *v.a.* klimpern, klimpern lassen (*coins etc.*). — *s.* das Geklimper.

job [dʒɔb], *s.* die Arbeit, Anstellung; die Stellung; das Geschäft; — *in hand*, die Beschäftigung.

jobber [ˈdʒɔbə], *s.* der Makler, Spekulant (*stock exchange*).

jockey [ˈdʒɔki], *s.* der Jockei, Reiter.

jocular [ˈdʒɔkjulə], *adj.* scherzhaft, lustig.

jocund [ˈdʒɔkənd], *adj.* munter, heiter.

jog [dʒɔg], *v.a.* stoßen, antreiben. — *v.n.* gemächlich traben, trotten. — *s.* der Trott.

join [dʒɔin], *v.a.* verbinden, zusammenfügen; (*club etc.*) beitreten (*Dat.*). — *v.n.* (*rivers*) zusammenfließen (mit, *Dat.*); (*Comm.*) sich vereinigen (mit, *Dat.*).

joiner [ˈdʒɔinə], *s.* der Tischler, Schreiner.

joint [dʒɔint], *s.* (*Anat.*) das Gelenk; das Stück Fleisch, der Braten (*meat*); (*sl.*) das Lokal, die Spelunke. — *adj.* vereint, gemeinsam; (*Comm.*) — *stock company*, die Aktiengesellschaft; — *heir*, der Miterbe.

joist [dʒɔist], *s.* (*Carp.*) der Querbalken.

joke [dʒouk], *s.* der Scherz, Witz.

jollity [ˈdʒɔliti], *s.* die Heiterkeit.

jolly [ˈdʒɔli], *adj.* fröhlich, heiter, lustig.

jolt [dʒoult], *v.a.* schütteln, erschüttern (*shake up*). — *s.* der Stoß.

jostle [dʒɔsl], *v.a.* stoßen, drängen. — *v.n.* drängeln.

jot [dʒɔt], *s.* der Punkt, das Iota. — *v.a.* — (*down*), notieren, niederschreiben.

journal [ˈdʒəːnəl], *s.* die Zeitschrift (*periodical*).

journalism [ˈdʒəːnəlizm], *s.* das Zeitungswesen, der Journalistenberuf.

journalist [ˈdʒəːnəlist], *s.* der Journalist.

journey [ˈdʒəːni], *s.* die Reise.

joust [dʒuːst], *s.* das Turnier.

jovial [ˈdʒouviəl], *adj.* jovial, freundlich; lustig (*gay*).

joy [dʒɔi], *s.* die Freude.

jubilant [ˈdʒuːbilənt], *adj.* frohlockend.

jubilation [dʒuːbiˈleiʃən], *s.* der Jubel.

jubilee [ˈdʒuːbiliː], *s.* das Jubiläum.

Judaism [ˈdʒuːdeiizm], *s.* das Judentum.

judge [dʒʌdʒ], *s.* der Richter. — *v.a.* richten, beurteilen, entscheiden.

judgment [ˈdʒʌdʒmənt], *s.* das Urteil; das Urteilsvermögen (*discretion*), die Urteilskraft.

judicial [dʒuːˈdiʃəl], *adj.* richterlich, gerichtlich.

judicious [dʒuːˈdiʃəs], *adj.* klug, scharfsinnig.

jug [dʒʌg], *s.* der Krug.

juggle [dʒʌgl], *v.n.* jonglieren, gaukeln.

juggler [ˈdʒʌglə], *s.* der Jongleur.

Jugoslav *see* **Yugoslav.**

jugular [ˈdʒuːg- *or* ˈdʒʌgjulə], *adj.* Kehl-, Hals-, Gurgel-. — *s.* (*vein*) die Halsader.

juice [dʒuːs], *s.* der Saft.

July [dʒuˈlai]. der Juli.

jumble [dʒʌmbl], *v.a.* zusammenmischen, vermischen. — *s.* das gemischte Zeug; — *sale*, der Verkauf, Ausverkauf gebrauchter Dinge, Ramschverkauf.

jump [dʒʌmp], *v.n.* springen. — *s.* der Sprung.

junction [ˈdʒʌŋkʃən], *s.* (*Railw.*) der Knotenpunkt; die Kreuzung.

juncture [ˈdʒʌŋktʃə], *s.* der (kritische) Zeitpunkt.

June [dʒuːn]. der Juni.

jungle [dʒʌŋgl], *s.* der Dschungel.

junior [ˈdʒuːnjə], *adj.* jünger; Unter-.

juniper [ˈdʒuːnipə], *s.* (*Bot.*) der Wacholder.

junk [dʒʌŋk], *s.* (*coll.*) das alte Zeug, alte Möbelstücke, *n. pl.*

junket [ˈdʒʌŋkit], *s.* der Schmaus, das Fest; (*Cul.*) dicke Milch mit Sahne. — *v.n.* schmausen, feiern (*celebrate*).

juridical [dʒuəˈridikəl], *adj.* rechtlich; gerichtlich (*in Court*).

jurisdiction [dʒuərizˈdikʃən], *s.* die Gerichtsbarkeit.

juror [ˈdʒuərə], *s.* der, die Geschworene.

jury [ˈdʒuəri], *s.* die Jury, das Geschworenengericht.

just [dʒʌst], *adj.* gerecht; rechtschaffen (*decent*); gehörig (*proper*). — *adv.* soeben, eben; — *as*, eben als, gerade wie.

justice [ˈdʒʌstis], *s.* die Gerechtigkeit; der Richter (*judge*).

justifiable [ˈdʒʌstifaiəbl], *adj.* zu rechtfertigen, berechtigt.

justify [ˈdʒʌstifai], *v.a.* rechtfertigen.

jut [dʒʌt], *v.n.* — (*out*), hervorragen. — *s.* der Vorsprung.

jute [dʒuːt], *s.* die Jute.

juvenile [ˈdʒuːvənail], *adj.* jugendlich, unreif.

juxtaposition [dʒʌkstəpəˈziʃən], *s.* die Nebeneinanderstellung, Gegenüberstellung.

K

K [kei]. das K.
kale [keil], *s.* (*Bot.*) der Krauskohl.
kaleidoscope [kə'laidəskoup], *s.* das Kaleidoskop.
kangaroo [kæŋgə'ru:], *s.* (*Zool.*) das Känguruh.
keel [ki:l], *s.* der Kiel; *on an even —,* bei ruhiger See; (*also fig.*) ruhig. — *v.n. — over,* umkippen.
keen [ki:n], *adj.* eifrig (*intent*); scharfsinnig (*perspicacious*); scharf (*blade*).
keenness ['ki:nnis], *s.* der Eifer; Scharfsinn; die Schärfe (*blade*).
keep [ki:p], *v.a. irr.* halten (*hold*); behalten (*retain*); führen (*a shop*); hüten (*gate, dog etc.*). — *v.n. — doing,* in etwas fortfahren, — *going,* weitergehen; — *away,* sich fernhalten; — *in, indoors,* zu Hause bleiben; — *off,* abhalten; sich fernhalten; — *out,* draußen bleiben; — *up,* aufrechterhalten. — *s.* das Burgverlies; der Unterhalt.
keeper ['ki:pə], *s.* der Hüter, Wärter; Museumsbeamte.
keeping ['ki:piŋ], *s.* die Verwahrung; *in safe —,* in guten Händen, in guter Obhut.
keepsake ['ki:pseik], *s.* das Andenken.
keg [keg], *s.* das Fäßchen.
ken [ken], *s.* die Kenntnis; *in my —,* meines Wissens. — *v.a.* (*Scottish*) kennen.
kennel [kenl], *s.* die Hundehütte.
kerb(stone) ['kə:b(stoun)], *s.* der Prellstein.
kerchief ['kə:tʃif], *s.* das Kopftuch, Halstuch.
kernel [kə:nl], *s.* der Kern.
kettle [ketl], *s.* der Kessel; — *drum,* die Kesselpauke.
key [ki:], *s.* der Schlüssel; (*Mus.*) die Tonart; die Taste (*on piano etc.*); — *man,* eine wichtige Person, Person in einer Schlüsselstellung. — *v.a. — (in),* einfügen, befestigen.
keyboard ['ki:bɔ:d], *s.* die Klaviatur; Tastatur (*typewriter*); — *instrument,* das Tasteninstrument.
keyhole ['ki:houl], *s.* das Schlüsselloch.
keystone ['ki:stoun], *s.* der Schlußstein.
kick [kik], *v.a., v.n.* mit dem Fuße stoßen *or* treten; — *against s.th.,* sich wehren. — *s.* der Fußstoß, Tritt; (*Footb.*) — *off,* der Ankick; *free —,* der Freistoß; *penalty —,* der Strafstoß, der Elfmeterstoß.
kid (1) [kid], *s.* (*Zool.*) das Geißlein, Zicklein; *with — gloves,* mit Glacéhandschuhen; (*coll.*) das Kind.
kid (2) [kid], *v.a.* (*Am. coll.*) zum Narren haben, aufziehen (*tease*).

kidnap ['kidnæp], *v.a.* entführen.
kidney ['kidni], *s.* (*Anat.*) die Niere; — *bean,* die französische Bohne.
kill [kil], *v.a.* töten; schlachten (*animal*).
kiln [kiln], *s.* der Darrofen; der Ziegelofen (*tiles, bricks*).
kilt [kilt], *s.* der Schottenrock.
kin [kin], *s.* die Verwandtschaft; *kith and —,* die Verwandten, *m. pl.*
kind [kaind], *s.* die Art, Gattung, Art und Weise. — *adj.* freundlich, gütig, liebenswürdig.
kindle [kindl], *v.a.* anzünden, anfachen.
kindliness, kindness ['kaindlinis, 'kaindnis], *s.* die Güte, Freundlichkeit.
kindred ['kindrid], *adj.* verwandt.
king [kiŋ], *s.* der König.
kingdom ['kiŋdəm], *s.* das Königreich.
kink [kiŋk], *s.* der Knoten; (*coll.*) der Vogel, die Grille (*obsession etc.*).
kinship ['kinʃip], *s.* die Sippe, Verwandtschaft.
kipper ['kipə], *s.* der geräucherte Hering.
kiss [kis], *v.a.* küssen. — *s.* der Kuß.
kit [kit], *s.* (*Mil.*) die Ausrüstung.
kitbag ['kitbæg], *s.* der Tornister.
kitchen ['kitʃən], *s.* die Küche; — *garden,* der Gemüsegarten.
kite [kait], *s.* der Drache, Papierdrache; *fly a —,* einen Drachen steigen lassen; (*Orn.*) der Gabelweih, der (rote) Milan; (*sl.*) der Schwindler.
kith [kiθ], *s.* now only in — *and kin,* die Verwandten, *m. pl.*
kitten [kitn], *s.* das Kätzchen.
knack [næk], *s.* der Kniff, Kunstgriff.
knacker ['nækə], *s.* der Abdecker (*horse*).
knapsack ['næpsæk], *s.* der Rucksack, Tornister.
knave [neiv], *s.* der Kerl, Schurke; Bube (*cards*).
knead [ni:d], *v.a.* kneten.
knee [ni:], *s.* (*Anat.*) das Knie.
kneel [ni:l], *v.n. irr.* knieen, niederknieen.
knell [nel], *s.* die Totenglocke.
knick-knack ['niknæk], *s.* die Nippsache.
knife [naif], *s.* das Messer. — *v.a.* erstechen.
knight [nait], *s.* der Ritter; der Springer (*chess*).
knit [nit], *v.a., v.n. reg. & irr.* stricken; *knitting needle,* die Stricknadel.
knob [nɔb], *s.* der (Tür)knopf, die Türklinke; der Knorren (*wood*).
knock [nɔk], *v.n.* klopfen, schlagen. — *s.* der Schlag, Stoß.
knoll [noul], *s.* der kleine Hügel.
knot [nɔt], *s.* der Knoten; die Schwierigkeit (*difficulty*).
know [nou], *v.a. irr.* kennen (*be acquainted with*); wissen (*possess knowledge (of)*).
knowing ['nouiŋ], *adj.* wissend.
knowledge ['nɔlidʒ], *s.* die Kenntnis (*acquaintance with*); das Wissen (*by*

study, information etc.); die Kenntnisse (*of language etc.*).
knuckle [nʌkl], *s.* (*Anat.*) der Knöchel.
— *v.n.* — *under*, sich fügen.
Kremlin ['kremlin], *s.* der Kreml.
kudos ['kjuːdɔs], *s.* der Ruhm, das
Ansehen.

L

L [el]. das L.
label [leibl], *s.* die Etikette, das Schildchen.
labial ['leibiəl], *adj.* (*Phonet.*) labial,
Lippen-. — *s.* (*Phonet.*) der Lippenlaut.
laboratory [lə'bɔrətəri, (*Am.*) 'læbərə-
təri], *s.* das Laboratorium, (*coll.*) das
Labor.
laborious [lə'bɔːriəs], *adj.* mühsam.
labour ['leibə], *s.* die Arbeit, Mühe;
Labour Party, die Arbeiterpartei;
(*Med.*) die Geburtswehen, *f. pl.* —
v.n. sich abmühen, leiden; sich
anstrengen.
labourer ['leibərə], *s.* der Arbeiter,
Taglöhner.
lace [leis], *s.* die Spitze, Tresse. — *v.a.*
verbrämen (*trim with lace*); zu-
schnüren (*shoe*); stärken (*coffee with
rum etc.*).
lacerate ['læsəreit], *v.a.* zerreißen.
lack [læk], *v.a.* ermangeln (*Genit.*). —
v.n. fehlen (an, *Dat.*). — *s.* der Mangel,
das Fehlen.
lackadaisical [lækə'deizikəl], *adj.*
schlaff, (*coll.*) schlapp, unbekümmert.
lackey ['læki], *s.* der Lakai, Diener,
Bediente.
laconic [lə'kɔnik], *adj.* lakonisch.
lacquer ['lækə], *s.* der Lack. — *v.a.*
lackieren.
lad [læd], *s.* der Bursche, Junge.
ladder ['lædə], *s.* die Leiter.
lading ['leidiŋ], *s.* (*Comm.*) das Laden;
die Fracht; *bill of —*, der Frachtbrief.
ladle [leidl], *s.* der Schöpflöffel, Sup-
penlöffel; die Kelle. — *v.a.* ausschöpfen, austeilen.
lady ['leidi], *s.* die Dame; — *-in-waiting*,
die Hofdame.
ladybird ['leidibəːd], *s.* (*Ent.*) der
Marienkäfer.
ladyship ['leidiʃip], *s.* (*Title*) gnädige
Frau.
lag [læg], *v.n.* zurückbleiben. — *v.a.*
verkleiden, isolieren (*tank*).
laggard ['lægəd], *s.* der Zauderer. —
adj. zögernd, zaudernd.
lagoon [lə'guːn], *s.* die Lagune.
lair [lɛə], *s.* das Lager (*of animal*).
laird [lɛəd], *s.* der schottische Guts-
herr.

laity ['leiiti], *s.* die Laien, *m. pl.*
lake [leik], *s.* der See.
lamb [læm], *s.* (*Zool.*) das Lamm. —
v.n. lammen.
lambent ['læmbənt], *adj.* brennend,
lodernd, strahlend.
lame [leim], *adj.* lahm. — *v.a.* lähmen.
lament [lə'ment], *v.a., v.n.* betrauern,
beweinen. — *s.* das Klagelied, die
Wehklage.
lamp [læmp], *s.* die Lampe; — *-post*,
der Laternenpfahl.
lampoon [læm'puːn], *v.a.* schmähen,
lächerlich machen. — *s.* die Schmähschrift.
lamprey ['læmpri], *s.* (*Zool.*) das
Neunauge.
lance [lɑːns], *s.* (*Mil.*) die Lanze. —
v.a. durchbohren; (*Med.*) lancieren.
lancer ['lɑːnsə], *s.* (*Mil.*) der Ulan.
lancet ['lɑːnsit], *s.* (*Med.*) die Lanzette.
land [lænd], *s.* das Land; das Grundstück (*plot*); — *tax*, die Grundsteuer.
— *v.a.* ans Land bringen, fangen
(*fish*). — *v.n.* landen.
landlord ['lændlɔːd], *s.* der Eigentümer,
der Hausherr; Wirt (*pub*).
landmark ['lændmɑːk], *s.* der Grenz-
stein, das Wahrzeichen.
landscape ['lændskeip], *s.* die Landschaft.
landslide, landslip ['lændslaid, 'lænd-
slip], *s.* der Erdrutsch.
lane [lein], *s.* der Heckenweg, Pfad; die
Gasse; (*Motor.*) die Fahrbahn.
language ['læŋgwidʒ], *s.* die Sprache.
languid ['læŋgwid], *adj.* flau, matt.
languor ['læŋgə], *s.* die Mattigkeit,
Flauheit.
lank [læŋk], *adj.* mager, schlank.
lantern ['læntən], *s.* die Laterne.
Laotian ['lauʃən], *adj.* laotisch. — *s.* der
Laote.
lap (1) [læp], *s.* der Schoß.
lap (2) [læp], *s.* das Plätschern (*of
waves*). — *v.a.* auflecken (*lick up*). —
v.n. plätschern.
lapel [lə'pel], *s.* der Aufschlag (*of
jacket*).
lapidary ['læpidəri], *adj.* lapidarisch;
wuchtig.
lapse [læps], *v.n.* gleiten, fallen; verlaufen (*time*). — *s.* der Verlauf (*time*);
der Fehler (*mistake*); das Verfallen
(*into laziness etc.*).
lapwing ['læpwiŋ], *s.* (*Orn.*) der Kiebitz.
larceny ['lɑːsəni], *s.* der Diebstahl.
larch [lɑːtʃ], *s.* (*Bot.*) die Lärche.
lard [lɑːd], *s.* das Schweinefett, Schweineschmalz.
larder ['lɑːdə], *s.* die Speisekammer.
large [lɑːdʒ], *adj.* groß; weit; dick, stark.
largesse ['lɑːdʒes], *s.* die Freigebigkeit
(*generosity*); die Schenkung (*donation*).
lark (1) [lɑːk], *s.* (*Orn.*) die Lerche.
lark (2) [lɑːk], *s.* (*coll.*) der Scherz.
— *v.n.* scherzen.
larkspur ['lɑːkspəː], *s.* (*Bot.*) der
Rittersporn.
larva ['lɑːvə], *s.* (*Zool.*) die Larve.

larynx ['læriŋks], s. (*Anat.*) der Kehlkopf.

lascivious [lə'siviəs], adj. wollüstig.

lash [læʃ], s. die Wimper (*eye*); die Peitschenschnur (*whip*), der Peitschenhieb (*stroke of whip*). — v.a. peitschen.

lass [læs], s. (*coll.*) das Mädchen.

lassitude ['læsitju:d], s. die Mattigkeit.

lasso [lə'su: or 'læsou], s. das Lasso. — v.a. mit einem Lasso fangen.

last (1) [lɑ:st], adj. letzt, vorig, äußerst; *at long* —, endlich.

last (2) [lɑ:st], s. der Leisten (*shoemaking*).

last (3) [lɑ:st], v.n. dauern, anhalten; hinreichen (*be sufficient*).

lastly ['lɑ:stli], adv. zuletzt.

latch [lætʃ], v.a. verschließen.

latchkey ['lætʃki:], s. der Hausschlüssel.

late [leit], adj. spät; verspätet; verstorben, selig (*deceased*); neulich (*recent*); *the train is* —, der Zug hat Verspätung; *of late*, jüngst.

latent ['leitənt], adj. (*Med.*) latent; verborgen.

lateral ['lætərəl], adj. seitlich, Seiten-.

lath [lɑ:θ], s. die Latte.

lathe [leið], s. die Drehbank.

lather ['læðə], s. der Seifenschaum. — v.n., v.a. (sich) einseifen.

Latin ['lætin], adj. lateinisch. — s. das Latein, die lateinische Sprache.

latitude ['lætitju:d], s. die geographische Breite; die Weite (*width*); (*fig.*) der Spielraum (*scope*).

latter ['lætə], adj. letzter; später (*later*). — s. der Letztere.

latterly ['lætəli], adv. neulich, neuerdings.

lattice ['lætis], s. das Gitter. — v.a. vergittern.

Latvian ['lætviən], adj. lettisch. — s. der Lette.

laud [lɔ:d], v.a. loben, preisen.

laudable ['lɔ:dəbl], adj. lobenswert.

laudatory ['lɔ:dətəri], adj. belobend.

laugh [lɑ:f], v.n. lachen; —*ing stock*, der Gegenstand des Gelächters.

laughter ['lɑ:ftə], s. das Lachen, Gelächter.

launch [lɔ:ntʃ], s. die Barkasse. — v.a. vom Stapel lassen.

launching ['lɔ:ntʃiŋ], s. der Stapellauf.

laundress ['lɔ:ndris], s. die Wäscherin.

laundry ['lɔ:ndri], s. die Wäsche (*clothes*); Wäscherei (*place*).

laureate ['lɔ:riit], s. der Hofdichter.

laurel ['lɔrəl], s. (*Bot.*) der Lorbeer.

lavatory ['lævətri], s. das W.C., der Abort, Waschraum; die Toilette; *public* —, die Bedürfnisanstalt.

lavender ['lævəndə], s. (*Bot.*) der Lavendel.

lavish ['læviʃ], adj. freigebig, verschwenderisch. — v.a. verschwenden.

lavishness ['læviʃnis], s. die Freigebigkeit, Verschwendung.

law [lɔ:], s. das Gesetz (*statute*); das Recht (*justice*); die Jura, Jurisprudenz (*subject of study*).

lawful ['lɔ:ful], adj. gesetzlich, gesetzmäßig.

lawless ['lɔ:lis], adj. gesetzlos; unrechtmäßig (*illegal*).

lawn (1) [lɔ:n], s. der Rasen.

lawn (2) [lɔ:n], s. der Batist.

lawsuit ['lɔ:su:t], s. der Prozeß.

lawyer ['lɔ:jə], s. der Advokat, Rechtsanwalt, Jurist.

lax [læks], adj. locker, lax.

laxative ['læksətiv], s. das Abführmittel.

laxity ['læksiti], s. die Schlaffheit, Lockerheit (*of rope etc.*).

lay (1) [lei], v.a. irr. legen; setzen (*put*); stellen (*place*); bannen (*ghost*); — *up*, sammeln. — v.n. legen (*eggs*); wetten (*wager*); — *about one*, um sich schlagen.

lay (2) [lei], s. (*Poet.*) das Lied.

lay (3) [lei], adj. Laien-.

layer ['leiə], s. die Schicht; — *cake*, die Cremetorte.

layman ['leimən], s. der Laie.

laziness ['leizinis], s. die Faulheit.

lazy ['leizi], adj. faul, träge.

lea [li:], s. (*Poet.*) die Aue.

lead (1) [li:d], v.a., v.n. irr. führen, leiten; ausspielen (*cards*). — s. die Führung; (*Elec.*) Leitung.

lead (2) [led], s. das Blei; Bleilot (*plumbline*).

leader ['li:də], s. der Führer; (*Mus.*) der Konzertmeister; der Leitartikel (*leading article*).

leaf [li:f], s. (*Bot.*) das Blatt; (*Build.*) der Türflügel. — v.a. (*coll.*) — *through*, durchblättern.

leafy ['li:fi], adj. belaubt.

league (1) [li:g], s. drei englische Meilen, *f.pl.*

league (2) [li:g], s. das Bündnis (*pact*); *be in* —, verbündet sein; *League of Nations*, der Völkerbund.

leak [li:k], v.n. lecken, ein Loch haben. — s. das Loch; (*Naut.*) das Leck.

leaky ['li:ki], adj. leck.

lean (1) [li:n], v.n. irr.(sich)lehnen (an, *Acc.*), stützen (auf, *Acc.*).

lean (2) [li:n], adj. mager, hager.

leap [li:p], v.n. irr. springen. — s. der Sprung; — *year*, das Schaltjahr.

learn [lə:n], v.a. irr. lernen, erfahren.

learned ['lə:nid], adj. gelehrt.

learning ['lə:niŋ], s. die Gelehrsamkeit.

lease [li:s], s. die Pacht, der Mietvertrag (*of house*). — v.a. (ver)pachten.

leasehold ['li:should], s. die Pachtung.

leash [li:ʃ], v.a. koppeln, anbinden. — s. die Koppel.

least [li:st], adj. wenigst, geringst, mindest, kleinst. — s. *at (the)* —, wenigstens, mindestens.

leather ['leðə], s. das Leder. — adj. Leder-, ledern.

leave [li:v], v.a. irr. verlassen (*quit*); lassen (*let*); hinterlassen (*bequeath*). — v.n. Abschied nehmen, abreisen. — s. der Urlaub; der Abschied (*farewell*); die Erlaubnis (*permission*).

leaven

leaven ['levn], s. der Sauerteig. — v.a. säuern.

Lebanese [lebə'niːz], adj. libanesisch. — s. der Libanese.

lecture ['lektʃə], s. die Vorlesung; der Vortrag.

lecturer ['lektʃərə], s. (Univ.) der Dozent; der Vortragende (speaker).

ledge [ledʒ], s. der Sims (window).

ledger ['ledʒə], s. (Comm.) das Hauptbuch.

lee [liː], s. die Leeseite (shelter).

leech [liːtʃ], s. (Zool.) der Blutegel.

leek [liːk], s. (Bot.) der Lauch.

leer ['liə], s. das Starren; der Seitenblick. — v.n. schielen (at, auf, nach); starren.

lees [liːz], s. pl. der Bodensatz, die Hefe.

left [left], adj. link. — adv. inks. — s. die linke Seite.

leg [leg], s. (Anat.) das Bein; der Schaft.

legacy ['legəsi], s. das Vermächtnis, das Erbe, Erbgut.

legal ['liːgəl], adj. gesetzlich.

legality [li'gæliti], s. die Gesetzlichkeit.

legatee [legə'tiː], s. (Law) der Erbe, die Erbin.

legation [li'geiʃən], s. die Gesandtschaft.

legend ['ledʒənd], s. die Legende, Sage; die Inschrift (inscription).

legendary ['ledʒəndəri], adj. legendär, sagenhaft.

leggings ['leginz], s. pl. die Gamaschen.

legible ['ledʒibl], adj. leserlich.

legislation [ledʒis'leiʃən], s. die Gesetzgebung.

legislative ['ledʒislətiv], adj. gesetzgebend.

legislator ['ledʒisleitə], s. der Gesetzgeber.

legitimacy [li'dʒitiməsi], s. die Gesetzmäßigkeit; (Law) die eheliche Geburt (of birth).

legitimate [li'dʒitimit], adj. gesetzmäßig; (Law) ehelich (child). — [-meit], v.a. für gesetzlich erklären.

legitimize [li'dʒitimaiz], v.a. legitimieren.

leguminous [li'gjuːminəs], adj. Hülsen-; hülsentragend.

leisure ['leʒə], s. die Freizeit, Muße.

leisurely ['leʒəli], adj., adv. gelassen, gemächlich.

lemon ['lemən], s. (Bot.) die Zitrone.

lemonade [lemən'eid], s. die Limonade.

lend [lend], v.a. irr. leihen; —ing library, die Leihbibliothek.

length [leŋθ], s. die Länge (extent); die Dauer (duration); at —, ausführlich.

lengthen ['leŋθən], v.a., v.n. (sich) verlängern.

lengthy ['leŋθi], adj. langwierig, lang.

lenient ['liːniənt], adj. nachsichtig, milde.

lens [lenz], s. die Linse (optics); das Objektiv.

Lent [lent]. die Fastenzeit.

lentil ['lentil], s. (Bot.) die Linse.

leprosy ['leprəsi], s. der Aussatz, die Leprakrankheit.

leprous ['leprəs], adj. aussätzig.

lesion ['liːʒən], s. die Verletzung.

less [les], comp. adj., adv. weniger, kleiner.

lessee [le'siː], s. der Pächter, Mieter.

lessen [lesn], v.a., v.n. (sich) verringern, vermindern.

lesser ['lesə], comp. adj. geringer; kleiner.

lesson [lesn], s. die Lehrstunde, Lektion; (pl.) der Unterricht; (Rel.) der Bibeltext.

lessor ['lesə], s. der Eigentümer, Vermieter.

lest [lest], conj. damit nicht; aus Furcht, daß.

let [let], v.a. irr. lassen; zulassen; vermieten; (room); — down, blamieren, enttäuschen; off, abschießen. — s. without — or hindrance, ohne Hinderung.

lethal ['liːθəl], adj. tödlich.

letter ['letə], s. der Brief; der Buchstabe (character); — box, der Briefkasten; (pl.) die Literatur.

letterpress ['letəpres], s. die Kopierpresse.

lettuce ['letis], s. (Bot.) der Salat.

level [levl], adj. eben, gleich. — s. die Ebene; das Niveau. — v.a. ebnen, ausgleichen; (Build.) planieren.

lever ['liːvə], s. der Hebel.

levity ['leviti], s. der Leichtsinn.

levy ['levi], v.a. erheben (tax); auferlegen (penalty). — s. die Steuer.

lewd [ljuːd or luːd], adj. liederlich, gemein, unzüchtig.

liability [laiə'biliti], s. die Verantwortlichkeit; limited —, beschränkte Haftung; die Steuerpflichtigkeit (to tax), Zollpflichtigkeit (to duty).

liable ['laiəbl], adj. haftbar, zahlungspflichtig.

liar ['laiə], s. der Lügner.

libel ['laibəl], s. die Verleumdung. — v.a. verleumden, schmähen.

libellous ['laibələs], adj. verleumderisch.

liberal ['libərəl], adj. (Pol.) liberal; freigebig (generous); — arts, Geisteswissenschaften, f pl.

liberate ['libəreit], v.a. befreien, freisetzen; (Law) in Freiheit setzen.

Liberian [lai'biːriən], adj. liberisch. — s. der Liberier.

libertine ['libətiːn], s. der Wüstling.

liberty ['libəti], s. die Freiheit; die Erlaubnis (permission).

librarian [lai'brɛəriən], s. der Bibliothekar, die Bibliothekarin.

library ['laibrəri], s. die Bibliothek.

Libyan ['libjən], adj. libysch. — s. der Libyer.

licence ['laisəns], s. die Genehmigung, Erlaubnis (permit); driving —, der Führerschein; die Zügellosigkeit (licentiousness).

license ['laisəns], v.a. genehmigen, bewilligen; licensing laws, Ausschanksgesetze, n. pl. (for alcohol).

liquidate

licentiate [lai'senʃiit], s. der Lizenziat (degree).
licentious [lai'senʃəs], adj. ausschweifend, liederlich, locker (in morals).
lichen ['laikən, 'litʃən], s. (Bot.) die Flechte.
lichgate ['litʃgeit], s. das Friedhofstor.
lick [lik], v.a. lecken; (Am.) prügeln, verhauen.
lid [lid], s. das Augenlid; der Deckel.
lie [lai], (1) v.n. lügen. — s. die Lüge (untruth).
lie [lai], (2) v.n. irr. liegen; — down, sich legen, hinlegen; sich fügen (fig.).
lieu [lju:], s. in —, an Stelle, anstatt (Genit.).
lieutenant [lef'tenənt], s. der Leutnant.
life [laif], s. das Leben.
lifebelt ['laifbelt], s. der Rettungsgürtel.
lifeboat ['laifbout], s. das Rettungsboot.
lifetime ['laiftaim], s. die Lebenszeit, Zeit seines Lebens.
lift [lift], s. der Aufzug, Fahrstuhl; (coll.) give a — to, mitnehmen (im Auto). — v.a. heben; aufheben (abolish); (coll.) klauen, stehlen.
ligament ['ligəmənt], s. das Band; (Anat.) die Flechse, die Sehne.
ligature ['ligətʃə], s. (Typ.) die Ligatur; die Verbindung.
light [lait], adj. hell, licht; blond (hair); leicht (weight). — s. das Licht; give a —, ein Streichholz geben, Feuer geben. — v.a. irr. beleuchten (room); anzünden (fire). — v.n. irr. — (up), hell werden, leuchten; (fig.) aufleuchten.
lighten [laitn], v.a. erhellen (brighten); erleichtern (ease).
lighter ['laitə], s. das Feuerzeug (smoker's); (Naut.) das Lichterschiff.
lighthouse ['laithaus], s. der Leuchtturm.
lightning ['laitnin], s. der Blitz; — conductor, der Blitzableiter; — speed, die Blitzesschnelle.
ligneous ['ligniəs], adj. holzig.
lignite ['lignait], s. die Braunkohle.
like (1) [laik], v.a. gern haben; I — to sing, ich singe gern. — v.n. belieben, wollen; as you —, wie Sie wollen. — s. his —s and dislikes, seine Wünsche und Abneigungen.
like (2) [laik], adj. gleich, ähnlich. — s. his —, seinesgleichen. — prep. gleich, wie; just — him! das sieht ihm ähnlich! feel —, möchte gern; what is it —? wie sieht es aus?
likelihood ['laiklihud], s. die Möglichkeit; Wahrscheinlichkeit (probability).
likely ['laikli], adj. möglich; wahrscheinlich (probable).
liken [laikən], v.a. vergleichen.
likeness ['laiknis], s. die Ähnlichkeit.
likewise ['laikwaiz], adv. ebenso, gleichfalls, auch.
liking ['laikin], s. die Vorliebe (for, für, Acc.); Neigung (for, zu, Dat.); to my

—, nach meinem Geschmack or Wunsch.
lilac ['lailək], s. (Bot.) der Flieder.
lilt [lilt], v.a., v.n. trällern, summen. — s. die Melodie, Weise.
lily ['lili], (Bot.) s. die Lilie; — of the valley, das Maiglöckchen.
limb [lim], s. das Glied.
limber ['limbə], adj. geschmeidig.
lime (1) [laim], s. der Leim, Kalk (chalk).
lime (2) [laim], s. (Bot.) die Linde (tree); die Limone (fruit); — juice, der Limonensaft.
limestone ['laimstoun], s. der Kalkstein.
limit ['limit], s. die Grenze, das Ende. — v.a. begrenzen, beschränken.
limitation [limi'teiʃən], s. die Begrenzung.
limn [lim], v.a. (Art.) zeichnen, malen.
limp [limp], v.n. hinken. — adj. müde, schlaff.
limpid ['limpid], adj. klar, durchsichtig.
linden ['lindən], s. (Bot.) die Linde.
line (1) [lain], s. die Linie, Eisenbahnlinie (Railw.); die Zeile; der Strich; (Mil.) die Reihe; — of business, die Geschäftsbranche; (Genealogy) die Abstammung; take a strong —, entschlossen auftreten.
line (2) [lain], v.a. füttern (a garment).
lineage ['liniidʒ], s. die Abstammung.
lineament ['liniəmənt], s. die Gesichtszug.
linear ['liniə], adj. linear, geradlinig.
linen ['linin], s. die Leinwand; bed —, die Laken, Bettwäsche. — adj. leinen.
liner ['lainə], s. (Naut.) das Passagierschiff.
linger ['lingə], v.n. zögern; verweilen.
lingerie ['lɛ̃ʒəri:], s. die Damenunterwäsche.
linguist ['lingwist], s. der Sprachkundige, Philologe, Linguist.
liniment ['linimənt], s. (Med.) die Salbe.
lining ['lainin], s. das Futter (of garment).
link [link], s. das Glied (in chain); die Verbindung (connexion). — v.a. verbinden, verknüpfen.
linnet ['linit], s. (Orn.) der Hänfling.
linseed ['linsi:d], s. der Leinsamen; — oil, das Leinöl.
lint [lint], s. die Scharpie, das Verbandzeug.
lion ['laiən], s. (Zool.) der Löwe.
lioness ['laiənes], s. (Zool.) die Löwin.
lip [lip], s. (Anat., Bot.) die Lippe (mouth); der Rand (of jug).
lipstick ['lipstik], s. der Lippenstift.
liquefy ['likwifai], v.a., v.n. flüssig machen or werden.
liqueur [li'kjuə], s. der Likör.
liquid ['likwid], adj. flüssig. — s. die Flüssigkeit.
liquidate ['likwideit], v.a. liquidieren; (Comm.) flüssig machen (assets); bezahlen (pay off).

431

liquor

liquor ['likə], s. der Alkohol.
liquorice ['likəris], s. die Lakritze.
lisp [lisp], v.n. lispeln. — s. der Sprachfehler, das Anstoßen, Lispeln.
list [list], s. die Liste, das Verzeichnis; (*Naut.*) die Schlagseite.
listen [lisn], v.n. horchen, zuhören.
listless ['listlis], adj. teilnahmslos.
litany ['litəni], s. (*Eccl.*) die Litanei.
literal ['litərəl], adj. buchstäblich.
literary ['litərəri], adj. literarisch, Literatur-.
literature ['litrətʃə], s. die Literatur.
lithe [laið], adj. geschmeidig.
Lithuanian [liθju'einiən], adj. litauisch. — s. der Litauer.
litigate ['litigeit], v.n. einen Prozeß anstrengen, litigieren, prozessieren.
litigation [liti'geiʃən], s. die Litigation, der Prozeß.
litter ['litə], s. (*Zool.*) die Jungen, n. pl.; die Brut; die Sänfte (*carriage*); der Abfall, die Abfälle (*waste paper etc.*). — v.n. (*Zool.*) Junge haben, werfen. — v.a. Abfälle wegwerfen, unsauber machen.
little [litl], adj. klein (*size, value*); gering (*value*); — by —, nach und nach.
liturgy ['litədʒi], s. (*Eccl.*) die Liturgie.
live [liv], v.n. leben; wohnen (*dwell*).
livelihood ['laivlihud], s. der Lebensunterhalt.
liveliness ['laivlinis], s. die Lebhaftigkeit.
lively ['laivli], adj. lebhaft.
liven [laivn], v.a. — up, beleben.
liver ['livə], s. (*Anat.*) die Leber.
livery ['livəri], s. die Livree (*uniform*); — company, die Zunftgenossenschaft.
livid ['livid], adj. bleich, blaß.
living ['liviŋ], s. das Auskommen, der Unterhalt; die Lebensweise; (*Eccl.*) die Pfründe, Pfarrstelle.
lizard ['lizəd], s. (*Zool.*) die Eidechse.
lo! [lou], excl. (*obs.*) sieh, da! siehe!
load [loud], s. die Last, Belastung. — v.a. beladen, belasten. — v.n. laden, aufladen.
loadstone see **lodestone**.
loaf [louf], s. der Laib (*bread*); sugar —, der Zuckerhut. — v.n. herumlungern, nichts tun.
loafer ['loufə], s. der Faulenzer, Drückeberger.
loam [loum], s. der Lehm.
loan [loun], s. die Anleihe. — v.a. leihen.
loath [louθ], adj. unwillig, abgeneigt.
loathe [louð], v.a. verabscheuen, hassen.
loathing ['louðiŋ], s. der Abscheu, Ekel.
loathsome ['louθsəm], adj. abscheulich, ekelhaft.
lobby ['lɔbi], s. die Vorhalle. — v.a. (*Pol.*) einen beeinflußen.
lobe [loub], s. das Läppchen.
lobster ['lɔbstə], s. (*Zool.*) der Hummer.
local ['loukəl], adj. lokal, örtlich. — s. (*coll.*) das Stammgasthaus (*pub*).

locality [lo'kæliti], s. die Lokalität, die Örtlichkeit, der Ort.
localize ['loukəlaiz], v.a. lokalisieren, auf einen Ort beschränken.
locate [lo'keit], v.a. finden (*find*); ausfindig machen.
location [lo'keiʃən], s. die Plazierung (*position*); die Lage; der Standort; on —, auf dem Gelände, auf Außenaufnahme (*film*).
loch [lɔx], s. (*Scot.*) der See.
lock [lɔk], s. das Schloß (*on door*); die Schleuse (*on waterway*); die Locke (*hair*). — v.a. schließen, abschließen (*door*); hemmen (*wheel*). — v.n. sich schließen; — in, ineinandergreifen (*cogs*).
locker ['lɔkə], s. der Schließschrank, das Schließfach.
locket ['lɔkit], s. das Medaillon.
locksmith ['lɔksmiθ], s. der Schlosser.
lock-up ['lɔkʌp], s. der Arrest, die Haftzelle; (*coll.*) die Garage.
locust ['loukəst], s. (*Ent.*) die Heuschrecke.
lodestone ['loudstoun], s. der Magnetstein, Magnet.
lodge [lɔdʒ], v.n. wohnen; logieren (*temporary*). — v.a. beherbergen (*accommodate*); einbringen (*a complaint, protest*). — s. das Haus, das Häuschen; die Loge (*Freemasons*).
lodger ['lɔdʒə], s. der (Unter)mieter.
lodgings ['lɔdʒiŋz], s. pl. das möblierte Zimmer, die Wohnung.
loft [lɔft], s. der Boden, Dachboden.
lofty ['lɔfti], adj. hoch; erhaben; stolz (*proud*).
log [lɔg], s. der Holzklotz, das Scheit; —cabin, —house, das Blockhaus; (*Naut.*) das Log, das Schiffstagebuch. — v.a. (*Naut.*) eintragen.
loggerheads ['lɔgəhedz], s. pl. at —, in Widerspruch, Widerstreit, im Konflikt.
logic ['lɔdʒik], s. die Logik.
logical ['lɔdʒikəl], adj. logisch.
loin [lɔin], s. (*Anat.*) die Lende.
loincloth ['lɔinklɔθ], s. der Lendenschurz.
loiter ['lɔitə], v.n. herumlungern; bummeln.
loiterer ['lɔitərə], s. der Lungerer, Faulenzer.
loitering ['lɔitəriŋ], s. das Herumlungern, Herumstehen, Faulenzen.
loll [lɔl], v.n. herumlungern.
lollipop ['lɔlipɔp], s. das Zuckerwerk, die Süßigkeit; (*fig.*) der Leckerbissen.
loneliness ['lounlinis], s. die Einsamkeit.
lonely, (*Am.*) **lonesome** ['lounli, 'lounsəm], adj. einsam.
long [lɔŋ], adj. lang. — adv. — ago, vor langer Zeit; before —, in kurzer Zeit. — v.n. sich sehnen (*for*, nach, *Dat.*).
longitude ['lɔndʒitju:d], s. die Länge; (*Geog.*) der Längengrad.

longitudinal [lɔndʒi'tju:dinəl], *adj.* in der geographischen Länge, Längen-.

look [luk], *v.n.* blicken, sehen, schauen (*at*, auf, *Acc.*); — *to it*, dafür sorgen; — *out for*, Ausschau halten nach (*Dat.*); — *out!* paß auf! — *after s.o.*, sich um jemanden kümmern; — *into*, prüfen, untersuchen; — *forward to*, sich freuen (auf, *Acc.*); — *over*, durchsehen. — *s.* der Blick (*glance*); das Aussehen (*appearance*).

looking-glass ['lukiŋglɑ:s], *s.* der Spiegel.

look-out ['lukaut], *s.* der Ausblick; die Ausschau.

loom [lu:m], *s.* der Webstuhl. — *v.n.* in der Ferne auftauchen (*emerge*).

loon [lu:n], *s.* (*Orn.*) der Eisvogel, Eistaucher; (*coll.*) der Narr.

loony ['lu:ni], *adj.* (*coll.*) wahnsinnig, närrisch.

loop [lu:p], *s.* die Schlinge, das Schlingband; (*Railw.*) — *line*, die Schleife.

loophole ['lu:phoul], *s.* der Ausweg, die Hintertür.

loose [lu:s], *adj.* locker, lose; liederlich (*morals*). — *v.a.* lösen.

loosen [lu:sn], *v.a.* auflockern, locker machen.

lop [lɔp], *v.a.* stutzen (*trees*).

lopsided [lɔp'saidid], *adj.* einseitig.

loquacious [lo'kweiʃəs], *adj.* geschwätzig.

loquacity [lo'kwæsiti], *s.* die Schwatzhaftigkeit.

Lord [lɔ:d], *s.* (*Rel.*) the —, Gott der Herr; der Lord (*nobleman's title*); — *Mayor*, der Oberbürgermeister.

lord [lɔ:d], *s.* der Herr.

lordly ['lɔ:dli], *adj.* vornehm, stolz.

lore [lɔ:], *s.* die Kunde.

lose [lu:z], *v.a., v.n. irr.* verlieren; nachgehen (*of timepiece*).

loser ['lu:zə], *s.* der Verlierende.

loss [lɔs], *s.* der Verlust.

lot [lɔt], *s.* das Los; der Anteil (*share*); die Menge (*quantity*); die Partie (*auction*); (*Am.*) das Stück Land.

loth see **loath**.

lotion ['louʃən], *s.* das Waschmittel, das Wasser.

loud [laud], *adj.* laut; grell (*colour*).

lounge [laundʒ], *s.* der Gesellschaftsraum; (*Obs.*) die Chaiselongue; — *suit*, der Straßenanzug. — *v.n.* nichts tun, herumlungern, herumsitzen.

louse [laus], *s.* (*Zool.*) die Laus.

lout [laut], *s.* der Tölpel.

lovable ['lʌvəbl], *adj.* liebenswürdig, liebenswert.

love [lʌv], *s.* die Liebe; *for the* — *of God*, um Gottes Willen; *for* —, um nichts; *not for* — *nor money*, weder für Geld noch gute Worte, auf keinen Fall. — *v.a., v.n.* lieben; — *to*, gern tun.

lover ['lʌvə], *s.* der Liebhaber, der *or* die Geliebte.

low [lou], *adj.* niedrig; nieder, tief; leise; (*Mus.*) tief; (*spirits*) niedergeschlagen. — *v.n.* muhen (*of cattle*).

lowlands ['louləndz], *s. pl.* die Niederungen, *f. pl.*; die Ebene; das Unterland.

lowliness ['loulinis], *s.* die Demut, Bescheidenheit.

lowness ['lounis], *s.* die Niedrigkeit; Tiefe.

loyal ['lɔiəl], *adj.* treu, ergeben, loyal.

loyalty ['lɔiəlti], *s.* die Treue, Ergebenheit, Loyalität.

lozenge ['lɔzindʒ], *s.* die Pastille; (*Geom.*) die Raute.

lubricant ['lu:brikənt], *s.* das Schmiermittel, Schmieröl.

lubricate ['lu:brikeit], *v.a.* ölen, schmieren.

lucid ['lu:sid], *adj.* klar, deutlich.

lucidity [lu:'siditi], *s.* die Klarheit.

luck [lʌk], *s.* das Glück, der Glücksfall.

luckily ['lʌkili], *adv.* glücklicherweise.

lucky ['lʌki], *adj.* mit Glück gesegnet, glücklich.

lucrative ['lu:krətiv], *adj.* einträglich.

lucre ['lu:kə], *s.* der Gewinn.

ludicrous ['lu:dikrəs], *adj.* lächerlich, komisch.

lug [lʌg], *v.a.* schleifen, zerren; (*burden*) schleppen.

luggage ['lʌgidʒ], *s.* das Gepäck.

lugger ['lʌgə], *s.* (*Naut.*) der Logger, Lugger.

lugubrious [lu:'gju:briəs], *adj.* traurig.

lukewarm ['lu:kwɔ:m], *adj.* lauwarm.

lull [lʌl], *s.* die (Wind)stille. — *v.a.* einlullen, beschwichtigen.

lullaby ['lʌləbai], *s.* das Wiegenlied.

lumbago [lʌm'beigou], *s.* (*Med.*) der Hexenschuß.

lumbar ['lʌmbə], *adj.* (*Anat.*) zu den Lenden gehörig, Lenden-.

lumber ['lʌmbə], *s.* der Kram, das alte Zeug; (*timber*) das Bauholz; — *room*, die Rumpelkammer.

luminous ['lu:minəs], *adj.* leuchtend, Leucht-.

lump [lʌmp], *s.* der Klumpen, Haufen; — *sugar*, der Würfelzucker; — *sum*, die Pauschalsumme. — *v.a.* (*together*), zusammenwerfen.

lumpy ['lʌmpi], *adj.* klumpig.

lunacy ['lu:nəsi], *s.* der Wahnsinn.

lunatic ['lu:nətik], *adj.* wahnsinnig. — *s.* der Wahnsinnige; — *asylum*, das Irrenhaus, die Irrenanstalt.

lunch [lʌntʃ], *v.n.* zu Mittag essen. — *s.* (*also* **luncheon** ['lʌntʃən]) das Mittagessen.

lung [lʌŋ], *s.* (*Anat.*) die Lunge.

lunge [lʌndʒ], *v.n.* stoßen, stürzen. — *s.* der Stoß.

lurch [lə:tʃ], *s. leave in the* —, im Stiche lassen. — *v.n.* taumeln.

lure [luə], *v.a.* locken, ködern (*bait*). — *s.* der Köder (*bait*), die Lockung.

lurid ['ljuərid], *adj.* unheimlich, grell.

lurk [lə:k], *v.n.* lauern.

luscious ['lʌʃəs], *adj.* saftig, süß.

lush [lʌʃ], *adj.* üppig (*vegetation*); übermäßig.

lust

lust [lʌst], *s.* die Wollust, Sucht. — *v.n.* gelüsten (*for*, nach, *Dat.*).
lustre ['lʌstə], *s.* der Glanz.
lusty ['lʌsti], *adj.* kräftig, laut.
lute [lu:t], *s.* (*Mus.*) die Laute.
lutanist ['lu:tənist], *s.* (*Mus.*) der Lautenspieler.
Lutheran ['lu:θərən], *adj.* lutherisch. — *s.* der Lutheraner.
luxuriate [lʌg'zjuərieit, lʌk'sjuə-], *v.n.* schwelgen; (*Bot.*) üppig wachsen.
luxurious [lʌg'zjuəriəs, lʌk'sjuə-], *adj.* üppig; (*rich*) reich ausgeschmückt, prächtig, luxuriös.
luxury ['lʌkʃəri], *s.* der Luxus, Aufwand.
lymph [limf], *s.* die Lymphe.
lynx [links], *s.* (*Zool.*) der Luchs.
lyric ['lirik], *s.* die Lyrik.
lyrical ['lirikəl], *adj.* lyrisch.

M

M [em]. das M.
macaroon [mækə'ru:n], *s.* die Makrone.
mace [meis], *s.* das Zepter.
macerate ['mæsəreit], *v.a.* abzehren.
machination [mæki'neiʃən], *s.* die Machenschaft, Ränke, *m.pl.*
machine [mə'ʃi:n], *s.* die Maschine.
mackerel ['mækərəl], *s.* (*Zool.*) die Makrele.
mackintosh ['mækintɔʃ], *s.* der Regenmantel.
mad [mæd], *adj.* verrückt, wahnsinnig.
madam ['mædəm], *s.* (*addr.*) gnädige Frau.
madden [mædn], *v.a.* verrückt machen.
madman ['mædmən], *s.* der Wahnsinnige.
madness ['mædnis], *s.* der Wahnsinn.
magazine [mægə'zi:n], *s.* die (illustrierte) Zeitschrift; (*gun*) der Ladestock; der Lagerraum (*storeroom*).
maggot ['mægət], *s.* (*Ent.*) die Made.
magic ['mædʒik], *adj.* zauberhaft; — *lantern*, die Laterna Magica. — *s.* der Zauber; die Magie, Zauberei.
magician [mə'dʒiʃən], *s.* der Zauberer.
magistracy ['mædʒistrəsi], *s.* die Obrigkeit (*authority*).
magistrate ['mædʒistr(e)it], *s.* der Richter.
magnanimity [mægnə'nimiti], *s.* der Großmut.
magnanimous [mæg'næniməs], *adj.* großmütig.
magnate ['mægneit], *s.* der Magnat, Großunternehmer.
magnet ['mægnit], *s.* der Magnet.
magnetic [mæg'netik], *adj.* magnetisch.
magnetize ['mægnitaiz], *v.a.* magnetisieren.

magnificence [mæg'nifisəns], *s.* die Herrlichkeit.
magnificent [mæg'nifisənt], *adj.* herrlich, großartig.
magnify ['mægnifai], *v.a.* vergrößern (*make larger*); (*Rel.*) verherrlichen.
magnitude ['mægnitju:d], *s.* die Größe; *order of* —, die Größenordnung.
magpie ['mægpai], *s.* (*Orn.*) die Elster.
Magyar ['mægjɑ:], *adj.* madjarisch. — *s.* der Magyar, Madjar.
mahogany [mə'hɔgəni], *s.* das Mahagoni(holz).
maid [meid], *s.* (*Poet.*) das Mädchen; das Stubenmädchen (*servant*).
maiden [meidn], *s.* (*Poet.*) die Jungfrau, das Mädchen; — *aunt*, die unverheiratete Tante.
mail (1) [meil], *s.* die Post. — *v.a.* aufgeben, mit der Post senden.
mail (2) [meil], *s.* (*Mil.*) der Panzer.
maim [meim], *v.a.* verstümmeln, lähmen.
main (1) [mein], *adj.* hauptsächlich, Haupt-; (*Railw.*) — *line*, die Hauptstrecke. — *s.* der Hauptteil; *in the* —, hauptsächlich; (*Poet.*) das Weltmeer; (*pl.*) das Hauptrohr, die Hauptleitung.
main (2) [mein], *s.* *with might and* —, mit allen Kräften.
mainstay ['meinstei], *s.* die Hauptgrundlage, Hauptstütze.
maintain [mein'tein], *v.a.* erhalten, unterhalten (*keep*); behaupten (*assert*).
maintenance ['meintənəns], *s.* der Unterhalt, die Unterhaltskosten, *pl.* die Erhaltung.
maize [meiz], *s.* (*Bot.*) der Mais.
majestic [mə'dʒestik], *adj.* majestätisch, prunkvoll.
majesty ['mædʒisti], *s.* die Majestät.
major ['meidʒə], *adj.* größer, älter (*elder broᵢₐ ᵣ*); wichtig (*more important*). — *s.* (*Mil.*) der Major; (*Law*) der Münᵢ ge. — *v.n.* (*Am.*) sich spezialisieren auf.
majority '.nə'dʒɔriti], *s.* die Mehrheit (*in num ers*); (*Law*) die Mündigkeit; (*Mil.*) ᵢer Majorsrang.
make [meik], *v.a. irr.* machen, schaffen, herstellen (*produce*); (*coll.*) verdienen (*money*); *he has made it!* (*coll.*) er hat's geschafft!; — *out*, ausfüllen (*cheque etc.*); entziffern (*decipher*); — *up*, erfinden (*invent*); schminken (*o.'s face*). — *v.n. what do you* — *of him?* was halten Sie von ihm? — *s.* die Marke.
make-believe ['meikbəli:v], *s.* der Vorwand. — *adj.* vorgeblich.
maladjustment [mælə'dʒʌstmənt], *s.* die Unfähigkeit sich anzupassen; die falsche Einstellung; das Missverhältnis.
maladroit [mælə'drɔit], *adj.* ungeschickt, ungewandt.
malady ['mælədi], *s.* das Leiden, die Krankheit.

Malagasy [mælə'gæsi], *adj.* madagassich. — *s.* der Madagasse.
Malaysian [mə'leiziən], *adj.* malaysisch. — *s.* der Malaysier.
malcontent ['mælkəntent], *adj.* mißvergnügt.
male [meil], *adj.* männlich; — *screw,* die Schraubenspindel. — *s.* der Mann; (*Zool.*) das Männchen.
malefactor ['mælifæktə], *s.* der Übeltäter.
malice ['mælis], *s.* die Bosheit.
malicious [mə'liʃəs], *adj.* boshaft, böswillig.
malign [mə'lain], *v.a.* lästern, verleumden.
malignant [mə'lignənt], *adj.* bösartig.
malignity [mə'ligniti], *s.* die Bösartigkeit.
malinger [mə'liŋgə], *v.n.* sich krank stellen.
malleable ['mæliəbl], *adj.* (*Metall.*) leicht zu hämmern; (*fig.*) geschmeidig.
mallet ['mælit], *s.* der Schlegel, Holzhammer.
mallow ['mælou], *s.* (*Bot.*) die Malve.
malpractice [mæl'præktis], *s.* das gesetzwidrige Handeln, der Mißbrauch; die Amtsvergehung.
malt [mɔ:lt], *s.* das Malz.
Maltese [mɔ:l'ti:z], *adj.* maltesisch. — *s.* der Malteser.
maltreat [mæl'tri:t], *v.a.* mißhandeln.
mammal ['mæməl], *s.* (*Zool.*) das Säugetier.
man [mæn], *s.* der Mann (*adult male*); der Mensch (*human being*); — *of war,* das Kriegsschiff. — *v.a.* bemannen.
manacle ['mænəkl], *s.* die Handschelle. — *v.a.* fesseln.
manage ['mænidʒ], *v.a.* leiten, handhaben, verwalten; *how did you — it?* wie haben Sie's fertiggebracht?
management ['mænidʒmənt], *s.* die Leitung, Führung.
manager ['mænədʒə], *s.* der Leiter, Geschäftsführer, Manager.
mandarin *see* **mandatory**.
mandate ['mændeit], *s.* das Mandat.
mandatory ['mændətəri], *adj.* befehlend, bevollmächtigt, beauftragt. — *s.* der Bevollmächtigte, Beauftragte.
mandrake ['mændreik], *s.* der Alraun.
mane [mein], *s.* die Mähne.
manganese ['mæŋgəni:z], *s.* (*Chem.*) das Mangan.
mange [meindʒ], *s.* die Räude.
manger ['meindʒə], *s.* die Krippe.
mangle (1) [mæŋgl], *s.* die Mangel. — *v.a.* rollen, mangeln (*laundry*).
mangle (2) [mæŋgl], *v.a.* verstümmeln (*disfigure*).
mango ['mæŋgou], *s.* (*Bot.*) die Mangofrucht.
manhood ['mænhud], *s.* die Mannbarkeit, das Mannesalter.
mania ['meiniə], *s.* der Wahnsinn, die Manie.
maniac ['meiniæk], *s.* der Wahnsinnige. — *adj.* wahnsinnig.

manifest ['mænifest], *adj.* deutlich, klar, offenbar.
manifestation [mænifes'teiʃən], *s.* die Offenbarung.
manifesto [mæni'festou], *s.* das Manifest.
manifold ['mænifould], *adj.* mannigfach.
manipulate [mə'nipjuleit], *v.a.* manipulieren, handhaben.
mankind [mæn'kaind], *s.* die Menschheit.
manly ['mænli], *adj.* mannhaft, männlich.
manner ['mænə], *s.* die Art, Sitte (*custom*); die Manier (*bearing*); das Benehmen (*behaviour*); (*pl.*) gute Sitten.
mannered ['mænəd], *adj.* gesittet, geartet; maniert, gekünstelt (*artificial*).
manor ['mænə], *s.* — *house,* das Herrenhaus, Schloß.
manorial [mə'nɔ:riəl], *adj.* des Herrenhauses, herrschaftlich.
manservant ['mænsə:vənt], *s.* der Bediente, Diener.
mansion ['mænʃən], *s.* das (herrschaftliche) Wohnhaus, Herrenhaus.
manslaughter ['mænslɔ:tə], *s.* der Totschlag.
mantelpiece ['mæntlpi:s], *s.* der Kaminsims.
mantle [mæntl], *s.* (*gas*) der Glühstrumpf; (*Tail.*) der Mantel. — *v.a.* verhüllen (*cloak*).
manual ['mænjuəl], *s.* das Handbuch; (*Mus.*) das Handregister. — *adj.* Hand-.
manufacture [mænju'fæktʃə], *s.* die Herstellung, Erzeugung (*production*); (*Comm.*) das Fabrikat (*product*).
manufacturer [mænju'fæktʃərə], *s.* der Fabrikant, Erzeuger.
manure [mə'njuə], *s.* der Dünger; der Mist. — *v.a.* düngen.
manuscript ['mænjuskript], *s.* die Handschrift, das Manuskript.
many ['meni], *adj.* viele; *as — as,* ganze ... (*emphatically*); — *a,* mancher.
map [mæp], *s.* die Landkarte. — *v.a.* — (*out*), nach der Karte planen.
maple [meipl], *s.* (*Bot.*) der Ahorn.
mar [ma:], *v.a.* verderben.
marauder [mə'rɔ:də], *s.* der Plünderer.
marble [ma:bl], *s.* der Marmor (*rock*); (*pl.*) die Murmel (*game*). — *adj.* marmorn.
March [ma:tʃ], *s.* der März.
march [ma:tʃ], *s.* der Marsch. — *v.n.* marschieren; *steal a — on s.o.,* jemandem zuvorkommen.
marchioness [ma:ʃə'nes], *s.* die Marquise.
mare [mɛə], *s.* (*Zool.*) die Stute.
margin ['ma:dʒin], *s.* der Rand.
marginal ['ma:dʒinəl], *adj.* Rand-, am Rande gelegen.
marigold ['mærigould], *s.* (*Bot.*) die Dotterblume.

marine

marine [mə'ri:n], *adj.* Marine-, See-. — *s.* (*Mil.*) der Seesoldat; *tell that to the Marines!* der Großmutter erzählen.
mariner ['mærinə], *s.* der Seemann.
marital ['mæritəl], *adj.* ehelich.
maritime ['mæritaim], *adj.* Meeres-, See-.
mark [ma:k], *s.* das Zeichen (*sign*); (*Sch.*) die Zensur, Note; (*Comm.*) die Marke; *wide of the —*, auf dem Holzwege. — *v.a.* markieren (*make sign on*); — *my words*, merk dir das! paß auf! (*Comm.*) — *down*, den Preis heruntersetzen; ins Auge fassen (*observe closely*); *a —ed man*, ein Gezeichneter.
market ['ma:kit], *s.* der Markt. — *v.a.* auf den Markt bringen.
marksman ['ma:ksmən], *s.* der Schütze.
marl [ma:l], *s.* der Mergel.
marmalade ['ma:məleid], *s.* die Orangenmarmelade.
marmot ['ma:mət], *s.* (*Zool.*) das Murmeltier.
maroon (1) [mə'ru:n], *adj.* kastanienbraun, rotbraun.
maroon (2) [mə'ru:n], *v.a.* aussetzen.
marquee [ma:'ki:], *s.* das große Zelt.
marquess, marquis ['ma:kwis], *s.* der Marquis.
marriage ['mærid3], *s.* die Ehe, Heirat; die Hochzeit (*wedding*).
marriageable ['mærid3əbl], *adj.* heiratsfähig.
married ['mærid], *adj.* verheiratet.
marrow ['mærou], *s.* (*Anat.*) das Mark; (*Bot.*) der Kürbis.
marry ['mæri], *v.a.* heiraten; trauen (*perform marriage ceremony*); — *off*, verheiraten (*o.'s daughter*). — *v.n.* sich verheiraten.
marsh [ma:ʃ], *s.* der Morast, Sumpf.
marshal ['ma:ʃəl], *s.* der Marschall.
marshy ['ma:ʃi], *adj.* morastig, sumpfig.
marten ['ma:tin], *s.* (*Zool.*) der Marder.
martial ['ma:ʃəl], *adj.* Kriegs-, kriegerisch.
martin ['ma:tin], *s.* (*Orn.*) die Mauerschwalbe.
martyr ['ma:tə], *s.* der Märtyrer.
martyrdom ['ma:tədəm], *s.* das Märtyrertum oder der Märtyrertod.
marvel [ma:vl], *v.n.* staunen (*at*, über, *Acc.*).
marvellous ['ma:v(ə)ləs], *adj.* wunderbar, erstaunlich.
masculine ['mæskjulin], *adj.* männlich. — *s.* (*Gram.*) das Maskulinum, das männliche Geschlecht.
mash [mæʃ], *v.a.* zerquetschen, zerdrücken. — *s.* der Brei.
mask [ma:sk], *v.a., v.n.* maskieren, sich vermummen. — *s.* die Maske.
mason ['meisən], *s.* der Maurer.
masonic [mə'sɔnik], *adj.* freimaurerisch.
masonry ['meisənri], *s.* das Mauerwerk.
masquerade [mæskə'reid], *s.* der Mummenschanz, die Maskerade.
Mass [mæs, ma:s], *s.* (*Eccl.*) die Messe; *Low Mass*, die stille Messe; *High*

Mass, das Hochamt; *Requiem Mass*, die Seelenmesse.
mass [mæs], *s.* die Masse; die Menge. — *v.a., v.n.* (sich) massen, ansammeln.
massacre ['mæsəkə], *s.* das Blutbad.
massive ['mæsiv], *adj.* massiv, schwer.
mast [ma:st], *s.* der Mast. — *v.a.* (*Naut.*) bemasten.
Master ['ma:stə], *s.* (*Univ.*) der Magister; der junge Herr (*before boy's name*).
master ['ma:stə], *s.* der Meister (*of a craft*); der Herr, Arbeitgeber (*employer*); — *key*, der Hauptschlüssel. — *v.a.* meistern, beherrschen.
masticate ['mæstikeit] *v.a.* kauen.
mastiff ['mæstif], *s.* (*Zool.*) der Kettenhund, Mastiff.
mat [mæt], *s.* die Matte.
match (1) [mætʃ], *s.* das Streichholz, Zündholz.
match (2) [mætʃ], *s.* der ebenbürtige Partner (*suitable partner*); *find o.'s —*, seinesgleichen finden; (*Sport*) das Wettspiel, der Wettkampf; Fußballkampf; (*Cricket*) das Cricketspiel. — *v.a., v.n.* passen zu, anpassen; ebenbürtig sein (*be equal*).
matchless ['mætʃlis], *adj.* unvergleichlich, ohnegleichen.
mate (1) [meit], *s.* der Gefährte, Genosse; (*Naut.*) der Maat, Steuermann; (*coll.*) Freund. — *v.n.* sich paaren, sich verheiraten.
mate (2) [meit], *v.a.* (*Chess*) matt setzen.
material [mə'tiəriəl], *s.* das Material, der Stoff. — *adj.* wesentlich (*essential*); materiell (*tangible*).
materialism [mə'tiəriəlizm], *s.* der Materialismus.
maternal [mə'tə:nəl], *adj.* mütterlich.
maternity [mə'tə:niti], *s.* die Mutterschaft; — *ward*, die Geburtsklinik.
mathematical [mæθə'mætikəl], *adj.* mathematisch.
mathematics [mæθə'mætiks], *s.* die Mathematik.
matins ['mætinz], *s.* (*Eccl.*) die Frühmette.
matriculate [mə'trikjuleit], *v.n.* sich immatrikulieren (lassen).
matrimonial [mætri'mouniəl], *adj.* Ehe-, ehelich.
matrimony ['mætriməni], *s.* die Ehe.
matron ['meitrən], *s.* die Oberschwester, Oberin (*in hospital etc.*); die Matrone (*older woman*).
matter ['mætə], *s.* der Stoff (*substance*); die Sache, der Gegenstand (*subject*); die Angelegenheit (*case*); *printed —*, Drucksache; *what is the —?* was ist los?; *the heart of the —*, des Pudels Kern; *as a — of fact*, tatsächlich, ernst gesprochen. — *v.n.* bedeutsam sein, wichtig sein.
mattock ['mætək], *s.* die Haue.
mattress ['mætrəs], *s.* die Matratze.
mature [mə'tjuə], *adj.* reif; (*fig.*) gereift. — *v.a., v.n.* reifen, zur Reife bringen; (*Comm.*) fällig werden.

matured [mə'tjuəd], *adj.* abgelagert.
maturity [mə'tjuəriti], *s.* die Reife; (*Comm.*) die Fälligkeit.
maudlin ['mɔ:dlin], *adj.* rührselig, sentimental.
maul [mɔ:l], *v.a.* mißhandeln.
Maundy Thursday ['mɔ:ndi'θə:zd(e)i], der Gründonnerstag.
mauve [mouv], *adj.* malvenfarbig; violett.
maw [mɔ:], *s.* (*Zool.*) der Magen.
mawkish ['mɔ:kiʃ], *adj.* abgeschmackt, sentimental, rührselig.
maxim ['mæksim], *s.* der Grundsatz.
May [mei]. der Mai.
may (1) [mei], *v.n. aux. irr.* mögen, können; (*permissive*) dürfen.
may (2) [mei], *s.* (*Bot.*) der Weißdorn.
mayor [mɛə], *s.* der Bürgermeister.
maypole ['meipoul], *s.* der Maibaum.
maze [meiz], *s.* das Labyrinth.
me [mi:], *pers. pron.* (*Acc.*) mich; (*Dat.*) mir.
mead [mi:d], *s.* der Met.
meadow ['medou], *s.* die Wiese.
meagre ['mi:gə], *adj.* mager, karg (*lean, poor*); dürftig.
meal (1) [mi:l], *s.* das Mahl, Essen, die Mahlzeit.
meal (2) [mi:l], *s.* das Mehl (*flour*).
mealy ['mi:li], *adj.* mehlig; — -mouthed, frömmelnd; kleinlaut (*shy*).
mean (1) [mi:n], *v.a. irr.* bedeuten (*signify*); meinen (*wish to express*); vorhaben (*intend*).
mean (2) [mi:n], *adj.* mittelmäßig, Mittel- (*average*). — *s.* die Mitte.
mean (3) [mi:n], *adj.* gemein, niedrig (*despicable*); geizig.
meander [mi'ændə], *s.* die Windung, das Wellenmuster. — *v.n.* sich winden, sich schlängeln.
meaning ['mi:niŋ], *s.* die Bedeutung (*significance, connotation*); der Sinn.
meaningless ['mi:niŋlis], *adj.* bedeutungslos.
means [mi:nz], *s.* das Mittel; by all —, auf jeden Fall, unbedingt; by no —, keinesfalls; by—of, mittels (*Genit.*).
meantime, meanwhile ['mi:ntaim, 'mi:nwail], *s.* die Zwischenzeit.—*adv.* in der Zwischenzeit, indessen.
measles [mi:zlz], *s.* (*Med.*) die Masern, *f. pl.*; German —, die Röteln, *m. pl.*
measurable ['meʒərəbl], *adj.* meßbar.
measure ['meʒə], *s.* das Maß; der Maßstab (*scale*); (*Mus.*) der Takt; das Zeitmaß.—*v.a.* messen, abmessen.
meat [mi:t], *s.* das Fleisch.
mechanic [mi'kænik], *s.* der Mechaniker.
mechanical [mi'kænikəl], *adj.* mechanisch, automatisch; — *engineering*, der Maschinenbau.
mechanics [mi'kæniks], *s.* die Mechanik.
medal [medl], *s.* die Medaille, der Orden.
meddle [medl], *v.n.* sich einmischen (in, *in*, *Acc.*).

mediæval, medieval [medi'i:vəl], *adj.* mittelalterlich.
mediate ['mi:dieit], *v.n.* vermitteln, intervenieren. — *adj.* mittelbar.
mediator ['mi:dieitə], *s.* der Vermittler.
medical ['medikəl], *adj.* medizinisch, ärztlich; — *orderly*, der Krankenwärter.
medicate ['medikeit], *v.a.* medizinisch behandeln.
medicine ['medsən], *s.* die Medizin, Arznei.
medieval *see* **mediæval**.
mediocre ['mi:dioukə], *adj.* mittelmäßig.
mediocrity [mi:di'ɔkriti], *s.* die Mittelmäßigkeit.
meditate ['mediteit], *v.n.* nachdenken, sinnen.
meditation [medi'teiʃən], *s.* das Sinnen, Nachdenken.
Mediterranean [meditə'reinən], *adj.* mittelländisch. — *s.* das Mittelmeer, mittelländische Meer.
medium ['mi:djəm], *s.* das Medium; das Mittel (*means*). — *adj.* mittelgroß.
medlar ['medlə], *s.* (*Bot.*) die Mispel.
medley ['medli], *s.* (*Mus.*) das Potpourri; das Gemisch (*mixture*).
meek [mi:k], *adj.* sanft, mild.
meet [mi:t], *v.a., v.n. irr.* treffen (*Acc.*), sich treffen (mit, *Dat.*), begegnen (*Dat.*). — *s.* (*Hunt.*) die Jagd.
meeting ['mi:tiŋ], *s.* das Zusammentreffen; die Tagung, Sitzung (*conference*).
melancholy ['melənkɔli], *adj.* melancholisch, schwermütig. — *s.* die Melancholie, die Schwermut.
mellifluous [me'lifluəs], *adj.* lieblich, süß (*of sounds*).
mellow ['melou], *adj.* mild, weich, mürbe (*fruit etc.*); freundlich (*mood*). — *v.a.* mürbe machen, reifen lassen. — *v.n.* weich werden.
melodious [mə'loudiəs], *adj.* klangvoll, wohlklingend, melodisch.
melodrama ['melədra:mə], *s.* das Melodrama.
melody ['melədi], *s.* die Melodie.
melon ['melən], *s.* (*Bot.*) die Melone.
melt [melt], *v.a., v.n. reg. & irr.* schmelzen.
member ['membə], *s.* das Mitglied (*of club*); (*Parl.*) der Abgeordnete, das Glied.
membrane ['membrein], *s.* die Membran; (*Anat.*) das Häutchen.
memento [mi'mentou], *s.* das Andenken.
memoir ['memwɑ:], *s.* die Denkschrift; (*pl.*) die Memoiren, *n. pl.*
memorable ['memərəbl], *adj.* denkwürdig.
memorandum [memə'rændəm], *s.* das Memorandum, die Denkschrift.
memorial [mi'mɔ:riəl], *s.* das Denkmal (*monument*). — *adj.* Gedenk-, zum Gedenken, Gedächtnis-.

memory ['meməri], s. die Erinnerung; das Gedächtnis (*faculty*); das Andenken (*remembrance*).

menace ['menis], s. die Drohung. — *v.a.* bedrohen.

mend [mend], *v.a.* reparieren; verbessern, ausbessern. — *v.n.* sich bessern.

mendacious [men'deiʃəs], *adj.* lügnerisch, verlogen (*lying*).

mendacity [men'dæsiti], s. die Lügenhaftigkeit, Verlogenheit.

mendicant ['mendikənt], *adj.* bettlerisch. — s. der Bettler.

mendicity [men'disiti], s. die Bettelei.

menial ['mi:niəl], *adj.* gemein, grob (*job*).

mental [mentl], *adj.* geistig; (*coll.*) geisteskrank.

mention ['menʃən], *v.a.* erwähnen; *don't — it*, gern geschehen! — s. die Erwähnung.

mentor ['mentə], s. der Ratgeber.

menu ['menju:], s. die Speisekarte.

mercantile ['mə:kəntail], *adj.* Handels-, kaufmännisch.

mercenary ['mə:sənəri], *adj.* für Geld zu haben, käuflich, feil; materiell eingestellt. — s. der Söldner.

mercer ['mə:sə], s. der Seidenhändler.

mercerised ['mə:səraizd], *adj.* (*Textile*) merzerisiert.

merchandise ['mə:tʃəndaiz], s. die Ware.

merchant ['mə:tʃənt], s. der Kaufmann.

merchantman ['mə:tʃəntmən], s. (*Naut.*) das Handelsschiff, Frachtschiff.

merciful ['mə:siful], *adj.* barmherzig, gnädig.

Mercury ['mə:kjuəri]. (*Myth.*) Merkur, *m.*

mercury ['mə:kjuəri], s. (*Chem.*) das Quecksilber.

mercy ['mə:si], s. die Barmherzigkeit, Gnade.

mere (1) [miə], *adj.* bloß, allein.

mere (2) [miə], s. der Teich.

meretricious [meri'triʃəs], *adj.* falsch, täuschend.

merge [mə:dʒ], *v.n.* aufgehen lassen, verschmelzen (*combine*).

merger ['mə:dʒə], s. (*Comm.*) die Fusion, Vereinigung, Zusammenlegung.

meridian [mə'ridiən], s. der Meridian; (*fig.*) der Gipfel.

merit ['merit], s. das Verdienst, der Wert. — *v.a.* verdienen.

meritorious [meri'tɔ:riəs], *adj.* verdienstlich.

mermaid ['mə:meid], s. die Wasserjungfer, Nixe.

merriment ['merimənt], s. die Belustigung, das Fröhlichsein, die Fröhlichkeit.

merry ['meri], *adj.* froh, fröhlich; *— go-round*, das Karussel.

mesh [meʃ], s. das Netz; die Masche (*knitting*). — *v.a.* einfangen.

mess (1) [mes], s. (*Mil.*) die Offiziersmesse.

mess (2) [mes], s. die Unordnung (*disorder*).

message ['mesidʒ], s. die Nachricht, Mitteilung, Botschaft.

messenger ['mesindʒə], s. der Bote.

Messiah [mi'saiə], s. der Messias.

metal [metl], s. das Metall.

metallurgy ['metələ:dʒi], s. die Metallurgie, Hüttenkunde.

metaphor ['metəfɔ:], s. die Metapher.

metaphorical [metə'fɔrikəl], *adj.* bildlich.

meter ['mi:tə], s. der Messer, Zähler (*gauge*); (*Am.*) *see* **metre** (1).

methinks [mi'θiŋks], *v. impers.* (*obs.*) mich dünkt, ich meine, mir scheint.

method ['meθəd], s. die Methode.

methodical [mi'θɔdikəl], *adj.* methodisch, systematisch.

methylate ['meθileit], *v.a.* (*Chem.*) denaturieren.

metre (1) ['mi:tə], s. der *or* das Meter (*unit of measurement*).

metre (2) ['mi:tə], s. (*Poet.*) das Versmaß.

metric ['metrik], *adj.* metrisch (*system of measurement*).

metrical ['metrikəl], *adj.* (*Poet.*) im Metrum, metrisch, Vers-.

metropolis [mi'trɔpəlis], s. die Metropole.

metropolitan [metrə'politən], *adj.* hauptstädtisch. — s. (*Eccl.*) der Erzbischof.

mettle [metl], s. der Mut (*courage*); *put s.o. on his —*, einen anspornen.

mew [mju:], *v.n.* das Miauen (*of cat*). — *v.n.* miauen.

mews [mju:z], s. *pl.* die Stallung.

Mexican ['meksikən], *adj.* mexikanisch. — s. der Mexikaner.

microphone ['maikrəfoun], s. das Mikrophon.

mid- [mid], *prefix.* mittel, Mittel-, mittler.

midday [mid'dei], s. der Mittag.

middle [midl], s. die Mitte, das Zentrum.

middling ['midliŋ], *adj.* (*coll.*) mittelmäßig.

midget ['midʒit], s. der Zwerg (*dwarf*).

midnight ['midnait], s. die Mitternacht.

midriff ['midrif], s. das Zwerchfell.

midshipman ['midʃipmən], s. (*Naut.*) der Seekadett.

midwife ['midwaif], s. die Hebamme.

mien [mi:n], s. die Miene.

might [mait], s. die Macht, Gewalt.

mighty ['maiti], *adj.* mächtig, stark.

mignonette [minjə'net], s. (*Bot.*) die Reseda.

migrate [mai'greit], *v.n.* wandern, migrieren; (*birds*) ziehen.

migratory ['maigrətəri], *adj.* Zug-, Wander-.

Milanese [milə'n:iz], *adj.* mailändisch.
— *s.* der Mailänder.
mild [maild], *adj.* mild, sanft.
mildew ['mildju:], *s.* der Meltau.
mile [mail], *s.* die (englische) Meile.
mileage ['mailidʒ], *s.* die Meilenzahl.
milfoil ['milfoil], *s.* (*Bot.*) die Schafgarbe (*yarrow*).
military ['militəri], *adj.* militärisch. —
s. das Militär.
militia [mi'liʃə], *s.* die Miliz.
milk [milk], *v.a.* melken. — *s.* die Milch.
milksop ['milksɔp], *s.* die Memme.
milky ['milki], *adj.* milchig; *Milky Way*,
die Milchstraße.
mill [mil], *s.* die Mühle; die Spinnerei
(*textile*); *rolling* —, das Walzwerk;
run of the —, gewöhnlich; *through the*
—, wohl erfahren, lebenserfahren.
— *v.a.* mahlen (*flour*); rollen, walzen
(*steel*); rändern (*coins*); —*ed edge*, die
Rändelkante. —*v.n.* — (*around*), sich
drängen.
miller ['milə], *s.* der Müller.
millet ['milit], *s.* die Hirse.
milliner ['milinə], *s.* die Modistin,
Putzmacherin.
millinery ['milinəri], *s.* die Putzwaren,
Modewaren, *f. pl.*
million ['miljən], *s.* die Million.
milt [milt], *s.* die Fischmilch; (*Anat.*)
die Milz.
mimic ['mimik], *s.* der Mimiker. —
v.a. nachahmen.
mimicry ['mimikri], *s.* die Nachahmung; (*Zool.*) die Anpassung (*in
colour*).
mince [mins], *v.a.* kleinhacken (*meat*);
— *o.'s words*, affektiert sprechen; *not
— o.'s words*, kein Blatt vor den Mund
nehmen; — *s.* gehacktes Fleisch; —
pie, die Dörrobstpastete.
mincemeat ['minsmi:t], *s.* die (gehackte)
Dörrobstmischung.
mincing ['minsiŋ], *adj.* affektiert; —
steps, trippelnde Schritte.
mind [maind], *s.* der Geist, das Gemüt;
die Meinung; der Sinn; der Verstand;
what is on your —? was bedrückt Sie?;
bear in —, daran denken; *have a* —,
Lust haben; *make up o.'s* —, sich
entschließen; *with an open* —, unparteiisch. — *v.a.* beachten, achten
(auf, *Acc.*). — *v.n. do you* —? macht
es Ihnen etwas aus? *never* —, macht
nichts; *I don't* —, mir ist's recht,
meinetwegen.
minded ['maindid], *adj.* gesinnt, eingestellt.
mine (1) [main], *poss. pron.* mein,
meinig.
mine (2) [main], *s.* das Bergwerk
(*general*), die Grube (*coal*). — *v.a.*
abbauen, graben (*Acc.*, nach, *Dat.*).
miner ['mainə], *s.* der Bergmann,
Bergarbeiter; (*coll.*) der Kumpel.
mineral ['minərəl], *s.* das Mineral;
(*pl.*) Mineralwasser.
mingle [miŋgl], *v.a.,v.n.* (sich) mischen.

minimize ['minimaiz], *v.a.* (möglichst) klein machen.
mining ['mainiŋ], *s.* die Hüttenkunde
(*theory*); der Bergbau.
minion ['minjən], *s.* der Liebling.
minister ['ministə], *s.* (*Pol.*) der Minister; *Prime Minister*, der Ministerpräsident; (*Eccl.*) der Geistliche,
Pfarrer. — *v.n.* einen Gottesdienst
abhalten; dienen (*to*, *Dat.*).
ministration [minis'treiʃən], *s.* der
Dienst, die Dienstleistung.
ministry ['ministri], *s.* das Ministerium
(*department of state*); (*Eccl.*) der Beruf
or das Amt des Geistlichen.
minnow ['minou], *s.* (*Zool.*) die Elritze.
minor ['mainə], *adj.* kleiner, geringer;
(*Sch.*) jünger (*after boy's name*). — *s.*
(*Law*) der Minderjährige, Unmündige.
minority [mai'nɔriti], *s.* die Minorität
(*in numbers*); (*Law*) die Unmündigkeit.
minster ['minstə], *s.* (*Eccl.*) das Münster.
minstrel ['minstrəl], *s.* der Spielmann.
mint (1) [mint], *s.* (*Bot.*) die Minze.
mint (2) [mint], *s.* die Münzstätte.
— *v.a.* münzen.
minuet [minju'et], *s.* (*Mus.*) das
Menuett.
minute (1) ['minit], *s.* die Minute
(*time*); (*pl.*) das Protokoll (*of meeting*).
— *v.a.* zu Protokoll nehmen, protokollieren.
minute (2) [mai'nju:t], *adj.* winzig, klein.
minutiae [mi'nju:ʃii], *s.pl.* die Details,
n. pl., die Einzelheiten, *f. pl.*
miracle ['mirəkl], *s.* das Wunder.
miraculous [mi'rækjuləs], *adj.* wunderbar; wundertätig.
mirage [mi'ra:ʒ], *s.* die Luftspiegelung,
die Fata Morgana.
mire [maiə], *s.* der Schlamm, Kot.
mirror ['mirə], *s.* der Spiegel. — *v.a.*
reflektieren, spiegeln.
mirth [mə:θ], *s.* der Frohsinn.
misadventure [misəd'ventʃə], *s.* das
Mißgeschick.
misalliance [misə'laiəns], *s.* die Mißheirat, Mesalliance.
misapply [misə'plai], *v.a.* falsch anwenden.
misapprehend [misæpri'hend], *v.a.*
mißverstehen.
misapprehension [misæpri'henʃən], *s.*
das Mißverständnis.
misappropriate [misə'prouprieit], *v.a.*
unrechtmäßig erwerben, unterschlagen.
misbehave [misbi'heiv], *v.n.* sich
schlecht benehmen.
miscalculate [mis'kælkjuleit], *v.a.,v.n.*
sich verrechnen.
miscarriage [mis'kæridʒ], *s.* das Mißlingen; (*Med.*) die Fehlgeburt.
miscarry [mis'kæri], *v.n.* mißlingen;
(*Med.*) fehlgebären.
miscellaneous [misə'leiniəs], *adj.* vermischt.

miscellany [mi'seləni], *s.* der Sammelband (*of writers*); die Mischung, das Gemisch.

mischief ['mistʃif], *s.* der Unfug; *out to make* —, darauf aus, Unfug zu stiften; — *maker*, der Unheilstifter.

mischievous ['mistʃivəs], *adj.* boshaft.

misconceive [miskən'si:v], *v.a.* mißverstehen.

misconception [miskən'sepʃən], *s.* das Mißverständnis.

misconduct [mis'kɔndʌkt], *s.* das unkorrekte Verhalten; der Fehltritt.

misconstruction [miskən'strʌkʃən], *s.* die Mißdeutung.

misconstrue [miskən'stru:], *v.a.* mißdeuten.

misdeed [mis'di:d], *s.* die Missetat.

misdemeanour [misdi'mi:nə], *s.* (*Law.*) das Vergehen; die Missetat.

miser ['maizə], *s.* der Geizhals.

miserable ['mizərəbl], *adj.* elend, kläglich (*wretched*); nichtswürdig (*base*).

miserly ['maizəli], *adj.* geizig.

misery ['mizəri], *s.* das Elend, die Not.

misfortune [mis'fɔ:tʃən], *s.* das Unglück.

misgiving [mis'givin], *s.* die Befürchtung, der Zweifel (*doubt*).

misguide [mis'gaid], *v.a.* irreführen, verleiten.

mishap [mis'hæp], *s.* der Unfall.

misinform [misin'fɔ:m], *v.a.* falsch informieren, falsch unterrichten.

misinterpret [misin'tə:prit], *v.a.* mißdeuten.

misjudge [mis'dʒʌdʒ], *v.a.* falsch beurteilen.

mislay [mis'lei], *v.a. irr.* verlegen.

mislead [mis'li:d], *v.a. irr.* verführen, irreführen.

misnomer [mis'noumə], *s.* der falsche Name.

misogynist [mi'sɔdʒinist], *s.* der Weiberfeind.

misplace [mis'pleis], *v.a.* übel anbringen (*remark*); verlegen (*thing*).

misprint [mis'print], *v.a.* verdrucken, falsch drucken. — ['misprint], *s.* der Druckfehler.

misquote [mis'kwout], *v.a.* falsch zitieren.

misrepresent [misrepri'zent], *v.a.* falsch darstellen.

misrule [mis'ru:l], *s.* die schlechte Regierung; die Unordnung (*disorder*).

miss (1) [mis], *s.* das Fräulein.

miss (2) [mis], *v.a.* vermissen (*yearn for*); versäumen (*a train, lesson etc.*); verfehlen (*target*); — *the boat,* den Anschluß verpassen; *be missing,* fehlen.

missal [misl], *s.* (*Eccl.*) das Meßbuch.

misshapen [mis'ʃeipən], *adj.* mißgestaltet.

missile ['misail], *s.* das Geschoß; *ballistic* —, das Raketengeschoß; *guided* —, ferngesteuertes Raketengeschoss.

mission ['miʃən], *s.* die Mission; Sendung; der Auftrag (*task*).

missionary ['miʃənəri], *adj.* Missions-. — *s.* der Missionar.

missive ['misiv], *s.* das Sendschreiben.

misspell [mis'spel], *v.a.* falsch buchstabieren, falsch schreiben.

mist [mist], *s.* der Dunst; Nebel (*fog*).

mistake [mis'teik], *s.* der Fehler. — *v.a. irr.* verkennen.

mistaken [mis'teikn], *adj.* im Unrecht; irrig; *be* —, sich irren.

mistimed [mis'taimd], *adj.* zur Unzeit, unzeitig.

mistletoe ['misltou], *s.* (*Bot.*) die Mistel, der Mistelzweig.

mistress ['mistrəs], *s.* die Herrin; Hausfrau; Geliebte (*paramour*); Lehrerin (*Sch.*).

mistrust [mis'trʌst], *v.a.* mißtrauen.

misunderstand [misʌndə'stænd], *v.a. irr.* mißverstehen.

misuse [mis'ju:z], *v.a.* mißbrauchen.

mite (1) [mait], *s.* (*Zool.*) die Milbe.

mite (2) [mait], *s.* das Scherflein (*coin*); (*coll.*) das Kindchen; das Kerlchen.

mitigate ['mitigeit], *v.a.* mildern.

mitre ['maitə], *s.* die Bischofsmütze, Mitra.

mitten [mitn], *s.* der Fäustling, Fausthandschuh.

mix [miks], *v.a.* mischen, vermischen. — *v.n.* verkehren.

mixed [miksd], *adj. a* — *blessing,* eine fragliche Wohltat.

mizzle [mizl], *v.n.* sprühen, rieseln.

mnemonics [ni'mɔniks], *s.* die Gedächtniskunst.

moan [moun], *v.n.* stöhnen (*wail*); klagen (*complain*). — *s.* (*coll.*) die Klage.

moat [mout], *s.* der Burggraben, Wassergraben.

mob [mɔb], *s.* der Pöbel.

mobility [mo'biliti], *s.* die Beweglichkeit.

mobilize ['moubilaiz], *v.a.* mobilisieren.

mock [mɔk], *v.a.* verspotten (*tease*); täuschen (*mislead*). — *v.n.* spotten. — *s.* der Spott, die Täuschung. — *adj.* Schein-; — *heroic,* komischheroisch.

modal [moudl], *adj.* (*Gram.*) modal, der Aussageweise nach; (*Mus.*) dem Modus nach.

mode [moud], *s.* (*Mus.*) der Modus, die Art; die Mode (*fashion*).

model [mɔdl], *s.* das Modell; das Muster (*pattern*). — *v.a.* ein Modell lieren.

moderate ['mɔdərit], *adj.* mäßig; (*climate*) gemäßigt. — [-reit]. *v.a.* mäßigen; abändern.

modern ['mɔdən], *adj.* modern.

modernize ['mɔdənaiz], *v.a.* modernisieren.

modest ['mɔdist], *adj.* bescheiden.

modesty ['mɔdisti], *s.* die Bescheidenheit.

modify ['mɔdifai], *v.a.* abändern, modifizieren.

modish ['moudiʃ], *adj.* nach der neuesten Mode, modisch.
modulate ['mɔdjuleit], *v.a.* modulieren.
moil [mɔil], *v.n.* sich plagen.
moist [mɔist], *adj.* feucht.
moisten [mɔisn], *v.a.* befeuchten.
moisture ['mɔistʃə], *s.* die Feuchtigkeit.
molasses [mo'læsiz], *s.* die Melasse.
mole (1) [moul], *s.* (*Zool.*) der Maulwurf.
mole (2) [moul], *s.* das Muttermal (*skin mark*).
mole (3) [moul], *s.* der Seedamm, Hafendamm.
molecular [mo'lekjulə], *adj.* molekular.
molecule ['mɔl-, 'moulikju:l], *s.* das Molekül.
molest [mo'lest], *v.a.* belästigen.
mollify ['mɔlifai], *v.a.* besänftigen.
mollusc ['mɔləsk], *s.* (*Zool.*) die Molluske.
molt *see under* **moult**.
molten ['moultən], *adj.* geschmolzen.
moment ['moumənt], *s.* der Augenblick, Moment (*instant*); die Wichtigkeit (*importance*).
momentary ['mouməntəri], *adj.* momentan, einen Augenblick lang.
momentum [mo'mentəm], *s.* das Moment, die Triebkraft.
monarch ['mɔnək], *s.* der Monarch.
monarchy ['mɔnəki], *s.* die Monarchie.
monastery ['mɔnəstri], *s.* das (Mönchs-)kloster.
monastic [mə'næstik], *adj.* klösterlich.
Monday ['mʌndi], der Montag.
money ['mʌni], *s.* das Geld; *ready* —, bares Geld; *make* —, Geld verdienen; — *order*, die Postanweisung.
Mongolian [mɔŋ'goulian], *adj.* mongolisch. — *s.* der Mongole.
mongrel ['mʌŋgrəl], *s.* (*Zool.*) der Mischling.
monitor ['mɔnitə], *s.* der Ermahner; (*Rad.*) der Abhörer.
monitoring ['mɔnitəriŋ], *adj.* — *service*, der Abhördienst.
monk [mʌŋk], *s.* (*Eccl.*) der Mönch.
monkey ['mʌŋki], *s.* (*Zool.*) der Affe.
monomania [mɔno'meiniə], *s.* die Monomanie, fixe Idee.
monopolize [mə'nɔpəlaiz], *v.a.* monopolisieren.
monopoly [mə'nɔpəli], *s.* das Monopol.
monosyllabic [mɔnəsi'læbik], *adj.* einsilbig.
monotonous [mə'nɔtənəs], *adj.* monoton, eintönig.
monsoon [mɔn'su:n], *s.* der Monsun.
monster ['mɔnstə], *s.* das Ungeheuer.
monstrance ['mɔnstrəns], *s.* (*Eccl.*) die Monstranz.
monstrosity [mɔns'trɔsiti], *s.* die Ungeheuerlichkeit.
monstrous ['mɔnstrəs], *adj.* ungeheuerlich.
month [mʌnθ], *s.* der Monat.
monthly ['mʌnθli], *adj.* monatlich, Monats-.

mood [mu:d], *s.* die Stimmung, Laune; (*Gram., Mus.*) der Modus.
moodiness ['mu:dinis], *s.* die Launenhaftigkeit.
moody ['mu:di], *adj.* launenhaft.
moon [mu:n], *s.* der Mond.
moonlight ['mu:nlait], *s.* das Mondlicht, der Mondschein.
moonshine ['mu:nʃain], *s.* der Mondschein; (*fig.*) Unsinn.
moonstruck ['mu:nstrʌk], *adj.* mondsüchtig; verliebt.
Moor [muə], *s.* der Mohr.
moor [muə], *s.* das Moor, Heideland.
moorage ['muəridʒ], *s.* der Ankerplatz.
moorhen ['mɔ:hen], *s.* (*Orn.*) das Moorhuhn, Wildhuhn.
moorish ['muəriʃ], *adj.* maurisch.
moot [mu:t], *v.a.* erörtern, besprechen. — *adj.* a — *point*, ein strittiger Punkt.
mop [mɔp], *s.* der Wischlappen, Mop. — *v.a.* aufwischen (*floor*), wischen (*brow*).
mope [moup], *v.n.* traurig sein.
moral ['mɔrəl], *adj.* moralisch (*high principled*); sittlich (*decent*). — *s.* die Moral (*precept*); (*pl.*) die Sitten, *f. pl.*; die Sittlichkeit.
moralize ['mɔrəlaiz], *v.n.* moralisieren, Moral predigen (*Dat.*).
morass [mo'ræs], *s.* der Morast.
morbid ['mɔ:bid], *adj.* krankhaft.
more [mɔ:], *comp. adj.*, *adv.* mehr; *once* —, noch einmal; *all the* —, umso mehr; *the* — *the better*, je mehr desto besser.
moreover [mɔ:'rouvə], *adv.* zudem, überdies, weiterhin.
morning ['mɔ:niŋ], *s.* der Morgen, Vormittag; — *coat*, der Cutaway, Frack.
Moroccan [mə'rɔkən], *adj.* marokkanisch. — *s.* der Marokkaner.
Morocco [mə'rɔkou]. Marokko, *n.*
morocco [mə'rɔkou], *s.* der Saffian, das Maroquinleder.
moron ['mɔ:rɔn], *s.* der Schwachsinnige.
morose [mə'rous], *adj.* mürrisch.
morrow ['mɔrou], *s.* (*Poet.*) der Morgen.
morsel ['mɔ:sl], *s.* der Bissen, das Stück.
mortal ['mɔ:tl], *adj.* sterblich, tödlich; — *sin*, die Todsünde. — *s.* der Sterbliche, der Mensch.
mortality [mɔ:'tæliti], *s.* die Sterblichkeit.
mortar ['mɔ:tə], *s.* (*Build.*) der Mörtel; (*Mil.*) der Mörser.
mortgage ['mɔ:gidʒ], *s.* die Hypothek. — *v.a.* verpfänden; eine Hypothek aufnehmen (auf, *Acc.*).
mortgagee [mɔ:gi'dʒi:], *s.* der Hypothekengläubiger.
mortician [mɔ:'tiʃən], *s.* (*Am.*) *see* **undertaker**.
mortify ['mɔ:tifai], *v.a.* kasteien (*chasten*); kränken (*humiliate*).
mortise ['mɔ:tis], *s.* (*Build.*) das Zapfenloch.

mortuary

mortuary ['mɔːtjuəri], s. die Leichenhalle.
mosque [mɔsk], s. (Rel.) die Moschee.
mosquito [mɔs'kiːtou], s. (Ent.) der Moskito.
moss [mɔs], s. (Bot.) das Moos.
most [moust], superl. adj. meist; (pl.) die meisten. — adv. meist, meistens; höchst (before adjectives).
mostly ['moustli], adv. meistenteils.
mote [mout], s. das Stäubchen.
moth [mɔθ], s. (Ent.) die Motte.
mother ['mʌðə], s. die Mutter; —-in-law, die Schwiegermutter; —-of-pearl, die Perlmutter.
motherly ['mʌðəli], adj. mütterlich.
motion ['mouʃən], s. die Bewegung, der Gang; (Parl., Rhet.) der Antrag. — v.a. bewegen. — v.n. zuwinken (Dat.).
motive ['moutiv], s. das Motiv, der Beweggrund.
motley ['mɔtli], adj. scheckig, bunt.
motor ['moutə], s. der Motor.
motoring ['moutəriŋ], s. das Autofahren, der Autosport.
mottled [mɔtld], adj. gescheckt, gesprenkelt.
motto ['mɔtou], s. das Motto, der Wahlspruch.
mould (1) [mould], s. die Form; Gußform (casting); die Schablone. — v.a. formen; (Metall.) gießen, formen.
mould (2) [mould], s. der Schimmel (fungus); (Hort.) die Gartenerde. — v.n. schimmeln.
moulder (1) ['mouldə], s. der Bildner; (Metall.) der Gießer.
moulder (2) ['mouldə], v.n. vermodern.
mouldy ['mouldi], adj. moderig, schimmelig.
moult, (Am.) **molt** [moult], v.n. (Zool.) sich mausern.
mound [maund], s. der Erdhügel.
mount [maunt], v.a. besteigen (horse, hill); montieren, anbringen (apparatus). — v.n. sich belaufen (bill), betragen. — s. (Poet.) der Berg.
mountain ['mauntin], s. der Berg.
mountaineer [maunti'niə], s. der Bergsteiger.
mountainous ['mauntinəs], adj. gebirgig.
mourn [mɔːn], v.a., v.n. (be)trauern.
mourner ['mɔːnə], s. der Leidtragende.
mournful ['mɔːnful], adj. traurig.
mourning ['mɔːniŋ], s. die Trauer.
mouse [maus], s. (Zool.) die Maus.
moustache [mə'staːʃ], s. der Schnurrbart.
mouth [mauθ], s. (Anat.) der Mund; (Geog.) die Mündung.
movable ['muːvəbl], adj. beweglich, verschiebbar.
move [muːv], v.a. bewegen; (emotionally) rühren; den Antrag stellen (a motion). — v.n. umziehen; übersiedeln (change residence).
movement ['muːvmənt], s. die Bewegung (motion); (Mus.) der Satz; das Gehwerk (mechanism).

movies ['muːviz], s. pl. (coll.) das Kino, der Film.
mow [mou], v.a. irr. mähen.
much [mʌtʃ], adj. viel. — adv. sehr, bei weitem; as — as, ganze ...; as — again, noch einmal so viel.
mud [mʌd], s. der Schmutz, Schlamm.
muddle [mʌdl], v.a. verwirren. — s. die Verwirrung.
muff (1) [mʌf], s. der Muff.
muff (2) [mʌf], v.a. verderben (mar).
muffin ['mʌfin], s. der dünne Kuchen, der Butterkuchen.
muffle [mʌfl], v.a. umwickeln; dämpfen (a sound).
muffler ['mʌflə], s. das Halstuch; (Motor.) der Schalldämpfer.
mug [mʌg], s. der Krug; (coll.) der Tölpel.
muggy ['mʌgi], adj. schwül; feucht (humid).
mulatto [mju'lætou], s. der Mulatte.
mulberry ['mʌlbəri], s. (Bot.) die Maulbeere.
mule [mjuːl], s. (Zool.) das Maultier, der Maulesel.
muleteer [mjuːli'tiə], s. der Mauleseltreiber.
mulish ['mjuːliʃ], adj. störrisch.
mull (1) [mʌl], v.a. würzen (add spices to); mulled wine, der Glühwein.
mull (2) [mʌl], v.a., v.n. — over, überlegen, überdenken.
multifarious [mʌlti'fɛəriəs], adj. mannigfaltig.
multiple ['mʌltipl], s. das Vielfache. — adj. vielfach.
multiply ['mʌltiplai], v.a., v.n. multiplizieren, (sich) vervielfachen.
multitude ['mʌltitjuːd], s. die Menge.
multitudinous [mʌlti'tjuːdinəs], adj. zahlreich, massenhaft.
mumble [mʌmbl], v.a., v.n. murmeln.
mummery ['mʌməri], s. der Mummenschanz.
mummy (1) ['mʌmi], s. die Mumie.
mummy (2) ['mʌmi], s. (coll.) die Mutti.
mumps [mʌmps], s. (Med.) der Ziegenpeter.
munch [mʌntʃ], v.a., v.n. kauen.
mundane ['mʌndein], adj. weltlich.
municipal [mju'nisipəl], adj. städtisch.
municipality [mjunisi'pæliti], s. die Stadtgemeinde.
munificence [mju'nifisəns], s. die Freigebigkeit.
munificent [mju'nifisənt], adj. freigebig.
mural ['mjuərəl], s. die Wandmalerei; das Wandgemälde. — adj. Wand-.
murder ['məːdə], s. der Mord. — v.a. ermorden, morden.
murderer ['məːdərə], s. der Mörder.
murderous ['məːdərəs], adj. mörderisch.
murky ['məːki], adj. trübe, unklar.
murmur ['məːmə], s. das Gemurmel.
muscle [mʌsl], s. (Anat.) der Muskel.
muscular ['mʌskjulə], adj. (Anat.) muskulös, Muskel-.

muse (1) [mju:z], *v.n.* nachdenken, sinnen.

muse (2) [mju:z], *s.* (*Myth.*) die Muse.

museum [mju:'ziəm], *s.* das Museum.

mushroom ['mʌʃrum], *s.* (*Bot.*) der (eßbare) Pilz.

music ['mju:zik], *s.* die Musik; — *stand,* das Notenpult.

musician [mju:'ziʃən], *s.* der Musiker.

musk [mʌsk], *s.* der Moschus, Bisam.

musket ['mʌskit], *s.* die Muskete, Flinte.

muslin ['mʌzlin], *s.* der Musselin.

mussel [mʌsl], *s.* (*Zool.*) die Muschel.

must [mʌst], *v. aux. irr.* müssen; (*with neg.*) dürfen.

mustard ['mʌstəd], *s.* der Senf.

muster ['mʌstə], *v.a.* mustern. — *v.n.* sich sammeln. — *s.* die Musterung; *pass* —, die Prüfung bestehen.

musty ['mʌsti], *adj.* dumpf, dumpfig, muffig.

mutable ['mju:təbl], *adj.* veränderlich.

mutation [mju:'teiʃən], *s.* die Veränderung; (*Maths., Genetics*) die Mutation.

mute [mju:t], *adj.* stumm. — *v.a.* (*Mus.*) dämpfen. — *s.* (*Mus.*) der Dämpfer.

mutilate ['mju:tileit], *v.a.* verstümmeln.

mutinous ['mju:tinəs], *adj.* aufrührerisch.

mutiny ['mju:tini], *s.* die Meuterei.

mutter ['mʌtə], *v.a., v.n.* murmeln.

mutton [mʌtn], *s.* das Hammelfleisch; — *chop,* das Hammelkotelett.

mutual ['mju:tjuəl], *adj.* gegenseitig.

muzzle [mʌzl], *s.* der Maulkorb (*of dog*); die Mündung (*of rifle*).

my [mai], *poss. adj.* mein.

myrrh [mə:], *s.* die Myrrhe.

myrtle [mə:tl], *s.* (*Bot.*) die Myrte.

myself [mai'self], *pron.* ich selbst; (*refl.*) mir, mich.

mysterious [mis'tiəriəs], *adj.* geheimnisvoll.

mystery ['mistəri], *s.* das Geheimnis.

mystic ['mistik], *s.* der Mystiker.

mystic(al) ['mistik(əl)], *adj.* mystisch, geheimnisvoll, dunkel.

mystification [mistifi'keiʃən], *s.* die Täuschung, Irreführung.

mystify ['mistifai], *v.a.* täuschen, verblüffen.

myth [miθ], *s.* der Mythos, die Mythe, Sage.

N

N [en]. das N.

nag (1) [næg], *v.a.* nörgeln.

nag (2) [næg], *s.* der Gaul.

nail [neil], *s.* der Nagel. — *v.a.* annageln.

naïve ['naii:v], *adj.* naiv.

naïveté, naïvety [nai'i:vti], *s.* die Naivität, Einfalt.

naked ['neikid], *adj.* nackt.

name [neim], *s.* der Name. — *v.a.* nennen, heißen.

nameless ['neimlis], *adj.* namenlos.

namely ['neimli], *adv.* nämlich.

namesake ['neimseik], *s.* der Namensvetter.

nap [næp], *s.* das Schläfchen. — *v.n.* schlummern, einnicken.

nape [neip], *s.* (*Anat.*) das Genick.

napkin ['næpkin], *s.* die Serviette; Windel (*baby's*).

narrate [nə'reit], *v.a.* erzählen.

narrative ['nærətiv], *s.* die Erzählung, Geschichte.

narrator [nə'reitə], *s.* der Erzähler; (*Rad.*) der Sprecher.

narrow ['nærou], *adj.* eng, schmal; — *gauge,* die Schmalspur; — *minded,* engstirnig.

nasty ['nɑ:sti], *adj.* widerlich, unangenehm.

natal [neitl], *adj.* Geburts-.

nation ['neiʃən], *s.* die Nation, das Volk.

nationality [næʃə'næliti], *s.* die Staatsangehörigkeit, Nationalität.

native ['neitiv], *adj.* einheimisch, eingeboren. — *s.* der Eingeborene.

natural ['nætʃərəl], *adj.* natürlich.

naturalist ['nætʃərəlist], *s.* der Naturforscher.

naturalization [nætʃərəlai'zeiʃən], *s.* die Naturalisierung, Einbürgerung.

naturalize ['nætʃərəlaiz], *v.a., v.n.* naturalisieren, einbürgern.

nature ['neitʃə], *s.* die Natur, das Wesen.

naught [nɔ:t], *s.* die Null.

naughty ['nɔ:ti], *adj.* unartig.

nausea ['nɔ:siə], *s.* (*Med.*) der Brechreiz, das Erbrechen.

nautical ['nɔ:tikəl], *adj.* nautisch, Schiffs-.

naval ['neivəl], *adj.* Marine-.

nave [neiv], *s.* (*Archit.*) das Schiff.

navigable ['nævigəbl], *adj.* schiffbar.

navigate ['nævigeit], *v.a., v.n.* steuern.

navigation [nævi'geiʃən], *s.* die Schiffahrt (*shipping*); das Steuern, die Navigation.

navy ['neivi], *s.* die Flotte, Marine.

Neopolitan [niə'pɔlitən], *adj.* neapolitanisch. — *s.* der Neapolitaner.

near [niə], *adj., adv.* nahe, in der Nähe. — *prep.* nahe (*an zu*).

nearly ['niəli], *adv.* beinahe, fast.

nearness ['niənis], *s.* die Nähe.

neat [ni:t], *adj.* nett, sauber (*tidy*); rein, unvermischt, pur (*unmixed*).

neatness ['ni:tnis], *s.* die Sauberkeit.

necessary ['nesəsəri], *adj.* notwendig.

necessity [ni'sesiti], *s.* die Not, Notwendigkeit; (*pl.*) das zum Leben Nötige.

neck [nek], *s.* (*Anat.*) der Hals; *stick o.'s* — *out,* es riskieren. — *v.n.* (*Am. sl.*) knutschen.

necklace ['neklis], s. das Halsband, die Halskette.
necktie ['nektai], s. der Schlips, die Krawatte.
need [ni:d], s. die Not, der Bedarf. — *v.a.* brauchen, nötig haben.
needful ['ni:dful], *adj.* notwendig.
needle [ni:dl], s. die Nadel. — *v.a. (coll.)* sticheln, ärgern *(annoy)*.
needy ['ni:di], *adj.* in Not befindlich, arm, bedürftig.
nefarious [ni'fɛəriəs], *adj.* nichtswürdig, schändlich.
negative ['negətiv], *adj.* negativ, verneinend. — s. *(Phot.)* das Negativ; die Verneinung *(denial); in the —,* verneinend.
neglect [ni'glekt], *v.a.* vernachlässigen, außer acht lassen. — s. die Vernachlässigung.
neglectful [ni'glektful], *adj.* nachlässig.
negligence ['neglidʒəns], s. die Nachlässigkeit.
negotiate [ni'goufieit], *v.a., v.n.* verhandeln, unterhandeln.
negotiation [nigoufi'eifən], s. die Unterhandlung.
Negro ['ni:grou], s. der Neger.
neigh [nei], *v.n.* wiehern.
neighbour ['neibə], s. der Nachbar.
neighbourhood ['neibəhud], s. die Nachbarschaft, Umgebung.
neighbouring ['neibəriŋ], *adj.* Nachbar-, benachbart.
neighbourliness ['neibəlinis], s. das gute nachbarliche Verhältnis, die Geselligkeit.
neither ['naiðə *or* 'ni:ðə], *adj., pron.* keiner (von beiden). — *conj.* auch nicht; — . . . *nor,* weder . . . noch.
Nepalese [nepə'li:z], *adj.* nepalesisch. — s. der Nepalese.
nephew ['nefju *or* 'nevju], s. der Neffe.
nerve [nə:v], s. der Nerv; der Mut *(courage);* die Frechheit *(impudence); (pl.)* die Angst, Nervosität.
nervous ['nə:vəs], *adj.* nervös; — *of,* furchtsam vor *(Dat.);* ängstlich wegen *(Genit.).*
nest [nest], s. das Nest; *(fig.)* — *egg,* die Ersparnisse, *f.pl.* — *v.n.* nisten.
nestle [nesl], *v.n.* sich anschmiegen.
net (1) [net], s. das Netz. — *v.a.* (Fische) fangen, ins Netz bekommen.
net (2) [net], *adj.* netto; ohne Verpackung; — *weight,* das Nettogewicht.
nettle [netl], s. *(Bot.)* die Nessel. — *v.a.* sticheln, ärgern.
neurosis [njuə'rousis], s. *(Med.)* die Neurose.
neutrality [nju:'træliti], s. die Neutralität.
never ['nevə], *adv.* nie, niemals; — *mind,* mach Dir (machen Sie sich) nichts draus!
nevertheless [nevəðə'les], *conj.* trotzdem, nichtsdestoweniger.
new [nju:], *adj.* neu; *New Year's Day,* der Neujahrstag; *New Zealander,* der

Neuseeländer. — s. *(pl.)* die Nachrichten, *f. pl.*
newspaper ['nju:speipə], s. die Zeitung.
next [nekst], *adj.* nächst. — *adv.* danach.
nib [nib], s. die Spitze *(of pen).*
nibble [nibl], *v.a., v.n.* knabbern, nagen *(at, an, Dat.).*
nice [nais], *adj.* fein *(scrupulous);* nett, angenehm *(pleasant).*
nicety ['naisəti], s. die Feinheit *(of distinction etc.).*
nickel [nikl], s. das Nickel; *(Am.)* das Fünfcentstück.
nickname ['nikneim], s. der Spitzname.
niece [ni:s], s. die Nichte.
Nigerian [nai'dʒiəriən], *adj.* nigerisch. — s. der Nigerier.
niggardly ['nigədli], *adj.* geizig.
nigh [nai], *adj., adv. (Poet.)* nahe.
night [nait], s. die Nacht; *last —,* gestern abend; *the — before last,* vorgestern abend; *at —,* nachts.
nightingale ['naitiŋgeil], s. *(Orn.)* die Nachtigall.
nightmare ['naitmɛə], s. der Alpdruck.
nimble [nimbl], *adj.* flink; geschickt *(deft).*
nine [nain], *num. adj.* neun.
nineteen [nain'ti:n], *num. adj.* neunzehn.
ninety ['nainti], *num. adj.* neunzig.
ninth [nainθ], *num. adj.* neunte.
nip [nip], *v.a.* zwicken.
nipple [nipl], s. *(Anat.)* die Brustwarze.
nitrogen ['naitrədʒən], s. *(Chem.)* der Stickstoff.
no [nou], *part.* nein. — *adj.* kein. — *adv.* nicht; — *one,* niemand.
nobility [no'biliti], s. der Adel.
noble [noubl], *adj.* edel; großmütig *(magnanimous);* adlig *(well born).*
nobody ['noubədi], *pron.* niemand.
nod [nɔd], *v.n.* nicken.
noise [nɔiz], s. der Lärm, das Geräusch.
noiseless ['nɔizlis], *adj.* geräuschlos.
noisy ['nɔizi], *adj.* laut, lärmend.
nominal ['nɔminəl], *adj.* nominell.
nominate ['nɔmineit], *v.a.* nennen *(name);* ernennen *(appoint).*
nomination [nɔmi'neifən], s. die Nennung, Ernennung.
none [nʌn], *pron.* keiner, niemand.
nonsense ['nɔnsəns], s. der Unsinn.
nook [nuk], s. die Ecke, der Winkel.
noon [nu:n], s. der Mittag.
noose [nu:s], s. die Schlinge.
nor [nɔ:], *conj.* auch nicht; *neither . . . —,* weder . . . noch.
normal ['nɔ:məl], *adj.* normal.
normalize ['nɔ:məlaiz], *v.a.* normalisieren.
Norman ['nɔ:mən], *adj.* normannisch. — s. der Normanne.
north [nɔ:θ], s. der Norden. — *adj.* nördlich.
northerly, northern ['nɔ:ðəli, 'nɔ:ðən], *adj.* nördlich, von Norden.
Norwegian [nɔ:'wi:dʒən], *adj.* norwegisch. — s. der Norweger.
nose [nouz], s. *(Anat.)* die Nase; — *dive,* der Sturzflug.

nosey ['nouzi], *adj.* (*coll.*) neugierig.
nostalgia [nɔs'tældʒə], *s.* das Heimweh, die Sehnsucht.
nostril ['nɔstril], *s.* (*Anat.*) das Nasenloch.
not [nɔt], *adv.* nicht; — *at all*, keineswegs.
notable ['noutəbl], *adj.* berühmt, wohlbekannt; bemerkenswert.
notary ['noutəri], *s.* der Notar.
notch [nɔtʃ], *s.* die Kerbe. — *v.a.* kerben, einkerben.
note [nout], *s.* die Notiz, der Zettel; (*Mus.*) die Note; die Bedeutung; *take —s*, Notizen machen; *take — of*, zur Kenntnis nehmen. — *v.a.* notieren, aufzeichnen.
notepaper ['noutpeipə], *s.* das Briefpapier.
noteworthy ['noutwə:ði], *adj.* beachtenswert.
nothing ['nʌθiŋ], *pron. s.* nichts; *for —*, umsonst; *good for —*, der Taugenichts.
notice ['noutis], *s.* die Kenntnis (*attention*); die Anzeige (*in press etc.*); Notiz; Bekanntmachung; *give —*, kündigen. — *v.a.* bemerken.
noticeable ['noutisəbl], *adj.* bemerkbar.
notification [noutifi'keiʃən], *s.* die Benachrichtigung, Bekanntmachung.
notify ['noutifai], *v.a.* benachrichtigen, informieren.
notion ['nouʃən], *s.* der Begriff (*concept*); die Idee (*idea*); die Meinung (*opinion*).
notoriety [noutə'raiiti], *s.* der üble Ruf.
notorious [no'tɔ:riəs], *adj.* berüchtigt.
notwithstanding [nɔtwið'stændiŋ], *prep.* ungeachtet (*Genit.*). — *adv.* trotzdem, dennoch. — *conj.* — *that*, obgleich.
nought [nɔ:t], *s.* die Null (*figure 0*); nichts (*nothing*).
noun [naun], *s.* (*Gram.*) das Hauptwort, Substantiv.
nourish ['nʌriʃ], *v.a.* nähren; ernähren.
nourishment ['nʌriʃmənt], *s.* die Nahrung.
Nova Scotian ['nouvə'skouʃən], *adj.* neuschottisch. [Neuschottland]
novel [nɔvl], *s.* (*Lit.*) der Roman. — *adj.* neu; neuartig (*modern*).
novelty ['nɔvlti], *s.* die Neuheit.
November [no'vembə]. der November.
novice ['nɔvis], *s.* der Neuling (*greenhorn*); (*Eccl.*) der, die Novize.
novitiate [no'viʃiit], *s.* die Lehrzeit; (*Eccl.*) das Noviziat.
now [nau], *adv.* nun, jetzt; — *and then*, dann und wann, hin und wieder. — *conj.* — (*that*), da nun.
nowadays ['nauədeiz], *adv.* heutzutage.
nowhere ['nouhwɛə], *aav.* nirgends.
noxious ['nɔkʃəs], *adj.* (*Med., Bot.*) schädlich.
nozzle [nɔzl], *s.* die Düse; (*sl.*) die Schnauze.
nuclear ['nju:kliə], *adj.* (*Phys.*) nuklear, Kern-.
nucleus ['nju:kliəs], *s.* der Kern.

nude [nju:d], *adj.* nackt, bloß.
nudge [nʌdʒ], *v.a.* leicht anstoßen.
nudity ['nju:diti], *s.* die Nacktheit.
nugget ['nʌgit], *s.* der Klumpen.
nuisance ['nju:səns], *s.* die Plage, Lästigkeit; das Ärgernis (*annoyance*).
null [nʌl], *adj.* null und nichtig; ungültig.
nullify ['nʌlifai], *v.a.* annullieren, ungültig machen.
nullity ['nʌliti], *s.* die Ungültigkeit.
numb [nʌm], *adj.* erstarrt, gefühllos. — *v.a.* erstarren lassen.
number ['nʌmbə], *s.* die Zahl, Nummer (*quantity*); *cardinal —*, die Grundzahl; *ordinal —*, die Ordnungszahl. — *v.a.* nummerieren; zählen (*count*).
numbness ['nʌmnis], *s.* die Erstarrung.
numeral ['nju:mərəl], *s.* (*Gram.*) das Zahlwort.
numerical [nju:'merikəl], *adj.* (*Maths.*) Zahlen-, numerisch.
numerous ['nju:mərəs], *adj.* zahlreich.
numismatics [nju:miz'mætiks], *s.* die Münzkunde.
numskull ['nʌmskʌl], *s.* der Dummkopf.
nun [nʌn], *s.* (*Eccl.*) die Nonne.
nunnery ['nʌnəri], *s.* (*Eccl.*) das Nonnenkloster.
nuptials ['nʌpʃəlz], *s. pl.* (*Lit., Poet.*) die Hochzeit, das Hochzeitsfest.
nurse [nə:s], *s.* die Krankenschwester, Pflegerin; die Amme (*wet nurse*). — *v.a.* pflegen.
nursery ['nə:səri], *s.* das Kinderzimmer; (*Bot.*) die Pflanzschule, Baumschule (*for trees*); — *school*, der Kindergarten.
nurture ['nə:tʃə], *v.a.* nähren, aufziehen.
nut [nʌt], *s.* (*Bot.*) die Nuß; (*Tech.*) die Schraubenmutter; (*Am. coll.*) *nuts*, verrückt.
nutcracker ['nʌtkrækə], *s.* (*usually pl.*) der Nußknacker.
nutmeg ['nʌtmeg], *s.* (*Cul.*) die Muskatnuß.
nutriment ['nju:trimənt], *s.* die Nahrung; (*animals*) das Futter.
nutrition [nju:'triʃən], *s.* die Ernährung.
nutritious [nju:'triʃəs], *adj.* nahrhaft.
nutshell ['nʌtʃel], *s.* die Nußschale; (*fig.*) *put in a —*, kurz ausdrücken.
nymph [nimf], *s.* (*Myth.*) die Nymphe.

O

O [ou]. das O. — *int.* oh!
oaf [ouf], *s.* der Tölpel.
oak [ouk], *s.* (*Bot.*) die Eiche.
oaken ['oukən], *adj.* eichen, aus Eichenholz.

oar [ɔ:], *s.* das Ruder; *put o.'s — in,* sich einmengen.

oasis [ou'eisis], *s.* die Oase.

oath [ouθ], *s.* der Eid; der Fluch (*curse*); *commissioner for —s,* der öffentliche Notar; *take an —,* einen Eid schwören *or* leisten.

oats [outs], *s. pl.* (*Bot.*) der Hafer; *sow o.'s wild —s,* sich austoben, sich die Hörner ablaufen.

obdurate ['ɔbdjurit], *adj.* halsstarrig.

obedience [o'bi:djəns], *s.* der Gehorsam.

obedient [o'bi:djənt], *adj.* gehorsam.

obeisance [o'beisəns], *s.* die Verbeugung, Ehrfurchtsbezeigung.

obese [o'bi:s], *adj.* fettleibig, beleibt.

obey [o'bei], *v.a., v.n.* gehorchen (*Dat.*).

obituary [o'bitjuəri], *s.* der Nachruf, der Nekrolog.

object ['ɔbdʒikt], *s.* der Gegenstand (*thing*); (*Gram.*) das Objekt; der Zweck (*objective, purpose*). — [əb-'dʒekt], *v.n.* — *to,* einwenden (*gainsay*); vorhalten (*remonstrate*).

objection [əb'dʒekʃən], *s.* der Einwand.

objectionable [əb'dʒekʃənəbl], *adj.* anstößig.

objective [əb'dʒektiv], *adj.* objektiv, unparteiisch. — *s.* das Ziel (*aim*).

obligation [ɔbli'geiʃən], *s.* die Verpflichtung.

obligatory [o'bligətəri, 'ɔblig-], *adj.* verbindlich, obligatorisch.

oblige [o'blaidʒ], *v.a.* verpflichten; *much obliged,* vielen Dank; *can you — me?* können Sie mir aushelfen?

obliging [o'blaidʒiŋ], *adj.* gefällig, zuvorkommend.

oblique [o'bli:k], *adj.* schräg, schief; (*fig.*) indirekt.

obliterate [o'blitəreit], *v.a.* auslöschen (*extinguish*); vertilgen (*destroy*).

oblivion [o'bliviən], *s.* die Vergessenheit.

oblivious [o'bliviəs], *adj.* vergeßlich.

oblong ['ɔblɔŋ], *adj.* länglich. — *s.* das Rechteck.

obloquy ['ɔbləkwi], *s.* die Schmähung, Schande.

obnoxious [ɔb'nɔkʃəs], *adj.* verhaßt, scheußlich.

obscene [ɔb'si:n], *adj.* anstößig, obszön.

obscenity [ɔb'sen-, ɔb'si:niti], *s.* die Obszönität.

obscure [əb'skjuə], *adj.* dunkel (*dark*); unbekannt (*unknown*).

obscurity [əb'skjuəriti], *s.* die Dunkelheit (*darkness*); die Unbekanntheit.

obsequies ['ɔbsikwiz], *s. pl.* das Leichenbegängnis.

obsequious [əb'si:kwiəs], *adj.* unterwürfig.

observance [əb'zə:vəns], *s.* die Befolgung, Beobachtung, das Einhalten (*Law etc.*).

observant [əb'zə:vənt], *adj.* aufmerksam; achtsam.

observation [ɔbzə'veiʃən], *s.* die Beobachtung (*watching*); die Bemerkung (*remark*).

observatory [əb'zə:vətri], *s.* die Sternwarte.

observe [əb'zə:v], *v.a.* beobachten (*watch*); bemerken (*notice, remark on*).

obsession [əb'seʃən], *s.* die Besessenheit, fixe Idee.

obsolete ['ɔbsəli:t], *adj.* veraltet.

obstacle ['ɔbstəkl], *s.* das Hindernis.

obstinacy ['ɔbstinəsi], *s.* die Hartnäckigkeit.

obstinate ['ɔbstinit], *adj.* hartnäckig.

obstruct [əb'strʌkt], *v.a.* hemmen, hindern.

obstruction [əb'strʌkʃən], *s.* das Hindernis, die Hemmung, Verstopfung.

obtain [əb'tein], *v.a.* erhalten, erlangen; bekommen (*get*).

obtrude [əb'tru:d], *v.n.* sich aufdrängen. — *v.a.* aufdrängen.

obtrusive [əb'tru:siv], *adj.* aufdringlich.

obtuse [əb'tju:s], *adj.* stumpf; dumm (*stupid*).

obviate ['ɔbvieit], *v.a.* vorbeugen (*Dat.*).

obvious ['ɔbviəs], *adj.* klar, offenbar, selbstverständlich.

occasion [o'keiʒən], *s.* die Gelegenheit (*chance*); der Anlaß; der Veranlassung (*cause*). — *v.a.* veranlassen; verursachen (*cause*).

occasional [o'keiʒənəl], *adj.* gelegentlich.

occident ['ɔksidənt], *s.* das Abendland, der Westen.

occult [ɔ'kʌlt], *adj.* geheim, Okkult-.

occupancy ['ɔkjupənsi], *s.* der Besitz, das Innehaben (*holding*).

occupant ['ɔkjupənt], *s.* der Inhaber; der Bewohner (*of house*), Insasse.

occupation [ɔkju'peiʃən], *s.* die Besetzung; (*Mil.*) *army of —,* die Besatzung; der Beruf, die Beschäftigung (*job*); — *with,* das Befassen mit (*Dat.*).

occupy ['ɔkjupai], *v.a.* (*Mil.*) besetzen, in Besitz nehmen; beschäftigen (*engage*); bekleiden (*office*).

occur [ə'kə:], *v.n.* geschehen, sich ereignen; — *to s.o.,* jemandem einfallen.

occurrence [ə'kʌrəns], *s.* das Geschehen, Ereignis, der Vorfall.

ocean ['ouʃən], *s.* der Ozean, die See, das Meer. — *adj.* Meeres-.

octagon ['ɔktəgən], *s.* das Achteck.

octagonal [ɔk'tægənəl], *adj.* achteckig.

October [ɔk'toubə], *s.* der Oktober.

octogenarian [ɔktodʒi'nɛəriən], *s.* der Achtzigjährige.

ocular ['ɔkjulə], *adj.* Augen-.

oculist ['ɔkjulist], *s.* (*Med.*) der Augenarzt.

odd [ɔd], *adj.* ungerade; seltsam (*queer*); einzeln (*solitary*). — *s.* (*pl.*) die Wahrscheinlichkeit.

oddity ['ɔditi], *s.* die Seltenheit, Sonderbarkeit.

oddment ['ɔdmənt], *s.* (*pl.*) die Reste, *m. pl.*

ode [oud], *s.* (*Poet.*) die Ode.

odious ['oudiəs], *adj.* verhaßt, widerwärtig.

odium ['oudiəm], *s.* der Haß.
odorous ['oudərəs], *adj.* duftend, duftig.
odour ['oudə], *s.* der Geruch, Duft.
of [ɔv], *prep.* von (*Dat.*); aus (*out of*) (*Dat.*); — *course*, natürlich.
off [ɔf, ɔːf], *adv.* fort, weg; entfernt; *make* —, sich davonmachen; *far* —, weit weg; — *and on*, ab und zu; *well* —, wohlhabend. — *prep.* von (*from*); fort von; entfernt von (*distant from*).
offal [ɔfl], *s.* der Abfall.
offence [o'fens], *s.* (*Law*) das Vergehen; die Beleidigung (*insult*).
offend [o'fend], *v.a.* beleidigen (*insult*). — *v.n.* (*Law*) sich vergehen (gegen, *Acc.*).
offensive [o'fensiv], *adj.* beleidigend (*insulting*); anstößig (*indecent*). — *s.* die Offensive, der Angriff (*against*, auf, *Acc.*).
offer ['ɔfə], *v.a.* bieten (*auction*); anbieten (*hold out*). — *s.* das Anerbieten; (*Comm.*) das Angebot, der Antrag.
offering ['ɔfəriŋ], *s.* das Opfer.
office ['ɔfis], *s.* das Amt; die Stellung (*position*); die Funktion (*duties*); das Büro; (*Eccl.*) der Gottesdienst; *high* —, das hohe Amt; — *bearer*, der Amtswalter.
officer ['ɔfisə], *s.* (*Mil.*) der Offizier; der Beamte (*functionary*); *honorary* —, der ehrenamtliche Beamte, der Beamte im Ehrenamt.
official [o'fiʃəl], *adj.* offiziell, amtlich. — *s.* der Beamte.
officiate [o'fiʃieit], *v.n.* amtieren; fungieren.
officious [o'fiʃəs], *adj.* zudringlich, (übertrieben) dienstfertig.
offing ['ɔfiŋ], *s.* (*Naut.*) die hohe See; *in the* —, bevorstehend.
offset [ɔf'set], *v.a.* (*Comm.*) ausgleichen; (*Typ.*) offset drucken, im Offset drucken; (*fig.*) unschädlich machen, wettmachen. — *s.* ['ɔfset], *s.* (*Comm.*) die Gegenrechnung, der Ausgleich; (*Typ.*) der Offsetdruck.
offshoot ['ɔfʃuːt], *s.* der Sprößling.
offspring ['ɔfspriŋ], *s.* die Nachkommenschaft.
often, (*Poet.*) **oft** [ɔfn, ɔft], *adv.* oft, häufig.
ogle [ougl], *v.a.*, *v.n.* äugeln, beäugeln, glotzen, anglotzen.
ogre ['ougə], *s.* der Menschenfresser.
oil [ɔil], *s.* das Öl. — *v.a.* einölen, einschmieren.
oilcloth ['ɔiklɔθ], *s.* das Wachstuch.
ointment ['ɔintmənt], *s.* die Salbe.
old [ould], *adj.* alt; —*fashioned*, altmodisch.
olive ['ɔliv], *s.* (*Bot.*) die Olive; *the Mount of Olives*, der Ölberg.
Olympic [o'limpik], *adj.* olympisch; *the* — *Games*, die Olympischen Spiele.
omelette ['ɔməlit], *s.* (*Cul.*) das Omelett, der Eierkuchen.
omen ['oumən], *s.* das (böse) Vorzeichen, das Omen.

ominous ['ɔminəs], *adj.* von schlimmer Vorbedeutung, ominös.
omission [o'miʃən], *s.* die Unterlassung; (*Typ.*) die Auslassung.
omit [o'mit], *v.a.* unterlassen (*leave undone*); auslassen (*leave out*).
omnibus ['ɔmnibəs], *s.* der Omnibus, der Autobus.
omnipotent [ɔm'nipətənt], *adj.* allmächtig.
omniscient [ɔm'nisiənt], *adj.* allwissend.
on [ɔn], *prep.* an; auf; über; vor; bei; zu; nach; um; *call* — (*s.o.*), vorsprechen (bei, *Dat.*); — *fire*, in Flammen; — *condition*, unter der Bedingung (*Comm.*); — *account*, a Konto; — *high*, hoch oben; — *my honour*, auf mein Ehrenwort; — *purpose*, absichtlich; — *sale*, zum Verkauf. — *adv.* weiter, fort (*forward*); gültig, zutreffend (*correct*, *valid*); *get* —, vorwärtskommen; *get* — *with s.th.*, weitermachen; *get* — *with s.o.*, auskommen (mit, *Dat.*).
once [wʌns], *adv.* einmal; einst (*long ago*); — *more*, nochmals, noch einmal; — *and for all*, ein für alle Mal; *at* —, sogleich; — *in a while*, ab und zu. — *conj.* sobald.
one [wʌn], *num. adj.* ein, eine, ein; — *way street*, die Einbahnstraße. — *pron.* man (*impersonal*). — *s. little* —, der Kleine; — *by* —, eins nach dem anderen, einzeln.
onerous ['ɔnərəs], *adj.* beschwerlich.
onion ['ʌnjən], *s.* (*Bot.*) die Zwiebel.
onlooker ['ɔnlukə], *s.* der Zuschauer.
only ['ounli], *adj.* einzig, allein. — *adv.* nur, bloß. — *conj.* jedoch.
onset ['ɔnset], *s.* der Angriff (*attack*); der Anfang (*beginning*).
onslaught ['ɔnslɔːt], *s.* der Angriff, Überfall.
onward ['ɔnwəd], *adj.* fortschreitend. — *adv.* (*also* **onwards**) vorwärts.
ooze [uːz], *s.* der Schlamm. — *v.n.* träufeln, sickern.
opacity [o'pæsiti], *s.* (*Phys.*) die Dunkelheit, Undurchsichtigkeit.
opal [oupl], *s.* der Opal.
opaque [o'peik], *adj.* (*Phys.*) dunkel, undurchsichtig.
open [oupn], *adj.* offen; offenherzig (*frank*); — *to suggestions*, einem Vorschlag zugänglich. — *v.a.* öffnen; eröffnen (*start*); — *an account*, ein Konto eröffnen. — *v.n.* sich öffnen, sich auftun.
opening ['oupniŋ], *s.* das Öffnen; die freie Stelle; die Gelegenheit (*opportunity*). — *adj.* einleitend; — *gambit*, (*Chess*) der Eröffnungszug.
openness ['oupənnis], *s.* die Offenheit, Ehrlichkeit (*frankness*).
opera ['ɔpərə], *s.* (*Mus.*) die Oper; *comic* —, die komische Oper; — *hat*, der Zylinderhut, Klapphut.
operatic [ɔpə'rætik], *adj.* (*Mus.*) Opern-.

operate ['ɔpəreit], *v.a.*, *v.n.* (*Engin.*) bedienen; (*Med.*) operieren (*on*, *Acc.*).
operation [ɔpə'reiʃən], *s.* (*Med..* *Mil.*) die Operation; die Bedienung (*of engine etc.*).
operative ['ɔpərətiv], *adj.* wirksam (*effective*). — *s.* der Arbeiter.
opiate ['oupiit], *s.* das Schlafmittel. — *adj.* einschläfernd.
opine [o'pain], *v.n.* meinen.
opinion [o'pinjən], *s.* die Meinung; *in my* —, meiner Meinung nach.
opinionated [o'pinjəneitid], *adj.* von sich eingenommen, selbstgefällig.
opium ['oupjəm], *s.* das Opium.
opponent [ə'pounənt], *s.* der Gegner.
opportune ['ɔpətjuːn], *adj.* gelegen, günstig.
opportunity [ɔpə'tjuːniti], *s.* die Gelegenheit, Chance; die Möglichkeit.
oppose [ə'pouz], *v.a.* bekämpfen; widerstehen, entgegentreten (*Dat.*).
opposite ['ɔpəzit], *adj.* entgegengesetzt; gegenüberliegend; gegensätzlich (*contrary*). — *prep.* gegenüber (*Dat.*). — *s.* das Gegenteil.
opposition [ɔpə'ziʃən], *s.* (*Parl.*) die Opposition; der Widerstand.
oppress [ə'pres], *v.a.* unterdrücken.
oppression [ə'preʃən], *s.* die Unterdrückung.
oppressive [ə'presiv], *adj.* drückend, tyrannisch.
opprobrious [ə'proubriəs], *adj.* schändlich, schimpflich.
opprobrium [ə'proubriəm], *s.* die Schande.
optician [ɔp'tiʃən], *s.* der Optiker.
optics ['ɔptiks], *s.* die Optik.
optimism ['ɔptimizm], *s.* der Optimismus.
option ['ɔpʃən], *s.* die Wahl.
optional ['ɔpʃənəl], *adj.* Wahl-, frei, beliebig.
opulence ['ɔpjuləns], *s.* der Reichtum (an, *Dat.*), die Üppigkeit.
opulent ['ɔpjulənt], *adj.* reich, üppig.
or [ɔ:], *conj.* oder; noch (*after neg.*); *either . . .* —, entweder . . . oder.
oracle ['ɔrəkl], *s.* das Orakel.
oral ['ɔ:rəl], *adj.* mündlich. — *s.* die mündliche Prüfung.
orange ['ɔrindʒ,] *s.* (*Bot.*) die Orange, Apfelsine.
oration [ɔ'reiʃən], *s.* die feierliche Rede, Ansprache.
orator ['ɔrətə], *s.* der Redner.
oratorio [ɔrə'tɔ:riou], *s.* (*Mus.*) das Oratorium.
oratory ['ɔrətəri], *s.* (*Eccl.*) die Kapelle; (*Rhet.*) die Redekunst.
orb [ɔ:b], *s.* die Kugel; der Reichsapfel; (*Poet.*) der Himmelskörper.
orbit ['ɔ:bit], *s.* (*Astron.*) die Bahn (der Gestirne), Planetenbahn.
orchard ['ɔ:tʃəd], *s.* der Obstgarten.
orchestra ['ɔ:kistrə], *s.* (*Mus.*) das Orchester.
ordain [ɔ:'dein], *v.a.* ordinieren, anordnen; (*Eccl.*) zum Priester weihen.

ordeal ['ɔ:diəl], *s.* die Feuerprobe; Heimsuchung.
order ['ɔ:də], *s.* die Ordnung (*system*); die Verordnung (*command etc.*); (*Mil.*) der Befehl; (*Comm.*) die Bestellung; (*Biol.*) die Ordnung; der Orden (*Eccl.*; *also decoration*); *take* (*holy*) —*s*, ordiniert werden, Priester werden; *in* — *to*, um zu; *in* — *that*, so daß; *by* —, auf (den) Befehl. — *v.a.* befehlen, verordnen, anordnen; (*Comm.*) bestellen.
orderly ['ɔ:dəli], *adj.* ordentlich, ruhig. — *s.* (*Mil.*) die Ordonanz; (*Med.*) der Gehilfe, Krankenwärter.
ordinal ['ɔ:dinl], *adj.*, *s.* (*number*) die Ordnungszahl.
ordinance ['ɔ:dinəns], *s.* die Verordnung.
ordinary ['ɔ:dinəri], *adj.* gewöhnlich.
ordnance ['ɔ:dnəns], *s.* das schwere Geschütz; (*Mil.*, *Geog.*) — *survey*, die Landesvermessung.
ore [ɔ:], *s.* das Erz, Metall.
organ ['ɔ:gən], *s.* das Organ; (*Mus.*) die Orgel; — *grinder*, der Leierkastenmann.
organic [ɔ:'gænik], *adj.* organisch.
organisation [ɔ:gənai'zeiʃən], *s.* die Organisation.
organise ['ɔ:gənaiz], *v.a.* organisieren.
organism ['ɔ:gənizm], *s.* (*Biol.*) der Organismus.
organist ['ɔ:gənist], *s.* (*Mus.*) der Organist.
orgy ['ɔ:dʒi], *s.* die Orgie.
oriel ['ɔ:riəl], *s.* der Erker; — *window*, das Erkerfenster.
orient ['ɔ:riənt], *s.* der Orient, Osten.
oriental [ɔ:ri'entl], *adj.* östlich.
orifice ['ɔrifis], *s.* die Öffnung, Mündung.
origin ['ɔridʒin], *s.* der Ursprung, die Herkunft.
original [ə'ridʒinl], *adj.* Ursprungs-, ursprünglich; originell (*creative*). — *s.* das Original.
originality [əridʒi'næliti], *s.* die Originalität.
originate [ə'ridʒineit], *v.n.* entstehen, entspringen. — *v.a.* hervorbringen, entstehen lassen.
ornament ['ɔ:nəmənt], *s.* das Ornament; die Verzierung (*decoration*).
ornate [ɔ:'neit], *adj.* geziert, geschmückt.
orphan ['ɔ:fən], *s.* der, die Waise.
orphanage ['ɔ:fənidʒ], *s.* das Waisenhaus.
orthodoxy ['ɔ:θədɔksi], *s.* die Orthodoxie, die Rechtgläubigkeit.
orthography [ɔ:'θɔgrəfi], *s.* die Rechtschreibung.
orthopaedic [ɔ:θə'pi:dik], *adj.* orthopädisch.
oscillate ['ɔsileit], *v.n.* oszillieren, schwingen.
oscillatory ['ɔsileitəri], *adj.* schwingend, oszillierend.
osier ['ouʒiə], *s.* (*Bot.*) die Korbweide.
osprey ['ɔsprei], *s.* (*Orn.*) der Seeadler.

448

ossify [ˈɔsifai], *v.a.* verknöchern lassen; versteinern lassen (*stone*). — *v.n.* verknöchern; versteinern (*stone*).

ostensible [ɔsˈtensibl], *adj.* scheinbar, anscheinend, vorgeblich.

ostentation [ɔstenˈteiʃən], *s.* die Großtuerei, der Prunk.

ostentatious [ɔstenˈteiʃəs], *adj.* großtuerisch, prahlerisch, protzig.

ostler [ˈɔslə], *s.* (*obs.*) der Stallknecht.

ostracize [ˈɔstrəsaiz], *v.a.* verbannen, ausschließen.

ostrich [ˈɔstritʃ], *s.* (*Orn.*) der Strauß.

other [ˈʌðə], *adj.* ander. — *pron.*, *s.* *the* —, der, die, das andere.

otherwise [ˈʌðəwaiz], *conj.* sonst. — *adv.* andernfalls.

otter [ˈɔtə], *s.* (*Zool.*) die Otter.

ought [ɔːt], *v. aux. defect.* sollte, müßte.

ounce [auns], *s.* die Unze.

our [ˈauə], *poss. adj.* unser, uns(e)re, unser.

ours [ˈauəz], *poss. pron.* unsrig, unser, uns(e)re, unser.

ourselves [auəˈselvz], *pers. pron.* wir, wir selbst, uns selbst; (*refl.*) uns.

ousel [uːzl], *s.* (*Orn.*) die Amsel.

out [aut], *adv.* aus; draußen (*outside*); außerhalb (*outside, externally*); heraus; hinaus (*outward, away from the speaker*). — *prep.* —*of*, aus, von (*Dat.*).

outer [ˈautə], *adj.* äußer.

outfit [ˈautfit], *s.* die Ausrüstung.

outing [ˈautiŋ], *s.* der Ausflug.

outhouse [ˈauthaus], *s.* das Nebengebäude, der Anbau.

outlaw [ˈautlɔː], *s.* der Verbannte, der Vogelfreie.

outlay [ˈautlei], *s.* (*Comm.*) die Auslagen, die Spesen, *f. pl.*

outlet [ˈautlit], *s.* der Ausfluß, Abfluß; (*fig.*) das Ventil.

outline [ˈautlain], *s.* der Umriß, Entwurf. — [autˈlain], *v.a.* skizzieren, umreißen, kurz beschreiben.

outlive [autˈliv], *v.a.* überleben.

outlook [ˈautluk], *s.* die Aussicht, der Ausblick; die Weltanschauung (*philosophy*).

outlying [ˈautlaiiŋ], *adj.* außenliegend, außerhalb liegend, entlegen.

outnumber [autˈnʌmbə], *v.a.* an Zahl übertreffen.

outpatient [ˈautpeiʃənt], *s.* der ambulante Patient.

outrage [ˈautreidʒ], *s.* die Beleidigung (*insult*); die Gewalttat. — [autˈreidʒ], *v.a.* verletzen, beleidigen, schänden.

outrageous [autˈreidʒəs], *adj.* schändlich, schimpflich, unerhört; übertrieben (*exaggerated*).

outright [ˈautrait], *adj.* völlig. — [autˈrait], *adv.* gerade heraus, gänzlich.

outrun [autˈrʌn], *v.a. irr.* überholen, einholen.

outset [ˈautset], *s.* der Anfang.

outshine [autˈʃain], *v.a. irr.* übertreffen.

outside [autˈsaid], *adv.* außen, draußen. — [ˈautsaid], *prep.* außerhalb (*Genit.*).

— *adj.* äußere, außenstehend. — *s.* das Äußere, die Außenseite.

outskirts [ˈautskəːts], *s. pl.* die Umgebung, Vorstadt.

outstanding [autˈstændiŋ], *adj.* hervorragend (*excellent*); noch unbeglichen (*unpaid*); unerledigt (*undone*).

outstay [autˈstei], *v.a.* länger bleiben, zu lange bleiben.

outvote [autˈvout], *v.a.* überstimmen.

outward [ˈautwəd], *adj.* äußere, äußerlich, außerhalb befindlich. — *adv.* (*also* **outwards**) auswärts, nach außen.

outweigh [autˈwei], *v.a.* schwerer wiegen als, überwiegen.

outwit [autˈwit], *v.a.* überlisten.

oval [ouvl], *adj.* oval. — *s.* das Oval.

ovary [ˈouvəri], *s.* (*Anat.*) der Eierstock.

ovation [oˈveiʃən], *s.* die Huldigung, Ovation.

oven [ʌvn], *s.* der Backofen; (kleine) Schmelzofen.

over [ˈouvə], *prep.* über; oberhalb. — *adv.* über; herüber; drüben; — *there*, drüben; hinüber (*across*); vorüber (*past*).

overact [ouvərˈækt], *v.n.* übertreiben.

overawe [ouvərˈɔː], *v.a.* einschüchtern.

overbalance [ouvəˈbæləns], *v.a.* überwiegen. — *v.n.* überkippen.

overbear [ouvəˈbɛə], *v.a. irr.* überwältigen.

overbearing [ouvəˈbɛəriŋ], *adj.* anmaßend.

overboard [ˈouvəbɔːd], *adv.* über Bord.

overburden [ouvəˈbəːdn], *v.a.* überlasten.

overcast [ouvəˈkɑːst], *adj.* bewölkt.

overcharge [ouvəˈtʃɑːdʒ], *v.a.* zu viel berechnen (*pers., Dat.*), übervorteilen; überladen (*overload*). — *s.* die Übervorteilung; (*Tech.*) der Überdruck.

overcoat [ˈouvəkout], *s.* der Mantel; *light* —, der Überzieher.

overcome [ouvəˈkʌm], *v.a., v.n. irr.* überwinden.

overdo [ouvəˈduː], *v.a. irr.* übertreiben.

overdone [ouvəˈdʌn], *adj.* übergar, zu lange gekocht.

overdrive [ouvəˈdraiv], *v.a. irr.* abhetzen, zu weit treiben. — [ˈouvədraiv] *s.* (*Motor.*) der Schnellgang.

overdue [ouvəˈdjuː], *adj.* überfällig, verfallen.

overflow [ouvəˈflou], *v.a., v.n.* überfließen; überfluten (*banks*). — [ˈouvəflou], *s.* der Überfluß (*flood*); die Überschwemmung.

overgrow [ouvəˈgrou], *v.a. irr.* überwachsen, überwuchern. — *v.n.* zu groß werden.

overhang [ouvəˈhæŋ], *v.a. irr.* überhängen.

overhaul [ouvəˈhɔːl], *v.a.* überholen. — [ˈouvəhɔːl], *s.* die Überholung.

overhead [ouvəˈhed], *adv.* droben, oben (*above*). — [ˈouvəhed], *s.* (*pl.*) (*Comm.*) laufende Unkosten, *pl.*

overhear [ouvə'hiə], *v.a. irr.* zufällig
hören.
overjoyed [ouvə'dʒɔid], *adj.* entzückt.
overlap [ouvə'læp], *v.n.* überschneiden,
zusammenfallen (*dates etc.*). — ['ouvə-
læp], *s.* die Überschneidung, das
Zusammenfallen.
overload [ouvə'loud], *v.a.* überlasten;
(*Elec.*) überladen.
overlook [ouvə'luk], *v.a.* übersehen;
verzeihen (*disregard*).
overmuch [ouvə'mʌtʃ], *adv.* allzusehr.
overpay [ouvə'pei], *v.a., v.n.* zu viel
bezahlen.
overpopulated [ouvə'pɔpjuleitid], *adj.*
übervölkert.
overpower [ouvə'pauə], *v.a.* überwältigen.
overrate [ouvə'reit], *v.a.* überschätzen.
overreach [ouvə'ri:tʃ], *v.a.* übervorteilen.
override [ouvə'raid], *v.a. irr.* über-
reiten; unterdrücken (*suppress*).
overrule [ouvə'ru:l], *v.a.* nicht gelten
lassen, verwerfen.
overseer ['ouvəsiə], *s.* der Aufseher.
oversleep [ouvə'sli:p], *v.n. irr.* sich verschlafen.
overstep [ouvə'step], *v.a.* überschreiten.
overstrain [ouvə'strein], *v.a., v.n.*
(sich) zu sehr anstrengen, überanstrengen.
overt ['ouvə:t], *adj.* offenkundig;
öffentlich (*public*).
overtake [ouvə'teik], *v.a. irr.* einholen;
(*Mot.*) überholen.
overtax [ouvə'tæks], *v.a.* zu hoch
besteuern; (*fig.*) überanstrengen
(*strain*).
overthrow [ouvə'θrou], *v.a. irr.* umstürzen; (*Pol.*) stürzen. — ['ouvəθrou],
s. der Sturz.
overtime ['ouvətaim], *s.* Überstunden,
f. pl.
overture ['ouvətjuə], *s.* die Ouvertüre.
overturn ['ouvətə:n], *v.a.* umstürzen.
— *v.n.* überschlagen.
overweening ['ouvə'wi:niŋ], *adj.* eingebildet.
overweight [ouvə'weit], *s.* das Übergewicht.
overwhelm [ouvə'welm], *v.a.* überwältigen.
overwork [ouvə'wə:k], *v.n.* sich überarbeiten.
overwrought [ouvə'rɔ:t], *adj.* übermäßig erregt, aufgeregt, überreizt.
owe [ou], *v.a.* schulden. — *v.n.* verdanken (*be in debt*).
owing ['ouiŋ], *pred. adj.* — *to*, dank
(*Dat.*), zufolge (*Dat.*).
owl [aul], *s.* (*Orn.*) die Eule.
own (1) [oun], *v.a.* besitzen (*possess*).
— *adj.* eigen.
own (2) [oun], *v.a.* anerkennen (*acknowledge*).
owner ['ounə], *s.* der Besitzer, Eigentümer.
ox [ɔks], *s.* (*Zool.*) der Ochse.
oxidate ['ɔksideit] *see* **oxidise.**

oxide ['ɔksaid], *s.* (*Chem.*) das Oxyd.
oxidise ['ɔksidaiz], *v.a., v.n.* (*Chem.*)
oxydieren.
oxtail ['ɔksteil], *s.* der Ochsenschwanz.
oxygen ['ɔksidʒən], *s.* (*Chem.*) der
Sauerstoff.
oyster ['ɔistə], *s.* (*Zool.*) die Auster.
ozone ['ouzoun], *s.* (*Chem.*) das Ozon.

P

P [pi:]. das P.
pa [pɑ:], *s.* (*coll.*) Papa, der Vater.
pace [peis], *s.* der Gang, Schritt (*step*);
das Tempo (*rate*). — *v.n.* — *up and
down,* auf- und abschreiten. — *v.a.*
einschulen (*horse*).
Pacific, The [pə'sifik, θə]. der Stille
Ozean.
pacific [pə'sifik], *adj.* friedlich, still.
pacify ['pæsifai], *v.a.* Frieden stiften,
beruhigen.
pack [pæk], *s.* das *or* der Pack; der
Ballen (*bale*); das Rudel (*wolves*); das
Spiel (*cards*); das Paket, die Packung.
— *v.a.* packen (*a case*); parteiisch zusammensetzen; die Karten schlecht
mischen (*cheat at cards*); *packed like
sardines,* dichtgedrängt, eingepfercht.
— *v.n.* packen; seine Sachen einpacken.
package ['pækidʒ], *s.* der Ballen (*bale*);
das Gepäckstück, Paket.
packet ['pækit], *s.* das Paket; (*Naut.*)
— *boat,* das Paketboot, Postschiff.
pact [pækt], *s.* der Pakt, Vertrag.
pad [pæd], *s.* das Polster, Kissen; der
Notizblock (*writing block*). —
v.a. auspolstern; *padded cell,* die
Gummizelle.
padding ['pædiŋ], *s.* (*Tail.*) das Futter;
(*fig.*) die (nichtssagende) Ausfüllung,
das leere Geschwätz.
paddle [pædl], *v.a., v.n.* rudern, paddeln. — *s.* das Paddel, (Doppel)ruder,
das Schaufelruder; — *steamer,* der
Raddampfer.
paddock ['pædək], *s.* der Sattelplatz;
das Gehege.
padlock ['pædlɔk], *s.* das Vorhängeschloß, Vorlegeschloß.
pagan ['peigən], *adj.* heidnisch. — *s.*
der Heide.
paganism ['peigənizm], *s.* das Heidentum.
page (1) [peidʒ], *s.* der Page (*court
attendant*); Hoteljunge (*hotel boy*). —
v.a. durch Pagen suchen lassen.
page (2) [peidʒ], *s.* die Seite (*of book*). —
v.a. paginieren (*book*).
pageant ['pædʒənt], *s.* der Aufzug, der
Prunkzug; das Schaustück (*dramatic*).
pail [peil], *s.* der Eimer.

450

pain [pein], *s.* der Schmerz, die Pein; (*pl.*) die Mühe; *go to a lot of* —*s*, sich große Mühe geben. — *v.a.* schmerzen; bekümmern (*mentally*).

paint [peint], *s.* die Farbe (*dye*); die Schminke (*make-up*). — *v.a.* anstreichen, malen.

painter ['peintə], *s.* der Maler.

painting ['peintiŋ], *s.* das Gemälde.

pair [pɛə], *s.* das Paar; *two* —*s of shoes*, zwei Paar Schuhe; *a* — *of spectacles*, die Brille; *a* — *of scissors*, die Schere. — *v.a.* paaren. — *v.n.* sich paaren.

pajamas [pə'dʒɑːməz] *see under* **pyjamas.**

Pakistani [pɑːkiˈstɑːni], *adj.* pakistanisch. — *s.* der Pakistaner.

palace ['pæləs], *s.* der Palast.

palatable ['pælətəbl], *adj.* schmackhaft.

palatal ['pælətl], *adj.* (*Phonet.*) palatal, Gaumen-, Vordergaumen-. — *s.* (*Phonet.*) der Gaumenlaut.

palate ['pælit], *s.* der Gaumen.

Palatinate, The [pə'lætinit, ðə], die Pfalz, Pfalzgrafschaft.

palaver [pə'lɑːvə], *s.* die Unterredung; das Palaver.

pale (1) [peil], *adj.* blaß, bleich.

pale (2) [peil], *s.* der Pfahl; *beyond the* —, unkultiviert.

Palestinian [pælisˈtiniən], *adj.* palästinisch. — *s.* der Palästiner.

palette ['pælit], *s.* die Palette (*see also* **pallet** (1)).

paling ['peiliŋ], *s.* der Lattenzaun; (*pl.*) der Pfahlbau.

pall (1) [pɔːl], *s.* das Leichentuch.

pall (2) [pɔːl], *v.n.* schal werden (*become stale*).

pallet (1) ['pælit], *s.* die Palette (*painter's*); — *knife*, das Streichmesser (*potter's etc.*).

pallet (2) ['pælit], *s.* der Strohsack.

palliative ['pæliətiv], *s.* linderndes Mittel; (*fig.*) die Beschönigung.

pallid ['pælid], *adj.* blaß, bleich.

pallor ['pælə], *s.* die Blässe.

palm (1) [pɑːm], *s.* die Handfläche. — *v.a.* — (*off*) *on to s.o.*, an jemanden loswerden, jemandem etwas andrehen.

palm (2) [pɑːm], *s.* (*Bot.*) die Palme; *Palm Sunday*, Palmsonntag.

palmer ['pɑːmə], *s.* (*obs.*) der Pilger (*pilgrim*).

palmist ['pɑːmist], *s.* der Handleser, Wahrsager.

palmistry ['pɑːmistri], *s.* die Handwahrsagerei.

palmy ['pɑːmi], *adj.* glorreich.

palpable ['pælpəbl], *adj.* handgreiflich, greifbar, klar.

palpitate ['pælpiteit], *v.n.* klopfen (*of heart*).

palsied ['pɔːlzid], *adj.* (*Med.*) gelähmt.

palsy ['pɔːlzi], *s.* (*Med.*) die Lähmung.

paltry ['pɔːltri], *adj.* erbärmlich, armselig.

pamper ['pæmpə], *v.a.* verwöhnen.

pan (1) [pæn], *s.* die Pfanne. — *v.n.* —

out, sich ausbreiten, sich weiten.

pan (2) [pæn], *v.a.* (*Phot.*) kreisen, im Bogen führen.

panacea [pænəˈsiə], *s.* das Universalmittel.

pancake ['pænkeik], *s.* der Pfannkuchen.

pander ['pændə], *v.n.* fröhnen (*Dat.*), nachgeben.

pane [pein], *s.* die Glasscheibe.

panel ['pænl], *s.* die Holzfüllung, Täfelung (*in room*); die Liste; die Kommission (*of experts etc.*).

pang [pæŋ], *s.* die Angst, Pein; der Schmerz, Stich (*stab of pain*).

panic ['pænik], *s.* die Panik, der Schrecken.

panoply ['pænəpli], *s.* (*Poet.*) die Rüstung.

pansy ['pænzi], *s.* (*Bot.*) das Stiefmütterchen; (*sl.*) der Weichling, Feigling.

pant [pænt], *v.n.* keuchen, schwer atmen.

pantaloons [pæntəˈluːnz] (*usually abbr.* **pants** [pænts]), *s. pl.* die Unterhosen, Hosen, *f.pl.*

panther ['pænθə], *s.* (*Zool.*) der Panther.

pantomime ['pæntəmaim], *s.* die Pantomime, das Weihnachtsstück.

pantry ['pæntri], *s.* die Speisekammer.

pap [pæp], *s.* der Kinderbrei.

papacy ['peipəsi], *s.* das Papsttum.

papal ['peipəl], *adj.* päpstlich.

paper ['peipə], *s.* das Papier (*material*); die Zeitung (*daily* —); die Abhandlung (*essay*); — *knife*, der Brieföffner. — *v.a.* tapezieren (*a room*).

paperhanger ['peipəhæŋə], *s.* der Tapezierer.

paperweight ['peipəweit], *s.* der Briefbeschwerer.

par [pɑː], *s.* die Gleichheit, das Pari.

parable ['pærəbl], *s.* die Parabel, das Gleichnis.

parabola [pəˈræbələ], *s.* (*Geom.*) die Parabel.

parabolic [pærəˈbɔlik], *adj.* parabolisch, gleichnishaft.

parachute ['pærəʃuːt], *s.* (*Aviat.*) der Fallschirm.

parade [pə'reid], *s.* die Parade, der Aufmarsch. — *v.a.* herausstellen; zur Schau tragen (*show off*). — *v.n.* (*Mil.*) vorbeimarschieren.

paradise ['pærədais], *s.* das Paradies.

paraffin ['pærəfin], *s.* das Paraffin.

paragon ['pærəgən], *s.* das Musterkind, Musterbeispiel, Vorbild.

paragraph ['pærəgrɑːf], *s.* der Abschnitt, Absatz, Paragraph.

Paraguayan [pærəˈgwaiən], *adj.* paraguayisch. — *s.* der Paraguayer.

parallel ['pærəlel], *adj.* parallel. — *s.* die Parallele.

paralyse ['pærəlaiz], *v.a.* lähmen.

paralysis [pəˈrælisis], *s.* die Lähmung.

paramount ['pærəmaunt], *adj.* oberst.

paramour ['pærəmuə], *s.* der *or* die Geliebte.

451

parapet ['pærəpit], s. das Geländer, die Brüstung.

paraphrase ['pærəfreiz], s. die Umschreibung. — v.a. umschreiben.

parasite ['pærəsait], s. der Schmarotzer, Parasit.

parasol ['pærəsɔl], s. der Sonnenschirm.

parboil ['pɑːbɔil], v.a. aufkochen lassen.

parcel [pɑːsl], s. das Paket; Bündel (bundle). — v.a. — up, einpacken.

parch [pɑːtʃ], v.a. austrocknen.

parchment ['pɑːtʃmənt], s. das Pergament.

pardon [pɑːdn], v.a. vergeben, verzeihen (Dat.); begnadigen (Acc.) (give amnesty). — s. der Pardon, die Verzeihung; —!, I beg your —! bitte um Entschuldigung; I beg your —? wie bitte?

pare [pɛə], v.a. beschneiden (nails); schälen (fruit).

parent ['pɛərənt], s. der Vater, die Mutter, (pl.) die Eltern, pl.

parentage ['pɛərəntidʒ], s. die Abkunft, Herkunft.

parenthesis [pə'renθisis], s. die Parenthese, die Klammer.

parish ['pæriʃ], s. das Kirchspiel, die Gemeinde, die Pfarre.

parishioner [pə'riʃənə], s. das Gemeindemitglied.

Parisian [pə'riziən], adj. parisisch. — s. der Pariser.

park [pɑːk], s. der Park; (Motor.) der Wagenpark, Parkplatz. — v.a., v.n. parken.

parking ['pɑːkiŋ], s. (Motor.) das Parken; — meter, die Parkuhr, der Parkometer.

parley ['pɑːli], s. die Unterredung, Verhandlung. — v.n. verhandeln.

parliament ['pɑːləmənt], s. das Parlament.

parlour ['pɑːlə], s. das Wohnzimmer, die gute Stube; —maid, das Dienstmädchen; — trick, das Kunststück.

parochial [pə'roukiəl], adj. Pfarr-, Gemeinde-; (fig.) engstirnig.

parody ['pærədi], s. die Parodie. — v.a. parodieren.

parole [pə'roul], s. das Ehrenwort; (Mil.) das Losungswort.

paroxysm ['pærəksizm], s. der heftige Anfall.

parquet ['pɑːki], s. das Parkett; — floor, der Parkettfußboden.

parrot ['pærət], s. (Orn.) der Papagei.

parry ['pæri], v.a. parieren, abwehren.

parse [pɑːs, pɑːz], v.a. (Gram.) analysieren.

parsimony ['pɑːsiməni], s. die Sparsamkeit.

parsley ['pɑːsli], s. (Bot.) die Petersilie.

parson [pɑːsn], s. der Pastor, Pfarrer.

parsonage ['pɑːsənidʒ], s. das Pfarrhaus.

part [pɑːt], s. der Teil; Anteil (share); (Theat.) die Rolle; (Mus.) die Stimme;

(Geog.) die Gegend; for his —, seinerseits. — v.n. (with), sich trennen (von, Dat.); — company, auseinandergehen.

partake [pɑː'teik], v.n. teilnehmen, teilhaben (in, an, Dat.).

partial [pɑːʃl], adj. Teil-; parteiisch (subjective); —, to, eingenommen für.

participate [pɑː'tisipeit], v.n. teilnehmen (in, an, Dat.).

participation [pɑːtisi'peiʃən], s. die Teilnahme.

participle ['pɑːtisipl], s. (Gram.) das Mittelwort, Partizip(ium).

particle ['pɑːtikl], s. die Partikel, das Teilchen.

particular [pə'tikjulə], adj. besonder (special); einzel (individual); sonderbar (queer); ungewöhnlich; genau. — s. (pl.) die Details, n. pl., Einzelheiten, f. pl.

parting ['pɑːtiŋ], s. der Abschied (taking leave); der Scheitel (hair).

partisan [pɑːti'zæn], s. der Partisane, Parteigänger.

partition [pɑː'tiʃən], s. die Teilung (division); die Scheidewand (dividing wall). — v.a. teilen; aufteilen (divide up).

partly ['pɑːtli], adv. zum Teil, teils.

partner ['pɑːtnə], s. der Partner; Teilhaber (in business etc.).

partnership ['pɑːtnəʃip], s. die Partnerschaft.

partridge ['pɑːtridʒ], s. (Orn.) das Rebhuhn.

party ['pɑːti], s. (Pol.) die Partei; (Law) die Partei, Seite; die Gesellschaft, die Party (social gathering); throw or give a —, einen Gesellschaftsabend (or eine Party) geben; guilty —, der schuldige Teil; (Build.) — wall, die Brandmauer.

Paschal ['pɑːskəl], adj. Oster-.

pass [pɑːs], v.a. passieren; vorbeigehen (an, Dat.); durchlassen (let through); (Law) — sentence, das Urteil fällen. — v.n. fortgehen, vergehen, geschehen (happen); vorübergehen (of time); — for, gelten; (Sch.) durchkommen (exam); come to —, sich ereignen. — s. der Paß; (Theat.) die Freikarte.

passable ['pɑːsəbl], adj. gangbar; (fig.) leidlich, erträglich.

passage ['pæsidʒ], s. der Durchgang (thoroughfare); das Vergehen (of time); die Seereise; die Stelle (book).

passenger ['pæsindʒə], s. der Reisende, Passagier; — train, der Personenzug.

passer-by ['pɑːsəbai], s. der Passant, Vorübergehende.

passing ['pɑːsiŋ], s. das Vorbeigehen, das Vorübergehen; (Parl.) das Durchgehen; das Hinscheiden (death). — adj. vorübergehend, zeitweilig.

Passion ['pæsidʒ], s. (Eccl.) das Leiden; (Mus.) die Passion; — Week, die Karwoche; — flower, die Passionsblume.

passion ['pæʃən], s. die Leidenschaft;

fly into a —, aufbrausen.

passive ['pæsiv], *adj.* passiv. — *s.* (*Gram.*) das Passiv(um).

Passover ['pɑ:souvə], *s.* (*Rel.*) das Passahfest.

passport ['pɑ:spɔ:t], *s.* der Reisepaß.

past [pɑ:st], *adj.* vergangen. — *adv.* vorbei. — *prep.* nach (*time*). — *s.* die Vergangenheit; (*Gram.*) das Imperfekt, Präteritum.

paste [peist], *s.* die Paste, der Brei; der Kleister (*glue*). — *v.a.* kleben, kleistern.

pasteboard ['peistbɔ:d], *s.* die Pappe.

pastime ['pɑ:staim], *s.* der Zeitvertreib.

pastor ['pɑ:stə], *s.* (*Rel.*) der Seelsorger, Pfarrer.

pastoral ['pɑ:stərəl], *adj.* Hirten-, pastoral. — *s.* (*Poet*) das Hirtengedicht.

pastry ['peistri], *s.* (*Cul.*) die Pastete; das Gebäck; — *cook,* der Konditor, Zuckerbäcker.

pasture ['pɑ:stʃə], *s.* die Weide, das Grasland. — *v.n.* weiden, grasen.

pasty ['pɑ:sti, 'pæsti], *s.* (*Cul.*) die Pastete. — ['peisti], *adj.* teigig.

pat [pæt], *s.* der Klaps; der Schlag (*slap*). — *v.a.* leicht schlagen, streicheln (*gently*).

patch [pætʃ], *v.a.* flicken, ausbessern. — *s.* der Fleck (*mending material*); der Flecken (*land*); (*coll.*) no — *on him,* kein Vergleich mit ihm; nicht zu vergleichen mit ihm.

patent ['peitənt *or* 'pætənt], *adj.* offen, klar, patent; — *leather,* das Glanzleder. — *s.* das Patent.

patentee [peitən'ti:], *s.* der Patentinhaber.

paternal [pə'tə:nəl], *adj.* väterlich.

path [pɑ:θ], *s.* der Pfad, Weg, Fußsteig.

pathetic [pə'θetik], *adj.* pathetisch, rührend; armselig.

pathology [pə'θɔlədʒi], *s.* (*Med.*) die Pathologie.

pathway ['pɑ:θwei], *s.* der Fußweg, Fußsteig.

patience ['peiʃəns], *s.* die Geduld; die Patience (*card game*).

patient ['peiʃənt], *adj.* geduldig. — *s.* (*Med.*) der Patient.

patrician [pə'triʃən], *adj.* patrizisch. — *s.* der Patrizier.

patrimony ['pætrɪmənɪ], *s.* das (väterliche) Erbgut.

patriot ['peitriət, 'pætriət], *s.* der Patriot.

patriotism ['peitriətizm, 'pæt-], *s.* die Vaterlandsliebe, der Patriotismus.

patrol [pə'troul], *s.* die Patrouille, Streife. — *v.n.* auf Patrouille gehen.

patron ['peitrən], *s.* der Schutzherr, der Gönner; (*Comm.*) der Kunde; — *saint,* der Schutzheilige.

patronage ['pætrənidʒ], *s.* die Gönnerschaft, Huld.

patronize ['pætrənaiz], *v.a.* besuchen (*frequent*); begünstigen (*favour*).

patronizing ['pætrənaiziŋ], *adj.* herablassend.

patten [pætn], *s.* (*Archit.*) der Sockel; der Holzschuh (*clog*).

patter (1) ['pætə], *s.* das Geplätscher (*rain etc.*). — *v.n.* plätschern.

patter (2) ['pætə], *s.* das Geplauder (*chatter*). — *v.n.* schwätzen.

pattern ['pætən], *s.* das Muster; die Schablone (*in material*).

paucity ['pɔ:siti], *s.* die geringe Anzahl, der Mangel.

paunch [pɔ:ntʃ], *s.* der Wanst.

pauper ['pɔ:pə], *s.* der Arme.

pauperize ['pɔ:pəraiz], *v.a.* arm machen, verarmen lassen.

pause [pɔ:z], *s.* die Pause. — *v.n.* innehalten.

pave [peiv], *v.a.* pflastern.

pavement ['peivmənt], *s.* das Pflaster; der Bürgersteig, Gehsteig.

pavilion [pə'viljən], *s.* das Gartenhaus; der Pavillon.

paw [pɔ:], *s.* die Pfote; die Tatze. — *v.a.* streicheln, betasten.

pawn (1) [pɔ:n], *s.* das Pfand. — *v.a.* verpfänden.

pawn (2) [pɔ:n], *s.* (*Chess*) der Bauer.

pawnbroker ['pɔ:nbroukə], *s.* der Pfandleiher.

pay [pei], *v.a. irr.* zahlen; bezahlen, begleichen (*bill*); — *attention,* aufpassen, Aufmerksamkeit schenken; — *o.'s respects,* Respekt zollen. — *v.n.* sich bezahlt machen, sich lohnen (*it —s to . . .*). — *s.* (*Mil.*) der Sold; (*Comm.*) der Lohn (*wage*), die Bezahlung (*payment*).

payable ['peiəbl], *adj.* zahlbar, zu bezahlen.

payee [pei'i:], *s.* der Empfänger, Präsentant.

payer ['peiə], *s.* der Zahler; (*Comm.*) der Trassat.

payment ['peimənt], *s.* die Bezahlung, Begleichung (*of sum*).

pea [pi:], *s.* (*Bot.*) die Erbse (*see also* **peas**(**e**).

peace [pi:s], *s.* der Friede(n); die Ruhe (*restfulness*).

peaceable ['pi:səbl], *adj.* friedlich; friedliebend.

peaceful ['pi:sful], *adj.* friedlich, ruhig (*restful*).

peach [pi:tʃ], *s.* (*Bot.*) der *or* (*Austr.*) die Pfirsich.

peacock ['pi:kɔk], *s.* (*Orn.*) der Pfau.

peahen ['pi:hen], *s.* (*Orn.*) die Pfauhenne.

peak [pi:k], *s.* der Gipfel, die Spitze; der Schirm (*of cap*); — *hour,* die Stunde des Hochbetriebs, Hauptverkehrsstunde.

peal [pi:l], *v.a.* läuten. — *v.n.* erschallen. — *s.* das Läuten, Geläute.

peanut ['pi:nʌt], *s.* (*Bot.*) die Erdnuß.

pear [pɛə], *s.* (*Bot.*) die Birne.

pearl [pə:l], *s.* die Perle; — *barley,* die Perlgraupen, *f. pl.*; *mother of* —, die Perlmutter.

peasant ['pezənt], *s.* der Bauer.
peasantry ['pezəntri], *s.* das Bauern-volk, die Bauernschaft.
peas(e) [pi:z], *s. pl. pease pudding,* der Erbsenbrei, das Erbsenpüree.
peat [pi:t], *s.* der Torf.
pebble [pebl], *s.* der Kiesel(stein).
peck (1) [pek], *s.* der Viertelscheffel (=9 litres.)
peck (2) [pek], *s.* das Picken (*of hen*); (*coll.*) der Kuß. — *v.a.* hacken, hauen.
pecker ['pekə], *s.* die Picke, Haue; *keep your — up!* Mut bewahren!
peckish ['pekiʃ], *adj.* hungrig.
pectoral ['pektərəl], *adj.* Brust-. — *s.* das Brustmittel.
peculiar [pi'kju:liə], *adj.* eigenartig, eigentümlich (*strange*); — *to,* eigen (*Dat.*); besonder (*special*).
peculiarity [pikju:li'æriti], *s.* die Eigentümlichkeit, Eigenartigkeit.
pecuniary [pi'kju:niəri], *adj.* Geld-, geldlich, finanziell, pekuniär.
pedagogue ['pedəgɔg], *s.* der Pädagog(e), Erzieher.
pedal [pedl] *s.* das Pedal; (*Motor.*) der Fußhebel. — *v.n.* radfahren; (*coll.*) radeln.
pedant ['pedənt], *s.* der Pedant.
pedantic [pi'dæntik], *adj.* pedantisch.
pedantry ['pedəntri], *s.* die Pedanterie.
peddle [pedl], *v.a.* hausieren.
peddling ['pedliŋ], *adj.* kleinlich, unbedeutend.
pedestal ['pedistl], *s.* der Sockel.
pedestrian [pi'destriən], *s.* der Fußgänger. — *adj.* Fuß-, Fußgänger-.
pedigree ['pedigri:], *s.* der Stammbaum.
pediment ['pedimənt], *s.* (*Archit.*) der Ziergiebel.
pedlar ['pedlə], *s.* der Hausierer.
peel [pi:l], *s.* die Schale (*of fruit*). — *v.a.* schälen. — *v.n.* sich schälen.
peep [pi:p], *v.n.* gucken. — *s.* der (schnelle) Blick, das Gucken; — *show,* der Guckkasten.
peer (1) [piə], *s.* (*Parl.*) der Pair, Lord; der Ebenbürtige (*equal*).
peer (2) [piə], *v.n.* gucken, blicken, schauen.
peerage ['piəridʒ], *s.* der (Reichs)adel.
peeress ['piəres], *s.* die Gattin eines Pairs.
peerless ['piəlis], *adj.* unvergleichlich.
peevish ['pi:viʃ], *adj.* mürrisch.
pe(e)wit ['pi:wit], *s.* (*Orn.*) der Kiebitz.
peg ['peg], *s.* der Pflock (*stake*); der Holzstift (*in wall*); *clothes —,* die Wäscheklammer. — *v.a.* anpflocken (*to ground*).
pelican ['pelikən], *s.* (*Orn.*) der Pelikan.
pellet ['pelit], *s.* das Kügelchen.
pell-mell ['pel'mel], *adv.* durcheinander.
pelt (1) [pelt], *v.a.* — *with,* bewerfen mit, — *a person with,* werfen nach einem (*Acc.*). — *v.n.* strömen (*rain etc.*); rennen (*hasten*).
pelt (2) [pelt], *s.* der Pelz (*of animal*).

pen (1) [pen], *s. quill —,* die Feder; *fountain —,* die Füllfeder; *ballpoint —,* der Kugelschreiber. — *v.a.* schreiben; verfassen (*compose*).
pen (2) [pen], *s.* das Gehege. — *v.a.* einschliessen (*sheep*).
penal ['pi:nəl], *adj.* Straf-; — *servitude,* die Zuchthausstrafe.
penalize ['pi:nəlaiz], *v.a.* bestrafen.
penalty ['penəlti], *s.* die Strafe.
penance ['penəns], *s.* die Buße.
pence [pens] *see under* **penny.**
pencil ['pensl], *s.* der Bleistift; der Stift; (*Geom.*) der Strahl. — *v.a.* niederschreiben, notieren.
pendant ['pendənt], *s.* das Ohrgehänge; (*fig.*) das Gegenstück.
pendent ['pendənt], *adj.* hängend, schwebend.
pending ['pendiŋ], *adj.* in der Schwebe; unentschieden (*undecided*). — *prep.* während (*during*); bis (zu) (*until*).
pendulum ['pendjuləm], *s.* das Pendel.
penetrate ['penitreit], *v.a.* durchdringen.
peninsula [pi'ninsjulə], *s.* die Halbinsel.
penitent ['penitənt], *s.* der Büßer. — *adj.* bußfertig.
penitentiary [peni'tenʃəri], *s.* (*Am.*) das Zuchthaus (*prison*).
penknife ['pennaif], *s.* das Taschenmesser.
pennant ['penənt], *s.* der Wimpel, das Fähnchen.
penniless ['penilis], *adj.* mittellos, ohne einen Heller Geld, arm.
pennon ['penən] *see* **pennant.**
penny ['peni], *s.* (*pl.* **pence** [pens], **pennies** ['peniz]) der Penny; (*Am.*) das Centstück; — *farthing,* das Hochrad; — *whistle,* die Blechpfeife; *a pretty —,* hübsches Geld.
pension ['penʃən], *s.* die Pension; das Ruhegehalt. — *v.a.* (*off*) pensionieren, in den Ruhestand versetzen.
pensive ['pensiv], *adj.* nachdenklich.
Pentecost ['pentikɔst]. das *or* (*pl.*) die Pfingsten.
penthouse ['penthaus], *s.* das Wetterdach.
penurious [pi'njuəriəs], *adj.* unbemittelt, arm (*poor*); dürftig, karg (*meagre*).
penury ['penjuəri], *s.* die Not, Armut.
peony ['piəni], *s.* (*Bot.*) die Päonie, Pfingstrose.
people [pi:pl], *s. pl.* das Volk (*nation*); die Leute, Menschen (*pl.*). — *v.a.* bevölkern.
pepper ['pepə], *s.* der Pfeffer. — *v.a.* pfeffern.
per [pə:], *prep.* pro; per; durch; *as — account,* laut Rechnung.
peradventure [pə:rəd'ventʃə], *adv.* (*obs.*) von ungefähr; vielleicht (*perhaps*).
perambulator [pə'ræmbjuleitə] (*abbr. coll.*) **pram** [præm]), *s.* der Kinderwagen.

perceive [pə'si:v], *v.a.* wahrnehmen, merken.

percentage [pə'sentidʒ], *s.* der Prozentsatz (*of interest*); Prozente, *n. pl.*

perceptible [pə'septibl], *adj.* wahrnehmbar, merklich.

perception [pə'sepʃən], *s.* die Wahrnehmung, Empfindung.

perch (1) [pə:tʃ], *v.n.* aufsitzen; sitzen (*of birds*). — *s.* die Stange.

perch (2) [pə:tʃ], *s.* (*Zool.*) der Barsch.

perchance [pə'tʃɑ:ns], *adv.* vielleicht.

percolate ['pə:kəleit], *v.n.* durchsickern, durchtröpfeln.

percolator ['pə:kəleitə], *s.* die Kaffeemaschine.

percussion [pə'kʌʃən], *s.* (*Mus.*) das Schlagzeug.

peremptory ['perəmptəri, pə'remptəri], *adj.* entschieden, bestimmt (*decided*); absprechend.

perennial [pə'reniəl], *adj.* (*Bot.*) perennierend; Dauer-.

perfect ['pə:fikt], *adj.* vollkommen, vollendet, perfekt. — *s.* (*tense*) (*Gram.*) das Perfekt(um). — [pə'fekt], *v.a.* vollenden.

perfection [pə'fekʃən], *s.* die Vollendung, Vollkommenheit; *to* —, vollkommen.

perfidious [pə'fidiəs], *adj.* treulos, untreu; tückisch.

perfidy ['pə:fidi], *s.* die Treulosigkeit.

perforate ['pə:fəreit], *v.a.* durchlöchern, perforieren (*paper*); durchbohren (*pierce*).

perforce [pə'fɔ:s], *adv.* mit Gewalt, notgedrungen.

perform [pə'fɔ:m], *v.a.* ausführen (*carry out*); (*Theat.*) aufführen. — *v.n.* spielen, auftreten (*of actor*).

performance [pə'fɔ:məns], *s.* die Ausführung, Verrichtung (*execution of duty etc.*); (*Theat.*) die Aufführung.

perfume ['pə:fju:m], *s.* das Parfüm; der Duft (*scent*). — *v.a.* parfümieren.

perfunctory [pə'fʌŋktəri], *adj.* nachlässig, oberflächlich, flüchtig.

perhaps [pə'hæps], *adv.* vielleicht.

peril ['peril], *s.* die Gefahr.

period ['piəriəd], *s.* die Periode (*time*); der Zeitraum (*span*); (*Am.*) der Punkt (*full stop*).

periodical [piəri'ɔdikəl], *adj.* periodisch. — *s.* die Zeitschrift.

perish ['periʃ], *v.n.* zugrunde gehen, umkommen.

perishable ['periʃəbl], *adj.* vergänglich; (leicht) verderblich (*of food*).

periwig ['periwig], *s.* die Perücke.

periwinkle (1) ['periwiŋkl], *s.* (*Zool.*) die Uferschnecke.

periwinkle (2) ['periwiŋkl], (*Bot.*) das Immergrün.

perjure ['pə:dʒə], *v.r.* meineidig werden.

perjurer ['pə:dʒərə], *s.* der Meineidige.

perjury ['pə:dʒəri], *s.* der Meineid.

permanence, permanency ['pə:mə-nəns, 'pə:mənənsi], *s.* die Dauer, Beständigkeit.

permanent ['pə:mənənt], *adj.* Dauer-, dauerhaft, beständig; — *wave*, die Dauerwelle.

permeability [pə:miə'biliti], *s.* die Durchdringbarkeit, Durchlässigkeit.

permeable ['pə:miəbl], *adj.* durchdringlich.

permeate ['pə:mieit], *v.a.* durchdringen.

permissible [pə'misibl], *adj.* zulässig, statthaft.

permission [pə'miʃən], *s.* die Erlaubnis.

permit [pə'mit], *v.a.* zulassen, erlauben; — ['pə:mit], *s.* die Erlaubnis; (*official*) die Genehmigung.

permutation [pə:mju'teiʃən], *s.* (*Maths.*) die Permutation.

pernicious [pə'niʃəs], *adj.* verderblich, schädlich, bösartig.

perorate ['perəreit], *v.n.* eine (lange) Rede beschließen.

perpendicular [pə:pən'dikjulə], *adj.* senkrecht. — *s.* die Senkrechte.

perpetrate ['pə:pitreit], *v.a.* begehen (*commit*).

perpetration [pə:pi'treiʃən], *s.* die Verübung, Begehung.

perpetrator ['pə:pitreitə], *s.* der Begeher, Täter.

perpetual [pə'petjuəl], *adj.* (an-)dauernd; ewig.

perpetuate [pə'petjueit], *v.a.* verewigen.

perpetuity [pə:pi'tju:iti], *s.* die Ewigkeit.

perplex [pə'pleks], *v.a.* bestürzen, verblüffen.

perplexity [pə'pleksiti], *s.* die Bestürzung, Verwirrung.

persecute ['pə:sikju:t], *v.a.* verfolgen.

persecution [pə:si'kju:ʃən], *s.* die Verfolgung.

perseverance [pə:si'viərəns], *s.* die Ausdauer, Beharrlichkeit.

persevere [pə:si'viə], *v.n.* beharren (*in*, *bei*, *Dat.*).

Persian ['pə:ʃən], *adj.* persisch. — *s.* der Perser.

persist [pə'sist], *v.n.* beharren (*in*, auf, *Dat.*).

persistence [pə'sistəns], *s.* die Beharrlichkeit.

person ['pə:sən], *s.* die Person; *in* —, persönlich.

personal ['pə:sənəl], *adj.* persönlich.

personality [pə:sə'næliti], *s.* die Persönlichkeit.

personify [pə'sɔnifai], *v.a.* verkörpern.

personnel [pə:sə'nel], *s.* das Personal; (*Comm.*) — *manager*, der Personalchef.

perspective [pə'spektiv], *s.* die Perspektive. — *adj.* perspektivisch.

perspicacious [pə:spi'keiʃəs], *adj.* scharfsichtig, scharfsinnig.

perspicacity [pə:spi'kæsiti], *s.* der Scharfblick, Scharfsinn.

perspicuity [pə:spi'kju:iti], *s.* die Durchsichtigkeit, Klarheit.

455

perspicuous

perspicuous [pə'spikjuəs], *adj.* deutlich, klar.
perspiration [pə:spi'reiʃən], *s.* der Schweiß.
perspire [pə'spaiə], *v.n.* schwitzen.
persuade [pə'sweid], *v.a.* überreden.
persuasion [pə'sweiʒən], *s.* die Überredung.
persuasive [pə'sweiziv], *adj.* überzeugend, überredend.
pert [pə:t], *adj.* naseweis, keck.
pertain [pə'tein], *v.n.* (an)gehören (*to Dat.*).
pertinacious [pə:ti'neiʃəs], *adj.* beharrlich, halsstarrig.
pertinacity [pə:ti'næsiti], *s.* die Beharrlichkeit, Halsstarrigkeit.
pertinence, pertinency ['pə:tinəns, 'pə:tinənsi], *s.* die Angemessenheit.
pertinent ['pə:tinənt], *adj.* angemessen, passend.
pertness ['pə:tnis], *s.* die Keckheit, der Vorwitz.
perturb [pə'tə:b], *v.a.* verwirren, stören, beunruhigen.
perturbation [pə:tə'beiʃən], *s.* die Verwirrung, Störung, Beunruhigung.
peruke [pə'ru:k], *s.* die Perücke.
peruse [pə'ru:z], *v.a.* durchlesen.
Peruvian [pə'ru:viən], *adj.* peruanisch. — *s.* der Peruaner.
pervade [pə'veid], *v.a.* durchdringen.
perverse [pə'və:s], *adj.* verkehrt.
perversion [pə'və:ʃən], *s.* die Perversion.
perversity [pə'və:siti], *s.* die Verdorbenheit, Widernatürlichkeit.
pervert [pə'və:t], *v.a.* verkehren, verderben. — ['pə:və:t], *s.* der Verdorbene, der perverse Mensch.
perverted [pə'və:tid], *adj.* pervers (*sexually*).
pervious ['pə:viəs], *adj.* zugänglich, passierbar; durchlässig.
pessimist ['pesimist], *s.* der Pessimist.
pest [pest], *s.* (*Med.*) die Pest; (*fig.*) die Plage.
pester ['pestə], *v.a.* quälen, auf die Nerven gehen (*Dat.*).
pestiferous [pes'tifərəs], *adj.* verpestend.
pestilence ['pestiləns], *s.* (*Med.*) die Pest, Seuche.
pestle [pesl], *s.* die Mörserkeule.
pet [pet], *s.* das Haustier; der Liebling; — *name*, der Kosename. — *v.a.* liebkosen, streicheln.
petition [pi'tiʃən], *s.* die Bittschrift. — *v.a.* mit einer Bittschrift herantreten an (*Acc.*).
petrel ['petrəl], *s.* (*Orn.*) der Sturmvogel.
petrification [petrifi'keiʃən], *s.* die Versteinerung.
petrify ['petrifai], *v.a.* versteinern; (*fig.*) starr machen, bestürzen; *petrified with fright*, starr vor Entsetzen. — *v.n.* zu Stein werden.
petrol ['petrəl], *s.* das Benzin; (*crude oil*) das Petroleum; — *station*, die Tankstelle.

petticoat ['petikout], *s.* der Unterrock.
pettifogging ['petifɔgiŋ], *adj.* Winkel-, kleinlich, schikanös (*petty*).
pettiness ['petinis], *s.* die Kleinlichkeit.
pettish ['petiʃ], *adj.* verdrießlich.
petty ['peti], *adj.* klein, gering, kleinlich.
petulance ['petjuləns], *s.* die Launenhaftigkeit, Gereiztheit.
petulant ['petjulənt], *adj.* launenhaft.
pew [pju:], *s.* (*Eccl.*) der Kirchensitz; (*coll.*) der Sitz, Stuhl.
pewit ['pi:wit] *see* **pe(e)wit**.
pewter ['pju:tə], *s.* das Zinn; die Zinnwaren, *f. pl.* (*wares*).
pewterer ['pju:tərə], *s.* der Zinngießer.
phantom ['fæntəm], *s.* das Phantom, Trugbild; das Gespenst (*ghost*).
Pharisee ['færisi], *s.* der Pharisäer.
pharmaceutical [fɑ:mə'sju:tikəl], *adj.* pharmazeutisch.
pharmacy ['fɑ:məsi], *s.* die Apothekerkunst (*dispensing*); die Apotheke (*dispensary*); die Pharmazeutik (*discipline*).
phase [feiz], *s.* die Phase.
pheasant ['fezənt], *s.* (*Orn.*) der Fasan.
phenomenal [fi'nɔminəl], *adj.* außerordentlich, phänomenal.
phenomenon [fi'nɔminən], *s.* das Phänomen.
phial ['faiəl], *s.* die Phiole, das Fläschchen.
philanthropist [fi'lænθrəpist], *s.* der Philanthrop.
philanthropy [fi'lænθrəpi], *s.* die Philanthropie.
philatelist [fi'lætəlist], *s.* der Philatelist, Markensammler.
philately [fi'lætəli], *s.* das Markensammeln, die Philatelie, Briefmarkenkunde.
Philippine ['filipi:n], *adj.* philippinisch.
Philistine ['filistain], *s.* der Philister; (*fig.*) der Spießbürger.
philologist [fi'lɔlədʒist], *s.* der Philologe.
philology [fi'lɔlədʒi], *s.* die Philologie.
philosopher [fi'lɔsəfə], *s.* der Philosoph.
philosophize [fi'lɔsəfaiz], *v.n.* philosophieren.
philosophy [fi'lɔsəfi], *s.* die Philosophie.
phlegm [flem], *s.* das Phlegma (*mood*); (*Med.*) der Schleim.
phlegmatic [fleg'mætik], *adj.* phlegmatisch, gelassen.
phone [foun] *see under* **telephone**.
phonetics [fə'netiks], *s.* die Phonetik.
phosphorescent [fɔsfə'resənt], *adj.* phosphoreszierend, leuchtend.
phosphorus ['fɔsfərəs], *s.* (*Chem.*) der Phosphor.
photograph ['foutəgræf *or* -grɑ:f], *s.* die Photographie, das Lichtbild (*picture*). — *v.a.* photographieren, aufnehmen, (*coll.*) knipsen.
photographer [fə'tɔgrəfə], *s.* der Photograph.

photography [fə'tɔgrəfi], s. die Photographie.

phrase [freiz], s. die Phrase. — v.a. phrasieren, fassen, ausdrücken.

phrenology [fre'nɔlədʒi], s. die Phrenologie, Schädellehre.

phthisis ['θaisis], s. (Med.) die Schwindsucht.

physic ['fizik], s. (obs.) die Medizin, Arznei.

physical ['fizikəl], adj. körperlich (bodily); physikalisch (of physics).

physician [fi'ziʃən], s. der Arzt.

physics ['fiziks], s. die Physik.

physiognomy [fizi'ɔnəmi or -'ɔgnəmi], s. die Physiognomie, die Gesichtsbildung.

physiologist [fizi'ɔlədʒist], s. der Physiolog.

physiology [fizi'ɔlədʒi], s. die Physiologie.

piano(forte) ['pjænou('fɔːti)], s. das Klavier.

pick [pik], v.a. pflücken (flowers); hacken (hack); — up, auflesen; auswählen (select); gewaltsam öffnen (a lock); anfangen (a quarrel). — v.n. why — on me? warum gerade mich auswählen? — s. die Picke, Spitzhacke (axe); die Auswahl; — of the bunch, (coll.) das Beste von allen.

picket ['pikit], s. die Wache; der Streikposten (of strikers); der Pflock (wood). — v.a. bewachen. — v.n. Wache stehen.

pickle [pikl], s. (Cul.) der Pökel, das Gepökelte; (coll.) die unangenehme Lage (calamity). — v.a. einpökeln.

pickpocket ['pikpɔkit], s. der Taschendieb.

picnic ['piknik], s. das Picknick. — v.n. picknicken.

pictorial [pik'tɔːriəl], adj. illustriert.

picture ['piktʃə], s. das Bild; — book, das Bilderbuch; — postcard, die Ansichtskarte; pretty as a —, bildhübsch; der Film; (pl.) das Kino. — v.a. sich vorstellen.

picturesque [piktʃə'resk], adj. pittoresk, malerisch.

pie [pai], s. (Cul.) die Pastete (savoury); das Törtchen (sweet).

piebald ['paibɔːld], adj. scheckig. — s. der Schecke (horse).

piece [piːs], s. das Stück. — v.a. — together, zusammenflicken (mend), zusammensetzen (compose).

piecemeal ['piːsmiːl], adv. stückweise.

pied [paid] see piebald.

pier [piə], s. der Hafendamm; der Pfeiler (column).

pierce [piəs], v.a. durchstechen, durchbohren.

pierglass ['piəglɑːs], s. der Pfeilerspiegel.

piety ['paiəti], s. die Pietät, Frömmigkeit.

pig [pig], s. (Zool.) das Schwein.

pigeon ['pidʒən], s. (Orn.) die Taube.

pigeonhole ['pidʒənhoul], s. das Fach.

pigheaded [pig'hedid], adj. starrköpfig, dickköpfig.

piglet ['piglit], s. (Zool.) das Ferkel.

pigment ['pigmənt], s. das Pigment, der (natürliche) Farbstoff.

pigtail ['pigteil], s. der Haarzopf.

pike [paik], s. (Zool.) der Hecht; die Pike (weapon).

pile (1) [pail], s. der Haufen, Stoß (paper). — v.a. aufhäufen.

pile (2) [pail], s. (Archit.) der Pfahl; Pfeiler (stone).

pile (3) [pail], s. (Text.) der Teppichflausch (carpet), die Noppe (cloth).

piles [pailz], s. pl. (Med. coll.) die Haemorrhoiden, pl.

pilfer ['pilfə], v.a. stehlen, mausen.

pilferer ['pilfərə], s. der Dieb.

pilgrim ['pilgrim], s. der Pilger.

pill [pil], s. (Med.) die Pille.

pillage ['pilidʒ], s. die Plünderung. — v.a. ausplündern.

pillar ['pilə], s. der Pfeiler, die Säule; — box, der Briefkasten.

pillion ['piljən], s. der zweite Sitz, Sozius (motorcycle).

pillory ['piləri], s. der Pranger. — v.a. anprangern.

pillow ['pilou], s. das Kopfkissen.

pilot ['pailət], s. der Pilot; (Naut.) der Lotse. — v.a. (Aviat.) steuern, (Naut.) lotsen.

pimento [pi'mentou], s. (Bot.) der Jamaikapfeffer.

pimp [pimp], s. der Kuppler.

pimple [pimpl], s. der Pickel; (pl.) der Ausschlag.

pin [pin], s. die Stecknadel; (Engin.) der Bolzen, Stift; (skittles) der Kegel. — v.a. — down, festlegen.

pinafore ['pinəfɔː], s. die Schürze, Kinderschürze.

pincers ['pinsəz], s. pl. die Kneifzange, Zange.

pinch [pintʃ], v.a. kneifen, zwicken; (coll.) klauen, stehlen. — v.n. sparen, darben. — s. die Prise (tobacco); at a —, wenn es sein muß.

pine (1) [pain], s. (Bot.) die Kiefer, Föhre.

pine (2) [pain], v.n. — for, schmachten (nach, Dat.), sich sehnen.

pineapple ['painæpl], s. (Bot.) die Ananas.

pinion ['pinjən], s. der Flügel (wing); (Poet.) die Schwinge; (Mech.) das Zahnrad; — shaft, die Ritzelwelle; — spindle, die Zahnradwelle. — v.a. binden, fesseln.

pink [piŋk], adj. rosa. — s. (Bot.) die (rosa) Nelke; (Hunt.) der (rote) Jagdrock; in the — (of condition), in bester Gesundheit, in bester Form.

pinnacle ['pinəkl], s. die Zinne, Spitze; (fig.) der Gipfel.

pint [paint], s. die Pinte (0.57 litre); (beer) der Schoppen.

pioneer [paiə'niə], s. der Pionier. — v.a. bahnbrechend sein, bahnen.

pious ['paiəs], adj. fromm.

pip [pip], *s.* der Obstkern; (*Mil. coll.*) der Leutnantsstern.
pipe [paip], *s.* die Pfeife; (*Engin.*) das Rohr; die Röhre; (*Mus.*) die Pfeife. — *v.a.* pfeifen; durch Rohre leiten.
piping ['paipiŋ], *adj.* — *hot*, kochend heiß.
pipkin ['pipkin], *s.* das Töpfchen.
piquant ['pi:kənt], *adj.* pikant; scharf (*taste*).
pique [pi:k], *s.* der Groll. — *v.a.* reizen.
piracy ['pairəsi], *s.* die Seeräuberei.
pirate ['pairit], *s.* der Pirat, Seeräuber. — [pai'reit], *v.a.* (*fig.*) plagieren, ohne Erlaubnis drucken (*books*).
pistil ['pistil], *s.* (*Bot.*) der Stempel.
pistol ['pistəl], *s.* die Pistole.
piston ['pistən], *s.* (*Mech.*) der Kolben.
pit [pit], *s.* die Grube; (*Min.*) der Schacht, das Bergwerk; (*Theat., Mus.*) der Orchesterraum; (*Theat.*) das Parterre.
pitch (1) [pitʃ], *s.* der Grad, Gipfel (*height*); (*Mus.*) der Ton, die Tonhöhe (*level*); (*Sport*) das Spielfeld. — *v.a.* werfen; feststecken; (*Mus.*) stimmen; befestigen; (*tent*) (ein Zelt) aufschlagen; — *in*, sich ins Zeug legen.
pitch (2) [pitʃ], *s.* das Pech (*tar*); — *dark*, pechschwarz.
pitchblende ['pitʃblend], *s.* die Pechblende.
pitcher ['pitʃə], *s.* der Krug.
pitchfork ['pitʃfɔ:k], *s.* die Heugabel.
piteous ['pitiəs], *adj.* erbärmlich.
pitfall ['pitfɔ:l], *s.* die Falle.
pith [piθ], *s.* das Mark; (*fig.*) der Kern, das Wesentliche; die Kraft (*strength*).
pithy ['piθi], *adj.* markig, kräftig; prägnant.
pitiable ['pitiəbl], *adj.* erbärmlich.
pitiful ['pitiful], *adj.* erbärmlich (*pitiable*); mitleidig (*sympathetic*).
pitiless ['pitilis], *adj.* erbarmungslos, grausam.
pittance ['pitəns], *s.* der Hungerlohn, das Bißchen, die Kleinigkeit.
pity ['piti], *s.* das Mitleid. — *v.a.* bemitleiden, bedauern.
pivot ['pivət], *s.* (*Mech.*) der Drehpunkt, Zapfen; (*fig.*) der Mittelpunkt, Angelpunkt. — *v.n.* zum Mittelpunkt haben, sich drehen (um).
placard ['plækɑ:d], *s.* das Plakat.
placate [plə'keit], *v.a.* versöhnen.
place [pleis], *s.* der Platz, Ort, die Stelle; — *name*, der Ortsname; (*rank*) der Rang, die Rangstufe. — *v.a.* plazieren (*in a job*); legen, setzen, stellen; — *an order*, einen Auftrag geben.
placid ['plæsid], *adj.* gelassen, sanft, gutmütig.
plagiarism ['pleidʒiərizm], *s.* das Plagiat, das Plagiieren.
plague [pleig], *s.* (*Med.*) die Pest, Seuche; (*fig.*) die Plage. — *v.a.* belästigen, plagen.
plaice [pleis], *s.* (*Zool.*) die Scholle.
plain [plein], *s.* die Ebene, Fläche. — *adj.* eben, flach (*even*); schlicht,

einfach, klar; — *dealing*, ehrliche Handlungsweise; — *speaking*, offenes Sprechen, aufrichtiges Reden; (*Mus.*) — *song*, der einstimmige Chorgesang, die gregorianische Kirchenmusik.
plaintiff ['pleintif], *s.* (*Law*) der Kläger.
plaintive ['pleintiv], *adj.* klagend.
plait [plæt], *s.* der Zopf, die Flechte. — *v.a.* flechten (*hair*); falten.
plan [plæn], *s.* der Plan, Grundriß. — *v.a.* planen, entwerfen.
plane (1) [plein], *v.a.* hobeln (*wood*). — *s.* die Fläche (*surface*); die Stufe (*level*); (*coll.*) das Flugzeug (*aeroplane*).
plane (2) *see* **plane-tree.**
planet ['plænit], *s.* (*Astron.*) der Planet.
plane-tree ['pleintri:], *s.* (*Bot.*) die Platane.
planish ['plæniʃ], *v.a.* (*woodwork*) polieren, glätten.
plank [plæŋk], *s.* die Planke; (*Pol.*) der Programmpunkt.
plant [plɑ:nt], *s.* (*Bot.*) die Pflanze; (*Ind.*) die Anlage, der Betrieb. — *v.a.* anpflanzen, anlegen; — *suspicion*, Verdacht einflößen (*of, against*, gegen, *Acc.*).
plantain ['plæntein], *s.* (*Bot.*) der Wegerich; (*fruit*) der Pisang.
plantation [plæn'teiʃən], *s.* die Pflanzung, Plantage.
plaster ['plɑ:stə], *s.* das Pflaster (*adhesive*); (*Build.*) der Mörtel, der Mauerbewurf; — *cast*, der Gipsabdruck; — *of Paris*, der Stuck, der feine Gipsmörtel. — *v.a.* bepflastern, verputzen; (*fig.*) dick auftragen.
plastic ['plæstik], *adj.* plastisch; (*malleable*) formbar; — *surgery*, plastische Chirurgie. — *s.* der Kunststoff.
Plate, River [pleit, 'rivə]. der La Plata Strom.
plate [pleit], *s.* der Teller (*dish*), die Platte, Scheibe; (*coll.*) — *glass*, das Spiegelglas; das Geschirr (*service of crockery*); *gold* —, das Goldgeschirr. — *v.a.* überziehen, versilbern, verchromen.
platform ['plætfɔ:m], *s.* (*Railw.*) der Bahnsteig; die Bühne, das Podium.
platinum ['plætinəm], *s.* das Platin.
platitude ['plætitju:d], *s.* die Plattheit, der Gemeinplatz.
platitudinous [plæti'tju:dinəs], *adj.* nichtssagend.
platoon [plə'tu:n], *s.* (*Mil.*) der Zug.
plaudit ['plɔ:dit], *s.* der Beifall.
plausible ['plɔ:zibl], *adj.* wahrscheinlich, glaubwürdig, einleuchtend.
play [plei], *s.* das Spiel (*game*); (*Theat.*) das Stück. — *v.a., v.n.* spielen.
player ['pleiə], *s.* der Spieler; (*Theat.*) der Schauspieler.
playful ['pleiful], *adj.* spielerisch, spielend.
playground ['pleigraund], *s.* der Spielplatz.
playhouse ['pleihaus], *s.* das Schauspielhaus.

playmate ['pleimeit], s. der Spielgefährte.

playwright ['pleirait], s. der Dramatiker, Schauspieldichter.

plea [pli:], s. die Bitte; das Gesuch; der Vorwand.

plead [pli:d], v.a., v.n. plädieren, sich berufen auf; vorschützen (claim).

pleasant ['plezənt], adj. angenehm, freundlich.

pleasantry ['plezəntri], s. das freundliche Wort, der Scherz (joke).

please [pli:z], v.a., v.n. gefallen; einen Gefallen tun (do a favour); —! bitte, haben Sie die Güte!; if you —, wenn Sie nichts dagegen haben.

pleasing ['pli:ziŋ], adj. einnehmend, angenehm.

pleasure ['pleʒə], s. das Vergnügen; at your —, nach Belieben; take — in, Vergnügen finden an (Dat.).

pleat [pli:t], v.a. plissieren. — s. die Falte, das Plissee.

pledge [pledʒ], s. das Pfand, die Bürgschaft (guarantee); das Versprechen (promise). — v.a. sich verbürgen, versprechen; zutrinken (drink to).

plenary ['pli:nəri], adj. Plenar-, vollständig.

plenipotentiary [plenipo'tenʃəri], s. der Bevollmächtigte.

plenitude ['plenitju:d], s. die Fülle.

plenteous, plentiful ['plentiəs, 'plentiful], adj. reichlich, in Fülle.

plenty ['plenti], s. die Fülle.

pleurisy ['pluərəsi], s. (Med.) die Brustfellentzündung.

pliable, pliant ['plaiəbl, 'plaiənt], adj. geschmeidig, biegsam.

pliers ['plaiəz], s. pl. die Drahtzange.

plight (1) [plait], s. die Notlage.

plight (2) [plait], v.a. feierlich versprechen.

plod [plɔd], v.n. schwerfällig gehen (walk); sich plagen (work hard).

plot (1) [plɔt], s. das Stück Land, der Bauplatz.

plot (2) [plɔt], s. das Komplott, die Verschwörung; die Handlung (book, play etc.). — v.a. aushecken (ambush etc.), planen.

plough, plow [plau], s. der Pflug. — v.a. pflügen; (coll.) be —ed, durchfallen (in, in, Dat.).

ploughshare ['plauʃeə], s. die Pflugschar.

plover ['plʌvə], s. (Orn.) der Kiebitz, Regenpfeifer.

plow see under **plough**.

pluck (1) [plʌk], v.a. pflücken (flowers); rupfen (feathers); — up courage, Mut fassen.

pluck (2) [plʌk], s. (coll.) der Mut.

plucky ['plʌki], adj. mutig.

plug [plʌg], s. (Elec.) der Stecker; der Stöpsel (stopper); sparking —, (Motor.) die Zündkerze. — v.a. stöpseln, zustopfen (block); (fig.) betonen, herausstellen (repeat for advertisement).

plum [plʌm], s. (Bot.) die Pflaume; (coll.) das Beste.

plumage ['plu:midʒ], s. (Orn.) das Gefieder.

plumb [plʌm], s. das Senkblei, Lot; — -rule, die Senkwaage. — adv. · senkrecht, gerade, lotrecht.

plume [plu:m], s. die (Schmuck) feder.

plump [plʌmp], adj. dick, drall.

plunder ['plʌndə], v.a., v.n. plündern. — s. die Beute, der Raub.

plunge [plʌndʒ], v.a., v.n. untertauchen, stoßen, hinabstürzen.

plunger ['plʌndʒə], s. der Taucher; (Engin.) der Tauchkolben.

pluperfect [plu:'pə:fikt], s. (Gram.) das Plusquamperfektum.

plural ['pluərəl], s. (Gram.) der Plural, die Mehrzahl.

plurality [pluə'ræliti], s. die Mehrzahl, der Plural.

plus [plʌs], prep. plus, zuzüglich.

plush [plʌʃ], s. (Text.) der Plüsch.

ply [plai], s. die Falte (fold), Lage (layer). — v.a. ausüben (trade).

plywood ['plaiwud], s. das Sperrholz, die Sperrholzplatte.

pneumonia [nju'mouniə], s. (Med.) die Lungenentzündung.

poach (1) [poutʃ], v.n. wildern; — on, übergreifen auf.

poach (2) [poutʃ], v.a. ohne Schale kochen; poached eggs, verlorene Eier, n. pl.

poacher ['poutʃə], s. der Wilderer, Wilddieb.

pocket ['pɔkit], s. die Tasche; — book, die Brieftasche; das Taschenbuch; — money, das Taschengeld.

pod [pɔd], s. (Bot.) die Schote.

poem ['pouim], s. das Gedicht.

poet ['pouit], s. der Dichter.

poetic(al) [pou'etik(l)], adj. dichterisch.

poignancy ['pɔinjənsi], s. die Schärfe.

poignant ['pɔinjənt], adj. scharf, beißend, schmerzlich.

point [pɔint], s. der Punkt (of remark, sentence); die Sache; der Zweck; die Spitze (of pencil etc.); make a —, es sich zur Aufgabe machen; in — of fact, tatsächlich; come to the —, zur Sache kommen. — v.a., v.n. spitzen, zuspitzen (pencil); — out, zeigen, (hin)deuten; — to, hinweisen auf; — the moral, die Moral erklären.

pointblank ['pɔint'blæŋk], adj., adv. schnurgerade, direkt.

pointed ['pɔintid], adj. scharf, spitzig, deutlich (remark).

pointer ['pɔintə], s. der Zeiger; (fig.) der Fingerzeig (hint).

poise [pɔiz], s. das Gleichgewicht; (fig.) angemessenes Benehmen, die Grazie. — v.a. abwägen; im Gleichgewicht halten. — v.n. schweben; —d for action, tatbereit.

poison [pɔizn], s. das Gift. — v.a. vergiften.

459

poke

poke (1) [pouk], *v.a.* schüren (*fire*); stoßen; — *fun at*, sich lustig machen über. — *s.* der Stoß; — *in the ribs*, ein Rippenstoß.

poke (2) [pouk], *s.* der Sack; *a pig in a* —, die Katze im Sack.

poker (1) ['poukə], *s.* der Schürhaken, das Schüreisen.

poker (2) ['poukə], *s.* (*Cards*) das Pokerspiel.

polar ['poulə], *adj.* (*Geog.*) Polar-; (*Phys.*) polar.

polarity [po'læriti], *s.* die Polarität.

Pole [poul], *s.* der Pole.

pole (1) [poul], *s.* (*Geog.*) der Pol.

pole (2) [poul], *s.* die Stange (*rod*); der Pfahl (*upright*).

poleaxe ['poulæks], *s.* die Streitaxt.

polecat ['poulkæt], *s.* (*Zool.*) der Iltis.

polemic [pə'lemik], *s.* die Polemik, der Streit.

police [pə'li:s], *s.* die Polizei. — *v.a.* polizeilich beaufsichtigen.

policeman [pə'li:smən], *s.* der Polizist.

policy (1) ['polisi], *s.* die Politik.

policy (2) ['polisi], *s.* (*Insurance*) die Police.

Polish ['pouliʃ], *adj.* polnisch.

polish ['poliʃ], *v.a.* polieren. — *s.* die Politur, der Glanz.

polished ['poliʃd], *adj.* glatt (*smooth*); (*fig.*) wohlerzogen, fein (*manners*).

polite [pə'lait], *adj.* höflich.

politeness [pə'laitnis], *s.* die Höflichkeit.

politic ['politik], *adj.* politisch; schlau (*cunning*).

political [pə'litikəl], *adj.* politisch; staatskundig.

politician [poli'tiʃən], *s.* der Politiker, Staatsmann.

politics ['politiks], *s.* (*sometimes pl.*) die Politik, politische Gesinnung.

poll [poul], *s.* die Wahl (*election*). — *v.n.* abstimmen, wählen, seine Stimme abgeben.

pollard ['poləd], *s.* (*Bot.*) der gekappte Baum; (*Zool.*) das hornlose Tier.

pollen ['polən], *s.* (*Bot.*) der Blütenstaub.

pollinate ['polineit], *v.a.* (*Bot.*) bestäuben.

polling ['pouliŋ], *s.* die Wahl, der Wahlgang (*election*); — *station*, das Wahllokal.

pollute [pə'lju:t], *v.a.* verunreinigen.

pollution [pə'lju:ʃən], *s.* die Verunreinigung.

poltroon [pol'tru:n], *s.* die Memme.

poly- ['poli], *pref.* viel-.

Polynesian [poli'ni:ziən], *adj.* polynesisch. — *s.* der Polynesier.

polytechnic [poli'teknik], *s.* das Technikum; polytechnische Fachschule.

pomegranate ['pom-, 'pʌmgrænit], *s.* (*Bot.*) der Granatapfel.

Pomeranian [pomə'reiniən], *adj.* pommerisch. — *s.* der Pommer; der Spitz (*dog*).

pommel [pʌml], *s.* der Sattelknopf; der Knauf (*sword*). — *v.a.* schlagen.

pomp [pomp], *s.* der Pomp, das Gepränge.

pompous ['pompəs], *adj.* hochtrabend, prahlerisch; (*manner*) schwerfällig, wichtigtuerisch.

pond [pond], *s.* der Teich.

ponder ['pondə], *v.a.*, *v.n.* bedenken, überlegen.

ponderous ['pondərəs], *adj.* schwer, schwerfällig.

pontiff ['pontif], *s.* der Hohepriester; der Papst.

pontifical [pon'tifikəl], *adj.* bischöflich, päpstlich. — *s. pl.* die bischöfliche Amtstracht.

pontificate [pon'tifikit], *s.* das (*or* der) Pontifikat. — [-keit], *v.n.* (*coll.*) predigen.

pontoon (1) [pon'tu:n], *s.* die Schiffsbrücke, der Brückenkahn.

pontoon (2) [pon'tu:n], *s.* (*cards*) das Einundzwanzig, Vingt-et-un.

pony ['pouni], *s.* (*Zool.*) der *or* das Pony.

poodle [pu:dl], *s.* (*Zool.*) der Pudel.

pooh-pooh [pu:'pu:], *v.a.* verspotten.

pool (1) [pu:l], *s.* die Lache, der Pfuhl.

pool (2) [pu:l], *s.* (*fig.*) der gemeinsame Einsatz (*money, forces etc.*). — *v.a.* zusammenschließen.

poop [pu:p], *s.* (*Naut.*) das Heck, Hinterteil.

poor [puə], *adj.* arm, dürftig; *in* — *health*, bei schwacher Gesundheit; (*fig.*) armselig, schlecht.

pop [pop], *v.n.* knallen, explodieren. — *v.a.* (*coll.*) schnell versetzen, verpfänden.

Pope [poup], *s.* (*Eccl.*) der Papst.

poplar ['poplə], *s.* (*Bot.*) die Pappel.

poppy ['popi], *s.* (*Bot.*) der Mohn.

populace ['popjulis], *s.* der Pöbel.

popular ['popjulə], *adj.* volkstümlich, beliebt.

popularity [popju'læriti], *s.* die Beliebtheit.

populate ['popjuleit], *v.a.* bevölkern.

population [popju'leiʃən], *s.* die Bevölkerung.

populous ['popjuləs], *adj.* dicht bevölkert.

porcelain ['po:slin], *s.* das Porzellan, das Geschirr.

porch [po:tʃ], *s.* die Eingangshalle, Vorhalle.

porcupine ['po:kjupain], *s.* (*Zool.*) das Stachelschwein.

pore (1) [po:], *s.* die Pore.

pore (2) [po:], *v.n.* sich vertiefen (*over, in*), brüten (*über*).

pork [po:k], *s.* das Schweinefleisch.

porosity [po:'rositi], *s.* die Porosität.

porous ['po:rəs], *adj.* porös.

porpoise ['po:pəs], *s.* (*Zool.*) der Tümmler, das Meerschwein.

porridge ['poridʒ], *s.* (*Cul.*) der Haferbrei.

porringer ['porindʒə], *s.* (*Cul.*) der Napf.

port (1) [po:t], *s.* der Hafen.

port (2) [po:t], *s.* der Portwein (*wine*).

portable ['pɔːtəbl], *adj.* tragbar; Koffer- (*radio etc.*).

portcullis [pɔːt'kʌlis], *s.* das Fallgatter.

portend [pɔː'tend], *v.a.* vorbedeuten, ahnen lassen.

portent ['pɔːtent], *s.* die Vorbedeutung.

porter ['pɔːtə], *s.* (*Railw.*) der Gepäckträger; der Pförtner, Portier (*caretaker, janitor*); das Porterbier (*beer*).

porterage ['pɔːtəridʒ], *s.* der Trägerlohn, die Zustellkosten, *f. pl.*

portfolio [pɔːt'fouliou], *s.* die Mappe; (*Pol.*) das Ressort; das Portefeuille.

portico ['pɔːtikou], *s.* (*Archit.*) die Säulenhalle.

portion ['pɔːʃən], *s.* die Portion, der Anteil. — *v.a.* aufteilen, austeilen (*share out*).

portliness ['pɔːtlinis], *s.* die Stattlichkeit (*dignity*); Behäbigkeit (*corpulence*).

portly ['pɔːtli], *adj.* stattlich (*dignified*); behäbig (*corpulent*).

portmanteau [pɔːt'mæntou], *s.* der Handkoffer.

portrait ['pɔːtrit], *s.* (*Art*) das Bildnis, Porträt.

portray [pɔː'trei], *v.a.* im Bilde darstellen, porträtieren; (*fig.*) schildern, darstellen (*describe*).

Portuguese [pɔːtju'giːz], *adj.* portugiesisch. — *s.* der Portugiese.

pose [pouz], *s.* die Haltung, Stellung (*of model etc.*). — *v.a.* in Pose stellen; aufwerfen (*question*). — *v.n.* (*as model*) stehen, sitzen; — *as*, posieren, sich ausgeben als (*pretend to be*).

poser ['pouzə], *s.* die schwierige Frage.

position [pə'ziʃən], *s.* die Lage (*situation*); die Stellung (*job*); der Stand, Rang (*rank*); (*Astron., Mil.*) die Position.

positive ['pɔzitiv], *adj.* positiv; (*fig.*) ausdrücklich, sicher (*sure*).

possess [pə'zes], *v.a.* besitzen.

possession [pə'zeʃən], *s.* der Besitz, Besitztum.

possessive [pə'zesiv], *adj.* (*Gram.*) besitzanzeigend, possessiv; (*fig.*) besitzgierig.

possibility [pɔsi'biliti], *s.* die Möglichkeit.

possible ['pɔsibl], *adj.* möglich.

post (1) [poust], *s.* der Pfosten (*pillar*).

post (2) [poust], *s.* die Post (*mail*); der Posten (*job*). — *v.a.* zur Post geben; (*coll.*) einstecken (*letter*).

postage ['poustidʒ], *s.* das Porto; — *stamp*, die Briefmarke.

postal [poustl], *adj.* Post-.

poster ['poustə], *s.* das Plakat.

posterity [pɔs'teriti], *s.* die Nachwelt.

posthumous ['pɔstjuməs], *adj.* hinterlassen, nach dem Tode, postum.

postman ['poustmən], *s.* der Briefträger.

postmark ['poustmaːk], *s.* der Poststempel.

post-mortem [poust'mɔːtəm], *s.* — — —

(*examination*), die Obduktion, Leichenschau.

post-office ['poustɔfis], *s.* das Postamt.

postpone [poust'poun], *v.a.* verschieben, aufschieben.

postscript ['poustskript], *s.* die Nachschrift.

postulate ['pɔstjuleit], *v.a.* postulieren, voraussetzen.

posture ['pɔstʃə], *s.* die Positur, Haltung (*of body*).

pot [pɔt], *s.* der Topf; die Kanne (*beer*); (*coll.*) go to —, zugrunde gehen. — *v.a.* einkochen, einmachen; (*fig.*) kürzen.

potash ['pɔtæʃ], *s.* (*Chem*) die Pottasche.

potassium [pə'tæsiəm], *s.* (*Chem.*) das Kalium.

potato [pə'teitou], *s.* (*Bot.*) die Kartoffel.

potent ['poutənt], *adj.* kräftig, stark, wirksam.

potential [pə'tenʃəl], *s.* das Potential. — *adj.* möglich, potentiell (*possible*).

potter ['pɔtə], *s.* der Töpfer.

pottery ['pɔtəri], *s.* die Töpferei; die Töpferwaren, Tonwaren, *f. pl.* (*goods*).

pouch [pautʃ], *s.* der Beutel.

poulterer ['poultərə], *s.* der Geflügelhändler.

poultice ['poultis], *s.* der Umschlag.

poultry ['poultri], *s.* das Geflügel.

pounce (1) [pauns], *s.*(*obs.*) die Klaue. — *v.n.* — *upon*, herfallen (über, *Acc.*).

pounce (2) [pauns], *s.* das Bimssteinpulver. — *v.a.* (mit Bimsstein) abreiben.

pound (1) [paund], *s.* das Pfund; das Pfund Sterling.

pound (2) [paund], *v.a.* zerstoßen.

poundage ['paundidʒ], *s.* das Pfundgeld, die Gebühr pro Pfund.

pour [pɔː], *v.a.* gießen, schütten, einschenken. — *v.n.* strömen.

pout [paut], *v.n.* schmollen.

poverty ['pɔvəti], *s.* die Armut.

powder ['paudə], *s.* (*Mil.*) das Pulver; der Puder (*face etc.*). — *v.a.* zu Pulver machen, stoßen; (*face*) pudern.

power [pauə], *s.* die Macht, Gewalt; Kraft; Fähigkeit; — *of attorney*, die Vollmacht; (*Maths.*) die Potenz; (*Elec.*) der Strom; — *house*, — *station*, das Elektrizitätswerk; — *cut*, die Stromstörung.

powerful ['pauəful], *adj.* kräftig, mächtig, einflußreich.

powerless ['pauəlis], *adj.* kraftlos, machtlos.

pox [pɔks], *s.* (*Med.*) die Pocken, *f. pl.*; die Syphilis.

practicable ['præktikəbl], *adj.* ausführbar, tunlich.

practical ['præktikəl], *adj.* praktisch.

practice ['præktis], *s.* die Ausübung (*doing, carrying out*); die Praxis.

practise ['præktis], *v.a.* ausführen, ausüben (*a profession etc.*); üben (*rehearse*). — *v.n.* sich üben.

practised ['præktisd], *adj.* geübt, geschult (in).

practitioner [præk'tiʃənə], *s.* (*Med.*) praktischer Arzt; (*Law*) Advokat.

pragmatic [præg'mætik], *adj.* pragmatisch.

prairie ['prɛəri], *s.* die Prärie.

praise [preiz], *v.a.* preisen, loben. — *s.* das Lob.

pram *see under* **perambulator.**

prance [prɑːns], *v.n.* sich bäumen; (*fig.*) sich brüsten (*brag*).

prank [præŋk], *s.* der Streich.

prate [preit], *v.n.* plappern, schwatzen.

prattle [prætl], *v.n.* plaudern, schwatzen. — *s.* das Geschwätz.

prawn [prɔːn], *s.* (*Zool.*) die Steingarnele.

pray [prei], *v.n.* beten. — *v.a.* bitten, ersuchen (*beseech*).

prayer [prɛə], *s.* das Gebet.

preach [priːtʃ], *v.a.*, *v.n.* predigen.

preacher ['priːtʃə], *s.* der Prediger.

preamble [priː'æmbl], *s.* die Vorrede, der Einleitungsparagraph.

precarious [pri'kɛəriəs], *adj.* unsicher, prekär.

precaution [pri'kɔːʃən], *s.* die Vorsichtsmaßregel.

precede [pri'siːd], *v.a.*, *v.n.* vorausgehen, den Vortritt haben.

precedence ['presidəns *or* pri'siːdəns], *s.* der Vortritt, Vorrang.

precedent ['presidənt], *s.* der Präzedenzfall.

precept ['priːsept], *s.* ·die Vorschrift, Regel.

preceptor [pri'septə], *s.* der Lehrer, Lehrmeister.

precinct ['priːsiŋkt], *s.* das Gebiet, der Bezirk; (*pl.*) die Grenzen, *f. pl.*

precious ['preʃəs], *adj.* wertvoll, kostbar; — *metal*, das Edelmetall.

precipice ['presipis], *s.* der Abgrund.

precipitous [pri'sipitəs], *adj.* jäh, abschüssig.

precise [pri'sais], *adj.* genau, bestimmt.

precision [pri'siʒən], *s.* die Präzision, Genauigkeit; (*Engin.*) — *tool*, das Präzisionswerkzeug.

preclude [pri'kluːd], *v.a.* ausschließen.

precocious [pri'kouʃəs], *adj.* frühreif.

preconceive [priːkən'siːv], *v.a.* vorher denken.

preconceived [priːkən'siːvd], *adj.* vorgefaßt.

preconception [priːkən'sepʃən], *s.* das Vorurteil.

precursor [pri'kəːsə], *s.* der Vorläufer.

predatory ['predətəri], *adj.* räuberisch, Raub-.

predecessor ['priːdisesə], *s.* der Vorgänger.

predestin(at)e [priː'destin(eit)], *v.a.* vorher bestimmen; (*Theol.*) prädestinieren.

predicament [pri'dikəmənt], *s.* die Verlegenheit.

predicate ['predikit], *s.* (*Gram.*) das Prädikat. — [-keit], *v.a.* behaupten.

predict [pri'dikt], *v.a.* voraussagen, vorhersagen.

prediction [pri'dikʃən], *s.* die Vorhersage (*weather etc.*); die Weissagung (*prophecy*).

predilection [priːdi'lekʃən], *s.* die Vorliebe.

predispose [priːdis'pouz], *v.a.* vorbereiten; empfänglich machen.

predominant [pri'dɔminənt], *adj.* vorherrschend.

predominate [pri'dɔmineit], *v.n.* vorherrschen.

pre-eminence [priː'eminəns], *s.* der Vorrang.

prefabricate [priː'fæbrikeit], *v.a.* vorfabrizieren, als Fertigteil herstellen, in der Fabrik herstellen.

prefabrication [priːfæbri'keiʃən], *s.* die Vorfabrizierung.

preface ['prefis], *s.* das Vorwort.

prefatory ['prefətəri], *adj.* einleitend.

prefect ['priːfekt], *s.* der Präfekt.

prefer [pri'fəː], *v.a.* vorziehen.

preference ['prefərəns], *s.* der Vorzug (*Comm.*) — *share*, die Vorzugsaktie.

preferment [pri'fəːmənt], *s.* die Beförderung.

prefix ['priːfiks], *s.* die Vorsilbe. — [priː'fiks], *v.a.* vorsetzen.

pregnancy ['pregnənsi], *s.* die Schwangerschaft.

pregnant ['pregnənt], *adj.* schwanger.

prejudge [priː'dʒʌdʒ], *v.a.* vorher urteilen, voreilig urteilen.

prejudice ['predʒudis], *s.* das Vorurteil. — *v.a.* beeinträchtigen.

prejudicial [predʒu'diʃəl], *adj.* schädlich.

prelate ['prelit], *s.* (*Eccl.*) der Prälat.

preliminary [pri'liminəri], *adj.* vorläufig, Präliminar-. —*s.* (*pl.*) die Vorbereitungen, *f. pl.*

prelude ['prelju:d], *s.* das Vorspiel.

premature ['premətʃə], *adj.* vorschnell, übereilt, vorzeitig.

premeditate [priː'mediteit], *v.a.* (*Law*) vorher überlegen.

Premier ['premiə], *s.* der Premierminister.

premise (1) ['premis], *s.* (*Log.*) die Prämisse; (*pl.*) das Haus, Grundstück; die Stätte, der Ort; das Lokal (*inn etc.*).

premise (2) [priː'maiz], *v.a.* vorausschicken.

premium ['priːmiəm], *s.* die Prämie.

premonition [priːmə'niʃən], *s.* die Vorahnung.

preoccupation [priːɔkju'peiʃən], *s.* die Zerstreutheit.

preoccupied [priː'ɔkjupaid], *adj.* besorgt; zerstreut (*absent-minded*).

preparation [prepə'reiʃən], *s.* die Vorbereitung; Zubereitung (*of meals*).

preparatory [pri'pærətri], *adj.* vorbereitend; — *school*, die Vorschule.

prepare [pri'pɛə], *v.a.*, *v.n.* vorbereiten (*for*, auf); zubereiten (*meals*).

prepay [priː'pei], *v.a. irr.* vorausbezahlen; (*post*) frankieren.

preponderant [pri'pɔndərənt], *adj.* überwiegend.

preponderate [pri'pɔndəreit], *v.a.,* *v.n.* überwiegen.

preposition [prepə'ziʃən], *s.* (*Gram.*) die Präposition.

prepossess [pri:pə'zes], *v.a.* einnehmen, beeindrucken.

preposterous [pri'pɔstərəs], *adj.* töricht, lächerlich, unerhört.

prerogative [pri'rɔgətiv], *s.* das Vorrecht.

presage [pri'seidʒ], *v.a.* prophezeien. — ['presidʒ], *s.* die Prophezeiung.

prescient ['preʃiənt, 'pri:-], *adj.* vorahnend, vorherwissend.

prescribe [pri'skraib], *v.a., v.n.* vorschreiben; (*Med.*) verschreiben, verordnen.

prescription [pri'skripʃən], *s.* die Vorschrift(*precept*); (*Med.*) das Rezept.

presence ['prezəns], *s.* die Gegenwart, Anwesenheit (*attendance*); das Äußere (*appearance*); — *of mind,* die Geistesgegenwart.

present (1) ['prezənt], *adj.* anwesend, gegenwärtig; jetzig. — *s.* (*Gram.*) das Präsens, die Gegenwart; (*time*) die Gegenwart, heutige Zeit.

present (2) [pri'zənt], *v.a.* darstellen (*on stage*); vorstellen (*introduce*); präsentieren (*arms*); schenken, geben (*gifts*). — ['prezənt], *s.* das Geschenk (*gift*).

presentation [prezən'teiʃən], *s.* die Darstellung (*stage, art*); die Vorstellung (*introduction*); die Überreichung (*of gift*).

presentiment [pri'zentimənt], *s.* das Vorgefühl, die Vorahnung.

presently ['prezəntli], *adv.* bald, sogleich.

preservation [prezə'veiʃən], *s.* die Erhaltung, Bewahrung.

preservative [pri'zə:vətiv], *s.* das Konservierungsmittel.

preserve [pri'zə:v], *v.a.* bewahren, erhalten; (*fruit*) einmachen. — *s.* (*Hunt.*) das Jagdgehege, Jagdrevier, (*pl.*) die Konserven, *f. pl.*

preside [pri'zaid], *v.n.* (*over*) den Vorsitz führen.

president ['prezidənt], *s.* der Präsident.

press [pres], *v.a., v.n.* drücken (*push*); bügeln, plätten (*iron*); nötigen (*force*); dringend bitten (*entreat*). — *s.* die Presse (*newspapers, printing*); der Schrank (*cupboard*); das Gedränge (*crowd*).

pressing ['presiŋ], *adj.* dringend.

pressure ['preʃə], *s.* der Druck.

prestige [pres'ti:ʒ], *s.* das Prestige, Ansehen.

presumable [pri'zju:məbl], *adj.* mutmaßlich, vermutlich.

presume [pri'zju:m], *v.a., v.n.* vermuten; — *on,* sich anmaßen.

presumption [pri'zʌmpʃən], *s.* die Annahme; die Anmaßung (*arrogance*).

presumptive [pri'zʌmptiv], *adj.* mutmaßlich.

presumptuous [pri'zʌmptjuəs], *adj.* anmaßend, dreist, vermessen.

presuppose [pri:sə'pouz], *v.a.* voraussetzen.

pretence [pri'tens], *s.* der Vorwand.

pretend [pri'tend], *v.a., v.n.* vortäuschen, vorgeben.

pretension [pri'tenʃən], *s.* die Anmaßung, der Anspruch (*to,* auf).

pretentious [pri'tenʃəs], *adj.* anspruchsvoll.

preterite ['pretərit], *s.* (*Gram.*) das Präteritum.

pretext ['pri:tekst], *s.* der Vorwand.

pretty ['priti], *adj.* hübsch, nett. — *adv.* (*coll.*) ziemlich.

prevail [pri'veil], *v.n.* vorherrschen, die Oberhand haben.

prevalence ['prevələns], *s.* das Vorherrschen.

prevaricate [pri'værikeit], *v.n.* Ausflüchte machen.

prevent [pri'vent], *v.a.* verhindern.

prevention [pri'venʃən], *s.* die Verhinderung.

preventive [pri'ventiv], *adj.* vorbeugend.

previous ['pri:viəs], *adj.* vorhergehend.

prey [prei], *s.* die Beute, der Raub. — *v.n.* rauben, nachstellen.

price [prais], *s.* der Preis, Wert.

priceless ['praislis], *adj.* unschätzbar, unbezahlbar.

prick [prik], *s.* der Stachel, Stich (*stab*). — *v.a.* stechen (*stab*); punktieren (*puncture*).

prickle [prikl], *s.* (*Bot.*) der Stachel.

pride [praid], *s.* der Stolz. — *v.r.* — *o.s.,* sich brüsten, stolz sein (*on, Acc.*).

priest [pri:st], *s.* (*Eccl.*) der Priester.

prig [prig], *s.* der eingebildete Tropf; Tugendheld.

priggish ['prigiʃ], *adj.* dünkelhaft, selbstgefällig.

prim [prim], *adj.* steif, spröde.

primacy ['praiməsi], *s.* der, das Primat.

primaeval [prai'mi:vəl], *adj.* Ur-, anfänglich, ursprünglich.

primary ['praiməri], *adj.* erst, ursprünglich; Haupt- (*main*). — *s.* (*pl.*) (*Am.*) die Vorwahlen, *f. pl.* (*Presidential elections*).

prime [praim], *adj.* erst, wichtigst. — *s.* die Blüte, Vollendung, Vollkraft.

primer ['praimə], *s.* das Elementarbuch, die Fibel.

primitive ['primitiv], *adj.* primitiv; ursprünglich (*original*).

primness ['primnis], *s.* die Geziertheit, Steifheit.

primrose ['primrouz], *s.* (*Bot.*) die Primel.

prince [prins], *s.* der Prinz; Fürst (*rank*).

princess [prin'ses], *s.* die Prinzessin.

principal ['prinsipl], *s.* der Direktor (*business*); Rektor (*school etc.*); (*Comm.*) das Kapital; (*Mus.*) der erste Spieler. — *adj.* erst, Haupt-.

principality [prinsi'pæliti], *s.* das Fürstentum.

463

principle

principle ['prinsipl], *s.* das Prinzip, der Grundsatz.

print [print], *v.a.* drucken, abdrucken. — *s.* (*Typ.*, *Art*) der Druck; *out of* —, vergriffen.

printer ['printə], *s.* der (Buch-)drucker.

prior [praiə], *adj.* früher, eher; — *to*, vor (*Dat.*). — *s.* (*Eccl.*) der Prior.

priority [prai'ɔriti], *s.* die Priorität, der Vorrang.

prise [praiz], *v.a.* — *open*, gewaltsam öffnen, aufbrechen.

prism [prizm], *s.* das Prisma.

prison [prizn], *s.* das Gefängnis.

prisoner ['prizənə], *s.* der Gefangene, Sträfling.

pristine ['pristain], *adj.* ehemalig, vormalig, ursprünglich.

privacy ['praivəsi *or* 'privəsi], *s.* die Zurückgezogenheit, Stille.

private ['praivit], *adj.* privat, persönlich, vertraulich (*confidential*). — *s.* (*Mil.*) der Gemeine, Landser.

privation [prai'veiʃən], *s.* der Mangel, die Entbehrung (*lack*); die Beraubung (*deprivation*).

privilege ['privilidʒ], *s.* das Privileg, Vorrecht. — *v.a.* ausnehmen, privilegieren.

privy ['privi], *s.* der Abtritt, Abort. — *adj.* — *to*, mitwissend; *Privy Council*, der Staatsrat.

prize [praiz], *s.* der Preis, die Belohnung; — *v.a.* hochschätzen.

prizewinner ['praizwinə], *s.* der Preisträger; *Nobel* —, der Nobelpreisträger.

probability [prɔbə'biliti], *s.* die Wahrscheinlichkeit.

probable ['prɔbəbl], *adj.* wahrscheinlich.

probate ['proubeit], *s.* (*Law*) die Testamentsbestätigung.

probation [pro'beiʃən], *s.* die Bewährung, Bewährungsfrist (*period*).

probationary [pro'beiʃənəri], *adj.* Bewährungs-.

probe [proub], *v.a.* sondieren, untersuchen. — *s.* die Sonde, Prüfung.

probity ['proubiti], *s.* die Redlichkeit, Anständigkeit.

problem ['prɔbləm], *s.* das Problem.

problematic [prɔblə'mætik], *adj.* zweifelhaft, problematisch.

proboscis [prə'bɔsis], *s.*(*Ent.*) der Rüssel.

procedure [prə'si:dʒə], *s.* der Vorgang, das Verfahren.

proceed [prə'si:d], *v.n.* vorgehen, verfahren.

proceeds ['prousi:dz], *s. pl.* der Ertrag.

process (1) ['prouses], *s.* der Vorgang, Prozeß. — *v.a.* verarbeiten, fertigen.

process (2) [pro'ses], *v.n.* in einem Zuge gehen.

procession [prə'seʃən], *s.* der (feierliche) Umzug, die Prozession.

proclaim [prə'kleim], *v.a.* (*Pol.*) proklamieren, ausrufen.

proclamation [prɔklə'meiʃən], *s.* (*Pol.*) die Ausrufung, Proklamation.

proclivity [prə'kliviti], *s.* der Hang, die Neigung (*tendency*).

procrastinate [prə'kræstineit], *v.a.* aufschieben. — *v.n.* zögern, zaudern.

procreate ['proukrieit], *v.a.* zeugen, hervorbringen.

procurable [prə'kjuərəbl], *adj.* zu verschaffen, erhältlich.

procure [prə'kjuə], *v.a.* verschaffen, besorgen.

prod [prɔd], *v.a.* stoßen.

prodigal ['prɔdigəl], *adj.* verschwenderisch, vergeudend; — *son*, der verlorene Sohn.

prodigious [prə'didʒəs], *adj.* erstaunlich, ungeheuer.

prodigy ['prɔdidʒi], *s.* das Wunderkind.

produce [prə'dju:s], *v.a.* erzeugen, produzieren. — ['prɔdju:s], *s.* das Produkt, Erzeugnis.

producer [prə'dju:sə], *s.* der Erzeuger; (*Theat.*, *Cinema*) der Regisseur.

product ['prɔdʌkt], *s.* das Produkt, Erzeugnis.

production [prə'dʌkʃən], *s.* die Produktion; die Erzeugung (*industrial*); das Zeigen, Vorweisen (*of documents*); (*Theat.*) die Regie.

productive [prə'dʌktiv], *adj.* produktiv, schöpferisch (*mind*); fruchtbar (*soil*).

profane [prə'fein], *adj.* profan; ruchlos.

profanity [prə'fæniti], *s.* die Profanierung; das Lästern.

profess [prə'fes], *v.a.*, *v.n.* bekennen, erklären, sich bekennen zu.

profession [prə'feʃən], *s.* der (höhere) Beruf; (*Eccl.*) das Bekenntnis; die Beteuerung (*protestation*).

professional [prə'feʃənəl], *adj.* beruflich, berufsmäßig.

professor [prə'fesə], *s.* der (Universitäts) Professor.

professorship [prə'fesəʃip], *s.* die Professur.

proffer ['prɔfə], *v.a.* anbieten (*offer*).

proficiency [prə'fiʃənsi], *s.* die Tüchtigkeit; (*skill*) die Beherrschung.

proficient [prə'fiʃənt], *adj.* bewandert, tüchtig; (*in language*) fließend.

profile ['proufail], *s.* das Profil.

profit ['prɔfit], *s.* der Profit, Gewinn, Nutzen. — *v.n.* Nutzen ziehen. — *v.a.* von Nutzen sein (*Dat.*).

profound [prə'faund], *adj.* tief; gründlich (*thorough*).

profuse [prə'fju:s], *adj.* reichlich, verschwenderisch.

profusion [prə'fju:ʒen], *s.* der Überfluß.

progeny ['prɔdʒəni], *s.* der Nachkomme; die Nachkommenschaft.

prognosticate [prɔg'nɔstikeit], *v.a.* vorhersagen.

prognostication [prɔgnɔsti'keiʃən], *s.* die Voraussage.

programme (*Am.*) **program** ['prougræm], *s.* das Programm.

progress ['prougres], *s.* der Fortschritt. — [prou'gres], *v.n.* fortschreiten, Fortschritte machen.

progression [proˈgreʃən], s. (Maths.) die Reihe, Progression.
progressive [proˈgresiv], adj. fortschrittlich (modern); fortschreitend (continuous); progressiv.
prohibit [prouˈhibit], v.a. verbieten.
prohibition [prouiˈbiʃən], s. das Verbot.
project [prəˈdʒekt], v.a. projizieren; entwerfen. — [ˈprɔdʒekt], s. das Projekt, der Plan.
projectile [prəˈdʒektail], s. das Geschoß.
projection [prəˈdʒekʃən], s. die Projektion (film); der Entwurf (plan); der Vorsprung (jutting out).
proletarian [prouliˈtɛəriən], adj. proletarisch. — s. der Prolet(arier).
prolific [prəˈlifik], adj. fruchtbar.
prolix [ˈprouliks], adj. weitschweifig.
prologue [ˈproulɔg], s. der Prolog.
prolong [prəˈlɔŋ], v.a. verlängern, prolongieren.
prominent [ˈprɔminənt], adj. prominent, hervorragend.
promiscuous [prəˈmiskjuəs], adj. unterschiedslos (indiscriminate); vermischt (mixed).
promise [ˈprɔmis], v.a. versprechen. — v.n. Erwartungen erwecken. — s. das Versprechen.
promissory [ˈprɔmisəri], adj. versprechend; (Comm.) — note, der Schuldschein.
promontory [ˈprɔməntəri], s. das Vorgebirge.
promote [prəˈmout], v.a. befördern; fördern (foster).
promotion [prəˈmouʃən], s. die Beförderung (advancement); Förderung (fostering); (Am.) die Reklame (publicity).
prompt [prɔmpt], adj. prompt, pünktlich. — v.a. (Theat.) soufflieren; treiben (inspire).
prompter [ˈprɔmptə], s. (Theat.) der Souffleur.
promptitude [ˈprɔmptitjuːd], s. die Promptheit, Pünktlichkeit.
promulgate [ˈprɔməlgeit], v.a. bekanntmachen, verbreiten.
prone [proun], adj. geneigt, neigend.
prong [prɔŋ], s. die Zinke, Gabel.
pronominal [proˈnɔminəl], adj. (Gram.) pronominal.
pronoun [ˈprounaun], s. das Fürwort, Pronomen.
pronounce [prəˈnauns], v.a., v.n. aussprechen (words); feierlich erklären (proclaim).
pronunciation [prənʌnsiˈeiʃən], s. die Aussprache.
proof [pruːf], s. der Beweis, die Probe; (Typ.) der Korrekturbogen. — v.a. (Engin., Chem.) imprägnieren.
prop [prɔp], s. die Stütze, der Stützpfahl. — v.a. stützen.
propaganda [prɔpəˈgændə], s. die Propaganda, Reklame.
propagate [ˈprɔpəgeit], v.a. propagieren; (Bot.) fortpflanzen.

propel [prəˈpel], v.a. forttreiben, vorwärtstreiben.
propeller [prəˈpelə], s. der Propeller, die Schraube.
propensity [prəˈpensiti], s. die Neigung, der Hang.
proper [ˈprɔpə], adj. schicklich (manners); eigentümlich, eigen (peculiar).
property [ˈprɔpəti], s. das Eigentum (possession); die Eigenschaft (quality).
prophecy [ˈprɔfisi], s. die Prophezeiung, Weissagung.
prophesy [ˈprɔfisai], v.a. prophezeien.
propitiate [prəˈpiʃieit], v.a. versöhnen.
propitiation [prəpiʃiˈeiʃən], s. die Versöhnung.
propitious [prəˈpiʃəs], adj. gnädig, günstig, geneigt.
proportion [prəˈpɔːʃən], s. das Verhältnis; die Proportion; der Anteil (portion); das Ebenmaß (in art).
proportionate [prəˈpɔːʃənit], adj. im Verhältnis, verhältnismäßig, proportioniert.
proposal [prəˈpouzəl], s. der Vorschlag, Antrag.
propose [prəˈpouz], v.a. antragen, beantragen, vorschlagen. — v.n. — to a lady, einen Heiratsantrag machen.
proposition [prɔpəˈziʃən], s. der Vorschlag, Antrag; die Idee.
propound [prəˈpaund], v.a. vorlegen, vorbringen (a theory etc.).
proprietor [prəˈpraiətə], s. der Eigentümer.
propriety [prəˈpraiəti], s. die Schicklichkeit.
propulsion [prəˈpʌlʃən], s. der Antrieb.
prorogue [prəˈroug], v.a. vertagen.
prosaic [prəˈzeiik], adj. prosaisch, nüchtern.
proscribe [proˈskraib], v.a. verbieten, ächten.
proscription [proˈskripʃən], s. die Verbannung, das Verbot.
prose [prouz], s. die Prosa.
prosecute [ˈprɔsikjuːt], v.a. verfolgen; (Law) gerichtlich verfolgen, anklagen.
prosecutor [ˈprɔsikjuːtə], s. (public) der Staatsanwalt; der Kläger.
proselyte [ˈprɔsəlait], s. der Neubekehrte, Proselyt.
prospect [ˈprɔspekt], s. die Aussicht; (pl.) die Aussichten, Chancen, f.pl. — [prɔsˈpekt], v.n. suchen (for, nach, Dat.).
prospectus [prəˈspektəs], s. der Prospekt.
prosper [ˈprɔspə], v.n. gedeihen, blühen. — v.a. segnen.
prosperity [prɔsˈperiti], s. der Wohlstand; der Reichtum; das Gedeihen (thriving).
prosperous [ˈprɔspərəs], adj. glücklich, wohlhabend.
prostitute [ˈprɔstitjuːt], s. die Prostituierte, Dirne. — v.a. erniedrigen.
prostrate [ˈprɔstreit], adj. hingestreckt, niedergeworfen, fußfällig. — [prɔsˈtreit], v.a. niederwerfen.

prosy ['prouzi], *adj.* prosaisch, weitschweifig, langweilig.
protect [prə'tekt], *v.a.* beschützen.
protection [prə'tekʃən], *s.* der Schutz; die Protektion (*favour*).
protective [prə'tektiv], *adj.* Schutz-, schützend.
protector [prə'tektə], *s.* der Beschützer; (*Engin.*) der Schutz.
protest [prə'test], *v.a., v.n.* protestieren, einwenden. — ['proutest], *s.* der Protest, Einspruch.
Protestant ['prɔtistənt], *adj.* protestantisch. — *s.* der Protestant.
protestation [prɔtes'teiʃən], *s.* die Beteuerung, Verwahrung.
protocol ['proutəkɔl], *s.* das Protokoll.
prototype ['proutotaip], *s.* das Urbild, Modell, der Prototyp.
protract [prə'trækt], *v.a.* in die Länge ziehen; hinausziehen.
protractor [prə'træktə], *s.* der Winkelmesser, Transporteur, die Schmiege.
protrude [prə'tru:d], *v.n.* herausragen, hervorstehen, vordringen.
protuberance [prə'tju:bərəns], *s.* der Höcker, der Auswuchs, die Protuberanz.
proud [praud], *adj.* stolz (*of*, auf, *Acc.*).
prove [pru:v], *v.a.* beweisen. — *v.n.* sich erweisen (*turn out*).
provender ['prɔvində], *s.* das Viehfutter.
proverb ['prɔvə:b], *s.* das Sprichwort.
proverbial [prə'və:biəl], *adj.* sprichwörtlich.
provide [prə'vaid], *v.a., v.n.* vorsehen, versorgen, verschaffen.
provided [prə'vaidid], *conj.* vorausgesetzt.
providence ['prɔvidəns], *s.* die Vorsehung.
provident ['prɔvidənt], *adj.* vorsorglich.
providential [prɔvi'denʃəl], *adj.* von der Vorsehung bestimmt.
province ['prɔvins], *s.* die Provinz, das Gebiet (*also fig.*).
provincial [prə'vinʃəl], *adj.* ländlich, Provinz-; provinziell.
provision [prə'viʒən], *s.* die Versorgung (*supply*); der Vorrat (*stock*); (*pl.*) die Lebensmittel (*victuals*).
provisional [prə'viʒənəl], *adj.* vorläufig.
proviso [prə'vaizou], *s.* der Vorbehalt.
provocation [prɔvo'keiʃən], *s.* die Herausforderung.
provoke [prə'vouk], *v.a.* herausfordern, provozieren.
prow [prau], *s.* (*Naut.*) der Bug.
prowess ['praues], *s.* die Stärke (*physical*); die körperliche Tüchtigkeit; Tapferkeit.
prowl [praul], *v.n.* herumstreichen.
proximity [prɔk'simiti], *s.* die Nähe.
proxy ['prɔksi], *s.* der Stellvertreter.
prudence ['pru:dəns], *s.* die Klugheit, Vorsicht.
prudent ['pru:dənt], *adj.* klug, vorsichtig.

prudery ['pru:dəri], *s.* die Sprödigkeit.
prudish ['pru:diʃ], *adj.* prüde, spröde, zimperlich.
prune (1) [pru:n], *s.* (*Cul.*) die Backpflaume.
prune (2) [pru:n], *v.a.* beschneiden, stutzen.
Prussian ['prʌʃən], *adj.* preußisch; — *blue*, das Berlinerblau. — *s.* der Preuße.
prussic ['prʌsik], *adj.* blausauer; — *acid*, die Blausäure.
pry [prai], *v.n.* spähen, ausforschen.
psalm [sɑ:m], *s.* der Psalm.
psychology [sai'kɔlədʒi], *s.* die Psychologie.
pub [pʌb], *s.* das Wirtshaus, die Kneipe.
puberty ['pju:bəti], *s.* die Pubertät, Mannbarkeit.
public ['pʌblik], *adj.* öffentlich. — *s.* das Publikum; die Öffentlichkeit.
publican ['pʌblikən], *s.* der Gastwirt.
publication [pʌbli'keiʃən], *s.* die Veröffentlichung, Herausgabe.
publicity [pʌb'lisiti], *s.* die Werbung, die Reklame; — *manager*, der Reklamechef, Werbeleiter.
publicize ['pʌblisaiz], *v.a.* weithin bekannt machen, publizieren.
publish ['pʌbliʃ], *v.a.* veröffentlichen; verlegen (*books*); —*ing house*, der Verlag.
publisher ['pʌbliʃə], *s.* der Verleger.
pucker ['pʌkə], *v.a.* falten; runzeln (*wrinkle*). — *s.* die Falte.
pudding ['pudiŋ], *s.* der Pudding.
puddle [pʌdl], *s.* die Pfütze. — *v.a.* puddeln (*iron*).
puerile ['pjuərail], *adj.* kindisch, knabenhaft.
puff [pʌf], *v.a., v.n.* puffen, paffen, blasen; —*ed-up*, aufgebläht, stolz. — *s.* der Windstoß; — *pastry*, der Blätterteig.
pug [pʌg], *s.* (*Zool.*) der Mops.
pugnacious [pʌg'neiʃəs], *adj.* kampfsüchtig, kampflustig.
puisne ['pju:ni], *adj.* (*Law*) jünger, Unter-.
puissant ['pwi:sənt], *adj.* mächtig, stark.
puke [pju:k], *v.n.* sich erbrechen.
pull [pul], *v.a., v.n.* ziehen, reißen; zerren. — *s.* der Zug, Ruck.
pullet ['pulit], *s.* (*Orn.*) das Hühnchen.
pulley ['puli], *s.* der Flaschenzug.
pulmonary, pulmonic ['pʌlmənəri, pʌl'mɔnik], *adj.* Lungen-.
pulp [pʌlp], *s.* der Brei; das Fleisch (*of fruit*); das Mark (*marrow*); die Pulpa (*tooth*). — *v.a.* zerstampfen, zu Brei stampfen.
pulpit ['pulpit], *s.* (*Eccl.*) die Kanzel.
pulsate [pʌl'seit], *v.n.* pulsieren, schlagen.
pulse (1) [pʌls], *s.* der Puls.
pulse (2) [pʌls], *s.* (*Bot.*) die Hülsenfrüchte, *f. pl.*
pulverize ['pʌlvəraiz], *v.a.* zu Pulver stoßen, zerstoßen.

pumice ['pʌmis], *s.* der Bimsstein.
pump (1) [pʌmp], *s.* die Pumpe. — *v.a.*, *v.n.* pumpen; ausfragen (*question*).
pump (2) [pʌmp], *s.* der Tanzschuh (*dancing shoe*).
pumpkin ['pʌmpkin], *s.* (*Bot.*) der Kürbis.
pun [pʌn], *s.* das Wortspiel. — *v.n.* Wortspiele machen.
Punch [pʌntʃ]. das Kasperle; — *and Judy*, Hanswurst und seine Frau.
punch (1) [pʌntʃ], *v.a.* schlagen, boxen (*box*). — *s.* der Schlag (*hit*); der Faustschlag (*boxing*).
punch (2) [pʌntʃ], *v.a.* lochen (*card*). — *s.* der Pfriem (*tool*).
punch (3) [pʌntʃ], *s.* der Punsch (*drink*).
punchy ['pʌntʃi], *adj.* kurz, dick, untersetzt.
punctilious [pʌŋk'tiliəs], *adj.* sorgfältig, spitzfindig.
punctual ['pʌŋktjuəl], *adj.* pünktlich.
punctuate ['pʌŋktjueit], *v.a.* (*Gram.*) interpunktieren; (*fig.*) betonen.
punctuation [pʌŋktju'eiʃən], *s.* (*Gram.*) die Interpunktion.
puncture ['pʌŋktʃə], *s.* (*Motor.*) der Reifendefekt, die Panne; (*Med.*) die Punktur, der Einstich. — *v.a.* (*Med.*) punktieren.
pungent ['pʌndʒənt], *adj.* scharf, stechend.
punish ['pʌniʃ], *v.a.* bestrafen (*s.o.*); strafen.
punishable ['pʌniʃəbl], *adj.* strafbar.
punishment ['pʌniʃmənt], *s.* die Strafe, Bestrafung.
punt [pʌnt],*s.* das kleine Boot, Flachboot.
puny ['pju:ni], *adj.* schwach, winzig.
pup [pʌp], *s.* der junge Hund; *be sold a* —, einen schlechten Kauf machen. — *v.n.* Junge werfen.
pupil (1) ['pju:pil], *s.* der Schüler.
pupil (2) ['pju:pil], *s.* die Pupille (*eye*).
pupil(l)age ['pju:pilidʒ], *s.* die Minderjährigkeit (*of minor*).
puppet ['pʌpit], *s.* die Puppe, Marionette; der Strohmann (*human tool*).
puppy ['pʌpi] *see* **pup.**
purblind ['pə:blaind], *adj.* halbblind.
purchase ['pə:tʃis], *s.* der Kauf, Einkauf. — *v.a.* kaufen.
pure ['pjuə], *adj.* pur, rein.
purge [pə:dʒ], *v.a.* reinigen. — *s.* die Reinigung; (*Pol.*) die Säuberung.
purify ['pjuərifai],*v.a.* läutern, reinigen.
purl (1) [pə:l], *s.* die Borte; (*knitting*) die Häkelkante.
purl (2) [pə:l], *v.n.* sich drehen, wirbeln; (*sl.*) umkippen.
purl (3) [pə:l], *s.* das Murmeln, Rieseln (*of brook*). — *v.n.* murmeln, rieseln.
purloin [pə:'lɔin], *v.a.* stehlen.
purple ['pə:pl], *adj.* purpurn; — *patch*, die Glanzstelle. — *s.* der Purpur.
purport [pə:'pɔ:t], *v.a.* bedeuten, Sinn haben. — ['pə:pət], *s.* der Sinn, die Bedeutung.
purpose ['pə:pəs], *s.* die Absicht, der Zweck.

purposeful ['pə:pəsful], *adj.* zweckbewußt, energisch, zielbewußt.
purr [pə:], *v.n.* schnurren (*of cat*).
purse [pə:s], *s.* die Börse, Geldtasche; das Portemonnaie.
pursuance [pə'sju:əns], *s.* (*Law*) die Verfolgung, Ausführung.
pursuant [pə'sju:ənt], *adj.* (*Law*) zufolge, gemäß (*to, Dat.*).
pursue [pə'sju:], *v.a.* verfolgen.
pursuit [pə'sju:t], *s.* die Verfolgung; (*pl.*) die Geschäfte, *n. pl.*; Beschäftigung.
purvey [pə'vei], *v.a.* versorgen, liefern.
purview ['pə:vju:], *s.* der Spielraum; das Blickfeld.
push [puʃ], *v.a.* stoßen, drücken, schieben, drängen; *be —ed for*, in der Klemme sein. — *s.* der Stoß, Schub, das Drängen; *at a* —, wenn absolut nötig.
pusillanimous [pju:si'læniməs], *adj.* kleinmütig.
puss, pussy [pus, 'pusi], *s.* (*coll.*) die Katze, das Kätzchen, Miezchen.
put [put], *v.a. irr.* setzen (*set*), legen (*lay*), stellen (*stand*); — *off*, aufschieben, aus der Fassung bringen (*deflect*); — *on*, anziehen, auflegen; — *it on thickly*, es dick auftragen. — *v.n.* (*Naut.*) — *in*, anlegen.
putrefy ['pju:trifai], *v.a.*, *v.n.* faul werden (*rot*), verwesen.
putrid ['pju:trid], *adj.* faul (*rotten*).
puttee ['pʌti:], *s.* (*Mil.*) die Wickelgamasche.
putty ['pʌti], *s.* der Kitt.
puzzle [pʌzl], *s.* das Rätsel. — *v.a.* zu denken geben (*Dat.*).
pygmy ['pigmi], *s.* der Pygmäe.
pyjamas, (*Am.*) **pajamas** [pi'dʒɑ:məz, pə-], *s. pl.* der Schlafanzug.
pyramid ['pirəmid], *s.* die Pyramide.
pyre [paiə], *s.* der Scheiterhaufen.
pyrotechnics [paiəro'tekniks], *s. pl.* das Feuerwerk, die Feuerwerkskunst.
python ['paiθən], *s.* (*Zool.*) die Riesenschlange.

Q

Q [kju:]. das Q.
qua [kwei], *conj.* als.
quack [kwæk], *v.n.* quaken; (*coll.*) quacksalbern. — *s.* der Quacksalber.
quadrangle ['kwɔdræŋgl], *s.* (*abbr.* **quad** [kwɔd]), das Viereck; der Hof (*in college etc*).
quadrant ['kwɔdrənt], *s.* der Quadrant, Viertelkreis; (*Engin.*) der Winkelmesser.
quadrille [kwɔ'dril], *s.* die Quadrille, der Kontertanz.

467

quadruped

quadruped ['kwɔdruped], *s.* (*Zool.*) das vierfüßige Tier.

quadruple ['kwɔdrupl], *adj.* vierfach.

quaff [kwæf], *v.a.* schlucken. — *v.n.* zechen (*drink heavily*).

quagmire ['kwægmaiə], *s.* der Sumpf.

quail (1) [kweil], *s.* (*Orn.*) die Wachtel.

quail (2) [kweil], *v.n.* verzagen.

quaint [kweint], *adj.* seltsam, wunderlich, eigenartig.

quake [kweik], *v.n.* erzittern, beben.

Quaker ['kweikə], *s.* der Quäker.

qualification [kwɔlifi'keiʃən], *s.* die Befähigung, Qualifikation (*ability*); die Einschränkung (*proviso*).

qualify ['kwɔlifai], *v.a.* befähigen (*make able*); beschränken, mäßigen, qualifizieren (*modify*). — *v.n.* sich qualifizieren, das Studium abschließen.

qualitative ['kwɔlitətiv], *adj.* qualitätsmäßig, Wert-, qualitativ.

quality ['kwɔliti], *s.* die Qualität (*high class*); der Wert (*standard*).

qualm [kwɑ:m], *s.* der Skrupel.

quantitative ['kwɔntitətiv], *adj.* quantitativ.

quantity ['kwɔntiti], *s.* die Quantität, Menge.

quantum ['kwɔntəm], *s.* die Menge; das Quantum; — *theory*, die Quantentheorie.

quarantine ['kwɔrənti:n], *s.* die Quarantäne.

quarrel ['kwɔrəl], *s.* der Streit, Zwist. — *v.n.* streiten, zanken.

quarry (1) ['kwɔri], *s.* der Steinbruch.

quarry (2) ['kwɔri], *s.* die Beute (*prey*).

quart [kwɔ:t], *s.* das Viertelmaß (*1.15 litre*).

quarter ['kwɔ:tə], *s.* das Viertel (jahr); (*Arith.*) das Viertel (*also of town*); (*pl.*) das Quartier.

quartermaster ['kwɔ:təmɑ:stə], *s.* (*Mil.*) der Feldzeugmeister.

quartet(te) [kwɔ:'tet], *s.* das Quartett.

quarto ['kwɔ:tou], *s.* das Quartformat.

quartz [kwɔ:ts], *s.* der Quartz.

quash [kwɔʃ], *v.a.* unterdrücken (*suppress*); (*Law*) annullieren.

quaver ['kweivə], *s.* (*Mus.*) die Achtelnote; der Triller (*trill*). — *v.n.* tremolieren, trillern.

quay [ki:], *s.* der Kai, Hafendamm.

queen [kwi:n], *s.* die Königin.

queer [kwiə], *adj.* seltsam, sonderlich.

quell [kwel], *v.a.* unterdrücken.

quench [kwentʃ], *v.a.* löschen; stillen (*thirst*).

querulous ['kweruləs], *adj.* mürrisch, jämmerlich; zänkisch.

query ['kwiəri], *s.* die Frage. — *v.a.* in Frage stellen.

quest [kwest], *s.* das Suchen, Streben; die Suche.

question ['kwestʃən], *s.* die Frage; — *mark*, das Fragezeichen. — *v.a.* fragen, in Frage stellen; ausfragen (*s.o.*).

questionable ['kwestʃənəbl], *adj.* zweifelhaft, fraglich, bedenklich.

queue [kju:], *s.* die Schlange, das Anstellen. — *v.n.* Schlange stehen.

quibble [kwibl], *s.* die Ausflucht. — *v.n.* um Worte streiten.

quick [kwik], *adj.* schnell (*fast*); lebendig (*live*).

quicken ['kwikən], *v.a.* beleben, anfeuern.

quicklime ['kwiklaim], *s.* der ungelöschte Kalk.

quicksand ['kwiksænd], *s.* der Flugsand.

quicksilver ['kwiksilvə], *s.* (*Chem.*) das Quecksilber.

quid (1) [kwid], *s.* (*sl.*) das Pfund Sterling.

quid (2) [kwid], *s.* (*Lat.*) etwas; — *pro quo*, Gleiches mit Gleichem.

quiescence [kwi'esəns], *s.* die Ruhe.

quiet ['kwaiət], *adj.* ruhig.

quietism ['kwaiətizm], *s.* der Quietismus.

quietness ['kwaiətnis], *s.* die Ruhe, Stille.

quill [kwil], *s.* der Federkiel, die Feder. — *v.a.* falten, fälteln.

quilt [kwilt], *s.* die Steppdecke.

quince [kwins], *s.* (*Bot.*) die Quitte.

quinine [kwi'ni:n], *s.* (*Med.*) das Chinin.

quinquennial [kwiŋ'kweniəl], *adj.* fünfjährig, fünfjährlich, alle fünf Jahre.

quinsy ['kwinzi], *s.* (*Med.*) die Bräune.

quint [kwint], *s.* (*Mus.*) die Quinte.

quintessence [kwin'tesəns], *s.* die Quintessenz, der Kern, der Inbegriff.

quintuple ['kwintjupl], *adj.* fünffach.

quip [kwip], *s.* die Stichelei; die witzige Bemerkung.

quire [kwaiə], *s.* das Buch Papier.

quirk [kwə:k], *s.* die (unerwartete) Wendung; Spitzfindigkeit.

quit [kwit], *v.a., v.n.* verlassen; weggehen; (*Am.*) aufhören. — *adj.* (*pl.*) (**quits**) quitt, bezahlt.

quite [kwait], *adv.* ganz, völlig.

quiver (1) ['kwivə], *s.* der Köcher.

quiver (2) ['kwivə], *v.n.* erzittern, schauern.

quiz [kwiz], *s.* das Fragespiel, Quizprogramm (*Radio etc.*).

quoit [kɔit], *s.* die Wurfscheibe.

quorum ['kwɔ:rəm], *s.* die beschlußfähige Anzahl.

quota ['kwoutə], *s.* die Quote.

quotation [kwo'teiʃən], *s.* das Zitat; (*Comm.*) der Kostenanschlag, die Notierung.

quote [kwout], *v.a.* zitieren; (*Comm.*) einen Preis zitieren, notieren.

R

R [ɑ:(r)]. das R.

rabbet ['ræbit], *s.* die Fuge, Nute. — *v.a.* einfugen.

rabbi ['ræbai], s. (*Rel.*) der Rabbiner.
rabbit ['ræbit], s. (*Zool.*) das Kaninchen.
rabble [ræbl], s. der Pöbel.
rabid ['ræbid], adj. wütend, rasend.
race (1) [reis], s. die Rasse; das Geschlecht (*stock*).
race (2) [reis], s. das Rennen (*horses etc.*); der Wettlauf (*run*); — *course*, die Rennbahn. — v.a., v.n. um die Wette laufen.
racial ['reiʃəl], adj. rassisch.
raciness ['reisinis], s. das Rassige, die Urwüchsigkeit.
rack [ræk], s. die Folterbank; das Reck (*gymnasium*); (*Railw.*) das Gepäcknetz. — v.a. recken, strecken; — o.'s *brains*, sich den Kopf zerbrechen.
racket (1), **racquet** ['rækit], s. der Tennisschläger.
racket (2) ['rækit], s. der Lärm (*noise, din*).
racket (3) ['rækit], s. (*coll.*) der Schwindel.
racketeer [ræki'tiə], s. der Schwindler.
racy ['reisi], adj. stark; pikant.
radar, ['reidɑ:], s. das Radar.
radiance ['reidiəns], s. der Glanz, das Strahlen.
radiant ['reidiənt], adj. strahlend.
radiate ['reidieit], v.a., v.n. strahlen, ausstrahlen.
radiator ['reidieitə], s. der Heizapparat, Heizkörper; (*Motor.*) der Kühler.
radical ['rædikəl], adj. (*Pol.*) radikal; gründlich (*thorough*). — s. (*Pol.*) der Radikale; (*Phonet.*) der Grundlaut, Wurzellaut.
radio ['reidiou], s. das Radio, der Rundfunk.
radioactive [reidiou'æktiv], adj. radioaktiv.
radish ['rædiʃ], s. (*Bot.*) der Rettich.
radius ['reidiəs], s. der Radius, Halbmesser; (*Phys., Maths.*) der Strahl (*line*).
raffle [ræfl], s. die Auslosung. — v.a. auslosen, ausspielen.
raft [rɑ:ft], s. das Floß.
rafter ['rɑ:ftə], s. der Dachsparren.
rag (1) [ræg], s. der Lumpen.
rag (2) [ræg], v.a. necken, zum Besten haben (*tease*).
ragamuffin ['rægəmʌfin], s. der Lumpenkerl.
rage [reidʒ], s. die Wut, Raserei; die Manie, Mode (*fashion*). — v.n. wüten, rasen.
ragged ['rægid], adj. zerlumpt; zackig, rauh (*rough*).
ragout [ra'gu:], s. (*Cul.*) das Ragout.
raid [reid], s. der Streifzug, die Razzia; der Angriff. — v.a. überfallen.
rail (1) [reil], s. (*Railw.*) die Schiene; by —, mit der Eisenbahn.
rail (2) [reil], v.n. schmähen; spotten (*Genit.*).
railing ['reiliŋ], s. das Geländer, Gitter.
raillery ['reiləri], s. die Spötteli, das Schmähen.

railway, (*Am.*) **railroad** ['reilwei, 'reilroud], s. die Eisenbahn.
raiment ['reimənt], s. (*Poet.*) die Kleidung.
rain [rein], s. der Regen. — v.n. regnen.
rainbow ['reinbou], s. der Regenbogen.
raincoat ['reinkout], s. der Regenmantel.
raise [reiz], v.a. heben (*lift*); steigern (*prices*); aufbringen (*army, money*); züchten (*breed*); aufziehen (*children*). — s. (*Am.*) die Steigerung, Erhöhung (*salary*).
raisin ['reizin], s. (*Bot.*) die Rosine.
rake (1) [reik], s. der Rechen (*tool*). — v.a. zusammenrechen, harken; bestreichen (*fire at*).
rake (2) [reik], s. der Schlemmer (*roué*).
rakish ['reikiʃ], adj. liederlich.
rally ['ræli], v.a. sammeln, versammeln. — v.n. sich versammeln, sich scharen. — s. die Massenversammlung, Kundgebung; das Treffen.
ram [ræm], s. der Widder; (*Mil.*) die Ramme. — v.a. rammen.
ramble [ræmbl], v.n. (im Grünen) wandern; herumschweifen; einen Ausflug machen. — s. der Ausflug.
rambler ['ræmblə], s. der Wanderer (*hiker*); (*Bot.*) die Heckenrose.
ramification [ræmifi'keiʃən], s. die Verzweigung, Verästelung (*also fig.*); (*pl.*) Zweige, m. pl. (*also fig.*).
ramp [ræmp], v.n. sich ranken (*of plants*). — s. die Rampe.
rampant ['ræmpənt], adj. zügellos, grassierend (*wild*); (*Her.*) sich bäumend.
rampart ['ræmpa:t], s. der Wall.
ramshackle ['ræmʃækl], adj. wackelig, baufällig.
rancid ['rænsid], adj. ranzig.
rancour ['ræŋkə], s. der Groll, die Erbitterung.
random ['rændəm], s. at —, aufs Geratewohl. — adj. zufällig, Zufalls-.
range [reindʒ], s. die Reihe (*row, series*); (*Geog.*) die Bergkette; der Küchenherd (*stove*); (*Mil.*) die Schießstätte (*shooting ground*); die Schußweite, Reichweite (*distance*). — v.n. sich reihen; sich erstrecken (*stretch*). — v.a. rangieren, anordnen, durchstreifen.
rangefinder ['reindʒfaində], s. (*Phot.*) der Entfernungsmesser.
ranger ['reindʒə], s. der Förster, Forstgehilfe; (*Mil.*) der leichte Reiter.
rank (1) [ræŋk], s. die Klasse; der Rang (*order*); — and *file*, die Mannschaft (*of members*); die Mitgliedschaft, Masse. — v.n. sich reihen; gelten.
rank (2) [ræŋk], adj. übermäßig, üppig, allzu stark; ranzig (*of fat etc.*).
rankle [ræŋkl], v.n. nagen.
ransack ['rænsæk], v.a. plündern.
ransom ['rænsəm], s. das Lösegeld; hold to —, (gegen Lösegeld) gefangen halten. — v.a. loskaufen.

rant [rænt], *v.n.* wüten; großtun; groß-
sprechen.
rap [ræp], *v.a.*, *v.n.* schlagen, klopfen.
rapacious [rə'peiʃəs], *adj.* raubgierig.
rape (1) [reip], *v.a.* vergewaltigen. — *s.*
die Vergewaltigung.
rape (2) [reip], *s.* (*Bot.*) der Raps.
rapid ['ræpid], *adj.* rasch, schnell,
reißend (*river*). — *s.* (*pl.*) die Stromschnelle.
rapier ['reipiə], *s.* der Degen; (*fencing*)
das Rapiér.
rapine ['ræpain], *s.* (*Poet.*) der Raub.
rapt [ræpt], *adj.* entzückt; versunken.
rapture ['ræptʃə], *s.* das Entzücken.
rare (1) [rɛə], *adj.* selten.
rare (2) [rɛə], *adj.* (*meat*) rar.
rarity ['rɛəriti], *s.* die Seltenheit.
rascal ['rɑːskəl], *s.* der Schurke.
rash (1) [ræʃ], *adj.* unbesonnen.
rash (2) [ræʃ], *s.* der Ausschlag (*skin*).
rasher ['ræʃə], *s.* die Speckschnitte.
rasp [rɑːsp], *s.* die Raspel, Feile. —
v.a., *v.n.* raspeln; heiser sein (*speech*).
raspberry ['rɑːzbəri], *s.* (*Bot.*) die
Himbeere.
rat [ræt], *s.* (*Zool.*) die Ratte; (*fig.*) der
Verräter.
ratable ['reitəbl], *adj.* steuerpflichtig.
rate (1) [reit], *s.* das Mass; der Tarif;
die Geschwindigkeit (*speed*); Gemein-
deabgabe (*tax*); das Verhältnis (*proportion*). — *v.a.* schätzen (*estimate*);
(*Am.*) einschätzen, halten für.
rate (2) [reit], *v.a.* schelten (*berate*).
rather ['rɑːðə], *adv.* vielmehr, eher,
lieber (*in comparisons*); — *good*, ziemlich gut.
ratification [rætifi'keiʃən], *s.* die Bestätigung; (*Pol.*) die Ratifizierung.
ratify ['rætifai], *v.a.* bestätigen; (*Pol.*)
ratifizieren.
ratio ['reiʃiou], *s.* das Verhältnis.
ration ['ræʃən], *s.* die Ration.
rational ['ræʃənəl], *adj.* Vernunfts-,
rationell, vernunftgemäß.
rattle [rætl], *s.* das Geklapper (*noise*);
die Klapper (*toy etc.*); *death* —, das
Todesröcheln. — *v.a.* klappern,
Lärm machen; (*fig.*) aus der Fassung
bringen; — *off*, herunterleiern. —
v.n. rasseln, klappern.
raucous ['rɔːkəs], *adj.* heiser, rauh.
ravage ['rævidʒ], *v.a.* verheeren. — *s.*
(*pl.*) die Verheerung, Verwüstung.
rave [reiv], *v.n.* vernarrt sein (*about*, in);
schwärmen (*für*).
raven [reivn], *s.* (*Orn.*) der Rabe.
ravenous ['rævənəs], *adj.* gefräßig,
gierig.
ravine [rə'viːn], *s.* die Schlucht.
ravish ['ræviʃ], *v.a.* schänden, entehren; (*delight*) entzücken.
raw [rɔː], *adj.* rauh (*rough*), roh (*meat*);
jung, grün (*novice*); *a* — *deal*, die
unfaire Behandlung.
ray (1) [rei], *s.* (*Phys.*) der Strahl. —
v.n. strahlen.
ray (2) [rei], *s.* (*Zool.*) der Rochen.
raze [reiz], *v.a.* radieren (*erase*); zer-

stören (*destroy*).
razor ['reizə], *s.* der Rasierapparat;
— *strop*, der Streichriemen.
re* [riː], *pref.* wieder —, noch einmal,
zurück-.

* In the following pages, only those
compounds are listed in which the
meaning is different from the root
word or where no simple stem exists.

reach [riːtʃ], *v.a.* reichen, erlangen
(*attain*); reichen (*hand*); erreichen.
— *s.* der Bereich, (*fig.*) die Weite.
react [riˈækt], *v.n.* reagieren (*to, auf,
Acc.*).
read (1) [riːd], *v.a.*, *v.n. irr.* lesen; anzeigen (*meter etc.*); — *for a degree*,
studieren.
read (2) [red], *adj. well*—, belesen.
readable ['riːdəbl], *adj.* gut zu lesen,
lesenswert; leserlich (*legible*).
reader ['riːdə], *s.* der Leser; (*Univ.*)
der außerordentliche Professor; (*fig.*)
das Lesebuch.
readiness ['redinis], *s.* die Bereitschaft,
Bereitwilligkeit.
ready ['redi], *adj.* bereit, fertig; prompt;
— *money*, das Bargeld.
real [riəl], *adj.* wirklich, wahr, tatsächlich; echt; — *estate*, der Grundbesitz.
realistic [riəˈlistik], *adj.* realistisch.
reality [riˈæliti], *s.* die Wirklichkeit.
realize ['riəlaiz], *v.a.* (*understand*) begreifen; (*sell*) veräußern; verwirklichen.
realm [relm], *s.* das Reich.
reap [riːp], *v.a.* ernten.
rear (1) [riə], *adj.* hinter, nach-. — *s.*
der Hintergrund; (*Mil.*) die Nachhut.
rear (2) [riə], *v.a.* aufziehen, erziehen
(*bring up*). — *v.n.* sich bäumen.
reason ['riːzən], *s.* die Ursache, der
Grund (*cause*); die Vernunft (*reasonableness*). — *v.n.* argumentieren,
debattieren.
reasonable ['riːzənəbl], *adj.* vernünftig;
verständig.
reasonably ['riːzənəbli], *adv.* ziemlich,
verhältnismäßig.
rebate ['riːbeit], *s.* der Rabatt.
rebel [rebl], *s.* der Rebell. — [riˈbel],
v.n. sich empören.
rebound [riˈbaund], *v.n.* zurückprallen.
— ['riːbaund], *s.* der Rückprall.
rebuff [riˈbʌf], *s.* die Abweisung. —
v.a. abweisen, zurückweisen.
rebuke [riˈbjuːk], *v.a.* zurechtweisen,
tadeln. — *s.* der Tadel, die Kritik (an).
rebut [riˈbʌt], *v.a.* widerlegen.
rebuttal [riˈbʌtl], *s.* die Widerlegung.
recalcitrant [riˈkælsitrənt], *adj.* widerspenstig, störrisch.
recall [riˈkɔːl], *v.a.* zurückrufen; (*remember*) sich erinnern.
recant [riˈkænt], *v.a.*, *v.n.* widerrufen.
recapitulate [riːkəˈpitjuleit], *v.a.* re-
kapitulieren, wiederholen.
recast [riˈkɑːst], *v.a.* neu fassen, umarbeiten.
recede [riˈsiːd], *v.n.* zurückgehen;
heruntergehen (*prices etc.*).

receipt [ri'si:t], *s.* die Empfangsbestätigung, Quittung. — *v.a.* quittieren.
receive [ri'si:v], *v.a.* erhalten, empfangen; (*Law*) Diebesgut annehmen.
receiver [ri'si:və], *s.* der Empfänger; (*Law*) der Hehler; (*Telephone*) der Hörer; (*Rad.*) der Apparat.
recent ['ri:sənt], *adj.* jüngst, neuest.
recently ['ri:səntli], *adv.* vor kurzem.
reception [ri'sepʃən], *s.* der Empfang.
receptive [ri'septiv]. *adj.* empfänglich.
recess [ri'ses], *s.* (*Parl.*) die Ferien, *pl.*; die Pause; die Nische (*nook*).
recession [ri'seʃən], *s.* (*Econ.*) die Rezession, die Baisse.
recipe ['resipi], *s.* (*Cul.*) das Rezept.
recipient [ri'sipiənt], *s.* der Empfänger (*of donation etc.*).
reciprocal [ri'siprəkəl], *adj.* gegenseitig, wechselseitig.
reciprocate [ri'siprəkeit], *v.a.*, *v.n.* erwidern, vergelten.
recital [ri'saitl], *s.* der Vortrag; (*Mus.*) das Solokonzert, Kammerkonzert.
recite [ri'sait], *v.a.* vortragen; (*story*) erzählen, aufsagen.
reckless ['reklis], *adj.* leichtsinnig.
reckon ['rekən], *v.n.* rechnen (*on*, mit, *Dat.*); dafür halten, denken (*think*).
reclamation [reklə'meiʃən], *s.* (*Agr.*) die Urbarmachung; (*fig.*) die Beschwerde, Reklamation.
recline [ri'klain], *v.n.* sich zurücklehnen.
recluse [ri'klu:s], *s.* der Einsiedler.
recognition [rekəg'niʃən], *s.* die Anerkennung.
recognize ['rekəgnaiz], *v.a.* anerkennen (als) (*acknowledge*); erkennen (*know again*).
recoil [ri'kɔil], *v.n.* zurückprallen, zurückfahren.
recollect [rekə'lekt], *v.a.* sich erinnern (an, *Acc.*).
recollection [rekə'lekʃən], *s.* die Erinnerung, das Gedächtnis.
recommend [rekə'mend], *v.a.* empfehlen.
recompense ['rekəmpens], *v.a.* vergelten, entschädigen, belohnen.
reconcile ['rekənsail], *v.a.* versöhnen.
reconciliation [rekənsili'eiʃən], *s.* die Versöhnung.
recondite ['rekəndait], *adj.* dunkel, verborgen, wenig bekannt.
reconnoitre [rekə'nɔitə], *v.a.* auskundschaften.
record [ri'kɔːd], *v.a.* notieren, eintragen (*enter*), festhalten; aufnehmen (*tape etc.*). — ['rekɔːd], *s.* die Aufzeichnung (*in writing*); die Schallplatte (*gramophone*); (*Sports*) der Rekord.
recorder [ri'kɔːdə], *s.* der Protokollführer; (*Law*) der Richter; Syndikus, Registrator; (*Mus.*) die Blockflöte.
recount [ri'kaunt], *v.a.* erzählen.
recourse [ri'kɔːs], *s.* die Zuflucht.
recover [ri'kʌvə], *v.a.* wiedererlangen. — *v.n.* sich erholen.

recovery [ri'kʌvəri], *s.* die Wiedererlangung (*regaining*); (*Med.*) die Genesung, Erholung.
recreation [rekri'eiʃən], *s.* die Erholung.
recrimination [rekrimi'neiʃən], *s.* die Gegenklage.
recruit [ri'kru:t], *v.a.* rekrutieren, anwerben. — *s.* der Rekrut.
rectangle ['rektæŋgl], *s.* das Rechteck.
rectify ['rektifai], *v.a.* richtigstellen; (*Elec.*) gleichrichten, umformen.
rectilinear [rekti'liniə], *adj.* geradlinig.
rectitude ['rektitju:d], *s.* die Aufrichtigkeit.
rector ['rektə], *s.* (*Eccl.*) der Pfarrer; der Rektor, Vorstand (*institution*).
recuperate [ri'kju:pəreit], *v.n.* sich erholen.
recur [ri'kə:], *v.n.* sich wieder ereignen, sich wiederholen.
recurrence [ri'kʌrəns], *s.* die Wiederholung.
red [red], *adj.* rot; — *hot*, glühend heiß.
redbreast ['redbrest], *s.* (*Orn.*) das Rotkehlchen.
redeem [ri'di:m], *v.a.* erlösen.
redemption [ri'dempʃən], *s.* die Erlösung.
redolent ['redolənt], *adj.* duftend.
redound [ri'daund], *v.n.* gereichen, sich erweisen.
redress [ri'dres], *v.a.* abhelfen (*Dat.*); wieder herstellen. — *s.* die Abhilfe.
reduce [ri'dju:s], *v.a.* vermindern, herabsetzen; (*fig.*) degradieren. — *v.n.* (*weight*) abnehmen.
reduction [ri'dʌkʃən], *s.* die Herabsetzung (*price etc.*); die Verminderung (*decrease*); (*Chem.*) die Reduktion.
redundant [ri'dʌndənt], *adj.* überflüssig.
reduplicate [ri:'dju:plikeit], *v.a.* verdoppeln.
reed [ri:d], *s.* (*Bot.*) das Schilfrohr; (*Mus.*) die Rohrpfeife.
reef [ri:f], *s.* das Riff, Felsenriff; (*Naut.*) das Reff.
reek [ri:k], *v.n.* rauchen, dampfen, riechen. — *s.* der Rauch, Dampf, der Gestank.
reel [ri:l], *s.* die Spule, Rolle, Haspel. — *v.a.* — *off*, abrollen; (*fig.*) mechanisch hersagen. —*v.n.* taumeln.
refectory [ri'fektəri], *s.* der Speisesaal; das Refektorium (*in monastery etc.*).
refer [ri'fə:], *v.n.* — *to s.th.*, weiterleiten; überweisen; — *to*, sich beziehen (auf, *Acc.*).
referee [refə'ri:], *s.* der Referent; (*Sport*) der Schiedsrichter.
reference ['refərəns], *s. with* — *to*, in or mit Bezug auf; die Referenz, Empfehlung; Verweisung (*to*, auf); — *library*, die Nachschlagebibliothek; — *index*, das (Nachschlags)verzeichnis.
refine [ri'fain], *v.a.* (*Chem.*) raffinieren; (*manners*) verfeinern; (*products*) läutern, veredeln.

reflect

reflect [ri'flekt], *v.a.* widerspiegeln (*mirror*); ein Licht werfen (auf, *Acc.*). — *v.n.* — *on*, überlegen (*think over*).

reflection, reflexion [ri'flekʃən], *s.* die Überlegung, das Nachdenken; die Spiegelung, Reflexion.

reform [ri:'fɔ:m], *s.* die Reform, Verbesserung. — *v.a.* reformieren; ['ri:'fɔ:m] (sich) neu bilden. — *v.n.* sich bessern.

refractory [ri'fræktəri], *adj.* widerspenstig.

refrain (1) [ri'frein], *v.n.* — *from*, sich enthalten (*Genit.*); absehen von (*Dat.*).

refrain (2) [ri'frein], *s.* (*Mus., Poet.*) der Kehrreim.

refresh [ri'freʃ], *v.a.* erfrischen.

refrigerator [ri'fridʒəreitə], *s.* der Kühlschrank.

refuge ['refju:dʒ], *s.* die Zuflucht.

refugee [refju'dʒi:], *s.* der Flüchtling. — *adj.* Flüchtlings-.

refund [ri:'fʌnd], *v.a.* ersetzen, zurückzahlen. — ['ri:fʌnd], *s.* die Rückvergütung.

refusal [ri'fju:zəl], *s.* die Verweigerung.

refuse [ri'fju:z], *v.a.* verweigern, abschlagen. — *v.n.* — *to*, sich weigern. — ['refju:s], *s.* der Müll.

refute [ri'fju:t], *v.a.* widerlegen.

regal [ri'gəl], *adj.* königlich.

regale [ri'geil], *v.a.* bewirten.

regalia [ri'geiliə], *s. pl.* die Kronjuwelen, *n. pl.*; (*fig.*) die Amtstracht, der Amtsschmuck.

regard [ri'gɑ:d], *v.a.* ansehen (*as*, als); beachten (*heed*); *as* —*s*, was ... betrifft. — *s.* die Hochachtung, Achtung (*esteem*);(*pl.*)die Grüsse,*m.pl.*

regarding [ri'gɑ:diŋ], *prep.* bezüglich, mit Bezug auf.

regardless [ri'gɑ:dlis], *adj.* rücksichtslos, ohne Rücksicht auf.

regency ['ri:dʒənsi], *s.* die Regentschaft.

regent ['ri:dʒənt], *s.* der Regent.

regiment ['redʒimənt], *s.* (*Mil.*) das Regiment. — [-ment], *v.a.* (*fig.*) regimentieren.

region ['ri:dʒən], *s.* die Gegend.

regional ['ri:dʒənəl], *adj.* örtlich, lokal, Bezirks-.

register ['redʒistə], *s.* das Register, die Liste. — *v.n.* sich eintragen.

registrar ['redʒistrɑ:], *s.* der Registrator; der Standesbeamte (*births etc.*); der Kanzleidirektor (*institution*).

registry ['redʒistri], *s.* die Registratur.

regret [ri'gret], *v.a.* bereuen, bedauern. — *s.* die Reue; das Bedauern (*in formal apology*); *with* —, mit Bedauern.

regular ['regjulə], *adj.* regelmäßig; (*Am.*) anständig. — *s.* (*Mil.*) der Berufssoldat.

regulate ['regjuleit], *v.a.* regulieren, regeln.

regulation [regju'leiʃən], *s.* die Regelung; die Anordnung (*order*).

rehabilitate [ri:hə'biliteit], *v.a.* rehabilitieren.

rehearsal [ri'hə:sl], *s.* (*Theat., Mus.*) die Probe.

rehearse [ri'hə:s], *v.a.* proben, wiederholen.

reign [rein], *v.n.* herrschen, regieren. — *s.* die Herrschaft, Regierung.

rein [rein], *s.* der Zügel, der Zaum.

reindeer ['reindiə], *s.* (*Zool.*) das Ren, Rentier.

reinforce [ri:in'fɔ:s], *v.a.* betonen, verstärken.

reinforced [ri:in'fɔ:sd], *adj.* verstärkt; — *concrete*, der Eisenbeton.

reject [ri'dʒekt], *v.a.* ausschlagen, verwerfen.

rejection [ri'dʒekʃən], *s.* die Ablehnung, Verwerfung.

rejoice [ri'dʒɔis], *v.n.* sich freuen.

rejoin ['ri:'dʒɔin],*v.a.* wiedervereinigen. — [ri'dʒɔin], *v.n.* erwidern.

rejoinder [ri'dʒɔində], *s.* die Erwiderung.

relapse [ri'læps], *s.* der Rückfall. — *v.n.* fallen, zurückfallen.

relation [ri'leiʃən], *s.* die Beziehung (*connexion*); der, die Verwandte (*relative*); (*pl.*) die Verwandtschaft (*family*).

relative [ri'lətiv], *adj.* relativ; verhältnismäßig (*in proportion*). — *s.* der, die Verwandte.

relax [ri'læks], *v.n.* sich ausruhen; nachlassen. — *v.a.* entspannen.

relay [ri'lei], *v.a.* (*Rad.*) übertragen. — ['ri:lei], *s.* — *race*, der Staffellauf.

release [ri'li:s], *v.a.* freilassen, freisetzen (*prisoner*); freigeben (*news*). — *s.* die Freigabe (*news etc.*); die Freisetzung (*liberation*).

relegate ['religeit], *v.a.* verweisen, zurückweisen.

relent [ri'lent], *v.n.* nachgeben.

relentless [ri'lentlis], *adj.* unerbittlich, unnachgiebig.

relevance ['reləvəns], *s.* die Wichtigkeit.

relevant ['reləvənt], *adj.* wichtig, sachdienlich.

reliable [ri'laiəbl], *adj.* verläßlich, zuverlässig.

reliance [ri'laiəns], *s.* das Vertrauen.

relic ['relik], *s.* das Überbleibsel; das Andenken; (*Eccl.*) die Reliquie.

relief (1) [ri'li:f], *s.* die Erleichterung, Linderung, (*easement*); die Ablösung (*guard etc.*); die Aushilfe (*extra staff etc.*).

relief (2) [ri'li:f], *s.* (*Art*) das Relief.

relieve [ri'li:v], *v.a.* erleichtern; lindern (*pain*); ablösen (*from duty*).

religion [ri'lidʒən], *s.* die Religion.

religious [ri'lidʒəs], *adj.* religiös, gläubig, fromm.

relinquish [ri'liŋkwiʃ], *v.a.* verlassen, aufgeben.

relish ['reliʃ], v.a. Geschmack finden
an. — v.n. schmecken. — s. der Geschmack, die Würze.
reluctance [ri'lʌktəns], s. der Widerwille, das Zögern.
reluctant [ri'lʌktənt], adj. widerwillig,
widerstrebend.
rely [ri'lai], v.n. sich verlassen (on, auf);
vertrauen (auf).
remain [ri'mein], v.n. bleiben, zurückbleiben, übrigbleiben.
remainder [ri'meində], s. der Rest.
remand [ri'mɑːnd], v.a. — in custody,
in die Untersuchungshaft zurück-
schicken. — s. — home, die Besserungsanstalt.
remark [ri'mɑːk], s. die Bemerkung.
— v.a. bemerken.
remarkable [ri'mɑːkəbl], adj. bemerkenswert, außerordentlich.
remedial [rə'miːdiəl], adj. Heil-, ab-
helfend.
remedy ['remədi], s. das Heilmittel,
Hilfsmittel. — v.a. abhelfen (Dat.).
remember [ri'membə], v.a. sich erinnern an; — s.o. to s.o. else, jemanden
von jemandem grüßen lassen.
remembrance [ri'membrəns], s. die
Erinnerung.
remind [ri'maind], v.a. erinnern (of,
an), mahnen.
reminiscence [remi'nisəns], s. die
Erinnerung.
remiss [ri'mis], adj. nachlässig.
remission [ri'miʃən], s. der Nachlaß;
(Rel.) die Vergebung (of sins).
remit [ri'mit], v.a. (Comm.) überweisen,
einsenden; erlassen (forgive).
remittance [ri'mitəns], s. (Comm.) die
Rimesse, die Überweisung.
remnant ['remnənt], s. der Überrest.
remonstrate ['remənstreit], v.n. Vor-
stellungen machen.
remorse [ri'mɔːs], s. die Reue.
remote [ri'mout], adj. fern, entlegen.
removal [ri'muːvəl], s. das Wegschaffen
(taking away); die Übersiedlung, der
Umzug.
remove [ri'muːv], v.a. entfernen. —
v.n. umziehen. — s. (Sch.) die Ver-
setzungsklasse; der Verwandtschafts-
grad (relationship).
removed [ri'muːvd], adj. entfernt;
cousin once —, der Vetter ersten
Grades.
remuneration [rimjuːnə'reiʃən], s. die
Besoldung, Entlöhnung.
rend [rend], v.a. reißen, entlegen.
render ['rendə], v.a. leisten (service);
übersetzen (translate); wiedergeben;
(Comm.) — account, Rechnung vorlegen.
rendering ['rendəriŋ], s. die Wiedergabe, der Vortrag (of song etc.);
(Comm.) der Vorlage; die Übersetzung (translation).
renegade ['renigeid], s. der Abtrün-
nige.
renewal [ri'njuːəl], s. die Erneuerung;
die Verlängerung (extension).

rennet ['renit], s. das Lab.
renounce [ri'nauns], v.a. entsagen
(Dat.), verzichten auf (Acc.).
renown [ri'naun], s. der Ruhm.
rent (1) [rent], v.a. mieten, pachten.
— s. die Miete, Pacht (of land, farm).
rent (2) [rent], s. der Riß (tear).
rental [rentl], s. die Miete.
renunciation [rinʌnsi'eiʃən], s. die
Entsagung, der Verzicht.
repair [ri'pɛə], v.a. ausbessern, reparieren. — s. die Reparatur; beyond
—, nicht reparierbar.
reparations [repə'reiʃənz], s. pl. (Pol.)
die Reparationen, Wiedergutma-
chungskosten, f. pl.
repartee [repɑː'tiː], s. die treffende
Antwort.
repast [ri'pɑːst], s. die Mahlzeit.
repeal [ri'piːl], v.a. (Parl.) aufheben,
widerrufen. — s. die Aufhebung.
repeat [ri'piːt], v.a. wiederholen.
repent [ri'pent], v.a. bereuen.
repercussion [riːpə'kʌʃən], s. der
Rückstoß, die Rückwirkung.
repertory ['repətəri], s. (Theat. etc.) das
Repertoire, der Spielplan.
repetition [repi'tiʃən], s. die Wiederholung.
replace [riː'pleis], v.a. ersetzen.
replete [ri'pliːt], adj. voll, angefüllt.
reply [ri'plai], v.n. antworten, erwidern.
— s. die Antwort.
report [ri'pɔːt], v.a., v.n. berichten. —
s. der Bericht; (Sch.) das Zeugnis;
der Knall (of explosion).
repose [ri'pouz], v.n. ruhen. — v.a.
setzen (in, auf). — s. die Ruhe, der
Friede.
repository [ri'pɔzitəri], s. die Niederlage, Aufbewahrungsstätte, Fund-
stätte.
reprehensible [repri'hensibl], adj. tadelnswert.
represent [repri'zent], v.a. repräsen-
tieren, vertreten.
representative [repri'zentətiv], adj.
repräsentativ, typisch. — s. der
Stellvertreter; (Pol.) der Repräsentant.
repress [ri'pres], v.a. unterdrücken.
reprieve [ri'priːv], v.a. begnadigen.
— s. die Gnadenfrist.
reprimand [repri'mɑːnd], v.a. verweisen, tadeln. — s. der Tadel.
reprint [riː'print], v.a. neu drucken.
— ['riːprint], s. der Neudruck.
reprisal [ri'praizəl], s. die Vergeltungs-
maßregel; (pl.) die Repressalien, f. pl.
reproach [ri'proutʃ], v.a. vorwerfen
(Dat.), tadeln. — s. der Vorwurf,
Tadel.
reprobate ['reprəbeit], adj. ruchlos,
verworfen.
reproduce [riːprə'djuːs], v.a. reproduzieren, erzeugen.
reproof [ri'pruːf], s. der Vorwurf,
Tadel.
reprove [ri'pruːv], v.a. tadeln, rügen
(a person), mißbilligen (a practice).

473

republic

republic [ri'pʌblik], s. die Republik.

repudiate [ri'pju:dieit], v.a. zurück-weisen, verwerfen.

repugnant [ri'pʌgnənt], adj. wider-wärtig, ekelhaft.

repulse [ri'pʌls], v.a. (Mil.) zurück-schlagen; abweisen (s.o.). — s. (Mil.) das Zurückschlagen; (fig.) die Zurückweisung.

repulsive [ri'pʌlsiv], adj. widerwärtig.

reputation [repju'teiʃən], s. der (gute) Ruf.

request [ri'kwest], v.a. ersuchen. — s. das Ersuchen, Ansuchen, die Bitte.

requiem ['rekwiəm], s. (Eccl.) das Requiem, die Totenmesse.

require [ri'kwaiə], v.a. fordern, ver-langen, brauchen.

requirement [ri'kwaiəmənt], s. die Anforderung, das Erfordernis.

requisite ['rekwizit], adj. erforderlich.

requisition [rekwi'ziʃən], s. (Mil.) die Requisition; die Forderung.

requite [ri'kwait], v.a. vergelten.

rescind [ri'sind], v.a. für ungültig erklären, aufheben.

rescue ['reskju:], v.a. retten. — s. die Rettung.

research [ri'sə:tʃ], v.n. forschen, For-schung treiben. — s. die Forschung.

resemble [ri'zembl], v.a. ähnlich sein (Dat.), gleichen (Dat.).

resent [ri'zent], v.a. übelnehmen.

resentful [ri'zentful], adj. nachträge-risch; empfindlich (over-sensitive).

resentment [ri'zentmənt], s. die Emp-findlichkeit; der Groll (spite).

reservation [rezə'veiʃən], s. die Reser-vierung (of seat); der Vorbehalt (doubt).

reserve [ri'zə:v], v.a. reservieren, be-legen (seat); (fig.) vorbehalten (o.'s position). — s. die Reserve, die Verschlossenheit (shyness); die Ein-schränkung (limitation); die Reserven, f. pl. (money).

reside [ri'zaid], v.n. wohnen.

resident ['rezidənt], adj. wohnhaft. — s. der Ansässige.

residual [ri'zidjuəl], adj. übrig blei-bend.

residue ['rezidju:], s. der Rückstand, Rest.

resign [ri'zain], v.a. abtreten, aufgeben; (ein Amt) niederlegen. — v.n. ab-danken. — v.r. — o.s. to, sich in etwas fügen, zurücktreten.

resignation [rezig'neiʃən], s. die Resig-nation, der Rücktritt (from office); die Fügung, Resignation (attitude).

resin ['rezin], s. das Harz.

resist [ri'zist], v.a., v.n. widerstehen, Widerstand leisten (Dat.).

resistance [ri'zistəns], s. der Wider-stand.

resolute ['rezəlju:t], adj. entschlossen.

resolution [rezə'lju:ʃən], s. die Ent-schlossenheit (determination); die Ent-scheidung (decision); der Vorsatz, Entschluß (vow).

resolve [ri'zɔlv], v.a. auflösen (solve); beschließen (conclude). — v.n. ent-scheiden (decide). — s. der Be-schluß, die Entscheidung.

resonance ['rezənəns], s. die Reso-nanz.

resort [ri'zɔ:t], v.n. — to, seine Zuflucht nehmen (zu). — s. seaside —, das Seebad, health —, der Kurort (spa).

resound [ri'zaund], v.n. widerhallen.

resource [ri'sɔ:s], s. das Hilfsmittel; (pl.) die Mittel, n. pl.

respect [ri'spekt], v.a. respektieren, achten; berücksichtigen (have regard to). — s. der Respekt, die Achtung; with — to, mit Bezug auf; in — of, bezüglich (Genit.).

respectability [rispektə'biliti], s. die Anständigkeit; Achtbarkeit.

respective [ris'pektiv], adj. respektiv.

respectively [ris'pektivli], adv. bezie-hungsweise.

respiration [respi'reiʃən], s. die At-mung.

respiratory [ris'paiərətri or 'respirei-təri], adj. Atmungs-.

respire [ri'spaiə], v.n. atmen.

respite ['respit], s. die Frist, der Auf-schub.

resplendent [ri'splendənt], adj. glän-zend.

respond [ri'spɔnd], v.n. antworten, eingehen (to, auf).

respondent [ri'spɔndənt], s. (Law) der Beklagte.

response [ri'spɔns], s. die Antwort, Aufnahme, Reaktion; (fig.) der Widerhall.

responsibility [rispɔnsi'biliti], s. die Verantwortung, Verantwortlichkeit.

responsible [ri'spɔnsibl], adj. verant-wortlich.

responsive [ri'spɔnsiv], adj. empfäng-lich, zugänglich.

rest (1) [rest], v.n. ruhen, rasten. — s. die Ruhe, Rast; (Mus.) die Pause.

rest (2) [rest], v.n. bleiben (stay); — assured, sei (seien Sie) versichert. — s. der Rest; die übrigen, pl.

restaurant ['restərã], s. das Restaurant.

restful ['restful], adj. ruhig.

restitution [resti'tju:ʃən], s. die Wieder-gutmachung.

restive ['restiv], adj. unruhig, ruhelos.

restless ['restlis], adj. rastlos, un-ruhig.

restoration [restə:'reiʃən], s. die Wie-derherstellung; (Hist.) die Restaura-tion.

restore [ri'stɔ:], v.a. wiederherstellen.

restrain [ri'strein], v.a. zurückhalten, einschränken.

restraint [ri'streint], s. die Zurückhal-tung.

restrict [ri'strikt], v.a. beschränken.

restriction [ri'strikʃən], s. die Ein-schränkung.

restrictive [ri'striktiv], adj. einschrän-kend.

result [ri'zʌlt], *v.n.* folgen, sich ergeben; (*come about*) erfolgen. — *s.* das Ergebnis, Resultat; (*consequence*) die Folge.

resume [ri'zju:m], *v.a.* wiederaufnehmen; (*narrative*) fortsetzen. — *v.n.* fortfahren.

résumé ['rezjumei], *s.* das Resümee, die Zusammenfassung.

resumption [ri'zʌmpʃən], *s.* die Wiederaufnahme.

resurrection [rezə'rekʃən], *s.* (*Rel.*) die Auferstehung.

resuscitate [ri'sʌsiteit], *v.a.* wiederbeleben.

retail ['ri:teil], *s.* der Kleinhandel, Einzelhandel. — [ri'teil], *v.a.* im Detail handeln, verkaufen.

retain [ri'tein], *v.a.* behalten.

retainer [ri'teinə], *s.* der Diener; Gefolgsmann; der Vorschuß (*fee*).

retake [ri:'teik], *v.a. irr.* (*Mil.*) wieder erobern; (*Phot., Film*) noch einmal aufnehmen. — *s.* (*Am.*) die Neuaufnahme (*Phot., Film*).

retaliate [ri'tælieit], *v.n.* sich rächen, vergelten.

retard [ri'ta:d], *v.a.* verzögern, verlangsamen.

retch [retʃ], *v.n.* sich erbrechen.

retentive [ri'tentiv], *adj.* behaltend, gut (*memory*).

reticent ['retisənt], *adj.* schweigsam, einsilbig.

retina ['retinə], *s.* (*Anat.*) die Netzhaut.

retinue ['retinju:], *s.* das Gefolge.

retire [ri'taiə], *v.n.* sich zurückziehen (*withdraw*); in den Ruhestand treten (*from work*). — *v.a.* pensionieren.

retirement [ri'taiəmənt], *s.* die Pension, der Ruhestand; die Zurückgezogenheit (*seclusion*).

retort [ri'tɔ:t], *s.* (*Chem.*) die Retorte; die scharfe Antwort (*debate*). — *v.n.* scharf erwidern.

retouch [ri:'tʌtʃ], *v.a.* (*Phot.*) retouchieren.

retrace [ri:'treis], *v.a.* zurückverfolgen.

retreat [ri'tri:t], *v.n.* sich zurückziehen. — *s.* der Rückzug (*Mil.*); die Zufluchtsort.

retrench [ri'trentʃ], *v.a.* einschränken (*restrict*); verkürzen (*shorten*). — *v.n.* sich einschränken.

retribution [retri'bju:ʃən], *s.* die Vergeltung.

retrieve [ri'tri:v], *v.a.* wieder bekommen, wieder gewinnen.

retriever [ri'tri:və], *s.* (*Zool.*) der Apportierhund, Stöberhund.

retrograde ['retrogreid], *adj.* rückgängig, rückwärts.

retrospect ['retrospekt], *s.* der Rückblick.

retrospective [retro'spektiv], *adj.* rückblickend.

return [ri'tə:n], *v.a.* zurückgeben; erwidern (*reciprocate*); abordnen, entsenden (*to Parl.*); (*figures*) einsenden. — *v.n.* zurückkehren, zurückkommen.

— *s.* die Rückkehr; (*Fin.*) der Gewinn; (*Parl.*) die Entsendung, Mandatierung; (*pl.*) (*figures*) die Einsendung; by — *of post*, umgehend, postwendend; — *ticket*, die Rückfahrkarte.

reunion [ri:'ju:niən], *s.* die Wiedervereinigung.

reveal [ri'vi:l], *v.a.* enthüllen, offenbaren (*show*); verraten (*betray*).

reveille [ri'væli], *s.* (*Mil.*) das Wecken, Wecksignal.

revel [revl], *v.n.* schwelgen.

revelation [revə'leiʃən], *s.* die Offenbarung.

revelry ['revəlri], *s.* die Schwelgerei.

revenge [ri'vendʒ], *s.* die Rache, Revanche. — *v.r.* (*also be revenged*) sich rächen (*on*, an, *Dat.*).

revenue ['revənju:], *s.* das Einkommen; *Inland* —, die Steuereinnahmen.

reverberate [ri'və:bəreit], *v.n.* widerhallen.

revere [ri'viə], *v.a.* verehren.

reverence ['revərəns], *s.* die Ehrerbietung, der Respekt; *show* —, Ehrerbietung zollen.

Reverend ['revərənd]. (*abbr.* **Rev.**) (*Eccl.*) *The* —, Seine Ehrwürden; *The Very* —, Seine Hochwürden.

reverent, reverential ['revərənt, revə'renʃəl], *adj.* ehrerbietig.

reverie ['revəri], *s.* die Träumerei.

reversal [ri'və:səl], *s.* die Umkehrung, Umstoßung.

reverse [ri'və:s], *v.a., v.n.* umkehren, umdrehen. — *s.* das Gegenteil (*contrary*); die Kehrseite (*of coin*).

revert [ri'və:t], *v.a., v.n.* umkehren, zurückkehren.

review [ri'vju:], *v.a.* durchsehen, prüfen (*examine*); rezensieren (*book etc.*). — *s.* die Revision; (*Mil.*) die Parade, Truppenmusterung; die Rezension, Besprechung (*book etc.*).

revile [ri'vail], *v.a., v.n.* schmähen.

revise [ri'vaiz], *v.a.* korrigieren (*correct*); wiederholen (*recapitulate*); umarbeiten (*modify*).

revision [ri'viʒən], *s.* die Revision; Korrektur; Umarbeitung; Wiederholung (*recapitulation*).

revolt [ri'voult], *v.n.* sich empören, revoltieren. — *v.a.* empören. — *s.* die Empörung.

revolting [ri'voultiŋ], *adj.* ekelhaft, empörend.

revolution [revə'lju:ʃən], *s.* (*Pol.*) die Revolution; (*Motor.*) die Umdrehung.

revolve [ri'vɔlv], *v.n.* rotieren, sich drehen.

revolver [ri'vɔlvə], *s.* der Revolver.

revue [ri'vju:], *s.* (*Theat.*) die Revue.

revulsion [ri'vʌlʃən], *s.* der Ekel; der Umschwung.

reward [ri'wɔ:d], *v.a.* belohnen (*person*); vergelten (*deed*). — *s.* die Belohnung.

rheumatic [ru:'mætik], *adj.* (*Med.*) rheumatisch.

rheumatism ['ru:mətizm], *s.* (*Med.*) der Rheumatismus.

rhetoric ['retərik], *s.* die Redekunst.

Rhodesian [ro'di:ʃən, -'di:ʒən], *adj.* rhodesisch. — *s.* der Rhodesier.

rhododendron [roudo'dendrən], *s.* (*Bot.*) die Alpenrose.

rhubarb ['ru:ba:b], *s.* (*Bot.*) der Rhabarber.

rhyme [raim], *s.* der Reim; *no — nor reason*, sinnlos.

rhythm [riðm], *s.* der Rhythmus.

rib [rib], *s.* (*Anat.*) die Rippe.

ribald ['ribəld], *adj.* liederlich; (*joke*) unanständig.

ribbon ['ribən], *s.* das Band.

rice [rais], *s.* der Reis.

rich [ritʃ], *adj.* reich; fruchtbar (*fertile*).

rick [rik], *s.* der Schober.

rickets ['rikits], *s.* (*Med.*) die englische Krankheit, die Rachitis.

rickety ['rikiti], *adj.* gebrechlich, wackelig, baufällig.

rid [rid], *v.a. irr.* befreien, freimachen (*of*, von); — *o.s.*, sich entledigen (*of*, *Genit.*); *get — of*, loswerden (*Acc.*); *be — of*, los sein (*Acc.*).

riddance ['ridəns], *s.* die Befreiung, das Loswerden.

riddle (1) [ridl], *s.* das Rätsel (*puzzle*).

riddle (2) [ridl], *s.* das grobe Sieb (*sieve*). — *v.a.* sieben (*sieve*); durchlöchern.

ride [raid], *v.a., v.n. irr.* reiten (*on horse*), fahren (*on bicycle etc.*); — *at anchor*, vor Anker liegen. — *s.* der Ritt (*on horse*), die Fahrt (*in vehicle*).

rider ['raidə], *s.* der Reiter (*horseman*); der Fahrer (*cyclist etc.*); der Zusatz (*addition*).

ridge [ridʒ], *s.* der Rücken (*edge*); die Bergkette; die Furche (*furrow*). — *v.a.* furchen.

ridicule ['ridikju:l], *s.* der Spott. — *v.a.* lächerlich machen.

ridiculous [ri'dikjuləs], *adj.* lächerlich.

rife [raif], *adj.* häufig, weitverbreitet.

rifle (1) [raifl], *s.* die Büchse, das Gewehr.

rifle (2) [raifl], *v.a.* ausplündern.

rift [rift], *s.* der Riß, Spalt, die Spalte. — *v.a.* spalten.

rig [rig], *s.* (*Naut.*) die Takelung; (*fig.*) — *out*, die Ausstattung. — *v.a.* (*Naut.*) (auf)takeln; (*Am.*) fälschen (*fake*); — *out*, ausstatten.

right [rait], *adj.* recht; richtig; wahr; gesund; korrekt; — *hand*, rechtsseitig; *you are —*, Sie haben recht; *that's —*, das stimmt. — *s.* das Recht; *by right(s)*, rechtmäßig; *drive on the —*, rechts fahren.

righteous ['raitʃəs], *adj.* rechtschaffen, aufrecht.

rightful ['raitful], *adj.* rechtmäßig.

rigid ['ridʒid], *adj.* steif; unbeugsam; streng (*severe*).

rigidity [ri'dʒiditi], *s.* die Steifheit, Unnachgiebigkeit; die Strenge.

rigmarole ['rigməroul], *s.* die Salbaderei, das Gewäsch.

rigorous ['rigərəs], *adj.* streng; genau.

rigour ['rigə], *s.* die Strenge; die Härte.

rill [ril], *s.* (*Poet.*) das Bächlein.

rim [rim], *s.* der Rand, die Felge.

rime [raim], *s.* (*Poet.*) der Reif.

rind [raind], *s.* die Rinde.

ring (1) [riŋ], *s.* der Ring.

ring (2) [riŋ], *s.* der Schall, das Läuten (*bell*); der Anruf (*telephone*); das Geläute (*bells*). — *v.a. irr.* läuten, klingeln (*bell*). — *v.n.* läuten; ertönen, tönen (*call, voice*).

ringleader ['riŋli:də], *s.* der Rädelsführer.

rink [riŋk], *s.* die Eisbahn; Rollschuhbahn.

rinse [rins], *v.a.* spülen, waschen. — *s.* das Abspülen.

riot ['raiət], *s.* der Aufruhr. — *v.n.* Aufruhr stiften; meutern.

rip [rip], *v.a.* reißen, aufreißen. — *s.* der Riß.

ripe [raip], *adj.* reif.

ripen ['raipən], *v.n.* reifen. — *v.a.* reifen lassen.

ripple [ripl], *s.* die Welle, Kräuselwelle (*water*). — *v.n.* kräuseln (*water*); (*Bot.*) riffeln.

rise [raiz], *v.n. irr.* aufstehen (*get up*); aufsteigen (*ascend*); anschwellen (*swell*); steigen (*price*). — *s.* die Erhöhung; (*Comm.*) der Anstieg; die Steigerung, Erhöhung (*salary*); der Ursprung (*origin*).

rising ['raiziŋ], *s.* der Aufstand (*rebellion*).

risk [risk], *s.* das Risiko. — *v.a.* wagen, riskieren.

rite [rait], *s.* der Ritus.

ritual ['ritjuəl], *s.* das Ritual.

rival [raivl], *s.* der Rivale, Nebenbuhler. — *adj.* nebenbuhlerisch, konkurrierend. — *v.a.* konkurrieren, wetteifern.

river ['rivə], *s.* der Fluß.

rivet ['rivit], *s.* die Niete. — *v.a.* nieten.

roach [routʃ], *s.* (*Zool.*) die Plötze.

road [roud], *s.* die Straße; der Weg.

roam [roum], *v.n.* herumstreifen.

roan [roun], *s.* der Rotschimmel (*horse*).

roar [rɔ:], *v.n.* brüllen (*animals*); brausen (*storm*). — *s.* das Gebrüll (*animal*); das Getöse, Brausen, Rauschen.

roast [roust], *v.a., v.n.* braten, rösten. — *s.* der Braten.

rob [rɔb], *v.a.* berauben.

robbery ['rɔbəri], *s.* der Raub, die Räuberei.

robe [roub], *s.* die Robe.

robin ['rɔbin], *s.* (*Orn.*) das Rotkehlchen.

rock [rɔk], *s.* der Felsen, die Klippe. — *v.a.* schaukeln, wiegen. — *v.n.* wackeln, taumeln.

rocket ['rɔkit], *s.* die Rakete; (*sl.*) die Rüge. — *v.n.* hochfliegen; hochgehen (*prices*).

rocky ['rɔki], *adj.* felsig.

rod [rɔd], *s.* die Rute; (*fishing*) die Angelrute; die Stange (*pole*).

rodent ['roudənt], *s.* (*Zool.*) das Nagetier.

roe (1) [rou], *s.* der Fischrogen.

roe (2) [rou], *s.* (*Zool.*) das Reh, die Hirschkuh.

rogation [ro'geiʃən], *s.* das Gebet, die Litanei; *Rogation Sunday*, der Sonntag Rogate.

rogue [roug], *s.* der Schelm.

role [roul]. *s.* (*Theat.*, *fig.*) die Rolle.

roll [roul], *s.* die Liste; — *call*, der Aufruf, die Parade; die Rolle; die Semmel, das Brötchen (*bread*). — *v.a.* rollen; wälzen. — *v.n.* rollen; sich wälzen; sich drehen; schlingen (*ship*); schlenkern (*person*).

roller ['roulə], *s.* die Rolle; — *bandage*, das Wickelband; — *skates*, die Rollschuhe.

rollick ['rɔlik], *v.n.* herumtollen, lustig sein.

rolling stock ['rouliŋ stɔk], *s.* (*Railw.*) der Wagenbestand.

romance [rou'mæns], *s.* die Romanze.

romantic [rou'mæntik], *adj.* romantisch.

romp [rɔmp], *s.* der Wildfang, das Tollen. — *v.n.* toben.

roof [ru:f], *s.* das Dach. — *v.a.* decken.

rook (1) [ruk], *s.* (*Orn.*) die Saatkrähe.

rook (2) [ruk], *s.* (*Chess*) der Turm.

room [ru:m, rum], *s.* der Raum, das Zimmer. — *v.n.* (*Am.*) ein Zimmer teilen (*with*, mit).

roomy ['ru:mi], *adj.* geräumig.

roost [ru:st], *s.* der Hühnerstall. — *v.n.* aufsitzen, schlafen.

root [ru:t], *s.* die Wurzel. — *v.n.* wurzeln.

rooted ['ru:tid], *adj.* eingewurzelt.

rope [roup], *s.* das Seil. — *v.a.* anseilen (*in climbing*); (*coll.*) — *in*, verwickeln, hereinziehen.

rosary ['rouzəri], *s.* (*Rel.*) der Rosenkranz.

rose [rouz], *s.* (*Bot.*) die Rose.

Rosemary ['rouzməri]. Rosemarie.

rosemary ['rouzməri], *s.* (*Bot.*) der Rosmarin.

rosin ['rɔzin] *see* **resin.**

rosy ['rouzi], *adj.* rosig.

rot [rɔt], *v.n.* faulen, modern. — *s.* die Fäulnis,Verwesung; (*coll.*) der Unsinn.

rotate [ro'teit], *v.a.*, *v.n.* (sich) drehen, rotieren.

rote [rout], *s. by* —, mechanisch, auswendig.

rotten [rɔtn], *adj.* faul, verdorben, schlecht.

rotund [ro'tʌnd], *adj.* rundlich, rund.

rough [rʌf], *adj.* rauh, grob; flüchtig, ungefähr (*approximate*); ungehobelt (*ill-mannered*).

roughshod ['rʌfʃɔd], *adj.* rücksichtslos.

round [raund], *adj.* rund. — *s.* die Runde. — *prep.* (rund) um; um ... herum. — *adv.* (rings)herum; (*around*) ungefähr; etwa (*approximately*).

roundabout ['raundəbaut], *s.* das Karussel. — *adj.* umständlich.

Roundhead ['raundhed], *s.* (*Eng. Hist.*) der Puritaner.

rouse [rauz], *v.a.* erwecken.

rout [raut], *s.* (*Mil.*) die wilde Flucht. — *v.a.* in die Flucht jagen.

route [ru:t], *s.* der Weg; die Route.

rover ['rouvə], *s.* der Wanderer, ältere Pfadfinder (*scout*); der Seeräuber (*pirate*).

row (1) [rou], *s.* die Reihe.

row (2) [rau], *s.* der Lärm, Streit. — *v.n.* (*coll.*) lärmend streiten, zanken.

row (3) [rou], *v.n.* rudern.

rowdy ['raudi], *s.* der Raufbold. — *adj.* laut, lärmend.

royal ['rɔiəl], *adj.* königlich.

royalty ['rɔiəlti], *s.* das Mitglied des Königshauses, die königliche Hoheit; (*pl.*) (*Law*) die Tantieme.

rub [rʌb], *v.a.*, *v.n.* (sich) reiben. — *s.* die Reibung; die heikle Stelle, das Problem.

rubber (1) ['rʌbə], *s.* der Gummi; Radiergummi.

rubber (2) ['rʌbə], *s.* (*Whist*) der Robber.

rubbish ['rʌbiʃ], *s.* der Abfall, Mist; (*fig.*) der Schund (*book*), der Unsinn (*nonsense*).

ruby ['ru:bi], *s.* der Rubin.

rudder ['rʌdə], *s.* das Steuerruder.

ruddy ['rʌdi], *adj.* rötlich.

rude [ru:d], *adj.* roh; grob; ungebildet; unhöflich.

rudiment ['ru:dimənt], *s.* die Anfangsgründe, die Grundlage.

rue (1) [ru:], *s.* (*Bot.*) die Raute.

rue (2) [ru:], *v.a.* beklagen, bereuen.

ruff [rʌf], *s.* die Halskrause.

ruffian ['rʌfiən], *s.* der Raufbold.

ruffle [rʌfl], *v.a.* zerzausen (*hair*); verwirren (*muddle*). — *s.* die Krause (*on dress*); die Aufregung.

rug [rʌg], *s.* die Wolldecke, der Vorleger.

rugged ['rʌgid], *adj.* rauh; uneben.

ruin ['ru:in], *s.* die Ruine; (*fig.*) der Zusammenbruch. — *v.a.* ruinieren.

rule [ru:l], *s.* die Regel, Vorschrift; die Herrschaft; *slide* —, der Rechenschieber. — *v.a.* beherrschen; regeln; lin(i)ieren (*draw lines on*). — *v.n.* herrschen (*reign*; *be valid*); lin(i)ieren (*draw lines*); entscheiden (*decide*).

ruling ['ru:liŋ], *s.* die Regelung, Entscheidung.

rum (1) [rʌm], *s.* der Rum.

rum (2) [rʌm], *adj.* (*sl.*) seltsam.

Rumanian [ru:'meiniən], *adj.* rumänisch. — *s.* der Rumäne.

rumble [rʌmbl], *v.n.* poltern, rasseln, rumpeln; (*stomach*) knurren.

ruminate ['ru:mineit], *v.n.* wiederkäuen; nachsinnen.

rummage ['rʌmidʒ], *v.a.*, *v.n.* durchstöbern.

rumour ['ru:mə], *s.* das Gerücht.

rump [rʌmp], *s.* der Rumpf, Steiß; — *steak*, das Rumpsteak.

run

run [rʌn], *v.n. irr.* laufen, rennen; eilen; verkehren (*bus*); fließen (*flow*); (*Theat.*) gegeben werden; lauten (*text*). — *s.* der Lauf, das Rennen; (*Theat.*) die Spieldauer; *in the long* —, am Ende, auf die Dauer.

runaway ['rʌnəwei], *adj.* entlaufen. — *s.* der Ausreißer.

rung [rʌŋ], *s.* die Sprosse.

runway ['rʌnwei], *s.* (*Aviat.*) die Rollbahn, Startbahn, Landebahn.

rupture ['rʌptʃə], *s.* (*Med.*) der Leistenbruch.

rural ['ruərəl], *adj.* ländlich.

rush (1) [rʌʃ], *s.* (*Bot.*) die Binse.

rush (2) [rʌʃ], *s.* der Ansturm, Andrang; die Hetze; der Hochbetrieb. — *v.n.* stürzen, in Eile sein.

Russian ['rʌʃən], *adj.* russisch. — *s.* der Russe.

rust [rʌst], *s.* der Rost. — *v.n.* verrosten.

rustic ['rʌstik], *adj.* ländlich.

rut (1) [rʌt], *s.* die Spur; das Geleise.

rut (2) [rʌt], *s.* (*animals*) die Brunst.

ruthless ['ruːθlis], *adj.* grausam, rücksichtslos.

rye [rai], *s.* (*Bot.*) der Roggen.

S

S [es]. das S.

sable [seibl], *s.* der Zobel. — *adj.* schwarz.

sabotage ['sæbotɑːʒ], *s.* die Sabotage. — *v.a.* sabotieren.

sabre ['seibə], *s.* der Säbel.

sack (1) [sæk], *s.* der Sack; (*coll.*) die Entlassung (*get the* —). — *v.a.* (*coll.*) entlassen.

sack (2) [sæk], *v.a.* plündern (*pillage*).

sack (3) [sæk], *s.* (*obs.*) der Weißwein.

sacrament ['sækrəmənt], *s.* das Sakrament.

sacred ['seikrid], *adj.* heilig.

sacrifice ['sækrifais], *s.* das Opfer. — *v.a.* opfern.

sacrilege ['sækrilidʒ], *s.* das Sakrileg, der Frevel.

sad [sæd], *adj.* traurig.

sadden [sædn], *v.a.* betrüben.

saddle [sædl], *s.* der Sattel. — *v.a.* satteln; (*coll.*) — *s.o. with s.th.*, einem etwas aufhalsen.

safe [seif], *adj.* sicher (*secure*); wohlbehalten (*arrival etc.*). — *s.* der Geldschrank, das Safe.

safeguard ['seifgɑːd], *v.a.* beschützen, garantieren. — *s.* der Schutz, die Sicherheit.

safety ['seifti], *s.* die Sicherheit.

saffron ['sæfrən], *s.* der Safran. — *adj.* safrangelb.

sagacious [sə'geiʃəs], *adj.* scharfsinnig.

sagacity [sə'gæsiti], *s.* der Scharfsinn.

sage (1) [seidʒ], *s.* (*Bot.*) der, die Salbei.

sage (2) [seidʒ], *s.* der Weise. — *adj.* weise, klug.

sail [seil], *s.* das Segel. — *v.n.* segeln, (*Naut.*) fahren.

sailor ['seilə], *s.* der Matrose, Seemann.

Saint [seint, sənt]. (*abbr.* **S.** *or* **St.**) Sankt (*before name*).

saint [seint], *s.* der *or* die Heilige.

sake [seik], *s. for my son's* —, um meines Sohnes willen; *for the* — *of peace*, um des Friedens willen.

salacious [sə'leiʃəs], *adj.* geil; zotig (*joke*).

salad ['sæləd], *s.* der Salat.

salary ['sæləri], *s.* das Gehalt.

sale [seil], *s.* der Verkauf; *annual* —, (*Comm.*) der Ausverkauf.

salesman ['seilzmən], *s.* der Verkäufer.

salient ['seiliənt], *adj.* hervorspringend, wichtig, Haupt-.

saline ['seilain], *s.* die Salzquelle. — *adj.* salzhaltig.

saliva [sə'laivə], *s.* der Speichel.

sallow ['sælou], *adj.* blaß, bleich.

sally ['sæli], *s.* der Ausfall, (*fig.*) der komische Einfall. — *v.n.* ausfallen; — *forth*, losgehen.

salmon ['sæmən], *s.* (*Zool.*) der Lachs.

saloon [sə'luːn], *s.* der Salon; (*Am.*) das Wirtshaus, die Kneipe.

salt [sɔːlt], *s.* das Salz; — *cellar*, das Salzfäßchen; (*coll.*) *old* —, der alte Matrose. — *v.a.* salzen.

saltpetre [sɔːlt'piːtə], *s.* der Salpeter.

salubrious [sə'ljuːbriəs], *adj.* gesund (*climate, neighbourhood*).

salutary ['sæljutəri], *adj.* heilsam (*lesson, experience*).

salute [sə'ljuːt], *v.a.* grüßen. — *s.* der Gruß, (*Mil.*) Salut.

salvage ['sælvidʒ], *s.* die Bergung, Rettung; das Bergegut. — *v.a.* retten, bergen.

salvation [sæl'veiʃən], *s.* die Rettung; (*Rel.*) die Erlösung, das Heil.

salve [sælv, sɑːv], *v.a.* einsalben; heilen. — *s.* die Salbe.

salver ['sælvə], *s.* der Präsentierteller.

salvo ['sælvou], *s.* (*Mil.*) die Salve.

Samaritan [sə'mæritən], *s.* der Samariter; (*fig.*) der Wohltäter.

same [seim], *adj.* der-, die-, dasselbe.

sample [sɑːmpl], *s.* die Probe, das Muster (*test, pack etc.*). — *v.a.* probieren; kosten (*food*).

sampler ['sɑːmplə], *s.* das Stickmuster.

sanctify ['sæŋktifai], *v.a.* heiligen.

sanctimonious [sæŋkti'mouniəs], *adj.* scheinheilig.

sanction ['sæŋkʃən], *s.* (*Pol.*) die Sanktion; (*fig.*) Genehmigung. — *v.a.* genehmigen, sanktionieren.

sanctuary ['sæŋktjuəri], *s.* das Heiligtum.

sand [sænd], *s.* der Sand. — *v.a.* sanden, bestreuen; (*floors*) abreiben.

sandal [sændl], *s.* die Sandale.

sandwich ['sænwitʃ], *s.* das belegte (Butter)brot.
sane [sein], *adj.* gesund (*mind*); vernünftig.
sanguine ['sæŋgwin], *adj.* optimistisch.
sanitary ['sænitəri], *adj.* Gesundheits-, Sanitäts-; — *towel*, die (Damen)binde.
sanity ['sæniti], *s.* die Vernunft, der gesunde Menschenverstand; (*Law*) die Zurechnungsfähigkeit.
Santa Claus [sæntə'klɔ:z]. der heilige Nikolaus, Knecht Ruprecht.
sap (1) [sæp], *s.* der Saft; (*fig.*) die Lebenskraft.
sap (2) [sæp], *v.a.* untergraben, schwächen.
sapling ['sæpliŋ], *s.* (*Bot.*) das Bäumchen, der junge Baum.
sapper ['sæpə], *s.* (*Mil.*) der Sappeur; der Schanzgräber, Pionier.
sapphire ['sæfaiə], *s.* der Saphir.
sarcasm ['sɑ:kæzm], *s.* der Sarkasmus.
sarcastic [sɑ:'kæstik], *adj.* sarkastisch.
sash (1) [sæʃ], *s.* die Schärpe.
sash (2) [sæʃ], *s.* — *window*, das Schiebefenster; — *cord*, die Fensterschnur.
Satan ['seitən]. der Satan.
satchel ['sætʃəl], *s.* die Leder(schul)-tasche.
sate [seit], *v.a.* sättigen.
satellite ['sætəlait], *s.* der Satellit, Trabant.
satin ['sætin], *s.* (*Text.*) der Atlas.
satire ['sætaiə], *s.* die Satire.
satisfaction [sætis'fækʃən], *s.* die Befriedigung, Zufriedenheit.
satisfactory [sætis'fæktri], *adj.* befriedigend, genügend; zufriedenstellend.
satisfy ['sætisfai], *v.a.* befriedigen, sättigen; (*fig.*) zufriedenstellen.
saturate ['sætʃureit], *v.a.* (*Chem.*) saturieren, sättigen.
Saturday ['sætədei]. der Samstag, Sonnabend.
sauce [sɔ:s], *s.* (*Cul.*) die Sauce, Tunke; (*coll.*) die Unverschämtheit.
saucepan ['sɔ:spæn], *s.* (*Cul.*) der Kochtopf.
saucer ['sɔ:sə], *s.* die Untertasse.
saucy ['sɔ:si], *adj.* (*coll.*) unverschämt, frech.
saunter ['sɔ:ntə], *v.n.* schlendern, spazieren.
sausage ['sɔsidʒ], *s.* die Wurst.
savage ['sævidʒ], *adj.* wild. — *s.* der Wilde.
save [seiv], *v.a.* retten (*life*); (*Theol.*) erlösen; sparen (*money*); sich ersparen (*trouble, labour*); aufheben (*keep*). — *v.n.* sparen, sparsam sein. — *prep., conj.* außer, außer daß, ausgenommen.
saving ['seiviŋ], *s.* das Ersparnis; *savings bank*, die Sparkasse.
saviour ['seivjə], *s.* der Retter; (*Rel.*) der Heiland.
savour ['seivə], *s.* der Geschmack; die Würze. — *v.n.* schmecken (*of*, nach, *Dat.*).

savoury ['seivəri], *adj.* schmackhaft. — *s.* pikantes Vor- *or* Nachgericht.
saw (1) [sɔ:], *v.a.* sägen. — *s.* die Säge.
saw (2) [sɔ:], *s.* (*obs.*) das Sprichwort.
sawyer ['sɔ:jə], *s.* der Sägearbeiter, Säger.
Saxon ['sæksən], *adj.* sächsisch. — *s.* der Sachse.
say [sei], *v.a. irr.* sagen; (*lines, prayer*) hersagen. — *v.n.* (*Am. coll.*) —! sagen Sie mal! — *s.* das entscheidende Wort.
saying ['seiiŋ], *s.* das Sprichwort, der Spruch.
scab [skæb], *s.* der Schorf, die Krätze.
scabbard ['skæbəd], *s.* die Degenscheide.
scaffold ['skæfəld], *s.* (*Build.*) das Gerüst; das Schafott (*place of execution*).
scald [skɔ:ld], *v.a.* verbrühen; —*ing hot*, brühheiß.
scale (1) [skeil], *s.* die Waagschale (*balance*).
scale (2) [skeil], *s.* (*Mus.*) die Skala, Tonleiter.
scale (3) [skeil], *s.* (*Geog. etc.*) die Skala, das Ausmaß, der Maßstab; *on a large* —, im großen (Maßstabe). — *v.a.* erklettern (*climb*); — *down*, im Maßstab verringern.
scale (4) [skeil], *s.* (*fish etc.*) die Schuppe. — *v.a.* schuppen, abschälen (*remove* —*s*).
scallop ['skɔləp], *s.* (*Zool.*) die Kammuschel.
scalp [skælp], *s.* (*Anat.*) die Kopfhaut. — *v.a.* skalpieren, die Kopfhaut abziehen.
scamp [skæmp], *s.* (*coll.*) der Taugenichts.
scan [skæn], *v.a.* (*Poet.*) skandieren; (*Rad.*) absuchen.
scandalize ['skændəlaiz], *v.a.* empören, verärgern.
scant [skænt], *adj.* selten; knapp, sparsam.
Scandinavian [skændi'neivjən], *adj.* skandinavisch. — *s.* der Skandinavier.
scanty ['skænti], *adj.* spärlich, knapp.
scapegoat ['skeipgout], *s.* der Sündenbock.
scar [skɑ:], *s.* die Narbe.
scarce [skeəs], *adj.* selten, spärlich.
scarcely ['skeəsli], *adv.* kaum.
scarcity ['skeəsiti], *s.* die Seltenheit, Knappheit.
scare [skeə], *v.a.* erschrecken, ängstigen. — *s.* der Schreck.
scarecrow ['skeəkrou], *s.* die Vogelscheuche.
scarf [skɑ:f], *s.* der Schal, das Halstuch.
scarlet ['skɑ:lit], *adj.* scharlachrot. — *s.* der Scharlach.
scarp [skɑ:p], *s.* die Böschung.
scatter ['skætə], *v.a., v.n.* (sich) zerstreuen, (sich) verbreiten; streuen.
scavenge ['skævindʒ], *v.a.* ausreinigen, auswaschen; säubern.
scavenger ['skævindʒə], *s.* der Straßenkehrer; Aasgeier.

479

scene

scene [si:n], s. die Szene, der Schauplatz; *behind the —s,* hinter den Kulissen; *— shifter,* der Kulissenschieber.

scenery ['si:nəri], s. die Landschaft (*nature*); (*Theat.*) das Bühnenbild, die Kulissen, *f. pl.*

scent [sent], s. der Geruch, Duft, das Parfüm (*perfume*); die Witterung, Fährte (*trail of hunted animal*).

sceptic ['skeptik], s. der Skeptiker.

sceptre ['septə], s. das Zepter.

schedule ['ʃedju:l, (*Am.*) 'ske-], s. der Plan; die Liste; der (Fahr-, Stunden-) plan; (*Law*) der Zusatz (*in documents*). *— v.a. (Am.)* einteilen, zuteilen (*apportion*); aufzeichnen.

scheme [ski:m], s. das Schema; der Plan; *— of things,* in der Gesamtplanung. *— v.n.* aushecken; Ränke schmieden.

scholar ['skɔlə], s. der Gelehrte, der Wissenschaftler; der Schuljunge, Schüler; (*Univ.*) der Stipendiat.

scholarly ['skɔləli], *adj.* gelehrt.

scholarship ['skɔləʃip], s. die Gelehrsamkeit (*learning*); das Stipendium (*award*).

scholastic [skɔ'læstik], *adj.* scholastisch. — s. der Scholastiker.

school [sku:l], s. die Schule. *— v.a.* abrichten; schulen; erziehen.

schoolboy ['sku:lbɔi], s. der Schüler.

schoolgirl ['sku:lgə:l], s. die Schülerin.

schoolmaster ['sku:lmɑ:stə], s. der Lehrer.

schoolmistress ['sku:lmistrəs], s. die Lehrerin.

schooner ['sku:nə], s. (*Naut.*) der Schoner.

science ['saiəns], s. die Wissenschaft, Naturwissenschaft (*natural — s*).

scientific [saiən'tifik], *adj.* wissenschaftlich, naturwissenschaftlich.

scientist ['saiəntist], s. der Gelehrte; Naturwissenschaftler, Naturforscher.

scintillate ['sintileit], *v.n.* funkeln, glänzen.

scion ['saiən], s. der Sprößling.

scissors ['sizəz], s. *pl.* die Schere.

scoff [skɔf], *v.a.* verspotten, verhöhnen. *— v.n.* spotten. — s. der Spott, Hohn.

scold [skould], *v.a.* schelten. *— v.n.* zanken.

scoop [sku:p], *v.a.* aushöhlen (*hollow out*); ausschöpfen (*ladle out*). — s. die Schippe, Schöpfkelle; (*fig.*) die Sensation, Erstmeldung.

scope [skoup], s. der Wirkungskreis, Spielraum.

scooter ['sku:tə], s. der (Motor)roller.

scorch [skɔ:tʃ], *v.a.* versengen, verbrennen. *— v.n.* versengt werden; (*coll.*) dahinrasen (*speed*).

score [skɔ:], s. die Zwanzig; die Rechnung; (*Mus.*) die Partitur; das Spielergebnis (*in game*).

scorn [skɔ:n], *v.a.* verachten. — s. der Spott (*scoffing*); die Geringschätzung, Verachtung.

Scot, Scotsman [skɔt, 'skɔtsmən], s. der Schotte.

Scotch [skɔtʃ], s. der Whisky.

scotch [skɔtʃ], *v.a.* ritzen; (*fig.*) vernichten.

Scotswoman ['skɔtswumən], s. die Schottin.

Scottish ['skɔtiʃ], *adj.* schottisch.

scoundrel ['skaundrəl], s. der Schurke.

scour ['skauə], *v.a.* scheuern, reinigen.

scourge [skə:dʒ], s. die Geißel. *— v.a.* geißeln.

scout [skaut], s. der Kundschafter; (*Boy Scout*) der Pfadfinder.

scowl [skaul], *v.n.* finster dreinsehen. — s. das finstere Gesicht.

scraggy ['skrægi], *adj.* hager, dürr.

scramble ['skræmbl], *v.n.* klettern. *— v.a.* verrühren; *scrambled eggs,* das Rührei.

scrap [skræp], s. das Stückchen, der Brocken, Fetzen; *— merchant,* der Altwarenhändler. *— v.a.* zum alten Eisen werfen, verschrotten.

scrapbook ['skræpbuk], s. das Sammelbuch, Bilderbuch.

scrape [skreip], *v.a., v.n.* (sich) schaben, kratzen; (*coll.*) *— up,* auflesen. — s. (*coll.*) die Klemme (*difficulty*).

scraper ['skreipə], s. der Fußabstreifer.

scratch [skrætʃ], *v.a., v.n.* kratzen; sich kratzen; (*Sport*) zurückziehen. — s. der Kratzer; *come up to —,* seinen Mann stellen.

scrawl [skrɔ:l], *v.a., v.n.* kritzeln (*scribble*); (*coll.*) unleserlich schreiben. — s. das Gekritzel.

scream [skri:m], *v.n.* schreien; kreischen. — s. der Schrei; (*coll.*) zum Schreien, zum Lachen.

screech [skri:tʃ], *v.n.* schreien, kreischen (*hoarsely*). — s. das Gekreisch.

screen [skri:n], s. der Schirm (*protection*); (*Cinema*) die Leinwand. *— v.a.* abschirmen (*shade*); (*Film*) durchspielen, vorführen; (*question*) untersuchen; ausfragen.

screening ['skri:niŋ], s. (*Cinema*) die Vorführung; (*Pol.*) die Befragung, Untersuchung.

screw [skru:], *v.a.* schrauben. — s. die Schraube.

screwdriver ['skru:draivə], s. der Schraubenzieher.

scribble [skribl], *v.a., v.n.* kritzeln, (unleserlich) schreiben. — s. das Gekritzel.

scribe [skraib], s. der Schreiber.

script [skript], s. das Manuskript; (*Film*) das Drehbuch.

scripture ['skriptʃə], s. die Heilige Schrift.

scroll [skroul], s. die Schriftrolle; (*Typ.*) der Schnörkel; die Urkunde (*document etc.*).

scrub [skrʌb], *v.a.* schrubben, reiben, scheuern.

scruff [skrʌf], s. (*of the neck*) das Genick.

scruple [skru:pl], s. der Skrupel.

scrupulous ['skru:pjuləs], *adj.* genau, gewissenhaft; allzu bedenklich.

480

scrutinize ['skru:tinaiz], v.a. genau
prüfen, untersuchen.

scrutiny ['skru:tini], s. die genaue
Prüfung; die Untersuchung.

scuffle [skʌfl], v.n. sich raufen. — s. die
Balgerei, Rauferei.

scull [skʌl], s. das kurze Ruder.

scullery ['skʌləri], s. die Abwasch-
küche.

scullion ['skʌliən], s. (obs.) der Küchen-
junge.

sculptor ['skʌlptə], s. der Bildhauer.

sculpture ['skʌlptʃə], s. die Bildhauerei
(activity); die Skulptur (piece).

scum [skʌm], s. der Abschaum.

scurf [skə:f], s. der Schorf, Grind.

scurrilous ['skʌriləs], adj. gemein.

scurvy ['skə:vi], s. (Med.) der Skorbut.
— adj. niederträchtig.

scutcheon ['skʌtʃən] see escutcheon.

scuttle (1) [skʌtl], s. (Naut.) die Spring-
luke. — v.a. (Naut.) ein Schiff zum
Sinken bringen, versenken.

scuttle (2) [skʌtl], s. der Kohleneimer.

scuttle (3) [skʌtl], v.n. eilen (hurry).

scythe [saið], s. die Sense.

sea [si:], s. die See, das Meer.

seal (1) [si:l], s. das Siegel, Petschaft.
— v.a. (be)siegeln.

seal (2) [si:l], s. (Zool.) der Seehund,
die Robbe.

seam [si:m], s. der Saum; die Naht;
(Min.) die Ader, das Flöz; (Metall.)
die Naht. — v.a. einsäumen.

seamstress ['si:mstrəs], s. die Näherin.

sear [siə], v.a. sengen (burn); trocknen;
verdorren. — adj. see sere.

search [sə:tʃ], v.n. suchen (for, nach,
Dat.); forschen (for, nach, Dat.).
— v.a. untersuchen, durchsuchen
(house, case etc.). — s. die Suche
(for person); die Untersuchung (of
house etc.).

searchlight ['sə:tʃlait], s. der Scheinwerfer.

seasick ['si:sik], adj. seekrank.

seaside ['si:said], s. die Küste, der Strand.

season [si:zn], s. die Jahreszeit, Saison;
— ticket, die Dauerkarte. — v.a.
würzen (spice). — v.n. reifen (mature).

seasoning ['si:zniŋ], s. die Würze.

seat [si:t], s. der Sitz, Sitzplatz, Stuhl.
— v.a. setzen; fassen (of room capacity); be —ed, Platz nehmen.

seaweed ['si:wi:d], s. (Bot.) der Seetang.

secession [si'seʃən], s. die Loslösung,
Trennung, Spaltung.

seclude [si'klu:d], v.a. abschließen,
absondern.

seclusion [si'klu:ʒən], s.die Abgeschlos-
senheit.

second ['sekənd], num. adj. zweit;
(repeat) noch ein. — s. die Sekunde
(time); (Sport) der Sekundant. —
v.a. sekundieren (Dat.), beipflichten;
[si'kɔnd] abkommandieren (zu).

secondary ['sekəndri], adj. zweitrangig,
sekundär.

secondhand ['sekəndhænd], adj. antiquarisch, gebraucht.

secrecy ['si:krəsi], s. die Heimlichkeit;
pledge to —, die Verschwiegenheit.

secret ['si:krit], s. das Geheimnis. —
adj. geheim.

secretary ['sekrətəri], s. der Sekretär,
die Sekretärin.

secrete [si'kri:t], v.a. ausscheiden,
absondern.

secretion [si'kri:ʃən], s. die Ausscheidung; (Med.) das Sekret.

sect [sekt], s. die Sekte.

section ['sekʃən], s. die Sektion, Abteilung (department); der Teil (part);
Abschnitt (in book etc.).

secular ['sekjulə], adj. weltlich, säkulär.

secure [sə'kjuə], adj. sicher, gesichert.
— v.a. sichern (make safe); besorgen
(obtain).

security [sə'kjuəriti], s. die Sicherheit;
(Comm.) die Garantie, Bürgschaft;
(pl.) die Staatspapiere, Wertpapiere,
n. pl., Aktien, f. pl.

sedate [si'deit], adj. gesetzt, ruhig
(placid).

sedative ['sedətiv], adj. beruhigend.
— s. das Beruhigungsmittel.

sedentary ['sedəntri], adj. sitzend,
Sitz-.

sediment ['sedimənt], s. der Bodensatz; (Geol.) das Sediment.

sedition [si'diʃən], s. der Aufstand.

seditious [si'diʃəs], adj. aufrührerisch.

seduce [si'dju:s], v.a. verführen.

sedulous ['sedjuləs], adj. emsig, fleißig.

see (1) [si:], s. (Eccl.) das (Erz)bistum;
Holy See, der Heilige Stuhl.

see (2) [si:], v.a., v.n. irr. sehen; einsehen, verstehen (understand).

seed [si:d], s. die Saat; der Same (grain).
— v.a. (Sport) aussetzen, setzen.

seediness ['si:dinis], s. die Schäbigkeit;
Armseligkeit, das Elend.

seedy ['si:di], adj. elend; schäbig.

seeing ['si:iŋ], conj. — that, da doch.

seek [si:k], v.a. irr. suchen (object). —
v.n. trachten (to, infin.).

seem [si:m], v.n. scheinen, erscheinen.

seemly ['si:mli], adj. schicklich, anständig.

seer [siə], s. der Prophet.

seesaw ['si:sɔ:], s. die Schaukel.

seethe [si:ð], v.n. kochen, (fig.) sieden.

segment ['segmənt], s. (Geom.) der
Abschnitt.

segregate ['segrigeit], v.a. absondern.

segregation [segri'geiʃən], s. racial —,
die Rassentrennung.

seize [si:z], v.a. ergreifen, packen
(arrest, grasp); beschlagnahmen (impound).

seizure ['si:ʒə], s. die Beschlagnahme
(of goods); (Med.) der Anfall.

seldom ['seldəm], adv. selten.

select [si'lekt], v.a. auswählen; auslesen.
— adj. auserlesen.

selection [si'lekʃən], s. die Wahl, Auswahl.

self [self], s. das Selbst; — consciousness, die Befangenheit; — denial, die
Selbstverleugnung, Selbstaufopferung.

selfish

selfish ['selfiʃ], *adj.* egoistisch, selbstsüchtig.
sell [sel], *v.a. irr.* verkaufen; (*sl.*) — (*s.o.*) *out*, jemanden verraten.
semblance ['semblǝns], *s.* der Anschein, die Ähnlichkeit.
semi- ['semi], *pref.* halb.
semibreve ['semibri:v], *s.* (*Mus.*) die ganze Note.
semicircle ['semisǝ:kl], *s.* der Halbkreis.
semicolon ['semikoulǝn], *s.* der Strichpunkt.
semiquaver ['semikweivǝ], *s.* (*Mus.*) die Sechzehntelnote.
senate ['senit], *s.* der Senat.
send [send], *v.a. irr.* senden, schicken; — *for*, holen lassen; — *off*, die Abschiedsfeier.
Senegalese [senigǝ'li:z], *adj.* senegal-. — *s.* der Senegalese.
senile ['si:nail], *adj.* altersschwach.
senior ['si:njǝ], *adj.* älter; dienstälter (*in position*).
seniority [si:ni'ɔriti], *s.* der Rangvortritt, das Dienstalter.
sensation [sen'seiʃǝn], *s.* die Empfindung; Sensation.
sensational [sen'seiʃǝnǝl], *adj.* sensationell.
sense [sens], *v.a.* fühlen, empfinden. — *s.* der Sinn; das Empfinden, Gefühl; *common* —, gesunder Menschenverstand.
senseless ['senslis], *adj.* sinnlos.
sensibility [sensi'biliti], *s.* die Empfindlichkeit.
sensible ['sensibl], *adj.* vernünftig.
sensitive ['sensitiv], *adj.* feinfühlend, empfindlich.
sensitize ['sensitaiz], *v.a.* (*Phot. etc.*) empfindlich machen.
sensual ['sensjuǝl], *adj.* sinnlich, wollüstig.
sensuous ['sensjuǝs], *adj.* sinnlich.
sentence ['sentǝns], *s.* (*Gram.*) der Satz; (*Law*) das Urteil. — *v.a.* verurteilen.
sententious [sen'tenʃǝs], *adj.* spruchreich; affektiert.
sentiment ['sentimǝnt], *s.* die Empfindung, das Gefühl; die Meinung (*opinion*).
sentimental [senti'mentl], *adj.* sentimental, gefühlvoll; empfindsam.
sentinel ['sentinǝl], *s.* (*Mil.*) die Schildwache, Wache.
separable ['sepǝrǝbl], *adj.* trennbar.
separate ['sepǝreit], *v.a.* trennen. — [-rit], *adj.* getrennt.
separation [sepǝ'reiʃǝn], *s.* die Trennung.
September [sep'tembǝ]. der September.
sequel ['si:kwǝl], *s.* die Folge, Fortsetzung (*serial*).
sequence ['si:kwǝns], *s.* die Ordnung, Reihenfolge, Aufeinanderfolge.
sequester [si'kwestǝ], *v.a.* absondern, entfernen.

sere [siǝ], *adj.* trocken, dürr.
serene [si'ri:n], *adj.* heiter; gelassen, ruhig (*quiet*).
serf [sǝ:f], *s.* der Leibeigene.
sergeant ['sɑ:dʒǝnt], *s.* (*Mil.*) der Feldwebel.
series ['siǝri:z *or* 'siǝrii:z], *s.* die Reihe.
serious ['siǝriǝs], *adj.* ernst, seriös.
sermon ['sǝ:mǝn], *s.* die Predigt.
serpent ['sǝ:pǝnt], *s.* (*Zool.*) die Schlange.
serpentine ['sǝ:pǝntain], *adj.* schlangenartig, sich schlängelnd.
serrated [se'reitid], *adj.* (*Bot., Engin.*) zackig, gezackt.
serried ['serid], *adj.* dichtgedrängt.
servant ['sǝ:vǝnt], *s.* der Bediente, Diener; die Magd, das Mädchen, Dienstmädchen.
serve [sǝ:v], *v.a., v.n.* dienen (*Dat.*); (*Law*) abbüßen, absitzen (*sentence*); servieren (*food*); (*Tennis*) angeben.
service ['sǝ:vis], *s.* der Dienst, die Bedienung; (*Mil.*) der Militärdienst; das Service, Geschirr, Porzellan (*china*).
serviceable ['sǝ:visǝbl], *adj.* brauchbar, dienlich, benutzbar.
servile ['sǝ:vail], *adj.* knechtisch.
servility [sǝ:'viliti], *s.* die Kriecherei.
servitude ['sǝ:vitju:d], *s.* die Knechtschaft.
session ['seʃǝn], *s.* die Sitzung; das Studienjahr, Hochschuljahr.
set [set], *v.a. irr.* setzen; stellen (*stand*); legen (*lay*); ordnen (— *out*); — *a saw*, eine Sage schärfen, wetzen; fassen (*stone*); — *fire to*, in Brand setzen; — *aside*, beiseitelegen; — *to music*, vertonen; — *about*, anfangen, sich anschicken; herfallen über (*s.o.*); — *up*, einrichten. — *v.n.* — *forth*, *forward*, aufbrechen; — *out to*, streben, trachten; (*sun*) untergehen; fest werden (*solidify*). — *s.* der Satz (*complete collection*); die Garnitur (*garments*); der Kreis, die Clique (*circle of people*); (*Theat.*) das Bühnenbild.
settee [se'ti:], *s.* das Sofa.
setter ['setǝ], *s.* (*Zool.*) der Vorstehhund; *red* —, der Hühnerhund.
setting ['setiŋ], *s.* das Setzen; die Szene (*of play etc.*); die Sonnenuntergang (*of the sun*); (*Typ.*) — *up*, die Auslegung, Aufstellung.
settle (1) [setl], *v.a.* ordnen, schlichten; (*Comm.*) begleichen, bezahlen. — *v.n.* sich niederlassen, siedeln; (*weather*) sich aufklären.
settle (2) [setl], *s.* der Ruhesitz.
settlement ['setlmǝnt], *s.* (*Comm.*) die Begleichung; die Siedlung (*habitation*).
seven [sevn], *num. adj.* sieben.
seventeen ['sevnti:n], *num.adj.* siebzehn.
seventh [sevnθ], *num. adj.* siebente.
seventy ['sevnti], *num. adj.* siebzig.
sever ['sevǝ], *v.a.* trennen.
several ['sevǝrǝl], *adj. pl.* verschiedene, mehrere.

severance ['sevərəns], s. die Trennung.
severe [si'viə], adj. streng.
severity [si'veriti], s. die Strenge.
sew [sou], v.a., v.n. nähen.
sewage ['sju:idʒ], s. das Abfuhrwasser, Kloakenwasser, Kanalwasser.
sewer (1) ['sju:ə], s. die Kanalanlage, der Abzugskanal.
sewer (2) ['souə], s. der Näher, die Näherin.
sewing ['souiŋ], s. das Nähen; — machine, die Nähmaschine.
sex [seks], s. das Geschlecht.
sexagenarian [seksədʒə'nɛəriən], s. der Sechzigjährige.
sextant ['sekstənt], s. der Sextant.
sexton ['sekstən], s. (Eccl.) der Küster, Totengräber.
sexual ['sekʃuəl], adj. geschlechtlich, sexuell.
shabby ['ʃæbi], adj. schäbig; (fig.) erbärmlich.
shackle [ʃækl], v.a. fesseln. — s. (usually pl.) die Fesseln, f. pl.
shade [ʃeid], s. der Schatten; (pl.) (Am.) die Jalousien, f. pl. (blinds). — v.a. beschatten; (Art) schattieren, verdunkeln.
shadow ['ʃædou], s. der Schatten. — v.a. verfolgen.
shady ['ʃeidi], adj. schattig; (fig.) verdächtig.
shaft [ʃɑ:ft], s. der Schaft (handle); (Min.) der Schacht; die Deichsel (cart); der Pfeil (arrow).
shag [ʃæg], s. der Tabak.
shaggy ['ʃægi], adj. zottig.
shake [ʃeik], v.a. irr. schütteln; rütteln; (fig.) erschüttern. — v.n. zittern (tremble); wanken (waver). — s. das Zittern, Beben; (Mus.) der Triller.
shaky ['ʃeiki], adj. zitternd, wankend; rissig, wackelig (wobbly); (fig.) unsicher (insecure).
shall [ʃæl], v. aux. sollen (be supposed to); werden (future).
shallow ['ʃælou], adj. flach, seicht. — s. die Untiefe (sea).
sham [ʃæm], adj. falsch, unecht. — v.a. vortäuschen.
shambles [ʃæmblz], s. die Unordnung; (fig.) das Schlachtfeld.
shame [ʃeim], s. die Scham (remorse); die Schande (dishonour); what a —! wie schade! — v.a. beschämen.
shamefaced ['ʃeimfeisd],adj.verschämt.
shameful ['ʃeimful], adj. schändlich (despicable).
shampoo [ʃæm'pu:], s. das Haarwaschmittel. — v.a. das Haar waschen.
shamrock ['ʃæmrɔk], s. (Bot.) der irische Klee.
shank [ʃæŋk], s. der Unterschenkel; (coll.) on Shanks's pony, zu Fuß.
shanty (1) ['ʃænti], s. die Hütte.
shanty (2) ['ʃænti], s. sea —, das Matrosenlied.
shape [ʃeip], s. die Gestalt, Figur, Form. — v.a. gestalten, formen. — v.n. Gestalt annehmen.

shapely ['ʃeipli], adj. wohlgestaltet, schön gestaltet.
share [ʃɛə], v.a., v.n. (sich) teilen. — s. der Teil, Anteil; (Comm.) die Aktie (in company).
shareholder ['ʃɛəhouldə], s. der Aktionär.
shark [ʃɑ:k], s. (Zool.) der Haifisch, Hai; (fig.) der Wucherer (profiteer), Hochstapler.
sharp [ʃɑ:p], adj. scharf; (fig.) intelligent. — s. (Mus.) das Kreuz.
sharpen [ʃɑ:pn], v.a. schärfen; spitzen (pencil).
sharpener ['ʃɑ:pnə], s. pencil —, der Bleistiftspitzer.
shatter ['ʃætə], v.a. zerschmettern. — v.n. zerbrechen.
shave [ʃeiv], v.a., v.n. (sich) rasieren; abschaben (pare). — s. die Rasur, das Rasieren.
shavings ['ʃeiviŋz], s. pl. die Hobelspäne, m. pl.
shawl [ʃɔ:l], s. der Schal, das Umschlagetuch.
she [ʃi:], pers. pron. sie.
sheaf [ʃi:f], s. die Garbe.
shear [ʃiə], v.a. scheren (sheep etc.).
shears [ʃiəz], s. pl. die Schere.
sheath [ʃi:θ], s. die Scheide.
sheathe [ʃi:ð], v.a. in die Scheide stecken.
shed (1) [ʃed], s. der Schuppen.
shed (2) [ʃed], v.a. irr. vergießen (blood, tears); ausschütten.
sheen [ʃi:n], s. der Glanz.
sheep [ʃi:p], s. (Zool.) das Schaf.
sheer (1) [ʃiə], adj. rein, lauter; senkrecht.
sheer (2) [ʃiə], v.n. (Naut.) gieren, abgieren.
sheet [ʃi:t], s. das Bettuch; das Blatt, der Bogen (paper); die Platte (metal); — metal, — iron, das Eisenblech; — lightning, das Wetterleuchten.
shelf [ʃelf], s. das Brett, Regal; der Sims (mantel); (Geog.) die Sandbank; (coll.) on the —, sitzengeblieben.
shell [ʃel], s. die Schale (case); die Muschel (mussel); (Mil.) die Bombe, Granate. — v.a. schälen (peas); bombardieren, beschiessen (town).
shelter ['ʃeltə], s. das Obdach (lodging); der Unterstand, Schuppen; der Schutz (protection). — v.a. Obdach gewähren (Dat.); beschützen (protect). — v.n. sich schützen, unterstellen.
shelve [ʃelv], v.a. auf ein Brett legen; (fig.) aufschieben (postpone).
shelving ['ʃelviŋ], s. das Regal.
shepherd ['ʃepəd], s. der Schäfer, Hirt.
sheriff ['ʃerif], s. der Sheriff.
shew [ʃou] see **show**.
shield [ʃi:ld], s. der Schild. — v.a. schützen.
shift [ʃift], v.a. verschieben. — v.n. die Lage ändern. — s. die Veränderung, der Wechsel; (Industry) die Schicht.
shifty ['ʃifti], adj. unstet; durchtrieben.

shin

shin [ʃin], *s.* (*Anat.*) das Schienbein.
shindy [ʃindi], *s.* der Lärm.
shine [ʃain], *v.n. irr.* scheinen (*sun*); glänzen. — *s.* der Glanz.
shingle (1) [ʃiŋgl], *s.* (*Build.*) die Schindel; (*Hair*) der Herrenschnitt.
shingle (2) [ʃiŋgl], *s.* (*Geol.*) der Kiesel.
shingles [ʃiŋglz], *s. pl.* (*Med.*) die Gürtelrose.
ship [ʃip], *s.* das Schiff. — *v.a.* verschiffen, (*Comm.*) versenden.
shipping [ʃipiŋ], *s.* die Schiffahrt; (*Comm.*) der Versand, die Verfrachtung, Verschiffung.
shire [ʃaiə], *s.* die Grafschaft.
shirk [ʃəːk], *v.a.* vermeiden, sich drücken (vor, *Dat.*).
shirt [ʃəːt], *s.* das Hemd.
shirting [ʃəːtiŋ], *s.* der Hemdenstoff.
shiver [ʃivə], *v.n.* zittern, beben. — *s.* der Schauer, Schauder.
shoal [ʃoul], *s.* der Schwarm; (*Naut.*) die Untiefe.
shock (1) [ʃɔk], *v.a.* entsetzen; erschrecken; schockieren. — *s.* der Schock, das Entsetzen.
shock (2) [ʃɔk], *s.* — *of hair*, zottiges Haar.
shoddy [ʃɔdi], *adj.* schlecht, wertlos.
shoe [ʃuː], *s.* der Schuh. — *v.a.* beschuhen; (*horse*) beschlagen.
shoelace, shoestring [ʃuːleis, ʃuːstriŋ], *s.* der Schuhsenkel, (*Austr.*) das Schuhschnürl; *on a shoestring*, fast ohne Geld.
shoeshine [ʃuːʃain], *s.* (*Am.*) der Schuhputzer.
shoestring *see under* **shoelace**.
shoot [ʃuːt], *v.a. irr.* schießen. — *v.n.* sprossen, hervorschießen; (*film*) aufnehmen. — *s.* (*Bot.*) der Sproß.
shooting [ʃuːtiŋ], *s.* das Schießen; — *range*, der Schießstand. — *adj.* — *star*, die Sternschnuppe.
shop [ʃɔp], *s.* der Laden, das Geschäft; (*work*) die Werkstatt; *talk* —, fachsimpeln; — *window*, das Schaufenster. — *v.n.* einkaufen.
shopkeeper [ʃɔpkiːpə], *s.* der Kaufmann, Krämer.
shoplifter [ʃɔplistə], *s.* der Ladendieb.
shore [ʃɔː], *s.* das Gestade, die Küste; die Stütze. — *v.a.* — *up*, stützen.
short [ʃɔːt], *adj.* kurz, klein, knapp; (*curt*) kurz angebunden; — *of money*, in Geldnot; *run* —, knapp werden; —*sighted*, kurzsichtig; *be on* — *time working*, kurz arbeiten. — *s.* (*Elect.*) (*coll.*) der Kurzschluß (*short circuit*); (*pl.*) die Kniehose, kurze Hose.
shortcoming [ʃɔːtkamiŋ], *s.* der Fehler, Mangel.
shorten [ʃɔːtn], *v.a.* verkürzen, abkürzen. — *v.n.* kürzer werden.
shorthand [ʃɔːthænd], *s.* die Stenographie; — *typist*, die Stenotypistin.
shot [ʃɔt], *s.* der Schuß; (*man*) der Schütze.

shoulder [ʃouldə], *s.* (*Anat.*) die Schulter. — *v.a.* schultern, auf sich nehmen, auf die Achsel nehmen.
shout [ʃaut], *v.n.* schreien, rufen. — *s.* der Schrei, Ruf.
shove [ʃʌv], *v.a.* schieben, stoßen. — *s.* der Schub, Stoß.
shovel [ʃʌvl], *s.* die Schaufel. — *v.a.* schaufeln.
show [ʃou], *v.a. irr.* zeigen; (*fig.*) dartun. — *v.n.* sich zeigen, zu sehen sein; — *off*, prahlen, protzen. — *v.r.* — *o.s. to be*, sich erweisen als. — *s.* (*Theat.*) die Schau, Aufführung.
shower [ʃauə], *s.* der Schauer (*rain*); (*fig.*) die Fülle, der Überfluß; — (*bath*), die Dusche; *take a* —(*bath*), brausen. — *v.a., v.n.* herabregnen; überschütten.
showing [ʃouiŋ], *s.* die Vorführung, der Beweis.
showy [ʃoui], *adj.* protzig, angeberisch.
shred [ʃred], *s.* der Fetzen; (*fig.*) die Spur (*of evidence*). — *v.a.* zerreißen, zerfetzen.
shrew [ʃruː], *s.* die Spitzmaus; (*fig.*) das zänkische Weib.
shrewd [ʃruːd], *adj.* schlau, verschlagen, listig.
shriek [ʃriːk], *v.n.* kreischen. — *s.* der Schrei, das Gekreisch.
shrift [ʃrift], *s. give s.o. short* —, mit einem kurzen Prozeß machen.
shrill [ʃril], *adj.* schrill, gellend, durchdringend.
shrimp [ʃrimp], *s.* (*Zool.*) die Garnele.
shrine [ʃrain], *s.* der (Reliquien)schrein; der Altar.
shrink [ʃriŋk], *v.n. irr.* eingehen, einschrumpfen. — *v.a.* eingehen lassen.
shrinkage [ʃriŋkidʒ], *s.* das Eingehen (*fabric*); (*Geol.*) die Schrumpfung.
shrivel [ʃrivl], *v.n.* einschrumpfen, sich runzeln.
shroud [ʃraud], *s.* das Leichentuch. — *v.a.* einhüllen.
Shrove [ʃrouv] **Tuesday**. die Fastnacht.
shrub [ʃrʌb], *s.* (*Bot.*) der Strauch, die Staude.
shrug [ʃrʌg], *v.a.* (*shoulders*) die Achseln zucken. — *s.* das Achselzucken.
shudder [ʃʌdə], *s.* der Schauder. — *v.n.* schaudern.
shuffle [ʃʌfl], *v.a.* (*cards*) mischen. — *v.n.* schlürfen, schleppend gehen.
shun [ʃʌn], *v.a.* meiden.
shunt [ʃʌnt], *v.a., v.n.* rangieren.
shut [ʃʌt], *v.a. irr.* schließen. — *v.n.* sich schließen, zugehen; (*coll.*) — *up!* halt's Maul!
shutter [ʃʌtə], *s.* der Fensterladen.
shuttle [ʃʌtl], *s.* (*Mech.*) das Weberschiff.
shuttlecock [ʃʌtlkɔk], *s.* der Federball.
shy (1) [ʃai], *adj.* scheu, schüchtern. — *v.n.* scheuen (*of horses*).
shy (2) [ʃai], *s.* der Wurf.
sick [sik], *adj.* krank; unwohl, übel; leidend (*suffering*); (*fig.*) — *of*, überdrüssig (*Genit.*).

484

sicken [sikn], *v.n.* krank werden *or* sein; sich ekeln (*be nauseated*). — *v.a.* anekeln.

sickle [sikl], *s.* die Sichel.

sickness ['siknis], *s.* die Krankheit.

side [said], *s.* die Seite. — *v.n.* — *with*, Partei ergreifen für.

sideboard ['saidbɔ:d], *s.* das Büffet, die Anrichte.

sidereal [sai'diəriəl], *adj.* (*Maths.*, *Phys.*) Sternen-, Stern-.

sidewalk ['saidwɔ:k] (*Am.*) *see* **pavement**.

siding ['saidiŋ],*s.*(*Railw.*)das Nebengleis.

sidle [saidl], *v.n.* — *up to*, sich heranmachen.

siege [si:dʒ], *s.* die Belagerung.

sieve [siv], *s.* das Sieb. — *v.a.* sieben.

sift [sift], *v.a.* sieben; (*fig.*) prüfen.

sigh [sai], *v.n.* seufzen. — *s.* der Seufzer.

sight [sait], *s.* die Sicht (*view*); die Sehkraft (*sense of*); der Anblick; *at* —, auf den ersten Blick; *out of* —, *out of mind*, aus den Augen, aus dem Sinn; (*pl.*) die Sehenswürdigkeiten, *f. pl.*; —*seeing*, die Besichtigung (der Sehenswürdigkeiten). — *v.a.* sichten.

sign [sain], *s.* das Zeichen; der Wink (*hint*); das Aushängeschild (*of pub, shop etc*). — *v.a.* unterschreiben, unterzeichnen. — *v.n.* winken.

signal ['signəl], *s.* das Signal.

signboard ['sainbɔ:d], *s.* das Aushängeschild.

signet ['signit], *s.* das Siegel; — *ring*, der Siegelring.

significance [sig'nifikəns], *s.* die Bedeutung, der Sinn.

significant [sig'nifikənt], *adj.* bedeutend, wichtig.

signify ['signifai], *v.a.* bedeuten (*mean*); anzeigen (*denote*).

silence ['sailəns], *s.* das Schweigen, die Ruhe.

silent ['sailənt], *adj.* still; schweigsam (*taciturn*).

Silesian [sai'li:ʃən], *adj.* schlesisch. — *s.* der Schlesier.

silk [silk], *s.* (*Text.*) die Seide.

silkworm ['silkwɔ:m], *s.* (*Ent.*) die Seidenraupe.

sill [sil], *s.* die Schwelle; *window* —, das Fensterbrett.

silly ['sili], *adj.* albern, dumm.

silver ['silvə], *s.* das Silber. — *v.a.* versilbern. — *adj.* silbern.

similar ['similə], *adj.* ähnlich.

simile ['simili], *s.* (*Lit.*) das Gleichnis.

simmer ['simə], *v.n.*, *v.a.* langsam kochen.

simper ['simpə], *v.n.* lächeln, grinsen.

simple [simpl], *adj.* einfach; (*fig.*) einfältig.

simpleton ['simpltən], *s.* der Einfaltspinsel, Tor.

simplicity [sim'plisiti], *s.* die Einfachheit; (*fig.*) die Einfalt.

simplify ['simplifai], *v.a.* vereinfachen.

simulate ['simjuleit], *v.a.* nachahmen, heucheln, vortäuschen.

simultaneous [siməl'teinjəs], *adj.* gleichzeitig.

sin [sin], *s.* die Sünde. — *v.n.* sündigen.

since [sins], *prep.* seit (*Dat.*). — *conj.* seit (*time*); weil, da (*cause*). — *adv.* seither, seitdem.

sincere [sin'siə], *adj.* aufrichtig.

sincerely [sin'siəli], *adv. yours* —, Ihr ergebener (*letters*).

sincerity [sin'seriti], *s.* die Aufrichtigkeit.

sine [sain], *s.* (*Maths.*) der Sinus, die Sinuskurve.

sinecure ['sainikjuə], *s.* der Ruheposten, die Sinekure.

sinew ['sinju:], *s.* (*Anat.*) die Sehne, der Nerv.

sinful ['sinful], *adj.* sündig, sündhaft.

sing [siŋ], *v.a.*, *v.n. irr.* singen; — *of*, besingen.

singe [sindʒ], *v.a.* sengen.

Singhalese [siŋgə'li:z], *adj.* singhalesisch. — *s.* der Singhalese, die Singhalesin.

single [siŋgl], *adj.* einzeln; ledig (*unmarried*); *single-handed*, allein. — *v.a.* — *out*, auswählen.

singlet ['siŋglit], *s.* die Unterjacke.

singly ['siŋgli], *adv.* einzeln (*one by one*).

singular ['siŋgjulə], *adj.* einzigartig, einzig. — *s.* (*Gram.*) die Einzahl.

sinister ['sinistə], *adj.* böse, unheimlich, finster.

sink [siŋk], *v.a. irr.* versenken; (*fig.*) (*differences etc.*) begraben. — *v.n.* versinken; (*Naut.*) sinken, versinken. — *s.* das Abwaschbecken, Ausgußbecken.

sinker ['siŋkə], *s.* der Schachtarbeiter (*man*); (*Naut.*) das Senkblei.

sinuous ['sinjuəs], *adj.* gewunden.

sinus ['sainəs], *s.* (*Anat.*) die Knochenhöhle; die Bucht.

sip [sip], *v.a.* schlürfen, nippen. — *s.* das Schlückchen.

siphon ['saifən], *s.* (*Phys.*) der Heber; die Siphonflasche. — *v.a.* auspumpen.

Sir (1) [sə:] (*title preceding Christian name*) Herr von... (*baronet or knight*).

sir (2) [sə:], *s.* Herr (*respectful form of address*); *dear* —, sehr geehrter Herr (*in letters*).

sire [saiə], *s.* der Ahnherr, Vater. — *v.a.* zeugen (*horses etc.*).

siren ['saiərən], *s.* die Sirene.

sirloin ['sə:lɔin], *s.* das Lendenstück.

siskin ['siskin], *s.* (*Orn.*) der Zeisig.

sister ['sistə], *s.* die Schwester; (*Eccl.*) Nonne; —*in-law*, die Schwägerin.

sit [sit], *v.n. irr.* sitzen. — *v.a.* — *an examination*, eine Prüfung machen.

site [sait], *s.* die Lage, der Platz.

sitting ['sitiŋ], *s.* die Sitzung; — *room*, das Wohnzimmer.

situated ['sitjueitid], *adj.* gelegen.

situation [sitju'eifən], *s.* die Lage, Situation; der Posten, die Stellung (*post*).

six [siks], *num. adj.* sechs; *be at —es and sevens*, durcheinander, uneinig sein.
sixteen [siks'ti:n], *num. adj.* sechzehn.
sixth [siksθ], *num. adj.* sechste.
sixty ['siksti], *num. adj.* sechzig.
size [saiz], *s.* die Größe, das Maß; (*fig.*) der Umfang.
skate (1) [skeit], *s.* der Schlittschuh. — *v.n.* Schlittschuh laufen.
skate (2) [skeit], *s.* (*Zool.*) der Glattrochen.
skeleton ['skelitən], *s.* das Skelett, Knochengerüst; — *key*, der Dietrich.
sketch [sketʃ], *s.* die Skizze, der Entwurf. — *v.a.* skizzieren, entwerfen. — *v.n.* Skizzen entwerfen.
sketchy ['sketʃi], *adj.* flüchtig.
skew [skju:], *adj.* schief, schräg.
skewer ['skju:ə], *s.* der Fleischspieß.
ski [ski:], *s.* der Schi.
skid [skid], *v.n.* gleiten, schleudern, rutschen. — *v.a.* hemmen, bremsen (*wheel*). — *s.* der Hemmschuh, die Bremse (*of wheel*).
skiff [skif], *s.* (*Naut.*) der Nachen, Kahn.
skilful ['skilful], *adj.* geschickt, gewandt; (*fig.*) erfahren.
skill [skil], *s.* die Geschicklichkeit, Gewandtheit; (*fig.*) die Erfahrung.
skim [skim], *v.a.* abschöpfen, abschäumen.
skimp [skimp], *v.a.* knausern, sparsam sein (mit, *Dat.*).
skimpy ['skimpi], *adj.* knapp.
skin [skin], *s.* die Haut; die Schale (*fruit*); — *deep*, oberflächlich. — *v.a.* häuten, schinden.
skinflint ['skinflint], *s.* der Geizhals.
skinner ['skinə], *s.* der Kürschner.
skip [skip], *v.n.* springen, hüpfen. — *v.a.* (*coll.*) auslassen, überspringen. — *s.* der Sprung.
skipper ['skipə], *s.* (*Naut.*) der Kapitän; (*coll.*) der Chef.
skipping rope ['skipiŋ roup], *s.* das Springseil.
skirmish ['skə:miʃ], *s.* das Scharmützel. — *v.n.* scharmützeln.
skirt [skə:t], *s.* der Rock, Rockschoß (*woman's garment*); der Saum (*edge*). — *v.a.* einsäumen (*seam, edge*); grenzen, am Rande entlang gehen.
skirting (**board**) ['skə:tiŋ (bɔ:d)], *s.* die Fußleiste.
skit [skit], *s.* die Stichelei, die Parodie, Satire.
skittish ['skitiʃ], *adj.* leichtfertig.
skulk [skʌlk], *v.n.* lauern, herumlungern.
skull [skʌl], *s.* der Schädel; — *and crossbones*, der Totenkopf.
skunk [skʌŋk], *s.* (*Zool.*) das Stinktier; (*coll.*) der Schuft.
sky [skai], *s.* der (sichtbare) Himmel.
skylark ['skaila:k], *s.* (*Orn.*) die Feldlerche.
skylarking ['skaila:kiŋ], *s.* das Possenreißen, die Streiche.
skyline ['skailain], *s.* der Horizont.
skyscraper ['skaiskreipə], *s.* der Wolkenkratzer.

slab [slæb], *s.* die Platte (*stone*); die Tafel, das Stück.
slack [slæk], *adj.* schlaff (*feeble*); locker (*loose*). — *s.* der Kohlengrus. — *v.n.* nachlassen, locker werden, faulenzen.
slacken [slækn], *v.a., v.n.* locker werden, nachlassen.
slackness ['slæknis], *s.* die Schlaffheit, Faulheit.
slag [slæg], *s.* die Schlacke.
slake [sleik], *v.a.* dämpfen, löschen, stillen.
slam (1) [slæm], *v.a.* zuwerfen, zuschlagen (*door*). — *s.* der Schlag.
slam (2) [slæm], *v.a.* (*Cards*) Schlemm ansagen, Schlemm machen. — *s.* (*Cards*) der Stich.
slander ['sla:ndə], *v.a.* verleumden. — *s.* die Verleumdung.
slanderer ['sla:ndərə], *s.* der Verleumder.
slang [slæŋ], *s.* der Slang.
slant [sla:nt], *s.* die schräge Richtung, der Winkel (*angle*).
slap [slæp], *v.a.* schlagen. — *s.* der Klaps, Schlag.
slapdash ['slæpdæʃ], *adj.* oberflächlich.
slash [slæʃ], *v.a.* schlitzen, aufschlitzen; (*coll.*) (*Comm.*) herunterbringen (*prices*). — *s.* der Hieb, Schlag.
slate [sleit], *s.* der Schiefer. — *v.a.* mit Schiefer decken; (*fig.*) ankreiden, ausschelten (*scold*).
slattern ['slætə:n], *s.* die Schlampe.
slaughter ['slɔ:tə], *v.a.* schlachten; niedermetzeln. — *s.* das Schlachten; das Gemetzel.
slave [sleiv], *s.* der Sklave; — *driver*, der Sklavenaufseher. — *v.n.* — (*away*), sich placken, sich rackern.
slavery ['sleivəri], *s.* die Sklaverei.
slavish ['sleiviʃ], *adj.* sklavisch.
slay [slei], *v.a.* erschlagen, töten.
sled, sledge [sled, sledʒ], *s.* der Schlitten.
sleek [sli:k], *adj.* glatt. — *v.a.* glätten.
sleep [sli:p], *v.n. irr.* schlafen. — *s.* der Schlaf.
sleeper ['sli:pə], *s.* der Schläfer; (*Railw.*) die Bahnschwelle; der Schlafwagen (*sleeping car*).
sleepwalker ['sli:pwɔ:kə], *s.* der Nachtwandler.
sleet [sli:t], *s.* der Graupelregen.
sleeve [sli:v], *s.* der Ärmel; der Umschlag (*of record*); *have up o.'s —*, eine Überraschung bereithalten; *laugh in o.'s —*, sich ins Fäustchen lachen.
sleigh [slei], *s.* der Schlitten; — *ride*, die Schlittenfahrt.
sleight [slait], *s.—of hand*, der Taschenspielerstreich; der Trick.
slender ['slendə], *adj.* schlank, dünn, gering.
slice [slais], *s.* die Schnitte, Scheibe. — *v.a.* in Scheiben schneiden.
slick [slik], *adj.* glatt.
slide [slaid], *v.n. irr.* gleiten, rutschen (*glide*). — *v.a.* einschieben. — *s.* die Rutschbahn; (*Phot.*) das Dia, Diapositiv; — *rule*, der Rechenschieber.

slight [slait], *adj.* leicht (*light*), gering (*small*); (*fig.*) schwach, dünn(*weak*). — *s.* die Geringschätzung, Respektlosigkeit. — *v.a.* mißachten, geringschätzig behandeln.

slim [slim], *adj.* schlank.

slime [slaim], *s.* der Schleim (*phlegm*); der Schlamm (*mud*).

sling [sliŋ], *v.a. irr.* schleudern, werfen. — *s.* die Schleuder; (*Med.*) die Binde; der Wurf (*throw*).

slink [sliŋk], *v.n. irr.* schleichen.

slip [slip], *v.n.* ausgleiten; — *away*, entschlüpfen; — *up*, einen Fehltritt begehen (*err*). — *v.a.* gleiten lassen, schieben. — *s.* das Ausgleiten; (*fig.*) der Fehltritt; der Fehler (*mistake*); der Unterrock (*petticoat*); *give s.o. the* —, einem entgehen, entschlüpfen.

slipper [ˈslipə], *s.* der Pantoffel, Hausschuh.

slippery [ˈslipəri], *adj.* schlüpfrig, glatt.

slipshod [ˈslipʃɔd], *adj.* nachlässig.

slit [slit], *v.a.* schlitzen, spalten. — *s.* der Schlitz, Spalt.

slither [ˈsliðə], *v.n.* gleiten, rutschen.

sloe [slou], *s.* (*Bot.*) die Schlehe.

slogan [ˈslougən], *s.* das Schlagwort.

sloop [slu:p], *s.* (*Naut.*) die Schaluppe.

slop [slɔp], *s.* das Spülicht, Spülwasser.

slope [sloup], *s.* der Abhang, die Abdachung. — *v.n.* sich neigen. — *v.a.* abschrägen.

sloppy [ˈslɔpi], *adj.* unordentlich, nachlässig.

slot [slɔt], *s.* der Spalt, Schlitz (*slit*); die Kerbe (*notch*); — *machine*, der Automat.

sloth [slouθ], *s.* die Trägheit; (*Zool.*) das Faultier.

slouch [slautʃ], *v.n.* umherschlendern; sich schlaff halten.

slough [slau], *s.* der Morast, Sumpf.

slovenly [ˈslʌvnli], *adj.* schlampig, schmutzig.

slow [slou], *adj.* langsam; (*Phot.*) — *motion*, die Zeitlupenaufnahme. — *v.n.* — *down*, langsamer fahren or laufen.

slow-worm [ˈslouwə:m], *s.* (*Zool.*) die Blindschleiche.

sludge [slʌdʒ], *s.* der Schlamm, Schmutz.

slug [slʌg], *s.* (*Zool.*) die Wegschnecke; (*Am.*) die Kugel.

sluggish [ˈslʌgiʃ], *adj.* träg(e).

sluice [slu:s], *s.* die Schleuse. — *v.a.* ablassen (*drain*); begießen (*water*).

slum [slʌm], *s.* das Elendsviertel; Haus im Elendsviertel.

slumber [ˈslʌmbə], *s.* der Schlummer. — *v.n.* schlummern.

slump [slʌmp], *s.* (*Comm.*) der Tiefstand der Konjunktur; der Preissturz. — *v.n.* stürzen.

slur [slə:], *v.a.* undeutlich sprechen. — *s.* der Schandfleck, die Beleidigung; das Bindezeichen.

slush [slʌʃ], *s.* der Matsch, Schlamm; (*Lit.*) der Kitsch, die Schundliteratur.

slut [slʌt], *s.* die Schlampe.

sly [slai], *adj.* schlau, listig.

smack [smæk], *v.n.* schmecken (*of*, nach, *Dat.*). — *v.a.* schmatzen, lecken. — *s.* der Klaps. — *adv.* (*coll.*) — *in the middle*, gerade in der Mitte.

small [smɔ:l], *adj.* klein; (*fig.*) kleinlich (*petty*); — *talk*, das Geplauder.

smallpox [ˈsmɔ:lpɔks], *s.* (*Med.*) die Blattern, *f. pl.*

smart [sma:t], *adj.* schneidig; elegant, schick (*well-dressed*). — *v.n.* schmerzen. — *s.* der Schmerz.

smash [smæʃ], *v.a.* zertrümmern, in Stücke schlagen.— *v.n.* zerschmettern; (*fig.*) zusammenbrechen. — *s.* der Krach.

smattering [ˈsmætəriŋ], *s.* die oberflächliche Kenntnis.

smear [smiə], *v.a.* beschmieren; (*Am. coll.*) den Charakter angreifen, verleumden. — *s.* die Beschmierung, Befleckung.

smell [smel], *v.a. irr.* riechen. — *v.n.* riechen (nach, *Dat.*). — *s.* der Geruch.

smelt (1) [smelt], *v.a.* (*Metall.*) schmelzen.

smelt (2) [smelt], *s.* (*Zool.*) der Stintfisch.

smile [smail], *v.n.* lächeln. — *s.* das Lächeln.

smirk [smə:k], *v.n.* grinsen. — *s.* das Grinsen, die Grimasse.

smite [smait], *v.a. irr.* treffen, schlagen.

smith [smiθ], *s.* der Schmied.

smitten [smitn], *adj.* verliebt.

smock [smɔk], *s.* der Arbeitskittel.

smoke [smouk], *v.a., v.n.* rauchen; räuchern (*fish etc.*). — *s.* der Rauch.

smoked [smoukd], *adj.* — *ham*, der Räucherschinken.

smooth [smu:ð], *adj.* glatt, sanft (*to touch*); (*fig.*) glatt, geschmeidig, wendig. — *v.a.* glätten, ebnen.

smother [ˈsmʌðə], *v.a.* ersticken.

smoulder [ˈsmouldə], *v.n.* schwelen.

smudge [smʌdʒ], *v.a.* beschmutzen. — *v.n.* schmieren, schmutzen. — *s.* der Schmutzfleck, Schmutz.

smug [smʌg], *adj.* selbstgefällig.

smuggle [ˈsmʌgl], *v.a.* schmuggeln.

smuggler [ˈsmʌglə], *s.* der Schmuggler.

smut [smʌt], *v.a., v.n.* beschmutzen. — *s.* (*fig.*) der Schmutz.

snack [snæk], *s.* der Imbiß.

snaffle [snæfl], *s.* die Trense.

snag [snæg], *s.* die Schwierigkeit; der Haken.

snail [sneil], *s.* (*Zool.*) die Schnecke.

snake [sneik], *s.* (*Zool.*) die Schlange.

snap [snæp], *v.n.* schnappen (*at*, nach, *Dat.*); (*fig.*) einen anfahren (*shout at s.o.*). — *v.a.* (er)schnappen; (*Phot.*) knipsen. — *s.* (*abbr. for* **snapshot** [ˈsnæpʃɔt]) (*Phot.*) das Photo.

snare [snεə], *s.* die Schlinge. — *v.a. see* **ensnare**.

snarl [sna:l], *v.n.* knurren (*dog*); — *at s.o.*, einen anfahren, anschnauzen.

487

snatch

snatch [snætʃ], *v.a.* erschnappen, erhaschen.

sneak [sni:k], *v.n.* kriechen, schleichen. — *s.* der Kriecher.

sneer [sniə], *v.n.* höhnen, verhöhnen (*at, Acc.*). — *s.* der Spott.

sneeze [sni:z], *v.n.* niesen. — *s.* das Niesen.

sniff [snif], *v.a., v.n.* schnüffeln.

snigger ['snigə], *v.n.* kichern. — *s.* das Kichern.

snip [snip], *v.a.* schneiden, schnippeln.

snipe (1) [snaip], *s.* (*Orn.*) die Schnepfe.

snipe (2) [snaip], *v.n.* schießen.

snivel [snivl], *v.n.* schluchzen (*from weeping*); verschnupft sein (*with a cold*).

snob [snɔb], *s.* der Snob.

snobbish ['snɔbiʃ], *adj.* vornehm tuend; protzig, snobbistisch.

snooze [snu:z], *s.* das Schläfchen. — *v.n.* einschlafen, ein Schläfchen machen.

snore [snɔ:], *v.n.* schnarchen. — *s.* das Schnarchen.

snort [snɔ:t], *v.n.* schnaufen; schnarchen (*snore*).

snout [snaut], *s.* die Schnauze, der Rüssel.

snow [snou], *s.* der Schnee. — *v.n.* schneien.

snowdrift ['snoudrift], *s.* das Schneegestöber.

snowdrop ['snoudrɔp], *s.* (*Bot.*) das Schneeglöckchen.

snub [snʌb], *v.a.* kurz abfertigen; (*fig.*) schneiden (*ignore*). — *adj.* — *nosed,* stumpfnasig. — *s.* die Geringschätzung, das Ignorieren.

snuff [snʌf], *s.* der Schnupftabak. — *v.a.* ausblasen (*candle*).

snug [snʌg], *adj.* behaglich; geborgen (*protected*).

so [sou], *adv.* so, also; *not — as,* nicht so wie. — *conj.* so.

soak [souk], *v.a.* einweichen, durchtränken. — *v.n.* weichen, durchsickern (*in(to)*, in, *Acc.*). — *s.* der Regenguß.

soap [soup], *s.* die Seife. — *v.a.* einseifen.

soar [sɔ:], *v.n.* sich aufschwingen, schweben.

sob [sɔb], *v.n.* schluchzen. — *s.* das Schluchzen.

sober ['soubə], *adj.* nüchtern. — *v.a., v.n.* — (*down*), (sich) ernüchtern.

sobriety [so'braiəti], *s.* die Nüchternheit.

soccer ['sɔkə], *s.* (*Sport*) das Fußballspiel.

sociable ['souʃəbl], *adj.* gesellig.

social ['souʃəl], *adj.* sozial, gesellschaftlich. — *s.* die Gesellschaft (*party*).

socialism ['souʃəlizm], *s.* (*Pol.*) der Sozialismus.

socialist ['souʃəlist], *adj.* (*Pol.*) sozialistisch, Sozial-. — *s.* der Sozialist.

society [sə'saiəti], *s.* die Gesellschaft (*human —*); der Verein (*association*); (*Comm.*) die (Handels)gesellschaft.

sock (1) [sɔk], *s.* der Strumpf.

sock (2) [sɔk], *v.a.* (*sl.*) schlagen, boxen.

socket ['sɔkit], *s. eye —,* die Augenhöhle; (*Elec.*) die Steckdose.

sod [sɔd], *s.* der Rasen, die Erde.

sodden [sɔdn], *adj.* durchweicht.

sofa ['soufə], *s.* das Sofa.

soft [sɔft], *adj.* weich, sanft; einfältig (*stupid*).

soften [sɔfn], *v.a.* weich machen, erweichen. — *v.n.* weich werden, erweichen.

soil [sɔil], *s.* der Boden, die Erde. — *v.a.* beschmutzen.

sojourn ['sʌdʒən *or* 'sɔdʒən], *s.* der Aufenthalt. — *v.n.* sich aufhalten.

solace ['sɔlis], *s.* der Trost.

solar ['soulə], *adj.* Sonnen-.

solder ['sɔldə *or* 'sɔ:də], *v.a.* löten. — *s.* das Lötmittel.

soldier ['souldʒə], *s.* der Soldat. — *v.n.* dienen, Soldat sein.

sole (1) [soul], *s.* (*Zool.*) die Seezunge.

sole (2) [soul], *s.* die Sohle (*foot*).

sole (3) [soul], *adj.* allein, einzig.

solecism ['sɔlisizm], *s.* der Sprachschnitzer.

solemn ['sɔləm], *adj.* feierlich.

solemnize ['sɔləmnaiz], *v.a.* feiern, feierlich begehen.

solicit [sə'lisit], *v.a.* direkt erbitten, angehen, anhalten (*for*, um).

solicitor [sə'lisitə], *s.* (*Law*) der Anwalt, Rechtsanwalt.

solicitous [sə'lisitəs], *adj.* besorgt.

solid ['sɔlid], *adj.* fest; solide; (*fig.*) gediegen; massiv (*bulky*).

solidify [sə'lidifai], *v.a.* verdichten, fest machen. — *v.n.* sich verfestigen.

soliloquy [sə'liləkwi], *s.* das Selbstgespräch, der Monolog.

solitaire [sɔli'teə], *s.* der Solitär; (*Am.*) die Patience.

solitary ['sɔlitəri], *adj.* einzeln (*single*); einsam (*lonely*).

solitude ['sɔlitju:d], *s.* die Einsamkeit.

solstice ['sɔlstis], *s.* die Sonnenwende.

soluble ['sɔljubl], *adj.* (*Chem.*) löslich; lösbar.

solution [sə'lju:ʃən], *s.* die Lösung.

solvable ['sɔlvəbl], *adj.* (auf)lösbar (*problem, puzzle*).

solve [sɔlv], *v.a.* lösen (*problem, puzzle*).

solvent ['sɔlvənt], *adj.* (*Chem.*) auflösend; (*Comm.*) zahlungsfähig. — *s.* das Lösungsmittel.

sombre ['sɔmbə], *adj.* düster; schwermütig, traurig.

some [sʌm], *adj.* irgend ein, etwas; (*pl.*) einige, manche; etliche.

somebody ['sʌmbɔdi], *s.* jemand.

somersault ['sʌməsɔːlt], *s.* der Purzelbaum.

sometimes ['sʌmtaimz], *adv.* manchmal, zuweilen.

somewhat ['sʌmwɔt], *adv.* etwas, ziemlich.

somewhere ['sʌmwɛə], *adv.* irgendwo(hin).

somnambulist [sɔm'næmbjulist], *s.* der Nachtwandler.

somnolent ['sɔmnələnt], *adj.* schläfrig, schlafsüchtig.

son [sʌn], *s.* der Sohn; —-in-law, der Schwiegersohn.

song [sɔŋ], *s.* (*Mus.*) das Lied; der Gesang; *for a* —, spottbillig.

sonnet ['sɔnit], *s.* (*Poet.*) das Sonett.

sonorous ['sɔnərəs], *adj.* wohlklingend.

soon [su:n], *adv.* bald.

sooner ['su:nə], *comp. adv.* lieber (*rather*); früher, eher (*earlier*); *no* — *said than done,* gesagt, getan.

soot [sut], *s.* der Ruß.

soothe [su:ð], *v.a.* besänftigen.

soothsayer ['su:θseiə], *s.* der Wahrsager.

sop [sɔp], *s.* der eingetunkte Bissen; (*fig.*) die Bestechung (*bribe*).

soporific [sɔpə'rifik], *adj.* einschläfernd.

soprano [sə'prɑ:nou], *s.* (*Mus.*) der Sopran.

sorcerer ['sɔ:sərə], *s.* der Zauberer.

sorceress ['sɔ:sərəs], *s.* die Hexe.

sorcery ['sɔ:səri], *s.* die Zauberei, Hexerei.

sordid ['sɔ:did], *adj.* schmutzig; gemein.

sore [sɔ:], *adj.* wund, schmerzhaft; empfindlich. — *s.* die wunde Stelle.

sorrel (1) ['sɔrəl], *s.* (*Bot.*) der Sauerampfer.

sorrel (2) ['sɔrəl], *s.* (*Zool.*) der Rotfuchs.

sorrow ['sɔrou], *s.* der Kummer, das Leid, der Gram.

sorry ['sɔri], *adj.* traurig; *I am* —, es tut mir leid.

sort [sɔ:t], *s.* die Art, Gattung, Sorte. — *v.a.* aussortieren.

sortie ['sɔ:ti:], *s.* (*Mil.*) der Ausfall.

sot [sɔt], *s.* der Trunkenbold.

soul [soul], *s.* die Seele; *not a* —, niemand, keine Menschenseele.

sound (1) [saund], *v.n., v.a.* tönen, klingen, erklingen lassen. — *s.* der Klang, Ton, Laut.

sound (2) [saund], *adj.* gesund; (*fig.*) vernünftig (*plan etc.*); solide.

soup [su:p], *s.* die Suppe.

sour [sauə], *adj.* sauer; (*fig.*) mürrisch.

source [sɔ:s], *s.* die Quelle; der Ursprung (*origin*).

souse [saus], *v.a.* einpökeln, einsalzen.

south [sauθ], *s.* der Süden.

South African [sauθ 'æfrikən], *adj.* südafrikanisch. — *s.* der Südafrikaner.

southern ['sʌðən], *adj.* südlich, Süd-.

sou(th)-wester [sau(θ)'westə], *s.* (*Naut.*) der Südwester.

souvenir ['su:vəniə], *s.* das Andenken.

sovereign ['sɔvrin], *s.* der Herrscher (*ruler*); das Goldstück (*£1 coin*). — *adj.* allerhöchst, souverän.

Soviet ['souviit], *adj.* sowjetisch. — *s.* der Sowjet.

sow (1) [sau], *s.* (*Zool.*) die Sau.

sow (2) [sou], *v.a. irr.* säen, ausstreuen (*cast*).

spa [spɑ:], *s.* das Bad; der Kurort.

space [speis], *s.* der Zwischenraum (*interval*); der Raum, das Weltall, der Kosmos (*interplanetary*); der Platz (*room*). — *v.a.* sperren, richtig plazieren.

spacious ['speiʃəs], *adj.* geräumig.

spade [speid], *s.* der Spaten; *call a* — *a* —, das Kind beim rechten Namen nennen; (*Cards*) das Pik.

span [spæn], *s.* die Spanne (*time*); die Spannweite. — *v.a.* überspannen (*bridge*); ausmessen.

spangle [spæŋgl], *s.* der Flitter. — *v.a.* beflittern, schmücken.

Spaniard ['spænjəd], *s.* der Spanier.

spaniel ['spænjəl], *s.*(*Zool.*) der Wachtelhund.

Spanish ['spæniʃ], *adj.* spanisch.

spanner ['spænə], *s.* der Schraubenschlüssel.

spar (1) [spɑ:], *s.* (*Naut.*) der Sparren.

spar (2) [spɑ:], *s.* (*Geol.*) der Spat.

spar (3) [spɑ:], *v.n.* boxen.

spare [spɛə], *v.a.* schonen (*save*); sparsam sein; übrig haben. — *v.n.* sparsam sein. — *adj.* übrig (*extra*); mager, hager (*lean*); Reserve— (*tyre etc.*).

sparing ['spɛəriŋ], *adj.* sparsam, karg.

spark [spɑ:k], *s.* der Funken; (*fig.*) der helle Kopf.

sparkle [spɑ:kl], *v.n.* glänzen, funkeln. — *s.* das Funkeln.

sparrow ['spærou], *s.* (*Orn.*) der Sperling.

sparrowhawk ['spærouhɔ:k], *s.* (*Orn.*) der Sperber.

sparse [spɑ:s], *adj.* spärlich, dünn.

spasm [spæzm], *s.* der Krampf.

spasmodic [spæz'mɔdik], *adj.* krampfhaft; (*fig.*) ab und zu auftretend.

spats [spæts], *s. pl.* die Gamaschen, *f.pl.*

spatter ['spætə], *v.a.* bespritzen, besudeln.

spatula ['spætjulə], *s.* der Spachtel.

spawn [spɔ:n], *s.* der Laich, die Brut.

speak [spi:k], *v.a., v.n. irr.* sprechen, reden; — *out,* frei heraussprechen.

speaker ['spi:kə], *s.* der Sprecher.

spear [spiə], *s.* der Spieß, Speer, die Lanze. — *v.a.* aufspießen.

special [speʃl], *adj.* besonder, speziell, Sonder-.

specific [spi'sifik], *adj.* spezifisch, eigentümlich.

specify ['spesifai], *v.a.* spezifizieren.

specimen ['spesimən], *s.* die Probe, (*Comm.*) das Muster.

specious ['spi:ʃəs], *adj.* bestechend, trügerisch.

speck [spek], *s.* der Fleck.

speckle [spekl], *s.* der Tüpfel, Sprenkel. — *v.a.* sprenkeln.

spectacle ['spektəkl], *s.* das Schauspiel, der Anblick; (*pl.*) die Brille.

spectator [spek'teitə], *s.* der Zuschauer.

spectre ['spektə], *s.* das Gespenst.

speculate ['spekjuleit], *v.n.* nachsinnen, grübeln (*ponder*); spekulieren.

speculative ['spekjulətiv], *adj.* speku-
lativ; sinnend.

speech [spi:tʃ], *s.* die Rede, Ansprache;
das Sprechen (*articulation*); *figure of*
—, die Redewendung; *make a* —,
eine Rede halten.

speechify ['spi:tʃifai], *v.n.* viele Worte
machen, unermüdlich reden.

speed [spi:d], *s.* die Eile; die Geschwindigkeit (*velocity*); (*Mus.*) das Tempo.
— *v.a.* (eilig) fortschicken. — *v.n.*
eilen, schnell fahren; — *up*, sich
beeilen.

spell (1) [spel], *s.* der Zauber (*enchantment*). — *v.a.* buchstabieren (*verbally*);
richtig schreiben (*in writing*).

spell (2) [spel], *s.* die Zeitlang, Zeit
(*period*).

spellbound ['spelbaund], *adj.* bezau-
bert, gebannt.

spend [spend], *v.a. irr.* ausgeben
(*money*); verbringen (*time*); — ausgeben-
den (*energy*); erschöpfen (*exhaust*).

spendthrift ['spendθrift], *s.* der Ver-
schwender.

spew [spju:], *v.a.* speien; ausspeien.

sphere [sfiə], *s.* die Sphäre (*also fig.*);
(*Geom.*) die Kugel.

spice [spais], *s.* die Würze (*seasoning*);
das Gewürz (*herb*). — *v.a.* würzen.

spider ['spaidə], *s.* (*Zool.*) die Spinne.

spigot ['spigət], *s.* (*Mech.*) der Zapfen.

spike [spaik], *s.* die Spitze, der lange
Nagel; (*fig.*) der Dorn. — *v.a.* durchbohren, spießen; (*Mil.*) vernageln
(*a gun*).

spill (1) [spil], *v.a. irr.* ausschütten,
vergießen; (*Am. coll.*) — *the beans*,
mit der Sprache herausrücken, alles
verraten; *it's no good crying over spilt
milk*, was geschehen ist, ist geschehen.

spill (2) [spil], *s.* der Fidibus.

spin [spin], *v.a. irr.* spinnen, drehen,
wirbeln. — *v.n.* wirbeln, sich schnell
drehen; — *dry*, schleudern. — *s.* die
schnelle Drehung; — *drier*, die
Wäscheschleuder.

spinach ['spinidʒ], *s.* (*Bot.*) der Spinat.

spinal ['spainəl], *adj.* Rückgrats-.

spine [spain], *s.* (*Anat.*) die Wirbelsäule;
der Rücken (*of book*).

spinney ['spini], *s.* das Gestrüpp.

spinster ['spinstə], *s.* die (alte) Jungfer;
die unverheiratete Dame.

spiral ['spaiərəl], *adj.* Spiral-, gewunden. — *s.* (*Geom.*) die Spirale.

spirant ['spaiərənt], *s.* (*Phonet.*) der
Spirant.

spire [spaiə], *s.* (*Archit.*) die Turmspitze.

spirit ['spirit], *s.* der Geist; das Gespenst (*ghost*); der Mut (*courage*); die
Stimmung, Verfassung (*mood*); das
geistige Getränk (*drink*), (*pl.*) Spirituosen, *pl.*; *in high* —s, in guter Stimmung, Laune. — *v.a.* — *away*, entführen, verschwinden lassen.

spiritual ['spiritjual], *adj.* geistig (*mental*); (*Rel.*) geistlich. — *s.* (*Mus.*) das
Negerlied.

spit (1) [spit], *s.* der Spieß, Bratspieß.
— *v.a.* aufspießen.

spit (2) [spit], *v.n. irr.* ausspucken. — *s.*
die Spucke.

spite [spait], *s.* der Groll; *in* — *of*, trotz
(*Genit.*). — *v.a.* ärgern.

spiteful ['spaitful], *adj.* boshaft.

spittle [spitl], *s.* der Speichel.

spittoon, [spi'tu:n], *s.* der Spucknapf.

splash [splæʃ], *s.* der Spritzer; *make a*
—, Aufsehen erregen. — *v.a., v.n.*
spritzen; (*fig.*) um sich werfen
(*money etc.*).

splay [splei], *v.a.* ausrenken, verrenken.

spleen [spli:n], *s.* (*Anat.*) die Milz;
(*fig.*) der Spleen, die Laune, Marotte.

splendour ['splendə], *s.* die Pracht, der
Glanz.

splice [splais], *v.a.* splissen; (*Naut.*) —
the mainbrace, das Hauptfaß öffnen!

splint [splint], *s.* (*Med.*) die Schiene.

splinter ['splintə], *s.* der Span; der
Splitter (*fragment*).

split [split], *v.a. irr.* spalten; (*fig.*)
verteilen, teilen (*divide*). — *v.n.* sich
trennen; (*coll.*) — *on s.o.*, einen
verraten. — *adj.* — *second timing*, auf
den Bruchteil einer Sekunde. — *s.*
die Spaltung.

splutter ['splʌtə], *v.n.* sprudeln. — *s.*
das Sprudeln.

spoil [spoil], *v.a. irr.* verderben; (*child*)
verwöhnen; (*Mil.*) plündern, berau-
ben. — *v.n.* verderben. — *s.* (*pl.*) die
Beute.

spoilsport ['spoilspo:t], *s.* der Spielverderber.

spoke [spouk], *s.* die Speiche; die
Sprosse.

spokesman ['spouksmən], *s.* der Wortführer, Sprecher.

sponge [spʌndʒ], *s.* der Schwamm; —
cake, die Sandtorte. — *v.a.* mit dem
Schwamm wischen. — *v.n.* (*coll.*)
schmarotzen (*on*, bei, *Dat.*).

sponger ['spʌndʒə], *s.* (*coll.*) der
Schmarotzer (*parasite*).

sponsor ['sponsə], *s.* der Bürge (*guarantor*); der Förderer; Pate. — *v.a.*
fördern, unterstützen.

spontaneous [spon'teiniəs], *adj.* spontan, freiwillig.

spook [spuk], *s.* der Spuk, Geist, das
Gespenst.

spool [spu:l], *s.* die Spule. — *v.a.* auf-
spulen.

spoon [spu:n], *s.* der Löffel. — *v.a.* mit
dem Löffel essen, löffeln.

sport [spo:t], *s.* der Sport; (*fig.*) der
Scherz. — *v.a.* tragen (*wear*). — *v.n.*
scherzen.

spot [spot], *s.* die Stelle, der Ort, Platz;
(*stain*) der Fleck; (*fig.*) der Schandfleck (*on o.'s honour*); *on the* —,
sogleich; auf der Stelle; *in a* —, (*Am.
coll.*) in Verlegenheit; — *cash*, Barzahlung, *f.* — *v.a.* entdecken, finden.

spotted ['spotid], *adj.* fleckig, gefleckt;
befleckt; pickelig.

spouse [spauz], *s.* der Gatte; die Gattin.

spout [spaut], *v.a.*, *v.n.* ausspeien, sprudeln, sprudeln lassen; (*sl.*) predigen, schwatzen. — *s.* die Tülle (*teapot etc.*); die Abflußröhre.

sprain [sprein], *v.a.* (*Med.*) verrenken. — *s.* die Verrenkung.

sprat [spræt], *s.* (*Zool.*) die Sprotte.

sprawl [sprɔ:l], *v.n.* sich spreizen, ausbreiten.

spray [sprei], *v.a.*, *v.n.* sprühen spritzen. — *s.* die Sprühe; der Sprühregen.

spread [spred], *v.a.*, *v.n. irr.* ausbreiten; verbreiten (*get abroad*); streichen (*overlay with*). — *s.* die Ausbreitung; Verbreitung.

spree [spri:], *s.* das Vergnügen, der lustige Abend, Bummel.

sprig [sprig], *s.* der Zweig, Sprößling.

sprightly ['spraitli], *adj.* munter, lebhaft.

spring [spriŋ], *s.* die Quelle (*water*); der Ursprung (*origin*); der Frühling (*season*); (*Mech.*) die Feder, Sprungfeder, Spirale. — *v.n. irr.* springen (*jump*); entspringen (*originate*). — *v.a.* — *a surprise*, eine Überraschung bereiten.

springe [sprindʒ], *s.* der Sprenkel.

sprinkle [spriŋkl], *v.a.* (be)sprengen; (*Hort.*) berieseln.

sprint [sprint], *s.* der Kurzstreckenlauf, Wettlauf.

sprite [sprait], *s.* der Geist, Kobold.

sprout [spraut], *s.* (*Bot.*) die Sprosse, der Sprößling; *Brussels* —*s*, der Rosenkohl.

spruce (1) [spru:s], *adj.* sauber, geputzt; schmuck.

spruce (2) [spru:s], *s.* (*Bot.*) die Fichte, Rottanne.

spume [spju:m], *s.* der Schaum.

spur [spə:], *s.* der Sporn (*goad*); (*fig.*) der Stachel; der Ansporn, Antrieb; (*Geog.*) der Ausläufer (*of range*). — *v.a.* anspornen.

spurious ['spjuəriəs], *adj.* unecht, falsch.

spurn [spə:n], *v.a.* verschmähen, verachten.

spurt [spə:t], *v.a.* spritzen. — *v.n.* sich anstrengen. — *s.* die Anstrengung.

sputter ['spʌtə], *v.a.* herausprudeln. — *v.n.* sprühen, sprudeln.

spy [spai], *s.* der Spion. — *v.n.* spionieren (*on, bei, Dat.*).

squabble [skwɔbl], *v.n.* zanken. — *s.* der Zank, Streit.

squad [skwɔd], *s.* der Trupp.

squadron ['skwɔdrən], *s.* die Schwadron, das Geschwader.

squalid ['skwɔlid], *adj.* schmutzig, elend, eklig.

squall [skwɔ:l], *s.* der Windstoß.

squalor ['skwɔlə], *s.* der Schmutz.

squander ['skwɔndə], *v.a.* verschwenden, vergeuden.

square [skwɛə], *s.* das Quadrat; der Platz; (*coll.*) der Philister, Spießer. — *v.a.* ausrichten; (*coll.*) ins Reine bringen. — *adj.* viereckig; quadratisch; redlich (*honest*); quitt (*quits*).

squash (1) [skwɔʃ], *v.a.* zerquetschen, zerdrücken (*press together*). — *s.* das Gedränge (*crowd*); der Fruchtsaft (*drink*).

squash (2) [skwɔʃ], *s.* (*Sport*) eine Art Racketspiel.

squat [skwɔt], *v.n.* kauern; sich niederlassen. — *adj.* stämmig, untersetzt.

squatter ['skwɔtə], *s.* der Ansiedler.

squaw [skwɔ:], *s.* die Indianerfrau.

squeak [skwi:k], *v.n.* quieken, quietschen. — *s.* das Gequiek.

squeal [skwi:l], *v.n.* quieken; (*Am. coll.*) verraten, preisgeben.

squeamish ['skwi:miʃ], *adj.* empfindlich, zimperlich.

squeeze [skwi:z], *v.a.* drücken, quetschen. — *s.* das Gedränge.

squib [skwib], *s.* der Frosch (*firework*); (*Lit.*) das Spottgedicht.

squint [skwint], *v.n.* schielen. — *s.* das Schielen.

squire [skwaiə], *s.* der Landedelmann, Junker.

squirrel ['skwirəl], *s.* (*Zool.*) das Eichhörnchen.

squirt [skwə:t], *v.a.* spritzen. — *s.* der Spritzer, Wasserstrahl; (*sl.*) der Wicht.

stab [stæb], *v.a.* erstechen, erdolchen. — *s.* der Dolchstich, Dolchstoß.

stability [stə'biliti], *s.* die Beständigkeit, Stabilität.

stable (1) [steibl], *adj.* fest, beständig; (*Phys.*) stabil.

stable (2) [steibl], *s.* der Stall.

stack [stæk], *s.* der Stoß (*pile*); der Schornstein (*chimneys*). — *v.a.* aufschichten.

staff [sta:f], *s.* der Stab, Stock; (*Mil.*) der Stab, Generalstab; (*Sch.*) der Lehrkörper; das Personal. — *v.a.* besetzen.

stag [stæg], *s.* (*Zool.*) der Hirsch; — *party*, die Herrengesellschaft.

stage [steidʒ], *s.* (*Theat.*) die Bühne; die Stufe, das Stadium (*phase*); (*fig.*) der Schauplatz; *fare* —, die Teilstrecke. — *v.a.* (*Theat.*) inszenieren, abhalten (*hold*).

stagecoach ['steidʒkoutʃ], *s.* die Postkutsche.

stagger ['stægə], *v.n.* schwanken, wanken, taumeln. — *v.a.* (*coll.*) verblüffen (*astonish*); staffeln (*graduate*).

stagnate [stæg'neit], *v.n.* stocken, stillstehen.

staid [steid], *adj.* gesetzt, gelassen.

stain [stein], *s.* der Fleck, Makel. — *v.a.* beflecken; beizen; färben (*dye*).

stained [steind], *adj.* — *glass window*, buntes Fenster.

stainless ['steinlis], *adj.* rostfrei.

stair [stɛə], *s.* die Stufe, Stiege.

staircase ['stɛəkeis], *s.* das Treppenhaus; die Treppe.

stake [steik], *s.* der Pfahl, Pfosten; Scheiterhaufen; (*Gambling*) der Einsatz; *at* —, auf dem Spiel. — *v.a.* aufs Spiel setzen.

stale [steil], *adj.* abgestanden, schal.

stalemate ['steilmeit], *s.* (*Chess*) das Patt; der Stillstand.

stalk (1) [stɔ:k], *s.* (*Bot.*) der Stengel, Halm.

stalk (2) [stɔ:k], *v.n.* stolzieren, steif gehen. — *v.a.* pirschen (*hunt*).

stall [stɔ:l], *s.* die Bude (*booth*), der Stand (*stand*); (*Eccl.*) der Chorstuhl; (*Theat.*) der Sperrsitz; Parterresitz. — *v.n.* (*Motor.*) stehenbleiben.

stallion ['stæljən], *s.* (*Zool.*) der Hengst.

stalwart ['stɔ:lwət], *adj.* kräftig, stark, verläßlich.

stamina ['stæminə], *s.* die Ausdauer, Widerstandskraft.

stammer ['stæmə], *v.n.* stammeln, stottern.

stamp [stæmp], *s.* der Stempel (*rubber* —); die Marke (*postage*); die Stampfe, Stanze (*die* —). — *v.a.* stempeln; (*Mech.*) stanzen; frankieren (*letters*). — *v.n.* stampfen.

stampede [stæm'pi:d], *s.* die wilde Flucht. — *v.n.* in wilder Flucht davonlaufen.

stand [stænd], *v.n. irr.* stehen. — *v.a.* aushalten, standhalten (*Dat.*). — *s.* der Ständer (*hats etc.*); der Stand (*stall*); (*fig.*) die Stellung.

standard ['stændəd], *s.* der Standard (*level*); (*Mil.*) die Standarte; der Maßstab (*yardstick*). — *adj.* normal.

standing ['stændiŋ], *s.* der Rang, das Ansehen. — *adj.* — *orders*, die Geschäftsordnung; (*Mil.*) die Vorschriften, *f. pl.*, Dauerbefehle, *m. pl.*

standpoint ['stændpɔint], *s.* der Standpunkt (*point of view*).

standstill ['stændstil], *s.* der Stillstand.

stanza ['stænzə], *s.* (*Poet.*) die Stanze, Strophe.

staple [steipl], *s.* das Haupterzeugnis; der Stapelplatz. — *adj.* Haupt-. — *v.a.* stapeln; heften (*paper*).

stapler ['steiplə], *s.* die Heftmaschine.

star [sta:], *s.* der Stern; (*Theat. etc.*) der Star. — *v.n.* (*Theat. etc.*) die Hauptrolle spielen.

starboard ['sta:bəd], *s.* das Steuerbord.

starch [sta:tʃ], *s.* die Stärke (*laundry*). — *v.a.* stärken.

stare [stɛə], *v.n.* starren. — *s.* der starre Blick, das Starren.

stark [sta:k], *adj.* völlig, ganz.

starling ['sta:liŋ], *s.* (*Orn.*) der Star.

start [sta:t], *v.n.* anfangen; aufbrechen; auffahren, aufspringen; stutzen (*jerk*); abfahren (*depart*). — *v.a.* starten (*car etc.*),in Gang setzen. — *s.* der Anfang; (*Sport*) der Start, Anlauf; der Aufbruch (*departure*); *by fits and* —*s*, ruckweise.

starter ['sta:tə], *s.* (*Sport*) der Starter, Teilnehmer (*participant*); das Rennpferd (*horse*); (*Motor.*) der Anlasser.

startle [sta:tl], *v.a.* erschrecken.

starve [sta:v], *v.n.* verhungern, hungern. — *v.a.* aushungern.

state [steit], *s.* der Zustand, die Lage;

(*Pol.*) der Staat; (*personal*) der Stand (*single etc.*). — *v.a.* erklären, darlegen.

stately ['steitli], *adj.* stattlich, prachtvoll.

statement ['steitmənt], *s.* die Feststellung; *bank* —, der Kontoauszug.

statesman ['steitsmən], *s.* der Staatsmann, Politiker.

statics ['stætiks], *s.* die Statik.

station ['steiʃən], *s.* (*Railw.*) die Station; der Bahnhof; die Stellung, der Rang (*position*); (*Mil.*) die Stationierung. — *v.a.* (*Mil.*) aufstellen, stationieren; (*fig.*) hinstellen.

stationary ['steiʃənri], *adj.* stationär, stillstehend.

stationer ['steiʃənə], *s.* der Papierhändler.

stationery ['steiʃənri], *s.* das Briefpapier, Schreibpapier; die Papierwaren, *f. pl.*

statuary ['stætjuəri], *s.* die Bildhauerkunst.

statue ['stætju:], *s.* das Standbild.

status ['steitəs], *s.* die Stellung (*rank, position*).

statute ['stætju:t], *s.* das Statut; — *law*, das Landesrecht, Gesetzesrecht.

staunch [stɔ:ntʃ], *adj.* zuverlässig.

stave [steiv], *s.* die Faßdaube (*of vat*); (*Poet.*) die Strophe; (*Mus.*) die Linie. — *v.a.* — *off*, abwehren.

stay [stei], *v.n.* bleiben, verweilen, wohnen. — *v.a.* hindern, aufhalten. — *s.* der Aufenthalt; (*pl.*) das Korsett.

stead [sted], *s.* die Stelle; *in his* —, an seiner Statt.

steadfast ['stedfa:st], *adj.* standhaft,fest.

steadiness ['stedinis], *s.* die Beständigkeit.

steady ['stedi], *adj.* fest, sicher; beständig, treu.

steak [steik], *s.* das Steak.

steal [sti:l], *v.a. irr.* stehlen. — *v.n.* sich stehlen, schleichen.

stealth [stelθ], *s.* die Heimlichkeit.

stealthy ['stelθi], *adj.* heimlich, verstohlen.

steam [sti:m], *s.* der Dampf; *get up* —, in Gang bringen *or* kommen; — *boiler*, der Dampfkessel. — *v.n.* dampfen; davondampfen. — *v.a.* dämpfen, (*Cul.*) dünsten.

steed [sti:d], *s.* das Schlachtroß.

steel [sti:l], *s.* der Stahl. — *adj.* stählern. — *v.n.* — *o.s.*, sich stählen.

steep (1) [sti:p], *adj.* steil; (*fig.*) hoch; (*coll.*) gesalzen (*price*).

steep (2) [sti:p], *v.a.* einweichen, sättigen.

steeple [sti:pl], *s.* (*Archit.*) der Kirchturm.

steeplechase ['sti:pltʃeis], *s.* das Hindernisrennen.

steeplejack ['sti:pldʒæk], *s.* der Turmdecker.

steer (1) [stiə], *s.* (*Zool.*) der junge Stier.

steer (2) [stiə], *v.a.* steuern (*guide*).

steerage ['stiəridʒ], *s.* die Steuerung; (*Naut.*) das Zwischendeck.

stellar [′stelə], *adj.* Stern-, Sternen-.
stem (1) [stem], *s.* der Stamm; (*Phonet.*) der Stamm; der Stiel, die Wurzel. — *v.n.* — *from*, kommen von, abstammen.
stem (2) [stem], *v.a.* sich entgegenstemmen (*Dat.*); (*fig.*) eindämmen.
stench [stentʃ], *s.* der Gestank.
stencil [′stensil], *s.* die Schablone, Matrize; *cut a* —, auf Matrize schreiben.
step [step], *s.* der Schritt, Tritt; (*of ladder*) die Sprosse; (*of stairs*) die Stufe. — *v.n.* treten, schreiten (*stride*). — *v.a.* (*coll.*) — *up*, beschleunigen.
step- [step], *pref.* Stief- (*brother, mother etc.*).
stereo- [′stiəriou], *pref.* Stereo-.
sterile [′sterail], *adj.* steril.
sterling [′stə:liŋ], *adj.* echt, vollwertig; *pound* —, ein Pfund Sterling.
stern (1) [stə:n], *adj.* streng.
stern (2) [stə:n], *s.* (*Naut.*) das Heck.
stevedore [′sti:vədɔ:], *s.* der Hafenarbeiter.
stew [stju:], *s.* (*Cul.*) das Schmorfleisch, das Gulasch.
steward [′stjuːəd], *s.* der Verwalter; der Haushofmeister; (*Naut.*) der Steward.
stick [stik], *s.* der Stock, Stecken. — *v.a.* stecken (*insert*); kleben (*glue*). — *v.n.* stecken, haften bleiben; (*fig., coll.*) — *to s.o.*, zu jemanderι halten (*be loyal*).
sticky [′stiki], *adj.* klebrig; (*fig.*) prekär, schwierig (*difficult*); *come to a* — *end*, ein böses Ende nehmen.
stiff [stif], *adj.* steif; schwer, schwierig (*examination*); formell (*manner*).
stiffen [stifn], *v.a.* steifen, versteifen. — *v.n.* steif werden, sich versteifen.
stifle [staifl], *v.a., v.n.* ersticken; (*fig.*) unterdrücken.
stigmatize [′stigmətaiz], *v.a.* stigmatisieren, brandmarken.
stile [stail], *s.* der Zauntritt, Übergang.
still (1) [stil], *adj.* still, ruhig. — *adv.* immer noch. — *conj.* doch, dennoch. — *v.a.* stillen, beruhigen.
still (2) [stil], *s.* die Destillierflasche, der Destillierkolben.
stilt [stilt], *s.* die Stelze.
stilted [′stiltid], *adj.* auf Stelzen; (*fig.*) hochtrabend, geschraubt.
stimulant [′stimjulənt], *s.* das Reizmittel. — *adj.* anreizend, anregend.
stimulate [′stimjuleit], *v.a.* anreizen, stimulieren, anregen.
stimulus [′stimjuləs], *s.* der Reiz, die Anregung.
sting [stiŋ], *v.a. irr.* stechen; (*fig.*) kränken, verwunden. — *v.n. irr.* stechen, brennen, schmerzen. — *s.* der Stachel (*prick*); der Stich (*stab*).
stink [stiŋk], *v.n. irr.* stinken. — *s.* der Gestank.
stint [stint], *s.* die Einschränkung (*limit*); das Maß, Tagespensum. — *v.a.* beschränken, einschränken.

stipend [′staipend], *s.* die Besoldung, das Gehalt.
stipendiary [stai′pendiəri], *adj.* besoldet, bezahlt.
stipulate [′stipjuleit], *v.a.* festsetzen, ausbedingen.
stir [stə:], *v.a.* rühren, bewegen. — *v.n.* sich rühren. — *s.* die Aufregung; *cause a* —, Aufsehen erregen.
stirrup [′stirəp], *s.* der Steigbügel.
stitch [stitʃ], *v.a.* sticken, nähen. — *s.* der Stich; der stechende Schmerz, der Seitenstich (*pain*).
stoat [stout], *s.* (*Zool.*) das Hermelin.
stock [stɔk], *s.* das Lager; *in* —, auf Lager; vorrätig; der Stamm, die Familie; (*Fin.*) das Kapital; — *exchange*, die Börse; (*pl.*) die Börsenpapiere, *n. pl.*, Aktien, *f.pl.* — *v.a.* halten, führen.
stockade [stɔ′keid], *s.* das Staket.
stockbroker [′stɔkbroukə], *s.* (*Fin.*) der Börsenmakler.
stockholder [′stɔkhouldə], *s.* (*Fin., Am.*) der Aktionär.
stocking [′stɔkiŋ], *s.* der Strumpf.
stocktaking [′stɔkteikiŋ], *s.* die Inventuraufnahme.
stoical [′stouikəl], *adj.* stoisch.
stoke [stouk], *v.a.* schüren.
stoker [′stoukə], *s.* der Heizer.
stole [stoul], *s.* (*Eccl.*) die Stola; der Pelzkragen (*fur*).
stolid [′stɔlid], *adj.* schwerfällig, gleichgültig.
stomach [′stʌmək], *s.* der Magen; (*fig.*) der Appetit.
stone [stoun], *s.* der Stein; der Kern (*fruit*). — *v.a.* steinigen (*throw* —*s at*); entsteinen (*fruit*).
stony [′stouni], *adj.* steinig; (*sl.*) — *broke*, pleite.
stool [stu:l], *s.* der Schemel, Hocker; (*Med.*) der Stuhlgang.
stoop [stu:p], *v.n.* sich bücken; (*fig.*) sich herablassen.
stooping [′stu:piŋ], *adj.* gebückt.
stop [stɔp], *v.a.* halten, stoppen; aufhören; aufhalten (*halt*); — *up*, verstopfen, versperren (*block*); (*tooth*) plombieren. — *v.n.* stehen bleiben (*stand*); sich aufhalten (*stay*). — *s.* der Halt, die Haltestelle (*of bus etc.*); das Aufhalten, Innehalten (*stoppage*); das Register (*organ*); (*Gram.*) der Punkt.
stoppage [′stɔpidʒ], *s.* die Stockung, Hemmung (*hindrance*); die Arbeitseinstellung (*strike*).
stopper [′stɔpə], *s.* der Stöpsel.
storage [′stɔ:ridʒ], *s.* das Lagern.
store [stɔ:], *s.* der Vorrat, das Lagerhaus, Magazin; (*Am.*) das Kaufhaus; (*fig.*) die Menge (*of anecdotes etc.*). — *v.a.* lagern.
storey [′stɔ:ri], *s.* das Stockwerk.
stork [stɔ:k], *s.* (*Orn.*) der Storch.
storm [stɔ:m], *s.* der Sturm, das Gewitter.
story [′stɔ:ri], *s.* die Geschichte, Erzählung (*narrative*).

stout [staut], *adj.* fest; stark, kräftig.
— *s.* das starke Bier.
stove [stouv], *s.* der Ofen.
stow [stou], *v.a.* verstauen, packen. —
v.n. — *away*, als blinder Passagier
fahren.
stowaway ['stouəwei], *s.* der blinde
Passagier.
straddle [strædl], *v.n.* rittlings sitzen.
straggle [strægl], *v.n.* umherschweifen,
streifen; (*Bot.*) wuchern.
straight [streit], *adj.* gerade, offen. —
adv. — *away*, sofort, sogleich.
straighten [streitn], *v.a.* ausrichten,
gerade richten. — *v.n.* sich ausrichten.
strain [strein], *s.* die Anstrengung,
Anspannung; (*Mus.*) der Ton, Stil;
der Hang. — *v.a.* anstrengen, filtrieren; seihen. — *v.n.* sich anstrengen.
strainer ['streinə], *s.* der Seiher, der
Filter, das Sieb.
strait [streit], *adj.* eng. — *s.* (*usually
pl.*) die Enge, Meerenge.
strand (1) [strænd], *s.* der Strand.
strand (2) [strænd], *s.* die Litze (*of
rope, string*).
strange [streindʒ], *adj.* fremd (*unknown*); seltsam (*queer*).
stranger ['streindʒə], *s.* der Fremdling,
Fremde; der Unbekannte.
strangle [stræŋgl], *v.a.* erdrosseln,
erwürgen.
strangulation [stræŋgju'leiʃən], *s.* die
Erdrosselung, Erwürgung.
strap [stræp], *v.a.* festschnallen, anschnallen. — *s.* der Gurt, Riemen.
strapping ['stræpiŋ], *adj.* stark, stämmig.
strata *see under* **stratum**.
stratagem ['strætədʒəm], *s.* die List;
(*Mil.*) der Plan.
strategy ['strætədʒi], *s.* die Strategie.
stratification [strætifi'keiʃən], *s.* die
Schichtung; (*Geol.*) die Lagerung.
stratum ['streitəm], *s.* (*pl.* **strata**
['streitə]) die Schicht, Lage.
straw [strɔ:], *s.* das Stroh; *that's the
last* —, das ist die Höhe!
strawberry ['strɔ:bəri], *s.* (*Bot.*) die
Erdbeere.
stray [strei], *v.n.* irregehen, schweifen;
sich verirren. — *adj.* irr, verirrt.
streak [stri:k], *s.* der Strich; der Streifen; (*fig.*) der Anflug.
streaky ['stri:ki], *adj.* gestreift; (*bacon*)
durchwachsen.
stream [stri:m], *v.n.* strömen, wehen
(*in the wind*). — *s.* die Strömung
(*flow*); der Bach (*brook*), der Strom
(*river*).
streamer ['stri:mə], *s.* der Wimpel, das
Band, die Papierschlange.
street [stri:t], *s.* die Straße; —*s ahead*,
weit voraus.
streetcar ['stri:tkɑ:], *s.* (*Am.*) *see* **tram**.
streetlamp ['stri:tlæmp], *s.* die Straßen-
laterne.
strength [streŋθ], *s.* die Stärke; die
Kraft.

strengthen ['streŋθən], *v.a.* stärken;
(*fig.*) bekräftigen (*support*).
strenuous ['strenjuəs], *adj.* anstrengend.
stress [stres], *v.a.* (*Phonet.*) betonen;
(*fig.*) hervorheben. — *s.* die Betonung
(*emphasis*); der Druck (*pressure*).
stretch [stretʃ], *v.a., v.n.* spannen; strecken,
ausstrecken; — *a point*, eine Aus-
nahme machen. — *s.* die Strecke
(*distance*); (*coll.*) die Zuchthausstrafe
(*penal sentence*).
stretcher ['stretʃə], *s.* die Tragbahre.
strew [stru:], *v.a.* streuen, ausstreuen.
strict [strikt], *adj.* streng (*severe*);
genau (*exact*).
stricture ['striktʃə], *s.* der Tadel, die
Kritik; (*pl.*) die kritische Rede.
stride [straid], *v.n. irr.* schreiten. — *s.*
der Schritt; *take in o.'s* —, leicht
bewältigen.
strident ['straidənt], *adj.* laut, lärmend;
grell.
strife [straif], *s.* der Streit, Zank.
strike [straik], *v.a., v.n. irr.* schlagen;
abmachen (*bargain*); (*Mus.*) — *up*,
anstimmen (*song*), aufspielen (*instrument*); beginnen; — *the eye*, auffallen;
streiken, in Streik treten. — *s.* der
Streik, die Arbeitseinstellung.
striking ['straikiŋ], *adj.* auffallend.
string [striŋ], *s.* die Schnur; (*Mus.*) die
Saite; — *quartet*, das Streichquartett;
die Reihe (*series*). — *v.a.* anreihen
(*beads etc.*); — *together*, verbinden. —
v.n. — *along*, sich anschließen.
stringency ['strindʒənsi], *s.* die Strenge
(*severity*); die Knappheit (*shortage*).
stringent ['strindʒənt], *adj.* streng
(*severe*); knapp (*short*).
strip [strip], *s.* der Streifen. — *v.a., v.n.*
abstreifen, (sich) entkleiden; (sich)
entblößen.
stripe [straip], *s.* der (Farb)streifen;
die Strieme (*mark on body*). — *v.a.*
streifen, bestreifen.
strive [straiv], *v.n. irr.* sich bemühen
(*for*, um, *Acc.*), streben (*for*, nach,
Dat.).
stroke (1) [strouk], *v.a.* streicheln.
stroke (2) [strouk], *s.* der Strich (*brush*);
der Streich (*sword*), der Stoß (*blow*);
(*Med.*) der Schlaganfall.
stroll [stroul], *v.n.* schlendern.
strolling ['strouliŋ], *adj.* — *players*, die
Wandertruppe.
strong [strɔŋ], *adj.* stark.
strongbox ['strɔŋbɔks], *s.* die Geldkas-
sette.
strongroom ['strɔŋrum], *s.* der Geld-
tresor.
strop [strɔp], *s.* der Streichriemen.
structure ['strʌktʃə], *s.* der Bau, Aufbau; die Struktur.
struggle [strʌgl], *s.* der Kampf, das
Ringen. — *v.n.* kämpfen, ringen.
strut [strʌt], *v.n.* stolzieren.
stub [stʌb], *s.* der Stumpf, Stummel
(*cigarette*). — *v.a.* — *out*, ausmachen,
auslöschen (*cigarette etc.*).

stubble [stʌbl], *s.* die Stoppel, das Stoppelfeld; die (Bart)stoppeln, *f. pl.* (*beard*).

stubborn ['stʌbən], *adj.* eigensinnig, hartnäckig.

stucco ['stʌkou], *s.* die Stuckarbeit.

stud (1) [stʌd], *s.* der Hemdenknopf, Kragenknopf (*collar* —). — *v.a.* beschlagen (*nail*); besetzen (*bejewel*).

stud (2) [stʌd], *s.* das Gestüt (*horses*).

student ['stju:dənt], *s.* der Student.

studied ['stʌdid], *adj.* geziert, absichtlich (*deliberate*); gelehrt (*learned*).

studio ['stju:diou], *s.* (*Phot.*) das Atelier; (*Film, Rad.*) das Studio.

studious ['stju:diəs], *adj.* beflissen, fleißig; lernbegierig.

study ['stʌdi], *v.a., v.n.* studieren. — *s.* das Studium; das Arbeitszimmer (*room*); (*Mus. etc.*) die Studie; (*Art*) der Entwurf; die Untersuchung (*investigation*).

stuff [stʌf], *s.* der Stoff, das Material; (*coll.*) das Zeug (*rubbish*). — *v.a.* stopfen, ausstopfen (*animals*); (*Cul.*) füllen.

stuffing ['stʌfiŋ], *s.* die Füllung, das Füllsel.

stultify ['stʌltifai], *v.a.* dumm machen.

stumble [stʌmbl], *v.n.* stolpern; — *upon*, zufällig stoßen (auf, *Acc.*).

stumbling ['stʌmbliŋ], *s.* das Stolpern; — *block*, das Hindernis, der Stein des Anstoßes.

stump [stʌmp], *s.* der Stumpf. — *v.a.* verblüffen; abstumpfen. — *v.n.* schwerfällig gehen.

stun [stʌn], *v.a.* betäuben, verdutzen.

stunning ['stʌniŋ], *adj.* betörend, fabelhaft, überwältigend.

stunt (1) [stʌnt], *v.a.* am Wachstum behindern, klein halten.

stunt (2) [stʌnt], *s.* der Trick, das Kunststück; (*Aviat.*) der Kunstflug.

stupefy ['stju:pifai], *v.a.* betäuben.

stupendous [stju:'pendəs], *adj.* erstaunlich.

stupid ['stju:pid], *adj.* dumm.

stupor ['stju:pə], *s.* die Erstarrung, Lähmung (*of mind*).

sturdy ['stə:di], *adj.* derb, stark, stämmig.

sturgeon ['stə:dʒən], *s.* (*Zool.*) der Stör.

stutter ['stʌtə], *v.n.* stottern.

sty [stai], *s.* der Schweinestall.

sty(e) [stai], *s.* (*Med.*) das Gerstenkorn (*on eyelid*).

style [stail], *s.* (*Lit.*) der Stil; der Griffel (*stylus*); die Mode (*fashion*); die Anrede (*address*). — *v.a.* anreden.

stylish ['stailiʃ], *adj.* elegant, modern.

suave [sweiv, swɑːv], *adj.* höflich, gewinnend.

sub- [sʌb], *pref.* Unter-.

subaltern ['sʌbəltən], *s.* (*Mil.*) der Leutnant, Oberleutnant.

subject ['sʌbdʒikt], *s.* (*Gram.*) das Subjekt; (*Pol.*) der Untertan; der Gegenstand. — *adj.* untertan (*to,*

Dat.); — *to,* abhängig von. — [sʌb'dʒekt], *v.a.* unterwerfen (*to, Dat.*); aussetzen (*Dat.*).

subjunctive [səb'dʒʌŋktiv], *s.* (*Gram.*) der Konjunktiv.

sublet [sʌb'let], *v.a.* in Untermiete vermieten, untervermieten.

sublimate ['sʌblimeit], *v.a.* sublimieren.

submarine ['sʌbməri:n], *s.* das Unterseeboot.

submission [səb'miʃən], *s.* die Unterwerfung (*subjection*); der Vorschlag (*suggestion*).

submit [səb'mit], *v.a.* unterwerfen (*subjugate*); vorlegen. — *v.n.* sich beugen (*to, Dat.*).

suborn [sʌ'bɔːn], *v.a.* anstiften; bestechen (*corrupt*).

subpoena [sʌb'piːnə], *s.* (*Law*) die Vorladung.

subscribe [səb'skraib], *v.a.* unterschreiben. — *v.n.* zeichnen (*to, zu*); abonnieren (*paper*).

subscription [səb'skripʃən], *s.* das Abonnement (*to, Genit.*); (*club*) der Beitrag.

subsequent ['sʌbsikwənt], *adj.* folgend.

subservient [sʌb'səːviənt], *adj.* unterwürfig.

subside [səb'said], *v.n.* sinken; abnehmen (*decrease*).

subsidence [sʌb'saidəns, 'sʌbsidəns], *s.* das Sinken, Sichsetzen.

subsidiary [sʌb'sidjəri], *adj.* Hilfs-, Neben-.

subsidize ['sʌbsidaiz], *v.a.* unterstützen (*with money*), subventionieren.

subsidy ['sʌbsidi], *s.* die Unterstützung, Subvention.

subsist [səb'sist], *v.n.* leben, existieren.

subsistence [səb'sistəns], *s.* das Dasein, Auskommen; der Lebensunterhalt.

substance ['sʌbstəns], *s.* das Wesen, der Stoff, die Substanz.

substantial [səb'stænʃəl], *adj.* wesentlich, beträchtlich.

substantiate [səb'stænʃieit], *v.a.* dartun, nachweisen, bestätigen.

substantive ['sʌbstəntiv], *s.* (*Gram.*) das Substantiv, Hauptwort. — *adj.* (*Mil.*) effektiv, wirklich.

substitute ['sʌbstitju:t], *v.a.* ersetzen, an die Stelle setzen. — *s.* der Ersatzmann, Vertreter.

subterfuge ['sʌbtəfjuːdʒ], *s.* die Ausflucht.

subtle [sʌtl], *adj.* fein, schlau, subtil.

subtract [səb'trækt], *v.a.* abziehen; (*Maths.*) subtrahieren.

suburb ['sʌbəːb], *s.* die Vorstadt, der Vorort.

subversion [səb'vəːʃən], *s.* (*Pol.*) der Umsturz.

subversive [səb'vəːsiv], *adj.* umstürzlerisch, umstürzend.

subway ['sʌbwei], *s.* die Unterführung; (*Am.*) die Untergrundbahn.

succeed [sək'siːd], *v.n.* erfolgreich sein, Erfolg haben. — nachfolgen (*Dat.*) (*follow*).

success

success [sək'ses], *s.* der Erfolg.
successful [sək'sesful], *adj.* erfolgreich.
succession [sək'seʃən], *s.* die Nachfolge.
successive [sək'sesiv], *adj.* der Reihe nach, aufeinanderfolgend.
succinct [sək'siŋkt], *adj.* bündig, kurz.
succour ['sʌkə], *v.a.* beistehen (*Dat.*), helfen (*Dat.*).
succulent ['sʌkjulənt], *adj.* saftig.
succumb [sə'kʌm], *v.n.* unterliegen (*to, Dat.*).
such [sʌtʃ], *adj.* solch, derartig. — *pron.* ein solcher; — *as*, diejenigen, alle die.
suchlike ['sʌtʃlaik], *pron.* (*coll.*) dergleichen.
suck [sʌk], *v.a., v.n.* saugen.
suckle [sʌkl], *v.a.* säugen, stillen.
suction ['sʌkʃən], *s.* das Saugen; (*Engin.*) Saug-.
Sudanese [su:də'ni:z], *adj.* sudanisch, sudanesisch. — *s.* der Sudan(es)er.
sudden [sʌdn], *adj.* plötzlich.
suds [sʌdz], *s. pl.* das Seifenwasser.
sue [sju:], *v.a.* gerichtlich belangen, verklagen.
suède [sweid], *s.* das Wildleder.
suet ['su:it], *s.* das Nierenfett.
suffer ['sʌfə], *v.a.* ertragen, dulden. — *v.n.* leiden (*from*, an).
sufferance ['sʌfərəns], *s.* die Duldung; *on* —, nur widerwillig.
suffice [sə'fais], *v.n.* genügen, langen, (aus)reichen.
sufficient [sə'fiʃənt], *adj.* genügend, hinreichend.
suffocate ['sʌfəkeit], *v.a., v.n.* ersticken.
suffragan ['sʌfrəgən], *s.* (*Eccl.*) der Weihbischof.
suffrage ['sʌfridʒ], *s.* das Wahlrecht, Stimmrecht.
suffuse [sə'fju:z], *v.a.* übergießen, überfließen.
sugar ['ʃugə], *s.* der Zucker; — *basin*, die Zuckerdose.
suggest [sə'dʒest], *v.a.* vorschlagen, anregen.
suggestion [sə'dʒestʃən], *s.* der Vorschlag.
suggestive [sə'dʒestiv], *adj.* zweideutig.
suicide ['sju:isaid], *s.* der Selbstmord, Freitod.
suit [su:t], *s.* das Gesuch, die Bitte (*request*); die Farbe (*cards*); (*Law*) der Prozeß; der Anzug (*clothes*). — *v.n.* passen (*Dat.*) (*be convenient to*); passen zu (*look well with*). — *v.a.* anpassen (*match*).
suitcase ['su:tkeis], *s.* der Handkoffer.
suitable ['su:təbl], *adj.* passend.
suite [swi:t], *s.* das Gefolge (*following*); die Zimmerflucht (*rooms*); die Reihe (*cards*).
suitor ['su:tə], *s.* der Brautwerber, Freier.
sulk [sʌlk], *v.n.* schmollen.
sullen ['sʌlən], *adj.* düster, mürrisch.
sully ['sʌli], *v.a.* beschmutzen.
sulphur ['sʌlfə], *s.* (*Chem.*) der Schwefel.

Sultan ['sʌltən], *s.* der Sultan.
Sultana [sʌl'tɑ:nə], *s.* die Sultanin.
sultana [sʌl'tɑ:nə], *s.* (*Bot.*) die Sultanine.
sultry ['sʌltri], *adj.* schwül.
sum [sʌm], *s.* die Summe; (*fig.*) der Inbegriff. — *v.a., v.n.* — *up*, zusammenfassen.
summary ['sʌməri], *s.* die Zusammenfassung, der Auszug. — *adj.* summarisch.
summer ['sʌmə], *s.* der Sommer; *Indian* —, der Spätsommer, Altweibersommer, Nachsommer.
summit ['sʌmit], *s.* der Gipfel, die Spitze.
summon(s) ['sʌmən(z)], *v.a.* (*Law*) vorladen. — *s.* (**summons**) die Vorladung.
sump [sʌmp], *s.* (*Motor.*) die Ölwanne.
sumptuous ['sʌmptjuəs], *adj.* prächtig, mit Aufwand, kostbar.
sun [sʌn], *s.* die Sonne. — *v.r.* sich sonnen.
sunburn ['sʌnbə:n], *s.* der Sonnenbrand.
Sunday ['sʌnd(e)i]. der Sonntag.
sundial ['sʌndaiəl], *s.* die Sonnenuhr.
sundown ['sʌndaun] *see* **sunset**.
sundry ['sʌndri], *adj.* mehrere, verschiedene. — *s.* (*pl.*) Gemischtwaren, *f. pl.*
sunny ['sʌni], *adj.* sonnig.
sunrise ['sʌnraiz], *s.* der Sonnenaufgang.
sunset ['sʌnset], *s.* der Sonnenuntergang.
sunshade ['sʌnʃeid], *s.* das Sonnendach, der Sonnenschirm (*parasol*).
super ['su:pə], *s.* (*Theat.*) der Statist. — *adj.* (*coll.*) fein, famos.
super- ['su:pə], *pref.* über-, hinzu-.
superannuation [su:pərænju'eiʃən], *s.* die Pensionierung.
superb [su'pə:b], *adj.* hervorragend, herrlich.
supercilious [su:pə'siliəs], *adj.* hochmütig, anmaßend.
superficial [su:pə'fiʃəl], *adj.* oberflächlich.
superfluous [su:'pə:fluəs], *adj.* überflüssig.
superintendent [su:pərin'tendənt], *s.* der Oberaufseher.
superior [su:'piəriə], *adj.* ober, höher. — *s.* der Vorgesetzte.
superiority [su:piəri'ɔriti], *s.* die Überlegenheit.
superlative [su:'pə:lətiv], *s.* (*Gram.*) der Superlativ. — *adj.* ausnehmend gut.
supermarket ['su:pəmɑ:kit], *s.* das Selbstbedienungsgeschäft, SB-Geschäft, der grosse Lebensmittelladen.
supersede [su:pə'si:d], *v.a.* verdrängen.
superstition [su:pə'stiʃən], *s.* der Aberglaube.
superstitious [su:pə'stiʃəs], *adj.* abergläubisch.
supervise ['su:pəvaiz], *v.a.* beaufsichtigen, überwachen.

supine [su'pain], *adj.* auf dem Rücken liegend. — ['su:pain], *s.* (*Gram.*) das Supinum.
supper ['sʌpə], *s.* das Abendessen; *Last Supper*, das Heilige Abendmahl.
supplant [sə'plɑ:nt], *v.a.* verdrängen.
supple [sʌpl], *adj.* geschmeidig, biegsam.
supplement ['sʌplimənt], *s.* die Beilage (*paper*); der Zusatz.
supplementary [sʌpli'mentri], *adj.* zusätzlich.
supplier [sə'plaiə], *s.* der Lieferant.
supply [sə'plai], *v.a.* liefern (*s. th.*); beliefern, versorgen (*s.o.*). — *s.* die Versorgung.
support [sə'pɔ:t], *v.a.* unterstützen. — *s.* die Stütze (*prop*); die Unterstützung (*financial etc.*).
suppose [sə'pouz], *v.a.* annehmen, vermuten.
supposition [sʌpə'ziʃən], *s.* die Annahme, Vermutung, Voraussetzung.
suppress [sə'pres], *v.a.* unterdrücken.
suppurate ['sʌpjureit], *v.n.* eitern.
supremacy [su'premasi], *s.* die Überlegenheit (*pre-eminence*); Obergewalt (*power*).
supreme [su'pri:m], *adj.* höchst, oberst.
surcharge ['sə:tʃɑ:dʒ], *s.* die Sonderzahlung, der Aufschlag, Zuschlag.
sure [ʃuə], *adj.* sicher; *to be —*, sicherlich; *make —*, sich überzeugen.
surety ['ʃuəti], *s.* (*Law*) die Kaution.
surf [sə:f], *s.* die Brandung.
surface ['sə:fis], *s.* die Oberfläche.
surfeit ['sə:fit], *s.* die Übersättigung, das Übermaß. — *v.a.* übersättigen.
surge [sə:dʒ], *v.n.* wogen, rauschen. — *s.* die Woge, das Aufwallen.
surgeon ['sə:dʒən], *s.* (*Med.*) der Chirurg.
surgery ['sə:dʒəri], *s.* (*Med.*) die Chirurgie (*subject*); — *hours*, die Sprechstunde.
surgical ['sə:dʒikəl], *adj.* chirurgisch.
surly ['sə:li], *adj.* mürrisch.
surmise [sə:'maiz], *v.a.* mutmaßen, vermuten. — *s.* die Mutmaßung, Vermutung.
surmount [sə'maunt], *v.a.* übersteigen; überwinden (*overcome*).
surname ['sə:neim], *s.* der Zuname.
surpass [sə'pɑ:s], *v.a.* übertreffen.
surplice ['sə:plis], *s.* das Chorhemd.
surplus ['sə:pləs], *s.* der Überfluß.
surprise [sə'praiz], *s.* die Überraschung. — *v.a.* überraschen.
surrender [sə'rendə], *v.a.* übergeben, aufgeben. — *v.n.* sich ergeben. — *s.* die Waffenstreckung, Kapitulation.
surreptitious [sʌrəp'tiʃəs], *adj.* heimlich.
surround [sə'raund], *v.a.* umgeben, einschließen.
surroundings [sə'raundiŋz], *s. pl.* die Umgegend, Umgebung.
survey ['sə:vei], *s.* die Übersicht; die Vermessung. — [sə'vei], *v.a.* überblicken; vermessen.

surveyor [sə'veiə], *s.* der Vermesser, Feldmesser.
survival [sə'vaivəl], *s.* das Überleben.
survive [sə'vaiv], *v.a., v.n.* überleben, überstehen.
susceptibility [səsepti'biliti], *s.* die Empfänglichkeit.
susceptible [sə'septibl], *adj.* empfänglich, empfindlich.
suspect [səs'pekt], *v.a.* verdächtigen. — ['sʌspekt], *adj.* verdächtig. — *s.* die Verdachtsperson, der Verdächtige.
suspend [səs'pend], *v.a.* aufhängen; unterbrechen (*procedure*); einstellen (*work*).
suspense [səs'pens], *s.* die Spannung (*tension*); Ungewißheit (*uncertainty*).
suspension [səs'penʃən], *s.* (*Law*) die Suspension; die Einstellung (*stoppage*); die Aufhängung, Suspension; (*Motor.*) die Federung; — *bridge*, die Kettenbrücke, Hängebrücke.
suspicion [səs'piʃən], *s.* der Verdacht, Argwohn.
suspicious [səs'piʃəs], *adj.* verdächtig; argwöhnisch.
sustain [səs'tein], *v.a.* erleiden (*suffer*); ertragen (*bear*); aufrechterhalten (*maintain*).
sustenance ['sʌstinəns], *s.* der Unterhalt (*maintenance*); die Nahrung (*food*).
suture ['sju:tʃə], *s.* (*Med.*) die Naht.
suzerain ['sju:zərein], *s.* der Oberherr, Oberlehnsherr.
swab [swɔb], *s.* (*Med.*) die Laborprobe, der Abstrich; der Schrubber (*scrubber*). — *v.a.* (*Med.*) eine Probe entnehmen; schrubben (*scrub*).
swaddle [swɔdl], *s.* die Windel.
swaddling ['swɔdliŋ], *adj.* — *clothes*, die Windeln, *f. pl.*
swagger ['swægə], *v.n.* großtun. — *s.* das Großtun, Renommieren.
swallow (1) ['swolou], *s.* (*Orn.*) die Schwalbe.
swallow (2) ['swolou], *v.a.* schlucken; verschlingen (*devour*).
swamp [swɔmp], *s.* der Sumpf. — *v.a.* versenken; (*fig.*) überschütten.
swan [swɔn], *s.* (*Orn.*) der Schwan.
swank [swæŋk], *v.n.* großtun, angeben, aufschneiden. — *s.* der Großtuer.
swap, swop [swɔp], *v.a.* eintauschen, tauschen. — *v.n.* tauschen. — *s.* der Tausch.
sward [swɔ:d], *s.* (*Poet.*) der Rasen.
swarm [swɔ:m], *v.n.* schwärmen. — *s.* der Schwarm.
swarthy ['swɔ:ði], *adj.* dunkel, dunkelbraun.
swashbuckler ['swɔʃbʌklə], *s.* der Aufschneider, Angeber, Renommist.
swastika ['swɔstikə], *s.* das Hakenkreuz.
swathe [sweið], *v.a.* einhüllen, einwickeln.
sway [swei], *v.a.* schwenken; beeinflußen. — *v.n.* schwanken, sich schwingen. — *s.* der Einfluß, die Macht.

swear [swɛə], *v.a.*, *v.n. irr.* schwören (*an oath*); fluchen (*curse*).
sweat [swet], *v.n.* schwitzen. — *s.* der Schweiß.
Swede [swi:d], *s.* der Schwede.
Swedish ['swi:diʃ], *adj.* schwedisch.
sweep [swi:p], *v.a.*, *v.n. irr.* fegen, kehren; *a new broom —s clean*, neue Besen kehren gut. — *s.* der Schornsteinfeger (*chimney —*).
sweet [swi:t], *adj.* süß. — *s.* der Nachtisch; (*pl.*) Süßigkeiten, *f. pl.*
swell [swel], *v.a. irr.* anschwellen lassen. — *v.n.* anschwellen. — *adj.*, *adv.* (*Am. sl.*) ausgezeichnet. — *s.* (*sl.*) der feine Kerl.
swelter ['sweltə], *v.n.* vor Hitze vergehen.
swerve [swə:v], *v.n.* abschweifen, abbiegen.
swift (1) [swift], *adj.* schnell, behende, rasch.
swift (2) [swift], *s.* (*Orn.*) die Turmschwalbe.
swill [swil], *v.a.* spülen (*rinse*); (*sl.*) saufen (*drink heavily*). — *s.* das Spülicht (*dishwater*); (*coll.*) das Gesöff.
swim [swim], *v.n. irr.* schwimmen. — *s.* das Schwimmen.
swindle [swindl], *v.a.* beschwindeln. — *s.* der Schwindel.
swine [swain], *s. pl.* die Schweine; (*sing.*) der Schweinehund, das Schwein.
swing [swiŋ], *v.a.*, *v.n. irr.* schwingen, schaukeln. — *s.* der Schwung; die Schaukel.
swipe [swaip], *v.a.* schlagen; (*fig.*) stehlen. — *s.* der Schlag.
swirl [swə:l], *v.a.*, *v.n.* wirbeln (*in air*). — *s.* der Wirbel.
Swiss [swis], *s.* der Schweizer. — *adj.* schweizerisch, Schweizer-.
switch [switʃ], *v.a.* (*Elec.*) — *on*, andrehen, einschalten; — *off*, abschalten; (*fig.*) wechseln, vertauschen (*change*). — *v.n.* umstellen, umschalten. — *s.* (*Elec.*) der Schalter.
switchboard ['switʃbɔ:d], *s.* die Telephonzentrale, das Schaltbrett.
switchgear ['switʃgiə], *s.* (*Elec.*) das Schaltgerät, die Schaltung.
swivel [swivl], *v.n.* drehen. — *s.* der Drehring; — *chair*, der Drehstuhl.
swoon [swu:n], *v.n.* in Ohnmacht fallen. — *s.* die Ohnmacht.
swoop [swu:p], *s.* der Stoß. — *v.n.* (herab)stoßen; stürzen; (nieder)schießen.
swop *see* **swap.**
sword [sɔ:d], *s.* das Schwert.
syllable ['siləbl], *s.* die Silbe.
syllabus ['siləbəs], *s.* das Verzeichnis, der Lehrplan.
symbol ['simbəl], *s.* das Symbol, Sinnbild.
sympathetic [simpə'θetik], *adj.* mitfühlend, teilnehmend; sympathisch.
sympathy ['simpəθi], *s.* die Sympathie, das Mitgefühl.

symphony ['simfəni], *s.* (*Mus.*) die Symphonie.
synchronize ['siŋkrənaiz], *v.a.* synchronisieren.
syndicate ['sindikit], *s.* die Arbeitsgruppe, das Syndikat.
synod ['sinəd], *s.* die Synode, Kirchentagung.
synonymous [si'nɔniməs], *adj.* synonym.
synopsis [si'nɔpsis], *s.* die Zusammenfassung, Übersicht.
Syrian ['siriən], *adj.* syrisch. — *s.* der Syrer.
syringe ['sirindʒ], *s.* die Spritze.
syrup ['sirəp], *s.* der Sirup.
system ['sistəm], *s.* das System.
systematize ['sistəmətaiz], *v.a.* ordnen, in ein System bringen.

T

T [ti:]. das T.
tab [tæb], *s.* das Schildchen, der Streifen.
tabard ['tæbəd], *s.* der Wappenrock, Heroldsrock.
tabby ['tæbi], *s.* (*cat*) die getigerte Katze.
table [teibl], *s.* der Tisch; (*Maths.*) die Tabelle, das Einmaleins. — *v.a.* (*Parl.*) einen Entwurf einbringen; (*Am.*) auf die lange Bank schieben.
tablecloth ['teiblklɔθ], *s.* das Tischtuch.
tablemat ['teiblmæt], *s.* der Untersatz.
tablenapkin ['teiblnæpkin], *s.* die Serviette.
tablespoon ['teiblspu:n], *s.* der Eßlöffel.
tablet ['tæblit], *s.* die Tablette (*pill*); die Schreibtafel, der Block (*writing*).
taboo [tə'bu:], *s.* das Verbot, Tabu.
tabular ['tæbjulə], *adj.* tabellarisch; wie eine Tafel.
tacit ['tæsit], *adj.* stillschweigend.
taciturn ['tæsitə:n], *adj.* schweigsam, einsilbig.
tack [tæk], *s.* der Stift; der Stich (*sewing*). — *v.a.* nageln; heften (*sew*).
tackle [tækl], *v.a.* (*Naut.*) takeln; (*Footb.*, *fig.*) angreifen; anpacken. — *s.* (*Naut.*) das Takel; (*fig.*) das Zeug; (*Footb.*) das Angreifen.
tact [tækt], *s.* der Takt; das Zartgefühl.
tactics ['tæktiks], *s. pl.* die Taktik.
tadpole ['tædpoul], *s.* (*Zool.*) die Kaulquappe.
taffeta ['tæfitə], *s.* (*Text.*) der Taft.
tag [tæg], *s.* der Anhängezettel; das Sprichwort (*saying*). — *v.a.* anhängen. — *v.n.* — *on to*, sich anschließen.

tail [teil], *s.* der Schwanz; (*fig.*) das Ende; (*pl.*) der Frack (*tailcoat*). — *v.a.* (*Am.*) folgen (*Dat.*).

tailor ['teilə], *s.* der Schneider; —*made*, geschneidert, nach Maß gemacht. — *v.a.* schneidern.

taint [teint], *v.a.* beflecken; verderben (*corrupt*). — *s.* der Fleck.

take [teik], *v.a. irr.* nehmen; bringen, ergreifen (*seize*); erfordern (*require*); — *up*, aufnehmen, beginnen; ertragen (*suffer*, *tolerate*); — *breath*, Atem holen; — *care*, sich in acht nehmen; — *offence at*, Anstoß nehmen an; — *place*, stattfinden; — *for*, halten für. — *v.n.* wirken (*be effective*); — *to*, Gefallen finden (an, *Dat.*); — *to flight* or *o.'s heels*, sich aus dem Staube machen; — *after*, ähnlich sein.

takings ['teikiŋz], *s.* (*pl.*) die Einnahmen, *f. pl.*

tale [teil], *s.* das Märchen, die Geschichte.

talent ['tælənt], *s.* das Talent, die Begabung.

talented ['tæləntid], *adj.* talentiert, begabt.

talk [tɔ:k], *v.a., v.n.* reden, sprechen. — *s.* das Gespräch (*discussion*); der Vortrag (*lecture*); das Reden, Gerede (*speaking*).

talkative ['tɔ:kətiv], *adj.* geschwätzig, redselig, gesprächig.

tall [tɔ:l], *adj.* hoch (*high*); groß (*grown high*); *a — order*, eine schwierige Aufgabe; *a — story*, eine Aufschneiderei, das Seemannsgarn.

tallow ['tælou], *s.* der Talg.

tally ['tæli], *v.n.* passen (*match*); stimmen (*be correct*).

talon ['tælən], *s.* die Klaue, Kralle.

tame [teim], *adj.* zahm. — *v.a.* zähmen.

tamper ['tæmpə], *v.n.* hineinpfuschen (*with*, in, *Acc.*).

tan [tæn], *s.* die Lohe; die braune Farbe; der Sonnenbrand (*sun*). — *v.a.* bräunen; (*leather*) gerben; (*fig.*) verbleuen (*beat*).

tang [tæŋ], *s.* der Seetang; (*fig.*) der Beigeschmack.

tangible ['tændʒibl], *adj.* greifbar.

tangle [tæŋgl], *v.a.* verwickeln (*entangle*). — *s.* die Verwirrung, Verwicklung.

tank [tæŋk], *s.* der Tank; (*Mil.*) der Panzer; der Wasserspeicher (*cistern*). — *v.a., v.n.* tanken.

tankard ['tæŋkəd], *s.* der Maßkrug, Bierkrug.

tanner (1) ['tænə], *s.* der Gerber.

tanner (2) ['tænə], *s.* (*sl.*) das Sechspencestück.

tantalize ['tæntəlaiz], *v.a.* quälen.

tantamount ['tæntəmaunt], *adj.* gleich, gleichwertig.

tap [tæp], *v.a.* anzapfen (*barrel*); klopfen; tippen (*on shoulder etc.*); (*fig.*) anpumpen (*for money*). — *s.* der Hahn; der Zapfen (*barrel*); der leichte Schlag (*on shoulder etc.*).

tape [teip], *s.* das Band; *red* —, die Bürokratie, der Bürokratismus; — *measure*, das Bandmaß; — *recorder*, das Tonbandgerät.

taper ['teipə], *v.n.* spitz zulaufen. — *v.a.* spitzen. — *s.* die (spitze) Kerze.

tapestry ['tæpistri], *s.* die Tapete, der Wandteppich.

tapeworm ['teipwə:m], *s.* der Bandwurm.

taproot ['tæpru:t], *s.* die Pfahlwurzel, Hauptwurzel.

tar [tɑ:], *s.* der Teer; (*Naut. sl.*) der Matrose. — *v.a.* teeren.

tardy ['tɑ:di], *adj.* träge (*sluggish*), langsam.

tare (1) [tɛə], das Taragewicht, die Tara (*weight*). — *v.a.* auswägen, tarieren.

tare (2) [tɛə], *s.* (*Bot.*) die Wicke.

target ['tɑ:git], *s.* das Ziel; die Zielscheibe (*board*).

tariff ['tærif], *s.* der Tarif.

tarnish ['tɑ:niʃ], *v.a.* trüben. — *v.n.* anlaufen.

tarpaulin [tɑ:'pɔ:lin], *s.* die Persenning.

tarry (1) ['tæri], *v.n.* zögern (*hesitate*); warten (*wait*).

tarry (2) ['tɑ:ri], *adj.* teerig.

tart (1) [tɑ:t], *s.* die Torte.

tart (2) [tɑ:t], *adj.* herb, sauer.

tart (3) [tɑ:t], *s.* (*sl.*) die Dirne.

Tartar ['tɑ:tə], *s.* der Tatar; (*fig.*) der Tyrann.

tartar ['tɑ:tə], *s.* (*Chem.*) der Weinstein.

task [tɑ:sk], *s.* die Aufgabe, das Tagewerk; *take to —*, zur Rechenschaft ziehen.

tassel [tæsl], *s.* die Quaste.

taste [teist], *v.a.* schmecken; versuchen, kosten. — *s.* die Probe (*tasting*); der Geschmack (*flavour*).

tasteful ['teistful], *adj.* geschmackvoll.

tasteless ['teistlis], *adj.* geschmacklos.

tasty ['teisti], *adj.* schmackhaft.

tatter ['tætə], *s.* der Lumpen. — *v.a.* in Fetzen reißen, zerfetzen.

tattle [tætl], *v.n.* schwatzen. — *s.* das Geschwätz.

tattoo (1) [tə'tu:], *s.* (*Mil.*) der Zapfenstreich, das militärische Schaustück, die Parade.

tattoo (2) [tə'tu:], *v.a.* tätowieren. — *s.* die Tätowierung.

taunt [tɔ:nt], *v.a.* höhnen, schmähen. — *s.* der Hohn, Spott.

tavern ['tævən], *s.* die Schenke.

tawdry ['tɔ:dri], *adj.* kitschig, flitterhaft.

tawny ['tɔ:ni], *adj.* braungelb, lohfarbig.

tax [tæks], *s.* die Abgabe, Steuer; Besteuerung (*taxation*). — *v.a.* besteuern; (*fig.*) anstrengen, ermüden (*strain*).

taxi ['tæksi], *s.* das Taxi.

tea [ti:], *s.* der Tee.

teach [ti:tʃ], *v.a., v.n. irr.* lehren, unterrichten.

teacher ['ti:tʃə], *s.* der Lehrer, die Lehrerin.

team

team [ti:m], s. (*Sport*) die Mannschaft; das Gespann (*horses*); (*fig.*) der Stab; — *spirit*, der Korpsgeist.

tear (1) [tɛə], s. der Riß (*rent*). — *v.a. irr.* zerreißen (*rend*).

tear (2) [tiə], s. die Träne.

tearing [ˈtɛəriŋ], adj. — *hurry*, rasende Eile.

tease [ti:z], v.a. necken (*mock*); aufrauhen (*roughen*).

teat [ti:t], s. die Brustwarze, Zitze.

technical [ˈteknikəl], adj. technisch.

technique [tekˈni:k], s. die Technik, Methode.

techy *see* **tetchy**.

tedious [ˈti:diəs], adj. langweilig, lästig.

tedium [ˈti:diəm], s. der Überdruß, die Langeweile.

tee [ti:], s. (*Sport*) der Golfballhalter.

teem [ti:m], v.n. wimmeln.

teenager [ˈti:neidʒə], s. der, die Jugendliche; Teenager.

teeth *see under* **tooth**.

teethe [ti:ð], v.n. Zähne bekommen, zahnen.

teetotal [ti:ˈtoutl], adj. abstinent, antialkoholisch.

teetotaller [ti:ˈtoutlə], s. der Antialkoholiker.

telegram [ˈteligræm], s. das Telegramm.

telephone [ˈtelifoun], s. (*abbr.* **phone**) das Telephon; — *booth*, die Fernsprechzelle; — *exchange*, das Fernsprechamt.

television [teliˈviʒən], s. die Fernsehen; — *set*, der Fernsehapparat.

tell [tel], v.a. irr. erzählen, berichten (*relate*); verraten (*reveal*).

tell-tale [ˈtelteil], s. der Angeber, Zuträger. — adj. sprechend; Warnungs-.

teller [ˈtelə], s. der Zähler, der Kassier (*cashier*).

temerity [tiˈmeriti], s. die Verwegenheit, Tollkühnheit.

temper [ˈtempə], v.a. vermischen (*mix*); mäßigen (*moderate*); (*Metall.*) härten. — s. die üble Stimmung, Wut, Laune; (*Metall.*) die Härte.

temperance [ˈtempərəns], s. die Mäßigkeit, Enthaltsamkeit.

temperate [ˈtempərit], adj. gemäßigt, temperiert.

temperature [ˈtemprətʃə], s. die Temperatur.

tempest [ˈtempist], s. der Sturm.

tempestuous [temˈpestjuəs], adj. stürmisch.

temple (1) [templ], s. der Tempel.

temple (2) [templ], s. (*Anat.*) die Schläfe (*side of brow*).

temporal [ˈtempərəl], adj. weltlich, zeitlich.

temporary [ˈtempərəri], adj. zeitweilig, vorläufig, provisorisch.

temporize [ˈtempəraiz], v.n. zögern, Zeit zu gewinnen suchen.

tempt [tempt], v.a. versuchen.

temptation [tempˈteiʃən], s. die Versuchung.

ten [ten], num. adj. zehn.

tenth [tenθ], num. adj. zehnte. — s. der Zehnte.

tenable [ˈtenəbl], adj. haltbar.

tenacious [tiˈneiʃəs], adj. zähe, festhaltend, hartnäckig.

tenacity [tiˈnæsiti], s. die Zähigkeit, Ausdauer.

tenancy [ˈtenənsi], s. das Mietverhältnis; die Mietdauer.

tenant [ˈtenənt], s. der Mieter, Pächter.

tench [tentʃ], s. (*Zool.*) die Schleie.

tend (1) [tend], v.a., v.n. warten, pflegen (*nurse*).

tend (2) [tend], v.n. neigen, gerichtet sein (*be inclined*).

tendency [ˈtendənsi], s. die Tendenz, Neigung.

tender (1) [ˈtendə], s. das Angebot (*offer*); *legal* —, das Zahlungsmittel. — v.a. einreichen.

tender (2) [ˈtendə], adj. sanft (*affectionate*); zart, zärtlich, weich (*delicate*).

tender (3) [ˈtendə], s. (*Railw.*) der Tender.

tendon [ˈtendən], s. (*Anat.*) die Sehne, Flechse.

tendril [ˈtendril], s. (*Bot.*) die Ranke.

tenement [ˈtenimənt], s. die Mietswohnung, die Mietskaserne.

tenet [ˈtenit], s. der Grundsatz (*principle*); die Lehre (*doctrine*).

tenfold [ˈtenfould], adj. zehnfach.

tennis [ˈtenis], s. das Tennis.

tenor [ˈtenə], s. (*Mus.*) der Tenor; der Sinn, Inhalt (*meaning*).

tense (1) [tens], adj. gespannt; straff (*taut*).

tense (2) [tens], s. (*Gram.*) die Zeitform.

tension [ˈtenʃən], s. die Spannung.

tent [tent], s. das Zelt.

tentacle [ˈtentəkl], s. (*Zool.*) das Fühlhorn, der Fühler.

tentative [ˈtentətiv], adj. versuchend, vorsichtig; (*fig.*) vorläufig.

tenterhooks [ˈtentəhuks], s. pl. die Spannhaken, m. pl.; *be on* —, in größter Spannung sein.

tenuous [ˈtenjuəs], adj. dünn, fadenscheinig, spärlich.

tenure [ˈtenjuə], s. der Mietbesitz, die Mietvertragslänge, das Mietrecht; — *of office*, die Amtsdauer.

tepid [ˈtepid], adj. lau, lauwarm.

term [tə:m], s. der Ausdruck (*expression*); die Bedingung (*condition*); der Termin, die Frist (*period*); (*Sch.*) das Semester, Trimester; *be on good* —*s with* (*s.o.*), auf gutem Fuß stehen mit. — v.a. benennen, bezeichen.

terminate [ˈtə:mineit], v.a. beenden, zu Ende bringen. — v.n. zu Ende kommen.

terminus [ˈtə:minəs], s. die Endstation.

terrace [ˈteris], s. die Terrasse.

terrestrial [təˈrestriəl], adj. irdisch.

terrible [ˈteribl], adj. schrecklich, furchtbar.

terrific [təˈrifik], adj. fürchterlich; (*coll.*) ungeheuer.

terrify ['terifai], v.a. erschrecken.
territory ['teritəri], s. das Gebiet.
terror ['terə], s. der Schrecken.
terse [tə:s], adj. bündig, kurz.
tertiary ['tə:ʃəri], adj. tertiär.
test [test], s. die Prüfung; (Chem.) die Probe; — -tube, das Reagensglas or Reagenzglas. — v.a. prüfen.
testament ['testəmənt], s. das Testament.
testator [tes'teitə], s. der Erblasser.
testicle ['testikl], s. (Anat.) die Hode.
testify ['testifai], v.a. bezeugen.
testimonial [testi'mouniəl], s. das Zeugnis.
testimony ['testiməni], s. das Zeugnis, die Zeugenaussage (oral).
testiness ['testinis], s. die Verdrießlichkeit.
testy ['testi], adj. verdrießlich, reizbar.
tetanus ['tetənəs], s. (Med.) der Starrkrampf.
tetchy, techy ['tetʃi], adj. mürrisch, reizbar.
tether ['teðə], s. das Spannseil; (fig.) at the end of o.'s —, am Ende seiner Geduld. — v.a. anbinden.
text ['tekst], s. der Text, Wortlaut.
textile ['tekstail], s. die Textilware, der Webstoff.
textual ['tekstjuəl], adj. textlich, Text-.
texture ['tekstʃə], s. das Gewebe, die Struktur.
Thai [tai], adj. Thai-, siamesisch. — s. pl. die Thaivölker, pl.
than [ðæn], conj. als (after comparatives).
thank [θæŋk], v.a. danken (Dat.). — s. (pl.) der Dank.
that [ðæt], dem. adj. der, die, das, jener. — dem. pron. der, die, das; (absolute, no pl.) das. — rel. pron. der, die, das, welcher, was. — conj. daß; damit (in order —).
thatch [θætʃ], v.a. decken (mit Stroh). — s. das Strohdach.
thaw [θɔ:], v.n. tauen; auftauen. — s. das Tauwetter.
the [ðə, before vowel ði], def. art. der, die, das. — adv. — bigger — better, je grösser desto or umso besser.
theatre ['θiətə], s. das Theater; (fig.) der Schauplatz.
theatrical [θi'ætrikəl], adj. bühnenhaft (of the stage); theatralisch; Bühnen-, Theater-.
theft [θeft], s. der Diebstahl.
their [ðɛə], poss. adj. ihr.
theirs [ðɛəz], poss. pron. der, die, das ihrige, der, die, das ihre.
them [ðem], pers. pron. sie, ihnen.
theme [θi:m], s. das Thema; (Mus.) das Thema, Motiv.
then [ðen], adv. dann, damals; by —, till —, bis dahin. — conj. dann, denn. — adj. damalig.
thence [ðens], adv. von da; daher.
theology [θi'ɔlədʒi], s. die Theologie.
theorem ['θiərəm], s. (Maths.) der Lehrsatz, Grundsatz.
theorize ['θiəraiz], v.n. theoretisieren.

therapeutics [θerə'pju:tiks], s. pl. die Heilkunde.
therapy ['θerəpi], s. die Therapie.
there [ðɛə], adv. dort, da; dorthin, dahin (thereto); — is, — are, es gibt; here and —, hier und da.
thereabout(s) [ðɛərəbaut(s)], adv. ungefähr, da herum.
thereafter [ðɛər'ɑ:ftə], adv. hernach, danach.
thereby [ðɛə'bai], adv. dadurch.
therefore ['ðɛəfɔ:], adv. darum, deshalb.
thermal, thermic ['θə:məl, 'θə:mik], adj. thermisch; warm; Wärme-.
thermometer [θə'mɔmitə], s. das Thermometer.
these [ði:z], dem. adj. & pron. pl. diese.
thesis ['θi:sis], s. die These; die Dissertation.
they [ðei], pers. pron. pl. sie.
thick [θik], adj. dick; dicht; (fig.) dick befreundet; — as thieves, wie eine Diebsbande.
thicken ['θikən], v.a. verdicken. — v.n. dick werden.
thicket ['θikit], s. das Dickicht.
thickness ['θiknis], s. die Dicke.
thief [θi:f], s. der Dieb.
thieve [θi:v], v.n. stehlen.
thigh [θai], s. (Anat.) der Oberschenkel.
thimble [θimbl], s. der Fingerhut.
thin [θin], adj. dünn. — v.a., v.n. (sich) verdünnen.
thine [ðain], poss. pron. (Poet.) dein, der, die, das deinige.
thing [θiŋ], s. das Ding; die Sache (matter).
think [θiŋk], v.a., v.n. irr. denken; meinen, glauben.
thinker ['θiŋkə], s. der Denker.
third [θə:d], num. adj. der, die, das dritte. — s. das Drittel.
thirdly ['θə:dli], adv. drittens.
thirst [θə:st], s. der Durst (for, nach). — v.n. dürsten.
thirsty ['θə:sti], adj. durstig; be —, Durst haben.
thirteen [θə:'ti:n], num. adj. dreizehn.
thirty ['θə:ti], num. adj. dreißig.
this [ðis], dem. adj. dieser, diese, dieses. — dem. pron. dieser, diese; dieses; dies.
thistle [θisl], s. (Bot.) die Distel.
thither ['ðiðə], adv. dahin, dorthin.
tho' [ðou] see under **though**.
thong [θɔŋ], s. der Riemen (strap); die Peitschenschnur.
thorn [θɔ:n], s. (Bot.) der Dorn.
thorough ['θʌrə], adj. gründlich; völlig (complete).
thoroughbred ['θʌrəbred], s. das Vollblut, der Vollblüter. — adj. Vollblut-.
thoroughfare ['θʌrəfɛə], s. der Durchgang (path); die Durchfahrt.
those [ðouz], dem. adj. pl. die, jene. — dem. pron. pl. jene, diejenigen.
thou [ðau], pers. pron. (Poet.) du.
though [ðou], conj. (abbr. tho') obgleich, obwohl, wenn auch (even if). — adv. doch, zwar.

thought

thought [θɔːt], *s.* der Gedanke; *also past tense and participle of* **think** *q.v.*
thoughtful [ˈθɔːtful], *adj.* rücksichtsvoll, nachdenklich.
thoughtless [ˈθɔːtlis], *adj.* gedankenlos.
thousand [ˈθauzənd], *num. adj.* a —, tausend. — *s.* das Tausend.
thrash [θræʃ], *v.a.* dreschen (*corn*); prügeln (*s.o.*).
thread [θred], *s.* der Faden. — *v.a.* einfädeln. — *v.n.* sich schlängeln, sich winden.
threadbare [ˈθredbɛə], *adj.* fadenscheinig.
threat [θret], *s.* die Drohung.
threaten [θretn], *v.a.* drohen, androhen (*Dat.*).
three [θriː], *num. adj.* drei.
threescore [ˈθriːskɔː], *num. adj.* sechzig.
thresh [θreʃ], *v.a.* dreschen (*corn*). — *See also* **thrash.**
threshold [ˈθreʃould], *s.* die Schwelle (*of door*).
thrice [θrais], *num. adv.* dreimal.
thrift [θrift], *s.* die Sparsamkeit; (*Bot.*) die Grasnelke, Meernelke.
thrill [θril], *v.a.* packen (*grip*). — *v.n.* erschauern, zittern (vor, *Dat.*). — *s.* der Schauer; die Spannung.
thriller [ˈθrilə], *s.* der Thriller, der spannende Roman *or* Film etc.
thrive [θraiv], *v.n.* gedeihen (*also fig.*); (*fig.*) gut weiterkommen, Glück haben.
thriving [ˈθraiviŋ], *adj.* blühend, (*Comm.*) gut gehend.
throat [θrout], *s.* (*Anat.*) der Schlund, die Kehle.
throb [θrɔb], *v.n.* pochen, klopfen.
throes [θrouz], *s. pl.* die Wehen, *f. pl.*; die Schmerzen, *m. pl.*
throne [θroun], *s.* der Thron.
throng [θrɔŋ], *s.* die Menge, das Gedränge. — *v.a., v.n.* (sich) drängen.
throttle [θrɔtl], *s.* die Kehle, Luftröhre; (*Mech.*) das Drosselventil; (*Motor.*) open the —, Gas geben.
through [θruː], *prep.* durch (*Acc.*); mittels (*Genit.*) (*by means of*). — *adv.* (mitten) durch.
throughout [θruːˈaut], *prep.* ganz (hin)durch (*space*); während, hindurch (*time*). — *adv.* durchaus, in jeder Beziehung.
throw [θrou], *v.a. irr.* werfen; — *open,* eröffnen. — *s.* der Wurf.
thrush [θrʌʃ], *s.* (*Orn.*) die Drossel.
thrust [θrʌst], *v.a.* stoßen, drängen. — *v.n.* stoßen (*at,* nach); sich drängen. — *s.* der Stoß, Angriff; *cut and* —, Hieb und Gegenhieb.
thud [θʌd], *s.* der Schlag, das Dröhnen, der dumpfe Ton. — *v.n.* dröhnen, aufschlagen.
thumb [θʌm], *s.* (*Anat.*) der Daumen; *rule of* —, die Faustregel; (*Am.*) *tack* see **drawing pin.** — *v.a.* durchblättern (*book*); —*a lift,* per Anhalter fahren.
thump [θʌmp], *v.a.* schlagen, puffen. —

v.n. schlagen (*on,* auf; *against,* gegen). —*s.* der Schlag, Stoß.
thunder [ˈθʌndə], *s.* der Donner. — *v.n.* donnern.
thunderstruck [ˈθʌndəstrʌk], *adj.* wie vom Donner gerührt.
Thursday [ˈθɔːzdi]. der Donnerstag.
Thuringian [θuəˈrindʒiən], *adj.* thüringisch. — *s.* der Thüringer.
thus [ðʌs], *adv.* so, auf diese Weise (*in this way*).
thwart [θwɔːt], *v.a.* vereiteln, durchkreuzen.
thy [ðai], *poss. adj.* (*Poet.*) dein, deine, dein.
thyme [taim], *s.* (*Bot.*) der Thymian.
tic [tik], *s.* (*Med.*) das Zucken.
tick (1) [tik], *s.* das Ticken (*watch*). — *v.n.* ticken.
tick (2) [tik], *s.* (*coll.*) der Kredit, Borg.
ticket [ˈtikit], *s.* die Fahrkarte (*travel*); die Eintrittskarte (*entry*); (*Am.*) der Strafzettel (*driving*).
ticking (1) [ˈtikiŋ], *s.* das Ticken (*of watch*).
ticking (2) [ˈtikiŋ], *s.* (*Text.*) der Zwillich.
tickle [tikl], *v.a., v.n.* kitzeln. — *s.* das Kitzeln.
ticklish [ˈtikliʃ], *adj.* kitzlig.
tidal [taidl], *adj.* Gezeiten-, Ebbe-, Flut-.
tide [taid], *s.* die Gezeiten, *f.pl.*, die Ebbe und Flut. — *v.a.* — *over,* hinweghelfen (über, *Acc.*).
tidiness [ˈtaidinis], *s.* die Sauberkeit, Ordnung.
tidings [ˈtaidiŋz], *s. pl.* (*Poet.*) die Nachricht.
tidy [ˈtaidi], *adj.* nett, sauber, ordentlich. — *v.a.* — *up,* sauber machen.
tie [tai], *v.a.* binden, knüpfen. — *v.n.* (*Sport*) unentschieden sein. — *s.* die Binde, Krawatte; (*Sport*) das Unentschieden.
tier [tiə], *s.* der Rang, die Reihe, Sitzreihe.
tiger [ˈtaigə], *s.* (*Zool.*) der Tiger.
tight [tait], *adj.* fest, eng, dicht (*close*); (*coll.*) betrunken (*drunk*); — *fisted,* geizig (*stingy*). — *s. pl.* die Trikothosen, *f.pl.*
tighten [taitn], *v.a.* festziehen.
tile [tail], *s.* der Ziegel (*roof etc.*); die Kachel (*glazed*). — *v.a.* kacheln, ziegeln.
till (1) [til], *prep., conj.* bis.
till (2) [til], *v.a.* aufbauen, beackern (*land*).
till (3) [til], *s.* die Ladenkasse.
tilt [tilt], *v.a.* kippen, neigen, umschlagen (*tip over*). — *v.n.* sich neigen, kippen, kentern. — *s.* die Neigung.
timber [ˈtimbə], *s.* das Holz, Bauholz.
time [taim], *s.* die Zeit; (*Mus.*) das Tempo, Zeitmaß; *in* —, zur rechten Zeit; *every* —, jedesmal; *what is the* —? wievel Uhr ist es ? — *v.a.* zeitlich messen, rechtzeitig einrichten.
timely [ˈtaimli], *adj.* rechtzeitig.

timetable ['taimteibl], *s.* (*Railw.*) der Fahrplan; (*Sch.*) der Stundenplan.

timid ['timid], *adj.* furchtsam.

timpani ['timpəni], *s. pl.* (*Mus.*) die Kesselpauken, *f. pl.*

tin [tin], *s.* das Zinn, Weißblech; die Dose, Büchse (*preserved foods*); — *opener,* der Büchsenöffner.

tincture ['tiŋktʃə], *s.* die Tinktur, das Färbungsmittel.

tinder ['tində], *s.* der Zunder.

tinfoil ['tinfɔil], *s.* das Stanniol.

tinge [tindʒ], *v.a.* färben, anfärben. — *s.* die Färbung, leichte Farbe; (*fig.*) die Spur.

tingle ['tiŋgl], *v.n.* klingen (*bells*); (*Anat.*) prickeln. — *s.* das Klingen; Prickeln.

tinker ['tiŋkə], *s.* der Kesselflicker. — *v.n.* basteln.

tinkle [tiŋkl], *v.a.* klingeln.

tinsel ['tinsəl], *s.* das Lametta, Flittergold.

tint [tint], *v.a.* färben. — *s.* die Farbe; der Farbton.

tiny ['taini], *adj.* winzig.

tip (1) [tip], *v.a.* kippen; (*coll.*) ein Trinkgeld geben (*Dat.*). — *s.* (*Sport etc.*) (*coll.*) der Tip; das Trinkgeld (*gratuity*).

tip (2) [tip], *s.* die Spitze; das Mundstück (*cigarette*).

tipple [tipl], *v.n.* (viel) trinken, zechen.

tipsy ['tipsi], *adj.* beschwipst.

tiptoe ['tiptou], *s. on* —, auf Zehenspitzen.

tiptop ['tiptɔp], *adj.* (*coll.*) erstklassig.

tirade [ti'reid *or* tai'reid], *s.* der Wortschwall, die Tirade.

tire (1) [taiə], *v.a., v.n.* ermüden.

tire (2) *see under* **tyre**.

tired ['taiəd], *adj.* müde.

tiresome ['taiəsəm], *adj.* langweilig (*boring*); auf die Nerven gehend (*annoying*).

tissue ['tiʃu:], *s.* das Gewebe; — *paper,* das Seidenpapier.

titbit ['titbit], *s.* der Leckerbissen.

tithe [taið], *s.* der Zehnte.

title [taitl], *s.* der Titel, die Überschrift; (*fig.*) der Anspruch (*claim*).

titmouse ['titmaus], *s.* (*Orn.*) die Meise.

titter ['titə], *v.n.* kichern. — *s.* das Kichern.

tittle [titl], *s.* das Tüpfelchen; — *tattle,* das Geschwätz.

titular ['titjulə], *adj.* Titular-.

to [tu], *prep.* zu (*Dat.*), gegen (*Acc.*); bis (*until, as far as*), nach, an, auf; *in order* —, um zu. — [tu:], *adv.* zu; — *and fro,* hin und her.

toad [toud], *s.* (*Zool.*) die Kröte.

toadstool ['toudstu:l], *s.* (*Bot.*) der Giftpilz.

toady ['toudi], *v.n.* kriechen. — *s.* der Kriecher.

toast [toust], *s.* der Toast, das Röstbrot; der Trinkspruch. — *v.a.* toasten,

rösten; trinken auf; — *s.o.,* einen Trinkspruch ausbringen auf einen.

tobacco [tə'bækou], *s.* der Tabak.

toboggan [tə'bɔgən], *s.* der Rodel, der Schlitten. — *v.n.* rodeln, Schlitten fahren.

tocsin ['tɔksin], *s.* die Sturmglocke.

today [tə'dei], *adv.* heute.

toddle ['tɔdl], *v.n.* watscheln; abschieben (— *off.*).

toddler ['tɔdlə], *s.* (*coll.*) das kleine Kind (das gehen lernt).

toe [tou], *s.* (*Anat.*) die Zehe.

toffee ['tɔfi], *s.* der Sahnebonbon.

together [tə'geðə], *adv.* zusammen.

toil [tɔil], *v.n.* hart arbeiten. — *s.* die schwere, harte Arbeit.

toilet ['tɔilit], *s.* das Anziehen, Ankleiden; die Toilette, der Abort, das Klosett (*lavatory*).

token ['toukən], *s.* das Zeichen (*sign*); der Beweis (*proof*); das Andenken (*keepsake*).

tolerable ['tɔlərəbl], *adj.* erträglich, leidlich.

tolerance ['tɔlərəns], *s.* die Toleranz, Duldsamkeit; (*Tech.*) die Toleranz.

tolerant ['tɔlərənt], *adj.* tolerant, duldsam.

tolerate ['tɔləreit], *v.a.* ertragen, dulden.

toll [toul], *v.a., v.n.* läuten. — *s.* der Zoll; — *gate,* — *bar,* der Schlagbaum.

tomato [tə'ma:tou], *s.* (*Bot.*) die Tomate.

tomb [tu:m], *s.* das Grab, Grabmal.

tomboy ['tɔmbɔi], *s.* der Wildfang.

tomcat ['tɔmkæt], *s.* (*Zool.*) der Kater.

tome [toum], *s.* der große Band, (*coll.*) der Wälzer.

tomfoolery [tɔm'fu:ləri], *s.* die Narretei.

Tommy ['tɔmi], *s.* (*Mil.*) (*coll.*) der englische Soldat.

tomorrow [tə'mɔrou], *adv.* morgen; — *morning,* morgen früh; *the day after* —, übermorgen.

ton [tʌn], *s.* die Tonne.

tone [toun], *s.* der Ton, Klang; (*fig.*) die Stimmung (*mood*). — *v.a.* — *down,* abtönen, abstimmen.

tongs [tɔŋz], *s. pl.* die Zange.

tongue [tʌŋ], *s.* (*Anat.*) die Zunge.

tonic ['tɔnik], *s.* das Stärkungsmittel. — *adj.* tonisch, stärkend.

tonight [tu'nait], *adv.* heute abend, heute nacht.

tonnage ['tʌnidʒ], *s.* die Tonnage, das Tonnengeld.

tonsil ['tɔnsil], *s.* (*Anat.*) die Mandel.

tonsilitis [tɔnsi'laitis], *s.* (*Med.*) die Mandelentzündung.

tonsure ['tɔnʃə], *s.* die Tonsur.

too [tu:], *adv.* allzu, zu, allzusehr; auch (*also*).

tool [tu:l], *s.* das Werkzeug, das Gerät; *machine* —, die Werkzeugmaschine.

tooth [tu:θ], *s.* (*pl.* **teeth** [ti:θ]) der Zahn.

toothache ['tu:θeik], *s.* das Zahnweh.

toothbrush ['tu:θbrʌʃ], *s.* die Zahnbürste.

toothpaste ['tu:θpeist], s. die Zahnpaste.
top (1) [tɔp], s. die Spitze; der Gipfel
(*mountain*); der Wipfel (*tree*); der
Giebel (*house*); die Oberfläche (*surface*); big —, das Zirkuszeltdach; —
hat, der Zylinder. — v.a. übertreffen
(*surpass*); bedecken (*cover*).
top (2) [tɔp], s. der Kreisel (*spinning* —).
topaz ['toupæz], s. der Topas.
tope [toup], v.n. zechen, saufen.
toper ['toupə], s. der Zecher.
topic ['tɔpik], s. das Thema, der
Gegenstand.
topical ['tɔpikəl], adj. aktuell (*up to date*).
topmost ['tɔpmoust], adj. höchst,
oberst.
topsy-turvy ['tɔpsi 'tə:vi], adv. durcheinander, auf den Kopf gestellt.
torch [tɔ:tʃ], s. die Fackel; (*Elec.*) die
Taschenlampe.
torment ['tɔ:mənt], s. die Qual, Marter.
— [tɔ:'ment], v.a. quälen, martern,
peinigen.
tornado [tɔ:'neidou], s. der Wirbelsturm.
torpid ['tɔ:pid], adj. starr, betäubt;
(*fig.*) stumpfsinnig.
torpor ['tɔ:pə], s. die Starre; die
Stumpfheit, Stumpfsinnigkeit.
torrent ['tɔrənt], s. der Gießbach, der
reißende) Strom.
torrid ['tɔrid], adj. brennend heiß,
verbrannt.
torsion ['tɔ:ʃən], s. die Drehung,
Windung.
tortoise ['tɔ:təs], s. (*Zool.*) die Schildkröte.
tortoiseshell ['tɔ:təʃel], s. das Schildpatt.
tortuous ['tɔ:tjuəs], adj. gewunden.
torture ['tɔ:tʃə], s. die Folter; (*fig.*) die
Folterqualen, f. pl. — v.a. foltern.
Tory ['tɔ:ri], s. (*Pol.*) der englische
Konservative.
toss [tɔs], s. der Wurf (*of coin, etc.*);
argue the —, sich streiten. — v.a.
werfen. — v.n. — up, losen.
total [toutl], adj. ganz, gänzlich, total.
— s. die Gesamtsumme. — v.a. sich
(im ganzen) belaufen auf.
totality [tou'tæliti], s. die Gesamtheit.
totter ['tɔtə], v.n. wanken, schwanken,
torkeln.
touch [tʌtʃ], v.a. berühren; anfassen;
(*coll.*) anpumpen (*for money*); — up,
auffrischen. — s. die Berührung
(*contact*); (*Mus.*) der Anschlag.
touching ['tʌtʃiŋ], adj. rührend, ergreifend.
touchline ['tʌtʃlain], s. (*Sport*) der Rand
des Spielfeldes, die Seitenlinie.
touchy ['tʌtʃi], adj. empfindlich.
tough [tʌf], adj. zäh, widerstandsfähig
(*resistant*); get —, grob werden; —
luck, Pech! — s. (*Am. coll.*) der
Grobian.
tour [tuə], s. die Tour, Reise; (*Theat.*)
die Tournee. — v.a., v.n. touren,
bereisen.

tourist ['tuərist], s. der Tourist.
tournament ['tuə- or 'tɔ:nəmənt], s. der
Wettkampf, das Turnier.
tout [taut], v.n. Kunden suchen,
anlocken. — s. der Kundenfänger.
tow [tou], s. das Schlepptau. — v.a.
ziehen, schleppen.
toward(s) [tu'wɔ:d(z), tɔ:d(z)], prep.
gegen; gegenüber; zu . . . hin; auf . . .
zu; für.
towel ['tauəl], s. das Handtuch.
towelling ['tauəliŋ], s. der Hand-
tuchdrell; Turkish —, das Frottiertuch.
tower [tauə], s. der Turm, Zwinger. —
v.n. emporragen, hervorragen
(über).
towing path ['tou(iŋ) pɑ:θ] see
towpath.
town [taun], s. die Stadt; — crier, der
Ausrufer; — hall, das Rathaus (*offices*).
townsman ['taunzmən], s. der Städter.
towpath ['toupɑ:θ], s. der Treidelpfad.
toy [tɔi], s. das Spielzeug; (*pl.*) Spiel-
sachen, Speilwaren, f. pl.; — shop, der
Speilwarenladen. — v.n. spielen.
trace [treis], s. die Spur. — v.a. suchen,
aufspüren; pausen (*through paper*).
track [træk], s. die Spur, Fährte (*path*);
(*Railw.*) das Geleis(e).
tract [trækt], s. der Traktat (*pamphlet*);
die Strecke (*stretch*).
traction ['trækʃən], s. das Ziehen
(*pulling*); (*Tech.*) der Zug.
tractor ['træktə], s. der Traktor.
trade [treid], s. der Handel (*commerce*);
das Gewerbe (*craft*); — wind, der Passatwind; — union, die Gewerkschaft.
— v.a. — in, in Zahlung geben. —
v.n. handeln, Handel treiben; — in,
eintauschen.
trademark ['treidmɑ:k], s. die (Schutz)-
marke, das Warenzeichen.
tradesman ['treidzmən], s. der Lieferant.
traduce [trə'dju:s], v.a. verleumden.
traffic ['træfik], s. der Verkehr; (*Comm.*)
der Handel; — light, die Verkehrs-
ampel.
trafficator ['træfikeitə], s. (*Motor.*) der
Winker.
tragedy ['trædʒədi], s. die Tragödie,
das Trauerspiel.
tragic ['trædʒik], adj. tragisch.
tradition [trə'diʃən], s. die Tradition.
traditional [trə'diʃənəl], adj. traditionell.
trail [treil], s. die Spur, Fährte; (*Am.*)
der Pfad. — v.a. nach sich ziehen,
schleppen; (*Am.*) nachfolgen (*Dat.*).
trailer ['treilə], s. (*Motor.*) der Anhänger; (*Film*) die Voranzeige.
train [trein], v.a. ausbilden; (*Sport*)
trainieren, abrichten, dressieren
(*animal*). — v.n. (*Sport*) sich vorbereiten; sich ausbilden (*for profession*). — s. (*Railw.*) der Zug; (*Mil.*)
der Zug, Transport; die Schleppe
(*bridal gown, etc.*); — of thought, die
Gedankenfolge.

training ['treiniŋ], *s.* die Erziehung; Ausbildung; — *college,* das Lehrerseminar, die pädagogische Hochschule.

trait [trei, treit], *s.* der Zug, Wesenszug.

traitor ['treitə], *s.* der Verräter.

tram(car) ['træm(kɑ:)], *s.* die Straßenbahn, der Strassenbahnwagen.

trammelled [træmld], *adj.* gebunden, gefesselt.

tramp [træmp], *s.* der Landstreicher, Strolch. — *v.n.* trampeln; (zu Fuß) wandern.

trample [træmpl], *v.a.* niedertrampeln. — *v.n.* trampeln, treten.

tramway ['træmwei], *s.* die Strassenbahn.

trance [trɑ:ns], *s.* die Verzückung.

tranquil ['træŋkwil], *adj.* ruhig, still, friedlich.

tranquillizer ['træŋkwilaizə], *s.* (*Med.*) das Beruhigungsmittel.

transact [træn'zækt], *v.a.* abmachen; verrichten (*conclude*), erledigen.

transaction [træn'zækʃən], *s.* die Verhandlung, Abmachung, Durchführung.

transcend [træn'send], *v.a.* übersteigen.

transcendental [trænsen'dentl], *adj.* transzendental.

transcribe [træn'skraib], *v.a.* übertragen; umschreiben (*cipher etc.*); abschreiben.

transcription [træn'skripʃən], *s.* die Umschrift; die Abschrift (*copy*).

transept ['trænsept], *s.* (*Archit.*) das Querschiff.

transfer [træns'fə:], *v.a.* versetzen, überführen; übertragen; überweisen (*money*). — *v.n.* verlegt werden. — ['trænsfə:], *s.* der Wechsel, Transfer; die Versetzung; Überweisung.

transfigure [træns'figə], *v.a.* verklären.

transfix [træns'fiks], *v.a.* durchbohren.

transform [træns'fɔ:m], *v.a.* verändern, umwandeln. — *v.r.* sich verwandeln.

transgress [træns'gres], *v.a.* überschreiten (*trespass on*). — *v.n.* sich vergehen.

transient ['trænsiənt], *adj.* vergänglich.

transit ['trænsit, 'trænzit], *s.* der Durchgang; die Durchfahrt, Durchfuhr (*travel*); (*Comm.*) der Transit. — *v.n.* (*Am.*) durchfahren (*of goods*).

transitive ['trænsitiv], *adj.* (*Gram.*) transitiv.

transitory ['trænsitəri], *adj.* vergänglich, flüchtig.

translate ['trænsleit], *v.a.* übersetzen; versetzen (*office*).

translation [træns'leiʃən], *s.* die Übersetzung, die Übertragung.

translucent [trænz'lju:sənt], *adj.* durchscheinend.

transmission [trænz'miʃən], *s.* die Übersendung, Übermittlung; (*Rad.*) die Sendung; (*Motor.*) die Transmission.

transmit [trænz'mit], *v.a.* übersenden, übermitteln; (*Rad., T.V.*) übertragen, senden.

transmutation [trænzmju'teiʃən], *s.* die Verwandlung.

transparent [træns'pɛərənt], *adj.* durchsichtig.

transpire [træns'paiə, trænz–], *v.n.* bekannt werden.

transplant [træns'plɑ:nt, trænz–], *v.a.* verpflanzen; (*Med.*) übertragen.

transport [træns'pɔ:t], *v.a.* transportieren; (*fig.*) entzücken. — ['trænspɔ:t], *s.* der Transport; die Versendung (*sending*); (*fig.*) die Entzückung.

transpose [træns'pouz], *v.a.* (*Mus.*) transponieren.

transverse [trænz'və:s], *adj.* quer; schräg (*oblique*).

trap [træp], *v.a.* in eine Falle führen; ertappen (*detect*). — *s.* die Falle; der Einspänner (*gig*).

trapeze [trə'pi:z], *s.* das Trapez.

trapper ['træpə], *s.* der Fallensteller.

trappings ['træpiŋz], *s. pl.* der Schmuck; (*fig.*) die Äußerlichkeiten, *f. pl.*

trash [træʃ], *s.* (*Lit.*) der Schund; der Kitsch; das wertlose Zeug.

trashy ['træʃi], *adj.* wertlos, kitschig.

travail ['træveil], *s.* die Wehen, Sorgen, die Mühe.

travel [trævl], *v.n.* reisen. — *v.a.* bereisen. — *s.* das Reisen; — *agency,* das Reisebüro.

traveller ['trævələ], *s.* der Reisende; (*Comm.*) der Handelsreisende, Vertreter.

traverse ['trævə:s], *adj.* quer. — *s.* die Traverse, der Querbalken. — [trə'və:s], *v.a.* durchqueren; (*fig.*) durchwandern.

trawl [trɔ:l], *v.n.* (mit Schleppnetz) fischen.

trawler ['trɔ:lə], *s.* das Fischerboot, der Fischdampfer.

tray [trei], *s.* das Tablett.

treacherous ['tretʃərəs], *adj.* verräterisch; (*fig.*) gefährlich.

treachery ['tretʃəri], *s.* der Verrat.

treacle [tri:kl], *s.* der Sirup.

tread [tred], *v.a., v.n. irr.* (be)treten, auftreten. — *s.* der Tritt, Schritt; die Lauffläche (*of a tyre*).

treason [tri:zn], *s.* der Verrat.

treasure ['treʒə], *s.* der Schatz.

treasurer ['treʒərə], *s.* der Schatzmeister.

treasury ['treʒəri], *s.* die Schatzkammer; (*U.K.*) *the Treasury,* das Schatzamt, Finanzministerium.

treat [tri:t], *v.a.* behandeln; bewirten (*as host*). — *v.n.* (*Pol.*) unterhandeln (*negotiate*). — *s.* der Genuß (*pleasure*).

treatise ['tri:tis], *s.* die Abhandlung.

treatment ['tri:tmənt], *s.* die Behandlung.

treaty ['tri:ti], *s.* der Vertrag.

treble [trebl], *s.* (*Mus.*) die Sopranstimme, Knabenstimme, der Diskant; (*Maths.*) das Dreifache. — *v.a.* verdreifachen.

tree

tree [tri:], *s.* (*Bot.*) der Baum.
trefoil ['tri:foil], *s.* (*Bot.*) der drei-blätt(e)rige Klee; das Dreiblatt.
trellis ['trelis], *s.* das Gitter.
tremble [trembl], *v.n.* zittern. — *s.* das Zittern.
tremendous [tri'mendəs], *adj.* unge-heuer (groß); schrecklich.
tremor ['tremə], *s.* das Zittern; (*Geol.*) das Beben; (*Med.*) das Zucken.
trench [trentʃ], *s.* der Graben.
trenchant ['trentʃənt], *adj.* einschnei-dend, scharf.
trend [trend], *s.* die Tendenz; (*Comm.*) der Trend.
trepidation [trepi'deiʃən], *s.* die Angst, das Zittern.
trespass ['trespəs], *v.n.* sich vergehen, übertreten (*law*); — *on*, unbefugt betreten. — *s.* die Übertretung.
tress [tres], *s.* die Flechte, Haarlocke.
trestle ['tresl], *s.* das Gestell; — *table*, der Klapptisch.
trial ['traiəl], *s.* die Probe, der Versuch; (*Law*) die Verhandlung, der Prozeß, das Verhör.
triangle ['traiæŋgl], *s.* das Dreieck; (*Mus.*) der Triangel.
tribe [traib], *s.* der Stamm.
tribulation [tribju'leiʃən], *s.* die Trüb-sal, Drangsal.
tribunal [trai'bju:nəl], *s.* das Tribunal, der Gerichtshof.
tributary ['tribjutəri], *adj.* Neben-. — *s.* der Nebenfluß.
tribute ['tribju:t], *s.* der Tribut.
trice [trais], *s. in a* —, im Nu.
trick [trik], *s.* der Kniff, Trick. — *v.a.* betrügen.
trickery ['trikəri], *s.* der Betrug.
trickle [trikl], *v.n.* tröpfeln, sickern. — *s.* das Tröpfeln.
tricky ['triki], *adj.* verwickelt; (*fig.*) bedenklich, heikel.
tricycle ['traisikl], *s.* das Dreirad.
tried [traid], *adj.* erprobt, bewährt.
triennial [trai'eniəl], *adj.* dreijährlich.
trifle [traifl], *v.n.* scherzen, spielen. — *s.* die Kleinigkeit; (*Cul.*) der süße Auflauf.
trigger ['trigə], *s.* der Drücker. — *v.a.* — *off*, auslösen.
trilateral [trai'lætərəl], *adj.* drei-seitig.
trill [tril], *s.* (*Mus.*) der Triller. — *v.a.*, *v.n.* trillern.
trim [trim], *adj.* niedlich, schmuck; nett (*dress*). — *v.a.* beschneiden; (*Naut.*) — *sails*, einziehen. — *s.* die Ausrüstung; (*Naut.*) das Gleichge-wicht.
trimmer ['trimə], *s.* die Putzmacherin; (*fig.*) der Opportunist.
trimmings ['triminz], *s. pl.* (*fig.*) der Kleinkram; (*Tail.*) der Besatz.
Trinity ['triniti], *s.* (*Theol.*) die Drei-faltigkeit, Dreieinigkeit.
trinket ['triŋkit], *s.* das Geschmeide; (*pl.*) Schmucksachen, *f. pl.*
trip [trip], *s.* der Ausflug, die Reise. —

v.a. — *up*, ein Bein stellen (*Dat.*). — *v.n.* stolpern.
tripe ['traip], *s.* die Kaldaunen, *f. pl.*; (*fig.*) der Unsinn.
triple [tripl], *adj.* dreifach.
triplet ['triplit], *s.* der Drilling; (*Mus.*) die Triole; (*Poet.*) der Dreireim.
tripod ['traipɔd], *s.* der Dreifuß.
tripos ['traipɔs], *s.* das Schlußexamen (*Cambridge Univ.*).
trite [trait], *adj.* abgedroschen.
triumph ['traiʌmf], *s.* der Triumph. — *v.n.* triumphieren.
triumphant [trai'ʌmfənt], *adj.* trium-phierend.
trivial ['triviəl], *adj.* trivial, platt, alltäglich.
troll (1) [troul], *v.n.* trällern (*hum*); fischen. — *s.* der Rundgesang (*song*).
troll (2) [troul], *s.* der Kobold (*gnome*).
trolley ['trɔli], *s.* der Teewagen (*furni-ture*); (*Tech.*) die Dräsine, der Karren.
trollop ['trɔləp], *s.* die Schlampe.
trombone [trɔm'boun], *s.* (*Mus.*) die Posaune.
troop [tru:p], *s.* der Haufe; (*Mil.*) die Truppe, der Trupp. — *v.n.* sich sammeln. — *v.a. Trooping the Colour*, die Fahnenparade.
trophy ['troufi], *s.* die Trophäe, das Siegeszeichen.
tropic ['trɔpik], *s.* (*Geog.*) der Wende-kreis; (*pl.*) die Tropen, *f. pl.*
tropical ['trɔpikəl], *adj.* tropisch.
trot [trɔt], *v.n.* traben. — *s.* der Trab, Trott.
troth [trouθ], *s.* (*obs.*) die Treue; *pledge o.'s* —, Treue geloben.
trouble [trʌbl], *s.* die Mühe, Sorge (*worry*); der Kummer (*sadness*); die Störung (*disturbance*). — *v.a.* be-mühen (*ask favour of*); bekümmern (*worry*); stören (*disturb*).
troublesome ['trʌblsəm], *adj.* ärgerlich, schwierig, unangenehm.
trough [trɔf], *s.* der Trog; (*Met.*) das Tief.
trounce [trauns], *v.a.* verprügeln.
trouncing ['traunsiŋ], *s.* die Tracht Prügel.
trousers ['trauzəz], *s. pl.* die Hosen, *f.pl.*
trout [traut], *s.* (*Zool.*) die Forelle.
trowel ['trauəl], *s.* die Kelle.
troy(weight) ['trɔi(weit)], *s.* das Troy-gewicht.
truant ['tru:ənt], *s.* (*Sch.*) der Schul-schwänzer; *play* —, die Schule schwänzen.
truce [tru:s], *s.* der Waffenstillstand.
truck (1) [trʌk], *s.* (*Rail.*) der Güter-wagen; (*Am.*) *see* **lorry**.
truck (2) [trʌk], *s. have no* — *with*, nichts zu tun haben mit.
truculent ['trʌkjulənt], *adj.* streit-süchtig.
trudge [trʌdʒ], *v.n.* sich schleppen.
true [tru:], *adj.* wahr; treu (*faithful*); echt (*genuine*); richtig (*correct*).

truffle [trʌfl], *s.* die Trüffel.

truism ['truːizm], *s.* der Gemeinplatz, die Binsenwahrheit.

truly ['truːli], *adv. yours* —, Ihr ergebener.

trump [trʌmp], *s.* der Trumpf; — *card*, die Trumpfkarte. — *v.a.* — *up*, erfinden, erdichten.

trumpery ['trʌmpəri], *s.* der Plunder, Schund. — *adj.* wertlos, belanglos.

trumpet ['trʌmpit], *s.* (*Mus.*) die Trompete. — *v.a.* stolz austrompeten, ausposaunen. — *v.n.* trompeten.

truncate [trʌŋ'keit], *v.a.* verstümmeln, stutzen.

truncheon ['trʌnʃən], *s.* der Knüppel. — *v.a.* durchprügeln.

trundle [trʌndl], *v.n.* trudeln; sich wälzen. — *v.a. — a hoop*, Reifen schlagen.

trunk [trʌŋk], *s.* der Stamm (*tree*); der Rüssel (*of elephant*); der (große) Koffer (*chest*); — *call*, das Ferngespräch.

truss [trʌs], *s.* das Band, Bruchband. — *v.a.* zäumen, stützen; aufschürzen.

trust [trʌst], *v.a., v.n.* trauen (*Dat.*), vertrauen (*Dat.*); anvertrauen (*Dat., Acc.*). — *s.* das Vertrauen; *in* —, zu treuen Händen, als Treuhänder; (*Comm.*) der Trust.

trustworthy ['trʌstwəːði], *adj.* zuverlässig.

truth [truːθ], *s.* die Wahrheit.

truthful ['truːθful], *adj.* wahrhaftig.

try [trai], *v.a. irr.* versuchen (*s. th.*); (*Law*) verhören; — *on* (*clothes*), anprobieren; — *out*, ausprobieren. — *v.n.* versuchen, sich bemühen. — *s.* der Versuch (*attempt*); (*Rugby*) der Try.

Tsar [zɑː], *s.* der Zar.

tub [tʌb], *s.* das Faß; die Wanne (*bath*); (*Naut.*) das Übungsboot.

tube [tjuːb], *s.* die Tube (*paste etc.*); die Röhre (*pipe, also Elec.*); der Schlauch (*tyre*); das Rohr (*tubing*); (*Transport*) die Londoner Untergrundbahn.

tuberous ['tjuːbərəs], *adj.* knollenartig, knollig.

tubular ['tjuːbjulə], *adj.* röhrenförmig.

tuck [tʌk], *s.* (*Tail.*) die Falte; (*Sch. sl.*) der Leckerbissen. — *v.a. — up*, zudecken; — *in*, einschlagen. — *v.n.* (*sl.*) — *in*, tüchtig zugreifen.

tucker ['tʌkə], *s.* (*sl.*) das Essen.

tuckshop ['tʌkʃɔp], *s.* der Schulladen.

Tuesday ['tjuːzdi]. der Dienstag.

tuft [tʌft], *s.* der Büschel.

tug [tʌg], *v.a.* ziehen, zerren. — *s.* (*Naut.*) der Schlepper; — *of war*, das Tauziehen.

tuition [tjuːˈiʃən], *s.* der Unterricht, Privatunterricht.

tulip ['tjuːlip], *s.* (*Bot.*) die Tulpe.

tumble [tʌmbl], *v.n.* purzeln. — *s.* der Sturz, Fall.

tumbril ['tʌmbril], *s.* der Karren.

tumid ['tjuːmid], *adj.* geschwollen.

tumour ['tjuːmə], *s.* (*Med.*) die Geschwulst, der Tumor.

tumult ['tjuːmʌlt], *s.* der Tumult, Auflauf; der Lärm (*noise*).

tun [tʌn], *s.* die Tonne, das Faß.

tune [tjuːn], *s.* die Melodie. — *v.a.* stimmen; (*Rad.*) — *in* (*to*), einstellen (auf).

tuneful ['tjuːnful], *adj.* melodisch.

tuner ['tjuːnə]. *s.* der (Klavier)stimmer.

tunic ['tjuːnik], *s.* der Kittel.

tuning ['tjuːniŋ], *s.* das Stimmen; die Abstimmung (*also Rad.*); — *fork*, die Stimmgabel.

tunnel [tʌnl], *s.* der Tunnel. — *v.n.* graben, einen Tunnel bauen.

turbid ['təːbid], *adj.* trüb, dick.

turbot ['təːbət], *s.* (*Zool.*) der Steinbutt.

turbulence ['təːbjuləns], *s.* der Sturm, das Ungestüm; (*Aviat.*) die Turbulenz.

tureen [tjuəˈriːn], *s.* die Suppenterrine, Suppenschüssel.

turf [təːf], *s.* der Rasen; (*Sport*) die Rennbahn, der Turf. — *v.a.* mit Rasen belegen; (*sl.*) — *out*, hinausschmeißen.

turgid ['təːdʒid], *adj.* schwülstig (*style*).

Turk [təːk], *s.* der Türke.

turkey ['təːki], *s.* (*Orn.*) der Truthahn.

Turkish ['təːkiʃ], *adj.* türkisch.

turmoil ['təːmɔil], *s.* die Unruhe, der Aufruhr.

turn [təːn], *v.a.* wenden, drehen, kehren (*to*); — *down*, ablehnen; (*coll.*) — *in*, abgeben (*hand over*); — *on*, andrehen (*tap etc.*); — *off*, ausdrehen; — *out*, produzieren. — *v.n.* sich drehen, sich ändern; werden; — *on s.o.*, jemanden verraten; (*coll.*) — *out*, ausrücken; (*coll.*) — *up*, auftauchen. — *s.* die Drehung, Windung; der Hang; die Reihe; die Nummer (*act*); *it is my* —, ich bin an der Reihe.

turncoat ['təːnkout], *s.* der Überläufer.

turner ['təːnə], *s.* der Drechsler.

turnip ['təːnip], *s.* (*Bot.*) die Rübe.

turnpike ['təːnpaik], *s.* der Schlagbaum.

turnstile ['təːnstail], *s.* das Drehkreuz.

turntable ['təːnteibl], *s.* die Drehscheibe.

turpentine ['təːpəntain], *s.* der *or* das Terpentin.

turquoise ['təːkwɔiz *or* 'təːkɔiz], *s.* der Türkis.

turret ['tʌrit], *s.* (*Archit.*) der Turm, das Türmchen.

turtle [təːtl], *s.* (*Zool.*) die Schildkröte; (*Orn.*) -*dove*, die Turteltaube.

tusk [tʌsk], *s.* (*Zool.*) der Stoßzahn.

tussle [tʌsl], *s.* der Streit, die Rauferei.

tutelage ['tjuːtilidʒ], *s.* die Vormundschaft.

tutor ['tjuːtə], *s.* der Privatlehrer; der Tutor, Studienleiter. — *v.a.* unterrichten.

twaddle [twɔdl], *s.* das Geschwätz. — *v.n.* schwätzen.

twang [twæŋ], *s.* der scharfe Ton. — *v.n.* scharf klingen.

tweed [twiːd], *s.* (*Text.*) der Tweed.

twelfth [twelfθ], *num.adj.* zwölft; *Twelfth Night*, das Fest der Heiligen Drei Könige (*6th January*).

507

twelve [twelv], *num. adj.* zwölf.

twenty ['twenti], *num. adj.* zwanzig.

twice [twais], *num. adv.* zweimal, doppelt.

twig [twig], *s.* (*Bot.*) der Zweig, die Rute.

twilight ['twailait], *s.* das Zwielicht, die Dämmerung.

twill [twil], *s.* (*Text.*) der Köper. — *v.a.* köpern.

twin [twin], *s.* der Zwilling.

twine [twain], *s.* der Bindfaden, die Schnur. — *v.a.* drehen, zwirnen. — *v.n.* sich verflechten; sich winden (*plant*).

twinge [twindʒ], *s.* der Zwick, Stich.

twinkle [twiŋkl], *v.n.* blinzeln, blinken. — *s.* das Zwinkern, der Blick.

twirl [twə:l], *s.* der Wirbel. — *v.a.* schnell drehen, wirbeln.

twist [twist], *v.a.* flechten, drehen; verdrehen. — *s.* die Drehung, Krümmung; das Geflecht; (*fig.*) die Wendung (*sudden change*).

twitch [twitʃ], *v.a.* zupfen, zucken. — *v.n.* zucken. — *s.* das Zucken, der Krampf.

twitter ['twitə], *v.n.* zwitschern; (*fig.*) zittern. — *s.* das Gezwitscher; (*fig.*) die Angst.

two [tu:], *num. adj.* zwei; — *-faced*, falsch.

twofold ['tu:fould], *adj.* zweifach.

tympanum ['timpənəm], *s.* (*Med.*) das Trommelfell.

type [taip], *s.* (*Typ.*) die Type; (*Psych.*) der Typ, Typus. — *v.a., v.n.* tippen; mit der Maschine schreiben.

typewriter ['taipraitə], *s.* die Schreibmaschine.

typhoid ['taifɔid], *s.* (*Med.*) der (Unterleibs)typhus. — *adj.* typhusartig.

typist ['taipist], *s.* der (die) Maschinenschreiber(in).

typhoon [tai'fu:n], *s.* der Taifun.

typical ['tipikəl], *adj.* typisch, charakteristisch.

typography [tai'pɔgrəfi], *s.* die Typographie, Buchdruckerkunst.

tyrannical [ti'rænikəl], *adj.* tyrannisch.

tyranny ['tirəni], *s.* die Tyrannei.

tyrant ['taiərənt], *s.* der Tyrann.

tyre, (*Am.*) **tire** ['taiə], *s.* der Reifen.

tyro ['taiərou], *s.* der Anfänger.

Tyrolese [tiro'li:z], *adj.* tirolisch, Tiroler-. — *s.* der Tiroler.

U

U [ju:]. das U.

ubiquitous [ju'bikwitəs], *adj.* überall da, überall zu finden.

udder ['ʌdə], *s.* (*Zool.*) das Euter.

ugly ['ʌgli], *adj.* häßlich.

Ukrainian [ju:'kreiniən], *adj.* ukrainisch. — *s.* der Ukrainer.

ulcer ['ʌlsə], *s.* (*Med.*) das Geschwür.

ulcerate ['ʌlsəreit], *v.n.* (*Med.*) schwären.

ulcerous ['ʌlsərəs], *adj.* (*Med.*) geschwürig.

ulterior [ʌl'tiəriə], *adj.* weiter, ferner, weiterliegend.

ultimate ['ʌltimit], *adj.* letzt, endlich, äußerst.

ultimatum [ʌlti'meitəm], *s.* das Ultimatum.

umbrage ['ʌmbridʒ], *s.* der Schatten; *take —*, Anstoß nehmen (an, *Dat.*).

umbrella [ʌm'brelə], *s.* der Schirm, Regenschirm.

umpire ['ʌmpaiə], *s.* (*Sport*) der Schiedsrichter.

umpteen ['ʌmpti:n], *adj.* zahlreiche, verschiedene.

un- [ʌn], *negating pref.* un-, nicht-; *with verbs*, auf-, ent-, los-, ver-; *where a word is not given, see the simple form.*

unable [ʌn'eibl], *adj.* unfähig; *be —*, nicht können.

unaccustomed [ʌnə'kʌstəmd], *adj.* ungewohnt.

unaided [ʌn'eidid], *adj.* allein, ohne Hilfe.

unaware [ʌnə'wɛə], *adj.* unbewußt.

uncertain [ʌn'sə:tin], *adj.* unsicher.

uncle [ʌŋkl], *s.* der Onkel.

unconscious [ʌn'kɔnʃəs], *adj.* bewußtlos; unbewußt.

uncouth [ʌn'ku:θ], *adj.* ungehobelt, roh.

unction ['ʌŋkʃən], *s.* die Salbung (*anointing*); die Salbe; *Extreme Unction,* (*Eccl.*) die Letzte Ölung.

unctuous ['ʌŋktjuəs], *adj.* salbungsvoll.

under ['ʌndə], *prep.* unter. — *adv.* darunter, unten (*underneath*); *pref.* (*compounds*) unter-.

undercarriage ['ʌndəkæridʒ], *s.* (*Aviat.*) das Fahrwerk.

underfed [ʌndə'fed], *adj.* unterernährt.

undergo [ʌndə'gou], *v.a. irr.* durchmachen, erdulden.

undergraduate [ʌndə'grædjuit], *s.* (*Univ.*) der Student.

underground ['ʌndəgraund], *adj.* unterirdisch; *railway* die Untergrundbahn. — [ʌndə'graund], *adv.* unterirdisch.

underhand [ʌndə'hænd], *adj.* heimlich, hinterlistig.

underline [ʌndə'lain], *v.a.* unterstreichen.

undermine [ʌndə'main], *v.a.* untergraben.

underneath [ʌndə'ni:θ], *adv.* unten, darunter. — ['ʌndəni:θ], *prep.* unter.

undersigned ['ʌndəsaind], *adj.* unterzeichnet. —*s.* der Unterzeichnete.

understand [ʌndə'stænd], *v.a. irr.* verstehen, begreifen.

understatement ['ʌndəsteitmənt], *s.* die zu bescheidene Festellung, Unterbewertung.

undertaker ['ʌndəteikə], s. der Leichenbestatter.

undertaking [ʌndə'teikiŋ], s. das Unternehmen (*business*); das Versprechen (*promise*).

undertone ['ʌndətoun], s. der Unterton.

underwrite [ʌndə'rait], v.a. irr. (*Comm.*) versichern.

underwriter ['ʌndəraitə], s. (*Comm.*) der Assekurant, Versicherer, Mitversicherer.

undeserved [ʌndi'zə:vd], adj. unverdient.

undeserving [ʌndi'zə:viŋ], adj. unwürdig.

undignified [ʌn'dignifaid], adj. würdelos.

undiscerning [ʌndi'zə:niŋ], adj. geschmacklos.

undiscriminating [ʌndis'krimineitiŋ], adj. unterschiedslos, unkritisch.

undisputed [ʌndis'pju:tid], adj. unbestritten.

undo [ʌn'du:], v.a. irr. zerstören (*destroy*); öffnen (*open*).

undoubted [ʌn'dautid], adj. zweifellos.

undress [ʌn'dres], v.a., v.n. — (sich)ausziehen. — ['ʌndres], s. das Hauskleid.

undue [ʌn'dju:], adj. unangemessen.

undulate ['ʌndjuleit], v.n. wallen, Wellen schlagen.

unduly [ʌn'dju:li], adv. ungebührlich, übermäßig.

unearth [ʌn'ə:θ], v.a. ausgraben.

unearthly [ʌn'ə:θli], adj. überirdisch.

uneasy [ʌn'i:zi], adj. unruhig, unbehaglich.

unemployed [ʌnim'plɔid], adj. arbeitslos.

unemployment [ʌnim'plɔimənt], s. die Arbeitslosigkeit.

unending [ʌn'endiŋ], adj. endlos.

uneven [ʌn'i:vən], adj. uneben; ungerade.

unexceptionable [ʌnik'sepʃənəbl], adj. tadellos.

unexpired [ʌniks'paiəd], adj. noch nicht abgelaufen, noch gültig.

unfair [ʌn'fɛə], adj. unfair; unehrlich.

unfeeling [ʌn'fi:liŋ], adj. gefühllos.

unfit [ʌn'fit], adj. (Mil., Med.) untauglich, schwach; (*food etc.*) ungenießbar.

unfold [ʌn'fould], v.a. entfalten.

unforeseen [ʌnfɔ:'si:n], adj. unerwartet.

unfounded [ʌn'faundid], adj. grundlos.

unfurnished [ʌn'fə:niʃd], adj. unmöbliert.

ungrudging [ʌn'grʌdʒiŋ], adj. bereitwillig.

unhappy [ʌn'hæpi], adj. unglücklich.

unhinge [ʌn'hindʒ], v.a. aus den Angeln heben.

unicorn ['ju:nikɔ:n], s. (Myth.) das Einhorn.

uniform ['ju:nifɔ:m], s. die Uniform. — adj. gleichförmig, einförmig.

union ['ju:niən], s. die Vereinigung; trade —, die Gewerkschaft; Union Jack, die britische Nationalflagge.

unique [ju'ni:k], adj. einzigartig.

unison ['ju:nisən], s. (Mus.) der Einklang, die Harmonie.

unit ['ju:nit], s. die Einheit (*measure etc.*).

unite [ju'nait], v.a. vereinen. — v.n. sich vereinen, verbünden.

unity ['ju:niti], s. die Einigkeit.

universal [ju:ni'və:səl], adj. allgemein.

universe ['ju:nivə:s], s. das Weltall.

university [ju:ni'və:siti], s. die Universität, Hochschule; — degree, der akademische Grad.

unkempt [ʌn'kempt], adj. ungekämmt, ungepflegt.

unleavened [ʌn'levənd], adj. ungesäuert.

unless [ʌn'les], conj. außer, wenn nicht, es sei denn.

unlettered [ʌn'letəd], adj. ungebildet.

unlicensed [ʌn'laisənsd], adj. nicht (für Alkoholverkauf) lizenziert.

unlike [ʌn'laik], adj. ungleich. — ['ʌnlaik], prep. anders als, verschieden von.

unlikely [ʌn'laikli], adj., adv. unwahrscheinlich.

unlock [ʌn'lɔk], v.a. aufschließen.

unmask [ʌn'mɑ:sk], v.a. entlarven.

unpack [ʌn'pæk], v.a., v.n. auspacken.

unpleasant [ʌn'pleznt], adj. unangenehm.

unreliable [ʌnri'laiəbl], adj. unzuverlässig.

unremitting [ʌnri'mitiŋ], adj. unablässig.

unrepentant [ʌnri'pentənt], adj.reuelos.

unrest [ʌn'rest], s. die Unruhe.

unsafe [ʌn'seif], adj. unsicher.

unscathed [ʌn'skeiðd], adj. unversehrt.

unscrew [ʌn'skru:], v.a. abschrauben.

unscrupulous [ʌn'skru:pjuləs], adj. skrupellos, gewissenlos.

unseat [ʌn'si:t], v.a. aus dem Sattel heben; absetzen.

unselfish [ʌn'selfiʃ], adj. selbstlos.

unsettle [ʌn'setl], v.a. verwirren; (fig.) aus dem Konzept bringen.

unsew [ʌn'sou], v.a. auftrennen.

unshrinking [ʌn'ʃrinkiŋ], adj. unverzagt.

unsophisticated [ʌnsə'fistikeitid], adj. naiv, natürlich.

unsparing [ʌn'spɛəriŋ], adj. schonungslos.

unstable [ʌn'steibl], adj. unsicher; labil.

unstitch [ʌn'stitʃ], v.a. auftrennen.

unstop [ʌn'stɔp], v.a. aufstöpseln, öffnen (a bottle).

unstudied [ʌn'stʌdid], adj. ungekünstelt.

unsuccessful [ʌnsək'sesful], adj. erfolglos.

unsuspecting [ʌnsə'spektiŋ], adj. arglos.

untie [ʌn'tai], v.a. losbinden.

until [ʌn'til], prep., conj. bis.

509

untimely

untimely [ʌn'taimli], *adj.* vorzeitig, unzeitig.
untiring [ʌn'taiərin], *adj.* unermüdlich.
unto ['ʌntu], *prep.* (*Poet.*) zu.
untold [ʌn'tould], *adj.* ungezählt, unermeßlich.
untoward [ʌn'tɔːd *or* ʌn'touəd], *adj.* unangenehm; widerspenstig (*recalcitrant*).
untrustworthy [ʌn'trʌstwəːði], *adj.* unzuverlässig.
unveil [ʌn'veil], *v.a.* enthüllen.
unwieldy [ʌn'wiːldi], *adj.* sperrig, schwerfällig.
unwind [ʌn'waind], *v.a.* abwickeln.
unwitting [ʌn'witiŋ], *adj.* unwissentlich, unbewusst.
unwonted [ʌn'wountid], *adj.* ungewohnt.
unwrap [ʌn'ræp], *v.a.* auspacken, auswickeln.
unyielding [ʌn'jiːldiŋ], *adj.* unnachgiebig; hartnäckig.
unyoke [ʌn'jouk], *v.a.* ausspannen.
up [ʌp], *adv.* auf, aufwärts (*upward*); aufgestanden (*out of bed*); — (*there*), oben; *what's up?* was ist los? — *to*, bis zu; *be — to s.th.*, auf etwas aus sein, etwas im Schilde führen; *it's — to you*, es liegt an dir. — *prep.* auf, hinauf. — *s. ups and downs*, das wechselnde Schicksal, Auf und Ab.
upbraid [ʌp'breid], *v.a.* tadeln.
upheaval [ʌp'hiːvl], *s.* das Chaos, Durcheinander, die Umwälzung.
uphill [ʌp'hil], *adv.* bergauf(wärts). — ['ʌphil], *adj.* (an)steigend; (*fig.*) mühsam.
uphold [ʌp'hould], *v.a.* aufrechterhalten.
upholster [ʌp'houlstə], *v.a.* polstern.
upholstery [ʌp'houlstəri], *s.* die Polsterung.
upon [ʌ'pɔn] *see* on.
upper ['ʌpə], *adj.* ober, höher; — *hand*, die Oberhand.
uppish ['ʌpiʃ], *adj.* anmaßend.
upright ['ʌprait], *adj.* aufrecht, gerade; (*fig.*) aufrichtig, rechtschaffen.
uproar ['ʌprɔː], *s.* der Lärm, Aufruhr.
uproot [ʌp'ruːt], *v.a.* entwurzeln.
upset [ʌp'set], *v.a.* umwerfen; (*fig.*) aus der Fassung bringen. — ['ʌpset], *s.* das Umwerfen; (*fig.*) die Bestürzung.
upshot ['ʌpʃɔt], *s.* der Ausgang, das Ergebnis.
upside ['ʌpsaid], *s.* die Oberseite; — *down*, auf den Kopf gestellt.
upstairs [ʌp'stɛəz], *adv.* oben, nach oben.
upstart ['ʌpstɑːt], *s.* der Parvenü, Emporkömmling.
upward ['ʌpwəd], *adj.* steigend, aufwärtsgehend. — *adv.* (*also* upwards*) aufwärts; — *of*, mehr als.
urban ['əːbən], *adj.* städtisch.
urbane [əː'bein], *adj.* zivilisiert.
urbanity [əː'bæniti], *s.* die Bildung, der Schliff.
urchin ['əːtʃin], *s.* der Schelm; (*Zool.*) sea —, der Seeigel.

urge [əːdʒ], *v.a.* drängen. — *s.* der Drang.
urgent ['əːdʒənt], *adj.* dringend, drängend, dringlich.
urine ['juərin], *s.* der Urin.
urn [əːn], *s.* die Urne.
Uruguayan [juːruˈgwaiən], *adj.* uruguayisch. — *s.* der Uruguayer.
us [ʌs], *pers. pron.* uns.
usage ['juːsidʒ], *s.* der (Sprach)gebrauch; die Sitte.
use [juːz], *v.a.* gebrauchen, benutzen. — [juːs], *s.* der Gebrauch, die Benutzung; der Nutzen (*usefulness*).
usher ['ʌʃə], *s.* der Türhüter, Platzanweiser. — *v.a. — in*, anmelden, einführen.
usherette [ʌʃə'ret], *s.* die Platzanweiserin, Programmverkäuferin.
usual ['juːʒuəl], *adj.* gewöhnlich, üblich.
usurer ['juːʒərə *or* 'juːzjuərə], *s.* der Wucherer.
usurp [juːˈzəːp], *v.a.* an sich reißen, usurpieren.
usury ['juːʒjuəri], *s.* der Wucher.
utensil [juː'tensil], *s.* das Gerät, Werkzeug.
utility [juː'tiliti], *s.* die Nützlichkeit (*usefulness*); der Nutzen; *public —*, (die) öffentliche Einrichtung.
utilize ['juːtilaiz], *v.a.* nutzbar machen, ausbeuten, ausnützen.
utmost ['ʌtmoust], *adj.* äußerst, weitest, höchst. — *s.* das Höchste, Äußerste.
utter ['ʌtə], *adj.* äußerst, gänzlich. — *v.a.* äußern, aussprechen.
utterly ['ʌtəli], *adv.* äußerst, völlig.
uvula ['juːvjulə], *s.* (*Anat.*) das Zäpfchen.

V

V [viː]. das V.
vacancy ['veikənsi], *s.* die freie Stelle, die Vakanz.
vacant ['veikənt], *adj.* frei; leer.
vacate [və'keit], *v.a.* frei machen.
vacation [vəˈkeiʃən], *s.* die Niederlegung (*of a post*); die Ferien, *pl.* (*school*); der Urlaub (*holiday*).
vaccinate ['væksineit], *v.a.* (*Med.*) impfen.
vaccine ['væksiːn], *s.* (*Med.*) der Impfstoff.
vacillate ['væsileit], *v.n.* schwanken.
vacuity [vəˈkjuːiti], *s.* die Leere.
vacuous ['vækjuəs], *adj.* leer.
vacuum ['vækjuəm], *s.* das Vakuum; — *cleaner*, der Staubsauger.
vagabond ['vægəbɔnd], *s.* der Landstreicher.
vagary [və'gɛəri], *s.* die Laune, Grille.

vagrant ['veigrənt], *adj.* herumstreichend. — *s.* der Landstreicher.

vague [veig], *adj.* vage, unbestimmt, unklar.

vain [vein], *adj.* nichtig, vergeblich, eitel; *in* —, vergebens, umsonst.

vale [veil], *s.* (*Poet.*) das Tal.

valerian [və'liəriən], *s.* (*Bot.*) der Baldrian.

valet ['vælei, 'vælit], *s.* der Diener.

valiant ['væljənt], *adj.* mutig, tapfer.

valid ['vælid], *adj.* gültig, stichhaltig.

valley ['væli], *s.* das Tal.

valuable ['væljuəbl], *adj.* wertvoll, kostbar.

valuation [vælju'eiʃən], *s.* die Schätzung.

value ['vælju:], *s.* der Wert. — *v.a.* wertschätzen, schätzen.

valve [vælv], *s.* (*Mech.*) das Ventil; (*Rad.*) die Röhre.

vamp (1) [væmp], *s.* das Oberleder.

vamp (2) [væmp], *s.* (*Am. coll.*) der Vamp.

vampire ['væmpaiə], *s.* der Vampir.

van [væn], *s.* der Lieferwagen.

vane [vein], *s.* die Wetterfahne.

vanguard ['vænga:d], *s.* die Vorhut, der Vortrupp.

vanilla [və'nilə], *s.* die Vanille.

vanish ['væniʃ], *v.n.* verschwinden.

vanity ['væniti], *s.* die Nichtigkeit; die Eitelkeit (*conceit*).

vanquish ['væŋkwiʃ], *v.a.* besiegen.

vantage ['va:ntidʒ], *s.* der Vorteil; — *point*, die günstige Position.

vapid ['væpid], *adj.* leer, schal.

vapour ['veipə], *s.* der Dunst; (*Chem.*) der Dampf.

variable ['veəriəbl], *adj.* variabel, veränderlich.

variance ['veəriəns], *s.* die Uneinigkeit.

variation [veəri'eiʃən], *s.* die Variation; die Veränderung, Abweichung.

varicose ['værikəs], *adj.* Krampf-, krampfaderig.

variegated ['veərigeitid], *adj.* bunt, vielfarbig.

variety [və'raiəti], *s.* die Mannigfaltigkeit; (*Bot.*) die Varietät, Abart; (*Theat.*) das Varieté, das Varietétheater.

various ['veəriəs], *adj.* verschieden, mannigfaltig.

varnish ['va:niʃ], *s.* der Firnis, der Lack. — *v.a.* mit Firnis anstreichen, lackieren.

vary ['veəri], *v.a.* abändern. — *v.n.* sich ändern, variieren.

vase [va:z], *s.* die Vase.

vassal [væsl], *s.* der Vasall, Lehnsmann.

vast [va:st], *adj.* ungeheuer, groß.

vat [væt], *s.* die Kufe, das große Faß.

vault [vɔ:lt], *s.* das Gewölbe; die Gruft (*grave*); (*Sport*) der Sprung, *pole* —, der Stabhochsprung. — *v.n.* springen.

vaunt [vɔ:nt], *v.a.* rühmen. — *v.n.* prahlen, sich rühmen. — *s.* die Prahlerei.

veal [vi:l], *s.* das Kalbfleisch.

veer [viə], *v.n.* sich drehen.

vegetable ['vedʒitəbl̩], ɔ. das Gemüse.

vegetarian [vedʒi'teəriən], *adj.* vegetarisch. — *s.* der Vegetarier.

vegetate ['vedʒiteit], *v.n.* vegetieren.

vehemence ['vi:əməns], *s.* die Vehemenz, Heftigkeit.

vehicle ['vi:ikl], *s.* das Fahrzeug, Fuhrwerk; (*Motor.*) der Wagen.

veil [veil], *s.* der Schleier. — *v.a.* verschleiern.

vein [vein], *s.* die Ader.

vellum ['veləm], *s.* das feine Pergamentpapier.

velocity [vi'lɔsiti], *s.* die Geschwindigkeit, Schnelligkeit.

velvet ['velvit], *s.* (*Text.*) der Samt.

venal ['vi:nəl], *adj.* käuflich.

vend [vend], *v.a.* verkaufen; —*ing machine*, der Automat.

veneer [və'niə], *s.* das Furnier. — *v.a.* furnieren.

venerable ['venərəbl], *adj.* ehrwürdig.

venerate ['venəreit], *v.a.* verehren.

venereal [və'niəriəl], *adj.* Geschlechts-.

Venezuelan [veni'zweilən], *adj.* venezolanisch. — *s.* der Venezolaner.

vengeance ['vendʒəns], *s.* die Rache.

venison ['venizn *or* venzn], *s.* das Wildpret.

venom ['venəm], *s.* das Gift.

vent [vent], *v.a.* Luft machen (*Dat.*). — *s.* das Luftloch, die Öffnung.

ventilate ['ventileit], *v.a.* ventilieren, lüften.

ventricle ['ventrikl], *s.* (*Anat.*) die Herzkammer.

ventriloquist [ven'triləkwist], *s.* der Bauchredner.

venture ['ventʃə], *s.* das Wagnis, Unternehmen. — *v.a.* wagen, riskieren. — *v.n.* sich erlauben, (sich) wagen.

venue ['venju:], *s.* der Treffpunkt, Versammlungsort.

veracity [və'ræsiti], *s.* die Glaubwürdigkeit, Wahrhaftigkeit.

verbose [və:'bous], *adj.* wortreich, weitschweifig.

verdant ['və:dənt], *adj.* grünend, grün.

verdict ['və:dikt], *s.* das Urteil, die Entscheidung.

verdigris ['və:digri:s], *s.* der Grünspan.

verdure ['və:djə], *s.* das Grün.

verge [və:dʒ], *s.* der Rand, die Einfassung. — *v.n.* grenzen (*on*, an, *Acc.*).

verify ['verifai], *v.a.* bestätigen; (*Law*) beglaubigen.

verily ['verili], *adv.* (*Bibl.*) wahrlich.

veritable ['veritəbl], *adj.* wahr, echt.

vermicelli [və:mi'seli], *s.* die Nudeln, *f. pl.*

vermilion [və'miljən], *s.* das Zinnober (*paint*).

vermin ['və:min], *s. pl.* das Ungeziefer.

vermouth ['və:mu:θ, -mu:t], *s.* der Wermut.

vernacular [və'nækjulə], *s.* die Landessprache. — *adj.* einheimisch.

vernal ['və:nəl], *adj.* frühlingsartig, Frühlings-.

versatile

versatile [ˈvəːsətail], *adj.* gewandt; vielseitig.

verse [vəːs], *s.* der Vers; (*Poet.*) die Strophe.

versed [vəːsd], *adj.* bewandert.

version [ˈvəːʃən], *s.* die Version, Fassung, Lesart; (*fig.*) die Darstellung.

vertebrate [ˈvəːtibrət], *s.* (*Zool.*) das Wirbeltier. — *adj.* mit Rückenwirbeln versehen.

vertex [ˈvəːteks], *s.* der Zenit.

vertigo [ˈvəːtigou], *s.* (*Med.*) der Schwindel, das Schwindelgefühl.

verve [vəːv], *s.* der Schwung.

very [ˈveri], *adv.* sehr. — *adj.* echt, wirklich, wahrhaftig.

vespers [ˈvespəz], *s. pl.* (*Eccl.*) der Abendgottesdienst, die Vesper.

vessel [vesl], *s.* das Gefäß (*container*); (*Naut.*) das Fahrzeug, Schiff.

vest [vest], *s.* das Gewand; (*Tail.*) die Weste; das Unterhemd (*undergarment*). — *v.a.* übertragen.

vested [ˈvestid], *adj.* — *interests*, das Eigeninteresse.

vestige [ˈvestidʒ], *s.* die Spur.

vestment [ˈvestmənt], *s.* (*Eccl.*) das Meßgewand.

vestry [ˈvestri], *s.* (*Eccl.*) die Sakristei.

vetch [vetʃ], *s.* (*Bot.*) die Wicke.

veterinary [ˈvetərinri], *adj.* tierärztlich; — *surgeon*, der Tierarzt.

veto [ˈviːtou], *s.* (*Pol.*) der Einspruch, das Veto.

vex [veks], *v.a.* quälen, plagen.

vexation [vekˈseiʃən], *s.* die Plage, der Verdruß.

via [vaiə], *prep.* über.

vibrate [vaiˈbreit], *v.n.* schwingen, vibrieren.

vicar [ˈvikə], *s.* (*Eccl.*) der Pfarrer, Vikar.

vicarious [viˈkɛəriəs], *adj.* stellvertretend.

vice (1) [vais], *s.* das Laster (*immorality*).

vice (2) [vais], *s.* (*Mech.*) der Schraubstock.

vice- [vais], *pref.* Vize-, zweiter (*chairman etc.*).

vicinity [viˈsiniti], *s.* die Nachbarschaft, Nähe.

vicious [ˈviʃəs], *adj.* böse, bösartig.

vicissitude [viˈsisitjuːd], *s.* der Wechsel, Wandel; (*pl.*) Wechselfälle, *m. pl.*

victim [ˈviktim], *s.* das Opfer.

victuals [vitlz], *s. pl.* die Lebensmittel, *n. pl.*

vie [vai], *v.n.* wetteifern.

Vietnamese [vjetnəˈmiːz], *adj.* vietnamesisch. — *s.* der Vietnamese.

view [vjuː], *s.* der Anblick, die Aussicht (*panorama*); die Ansicht (*opinion*); die Absicht (*intention*). — *v.a.* betrachten; besichtigen (*inspect*).

vigil [ˈvidʒil], *s.* die Nachtwache.

vigilance [ˈvidʒiləns], *s.* die Wachsamkeit.

vigorous [ˈvigərəs], *adj.* kräftig, rüstig, energisch.

vigour [ˈvigə], *s.* die Kraft, Energie.

vile [vail], *adj.* schlecht, niedrig.

vilify [ˈvilifai], *v.a.* beschimpfen, erniedrigen.

villa [ˈvilə], *s.* das Landhaus, die Villa.

village [ˈvilidʒ], *s.* das Dorf.

villain [ˈvilən], *s.* der Schurke.

villainous [ˈvilənəs], *adj.* niederträchtig.

villainy [ˈviləni], *s.* die Niedertracht, Schändlichkeit.

vindicate [ˈvindikeit], *v.a.* behaupten, verteidigen; rechtfertigen (*justify*).

vindictive [vinˈdiktiv], *adj.* rachsüchtig.

vine [vain], *s.* (*Bot.*) der Weinstock, die Rebe.

vinegar [ˈvinigə], *s.* der Essig.

vintage [ˈvintidʒ], *s.* die Weinernte; der Jahrgang (*also fig.*).

vintner [ˈvintnə], *s.* der Weinbauer, Winzer.

viola [viˈoulə], *s.* (*Mus.*) die Viola, Bratsche.

violate [ˈvaiəleit], *v.a.* verletzen, schänden.

violence [ˈvaiələns], *s.* die Gewalt; die Gewalttätigkeit.

violent [ˈvaiələnt], *adj.* gewalttätig (*brutal*); heftig (*vehement*).

violet [ˈvaiəlit], *s.* (*Bot.*) das Veilchen. — *adj.* veilchenblau, violett.

violin [vaiəˈlin], *s.* (*Mus.*) die Violine, Geige.

viper [ˈvaipə], *s.* (*Zool.*) die Viper, Natter.

virago [viˈrɑːgou], *s.* das Mannweib.

virgin [ˈvəːdʒin], *s.* die Jungfrau.

virile [ˈvirail], *adj.* männlich, kräftig.

virtual [ˈvəːtjuəl], *adj.* eigentlich.

virtue [ˈvəːtjuː], *s.* die Tugend; *by* — *of*, kraft (*Genit.*).

virtuoso [vəːtjuˈousou], *s.* der Virtuose.

virtuous [ˈvəːtjuəs], *adj.* tugendhaft.

virulent [ˈvirulənt], *adj.* bösartig, giftig.

virus [ˈvaiərəs], *s.* (*Med.*) das Gift, Virus.

viscosity [visˈkɔsiti], *s.* die Zähigkeit, Zähflüssigkeit.

viscount [ˈvaikaunt], *s.* der Vicomte.

viscous [ˈviskəs], *adj.* zähflüssig, klebrig.

visibility [viziˈbiliti], *s.* die Sichtbarkeit, Sicht.

visible [ˈvizibl], *adj.* sichtbar.

vision [ˈviʒən], *s.* die Sehkraft; (*fig.*) die Vision (*dream*); die Erscheinung (*apparition*).

visionary [ˈviʒnri], *s.* der Träumer, (*Poet.*) der Seher. — *adj.* visionär, phantastisch, seherisch.

visit [ˈvizit], *s.* der Besuch. — *v.a.* besuchen.

visitation [viziˈteiʃən], *s.* die Heimsuchung.

visor [ˈvaizə], *s.* das Visier.

vista [ˈvistə], *s.* (*Art*) die Aussicht, der Ausblick.

visual [ˈviʒuəl], *adj.* visuell, Seh-.

vital [vaitl], *adj.* lebenswichtig; (*fig.*) wesentlich.

vitality [vaiˈtæliti], *s.* die Lebenskraft, Vitalität.

vitiate ['viʃieit], v.a. verderben, umstoßen.

vitreous ['vitriəs], adj. gläsern, glasartig.

vitrify ['vitrifai], v.a. verglasen.

vivacious [vi'veiʃəs], adj. lebhaft, munter.

viva (voce) ['vaivə ('vousi)], s. die mündliche Prüfung.

vivacity [vi'væsiti], s. die Lebhaftigkeit.

vivid ['vivid], adj. lebhaft.

vixen ['viksən], s. (Zool.) die Füchsin; (fig.) das zänkische Weib.

vizier [vi'ziə], s. der Wesir.

vocabulary [vo'kæbjuləri], s. das Vokabular; der Wortschatz.

vocal ['voukəl], adj. laut; (Mus.) Stimm-, Sing-.

vocation [vo'keiʃən], s. die Berufung (call); der Beruf (occupation).

vociferous [vo'sifərəs], adj. schreiend, laut.

vogue [voug], s. die Mode.

voice [vɔis], s. die Stimme.

void [vɔid], adj. leer (empty); ungültig, (invalid); null and —, null und nichtig. — s. die Leere.

volatile ['vɔlətail], adj. flüchtig.

volcanic [vɔl'kænik], adj. vulkanisch.

volcano [vɔl'keinou], s. der Vulkan.

volition [və'liʃən], s. der Wille.

volley ['vɔli], s. (Mil.) die Salve; (Footb.) der Volleyschuß; (Tennis) der Flugball.

volt [voult], s. (Elec.) das Volt.

voltage ['voultidʒ], s. die Spannung.

voluble ['vɔljubl], adj. gesprächig, zungenfertig.

volume ['vɔlju:m], s. (Phys.) das Volumen; der Band (book); (fig.) der Umfang.

voluminous [və'lju:minəs], adj. umfangreich.

voluntary ['vɔləntri], adj. freiwillig. — s. (Mus.) das Orgelsolo.

volunteer [vɔlən'tiə], s. der Freiwillige. — v.n. sich freiwillig melden.

voluptuous [və'lʌptjuəs], adj. wollüstig, lüstern.

vomit ['vɔmit], v.a., v.n. (sich) erbrechen, übergeben.

voracious [vo'reiʃəs], adj. gierig, gefräßig.

vortex ['vɔ:teks], s. der Wirbel, Strudel.

vote [vout], v.n. (Pol.) wählen, abstimmen, die Stimme abgeben. — s. (Pol.) die Stimme.

voter ['voutə], s. der Wähler.

votive ['voutiv], adj. (Eccl.) geweiht, gelobt; Votiv-.

vouch [vautʃ], v.a., v.n. (sich) verbürgen, einstehen(für).

voucher ['vautʃə], s. der Beleg; (Comm.) der Gutschein.

vouchsafe [vautʃ'seif], v.a. bewilligen, gewähren. — v.n. geruhen, sich herablassen.

vow [vau], s. das Gelübde. — v.a. schwören, geloben.

vowel ['vauəl], s. der Vokal.

voyage ['vɔiidʒ], s. die Seereise. — v.n. zur See reisen.

vulcanize ['vʌlkənaiz], v.a. vulkanisieren.

vulgar ['vʌlgə], adj. gemein, pöbelhaft, ordinär, vulgär.

vulnerable ['vʌlnərəbl], adj. verwundbar, verletzbar.

vulture ['vʌltʃə], s. (Orn.) der Geier.

W

W ['dʌblju:]. das W.

wabble see **wobble**.

wad [wɔd], s. das Bündel (notes); der Bausch (cotton wool).

waddle [wɔdl], v.n. watscheln.

wade [weid], v.n. waten, durchwaten.

wafer ['weifə], s. die Oblate, die Waffel; (Eccl.) die Hostie.

waffle [wɔfl], s. (Cul.) die Waffel. — v.n. (coll.) schwafeln.

waft [wæft], v.a. wegwehen.

wag (1) [wæg], v.a. wedeln, schütteln.

wag (2) [wæg], s. der Spaßvogel.

wage (1) [weidʒ], v.a. unternehmen; — war, Krieg führen.

wage (2) ['weidʒ], s. (often in pl.) der Lohn.

wager ['weidʒə], v.a. wetten. — s. die Wette.

waggish ['wægiʃ], adj. spaßhaft, mutwillig, schelmisch.

wag(g)on ['wægən], s. der Wagen, Güterwagen.

wagtail ['wægteil], s. (Orn.) die Bachstelze.

waif [weif], s. das verwahrloste Kind; das herrenlose Gut.

wail [weil], v.n. wehklagen. — s. das Wehklagen, die Klage.

waist [weist], s. (Anat.) die Taille.

waistcoat ['weiskout, 'weskət], s. die Weste, das Wams.

wait [weit], v.n. warten; — for, warten auf; — upon, bedienen. — v.a. erwarten.

waiter ['weitə], s. der Kellner; head —, der Oberkellner, (coll.) der Ober.

waiting room ['weitiŋ rum], s. das Wartezimmer; (Railw.) der Wartesaal.

waive [weiv], v.a. aufgeben, verzichten (auf, Acc.).

wake (1) [weik], v.n. irr. wachen, aufwachen, wach sein. — v.a. aufwecken.

wake (2) [weik], s. (Naut.) das Kielwasser; (fig.) die Spur; in the — of, in den Fußstapfen (Genit.).

waken ['weikən], v.a. aufwecken. — v.n. aufwachen.

walk [wɔ:k], v.n. (zu Fuß) gehen. — s. der Gang (gait); der Spaziergang.

wall

wall [wɔːl], s. die Wand, Mauer.
wallet ['wɔlit], s. die Brieftasche.
wallflower ['wɔːlflauə], s. (Bot.) der Goldlack; (fig.) das Mauerblümchen.
wallow ['wɔlou], v.n. schwelgen; sich wälzen.
walnut ['wɔːlnʌt], s. (Bot.) die Walnuß.
walrus ['wɔːlrəs], s. (Zool.) das Walroß.
waltz [wɔːlts], s. der Walzer.
wan [wɔn], adj. blaß, bleich.
wand [wɔnd], s. der Stab.
wander ['wɔndə], v.n. wandern, durchwandern; (fig.) — from the subject, vom Thema abkommen.
wane [wein], v.n. abnehmen, verfallen.
want [wɔnt], v.a. brauchen, wollen, nötig haben, wünschen. — v.n. mangeln, fehlen. — s. die Not.
wanton ['wɔntən], adj. mutwillig, ausgelassen.
war [wɔː], s. der Krieg.
warble [wɔːbl], v.a., v.n. singen; (Mus.) trillern.
warbler ['wɔːblə], s. (Orn.) der Singvogel.
ward [wɔːd], s. die Verwahrung; das or der Mündel (child in care); (Pol.) der Wahlbezirk; die Station (hospital). — v.a. — off, abwehren.
warden [wɔːdn], s. der Vorstand, Vorsteher; Rektor.
warder ['wɔːdə], s. der Wächter; (in prison) der Wärter, Gefängniswärter.
wardrobe ['wɔːdroub], s. der Kleiderschrank.
ware [wɛə], s. die Ware.
warehouse ['wɛəhaus], s. das Warenlager.
warfare ['wɔːfɛə], s. der Krieg, die Kriegsführung.
warlike ['wɔːlaik], adj. kriegerisch.
warm [wɔːm], adj. warm.
warn [wɔːn], v.a. warnen, ermahnen.
warning ['wɔːniŋ], s. die Warnung.
warp [wɔːp], v.a. krümmen, verziehen (of wood); (fig.) verderben; verzerren, verdrehen. — v.n. sich werfen, krümmen.
warrant ['wɔrənt], s. (Law) der Haftbefehl; — officer, der Unteroffizier; (Comm.) die Vollmacht, Bürgschaft. — v.a. garantieren (vouch for); versichern (assure).
warranty ['wɔrənti], s. (Law) die Gewähr; Garantie.
warren ['wɔrən], s. das Gehege.
warrior ['wɔriə], s. der Krieger.
wart [wɔːt], s. (Med.) die Warze.
wary ['wɛəri], adj. vorsichtig, achtsam (careful).
wash [wɔʃ], v.a., v.n. (sich) waschen; — up, spülen, abwaschen. — s. die Wäsche (laundry).
wasp [wɔsp], s. (Ent.) die Wespe.
waspish ['wɔspiʃ], adj. reizbar, zänkisch, bissig.
wassail ['wɔsl], s. das Trinkgelage. — v.n. zechen.
waste [weist], v.a. zerstören, verwüsten;

verschwenden. — adj. wüst, öde. — s. die Verschwendung (process); der Abfall (product); — paper, die Makulatur; — paper basket, der Papierkorb.
wasteful ['weistful], adj. verschwenderisch.
watch [wɔtʃ], v.a. bewachen; beobachten (observe); hüten (guard). — s. die Wache (guard); die Uhr, Taschenuhr (time-piece).
watchful ['wɔtʃful], adj. wachsam.
watchman ['wɔtʃmən], s. der Nachtwächter.
water ['wɔːtə], s. das Wasser; (pl.) die Kur; — colour, das Aquarell; — gauge, der Pegel. — v.a. wässern; begießen (flowers).
watercress ['wɔːtəkres], s. (Bot.) die Brunnenkresse.
waterproof ['wɔːtəpruːf], adj. wasserdicht.
watt [wɔt], s. (Elec.) das Watt.
wattle [wɔtl], s. (Bot.) die Hürde.
wave [weiv], s. die Welle; permanent —, die Dauerwelle. — v.n. zuwinken (Dat.); wehen; winken. — v.a. schwenken (handkerchief).
waver ['weivə], v.n. schwanken, unentschlossen sein.
wax [wæks], s. das Wachs, der Siegellack. — v.a. wachsen, bohnern.
waxen [wæksn], adj. aus Wachs, wächsern.
way [wei], s. der Weg (road etc.); die Strecke; Richtung; in no —, keineswegs; (pl.) die Art und Weise; Milky Way, die Milchstraße.
wayward ['weiwəd], adj. eigensinnig.
we [wiː], pers. pron. wir.
weak [wiːk], adj. schwach, kraftlos.
weaken ['wiːkən], v.a. schwächen. — v.n. schwach werden.
weakling ['wiːkliŋ], s. der Schwächling.
wealth [welθ], s. der Wohlstand, Reichtum.
wealthy ['welθi], adj. wohlhabend, reich.
wean [wiːn], v.a. entwöhnen.
weapon ['wepən], s. die Waffe.
wear [wɛə], v.a. irr. tragen (clothes). — v.n. — off, sich abnagen, schäbig werden; — out, sich erschöpfen. — s. die Abnutzung.
weariness ['wiərinis], s. die Müdigkeit, der Überdruß.
weary ['wiəri], adj. müde, überdrüssig.
weasel [wiːzl], s. (Zool.) das Wiesel.
weather ['weðə], s. das Wetter. — v.a. überstehen. — v.n. (Geol.) verwittern.
weatherbeaten ['weðəbiːtn], adj. abgehärtet, wetterhart.
weathercock ['weðəkɔk], s. der Wetterhahn; (fig.) wetterwendischer Mensch.
weave [wiːv], v.a. irr. (Text.) weben, — s. das Gewebe.
web [web], s. das Gewebe.
wed [wed], v.a. heiraten; trauen (a couple). — v.n. (sich ver)heiraten.
wedding ['wediŋ], s. die Hochzeit; Trauung (ceremony).

wedge [wedʒ], *s.* der Keil. — *v.a.* keilen.

wedlock ['wedlɔk], *s.* die Ehe.

Wednesday ['wenzd(e)i]. der Mittwoch.

wee [wi:], *adj.* (*Scot.*) winzig, klein.

weed [wi:d], *s.* das Unkraut. — *v.a.* ausjäten, jäten.

week [wi:k], *s.* die Woche.

weep [wi:p], *v.n. irr.* weinen; *—ing willow,* die Trauerweide.

weigh [wei], *v.a.* wiegen, wägen; (*fig.*) abwägen, beurteilen; (*Naut.*) — *anchor,* den Anker lichten. — *v.n.* wiegen.

weighing machine ['weiiŋ mə'ʃi:n], *s.* die Waage.

weight [weit], *s.* das Gewicht; *gross —,* das Bruttogewicht; *net —,* das Nettogewicht.

weighty ['weiti], *adj.* (ge)wichtig; (*fig.*) schwer.

weir [wiə], *s.* das Wehr.

weird [wiəd], *adj.* unheimlich.

welcome ['welkəm], *adj.* willkommen. — *s.* der *or* das Willkommen. — *v.a.* willkommen heißen, begrüßen.

weld [weld], *v.a.* schweißen.

welfare ['welfɛə], *s.* die Wohlfahrt, soziale Fürsorge.

well (1) [wel], *s.* der Brunnen. — *v.n.* hervorsprudeln.

well (2) [wel], *adv.* gut, wohl; durchaus; — *bred,* wohlerzogen. — *pred. adj.* gesund, wohl.

Welsh [welʃ], *adj.* walisisch. — *s. pl.* die Waliser, *m.pl.*

Welshman ['welʃmən], *s.* der Waliser.

welt [welt], *s.* der Rand, die Einfassung.

welter ['weltə], *s.* die Masse, das Chaos. — *v.n.* sich wälzen.

wen [wen], *s.* (*Med.*) die Schwellung.

wench [wentʃ], *s.* die Magd, das Mädchen.

west [west], *s.* der Westen. — *adj.* (*also* **westerly, western** ['westəli, 'westən]) westlich.

Westphalian [west'feiliən], *adj.* westfälisch. — *s.* der Westfale.

wet [wet], *adj.* naß, feucht; — *paint,* frisch gestrichen. — *v.a.* anfeuchten, benetzen, naß machen.

whack [hwæk], *v.a.* durchprügeln. — *s.* die Tracht Prügel, der Schlag.

whale [hweil], *s.* (*Zool.*) der Walfisch.

whalebone ['hweilboun], *s.* das Fischbein.

wharf [hwɔ:f], *s.* der Kai.

wharfinger ['hwɔ:findʒə], *s.* der Kaimeister.

what [hwɔt], *rel. & interr. pron.* was; welcher, welche, welches; was für.

what(so)ever [hwɔt(sou)'evə], *rel. pron.* was auch immer. — *adj.* einerlei welche-r, -s, -n.

wheat [hwi:t], *s.* (*Bot.*) der Weizen.

wheedle [hwi:dl], *v.a.* beschwatzen.

wheel [hwi:l], *s.* das Rad; die Umdrehung, Drehung. — *v.a., v.n.* drehen, sich drehen, schieben.

wheelbarrow ['hwi:lbærou], *s.* der Schubkarren.

wheeze [hwi:z], *v.n.* keuchen, schnaufen. — *s.* das Keuchen.

whelp [hwelp], *s.* (*Zool.*) das Junge, der junge Hund. — *v.n.* Junge werfen.

when [hwen], *adv.* (*interr.*) wann? — *conj.* als (*in past*), wenn, während.

whence [hwens], *adv.* woher, von wo.

where [hwɛə], *adv.* wo, wohin; (*interr.*) wo? wohin?

whereabout(s) ['hwɛərəbaut(s)], *adv.* wo, wo etwa. — *s.* (**whereabouts**) der zeitweilige Aufenthalt *or* Wohnort.

whereas [hwɛər'æz], *conj.* wohingegen, während.

whereupon [hwɛərə'pɔn], *conj.* woraufhin.

wherewithal ['hwɛəwiðɔ:l], *s.* die gesamte Habe, das Nötige. — *adv.* (*obs.*) womit.

whet [hwet], *v.a.* wetzen, schleifen.

whether ['hweðə], *conj.* ob.

whey [hwei], *s.* die Molke.

which [hwitʃ], *rel. & interr. pron.* welcher, welche, welches; der, die, das.

whiff [hwif], *s.* der Hauch, Luftzug.

while [hwail], *s.* die Weile, Zeit. — *v.a.* — *away the time,* dahinbringen, vertreiben. — *conj.* (*also* **whilst**) während, so lange als.

whim [hwim], *s.* die Laune, Grille.

whimper ['hwimpə], *v.n.* winseln.

whimsical ['hwimzikəl], *adj.* grillenhaft.

whine [hwain], *v.n.* weinen, wimmern, klagen. — *s.* das Gewimmer, Gejammer.

whinny ['hwini], *v.n.* wiehern.

whip [hwip], *s.* die Peitsche; (*Pol.*) der Einpeitscher. — *v.a.* peitschen.

whir [hwə:], *v.n.* schwirren. — *s.* das Schwirren.

whirl [hwə:l], *s.* der Wirbel, Strudel. — *v.a., v.n.* wirbeln.

whirligig ['hwə:ligig], *s.* der Karussel.

whirlpool ['hwə:lpu:l], *s.* der Strudel.

whirr *see* whir.

whisk [hwisk], *v.a.* fegen; schlagen; —*away or off,* schnell wegtun (*a th.*), schnell fortnehmen (*a p.*). — *v.n.* — *away,* dahinhuschen. — *s.* der Schläger.

whiskers ['hwiskəz], *s.* der Backenbart, Bart.

whisky ['hwiski], *s.* der Whisky.

whisper ['hwispə], *s.* das Geflüster. *v.a., v.n.* flüstern.

whistle [hwisl], *s.* die Pfeife (*instrument*); der Pfiff (*sound*). — *v.a., v.n.* pfeifen.

whit [hwit], *s.* die Kleinigkeit; *not a —,* nicht im geringsten.

white [hwait], *adj.* weiß; — *lead,* das Bleiweiß; — *lie,* die Notlüge.

whitebait ['hwaitbeit], *s.* (*Zool.*) der Breitling.

whiten [hwaitn], *v.a.* weißen, bleichen.

whitewash ['hwaitwɔʃ], *s.* die Tünche. — *v.a.* reinwaschen.

whither

whither ['hwiðə], *adv.* wohin; dahin wo.

whiting ['hwaitiŋ], *s.* (*Zool.*) der Weißfisch; die Schlämmkreide (*chalk*).

whitlow ['hwitlou], *s.* (*Med.*) das Nagelgeschwür.

Whitsun(tide) ['hwitsən(taid)], *s.* (das) Pfingsten; *Whit Sunday*, der Pfingstsonntag.

whittle [hwitl], *v.a.* schnitzen, abschaben.

whiz [hwiz], *v.n.* zischen; (*fig.*) vorbeiflitzen.

who [hu:], *interr. pron.* wer?, welcher?, welche? — *rel. pron.* welcher, welche, welches, der, die, das.

whoever [hu:'evə], *rel. pron.* wer auch immer.

whole [houl], *adj.* ganz, völlig. — *s.* das Ganze.

wholesale ['houlseil], *adv.* im Engros. — *adj.* Engros-, Großhandels-.

wholesome ['houlsəm], *adj.* gesund.

whoop [hu:p], *s.* das Geschrei; — *v.n.* laut keuchen; —*ing cough*, der Keuchhusten.

whortleberry ['hwə:tlbəri], *s.* (*Bot.*) die Heidelbeere.

whose [hu:z], *pron.* wessen, dessen, deren.

whosoever [hu:sou'evə] *see* **whoever.**

why [hwai], *rel. & interr. adv.* warum?

wick [wik], *s.* der Docht.

wicked ['wikid], *adj.* böse, schlecht.

wicker ['wikə], *adj.* Rohr-, geflochten.

wicket ['wikit], *s.* das Pförtchen.

wide [waid], *adj.* weit, breit; (*fig.*) umfangreich, groß, reich(*experience*). — *adv. far and* —, weit und breit; — *awake*, völlig wach.

widen [waidn], *v.a.,* erweitern.

widgeon ['widʒən], *s.* die Pfeifente.

widow ['widou], *s.* die Witwe.

widower ['widouə], *s.* der Witwer.

width [widθ], *s.* die Weite, Breite.

wield [wi:ld], *v.a.* schwingen; — *power*, die Macht ausüben.

wife [waif], *s.* die Frau, Gattin.

wig [wig], *s.* die Perücke.

wild [waild], *adj.* wild.

wilderness ['wildənis], *s.* die Wildnis.

wildfire ['waildfaiə], *s.* das Lauffeuer.

wilful ['wilful], *adj.* absichtlich; vorsätzlich.

wiliness ['wailinis], *s.* die Schlauheit, Arglist.

will [wil], *s.* der Wille; (*Law*) der letzte Wille, das Testament. — *v.n.* wollen. — *v.a.* (*Law*) vermachen, hinterlassen.

willing ['wiliŋ], *adj.* bereitwillig.

will-o'-the-wisp [wiləðə'wisp], *s.* das Irrlicht.

willow ['wilou], *s.* (*Bot.*) die Weide.

wily ['waili], *adj.* schlau, verschmitzt.

wimple [wimpl], *s.* der Schleier.

win [win], *v.a., v.n.* *irr.* gewinnen, siegen, erringen.

wince [wins], *v.n.* zucken, zusammenzucken.

winch [wintʃ], *s.* die Kurbel, Winde.

wind (1) [wind], *s.* der Wind; der Atem (*breath*); *get* — *of s.th.*, von etwas hören.

wind (2) [waind], *v.a. irr.* winden; wenden, drehen (*turn*); — (*up*), aufziehen (*timepiece*); — *up*, (*business, debate*) beenden. — *v.n.* sich schlängeln, winden.

windfall ['windfɔ:l], *s.* das Fallobst (*fruit*); (*fig.*) der Glücksfall.

windlass ['windləs], *s.* die Winde.

window ['windou], *s.* das Fenster; — *sill*, das Fensterbrett.

windpipe ['windpaip], *s.* (*Anat.*) die Luftröhre.

windscreen ['windskri:n], *s.* (*Motor.*) die Windschutzscheibe.

windshield ['windʃi:ld] (*Am.*) *see* **windscreen.**

windy ['windi], *adj.* windig.

wine [wain], *s.* der Wein; — *merchant*, der Weinhändler.

wing [wiŋ], *s.* der Flügel; (*Poet.*) die Schwinge.

wink [wiŋk], *s.* das Zwinkern; der Augenblick. — *v.n.* blinzeln, zwinkern.

winner ['winə], *s.* der Sieger, Gewinner.

winning ['winiŋ], *adj.* einnehmend.

winsome ['winsəm], *adj.* reizend, einnehmend.

winter ['wintə], *s.* der Winter.

wintry ['wintri], *adj.* winterlich.

wipe [waip], *v.a.* wischen, abwischen.

wire [waiə], *s.* der Draht; (*coll.*) das Telegramm; *barbed* —, der Stacheldraht. — *v.a.* verbinden; (*fig.*) telegraphieren. — *v.n.* telegraphieren.

wireless ['waiəlis], *s.* das Radio. — *adj.* drahtlos.

wirepuller ['waiəpulə], *s.* der Puppenspieler; (*fig.*) der Intrigant.

wiry ['waiəri], *adj.* zäh, stark.

wisdom ['wizdəm], *s.* die Weisheit.

wise [waiz], *adj.* weise, verständig, klug.

wiseacre ['waizeikə], *s.* der Allzuschlaue, Naseweis.

wish [wiʃ], *v.a., v.n.* wünschen. — *s.* der Wunsch.

wistful ['wistful], *adj.* nachdenklich (*pensive*); wehmütig (*sad*).

wit [wit], *s.* der Witz; Geist; Verstand; der witzige Mensch; der Witzbold.

witch [witʃ], *s.* die Hexe, Zauberin.

witchcraft ['witʃkra:ft], *s.* die Zauberkunst, Hexerei.

with [wið], *prep.* mit, mitsamt, bei, durch, von.

withal [wi'ðɔ:l], *adv.* obendrein.

withdraw [wið'drɔ:], *v.a., v.n. irr.* (sich) zurückziehen; widerrufen; abheben (*money from bank*).

withdrawal [wið'drɔ:əl], *s.* der Rückzug; (*Comm. etc.*) die Widerrufung; Abhebung (*bank*).

wither ['wiðə], *v.a.* welk machen. — *v.n.* verwelken; ausdorren, verdorren (*dry up*); (*fig.*) vergehen.

withhold [wið'hould], *v.a. irr.* zurückhalten, vorenthalten.

516

within [wi'ðin], *prep.* innerhalb; (*time*) binnen (*Genit.*). — *adv.* darin, drinnen.

without [wi'ðaut], *prep.* ohne; (*obs.*) außerhalb (*outside*); *do* —, entbehren. — *adv.* draußen, außen.

withstand [wið'stænd], *v.a. irr.* widerstehen (*Dat.*).

withy ['wiði], *s.* der Weidenzweig.

witless ['witlis], *adj.* einfältig.

witness ['witnis], *s.* der Zeuge. — *v.a.* bezeugen, Zeuge sein von. — *v.n.* zeugen, Zeuge sein.

witticism ['witisizm], *s.* das Bonmot, die witzige Bemerkung.

witty ['witi], *adj.* witzig, geistreich.

wizard ['wizəd], *s.* der Zauberer.

wizened ['wizənd], *adj.* verwelkt, vertrocknet, runzlig.

wobble [wɔbl], *v.n.* wackeln.

woe [wou], *s.* (*Poet.*) das Weh, Leid.

wolf [wulf], *s.* (*Zool.*) der Wolf.

woman ['wumən], *s.* die Frau, das Weib.

womanly ['wumənli], *adj.* weiblich.

womb [wu:m], *s.* der Mutterleib, Schoß; (*Anat.*) die Gebärmutter.

wonder ['wʌndə], *s.* das Wunder. — *v.n.* sich wundern (*be amazed*); gern wissen mögen (*like to know*); sich fragen.

wonderful ['wʌndəful], *adj.* wunderbar.

wondrous ['wʌndrəs], *adj.* (*Poet.*) wunderbar.

wont [wount], *s.* die Gewohnheit. — *pred. adj.* gewohnt.

won't [wount] = **will not**.

woo [wu:], *v.a.* freien, werben (um).

wood [wud], *s.* das Holz (*timber*); der Wald (*forest*).

woodbine ['wudbain], *s.* das Geißblatt.

woodcock ['wudkɔk], *s.* (*Orn.*) die Waldschnepfe.

woodcut ['wudkʌt], *s.* (*Art*) der Holzschnitt.

wooded ['wudid], *adj.* bewaldet.

wooden [wudn], *adj.* hölzern, Holz–.

woodlark ['wudla:k], *s.* (*Orn.*) die Heidelerche.

woodpecker ['wudpekə], *s.* (*Orn.*) der Specht.

woodruff ['wudrʌf], *s.* (*Bot.*) der Waldmeister.

woof [wu:f], *s.* (*Text.*) der Einschlag, das Gewebe.

wool [wul], *s.* die Wolle; — *gathering*, zerstreut.

woollen ['wulən], *adj.* wollen, aus Wolle.

woolly ['wuli], *adj.* wollig; (*fig.*) unklar, verschwommen.

word [wə:d], *s.* das Wort; *send* —, Botschaft senden. — *v.a.* ausdrücken.

wording ['wə:diŋ], *s.* die Fassung, der Stil.

work [wə:k], *s.* die Arbeit; *out of* —, arbeitslos; das Werk (*opus*); (*pl.*) die Fabrik. — *v.a., v.n.* arbeiten, bearbeiten; (*engine*) funktionieren.

worker ['wə:kə], *s.* der Arbeiter.

workhouse ['wə:khaus], *s.* das Armenhaus.

workshop ['wə:kʃɔp], *s.* die Werkstatt.

world [wə:ld], *s.* die Welt.

worldly ['wə:ldli], *adj.* weltlich, zeitlich.

worm [wə:m], *s.* (*Zool.*) der Wurm. — *v.a.* — *o.'s way*, sich einschleichen. — *v.n.* sich einschleichen.

wormeaten ['wə:mi:tn], *adj.* wurmstichig.

worry ['wʌri], *v.a., v.n.* plagen, quälen, sorgen, ängstigen; sich beunruhigen; *don't* —, bitte machen Sie sich keine Mühe. — *s.* die Plage, Mühe, Qual, Sorge (*about*, um, *Acc.*).

worse [wə:s], *comp. adj., adv.* schlechter, schlimmer.

worship ['wə:ʃip], *s.* die Verehrung; der Gottesdienst (*divine* —).

worst [wə:st], *superl. adj.* schlechtest, schlimmst. — *adv.* am schlimmsten *or* schlechtesten. — *s.* das Schlimmste.

worsted ['wustid], *s.* (*Text.*) das Kammgarn.

worth [wə:θ], *adj.* wert. — *s.* der Wert.

worthy ['wə:ði], *adj.* würdig, wert, verdient.

would [wud] *past tense of* **will**, *q.v.*

wound [wu:nd], *s.* die Wunde. — *v.a.* verwunden.

wraith [reiθ], *s.* das Gespenst.

wrangle [ræŋgl], *v.n.* zanken, streiten. — *s.* der Zank, Streit.

wrap [ræp], *v.a.* einwickeln, einhüllen. — *s.* (*Am.*) der Mantel (*coat*), Pelz (*fur*), Schal (*stole*).

wrapper ['ræpə], *s.* der Umschlag, die Hülle.

wrath [rɔ:θ], *s.* der Zorn, Grimm.

wreak ‚[ri:k], *v.a.* (*Lit.*) auslassen, üben.

wreath [ri:θ], *s.* der Kranz.

wreathe [ri:ð], *v.a.* winden, bekränzen.

wreck [rek], *s.* der Schiffbruch; das Wrack (*debris*). — *v.a.* zerstören, zertrümmern, (*fig.*) verderben.

wren [ren], *s.* (*Orn.*) der Zaunkönig.

wrench [rentʃ], *v.a.* entreißen (*tear from*); verdrehen. — *s.* heftiger Ruck; (*fig.*) der (Trennungs)schmerz.

wrest [rest], *v.a.* zerren.

wrestle [resl], *v.n.* ringen, im Ringkampf kämpfen.

wrestling ['resliŋ], *s.* der Ringkampf.

wretch [retʃ], *s.* der Schuft, Lump (*scoundrel*).

wretched ['retʃid], *adj.* elend.

wriggle [rigl], *v.n.* sich winden, schlängeln.

wring [riŋ], *v.a. irr.* auswinden, ausringen.

wrinkle [riŋkl], *s.* die Hautfalte, Runzel. — *v.a.* runzeln (*brow*); rümpfen (*nose*).

wrist [rist], *s.* (*Anat.*) das Handgelenk.

wristwatch ['ristwɔtʃ], *s.* die Armbanduhr.

writ [rit], *s.* die Schrift; (*Law*) die Vorladung.

write

write [rait], *v.a.*, *v.n. irr.* schreiben, verfassen.
writer ['raitə], *s.* der Schreiber; (*Lit.*) der Schriftsteller.
writhe [raið], *v.n.* sich winden.
writing ['raitiŋ], *s.* die Schrift; der Stil (*style*).
wrong [rɔŋ], *adj.* falsch, verkehrt; *to be* —, unrecht haben. — *s.* das Unrecht. — *v.a.* Unrecht *or* Schaden tun (*Dat.*).
wrongful ['rɔŋful], *adj.* unrechtmäßig.
wrongheaded [rɔŋ'hedid], *adj.* querköpfig.
wroth [rouθ], *adj.* (*Lit.*) zornig.
wrought [rɔːt], *adj.* (*work*) gearbeitet; — *iron*, das Schmiedeeisen.
wry [rai], *adj.* verkehrt, krumm, schief, verdreht.

X

X [eks]. das X.
X-ray ['eksrei], *s.* (der) Röntgenstrahl.
xylophone ['zailəfoun], *s.* (*Mus.*) das Xylophon.

Y

Y [wai]. das Y, Ypsilon.
yacht [jɔt], *s.* (*Naut.*) die Jacht.
yachtsman ['jɔtsmən], *s.* (*Naut.*) der Segelsportler.
yap [jæp], *v.n.* kläffen.
yard (1) [jɑːd], *s.* der Hof.
yard (2) [jɑːd], *s.* die englische Elle, der Yard.
yarn [jɑːn], *s.* das Garn; (*coll.*) die Geschichte (*tale*).
yarrow ['jærou], *s.* (*Bot.*) die Schafgarbe.
yawl [jɔːl], *s.* (*Naut.*) die Yawl.
yawn [jɔːn], *v.n.* gähnen. — *s.* das Gähnen.
ye [jiː], *pron.* (*obs.*) *see* you.
year [jə: *or* jiə], *s.* das Jahr; *every other* —, alle zwei Jahre.
yearly ['jiəli], *adj.*, *adv.* jährlich.
yearn [jə:n], *v.n.* sich sehnen (nach, *Dat.*).
yeast [jiːst], *s.* die Hefe.
yell [jel], *v.n.* gellen, schreien. — *s.* der Schrei.
yellow ['jelou], *adj.* gelb; (*sl.*) feige.
yelp [jelp], *v.n.* kläffen, bellen. — *s.* das Gebelle.
yeoman ['joumən], *s.* der Freisasse; (*Mil.*) der Leibgardist (*Yeoman of the Guard*).

yes [jes], *adv.* ja; jawohl.
yesterday ['jestəd(e)i], *adv.* gestern; *the day before* —, vorgestern.
yet [jet], *conj.* doch, dennoch. — *adv.* noch, außerdem; *as* —, bisher; *not* —, noch nicht.
yew [juː], *s.* (*Bot.*) die Eibe.
yield [jiːld], *v.a.* hervorbringen, ergeben; abwerfen (*profit*). — *v.n.* nachgeben (*to, Dat.*). — *s.* der Ertrag.
yoke [jouk], *s.* das Joch (Ochsen). — *v.a.* einspannen, anspannen.
yolk [jouk], *s.* das Eidotter.
yon, yonder [jɔn, 'jɔndə], *dem. adj.* (*obs.*) jener, jene, jenes; der *or* die *or* das da drüben.
yore [jɔː], *adv.* (*obs.*) *of* —, von damals; ehedem.
you [juː], *pers. pron.* du, dich, ihr, euch; (*formal*) sie (*in letters*, Du, Dich *etc.*).
young [jʌŋ], *adj.* jung. — *s.* (*Zool.*) das Junge.
your [juə], *poss. adj.* dein, deine, dein; euer, eure, euer; (*formal*) ihr, ihre, ihr (*in letters* Dein, Euer *etc.*).
yours [jɔːz], *poss. pron.* deinig, eurig; der, die *or* das ihrige (*in letters* Deinig, der Ihrige *etc.*).
yourself [juə'self], *pers. pron.* du selbst, Sie selbst; ihr selbst; dich (selbst), euch (selbst) (*in letters* Du selbst, Dich (selbst) *etc.*).
youth [juːθ], *s.* die Jugend.
youthful ['juːθful], *adj.* jugendlich.
Yugoslav [ju:go'slɑ:v], *adj.* jugoslawisch. — *s.* der Jugoslawe.
Yule, Yuletide [juːl, 'juːltaid], *s.* das Julfest, die Weihnachtszeit.

Z

Z [zed, (*Am.*) ziː]. das Z.
zany ['zeini], *s.* der Hanswurst.
zeal [ziːl], *s.* der Eifer.
zealous ['zeləs], *adj.* eifrig.
zebra ['ziːbrə], *s.* (*Zool.*) das Zebra.
zenith ['zeniθ], *s.* der Zenit, Scheitelpunkt.
zero ['ziərou], *s.* der Nullpunkt, die (Ziffer) Null; — *hour*, die festgesetzte Stunde; festgesetzter Zeitpunkt.
zest [zest], *s.* die Lust; der Genuß; die Würze.
zigzag ['zigzæg], *s.* der Zickzack. — *adj.* Zickzack-.
zinc [ziŋk], *s.* das Zink.
zip(per) ['zip(ə)], *s.* der Reißverschluß (*zip fastener*).
zone [zoun], *s.* die Zone.
zoological gardens [zouə'lɔdʒikəl gɑːdnz], *s.* (*abbr.* **zoo** [zuː]) zoologischer Garten, der Zoo, Tiergarten.

German Irregular Verbs

Infin.	Pres. Indic. 3rd Pers. Sing.	Imperf. Indic.	Imperf. Subj.
backen	bäckt	backte (buk)	backte
befehlen	befiehlt	befahl	beföhle
beginnen	beginnt	begann	begönne
beißen	beißt	biß	bisse
bergen	birgt	barg	bürge
bersten	birst	barst	börste
bewegen	bewegt	bewog	bewöge
biegen	biegt	bog	böge
bieten	bietet	bot	böte
binden	bindet	band	bände
bitten	bittet	bat	bäte
blasen	bläst	blies	bliese
bleiben	bleibt	blieb	bliebe
braten	brät	briet	briete
brechen	bricht	brach	bräche
brennen	brennt	brannte	brennte
bringen	bringt	brachte	brächte
denken	denkt	dachte	dächte
dreschen	drischt	drosch	dräsche
dringen	dringt	drang	dränge
dürfen	darf	durfte	dürfte
empfangen	empfängt	empfing	empfinge
empfehlen	empfiehlt	empfahl	empföhle
empfinden	empfindet	empfand	empfände
erlöschen	erlischt	erlosch	erlösche

German Irregular Verbs

Imper.	Past Participle	English
backe	gebacken	bake
befiehl	befohlen	order, command
beginn(e)	begonnen	begin
beiß(e)	gebissen	bite
birg	geborgen	save, conceal
birst	geborsten	burst
beweg(e)	bewogen	induce
bieg(e)	gebogen	bend
biet(e)	geboten	offer
bind(e)	gebunden	tie, bind
bitte	gebeten	request
blas(e)	geblasen	blow
bleib(e)	geblieben	remain
brat(e)	gebraten	roast
brich	gebrochen	break
brenne	gebrannt	burn
bring(e)	gebracht	bring
denk(e)	gedacht	think
drisch	gedroschen	thrash
dring(e)	gedrungen	press forward
	gedurft	be permitted
empfang(e)	empfangen	receive
empfiehl	empfohlen	(re)commend
empfind(e)	empfunden	feel, perceive
erlisch	erloschen	extinguish

German Irregular Verbs

Infin.	Pres. Indic. 3rd Pers. Sing.	Imperf. Indic.	Imperf. Subj.
erschrecken (*v.n.*)	erschrickt	erschrak	erschräke
essen	ißt	aß	äße
fahren	fährt	fuhr	führe
fallen	fällt	fiel	fiele
fangen	fängt	fing	finge
fechten	ficht	focht	föchte
finden	findet	fand	fände
flechten	flicht	flocht	flöchte
fliegen	fliegt	flog	flöge
fliehen	flieht	floh	flöhe
fließen	fließt	floß	flösse
fressen	frißt	fraß	fräße
frieren	friert	fror	fröre
gebären	gebiert	gebar	gebäre
geben	gibt	gab	gäbe
gedeihen	gedeiht	gedieh	gediehe
gehen	geht	ging	ginge
gelingen (*impers.*)	(mir) gelingt	gelang	gelänge
gelten	gilt	galt	gälte
genesen	genest	genas	genäse
genießen	genießt	genoß	genösse
geschehen (*impers.*)	(mir) geschieht	geschah	geschähe
gewinnen	gewinnt	gewann	gewönne
gießen	gießt	goß	gösse
gleichen	gleicht	glich	gliche
gleiten	gleitet	glitt	glitte
graben	gräbt	grub	grübe
greifen	greift	griff	griffe

German Irregular Verbs

Imper.	Past Participle	English
erschrick	erschrocken	be frightened
iß	gegessen	eat
fahr(e)	gefahren	travel
fall(e)	gefallen	fall
fang(e)	gefangen	catch
ficht	gefochten	fight
find(e)	gefunden	find
flicht	geflochten	twine together
flieg(e)	geflogen	fly
flieh(e)	geflohen	flee
fließ(e)	geflossen	flow
friß	gefressen	eat (of animals)
frier(e)	gefroren	freeze
gebier	geboren	give birth to
gib	gegeben	give
gedeih(e)	gediehen	thrive
geh(e)	gegangen	go
geling(e)	gelungen	succeed
gilt	gegolten	be worth, be valid
genese	genesen	recover
genieß(e)	genossen	enjoy
	geschehen	happen
gewinn(e)	gewonnen	win
gieß(e)	gegossen	pour
gleich(e)	geglichen	equal, resemble
gleit(e)	geglitten	glide
grab(e)	gegraben	dig
greif(e)	gegriffen	grasp

German Irregular Verbs

Infin.	Pres. Indic. 3rd Pers. Sing.	Imperf. Indic.	Imperf. Subj.
haben	hat	hatte	hätte
halten	hält	hielt	hielte
hangen (v.n.)	hängt	hing	hinge
heben	hebt	hob	höbe
heißen	heißt	hieß	hieße
helfen	hilft	half	hülfe
kennen	kennt	kannte	kennte
klimmen	klimmt	klomm	klömme
klingen	klingt	klang	klänge
kneifen	kneift	kniff	kniffe
kommen	kommt	kam	käme
können	kann	konnte	könnte
kriechen	kriecht	kroch	kröche
laden	lädt	lud	lüde
lassen	läßt	ließ	ließe
laufen	läuft	lief	liefe
leiden	leidet	litt	litte
leihen	leiht	lieh	liehe
lesen	liest	las	läse
liegen	liegt	lag	läge
lügen	lügt	log	löge
mahlen	mahlt	mahlte	mahlte
meiden	meidet	mied	miede
messen	mißt	maß	mäße
mißlingen (impers.)	(mir) mißlingt	mißlang	mißlänge
mögen	mag	mochte	möchte
müssen	muß	mußte	müßte
nehmen	nimmt	nahm	nähme

German Irregular Verbs

Imper.	Past Participle	English
habe	gehabt	have
halt(e)	gehalten	hold
häng(e)	gehangen	hang
hebe	gehoben	lift
heiß(e)	geheißen	be called
hilf	geholfen	help
kenn(e)	gekannt	know
klimm(e)	geklommen	climb
kling(e)	geklungen	ring, sound
kneif(e)	gekniffen	pinch
komm(e)	gekommen	come
	gekonnt	be able
kriech(e)	gekrochen	creep
lad(e)	geladen	load
laß	gelassen	let
lauf(e)	gelaufen	run
leid(e)	gelitten	suffer
leih(e)	geliehen	lend
lies	gelesen	read
lieg(e)	gelegen	lie
lüg(e)	gelogen	lie, be untruthful
mahle	gemahlen	grind
meid(e)	gemieden	avoid
miß	gemessen	measure
	mißlungen	fail
	gemocht	wish, be willing
	gemußt	have to
nimm	genommen	take

German Irregular Verbs

Infin.	Pres. Indic. 3rd Pers. Sing.	Imperf. Indic.	Imperf. Subj.
nennen	nennt	nannte	nennte
pfeifen	pfeift	pfiff	pfiffe
preisen	preist	pries	priese
quellen (v.n.)	quillt	quoll	quölle
raten	rät	riet	riete
reiben	reibt	rieb	riebe
reißen	reißt	riß	risse
reiten	reitet	ritt	ritte
rennen	rennt	rannte	rennte
riechen	riecht	roch	röche
ringen	ringt	rang	ränge
rinnen	rinnt	rann	rönne
rufen	ruft	rief	riefe
saufen	säuft	soff	söffe
saugen	saugt	sog	söge
schaffen	schafft	schuf	schüfe
scheiden	scheidet	schied	schiede
scheinen	scheint	schien	schiene
schelten	schilt	schalt	schölte
schieben	schiebt	schob	schöbe
schießen	schießt	schoß	schösse
schinden	schindet	schund	schünde
schlafen	schläft	schlief	schliefe
schlagen	schlägt	schlug	schlüge
schleichen	schleicht	schlich	schliche
schleifen	schleift	schliff	schliffe
schließen	schließt	schloß	schlösse
schlingen	schlingt	schlang	schlänge

German Irregular Verbs

Imper.	Past Participle	English
nenne	genannt	name
pfeif(e)	gepfiffen	whistle
preis(e)	gepriesen	praise
quill	gequollen	spring
rat(e)	geraten	counsel
reib(e)	gerieben	rub
reiß(e)	gerissen	tear
reit(e)	geritten	ride
renn(e)	gerannt	run
riech(e)	gerochen	smell
ring(e)	gerungen	struggle
rinn(e)	geronnen	flow
ruf(e)	gerufen	call
sauf(e)	gesoffen	drink (to excess)
saug(e)	gesogen	suck
schaff(e)	geschaffen	create
scheid(e)	geschieden	separate
schein(e)	geschienen	appear
schilt	gescholten	scold
schieb(e)	geschoben	shove
schieß(e)	geschossen	shoot
schind(e)	geschunden	skin
schlaf(e)	geschlafen	sleep
schlag(e)	geschlagen	beat
schleich(e)	geschlichen	slink, creep
schleif(e)	geschliffen	slide, polish
schließ(e)	geschlossen	shut, close
schling(e)	geschlungen	wind, devour

German Irregular Verbs

Infin.	Pres. Indic. 3rd Pers. Sing.	Imperf. Indic.	Imperf. Subj.
schmeißen	schmeißt	schmiß	schmisse
schmelzen (v.n.)	schmilzt	schmolz	schmölze
schneiden	schneidet	schnitt	schnitte
schrecken (v.n.)	schrickt	schrak	schräke
schreiben	schreibt	schrieb	schriebe
schreien	schreit	schrie	schriee
schreiten	schreitet	schritt	schritte
schweigen	schweigt	schwieg	schwiege
schwellen	schwillt	schwoll	schwölle
schwimmen	schwimmt	schwamm	schwömme
schwinden	schwindet	schwand	schwände
schwingen	schwingt	schwang	schwänge
schwören	schwört	schwur	schwüre
sehen	sieht	sah	sähe
sein	ist	war	wäre
senden	sendet	sandte or sendete	sendete
singen	singt	sang	sänge
sinken	sinkt	sank	sänke
sinnen	sinnt	sann	sänne
sitzen	sitzt	saß	säße
sollen	soll	sollte	sollte
speien	speit	spie	spiee
spinnen	spinnt	spann	spönne
sprechen	spricht	sprach	spräche
sprießen	sprießt	sproß	sprösse
springen	springt	sprang	spränge
stechen	sticht	stach	stäche
stehen	steht	stand	stände

German Irregular Verbs

Imper.	Past Participle	English
schmeiß(e)	geschmissen	hurl
schmilz	geschmolzen	melt
schneid(e)	geschnitten	cut
schrick	(erschrocken)	frighten
schreib(e)	geschrieben	write
schrei(e)	geschrien	cry
schreit(e)	geschritten	stride
schweig(e)	geschwiegen	be silent
schwill	geschwollen	swell
schwimm(e)	geschwommen	swim
schwind(e)	geschwunden	vanish
schwing(e)	geschwungen	swing
schwör(e)	geschworen	swear
sieh	gesehen	see
sei	gewesen	be
send(e)	gesandt *or* gesendet	send
sing(e)	gesungen	sing
sink(e)	gesunken	sink
sinn(e)	gesonnen	meditate
sitz(e)	gesessen	sit
	gesollt	be obliged
spei(e)	gespieen	spit
spinn(e)	gesponnen	spin
sprich	gesprochen	speak
sprieß(e)	gesprossen	sprout
spring(e)	gesprungen	leap
stich	gestochen	prick
steh(e)	gestanden	stand

German Irregular Verbs

Infin.	Pres. Indic. 3rd Pers. Sing.	Imperf. Indic.	Imperf. Subj.
stehlen	stiehlt	stahl	stöhle
steigen	steigt	stieg	stiege
sterben	stirbt	starb	stürbe
stinken	stinkt	stank	stänke
stoßen	stößt	stieß	stieße
streichen	streicht	strich	striche
streiten	streitet	stritt	stritte
tragen	trägt	trug	trüge
treffen	trifft	traf	träfe
treiben	treibt	trieb	triebe
treten	tritt	trat	träte
trinken	trinkt	trank	tränke
trügen	trügt	trog	tröge
tun	tut	tat	täte
verderben	verdirbt	verdarb	verdürbe
verdrießen	verdrießt	verdroß	verdrösse
vergessen	vergißt	vergaß	vergäße
verlieren	verliert	verlor	verlöre
wachsen	wächst	wuchs	wüchse
wägen	wägt	wog	wöge
waschen	wäscht	wusch	wüsche
weichen	weicht	wich	wiche
weisen	weist	wies	wiese
werben	wirbt	warb	würbe
werden	wird	wurde	würde
werfen	wirft	warf	würfe
wiegen	wiegt	wog	wöge
winden (v.a.)	windet	wand	wände

German Irregular Verbs

Imper.	Past Participle	English
stiehl	gestohlen	steal
steig(e)	gestiegen	climb
stirb	gestorben	die
stink(e)	gestunken	stink
stoß(e)	gestoßen	push
streich(e)	gestrichen	stroke, touch
streit(e)	gestritten	quarrel, fight
trag(e)	getragen	carry
triff	getroffen	meet
treib(e)	getrieben	drive
tritt	getreten	step
trink(e)	getrunken	drink
trüg(e)	getrogen	deceive
tu(e)	getan	do
verdirb	verdorben (and verderbt)	spoil
verdrieß(e)	verdrossen	grieve
vergiß	vergessen	forget
verlier(e)	verloren	lose
wachs(e)	gewachsen	grow
wäg(e)	gewogen	weigh
wasch(e)	gewaschen	wash
weich(e)	gewichen	yield
weis(e)	gewiesen	show
wirb	geworben	court
werde	geworden	become
wirf	geworfen	throw
wieg(e)	gewogen	weigh
wind(e)	gewunden	wind

German Irregular Verbs

Infin.	Pres. Indic. 3rd. Pers. Sing.	Imperf. Indic.	Imperf. Subj.
wissen	weiß	wußte	wüßte
wollen	will	wollte	wollte
zeihen	zeiht	zieh	ziehe
ziehen	zieht	zog	zöge
zwingen	zwingt	zwang	zwänge

German Irregular Verbs

Imper.	Past Participle	English
wisse	gewußt	know
wolle	gewollt	wish, want
zeih(e)	geziehen	accuse
zieh(e)	gezogen	draw, pull
zwing(e)	gezwungen	force, compel

English Irregular Verbs

Infin.	Past Indic.	Past Participle	German
abide	abode	abode	bleiben
arise	arose	arisen	aufstehen
awake	awoke	awoke	aufwecken
be	was, were	been	sein
bear	bore	borne	tragen
beat	beat	beaten	schlagen
become	became	become	werden
beget	begot	begotten	zeugen
begin	began	begun	beginnen
bend	bent	bent	biegen
bereave	bereaved, bereft	bereaved, bereft	berauben
beseech	besought	besought	bitten
bid	bade, bid	bidden, bid	gebieten
bide	bided, bode	bided	verbleiben
bind	bound	bound	binden
bite	bit	bitten	beißen
bleed	bled	bled	bluten
blow	blew	blown	blasen
break	broke	broken	brechen
breed	bred	bred	zeugen
bring	brought	brought	bringen
build	built	built	bauen
burn	burnt, burned	burnt, burned	brennen
burst	burst	burst	bersten
buy	bought	bought	kaufen

English Irregular Verbs

Infin.	Past Indic.	Past Participle	German
can (*pres. indic.*)	could	—	können
cast	cast	cast	werfen
catch	caught	caught	fangen
chide	chid	chidden, chid	schelten
choose	chose	chosen	wählen
cleave	cleft, clove	cleft, cloven	spalten
cling	clung	clung	sich anklammern
clothe	clothed, clad	clothed, clad	kleiden
come	came	come	kommen
cost	cost	cost	kosten
creep	crept	crept	kriechen
crow	crowed, crew	crowed	krähen
cut	cut	cut	schneiden
dare	dared, durst	dared	wagen
deal	dealt	dealt	austeilen, handeln
dig	dug	dug	graben
do	did	done	tun
draw	drew	drawn	ziehen
dream	dreamt, dreamed	dreamt, dreamed	träumen
drink	drank	drunk	trinken
drive	drove	driven	treiben
dwell	dwelt	dwelt	wohnen
eat	ate	eaten	essen
fall	fell	fallen	fallen
feed	fed	fed	füttern
feel	felt	felt	fühlen
fight	fought	fought	kämpfen
find	found	found	finden

English Irregular Verbs

Infin.	Past Indic.	Past Participle	German
flee	fled	fled	fliehen
fling	flung	flung	schleudern
fly	flew	flown	fliegen
forbid	forbad(e)	forbidden	verbieten
forget	forgot	forgotten	vergessen
forgive	forgave	forgiven	vergeben
forsake	forsook	forsaken	verlassen
freeze	froze	frozen	frieren
get	got	got	bekommen
gird	girded, girt	girden, girt	gürten
give	gave	given	geben
go	went	gone	gehen
grind	ground	ground	mahlen
grow	grew	grown	wachsen
hang	hung	hung	hängen
have	had	had	haben
hear	heard	heard	hören
heave	heaved, hove	heaved, hove	heben
hew	hewed	hewn, hewed	hauen
hide	hid	hidden, hid	verstecken
hit	hit	hit	schlagen
hold	held	held	halten
hurt	hurt	hurt	verletzen
keep	kept	kept	halten
kneel	knelt	knelt	knien
knit	knitted, knit	knitted, knit	stricken
know	knew	known	kennen, wissen
lay	laid	laid	legen

English Irregular Verbs

Infin.	Past Indic.	Past Participle	German
lead	led	led	führen
lean	leant, leaned	leant, leaned	lehnen
leap	leaped, leapt	leaped, leapt	springen
learn	learned, learnt	learned, learnt	lernen
leave	left	left	lassen
lend	lent	lent	leihen
let	let	let	lassen
lie (= recline)	lay	lain	liegen
light	lit, lighted	lit, lighted	beleuchten
lost	lost	lost	verlieren
make	made	made	machen
may (*pres. indic.*)	might	—	mögen
mean	meant	meant	meinen
meet	met	met	treffen, begegnen
melt	melted	melted, molten	schmelzen
mow	mowed	mown	mähen
must (*pres. indic.*)	—	—	müssen
pay	paid	paid	zahlen
put	put	put	stellen
quit	quit(ted)	quit(ted)	verlassen
—	quoth	—	sagte
read	read	read	lesen
rend	rent	rent	reissen
rid	rid	rid	befreien
ride	rode	ridden	reiten, fahren
ring	rang	rung	klingeln
rise	rose	risen	aufstehen
run	ran	run	laufen

English Irregular Verbs

Infin.	Past Indic.	Past Participle	German
saw	sawed	sawn	sägen
say	said	said	sagen
see	saw	seen	sehen
seek	sought	sought	suchen
sell	sold	sold	verkaufen
send	sent	sent	senden
set	set	set	setzen
shake	shook	shaken	schütteln
shall (*pres. indic.*)	should	—	werden, sollen
shape	shaped	shaped, shapen	formen
shear	sheared	shorn	scheren
shed	shed	shed	vergiessen
shine	shone	shone	scheinen
shoe	shod	shod	beschuhen
shoot	shot	shot	schiessen
show	showed	shown	zeigen
shrink	shrank	shrunk	schrumpfen
shut	shut	shut	schliessen
sing	sang	sung	singen
sink	sank	sunk	sinken
sit	sat	sat	sitzen
slay	slew	slain	erschlagen
sleep	slept	slept	schlafen
slide	slid	slid	gleiten
sling	slung	slung	schleudern
slink	slunk	slunk	schleichen
slit	slit	slit	schlitzen
smell	smelt, smelled	smelt, smelled	riechen

English Irregular Verbs

Infin.	Past Indic.	Past Participle	German
smit	smote	smitten	schlagen
sow	sowed	sown, sowed	säen
speak	spoke	spoken	sprechen
speed	sped, speeded	sped, speeded	eilen
spell	spelt, spelled	spelt, spelled	buchstabieren
spend	spent	spent	ausgeben
spill	spilled, spilt	spilled, spilt	verschütten
spin	spun, span	spun	spinnen
spit	spat	spat	speien
split	split	split	spalten
spread	spread	spread	ausbreiten
spring	sprang	sprung	springen
stand	stood	stood	stehen
steal	stole	stolen	stehlen
stick	stuck	stuck	stecken
sting	stung	stung	stechen
stink	stank, stunk	stunk	stinken
strew	strewed	strewed, strewn	streuen
stride	strode	stridden	schreiten
strike	struck	struck, stricken	schlagen
string	strung	strung	(auf)reihen
strive	strove	striven	streben
swear	swore	sworn	schwören
sweep	swept	swept	kehren
swell	swelled	swollen, **swelled**	schwellen
swim	swam	swum	schwimmen
swing	swung	swung	schwingen
take	took	taken	nehmen

English Irregular Verbs

Infin.	Past Indic.	Past Participle	German
teach	taught	taught	lehren
tear	tore	torn	zerreißen
tell	told	told	erzählen
think	thought	thought	denken
thrive	thrived, throve	thrived, thriven	gedeihen
throw	threw	thrown	werfen
thrust	thrust	thrust	stoßen
tread	trod	trodden	treten
wake	woke, waked	waked, woken woke	wachen
wear	wore	worn	tragen
weave	wove	woven	weben
weep	wept	wept	weinen
will	would	—	wollen
win	won	won	gewinnen
wind	wound	wound	winden
work	worked, wrought	worked, wrought	arbeiten
wring	wrung	wrung	ringen
write	wrote	written	schreiben

Numerical Tables

Cardinal Numbers

0	nought, zero	null
1	one	eins
2	two	zwei
3	three	drei
4	four	vier
5	five	fünf
6	six	sechs
7	seven	sieben
8	eight	acht
9	nine	neun
10	ten	zehn
11	eleven	elf
12	twelve	zwölf
13	thirteen	dreizehn
14	fourteen	vierzehn
15	fifteen	fünfzehn
16	sixteen	sechzehn
17	seventeen	siebzehn
18	eighteen	achtzehn
19	nineteen	neunzehn
20	twenty	zwanzig
21	twenty-one	einundzwanzig
22	twenty-two	zweiundzwanzig
25	twenty-five	fünfundzwanzig
30	thirty	dreißig
36	thirty-six	sechsunddreißig
40	forty	vierzig
50	fifty	fünfzig
60	sixty	sechzig
70	seventy	siebzig
80	eighty	achtzig
90	ninety	neunzig
100	(one)hundred	hundert
101	(a)hundred and one	hundert(und)eins
102	(a)hundred and two	hundert(und)zwei
200	two hundred	zweihundert
300	three hundred	dreihundert
600	six hundred	sechshundert
625	six hundred and twenty-five	sechshundertfünf-undzwanzig
1000	(a)thousand	tausend
1965	nineteen hundred and sixty-five	neunzehnhundert-fünfundsechzig
2000	two thousand	zweitausend
1,000,000	a million	eine Million
2,000,000	two million	zwei Millionen

Various suffixes may be added to German numerals, the commonest of which are cited in the following examples:

zehnfach	tenfold
dreisilbig	trisyllabic
vierstimmig	four-part (*i.e.* for four voices)
sechsteilig	in six parts

Ordinal Numbers

1st	first	erste (abbr. 1.)
2nd	second	zweite (abbr. 2.)
3rd	third	dritte (abbr. 3.)
4th	fourth	vierte
5th	fifth	fünfte
6th	sixth	sechste
7th	seventh	siebte
8th	eighth	achte
9th	ninth	neunte
10th	tenth	zehnte
11th	eleventh	elfte
12th	twelfth	zwölfte
13th	thirteenth	dreizehnte
14th	fourteenth	vierzehnte
15th	fifteenth	fünfzehnte
16th	sixteenth	sechzehnte
17th	seventeenth	siebzehnte
18th	eighteenth	achtzehnte
19th	nineteenth	neunzehnte
20th	twentieth	zwanzigste
21st	twenty-first	einundzwanzigste
22nd	twenty-second	zweiundzwanzigste
25th	twenty-fifth	fünfundzwanzigste
30th	thirtieth	dreißigste
40th	fortieth	vierzigste
50th	fiftieth	fünfzigste
60th	sixtieth	sechzigste
70th	seventieth	siebzigste
80th	eightieth	achtzigste
90th	ninetieth	neunzigste
100th	hundredth	hundertste
102nd	hundred and second	hundert(und)zweite
200th	two hundredth	zweihundertste
300th	three hundredth	dreihundertste
625th	six hundred and twenty-fifth	sechshundertfünf-undzwanzigste
1000th	thousandth	tausendste
2000th	two thousandth	zweitausendste
1,000,000th	millionth	millionste

Fractions etc.

$\frac{1}{4}$	a quarter	ein Viertel
$\frac{1}{3}$	a third	ein Drittel
$\frac{1}{2}$	a half	(ein)halb
$\frac{2}{3}$	two thirds	zwei Drittel
$\frac{3}{4}$	three quarters	drei Viertel
$1\frac{1}{4}$	one and a quarter	ein ein Viertel
$1\frac{1}{2}$	one and a half	anderthalb
$5\frac{1}{2}$	five and a half	fünfeinhalb
$7\frac{2}{5}$	seven and two-fifths	sieben zwei Fünftel
$\frac{15}{20}$	fifteen-twentieths	fünfzehn Zwanzigstel
.7	point seven	0,7 Null Komma sieben